Profiles of Indiana

2016
Fourth Edition

Profiles of Indiana

A UNIVERSAL REFERENCE BOOK

Grey House Publishing

PUBLISHER: Leslie Mackenzie
EDITORIAL DIRECTOR: Laura Mars
EDITOR: David Garoogian
MARKETING DIRECTOR: Jessica Moody

Grey House Publishing, Inc.
4919 Route 22
Amenia, NY 12501
518.789.8700
FAX 845.373.6390
www.greyhouse.com
e-mail: books @greyhouse.com

While every effort has been made to ensure the reliability of the information presented in this publication, Grey House Publishing neither guarantees the accuracy of the data contained herein nor assumes any responsibility for errors, omissions or discrepancies. Grey House accepts no payment for listing; inclusion in the publication of any organization, agency, institution, publication, service or individual does not imply endorsement of the editors or publisher.

Errors brought to the attention of the publisher and verified to the satisfaction of the publisher will be corrected in future editions.

Except by express prior written permission of the Copyright Proprietor no part of this work may be copied by any means of publication or communication now known or developed hereafter including, but not limited to, use in any directory or compilation or other print publication, in any information storage and retrieval system, in any other electronic device, or in any visual or audio-visual device or product.

This publication is an original and creative work, copyrighted by Grey House Publishing, Inc. and is fully protected by all applicable copyright laws, as well as by laws covering misappropriation, trade secrets and unfair competition.

Grey House has added value to the underlying factual material through one or more of the following efforts: unique and original selection; expression; arrangement; coordination; and classification.

Grey House Publishing, Inc. will defend its rights in this publication.

©2016 Grey House Publishing, Inc.
All rights reserved

First edition published 2007
Printed in Canada

ISBN: 978-1-61925-901-0

Table of Contents

Introduction
    Introduction vii

User Guide
    Profiles
        Places Covered ix
        Data Explanation and Sources—County Profiles xi
        Data Explanation and Sources—Community Profiles xix
    Education Section xxv
    Ancestry and Ethnicity Section xxviii
    Climate Section xxxvi

About Indiana
    Key Facts, State Emblems, and Location Map 2
    Photo Gallery 3
    A Brief History of Indiana 10
    Timeline of Indiana History 14
    Government
        A Guide to Indiana State Government 18
        Congressional Districts (113th Congress) 22
        Percent of Population Who Voted for Barack Obama in 2012 by County ... 23
        Core Based Statistical Areas (CBSAs) and Counties 24
    Land and Natural Resources
        State Summary 25
        Populated Places, Transportation and Physical Features 26
        Federal Lands and Indian Reservations 27
        Satellite View 28
        Indiana Hazard Events and Losses, 1960-2012 29
    Energy
        Indiana Energy Profile 30
    Demographic Maps
        Population 33
        Percent White 34
        Percent Black 35
        Percent Asian 36
        Percent Hispanic 37
        Median Age 38
        Median Household Income 39
        Median Home Value 40
        High School Graduates 41
        College Graduates 42

Profiles
    Alphabetical by County/Place 44
    Place Name Index 209

Comparative Statistics
    Comparative statistics of 100 largest communities 215

Community Rankings
    Rankings of top/bottom 150 communities with population of 2,500 or more 245

Education
    Indiana Public School Educational Profile 372
    School District Rankings 373

National Assessment of Educational Progress (NAEP) 387
State Report Card... 395

Ancestry and Ethnicity
Indiana State Profile 400
County Profiles 401
Place Profiles... 493
Ancestry Group Rankings 508
Hispanic Origin Rankings 528
Racial Group Rankings 533

Climate
Indiana Physical Features and Climate Narrative 551
Reference Map of Indiana 552
Relief Map of Indiana 553
Weather Stations Map 554
Weather Stations by County 555
Weather Stations by City... 556
Weather Stations by Elevation...................................... 557
National Weather Service Stations 558
Cooperative Weather Stations 562
Weather Station Rankings 572
Significant Storm Events... 583

Introduction

This is the fourth edition of *Profiles of Indiana—Facts, Figures & Statistics for 786 Populated Places in Indiana*. As with the other titles in our *State Profiles* series, it was built with content from Grey House Publishing's award-winning *Profiles of America*—a 4-volume compilation of data on more than 43,000 places in the United States. We have updated and included the Indiana chapter from *Profiles of America,* and added several new chapters of demographic information and ranking sections, so that *Profiles of Indiana* is the most comprehensive portrait of the state of Indiana ever published.

Profiles of Indiana provides data on all populated communities and counties in the states for which the US Census provides individual statistics. This edition also includes profiles of 106 unincorporated places based on US Census data by zip code.

This premier reference work includes seven major sections that cover everything from **Education** to **Ethnic Backgrounds** to **Climate**. All sections include **Comparative Statistics** or **Rankings**. Here is an overview of each section:

1. About Indiana
This 4-color section gives the researcher a real sense of the state and its history. It includes a Photo Gallery, and comprehensive sections on Indiana's History, Government, Land and Natural Resources, Energy and Demographic Maps. With charts and maps, these 42 pages help to anchor the researcher to the state, both physically and politically.

2. Profiles
This section, organized by county, gives detailed profiles of 786 places plus 92 counties, based on Census 2010 and data from the American Community Survey. We have added current government statistics and original research, so that these profiles pull together statistical and descriptive information on every Census-recognized place in each state. Major fields of information include:

Geography	*Housing*	*Education*	*Religion*
Ancestry	*Transportation*	*Population*	*Climate*
Economy	*Industry*	*Health*	

NEW categories to this edition include data on public and private health insurance, language spoken at home, people with disabilities and veterans. In addition to place profiles, this section includes a **Place Name Index**.

3. Comparative Statistics
This section include tables that compare Indiana's 100 largest communities by dozens of data points.

4. Community Rankings
This **NEW** section include tables that rank the top and bottom 150 communities with population over 2,500, in dozens of categories.

5. Education
This section begins with an **Educational State Profile,** summarizing number of schools, students, diplomas granted and educational dollars spent. Following the state profile are **School District Rankings** on 16 topics ranging from *Teacher/Student Ratios* to *High School Drop-Out Rates*. Following these rankings are statewide *National Assessment of Educational Progress (NAEP)* results and data from the *Indiana Statewide Testing for Educational Progress-Plus (ISTEP+)*—an overview of student performance by subject, including easy-to-read charts and graphs.

6. Ancestry and Ethnicity
This section provides a detailed look at the ancestral, Hispanic and racial makeup of Indiana's 200+ ethnic categories. Data is ranked three ways: 1) by number, based on all places regardless of population; 2) by percent, based on all places regardless of population; 3) by percent, based on places with populations of

50,000 or more. You will discover, for example, that the city of Crown Point has the greatest number of Macedonians in the state (901), and that 84.6% of the population of Raglesville are of French ancestry.

7. Climate

Each state chapter includes a State Summary, three colorful maps and profiles of both National and Cooperative Weather Stations. In addition, you'll find Weather Station Rankings with hundreds of interesting details, such as South Bend Michiana Regional reporting the highest annual snowfall with 67.3 inches.

This section also includes Significant Storm Event data from January 2000 through December 2009. Here you will learn that a flood caused $150 million in property damage in Bartholomew County in June 2008 and that an F3 tornado was responsible for 20 deaths in Vanderburgh County in November 2005.

Note: The extensive **User Guide** that follows this introduction is segmented into four sections and examines, in some detail, each data field in the individual profiles and comparative sections for all chapters. It provides sources for all data points and statistical definitions as necessary.

User Guide

Places Covered

All 92 counties.

568 incorporated municipalities. Includes 119 cities and 449 towns.

112 Census Designated Places (CDP). The U.S. Bureau of the Census defines a CDP as "a statistical entity, defined for each decennial census according to Census Bureau guidelines, comprising a densely settled concentration of population that is not within an incorporated place, but is locally identified by a name. CDPs are delineated cooperatively by state and local officials and the Census Bureau, following Census Bureau guidelines."

106 unincorporated communities. The communities included have statistics for their ZIP Code Tabulation Area (ZCTA) available from the Census Bureau. They are referred to as "postal areas." A ZCTA is a statistical entity developed by the Census Bureau to approximate the delivery area for a US Postal Service 5-digit or 3-digit ZIP Code in the US and Puerto Rico. A ZCTA is an aggregation of census blocks that have the same predominant ZIP Code associated with the mailing addresses in the Census Bureau's Master Address File. Thus, the Postal Service's delivery areas have been adjusted to encompass whole census blocks so that the Census Bureau can tabulate census data for the ZCTAs. ZCTAs do not include all ZIP Codes used for mail delivery and therefore do not precisely depict the area within which mail deliveries associated with that ZIP Code occur. Additionally, some areas that are known by a unique name, although they are part of a larger incorporated place, are also included as "postal areas."

For a more in-depth discussion of geographic areas, please refer to the Census Bureau's Geographic Areas Reference Manual at http://www.census.gov/geo/www/garm.html.

IMPORTANT NOTES

- Since the last decennial census, the U.S. Census replaced the long-form sample with the American Community Survey (ACS), which uses a series of monthly samples to produce annually updated estimates for the same areas. ACS estimates are based on data from a sample of housing units (3.54 million in 2013) and people in the population, not the full population. ACS sampling error (uncertainty of data) is greater for those areas with smaller populations. In an effort to provide the most accurate data, *Profiles of Indiana* reports ACS data for counties and communities with populations of 2,500 or more. The profiles for these places (2,500 or more population) also include data from Census 2010, including: population; population growth; population density; race; Hispanic origin; average household size; median age; age under 18; age 65 and over; males per 100 females; homeownership rate; homeowner vacancy rate; and rental vacancy rate. Profiles for counties and communities with 2,500 or less population show data from the Census 2010 only.
- *Profiles of Indiana* uses the term "community" to refer to all places except counties. The term "county" is used to refer to counties and county-equivalents. All places are defined as of the 2010 Census.
- If a community spans multiple counties, the community will be shown in the county that contains its largest population.
- In each community profile, only school districts that have schools that are physically located within the community are shown. In addition, statistics for each school district cover the entire district, regardless of the physical location of the schools within the district.
- Special care should be taken when interpreting certain statistics for communities containing large colleges or universities. College students were counted as residents of the area in which they were living while attending college (as they have been since the 1950 census). One effect this may have is skewing the figures for population, income, housing, and educational attainment.

- Some information (e.g. income) is available for both counties and individual communities. Other information is available for just counties (e.g. election results), or just individual communities (e.g. local newspapers). Refer to the "Data Explanation and Sources" section for a complete listing.
- Some statistical information is available only for larger communities. In addition, the larger places are more apt to have services such as newspapers, airports, school districts, etc.
- For the most complete information on any community, users should also check the entry for the county in which the community is located. In addition, more information and services will be listed under the larger places in the county.

Data Explanation and Sources—County Profiles

PHYSICAL AND GEOGRAPHICAL CHARACTERISTICS

Physical Location: Describes the physical location of the county. *Source: Columbia University Press, The Columbia Gazetteer of North America and original research.*

Land and Water Area: Land and water area in square miles. *Source: U.S. Census Bureau, Census 2010*

Latitude and Longitude: Latitude and longitude in degrees. *Source: U.S. Census Bureau, Census 2010*

Time Zone: Lists the time zone. *Source: Original research*

Year Organized: Year the county government was organized. *Source: National Association of Counties*

County Seat: Lists the county seat. If a county has more than one seat, then both are listed. *Source: National Association of Counties*

Metropolitan Area: Indicates the metropolitan area the county is located in. Also lists all the component counties of that metropolitan area. The Office of Management and Budget (OMB) defines metropolitan and micropolitan statistical areas. The most current definitions are as of February 2013. *Source: U.S. Census Bureau*

Climate: Includes all weather stations located within the county. Indicates the station name and elevation as well as the monthly average high and low temperatures, average precipitation, and average snowfall. The period of record is generally 1980-2009, however, certain weather stations contain averages going back as far as 1900. *Source: Grey House Publishing, Weather America: A Thirty-Year Summary of Statistical Weather Data and Rankings, 2010*

POPULATION

Population: 2010 figures are a 100% count of population. *Source: U.S. Census Bureau, Census 2010*

Population Growth: The increase or decrease in population between 2000 and 2010. *Source: U.S. Census Bureau, Census 2000, Census 2010*

Population Density: Total 2010 population divided by the land area in square miles. *Source: U.S. Census Bureau, U.S. Census Bureau, Census 2010*

Race/Hispanic Origin: Figures include the U.S. Census Bureau categories of White alone; Black/African American alone; Asian alone; American Indian/Alaska Native alone; Native Hawaiian/Other Pacific Islander alone; two or more races; and Hispanic of any race. Alone refers to the fact that these figures are not in combination with any other race. *Source: U.S. Census Bureau, Census 2010*

The concept of race, as used by the Census Bureau, reflects self-identification by people according to the race or races with which they most closely identify. These categories are socio-political constructs and should not be interpreted as being scientific or anthropological in nature. Furthermore, the race categories include both racial and national-origin groups.

- **White.** A person having origins in any of the original peoples of Europe, the Middle East, or North Africa. It includes people who indicated their race(s) as "White" or reported entries such as Irish, German, Italian, Lebanese, Arab, Moroccan, or Caucasian.
- **Black/African American.** A person having origins in any of the Black racial groups of Africa. It includes people who indicated their race(s) as "Black, African Am., or Negro" or reported entries such as African American, Kenyan, Nigerian, or Haitian.
- **Asian.** A person having origins in any of the original peoples of the Far East, Southeast Asia, or the Indian subcontinent, including, for example, Cambodia, China, India, Japan, Korea, Malaysia, Pakistan, the Philippine Islands, Thailand, and Vietnam. It includes people who indicated their race(s) as "Asian" or reported entries such as "Asian Indian," "Chinese," "Filipino," "Korean," "Japanese," "Vietnamese," and "Other Asian" or provided other detailed Asian responses.
- **American Indian/Alaska Native.** A person having origins in any of the original peoples of North and South America (including Central America) and who maintains tribal affiliation or community attachment. This category includes people who indicated their race(s) as "American Indian or Alaska Native" or

reported their enrolled or principal tribe, such as Navajo, Blackfeet, Inupiat, Yup'ik, or Central American Indian groups or South American Indian groups.

- **Native Hawaiian/Other Pacific Islander.** A person having origins in any of the original peoples of Hawaii, Guam, Samoa, or other Pacific Islands. It includes people who indicated their race(s) as "Pacific Islander" or reported entries such as "Native Hawaiian," "Guamanian or Chamorro," "Samoan," and "Other Pacific Islander" or provided other detailed Pacific Islander responses..
- **Two or More Races.** People may choose to provide two or more races either by checking two or more race response check boxes, by providing multiple responses, or by some combination of check boxes and other responses. The race response categories shown on the questionnaire are collapsed into the five minimum race groups identified by OMB, and the Census Bureau's "Some Other Race" category.
- **Hispanic.** The data on the Hispanic or Latino population were derived from answers to a question that was asked of all people. The terms "Spanish," "Hispanic origin," and "Latino" are used interchangeably. Some respondents identify with all three terms while others may identify with only one of these three specific terms. Hispanics or Latinos who identify with the terms "Spanish," "Hispanic," or "Latino" are those who classify themselves in one of the specific Spanish, Hispanic, or Latino categories listed on the questionnaire ("Mexican," "Puerto Rican," or "Cuban") as well as those who indicate that they are "other Spanish/Hispanic/Latino." People who do not identify with one of the specific origins listed on the questionnaire but indicate that they are "other Spanish/Hispanic/Latino" are those whose origins are from Spain, the Spanish-speaking countries of Central or South America, the Dominican Republic, or people identifying themselves generally as Spanish, Spanish-American, Hispanic, Hispano, Latino, and so on. All write-in responses to the "other Spanish/Hispanic/Latino" category were coded. Origin can be viewed as the heritage, nationality group, lineage, or country of birth of the person or the person's parents or ancestors before their arrival in the United States. People who identify their origin as Spanish, Hispanic, or Latino may be of any race.

Average Household Size: Number of persons in the average household. *Source: U.S. Census Bureau, Census 2010*

Median Age: Median age of the population. *Source: U.S. Census Bureau, Census 2010*

Age Under 18: Percent of the total population under 18 years old. *Source: U.S. Census Bureau, Census 2010*

Age 65 and Over: Percent of the total population age 65 and over. *Source: U.S. Census Bureau, Census 2010*

Males per 100 Females: Number of males per 100 females. *Source: U.S. Census Bureau, Census 2010*

Marital Status: Percentage of population never married, now married, separated, widowed, or divorced. *Source: U.S. Census Bureau, American Community Survey, 2009-2013 Five-Year Estimates*

The marital status classification refers to the status at the time of enumeration. Data on marital status are tabulated only for the population 15 years old and over. Each person was asked whether they were "Now married," "Widowed," "Separated," "Divorced," or "Never married." Couples who live together (for example, people in common-law marriages) were able to report the marital status they considered to be the most appropriate.

- **Never married.** Never married includes all people who have never been married, including people whose only marriage(s) was annulled.
- **Now married.** All people whose current marriage has not ended by widowhood or divorce. This category includes people defined as "separated."
- **Separated.** Includes people legally separated or otherwise absent from their spouse because of marital discord. Those without a final divorce decree are classified as "separated." This category also includes people who have been deserted or who have parted because they no longer want to live together, but who have not obtained a divorce.
- **Widowed.** This category includes widows and widowers who have not remarried.
- **Divorced.** This category includes people who are legally divorced and who have not remarried.

Foreign Born: Percentage of population who were not U.S. citizens at birth. Foreign-born people are those who indicated they were either a U.S. citizen by naturalization or they were not a citizen of the United States. *Source: U.S. Census Bureau, American Community Survey, 2009-2013 Five-Year Estimates*

Speak English Only: Percent of population that reported speaking only English at home. *Source: U.S. Census Bureau, American Community Survey, 2009-2013 Five-Year Estimates*

With Disability: Percent of the civilian noninstitutionalized population that reported having a disability. Disability status is determined from from six types of difficulty: vision, hearing, cognitive, ambulatory, self-care, and independent living. For children under 5 years old, hearing and vision difficulty are used to determine disability status. For children between the ages of 5 and 14, disability status is determined from hearing, vision, cognitive, ambulatory, and self-care difficulties. For people aged 15 years and older, they are considered to have a disability if they have difficulty with any one of the six difficulty types. *Source: U.S. Census Bureau, American Community Survey, 2009-2013 Five-Year Estimates*

Veterans: Percent of the civilian population 18 years and over who have served (even for a short time), but are not currently serving, on active duty in the U.S. Army, Navy, Air Force, Marine Corps, or the Coast Guard, or who served in the U.S. Merchant Marine during World War II. People who served in the National Guard or Reserves are classified as veterans only if they were ever called or ordered to active duty, not counting the 4-6 months for initial training or yearly summer camps. All other civilians are classified as nonveterans. Note: While it is possible for 17 year olds to be veterans of the Armed Forces, ACS data products are restricted to the population 18 years and older. *Source: U.S. Census Bureau, American Community Survey, 2009-2013 Five-Year Estimates*

Ancestry: Largest ancestry groups reported (up to five). The data includes persons who report multiple ancestries. For example, if a person reported being Irish and Italian, they would be included in both categories. Thus, the sum of the percentages may be greater than 100%. *Source: U.S. Census Bureau, American Community Survey, 2009-2013 Five-Year Estimates*

The data represent self-classification by people according to the ancestry group or groups with which they most closely identify. Ancestry refers to a person's ethnic origin or descent, "roots," heritage, or the place of birth of the person, the person's parents, or their ancestors before their arrival in the United States. Some ethnic identities, such as Egyptian or Polish, can be traced to geographic areas outside the United States, while other ethnicities such as Pennsylvania German or Cajun evolved in the United States.

The ancestry question was intended to provide data for groups that were not included in the Hispanic origin and race questions. Therefore, although data on all groups are collected, the ancestry data shown in these tabulations are for non-Hispanic and non-race groups. *See* Race/Hispanic Origin for information on Hispanic and race groups.

RELIGION

Religion: Lists the largest religious groups (up to six) based on the number of adherents divided by the population of the county. Adherents are defined as "all members, including full members, their children and the estimated number of other regular participants who are not considered as communicant, confirmed or full members." *Source: American Religious Bodies, 2010 U.S. Religion Census: Religious Congregations & Membership Study*

ECONOMY

Unemployment Rate: Unemployment rate as of October 2014. Includes all civilians age 16 or over who were unemployed and looking for work. *Source: U.S. Department of Labor, Bureau of Labor Statistics, Local Area Unemployment Statistics*

Leading Industries: Lists the three largest industries (excluding government) based on the number of employees. *Source: U.S. Census Bureau, County Business Patterns 2012*

Farms: The total number of farms and the total acreage they occupy. *Source: U.S. Department of Agriculture, National Agricultural Statistics Service, 2012 Census of Agriculture*

Company Size: The numbers of companies at various employee headcounts. Includes private employers only. *Source: U.S. Census Bureau, County Business Patterns 2012*

- **Employ 1,000 or more persons.** The numbers of companies that employ 1,000 or more persons.
- **Employ 500-999 persons.** The numbers of companies that employ 500 to 999 persons.
- **Employ 100-499 persons.** The numbers of companies that employ 100 to 499 persons.
- **Employ 1-99 persons.** The numbers of companies that employ 1 to 99 persons.

Business Ownership: Number of businesses that are majority-owned by women or various minority groups. *Source: U.S. Census Bureau, 2007 Economic Census, Survey of Business Owners: Black-Owned Firms, 2007 (latest statistics available at time of publication)*

- **Women-Owned.** Number of businesses that are majority-owned by a woman. Majority ownership is defined as having 51 percent or more of the stock or equity in the business.
- **Black-Owned.** Number of businesses that are majority-owned by a Black or African-American person(s). Majority ownership is defined as having 51 percent or more of the stock or equity in the business. Black or African American is defined as a person having origins in any of the black racial groups of Africa, including those who consider themselves to be "Haitian."
- **Hispanic-Owned.** Number of businesses that are majority-owned by a person(s) of Hispanic or Latino origin. Majority ownership is defined as having 51 percent or more of the stock or equity in the business. Hispanic or Latino origin is defined as a person of Cuban, Mexican, Puerto Rican, South or Central American, or other Spanish culture or origin, regardless of race.
- **Asian-Owned.** Number of businesses that are majority-owned by an Asian person(s). Majority ownership is defined as having 51 percent or more of the stock or equity in the business.

EMPLOYMENT

Employment by Occupation: Percentage of the employed civilian population 16 years and over in management, professional, service, sales, farming, construction, and production occupations. *Source: U.S. Census Bureau, American Community Survey, 2009-2013 Five-Year Estimates*

- Management, business, and financial occupations include:
    Management occupations
    Business and financial operations occupations

- Computer, engineering, and science occupations include:
    Computer and mathematical occupations
    Architecture and engineering occupations
    Life, physical, and social science occupations

- Education, legal, community service, arts, and media occupations include:
    Community and social service occupations
    Legal occupations
    Education, training, and library occupations
    Arts, design, entertainment, sports, and media occupations

- Healthcare practitioners and technical occupations include:
    Health diagnosing and treating practitioners and other technical occupations
    Health technologists and technicians

- Service occupations include:
    Healthcare support occupations
    Protective service occupations:
        Fire fighting and prevention, and other protective service workers including supervisors
        Law enforcement workers including supervisors
    Food preparation and serving related occupations
    Building and grounds cleaning and maintenance occupations
    Personal care and service occupations

- Sales and office occupations include:
    Sales and related occupations
    Office and administrative support occupations

- Natural resources, construction, and maintenance occupations include:
    Farming, fishing, and forestry occupations
    Construction and extraction occupations
    Installation, maintenance, and repair occupations

- Production, transportation, and material moving occupations include:
    Production occupations
    Transportation occupations
    Material moving occupations

INCOME

Per Capita Income: Per capita income is the mean income computed for every man, woman, and child in a particular group. It is derived by dividing the total income of a particular group by the total population in that group. Per capita income is rounded to the nearest whole dollar. *Source: U.S. Census Bureau, American Community Survey, 2009-2013 Five-Year Estimates*

Median Household Income: Includes the income of the householder and all other individuals 15 years old and over in the household, whether they are related to the householder or not. The median divides the income distribution into two equal parts: one-half of the cases falling below the median income and one-half above the median. For households, the median income is based on the distribution of the total number of households including those with no income. Median income for households is computed on the basis of a standard distribution and is rounded to the nearest whole dollar. *Source: U.S. Census Bureau, American Community Survey, 2009-2013 Five-Year Estimates*

Average Household Income: Average household income is obtained by dividing total household income by the total number of households. *Source: U.S. Census Bureau, American Community Survey, 2009-2013 Five-Year Estimates*

Percent of Households with Income of $100,000 or more: Percent of households with income of $100,000 or more. *Source: U.S. Census Bureau, American Community Survey, 2009-2013 Five-Year Estimates*

Poverty Rate: Percentage of population with income below the poverty level. Based on individuals for whom poverty status is determined. Poverty status was determined for all people except institutionalized people, people in military group quarters, people in college dormitories, and unrelated individuals under 15 years old. *Source: U.S. Census Bureau, American Community Survey, 2009-2013 Five-Year Estimates*

EDUCATIONAL ATTAINMENT

Figures show the percent of population age 25 and over with the following levels of educational attainment. *Source: U.S. Census Bureau, American Community Survey, 2009-2013 Five-Year Estimates*

- **High school diploma or higher.** Includes people whose highest degree is a high school diploma or its equivalent (GED), people who attended college but did not receive a degree, and people who received a college, university, or professional degree.
- **Bachelor's degree or higher.** Includes people who received a bachelor's, master's, doctorate, or professional degree.
- **Graduate/professional degree or higher.** Includes people who received a master's, doctorate, or professional degree.

HOUSING

Homeownership Rate: Percentage of housing units that are owner-occupied. *Source: U.S. Census Bureau, Census 2010*

Median Home Value: Median value in dollars of all owner-occupied housing units as reported by the owner. *Source: U.S. Census Bureau, American Community Survey, 2009-2013 Five-Year Estimates*

Median Year Structure Built: Year structure built refers to when the building was first constructed, not when it was remodeled, added to, or converted. For mobile homes, houseboats, RVs, etc, the manufacturer's model year was assumed to be the year built. The data relate to the number of units built during the specified periods that were still in existence at the time of enumeration. *Source: U.S. Census Bureau, American Community Survey, 2009-2013 Five-Year Estimates*

Homeowner Vacancy Rate: Proportion of the homeowner inventory that is vacant "for sale." It is computed by dividing the number of vacant units "for sale only" by the sum of the owner-occupied units, vacant units that are "for sale only," and vacant units that have been sold but not yet occupied, and then multiplying by 100. This measure is rounded to the nearest tenth. *Source: U.S. Census Bureau, Census 2010*

Median Gross Rent: Median monthly gross rent in dollars on specified renter-occupied and specified vacant-for-rent units. Specified renter-occupied and specified vacant-for-rent units exclude 1-family houses on 10 acres or more. Gross rent is the contract rent plus the estimated average monthly cost of utilities (electricity, gas, and water and sewer) and fuels (oil, coal, kerosene, wood, etc.) if these are paid by the renter (or paid for the renter by someone else). Gross rent is intended to eliminate differentials that result from varying practices with respect to the inclusion of utilities and fuels as part of the rental payment. Contract rent is the monthly rent agreed to or contracted for, regardless of any furnishings, utilities, fees, meals, or services that may be included. For vacant units, it is the monthly rent asked for the rental unit at the time of enumeration. *Source: U.S. Census Bureau, American Community Survey, 2009-2013 Five-Year Estimates*

Rental Vacancy Rate: Proportion of the rental inventory that is vacant "for rent." It is computed by dividing the number of vacant units "for rent" by the sum of the renter-occupied units, vacant units that are "for rent," and vacant units that have been rented but not yet occupied, and then multiplying by 100. This measure is rounded to the nearest tenth. *Source: U.S. Census Bureau, Census 2010*

VITAL STATISTICS

Birth Rate: Estimated number of births per 10,000 population in 2013. *Source: U.S. Census Bureau, Annual Components of Population Change, July 1, 2010 - July 1, 2013*

Death Rate: Estimated number of deaths per 10,000 population in 2013. *Source: U.S. Census Bureau, Annual Components of Population Change, July 1, 2010 - July 1, 2013*

Age-adjusted Cancer Mortality Rate: Number of age-adjusted deaths from cancer per 100,000 population in 2011. Cancer is defined as International Classification of Disease (ICD) codes C00–D48.9 Neoplasms. *Source: Centers for Disease Control, CDC Wonder, 2011*

Age-adjusted death rates are weighted averages of the age-specific death rates, where the weights represent a fixed population by age. They are used because the rates of almost all causes of death vary by age. Age adjustment is a technique for "removing" the effects of age from crude rates, so as to allow meaningful comparisons across populations with different underlying age structures. For example, comparing the crude rate of heart disease in Virginia to that of California is misleading, because the relatively older population in Virginia will lead to a higher crude death rate, even if the age-specific rates of heart disease in Virginia and California are the same. For such a comparison, age-adjusted rates would be preferable. Age-adjusted rates should be viewed as relative indexes rather than as direct or actual measures of mortality risk.

Death rates based on counts of twenty or less (≤ 20) are flagged as "Unreliable". Death rates based on fewer than three years of data for counties with populations of less than 100,000 in the 2000 Census counts, are also flagged as "Unreliable" if the number of deaths is five or less (≤ 5).

HEALTH INSURANCE

Health insurance coverage in the ACS and other Census Bureau surveys define coverage to include plans and programs that provide comprehensive health coverage. Plans that provide insurance for specific conditions or situations such as cancer and long-term care policies are not considered coverage. Likewise, other types of insurance like dental, vision, life, and disability insurance are not considered health insurance coverage.

For reporting purposes, the Census Bureau broadly classifies health insurance coverage as private health insurance or public coverage. Private health insurance is a plan provided through an employer or union, a plan purchased by an individual from a private company, or TRICARE or other military health care. Public health coverage includes the federal programs Medicare, Medicaid, and VA Health Care (provided through the Department of Veterans Affairs); the Children's Health Insurance Program (CHIP); and individual state health plans. The types of health insurance are not mutually exclusive; people may be covered by more than one at the same time. People who had no reported health coverage, or those whose only health coverage was Indian Health Service, were considered uninsured. *Source: U.S. Census Bureau, American Community Survey, 2009-2013 Five-Year Estimates*

- **Have Insurance:** Percent of the civilian noninstitutionalized population with any type of comprehensive health insurance.
- **Have Private Insurance.** Percent of the civilian noninstitutionalized population with private health insurance. A person may report that they have both public and private health insurance, thus, the sum of the percentages may be greater than 100%.
- **Have Public Insurance.** Percent of the civilian noninstitutionalized population with public health insurance. A person may report that they have both public and private health insurance, thus, the sum of the percentages may be greater than 100%.
- **Do Not Have Insurance.** Percent of the civilian noninstitutionalized population with no health insurance.
- **Children Under 18 With No Insurance.** Percent of the civilian noninstitutionalized population under age 18 with no health insurance.

HEALTH CARE

Number of physicians, hospital beds and hospital admission per 10,000 population. *Source: Area Resource File (ARF) 2012-2013. U.S. Department of Health and Human Services, Health Resources and Services Administration, Bureau of Health Professions, Rockville, MD.*

- **Number of Physicians.** The number of active, non-federal physicians (MDs and DOs) per 10,000 population in 2011.
- **Number of Hospital Beds.** The number of hospital beds per 10,000 population in 2010.
- **Number of Hospital Admissions.** The number of hospital admissions per 10,000 population in 2010.

AIR QUALITY INDEX

The percentage of days in 2013 the AQI fell into the Good (0-50), Moderate (51-100), Unhealthy for Sensitive Groups (101-150), Unhealthy (151-200), Very Unhealthy (201-300), and Hazardous (300+) ranges. If a range does not appear, its value is zero. Data covers January 2013 through December 2013. *Source: AirData: Access to Air Pollution Data, U.S. Environmental Protection Agency, Office of Air and Radiation*

The AQI is an index for reporting daily air quality. It tells you how clean or polluted your air is, and what associated health concerns you should be aware of. The AQI focuses on health effects that can happen within a few hours or days after breathing polluted air. EPA uses the AQI for five major air pollutants regulated by the Clean Air Act: ground-level ozone, particulate matter, carbon monoxide, sulfur dioxide, and nitrogen dioxide. For each of these pollutants, EPA has established national air quality standards to protect against harmful health effects.

The AQI runs from 0 to 500. The higher the AQI value, the greater the level of air pollution and the greater the health danger. For example, an AQI value of 50 represents good air quality and little potential to affect public health, while an AQI value over 300 represents hazardous air quality. An AQI value of 100 generally corresponds to the national air quality standard for the pollutant, which is the level EPA has set to protect public health. So, AQI values below 100 are generally thought of as satisfactory. When AQI values are above 100, air quality is considered to be unhealthy—at first for certain sensitive groups of people, then for everyone as AQI values get higher. Each category corresponds to a different level of health concern. For example, when the AQI for a pollutant is between 51 and 100, the health concern is "Moderate." Here are the six levels of health concern and what they mean:

- "Good" The AQI value for your community is between 0 and 50. Air quality is considered satisfactory and air pollution poses little or no risk.
- "Moderate" The AQI for your community is between 51 and 100. Air quality is acceptable; however, for some pollutants there may be a moderate health concern for a very small number of individuals. For example, people who are unusually sensitive to ozone may experience respiratory symptoms.
- "Unhealthy for Sensitive Groups" Certain groups of people are particularly sensitive to the harmful effects of certain air pollutants. This means they are likely to be affected at lower levels than the general public. For example, children and adults who are active outdoors and people with respiratory disease are at greater risk from exposure to ozone, while people with heart disease are at greater risk from carbon monoxide. Some people may be sensitive to more than one pollutant. When AQI values are between 101 and 150, members of sensitive groups may experience health effects. The general public is not likely to be affected when the AQI is in this range.
- "Unhealthy" AQI values are between 151 and 200. Everyone may begin to experience health effects. Members of sensitive groups may experience more serious health effects.
- "Very Unhealthy" AQI values between 201 and 300 trigger a health alert, meaning everyone may experience more serious health effects.
- "Hazardous" AQI values over 300 trigger health warnings of emergency conditions. The entire population is more likely to be affected.

TRANSPORTATION

Commute to Work: Percentage of workers 16 years old and over that use the following means of transportation to commute to work: car; public transportation; walk; work from home. The means of transportation data for some areas may show workers using modes of public transportation that are not available in those areas (e.g. subway or elevated riders in a metropolitan area where there actually is no subway or elevated service). This result is largely due to people who worked during the reference week at a location that was different from their usual place of work (such as people away from home on business in an area where subway service was available) and people who used more than one means of transportation each day but whose principal means was unavailable where they lived (e.g. residents of non-metropolitan areas who drove to the fringe of a metropolitan area and took the commuter railroad most of the distance to work). *Source: U.S. Census Bureau, American Community Survey, 2009-2013 Five-Year Estimates*

Median Travel Time to Work: Median travel time to work for workers 16 years old and over. Travel time to work refers to the total number of minutes that it usually took the person to get from home to work each day during the reference week. The elapsed time includes time spent waiting for public transportation, picking up passengers in carpools, and time spent in other activities related to getting to work. *Source: U.S. Census Bureau, American Community Survey, 2009-2013 Five-Year Estimates*

PRESIDENTIAL ELECTION

2012 Presidential election results. *Source: Dave Leip's Atlas of U.S. Presidential Elections*

NATIONAL AND STATE PARKS

Lists National/State parks located in the area. *Source: U.S. Geological Survey, Geographic Names Information System*

ADDITIONAL INFORMATION CONTACTS

General telephone number and website address (if available) of local government.

Data Explanation and Sources—Community Profiles

PHYSICAL AND GEOGRAPHICAL CHARACTERISTICS

Place Type: Lists the type of place (city, town, village, borough, Census-Designated Place (CDP), township, charter township, plantation, gore, district, grant, location, purchase, municipality, reservation, unorganized territory, or unincorporated postal area). *Source: U.S. Census Bureau, Census 2010 and U.S. Postal Service, City State File*

ZCTA: *This only appears within unincorporated postal areas.* The statistics that follow cover the corresponding ZIP Code Tabulation Area (ZCTA). A ZCTA is a statistical entity developed by the Census Bureau to approximate the delivery area for a US Postal Service 5-digit or 3-digit ZIP Code in the US and Puerto Rico. A ZCTA is an aggregation of census blocks that have the same predominant ZIP Code associated with the mailing addresses in the Census Bureau's Master Address File. Thus, the Postal Service's delivery areas have been adjusted to encompass whole census blocks so that the Census Bureau can tabulate census data for the ZCTAs. ZCTAs do not include all ZIP Codes used for mail delivery and therefore do not precisely depict the area within which mail deliveries associated with that ZIP Code occur. Additionally, some areas that are known by a unique name, although they are part of a larger incorporated place, are also included as "postal areas."

Land and Water Area: Land and water area in square miles. *Source: U.S. Census Bureau, Census 2010*

Latitude and Longitude: Latitude and longitude in degrees. *Source: U.S. Census Bureau, Census 2010.*

Elevation: Elevation in feet. *Source: U.S. Geological Survey, Geographic Names Information System (GNIS)*

HISTORY

Historical information. *Source: Columbia University Press, The Columbia Gazetteer of North America; Original research*

POPULATION

Population: 2010 figures are a 100% count of population. *Source: U.S. Census Bureau, Census 2010*

Population Growth: The increase or decrease in population between 2000 and 2010. *Source: U.S. Census Bureau, Census 2000, Census 2010*

Population Density: Total 2010 population divided by the land area in square miles. *Source: U.S. Census Bureau, U.S. Census Bureau, Census 2010*

Race/Hispanic Origin: Figures include the U.S. Census Bureau categories of White alone; Black/African American alone; Asian alone; American Indian/Alaska Native alone; Native Hawaiian/Other Pacific Islander alone; two or more races; and Hispanic of any race. Alone refers to the fact that these figures are not in combination with any other race. *Source: U.S. Census Bureau, Census 2010*

The concept of race, as used by the Census Bureau, reflects self-identification by people according to the race or races with which they most closely identify. These categories are socio-political constructs and should not be interpreted as being scientific or anthropological in nature. Furthermore, the race categories include both racial and national-origin groups.

- **White.** A person having origins in any of the original peoples of Europe, the Middle East, or North Africa. It includes people who indicated their race(s) as "White" or reported entries such as Irish, German, Italian, Lebanese, Arab, Moroccan, or Caucasian.
- **Black/African American.** A person having origins in any of the Black racial groups of Africa. It includes people who indicated their race(s) as "Black, African Am., or Negro" or reported entries such as African American, Kenyan, Nigerian, or Haitian.
- **Asian.** A person having origins in any of the original peoples of the Far East, Southeast Asia, or the Indian subcontinent, including, for example, Cambodia, China, India, Japan, Korea, Malaysia, Pakistan, the Philippine Islands, Thailand, and Vietnam. It includes people who indicated their race(s) as "Asian" or reported entries such as "Asian Indian," "Chinese," "Filipino," "Korean," "Japanese," "Vietnamese," and "Other Asian" or provided other detailed Asian responses.
- **American Indian/Alaska Native.** A person having origins in any of the original peoples of North and South America (including Central America) and who maintains tribal affiliation or community attachment.

This category includes people who indicated their race(s) as "American Indian or Alaska Native" or reported their enrolled or principal tribe, such as Navajo, Blackfeet, Inupiat, Yup'ik, or Central American Indian groups or South American Indian groups.

- **Native Hawaiian/Other Pacific Islander.** A person having origins in any of the original peoples of Hawaii, Guam, Samoa, or other Pacific Islands. It includes people who indicated their race(s) as "Pacific Islander" or reported entries such as "Native Hawaiian," "Guamanian or Chamorro," "Samoan," and "Other Pacific Islander" or provided other detailed Pacific Islander responses..
- **Two or More Races.** People may choose to provide two or more races either by checking two or more race response check boxes, by providing multiple responses, or by some combination of check boxes and other responses. The race response categories shown on the questionnaire are collapsed into the five minimum race groups identified by OMB, and the Census Bureau's "Some Other Race" category.
- **Hispanic.** The data on the Hispanic or Latino population were derived from answers to a question that was asked of all people. The terms "Spanish," "Hispanic origin," and "Latino" are used interchangeably. Some respondents identify with all three terms while others may identify with only one of these three specific terms. Hispanics or Latinos who identify with the terms "Spanish," "Hispanic," or "Latino" are those who classify themselves in one of the specific Spanish, Hispanic, or Latino categories listed on the questionnaire ("Mexican," "Puerto Rican," or "Cuban") as well as those who indicate that they are "other Spanish/Hispanic/Latino." People who do not identify with one of the specific origins listed on the questionnaire but indicate that they are "other Spanish/Hispanic/Latino" are those whose origins are from Spain, the Spanish-speaking countries of Central or South America, the Dominican Republic, or people identifying themselves generally as Spanish, Spanish-American, Hispanic, Hispano, Latino, and so on. All write-in responses to the "other Spanish/Hispanic/Latino" category were coded. Origin can be viewed as the heritage, nationality group, lineage, or country of birth of the person or the person's parents or ancestors before their arrival in the United States. People who identify their origin as Spanish, Hispanic, or Latino may be of any race.

Average Household Size: Number of persons in the average household. *Source: U.S. Census Bureau, Census 2010*

Median Age: Median age of the population. *Source: U.S. Census Bureau, Census 2010*

Age Under 18: Percent of the total population under 18 years old. *Source: U.S. Census Bureau, Census 2010*

Age 65 and Over: Percent of the total population age 65 and over. *Source: U.S. Census Bureau, Census 2010*

Males per 100 Females: Number of males per 100 females. *Source: U.S. Census Bureau, Census 2010*

Marital Status: Percentage of population never married, now married, separated, widowed, or divorced. *Source: U.S. Census Bureau, American Community Survey, 2009-2013 Five-Year Estimates*

The marital status classification refers to the status at the time of enumeration. Data on marital status are tabulated only for the population 15 years old and over. Each person was asked whether they were "Now married," "Widowed," "Separated," "Divorced," or "Never married." Couples who live together (for example, people in common-law marriages) were able to report the marital status they considered to be the most appropriate.

- **Never married.** Never married includes all people who have never been married, including people whose only marriage(s) was annulled.
- **Now married.** All people whose current marriage has not ended by widowhood or divorce. This category includes people defined as "separated."
- **Separated.** Includes people legally separated or otherwise absent from their spouse because of marital discord. Those without a final divorce decree are classified as "separated." This category also includes people who have been deserted or who have parted because they no longer want to live together, but who have not obtained a divorce.
- **Widowed.** This category includes widows and widowers who have not remarried.
- **Divorced.** This category includes people who are legally divorced and who have not remarried.

Foreign Born: Percentage of population who were not U.S. citizens at birth. Foreign-born people are those who indicated they were either a U.S. citizen by naturalization or they were not a citizen of the United States. *Source: U.S. Census Bureau, American Community Survey, 2009-2013 Five-Year Estimates*

Speak English Only: Percent of population that reported speaking only English at home. *Source: U.S. Census Bureau, American Community Survey, 2009-2013 Five-Year Estimates*

With Disability: Percent of the civilian noninstitutionalized population that reported having a disability. Disability status is determined from from six types of difficulty: vision, hearing, cognitive, ambulatory, self-care, and independent living. For children under 5 years old, hearing and vision difficulty are used to determine disability status. For children between the ages of 5 and 14, disability status is determined from hearing, vision, cognitive, ambulatory, and self-care difficulties. For people aged 15 years and older, they are considered to have a disability if they have difficulty with any one of the six difficulty types. *Source: U.S. Census Bureau, American Community Survey, 2009-2013 Five-Year Estimates*

Veterans: Percent of the civilian population 18 years and over who have served (even for a short time), but are not currently serving, on active duty in the U.S. Army, Navy, Air Force, Marine Corps, or the Coast Guard, or who served in the U.S. Merchant Marine during World War II. People who served in the National Guard or Reserves are classified as veterans only if they were ever called or ordered to active duty, not counting the 4-6 months for initial training or yearly summer camps. All other civilians are classified as nonveterans. Note: While it is possible for 17 year olds to be veterans of the Armed Forces, ACS data products are restricted to the population 18 years and older. *Source: U.S. Census Bureau, American Community Survey, 2009-2013 Five-Year Estimates*

Ancestry: Largest ancestry groups reported (up to five). The data includes persons who report multiple ancestries. For example, if a person reported being Irish and Italian, they would be included in both categories. Thus, the sum of the percentages may be greater than 100%. *Source: U.S. Census Bureau, American Community Survey, 2009-2013 Five-Year Estimates*

The data represent self-classification by people according to the ancestry group or groups with which they most closely identify. Ancestry refers to a person's ethnic origin or descent, "roots," heritage, or the place of birth of the person, the person's parents, or their ancestors before their arrival in the United States. Some ethnic identities, such as Egyptian or Polish, can be traced to geographic areas outside the United States, while other ethnicities such as Pennsylvania German or Cajun evolved in the United States.

The ancestry question was intended to provide data for groups that were not included in the Hispanic origin and race questions. Therefore, although data on all groups are collected, the ancestry data shown in these tabulations are for non-Hispanic and non-race groups. *See* Race/Hispanic Origin for information on Hispanic and race groups.

EMPLOYMENT

Employment by Occupation: Percentage of the employed civilian population 16 years and over in management, professional, service, sales, farming, construction, and production occupations. *Source: U.S. Census Bureau, American Community Survey, 2009-2013 Five-Year Estimates*

- Management, business, and financial occupations include:
    Management occupations
    Business and financial operations occupations

- Computer, engineering, and science occupations include:
    Computer and mathematical occupations
    Architecture and engineering occupations
    Life, physical, and social science occupations

- Education, legal, community service, arts, and media occupations include:
    Community and social service occupations
    Legal occupations
    Education, training, and library occupations
    Arts, design, entertainment, sports, and media occupations

- Healthcare practitioners and technical occupations include:
    Health diagnosing and treating practitioners and other technical occupations
    Health technologists and technicians

- Service occupations include:
    Healthcare support occupations
    Protective service occupations:
        Fire fighting and prevention, and other protective service workers including supervisors
        Law enforcement workers including supervisors
    Food preparation and serving related occupations
    Building and grounds cleaning and maintenance occupations
    Personal care and service occupations

- Sales and office occupations include:
  Sales and related occupations
  Office and administrative support occupations

- Natural resources, construction, and maintenance occupations include:
  Farming, fishing, and forestry occupations
  Construction and extraction occupations
  Installation, maintenance, and repair occupations

- Production, transportation, and material moving occupations include:
  Production occupations
  Transportation occupations
  Material moving occupations

INCOME

Per Capita Income: Per capita income is the mean income computed for every man, woman, and child in a particular group. It is derived by dividing the total income of a particular group by the total population in that group. Per capita income is rounded to the nearest whole dollar. *Source: U.S. Census Bureau, American Community Survey, 2009-2013 Five-Year Estimates*

Median Household Income: Includes the income of the householder and all other individuals 15 years old and over in the household, whether they are related to the householder or not. The median divides the income distribution into two equal parts: one-half of the cases falling below the median income and one-half above the median. For households, the median income is based on the distribution of the total number of households including those with no income. Median income for households is computed on the basis of a standard distribution and is rounded to the nearest whole dollar. *Source: U.S. Census Bureau, American Community Survey, 2009-2013 Five-Year Estimates*

Average Household Income: Average household income is obtained by dividing total household income by the total number of households. *Source: U.S. Census Bureau, American Community Survey, 2009-2013 Five-Year Estimates*

Percent of Households with Income of $100,000 or more: Percent of households with income of $100,000 or more. *Source: U.S. Census Bureau, American Community Survey, 2009-2013 Five-Year Estimates*

Poverty Rate: Percentage of population with income below the poverty level. Based on individuals for whom poverty status is determined. Poverty status was determined for all people except institutionalized people, people in military group quarters, people in college dormitories, and unrelated individuals under 15 years old. *Source: U.S. Census Bureau, American Community Survey, 2009-2013 Five-Year Estimates*

EDUCATIONAL ATTAINMENT

Figures show the percent of population age 25 and over with the following levels of educational attainment. *Source: U.S. Census Bureau, American Community Survey, 2009-2013 Five-Year Estimates*

- **High school diploma or higher.** Includes people whose highest degree is a high school diploma or its equivalent (GED), people who attended college but did not receive a degree, and people who received a college, university, or professional degree.
- **Bachelor's degree or higher.** Includes people who received a bachelor's, master's, doctorate, or professional degree.
- **Graduate/professional degree or higher.** Includes people who received a master's, doctorate, or professional degree.

SCHOOL DISTRICTS

Lists the name of each school district, the grade range (PK=pre-kindergarten; KG=kindergarten), the student enrollment, and the district headquarters' phone number. In each community profile, only school districts that have schools that are physically located within the community are shown. In addition, statistics for each school district cover the entire district, regardless of the physical location of the schools within the district. *Source: U.S. Department of Education, National Center for Educational Statistics, Directory of Public Elementary and Secondary Education Agencies, 2012-13*

COLLEGES

Four-year Colleges: Lists the name of each four-year college, the type of institution (private or public; for-profit or non-profit; religious affiliation; historically black), the total estimated student enrollment in 2013, the general telephone number, and the annual tuition and fees for full-time, first-time undergraduate students (in-state and out-of-state). *Source: U.S. Department of Education, National Center for Educational Statistics, IPEDS College Data, 2013-14*

Two-year Colleges: Lists the name of each two-year college, the type of institution (private or public; for-profit or non-profit; religious affiliation; historically black), the total estimated student enrollment in 2013, the general telephone number, and the annual tuition and fees for full-time, first-time undergraduate students (in-state and out-of-state). *Source: U.S. Department of Education, National Center for Educational Statistics, IPEDS College Data, 2013-14*

Vocational/Technical Schools: Lists the name of each vocational/technical school, the type of institution (private or public; for-profit or non-profit; religious affiliation; historically black), the total estimated student enrollment in 2013, the general telephone number, and the annual tuition and fees for full-time students. *Source: U.S. Department of Education, National Center for Educational Statistics, IPEDS College Data, 2013-14*

HOUSING

Homeownership Rate: Percentage of housing units that are owner-occupied. *Source: U.S. Census Bureau, Census 2010*

Median Home Value: Median value in dollars of all owner-occupied housing units as reported by the owner. *Source: U.S. Census Bureau, American Community Survey, 2009-2013 Five-Year Estimates*

Median Year Structure Built: Year structure built refers to when the building was first constructed, not when it was remodeled, added to, or converted. For mobile homes, houseboats, RVs, etc, the manufacturer's model year was assumed to be the year built. The data relate to the number of units built during the specified periods that were still in existence at the time of enumeration. *Source: U.S. Census Bureau, American Community Survey, 2009-2013 Five-Year Estimates*

Homeowner Vacancy Rate: Proportion of the homeowner inventory that is vacant "for sale." It is computed by dividing the number of vacant units "for sale only" by the sum of the owner-occupied units, vacant units that are "for sale only," and vacant units that have been sold but not yet occupied, and then multiplying by 100. This measure is rounded to the nearest tenth. *Source: U.S. Census Bureau, Census 2010*

Median Gross Rent: Median monthly gross rent in dollars on specified renter-occupied and specified vacant-for-rent units. Specified renter-occupied and specified vacant-for-rent units exclude 1-family houses on 10 acres or more. Gross rent is the contract rent plus the estimated average monthly cost of utilities (electricity, gas, and water and sewer) and fuels (oil, coal, kerosene, wood, etc.) if these are paid by the renter (or paid for the renter by someone else). Gross rent is intended to eliminate differentials that result from varying practices with respect to the inclusion of utilities and fuels as part of the rental payment. Contract rent is the monthly rent agreed to or contracted for, regardless of any furnishings, utilities, fees, meals, or services that may be included. For vacant units, it is the monthly rent asked for the rental unit at the time of enumeration. *Source: U.S. Census Bureau, American Community Survey, 2009-2013 Five-Year Estimates*

Rental Vacancy Rate: Proportion of the rental inventory that is vacant "for rent." It is computed by dividing the number of vacant units "for rent" by the sum of the renter-occupied units, vacant units that are "for rent," and vacant units that have been rented but not yet occupied, and then multiplying by 100. This measure is rounded to the nearest tenth. *Source: U.S. Census Bureau, Census 2010*

HEALTH INSURANCE

Health insurance coverage in the ACS and other Census Bureau surveys define coverage to include plans and programs that provide comprehensive health coverage. Plans that provide insurance for specific conditions or situations such as cancer and long-term care policies are not considered coverage. Likewise, other types of insurance like dental, vision, life, and disability insurance are not considered health insurance coverage.

For reporting purposes, the Census Bureau broadly classifies health insurance coverage as private health insurance or public coverage. Private health insurance is a plan provided through an employer or union, a plan purchased by an individual from a private company, or TRICARE or other military health care. Public health coverage includes the federal programs Medicare, Medicaid, and VA Health Care (provided through the Department of Veterans Affairs); the Children's Health Insurance Program (CHIP); and individual state health plans. The types of health insurance are not mutually exclusive; people may be covered by more than one at the same time. People who had no reported health coverage, or those whose only health coverage was Indian Health Service, were considered uninsured. *Source: U.S. Census Bureau, American Community Survey, 2009-2013 Five-Year Estimates*

- **Have Insurance:** Percent of the civilian noninstitutionalized population with any type of comprehensive health insurance.
- **Have Private Insurance.** Percent of the civilian noninstitutionalized population with private health insurance. A person may report that they have both public and private health insurance, thus, the sum of the percentages may be greater than 100%.
- **Have Public Insurance.** Percent of the civilian noninstitutionalized population with public health insurance. A person may report that they have both public and private health insurance, thus, the sum of the percentages may be greater than 100%.
- **Do Not Have Insurance.** Percent of the civilian noninstitutionalized population with no health insurance.
- **Children Under 18 With No Insurance.** Percent of the civilian noninstitutionalized population under age 18 with no health insurance.

HOSPITALS

Lists the hospital name and the number of licensed beds. *Source: Grey House Publishing, The Comparative Guide to American Hospitals, 2014*

NEWSPAPERS

List of daily and weekly newspapers with circulation figures. *Source: Gebbie Press, 2015 All-In-One Media Directory*

SAFETY

Violent Crime Rate: Number of violent crimes reported per 10,000 population. Violent crimes include murder, forcible rape, robbery, and aggravated assault. *Source: Federal Bureau of Investigation, Uniform Crime Reports 2013*

Property Crime Rate: Number of property crimes reported per 10,000 population. Property crimes include burglary, larceny-theft, and motor vehicle theft. *Source: Federal Bureau of Investigation, Uniform Crime Reports 2013*

TRANSPORTATION

Commute to Work: Percentage of workers 16 years old and over that use the following means of transportation to commute to work: car; public transportation; walk; work from home. The means of transportation data for some areas may show workers using modes of public transportation that are not available in those areas (e.g. subway or elevated riders in a metropolitan area where there actually is no subway or elevated service). This result is largely due to people who worked during the reference week at a location that was different from their usual place of work (such as people away from home on business in an area where subway service was available) and people who used more than one means of transportation each day but whose principal means was unavailable where they lived (e.g. residents of non-metropolitan areas who drove to the fringe of a metropolitan area and took the commuter railroad most of the distance to work). *Source: U.S. Census Bureau, American Community Survey, 2009-2013 Five-Year Estimates*

Median Travel Time to Work: Median travel time to work for workers 16 years old and over. Travel time to work refers to the total number of minutes that it usually took the person to get from home to work each day during the reference week. The elapsed time includes time spent waiting for public transportation, picking up passengers in carpools, and time spent in other activities related to getting to work. *Source: U.S. Census Bureau, American Community Survey, 2009-2013 Five-Year Estimates*

Amtrak: Indicates if Amtrak rail or bus service is available. Please note that the cities being served continually change. *Source: National Railroad Passenger Corporation, Amtrak National Timetable, 2015*

AIRPORTS

Lists the local airport(s) along with type of service and hub size. *Source: U.S. Department of Transportation, Bureau of Transportation Statistics*

ADDITIONAL INFORMATION CONTACTS

General telephone number and website address (if available) of local government.

Education Section

School District Rankings

Number of Schools: Total number of schools in the district. *Source: U.S. Department of Education, National Center for Education Statistics, Common Core of Data, Public Elementary/Secondary School Universe Survey: School Year 2011-2012.*

Number of Teachers: Teachers are defined as individuals who provide instruction to pre-kindergarten, kindergarten, grades 1 through 12, or ungraded classes, or individuals who teach in an environment other than a classroom setting, and who maintain daily student attendance records. Numbers reported are full-time equivalents (FTE). *Source: U.S. Department of Education, National Center for Education Statistics, Common Core of Data, Local Education Agency (School District) Universe Survey: School Year 2011-2012.*

Number of Students: A student is an individual for whom instruction is provided in an elementary or secondary education program that is not an adult education program and is under the jurisdiction of a school, school system, or other education institution. *Sources: U.S. Department of Education, National Center for Education Statistics, Common Core of Data, Local Education Agency (School District) Universe Survey: School Year 2011-2012 and Public Elementary/Secondary School Universe Survey: School Year 2011-2012*

Individual Education Program (IEP) Students: A written instructional plan for students with disabilities designated as special education students under IDEA-Part B. The written instructional plan includes a statement of present levels of educational performance of a child; statement of annual goals, including short-term instructional objectives; statement of specific educational services to be provided and the extent to which the child will be able to participate in regular educational programs; the projected date for initiation and anticipated duration of services; the appropriate objectives, criteria and evaluation procedures; and the schedules for determining, on at least an annual basis, whether instructional objectives are being achieved. *Source: U.S. Department of Education, National Center for Education Statistics, Common Core of Data, Local Education Agency (School District) Universe Survey: School Year 2011-2012*

English Language Learner (ELL) Students: Formerly referred to as Limited English Proficient (LEP). Students being served in appropriate programs of language assistance (e.g., English as a Second Language, High Intensity Language Training, bilingual education). Does not include pupils enrolled in a class to learn a language other than English. Also Limited-English-Proficient students are individuals who were not born in the United States or whose native language is a language other than English; or individuals who come from environments where a language other than English is dominant; or individuals who are American Indians and Alaskan Natives and who come from environments where a language other than English has had a significant impact on their level of English language proficiency; and who, by reason thereof, have sufficient difficulty speaking, reading, writing, or understanding the English language, to deny such individuals the opportunity to learn successfully in classrooms where the language of instruction is English or to participate fully in our society. *Source: U.S. Department of Education, National Center for Education Statistics, Common Core of Data, Local Education Agency (School District) Universe Survey: School Year 2011-2012*

Students Eligible for Free Lunch Program: The free lunch program is defined as a program under the National School Lunch Act that provides cash subsidies for free lunches to students based on family size and income criteria. *Source: U.S. Department of Education, National Center for Education Statistics, Common Core of Data, Public Elementary/Secondary School Universe Survey: School Year 2011-2012*

Students Eligible for Reduced-Price Lunch Program: A student who is eligible to participate in the Reduced-Price Lunch Program under the National School Lunch Act. *Source: U.S. Department of Education, National Center for Education Statistics, Common Core of Data, Public Elementary/Secondary School Universe Survey: School Year 2011-2012*

Student/Teacher Ratio: The number of students divided by the number of teachers (FTE). See Number of Students and Number of Teachers above for for information.

Student/Librarian Ratio: The number of students divided by the number of library and media support staff. Library and media support staff are defined as staff members who render other professional library and media services; also includes library aides and those involved in library/media support. Their duties include selecting, preparing, caring for, and making available to instructional staff, equipment, films, filmstrips, transparencies, tapes, TV programs, and similar materials maintained separately or as part of an instructional materials center. Also included are activities in the audio-visual center, TV studio, related-work-study areas, and services provided by audio-visual personnel.

Numbers are based on full-time equivalents. *Source: U.S. Department of Education, National Center for Education Statistics, Common Core of Data, Local Education Agency (School District) Universe Survey: School Year 2011-2012.*

Student/Counselor Ratio: The number of students divided by the number of guidance counselors. Guidance counselors are professional staff assigned specific duties and school time for any of the following activities in an elementary or secondary setting: counseling with students and parents; consulting with other staff members on learning problems; evaluating student abilities; assisting students in making educational and career choices; assisting students in personal and social development; providing referral assistance; and/or working with other staff members in planning and conducting guidance programs for students. The state applies its own standards in apportioning the aggregate of guidance counselors/directors into the elementary and secondary level components. Numbers reported are full-time equivalents. *Source: U.S. Department of Education, National Center for Education Statistics, Common Core of Data, Local Education Agency (School District) Universe Survey: School Year 2011-2012.*

Current Spending per Student: Expenditure for Instruction, Support Services, and Other Elementary/Secondary Programs. Includes salaries, employee benefits, purchased services, and supplies, as well as payments made by states on behalf of school districts. Also includes transfers made by school districts into their own retirement system. Excludes expenditure for Non-Elementary/Secondary Programs, debt service, capital outlay, and transfers to other governments or school districts. This item is formally called "Current Expenditures for Public Elementary/Secondary Education."

Instruction: Includes payments from all funds for salaries, employee benefits, supplies, materials, and contractual services for elementary/secondary instruction. It excludes capital outlay, debt service, and interfund transfers for elementary/secondary instruction. Instruction covers regular, special, and vocational programs offered in both the regular school year and summer school. It excludes instructional support activities as well as adult education and community services. Instruction salaries includes salaries for teachers and teacher aides and assistants.

Support Services: Relates to support services functions (series 2000) defined in Financial Accounting for Local and State School Systems (National Center for Education Statistics 2000). Includes payments from all funds for salaries, employee benefits, supplies, materials, and contractual services. It excludes capital outlay, debt service, and interfund transfers. It includes expenditure for the following functions:

- Business/Central/Other Support Services
- General Administration
- Instructional Staff Support
- Operation and Maintenance
- Pupil Support Services
- Pupil Transportation Services
- School Administration
- Nonspecified Support Services

Values shown are dollars per pupil per year. They were calculated by dividing the total dollar amounts by the fall membership. Fall membership is comprised of the total student enrollment on October 1 (or the closest school day to October 1) for all grade levels (including prekindergarten and kindergarten) and ungraded pupils. Membership includes students both present and absent on the measurement day. *Source: U.S. Department of Education, National Center for Education Statistics, Common Core of Data, School District Finance Survey (F-33), Fiscal Year 2011.*

Drop-out Rate: A dropout is a student who was enrolled in school at some time during the previous school year; was not enrolled at the beginning of the current school year; has not graduated from high school or completed a state or district approved educational program; and does not meet any of the following exclusionary conditions: has transferred to another public school district, private school, or state- or district-approved educational program; is temporarily absent due to suspension or school-approved illness; or has died. The values shown cover grades 9 through 12. *Note: Drop-out rates are no longer available to the general public disaggregated by grade, race/ethnicity, and gender at the school district level. Beginning with the 2005–06 school year the CCD is reporting dropout data aggregated from the local education agency (district) level to the state level. This allows data users to compare event dropout rates across states, regions, and other jurisdictions. Source: U.S. Department of Education, National Center for Education Statistics, Common Core of Data, Local Education Agency (School District) Universe Survey Dropout and Completion Data, 2008-2009; U.S. Department of Education, National Center for Education Statistics, Common Core of Data, State Dropout and Completion Data File, 2009-2010*

Average Freshman Graduation Rate (AFGR): The AFGR is the number of regular diploma recipients in a given year divided by the average of the membership in grades 8, 9, and 10, reported 5, 4, and 3 years earlier, respectively. For example, the denominator of the 2008–09 AFGR is the average of the 8th-grade membership in 2004–05, 9th-grade membership in 2005–06, and 10th-grade membership in 2006–07. Ungraded students are prorated into these grades. Averaging these three grades provides an estimate of the number of first-time freshmen in the class of 2005–06 freshmen in order to estimate the on-time graduation rate for 2008–09.

Caution in interpreting the AFGR. Although the AFGR was selected as the best of the available alternatives, several factors make it fall short of a true on-time graduation rate. First, the AFGR does not take into account any imbalances in the number of students moving in and out of the nation or individual states over the high school years. As a result, the averaged freshman class is at best an approximation of the actual number of freshmen, where differences in the rates of transfers, retention, and dropping out in the three grades affect the average. Second, by including all graduates in a specific year, the graduates may include students who repeated a grade in high school or completed high school early and thus are not on-time graduates in that year. *Source: U.S. Department of Education, National Center for Education Statistics, Common Core of Data, Local Education Agency (School District) Universe Survey Dropout and Completion Data, 2008-2009; U.S. Department of Education, National Center for Education Statistics, Common Core of Data, State Dropout and Completion Data File, 2009-2010*

Number of Diploma Recipients: A student who has received a diploma during the previous school year or subsequent summer school. This category includes regular diploma recipients and other diploma recipients. A High School Diploma is a formal document certifying the successful completion of a secondary school program prescribed by the state education agency or other appropriate body. *Note: Diploma counts are no longer available to the general public disaggregated by grade, race/ethnicity, and gender at the school district level. Source: U.S. Department of Education, National Center for Education Statistics, Common Core of Data, Local Education Agency (School District) Universe Survey Dropout and Completion Data, 2008-2009; U.S. Department of Education, National Center for Education Statistics, Common Core of Data, State Dropout and Completion Data File, 2009-2010*

Note: n/a indicates data not available.

State Educational Profile

Please refer to the District Rankings section in the front of this User Guide for an explanation of data for all items except for the following:

Average Salary: The average salary for classroom teachers in 2013-2014. *Source: National Education Association, Rankings & Estimates: Rankings of the States 2013 and Estimates of School Statistics 2014*

College Entrance Exam Scores:

Scholastic Aptitude Test (SAT). *Note: Data covers all students during the 2013 school year. The College Board strongly discourages the comparison or ranking of states on the basis of SAT scores alone. Source: The College Board*

American College Testing Program (ACT). *Note: Data covers all students during the 2013 school year. Source: ACT, 2013 ACT National and State Scores*

National Assessment of Educational Progress (NAEP)

The National Assessment of Educational Progress (NAEP), also known as "the Nation's Report Card," is the only nationally representative and continuing assessment of what America's students know and can do in various subject areas. As a result of the "No Child Left Behind" legislation, all states are required to participate in NAEP.

For more information, visit the U.S. Department of Education, National Center for Education Statistics at http://nces.ed.gov/nationsreportcard.

Ancestry and Ethnicity Section

Places Covered

The ancestry and ethnicity profile section of this book covers the state and all counties and places with populations of 50,000 or more. Places included fall into one of the following categories:

Incorporated Places. Depending on the state, places are incorporated as either cities, towns, villages, boroughs, municipalities, independent cities, or corporations. A few municipalities have a form of government combined with another entity (e.g. county) and are listed as special cities or consolidated, unified, or metropolitan governments.

Census Designated Places (CDP). The U.S. Census Bureau defines a CDP as "a statistical entity," defined for each decennial census according to Census Bureau guidelines, comprising a densely settled concentration of population that is not within an incorporated place, but is locally identified by a name. CDPs are delineated cooperatively by state and local officials and the Census Bureau, following Census Bureau guidelines.

Minor Civil Divisions (called charter townships, districts, gores, grants, locations, plantations, purchases, reservations, towns, townships, and unorganized territories) for the states where the Census Bureau has determined that they serve as general-purpose governments. Those states are Connecticut, Maine, Massachusetts, Michigan, Minnesota, New Hampshire, New Jersey, New York, Pennsylvania, Rhode Island, Vermont, and Wisconsin. In some states incorporated municipalities are part of minor civil divisions and in some states they are independent of them.

Note: Several states have incorporated municipalities and minor civil divisions in the same county with the same name. Those communities are given separate entries (e.g. Burlington, New Jersey, in Burlington County will be listed under both the city and township of Burlington). A few states have Census Designated Places and minor civil divisions in the same county with the same name. Those communities are given separate entries (e.g. Bridgewater, Massachusetts, in Plymouth County will be listed under both the CDP and town of Bridgewater).

Source of Data

The ethnicities shown in this book were compiled from two different sources. Data for Race and Hispanic Origin was taken from Census 2010 Summary File 1 (SF1) while Ancestry data was taken from the American Community Survey (ACS) 2006-2010 Five-Year Estimate. The distinction is important because SF1 contains 100-percent data, which is the information compiled from the questions asked of all people and about every housing unit. ACS estimates are compiled from a sampling of households. The 2006-2010 Five-Year Estimate is based on data collected from January 1, 2006 to December 31, 2010.

The American Community Survey (ACS) is a relatively new survey conducted by the U.S. Census Bureau. It uses a series of monthly samples to produce annually updated data for the same small areas (census tracts and block groups) formerly surveyed via the decennial census long-form sample. While some version of this survey has been in the field since 1999, it was not fully implemented in terms of coverage until 2006. In 2005 it was expanded to cover all counties in the country and the 1-in-40 households sampling rate was first applied. The full implementation of the (household) sampling strategy for ACS entails having the survey mailed to about 250,000 households nationwide every month of every year and was begun in January 2005. In January 2006 sampling of group quarters was added to complete the sample as planned. In any given year about 2.5% (1 in 40) of U.S. households will receive the survey. Over any 5-year period about 1 in 8 households should receive the survey (as compared to about 1 in 6 that received the census long form in the 2000 census). Since receiving the survey is not the same as responding to it, the Bureau has adopted a strategy of sampling for non-response, resulting in something closer to 1 in 11 households actually participating in the survey over any 5-year period. For more information about the American Community Survey visit http://www.census.gov/acs/www.

Ancestry

Ancestry refers to a person's ethnic origin, heritage, descent, or "roots," which may reflect their place of birth or that of previous generations of their family. Some ethnic identities, such as "Egyptian" or "Polish" can be traced to geographic areas outside the United States, while other ethnicities such as "Pennsylvania German" or "Cajun" evolved in the United States.

The intent of the ancestry question in the ACS was not to measure the degree of attachment the respondent had to a particular ethnicity, but simply to establish that the respondent had a connection to and self-identified with a particular ethnic group. For example, a response of "Irish" might reflect total involvement in an Irish community or only a memory of ancestors several generations removed from the respondent.

The Census Bureau coded the responses into a numeric representation of over 1,000 categories. Responses initially were processed through an automated coding system; then, those that were not automatically assigned a code were coded by individuals trained in coding ancestry responses. The code list reflects the results of the Census Bureau's own research and consultations with many ethnic experts. Many decisions were made to determine the classification of responses. These decisions affected the grouping of the tabulated data. For example, the "Indonesian" category includes the responses of "Indonesian," "Celebesian," "Moluccan," and a number of other responses.

Ancestries Covered

Afghan	Palestinian	French, ex. Basque	Scottish
African, Sub-Saharan	Syrian	French Canadian	Serbian
African	Other Arab	German	Slavic
Cape Verdean	Armenian	German Russian	Slovak
Ethiopian	Assyrian/Chaldean/Syriac	Greek	Slovene
Ghanaian	Australian	Guyanese	Soviet Union
Kenyan	Austrian	Hungarian	Swedish
Liberian	Basque	Icelander	Swiss
Nigerian	Belgian	Iranian	Turkish
Senegalese	Brazilian	Irish	Ukrainian
Sierra Leonean	British	Israeli	Welsh
Somalian	Bulgarian	Italian	West Indian, ex.
South African	Cajun	Latvian	Hispanic
Sudanese	Canadian	Lithuanian	Bahamian
Ugandan	Carpatho Rusyn	Luxemburger	Barbadian
Zimbabwean	Celtic	Macedonian	Belizean
Other Sub-Saharan African	Croatian	Maltese	Bermudan
Albanian	Cypriot	New Zealander	British West Indian
Alsatian	Czech	Northern European	Dutch West Indian
American	Czechoslovakian	Norwegian	Haitian
Arab	Danish	Pennsylvania German	Jamaican
Arab	Dutch	Polish	Trinidadian/
Egyptian	Eastern European	Portuguese	Tobagonian
Iraqi	English	Romanian	U.S. Virgin Islander
Jordanian	Estonian	Russian	West Indian
Lebanese	European	Scandinavian	Other West Indian
Moroccan	Finnish	Scotch-Irish	Yugoslavian

The ancestry question allowed respondents to report one or more ancestry groups. Generally, only the first two responses reported were coded. If a response was in terms of a dual ancestry, for example, "Irish English," the person was assigned two codes, in this case one for Irish and another for English. However, in certain cases, multiple responses such as "French Canadian," "Scotch-Irish," "Greek Cypriot," and "Black Dutch" were assigned a single code reflecting their status as unique groups. If a person reported one of these unique groups in addition to another group, for example, "Scotch-Irish English," resulting in three terms, that person received one code for the unique group (Scotch-Irish) and another one for the remaining group (English). If a person reported "English Irish French," only English and Irish were coded. If there were more than two ancestries listed and one of the ancestries was a part of another, such as "German Bavarian Hawaiian," the responses were coded using the more detailed groups (Bavarian and Hawaiian).

The Census Bureau accepted "American" as a unique ethnicity if it was given alone or with one other ancestry. There were some groups such as "American Indian," "Mexican American," and "African American" that were coded and identified separately.

The ancestry question is asked for every person in the American Community Survey, regardless of age, place of birth, Hispanic origin, or race.

Although some people consider religious affiliation a component of ethnic identity, the ancestry question was not designed to collect any information concerning religion. Thus, if a religion was given as an answer to the ancestry question, it was listed in the "Other groups" category which is not shown in this book.

Ancestry should not be confused with a person's place of birth, although a person's place of birth and ancestry may be the same.

Hispanic Origin

The data on the Hispanic or Latino population were derived from answers to a Census 2010 question that was asked of all people. The terms "Spanish," "Hispanic origin," and "Latino" are used interchangeably. Some respondents identify with all three terms while others may identify with only one of these three specific terms. Hispanics or Latinos who identify with the terms "Spanish," "Hispanic," or "Latino" are those who classify themselves in one of the specific Spanish, Hispanic, or Latino categories listed on the questionnaire ("Mexican," "Puerto Rican," or "Cuban") as well as those who indicate that they are "other Spanish/Hispanic/Latino." People who do not identify with one of the specific origins listed on the questionnaire but indicate that they are "other Spanish/Hispanic/Latino" are those whose origins are from Spain, the Spanish-speaking countries of Central or South America, the Dominican Republic, or people identifying themselves generally as Spanish, Spanish-American, Hispanic, Hispano, Latino, and so on. All write-in responses to the "other Spanish/Hispanic/Latino" category were coded.

Hispanic Origins Covered

Hispanic or Latino	Salvadoran	Argentinean	Uruguayan
Central American, ex. Mexican	Other Central American	Bolivian	Venezuelan
Costa Rican	Cuban	Chilean	Other South American
Guatemalan	Dominican Republic	Colombian	Other Hispanic or Latino
Honduran	Mexican	Ecuadorian	
Nicaraguan	Puerto Rican	Paraguayan	
Panamanian	South American	Peruvian	

Origin can be viewed as the heritage, nationality group, lineage, or country of birth of the person or the person's parents or ancestors before their arrival in the United States. People who identify their origin as Hispanic, Latino, or Spanish may be of any race.

Ethnicities Based on Race

The data on race were derived from answers to the Census 2010 question on race that was asked of individuals in the United States. The Census Bureau collects racial data in accordance with guidelines provided by the U.S. Office of Management and Budget (OMB), and these data are based on self-identification.

The racial categories included in the census questionnaire generally reflect a social definition of race recognized in this country and not an attempt to define race biologically, anthropologically, or genetically. In addition, it is recognized that the categories of the race item include racial and national origin or sociocultural groups. People may choose to report more than one race to indicate their racial mixture, such as "American Indian" and "White." People who identify their origin as Hispanic, Latino, or Spanish may be of any race.

Racial Groups Covered

African-American/Black	Crow	Spanish American Indian	Korean
Not Hispanic	Delaware	Tlingit-Haida *(Alaska Native)*	Laotian
Hispanic	Hopi	Tohono O'Odham	Malaysian
American Indian/Alaska Native	Houma	Tsimshian *(Alaska Native)*	Nepalese
Not Hispanic	Inupiat *(Alaska Native)*	Ute	Pakistani
Hispanic	Iroquois	Yakama	Sri Lankan
Alaska Athabascan *(Ala. Nat.)*	Kiowa	Yaqui	Taiwanese
Aleut *(Alaska Native)*	Lumbee	Yuman	Thai
Apache	Menominee	Yup'ik *(Alaska Native)*	Vietnamese
Arapaho	Mexican American Indian	**Asian**	**Hawaii Native/Pacific Islander**
Blackfeet	Navajo	*Not Hispanic*	*Not Hispanic*
Canadian/French Am. Indian	Osage	*Hispanic*	*Hispanic*
Central American Indian	Ottawa	Bangladeshi	Fijian
Cherokee	Paiute	Bhutanese	Guamanian/Chamorro
Cheyenne	Pima	Burmese	Marshallese
Chickasaw	Potawatomi	Cambodian	Native Hawaiian
Chippewa	Pueblo	Chinese, ex. Taiwanese	Samoan
Choctaw	Puget Sound Salish	Filipino	Tongan
Colville	Seminole	Hmong	**White**
Comanche	Shoshone	Indian	*Not Hispanic*
Cree	Sioux	Indonesian	*Hispanic*
Creek	South American Indian	Japanese	

African American or Black: A person having origins in any of the Black racial groups of Africa. It includes people who indicated their race(s) as "Black, African Am., or Negro" or reported entries such as African American, Kenyan, Nigerian, or Haitian.

American Indian or Alaska Native: A person having origins in any of the original peoples of North and South America (including Central America) and who maintains tribal affiliation or community attachment. This category includes people who indicated their race(s) as "American Indian or Alaska Native" or reported their enrolled or principal tribe, such as Navajo, Blackfeet, Inupiat, Yup'ik, or Central American Indian groups or South American Indian groups.

Asian: A person having origins in any of the original peoples of the Far East, Southeast Asia, or the Indian subcontinent, including, for example, Cambodia, China, India, Japan, Korea, Malaysia, Pakistan, the Philippine Islands, Thailand, and Vietnam. It includes people who indicated their race(s) as "Asian" or reported entries such as "Asian Indian," "Chinese," "Filipino," "Korean," "Japanese," "Vietnamese," and "Other Asian" or provided other detailed Asian responses.

Native Hawaiian or Other Pacific Islander: A person having origins in any of the original peoples of Hawaii, Guam, Samoa, or other Pacific Islands. It includes people who indicated their race(s) as "Pacific Islander" or reported entries such as "Native Hawaiian," "Guamanian or Chamorro," "Samoan," and "Other Pacific Islander" or provided other detailed Pacific Islander responses.

White: A person having origins in any of the original peoples of Europe, the Middle East, or North Africa. It includes people who indicated their race(s) as "White" or reported entries such as Irish, German, Italian, Lebanese, Arab, Moroccan, or Caucasian.

Profiles

Each profile shows the name of the place, the county (if a place spans more than one county, the county that holds the majority of the population is shown), and the 2010 population (based on 100-percent data from Census 2010 Summary File 1). The rest of each profile is comprised of all 218 ethnicities grouped into three sections: ancestry; Hispanic origin; and race.

Column one displays the ancestry/Hispanic origin/race name, column two displays the number of people reporting each ancestry/Hispanic origin/race, and column three is the percent of the total population reporting each ancestry/Hispanic origin/race. The population figure shown is used to calculate the value in the "%" column for ethnicities based on race and Hispanic origin. The 2006-2010 estimated population figure from the American Community Survey (not shown) is used to calculate the value in the "%" column for all other ancestries.

For ethnicities in the ancestries group, the value in the "Number" column includes multiple ancestries reported. For example, if a person reported a multiple ancestry such as "French Danish," that response was counted twice in the tabulations, once in the French category and again in the Danish category. Thus, the sum of the counts is not the total population but the total of all responses. Numbers in parentheses indicate the number of people reporting a single ancestry. People reporting a single ancestry includes all people who reported only one ethnic group such as "German." Also included in this category are people with only a multiple-term response such as "Scotch-Irish" who are assigned a single code because they represent one distinct group. For example, the count for German would be interpreted as "The number of people who reported that German was their only ancestry."

For ethnicities based on Hispanic origin, the value in the "Number" column represents the number of people who reported being Mexican, Puerto Rican, Cuban or other Spanish/Hispanic/ Latino (all written-in responses were coded). All ethnicities based on Hispanic origin can be of any race.

For ethnicities based on race data the value in the "Number" column represents the total number of people who reported each category alone or in combination with one or more other race categories. This number represents the maximum number of people reporting and therefore the individual race categories may add up to more than the total population because people may be included in more than one category. The figures in parentheses show the number of people that reported that particular ethnicity alone, not in combination with any other race. For example, in Alabama, the entry for Korean shows 8,320 in parentheses and 10,624 in the "Number" column. This means that 8,320 people reported being Korean alone and 10,624 people reported being Korean alone or in combination with one or more other races.

Rankings

In the rankings section, each ethnicity has three tables. The first table shows the top 10 places sorted by ethnic population (based on all places, regardless of total population), the second table shows the top 10 places sorted by percent of the total population (based on all places, regardless of total population), the third table shows the top 10 places sorted by percent of the total population (based on places with total population of 50,000 or more).

Within each table, column one displays the place name, the state, and the county (if a place spans more than one county, the county that holds the majority of the population is shown). Column one in the first table displays the state only. Column two displays the number of people reporting each ancestry (includes people reporting multiple ancestries), Hispanic origin, or race (alone or in combination with any other race). Column three is the percent of the total population reporting each ancestry, Hispanic origin or race. For tables representing ethnicities based on race or Hispanic origin, the 100-percent population figure from SF1 is used to calculate the value in the "%" column. For all other ancestries, the 2006-2010 five-year estimated population figure from the American Community Survey is used to calculate the value in the "%" column.

Alphabetical Ethnicity Cross-Reference Guide

Afghan *see* Ancestry–Afghan
African *see* Ancestry–African, Sub-Saharan: African
African-American *see* Race–African-American/Black
African-American: Hispanic *see* Race–African-American/Black: Hispanic
African-American: Not Hispanic *see* Race–African-American/Black: Not Hispanic
Alaska Athabascan *see* Race–Alaska Native: Alaska Athabascan
Alaska Native *see* Race–American Indian/Alaska Native
Alaska Native: Hispanic *see* Race–American Indian/Alaska Native: Hispanic
Alaska Native: Not Hispanic *see* Race–American Indian/Alaska Native: Not Hispanic
Albanian *see* Ancestry–Albanian
Aleut *see* Race–Alaska Native: Aleut
Alsatian *see* Ancestry–Alsatian
American *see* Ancestry–American
American Indian *see* Race–American Indian/Alaska Native
American Indian: Hispanic *see* Race–American Indian/Alaska Native: Hispanic
American Indian: Not Hispanic *see* Race–American Indian/Alaska Native: Not Hispanic
Apache *see* Race–American Indian: Apache
Arab *see* Ancestry–Arab: Arab
Arab: Other *see* Ancestry–Arab: Other
Arapaho *see* Race–American Indian: Arapaho
Argentinean *see* Hispanic Origin–South American: Argentinean
Armenian *see* Ancestry–Armenian
Asian *see* Race–Asian
Asian Indian *see* Race–Asian: Indian
Asian: Hispanic *see* Race–Asian: Hispanic
Asian: Not Hispanic *see* Race–Asian: Not Hispanic
Assyrian *see* Ancestry–Assyrian/Chaldean/Syriac
Australian *see* Ancestry–Australian
Austrian *see* Ancestry–Austrian
Bahamian *see* Ancestry–West Indian: Bahamian, except Hispanic
Bangladeshi *see* Race–Asian: Bangladeshi
Barbadian *see* Ancestry–West Indian: Barbadian, except Hispanic
Basque *see* Ancestry–Basque
Belgian *see* Ancestry–Belgian
Belizean *see* Ancestry–West Indian: Belizean, except Hispanic
Bermudan *see* Ancestry–West Indian: Bermudan, except Hispanic
Bhutanese *see* Race–Asian: Bhutanese
Black *see* Race–African-American/Black
Black: Hispanic *see* Race–African-American/Black: Hispanic
Black: Not Hispanic *see* Race–African-American/Black: Not Hispanic
Blackfeet *see* Race–American Indian: Blackfeet
Bolivian *see* Hispanic Origin–South American: Bolivian
Brazilian *see* Ancestry–Brazilian
British *see* Ancestry–British

British West Indian *see* Ancestry–West Indian: British West Indian, except Hispanic
Bulgarian *see* Ancestry–Bulgarian
Burmese *see* Race–Asian: Burmese
Cajun *see* Ancestry–Cajun
Cambodian *see* Race–Asian: Cambodian
Canadian *see* Ancestry–Canadian
Canadian/French American Indian *see* Race–American Indian: Canadian/French American Indian
Cape Verdean *see* Ancestry–African, Sub-Saharan: Cape Verdean
Carpatho Rusyn *see* Ancestry–Carpatho Rusyn
Celtic *see* Ancestry–Celtic
Central American *see* Hispanic Origin–Central American, except Mexican
Central American Indian *see* Race–American Indian: Central American Indian
Central American: Other *see* Hispanic Origin–Central American: Other Central American
Chaldean *see* Ancestry–Assyrian/Chaldean/Syriac
Chamorro *see* Race–Hawaii Native/Pacific Islander: Guamanian or Chamorro
Cherokee *see* Race–American Indian: Cherokee
Cheyenne *see* Race–American Indian: Cheyenne
Chickasaw *see* Race–American Indian: Chickasaw
Chilean *see* Hispanic Origin–South American: Chilean
Chinese (except Taiwanese) *see* Race–Asian: Chinese, except Taiwanese
Chippewa *see* Race–American Indian: Chippewa
Choctaw *see* Race–American Indian: Choctaw
Colombian *see* Hispanic Origin–South American: Colombian
Colville *see* Race–American Indian: Colville
Comanche *see* Race–American Indian: Comanche
Costa Rican *see* Hispanic Origin–Central American: Costa Rican
Cree *see* Race–American Indian: Cree
Creek *see* Race–American Indian: Creek
Croatian *see* Ancestry–Croatian
Crow *see* Race–American Indian: Crow
Cuban *see* Hispanic Origin–Cuban
Cypriot *see* Ancestry–Cypriot
Czech *see* Ancestry–Czech
Czechoslovakian *see* Ancestry–Czechoslovakian
Danish *see* Ancestry–Danish
Delaware *see* Race–American Indian: Delaware
Dominican Republic *see* Hispanic Origin–Dominican Republic
Dutch *see* Ancestry–Dutch
Dutch West Indian *see* Ancestry–West Indian: Dutch West Indian, except Hispanic
Eastern European *see* Ancestry–Eastern European
Ecuadorian *see* Hispanic Origin–South American: Ecuadorian
Egyptian *see* Ancestry–Arab: Egyptian
English *see* Ancestry–English
Eskimo *see* Race–Alaska Native: Inupiat
Estonian *see* Ancestry–Estonian
Ethiopian *see* Ancestry–African, Sub-Saharan: Ethiopian
European *see* Ancestry–European
Fijian *see* Race–Hawaii Native/Pacific Islander: Fijian
Filipino *see* Race–Asian: Filipino
Finnish *see* Ancestry–Finnish
French (except Basque) *see* Ancestry–French, except Basque
French Canadian *see* Ancestry–French Canadian
German *see* Ancestry–German
German Russian *see* Ancestry–German Russian
Ghanaian *see* Ancestry–African, Sub-Saharan: Ghanaian
Greek *see* Ancestry–Greek
Guamanian *see* Race–Hawaii Native/Pacific Islander: Guamanian or Chamorro
Guatemalan *see* Hispanic Origin–Central American: Guatemalan
Guyanese *see* Ancestry–Guyanese
Haitian *see* Ancestry–West Indian: Haitian, except Hispanic
Hawaii Native *see* Race–Hawaii Native/Pacific Islander
Hawaii Native: Hispanic *see* Race–Hawaii Native/Pacific Islander: Hispanic

Hawaii Native: Not Hispanic *see* Race–Hawaii Native/Pacific Islander: Not Hispanic
Hispanic or Latino: *see* Hispanic Origin–Hispanic or Latino (of any race)
Hispanic or Latino: Other *see* Hispanic Origin–Other Hispanic or Latino
Hmong *see* Race–Asian: Hmong
Honduran *see* Hispanic Origin–Central American: Honduran
Hopi *see* Race–American Indian: Hopi
Houma *see* Race–American Indian: Houma
Hungarian *see* Ancestry–Hungarian
Icelander *see* Ancestry–Icelander
Indonesian *see* Race–Asian: Indonesian
Inupiat *see* Race–Alaska Native: Inupiat
Iranian *see* Ancestry–Iranian
Iraqi *see* Ancestry–Arab: Iraqi
Irish *see* Ancestry–Irish
Iroquois *see* Race–American Indian: Iroquois
Israeli *see* Ancestry–Israeli
Italian *see* Ancestry–Italian
Jamaican *see* Ancestry–West Indian: Jamaican, except Hispanic
Japanese *see* Race–Asian: Japanese
Jordanian *see* Ancestry–Arab: Jordanian
Kenyan *see* Ancestry–African, Sub-Saharan: Kenyan
Kiowa *see* Race–American Indian: Kiowa
Korean *see* Race–Asian: Korean
Laotian *see* Race–Asian: Laotian
Latvian *see* Ancestry–Latvian
Lebanese *see* Ancestry–Arab: Lebanese
Liberian *see* Ancestry–African, Sub-Saharan: Liberian
Lithuanian *see* Ancestry–Lithuanian
Lumbee *see* Race–American Indian: Lumbee
Luxemburger *see* Ancestry–Luxemburger
Macedonian *see* Ancestry–Macedonian
Malaysian *see* Race–Asian: Malaysian
Maltese *see* Ancestry–Maltese
Marshallese *see* Race–Hawaii Native/Pacific Islander: Marshallese
Menominee *see* Race–American Indian: Menominee
Mexican *see* Hispanic Origin–Mexican
Mexican American Indian *see* Race–American Indian: Mexican American Indian
Moroccan *see* Ancestry–Arab: Moroccan
Native Hawaiian *see* Race–Hawaii Native/Pacific Islander: Native Hawaiian
Navajo *see* Race–American Indian: Navajo
Nepalese *see* Race–Asian: Nepalese
New Zealander *see* Ancestry–New Zealander
Nicaraguan *see* Hispanic Origin–Central American: Nicaraguan
Nigerian *see* Ancestry–African, Sub-Saharan: Nigerian
Northern European *see* Ancestry–Northern European
Norwegian *see* Ancestry–Norwegian
Osage *see* Race–American Indian: Osage
Ottawa *see* Race–American Indian: Ottawa
Pacific Islander *see* Race–Hawaii Native/Pacific Islander
Pacific Islander: Hispanic *see* Race–Hawaii Native/Pacific Islander: Hispanic
Pacific Islander: Not Hispanic *see* Race–Hawaii Native/Pacific Islander: Not Hispanic
Paiute *see* Race–American Indian: Paiute
Pakistani *see* Race–Asian: Pakistani
Palestinian *see* Ancestry–Arab: Palestinian
Panamanian *see* Hispanic Origin–Central American: Panamanian
Paraguayan *see* Hispanic Origin–South American: Paraguayan
Pennsylvania German *see* Ancestry–Pennsylvania German
Peruvian *see* Hispanic Origin–South American: Peruvian
Pima *see* Race–American Indian: Pima
Polish *see* Ancestry–Polish
Portuguese *see* Ancestry–Portuguese
Potawatomi *see* Race–American Indian: Potawatomi

Pueblo see Race–American Indian: Pueblo
Puerto Rican see Hispanic Origin–Puerto Rican
Puget Sound Salish see Race–American Indian: Puget Sound Salish
Romanian see Ancestry–Romanian
Russian see Ancestry–Russian
Salvadoran see Hispanic Origin–Central American: Salvadoran
Samoan see Race–Hawaii Native/Pacific Islander: Samoan
Scandinavian see Ancestry–Scandinavian
Scotch-Irish see Ancestry–Scotch-Irish
Scottish see Ancestry–Scottish
Seminole see Race–American Indian: Seminole
Senegalese see Ancestry–African, Sub-Saharan: Senegalese
Serbian see Ancestry–Serbian
Shoshone see Race–American Indian: Shoshone
Sierra Leonean see Ancestry–African, Sub-Saharan: Sierra Leonean
Sioux see Race–American Indian: Sioux
Slavic see Ancestry–Slavic
Slovak see Ancestry–Slovak
Slovene see Ancestry–Slovene
Somalian see Ancestry–African, Sub-Saharan: Somalian
South African see Ancestry–African, Sub-Saharan: South African
South American see Hispanic Origin–South American
South American Indian see Race–American Indian: South American Indian
South American: Other see Hispanic Origin–South American: Other South American
Soviet Union see Ancestry–Soviet Union
Spanish American Indian see Race–American Indian: Spanish American Indian
Sri Lankan see Race–Asian: Sri Lankan
Sub-Saharan African see Ancestry–African, Sub-Saharan
Sub-Saharan African: Other see Ancestry–African, Sub-Saharan: Other
Sudanese see Ancestry–African, Sub-Saharan: Sudanese
Swedish see Ancestry–Swedish
Swiss see Ancestry–Swiss
Syriac see Ancestry–Assyrian/Chaldean/Syriac
Syrian see Ancestry–Arab: Syrian
Taiwanese see Race–Asian: Taiwanese
Thai see Race–Asian: Thai
Tlingit-Haida see Race–Alaska Native: Tlingit-Haida
Tohono O'Odham see Race–American Indian: Tohono O'Odham
Tongan see Race–Hawaii Native/Pacific Islander: Tongan
Trinidadian and Tobagonian see Ancestry–West Indian: Trinidadian and Tobagonian, except Hispanic
Tsimshian see Race–Alaska Native: Tsimshian
Turkish see Ancestry–Turkish
U.S. Virgin Islander see Ancestry–West Indian: U.S. Virgin Islander, except Hispanic
Ugandan see Ancestry–African, Sub-Saharan: Ugandan
Ukrainian see Ancestry–Ukrainian
Uruguayan see Hispanic Origin–South American: Uruguayan
Ute see Race–American Indian: Ute
Venezuelan see Hispanic Origin–South American: Venezuelan
Vietnamese see Race–Asian: Vietnamese
Welsh see Ancestry–Welsh
West Indian see Ancestry–West Indian: West Indian, except Hispanic
West Indian (except Hispanic) see Ancestry–West Indian, except Hispanic
West Indian: Other see Ancestry–West Indian: Other, except Hispanic
White see Race–White
White: Hispanic see Race–White: Hispanic
White: Not Hispanic see Race–White: Not Hispanic
Yakama see Race–American Indian: Yakama
Yaqui see Race–American Indian: Yaqui
Yugoslavian see Ancestry–Yugoslavian
Yuman see Race–American Indian: Yuman
Yup'ik see Race–Alaska Native: Yup'ik
Zimbabwean see Ancestry–African, Sub-Saharan: Zimbabwean

Climate Section

SOURCES OF THE DATA

The National Climactic Data Center (NCDC) has two main classes or types of weather stations; first-order stations which are staffed by professional meteorologists and cooperative stations which are staffed by volunteers. All National Weather Service (NWS) stations included in this book are first-order stations.

The data in the climate section is compiled from several sources. The majority comes from the original NCDC computer tapes (DSI-3220 Summary of Month Cooperative). This data was used to create the entire table for each cooperative station and part of each National Weather Service station. The remainder of the data for each NWS station comes from the International Station Meteorological Climate Summary, Version 4.0, September 1996, which is also available from the NCDC.

Storm events come from the NCDC Storm Events Database which is accessible over the Internet at https://www.ncdc.noaa.gov/stormevents.

WEATHER STATION TABLES

The weather station tables are grouped by type (National Weather Service and Cooperative) and then arranged alphabetically. The station name is almost always a place name, and is shown here just as it appears in NCDC data. The station name is followed by the county in which the station is located (or by county equivalent name), the elevation of the station (at the time beginning of the thirty year period) and the latitude and longitude.

The National Weather Service Station tables contain 32 data elements which were compiled from two different sources, the International Station Meteorological Climate Summary (ISMCS) and NCDC DSI-3220 data tapes. The following 13 elements are from the ISMCS: maximum precipitation, minimum precipitation, maximum snowfall, maximum 24-hour snowfall, thunderstorm days, foggy days, predominant sky cover, relative humidity (morning and afternoon), dewpoint, wind speed and direction, and maximum wind gust. The remaining 19 elements come from the DSI-3220 data tapes. The period of record (POR) for data from the DSI-3220 data tapes is 1980-2009. The POR for ISMCS data varies from station to station and appears in a note below each station.

The Cooperative Station tables contain 19 data elements which were all compiled from the DSI-3220 data tapes with a POR of 1980-2009.

WEATHER ELEMENTS (NWS AND COOPERATIVE STATIONS)

The following elements were compiled by the editor from the NCDC DSI-3220 data tapes using a period of record of 1980-2009.

The average temperatures (maximum, minimum, and mean) are the average (see Methodology below) of those temperatures for all available values for a given month. For example, for a given station the average maximum temperature for July is the arithmetic average of all available maximum July temperatures for that station. (Maximum means the highest recorded temperature, minimum means the lowest recorded temperature, and mean means an arithmetic average temperature.)

The extreme maximum temperature is the highest temperature recorded in each month over the period 1980-2009. The extreme minimum temperature is the lowest temperature recorded in each month over the same time period. The extreme maximum daily precipitation is the largest amount of precipitation recorded over a 24-hour period in each month from 1980-2009. The maximum snow depth is the maximum snow depth recorded in each month over the period 1980-2009.

The days for maximum temperature and minimum temperature are the average number of days those criteria were met for all available instances. The symbol ≥ means greater than or equal to, the symbol ≤ means less than or equal to. For example, for a given station, the number of days the maximum temperature was greater than or equal to 90°F in July, is just an arithmetic average of the number of days in all the available Julys for that station.

Heating and cooling degree days are based on the median temperature for a given day and its variance from 65°F. For example, for a given station if the day's high temperature was 50°F and the day's low temperature was 30°F, the median (midpoint) temperature was 40°F. 40°F is 25 degrees below 65°F, hence on this day there would be 25 heating degree days. This also applies for cooling degree days. For example, for a given station if the day's high temperature was 80°F and the day's low temperature was 70°F, the median (midpoint) temperature was 75°F. 75°F is 10 degrees above 65°F, hence on this day there would be 10 cooling degree days. All heating and/or cooling degree days in a month are summed for the month giving respective totals for each element for that month. These sums for a given month for a given station over the past thirty years are again summed and then arithmetically averaged. It should be noted that the heating and cooling degree days do not cancel each other out. It is possible to have both for a given station in the same month.

Precipitation data is computed the same as heating and cooling degree days. Mean precipitation and mean snowfall are arithmetic averages of cumulative totals for the month. All available values for the thirty year period for a given month for a given station are summed and then divided by the number of values. The same is true for days of greater than or equal to 0.1", 0.5",and 1.0" of precipitation, and days of greater than or equal to 1.0" of snow depth on the ground. The word trace appears for precipitation and snowfall amounts that are too small to measure.

Finally, remember that all values presented in the tables and the rankings are averages, maximums, or minimums of available data (see Methodology below) for that specific data element for the last thirty years (1980-2009).

WEATHER ELEMENTS (NWS STATIONS ONLY)

The following elements were taken directly from the International Station Meteorological Climate Summary. The periods of records vary per station and are noted at the bottom of each table.

Maximum precipitation, minimum precipitation, maximum snowfall, maximum snow depth, maximum 24-hour snowfall, thunderstorm days, foggy days, relative humidity (morning and afternoon), dewpoint, prevailing wind speed and direction, and maximum wind gust are all self-explanatory.

The word trace appears for precipitation and snowfall amounts that are too small to measure.

Predominant sky cover contains four possible entries: CLR (clear); SCT (scattered); BRK (broken); and OVR (overcast).

INCLUSION CRITERIA—HOW STATIONS WERE SELECTED

The basic criteria is that a station must have data for temperature, precipitation, heating and cooling degree days of sufficient quantity in order to create a meaningful average. More specifically, the definition of sufficiency here has two parts. First, there must be 22 values for a given data element, and second, ten of the nineteen elements included in the table must pass this sufficiency test. For example, in regard to mean maximum temperature (the first element on every data table), a given station needs to have a value for every month of at least 22 of the last thirty years in order to meet the criteria, and, in addition, every station included must have at least ten of the nineteen elements with at least this minimal level of completeness in order to fulfill the criteria. We then removed stations that were geographically close together, giving preference to stations with better data quality.

METHODOLOGY

The following discussion applies only to data compiled from the NCDC DSI-3220 data tapes and excludes weather elements that are extreme maximums or minimums.

The data is based on an arithmetic average of all available data for a specific data element at a given station. For example, the average maximum daily high temperature during July for any given station was abstracted from NCDC source tapes for the thirty Julys, starting in July, 1980 and ending in July, 2009. These thirty figures were then summed and divided by thirty to produce an arithmetic average. As might be expected, there were not thirty values for every data element on every table. For a variety of reasons, NCDC data is sometimes incomplete. Thus the following standards were established.

For those data elements where there were 26-30 values, the data was taken to be essentially complete and an average was computed. For data elements where there were 22-25 values, the data was taken as being partly complete but still valid enough to use to compute an average. Such averages are shown in ***bold italic*** type to indicate that there was less than 26 values. For the few data elements where there were not even 22 values, no average was computed and 'na' appears in the space. If any of the twelve months for a given data element reported a value of 'na', no annual average was computed and the annual average was reported as 'na' as well.

Thus the basic computational methodology used is designed to provide an arithmetic average. Because of this, such a pure arithmetic average is somewhat different from the special type of average (called a "normal") which NCDC procedures produces and appears in federal publications.

Perhaps the best outline of the contrasting normalization methodology is found in the following paragraph (which appears as part of an NCDC technical document titled, CLIM81 1961-1990 NORMALS TD-9641 prepared by Lewis France of NCDC in May, 1992):

Normals have been defined as the arithmetic mean of a climatological element computed over a long time period. International agreements eventually led to the decision that the appropriate time period would be three consecutive decades (Guttman, 1989). The data record should be consistent (have no changes in location, instruments, observation practices, etc.; these are identified here as "exposure changes") and have no missing values so a normal will reflect the actual average climatic conditions. If any significant exposure changes have occurred, the data record is said to be "inhomogeneous," and the normal may not reflect a true climatic average. Such data need to be adjusted to remove the nonclimatic inhomogeneities. The resulting (adjusted) record is then said to be "homogeneous." If no exposure changes have occurred at a station, the normal is calculated simply by averaging the appropriate 30 values from the 1961-1990 record.

In the main, there are two "inhomogeneities" that NCDC is correcting for with normalization: adjusting for variances in time of day of observation (at the so-called First Order stations data is based on midnight to midnight observation times and this practice is not necessarily followed at cooperative stations which are staffed by volunteers), and second, estimating data that is either missing or incongruent.

The editors had some concerns regarding the comparative results of the two methodologies. Would our methodology produce strikingly different results than NCDC's? To allay concerns, results of the two processes were compared for the time period normalized results are available (1971-2000). In short, what was found was that the answer to this question is no. Never the less, users should be aware that because of both the time period covered (1980-2009) and the methodology used, data is not compatible with data from other sources.

POTENTIAL CAUTIONS

First, as with any statistical reference work of this type, users need to be aware of the source of the data. The information here comes from NOAA, and it is the most comprehensive and reliable core data available. Although it is the best, it is not perfect. Most weather stations are staffed by volunteers, times of observation sometimes vary, stations occasionally are moved (especially over a thirty year period), equipment is changed or upgraded, and all of these factors affect the uniformity of the data. The editors do not attempt to correct for these factors, and this data is not intended for either climatologists or atmospheric scientists. Users with concerns about data collection and reporting protocols are both referred to NCDC technical documentation.

Second, users need to be aware of the methodology here which is described above. Although this methodology has produced fully satisfactory results, it is not directly compatible with other methodologies, hence variances in the results published here and those which appear in other publications will doubtlessly arise.

Third, is the trap of that informal logical fallacy known as "hasty generalization," and its corollaries. This may involve presuming the future will be like the past (specifically, next year will be an average year), or it may involve misunderstanding the limitations of an arithmetic average, but more interestingly, it may involve those mistakes made most innocently by generalizing informally on too broad a basis. As weather is highly localized, the data should be taken in that context. A weather station collects data about climatic conditions at that spot, and that spot may or may not be an effective paradigm for an entire town or area.

About Indiana

Governor	**Michael Richard "Mike" Pence (R)**
Lieutenant Governor	**Sue Ellspermann (R)**
State Capital	Indianapolis
Date of Statehood	December 11, 1816 (19th state)
Before Statehood	Indiana Territory
Largest City	Indianapolis
Demonym	Hoosier (official)
Highest Point	Hoosier Hill (1,257 feet)
Lowest Point	Confluence of Ohio River and Wabash River (320 feet)
Time Zone	Eastern (80 counties); Central (12 counties)
State Emblems	
State Bird	Cardinal *(Richmondena cardinalis cardinalis)*
State Flower	Peony *(Paeonia)*
State Motto	"The Crossroads of America"
State Nickname	"The Hoosier State"
State Poem	"Indiana" by Arthur Franklin Mapes
State River	Wabash River
State Song	"On the Banks of the Wabash, Far Away" by Paul Dresser
State Stone	Salem Limestone
State Tree	Tulip Tree *(Liriodendron tulipifera)*

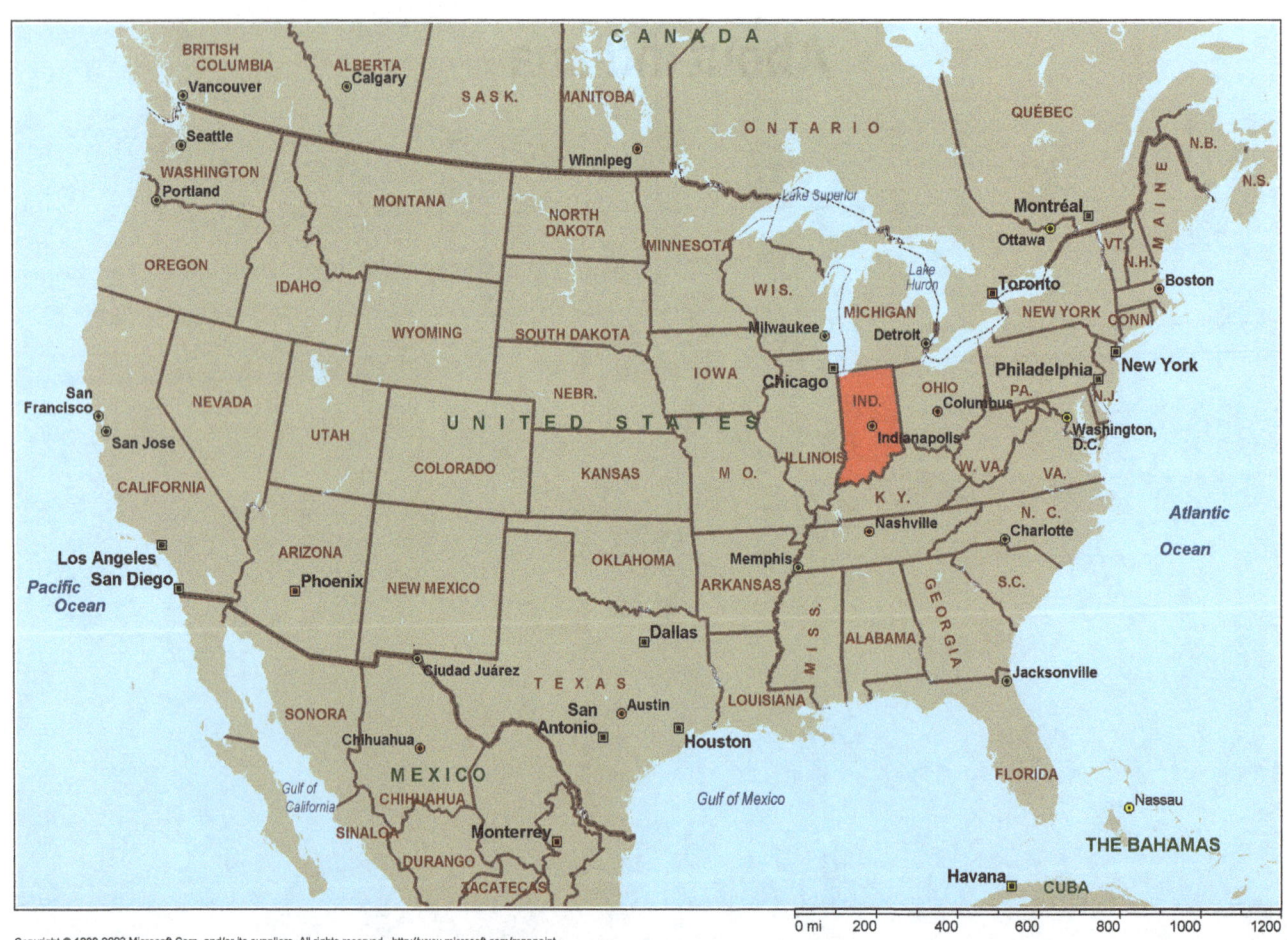

Profiles of Indiana — Photo Gallery 3

Indianapolis, top, is the capital of Indiana and the 12th largest city in the United States. The bottom photo shows University Hall of Purdue University in West Layfayette, Indiana. Founded in 1869, Purdue is a member of the Big Ten Conference and a world class research institution. Source: Wikimedia Commons; Author: Abhijitsathe.

Fort Wayne is the county seat of Allen County and the second largest city in Indiana. The top photo shows the Fort Wayne Courthouse. The Spencer Park Dentzel Carousel, bottom, was brought to Indiana in 1917. The carousel, a National Historic Landmark, is housed in The Children's Museum of Indianapolis, and its animals were built before 1900. Source: Wikimedia Commons; Author: Kevin Burkett.

Indiana has its share of natural beauty. Brown County State Park, top, one of the larger state parks in the United States, is Indiana's most visited, and known for scenic views of the hills of southern Indiana. Indiana Dunes National Lakeshore, bottom, runs for nearly 25 miles along the southern shore of Lake Michigan in Beverly Shores in northwest Indiana, and includes the Indiana Dunes State Park.

The William Henry Harrison Mansion and Museum in Vincennes, above, was built in 1804 for Harrison during his term as Governor, and dubbed Gouseland for the many grouse in the area. The vast domed atrium of the West Baden Springs Hotel, bottom, built in 1902, was the largest free-spanning dome in the world until 1913 and in the US until 1955. Both the resort, known for its mineral baths, and Grouseland are National Historic Landmarks. Source: Wikimedia Commons; Author: Sarah Wilkerson Poole, Bedford, USA.

The Indiana Soldiers' and Sailors' Monument, just over 284 feet, stands in Monument Circle in the center of Indianapolis. Designed by German architect Bruno Schmitz, it was completed in 1901 to honor Hoosiers who served from the American Revolution to the Spanish American War.

The Indianapolis Motor Speedway hosts the Indy 500, the largest single-day sporting event in the world with more than 257,000 permanent seats. Called the Brickyard because it was paved with 3.2 million bricks in 1909, the track is now paved in asphalt, except for a one-yard strip at the start/finish line. This photo shows the track's scoring pylon.

This Basilica of the Sacred Heart is part of the University of Nortre Dame, a Catholic research university just north of the city of South Bend. Founded in 1842 as an all-male institution, it began enrolling women in 1972. It is considered one of the "Big Three" universities in American Roman Catholic higher education and its athletic teams are members of the NCAA Division I, and known as the Fighting Irish. Source: Wikimedia Commons; Author: Michael Fernandes.

A Brief History of Indiana

Aboriginal Inhabitants

The first inhabitants in what is now Indiana were the Paleo-Indians, who arrived about 8000 BC after the melting of the glaciers at the end of the Ice Age. Divided into small groups, the Paleo-Indians were nomads who hunted large game such as mastodons. They created stone tools made out of chert by chipping, knapping and flaking. The Archaic period, which began between 5000 and 4000 BC, covered the next phase of indigenous culture. The people developed new tools as well as techniques to cook food, an important step in civilization. Such new tools included different types of spear points and knives, with various forms of notches. They made ground-stone tools such as stone axes, woodworking tools and grinding stones. During the latter part of the period, they built earthwork mounds and middens, which showed that settlements were becoming more permanent. The Archaic period ended at about 1500 BC, although some Archaic people lived until 700 BC. Afterward, the Woodland period took place in Indiana, where various new cultural attributes appeared. During this period, the people created ceramics and pottery, and extended their cultivation of plants. An early Woodland period group named the Adena people had elegant burial rituals, featuring log tombs beneath earth mounds. In the middle portion of the Woodland period, the Hopewell people began developing long-range trade of goods. Nearing the end of the stage, the people developed highly productive cultivation and adaptation of agriculture, growing such crops as corn and squash. The Woodland period ended around 1000 AD. The Mississippian culture emerged, lasting from 1000 until the 15th century, shortly before the arrival of Europeans. During this stage, the people created large urban settlements designed according to their cosmology, with large mounds and plazas defining ceremonial and public spaces. The concentrated settlements depended on the agricultural surpluses. One such complex was the Angel Mounds. They had large public areas such as plazas and platform mounds, where leaders lived or conducted rituals. Mississippian civilization collapsed in Indiana during the mid-15th century for reasons that remain unclear. The historic Native American tribes in the area at the time of European encounter spoke different languages of the Algonquian family. They included the Shawnee, Miami, and Illini. Later they were joined by refugee tribes from eastern regions including the Delaware who settled in the White and Whitewater River Valleys.

European Exploration and Sovereignty

In 1679 the French explorer René-Robert Cavelier, Sieur de La Salle was the first European to cross into Indiana after reaching present-day South Bend at the Saint Joseph River. He returned the following year to learn about the region. French-Canadian fur traders soon arrived, bringing blankets, jewelry, tools, whiskey and weapons to trade for skins with the Native Americans. By 1702, Sieur Juchereau established the first trading post near Vincennes. In 1715, Sieur de Vincennes built Fort Miami at Kekionga, now Fort Wayne. In 1717, another Canadian, Picote de Beletre, built Fort Ouiatenon on the Wabash River, to try to control Native American trade routes from Lake Erie to the Mississippi River. In 1732, Sieur de Vincennes built a second fur trading post at Vincennes. French Canadian settlers, who had left the earlier post because of hostilities, returned in larger numbers. In a period of a few years, British colonists arrived from the East and contended against the Canadians for control of the lucrative fur trade. Fighting between the French and British colonists occurred throughout the 1750s as a result.

The Native American tribes of Indiana sided with the French Canadians during the French and Indian War (also known as the Seven Years' War). With British victory in 1763, the French were forced to cede all their lands in North America east of the Mississippi River and north and west of the colonies to the British crown.

The tribes in Indiana did not give up; they destroyed Fort Ouiatenon and Fort Miami during Pontiac's Rebellion. The British royal proclamation of 1763 designated the land west of the Appalachians for Indian use, and excluded British colonists from the area, which the Crown called Indian Territory. In 1775, the American Revolutionary War began as the colonists sought for more self-government and independence from the British. The majority of the fighting took place near the East Coast, but the Patriot military officer George Rogers Clark called for an army to help fight the British in the west. Clark's army won significant battles and took over Vincennes and Fort Sackville on February 25, 1779. During the war, Clark managed to cut off British troops who were attacking the eastern colonists from the west. His success is often credited for changing the course of the American Revolutionary War. At the end of the war, through the Treaty of Paris, the British crown ceded their claims to the land south of the Great Lakes to the newly formed United States, including American Indian lands.

The Frontier

In 1787 the US defined present-day Indiana as part of its Northwest Territory. In 1800, Congress separated Ohio from the Northwest Territory, designating the rest of the land as the Indiana Territory. President Thomas Jefferson chose William Henry Harrison as the governor of the territory and Vincennes was established as the capital. After Michigan Territory was separated and the Illinois Territory was formed, Indiana was reduced to its current size and geography.

Starting with the Battle of Fallen Timbers in 1794 and Treaty of Greenville, 1795, Indian titles to Indiana lands were extinguished by usurpation, purchase, or war and treaty. About half the state was acquired in the St. Mary's Purchase from the Miami in 1818. Purchases weren't complete until the Treaty of Mississinwas in 1826 acquired the last of the reserved Indian lands in the northeast.

A portrait of the Indiana frontier about 1810: The frontier was defined by the treaty of Fort Wayne in 1809, adding much of southwestern lands around Vincinnes and southeastern lands adjacent to Cincinnati, to areas along the Ohio River as part of U.S. territory. Settlements were military outposts, Fort Ouiatenon in the northwest and Fort Miami (later Fort Wayne) in the northeast, Fort Knox and Vincinnes settlement on the lower Wabash, Clarksville (across from Louisville), Vevay, and Corydon along the Ohio River, the Quaker Colony in Richmond on the eastern border, and Conner's Post (later Connersville) on the east central frontier. Indianapolis wouldn't be a populated place for 15 more years, and central and northern Indiana Territory remained savage wilderness. Indian presence was waning, but still a threat to settlement. Only two counties, Clark and Dearborn in the extreme southeast, had been organized. Land titles issued out of Cincinnati were sparse. Migration was chiefly by flatboat on the Ohio River westerly, and wagon trails up the Wabash/White River Valleys (west) and Whitewater River Valleys (east).

In 1810, the Shawnee chief Tecumseh and his brother Tenskwatawa encouraged other tribes in the territory to resist European settlement. Tensions rose and the US authorized Harrison to launch a preemptive expedition against Tecumseh's Confederacy; the US gained victory at the Battle of Tippecanoe on November 7, 1811. Tecumseh was killed in 1813 during the Battle of Thames. After his death, armed resistance to United States control ended in the region. Most Native American tribes in the state were later removed to west of the Mississippi River in the 1820s and 1830s after US negotiations and purchase of their lands.

Statehood and Settlement

In order to decrease the threat of Indian raids following the Battle of Tippecanoe, Corydon, a town in the far southern part of Indiana, was named the second capital of the Indiana Territory in May 1813. Two years later, a petition for statehood was approved by the territorial general assembly and sent to Congress. An Enabling Act was passed to provide an election of delegates to write a constitution for Indiana. On June 10, 1816, delegates assembled at Corydon to write the constitution, which was completed in 19 days. President James Madison approved Indiana's admission into the union as the nineteenth state on December 11, 1816. In 1825, the state capital was moved from Corydon to Indianapolis.

Many European immigrants went west to settle in Indiana in the early 19th century. The largest immigrant group to settle in Indiana were Germans, as well as numerous immigrants from Ireland and England. Americans who were primarily ethnically English migrated from the Northern Tier of New York and New England, as well as the mid-Atlantic state of Pennsylvania. The arrival of steamboats on the Ohio River in 1811, and the National Road at Richmond in 1829 greatly facilitated settlement of northern and western Indiana.

Following statehood, the new government worked to transform Indiana from a frontier into a developed, well-populated, and thriving state, beginning significant demographic and economic changes. The state's founders initiated a program, Indiana Mammoth Internal Improvement Act, that led to the construction of roads, canals, railroads and state-funded public schools. The plans bankrupted the state and were a financial disaster, but increased land and produce value more than fourfold. In response to the crisis and in order to avert another, in 1851, a second constitution was adopted. Among its provisions were a prohibition on public debt and extension of suffrage to African-Americans.

Civil War

During the American Civil War, Indiana became politically influential and played an important role in the affairs of the nation. As the first western state to mobilize for the United States in the war, Indiana had soldiers participating in all of the major engagements. The state provided 126 infantry regiments, 26 batteries of artillery and 13 regiments of cavalry to the cause of the Union. In 1861, Indiana was assigned a quota of 7,500 men to join the Union Army. So many volunteered in the first call that thousands had to be turned away. Before the war ended, Indiana contributed 208,367 men to fight and serve in the war. Casualties were over 35% among these men: 24,416 lost their lives in the conflict and over 50,000 more were wounded. The only Civil War battle fought in Indiana was the Battle of Corydon, which occurred during Morgan's Raid. The battle left 15 dead, 40 wounded, and 355 captured.

Indiana remained a largely agricultural state; post-war industries included food processing, such as milling grain, distilling it into alcohol, and meatpacking; building of wagons, buggies, farm machinery, and hardware.

Early 20th century

With the onset of the industrial revolution, Indiana industry began to grow at an accelerated rate across the northern part of the state. With industrialization, workers developed labor unions and suffrage movements arose in relation to the progress of women. The Indiana Gas Boom led to rapid industrialization during the late 19th century by providing cheap fuel to the region. In the early 20th century, Indiana developed into a strong manufacturing state with ties to the new auto industry. Haynes-Apperson, the nation's first commercially successful auto company, operated in Kokomo until 1925. The construction of the Indianapolis Motor Speedway and the start of auto-related industries were also related to the auto industry boom.

During the 1930s, Indiana, like the rest of the nation, was affected by the Great Depression. The economic downturn had a wide-ranging negative impact on Indiana, such as the decline of urbanization. The Dust Bowl further to the west resulted in many migrants fleeing into the more industrialized Midwest. Governor Paul V. McNutt's administration struggled to build a state-funded welfare system to help the overwhelmed private charities. During his administration, spending and taxes were both cut drastically in response to the Depression, and the state government was completely reorganized. McNutt ended Prohibition in the state and enacted the state's first income tax. On several occasions, he declared martial law to put an end to worker strikes. World War II helped lift the economy in Indiana, as the war required steel, food and other goods that were produced in the state. Roughly 10 percent of Indiana's population joined the armed forces, while hundreds of industries earned war production contracts and began making war material. Indiana manufactured 4.5 percent of total United States military armaments produced during World War II, ranking eighth among the 48 states. The expansion of industry to meet war demands helped end the Great Depression.

Modern Era

With the conclusion of World War II, Indiana rebounded to levels of production prior to the Great Depression. Industry became the primary employer, a trend that continued into the 1960s. Urbanization during the 1950s and 1960s led to substantial growth in the state's cities. The auto, steel and pharmaceutical industries topped Indiana's major businesses. Indiana's population continued to grow during the years after the war, exceeding five million by the 1970 census. In the 1960s, the administration of Matthew E. Welsh adopted its first sales tax of two percent. Indiana schools were desegregated in 1949. In 1950, the Census Bureau reported Indiana's population as 95.5% white and 4.4% black. Governor Welsh also worked with the General Assembly to pass the Indiana Civil Rights Bill, granting equal protection to minorities in seeking employment.

Beginning in 1970, a series of amendments to the state constitution were proposed. With adoption, the Indiana Court of Appeals was created and the procedure of appointing justices on the courts was adjusted.

The 1973 oil crisis created a recession that hurt the automotive industry in Indiana. Companies such as Delco Electronics and Delphi began a long series of downsizing that contributed to high unemployment rates in manufacturing in Anderson, Muncie, and Kokomo. The restructuring and deindustrialization trend continued until the 1980s, when the national and state economy began to diversify and recover.

Source: Wikipedia

Timeline of Indiana History

1614-1615
Samuel de Champlain, New France governor, explored Maumee River region

1671
Simon de Saint-Lusson claimed most of the area for France

1679
Rene-Robert Cavelier de La Salle, Louis de Baude de Frontenac, planned for control of Maumee-Wabash trade route; plans included relocation of Miami Indians to headwaters of Maumee River

1728-1732
Vincennes established on Wabash River by France, first European settlement in area

1747
British convinced Huron Indian Chief, King Nicolas, to attack French-owned Fort Miami

1752-1753
Smallpox epidemic devastated local Indian population

1754-1763
France and Indian War

1763
England gained control of Vincennes and Indiana area; Proclamation of 1763 forbade settlement west of Appalachian Mountains; British sent Indian war parties to attack settlers who disobeyed proclamation

1772
General Gage ordered France to leave settlements in Wabash Valley, demanded land deeds

1774
British Parliament passed Quebec Act, French settlements, including Indiana, were included in province of Quebec

1775-1783
Revolutionary War

1777
British encouraged Indians to attack settlers George Rogers Clark

1778
Colonel George Rogers Clark's expedition captured Fort Sackville at Vincennes; Indiana became part of Virginia; British Governor Henry Hamilton overtook Fort Sackville

1779
British at Fort Sackville surrendered to Colonel George Rogers Clark, his expedition and Francis Vigo

1783
Treaty of Paris gave modern-day Indiana lands to United States

1787
Continental Congress created Northwest Territory; territory to be governed by a governor, three judges; laws prohibited slavery, encouraged public education, guaranteed religious freedom and civil rights

1794
Anthony Wayne overwhelmed Shawnee Indians, led by Tecumseh, in battle near rapids of Maumee River; Anthony Wayne established fort, named Fort Wayne

1800
Indiana Territory established from Northwest Territory; William Henry Harrison first Governor; Vincennes named capital

1803
Indians signed treaties ceding land in Indiana

1805
Michigan Territory separated from Indiana Territory

1809
Illinois Territory separated from Indiana Territory

1811
Chief Tecumseh and Indians defeated in Battle of Tippecanoe

1812-1814
War of 1812

1813
Chief Tecumseh killed at Battle of the Thames; Indiana Territory capital moved to Corydon

1814
Treaty of Ghent ended War of 1812

1816
Indiana became 19th U. S. state; Jonathan Jennings first Governor; Abraham Lincoln and family moved to Indiana

1818
Indians gave up claims to portion of central Indiana, "New Purchase"

1825
State capital moved to Indianapolis

1835
Wabash and Erie Canal opened from Fort Wayne to Huntington

1842
University of Notre Dame founded

1851
State Consitution adopted, included measure protecting property rights of married women

1861-1865
Civil War

1889
Standard Oil Co. built refinery in Whiting

1897
Tribal status of Miami Indians terminated

1906
U. S. Steel Company built plant, founded Gary

1908
Serial killer, Belle Gunness, died in fire at her farm in LaPorte

1911
First Indy 500 auto race occurred

1915
Workmen's Compensation Act enacted

1925
Tri-State tornado struck Indiana, Illinois, Missouri; many dead

1930
Mob broke into Marion jail, beat two young black men to death, hung them from tree

1937
Ohio River flooded causing severe damage in southern Indiana

1956
Northern Indiana Toll Road completed

1963
Studebaker Automobile Corporation ceased auto production at South Bend plant

1974
Series of 148 tornadoes struck the Midwest and Southern states (including Indiana); many killed with severe property damage

1980
Indianapolis businessman, Herbert Baumeister, killed 16 men, most gay

1984
NFL Baltimore Colts moved to Indianapolis

1985
AIDS patient, Ryan White, barred from attending public school

1987
Air Force jet crashed into Ramada Inn near Indianapolis Airport, ten killed

1988
Indianian J. Danforth Quayle, elected U. S. Vice President

1998
Explosion at Southern Energy Co. in Hammond killed 16

1999
Lilly Endowment Inc. presented $50 million grant to Hispanic Scholarship Fund

2001
Cicero's town president, nine others, charged with stealing $10 million in taxpayer monies; Oklahoma City bomber, Timothy McVeigh, executed at Federal Penitentiary in Terre Haute

2003
Governor Frank O'Bannon suffered massive stroke, died

2004
Indianapolis Colts' Peyton Manning broke Dan Marino's pass record

2005
Measles outbreak among school children; tornado struck Evansville, 22 killed, 200 injured

2007
Indianapolis Colts won Super Bowl XLI

2010
Eight teenagers shot at skating rink during concert in Gary

2011
Five people killed, more than 40 injured in stage collapse at Indiana State Fair

2012
Series of powerful storms and tornadoes left 13 dead, destroyed town of Marysville

Indiana Governor Mitch Daniels signed legislation making Indiana the 23rd right-to-work state

New York Giants quarterback Eli Manning led his team to a 21-17 victory over the New England Patriots in Super Bowl XLVI at Lucas Oil Stadium in Indianapolis.

BP agreed to spend over $400 million to settle legal complaints about chronic pollution problems at its refinery in northwest Indiana.

Mike Pence, a Republican congressman, was elected state governor.

2013
Floodwaters swelled the Mississippi River and other Midwestern rivers following days of torrential rains. Two flood related deaths were in Indiana.

2014
U.S. health officials reported the first time that Middle East respiratory syndrome (MERS) spread from one person to another in the U.S. when an Indiana man (the first US case of MERS) spread the virus to an Illinois man.

The U.S. Supreme court denied review of cases that limited marriage to opposite sex couples, in effect, granting equal marriage rights to gays and lesbians in Indiana and four other states.

2015
Theodore Hesburgh (b.1917), former president of Notre Dame University (1952-1987), died. He was awarded the Presidential Medal of Freedom in 1964 and the Congressional Gold Medal in 2000.

Indiana governor Mike Pence signed into law a religious objections bill that opponents worry could allow discrimination against gays and lesbians.

Source: http://www.worldatlas.com, December 3, 2015; Original research

A Guide to Indiana State Government

The government of Indiana is established and regulated by the Constitution of Indiana. The state-level government consists of three branches, the judicial branch, the legislative branch, and the executive branch. The three branches balance share power and jointly govern the state of Indiana. County and local governments are also constitutional bodies with limited authority to levy taxes, pass legislation, and create and maintain local public infrastructure.

The government of Indiana was first formed in December 1816 and replaced the government of the Indiana Territory. The early government came under criticism beginning as early as the 1820s for having many public offices filled by appointment and lack of delegation of authority to lower officials, requiring state level legislation for things like divorce approval. In 1851 a new constitution was adopted by the state remedying many of these problems and opening more offices to public election. Significant government reforms were enacted again in 1971 when the state courts were reorganized and new powers were granted to the governor which had historically been a weak institution.

Elections to fill positions in Indiana's government are held biennally on Election Day, with special elections being occasionally held to fill unexpected vacancies. State representatives serve two-year terms, while all other elected state, county, and municipal officials serve four-year terms. Most of the positions in the government bureaucracy are filled through the state merit system or the state patronage system.

The government provides a wide range of services including law enforcement, infrastructure construction and maintenance, licensing and registration of numerous things, tax collection, fire protection, business and utility regulation, utility services, and park and conversation maintenance efforts.

The government of Indiana sits in the state capital of Indianapolis. Each of the three branches operates out of the Indiana Statehouse. The state maintains several office buildings that hold many of its bureaus and departments. Most of the state's bureaus are located in the Indiana Government Center North, a high-rise tower in downtown Indianapolis.

Legislature

The Indiana General Assembly is the legislative branch of the state of Indiana. It is a bicameral legislature that consists of a lower house, the Indiana House of Representatives, and an upper house, the Indiana Senate. The General Assembly meets annually at the Indiana State House in Indianapolis.

Members of the General Assembly are elected from districts that are realigned every ten years. Representatives serve two-year terms; senators serve four-year terms. Both houses must pass a bill before it can be submitted to the governor and enacted into law.

Judiciary

The Supreme Court of Indiana is the highest judicial body in Indiana. The court oversees the lower courts and commissions that jointly make up the judicial branch. The other courts include the Indiana Tax Court, the Indiana Court of Appeals, and circuit, superior, and city or town courts.[2] The courts are assisted by several commissions that are also part of the judicial branch, including the Judicial Nominating Commission.

Executive

The Governor of Indiana is the chief executive officer of the government of Indiana. Elected to a four-year term, the Governor is responsible for overseeing the day-to-day management of the functions of the state government.

The governor is assisted by other officials elected to the executive branch including the Lieutenant Governor and the Attorney General.

Checks and Balances

The Constitution of Indiana has several checks and balances built into its clauses to prevent any one branch of the government from becoming dominant. The governor has the power to veto any bill passed by the General Assembly. The General Assembly has the power to override a veto with a simple majority. The courts have the authority to declare laws unconstitutional and revoke them, while the General Assembly has the power to initiate an amendment to the constitution to override the decision of the courts. The courts judges are appointed by a commission made of representatives of the governor and the courts, and their jurisdictions can be regulated by the General Assembly.

How a Bill Becomes a Law—Constitutional Requirements

Introduction

"The style of every law shall be: "Be it enacted by the General Assembly of the State of Indiana"; and no law shall be enacted, except by bill. Bills may originate in either House, but may be amended or rejected in the other; except that bills for raising revenue shall originate in the House of Representatives" Art. 4. Sec. 1; Art. 4, Sec. 17

Consideration

"Every bill shall be read, by title, on three several days, in each House; unless, in case of emergency, two-thirds of the House where such bill may be pending shall, by a vote of yeas and nays, deem it expedient to dispense with this rule; but the reading of a bill, by title, on its final passage, shall, in no case, be dispensed with; and the vote on the passage of every bill or joint resolution shall be taken by yeas and nays" Art. 4. Sec. 18

Passage

"A majority of all the members elected to each House, shall be necessary to pass every bill or joint resolution; and all bills and joint resolutions so passed, shall be signed by the Presiding Officers of the respective Houses" Art. 4, Sec. 25

Presentment

"Every bill which shall have passed the General Assembly shall be presented to the Governor" Art. 5, Sec. 14

Filing

"Every bill presented to the Governor which is signed by him or on which he fails to act within said seven days after presentment shall be filed with the Secretary of State within ten days of presentmentàIn the event a bill is passed over the Governor's veto, such bill shall be filed with the Secretary of State without further presentment to the Governor" Art. 5, Sec. 17

Circulation

"No act shall take effect, until the same shall have been published and circulated in the several counties of the State, by authority, except in case of emergency, which emergency shall be declared in the preamble, or in the body, of the law" Art. 5, Sec. 17

County Government

County governments are made up of two bodies:

County Council—A county council of seven to fifteen members controls all spending and revenue of the county government. Four of the representatives are elected from county districts; the other three representatives are elected at large. The council members serve four year terms. They are responsible for setting salaries, the annual budget, and special spending. The council also has limited authority to impose local taxes, usually in the form of an income tax that is subject to state level approval, excise taxes, or service taxes, like those on dining or lodging.

Commissioners—The executive body consists of three to five commissioners. The commissioners are elected county wide, usually in staggered terms, and serve four-year terms. One of the commissioners, typically the most senior, serves as president. They are charged with executing the acts legislated by the council and managing the day-to-day functions of the county government.

Counties also have employee boards to oversee different aspects of the county. These boards are usually filled by direct election from the public, appointment by the commission, or a combination of both methods. Boards typically oversee management of water facilities, public roads, and new projects, among others tasks. Each school district has a board that is elected by public election. County school boards are responsible for funding and management of the public school system within their district. The majority of school funding comes from property taxes imposed by the board on the district. The tax rate is subject to state level approval and is capped, by law, at 1% of property value.

Court: Each county forms a Judicial Circuit of the state, and has a Circuit Court. Some counties also have Superior Courts. These are the courts of general jurisdiction. Marion County also has dedicated small claims courts.

County Officials: The county has several other elected offices, including sheriff, coroner, auditor, treasurer, recorder, surveyor, and circuit court clerk. Each of these elected officers serves a term of four years and oversees a different part of the county government. Members elected to county government positions are required to declare party affiliations and to be residents of the county.

Town Government

Many small communities in Indiana are incorporated as towns. A town has a council-manager form of government, with a three- or five-member Town Council serving as primarily the legislature function of government. For practical reasons, the Town Council may share in some of the executive functions. However, under statute, the role of the executive officer belongs to the President of the Town Council. The President of the Town Council is an elected member of the town selected by his fellow town councilmen to lead the council. The council may appoint a non-partisan town manager to oversee the day-to-day operations of the municipal government. The council is responsible for setting the town's budget and tax rates, and appointing all town employees.

Unlike some states, Indiana council members must declare a political party affiliation, if any, when they file to run for office. Upon election in November, they are sworn in before January 1 of the following year and serve a four-year term. There are no state term limits affecting how many times a candidate may run for reelection to office.

A town also elects a clerk/treasurer, who manages the town's finances. As an elected official, the clerk/treasurer is solely executive in function and operates independently of the town council, but operates within the council-approved budget.

City Government

Most larger communities are incorporated as cities. A city can be either a third-class city or a second-class city (the first-class designation is reserved for Indianapolis). An Indiana city has a mayor-council form of government, but a third-class city may appoint a city manager. The mayor, elected to a four-year term, serves as the executive. Most mayors in Indiana are elected in partisan elections. The legislative branch consists of a five-, seven-, or nine-member City Council. Council members serve four-year terms, and may be elected by geographic districts or at-large. Most cities in Indiana use districts.

Township Government

A township trustee administers the civil government of the township. The trustee is elected by the residents of the township to a term of four years. The trustee is responsible for providing fire protection and ambulance service to unincorporated areas, providing relief for those living in poverty and burial of the indigent, maintaining cemeteries and burial grounds, resolving fencing disputes between neighbors, investigating claims of livestock killed by dogs, controlling weeds, managing the township budget and financial records, and preparing an annual financial report. The trustee also acts as the property tax assessor. Other public matters in which a trustee may sometimes be involved include zoning, parks, libraries, schools, shelters and community centers.

The trustee is assisted by a three-member Township Board whose members are elected to four-year terms. Duties of the board include adopting the annual budget, serving as a board of finance and approving township contracts. In January of each year, the trustee presents to the board an annual report showing the receipts, expenditures, investments and debts of the township. The approved report is then published in local papers for public inspection.

Source: State of Indiana, http://www.in.gov; Wikipedia, http://en.wikipedia.org/wiki/Government_of_Indiana

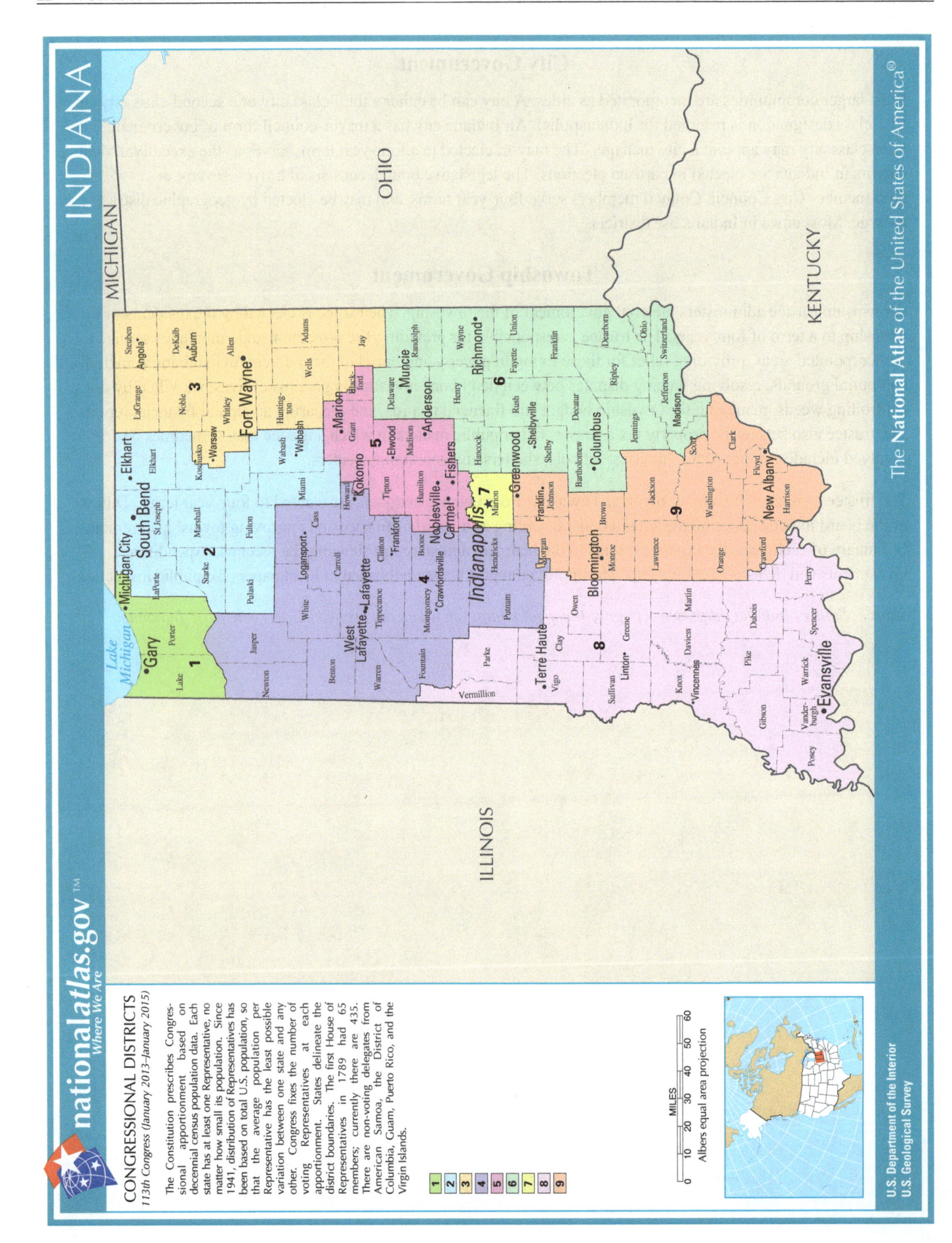

CONGRESSIONAL DISTRICTS
113th Congress (January 2013-January 2015)

The Constitution prescribes Congressional apportionment based on decennial census population data. Each state has at least one Representative, no matter how small its population. Since 1941, distribution of Representatives has been based on total U.S. population, so that the average population per Representative has the least possible variation between one state and any other. Congress fixes the number of voting Representatives at each apportionment. States delineate the district boundaries. The first House of Representatives in 1789 had 65 members; currently there are 435. There are non-voting delegates from American Samoa, the District of Columbia, Guam, Puerto Rico, and the Virgin Islands.

The National Atlas of the United States of America
U.S. Department of the Interior
U.S. Geological Survey

Profiles of Indiana   A Guide to Indiana State Government   23

Percent of Population Who Voted for Barack Obama in 2012

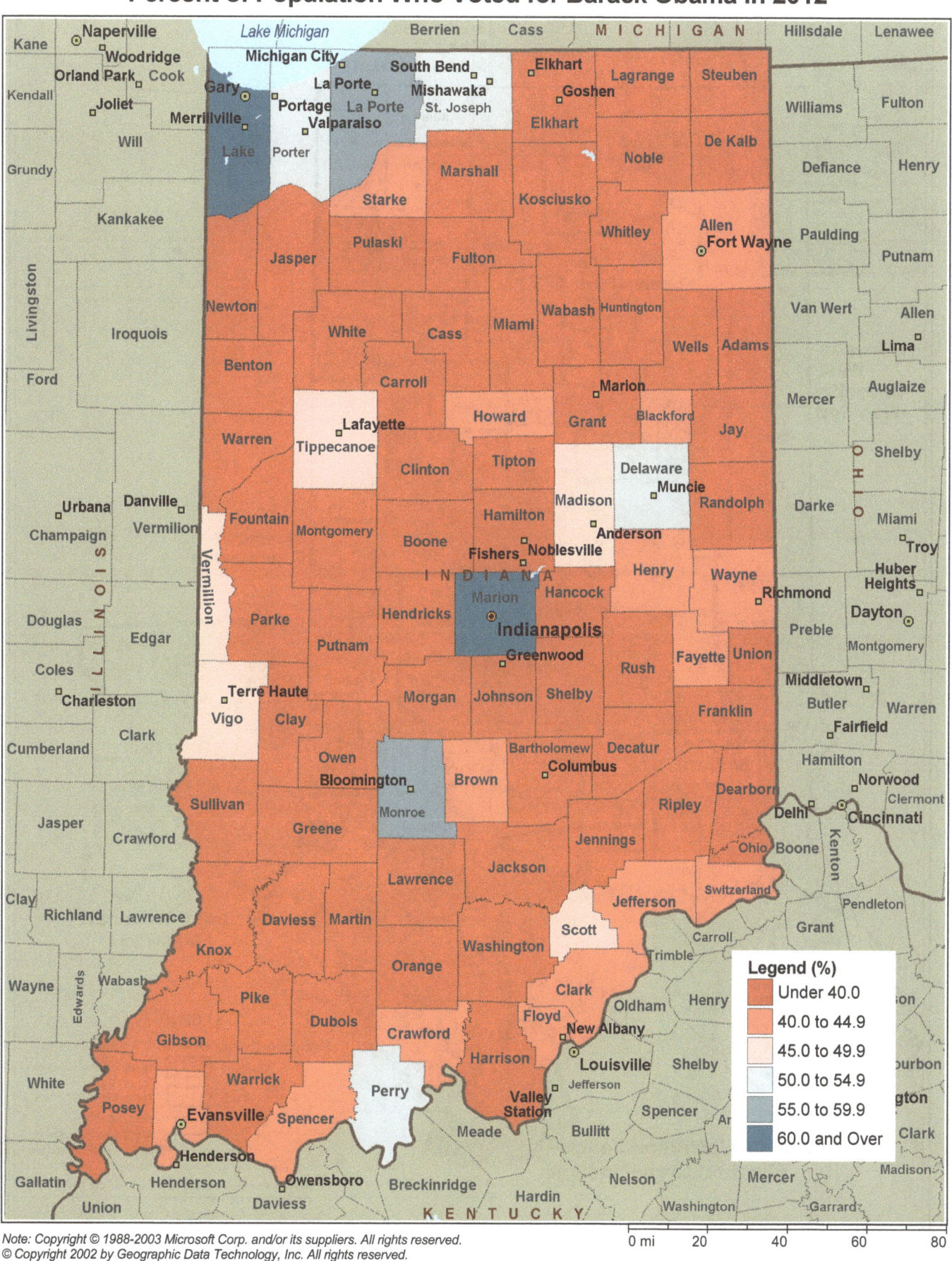

Legend (%)
- Under 40.0
- 40.0 to 44.9
- 45.0 to 49.9
- 50.0 to 54.9
- 55.0 to 59.9
- 60.0 and Over

0 mi 20 40 60 80

Note: Copyright © 1988-2003 Microsoft Corp. and/or its suppliers. All rights reserved.
© Copyright 2002 by Geographic Data Technology, Inc. All rights reserved.
© 2002 Navigation Technologies. All rights reserved.

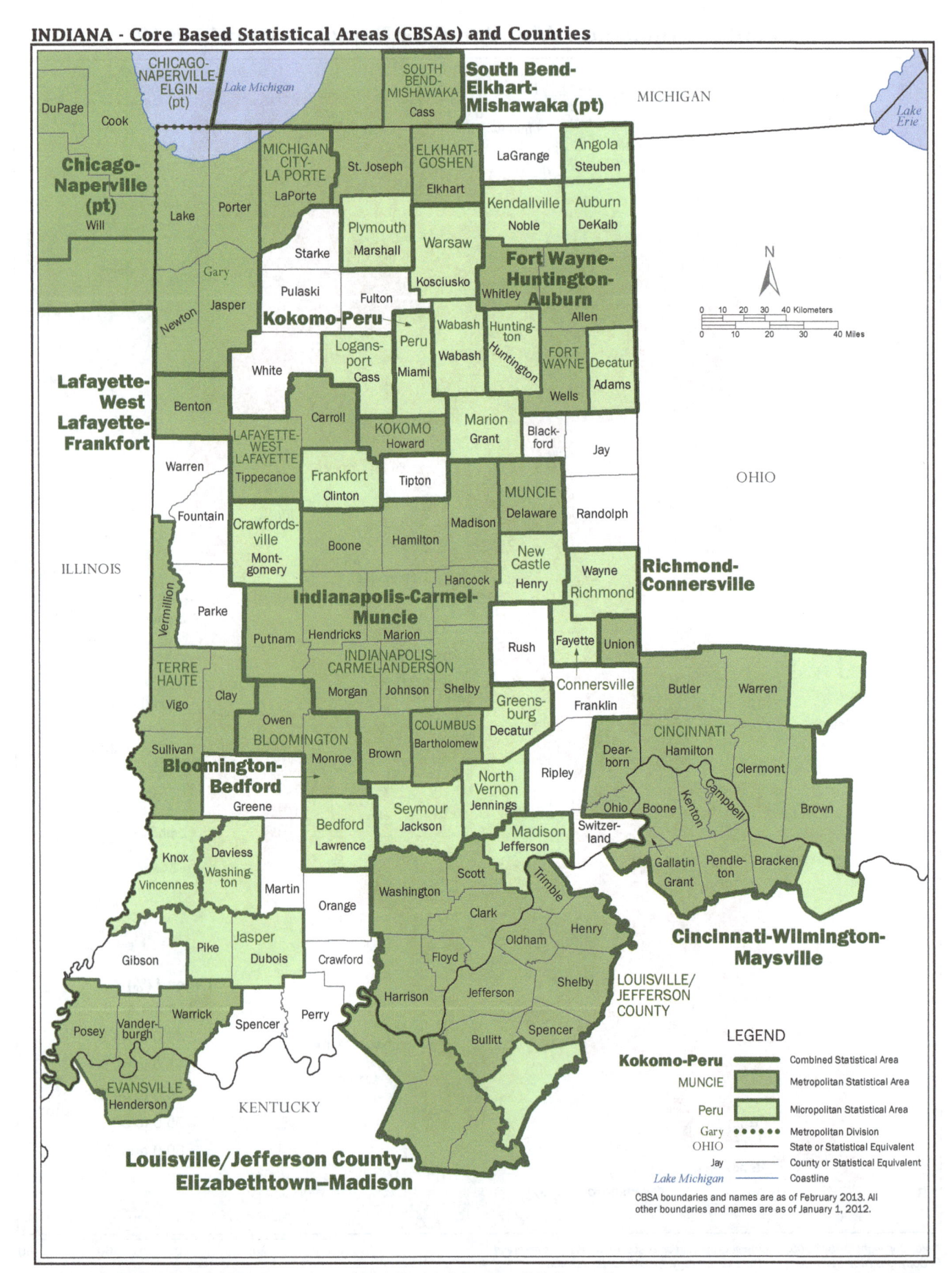

INDIANA - Core Based Statistical Areas (CBSAs) and Counties

U.S. DEPARTMENT OF COMMERCE Economics and Statistics Administration U.S. Census Bureau

Land and Natural Resources

Topic	Value	Time Period
Total Surface Area (acres)	23,158,400	2010
Land	22,778,400	2010
Federal Land	472,400	2010
Non-Federal Land, Developed	2,512,400	2010
Non-Federal Land, Rural	19,793,600	2010
Cropland	13,295,300	2010
Conservation Reserve Program (CRP) Land	164,500	2010
Pastureland	1,747,800	2010
Rangeland	0	2010
Forest Land	3,927,200	2010
Other Rural Land	658,800	2010
Water	380,000	2010
World Heritage Sites	0	FY Ending 9/30/2014
National Heritage Areas	0	FY Ending 9/30/2014
National Natural Landmarks	30	FY Ending 9/30/2014
National Historic Landmarks	40	FY Ending 9/30/2014
National Register of Historic Places Listings	1,828	FY Ending 9/30/2014
National Parks	3	FY Ending 9/30/2014
Visitors to National Parks	1,778,385	FY Ending 9/30/2014
Archeological Sites in National Parks	223	FY Ending 9/30/2014
Threatened and Endangered Species in National Parks	6	FY Ending 9/30/2014
Places Recorded by Heritage Documentation Programs	461	FY Ending 9/30/2014
Economic Benefit from National Park Tourism	$76,500,000	FY Ending 9/30/2014
Historic Preservation Grants	$24,498,604	Since 1969
Historic Rehabilitation Projects Stimulated by Tax Incentives	$792,179,201	Since 1995
Land & Water Conservation Fund Grants	$86,845,320	Since 1965
Acres Transferred by Federal Lands to Local Parks	15,998	Since 1948

Sources: *United States Department of Agriculture, Natural Resources Conservation Service, National Resources Inventory; U.S. Department of the Interior, National Park Service, State Profiles*

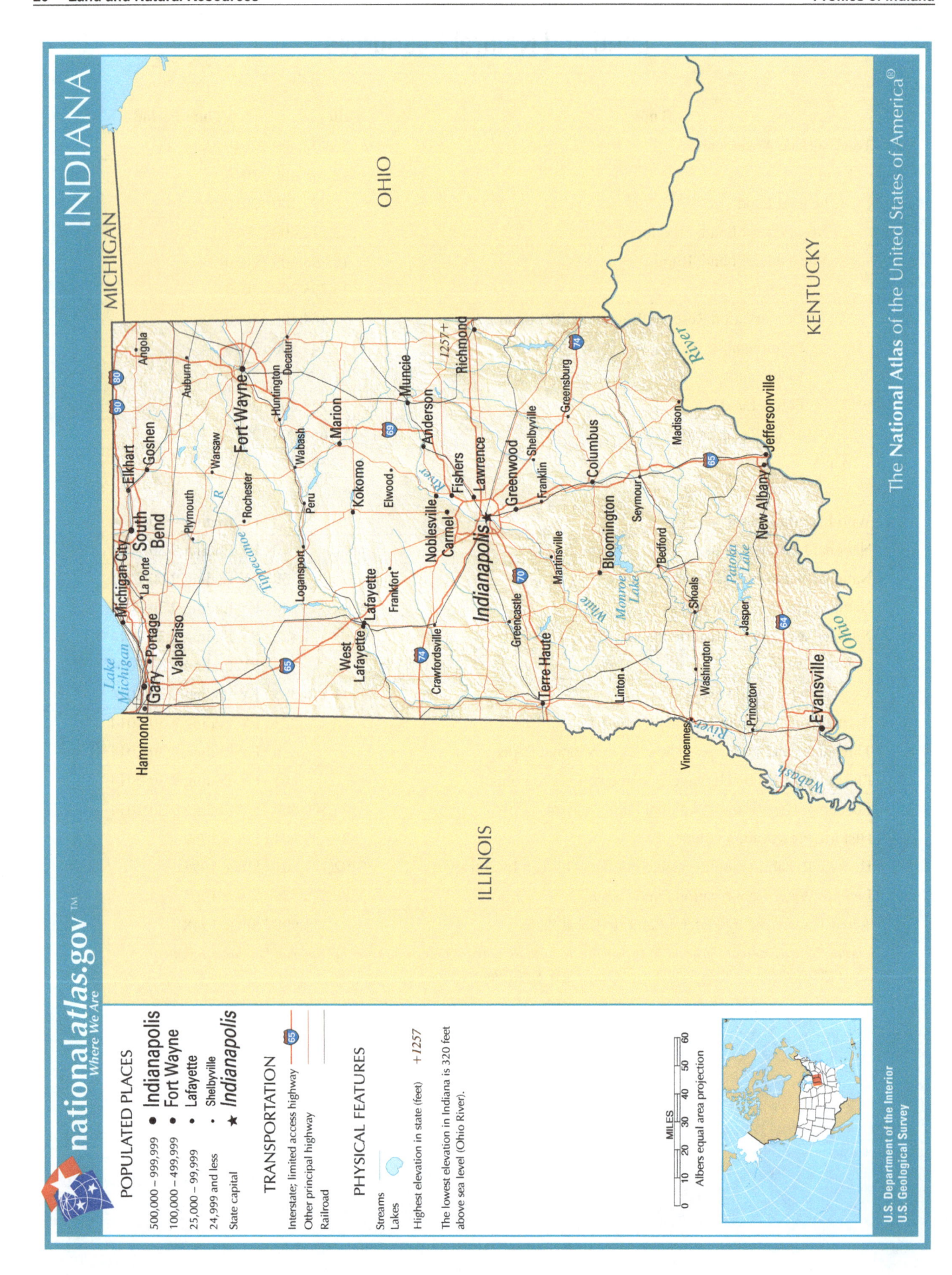

Land and Natural Resources

Profiles of Indiana

INDIANA

nationalatlas.gov — Where We Are

POPULATED PLACES
- 500,000 – 999,999 ● Indianapolis
- 100,000 – 499,999 ● Fort Wayne
- 25,000 – 99,999 ● Lafayette
- 24,999 and less ● Shelbyville
- State capital ★ *Indianapolis*

TRANSPORTATION
- Interstate; limited access highway
- Other principal highway
- Railroad

PHYSICAL FEATURES
- Streams
- Lakes
- Highest elevation in state (feet) +1257

The lowest elevation in Indiana is 320 feet above sea level (Ohio River).

The **National Atlas** of the United States of America

U.S. Department of the Interior
U.S. Geological Survey

Albers equal area projection
MILES 0 10 20 30 40 50 60

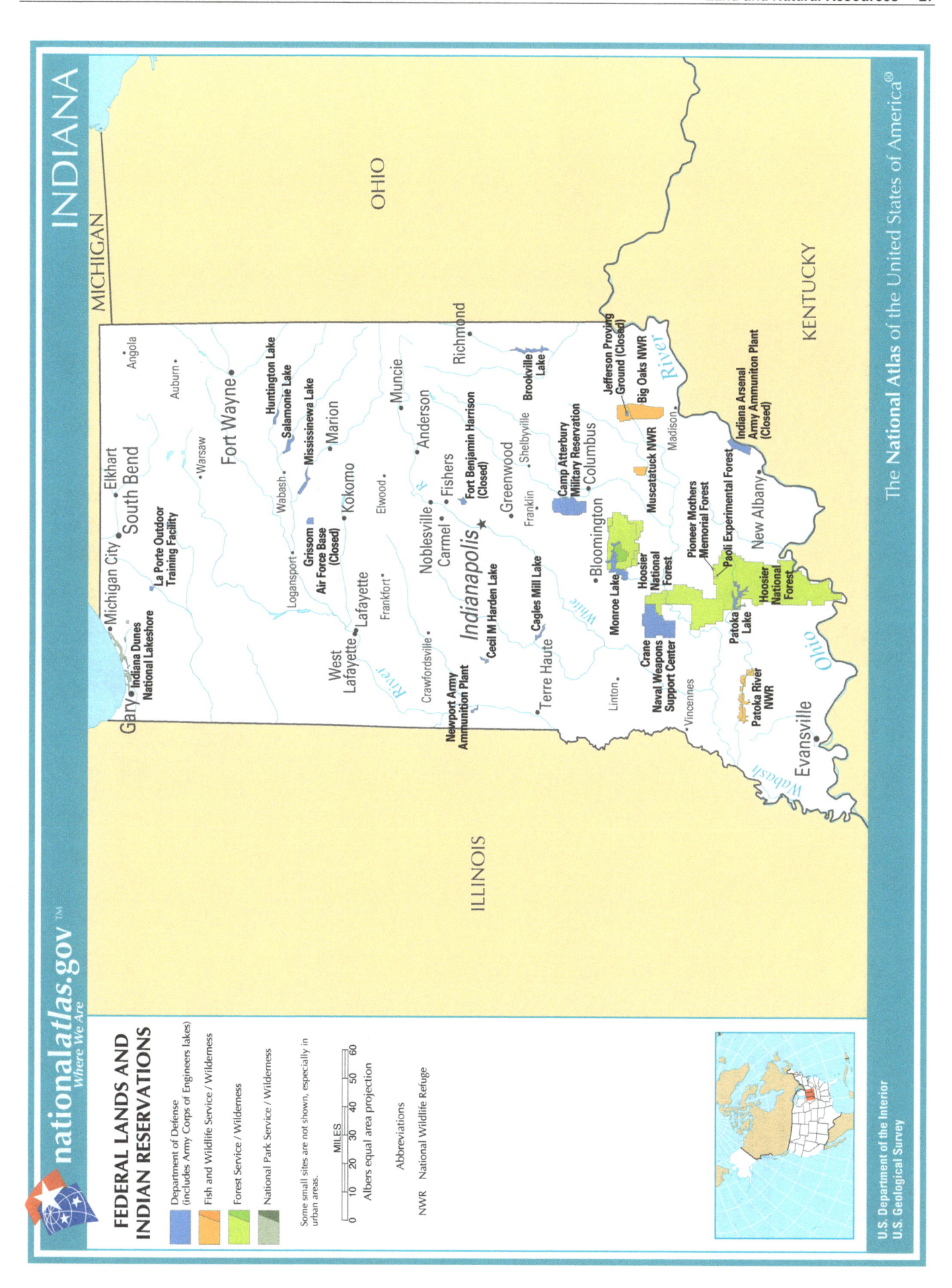

Profiles of Indiana — Land and Natural Resources 27

FEDERAL LANDS AND INDIAN RESERVATIONS

Legend:
- Department of Defense (includes Army Corps of Engineers lakes)
- Fish and Wildlife Service / Wilderness
- Forest Service / Wilderness
- National Park Service / Wilderness

Some small sites are not shown, especially in urban areas.

MILES: 0 10 20 30 40 50 60
Albers equal area projection

Abbreviations
NWR National Wildlife Refuge

U.S. Department of the Interior
U.S. Geological Survey

The National Atlas of the United States of America®

nationalatlas.gov — Where We Are

Locations shown on map:

Cities: Gary, Michigan City, South Bend, Elkhart, Angola, Auburn, Fort Wayne, Warsaw, Logansport, Lafayette, West Lafayette, Frankfort, Crawfordsville, Kokomo, Elwood, Marion, Muncie, Anderson, Noblesville, Carmel, Fishers, Indianapolis, Greenwood, Shelbyville, Richmond, Franklin, Terre Haute, Bloomington, Columbus, Linton, Vincennes, Madison, New Albany, Evansville

Federal lands/features: Indiana Dunes National Lakeshore, La Porte Outdoor Training Facility, Grissom Air Force Base (Closed), Huntington Lake, Salamonie Lake, Mississinewa Lake, Fort Benjamin Harrison (Closed), Cecil M Harden Lake, Cagles Mill Lake, Newport Army Ammunition Plant, Camp Atterbury Military Reservation, Brookville Lake, Muscatatuck NWR, Jefferson Proving Ground (Closed), Big Oaks NWR, Monroe Lake, Hoosier National Forest, Crane Naval Weapons Support Center, Pioneer Mothers Memorial Forest, Paoli Experimental Forest, Patoka Lake, Patoka River NWR, Indiana Arsenal Army Ammunition Plant (Closed)

Rivers: Wabash, White, Ohio

Bordering states: Michigan, Ohio, Illinois, Kentucky

Land and Natural Resources

Profiles of Indiana

INDIANA

MICHIGAN · **OHIO** · **KENTUCKY** · **ILLINOIS**

Lake Michigan · Ohio River · Wabash River

SATELLITE VIEW

In 1972, Landsat began transmitting views of our planet back to Earth. The first Landsat and its five successors (two of them are in operation now) have delivered millions of images from a satellite orbiting 438 miles above the Earth. Landsat's orbit enables a new image to be recorded every sixteen days of any area on the Earth's surface. The satellite view on this map was created from a mosaic of many Landsat images joined together. Colors were selected to better show variations in the landscape. Relief shading was added to enhance the terrain and make the landforms of each state more apparent.

MILES: 0 10 20 30 40 50 60
Albers equal area projection

nationalatlas.gov — Where We Are

The National Atlas of the United States of America®

U.S. Department of the Interior
U.S. Geological Survey

Indiana Hazard Events and Losses, 1960-2012

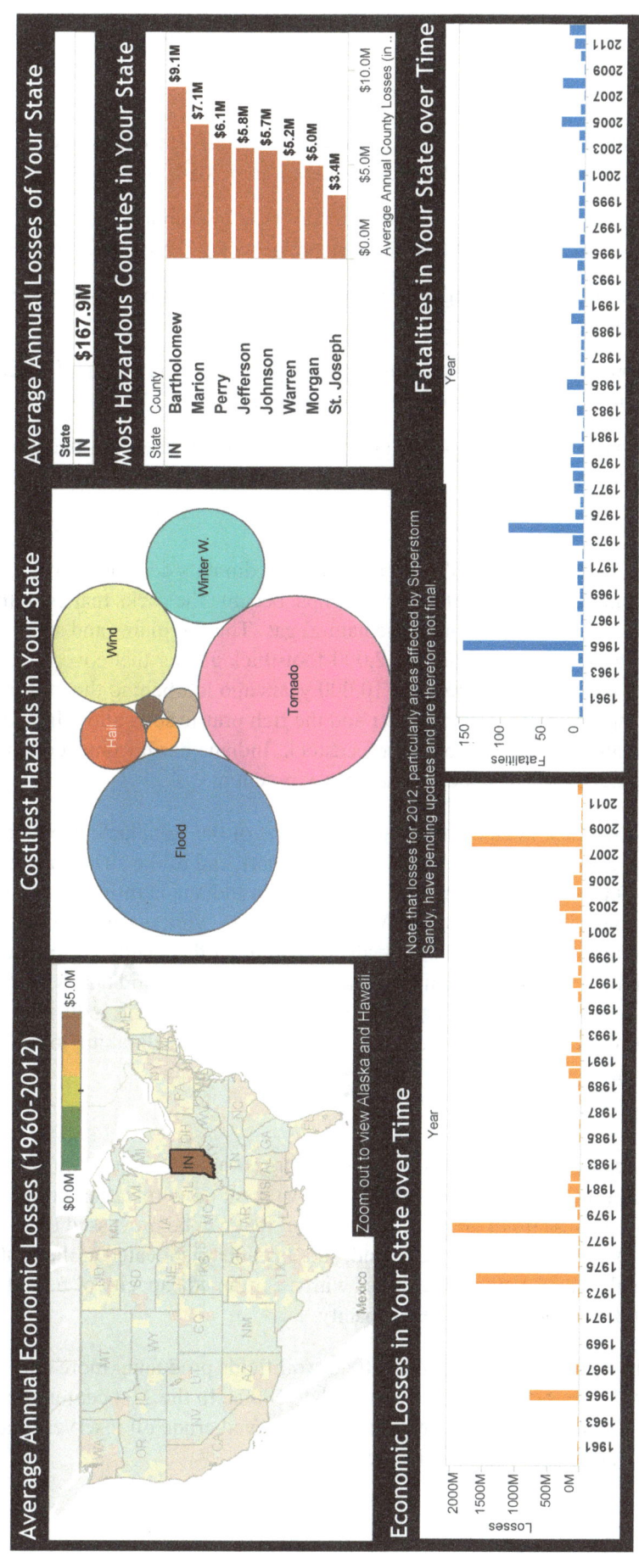

Average Annual Economic Losses (1960-2012)

Costliest Hazards in Your State

Flood, Tornado, Wind, Winter W., Hail

Average Annual Losses of Your State

State	
IN	$167.9M

Most Hazardous Counties in Your State

State	County	Average Annual County Losses
IN	Bartholomew	$9.1M
	Marion	$7.1M
	Perry	$6.1M
	Jefferson	$5.8M
	Johnson	$5.7M
	Warren	$5.2M
	Morgan	$5.0M
	St. Joseph	$3.4M

Economic Losses in Your State over Time

Note that losses for 2012, particularly areas affected by Superstorm Sandy, have pending updates and are therefore not final.

Fatalities in Your State over Time

Source: Hazards & Vulnerability Research Institute (2015). The Spatial Hazard Events and Losses Database for the United States, Version 14.0 [Online Database]. Columbia, SC: University of South Carolina. Available from http://www.sheldus.org

Indiana Energy Profile

Quick Facts

- Indiana ranked eighth among the states in coal production in 2013. Coal-fired electric power plants provided about 85% of Indiana's net electricity generation in 2014.
- Indiana's industrial sector, which includes manufacturers of aluminum, chemicals, glass, metal casting, and steel, consumed more energy in 2012 than the residential sector and commercial sector combined.
- As of January 2014, Indiana's Whiting oil refinery had the largest processing capacity of any refinery outside the Gulf Coast region.
- Indiana is a major producer of ethanol. As of February 2015, Indiana's ethanol plants were capable of producing more than 1.2 billion gallons of ethanol per year.
- The largest geothermal heating and cooling system in the United States has been installed at Ball State University in Muncie, Indiana.

Overview

Indiana is on the eastern edge of the nation's Interior Plains. Sediments deposited over millions of years, when the state was covered by inland seas and later lush swamps, became the rocks that contain the state's fossil fuel reserves, predominantly coal but also oil and some natural gas. The flat plains and slightly rolling land in the northern two-thirds of the state are the result of a 2,000-foot-thick glacier that covered much of the state during the Ice Ages. The retreat of the glacier more than 10,000 years ago left behind the topsoil that now supports Indiana's agriculture. Ample rainfall in the summer and the rich prairie soils allow Indiana farmers to produce abundant corn and soybean crops. Using corn as a feedstock, Indiana has become a major ethanol-producing state. Indiana's open farmland has substantial wind energy potential.

Although the state is the smallest in land area of any state west of the Appalachian Mountains, it has a varied climate because of its length from north to south. At the northern end of the state, Indiana experiences lake-effect snows and winds off Lake Michigan. The climate in Indiana is influenced both by polar air from Canada and by warm, moist air from the Gulf of Mexico. Indiana's winters can be bitterly cold, and active spring weather often includes tornadoes. The state also has summer days with oppressive humidity and heat. In part because of the weather extremes, residential energy use per capita in Indiana is well above the national average. The industrial sector is the state's largest energy consumer. Indiana's industrial activities include the energy-intensive chemical, petroleum, transportation equipment, and steelmaking industries. The state consumes more energy than it produces.

Petroleum

The Whiting refinery, located in northwest Indiana, is the largest inland crude oil refinery in the nation; only six Gulf Coast refineries can process more crude oil per day. A recent modernization project at the Whiting refinery has significantly increased the share of heavy, sour crude oil that can be processed there from about one-fifth of the crude oil feedstock to about four-fifths. A second, small refinery is located at the southern tip of the state at Mount Vernon. Indiana also has 14 ethanol facilities with a combined capacity of more than 1 billion gallons per year, equal to about 8% of the nation's total capacity.

Trenton Field, one of the nation's earliest giant oil fields (oil fields producing more than 100 million barrels of crude oil) was discovered in east-central Indiana in the late 1800s. In the 21st century, crude oil is produced from fields in southwestern Indiana. The state has the least proved crude oil reserves of any of the oil-producing states and produces only about 2.5 million barrels of oil per year.

Indiana is a major consumer of petroleum and petroleum products, which enter the state via three major crude oil pipelines and six major petroleum product pipelines. The majority of Indiana's petroleum consumption is in the form of motor gasoline, followed by distillate fuel oil, including diesel fuels. Although conventional motor gasoline is used throughout most of Indiana, reformulated motor gasoline blended with ethanol is required in the northwestern corner of the state in the greater Chicago metropolitan area. In addition, motor gasoline formulated to reduce emissions that contribute to ground-level ozone is required during the summer months on Indiana's southeastern border near Louisville, Kentucky. Distillate fuel sales to the residential sector have been declining steadily over the past three decades. Currently less than 1% of Indiana households use fuel oil or kerosene for home heating, and 7% use liquefied petroleum gases (LPG).

Natural Gas

Early discoveries of natural gas in the late 1870s attracted industry to the east central part of Indiana, but unregulated development squandered much of the resource. Renewed interest in the New Albany Shale gas play since the mid-1990s, as well as potential coalbed methane resources, could add significant new natural gas reserves. Indiana's natural gas production is modest, but it has increased in the past two decades. However, production in the state is much lower than demand, and interstate pipelines supply Indiana with natural gas from the U.S. Gulf Coast and western Canada. Natural gas enters Indiana primarily via Illinois and Kentucky, and the majority of the natural gas is sent on to Ohio and Michigan. Indiana is crossed by many major interstate natural gas pipelines, but it does not have any natural gas market centers. The state has 22 natural gas storage fields with a total working capacity of about 33 billion cubic feet of natural gas.

The industrial sector is the largest consumer of natural gas in Indiana. The sector uses more natural gas than all other sectors combined. The residential sector accounts for only one-fifth of the natural gas consumed in Indiana, even though almost two-thirds of households use natural gas for home heating. The electric power sector increased its use of natural gas for power generation dramatically from 2009 through 2012, when it peaked at a level equal to residential use.

Coal

Indiana is one of the top 10 coal-producing states in the nation. Bituminous coal is produced from 18 surface and 9 underground mines located within the Illinois Basin in southwestern Indiana. About two-thirds of the coal produced in Indiana is consumed in state, but production does not meet demand, and two-fifths of the coal delivered to Indiana consumers is from other states. Coal arrives by rail, barge, or truck from Illinois, Wyoming, West Virginia, Kentucky, Virginia, Alabama, and Pennsylvania, with small amounts from Colorado, Utah, and Ohio.

Indiana's coal consumption is second only to that of Texas. Although large amounts of coal are used for electricity generation, substantial amounts are also used by Indiana's industrial sector. Indiana leads the nation in the use of coal by the industrial sector. About one-tenth of the coal used in state is delivered to coking plants, where coke production begins with pulverized bituminous coal. Coke plants serve the state's steel industry, and Indiana is a leader in steel manufacturing. The coal delivered to Indiana's coke plants comes primarily from West Virginia and Virginia, but deliveries also arrive from Alabama, Kentucky, and Pennsylvania.

Electricity

Almost all of Indiana's electricity generation is fueled by coal, and 9 of the state's 10 largest power plants are coal-fired. Natural gas accounts for the majority of the remainder of the state's net electricity generation, but wind is providing a small but increasing share. Indiana does not have any nuclear power plants.

Retail sales of electricity to Indiana's industrial sector are among the highest in the nation, after Texas, Ohio, Pennsylvania, and California. However, residential use of electricity in the state is closer to the national median, and per capita residential electricity consumption in Indiana is lower than in 19 other states. Slightly more than one-fourth of Indiana households rely on electricity as their main source of energy for home heating.

Renewable Energy

Wind has become the primary renewable resource used for electric power generation in Indiana. In 2008, Indiana's first utility-scale wind project, the Benton County Wind Farm, was installed in the northwestern part of the state. Currently the state has more than 1,700 megawatts of installed wind capacity including the 500-megawatt Meadow Lake Wind Farms, the eighth-largest wind project in the nation. In 2014, about 3% of Indiana's electric power was generated by wind turbines. The rest of Indiana's renewable generation comes primarily from hydroelectric power facilities, with some from biomass and solar. Less than 5% of Indiana's net electricity generation comes from renewable fuels including hydroelectric power.

Ball State University in Muncie, Indiana, has installed the nation's largest geothermal heating and cooling system. The system replaced four aging coal-fired boilers and provides renewable power to heat and cool 47 university buildings. It is estimated that $2 million in operating costs will be saved each year, and that the university's carbon footprint will be cut in half. The project was completed in 2014.

In 2011, Indiana's legislature created a voluntary clean energy portfolio standard that took effect on January 1, 2012. Electric utilities and retail power suppliers are eligible for incentives if they meet the program goals of obtaining increasing amounts of their electricity supply from clean energy in each of three goal periods. The ultimate goal is for suppliers to obtain 10% of their electricity from clean energy sources in the year 2025. Technologies that qualify as clean energy include not only renewable resources, but also coalbed methane, clean-coal technology, nuclear energy, combined heat and power systems, and natural gas that displaces electricity from coal. At least half of the qualifying energy obtained by Indiana's participating electric utilities must come from within the state.

Source: U.S. Energy Information Administration, State Profile and Energy Estimates, March 19, 2015

Profiles of Indiana — Demographic Maps 33

Population

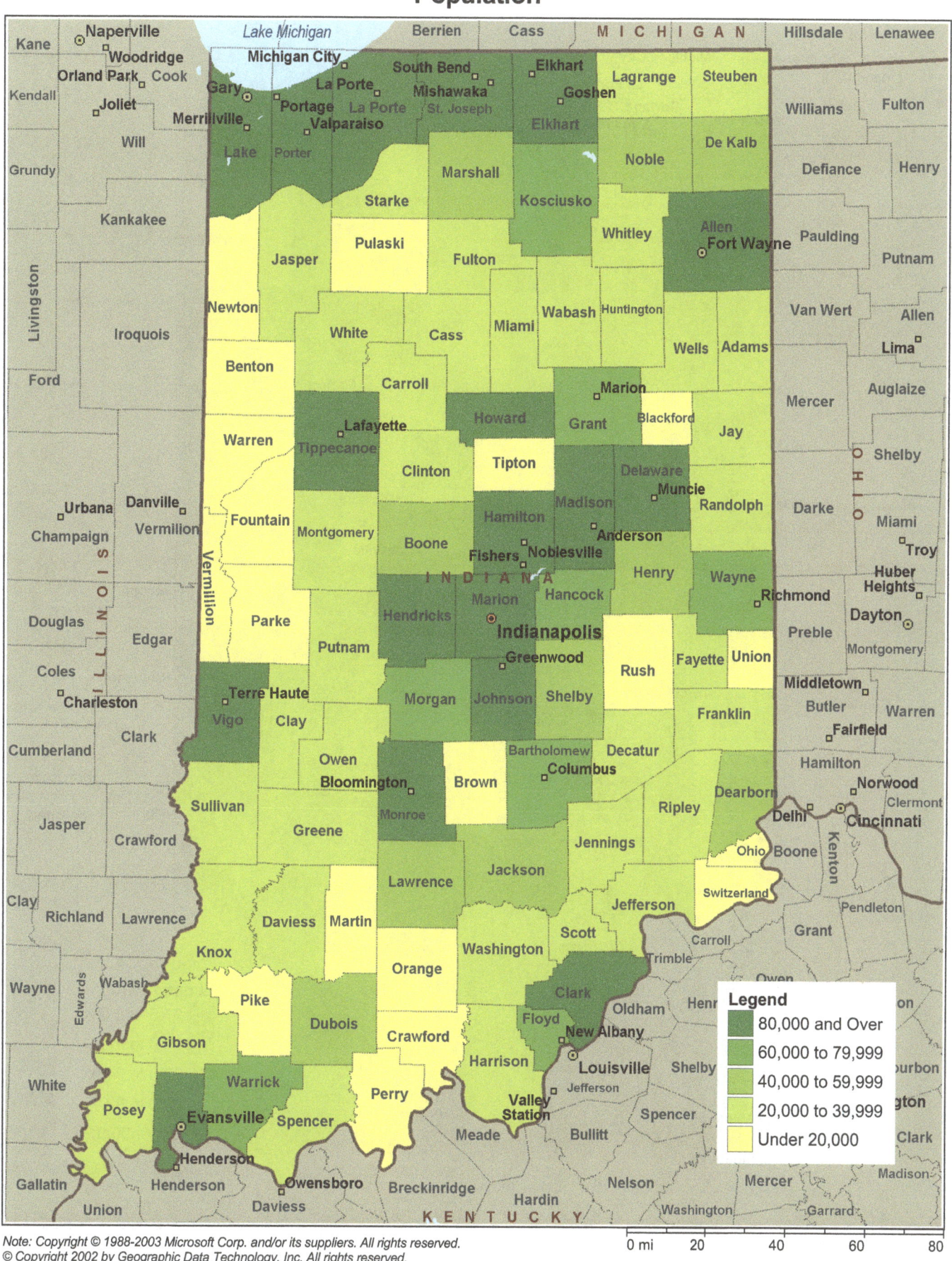

Legend
- 80,000 and Over
- 60,000 to 79,999
- 40,000 to 59,999
- 20,000 to 39,999
- Under 20,000

Percent White

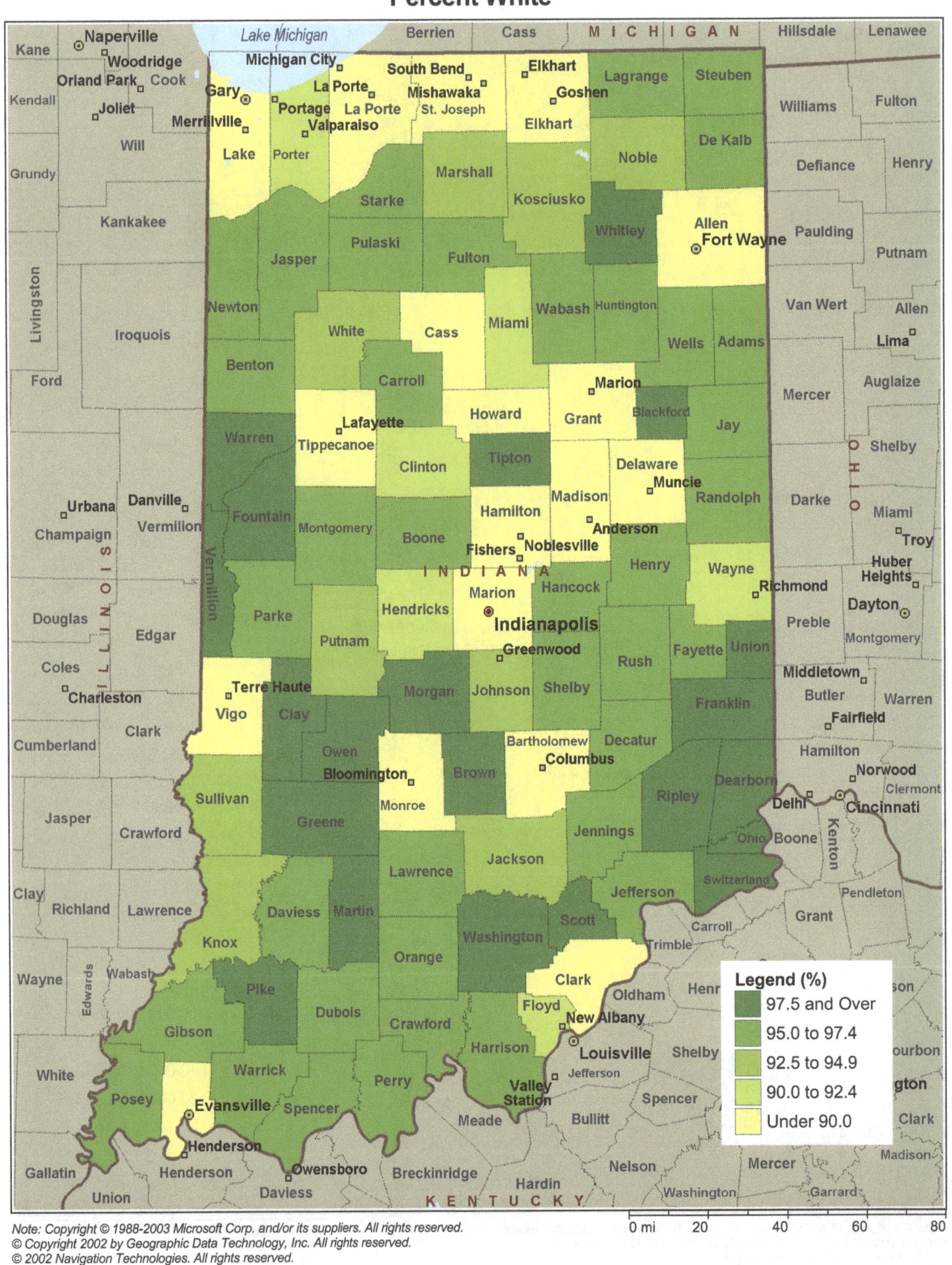

Legend (%)
- 97.5 and Over
- 95.0 to 97.4
- 92.5 to 94.9
- 90.0 to 92.4
- Under 90.0

Percent Black

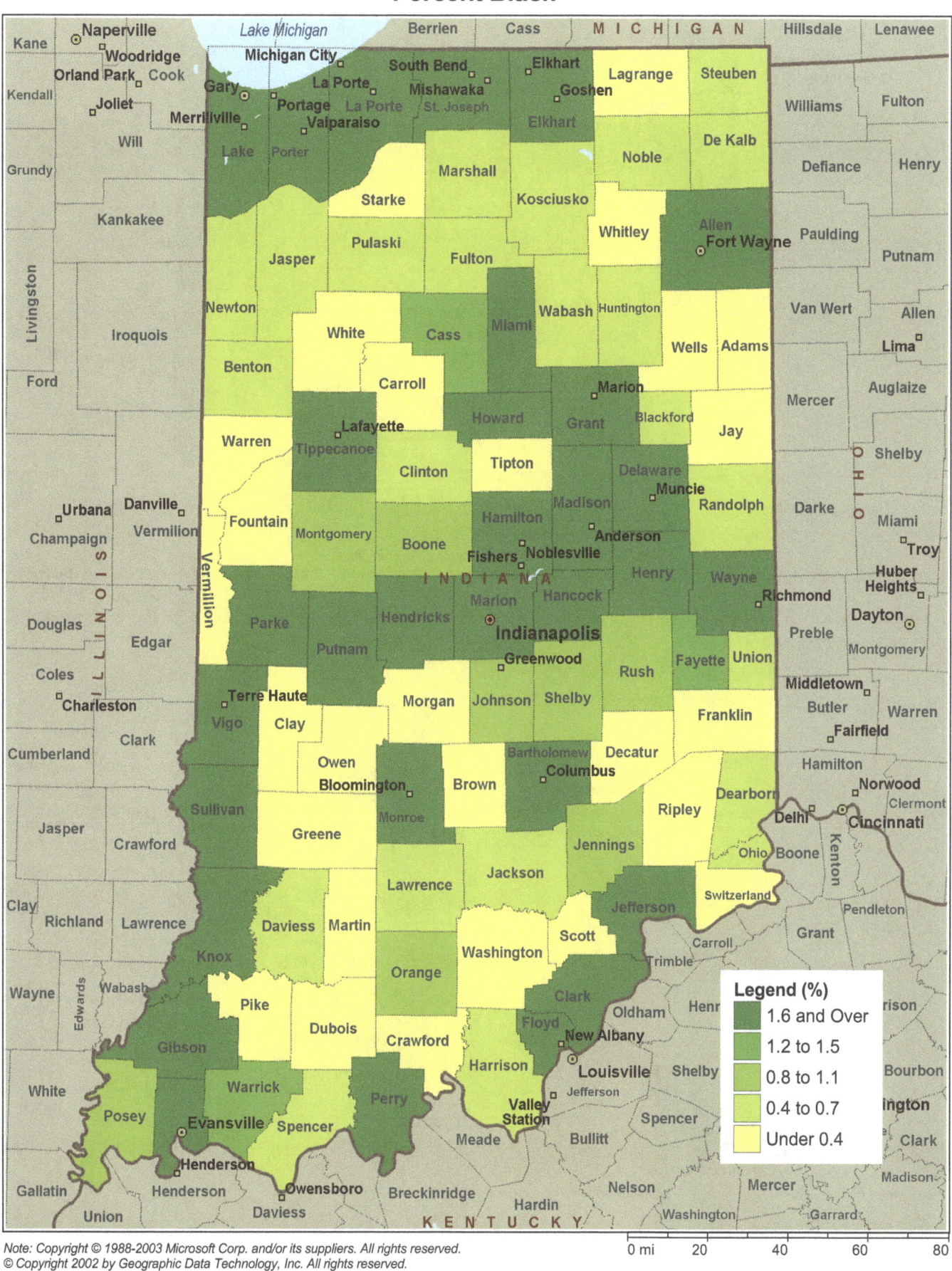

Legend (%)
- 1.6 and Over
- 1.2 to 1.5
- 0.8 to 1.1
- 0.4 to 0.7
- Under 0.4

Profiles of Indiana — Demographic Maps 35

Note: Copyright © 1988-2003 Microsoft Corp. and/or its suppliers. All rights reserved.
© Copyright 2002 by Geographic Data Technology, Inc. All rights reserved.
© 2002 Navigation Technologies. All rights reserved.

Demographic Maps

Percent Asian

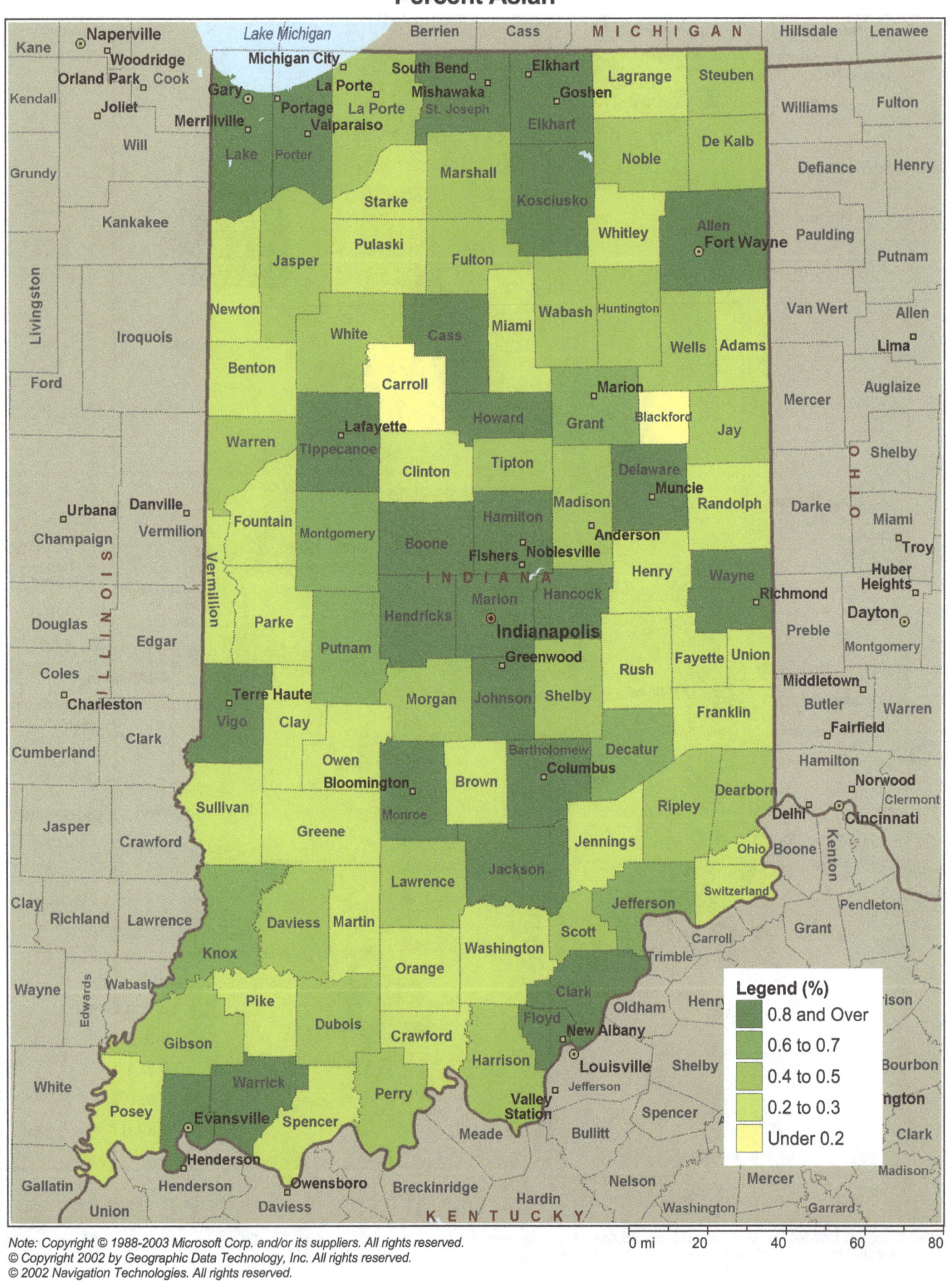

Legend (%)
- 0.8 and Over
- 0.6 to 0.7
- 0.4 to 0.5
- 0.2 to 0.3
- Under 0.2

Note: Copyright © 1988-2003 Microsoft Corp. and/or its suppliers. All rights reserved.
© Copyright 2002 by Geographic Data Technology, Inc. All rights reserved.
© 2002 Navigation Technologies. All rights reserved.

Percent Hispanic

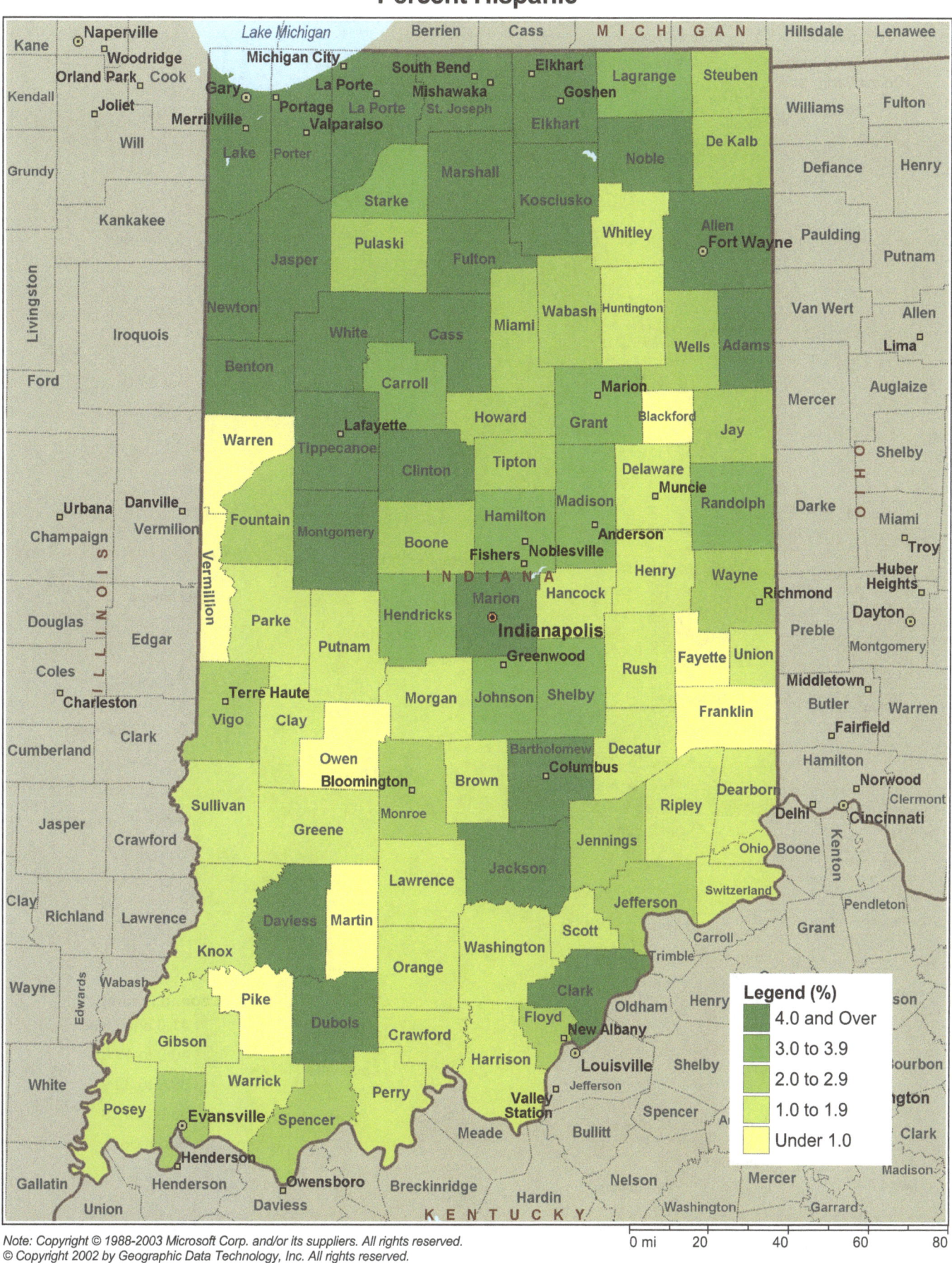

Profiles of Indiana — Demographic Maps 37

Legend (%)
- 4.0 and Over
- 3.0 to 3.9
- 2.0 to 2.9
- 1.0 to 1.9
- Under 1.0

Demographic Maps

Median Age

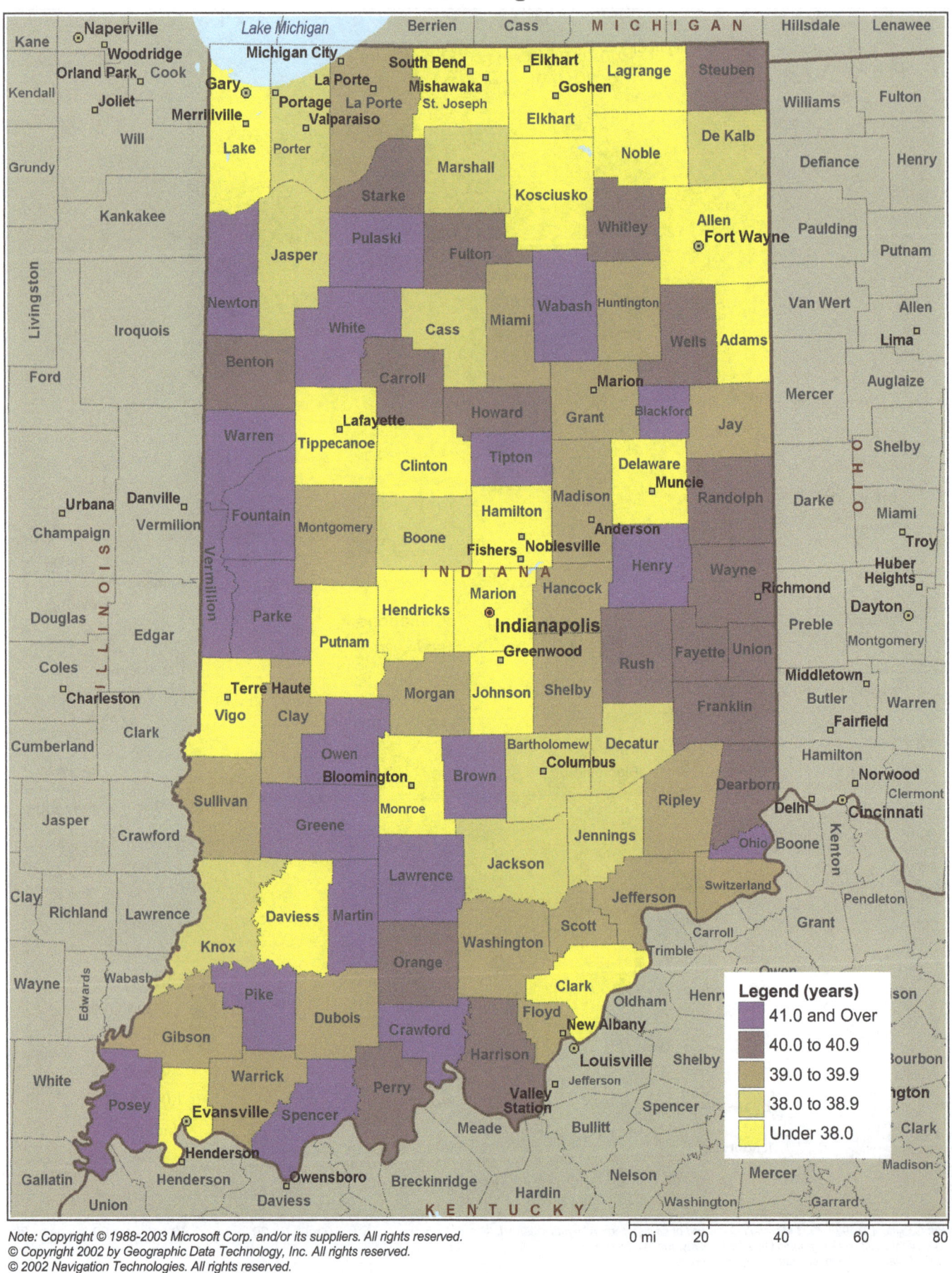

Legend (years)
- 41.0 and Over
- 40.0 to 40.9
- 39.0 to 39.9
- 38.0 to 38.9
- Under 38.0

Note: Copyright © 1988-2003 Microsoft Corp. and/or its suppliers. All rights reserved.
© Copyright 2002 by Geographic Data Technology, Inc. All rights reserved.
© 2002 Navigation Technologies. All rights reserved.

Profiles of Indiana • Demographic Maps 39

Median Household Income

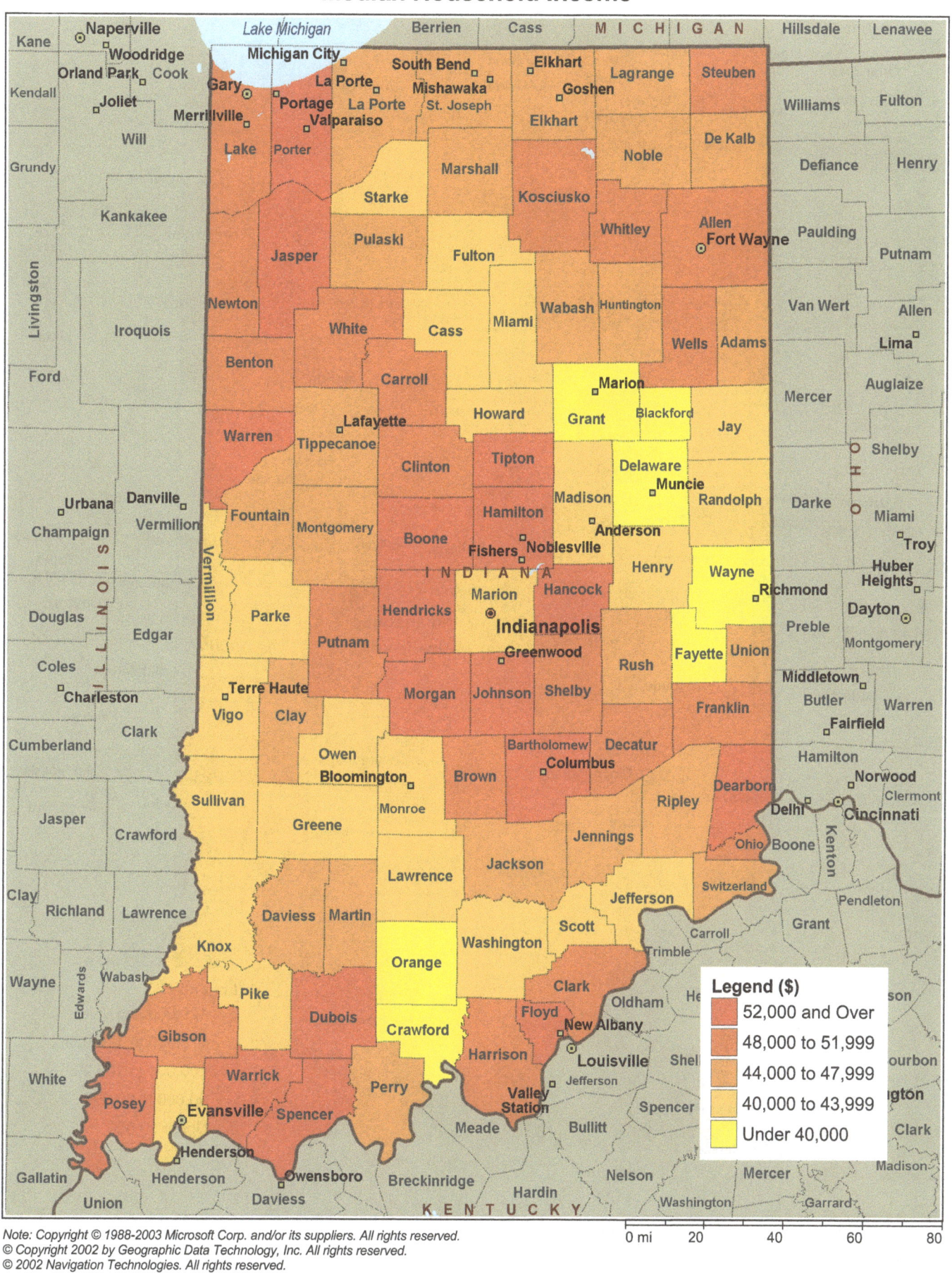

Legend ($)
- 52,000 and Over
- 48,000 to 51,999
- 44,000 to 47,999
- 40,000 to 43,999
- Under 40,000

Median Home Value

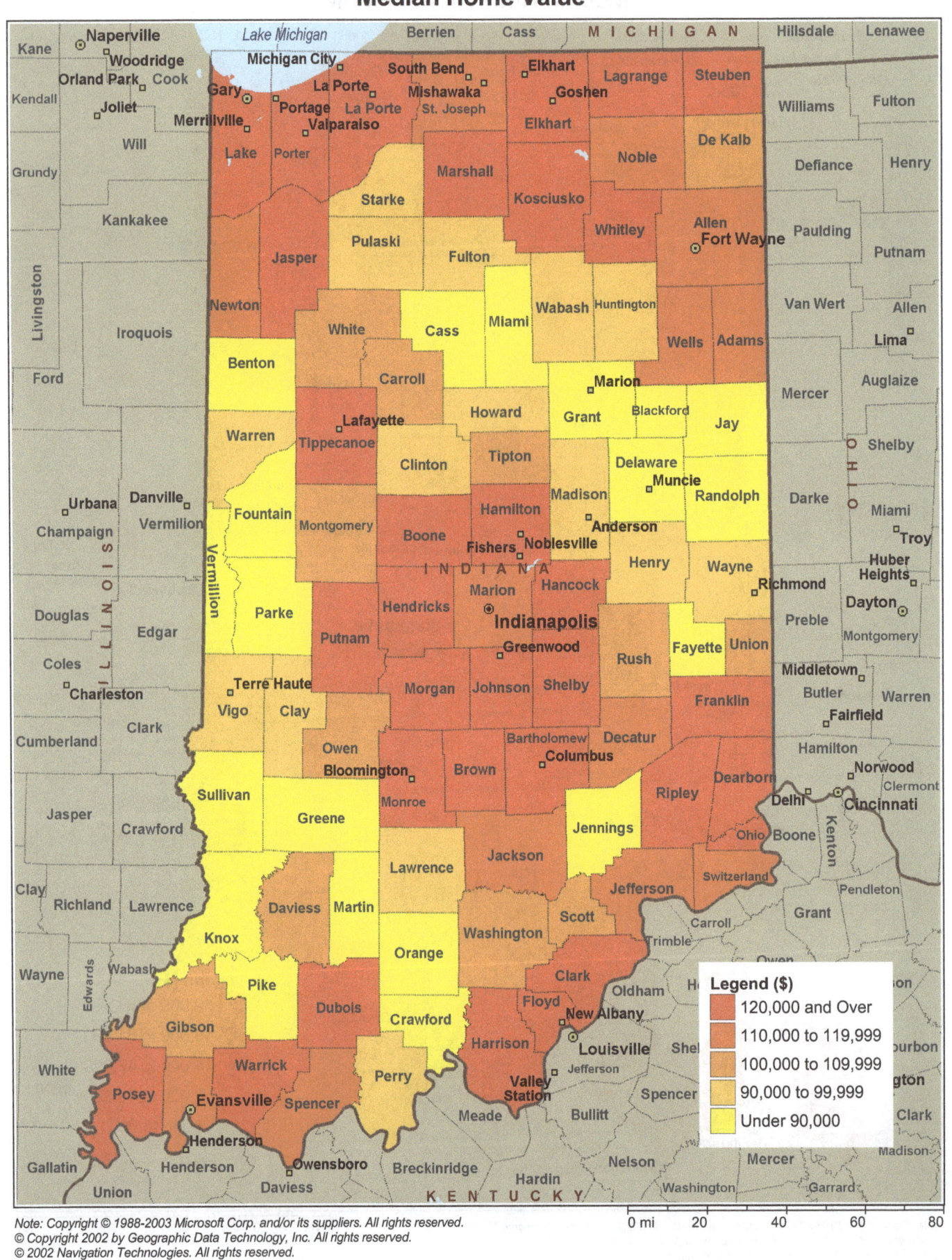

Legend ($)
- 120,000 and Over
- 110,000 to 119,999
- 100,000 to 109,999
- 90,000 to 99,999
- Under 90,000

Profiles of Indiana — Demographic Maps 41

High School Graduates*

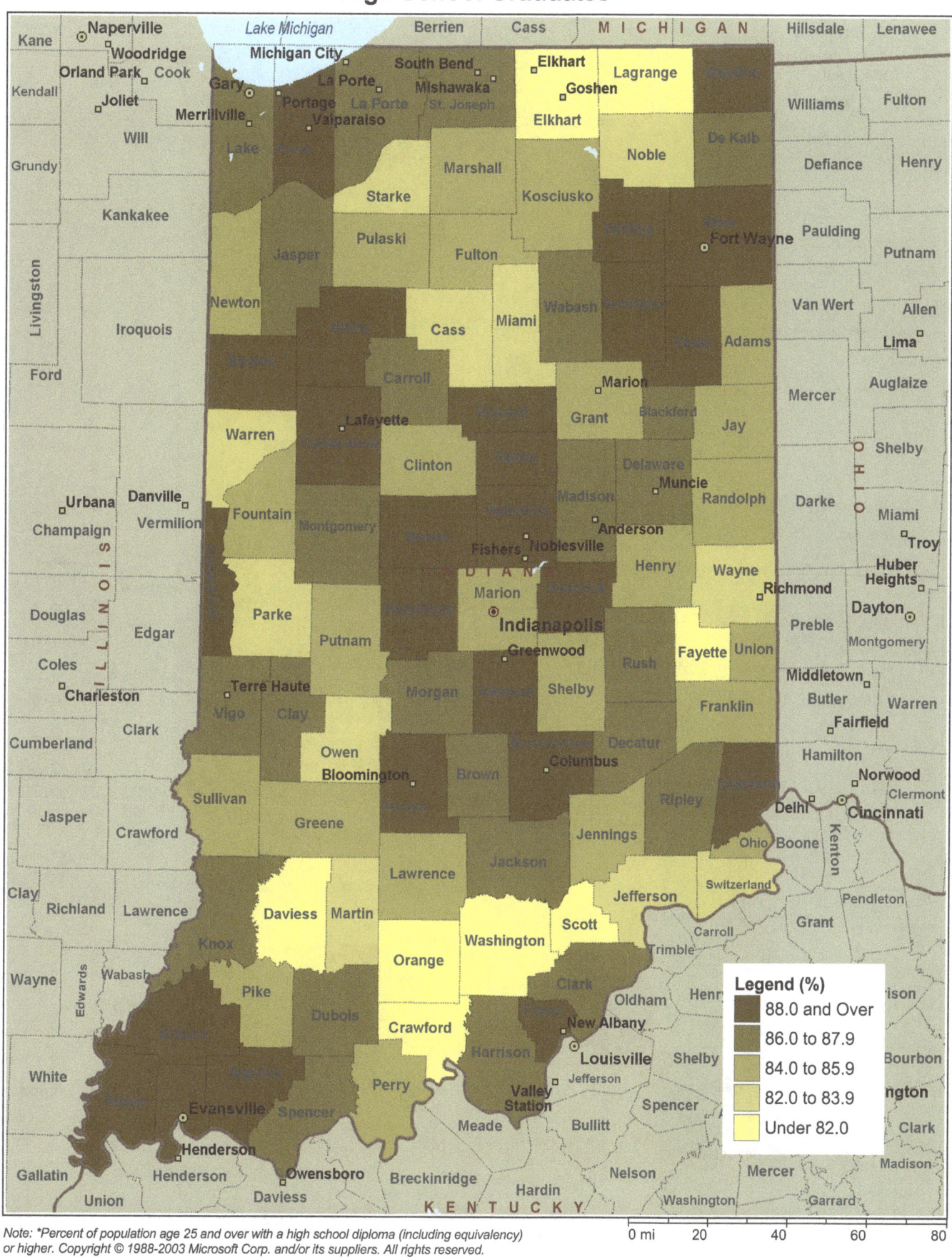

Legend (%)
- 88.0 and Over
- 86.0 to 87.9
- 84.0 to 85.9
- 82.0 to 83.9
- Under 82.0

Note: *Percent of population age 25 and over with a high school diploma (including equivalency) or higher. Copyright © 1988-2003 Microsoft Corp. and/or its suppliers. All rights reserved.
© Copyright 2002 by Geographic Data Technology, Inc. All rights reserved.
© 2002 Navigation Technologies. All rights reserved.

College Graduates*

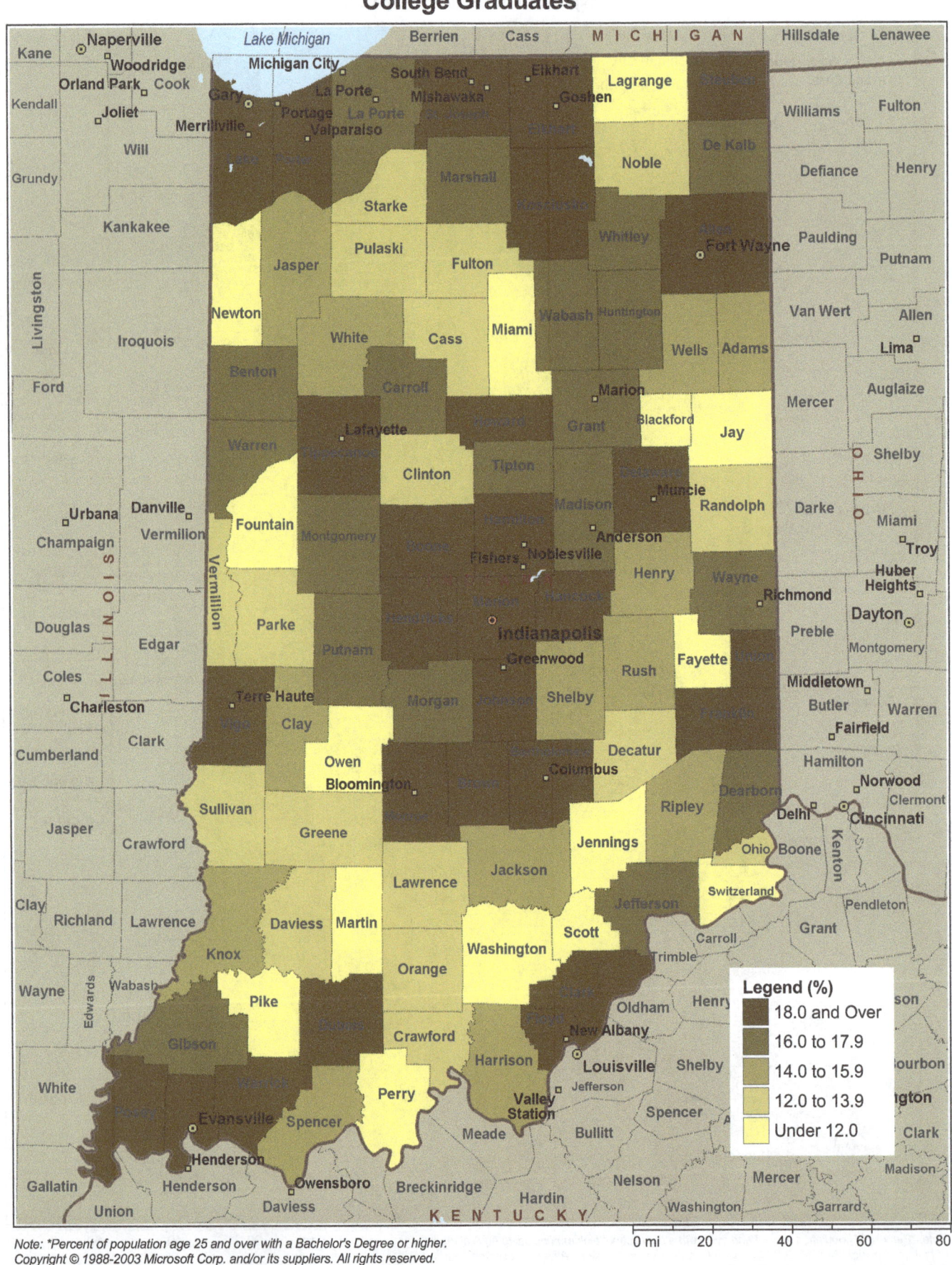

Legend (%)
- 18.0 and Over
- 16.0 to 17.9
- 14.0 to 15.9
- 12.0 to 13.9
- Under 12.0

Note: *Percent of population age 25 and over with a Bachelor's Degree or higher.
Copyright © 1988-2003 Microsoft Corp. and/or its suppliers. All rights reserved.
© Copyright 2002 by Geographic Data Technology, Inc. All rights reserved.
© 2002 Navigation Technologies. All rights reserved.

Profiles

Adams County

Located in eastern Indiana; bounded on the east by Ohio. Covers a land area of 339.028 square miles, a water area of 0.938 square miles, and is located in the Eastern Time Zone at 40.75° N. Lat., 84.94° W. Long. The county was founded in 1835. County seat is Decatur.

Adams County is part of the Decatur, IN Micropolitan Statistical Area. The entire metro area includes: Adams County, IN

Weather Station: Berne — Elevation: 859 feet

	Jan	Feb	Mar	Apr	May	Jun	Jul	Aug	Sep	Oct	Nov	Dec
High	34	37	48	61	72	81	85	83	77	64	50	37
Low	19	21	30	40	51	61	65	63	55	44	34	24
Precip	2.4	2.3	2.8	3.8	3.9	4.3	4.4	3.6	2.8	2.9	3.1	2.8
Snow	8.2	7.3	4.1	0.8	0.0	0.0	0.0	0.0	0.0	0.3	1.6	5.9

High and Low temperatures in degrees Fahrenheit; Precipitation and Snow in inches

Population: 34,387; Growth (since 2000): 2.3%; Density: 101.4 persons per square mile; Race: 97.0% White, 0.3% Black/African American, 0.2% Asian, 0.2% American Indian/Alaska Native, 0.0% Native Hawaiian/Other Pacific Islander, 0.9% two or more races, 4.1% Hispanic of any race; Average household size: 2.83; Median age: 34.0; Age under 18: 31.2%; Age 65 and over: 13.8%; Males per 100 females: 97.8; Marriage status: 24.4% never married, 59.8% now married, 1.0% separated, 7.0% widowed, 8.8% divorced; Foreign born: 0.7%; Speak English only: 83.2%; With disability: 11.1%; Veterans: 7.5%; Ancestry: 37.7% German, 11.7% American, 11.3% Swiss, 7.9% Irish, 6.5% English
Religion: Six largest groups: 24.4% European Free-Church, 11.7% Lutheran, 10.5% Catholicism, 7.8% Non-denominational Protestant, 7.0% Methodist/Pietist, 5.9% Holiness
Economy: Unemployment rate: 4.6%; Leading industries: 18.2% retail trade; 15.6% other services (except public administration); 9.9% construction; Farms: 1,476 totaling 210,227 acres; Company size: 0 employ 1,000 or more persons, 1 employs 500 to 999 persons, 19 employ 100 to 499 persons, 705 employ less than 100 persons; Business ownership: 591 women-owned, n/a Black-owned, n/a Hispanic-owned, n/a Asian-owned
Employment: 9.9% management, business, and financial, 3.1% computer, engineering, and science, 7.3% education, legal, community service, arts, and media, 4.3% healthcare practitioners, 15.9% service, 22.5% sales and office, 13.5% natural resources, construction, and maintenance, 23.6% production, transportation, and material moving
Income: Per capita: $20,160; Median household: $46,695; Average household: $56,982; Households with income of $100,000 or more: 11.8%; Poverty rate: 18.1%
Educational Attainment: High school diploma or higher: 84.3%; Bachelor's degree or higher: 14.7%; Graduate/professional degree or higher: 5.3%
Housing: Homeownership rate: 76.6%; Median home value: $116,100; Median year structure built: 1967; Homeowner vacancy rate: 2.3%; Median gross rent: $570 per month; Rental vacancy rate: 12.5%
Vital Statistics: Birth rate: 187.2 per 10,000 population; Death rate: 73.4 per 10,000 population; Age-adjusted cancer mortality rate: 172.7 deaths per 100,000 population
Health Insurance: 74.8% have insurance; 61.1% have private insurance; 25.2% have public insurance; 25.2% do not have insurance; 35.0% of children under 18 do not have insurance
Health Care: Physicians: 4.7 per 10,000 population; Hospital beds: 66.7 per 10,000 population; Hospital admissions: 719.2 per 10,000 population
Transportation: Commute: 91.6% car, 0.0% public transportation, 1.6% walk, 4.9% work from home; Median travel time to work: 21.5 minutes
Presidential Election: 29.2% Obama, 68.7% Romney (2012)
National and State Parks: Limberlost State Memorial
Additional Information Contacts
Adams Government . . . . (219) 724-5300
http://www.co.adams.in.us

Adams County Communities

BERNE (city). Covers a land area of 2.078 square miles and a water area of <.001 square miles. Located at 40.66° N. Lat; 84.96° W. Long. Elevation is 846 feet.
History: Mennonite immigrants from Berne, Switzerland, settled here in 1852 and named Berne for their former home. The Mennonite Book Concern was established here in 1882.
Population: 3,999; Growth (since 2000): -3.6%; Density: 1,924.7 persons per square mile; Race: 96.5% White, 0.5% Black/African American, 0.6% Asian, 0.1% American Indian/Alaska Native, 0.0% Native Hawaiian/Other Pacific Islander, 1.0% Two or more races, 4.0% Hispanic of any race; Average household size: 2.35; Median age: 42.0; Age under 18: 24.1%; Age 65 and over: 24.0%; Males per 100 females: 85.6; Marriage status: 24.0% never married, 51.7% now married, 0.8% separated, 13.3% widowed, 11.1% divorced; Foreign born: 0.4%; Speak English only: 97.3%; With disability: 14.7%; Veterans: 5.0%; Ancestry: 35.8% German, 25.2% Swiss, 9.2% Irish, 8.9% English, 6.3% American
Employment: 8.3% management, business, and financial, 2.0% computer, engineering, and science, 11.1% education, legal, community service, arts, and media, 6.4% healthcare practitioners, 19.9% service, 24.6% sales and office, 6.0% natural resources, construction, and maintenance, 21.6% production, transportation, and material moving
Income: Per capita: $26,069; Median household: $38,671; Average household: $62,817; Households with income of $100,000 or more: 14.8%; Poverty rate: 14.3%
Educational Attainment: High school diploma or higher: 90.6%; Bachelor's degree or higher: 24.2%; Graduate/professional degree or higher: 8.7%

School District(s)
South Adams Schools (KG-12)
    2012-13 Enrollment: 1,351 . . . . (260) 589-3133
Housing: Homeownership rate: 65.8%; Median home value: $91,900; Median year structure built: 1970; Homeowner vacancy rate: 3.6%; Median gross rent: $702 per month; Rental vacancy rate: 15.4%
Health Insurance: 90.1% have insurance; 72.0% have private insurance; 39.0% have public insurance; 9.9% do not have insurance; 10.5% of children under 18 do not have insurance
Safety: Violent crime rate: 2.5 per 10,000 population; Property crime rate: 78.2 per 10,000 population
Newspapers: Berne Tri-Weekly News (weekly circulation 2500)
Transportation: Commute: 94.0% car, 0.0% public transportation, 2.6% walk, 0.0% work from home; Median travel time to work: 14.3 minutes
Additional Information Contacts
City of Berne . . . . (260) 589-8526
http://www.cityofberne.com

DECATUR (city). County seat. Covers a land area of 5.777 square miles and a water area of 0.006 square miles. Located at 40.83° N. Lat; 84.93° W. Long. Elevation is 801 feet.
History: Decatur was named for Stephen Decatur, American naval hero. Novelist Gene Stratton Porter (1868-1924) lived here for three years.
Population: 9,405; Growth (since 2000): -1.3%; Density: 1,627.9 persons per square mile; Race: 94.7% White, 0.5% Black/African American, 0.4% Asian, 0.4% American Indian/Alaska Native, 0.0% Native Hawaiian/Other Pacific Islander, 1.4% Two or more races, 8.4% Hispanic of any race; Average household size: 2.32; Median age: 37.2; Age under 18: 24.7%; Age 65 and over: 14.6%; Males per 100 females: 93.8; Marriage status: 25.0% never married, 54.7% now married, 1.3% separated, 7.9% widowed, 12.3% divorced; Foreign born: 1.0%; Speak English only: 93.5%; With disability: 16.0%; Veterans: 7.0%; Ancestry: 37.6% German, 12.8% American, 10.9% Irish, 7.5% English, 2.5% Swiss
Employment: 6.7% management, business, and financial, 2.5% computer, engineering, and science, 7.4% education, legal, community service, arts, and media, 5.4% healthcare practitioners, 18.9% service, 25.6% sales and office, 8.7% natural resources, construction, and maintenance, 24.8% production, transportation, and material moving
Income: Per capita: $20,909; Median household: $41,949; Average household: $50,891; Households with income of $100,000 or more: 10.5%; Poverty rate: 17.0%
Educational Attainment: High school diploma or higher: 86.4%; Bachelor's degree or higher: 13.9%; Graduate/professional degree or higher: 4.5%

School District(s)
North Adams Community Schools (KG-12)
    2012-13 Enrollment: 1,826 . . . . (260) 724-7146
Housing: Homeownership rate: 64.8%; Median home value: $93,800; Median year structure built: 1959; Homeowner vacancy rate: 3.8%; Median gross rent: $541 per month; Rental vacancy rate: 10.8%
Health Insurance: 86.7% have insurance; 69.6% have private insurance; 28.0% have public insurance; 13.3% do not have insurance; 9.8% of children under 18 do not have insurance
Hospitals: Adams Memorial Hospital (87 beds)

Safety: Violent crime rate: 10.7 per 10,000 population; Property crime rate: 199.0 per 10,000 population
Newspapers: Decatur Daily Democrat (daily circulation 5100)
Transportation: Commute: 95.7% car, 0.0% public transportation, 1.4% walk, 1.6% work from home; Median travel time to work: 18.4 minutes
Additional Information Contacts
City of Decatur.................................... (260) 724-7171
   http://www.decaturin.org

GENEVA (town).
Covers a land area of 1.087 square miles and a water area of 0.140 square miles. Located at 40.60° N. Lat; 84.96° W. Long. Elevation is 846 feet.
History: Geneva was the home of novelist Gene Stratton Porter from 1893 to 1913. Her books were set in the Limberlost Swamps here.
Population: 1,293; Growth (since 2000): -5.5%; Density: 1,190.0 persons per square mile; Race: 94.6% White, 0.6% Black/African American, 0.2% Asian, 0.2% American Indian/Alaska Native, 0.0% Native Hawaiian/Other Pacific Islander, 1.2% Two or more races, 5.4% Hispanic of any race; Average household size: 2.27; Median age: 41.1; Age under 18: 23.9%; Age 65 and over: 18.0%; Males per 100 females: 93.9
Housing: Homeownership rate: 68.8%; Homeowner vacancy rate: 3.0%; Rental vacancy rate: 11.7%

MONROE (town).
Covers a land area of 0.630 square miles and a water area of 0 square miles. Located at 40.75° N. Lat; 84.94° W. Long. Elevation is 823 feet.
Population: 842; Growth (since 2000): 14.7%; Density: 1,336.1 persons per square mile; Race: 99.0% White, 0.0% Black/African American, 0.2% Asian, 0.0% American Indian/Alaska Native, 0.0% Native Hawaiian/Other Pacific Islander, 0.6% Two or more races, 2.3% Hispanic of any race; Average household size: 2.72; Median age: 34.7; Age under 18: 30.4%; Age 65 and over: 14.8%; Males per 100 females: 89.6
School District(s)
Adams Central Community Schools (KG-12)
   2012-13 Enrollment: 1,214 .... (260) 692-6193
Housing: Homeownership rate: 84.6%; Homeowner vacancy rate: 0.7%; Rental vacancy rate: 4.0%

Allen County

Located in northeastern Indiana; bounded on the east by Ohio; crossed by the Saint Joseph, Saint Marys, and Maumee Rivers. Covers a land area of 657.308 square miles, a water area of 2.714 square miles, and is located in the Eastern Time Zone at 41.09° N. Lat., 85.07° W. Long. The county was founded in 1823. County seat is Fort Wayne.

Allen County is part of the Fort Wayne, IN Metropolitan Statistical Area. The entire metro area includes: Allen County, IN; Wells County, IN; Whitley County, IN

Weather Station: Fort Wayne Baer Field Elevation: 791 feet

	Jan	Feb	Mar	Apr	May	Jun	Jul	Aug	Sep	Oct	Nov	Dec
High	32	36	48	61	72	81	84	82	76	63	50	36
Low	18	21	29	39	49	59	63	61	53	42	33	23
Precip	2.3	2.1	2.8	3.5	4.1	4.2	4.3	3.7	2.8	2.9	3.0	2.8
Snow	10.2	7.8	4.1	1.1	tr	tr	tr	tr	tr	0.4	2.0	8.2

High and Low temperatures in degrees Fahrenheit; Precipitation and Snow in inches

Population: 355,329; Growth (since 2000): 7.1%; Density: 540.6 persons per square mile; Race: 79.3% White, 11.7% Black/African American, 2.7% Asian, 0.4% American Indian/Alaska Native, 0.1% Native Hawaiian/Other Pacific Islander, 2.9% two or more races, 6.5% Hispanic of any race; Average household size: 2.53; Median age: 35.3; Age under 18: 27.0%; Age 65 and over: 11.9%; Males per 100 females: 95.1; Marriage status: 30.6% never married, 51.9% now married, 1.4% separated, 5.7% widowed, 11.8% divorced; Foreign born: 6.2%; Speak English only: 90.3%; With disability: 10.9%; Veterans: 8.9%; Ancestry: 30.3% German, 12.6% American, 9.4% Irish, 7.3% English, 3.7% French
Religion: Six largest groups: 16.0% Catholicism, 9.2% Lutheran, 7.3% Non-denominational Protestant, 6.5% Baptist, 4.7% Methodist/Pietist, 3.6% Holiness
Economy: Unemployment rate: 4.9%; Leading industries: 14.2% retail trade; 10.8% other services (except public administration); 10.4% health care and social assistance; Farms: 1,725 totaling 270,808 acres; Company size: 9 employ 1,000 or more persons, 14 employ 500 to 999 persons, 232 employ 100 to 499 persons, 8,796 employ less than 100 persons;
Business ownership: 7,389 women-owned, n/a Black-owned, n/a Hispanic-owned, 532 Asian-owned
Employment: 13.1% management, business, and financial, 4.9% computer, engineering, and science, 10.3% education, legal, community service, arts, and media, 6.1% healthcare practitioners, 16.8% service, 25.2% sales and office, 7.2% natural resources, construction, and maintenance, 16.5% production, transportation, and material moving
Income: Per capita: $25,279; Median household: $49,370; Average household: $64,359; Households with income of $100,000 or more: 16.4%; Poverty rate: 15.3%
Educational Attainment: High school diploma or higher: 89.0%; Bachelor's degree or higher: 26.3%; Graduate/professional degree or higher: 8.9%
Housing: Homeownership rate: 69.5%; Median home value: $112,700; Median year structure built: 1971; Homeowner vacancy rate: 2.6%; Median gross rent: $668 per month; Rental vacancy rate: 12.5%
Vital Statistics: Birth rate: 145.0 per 10,000 population; Death rate: 79.8 per 10,000 population; Age-adjusted cancer mortality rate: 180.4 deaths per 100,000 population
Health Insurance: 85.2% have insurance; 67.2% have private insurance; 27.6% have public insurance; 14.8% do not have insurance; 9.3% of children under 18 do not have insurance
Health Care: Physicians: 25.5 per 10,000 population; Hospital beds: 44.4 per 10,000 population; Hospital admissions: 1,774.7 per 10,000 population
Air Quality Index: 69.3% good, 30.7% moderate, 0.0% unhealthy for sensitive individuals, 0.0% unhealthy (percent of days)
Transportation: Commute: 93.0% car, 0.6% public transportation, 1.3% walk, 4.0% work from home; Median travel time to work: 20.3 minutes
Presidential Election: 40.9% Obama, 57.6% Romney (2012)
Additional Information Contacts
Allen Government .... (219) 449-3155
   http://www.allencounty.us

Allen County Communities

ARCOLA (unincorporated postal area)
ZCTA: 46704
   Covers a land area of 0.020 square miles and a water area of 0 square miles. Located at 41.10° N. Lat; 85.29° W. Long. Elevation is 843 feet.
   Population: 60; Growth (since 2000): n/a; Density: 2,965.2 persons per square mile; Race: 98.3% White, 0.0% Black/African American, 1.7% Asian, 0.0% American Indian/Alaska Native, 0.0% Native Hawaiian/Other Pacific Islander, 0.0% Two or more races, 0.0% Hispanic of any race; Average household size: 2.07; Median age: 44.3; Age under 18: 16.7%; Age 65 and over: 18.3%; Males per 100 females: 114.3
School District(s)
Northwest Allen County Schools (KG-12)
   2012-13 Enrollment: 6,701 .... (260) 637-3155
   Housing: Homeownership rate: 75.8%; Homeowner vacancy rate: 4.3%; Rental vacancy rate: 50.0%

FORT WAYNE (city).
County seat. Covers a land area of 110.618 square miles and a water area of 0.214 square miles. Located at 41.09° N. Lat; 85.14° W. Long. Elevation is 810 feet.
History: The first fort at the site of Fort Wayne was Fort Miami, established in the 1680's by the French. Another stockade was built by Anthony Wayne in 1794. By 1819 a trading post and gristmill were started and more settlers appeared. When Allen County was organized in 1824, Fort Wayne was named as county seat. It was incorporated in 1829. The building of the Wabash & Erie Canal between 1832 and 1840 was a boost for Fort Wayne's economy. Fort Wayne may have claims to the first baseball game played under the lights at its League Park, where in 1883 an arc-lighting system illuminated the field for a game between a professional team from Quincy, Illinois, and a team of students from a Fort Wayne college.
Population: 253,691; Growth (since 2000): 23.3%; Density: 2,293.4 persons per square mile; Race: 73.6% White, 15.4% Black/African American, 3.3% Asian, 0.4% American Indian/Alaska Native, 0.1% Native Hawaiian/Other Pacific Islander, 3.5% Two or more races, 8.0% Hispanic of any race; Average household size: 2.44; Median age: 34.5; Age under 18: 26.4%; Age 65 and over: 12.0%; Males per 100 females: 93.8; Marriage status: 33.6% never married, 47.3% now married, 1.6% separated, 6.1% widowed, 12.9% divorced; Foreign born: 7.6%; Speak

English only: 89.0%; With disability: 11.7%; Veterans: 8.9%; Ancestry: 27.1% German, 11.9% American, 9.6% Irish, 6.9% English, 3.7% African
Employment: 11.8% management, business, and financial, 5.1% computer, engineering, and science, 10.7% education, legal, community service, arts, and media, 5.7% healthcare practitioners, 18.0% service, 25.5% sales and office, 6.3% natural resources, construction, and maintenance, 16.8% production, transportation, and material moving
Income: Per capita: $23,400; Median household: $43,969; Average household: $57,768; Households with income of $100,000 or more: 13.5%; Poverty rate: 18.7%
Educational Attainment: High school diploma or higher: 87.9%; Bachelor's degree or higher: 25.6%; Graduate/professional degree or higher: 8.5%

School District(s)
East Allen County Schools (PK-12)
    2012-13 Enrollment: 9,294 . . . . (260) 446-0100
Fort Wayne Community Schools (PK-12)
    2012-13 Enrollment: 30,407 . . . . (260) 467-2025
Imagine Master Academy (KG-08)
    2012-13 Enrollment: 716. . . . . (260) 420-8395
Imagine Master On Broadway (KG-05)
    2012-13 Enrollment: 366. . . . . (260) 420-8395
M S D Southwest Allen County (KG-12)
    2012-13 Enrollment: 6,940 . . . . (260) 431-2010
Northwest Allen County Schools (KG-12)
    2012-13 Enrollment: 6,701 . . . . (260) 637-3155
Timothy L Johnson Academy (KG-08)
    2012-13 Enrollment: 314. . . . . (260) 441-8727

Four-year College(s)
Brown Mackie College-Fort Wayne (Private, For-profit)
    Fall 2013 Enrollment: 659. . . . . (260) 484-4400
    2013-14 Tuition: In-state $12,114; Out-of-state $12,114
Concordia Theological Seminary (Private, Not-for-profit, Lutheran Church - Missouri Synod)
    Fall 2013 Enrollment: 301. . . . . (260) 452-2100
ITT Technical Institute-Fort Wayne (Private, For-profit)
    Fall 2013 Enrollment: 283. . . . . (260) 497-6200
    2013-14 Tuition: In-state $18,048; Out-of-state $18,048
Indiana Institute of Technology (Private, Not-for-profit)
    Fall 2013 Enrollment: 6,307 . . . . (800) 937-2448
    2013-14 Tuition: In-state $24,860; Out-of-state $24,860
Indiana University-Purdue University-Fort Wayne (Public)
    Fall 2013 Enrollment: 13,459 . . . . (260) 481-6100
    2013-14 Tuition: In-state $7,013; Out-of-state $16,845
International Business College-Fort Wayne (Private, For-profit)
    Fall 2013 Enrollment: 406. . . . . (260) 459-4500
    2013-14 Tuition: In-state $13,880; Out-of-state $13,880
Trine University-Regional/Non-Traditional Campuses (Private, Not-for-profit)
    Fall 2013 Enrollment: 541. . . . . (260) 483-4949
    2013-14 Tuition: In-state $9,840; Out-of-state $9,840
University of Saint Francis-Fort Wayne (Private, Not-for-profit, Roman Catholic)
    Fall 2013 Enrollment: 2,381 . . . . (260) 399-7700
    2013-14 Tuition: In-state $25,180; Out-of-state $25,180

Two-year College(s)
Masters of Cosmetology College (Private, For-profit)
    Fall 2013 Enrollment: 96. . . . . (260) 747-6667
MedTech College-Ft Wayne Campus (Private, For-profit)
    Fall 2013 Enrollment: 357. . . . . (260) 436-3272

Vocational/Technical School(s)
Ravenscroft Beauty College (Private, For-profit)
    Fall 2013 Enrollment: 187. . . . . (260) 486-8868
    2013-14 Tuition: $11,800
Ross Medical Education Center-Fort Wayne (Private, For-profit)
    Fall 2013 Enrollment: 138. . . . . (260) 471-4840
    2013-14 Tuition: $15,680
Rudae's School of Beauty Culture-Ft Wayne (Private, For-profit)
    Fall 2013 Enrollment: 138. . . . . (260) 483-2466
    2013-14 Tuition: $12,375

Housing: Homeownership rate: 63.3%; Median home value: $99,900; Median year structure built: 1968; Homeowner vacancy rate: 2.9%; Median gross rent: $656 per month; Rental vacancy rate: 12.5%

Health Insurance: 83.7% have insurance; 62.6% have private insurance; 30.7% have public insurance; 16.3% do not have insurance; 9.3% of children under 18 do not have insurance
Hospitals: Dupont Hospital (131 beds); Lutheran Hospital of Indiana (435 beds); Orthopaedic Hospital at Parkview North (37 beds); Parkview Regional Medical Center (656 beds); Saint Joseph Hospital (191 beds); The Orthopaedic Hospital of Lutheran Health Network (39 beds)
Safety: Violent crime rate: 37.2 per 10,000 population; Property crime rate: 384.9 per 10,000 population
Newspapers: Fort Wayne Ink (weekly circulation 25000); Fort Wayne Reader (weekly circulation 25000); Journal Gazette (daily circulation 49000); News-Sentinel (daily circulation 27300); Waynedale News (weekly circulation 10000)
Transportation: Commute: 93.2% car, 0.9% public transportation, 1.4% walk, 3.3% work from home; Median travel time to work: 19.7 minutes
Airports: Fort Wayne International (primary service/non-hub)
Additional Information Contacts
City of Fort Wayne. . . . . (260) 427-1221
    http://www.cityoffortwayne.org

GRABILL (town). Covers a land area of 0.602 square miles and a water area of 0 square miles. Located at 41.21° N. Lat; 84.97° W. Long. Elevation is 817 feet.
Population: 1,053; Growth (since 2000): -5.4%; Density: 1,748.0 persons per square mile; Race: 96.8% White, 0.6% Black/African American, 0.5% Asian, 0.7% American Indian/Alaska Native, 0.0% Native Hawaiian/Other Pacific Islander, 1.2% Two or more races, 1.6% Hispanic of any race; Average household size: 2.61; Median age: 32.8; Age under 18: 30.9%; Age 65 and over: 11.3%; Males per 100 females: 92.9
Housing: Homeownership rate: 82.1%; Homeowner vacancy rate: 2.3%; Rental vacancy rate: 21.7%
Newspapers: East Allen Courier (weekly circulation 7200)
Additional Information Contacts
Town of Grabill . . . . (260) 627-5227
    http://grabill.net

HARLAN (CDP). Covers a land area of 3.104 square miles and a water area of 0 square miles. Located at 41.20° N. Lat; 84.92° W. Long. Elevation is 784 feet.
Population: 1,634; Growth (since 2000): n/a; Density: 526.4 persons per square mile; Race: 97.4% White, 0.4% Black/African American, 0.1% Asian, 0.1% American Indian/Alaska Native, 0.0% Native Hawaiian/Other Pacific Islander, 1.5% Two or more races, 2.8% Hispanic of any race; Average household size: 2.84; Median age: 31.1; Age under 18: 31.5%; Age 65 and over: 10.6%; Males per 100 females: 100.0
Housing: Homeownership rate: 82.1%; Homeowner vacancy rate: 4.3%; Rental vacancy rate: 5.4%

HOAGLAND (CDP). Covers a land area of 3.398 square miles and a water area of 0 square miles. Located at 40.95° N. Lat; 85.00° W. Long. Elevation is 823 feet.
Population: 821; Growth (since 2000): n/a; Density: 241.6 persons per square mile; Race: 97.7% White, 0.1% Black/African American, 0.0% Asian, 0.6% American Indian/Alaska Native, 0.1% Native Hawaiian/Other Pacific Islander, 1.2% Two or more races, 0.6% Hispanic of any race; Average household size: 2.56; Median age: 39.3; Age under 18: 25.3%; Age 65 and over: 13.9%; Males per 100 females: 96.9

School District(s)
East Allen County Schools (PK-12)
    2012-13 Enrollment: 9,294 . . . . (260) 446-0100
Housing: Homeownership rate: 87.8%; Homeowner vacancy rate: 2.8%; Rental vacancy rate: 2.5%

HUNTERTOWN (town). Covers a land area of 3.802 square miles and a water area of 0.010 square miles. Located at 41.21° N. Lat; 85.17° W. Long. Elevation is 833 feet.
History: Settled 1830s.
Population: 4,810; Growth (since 2000): 171.6%; Density: 1,265.0 persons per square mile; Race: 93.6% White, 1.4% Black/African American, 2.0% Asian, 0.4% American Indian/Alaska Native, 0.0% Native Hawaiian/Other Pacific Islander, 1.9% Two or more races, 2.3% Hispanic of any race; Average household size: 2.79; Median age: 31.5; Age under 18: 31.9%; Age 65 and over: 6.4%; Males per 100 females: 96.7; Marriage status: 21.2% never married, 61.7% now married, 0.0% separated, 4.5% widowed, 12.6% divorced; Foreign born: 2.5%; Speak English only: 94.9%;

With disability: 7.4%; Veterans: 10.7%; Ancestry: 29.0% German, 17.1% American, 11.8% Irish, 10.7% English, 4.2% Italian
Employment: 22.5% management, business, and financial, 7.8% computer, engineering, and science, 9.0% education, legal, community service, arts, and media, 6.9% healthcare practitioners, 13.8% service, 20.4% sales and office, 6.9% natural resources, construction, and maintenance, 12.8% production, transportation, and material moving
Income: Per capita: $28,595; Median household: $73,636; Average household: $86,663; Households with income of $100,000 or more: 22.9%; Poverty rate: 2.9%
Educational Attainment: High school diploma or higher: 96.3%; Bachelor's degree or higher: 30.5%; Graduate/professional degree or higher: 9.9%

School District(s)
Northwest Allen County Schools (KG-12)
    2012-13 Enrollment: 6,701 . . . . (260) 637-3155
Housing: Homeownership rate: 87.5%; Median home value: $134,200; Median year structure built: 2000; Homeowner vacancy rate: 2.8%; Median gross rent: $825 per month; Rental vacancy rate: 6.9%
Health Insurance: 94.6% have insurance; 89.7% have private insurance; 13.6% have public insurance; 5.4% do not have insurance; 3.2% of children under 18 do not have insurance
Newspapers: Northwest News (weekly circulation 1500)
Transportation: Commute: 98.7% car, 0.0% public transportation, 0.2% walk, 0.3% work from home; Median travel time to work: 24.3 minutes
Additional Information Contacts
Town of Huntertown . . . . (260) 637-5058
    http://www.huntertown.org

LEO-CEDARVILLE (town).
Covers a land area of 3.713 square miles and a water area of 0.136 square miles. Located at 41.22° N. Lat; 85.02° W. Long. Elevation is 797 feet.
History: Leo-Cedarville was formed by the incorporation of the villages of Leo and Cedarville into a town in the mid-1990s in a defensive move against the rapidly expanding Fort Wayne, whose city limits currently sit five miles from the town.
Population: 3,603; Growth (since 2000): 29.5%; Density: 970.3 persons per square mile; Race: 97.1% White, 0.1% Black/African American, 0.8% Asian, 0.2% American Indian/Alaska Native, 0.0% Native Hawaiian/Other Pacific Islander, 1.2% Two or more races, 1.6% Hispanic of any race; Average household size: 3.04; Median age: 38.1; Age under 18: 32.3%; Age 65 and over: 9.4%; Males per 100 females: 99.4; Marriage status: 22.1% never married, 67.4% now married, 0.4% separated, 2.6% widowed, 7.9% divorced; Foreign born: 1.3%; Speak English only: 97.9%; With disability: 8.4%; Veterans: 8.1%; Ancestry: 42.0% German, 22.6% American, 9.2% English, 7.4% Irish, 3.5% French
Employment: 14.9% management, business, and financial, 4.6% computer, engineering, and science, 10.2% education, legal, community service, arts, and media, 9.3% healthcare practitioners, 16.1% service, 27.8% sales and office, 4.4% natural resources, construction, and maintenance, 12.6% production, transportation, and material moving
Income: Per capita: $23,639; Median household: $62,865; Average household: $73,218; Households with income of $100,000 or more: 22.6%; Poverty rate: 4.3%
Educational Attainment: High school diploma or higher: 96.7%; Bachelor's degree or higher: 31.8%; Graduate/professional degree or higher: 7.7%

School District(s)
East Allen County Schools (PK-12)
    2012-13 Enrollment: 9,294 . . . . (260) 446-0100
Housing: Homeownership rate: 90.6%; Median home value: $159,600; Median year structure built: 1991; Homeowner vacancy rate: 0.8%; Median gross rent: $930 per month; Rental vacancy rate: 6.7%
Health Insurance: 94.8% have insurance; 82.4% have private insurance; 18.7% have public insurance; 5.2% do not have insurance; 2.6% of children under 18 do not have insurance
Transportation: Commute: 95.7% car, 0.0% public transportation, 0.3% walk, 3.7% work from home; Median travel time to work: 21.4 minutes
Additional Information Contacts
Town of Leo-Cedarville . . . . (260) 627-6321
    http://www.leocedarville.com

MONROEVILLE (town).
Covers a land area of 0.744 square miles and a water area of 0 square miles. Located at 40.97° N. Lat; 84.87° W. Long. Elevation is 791 feet.
History: Settled 1841, incorporated 1865.
Population: 1,235; Growth (since 2000): -0.1%; Density: 1,659.2 persons per square mile; Race: 98.9% White, 0.0% Black/African American, 0.0% Asian, 0.0% American Indian/Alaska Native, 0.1% Native Hawaiian/Other Pacific Islander, 0.6% Two or more races, 1.9% Hispanic of any race; Average household size: 2.40; Median age: 42.3; Age under 18: 22.2%; Age 65 and over: 19.9%; Males per 100 females: 89.1

School District(s)
East Allen County Schools (PK-12)
    2012-13 Enrollment: 9,294 . . . . (260) 446-0100
Housing: Homeownership rate: 79.4%; Homeowner vacancy rate: 2.7%; Rental vacancy rate: 13.6%
Newspapers: The Monroeville News (weekly circulation 1200)

NEW HAVEN (city).
Covers a land area of 9.867 square miles and a water area of 0.005 square miles. Located at 41.06° N. Lat; 85.03° W. Long. Elevation is 758 feet.
History: New Haven was settled when the Wabash & Erie Canal was built. Its first residents, who came from New England, named it for the city in Connecticut.
Population: 14,794; Growth (since 2000): 19.2%; Density: 1,499.3 persons per square mile; Race: 93.2% White, 3.3% Black/African American, 0.4% Asian, 0.4% American Indian/Alaska Native, 0.1% Native Hawaiian/Other Pacific Islander, 1.7% Two or more races, 3.1% Hispanic of any race; Average household size: 2.52; Median age: 37.5; Age under 18: 26.2%; Age 65 and over: 13.9%; Males per 100 females: 92.7; Marriage status: 25.2% never married, 55.0% now married, 1.2% separated, 6.1% widowed, 13.7% divorced; Foreign born: 1.8%; Speak English only: 94.9%; With disability: 10.9%; Veterans: 10.4%; Ancestry: 33.9% German, 16.1% American, 9.7% Irish, 9.2% English, 5.5% French
Employment: 12.2% management, business, and financial, 4.2% computer, engineering, and science, 9.8% education, legal, community service, arts, and media, 4.3% healthcare practitioners, 16.3% service, 25.0% sales and office, 8.7% natural resources, construction, and maintenance, 19.5% production, transportation, and material moving
Income: Per capita: $23,192; Median household: $47,931; Average household: $57,895; Households with income of $100,000 or more: 13.0%; Poverty rate: 14.2%
Educational Attainment: High school diploma or higher: 88.6%; Bachelor's degree or higher: 19.1%; Graduate/professional degree or higher: 5.3%

School District(s)
East Allen County Schools (PK-12)
    2012-13 Enrollment: 9,294 . . . . (260) 446-0100
Housing: Homeownership rate: 75.4%; Median home value: $92,200; Median year structure built: 1970; Homeowner vacancy rate: 1.9%; Median gross rent: $700 per month; Rental vacancy rate: 10.8%
Health Insurance: 85.3% have insurance; 69.5% have private insurance; 27.8% have public insurance; 14.7% do not have insurance; 7.4% of children under 18 do not have insurance
Safety: Violent crime rate: 15.4 per 10,000 population; Property crime rate: 341.6 per 10,000 population
Transportation: Commute: 93.0% car, 0.1% public transportation, 2.6% walk, 3.1% work from home; Median travel time to work: 19.3 minutes
Additional Information Contacts
City of New Haven . . . . (260) 748-7000
    http://www.newhavenin.org

SPENCERVILLE (unincorporated postal area)
ZCTA: 46788
    Covers a land area of 35.517 square miles and a water area of 0.335 square miles. Located at 41.27° N. Lat; 84.91° W. Long..
    Population: 3,260; Growth (since 2000): 15.0%; Density: 91.8 persons per square mile; Race: 97.9% White, 0.3% Black/African American, 0.4% Asian, 0.4% American Indian/Alaska Native, 0.0% Native Hawaiian/Other Pacific Islander, 0.8% Two or more races, 1.5% Hispanic of any race; Average household size: 3.13; Median age: 36.7; Age under 18: 30.6%; Age 65 and over: 9.4%; Males per 100 females: 108.4; Marriage status: 27.3% never married, 56.2% now married, 0.5% separated, 6.4% widowed, 10.2% divorced; Foreign born: 1.7%; Speak English only: 87.1%; With disability: 11.6%; Veterans: 10.9%; Ancestry: 39.3% German, 22.7% American, 7.8% Irish, 5.6% English, 2.5% Italian

Employment: 15.4% management, business, and financial, 5.4% computer, engineering, and science, 10.5% education, legal, community service, arts, and media, 4.6% healthcare practitioners, 17.8% service, 15.7% sales and office, 10.0% natural resources, construction, and maintenance, 20.6% production, transportation, and material moving
Income: Per capita: $23,638; Median household: $55,191; Average household: $66,740; Households with income of $100,000 or more: 18.8%; Poverty rate: 8.4%
Educational Attainment: High school diploma or higher: 93.3%; Bachelor's degree or higher: 22.7%; Graduate/professional degree or higher: 5.7%
Housing: Homeownership rate: 91.7%; Median home value: $170,100; Median year structure built: 1982; Homeowner vacancy rate: 0.6%; Median gross rent: $591 per month; Rental vacancy rate: 5.3%
Health Insurance: 84.6% have insurance; 72.9% have private insurance; 20.0% have public insurance; 15.4% do not have insurance; 18.0% of children under 18 do not have insurance
Transportation: Commute: 84.8% car, 1.1% public transportation, 0.7% walk, 13.4% work from home; Median travel time to work: 26.4 minutes

WOODBURN (city).
Covers a land area of 0.931 square miles and a water area of 0 square miles. Located at 41.13° N. Lat; 84.86° W. Long. Elevation is 748 feet.
History: Laid out 1865. Until 1936, called Shirley City.
Population: 1,520; Growth (since 2000): -3.7%; Density: 1,633.0 persons per square mile; Race: 98.6% White, 0.0% Black/African American, 0.1% Asian, 0.2% American Indian/Alaska Native, 0.1% Native Hawaiian/Other Pacific Islander, 0.7% Two or more races, 1.1% Hispanic of any race; Average household size: 2.60; Median age: 32.9; Age under 18: 28.0%; Age 65 and over: 10.5%; Males per 100 females: 103.8

School District(s)
East Allen County Schools (PK-12)
    2012-13 Enrollment: 9,294 . . . . (260) 446-0100
Housing: Homeownership rate: 80.5%; Homeowner vacancy rate: 3.1%; Rental vacancy rate: 11.6%

YODER (unincorporated postal area)
ZCTA: 46798
Covers a land area of 20.604 square miles and a water area of <.001 square miles. Located at 40.94° N. Lat; 85.21° W. Long. Elevation is 810 feet.
Population: 1,661; Growth (since 2000): -11.3%; Density: 80.6 persons per square mile; Race: 94.9% White, 1.9% Black/African American, 0.5% Asian, 0.5% American Indian/Alaska Native, 0.1% Native Hawaiian/Other Pacific Islander, 1.3% Two or more races, 2.5% Hispanic of any race; Average household size: 2.52; Median age: 42.2; Age under 18: 25.1%; Age 65 and over: 13.5%; Males per 100 females: 103.1
Housing: Homeownership rate: 83.6%; Homeowner vacancy rate: 0.9%; Rental vacancy rate: 27.9%

Bartholomew County

Located in south central Indiana; drained by the East Fork of the White River. Covers a land area of 406.908 square miles, a water area of 2.617 square miles, and is located in the Eastern Time Zone at 39.21° N. Lat., 85.90° W. Long. The county was founded in 1821. County seat is Columbus.

Bartholomew County is part of the Columbus, IN Metropolitan Statistical Area. The entire metro area includes: Bartholomew County, IN

Weather Station: Columbus											Elevation: 621 feet	
	Jan	Feb	Mar	Apr	May	Jun	Jul	Aug	Sep	Oct	Nov	Dec
High	38	42	52	64	74	82	85	85	78	67	54	41
Low	21	23	31	42	52	62	65	63	55	43	34	25
Precip	2.9	2.6	3.7	4.5	5.3	3.9	4.1	3.7	3.1	3.2	3.7	3.5
Snow	5.1	3.5	2.1	0.1	tr	0.0	0.0	0.0	0.0	0.1	0.1	3.4

High and Low temperatures in degrees Fahrenheit; Precipitation and Snow in inches

Population: 76,794; Growth (since 2000): 7.5%; Density: 188.7 persons per square mile; Race: 89.6% White, 1.8% Black/African American, 3.4% Asian, 0.3% American Indian/Alaska Native, 0.1% Native Hawaiian/Other Pacific Islander, 1.6% two or more races, 6.2% Hispanic of any race; Average household size: 2.53; Median age: 38.2; Age under 18: 25.2%; Age 65 and over: 14.0%; Males per 100 females: 97.6; Marriage status: 24.1% never married, 56.6% now married, 1.4% separated, 6.4% widowed, 12.9% divorced; Foreign born: 7.6%; Speak English only: 90.4%; With disability: 11.8%; Veterans: 9.4%; Ancestry: 23.5% German, 18.7% American, 11.5% English, 10.5% Irish, 2.5% Scottish
Religion: Six largest groups: 15.1% Baptist, 8.9% Lutheran, 6.0% Catholicism, 6.0% Methodist/Pietist, 5.1% Non-denominational Protestant, 2.1% Holiness
Economy: Unemployment rate: 4.0%; Leading industries: 16.5% retail trade; 11.8% health care and social assistance; 10.8% accommodation and food services; Farms: 623 totaling 171,601 acres; Company size: 6 employ 1,000 or more persons, 8 employ 500 to 999 persons, 54 employ 100 to 499 persons, 1,809 employ less than 100 persons; Business ownership: 1,697 women-owned, 48 Black-owned, n/a Hispanic-owned, 161 Asian-owned
Employment: 15.3% management, business, and financial, 9.0% computer, engineering, and science, 8.3% education, legal, community service, arts, and media, 5.7% healthcare practitioners, 15.5% service, 21.0% sales and office, 6.8% natural resources, construction, and maintenance, 18.5% production, transportation, and material moving
Income: Per capita: $27,359; Median household: $54,165; Average household: $69,369; Households with income of $100,000 or more: 20.7%; Poverty rate: 12.2%
Educational Attainment: High school diploma or higher: 89.1%; Bachelor's degree or higher: 26.5%; Graduate/professional degree or higher: 10.4%
Housing: Homeownership rate: 71.6%; Median home value: $134,900; Median year structure built: 1972; Homeowner vacancy rate: 2.6%; Median gross rent: $786 per month; Rental vacancy rate: 14.4%
Vital Statistics: Birth rate: 129.9 per 10,000 population; Death rate: 82.7 per 10,000 population; Age-adjusted cancer mortality rate: 184.7 deaths per 100,000 population
Health Insurance: 87.3% have insurance; 74.6% have private insurance; 25.4% have public insurance; 12.7% do not have insurance; 9.6% of children under 18 do not have insurance
Health Care: Physicians: 22.0 per 10,000 population; Hospital beds: 25.5 per 10,000 population; Hospital admissions: 1,157.5 per 10,000 population
Air Quality Index: 89.7% good, 10.3% moderate, 0.0% unhealthy for sensitive individuals, 0.0% unhealthy (percent of days)
Transportation: Commute: 93.7% car, 0.5% public transportation, 1.5% walk, 2.7% work from home; Median travel time to work: 19.1 minutes
Presidential Election: 36.2% Obama, 61.7% Romney (2012)
Additional Information Contacts
Bartholomew Government . . . . (812) 376-2510
   http://www.bartholomewco.com

Bartholomew County Communities

CLIFFORD (town).
Covers a land area of 0.105 square miles and a water area of 0 square miles. Located at 39.28° N. Lat; 85.87° W. Long. Elevation is 659 feet.
Population: 233; Growth (since 2000): -19.9%; Density: 2,211.6 persons per square mile; Race: 99.1% White, 0.0% Black/African American, 0.0% Asian, 0.4% American Indian/Alaska Native, 0.0% Native Hawaiian/Other Pacific Islander, 0.0% Two or more races, 1.7% Hispanic of any race; Average household size: 2.48; Median age: 35.6; Age under 18: 30.5%; Age 65 and over: 10.3%; Males per 100 females: 119.8
Housing: Homeownership rate: 62.8%; Homeowner vacancy rate: 3.0%; Rental vacancy rate: 7.9%

COLUMBUS (city).
County seat. Covers a land area of 27.497 square miles and a water area of 0.386 square miles. Located at 39.21° N. Lat; 85.92° W. Long. Elevation is 627 feet.
History: Columbus was settled by General John Tipton, John Lindsay, and Luke Bonesteel in 1820, and was called Tiptonia. In 1821 General Tipton offered land for a county seat if the new town were named for him. The county commissioners accepted the land, but named the town Columbus.
Population: 44,061; Growth (since 2000): 12.8%; Density: 1,602.4 persons per square mile; Race: 86.9% White, 2.7% Black/African American, 5.6% Asian, 0.2% American Indian/Alaska Native, 0.1% Native Hawaiian/Other Pacific Islander, 2.0% Two or more races, 5.8% Hispanic of any race; Average household size: 2.43; Median age: 37.1; Age under 18: 25.2%; Age 65 and over: 14.4%; Males per 100 females: 93.9; Marriage status: 26.7% never married, 52.7% now married, 1.6% separated, 6.9% widowed, 13.8% divorced; Foreign born: 10.0%; Speak English only: 89.3%; With disability: 12.4%; Veterans: 8.7%; Ancestry:

24.1% German, 17.0% American, 12.3% English, 10.5% Irish, 2.5% Scottish
Employment: 17.0% management, business, and financial, 10.8% computer, engineering, and science, 9.3% education, legal, community service, arts, and media, 6.6% healthcare practitioners, 15.0% service, 19.9% sales and office, 5.1% natural resources, construction, and maintenance, 16.4% production, transportation, and material moving
Income: Per capita: $28,739; Median household: $53,045; Average household: $69,804; Households with income of $100,000 or more: 22.1%; Poverty rate: 11.6%
Educational Attainment: High school diploma or higher: 90.1%; Bachelor's degree or higher: 31.9%; Graduate/professional degree or higher: 13.9%

School District(s)
Bartholomew Con School Corp (PK-12)
    2012-13 Enrollment: 11,416 . . . . (812) 376-4220
International School of Columbus (07-11)
    2012-13 Enrollment: 128. . . . . (812) 314-7078
Housing: Homeownership rate: 62.6%; Median home value: $140,900; Median year structure built: 1972; Homeowner vacancy rate: 2.9%; Median gross rent: $794 per month; Rental vacancy rate: 14.2%
Health Insurance: 87.9% have insurance; 75.2% have private insurance; 25.1% have public insurance; 12.1% do not have insurance; 9.6% of children under 18 do not have insurance
Hospitals: Columbus Regional Hospital (225 beds)
Safety: Violent crime rate: 17.9 per 10,000 population; Property crime rate: 463.0 per 10,000 population
Newspapers: The Republic (daily circulation 21200)
Transportation: Commute: 93.8% car, 0.7% public transportation, 1.1% walk, 2.7% work from home; Median travel time to work: 17.2 minutes
Airports: Columbus Municipal (general aviation)
Additional Information Contacts
City of Columbus . . . . (812) 376-2510
http://www.columbus.in.gov

ELIZABETHTOWN (town).
Covers a land area of 0.253 square miles and a water area of 0 square miles. Located at 39.14° N. Lat; 85.81° W. Long. Elevation is 636 feet.
Population: 504; Growth (since 2000): 28.9%; Density: 1,989.6 persons per square mile; Race: 91.1% White, 1.0% Black/African American, 0.0% Asian, 0.0% American Indian/Alaska Native, 0.0% Native Hawaiian/Other Pacific Islander, 0.8% Two or more races, 9.5% Hispanic of any race; Average household size: 2.90; Median age: 31.4; Age under 18: 30.4%; Age 65 and over: 8.9%; Males per 100 females: 96.9
Housing: Homeownership rate: 70.1%; Homeowner vacancy rate: 2.4%; Rental vacancy rate: 13.3%

HARTSVILLE (town).
Covers a land area of 0.344 square miles and a water area of 0 square miles. Located at 39.27° N. Lat; 85.70° W. Long. Elevation is 758 feet.
History: Hartsville was the first location of Hartsville College, founded in 1850 by the United Brethren denomination but moved to Huntington in 1898.
Population: 362; Growth (since 2000): -3.7%; Density: 1,052.9 persons per square mile; Race: 97.0% White, 1.1% Black/African American, 0.0% Asian, 0.0% American Indian/Alaska Native, 0.0% Native Hawaiian/Other Pacific Islander, 1.9% Two or more races, 1.1% Hispanic of any race; Average household size: 2.74; Median age: 36.5; Age under 18: 26.8%; Age 65 and over: 12.7%; Males per 100 females: 88.5
Housing: Homeownership rate: 79.5%; Homeowner vacancy rate: 1.8%; Rental vacancy rate: 15.6%

HOPE (town).
Covers a land area of 0.951 square miles and a water area of 0 square miles. Located at 39.30° N. Lat; 85.77° W. Long. Elevation is 715 feet.
Population: 2,102; Growth (since 2000): -1.8%; Density: 2,210.6 persons per square mile; Race: 97.1% White, 0.6% Black/African American, 0.4% Asian, 0.1% American Indian/Alaska Native, 0.0% Native Hawaiian/Other Pacific Islander, 1.3% Two or more races, 1.8% Hispanic of any race; Average household size: 2.64; Median age: 35.6; Age under 18: 25.7%; Age 65 and over: 11.2%; Males per 100 females: 99.4

School District(s)
Flat Rock-Hawcreek School Corp (KG-12)
    2012-13 Enrollment: 902. . . . . (812) 546-2000
Housing: Homeownership rate: 70.9%; Homeowner vacancy rate: 2.7%; Rental vacancy rate: 13.9%
Newspapers: Star Journal (weekly circulation 1000)
Additional Information Contacts
Town of Hope . . . . (812) 546-4673
http://www.hopechamber.com

JONESVILLE (town).
Covers a land area of 0.128 square miles and a water area of 0 square miles. Located at 39.06° N. Lat; 85.89° W. Long. Elevation is 594 feet.
History: Laid out 1851.
Population: 177; Growth (since 2000): -19.5%; Density: 1,382.1 persons per square mile; Race: 92.7% White, 0.0% Black/African American, 0.0% Asian, 2.3% American Indian/Alaska Native, 0.0% Native Hawaiian/Other Pacific Islander, 1.7% Two or more races, 4.0% Hispanic of any race; Average household size: 2.30; Median age: 45.1; Age under 18: 17.5%; Age 65 and over: 19.2%; Males per 100 females: 101.1
Housing: Homeownership rate: 76.7%; Homeowner vacancy rate: 1.6%; Rental vacancy rate: 10.0%

TAYLORSVILLE (CDP).
Covers a land area of 1.064 square miles and a water area of 0 square miles. Located at 39.30° N. Lat; 85.95° W. Long. Elevation is 653 feet.
History: Laid out 1849.
Population: 919; Growth (since 2000): -1.8%; Density: 863.5 persons per square mile; Race: 96.2% White, 1.1% Black/African American, 0.4% Asian, 0.2% American Indian/Alaska Native, 0.0% Native Hawaiian/Other Pacific Islander, 0.5% Two or more races, 2.9% Hispanic of any race; Average household size: 2.55; Median age: 41.4; Age under 18: 23.5%; Age 65 and over: 16.6%; Males per 100 females: 98.5

School District(s)
Bartholomew Con School Corp (PK-12)
    2012-13 Enrollment: 11,416 . . . . (812) 376-4220
Housing: Homeownership rate: 79.5%; Homeowner vacancy rate: 3.0%; Rental vacancy rate: 6.3%

Benton County

Located in western Indiana; bounded on the west by Illinois. Covers a land area of 406.417 square miles, a water area of 0.091 square miles, and is located in the Eastern Time Zone at 40.61° N. Lat., 87.32° W. Long. The county was founded in 1840. County seat is Fowler.

Benton County is part of the Lafayette-West Lafayette, IN Metropolitan Statistical Area. The entire metro area includes: Benton County, IN; Carroll County, IN; Tippecanoe County, IN

Population: 8,854; Growth (since 2000): -6.0%; Density: 21.8 persons per square mile; Race: 95.9% White, 0.5% Black/African American, 0.2% Asian, 0.1% American Indian/Alaska Native, 0.0% Native Hawaiian/Other Pacific Islander, 1.1% two or more races, 4.9% Hispanic of any race; Average household size: 2.52; Median age: 40.1; Age under 18: 25.8%; Age 65 and over: 15.7%; Males per 100 females: 98.1; Marriage status: 23.9% never married, 54.3% now married, 0.6% separated, 8.2% widowed, 13.6% divorced; Foreign born: 1.6%; Speak English only: 95.3%; With disability: 17.2%; Veterans: 9.7%; Ancestry: 28.4% German, 14.4% Irish, 11.5% American, 6.9% English, 6.3% French
Religion: Five largest groups: 33.7% Methodist/Pietist, 30.6% Catholicism, 11.6% Baptist, 1.7% Presbyterian-Reformed, 1.2% Holiness
Economy: Unemployment rate: 5.3%; Leading industries: 16.0% retail trade; 13.4% transportation and warehousing; 11.3% other services (except public administration); Farms: 381 totaling 254,245 acres; Company size: 0 employ 1,000 or more persons, 0 employ 500 to 999 persons, 0 employ 100 to 499 persons, 194 employ less than 100 persons; Business ownership: n/a women-owned, n/a Black-owned, n/a Hispanic-owned, n/a Asian-owned
Employment: 14.8% management, business, and financial, 1.4% computer, engineering, and science, 6.8% education, legal, community service, arts, and media, 4.5% healthcare practitioners, 16.3% service, 20.5% sales and office, 14.9% natural resources, construction, and maintenance, 20.7% production, transportation, and material moving
Income: Per capita: $23,049; Median household: $48,711; Average household: $58,250; Households with income of $100,000 or more: 15.4%; Poverty rate: 11.1%

Educational Attainment: High school diploma or higher: 88.9%; Bachelor's degree or higher: 16.0%; Graduate/professional degree or higher: 4.9%
Housing: Homeownership rate: 74.6%; Median home value: $84,300; Median year structure built: 1949; Homeowner vacancy rate: 2.4%; Median gross rent: $721 per month; Rental vacancy rate: 14.1%
Vital Statistics: Birth rate: 118.6 per 10,000 population; Death rate: 97.0 per 10,000 population; Age-adjusted cancer mortality rate: 186.3 deaths per 100,000 population
Health Insurance: 85.4% have insurance; 65.4% have private insurance; 33.0% have public insurance; 14.6% do not have insurance; 8.2% of children under 18 do not have insurance
Health Care: Physicians: 3.4 per 10,000 population; Hospital beds: 0.0 per 10,000 population; Hospital admissions: 0.0 per 10,000 population
Transportation: Commute: 89.0% car, 0.5% public transportation, 4.4% walk, 5.3% work from home; Median travel time to work: 24.9 minutes
Presidential Election: 32.4% Obama, 65.1% Romney (2012)
Additional Information Contacts
Benton Government .... (765) 884-0930
  http://www.bentoncounty.in.gov

Benton County Communities

AMBIA (town). Covers a land area of 0.148 square miles and a water area of 0 square miles. Located at 40.49° N. Lat; 87.52° W. Long. Elevation is 735 feet.
Population: 239; Growth (since 2000): 21.3%; Density: 1,615.0 persons per square mile; Race: 77.0% White, 0.0% Black/African American, 0.0% Asian, 0.0% American Indian/Alaska Native, 0.0% Native Hawaiian/Other Pacific Islander, 2.5% Two or more races, 43.5% Hispanic of any race; Average household size: 3.06; Median age: 31.4; Age under 18: 34.3%; Age 65 and over: 8.8%; Males per 100 females: 102.5
Housing: Homeownership rate: 74.4%; Homeowner vacancy rate: 0.0%; Rental vacancy rate: 0.0%

BOSWELL (town). Covers a land area of 0.927 square miles and a water area of 0 square miles. Located at 40.52° N. Lat; 87.37° W. Long. Elevation is 755 feet.
Population: 778; Growth (since 2000): -5.9%; Density: 839.6 persons per square mile; Race: 87.9% White, 0.6% Black/African American, 0.1% Asian, 0.3% American Indian/Alaska Native, 0.0% Native Hawaiian/Other Pacific Islander, 0.9% Two or more races, 15.0% Hispanic of any race; Average household size: 2.51; Median age: 38.1; Age under 18: 27.6%; Age 65 and over: 16.2%; Males per 100 females: 92.1
School District(s)
Benton Community School Corp (KG-12)
  2012-13 Enrollment: 1,850 .... (765) 884-0850
Housing: Homeownership rate: 75.5%; Homeowner vacancy rate: 3.3%; Rental vacancy rate: 17.0%

EARL PARK (town). Covers a land area of 0.941 square miles and a water area of 0 square miles. Located at 40.69° N. Lat; 87.42° W. Long. Elevation is 810 feet.
History: Laid out 1872.
Population: 348; Growth (since 2000): -28.2%; Density: 369.8 persons per square mile; Race: 98.3% White, 0.0% Black/African American, 0.0% Asian, 0.0% American Indian/Alaska Native, 0.0% Native Hawaiian/Other Pacific Islander, 0.3% Two or more races, 2.6% Hispanic of any race; Average household size: 2.35; Median age: 42.0; Age under 18: 20.1%; Age 65 and over: 14.7%; Males per 100 females: 113.5
Housing: Homeownership rate: 77.6%; Homeowner vacancy rate: 4.2%; Rental vacancy rate: 19.0%

FOWLER (town). County seat. Covers a land area of 1.397 square miles and a water area of 0.006 square miles. Located at 40.62° N. Lat; 87.32° W. Long. Elevation is 823 feet.
History: Laid out 1872.
Population: 2,317; Growth (since 2000): -4.1%; Density: 1,658.8 persons per square mile; Race: 96.7% White, 0.6% Black/African American, 0.1% Asian, 0.1% American Indian/Alaska Native, 0.0% Native Hawaiian/Other Pacific Islander, 1.6% Two or more races, 3.9% Hispanic of any race; Average household size: 2.40; Median age: 41.8; Age under 18: 25.1%; Age 65 and over: 20.0%; Males per 100 females: 92.0
Housing: Homeownership rate: 68.7%; Homeowner vacancy rate: 3.4%; Rental vacancy rate: 13.9%

Newspapers: Benton Review (weekly circulation 3000)
Additional Information Contacts
Town of Fowler .... (765) 742-4044
  http://www.lafayettechamber.com

OTTERBEIN (town). Covers a land area of 0.611 square miles and a water area of 0 square miles. Located at 40.49° N. Lat; 87.09° W. Long. Elevation is 709 feet.
History: Laid out 1872.
Population: 1,262; Growth (since 2000): -3.8%; Density: 2,067.1 persons per square mile; Race: 96.8% White, 0.7% Black/African American, 0.1% Asian, 0.3% American Indian/Alaska Native, 0.1% Native Hawaiian/Other Pacific Islander, 1.2% Two or more races, 3.1% Hispanic of any race; Average household size: 2.51; Median age: 32.4; Age under 18: 28.0%; Age 65 and over: 11.1%; Males per 100 females: 96.9
School District(s)
Benton Community School Corp (KG-12)
  2012-13 Enrollment: 1,850 .... (765) 884-0850
Housing: Homeownership rate: 66.7%; Homeowner vacancy rate: 2.0%; Rental vacancy rate: 12.1%

OXFORD (town). Covers a land area of 0.541 square miles and a water area of 0 square miles. Located at 40.52° N. Lat; 87.25° W. Long. Elevation is 741 feet.
History: In 1896 in Oxford a racehorse named Dan Patch was born, and brought a measure of fame to the town for the records he set. For a time, Oxford was the seat of Benton County.
Population: 1,162; Growth (since 2000): -8.6%; Density: 2,148.3 persons per square mile; Race: 98.4% White, 0.1% Black/African American, 0.1% Asian, 0.5% American Indian/Alaska Native, 0.0% Native Hawaiian/Other Pacific Islander, 0.6% Two or more races, 0.7% Hispanic of any race; Average household size: 2.43; Median age: 39.6; Age under 18: 25.0%; Age 65 and over: 15.6%; Males per 100 females: 95.3
School District(s)
Benton Community School Corp (KG-12)
  2012-13 Enrollment: 1,850 .... (765) 884-0850
Housing: Homeownership rate: 73.9%; Homeowner vacancy rate: 3.3%; Rental vacancy rate: 15.4%

Blackford County

Located in eastern Indiana; drained by the Salamonie River. Covers a land area of 165.080 square miles, a water area of 0.503 square miles, and is located in the Eastern Time Zone at 40.47° N. Lat., 85.32° W. Long. The county was founded in 1838. County seat is Hartford City.

Weather Station: Hartford City 4 ESE   Elevation: 941 feet

	Jan	Feb	Mar	Apr	May	Jun	Jul	Aug	Sep	Oct	Nov	Dec
High	32	37	48	61	71	80	83	82	76	64	51	37
Low	17	21	29	40	51	60	63	62	54	42	34	22
Precip	2.3	2.1	2.8	3.5	4.2	4.1	4.2	4.1	3.0	2.7	3.3	2.9
Snow	8.4	7.1	3.9	0.9	0.0	0.0	0.0	0.0	0.0	0.4	1.5	7.0

High and Low temperatures in degrees Fahrenheit; Precipitation and Snow in inches

Population: 12,766; Growth (since 2000): -9.1%; Density: 77.3 persons per square mile; Race: 97.7% White, 0.4% Black/African American, 0.1% Asian, 0.2% American Indian/Alaska Native, 0.0% Native Hawaiian/Other Pacific Islander, 1.3% two or more races, 0.9% Hispanic of any race; Average household size: 2.41; Median age: 42.4; Age under 18: 22.8%; Age 65 and over: 17.8%; Males per 100 females: 97.2; Marriage status: 23.4% never married, 53.7% now married, 1.2% separated, 7.9% widowed, 15.0% divorced; Foreign born: 0.9%; Speak English only: 98.4%; With disability: 20.5%; Veterans: 11.6%; Ancestry: 21.5% German, 14.3% American, 11.0% Irish, 9.9% English, 2.2% Dutch
Religion: Six largest groups: 7.5% Methodist/Pietist, 6.9% Baptist, 4.9% Holiness, 3.2% Non-denominational Protestant, 3.1% Catholicism, 2.5% Lutheran
Economy: Unemployment rate: 5.9%; Leading industries: 16.7% other services (except public administration); 15.4% retail trade; 10.0% manufacturing; Farms: 263 totaling 88,010 acres; Company size: 0 employ 1,000 or more persons, 0 employ 500 to 999 persons, 5 employ 100 to 499 persons, 235 employ less than 100 persons; Business ownership: n/a women-owned, n/a Black-owned, n/a Hispanic-owned, n/a Asian-owned
Employment: 10.2% management, business, and financial, 0.5% computer, engineering, and science, 6.0% education, legal, community

service, arts, and media, 4.5% healthcare practitioners, 18.6% service, 24.0% sales and office, 6.7% natural resources, construction, and maintenance, 29.5% production, transportation, and material moving
Income: Per capita: $20,322; Median household: $39,225; Average household: $49,741; Households with income of $100,000 or more: 7.7%; Poverty rate: 16.0%
Educational Attainment: High school diploma or higher: 86.0%; Bachelor's degree or higher: 9.8%; Graduate/professional degree or higher: 3.3%
Housing: Homeownership rate: 75.0%; Median home value: $70,400; Median year structure built: 1961; Homeowner vacancy rate: 3.2%; Median gross rent: $595 per month; Rental vacancy rate: 8.5%
Vital Statistics: Birth rate: 113.0 per 10,000 population; Death rate: 134.6 per 10,000 population; Age-adjusted cancer mortality rate: 170.4 deaths per 100,000 population
Health Insurance: 82.8% have insurance; 61.0% have private insurance; 38.3% have public insurance; 17.2% do not have insurance; 9.6% of children under 18 do not have insurance
Health Care: Physicians: 4.8 per 10,000 population; Hospital beds: 11.8 per 10,000 population; Hospital admissions: 392.6 per 10,000 population
Transportation: Commute: 93.1% car, 0.3% public transportation, 2.6% walk, 2.7% work from home; Median travel time to work: 24.4 minutes
Presidential Election: 40.6% Obama, 57.2% Romney (2012)
Additional Information Contacts
Blackford Government . . . . (765) 348-1620
http://www.blackfordcounty.com

Blackford County Communities

HARTFORD CITY (city). County seat. Covers a land area of 3.875 square miles and a water area of 0.021 square miles. Located at 40.45° N. Lat; 85.37° W. Long. Elevation is 919 feet.
History: Settled 1832, laid out 1839.
Population: 6,220; Growth (since 2000): -10.2%; Density: 1,605.0 persons per square mile; Race: 97.3% White, 0.3% Black/African American, 0.1% Asian, 0.2% American Indian/Alaska Native, 0.1% Native Hawaiian/Other Pacific Islander, 1.7% Two or more races, 1.2% Hispanic of any race; Average household size: 2.32; Median age: 41.3; Age under 18: 23.1%; Age 65 and over: 18.4%; Males per 100 females: 90.7; Marriage status: 23.6% never married, 52.8% now married, 1.1% separated, 7.1% widowed, 16.4% divorced; Foreign born: 0.5%; Speak English only: 98.9%; With disability: 22.9%; Veterans: 12.2%; Ancestry: 18.4% German, 14.9% American, 13.9% Irish, 10.1% English, 2.0% French
Employment: 10.3% management, business, and financial, 0.0% computer, engineering, and science, 4.8% education, legal, community service, arts, and media, 5.0% healthcare practitioners, 24.1% service, 21.6% sales and office, 4.0% natural resources, construction, and maintenance, 30.2% production, transportation, and material moving
Income: Per capita: $18,902; Median household: $39,344; Average household: $46,042; Households with income of $100,000 or more: 5.0%; Poverty rate: 16.9%
Educational Attainment: High school diploma or higher: 86.4%; Bachelor's degree or higher: 8.7%; Graduate/professional degree or higher: 3.1%
School District(s)
Blackford County Schools (KG-12)
2012-13 Enrollment: 1,806 . . . . (765) 348-7550
Housing: Homeownership rate: 69.6%; Median home value: $60,700; Median year structure built: 1960; Homeowner vacancy rate: 5.2%; Median gross rent: $598 per month; Rental vacancy rate: 10.6%
Health Insurance: 78.6% have insurance; 58.0% have private insurance; 38.9% have public insurance; 21.4% do not have insurance; 14.8% of children under 18 do not have insurance
Hospitals: Indiana University Health Blackford Hospital (15 beds)
Safety: Violent crime rate: 9.9 per 10,000 population; Property crime rate: 408.1 per 10,000 population
Newspapers: News-Times (daily circulation 1500)
Transportation: Commute: 94.0% car, 0.0% public transportation, 3.2% walk, 1.1% work from home; Median travel time to work: 21.9 minutes
Additional Information Contacts
City of Hartford City . . . . (765) 348-1872
http://www.hartfordcity.net

MONTPELIER (city). Covers a land area of 1.542 square miles and a water area of 0 square miles. Located at 40.55° N. Lat; 85.29° W. Long. Elevation is 869 feet.
History: Settled 1836, laid out 1837, incorporated 1937.
Population: 1,805; Growth (since 2000): -6.4%; Density: 1,170.9 persons per square mile; Race: 97.9% White, 0.3% Black/African American, 0.1% Asian, 0.3% American Indian/Alaska Native, 0.0% Native Hawaiian/Other Pacific Islander, 1.2% Two or more races, 0.9% Hispanic of any race; Average household size: 2.55; Median age: 36.3; Age under 18: 28.1%; Age 65 and over: 13.1%; Males per 100 females: 100.6
School District(s)
Blackford County Schools (KG-12)
2012-13 Enrollment: 1,806 . . . . (765) 348-7550
Housing: Homeownership rate: 62.7%; Homeowner vacancy rate: 1.8%; Rental vacancy rate: 6.3%

SHAMROCK LAKES (town). Covers a land area of 0.263 square miles and a water area of 0.056 square miles. Located at 40.41° N. Lat; 85.43° W. Long. Elevation is 889 feet.
Population: 231; Growth (since 2000): 37.5%; Density: 878.0 persons per square mile; Race: 98.7% White, 0.0% Black/African American, 1.3% Asian, 0.0% American Indian/Alaska Native, 0.0% Native Hawaiian/Other Pacific Islander, 0.0% Two or more races, 0.0% Hispanic of any race; Average household size: 2.46; Median age: 48.8; Age under 18: 20.8%; Age 65 and over: 15.2%; Males per 100 females: 94.1
Housing: Homeownership rate: 94.7%; Homeowner vacancy rate: 4.3%; Rental vacancy rate: 0.0%

Boone County

Located in central Indiana; drained by Sugar and Raccoon Creeks and the Eel River. Covers a land area of 422.913 square miles, a water area of 0.339 square miles, and is located in the Eastern Time Zone at 40.05° N. Lat., 86.47° W. Long. The county was founded in 1830. County seat is Lebanon.

Boone County is part of the Indianapolis-Carmel-Anderson, IN Metropolitan Statistical Area. The entire metro area includes: Boone County, IN; Brown County, IN; Hamilton County, IN; Hancock County, IN; Hendricks County, IN; Johnson County, IN; Madison County, IN; Marion County, IN; Morgan County, IN; Putnam County, IN; Shelby County, IN

Weather Station: Whitestown | | | | | | | | | | | Elevation: 935 feet
	Jan	Feb	Mar	Apr	May	Jun	Jul	Aug	Sep	Oct	Nov	Dec
High	35	40	51	64	74	83	86	84	79	66	52	39
Low	19	22	31	41	51	60	64	62	54	43	34	24
Precip	2.7	2.6	3.4	3.9	4.8	4.1	4.3	3.3	3.4	3.1	3.7	3.3
Snow	8.0	6.4	2.4	0.3	0.0	0.0	0.0	0.0	0.0	0.3	0.7	5.8

High and Low temperatures in degrees Fahrenheit; Precipitation and Snow in inches

Population: 56,640; Growth (since 2000): 22.8%; Density: 133.9 persons per square mile; Race: 95.3% White, 0.9% Black/African American, 1.7% Asian, 0.2% American Indian/Alaska Native, 0.0% Native Hawaiian/Other Pacific Islander, 1.4% two or more races, 2.2% Hispanic of any race; Average household size: 2.65; Median age: 38.6; Age under 18: 28.1%; Age 65 and over: 11.7%; Males per 100 females: 96.8; Marriage status: 20.6% never married, 62.9% now married, 1.0% separated, 5.5% widowed, 11.0% divorced; Foreign born: 3.4%; Speak English only: 95.6%; With disability: 8.1%; Veterans: 8.0%; Ancestry: 27.3% German, 18.7% English, 13.3% Irish, 9.8% American, 3.2% Italian
Religion: Six largest groups: 16.5% Catholicism, 15.5% Baptist, 7.8% Non-denominational Protestant, 6.6% Methodist/Pietist, 5.3% Presbyterian-Reformed, 2.8% Lutheran
Economy: Unemployment rate: 4.2%; Leading industries: 12.2% professional, scientific, and technical services; 11.5% retail trade; 10.6% construction; Farms: 607 totaling 221,703 acres; Company size: 0 employ 1,000 or more persons, 2 employ 500 to 999 persons, 23 employ 100 to 499 persons, 1,371 employs less than 100 persons; Business ownership: 1,315 women-owned, n/a Black-owned, n/a Hispanic-owned, n/a Asian-owned
Employment: 18.6% management, business, and financial, 6.0% computer, engineering, and science, 10.6% education, legal, community service, arts, and media, 9.0% healthcare practitioners, 13.3% service, 22.5% sales and office, 8.8% natural resources, construction, and maintenance, 11.1% production, transportation, and material moving

Income: Per capita: $37,482; Median household: $67,255; Average household: $98,989; Households with income of $100,000 or more: 31.4%; Poverty rate: 7.5%
Educational Attainment: High school diploma or higher: 93.5%; Bachelor's degree or higher: 41.0%; Graduate/professional degree or higher: 17.2%
Housing: Homeownership rate: 78.2%; Median home value: $179,000; Median year structure built: 1980; Homeowner vacancy rate: 2.3%; Median gross rent: $790 per month; Rental vacancy rate: 11.2%
Vital Statistics: Birth rate: 120.2 per 10,000 population; Death rate: 72.1 per 10,000 population; Age-adjusted cancer mortality rate: 190.8 deaths per 100,000 population
Health Insurance: 91.1% have insurance; 82.2% have private insurance; 19.1% have public insurance; 8.9% do not have insurance; 3.7% of children under 18 do not have insurance
Health Care: Physicians: 71.4 per 10,000 population; Hospital beds: 9.0 per 10,000 population; Hospital admissions: 450.8 per 10,000 population
Air Quality Index: 91.3% good, 8.7% moderate, 0.0% unhealthy for sensitive individuals, 0.0% unhealthy (percent of days)
Transportation: Commute: 92.4% car, 0.2% public transportation, 0.8% walk, 4.8% work from home; Median travel time to work: 24.1 minutes
Presidential Election: 30.0% Obama, 67.8% Romney (2012)
Additional Information Contacts
Boone Government . . . . (765) 482-2940
http://www.boonecounty.in.gov

Boone County Communities

ADVANCE (town). Covers a land area of 0.622 square miles and a water area of 0 square miles. Located at 40.00° N. Lat; 86.62° W. Long. Elevation is 932 feet.
Population: 477; Growth (since 2000): -15.1%; Density: 766.5 persons per square mile; Race: 97.1% White, 0.4% Black/African American, 0.6% Asian, 0.2% American Indian/Alaska Native, 0.0% Native Hawaiian/Other Pacific Islander, 1.5% Two or more races, 0.8% Hispanic of any race; Average household size: 2.96; Median age: 32.9; Age under 18: 32.5%; Age 65 and over: 9.9%; Males per 100 females: 107.4
Housing: Homeownership rate: 82.6%; Homeowner vacancy rate: 1.5%; Rental vacancy rate: 17.1%

JAMESTOWN (town). Covers a land area of 0.876 square miles and a water area of 0 square miles. Located at 39.93° N. Lat; 86.63° W. Long. Elevation is 955 feet.
History: Jamestown developed as a stop on the stagecoach route, and later as a station on the New York Central Railroad.
Population: 958; Growth (since 2000): 8.1%; Density: 1,094.0 persons per square mile; Race: 98.9% White, 0.0% Black/African American, 0.5% Asian, 0.0% American Indian/Alaska Native, 0.0% Native Hawaiian/Other Pacific Islander, 0.6% Two or more races, 0.7% Hispanic of any race; Average household size: 2.43; Median age: 36.5; Age under 18: 26.6%; Age 65 and over: 11.7%; Males per 100 females: 87.8
School District(s)
Western Boone County Com SD (PK-12)
    2012-13 Enrollment: 1,761 . . . . (765) 482-6333
Housing: Homeownership rate: 72.1%; Homeowner vacancy rate: 2.7%; Rental vacancy rate: 6.0%

LEBANON (city). County seat. Covers a land area of 15.555 square miles and a water area of 0.016 square miles. Located at 40.03° N. Lat; 86.46° W. Long. Elevation is 942 feet.
History: Named for the Biblical mountain of cedars, although the trees in the area are primarily hickory trees. Lebanon received its biblical name because the forests surrounding it reminded one of its founders of the Cedars of Lebanon. Lebanon was the home of Samuel M. Ralston (1857-1925), governor of Indiana and U.S. senator.
Population: 15,792; Growth (since 2000): 11.0%; Density: 1,015.3 persons per square mile; Race: 96.1% White, 0.5% Black/African American, 0.6% Asian, 0.2% American Indian/Alaska Native, 0.0% Native Hawaiian/Other Pacific Islander, 1.5% Two or more races, 3.1% Hispanic of any race; Average household size: 2.38; Median age: 37.5; Age under 18: 24.5%; Age 65 and over: 14.7%; Males per 100 females: 92.2; Marriage status: 22.6% never married, 50.3% now married, 1.4% separated, 8.4% widowed, 18.7% divorced; Foreign born: 3.2%; Speak English only: 95.6%; With disability: 12.8%; Veterans: 8.7%; Ancestry: 25.4% German, 22.6% English, 13.2% Irish, 7.4% American, 3.7% Scottish
Employment: 11.3% management, business, and financial, 4.5% computer, engineering, and science, 5.3% education, legal, community service, arts, and media, 6.0% healthcare practitioners, 19.1% service, 24.6% sales and office, 13.0% natural resources, construction, and maintenance, 16.2% production, transportation, and material moving
Income: Per capita: $23,673; Median household: $43,154; Average household: $56,213; Households with income of $100,000 or more: 10.8%; Poverty rate: 14.9%
Educational Attainment: High school diploma or higher: 87.2%; Bachelor's degree or higher: 18.4%; Graduate/professional degree or higher: 5.6%
School District(s)
Lebanon Community School Corp (KG-12)
    2012-13 Enrollment: 3,557 . . . . (765) 482-0380
Housing: Homeownership rate: 64.6%; Median home value: $112,700; Median year structure built: 1973; Homeowner vacancy rate: 3.3%; Median gross rent: $667 per month; Rental vacancy rate: 10.8%
Health Insurance: 83.0% have insurance; 67.2% have private insurance; 27.0% have public insurance; 17.0% do not have insurance; 8.8% of children under 18 do not have insurance
Hospitals: Witham Health Services (80 beds)
Newspapers: Sun Times (weekly circulation 7000); The Reporter (daily circulation 5300)
Transportation: Commute: 94.3% car, 0.0% public transportation, 0.9% walk, 2.2% work from home; Median travel time to work: 21.8 minutes
Additional Information Contacts
City of Lebanon . . . . (765) 482-1218
http://www.cityoflebanon.org

THORNTOWN (town). Covers a land area of 0.603 square miles and a water area of 0 square miles. Located at 40.13° N. Lat; 86.61° W. Long. Elevation is 853 feet.
History: Thorntown was called Keewaskee, meaning "place of thorns," when a trading post was established here by Jesuit missionaries. Thorntown was platted in 1829 by Cornelius Westfall.
Population: 1,520; Growth (since 2000): -2.7%; Density: 2,522.3 persons per square mile; Race: 99.1% White, 0.1% Black/African American, 0.0% Asian, 0.2% American Indian/Alaska Native, 0.0% Native Hawaiian/Other Pacific Islander, 0.5% Two or more races, 0.7% Hispanic of any race; Average household size: 2.73; Median age: 37.5; Age under 18: 26.0%; Age 65 and over: 13.0%; Males per 100 females: 91.4
School District(s)
Western Boone County Com SD (PK-12)
    2012-13 Enrollment: 1,761 . . . . (765) 482-6333
Housing: Homeownership rate: 70.5%; Homeowner vacancy rate: 3.2%; Rental vacancy rate: 7.3%

ULEN (town). Covers a land area of 0.063 square miles and a water area of 0 square miles. Located at 40.06° N. Lat; 86.46° W. Long. Elevation is 945 feet.
Population: 117; Growth (since 2000): -4.9%; Density: 1,859.6 persons per square mile; Race: 100.0% White, 0.0% Black/African American, 0.0% Asian, 0.0% American Indian/Alaska Native, 0.0% Native Hawaiian/Other Pacific Islander, 0.0% Two or more races, 0.9% Hispanic of any race; Average household size: 2.39; Median age: 51.8; Age under 18: 19.7%; Age 65 and over: 26.5%; Males per 100 females: 105.3
Housing: Homeownership rate: 98.0%; Homeowner vacancy rate: 4.0%; Rental vacancy rate: 0.0%

WHITESTOWN (town). Covers a land area of 10.458 square miles and a water area of 0 square miles. Located at 39.96° N. Lat; 86.37° W. Long. Elevation is 938 feet.
History: Laid out 1851.
Population: 2,867; Growth (since 2000): 508.7%; Density: 274.1 persons per square mile; Race: 90.9% White, 2.8% Black/African American, 2.9% Asian, 0.1% American Indian/Alaska Native, 0.0% Native Hawaiian/Other Pacific Islander, 2.2% Two or more races, 3.5% Hispanic of any race; Average household size: 2.72; Median age: 30.0; Age under 18: 30.6%; Age 65 and over: 4.3%; Males per 100 females: 101.9; Marriage status: 25.5% never married, 64.3% now married, 0.9% separated, 1.4% widowed, 8.8% divorced; Foreign born: 2.6%; Speak English only: 94.8%; With disability: 4.2%; Veterans: 4.4%; Ancestry: 30.1% German, 12.8% Irish, 10.7% English, 8.5% American, 4.5% Italian

Employment: 19.3% management, business, and financial, 11.1% computer, engineering, and science, 9.8% education, legal, community service, arts, and media, 11.8% healthcare practitioners, 13.2% service, 21.3% sales and office, 7.6% natural resources, construction, and maintenance, 5.9% production, transportation, and material moving
Income: Per capita: $33,428; Median household: $74,638; Average household: $91,625; Households with income of $100,000 or more: 31.4%; Poverty rate: 9.8%
Educational Attainment: High school diploma or higher: 95.6%; Bachelor's degree or higher: 51.5%; Graduate/professional degree or higher: 16.1%

School District(s)
Zionsville Community Schools (PK-12)
    2012-13 Enrollment: 5,924 . . . . (317) 873-2858
Housing: Homeownership rate: 85.3%; Median home value: $163,100; Median year structure built: 2005; Homeowner vacancy rate: 2.8%; Median gross rent: $1,221 per month; Rental vacancy rate: 13.7%
Health Insurance: 91.9% have insurance; 83.3% have private insurance; 13.0% have public insurance; 8.1% do not have insurance; 3.7% of children under 18 do not have insurance
Safety: Violent crime rate: 50.3 per 10,000 population; Property crime rate: 301.7 per 10,000 population
Transportation: Commute: 95.7% car, 0.6% public transportation, 0.3% walk, 3.4% work from home; Median travel time to work: 26.6 minutes

ZIONSVILLE (town). Covers a land area of 10.257 square miles and a water area of 0.038 square miles. Located at 39.96° N. Lat; 86.27° W. Long. Elevation is 843 feet.
History: On his way to his inauguration in Washington in 1861, Abraham Lincoln spoke from the back of a train in Zionsville, saying, "I would like to spend more time here, but there is an event to take place in Washington which cannot start until I get there."
Population: 14,160; Growth (since 2000): 61.4%; Density: 1,380.5 persons per square mile; Race: 94.0% White, 1.2% Black/African American, 2.7% Asian, 0.1% American Indian/Alaska Native, 0.0% Native Hawaiian/Other Pacific Islander, 1.4% Two or more races, 2.1% Hispanic of any race; Average household size: 2.75; Median age: 39.6; Age under 18: 31.6%; Age 65 and over: 10.9%; Males per 100 females: 94.9; Marriage status: 19.2% never married, 68.4% now married, 0.9% separated, 4.5% widowed, 7.9% divorced; Foreign born: 5.4%; Speak English only: 94.2%; With disability: 4.1%; Veterans: 6.2%; Ancestry: 29.1% German, 17.5% English, 14.1% Irish, 7.9% American, 5.0% Italian
Employment: 25.6% management, business, and financial, 7.6% computer, engineering, and science, 15.7% education, legal, community service, arts, and media, 12.3% healthcare practitioners, 8.7% service, 21.2% sales and office, 3.4% natural resources, construction, and maintenance, 5.7% production, transportation, and material moving
Income: Per capita: $52,793; Median household: $106,071; Average household: $150,719; Households with income of $100,000 or more: 53.9%; Poverty rate: 2.6%
Educational Attainment: High school diploma or higher: 97.6%; Bachelor's degree or higher: 66.9%; Graduate/professional degree or higher: 31.7%

School District(s)
Zionsville Community Schools (PK-12)
    2012-13 Enrollment: 5,924 . . . . (317) 873-2858
Housing: Homeownership rate: 77.5%; Median home value: $336,700; Median year structure built: 1992; Homeowner vacancy rate: 2.1%; Median gross rent: $1,155 per month; Rental vacancy rate: 16.0%
Health Insurance: 96.3% have insurance; 92.2% have private insurance; 11.8% have public insurance; 3.7% do not have insurance; 0.5% of children under 18 do not have insurance
Safety: Violent crime rate: 0.8 per 10,000 population; Property crime rate: 25.8 per 10,000 population
Newspapers: Zionsville Times Sentinel (weekly circulation 4200)
Transportation: Commute: 91.1% car, 0.2% public transportation, 0.4% walk, 7.0% work from home; Median travel time to work: 23.8 minutes
Airports: Indianapolis Executive (general aviation)
Additional Information Contacts
Town of Zionsville . . . . (317) 873-5410
    http://www.zionsville-in.gov

Brown County

Located in south central Indiana; drained by Salt Creek and its north fork. Covers a land area of 311.981 square miles, a water area of 4.650 square miles, and is located in the Eastern Time Zone at 39.19° N. Lat., 86.24° W. Long. The county was founded in 1836. County seat is Nashville.

Brown County is part of the Indianapolis-Carmel-Anderson, IN Metropolitan Statistical Area. The entire metro area includes: Boone County, IN; Brown County, IN; Hamilton County, IN; Hancock County, IN; Hendricks County, IN; Johnson County, IN; Madison County, IN; Marion County, IN; Morgan County, IN; Putnam County, IN; Shelby County, IN

Population: 15,242; Growth (since 2000): 1.9%; Density: 48.9 persons per square mile; Race: 97.6% White, 0.3% Black/African American, 0.3% Asian, 0.3% American Indian/Alaska Native, 0.0% Native Hawaiian/Other Pacific Islander, 1.1% two or more races, 1.2% Hispanic of any race; Average household size: 2.43; Median age: 46.7; Age under 18: 20.8%; Age 65 and over: 17.2%; Males per 100 females: 98.5; Marriage status: 20.2% never married, 55.3% now married, 0.9% separated, 6.1% widowed, 18.4% divorced; Foreign born: 0.9%; Speak English only: 96.6%; With disability: 12.1%; Veterans: 14.2%; Ancestry: 23.8% German, 22.0% American, 12.6% Irish, 10.7% English, 3.0% Dutch
Religion: Six largest groups: 8.7% Baptist, 4.9% Catholicism, 3.3% Non-denominational Protestant, 3.1% Methodist/Pietist, 1.9% Holiness, 0.4% Presbyterian-Reformed
Economy: Unemployment rate: 4.6%; Leading industries: 21.7% retail trade; 13.9% construction; 9.6% accommodation and food services; Farms: 173 totaling 14,590 acres; Company size: 0 employ 1,000 or more persons, 0 employ 500 to 999 persons, 1 employs 100 to 499 persons, 344 employ less than 100 persons; Business ownership: 534 women-owned, n/a Black-owned, n/a Hispanic-owned, n/a Asian-owned
Employment: 14.4% management, business, and financial, 2.4% computer, engineering, and science, 9.3% education, legal, community service, arts, and media, 6.8% healthcare practitioners, 22.1% service, 17.3% sales and office, 11.2% natural resources, construction, and maintenance, 16.5% production, transportation, and material moving
Income: Per capita: $25,833; Median household: $51,568; Average household: $63,457; Households with income of $100,000 or more: 19.1%; Poverty rate: 14.6%
Educational Attainment: High school diploma or higher: 87.1%; Bachelor's degree or higher: 21.1%; Graduate/professional degree or higher: 9.3%
Housing: Homeownership rate: 83.8%; Median home value: $157,400; Median year structure built: 1977; Homeowner vacancy rate: 3.2%; Median gross rent: $887 per month; Rental vacancy rate: 8.4%
Vital Statistics: Birth rate: 80.5 per 10,000 population; Death rate: 89.9 per 10,000 population; Age-adjusted cancer mortality rate: 171.3 deaths per 100,000 population
Health Insurance: 86.0% have insurance; 67.3% have private insurance; 35.8% have public insurance; 14.0% do not have insurance; 7.0% of children under 18 do not have insurance
Health Care: Physicians: 6.6 per 10,000 population; Hospital beds: 0.0 per 10,000 population; Hospital admissions: 0.0 per 10,000 population
Transportation: Commute: 91.9% car, 0.7% public transportation, 1.7% walk, 4.9% work from home; Median travel time to work: 35.9 minutes
Presidential Election: 40.3% Obama, 57.0% Romney (2012)
National and State Parks: Brown County State Park; Middle Fork State Wildlife Refuge; TC Steele State Memorial; Yellowwood State Forest
Additional Information Contacts
Brown Government . . . . (812) 988-7064
    http://www.browncounty-in.gov

Brown County Communities

CORDRY SWEETWATER LAKES (CDP). Covers a land area of 2.755 square miles and a water area of 0.644 square miles. Located at 39.31° N. Lat; 86.12° W. Long. Elevation is 919 feet.
Population: 1,128; Growth (since 2000): n/a; Density: 409.5 persons per square mile; Race: 98.5% White, 0.3% Black/African American, 0.2% Asian, 0.3% American Indian/Alaska Native, 0.0% Native Hawaiian/Other Pacific Islander, 0.5% Two or more races, 0.5% Hispanic of any race; Average household size: 2.28; Median age: 50.8; Age under 18: 16.0%; Age 65 and over: 19.9%; Males per 100 females: 100.0

Housing: Homeownership rate: 95.5%; Homeowner vacancy rate: 6.5%; Rental vacancy rate: 8.0%

NASHVILLE (town). County seat. Covers a land area of 1.011 square miles and a water area of 0.005 square miles. Located at 39.21° N. Lat; 86.24° W. Long. Elevation is 594 feet.

History: Local tradition in Nashville tells of the Liars' Bench on the courthouse lawn which accommodated six tellers of tall and unlikely tales. When a bigger and better story was told by someone standing, one of the seated liars would be pushed off the end of the bench to make room for the bigger liar.

Population: 803; Growth (since 2000): -2.7%; Density: 794.6 persons per square mile; Race: 98.1% White, 0.4% Black/African American, 0.1% Asian, 0.2% American Indian/Alaska Native, 0.0% Native Hawaiian/Other Pacific Islander, 0.5% Two or more races, 0.7% Hispanic of any race; Average household size: 1.90; Median age: 59.7; Age under 18: 14.7%; Age 65 and over: 40.0%; Males per 100 females: 69.4

School District(s)
Brown County School Corporation (KG-12)
    2012-13 Enrollment: 2,036 . . . . (812) 988-6601

Housing: Homeownership rate: 58.2%; Homeowner vacancy rate: 5.8%; Rental vacancy rate: 3.8%

Newspapers: Brown County Democrat (weekly circulation 4400)

NINEVEH (unincorporated postal area)
ZCTA: 46164

Covers a land area of 23.488 square miles and a water area of 0.928 square miles. Located at 39.32° N. Lat; 86.11° W. Long..

Population: 3,957; Growth (since 2000): -4.3%; Density: 168.5 persons per square mile; Race: 98.4% White, 0.3% Black/African American, 0.2% Asian, 0.2% American Indian/Alaska Native, 0.0% Native Hawaiian/Other Pacific Islander, 0.8% Two or more races, 0.9% Hispanic of any race; Average household size: 2.55; Median age: 43.4; Age under 18: 23.1%; Age 65 and over: 14.0%; Males per 100 females: 100.8; Marriage status: 18.7% never married, 62.0% now married, 1.2% separated, 4.4% widowed, 14.9% divorced; Foreign born: 0.7%; Speak English only: 98.1%; With disability: 13.0%; Veterans: 12.8%; Ancestry: 22.9% German, 15.5% American, 13.5% Irish, 8.6% English, 3.0% French

Employment: 6.8% management, business, and financial, 4.6% computer, engineering, and science, 10.4% education, legal, community service, arts, and media, 1.9% healthcare practitioners, 16.6% service, 26.5% sales and office, 13.4% natural resources, construction, and maintenance, 19.9% production, transportation, and material moving

Income: Per capita: $30,865; Median household: $55,059; Average household: $73,689; Households with income of $100,000 or more: 19.5%; Poverty rate: 7.9%

Educational Attainment: High school diploma or higher: 89.5%; Bachelor's degree or higher: 16.7%; Graduate/professional degree or higher: 7.4%

School District(s)
Brown County School Corporation (KG-12)
    2012-13 Enrollment: 2,036 . . . . (812) 988-6601

Housing: Homeownership rate: 89.1%; Median home value: $141,800; Median year structure built: 1974; Homeowner vacancy rate: 4.9%; Median gross rent: $911 per month; Rental vacancy rate: 8.1%

Health Insurance: 88.5% have insurance; 74.9% have private insurance; 27.7% have public insurance; 11.5% do not have insurance; 5.2% of children under 18 do not have insurance

Transportation: Commute: 96.5% car, 0.0% public transportation, 0.5% walk, 2.3% work from home; Median travel time to work: 35.3 minutes

Carroll County

Located in northwest central Indiana; crossed by the Wabash River; drained by the Tippecanoe River. Covers a land area of 372.224 square miles, a water area of 2.795 square miles, and is located in the Eastern Time Zone at 40.58° N. Lat., 86.57° W. Long. The county was founded in 1828. County seat is Delphi.

Carroll County is part of the Lafayette-West Lafayette, IN Metropolitan Statistical Area. The entire metro area includes: Benton County, IN; Carroll County, IN; Tippecanoe County, IN

Weather Station: Delphi 3 S   Elevation: 670 feet

	Jan	Feb	Mar	Apr	May	Jun	Jul	Aug	Sep	Oct	Nov	Dec
High	35	39	51	64	74	83	85	84	78	66	52	38
Low	19	22	31	41	51	60	63	61	53	43	35	24
Precip	2.2	2.1	2.8	3.5	4.4	4.0	4.6	3.7	2.7	3.0	3.1	2.6
Snow	5.6	4.8	2.4	0.6	tr	0.0	0.0	0.0	0.0	0.2	0.5	4.6

High and Low temperatures in degrees Fahrenheit; Precipitation and Snow in inches

Population: 20,155; Growth (since 2000): 0.0%; Density: 54.1 persons per square mile; Race: 96.8% White, 0.2% Black/African American, 0.1% Asian, 0.2% American Indian/Alaska Native, 0.0% Native Hawaiian/Other Pacific Islander, 1.0% two or more races, 3.5% Hispanic of any race; Average household size: 2.54; Median age: 40.9; Age under 18: 24.6%; Age 65 and over: 15.8%; Males per 100 females: 100.4; Marriage status: 22.5% never married, 58.4% now married, 0.6% separated, 6.2% widowed, 12.9% divorced; Foreign born: 2.5%; Speak English only: 95.4%; With disability: 13.8%; Veterans: 11.1%; Ancestry: 26.6% German, 14.8% American, 12.7% Irish, 10.0% English, 3.1% Dutch

Religion: Six largest groups: 9.3% Catholicism, 8.7% Baptist, 7.2% Methodist/Pietist, 3.2% Pentecostal, 2.9% Presbyterian-Reformed, 2.8% Non-denominational Protestant

Economy: Unemployment rate: 4.8%; Leading industries: 17.4% construction; 13.3% retail trade; 12.8% other services (except public administration); Farms: 491 totaling 204,090 acres; Company size: 1 employs 1,000 or more persons, 0 employ 500 to 999 persons, 0 employ 100 to 499 persons, 383 employ less than 100 persons; Business ownership: n/a women-owned, n/a Black-owned, n/a Hispanic-owned, n/a Asian-owned

Employment: 12.1% management, business, and financial, 1.7% computer, engineering, and science, 8.1% education, legal, community service, arts, and media, 5.7% healthcare practitioners, 15.8% service, 21.7% sales and office, 12.1% natural resources, construction, and maintenance, 22.9% production, transportation, and material moving

Income: Per capita: $24,531; Median household: $50,542; Average household: $60,718; Households with income of $100,000 or more: 15.0%; Poverty rate: 10.7%

Educational Attainment: High school diploma or higher: 87.7%; Bachelor's degree or higher: 16.0%; Graduate/professional degree or higher: 5.3%

Housing: Homeownership rate: 79.6%; Median home value: $103,900; Median year structure built: 1963; Homeowner vacancy rate: 2.8%; Median gross rent: $644 per month; Rental vacancy rate: 10.6%

Vital Statistics: Birth rate: 105.0 per 10,000 population; Death rate: 88.6 per 10,000 population; Age-adjusted cancer mortality rate: 197.9 deaths per 100,000 population

Health Insurance: 86.8% have insurance; 74.1% have private insurance; 26.8% have public insurance; 13.2% do not have insurance; 7.3% of children under 18 do not have insurance

Health Care: Physicians: 3.5 per 10,000 population; Hospital beds: 0.0 per 10,000 population; Hospital admissions: 0.0 per 10,000 population

Air Quality Index: 89.0% good, 11.0% moderate, 0.0% unhealthy for sensitive individuals, 0.0% unhealthy (percent of days)

Transportation: Commute: 91.5% car, 0.1% public transportation, 2.7% walk, 5.1% work from home; Median travel time to work: 25.7 minutes

Presidential Election: 33.7% Obama, 64.0% Romney (2012)

Additional Information Contacts
Carroll Government . . . . (765) 564-3172
http://www.carrollcountygovernment.org

Carroll County Communities

BRINGHURST (unincorporated postal area)
ZCTA: 46913

Covers a land area of 32.901 square miles and a water area of 0 square miles. Located at 40.50° N. Lat; 86.50° W. Long. Elevation is 722 feet.

Population: 1,329; Growth (since 2000): -3.6%; Density: 40.4 persons per square mile; Race: 97.4% White, 0.1% Black/African American, 0.2% Asian, 0.1% American Indian/Alaska Native, 0.0% Native Hawaiian/Other Pacific Islander, 0.9% Two or more races, 1.8% Hispanic of any race; Average household size: 2.73; Median age: 39.9; Age under 18: 26.5%; Age 65 and over: 13.0%; Males per 100 females: 113.7

Housing: Homeownership rate: 90.1%; Homeowner vacancy rate: 1.1%; Rental vacancy rate: 5.9%

BURLINGTON (town). Covers a land area of 0.596 square miles and a water area of 0 square miles. Located at 40.48° N. Lat; 86.39° W. Long. Elevation is 784 feet.
History: Burlington was founded in 1832 as a stagecoach and tavern stop on the Michigan Road. It was named for Wyandotte Chief Burlington.
Population: 603; Growth (since 2000): 35.8%; Density: 1,011.9 persons per square mile; Race: 98.8% White, 0.5% Black/African American, 0.2% Asian, 0.0% American Indian/Alaska Native, 0.0% Native Hawaiian/Other Pacific Islander, 0.5% Two or more races, 2.0% Hispanic of any race; Average household size: 2.34; Median age: 40.6; Age under 18: 23.5%; Age 65 and over: 21.7%; Males per 100 females: 84.4
Housing: Homeownership rate: 76.4%; Homeowner vacancy rate: 4.4%; Rental vacancy rate: 7.6%

CAMDEN (town). Covers a land area of 0.261 square miles and a water area of <.001 square miles. Located at 40.61° N. Lat; 86.54° W. Long. Elevation is 669 feet.
Population: 611; Growth (since 2000): 5.0%; Density: 2,340.0 persons per square mile; Race: 98.2% White, 0.3% Black/African American, 0.0% Asian, 0.2% American Indian/Alaska Native, 0.0% Native Hawaiian/Other Pacific Islander, 1.3% Two or more races, 0.0% Hispanic of any race; Average household size: 2.45; Median age: 40.2; Age under 18: 25.2%; Age 65 and over: 17.8%; Males per 100 females: 90.9
Housing: Homeownership rate: 78.7%; Homeowner vacancy rate: 3.4%; Rental vacancy rate: 6.8%

CUTLER (unincorporated postal area)
ZCTA: 46920
Covers a land area of 31.474 square miles and a water area of 0 square miles. Located at 40.46° N. Lat; 86.49° W. Long. Elevation is 745 feet.
Population: 1,045; Growth (since 2000): -29.7%; Density: 33.2 persons per square mile; Race: 98.2% White, 0.0% Black/African American, 0.0% Asian, 0.6% American Indian/Alaska Native, 0.0% Native Hawaiian/Other Pacific Islander, 1.0% Two or more races, 2.0% Hispanic of any race; Average household size: 2.69; Median age: 38.6; Age under 18: 26.8%; Age 65 and over: 13.1%; Males per 100 females: 106.9
Housing: Homeownership rate: 85.6%; Homeowner vacancy rate: 1.2%; Rental vacancy rate: 6.7%

DELPHI (city). County seat. Covers a land area of 2.726 square miles and a water area of 0 square miles. Located at 40.58° N. Lat; 86.67° W. Long. Elevation is 568 feet.
History: Delphi was named by Samuel Milroy (1780-1845), a member of the State Constitutional Convention of 1816, who sold the first town lots in 1828. Poet James Whitcomb Riley was a resident here.
Population: 2,893; Growth (since 2000): -4.0%; Density: 1,061.3 persons per square mile; Race: 91.7% White, 0.4% Black/African American, 0.2% Asian, 0.2% American Indian/Alaska Native, 0.0% Native Hawaiian/Other Pacific Islander, 1.9% Two or more races, 11.3% Hispanic of any race; Average household size: 2.46; Median age: 37.5; Age under 18: 25.9%; Age 65 and over: 18.0%; Males per 100 females: 91.8; Marriage status: 28.7% never married, 43.8% now married, 0.3% separated, 8.2% widowed, 19.4% divorced; Foreign born: 6.8%; Speak English only: 87.7%; With disability: 15.3%; Veterans: 11.0%; Ancestry: 18.5% German, 15.1% American, 14.7% Irish, 6.0% English, 3.6% Italian
Employment: 4.9% management, business, and financial, 0.0% computer, engineering, and science, 10.2% education, legal, community service, arts, and media, 2.1% healthcare practitioners, 19.4% service, 22.5% sales and office, 18.2% natural resources, construction, and maintenance, 22.6% production, transportation, and material moving
Income: Per capita: $18,796; Median household: $39,621; Average household: $46,881; Households with income of $100,000 or more: 10.4%; Poverty rate: 14.5%
Educational Attainment: High school diploma or higher: 79.5%; Bachelor's degree or higher: 12.5%; Graduate/professional degree or higher: 6.4%
School District(s)
Delphi Community School Corp (KG-12)
 2012-13 Enrollment: 1,603 . . . . (765) 564-2100
Housing: Homeownership rate: 61.0%; Median home value: $82,900; Median year structure built: 1953; Homeowner vacancy rate: 3.5%; Median gross rent: $620 per month; Rental vacancy rate: 8.2%

Health Insurance: 84.7% have insurance; 67.5% have private insurance; 32.4% have public insurance; 15.3% do not have insurance; 0.0% of children under 18 do not have insurance
Safety: Violent crime rate: 45.0 per 10,000 population; Property crime rate: 214.8 per 10,000 population
Transportation: Commute: 86.8% car, 0.0% public transportation, 9.6% walk, 3.2% work from home; Median travel time to work: 21.6 minutes
Additional Information Contacts
City of Delphi . . . . (765) 564-2097
 http://www.cityofdelphi.org

FLORA (town). Covers a land area of 1.058 square miles and a water area of 0 square miles. Located at 40.55° N. Lat; 86.52° W. Long. Elevation is 705 feet.
History: Laid out 1872, incorporated 1898.
Population: 2,036; Growth (since 2000): -8.6%; Density: 1,924.1 persons per square mile; Race: 97.5% White, 0.3% Black/African American, 0.0% Asian, 0.0% American Indian/Alaska Native, 0.0% Native Hawaiian/Other Pacific Islander, 0.9% Two or more races, 2.6% Hispanic of any race; Average household size: 2.37; Median age: 40.4; Age under 18: 25.5%; Age 65 and over: 19.2%; Males per 100 females: 87.8
School District(s)
Carroll Consolidated Sch Corp (KG-12)
 2012-13 Enrollment: 1,124 . . . . (574) 967-4113
Housing: Homeownership rate: 67.3%; Homeowner vacancy rate: 3.5%; Rental vacancy rate: 19.5%
Newspapers: Carroll County Comet (weekly circulation 5000)
Additional Information Contacts
Town of Flora . . . . (574) 967-4844
 http://www.townofflora.org

YEOMAN (town). Covers a land area of 0.122 square miles and a water area of 0 square miles. Located at 40.67° N. Lat; 86.72° W. Long. Elevation is 663 feet.
History: Laid out 1880.
Population: 139; Growth (since 2000): 44.8%; Density: 1,141.7 persons per square mile; Race: 100.0% White, 0.0% Black/African American, 0.0% Asian, 0.0% American Indian/Alaska Native, 0.0% Native Hawaiian/Other Pacific Islander, 0.0% Two or more races, 0.0% Hispanic of any race; Average household size: 2.73; Median age: 27.1; Age under 18: 28.8%; Age 65 and over: 4.3%; Males per 100 females: 98.6
Housing: Homeownership rate: 80.4%; Homeowner vacancy rate: 0.0%; Rental vacancy rate: 0.0%

Cass County

Located in north central Indiana; intersected by the Wabash River; drained by the Eel River and Deer Creek. Covers a land area of 412.155 square miles, a water area of 2.693 square miles, and is located in the Eastern Time Zone at 40.75° N. Lat., 86.36° W. Long. The county was founded in 1828. County seat is Logansport.

Cass County is part of the Logansport, IN Micropolitan Statistical Area. The entire metro area includes: Cass County, IN

Population: 38,966; Growth (since 2000): -4.8%; Density: 94.5 persons per square mile; Race: 88.2% White, 1.5% Black/African American, 1.1% Asian, 0.5% American Indian/Alaska Native, 0.1% Native Hawaiian/Other Pacific Islander, 1.6% two or more races, 12.6% Hispanic of any race; Average household size: 2.55; Median age: 38.7; Age under 18: 25.9%; Age 65 and over: 15.1%; Males per 100 females: 99.9; Marriage status: 26.2% never married, 54.8% now married, 1.6% separated, 6.5% widowed, 12.5% divorced; Foreign born: 8.3%; Speak English only: 86.6%; With disability: 13.7%; Veterans: 10.8%; Ancestry: 22.2% German, 18.2% American, 11.0% Irish, 7.7% English, 3.0% Italian
Religion: Six largest groups: 11.8% Catholicism, 8.1% Methodist/Pietist, 7.3% Baptist, 4.7% Non-denominational Protestant, 3.4% Pentecostal, 2.6% Holiness
Economy: Unemployment rate: 5.2%; Leading industries: 15.8% retail trade; 13.4% other services (except public administration); 10.5% accommodation and food services; Farms: 688 totaling 200,257 acres; Company size: 1 employs 1,000 or more persons, 1 employs 500 to 999 persons, 17 employ 100 to 499 persons, 730 employ less than 100 persons; Business ownership: 449 women-owned, n/a Black-owned, n/a Hispanic-owned, n/a Asian-owned

Employment: 9.0% management, business, and financial, 1.4% computer, engineering, and science, 8.5% education, legal, community service, arts, and media, 5.6% healthcare practitioners, 18.0% service, 19.1% sales and office, 9.2% natural resources, construction, and maintenance, 29.1% production, transportation, and material moving
Income: Per capita: $21,700; Median household: $41,940; Average household: $55,509; Households with income of $100,000 or more: 9.3%; Poverty rate: 16.5%
Educational Attainment: High school diploma or higher: 83.1%; Bachelor's degree or higher: 13.7%; Graduate/professional degree or higher: 4.6%
Housing: Homeownership rate: 74.0%; Median home value: $81,900; Median year structure built: 1953; Homeowner vacancy rate: 2.7%; Median gross rent: $599 per month; Rental vacancy rate: 9.5%
Vital Statistics: Birth rate: 131.0 per 10,000 population; Death rate: 103.5 per 10,000 population; Age-adjusted cancer mortality rate: 202.9 deaths per 100,000 population
Health Insurance: 83.4% have insurance; 67.0% have private insurance; 30.3% have public insurance; 16.6% do not have insurance; 9.3% of children under 18 do not have insurance
Health Care: Physicians: 11.1 per 10,000 population; Hospital beds: 123.2 per 10,000 population; Hospital admissions: 781.4 per 10,000 population
Transportation: Commute: 93.0% car, 0.9% public transportation, 1.6% walk, 2.5% work from home; Median travel time to work: 20.1 minutes
Presidential Election: 19.9% Obama, 76.9% Romney (2012)
Additional Information Contacts
Cass Government . . . . (219) 753-7720
http://www.co.cass.in.us

Cass County Communities

GALVESTON (town).
Covers a land area of 0.525 square miles and a water area of 0 square miles. Located at 40.58° N. Lat; 86.19° W. Long. Elevation is 801 feet.
Population: 1,311; Growth (since 2000): -14.4%; Density: 2,497.8 persons per square mile; Race: 96.9% White, 0.5% Black/African American, 0.5% Asian, 0.3% American Indian/Alaska Native, 0.0% Native Hawaiian/Other Pacific Islander, 1.4% Two or more races, 1.6% Hispanic of any race; Average household size: 2.37; Median age: 39.6; Age under 18: 24.9%; Age 65 and over: 13.9%; Males per 100 females: 94.2
School District(s)
Southeastern School Corp (KG-12)
    2012-13 Enrollment: 1,466 . . . . (574) 626-2525
Housing: Homeownership rate: 80.6%; Homeowner vacancy rate: 2.8%; Rental vacancy rate: 20.0%

LOGANSPORT (city).
County seat. Covers a land area of 8.748 square miles and a water area of 0.222 square miles. Located at 40.75° N. Lat; 86.36° W. Long. Elevation is 640 feet.
History: Logansport began as a trading post situated at the junction of the Wabash and Eel Rivers. The first permanent settler was Alexander Chamberlain, who built the Log Pioneer Inn in 1828.
Population: 18,396; Growth (since 2000): -6.5%; Density: 2,103.0 persons per square mile; Race: 80.7% White, 2.3% Black/African American, 1.7% Asian, 0.8% American Indian/Alaska Native, 0.1% Native Hawaiian/Other Pacific Islander, 2.2% Two or more races, 21.6% Hispanic of any race; Average household size: 2.57; Median age: 34.2; Age under 18: 27.8%; Age 65 and over: 13.9%; Males per 100 females: 97.2; Marriage status: 32.4% never married, 45.3% now married, 2.6% separated, 7.5% widowed, 14.7% divorced; Foreign born: 14.8%; Speak English only: 78.4%; With disability: 15.6%; Veterans: 9.3%; Ancestry: 18.1% German, 16.1% American, 9.9% Irish, 7.9% English, 3.3% Italian
Employment: 6.2% management, business, and financial, 0.4% computer, engineering, and science, 8.5% education, legal, community service, arts, and media, 4.5% healthcare practitioners, 18.9% service, 18.9% sales and office, 8.1% natural resources, construction, and maintenance, 34.5% production, transportation, and material moving
Income: Per capita: $17,207; Median household: $32,838; Average household: $44,124; Households with income of $100,000 or more: 4.9%; Poverty rate: 22.1%
Educational Attainment: High school diploma or higher: 75.7%; Bachelor's degree or higher: 11.9%; Graduate/professional degree or higher: 3.1%
School District(s)
In Department of Correction (06-12)
    2012-13 Enrollment: 484 . . . . (317) 233-3111
Logansport Community Sch Corp (PK-12)
    2012-13 Enrollment: 4,161 . . . . (574) 722-2911
Housing: Homeownership rate: 60.4%; Median home value: $65,100; Median year structure built: 1941; Homeowner vacancy rate: 4.5%; Median gross rent: $606 per month; Rental vacancy rate: 9.8%
Health Insurance: 77.9% have insurance; 55.5% have private insurance; 34.1% have public insurance; 22.1% do not have insurance; 11.3% of children under 18 do not have insurance
Hospitals: Memorial Hospital (104 beds)
Newspapers: Pharos-Tribune (daily circulation 9300)
Transportation: Commute: 92.8% car, 1.6% public transportation, 1.4% walk, 1.5% work from home; Median travel time to work: 18.7 minutes
Additional Information Contacts
City of Logansport . . . . (574) 753-4745
http://www.cityoflogansport.org

LUCERNE (unincorporated postal area)
ZCTA: 46950
Covers a land area of 28.105 square miles and a water area of 0.002 square miles. Located at 40.89° N. Lat; 86.36° W. Long. Elevation is 801 feet.
Population: 643; Growth (since 2000): -3.3%; Density: 22.9 persons per square mile; Race: 96.4% White, 0.0% Black/African American, 0.5% Asian, 0.3% American Indian/Alaska Native, 0.0% Native Hawaiian/Other Pacific Islander, 1.2% Two or more races, 2.5% Hispanic of any race; Average household size: 2.52; Median age: 42.9; Age under 18: 24.6%; Age 65 and over: 17.1%; Males per 100 females: 96.6
Housing: Homeownership rate: 85.9%; Homeowner vacancy rate: 2.7%; Rental vacancy rate: 12.2%

NEW WAVERLY (unincorporated postal area)
ZCTA: 46961
Covers a land area of 0.484 square miles and a water area of 0 square miles. Located at 40.77° N. Lat; 86.19° W. Long. Elevation is 682 feet.
Population: 99; Growth (since 2000): 23.8%; Density: 204.4 persons per square mile; Race: 98.0% White, 0.0% Black/African American, 0.0% Asian, 2.0% American Indian/Alaska Native, 0.0% Native Hawaiian/Other Pacific Islander, 0.0% Two or more races, 0.0% Hispanic of any race; Average household size: 2.15; Median age: 41.1; Age under 18: 20.2%; Age 65 and over: 18.2%; Males per 100 females: 125.0
Housing: Homeownership rate: 76.1%; Homeowner vacancy rate: 2.8%; Rental vacancy rate: 8.3%

ONWARD (town).
Covers a land area of 0.099 square miles and a water area of 0 square miles. Located at 40.69° N. Lat; 86.20° W. Long. Elevation is 768 feet.
Population: 100; Growth (since 2000): 23.5%; Density: 1,014.2 persons per square mile; Race: 98.0% White, 0.0% Black/African American, 2.0% Asian, 0.0% American Indian/Alaska Native, 0.0% Native Hawaiian/Other Pacific Islander, 0.0% Two or more races, 0.0% Hispanic of any race; Average household size: 2.56; Median age: 32.0; Age under 18: 32.0%; Age 65 and over: 14.0%; Males per 100 females: 104.1
Housing: Homeownership rate: 61.5%; Homeowner vacancy rate: 0.0%; Rental vacancy rate: 6.3%

ROYAL CENTER (town).
Covers a land area of 0.596 square miles and a water area of 0 square miles. Located at 40.86° N. Lat; 86.50° W. Long. Elevation is 735 feet.
History: Laid out 1846.
Population: 861; Growth (since 2000): 3.5%; Density: 1,445.8 persons per square mile; Race: 97.4% White, 0.8% Black/African American, 0.5% Asian, 0.3% American Indian/Alaska Native, 0.0% Native Hawaiian/Other Pacific Islander, 0.9% Two or more races, 1.3% Hispanic of any race; Average household size: 2.52; Median age: 38.0; Age under 18: 27.3%; Age 65 and over: 15.4%; Males per 100 females: 99.8
School District(s)
Pioneer Regional School Corp (KG-12)
    2012-13 Enrollment: 926 . . . . (574) 643-2605
Housing: Homeownership rate: 77.2%; Homeowner vacancy rate: 3.3%; Rental vacancy rate: 7.1%

Newspapers: Royal Centre Record (weekly circulation 1000)

TWELVE MILE (unincorporated postal area)
ZCTA: 46988
Covers a land area of 26.403 square miles and a water area of 0.029 square miles. Located at 40.88° N. Lat; 86.23° W. Long. Elevation is 794 feet.
Population: 823; Growth (since 2000): -25.5%; Density: 31.2 persons per square mile; Race: 96.2% White, 0.2% Black/African American, 0.0% Asian, 0.2% American Indian/Alaska Native, 0.1% Native Hawaiian/Other Pacific Islander, 1.1% Two or more races, 3.5% Hispanic of any race; Average household size: 2.60; Median age: 40.5; Age under 18: 26.0%; Age 65 and over: 16.5%; Males per 100 females: 99.8
Housing: Homeownership rate: 80.7%; Homeowner vacancy rate: 3.4%; Rental vacancy rate: 21.3%

WALTON (town).
Covers a land area of 0.426 square miles and a water area of 0 square miles. Located at 40.66° N. Lat; 86.24° W. Long. Elevation is 771 feet.
History: Laid out 1852.
Population: 1,049; Growth (since 2000): -1.9%; Density: 2,460.8 persons per square mile; Race: 93.2% White, 0.3% Black/African American, 0.3% Asian, 0.1% American Indian/Alaska Native, 0.0% Native Hawaiian/Other Pacific Islander, 1.6% Two or more races, 9.5% Hispanic of any race; Average household size: 2.57; Median age: 36.4; Age under 18: 27.5%; Age 65 and over: 15.0%; Males per 100 females: 87.3
School District(s)
Southeastern School Corp (KG-12)
    2012-13 Enrollment: 1,466 . . . . (574) 626-2525
Housing: Homeownership rate: 74.2%; Homeowner vacancy rate: 1.3%; Rental vacancy rate: 5.3%

YOUNG AMERICA (unincorporated postal area)
ZCTA: 46998
Covers a land area of 0.082 square miles and a water area of 0 square miles. Located at 40.57° N. Lat; 86.35° W. Long. Elevation is 768 feet.
Population: 112; Growth (since 2000): -2.6%; Density: 1,371.3 persons per square mile; Race: 98.2% White, 0.0% Black/African American, 0.0% Asian, 0.0% American Indian/Alaska Native, 0.0% Native Hawaiian/Other Pacific Islander, 1.8% Two or more races, 1.8% Hispanic of any race; Average household size: 2.24; Median age: 43.5; Age under 18: 17.9%; Age 65 and over: 15.2%; Males per 100 females: 72.3
Housing: Homeownership rate: 84.0%; Homeowner vacancy rate: 0.0%; Rental vacancy rate: 20.0%

Clark County

Located in southeastern Indiana; bounded on the southeast by the Ohio River and the Kentucky border; drained by Silver Creek. Covers a land area of 372.855 square miles, a water area of 3.596 square miles, and is located in the Eastern Time Zone at 38.48° N. Lat., 85.71° W. Long. The county was founded in 1801. County seat is Jeffersonville.

Clark County is part of the Louisville/Jefferson County, KY-IN Metropolitan Statistical Area. The entire metro area includes: Clark County, IN; Floyd County, IN; Harrison County, IN; Scott County, IN; Washington County, IN; Bullitt County, KY; Henry County, KY; Jefferson County, KY; Oldham County, KY; Shelby County, KY; Spencer County, KY; Trimble County, KY

Population: 110,232; Growth (since 2000): 14.3%; Density: 295.6 persons per square mile; Race: 87.1% White, 6.9% Black/African American, 0.8% Asian, 0.3% American Indian/Alaska Native, 0.0% Native Hawaiian/Other Pacific Islander, 2.2% two or more races, 4.9% Hispanic of any race; Average household size: 2.46; Median age: 37.9; Age under 18: 23.7%; Age 65 and over: 12.8%; Males per 100 females: 96.0; Marriage status: 27.9% never married, 51.1% now married, 1.6% separated, 6.5% widowed, 14.5% divorced; Foreign born: 3.7%; Speak English only: 94.8%; With disability: 15.1%; Veterans: 10.5%; Ancestry: 22.9% German, 14.3% Irish, 12.7% American, 8.9% English, 2.3% French
Religion: Six largest groups: 13.2% Baptist, 9.2% Catholicism, 5.6% Non-denominational Protestant, 3.3% Methodist/Pietist, 0.8% Presbyterian-Reformed, 0.6% Holiness
Economy: Unemployment rate: 5.1%; Leading industries: 17.7% retail trade; 10.5% other services (except public administration); 10.0% health care and social assistance; Farms: 515 totaling 78,545 acres; Company size: 2 employ 1,000 or more persons, 2 employ 500 to 999 persons, 77 employ 100 to 499 persons, 2,314 employ less than 100 persons; Business ownership: 2,255 women-owned, n/a Black-owned, 87 Hispanic-owned, n/a Asian-owned
Employment: 12.3% management, business, and financial, 3.5% computer, engineering, and science, 6.7% education, legal, community service, arts, and media, 6.6% healthcare practitioners, 17.4% service, 27.7% sales and office, 8.2% natural resources, construction, and maintenance, 17.6% production, transportation, and material moving
Income: Per capita: $24,312; Median household: $50,496; Average household: $60,836; Households with income of $100,000 or more: 14.7%; Poverty rate: 12.2%
Educational Attainment: High school diploma or higher: 86.2%; Bachelor's degree or higher: 18.9%; Graduate/professional degree or higher: 6.2%
Housing: Homeownership rate: 70.1%; Median home value: $127,400; Median year structure built: 1976; Homeowner vacancy rate: 2.8%; Median gross rent: $739 per month; Rental vacancy rate: 8.1%
Vital Statistics: Birth rate: 126.8 per 10,000 population; Death rate: 94.8 per 10,000 population; Age-adjusted cancer mortality rate: 173.2 deaths per 100,000 population
Health Insurance: 86.0% have insurance; 71.0% have private insurance; 27.1% have public insurance; 14.0% do not have insurance; 9.1% of children under 18 do not have insurance
Health Care: Physicians: 12.8 per 10,000 population; Hospital beds: 33.7 per 10,000 population; Hospital admissions: 1,840.6 per 10,000 population
Air Quality Index: 57.4% good, 42.6% moderate, 0.0% unhealthy for sensitive individuals, 0.0% unhealthy (percent of days)
Transportation: Commute: 95.7% car, 0.4% public transportation, 1.0% walk, 2.1% work from home; Median travel time to work: 24.1 minutes
Presidential Election: 44.1% Obama, 54.0% Romney (2012)
National and State Parks: Deam Lake State Recreation Area; Falls of the Ohio State Park
Additional Information Contacts
Clark Government . . . . (812) 285-6200
    http://www.clarkcountyconnect.net

Clark County Communities

BORDEN (town).
Covers a land area of 1.392 square miles and a water area of <.001 square miles. Located at 38.47° N. Lat; 85.95° W. Long. Elevation is 561 feet.
Population: 808; Growth (since 2000): -1.2%; Density: 580.6 persons per square mile; Race: 98.9% White, 0.0% Black/African American, 0.0% Asian, 0.0% American Indian/Alaska Native, 0.0% Native Hawaiian/Other Pacific Islander, 0.6% Two or more races, 1.1% Hispanic of any race; Average household size: 2.52; Median age: 35.3; Age under 18: 26.4%; Age 65 and over: 12.6%; Males per 100 females: 94.2
School District(s)
West Clark Community Schools (PK-12)
    2012-13 Enrollment: 4,619 . . . . (812) 246-3375
Housing: Homeownership rate: 75.1%; Homeowner vacancy rate: 2.0%; Rental vacancy rate: 14.7%

CHARLESTOWN (city).
Covers a land area of 11.446 square miles and a water area of 0.039 square miles. Located at 38.43° N. Lat; 85.67° W. Long. Elevation is 591 feet.
History: Charleston was platted in 1808, and served as the seat of Clark County from 1811 to 1878. In 1940 the E.I. du Pont de Nemours Company built a plant here, followed by the Goodyear Tire and Rubber Company's plant.
Population: 7,585; Growth (since 2000): 26.6%; Density: 662.7 persons per square mile; Race: 89.9% White, 2.1% Black/African American, 0.3% Asian, 0.3% American Indian/Alaska Native, 0.0% Native Hawaiian/Other Pacific Islander, 2.1% Two or more races, 8.3% Hispanic of any race; Average household size: 2.63; Median age: 35.2; Age under 18: 28.4%; Age 65 and over: 11.2%; Males per 100 females: 90.5; Marriage status: 32.6% never married, 44.8% now married, 1.7% separated, 6.2% widowed, 16.4% divorced; Foreign born: 4.9%; Speak English only: 92.6%; With disability: 14.2%; Veterans: 8.4%; Ancestry: 23.4% German, 15.6% Irish, 13.9% American, 9.7% English, 3.5% Dutch

Employment: 9.8% management, business, and financial, 2.2% computer, engineering, and science, 4.5% education, legal, community service, arts, and media, 5.2% healthcare practitioners, 15.9% service, 31.2% sales and office, 7.0% natural resources, construction, and maintenance, 24.2% production, transportation, and material moving
Income: Per capita: $19,981; Median household: $40,034; Average household: $51,301; Households with income of $100,000 or more: 11.8%; Poverty rate: 19.8%
Educational Attainment: High school diploma or higher: 85.8%; Bachelor's degree or higher: 13.3%; Graduate/professional degree or higher: 4.9%

School District(s)
Greater Clark County Schools (PK-12)
    2012-13 Enrollment: 10,529 . . . . (812) 283-0701

Housing: Homeownership rate: 61.4%; Median home value: $110,600; Median year structure built: 1970; Homeowner vacancy rate: 3.5%; Median gross rent: $618 per month; Rental vacancy rate: 8.3%
Health Insurance: 84.2% have insurance; 64.3% have private insurance; 30.5% have public insurance; 15.8% do not have insurance; 6.0% of children under 18 do not have insurance
Hospitals: Saint Catherine Regional Hospital (96 beds)
Newspapers: The Leader (weekly circulation 13000)
Transportation: Commute: 95.8% car, 0.6% public transportation, 0.4% walk, 1.6% work from home; Median travel time to work: 25.0 minutes
Additional Information Contacts
City of Charlestown . . . . (812) 256-3422
http://www.cityofcharlestown.com

CLARKSVILLE (town).
Covers a land area of 9.973 square miles and a water area of 0.203 square miles. Located at 38.32° N. Lat; 85.77° W. Long. Elevation is 456 feet.
History: Named for General George Rogers Clark, who founded the town in 1784. Clarksville was founded in 1784 by George Rogers Clark on land given to Clark by the State of Virginia in reward for his military service. Clarksville was the site of the duel between Henry Clay and Humphrey Marshall in which each was wounded.
Population: 21,724; Growth (since 2000): 1.5%; Density: 2,178.2 persons per square mile; Race: 85.1% White, 5.6% Black/African American, 0.7% Asian, 0.3% American Indian/Alaska Native, 0.0% Native Hawaiian/Other Pacific Islander, 2.5% Two or more races, 9.5% Hispanic of any race; Average household size: 2.34; Median age: 37.3; Age under 18: 22.9%; Age 65 and over: 15.2%; Males per 100 females: 92.4; Marriage status: 29.5% never married, 45.9% now married, 1.6% separated, 9.3% widowed, 15.3% divorced; Foreign born: 6.3%; Speak English only: 90.9%; With disability: 14.4%; Veterans: 9.6%; Ancestry: 20.0% German, 12.6% Irish, 10.7% American, 6.9% English, 2.3% French
Employment: 13.9% management, business, and financial, 2.9% computer, engineering, and science, 6.4% education, legal, community service, arts, and media, 5.7% healthcare practitioners, 20.5% service, 26.5% sales and office, 6.4% natural resources, construction, and maintenance, 17.8% production, transportation, and material moving
Income: Per capita: $21,662; Median household: $43,715; Average household: $51,922; Households with income of $100,000 or more: 10.6%; Poverty rate: 14.2%
Educational Attainment: High school diploma or higher: 84.6%; Bachelor's degree or higher: 19.4%; Graduate/professional degree or higher: 5.1%

School District(s)
Clarksville Com School Corp (PK-12)
    2012-13 Enrollment: 1,332 . . . . (812) 282-7753
Greater Clark County Schools (PK-12)
    2012-13 Enrollment: 10,529 . . . . (812) 283-0701

Two-year College(s)
PJ's College of Cosmetology-Clarksville (Private, For-profit)
    Fall 2013 Enrollment: 116 . . . . (317) 846-8999

Housing: Homeownership rate: 59.8%; Median home value: $114,200; Median year structure built: 1970; Homeowner vacancy rate: 2.7%; Median gross rent: $755 per month; Rental vacancy rate: 7.3%
Health Insurance: 81.5% have insurance; 62.7% have private insurance; 29.7% have public insurance; 18.5% do not have insurance; 12.7% of children under 18 do not have insurance
Hospitals: Kentuckiana Medical Center (34 beds)
Safety: Violent crime rate: 55.8 per 10,000 population; Property crime rate: 699.3 per 10,000 population

Transportation: Commute: 96.0% car, 0.6% public transportation, 0.7% walk, 1.7% work from home; Median travel time to work: 21.5 minutes
Additional Information Contacts
Town of Clarksville . . . . (812) 283-1500
http://town.clarksville.in.us

HENRYVILLE (CDP).
Covers a land area of 2.847 square miles and a water area of 0.003 square miles. Located at 38.54° N. Lat; 85.77° W. Long. Elevation is 518 feet.
Population: 1,905; Growth (since 2000): 23.3%; Density: 669.1 persons per square mile; Race: 98.1% White, 0.0% Black/African American, 0.4% Asian, 0.0% American Indian/Alaska Native, 0.0% Native Hawaiian/Other Pacific Islander, 0.9% Two or more races, 1.6% Hispanic of any race; Average household size: 2.62; Median age: 35.0; Age under 18: 25.5%; Age 65 and over: 10.7%; Males per 100 females: 97.2

School District(s)
West Clark Community Schools (PK-12)
    2012-13 Enrollment: 4,619 . . . . (812) 246-3375

Housing: Homeownership rate: 71.6%; Homeowner vacancy rate: 2.8%; Rental vacancy rate: 6.8%

JEFFERSONVILLE (city).
County seat. Covers a land area of 34.064 square miles and a water area of 0.294 square miles. Located at 38.33° N. Lat; 85.70° W. Long. Elevation is 446 feet.
History: Jeffersonville was platted in 1802 and named by William Henry Harrison for Thomas Jefferson, who had suggested the plan. The Howard Shipyards were founded in 1834 and influenced the economy of Jeffersonville for a century. The city sustained heavy damage in the 1937 flooding of the Ohio River.
Population: 44,953; Growth (since 2000): 64.3%; Density: 1,319.7 persons per square mile; Race: 80.4% White, 13.2% Black/African American, 1.1% Asian, 0.3% American Indian/Alaska Native, 0.0% Native Hawaiian/Other Pacific Islander, 3.0% Two or more races, 4.1% Hispanic of any race; Average household size: 2.37; Median age: 37.3; Age under 18: 23.2%; Age 65 and over: 11.9%; Males per 100 females: 95.4; Marriage status: 30.9% never married, 47.4% now married, 1.8% separated, 6.3% widowed, 15.4% divorced; Foreign born: 3.6%; Speak English only: 95.1%; With disability: 16.4%; Veterans: 10.4%; Ancestry: 22.5% German, 13.8% Irish, 12.0% American, 8.1% English, 2.1% French
Employment: 11.3% management, business, and financial, 3.9% computer, engineering, and science, 6.9% education, legal, community service, arts, and media, 6.4% healthcare practitioners, 18.9% service, 27.6% sales and office, 7.4% natural resources, construction, and maintenance, 17.4% production, transportation, and material moving
Income: Per capita: $24,781; Median household: $50,020; Average household: $60,227; Households with income of $100,000 or more: 15.1%; Poverty rate: 12.3%
Educational Attainment: High school diploma or higher: 87.1%; Bachelor's degree or higher: 20.8%; Graduate/professional degree or higher: 7.3%

School District(s)
Greater Clark County Schools (PK-12)
    2012-13 Enrollment: 10,529 . . . . (812) 283-0701

Four-year College(s)
Mid-America College of Funeral Service (Private, Not-for-profit)
    Fall 2013 Enrollment: 63 . . . . (812) 288-8878
    2013-14 Tuition: In-state $10,550; Out-of-state $10,550
Ottawa University-Jeffersonville (Private, Not-for-profit, American Baptist)
    Fall 2013 Enrollment: 114 . . . . (812) 280-7271

Vocational/Technical School(s)
Ideal Beauty Academy (Private, For-profit)
    Fall 2013 Enrollment: 33 . . . . (812) 282-1371
    2013-14 Tuition: $12,850

Housing: Homeownership rate: 66.9%; Median home value: $126,300; Median year structure built: 1976; Homeowner vacancy rate: 2.3%; Median gross rent: $730 per month; Rental vacancy rate: 8.7%
Health Insurance: 86.3% have insurance; 71.1% have private insurance; 28.3% have public insurance; 13.7% do not have insurance; 7.7% of children under 18 do not have insurance
Hospitals: Clark Memorial Hospital (241 beds)
Safety: Violent crime rate: 76.1 per 10,000 population; Property crime rate: 366.0 per 10,000 population
Newspapers: Evening News (daily circulation 7200)
Transportation: Commute: 94.5% car, 0.3% public transportation, 1.8% walk, 2.3% work from home; Median travel time to work: 21.5 minutes

Airports: Clark Regional (general aviation)
Additional Information Contacts
City of Jeffersonville . . . . (812) 285-6427
   http://www.cityofjeff.net

MARYSVILLE (unincorporated postal area)
ZCTA: 47141
   Covers a land area of 34.119 square miles and a water area of 0.156 square miles. Located at 38.55° N. Lat; 85.61° W. Long. Elevation is 712 feet.
   Population: 1,668; Growth (since 2000): 18.0%; Density: 48.9 persons per square mile; Race: 97.4% White, 0.7% Black/African American, 0.5% Asian, 0.2% American Indian/Alaska Native, 0.0% Native Hawaiian/Other Pacific Islander, 0.6% Two or more races, 1.1% Hispanic of any race; Average household size: 2.68; Median age: 40.7; Age under 18: 24.8%; Age 65 and over: 12.0%; Males per 100 females: 101.0
   Housing: Homeownership rate: 88.4%; Homeowner vacancy rate: 3.5%; Rental vacancy rate: 3.9%

MEMPHIS (CDP).
Covers a land area of 2.598 square miles and a water area of 0.023 square miles. Located at 38.49° N. Lat; 85.77° W. Long. Elevation is 486 feet.
   Population: 695; Growth (since 2000): 73.8%; Density: 267.5 persons per square mile; Race: 96.5% White, 1.7% Black/African American, 0.0% Asian, 0.0% American Indian/Alaska Native, 0.0% Native Hawaiian/Other Pacific Islander, 0.6% Two or more races, 1.4% Hispanic of any race; Average household size: 2.50; Median age: 32.8; Age under 18: 25.0%; Age 65 and over: 8.2%; Males per 100 females: 92.0
   Housing: Homeownership rate: 74.5%; Homeowner vacancy rate: 2.8%; Rental vacancy rate: 7.8%

NABB (unincorporated postal area)
ZCTA: 47147
   Covers a land area of 27.811 square miles and a water area of 0.074 square miles. Located at 38.59° N. Lat; 85.55° W. Long..
   Population: 945; Growth (since 2000): -11.0%; Density: 34.0 persons per square mile; Race: 99.6% White, 0.0% Black/African American, 0.0% Asian, 0.0% American Indian/Alaska Native, 0.0% Native Hawaiian/Other Pacific Islander, 0.0% Two or more races, 1.1% Hispanic of any race; Average household size: 2.55; Median age: 44.0; Age under 18: 21.7%; Age 65 and over: 14.8%; Males per 100 females: 96.9
   Housing: Homeownership rate: 84.7%; Homeowner vacancy rate: 1.9%; Rental vacancy rate: 4.9%

NEW WASHINGTON (CDP).
Covers a land area of 5.207 square miles and a water area of 0.015 square miles. Located at 38.57° N. Lat; 85.56° W. Long. Elevation is 718 feet.
   Population: 566; Growth (since 2000): 3.5%; Density: 108.7 persons per square mile; Race: 99.1% White, 0.2% Black/African American, 0.0% Asian, 0.0% American Indian/Alaska Native, 0.0% Native Hawaiian/Other Pacific Islander, 0.5% Two or more races, 0.9% Hispanic of any race; Average household size: 2.38; Median age: 40.0; Age under 18: 23.7%; Age 65 and over: 17.5%; Males per 100 females: 84.4
   School District(s)
   Greater Clark County Schools (PK-12)
      2012-13 Enrollment: 10,529 . . . . (812) 283-0701
   Housing: Homeownership rate: 75.6%; Homeowner vacancy rate: 1.1%; Rental vacancy rate: 7.8%

OTISCO (unincorporated postal area)
ZCTA: 47163
   Covers a land area of 20.827 square miles and a water area of 0.136 square miles. Located at 38.53° N. Lat; 85.67° W. Long. Elevation is 673 feet.
   Population: 1,746; Growth (since 2000): 0.8%; Density: 83.8 persons per square mile; Race: 96.7% White, 0.3% Black/African American, 0.1% Asian, 0.1% American Indian/Alaska Native, 0.0% Native Hawaiian/Other Pacific Islander, 1.2% Two or more races, 2.2% Hispanic of any race; Average household size: 2.72; Median age: 42.4; Age under 18: 22.8%; Age 65 and over: 13.8%; Males per 100 females: 105.4
   Housing: Homeownership rate: 89.9%; Homeowner vacancy rate: 1.2%; Rental vacancy rate: 11.0%

SELLERSBURG (town).
Covers a land area of 3.943 square miles and a water area of 0.030 square miles. Located at 38.39° N. Lat; 85.76° W. Long. Elevation is 486 feet.
   History: Laid out 1846.
   Population: 6,128; Growth (since 2000): 0.9%; Density: 1,554.3 persons per square mile; Race: 94.2% White, 0.8% Black/African American, 0.3% Asian, 0.3% American Indian/Alaska Native, 0.0% Native Hawaiian/Other Pacific Islander, 1.6% Two or more races, 5.5% Hispanic of any race; Average household size: 2.48; Median age: 38.0; Age under 18: 24.6%; Age 65 and over: 14.7%; Males per 100 females: 94.4; Marriage status: 18.5% never married, 55.1% now married, 0.7% separated, 8.5% widowed, 17.8% divorced; Foreign born: 3.4%; Speak English only: 95.5%; With disability: 12.3%; Veterans: 10.5%; Ancestry: 22.1% German, 17.1% Irish, 12.5% American, 11.9% English, 2.7% Dutch
   Employment: 11.1% management, business, and financial, 2.5% computer, engineering, and science, 4.8% education, legal, community service, arts, and media, 2.8% healthcare practitioners, 11.9% service, 32.5% sales and office, 12.1% natural resources, construction, and maintenance, 22.2% production, transportation, and material moving
   Income: Per capita: $23,204; Median household: $52,259; Average household: $59,135; Households with income of $100,000 or more: 10.2%; Poverty rate: 10.3%
   Educational Attainment: High school diploma or higher: 87.1%; Bachelor's degree or higher: 13.2%; Graduate/professional degree or higher: 5.7%
   School District(s)
   Rock Creek Community Academy (KG-12)
      2012-13 Enrollment: 426 . . . . (812) 246-9271
   West Clark Community Schools (PK-12)
      2012-13 Enrollment: 4,619 . . . . (812) 246-3375
   Housing: Homeownership rate: 76.7%; Median home value: $109,300; Median year structure built: 1970; Homeowner vacancy rate: 2.4%; Median gross rent: $975 per month; Rental vacancy rate: 6.7%
   Health Insurance: 82.7% have insurance; 70.8% have private insurance; 22.4% have public insurance; 17.3% do not have insurance; 15.8% of children under 18 do not have insurance
   Safety: Violent crime rate: n/a per 10,000 population; Property crime rate: 177.2 per 10,000 population
   Transportation: Commute: 96.4% car, 0.7% public transportation, 0.4% walk, 2.2% work from home; Median travel time to work: 21.3 minutes
   Additional Information Contacts
   Town of Sellersburg . . . . (812) 246-7049
      http://www.sellersburg.org

UTICA (town).
Covers a land area of 1.266 square miles and a water area of 0.178 square miles. Located at 38.34° N. Lat; 85.66° W. Long. Elevation is 443 feet.
   History: Laid out 1816.
   Population: 776; Growth (since 2000): 31.3%; Density: 612.8 persons per square mile; Race: 89.6% White, 3.4% Black/African American, 1.9% Asian, 0.8% American Indian/Alaska Native, 0.0% Native Hawaiian/Other Pacific Islander, 2.4% Two or more races, 3.4% Hispanic of any race; Average household size: 2.37; Median age: 43.3; Age under 18: 19.3%; Age 65 and over: 14.2%; Males per 100 females: 91.1
   Housing: Homeownership rate: 79.6%; Homeowner vacancy rate: 4.3%; Rental vacancy rate: 6.9%

Clay County

Located in western Indiana; drained by the Eel River and Small Birch Creek. Covers a land area of 357.542 square miles, a water area of 2.780 square miles, and is located in the Eastern Time Zone at 39.39° N. Lat., 87.12° W. Long. The county was founded in 1825. County seat is Brazil.

Clay County is part of the Terre Haute, IN Metropolitan Statistical Area. The entire metro area includes: Clay County, IN; Sullivan County, IN; Vermillion County, IN; Vigo County, IN

Population: 26,890; Growth (since 2000): 1.3%; Density: 75.2 persons per square mile; Race: 97.8% White, 0.3% Black/African American, 0.2% Asian, 0.2% American Indian/Alaska Native, 0.0% Native Hawaiian/Other Pacific Islander, 0.9% two or more races, 1.1% Hispanic of any race; Average household size: 2.54; Median age: 39.9; Age under 18: 24.0%; Age 65 and over: 15.1%; Males per 100 females: 96.9; Marriage status: 21.4% never married, 58.7% now married, 0.9% separated, 7.5%

widowed, 12.4% divorced; Foreign born: 0.5%; Speak English only: 98.5%; With disability: 16.9%; Veterans: 9.7%; Ancestry: 26.1% German, 21.0% American, 12.1% Irish, 9.8% English, 3.6% Dutch
Religion: Six largest groups: 13.9% Non-denominational Protestant, 11.6% Baptist, 7.8% Methodist/Pietist, 3.6% Presbyterian-Reformed, 2.3% Holiness, 1.5% Pentecostal
Economy: Unemployment rate: 6.2%; Leading industries: 17.4% retail trade; 15.7% other services (except public administration); 10.7% construction; Farms: 579 totaling 162,883 acres; Company size: 1 employs 1,000 or more persons, 0 employ 500 to 999 persons, 7 employ 100 to 499 persons, 470 employ less than 100 persons; Business ownership: 504 women-owned, n/a Black-owned, n/a Hispanic-owned, n/a Asian-owned
Employment: 10.0% management, business, and financial, 2.9% computer, engineering, and science, 8.8% education, legal, community service, arts, and media, 6.0% healthcare practitioners, 19.5% service, 22.0% sales and office, 10.5% natural resources, construction, and maintenance, 20.2% production, transportation, and material moving
Income: Per capita: $21,474; Median household: $46,430; Average household: $55,760; Households with income of $100,000 or more: 12.9%; Poverty rate: 15.8%
Educational Attainment: High school diploma or higher: 86.6%; Bachelor's degree or higher: 14.0%; Graduate/professional degree or higher: 4.6%
Housing: Homeownership rate: 75.6%; Median home value: $91,300; Median year structure built: 1968; Homeowner vacancy rate: 2.1%; Median gross rent: $650 per month; Rental vacancy rate: 7.5%
Vital Statistics: Birth rate: 113.4 per 10,000 population; Death rate: 101.1 per 10,000 population; Age-adjusted cancer mortality rate: 239.4 deaths per 100,000 population
Health Insurance: 85.4% have insurance; 66.5% have private insurance; 31.7% have public insurance; 14.6% do not have insurance; 8.6% of children under 18 do not have insurance
Health Care: Physicians: 7.1 per 10,000 population; Hospital beds: 9.3 per 10,000 population; Hospital admissions: 223.9 per 10,000 population
Transportation: Commute: 94.2% car, 0.1% public transportation, 1.9% walk, 3.1% work from home; Median travel time to work: 27.0 minutes
Presidential Election: 33.2% Obama, 64.7% Romney (2012)
National and State Parks: Shakamak State Park
Additional Information Contacts
Clay Government . . . . (812) 448-9025
http://www.claycountyin.gov

Clay County Communities

BRAZIL (city). County seat. Covers a land area of 3.027 square miles and a water area of 0.028 square miles. Located at 39.52° N. Lat; 87.12° W. Long. Elevation is 653 feet.
History: Brazil's development was based on its coal mines and clay plants, which manufactured glazed building bricks and tiles. Brazil was named for the country in South America, the name suggested by resident William Stewart who had just read a magazine article about Brazil.
Population: 7,912; Growth (since 2000): -3.4%; Density: 2,613.8 persons per square mile; Race: 97.1% White, 0.6% Black/African American, 0.5% Asian, 0.1% American Indian/Alaska Native, 0.0% Native Hawaiian/Other Pacific Islander, 1.0% Two or more races, 1.6% Hispanic of any race; Average household size: 2.46; Median age: 36.2; Age under 18: 26.0%; Age 65 and over: 14.4%; Males per 100 females: 92.3; Marriage status: 27.8% never married, 46.3% now married, 1.3% separated, 6.9% widowed, 18.9% divorced; Foreign born: 0.6%; Speak English only: 98.8%; With disability: 17.8%; Veterans: 9.0%; Ancestry: 22.8% American, 19.7% German, 11.7% Irish, 7.4% English, 5.4% French
Employment: 12.0% management, business, and financial, 2.9% computer, engineering, and science, 6.2% education, legal, community service, arts, and media, 6.9% healthcare practitioners, 22.7% service, 21.6% sales and office, 5.7% natural resources, construction, and maintenance, 22.1% production, transportation, and material moving
Income: Per capita: $16,194; Median household: $29,981; Average household: $41,019; Households with income of $100,000 or more: 5.8%; Poverty rate: 28.7%
Educational Attainment: High school diploma or higher: 76.6%; Bachelor's degree or higher: 9.5%; Graduate/professional degree or higher: 3.6%

School District(s)
Clay Community Schools (PK-12)
    2012-13 Enrollment: 4,405 . . . . (812) 443-4461

Housing: Homeownership rate: 57.2%; Median home value: $72,500; Median year structure built: 1957; Homeowner vacancy rate: 3.8%; Median gross rent: $641 per month; Rental vacancy rate: 7.3%
Health Insurance: 80.4% have insurance; 49.9% have private insurance; 41.4% have public insurance; 19.6% do not have insurance; 9.3% of children under 18 do not have insurance
Hospitals: Saint Vincent Clay Hospital (58 beds)
Newspapers: Brazil Times (daily circulation 4600)
Transportation: Commute: 96.7% car, 0.0% public transportation, 1.8% walk, 1.0% work from home; Median travel time to work: 22.5 minutes
Additional Information Contacts
City of Brazil . . . . (812) 443-2221
http://brazil.in.gov

CARBON (town). Covers a land area of 0.159 square miles and a water area of 0 square miles. Located at 39.60° N. Lat; 87.11° W. Long. Elevation is 692 feet.
Population: 397; Growth (since 2000): 18.9%; Density: 2,493.4 persons per square mile; Race: 96.7% White, 0.0% Black/African American, 0.0% Asian, 0.0% American Indian/Alaska Native, 0.0% Native Hawaiian/Other Pacific Islander, 1.0% Two or more races, 3.0% Hispanic of any race; Average household size: 2.88; Median age: 35.6; Age under 18: 30.7%; Age 65 and over: 9.1%; Males per 100 females: 102.6
Housing: Homeownership rate: 84.1%; Homeowner vacancy rate: 2.5%; Rental vacancy rate: 8.3%

CENTER POINT (town). Covers a land area of 0.740 square miles and a water area of 0.022 square miles. Located at 39.42° N. Lat; 87.08° W. Long. Elevation is 656 feet.
Population: 242; Growth (since 2000): -17.1%; Density: 326.9 persons per square mile; Race: 98.3% White, 0.4% Black/African American, 1.2% Asian, 0.0% American Indian/Alaska Native, 0.0% Native Hawaiian/Other Pacific Islander, 0.0% Two or more races, 0.0% Hispanic of any race; Average household size: 2.33; Median age: 40.0; Age under 18: 20.2%; Age 65 and over: 14.9%; Males per 100 females: 83.3
Housing: Homeownership rate: 73.1%; Homeowner vacancy rate: 0.0%; Rental vacancy rate: 9.7%

CENTERPOINT (unincorporated postal area)
ZCTA: 47840
    Covers a land area of 53.117 square miles and a water area of 0.550 square miles. Located at 39.41° N. Lat; 87.06° W. Long..
Population: 1,500; Growth (since 2000): -10.6%; Density: 28.2 persons per square mile; Race: 98.8% White, 0.3% Black/African American, 0.3% Asian, 0.1% American Indian/Alaska Native, 0.0% Native Hawaiian/Other Pacific Islander, 0.3% Two or more races, 0.5% Hispanic of any race; Average household size: 2.53; Median age: 42.5; Age under 18: 21.3%; Age 65 and over: 15.9%; Males per 100 females: 98.7
Housing: Homeownership rate: 83.8%; Homeowner vacancy rate: 1.8%; Rental vacancy rate: 8.6%

CLAY CITY (town). Covers a land area of 0.540 square miles and a water area of 0 square miles. Located at 39.28° N. Lat; 87.11° W. Long. Elevation is 594 feet.
History: Settled 1873, incorporated 1888.
Population: 861; Growth (since 2000): -15.5%; Density: 1,593.7 persons per square mile; Race: 99.2% White, 0.0% Black/African American, 0.1% Asian, 0.0% American Indian/Alaska Native, 0.0% Native Hawaiian/Other Pacific Islander, 0.7% Two or more races, 0.7% Hispanic of any race; Average household size: 2.39; Median age: 39.2; Age under 18: 24.5%; Age 65 and over: 19.6%; Males per 100 females: 80.5

School District(s)
Clay Community Schools (PK-12)
    2012-13 Enrollment: 4,405 . . . . (812) 443-4461

Housing: Homeownership rate: 68.1%; Homeowner vacancy rate: 4.2%; Rental vacancy rate: 12.7%
Newspapers: Clay City News (weekly circulation 2000)
Additional Information Contacts
Town of Clay City . . . . (812) 939-2345
http://www.claycity.net

COALMONT (CDP). Covers a land area of 1.501 square miles and a water area of 0.003 square miles. Located at 39.19° N. Lat; 87.22° W. Long. Elevation is 630 feet.
Population: 402; Growth (since 2000): n/a; Density: 267.8 persons per square mile; Race: 95.8% White, 0.2% Black/African American, 0.0% Asian, 1.7% American Indian/Alaska Native, 0.0% Native Hawaiian/Other Pacific Islander, 2.0% Two or more races, 0.5% Hispanic of any race; Average household size: 2.58; Median age: 39.7; Age under 18: 23.4%; Age 65 and over: 14.7%; Males per 100 females: 103.0
Housing: Homeownership rate: 81.4%; Homeowner vacancy rate: 2.3%; Rental vacancy rate: 14.7%

CORY (unincorporated postal area)
ZCTA: 47846
Covers a land area of 31.521 square miles and a water area of 0.157 square miles. Located at 39.38° N. Lat; 87.19° W. Long. Elevation is 630 feet.
Population: 638; Growth (since 2000): -12.0%; Density: 20.2 persons per square mile; Race: 96.4% White, 0.2% Black/African American, 0.0% Asian, 0.0% American Indian/Alaska Native, 0.0% Native Hawaiian/Other Pacific Islander, 1.3% Two or more races, 2.7% Hispanic of any race; Average household size: 2.50; Median age: 42.3; Age under 18: 22.6%; Age 65 and over: 17.4%; Males per 100 females: 98.8
Housing: Homeownership rate: 84.7%; Homeowner vacancy rate: 0.4%; Rental vacancy rate: 2.5%

HARMONY (town). Covers a land area of 0.745 square miles and a water area of 0 square miles. Located at 39.53° N. Lat; 87.07° W. Long. Elevation is 659 feet.
History: Harmony was once a prosperous coal-mining town.
Population: 656; Growth (since 2000): 11.4%; Density: 880.6 persons per square mile; Race: 97.6% White, 0.8% Black/African American, 0.3% Asian, 0.0% American Indian/Alaska Native, 0.0% Native Hawaiian/Other Pacific Islander, 0.5% Two or more races, 1.2% Hispanic of any race; Average household size: 2.48; Median age: 38.6; Age under 18: 25.2%; Age 65 and over: 13.6%; Males per 100 females: 82.7
Housing: Homeownership rate: 73.2%; Homeowner vacancy rate: 2.5%; Rental vacancy rate: 7.8%

KNIGHTSVILLE (town). Covers a land area of 1.038 square miles and a water area of 0 square miles. Located at 39.53° N. Lat; 87.09° W. Long. Elevation is 669 feet.
Population: 872; Growth (since 2000): 39.7%; Density: 839.9 persons per square mile; Race: 96.6% White, 1.3% Black/African American, 0.2% Asian, 0.2% American Indian/Alaska Native, 0.1% Native Hawaiian/Other Pacific Islander, 1.6% Two or more races, 0.7% Hispanic of any race; Average household size: 2.61; Median age: 41.3; Age under 18: 20.1%; Age 65 and over: 20.6%; Males per 100 females: 100.5
Housing: Homeownership rate: 84.3%; Homeowner vacancy rate: 0.8%; Rental vacancy rate: 13.7%

STAUNTON (town). Covers a land area of 0.345 square miles and a water area of 0 square miles. Located at 39.49° N. Lat; 87.19° W. Long. Elevation is 646 feet.
History: Founded 1851.
Population: 534; Growth (since 2000): -2.9%; Density: 1,550.0 persons per square mile; Race: 98.3% White, 0.0% Black/African American, 0.0% Asian, 0.0% American Indian/Alaska Native, 0.0% Native Hawaiian/Other Pacific Islander, 0.2% Two or more races, 2.1% Hispanic of any race; Average household size: 2.68; Median age: 36.6; Age under 18: 29.2%; Age 65 and over: 11.8%; Males per 100 females: 100.8
Housing: Homeownership rate: 78.9%; Homeowner vacancy rate: 0.6%; Rental vacancy rate: 6.5%

Clinton County

Located in central Indiana; drained by Sugar Creek. Covers a land area of 405.070 square miles, a water area of 0.178 square miles, and is located in the Eastern Time Zone at 40.31° N. Lat., 86.48° W. Long. The county was founded in 1830. County seat is Frankfort.

Clinton County is part of the Frankfort, IN Micropolitan Statistical Area. The entire metro area includes: Clinton County, IN

Weather Station: Frankfort Disposal Plant — Elevation: 834 feet

	Jan	Feb	Mar	Apr	May	Jun	Jul	Aug	Sep	Oct	Nov	Dec
High	34	38	49	62	72	81	84	82	77	64	51	37
Low	19	22	30	40	50	60	63	62	54	43	34	23
Precip	2.3	2.2	3.0	3.7	4.3	4.4	4.3	3.9	3.0	3.1	3.5	2.9
Snow	7.5	6.1	2.7	0.4	tr	0.0	0.0	0.0	0.0	0.4	0.5	5.0

High and Low temperatures in degrees Fahrenheit; Precipitation and Snow in inches

Population: 33,224; Growth (since 2000): -1.9%; Density: 82.0 persons per square mile; Race: 91.0% White, 0.4% Black/African American, 0.2% Asian, 0.2% American Indian/Alaska Native, 0.0% Native Hawaiian/Other Pacific Islander, 1.3% two or more races, 13.2% Hispanic of any race; Average household size: 2.68; Median age: 37.5; Age under 18: 26.6%; Age 65 and over: 14.4%; Males per 100 females: 97.8; Marriage status: 23.9% never married, 55.9% now married, 1.7% separated, 7.2% widowed, 13.1% divorced; Foreign born: 6.5%; Speak English only: 87.5%; With disability: 13.1%; Veterans: 8.4%; Ancestry: 24.1% German, 10.9% American, 10.5% Irish, 8.2% English, 2.2% Scottish
Religion: Six largest groups: 15.5% Catholicism, 12.9% Baptist, 6.9% Methodist/Pietist, 2.5% Holiness, 2.2% Presbyterian-Reformed, 1.6% Non-denominational Protestant
Economy: Unemployment rate: 4.8%; Leading industries: 17.2% retail trade; 14.7% other services (except public administration); 10.6% construction; Farms: 597 totaling 223,428 acres; Company size: 0 employ 1,000 or more persons, 2 employ 500 to 999 persons, 16 employ 100 to 499 persons, 574 employ less than 100 persons; Business ownership: 598 women-owned, n/a Black-owned, 31 Hispanic-owned, n/a Asian-owned
Employment: 8.3% management, business, and financial, 2.5% computer, engineering, and science, 7.0% education, legal, community service, arts, and media, 3.9% healthcare practitioners, 13.4% service, 20.9% sales and office, 10.1% natural resources, construction, and maintenance, 33.9% production, transportation, and material moving
Income: Per capita: $21,554; Median household: $48,953; Average household: $58,130; Households with income of $100,000 or more: 13.6%; Poverty rate: 13.9%
Educational Attainment: High school diploma or higher: 84.7%; Bachelor's degree or higher: 13.0%; Graduate/professional degree or higher: 4.2%
Housing: Homeownership rate: 72.0%; Median home value: $97,300; Median year structure built: 1954; Homeowner vacancy rate: 2.4%; Median gross rent: $682 per month; Rental vacancy rate: 11.9%
Vital Statistics: Birth rate: 118.5 per 10,000 population; Death rate: 92.7 per 10,000 population; Age-adjusted cancer mortality rate: 166.6 deaths per 100,000 population
Health Insurance: 84.3% have insurance; 67.5% have private insurance; 29.4% have public insurance; 15.7% do not have insurance; 7.6% of children under 18 do not have insurance
Health Care: Physicians: 6.1 per 10,000 population; Hospital beds: 7.6 per 10,000 population; Hospital admissions: 301.6 per 10,000 population
Transportation: Commute: 94.0% car, 0.0% public transportation, 0.9% walk, 2.6% work from home; Median travel time to work: 22.1 minutes
Presidential Election: 33.5% Obama, 64.1% Romney (2012)
Additional Information Contacts
Clinton Government .... (765) 654-5715
http://www.clintonco.com

Clinton County Communities

COLFAX (town). Covers a land area of 0.363 square miles and a water area of 0 square miles. Located at 40.19° N. Lat; 86.67° W. Long. Elevation is 846 feet.
Population: 691; Growth (since 2000): -10.0%; Density: 1,901.7 persons per square mile; Race: 96.1% White, 0.4% Black/African American, 0.7% Asian, 0.0% American Indian/Alaska Native, 0.0% Native Hawaiian/Other Pacific Islander, 2.5% Two or more races, 3.2% Hispanic of any race; Average household size: 2.58; Median age: 40.1; Age under 18: 25.2%; Age 65 and over: 15.2%; Males per 100 females: 89.3
Housing: Homeownership rate: 73.9%; Homeowner vacancy rate: 5.2%; Rental vacancy rate: 27.1%

FOREST (unincorporated postal area)
ZCTA: 46039
Covers a land area of 27.071 square miles and a water area of 0 square miles. Located at 40.37° N. Lat; 86.31° W. Long. Elevation is 883 feet.

Population: 745; Growth (since 2000): -11.2%; Density: 27.5 persons per square mile; Race: 98.9% White, 0.0% Black/African American, 0.0% Asian, 0.0% American Indian/Alaska Native, 0.0% Native Hawaiian/Other Pacific Islander, 0.1% Two or more races, 2.0% Hispanic of any race; Average household size: 2.60; Median age: 40.3; Age under 18: 24.8%; Age 65 and over: 15.2%; Males per 100 females: 102.4
Housing: Homeownership rate: 87.1%; Homeowner vacancy rate: 2.0%; Rental vacancy rate: 14.0%

FRANKFORT (city). County seat. Covers a land area of 6.311 square miles and a water area of 0 square miles. Located at 40.28° N. Lat; 86.51° W. Long. Elevation is 850 feet.
History: Frankfort was named for Frankfurt am Main, Germany, the home of the grandfather of the Pence brothers who owned the land on which the city was founded. Frankfort developed as the county seat of Clinton County.
Population: 16,422; Growth (since 2000): -1.4%; Density: 2,602.0 persons per square mile; Race: 83.9% White, 0.6% Black/African American, 0.2% Asian, 0.3% American Indian/Alaska Native, 0.0% Native Hawaiian/Other Pacific Islander, 1.8% Two or more races, 25.0% Hispanic of any race; Average household size: 2.71; Median age: 33.5; Age under 18: 28.2%; Age 65 and over: 13.8%; Males per 100 females: 97.1; Marriage status: 28.5% never married, 47.9% now married, 2.2% separated, 8.2% widowed, 15.4% divorced; Foreign born: 12.0%; Speak English only: 77.0%; With disability: 13.3%; Veterans: 8.2%; Ancestry: 19.6% German, 9.4% American, 8.9% Irish, 7.9% English, 1.6% Italian
Employment: 4.0% management, business, and financial, 1.3% computer, engineering, and science, 5.5% education, legal, community service, arts, and media, 3.6% healthcare practitioners, 15.9% service, 19.2% sales and office, 9.0% natural resources, construction, and maintenance, 41.4% production, transportation, and material moving
Income: Per capita: $17,641; Median household: $40,368; Average household: $48,045; Households with income of $100,000 or more: 7.9%; Poverty rate: 18.1%
Educational Attainment: High school diploma or higher: 77.4%; Bachelor's degree or higher: 10.5%; Graduate/professional degree or higher: 3.7%

School District(s)
Clinton Prairie School Corp (KG-12)
    2012-13 Enrollment: 1,048 . . . . (765) 659-1339
Community Schools of Frankfort (PK-12)
    2012-13 Enrollment: 3,111 . . . . (765) 654-5585
Housing: Homeownership rate: 60.3%; Median home value: $82,300; Median year structure built: 1950; Homeowner vacancy rate: 3.4%; Median gross rent: $650 per month; Rental vacancy rate: 12.4%
Health Insurance: 79.4% have insurance; 56.6% have private insurance; 34.4% have public insurance; 20.6% do not have insurance; 7.0% of children under 18 do not have insurance
Hospitals: Saint Vincent Frankfort Hospital (25 beds)
Newspapers: Frankfort Times (weekly circulation 2600); The Times (daily circulation 6200)
Transportation: Commute: 94.4% car, 0.0% public transportation, 0.5% walk, 1.0% work from home; Median travel time to work: 19.3 minutes
Airports: Frankfort Municipal (general aviation)
Additional Information Contacts
City of Frankfort. . . . . (765) 654-5715
   http://frankfort-in.gov

KIRKLIN (town). Covers a land area of 0.341 square miles and a water area of 0 square miles. Located at 40.19° N. Lat; 86.36° W. Long. Elevation is 919 feet.
History: Kirklin was established at the junction of the Michigan Road with a state road. Nathan Kirklin bought the land here in 1828 and built a tavern.
Population: 788; Growth (since 2000): 2.9%; Density: 2,308.3 persons per square mile; Race: 98.5% White, 0.1% Black/African American, 0.1% Asian, 0.0% American Indian/Alaska Native, 0.0% Native Hawaiian/Other Pacific Islander, 0.8% Two or more races, 1.3% Hispanic of any race; Average household size: 2.74; Median age: 34.1; Age under 18: 31.1%; Age 65 and over: 10.4%; Males per 100 females: 98.5
Housing: Homeownership rate: 67.0%; Homeowner vacancy rate: 5.8%; Rental vacancy rate: 5.9%

MICHIGANTOWN (town). Covers a land area of 0.264 square miles and a water area of 0 square miles. Located at 40.33° N. Lat; 86.39° W. Long. Elevation is 876 feet.
History: Michigantown was founded in 1830 and named for the Michigan Road, for which it served as a stage stop.
Population: 467; Growth (since 2000): 15.0%; Density: 1,767.0 persons per square mile; Race: 97.9% White, 0.4% Black/African American, 0.4% Asian, 0.0% American Indian/Alaska Native, 0.0% Native Hawaiian/Other Pacific Islander, 0.9% Two or more races, 2.6% Hispanic of any race; Average household size: 2.55; Median age: 34.1; Age under 18: 27.0%; Age 65 and over: 13.7%; Males per 100 females: 92.2

School District(s)
Clinton Central School Corp (KG-12)
    2012-13 Enrollment: 1,019 . . . . (765) 249-2515
Housing: Homeownership rate: 60.1%; Homeowner vacancy rate: 0.0%; Rental vacancy rate: 12.0%

MULBERRY (town). Covers a land area of 0.589 square miles and a water area of 0 square miles. Located at 40.35° N. Lat; 86.67° W. Long. Elevation is 784 feet.
History: Laid out 1858.
Population: 1,254; Growth (since 2000): -9.6%; Density: 2,127.4 persons per square mile; Race: 98.4% White, 0.2% Black/African American, 0.0% Asian, 0.4% American Indian/Alaska Native, 0.1% Native Hawaiian/Other Pacific Islander, 0.9% Two or more races, 1.0% Hispanic of any race; Average household size: 2.41; Median age: 44.9; Age under 18: 20.4%; Age 65 and over: 24.6%; Males per 100 females: 80.4
Housing: Homeownership rate: 71.4%; Homeowner vacancy rate: 1.2%; Rental vacancy rate: 14.7%

ROSSVILLE (town). Covers a land area of 0.525 square miles and a water area of 0 square miles. Located at 40.42° N. Lat; 86.60° W. Long. Elevation is 725 feet.
History: Laid out 1834.
Population: 1,653; Growth (since 2000): 9.3%; Density: 3,149.8 persons per square mile; Race: 97.5% White, 0.4% Black/African American, 0.5% Asian, 0.2% American Indian/Alaska Native, 0.0% Native Hawaiian/Other Pacific Islander, 0.8% Two or more races, 0.8% Hispanic of any race; Average household size: 2.56; Median age: 39.6; Age under 18: 26.0%; Age 65 and over: 18.9%; Males per 100 females: 83.5

School District(s)
Rossville Con SD (KG-12)
    2012-13 Enrollment: 1,005 . . . . (765) 379-2990
Housing: Homeownership rate: 73.5%; Homeowner vacancy rate: 1.1%; Rental vacancy rate: 6.4%

Crawford County

Located in southern Indiana; bounded on the south by the Ohio River and the Kentucky border; drained by the Blue and Little Blue Rivers. Covers a land area of 305.643 square miles, a water area of 3.076 square miles, and is located in the Eastern Time Zone at 38.29° N. Lat., 86.44° W. Long. The county was founded in 1818. County seat is English.

Weather Station: English 4 S   Elevation: 509 feet

	Jan	Feb	Mar	Apr	May	Jun	Jul	Aug	Sep	Oct	Nov	Dec
High	42	48	58	68	77	84	88	87	81	70	58	45
Low	22	25	32	41	50	59	63	61	53	41	34	25
Precip	3.5	3.5	4.5	4.5	5.7	4.5	4.0	3.3	3.6	3.5	4.2	3.9
Snow	1.0	na	0.1	tr	0.0	0.0	0.0	0.0	0.0	tr	tr	2.0

High and Low temperatures in degrees Fahrenheit; Precipitation and Snow in inches

Population: 10,713; Growth (since 2000): -0.3%; Density: 35.1 persons per square mile; Race: 97.4% White, 0.2% Black/African American, 0.2% Asian, 0.4% American Indian/Alaska Native, 0.1% Native Hawaiian/Other Pacific Islander, 1.1% two or more races, 1.2% Hispanic of any race; Average household size: 2.48; Median age: 41.8; Age under 18: 23.3%; Age 65 and over: 15.0%; Males per 100 females: 103.0; Marriage status: 21.4% never married, 57.7% now married, 1.4% separated, 6.1% widowed, 14.9% divorced; Foreign born: 0.7%; Speak English only: 99.0%; With disability: 21.5%; Veterans: 10.0%; Ancestry: 21.7% German, 13.7% Irish, 11.2% American, 8.3% English, 2.4% Dutch
Religion: Six largest groups: 15.2% Baptist, 6.0% Non-denominational Protestant, 5.2% Methodist/Pietist, 3.2% Latter-day Saints, 2.6% Holiness, 1.8% Catholicism

Economy: Unemployment rate: 6.0%; Leading industries: 18.8% retail trade; 16.4% accommodation and food services; 13.3% construction; Farms: 338 totaling 46,404 acres; Company size: 0 employ 1,000 or more persons, 0 employ 500 to 999 persons, 2 employ 100 to 499 persons, 126 employ less than 100 persons; Business ownership: n/a women-owned, n/a Black-owned, n/a Hispanic-owned, n/a Asian-owned

Employment: 6.0% management, business, and financial, 0.7% computer, engineering, and science, 6.7% education, legal, community service, arts, and media, 6.7% healthcare practitioners, 18.8% service, 18.6% sales and office, 10.6% natural resources, construction, and maintenance, 31.8% production, transportation, and material moving

Income: Per capita: $20,504; Median household: $39,700; Average household: $49,750; Households with income of $100,000 or more: 9.3%; Poverty rate: 19.6%

Educational Attainment: High school diploma or higher: 80.8%; Bachelor's degree or higher: 12.1%; Graduate/professional degree or higher: 6.1%

Housing: Homeownership rate: 82.6%; Median home value: $83,300; Median year structure built: 1985; Homeowner vacancy rate: 3.0%; Median gross rent: $555 per month; Rental vacancy rate: 9.1%

Vital Statistics: Birth rate: 102.6 per 10,000 population; Death rate: 101.7 per 10,000 population; Age-adjusted cancer mortality rate: 223.5 deaths per 100,000 population

Health Insurance: 86.1% have insurance; 61.3% have private insurance; 37.3% have public insurance; 13.9% do not have insurance; 9.8% of children under 18 do not have insurance

Health Care: Physicians: 0.0 per 10,000 population; Hospital beds: 0.0 per 10,000 population; Hospital admissions: 0.0 per 10,000 population

Transportation: Commute: 93.4% car, 0.0% public transportation, 1.4% walk, 3.8% work from home; Median travel time to work: 33.2 minutes

Presidential Election: 44.5% Obama, 52.7% Romney (2012)

National and State Parks: Hilands Overlook State Park

Additional Information Contacts
Crawford Government . . . . (812) 338-2565

Crawford County Communities

ALTON
(town). Covers a land area of 0.172 square miles and a water area of 0.018 square miles. Located at 38.12° N. Lat; 86.42° W. Long. Elevation is 427 feet.

Population: 55; Growth (since 2000): 3.8%; Density: 319.8 persons per square mile; Race: 96.4% White, 0.0% Black/African American, 0.0% Asian, 0.0% American Indian/Alaska Native, 0.0% Native Hawaiian/Other Pacific Islander, 0.0% Two or more races, 3.6% Hispanic of any race; Average household size: 2.20; Median age: 53.2; Age under 18: 10.9%; Age 65 and over: 23.6%; Males per 100 females: 129.2

Housing: Homeownership rate: 84.0%; Homeowner vacancy rate: 0.0%; Rental vacancy rate: 0.0%

ECKERTY
(unincorporated postal area)
ZCTA: 47116

Covers a land area of 30.021 square miles and a water area of 0.662 square miles. Located at 38.32° N. Lat; 86.62° W. Long. Elevation is 745 feet.

Population: 805; Growth (since 2000): -5.7%; Density: 26.8 persons per square mile; Race: 97.6% White, 0.1% Black/African American, 0.1% Asian, 0.7% American Indian/Alaska Native, 0.0% Native Hawaiian/Other Pacific Islander, 1.4% Two or more races, 0.4% Hispanic of any race; Average household size: 2.32; Median age: 45.2; Age under 18: 20.0%; Age 65 and over: 15.8%; Males per 100 females: 111.3

School District(s)
Crawford County Com School Corp (KG-12)
 2012-13 Enrollment: 1,545 . . . . (812) 365-2135

Housing: Homeownership rate: 85.8%; Homeowner vacancy rate: 2.3%; Rental vacancy rate: 10.5%

ENGLISH
(town). County seat. Covers a land area of 3.044 square miles and a water area of 0 square miles. Located at 38.34° N. Lat; 86.46° W. Long. Elevation is 505 feet.

History: The town of English was laid out in 1839, and grew when it became the county seat in 1893. The town was named for William Hayden English, a U.S. congressman from Indiana.

Population: 645; Growth (since 2000): -4.2%; Density: 211.9 persons per square mile; Race: 97.5% White, 0.3% Black/African American, 0.2% Asian, 0.6% American Indian/Alaska Native, 0.0% Native Hawaiian/Other Pacific Islander, 1.1% Two or more races, 0.8% Hispanic of any race; Average household size: 2.26; Median age: 43.6; Age under 18: 20.9%; Age 65 and over: 20.0%; Males per 100 females: 89.7

School District(s)
Crawford County Com School Corp (KG-12)
 2012-13 Enrollment: 1,545 . . . . (812) 365-2135

Housing: Homeownership rate: 65.9%; Homeowner vacancy rate: 5.4%; Rental vacancy rate: 7.6%

GRANTSBURG (unincorporated postal area)
ZCTA: 47123

Covers a land area of 7.400 square miles and a water area of 0 square miles. Located at 38.27° N. Lat; 86.48° W. Long. Elevation is 614 feet.

Population: 189; Growth (since 2000): 530.0%; Density: 25.5 persons per square mile; Race: 95.8% White, 0.0% Black/African American, 0.0% Asian, 0.0% American Indian/Alaska Native, 0.0% Native Hawaiian/Other Pacific Islander, 1.6% Two or more races, 7.9% Hispanic of any race; Average household size: 2.36; Median age: 46.3; Age under 18: 22.2%; Age 65 and over: 20.6%; Males per 100 females: 94.8

Housing: Homeownership rate: 82.6%; Homeowner vacancy rate: 2.9%; Rental vacancy rate: 0.0%

LEAVENWORTH
(town). Covers a land area of 0.822 square miles and a water area of 0.048 square miles. Located at 38.20° N. Lat; 86.35° W. Long. Elevation is 659 feet.

History: Leavenworth was founded in 1818 and served as Crawford County's seat from 1843 to 1893. A boat-building industry was established in 1830 by David Lyon, and Leavenworth became a shipping point on the Ohio River. The 1937 flooding of the Ohio River destroyed most of the town, which was rebuilt on the hills behind the original site.

Population: 238; Growth (since 2000): -32.6%; Density: 289.4 persons per square mile; Race: 95.0% White, 2.5% Black/African American, 0.0% Asian, 0.0% American Indian/Alaska Native, 1.7% Native Hawaiian/Other Pacific Islander, 0.8% Two or more races, 1.3% Hispanic of any race; Average household size: 2.06; Median age: 56.5; Age under 18: 13.9%; Age 65 and over: 35.3%; Males per 100 females: 68.8

School District(s)
Crawford County Com School Corp (KG-12)
 2012-13 Enrollment: 1,545 . . . . (812) 365-2135

Housing: Homeownership rate: 72.7%; Homeowner vacancy rate: 13.5%; Rental vacancy rate: 22.6%

MARENGO
(town). Covers a land area of 0.774 square miles and a water area of 0 square miles. Located at 38.37° N. Lat; 86.34° W. Long. Elevation is 597 feet.

History: Marengo grew as a resort village in an area of coldwater springs and caves. Quarrying was an early industry.

Population: 828; Growth (since 2000): -0.1%; Density: 1,069.2 persons per square mile; Race: 95.4% White, 0.1% Black/African American, 0.0% Asian, 0.8% American Indian/Alaska Native, 0.5% Native Hawaiian/Other Pacific Islander, 2.7% Two or more races, 2.1% Hispanic of any race; Average household size: 2.34; Median age: 36.2; Age under 18: 26.7%; Age 65 and over: 14.5%; Males per 100 females: 91.7

School District(s)
Crawford County Com School Corp (KG-12)
 2012-13 Enrollment: 1,545 . . . . (812) 365-2135

Housing: Homeownership rate: 56.8%; Homeowner vacancy rate: 6.7%; Rental vacancy rate: 9.9%

MILLTOWN
(town). Covers a land area of 1.412 square miles and a water area of 0 square miles. Located at 38.34° N. Lat; 86.27° W. Long. Elevation is 620 feet.

Population: 818; Growth (since 2000): -12.2%; Density: 579.2 persons per square mile; Race: 97.7% White, 0.0% Black/African American, 0.4% Asian, 0.1% American Indian/Alaska Native, 0.0% Native Hawaiian/Other Pacific Islander, 1.8% Two or more races, 0.0% Hispanic of any race; Average household size: 2.41; Median age: 39.2; Age under 18: 24.8%; Age 65 and over: 17.2%; Males per 100 females: 92.9

School District(s)
Crawford County Com School Corp (KG-12)
 2012-13 Enrollment: 1,545 . . . . (812) 365-2135

Housing: Homeownership rate: 73.2%; Homeowner vacancy rate: 6.4%; Rental vacancy rate: 13.3%

TASWELL (unincorporated postal area)
ZCTA: 47175
Covers a land area of 22.449 square miles and a water area of 2.067 square miles. Located at 38.38° N. Lat; 86.57° W. Long. Elevation is 778 feet.
Population: 909; Growth (since 2000): 11.0%; Density: 40.5 persons per square mile; Race: 97.5% White, 0.1% Black/African American, 0.0% Asian, 0.0% American Indian/Alaska Native, 0.0% Native Hawaiian/Other Pacific Islander, 1.1% Two or more races, 1.4% Hispanic of any race; Average household size: 2.48; Median age: 41.8; Age under 18: 22.2%; Age 65 and over: 15.8%; Males per 100 females: 110.9
Housing: Homeownership rate: 88.3%; Homeowner vacancy rate: 2.4%; Rental vacancy rate: 21.4%

Daviess County

Located in southwestern Indiana; bounded on the south by the East Fork of the White River, on the west by the West Fork of the White River. Covers a land area of 429.487 square miles, a water area of 7.387 square miles, and is located in the Eastern Time Zone at 38.70° N. Lat., 87.08° W. Long. The county was founded in 1816. County seat is Washington.

Daviess County is part of the Washington, IN Micropolitan Statistical Area. The entire metro area includes: Daviess County, IN

Weather Station: Washington   Elevation: 524 feet

	Jan	Feb	Mar	Apr	May	Jun	Jul	Aug	Sep	Oct	Nov	Dec
High	40	45	56	68	77	85	88	87	80	69	56	43
Low	25	27	36	45	55	64	67	66	58	47	38	28
Precip	3.1	2.9	4.2	4.4	5.8	4.4	4.7	3.2	3.3	3.8	4.3	3.6
Snow	3.1	2.7	1.3	0.1	tr	0.0	0.0	0.0	0.0	0.1	0.1	2.6

High and Low temperatures in degrees Fahrenheit; Precipitation and Snow in inches

Population: 31,648; Growth (since 2000): 6.1%; Density: 73.7 persons per square mile; Race: 95.0% White, 0.5% Black/African American, 0.5% Asian, 0.2% American Indian/Alaska Native, 0.0% Native Hawaiian/Other Pacific Islander, 1.1% two or more races, 4.2% Hispanic of any race; Average household size: 2.74; Median age: 35.4; Age under 18: 28.8%; Age 65 and over: 14.1%; Males per 100 females: 99.3; Marriage status: 22.8% never married, 58.3% now married, 1.4% separated, 7.2% widowed, 11.7% divorced; Foreign born: 2.2%; Speak English only: 85.3%; With disability: 13.1%; Veterans: 8.5%; Ancestry: 29.9% German, 14.3% American, 12.1% Irish, 8.8% English, 2.2% French
Religion: Six largest groups: 16.7% European Free-Church, 15.9% Baptist, 8.5% Catholicism, 6.3% Methodist/Pietist, 3.6% Non-denominational Protestant, 1.9% Holiness
Economy: Unemployment rate: 4.3%; Leading industries: 19.6% construction; 14.6% retail trade; 13.1% other services (except public administration); Farms: 1,325 totaling 225,156 acres; Company size: 0 employ 1,000 or more persons, 2 employ 500 to 999 persons, 12 employ 100 to 499 persons, 827 employ less than 100 persons; Business ownership: 413 women-owned, n/a Black-owned, n/a Hispanic-owned, n/a Asian-owned
Employment: 9.6% management, business, and financial, 2.7% computer, engineering, and science, 5.7% education, legal, community service, arts, and media, 5.3% healthcare practitioners, 16.3% service, 18.6% sales and office, 16.7% natural resources, construction, and maintenance, 25.0% production, transportation, and material moving
Income: Per capita: $21,416; Median household: $47,165; Average household: $59,051; Households with income of $100,000 or more: 12.6%; Poverty rate: 12.9%
Educational Attainment: High school diploma or higher: 77.5%; Bachelor's degree or higher: 12.4%; Graduate/professional degree or higher: 5.4%
Housing: Homeownership rate: 74.7%; Median home value: $105,500; Median year structure built: 1964; Homeowner vacancy rate: 2.1%; Median gross rent: $584 per month; Rental vacancy rate: 8.8%
Vital Statistics: Birth rate: 173.1 per 10,000 population; Death rate: 98.4 per 10,000 population; Age-adjusted cancer mortality rate: 181.2 deaths per 100,000 population
Health Insurance: 78.3% have insurance; 60.9% have private insurance; 28.7% have public insurance; 21.7% do not have insurance; 22.4% of children under 18 do not have insurance
Health Care: Physicians: 8.4 per 10,000 population; Hospital beds: 25.0 per 10,000 population; Hospital admissions: 932.0 per 10,000 population
Air Quality Index: 89.8% good, 5.1% moderate, 4.8% unhealthy for sensitive individuals, 0.3% unhealthy (percent of days)
Transportation: Commute: 90.5% car, 0.3% public transportation, 3.0% walk, 4.1% work from home; Median travel time to work: 21.0 minutes
Presidential Election: 23.8% Obama, 74.5% Romney (2012)
National and State Parks: Glendale State Fish and Wildlife Area
Additional Information Contacts
Daviess Government................................. (812) 254-5262
http://www.daviess.org

Daviess County Communities

ALFORDSVILLE (town). Covers a land area of 0.068 square miles and a water area of <.001 square miles. Located at 38.56° N. Lat; 86.95° W. Long. Elevation is 512 feet.
History: Laid out 1845.
Population: 101; Growth (since 2000): -9.8%; Density: 1,494.8 persons per square mile; Race: 99.0% White, 0.0% Black/African American, 0.0% Asian, 0.0% American Indian/Alaska Native, 0.0% Native Hawaiian/Other Pacific Islander, 1.0% Two or more races, 0.0% Hispanic of any race; Average household size: 2.73; Median age: 38.8; Age under 18: 24.8%; Age 65 and over: 13.9%; Males per 100 females: 110.4
Housing: Homeownership rate: 91.8%; Homeowner vacancy rate: 0.0%; Rental vacancy rate: 0.0%

CANNELBURG (town). Covers a land area of 0.189 square miles and a water area of 0 square miles. Located at 38.67° N. Lat; 87.00° W. Long. Elevation is 528 feet.
Population: 135; Growth (since 2000): -3.6%; Density: 714.4 persons per square mile; Race: 99.3% White, 0.0% Black/African American, 0.0% Asian, 0.0% American Indian/Alaska Native, 0.0% Native Hawaiian/Other Pacific Islander, 0.7% Two or more races, 0.7% Hispanic of any race; Average household size: 2.37; Median age: 44.2; Age under 18: 21.5%; Age 65 and over: 20.0%; Males per 100 females: 114.3
Housing: Homeownership rate: 86.0%; Homeowner vacancy rate: 0.0%; Rental vacancy rate: 0.0%

ELNORA (town). Covers a land area of 0.948 square miles and a water area of 0 square miles. Located at 38.88° N. Lat; 87.08° W. Long. Elevation is 479 feet.
Population: 640; Growth (since 2000): -11.2%; Density: 675.3 persons per square mile; Race: 96.9% White, 0.5% Black/African American, 0.6% Asian, 0.3% American Indian/Alaska Native, 0.0% Native Hawaiian/Other Pacific Islander, 1.4% Two or more races, 1.7% Hispanic of any race; Average household size: 2.57; Median age: 39.4; Age under 18: 26.9%; Age 65 and over: 16.4%; Males per 100 females: 87.1
School District(s)
North Daviess Com Schools (KG-12)
    2012-13 Enrollment: 1,085 .... (812) 636-8000
Housing: Homeownership rate: 76.7%; Homeowner vacancy rate: 6.2%; Rental vacancy rate: 18.1%

MONTGOMERY (town). Covers a land area of 0.241 square miles and a water area of 0.002 square miles. Located at 38.67° N. Lat; 87.05° W. Long. Elevation is 528 feet.
History: Montgomery grew up around St. Peter's Church which was founded in 1818.
Population: 343; Growth (since 2000): -6.8%; Density: 1,420.5 persons per square mile; Race: 99.4% White, 0.0% Black/African American, 0.0% Asian, 0.0% American Indian/Alaska Native, 0.0% Native Hawaiian/Other Pacific Islander, 0.6% Two or more races, 0.6% Hispanic of any race; Average household size: 2.50; Median age: 36.6; Age under 18: 25.4%; Age 65 and over: 11.1%; Males per 100 females: 101.8
School District(s)
Barr-Reeve Com Schools Inc (KG-12)
    2012-13 Enrollment: 736 .... (812) 486-3220
Housing: Homeownership rate: 78.8%; Homeowner vacancy rate: 0.9%; Rental vacancy rate: 21.1%

ODON (town). Covers a land area of 0.954 square miles and a water area of 0.009 square miles. Located at 38.84° N. Lat; 86.99° W. Long. Elevation is 548 feet.
History: Odon grew as a farm town on a site at a spring where George Rogers Clark and his soldiers stopped for water and to hunt buffalo.
Population: 1,354; Growth (since 2000): -1.6%; Density: 1,419.7 persons per square mile; Race: 98.3% White, 0.0% Black/African American, 0.3% Asian, 0.6% American Indian/Alaska Native, 0.0% Native Hawaiian/Other Pacific Islander, 0.8% Two or more races, 0.3% Hispanic of any race; Average household size: 2.18; Median age: 45.1; Age under 18: 23.8%; Age 65 and over: 24.0%; Males per 100 females: 84.0
Housing: Homeownership rate: 66.6%; Homeowner vacancy rate: 4.0%; Rental vacancy rate: 13.3%
Newspapers: The Journal (weekly circulation 2800)

PLAINVILLE (town). Covers a land area of 0.351 square miles and a water area of 0 square miles. Located at 38.80° N. Lat; 87.15° W. Long. Elevation is 469 feet.
Population: 476; Growth (since 2000): -7.2%; Density: 1,356.9 persons per square mile; Race: 97.7% White, 0.4% Black/African American, 1.1% Asian, 0.0% American Indian/Alaska Native, 0.0% Native Hawaiian/Other Pacific Islander, 0.8% Two or more races, 0.4% Hispanic of any race; Average household size: 2.41; Median age: 39.4; Age under 18: 27.3%; Age 65 and over: 18.1%; Males per 100 females: 100.8
Housing: Homeownership rate: 72.7%; Homeowner vacancy rate: 5.3%; Rental vacancy rate: 12.9%

RAGLESVILLE (CDP). Covers a land area of 0.854 square miles and a water area of 0.003 square miles. Located at 38.80° N. Lat; 86.96° W. Long. Elevation is 614 feet.
Population: 141; Growth (since 2000): n/a; Density: 165.1 persons per square mile; Race: 100.0% White, 0.0% Black/African American, 0.0% Asian, 0.0% American Indian/Alaska Native, 0.0% Native Hawaiian/Other Pacific Islander, 0.0% Two or more races, 0.7% Hispanic of any race; Average household size: 3.36; Median age: 26.5; Age under 18: 32.6%; Age 65 and over: 9.2%; Males per 100 females: 116.9
Housing: Homeownership rate: 80.9%; Homeowner vacancy rate: 0.0%; Rental vacancy rate: 0.0%

WASHINGTON (city). County seat. Covers a land area of 4.731 square miles and a water area of 0.037 square miles. Located at 38.66° N. Lat; 87.17° W. Long. Elevation is 502 feet.
History: Washington was founded by Emmanuel Van Trees, who settled here in 1817 on the site where Fort Flora had been built in 1805. The town developed around the Baltimore & Ohio Railroad shops, and became a trading and industrial center.
Population: 11,509; Growth (since 2000): 1.1%; Density: 2,432.9 persons per square mile; Race: 89.2% White, 1.1% Black/African American, 1.1% Asian, 0.3% American Indian/Alaska Native, 0.1% Native Hawaiian/Other Pacific Islander, 1.9% Two or more races, 9.6% Hispanic of any race; Average household size: 2.43; Median age: 37.3; Age under 18: 25.5%; Age 65 and over: 15.9%; Males per 100 females: 92.9; Marriage status: 23.7% never married, 48.5% now married, 2.0% separated, 9.7% widowed, 18.1% divorced; Foreign born: 5.3%; Speak English only: 91.0%; With disability: 18.5%; Veterans: 10.4%; Ancestry: 22.3% German, 15.5% American, 13.2% Irish, 7.5% English, 1.8% French
Employment: 8.7% management, business, and financial, 0.8% computer, engineering, and science, 6.2% education, legal, community service, arts, and media, 5.1% healthcare practitioners, 21.9% service, 18.2% sales and office, 12.6% natural resources, construction, and maintenance, 26.4% production, transportation, and material moving
Income: Per capita: $21,352; Median household: $42,287; Average household: $54,332; Households with income of $100,000 or more: 9.1%; Poverty rate: 19.0%
Educational Attainment: High school diploma or higher: 82.3%; Bachelor's degree or higher: 14.0%; Graduate/professional degree or higher: 6.0%

School District(s)
Twin Rivers Career & Tech Ed Area (09-12)
    2012-13 Enrollment: n/a . . . . (812) 882-0801
Washington Com Schools (KG-12)
    2012-13 Enrollment: 2,490 . . . . (812) 254-5536

Housing: Homeownership rate: 60.5%; Median home value: $76,700; Median year structure built: 1954; Homeowner vacancy rate: 3.5%; Median gross rent: $568 per month; Rental vacancy rate: 7.8%
Health Insurance: 86.3% have insurance; 60.7% have private insurance; 36.5% have public insurance; 13.7% do not have insurance; 3.1% of children under 18 do not have insurance
Hospitals: Daviess Community Hospital (120 beds)
Safety: Violent crime rate: 36.4 per 10,000 population; Property crime rate: 639.1 per 10,000 population
Newspapers: Washington Times-Herald (daily circulation 8800)
Transportation: Commute: 95.2% car, 0.5% public transportation, 2.0% walk, 1.0% work from home; Median travel time to work: 16.0 minutes
Additional Information Contacts
City of Washington . . . . (812) 254-6143
   http://www.washingtonin.us

Dearborn County

Located in southeastern Indiana; bounded on the east by Ohio, and on the southeast by the Ohio River and the Kentucky border; drained by the Whitewater River. Covers a land area of 305.034 square miles, a water area of 2.382 square miles, and is located in the Eastern Time Zone at 39.15° N. Lat., 84.97° W. Long. The county was founded in 1803. County seat is Lawrenceburg.

Dearborn County is part of the Cincinnati, OH-KY-IN Metropolitan Statistical Area. The entire metro area includes: Dearborn County, IN; Ohio County, IN; Union County, IN; Boone County, KY; Bracken County, KY; Campbell County, KY; Gallatin County, KY; Grant County, KY; Kenton County, KY; Pendleton County, KY; Brown County, OH; Butler County, OH; Clermont County, OH; Hamilton County, OH; Warren County, OH

Population: 50,047; Growth (since 2000): 8.5%; Density: 164.1 persons per square mile; Race: 97.5% White, 0.6% Black/African American, 0.4% Asian, 0.2% American Indian/Alaska Native, 0.1% Native Hawaiian/Other Pacific Islander, 1.0% two or more races, 1.0% Hispanic of any race; Average household size: 2.64; Median age: 40.0; Age under 18: 25.0%; Age 65 and over: 13.1%; Males per 100 females: 98.8; Marriage status: 24.3% never married, 57.7% now married, 1.4% separated, 5.4% widowed, 12.6% divorced; Foreign born: 1.1%; Speak English only: 97.8%; With disability: 12.1%; Veterans: 9.9%; Ancestry: 45.7% German, 19.1% Irish, 10.9% English, 10.4% American, 4.1% Italian
Religion: Six largest groups: 18.6% Catholicism, 8.5% Baptist, 5.2% Lutheran, 3.8% Methodist/Pietist, 1.9% Non-denominational Protestant, 0.9% Presbyterian-Reformed
Economy: Unemployment rate: 5.1%; Leading industries: 14.8% retail trade; 12.5% health care and social assistance; 12.1% construction; Farms: 561 totaling 56,573 acres; Company size: 1 employs 1,000 or more persons, 2 employ 500 to 999 persons, 16 employ 100 to 499 persons, 924 employ less than 100 persons; Business ownership: 743 women-owned, n/a Black-owned, n/a Hispanic-owned, n/a Asian-owned
Employment: 11.7% management, business, and financial, 3.4% computer, engineering, and science, 7.3% education, legal, community service, arts, and media, 4.9% healthcare practitioners, 16.8% service, 24.7% sales and office, 11.9% natural resources, construction, and maintenance, 19.2% production, transportation, and material moving
Income: Per capita: $27,058; Median household: $56,946; Average household: $71,112; Households with income of $100,000 or more: 19.7%; Poverty rate: 9.1%
Educational Attainment: High school diploma or higher: 89.0%; Bachelor's degree or higher: 17.6%; Graduate/professional degree or higher: 5.8%
Housing: Homeownership rate: 78.4%; Median home value: $160,400; Median year structure built: 1979; Homeowner vacancy rate: 2.3%; Median gross rent: $713 per month; Rental vacancy rate: 7.5%
Vital Statistics: Birth rate: 109.6 per 10,000 population; Death rate: 82.2 per 10,000 population; Age-adjusted cancer mortality rate: 237.1 deaths per 100,000 population
Health Insurance: 89.3% have insurance; 74.9% have private insurance; 26.4% have public insurance; 10.7% do not have insurance; 6.8% of children under 18 do not have insurance
Health Care: Physicians: 11.0 per 10,000 population; Hospital beds: 18.4 per 10,000 population; Hospital admissions: 955.5 per 10,000 population
Transportation: Commute: 94.1% car, 0.4% public transportation, 1.6% walk, 3.1% work from home; Median travel time to work: 29.3 minutes
Presidential Election: 29.2% Obama, 68.9% Romney (2012)
Additional Information Contacts

Dearborn Government.............................. (812) 537-8867
http://www.dearborncounty.org

Dearborn County Communities

AURORA (city). Covers a land area of 2.761 square miles and a water area of 0.327 square miles. Located at 39.07° N. Lat; 84.90° W. Long. Elevation is 486 feet.
History: Aurora was founded in 1819 along the Ohio River. Judge Jesse Holman of the Indiana Supreme Court suggested that the town be named for the goddess of the dawn. Aurora was severely damaged in the 1937 flood of the Ohio River.
Population: 3,750; Growth (since 2000): -5.4%; Density: 1,358.4 persons per square mile; Race: 97.5% White, 0.5% Black/African American, 0.3% Asian, 0.3% American Indian/Alaska Native, 0.0% Native Hawaiian/Other Pacific Islander, 0.7% Two or more races, 1.5% Hispanic of any race; Average household size: 2.55; Median age: 36.2; Age under 18: 26.6%; Age 65 and over: 12.9%; Males per 100 females: 97.4; Marriage status: 30.5% never married, 49.5% now married, 3.5% separated, 6.1% widowed, 13.9% divorced; Foreign born: 1.2%; Speak English only: 97.6%; With disability: 20.1%; Veterans: 13.1%; Ancestry: 42.6% German, 20.4% Irish, 13.0% English, 10.8% American, 5.0% Dutch
Employment: 8.2% management, business, and financial, 4.1% computer, engineering, and science, 2.2% education, legal, community service, arts, and media, 5.4% healthcare practitioners, 28.4% service, 23.1% sales and office, 15.1% natural resources, construction, and maintenance, 13.5% production, transportation, and material moving
Income: Per capita: $19,720; Median household: $41,090; Average household: $47,658; Households with income of $100,000 or more: 6.5%; Poverty rate: 14.1%
Educational Attainment: High school diploma or higher: 81.0%; Bachelor's degree or higher: 8.9%; Graduate/professional degree or higher: 4.2%
School District(s)
South Dearborn Com School Corp (KG-12)
    2012-13 Enrollment: 2,818 .... (812) 926-2090
Housing: Homeownership rate: 56.4%; Median home value: $114,800; Median year structure built: 1947; Homeowner vacancy rate: 4.0%; Median gross rent: $753 per month; Rental vacancy rate: 11.0%
Health Insurance: 84.8% have insurance; 61.8% have private insurance; 36.4% have public insurance; 15.2% do not have insurance; 12.0% of children under 18 do not have insurance
Safety: Violent crime rate: 53.7 per 10,000 population; Property crime rate: 572.4 per 10,000 population
Transportation: Commute: 94.8% car, 0.4% public transportation, 2.4% walk, 1.7% work from home; Median travel time to work: 24.8 minutes
Additional Information Contacts
City of Aurora .... (812) 926-1777
http://www.aurora.in.us

BRIGHT (CDP). Covers a land area of 12.548 square miles and a water area of 0.018 square miles. Located at 39.22° N. Lat; 84.86° W. Long. Elevation is 922 feet.
History: Bright is a community in Dearborn County, which was formed in 1803. It was named for Dr. Henry Dearborn (DR), an officer in the Revolutionary War and the War of 1812.
Population: 5,693; Growth (since 2000): 5.3%; Density: 453.7 persons per square mile; Race: 98.3% White, 0.3% Black/African American, 0.3% Asian, 0.1% American Indian/Alaska Native, 0.0% Native Hawaiian/Other Pacific Islander, 0.6% Two or more races, 0.7% Hispanic of any race; Average household size: 2.77; Median age: 39.0; Age under 18: 26.5%; Age 65 and over: 11.3%; Males per 100 females: 98.3; Marriage status: 23.6% never married, 58.0% now married, 1.1% separated, 6.9% widowed, 11.6% divorced; Foreign born: 1.5%; Speak English only: 97.5%; With disability: 8.9%; Veterans: 8.4%; Ancestry: 49.8% German, 16.8% Irish, 9.6% English, 9.1% American, 7.6% Italian
Employment: 13.5% management, business, and financial, 4.3% computer, engineering, and science, 10.5% education, legal, community service, arts, and media, 5.0% healthcare practitioners, 14.4% service, 24.6% sales and office, 11.6% natural resources, construction, and maintenance, 16.0% production, transportation, and material moving
Income: Per capita: $30,720; Median household: $65,900; Average household: $82,199; Households with income of $100,000 or more: 26.0%; Poverty rate: 2.9%

Educational Attainment: High school diploma or higher: 98.6%; Bachelor's degree or higher: 23.1%; Graduate/professional degree or higher: 7.2%
Housing: Homeownership rate: 85.0%; Median home value: $170,900; Median year structure built: 1984; Homeowner vacancy rate: 1.2%; Median gross rent: $617 per month; Rental vacancy rate: 7.4%
Health Insurance: 94.1% have insurance; 82.9% have private insurance; 21.8% have public insurance; 5.9% do not have insurance; 2.1% of children under 18 do not have insurance
Transportation: Commute: 95.6% car, 0.0% public transportation, 1.5% walk, 2.6% work from home; Median travel time to work: 30.6 minutes

DILLSBORO (town). Covers a land area of 1.000 square miles and a water area of 0 square miles. Located at 39.02° N. Lat; 85.06° W. Long. Elevation is 869 feet.
Population: 1,327; Growth (since 2000): -7.6%; Density: 1,326.6 persons per square mile; Race: 98.6% White, 0.2% Black/African American, 0.0% Asian, 0.2% American Indian/Alaska Native, 0.5% Native Hawaiian/Other Pacific Islander, 0.7% Two or more races, 0.2% Hispanic of any race; Average household size: 2.34; Median age: 42.2; Age under 18: 23.1%; Age 65 and over: 24.2%; Males per 100 females: 80.5
School District(s)
South Dearborn Com School Corp (KG-12)
    2012-13 Enrollment: 2,818 .... (812) 926-2090
Housing: Homeownership rate: 49.0%; Homeowner vacancy rate: 3.8%; Rental vacancy rate: 10.4%

GREENDALE (city). Covers a land area of 5.712 square miles and a water area of 0.075 square miles. Located at 39.15° N. Lat; 84.83° W. Long. Elevation is 528 feet.
History: Greendale became associated with the distilling of whiskey in 1809, when the local manufacture of distilled liquors began. The Joseph E. Seagram Company purchased a plant in Greendale in 1933.
Population: 4,520; Growth (since 2000): 5.2%; Density: 791.3 persons per square mile; Race: 95.6% White, 1.0% Black/African American, 0.8% Asian, 0.2% American Indian/Alaska Native, 0.0% Native Hawaiian/Other Pacific Islander, 1.8% Two or more races, 1.6% Hispanic of any race; Average household size: 2.50; Median age: 40.1; Age under 18: 24.4%; Age 65 and over: 15.3%; Males per 100 females: 91.6; Marriage status: 30.8% never married, 51.3% now married, 1.1% separated, 6.4% widowed, 11.4% divorced; Foreign born: 1.3%; Speak English only: 96.7%; With disability: 12.7%; Veterans: 8.0%; Ancestry: 42.1% German, 21.4% Irish, 12.8% English, 12.2% American, 2.6% French
Employment: 14.3% management, business, and financial, 2.6% computer, engineering, and science, 9.9% education, legal, community service, arts, and media, 8.7% healthcare practitioners, 15.0% service, 30.1% sales and office, 5.4% natural resources, construction, and maintenance, 14.1% production, transportation, and material moving
Income: Per capita: $26,305; Median household: $52,188; Average household: $64,704; Households with income of $100,000 or more: 21.9%; Poverty rate: 14.1%
Educational Attainment: High school diploma or higher: 90.8%; Bachelor's degree or higher: 26.6%; Graduate/professional degree or higher: 8.5%
Housing: Homeownership rate: 76.5%; Median home value: $136,300; Median year structure built: 1959; Homeowner vacancy rate: 2.5%; Median gross rent: $674 per month; Rental vacancy rate: 6.4%
Health Insurance: 87.8% have insurance; 71.2% have private insurance; 28.4% have public insurance; 12.2% do not have insurance; 3.0% of children under 18 do not have insurance
Transportation: Commute: 97.8% car, 0.0% public transportation, 0.7% walk, 0.9% work from home; Median travel time to work: 23.6 minutes
Additional Information Contacts
City of Greendale .... (812) 537-9219
http://cityofgreendale.net

GUILFORD (unincorporated postal area)
ZCTA: 47022
    Covers a land area of 34.003 square miles and a water area of 0 square miles. Located at 39.20° N. Lat; 84.95° W. Long. Elevation is 499 feet.
    Population: 3,358; Growth (since 2000): 10.3%; Density: 98.8 persons per square mile; Race: 99.0% White, 0.1% Black/African American, 0.3% Asian, 0.2% American Indian/Alaska Native, 0.0% Native Hawaiian/Other Pacific Islander, 0.3% Two or more races, 0.4% Hispanic of any race; Average household size: 2.87; Median age: 40.3;

Age under 18: 27.3%; Age 65 and over: 10.7%; Males per 100 females: 104.8; Marriage status: 17.2% never married, 71.3% now married, 0.7% separated, 4.1% widowed, 7.5% divorced; Foreign born: 1.2%; Speak English only: 98.0%; With disability: 6.7%; Veterans: 9.2%; Ancestry: 48.8% German, 24.9% Irish, 13.7% English, 6.6% American, 6.3% Italian
Employment: 12.4% management, business, and financial, 1.8% computer, engineering, and science, 5.9% education, legal, community service, arts, and media, 5.8% healthcare practitioners, 11.0% service, 26.7% sales and office, 15.2% natural resources, construction, and maintenance, 21.3% production, transportation, and material moving
Income: Per capita: $28,915; Median household: $74,500; Average household: $80,806; Households with income of $100,000 or more: 27.0%; Poverty rate: 2.2%
Educational Attainment: High school diploma or higher: 91.5%; Bachelor's degree or higher: 24.6%; Graduate/professional degree or higher: 8.2%

School District(s)
Sunman-Dearborn Com Sch Corp (KG-12)
    2012-13 Enrollment: 4,133 . . . . (812) 623-2291
Housing: Homeownership rate: 93.2%; Median home value: $190,400; Median year structure built: 1988; Homeowner vacancy rate: 0.8%; Median gross rent: $825 per month; Rental vacancy rate: 5.8%
Health Insurance: 95.3% have insurance; 86.4% have private insurance; 18.6% have public insurance; 4.7% do not have insurance; 3.6% of children under 18 do not have insurance
Transportation: Commute: 97.4% car, 0.0% public transportation, 0.0% walk, 2.6% work from home; Median travel time to work: 34.6 minutes

HIDDEN VALLEY (CDP). Covers a land area of 4.138 square miles and a water area of 0.270 square miles. Located at 39.17° N. Lat; 84.84° W. Long. Elevation is 548 feet.
History: The community of Hidden Valley and lake of the same name was built by James Jacob Rupel, legendary land developer. Active in the Greater Dayton area and Indiana for over 50 years and the former owner of Centre City Offices and the Carillon House in Downtown Dayton.
Population: 5,387; Growth (since 2000): 22.0%; Density: 1,301.8 persons per square mile; Race: 97.6% White, 0.2% Black/African American, 0.5% Asian, 0.1% American Indian/Alaska Native, 0.0% Native Hawaiian/Other Pacific Islander, 1.0% Two or more races, 1.4% Hispanic of any race; Average household size: 2.82; Median age: 39.9; Age under 18: 26.4%; Age 65 and over: 11.2%; Males per 100 females: 101.4; Marriage status: 19.2% never married, 69.0% now married, 0.6% separated, 3.8% widowed, 8.1% divorced; Foreign born: 1.8%; Speak English only: 96.5%; With disability: 9.5%; Veterans: 12.8%; Ancestry: 46.0% German, 13.1% Irish, 11.9% English, 7.8% American, 5.4% Italian
Employment: 10.3% management, business, and financial, 6.0% computer, engineering, and science, 8.6% education, legal, community service, arts, and media, 5.7% healthcare practitioners, 13.5% service, 30.8% sales and office, 12.2% natural resources, construction, and maintenance, 12.9% production, transportation, and material moving
Income: Per capita: $43,419; Median household: $79,896; Average household: $121,052; Households with income of $100,000 or more: 35.2%; Poverty rate: 5.8%
Educational Attainment: High school diploma or higher: 94.6%; Bachelor's degree or higher: 25.7%; Graduate/professional degree or higher: 9.7%
Housing: Homeownership rate: 93.9%; Median home value: $188,100; Median year structure built: 1994; Homeowner vacancy rate: 2.1%; Median gross rent: $1,385 per month; Rental vacancy rate: 6.3%
Health Insurance: 94.2% have insurance; 84.8% have private insurance; 21.9% have public insurance; 5.8% do not have insurance; 5.7% of children under 18 do not have insurance
Transportation: Commute: 94.8% car, 0.0% public transportation, 0.0% walk, 4.2% work from home; Median travel time to work: 33.8 minutes

LAWRENCEBURG (city). County seat. Covers a land area of 4.941 square miles and a water area of 0.270 square miles. Located at 39.10° N. Lat; 84.87° W. Long. Elevation is 479 feet.
History: Lawrenceburg was founded in 1801 by Captain Samuel C. Vance. It developed as a port on the Ohio River. In 1937 the river flooded the town, reaching a crest of 82.6 feet. Lawrenceburg was the site of the church where Henry Ward Beecher was pastor in 1837.
Population: 5,042; Growth (since 2000): 7.6%; Density: 1,020.4 persons per square mile; Race: 93.5% White, 3.0% Black/African American, 0.8% Asian, 0.3% American Indian/Alaska Native, 0.0% Native Hawaiian/Other Pacific Islander, 2.2% Two or more races, 1.2% Hispanic of any race; Average household size: 2.26; Median age: 35.5; Age under 18: 24.1%; Age 65 and over: 14.7%; Males per 100 females: 96.3; Marriage status: 27.3% never married, 45.1% now married, 3.4% separated, 6.8% widowed, 20.9% divorced; Foreign born: 0.5%; Speak English only: 98.3%; With disability: 19.1%; Veterans: 10.9%; Ancestry: 34.3% German, 21.3% Irish, 12.3% American, 7.4% Italian, 7.1% English
Employment: 4.8% management, business, and financial, 1.2% computer, engineering, and science, 4.6% education, legal, community service, arts, and media, 3.4% healthcare practitioners, 22.0% service, 24.7% sales and office, 9.8% natural resources, construction, and maintenance, 29.5% production, transportation, and material moving
Income: Per capita: $16,123; Median household: $34,270; Average household: $39,148; Households with income of $100,000 or more: 5.2%; Poverty rate: 16.9%
Educational Attainment: High school diploma or higher: 74.7%; Bachelor's degree or higher: 7.4%; Graduate/professional degree or higher: 2.4%

School District(s)
Lawrenceburg Com School Corp (PK-12)
    2012-13 Enrollment: 1,936 . . . . (812) 537-7201
Sunman-Dearborn Com Sch Corp (KG-12)
    2012-13 Enrollment: 4,133 . . . . (812) 623-2291
Housing: Homeownership rate: 39.7%; Median home value: $123,600; Median year structure built: 1969; Homeowner vacancy rate: 7.4%; Median gross rent: $667 per month; Rental vacancy rate: 6.1%
Health Insurance: 87.1% have insurance; 63.4% have private insurance; 39.9% have public insurance; 12.9% do not have insurance; 2.9% of children under 18 do not have insurance
Hospitals: Dearborn County Hospital (144 beds)
Safety: Violent crime rate: 16.0 per 10,000 population; Property crime rate: 357.1 per 10,000 population
Newspapers: Register Publications (weekly circulation 14000)
Transportation: Commute: 88.7% car, 0.0% public transportation, 7.7% walk, 3.6% work from home; Median travel time to work: 20.3 minutes
Additional Information Contacts
City of Lawrenceburg . . . . (812) 532-3573
    http://www.lawrenceburg-in.com

MOORES HILL (town). Covers a land area of 0.539 square miles and a water area of 0 square miles. Located at 39.11° N. Lat; 85.09° W. Long. Elevation is 991 feet.
History: Laid out 1838.
Population: 597; Growth (since 2000): -6.0%; Density: 1,108.2 persons per square mile; Race: 97.8% White, 0.2% Black/African American, 0.2% Asian, 0.0% American Indian/Alaska Native, 0.0% Native Hawaiian/Other Pacific Islander, 1.2% Two or more races, 0.3% Hispanic of any race; Average household size: 2.68; Median age: 37.5; Age under 18: 28.5%; Age 65 and over: 10.1%; Males per 100 females: 90.1

School District(s)
South Dearborn Com School Corp (KG-12)
    2012-13 Enrollment: 2,818 . . . . (812) 926-2090
Housing: Homeownership rate: 80.3%; Homeowner vacancy rate: 4.8%; Rental vacancy rate: 11.8%

SAINT LEON (town). Covers a land area of 6.982 square miles and a water area of 0.009 square miles. Located at 39.30° N. Lat; 84.97° W. Long. Elevation is 1,010 feet.
Population: 678; Growth (since 2000): 75.2%; Density: 97.1 persons per square mile; Race: 98.1% White, 0.1% Black/African American, 0.6% Asian, 0.0% American Indian/Alaska Native, 0.0% Native Hawaiian/Other Pacific Islander, 0.7% Two or more races, 0.3% Hispanic of any race; Average household size: 2.69; Median age: 36.2; Age under 18: 26.8%; Age 65 and over: 13.1%; Males per 100 females: 100.0

School District(s)
Sunman-Dearborn Com Sch Corp (KG-12)
    2012-13 Enrollment: 4,133 . . . . (812) 623-2291
Housing: Homeownership rate: 69.5%; Homeowner vacancy rate: 1.1%; Rental vacancy rate: 4.9%

WEST HARRISON (town). Covers a land area of 0.215 square miles and a water area of 0.008 square miles. Located at 39.26° N. Lat; 84.82° W. Long. Elevation is 518 feet.

History: West Harrison was founded in 1813. General John Hunt Morgan and his Confederate cavalry raided West Harrison in 1863 before moving on to Ohio.

Population: 289; Growth (since 2000): 1.8%; Density: 1,341.4 persons per square mile; Race: 99.0% White, 0.3% Black/African American, 0.3% Asian, 0.3% American Indian/Alaska Native, 0.0% Native Hawaiian/Other Pacific Islander, 0.0% Two or more races, 0.3% Hispanic of any race; Average household size: 2.13; Median age: 42.2; Age under 18: 17.3%; Age 65 and over: 12.5%; Males per 100 females: 110.9

School District(s)
Sunman-Dearborn Com Sch Corp (KG-12)
    2012-13 Enrollment: 4,133 . . . . (812) 623-2291

Housing: Homeownership rate: 44.9%; Homeowner vacancy rate: 3.2%; Rental vacancy rate: 23.0%

Decatur County

Located in southeast central Indiana; drained by Flatrock, Small Duck, Clifty, and Sand Creeks. Covers a land area of 372.568 square miles, a water area of 0.755 square miles, and is located in the Eastern Time Zone at 39.31° N. Lat., 85.50° W. Long. The county was founded in 1821. County seat is Greensburg.

Decatur County is part of the Greensburg, IN Micropolitan Statistical Area. The entire metro area includes: Decatur County, IN

Weather Station: Greensburg   Elevation: 935 feet

	Jan	Feb	Mar	Apr	May	Jun	Jul	Aug	Sep	Oct	Nov	Dec
High	36	40	51	63	73	82	85	84	77	65	52	40
Low	21	24	32	43	53	62	66	64	56	44	35	25
Precip	2.9	2.5	3.7	4.4	5.5	4.5	4.0	3.9	3.1	3.2	3.7	3.4
Snow	5.5	3.8	2.2	0.3	tr	0.0	0.0	0.0	0.0	0.2	0.2	4.2

High and Low temperatures in degrees Fahrenheit; Precipitation and Snow in inches

Population: 25,740; Growth (since 2000): 4.8%; Density: 69.1 persons per square mile; Race: 97.3% White, 0.3% Black/African American, 0.7% Asian, 0.2% American Indian/Alaska Native, 0.0% Native Hawaiian/Other Pacific Islander, 0.9% two or more races, 1.7% Hispanic of any race; Average household size: 2.54; Median age: 38.7; Age under 18: 25.5%; Age 65 and over: 14.4%; Males per 100 females: 98.2; Marriage status: 24.9% never married, 56.2% now married, 1.4% separated, 6.3% widowed, 12.7% divorced; Foreign born: 1.9%; Speak English only: 97.8%; With disability: 13.7%; Veterans: 10.1%; Ancestry: 29.2% German, 19.4% American, 10.6% Irish, 8.2% English, 3.0% French

Religion: Six largest groups: 25.3% Catholicism, 18.7% Baptist, 4.9% Methodist/Pietist, 3.1% Non-denominational Protestant, 2.7% Holiness, 1.4% Presbyterian-Reformed

Economy: Unemployment rate: 4.7%; Leading industries: 17.7% retail trade; 10.0% other services (except public administration); 9.5% construction; Farms: 610 totaling 186,528 acres; Company size: 1 employs 1,000 or more persons, 2 employs 500 to 999 persons, 14 employ 100 to 499 persons, 604 employ less than 100 persons; Business ownership: 550 women-owned, n/a Black-owned, n/a Hispanic-owned, n/a Asian-owned

Employment: 10.7% management, business, and financial; 3.3% computer, engineering, and science, 7.3% education, legal, community service, arts, and media, 4.4% healthcare practitioners, 15.2% service, 20.8% sales and office, 10.3% natural resources, construction, and maintenance, 28.0% production, transportation, and material moving

Income: Per capita: $22,046; Median household: $48,047; Average household: $56,518; Households with income of $100,000 or more: 12.3%; Poverty rate: 14.1%

Educational Attainment: High school diploma or higher: 87.1%; Bachelor's degree or higher: 13.7%; Graduate/professional degree or higher: 5.2%

Housing: Homeownership rate: 70.5%; Median home value: $112,000; Median year structure built: 1968; Homeowner vacancy rate: 2.7%; Median gross rent: $711 per month; Rental vacancy rate: 10.7%

Vital Statistics: Birth rate: 125.6 per 10,000 population; Death rate: 95.9 per 10,000 population; Age-adjusted cancer mortality rate: 187.2 deaths per 100,000 population

Health Insurance: 85.1% have insurance; 66.2% have private insurance; 31.4% have public insurance; 14.9% do not have insurance; 10.3% of children under 18 do not have insurance

Health Care: Physicians: 6.9 per 10,000 population; Hospital beds: 9.7 per 10,000 population; Hospital admissions: 447.5 per 10,000 population

Transportation: Commute: 93.6% car, 0.4% public transportation, 1.4% walk, 3.4% work from home; Median travel time to work: 23.2 minutes

Presidential Election: 28.5% Obama, 69.1% Romney (2012)

National and State Parks: Greenburg Reservoir State Fishing Area

Additional Information Contacts
Decatur Government . . . . (812) 663-2570
    http://www.decaturcounty.in.gov

Decatur County Communities

CLARKSBURG (CDP). Covers a land area of 0.479 square miles and a water area of 0 square miles. Located at 39.44° N. Lat; 85.35° W. Long. Elevation is 1,053 feet.

Population: 149; Growth (since 2000): n/a; Density: 311.0 persons per square mile; Race: 99.3% White, 0.0% Black/African American, 0.0% Asian, 0.0% American Indian/Alaska Native, 0.0% Native Hawaiian/Other Pacific Islander, 0.7% Two or more races, 0.0% Hispanic of any race; Average household size: 2.87; Median age: 42.2; Age under 18: 24.2%; Age 65 and over: 20.1%; Males per 100 females: 119.1

Housing: Homeownership rate: 73.0%; Homeowner vacancy rate: 5.0%; Rental vacancy rate: 0.0%

GREENSBURG (city). County seat. Covers a land area of 9.270 square miles and a water area of 0.045 square miles. Located at 39.35° N. Lat; 85.50° W. Long. Elevation is 958 feet.

History: Greensburg developed as a residential center.

Population: 11,492; Growth (since 2000): 12.0%; Density: 1,239.8 persons per square mile; Race: 96.1% White, 0.4% Black/African American, 1.3% Asian, 0.2% American Indian/Alaska Native, 0.0% Native Hawaiian/Other Pacific Islander, 0.9% Two or more races, 2.4% Hispanic of any race; Average household size: 2.38; Median age: 37.0; Age under 18: 25.0%; Age 65 and over: 15.6%; Males per 100 females: 91.9; Marriage status: 27.5% never married, 48.7% now married, 1.5% separated, 8.1% widowed, 15.7% divorced; Foreign born: 3.2%; Speak English only: 96.7%; With disability: 16.0%; Veterans: 8.4%; Ancestry: 30.4% German, 19.1% American, 11.6% Irish, 6.9% English, 2.5% French

Employment: 9.6% management, business, and financial, 5.5% computer, engineering, and science, 7.3% education, legal, community service, arts, and media, 5.3% healthcare practitioners, 17.5% service, 20.4% sales and office, 7.0% natural resources, construction, and maintenance, 27.4% production, transportation, and material moving

Income: Per capita: $20,677; Median household: $42,840; Average household: $49,865; Households with income of $100,000 or more: 9.8%; Poverty rate: 18.5%

Educational Attainment: High school diploma or higher: 87.2%; Bachelor's degree or higher: 14.6%; Graduate/professional degree or higher: 5.0%

School District(s)
Decatur County Com Schools (KG-12)
    2012-13 Enrollment: 2,147 . . . . (812) 663-4595
Greensburg Community Schools (KG-12)
    2012-13 Enrollment: 2,261 . . . . (812) 663-4774

Housing: Homeownership rate: 58.5%; Median home value: $103,300; Median year structure built: 1970; Homeowner vacancy rate: 3.3%; Median gross rent: $712 per month; Rental vacancy rate: 11.6%

Health Insurance: 84.4% have insurance; 62.4% have private insurance; 33.5% have public insurance; 15.6% do not have insurance; 9.0% of children under 18 do not have insurance

Hospitals: Decatur County Memorial Hospital (115 beds)

Safety: Violent crime rate: 27.4 per 10,000 population; Property crime rate: 50.5 per 10,000 population

Newspapers: Greensburg Daily News (daily circulation 5600); Greensburg Times (weekly circulation 700)

Transportation: Commute: 94.6% car, 0.4% public transportation, 2.5% walk, 1.5% work from home; Median travel time to work: 19.5 minutes

Additional Information Contacts
City of Greensburg . . . . (812) 663-8582
    http://www.cityofgreensburg.com

LAKE SANTEE (CDP). Covers a land area of 2.467 square miles and a water area of 0.356 square miles. Located at 39.41° N. Lat; 85.31° W. Long.
Population: 820; Growth (since 2000): n/a; Density: 332.4 persons per square mile; Race: 97.1% White, 1.2% Black/African American, 0.1% Asian, 0.1% American Indian/Alaska Native, 0.0% Native Hawaiian/Other Pacific Islander, 1.5% Two or more races, 1.5% Hispanic of any race; Average household size: 2.62; Median age: 43.0; Age under 18: 25.5%; Age 65 and over: 14.5%; Males per 100 females: 101.5
Housing: Homeownership rate: 90.1%; Homeowner vacancy rate: 5.7%; Rental vacancy rate: 8.8%

MILLHOUSEN (town). Covers a land area of 1.010 square miles and a water area of 0 square miles. Located at 39.21° N. Lat; 85.44° W. Long. Elevation is 896 feet.
History: Settled 1838, plotted 1858.
Population: 127; Growth (since 2000): -6.6%; Density: 125.8 persons per square mile; Race: 99.2% White, 0.0% Black/African American, 0.0% Asian, 0.0% American Indian/Alaska Native, 0.0% Native Hawaiian/Other Pacific Islander, 0.8% Two or more races, 0.0% Hispanic of any race; Average household size: 2.44; Median age: 32.9; Age under 18: 28.3%; Age 65 and over: 11.8%; Males per 100 females: 98.4
Housing: Homeownership rate: 84.6%; Homeowner vacancy rate: 2.2%; Rental vacancy rate: 11.1%

NEW POINT (town). Covers a land area of 0.217 square miles and a water area of 0 square miles. Located at 39.31° N. Lat; 85.33° W. Long. Elevation is 974 feet.
Population: 331; Growth (since 2000): 14.1%; Density: 1,521.9 persons per square mile; Race: 99.4% White, 0.0% Black/African American, 0.3% Asian, 0.0% American Indian/Alaska Native, 0.0% Native Hawaiian/Other Pacific Islander, 0.3% Two or more races, 0.6% Hispanic of any race; Average household size: 2.67; Median age: 36.6; Age under 18: 28.1%; Age 65 and over: 15.1%; Males per 100 females: 105.6
Housing: Homeownership rate: 74.1%; Homeowner vacancy rate: 2.1%; Rental vacancy rate: 11.1%

SAINT PAUL (town). Covers a land area of 0.312 square miles and a water area of 0 square miles. Located at 39.43° N. Lat; 85.63° W. Long. Elevation is 856 feet.
Population: 1,031; Growth (since 2000): 0.9%; Density: 3,301.0 persons per square mile; Race: 98.3% White, 0.3% Black/African American, 0.0% Asian, 0.1% American Indian/Alaska Native, 0.1% Native Hawaiian/Other Pacific Islander, 1.0% Two or more races, 1.5% Hispanic of any race; Average household size: 2.68; Median age: 35.7; Age under 18: 27.0%; Age 65 and over: 11.6%; Males per 100 females: 97.1
Housing: Homeownership rate: 74.7%; Homeowner vacancy rate: 2.7%; Rental vacancy rate: 17.8%

WESTPORT (town). Covers a land area of 1.320 square miles and a water area of 0.013 square miles. Located at 39.18° N. Lat; 85.58° W. Long. Elevation is 814 feet.
History: Laid out 1836.
Population: 1,379; Growth (since 2000): -9.0%; Density: 1,044.9 persons per square mile; Race: 98.5% White, 0.1% Black/African American, 0.1% Asian, 0.2% American Indian/Alaska Native, 0.0% Native Hawaiian/Other Pacific Islander, 1.1% Two or more races, 0.9% Hispanic of any race; Average household size: 2.52; Median age: 36.4; Age under 18: 27.6%; Age 65 and over: 14.1%; Males per 100 females: 94.2
Housing: Homeownership rate: 68.7%; Homeowner vacancy rate: 6.4%; Rental vacancy rate: 9.0%

DeKalb County

Located in northeastern Indiana; bounded on the east by Ohio; drained by the Saint Joseph River and Cedar and Fish Creeks. Covers a land area of 362.824 square miles, a water area of 1.026 square miles, and is located in the Eastern Time Zone at 41.40° N. Lat., 85.00° W. Long. The county was founded in 1835. County seat is Auburn.

DeKalb County is part of the Auburn, IN Micropolitan Statistical Area. The entire metro area includes: DeKalb County, IN

Population: 42,223; Growth (since 2000): 4.8%; Density: 116.4 persons per square mile; Race: 96.9% White, 0.4% Black/African American, 0.5% Asian, 0.2% American Indian/Alaska Native, 0.0% Native Hawaiian/Other Pacific Islander, 1.2% two or more races, 2.4% Hispanic of any race; Average household size: 2.61; Median age: 38.1; Age under 18: 26.4%; Age 65 and over: 13.1%; Males per 100 females: 98.4; Marriage status: 24.8% never married, 56.0% now married, 1.3% separated, 6.4% widowed, 12.8% divorced; Foreign born: 1.1%; Speak English only: 97.2%; With disability: 16.0%; Veterans: 9.8%; Ancestry: 35.7% German, 12.3% Irish, 11.8% American, 8.1% English, 2.8% French
Religion: Six largest groups: 12.5% Catholicism, 6.6% Baptist, 5.9% Methodist/Pietist, 5.7% Holiness, 3.5% Non-denominational Protestant, 3.0% Lutheran
Economy: Unemployment rate: 5.0%; Leading industries: 12.8% retail trade; 12.0% other services (except public administration); 11.5% manufacturing; Farms: 924 totaling 160,894 acres; Company size: 0 employ 1,000 or more persons, 3 employ 500 to 999 persons, 36 employ 100 to 499 persons, 927 employ less than 100 persons; Business ownership: 597 women-owned, n/a Black-owned, n/a Hispanic-owned, n/a Asian-owned
Employment: 10.7% management, business, and financial, 4.7% computer, engineering, and science, 7.9% education, legal, community service, arts, and media, 5.0% healthcare practitioners, 14.3% service, 21.2% sales and office, 8.4% natural resources, construction, and maintenance, 27.8% production, transportation, and material moving
Income: Per capita: $22,827; Median household: $47,247; Average household: $58,744; Households with income of $100,000 or more: 13.6%; Poverty rate: 12.4%
Educational Attainment: High school diploma or higher: 87.9%; Bachelor's degree or higher: 16.3%; Graduate/professional degree or higher: 5.5%
Housing: Homeownership rate: 78.7%; Median home value: $107,800; Median year structure built: 1971; Homeowner vacancy rate: 2.9%; Median gross rent: $630 per month; Rental vacancy rate: 11.0%
Vital Statistics: Birth rate: 116.3 per 10,000 population; Death rate: 89.8 per 10,000 population; Age-adjusted cancer mortality rate: 204.4 deaths per 100,000 population
Health Insurance: 86.3% have insurance; 69.8% have private insurance; 28.7% have public insurance; 13.7% do not have insurance; 6.8% of children under 18 do not have insurance
Health Care: Physicians: 8.3 per 10,000 population; Hospital beds: 12.5 per 10,000 population; Hospital admissions: 434.0 per 10,000 population
Transportation: Commute: 93.5% car, 0.3% public transportation, 1.9% walk, 2.7% work from home; Median travel time to work: 21.0 minutes
Presidential Election: 33.2% Obama, 64.8% Romney (2012)
Additional Information Contacts
DeKalb Government . . . . (219) 925-2362
http://www.co.dekalb.in.us

DeKalb County Communities

ALTONA (town). Covers a land area of 0.217 square miles and a water area of 0 square miles. Located at 41.35° N. Lat; 85.15° W. Long. Elevation is 899 feet.
Population: 197; Growth (since 2000): -0.5%; Density: 906.4 persons per square mile; Race: 98.5% White, 0.0% Black/African American, 0.0% Asian, 0.5% American Indian/Alaska Native, 0.0% Native Hawaiian/Other Pacific Islander, 1.0% Two or more races, 1.0% Hispanic of any race; Average household size: 2.19; Median age: 41.1; Age under 18: 20.3%; Age 65 and over: 17.8%; Males per 100 females: 107.4
Housing: Homeownership rate: 75.5%; Homeowner vacancy rate: 0.0%; Rental vacancy rate: 12.0%

ASHLEY (town). Covers a land area of 1.808 square miles and a water area of 0 square miles. Located at 41.52° N. Lat; 85.06° W. Long. Elevation is 1,010 feet.
Population: 983; Growth (since 2000): -2.7%; Density: 543.7 persons per square mile; Race: 95.6% White, 0.2% Black/African American, 0.3% Asian, 0.5% American Indian/Alaska Native, 0.0% Native Hawaiian/Other Pacific Islander, 1.7% Two or more races, 3.4% Hispanic of any race; Average household size: 2.60; Median age: 34.0; Age under 18: 30.5%; Age 65 and over: 10.8%; Males per 100 females: 103.5
School District(s)
Dekalb County Ctl United SD (KG-12)
    2012-13 Enrollment: 3,792 . . . . (260) 920-1011
Housing: Homeownership rate: 65.9%; Homeowner vacancy rate: 3.1%; Rental vacancy rate: 23.7%

Additional Information Contacts
Town of Ashley .... (260) 587-3982
  http://www.ashley.in.gov

AUBURN (city).
County seat. Covers a land area of 7.104 square miles and a water area of 0 square miles. Located at 41.37° N. Lat; 85.05° W. Long. Elevation is 866 feet.
History: Auburn developed as a trading center for the surrounding farmlands, and as the seat of DeKalb County.
Population: 12,731; Growth (since 2000): 5.4%; Density: 1,792.0 persons per square mile; Race: 96.9% White, 0.4% Black/African American, 0.7% Asian, 0.2% American Indian/Alaska Native, 0.0% Native Hawaiian/Other Pacific Islander, 1.0% Two or more races, 2.6% Hispanic of any race; Average household size: 2.38; Median age: 37.9; Age under 18: 25.3%; Age 65 and over: 15.6%; Males per 100 females: 92.8; Marriage status: 28.2% never married, 51.6% now married, 0.9% separated, 7.9% widowed, 12.3% divorced; Foreign born: 1.0%; Speak English only: 97.9%; With disability: 17.0%; Veterans: 8.1%; Ancestry: 38.2% German, 15.4% Irish, 10.6% American, 9.1% English, 3.2% Scottish
Employment: 11.3% management, business, and financial, 5.8% computer, engineering, and science, 11.0% education, legal, community service, arts, and media, 4.9% healthcare practitioners, 15.6% service, 23.1% sales and office, 3.9% natural resources, construction, and maintenance, 24.5% production, transportation, and material moving
Income: Per capita: $23,963; Median household: $42,855; Average household: $57,496; Households with income of $100,000 or more: 14.8%; Poverty rate: 13.5%
Educational Attainment: High school diploma or higher: 89.2%; Bachelor's degree or higher: 22.4%; Graduate/professional degree or higher: 8.6%
School District(s)
Dekalb County Ctl United SD (KG-12)
  2012-13 Enrollment: 3,792 .... (260) 920-1011
Housing: Homeownership rate: 72.2%; Median home value: $104,800; Median year structure built: 1975; Homeowner vacancy rate: 4.0%; Median gross rent: $613 per month; Rental vacancy rate: 9.7%
Health Insurance: 85.7% have insurance; 72.3% have private insurance; 27.6% have public insurance; 14.3% do not have insurance; 9.8% of children under 18 do not have insurance
Hospitals: Dekalb Health (47 beds)
Safety: Violent crime rate: 8.6 per 10,000 population; Property crime rate: 194.5 per 10,000 population
Newspapers: Evening Star (daily circulation 6800)
Transportation: Commute: 92.8% car, 0.0% public transportation, 0.9% walk, 3.9% work from home; Median travel time to work: 18.2 minutes
Additional Information Contacts
City of Auburn .... (260) 925-6450
  http://www.ci.auburn.in.us

BUTLER (city).
Covers a land area of 2.093 square miles and a water area of 0 square miles. Located at 41.43° N. Lat; 84.87° W. Long. Elevation is 866 feet.
Population: 2,684; Growth (since 2000): -1.5%; Density: 1,282.3 persons per square mile; Race: 94.9% White, 0.5% Black/African American, 0.2% Asian, 0.4% American Indian/Alaska Native, 0.0% Native Hawaiian/Other Pacific Islander, 1.8% Two or more races, 4.3% Hispanic of any race; Average household size: 2.71; Median age: 33.7; Age under 18: 29.3%; Age 65 and over: 11.9%; Males per 100 females: 99.4; Marriage status: 31.7% never married, 45.9% now married, 3.1% separated, 6.5% widowed, 15.8% divorced; Foreign born: 0.4%; Speak English only: 98.9%; With disability: 16.2%; Veterans: 9.9%; Ancestry: 34.7% German, 18.5% Irish, 10.5% American, 3.8% English, 3.5% French
Employment: 3.9% management, business, and financial, 0.9% computer, engineering, and science, 4.1% education, legal, community service, arts, and media, 2.7% healthcare practitioners, 23.4% service, 15.6% sales and office, 5.4% natural resources, construction, and maintenance, 44.0% production, transportation, and material moving
Income: Per capita: $16,250; Median household: $35,469; Average household: $43,572; Households with income of $100,000 or more: 8.6%; Poverty rate: 22.8%
Educational Attainment: High school diploma or higher: 80.1%; Bachelor's degree or higher: 6.4%; Graduate/professional degree or higher: 3.4%
School District(s)
Dekalb County Eastern Com SD (KG-12)
  2012-13 Enrollment: 1,364 .... (260) 868-2125
Housing: Homeownership rate: 65.8%; Median home value: $68,600; Median year structure built: 1960; Homeowner vacancy rate: 5.7%; Median gross rent: $639 per month; Rental vacancy rate: 17.4%
Health Insurance: 78.8% have insurance; 49.2% have private insurance; 39.5% have public insurance; 21.2% do not have insurance; 5.4% of children under 18 do not have insurance
Newspapers: Butler Bulletin (weekly circulation 1000)
Transportation: Commute: 93.4% car, 0.5% public transportation, 5.2% walk, 0.9% work from home; Median travel time to work: 20.3 minutes
Additional Information Contacts
City of Butler .... (260) 868-5200
  http://www.butler.in.us

CORUNNA (town).
Covers a land area of 0.173 square miles and a water area of 0 square miles. Located at 41.44° N. Lat; 85.14° W. Long. Elevation is 974 feet.
Population: 254; Growth (since 2000): 0.0%; Density: 1,467.4 persons per square mile; Race: 94.9% White, 0.4% Black/African American, 0.4% Asian, 0.4% American Indian/Alaska Native, 0.0% Native Hawaiian/Other Pacific Islander, 1.6% Two or more races, 4.3% Hispanic of any race; Average household size: 2.89; Median age: 34.3; Age under 18: 29.5%; Age 65 and over: 10.2%; Males per 100 females: 96.9
Housing: Homeownership rate: 81.8%; Homeowner vacancy rate: 2.7%; Rental vacancy rate: 0.0%

GARRETT (city).
Covers a land area of 3.851 square miles and a water area of 0 square miles. Located at 41.35° N. Lat; 85.12° W. Long. Elevation is 883 feet.
History: Garrett developed around the Baltimore & Ohio Railroad shops and roundhouse, and served the surrounding farms.
Population: 6,286; Growth (since 2000): 8.3%; Density: 1,632.5 persons per square mile; Race: 95.9% White, 0.4% Black/African American, 0.4% Asian, 0.4% American Indian/Alaska Native, 0.1% Native Hawaiian/Other Pacific Islander, 1.5% Two or more races, 3.5% Hispanic of any race; Average household size: 2.67; Median age: 33.7; Age under 18: 29.2%; Age 65 and over: 11.2%; Males per 100 females: 92.1; Marriage status: 22.9% never married, 55.3% now married, 1.6% separated, 6.1% widowed, 15.7% divorced; Foreign born: 0.5%; Speak English only: 95.8%; With disability: 15.4%; Veterans: 9.8%; Ancestry: 33.2% German, 12.4% American, 9.5% Irish, 5.3% English, 4.5% Polish
Employment: 8.0% management, business, and financial, 3.5% computer, engineering, and science, 7.9% education, legal, community service, arts, and media, 4.0% healthcare practitioners, 18.8% service, 16.8% sales and office, 11.5% natural resources, construction, and maintenance, 29.6% production, transportation, and material moving
Income: Per capita: $18,359; Median household: $42,719; Average household: $48,436; Households with income of $100,000 or more: 7.1%; Poverty rate: 12.2%
Educational Attainment: High school diploma or higher: 84.4%; Bachelor's degree or higher: 11.4%; Graduate/professional degree or higher: 2.4%
School District(s)
Garrett-Keyser-Butler Com (KG-12)
  2012-13 Enrollment: 1,787 .... (260) 357-3185
Housing: Homeownership rate: 73.5%; Median home value: $82,300; Median year structure built: 1970; Homeowner vacancy rate: 3.4%; Median gross rent: $636 per month; Rental vacancy rate: 8.7%
Health Insurance: 89.1% have insurance; 67.8% have private insurance; 31.9% have public insurance; 10.9% do not have insurance; 1.0% of children under 18 do not have insurance
Safety: Violent crime rate: 3.2 per 10,000 population; Property crime rate: 446.7 per 10,000 population
Newspapers: Garrett Clipper (weekly circulation 1800)
Transportation: Commute: 97.1% car, 0.0% public transportation, 2.5% walk, 0.3% work from home; Median travel time to work: 20.6 minutes
Additional Information Contacts
City of Garrett .... (260) 357-4151
  http://www.garrettindiana.us

SAINT JOE (town). Covers a land area of 0.273 square miles and a water area of 0 square miles. Located at 41.31° N. Lat; 84.90° W. Long. Elevation is 820 feet.
Population: 460; Growth (since 2000): -3.8%; Density: 1,682.0 persons per square mile; Race: 95.9% White, 0.0% Black/African American, 0.9% Asian, 0.0% American Indian/Alaska Native, 0.0% Native Hawaiian/Other Pacific Islander, 2.8% Two or more races, 3.7% Hispanic of any race; Average household size: 2.93; Median age: 33.1; Age under 18: 32.6%; Age 65 and over: 10.9%; Males per 100 females: 103.5
School District(s)
Dekalb County Eastern Com SD (KG-12)
    2012-13 Enrollment: 1,364 . . . . (260) 868-2125
Housing: Homeownership rate: 73.2%; Homeowner vacancy rate: 4.9%; Rental vacancy rate: 10.6%

WATERLOO (town). Covers a land area of 1.739 square miles and a water area of 0 square miles. Located at 41.43° N. Lat; 85.03° W. Long. Elevation is 906 feet.
Population: 2,242; Growth (since 2000): 1.9%; Density: 1,289.3 persons per square mile; Race: 95.3% White, 0.5% Black/African American, 0.0% Asian, 0.1% American Indian/Alaska Native, 0.0% Native Hawaiian/Other Pacific Islander, 2.4% Two or more races, 3.8% Hispanic of any race; Average household size: 2.77; Median age: 31.5; Age under 18: 30.0%; Age 65 and over: 8.0%; Males per 100 females: 102.3
School District(s)
Dekalb County Ctl United SD (KG-12)
    2012-13 Enrollment: 3,792 . . . . (260) 920-1011
Housing: Homeownership rate: 73.8%; Homeowner vacancy rate: 4.0%; Rental vacancy rate: 19.6%
Safety: Violent crime rate: 49.1 per 10,000 population; Property crime rate: 348.2 per 10,000 population
Additional Information Contacts
Town of Waterloo . . . . (260) 837-7428
http://mywaterlooindiana.com

Delaware County

Located in eastern Indiana; drained by the Mississinewa River and the West Fork of the White River. Covers a land area of 392.124 square miles, a water area of 3.785 square miles, and is located in the Eastern Time Zone at 40.23° N. Lat., 85.40° W. Long. The county was founded in 1827. County seat is Muncie.

Delaware County is part of the Muncie, IN Metropolitan Statistical Area. The entire metro area includes: Delaware County, IN

Weather Station: Muncie Delaware Cnty   Elevation: 978 feet

	Jan	Feb	Mar	Apr	May	Jun	Jul	Aug	Sep	Oct	Nov	Dec
High	33	38	48	61	72	81	85	83	77	64	51	38
Low	17	21	29	39	51	60	64	61	53	42	33	22
Precip	1.9	2.1	2.9	3.5	4.6	4.5	4.6	3.1	3.3	2.7	3.5	2.9
Snow	7.5	6.0	2.7	0.5	tr	0.0	0.0	0.0	0.0	0.3	1.0	6.1

High and Low temperatures in degrees Fahrenheit; Precipitation and Snow in inches

Population: 117,671; Growth (since 2000): -0.9%; Density: 300.1 persons per square mile; Race: 89.1% White, 6.9% Black/African American, 1.0% Asian, 0.3% American Indian/Alaska Native, 0.1% Native Hawaiian/Other Pacific Islander, 2.1% two or more races, 1.8% Hispanic of any race; Average household size: 2.34; Median age: 34.8; Age under 18: 20.0%; Age 65 and over: 14.7%; Males per 100 females: 92.7; Marriage status: 37.5% never married, 44.5% now married, 1.5% separated, 6.2% widowed, 11.9% divorced; Foreign born: 2.0%; Speak English only: 97.1%; With disability: 17.2%; Veterans: 9.1%; Ancestry: 21.2% German, 13.2% Irish, 10.8% American, 10.8% English, 2.2% French
Religion: Six largest groups: 5.5% Methodist/Pietist, 4.9% Baptist, 4.8% Non-denominational Protestant, 3.7% Holiness, 3.5% Catholicism, 2.0% Presbyterian-Reformed
Economy: Unemployment rate: 6.2%; Leading industries: 18.0% retail trade; 13.9% health care and social assistance; 12.7% other services (except public administration); Farms: 610 totaling 175,266 acres; Company size: 1 employs 1,000 or more persons, 0 employ 500 to 999 persons, 55 employ 100 to 499 persons, 2,321 employs less than 100 persons; Business ownership: 2,125 women-owned, 159 Black-owned, n/a Hispanic-owned, n/a Asian-owned
Employment: 10.7% management, business, and financial, 3.0% computer, engineering, and science, 12.2% education, legal, community service, arts, and media, 6.0% healthcare practitioners, 22.7% service, 24.2% sales and office, 6.9% natural resources, construction, and maintenance, 14.3% production, transportation, and material moving
Income: Per capita: $20,854; Median household: $37,474; Average household: $51,500; Households with income of $100,000 or more: 10.9%; Poverty rate: 22.3%
Educational Attainment: High school diploma or higher: 86.9%; Bachelor's degree or higher: 22.5%; Graduate/professional degree or higher: 10.1%
Housing: Homeownership rate: 64.4%; Median home value: $89,600; Median year structure built: 1963; Homeowner vacancy rate: 3.0%; Median gross rent: $675 per month; Rental vacancy rate: 10.6%
Vital Statistics: Birth rate: 107.8 per 10,000 population; Death rate: 98.7 per 10,000 population; Age-adjusted cancer mortality rate: 163.4 deaths per 100,000 population
Health Insurance: 86.2% have insurance; 68.1% have private insurance; 31.4% have public insurance; 13.8% do not have insurance; 6.2% of children under 18 do not have insurance
Health Care: Physicians: 25.2 per 10,000 population; Hospital beds: 32.2 per 10,000 population; Hospital admissions: 1,637.5 per 10,000 population
Air Quality Index: 83.3% good, 16.7% moderate, 0.0% unhealthy for sensitive individuals, 0.0% unhealthy (percent of days)
Transportation: Commute: 89.3% car, 1.5% public transportation, 5.0% walk, 2.8% work from home; Median travel time to work: 20.1 minutes
Presidential Election: 50.4% Obama, 47.3% Romney (2012)
Additional Information Contacts
Delaware Government . . . . (765) 747-7726
http://www.co.delaware.in.us

Delaware County Communities

ALBANY (town). Covers a land area of 1.752 square miles and a water area of 0.007 square miles. Located at 40.31° N. Lat; 85.23° W. Long. Elevation is 938 feet.
Population: 2,165; Growth (since 2000): -8.6%; Density: 1,235.5 persons per square mile; Race: 97.2% White, 0.6% Black/African American, 0.2% Asian, 0.0% American Indian/Alaska Native, 0.0% Native Hawaiian/Other Pacific Islander, 1.6% Two or more races, 1.1% Hispanic of any race; Average household size: 2.34; Median age: 40.3; Age under 18: 24.8%; Age 65 and over: 15.5%; Males per 100 females: 90.4
School District(s)
Delaware Community School Corp (KG-12)
    2012-13 Enrollment: 2,591 . . . . (765) 284-5074
Housing: Homeownership rate: 71.2%; Homeowner vacancy rate: 2.5%; Rental vacancy rate: 16.9%
Additional Information Contacts
Town of Albany . . . . (765) 288-6681
http://www.muncie.com/Chamber-of-Commerce.aspx

DALEVILLE (town). Covers a land area of 2.051 square miles and a water area of 0.022 square miles. Located at 40.12° N. Lat; 85.56° W. Long. Elevation is 912 feet.
History: When Daleville was platted in 1838, it was expected that a canal would be built here. Instead, the railroad came in 1852.
Population: 1,647; Growth (since 2000): -0.7%; Density: 803.2 persons per square mile; Race: 97.6% White, 0.4% Black/African American, 0.7% Asian, 0.1% American Indian/Alaska Native, 0.1% Native Hawaiian/Other Pacific Islander, 1.0% Two or more races, 0.5% Hispanic of any race; Average household size: 2.45; Median age: 40.0; Age under 18: 22.9%; Age 65 and over: 14.7%; Males per 100 females: 91.7
School District(s)
Daleville Community Schools (KG-12)
    2012-13 Enrollment: 824 . . . . (765) 378-3329
Housing: Homeownership rate: 72.3%; Homeowner vacancy rate: 2.8%; Rental vacancy rate: 6.1%

EATON (town). Covers a land area of 3.698 square miles and a water area of 0.063 square miles. Located at 40.32° N. Lat; 85.36° W. Long. Elevation is 909 feet.
Population: 1,805; Growth (since 2000): 12.6%; Density: 488.1 persons per square mile; Race: 97.8% White, 0.1% Black/African American, 0.1% Asian, 0.3% American Indian/Alaska Native, 0.0% Native Hawaiian/Other Pacific Islander, 1.3% Two or more races, 1.8% Hispanic of any race;

Average household size: 2.59; Median age: 36.3; Age under 18: 27.4%; Age 65 and over: 14.2%; Males per 100 females: 104.6

School District(s)
Delaware Community School Corp (KG-12)
    2012-13 Enrollment: 2,591 . . . . (765) 284-5074
Housing: Homeownership rate: 76.5%; Homeowner vacancy rate: 2.8%; Rental vacancy rate: 27.1%

GASTON (town).
Covers a land area of 0.351 square miles and a water area of 0 square miles. Located at 40.31° N. Lat; 85.50° W. Long. Elevation is 896 feet.
Population: 871; Growth (since 2000): -13.8%; Density: 2,483.5 persons per square mile; Race: 97.0% White, 0.1% Black/African American, 0.1% Asian, 0.0% American Indian/Alaska Native, 0.0% Native Hawaiian/Other Pacific Islander, 2.2% Two or more races, 2.9% Hispanic of any race; Average household size: 2.63; Median age: 34.4; Age under 18: 29.6%; Age 65 and over: 10.3%; Males per 100 females: 92.3

School District(s)
Wes-Del Community Schools (KG-12)
    2012-13 Enrollment: 825. . . . . (765) 358-4006
Housing: Homeownership rate: 77.7%; Homeowner vacancy rate: 6.8%; Rental vacancy rate: 20.4%

MUNCIE (city).
County seat. Covers a land area of 27.196 square miles and a water area of 0.192 square miles. Located at 40.20° N. Lat; 85.39° W. Long. Elevation is 951 feet.
History: A railroad station and some factories were the impetus for the growth of Muncie, which was platted in 1827 and called Munseytown. Incorporation as a town came in 1847, and by 1865 Muncie was declared a city. About 1887 natural gas wells began to bring many new industries to Muncie. One of these was the Ball Brothers Company, producers of canning jars.
Population: 70,085; Growth (since 2000): 3.9%; Density: 2,577.0 persons per square mile; Race: 84.0% White, 10.9% Black/African American, 1.2% Asian, 0.3% American Indian/Alaska Native, 0.1% Native Hawaiian/Other Pacific Islander, 2.8% Two or more races, 2.3% Hispanic of any race; Average household size: 2.22; Median age: 28.1; Age under 18: 17.8%; Age 65 and over: 13.0%; Males per 100 females: 90.6; Marriage status: 48.2% never married, 32.8% now married, 1.5% separated, 6.0% widowed, 13.1% divorced; Foreign born: 2.8%; Speak English only: 96.2%; With disability: 18.4%; Veterans: 7.9%; Ancestry: 20.0% German, 13.0% Irish, 9.2% English, 9.0% American, 2.7% Italian
Employment: 9.3% management, business, and financial, 2.3% computer, engineering, and science, 13.6% education, legal, community service, arts, and media, 4.9% healthcare practitioners, 26.4% service, 24.4% sales and office, 5.1% natural resources, construction, and maintenance, 14.0% production, transportation, and material moving
Income: Per capita: $17,066; Median household: $29,287; Average household: $40,856; Households with income of $100,000 or more: 6.6%; Poverty rate: 33.4%
Educational Attainment: High school diploma or higher: 83.5%; Bachelor's degree or higher: 22.4%; Graduate/professional degree or higher: 10.8%

School District(s)
Burris Laboratory School (KG-12)
    2012-13 Enrollment: 612. . . . . (765) 285-8488
Cowan Community School Corp (KG-12)
    2012-13 Enrollment: 780. . . . . (765) 289-4866
Delaware Community School Corp (KG-12)
    2012-13 Enrollment: 2,591 . . . . (765) 284-5074
Hoosier Academy - Muncie (KG-08)
    2012-13 Enrollment: 129. . . . . (317) 288-9633
In Acad for Sci Math Humanities (11-12)
    2012-13 Enrollment: 302. . . . . (765) 285-8488
Muncie Community Schools (PK-12)
    2012-13 Enrollment: 6,784 . . . . (765) 747-5205

Four-year College(s)
Ball State University (Public)
    Fall 2013 Enrollment: 20,503 . . . . (765) 289-1241
    2013-14 Tuition: In-state $9,160; Out-of-state $24,124
Housing: Homeownership rate: 51.4%; Median home value: $73,200; Median year structure built: 1959; Homeowner vacancy rate: 3.8%; Median gross rent: $670 per month; Rental vacancy rate: 10.1%

Health Insurance: 83.5% have insurance; 62.8% have private insurance; 32.1% have public insurance; 16.5% do not have insurance; 7.7% of children under 18 do not have insurance
Hospitals: Indiana University Health Ball Memorial Hospital (350 beds)
Safety: Violent crime rate: 41.1 per 10,000 population; Property crime rate: 429.2 per 10,000 population
Newspapers: Star-Press (daily circulation 32000)
Transportation: Commute: 85.4% car, 2.6% public transportation, 7.9% walk, 2.1% work from home; Median travel time to work: 17.7 minutes
Airports: Delaware County Regional (general aviation)
Additional Information Contacts
City of Muncie . . . . (765) 747-4831
    http://www.cityofmuncie.com

OAKVILLE (unincorporated postal area)
ZCTA: 47367
    Covers a land area of 0.720 square miles and a water area of 0 square miles. Located at 40.08° N. Lat; 85.39° W. Long. Elevation is 1,010 feet.
    Population: 191; Growth (since 2000): n/a; Density: 265.4 persons per square mile; Race: 97.4% White, 0.0% Black/African American, 0.5% Asian, 1.0% American Indian/Alaska Native, 0.0% Native Hawaiian/Other Pacific Islander, 0.0% Two or more races, 2.6% Hispanic of any race; Average household size: 2.67; Median age: 38.4; Age under 18: 28.8%; Age 65 and over: 22.5%; Males per 100 females: 99.0
    Housing: Homeownership rate: 90.0%; Homeowner vacancy rate: 1.6%; Rental vacancy rate: 12.5%

SELMA (town).
Covers a land area of 0.909 square miles and a water area of 0.002 square miles. Located at 40.19° N. Lat; 85.27° W. Long. Elevation is 1,004 feet.
Population: 866; Growth (since 2000): -1.6%; Density: 952.4 persons per square mile; Race: 97.2% White, 0.7% Black/African American, 0.2% Asian, 0.5% American Indian/Alaska Native, 0.2% Native Hawaiian/Other Pacific Islander, 1.0% Two or more races, 0.9% Hispanic of any race; Average household size: 2.55; Median age: 39.0; Age under 18: 26.0%; Age 65 and over: 14.2%; Males per 100 females: 89.5

School District(s)
Liberty-Perry Com School Corp (KG-12)
    2012-13 Enrollment: 1,103 . . . . (765) 282-5615
Housing: Homeownership rate: 71.2%; Homeowner vacancy rate: 0.8%; Rental vacancy rate: 9.3%

YORKTOWN (town).
Covers a land area of 8.779 square miles and a water area of 0.083 square miles. Located at 40.19° N. Lat; 85.47° W. Long. Elevation is 915 feet.
Population: 9,405; Growth (since 2000): 96.6%; Density: 1,071.3 persons per square mile; Race: 95.3% White, 1.6% Black/African American, 1.5% Asian, 0.2% American Indian/Alaska Native, 0.0% Native Hawaiian/Other Pacific Islander, 1.0% Two or more races, 1.3% Hispanic of any race; Average household size: 2.55; Median age: 41.2; Age under 18: 25.7%; Age 65 and over: 17.0%; Males per 100 females: 90.5; Marriage status: 18.4% never married, 64.7% now married, 0.9% separated, 6.9% widowed, 10.0% divorced; Foreign born: 1.4%; Speak English only: 98.2%; With disability: 14.3%; Veterans: 12.4%; Ancestry: 31.7% German, 18.9% Irish, 14.2% English, 12.8% American, 2.6% Dutch
Employment: 15.8% management, business, and financial, 4.6% computer, engineering, and science, 12.3% education, legal, community service, arts, and media, 8.5% healthcare practitioners, 15.3% service, 27.1% sales and office, 6.2% natural resources, construction, and maintenance, 10.1% production, transportation, and material moving
Income: Per capita: $28,405; Median household: $58,880; Average household: $73,736; Households with income of $100,000 or more: 22.8%; Poverty rate: 6.0%
Educational Attainment: High school diploma or higher: 94.7%; Bachelor's degree or higher: 33.1%; Graduate/professional degree or higher: 13.0%

School District(s)
Yorktown Community Schools (KG-12)
    2012-13 Enrollment: 2,309 . . . . (765) 759-2720
Housing: Homeownership rate: 80.8%; Median home value: $125,000; Median year structure built: 1971; Homeowner vacancy rate: 3.2%; Median gross rent: $710 per month; Rental vacancy rate: 8.8%

Health Insurance: 93.5% have insurance; 78.0% have private insurance; 32.5% have public insurance; 6.5% do not have insurance; 2.1% of children under 18 do not have insurance
Transportation: Commute: 94.6% car, 0.0% public transportation, 0.5% walk, 3.6% work from home; Median travel time to work: 19.5 minutes
Additional Information Contacts
Town of Yorktown .... (765) 759-4002
http://www.yorktownindiana.org

Dubois County

Located in southwestern Indiana; bounded on the north by the East Fork of the White River; drained by the Patoka River. Covers a land area of 427.269 square miles, a water area of 8.064 square miles, and is located in the Eastern Time Zone at 38.37° N. Lat., 86.87° W. Long. The county was founded in 1817. County seat is Jasper.

Dubois County is part of the Jasper, IN Micropolitan Statistical Area. The entire metro area includes: Dubois County, IN; Pike County, IN

Weather Station: Dubois S Ind Forage Frm   Elevation: 689 feet

	Jan	Feb	Mar	Apr	May	Jun	Jul	Aug	Sep	Oct	Nov	Dec
High	40	44	54	65	75	83	86	86	79	68	56	43
Low	22	24	33	43	53	62	65	64	56	44	36	25
Precip	3.3	3.0	4.2	4.6	5.8	4.3	4.3	3.2	3.9	3.7	4.0	3.7
Snow	2.4	2.7	1.6	tr	0.0	0.0	0.0	0.0	0.0	0.2	tr	2.3

High and Low temperatures in degrees Fahrenheit; Precipitation and Snow in inches

Population: 41,889; Growth (since 2000): 5.6%; Density: 98.0 persons per square mile; Race: 95.1% White, 0.3% Black/African American, 0.5% Asian, 0.2% American Indian/Alaska Native, 0.0% Native Hawaiian/Other Pacific Islander, 0.9% two or more races, 6.0% Hispanic of any race; Average household size: 2.54; Median age: 39.9; Age under 18: 25.5%; Age 65 and over: 14.5%; Males per 100 females: 97.0; Marriage status: 23.5% never married, 60.2% now married, 1.2% separated, 6.4% widowed, 9.8% divorced; Foreign born: 3.6%; Speak English only: 92.1%; With disability: 9.3%; Veterans: 10.1%; Ancestry: 56.3% German, 10.8% American, 7.3% Irish, 6.4% English, 1.8% French
Religion: Six largest groups: 52.5% Catholicism, 5.8% Lutheran, 4.2% Baptist, 4.0% Methodist/Pietist, 3.7% Presbyterian-Reformed, 1.9% Non-denominational Protestant
Economy: Unemployment rate: 3.8%; Leading industries: 17.0% retail trade; 11.3% construction; 9.9% health care and social assistance; Farms: 720 totaling 174,877 acres; Company size: 1 employs 1,000 or more persons, 8 employ 500 to 999 persons, 33 employ 100 to 499 persons, 1,227 employ less than 100 persons; Business ownership: 939 women-owned, n/a Black-owned, n/a Hispanic-owned, n/a Asian-owned
Employment: 12.1% management, business, and financial, 3.2% computer, engineering, and science, 6.8% education, legal, community service, arts, and media, 5.7% healthcare practitioners, 12.4% service, 24.3% sales and office, 9.0% natural resources, construction, and maintenance, 26.5% production, transportation, and material moving
Income: Per capita: $25,589; Median household: $54,780; Average household: $65,584; Households with income of $100,000 or more: 16.3%; Poverty rate: 8.3%
Educational Attainment: High school diploma or higher: 86.9%; Bachelor's degree or higher: 18.9%; Graduate/professional degree or higher: 6.8%
Housing: Homeownership rate: 76.9%; Median home value: $133,200; Median year structure built: 1976; Homeowner vacancy rate: 1.9%; Median gross rent: $626 per month; Rental vacancy rate: 5.9%
Vital Statistics: Birth rate: 119.0 per 10,000 population; Death rate: 89.9 per 10,000 population; Age-adjusted cancer mortality rate: 192.2 deaths per 100,000 population
Health Insurance: 91.0% have insurance; 79.3% have private insurance; 23.7% have public insurance; 9.0% do not have insurance; 6.5% of children under 18 do not have insurance
Health Care: Physicians: 19.7 per 10,000 population; Hospital beds: 32.0 per 10,000 population; Hospital admissions: 1,632.4 per 10,000 population
Air Quality Index: 59.2% good, 40.8% moderate, 0.0% unhealthy for sensitive individuals, 0.0% unhealthy (percent of days)
Transportation: Commute: 93.1% car, 0.2% public transportation, 2.1% walk, 4.0% work from home; Median travel time to work: 19.8 minutes
Presidential Election: 35.2% Obama, 62.9% Romney (2012)
National and State Parks: Lick Fork State Recreation Area
Additional Information Contacts

Dubois Government .... (812) 481-7000
http://www.duboiscountyin.org

Dubois County Communities

BIRDSEYE (town).
Covers a land area of 0.637 square miles and a water area of <.001 square miles. Located at 38.31° N. Lat; 86.70° W. Long. Elevation is 722 feet.
History: Laid out 1880.
Population: 416; Growth (since 2000): -10.5%; Density: 652.7 persons per square mile; Race: 98.8% White, 0.5% Black/African American, 0.0% Asian, 0.0% American Indian/Alaska Native, 0.0% Native Hawaiian/Other Pacific Islander, 0.7% Two or more races, 0.5% Hispanic of any race; Average household size: 2.40; Median age: 38.0; Age under 18: 26.9%; Age 65 and over: 14.9%; Males per 100 females: 88.2
School District(s)
Southeast Dubois County Sch Corp (PK-12)
　2012-13 Enrollment: 1,385 .... (812) 367-1653
Housing: Homeownership rate: 60.7%; Homeowner vacancy rate: 2.7%; Rental vacancy rate: 8.0%

CELESTINE (unincorporated postal area)
ZCTA: 47521
　Covers a land area of 18.851 square miles and a water area of 3.197 square miles. Located at 38.40° N. Lat; 86.72° W. Long. Elevation is 594 feet.
Population: 927; Growth (since 2000): 16.3%; Density: 49.2 persons per square mile; Race: 98.8% White, 0.2% Black/African American, 0.0% Asian, 0.0% American Indian/Alaska Native, 0.0% Native Hawaiian/Other Pacific Islander, 0.5% Two or more races, 0.5% Hispanic of any race; Average household size: 2.91; Median age: 35.0; Age under 18: 30.4%; Age 65 and over: 10.2%; Males per 100 females: 97.7
School District(s)
Northeast Dubois County Sch Corp (PK-12)
　2012-13 Enrollment: 1,017 .... (812) 678-2781
Housing: Homeownership rate: 90.2%; Homeowner vacancy rate: 0.7%; Rental vacancy rate: 0.0%

DUBOIS (CDP).
Covers a land area of 1.573 square miles and a water area of 0.025 square miles. Located at 38.45° N. Lat; 86.80° W. Long. Elevation is 505 feet.
Population: 488; Growth (since 2000): n/a; Density: 310.3 persons per square mile; Race: 98.2% White, 0.2% Black/African American, 0.0% Asian, 0.2% American Indian/Alaska Native, 0.0% Native Hawaiian/Other Pacific Islander, 0.0% Two or more races, 2.5% Hispanic of any race; Average household size: 2.50; Median age: 35.4; Age under 18: 28.9%; Age 65 and over: 15.0%; Males per 100 females: 103.3
School District(s)
Northeast Dubois County Sch Corp (PK-12)
　2012-13 Enrollment: 1,017 .... (812) 678-2781
Housing: Homeownership rate: 77.5%; Homeowner vacancy rate: 0.7%; Rental vacancy rate: 25.0%

FERDINAND (town).
Covers a land area of 2.271 square miles and a water area of 0.038 square miles. Located at 38.23° N. Lat; 86.86° W. Long. Elevation is 538 feet.
History: Ferdinand was settled by German Catholics. It was the southern terminus of the Ferdinand Railroad, the shortest steam line in Indiana, with one locomotive making the eight-mile trip north to Huntingburg twice a day.
Population: 2,157; Growth (since 2000): -5.3%; Density: 949.7 persons per square mile; Race: 98.2% White, 0.1% Black/African American, 0.2% Asian, 0.0% American Indian/Alaska Native, 0.0% Native Hawaiian/Other Pacific Islander, 1.0% Two or more races, 1.6% Hispanic of any race; Average household size: 2.38; Median age: 45.1; Age under 18: 21.0%; Age 65 and over: 25.2%; Males per 100 females: 80.1
School District(s)
North Spencer County Sch Corp (PK-12)
　2012-13 Enrollment: 1,940 .... (812) 937-2400
Southeast Dubois County Sch Corp (PK-12)
　2012-13 Enrollment: 1,385 .... (812) 367-1653
Housing: Homeownership rate: 75.9%; Homeowner vacancy rate: 1.3%; Rental vacancy rate: 3.4%
Newspapers: Ferdinand News (weekly circulation 3100)
Additional Information Contacts

Town of Ferdinand .... (812) 367-2280
http://www.ferdinandindiana.org

HOLLAND (town). Covers a land area of 0.315 square miles and a water area of 0.001 square miles. Located at 38.25° N. Lat; 87.04° W. Long. Elevation is 528 feet.
Population: 626; Growth (since 2000): -9.9%; Density: 1,990.2 persons per square mile; Race: 96.0% White, 0.2% Black/African American, 0.3% Asian, 0.6% American Indian/Alaska Native, 0.2% Native Hawaiian/Other Pacific Islander, 0.5% Two or more races, 3.7% Hispanic of any race; Average household size: 2.48; Median age: 37.9; Age under 18: 26.0%; Age 65 and over: 16.6%; Males per 100 females: 93.2
School District(s)
Southwest Dubois County Sch Corp (KG-12)
    2012-13 Enrollment: 1,740 .... (812) 683-3971
Housing: Homeownership rate: 77.8%; Homeowner vacancy rate: 5.3%; Rental vacancy rate: 3.4%

HUNTINGBURG (city). Covers a land area of 5.061 square miles and a water area of 0.213 square miles. Located at 38.30° N. Lat; 86.96° W. Long. Elevation is 489 feet.
History: Huntingburg, settled by German immigrants, developed around clay mines and poettery works.
Population: 6,057; Growth (since 2000): 8.2%; Density: 1,196.7 persons per square mile; Race: 87.3% White, 0.5% Black/African American, 0.3% Asian, 0.2% American Indian/Alaska Native, 0.0% Native Hawaiian/Other Pacific Islander, 1.8% Two or more races, 18.5% Hispanic of any race; Average household size: 2.55; Median age: 35.1; Age under 18: 27.9%; Age 65 and over: 13.5%; Males per 100 females: 91.2; Marriage status: 25.2% never married, 57.5% now married, 2.4% separated, 7.6% widowed, 9.7% divorced; Foreign born: 13.4%; Speak English only: 81.3%; With disability: 12.7%; Veterans: 10.4%; Ancestry: 40.9% German, 10.4% American, 8.1% English, 7.4% Irish, 1.4% French Canadian
Employment: 9.4% management, business, and financial, 3.5% computer, engineering, and science, 4.6% education, legal, community service, arts, and media, 8.2% healthcare practitioners, 15.6% service, 18.5% sales and office, 7.3% natural resources, construction, and maintenance, 32.9% production, transportation, and material moving
Income: Per capita: $18,813; Median household: $42,903; Average household: $51,236; Households with income of $100,000 or more: 9.6%; Poverty rate: 21.6%
Educational Attainment: High school diploma or higher: 73.3%; Bachelor's degree or higher: 14.1%; Graduate/professional degree or higher: 4.2%
School District(s)
Southeast Dubois County Sch Corp (PK-12)
    2012-13 Enrollment: 1,385 .... (812) 367-1653
Southwest Dubois County Sch Corp (KG-12)
    2012-13 Enrollment: 1,740 .... (812) 683-3971
Housing: Homeownership rate: 65.9%; Median home value: $107,900; Median year structure built: 1962; Homeowner vacancy rate: 2.6%; Median gross rent: $589 per month; Rental vacancy rate: 5.7%
Health Insurance: 79.4% have insurance; 55.5% have private insurance; 34.0% have public insurance; 20.6% do not have insurance; 12.1% of children under 18 do not have insurance
Newspapers: Huntingburg Press (weekly circulation 2000)
Transportation: Commute: 90.8% car, 1.2% public transportation, 2.0% walk, 5.4% work from home; Median travel time to work: 22.2 minutes
Airports: Huntingburg (general aviation)
Additional Information Contacts
City of Huntingburg .... (812) 683-2211
http://www.huntingburg-in.gov

JASPER (city). County seat. Covers a land area of 13.105 square miles and a water area of 0.091 square miles. Located at 38.39° N. Lat; 86.94° W. Long. Elevation is 466 feet.
History: Jasper was settled by German Catholics in 1838, on a site where a town had been founded about 20 years earlier. An early industry was desk manufacturing.
Population: 15,038; Growth (since 2000): 24.3%; Density: 1,147.5 persons per square mile; Race: 93.6% White, 0.4% Black/African American, 0.9% Asian, 0.2% American Indian/Alaska Native, 0.0% Native Hawaiian/Other Pacific Islander, 0.9% Two or more races, 7.7% Hispanic of any race; Average household size: 2.41; Median age: 39.3; Age under 18: 24.9%; Age 65 and over: 15.6%; Males per 100 females: 96.7;
Marriage status: 25.3% never married, 55.1% now married, 1.5% separated, 7.0% widowed, 12.7% divorced; Foreign born: 4.2%; Speak English only: 89.3%; With disability: 7.6%; Veterans: 10.3%; Ancestry: 48.4% German, 9.9% Irish, 9.9% American, 6.3% English, 2.6% Italian
Employment: 11.9% management, business, and financial, 3.2% computer, engineering, and science, 9.0% education, legal, community service, arts, and media, 4.6% healthcare practitioners, 11.9% service, 29.4% sales and office, 5.3% natural resources, construction, and maintenance, 24.5% production, transportation, and material moving
Income: Per capita: $28,540; Median household: $53,968; Average household: $68,905; Households with income of $100,000 or more: 16.1%; Poverty rate: 7.6%
Educational Attainment: High school diploma or higher: 87.1%; Bachelor's degree or higher: 21.7%; Graduate/professional degree or higher: 6.7%
School District(s)
Greater Jasper Con Schs (PK-12)
    2012-13 Enrollment: 3,274 .... (812) 482-1801
Housing: Homeownership rate: 67.3%; Median home value: $128,600; Median year structure built: 1978; Homeowner vacancy rate: 2.6%; Median gross rent: $638 per month; Rental vacancy rate: 6.2%
Health Insurance: 92.5% have insurance; 82.2% have private insurance; 24.1% have public insurance; 7.5% do not have insurance; 5.0% of children under 18 do not have insurance
Hospitals: Memorial Hospital & Health Care Center (131 beds)
Safety: Violent crime rate: 31.6 per 10,000 population; Property crime rate: 88.8 per 10,000 population
Newspapers: The Herald (daily circulation 12600)
Transportation: Commute: 93.5% car, 0.0% public transportation, 1.8% walk, 3.9% work from home; Median travel time to work: 16.5 minutes
Additional Information Contacts
City of Jasper .... (812) 482-6944
http://www.jasperindiana.gov

SAINT ANTHONY (unincorporated postal area)
ZCTA: 47575
    Covers a land area of 21.176 square miles and a water area of 0.180 square miles. Located at 38.32° N. Lat; 86.80° W. Long. Elevation is 545 feet.
    Population: 976; Growth (since 2000): 0.6%; Density: 46.1 persons per square mile; Race: 98.6% White, 0.4% Black/African American, 0.0% Asian, 0.0% American Indian/Alaska Native, 0.0% Native Hawaiian/Other Pacific Islander, 0.5% Two or more races, 0.7% Hispanic of any race; Average household size: 2.59; Median age: 40.6; Age under 18: 24.9%; Age 65 and over: 11.6%; Males per 100 females: 98.0
    Housing: Homeownership rate: 90.5%; Homeowner vacancy rate: 1.4%; Rental vacancy rate: 5.1%

SCHNELLVILLE (unincorporated postal area)
ZCTA: 47580
    Covers a land area of 5.015 square miles and a water area of 0.013 square miles. Located at 38.36° N. Lat; 86.77° W. Long. Elevation is 653 feet.
    Population: 289; Growth (since 2000): 70.0%; Density: 57.6 persons per square mile; Race: 99.0% White, 0.3% Black/African American, 0.3% Asian, 0.0% American Indian/Alaska Native, 0.0% Native Hawaiian/Other Pacific Islander, 0.3% Two or more races, 0.0% Hispanic of any race; Average household size: 2.81; Median age: 32.8; Age under 18: 28.0%; Age 65 and over: 8.3%; Males per 100 females: 112.5
    Housing: Homeownership rate: 89.3%; Homeowner vacancy rate: 1.1%; Rental vacancy rate: 0.0%

Elkhart County

Located in northern Indiana; bounded on the north by Michigan; drained by the Elkhart and Saint Joseph Rivers. Covers a land area of 463.170 square miles, a water area of 4.800 square miles, and is located in the Eastern Time Zone at 41.60° N. Lat., 85.86° W. Long. The county was founded in 1830. County seat is Goshen.

Elkhart County is part of the Elkhart-Goshen, IN Metropolitan Statistical Area. The entire metro area includes: Elkhart County, IN

Weather Station: Goshen College   Elevation: 875 feet

	Jan	Feb	Mar	Apr	May	Jun	Jul	Aug	Sep	Oct	Nov	Dec
High	32	36	47	61	72	81	84	82	75	63	49	36
Low	18	21	29	39	49	59	63	61	54	43	34	23
Precip	2.2	2.1	2.5	3.5	3.9	4.0	4.3	4.2	3.5	3.2	3.0	2.7
Snow	10.9	9.0	5.0	1.3	tr	0.0	0.0	0.0	0.0	0.4	3.1	10.6

High and Low temperatures in degrees Fahrenheit; Precipitation and Snow in inches

Population: 197,559; Growth (since 2000): 8.1%; Density: 426.5 persons per square mile; Race: 82.9% White, 5.7% Black/African American, 1.0% Asian, 0.4% American Indian/Alaska Native, 0.0% Native Hawaiian/Other Pacific Islander, 2.5% two or more races, 14.1% Hispanic of any race; Average household size: 2.76; Median age: 34.9; Age under 18: 28.4%; Age 65 and over: 12.1%; Males per 100 females: 97.4%; Marriage status: 28.1% never married, 55.1% now married, 1.7% separated, 5.5% widowed, 11.3% divorced; Foreign born: 8.5%; Speak English only: 81.9%; With disability: 12.5%; Veterans: 7.9%; Ancestry: 25.2% German, 10.9% American, 9.2% Irish, 6.0% English, 2.8% Dutch
Religion: Six largest groups: 10.4% European Free-Church, 6.9% Non-denominational Protestant, 6.3% Holiness, 5.4% Catholicism, 4.8% Methodist/Pietist, 2.3% Baptist
Economy: Unemployment rate: 4.8%; Leading industries: 16.4% manufacturing; 13.8% retail trade; 11.2% other services (except public administration); Farms: 1,724 totaling 172,847 acres; Company size: 8 employ 1,000 or more persons, 14 employ 500 to 999 persons, 191 employs 100 to 499 persons, 4,636 employ less than 100 persons; Business ownership: 3,639 women-owned, 398 Black-owned, 317 Hispanic-owned, 308 Asian-owned
Employment: 11.1% management, business, and financial, 2.8% computer, engineering, and science, 7.0% education, legal, community service, arts, and media, 4.2% healthcare practitioners, 14.7% service, 23.0% sales and office, 7.2% natural resources, construction, and maintenance, 30.2% production, transportation, and material moving
Income: Per capita: $21,109; Median household: $45,693; Average household: $58,065; Households with income of $100,000 or more: 12.7%; Poverty rate: 16.7%
Educational Attainment: High school diploma or higher: 80.5%; Bachelor's degree or higher: 18.2%; Graduate/professional degree or higher: 5.9%
Housing: Homeownership rate: 70.1%; Median home value: $121,700; Median year structure built: 1975; Homeowner vacancy rate: 2.7%; Median gross rent: $708 per month; Rental vacancy rate: 13.3%
Vital Statistics: Birth rate: 146.4 per 10,000 population; Death rate: 75.9 per 10,000 population; Age-adjusted cancer mortality rate: 188.8 deaths per 100,000 population
Health Insurance: 79.6% have insurance; 60.2% have private insurance; 29.9% have public insurance; 20.4% do not have insurance; 15.8% of children under 18 do not have insurance
Health Care: Physicians: 13.8 per 10,000 population; Hospital beds: 22.3 per 10,000 population; Hospital admissions: 956.5 per 10,000 population
Air Quality Index: 57.1% good, 42.0% moderate, 0.9% unhealthy for sensitive individuals, 0.0% unhealthy (percent of days)
Transportation: Commute: 92.2% car, 0.5% public transportation, 1.8% walk, 2.3% work from home; Median travel time to work: 19.4 minutes
Presidential Election: 36.0% Obama, 62.5% Romney (2012)
Additional Information Contacts
Elkhart Government .... (574) 535-6743
http://www.elkhartcountyindiana.com

Elkhart County Communities

BRISTOL (town). Covers a land area of 3.694 square miles and a water area of 0.130 square miles. Located at 41.72° N. Lat; 85.83° W. Long. Elevation is 774 feet.
Population: 1,602; Growth (since 2000): 15.9%; Density: 433.7 persons per square mile; Race: 87.9% White, 2.1% Black/African American, 1.5% Asian, 0.7% American Indian/Alaska Native, 0.0% Native Hawaiian/Other Pacific Islander, 3.1% Two or more races, 10.2% Hispanic of any race; Average household size: 2.62; Median age: 36.4; Age under 18: 27.0%; Age 65 and over: 14.4%; Males per 100 females: 98.5
School District(s)
Elkhart Community Schools (KG-12)
    2012-13 Enrollment: 13,108 .... (574) 262-5516
Middlebury Community Schools (KG-12)
    2012-13 Enrollment: 4,367 .... (574) 825-9425

Housing: Homeownership rate: 69.9%; Homeowner vacancy rate: 2.7%; Rental vacancy rate: 28.6%

DUNLAP (CDP). Covers a land area of 4.900 square miles and a water area of 0.010 square miles. Located at 41.63° N. Lat; 85.92° W. Long. Elevation is 778 feet.
Population: 6,235; Growth (since 2000): 5.9%; Density: 1,272.3 persons per square mile; Race: 86.3% White, 4.0% Black/African American, 1.3% Asian, 0.2% American Indian/Alaska Native, 0.0% Native Hawaiian/Other Pacific Islander, 2.1% Two or more races, 10.6% Hispanic of any race; Average household size: 2.86; Median age: 38.4; Age under 18: 27.7%; Age 65 and over: 13.0%; Males per 100 females: 97.1; Marriage status: 23.3% never married, 64.5% now married, 2.2% separated, 4.0% widowed, 8.2% divorced; Foreign born: 5.9%; Speak English only: 90.1%; With disability: 10.7%; Veterans: 9.0%; Ancestry: 30.9% German, 10.8% Irish, 8.8% American, 7.4% English, 5.8% Polish
Employment: 13.5% management, business, and financial, 4.1% computer, engineering, and science, 8.0% education, legal, community service, arts, and media, 5.3% healthcare practitioners, 11.3% service, 23.3% sales and office, 6.7% natural resources, construction, and maintenance, 27.8% production, transportation, and material moving
Income: Per capita: $22,914; Median household: $56,301; Average household: $66,581; Households with income of $100,000 or more: 18.6%; Poverty rate: 13.2%
Educational Attainment: High school diploma or higher: 84.4%; Bachelor's degree or higher: 21.1%; Graduate/professional degree or higher: 8.1%
Housing: Homeownership rate: 89.8%; Median home value: $125,000; Median year structure built: 1976; Homeowner vacancy rate: 1.9%; Median gross rent: $946 per month; Rental vacancy rate: 6.3%
Health Insurance: 80.4% have insurance; 66.7% have private insurance; 24.8% have public insurance; 19.6% do not have insurance; 14.8% of children under 18 do not have insurance
Transportation: Commute: 98.0% car, 0.0% public transportation, 0.4% walk, 1.6% work from home; Median travel time to work: 18.6 minutes

ELKHART (city). Covers a land area of 23.453 square miles and a water area of 0.967 square miles. Located at 41.69° N. Lat; 85.97° W. Long. Elevation is 751 feet.
History: Elkhart was named for an island, thought by some to be shaped like an elk's heart, at the place where two rivers meet. The town was platted in 1832 by Dr. Havilah Beardsley. Elkhart grew when the Michigan Southern Railway Company built its shops here in 1870. It was incorporated in 1873. The musical instrument company begun here in 1875 by Charles G. Conn became the largest band instrument manufacturer in the world.
Population: 50,949; Growth (since 2000): -1.8%; Density: 2,172.4 persons per square mile; Race: 66.1% White, 15.4% Black/African American, 0.9% Asian, 0.6% American Indian/Alaska Native, 0.1% Native Hawaiian/Other Pacific Islander, 4.1% Two or more races, 22.5% Hispanic of any race; Average household size: 2.60; Median age: 32.7; Age under 18: 29.1%; Age 65 and over: 11.5%; Males per 100 females: 93.0; Marriage status: 36.1% never married, 43.1% now married, 2.4% separated, 6.2% widowed, 14.6% divorced; Foreign born: 13.9%; Speak English only: 76.8%; With disability: 14.6%; Veterans: 8.6%; Ancestry: 17.8% German, 9.3% American, 8.1% Irish, 5.3% English, 3.4% Italian
Employment: 7.4% management, business, and financial, 2.7% computer, engineering, and science, 6.3% education, legal, community service, arts, and media, 2.9% healthcare practitioners, 17.7% service, 18.6% sales and office, 5.3% natural resources, construction, and maintenance, 39.1% production, transportation, and material moving
Income: Per capita: $16,770; Median household: $34,443; Average household: $43,008; Households with income of $100,000 or more: 5.5%; Poverty rate: 28.5%
Educational Attainment: High school diploma or higher: 75.5%; Bachelor's degree or higher: 14.0%; Graduate/professional degree or higher: 4.6%
School District(s)
Baugo Community Schools (KG-12)
    2012-13 Enrollment: 1,952 .... (574) 293-8583
Concord Community Schools (KG-12)
    2012-13 Enrollment: 4,975 .... (574) 875-5161
Elkhart Community Schools (KG-12)
    2012-13 Enrollment: 13,108 .... (574) 262-5516

Four-year College(s)
Anabaptist Mennonite Biblical Seminary (Private, Not-for-profit, Mennonite Church)
    Fall 2013 Enrollment: 101 . . . . (574) 295-3726
Housing: Homeownership rate: 50.8%; Median home value: $85,900; Median year structure built: 1960; Homeowner vacancy rate: 3.9%; Median gross rent: $671 per month; Rental vacancy rate: 15.8%
Health Insurance: 75.7% have insurance; 47.1% have private insurance; 39.0% have public insurance; 24.3% do not have insurance; 12.6% of children under 18 do not have insurance
Hospitals: Elkhart General Hospital (365 beds)
Newspapers: Elkhart Truth (daily circulation 29000)
Transportation: Commute: 91.9% car, 1.4% public transportation, 1.9% walk, 0.7% work from home; Median travel time to work: 19.7 minutes; Amtrak: Train service available.
Airports: Elkhart Municipal (general aviation)
Additional Information Contacts
City of Elkhart . . . . (574) 522-5272
    http://www.elkhartindiana.org

GOSHEN (city). County seat. Covers a land area of 16.229 square miles and a water area of 0.355 square miles. Located at 41.57° N. Lat; 85.83° W. Long. Elevation is 801 feet.
History: Goshen was established by Mennonite settlers, who in 1894 founded Elkhart Academy which became Goshen College.
Population: 31,719; Growth (since 2000): 8.0%; Density: 1,954.4 persons per square mile; Race: 78.2% White, 2.6% Black/African American, 1.2% Asian, 0.5% American Indian/Alaska Native, 0.0% Native Hawaiian/Other Pacific Islander, 2.7% Two or more races, 28.1% Hispanic of any race; Average household size: 2.67; Median age: 32.4; Age under 18: 27.4%; Age 65 and over: 14.9%; Males per 100 females: 95.5; Marriage status: 28.6% never married, 52.3% now married, 1.9% separated, 7.1% widowed, 12.0% divorced; Foreign born: 15.8%; Speak English only: 72.7%; With disability: 12.5%; Veterans: 6.7%; Ancestry: 23.2% German, 9.6% American, 7.9% Irish, 5.6% English, 3.8% Swiss
Employment: 8.2% management, business, and financial, 2.5% computer, engineering, and science, 9.7% education, legal, community service, arts, and media, 3.8% healthcare practitioners, 16.0% service, 20.4% sales and office, 10.9% natural resources, construction, and maintenance, 28.5% production, transportation, and material moving
Income: Per capita: $19,369; Median household: $41,579; Average household: $50,917; Households with income of $100,000 or more: 9.0%; Poverty rate: 20.8%
Educational Attainment: High school diploma or higher: 77.2%; Bachelor's degree or higher: 21.1%; Graduate/professional degree or higher: 7.8%
School District(s)
Fairfield Community Schools (KG-12)
    2012-13 Enrollment: 2,063 . . . . (574) 831-2188
Goshen Community Schools (KG-12)
    2012-13 Enrollment: 6,524 . . . . (574) 533-8631
Middlebury Community Schools (KG-12)
    2012-13 Enrollment: 4,367 . . . . (574) 825-9425
Four-year College(s)
Goshen College (Private, Not-for-profit, Mennonite Church)
    Fall 2013 Enrollment: 888 . . . . (574) 535-7000
    2013-14 Tuition: In-state $28,500; Out-of-state $28,500
Housing: Homeownership rate: 58.6%; Median home value: $107,800; Median year structure built: 1978; Homeowner vacancy rate: 3.7%; Median gross rent: $734 per month; Rental vacancy rate: 11.6%
Health Insurance: 78.5% have insurance; 56.8% have private insurance; 33.9% have public insurance; 21.5% do not have insurance; 13.5% of children under 18 do not have insurance
Hospitals: IU Health Goshen Hospital (115 beds)
Safety: Violent crime rate: 9.3 per 10,000 population; Property crime rate: 341.0 per 10,000 population
Newspapers: Goshen News (daily circulation 16100)
Transportation: Commute: 90.2% car, 0.9% public transportation, 4.3% walk, 2.0% work from home; Median travel time to work: 17.4 minutes
Airports: Goshen Municipal (general aviation)
Additional Information Contacts
City of Goshen . . . . (574) 533-8625
    http://www.goshenindiana.org

MIDDLEBURY (town). Covers a land area of 3.755 square miles and a water area of 0.022 square miles. Located at 41.67° N. Lat; 85.71° W. Long. Elevation is 837 feet.
History: Laid out 1835.
Population: 3,420; Growth (since 2000): 15.7%; Density: 910.7 persons per square mile; Race: 95.6% White, 0.6% Black/African American, 1.2% Asian, 0.1% American Indian/Alaska Native, 0.0% Native Hawaiian/Other Pacific Islander, 1.5% Two or more races, 3.2% Hispanic of any race; Average household size: 2.70; Median age: 36.7; Age under 18: 29.0%; Age 65 and over: 13.5%; Males per 100 females: 94.6; Marriage status: 21.4% never married, 64.4% now married, 0.7% separated, 5.0% widowed, 9.2% divorced; Foreign born: 0.7%; Speak English only: 93.2%; With disability: 10.0%; Veterans: 3.5%; Ancestry: 37.4% German, 15.2% Irish, 8.2% American, 7.3% English, 4.0% Dutch
Employment: 9.8% management, business, and financial, 2.7% computer, engineering, and science, 13.5% education, legal, community service, arts, and media, 0.3% healthcare practitioners, 14.1% service, 27.7% sales and office, 8.2% natural resources, construction, and maintenance, 23.6% production, transportation, and material moving
Income: Per capita: $28,231; Median household: $55,118; Average household: $78,291; Households with income of $100,000 or more: 15.0%; Poverty rate: 9.7%
Educational Attainment: High school diploma or higher: 88.2%; Bachelor's degree or higher: 20.4%; Graduate/professional degree or higher: 8.8%
School District(s)
Middlebury Community Schools (KG-12)
    2012-13 Enrollment: 4,367 . . . . (574) 825-9425
Housing: Homeownership rate: 70.9%; Median home value: $125,000; Median year structure built: 1990; Homeowner vacancy rate: 4.4%; Median gross rent: $823 per month; Rental vacancy rate: 4.2%
Health Insurance: 90.2% have insurance; 78.1% have private insurance; 36.6% have public insurance; 9.8% do not have insurance; 14.5% of children under 18 do not have insurance
Transportation: Commute: 93.8% car, 0.0% public transportation, 3.3% walk, 2.5% work from home; Median travel time to work: 16.6 minutes
Additional Information Contacts
Town of Middlebury . . . . (574) 825-1499
    http://www.middleburyin.org/publishsite/index.cfm

MILLERSBURG (town). Covers a land area of 0.544 square miles and a water area of 0 square miles. Located at 41.53° N. Lat; 85.70° W. Long. Elevation is 886 feet.
History: Laid out 1855.
Population: 903; Growth (since 2000): 4.0%; Density: 1,660.0 persons per square mile; Race: 97.0% White, 0.6% Black/African American, 0.0% Asian, 0.9% American Indian/Alaska Native, 0.0% Native Hawaiian/Other Pacific Islander, 0.4% Two or more races, 4.4% Hispanic of any race; Average household size: 2.79; Median age: 33.1; Age under 18: 30.1%; Age 65 and over: 9.2%; Males per 100 females: 104.3
School District(s)
Fairfield Community Schools (KG-12)
    2012-13 Enrollment: 2,063 . . . . (574) 831-2188
Housing: Homeownership rate: 71.3%; Homeowner vacancy rate: 2.9%; Rental vacancy rate: 6.1%

NAPPANEE (city). Covers a land area of 4.149 square miles and a water area of 0 square miles. Located at 41.45° N. Lat; 86.00° W. Long. Elevation is 876 feet.
History: Nappanee grew up along the Baltimore & Ohio Railroad. Furniture manufacturing was an early industry in Nappanee, which was platted in 1874.
Population: 6,648; Growth (since 2000): -0.9%; Density: 1,602.5 persons per square mile; Race: 94.8% White, 0.7% Black/African American, 0.2% Asian, 0.3% American Indian/Alaska Native, 0.1% Native Hawaiian/Other Pacific Islander, 1.5% Two or more races, 6.2% Hispanic of any race; Average household size: 2.60; Median age: 34.8; Age under 18: 27.9%; Age 65 and over: 12.5%; Males per 100 females: 95.5; Marriage status: 21.1% never married, 64.3% now married, 1.8% separated, 4.6% widowed, 10.0% divorced; Foreign born: 1.6%; Speak English only: 91.6%; With disability: 9.9%; Veterans: 6.9%; Ancestry: 39.7% German, 11.4% American, 10.6% Irish, 5.8% English, 4.0% French
Employment: 8.9% management, business, and financial, 2.1% computer, engineering, and science, 6.3% education, legal, community service, arts, and media, 2.4% healthcare practitioners, 14.9% service, 29.3% sales and

office, 7.3% natural resources, construction, and maintenance, 28.8% production, transportation, and material moving
Income: Per capita: $19,498; Median household: $45,813; Average household: $53,935; Households with income of $100,000 or more: 9.9%; Poverty rate: 13.7%
Educational Attainment: High school diploma or higher: 83.6%; Bachelor's degree or higher: 16.7%; Graduate/professional degree or higher: 4.7%

School District(s)
Wa-Nee Community Schools (KG-12)
   2012-13 Enrollment: 3,084 . . . . (574) 773-3131
Housing: Homeownership rate: 64.0%; Median home value: $129,900; Median year structure built: 1976; Homeowner vacancy rate: 3.5%; Median gross rent: $630 per month; Rental vacancy rate: 15.4%
Health Insurance: 83.6% have insurance; 66.1% have private insurance; 29.2% have public insurance; 16.4% do not have insurance; 9.4% of children under 18 do not have insurance
Safety: Violent crime rate: 4.5 per 10,000 population; Property crime rate: 168.8 per 10,000 population
Transportation: Commute: 95.9% car, 0.0% public transportation, 2.1% walk, 1.5% work from home; Median travel time to work: 21.3 minutes
Additional Information Contacts
City of Nappanee. . . . . (574) 773-2112
   http://www.nappanee.org

NEW PARIS (CDP).
Covers a land area of 1.333 square miles and a water area of 0 square miles. Located at 41.50° N. Lat; 85.82° W. Long. Elevation is 820 feet.
History: Laid out 1838.
Population: 1,494; Growth (since 2000): 48.5%; Density: 1,121.1 persons per square mile; Race: 98.1% White, 0.1% Black/African American, 0.1% Asian, 0.2% American Indian/Alaska Native, 0.0% Native Hawaiian/Other Pacific Islander, 0.7% Two or more races, 3.2% Hispanic of any race; Average household size: 2.83; Median age: 32.4; Age under 18: 30.3%; Age 65 and over: 9.8%; Males per 100 females: 99.2

School District(s)
Fairfield Community Schools (KG-12)
   2012-13 Enrollment: 2,063 . . . . (574) 831-2188
Housing: Homeownership rate: 78.3%; Homeowner vacancy rate: 0.7%; Rental vacancy rate: 7.3%

SIMONTON LAKE (CDP).
Covers a land area of 3.564 square miles and a water area of 0.471 square miles. Located at 41.75° N. Lat; 85.97° W. Long. Elevation is 784 feet.
Population: 4,678; Growth (since 2000): 15.4%; Density: 1,312.7 persons per square mile; Race: 87.8% White, 4.9% Black/African American, 2.8% Asian, 0.3% American Indian/Alaska Native, 0.0% Native Hawaiian/Other Pacific Islander, 2.6% Two or more races, 4.7% Hispanic of any race; Average household size: 2.52; Median age: 41.1; Age under 18: 23.5%; Age 65 and over: 14.4%; Males per 100 females: 96.7; Marriage status: 28.4% never married, 49.5% now married, 0.4% separated, 8.8% widowed, 13.3% divorced; Foreign born: 2.7%; Speak English only: 92.9%; With disability: 16.9%; Veterans: 9.8%; Ancestry: 37.3% German, 12.8% Irish, 10.5% English, 8.1% American, 5.1% Hungarian
Employment: 14.9% management, business, and financial, 2.6% computer, engineering, and science, 7.3% education, legal, community service, arts, and media, 6.5% healthcare practitioners, 15.7% service, 25.9% sales and office, 5.9% natural resources, construction, and maintenance, 21.2% production, transportation, and material moving
Income: Per capita: $25,618; Median household: $49,583; Average household: $60,902; Households with income of $100,000 or more: 13.8%; Poverty rate: 13.2%
Educational Attainment: High school diploma or higher: 91.8%; Bachelor's degree or higher: 23.1%; Graduate/professional degree or higher: 6.3%
Housing: Homeownership rate: 75.5%; Median home value: $141,600; Median year structure built: 1977; Homeowner vacancy rate: 2.5%; Median gross rent: $703 per month; Rental vacancy rate: 4.2%
Health Insurance: 85.3% have insurance; 72.7% have private insurance; 32.5% have public insurance; 14.7% do not have insurance; 12.4% of children under 18 do not have insurance
Transportation: Commute: 99.1% car, 0.0% public transportation, 0.0% walk, 0.9% work from home; Median travel time to work: 19.6 minutes

WAKARUSA (town).
Covers a land area of 2.204 square miles and a water area of 0.077 square miles. Located at 41.53° N. Lat; 86.01° W. Long. Elevation is 846 feet.
History: Laid out 1852.
Population: 1,758; Growth (since 2000): 8.7%; Density: 797.6 persons per square mile; Race: 96.0% White, 1.0% Black/African American, 1.0% Asian, 0.1% American Indian/Alaska Native, 0.0% Native Hawaiian/Other Pacific Islander, 1.1% Two or more races, 2.4% Hispanic of any race; Average household size: 2.48; Median age: 42.0; Age under 18: 24.9%; Age 65 and over: 22.2%; Males per 100 females: 84.5

School District(s)
Penn-Harris-Madison Sch Corp (KG-12)
   2012-13 Enrollment: 10,420 . . . . (574) 259-7941
Wa-Nee Community Schools (KG-12)
   2012-13 Enrollment: 3,084 . . . . (574) 773-3131
Housing: Homeownership rate: 71.9%; Homeowner vacancy rate: 1.4%; Rental vacancy rate: 14.9%
Newspapers: Wakarusa Tribune (weekly circulation 1400)

Fayette County

Located in eastern Indiana; drained by the Whitewater River. Covers a land area of 215.014 square miles, a water area of 0.148 square miles, and is located in the Eastern Time Zone at 39.64° N. Lat., 85.19° W. Long. The county was founded in 1818. County seat is Connersville.

Fayette County is part of the Connersville, IN Micropolitan Statistical Area. The entire metro area includes: Fayette County, IN

Population: 24,277; Growth (since 2000): -5.1%; Density: 112.9 persons per square mile; Race: 96.9% White, 1.3% Black/African American, 0.3% Asian, 0.1% American Indian/Alaska Native, 0.0% Native Hawaiian/Other Pacific Islander, 1.0% two or more races, 0.9% Hispanic of any race; Average household size: 2.46; Median age: 40.8; Age under 18: 24.0%; Age 65 and over: 16.7%; Males per 100 females: 96.0; Marriage status: 21.6% never married, 54.6% now married, 2.7% separated, 7.5% widowed, 16.4% divorced; Foreign born: 0.7%; Speak English only: 97.7%; With disability: 19.4%; Veterans: 11.6%; Ancestry: 20.2% German, 14.6% American, 10.5% Irish, 7.8% English, 1.9% Scottish
Religion: Six largest groups: 12.7% Non-denominational Protestant, 10.1% Baptist, 8.5% Catholicism, 5.5% Methodist/Pietist, 2.4% Holiness, 1.3% Latter-day Saints
Economy: Unemployment rate: 7.2%; Leading industries: 16.6% retail trade; 14.6% other services (except public administration); 13.5% health care and social assistance; Farms: 347 totaling 78,242 acres; Company size: 0 employ 1,000 or more persons, 0 employ 500 to 999 persons, 11 employs 100 to 499 persons, 441 employs less than 100 persons; Business ownership: 386 women-owned, n/a Black-owned, n/a Hispanic-owned, n/a Asian-owned
Employment: 9.2% management, business, and financial, 2.1% computer, engineering, and science, 6.6% education, legal, community service, arts, and media, 7.3% healthcare practitioners, 21.1% service, 22.5% sales and office, 8.6% natural resources, construction, and maintenance, 22.7% production, transportation, and material moving
Income: Per capita: $18,757; Median household: $37,391; Average household: $46,082; Households with income of $100,000 or more: 8.3%; Poverty rate: 23.0%
Educational Attainment: High school diploma or higher: 77.3%; Bachelor's degree or higher: 8.9%; Graduate/professional degree or higher: 3.2%
Housing: Homeownership rate: 70.2%; Median home value: $81,700; Median year structure built: 1960; Homeowner vacancy rate: 2.3%; Median gross rent: $638 per month; Rental vacancy rate: 12.0%
Vital Statistics: Birth rate: 99.7 per 10,000 population; Death rate: 114.8 per 10,000 population; Age-adjusted cancer mortality rate: 216.3 deaths per 100,000 population
Health Insurance: 82.2% have insurance; 55.1% have private insurance; 41.2% have public insurance; 17.8% do not have insurance; 7.0% of children under 18 do not have insurance
Health Care: Physicians: 8.3 per 10,000 population; Hospital beds: 30.2 per 10,000 population; Hospital admissions: 938.0 per 10,000 population
Transportation: Commute: 94.4% car, 0.4% public transportation, 1.9% walk, 1.7% work from home; Median travel time to work: 25.0 minutes
Presidential Election: 40.3% Obama, 57.2% Romney (2012)
Additional Information Contacts

Fayette Government .... (765) 825-8987
http://www.co.fayette.in.us

Fayette County Communities

CONNERSVILLE (city). County seat. Covers a land area of 7.745 square miles and a water area of 0.015 square miles. Located at 39.66° N. Lat; 85.14° W. Long. Elevation is 823 feet.
History: Settlement at Connersville began in 1808 when John Conner established a fur-trading post here. He founded the town of Connersville in 1813 and served as its first sheriff, in addition to operating the gristmill, sawmill, tavern, and store.
Population: 13,481; Growth (since 2000): -12.5%; Density: 1,740.7 persons per square mile; Race: 95.7% White, 2.1% Black/African American, 0.3% Asian, 0.2% American Indian/Alaska Native, 0.0% Native Hawaiian/Other Pacific Islander, 1.3% Two or more races, 1.0% Hispanic of any race; Average household size: 2.37; Median age: 39.4; Age under 18: 24.2%; Age 65 and over: 17.7%; Males per 100 females: 91.0; Marriage status: 23.4% never married, 47.7% now married, 3.2% separated, 9.2% widowed, 19.6% divorced; Foreign born: 1.1%; Speak English only: 96.5%; With disability: 20.5%; Veterans: 12.3%; Ancestry: 16.8% German, 13.0% American, 10.3% Irish, 7.7% English, 1.5% French
Employment: 6.7% management, business, and financial, 1.5% computer, engineering, and science, 5.3% education, legal, community service, arts, and media, 7.6% healthcare practitioners, 23.5% service, 24.6% sales and office, 6.6% natural resources, construction, and maintenance, 24.1% production, transportation, and material moving
Income: Per capita: $16,825; Median household: $30,952; Average household: $40,044; Households with income of $100,000 or more: 4.8%; Poverty rate: 27.9%
Educational Attainment: High school diploma or higher: 75.4%; Bachelor's degree or higher: 6.9%; Graduate/professional degree or higher: 2.5%

School District(s)
Fayette County School Corp (PK-12)
    2012-13 Enrollment: 3,913 .... (765) 825-2178
Housing: Homeownership rate: 60.4%; Median home value: $68,900; Median year structure built: 1950; Homeowner vacancy rate: 3.3%; Median gross rent: $630 per month; Rental vacancy rate: 13.7%
Health Insurance: 79.8% have insurance; 47.1% have private insurance; 47.3% have public insurance; 20.2% do not have insurance; 6.4% of children under 18 do not have insurance
Hospitals: Fayette Regional Health System (140 beds)
Newspapers: Connersville News-Examiner (daily circulation 6500)
Transportation: Commute: 92.9% car, 0.6% public transportation, 1.8% walk, 2.0% work from home; Median travel time to work: 25.3 minutes; Amtrak: Train service available.

Floyd County

Located in southern Indiana; hilly region, bounded on the south by the Ohio River and the Kentucky border; drained by tributaries of the Ohio River. Covers a land area of 147.935 square miles, a water area of 1.023 square miles, and is located in the Eastern Time Zone at 38.32° N. Lat., 85.91° W. Long. The county was founded in 1819. County seat is New Albany.

Floyd County is part of the Louisville/Jefferson County, KY-IN Metropolitan Statistical Area. The entire metro area includes: Clark County, IN; Floyd County, IN; Harrison County, IN; Scott County, IN; Washington County, IN; Bullitt County, KY; Henry County, KY; Jefferson County, KY; Oldham County, KY; Shelby County, KY; Spencer County, KY; Trimble County, KY

Population: 74,578; Growth (since 2000): 5.3%; Density: 504.1 persons per square mile; Race: 90.4% White, 5.2% Black/African American, 0.9% Asian, 0.2% American Indian/Alaska Native, 0.0% Native Hawaiian/Other Pacific Islander, 2.1% two or more races, 2.6% Hispanic of any race; Average household size: 2.48; Median age: 39.1; Age under 18: 24.0%; Age 65 and over: 13.0%; Males per 100 females: 94.0; Marriage status: 27.5% never married, 52.4% now married, 1.7% separated, 6.8% widowed, 13.3% divorced; Foreign born: 2.8%; Speak English only: 95.8%; With disability: 13.4%; Veterans: 10.7%; Ancestry: 26.5% German, 14.8% American, 14.0% Irish, 10.6% English, 3.4% French

Religion: Six largest groups: 22.8% Baptist, 16.4% Catholicism, 6.4% Methodist/Pietist, 3.4% Non-denominational Protestant, 2.2% Holiness, 2.0% Lutheran
Economy: Unemployment rate: 5.0%; Leading industries: 13.5% health care and social assistance; 11.9% retail trade; 11.2% professional, scientific, and technical services; Farms: 277 totaling 21,463 acres; Company size: 3 employ 1,000 or more persons, 2 employ 500 to 999 persons, 32 employ 100 to 499 persons, 1,721 employs less than 100 persons; Business ownership: 2,188 women-owned, 200 Black-owned, n/a Hispanic-owned, n/a Asian-owned
Employment: 13.7% management, business, and financial, 4.8% computer, engineering, and science, 9.3% education, legal, community service, arts, and media, 5.7% healthcare practitioners, 15.7% service, 27.5% sales and office, 7.9% natural resources, construction, and maintenance, 15.4% production, transportation, and material moving
Income: Per capita: $27,185; Median household: $53,961; Average household: $68,257; Households with income of $100,000 or more: 19.8%; Poverty rate: 13.3%
Educational Attainment: High school diploma or higher: 88.0%; Bachelor's degree or higher: 22.6%; Graduate/professional degree or higher: 7.4%
Housing: Homeownership rate: 71.3%; Median home value: $150,400; Median year structure built: 1973; Homeowner vacancy rate: 2.7%; Median gross rent: $718 per month; Rental vacancy rate: 8.8%
Vital Statistics: Birth rate: 117.4 per 10,000 population; Death rate: 90.2 per 10,000 population; Age-adjusted cancer mortality rate: 166.5 deaths per 100,000 population
Health Insurance: 87.7% have insurance; 74.3% have private insurance; 25.7% have public insurance; 12.3% do not have insurance; 8.2% of children under 18 do not have insurance
Health Care: Physicians: 19.9 per 10,000 population; Hospital beds: 37.7 per 10,000 population; Hospital admissions: 2,178.5 per 10,000 population
Air Quality Index: 71.2% good, 28.8% moderate, 0.0% unhealthy for sensitive individuals, 0.0% unhealthy (percent of days)
Transportation: Commute: 95.3% car, 0.8% public transportation, 0.9% walk, 2.4% work from home; Median travel time to work: 22.7 minutes
Presidential Election: 42.0% Obama, 56.3% Romney (2012)
Additional Information Contacts
Floyd Government. .... (812) 948-5466
    http://www.floydcounty.in.gov

Floyd County Communities

FLOYDS KNOBS (unincorporated postal area)
ZCTA: 47119
    Covers a land area of 43.110 square miles and a water area of 0.257 square miles. Located at 38.37° N. Lat; 85.88° W. Long. Elevation is 771 feet.
Population: 10,911; Growth (since 2000): 11.6%; Density: 253.1 persons per square mile; Race: 96.8% White, 0.8% Black/African American, 1.1% Asian, 0.2% American Indian/Alaska Native, 0.0% Native Hawaiian/Other Pacific Islander, 0.9% Two or more races, 1.1% Hispanic of any race; Average household size: 2.72; Median age: 42.9; Age under 18: 24.3%; Age 65 and over: 13.2%; Males per 100 females: 98.5; Marriage status: 20.6% never married, 60.8% now married, 0.1% separated, 6.5% widowed, 12.1% divorced; Foreign born: 1.9%; Speak English only: 98.1%; With disability: 8.8%; Veterans: 10.8%; Ancestry: 36.2% German, 19.3% Irish, 12.0% English, 11.5% American, 5.5% French
Employment: 19.3% management, business, and financial, 6.0% computer, engineering, and science, 7.0% education, legal, community service, arts, and media, 8.1% healthcare practitioners, 9.0% service, 27.6% sales and office, 10.6% natural resources, construction, and maintenance, 12.2% production, transportation, and material moving
Income: Per capita: $37,270; Median household: $80,434; Average household: $101,451; Households with income of $100,000 or more: 37.6%; Poverty rate: 3.5%
Educational Attainment: High school diploma or higher: 93.9%; Bachelor's degree or higher: 30.1%; Graduate/professional degree or higher: 9.9%

School District(s)
New Albany-Floyd County Con Sch (PK-12)
    2012-13 Enrollment: 11,293 .... (812) 949-4200

Housing: Homeownership rate: 91.3%; Median home value: $217,800; Median year structure built: 1981; Homeowner vacancy rate: 1.6%; Median gross rent: $881 per month; Rental vacancy rate: 5.7%
Health Insurance: 91.9% have insurance; 86.7% have private insurance; 18.3% have public insurance; 8.1% do not have insurance; 8.5% of children under 18 do not have insurance
Transportation: Commute: 96.1% car, 0.7% public transportation, 0.0% walk, 3.2% work from home; Median travel time to work: 26.0 minutes

GALENA (CDP).
Covers a land area of 2.671 square miles and a water area of 0.008 square miles. Located at 38.36° N. Lat; 85.94° W. Long. Elevation is 810 feet.
History: Galena was laid out in 1836, when it was called Germantown for the German immigrants who settled here. The Galena Mill, built in 1857, was a steam-powered flour mill.
Population: 1,818; Growth (since 2000): -0.7%; Density: 680.8 persons per square mile; Race: 98.6% White, 0.0% Black/African American, 0.6% Asian, 0.2% American Indian/Alaska Native, 0.0% Native Hawaiian/Other Pacific Islander, 0.6% Two or more races, 0.7% Hispanic of any race; Average household size: 2.85; Median age: 38.2; Age under 18: 27.0%; Age 65 and over: 9.8%; Males per 100 females: 95.3
Housing: Homeownership rate: 87.6%; Homeowner vacancy rate: 1.4%; Rental vacancy rate: 7.1%

GEORGETOWN (town).
Covers a land area of 2.049 square miles and a water area of 0.018 square miles. Located at 38.30° N. Lat; 85.96° W. Long. Elevation is 722 feet.
Population: 2,876; Growth (since 2000): 29.1%; Density: 1,403.5 persons per square mile; Race: 97.3% White, 0.3% Black/African American, 0.6% Asian, 0.3% American Indian/Alaska Native, 0.0% Native Hawaiian/Other Pacific Islander, 1.1% Two or more races, 1.9% Hispanic of any race; Average household size: 2.64; Median age: 35.4; Age under 18: 27.7%; Age 65 and over: 9.0%; Males per 100 females: 93.4; Marriage status: 21.6% never married, 56.2% now married, 2.4% separated, 6.1% widowed, 16.0% divorced; Foreign born: 0.8%; Speak English only: 97.4%; With disability: 8.7%; Veterans: 10.0%; Ancestry: 32.9% German, 20.7% Irish, 10.2% American, 9.3% English, 7.7% Italian
Employment: 18.7% management, business, and financial, 6.1% computer, engineering, and science, 12.0% education, legal, community service, arts, and media, 6.6% healthcare practitioners, 8.7% service, 25.5% sales and office, 5.1% natural resources, construction, and maintenance, 17.6% production, transportation, and material moving
Income: Per capita: $32,148; Median household: $67,898; Average household: $83,141; Households with income of $100,000 or more: 21.9%; Poverty rate: 4.6%
Educational Attainment: High school diploma or higher: 93.2%; Bachelor's degree or higher: 34.3%; Graduate/professional degree or higher: 9.8%
School District(s)
New Albany-Floyd County Con Sch (PK-12)
 2012-13 Enrollment: 11,293 . . . . (812) 949-4200
Housing: Homeownership rate: 81.9%; Median home value: $153,900; Median year structure built: 1979; Homeowner vacancy rate: 2.9%; Median gross rent: $777 per month; Rental vacancy rate: 6.6%
Health Insurance: 94.4% have insurance; 85.6% have private insurance; 18.1% have public insurance; 5.6% do not have insurance; 1.3% of children under 18 do not have insurance
Transportation: Commute: 96.7% car, 0.0% public transportation, 0.6% walk, 2.3% work from home; Median travel time to work: 29.4 minutes
Additional Information Contacts
Town of Georgetown . . . . (812) 951-3012
 http://georgetown.in.gov

GREENVILLE (town).
Covers a land area of 0.780 square miles and a water area of <.001 square miles. Located at 38.37° N. Lat; 85.98° W. Long. Elevation is 827 feet.
History: Greenville was settled in 1807 and laid out in 1816 as a station on the Old Stage Road. A ready supply of white-oak timber led to the town becoming a center for the production of barrels, wine kegs, and wooden clocks.
Population: 595; Growth (since 2000): 0.7%; Density: 763.1 persons per square mile; Race: 95.5% White, 1.5% Black/African American, 0.8% Asian, 0.8% American Indian/Alaska Native, 0.0% Native Hawaiian/Other Pacific Islander, 0.8% Two or more races, 2.0% Hispanic of any race;

Average household size: 2.72; Median age: 39.4; Age under 18: 26.9%; Age 65 and over: 11.9%; Males per 100 females: 104.5
School District(s)
New Albany-Floyd County Con Sch (PK-12)
 2012-13 Enrollment: 11,293 . . . . (812) 949-4200
Housing: Homeownership rate: 82.2%; Homeowner vacancy rate: 2.7%; Rental vacancy rate: 0.0%

NEW ALBANY (city).
County seat. Covers a land area of 14.939 square miles and a water area of 0.171 square miles. Located at 38.31° N. Lat; 85.83° W. Long. Elevation is 449 feet.
History: New Albany began as a river town, utilizing its location on the Ohio River for shipping and industry. The town was platted in 1813 by three brothers from New York, who named it for the capital of their former home state. New Albany received its city charter in 1838. Shipyards here built many vessels in the mid-1800's, including the "Robert E. Lee" built in 1866 for Captain John W. Cannon.
Population: 36,372; Growth (since 2000): -3.3%; Density: 2,434.8 persons per square mile; Race: 85.8% White, 8.7% Black/African American, 0.7% Asian, 0.2% American Indian/Alaska Native, 0.0% Native Hawaiian/Other Pacific Islander, 2.9% Two or more races, 3.7% Hispanic of any race; Average household size: 2.27; Median age: 37.1; Age under 18: 22.9%; Age 65 and over: 13.9%; Males per 100 females: 90.5; Marriage status: 32.7% never married, 42.4% now married, 2.5% separated, 8.4% widowed, 16.5% divorced; Foreign born: 2.3%; Speak English only: 95.6%; With disability: 17.4%; Veterans: 10.7%; Ancestry: 22.3% German, 15.4% American, 11.4% Irish, 9.5% English, 3.1% French
Employment: 9.8% management, business, and financial, 3.3% computer, engineering, and science, 9.1% education, legal, community service, arts, and media, 4.0% healthcare practitioners, 21.6% service, 27.4% sales and office, 7.1% natural resources, construction, and maintenance, 17.6% production, transportation, and material moving
Income: Per capita: $21,183; Median household: $39,607; Average household: $48,539; Households with income of $100,000 or more: 8.4%; Poverty rate: 22.2%
Educational Attainment: High school diploma or higher: 83.2%; Bachelor's degree or higher: 16.1%; Graduate/professional degree or higher: 4.6%
School District(s)
Community Montessori Inc (KG-12)
 2012-13 Enrollment: 520 . . . . (812) 948-1000
New Albany-Floyd County Con Sch (PK-12)
 2012-13 Enrollment: 11,293 . . . . (812) 949-4200
Four-year College(s)
Indiana University-Southeast (Public)
 Fall 2013 Enrollment: 6,733 . . . . (812) 941-2000
 2013-14 Tuition: In-state $6,700; Out-of-state $17,778
Housing: Homeownership rate: 56.1%; Median home value: $110,100; Median year structure built: 1959; Homeowner vacancy rate: 3.9%; Median gross rent: $697 per month; Rental vacancy rate: 9.4%
Health Insurance: 83.3% have insurance; 61.9% have private insurance; 34.5% have public insurance; 16.7% do not have insurance; 10.5% of children under 18 do not have insurance
Hospitals: Floyd Memorial Hospital & Health Services (245 beds); Physicians' Medical Center
Safety: Violent crime rate: 23.8 per 10,000 population; Property crime rate: 548.6 per 10,000 population
Newspapers: Tribune (daily circulation 12200)
Transportation: Commute: 94.0% car, 1.2% public transportation, 1.7% walk, 2.0% work from home; Median travel time to work: 20.1 minutes
Additional Information Contacts
City of New Albany . . . . (812) 948-5333
 http://www.cityofnewalbany.com

Fountain County

Located in western Indiana; bounded on the west and north by the Wabash River; drained by Coal Creek. Covers a land area of 395.656 square miles, a water area of 2.224 square miles, and is located in the Eastern Time Zone at 40.12° N. Lat., 87.23° W. Long. The county was founded in 1825. County seat is Covington.
Population: 17,240; Growth (since 2000): -4.0%; Density: 43.6 persons per square mile; Race: 97.5% White, 0.2% Black/African American, 0.2% Asian, 0.3% American Indian/Alaska Native, 0.0% Native Hawaiian/Other Pacific Islander, 1.0% two or more races, 2.2% Hispanic of any race;

Average household size: 2.46; Median age: 41.6; Age under 18: 24.2%; Age 65 and over: 17.7%; Males per 100 females: 98.0; Marriage status: 21.4% never married, 55.9% now married, 0.9% separated, 8.4% widowed, 14.2% divorced; Foreign born: 1.3%; Speak English only: 97.2%; With disability: 15.6%; Veterans: 9.6%; Ancestry: 20.5% German, 16.5% American, 13.4% Irish, 11.1% English, 2.2% Scottish
Religion: Six largest groups: 11.1% Baptist, 4.4% Holiness, 4.2% Non-denominational Protestant, 3.7% Methodist/Pietist, 3.5% Catholicism, 2.5% Pentecostal
Economy: Unemployment rate: 6.6%; Leading industries: 19.6% retail trade; 14.7% other services (except public administration); 11.9% accommodation and food services; Farms: 460 totaling 214,412 acres; Company size: 0 employ 1,000 or more persons, 2 employ 500 to 999 persons, 4 employ 100 to 499 persons, 321 employs less than 100 persons; Business ownership: n/a women-owned, n/a Black-owned, n/a Hispanic-owned, n/a Asian-owned
Employment: 11.0% management, business, and financial, 3.0% computer, engineering, and science, 6.5% education, legal, community service, arts, and media, 5.0% healthcare practitioners, 15.0% service, 17.1% sales and office, 11.6% natural resources, construction, and maintenance, 30.8% production, transportation, and material moving
Income: Per capita: $23,063; Median household: $45,884; Average household: $56,429; Households with income of $100,000 or more: 14.0%; Poverty rate: 11.9%
Educational Attainment: High school diploma or higher: 85.5%; Bachelor's degree or higher: 11.9%; Graduate/professional degree or higher: 4.3%
Housing: Homeownership rate: 76.6%; Median home value: $88,800; Median year structure built: 1961; Homeowner vacancy rate: 2.3%; Median gross rent: $617 per month; Rental vacancy rate: 9.0%
Vital Statistics: Birth rate: 107.8 per 10,000 population; Death rate: 109.0 per 10,000 population; Age-adjusted cancer mortality rate: 223.8 deaths per 100,000 population
Health Insurance: 87.7% have insurance; 70.9% have private insurance; 31.8% have public insurance; 12.3% do not have insurance; 7.9% of children under 18 do not have insurance
Health Care: Physicians: 2.9 per 10,000 population; Hospital beds: 0.0 per 10,000 population; Hospital admissions: 0.0 per 10,000 population
Air Quality Index: 99.5% good, 0.5% moderate, 0.0% unhealthy for sensitive individuals, 0.0% unhealthy (percent of days)
Transportation: Commute: 92.2% car, 0.0% public transportation, 3.7% walk, 2.7% work from home; Median travel time to work: 25.7 minutes
Presidential Election: 31.4% Obama, 65.6% Romney (2012)
National and State Parks: Shades State Park
Additional Information Contacts
Fountain Government . . . . (765) 793-2243
http://www.co.fountain.in.us

Fountain County Communities

ATTICA (city). Covers a land area of 1.600 square miles and a water area of 0 square miles. Located at 40.29° N. Lat; 87.24° W. Long. Elevation is 541 feet.
History: Attica developed in the late 1840's when the Wabash & Erie Canal was extended here. A prominent resident of Attica was Dr. John Evans (1814-1897), a physician who later served as Territorial Governor of Colorado and as a U.S. senator.
Population: 3,245; Growth (since 2000): -7.0%; Density: 2,028.3 persons per square mile; Race: 97.8% White, 0.1% Black/African American, 0.3% Asian, 0.2% American Indian/Alaska Native, 0.0% Native Hawaiian/Other Pacific Islander, 1.0% Two or more races, 2.4% Hispanic of any race; Average household size: 2.45; Median age: 38.9; Age under 18: 25.2%; Age 65 and over: 17.2%; Males per 100 females: 95.7; Marriage status: 25.2% never married, 41.4% now married, 0.2% separated, 13.5% widowed, 20.0% divorced; Foreign born: 1.7%; Speak English only: 95.2%; With disability: 20.1%; Veterans: 8.1%; Ancestry: 17.2% German, 15.1% American, 11.7% Irish, 10.4% English, 4.6% Polish
Employment: 8.2% management, business, and financial, 3.4% computer, engineering, and science, 10.2% education, legal, community service, arts, and media, 5.5% healthcare practitioners, 13.6% service, 14.7% sales and office, 7.6% natural resources, construction, and maintenance, 36.8% production, transportation, and material moving
Income: Per capita: $20,864; Median household: $36,250; Average household: $49,092; Households with income of $100,000 or more: 10.8%; Poverty rate: 14.0%

Educational Attainment: High school diploma or higher: 83.2%; Bachelor's degree or higher: 12.7%; Graduate/professional degree or higher: 5.7%
School District(s)
Attica Consolidated Sch Corp (PK-12)
    2012-13 Enrollment: 890. . . . . (765) 762-7000
Housing: Homeownership rate: 66.3%; Median home value: $83,900; Median year structure built: 1954; Homeowner vacancy rate: 2.8%; Median gross rent: $591 per month; Rental vacancy rate: 11.4%
Health Insurance: 87.3% have insurance; 67.0% have private insurance; 36.5% have public insurance; 12.7% do not have insurance; 5.0% of children under 18 do not have insurance
Newspapers: Fountain County Neighbor (weekly circulation 2200)
Transportation: Commute: 91.6% car, 0.0% public transportation, 5.0% walk, 1.9% work from home; Median travel time to work: 21.2 minutes
Additional Information Contacts
City of Attica . . . . (765) 761-7074
    http://www.wcchamber.net; http://www.atticaonline.com

COVINGTON (city). County seat. Covers a land area of 1.176 square miles and a water area of 0 square miles. Located at 40.14° N. Lat; 87.39° W. Long. Elevation is 564 feet.
History: Covington was laid out in 1826 along the east bank of the Wabash River. A prominent resident was Edward A. Hannegan (1807-1859), U.S. senator and minister to Prussia, where he is said to have dazzled the court. Back home, Hannegan's bid for the presidency was ended when he stabbed his brother-in-law to death.
Population: 2,645; Growth (since 2000): 3.1%; Density: 2,249.3 persons per square mile; Race: 97.6% White, 0.2% Black/African American, 0.3% Asian, 0.5% American Indian/Alaska Native, 0.0% Native Hawaiian/Other Pacific Islander, 1.1% Two or more races, 1.1% Hispanic of any race; Average household size: 2.25; Median age: 44.0; Age under 18: 22.4%; Age 65 and over: 23.6%; Males per 100 females: 88.1; Marriage status: 20.5% never married, 61.4% now married, 1.2% separated, 8.3% widowed, 9.8% divorced; Foreign born: 0.5%; Speak English only: 98.6%; With disability: 11.6%; Veterans: 12.8%; Ancestry: 21.7% German, 16.0% American, 14.1% English, 9.0% Irish, 2.1% Scotch-Irish
Employment: 8.7% management, business, and financial, 0.7% computer, engineering, and science, 12.7% education, legal, community service, arts, and media, 4.6% healthcare practitioners, 21.1% service, 24.4% sales and office, 12.2% natural resources, construction, and maintenance, 15.6% production, transportation, and material moving
Income: Per capita: $25,767; Median household: $51,742; Average household: $62,131; Households with income of $100,000 or more: 15.1%; Poverty rate: 7.5%
Educational Attainment: High school diploma or higher: 91.0%; Bachelor's degree or higher: 16.7%; Graduate/professional degree or higher: 5.9%
School District(s)
Covington Community Sch Corp (PK-12)
    2012-13 Enrollment: 980. . . . . (765) 793-4877
Housing: Homeownership rate: 70.9%; Median home value: $96,000; Median year structure built: 1962; Homeowner vacancy rate: 1.7%; Median gross rent: $618 per month; Rental vacancy rate: 7.9%
Health Insurance: 91.2% have insurance; 76.4% have private insurance; 34.2% have public insurance; 8.8% do not have insurance; 2.3% of children under 18 do not have insurance
Transportation: Commute: 85.3% car, 0.0% public transportation, 7.8% walk, 5.4% work from home; Median travel time to work: 21.0 minutes
Additional Information Contacts
City of Covington. . . . . (765) 761-7074
    http://www.wcchamber.net

HILLSBORO (town). Covers a land area of 0.313 square miles and a water area of 0 square miles. Located at 40.11° N. Lat; 87.16° W. Long. Elevation is 709 feet.
History: Early industry in Hillsboro was based on the clay soil used in the manufacture of tiles and bricks.
Population: 538; Growth (since 2000): 10.0%; Density: 1,717.9 persons per square mile; Race: 96.1% White, 0.2% Black/African American, 0.0% Asian, 0.7% American Indian/Alaska Native, 0.0% Native Hawaiian/Other Pacific Islander, 1.1% Two or more races, 5.4% Hispanic of any race; Average household size: 2.60; Median age: 38.2; Age under 18: 27.5%; Age 65 and over: 13.0%; Males per 100 females: 94.9

Housing: Homeownership rate: 71.9%; Homeowner vacancy rate: 3.2%; Rental vacancy rate: 9.2%

KINGMAN (town). Covers a land area of 0.818 square miles and a water area of 0 square miles. Located at 39.97° N. Lat; 87.28° W. Long. Elevation is 702 feet.
Population: 511; Growth (since 2000): -5.0%; Density: 624.9 persons per square mile; Race: 97.7% White, 0.0% Black/African American, 0.0% Asian, 0.0% American Indian/Alaska Native, 0.0% Native Hawaiian/Other Pacific Islander, 2.0% Two or more races, 1.4% Hispanic of any race; Average household size: 2.41; Median age: 38.7; Age under 18: 26.4%; Age 65 and over: 17.8%; Males per 100 females: 99.6
Housing: Homeownership rate: 64.2%; Homeowner vacancy rate: 2.1%; Rental vacancy rate: 16.7%

MELLOTT (town). Covers a land area of 0.171 square miles and a water area of 0 square miles. Located at 40.16° N. Lat; 87.15° W. Long. Elevation is 705 feet.
Population: 197; Growth (since 2000): -4.8%; Density: 1,152.8 persons per square mile; Race: 99.0% White, 0.0% Black/African American, 0.0% Asian, 0.0% American Indian/Alaska Native, 0.0% Native Hawaiian/Other Pacific Islander, 1.0% Two or more races, 2.5% Hispanic of any race; Average household size: 2.24; Median age: 42.8; Age under 18: 22.8%; Age 65 and over: 24.4%; Males per 100 females: 84.1
Housing: Homeownership rate: 73.9%; Homeowner vacancy rate: 0.0%; Rental vacancy rate: 17.9%

NEWTOWN (town). Covers a land area of 0.504 square miles and a water area of 0 square miles. Located at 40.20° N. Lat; 87.15° W. Long. Elevation is 709 feet.
Population: 256; Growth (since 2000): 58.0%; Density: 507.5 persons per square mile; Race: 95.3% White, 2.0% Black/African American, 0.0% Asian, 0.8% American Indian/Alaska Native, 0.0% Native Hawaiian/Other Pacific Islander, 2.0% Two or more races, 1.6% Hispanic of any race; Average household size: 2.75; Median age: 35.4; Age under 18: 28.5%; Age 65 and over: 8.6%; Males per 100 females: 128.6
Housing: Homeownership rate: 76.3%; Homeowner vacancy rate: 7.7%; Rental vacancy rate: 12.0%

VEEDERSBURG (town). Covers a land area of 2.717 square miles and a water area of 0 square miles. Located at 40.11° N. Lat; 87.26° W. Long. Elevation is 633 feet.
History: Veedersburg was a brick manufacturing center. The Veedersburg Paver Company furnished the brick for paving the Indianapolis Motor Speedway.
Population: 2,180; Growth (since 2000): -5.2%; Density: 802.5 persons per square mile; Race: 94.8% White, 0.1% Black/African American, 0.1% Asian, 0.5% American Indian/Alaska Native, 0.0% Native Hawaiian/Other Pacific Islander, 1.0% Two or more races, 6.2% Hispanic of any race; Average household size: 2.48; Median age: 39.2; Age under 18: 25.2%; Age 65 and over: 16.4%; Males per 100 females: 94.5

School District(s)
Southeast Fountain School Corp (KG-12)
    2012-13 Enrollment: 1,168 . . . . (765) 294-2254
Housing: Homeownership rate: 69.6%; Homeowner vacancy rate: 4.1%; Rental vacancy rate: 8.5%
Additional Information Contacts
Town of Veedersburg . . . . (765) 362-6800
    http://www.crawfordsvillechamber.com

WALLACE (town). Covers a land area of 0.085 square miles and a water area of 0 square miles. Located at 39.99° N. Lat; 87.15° W. Long. Elevation is 702 feet.
History: Laid out 1832.
Population: 105; Growth (since 2000): 5.0%; Density: 1,231.0 persons per square mile; Race: 100.0% White, 0.0% Black/African American, 0.0% Asian, 0.0% American Indian/Alaska Native, 0.0% Native Hawaiian/Other Pacific Islander, 0.0% Two or more races, 0.0% Hispanic of any race; Average household size: 2.02; Median age: 45.5; Age under 18: 18.1%; Age 65 and over: 22.9%; Males per 100 females: 94.4
Housing: Homeownership rate: 80.8%; Homeowner vacancy rate: 0.0%; Rental vacancy rate: 0.0%

Franklin County

Located in southeastern Indiana; bounded on the east by Ohio; drained by the Whitewater River and its East Fork. Covers a land area of 384.430 square miles, a water area of 6.620 square miles, and is located in the Eastern Time Zone at 39.41° N. Lat., 85.07° W. Long. The county was founded in 1810. County seat is Brookville.

Weather Station: Brookville   Elevation: 629 feet

	Jan	Feb	Mar	Apr	May	Jun	Jul	Aug	Sep	Oct	Nov	Dec
High	38	42	53	65	75	83	87	86	80	67	55	41
Low	20	22	29	40	50	59	63	62	53	41	33	24
Precip	3.0	2.6	3.6	4.1	5.1	3.7	4.4	3.4	2.6	3.2	3.6	3.4
Snow	4.2	4.0	1.5	0.1	tr	0.0	0.0	0.0	0.0	0.1	0.6	3.7

High and Low temperatures in degrees Fahrenheit; Precipitation and Snow in inches

Population: 23,087; Growth (since 2000): 4.2%; Density: 60.1 persons per square mile; Race: 98.3% White, 0.2% Black/African American, 0.2% Asian, 0.1% American Indian/Alaska Native, 0.0% Native Hawaiian/Other Pacific Islander, 0.8% two or more races, 0.9% Hispanic of any race; Average household size: 2.67; Median age: 40.0; Age under 18: 26.1%; Age 65 and over: 14.1%; Males per 100 females: 99.9; Marriage status: 23.6% never married, 61.4% now married, 1.1% separated, 5.5% widowed, 9.5% divorced; Foreign born: 0.8%; Speak English only: 98.1%; With disability: 12.5%; Veterans: 8.5%; Ancestry: 38.3% German, 16.3% American, 11.8% Irish, 7.8% English, 2.1% French
Religion: Six largest groups: 20.5% Catholicism, 9.1% Baptist, 4.3% Methodist/Pietist, 4.0% Presbyterian-Reformed, 2.5% Lutheran, 1.3% Non-denominational Protestant
Economy: Unemployment rate: 5.2%; Leading industries: 16.6% retail trade; 13.5% other services (except public administration); 13.3% construction; Farms: 727 totaling 124,960 acres; Company size: 1 employs 1,000 or more persons, 0 employ 500 to 999 persons, 6 employ 100 to 499 persons, 408 employ less than 100 persons; Business ownership: 308 women-owned, n/a Black-owned, n/a Hispanic-owned, n/a Asian-owned
Employment: 13.0% management, business, and financial, 2.9% computer, engineering, and science, 8.6% education, legal, community service, arts, and media, 6.4% healthcare practitioners, 14.5% service, 21.7% sales and office, 13.1% natural resources, construction, and maintenance, 19.8% production, transportation, and material moving
Income: Per capita: $24,085; Median household: $49,516; Average household: $63,547; Households with income of $100,000 or more: 15.3%; Poverty rate: 13.5%
Educational Attainment: High school diploma or higher: 85.4%; Bachelor's degree or higher: 18.1%; Graduate/professional degree or higher: 6.4%
Housing: Homeownership rate: 80.4%; Median home value: $150,100; Median year structure built: 1976; Homeowner vacancy rate: 1.7%; Median gross rent: $626 per month; Rental vacancy rate: 7.0%
Vital Statistics: Birth rate: 111.1 per 10,000 population; Death rate: 82.3 per 10,000 population; Age-adjusted cancer mortality rate: 197.3 deaths per 100,000 population
Health Insurance: 89.5% have insurance; 73.6% have private insurance; 29.0% have public insurance; 10.5% do not have insurance; 5.8% of children under 18 do not have insurance
Health Care: Physicians: 2.2 per 10,000 population; Hospital beds: 0.0 per 10,000 population; Hospital admissions: 0.0 per 10,000 population
Transportation: Commute: 92.5% car, 0.1% public transportation, 1.8% walk, 4.6% work from home; Median travel time to work: 31.4 minutes
Presidential Election: 27.6% Obama, 70.3% Romney (2012)
National and State Parks: Mounds State Recreation Area
Additional Information Contacts
Franklin Government. . . . . (765) 647-4985
    http://www.franklincounty.in.gov

Franklin County Communities

BATH (unincorporated postal area)
ZCTA: 47010
    Covers a land area of 10.764 square miles and a water area of 0.043 square miles. Located at 39.50° N. Lat; 84.85° W. Long. Elevation is 1,010 feet.
    Population: 306; Growth (since 2000): -23.3%; Density: 28.4 persons per square mile; Race: 99.7% White, 0.0% Black/African American, 0.0% Asian, 0.0% American Indian/Alaska Native, 0.0% Native Hawaiian/Other Pacific Islander, 0.3% Two or more races, 0.0%

Hispanic of any race; Average household size: 2.71; Median age: 42.8; Age under 18: 22.5%; Age 65 and over: 10.8%; Males per 100 females: 112.5
Housing: Homeownership rate: 82.3%; Homeowner vacancy rate: 3.1%; Rental vacancy rate: 9.1%

BROOKVILLE (town). County seat. Covers a land area of 1.498 square miles and a water area of 0.043 square miles. Located at 39.42° N. Lat; 85.01° W. Long. Elevation is 666 feet.

History: Brookville was laid out in 1808 on a site selected by Amos Butler and Jesse Brooks Thomas. They called their settlement Brooksville in honor of Thomas' mother, whose maiden name was Brooks. The "s" was removed when Franklin County was organized a few years later and Brookville became the county seat. Thomas became a U.S. senator from Illinois and was instrumental in the Missouri Compromise of 1820.
Population: 2,596; Growth (since 2000): -2.1%; Density: 1,732.5 persons per square mile; Race: 97.5% White, 0.3% Black/African American, 0.2% Asian, 0.3% American Indian/Alaska Native, 0.0% Native Hawaiian/Other Pacific Islander, 0.9% Two or more races, 1.6% Hispanic of any race; Average household size: 2.24; Median age: 39.6; Age under 18: 24.1%; Age 65 and over: 20.2%; Males per 100 females: 87.8; Marriage status: 26.2% never married, 48.9% now married, 0.9% separated, 9.1% widowed, 15.8% divorced; Foreign born: 0.7%; Speak English only: 98.9%; With disability: 19.5%; Veterans: 9.4%; Ancestry: 36.5% German, 23.3% American, 15.5% Irish, 8.7% English, 1.5% Russian
Employment: 11.1% management, business, and financial, 2.8% computer, engineering, and science, 7.3% education, legal, community service, arts, and media, 9.2% healthcare practitioners, 13.5% service, 28.0% sales and office, 3.5% natural resources, construction, and maintenance, 24.7% production, transportation, and material moving
Income: Per capita: $21,691; Median household: $30,833; Average household: $45,704; Households with income of $100,000 or more: 7.9%; Poverty rate: 19.4%
Educational Attainment: High school diploma or higher: 85.2%; Bachelor's degree or higher: 18.8%; Graduate/professional degree or higher: 5.0%

School District(s)
Franklin County Com Sch Corp (PK-12)
    2012-13 Enrollment: 2,863 . . . . (765) 647-4128
Housing: Homeownership rate: 56.3%; Median home value: $113,000; Median year structure built: 1958; Homeowner vacancy rate: 4.1%; Median gross rent: $554 per month; Rental vacancy rate: 7.5%
Health Insurance: 87.1% have insurance; 63.9% have private insurance; 44.8% have public insurance; 12.9% do not have insurance; 6.0% of children under 18 do not have insurance
Newspapers: Brookville American-Democrat (weekly circulation 1200)
Transportation: Commute: 91.7% car, 0.0% public transportation, 3.3% walk, 3.6% work from home; Median travel time to work: 27.2 minutes
Additional Information Contacts
Town of Brookville . . . . (866) 647-6555
   http://www.franklincountyin.com

CEDAR GROVE (town). Covers a land area of 0.150 square miles and a water area of <.001 square miles. Located at 39.36° N. Lat; 84.94° W. Long. Elevation is 600 feet.

Population: 156; Growth (since 2000): -15.7%; Density: 1,040.3 persons per square mile; Race: 98.7% White, 0.0% Black/African American, 0.0% Asian, 0.0% American Indian/Alaska Native, 0.0% Native Hawaiian/Other Pacific Islander, 1.3% Two or more races, 0.0% Hispanic of any race; Average household size: 2.08; Median age: 44.5; Age under 18: 19.2%; Age 65 and over: 14.1%; Males per 100 females: 90.2

School District(s)
Franklin County Com Sch Corp (PK-12)
    2012-13 Enrollment: 2,863 . . . . (765) 647-4128
Housing: Homeownership rate: 72.0%; Homeowner vacancy rate: 0.0%; Rental vacancy rate: 12.5%

LAUREL (town). Covers a land area of 0.241 square miles and a water area of <.001 square miles. Located at 39.50° N. Lat; 85.19° W. Long. Elevation is 728 feet.

History: Laurel was founded in 1836 by James Conwell, who named it for Laurel, Delaware. It began as a farming community, becoming a mill town and shipping center during the canal period.
Population: 512; Growth (since 2000): -11.6%; Density: 2,122.1 persons per square mile; Race: 98.4% White, 0.2% Black/African American, 0.0% Asian, 0.6% American Indian/Alaska Native, 0.0% Native Hawaiian/Other Pacific Islander, 0.6% Two or more races, 2.5% Hispanic of any race; Average household size: 2.61; Median age: 34.8; Age under 18: 27.0%; Age 65 and over: 13.7%; Males per 100 females: 104.0

School District(s)
Franklin County Com Sch Corp (PK-12)
    2012-13 Enrollment: 2,863 . . . . (765) 647-4128
Housing: Homeownership rate: 64.8%; Homeowner vacancy rate: 0.8%; Rental vacancy rate: 8.0%

METAMORA (CDP). Covers a land area of 0.336 square miles and a water area of 0 square miles. Located at 39.45° N. Lat; 85.14° W. Long. Elevation is 718 feet.

Population: 188; Growth (since 2000): n/a; Density: 559.9 persons per square mile; Race: 93.6% White, 0.0% Black/African American, 0.0% Asian, 0.5% American Indian/Alaska Native, 0.0% Native Hawaiian/Other Pacific Islander, 0.5% Two or more races, 5.3% Hispanic of any race; Average household size: 2.41; Median age: 48.5; Age under 18: 16.5%; Age 65 and over: 23.9%; Males per 100 females: 72.5
Housing: Homeownership rate: 80.8%; Homeowner vacancy rate: 4.5%; Rental vacancy rate: 11.8%

MOUNT CARMEL (town). Covers a land area of 0.045 square miles and a water area of 0 square miles. Located at 39.41° N. Lat; 84.88° W. Long. Elevation is 1,020 feet.

Population: 86; Growth (since 2000): -18.9%; Density: 1,895.6 persons per square mile; Race: 97.7% White, 0.0% Black/African American, 0.0% Asian, 0.0% American Indian/Alaska Native, 0.0% Native Hawaiian/Other Pacific Islander, 2.3% Two or more races, 0.0% Hispanic of any race; Average household size: 2.77; Median age: 35.0; Age under 18: 31.4%; Age 65 and over: 11.6%; Males per 100 females: 83.0
Housing: Homeownership rate: 64.5%; Homeowner vacancy rate: 0.0%; Rental vacancy rate: 0.0%

NEW TRENTON (CDP). Covers a land area of 0.441 square miles and a water area of 0 square miles. Located at 39.31° N. Lat; 84.90° W. Long. Elevation is 614 feet.

Population: 252; Growth (since 2000): n/a; Density: 571.1 persons per square mile; Race: 98.8% White, 0.0% Black/African American, 0.0% Asian, 0.0% American Indian/Alaska Native, 0.0% Native Hawaiian/Other Pacific Islander, 1.2% Two or more races, 0.4% Hispanic of any race; Average household size: 2.40; Median age: 38.8; Age under 18: 25.0%; Age 65 and over: 13.1%; Males per 100 females: 93.8
Housing: Homeownership rate: 76.2%; Homeowner vacancy rate: 3.6%; Rental vacancy rate: 10.7%

OLDENBURG (town). Covers a land area of 0.434 square miles and a water area of 0.002 square miles. Located at 39.34° N. Lat; 85.20° W. Long. Elevation is 889 feet.

History: Oldenburg was founded in 1837 by German immigrants. It was once a brick manufacturing center.
Population: 674; Growth (since 2000): 4.2%; Density: 1,554.3 persons per square mile; Race: 98.5% White, 0.1% Black/African American, 0.0% Asian, 0.0% American Indian/Alaska Native, 0.0% Native Hawaiian/Other Pacific Islander, 0.7% Two or more races, 1.9% Hispanic of any race; Average household size: 2.39; Median age: 51.0; Age under 18: 20.6%; Age 65 and over: 29.5%; Males per 100 females: 64.8
Housing: Homeownership rate: 67.2%; Homeowner vacancy rate: 2.5%; Rental vacancy rate: 13.3%

Fulton County

Located in northern Indiana; drained by the Tippecanoe River. Covers a land area of 368.388 square miles, a water area of 2.877 square miles, and is located in the Eastern Time Zone at 41.05° N. Lat., 86.27° W. Long. The county was founded in 1835. County seat is Rochester.

Weather Station: Rochester   Elevation: 770 feet

	Jan	Feb	Mar	Apr	May	Jun	Jul	Aug	Sep	Oct	Nov	Dec
High	32	36	47	60	71	80	83	82	75	62	49	36
Low	17	19	28	38	49	59	62	61	52	41	32	21
Precip	2.5	2.0	2.6	3.8	4.5	3.9	4.6	4.0	3.2	3.3	3.4	2.8
Snow	10.9	8.2	3.2	0.9	0.0	0.0	0.0	0.0	0.0	0.3	1.4	7.1

High and Low temperatures in degrees Fahrenheit; Precipitation and Snow in inches

Population: 20,836; Growth (since 2000): 1.6%; Density: 56.6 persons per square mile; Race: 95.0% White, 0.7% Black/African American, 0.5% Asian, 0.5% American Indian/Alaska Native, 0.0% Native Hawaiian/Other Pacific Islander, 1.1% two or more races, 4.2% Hispanic of any race; Average household size: 2.50; Median age: 40.3; Age under 18: 24.8%; Age 65 and over: 16.5%; Males per 100 females: 98.9; Marriage status: 23.3% never married, 58.9% now married, 1.2% separated, 7.2% widowed, 10.5% divorced; Foreign born: 2.9%; Speak English only: 92.5%; With disability: 16.9%; Veterans: 10.5%; Ancestry: 24.1% German, 21.4% American, 9.0% Irish, 8.8% English, 2.9% Polish
Religion: Six largest groups: 8.7% Methodist/Pietist, 6.5% Baptist, 5.4% Catholicism, 4.9% Non-denominational Protestant, 3.3% Holiness, 2.1% Pentecostal
Economy: Unemployment rate: 5.2%; Leading industries: 16.8% retail trade; 14.7% other services (except public administration); 9.6% health care and social assistance; Farms: 653 totaling 188,411 acres; Company size: 0 employ 1,000 or more persons, 0 employ 500 to 999 persons, 11 employs 100 to 499 persons, 458 employ less than 100 persons; Business ownership: 570 women-owned, n/a Black-owned, n/a Hispanic-owned, n/a Asian-owned
Employment: 10.9% management, business, and financial, 1.9% computer, engineering, and science, 8.9% education, legal, community service, arts, and media, 4.4% healthcare practitioners, 14.7% service, 18.0% sales and office, 12.6% natural resources, construction, and maintenance, 28.5% production, transportation, and material moving
Income: Per capita: $21,226; Median household: $40,168; Average household: $52,804; Households with income of $100,000 or more: 11.5%; Poverty rate: 15.5%
Educational Attainment: High school diploma or higher: 84.1%; Bachelor's degree or higher: 12.7%; Graduate/professional degree or higher: 4.3%
Housing: Homeownership rate: 75.9%; Median home value: $95,600; Median year structure built: 1971; Homeowner vacancy rate: 2.6%; Median gross rent: $608 per month; Rental vacancy rate: 9.8%
Vital Statistics: Birth rate: 108.6 per 10,000 population; Death rate: 96.8 per 10,000 population; Age-adjusted cancer mortality rate: 230.4 deaths per 100,000 population
Health Insurance: 84.9% have insurance; 66.1% have private insurance; 32.5% have public insurance; 15.1% do not have insurance; 12.5% of children under 18 do not have insurance
Health Care: Physicians: 7.7 per 10,000 population; Hospital beds: 12.0 per 10,000 population; Hospital admissions: 450.1 per 10,000 population
Transportation: Commute: 90.6% car, 0.4% public transportation, 2.5% walk, 4.7% work from home; Median travel time to work: 22.7 minutes
Presidential Election: 32.3% Obama, 65.4% Romney (2012)
Additional Information Contacts
Fulton Government . . . . (574) 223-2912
http://www.co.fulton.in.us

Fulton County Communities

AKRON (town). Covers a land area of 0.457 square miles and a water area of 0 square miles. Located at 41.04° N. Lat; 86.02° W. Long. Elevation is 853 feet.
Population: 1,167; Growth (since 2000): 8.5%; Density: 2,553.2 persons per square mile; Race: 74.2% White, 0.0% Black/African American, 0.0% Asian, 1.9% American Indian/Alaska Native, 0.0% Native Hawaiian/Other Pacific Islander, 1.5% Two or more races, 30.1% Hispanic of any race; Average household size: 2.84; Median age: 33.0; Age under 18: 29.6%; Age 65 and over: 14.7%; Males per 100 females: 95.5
School District(s)
Tippecanoe Valley School Corp (KG-12)
    2012-13 Enrollment: 1,980 . . . . (574) 353-7741
Housing: Homeownership rate: 64.3%; Homeowner vacancy rate: 4.3%; Rental vacancy rate: 14.5%

FULTON (town). Covers a land area of 0.178 square miles and a water area of 0 square miles. Located at 40.95° N. Lat; 86.26° W. Long. Elevation is 794 feet.
Population: 333; Growth (since 2000): 2.1%; Density: 1,874.8 persons per square mile; Race: 98.2% White, 0.0% Black/African American, 0.0% Asian, 0.0% American Indian/Alaska Native, 0.0% Native Hawaiian/Other Pacific Islander, 0.0% Two or more races, 2.1% Hispanic of any race; Average household size: 2.60; Median age: 36.9; Age under 18: 30.3%; Age 65 and over: 15.6%; Males per 100 females: 103.0

School District(s)
Caston School Corporation (KG-12)
    2012-13 Enrollment: 749 . . . . (574) 857-2035
Housing: Homeownership rate: 78.1%; Homeowner vacancy rate: 2.9%; Rental vacancy rate: 17.6%

KEWANNA (town). Covers a land area of 0.531 square miles and a water area of 0 square miles. Located at 41.02° N. Lat; 86.41° W. Long. Elevation is 784 feet.
Population: 613; Growth (since 2000): -0.2%; Density: 1,155.5 persons per square mile; Race: 96.2% White, 1.1% Black/African American, 0.2% Asian, 0.3% American Indian/Alaska Native, 0.0% Native Hawaiian/Other Pacific Islander, 2.0% Two or more races, 2.1% Hispanic of any race; Average household size: 2.44; Median age: 35.2; Age under 18: 28.4%; Age 65 and over: 13.2%; Males per 100 females: 92.8
Housing: Homeownership rate: 71.7%; Homeowner vacancy rate: 3.2%; Rental vacancy rate: 12.3%
Newspapers: The Observer (weekly circulation 600)

ROCHESTER (city). County seat. Covers a land area of 4.691 square miles and a water area of 1.111 square miles. Located at 41.06° N. Lat; 86.20° W. Long. Elevation is 781 feet.
History: Rochester was founded in 1831 as a trading post, and became a resort town on Lake Manitou.
Population: 6,218; Growth (since 2000): -3.1%; Density: 1,325.6 persons per square mile; Race: 95.9% White, 0.6% Black/African American, 0.9% Asian, 0.4% American Indian/Alaska Native, 0.0% Native Hawaiian/Other Pacific Islander, 1.2% Two or more races, 3.4% Hispanic of any race; Average household size: 2.26; Median age: 41.6; Age under 18: 22.5%; Age 65 and over: 19.5%; Males per 100 females: 91.9; Marriage status: 22.6% never married, 51.6% now married, 1.5% separated, 10.8% widowed, 15.0% divorced; Foreign born: 2.0%; Speak English only: 95.2%; With disability: 22.6%; Veterans: 10.2%; Ancestry: 24.6% German, 20.5% American, 10.2% English, 9.6% Irish, 4.3% Polish
Employment: 10.2% management, business, and financial, 2.5% computer, engineering, and science, 10.0% education, legal, community service, arts, and media, 3.3% healthcare practitioners, 14.6% service, 16.3% sales and office, 8.7% natural resources, construction, and maintenance, 34.5% production, transportation, and material moving
Income: Per capita: $22,795; Median household: $29,731; Average household: $49,076; Households with income of $100,000 or more: 10.4%; Poverty rate: 20.7%
Educational Attainment: High school diploma or higher: 84.4%; Bachelor's degree or higher: 18.1%; Graduate/professional degree or higher: 7.5%
School District(s)
Rochester Community Sch Corp (PK-12)
    2012-13 Enrollment: 1,879 . . . . (574) 223-2159
Housing: Homeownership rate: 62.4%; Median home value: $89,500; Median year structure built: 1965; Homeowner vacancy rate: 3.4%; Median gross rent: $623 per month; Rental vacancy rate: 9.9%
Health Insurance: 85.5% have insurance; 54.6% have private insurance; 46.1% have public insurance; 14.5% do not have insurance; 12.3% of children under 18 do not have insurance
Hospitals: Woodlawn Hospital
Newspapers: Rochester Sentinel (daily circulation 3800)
Transportation: Commute: 87.1% car, 0.1% public transportation, 4.0% walk, 6.9% work from home; Median travel time to work: 19.4 minutes
Airports: Fulton County (general aviation)
Additional Information Contacts
City of Rochester. . . . . (574) 223-2510
http://www.rochester.in.us

Gibson County

Located in southwestern Indiana; bounded on the west by the Wabash River and the Illinois border, and on the north by the White River; also drained by the Patoka and Black Rivers. Covers a land area of 487.486 square miles, a water area of 11.679 square miles, and is located in the Central Time Zone at 38.32° N. Lat., 87.58° W. Long. The county was founded in 1813. County seat is Princeton.

Weather Station: Princeton 1 W   Elevation: 479 feet

	Jan	Feb	Mar	Apr	May	Jun	Jul	Aug	Sep	Oct	Nov	Dec
High	39	44	55	66	76	85	88	87	80	68	54	42
Low	23	27	35	45	55	64	68	66	58	46	37	27
Precip	3.1	3.0	4.5	4.4	5.9	3.9	4.2	3.7	3.8	3.8	4.4	3.7
Snow	3.0	3.5	0.8	0.1	0.0	0.0	0.0	0.0	0.0	0.1	0.2	3.3

High and Low temperatures in degrees Fahrenheit; Precipitation and Snow in inches

Population: 33,503; Growth (since 2000): 3.1%; Density: 68.7 persons per square mile; Race: 95.5% White, 1.8% Black/African American, 0.5% Asian, 0.2% American Indian/Alaska Native, 0.0% Native Hawaiian/Other Pacific Islander, 1.6% two or more races, 1.3% Hispanic of any race; Average household size: 2.47; Median age: 39.9; Age under 18: 24.3%; Age 65 and over: 15.3%; Males per 100 females: 97.9; Marriage status: 23.0% never married, 58.6% now married, 1.1% separated, 6.2% widowed, 12.2% divorced; Foreign born: 1.0%; Speak English only: 98.0%; With disability: 13.4%; Veterans: 9.7%; Ancestry: 28.7% German, 17.6% American, 13.7% Irish, 12.3% English, 2.5% French
Religion: Six largest groups: 18.6% Catholicism, 7.2% Methodist/Pietist, 3.8% Holiness, 3.6% Pentecostal, 2.8% Non-denominational Protestant, 2.8% Baptist
Economy: Unemployment rate: 5.1%; Leading industries: 16.9% retail trade; 14.4% other services (except public administration); 10.7% health care and social assistance; Farms: 589 totaling 268,146 acres; Company size: 1 employs 1,000 or more persons, 2 employ 500 to 999 persons, 18 employ 100 to 499 persons, 701 employs less than 100 persons; Business ownership: 570 women-owned, n/a Black-owned, n/a Hispanic-owned, n/a Asian-owned
Employment: 11.6% management, business, and financial, 3.4% computer, engineering, and science, 7.2% education, legal, community service, arts, and media, 4.6% healthcare practitioners, 16.8% service, 17.7% sales and office, 11.9% natural resources, construction, and maintenance, 26.8% production, transportation, and material moving
Income: Per capita: $24,258; Median household: $49,329; Average household: $61,416; Households with income of $100,000 or more: 16.7%; Poverty rate: 11.5%
Educational Attainment: High school diploma or higher: 90.1%; Bachelor's degree or higher: 16.1%; Graduate/professional degree or higher: 4.3%
Housing: Homeownership rate: 76.7%; Median home value: $104,400; Median year structure built: 1968; Homeowner vacancy rate: 2.1%; Median gross rent: $615 per month; Rental vacancy rate: 9.3%
Vital Statistics: Birth rate: 130.3 per 10,000 population; Death rate: 109.2 per 10,000 population; Age-adjusted cancer mortality rate: 175.3 deaths per 100,000 population
Health Insurance: 88.7% have insurance; 74.2% have private insurance; 27.9% have public insurance; 11.3% do not have insurance; 6.9% of children under 18 do not have insurance
Health Care: Physicians: 7.7 per 10,000 population; Hospital beds: 20.9 per 10,000 population; Hospital admissions: 224.5 per 10,000 population
Air Quality Index: 96.4% good, 3.0% moderate, 0.5% unhealthy for sensitive individuals, 0.0% unhealthy (percent of days)
Transportation: Commute: 93.1% car, 0.4% public transportation, 3.0% walk, 3.0% work from home; Median travel time to work: 21.2 minutes
Presidential Election: 33.5% Obama, 64.5% Romney (2012)
Additional Information Contacts
Gibson Government . . . . (812) 385-5286
http://www.gibsoncounty-in.gov

Gibson County Communities

FORT BRANCH (town). Covers a land area of 1.097 square miles and a water area of 0.011 square miles. Located at 38.25° N. Lat; 87.57° W. Long. Elevation is 449 feet.
History: The town of Fort Branch was named for Old Fort Branch, built in 1811.
Population: 2,771; Growth (since 2000): 19.4%; Density: 2,526.0 persons per square mile; Race: 96.8% White, 0.3% Black/African American, 1.2% Asian, 0.1% American Indian/Alaska Native, 0.0% Native Hawaiian/Other Pacific Islander, 0.9% Two or more races, 0.9% Hispanic of any race; Average household size: 2.38; Median age: 38.0; Age under 18: 24.4%; Age 65 and over: 14.4%; Males per 100 females: 99.4; Marriage status: 22.8% never married, 57.7% now married, 0.5% separated, 6.2% widowed, 13.2% divorced; Foreign born: 0.9%; Speak English only: 97.8%; With disability: 12.7%; Veterans: 10.6%; Ancestry: 42.6% German, 13.3% Irish, 12.9% English, 10.5% American, 2.0% French
Employment: 7.3% management, business, and financial, 3.3% computer, engineering, and science, 8.4% education, legal, community service, arts, and media, 5.3% healthcare practitioners, 25.6% service, 17.1% sales and office, 12.0% natural resources, construction, and maintenance, 21.0% production, transportation, and material moving
Income: Per capita: $23,002; Median household: $46,821; Average household: $56,223; Households with income of $100,000 or more: 15.0%; Poverty rate: 7.9%
Educational Attainment: High school diploma or higher: 93.6%; Bachelor's degree or higher: 16.5%; Graduate/professional degree or higher: 5.6%
School District(s)
South Gibson School Corp (KG-12)
    2012-13 Enrollment: 1,957 . . . . (812) 753-4230
Housing: Homeownership rate: 76.1%; Median home value: $106,200; Median year structure built: 1962; Homeowner vacancy rate: 2.4%; Median gross rent: $508 per month; Rental vacancy rate: 8.9%
Health Insurance: 91.8% have insurance; 78.1% have private insurance; 27.0% have public insurance; 8.2% do not have insurance; 3.7% of children under 18 do not have insurance
Newspapers: South Gibson Star Times (weekly circulation 5100)
Transportation: Commute: 95.9% car, 0.0% public transportation, 1.6% walk, 2.1% work from home; Median travel time to work: 19.5 minutes
Additional Information Contacts
Town of Fort Branch . . . . (812) 385-2134
    http://www.gibsoncountychamber.org

FRANCISCO (town). Covers a land area of 0.495 square miles and a water area of 0.004 square miles. Located at 38.33° N. Lat; 87.45° W. Long. Elevation is 469 feet.
History: Francisco developed when the Wabash & Erie Canal was built, and was named for a Spanish laborer on the canal.
Population: 469; Growth (since 2000): -13.6%; Density: 946.6 persons per square mile; Race: 97.0% White, 0.2% Black/African American, 0.2% Asian, 0.2% American Indian/Alaska Native, 0.0% Native Hawaiian/Other Pacific Islander, 2.3% Two or more races, 0.9% Hispanic of any race; Average household size: 2.48; Median age: 39.6; Age under 18: 25.8%; Age 65 and over: 16.2%; Males per 100 females: 91.4
School District(s)
East Gibson School Corporation (KG-12)
    2012-13 Enrollment: 946 . . . . (812) 749-4755
Housing: Homeownership rate: 87.9%; Homeowner vacancy rate: 7.7%; Rental vacancy rate: 23.3%

HAUBSTADT (town). Covers a land area of 0.704 square miles and a water area of 0.007 square miles. Located at 38.20° N. Lat; 87.58° W. Long. Elevation is 472 feet.
Population: 1,577; Growth (since 2000): 3.1%; Density: 2,240.1 persons per square mile; Race: 98.2% White, 0.6% Black/African American, 0.2% Asian, 0.2% American Indian/Alaska Native, 0.0% Native Hawaiian/Other Pacific Islander, 0.6% Two or more races, 0.6% Hispanic of any race; Average household size: 2.35; Median age: 41.1; Age under 18: 23.0%; Age 65 and over: 16.7%; Males per 100 females: 101.4
School District(s)
South Gibson School Corp (KG-12)
    2012-13 Enrollment: 1,957 . . . . (812) 753-4230
Housing: Homeownership rate: 77.5%; Homeowner vacancy rate: 1.1%; Rental vacancy rate: 9.0%

HAZLETON (town). Covers a land area of 0.333 square miles and a water area of <.001 square miles. Located at 38.49° N. Lat; 87.54° W. Long. Elevation is 453 feet.
History: Also spelled Hazelton.
Population: 263; Growth (since 2000): -8.7%; Density: 789.5 persons per square mile; Race: 97.3% White, 2.3% Black/African American, 0.0% Asian, 0.0% American Indian/Alaska Native, 0.0% Native Hawaiian/Other Pacific Islander, 0.4% Two or more races, 0.4% Hispanic of any race; Average household size: 2.44; Median age: 44.9; Age under 18: 21.3%; Age 65 and over: 14.4%; Males per 100 females: 100.8
Housing: Homeownership rate: 82.4%; Homeowner vacancy rate: 0.0%; Rental vacancy rate: 0.0%

MACKEY (town). Covers a land area of 0.086 square miles and a water area of 0 square miles. Located at 38.25° N. Lat; 87.39° W. Long. Elevation is 449 feet.
Population: 106; Growth (since 2000): -25.4%; Density: 1,228.0 persons per square mile; Race: 98.1% White, 0.0% Black/African American, 0.0% Asian, 0.0% American Indian/Alaska Native, 0.0% Native Hawaiian/Other Pacific Islander, 1.9% Two or more races, 0.0% Hispanic of any race; Average household size: 2.36; Median age: 37.5; Age under 18: 19.8%; Age 65 and over: 14.2%; Males per 100 females: 103.8
School District(s)
East Gibson School Corporation (KG-12)
   2012-13 Enrollment: 946. . . . . (812) 749-4755
Housing: Homeownership rate: 75.6%; Homeowner vacancy rate: 2.8%; Rental vacancy rate: 0.0%

OAKLAND CITY (city). Covers a land area of 1.131 square miles and a water area of 0.002 square miles. Located at 38.34° N. Lat; 87.35° W. Long. Elevation is 463 feet.
History: Oakland City developed around Oakland City College, established by the Baptist church in 1891.
Population: 2,429; Growth (since 2000): -6.1%; Density: 2,148.0 persons per square mile; Race: 97.2% White, 0.4% Black/African American, 0.6% Asian, 0.2% American Indian/Alaska Native, 0.0% Native Hawaiian/Other Pacific Islander, 1.1% Two or more races, 2.0% Hispanic of any race; Average household size: 2.22; Median age: 36.1; Age under 18: 20.6%; Age 65 and over: 17.5%; Males per 100 females: 89.5
School District(s)
East Gibson School Corporation (KG-12)
   2012-13 Enrollment: 946. . . . . (812) 749-4755
Four-year College(s)
Oakland City University (Private, Not-for-profit, Baptist)
   Fall 2013 Enrollment: 2,418 . . . . (812) 749-4781
   2013-14 Tuition: In-state $19,200; Out-of-state $19,200
Housing: Homeownership rate: 63.1%; Homeowner vacancy rate: 3.3%; Rental vacancy rate: 13.5%
Additional Information Contacts
City of Oakland City. . . . . (812) 385-2134
   http://www.gibsoncountychamber.org

OWENSVILLE (town). Covers a land area of 0.589 square miles and a water area of 0 square miles. Located at 38.27° N. Lat; 87.69° W. Long. Elevation is 509 feet.
History: Laid out 1817; incorporated 1881.
Population: 1,284; Growth (since 2000): -2.9%; Density: 2,181.0 persons per square mile; Race: 97.9% White, 0.2% Black/African American, 0.2% Asian, 0.7% American Indian/Alaska Native, 0.0% Native Hawaiian/Other Pacific Islander, 0.9% Two or more races, 1.2% Hispanic of any race; Average household size: 2.41; Median age: 40.6; Age under 18: 24.0%; Age 65 and over: 19.9%; Males per 100 females: 90.5
School District(s)
South Gibson School Corp (KG-12)
   2012-13 Enrollment: 1,957 . . . . (812) 753-4230
Housing: Homeownership rate: 70.4%; Homeowner vacancy rate: 1.6%; Rental vacancy rate: 6.8%

PATOKA (town). Covers a land area of 1.121 square miles and a water area of 0.019 square miles. Located at 38.40° N. Lat; 87.59° W. Long. Elevation is 436 feet.
History: Patoka was settled in 1789 on the Patoka River, and platted in 1813. It was a stagecoach stop on the Vincennes-Evansville line. The name is of Indian origin meaning "logs on the bottom."
Population: 735; Growth (since 2000): -1.9%; Density: 655.7 persons per square mile; Race: 95.8% White, 1.1% Black/African American, 0.3% Asian, 0.4% American Indian/Alaska Native, 0.0% Native Hawaiian/Other Pacific Islander, 2.0% Two or more races, 1.0% Hispanic of any race; Average household size: 2.49; Median age: 41.4; Age under 18: 24.6%; Age 65 and over: 16.7%; Males per 100 females: 114.9
Housing: Homeownership rate: 84.4%; Homeowner vacancy rate: 1.6%; Rental vacancy rate: 21.3%

PRINCETON (city). County seat. Covers a land area of 5.070 square miles and a water area of 0.005 square miles. Located at 38.36° N. Lat; 87.58° W. Long. Elevation is 499 feet.
History: Princeton was founded in 1814 and named for Captain William Prince. An early industry was Evans Mill, a wool-carding mill which had Abraham Lincoln as a customer in 1827.
Population: 8,644; Growth (since 2000): 5.7%; Density: 1,704.9 persons per square mile; Race: 90.4% White, 4.6% Black/African American, 0.7% Asian, 0.2% American Indian/Alaska Native, 0.0% Native Hawaiian/Other Pacific Islander, 3.0% Two or more races, 2.5% Hispanic of any race; Average household size: 2.34; Median age: 37.2; Age under 18: 25.0%; Age 65 and over: 16.1%; Males per 100 females: 91.1; Marriage status: 27.9% never married, 50.7% now married, 1.9% separated, 6.6% widowed, 14.9% divorced; Foreign born: 2.0%; Speak English only: 96.8%; With disability: 16.5%; Veterans: 11.2%; Ancestry: 18.6% German, 15.5% American, 13.5% Irish, 11.3% English, 2.7% French
Employment: 10.0% management, business, and financial, 1.5% computer, engineering, and science, 7.0% education, legal, community service, arts, and media, 2.6% healthcare practitioners, 20.6% service, 17.4% sales and office, 9.9% natural resources, construction, and maintenance, 31.1% production, transportation, and material moving
Income: Per capita: $20,981; Median household: $41,099; Average household: $51,524; Households with income of $100,000 or more: 10.3%; Poverty rate: 16.4%
Educational Attainment: High school diploma or higher: 88.3%; Bachelor's degree or higher: 13.6%; Graduate/professional degree or higher: 2.1%
School District(s)
North Gibson School Corp (KG-12)
   2012-13 Enrollment: 2,055 . . . . (812) 385-4851
Housing: Homeownership rate: 58.9%; Median home value: $82,400; Median year structure built: 1961; Homeowner vacancy rate: 4.4%; Median gross rent: $643 per month; Rental vacancy rate: 9.2%
Health Insurance: 86.4% have insurance; 65.1% have private insurance; 37.5% have public insurance; 13.6% do not have insurance; 5.8% of children under 18 do not have insurance
Hospitals: Gibson General Hospital (109 beds)
Newspapers: Oakland City Journal (weekly circulation 800); Princeton Daily Clarion (daily circulation 6300)
Transportation: Commute: 93.2% car, 0.5% public transportation, 4.7% walk, 1.5% work from home; Median travel time to work: 15.6 minutes
Additional Information Contacts
City of Princeton . . . . (812) 385-2134
   http://www.gibsoncountychamber.org

SOMERVILLE (town). Covers a land area of 0.315 square miles and a water area of 0.002 square miles. Located at 38.28° N. Lat; 87.38° W. Long. Elevation is 469 feet.
Population: 293; Growth (since 2000): -6.1%; Density: 930.4 persons per square mile; Race: 98.6% White, 0.3% Black/African American, 0.0% Asian, 0.3% American Indian/Alaska Native, 0.0% Native Hawaiian/Other Pacific Islander, 0.3% Two or more races, 2.4% Hispanic of any race; Average household size: 2.66; Median age: 36.9; Age under 18: 28.3%; Age 65 and over: 16.4%; Males per 100 females: 103.5
Housing: Homeownership rate: 82.7%; Homeowner vacancy rate: 1.1%; Rental vacancy rate: 0.0%

Grant County

Located in east central Indiana; drained by the Mississinewa River. Covers a land area of 414.074 square miles, a water area of 0.824 square miles, and is located in the Eastern Time Zone at 40.52° N. Lat., 85.65° W. Long. The county was founded in 1831. County seat is Marion.

Grant County is part of the Marion, IN Micropolitan Statistical Area. The entire metro area includes: Grant County, IN

Weather Station: Marion 2 N   Elevation: 790 feet

	Jan	Feb	Mar	Apr	May	Jun	Jul	Aug	Sep	Oct	Nov	Dec
High	33	37	48	61	72	81	84	82	77	64	51	37
Low	18	20	28	38	49	59	63	61	53	42	33	23
Precip	2.4	2.3	3.0	3.7	4.8	3.8	4.7	3.7	2.9	3.1	3.3	3.0
Snow	7.5	6.9	3.2	0.6	0.0	0.0	0.0	0.0	0.0	0.4	0.9	5.4

High and Low temperatures in degrees Fahrenheit; Precipitation and Snow in inches

Population: 70,061; Growth (since 2000): -4.6%; Density: 169.2 persons per square mile; Race: 88.2% White, 7.0% Black/African American, 0.6% Asian, 0.3% American Indian/Alaska Native, 0.0% Native Hawaiian/Other Pacific Islander, 2.4% two or more races, 3.6% Hispanic of any race; Average household size: 2.39; Median age: 39.5; Age under 18: 21.7%; Age 65 and over: 16.2%; Males per 100 females: 92.6; Marriage status: 30.5% never married, 48.5% now married, 1.4% separated, 7.4% widowed, 13.6% divorced; Foreign born: 1.5%; Speak English only: 97.1%; With disability: 17.1%; Veterans: 10.8%; Ancestry: 21.1% German, 11.5% American, 10.8% Irish, 8.6% English, 2.1% Dutch
Religion: Six largest groups: 8.9% Methodist/Pietist, 8.8% Holiness, 6.7% Baptist, 6.3% Non-denominational Protestant, 3.3% Catholicism, 1.6% European Free-Church
Economy: Unemployment rate: 6.4%; Leading industries: 18.5% retail trade; 14.4% other services (except public administration); 14.3% health care and social assistance; Farms: 500 totaling 183,380 acres; Company size: 5 employ 1,000 or more persons, 3 employ 500 to 999 persons, 26 employ 100 to 499 persons, 1,298 employ less than 100 persons; Business ownership: n/a women-owned, 114 Black-owned, n/a Hispanic-owned, 54 Asian-owned
Employment: 11.0% management, business, and financial, 2.0% computer, engineering, and science, 9.8% education, legal, community service, arts, and media, 6.1% healthcare practitioners, 19.2% service, 26.5% sales and office, 7.7% natural resources, construction, and maintenance, 17.7% production, transportation, and material moving
Income: Per capita: $20,516; Median household: $39,747; Average household: $51,236; Households with income of $100,000 or more: 9.5%; Poverty rate: 18.6%
Educational Attainment: High school diploma or higher: 85.7%; Bachelor's degree or higher: 16.8%; Graduate/professional degree or higher: 6.6%
Housing: Homeownership rate: 70.0%; Median home value: $80,100; Median year structure built: 1962; Homeowner vacancy rate: 2.5%; Median gross rent: $610 per month; Rental vacancy rate: 12.9%
Vital Statistics: Birth rate: 114.3 per 10,000 population; Death rate: 112.4 per 10,000 population; Age-adjusted cancer mortality rate: 186.5 deaths per 100,000 population
Health Insurance: 85.4% have insurance; 64.1% have private insurance; 36.1% have public insurance; 14.6% do not have insurance; 8.3% of children under 18 do not have insurance
Health Care: Physicians: 12.7 per 10,000 population; Hospital beds: 16.5 per 10,000 population; Hospital admissions: 741.5 per 10,000 population
Transportation: Commute: 87.7% car, 0.2% public transportation, 4.0% walk, 6.8% work from home; Median travel time to work: 18.9 minutes
Presidential Election: 38.0% Obama, 60.0% Romney (2012)
Additional Information Contacts
Grant Government. . . . . (765) 668-8871
http://www.grantcounty.net

Grant County Communities

FAIRMOUNT (town). Covers a land area of 1.583 square miles and a water area of 0 square miles. Located at 40.42° N. Lat; 85.65° W. Long. Elevation is 873 feet.
History: Fairmount developed around the Wesleyan Camp Meeting Grounds, site of state and national conferences of the Methodist Church.
Population: 2,954; Growth (since 2000): -1.3%; Density: 1,866.4 persons per square mile; Race: 98.6% White, 0.1% Black/African American, 0.2% Asian, 0.2% American Indian/Alaska Native, 0.0% Native Hawaiian/Other Pacific Islander, 0.7% Two or more races, 0.9% Hispanic of any race; Average household size: 2.38; Median age: 40.3; Age under 18: 23.9%; Age 65 and over: 16.5%; Males per 100 females: 94.3; Marriage status: 23.5% never married, 55.9% now married, 2.4% separated, 8.6% widowed, 12.1% divorced; Foreign born: 0.0%; Speak English only: 99.0%; With disability: 19.0%; Veterans: 9.1%; Ancestry: 25.9% German, 16.9% Irish, 11.8% American, 10.4% English, 4.6% French
Employment: 8.9% management, business, and financial, 1.4% computer, engineering, and science, 5.2% education, legal, community service, arts, and media, 2.0% healthcare practitioners, 30.3% service, 28.1% sales and office, 10.3% natural resources, construction, and maintenance, 13.6% production, transportation, and material moving
Income: Per capita: $18,942; Median household: $43,080; Average household: $49,656; Households with income of $100,000 or more: 8.0%; Poverty rate: 16.6%
Educational Attainment: High school diploma or higher: 84.4%; Bachelor's degree or higher: 14.0%; Graduate/professional degree or higher: 7.0%

School District(s)
Madison-Grant United Sch Corp (KG-12)
    2012-13 Enrollment: 1,408 . . . . (765) 948-4143
Housing: Homeownership rate: 75.4%; Median home value: $74,300; Median year structure built: 1960; Homeowner vacancy rate: 1.3%; Median gross rent: $653 per month; Rental vacancy rate: 9.7%
Health Insurance: 86.9% have insurance; 68.4% have private insurance; 31.0% have public insurance; 13.1% do not have insurance; 7.8% of children under 18 do not have insurance
Safety: Violent crime rate: 13.8 per 10,000 population; Property crime rate: 31.0 per 10,000 population
Newspapers: Fairmount News Sun (weekly circulation 4400)
Transportation: Commute: 93.6% car, 0.0% public transportation, 0.0% walk, 4.4% work from home; Median travel time to work: 21.7 minutes
Additional Information Contacts
Town of Fairmount . . . . (765) 664-5107
http://marionchamber.org

FOWLERTON (town). Covers a land area of 0.196 square miles and a water area of 0 square miles. Located at 40.41° N. Lat; 85.57° W. Long. Elevation is 883 feet.
Population: 261; Growth (since 2000): -12.4%; Density: 1,334.5 persons per square mile; Race: 98.9% White, 0.0% Black/African American, 0.0% Asian, 0.0% American Indian/Alaska Native, 0.0% Native Hawaiian/Other Pacific Islander, 1.1% Two or more races, 0.4% Hispanic of any race; Average household size: 2.61; Median age: 43.9; Age under 18: 25.7%; Age 65 and over: 17.6%; Males per 100 females: 103.9
Housing: Homeownership rate: 77.0%; Homeowner vacancy rate: 4.9%; Rental vacancy rate: 22.6%

GAS CITY (city). Covers a land area of 4.556 square miles and a water area of 0 square miles. Located at 40.49° N. Lat; 85.60° W. Long. Elevation is 856 feet.
History: Natural gas was discovered here in 1887, giving brief fortune to Gas City. The Owens-Illinois Glass Company Plant was founded here during the gas boom.
Population: 5,965; Growth (since 2000): 0.4%; Density: 1,309.1 persons per square mile; Race: 96.2% White, 0.9% Black/African American, 0.4% Asian, 0.3% American Indian/Alaska Native, 0.0% Native Hawaiian/Other Pacific Islander, 1.7% Two or more races, 2.4% Hispanic of any race; Average household size: 2.45; Median age: 39.4; Age under 18: 24.6%; Age 65 and over: 15.4%; Males per 100 females: 93.0; Marriage status: 25.6% never married, 50.3% now married, 1.8% separated, 6.0% widowed, 18.1% divorced; Foreign born: 0.8%; Speak English only: 98.8%; With disability: 16.6%; Veterans: 13.3%; Ancestry: 17.6% American, 15.5% German, 14.1% Irish, 7.8% English, 2.0% Dutch
Employment: 4.2% management, business, and financial, 0.5% computer, engineering, and science, 11.2% education, legal, community service, arts, and media, 6.4% healthcare practitioners, 15.1% service, 30.8% sales and office, 7.8% natural resources, construction, and maintenance, 24.1% production, transportation, and material moving
Income: Per capita: $20,295; Median household: $42,100; Average household: $51,077; Households with income of $100,000 or more: 8.3%; Poverty rate: 22.3%
Educational Attainment: High school diploma or higher: 86.1%; Bachelor's degree or higher: 11.5%; Graduate/professional degree or higher: 2.9%

School District(s)
Mississinewa Community School Corp (PK-12)
    2012-13 Enrollment: 2,520 . . . . (765) 674-8528
Housing: Homeownership rate: 71.5%; Median home value: $78,000; Median year structure built: 1967; Homeowner vacancy rate: 2.4%; Median gross rent: $671 per month; Rental vacancy rate: 7.2%
Health Insurance: 81.4% have insurance; 56.7% have private insurance; 36.9% have public insurance; 18.6% do not have insurance; 19.0% of children under 18 do not have insurance
Newspapers: Indiana Newspaper Group (weekly circulation 5000)
Transportation: Commute: 92.8% car, 0.9% public transportation, 3.7% walk, 2.3% work from home; Median travel time to work: 18.3 minutes
Additional Information Contacts
City of Gas City . . . . (765) 677-3079
http://www.gascityindiana.com

HERBST (CDP). Covers a land area of 1.305 square miles and a water area of 0 square miles. Located at 40.51° N. Lat; 85.78° W. Long. Elevation is 856 feet.
Population: 112; Growth (since 2000): n/a; Density: 85.8 persons per square mile; Race: 100.0% White, 0.0% Black/African American, 0.0% Asian, 0.0% American Indian/Alaska Native, 0.0% Native Hawaiian/Other Pacific Islander, 0.0% Two or more races, 0.0% Hispanic of any race; Average household size: 2.49; Median age: 47.5; Age under 18: 17.9%; Age 65 and over: 25.0%; Males per 100 females: 96.5
Housing: Homeownership rate: 82.2%; Homeowner vacancy rate: 0.0%; Rental vacancy rate: 0.0%

JALAPA (CDP). Covers a land area of 3.177 square miles and a water area of 0 square miles. Located at 40.63° N. Lat; 85.75° W. Long. Elevation is 817 feet.
Population: 171; Growth (since 2000): n/a; Density: 53.8 persons per square mile; Race: 98.2% White, 0.0% Black/African American, 0.6% Asian, 0.0% American Indian/Alaska Native, 0.0% Native Hawaiian/Other Pacific Islander, 1.2% Two or more races, 0.6% Hispanic of any race; Average household size: 2.51; Median age: 49.2; Age under 18: 17.0%; Age 65 and over: 17.5%; Males per 100 females: 92.1
Housing: Homeownership rate: 89.7%; Homeowner vacancy rate: 0.0%; Rental vacancy rate: 12.5%

JONESBORO (city). Covers a land area of 0.891 square miles and a water area of 0 square miles. Located at 40.48° N. Lat; 85.63° W. Long. Elevation is 853 feet.
History: Jonesboro was founded in 1837 by Obadiah Jones. Its location on the Mississinewa River made it a trading center.
Population: 1,756; Growth (since 2000): -6.9%; Density: 1,971.6 persons per square mile; Race: 97.7% White, 0.1% Black/African American, 0.0% Asian, 0.5% American Indian/Alaska Native, 0.0% Native Hawaiian/Other Pacific Islander, 1.2% Two or more races, 2.4% Hispanic of any race; Average household size: 2.57; Median age: 39.0; Age under 18: 25.8%; Age 65 and over: 14.9%; Males per 100 females: 94.2
School District(s)
Mississinewa Community School Corp (PK-12)
    2012-13 Enrollment: 2,520 . . . . (765) 674-8528
Housing: Homeownership rate: 76.4%; Homeowner vacancy rate: 1.7%; Rental vacancy rate: 17.4%

LANDESS (CDP). Covers a land area of 1.392 square miles and a water area of 0 square miles. Located at 40.61° N. Lat; 85.56° W. Long. Elevation is 869 feet.
Population: 188; Growth (since 2000): n/a; Density: 135.1 persons per square mile; Race: 97.3% White, 0.0% Black/African American, 0.0% Asian, 0.0% American Indian/Alaska Native, 0.0% Native Hawaiian/Other Pacific Islander, 0.5% Two or more races, 2.7% Hispanic of any race; Average household size: 2.69; Median age: 40.0; Age under 18: 27.7%; Age 65 and over: 10.6%; Males per 100 females: 126.5
Housing: Homeownership rate: 80.0%; Homeowner vacancy rate: 3.3%; Rental vacancy rate: 6.7%

MARION (city). County seat. Covers a land area of 15.711 square miles and a water area of 0.084 square miles. Located at 40.55° N. Lat; 85.66° W. Long. Elevation is 814 feet.
History: The first settlers came to Marion in 1826. The town was laid out in 1831 and named for General Francis Marion, cavalry officer in the American Revolution. Marion grew rapidly when natural gas and oil were discovered here in the 1880's, but the boom was short-lived. Diversified industry replaced the oil wells.
Population: 29,948; Growth (since 2000): -4.4%; Density: 1,906.2 persons per square mile; Race: 78.1% White, 14.7% Black/African American, 0.7% Asian, 0.4% American Indian/Alaska Native, 0.0% Native Hawaiian/Other Pacific Islander, 3.6% Two or more races, 5.5% Hispanic of any race; Average household size: 2.25; Median age: 36.2; Age under 18: 21.1%; Age 65 and over: 16.0%; Males per 100 females: 88.8; Marriage status: 37.6% never married, 37.5% now married, 1.9% separated, 9.1% widowed, 15.8% divorced; Foreign born: 1.8%; Speak English only: 96.4%; With disability: 19.6%; Veterans: 9.5%; Ancestry: 19.2% German, 9.8% American, 8.5% Irish, 7.8% English, 2.1% Dutch
Employment: 11.4% management, business, and financial, 2.0% computer, engineering, and science, 8.5% education, legal, community service, arts, and media, 5.9% healthcare practitioners, 21.5% service, 27.8% sales and office, 5.3% natural resources, construction, and maintenance, 17.6% production, transportation, and material moving
Income: Per capita: $17,808; Median household: $31,391; Average household: $41,914; Households with income of $100,000 or more: 6.5%; Poverty rate: 26.0%
Educational Attainment: High school diploma or higher: 81.1%; Bachelor's degree or higher: 14.9%; Graduate/professional degree or higher: 5.9%
School District(s)
Dr Robert H Faulkner Academy (KG-06)
    2012-13 Enrollment: 194 . . . . (765) 662-9910
Eastbrook Community Sch Corp (PK-12)
    2012-13 Enrollment: 1,630 . . . . (765) 664-0624
Marion Community Schools (PK-12)
    2012-13 Enrollment: 3,842 . . . . (765) 662-2546
Four-year College(s)
Indiana Wesleyan University (Private, Not-for-profit, Wesleyan)
    Fall 2013 Enrollment: 14,959 . . . . (765) 674-6901
    2013-14 Tuition: In-state $23,628; Out-of-state $23,628
Vocational/Technical School(s)
Marion Community Schools-Tucker Career & Technology Center (Public)
    Fall 2013 Enrollment: 6 . . . . (765) 664-9091
    2013-14 Tuition: $9,987
Housing: Homeownership rate: 56.6%; Median home value: $65,200; Median year structure built: 1957; Homeowner vacancy rate: 3.7%; Median gross rent: $579 per month; Rental vacancy rate: 13.7%
Health Insurance: 83.5% have insurance; 55.4% have private insurance; 42.7% have public insurance; 16.5% do not have insurance; 6.9% of children under 18 do not have insurance
Hospitals: Marion General Hospital (191 beds); VA Northern Indiana Healthcare System - Marion
Safety: Violent crime rate: 27.1 per 10,000 population; Property crime rate: 388.5 per 10,000 population
Newspapers: Chronicle-Tribune (daily circulation 17100)
Transportation: Commute: 84.6% car, 0.2% public transportation, 5.7% walk, 7.8% work from home; Median travel time to work: 16.5 minutes
Airports: Marion Municipal (general aviation)
Additional Information Contacts
City of Marion . . . . (765) 662-9931
    http://www.marionindiana.us

MATTHEWS (town). Covers a land area of 0.352 square miles and a water area of 0 square miles. Located at 40.39° N. Lat; 85.50° W. Long. Elevation is 879 feet.
History: Matthews was established in 1833 with a gristmill, sawmill, blacksmith shop, and general store.
Population: 596; Growth (since 2000): 0.2%; Density: 1,691.4 persons per square mile; Race: 98.0% White, 0.8% Black/African American, 0.0% Asian, 0.2% American Indian/Alaska Native, 0.0% Native Hawaiian/Other Pacific Islander, 1.0% Two or more races, 0.2% Hispanic of any race; Average household size: 2.55; Median age: 40.6; Age under 18: 26.5%; Age 65 and over: 18.6%; Males per 100 females: 95.4
Housing: Homeownership rate: 79.9%; Homeowner vacancy rate: 2.1%; Rental vacancy rate: 9.6%

MIER (CDP). Covers a land area of 0.239 square miles and a water area of 0 square miles. Located at 40.57° N. Lat; 85.82° W. Long. Elevation is 823 feet.
Population: 78; Growth (since 2000): n/a; Density: 326.0 persons per square mile; Race: 98.7% White, 0.0% Black/African American, 0.0% Asian, 0.0% American Indian/Alaska Native, 0.0% Native Hawaiian/Other Pacific Islander, 0.0% Two or more races, 1.3% Hispanic of any race; Average household size: 2.44; Median age: 48.0; Age under 18: 15.4%; Age 65 and over: 20.5%; Males per 100 females: 129.4
Housing: Homeownership rate: 78.2%; Homeowner vacancy rate: 0.0%; Rental vacancy rate: 22.2%

POINT ISABEL (CDP). Covers a land area of 3.401 square miles and a water area of 0 square miles. Located at 40.42° N. Lat; 85.82° W. Long. Elevation is 883 feet.
Population: 91; Growth (since 2000): n/a; Density: 26.8 persons per square mile; Race: 86.8% White, 0.0% Black/African American, 0.0% Asian, 0.0% American Indian/Alaska Native, 0.0% Native Hawaiian/Other Pacific Islander, 8.8% Two or more races, 9.9% Hispanic of any race;

Average household size: 2.60; Median age: 43.4; Age under 18: 20.9%; Age 65 and over: 13.2%; Males per 100 females: 97.8
Housing: Homeownership rate: 80.0%; Homeowner vacancy rate: 3.4%; Rental vacancy rate: 0.0%

SIMS (CDP). Covers a land area of 0.998 square miles and a water area of 0 square miles. Located at 40.50° N. Lat; 85.85° W. Long. Elevation is 860 feet.
Population: 156; Growth (since 2000): n/a; Density: 156.3 persons per square mile; Race: 95.5% White, 0.0% Black/African American, 0.6% Asian, 0.6% American Indian/Alaska Native, 0.0% Native Hawaiian/Other Pacific Islander, 0.0% Two or more races, 4.5% Hispanic of any race; Average household size: 2.29; Median age: 49.0; Age under 18: 19.2%; Age 65 and over: 16.7%; Males per 100 females: 113.7
Housing: Homeownership rate: 80.9%; Homeowner vacancy rate: 1.7%; Rental vacancy rate: 0.0%

SWAYZEE (town). Covers a land area of 0.469 square miles and a water area of 0 square miles. Located at 40.51° N. Lat; 85.82° W. Long. Elevation is 863 feet.
Population: 981; Growth (since 2000): -3.0%; Density: 2,093.4 persons per square mile; Race: 97.7% White, 0.3% Black/African American, 0.1% Asian, 0.3% American Indian/Alaska Native, 0.0% Native Hawaiian/Other Pacific Islander, 1.4% Two or more races, 1.3% Hispanic of any race; Average household size: 2.50; Median age: 40.0; Age under 18: 25.8%; Age 65 and over: 16.3%; Males per 100 females: 94.6
School District(s)
Oak Hill United School Corp (PK-12)
   2012-13 Enrollment: 1,597 . . . . (765) 395-3341
Housing: Homeownership rate: 85.3%; Homeowner vacancy rate: 2.9%; Rental vacancy rate: 13.4%

SWEETSER (town). Covers a land area of 1.014 square miles and a water area of 0.003 square miles. Located at 40.57° N. Lat; 85.77° W. Long. Elevation is 850 feet.
History: Laid out 1871.
Population: 1,229; Growth (since 2000): 35.7%; Density: 1,211.6 persons per square mile; Race: 95.2% White, 0.4% Black/African American, 0.3% Asian, 0.7% American Indian/Alaska Native, 0.0% Native Hawaiian/Other Pacific Islander, 1.5% Two or more races, 4.5% Hispanic of any race; Average household size: 2.49; Median age: 40.5; Age under 18: 25.3%; Age 65 and over: 16.1%; Males per 100 females: 91.1
School District(s)
Oak Hill United School Corp (PK-12)
   2012-13 Enrollment: 1,597 . . . . (765) 395-3341
Housing: Homeownership rate: 77.0%; Homeowner vacancy rate: 2.8%; Rental vacancy rate: 4.2%

UPLAND (town). Covers a land area of 3.138 square miles and a water area of 0.012 square miles. Located at 40.46° N. Lat; 85.50° W. Long. Elevation is 935 feet.
History: Upland was laid out in 1867 when the railroad arrived and a sawmill was built. Many of the early settlers were Quakers.
Population: 3,845; Growth (since 2000): 1.1%; Density: 1,225.2 persons per square mile; Race: 94.6% White, 1.6% Black/African American, 1.2% Asian, 0.2% American Indian/Alaska Native, 0.1% Native Hawaiian/Other Pacific Islander, 1.5% Two or more races, 2.3% Hispanic of any race; Average household size: 2.60; Median age: 21.8; Age under 18: 14.1%; Age 65 and over: 9.5%; Males per 100 females: 91.2; Marriage status: 55.7% never married, 34.0% now married, 0.6% separated, 3.3% widowed, 7.0% divorced; Foreign born: 2.7%; Speak English only: 96.1%; With disability: 7.0%; Veterans: 5.6%; Ancestry: 27.0% German, 9.6% Irish, 9.2% English, 3.7% Dutch, 3.6% Italian
Employment: 9.1% management, business, and financial, 5.3% computer, engineering, and science, 23.2% education, legal, community service, arts, and media, 3.5% healthcare practitioners, 19.6% service, 28.6% sales and office, 3.6% natural resources, construction, and maintenance, 7.1% production, transportation, and material moving
Income: Per capita: $14,149; Median household: $48,333; Average household: $53,407; Households with income of $100,000 or more: 11.8%; Poverty rate: 13.9%
Educational Attainment: High school diploma or higher: 95.8%; Bachelor's degree or higher: 45.8%; Graduate/professional degree or higher: 20.4%

School District(s)
Eastbrook Community Sch Corp (PK-12)
   2012-13 Enrollment: 1,630 . . . . (765) 664-0624
Four-year College(s)
Taylor University (Private, Not-for-profit, Interdenominational)
   Fall 2013 Enrollment: 2,245 . . . . (765) 998-2751
   2013-14 Tuition: In-state $28,753; Out-of-state $28,753
Housing: Homeownership rate: 67.7%; Median home value: $121,100; Median year structure built: 1972; Homeowner vacancy rate: 1.8%; Median gross rent: $573 per month; Rental vacancy rate: 9.3%
Health Insurance: 91.1% have insurance; 84.1% have private insurance; 16.6% have public insurance; 8.9% do not have insurance; 8.3% of children under 18 do not have insurance
Transportation: Commute: 57.8% car, 0.1% public transportation, 12.9% walk, 27.0% work from home; Median travel time to work: 18.0 minutes
Additional Information Contacts
Town of Upland . . . . (765) 998-7439
   http://upland.in.gov

VAN BUREN (town). Covers a land area of 0.584 square miles and a water area of 0 square miles. Located at 40.62° N. Lat; 85.50° W. Long. Elevation is 850 feet.
Population: 864; Growth (since 2000): -7.6%; Density: 1,479.9 persons per square mile; Race: 98.0% White, 0.0% Black/African American, 0.3% Asian, 0.2% American Indian/Alaska Native, 0.0% Native Hawaiian/Other Pacific Islander, 1.0% Two or more races, 0.9% Hispanic of any race; Average household size: 2.42; Median age: 38.6; Age under 18: 26.6%; Age 65 and over: 13.8%; Males per 100 females: 88.6
School District(s)
Eastbrook Community Sch Corp (PK-12)
   2012-13 Enrollment: 1,630 . . . . (765) 664-0624
Housing: Homeownership rate: 73.2%; Homeowner vacancy rate: 2.6%; Rental vacancy rate: 11.0%

Greene County

Located in southwestern Indiana; drained by the West Fork of White River and the Eel River. Covers a land area of 542.495 square miles, a water area of 3.423 square miles, and is located in the Eastern Time Zone at 39.05° N. Lat., 87.01° W. Long. The county was founded in 1821. County seat is Bloomfield.
Population: 33,165; Growth (since 2000): 0.0%; Density: 61.1 persons per square mile; Race: 98.1% White, 0.1% Black/African American, 0.3% Asian, 0.3% American Indian/Alaska Native, 0.0% Native Hawaiian/Other Pacific Islander, 0.9% two or more races, 1.0% Hispanic of any race; Average household size: 2.44; Median age: 41.1; Age under 18: 23.8%; Age 65 and over: 16.0%; Males per 100 females: 99.7; Marriage status: 22.6% never married, 57.5% now married, 0.9% separated, 7.2% widowed, 12.6% divorced; Foreign born: 0.7%; Speak English only: 98.8%; With disability: 17.4%; Veterans: 12.1%; Ancestry: 19.2% German, 15.4% Irish, 14.4% American, 10.4% English, 2.3% Dutch
Religion: Six largest groups: 14.2% Baptist, 6.6% Non-denominational Protestant, 4.7% Methodist/Pietist, 4.1% Pentecostal, 2.6% Presbyterian-Reformed, 2.2% Catholicism
Economy: Unemployment rate: 6.2%; Leading industries: 17.2% retail trade; 14.2% other services (except public administration); 11.7% construction; Farms: 810 totaling 181,086 acres; Company size: 0 employ 1,000 or more persons, 0 employ 500 to 999 persons, 4 employ 100 to 499 persons, 601 employs less than 100 persons; Business ownership: n/a women-owned, n/a Black-owned, n/a Hispanic-owned, n/a Asian-owned
Employment: 10.2% management, business, and financial, 4.5% computer, engineering, and science, 8.0% education, legal, community service, arts, and media, 5.3% healthcare practitioners, 18.0% service, 20.7% sales and office, 13.7% natural resources, construction, and maintenance, 19.5% production, transportation, and material moving
Income: Per capita: $22,235; Median household: $43,980; Average household: $55,501; Households with income of $100,000 or more: 12.4%; Poverty rate: 14.0%
Educational Attainment: High school diploma or higher: 84.6%; Bachelor's degree or higher: 12.1%; Graduate/professional degree or higher: 4.6%
Housing: Homeownership rate: 78.2%; Median home value: $88,800; Median year structure built: 1972; Homeowner vacancy rate: 2.4%; Median gross rent: $577 per month; Rental vacancy rate: 9.9%

Vital Statistics: Birth rate: 110.7 per 10,000 population; Death rate: 121.1 per 10,000 population; Age-adjusted cancer mortality rate: 191.0 deaths per 100,000 population
Health Insurance: 85.9% have insurance; 65.8% have private insurance; 34.6% have public insurance; 14.1% do not have insurance; 10.3% of children under 18 do not have insurance
Health Care: Physicians: 4.5 per 10,000 population; Hospital beds: 7.6 per 10,000 population; Hospital admissions: 275.5 per 10,000 population
Air Quality Index: 79.9% good, 19.7% moderate, 0.4% unhealthy for sensitive individuals, 0.0% unhealthy (percent of days)
Transportation: Commute: 95.1% car, 0.2% public transportation, 2.1% walk, 1.5% work from home; Median travel time to work: 29.4 minutes
Presidential Election: 33.1% Obama, 64.6% Romney (2012)
Additional Information Contacts
Greene Government . . . . (812) 384-8532
http://www.co.greene.in.us

Greene County Communities

BLOOMFIELD
(town). County seat. Covers a land area of 1.377 square miles and a water area of 0 square miles. Located at 39.03° N. Lat; 86.94° W. Long. Elevation is 607 feet.
Population: 2,405; Growth (since 2000): -5.4%; Density: 1,746.5 persons per square mile; Race: 98.0% White, 0.5% Black/African American, 0.6% Asian, 0.0% American Indian/Alaska Native, 0.0% Native Hawaiian/Other Pacific Islander, 0.7% Two or more races, 1.3% Hispanic of any race; Average household size: 2.16; Median age: 39.7; Age under 18: 24.5%; Age 65 and over: 18.5%; Males per 100 females: 88.2
School District(s)
Bloomfield SD (KG-12)
    2012-13 Enrollment: 984. . . . . (812) 384-4507
Eastern Greene Schools (PK-12)
    2012-13 Enrollment: 1,303 . . . . (812) 825-5722
Housing: Homeownership rate: 59.4%; Homeowner vacancy rate: 3.1%; Rental vacancy rate: 11.4%
Additional Information Contacts
Town of Bloomfield . . . . (812) 384-4378
http://www.bloomfieldin.com

JASONVILLE
(city). Covers a land area of 1.309 square miles and a water area of <.001 square miles. Located at 39.16° N. Lat; 87.20° W. Long. Elevation is 633 feet.
History: Laid out 1859.
Population: 2,222; Growth (since 2000): -10.8%; Density: 1,697.3 persons per square mile; Race: 98.1% White, 0.2% Black/African American, 0.4% Asian, 0.1% American Indian/Alaska Native, 0.0% Native Hawaiian/Other Pacific Islander, 0.9% Two or more races, 0.8% Hispanic of any race; Average household size: 2.47; Median age: 38.4; Age under 18: 26.7%; Age 65 and over: 17.1%; Males per 100 females: 90.2
School District(s)
M S D Shakamak Schools (KG-12)
    2012-13 Enrollment: 824. . . . . (812) 665-3550
Housing: Homeownership rate: 65.2%; Homeowner vacancy rate: 4.4%; Rental vacancy rate: 10.1%
Additional Information Contacts
City of Jasonville . . . . (812) 665-3622
http://www.gojasonville.com/Home/contact-us-city-public-offices.php

LINTON
(city). Covers a land area of 3.022 square miles and a water area of 0 square miles. Located at 39.04° N. Lat; 87.16° W. Long. Elevation is 531 feet.
History: Linton developed as a coal-mining town.
Population: 5,413; Growth (since 2000): -6.3%; Density: 1,791.5 persons per square mile; Race: 97.7% White, 0.1% Black/African American, 0.4% Asian, 0.3% American Indian/Alaska Native, 0.0% Native Hawaiian/Other Pacific Islander, 1.2% Two or more races, 1.2% Hispanic of any race; Average household size: 2.30; Median age: 39.8; Age under 18: 23.4%; Age 65 and over: 19.2%; Males per 100 females: 91.1; Marriage status: 19.6% never married, 52.0% now married, 0.8% separated, 11.7% widowed, 16.7% divorced; Foreign born: 0.8%; Speak English only: 99.0%; With disability: 25.4%; Veterans: 12.0%; Ancestry: 19.3% German, 13.8% American, 12.5% Irish, 9.5% English, 3.2% Dutch
Employment: 10.8% management, business, and financial; 3.1% computer, engineering, and science; 9.7% education, legal, community service, arts, and media; 5.4% healthcare practitioners, 27.0% service, 16.8% sales and office, 9.9% natural resources, construction, and maintenance, 17.5% production, transportation, and material moving
Income: Per capita: $19,164; Median household: $36,391; Average household: $44,621; Households with income of $100,000 or more: 8.0%; Poverty rate: 17.6%
Educational Attainment: High school diploma or higher: 80.7%; Bachelor's degree or higher: 11.2%; Graduate/professional degree or higher: 4.1%
School District(s)
Greene-Sullivan Sp Ed Coop (KG-12)
    2012-13 Enrollment: n/a . . . . (812) 847-8497
Linton-Stockton School Corp (KG-12)
    2012-13 Enrollment: 1,369 . . . . (812) 847-6020
Housing: Homeownership rate: 66.9%; Median home value: $65,000; Median year structure built: 1964; Homeowner vacancy rate: 3.0%; Median gross rent: $576 per month; Rental vacancy rate: 9.6%
Health Insurance: 85.1% have insurance; 58.9% have private insurance; 42.9% have public insurance; 14.9% do not have insurance; 5.2% of children under 18 do not have insurance
Hospitals: Greene County General Hospital (76 beds)
Safety: Violent crime rate: 0.0 per 10,000 population; Property crime rate: 339.6 per 10,000 population
Newspapers: Greene Co. Daily World (daily circulation 3000)
Transportation: Commute: 94.0% car, 1.1% public transportation, 3.1% walk, 0.5% work from home; Median travel time to work: 22.4 minutes
Additional Information Contacts
City of Linton . . . . (812) 847-4846
http://www.lintonchamber.org

LYONS
(town). Covers a land area of 0.866 square miles and a water area of 0 square miles. Located at 38.99° N. Lat; 87.08° W. Long. Elevation is 531 feet.
Population: 742; Growth (since 2000): -0.8%; Density: 856.4 persons per square mile; Race: 98.1% White, 0.1% Black/African American, 0.3% Asian, 0.5% American Indian/Alaska Native, 0.0% Native Hawaiian/Other Pacific Islander, 0.8% Two or more races, 1.5% Hispanic of any race; Average household size: 2.53; Median age: 43.3; Age under 18: 22.1%; Age 65 and over: 24.3%; Males per 100 females: 96.8
School District(s)
White River Valley SD (KG-12)
    2012-13 Enrollment: 814. . . . . (812) 659-1424
Housing: Homeownership rate: 75.2%; Homeowner vacancy rate: 3.3%; Rental vacancy rate: 11.8%

NEWBERRY
(town). Covers a land area of 0.493 square miles and a water area of 0 square miles. Located at 38.92° N. Lat; 87.02° W. Long. Elevation is 548 feet.
History: Laid out 1822.
Population: 193; Growth (since 2000): -6.3%; Density: 391.5 persons per square mile; Race: 97.9% White, 0.0% Black/African American, 0.0% Asian, 1.0% American Indian/Alaska Native, 0.5% Native Hawaiian/Other Pacific Islander, 0.0% Two or more races, 2.6% Hispanic of any race; Average household size: 2.38; Median age: 47.8; Age under 18: 20.7%; Age 65 and over: 17.6%; Males per 100 females: 96.9
Housing: Homeownership rate: 82.7%; Homeowner vacancy rate: 5.6%; Rental vacancy rate: 6.7%

OWENSBURG
(CDP). Covers a land area of 5.919 square miles and a water area of 0.008 square miles. Located at 38.93° N. Lat; 86.72° W. Long. Elevation is 643 feet.
Population: 406; Growth (since 2000): n/a; Density: 68.6 persons per square mile; Race: 98.5% White, 0.0% Black/African American, 1.0% Asian, 0.0% American Indian/Alaska Native, 0.0% Native Hawaiian/Other Pacific Islander, 0.5% Two or more races, 0.2% Hispanic of any race; Average household size: 2.42; Median age: 40.5; Age under 18: 23.2%; Age 65 and over: 15.5%; Males per 100 females: 116.0
Housing: Homeownership rate: 82.1%; Homeowner vacancy rate: 2.8%; Rental vacancy rate: 9.1%

SCOTLAND
(CDP). Covers a land area of 0.576 square miles and a water area of 0 square miles. Located at 38.91° N. Lat; 86.90° W. Long. Elevation is 614 feet.
Population: 134; Growth (since 2000): n/a; Density: 232.5 persons per square mile; Race: 99.3% White, 0.0% Black/African American, 0.7% Asian, 0.0% American Indian/Alaska Native, 0.0% Native Hawaiian/Other

Pacific Islander, 0.0% Two or more races, 2.2% Hispanic of any race; Average household size: 2.44; Median age: 43.0; Age under 18: 25.4%; Age 65 and over: 16.4%; Males per 100 females: 94.2
Housing: Homeownership rate: 87.2%; Homeowner vacancy rate: 0.0%; Rental vacancy rate: 22.2%

SOLSBERRY (unincorporated postal area)
ZCTA: 47459

Covers a land area of 58.367 square miles and a water area of 0 square miles. Located at 39.11° N. Lat; 86.75° W. Long. Elevation is 778 feet.
Population: 3,795; Growth (since 2000): 9.1%; Density: 65.0 persons per square mile; Race: 97.7% White, 0.2% Black/African American, 0.2% Asian, 0.3% American Indian/Alaska Native, 0.0% Native Hawaiian/Other Pacific Islander, 1.3% Two or more races, 0.6% Hispanic of any race; Average household size: 2.62; Median age: 39.0; Age under 18: 26.4%; Age 65 and over: 11.8%; Males per 100 females: 101.5; Marriage status: 19.6% never married, 64.5% now married, 1.6% separated, 7.1% widowed, 8.8% divorced; Foreign born: 0.0%; Speak English only: 99.0%; With disability: 12.3%; Veterans: 10.5%; Ancestry: 28.0% German, 18.6% Irish, 14.3% English, 10.5% American, 3.8% Scottish
Employment: 10.3% management, business, and financial, 5.5% computer, engineering, and science, 5.2% education, legal, community service, arts, and media, 5.4% healthcare practitioners, 17.3% service, 20.1% sales and office, 18.9% natural resources, construction, and maintenance, 17.3% production, transportation, and material moving
Income: Per capita: $20,551; Median household: $47,500; Average household: $56,057; Households with income of $100,000 or more: 13.0%; Poverty rate: 10.5%
Educational Attainment: High school diploma or higher: 86.5%; Bachelor's degree or higher: 15.5%; Graduate/professional degree or higher: 6.0%
Housing: Homeownership rate: 87.8%; Median home value: $127,300; Median year structure built: 1982; Homeowner vacancy rate: 1.9%; Median gross rent: $606 per month; Rental vacancy rate: 12.9%
Health Insurance: 83.3% have insurance; 66.6% have private insurance; 28.1% have public insurance; 16.7% do not have insurance; 12.5% of children under 18 do not have insurance
Transportation: Commute: 97.3% car, 0.0% public transportation, 0.4% walk, 2.3% work from home; Median travel time to work: 29.6 minutes

SWITZ CITY (town).
Covers a land area of 0.225 square miles and a water area of 0 square miles. Located at 39.03° N. Lat; 87.05° W. Long. Elevation is 525 feet.
History: Switz City grew up around the nearby strip-mining coal fields.
Population: 293; Growth (since 2000): -5.8%; Density: 1,301.3 persons per square mile; Race: 97.3% White, 0.7% Black/African American, 0.3% Asian, 0.7% American Indian/Alaska Native, 0.0% Native Hawaiian/Other Pacific Islander, 0.3% Two or more races, 2.0% Hispanic of any race; Average household size: 2.38; Median age: 37.9; Age under 18: 26.6%; Age 65 and over: 17.7%; Males per 100 females: 99.3

School District(s)
White River Valley SD (KG-12)
    2012-13 Enrollment: 814 . . . . (812) 659-1424
Housing: Homeownership rate: 77.2%; Homeowner vacancy rate: 2.1%; Rental vacancy rate: 3.4%

WORTHINGTON (town).
Covers a land area of 0.808 square miles and a water area of 0 square miles. Located at 39.12° N. Lat; 86.98° W. Long. Elevation is 515 feet.
History: Laid out 1849.
Population: 1,463; Growth (since 2000): -1.2%; Density: 1,810.4 persons per square mile; Race: 98.5% White, 0.1% Black/African American, 0.1% Asian, 0.3% American Indian/Alaska Native, 0.0% Native Hawaiian/Other Pacific Islander, 0.5% Two or more races, 1.4% Hispanic of any race; Average household size: 2.34; Median age: 39.0; Age under 18: 24.1%; Age 65 and over: 18.1%; Males per 100 females: 91.7

School District(s)
White River Valley SD (KG-12)
    2012-13 Enrollment: 814 . . . . (812) 659-1424
Housing: Homeownership rate: 71.0%; Homeowner vacancy rate: 2.5%; Rental vacancy rate: 10.8%

Hamilton County

Located in central Indiana; drained by the West Fork of the White River, and by several creeks. Covers a land area of 394.267 square miles, a water area of 8.170 square miles, and is located in the Eastern Time Zone at 40.05° N. Lat., 86.02° W. Long. The county was founded in 1823. County seat is Noblesville.

Hamilton County is part of the Indianapolis-Carmel-Anderson, IN Metropolitan Statistical Area. The entire metro area includes: Boone County, IN; Brown County, IN; Hamilton County, IN; Hancock County, IN; Hendricks County, IN; Johnson County, IN; Madison County, IN; Marion County, IN; Morgan County, IN; Putnam County, IN; Shelby County, IN

Population: 274,569; Growth (since 2000): 50.3%; Density: 696.4 persons per square mile; Race: 88.5% White, 3.5% Black/African American, 4.8% Asian, 0.2% American Indian/Alaska Native, 0.0% Native Hawaiian/Other Pacific Islander, 1.8% two or more races, 3.4% Hispanic of any race; Average household size: 2.73; Median age: 35.6; Age under 18: 30.2%; Age 65 and over: 8.6%; Males per 100 females: 95.3; Marriage status: 22.9% never married, 63.9% now married, 0.9% separated, 3.6% widowed, 9.6% divorced; Foreign born: 7.2%; Speak English only: 90.7%; With disability: 7.0%; Veterans: 7.9%; Ancestry: 26.4% German, 13.3% Irish, 11.0% English, 8.3% American, 4.3% Italian
Religion: Six largest groups: 14.7% Catholicism, 7.7% Non-denominational Protestant, 6.2% Methodist/Pietist, 4.4% Baptist, 3.2% Lutheran, 1.1% Presbyterian-Reformed
Economy: Unemployment rate: 4.0%; Leading industries: 15.9% professional, scientific, and technical services; 11.3% health care and social assistance; 10.9% retail trade; Farms: 598 totaling 130,854 acres; Company size: 4 employ 1,000 or more persons, 9 employ 500 to 999 persons, 170 employ 100 to 499 persons, 7,811 employs less than 100 persons; Business ownership: 7,793 women-owned, 508 Black-owned, 383 Hispanic-owned, 862 Asian-owned
Employment: 21.9% management, business, and financial, 8.9% computer, engineering, and science, 12.2% education, legal, community service, arts, and media, 8.3% healthcare practitioners, 11.7% service, 26.3% sales and office, 4.6% natural resources, construction, and maintenance, 6.1% production, transportation, and material moving
Income: Per capita: $39,521; Median household: $82,468; Average household: $107,384; Households with income of $100,000 or more: 40.4%; Poverty rate: 5.1%
Educational Attainment: High school diploma or higher: 96.3%; Bachelor's degree or higher: 55.1%; Graduate/professional degree or higher: 19.8%
Housing: Homeownership rate: 80.1%; Median home value: $215,600; Median year structure built: 1995; Homeowner vacancy rate: 2.0%; Median gross rent: $963 per month; Rental vacancy rate: 11.3%
Vital Statistics: Birth rate: 133.2 per 10,000 population; Death rate: 46.8 per 10,000 population; Age-adjusted cancer mortality rate: 154.3 deaths per 100,000 population
Health Insurance: 92.1% have insurance; 86.0% have private insurance; 13.8% have public insurance; 7.9% do not have insurance; 4.9% of children under 18 do not have insurance
Health Care: Physicians: 53.9 per 10,000 population; Hospital beds: 19.0 per 10,000 population; Hospital admissions: 884.8 per 10,000 population
Air Quality Index: 95.6% good, 4.4% moderate, 0.0% unhealthy for sensitive individuals, 0.0% unhealthy (percent of days)
Transportation: Commute: 92.1% car, 0.3% public transportation, 0.9% walk, 5.8% work from home; Median travel time to work: 26.5 minutes
Presidential Election: 32.0% Obama, 66.3% Romney (2012)
Additional Information Contacts
Hamilton Government . . . . (317) 776-9719
    http://www.hamiltoncounty.in.gov

Hamilton County Communities

ARCADIA (town).
Covers a land area of 0.558 square miles and a water area of 0 square miles. Located at 40.17° N. Lat; 86.02° W. Long. Elevation is 856 feet.
Population: 1,666; Growth (since 2000): -4.6%; Density: 2,987.3 persons per square mile; Race: 97.7% White, 0.4% Black/African American, 0.2% Asian, 0.2% American Indian/Alaska Native, 0.0% Native Hawaiian/Other Pacific Islander, 1.2% Two or more races, 0.8% Hispanic of any race;

Average household size: 2.62; Median age: 36.0; Age under 18: 27.9%; Age 65 and over: 12.5%; Males per 100 females: 99.5

School District(s)
Hamilton Heights School Corp (KG-12)
   2012-13 Enrollment: 2,281 . . . . (317) 984-3538
Housing: Homeownership rate: 65.3%; Homeowner vacancy rate: 3.8%; Rental vacancy rate: 5.3%

ATLANTA (town). Covers a land area of 0.302 square miles and a water area of 0 square miles. Located at 40.21° N. Lat; 86.03° W. Long. Elevation is 863 feet.
Population: 725; Growth (since 2000): -4.7%; Density: 2,404.3 persons per square mile; Race: 97.8% White, 0.6% Black/African American, 0.0% Asian, 0.0% American Indian/Alaska Native, 0.0% Native Hawaiian/Other Pacific Islander, 0.3% Two or more races, 1.9% Hispanic of any race; Average household size: 2.69; Median age: 36.1; Age under 18: 27.0%; Age 65 and over: 10.1%; Males per 100 females: 95.9
Housing: Homeownership rate: 80.7%; Homeowner vacancy rate: 1.4%; Rental vacancy rate: 28.8%

CARMEL (city). Covers a land area of 47.463 square miles and a water area of 1.085 square miles. Located at 39.97° N. Lat; 86.15° W. Long. Elevation is 853 feet.
Population: 79,191; Growth (since 2000): 109.9%; Density: 1,668.5 persons per square mile; Race: 85.4% White, 3.0% Black/African American, 8.9% Asian, 0.2% American Indian/Alaska Native, 0.0% Native Hawaiian/Other Pacific Islander, 1.8% Two or more races, 2.5% Hispanic of any race; Average household size: 2.71; Median age: 39.2; Age under 18: 29.4%; Age 65 and over: 10.4%; Males per 100 females: 95.1; Marriage status: 21.8% never married, 67.5% now married, 0.7% separated, 3.5% widowed, 7.2% divorced; Foreign born: 11.8%; Speak English only: 86.0%; With disability: 6.3%; Veterans: 7.3%; Ancestry: 25.6% German, 12.8% Irish, 11.7% English, 7.5% American, 4.5% Italian
Employment: 24.3% management, business, and financial, 12.1% computer, engineering, and science, 14.1% education, legal, community service, arts, and media, 9.3% healthcare practitioners, 8.8% service, 24.6% sales and office, 2.8% natural resources, construction, and maintenance, 4.2% production, transportation, and material moving
Income: Per capita: $51,767; Median household: $106,121; Average household: $139,859; Households with income of $100,000 or more: 53.3%; Poverty rate: 3.6%
Educational Attainment: High school diploma or higher: 98.3%; Bachelor's degree or higher: 68.1%; Graduate/professional degree or higher: 30.2%

School District(s)
Carmel Clay Schools (PK-12)
   2012-13 Enrollment: 15,724 . . . . (317) 844-9961
Options Charter School - Carmel (09-12)
   2012-13 Enrollment: 160 . . . . (317) 815-2098
Housing: Homeownership rate: 80.5%; Median home value: $297,300; Median year structure built: 1993; Homeowner vacancy rate: 1.7%; Median gross rent: $1,077 per month; Rental vacancy rate: 10.8%
Health Insurance: 95.5% have insurance; 91.1% have private insurance; 13.0% have public insurance; 4.5% do not have insurance; 2.7% of children under 18 do not have insurance
Hospitals: Franciscan Saint Francis Health - Carmel; Indiana University Health North Hospital; Saint Vincent Carmel Hospital (100 beds)
Safety: Violent crime rate: 2.4 per 10,000 population; Property crime rate: 87.7 per 10,000 population
Transportation: Commute: 91.1% car, 0.4% public transportation, 1.0% walk, 6.6% work from home; Median travel time to work: 24.8 minutes
Additional Information Contacts
City of Carmel . . . . (317) 571-2400
   http://www.carmel.in.gov

CICERO (town). Covers a land area of 1.708 square miles and a water area of 0.412 square miles. Located at 40.12° N. Lat; 86.03° W. Long. Elevation is 833 feet.
History: Cicero, named for a Delaware chief, grew around a Seventh-Day Adventist academy nearby.
Population: 4,812; Growth (since 2000): 11.8%; Density: 2,817.3 persons per square mile; Race: 96.8% White, 0.6% Black/African American, 0.5% Asian, 0.6% American Indian/Alaska Native, 0.0% Native Hawaiian/Other Pacific Islander, 1.1% Two or more races, 1.5% Hispanic of any race; Average household size: 2.47; Median age: 39.8; Age under 18: 25.2%; Age 65 and over: 11.6%; Males per 100 females: 97.0; Marriage status: 20.5% never married, 54.7% now married, 0.4% separated, 7.3% widowed, 17.4% divorced; Foreign born: 1.1%; Speak English only: 95.8%; With disability: 11.1%; Veterans: 13.6%; Ancestry: 28.5% German, 12.9% Irish, 9.0% American, 8.9% English, 5.4% Polish
Employment: 12.3% management, business, and financial, 4.0% computer, engineering, and science, 2.0% education, legal, community service, arts, and media, 8.4% healthcare practitioners, 20.0% service, 27.3% sales and office, 9.7% natural resources, construction, and maintenance, 16.4% production, transportation, and material moving
Income: Per capita: $27,843; Median household: $53,048; Average household: $64,395; Households with income of $100,000 or more: 22.2%; Poverty rate: 11.5%
Educational Attainment: High school diploma or higher: 90.6%; Bachelor's degree or higher: 24.2%; Graduate/professional degree or higher: 4.9%
Housing: Homeownership rate: 78.3%; Median home value: $150,800; Median year structure built: 1979; Homeowner vacancy rate: 3.3%; Median gross rent: $783 per month; Rental vacancy rate: 8.2%
Health Insurance: 75.2% have insurance; 67.9% have private insurance; 21.6% have public insurance; 24.8% do not have insurance; 36.5% of children under 18 do not have insurance
Transportation: Commute: 92.0% car, 0.0% public transportation, 2.6% walk, 5.4% work from home; Median travel time to work: 30.3 minutes
Additional Information Contacts
Town of Cicero . . . . (317) 984-4900
   http://www.ciceroin.org

FISHERS (town). Covers a land area of 33.585 square miles and a water area of 2.249 square miles. Located at 39.96° N. Lat; 85.97° W. Long. Elevation is 817 feet.
Population: 76,794; Growth (since 2000): 103.0%; Density: 2,286.5 persons per square mile; Race: 85.6% White, 5.6% Black/African American, 5.5% Asian, 0.2% American Indian/Alaska Native, 0.0% Native Hawaiian/Other Pacific Islander, 2.1% Two or more races, 3.4% Hispanic of any race; Average household size: 2.82; Median age: 33.2; Age under 18: 33.0%; Age 65 and over: 5.5%; Males per 100 females: 94.5; Marriage status: 24.4% never married, 63.8% now married, 0.9% separated, 2.2% widowed, 9.5% divorced; Foreign born: 7.6%; Speak English only: 90.0%; With disability: 5.0%; Veterans: 6.9%; Ancestry: 26.1% German, 15.1% Irish, 10.4% English, 7.1% American, 3.9% French
Employment: 23.7% management, business, and financial, 10.0% computer, engineering, and science, 12.2% education, legal, community service, arts, and media, 9.3% healthcare practitioners, 10.7% service, 27.2% sales and office, 3.3% natural resources, construction, and maintenance, 3.7% production, transportation, and material moving
Income: Per capita: $38,577; Median household: $90,437; Average household: $110,390; Households with income of $100,000 or more: 44.1%; Poverty rate: 3.3%
Educational Attainment: High school diploma or higher: 97.9%; Bachelor's degree or higher: 59.7%; Graduate/professional degree or higher: 19.1%

School District(s)
Hamilton Southeastern Schools (KG-12)
   2012-13 Enrollment: 20,209 . . . . (317) 594-4100
Housing: Homeownership rate: 82.3%; Median home value: $209,700; Median year structure built: 1998; Homeowner vacancy rate: 1.6%; Median gross rent: $1,058 per month; Rental vacancy rate: 8.4%
Health Insurance: 92.7% have insurance; 88.1% have private insurance; 9.1% have public insurance; 7.3% do not have insurance; 3.2% of children under 18 do not have insurance
Hospitals: Saint Vincent Fishers Hospital
Safety: Violent crime rate: 1.9 per 10,000 population; Property crime rate: 99.1 per 10,000 population
Transportation: Commute: 92.2% car, 0.2% public transportation, 0.4% walk, 6.4% work from home; Median travel time to work: 27.4 minutes
Airports: Indianapolis Metropolitan (general aviation)
Additional Information Contacts
Town of Fishers. . . . . (317) 595-3140
   http://www.fishers.in.us

NOBLESVILLE (city). County seat. Covers a land area of 31.374 square miles and a water area of 1.415 square miles. Located at 40.04° N. Lat; 86.01° W. Long. Elevation is 764 feet.

History: Named for James Noble, first U.S. Senator from Indiana. Noblesville was founded in 1823 by William Conner who had built a trading post nearby in 1818. Noblesville became the seat of Hamilton County, and Conner became a state senator.

Population: 51,969; Growth (since 2000): 81.8%; Density: 1,656.4 persons per square mile; Race: 91.1% White, 3.6% Black/African American, 1.7% Asian, 0.2% American Indian/Alaska Native, 0.1% Native Hawaiian/Other Pacific Islander, 1.8% Two or more races, 4.3% Hispanic of any race; Average household size: 2.69; Median age: 33.0; Age under 18: 30.2%; Age 65 and over: 8.7%; Males per 100 females: 93.8; Marriage status: 22.7% never married, 60.9% now married, 1.0% separated, 5.1% widowed, 11.3% divorced; Foreign born: 4.1%; Speak English only: 93.4%; With disability: 7.6%; Veterans: 8.8%; Ancestry: 27.2% German, 12.5% Irish, 12.1% English, 7.8% American, 4.1% Italian

Employment: 19.5% management, business, and financial, 5.7% computer, engineering, and science, 12.6% education, legal, community service, arts, and media, 7.5% healthcare practitioners, 14.8% service, 27.6% sales and office, 4.3% natural resources, construction, and maintenance, 8.0% production, transportation, and material moving

Income: Per capita: $31,261; Median household: $66,644; Average household: $81,877; Households with income of $100,000 or more: 27.3%; Poverty rate: 7.4%

Educational Attainment: High school diploma or higher: 94.7%; Bachelor's degree or higher: 47.2%; Graduate/professional degree or higher: 14.6%

School District(s)
Hamilton Southeastern Schools (KG-12)
   2012-13 Enrollment: 20,209 . . . . (317) 594-4100
Noblesville Schools (PK-12)
   2012-13 Enrollment: 9,601 . . . . (317) 773-3171
Options Charter Sch - Noblesville (09-12)
   2012-13 Enrollment: 159 . . . . (317) 773-8659

Vocational/Technical School(s)
Hair Fashions By Kaye Beauty College-Noblesville (Private, For-profit)
   Fall 2013 Enrollment: 70 . . . . (317) 773-6189
   2013-14 Tuition: $14,650

Housing: Homeownership rate: 74.6%; Median home value: $168,500; Median year structure built: 1997; Homeowner vacancy rate: 2.6%; Median gross rent: $889 per month; Rental vacancy rate: 15.6%

Health Insurance: 90.7% have insurance; 82.5% have private insurance; 17.0% have public insurance; 9.3% do not have insurance; 6.4% of children under 18 do not have insurance

Hospitals: Riverview Hospital (161 beds)

Newspapers: Noblesville Daily Times (daily circulation 6000)

Transportation: Commute: 92.5% car, 0.1% public transportation, 1.2% walk, 5.5% work from home; Median travel time to work: 27.5 minutes

Additional Information Contacts
City of Noblesville . . . . (317) 776-6328
http://www.cityofnoblesville.org

SHERIDAN (town). Covers a land area of 2.137 square miles and a water area of 0.004 square miles. Located at 40.13° N. Lat; 86.22° W. Long. Elevation is 948 feet.

History: Laid out 1860.

Population: 2,665; Growth (since 2000): 5.8%; Density: 1,247.0 persons per square mile; Race: 95.3% White, 0.8% Black/African American, 0.4% Asian, 0.3% American Indian/Alaska Native, 0.0% Native Hawaiian/Other Pacific Islander, 1.7% Two or more races, 3.3% Hispanic of any race; Average household size: 2.62; Median age: 33.8; Age under 18: 29.3%; Age 65 and over: 11.0%; Males per 100 females: 100.2; Marriage status: 29.1% never married, 51.2% now married, 4.5% separated, 6.3% widowed, 13.4% divorced; Foreign born: 0.6%; Speak English only: 96.6%; With disability: 13.5%; Veterans: 11.6%; Ancestry: 20.0% American, 14.3% English, 13.1% German, 12.4% Irish, 3.3% Dutch

Employment: 10.2% management, business, and financial, 4.5% computer, engineering, and science, 5.9% education, legal, community service, arts, and media, 3.4% healthcare practitioners, 27.1% service, 23.2% sales and office, 11.2% natural resources, construction, and maintenance, 14.5% production, transportation, and material moving

Income: Per capita: $20,203; Median household: $44,974; Average household: $53,424; Households with income of $100,000 or more: 7.0%; Poverty rate: 15.7%

Educational Attainment: High school diploma or higher: 86.4%; Bachelor's degree or higher: 12.8%; Graduate/professional degree or higher: 3.9%

School District(s)
Sheridan Community Schools (KG-12)
   2012-13 Enrollment: 1,072 . . . . (317) 758-4172

Housing: Homeownership rate: 72.2%; Median home value: $101,500; Median year structure built: 1971; Homeowner vacancy rate: 4.5%; Median gross rent: $785 per month; Rental vacancy rate: 15.3%

Health Insurance: 85.0% have insurance; 66.6% have private insurance; 27.0% have public insurance; 15.0% do not have insurance; 11.0% of children under 18 do not have insurance

Transportation: Commute: 96.3% car, 0.2% public transportation, 0.8% walk, 2.7% work from home; Median travel time to work: 27.0 minutes

Additional Information Contacts
Town of Sheridan . . . . (317) 758-5293
http://www.sheridan.org

WESTFIELD (city). Covers a land area of 26.838 square miles and a water area of 0.241 square miles. Located at 40.03° N. Lat; 86.16° W. Long. Elevation is 886 feet.

History: Westfield was founded in 1834 by a group of Quakers, and was an important station on the Underground Railroad for slaves fleeing to the north.

Population: 30,068; Growth (since 2000): 223.6%; Density: 1,120.3 persons per square mile; Race: 90.9% White, 2.2% Black/African American, 2.5% Asian, 0.2% American Indian/Alaska Native, 0.0% Native Hawaiian/Other Pacific Islander, 1.6% Two or more races, 5.8% Hispanic of any race; Average household size: 2.85; Median age: 33.7; Age under 18: 31.9%; Age 65 and over: 6.8%; Males per 100 females: 95.7; Marriage status: 22.4% never married, 65.7% now married, 0.7% separated, 2.5% widowed, 9.4% divorced; Foreign born: 5.1%; Speak English only: 93.1%; With disability: 6.7%; Veterans: 7.4%; Ancestry: 27.5% German, 14.5% Irish, 10.6% English, 8.9% American, 6.3% Italian

Employment: 24.4% management, business, and financial, 9.1% computer, engineering, and science, 10.6% education, legal, community service, arts, and media, 9.0% healthcare practitioners, 11.6% service, 23.8% sales and office, 3.6% natural resources, construction, and maintenance, 7.8% production, transportation, and material moving

Income: Per capita: $36,068; Median household: $87,435; Average household: $101,700; Households with income of $100,000 or more: 42.8%; Poverty rate: 6.1%

Educational Attainment: High school diploma or higher: 95.9%; Bachelor's degree or higher: 56.6%; Graduate/professional degree or higher: 16.6%

School District(s)
Westfield-Washington Schools (PK-12)
   2012-13 Enrollment: 6,518 . . . . (317) 867-8000

Housing: Homeownership rate: 82.4%; Median home value: $217,400; Median year structure built: 2001; Homeowner vacancy rate: 2.5%; Median gross rent: $876 per month; Rental vacancy rate: 12.2%

Health Insurance: 93.6% have insurance; 87.4% have private insurance; 12.5% have public insurance; 6.4% do not have insurance; 3.0% of children under 18 do not have insurance

Safety: Violent crime rate: 6.4 per 10,000 population; Property crime rate: 149.2 per 10,000 population

Transportation: Commute: 93.4% car, 0.3% public transportation, 0.9% walk, 3.2% work from home; Median travel time to work: 26.1 minutes

Additional Information Contacts
Town of Westfield . . . . (317) 804-3020
http://www.westfield.in.gov

Hancock County

Located in central Indiana; drained by the Big Blue River and by Sugar and Brandywine Creeks. Covers a land area of 306.016 square miles, a water area of 1.009 square miles, and is located in the Eastern Time Zone at 39.82° N. Lat., 85.77° W. Long. The county was founded in 1827. County seat is Greenfield.

Hancock County is part of the Indianapolis-Carmel-Anderson, IN Metropolitan Statistical Area. The entire metro area includes: Boone County, IN; Brown County, IN; Hamilton County, IN; Hancock County, IN; Hendricks County, IN; Johnson County, IN; Madison County, IN; Marion County, IN; Morgan County, IN; Putnam County, IN; Shelby County, IN

Weather Station: Greenfield   Elevation: 865 feet

	Jan	Feb	Mar	Apr	May	Jun	Jul	Aug	Sep	Oct	Nov	Dec
High	35	39	50	62	72	81	85	84	78	65	52	38
Low	19	21	30	41	52	61	64	63	55	43	34	23
Precip	2.7	2.4	3.6	4.3	5.5	4.6	5.1	3.9	3.5	3.4	3.8	3.2
Snow	5.8	3.5	1.7	0.2	0.0	0.0	0.0	0.0	0.0	0.1	0.6	3.9

High and Low temperatures in degrees Fahrenheit; Precipitation and Snow in inches

Population: 70,002; Growth (since 2000): 26.4%; Density: 228.8 persons per square mile; Race: 95.2% White, 2.1% Black/African American, 0.8% Asian, 0.2% American Indian/Alaska Native, 0.0% Native Hawaiian/Other Pacific Islander, 1.2% two or more races, 1.7% Hispanic of any race; Average household size: 2.64; Median age: 39.1; Age under 18: 26.2%; Age 65 and over: 12.8%; Males per 100 females: 96.5; Marriage status: 24.1% never married, 58.6% now married, 1.3% separated, 5.1% widowed, 12.2% divorced; Foreign born: 1.5%; Speak English only: 97.8%; With disability: 12.2%; Veterans: 10.3%; Ancestry: 24.7% German, 13.6% Irish, 12.1% American, 11.8% English, 2.6% Scottish
Religion: Six largest groups: 10.7% Non-denominational Protestant, 8.2% Baptist, 6.6% Catholicism, 6.3% Methodist/Pietist, 2.7% Lutheran, 2.1% Holiness
Economy: Unemployment rate: 4.5%; Leading industries: 15.7% construction; 12.2% retail trade; 11.7% other services (except public administration); Farms: 604 totaling 165,861 acres; Company size: 1 employs 1,000 or more persons, 3 employ 500 to 999 persons, 19 employ 100 to 499 persons, 1,310 employ less than 100 persons; Business ownership: 1,772 women-owned, n/a Black-owned, n/a Hispanic-owned, n/a Asian-owned
Employment: 15.3% management, business, and financial, 5.5% computer, engineering, and science, 9.1% education, legal, community service, arts, and media, 7.4% healthcare practitioners, 15.0% service, 25.1% sales and office, 9.8% natural resources, construction, and maintenance, 12.7% production, transportation, and material moving
Income: Per capita: $28,111; Median household: $62,981; Average household: $73,897; Households with income of $100,000 or more: 22.8%; Poverty rate: 7.6%
Educational Attainment: High school diploma or higher: 92.6%; Bachelor's degree or higher: 26.3%; Graduate/professional degree or higher: 9.2%
Housing: Homeownership rate: 79.3%; Median home value: $155,400; Median year structure built: 1985; Homeowner vacancy rate: 2.0%; Median gross rent: $820 per month; Rental vacancy rate: 9.9%
Vital Statistics: Birth rate: 108.7 per 10,000 population; Death rate: 75.0 per 10,000 population; Age-adjusted cancer mortality rate: 192.0 deaths per 100,000 population
Health Insurance: 89.3% have insurance; 79.2% have private insurance; 23.3% have public insurance; 10.7% do not have insurance; 5.7% of children under 18 do not have insurance
Health Care: Physicians: 18.5 per 10,000 population; Hospital beds: 12.1 per 10,000 population; Hospital admissions: 492.3 per 10,000 population
Air Quality Index: 96.7% good, 3.3% moderate, 0.0% unhealthy for sensitive individuals, 0.0% unhealthy (percent of days)
Transportation: Commute: 93.6% car, 0.2% public transportation, 1.0% walk, 4.6% work from home; Median travel time to work: 26.3 minutes
Presidential Election: 28.4% Obama, 69.4% Romney (2012)
Additional Information Contacts
Hancock Government . . . . (317) 462-1102
http://www.hancockcoingov.org

Hancock County Communities

CHARLOTTESVILLE (unincorporated postal area)
ZCTA: 46117
Covers a land area of 11.790 square miles and a water area of 0.022 square miles. Located at 39.81° N. Lat; 85.62° W. Long. Elevation is 942 feet.
Population: 671; Growth (since 2000): 1.4%; Density: 56.9 persons per square mile; Race: 96.4% White, 0.1% Black/African American, 0.0% Asian, 0.7% American Indian/Alaska Native, 0.0% Native Hawaiian/Other Pacific Islander, 1.6% Two or more races, 1.5% Hispanic of any race; Average household size: 2.64; Median age: 43.1; Age under 18: 23.8%; Age 65 and over: 15.9%; Males per 100 females: 96.8

School District(s)
Eastern Hancock County Com Sch Corp (KG-12)
  2012-13 Enrollment: 1,112 . . . . (317) 467-0064
  Housing: Homeownership rate: 87.4%; Homeowner vacancy rate: 2.6%; Rental vacancy rate: 3.0%

FORTVILLE (town).
Covers a land area of 2.976 square miles and a water area of 0.007 square miles. Located at 39.92° N. Lat; 85.85° W. Long. Elevation is 856 feet.
History: Fortville was founded in 1849 by Cephas Fort.
Population: 3,929; Growth (since 2000): 14.1%; Density: 1,320.0 persons per square mile; Race: 96.2% White, 1.3% Black/African American, 0.1% Asian, 0.3% American Indian/Alaska Native, 0.0% Native Hawaiian/Other Pacific Islander, 1.3% Two or more races, 2.3% Hispanic of any race; Average household size: 2.53; Median age: 35.7; Age under 18: 28.3%; Age 65 and over: 11.6%; Males per 100 females: 94.5; Marriage status: 26.5% never married, 52.8% now married, 0.4% separated, 3.7% widowed, 16.9% divorced; Foreign born: 1.1%; Speak English only: 99.5%; With disability: 17.5%; Veterans: 10.6%; Ancestry: 16.0% German, 11.4% Irish, 9.7% American, 6.0% English, 3.7% Italian
Employment: 19.1% management, business, and financial, 2.6% computer, engineering, and science, 12.3% education, legal, community service, arts, and media, 4.1% healthcare practitioners, 16.7% service, 20.8% sales and office, 9.3% natural resources, construction, and maintenance, 15.1% production, transportation, and material moving
Income: Per capita: $20,967; Median household: $41,005; Average household: $54,880; Households with income of $100,000 or more: 12.5%; Poverty rate: 20.9%
Educational Attainment: High school diploma or higher: 90.1%; Bachelor's degree or higher: 21.8%; Graduate/professional degree or higher: 6.4%

School District(s)
Mt Vernon Community Sch Corp (KG-12)
  2012-13 Enrollment: 3,495 . . . . (317) 485-3100
Housing: Homeownership rate: 63.9%; Median home value: $118,900; Median year structure built: 1984; Homeowner vacancy rate: 2.5%; Median gross rent: $756 per month; Rental vacancy rate: 9.5%
Health Insurance: 87.7% have insurance; 66.1% have private insurance; 35.3% have public insurance; 12.3% do not have insurance; 0.7% of children under 18 do not have insurance
Transportation: Commute: 94.4% car, 0.1% public transportation, 2.0% walk, 2.3% work from home; Median travel time to work: 23.4 minutes
Additional Information Contacts
Town of Fortville . . . . (317) 485-4044
  http://www.fortvilleindiana.org

GREENFIELD (city). County seat.
Covers a land area of 12.551 square miles and a water area of 0.112 square miles. Located at 39.79° N. Lat; 85.77° W. Long. Elevation is 883 feet.
History: Named for John Green, an early settler. Greenfield was the birthplace in 1849 of poet James Whitcomb Riley. An early industry here was tomato canning.
Population: 20,602; Growth (since 2000): 41.1%; Density: 1,641.5 persons per square mile; Race: 96.6% White, 0.6% Black/African American, 0.8% Asian, 0.3% American Indian/Alaska Native, 0.0% Native Hawaiian/Other Pacific Islander, 1.3% Two or more races, 1.8% Hispanic of any race; Average household size: 2.51; Median age: 35.6; Age under 18: 26.4%; Age 65 and over: 14.0%; Males per 100 females: 92.7; Marriage status: 27.6% never married, 49.3% now married, 2.4% separated, 6.1% widowed, 17.0% divorced; Foreign born: 1.1%; Speak English only: 97.5%; With disability: 12.9%; Veterans: 9.5%; Ancestry: 22.9% German, 13.0% Irish, 11.6% American, 10.7% English, 1.8% European
Employment: 13.2% management, business, and financial, 4.5% computer, engineering, and science, 8.8% education, legal, community service, arts, and media, 5.1% healthcare practitioners, 17.3% service, 25.9% sales and office, 8.7% natural resources, construction, and maintenance, 16.5% production, transportation, and material moving
Income: Per capita: $23,112; Median household: $49,940; Average household: $58,482; Households with income of $100,000 or more: 13.7%; Poverty rate: 11.1%
Educational Attainment: High school diploma or higher: 88.2%; Bachelor's degree or higher: 19.7%; Graduate/professional degree or higher: 8.1%

School District(s)
Greenfield-Central Com Schools (PK-12)
  2012-13 Enrollment: 4,626 . . . . (317) 462-4434
Mt Vernon Community Sch Corp (KG-12)
  2012-13 Enrollment: 3,495 . . . . (317) 485-3100
Southern Hancock County Com Sch Corp (PK-12)
  2012-13 Enrollment: 3,268 . . . . (317) 861-4463
Housing: Homeownership rate: 66.1%; Median home value: $118,100; Median year structure built: 1989; Homeowner vacancy rate: 3.4%; Median gross rent: $814 per month; Rental vacancy rate: 12.1%
Health Insurance: 87.1% have insurance; 71.8% have private insurance; 28.2% have public insurance; 12.9% do not have insurance; 7.2% of children under 18 do not have insurance
Hospitals: Hancock Regional Hospital (94 beds)
Safety: Violent crime rate: 5.7 per 10,000 population; Property crime rate: 192.2 per 10,000 population
Newspapers: Daily Reporter (daily circulation 11400)
Transportation: Commute: 94.9% car, 0.0% public transportation, 1.8% walk, 2.5% work from home; Median travel time to work: 24.5 minutes
Additional Information Contacts
City of Greenfield. . . . . (317) 477-4300
  http://www.greenfieldin.org

MCCORDSVILLE (town). Covers a land area of 4.701 square miles and a water area of 0.009 square miles. Located at 39.90° N. Lat; 85.93° W. Long. Elevation is 850 feet.
History: Laid out 1865.
Population: 4,797; Growth (since 2000): 323.0%; Density: 1,020.4 persons per square mile; Race: 83.2% White, 10.3% Black/African American, 2.3% Asian, 0.3% American Indian/Alaska Native, 0.0% Native Hawaiian/Other Pacific Islander, 2.6% Two or more races, 4.4% Hispanic of any race; Average household size: 2.90; Median age: 32.7; Age under 18: 32.4%; Age 65 and over: 5.0%; Males per 100 females: 93.8; Marriage status: 28.1% never married, 56.2% now married, 1.8% separated, 2.0% widowed, 13.8% divorced; Foreign born: 3.4%; Speak English only: 94.9%; With disability: 5.7%; Veterans: 10.4%; Ancestry: 30.4% German, 21.9% Irish, 9.5% Polish, 9.0% English, 5.7% American
Employment: 20.2% management, business, and financial, 10.5% computer, engineering, and science, 12.0% education, legal, community service, arts, and media, 10.9% healthcare practitioners, 10.8% service, 27.0% sales and office, 6.3% natural resources, construction, and maintenance, 2.3% production, transportation, and material moving
Income: Per capita: $38,349; Median household: $80,417; Average household: $101,292; Households with income of $100,000 or more: 30.8%; Poverty rate: 7.5%
Educational Attainment: High school diploma or higher: 97.7%; Bachelor's degree or higher: 47.6%; Graduate/professional degree or higher: 11.3%
School District(s)
Geist Montessori Academy (KG-08)
  2012-13 Enrollment: 290. . . . . (317) 335-1158
Mt Vernon Community Sch Corp (KG-12)
  2012-13 Enrollment: 3,495 . . . . (317) 485-3100
Housing: Homeownership rate: 85.0%; Median home value: $182,500; Median year structure built: 2003; Homeowner vacancy rate: 1.7%; Median gross rent: $1,174 per month; Rental vacancy rate: 4.2%
Health Insurance: 82.3% have insurance; 80.7% have private insurance; 4.0% have public insurance; 17.7% do not have insurance; 11.4% of children under 18 do not have insurance
Transportation: Commute: 92.6% car, 0.0% public transportation, 0.7% walk, 6.7% work from home; Median travel time to work: 25.3 minutes
Airports: Indianapolis Regional (general aviation)

NEW PALESTINE (town). Covers a land area of 1.092 square miles and a water area of 0.005 square miles. Located at 39.73° N. Lat; 85.89° W. Long. Elevation is 837 feet.
History: Laid out 1838.
Population: 2,055; Growth (since 2000): 62.6%; Density: 1,881.8 persons per square mile; Race: 97.8% White, 0.0% Black/African American, 0.6% Asian, 0.2% American Indian/Alaska Native, 0.0% Native Hawaiian/Other Pacific Islander, 1.2% Two or more races, 1.0% Hispanic of any race; Average household size: 2.64; Median age: 37.2; Age under 18: 28.9%; Age 65 and over: 12.5%; Males per 100 females: 99.3

School District(s)
Southern Hancock County Com Sch Corp (PK-12)
  2012-13 Enrollment: 3,268 . . . . (317) 861-4463
Housing: Homeownership rate: 77.6%; Homeowner vacancy rate: 1.6%; Rental vacancy rate: 8.3%
Newspapers: New Palestine Press (weekly circulation 3000)

SHIRLEY (town). Covers a land area of 0.344 square miles and a water area of 0 square miles. Located at 39.89° N. Lat; 85.58° W. Long. Elevation is 1,027 feet.
Population: 830; Growth (since 2000): 3.0%; Density: 2,411.0 persons per square mile; Race: 97.7% White, 0.6% Black/African American, 0.4% Asian, 0.6% American Indian/Alaska Native, 0.0% Native Hawaiian/Other Pacific Islander, 0.5% Two or more races, 0.4% Hispanic of any race; Average household size: 2.53; Median age: 35.0; Age under 18: 28.9%; Age 65 and over: 13.6%; Males per 100 females: 97.1
Housing: Homeownership rate: 71.6%; Homeowner vacancy rate: 1.7%; Rental vacancy rate: 8.8%

SPRING LAKE (town). Covers a land area of 0.153 square miles and a water area of 0.011 square miles. Located at 39.78° N. Lat; 85.85° W. Long. Elevation is 850 feet.
History: Settled 1884, laid out 1912.
Population: 218; Growth (since 2000): -16.8%; Density: 1,428.0 persons per square mile; Race: 95.9% White, 0.5% Black/African American, 0.0% Asian, 0.5% American Indian/Alaska Native, 0.0% Native Hawaiian/Other Pacific Islander, 2.8% Two or more races, 0.9% Hispanic of any race; Average household size: 2.29; Median age: 47.0; Age under 18: 16.5%; Age 65 and over: 20.6%; Males per 100 females: 111.7
Housing: Homeownership rate: 91.5%; Homeowner vacancy rate: 1.1%; Rental vacancy rate: 0.0%

WILKINSON (town). Covers a land area of 0.232 square miles and a water area of 0 square miles. Located at 39.89° N. Lat; 85.61° W. Long. Elevation is 1,001 feet.
History: Laid out 1883.
Population: 449; Growth (since 2000): 26.1%; Density: 1,934.6 persons per square mile; Race: 99.3% White, 0.0% Black/African American, 0.0% Asian, 0.0% American Indian/Alaska Native, 0.0% Native Hawaiian/Other Pacific Islander, 0.7% Two or more races, 2.0% Hispanic of any race; Average household size: 2.55; Median age: 39.7; Age under 18: 25.2%; Age 65 and over: 14.7%; Males per 100 females: 106.9
Housing: Homeownership rate: 80.1%; Homeowner vacancy rate: 0.0%; Rental vacancy rate: 7.9%

Harrison County

Located in southern Indiana; bounded on the east, south, and southwest by the Ohio River and the Kentucky border, and on the west by the Blue River. Covers a land area of 484.516 square miles, a water area of 2.005 square miles, and is located in the Eastern Time Zone at 38.19° N. Lat., 86.10° W. Long. The county was founded in 1808. County seat is Corydon.

Harrison County is part of the Louisville/Jefferson County, KY-IN Metropolitan Statistical Area. The entire metro area includes: Clark County, IN; Floyd County, IN; Harrison County, IN; Scott County, IN; Washington County, IN; Bullitt County, KY; Henry County, KY; Jefferson County, KY; Oldham County, KY; Shelby County, KY; Spencer County, KY; Trimble County, KY

Population: 39,364; Growth (since 2000): 14.7%; Density: 81.2 persons per square mile; Race: 97.4% White, 0.5% Black/African American, 0.4% Asian, 0.2% American Indian/Alaska Native, 0.0% Native Hawaiian/Other Pacific Islander, 1.0% two or more races, 1.5% Hispanic of any race; Average household size: 2.56; Median age: 40.2; Age under 18: 23.6%; Age 65 and over: 13.8%; Males per 100 females: 100.0; Marriage status: 23.0% never married, 56.5% now married, 1.3% separated, 7.0% widowed, 13.5% divorced; Foreign born: 1.1%; Speak English only: 98.0%; With disability: 15.4%; Veterans: 11.1%; Ancestry: 28.1% German, 19.2% American, 11.7% Irish, 11.5% English, 2.6% French
Religion: Six largest groups: 11.3% Catholicism, 10.9% Methodist/Pietist, 8.3% Baptist, 2.5% Non-denominational Protestant, 2.5% Lutheran, 1.5% Pentecostal
Economy: Unemployment rate: 4.8%; Leading industries: 17.2% retail trade; 14.8% construction; 10.9% other services (except public

administration); Farms: 967 totaling 134,995 acres; Company size: 1 employs 1,000 or more persons, 0 employ 500 to 999 persons, 11 employs 100 to 499 persons, 658 employ less than 100 persons; Business ownership: 1,002 women-owned, 76 Black-owned, 49 Hispanic-owned, 38 Asian-owned

Employment: 10.9% management, business, and financial, 3.9% computer, engineering, and science, 7.4% education, legal, community service, arts, and media, 6.4% healthcare practitioners, 16.0% service, 23.8% sales and office, 10.3% natural resources, construction, and maintenance, 21.5% production, transportation, and material moving
Income: Per capita: $23,244; Median household: $50,510; Average household: $59,761; Households with income of $100,000 or more: 15.3%; Poverty rate: 13.2%
Educational Attainment: High school diploma or higher: 87.6%; Bachelor's degree or higher: 14.9%; Graduate/professional degree or higher: 5.1%
Housing: Homeownership rate: 81.7%; Median home value: $122,100; Median year structure built: 1982; Homeowner vacancy rate: 1.7%; Median gross rent: $690 per month; Rental vacancy rate: 8.9%
Vital Statistics: Birth rate: 103.7 per 10,000 population; Death rate: 83.2 per 10,000 population; Age-adjusted cancer mortality rate: 162.8 deaths per 100,000 population
Health Insurance: 88.7% have insurance; 74.1% have private insurance; 27.8% have public insurance; 11.3% do not have insurance; 5.0% of children under 18 do not have insurance
Health Care: Physicians: 6.6 per 10,000 population; Hospital beds: 6.4 per 10,000 population; Hospital admissions: 413.1 per 10,000 population
Transportation: Commute: 94.2% car, 0.2% public transportation, 0.4% walk, 3.7% work from home; Median travel time to work: 30.2 minutes
Presidential Election: 37.4% Obama, 60.2% Romney (2012)
Additional Information Contacts
Harrison Government . . . . (812) 738-8241
http://www.harrisoncounty.in.gov

Harrison County Communities

CENTRAL (unincorporated postal area)
ZCTA: 47110
Covers a land area of 5.799 square miles and a water area of 0 square miles. Located at 38.10° N. Lat; 86.19° W. Long. Elevation is 699 feet.
Population: 350; Growth (since 2000): n/a; Density: 60.4 persons per square mile; Race: 92.0% White, 0.3% Black/African American, 0.0% Asian, 0.3% American Indian/Alaska Native, 0.3% Native Hawaiian/Other Pacific Islander, 4.0% Two or more races, 4.0% Hispanic of any race; Average household size: 2.57; Median age: 36.8; Age under 18: 25.7%; Age 65 and over: 14.3%; Males per 100 females: 102.3
School District(s)
South Harrison Com Schools (PK-12)
    2012-13 Enrollment: 3,113 . . . . (812) 738-2168
Housing: Homeownership rate: 83.8%; Homeowner vacancy rate: 3.4%; Rental vacancy rate: 4.3%

CORYDON (town). County seat.
Covers a land area of 1.649 square miles and a water area of 0 square miles. Located at 38.21° N. Lat; 86.13° W. Long. Elevation is 587 feet.
History: Corydon was named by General William Henry Harrison, who owned the land on which the town was platted. Harrison chose the name for the young shepherd in the song "Pastoral Elegy," a favorite of the day. Corydon served as the capital of Indiana for a time, and was the site of the only Civil War battle fought in Indiana. The Battle of Corydon occurred in 1863, when General John Hunt Morgan and his Confederate troops crossed the Ohio River and invaded the town.
Population: 3,122; Growth (since 2000): 15.0%; Density: 1,892.8 persons per square mile; Race: 96.7% White, 0.7% Black/African American, 0.2% Asian, 0.2% American Indian/Alaska Native, 0.1% Native Hawaiian/Other Pacific Islander, 1.2% Two or more races, 2.6% Hispanic of any race; Average household size: 2.14; Median age: 40.8; Age under 18: 20.5%; Age 65 and over: 23.4%; Males per 100 females: 84.0; Marriage status: 25.9% never married, 35.4% now married, 1.9% separated, 13.5% widowed, 25.2% divorced; Foreign born: 0.0%; Speak English only: 97.8%; With disability: 17.8%; Veterans: 15.3%; Ancestry: 26.0% German, 18.0% Irish, 12.4% American, 6.4% English, 2.9% Italian
Employment: 9.3% management, business, and financial, 1.8% computer, engineering, and science, 10.7% education, legal, community service, arts, and media, 4.6% healthcare practitioners, 19.3% service, 22.7% sales and office, 4.8% natural resources, construction, and maintenance, 26.8% production, transportation, and material moving
Income: Per capita: $18,715; Median household: $32,120; Average household: $41,316; Households with income of $100,000 or more: 10.0%; Poverty rate: 34.1%
Educational Attainment: High school diploma or higher: 88.5%; Bachelor's degree or higher: 14.5%; Graduate/professional degree or higher: 5.4%
School District(s)
South Harrison Com Schools (PK-12)
    2012-13 Enrollment: 3,113 . . . . (812) 738-2168
Housing: Homeownership rate: 54.8%; Median home value: $87,800; Median year structure built: 1955; Homeowner vacancy rate: 2.4%; Median gross rent: $692 per month; Rental vacancy rate: 8.5%
Health Insurance: 84.4% have insurance; 55.9% have private insurance; 42.4% have public insurance; 15.6% do not have insurance; 6.5% of children under 18 do not have insurance
Hospitals: Harrison County Hospital (68 beds)
Newspapers: Clarion News & Corydon Democrat (weekly circulation 15000)
Transportation: Commute: 89.1% car, 0.0% public transportation, 4.8% walk, 5.1% work from home; Median travel time to work: 27.3 minutes
Additional Information Contacts
Town of Corydon. . . . . (812) 738-2138
http://www.thisisindiana.org

CRANDALL (town).
Covers a land area of 0.102 square miles and a water area of 0 square miles. Located at 38.29° N. Lat; 86.07° W. Long. Elevation is 653 feet.
Population: 152; Growth (since 2000): 16.0%; Density: 1,492.4 persons per square mile; Race: 98.0% White, 0.0% Black/African American, 0.7% Asian, 1.3% American Indian/Alaska Native, 0.0% Native Hawaiian/Other Pacific Islander, 0.0% Two or more races, 2.6% Hispanic of any race; Average household size: 2.30; Median age: 45.5; Age under 18: 25.0%; Age 65 and over: 17.8%; Males per 100 females: 100.0
Housing: Homeownership rate: 74.2%; Homeowner vacancy rate: 0.0%; Rental vacancy rate: 10.5%

DEPAUW (unincorporated postal area)
ZCTA: 47115
Covers a land area of 56.975 square miles and a water area of 0.216 square miles. Located at 38.35° N. Lat; 86.21° W. Long. Elevation is 650 feet.
Population: 2,622; Growth (since 2000): 11.5%; Density: 46.0 persons per square mile; Race: 98.4% White, 0.2% Black/African American, 0.4% Asian, 0.1% American Indian/Alaska Native, 0.0% Native Hawaiian/Other Pacific Islander, 0.8% Two or more races, 0.8% Hispanic of any race; Average household size: 2.54; Median age: 40.9; Age under 18: 23.8%; Age 65 and over: 13.1%; Males per 100 females: 102.3; Marriage status: 22.7% never married, 57.2% now married, 0.0% separated, 7.1% widowed, 13.0% divorced; Foreign born: 0.0%; Speak English only: 100.0%; With disability: 18.5%; Veterans: 11.7%; Ancestry: 28.4% German, 20.9% American, 10.4% English, 10.0% Irish, 3.4% British
Employment: 15.4% management, business, and financial, 0.2% computer, engineering, and science, 7.2% education, legal, community service, arts, and media, 2.2% healthcare practitioners, 10.3% service, 30.3% sales and office, 10.9% natural resources, construction, and maintenance, 23.5% production, transportation, and material moving
Income: Per capita: $22,474; Median household: $50,347; Average household: $55,245; Households with income of $100,000 or more: 16.3%; Poverty rate: 13.0%
Educational Attainment: High school diploma or higher: 83.9%; Bachelor's degree or higher: 16.2%; Graduate/professional degree or higher: 4.0%
Housing: Homeownership rate: 82.4%; Median home value: $127,200; Median year structure built: 1978; Homeowner vacancy rate: 2.2%; Median gross rent: $425 per month; Rental vacancy rate: 10.3%
Health Insurance: 85.8% have insurance; 78.0% have private insurance; 21.1% have public insurance; 14.2% do not have insurance; 5.4% of children under 18 do not have insurance
Transportation: Commute: 96.3% car, 0.0% public transportation, 0.0% walk, 3.2% work from home; Median travel time to work: 33.1 minutes

ELIZABETH (town). Covers a land area of 0.165 square miles and a water area of 0 square miles. Located at 38.12° N. Lat; 85.97° W. Long. Elevation is 728 feet.
Population: 162; Growth (since 2000): 18.2%; Density: 979.7 persons per square mile; Race: 96.3% White, 1.2% Black/African American, 0.0% Asian, 0.6% American Indian/Alaska Native, 0.0% Native Hawaiian/Other Pacific Islander, 0.6% Two or more races, 1.2% Hispanic of any race; Average household size: 2.61; Median age: 33.9; Age under 18: 27.2%; Age 65 and over: 19.1%; Males per 100 females: 97.6
School District(s)
South Harrison Com Schools (PK-12)
   2012-13 Enrollment: 3,113 .... (812) 738-2168
Housing: Homeownership rate: 75.8%; Homeowner vacancy rate: 7.8%; Rental vacancy rate: 0.0%

LACONIA (town). Covers a land area of 0.050 square miles and a water area of 0 square miles. Located at 38.03° N. Lat; 86.09° W. Long. Elevation is 663 feet.
History: Laid out 1816.
Population: 50; Growth (since 2000): 72.4%; Density: 1,007.4 persons per square mile; Race: 98.0% White, 0.0% Black/African American, 2.0% Asian, 0.0% American Indian/Alaska Native, 0.0% Native Hawaiian/Other Pacific Islander, 0.0% Two or more races, 0.0% Hispanic of any race; Average household size: 2.38; Median age: 41.0; Age under 18: 16.0%; Age 65 and over: 6.0%; Males per 100 females: 92.3
Housing: Homeownership rate: 52.4%; Homeowner vacancy rate: 15.4%; Rental vacancy rate: 0.0%

LANESVILLE (town). Covers a land area of 0.523 square miles and a water area of 0 square miles. Located at 38.23° N. Lat; 85.99° W. Long. Elevation is 699 feet.
History: Lanesville was settled in 1792 as a stage stop and trading center for surrounding farms. It was platted in 1817, and named for General Lane, a surveyor who was an early resident.
Population: 564; Growth (since 2000): -8.1%; Density: 1,078.6 persons per square mile; Race: 98.2% White, 0.4% Black/African American, 0.2% Asian, 0.0% American Indian/Alaska Native, 0.0% Native Hawaiian/Other Pacific Islander, 0.5% Two or more races, 0.9% Hispanic of any race; Average household size: 2.34; Median age: 40.9; Age under 18: 24.6%; Age 65 and over: 16.7%; Males per 100 females: 93.8
School District(s)
Lanesville Community School Corp (KG-12)
   2012-13 Enrollment: 662 .... (812) 952-2555
Housing: Homeownership rate: 76.7%; Homeowner vacancy rate: 3.1%; Rental vacancy rate: 28.8%

MAUCKPORT (town). Covers a land area of 0.189 square miles and a water area of 0.013 square miles. Located at 38.02° N. Lat; 86.20° W. Long. Elevation is 440 feet.
Population: 81; Growth (since 2000): -2.4%; Density: 428.7 persons per square mile; Race: 100.0% White, 0.0% Black/African American, 0.0% Asian, 0.0% American Indian/Alaska Native, 0.0% Native Hawaiian/Other Pacific Islander, 0.0% Two or more races, 0.0% Hispanic of any race; Average household size: 2.25; Median age: 34.2; Age under 18: 32.1%; Age 65 and over: 16.0%; Males per 100 females: 102.5
Housing: Homeownership rate: 58.3%; Homeowner vacancy rate: 4.5%; Rental vacancy rate: 21.1%

NEW AMSTERDAM (town). Covers a land area of 0.080 square miles and a water area of 0.024 square miles. Located at 38.10° N. Lat; 86.27° W. Long. Elevation is 449 feet.
Population: 27; Growth (since 2000): 2,600.0%; Density: 335.6 persons per square mile; Race: 85.2% White, 0.0% Black/African American, 0.0% Asian, 0.0% American Indian/Alaska Native, 0.0% Native Hawaiian/Other Pacific Islander, 3.7% Two or more races, 11.1% Hispanic of any race; Average household size: 2.45; Median age: 42.3; Age under 18: 29.6%; Age 65 and over: 18.5%; Males per 100 females: 125.0
Housing: Homeownership rate: 72.8%; Homeowner vacancy rate: 10.0%; Rental vacancy rate: 40.0%

NEW MIDDLETOWN (town). Covers a land area of 0.041 square miles and a water area of 0 square miles. Located at 38.16° N. Lat; 86.05° W. Long. Elevation is 702 feet.
Population: 93; Growth (since 2000): 20.8%; Density: 2,261.7 persons per square mile; Race: 95.7% White, 2.2% Black/African American, 0.0% Asian, 0.0% American Indian/Alaska Native, 0.0% Native Hawaiian/Other Pacific Islander, 2.2% Two or more races, 0.0% Hispanic of any race; Average household size: 2.91; Median age: 29.5; Age under 18: 29.0%; Age 65 and over: 7.5%; Males per 100 females: 121.4
School District(s)
South Harrison Com Schools (PK-12)
   2012-13 Enrollment: 3,113 .... (812) 738-2168
Housing: Homeownership rate: 81.2%; Homeowner vacancy rate: 3.7%; Rental vacancy rate: 0.0%

NEW SALISBURY (CDP). Covers a land area of 1.978 square miles and a water area of 0 square miles. Located at 38.31° N. Lat; 86.10° W. Long. Elevation is 728 feet.
Population: 613; Growth (since 2000): n/a; Density: 310.0 persons per square mile; Race: 97.9% White, 0.7% Black/African American, 0.7% Asian, 0.2% American Indian/Alaska Native, 0.0% Native Hawaiian/Other Pacific Islander, 0.5% Two or more races, 0.7% Hispanic of any race; Average household size: 2.52; Median age: 38.6; Age under 18: 21.9%; Age 65 and over: 16.8%; Males per 100 females: 100.3
Housing: Homeownership rate: 72.5%; Homeowner vacancy rate: 1.1%; Rental vacancy rate: 6.8%

PALMYRA (town). Covers a land area of 1.238 square miles and a water area of 0.042 square miles. Located at 38.41° N. Lat; 86.11° W. Long. Elevation is 771 feet.
History: Palmyra was founded in 1810 as a farming village.
Population: 930; Growth (since 2000): 46.9%; Density: 751.2 persons per square mile; Race: 96.1% White, 0.1% Black/African American, 1.6% Asian, 0.2% American Indian/Alaska Native, 0.0% Native Hawaiian/Other Pacific Islander, 1.9% Two or more races, 1.0% Hispanic of any race; Average household size: 2.40; Median age: 37.4; Age under 18: 24.2%; Age 65 and over: 14.4%; Males per 100 females: 92.1
School District(s)
North Harrison Com School Corp (KG-12)
   2012-13 Enrollment: 2,184 .... (812) 347-2407
Housing: Homeownership rate: 65.5%; Homeowner vacancy rate: 3.8%; Rental vacancy rate: 2.9%

RAMSEY (unincorporated postal area)
ZCTA: 47166
   Covers a land area of 12.842 square miles and a water area of 0 square miles. Located at 38.31° N. Lat; 86.17° W. Long. Elevation is 705 feet.
   Population: 1,302; Growth (since 2000): 4.6%; Density: 101.4 persons per square mile; Race: 98.8% White, 0.0% Black/African American, 0.2% Asian, 0.2% American Indian/Alaska Native, 0.0% Native Hawaiian/Other Pacific Islander, 0.3% Two or more races, 1.2% Hispanic of any race; Average household size: 2.57; Median age: 39.2; Age under 18: 24.2%; Age 65 and over: 13.7%; Males per 100 females: 99.4
School District(s)
North Harrison Com School Corp (KG-12)
   2012-13 Enrollment: 2,184 .... (812) 347-2407
   Housing: Homeownership rate: 85.4%; Homeowner vacancy rate: 0.9%; Rental vacancy rate: 6.3%

Hendricks County

Located in central Indiana; drained by the Eel and Whitelick Rivers and Mill Creek. Covers a land area of 406.911 square miles, a water area of 1.866 square miles, and is located in the Eastern Time Zone at 39.77° N. Lat., 86.51° W. Long. The county was founded in 1823. County seat is Danville.

Hendricks County is part of the Indianapolis-Carmel-Anderson, IN Metropolitan Statistical Area. The entire metro area includes: Boone County, IN; Brown County, IN; Hamilton County, IN; Hancock County, IN; Hendricks County, IN; Johnson County, IN; Madison County, IN; Marion County, IN; Morgan County, IN; Putnam County, IN; Shelby County, IN

Population: 145,448; Growth (since 2000): 39.7%; Density: 357.4 persons per square mile; Race: 90.1% White, 4.9% Black/African American, 2.1%

Asian, 0.2% American Indian/Alaska Native, 0.0% Native Hawaiian/Other Pacific Islander, 1.6% two or more races, 3.0% Hispanic of any race; Average household size: 2.71; Median age: 36.7; Age under 18: 27.4%; Age 65 and over: 10.7%; Males per 100 females: 99.4; Marriage status: 23.6% never married, 60.3% now married, 1.1% separated, 4.8% widowed, 11.2% divorced; Foreign born: 4.2%; Speak English only: 94.3%; With disability: 8.9%; Veterans: 9.7%; Ancestry: 25.9% German, 16.2% English, 14.5% Irish, 10.0% American, 3.0% Scottish
Religion: Six largest groups: 13.5% Baptist, 7.5% Catholicism, 6.4% Non-denominational Protestant, 5.2% Methodist/Pietist, 1.8% Lutheran, 1.5% Latter-day Saints
Economy: Unemployment rate: 4.5%; Leading industries: 15.0% retail trade; 10.6% construction; 10.5% health care and social assistance; Farms: 694 totaling 218,398 acres; Company size: 2 employ 1,000 or more persons, 6 employ 500 to 999 persons, 92 employ 100 to 499 persons, 2,836 employ less than 100 persons; Business ownership: 2,943 women-owned, 285 Black-owned, 104 Hispanic-owned, 451 Asian-owned
Employment: 17.1% management, business, and financial, 6.1% computer, engineering, and science, 9.2% education, legal, community service, arts, and media, 7.2% healthcare practitioners, 13.1% service, 26.1% sales and office, 8.7% natural resources, construction, and maintenance, 12.5% production, transportation, and material moving
Income: Per capita: $29,830; Median household: $68,297; Average household: $82,006; Households with income of $100,000 or more: 28.7%; Poverty rate: 5.0%
Educational Attainment: High school diploma or higher: 93.5%; Bachelor's degree or higher: 32.2%; Graduate/professional degree or higher: 9.1%
Housing: Homeownership rate: 80.5%; Median home value: $159,800; Median year structure built: 1993; Homeowner vacancy rate: 1.9%; Median gross rent: $906 per month; Rental vacancy rate: 8.0%
Vital Statistics: Birth rate: 117.8 per 10,000 population; Death rate: 60.6 per 10,000 population; Age-adjusted cancer mortality rate: 161.4 deaths per 100,000 population
Health Insurance: 90.7% have insurance; 82.6% have private insurance; 18.2% have public insurance; 9.3% do not have insurance; 6.3% of children under 18 do not have insurance
Health Care: Physicians: 16.0 per 10,000 population; Hospital beds: 16.7 per 10,000 population; Hospital admissions: 877.7 per 10,000 population
Air Quality Index: 98.9% good, 1.1% moderate, 0.0% unhealthy for sensitive individuals, 0.0% unhealthy (percent of days)
Transportation: Commute: 95.1% car, 0.1% public transportation, 0.7% walk, 3.0% work from home; Median travel time to work: 25.9 minutes
Presidential Election: 31.7% Obama, 66.5% Romney (2012)
Additional Information Contacts
Hendricks Government . . . . (317) 745-9221
http://www.co.hendricks.in.us

Hendricks County Communities

AMO (town). Covers a land area of 0.633 square miles and a water area of 0 square miles. Located at 39.69° N. Lat; 86.61° W. Long. Elevation is 820 feet.
Population: 401; Growth (since 2000): -3.1%; Density: 633.8 persons per square mile; Race: 98.8% White, 0.0% Black/African American, 0.0% Asian, 1.0% American Indian/Alaska Native, 0.0% Native Hawaiian/Other Pacific Islander, 0.2% Two or more races, 0.2% Hispanic of any race; Average household size: 2.84; Median age: 38.3; Age under 18: 29.2%; Age 65 and over: 16.0%; Males per 100 females: 99.5
School District(s)
Mill Creek Community Sch Corp (PK-12)
    2012-13 Enrollment: 1,515 . . . . (317) 539-9200
Housing: Homeownership rate: 82.2%; Homeowner vacancy rate: 0.8%; Rental vacancy rate: 3.8%

AVON (town). Covers a land area of 14.241 square miles and a water area of 0.102 square miles. Located at 39.77° N. Lat; 86.38° W. Long. Elevation is 833 feet.
History: Avon was incorporated in 1995. Previous town names included Hampton, White Lick, Smootsdale and New Philadelphia. The name Avon was placed on a sign by the railroad company.
Population: 12,446; Growth (since 2000): 99.2%; Density: 874.0 persons per square mile; Race: 86.7% White, 5.9% Black/African American, 3.3% Asian, 0.3% American Indian/Alaska Native, 0.1% Native Hawaiian/Other Pacific Islander, 2.2% Two or more races, 4.3% Hispanic of any race; Average household size: 2.77; Median age: 33.9; Age under 18: 30.2%; Age 65 and over: 8.0%; Males per 100 females: 93.4; Marriage status: 25.4% never married, 57.4% now married, 0.3% separated, 2.8% widowed, 14.4% divorced; Foreign born: 6.9%; Speak English only: 91.2%; With disability: 4.9%; Veterans: 11.0%; Ancestry: 26.6% German, 19.6% English, 14.8% Irish, 6.7% American, 3.0% African
Employment: 20.4% management, business, and financial, 5.9% computer, engineering, and science, 8.8% education, legal, community service, arts, and media, 8.6% healthcare practitioners, 10.9% service, 27.5% sales and office, 8.5% natural resources, construction, and maintenance, 9.5% production, transportation, and material moving
Income: Per capita: $29,362; Median household: $75,425; Average household: $86,635; Households with income of $100,000 or more: 37.0%; Poverty rate: 3.7%
Educational Attainment: High school diploma or higher: 95.8%; Bachelor's degree or higher: 32.0%; Graduate/professional degree or higher: 8.7%
School District(s)
Avon Community School Corp (KG-12)
    2012-13 Enrollment: 8,667 . . . . (317) 544-6000
Vocational/Technical School(s)
Avant Gard The School (Private, For-profit)
    Fall 2013 Enrollment: 47 . . . . (317) 272-1212
    2013-14 Tuition: $14,130
Housing: Homeownership rate: 79.7%; Median home value: $164,900; Median year structure built: 2001; Homeowner vacancy rate: 3.4%; Median gross rent: $878 per month; Rental vacancy rate: 6.7%
Health Insurance: 90.3% have insurance; 82.9% have private insurance; 15.1% have public insurance; 9.7% do not have insurance; 8.2% of children under 18 do not have insurance
Hospitals: IU Health West Hospital
Newspapers: Hendricks Co Flyer (weekly circulation 83000)
Transportation: Commute: 95.0% car, 0.0% public transportation, 0.0% walk, 3.9% work from home; Median travel time to work: 28.2 minutes
Additional Information Contacts
Town of Avon . . . . (317) 272-0948
    http://www.avongov.org

BROWNSBURG (town). Covers a land area of 11.076 square miles and a water area of 0.076 square miles. Located at 39.84° N. Lat; 86.39° W. Long. Elevation is 883 feet.
History: Brownsburg's first settler was James B. Brown, a Kentucky native, who settled in Brown Township in 1824. At the time the area was dense and unbroken wilderness with only hunters and trappers in the area.
Population: 21,285; Growth (since 2000): 46.6%; Density: 1,921.7 persons per square mile; Race: 93.4% White, 2.2% Black/African American, 1.6% Asian, 0.1% American Indian/Alaska Native, 0.1% Native Hawaiian/Other Pacific Islander, 1.4% Two or more races, 3.0% Hispanic of any race; Average household size: 2.64; Median age: 36.0; Age under 18: 28.4%; Age 65 and over: 12.0%; Males per 100 females: 92.2; Marriage status: 21.4% never married, 59.7% now married, 0.6% separated, 6.9% widowed, 12.1% divorced; Foreign born: 3.7%; Speak English only: 95.0%; With disability: 9.0%; Veterans: 9.1%; Ancestry: 22.4% German, 18.7% English, 15.9% Irish, 9.3% American, 2.9% Polish
Employment: 16.6% management, business, and financial, 6.2% computer, engineering, and science, 9.3% education, legal, community service, arts, and media, 8.4% healthcare practitioners, 14.3% service, 27.2% sales and office, 6.4% natural resources, construction, and maintenance, 11.7% production, transportation, and material moving
Income: Per capita: $31,829; Median household: $65,340; Average household: $82,255; Households with income of $100,000 or more: 24.7%; Poverty rate: 4.6%
Educational Attainment: High school diploma or higher: 94.0%; Bachelor's degree or higher: 37.0%; Graduate/professional degree or higher: 9.7%
School District(s)
Brownsburg Community Sch Corp (PK-12)
    2012-13 Enrollment: 7,832 . . . . (317) 852-5726
Housing: Homeownership rate: 78.4%; Median home value: $144,100; Median year structure built: 1995; Homeowner vacancy rate: 1.8%; Median gross rent: $896 per month; Rental vacancy rate: 7.6%
Health Insurance: 90.6% have insurance; 84.7% have private insurance; 16.1% have public insurance; 9.4% do not have insurance; 7.9% of children under 18 do not have insurance

Safety: Violent crime rate: 14.4 per 10,000 population; Property crime rate: 168.1 per 10,000 population
Transportation: Commute: 95.4% car, 0.0% public transportation, 0.6% walk, 2.9% work from home; Median travel time to work: 26.0 minutes
Additional Information Contacts
Town of Brownsburg .... (317) 852-1120
http://www.brownsburg.org

CLAYTON (town).
Covers a land area of 0.763 square miles and a water area of 0 square miles. Located at 39.69° N. Lat; 86.52° W. Long. Elevation is 876 feet.
Population: 972; Growth (since 2000): 40.3%; Density: 1,274.6 persons per square mile; Race: 98.7% White, 0.3% Black/African American, 0.0% Asian, 0.1% American Indian/Alaska Native, 0.0% Native Hawaiian/Other Pacific Islander, 0.8% Two or more races, 0.9% Hispanic of any race; Average household size: 2.72; Median age: 34.3; Age under 18: 29.0%; Age 65 and over: 10.4%; Males per 100 females: 105.9
School District(s)
Mill Creek Community Sch Corp (PK-12)
    2012-13 Enrollment: 1,515 .... (317) 539-9200
Housing: Homeownership rate: 69.8%; Homeowner vacancy rate: 4.2%; Rental vacancy rate: 0.9%

COATESVILLE (town).
Covers a land area of 0.653 square miles and a water area of 0.012 square miles. Located at 39.69° N. Lat; 86.67° W. Long. Elevation is 883 feet.
Population: 523; Growth (since 2000): 1.4%; Density: 800.4 persons per square mile; Race: 96.7% White, 0.0% Black/African American, 0.2% Asian, 0.0% American Indian/Alaska Native, 0.0% Native Hawaiian/Other Pacific Islander, 1.5% Two or more races, 1.3% Hispanic of any race; Average household size: 2.63; Median age: 41.4; Age under 18: 25.4%; Age 65 and over: 14.1%; Males per 100 females: 97.4
Housing: Homeownership rate: 78.9%; Homeowner vacancy rate: 4.3%; Rental vacancy rate: 0.0%

DANVILLE (town).
County seat. Covers a land area of 6.930 square miles and a water area of 0.046 square miles. Located at 39.76° N. Lat; 86.51° W. Long. Elevation is 955 feet.
History: Danville was settled in 1824 by Daniel Clark, a justice of the peace, for whom the town was named. In 1878 citizens of Danville carried off the desks, bookcases, and books of Central Normal College at Ladoga, and re-established it in Danville.
Population: 9,001; Growth (since 2000): 40.2%; Density: 1,298.8 persons per square mile; Race: 96.8% White, 0.8% Black/African American, 0.4% Asian, 0.2% American Indian/Alaska Native, 0.0% Native Hawaiian/Other Pacific Islander, 1.4% Two or more races, 1.8% Hispanic of any race; Average household size: 2.66; Median age: 34.3; Age under 18: 29.3%; Age 65 and over: 11.6%; Males per 100 females: 94.1; Marriage status: 21.6% never married, 57.0% now married, 0.9% separated, 5.8% widowed, 15.6% divorced; Foreign born: 0.5%; Speak English only: 97.7%; With disability: 10.2%; Veterans: 8.0%; Ancestry: 26.7% German, 22.3% Irish, 14.7% English, 10.0% American, 3.9% Dutch
Employment: 12.4% management, business, and financial, 3.6% computer, engineering, and science, 10.6% education, legal, community service, arts, and media, 6.3% healthcare practitioners, 17.8% service, 26.6% sales and office, 11.1% natural resources, construction, and maintenance, 11.6% production, transportation, and material moving
Income: Per capita: $27,095; Median household: $58,907; Average household: $72,462; Households with income of $100,000 or more: 21.9%; Poverty rate: 8.4%
Educational Attainment: High school diploma or higher: 91.2%; Bachelor's degree or higher: 26.1%; Graduate/professional degree or higher: 6.2%
School District(s)
Danville Community School Corp (PK-12)
    2012-13 Enrollment: 2,600 .... (317) 745-2212
Housing: Homeownership rate: 67.9%; Median home value: $150,200; Median year structure built: 1993; Homeowner vacancy rate: 1.8%; Median gross rent: $757 per month; Rental vacancy rate: 9.7%
Health Insurance: 90.4% have insurance; 77.7% have private insurance; 22.7% have public insurance; 9.6% do not have insurance; 2.6% of children under 18 do not have insurance
Hospitals: Hendricks Regional Health (141 beds)
Safety: Violent crime rate: 32.8 per 10,000 population; Property crime rate: 97.3 per 10,000 population
Newspapers: Danville Republican (weekly circulation 1600)
Transportation: Commute: 95.6% car, 0.4% public transportation, 1.2% walk, 2.0% work from home; Median travel time to work: 25.5 minutes
Additional Information Contacts
Town of Danville .... (317) 745-4180
http://www.danvilleindiana.org

LIZTON (town).
Covers a land area of 0.574 square miles and a water area of 0 square miles. Located at 39.88° N. Lat; 86.54° W. Long. Elevation is 958 feet.
History: The area in which Lizton was established in 1851 was swamp land, but a drainage system converted it into fertile farm land. James Whitcomb Riley wrote about Lizton in his poem, "The Lizton Humorist."
Population: 488; Growth (since 2000): 31.2%; Density: 850.6 persons per square mile; Race: 97.3% White, 0.0% Black/African American, 0.4% Asian, 0.0% American Indian/Alaska Native, 0.0% Native Hawaiian/Other Pacific Islander, 1.4% Two or more races, 1.4% Hispanic of any race; Average household size: 2.48; Median age: 32.1; Age under 18: 28.5%; Age 65 and over: 7.6%; Males per 100 females: 113.1
School District(s)
North West Hendricks Schools (KG-12)
    2012-13 Enrollment: 1,936 .... (317) 994-4100
Housing: Homeownership rate: 65.9%; Homeowner vacancy rate: 4.4%; Rental vacancy rate: 6.9%

NORTH SALEM (town).
Covers a land area of 0.260 square miles and a water area of 0 square miles. Located at 39.86° N. Lat; 86.64° W. Long. Elevation is 896 feet.
History: Laid out 1835.
Population: 518; Growth (since 2000): -12.4%; Density: 1,991.9 persons per square mile; Race: 98.1% White, 0.2% Black/African American, 0.4% Asian, 0.0% American Indian/Alaska Native, 0.0% Native Hawaiian/Other Pacific Islander, 1.2% Two or more races, 0.6% Hispanic of any race; Average household size: 2.48; Median age: 39.9; Age under 18: 23.9%; Age 65 and over: 13.1%; Males per 100 females: 101.6
School District(s)
North West Hendricks Schools (KG-12)
    2012-13 Enrollment: 1,936 .... (317) 994-4100
Housing: Homeownership rate: 75.1%; Homeowner vacancy rate: 3.1%; Rental vacancy rate: 7.1%

PITTSBORO (town).
Covers a land area of 2.951 square miles and a water area of 0 square miles. Located at 39.87° N. Lat; 86.46° W. Long. Elevation is 942 feet.
Population: 2,928; Growth (since 2000): 84.4%; Density: 992.2 persons per square mile; Race: 96.7% White, 0.4% Black/African American, 0.7% Asian, 0.4% American Indian/Alaska Native, 0.0% Native Hawaiian/Other Pacific Islander, 1.7% Two or more races, 1.4% Hispanic of any race; Average household size: 2.73; Median age: 36.3; Age under 18: 30.8%; Age 65 and over: 10.9%; Males per 100 females: 93.9; Marriage status: 22.6% never married, 63.5% now married, 1.9% separated, 4.1% widowed, 9.8% divorced; Foreign born: 3.9%; Speak English only: 94.9%; With disability: 8.5%; Veterans: 7.6%; Ancestry: 29.5% German, 18.7% Irish, 15.9% English, 12.5% American, 2.8% French
Employment: 19.3% management, business, and financial, 4.6% computer, engineering, and science, 6.6% education, legal, community service, arts, and media, 7.7% healthcare practitioners, 15.6% service, 21.3% sales and office, 14.7% natural resources, construction, and maintenance, 10.2% production, transportation, and material moving
Income: Per capita: $27,653; Median household: $78,348; Average household: $77,840; Households with income of $100,000 or more: 28.4%; Poverty rate: 7.2%
Educational Attainment: High school diploma or higher: 91.7%; Bachelor's degree or higher: 25.8%; Graduate/professional degree or higher: 7.0%
School District(s)
North West Hendricks Schools (KG-12)
    2012-13 Enrollment: 1,936 .... (317) 994-4100
Housing: Homeownership rate: 82.5%; Median home value: $154,500; Median year structure built: 1998; Homeowner vacancy rate: 2.0%; Median gross rent: $1,284 per month; Rental vacancy rate: 3.0%
Health Insurance: 88.4% have insurance; 78.9% have private insurance; 16.4% have public insurance; 11.6% do not have insurance; 7.3% of children under 18 do not have insurance

Transportation: Commute: 96.6% car, 0.0% public transportation, 1.1% walk, 1.3% work from home; Median travel time to work: 26.2 minutes

Additional Information Contacts

Town of Pittsboro . . . . (317) 892-3326
http://www.townofpittsboro.org

PLAINFIELD (town). Covers a land area of 22.274 square miles and a water area of 0.109 square miles. Located at 39.70° N. Lat; 86.37° W. Long. Elevation is 732 feet.

History: Named by Quaker settlers, "the plain people". Plainfield, which called itself the Village of Friendly Folk, developed as the headquarters of the Society of Friends. It was in Plainfield in 1842 that Martin Van Buren, campaigning for the 1844 election, was dumped into a mudhole when his carriage was purposely upset by residents who wanted him to pay attention to the need for road improvements.

Population: 27,631; Growth (since 2000): 50.2%; Density: 1,240.5 persons per square mile; Race: 85.2% White, 7.9% Black/African American, 3.3% Asian, 0.2% American Indian/Alaska Native, 0.0% Native Hawaiian/Other Pacific Islander, 1.8% Two or more races, 4.0% Hispanic of any race; Average household size: 2.57; Median age: 35.5; Age under 18: 24.5%; Age 65 and over: 11.3%; Males per 100 females: 111.7; Marriage status: 29.2% never married, 51.3% now married, 1.9% separated, 5.4% widowed, 14.1% divorced; Foreign born: 6.8%; Speak English only: 89.3%; With disability: 12.5%; Veterans: 10.7%; Ancestry: 22.5% German, 14.2% English, 13.0% Irish, 11.2% American, 3.6% Scottish

Employment: 16.1% management, business, and financial, 5.6% computer, engineering, and science, 9.9% education, legal, community service, arts, and media, 5.1% healthcare practitioners, 14.5% service, 26.9% sales and office, 8.1% natural resources, construction, and maintenance, 13.9% production, transportation, and material moving

Income: Per capita: $25,978; Median household: $59,036; Average household: $70,523; Households with income of $100,000 or more: 20.0%; Poverty rate: 8.1%

Educational Attainment: High school diploma or higher: 90.3%; Bachelor's degree or higher: 26.9%; Graduate/professional degree or higher: 8.1%

School District(s)

Plainfield Community Sch Corp (PK-12)
    2012-13 Enrollment: 4,954 . . . . (317) 839-2578

Housing: Homeownership rate: 69.0%; Median home value: $147,900; Median year structure built: 1990; Homeowner vacancy rate: 2.0%; Median gross rent: $898 per month; Rental vacancy rate: 7.0%

Health Insurance: 88.0% have insurance; 75.2% have private insurance; 24.5% have public insurance; 12.0% do not have insurance; 6.9% of children under 18 do not have insurance

Safety: Violent crime rate: 16.9 per 10,000 population; Property crime rate: 298.9 per 10,000 population

Transportation: Commute: 95.0% car, 0.2% public transportation, 0.8% walk, 2.0% work from home; Median travel time to work: 23.5 minutes

Additional Information Contacts

Town of Plainfield . . . . (317) 839-2561
http://townofplainfield.com

STILESVILLE (town). Covers a land area of 0.373 square miles and a water area of 0.006 square miles. Located at 39.64° N. Lat; 86.63° W. Long. Elevation is 804 feet.

History: Laid out 1828.

Population: 316; Growth (since 2000): 21.1%; Density: 847.5 persons per square mile; Race: 98.7% White, 0.3% Black/African American, 0.0% Asian, 0.0% American Indian/Alaska Native, 0.0% Native Hawaiian/Other Pacific Islander, 0.0% Two or more races, 2.8% Hispanic of any race; Average household size: 2.55; Median age: 41.9; Age under 18: 25.3%; Age 65 and over: 13.6%; Males per 100 females: 96.3

Housing: Homeownership rate: 80.7%; Homeowner vacancy rate: 3.8%; Rental vacancy rate: 0.0%

Henry County

Located in eastern Indiana; drained by the Big Blue River, Flatrock and Fall Creeks. Covers a land area of 391.876 square miles, a water area of 2.956 square miles, and is located in the Eastern Time Zone at 39.93° N. Lat., 85.40° W. Long. The county was founded in 1821. County seat is New Castle.

Henry County is part of the New Castle, IN Micropolitan Statistical Area. The entire metro area includes: Henry County, IN

Weather Station: New Castle 4 N — Elevation: 1,064 feet

	Jan	Feb	Mar	Apr	May	Jun	Jul	Aug	Sep	Oct	Nov	Dec
High	34	37	48	61	71	80	83	82	76	64	51	37
Low	18	20	28	38	49	58	61	60	52	41	33	22
Precip	2.5	2.3	3.0	4.0	5.1	4.5	5.0	3.4	2.9	3.1	3.5	2.9
Snow	6.3	4.4	1.8	0.2	tr	0.0	0.0	0.0	0.0	tr	0.7	4.7

High and Low temperatures in degrees Fahrenheit; Precipitation and Snow in inches

Population: 49,462; Growth (since 2000): 2.0%; Density: 126.2 persons per square mile; Race: 95.7% White, 2.2% Black/African American, 0.3% Asian, 0.1% American Indian/Alaska Native, 0.0% Native Hawaiian/Other Pacific Islander, 1.2% two or more races, 1.4% Hispanic of any race; Average household size: 2.43; Median age: 41.4; Age under 18: 22.3%; Age 65 and over: 16.2%; Males per 100 females: 102.9; Marriage status: 25.3% never married, 51.2% now married, 1.8% separated, 6.8% widowed, 16.6% divorced; Foreign born: 0.9%; Speak English only: 98.0%; With disability: 15.9%; Veterans: 11.1%; Ancestry: 18.9% German, 14.6% American, 11.8% Irish, 8.6% English, 1.8% Dutch

Religion: Six largest groups: 14.2% Baptist, 6.7% Holiness, 5.4% Non-denominational Protestant, 4.2% Methodist/Pietist, 2.3% Pentecostal, 2.1% European Free-Church

Economy: Unemployment rate: 6.0%; Leading industries: 18.1% retail trade; 14.2% other services (except public administration); 11.4% construction; Farms: 702 totaling 176,451 acres; Company size: 0 employ 1,000 or more persons, 2 employ 500 to 999 persons, 12 employ 100 to 499 persons, 825 employ less than 100 persons; Business ownership: 835 women-owned, n/a Black-owned, n/a Hispanic-owned, 32 Asian-owned

Employment: 11.8% management, business, and financial, 2.2% computer, engineering, and science, 8.4% education, legal, community service, arts, and media, 6.0% healthcare practitioners, 18.2% service, 23.2% sales and office, 9.3% natural resources, construction, and maintenance, 20.9% production, transportation, and material moving

Income: Per capita: $20,309; Median household: $40,679; Average household: $51,655; Households with income of $100,000 or more: 9.4%; Poverty rate: 17.0%

Educational Attainment: High school diploma or higher: 85.8%; Bachelor's degree or higher: 14.9%; Graduate/professional degree or higher: 5.0%

Housing: Homeownership rate: 73.7%; Median home value: $94,200; Median year structure built: 1959; Homeowner vacancy rate: 2.5%; Median gross rent: $621 per month; Rental vacancy rate: 11.7%

Vital Statistics: Birth rate: 90.1 per 10,000 population; Death rate: 110.7 per 10,000 population; Age-adjusted cancer mortality rate: 207.0 deaths per 100,000 population

Health Insurance: 83.9% have insurance; 67.1% have private insurance; 33.0% have public insurance; 16.1% do not have insurance; 9.7% of children under 18 do not have insurance

Health Care: Physicians: 8.1 per 10,000 population; Hospital beds: 18.2 per 10,000 population; Hospital admissions: 572.1 per 10,000 population

Air Quality Index: 70.8% good, 29.2% moderate, 0.0% unhealthy for sensitive individuals, 0.0% unhealthy (percent of days)

Transportation: Commute: 94.5% car, 0.3% public transportation, 1.2% walk, 3.1% work from home; Median travel time to work: 27.3 minutes

Presidential Election: 40.1% Obama, 57.0% Romney (2012)

Additional Information Contacts

Henry Government . . . . (765) 529-6401
http://www.henryco.net

Henry County Communities

BLOUNTSVILLE (town). Covers a land area of 0.112 square miles and a water area of 0.001 square miles. Located at 40.06° N. Lat; 85.24° W. Long. Elevation is 1,093 feet.

Population: 134; Growth (since 2000): -19.3%; Density: 1,193.6 persons per square mile; Race: 97.0% White, 0.0% Black/African American, 0.0% Asian, 0.0% American Indian/Alaska Native, 0.0% Native Hawaiian/Other Pacific Islander, 3.0% Two or more races, 0.0% Hispanic of any race; Average household size: 2.73; Median age: 38.3; Age under 18: 28.4%; Age 65 and over: 12.7%; Males per 100 females: 78.7

Housing: Homeownership rate: 81.6%; Homeowner vacancy rate: 10.9%; Rental vacancy rate: 0.0%

CADIZ (town). Covers a land area of 0.160 square miles and a water area of 0 square miles. Located at 39.95° N. Lat; 85.49° W. Long. Elevation is 1,093 feet.
Population: 150; Growth (since 2000): -6.8%; Density: 940.2 persons per square mile; Race: 100.0% White, 0.0% Black/African American, 0.0% Asian, 0.0% American Indian/Alaska Native, 0.0% Native Hawaiian/Other Pacific Islander, 0.0% Two or more races, 2.7% Hispanic of any race; Average household size: 2.94; Median age: 35.2; Age under 18: 32.0%; Age 65 and over: 6.7%; Males per 100 females: 94.8
Housing: Homeownership rate: 62.8%; Homeowner vacancy rate: 0.0%; Rental vacancy rate: 9.5%

DUNREITH (town). Covers a land area of 0.128 square miles and a water area of 0 square miles. Located at 39.80° N. Lat; 85.44° W. Long. Elevation is 1,043 feet.
History: Dunreith developed around the Pennsylvania Railroad station.
Population: 177; Growth (since 2000): -3.8%; Density: 1,386.7 persons per square mile; Race: 88.1% White, 0.6% Black/African American, 2.8% Asian, 0.6% American Indian/Alaska Native, 0.0% Native Hawaiian/Other Pacific Islander, 2.8% Two or more races, 4.5% Hispanic of any race; Average household size: 2.27; Median age: 46.5; Age under 18: 17.5%; Age 65 and over: 18.6%; Males per 100 females: 90.3
Housing: Homeownership rate: 78.2%; Homeowner vacancy rate: 0.0%; Rental vacancy rate: 5.6%

GREENSBORO (town). Covers a land area of 0.110 square miles and a water area of 0 square miles. Located at 39.88° N. Lat; 85.46° W. Long. Elevation is 981 feet.
Population: 143; Growth (since 2000): -17.8%; Density: 1,300.0 persons per square mile; Race: 100.0% White, 0.0% Black/African American, 0.0% Asian, 0.0% American Indian/Alaska Native, 0.0% Native Hawaiian/Other Pacific Islander, 0.0% Two or more races, 2.8% Hispanic of any race; Average household size: 2.34; Median age: 39.9; Age under 18: 23.1%; Age 65 and over: 16.1%; Males per 100 females: 107.2
Housing: Homeownership rate: 81.9%; Homeowner vacancy rate: 3.8%; Rental vacancy rate: 0.0%

KENNARD (town). Covers a land area of 0.421 square miles and a water area of <.001 square miles. Located at 39.91° N. Lat; 85.52° W. Long. Elevation is 1,040 feet.
Population: 471; Growth (since 2000): 3.5%; Density: 1,119.2 persons per square mile; Race: 99.2% White, 0.0% Black/African American, 0.6% Asian, 0.0% American Indian/Alaska Native, 0.0% Native Hawaiian/Other Pacific Islander, 0.2% Two or more races, 0.0% Hispanic of any race; Average household size: 2.94; Median age: 34.3; Age under 18: 30.6%; Age 65 and over: 12.5%; Males per 100 females: 104.8
School District(s)
C A Beard Memorial School Corp (KG-12)
    2012-13 Enrollment: 1,318 . . . . (765) 345-5101
Housing: Homeownership rate: 83.8%; Homeowner vacancy rate: 2.2%; Rental vacancy rate: 3.7%

KNIGHTSTOWN (town). Covers a land area of 1.029 square miles and a water area of 0.010 square miles. Located at 39.80° N. Lat; 85.53° W. Long. Elevation is 932 feet.
History: Knightstown was named for John Knight, an engineer who was involved in the construction of the National Road here.
Population: 2,182; Growth (since 2000): 1.6%; Density: 2,120.1 persons per square mile; Race: 98.0% White, 0.1% Black/African American, 0.1% Asian, 0.1% American Indian/Alaska Native, 0.1% Native Hawaiian/Other Pacific Islander, 1.1% Two or more races, 0.6% Hispanic of any race; Average household size: 2.43; Median age: 38.8; Age under 18: 25.4%; Age 65 and over: 16.0%; Males per 100 females: 91.4
School District(s)
C A Beard Memorial School Corp (KG-12)
    2012-13 Enrollment: 1,318 . . . . (765) 345-5101
Housing: Homeownership rate: 63.7%; Homeowner vacancy rate: 2.0%; Rental vacancy rate: 11.9%
Newspapers: Knightstown Banner (weekly circulation 2000)

LEWISVILLE (town). Covers a land area of 0.253 square miles and a water area of 0 square miles. Located at 39.81° N. Lat; 85.35° W. Long. Elevation is 1,053 feet.
History: Laid out 1829.
Population: 366; Growth (since 2000): -7.3%; Density: 1,443.8 persons per square mile; Race: 99.5% White, 0.0% Black/African American, 0.0% Asian, 0.0% American Indian/Alaska Native, 0.0% Native Hawaiian/Other Pacific Islander, 0.5% Two or more races, 1.4% Hispanic of any race; Average household size: 2.52; Median age: 42.4; Age under 18: 20.5%; Age 65 and over: 17.8%; Males per 100 females: 87.7
Housing: Homeownership rate: 71.7%; Homeowner vacancy rate: 1.9%; Rental vacancy rate: 12.8%

MIDDLETOWN (town). Covers a land area of 1.156 square miles and a water area of 0.002 square miles. Located at 40.06° N. Lat; 85.54° W. Long. Elevation is 978 feet.
History: Laid out 1829.
Population: 2,322; Growth (since 2000): -6.7%; Density: 2,008.1 persons per square mile; Race: 97.6% White, 0.3% Black/African American, 0.5% Asian, 0.1% American Indian/Alaska Native, 0.0% Native Hawaiian/Other Pacific Islander, 1.3% Two or more races, 0.8% Hispanic of any race; Average household size: 2.51; Median age: 36.6; Age under 18: 27.8%; Age 65 and over: 15.6%; Males per 100 females: 88.0
School District(s)
Shenandoah School Corporation (KG-12)
    2012-13 Enrollment: 1,394 . . . . (765) 354-2266
Housing: Homeownership rate: 68.1%; Homeowner vacancy rate: 1.6%; Rental vacancy rate: 11.2%
Newspapers: Middletown News (weekly circulation 2000)
Additional Information Contacts
Town of Middletown . . . . (765) 354-2268
  http://www.middletownin.com

MOORELAND (town). Covers a land area of 0.144 square miles and a water area of 0 square miles. Located at 40.00° N. Lat; 85.25° W. Long. Elevation is 1,122 feet.
History: Mooreland was named for early settler Philip Moore.
Population: 375; Growth (since 2000): -4.6%; Density: 2,609.2 persons per square mile; Race: 97.3% White, 0.0% Black/African American, 0.0% Asian, 0.0% American Indian/Alaska Native, 0.0% Native Hawaiian/Other Pacific Islander, 2.7% Two or more races, 1.6% Hispanic of any race; Average household size: 2.59; Median age: 37.4; Age under 18: 29.6%; Age 65 and over: 9.3%; Males per 100 females: 82.0
Housing: Homeownership rate: 75.9%; Homeowner vacancy rate: 5.2%; Rental vacancy rate: 12.5%

MOUNT SUMMIT (town). Covers a land area of 0.189 square miles and a water area of 0 square miles. Located at 40.00° N. Lat; 85.39° W. Long. Elevation is 1,093 feet.
History: Mount Summit is at one of the highest elevations in Henry County.
Population: 352; Growth (since 2000): 12.5%; Density: 1,865.0 persons per square mile; Race: 97.2% White, 0.0% Black/African American, 0.0% Asian, 0.3% American Indian/Alaska Native, 0.0% Native Hawaiian/Other Pacific Islander, 2.0% Two or more races, 2.3% Hispanic of any race; Average household size: 2.53; Median age: 42.1; Age under 18: 25.0%; Age 65 and over: 13.6%; Males per 100 females: 102.3
Housing: Homeownership rate: 79.9%; Homeowner vacancy rate: 3.4%; Rental vacancy rate: 9.7%

NEW CASTLE (city). County seat. Covers a land area of 7.295 square miles and a water area of 0.021 square miles. Located at 39.92° N. Lat; 85.37° W. Long. Elevation is 1,063 feet.
History: New Castle was the birthplace in 1867 of Wilbur Wright, who with his brother Orville flew the first heavier-than-air craft in 1903 in North Carolina. New Castle developed as an industrial city.
Population: 18,114; Growth (since 2000): 1.9%; Density: 2,483.2 persons per square mile; Race: 95.1% White, 1.9% Black/African American, 0.4% Asian, 0.2% American Indian/Alaska Native, 0.0% Native Hawaiian/Other Pacific Islander, 1.8% Two or more races, 1.7% Hispanic of any race; Average household size: 2.29; Median age: 39.5; Age under 18: 23.4%; Age 65 and over: 16.7%; Males per 100 females: 87.6; Marriage status: 27.9% never married, 44.0% now married, 2.1% separated, 7.7% widowed, 20.3% divorced; Foreign born: 1.2%; Speak English only: 96.6%; With disability: 19.1%; Veterans: 12.1%; Ancestry: 16.0% German, 13.9% American, 12.5% Irish, 7.2% English, 1.9% Scottish
Employment: 8.7% management, business, and financial, 1.8% computer, engineering, and science, 9.9% education, legal, community service, arts, and media, 4.7% healthcare practitioners, 20.0% service, 24.5% sales and

office, 8.1% natural resources, construction, and maintenance, 22.3% production, transportation, and material moving
Income: Per capita: $17,126; Median household: $32,859; Average household: $39,638; Households with income of $100,000 or more: 4.5%; Poverty rate: 25.0%
Educational Attainment: High school diploma or higher: 81.9%; Bachelor's degree or higher: 13.2%; Graduate/professional degree or higher: 5.1%

School District(s)
Blue River Valley Schools (KG-12)
    2012-13 Enrollment: 647 . . . . (765) 836-4816
New Castle Community Sch Corp (KG-12)
    2012-13 Enrollment: 3,493 . . . . (765) 521-7201
Housing: Homeownership rate: 59.7%; Median home value: $67,400; Median year structure built: 1956; Homeowner vacancy rate: 4.0%; Median gross rent: $618 per month; Rental vacancy rate: 13.0%
Health Insurance: 81.2% have insurance; 56.1% have private insurance; 40.4% have public insurance; 18.8% do not have insurance; 9.3% of children under 18 do not have insurance
Hospitals: Henry County Memorial Hospital (107 beds)
Newspapers: Courier-Times (daily circulation 9200)
Transportation: Commute: 94.7% car, 0.5% public transportation, 1.9% walk, 1.8% work from home; Median travel time to work: 22.6 minutes
Airports: New Castle-Henry Co Municipal (general aviation)
Additional Information Contacts
City of New Castle . . . . (765) 521-6803
    http://www.cityofnewcastle.net

SPICELAND (town).
Covers a land area of 0.503 square miles and a water area of 0 square miles. Located at 39.84° N. Lat; 85.44° W. Long. Elevation is 1,050 feet.
History: Spiceland was settled in 1828 by a group of Quakers from North Carolina. From Spiceland Academy, founded in 1834, came historian Charles Austin Beard.
Population: 890; Growth (since 2000): 10.3%; Density: 1,770.0 persons per square mile; Race: 98.5% White, 0.1% Black/African American, 0.2% Asian, 0.0% American Indian/Alaska Native, 0.0% Native Hawaiian/Other Pacific Islander, 0.4% Two or more races, 0.7% Hispanic of any race; Average household size: 2.52; Median age: 39.5; Age under 18: 26.9%; Age 65 and over: 16.5%; Males per 100 females: 96.0
Housing: Homeownership rate: 76.8%; Homeowner vacancy rate: 2.2%; Rental vacancy rate: 11.6%

SPRINGPORT (town).
Covers a land area of 0.120 square miles and a water area of 0 square miles. Located at 40.05° N. Lat; 85.39° W. Long. Elevation is 1,063 feet.
Population: 149; Growth (since 2000): -14.4%; Density: 1,239.9 persons per square mile; Race: 96.6% White, 0.0% Black/African American, 0.0% Asian, 0.0% American Indian/Alaska Native, 0.0% Native Hawaiian/Other Pacific Islander, 3.4% Two or more races, 0.0% Hispanic of any race; Average household size: 2.44; Median age: 41.2; Age under 18: 22.8%; Age 65 and over: 13.4%; Males per 100 females: 75.3
Housing: Homeownership rate: 86.8%; Homeowner vacancy rate: 5.4%; Rental vacancy rate: 11.1%

STRAUGHN (town).
Covers a land area of 0.141 square miles and a water area of 0 square miles. Located at 39.81° N. Lat; 85.29° W. Long. Elevation is 1,079 feet.
Population: 222; Growth (since 2000): -15.6%; Density: 1,576.8 persons per square mile; Race: 99.5% White, 0.0% Black/African American, 0.0% Asian, 0.0% American Indian/Alaska Native, 0.0% Native Hawaiian/Other Pacific Islander, 0.0% Two or more races, 0.5% Hispanic of any race; Average household size: 2.74; Median age: 40.0; Age under 18: 22.1%; Age 65 and over: 14.9%; Males per 100 females: 77.5

School District(s)
South Henry School Corp (KG-12)
    2012-13 Enrollment: 755 . . . . (765) 987-7882
Housing: Homeownership rate: 80.3%; Homeowner vacancy rate: 2.9%; Rental vacancy rate: 0.0%

SULPHUR SPRINGS (town).
Covers a land area of 0.693 square miles and a water area of <.001 square miles. Located at 40.00° N. Lat; 85.43° W. Long. Elevation is 1,063 feet.
History: Laid out 1853.

Population: 399; Growth (since 2000): 15.3%; Density: 575.6 persons per square mile; Race: 98.7% White, 0.0% Black/African American, 0.0% Asian, 0.0% American Indian/Alaska Native, 0.0% Native Hawaiian/Other Pacific Islander, 1.0% Two or more races, 0.0% Hispanic of any race; Average household size: 2.64; Median age: 37.9; Age under 18: 27.1%; Age 65 and over: 16.8%; Males per 100 females: 96.6
Housing: Homeownership rate: 84.8%; Homeowner vacancy rate: 3.8%; Rental vacancy rate: 4.2%

Howard County

Located in central Indiana; drained by Wildcat Creek. Covers a land area of 293.057 square miles, a water area of 0.865 square miles, and is located in the Eastern Time Zone at 40.48° N. Lat., 86.11° W. Long. The county was founded in 1844. County seat is Kokomo.

Howard County is part of the Kokomo, IN Metropolitan Statistical Area. The entire metro area includes: Howard County, IN

Weather Station: Kokomo 3 WSW   Elevation: 819 feet

	Jan	Feb	Mar	Apr	May	Jun	Jul	Aug	Sep	Oct	Nov	Dec
High	32	36	48	61	71	81	84	82	77	64	50	36
Low	16	19	27	38	49	59	62	60	52	41	32	21
Precip	2.6	2.5	3.0	3.9	4.5	4.4	4.8	4.0	3.5	3.3	3.6	3.2
Snow	11.1	10.4	5.2	1.1	tr	0.0	0.0	0.0	0.0	0.4	1.3	8.8

High and Low temperatures in degrees Fahrenheit; Precipitation and Snow in inches

Population: 82,752; Growth (since 2000): -2.6%; Density: 282.4 persons per square mile; Race: 88.6% White, 6.9% Black/African American, 0.9% Asian, 0.3% American Indian/Alaska Native, 0.0% Native Hawaiian/Other Pacific Islander, 2.5% two or more races, 2.7% Hispanic of any race; Average household size: 2.38; Median age: 40.7; Age under 18: 23.7%; Age 65 and over: 16.2%; Males per 100 females: 92.6; Marriage status: 24.4% never married, 55.0% now married, 1.3% separated, 6.7% widowed, 13.9% divorced; Foreign born: 2.0%; Speak English only: 95.8%; With disability: 15.9%; Veterans: 11.8%; Ancestry: 21.3% German, 19.1% American, 11.2% Irish, 10.1% English, 2.6% Italian
Religion: Six largest groups: 15.4% Non-denominational Protestant, 9.6% Baptist, 6.3% Catholicism, 6.0% Methodist/Pietist, 3.1% Holiness, 2.8% Pentecostal
Economy: Unemployment rate: 5.8%; Leading industries: 18.6% retail trade; 13.7% other services (except public administration); 13.1% health care and social assistance; Farms: 476 totaling 144,191 acres; Company size: 3 employ 1,000 or more persons, 5 employ 500 to 999 persons, 25 employ 100 to 499 persons, 1,742 employ less than 100 persons; Business ownership: 1,656 women-owned, n/a Black-owned, n/a Hispanic-owned, n/a Asian-owned
Employment: 10.7% management, business, and financial, 4.1% computer, engineering, and science, 9.1% education, legal, community service, arts, and media, 6.1% healthcare practitioners, 20.4% service, 22.4% sales and office, 7.8% natural resources, construction, and maintenance, 19.4% production, transportation, and material moving
Income: Per capita: $24,071; Median household: $43,590; Average household: $57,187; Households with income of $100,000 or more: 15.0%; Poverty rate: 16.7%
Educational Attainment: High school diploma or higher: 88.8%; Bachelor's degree or higher: 20.0%; Graduate/professional degree or higher: 7.5%
Housing: Homeownership rate: 70.5%; Median home value: $98,500; Median year structure built: 1965; Homeowner vacancy rate: 3.3%; Median gross rent: $637 per month; Rental vacancy rate: 12.8%
Vital Statistics: Birth rate: 114.9 per 10,000 population; Death rate: 107.9 per 10,000 population; Age-adjusted cancer mortality rate: 159.2 deaths per 100,000 population
Health Insurance: 86.7% have insurance; 68.4% have private insurance; 34.0% have public insurance; 13.3% do not have insurance; 7.7% of children under 18 do not have insurance
Health Care: Physicians: 16.5 per 10,000 population; Hospital beds: 38.5 per 10,000 population; Hospital admissions: 1,384.8 per 10,000 population
Transportation: Commute: 93.8% car, 0.4% public transportation, 1.6% walk, 2.4% work from home; Median travel time to work: 20.4 minutes
Presidential Election: 41.7% Obama, 56.0% Romney (2012)
Additional Information Contacts
Howard Government . . . . (765) 456-2234
    http://www.co.howard.in.us

Howard County Communities

GREENTOWN (town). Covers a land area of 1.366 square miles and a water area of 0 square miles. Located at 40.48° N. Lat; 85.96° W. Long. Elevation is 837 feet.
History: Greentown was named for Miami Chief Green. It was founded in 1848 by English, German, Scotch, and Dutch immigrants who received the land from the U.S. government.
Population: 2,415; Growth (since 2000): -5.1%; Density: 1,768.4 persons per square mile; Race: 97.1% White, 0.6% Black/African American, 1.0% Asian, 0.2% American Indian/Alaska Native, 0.0% Native Hawaiian/Other Pacific Islander, 0.7% Two or more races, 1.5% Hispanic of any race; Average household size: 2.40; Median age: 41.4; Age under 18: 25.1%; Age 65 and over: 20.1%; Males per 100 females: 85.2

School District(s)
Eastern Howard School Corp (KG-12)
    2012-13 Enrollment: 1,422 .... (765) 628-3391
Housing: Homeownership rate: 71.1%; Homeowner vacancy rate: 4.5%; Rental vacancy rate: 10.0%

Additional Information Contacts
Town of Greentown .... (765) 610-8461
    http://www.greentownindiana.org

KOKOMO (city). County seat. Covers a land area of 18.497 square miles and a water area of 0.059 square miles. Located at 40.48° N. Lat; 86.13° W. Long. Elevation is 810 feet.
History: Kokomo was platted in 1844. The coming of the railroad in 1853 and the discovery of natural gas in 1886 brought growth to the town. Kokomo was named for a Miami chief.
Population: 45,468; Growth (since 2000): -1.4%; Density: 2,458.1 persons per square mile; Race: 83.5% White, 10.7% Black/African American, 1.0% Asian, 0.4% American Indian/Alaska Native, 0.0% Native Hawaiian/Other Pacific Islander, 3.3% Two or more races, 3.3% Hispanic of any race; Average household size: 2.25; Median age: 38.2; Age under 18: 24.0%; Age 65 and over: 15.8%; Males per 100 females: 88.0; Marriage status: 26.0% never married, 49.3% now married, 1.5% separated, 7.6% widowed, 17.1% divorced; Foreign born: 2.3%; Speak English only: 95.5%; With disability: 17.6%; Veterans: 12.3%; Ancestry: 20.1% German, 18.6% American, 11.1% Irish, 9.5% English, 2.4% Italian
Employment: 9.1% management, business, and financial, 3.2% computer, engineering, and science, 8.3% education, legal, community service, arts, and media, 5.2% healthcare practitioners, 23.1% service, 24.1% sales and office, 7.3% natural resources, construction, and maintenance, 19.7% production, transportation, and material moving
Income: Per capita: $22,006; Median household: $37,215; Average household: $49,616; Households with income of $100,000 or more: 10.6%; Poverty rate: 20.6%
Educational Attainment: High school diploma or higher: 87.3%; Bachelor's degree or higher: 17.3%; Graduate/professional degree or higher: 6.3%

School District(s)
Kokomo-Center Twp Con Sch Corp (PK-12)
    2012-13 Enrollment: 6,279 .... (765) 455-8000
Northwestern School Corp (KG-12)
    2012-13 Enrollment: 1,695 .... (765) 452-3060
Taylor Community School Corp (PK-12)
    2012-13 Enrollment: 1,293 .... (765) 453-3035

Four-year College(s)
Indiana University-Kokomo (Public)
    Fall 2013 Enrollment: 4,178 .... (765) 453-2000
    2013-14 Tuition: In-state $6,675; Out-of-state $17,778

Vocational/Technical School(s)
Ross Medical Education Center-Kokomo (Private, For-profit)
    Fall 2013 Enrollment: 115 .... (765) 453-4864
    2013-14 Tuition: $15,680
Rudae's School of Beauty Culture-Kokomo (Private, For-profit)
    Fall 2013 Enrollment: 39 .... (800) 466-9744
    2013-14 Tuition: $12,375
The Salon Professional Academy-Kokomo (Private, For-profit)
    Fall 2013 Enrollment: 68 .... (765) 454-9840
    2013-14 Tuition: $15,990
Housing: Homeownership rate: 59.3%; Median home value: $84,000; Median year structure built: 1963; Homeowner vacancy rate: 4.4%; Median gross rent: $637 per month; Rental vacancy rate: 12.6%

Health Insurance: 84.5% have insurance; 62.7% have private insurance; 37.4% have public insurance; 15.5% do not have insurance; 8.6% of children under 18 do not have insurance
Hospitals: Community Howard Regional Health (150 beds); Saint Joseph Hospital & Health Center (156 beds)
Safety: Violent crime rate: 32.5 per 10,000 population; Property crime rate: 388.6 per 10,000 population
Newspapers: Kokomo Herald (weekly circulation 500); Kokomo Perspective (weekly circulation 31000); Kokomo Tribune (daily circulation 20900)
Transportation: Commute: 93.3% car, 0.6% public transportation, 2.0% walk, 2.4% work from home; Median travel time to work: 19.6 minutes
Airports: Kokomo Municipal (general aviation)

Additional Information Contacts
City of Kokomo .... (765) 456-7370
    http://www.cityofkokomo.org

RUSSIAVILLE (town). Covers a land area of 0.806 square miles and a water area of 0 square miles. Located at 40.42° N. Lat; 86.27° W. Long. Elevation is 846 feet.
History: Laid out 1845.
Population: 1,094; Growth (since 2000): 0.2%; Density: 1,356.9 persons per square mile; Race: 98.6% White, 0.2% Black/African American, 0.2% Asian, 0.2% American Indian/Alaska Native, 0.0% Native Hawaiian/Other Pacific Islander, 0.7% Two or more races, 1.3% Hispanic of any race; Average household size: 2.52; Median age: 37.1; Age under 18: 27.9%; Age 65 and over: 12.6%; Males per 100 females: 96.4

School District(s)
Western School Corp (KG-12)
    2012-13 Enrollment: 2,636 .... (765) 883-5576
Housing: Homeownership rate: 80.0%; Homeowner vacancy rate: 7.2%; Rental vacancy rate: 11.2%

Huntington County

Located in northeast central Indiana; drained by the Wabash, Salamonie, and Little Rivers. Covers a land area of 382.651 square miles, a water area of 5.071 square miles, and is located in the Eastern Time Zone at 40.83° N. Lat., 85.48° W. Long. The county was founded in 1832. County seat is Huntington.

Huntington County is part of the Huntington, IN Micropolitan Statistical Area. The entire metro area includes: Huntington County, IN

Weather Station: Huntington   Elevation: 725 feet

	Jan	Feb	Mar	Apr	May	Jun	Jul	Aug	Sep	Oct	Nov	Dec
High	33	37	48	61	72	82	85	84	77	64	50	37
Low	17	19	27	38	48	58	62	61	52	40	32	22
Precip	2.3	2.0	2.6	3.5	4.3	4.2	4.1	3.7	3.0	3.1	3.0	2.7
Snow	9.7	7.1	3.2	0.8	0.0	0.0	0.0	0.0	0.0	0.2	1.0	7.3

High and Low temperatures in degrees Fahrenheit; Precipitation and Snow in inches

Population: 37,124; Growth (since 2000): -2.5%; Density: 97.0 persons per square mile; Race: 97.1% White, 0.4% Black/African American, 0.4% Asian, 0.4% American Indian/Alaska Native, 0.0% Native Hawaiian/Other Pacific Islander, 1.1% two or more races, 1.7% Hispanic of any race; Average household size: 2.52; Median age: 39.0; Age under 18: 23.7%; Age 65 and over: 14.7%; Males per 100 females: 96.6; Marriage status: 25.7% never married, 56.3% now married, 1.0% separated, 6.5% widowed, 11.5% divorced; Foreign born: 1.5%; Speak English only: 97.7%; With disability: 13.4%; Veterans: 9.5%; Ancestry: 33.3% German, 13.8% Irish, 13.1% American, 10.0% English, 2.6% French
Religion: Six largest groups: 13.1% Catholicism, 9.9% Methodist/Pietist, 9.4% Holiness, 5.4% Baptist, 4.5% Non-denominational Protestant, 2.1% Lutheran
Economy: Unemployment rate: 4.9%; Leading industries: 15.6% retail trade; 14.4% other services (except public administration); 10.1% accommodation and food services; Farms: 695 totaling 188,848 acres; Company size: 0 employ 1,000 or more persons, 2 employ 500 to 999 persons, 17 employ 100 to 499 persons, 835 employ less than 100 persons; Business ownership: 535 women-owned, n/a Black-owned, n/a Hispanic-owned, n/a Asian-owned
Employment: 10.4% management, business, and financial, 3.5% computer, engineering, and science, 8.1% education, legal, community service, arts, and media, 4.8% healthcare practitioners, 17.5% service,

20.0% sales and office, 9.7% natural resources, construction, and maintenance, 26.1% production, transportation, and material moving
Income: Per capita: $22,601; Median household: $46,148; Average household: $57,099; Households with income of $100,000 or more: 12.9%; Poverty rate: 12.0%
Educational Attainment: High school diploma or higher: 88.5%; Bachelor's degree or higher: 16.9%; Graduate/professional degree or higher: 6.6%
Housing: Homeownership rate: 77.3%; Median home value: $97,100; Median year structure built: 1960; Homeowner vacancy rate: 3.4%; Median gross rent: $663 per month; Rental vacancy rate: 12.8%
Vital Statistics: Birth rate: 109.8 per 10,000 population; Death rate: 101.9 per 10,000 population; Age-adjusted cancer mortality rate: 206.7 deaths per 100,000 population
Health Insurance: 85.5% have insurance; 68.2% have private insurance; 29.4% have public insurance; 14.5% do not have insurance; 7.4% of children under 18 do not have insurance
Health Care: Physicians: 13.5 per 10,000 population; Hospital beds: 9.7 per 10,000 population; Hospital admissions: 513.0 per 10,000 population
Air Quality Index: 98.4% good, 1.6% moderate, 0.0% unhealthy for sensitive individuals, 0.0% unhealthy (percent of days)
Transportation: Commute: 92.5% car, 0.4% public transportation, 2.5% walk, 3.8% work from home; Median travel time to work: 20.8 minutes
Presidential Election: 29.2% Obama, 68.9% Romney (2012)
National and State Parks: Kil-So-Quah State Recreation Area; Little Turtle State Recreation Area; Markle State Recreation Area; Mount Etna State Recreation Area
Additional Information Contacts
Huntington Government . . . . (219) 358-4822
http://www.huntington.in.us

Huntington County Communities

ANDREWS (town). Covers a land area of 0.645 square miles and a water area of 0.007 square miles. Located at 40.86° N. Lat; 85.60° W. Long. Elevation is 715 feet.
History: Andrews was the birthplace of educator Ellwood Patterson Cubberley who graduated from Indiana University in 1891 and went on to be president of Vincennes University and instrumental in the early days of Stanford University.
Population: 1,149; Growth (since 2000): -10.9%; Density: 1,780.2 persons per square mile; Race: 96.3% White, 0.3% Black/African American, 0.3% Asian, 1.0% American Indian/Alaska Native, 0.0% Native Hawaiian/Other Pacific Islander, 1.8% Two or more races, 1.9% Hispanic of any race; Average household size: 2.64; Median age: 36.4; Age under 18: 27.7%; Age 65 and over: 12.3%; Males per 100 females: 104.4
School District(s)
Huntington County Com Sch Corp (PK-12)
 2012-13 Enrollment: 5,641 . . . . (260) 356-8312
Housing: Homeownership rate: 79.1%; Homeowner vacancy rate: 4.9%; Rental vacancy rate: 27.7%
Additional Information Contacts
Town of Andrews. . . . . (260) 356-5300
http://huntingtoncountychamber.com

HUNTINGTON (city). County seat. Covers a land area of 8.707 square miles and a water area of 0.134 square miles. Located at 40.88° N. Lat; 85.51° W. Long. Elevation is 748 feet.
History: Huntington was named in 1831 for Samuel Huntington, a member of the first Continental Congress. Previous to that the community was known as Wepecheange, meaning "place of flints." Huntington was the home of John R. Kissinger, on whom Dr. Walter Reed experimented with yellow fever tests in 1900 in Cuba.
Population: 17,391; Growth (since 2000): -0.3%; Density: 1,997.3 persons per square mile; Race: 96.4% White, 0.6% Black/African American, 0.5% Asian, 0.4% American Indian/Alaska Native, 0.0% Native Hawaiian/Other Pacific Islander, 1.4% Two or more races, 2.4% Hispanic of any race; Average household size: 2.48; Median age: 33.4; Age under 18: 24.8%; Age 65 and over: 13.5%; Males per 100 females: 91.3; Marriage status: 31.9% never married, 45.8% now married, 1.3% separated, 8.0% widowed, 14.3% divorced; Foreign born: 1.9%; Speak English only: 97.0%; With disability: 14.8%; Veterans: 8.4%; Ancestry: 31.7% German, 14.9% Irish, 14.1% American, 9.5% English, 3.1% French
Employment: 8.5% management, business, and financial, 2.7% computer, engineering, and science, 8.5% education, legal, community service, arts,
and media, 3.5% healthcare practitioners, 20.2% service, 19.0% sales and office, 8.2% natural resources, construction, and maintenance, 29.3% production, transportation, and material moving
Income: Per capita: $18,789; Median household: $37,043; Average household: $45,949; Households with income of $100,000 or more: 5.7%; Poverty rate: 16.7%
Educational Attainment: High school diploma or higher: 85.1%; Bachelor's degree or higher: 15.2%; Graduate/professional degree or higher: 5.3%
School District(s)
Huntington County Com Sch Corp (PK-12)
 2012-13 Enrollment: 5,641 . . . . (260) 356-8312
Four-year College(s)
Huntington University (Private, Not-for-profit, United Brethren Church)
 Fall 2013 Enrollment: 1,124 . . . . (260) 356-6000
 2013-14 Tuition: In-state $24,040; Out-of-state $24,040
Housing: Homeownership rate: 66.3%; Median home value: $75,000; Median year structure built: 1950; Homeowner vacancy rate: 4.7%; Median gross rent: $636 per month; Rental vacancy rate: 12.5%
Health Insurance: 82.6% have insurance; 60.3% have private insurance; 33.8% have public insurance; 17.4% do not have insurance; 6.0% of children under 18 do not have insurance
Hospitals: Parkview Huntington Hospital (36 beds)
Safety: Violent crime rate: 15.6 per 10,000 population; Property crime rate: 216.0 per 10,000 population
Newspapers: Huntington County TAB (weekly circulation 15500); Huntington Herald-Press (daily circulation 6400)
Transportation: Commute: 90.8% car, 0.3% public transportation, 4.1% walk, 3.3% work from home; Median travel time to work: 18.5 minutes
Additional Information Contacts
City of Huntington . . . . (260) 356-1400
http://www.huntington.in.us

MARKLE (town). Covers a land area of 1.222 square miles and a water area of 0.049 square miles. Located at 40.83° N. Lat; 85.34° W. Long. Elevation is 781 feet.
Population: 1,095; Growth (since 2000): -0.6%; Density: 896.3 persons per square mile; Race: 98.3% White, 0.8% Black/African American, 0.2% Asian, 0.0% American Indian/Alaska Native, 0.0% Native Hawaiian/Other Pacific Islander, 0.6% Two or more races, 1.2% Hispanic of any race; Average household size: 2.35; Median age: 43.0; Age under 18: 23.1%; Age 65 and over: 20.3%; Males per 100 females: 91.8
Housing: Homeownership rate: 70.4%; Homeowner vacancy rate: 1.6%; Rental vacancy rate: 10.5%

MOUNT ETNA (town). Covers a land area of 0.082 square miles and a water area of <.001 square miles. Located at 40.74° N. Lat; 85.56° W. Long. Elevation is 810 feet.
History: Mount Etna was founded in 1839, and named for Mt. Etna in Sicily.
Population: 94; Growth (since 2000): -14.5%; Density: 1,147.1 persons per square mile; Race: 96.8% White, 0.0% Black/African American, 0.0% Asian, 0.0% American Indian/Alaska Native, 2.1% Native Hawaiian/Other Pacific Islander, 0.0% Two or more races, 2.1% Hispanic of any race; Average household size: 2.24; Median age: 45.2; Age under 18: 17.0%; Age 65 and over: 16.0%; Males per 100 females: 113.6
Housing: Homeownership rate: 73.8%; Homeowner vacancy rate: 0.0%; Rental vacancy rate: 21.4%

ROANOKE (town). Covers a land area of 1.197 square miles and a water area of 0.006 square miles. Located at 40.96° N. Lat; 85.38° W. Long. Elevation is 758 feet.
History: Roanoke was known for the Roanoke Classical Seminary founded in 1861 by Frederick S. Reefy. The emphasis in culture provided by the seminary gave Roanoke the reputation as the Athens of Indiana.
Population: 1,722; Growth (since 2000): 15.2%; Density: 1,438.5 persons per square mile; Race: 97.1% White, 0.2% Black/African American, 0.5% Asian, 0.1% American Indian/Alaska Native, 0.0% Native Hawaiian/Other Pacific Islander, 1.7% Two or more races, 1.7% Hispanic of any race; Average household size: 2.52; Median age: 36.8; Age under 18: 26.1%; Age 65 and over: 11.8%; Males per 100 females: 94.6
School District(s)
Huntington County Com Sch Corp (PK-12)
 2012-13 Enrollment: 5,641 . . . . (260) 356-8312

M S D Southwest Allen County (KG-12)
    2012-13 Enrollment: 6,940 . . . . (260) 431-2010
Housing: Homeownership rate: 86.6%; Homeowner vacancy rate: 3.6%; Rental vacancy rate: 18.0%

WARREN (town).
Covers a land area of 1.143 square miles and a water area of 0.005 square miles. Located at 40.69° N. Lat; 85.42° W. Long. Elevation is 827 feet.
History: Laid out 1836.
Population: 1,239; Growth (since 2000): -2.6%; Density: 1,084.1 persons per square mile; Race: 98.8% White, 0.1% Black/African American, 0.2% Asian, 0.1% American Indian/Alaska Native, 0.0% Native Hawaiian/Other Pacific Islander, 0.8% Two or more races, 0.4% Hispanic of any race; Average household size: 2.41; Median age: 40.1; Age under 18: 24.9%; Age 65 and over: 19.0%; Males per 100 females: 97.6

School District(s)
Huntington County Com Sch Corp (PK-12)
    2012-13 Enrollment: 5,641 . . . . (260) 356-8312
Housing: Homeownership rate: 73.0%; Homeowner vacancy rate: 4.7%; Rental vacancy rate: 19.5%
Newspapers: Warren Weekly (weekly circulation 3200)

Jackson County

Located in southern Indiana; bounded on the south by the Muscatatuck River; drained by the East Fork of the White River. Covers a land area of 509.312 square miles, a water area of 4.601 square miles, and is located in the Eastern Time Zone at 38.91° N. Lat., 86.04° W. Long. The county was founded in 1815. County seat is Brownstown.

Jackson County is part of the Seymour, IN Micropolitan Statistical Area. The entire metro area includes: Jackson County, IN

Weather Station: Seymour 2 N   Elevation: 569 feet

	Jan	Feb	Mar	Apr	May	Jun	Jul	Aug	Sep	Oct	Nov	Dec
High	38	42	53	64	74	82	85	84	78	67	54	41
Low	21	23	31	41	51	61	64	62	53	41	33	24
Precip	3.2	2.8	3.9	4.7	5.5	4.2	4.3	4.5	3.2	3.8	3.8	3.6
Snow	3.0	3.1	2.0	tr	0.0	0.0	0.0	0.0	0.0	0.2	0.1	1.9

High and Low temperatures in degrees Fahrenheit; Precipitation and Snow in inches

Population: 42,376; Growth (since 2000): 2.5%; Density: 83.2 persons per square mile; Race: 94.5% White, 0.7% Black/African American, 0.8% Asian, 0.2% American Indian/Alaska Native, 0.1% Native Hawaiian/Other Pacific Islander, 1.3% two or more races, 5.7% Hispanic of any race; Average household size: 2.53; Median age: 38.7; Age under 18: 24.6%; Age 65 and over: 14.3%; Males per 100 females: 99.1; Marriage status: 22.5% never married, 55.3% now married, 1.5% separated, 7.3% widowed, 14.9% divorced; Foreign born: 5.6%; Speak English only: 92.9%; With disability: 12.5%; Veterans: 8.7%; Ancestry: 24.5% American, 23.2% German, 9.8% Irish, 7.4% English, 1.7% French
Religion: Six largest groups: 20.2% Baptist, 19.8% Lutheran, 5.1% Holiness, 3.5% Catholicism, 3.3% Methodist/Pietist, 2.6% Non-denominational Protestant
Economy: Unemployment rate: 4.4%; Leading industries: 18.3% retail trade; 11.6% other services (except public administration); 10.5% health care and social assistance; Farms: 744 totaling 183,878 acres; Company size: 1 employs 1,000 or more persons, 3 employ 500 to 999 persons, 28 employ 100 to 499 persons, 978 employ less than 100 persons; Business ownership: 650 women-owned, n/a Black-owned, n/a Hispanic-owned, n/a Asian-owned
Employment: 9.8% management, business, and financial, 5.1% computer, engineering, and science, 6.0% education, legal, community service, arts, and media, 5.5% healthcare practitioners, 16.2% service, 20.1% sales and office, 9.7% natural resources, construction, and maintenance, 27.7% production, transportation, and material moving
Income: Per capita: $22,568; Median household: $46,501; Average household: $56,180; Households with income of $100,000 or more: 11.3%; Poverty rate: 13.0%
Educational Attainment: High school diploma or higher: 86.2%; Bachelor's degree or higher: 14.5%; Graduate/professional degree or higher: 5.0%
Housing: Homeownership rate: 73.2%; Median home value: $117,100; Median year structure built: 1976; Homeowner vacancy rate: 2.6%; Median gross rent: $686 per month; Rental vacancy rate: 11.4%
Vital Statistics: Birth rate: 121.2 per 10,000 population; Death rate: 96.2 per 10,000 population; Age-adjusted cancer mortality rate: 237.7 deaths per 100,000 population
Health Insurance: 86.0% have insurance; 70.0% have private insurance; 28.6% have public insurance; 14.0% do not have insurance; 8.3% of children under 18 do not have insurance
Health Care: Physicians: 12.3 per 10,000 population; Hospital beds: 21.7 per 10,000 population; Hospital admissions: 867.7 per 10,000 population
Air Quality Index: 95.1% good, 4.9% moderate, 0.0% unhealthy for sensitive individuals, 0.0% unhealthy (percent of days)
Transportation: Commute: 93.6% car, 0.2% public transportation, 1.5% walk, 1.5% work from home; Median travel time to work: 20.3 minutes
Presidential Election: 34.9% Obama, 62.3% Romney (2012)
National and State Parks: Muscatatuck National Wildlife Refuge; Starve Hollow State Beach
Additional Information Contacts
Jackson Government . . . . (812) 358-6116
    http://www.jacksoncounty.in.gov

Jackson County Communities

BROWNSTOWN (town).
County seat. Covers a land area of 1.588 square miles and a water area of 0.006 square miles. Located at 38.88° N. Lat; 86.05° W. Long. Elevation is 623 feet.
History: Brownstown was founded in 1816 as a farm town and seat of Jackson County.
Population: 2,947; Growth (since 2000): -1.0%; Density: 1,855.7 persons per square mile; Race: 98.3% White, 0.1% Black/African American, 0.2% Asian, 0.3% American Indian/Alaska Native, 0.1% Native Hawaiian/Other Pacific Islander, 0.8% Two or more races, 1.0% Hispanic of any race; Average household size: 2.42; Median age: 38.7; Age under 18: 25.7%; Age 65 and over: 18.6%; Males per 100 females: 93.1; Marriage status: 23.4% never married, 50.2% now married, 1.8% separated, 12.0% widowed, 14.5% divorced; Foreign born: 2.0%; Speak English only: 97.4%; With disability: 11.8%; Veterans: 9.2%; Ancestry: 26.4% German, 24.9% American, 10.8% Irish, 5.6% English, 5.2% Dutch
Employment: 9.0% management, business, and financial, 2.5% computer, engineering, and science, 5.2% education, legal, community service, arts, and media, 9.2% healthcare practitioners, 21.0% service, 19.1% sales and office, 9.4% natural resources, construction, and maintenance, 24.6% production, transportation, and material moving
Income: Per capita: $21,438; Median household: $38,819; Average household: $48,162; Households with income of $100,000 or more: 4.4%; Poverty rate: 8.9%
Educational Attainment: High school diploma or higher: 89.3%; Bachelor's degree or higher: 10.2%; Graduate/professional degree or higher: 3.1%

School District(s)
Brownstown Cnt Com Sch Corp (PK-12)
    2012-13 Enrollment: 1,696 . . . . (812) 358-4271
Housing: Homeownership rate: 67.4%; Median home value: $115,200; Median year structure built: 1971; Homeowner vacancy rate: 3.2%; Median gross rent: $630 per month; Rental vacancy rate: 7.9%
Health Insurance: 85.4% have insurance; 72.6% have private insurance; 33.0% have public insurance; 14.6% do not have insurance; 9.8% of children under 18 do not have insurance
Newspapers: Jackson County Banner (weekly circulation 3000)
Transportation: Commute: 92.0% car, 0.0% public transportation, 3.1% walk, 1.5% work from home; Median travel time to work: 18.9 minutes
Additional Information Contacts
Town of Brownstown . . . . (812) 358-2930
    http://www.brownstownchamber.org

CROTHERSVILLE (town).
Covers a land area of 1.142 square miles and a water area of 0 square miles. Located at 38.79° N. Lat; 85.84° W. Long. Elevation is 558 feet.
Population: 1,591; Growth (since 2000): 1.3%; Density: 1,393.4 persons per square mile; Race: 96.2% White, 0.2% Black/African American, 0.4% Asian, 0.3% American Indian/Alaska Native, 0.0% Native Hawaiian/Other Pacific Islander, 1.5% Two or more races, 2.1% Hispanic of any race; Average household size: 2.55; Median age: 37.9; Age under 18: 24.8%; Age 65 and over: 15.5%; Males per 100 females: 94.7

School District(s)
Crothersville Community Schools (KG-12)
    2012-13 Enrollment: 551. . . . . (812) 793-2601

Housing: Homeownership rate: 75.4%; Homeowner vacancy rate: 6.4%; Rental vacancy rate: 13.1%
Newspapers: Crothersville Times (weekly circulation 2300)

FREETOWN (CDP).
Covers a land area of 0.724 square miles and a water area of 0.003 square miles. Located at 38.98° N. Lat; 86.13° W. Long. Elevation is 650 feet.
Population: 385; Growth (since 2000): n/a; Density: 531.6 persons per square mile; Race: 97.9% White, 0.0% Black/African American, 0.0% Asian, 0.3% American Indian/Alaska Native, 0.0% Native Hawaiian/Other Pacific Islander, 1.8% Two or more races, 0.0% Hispanic of any race; Average household size: 2.55; Median age: 36.1; Age under 18: 23.9%; Age 65 and over: 13.8%; Males per 100 females: 94.4
Housing: Homeownership rate: 75.5%; Homeowner vacancy rate: 5.7%; Rental vacancy rate: 19.1%

MEDORA (town).
Covers a land area of 0.329 square miles and a water area of 0.002 square miles. Located at 38.82° N. Lat; 86.17° W. Long. Elevation is 528 feet.
Population: 693; Growth (since 2000): 22.7%; Density: 2,105.8 persons per square mile; Race: 97.3% White, 0.1% Black/African American, 0.0% Asian, 0.1% American Indian/Alaska Native, 0.4% Native Hawaiian/Other Pacific Islander, 2.0% Two or more races, 1.0% Hispanic of any race; Average household size: 2.48; Median age: 38.6; Age under 18: 26.1%; Age 65 and over: 17.0%; Males per 100 females: 99.1
School District(s)
Medora Community School Corp (KG-12)
    2012-13 Enrollment: 243 . . . . (812) 966-2210
Housing: Homeownership rate: 79.2%; Homeowner vacancy rate: 2.6%; Rental vacancy rate: 21.3%

NORMAN (unincorporated postal area)
ZCTA: 47264
    Covers a land area of 98.863 square miles and a water area of 0.287 square miles. Located at 38.97° N. Lat; 86.25° W. Long. Elevation is 869 feet.
Population: 1,428; Growth (since 2000): 0.0%; Density: 14.4 persons per square mile; Race: 97.8% White, 0.2% Black/African American, 0.1% Asian, 0.4% American Indian/Alaska Native, 0.0% Native Hawaiian/Other Pacific Islander, 1.2% Two or more races, 1.3% Hispanic of any race; Average household size: 2.53; Median age: 44.3; Age under 18: 23.5%; Age 65 and over: 17.5%; Males per 100 females: 106.4
Housing: Homeownership rate: 86.1%; Homeowner vacancy rate: 3.2%; Rental vacancy rate: 8.2%

SEYMOUR (city).
Covers a land area of 11.422 square miles and a water area of 0.005 square miles. Located at 38.94° N. Lat; 85.89° W. Long. Elevation is 600 feet.
History: Seymour developed as a factory town at the junction of three railroads.
Population: 17,503; Growth (since 2000): -3.3%; Density: 1,532.4 persons per square mile; Race: 90.3% White, 1.3% Black/African American, 1.2% Asian, 0.2% American Indian/Alaska Native, 0.1% Native Hawaiian/Other Pacific Islander, 1.8% Two or more races, 11.5% Hispanic of any race; Average household size: 2.49; Median age: 35.5; Age under 18: 25.3%; Age 65 and over: 13.4%; Males per 100 females: 95.1; Marriage status: 24.1% never married, 52.1% now married, 1.6% separated, 7.5% widowed, 16.2% divorced; Foreign born: 10.6%; Speak English only: 86.4%; With disability: 14.4%; Veterans: 8.9%; Ancestry: 22.9% German, 21.4% American, 11.3% Irish, 8.2% English, 1.4% Italian
Employment: 8.6% management, business, and financial, 4.0% computer, engineering, and science, 5.0% education, legal, community service, arts, and media, 5.2% healthcare practitioners, 18.0% service, 22.2% sales and office, 9.1% natural resources, construction, and maintenance, 27.9% production, transportation, and material moving
Income: Per capita: $21,508; Median household: $42,044; Average household: $52,727; Households with income of $100,000 or more: 9.3%; Poverty rate: 16.3%
Educational Attainment: High school diploma or higher: 83.2%; Bachelor's degree or higher: 16.1%; Graduate/professional degree or higher: 5.1%
School District(s)
Seymour Community Schools (PK-12)
    2012-13 Enrollment: 4,250 . . . . (812) 522-3340
Housing: Homeownership rate: 61.4%; Median home value: $101,200; Median year structure built: 1973; Homeowner vacancy rate: 3.4%; Median gross rent: $720 per month; Rental vacancy rate: 13.1%
Health Insurance: 82.9% have insurance; 65.3% have private insurance; 27.9% have public insurance; 17.1% do not have insurance; 12.4% of children under 18 do not have insurance
Hospitals: Schneck Medical Center (166 beds)
Safety: Violent crime rate: 53.6 per 10,000 population; Property crime rate: 643.8 per 10,000 population
Newspapers: The Tribune (daily circulation 8900)
Transportation: Commute: 92.0% car, 0.2% public transportation, 1.2% walk, 1.3% work from home; Median travel time to work: 16.0 minutes
Airports: Freeman Municipal (general aviation)
Additional Information Contacts
City of Seymour . . . . (812) 522-4020
    http://www.seymourcity.com

VALLONIA (CDP).
Covers a land area of 0.761 square miles and a water area of <.001 square miles. Located at 38.85° N. Lat; 86.10° W. Long. Elevation is 535 feet.
Population: 336; Growth (since 2000): n/a; Density: 441.3 persons per square mile; Race: 98.5% White, 0.0% Black/African American, 0.3% Asian, 0.0% American Indian/Alaska Native, 0.0% Native Hawaiian/Other Pacific Islander, 1.2% Two or more races, 1.2% Hispanic of any race; Average household size: 2.49; Median age: 40.7; Age under 18: 24.4%; Age 65 and over: 14.6%; Males per 100 females: 108.7
Housing: Homeownership rate: 83.7%; Homeowner vacancy rate: 0.0%; Rental vacancy rate: 0.0%

Jasper County

Located in northwestern Indiana; bounded on the north by the Kankakee River; drained by the Iroquois River. Covers a land area of 559.625 square miles, a water area of 1.761 square miles, and is located in the Central Time Zone at 41.02° N. Lat., 87.12° W. Long. The county was founded in 1835. County seat is Rensselaer.

Jasper County is part of the Chicago-Naperville-Elgin, IL-IN-WI Metropolitan Statistical Area. The entire metro area includes: Chicago-Naperville-Arlington Heights, IL Metropolitan Division (Cook County, IL; DuPage County, IL; Grundy County, IL; Kendall County, IL; McHenry County, IL; Will County, IL); Elgin, IL Metropolitan Division (DeKalb County, IL; Kane County, IL); Gary, IN Metropolitan Division (Jasper County, IN; Lake County, IN; Newton County, IN; Porter County, IN); Lake County-Kenosha County, IL-WI Metropolitan Division (Lake County, IL; Kenosha County, WI)

Weather Station: Rensselaer   Elevation: 649 feet

	Jan	Feb	Mar	Apr	May	Jun	Jul	Aug	Sep	Oct	Nov	Dec
High	32	36	47	61	72	81	84	82	76	63	49	36
Low	16	19	29	40	50	60	64	62	53	41	33	21
Precip	2.3	1.9	2.9	3.6	4.4	4.1	4.6	3.5	3.2	3.5	3.3	2.7
Snow	9.0	6.6	2.7	0.3	0.0	0.0	0.0	0.0	0.0	0.1	0.5	5.5

High and Low temperatures in degrees Fahrenheit; Precipitation and Snow in inches

Population: 33,478; Growth (since 2000): 11.4%; Density: 59.8 persons per square mile; Race: 95.8% White, 0.6% Black/African American, 0.4% Asian, 0.2% American Indian/Alaska Native, 0.0% Native Hawaiian/Other Pacific Islander, 1.0% two or more races, 5.4% Hispanic of any race; Average household size: 2.66; Median age: 38.0; Age under 18: 25.7%; Age 65 and over: 14.0%; Males per 100 females: 99.1; Marriage status: 24.1% never married, 60.9% now married, 1.1% separated, 6.0% widowed, 9.0% divorced; Foreign born: 2.3%; Speak English only: 94.7%; With disability: 14.3%; Veterans: 10.1%; Ancestry: 25.7% German, 15.0% Irish, 9.0% Dutch, 8.2% English, 7.1% American
Religion: Six largest groups: 13.0% Catholicism, 8.0% Presbyterian-Reformed, 5.6% Baptist, 4.4% Methodist/Pietist, 3.2% Non-denominational Protestant, 2.4% Lutheran
Economy: Unemployment rate: 6.1%; Leading industries: 16.8% retail trade; 12.7% other services (except public administration); 12.2% construction; Farms: 615 totaling 282,831 acres; Company size: 0 employ 1,000 or more persons, 0 employ 500 to 999 persons, 16 employ 100 to 499 persons, 715 employ less than 100 persons; Business ownership: n/a women-owned, n/a Black-owned, n/a Hispanic-owned, n/a Asian-owned
Employment: 10.3% management, business, and financial, 2.2% computer, engineering, and science, 7.9% education, legal, community

service, arts, and media, 6.7% healthcare practitioners, 17.0% service, 19.7% sales and office, 18.5% natural resources, construction, and maintenance, 17.7% production, transportation, and material moving
Income: Per capita: $24,297; Median household: $57,500; Average household: $65,320; Households with income of $100,000 or more: 16.2%; Poverty rate: 7.7%
Educational Attainment: High school diploma or higher: 87.2%; Bachelor's degree or higher: 14.9%; Graduate/professional degree or higher: 4.8%
Housing: Homeownership rate: 76.9%; Median home value: $146,200; Median year structure built: 1978; Homeowner vacancy rate: 2.1%; Median gross rent: $688 per month; Rental vacancy rate: 7.2%
Vital Statistics: Birth rate: 116.5 per 10,000 population; Death rate: 92.8 per 10,000 population; Age-adjusted cancer mortality rate: 167.9 deaths per 100,000 population
Health Insurance: 88.5% have insurance; 75.5% have private insurance; 25.7% have public insurance; 11.5% do not have insurance; 5.3% of children under 18 do not have insurance
Health Care: Physicians: 5.4 per 10,000 population; Hospital beds: 12.6 per 10,000 population; Hospital admissions: 412.2 per 10,000 population
Air Quality Index: 98.9% good, 1.1% moderate, 0.0% unhealthy for sensitive individuals, 0.0% unhealthy (percent of days)
Transportation: Commute: 93.3% car, 0.2% public transportation, 3.2% walk, 2.2% work from home; Median travel time to work: 26.6 minutes
Presidential Election: 36.2% Obama, 61.7% Romney (2012)
Additional Information Contacts
Jasper Government............................ (219) 866-4926
  http://www.jaspercountyin.gov

Jasper County Communities

COLLEGEVILLE (CDP). Covers a land area of 1.132 square miles and a water area of 0 square miles. Located at 40.91° N. Lat; 87.16° W. Long. Elevation is 666 feet.
History: Seat of St. Joseph's College.
Population: 330; Growth (since 2000): -61.8%; Density: 291.4 persons per square mile; Race: 83.0% White, 11.8% Black/African American, 0.6% Asian, 0.3% American Indian/Alaska Native, 0.0% Native Hawaiian/Other Pacific Islander, 3.0% Two or more races, 4.5% Hispanic of any race; Average household size: 2.52; Median age: 20.6; Age under 18: 5.2%; Age 65 and over: 3.0%; Males per 100 females: 226.7
Housing: Homeownership rate: 88.9%; Homeowner vacancy rate: 0.0%; Rental vacancy rate: 0.0%

DE MOTTE (town). Covers a land area of 3.609 square miles and a water area of 0.003 square miles. Located at 41.20° N. Lat; 87.20° W. Long. Elevation is 669 feet.
Population: 3,814; Growth (since 2000): 17.9%; Density: 1,056.8 persons per square mile; Race: 96.2% White, 0.4% Black/African American, 0.4% Asian, 0.3% American Indian/Alaska Native, 0.0% Native Hawaiian/Other Pacific Islander, 1.3% Two or more races, 4.7% Hispanic of any race; Average household size: 2.42; Median age: 39.4; Age under 18: 24.4%; Age 65 and over: 20.7%; Males per 100 females: 87.1; Marriage status: 20.9% never married, 59.5% now married, 0.9% separated, 8.5% widowed, 11.0% divorced; Foreign born: 3.1%; Speak English only: 93.3%; With disability: 12.7%; Veterans: 13.2%; Ancestry: 29.5% German, 13.8% Dutch, 11.2% Polish, 8.7% English, 7.8% Irish
Employment: 7.7% management, business, and financial, 4.7% computer, engineering, and science, 6.5% education, legal, community service, arts, and media, 2.8% healthcare practitioners, 18.8% service, 28.4% sales and office, 25.3% natural resources, construction, and maintenance, 5.7% production, transportation, and material moving
Income: Per capita: $22,616; Median household: $52,098; Average household: $54,535; Households with income of $100,000 or more: 7.9%; Poverty rate: 9.4%
Educational Attainment: High school diploma or higher: 90.6%; Bachelor's degree or higher: 7.7%; Graduate/professional degree or higher: 3.3%
School District(s)
Kankakee Valley School Corp (KG-12)
  2012-13 Enrollment: 3,488...................... (219) 987-4711
North Newton School Corp (KG-12)
  2012-13 Enrollment: 1,478...................... (219) 285-2228

Housing: Homeownership rate: 68.6%; Median home value: $151,000; Median year structure built: 1992; Homeowner vacancy rate: 2.4%; Median gross rent: $686 per month; Rental vacancy rate: 7.7%
Health Insurance: 88.3% have insurance; 76.7% have private insurance; 28.8% have public insurance; 11.7% do not have insurance; 2.6% of children under 18 do not have insurance
Newspapers: Kankakee Valley Post News (weekly circulation 3300)
Transportation: Commute: 95.3% car, 0.0% public transportation, 2.2% walk, 1.7% work from home; Median travel time to work: 30.7 minutes
Additional Information Contacts
Town of De Motte.............................. (219) 987-3831
  http://www.townofdemotte.com

FAIR OAKS (unincorporated postal area)
ZCTA: 47943
  Covers a land area of 62.697 square miles and a water area of 0.057 square miles. Located at 41.06° N. Lat; 87.27° W. Long. Elevation is 702 feet.
Population: 932; Growth (since 2000): 22.1%; Density: 14.9 persons per square mile; Race: 86.8% White, 0.2% Black/African American, 0.2% Asian, 0.4% American Indian/Alaska Native, 0.0% Native Hawaiian/Other Pacific Islander, 1.0% Two or more races, 27.4% Hispanic of any race; Average household size: 3.10; Median age: 34.9; Age under 18: 30.6%; Age 65 and over: 11.5%; Males per 100 females: 116.2
Housing: Homeownership rate: 68.8%; Homeowner vacancy rate: 0.0%; Rental vacancy rate: 6.0%

REMINGTON (town). Covers a land area of 1.018 square miles and a water area of 0 square miles. Located at 40.77° N. Lat; 87.15° W. Long. Elevation is 735 feet.
History: Laid out 1860.
Population: 1,185; Growth (since 2000): -10.4%; Density: 1,163.9 persons per square mile; Race: 96.5% White, 0.6% Black/African American, 0.3% Asian, 0.1% American Indian/Alaska Native, 0.1% Native Hawaiian/Other Pacific Islander, 2.2% Two or more races, 3.1% Hispanic of any race; Average household size: 2.36; Median age: 39.8; Age under 18: 24.8%; Age 65 and over: 16.1%; Males per 100 females: 95.2
School District(s)
Tri-County School Corp (KG-12)
  2012-13 Enrollment: 762........................ (219) 279-2418
Housing: Homeownership rate: 67.4%; Homeowner vacancy rate: 4.1%; Rental vacancy rate: 7.3%

RENSSELAER (city). County seat. Covers a land area of 3.800 square miles and a water area of 0.060 square miles. Located at 40.93° N. Lat; 87.15° W. Long. Elevation is 663 feet.
History: Rensselaer was founded in 1837 by James Van Rensselaer, a merchant from New York who operated a gristmill here. Rensselaer soon became a trading center for the surrounding farming community.
Population: 5,859; Growth (since 2000): 10.7%; Density: 1,541.8 persons per square mile; Race: 95.4% White, 0.7% Black/African American, 0.4% Asian, 0.4% American Indian/Alaska Native, 0.1% Native Hawaiian/Other Pacific Islander, 1.3% Two or more races, 5.4% Hispanic of any race; Average household size: 2.42; Median age: 36.6; Age under 18: 25.5%; Age 65 and over: 16.4%; Males per 100 females: 92.2; Marriage status: 28.2% never married, 51.8% now married, 1.7% separated, 10.2% widowed, 9.8% divorced; Foreign born: 1.1%; Speak English only: 98.3%; With disability: 18.8%; Veterans: 9.5%; Ancestry: 20.4% German, 14.4% Irish, 10.4% English, 7.4% American, 3.5% Dutch
Employment: 12.1% management, business, and financial, 1.1% computer, engineering, and science, 8.2% education, legal, community service, arts, and media, 4.8% healthcare practitioners, 26.3% service, 18.3% sales and office, 11.8% natural resources, construction, and maintenance, 17.4% production, transportation, and material moving
Income: Per capita: $25,697; Median household: $44,178; Average household: $58,966; Households with income of $100,000 or more: 12.3%; Poverty rate: 12.3%
Educational Attainment: High school diploma or higher: 84.5%; Bachelor's degree or higher: 17.3%; Graduate/professional degree or higher: 6.7%
School District(s)
Rensselaer Central School Corp (PK-12)
  2012-13 Enrollment: 1,739...................... (219) 866-7822

Four-year College(s)
Saint Josephs College (Private, Not-for-profit, Roman Catholic)
Fall 2013 Enrollment: 1,163 . . . . (219) 866-6000
2013-14 Tuition: In-state $27,350; Out-of-state $27,350
Housing: Homeownership rate: 59.9%; Median home value: $111,600; Median year structure built: 1957; Homeowner vacancy rate: 4.4%; Median gross rent: $611 per month; Rental vacancy rate: 6.2%
Health Insurance: 88.9% have insurance; 75.1% have private insurance; 29.6% have public insurance; 11.1% do not have insurance; 7.9% of children under 18 do not have insurance
Hospitals: Jasper County Hospital (86 beds)
Safety: Violent crime rate: 44.0 per 10,000 population; Property crime rate: 369.2 per 10,000 population
Newspapers: Rensselaer Republican (daily circulation 2100)
Transportation: Commute: 90.6% car, 0.0% public transportation, 6.2% walk, 2.7% work from home; Median travel time to work: 16.5 minutes; Amtrak: Train service available.
Additional Information Contacts
City of Rensselaer . . . . (219) 866-5213
http://www.cityofrensselaerin.com

WHEATFIELD (town). Covers a land area of 0.558 square miles and a water area of 0 square miles. Located at 41.19° N. Lat; 87.05° W. Long. Elevation is 663 feet.
Population: 853; Growth (since 2000): 10.5%; Density: 1,529.6 persons per square mile; Race: 95.8% White, 0.8% Black/African American, 0.1% Asian, 0.0% American Indian/Alaska Native, 0.2% Native Hawaiian/Other Pacific Islander, 1.2% Two or more races, 5.9% Hispanic of any race; Average household size: 2.65; Median age: 31.8; Age under 18: 29.1%; Age 65 and over: 11.5%; Males per 100 females: 97.5
School District(s)
Kankakee Valley School Corp (KG-12)
2012-13 Enrollment: 3,488 . . . . (219) 987-4711
Housing: Homeownership rate: 65.9%; Homeowner vacancy rate: 0.9%; Rental vacancy rate: 11.8%

Jay County

Located in eastern Indiana; bounded on the east by Ohio; drained by the Salamonie River. Covers a land area of 383.905 square miles, a water area of 0.177 square miles, and is located in the Eastern Time Zone at 40.43° N. Lat., 85.00° W. Long. The county was founded in 1835. County seat is Portland.

Weather Station: Portland 1 SW   Elevation: 910 feet

	Jan	Feb	Mar	Apr	May	Jun	Jul	Aug	Sep	Oct	Nov	Dec
High	33	37	48	61	71	80	84	82	76	64	50	38
Low	17	19	28	38	49	59	62	60	52	41	32	22
Precip	1.8	2.0	2.4	3.5	4.1	3.9	4.7	3.7	2.6	2.6	2.9	2.4
Snow	6.3	5.3	2.6	0.3	0.0	0.0	0.0	0.0	0.0	0.2	0.7	4.5

High and Low temperatures in degrees Fahrenheit; Precipitation and Snow in inches

Population: 21,253; Growth (since 2000): -2.5%; Density: 55.4 persons per square mile; Race: 97.0% White, 0.3% Black/African American, 0.4% Asian, 0.1% American Indian/Alaska Native, 0.0% Native Hawaiian/Other Pacific Islander, 0.9% two or more races, 2.7% Hispanic of any race; Average household size: 2.58; Median age: 39.0; Age under 18: 26.6%; Age 65 and over: 15.4%; Males per 100 females: 97.4; Marriage status: 24.7% never married, 54.6% now married, 1.7% separated, 7.2% widowed, 13.5% divorced; Foreign born: 1.1%; Speak English only: 95.4%; With disability: 16.5%; Veterans: 8.9%; Ancestry: 27.8% German, 15.5% American, 10.4% English, 10.1% Irish, 1.6% French
Religion: Six largest groups: 10.8% Methodist/Pietist, 8.1% Catholicism, 6.1% Holiness, 5.6% European Free-Church, 2.0% Lutheran, 2.0% Non-denominational Protestant
Economy: Unemployment rate: 4.8%; Leading industries: 16.4% retail trade; 16.4% other services (except public administration); 9.7% construction; Farms: 836 totaling 175,770 acres; Company size: 0 employ 1,000 or more persons, 1 employs 500 to 999 persons, 11 employs 100 to 499 persons, 391 employs less than 100 persons; Business ownership: 309 women-owned, n/a Black-owned, n/a Hispanic-owned, n/a Asian-owned
Employment: 8.9% management, business, and financial; 1.2% computer, engineering, and science; 7.2% education, legal, community service, arts, and media; 5.8% healthcare practitioners; 13.5% service; 19.8% sales and office, 11.0% natural resources, construction, and maintenance, 32.6% production, transportation, and material moving
Income: Per capita: $19,236; Median household: $40,235; Average household: $49,157; Households with income of $100,000 or more: 7.7%; Poverty rate: 14.7%
Educational Attainment: High school diploma or higher: 84.1%; Bachelor's degree or higher: 10.0%; Graduate/professional degree or higher: 3.5%
Housing: Homeownership rate: 76.3%; Median home value: $79,300; Median year structure built: 1954; Homeowner vacancy rate: 2.2%; Median gross rent: $551 per month; Rental vacancy rate: 10.9%
Vital Statistics: Birth rate: 150.0 per 10,000 population; Death rate: 102.2 per 10,000 population; Age-adjusted cancer mortality rate: 192.0 deaths per 100,000 population
Health Insurance: 87.1% have insurance; 66.7% have private insurance; 33.4% have public insurance; 12.9% do not have insurance; 8.2% of children under 18 do not have insurance
Health Care: Physicians: 4.2 per 10,000 population; Hospital beds: 16.4 per 10,000 population; Hospital admissions: 546.9 per 10,000 population
Transportation: Commute: 93.4% car, 0.1% public transportation, 1.9% walk, 2.5% work from home; Median travel time to work: 20.6 minutes
Presidential Election: 38.8% Obama, 58.8% Romney (2012)
National and State Parks: Limberlost State Game Reserve
Additional Information Contacts
Jay Government . . . . (260) 726-4951
http://www.jaycounty.net

Jay County Communities

BRYANT (town). Covers a land area of 0.304 square miles and a water area of 0 square miles. Located at 40.54° N. Lat; 84.96° W. Long. Elevation is 873 feet.
Population: 252; Growth (since 2000): -7.4%; Density: 828.8 persons per square mile; Race: 97.2% White, 0.4% Black/African American, 0.8% Asian, 0.8% American Indian/Alaska Native, 0.0% Native Hawaiian/Other Pacific Islander, 0.8% Two or more races, 2.4% Hispanic of any race; Average household size: 2.55; Median age: 38.5; Age under 18: 24.2%; Age 65 and over: 14.3%; Males per 100 females: 96.9
School District(s)
Jay School Corp (KG-12)
2012-13 Enrollment: 3,503 . . . . (260) 726-9341
Housing: Homeownership rate: 82.9%; Homeowner vacancy rate: 3.3%; Rental vacancy rate: 14.3%

DUNKIRK (city). Covers a land area of 1.257 square miles and a water area of 0 square miles. Located at 40.37° N. Lat; 85.21° W. Long. Elevation is 948 feet.
Population: 2,362; Growth (since 2000): -10.7%; Density: 1,879.5 persons per square mile; Race: 98.6% White, 0.3% Black/African American, 0.0% Asian, 0.1% American Indian/Alaska Native, 0.0% Native Hawaiian/Other Pacific Islander, 0.6% Two or more races, 1.2% Hispanic of any race; Average household size: 2.46; Median age: 37.2; Age under 18: 26.3%; Age 65 and over: 14.2%; Males per 100 females: 94.7
School District(s)
Jay School Corp (KG-12)
2012-13 Enrollment: 3,503 . . . . (260) 726-9341
Housing: Homeownership rate: 70.7%; Homeowner vacancy rate: 2.9%; Rental vacancy rate: 11.5%
Newspapers: Dunkirk News & Sun (weekly circulation 1200)
Additional Information Contacts
City of Dunkirk . . . . (260) 726-4481
http://www.jaycountychamber.com

PENNVILLE (town). Covers a land area of 0.504 square miles and a water area of 0 square miles. Located at 40.49° N. Lat; 85.15° W. Long. Elevation is 876 feet.
Population: 701; Growth (since 2000): -0.7%; Density: 1,390.9 persons per square mile; Race: 97.1% White, 0.0% Black/African American, 0.4% Asian, 0.0% American Indian/Alaska Native, 0.0% Native Hawaiian/Other Pacific Islander, 0.6% Two or more races, 3.6% Hispanic of any race; Average household size: 2.40; Median age: 39.6; Age under 18: 25.5%; Age 65 and over: 18.7%; Males per 100 females: 90.0
School District(s)
Jay School Corp (KG-12)
2012-13 Enrollment: 3,503 . . . . (260) 726-9341

Housing: Homeownership rate: 74.7%; Homeowner vacancy rate: 0.0%; Rental vacancy rate: 4.9%

PORTLAND (city). County seat. Covers a land area of 4.651 square miles and a water area of 0.003 square miles. Located at 40.44° N. Lat; 84.98° W. Long. Elevation is 906 feet.
History: Portland was the birthplace of Elwood Haynes (1857-1925) who invented the first successful clutch-driven automobile.
Population: 6,223; Growth (since 2000): -3.3%; Density: 1,338.0 persons per square mile; Race: 94.5% White, 0.4% Black/African American, 0.5% Asian, 0.0% American Indian/Alaska Native, 0.0% Native Hawaiian/Other Pacific Islander, 1.5% Two or more races, 5.8% Hispanic of any race; Average household size: 2.32; Median age: 39.4; Age under 18: 23.7%; Age 65 and over: 17.9%; Males per 100 females: 87.8; Marriage status: 27.4% never married, 47.5% now married, 1.7% separated, 10.3% widowed, 14.8% divorced; Foreign born: 2.4%; Speak English only: 93.2%; With disability: 17.7%; Veterans: 8.2%; Ancestry: 26.4% German, 12.5% American, 11.9% English, 10.7% Irish, 2.4% Dutch
Employment: 6.6% management, business, and financial, 1.7% computer, engineering, and science, 5.9% education, legal, community service, arts, and media, 7.7% healthcare practitioners, 13.6% service, 18.5% sales and office, 7.0% natural resources, construction, and maintenance, 38.9% production, transportation, and material moving
Income: Per capita: $18,170; Median household: $34,944; Average household: $41,875; Households with income of $100,000 or more: 5.3%; Poverty rate: 14.3%
Educational Attainment: High school diploma or higher: 82.6%; Bachelor's degree or higher: 9.7%; Graduate/professional degree or higher: 4.0%

School District(s)
Jay School Corp (KG-12)
    2012-13 Enrollment: 3,503 . . . . (260) 726-9341
Housing: Homeownership rate: 64.1%; Median home value: $68,400; Median year structure built: 1953; Homeowner vacancy rate: 3.6%; Median gross rent: $526 per month; Rental vacancy rate: 13.6%
Health Insurance: 84.8% have insurance; 65.5% have private insurance; 33.4% have public insurance; 15.2% do not have insurance; 7.3% of children under 18 do not have insurance
Hospitals: Jay County Hospital (25 beds)
Safety: Violent crime rate: 1.6 per 10,000 population; Property crime rate: 388.7 per 10,000 population
Newspapers: Commercial-Review (daily circulation 4800)
Transportation: Commute: 92.5% car, 0.0% public transportation, 2.2% walk, 2.2% work from home; Median travel time to work: 15.3 minutes
Airports: Portland Municipal (general aviation)
Additional Information Contacts
City of Portland . . . . (260) 726-9395
    http://www.thecityofportland.net

REDKEY (town). Covers a land area of 0.936 square miles and a water area of 0.008 square miles. Located at 40.35° N. Lat; 85.15° W. Long. Elevation is 965 feet.
Population: 1,353; Growth (since 2000): -5.2%; Density: 1,446.0 persons per square mile; Race: 98.2% White, 0.2% Black/African American, 0.2% Asian, 0.0% American Indian/Alaska Native, 0.0% Native Hawaiian/Other Pacific Islander, 0.9% Two or more races, 1.4% Hispanic of any race; Average household size: 2.46; Median age: 37.1; Age under 18: 27.3%; Age 65 and over: 16.1%; Males per 100 females: 93.0

School District(s)
Jay School Corp (KG-12)
    2012-13 Enrollment: 3,503 . . . . (260) 726-9341
Housing: Homeownership rate: 69.3%; Homeowner vacancy rate: 1.5%; Rental vacancy rate: 4.4%

SALAMONIA (town). Covers a land area of 0.366 square miles and a water area of 0 square miles. Located at 40.38° N. Lat; 84.87° W. Long. Elevation is 971 feet.
Population: 157; Growth (since 2000): -0.6%; Density: 428.7 persons per square mile; Race: 98.7% White, 0.0% Black/African American, 0.0% Asian, 0.6% American Indian/Alaska Native, 0.0% Native Hawaiian/Other Pacific Islander, 0.6% Two or more races, 0.6% Hispanic of any race; Average household size: 3.02; Median age: 30.5; Age under 18: 33.8%; Age 65 and over: 7.6%; Males per 100 females: 98.7
Housing: Homeownership rate: 73.1%; Homeowner vacancy rate: 7.3%; Rental vacancy rate: 12.5%

Jefferson County

Located in southeastern Indiana; bounded on the south partly by the Ohio River and the Kentucky border; drained by Big Creek. Covers a land area of 360.631 square miles, a water area of 2.258 square miles, and is located in the Eastern Time Zone at 38.78° N. Lat., 85.44° W. Long. The county was founded in 1810. County seat is Madison.

Jefferson County is part of the Madison, IN Micropolitan Statistical Area. The entire metro area includes: Jefferson County, IN

Weather Station: Madison Sewage Plant   Elevation: 459 feet

	Jan	Feb	Mar	Apr	May	Jun	Jul	Aug	Sep	Oct	Nov	Dec
High	41	45	55	66	75	83	87	86	80	68	56	44
Low	24	26	34	43	53	62	66	65	58	46	37	28
Precip	3.4	3.0	4.2	4.3	5.3	4.2	4.6	4.1	3.2	3.8	3.7	3.8
Snow	4.3	3.9	1.3	0.1	tr	0.0	0.0	0.0	0.0	0.1	tr	3.4

High and Low temperatures in degrees Fahrenheit; Precipitation and Snow in inches

Population: 32,428; Growth (since 2000): 2.3%; Density: 89.9 persons per square mile; Race: 95.2% White, 1.7% Black/African American, 0.7% Asian, 0.2% American Indian/Alaska Native, 0.0% Native Hawaiian/Other Pacific Islander, 1.3% two or more races, 2.3% Hispanic of any race; Average household size: 2.42; Median age: 39.7; Age under 18: 22.6%; Age 65 and over: 14.6%; Males per 100 females: 93.1; Marriage status: 27.8% never married, 51.0% now married, 1.3% separated, 6.8% widowed, 14.4% divorced; Foreign born: 2.0%; Speak English only: 96.6%; With disability: 14.4%; Veterans: 10.6%; Ancestry: 20.1% German, 13.3% American, 12.2% Irish, 11.5% English, 2.8% French
Religion: Six largest groups: 23.9% Baptist, 7.7% Catholicism, 4.4% Methodist/Pietist, 2.3% Non-denominational Protestant, 1.5% Holiness, 1.2% Presbyterian-Reformed
Economy: Unemployment rate: 5.1%; Leading industries: 18.8% retail trade; 12.3% accommodation and food services; 12.1% other services (except public administration); Farms: 615 totaling 95,411 acres; Company size: 0 employ 1,000 or more persons, 3 employ 500 to 999 persons, 12 employ 100 to 499 persons, 660 employ less than 100 persons; Business ownership: n/a women-owned, n/a Black-owned, n/a Hispanic-owned, n/a Asian-owned
Employment: 8.0% management, business, and financial, 2.6% computer, engineering, and science, 10.0% education, legal, community service, arts, and media, 5.6% healthcare practitioners, 17.6% service, 22.8% sales and office, 11.1% natural resources, construction, and maintenance, 22.3% production, transportation, and material moving
Income: Per capita: $21,524; Median household: $43,795; Average household: $54,077; Households with income of $100,000 or more: 10.4%; Poverty rate: 13.6%
Educational Attainment: High school diploma or higher: 83.9%; Bachelor's degree or higher: 17.8%; Graduate/professional degree or higher: 7.7%
Housing: Homeownership rate: 72.8%; Median home value: $111,500; Median year structure built: 1973; Homeowner vacancy rate: 2.7%; Median gross rent: $652 per month; Rental vacancy rate: 10.7%
Vital Statistics: Birth rate: 106.6 per 10,000 population; Death rate: 102.3 per 10,000 population; Age-adjusted cancer mortality rate: 168.0 deaths per 100,000 population
Health Insurance: 84.5% have insurance; 66.7% have private insurance; 31.9% have public insurance; 15.5% do not have insurance; 8.8% of children under 18 do not have insurance
Health Care: Physicians: 14.5 per 10,000 population; Hospital beds: 71.8 per 10,000 population; Hospital admissions: 1,144.4 per 10,000 population
Transportation: Commute: 92.9% car, 0.2% public transportation, 2.6% walk, 3.4% work from home; Median travel time to work: 22.0 minutes
Presidential Election: 43.7% Obama, 54.1% Romney (2012)
National and State Parks: Clifty Falls State Park
Additional Information Contacts
Jefferson Government . . . . (812) 265-8922
    http://jeffersoncounty.in.gov

Jefferson County Communities

BROOKSBURG (town). Covers a land area of 0.102 square miles and a water area of 0.009 square miles. Located at 38.74° N. Lat; 85.25° W. Long. Elevation is 472 feet.
Population: 81; Growth (since 2000): 9.5%; Density: 797.2 persons per square mile; Race: 98.8% White, 1.2% Black/African American, 0.0%

Asian, 0.0% American Indian/Alaska Native, 0.0% Native Hawaiian/Other Pacific Islander, 0.0% Two or more races, 0.0% Hispanic of any race; Average household size: 2.53; Median age: 38.5; Age under 18: 27.2%; Age 65 and over: 12.3%; Males per 100 females: 102.5
Housing: Homeownership rate: 71.9%; Homeowner vacancy rate: 0.0%; Rental vacancy rate: 25.0%

CANAAN (CDP).
Covers a land area of 0.309 square miles and a water area of <.001 square miles. Located at 38.87° N. Lat; 85.30° W. Long. Elevation is 948 feet.
Population: 90; Growth (since 2000): n/a; Density: 291.2 persons per square mile; Race: 94.4% White, 0.0% Black/African American, 0.0% Asian, 0.0% American Indian/Alaska Native, 0.0% Native Hawaiian/Other Pacific Islander, 5.6% Two or more races, 1.1% Hispanic of any race; Average household size: 2.90; Median age: 33.0; Age under 18: 35.6%; Age 65 and over: 14.4%; Males per 100 females: 114.3
Housing: Homeownership rate: 67.7%; Homeowner vacancy rate: 0.0%; Rental vacancy rate: 9.1%

DEPUTY (CDP).
Covers a land area of 0.074 square miles and a water area of 0 square miles. Located at 38.80° N. Lat; 85.65° W. Long. Elevation is 627 feet.
Population: 86; Growth (since 2000): n/a; Density: 1,166.2 persons per square mile; Race: 96.5% White, 0.0% Black/African American, 0.0% Asian, 1.2% American Indian/Alaska Native, 0.0% Native Hawaiian/Other Pacific Islander, 2.3% Two or more races, 0.0% Hispanic of any race; Average household size: 2.32; Median age: 40.3; Age under 18: 25.6%; Age 65 and over: 14.0%; Males per 100 females: 65.4
School District(s)
Madison Consolidated Schools (KG-12)
    2012-13 Enrollment: 3,039 . . . . (812) 273-8511
Housing: Homeownership rate: 83.8%; Homeowner vacancy rate: 6.1%; Rental vacancy rate: 33.3%

DUPONT (town).
Covers a land area of 1.019 square miles and a water area of 0 square miles. Located at 38.89° N. Lat; 85.52° W. Long. Elevation is 791 feet.
History: Laid out 1849.
Population: 339; Growth (since 2000): -13.5%; Density: 332.8 persons per square mile; Race: 95.9% White, 2.1% Black/African American, 0.0% Asian, 0.0% American Indian/Alaska Native, 0.0% Native Hawaiian/Other Pacific Islander, 0.0% Two or more races, 2.7% Hispanic of any race; Average household size: 2.90; Median age: 33.9; Age under 18: 31.6%; Age 65 and over: 10.0%; Males per 100 females: 108.0
School District(s)
Madison Consolidated Schools (KG-12)
    2012-13 Enrollment: 3,039 . . . . (812) 273-8511
Housing: Homeownership rate: 80.3%; Homeowner vacancy rate: 7.8%; Rental vacancy rate: 25.8%

HANOVER (town).
Covers a land area of 2.308 square miles and a water area of 0.004 square miles. Located at 38.71° N. Lat; 85.47° W. Long. Elevation is 784 feet.
History: Hanover developed around Hanover College, founded in 1827 by the Presbyterian denomination as a manual labor academy.
Population: 3,546; Growth (since 2000): 25.1%; Density: 1,536.5 persons per square mile; Race: 94.9% White, 2.3% Black/African American, 0.8% Asian, 0.2% American Indian/Alaska Native, 0.0% Native Hawaiian/Other Pacific Islander, 1.3% Two or more races, 2.4% Hispanic of any race; Average household size: 2.43; Median age: 26.2; Age under 18: 18.6%; Age 65 and over: 12.0%; Males per 100 females: 90.7; Marriage status: 48.6% never married, 31.5% now married, 1.5% separated, 7.8% widowed, 12.1% divorced; Foreign born: 2.3%; Speak English only: 97.7%; With disability: 9.4%; Veterans: 7.4%; Ancestry: 20.7% German, 10.1% English, 10.1% Irish, 9.0% American, 3.3% Scottish
Employment: 6.4% management, business, and financial, 0.9% computer, engineering, and science, 9.9% education, legal, community service, arts, and media, 3.7% healthcare practitioners, 24.9% service, 22.1% sales and office, 10.6% natural resources, construction, and maintenance, 21.6% production, transportation, and material moving
Income: Per capita: $13,252; Median household: $38,536; Average household: $42,669; Households with income of $100,000 or more: 4.6%; Poverty rate: 25.4%

Educational Attainment: High school diploma or higher: 81.0%; Bachelor's degree or higher: 11.9%; Graduate/professional degree or higher: 4.7%
School District(s)
Southwestern-Jefferson County Con (KG-12)
    2012-13 Enrollment: 1,289 . . . . (812) 866-6255
Four-year College(s)
Hanover College (Private, Not-for-profit, Presbyterian Church (USA))
    Fall 2013 Enrollment: 1,163 . . . . (812) 866-7000
    2013-14 Tuition: In-state $31,760; Out-of-state $31,760
Housing: Homeownership rate: 58.7%; Median home value: $75,500; Median year structure built: 1973; Homeowner vacancy rate: 3.2%; Median gross rent: $680 per month; Rental vacancy rate: 13.9%
Health Insurance: 86.7% have insurance; 69.9% have private insurance; 26.0% have public insurance; 13.3% do not have insurance; 6.3% of children under 18 do not have insurance
Transportation: Commute: 80.5% car, 0.0% public transportation, 14.3% walk, 5.2% work from home; Median travel time to work: 17.2 minutes
Additional Information Contacts
Town of Hanover . . . . (812) 265-3135
    http://www.madisonchamber.org

KENT (CDP).
Covers a land area of 0.104 square miles and a water area of 0 square miles. Located at 38.74° N. Lat; 85.54° W. Long. Elevation is 712 feet.
Population: 70; Growth (since 2000): n/a; Density: 675.9 persons per square mile; Race: 98.6% White, 1.4% Black/African American, 0.0% Asian, 0.0% American Indian/Alaska Native, 0.0% Native Hawaiian/Other Pacific Islander, 0.0% Two or more races, 0.0% Hispanic of any race; Average household size: 2.50; Median age: 43.5; Age under 18: 20.0%; Age 65 and over: 11.4%; Males per 100 females: 112.1
Housing: Homeownership rate: 71.4%; Homeowner vacancy rate: 8.7%; Rental vacancy rate: 0.0%

LEXINGTON (unincorporated postal area)
ZCTA: 47138
    Covers a land area of 73.705 square miles and a water area of 0.535 square miles. Located at 38.68° N. Lat; 85.58° W. Long..
Population: 4,373; Growth (since 2000): 2.4%; Density: 59.3 persons per square mile; Race: 97.8% White, 0.6% Black/African American, 0.3% Asian, 0.1% American Indian/Alaska Native, 0.0% Native Hawaiian/Other Pacific Islander, 0.9% Two or more races, 1.4% Hispanic of any race; Average household size: 2.62; Median age: 40.8; Age under 18: 24.4%; Age 65 and over: 12.4%; Males per 100 females: 103.1; Marriage status: 20.3% never married, 64.3% now married, 1.4% separated, 4.3% widowed, 11.2% divorced; Foreign born: 0.5%; Speak English only: 99.4%; With disability: 19.3%; Veterans: 10.5%; Ancestry: 20.2% German, 15.6% English, 15.3% American, 12.6% Irish, 4.1% Polish
Employment: 12.7% management, business, and financial, 3.7% computer, engineering, and science, 10.4% education, legal, community service, arts, and media, 1.9% healthcare practitioners, 18.7% service, 16.9% sales and office, 8.3% natural resources, construction, and maintenance, 27.4% production, transportation, and material moving
Income: Per capita: $20,976; Median household: $48,447; Average household: $54,477; Households with income of $100,000 or more: 8.4%; Poverty rate: 13.4%
Educational Attainment: High school diploma or higher: 84.0%; Bachelor's degree or higher: 11.7%; Graduate/professional degree or higher: 2.3%
School District(s)
Scott County SD 2 (PK-12)
    2012-13 Enrollment: 2,808 . . . . (812) 752-8946
Housing: Homeownership rate: 85.7%; Median home value: $112,000; Median year structure built: 1982; Homeowner vacancy rate: 1.6%; Median gross rent: $775 per month; Rental vacancy rate: 6.3%
Health Insurance: 87.8% have insurance; 70.2% have private insurance; 31.2% have public insurance; 12.2% do not have insurance; 4.7% of children under 18 do not have insurance
Transportation: Commute: 97.0% car, 0.7% public transportation, 0.7% walk, 0.9% work from home; Median travel time to work: 26.6 minutes

MADISON (city). County seat. Covers a land area of 8.575 square miles and a water area of 0.272 square miles. Located at 38.76° N. Lat; 85.40° W. Long. Elevation is 489 feet.

History: Madison was settled in 1805, and the town was platted in 1809 by Colonel John Paul, a Revolutionary War soldier, who named it for President James Madison. Shipyards flourished here in the 1830's, and by 1850 Madison was the largest city in Indiana. Tobacco was an important part of the economy in the early 1900's.

Population: 11,967; Growth (since 2000): -0.3%; Density: 1,395.6 persons per square mile; Race: 93.5% White, 2.8% Black/African American, 1.2% Asian, 0.2% American Indian/Alaska Native, 0.0% Native Hawaiian/Other Pacific Islander, 1.6% Two or more races, 1.7% Hispanic of any race; Average household size: 2.18; Median age: 42.2; Age under 18: 21.0%; Age 65 and over: 17.2%; Males per 100 females: 81.2; Marriage status: 27.9% never married, 47.1% now married, 1.1% separated, 9.5% widowed, 15.4% divorced; Foreign born: 1.4%; Speak English only: 96.7%; With disability: 16.1%; Veterans: 8.8%; Ancestry: 20.0% German, 11.6% English, 11.1% Irish, 10.8% American, 3.4% Scottish

Employment: 8.5% management, business, and financial, 3.1% computer, engineering, and science, 12.6% education, legal, community service, arts, and media, 7.7% healthcare practitioners, 19.5% service, 24.0% sales and office, 8.8% natural resources, construction, and maintenance, 15.7% production, transportation, and material moving

Income: Per capita: $24,256; Median household: $45,882; Average household: $56,838; Households with income of $100,000 or more: 12.6%; Poverty rate: 10.2%

Educational Attainment: High school diploma or higher: 83.4%; Bachelor's degree or higher: 22.6%; Graduate/professional degree or higher: 11.3%

School District(s)
In Department of Correction (06-12)
    2012-13 Enrollment: 484 . . . . (317) 233-3111
Madison Consolidated Schools (KG-12)
    2012-13 Enrollment: 3,039 . . . . (812) 273-8511

Housing: Homeownership rate: 62.6%; Median home value: $117,800; Median year structure built: 1964; Homeowner vacancy rate: 3.9%; Median gross rent: $604 per month; Rental vacancy rate: 11.2%

Health Insurance: 85.7% have insurance; 68.9% have private insurance; 32.7% have public insurance; 14.3% do not have insurance; 11.2% of children under 18 do not have insurance

Hospitals: King's Daughters' Health (142 beds)

Newspapers: Madison Courier (daily circulation 8800)

Transportation: Commute: 92.1% car, 0.5% public transportation, 2.1% walk, 3.7% work from home; Median travel time to work: 18.7 minutes

Airports: Madison Municipal (general aviation)

Additional Information Contacts
City of Madison . . . . (812) 265-8300
    http://www.madison-in.gov

Jennings County

Located in southeastern Indiana; drained by Vernon, Graham, and Sand Creeks. Covers a land area of 376.583 square miles, a water area of 1.762 square miles, and is located in the Eastern Time Zone at 39.00° N. Lat., 85.63° W. Long. The county was founded in 1816. County seat is Vernon.

Jennings County is part of the North Vernon, IN Micropolitan Statistical Area. The entire metro area includes: Jennings County, IN

Weather Station: North Vernon 1 NW   Elevation: 745 feet

	Jan	Feb	Mar	Apr	May	Jun	Jul	Aug	Sep	Oct	Nov	Dec
High	40	45	55	67	75	83	86	85	79	68	55	43
Low	24	26	34	43	52	61	65	63	56	45	36	26
Precip	2.4	2.6	3.7	4.5	5.0	4.0	4.4	4.6	3.2	3.7	3.9	3.6
Snow	2.7	3.1	1.5	tr	tr	0.0	0.0	0.0	0.0	0.0	0.0	3.5

High and Low temperatures in degrees Fahrenheit; Precipitation and Snow in inches

Population: 28,525; Growth (since 2000): 3.5%; Density: 75.7 persons per square mile; Race: 96.8% White, 0.8% Black/African American, 0.2% Asian, 0.1% American Indian/Alaska Native, 0.0% Native Hawaiian/Other Pacific Islander, 1.2% two or more races, 2.0% Hispanic of any race; Average household size: 2.64; Median age: 38.4; Age under 18: 26.4%; Age 65 and over: 12.6%; Males per 100 females: 100.4; Marriage status: 24.4% never married, 54.7% now married, 1.3% separated, 6.9% widowed, 14.0% divorced; Foreign born: 1.2%; Speak English only: 97.2%; With disability: 14.8%; Veterans: 10.5%; Ancestry: 22.4% German, 16.7% American, 13.5% Irish, 8.0% English, 2.0% French

Religion: Six largest groups: 18.6% Baptist, 7.8% Catholicism, 3.1% Methodist/Pietist, 2.0% Latter-day Saints, 1.9% Holiness, 1.3% Non-denominational Protestant

Economy: Unemployment rate: 5.7%; Leading industries: 18.1% health care and social assistance; 16.6% retail trade; 10.7% construction; Farms: 528 totaling 123,391 acres; Company size: 0 employ 1,000 or more persons, 1 employs 500 to 999 persons, 13 employ 100 to 499 persons, 389 employ less than 100 persons; Business ownership: n/a women-owned, n/a Black-owned, n/a Hispanic-owned, 28 Asian-owned

Employment: 10.2% management, business, and financial, 2.5% computer, engineering, and science, 6.8% education, legal, community service, arts, and media, 6.0% healthcare practitioners, 19.3% service, 19.8% sales and office, 11.0% natural resources, construction, and maintenance, 24.5% production, transportation, and material moving

Income: Per capita: $20,109; Median household: $44,128; Average household: $52,493; Households with income of $100,000 or more: 10.5%; Poverty rate: 16.7%

Educational Attainment: High school diploma or higher: 85.3%; Bachelor's degree or higher: 9.6%; Graduate/professional degree or higher: 3.4%

Housing: Homeownership rate: 76.7%; Median home value: $89,700; Median year structure built: 1979; Homeowner vacancy rate: 2.3%; Median gross rent: $693 per month; Rental vacancy rate: 10.7%

Vital Statistics: Birth rate: 123.9 per 10,000 population; Death rate: 98.4 per 10,000 population; Age-adjusted cancer mortality rate: 199.3 deaths per 100,000 population

Health Insurance: 84.4% have insurance; 64.5% have private insurance; 32.7% have public insurance; 15.6% do not have insurance; 8.6% of children under 18 do not have insurance

Health Care: Physicians: 6.7 per 10,000 population; Hospital beds: 8.9 per 10,000 population; Hospital admissions: 133.3 per 10,000 population

Transportation: Commute: 94.0% car, 0.6% public transportation, 1.0% walk, 2.7% work from home; Median travel time to work: 25.5 minutes

Presidential Election: 37.3% Obama, 59.7% Romney (2012)

National and State Parks: Brush Creek State Fish and Wildlife Area; Crosley State Fish and Wildlife Area; Selmier State Forest

Additional Information Contacts
Jennings Government . . . . (812) 352-3005
    http://www.jenningscounty-in.gov

Jennings County Communities

BUTLERVILLE (CDP). Covers a land area of 0.378 square miles and a water area of 0 square miles. Located at 39.03° N. Lat; 85.51° W. Long. Elevation is 807 feet.

Population: 282; Growth (since 2000): n/a; Density: 745.1 persons per square mile; Race: 98.2% White, 0.0% Black/African American, 0.7% Asian, 0.4% American Indian/Alaska Native, 0.0% Native Hawaiian/Other Pacific Islander, 0.4% Two or more races, 1.1% Hispanic of any race; Average household size: 2.64; Median age: 37.6; Age under 18: 24.5%; Age 65 and over: 10.6%; Males per 100 females: 105.8

Housing: Homeownership rate: 76.6%; Homeowner vacancy rate: 4.6%; Rental vacancy rate: 21.9%

COMMISKEY (unincorporated postal area)
ZCTA: 47227
    Covers a land area of 49.146 square miles and a water area of 0.115 square miles. Located at 38.87° N. Lat; 85.65° W. Long. Elevation is 696 feet.

    Population: 1,598; Growth (since 2000): 16.6%; Density: 32.5 persons per square mile; Race: 99.3% White, 0.1% Black/African American, 0.1% Asian, 0.0% American Indian/Alaska Native, 0.0% Native Hawaiian/Other Pacific Islander, 0.4% Two or more races, 0.3% Hispanic of any race; Average household size: 2.65; Median age: 39.7; Age under 18: 25.1%; Age 65 and over: 13.0%; Males per 100 females: 102.5

School District(s)
Jennings County Schools (PK-12)
    2012-13 Enrollment: 4,774 . . . . (812) 346-4483
    Housing: Homeownership rate: 84.4%; Homeowner vacancy rate: 1.7%; Rental vacancy rate: 8.7%

COUNTRY SQUIRE LAKES (CDP). Covers a land area of 2.562 square miles and a water area of 0.139 square miles. Located at 39.04° N. Lat; 85.69° W. Long. Elevation is 702 feet.
Population: 3,571; Growth (since 2000): n/a; Density: 1,393.7 persons per square mile; Race: 93.0% White, 1.2% Black/African American, 0.2% Asian, 0.1% American Indian/Alaska Native, 0.0% Native Hawaiian/Other Pacific Islander, 2.2% Two or more races, 5.4% Hispanic of any race; Average household size: 2.73; Median age: 35.2; Age under 18: 29.2%; Age 65 and over: 11.2%; Males per 100 females: 102.3; Marriage status: 30.1% never married, 44.2% now married, 2.0% separated, 6.4% widowed, 19.2% divorced; Foreign born: 4.3%; Speak English only: 90.3%; With disability: 23.0%; Veterans: 14.4%; Ancestry: 15.7% American, 13.9% German, 11.0% Irish, 5.9% English, 2.9% French
Employment: 4.1% management, business, and financial, 3.5% computer, engineering, and science, 5.9% education, legal, community service, arts, and media, 1.9% healthcare practitioners, 24.5% service, 15.8% sales and office, 8.9% natural resources, construction, and maintenance, 35.5% production, transportation, and material moving
Income: Per capita: $13,779; Median household: $31,375; Average household: $35,009; Households with income of $100,000 or more: 0.9%; Poverty rate: 32.1%
Educational Attainment: High school diploma or higher: 69.9%; Bachelor's degree or higher: 2.7%; Graduate/professional degree or higher: n/a
Housing: Homeownership rate: 77.0%; Median home value: $28,800; Median year structure built: 1985; Homeowner vacancy rate: 4.6%; Median gross rent: $704 per month; Rental vacancy rate: 19.1%
Health Insurance: 73.1% have insurance; 37.3% have private insurance; 50.2% have public insurance; 26.9% do not have insurance; 13.0% of children under 18 do not have insurance
Transportation: Commute: 91.4% car, 0.0% public transportation, 1.2% walk, 3.6% work from home; Median travel time to work: 28.4 minutes

HAYDEN (CDP). Covers a land area of 2.474 square miles and a water area of 0 square miles. Located at 38.97° N. Lat; 85.74° W. Long. Elevation is 620 feet.
Population: 521; Growth (since 2000): n/a; Density: 210.6 persons per square mile; Race: 97.5% White, 0.8% Black/African American, 0.2% Asian, 0.4% American Indian/Alaska Native, 0.0% Native Hawaiian/Other Pacific Islander, 0.6% Two or more races, 2.7% Hispanic of any race; Average household size: 2.96; Median age: 34.6; Age under 18: 31.5%; Age 65 and over: 6.9%; Males per 100 females: 110.9
School District(s)
Jennings County Schools (PK-12)
   2012-13 Enrollment: 4,774 . . . . (812) 346-4483
Housing: Homeownership rate: 82.4%; Homeowner vacancy rate: 2.7%; Rental vacancy rate: 6.1%

NORTH VERNON (city). Covers a land area of 6.619 square miles and a water area of 0.010 square miles. Located at 39.01° N. Lat; 85.63° W. Long. Elevation is 718 feet.
History: North Vernon was platted in 1854 as a railroad town and trading center.
Population: 6,728; Growth (since 2000): 3.3%; Density: 1,016.5 persons per square mile; Race: 95.0% White, 1.5% Black/African American, 0.4% Asian, 0.2% American Indian/Alaska Native, 0.0% Native Hawaiian/Other Pacific Islander, 1.7% Two or more races, 2.4% Hispanic of any race; Average household size: 2.43; Median age: 35.6; Age under 18: 26.5%; Age 65 and over: 14.1%; Males per 100 females: 91.7; Marriage status: 26.4% never married, 46.6% now married, 2.0% separated, 8.1% widowed, 18.9% divorced; Foreign born: 0.6%; Speak English only: 98.2%; With disability: 17.7%; Veterans: 8.3%; Ancestry: 20.2% German, 16.6% American, 8.6% Irish, 8.0% English, 3.8% French
Employment: 4.5% management, business, and financial, 2.1% computer, engineering, and science, 6.2% education, legal, community service, arts, and media, 7.9% healthcare practitioners, 26.6% service, 19.6% sales and office, 7.0% natural resources, construction, and maintenance, 26.1% production, transportation, and material moving
Income: Per capita: $17,792; Median household: $35,106; Average household: $44,507; Households with income of $100,000 or more: 5.7%; Poverty rate: 28.3%
Educational Attainment: High school diploma or higher: 82.3%; Bachelor's degree or higher: 11.3%; Graduate/professional degree or higher: 5.7%

School District(s)
Jennings County Schools (PK-12)
   2012-13 Enrollment: 4,774 . . . . (812) 346-4483
Housing: Homeownership rate: 56.7%; Median home value: $78,400; Median year structure built: 1965; Homeowner vacancy rate: 3.5%; Median gross rent: $642 per month; Rental vacancy rate: 11.0%
Health Insurance: 79.0% have insurance; 52.1% have private insurance; 40.6% have public insurance; 21.0% do not have insurance; 12.5% of children under 18 do not have insurance
Hospitals: Saint Vincent Jennings Hospital (25 beds)
Safety: Violent crime rate: 33.1 per 10,000 population; Property crime rate: 590.4 per 10,000 population
Newspapers: North Vernon Plain Dealer (weekly circulation 7000); North Vernon Sun (weekly circulation 6000)
Transportation: Commute: 92.2% car, 0.0% public transportation, 2.2% walk, 3.3% work from home; Median travel time to work: 21.5 minutes
Additional Information Contacts
City of North Vernon . . . . (812) 346-5907
   http://www.northvernon-in.gov

PARIS CROSSING (unincorporated postal area)
ZCTA: 47270
   Covers a land area of 18.579 square miles and a water area of 0.058 square miles. Located at 38.84° N. Lat; 85.72° W. Long. Elevation is 623 feet.
Population: 807; Growth (since 2000): -1.5%; Density: 43.4 persons per square mile; Race: 99.6% White, 0.0% Black/African American, 0.0% Asian, 0.2% American Indian/Alaska Native, 0.0% Native Hawaiian/Other Pacific Islander, 0.1% Two or more races, 0.4% Hispanic of any race; Average household size: 2.60; Median age: 42.2; Age under 18: 22.3%; Age 65 and over: 15.4%; Males per 100 females: 104.3
Housing: Homeownership rate: 90.6%; Homeowner vacancy rate: 1.4%; Rental vacancy rate: 3.3%

SCIPIO (CDP). Covers a land area of 1.148 square miles and a water area of 0.020 square miles. Located at 39.07° N. Lat; 85.72° W. Long. Elevation is 679 feet.
Population: 153; Growth (since 2000): n/a; Density: 133.3 persons per square mile; Race: 100.0% White, 0.0% Black/African American, 0.0% Asian, 0.0% American Indian/Alaska Native, 0.0% Native Hawaiian/Other Pacific Islander, 0.0% Two or more races, 0.7% Hispanic of any race; Average household size: 2.39; Median age: 45.2; Age under 18: 22.2%; Age 65 and over: 15.0%; Males per 100 females: 86.6
School District(s)
Jennings County Schools (PK-12)
   2012-13 Enrollment: 4,774 . . . . (812) 346-4483
Housing: Homeownership rate: 89.0%; Homeowner vacancy rate: 1.7%; Rental vacancy rate: 0.0%

VERNON (town). County seat. Covers a land area of 0.238 square miles and a water area of 0 square miles. Located at 38.99° N. Lat; 85.61° W. Long. Elevation is 663 feet.
History: The land grant that established Vernon in 1815 stipulated that it should be the county seat forever.
Population: 318; Growth (since 2000): -3.6%; Density: 1,337.7 persons per square mile; Race: 97.5% White, 0.3% Black/African American, 0.3% Asian, 0.0% American Indian/Alaska Native, 0.0% Native Hawaiian/Other Pacific Islander, 1.6% Two or more races, 0.6% Hispanic of any race; Average household size: 2.37; Median age: 39.3; Age under 18: 26.4%; Age 65 and over: 13.8%; Males per 100 females: 92.7
Housing: Homeownership rate: 64.9%; Homeowner vacancy rate: 2.2%; Rental vacancy rate: 30.9%

Johnson County

Located in central Indiana; drained by the West Fork of the White River. Covers a land area of 320.427 square miles, a water area of 1.363 square miles, and is located in the Eastern Time Zone at 39.50° N. Lat., 86.09° W. Long. The county was founded in 1822. County seat is Franklin.

Johnson County is part of the Indianapolis-Carmel-Anderson, IN Metropolitan Statistical Area. The entire metro area includes: Boone County, IN; Brown County, IN; Hamilton County, IN; Hancock County, IN;

Hendricks County, IN; Johnson County, IN; Madison County, IN; Marion County, IN; Morgan County, IN; Putnam County, IN; Shelby County, IN

Population: 139,654; Growth (since 2000): 21.2%; Density: 435.8 persons per square mile; Race: 93.9% White, 1.1% Black/African American, 2.0% Asian, 0.2% American Indian/Alaska Native, 0.0% Native Hawaiian/Other Pacific Islander, 1.5% two or more races, 3.1% Hispanic of any race; Average household size: 2.63; Median age: 36.8; Age under 18: 26.4%; Age 65 and over: 12.3%; Males per 100 females: 96.8; Marriage status: 24.0% never married, 58.3% now married, 1.1% separated, 5.5% widowed, 12.3% divorced; Foreign born: 3.8%; Speak English only: 94.3%; With disability: 10.0%; Veterans: 9.5%; Ancestry: 25.8% German, 13.0% Irish, 11.5% American, 11.1% English, 3.0% Italian
Religion: Six largest groups: 13.0% Baptist, 12.7% Non-denominational Protestant, 8.3% Catholicism, 5.0% Pentecostal, 2.4% Methodist/Pietist, 1.5% Lutheran
Economy: Unemployment rate: 4.6%; Leading industries: 16.5% retail trade; 11.3% health care and social assistance; 10.9% construction; Farms: 562 totaling 144,646 acres; Company size: 0 employ 1,000 or more persons, 4 employ 500 to 999 persons, 65 employ 100 to 499 persons, 2,963 employ less than 100 persons; Business ownership: 3,185 women-owned, n/a Black-owned, 96 Hispanic-owned, 371 Asian-owned
Employment: 14.7% management, business, and financial, 4.9% computer, engineering, and science, 8.8% education, legal, community service, arts, and media, 6.7% healthcare practitioners, 14.9% service, 27.1% sales and office, 9.3% natural resources, construction, and maintenance, 13.5% production, transportation, and material moving
Income: Per capita: $28,575; Median household: $61,231; Average household: $76,423; Households with income of $100,000 or more: 24.4%; Poverty rate: 10.6%
Educational Attainment: High school diploma or higher: 91.0%; Bachelor's degree or higher: 26.8%; Graduate/professional degree or higher: 8.8%
Housing: Homeownership rate: 73.9%; Median home value: $144,300; Median year structure built: 1987; Homeowner vacancy rate: 2.1%; Median gross rent: $830 per month; Rental vacancy rate: 10.4%
Vital Statistics: Birth rate: 129.2 per 10,000 population; Death rate: 80.3 per 10,000 population; Age-adjusted cancer mortality rate: 173.1 deaths per 100,000 population
Health Insurance: 88.9% have insurance; 75.7% have private insurance; 23.9% have public insurance; 11.1% do not have insurance; 6.0% of children under 18 do not have insurance
Health Care: Physicians: 21.0 per 10,000 population; Hospital beds: 18.6 per 10,000 population; Hospital admissions: 379.7 per 10,000 population
Air Quality Index: 97.3% good, 2.7% moderate, 0.0% unhealthy for sensitive individuals, 0.0% unhealthy (percent of days)
Transportation: Commute: 93.2% car, 0.3% public transportation, 1.3% walk, 4.2% work from home; Median travel time to work: 26.1 minutes
Presidential Election: 29.8% Obama, 68.2% Romney (2012)
National and State Parks: Atterbury State Fish and Wildlife Area
Additional Information Contacts
Johnson Government . . . . (317) 346-4700
http://www.co.johnson.in.us

Johnson County Communities

BARGERSVILLE (town). Covers a land area of 4.926 square miles and a water area of 0 square miles. Located at 39.54° N. Lat; 86.16° W. Long. Elevation is 820 feet.
Population: 4,013; Growth (since 2000): 89.3%; Density: 814.7 persons per square mile; Race: 95.6% White, 1.1% Black/African American, 1.0% Asian, 0.3% American Indian/Alaska Native, 0.0% Native Hawaiian/Other Pacific Islander, 1.6% Two or more races, 2.1% Hispanic of any race; Average household size: 2.69; Median age: 33.2; Age under 18: 29.2%; Age 65 and over: 7.7%; Males per 100 females: 104.8; Marriage status: 15.6% never married, 68.8% now married, 2.0% separated, 4.7% widowed, 10.9% divorced; Foreign born: 3.0%; Speak English only: 93.1%; With disability: 7.0%; Veterans: 11.0%; Ancestry: 29.4% German, 16.7% Irish, 13.3% English, 12.0% American, 4.4% Italian
Employment: 16.8% management, business, and financial, 3.4% computer, engineering, and science, 6.3% education, legal, community service, arts, and media, 4.9% healthcare practitioners, 17.8% service, 29.3% sales and office, 7.3% natural resources, construction, and maintenance, 14.2% production, transportation, and material moving
Income: Per capita: $32,688; Median household: $73,205; Average household: $88,451; Households with income of $100,000 or more: 27.6%; Poverty rate: 11.6%
Educational Attainment: High school diploma or higher: 94.3%; Bachelor's degree or higher: 31.7%; Graduate/professional degree or higher: 9.0%
School District(s)
Center Grove Com Sch Corp (KG-12)
    2012-13 Enrollment: 7,587 . . . . (317) 881-9326
Franklin Community School Corp (KG-12)
    2012-13 Enrollment: 5,062 . . . . (317) 738-5800
Housing: Homeownership rate: 70.4%; Median home value: $169,700; Median year structure built: 1996; Homeowner vacancy rate: 2.9%; Median gross rent: $811 per month; Rental vacancy rate: 20.9%
Health Insurance: 93.2% have insurance; 85.4% have private insurance; 15.9% have public insurance; 6.8% do not have insurance; 0.5% of children under 18 do not have insurance
Transportation: Commute: 89.0% car, 0.0% public transportation, 0.9% walk, 8.5% work from home; Median travel time to work: 30.6 minutes
Additional Information Contacts
Town of Bargersville . . . . (317) 422-5115
http://www.townofbargersville.org

EDINBURGH (town). Covers a land area of 3.109 square miles and a water area of 0 square miles. Located at 39.35° N. Lat; 85.96° W. Long. Elevation is 673 feet.
Population: 4,480; Growth (since 2000): -0.6%; Density: 1,440.8 persons per square mile; Race: 95.2% White, 0.3% Black/African American, 0.1% Asian, 0.2% American Indian/Alaska Native, 0.0% Native Hawaiian/Other Pacific Islander, 1.1% Two or more races, 5.5% Hispanic of any race; Average household size: 2.55; Median age: 38.3; Age under 18: 24.5%; Age 65 and over: 12.0%; Males per 100 females: 99.6; Marriage status: 22.0% never married, 52.6% now married, 2.6% separated, 9.9% widowed, 15.4% divorced; Foreign born: 2.0%; Speak English only: 95.2%; With disability: 20.9%; Veterans: 8.8%; Ancestry: 15.6% American, 14.2% German, 5.9% Irish, 5.7% English, 2.7% Welsh
Employment: 6.4% management, business, and financial, 1.0% computer, engineering, and science, 5.9% education, legal, community service, arts, and media, 2.4% healthcare practitioners, 13.8% service, 23.2% sales and office, 10.0% natural resources, construction, and maintenance, 37.3% production, transportation, and material moving
Income: Per capita: $16,878; Median household: $37,500; Average household: $44,251; Households with income of $100,000 or more: 6.1%; Poverty rate: 23.7%
Educational Attainment: High school diploma or higher: 80.6%; Bachelor's degree or higher: 7.7%; Graduate/professional degree or higher: 2.3%
School District(s)
Edinburgh Community Sch Corp (PK-12)
    2012-13 Enrollment: 939 . . . . (812) 526-2681
Housing: Homeownership rate: 61.3%; Median home value: $84,300; Median year structure built: 1965; Homeowner vacancy rate: 3.3%; Median gross rent: $703 per month; Rental vacancy rate: 6.8%
Health Insurance: 83.5% have insurance; 53.7% have private insurance; 43.9% have public insurance; 16.5% do not have insurance; 6.7% of children under 18 do not have insurance
Safety: Violent crime rate: 31.0 per 10,000 population; Property crime rate: 1,009.1 per 10,000 population
Transportation: Commute: 90.8% car, 0.0% public transportation, 4.9% walk, 1.2% work from home; Median travel time to work: 17.9 minutes
Additional Information Contacts
Town of Edinburgh . . . . (812) 526-3511
http://www.edinburgh.in.us

FRANKLIN (city). County seat. Covers a land area of 13.006 square miles and a water area of 0 square miles. Located at 39.49° N. Lat; 86.05° W. Long. Elevation is 725 feet.
History: Named for Benjamin Franklin, American statesman and inventor. Franklin developed as a shipping center for grain and tomatoes. In 1834 Franklin College was established as the Indiana Baptist Manual Labor Institute.
Population: 23,712; Growth (since 2000): 21.8%; Density: 1,823.1 persons per square mile; Race: 94.9% White, 1.4% Black/African American, 0.8% Asian, 0.3% American Indian/Alaska Native, 0.0% Native Hawaiian/Other Pacific Islander, 1.6% Two or more races, 2.5% Hispanic

of any race; Average household size: 2.54; Median age: 34.6; Age under 18: 26.3%; Age 65 and over: 14.6%; Males per 100 females: 91.3; Marriage status: 26.9% never married, 51.5% now married, 2.0% separated, 7.1% widowed, 14.4% divorced; Foreign born: 1.9%; Speak English only: 96.1%; With disability: 13.4%; Veterans: 11.1%; Ancestry: 24.6% German, 13.0% American, 11.9% Irish, 9.7% English, 1.9% Scottish
Employment: 10.1% management, business, and financial, 2.9% computer, engineering, and science, 10.6% education, legal, community service, arts, and media, 4.9% healthcare practitioners, 18.1% service, 26.6% sales and office, 8.6% natural resources, construction, and maintenance, 18.2% production, transportation, and material moving
Income: Per capita: $23,537; Median household: $48,415; Average household: $62,447; Households with income of $100,000 or more: 17.7%; Poverty rate: 15.0%
Educational Attainment: High school diploma or higher: 88.5%; Bachelor's degree or higher: 20.9%; Graduate/professional degree or higher: 7.9%

School District(s)
Clark-Pleasant Com School Corp (KG-12)
    2012-13 Enrollment: 6,038 . . . . (317) 535-7579
Franklin Community School Corp (KG-12)
    2012-13 Enrollment: 5,062 . . . . (317) 738-5800

Four-year College(s)
Franklin College (Private, Not-for-profit, American Baptist)
    Fall 2013 Enrollment: 1,014 . . . . (317) 738-8000
    2013-14 Tuition: In-state $27,695; Out-of-state $27,695
Housing: Homeownership rate: 65.8%; Median home value: $115,700; Median year structure built: 1990; Homeowner vacancy rate: 2.7%; Median gross rent: $835 per month; Rental vacancy rate: 11.1%
Health Insurance: 89.6% have insurance; 72.6% have private insurance; 29.0% have public insurance; 10.4% do not have insurance; 4.0% of children under 18 do not have insurance
Hospitals: Johnson Memorial Hospital (161 beds)
Safety: Violent crime rate: 28.7 per 10,000 population; Property crime rate: 381.1 per 10,000 population
Newspapers: Daily Journal (daily circulation 17100)
Transportation: Commute: 91.4% car, 1.2% public transportation, 2.7% walk, 2.8% work from home; Median travel time to work: 23.8 minutes
Additional Information Contacts
City of Franklin . . . . (317) 736-3609
http://www.franklin.in.gov

GREENWOOD (city). Covers a land area of 21.230 square miles and a water area of <.001 square miles. Located at 39.61° N. Lat; 86.11° W. Long. Elevation is 804 feet.
History: Named for Samuel Greenwood who plotted the village in 1872. Greenwood developed as an industrial town with automobile-parts factories and a canning company.
Population: 49,791; Growth (since 2000): 38.2%; Density: 2,345.3 persons per square mile; Race: 90.1% White, 1.7% Black/African American, 3.7% Asian, 0.3% American Indian/Alaska Native, 0.1% Native Hawaiian/Other Pacific Islander, 2.1% Two or more races, 5.0% Hispanic of any race; Average household size: 2.51; Median age: 34.0; Age under 18: 26.6%; Age 65 and over: 11.6%; Males per 100 females: 93.9; Marriage status: 26.4% never married, 53.9% now married, 0.9% separated, 5.9% widowed, 13.9% divorced; Foreign born: 7.4%; Speak English only: 90.5%; With disability: 9.7%; Veterans: 9.6%; Ancestry: 25.8% German, 12.2% Irish, 11.1% English, 9.8% American, 3.5% Italian
Employment: 13.5% management, business, and financial, 6.2% computer, engineering, and science, 7.5% education, legal, community service, arts, and media, 7.1% healthcare practitioners, 14.9% service, 27.1% sales and office, 9.8% natural resources, construction, and maintenance, 14.0% production, transportation, and material moving
Income: Per capita: $26,646; Median household: $52,252; Average household: $66,335; Households with income of $100,000 or more: 19.4%; Poverty rate: 14.2%
Educational Attainment: High school diploma or higher: 89.6%; Bachelor's degree or higher: 26.4%; Graduate/professional degree or higher: 8.3%

School District(s)
Center Grove Com Sch Corp (KG-12)
    2012-13 Enrollment: 7,587 . . . . (317) 881-9326
Central Nine Career Center (09-12)
    2012-13 Enrollment: n/a . . . . (317) 888-4401
Clark-Pleasant Com School Corp (KG-12)
    2012-13 Enrollment: 6,038 . . . . (317) 535-7579
Greenwood Community Sch Corp (KG-12)
    2012-13 Enrollment: 3,821 . . . . (317) 889-4060

Two-year College(s)
MedTech College-Greenwood Campus (Private, For-profit)
    Fall 2013 Enrollment: 551 . . . . (317) 534-0322
Housing: Homeownership rate: 62.3%; Median home value: $131,900; Median year structure built: 1991; Homeowner vacancy rate: 2.5%; Median gross rent: $811 per month; Rental vacancy rate: 10.9%
Health Insurance: 84.8% have insurance; 69.2% have private insurance; 26.3% have public insurance; 15.2% do not have insurance; 9.4% of children under 18 do not have insurance
Safety: Violent crime rate: 37.6 per 10,000 population; Property crime rate: 358.6 per 10,000 population
Newspapers: Franklin Challenger (weekly circulation 3600); Southside Challenger (weekly circulation 4200)
Transportation: Commute: 95.8% car, 0.4% public transportation, 0.5% walk, 2.8% work from home; Median travel time to work: 25.8 minutes
Airports: Greenwood Municipal (general aviation)
Additional Information Contacts
City of Greenwood. . . . . (317) 881-8527
http://www.greenwood.in.gov

NEEDHAM (unincorporated postal area)
ZCTA: 46162
    Covers a land area of 11.233 square miles and a water area of 0.029 square miles. Located at 39.55° N. Lat; 85.95° W. Long. Elevation is 728 feet.
Population: 458; Growth (since 2000): 11.4%; Density: 40.8 persons per square mile; Race: 98.3% White, 0.2% Black/African American, 0.0% Asian, 0.0% American Indian/Alaska Native, 0.0% Native Hawaiian/Other Pacific Islander, 1.1% Two or more races, 0.9% Hispanic of any race; Average household size: 2.52; Median age: 44.7; Age under 18: 22.1%; Age 65 and over: 11.8%; Males per 100 females: 113.0
Housing: Homeownership rate: 78.5%; Homeowner vacancy rate: 0.7%; Rental vacancy rate: 9.1%

NEW WHITELAND (town). Covers a land area of 1.461 square miles and a water area of 0 square miles. Located at 39.56° N. Lat; 86.10° W. Long. Elevation is 807 feet.
Population: 5,472; Growth (since 2000): 19.5%; Density: 3,744.4 persons per square mile; Race: 96.6% White, 0.4% Black/African American, 1.0% Asian, 0.1% American Indian/Alaska Native, 0.0% Native Hawaiian/Other Pacific Islander, 1.4% Two or more races, 2.0% Hispanic of any race; Average household size: 2.87; Median age: 33.7; Age under 18: 29.8%; Age 65 and over: 10.4%; Males per 100 females: 94.6; Marriage status: 22.5% never married, 60.7% now married, 0.0% separated, 5.4% widowed, 11.5% divorced; Foreign born: 1.1%; Speak English only: 98.3%; With disability: 8.1%; Veterans: 7.7%; Ancestry: 19.5% German, 14.2% Irish, 8.6% English, 7.1% American, 2.7% Italian
Employment: 11.0% management, business, and financial, 2.6% computer, engineering, and science, 1.6% education, legal, community service, arts, and media, 5.3% healthcare practitioners, 19.2% service, 26.5% sales and office, 10.0% natural resources, construction, and maintenance, 23.7% production, transportation, and material moving
Income: Per capita: $20,431; Median household: $57,033; Average household: $58,028; Households with income of $100,000 or more: 8.0%; Poverty rate: 6.5%
Educational Attainment: High school diploma or higher: 91.9%; Bachelor's degree or higher: 8.8%; Graduate/professional degree or higher: 0.3%

School District(s)
Clark-Pleasant Com School Corp (KG-12)
    2012-13 Enrollment: 6,038 . . . . (317) 535-7579
Housing: Homeownership rate: 84.4%; Median home value: $95,300; Median year structure built: 1971; Homeowner vacancy rate: 2.5%; Median gross rent: $1,209 per month; Rental vacancy rate: 3.9%
Health Insurance: 87.3% have insurance; 72.6% have private insurance; 23.4% have public insurance; 12.7% do not have insurance; 1.5% of children under 18 do not have insurance
Safety: Violent crime rate: 10.6 per 10,000 population; Property crime rate: 45.9 per 10,000 population

Transportation: Commute: 98.5% car, 0.0% public transportation, 0.0% walk, 1.5% work from home; Median travel time to work: 26.5 minutes
Additional Information Contacts
Town of New Whiteland . . . . (317) 535-9487
http://www.townofnewwhiteland.com

PRINCES LAKES (town). Covers a land area of 1.348 square miles and a water area of 0.172 square miles. Located at 39.35° N. Lat; 86.11° W. Long. Elevation is 820 feet.
Population: 1,312; Growth (since 2000): -12.9%; Density: 973.6 persons per square mile; Race: 98.8% White, 0.2% Black/African American, 0.3% Asian, 0.4% American Indian/Alaska Native, 0.0% Native Hawaiian/Other Pacific Islander, 0.3% Two or more races, 0.9% Hispanic of any race; Average household size: 2.48; Median age: 42.5; Age under 18: 23.0%; Age 65 and over: 11.0%; Males per 100 females: 94.1
Housing: Homeownership rate: 87.0%; Homeowner vacancy rate: 6.7%; Rental vacancy rate: 8.0%

TRAFALGAR (town). Covers a land area of 2.638 square miles and a water area of 0 square miles. Located at 39.41° N. Lat; 86.15° W. Long. Elevation is 827 feet.
History: Laid out 1850.
Population: 1,101; Growth (since 2000): 38.0%; Density: 417.4 persons per square mile; Race: 96.3% White, 0.9% Black/African American, 0.5% Asian, 0.9% American Indian/Alaska Native, 0.0% Native Hawaiian/Other Pacific Islander, 1.1% Two or more races, 1.0% Hispanic of any race; Average household size: 2.83; Median age: 34.2; Age under 18: 30.2%; Age 65 and over: 8.2%; Males per 100 females: 97.3
School District(s)
Nineveh-Hensley-Jackson United (KG-12)
    2012-13 Enrollment: 1,850 . . . . (317) 878-2100
Housing: Homeownership rate: 77.6%; Homeowner vacancy rate: 3.8%; Rental vacancy rate: 6.5%

WHITELAND (town). Covers a land area of 3.219 square miles and a water area of 0 square miles. Located at 39.55° N. Lat; 86.08° W. Long. Elevation is 794 feet.
Population: 4,169; Growth (since 2000): 5.3%; Density: 1,294.9 persons per square mile; Race: 97.0% White, 0.4% Black/African American, 0.7% Asian, 0.2% American Indian/Alaska Native, 0.1% Native Hawaiian/Other Pacific Islander, 1.1% Two or more races, 1.8% Hispanic of any race; Average household size: 2.84; Median age: 37.3; Age under 18: 27.6%; Age 65 and over: 8.5%; Males per 100 females: 96.4; Marriage status: 17.6% never married, 63.2% now married, 1.4% separated, 5.5% widowed, 13.7% divorced; Foreign born: 1.5%; Speak English only: 98.9%; With disability: 13.2%; Veterans: 5.9%; Ancestry: 22.4% German, 12.4% Irish, 11.4% American, 10.2% English, 2.8% Scottish
Employment: 16.6% management, business, and financial, 3.3% computer, engineering, and science, 9.3% education, legal, community service, arts, and media, 2.9% healthcare practitioners, 16.3% service, 32.7% sales and office, 6.6% natural resources, construction, and maintenance, 12.3% production, transportation, and material moving
Income: Per capita: $26,400; Median household: $71,146; Average household: $72,336; Households with income of $100,000 or more: 21.3%; Poverty rate: 5.6%
Educational Attainment: High school diploma or higher: 90.3%; Bachelor's degree or higher: 21.0%; Graduate/professional degree or higher: 4.7%
School District(s)
Clark-Pleasant Com School Corp (KG-12)
    2012-13 Enrollment: 6,038 . . . . (317) 535-7579
Housing: Homeownership rate: 85.3%; Median home value: $126,300; Median year structure built: 1989; Homeowner vacancy rate: 1.4%; Median gross rent: $935 per month; Rental vacancy rate: 2.7%
Health Insurance: 92.8% have insurance; 82.3% have private insurance; 19.4% have public insurance; 7.2% do not have insurance; 2.3% of children under 18 do not have insurance
Transportation: Commute: 96.4% car, 0.0% public transportation, 0.7% walk, 3.0% work from home; Median travel time to work: 26.9 minutes
Additional Information Contacts
Town of Whiteland . . . . (317) 535-5531
http://townofwhiteland.com

Knox County

Located in southwestern Indiana; bounded on the west by the Wabash River and the Illinois border, on the east by the West Fork of the White River, and on the south by the White River. Covers a land area of 516.031 square miles, a water area of 8.014 square miles, and is located in the Eastern Time Zone at 38.69° N. Lat., 87.42° W. Long. The county was founded in 1790. County seat is Vincennes.

Knox County is part of the Vincennes, IN Micropolitan Statistical Area. The entire metro area includes: Knox County, IN

Weather Station: Freelandville   Elevation: 549 feet

	Jan	Feb	Mar	Apr	May	Jun	Jul	Aug	Sep	Oct	Nov	Dec
High	37	42	52	64	74	83	86	85	79	66	54	40
Low	22	25	33	43	54	63	66	64	56	45	36	25
Precip	2.8	2.7	3.7	4.2	5.7	3.8	4.8	3.2	3.5	3.9	4.1	3.3
Snow	4.5	3.5	1.5	tr	0.0	0.0	0.0	0.0	0.0	0.2	0.2	4.1

High and Low temperatures in degrees Fahrenheit; Precipitation and Snow in inches

Weather Station: Vincennes 5 NE   Elevation: 450 feet

	Jan	Feb	Mar	Apr	May	Jun	Jul	Aug	Sep	Oct	Nov	Dec
High	38	43	54	65	75	84	88	87	81	69	55	42
Low	22	24	33	43	54	63	66	64	56	44	35	25
Precip	2.7	2.6	3.7	4.4	5.7	4.3	4.4	3.4	3.5	4.0	4.3	3.4
Snow	2.0	1.3	0.7	tr	0.0	0.0	0.0	0.0	0.0	0.0	0.1	3.0

High and Low temperatures in degrees Fahrenheit; Precipitation and Snow in inches

Population: 38,440; Growth (since 2000): -2.1%; Density: 74.5 persons per square mile; Race: 94.9% White, 2.6% Black/African American, 0.6% Asian, 0.2% American Indian/Alaska Native, 0.0% Native Hawaiian/Other Pacific Islander, 1.2% two or more races, 1.5% Hispanic of any race; Average household size: 2.35; Median age: 38.5; Age under 18: 21.3%; Age 65 and over: 15.8%; Males per 100 females: 101.2; Marriage status: 29.4% never married, 50.3% now married, 1.0% separated, 7.1% widowed, 13.2% divorced; Foreign born: 1.3%; Speak English only: 97.9%; With disability: 14.3%; Veterans: 9.0%; Ancestry: 22.1% German, 21.0% American, 11.3% Irish, 8.4% English, 5.6% French
Religion: Six largest groups: 12.7% Catholicism, 12.0% Baptist, 7.1% Holiness, 4.6% Methodist/Pietist, 3.1% Presbyterian-Reformed, 2.6% Non-denominational Protestant
Economy: Unemployment rate: 4.5%; Leading industries: 17.2% retail trade; 12.9% other services (except public administration); 11.8% health care and social assistance; Farms: 496 totaling 329,289 acres; Company size: 1 employs 1,000 or more persons, 1 employs 500 to 999 persons, 15 employ 100 to 499 persons, 915 employ less than 100 persons; Business ownership: 572 women-owned, n/a Black-owned, n/a Hispanic-owned, 47 Asian-owned
Employment: 9.5% management, business, and financial, 3.1% computer, engineering, and science, 8.7% education, legal, community service, arts, and media, 5.7% healthcare practitioners, 19.4% service, 21.9% sales and office, 12.8% natural resources, construction, and maintenance, 19.0% production, transportation, and material moving
Income: Per capita: $21,047; Median household: $42,119; Average household: $52,344; Households with income of $100,000 or more: 11.3%; Poverty rate: 14.0%
Educational Attainment: High school diploma or higher: 86.2%; Bachelor's degree or higher: 14.1%; Graduate/professional degree or higher: 5.2%
Housing: Homeownership rate: 66.7%; Median home value: $84,100; Median year structure built: 1957; Homeowner vacancy rate: 2.2%; Median gross rent: $609 per month; Rental vacancy rate: 9.1%
Vital Statistics: Birth rate: 113.8 per 10,000 population; Death rate: 103.0 per 10,000 population; Age-adjusted cancer mortality rate: 211.3 deaths per 100,000 population
Health Insurance: 85.6% have insurance; 67.9% have private insurance; 31.0% have public insurance; 14.4% do not have insurance; 6.6% of children under 18 do not have insurance
Health Care: Physicians: 23.1 per 10,000 population; Hospital beds: 45.7 per 10,000 population; Hospital admissions: 1,989.1 per 10,000 population
Air Quality Index: 96.7% good, 3.3% moderate, 0.0% unhealthy for sensitive individuals, 0.0% unhealthy (percent of days)
Transportation: Commute: 93.7% car, 0.3% public transportation, 2.6% walk, 2.2% work from home; Median travel time to work: 19.6 minutes
Presidential Election: 34.5% Obama, 63.5% Romney (2012)

National and State Parks: George Rogers Clark National Historical Park; George Rogers Clark State Memorial; White Oak State Fishing Area
Additional Information Contacts
Knox Government .... (812) 885-2521
  http://www.knoxcounty.in.gov

Knox County Communities

BICKNELL (city). Covers a land area of 1.346 square miles and a water area of 0 square miles. Located at 38.77° N. Lat; 87.31° W. Long. Elevation is 515 feet.
History: Coal mining began in Bicknell in 1875, and was responsible for the growth of the community. The town was founded by a Bicknell, an ancestor of Ernest P. Bicknell (1862-1930) who directed American Red Cross activities abroad.
Population: 2,915; Growth (since 2000): -13.7%; Density: 2,165.4 persons per square mile; Race: 97.6% White, 0.5% Black/African American, 0.2% Asian, 0.2% American Indian/Alaska Native, 0.0% Native Hawaiian/Other Pacific Islander, 1.0% Two or more races, 1.9% Hispanic of any race; Average household size: 2.45; Median age: 38.7; Age under 18: 25.1%; Age 65 and over: 16.4%; Males per 100 females: 94.9; Marriage status: 25.9% never married, 47.0% now married, 1.6% separated, 9.4% widowed, 17.6% divorced; Foreign born: 0.4%; Speak English only: 99.5%; With disability: 21.8%; Veterans: 14.7%; Ancestry: 28.2% American, 17.9% German, 9.3% Irish, 4.4% English, 3.5% Scotch-Irish
Employment: 2.5% management, business, and financial, 3.9% computer, engineering, and science, 5.6% education, legal, community service, arts, and media, 3.5% healthcare practitioners, 25.6% service, 10.9% sales and office, 15.6% natural resources, construction, and maintenance, 32.3% production, transportation, and material moving
Income: Per capita: $17,856; Median household: $26,901; Average household: $41,783; Households with income of $100,000 or more: 7.2%; Poverty rate: 20.1%
Educational Attainment: High school diploma or higher: 81.5%; Bachelor's degree or higher: 6.1%; Graduate/professional degree or higher: 2.4%
School District(s)
North Knox School Corp (KG-12)
  2012-13 Enrollment: 1,352 .... (812) 735-4434
Housing: Homeownership rate: 63.8%; Median home value: $53,100; Median year structure built: Before 1940; Homeowner vacancy rate: 3.8%; Median gross rent: $513 per month; Rental vacancy rate: 17.3%
Health Insurance: 82.5% have insurance; 52.2% have private insurance; 42.6% have public insurance; 17.5% do not have insurance; 4.3% of children under 18 do not have insurance
Transportation: Commute: 98.1% car, 0.0% public transportation, 1.9% walk, 0.0% work from home; Median travel time to work: 27.1 minutes
Additional Information Contacts
City of Bicknell.................................... (812) 882-6440
  http://www.knoxcountychamber.com

BRUCEVILLE (town). Covers a land area of 0.343 square miles and a water area of 0 square miles. Located at 38.76° N. Lat; 87.42° W. Long. Elevation is 554 feet.
History: Bruceville was first settled by Major William Bruce in 1805, who built a fort on his land. The town was founded in 1811. Major Bruce operated a tavern and inn here, and raised his family of 25 children. Abraham Lincoln was a guest of Bruce in 1844.
Population: 478; Growth (since 2000): 1.9%; Density: 1,394.1 persons per square mile; Race: 95.6% White, 0.2% Black/African American, 1.0% Asian, 0.4% American Indian/Alaska Native, 0.0% Native Hawaiian/Other Pacific Islander, 1.3% Two or more races, 2.1% Hispanic of any race; Average household size: 2.48; Median age: 35.4; Age under 18: 26.8%; Age 65 and over: 10.5%; Males per 100 females: 92.0
School District(s)
North Knox School Corp (KG-12)
  2012-13 Enrollment: 1,352 .... (812) 735-4434
Housing: Homeownership rate: 76.7%; Homeowner vacancy rate: 4.4%; Rental vacancy rate: 8.2%

DECKER (town). Covers a land area of 0.181 square miles and a water area of 0 square miles. Located at 38.52° N. Lat; 87.52° W. Long. Elevation is 466 feet.
Population: 249; Growth (since 2000): -12.0%; Density: 1,378.9 persons per square mile; Race: 97.6% White, 1.2% Black/African American, 0.8% Asian, 0.0% American Indian/Alaska Native, 0.0% Native Hawaiian/Other Pacific Islander, 0.4% Two or more races, 0.0% Hispanic of any race; Average household size: 2.71; Median age: 39.3; Age under 18: 24.9%; Age 65 and over: 12.9%; Males per 100 females: 109.2
Housing: Homeownership rate: 78.2%; Homeowner vacancy rate: 1.4%; Rental vacancy rate: 13.0%

EDWARDSPORT (town). Covers a land area of 0.279 square miles and a water area of 0 square miles. Located at 38.81° N. Lat; 87.25° W. Long. Elevation is 499 feet.
History: Edwardsport developed as a docking place for the flatboats on the White River. Later, the Indiana Public Service Company used water power and coal from the nearby strip mines to generate electricity for many parts of southwestern Indiana.
Population: 303; Growth (since 2000): -16.5%; Density: 1,087.6 persons per square mile; Race: 98.3% White, 0.0% Black/African American, 0.0% Asian, 0.0% American Indian/Alaska Native, 0.3% Native Hawaiian/Other Pacific Islander, 0.7% Two or more races, 1.7% Hispanic of any race; Average household size: 2.37; Median age: 45.2; Age under 18: 19.5%; Age 65 and over: 15.2%; Males per 100 females: 103.4
Housing: Homeownership rate: 82.0%; Homeowner vacancy rate: 1.8%; Rental vacancy rate: 17.2%

EMISON (CDP). Covers a land area of 1.570 square miles and a water area of 0.009 square miles. Located at 38.80° N. Lat; 87.46° W. Long. Elevation is 463 feet.
Population: 154; Growth (since 2000): n/a; Density: 98.1 persons per square mile; Race: 98.1% White, 0.6% Black/African American, 0.0% Asian, 0.0% American Indian/Alaska Native, 0.0% Native Hawaiian/Other Pacific Islander, 1.3% Two or more races, 0.0% Hispanic of any race; Average household size: 2.44; Median age: 47.5; Age under 18: 22.7%; Age 65 and over: 16.9%; Males per 100 females: 102.6
Housing: Homeownership rate: 88.9%; Homeowner vacancy rate: 3.4%; Rental vacancy rate: 0.0%

FREELANDVILLE (CDP). Covers a land area of 5.570 square miles and a water area of 0 square miles. Located at 38.87° N. Lat; 87.31° W. Long. Elevation is 568 feet.
Population: 643; Growth (since 2000): n/a; Density: 115.4 persons per square mile; Race: 99.8% White, 0.2% Black/African American, 0.0% Asian, 0.0% American Indian/Alaska Native, 0.0% Native Hawaiian/Other Pacific Islander, 0.0% Two or more races, 0.0% Hispanic of any race; Average household size: 2.38; Median age: 43.6; Age under 18: 20.4%; Age 65 and over: 23.5%; Males per 100 females: 91.9
Housing: Homeownership rate: 78.4%; Homeowner vacancy rate: 1.5%; Rental vacancy rate: 6.8%

MONROE CITY (town). Covers a land area of 0.269 square miles and a water area of 0 square miles. Located at 38.61° N. Lat; 87.35° W. Long. Elevation is 522 feet.
Population: 545; Growth (since 2000): -0.5%; Density: 2,024.0 persons per square mile; Race: 98.7% White, 0.6% Black/African American, 0.0% Asian, 0.2% American Indian/Alaska Native, 0.0% Native Hawaiian/Other Pacific Islander, 0.0% Two or more races, 0.7% Hispanic of any race; Average household size: 2.51; Median age: 32.8; Age under 18: 28.8%; Age 65 and over: 13.2%; Males per 100 females: 89.9
Housing: Homeownership rate: 75.1%; Homeowner vacancy rate: 1.8%; Rental vacancy rate: 18.2%

OAKTOWN (town). Covers a land area of 0.272 square miles and a water area of 0 square miles. Located at 38.87° N. Lat; 87.44° W. Long. Elevation is 472 feet.
History: Laid out 1867.
Population: 608; Growth (since 2000): -3.9%; Density: 2,233.1 persons per square mile; Race: 98.0% White, 0.7% Black/African American, 0.5% Asian, 0.0% American Indian/Alaska Native, 0.0% Native Hawaiian/Other Pacific Islander, 0.8% Two or more races, 2.3% Hispanic of any race; Average household size: 2.25; Median age: 42.7; Age under 18: 20.6%; Age 65 and over: 22.0%; Males per 100 females: 82.0
Housing: Homeownership rate: 61.3%; Homeowner vacancy rate: 3.1%; Rental vacancy rate: 16.1%

RAGSDALE (CDP). Covers a land area of 2.228 square miles and a water area of 0 square miles. Located at 38.75° N. Lat; 87.32° W. Long. Elevation is 577 feet.
Population: 129; Growth (since 2000): n/a; Density: 57.9 persons per square mile; Race: 100.0% White, 0.0% Black/African American, 0.0% Asian, 0.0% American Indian/Alaska Native, 0.0% Native Hawaiian/Other Pacific Islander, 0.0% Two or more races, 1.6% Hispanic of any race; Average household size: 2.48; Median age: 45.8; Age under 18: 20.9%; Age 65 and over: 25.6%; Males per 100 females: 101.6
Housing: Homeownership rate: 94.2%; Homeowner vacancy rate: 2.0%; Rental vacancy rate: 20.0%

SANDBORN (town). Covers a land area of 0.391 square miles and a water area of 0 square miles. Located at 38.90° N. Lat; 87.18° W. Long. Elevation is 479 feet.
Population: 415; Growth (since 2000): -8.0%; Density: 1,060.5 persons per square mile; Race: 98.6% White, 0.2% Black/African American, 0.0% Asian, 1.0% American Indian/Alaska Native, 0.0% Native Hawaiian/Other Pacific Islander, 0.0% Two or more races, 0.7% Hispanic of any race; Average household size: 2.39; Median age: 42.1; Age under 18: 22.7%; Age 65 and over: 16.9%; Males per 100 females: 92.1
Housing: Homeownership rate: 85.1%; Homeowner vacancy rate: 2.6%; Rental vacancy rate: 3.7%

VINCENNES (city). County seat. Covers a land area of 7.412 square miles and a water area of 0.068 square miles. Located at 38.68° N. Lat; 87.51° W. Long. Elevation is 420 feet.
History: Vicennes had its beginnings about 1732, when Francois Morgane de Vincennes built a fort here. The French flag flew over Vincennes until 1763, when it was ceded to Great Britain by the Treaty of Paris. The American flag replaced the Union Jack in 1779 when George Rogers Clark captured Fort Sackville. Vincennes was the first seat of government for the Indiana Territory created in 1800, with William Henry Harrison as governor.
Population: 18,423; Growth (since 2000): -1.5%; Density: 2,485.7 persons per square mile; Race: 91.9% White, 4.7% Black/African American, 0.7% Asian, 0.3% American Indian/Alaska Native, 0.0% Native Hawaiian/Other Pacific Islander, 1.7% Two or more races, 1.9% Hispanic of any race; Average household size: 2.19; Median age: 33.0; Age under 18: 19.2%; Age 65 and over: 15.0%; Males per 100 females: 101.1; Marriage status: 36.8% never married, 41.3% now married, 1.2% separated, 8.0% widowed, 13.9% divorced; Foreign born: 1.0%; Speak English only: 98.2%; With disability: 14.6%; Veterans: 7.3%; Ancestry: 19.7% American, 18.7% German, 12.2% Irish, 7.4% English, 5.6% French
Employment: 10.4% management, business, and financial, 2.4% computer, engineering, and science, 9.1% education, legal, community service, arts, and media, 4.0% healthcare practitioners, 23.4% service, 23.0% sales and office, 7.6% natural resources, construction, and maintenance, 20.0% production, transportation, and material moving
Income: Per capita: $17,896; Median household: $35,165; Average household: $44,297; Households with income of $100,000 or more: 6.7%; Poverty rate: 20.5%
Educational Attainment: High school diploma or higher: 83.6%; Bachelor's degree or higher: 14.1%; Graduate/professional degree or higher: 5.1%

School District(s)
South Knox School Corp (KG-12)
    2012-13 Enrollment: 1,222 . . . . (812) 726-4440
Vincennes Community Sch Corp (KG-12)
    2012-13 Enrollment: 2,697 . . . . (812) 882-4844

Four-year College(s)
Vincennes University (Public)
    Fall 2013 Enrollment: 18,383 . . . . (812) 888-8888
    2013-14 Tuition: In-state $5,019; Out-of-state $11,867

Two-year College(s)
Good Samaritan Hospital School of Radiologic Technology (Public)
    Fall 2013 Enrollment: n/a . . . . (812) 885-8011

Vocational/Technical School(s)
Vincennes Beauty College (Private, For-profit)
    Fall 2013 Enrollment: 89 . . . . (812) 882-1086
    2013-14 Tuition: $11,020

Housing: Homeownership rate: 53.5%; Median home value: $74,000; Median year structure built: 1952; Homeowner vacancy rate: 3.1%; Median gross rent: $606 per month; Rental vacancy rate: 8.4%
Health Insurance: 83.8% have insurance; 64.5% have private insurance; 31.9% have public insurance; 16.2% do not have insurance; 9.0% of children under 18 do not have insurance
Hospitals: Good Samaritan Hospital
Newspapers: Vincennes Sun-Commercial (daily circulation 9500)
Transportation: Commute: 91.6% car, 0.5% public transportation, 4.4% walk, 1.2% work from home; Median travel time to work: 16.0 minutes
Additional Information Contacts
City of Vincennes . . . . (812) 882-6426
   http://www.vincennes.org

WESTPHALIA (CDP). Covers a land area of 2.062 square miles and a water area of 0 square miles. Located at 38.87° N. Lat; 87.23° W. Long. Elevation is 466 feet.
Population: 202; Growth (since 2000): n/a; Density: 98.0 persons per square mile; Race: 100.0% White, 0.0% Black/African American, 0.0% Asian, 0.0% American Indian/Alaska Native, 0.0% Native Hawaiian/Other Pacific Islander, 0.0% Two or more races, 0.0% Hispanic of any race; Average household size: 2.24; Median age: 45.0; Age under 18: 18.8%; Age 65 and over: 17.8%; Males per 100 females: 88.8
Housing: Homeownership rate: 76.7%; Homeowner vacancy rate: 0.0%; Rental vacancy rate: 4.3%

WHEATLAND (town). Covers a land area of 0.410 square miles and a water area of 0 square miles. Located at 38.66° N. Lat; 87.31° W. Long. Elevation is 492 feet.
History: Laid out 1858.
Population: 480; Growth (since 2000): -4.8%; Density: 1,171.9 persons per square mile; Race: 97.9% White, 0.2% Black/African American, 0.0% Asian, 0.2% American Indian/Alaska Native, 0.0% Native Hawaiian/Other Pacific Islander, 1.7% Two or more races, 2.9% Hispanic of any race; Average household size: 2.51; Median age: 36.0; Age under 18: 27.1%; Age 65 and over: 12.5%; Males per 100 females: 98.3
Housing: Homeownership rate: 68.6%; Homeowner vacancy rate: 2.9%; Rental vacancy rate: 7.7%

Kosciusko County

Located in northern Indiana; drained by the Tippecanoe and Eel Rivers; includes Wawasee and Winona Lakes. Covers a land area of 531.381 square miles, a water area of 23.012 square miles, and is located in the Eastern Time Zone at 41.24° N. Lat., 85.86° W. Long. The county was founded in 1835. County seat is Warsaw.

Kosciusko County is part of the Warsaw, IN Micropolitan Statistical Area. The entire metro area includes: Kosciusko County, IN

Weather Station: Warsaw   Elevation: 810 feet

	Jan	Feb	Mar	Apr	May	Jun	Jul	Aug	Sep	Oct	Nov	Dec
High	32	36	47	60	71	80	83	81	75	62	49	36
Low	18	20	29	39	49	59	63	61	53	42	33	22
Precip	2.1	1.7	2.2	3.6	4.2	4.3	4.1	4.4	3.1	3.3	2.9	2.6
Snow	na	na	1.7	0.3	0.0	0.0	0.0	0.0	0.0	tr	0.3	4.3

High and Low temperatures in degrees Fahrenheit; Precipitation and Snow in inches

Population: 77,358; Growth (since 2000): 4.5%; Density: 145.6 persons per square mile; Race: 93.3% White, 0.7% Black/African American, 0.8% Asian, 0.3% American Indian/Alaska Native, 0.0% Native Hawaiian/Other Pacific Islander, 1.4% two or more races, 7.3% Hispanic of any race; Average household size: 2.60; Median age: 37.7; Age under 18: 25.6%; Age 65 and over: 13.5%; Males per 100 females: 98.9; Marriage status: 23.9% never married, 59.2% now married, 1.1% separated, 6.7% widowed, 10.2% divorced; Foreign born: 4.1%; Speak English only: 89.4%; With disability: 11.7%; Veterans: 8.5%; Ancestry: 28.0% German, 13.3% American, 10.4% Irish, 9.3% English, 2.8% Dutch
Religion: Six largest groups: 8.4% Non-denominational Protestant, 6.2% Methodist/Pietist, 5.6% Catholicism, 4.8% European Free-Church, 2.9% Holiness, 1.6% Baptist
Economy: Unemployment rate: 4.2%; Leading industries: 15.6% retail trade; 12.8% other services (except public administration); 10.4% construction; Farms: 1,247 totaling 254,847 acres; Company size: 4 employ 1,000 or more persons, 4 employ 500 to 999 persons, 42 employ 100 to 499 persons, 1,866 employ less than 100 persons; Business ownership: 1,564 women-owned, n/a Black-owned, n/a Hispanic-owned, n/a Asian-owned

Employment: 11.3% management, business, and financial; 3.8% computer, engineering, and science; 8.9% education, legal, community service, arts, and media; 3.5% healthcare practitioners; 13.3% service; 20.8% sales and office; 7.6% natural resources, construction, and maintenance; 30.7% production, transportation, and material moving
Income: Per capita: $24,881; Median household: $50,859; Average household: $64,212; Households with income of $100,000 or more: 16.5%; Poverty rate: 11.9%
Educational Attainment: High school diploma or higher: 85.8%; Bachelor's degree or higher: 20.3%; Graduate/professional degree or higher: 7.3%
Housing: Homeownership rate: 76.4%; Median home value: $132,200; Median year structure built: 1974; Homeowner vacancy rate: 2.6%; Median gross rent: $682 per month; Rental vacancy rate: 11.6%
Vital Statistics: Birth rate: 127.9 per 10,000 population; Death rate: 82.5 per 10,000 population; Age-adjusted cancer mortality rate: 201.3 deaths per 100,000 population
Health Insurance: 84.5% have insurance; 69.3% have private insurance; 26.1% have public insurance; 15.5% do not have insurance; 12.0% of children under 18 do not have insurance
Health Care: Physicians: 8.8 per 10,000 population; Hospital beds: 11.4 per 10,000 population; Hospital admissions: 631.6 per 10,000 population
Transportation: Commute: 91.7% car, 0.2% public transportation, 2.6% walk, 3.5% work from home; Median travel time to work: 20.9 minutes
Presidential Election: 22.8% Obama, 75.0% Romney (2012)
National and State Parks: Tri-County State Fish and Game Area
Additional Information Contacts
Kosciusko Government . . . . (574) 372-2329
   http://www.kcgov.com

Kosciusko County Communities

ATWOOD (unincorporated postal area)
ZCTA: 46502
   Covers a land area of 0.056 square miles and a water area of 0 square miles. Located at 41.26° N. Lat; 85.98° W. Long. Elevation is 823 feet.
   Population: 115; Growth (since 2000): 85.5%; Density: 2,046.8 persons per square mile; Race: 86.1% White, 5.2% Black/African American, 1.7% Asian, 0.0% American Indian/Alaska Native, 0.0% Native Hawaiian/Other Pacific Islander, 1.7% Two or more races, 10.4% Hispanic of any race; Average household size: 2.74; Median age: 33.5; Age under 18: 27.0%; Age 65 and over: 13.0%; Males per 100 females: 94.9
   Housing: Homeownership rate: 85.7%; Homeowner vacancy rate: 2.7%; Rental vacancy rate: 0.0%

BURKET (town). Covers a land area of 0.071 square miles and a water area of 0 square miles. Located at 41.15° N. Lat; 85.97° W. Long. Elevation is 863 feet.
Population: 195; Growth (since 2000): 0.0%; Density: 2,733.8 persons per square mile; Race: 96.9% White, 0.0% Black/African American, 0.0% Asian, 2.6% American Indian/Alaska Native, 0.0% Native Hawaiian/Other Pacific Islander, 0.5% Two or more races, 3.6% Hispanic of any race; Average household size: 2.87; Median age: 34.3; Age under 18: 32.8%; Age 65 and over: 11.8%; Males per 100 females: 80.6
Housing: Homeownership rate: 83.9%; Homeowner vacancy rate: 1.7%; Rental vacancy rate: 15.4%

CLAYPOOL (town). Covers a land area of 0.244 square miles and a water area of 0.008 square miles. Located at 41.13° N. Lat; 85.88° W. Long. Elevation is 889 feet.
Population: 431; Growth (since 2000): 38.6%; Density: 1,768.4 persons per square mile; Race: 95.1% White, 0.2% Black/African American, 0.9% Asian, 0.7% American Indian/Alaska Native, 0.0% Native Hawaiian/Other Pacific Islander, 1.6% Two or more races, 5.1% Hispanic of any race; Average household size: 2.78; Median age: 33.0; Age under 18: 26.7%; Age 65 and over: 10.4%; Males per 100 females: 101.4
   School District(s)
Warsaw Community Schools (KG-12)
   2012-13 Enrollment: 7,004 . . . . (574) 371-5098
Housing: Homeownership rate: 71.6%; Homeowner vacancy rate: 2.6%; Rental vacancy rate: 13.5%

ETNA GREEN (town). Covers a land area of 0.512 square miles and a water area of <.001 square miles. Located at 41.28° N. Lat; 86.04° W. Long. Elevation is 817 feet.
Population: 586; Growth (since 2000): -11.6%; Density: 1,145.6 persons per square mile; Race: 97.8% White, 0.5% Black/African American, 0.3% Asian, 0.3% American Indian/Alaska Native, 0.0% Native Hawaiian/Other Pacific Islander, 0.5% Two or more races, 2.4% Hispanic of any race; Average household size: 2.64; Median age: 35.9; Age under 18: 27.3%; Age 65 and over: 11.9%; Males per 100 females: 99.3
Housing: Homeownership rate: 74.4%; Homeowner vacancy rate: 8.9%; Rental vacancy rate: 5.0%

LEESBURG (town). Covers a land area of 0.260 square miles and a water area of 0 square miles. Located at 41.33° N. Lat; 85.85° W. Long. Elevation is 856 feet.
History: Laid out 1835.
Population: 555; Growth (since 2000): -11.2%; Density: 2,130.9 persons per square mile; Race: 91.7% White, 0.2% Black/African American, 2.3% Asian, 0.2% American Indian/Alaska Native, 0.0% Native Hawaiian/Other Pacific Islander, 1.3% Two or more races, 7.7% Hispanic of any race; Average household size: 2.59; Median age: 38.3; Age under 18: 26.7%; Age 65 and over: 15.0%; Males per 100 females: 96.8
   School District(s)
Warsaw Community Schools (KG-12)
   2012-13 Enrollment: 7,004 . . . . (574) 371-5098
Housing: Homeownership rate: 82.7%; Homeowner vacancy rate: 1.7%; Rental vacancy rate: 7.5%

MENTONE (town). Covers a land area of 0.583 square miles and a water area of 0.012 square miles. Located at 41.17° N. Lat; 86.04° W. Long. Elevation is 840 feet.
Population: 1,001; Growth (since 2000): 11.5%; Density: 1,715.8 persons per square mile; Race: 94.1% White, 0.3% Black/African American, 0.0% Asian, 0.8% American Indian/Alaska Native, 0.0% Native Hawaiian/Other Pacific Islander, 1.7% Two or more races, 4.8% Hispanic of any race; Average household size: 2.71; Median age: 31.2; Age under 18: 28.8%; Age 65 and over: 11.2%; Males per 100 females: 98.6
   School District(s)
Tippecanoe Valley School Corp (KG-12)
   2012-13 Enrollment: 1,980 . . . . (574) 353-7741
Housing: Homeownership rate: 69.1%; Homeowner vacancy rate: 3.7%; Rental vacancy rate: 13.3%

MILFORD (town). Covers a land area of 1.102 square miles and a water area of 0.023 square miles. Located at 41.41° N. Lat; 85.85° W. Long. Elevation is 837 feet.
History: Laid out 1836.
Population: 1,562; Growth (since 2000): 0.8%; Density: 1,417.0 persons per square mile; Race: 88.3% White, 0.7% Black/African American, 0.3% Asian, 0.3% American Indian/Alaska Native, 0.0% Native Hawaiian/Other Pacific Islander, 1.7% Two or more races, 12.4% Hispanic of any race; Average household size: 2.47; Median age: 36.9; Age under 18: 27.1%; Age 65 and over: 16.3%; Males per 100 females: 96.7
   School District(s)
Wawasee Community School Corp (PK-12)
   2012-13 Enrollment: 3,113 . . . . (574) 457-3188
Housing: Homeownership rate: 67.1%; Homeowner vacancy rate: 1.4%; Rental vacancy rate: 6.0%
Newspapers: The Papers Inc (weekly circulation 71500)

NORTH WEBSTER (town). Covers a land area of 0.803 square miles and a water area of 0.016 square miles. Located at 41.32° N. Lat; 85.70° W. Long. Elevation is 883 feet.
Population: 1,146; Growth (since 2000): 7.4%; Density: 1,426.5 persons per square mile; Race: 96.3% White, 0.6% Black/African American, 0.3% Asian, 0.1% American Indian/Alaska Native, 0.0% Native Hawaiian/Other Pacific Islander, 1.7% Two or more races, 2.5% Hispanic of any race; Average household size: 2.29; Median age: 41.6; Age under 18: 21.4%; Age 65 and over: 18.2%; Males per 100 females: 93.6
   School District(s)
Wawasee Community School Corp (PK-12)
   2012-13 Enrollment: 3,113 . . . . (574) 457-3188
Housing: Homeownership rate: 67.5%; Homeowner vacancy rate: 0.6%; Rental vacancy rate: 9.9%

PIERCETON (town). Covers a land area of 1.198 square miles and a water area of 0.002 square miles. Located at 41.20° N. Lat; 85.70° W. Long. Elevation is 928 feet.
Population: 1,015; Growth (since 2000): 46.0%; Density: 847.5 persons per square mile; Race: 96.8% White, 0.0% Black/African American, 0.2% Asian, 0.3% American Indian/Alaska Native, 0.0% Native Hawaiian/Other Pacific Islander, 1.4% Two or more races, 6.1% Hispanic of any race; Average household size: 2.56; Median age: 35.7; Age under 18: 28.5%; Age 65 and over: 13.2%; Males per 100 females: 91.9
School District(s)
Whitko Community School Corp (PK-12)
    2012-13 Enrollment: 1,714 . . . . (574) 594-2658
Housing: Homeownership rate: 73.8%; Homeowner vacancy rate: 2.0%; Rental vacancy rate: 9.2%

SIDNEY (town). Covers a land area of 0.125 square miles and a water area of 0.005 square miles. Located at 41.11° N. Lat; 85.74° W. Long. Elevation is 915 feet.
Population: 83; Growth (since 2000): -50.6%; Density: 666.1 persons per square mile; Race: 100.0% White, 0.0% Black/African American, 0.0% Asian, 0.0% American Indian/Alaska Native, 0.0% Native Hawaiian/Other Pacific Islander, 0.0% Two or more races, 3.6% Hispanic of any race; Average household size: 2.44; Median age: 42.3; Age under 18: 25.3%; Age 65 and over: 22.9%; Males per 100 females: 84.4
Housing: Homeownership rate: 91.2%; Homeowner vacancy rate: 8.8%; Rental vacancy rate: 25.0%

SILVER LAKE (town). Covers a land area of 0.525 square miles and a water area of 0.001 square miles. Located at 41.07° N. Lat; 85.89° W. Long. Elevation is 906 feet.
History: Laid out 1859.
Population: 915; Growth (since 2000): 67.6%; Density: 1,742.1 persons per square mile; Race: 97.7% White, 0.9% Black/African American, 0.2% Asian, 0.2% American Indian/Alaska Native, 0.0% Native Hawaiian/Other Pacific Islander, 0.9% Two or more races, 1.9% Hispanic of any race; Average household size: 2.46; Median age: 38.1; Age under 18: 23.5%; Age 65 and over: 13.6%; Males per 100 females: 88.3
Housing: Homeownership rate: 79.5%; Homeowner vacancy rate: 3.0%; Rental vacancy rate: 16.1%

SYRACUSE (town). Covers a land area of 1.787 square miles and a water area of 0.366 square miles. Located at 41.42° N. Lat; 85.75° W. Long. Elevation is 879 feet.
History: Syracuse was settled as a summer resort town on Lakes Syracuse, Wawasee, and Papakeechee.
Population: 2,810; Growth (since 2000): -7.5%; Density: 1,572.4 persons per square mile; Race: 95.7% White, 0.6% Black/African American, 0.7% Asian, 0.1% American Indian/Alaska Native, 0.0% Native Hawaiian/Other Pacific Islander, 1.3% Two or more races, 5.2% Hispanic of any race; Average household size: 2.43; Median age: 37.4; Age under 18: 25.1%; Age 65 and over: 13.1%; Males per 100 females: 101.4; Marriage status: 21.6% never married, 54.9% now married, 0.2% separated, 7.4% widowed, 16.1% divorced; Foreign born: 3.9%; Speak English only: 90.6%; With disability: 12.1%; Veterans: 9.7%; Ancestry: 25.5% German, 15.5% American, 7.2% English, 5.7% Irish, 1.8% Swiss
Employment: 6.9% management, business, and financial, 2.1% computer, engineering, and science, 4.0% education, legal, community service, arts, and media, 6.2% healthcare practitioners, 17.2% service, 19.2% sales and office, 8.4% natural resources, construction, and maintenance, 36.0% production, transportation, and material moving
Income: Per capita: $20,398; Median household: $45,625; Average household: $54,211; Households with income of $100,000 or more: 12.8%; Poverty rate: 11.9%
Educational Attainment: High school diploma or higher: 85.6%; Bachelor's degree or higher: 12.4%; Graduate/professional degree or higher: 4.6%
School District(s)
Wawasee Community School Corp (PK-12)
    2012-13 Enrollment: 3,113 . . . . (574) 457-3188
Housing: Homeownership rate: 67.1%; Median home value: $107,600; Median year structure built: 1970; Homeowner vacancy rate: 3.6%; Median gross rent: $548 per month; Rental vacancy rate: 23.1%
Health Insurance: 77.7% have insurance; 62.0% have private insurance; 26.6% have public insurance; 22.3% do not have insurance; 19.2% of children under 18 do not have insurance
Transportation: Commute: 92.1% car, 0.0% public transportation, 6.8% walk, 1.1% work from home; Median travel time to work: 22.2 minutes
Additional Information Contacts
Town of Syracuse . . . . (574) 457-3216
  http://www.syracusein.org

WARSAW (city). County seat. Covers a land area of 11.576 square miles and a water area of 1.338 square miles. Located at 41.24° N. Lat; 85.85° W. Long. Elevation is 827 feet.
History: In its name, Warsaw remembers the Polish nationality of Thaddeus Kosciusko (1746-1817), for whom Kosciusko County was named. Kosciusko was an aide to General Washington during the Revolutionary War, in addition to being a Polish national hero.
Population: 13,559; Growth (since 2000): 9.2%; Density: 1,171.3 persons per square mile; Race: 89.5% White, 1.6% Black/African American, 2.2% Asian, 0.5% American Indian/Alaska Native, 0.0% Native Hawaiian/Other Pacific Islander, 2.0% Two or more races, 10.4% Hispanic of any race; Average household size: 2.38; Median age: 34.8; Age under 18: 25.2%; Age 65 and over: 13.4%; Males per 100 females: 96.4; Marriage status: 30.2% never married, 50.2% now married, 1.2% separated, 8.2% widowed, 11.4% divorced; Foreign born: 8.2%; Speak English only: 85.3%; With disability: 11.5%; Veterans: 8.4%; Ancestry: 20.0% German, 13.4% Irish, 11.0% American, 7.8% English, 3.4% Dutch
Employment: 9.9% management, business, and financial, 3.7% computer, engineering, and science, 10.5% education, legal, community service, arts, and media, 3.6% healthcare practitioners, 14.1% service, 22.0% sales and office, 4.4% natural resources, construction, and maintenance, 31.8% production, transportation, and material moving
Income: Per capita: $23,167; Median household: $42,648; Average household: $54,517; Households with income of $100,000 or more: 10.9%; Poverty rate: 15.0%
Educational Attainment: High school diploma or higher: 84.3%; Bachelor's degree or higher: 22.5%; Graduate/professional degree or higher: 9.7%
School District(s)
Warsaw Community Schools (KG-12)
    2012-13 Enrollment: 7,004 . . . . (574) 371-5098
Housing: Homeownership rate: 57.5%; Median home value: $115,900; Median year structure built: 1972; Homeowner vacancy rate: 3.2%; Median gross rent: $644 per month; Rental vacancy rate: 10.3%
Health Insurance: 84.2% have insurance; 66.5% have private insurance; 30.3% have public insurance; 15.8% do not have insurance; 7.1% of children under 18 do not have insurance
Hospitals: Kosciusko Community Hospital (72 beds)
Safety: Violent crime rate: 76.3 per 10,000 population; Property crime rate: 321.7 per 10,000 population
Newspapers: Times-Union (daily circulation 10900)
Transportation: Commute: 92.3% car, 0.5% public transportation, 3.1% walk, 2.0% work from home; Median travel time to work: 15.7 minutes
Airports: Warsaw Municipal (general aviation)
Additional Information Contacts
City of Warsaw . . . . (574) 372-9545
  http://warsaw.in.gov

WINONA LAKE (town). Covers a land area of 2.763 square miles and a water area of 0.490 square miles. Located at 41.22° N. Lat; 85.81° W. Long. Elevation is 817 feet.
History: Winona Lake is a vacation retreat area. Evangelist Billy Sunday built a tabernacle here that influenced the character of the town.
Population: 4,908; Growth (since 2000): 23.1%; Density: 1,776.5 persons per square mile; Race: 92.2% White, 1.5% Black/African American, 1.0% Asian, 0.1% American Indian/Alaska Native, 0.0% Native Hawaiian/Other Pacific Islander, 1.2% Two or more races, 7.4% Hispanic of any race; Average household size: 2.62; Median age: 28.3; Age under 18: 23.7%; Age 65 and over: 12.7%; Males per 100 females: 87.3; Marriage status: 30.1% never married, 55.7% now married, 1.2% separated, 8.1% widowed, 6.1% divorced; Foreign born: 5.4%; Speak English only: 93.1%; With disability: 14.3%; Veterans: 7.8%; Ancestry: 35.4% German, 13.4% English, 12.3% Irish, 5.2% American, 4.9% Dutch
Employment: 21.8% management, business, and financial, 3.5% computer, engineering, and science, 19.5% education, legal, community service, arts, and media, 4.0% healthcare practitioners, 12.1% service, 20.0% sales and office, 5.6% natural resources, construction, and maintenance, 13.5% production, transportation, and material moving

Income: Per capita: $27,874; Median household: $54,750; Average household: $77,226; Households with income of $100,000 or more: 28.9%; Poverty rate: 11.6%
Educational Attainment: High school diploma or higher: 91.2%; Bachelor's degree or higher: 46.9%; Graduate/professional degree or higher: 17.6%

School District(s)
Warsaw Community Schools (KG-12)
    2012-13 Enrollment: 7,004 . . . . (574) 371-5098

Four-year College(s)
Grace College and Theological Seminary (Private, Not-for-profit, Brethren Church)
    Fall 2013 Enrollment: 1,904 . . . . (574) 372-5100
    2013-14 Tuition: In-state $23,970; Out-of-state $23,970

Housing: Homeownership rate: 67.7%; Median home value: $166,100; Median year structure built: 1983; Homeowner vacancy rate: 2.3%; Median gross rent: $674 per month; Rental vacancy rate: 12.1%
Health Insurance: 89.2% have insurance; 80.3% have private insurance; 18.9% have public insurance; 10.8% do not have insurance; 8.7% of children under 18 do not have insurance
Safety: Violent crime rate: 24.3 per 10,000 population; Property crime rate: 54.7 per 10,000 population
Transportation: Commute: 82.5% car, 0.0% public transportation, 9.7% walk, 7.8% work from home; Median travel time to work: 18.9 minutes
Additional Information Contacts
Town of Winona Lake . . . . (574) 267-7581
    http://www.winonalake.net

LaGrange County

Located in northeastern Indiana; bounded on the north by Michigan; drained by the Pigeon and Short Little Elkhart Rivers. Covers a land area of 379.624 square miles, a water area of 7.078 square miles, and is located in the Eastern Time Zone at 41.64° N. Lat., 85.43° W. Long. The county was founded in 1832. County seat is Lagrange.

Weather Station: Lagrange Sewage Plant   Elevation: 895 feet

	Jan	Feb	Mar	Apr	May	Jun	Jul	Aug	Sep	Oct	Nov	Dec
High	30	35	45	59	70	79	83	81	74	61	48	35
Low	15	18	26	37	48	57	61	59	52	40	32	21
Precip	1.8	1.7	2.3	3.5	4.0	4.0	3.7	4.1	3.4	3.2	2.9	2.5
Snow	6.9	5.7	2.6	0.9	tr	0.0	0.0	0.0	0.0	0.5	1.4	5.9

High and Low temperatures in degrees Fahrenheit; Precipitation and Snow in inches

Population: 37,128; Growth (since 2000): 6.4%; Density: 97.8 persons per square mile; Race: 96.6% White, 0.3% Black/African American, 0.3% Asian, 0.2% American Indian/Alaska Native, 0.0% Native Hawaiian/Other Pacific Islander, 0.8% two or more races, 3.5% Hispanic of any race; Average household size: 3.17; Median age: 30.4; Age under 18: 34.5%; Age 65 and over: 11.6%; Males per 100 females: 101.8; Marriage status: 24.6% never married, 62.3% now married, 0.8% separated, 5.1% widowed, 8.0% divorced; Foreign born: 1.9%; Speak English only: 60.0%; With disability: 9.9%; Veterans: 7.2%; Ancestry: 32.1% German, 15.5% American, 6.8% English, 6.0% Irish, 5.8% Swiss
Religion: Six largest groups: 41.7% European Free-Church, 5.2% Methodist/Pietist, 3.0% Baptist, 1.9% Holiness, 1.8% Catholicism, 1.7% Non-denominational Protestant
Economy: Unemployment rate: 4.5%; Leading industries: 19.6% retail trade; 17.1% manufacturing; 11.6% construction; Farms: 2,419 totaling 204,092 acres; Company size: 0 employ 1,000 or more persons, 1 employs 500 to 999 persons, 20 employ 100 to 499 persons, 761 employs less than 100 persons; Business ownership: 757 women-owned, n/a Black-owned, n/a Hispanic-owned, n/a Asian-owned
Employment: 11.5% management, business, and financial, 0.8% computer, engineering, and science, 6.1% education, legal, community service, arts, and media, 2.4% healthcare practitioners, 14.1% service, 16.1% sales and office, 12.1% natural resources, construction, and maintenance, 37.0% production, transportation, and material moving
Income: Per capita: $19,356; Median household: $47,617; Average household: $60,164; Households with income of $100,000 or more: 13.8%; Poverty rate: 16.5%
Educational Attainment: High school diploma or higher: 62.1%; Bachelor's degree or higher: 10.3%; Graduate/professional degree or higher: 4.8%

Housing: Homeownership rate: 80.9%; Median home value: $160,200; Median year structure built: 1975; Homeowner vacancy rate: 2.7%; Median gross rent: $680 per month; Rental vacancy rate: 9.8%
Vital Statistics: Birth rate: 187.1 per 10,000 population; Death rate: 60.0 per 10,000 population; Age-adjusted cancer mortality rate: 184.7 deaths per 100,000 population
Health Insurance: 57.1% have insurance; 42.1% have private insurance; 24.0% have public insurance; 42.9% do not have insurance; 53.2% of children under 18 do not have insurance
Health Care: Physicians: 5.3 per 10,000 population; Hospital beds: 6.7 per 10,000 population; Hospital admissions: 320.3 per 10,000 population
Transportation: Commute: 77.3% car, 0.6% public transportation, 2.7% walk, 8.6% work from home; Median travel time to work: 22.5 minutes
Presidential Election: 31.1% Obama, 66.9% Romney (2012)
National and State Parks: Pigeon River State Fish and Wildlife Area
Additional Information Contacts
LaGrange Government . . . . (260) 499-6300
    http://www.lagrangecounty.org

LaGrange County Communities

HOWE (CDP). Covers a land area of 1.788 square miles and a water area of 0 square miles. Located at 41.72° N. Lat; 85.43° W. Long. Elevation is 883 feet.
Population: 807; Growth (since 2000): n/a; Density: 451.4 persons per square mile; Race: 82.9% White, 2.7% Black/African American, 3.0% Asian, 0.6% American Indian/Alaska Native, 0.0% Native Hawaiian/Other Pacific Islander, 2.2% Two or more races, 14.6% Hispanic of any race; Average household size: 2.66; Median age: 28.3; Age under 18: 34.9%; Age 65 and over: 9.5%; Males per 100 females: 131.9

School District(s)
Lakeland School Corporation (KG-12)
    2012-13 Enrollment: 2,178 . . . . (260) 499-2400
Housing: Homeownership rate: 71.2%; Homeowner vacancy rate: 2.7%; Rental vacancy rate: 2.7%

LAGRANGE (town). County seat. Covers a land area of 1.704 square miles and a water area of 0 square miles. Located at 41.65° N. Lat; 85.42° W. Long. Elevation is 932 feet.
History: LaGrange became the seat of LaGrange County in 1844. The town was named in 1836 for the Marquis de LaFayette's country residence near Paris, by the French immigrants who settled here. LaGrange was incorporated in 1855.
Population: 2,625; Growth (since 2000): -10.1%; Density: 1,540.7 persons per square mile; Race: 93.7% White, 0.6% Black/African American, 0.4% Asian, 0.4% American Indian/Alaska Native, 0.0% Native Hawaiian/Other Pacific Islander, 0.7% Two or more races, 9.5% Hispanic of any race; Average household size: 2.43; Median age: 37.7; Age under 18: 27.0%; Age 65 and over: 17.8%; Males per 100 females: 87.8; Marriage status: 22.4% never married, 38.9% now married, 1.6% separated, 14.0% widowed, 24.7% divorced; Foreign born: 3.9%; Speak English only: 87.5%; With disability: 21.6%; Veterans: 13.4%; Ancestry: 27.7% German, 11.1% English, 9.7% Irish, 8.8% American, 7.5% French
Employment: 3.0% management, business, and financial, 0.4% computer, engineering, and science, 8.5% education, legal, community service, arts, and media, 3.8% healthcare practitioners, 18.4% service, 20.3% sales and office, 13.9% natural resources, construction, and maintenance, 31.7% production, transportation, and material moving
Income: Per capita: $16,596; Median household: $34,279; Average household: $38,989; Households with income of $100,000 or more: 4.9%; Poverty rate: 24.6%
Educational Attainment: High school diploma or higher: 82.5%; Bachelor's degree or higher: 6.8%; Graduate/professional degree or higher: 3.9%

School District(s)
Lakeland School Corporation (KG-12)
    2012-13 Enrollment: 2,178 . . . . (260) 499-2400
Prairie Heights Com Sch Corp (KG-12)
    2012-13 Enrollment: 1,358 . . . . (260) 351-3214
Housing: Homeownership rate: 57.7%; Median home value: $93,300; Median year structure built: 1963; Homeowner vacancy rate: 4.7%; Median gross rent: $672 per month; Rental vacancy rate: 16.8%
Health Insurance: 73.3% have insurance; 48.2% have private insurance; 40.4% have public insurance; 26.7% do not have insurance; 22.5% of children under 18 do not have insurance

Hospitals: Parkview Lagrange Hospital (62 beds)
Newspapers: Lagrange Publishing (weekly circulation 34000)
Transportation: Commute: 86.7% car, 1.1% public transportation, 3.9% walk, 7.0% work from home; Median travel time to work: 22.0 minutes
Additional Information Contacts
Town of LaGrange. . . . . (260) 463-3241
http://www.lagrangein.org

SHIPSHEWANA (town).
Covers a land area of 1.180 square miles and a water area of 0 square miles. Located at 41.67° N. Lat; 85.58° W. Long. Elevation is 889 feet.
History: Shipshewana began as a trading center for Amish farmers in the area.
Population: 658; Growth (since 2000): 22.8%; Density: 557.7 persons per square mile; Race: 98.3% White, 0.2% Black/African American, 0.2% Asian, 0.5% American Indian/Alaska Native, 0.0% Native Hawaiian/Other Pacific Islander, 0.6% Two or more races, 0.8% Hispanic of any race; Average household size: 2.22; Median age: 37.7; Age under 18: 24.2%; Age 65 and over: 22.0%; Males per 100 females: 80.8

School District(s)
Westview School Corporation (KG-12)
    2012-13 Enrollment: 2,434 . . . . (260) 768-4404
Housing: Homeownership rate: 57.9%; Homeowner vacancy rate: 2.8%; Rental vacancy rate: 11.3%

SOUTH MILFORD (unincorporated postal area)
ZCTA: 46786
Covers a land area of 0.036 square miles and a water area of 0 square miles. Located at 41.53° N. Lat; 85.27° W. Long. Elevation is 978 feet.
Population: 102; Growth (since 2000): n/a; Density: 2,814.2 persons per square mile; Race: 93.1% White, 0.0% Black/African American, 0.0% Asian, 0.0% American Indian/Alaska Native, 1.0% Native Hawaiian/Other Pacific Islander, 5.9% Two or more races, 5.9% Hispanic of any race; Average household size: 2.43; Median age: 46.0; Age under 18: 17.6%; Age 65 and over: 19.6%; Males per 100 females: 82.1
Housing: Homeownership rate: 81.0%; Homeowner vacancy rate: 0.0%; Rental vacancy rate: 0.0%

TOPEKA (town).
Covers a land area of 1.737 square miles and a water area of 0 square miles. Located at 41.54° N. Lat; 85.55° W. Long. Elevation is 925 feet.
History: Laid out 1843.
Population: 1,153; Growth (since 2000): -0.5%; Density: 663.7 persons per square mile; Race: 94.4% White, 0.3% Black/African American, 1.0% Asian, 0.0% American Indian/Alaska Native, 0.0% Native Hawaiian/Other Pacific Islander, 2.7% Two or more races, 3.6% Hispanic of any race; Average household size: 2.74; Median age: 29.6; Age under 18: 33.9%; Age 65 and over: 8.2%; Males per 100 females: 91.5

School District(s)
Westview School Corporation (KG-12)
    2012-13 Enrollment: 2,434 . . . . (260) 768-4404
Housing: Homeownership rate: 62.7%; Homeowner vacancy rate: 5.0%; Rental vacancy rate: 8.1%

Lake County

Located in northwestern Indiana; bounded on the north by Lake Michigan, on the west by Illinois, and on the south by the Kankakee River; crossed by the Grand Calumet and Little Calumet Rivers. Covers a land area of 498.961 square miles, a water area of 127.599 square miles, and is located in the Central Time Zone at 41.47° N. Lat., 87.37° W. Long. The county was founded in 1836. County seat is Crown Point.

Lake County is part of the Chicago-Naperville-Elgin, IL-IN-WI Metropolitan Statistical Area. The entire metro area includes:
Chicago-Naperville-Arlington Heights, IL Metropolitan Division (Cook County, IL; DuPage County, IL; Grundy County, IL; Kendall County, IL; McHenry County, IL; Will County, IL); Elgin, IL Metropolitan Division (DeKalb County, IL; Kane County, IL); Gary, IN Metropolitan Division (Jasper County, IN; Lake County, IN; Newton County, IN; Porter County, IN); Lake County-Kenosha County, IL-WI Metropolitan Division (Lake County, IL; Kenosha County, WI)

Weather Station: Lowell   Elevation: 665 feet

	Jan	Feb	Mar	Apr	May	Jun	Jul	Aug	Sep	Oct	Nov	Dec
High	32	36	47	61	72	81	84	82	76	64	49	35
Low	15	18	28	38	48	58	62	60	52	40	31	19
Precip	1.9	1.7	2.7	3.7	4.3	4.5	3.9	4.2	3.2	3.4	3.4	2.5
Snow	9.4	9.1	3.6	0.3	tr	0.0	0.0	0.0	0.0	0.2	0.8	7.4

High and Low temperatures in degrees Fahrenheit; Precipitation and Snow in inches

Population: 496,005; Growth (since 2000): 2.4%; Density: 994.1 persons per square mile; Race: 64.4% White, 25.9% Black/African American, 1.2% Asian, 0.3% American Indian/Alaska Native, 0.0% Native Hawaiian/Other Pacific Islander, 2.4% two or more races, 16.7% Hispanic of any race; Average household size: 2.60; Median age: 37.4; Age under 18: 25.7%; Age 65 and over: 13.3%; Males per 100 females: 93.3; Marriage status: 34.1% never married, 47.3% now married, 2.0% separated, 7.2% widowed, 11.4% divorced; Foreign born: 6.7%; Speak English only: 85.5%; With disability: 13.6%; Veterans: 8.9%; Ancestry: 15.0% German, 11.0% Irish, 9.3% Polish, 5.2% English, 4.4% Italian
Religion: Six largest groups: 20.4% Catholicism, 12.6% Non-denominational Protestant, 6.3% Baptist, 3.2% Methodist/Pietist, 3.1% Presbyterian-Reformed, 2.8% Eastern Liturgical (Orthodox)
Economy: Unemployment rate: 7.2%; Leading industries 15.5% retail trade; 12.8% health care and social assistance; 12.5% other services (except public administration); Farms: 430 totaling 133,064 acres; Company size: 15 employ 1,000 or more persons, 9 employ 500 to 999 persons, 190 employ 100 to 499 persons, 9,635 employ less than 100 persons; Business ownership: 10,614 women-owned, 6,364 Black-owned, 2,300 Hispanic-owned, 846 Asian-owned
Employment: 10.9% management, business, and financial, 3.0% computer, engineering, and science, 9.3% education, legal, community service, arts, and media, 6.3% healthcare practitioners, 19.3% service, 24.0% sales and office, 10.0% natural resources, construction, and maintenance, 17.1% production, transportation, and material moving
Income: Per capita: $23,918; Median household: $49,035; Average household: $62,295; Households with income of $100,000 or more: 17.3%; Poverty rate: 17.8%
Educational Attainment: High school diploma or higher: 87.0%; Bachelor's degree or higher: 19.8%; Graduate/professional degree or higher: 6.7%
Housing: Homeownership rate: 69.3%; Median home value: $136,600; Median year structure built: 1962; Homeowner vacancy rate: 2.3%; Median gross rent: $799 per month; Rental vacancy rate: 9.8%
Vital Statistics: Birth rate: 123.0 per 10,000 population; Death rate: 95.0 per 10,000 population; Age-adjusted cancer mortality rate: 190.1 deaths per 100,000 population
Health Insurance: 85.3% have insurance; 64.5% have private insurance; 32.2% have public insurance; 14.7% do not have insurance; 6.6% of children under 18 do not have insurance
Health Care: Physicians: 17.2 per 10,000 population; Hospital beds: 45.6 per 10,000 population; Hospital admissions: 1,878.3 per 10,000 population
Air Quality Index: 45.2% good, 54.5% moderate, 0.3% unhealthy for sensitive individuals, 0.0% unhealthy (percent of days)
Transportation: Commute: 92.7% car, 2.8% public transportation, 1.5% walk, 2.0% work from home; Median travel time to work: 27.6 minutes
Presidential Election: 64.9% Obama, 33.9% Romney (2012)
National and State Parks: Hoosier Prairie State Nature Preserve
Additional Information Contacts
Lake Government . . . . (219) 755-3200
http://www.lakecountyin.org

Lake County Communities

CEDAR LAKE (town).
Covers a land area of 8.219 square miles and a water area of 1.387 square miles. Located at 41.37° N. Lat; 87.44° W. Long. Elevation is 709 feet.
Population: 11,560; Growth (since 2000): 24.6%; Density: 1,406.5 persons per square mile; Race: 94.9% White, 0.5% Black/African American, 0.4% Asian, 0.3% American Indian/Alaska Native, 0.0% Native Hawaiian/Other Pacific Islander, 1.7% Two or more races, 6.5% Hispanic of any race; Average household size: 2.75; Median age: 34.9; Age under 18: 26.6%; Age 65 and over: 8.6%; Males per 100 females: 102.8; Marriage status: 28.3% never married, 52.2% now married, 1.7% separated, 6.6% widowed, 13.0% divorced; Foreign born: 2.3%; Speak English only: 95.3%; With disability: 12.9%; Veterans: 7.8%; Ancestry: 27.5% German, 15.9% Polish, 15.0% Irish, 10.0% American, 9.6% English

Employment: 12.3% management, business, and financial, 2.2% computer, engineering, and science, 6.7% education, legal, community service, arts, and media, 5.3% healthcare practitioners, 16.4% service, 23.9% sales and office, 20.5% natural resources, construction, and maintenance, 12.6% production, transportation, and material moving
Income: Per capita: $24,893; Median household: $58,401; Average household: $66,505; Households with income of $100,000 or more: 15.3%; Poverty rate: 7.5%
Educational Attainment: High school diploma or higher: 88.0%; Bachelor's degree or higher: 13.4%; Graduate/professional degree or higher: 3.5%

School District(s)
Crown Point Community Sch Corp (KG-12)
    2012-13 Enrollment: 7,757 . . . . (219) 663-3371
Hanover Community School Corp (KG-12)
    2012-13 Enrollment: 2,138 . . . . (219) 374-3500
Housing: Homeownership rate: 77.1%; Median home value: $153,900; Median year structure built: 1973; Homeowner vacancy rate: 3.4%; Median gross rent: $856 per month; Rental vacancy rate: 8.2%
Health Insurance: 85.8% have insurance; 70.3% have private insurance; 24.9% have public insurance; 14.2% do not have insurance; 11.5% of children under 18 do not have insurance
Safety: Violent crime rate: 11.1 per 10,000 population; Property crime rate: 212.2 per 10,000 population
Transportation: Commute: 95.9% car, 0.6% public transportation, 0.2% walk, 2.4% work from home; Median travel time to work: 32.8 minutes
Additional Information Contacts
Town of Cedar Lake . . . . (219) 374-7000
    http://www.cedarlakein.org

CROWN POINT (city). County seat. Covers a land area of 17.713 square miles and a water area of 0.015 square miles. Located at 41.42° N. Lat; 87.35° W. Long. Elevation is 732 feet.
History: Named for Solon Robinson, a settler who was called King of the Squatters. Crown Point was founded by Solon Robinson, who came here from Connecticut in 1834 and built a cabin. Robinson, who served as Lake County's first justice of the peace, built the first courthouse for Lake County when Crown Point was chosen as the county seat. The town was first called Robinson's Prairie; the later name refers to Robinson's nickname of King of the Squatters.
Population: 27,317; Growth (since 2000): 37.9%; Density: 1,542.2 persons per square mile; Race: 88.2% White, 6.3% Black/African American, 1.8% Asian, 0.2% American Indian/Alaska Native, 0.0% Native Hawaiian/Other Pacific Islander, 1.6% Two or more races, 8.1% Hispanic of any race; Average household size: 2.45; Median age: 39.6; Age under 18: 21.2%; Age 65 and over: 16.1%; Males per 100 females: 100.0; Marriage status: 28.4% never married, 54.4% now married, 1.6% separated, 7.1% widowed, 10.1% divorced; Foreign born: 8.0%; Speak English only: 87.6%; With disability: 10.3%; Veterans: 9.0%; Ancestry: 25.2% German, 12.6% Irish, 10.5% Polish, 7.1% English, 6.8% American
Employment: 13.3% management, business, and financial, 5.1% computer, engineering, and science, 10.8% education, legal, community service, arts, and media, 11.4% healthcare practitioners, 14.4% service, 21.4% sales and office, 8.9% natural resources, construction, and maintenance, 14.9% production, transportation, and material moving
Income: Per capita: $31,177; Median household: $63,121; Average household: $78,090; Households with income of $100,000 or more: 25.5%; Poverty rate: 7.0%
Educational Attainment: High school diploma or higher: 92.4%; Bachelor's degree or higher: 30.2%; Graduate/professional degree or higher: 9.4%

School District(s)
Crown Point Community Sch Corp (KG-12)
    2012-13 Enrollment: 7,757 . . . . (219) 663-3371
Northwest Indiana Spec Ed Coop (KG-12)
    2012-13 Enrollment: 92 . . . . (219) 663-6500
Housing: Homeownership rate: 78.9%; Median home value: $172,500; Median year structure built: 1981; Homeowner vacancy rate: 2.0%; Median gross rent: $914 per month; Rental vacancy rate: 7.6%
Health Insurance: 89.2% have insurance; 79.4% have private insurance; 23.4% have public insurance; 10.8% do not have insurance; 4.4% of children under 18 do not have insurance
Hospitals: Franciscan Saint Anthony Health - Crown Point (411 beds); Pinnacle Hospital (18 beds)
Newspapers: Crown Point Star (weekly circulation 2700)
Transportation: Commute: 92.7% car, 1.6% public transportation, 1.5% walk, 2.9% work from home; Median travel time to work: 27.6 minutes
Additional Information Contacts
City of Crown Point . . . . (219) 662-3235
    http://www.crownpoint.in.gov

DYER (town). Covers a land area of 6.104 square miles and a water area of 0 square miles. Located at 41.50° N. Lat; 87.51° W. Long. Elevation is 640 feet.
History: On January 24, 1910, citizens of Dyer decided by a vote of 57 to 35 to incorporate as a town under the laws of the State of Indiana. The Town of Dyer was formally incorporated on February 8, 1910.
Population: 16,390; Growth (since 2000): 18.0%; Density: 2,685.1 persons per square mile; Race: 90.1% White, 2.5% Black/African American, 2.9% Asian, 0.2% American Indian/Alaska Native, 0.0% Native Hawaiian/Other Pacific Islander, 1.8% Two or more races, 9.3% Hispanic of any race; Average household size: 2.68; Median age: 42.9; Age under 18: 23.1%; Age 65 and over: 15.5%; Males per 100 females: 93.8; Marriage status: 26.8% never married, 59.6% now married, 0.8% separated, 7.0% widowed, 6.5% divorced; Foreign born: 5.9%; Speak English only: 91.7%; With disability: 10.4%; Veterans: 8.8%; Ancestry: 20.0% German, 18.4% Polish, 16.6% Irish, 10.4% English, 10.2% Italian
Employment: 14.4% management, business, and financial, 2.9% computer, engineering, and science, 9.8% education, legal, community service, arts, and media, 7.1% healthcare practitioners, 15.1% service, 26.9% sales and office, 8.9% natural resources, construction, and maintenance, 14.9% production, transportation, and material moving
Income: Per capita: $36,269; Median household: $76,457; Average household: $102,104; Households with income of $100,000 or more: 34.1%; Poverty rate: 2.6%
Educational Attainment: High school diploma or higher: 92.0%; Bachelor's degree or higher: 28.9%; Graduate/professional degree or higher: 8.5%

School District(s)
Lake Central School Corp (PK-12)
    2012-13 Enrollment: 10,009 . . . . (219) 558-2707
Housing: Homeownership rate: 91.2%; Median home value: $191,100; Median year structure built: 1980; Homeowner vacancy rate: 0.8%; Median gross rent: $921 per month; Rental vacancy rate: 4.0%
Health Insurance: 92.4% have insurance; 84.4% have private insurance; 21.0% have public insurance; 7.6% do not have insurance; 2.1% of children under 18 do not have insurance
Hospitals: Franciscan Saint Margaret Health - Dyer (794 beds)
Safety: Violent crime rate: 6.7 per 10,000 population; Property crime rate: 120.3 per 10,000 population
Transportation: Commute: 93.0% car, 5.1% public transportation, 0.3% walk, 1.4% work from home; Median travel time to work: 29.8 minutes; Amtrak: Train service available.
Additional Information Contacts
Town of Dyer . . . . (219) 865-2421
    http://www.townofdyer.com

EAST CHICAGO (city). Covers a land area of 14.088 square miles and a water area of 2.065 square miles. Located at 41.65° N. Lat; 87.45° W. Long. Elevation is 591 feet.
History: Named for its location east of the city of Chicago. East Chicago was incorporated as a town in 1889. Growth was slow until 1901, when a steel mill was built and work was begun on the Indiana Harbor and Ship Canal. Other industries followed, and East Chicago became an important petroleum refining area.
Population: 29,698; Growth (since 2000): -8.4%; Density: 2,108.1 persons per square mile; Race: 35.5% White, 42.9% Black/African American, 0.1% Asian, 0.6% American Indian/Alaska Native, 0.0% Native Hawaiian/Other Pacific Islander, 2.8% Two or more races, 50.9% Hispanic of any race; Average household size: 2.75; Median age: 30.9; Age under 18: 31.4%; Age 65 and over: 11.3%; Males per 100 females: 88.1; Marriage status: 47.3% never married, 33.8% now married, 3.5% separated, 7.4% widowed, 11.5% divorced; Foreign born: 15.1%; Speak English only: 62.2%; With disability: 15.1%; Veterans: 6.0%; Ancestry: 2.2% Polish, 1.8% Irish, 1.1% American, 1.1% German, 0.6% Hungarian
Employment: 5.8% management, business, and financial, 0.6% computer, engineering, and science, 5.1% education, legal, community service, arts, and media, 4.8% healthcare practitioners, 30.6% service, 22.5% sales and office, 8.5% natural resources, construction, and maintenance, 22.2% production, transportation, and material moving

Income: Per capita: $13,497; Median household: $27,583; Average household: $37,716; Households with income of $100,000 or more: 5.4%; Poverty rate: 35.7%
Educational Attainment: High school diploma or higher: 71.7%; Bachelor's degree or higher: 7.0%; Graduate/professional degree or higher: 2.1%

School District(s)
East Chicago Lighthouse Charter (KG-09)
    2012-13 Enrollment: 575 . . . . (219) 378-7451
East Chicago Urban Enterprise Acad (KG-08)
    2012-13 Enrollment: 446 . . . . (219) 392-3650
School City of East Chicago (PK-12)
    2012-13 Enrollment: 5,258 . . . . (219) 391-4100
Housing: Homeownership rate: 41.5%; Median home value: $82,900; Median year structure built: 1940; Homeowner vacancy rate: 3.6%; Median gross rent: $670 per month; Rental vacancy rate: 10.2%
Health Insurance: 79.1% have insurance; 39.2% have private insurance; 48.1% have public insurance; 20.9% do not have insurance; 9.3% of children under 18 do not have insurance
Hospitals: Saint Catherine Hospital (290 beds)
Safety: Violent crime rate: 66.7 per 10,000 population; Property crime rate: 497.3 per 10,000 population
Transportation: Commute: 88.2% car, 4.9% public transportation, 5.4% walk, 0.8% work from home; Median travel time to work: 21.7 minutes
Additional Information Contacts
City of East Chicago . . . . (219) 391-8491
    http://www.eastchicago.com

GARY (city). Covers a land area of 49.865 square miles and a water area of 7.310 square miles. Located at 41.60° N. Lat; 87.34° W. Long. Elevation is 600 feet.
History: Named for Judge Elbet H. Gary, chairman of the board of directors of U.S. Steel. The site of Gary was selected by the United States Steel Corporation in 1905 as the location of a new plant, as reported by Judge Elbert H. Gary in the Corporation's annual report. What was at first a work camp was expanded by the Gary Land Company into the city of Gary. Since the area was all sand where no grass would grow, soil had to be imported and trees and shrubs planted. Other industries soon joined the steel company, and Gary's industrial character was fixed.
Population: 80,294; Growth (since 2000): -21.9%; Density: 1,610.2 persons per square mile; Race: 10.7% White, 84.8% Black/African American, 0.2% Asian, 0.3% American Indian/Alaska Native, 0.0% Native Hawaiian/Other Pacific Islander, 2.1% Two or more races, 5.1% Hispanic of any race; Average household size: 2.54; Median age: 36.7; Age under 18: 28.1%; Age 65 and over: 14.5%; Males per 100 females: 85.1; Marriage status: 45.1% never married, 30.3% now married, 3.3% separated, 9.6% widowed, 15.0% divorced; Foreign born: 1.6%; Speak English only: 95.0%; With disability: 18.6%; Veterans: 9.8%; Ancestry: 2.8% Irish, 2.6% German, 1.8% English, 1.6% American, 1.5% African
Employment: 7.3% management, business, and financial, 1.6% computer, engineering, and science, 11.1% education, legal, community service, arts, and media, 4.5% healthcare practitioners, 27.9% service, 22.3% sales and office, 5.9% natural resources, construction, and maintenance, 19.5% production, transportation, and material moving
Income: Per capita: $15,931; Median household: $26,885; Average household: $38,600; Households with income of $100,000 or more: 6.4%; Poverty rate: 38.1%
Educational Attainment: High school diploma or higher: 82.9%; Bachelor's degree or higher: 12.3%; Graduate/professional degree or higher: 4.2%

School District(s)
21st Century Charter Sch of Gary (KG-12)
    2012-13 Enrollment: n/a . . . . (317) 536-1027
Aspire Charter Academy (KG-08)
    2012-13 Enrollment: 657 . . . . (219) 944-7400
Charter School of the Dunes (KG-08)
    2012-13 Enrollment: 464 . . . . (219) 939-9690
Gary Community School Corp (PK-12)
    2012-13 Enrollment: 8,873 . . . . (219) 881-5401
Gary Lighthouse Charter School (KG-11)
    2012-13 Enrollment: 716 . . . . (219) 880-1762
Kipp Lead College Prep Charter (05-10)
    2012-13 Enrollment: 298 . . . . (219) 979-9236
Lake Ridge Schools (KG-12)
    2012-13 Enrollment: 1,905 . . . . (219) 838-1819
Thea Bowman Leadership Academy (KG-12)
    2012-13 Enrollment: 1,464 . . . . (219) 883-4826
West Gary Lighthouse Charter (KG-10)
    2012-13 Enrollment: 613 . . . . (219) 977-9583

Four-year College(s)
Indiana University-Northwest (Public)
    Fall 2013 Enrollment: 6,387 . . . . (219) 980-6500
    2013-14 Tuition: In-state $6,739; Out-of-state $17,778

Vocational/Technical School(s)
Lil Lou's Barber College (Private, For-profit)
    Fall 2013 Enrollment: 62 . . . . (219) 884-9954
    2013-14 Tuition: $12,600

Housing: Homeownership rate: 52.7%; Median home value: $65,400; Median year structure built: 1955; Homeowner vacancy rate: 3.6%; Median gross rent: $711 per month; Rental vacancy rate: 14.5%
Health Insurance: 81.1% have insurance; 41.0% have private insurance; 52.1% have public insurance; 18.9% do not have insurance; 4.7% of children under 18 do not have insurance
Hospitals: Methodist Hospitals (469 beds)
Safety: Violent crime rate: 112.0 per 10,000 population; Property crime rate: 598.7 per 10,000 population
Transportation: Commute: 89.9% car, 3.7% public transportation, 3.2% walk, 1.9% work from home; Median travel time to work: 24.7 minutes
Airports: Gary/Chicago International (commercial service–non-primary)
Additional Information Contacts
City of Gary . . . . (219) 881-4730
    http://www.gary.in.us

GRIFFITH (town). Covers a land area of 7.733 square miles and a water area of 0 square miles. Located at 41.53° N. Lat; 87.42° W. Long. Elevation is 630 feet.
History: Named for Benjamin Griffith, a civil engineer for the railroad. Settled c.1854. Incorporated 1904.
Population: 16,893; Growth (since 2000): -2.5%; Density: 2,184.6 persons per square mile; Race: 75.8% White, 16.9% Black/African American, 0.8% Asian, 0.3% American Indian/Alaska Native, 0.0% Native Hawaiian/Other Pacific Islander, 2.4% Two or more races, 13.3% Hispanic of any race; Average household size: 2.53; Median age: 36.1; Age under 18: 24.3%; Age 65 and over: 11.2%; Males per 100 females: 90.9; Marriage status: 33.4% never married, 48.3% now married, 0.7% separated, 4.7% widowed, 13.6% divorced; Foreign born: 4.7%; Speak English only: 89.1%; With disability: 12.1%; Veterans: 9.1%; Ancestry: 20.6% German, 15.5% Irish, 9.4% Polish, 8.0% English, 4.6% Italian
Employment: 9.2% management, business, and financial, 3.9% computer, engineering, and science, 8.0% education, legal, community service, arts, and media, 3.9% healthcare practitioners, 21.8% service, 25.5% sales and office, 11.8% natural resources, construction, and maintenance, 15.9% production, transportation, and material moving
Income: Per capita: $25,247; Median household: $53,552; Average household: $64,871; Households with income of $100,000 or more: 17.5%; Poverty rate: 11.7%
Educational Attainment: High school diploma or higher: 90.5%; Bachelor's degree or higher: 16.7%; Graduate/professional degree or higher: 4.5%

School District(s)
Griffith Public Schools (KG-12)
    2012-13 Enrollment: 2,492 . . . . (219) 924-4250
Housing: Homeownership rate: 66.1%; Median home value: $140,900; Median year structure built: 1968; Homeowner vacancy rate: 1.3%; Median gross rent: $830 per month; Rental vacancy rate: 9.0%
Health Insurance: 88.2% have insurance; 74.4% have private insurance; 25.9% have public insurance; 11.8% do not have insurance; 6.0% of children under 18 do not have insurance
Safety: Violent crime rate: 18.0 per 10,000 population; Property crime rate: 338.9 per 10,000 population
Transportation: Commute: 93.9% car, 3.4% public transportation, 0.5% walk, 0.4% work from home; Median travel time to work: 25.7 minutes
Additional Information Contacts
Town of Griffith . . . . (219) 924-7500
    http://www.grffith.in.gov

HAMMOND

HAMMOND (city). Covers a land area of 22.776 square miles and a water area of 2.106 square miles. Located at 41.62° N. Lat; 87.49° W. Long. Elevation is 600 feet.

History: Named for George H. Hammond, a Detroit butcher who adapted the refrigeration boxcar. George H. Hammond, a Detroit butcher, opened a slaughterhouse in what was to become Hammond in 1869, when the refrigerator box was invented by the Davis brothers in Detroit and shipping of dressed beef became possible. Before Hammond was incorporated as a city in 1884, it had been known as Hohman for an early settler, and as State Line for its location on the Indiana-Illinois border. Hammond's slaughterhouse was the beginning of much industry in Hammond.

Population: 80,830; Growth (since 2000): -2.7%; Density: 3,549.0 persons per square mile; Race: 59.4% White, 22.5% Black/African American, 1.0% Asian, 0.5% American Indian/Alaska Native, 0.0% Native Hawaiian/Other Pacific Islander, 3.3% Two or more races, 34.1% Hispanic of any race; Average household size: 2.67; Median age: 33.3; Age under 18: 27.6%; Age 65 and over: 10.7%; Males per 100 females: 96.2; Marriage status: 39.1% never married, 43.3% now married, 3.0% separated, 6.3% widowed, 11.3% divorced; Foreign born: 12.0%; Speak English only: 73.0%; With disability: 14.4%; Veterans: 7.6%; Ancestry: 9.5% Irish, 9.3% German, 8.2% Polish, 3.6% English, 3.0% American

Employment: 6.9% management, business, and financial, 2.2% computer, engineering, and science, 8.3% education, legal, community service, arts, and media, 3.8% healthcare practitioners, 22.7% service, 24.5% sales and office, 9.6% natural resources, construction, and maintenance, 22.1% production, transportation, and material moving

Income: Per capita: $17,920; Median household: $38,365; Average household: $47,709; Households with income of $100,000 or more: 8.7%; Poverty rate: 22.9%

Educational Attainment: High school diploma or higher: 79.3%; Bachelor's degree or higher: 12.9%; Graduate/professional degree or higher: 4.0%

School District(s)
Hammond Academy of Science & Tech (06-10)
   2012-13 Enrollment: 469 . . . . (219) 852-0500
School City of Hammond (PK-12)
   2012-13 Enrollment: 13,670 . . . . (219) 933-2400

Four-year College(s)
Purdue University-Calumet Campus (Public)
   Fall 2013 Enrollment: 9,422 . . . . (219) 989-2400
   2013-14 Tuition: In-state $6,624; Out-of-state $14,966

Two-year College(s)
Kaplan College-Hammond (Private, For-profit)
   Fall 2013 Enrollment: 366 . . . . (219) 844-0100

Housing: Homeownership rate: 61.3%; Median home value: $92,400; Median year structure built: 1949; Homeowner vacancy rate: 2.6%; Median gross rent: $802 per month; Rental vacancy rate: 6.9%

Health Insurance: 79.3% have insurance; 53.4% have private insurance; 34.9% have public insurance; 20.7% do not have insurance; 8.7% of children under 18 do not have insurance

Hospitals: Franciscan Saint Margaret Health - Hammond (475 beds)

Safety: Violent crime rate: 82.4 per 10,000 population; Property crime rate: 407.8 per 10,000 population

Transportation: Commute: 91.7% car, 3.9% public transportation, 2.2% walk, 1.4% work from home; Median travel time to work: 27.0 minutes; Amtrak: Train service available.

Additional Information Contacts
City of Hammond . . . . (219) 853-6346
   http://www.gohammond.com/web

HIGHLAND

HIGHLAND (town). Covers a land area of 6.936 square miles and a water area of 0.023 square miles. Located at 41.55° N. Lat; 87.46° W. Long. Elevation is 623 feet.

History: Named originanlly Clough, then for its location on an area of high ground, in 1888. Highland was settled by people of Dutch descent, who established truck-gardening farms in the area.

Population: 23,727; Growth (since 2000): 0.8%; Density: 3,421.0 persons per square mile; Race: 88.6% White, 4.2% Black/African American, 1.6% Asian, 0.2% American Indian/Alaska Native, 0.0% Native Hawaiian/Other Pacific Islander, 2.0% Two or more races, 12.8% Hispanic of any race; Average household size: 2.39; Median age: 41.5; Age under 18: 20.9%; Age 65 and over: 17.3%; Males per 100 females: 92.3; Marriage status: 29.2% never married, 52.2% now married, 1.0% separated, 7.3% widowed, 11.3% divorced; Foreign born: 5.1%; Speak English only: 87.7%; With disability: 11.7%; Veterans: 9.1%; Ancestry: 19.5% German, 16.1% Polish, 14.3% Irish, 6.5% Dutch, 5.9% American

Employment: 13.3% management, business, and financial, 3.3% computer, engineering, and science, 11.0% education, legal, community service, arts, and media, 6.4% healthcare practitioners, 16.3% service, 25.1% sales and office, 10.1% natural resources, construction, and maintenance, 14.4% production, transportation, and material moving

Income: Per capita: $29,560; Median household: $61,353; Average household: $70,886; Households with income of $100,000 or more: 21.3%; Poverty rate: 5.7%

Educational Attainment: High school diploma or higher: 91.9%; Bachelor's degree or higher: 26.5%; Graduate/professional degree or higher: 8.2%

School District(s)
School Town of Highland (KG-12)
   2012-13 Enrollment: 3,242 . . . . (219) 922-5615

Vocational/Technical School(s)
Tricoci University of Beauty Culture-Highland (Private, For-profit)
   Fall 2013 Enrollment: 182 . . . . (219) 838-2004
   2013-14 Tuition: $18,800

Housing: Homeownership rate: 78.7%; Median home value: $153,900; Median year structure built: 1966; Homeowner vacancy rate: 1.1%; Median gross rent: $946 per month; Rental vacancy rate: 4.7%

Health Insurance: 90.1% have insurance; 77.8% have private insurance; 25.9% have public insurance; 9.9% do not have insurance; 7.1% of children under 18 do not have insurance

Safety: Violent crime rate: 3.9 per 10,000 population; Property crime rate: 324.3 per 10,000 population

Transportation: Commute: 94.6% car, 2.5% public transportation, 1.0% walk, 1.6% work from home; Median travel time to work: 25.6 minutes

Additional Information Contacts
Town of Highland . . . . (219) 838-1080
   http://www.highland.in.gov

HOBART

HOBART (city). Covers a land area of 26.331 square miles and a water area of 0.375 square miles. Located at 41.51° N. Lat; 87.28° W. Long. Elevation is 623 feet.

History: Hobart was founded by George Earle, an Englishman who built a home here and named the town for his brother. The town was platted in 1849.

Population: 29,059; Growth (since 2000): 14.6%; Density: 1,103.6 persons per square mile; Race: 85.3% White, 7.0% Black/African American, 1.0% Asian, 0.4% American Indian/Alaska Native, 0.0% Native Hawaiian/Other Pacific Islander, 2.4% Two or more races, 13.9% Hispanic of any race; Average household size: 2.48; Median age: 38.0; Age under 18: 23.1%; Age 65 and over: 14.4%; Males per 100 females: 94.2; Marriage status: 28.3% never married, 53.5% now married, 1.5% separated, 6.8% widowed, 11.5% divorced; Foreign born: 4.6%; Speak English only: 90.2%; With disability: 12.2%; Veterans: 11.9%; Ancestry: 19.7% German, 16.4% Irish, 9.4% Polish, 6.6% English, 5.0% Italian

Employment: 10.6% management, business, and financial, 3.0% computer, engineering, and science, 6.9% education, legal, community service, arts, and media, 5.4% healthcare practitioners, 19.9% service, 25.6% sales and office, 12.3% natural resources, construction, and maintenance, 16.3% production, transportation, and material moving

Income: Per capita: $25,392; Median household: $55,617; Average household: $61,955; Households with income of $100,000 or more: 14.9%; Poverty rate: 10.2%

Educational Attainment: High school diploma or higher: 88.7%; Bachelor's degree or higher: 15.4%; Graduate/professional degree or higher: 4.7%

School District(s)
River Forest Community Sch Corp (KG-12)
   2012-13 Enrollment: 1,530 . . . . (219) 962-2909
School City of Hobart (KG-12)
   2012-13 Enrollment: 3,969 . . . . (219) 942-8885

Two-year College(s)
College of Court Reporting Inc (Private, For-profit)
   Fall 2013 Enrollment: 265 . . . . (219) 942-1459
   2013-14 Tuition: In-state $13,550; Out-of-state $13,550

Housing: Homeownership rate: 73.3%; Median home value: $132,800; Median year structure built: 1967; Homeowner vacancy rate: 1.9%; Median gross rent: $838 per month; Rental vacancy rate: 8.1%

Health Insurance: 88.0% have insurance; 75.0% have private insurance; 26.3% have public insurance; 12.0% do not have insurance; 6.3% of children under 18 do not have insurance
Hospitals: Saint Mary Medical Center (190 beds)
Safety: Violent crime rate: 21.3 per 10,000 population; Property crime rate: 536.8 per 10,000 population
Transportation: Commute: 95.6% car, 1.7% public transportation, 0.3% walk, 2.0% work from home; Median travel time to work: 26.7 minutes
Additional Information Contacts
City of Hobart . . . . (219) 942-1940
http://www.city.hobart.in.us

LAKE DALECARLIA (CDP).
Covers a land area of 1.130 square miles and a water area of 0.257 square miles. Located at 41.34° N. Lat; 87.40° W. Long. Elevation is 712 feet.
Population: 1,355; Growth (since 2000): 5.4%; Density: 1,198.9 persons per square mile; Race: 97.3% White, 0.2% Black/African American, 0.1% Asian, 0.1% American Indian/Alaska Native, 0.0% Native Hawaiian/Other Pacific Islander, 1.1% Two or more races, 3.4% Hispanic of any race; Average household size: 2.58; Median age: 43.6; Age under 18: 21.8%; Age 65 and over: 14.0%; Males per 100 females: 111.1
Housing: Homeownership rate: 89.7%; Homeowner vacancy rate: 2.5%; Rental vacancy rate: 1.8%

LAKE STATION (city).
Covers a land area of 8.296 square miles and a water area of 0.131 square miles. Located at 41.58° N. Lat; 87.25° W. Long. Elevation is 620 feet.
Population: 12,572; Growth (since 2000): -9.9%; Density: 1,515.4 persons per square mile; Race: 79.7% White, 3.6% Black/African American, 0.3% Asian, 0.5% American Indian/Alaska Native, 0.0% Native Hawaiian/Other Pacific Islander, 4.1% Two or more races, 28.0% Hispanic of any race; Average household size: 2.72; Median age: 35.4; Age under 18: 26.4%; Age 65 and over: 10.7%; Males per 100 females: 99.9; Marriage status: 30.7% never married, 47.7% now married, 2.4% separated, 6.3% widowed, 15.3% divorced; Foreign born: 4.3%; Speak English only: 83.3%; With disability: 19.8%; Veterans: 8.8%; Ancestry: 18.2% German, 14.9% Irish, 7.0% Polish, 5.9% American, 5.4% Italian
Employment: 6.0% management, business, and financial, 1.3% computer, engineering, and science, 6.6% education, legal, community service, arts, and media, 4.7% healthcare practitioners, 23.1% service, 20.3% sales and office, 16.5% natural resources, construction, and maintenance, 21.4% production, transportation, and material moving
Income: Per capita: $16,970; Median household: $38,537; Average household: $44,380; Households with income of $100,000 or more: 7.4%; Poverty rate: 21.5%
Educational Attainment: High school diploma or higher: 79.1%; Bachelor's degree or higher: 5.6%; Graduate/professional degree or higher: 1.0%

School District(s)
Lake Station Community Schools (KG-12)
    2012-13 Enrollment: 1,520 . . . . (219) 962-1159
River Forest Community Sch Corp (KG-12)
    2012-13 Enrollment: 1,530 . . . . (219) 962-2909
Housing: Homeownership rate: 72.2%; Median home value: $81,200; Median year structure built: 1955; Homeowner vacancy rate: 3.7%; Median gross rent: $768 per month; Rental vacancy rate: 8.6%
Health Insurance: 75.8% have insurance; 52.9% have private insurance; 33.8% have public insurance; 24.2% do not have insurance; 14.4% of children under 18 do not have insurance
Safety: Violent crime rate: 40.5 per 10,000 population; Property crime rate: 471.0 per 10,000 population
Transportation: Commute: 95.8% car, 0.5% public transportation, 0.1% walk, 2.4% work from home; Median travel time to work: 24.9 minutes
Additional Information Contacts
City of Lake Station . . . . (219) 962-2081
http://www.lakestation.in.gov

LAKES OF THE FOUR SEASONS (CDP).
Covers a land area of 2.681 square miles and a water area of 0.416 square miles. Located at 41.40° N. Lat; 87.22° W. Long. Elevation is 764 feet.
History: Lakes of the Four Seasons (LOFS) is a private, gated community of about 10,000 residents located half-way between Crown Point and Valparaiso, Indiana. The community has its own private security force, four lakes, an 18 hole championship golf course, parks, playgrounds, athletic fields, tennis courts, beaches, a swimming pool, two restaurants, a clubhouse, and pro-shop. A set of restrictive covenants governs construction, maintenance, and general rules of the community through the POA.
Population: 7,033; Growth (since 2000): -3.5%; Density: 2,623.6 persons per square mile; Race: 93.4% White, 1.2% Black/African American, 1.0% Asian, 0.2% American Indian/Alaska Native, 0.1% Native Hawaiian/Other Pacific Islander, 1.9% Two or more races, 8.5% Hispanic of any race; Average household size: 2.76; Median age: 42.3; Age under 18: 23.3%; Age 65 and over: 14.5%; Males per 100 females: 96.0; Marriage status: 21.4% never married, 66.0% now married, 0.3% separated, 4.2% widowed, 8.5% divorced; Foreign born: 5.0%; Speak English only: 92.9%; With disability: 9.4%; Veterans: 12.5%; Ancestry: 27.9% German, 20.1% Irish, 16.4% Polish, 10.9% Italian, 8.9% English
Employment: 9.6% management, business, and financial, 6.1% computer, engineering, and science, 13.8% education, legal, community service, arts, and media, 10.2% healthcare practitioners, 14.1% service, 28.5% sales and office, 8.4% natural resources, construction, and maintenance, 9.3% production, transportation, and material moving
Income: Per capita: $34,342; Median household: $87,929; Average household: $94,008; Households with income of $100,000 or more: 37.6%; Poverty rate: 2.5%
Educational Attainment: High school diploma or higher: 94.3%; Bachelor's degree or higher: 29.7%; Graduate/professional degree or higher: 8.9%
Housing: Homeownership rate: 95.0%; Median home value: $179,700; Median year structure built: 1979; Homeowner vacancy rate: 1.7%; Median gross rent: n/a per month; Rental vacancy rate: 0.7%
Health Insurance: 91.4% have insurance; 86.0% have private insurance; 19.6% have public insurance; 8.6% do not have insurance; 5.9% of children under 18 do not have insurance
Transportation: Commute: 96.4% car, 2.3% public transportation, 0.0% walk, 1.3% work from home; Median travel time to work: 38.5 minutes

LOWELL (town).
Covers a land area of 5.180 square miles and a water area of 0.086 square miles. Located at 41.29° N. Lat; 87.42° W. Long. Elevation is 669 feet.
History: Settled 1849, laid out 1853.
Population: 9,276; Growth (since 2000): 23.6%; Density: 1,790.8 persons per square mile; Race: 95.9% White, 0.5% Black/African American, 0.3% Asian, 0.4% American Indian/Alaska Native, 0.1% Native Hawaiian/Other Pacific Islander, 1.2% Two or more races, 6.9% Hispanic of any race; Average household size: 2.71; Median age: 35.7; Age under 18: 26.6%; Age 65 and over: 11.7%; Males per 100 females: 96.9; Marriage status: 32.8% never married, 54.9% now married, 1.6% separated, 4.7% widowed, 7.6% divorced; Foreign born: 1.8%; Speak English only: 96.5%; With disability: 12.2%; Veterans: 10.2%; Ancestry: 34.2% German, 19.8% Irish, 9.4% Polish, 9.4% English, 8.8% American
Employment: 8.8% management, business, and financial, 3.7% computer, engineering, and science, 10.0% education, legal, community service, arts, and media, 8.3% healthcare practitioners, 14.4% service, 20.3% sales and office, 15.9% natural resources, construction, and maintenance, 18.7% production, transportation, and material moving
Income: Per capita: $23,592; Median household: $61,660; Average household: $69,914; Households with income of $100,000 or more: 19.2%; Poverty rate: 7.5%
Educational Attainment: High school diploma or higher: 94.1%; Bachelor's degree or higher: 18.1%; Graduate/professional degree or higher: 6.4%

School District(s)
Tri-Creek School Corporation (KG-12)
    2012-13 Enrollment: 3,556 . . . . (219) 696-6661
Housing: Homeownership rate: 77.9%; Median home value: $145,600; Median year structure built: 1977; Homeowner vacancy rate: 2.3%; Median gross rent: $883 per month; Rental vacancy rate: 9.2%
Health Insurance: 86.3% have insurance; 75.4% have private insurance; 20.2% have public insurance; 13.7% do not have insurance; 12.4% of children under 18 do not have insurance
Safety: Violent crime rate: 19.2 per 10,000 population; Property crime rate: 112.3 per 10,000 population
Newspapers: Pilcher Publishing (weekly circulation 8800)
Transportation: Commute: 96.2% car, 0.2% public transportation, 0.8% walk, 1.7% work from home; Median travel time to work: 35.1 minutes
Additional Information Contacts
Town of Lowell . . . . (219) 696-7794
http://www.lowell.net

MERRILLVILLE (town). Covers a land area of 33.216 square miles and a water area of 0.035 square miles. Located at 41.47° N. Lat; 87.32° W. Long. Elevation is 656 feet.
History: Named for Dudley Merrill, a local storekeeper. Merrillville was settled at the place where many smaller trails met with the Sauk Trail.
Population: 35,246; Growth (since 2000): 15.3%; Density: 1,061.1 persons per square mile; Race: 46.4% White, 44.5% Black/African American, 1.2% Asian, 0.2% American Indian/Alaska Native, 0.0% Native Hawaiian/Other Pacific Islander, 3.2% Two or more races, 12.9% Hispanic of any race; Average household size: 2.54; Median age: 36.7; Age under 18: 25.5%; Age 65 and over: 13.7%; Males per 100 females: 88.6; Marriage status: 35.1% never married, 44.0% now married, 2.1% separated, 7.1% widowed, 13.8% divorced; Foreign born: 5.9%; Speak English only: 88.4%; With disability: 14.9%; Veterans: 10.3%; Ancestry: 10.5% German, 7.2% Irish, 5.1% Polish, 4.0% English, 3.5% American
Employment: 8.1% management, business, and financial, 1.8% computer, engineering, and science, 8.8% education, legal, community service, arts, and media, 7.3% healthcare practitioners, 21.2% service, 25.4% sales and office, 7.3% natural resources, construction, and maintenance, 20.1% production, transportation, and material moving
Income: Per capita: $22,989; Median household: $51,389; Average household: $58,756; Households with income of $100,000 or more: 13.6%; Poverty rate: 16.7%
Educational Attainment: High school diploma or higher: 90.0%; Bachelor's degree or higher: 20.9%; Graduate/professional degree or higher: 7.8%

School District(s)
Merrillville Community School (KG-12)
    2012-13 Enrollment: 6,858 . . . . (219) 650-5300

Four-year College(s)
Brown Mackie College-Merrillville (Private, For-profit)
    Fall 2013 Enrollment: 619 . . . . (219) 769-3321
    2013-14 Tuition: In-state $12,114; Out-of-state $12,114
ITT Technical Institute-Merrillville (Private, For-profit)
    Fall 2013 Enrollment: 357 . . . . (219) 738-6100
    2013-14 Tuition: In-state $18,048; Out-of-state $18,048

Vocational/Technical School(s)
Everest College-Merrillville (Private, For-profit)
    Fall 2013 Enrollment: 645 . . . . (219) 756-6811
    2013-14 Tuition: $18,841
Merrillville Beauty College (Private, For-profit)
    Fall 2013 Enrollment: 62 . . . . (219) 769-2232
    2013-14 Tuition: $11,500
Regency Beauty Institute-Merrillville (Private, For-profit)
    Fall 2013 Enrollment: 146 . . . . (800) 787-6456
    2013-14 Tuition: $16,200
Success Schools (Private, For-profit)
    Fall 2013 Enrollment: 130 . . . . (219) 736-9999
    2013-14 Tuition: $18,000

Housing: Homeownership rate: 66.4%; Median home value: $130,400; Median year structure built: 1973; Homeowner vacancy rate: 3.2%; Median gross rent: $931 per month; Rental vacancy rate: 10.1%
Health Insurance: 85.5% have insurance; 65.3% have private insurance; 33.3% have public insurance; 14.5% do not have insurance; 6.3% of children under 18 do not have insurance
Safety: Violent crime rate: 27.7 per 10,000 population; Property crime rate: 373.9 per 10,000 population
Transportation: Commute: 93.8% car, 1.6% public transportation, 0.7% walk, 1.8% work from home; Median travel time to work: 27.2 minutes
Additional Information Contacts
Town of Merrillville. . . . . (219) 769-3501
    http://www.merrillville.in.gov

MUNSTER (town). Covers a land area of 7.570 square miles and a water area of 0.081 square miles. Located at 41.55° N. Lat; 87.50° W. Long. Elevation is 610 feet.
History: Named for Eldert Munster, who settled here in 1855. Settled 1855.
Population: 23,603; Growth (since 2000): 9.7%; Density: 3,117.9 persons per square mile; Race: 85.6% White, 3.5% Black/African American, 5.8% Asian, 0.2% American Indian/Alaska Native, 0.0% Native Hawaiian/Other Pacific Islander, 1.8% Two or more races, 10.2% Hispanic of any race; Average household size: 2.59; Median age: 44.8; Age under 18: 23.4%; Age 65 and over: 18.7%; Males per 100 females: 92.5; Marriage status: 26.1% never married, 56.3% now married, 1.6% separated, 10.3% widowed, 7.3% divorced; Foreign born: 10.8%; Speak English only: 81.3%; With disability: 10.7%; Veterans: 8.5%; Ancestry: 19.5% German, 16.2% Polish, 14.3% Irish, 7.6% English, 6.4% Italian
Employment: 17.8% management, business, and financial, 5.8% computer, engineering, and science, 12.6% education, legal, community service, arts, and media, 9.7% healthcare practitioners, 12.0% service, 24.6% sales and office, 7.3% natural resources, construction, and maintenance, 10.3% production, transportation, and material moving
Income: Per capita: $37,099; Median household: $72,583; Average household: $96,848; Households with income of $100,000 or more: 36.1%; Poverty rate: 6.6%
Educational Attainment: High school diploma or higher: 94.2%; Bachelor's degree or higher: 40.6%; Graduate/professional degree or higher: 16.7%

School District(s)
School Town of Munster (KG-12)
    2012-13 Enrollment: 4,158 . . . . (219) 836-9111

Housing: Homeownership rate: 86.8%; Median home value: $196,400; Median year structure built: 1971; Homeowner vacancy rate: 1.4%; Median gross rent: $962 per month; Rental vacancy rate: 5.9%
Health Insurance: 92.5% have insurance; 82.7% have private insurance; 22.7% have public insurance; 7.5% do not have insurance; 1.6% of children under 18 do not have insurance
Hospitals: Community Hospital (354 beds); Franciscan Healthcare - Munster (63 beds)
Newspapers: The Times (daily circulation 81200)
Transportation: Commute: 89.2% car, 5.0% public transportation, 0.7% walk, 4.5% work from home; Median travel time to work: 27.8 minutes
Additional Information Contacts
Town of Munster . . . . (219) 836-6900
    http://www.ci.munster.in.us

NEW CHICAGO (town). Covers a land area of 0.669 square miles and a water area of 0 square miles. Located at 41.56° N. Lat; 87.27° W. Long. Elevation is 636 feet.
History: New Chicago was the home of the United States Electric Carriage Company, which built the first electric buggy in 1898.
Population: 2,035; Growth (since 2000): -1.4%; Density: 3,040.0 persons per square mile; Race: 81.0% White, 2.2% Black/African American, 0.7% Asian, 0.7% American Indian/Alaska Native, 0.0% Native Hawaiian/Other Pacific Islander, 5.3% Two or more races, 27.4% Hispanic of any race; Average household size: 2.67; Median age: 33.9; Age under 18: 27.5%; Age 65 and over: 11.1%; Males per 100 females: 99.9
Housing: Homeownership rate: 70.6%; Homeowner vacancy rate: 4.1%; Rental vacancy rate: 17.3%

SAINT JOHN (town). Covers a land area of 11.387 square miles and a water area of 0.091 square miles. Located at 41.44° N. Lat; 87.47° W. Long. Elevation is 725 feet.
History: St. John was founded in 1837. It is generally agreed that the Town of St. John had its beginning when John Hack, a German immigrant farmer and his family arrived in 1837, in the area then known asWestern prairie or Prairie West.
Population: 14,850; Growth (since 2000): 77.2%; Density: 1,304.1 persons per square mile; Race: 93.5% White, 1.3% Black/African American, 1.3% Asian, 0.1% American Indian/Alaska Native, 0.1% Native Hawaiian/Other Pacific Islander, 1.2% Two or more races, 8.2% Hispanic of any race; Average household size: 2.94; Median age: 40.2; Age under 18: 27.3%; Age 65 and over: 11.3%; Males per 100 females: 99.6; Marriage status: 21.7% never married, 67.2% now married, 0.4% separated, 5.1% widowed, 6.0% divorced; Foreign born: 5.1%; Speak English only: 89.4%; With disability: 7.8%; Veterans: 8.1%; Ancestry: 25.2% German, 19.4% Polish, 17.5% Irish, 11.2% Italian, 6.8% Dutch
Employment: 21.7% management, business, and financial, 4.2% computer, engineering, and science, 13.5% education, legal, community service, arts, and media, 7.3% healthcare practitioners, 12.3% service, 22.2% sales and office, 8.8% natural resources, construction, and maintenance, 9.9% production, transportation, and material moving
Income: Per capita: $37,513; Median household: $94,526; Average household: $106,902; Households with income of $100,000 or more: 47.1%; Poverty rate: 3.9%
Educational Attainment: High school diploma or higher: 96.6%; Bachelor's degree or higher: 36.7%; Graduate/professional degree or higher: 11.6%

School District(s)
Lake Central School Corp (PK-12)
2012-13 Enrollment: 10,009 . . . . (219) 558-2707
Housing: Homeownership rate: 97.0%; Median home value: $250,300; Median year structure built: 1996; Homeowner vacancy rate: 2.0%; Median gross rent: $1,031 per month; Rental vacancy rate: 3.3%
Health Insurance: 93.4% have insurance; 88.3% have private insurance; 14.2% have public insurance; 6.6% do not have insurance; 4.1% of children under 18 do not have insurance
Transportation: Commute: 92.6% car, 2.4% public transportation, 0.0% walk, 3.6% work from home; Median travel time to work: 32.9 minutes
Additional Information Contacts
Town of Saint John . . . . (219) 365-6465
http://www.stjohnin.com

SCHERERVILLE (town).
Covers a land area of 14.712 square miles and a water area of 0.053 square miles. Located at 41.49° N. Lat; 87.44° W. Long. Elevation is 669 feet.
History: Named for Nicholas Scherer, who plotted the town in 1866. Laid out 1866.
Population: 29,243; Growth (since 2000): 17.7%; Density: 1,987.7 persons per square mile; Race: 86.8% White, 5.4% Black/African American, 2.8% Asian, 0.2% American Indian/Alaska Native, 0.0% Native Hawaiian/Other Pacific Islander, 1.8% Two or more races, 10.6% Hispanic of any race; Average household size: 2.45; Median age: 40.9; Age under 18: 22.1%; Age 65 and over: 14.0%; Males per 100 females: 94.2; Marriage status: 27.8% never married, 56.4% now married, 0.9% separated, 6.2% widowed, 9.5% divorced; Foreign born: 9.6%; Speak English only: 83.7%; With disability: 9.7%; Veterans: 8.1%; Ancestry: 21.8% German, 16.7% Polish, 13.9% Irish, 6.9% English, 5.6% American
Employment: 19.1% management, business, and financial, 4.5% computer, engineering, and science, 10.5% education, legal, community service, arts, and media, 9.4% healthcare practitioners, 12.4% service, 22.2% sales and office, 7.5% natural resources, construction, and maintenance, 14.4% production, transportation, and material moving
Income: Per capita: $33,969; Median household: $66,449; Average household: $82,777; Households with income of $100,000 or more: 30.0%; Poverty rate: 6.6%
Educational Attainment: High school diploma or higher: 93.0%; Bachelor's degree or higher: 32.4%; Graduate/professional degree or higher: 13.9%
School District(s)
Lake Central School Corp (PK-12)
2012-13 Enrollment: 10,009 . . . . (219) 558-2707
Vocational/Technical School(s)
Don Roberts School of Hair Design (Private, For-profit)
Fall 2013 Enrollment: 53 . . . . (219) 864-1600
2013-14 Tuition: $16,150
Housing: Homeownership rate: 78.1%; Median home value: $207,800; Median year structure built: 1987; Homeowner vacancy rate: 1.3%; Median gross rent: $832 per month; Rental vacancy rate: 7.0%
Health Insurance: 90.3% have insurance; 82.2% have private insurance; 20.7% have public insurance; 9.7% do not have insurance; 2.9% of children under 18 do not have insurance
Safety: Violent crime rate: 7.1 per 10,000 population; Property crime rate: 240.3 per 10,000 population
Transportation: Commute: 94.5% car, 2.0% public transportation, 0.5% walk, 1.7% work from home; Median travel time to work: 29.8 minutes
Additional Information Contacts
Town of Schererville . . . . (219) 322-2211
http://www.ci.schererville.in.us

SCHNEIDER (town).
Covers a land area of 0.861 square miles and a water area of 0 square miles. Located at 41.19° N. Lat; 87.45° W. Long. Elevation is 633 feet.
Population: 277; Growth (since 2000): -12.6%; Density: 321.6 persons per square mile; Race: 97.1% White, 0.0% Black/African American, 1.1% Asian, 1.1% American Indian/Alaska Native, 0.0% Native Hawaiian/Other Pacific Islander, 0.7% Two or more races, 2.5% Hispanic of any race; Average household size: 2.83; Median age: 33.5; Age under 18: 29.6%; Age 65 and over: 10.1%; Males per 100 females: 106.7
Housing: Homeownership rate: 77.5%; Homeowner vacancy rate: 5.0%; Rental vacancy rate: 15.4%

SHELBY (CDP).
Covers a land area of 1.287 square miles and a water area of 0 square miles. Located at 41.19° N. Lat; 87.34° W. Long. Elevation is 640 feet.
Population: 539; Growth (since 2000): n/a; Density: 418.7 persons per square mile; Race: 95.5% White, 1.7% Black/African American, 0.2% Asian, 0.7% American Indian/Alaska Native, 0.0% Native Hawaiian/Other Pacific Islander, 1.1% Two or more races, 0.9% Hispanic of any race; Average household size: 2.45; Median age: 42.6; Age under 18: 21.2%; Age 65 and over: 14.1%; Males per 100 females: 108.9
Housing: Homeownership rate: 80.9%; Homeowner vacancy rate: 2.2%; Rental vacancy rate: 0.0%

WHITING (city).
Covers a land area of 1.798 square miles and a water area of 1.429 square miles. Located at 41.68° N. Lat; 87.48° W. Long. Elevation is 587 feet.
History: Whiting was settled by German immigrants. For many years a Standard Oil Company plant, established in 1889, was the major industry.
Population: 4,997; Growth (since 2000): -2.7%; Density: 2,779.8 persons per square mile; Race: 76.3% White, 3.5% Black/African American, 0.7% Asian, 0.7% American Indian/Alaska Native, 0.0% Native Hawaiian/Other Pacific Islander, 3.2% Two or more races, 40.7% Hispanic of any race; Average household size: 2.63; Median age: 34.4; Age under 18: 26.9%; Age 65 and over: 11.6%; Males per 100 females: 96.6; Marriage status: 36.4% never married, 46.8% now married, 2.0% separated, 7.3% widowed, 9.5% divorced; Foreign born: 7.6%; Speak English only: 75.1%; With disability: 14.8%; Veterans: 9.5%; Ancestry: 17.2% Polish, 12.3% German, 11.2% Slovak, 10.4% Irish, 5.3% English
Employment: 8.5% management, business, and financial, 2.9% computer, engineering, and science, 8.0% education, legal, community service, arts, and media, 1.2% healthcare practitioners, 19.4% service, 25.5% sales and office, 6.3% natural resources, construction, and maintenance, 28.3% production, transportation, and material moving
Income: Per capita: $23,286; Median household: $49,563; Average household: $61,246; Households with income of $100,000 or more: 18.4%; Poverty rate: 12.9%
Educational Attainment: High school diploma or higher: 88.6%; Bachelor's degree or higher: 19.1%; Graduate/professional degree or higher: 6.4%
School District(s)
School City of Hammond (PK-12)
2012-13 Enrollment: 13,670 . . . . (219) 933-2400
Whiting School City (PK-12)
2012-13 Enrollment: 1,123 . . . . (219) 659-0656
Four-year College(s)
Calumet College of Saint Joseph (Private, Not-for-profit, Roman Catholic)
Fall 2013 Enrollment: 1,140 . . . . (219) 473-7770
2013-14 Tuition: In-state $15,620; Out-of-state $15,620
Housing: Homeownership rate: 55.5%; Median home value: $112,100; Median year structure built: Before 1940; Homeowner vacancy rate: 3.6%; Median gross rent: $727 per month; Rental vacancy rate: 4.8%
Health Insurance: 86.6% have insurance; 67.5% have private insurance; 28.0% have public insurance; 13.4% do not have insurance; 6.4% of children under 18 do not have insurance
Safety: Violent crime rate: 8.1 per 10,000 population; Property crime rate: 329.4 per 10,000 population
Transportation: Commute: 88.4% car, 1.4% public transportation, 6.8% walk, 0.9% work from home; Median travel time to work: 23.5 minutes; Amtrak: Train service available.
Additional Information Contacts
City of Whiting . . . . (219) 659-3100
http://whitingindiana.com

WINFIELD (town).
Covers a land area of 11.975 square miles and a water area of 0.066 square miles. Located at 41.41° N. Lat; 87.26° W. Long. Elevation is 709 feet.
History: The town was incorporated 1993, making it one of newest towns in Indiana. Prior to that time it had been part of Winfield Township as an unincorporated town. Winfield is named for General Winfield Scott.
Population: 4,383; Growth (since 2000): 90.7%; Density: 366.0 persons per square mile; Race: 88.5% White, 3.7% Black/African American, 3.5% Asian, 0.4% American Indian/Alaska Native, 0.0% Native Hawaiian/Other Pacific Islander, 1.3% Two or more races, 8.9% Hispanic of any race; Average household size: 3.00; Median age: 38.7; Age under 18: 29.0%; Age 65 and over: 13.0%; Males per 100 females: 95.0; Marriage status: 20.5% never married, 63.8% now married, 0.6% separated, 9.6%

widowed, 6.1% divorced; Foreign born: 8.0%; Speak English only: 85.7%; With disability: 10.8%; Veterans: 8.6%; Ancestry: 17.9% German, 14.1% Irish, 10.1% English, 10.0% Polish, 9.1% Italian
Employment: 24.2% management, business, and financial, 4.5% computer, engineering, and science, 10.3% education, legal, community service, arts, and media, 6.5% healthcare practitioners, 11.2% service, 19.6% sales and office, 9.5% natural resources, construction, and maintenance, 14.2% production, transportation, and material moving
Income: Per capita: $31,535; Median household: $76,123; Average household: $90,229; Households with income of $100,000 or more: 30.1%; Poverty rate: 4.6%
Educational Attainment: High school diploma or higher: 92.8%; Bachelor's degree or higher: 32.0%; Graduate/professional degree or higher: 10.9%
Housing: Homeownership rate: 90.4%; Median home value: $226,700; Median year structure built: 2001; Homeowner vacancy rate: 3.3%; Median gross rent: $746 per month; Rental vacancy rate: 7.4%
Health Insurance: 95.0% have insurance; 84.6% have private insurance; 21.6% have public insurance; 5.0% do not have insurance; 2.0% of children under 18 do not have insurance
Newspapers: Winfield American (weekly circulation 5000)
Transportation: Commute: 92.8% car, 0.8% public transportation, 1.7% walk, 4.8% work from home; Median travel time to work: 29.7 minutes
Additional Information Contacts
Town of Winfield . . . . (219) 662-2665
  http://www.winfieldgov.com

LaPorte County

Located in northwestern Indiana; bounded on the northwest by Lake Michigan, on the north by Michigan, and partly on the south by the Kankakee River. Covers a land area of 598.299 square miles, a water area of 14.960 square miles, and is located in the Central Time Zone at 41.55° N. Lat., 86.74° W. Long. The county was founded in 1832. County seat is La Porte.

LaPorte County is part of the Michigan City-La Porte, IN Metropolitan Statistical Area. The entire metro area includes: LaPorte County, IN

Weather Station: La Porte												Elevation: 810 feet
	Jan	Feb	Mar	Apr	May	Jun	Jul	Aug	Sep	Oct	Nov	Dec
High	31	35	46	58	70	79	82	80	74	62	48	35
Low	18	21	29	40	50	60	64	63	55	44	34	23
Precip	2.6	2.3	2.9	3.6	3.8	4.2	4.3	4.4	3.7	3.8	3.9	3.2
Snow	20.6	13.9	7.2	1.4	tr	0.0	0.0	0.0	0.0	0.4	3.8	14.9

High and Low temperatures in degrees Fahrenheit; Precipitation and Snow in inches

Population: 111,467; Growth (since 2000): 1.2%; Density: 186.3 persons per square mile; Race: 84.1% White, 10.8% Black/African American, 0.5% Asian, 0.3% American Indian/Alaska Native, 0.0% Native Hawaiian/Other Pacific Islander, 2.3% two or more races, 5.5% Hispanic of any race; Average household size: 2.48; Median age: 39.6; Age under 18: 22.8%; Age 65 and over: 14.2%; Males per 100 females: 107.1; Marriage status: 29.4% never married, 50.7% now married, 1.7% separated, 6.2% widowed, 13.6% divorced; Foreign born: 3.0%; Speak English only: 94.7%; With disability: 14.5%; Veterans: 10.4%; Ancestry: 27.4% German, 14.9% Irish, 11.7% Polish, 7.2% English, 6.6% American
Religion: Six largest groups: 13.3% Catholicism, 4.8% Lutheran, 3.9% Baptist, 3.5% Methodist/Pietist, 3.4% Non-denominational Protestant, 1.8% Presbyterian-Reformed
Economy: Unemployment rate: 6.7%; Leading industries: 19.6% retail trade; 11.6% other services (except public administration); 10.0% accommodation and food services; Farms: 731 totaling 227,865 acres; Company size: 3 employ 1,000 or more persons, 1 employs 500 to 999 persons, 46 employ 100 to 499 persons, 2,297 employ less than 100 persons; Business ownership: n/a women-owned, n/a Black-owned, 94 Hispanic-owned, 70 Asian-owned
Employment: 11.6% management, business, and financial, 2.4% computer, engineering, and science, 8.5% education, legal, community service, arts, and media, 4.7% healthcare practitioners, 18.2% service, 24.5% sales and office, 10.0% natural resources, construction, and maintenance, 20.1% production, transportation, and material moving
Income: Per capita: $22,852; Median household: $47,538; Average household: $59,211; Households with income of $100,000 or more: 14.5%; Poverty rate: 16.5%
Educational Attainment: High school diploma or higher: 86.5%; Bachelor's degree or higher: 17.3%; Graduate/professional degree or higher: 6.1%
Housing: Homeownership rate: 73.7%; Median home value: $122,800; Median year structure built: 1964; Homeowner vacancy rate: 2.2%; Median gross rent: $694 per month; Rental vacancy rate: 11.6%
Vital Statistics: Birth rate: 119.8 per 10,000 population; Death rate: 103.4 per 10,000 population; Age-adjusted cancer mortality rate: 193.7 deaths per 100,000 population
Health Insurance: 86.9% have insurance; 65.9% have private insurance; 32.8% have public insurance; 13.1% do not have insurance; 5.8% of children under 18 do not have insurance
Health Care: Physicians: 14.4 per 10,000 population; Hospital beds: 33.7 per 10,000 population; Hospital admissions: 1,255.2 per 10,000 population
Air Quality Index: 84.9% good, 14.5% moderate, 0.5% unhealthy for sensitive individuals, 0.0% unhealthy (percent of days)
Transportation: Commute: 93.6% car, 1.1% public transportation, 1.4% walk, 2.9% work from home; Median travel time to work: 22.3 minutes
Presidential Election: 55.2% Obama, 42.6% Romney (2012)
National and State Parks: Kingsbury State Fish and Wildlife Area
Additional Information Contacts
LaPorte Government . . . . (219) 326-6808
  http://www.laportecounty.org

LaPorte County Communities

FISH LAKE (CDP). Covers a land area of 1.541 square miles and a water area of 0.344 square miles. Located at 41.56° N. Lat; 86.55° W. Long. Elevation is 702 feet.
Population: 1,016; Growth (since 2000): n/a; Density: 659.4 persons per square mile; Race: 97.6% White, 0.5% Black/African American, 0.1% Asian, 0.2% American Indian/Alaska Native, 0.0% Native Hawaiian/Other Pacific Islander, 1.3% Two or more races, 2.4% Hispanic of any race; Average household size: 2.33; Median age: 46.1; Age under 18: 20.1%; Age 65 and over: 20.4%; Males per 100 females: 97.7
Housing: Homeownership rate: 85.3%; Homeowner vacancy rate: 3.4%; Rental vacancy rate: 7.2%

HANNA (CDP). Covers a land area of 0.978 square miles and a water area of 0 square miles. Located at 41.41° N. Lat; 86.78° W. Long. Elevation is 705 feet.
Population: 463; Growth (since 2000): n/a; Density: 473.3 persons per square mile; Race: 98.1% White, 0.0% Black/African American, 0.0% Asian, 0.2% American Indian/Alaska Native, 0.0% Native Hawaiian/Other Pacific Islander, 1.7% Two or more races, 0.9% Hispanic of any race; Average household size: 2.50; Median age: 42.8; Age under 18: 19.2%; Age 65 and over: 18.4%; Males per 100 females: 98.7
Housing: Homeownership rate: 81.1%; Homeowner vacancy rate: 0.7%; Rental vacancy rate: 0.0%

HUDSON LAKE (CDP). Covers a land area of 1.925 square miles and a water area of 0.759 square miles. Located at 41.72° N. Lat; 86.55° W. Long. Elevation is 771 feet.
Population: 1,297; Growth (since 2000): n/a; Density: 673.7 persons per square mile; Race: 97.1% White, 0.1% Black/African American, 0.1% Asian, 0.2% American Indian/Alaska Native, 0.0% Native Hawaiian/Other Pacific Islander, 1.6% Two or more races, 3.0% Hispanic of any race; Average household size: 2.47; Median age: 41.1; Age under 18: 23.0%; Age 65 and over: 14.5%; Males per 100 females: 105.2
Housing: Homeownership rate: 83.4%; Homeowner vacancy rate: 2.4%; Rental vacancy rate: 2.2%

KINGSBURY (town). Covers a land area of 0.573 square miles and a water area of 0 square miles. Located at 41.53° N. Lat; 86.70° W. Long. Elevation is 748 feet.
History: Kingsbury developed around the Wabash and the Grand Trunk Railroads in the mid-1800's.
Population: 242; Growth (since 2000): 5.7%; Density: 422.3 persons per square mile; Race: 97.1% White, 0.4% Black/African American, 0.0% Asian, 0.4% American Indian/Alaska Native, 0.0% Native Hawaiian/Other Pacific Islander, 0.0% Two or more races, 5.4% Hispanic of any race; Average household size: 2.66; Median age: 39.8; Age under 18: 25.2%; Age 65 and over: 16.1%; Males per 100 females: 98.4
Housing: Homeownership rate: 75.9%; Homeowner vacancy rate: 0.0%; Rental vacancy rate: 8.3%

KINGSFORD HEIGHTS (town). Covers a land area of 0.942 square miles and a water area of 0 square miles. Located at 41.48° N. Lat; 86.69° W. Long. Elevation is 725 feet.
Population: 1,435; Growth (since 2000): -1.2%; Density: 1,524.0 persons per square mile; Race: 86.3% White, 8.1% Black/African American, 0.3% Asian, 0.6% American Indian/Alaska Native, 0.0% Native Hawaiian/Other Pacific Islander, 3.7% Two or more races, 5.0% Hispanic of any race; Average household size: 2.82; Median age: 33.0; Age under 18: 30.2%; Age 65 and over: 10.9%; Males per 100 females: 89.8
School District(s)
Laporte Community School Corp (KG-12)
    2012-13 Enrollment: 6,382 . . . . (219) 362-7056
Housing: Homeownership rate: 67.4%; Homeowner vacancy rate: 2.3%; Rental vacancy rate: 3.5%

LA CROSSE (town). Covers a land area of 0.531 square miles and a water area of 0 square miles. Located at 41.32° N. Lat; 86.89° W. Long. Elevation is 676 feet.
Population: 551; Growth (since 2000): -1.8%; Density: 1,037.6 persons per square mile; Race: 99.5% White, 0.2% Black/African American, 0.0% Asian, 0.0% American Indian/Alaska Native, 0.0% Native Hawaiian/Other Pacific Islander, 0.4% Two or more races, 1.8% Hispanic of any race; Average household size: 2.43; Median age: 36.4; Age under 18: 22.7%; Age 65 and over: 10.7%; Males per 100 females: 96.8
School District(s)
Tri-Township Cons School Corp (KG-12)
    2012-13 Enrollment: 374 . . . . (219) 754-2709
Housing: Homeownership rate: 85.5%; Homeowner vacancy rate: 1.5%; Rental vacancy rate: 5.7%

LA PORTE (city). County seat. Covers a land area of 11.660 square miles and a water area of 0.710 square miles. Located at 41.61° N. Lat; 86.71° W. Long. Elevation is 814 feet.
History: La Porte was founded in 1830 when the Michigan Road was under construction. Its name is French for "the door," and through La Porte passed much commerce.
Population: 22,053; Growth (since 2000): 2.0%; Density: 1,891.3 persons per square mile; Race: 88.6% White, 3.0% Black/African American, 0.5% Asian, 0.3% American Indian/Alaska Native, 0.0% Native Hawaiian/Other Pacific Islander, 2.6% Two or more races, 11.2% Hispanic of any race; Average household size: 2.39; Median age: 36.2; Age under 18: 24.5%; Age 65 and over: 15.3%; Males per 100 females: 93.2; Marriage status: 28.7% never married, 49.3% now married, 1.5% separated, 7.7% widowed, 14.2% divorced; Foreign born: 5.9%; Speak English only: 90.1%; With disability: 15.6%; Veterans: 11.3%; Ancestry: 26.9% German, 16.4% Irish, 9.8% Polish, 8.1% English, 6.6% American
Employment: 7.3% management, business, and financial, 2.2% computer, engineering, and science, 8.9% education, legal, community service, arts, and media, 3.4% healthcare practitioners, 22.2% service, 26.7% sales and office, 7.6% natural resources, construction, and maintenance, 21.7% production, transportation, and material moving
Income: Per capita: $19,025; Median household: $34,597; Average household: $45,732; Households with income of $100,000 or more: 7.0%; Poverty rate: 21.9%
Educational Attainment: High school diploma or higher: 85.2%; Bachelor's degree or higher: 14.6%; Graduate/professional degree or higher: 4.6%
School District(s)
In Department of Correction (06-12)
    2012-13 Enrollment: 484 . . . . (317) 233-3111
Laporte Community School Corp (KG-12)
    2012-13 Enrollment: 6,382 . . . . (219) 362-7056
Renaissance Academy Charter School (KG-08)
    2012-13 Enrollment: 205 . . . . (219) 878-8711
Housing: Homeownership rate: 59.0%; Median home value: $91,600; Median year structure built: 1954; Homeowner vacancy rate: 3.1%; Median gross rent: $652 per month; Rental vacancy rate: 10.1%
Health Insurance: 82.3% have insurance; 58.4% have private insurance; 35.9% have public insurance; 17.7% do not have insurance; 8.3% of children under 18 do not have insurance
Hospitals: Indiana University Health La Porte Hospital (227 beds)
Safety: Violent crime rate: 19.9 per 10,000 population; Property crime rate: 393.0 per 10,000 population
Newspapers: Herald-Argus (daily circulation 12500)

Transportation: Commute: 95.3% car, 0.7% public transportation, 2.1% walk, 1.0% work from home; Median travel time to work: 18.6 minutes
Airports: La Porte Municipal (general aviation)
Additional Information Contacts
City of La Porte . . . . (219) 362-9512
    http://www.cityoflaporte.com

LONG BEACH (town). Covers a land area of 1.062 square miles and a water area of 2.086 square miles. Located at 41.75° N. Lat; 86.86° W. Long. Elevation is 620 feet.
Population: 1,179; Growth (since 2000): -24.4%; Density: 1,110.0 persons per square mile; Race: 96.8% White, 1.4% Black/African American, 1.1% Asian, 0.3% American Indian/Alaska Native, 0.0% Native Hawaiian/Other Pacific Islander, 0.2% Two or more races, 0.6% Hispanic of any race; Average household size: 2.12; Median age: 58.0; Age under 18: 14.2%; Age 65 and over: 32.1%; Males per 100 females: 93.0
Housing: Homeownership rate: 93.2%; Homeowner vacancy rate: 3.3%; Rental vacancy rate: 33.3%
Safety: Violent crime rate: 0.0 per 10,000 population; Property crime rate: 93.8 per 10,000 population

MICHIANA SHORES (town). Covers a land area of 0.351 square miles and a water area of 0 square miles. Located at 41.76° N. Lat; 86.82° W. Long. Elevation is 610 feet.
Population: 313; Growth (since 2000): -5.2%; Density: 891.6 persons per square mile; Race: 97.4% White, 0.0% Black/African American, 0.0% Asian, 0.3% American Indian/Alaska Native, 0.0% Native Hawaiian/Other Pacific Islander, 2.2% Two or more races, 2.9% Hispanic of any race; Average household size: 1.94; Median age: 57.8; Age under 18: 10.9%; Age 65 and over: 27.5%; Males per 100 females: 96.9
Housing: Homeownership rate: 91.3%; Homeowner vacancy rate: 3.9%; Rental vacancy rate: 16.7%

MICHIGAN CITY (city). Covers a land area of 19.588 square miles and a water area of 3.265 square miles. Located at 41.71° N. Lat; 86.88° W. Long. Elevation is 627 feet.
History: It was in Michigan City that Daniel Webster made a Fourth of July speech in 1837. The city was founded in 1832 at the northern end of the Michigan Road, on Lake Michigan. From the early 1840's it served as a port for shipping interests and later for a fishing fleet.
Population: 31,479; Growth (since 2000): -4.3%; Density: 1,607.1 persons per square mile; Race: 64.9% White, 28.1% Black/African American, 0.7% Asian, 0.4% American Indian/Alaska Native, 0.0% Native Hawaiian/Other Pacific Islander, 3.7% Two or more races, 5.9% Hispanic of any race; Average household size: 2.37; Median age: 37.1; Age under 18: 23.5%; Age 65 and over: 13.5%; Males per 100 females: 105.8; Marriage status: 37.9% never married, 38.7% now married, 2.5% separated, 7.3% widowed, 16.2% divorced; Foreign born: 3.8%; Speak English only: 94.2%; With disability: 18.0%; Veterans: 9.0%; Ancestry: 18.9% German, 13.0% Irish, 9.6% Polish, 4.9% English, 4.9% American
Employment: 10.7% management, business, and financial, 1.8% computer, engineering, and science, 7.8% education, legal, community service, arts, and media, 2.9% healthcare practitioners, 23.6% service, 24.8% sales and office, 7.4% natural resources, construction, and maintenance, 21.1% production, transportation, and material moving
Income: Per capita: $19,027; Median household: $35,601; Average household: $46,249; Households with income of $100,000 or more: 7.6%; Poverty rate: 26.3%
Educational Attainment: High school diploma or higher: 83.4%; Bachelor's degree or higher: 15.6%; Graduate/professional degree or higher: 5.7%
School District(s)
Michigan City Area Schools (PK-12)
    2012-13 Enrollment: 6,087 . . . . (219) 873-2000
Four-year College(s)
Brown Mackie College-Michigan City (Private, For-profit)
    Fall 2013 Enrollment: 290 . . . . (219) 877-3100
    2013-14 Tuition: In-state $12,114; Out-of-state $12,114
Housing: Homeownership rate: 58.8%; Median home value: $93,100; Median year structure built: 1959; Homeowner vacancy rate: 3.0%; Median gross rent: $690 per month; Rental vacancy rate: 12.8%
Health Insurance: 83.2% have insurance; 53.4% have private insurance; 41.7% have public insurance; 16.8% do not have insurance; 5.8% of children under 18 do not have insurance
Hospitals: Franciscan Saint Anthony Health - Michigan City (310 beds)

Newspapers: News-Dispatch (daily circulation 10700)
Transportation: Commute: 91.5% car, 2.5% public transportation, 2.2% walk, 3.2% work from home; Median travel time to work: 19.2 minutes; Amtrak: Train service available.
Additional Information Contacts
City of Michigan City . . . . (219) 873-1410
http://www.emichigancity.com

MILL CREEK (unincorporated postal area)
ZCTA: 46365
Covers a land area of 23.266 square miles and a water area of 0.328 square miles. Located at 41.61° N. Lat; 86.55° W. Long..
Population: 1,068; Growth (since 2000): 6.5%; Density: 45.9 persons per square mile; Race: 98.6% White, 0.8% Black/African American, 0.0% Asian, 0.0% American Indian/Alaska Native, 0.0% Native Hawaiian/Other Pacific Islander, 0.5% Two or more races, 1.5% Hispanic of any race; Average household size: 2.72; Median age: 42.3; Age under 18: 24.7%; Age 65 and over: 11.9%; Males per 100 females: 107.0
Housing: Homeownership rate: 88.5%; Homeowner vacancy rate: 0.9%; Rental vacancy rate: 11.8%

POTTAWATTAMIE PARK (town).
Covers a land area of 0.246 square miles and a water area of 0 square miles. Located at 41.72° N. Lat; 86.87° W. Long. Elevation is 620 feet.
Population: 235; Growth (since 2000): n/a; Density: 956.6 persons per square mile; Race: 92.3% White, 7.2% Black/African American, 0.0% Asian, 0.0% American Indian/Alaska Native, 0.0% Native Hawaiian/Other Pacific Islander, 0.4% Two or more races, 0.4% Hispanic of any race; Average household size: 2.23; Median age: 53.1; Age under 18: 18.7%; Age 65 and over: 25.1%; Males per 100 females: 91.1
Housing: Homeownership rate: 95.1%; Homeowner vacancy rate: 2.0%; Rental vacancy rate: 0.0%

ROLLING PRAIRIE (CDP).
Covers a land area of 1.053 square miles and a water area of 0.015 square miles. Located at 41.67° N. Lat; 86.62° W. Long. Elevation is 827 feet.
Population: 582; Growth (since 2000): n/a; Density: 552.8 persons per square mile; Race: 98.3% White, 0.3% Black/African American, 0.2% Asian, 0.2% American Indian/Alaska Native, 0.0% Native Hawaiian/Other Pacific Islander, 0.3% Two or more races, 1.2% Hispanic of any race; Average household size: 2.73; Median age: 39.3; Age under 18: 23.4%; Age 65 and over: 17.0%; Males per 100 females: 94.6
School District(s)
New Prairie United School Corp (KG-12)
2012-13 Enrollment: 2,844 . . . . (574) 654-7273
Housing: Homeownership rate: 86.9%; Homeowner vacancy rate: 2.1%; Rental vacancy rate: 0.0%

TRAIL CREEK (town).
Covers a land area of 1.212 square miles and a water area of 0 square miles. Located at 41.70° N. Lat; 86.86° W. Long. Elevation is 627 feet.
Population: 2,052; Growth (since 2000): -10.6%; Density: 1,693.7 persons per square mile; Race: 91.2% White, 5.5% Black/African American, 0.6% Asian, 0.2% American Indian/Alaska Native, 0.0% Native Hawaiian/Other Pacific Islander, 1.3% Two or more races, 3.3% Hispanic of any race; Average household size: 2.32; Median age: 46.5; Age under 18: 19.4%; Age 65 and over: 21.2%; Males per 100 females: 101.6
Housing: Homeownership rate: 90.2%; Homeowner vacancy rate: 1.7%; Rental vacancy rate: 7.5%
Additional Information Contacts
Town of Trail Creek. . . . . (219) 874-6221
http://www.michigancitychamber.com

UNION MILLS (unincorporated postal area)
ZCTA: 46382
Covers a land area of 48.759 square miles and a water area of 0.032 square miles. Located at 41.46° N. Lat; 86.76° W. Long. Elevation is 732 feet.
Population: 2,108; Growth (since 2000): 5.9%; Density: 43.2 persons per square mile; Race: 96.7% White, 0.5% Black/African American, 0.1% Asian, 0.0% American Indian/Alaska Native, 0.0% Native Hawaiian/Other Pacific Islander, 1.8% Two or more races, 2.8% Hispanic of any race; Average household size: 2.80; Median age: 40.0; Age under 18: 26.8%; Age 65 and over: 13.2%; Males per 100 females: 97.7
School District(s)
South Central Com School Corp (KG-12)
2012-13 Enrollment: 906. . . . . (219) 767-2263
Housing: Homeownership rate: 89.9%; Homeowner vacancy rate: 1.3%; Rental vacancy rate: 6.2%

WANATAH (town).
Covers a land area of 1.421 square miles and a water area of 0 square miles. Located at 41.43° N. Lat; 86.89° W. Long. Elevation is 732 feet.
History: Wanatah is named for an Indian chief whose name means "keep knee deep in mud."
Population: 1,048; Growth (since 2000): 3.5%; Density: 737.4 persons per square mile; Race: 96.9% White, 0.1% Black/African American, 0.2% Asian, 1.0% American Indian/Alaska Native, 0.1% Native Hawaiian/Other Pacific Islander, 1.5% Two or more races, 3.0% Hispanic of any race; Average household size: 2.40; Median age: 40.2; Age under 18: 22.9%; Age 65 and over: 12.5%; Males per 100 females: 100.0
School District(s)
Tri-Township Cons School Corp (KG-12)
2012-13 Enrollment: 374. . . . . (219) 754-2709
Housing: Homeownership rate: 84.2%; Homeowner vacancy rate: 0.8%; Rental vacancy rate: 10.4%

WESTVILLE (town).
Covers a land area of 3.088 square miles and a water area of 0 square miles. Located at 41.54° N. Lat; 86.91° W. Long. Elevation is 794 feet.
History: Settled 1836, laid out 1851.
Population: 5,853; Growth (since 2000): 176.6%; Density: 1,895.5 persons per square mile; Race: 72.1% White, 25.1% Black/African American, 0.3% Asian, 0.2% American Indian/Alaska Native, 0.0% Native Hawaiian/Other Pacific Islander, 0.7% Two or more races, 6.3% Hispanic of any race; Average household size: 2.45; Median age: 33.1; Age under 18: 12.0%; Age 65 and over: 5.5%; Males per 100 females: 333.2; Marriage status: 56.8% never married, 21.5% now married, 3.0% separated, 1.1% widowed, 20.6% divorced; Foreign born: 2.2%; Speak English only: 95.6%; With disability: 10.6%; Veterans: 6.9%; Ancestry: 17.3% German, 11.4% Irish, 3.5% English, 3.1% Polish, 2.9% Italian
Employment: 10.7% management, business, and financial, 3.5% computer, engineering, and science, 8.0% education, legal, community service, arts, and media, 5.8% healthcare practitioners, 14.9% service, 25.5% sales and office, 9.0% natural resources, construction, and maintenance, 22.5% production, transportation, and material moving
Income: Per capita: $7,153; Median household: $51,892; Average household: $57,029; Households with income of $100,000 or more: 11.1%; Poverty rate: 15.6%
Educational Attainment: High school diploma or higher: 69.2%; Bachelor's degree or higher: 6.3%; Graduate/professional degree or higher: 1.7%
School District(s)
M S D of New Durham Township (KG-12)
2012-13 Enrollment: 902. . . . . (219) 785-2239
Four-year College(s)
Purdue University-North Central Campus (Public)
Fall 2013 Enrollment: 6,102 . . . . (219) 785-5200
2013-14 Tuition: In-state $7,186; Out-of-state $17,105
Housing: Homeownership rate: 78.8%; Median home value: $108,200; Median year structure built: 1987; Homeowner vacancy rate: 1.8%; Median gross rent: $658 per month; Rental vacancy rate: 17.2%
Health Insurance: 87.1% have insurance; 58.3% have private insurance; 34.8% have public insurance; 12.9% do not have insurance; 0.0% of children under 18 do not have insurance
Newspapers: Regional News (weekly circulation 2000); Westville Indicator (weekly circulation 2000)
Transportation: Commute: 93.6% car, 1.0% public transportation, 1.7% walk, 2.2% work from home; Median travel time to work: 23.8 minutes
Additional Information Contacts
Town of Westville . . . . (219) 785-2123
http://westville.us

Lawrence County

Located in southern Indiana; drained by Salt Creek and the East Fork of the White River. Covers a land area of 449.168 square miles, a water area of 2.761 square miles, and is located in the Eastern Time Zone at 38.84° N. Lat., 86.49° W. Long. The county was founded in 1819. County seat is Bedford.

Lawrence County is part of the Bedford, IN Micropolitan Statistical Area. The entire metro area includes: Lawrence County, IN

Weather Station: Oolitic Purdue Exp Farm   Elevation: 649 feet

	Jan	Feb	Mar	Apr	May	Jun	Jul	Aug	Sep	Oct	Nov	Dec
High	38	43	53	64	74	82	85	85	79	67	55	42
Low	20	23	30	41	51	60	64	62	54	41	33	23
Precip	2.9	2.7	3.8	4.4	5.8	4.1	4.5	3.7	3.2	3.7	3.7	3.5
Snow	4.6	4.1	2.0	0.1	tr	0.0	0.0	0.0	0.0	0.1	0.1	3.9

High and Low temperatures in degrees Fahrenheit; Precipitation and Snow in inches

Population: 46,134; Growth (since 2000): 0.5%; Density: 102.7 persons per square mile; Race: 97.3% White, 0.4% Black/African American, 0.5% Asian, 0.3% American Indian/Alaska Native, 0.0% Native Hawaiian/Other Pacific Islander, 1.1% two or more races, 1.2% Hispanic of any race; Average household size: 2.42; Median age: 41.6; Age under 18: 23.6%; Age 65 and over: 16.4%; Males per 100 females: 97.7; Marriage status: 20.1% never married, 59.7% now married, 1.2% separated, 7.0% widowed, 13.3% divorced; Foreign born: 1.4%; Speak English only: 97.3%; With disability: 16.7%; Veterans: 11.9%; Ancestry: 16.8% German, 15.0% Irish, 14.2% American, 10.3% English, 2.6% French
Religion: Six largest groups: 21.5% Baptist, 7.8% Non-denominational Protestant, 4.1% Catholicism, 3.8% Holiness, 2.3% Methodist/Pietist, 1.4% Pentecostal
Economy: Unemployment rate: 6.8%; Leading industries: 18.7% retail trade; 14.8% other services (except public administration); 11.0% health care and social assistance; Farms: 800 totaling 134,689 acres; Company size: 0 employ 1,000 or more persons, 2 employ 500 to 999 persons, 18 employ 100 to 499 persons, 845 employ less than 100 persons; Business ownership: 701 women-owned, n/a Black-owned, 55 Hispanic-owned, 38 Asian-owned
Employment: 9.8% management, business, and financial, 4.5% computer, engineering, and science, 6.8% education, legal, community service, arts, and media, 6.7% healthcare practitioners, 20.3% service, 20.3% sales and office, 11.6% natural resources, construction, and maintenance, 20.0% production, transportation, and material moving
Income: Per capita: $22,169; Median household: $42,627; Average household: $54,165; Households with income of $100,000 or more: 11.7%; Poverty rate: 15.2%
Educational Attainment: High school diploma or higher: 84.1%; Bachelor's degree or higher: 13.7%; Graduate/professional degree or higher: 4.7%
Housing: Homeownership rate: 76.4%; Median home value: $98,200; Median year structure built: 1973; Homeowner vacancy rate: 2.8%; Median gross rent: $606 per month; Rental vacancy rate: 8.3%
Vital Statistics: Birth rate: 103.2 per 10,000 population; Death rate: 113.9 per 10,000 population; Age-adjusted cancer mortality rate: 181.7 deaths per 100,000 population
Health Insurance: 84.1% have insurance; 65.3% have private insurance; 33.7% have public insurance; 15.9% do not have insurance; 10.8% of children under 18 do not have insurance
Health Care: Physicians: 10.2 per 10,000 population; Hospital beds: 10.9 per 10,000 population; Hospital admissions: 594.7 per 10,000 population
Transportation: Commute: 94.8% car, 0.7% public transportation, 1.1% walk, 2.9% work from home; Median travel time to work: 26.0 minutes
Presidential Election: 32.4% Obama, 65.2% Romney (2012)
National and State Parks: Spring Mill State Park
Additional Information Contacts
Lawrence Government . . . . (812) 275-7543
  http://bedfordonline.com/government/lawrence

Lawrence County Communities

AVOCA (CDP). Covers a land area of 2.095 square miles and a water area of 0 square miles. Located at 38.92° N. Lat; 86.56° W. Long. Elevation is 623 feet.
Population: 583; Growth (since 2000): n/a; Density: 278.3 persons per square mile; Race: 96.7% White, 0.0% Black/African American, 0.7% Asian, 0.5% American Indian/Alaska Native, 0.0% Native Hawaiian/Other Pacific Islander, 1.5% Two or more races, 1.2% Hispanic of any race; Average household size: 2.35; Median age: 44.7; Age under 18: 19.6%; Age 65 and over: 14.9%; Males per 100 females: 97.6
Housing: Homeownership rate: 85.9%; Homeowner vacancy rate: 1.4%; Rental vacancy rate: 0.0%

BEDFORD (city). County seat. Covers a land area of 12.161 square miles and a water area of 0 square miles. Located at 38.86° N. Lat; 86.49° W. Long. Elevation is 686 feet.
History: Beford developed as the center of a limestone industry, providing stone for such buildings as the Empire State Building and the Chicago Museum of Fine Arts.
Population: 13,413; Growth (since 2000): -2.6%; Density: 1,102.9 persons per square mile; Race: 96.2% White, 0.8% Black/African American, 0.9% Asian, 0.3% American Indian/Alaska Native, 0.0% Native Hawaiian/Other Pacific Islander, 1.3% Two or more races, 1.8% Hispanic of any race; Average household size: 2.22; Median age: 41.5; Age under 18: 22.3%; Age 65 and over: 20.1%; Males per 100 females: 89.8; Marriage status: 22.6% never married, 49.2% now married, 1.5% separated, 10.5% widowed, 17.7% divorced; Foreign born: 2.7%; Speak English only: 95.8%; With disability: 20.1%; Veterans: 10.4%; Ancestry: 16.2% German, 13.6% Irish, 13.3% American, 8.3% English, 2.6% Italian
Employment: 10.0% management, business, and financial, 2.8% computer, engineering, and science, 6.2% education, legal, community service, arts, and media, 6.6% healthcare practitioners, 23.5% service, 23.4% sales and office, 10.3% natural resources, construction, and maintenance, 17.1% production, transportation, and material moving
Income: Per capita: $19,348; Median household: $34,706; Average household: $44,051; Households with income of $100,000 or more: 7.9%; Poverty rate: 21.4%
Educational Attainment: High school diploma or higher: 81.2%; Bachelor's degree or higher: 11.9%; Graduate/professional degree or higher: 3.8%

School District(s)
North Lawrence Com Schools (PK-12)
  2012-13 Enrollment: 5,193 . . . . (812) 279-3521
Housing: Homeownership rate: 61.6%; Median home value: $88,600; Median year structure built: 1954; Homeowner vacancy rate: 4.8%; Median gross rent: $611 per month; Rental vacancy rate: 9.0%
Health Insurance: 82.5% have insurance; 57.0% have private insurance; 41.2% have public insurance; 17.5% do not have insurance; 9.2% of children under 18 do not have insurance
Hospitals: Indiana University Health Bedford Hospital (49 beds); Saint Vincent Dunn Hospital (137 beds)
Safety: Violent crime rate: 52.2 per 10,000 population; Property crime rate: 337.3 per 10,000 population
Newspapers: Times-Mail (daily circulation 12600)
Transportation: Commute: 91.2% car, 1.3% public transportation, 2.3% walk, 4.2% work from home; Median travel time to work: 19.8 minutes
Airports: Virgil I Grissom Municipal (general aviation)
Additional Information Contacts
City of Bedford. . . . . (812) 279-6555
  http://www.bedford.in.us

HELTONVILLE (unincorporated postal area)
ZCTA: 47436
  Covers a land area of 45.799 square miles and a water area of 0.314 square miles. Located at 38.95° N. Lat; 86.39° W. Long. Elevation is 653 feet.
  Population: 1,663; Growth (since 2000): 35.0%; Density: 36.3 persons per square mile; Race: 97.1% White, 0.2% Black/African American, 0.4% Asian, 1.0% American Indian/Alaska Native, 0.0% Native Hawaiian/Other Pacific Islander, 1.0% Two or more races, 0.7% Hispanic of any race; Average household size: 2.53; Median age: 41.3; Age under 18: 23.7%; Age 65 and over: 14.4%; Males per 100 females: 109.4

School District(s)
North Lawrence Com Schools (PK-12)
  2012-13 Enrollment: 5,193 . . . . (812) 279-3521
  Housing: Homeownership rate: 85.7%; Homeowner vacancy rate: 2.2%; Rental vacancy rate: 5.9%

MITCHELL (city).
Covers a land area of 3.276 square miles and a water area of 0.005 square miles. Located at 38.74° N. Lat; 86.47° W. Long. Elevation is 682 feet.

History: The first settlers came to Mitchell in 1813. The town was platted about 1852 when the Louisville, New Albany, & Salem Railroad came through Lawrence County. The town was named for O.M. Mitchell, a construction engineer for the Ohio & Mississippi Railroad which crossed the original line in 1856.

Population: 4,350; Growth (since 2000): -4.8%; Density: 1,327.8 persons per square mile; Race: 97.6% White, 0.4% Black/African American, 0.3% Asian, 0.2% American Indian/Alaska Native, 0.1% Native Hawaiian/Other Pacific Islander, 0.8% Two or more races, 1.4% Hispanic of any race; Average household size: 2.38; Median age: 39.2; Age under 18: 24.9%; Age 65 and over: 17.1%; Males per 100 females: 86.9; Marriage status: 23.5% never married, 48.0% now married, 2.1% separated, 8.1% widowed, 20.5% divorced; Foreign born: 0.5%; Speak English only: 97.6%; With disability: 24.6%; Veterans: 10.9%; Ancestry: 16.4% American, 14.1% German, 10.7% Irish, 9.8% English, 2.4% French

Employment: 6.0% management, business, and financial, 2.2% computer, engineering, and science, 5.3% education, legal, community service, arts, and media, 6.2% healthcare practitioners, 28.7% service, 18.7% sales and office, 5.8% natural resources, construction, and maintenance, 27.1% production, transportation, and material moving

Income: Per capita: $17,618; Median household: $29,111; Average household: $39,792; Households with income of $100,000 or more: 5.4%; Poverty rate: 24.9%

Educational Attainment: High school diploma or higher: 75.2%; Bachelor's degree or higher: 10.4%; Graduate/professional degree or higher: 3.9%

School District(s)
Mitchell Community Schools (PK-12)
  2012-13 Enrollment: 1,774 . . . . (812) 849-4481

Housing: Homeownership rate: 65.4%; Median home value: $75,800; Median year structure built: 1964; Homeowner vacancy rate: 2.7%; Median gross rent: $551 per month; Rental vacancy rate: 6.5%

Health Insurance: 73.2% have insurance; 47.3% have private insurance; 38.5% have public insurance; 26.8% do not have insurance; 24.0% of children under 18 do not have insurance

Transportation: Commute: 93.7% car, 0.6% public transportation, 1.9% walk, 3.2% work from home; Median travel time to work: 25.9 minutes

Additional Information Contacts
City of Mitchell. . . . . (812) 849-3831
  http://www.mitchell-in.gov

OOLITIC (town).
Covers a land area of 0.783 square miles and a water area of 0 square miles. Located at 38.89° N. Lat; 86.53° W. Long. Elevation is 600 feet.

History: Oolitic was named for the oolitic texture of the limestone in the quarries that surround it, which provided the town with its early industry.

Population: 1,184; Growth (since 2000): 2.8%; Density: 1,512.8 persons per square mile; Race: 98.7% White, 0.3% Black/African American, 0.3% Asian, 0.0% American Indian/Alaska Native, 0.0% Native Hawaiian/Other Pacific Islander, 0.6% Two or more races, 1.0% Hispanic of any race; Average household size: 2.22; Median age: 41.0; Age under 18: 22.1%; Age 65 and over: 17.1%; Males per 100 females: 101.0

School District(s)
North Lawrence Com Schools (PK-12)
  2012-13 Enrollment: 5,193 . . . . (812) 279-3521

Housing: Homeownership rate: 67.8%; Homeowner vacancy rate: 2.4%; Rental vacancy rate: 11.8%

SPRINGVILLE (unincorporated postal area)
ZCTA: 47462

Covers a land area of 75.862 square miles and a water area of 0.040 square miles. Located at 38.96° N. Lat; 86.65° W. Long. Elevation is 640 feet.

Population: 4,871; Growth (since 2000): 0.8%; Density: 64.2 persons per square mile; Race: 97.7% White, 0.3% Black/African American, 0.4% Asian, 0.5% American Indian/Alaska Native, 0.0% Native Hawaiian/Other Pacific Islander, 1.1% Two or more races, 1.0% Hispanic of any race; Average household size: 2.60; Median age: 40.6; Age under 18: 24.8%; Age 65 and over: 11.7%; Males per 100 females: 107.3; Marriage status: 22.4% never married, 64.1% now married, 1.2% separated, 3.7% widowed, 9.9% divorced; Foreign born: 1.3%; Speak English only: 97.1%; With disability: 16.0%; Veterans: 10.0%; Ancestry: 21.3% German, 19.3% Irish, 13.9% American, 9.5% English, 4.8% Scottish

Employment: 13.5% management, business, and financial, 5.2% computer, engineering, and science, 8.6% education, legal, community service, arts, and media, 8.6% healthcare practitioners, 24.7% service, 17.7% sales and office, 7.3% natural resources, construction, and maintenance, 14.3% production, transportation, and material moving

Income: Per capita: $20,937; Median household: $46,164; Average household: $61,747; Households with income of $100,000 or more: 16.5%; Poverty rate: 15.7%

Educational Attainment: High school diploma or higher: 84.2%; Bachelor's degree or higher: 11.7%; Graduate/professional degree or higher: 4.6%

School District(s)
North Lawrence Com Schools (PK-12)
  2012-13 Enrollment: 5,193 . . . . (812) 279-3521

Housing: Homeownership rate: 88.2%; Median home value: $111,000; Median year structure built: 1986; Homeowner vacancy rate: 2.3%; Median gross rent: $627 per month; Rental vacancy rate: 10.4%

Health Insurance: 89.1% have insurance; 71.0% have private insurance; 32.9% have public insurance; 10.9% do not have insurance; 9.5% of children under 18 do not have insurance

Transportation: Commute: 98.9% car, 0.0% public transportation, 0.0% walk, 1.1% work from home; Median travel time to work: 29.0 minutes

TUNNELTON (unincorporated postal area)
ZCTA: 47467

Covers a land area of 0.055 square miles and a water area of 0 square miles. Located at 38.77° N. Lat; 86.34° W. Long. Elevation is 571 feet.

Population: 72; Growth (since 2000): 24.1%; Density: 1,315.1 persons per square mile; Race: 100.0% White, 0.0% Black/African American, 0.0% Asian, 0.0% American Indian/Alaska Native, 0.0% Native Hawaiian/Other Pacific Islander, 0.0% Two or more races, 0.0% Hispanic of any race; Average household size: 2.40; Median age: 33.5; Age under 18: 27.8%; Age 65 and over: 18.1%; Males per 100 females: 105.7

Housing: Homeownership rate: 73.4%; Homeowner vacancy rate: 14.3%; Rental vacancy rate: 11.1%

WILLIAMS (CDP).
Covers a land area of 3.577 square miles and a water area of 0.003 square miles. Located at 38.82° N. Lat; 86.64° W. Long. Elevation is 574 feet.

Population: 286; Growth (since 2000): n/a; Density: 80.0 persons per square mile; Race: 96.9% White, 0.0% Black/African American, 0.7% Asian, 0.3% American Indian/Alaska Native, 0.0% Native Hawaiian/Other Pacific Islander, 2.1% Two or more races, 0.3% Hispanic of any race; Average household size: 2.47; Median age: 41.0; Age under 18: 23.1%; Age 65 and over: 12.9%; Males per 100 females: 107.2

Housing: Homeownership rate: 72.4%; Homeowner vacancy rate: 3.4%; Rental vacancy rate: 2.9%

Madison County

Located in east central Indiana; drained by the West Fork of the White River and by many creeks. Covers a land area of 451.915 square miles, a water area of 0.989 square miles, and is located in the Eastern Time Zone at 40.17° N. Lat., 85.72° W. Long. The county was founded in 1823. County seat is Anderson.

Madison County is part of the Indianapolis-Carmel-Anderson, IN Metropolitan Statistical Area. The entire metro area includes: Boone County, IN; Brown County, IN; Hamilton County, IN; Hancock County, IN; Hendricks County, IN; Johnson County, IN; Madison County, IN; Marion County, IN; Morgan County, IN; Putnam County, IN; Shelby County, IN

Weather Station: Anderson Sewage Plant   Elevation: 845 feet

	Jan	Feb	Mar	Apr	May	Jun	Jul	Aug	Sep	Oct	Nov	Dec
High	34	39	49	62	72	81	84	82	76	64	51	38
Low	20	23	31	41	51	61	64	63	55	44	35	24
Precip	2.4	2.3	3.3	3.8	4.4	4.2	4.4	3.5	3.0	3.1	3.7	3.1
Snow	7.2	4.2	1.6	0.2	0.0	0.0	0.0	0.0	0.0	0.1	0.5	4.1

High and Low temperatures in degrees Fahrenheit; Precipitation and Snow in inches

Weather Station: Elwood Wastewater Plant Elevation: 839 feet

	Jan	Feb	Mar	Apr	May	Jun	Jul	Aug	Sep	Oct	Nov	Dec
High	33	38	49	62	72	81	85	83	77	64	51	38
Low	17	20	28	38	49	59	62	60	52	40	32	21
Precip	2.6	2.0	2.9	3.7	4.3	4.4	4.3	3.8	3.4	2.8	3.6	3.0
Snow	na	na	0.8	tr	0.0	0.0	0.0	0.0	0.0	tr	0.1	2.8

High and Low temperatures in degrees Fahrenheit; Precipitation and Snow in inches

Population: 131,636; Growth (since 2000): -1.3%; Density: 291.3 persons per square mile; Race: 87.7% White, 8.3% Black/African American, 0.4% Asian, 0.2% American Indian/Alaska Native, 0.0% Native Hawaiian/Other Pacific Islander, 1.8% two or more races, 3.2% Hispanic of any race; Average household size: 2.41; Median age: 39.2; Age under 18: 23.1%; Age 65 and over: 15.4%; Males per 100 females: 99.8; Marriage status: 27.8% never married, 49.4% now married, 1.4% separated, 7.2% widowed, 15.6% divorced; Foreign born: 2.0%; Speak English only: 96.8%; With disability: 17.3%; Veterans: 10.2%; Ancestry: 18.7% German, 14.0% American, 11.5% Irish, 9.2% English, 2.0% French
Religion: Six largest groups: 9.5% Baptist, 7.3% Holiness, 6.0% Catholicism, 5.7% Non-denominational Protestant, 3.6% Methodist/Pietist, 2.0% Pentecostal
Economy: Unemployment rate: 6.0%; Leading industries: 15.2% retail trade; 15.1% other services (except public administration); 11.0% health care and social assistance; Farms: 737 totaling 205,147 acres; Company size: 4 employ 1,000 or more persons, 2 employ 500 to 999 persons, 44 employ 100 to 499 persons, 2,223 employ less than 100 persons; Business ownership: 1,999 women-owned, n/a Black-owned, 53 Hispanic-owned, 68 Asian-owned
Employment: 10.3% management, business, and financial, 3.4% computer, engineering, and science, 8.4% education, legal, community service, arts, and media, 6.2% healthcare practitioners, 20.7% service, 25.6% sales and office, 9.3% natural resources, construction, and maintenance, 16.1% production, transportation, and material moving
Income: Per capita: $21,527; Median household: $43,120; Average household: $53,392; Households with income of $100,000 or more: 11.2%; Poverty rate: 17.3%
Educational Attainment: High school diploma or higher: 87.0%; Bachelor's degree or higher: 16.7%; Graduate/professional degree or higher: 5.3%
Housing: Homeownership rate: 70.9%; Median home value: $92,800; Median year structure built: 1963; Homeowner vacancy rate: 3.3%; Median gross rent: $688 per month; Rental vacancy rate: 14.3%
Vital Statistics: Birth rate: 116.0 per 10,000 population; Death rate: 106.8 per 10,000 population; Age-adjusted cancer mortality rate: 203.8 deaths per 100,000 population
Health Insurance: 84.1% have insurance; 64.5% have private insurance; 35.0% have public insurance; 15.9% do not have insurance; 10.6% of children under 18 do not have insurance
Health Care: Physicians: 12.4 per 10,000 population; Hospital beds: 29.2 per 10,000 population; Hospital admissions: 1,153.5 per 10,000 population
Air Quality Index: 65.3% good, 34.4% moderate, 0.3% unhealthy for sensitive individuals, 0.0% unhealthy (percent of days)
Transportation: Commute: 92.5% car, 0.4% public transportation, 2.8% walk, 3.0% work from home; Median travel time to work: 25.7 minutes
Presidential Election: 46.6% Obama, 51.1% Romney (2012)
National and State Parks: Mounds State Park
Additional Information Contacts
Madison Government . . . . (765) 641-9470
http://www.madisoncty.com

Madison County Communities

ALEXANDRIA (city). Covers a land area of 2.627 square miles and a water area of 0 square miles. Located at 40.26° N. Lat; 85.68° W. Long. Elevation is 869 feet.
History: In Alexandria the Johns-Manville Company operated the first rock-wool insulation factory in the world, utilizing the argillaceous limestone found here.
Population: 5,145; Growth (since 2000): -17.8%; Density: 1,958.3 persons per square mile; Race: 97.4% White, 0.3% Black/African American, 0.2% Asian, 0.1% American Indian/Alaska Native, 0.0% Native Hawaiian/Other Pacific Islander, 1.1% Two or more races, 1.7% Hispanic of any race; Average household size: 2.41; Median age: 38.2; Age under 18: 25.6%; Age 65 and over: 15.6%; Males per 100 females: 91.6; Marriage status: 22.2% never married, 49.2% now married, 1.0% separated, 10.7% widowed, 17.9% divorced; Foreign born: 0.4%; Speak English only: 98.2%; With disability: 17.5%; Veterans: 8.9%; Ancestry: 18.4% American, 13.0% German, 11.4% Irish, 9.6% English, 1.7% Welsh
Employment: 10.1% management, business, and financial, 3.2% computer, engineering, and science, 5.9% education, legal, community service, arts, and media, 7.2% healthcare practitioners, 18.4% service, 23.1% sales and office, 10.1% natural resources, construction, and maintenance, 21.9% production, transportation, and material moving
Income: Per capita: $19,614; Median household: $36,745; Average household: $44,429; Households with income of $100,000 or more: 10.0%; Poverty rate: 17.3
Educational Attainment: High school diploma or higher: 82.5%; Bachelor's degree or higher: 10.7%; Graduate/professional degree or higher: 3.5%
School District(s)
Alexandria Com School Corp (PK-12)
    2012-13 Enrollment: 1,538 . . . . (765) 724-4496
Vocational/Technical School(s)
Alexandria School of Scientific Therapeutics (Private, For-profit)
    Fall 2013 Enrollment: 30 . . . . (765) 724-9152
    2013-14 Tuition: $9,665
Housing: Homeownership rate: 64.2%; Median home value: $67,000; Median year structure built: 1954; Homeowner vacancy rate: 5.7%; Median gross rent: $599 per month; Rental vacancy rate: 15.2%
Health Insurance: 84.8% have insurance; 66.4% have private insurance; 36.1% have public insurance; 15.2% do not have insurance; 10.6% of children under 18 do not have insurance
Safety: Violent crime rate: 11.9 per 10,000 population; Property crime rate: 239.1 per 10,000 population
Newspapers: Alexandria Times-Tribune (weekly circulation 2100)
Transportation: Commute: 96.8% car, 0.0% public transportation, 1.5% walk, 1.7% work from home; Median travel time to work: 25.5 minutes
Additional Information Contacts
City of Alexandria . . . . (765) 724-2541
http://www.alexandriaindiana.net

ANDERSON (city). County seat. Covers a land area of 41.371 square miles and a water area of 0.109 square miles. Located at 40.09° N. Lat; 85.69° W. Long. Elevation is 879 feet.
History: Anderson was platted in 1823 and named for Delaware Chief Kikthawenund, who was called Captain Anderson by the settlers. It was incorporated as Andersontown in 1838, and reincorporated as a city in 1865. The discovery of natural gas in 1886 brought industrial development, followed by the automotive industry.
Population: 56,129; Growth (since 2000): -6.0%; Density: 1,356.7 persons per square mile; Race: 78.8% White, 15.2% Black/African American, 0.5% Asian, 0.3% American Indian/Alaska Native, 0.0% Native Hawaiian/Other Pacific Islander, 2.6% Two or more races, 4.8% Hispanic of any race; Average household size: 2.28; Median age: 37.8; Age under 18: 22.4%; Age 65 and over: 16.3%; Males per 100 females: 91.9; Marriage status: 33.0% never married, 40.9% now married, 1.7% separated, 8.2% widowed, 17.9% divorced; Foreign born: 3.1%; Speak English only: 95.7%; With disability: 20.1%; Veterans: 10.0%; Ancestry: 16.8% German, 11.6% American, 11.1% Irish, 7.9% English, 1.8% French
Employment: 9.0% management, business, and financial, 2.8% computer, engineering, and science, 7.1% education, legal, community service, arts, and media, 5.3% healthcare practitioners, 24.6% service, 26.3% sales and office, 9.1% natural resources, construction, and maintenance, 15.7% production, transportation, and material moving
Income: Per capita: $18,216; Median household: $33,574; Average household: $41,963; Households with income of $100,000 or more: 6.0%; Poverty rate: 25.8%
Educational Attainment: High school diploma or higher: 83.4%; Bachelor's degree or higher: 14.5%; Graduate/professional degree or higher: 4.8%
School District(s)
Anderson Community School Corp (KG-12)
    2012-13 Enrollment: 6,918 . . . . (765) 641-2028
Anderson Preparatory Academy (KG-12)
    2012-13 Enrollment: 931 . . . . (765) 649-8472
Four-year College(s)
Anderson University (Private, Not-for-profit, Church of God)
    Fall 2013 Enrollment: 2,442 . . . . (765) 649-9071
    2013-14 Tuition: In-state $26,280; Out-of-state $26,280

Vocational/Technical School(s)
Apex Academy of Hair Design Inc (Private, For-profit)
    Fall 2013 Enrollment: 9 . . . . (765) 642-7560
    2013-14 Tuition: $8,600
The Salon Professional Academy-Anderson (Private, For-profit)
    Fall 2013 Enrollment: 106 . . . . (765) 649-5555
    2013-14 Tuition: $14,549

Housing: Homeownership rate: 58.4%; Median home value: $73,600; Median year structure built: 1959; Homeowner vacancy rate: 4.5%; Median gross rent: $672 per month; Rental vacancy rate: 15.9%
Health Insurance: 79.3% have insurance; 53.0% have private insurance; 40.9% have public insurance; 20.7% do not have insurance; 13.2% of children under 18 do not have insurance
Hospitals: Community Hospital of Anderson & Madison County; Saint Vincent Anderson Regional Hospital (225 beds)
Safety: Violent crime rate: 36.1 per 10,000 population; Property crime rate: 481.2 per 10,000 population
Newspapers: Herald-Bulletin (daily circulation 22000)
Transportation: Commute: 90.5% car, 0.9% public transportation, 4.4% walk, 2.6% work from home; Median travel time to work: 22.8 minutes
Airports: Anderson Municipal-Darlington Field (general aviation)
Additional Information Contacts
City of Anderson . . . . (765) 648-6000
    http://www.cityofanderson.com

CHESTERFIELD (town).
Covers a land area of 1.323 square miles and a water area of 0 square miles. Located at 40.11° N. Lat; 85.59° W. Long. Elevation is 909 feet.
History: The Chesterfield Spiritualist Camp was built here in 1890 by Dr. J. Westerfield and his followers.
Population: 2,547; Growth (since 2000): -14.2%; Density: 1,925.8 persons per square mile; Race: 97.4% White, 0.4% Black/African American, 0.7% Asian, 0.2% American Indian/Alaska Native, 0.0% Native Hawaiian/Other Pacific Islander, 1.3% Two or more races, 1.1% Hispanic of any race; Average household size: 2.28; Median age: 39.5; Age under 18: 22.8%; Age 65 and over: 17.3%; Males per 100 females: 94.3; Marriage status: 28.8% never married, 46.7% now married, 0.9% separated, 6.3% widowed, 18.1% divorced; Foreign born: 1.4%; Speak English only: 98.7%; With disability: 21.2%; Veterans: 14.0%; Ancestry: 20.9% German, 13.9% Irish, 11.3% American, 11.3% English, 4.8% French
Employment: 5.8% management, business, and financial, 4.3% computer, engineering, and science, 3.9% education, legal, community service, arts, and media, 4.2% healthcare practitioners, 27.9% service, 33.4% sales and office, 6.5% natural resources, construction, and maintenance, 14.1% production, transportation, and material moving
Income: Per capita: $19,697; Median household: $34,423; Average household: $41,494; Households with income of $100,000 or more: 3.9%; Poverty rate: 11.3%
Educational Attainment: High school diploma or higher: 89.7%; Bachelor's degree or higher: 10.8%; Graduate/professional degree or higher: 3.7%
Housing: Homeownership rate: 72.6%; Median home value: $66,400; Median year structure built: 1961; Homeowner vacancy rate: 4.5%; Median gross rent: $610 per month; Rental vacancy rate: 20.2%
Health Insurance: 82.9% have insurance; 57.4% have private insurance; 42.1% have public insurance; 17.1% do not have insurance; 1.9% of children under 18 do not have insurance
Safety: Violent crime rate: 4.0 per 10,000 population; Property crime rate: 203.3 per 10,000 population
Transportation: Commute: 92.8% car, 0.0% public transportation, 3.9% walk, 1.4% work from home; Median travel time to work: 20.0 minutes
Additional Information Contacts
Town of Chesterfield . . . . (765) 378-3331
    http://www.chesterfield.in.gov

COUNTRY CLUB HEIGHTS (town).
Covers a land area of 0.283 square miles and a water area of 0 square miles. Located at 40.12° N. Lat; 85.69° W. Long. Elevation is 879 feet.
Population: 79; Growth (since 2000): -13.2%; Density: 278.9 persons per square mile; Race: 100.0% White, 0.0% Black/African American, 0.0% Asian, 0.0% American Indian/Alaska Native, 0.0% Native Hawaiian/Other Pacific Islander, 0.0% Two or more races, 0.0% Hispanic of any race; Average household size: 2.26; Median age: 57.9; Age under 18: 16.5%; Age 65 and over: 30.4%; Males per 100 females: 107.9

Housing: Homeownership rate: 100.0%; Homeowner vacancy rate: 7.9%; Rental vacancy rate: 0.0%

EDGEWOOD (town).
Covers a land area of 0.809 square miles and a water area of 0 square miles. Located at 40.10° N. Lat; 85.74° W. Long. Elevation is 879 feet.
History: Edgewood grew as a residential suburb for employees of the manufacturing plants in nearby Anderson.
Population: 1,913; Growth (since 2000): -3.8%; Density: 2,366.0 persons per square mile; Race: 92.9% White, 4.5% Black/African American, 0.3% Asian, 0.2% American Indian/Alaska Native, 0.0% Native Hawaiian/Other Pacific Islander, 1.2% Two or more races, 1.8% Hispanic of any race; Average household size: 2.24; Median age: 47.4; Age under 18: 20.2%; Age 65 and over: 21.3%; Males per 100 females: 88.8
Housing: Homeownership rate: 91.6%; Homeowner vacancy rate: 2.4%; Rental vacancy rate: 2.7%

ELWOOD (city).
Covers a land area of 3.774 square miles and a water area of 0 square miles. Located at 40.27° N. Lat; 85.84° W. Long. Elevation is 863 feet.
History: Elwood was the birthplace of Wendell L. Wilkie, presidential nominee in 1940, who lived here until 1919. His speech accepting the nomination was made in Elwood.
Population: 8,614; Growth (since 2000): -11.5%; Density: 2,282.5 persons per square mile; Race: 96.7% White, 0.2% Black/African American, 0.3% Asian, 0.2% American Indian/Alaska Native, 0.0% Native Hawaiian/Other Pacific Islander, 1.5% Two or more races, 3.3% Hispanic of any race; Average household size: 2.49; Median age: 38.6; Age under 18: 25.2%; Age 65 and over: 14.1%; Males per 100 females: 94.9; Marriage status: 24.7% never married, 53.5% now married, 2.6% separated, 6.5% widowed, 15.2% divorced; Foreign born: 1.8%; Speak English only: 95.9%; With disability: 20.6%; Veterans: 9.0%; Ancestry: 23.4% German, 15.6% American, 14.7% Irish, 6.7% English, 1.9% Italian
Employment: 9.5% management, business, and financial, 2.3% computer, engineering, and science, 7.9% education, legal, community service, arts, and media, 2.1% healthcare practitioners, 21.1% service, 20.9% sales and office, 5.7% natural resources, construction, and maintenance, 30.5% production, transportation, and material moving
Income: Per capita: $18,402; Median household: $35,625; Average household: $46,897; Households with income of $100,000 or more: 9.5%; Poverty rate: 18.2%
Educational Attainment: High school diploma or higher: 83.8%; Bachelor's degree or higher: 9.6%; Graduate/professional degree or higher: 1.8%
School District(s)
Elwood Community School Corp (PK-12)
    2012-13 Enrollment: 1,618 . . . . (765) 552-9861
Housing: Homeownership rate: 67.3%; Median home value: $73,200; Median year structure built: 1945; Homeowner vacancy rate: 5.3%; Median gross rent: $665 per month; Rental vacancy rate: 12.6%
Health Insurance: 85.0% have insurance; 57.7% have private insurance; 38.0% have public insurance; 15.0% do not have insurance; 12.4% of children under 18 do not have insurance
Hospitals: Saint Vincent Mercy Hospital (25 beds)
Safety: Violent crime rate: 8.2 per 10,000 population; Property crime rate: 335.6 per 10,000 population
Newspapers: Call-Leader (daily circulation 3100)
Transportation: Commute: 92.3% car, 0.0% public transportation, 1.9% walk, 2.9% work from home; Median travel time to work: 30.6 minutes
Additional Information Contacts
City of Elwood . . . . (765) 552-5078
    http://www.elwoodcity-in.org

FRANKTON (town).
Covers a land area of 1.054 square miles and a water area of 0 square miles. Located at 40.22° N. Lat; 85.77° W. Long. Elevation is 833 feet.
Population: 1,862; Growth (since 2000): -2.3%; Density: 1,766.0 persons per square mile; Race: 97.5% White, 0.4% Black/African American, 0.1% Asian, 0.1% American Indian/Alaska Native, 0.0% Native Hawaiian/Other Pacific Islander, 1.1% Two or more races, 2.2% Hispanic of any race; Average household size: 2.54; Median age: 38.2; Age under 18: 26.9%; Age 65 and over: 14.3%; Males per 100 females: 94.8
School District(s)
Frankton-Lapel Community Schs (PK-12)
    2012-13 Enrollment: 2,985 . . . . (765) 734-1261

Housing: Homeownership rate: 80.4%; Homeowner vacancy rate: 2.1%; Rental vacancy rate: 14.8%

INGALLS (town).
Covers a land area of 1.512 square miles and a water area of 0.033 square miles. Located at 39.96° N. Lat; 85.81° W. Long. Elevation is 866 feet.
Population: 2,394; Growth (since 2000): 105.0%; Density: 1,583.6 persons per square mile; Race: 92.4% White, 3.0% Black/African American, 0.3% Asian, 0.4% American Indian/Alaska Native, 0.0% Native Hawaiian/Other Pacific Islander, 2.3% Two or more races, 3.9% Hispanic of any race; Average household size: 2.87; Median age: 29.8; Age under 18: 32.9%; Age 65 and over: 7.6%; Males per 100 females: 98.2
Housing: Homeownership rate: 84.4%; Homeowner vacancy rate: 3.1%; Rental vacancy rate: 4.4%

LAPEL (town).
Covers a land area of 1.379 square miles and a water area of 0 square miles. Located at 40.07° N. Lat; 85.85° W. Long. Elevation is 860 feet.
History: Laid out 1876.
Population: 2,068; Growth (since 2000): 11.5%; Density: 1,499.6 persons per square mile; Race: 97.7% White, 0.2% Black/African American, 0.2% Asian, 0.3% American Indian/Alaska Native, 0.0% Native Hawaiian/Other Pacific Islander, 1.3% Two or more races, 0.8% Hispanic of any race; Average household size: 2.58; Median age: 37.3; Age under 18: 27.9%; Age 65 and over: 12.4%; Males per 100 females: 93.5
School District(s)
Frankton-Lapel Community Schs (PK-12)
   2012-13 Enrollment: 2,985 . . . . (765) 734-1261
Housing: Homeownership rate: 74.1%; Homeowner vacancy rate: 1.5%; Rental vacancy rate: 5.0%

MARKLEVILLE (town).
Covers a land area of 0.563 square miles and a water area of 0 square miles. Located at 39.98° N. Lat; 85.62° W. Long. Elevation is 951 feet.
History: Laid out 1852.
Population: 528; Growth (since 2000): 37.9%; Density: 938.0 persons per square mile; Race: 97.9% White, 0.2% Black/African American, 0.2% Asian, 0.0% American Indian/Alaska Native, 0.0% Native Hawaiian/Other Pacific Islander, 1.1% Two or more races, 0.9% Hispanic of any race; Average household size: 2.69; Median age: 35.7; Age under 18: 28.6%; Age 65 and over: 13.1%; Males per 100 females: 95.6
Housing: Homeownership rate: 83.1%; Homeowner vacancy rate: 4.1%; Rental vacancy rate: 2.9%

ORESTES (town).
Covers a land area of 0.623 square miles and a water area of 0 square miles. Located at 40.27° N. Lat; 85.73° W. Long. Elevation is 873 feet.
Population: 414; Growth (since 2000): 24.0%; Density: 664.2 persons per square mile; Race: 95.7% White, 0.2% Black/African American, 0.0% Asian, 0.5% American Indian/Alaska Native, 0.0% Native Hawaiian/Other Pacific Islander, 0.7% Two or more races, 4.8% Hispanic of any race; Average household size: 2.80; Median age: 35.8; Age under 18: 24.6%; Age 65 and over: 13.3%; Males per 100 females: 106.0
Housing: Homeownership rate: 69.6%; Homeowner vacancy rate: 6.4%; Rental vacancy rate: 18.2%

PENDLETON (town).
Covers a land area of 11.166 square miles and a water area of 0.067 square miles. Located at 40.01° N. Lat; 85.76° W. Long. Elevation is 846 feet.
History: Pendleton was the county seat in the 1820's.
Population: 4,253; Growth (since 2000): 9.8%; Density: 380.9 persons per square mile; Race: 96.6% White, 1.0% Black/African American, 0.8% Asian, 0.3% American Indian/Alaska Native, 0.1% Native Hawaiian/Other Pacific Islander, 0.9% Two or more races, 1.0% Hispanic of any race; Average household size: 2.37; Median age: 37.6; Age under 18: 26.4%; Age 65 and over: 15.0%; Males per 100 females: 89.7; Marriage status: 24.4% never married, 49.6% now married, 1.0% separated, 7.6% widowed, 18.4% divorced; Foreign born: 0.9%; Speak English only: 98.7%; With disability: 15.1%; Veterans: 13.5%; Ancestry: 21.7% German, 16.3% American, 12.0% Irish, 11.4% English, 3.6% Polish
Employment: 11.3% management, business, and financial, 3.5% computer, engineering, and science, 12.6% education, legal, community service, arts, and media, 8.6% healthcare practitioners, 21.2% service, 25.8% sales and office, 9.7% natural resources, construction, and maintenance, 7.2% production, transportation, and material moving

Income: Per capita: $28,215; Median household: $51,481; Average household: $71,531; Households with income of $100,000 or more: 21.2%; Poverty rate: 10.3%
Educational Attainment: High school diploma or higher: 91.7%; Bachelor's degree or higher: 25.9%; Graduate/professional degree or higher: 7.7%
School District(s)
In Department of Correction (06-12)
   2012-13 Enrollment: 484 . . . . (317) 233-3111
South Madison Com Sch Corp (PK-12)
   2012-13 Enrollment: 4,077 . . . . (765) 778-2152
Housing: Homeownership rate: 66.5%; Median home value: $136,400; Median year structure built: 1968; Homeowner vacancy rate: 1.8%; Median gross rent: $841 per month; Rental vacancy rate: 8.9%
Health Insurance: 87.6% have insurance; 67.3% have private insurance; 37.1% have public insurance; 12.4% do not have insurance; 5.3% of children under 18 do not have insurance
Newspapers: Times-Post (weekly circulation 1000)
Transportation: Commute: 97.3% car, 0.0% public transportation, 0.0% walk, 2.1% work from home; Median travel time to work: 27.1 minutes
Additional Information Contacts
Town of Pendleton . . . . (765) 778-7937
   http://www.town.pendleton.in.us

RIVER FOREST (town).
Covers a land area of 0.017 square miles and a water area of 0 square miles. Located at 40.11° N. Lat; 85.73° W. Long. Elevation is 873 feet.
Population: 22; Growth (since 2000): -21.4%; Density: 1,261.5 persons per square mile; Race: 100.0% White, 0.0% Black/African American, 0.0% Asian, 0.0% American Indian/Alaska Native, 0.0% Native Hawaiian/Other Pacific Islander, 0.0% Two or more races, 0.0% Hispanic of any race; Average household size: 2.44; Median age: 58.0; Age under 18: 9.1%; Age 65 and over: 22.7%; Males per 100 females: 144.4
Housing: Homeownership rate: 100.0%; Homeowner vacancy rate: 10.0%; Rental vacancy rate: 0.0%

SUMMITVILLE (town).
Covers a land area of 0.489 square miles and a water area of 0 square miles. Located at 40.34° N. Lat; 85.64° W. Long. Elevation is 883 feet.
History: Laid out 1867.
Population: 967; Growth (since 2000): -11.3%; Density: 1,977.5 persons per square mile; Race: 96.6% White, 0.7% Black/African American, 0.0% Asian, 0.1% American Indian/Alaska Native, 0.0% Native Hawaiian/Other Pacific Islander, 1.1% Two or more races, 2.1% Hispanic of any race; Average household size: 2.56; Median age: 39.6; Age under 18: 25.7%; Age 65 and over: 13.3%; Males per 100 females: 99.8
School District(s)
Madison-Grant United Sch Corp (KG-12)
   2012-13 Enrollment: 1,408 . . . . (765) 948-4143
Housing: Homeownership rate: 73.9%; Homeowner vacancy rate: 4.4%; Rental vacancy rate: 8.3%

WOODLAWN HEIGHTS (town).
Covers a land area of 0.116 square miles and a water area of 0 square miles. Located at 40.12° N. Lat; 85.70° W. Long. Elevation is 866 feet.
Population: 79; Growth (since 2000): 8.2%; Density: 683.2 persons per square mile; Race: 97.5% White, 0.0% Black/African American, 0.0% Asian, 0.0% American Indian/Alaska Native, 0.0% Native Hawaiian/Other Pacific Islander, 1.3% Two or more races, 3.8% Hispanic of any race; Average household size: 2.32; Median age: 56.3; Age under 18: 19.0%; Age 65 and over: 22.8%; Males per 100 females: 83.7
Housing: Homeownership rate: 88.2%; Homeowner vacancy rate: 0.0%; Rental vacancy rate: 0.0%

Marion County

Located in central Indiana; drained by the West Fork of the White River. Covers a land area of 396.298 square miles, a water area of 6.710 square miles, and is located in the Eastern Time Zone at 39.78° N. Lat., 86.14° W. Long. The county was founded in 1821. County seat is Indianapolis.

Marion County is part of the Indianapolis-Carmel-Anderson, IN Metropolitan Statistical Area. The entire metro area includes: Boone County, IN; Brown County, IN; Hamilton County, IN; Hancock County, IN;

Hendricks County, IN; Johnson County, IN; Madison County, IN; Marion County, IN; Morgan County, IN; Putnam County, IN; Shelby County, IN

Weather Station: Indianapolis Int'l Arpt   Elevation: 791 feet

	Jan	Feb	Mar	Apr	May	Jun	Jul	Aug	Sep	Oct	Nov	Dec
High	36	41	52	63	73	82	85	84	78	65	52	39
Low	21	24	32	42	52	62	66	64	56	45	35	25
Precip	2.7	2.4	3.6	3.8	5.0	4.1	4.6	3.4	3.2	3.1	3.6	3.1
Snow	8.5	6.4	2.7	0.3	tr	tr	0.0	tr	tr	0.4	0.8	6.4

High and Low temperatures in degrees Fahrenheit; Precipitation and Snow in inches

Weather Station: Indianapolis SE Side   Elevation: 845 feet

	Jan	Feb	Mar	Apr	May	Jun	Jul	Aug	Sep	Oct	Nov	Dec
High	35	39	50	62	72	81	84	83	77	65	52	39
Low	19	22	30	41	52	61	65	63	55	43	34	23
Precip	2.3	2.1	3.3	4.1	5.0	4.3	4.7	3.4	3.0	3.2	3.6	3.1
Snow	5.0	3.6	1.0	0.1	tr	0.0	0.0	0.0	0.0	0.2	0.2	3.3

High and Low temperatures in degrees Fahrenheit; Precipitation and Snow in inches

Population: 903,393; Growth (since 2000): 5.0%; Density: 2,279.6 persons per square mile; Race: 62.7% White, 26.7% Black/African American, 2.0% Asian, 0.3% American Indian/Alaska Native, 0.1% Native Hawaiian/Other Pacific Islander, 2.8% two or more races, 9.3% Hispanic of any race; Average household size: 2.42; Median age: 33.9; Age under 18: 25.1%; Age 65 and over: 10.6%; Males per 100 females: 93.2; Marriage status: 38.1% never married, 43.0% now married, 2.5% separated, 5.5% widowed, 13.4% divorced; Foreign born: 8.5%; Speak English only: 87.6%; With disability: 12.9%; Veterans: 8.3%; Ancestry: 17.1% German, 10.7% Irish, 7.2% English, 7.1% American, 3.3% African
Religion: Six largest groups: 11.1% Catholicism, 10.4% Baptist, 6.4% Non-denominational Protestant, 5.0% Methodist/Pietist, 2.1% Presbyterian-Reformed, 1.6% Pentecostal
Economy: Unemployment rate: 5.6%; Leading industries: 13.1% retail trade; 12.0% professional, scientific, and technical services; 10.7% health care and social assistance; Farms: 231 totaling 20,075 acres; Company size: 38 employ 1,000 or more persons, 45 employ 500 to 999 persons, 752 employ 100 to 499 persons, 21,885 employ less than 100 persons; Business ownership: 19,422 women-owned, 8,219 Black-owned, 1,539 Hispanic-owned, 1,660 Asian-owned
Employment: 13.8% management, business, and financial, 4.7% computer, engineering, and science, 9.7% education, legal, community service, arts, and media, 5.8% healthcare practitioners, 18.7% service, 26.0% sales and office, 7.4% natural resources, construction, and maintenance, 14.0% production, transportation, and material moving
Income: Per capita: $24,124; Median household: $42,334; Average household: $58,836; Households with income of $100,000 or more: 14.6%; Poverty rate: 20.4%
Educational Attainment: High school diploma or higher: 84.5%; Bachelor's degree or higher: 27.4%; Graduate/professional degree or higher: 9.3%
Housing: Homeownership rate: 56.5%; Median home value: $118,000; Median year structure built: 1969; Homeowner vacancy rate: 3.3%; Median gross rent: $768 per month; Rental vacancy rate: 12.5%
Vital Statistics: Birth rate: 156.3 per 10,000 population; Death rate: 81.0 per 10,000 population; Age-adjusted cancer mortality rate: 205.2 deaths per 100,000 population
Health Insurance: 82.9% have insurance; 59.9% have private insurance; 32.5% have public insurance; 17.1% do not have insurance; 8.9% of children under 18 do not have insurance
Health Care: Physicians: 38.6 per 10,000 population; Hospital beds: 50.7 per 10,000 population; Hospital admissions: 2,091.0 per 10,000 population
Air Quality Index: 30.4% good, 67.1% moderate, 2.5% unhealthy for sensitive individuals, 0.0% unhealthy (percent of days)
Transportation: Commute: 92.0% car, 1.9% public transportation, 1.9% walk, 2.9% work from home; Median travel time to work: 22.7 minutes
Presidential Election: 60.2% Obama, 38.1% Romney (2012)
National and State Parks: Fort Benjamin Harrison State Park and Nature Preserve; White River State Park
Additional Information Contacts
Marion Government . . . . (317) 327-4740
http://www.indygov.org

Marion County Communities

BEECH GROVE (city). Covers a land area of 4.395 square miles and a water area of 0 square miles. Located at 39.72° N. Lat; 86.09° W. Long. Elevation is 804 feet.
History: Named for the many local beech trees. Incorporated 1906.
Population: 14,192; Growth (since 2000): -4.6%; Density: 3,229.4 persons per square mile; Race: 91.5% White, 3.2% Black/African American, 0.7% Asian, 0.3% American Indian/Alaska Native, 0.0% Native Hawaiian/Other Pacific Islander, 2.1% Two or more races, 4.2% Hispanic of any race; Average household size: 2.36; Median age: 37.7; Age under 18: 24.6%; Age 65 and over: 14.9%; Males per 100 females: 86.8; Marriage status: 30.9% never married, 47.9% now married, 1.4% separated, 7.4% widowed, 13.7% divorced; Foreign born: 2.1%; Speak English only: 95.7%; With disability: 13.6%; Veterans: 9.2%; Ancestry: 23.8% German, 16.0% Irish, 11.0% American, 7.8% English, 3.9% Italian
Employment: 9.4% management, business, and financial, 3.0% computer, engineering, and science, 7.3% education, legal, community service, arts, and media, 4.3% healthcare practitioners, 17.8% service, 29.4% sales and office, 9.3% natural resources, construction, and maintenance, 19.5% production, transportation, and material moving
Income: Per capita: $20,095; Median household: $39,444; Average household: $49,189; Households with income of $100,000 or more: 8.8%; Poverty rate: 19.5%
Educational Attainment: High school diploma or higher: 86.4%; Bachelor's degree or higher: 15.5%; Graduate/professional degree or higher: 5.0%

School District(s)
Beech Grove City Schools (PK-12)
   2012-13 Enrollment: 2,784 . . . . (317) 788-4481
Housing: Homeownership rate: 55.7%; Median home value: $93,600; Median year structure built: 1960; Homeowner vacancy rate: 3.2%; Median gross rent: $730 per month; Rental vacancy rate: 10.3%
Health Insurance: 87.5% have insurance; 64.4% have private insurance; 35.9% have public insurance; 12.5% do not have insurance; 4.0% of children under 18 do not have insurance
Safety: Violent crime rate: 22.9 per 10,000 population; Property crime rate: 374.7 per 10,000 population
Transportation: Commute: 95.7% car, 0.3% public transportation, 1.2% walk, 2.2% work from home; Median travel time to work: 21.1 minutes
Additional Information Contacts
City of Beech Grove . . . . (317) 788-4977
http://www.beechgrove.com

CLERMONT (town). Covers a land area of 0.672 square miles and a water area of 0 square miles. Located at 39.82° N. Lat; 86.32° W. Long. Elevation is 833 feet.
History: When Clermont was platted in 1849 it was called Mechanicsburg, but the name was changed in 1855.
Population: 1,356; Growth (since 2000): -8.2%; Density: 2,018.1 persons per square mile; Race: 92.1% White, 4.2% Black/African American, 0.7% Asian, 0.2% American Indian/Alaska Native, 0.0% Native Hawaiian/Other Pacific Islander, 2.6% Two or more races, 2.5% Hispanic of any race; Average household size: 2.34; Median age: 45.0; Age under 18: 21.1%; Age 65 and over: 15.1%; Males per 100 females: 96.8
Housing: Homeownership rate: 81.5%; Homeowner vacancy rate: 1.6%; Rental vacancy rate: 9.3%

CROWS NEST (town). Covers a land area of 0.429 square miles and a water area of 0 square miles. Located at 39.86° N. Lat; 86.17° W. Long. Elevation is 774 feet.
History: Joined Indianapolis in 1970.
Population: 73; Growth (since 2000): -24.0%; Density: 170.0 persons per square mile; Race: 97.3% White, 2.7% Black/African American, 0.0% Asian, 0.0% American Indian/Alaska Native, 0.0% Native Hawaiian/Other Pacific Islander, 0.0% Two or more races, 1.4% Hispanic of any race; Average household size: 2.15; Median age: 60.3; Age under 18: 4.1%; Age 65 and over: 26.0%; Males per 100 females: 114.7
Housing: Homeownership rate: 88.3%; Homeowner vacancy rate: 6.3%; Rental vacancy rate: 0.0%

CUMBERLAND (town)
Covers a land area of 2.058 square miles and a water area of 0.010 square miles. Located at 39.79° N. Lat; 85.95° W. Long. Elevation is 853 feet.

History: The Town was officially platted on July 7, 1831 and originally had just six streets. The first Cumberland Post Office was established in 1842.

Population: 5,169; Growth (since 2000): -6.0%; Density: 2,511.3 persons per square mile; Race: 77.0% White, 16.8% Black/African American, 0.9% Asian, 0.6% American Indian/Alaska Native, 0.1% Native Hawaiian/Other Pacific Islander, 2.3% Two or more races, 5.3% Hispanic of any race; Average household size: 2.61; Median age: 38.4; Age under 18: 27.4%; Age 65 and over: 11.5%; Males per 100 females: 92.6; Marriage status: 31.2% never married, 54.2% now married, 4.3% separated, 2.6% widowed, 12.0% divorced; Foreign born: 2.6%; Speak English only: 94.9%; With disability: 12.6%; Veterans: 10.9%; Ancestry: 19.1% German, 13.7% Irish, 11.4% American, 7.9% English, 5.0% Scottish

Employment: 12.3% management, business, and financial, 4.4% computer, engineering, and science, 9.5% education, legal, community service, arts, and media, 6.3% healthcare practitioners, 11.8% service, 31.7% sales and office, 17.9% natural resources, construction, and maintenance, 6.2% production, transportation, and material moving

Income: Per capita: $21,549; Median household: $44,637; Average household: $54,021; Households with income of $100,000 or more: 9.5%; Poverty rate: 14.7%

Educational Attainment: High school diploma or higher: 86.0%; Bachelor's degree or higher: 18.6%; Graduate/professional degree or higher: 6.6%

Housing: Homeownership rate: 68.6%; Median home value: $138,500; Median year structure built: 1976; Homeowner vacancy rate: 2.7%; Median gross rent: $734 per month; Rental vacancy rate: 22.0%

Health Insurance: 91.1% have insurance; 60.5% have private insurance; 38.2% have public insurance; 8.9% do not have insurance; 2.6% of children under 18 do not have insurance

Safety: Violent crime rate: 38.3 per 10,000 population; Property crime rate: 368.0 per 10,000 population

Transportation: Commute: 92.6% car, 0.5% public transportation, 1.4% walk, 3.0% work from home; Median travel time to work: 27.6 minutes

Additional Information Contacts
Town of Cumberland . . . . (317) 894-6201
  http://www.town.cumberland.in.us

HOMECROFT (town)
Covers a land area of 0.242 square miles and a water area of 0 square miles. Located at 39.67° N. Lat; 86.13° W. Long. Elevation is 755 feet.

Population: 722; Growth (since 2000): -3.9%; Density: 2,988.8 persons per square mile; Race: 95.7% White, 0.8% Black/African American, 0.7% Asian, 0.7% American Indian/Alaska Native, 0.0% Native Hawaiian/Other Pacific Islander, 1.5% Two or more races, 1.1% Hispanic of any race; Average household size: 2.34; Median age: 41.2; Age under 18: 21.6%; Age 65 and over: 12.7%; Males per 100 females: 87.5

Housing: Homeownership rate: 88.7%; Homeowner vacancy rate: 2.1%; Rental vacancy rate: 2.8%

INDIANAPOLIS (city)
State capital. County seat. Covers a land area of 361.433 square miles and a water area of 6.592 square miles. Located at 39.78° N. Lat; 86.15° W. Long. Elevation is 718 feet.

History: Settlement began in Indianapolis in 1820, when several families built cabins here and called it Fall Creek. That same year, Fall Creek was selected as the site for Indiana's capital because of its location near the center of the state. The new city was named Indianapolis in 1821; the first legislature met here in 1825. Indianapolis was incorporated as a city in 1847. Henry Ward Beecher, well-known writer, preacher, and brother of Harriet Beecher Stowe, lived in Indianapolis at that time.

Population: 820,445; Growth (since 2000): 4.9%; Density: 2,270.0 persons per square mile; Race: 61.8% White, 27.5% Black/African American, 2.1% Asian, 0.3% American Indian/Alaska Native, 0.0% Native Hawaiian/Other Pacific Islander, 2.8% Two or more races, 9.4% Hispanic of any race; Average household size: 2.42; Median age: 33.7; Age under 18: 25.0%; Age 65 and over: 10.5%; Males per 100 females: 93.5; Marriage status: 38.7% never married, 42.4% now married, 2.5% separated, 5.5% widowed, 13.4% divorced; Foreign born: 8.7%; Speak English only: 87.4%; With disability: 12.9%; Veterans: 8.1%; Ancestry: 17.0% German, 10.4% Irish, 7.1% English, 7.0% American, 3.5% African

Employment: 13.6% management, business, and financial, 4.7% computer, engineering, and science, 9.8% education, legal, community service, arts, and media, 5.9% healthcare practitioners, 18.8% service, 25.9% sales and office, 7.3% natural resources, construction, and maintenance, 14.1% production, transportation, and material moving

Income: Per capita: $24,012; Median household: $41,962; Average household: $58,562; Households with income of $100,000 or more: 14.5%; Poverty rate: 20.9%

Educational Attainment: High school diploma or higher: 84.3%; Bachelor's degree or higher: 27.3%; Graduate/professional degree or higher: 9.4%

School District(s)
Andrew Academy (KG-08)
  2012-13 Enrollment: 217 . . . . (317) 236-7324
Andrew J Brown Academy (KG-08)
  2012-13 Enrollment: 667 . . . . (317) 891-0730
Carmel Clay Schools (PK-12)
  2012-13 Enrollment: 15,724 . . . . (317) 844-9961
Challenge Foundation Academy (KG-05)
  2012-13 Enrollment: 482 . . . . (317) 803-3182
Charles A Tindley Accelerated Schl (06-12)
  2012-13 Enrollment: 383 . . . . (317) 545-1745
Christel House Academy (KG-10)
  2012-13 Enrollment: 613 . . . . (317) 783-4690
Damar Charter Academy (01-12)
  2012-13 Enrollment: 160 . . . . (317) 455-7121
Excel Center for Adult Learners (09-12)
  2012-13 Enrollment: 1,221 . . . . (317) 524-4141
Fall Creek Academy (KG-12)
  2012-13 Enrollment: 471 . . . . (317) 536-1027
Flanner House Elementary School (KG-06)
  2012-13 Enrollment: 228 . . . . (317) 925-4231
Fountain Square Academy (05-12)
  2012-13 Enrollment: 245 . . . . (317) 951-1000
Franklin Township Com Sch Corp (PK-12)
  2012-13 Enrollment: 8,607 . . . . (317) 862-2411
Herron Charter (09-12)
  2012-13 Enrollment: 640 . . . . (317) 231-0010
Hoosier Acad Virtual Charter (KG-12)
  2012-13 Enrollment: 3,832 . . . . (317) 495-6494
Hoosier Academy - Indianapolis (KG-12)
  2012-13 Enrollment: 540 . . . . (317) 547-1400
Hope Academy (09-12)
  2012-13 Enrollment: 37 . . . . (317) 572-9356
Imagine Life Sciences Acad - East (KG-08)
  2012-13 Enrollment: 639 . . . . (317) 890-9100
Imagine Life Sciences Acad - West (KG-08)
  2012-13 Enrollment: 616 . . . . (317) 297-9100
In Connections Acad Virtual Pilot (KG-12)
  2012-13 Enrollment: 2,748 . . . . (317) 550-3188
In Department of Correction (06-12)
  2012-13 Enrollment: 484 . . . . (317) 233-3111
In Sch for the Blind & Vis Imprd (PK-12)
  2012-13 Enrollment: 158 . . . . (317) 253-1481
Indiana Math Science Academy North (KG-08)
  2012-13 Enrollment: 519 . . . . (317) 259-7300
Indiana Math and Science Academy (KG-12)
  2012-13 Enrollment: 541 . . . . (317) 298-0025
Indiana School for the Deaf (PK-12)
  2012-13 Enrollment: 333 . . . . (317) 924-8400
Indiana Virtual School (06-12)
  2012-13 Enrollment: 36 . . . . (317) 581-5355
Indianapolis Metropolitan High Sch (09-12)
  2012-13 Enrollment: 319 . . . . (317) 524-4501
Indianapolis Public Schools (PK-12)
  2012-13 Enrollment: 29,806 . . . . (317) 226-4411
Indpls Lighthouse Charter School (PK-11)
  2012-13 Enrollment: 663 . . . . (317) 897-2430
Irvington Community School (KG-12)
  2012-13 Enrollment: 1,028 . . . . (317) 357-5359
Kipp Indpls College Preparatory (05-08)
  2012-13 Enrollment: 282 . . . . (317) 637-9780
M S D Decatur Township (KG-12)
  2012-13 Enrollment: 6,270 . . . . (317) 856-5265
M S D Lawrence Township (PK-12)
  2012-13 Enrollment: 15,118 . . . . (317) 423-8200
M S D Perry Township (KG-12)
  2012-13 Enrollment: 14,473 . . . . (317) 789-3700

M S D Pike Township (PK-12)
   2012-13 Enrollment: 11,006 .... (317) 293-0393
M S D Warren Township (PK-12)
   2012-13 Enrollment: 11,897 .... (317) 869-4300
M S D Washington Township (PK-12)
   2012-13 Enrollment: 11,050 .... (317) 845-9400
M S D Wayne Township (PK-12)
   2012-13 Enrollment: 15,742 .... (317) 243-8251
Monument Lighthouse Charter School (KG-09)
   2012-13 Enrollment: 607 .... (317) 897-2472
Padua Academy (KG-07)
   2012-13 Enrollment: 186 .... (317) 236-1532
Paramount School of Excellence Inc (KG-08)
   2012-13 Enrollment: 536 .... (317) 775-6660
Se Neighborhood Sch of Excellence (KG-06)
   2012-13 Enrollment: 376 .... (317) 423-0204
Southside Sp Srvs of Marion County (PK-PK)
   2012-13 Enrollment: 112 .... (317) 789-1650

Four-year College(s)
American College of Education (Private, For-profit)
   Fall 2013 Enrollment: 3,021 .... (800) 280-0307
Brown Mackie College-Indianapolis (Private, For-profit)
   Fall 2013 Enrollment: 899 .... (317) 554-8300
   2013-14 Tuition: In-state $12,762; Out-of-state $12,762
Butler University (Private, Not-for-profit)
   Fall 2013 Enrollment: 4,827 .... (317) 940-8000
   2013-14 Tuition: In-state $34,368; Out-of-state $34,368
Chamberlain College of Nursing-Indiana (Private, For-profit)
   Fall 2013 Enrollment: 159 .... (317) 816-7335
   2013-14 Tuition: In-state $17,280; Out-of-state $17,280
Christian Theological Seminary (Private, Not-for-profit, Christian Church (Disciples of Christ))
   Fall 2013 Enrollment: 188 .... (317) 924-1331
Crossroads Bible College (Private, Not-for-profit, Baptist)
   Fall 2013 Enrollment: 257 .... (317) 789-8255
   2013-14 Tuition: In-state $12,350; Out-of-state $12,350
DeVry University-Indiana (Private, For-profit)
   Fall 2013 Enrollment: 467 .... (317) 581-8854
   2013-14 Tuition: In-state $16,010; Out-of-state $16,010
Harrison College-Indianapolis (Private, For-profit)
   Fall 2013 Enrollment: 3,726 .... (317) 447-6200
   2013-14 Tuition: In-state $16,740; Out-of-state $16,740
ITT Technical Institute-Indianapolis (Private, For-profit)
   Fall 2013 Enrollment: 4,397 .... (317) 875-8640
   2013-14 Tuition: In-state $16,842; Out-of-state $16,842
ITT Technical Institute-Indianapolis East (Private, For-profit)
   Fall 2013 Enrollment: 337 .... (317) 351-3800
   2013-14 Tuition: In-state $18,048; Out-of-state $18,048
Indiana University-Purdue University-Indianapolis (Public)
   Fall 2013 Enrollment: 30,488 .... (317) 274-5555
   2013-14 Tuition: In-state $8,756; Out-of-state $29,571
Marian University (Private, Not-for-profit, Roman Catholic)
   Fall 2013 Enrollment: 2,714 .... (317) 955-6000
   2013-14 Tuition: In-state $28,400; Out-of-state $28,400
Martin University (Private, Not-for-profit)
   Fall 2013 Enrollment: 506 .... (317) 543-3235
   2013-14 Tuition: In-state $11,960; Out-of-state $11,960
National American University-Indianapolis (Private, For-profit)
   Fall 2013 Enrollment: 198 .... (317) 810-8100
   2013-14 Tuition: In-state $12,891; Out-of-state $12,891
Strayer University-Indiana (Private, For-profit)
   Fall 2013 Enrollment: 142 .... (317) 810-0600
   2013-14 Tuition: In-state $15,495; Out-of-state $15,495
The Art Institute of Indianapolis (Private, For-profit)
   Fall 2013 Enrollment: 862 .... (317) 613-4800
   2013-14 Tuition: In-state $14,824; Out-of-state $14,824
University of Indianapolis (Private, Not-for-profit, United Methodist)
   Fall 2013 Enrollment: 5,452 .... (317) 788-3368
   2013-14 Tuition: In-state $24,660; Out-of-state $24,660
University of Phoenix-Indianapolis Campus (Private, For-profit)
   Fall 2013 Enrollment: 372 .... (866) 766-0766
   2013-14 Tuition: In-state $10,828; Out-of-state $10,828

Two-year College(s)
Aviation Institute of Maintenance-Indianapolis (Private, For-profit)
   Fall 2013 Enrollment: 157 .... (317) 243-4519
   2013-14 Tuition: In-state $18,007; Out-of-state $18,007
Fortis College-Indianapolis (Private, For-profit)
   Fall 2013 Enrollment: 172 .... (317) 808-4800
   2013-14 Tuition: In-state $19,957; Out-of-state $19,957
International Business College-Indianapolis (Private, For-profit)
   Fall 2013 Enrollment: 399 .... (317) 813-2300
   2013-14 Tuition: In-state $13,930; Out-of-state $13,930
Ivy Tech Community College (Public)
   Fall 2013 Enrollment: 98,778 .... (317) 921-4800
   2013-14 Tuition: In-state $3,605; Out-of-state $7,632
Kaplan College-Indianapolis (Private, For-profit)
   Fall 2013 Enrollment: 81 .... (317) 299-6001
Kaplan College-Indianapolis (Private, For-profit)
   Fall 2013 Enrollment: 478 .... (317) 782-0315
Lincoln College of Technology-Indianapolis (Private, For-profit)
   Fall 2013 Enrollment: 1,240 .... (317) 632-5553
MedTech College (Private, For-profit)
   Fall 2013 Enrollment: 603 .... (317) 845-0100

Vocational/Technical School(s)
Aveda Fredric's Institute-Indianapolis (Private, For-profit)
   Fall 2013 Enrollment: 208 .... (513) 533-0700
   2013-14 Tuition: $17,200
Empire Beauty School-Indianapolis (Private, For-profit)
   Fall 2013 Enrollment: 194 .... (800) 920-4593
   2013-14 Tuition: $15,645
Hair Fashions By Kaye Beauty College-Indianapolis (Private, For-profit)
   Fall 2013 Enrollment: 108 .... (317) 576-8000
   2013-14 Tuition: $15,650
J Everett Light Career Center (Public)
   Fall 2013 Enrollment: 40 .... (317) 259-5265
   2013-14 Tuition: In-state $15,000; Out-of-state $15,000
MyComputerCareer.com-Indianapolis (Private, For-profit)
   Fall 2013 Enrollment: 208 .... (317) 251-4600
   2013-14 Tuition: $11,280
Paul Mitchell the School-Indianapolis (Private, For-profit)
   Fall 2013 Enrollment: 174 .... (317) 885-0348
   2013-14 Tuition: $15,495
Regency Beauty Institute-Avon (Private, For-profit)
   Fall 2013 Enrollment: 41 .... (800) 787-6456
   2013-14 Tuition: $16,200
Regency Beauty Institute-Castleton (Private, For-profit)
   Fall 2013 Enrollment: 75 .... (800) 787-6456
   2013-14 Tuition: $16,200
Regency Beauty Institute-Greenwood (Private, For-profit)
   Fall 2013 Enrollment: 69 .... (800) 787-6456
   2013-14 Tuition: $16,200
Sanford-Brown College-Indianapolis (Private, For-profit)
   Fall 2013 Enrollment: 36 .... (317) 532-8300
Tricoci University of Beauty Culture-Indianapolis (Private, For-profit)
   Fall 2013 Enrollment: 111 .... (317) 841-9400
   2013-14 Tuition: $17,800

Housing: Homeownership rate: 55.8%; Median home value: $118,000; Median year structure built: 1969; Homeowner vacancy rate: 3.4%; Median gross rent: $770 per month; Rental vacancy rate: 12.3%
Health Insurance: 82.6% have insurance; 59.4% have private insurance; 32.6% have public insurance; 17.4% do not have insurance; 9.2% of children under 18 do not have insurance
Hospitals: Community Hospital East (1025 beds); Community Hospital North (282 beds); Community Hospital South; Community Westview Hospital (116 beds); Eskenazi Health (354 beds); Fairbanks; Franciscan Saint Francis Health - Indianapolis; Indiana Orthopaedic Hospital; Indiana University Health (1120 beds); Indianapolis VA Medical Center (170 beds); Saint Vincent Heart Center of Indiana (80 beds); Saint Vincent Hospital & Health Services (650 beds); The Indiana Heart Hospital (72 beds)
Safety: Violent crime rate: 123.3 per 10,000 population; Property crime rate: 524.6 per 10,000 population
Newspapers: Franklin Township Informer (weekly circulation 5000); Indianapolis Star (daily circulation 259000); Southside Times (weekly circulation 22500); West Indianapolis Community News (weekly circulation 15000)

Transportation: Commute: 91.8% car, 2.1% public transportation, 2.0% walk, 2.9% work from home; Median travel time to work: 22.6 minutes; Amtrak: Train service available.
Airports: Eagle Creek Airpark (general aviation); Indianapolis International (primary service/medium hub)
Additional Information Contacts
City of Indianapolis . . . . (317) 327-4740
http://www.indy.gov/Pages/Home.aspx

LAWRENCE (city).
Covers a land area of 20.132 square miles and a water area of 0.110 square miles. Located at 39.87° N. Lat; 85.99° W. Long. Elevation is 873 feet.
History: Named for Captain James Lawrence, U.S. Naval officer in the War of 1812. Fort Benjamin Harrison is here.
Population: 46,001; Growth (since 2000): 18.2%; Density: 2,285.0 persons per square mile; Race: 63.2% White, 25.8% Black/African American, 1.4% Asian, 0.4% American Indian/Alaska Native, 0.1% Native Hawaiian/Other Pacific Islander, 3.5% Two or more races, 11.2% Hispanic of any race; Average household size: 2.56; Median age: 34.2; Age under 18: 28.2%; Age 65 and over: 9.6%; Males per 100 females: 90.5; Marriage status: 31.6% never married, 49.8% now married, 2.3% separated, 5.3% widowed, 13.3% divorced; Foreign born: 7.4%; Speak English only: 87.8%; With disability: 11.0%; Veterans: 11.5%; Ancestry: 15.8% German, 12.3% Irish, 7.4% English, 6.6% American, 3.4% Italian
Employment: 17.7% management, business, and financial, 4.6% computer, engineering, and science, 8.8% education, legal, community service, arts, and media, 4.6% healthcare practitioners, 19.1% service, 27.1% sales and office, 7.0% natural resources, construction, and maintenance, 11.2% production, transportation, and material moving
Income: Per capita: $24,726; Median household: $51,384; Average household: $63,507; Households with income of $100,000 or more: 17.4%; Poverty rate: 15.1%
Educational Attainment: High school diploma or higher: 87.1%; Bachelor's degree or higher: 31.6%; Graduate/professional degree or higher: 9.3%
Housing: Homeownership rate: 69.5%; Median home value: $125,500; Median year structure built: 1990; Homeowner vacancy rate: 3.2%; Median gross rent: $804 per month; Rental vacancy rate: 12.9%
Health Insurance: 84.9% have insurance; 65.6% have private insurance; 28.9% have public insurance; 15.1% do not have insurance; 5.5% of children under 18 do not have insurance
Transportation: Commute: 94.5% car, 0.1% public transportation, 1.5% walk, 3.8% work from home; Median travel time to work: 24.8 minutes

MERIDIAN HILLS (town).
Covers a land area of 1.477 square miles and a water area of 0 square miles. Located at 39.89° N. Lat; 86.16° W. Long. Elevation is 794 feet.
History: Former municipality, merged with Indianapolis 1970.
Population: 1,616; Growth (since 2000): -5.7%; Density: 1,094.4 persons per square mile; Race: 95.9% White, 1.2% Black/African American, 1.1% Asian, 0.1% American Indian/Alaska Native, 0.1% Native Hawaiian/Other Pacific Islander, 1.2% Two or more races, 1.7% Hispanic of any race; Average household size: 2.51; Median age: 47.8; Age under 18: 24.3%; Age 65 and over: 19.3%; Males per 100 females: 96.4
Housing: Homeownership rate: 94.1%; Homeowner vacancy rate: 2.4%; Rental vacancy rate: 2.6%

NORTH CROWS NEST (town).
Covers a land area of 0.065 square miles and a water area of 0 square miles. Located at 39.87° N. Lat; 86.16° W. Long. Elevation is 781 feet.
Population: 45; Growth (since 2000): 7.1%; Density: 696.8 persons per square mile; Race: 100.0% White, 0.0% Black/African American, 0.0% Asian, 0.0% American Indian/Alaska Native, 0.0% Native Hawaiian/Other Pacific Islander, 0.0% Two or more races, 0.0% Hispanic of any race; Average household size: 2.37; Median age: 47.5; Age under 18: 22.2%; Age 65 and over: 24.4%; Males per 100 females: 104.5
Housing: Homeownership rate: 94.8%; Homeowner vacancy rate: 0.0%; Rental vacancy rate: 0.0%

ROCKY RIPPLE (town).
Covers a land area of 0.303 square miles and a water area of 0 square miles. Located at 39.85° N. Lat; 86.17° W. Long. Elevation is 705 feet.
Population: 606; Growth (since 2000): -14.9%; Density: 2,000.7 persons per square mile; Race: 89.1% White, 6.1% Black/African American, 0.8% Asian, 0.5% American Indian/Alaska Native, 0.0% Native Hawaiian/Other Pacific Islander, 2.5% Two or more races, 2.5% Hispanic of any race; Average household size: 2.08; Median age: 40.3; Age under 18: 18.2%; Age 65 and over: 13.7%; Males per 100 females: 97.4
Housing: Homeownership rate: 77.7%; Homeowner vacancy rate: 0.9%; Rental vacancy rate: 5.8%

SOUTHPORT (city).
Covers a land area of 0.628 square miles and a water area of 0 square miles. Located at 39.66° N. Lat; 86.12° W. Long. Elevation is 748 feet.
History: Laid out 1852.
Population: 1,712; Growth (since 2000): -7.6%; Density: 2,725.2 persons per square mile; Race: 94.1% White, 1.8% Black/African American, 1.1% Asian, 0.1% American Indian/Alaska Native, 0.0% Native Hawaiian/Other Pacific Islander, 1.2% Two or more races, 3.4% Hispanic of any race; Average household size: 2.46; Median age: 41.3; Age under 18: 22.1%; Age 65 and over: 15.7%; Males per 100 females: 92.6
Housing: Homeownership rate: 76.4%; Homeowner vacancy rate: 2.4%; Rental vacancy rate: 11.4%

SPEEDWAY (town).
Covers a land area of 4.758 square miles and a water area of 0.008 square miles. Located at 39.79° N. Lat; 86.25° W. Long. Elevation is 748 feet.
History: Named for Indianapolis Motor Speedway, located in the city. Speedway, laid out in 1912 by Carl Fisher, James T. Allison, and Frank H. Wheeler, gained fame as the home of the Indianapolis Motor Speedway.
Population: 11,812; Growth (since 2000): -8.3%; Density: 2,482.4 persons per square mile; Race: 74.2% White, 16.7% Black/African American, 2.0% Asian, 0.3% American Indian/Alaska Native, 0.0% Native Hawaiian/Other Pacific Islander, 2.3% Two or more races, 7.6% Hispanic of any race; Average household size: 2.13; Median age: 37.8; Age under 18: 21.7%; Age 65 and over: 14.8%; Males per 100 females: 93.6; Marriage status: 34.6% never married, 43.1% now married, 2.1% separated, 7.3% widowed, 15.0% divorced; Foreign born: 8.9%; Speak English only: 88.5%; With disability: 15.6%; Veterans: 10.0%; Ancestry: 20.3% German, 12.9% Irish, 12.2% English, 11.0% American, 2.5% Italian
Employment: 12.8% management, business, and financial, 5.1% computer, engineering, and science, 10.0% education, legal, community service, arts, and media, 5.5% healthcare practitioners, 18.6% service, 21.6% sales and office, 8.9% natural resources, construction, and maintenance, 17.4% production, transportation, and material moving
Income: Per capita: $25,181; Median household: $38,896; Average household: $49,903; Households with income of $100,000 or more: 10.8%; Poverty rate: 15.2%
Educational Attainment: High school diploma or higher: 88.6%; Bachelor's degree or higher: 24.5%; Graduate/professional degree or higher: 8.0%

School District(s)
School Town of Speedway (KG-12)
    2012-13 Enrollment: 1,689 . . . . (317) 244-0236
Vocational/Technical School(s)
Empire Beauty School-Speedway (Private, For-profit)
    Fall 2013 Enrollment: 170 . . . . (800) 920-4593
    2013-14 Tuition: $15,750
Housing: Homeownership rate: 48.5%; Median home value: $117,500; Median year structure built: 1961; Homeowner vacancy rate: 1.6%; Median gross rent: $721 per month; Rental vacancy rate: 22.2%
Health Insurance: 81.5% have insurance; 58.6% have private insurance; 33.3% have public insurance; 18.5% do not have insurance; 10.7% of children under 18 do not have insurance
Safety: Violent crime rate: 24.2 per 10,000 population; Property crime rate: 524.8 per 10,000 population
Newspapers: The Press Newspapers (weekly circulation 8500)
Transportation: Commute: 91.3% car, 3.0% public transportation, 0.9% walk, 3.6% work from home; Median travel time to work: 23.5 minutes
Additional Information Contacts
Town of Speedway . . . . (317) 246-4300
http://www.townofspeedway.org

SPRING HILL (town).
Covers a land area of 0.107 square miles and a water area of 0 square miles. Located at 39.83° N. Lat; 86.19° W. Long. Elevation is 761 feet.
Population: 98; Growth (since 2000): 1.0%; Density: 914.7 persons per square mile; Race: 78.6% White, 17.3% Black/African American, 0.0% Asian, 1.0% American Indian/Alaska Native, 0.0% Native Hawaiian/Other Pacific Islander, 3.1% Two or more races, 0.0% Hispanic of any race;

Average household size: 1.78; Median age: 64.7; Age under 18: 4.1%; Age 65 and over: 49.0%; Males per 100 females: 117.8
Housing: Homeownership rate: 96.4%; Homeowner vacancy rate: 3.6%; Rental vacancy rate: 0.0%

WARREN PARK (town).
Covers a land area of 0.450 square miles and a water area of 0 square miles. Located at 39.78° N. Lat; 86.05° W. Long. Elevation is 827 feet.
Population: 1,480; Growth (since 2000): -10.6%; Density: 3,292.4 persons per square mile; Race: 78.6% White, 16.1% Black/African American, 0.2% Asian, 0.1% American Indian/Alaska Native, 0.0% Native Hawaiian/Other Pacific Islander, 1.9% Two or more races, 7.3% Hispanic of any race; Average household size: 1.82; Median age: 50.5; Age under 18: 18.4%; Age 65 and over: 30.5%; Males per 100 females: 72.1
Housing: Homeownership rate: 31.4%; Homeowner vacancy rate: 2.6%; Rental vacancy rate: 24.5%

WEST NEWTON (unincorporated postal area)
ZCTA: 46183
Covers a land area of 0.031 square miles and a water area of 0 square miles. Located at 39.65° N. Lat; 86.28° W. Long. Elevation is 738 feet.
Population: 82; Growth (since 2000): n/a; Density: 2,655.4 persons per square mile; Race: 100.0% White, 0.0% Black/African American, 0.0% Asian, 0.0% American Indian/Alaska Native, 0.0% Native Hawaiian/Other Pacific Islander, 0.0% Two or more races, 3.7% Hispanic of any race; Average household size: 2.93; Median age: 29.3; Age under 18: 28.0%; Age 65 and over: 8.5%; Males per 100 females: 115.8

School District(s)
M S D Decatur Township (KG-12)
2012-13 Enrollment: 6,270 . . . . (317) 856-5265
Housing: Homeownership rate: 85.7%; Homeowner vacancy rate: 4.0%; Rental vacancy rate: 20.0%

WILLIAMS CREEK (town).
Covers a land area of 0.334 square miles and a water area of 0 square miles. Located at 39.90° N. Lat; 86.15° W. Long. Elevation is 774 feet.
Population: 407; Growth (since 2000): -1.5%; Density: 1,217.4 persons per square mile; Race: 96.1% White, 1.0% Black/African American, 1.5% Asian, 0.0% American Indian/Alaska Native, 0.0% Native Hawaiian/Other Pacific Islander, 1.0% Two or more races, 2.5% Hispanic of any race; Average household size: 2.79; Median age: 46.8; Age under 18: 30.2%; Age 65 and over: 20.4%; Males per 100 females: 97.6
Housing: Homeownership rate: 95.2%; Homeowner vacancy rate: 1.4%; Rental vacancy rate: 0.0%

WYNNEDALE (town).
Covers a land area of 0.159 square miles and a water area of 0 square miles. Located at 39.83° N. Lat; 86.20° W. Long. Elevation is 758 feet.
Population: 231; Growth (since 2000): -16.0%; Density: 1,448.8 persons per square mile; Race: 61.0% White, 35.9% Black/African American, 1.3% Asian, 0.0% American Indian/Alaska Native, 0.0% Native Hawaiian/Other Pacific Islander, 1.3% Two or more races, 0.9% Hispanic of any race; Average household size: 2.41; Median age: 52.4; Age under 18: 19.9%; Age 65 and over: 25.5%; Males per 100 females: 92.5
Housing: Homeownership rate: 96.9%; Homeowner vacancy rate: 1.1%; Rental vacancy rate: 0.0%

Marshall County

Located in northern Indiana; drained by the Yellow and Tippecanoe River; includes several lakes. Covers a land area of 443.628 square miles, a water area of 6.114 square miles, and is located in the Eastern Time Zone at 41.33° N. Lat., 86.27° W. Long. The county was founded in 1835. County seat is Plymouth.

Marshall County is part of the Plymouth, IN Micropolitan Statistical Area. The entire metro area includes: Marshall County, IN

Population: 47,051; Growth (since 2000): 4.3%; Density: 106.1 persons per square mile; Race: 93.5% White, 0.5% Black/African American, 0.5% Asian, 0.2% American Indian/Alaska Native, 0.0% Native Hawaiian/Other Pacific Islander, 1.5% two or more races, 8.4% Hispanic of any race; Average household size: 2.66; Median age: 38.4; Age under 18: 26.9%; Age 65 and over: 14.7%; Males per 100 females: 98.0; Marriage status: 24.7% never married, 57.0% now married, 1.6% separated, 6.2% widowed, 12.1% divorced; Foreign born: 4.2%; Speak English only: 89.2%; With disability: 12.8%; Veterans: 9.4%; Ancestry: 31.7% German, 10.6% Irish, 8.8% American, 8.5% English, 4.3% Polish
Religion: Six largest groups: 7.6% Methodist/Pietist, 5.3% Non-denominational Protestant, 5.3% European Free-Church, 4.3% Catholicism, 3.5% Holiness, 2.9% Lutheran
Economy: Unemployment rate: 5.2%; Leading industries: 16.4% retail trade; 13.2% other services (except public administration); 12.2% manufacturing; Farms: 878 totaling 206,306 acres; Company size: 0 employ 1,000 or more persons, 1 employs 500 to 999 persons, 27 employ 100 to 499 persons, 1,029 employ less than 100 persons; Business ownership: 1,026 women-owned, n/a Black-owned, n/a Hispanic-owned, n/a Asian-owned
Employment: 12.0% management, business, and financial, 1.7% computer, engineering, and science, 8.0% education, legal, community service, arts, and media, 5.1% healthcare practitioners, 14.0% service, 23.2% sales and office, 10.2% natural resources, construction, and maintenance, 25.8% production, transportation, and material moving
Income: Per capita: $21,933; Median household: $45,709; Average household: $57,529; Households with income of $100,000 or more: 13.0%; Poverty rate: 15.2%
Educational Attainment: High school diploma or higher: 84.4%; Bachelor's degree or higher: 16.6%; Graduate/professional degree or higher: 5.9%
Housing: Homeownership rate: 76.3%; Median home value: $124,600; Median year structure built: 1971; Homeowner vacancy rate: 2.7%; Median gross rent: $655 per month; Rental vacancy rate: 10.9%
Vital Statistics: Birth rate: 129.3 per 10,000 population; Death rate: 93.2 per 10,000 population; Age-adjusted cancer mortality rate: 158.1 deaths per 100,000 population
Health Insurance: 84.2% have insurance; 66.2% have private insurance; 29.4% have public insurance; 15.8% do not have insurance; 13.1% of children under 18 do not have insurance
Health Care: Physicians: 11.3 per 10,000 population; Hospital beds: 35.1 per 10,000 population; Hospital admissions: 1,253.1 per 10,000 population
Transportation: Commute: 91.1% car, 0.2% public transportation, 3.1% walk, 2.9% work from home; Median travel time to work: 21.3 minutes
Presidential Election: 34.6% Obama, 63.4% Romney (2012)
National and State Parks: Menominee State Wetlands
Additional Information Contacts
Marshall Government . . . . (574) 936-8922
http://www.co.marshall.in.us

Marshall County Communities

ARGOS (town).
Covers a land area of 1.159 square miles and a water area of 0.010 square miles. Located at 41.24° N. Lat; 86.25° W. Long. Elevation is 804 feet.
History: Argos began as a stagecoach stop on the Michigan Road. The name was chosen by Schuyler Colfax, vice-president under the Grant administration.
Population: 1,691; Growth (since 2000): 4.8%; Density: 1,459.5 persons per square mile; Race: 94.9% White, 0.3% Black/African American, 0.2% Asian, 0.5% American Indian/Alaska Native, 0.0% Native Hawaiian/Other Pacific Islander, 2.1% Two or more races, 4.6% Hispanic of any race; Average household size: 2.63; Median age: 33.1; Age under 18: 28.4%; Age 65 and over: 12.0%; Males per 100 females: 100.8

School District(s)
Argos Community Schools (KG-12)
2012-13 Enrollment: 635. . . . . (574) 892-5139
Housing: Homeownership rate: 67.9%; Homeowner vacancy rate: 4.0%; Rental vacancy rate: 14.2%

BOURBON (town).
Covers a land area of 0.992 square miles and a water area of 0.004 square miles. Located at 41.30° N. Lat; 86.12° W. Long. Elevation is 846 feet.
Population: 1,810; Growth (since 2000): 7.0%; Density: 1,824.7 persons per square mile; Race: 96.7% White, 0.3% Black/African American, 0.6% Asian, 0.1% American Indian/Alaska Native, 0.0% Native Hawaiian/Other Pacific Islander, 1.0% Two or more races, 5.0% Hispanic of any race; Average household size: 2.67; Median age: 32.7; Age under 18: 30.8%; Age 65 and over: 10.9%; Males per 100 females: 94.4

School District(s)
Triton School Corporation (KG-12)
2012-13 Enrollment: 961........................ (574) 342-2255
Housing: Homeownership rate: 69.5%; Homeowner vacancy rate: 1.7%; Rental vacancy rate: 11.5%
Additional Information Contacts
Town of Bourbon................................ (574) 342-4755
http://www.bourbon-in.gov

BREMEN (town).
Covers a land area of 2.715 square miles and a water area of 0.004 square miles. Located at 41.45° N. Lat; 86.15° W. Long. Elevation is 853 feet.
History: Bremen reports that its fire department was the 1882 and 1887 winner of the hose and engine maneuvers at the state championships.
Population: 4,588; Growth (since 2000): 2.3%; Density: 1,689.6 persons per square mile; Race: 86.5% White, 0.4% Black/African American, 0.3% Asian, 0.2% American Indian/Alaska Native, 0.0% Native Hawaiian/Other Pacific Islander, 1.5% Two or more races, 18.0% Hispanic of any race; Average household size: 2.58; Median age: 36.6; Age under 18: 27.6%; Age 65 and over: 16.0%; Males per 100 females: 91.5; Marriage status: 29.7% never married, 47.6% now married, 2.5% separated, 6.9% widowed, 15.9% divorced; Foreign born: 4.8%; Speak English only: 91.4%; With disability: 11.5%; Veterans: 7.5%; Ancestry: 27.1% German, 10.3% Irish, 8.8% American, 6.0% Italian, 5.6% English
Employment: 12.1% management, business, and financial, 1.2% computer, engineering, and science, 7.2% education, legal, community service, arts, and media, 3.6% healthcare practitioners, 13.4% service, 17.1% sales and office, 6.7% natural resources, construction, and maintenance, 38.5% production, transportation, and material moving
Income: Per capita: $18,786; Median household: $35,613; Average household: $47,599; Households with income of $100,000 or more: 8.7%; Poverty rate: 9.6%
Educational Attainment: High school diploma or higher: 82.4%; Bachelor's degree or higher: 13.2%; Graduate/professional degree or higher: 4.3%
School District(s)
Bremen Public Schools (KG-12)
2012-13 Enrollment: 1,430 .... (574) 546-3929
Housing: Homeownership rate: 67.6%; Median home value: $110,100; Median year structure built: 1960; Homeowner vacancy rate: 2.9%; Median gross rent: $600 per month; Rental vacancy rate: 12.8%
Health Insurance: 86.2% have insurance; 67.8% have private insurance; 30.1% have public insurance; 13.8% do not have insurance; 12.9% of children under 18 do not have insurance
Hospitals: Community Hospital of Bremen (24 beds); Doctors Neuromedical Hospital & Brain Institute
Safety: Violent crime rate: 32.6 per 10,000 population; Property crime rate: 128.3 per 10,000 population
Newspapers: Advance-News (weekly circulation 2200); Bremen Enquirer (weekly circulation 1800)
Transportation: Commute: 90.0% car, 0.0% public transportation, 6.4% walk, 2.6% work from home; Median travel time to work: 15.4 minutes
Additional Information Contacts
Town of Bremen................................ (574) 546-2471
http://www.bremenchamberofcommerce.com

CULVER (town).
Covers a land area of 0.899 square miles and a water area of 0 square miles. Located at 41.22° N. Lat; 86.42° W. Long. Elevation is 771 feet.
History: Culver developed as a resort town near Lake Maxinkuckee. It was named for Henry Harrison Culver of St. Louis who founded Culver Military Academy in 1894.
Population: 1,353; Growth (since 2000): -12.1%; Density: 1,504.7 persons per square mile; Race: 95.8% White, 1.2% Black/African American, 0.4% Asian, 0.0% American Indian/Alaska Native, 0.0% Native Hawaiian/Other Pacific Islander, 1.8% Two or more races, 2.4% Hispanic of any race; Average household size: 2.15; Median age: 47.7; Age under 18: 19.2%; Age 65 and over: 25.6%; Males per 100 females: 83.1
School District(s)
Culver Community Schools Corp (KG-12)
2012-13 Enrollment: 936........................ (574) 842-3364
Housing: Homeownership rate: 65.4%; Homeowner vacancy rate: 6.2%; Rental vacancy rate: 11.9%

LA PAZ (town).
Covers a land area of 0.383 square miles and a water area of 0 square miles. Located at 41.46° N. Lat; 86.31° W. Long. Elevation is 860 feet.
Population: 561; Growth (since 2000): 14.7%; Density: 1,463.0 persons per square mile; Race: 97.9% White, 0.2% Black/African American, 0.2% Asian, 0.2% American Indian/Alaska Native, 0.0% Native Hawaiian/Other Pacific Islander, 1.1% Two or more races, 4.3% Hispanic of any race; Average household size: 2.60; Median age: 35.1; Age under 18: 29.4%; Age 65 and over: 12.3%; Males per 100 females: 88.9
Housing: Homeownership rate: 66.6%; Homeowner vacancy rate: 5.8%; Rental vacancy rate: 6.4%

PLYMOUTH (city).
County seat. Covers a land area of 7.534 square miles and a water area of 0.040 square miles. Located at 41.35° N. Lat; 86.32° W. Long. Elevation is 797 feet.
History: Plymouth was founded in 1834 as a shipping center and county seat.
Population: 10,033; Growth (since 2000): 2.0%; Density: 1,331.7 persons per square mile; Race: 87.2% White, 0.9% Black/African American, 0.5% Asian, 0.6% American Indian/Alaska Native, 0.0% Native Hawaiian/Other Pacific Islander, 2.5% Two or more races, 20.0% Hispanic of any race; Average household size: 2.49; Median age: 34.3; Age under 18: 27.9%; Age 65 and over: 15.2%; Males per 100 females: 91.9; Marriage status: 27.7% never married, 49.6% now married, 2.7% separated, 7.9% widowed, 14.8% divorced; Foreign born: 13.3%; Speak English only: 76.8%; With disability: 15.0%; Veterans: 9.2%; Ancestry: 22.4% German, 8.2% Irish, 6.7% American, 6.6% English, 6.6% Polish
Employment: 4.2% management, business, and financial, 2.1% computer, engineering, and science, 6.9% education, legal, community service, arts, and media, 4.0% healthcare practitioners, 18.0% service, 26.6% sales and office, 8.5% natural resources, construction, and maintenance, 29.6% production, transportation, and material moving
Income: Per capita: $15,596; Median household: $32,486; Average household: $41,507; Households with income of $100,000 or more: 5.9%; Poverty rate: 31.6%
Educational Attainment: High school diploma or higher: 76.7%; Bachelor's degree or higher: 13.0%; Graduate/professional degree or higher: 3.3%
School District(s)
Plymouth Community School Corp (KG-12)
2012-13 Enrollment: 3,691 .... (574) 936-3115
Housing: Homeownership rate: 56.2%; Median home value: $85,700; Median year structure built: 1975; Homeowner vacancy rate: 5.8%; Median gross rent: $626 per month; Rental vacancy rate: 12.0%
Health Insurance: 80.6% have insurance; 51.8% have private insurance; 38.5% have public insurance; 19.4% do not have insurance; 9.7% of children under 18 do not have insurance
Hospitals: Saint Joseph Regional Medical Center - Plymouth (58 beds)
Safety: Violent crime rate: 7.0 per 10,000 population; Property crime rate: 314.9 per 10,000 population
Newspapers: Bourbon News-Mirror (weekly circulation 1300); Culver Citizen (weekly circulation 1800); Pilot-News (daily circulation 6200)
Transportation: Commute: 92.1% car, 0.0% public transportation, 3.3% walk, 2.5% work from home; Median travel time to work: 16.7 minutes
Airports: Plymouth Municipal (general aviation)
Additional Information Contacts
City of Plymouth .... (574) 936-2124
http://www.plymouthin.com

TIPPECANOE (unincorporated postal area)
ZCTA: 46570
Covers a land area of 20.438 square miles and a water area of 0.026 square miles. Located at 41.20° N. Lat; 86.12° W. Long. Elevation is 781 feet.
Population: 1,060; Growth (since 2000): 0.7%; Density: 51.9 persons per square mile; Race: 95.8% White, 0.6% Black/African American, 0.8% Asian, 0.4% American Indian/Alaska Native, 0.0% Native Hawaiian/Other Pacific Islander, 1.7% Two or more races, 3.1% Hispanic of any race; Average household size: 2.66; Median age: 40.5; Age under 18: 24.6%; Age 65 and over: 13.2%; Males per 100 females: 105.4
Housing: Homeownership rate: 89.2%; Homeowner vacancy rate: 2.7%; Rental vacancy rate: 15.7%

Martin County

Located in southwestern Indiana; drained by the Lost River and East Fork of the White River. Covers a land area of 335.737 square miles, a water area of 4.669 square miles, and is located in the Eastern Time Zone at 38.71° N. Lat., 86.80° W. Long. The county was founded in 1820. County seat is Shoals.

Weather Station: Shoals Hiway 50 Bridge   Elevation: 549 feet

	Jan	Feb	Mar	Apr	May	Jun	Jul	Aug	Sep	Oct	Nov	Dec
High	39	44	54	66	75	83	86	86	79	68	55	42
Low	21	23	31	41	51	60	64	62	54	42	34	25
Precip	3.1	3.0	4.3	4.5	6.1	4.3	4.4	2.9	3.6	3.7	4.2	3.8
Snow	4.1	4.1	1.9	0.1	0.0	0.0	0.0	0.0	0.0	0.1	tr	3.0

High and Low temperatures in degrees Fahrenheit; Precipitation and Snow in inches

Population: 10,334; Growth (since 2000): -0.3%; Density: 30.8 persons per square mile; Race: 98.4% White, 0.1% Black/African American, 0.3% Asian, 0.3% American Indian/Alaska Native, 0.0% Native Hawaiian/Other Pacific Islander, 0.7% two or more races, 0.7% Hispanic of any race; Average household size: 2.43; Median age: 41.8; Age under 18: 24.0%; Age 65 and over: 15.7%; Males per 100 females: 102.2; Marriage status: 23.0% never married, 53.9% now married, 0.8% separated, 6.8% widowed, 16.3% divorced; Foreign born: 0.8%; Speak English only: 97.6%; With disability: 11.8%; Veterans: 11.8%; Ancestry: 31.6% German, 20.2% Irish, 14.4% American, 12.9% English, 3.1% French
Religion: Six largest groups: 25.4% Catholicism, 9.0% Methodist/Pietist, 8.8% Baptist, 7.4% European Free-Church, 4.5% Non-denominational Protestant, 2.9% Lutheran
Economy: Unemployment rate: 4.5%; Leading industries: 18.3% retail trade; 13.4% accommodation and food services; 12.9% other services (except public administration); Farms: 283 totaling 62,544 acres; Company size: 0 employ 1,000 or more persons, 1 employs 500 to 999 persons, 1 employs 100 to 499 persons, 184 employ less than 100 persons; Business ownership: 201 women-owned, n/a Black-owned, n/a Hispanic-owned, n/a Asian-owned
Employment: 11.6% management, business, and financial, 3.8% computer, engineering, and science, 7.3% education, legal, community service, arts, and media, 7.8% healthcare practitioners, 13.3% service, 21.4% sales and office, 12.7% natural resources, construction, and maintenance, 22.1% production, transportation, and material moving
Income: Per capita: $22,817; Median household: $44,740; Average household: $55,067; Households with income of $100,000 or more: 12.6%; Poverty rate: 14.6%
Educational Attainment: High school diploma or higher: 82.9%; Bachelor's degree or higher: 10.8%; Graduate/professional degree or higher: 4.4%
Housing: Homeownership rate: 80.5%; Median home value: $88,500; Median year structure built: 1975; Homeowner vacancy rate: 1.0%; Median gross rent: $542 per month; Rental vacancy rate: 10.7%
Vital Statistics: Birth rate: 119.1 per 10,000 population; Death rate: 87.6 per 10,000 population; Age-adjusted cancer mortality rate: 190.8 deaths per 100,000 population
Health Insurance: 86.4% have insurance; 67.0% have private insurance; 33.4% have public insurance; 13.6% do not have insurance; 10.6% of children under 18 do not have insurance
Health Care: Physicians: 3.9 per 10,000 population; Hospital beds: 0.0 per 10,000 population; Hospital admissions: 0.0 per 10,000 population
Transportation: Commute: 94.7% car, 0.2% public transportation, 2.1% walk, 2.1% work from home; Median travel time to work: 25.4 minutes
Presidential Election: 28.5% Obama, 68.8% Romney (2012)
National and State Parks: Martin County State Forest; Martin State Forest
Additional Information Contacts
Martin Government . . . . (812) 295-4093

Martin County Communities

BURNS CITY (CDP). Covers a land area of 0.735 square miles and a water area of 0.005 square miles. Located at 38.82° N. Lat; 86.89° W. Long. Elevation is 712 feet.
Population: 117; Growth (since 2000): n/a; Density: 159.3 persons per square mile; Race: 99.1% White, 0.0% Black/African American, 0.9% Asian, 0.0% American Indian/Alaska Native, 0.0% Native Hawaiian/Other Pacific Islander, 0.0% Two or more races, 0.9% Hispanic of any race; Average household size: 2.25; Median age: 49.5; Age under 18: 17.1%; Age 65 and over: 17.1%; Males per 100 females: 105.3
Housing: Homeownership rate: 82.7%; Homeowner vacancy rate: 0.0%; Rental vacancy rate: 10.0%

CRANE (town). Covers a land area of 0.118 square miles and a water area of 0 square miles. Located at 38.89° N. Lat; 86.90° W. Long. Elevation is 614 feet.
Population: 184; Growth (since 2000): -9.4%; Density: 1,555.4 persons per square mile; Race: 96.7% White, 0.0% Black/African American, 3.3% Asian, 0.0% American Indian/Alaska Native, 0.0% Native Hawaiian/Other Pacific Islander, 0.0% Two or more races, 0.0% Hispanic of any race; Average household size: 2.30; Median age: 39.4; Age under 18: 26.1%; Age 65 and over: 16.3%; Males per 100 females: 93.7
Housing: Homeownership rate: 62.5%; Homeowner vacancy rate: 0.0%; Rental vacancy rate: 34.8%

DOVER HILL (CDP). Covers a land area of 0.776 square miles and a water area of <.001 square miles. Located at 38.72° N. Lat; 86.80° W. Long. Elevation is 663 feet.
Population: 114; Growth (since 2000): n/a; Density: 146.9 persons per square mile; Race: 97.4% White, 0.0% Black/African American, 0.0% Asian, 0.0% American Indian/Alaska Native, 0.0% Native Hawaiian/Other Pacific Islander, 2.6% Two or more races, 0.0% Hispanic of any race; Average household size: 2.53; Median age: 39.5; Age under 18: 23.7%; Age 65 and over: 17.5%; Males per 100 females: 93.2
Housing: Homeownership rate: 88.9%; Homeowner vacancy rate: 2.3%; Rental vacancy rate: 16.7%

LOOGOOTEE (city). Covers a land area of 1.567 square miles and a water area of 0.004 square miles. Located at 38.68° N. Lat; 86.91° W. Long. Elevation is 538 feet.
History: Loogootee grew when natural gas was found here in 1899, and several glass factories were established. The town was named for Lowe, an engineer on the first railroad, and Gootee, who owned the land on which the town was built.
Population: 2,751; Growth (since 2000): 0.4%; Density: 1,755.5 persons per square mile; Race: 98.3% White, 0.1% Black/African American, 0.3% Asian, 0.2% American Indian/Alaska Native, 0.0% Native Hawaiian/Other Pacific Islander, 0.5% Two or more races, 0.8% Hispanic of any race; Average household size: 2.25; Median age: 40.4; Age under 18: 23.4%; Age 65 and over: 17.1%; Males per 100 females: 91.3; Marriage status: 24.2% never married, 43.5% now married, 0.8% separated, 8.7% widowed, 23.6% divorced; Foreign born: 2.1%; Speak English only: 97.7%; With disability: 12.2%; Veterans: 12.6%; Ancestry: 25.4% Irish, 20.0% German, 16.4% American, 13.3% English, 3.6% Polish
Employment: 11.4% management, business, and financial, 3.8% computer, engineering, and science, 4.1% education, legal, community service, arts, and media, 6.8% healthcare practitioners, 18.9% service, 28.9% sales and office, 5.4% natural resources, construction, and maintenance, 20.6% production, transportation, and material moving
Income: Per capita: $19,761; Median household: $38,208; Average household: $46,369; Households with income of $100,000 or more: 6.4%; Poverty rate: 23.6%
Educational Attainment: High school diploma or higher: 79.4%; Bachelor's degree or higher: 8.9%; Graduate/professional degree or higher: 3.1%

School District(s)
Loogootee Community Sch Corp (KG-12)
    2012-13 Enrollment: 963. . . . . (812) 295-2595
Housing: Homeownership rate: 69.3%; Median home value: $81,700; Median year structure built: 1961; Homeowner vacancy rate: 1.5%; Median gross rent: $550 per month; Rental vacancy rate: 9.2%
Health Insurance: 88.7% have insurance; 59.8% have private insurance; 46.1% have public insurance; 11.3% do not have insurance; 8.5% of children under 18 do not have insurance
Newspapers: The Tribune (weekly circulation 3000)
Transportation: Commute: 97.0% car, 0.4% public transportation, 0.7% walk, 0.8% work from home; Median travel time to work: 18.2 minutes
Additional Information Contacts
City of Loogootee . . . . (812) 295-3200
    http://www.loogootee.com/government/loogooteegovernment.html

SHOALS (town). County seat. Covers a land area of 1.793 square miles and a water area of 0.093 square miles. Located at 38.67° N. Lat; 86.79° W. Long. Elevation is 505 feet.
History: Shoals was founded in 1816 and named for the shallow place in the White River that afforded a crossing. The area was known as a haven for moonshiners and bootleggers during prohibition.
Population: 756; Growth (since 2000): -6.3%; Density: 421.7 persons per square mile; Race: 97.4% White, 0.3% Black/African American, 0.3% Asian, 0.1% American Indian/Alaska Native, 0.0% Native Hawaiian/Other Pacific Islander, 1.6% Two or more races, 1.3% Hispanic of any race; Average household size: 2.01; Median age: 47.1; Age under 18: 20.1%; Age 65 and over: 24.6%; Males per 100 females: 96.4

School District(s)
Shoals Community School Corp (PK-12)
   2012-13 Enrollment: 582 . . . . (812) 247-2060
Housing: Homeownership rate: 67.3%; Homeowner vacancy rate: 2.3%; Rental vacancy rate: 5.3%
Newspapers: Shoals News (weekly circulation 2700)

Miami County

Located in north central Indiana; crossed by the Wabash, Mississinewa, and Eel Rivers. Covers a land area of 373.842 square miles, a water area of 3.546 square miles, and is located in the Eastern Time Zone at 40.77° N. Lat., 86.04° W. Long. The county was founded in 1832. County seat is Peru.

Miami County is part of the Peru, IN Micropolitan Statistical Area. The entire metro area includes: Miami County, IN

Population: 36,903; Growth (since 2000): 2.3%; Density: 98.7 persons per square mile; Race: 91.8% White, 4.5% Black/African American, 0.3% Asian, 0.9% American Indian/Alaska Native, 0.0% Native Hawaiian/Other Pacific Islander, 1.8% two or more races, 2.5% Hispanic of any race; Average household size: 2.49; Median age: 39.5; Age under 18: 22.7%; Age 65 and over: 14.0%; Males per 100 females: 114.4; Marriage status: 27.6% never married, 51.1% now married, 1.7% separated, 5.7% widowed, 15.7% divorced; Foreign born: 1.2%; Speak English only: 95.3%; With disability: 17.2%; Veterans: 12.2%; Ancestry: 27.4% American, 22.5% German, 11.2% Irish, 7.8% English, 2.2% Dutch
Religion: Six largest groups: 12.5% Baptist, 7.3% Methodist/Pietist, 3.2% Non-denominational Protestant, 3.1% European Free-Church, 3.0% Catholicism, 2.9% Pentecostal
Economy: Unemployment rate: 6.5%; Leading industries: 16.5% retail trade; 15.3% other services (except public administration); 9.7% accommodation and food services; Farms: 666 totaling 175,276 acres; Company size: 0 employ 1,000 or more persons, 0 employ 500 to 999 persons, 12 employ 100 to 499 persons, 556 employ less than 100 persons; Business ownership: 736 women-owned, n/a Black-owned, n/a Hispanic-owned, n/a Asian-owned
Employment: 8.8% management, business, and financial, 1.7% computer, engineering, and science, 7.6% education, legal, community service, arts, and media, 5.4% healthcare practitioners, 18.9% service, 19.7% sales and office, 13.2% natural resources, construction, and maintenance, 24.7% production, transportation, and material moving
Income: Per capita: $20,475; Median household: $42,023; Average household: $53,283; Households with income of $100,000 or more: 10.9%; Poverty rate: 17.2%
Educational Attainment: High school diploma or higher: 83.3%; Bachelor's degree or higher: 10.6%; Graduate/professional degree or higher: 4.0%
Housing: Homeownership rate: 74.0%; Median home value: $84,100; Median year structure built: 1958; Homeowner vacancy rate: 2.4%; Median gross rent: $632 per month; Rental vacancy rate: 15.5%
Vital Statistics: Birth rate: 101.5 per 10,000 population; Death rate: 91.6 per 10,000 population; Age-adjusted cancer mortality rate: 186.6 deaths per 100,000 population
Health Insurance: 85.4% have insurance; 62.4% have private insurance; 37.0% have public insurance; 14.6% do not have insurance; 6.0% of children under 18 do not have insurance
Health Care: Physicians: 6.0 per 10,000 population; Hospital beds: 6.8 per 10,000 population; Hospital admissions: 403.9 per 10,000 population
Transportation: Commute: 92.1% car, 0.3% public transportation, 1.9% walk, 3.5% work from home; Median travel time to work: 24.0 minutes
Presidential Election: 33.1% Obama, 64.0% Romney (2012)
National and State Parks: Frances Slocum State Forest
Additional Information Contacts
Miami Government . . . . (765) 472-3901
http://www.miamicountyin.gov

Miami County Communities

AMBOY (town). Covers a land area of 0.350 square miles and a water area of <.001 square miles. Located at 40.60° N. Lat; 85.93° W. Long. Elevation is 817 feet.
Population: 384; Growth (since 2000): 6.7%; Density: 1,096.1 persons per square mile; Race: 96.6% White, 0.5% Black/African American, 1.0% Asian, 0.0% American Indian/Alaska Native, 0.0% Native Hawaiian/Other Pacific Islander, 0.8% Two or more races, 0.8% Hispanic of any race; Average household size: 2.54; Median age: 40.5; Age under 18: 23.4%; Age 65 and over: 19.5%; Males per 100 females: 93.9
Housing: Homeownership rate: 83.4%; Homeowner vacancy rate: 3.8%; Rental vacancy rate: 10.7%

BUNKER HILL (town). Covers a land area of 0.419 square miles and a water area of <.001 square miles. Located at 40.66° N. Lat; 86.10° W. Long. Elevation is 820 feet.
Population: 888; Growth (since 2000): -10.0%; Density: 2,118.3 persons per square mile; Race: 93.7% White, 1.6% Black/African American, 0.8% Asian, 0.8% American Indian/Alaska Native, 0.0% Native Hawaiian/Other Pacific Islander, 2.5% Two or more races, 2.0% Hispanic of any race; Average household size: 2.43; Median age: 37.4; Age under 18: 25.7%; Age 65 and over: 14.3%; Males per 100 females: 93.5

School District(s)
Maconaquah School Corp (PK-12)
   2012-13 Enrollment: 2,231 . . . . (765) 689-9131
Housing: Homeownership rate: 69.1%; Homeowner vacancy rate: 4.5%; Rental vacancy rate: 27.1%

CONVERSE (town). Covers a land area of 0.896 square miles and a water area of 0.003 square miles. Located at 40.58° N. Lat; 85.87° W. Long. Elevation is 830 feet.
Population: 1,265; Growth (since 2000): 11.3%; Density: 1,411.3 persons per square mile; Race: 97.5% White, 0.1% Black/African American, 0.1% Asian, 0.2% American Indian/Alaska Native, 0.1% Native Hawaiian/Other Pacific Islander, 0.9% Two or more races, 4.2% Hispanic of any race; Average household size: 2.59; Median age: 36.9; Age under 18: 29.7%; Age 65 and over: 12.8%; Males per 100 females: 92.8

School District(s)
Oak Hill United School Corp (PK-12)
   2012-13 Enrollment: 1,597 . . . . (765) 395-3341
Housing: Homeownership rate: 74.6%; Homeowner vacancy rate: 1.6%; Rental vacancy rate: 15.6%

DENVER (town). Covers a land area of 0.233 square miles and a water area of 0 square miles. Located at 40.86° N. Lat; 86.08° W. Long. Elevation is 709 feet.
Population: 482; Growth (since 2000): -10.9%; Density: 2,069.5 persons per square mile; Race: 98.8% White, 0.2% Black/African American, 0.0% Asian, 0.6% American Indian/Alaska Native, 0.0% Native Hawaiian/Other Pacific Islander, 0.4% Two or more races, 1.2% Hispanic of any race; Average household size: 2.72; Median age: 37.6; Age under 18: 29.3%; Age 65 and over: 12.7%; Males per 100 females: 94.4

School District(s)
North Miami Community Schools (KG-12)
   2012-13 Enrollment: 1,033 . . . . (765) 985-3891
Housing: Homeownership rate: 89.8%; Homeowner vacancy rate: 2.4%; Rental vacancy rate: 10.0%

GRISSOM AFB (CDP). Covers a land area of 4.992 square miles and a water area of 0.003 square miles. Located at 40.66° N. Lat; 86.15° W. Long.
Population: 5,537; Growth (since 2000): 235.2%; Density: 1,109.3 persons per square mile; Race: 74.4% White, 22.5% Black/African American, 0.2% Asian, 0.3% American Indian/Alaska Native, 0.0% Native Hawaiian/Other Pacific Islander, 1.5% Two or more races, 4.6% Hispanic of any race; Average household size: 2.80; Median age: 34.2; Age under 18: 14.8%; Age 65 and over: 4.3%; Males per 100 females: 338.1; Marriage status: 31.6% never married, 38.7% now married, 3.4% separated, 4.6% widowed, 25.2% divorced; Foreign born: 1.6%; Speak

English only: 92.4%; With disability: 15.3%; Veterans: 12.4%; Ancestry: 28.7% American, 25.8% German, 21.9% Irish, 7.7% English, 3.4% French
Employment: 2.6% management, business, and financial, 0.0% computer, engineering, and science, 4.8% education, legal, community service, arts, and media, 7.9% healthcare practitioners, 13.1% service, 24.3% sales and office, 14.5% natural resources, construction, and maintenance, 32.7% production, transportation, and material moving
Income: Per capita: $15,476; Median household: $39,725; Average household: $46,154; Households with income of $100,000 or more: 8.7%; Poverty rate: 22.7%
Educational Attainment: High school diploma or higher: 77.6%; Bachelor's degree or higher: 5.8%; Graduate/professional degree or higher: 1.9%
Housing: Homeownership rate: 29.6%; Median home value: $80,700; Median year structure built: 1959; Homeowner vacancy rate: 4.9%; Median gross rent: $701 per month; Rental vacancy rate: 29.1%
Health Insurance: 85.5% have insurance; 60.8% have private insurance; 37.0% have public insurance; 14.5% do not have insurance; 4.4% of children under 18 do not have insurance
Transportation: Commute: 95.5% car, 0.0% public transportation, 0.0% walk, 1.3% work from home; Median travel time to work: 23.8 minutes

MACY (town).
Covers a land area of 0.134 square miles and a water area of 0 square miles. Located at 40.96° N. Lat; 86.13° W. Long. Elevation is 856 feet.
History: Laid out 1860.
Population: 209; Growth (since 2000): -15.7%; Density: 1,557.7 persons per square mile; Race: 98.1% White, 0.5% Black/African American, 0.0% Asian, 0.5% American Indian/Alaska Native, 0.0% Native Hawaiian/Other Pacific Islander, 1.0% Two or more races, 0.0% Hispanic of any race; Average household size: 2.75; Median age: 39.6; Age under 18: 25.4%; Age 65 and over: 14.8%; Males per 100 females: 101.0
Housing: Homeownership rate: 84.2%; Homeowner vacancy rate: 7.2%; Rental vacancy rate: 7.7%

MEXICO (CDP).
Covers a land area of 5.419 square miles and a water area of 0.066 square miles. Located at 40.81° N. Lat; 86.11° W. Long. Elevation is 702 feet.
History: Mexico was settled largely by German Baptists as a stagecoach stop between Indianapolis and Michigan City.
Population: 836; Growth (since 2000): -15.0%; Density: 154.3 persons per square mile; Race: 97.2% White, 0.2% Black/African American, 0.1% Asian, 1.3% American Indian/Alaska Native, 0.0% Native Hawaiian/Other Pacific Islander, 1.0% Two or more races, 0.8% Hispanic of any race; Average household size: 2.30; Median age: 46.3; Age under 18: 19.9%; Age 65 and over: 17.2%; Males per 100 females: 100.5
Housing: Homeownership rate: 83.7%; Homeowner vacancy rate: 0.0%; Rental vacancy rate: 7.8%

MIAMI (unincorporated postal area)
ZCTA: 46959
Covers a land area of 1.100 square miles and a water area of 0 square miles. Located at 40.62° N. Lat; 86.11° W. Long. Elevation is 791 feet.
Population: 231; Growth (since 2000): -10.1%; Density: 210.0 persons per square mile; Race: 92.6% White, 1.3% Black/African American, 0.0% Asian, 0.0% American Indian/Alaska Native, 0.0% Native Hawaiian/Other Pacific Islander, 3.9% Two or more races, 5.6% Hispanic of any race; Average household size: 2.24; Median age: 45.5; Age under 18: 19.9%; Age 65 and over: 17.3%; Males per 100 females: 92.5
Housing: Homeownership rate: 78.7%; Homeowner vacancy rate: 3.5%; Rental vacancy rate: 8.0%

PERU (city). County seat.
Covers a land area of 5.105 square miles and a water area of 0.073 square miles. Located at 40.76° N. Lat; 86.07° W. Long. Elevation is 653 feet.
History: Peru's reputation as the Circus City of the World, serving as winter quarters for many circuses, began in the late 1800's when Ben Wallace started the Hagenbeck-Wallace Circus.
Population: 11,417; Growth (since 2000): -12.1%; Density: 2,236.5 persons per square mile; Race: 93.1% White, 2.5% Black/African American, 0.4% Asian, 1.3% American Indian/Alaska Native, 0.0% Native Hawaiian/Other Pacific Islander, 2.3% Two or more races, 2.4% Hispanic of any race; Average household size: 2.36; Median age: 39.0; Age under 18: 24.5%; Age 65 and over: 15.6%; Males per 100 females: 90.4;
Marriage status: 31.5% never married, 43.3% now married, 1.9% separated, 7.3% widowed, 17.8% divorced; Foreign born: 0.9%; Speak English only: 97.8%; With disability: 20.3%; Veterans: 11.6%; Ancestry: 27.2% American, 19.2% German, 12.6% Irish, 7.3% English, 2.1% Dutch
Employment: 5.3% management, business, and financial, 1.5% computer, engineering, and science, 9.5% education, legal, community service, arts, and media, 6.1% healthcare practitioners, 24.6% service, 18.7% sales and office, 10.4% natural resources, construction, and maintenance, 23.8% production, transportation, and material moving
Income: Per capita: $18,035; Median household: $32,947; Average household: $44,303; Households with income of $100,000 or more: 5.6%; Poverty rate: 19.6%
Educational Attainment: High school diploma or higher: 78.0%; Bachelor's degree or higher: 8.4%; Graduate/professional degree or higher: 3.4%

School District(s)
Maconaquah School Corp (PK-12)
    2012-13 Enrollment: 2,231 . . . . (765) 689-9131
Peru Community Schools (PK-12)
    2012-13 Enrollment: 2,133 . . . . (765) 473-3081
Housing: Homeownership rate: 67.4%; Median home value: $57,000; Median year structure built: 1940; Homeowner vacancy rate: 3.7%; Median gross rent: $596 per month; Rental vacancy rate: 11.0%
Health Insurance: 82.5% have insurance; 51.4% have private insurance; 43.5% have public insurance; 17.5% do not have insurance; 5.4% of children under 18 do not have insurance
Hospitals: Dukes Memorial Hospital (158 beds)
Safety: Violent crime rate: 18.7 per 10,000 population; Property crime rate: 118.5 per 10,000 population
Newspapers: Peru Tribune (daily circulation 6400)
Transportation: Commute: 90.3% car, 0.4% public transportation, 3.5% walk, 1.8% work from home; Median travel time to work: 19.2 minutes
Airports: Grissom ARB (general aviation)
Additional Information Contacts
City of Peru . . . . (765) 472-2400
   http://www.cityofperu.org

Monroe County

Located in south central Indiana; drained by the West Fork of the White River, and several creeks. Covers a land area of 394.509 square miles, a water area of 16.812 square miles, and is located in the Eastern Time Zone at 39.16° N. Lat., 86.52° W. Long. The county was founded in 1818. County seat is Bloomington.

Monroe County is part of the Bloomington, IN Metropolitan Statistical Area. The entire metro area includes: Monroe County, IN; Owen County, IN

Weather Station: Bloomington Indiana Univ   Elevation: 830 feet

	Jan	Feb	Mar	Apr	May	Jun	Jul	Aug	Sep	Oct	Nov	Dec
High	37	42	52	64	74	82	85	85	78	66	54	41
Low	21	24	32	43	53	62	66	64	56	45	36	25
Precip	3.1	2.7	3.6	4.5	5.8	4.7	4.6	3.6	3.8	3.7	3.8	3.6
Snow	5.2	2.7	0.9	tr	0.0	0.0	0.0	0.0	0.0	0.2	0.1	3.9

High and Low temperatures in degrees Fahrenheit; Precipitation and Snow in inches

Population: 137,974; Growth (since 2000): 14.4%; Density: 349.7 persons per square mile; Race: 87.8% White, 3.3% Black/African American, 5.2% Asian, 0.3% American Indian/Alaska Native, 0.0% Native Hawaiian/Other Pacific Islander, 2.5% two or more races, 2.9% Hispanic of any race; Average household size: 2.24; Median age: 27.7; Age under 18: 16.3%; Age 65 and over: 10.2%; Males per 100 females: 99.6; Marriage status: 48.6% never married, 37.1% now married, 0.8% separated, 4.3% widowed, 10.1% divorced; Foreign born: 7.9%; Speak English only: 90.1%; With disability: 10.1%; Veterans: 6.4%; Ancestry: 24.2% German, 14.0% Irish, 11.2% English, 7.3% American, 4.0% Italian
Religion: Six largest groups: 7.5% Catholicism, 7.3% Baptist, 4.0% Methodist/Pietist, 3.5% Non-denominational Protestant, 1.5% Holiness, 1.3% Pentecostal
Economy: Unemployment rate: 5.1%; Leading industries: 15.5% retail trade; 12.4% accommodation and food services; 11.1% health care and social assistance; Farms: 462 totaling 52,762 acres; Company size: 3 employ 1,000 or more persons, 3 employ 500 to 999 persons, 58 employ 100 to 499 persons, 2,878 employ less than 100 persons; Business ownership: 2,659 women-owned, 188 Black-owned, 161 Hispanic-owned, 246 Asian-owned

Employment: 12.6% management, business, and financial, 5.9% computer, engineering, and science, 19.9% education, legal, community service, arts, and media, 4.3% healthcare practitioners, 19.4% service, 21.5% sales and office, 5.8% natural resources, construction, and maintenance, 10.5% production, transportation, and material moving
Income: Per capita: $23,032; Median household: $40,052; Average household: $57,267; Households with income of $100,000 or more: 14.9%; Poverty rate: 25.1%
Educational Attainment: High school diploma or higher: 91.9%; Bachelor's degree or higher: 43.4%; Graduate/professional degree or higher: 21.9%
Housing: Homeownership rate: 52.6%; Median home value: $156,300; Median year structure built: 1980; Homeowner vacancy rate: 2.1%; Median gross rent: $799 per month; Rental vacancy rate: 5.4%
Vital Statistics: Birth rate: 90.6 per 10,000 population; Death rate: 58.4 per 10,000 population; Age-adjusted cancer mortality rate: 178.2 deaths per 100,000 population
Health Insurance: 87.9% have insurance; 76.9% have private insurance; 20.1% have public insurance; 12.1% do not have insurance; 6.0% of children under 18 do not have insurance
Health Care: Physicians: 22.7 per 10,000 population; Hospital beds: 27.9 per 10,000 population; Hospital admissions: 1,112.4 per 10,000 population
Air Quality Index: 81.3% good, 18.7% moderate, 0.0% unhealthy for sensitive individuals, 0.0% unhealthy (percent of days)
Transportation: Commute: 80.0% car, 4.5% public transportation, 8.1% walk, 4.3% work from home; Median travel time to work: 18.2 minutes
Presidential Election: 56.9% Obama, 40.4% Romney (2012)
National and State Parks: Allens Creek State Recreation Area; Fairfax State Recreation Area; Morgan-Monroe State Forest; North Fork State Wildlife Refuge; Paynetown State Recreation Area
Additional Information Contacts
Monroe Government . . . . (812) 349-2550
http://www.co.monroe.in.us

Monroe County Communities

BLOOMINGTON (city). County seat. Covers a land area of 23.158 square miles and a water area of 0.199 square miles. Located at 39.16° N. Lat; 86.52° W. Long. Elevation is 771 feet.
History: Bloomington was settled in 1815 and developed around the stone quarries and mills. In 1820 Indiana University was founded here. Bloomington was named by a group of early settlers who enjoyed the many flowers on the hillsides.
Population: 80,405; Growth (since 2000): 16.0%; Density: 3,472.0 persons per square mile; Race: 83.0% White, 4.6% Black/African American, 8.0% Asian, 0.3% American Indian/Alaska Native, 0.1% Native Hawaiian/Other Pacific Islander, 3.0% Two or more races, 3.5% Hispanic of any race; Average household size: 2.09; Median age: 23.3; Age under 18: 11.4%; Age 65 and over: 7.9%; Males per 100 females: 101.1; Marriage status: 64.2% never married, 24.6% now married, 0.9% separated, 3.2% widowed, 8.0% divorced; Foreign born: 11.8%; Speak English only: 85.6%; With disability: 8.7%; Veterans: 4.0%; Ancestry: 23.7% German, 14.4% Irish, 10.3% English, 4.5% Italian, 4.3% Polish
Employment: 11.4% management, business, and financial, 5.7% computer, engineering, and science, 25.7% education, legal, community service, arts, and media, 3.3% healthcare practitioners, 22.3% service, 20.2% sales and office, 3.1% natural resources, construction, and maintenance, 8.3% production, transportation, and material moving
Income: Per capita: $18,987; Median household: $27,395; Average household: $47,606; Households with income of $100,000 or more: 11.6%; Poverty rate: 39.2%
Educational Attainment: High school diploma or higher: 92.9%; Bachelor's degree or higher: 56.6%; Graduate/professional degree or higher: 31.0%
School District(s)
Monroe County Com Sch Corp (PK-12)
    2012-13 Enrollment: 10,810 . . . . (812) 330-7700
Richland-Bean Blossom C S C (PK-12)
    2012-13 Enrollment: 2,665 . . . . (812) 876-7100
The Bloomington Project School (KG-09)
    2012-13 Enrollment: 269 . . . . (812) 558-0041
Four-year College(s)
Indiana University-Bloomington (Public)
    Fall 2013 Enrollment: 46,817 . . . . (812) 855-4848
    2013-14 Tuition: In-state $10,209; Out-of-state $32,350

Vocational/Technical School(s)
Hair Arts Academy (Private, For-profit)
    Fall 2013 Enrollment: 74 . . . . (812) 339-1117
    2013-14 Tuition: $11,900
Housing: Homeownership rate: 33.1%; Median home value: $171,900; Median year structure built: 1978; Homeowner vacancy rate: 2.0%; Median gross rent: $782 per month; Rental vacancy rate: 4.4%
Health Insurance: 87.7% have insurance; 77.5% have private insurance; 16.9% have public insurance; 12.3% do not have insurance; 4.3% of children under 18 do not have insurance
Hospitals: Indiana University Health Bloomington Hospital (355 beds); Monroe Hospital
Safety: Violent crime rate: 33.4 per 10,000 population; Property crime rate: 316.2 per 10,000 population
Newspapers: Herald-Times (daily circulation 27300)
Transportation: Commute: 69.7% car, 7.0% public transportation, 13.8% walk, 4.6% work from home; Median travel time to work: 15.3 minutes
Airports: Monroe County (general aviation)
Additional Information Contacts
City of Bloomington . . . . (812) 349-3400
http://bloomington.in.gov

ELLETTSVILLE (town). Covers a land area of 4.240 square miles and a water area of 0 square miles. Located at 39.23° N. Lat; 86.62° W. Long. Elevation is 696 feet.
History: Ellettsville developed around the stone quarries, some of which specialized in fine carving and ornamentation. Ellettsville was platted in 1837 and named for Edward Elletts who had operated a tavern here in the early 1800's.
Population: 6,378; Growth (since 2000): 25.6%; Density: 1,504.3 persons per square mile; Race: 95.5% White, 1.0% Black/African American, 0.6% Asian, 0.2% American Indian/Alaska Native, 0.0% Native Hawaiian/Other Pacific Islander, 1.9% Two or more races, 1.6% Hispanic of any race; Average household size: 2.43; Median age: 34.5; Age under 18: 26.5%; Age 65 and over: 12.1%; Males per 100 females: 87.5; Marriage status: 25.7% never married, 50.2% now married, 0.5% separated, 7.3% widowed, 16.8% divorced; Foreign born: 1.8%; Speak English only: 96.8%; With disability: 16.2%; Veterans: 7.7%; Ancestry: 34.6% German, 16.9% Irish, 10.6% American, 9.9% English, 4.1% French
Employment: 12.8% management, business, and financial, 3.2% computer, engineering, and science, 11.0% education, legal, community service, arts, and media, 5.6% healthcare practitioners, 18.9% service, 23.8% sales and office, 6.7% natural resources, construction, and maintenance, 17.9% production, transportation, and material moving
Income: Per capita: $20,532; Median household: $47,674; Average household: $49,849; Households with income of $100,000 or more: 9.3%; Poverty rate: 8.3%
Educational Attainment: High school diploma or higher: 85.9%; Bachelor's degree or higher: 23.8%; Graduate/professional degree or higher: 7.2%
School District(s)
Richland-Bean Blossom C S C (PK-12)
    2012-13 Enrollment: 2,665 . . . . (812) 876-7100
Housing: Homeownership rate: 70.8%; Median home value: $119,400; Median year structure built: 1983; Homeowner vacancy rate: 3.1%; Median gross rent: $733 per month; Rental vacancy rate: 5.3%
Health Insurance: 84.6% have insurance; 69.9% have private insurance; 28.0% have public insurance; 15.4% do not have insurance; 6.4% of children under 18 do not have insurance
Safety: Violent crime rate: 38.0 per 10,000 population; Property crime rate: 115.4 per 10,000 population
Newspapers: The Journal (weekly circulation 2500)
Transportation: Commute: 92.5% car, 0.0% public transportation, 3.6% walk, 3.6% work from home; Median travel time to work: 20.6 minutes
Additional Information Contacts
Town of Ellettsville. . . . . (812) 876-3860
http://ellettsville.in.us

HARRODSBURG (CDP). Covers a land area of 4.314 square miles and a water area of 0.036 square miles. Located at 39.02° N. Lat; 86.55° W. Long. Elevation is 558 feet.
Population: 691; Growth (since 2000): n/a; Density: 160.2 persons per square mile; Race: 95.9% White, 0.7% Black/African American, 0.0% Asian, 0.1% American Indian/Alaska Native, 0.0% Native Hawaiian/Other Pacific Islander, 3.2% Two or more races, 1.6% Hispanic of any race;

Average household size: 2.47; Median age: 40.6; Age under 18: 24.0%; Age 65 and over: 13.5%; Males per 100 females: 90.4
Housing: Homeownership rate: 84.7%; Homeowner vacancy rate: 2.1%; Rental vacancy rate: 8.5%

SMITHVILLE-SANDERS (CDP). Covers a land area of 10.720 square miles and a water area of 0 square miles. Located at 39.06° N. Lat; 86.51° W. Long.
Population: 3,184; Growth (since 2000): n/a; Density: 297.0 persons per square mile; Race: 95.9% White, 1.0% Black/African American, 1.1% Asian, 0.1% American Indian/Alaska Native, 0.0% Native Hawaiian/Other Pacific Islander, 1.7% Two or more races, 1.3% Hispanic of any race; Average household size: 2.35; Median age: 41.8; Age under 18: 23.1%; Age 65 and over: 11.5%; Males per 100 females: 101.6; Marriage status: 19.5% never married, 57.0% now married, 0.5% separated, 6.9% widowed, 16.6% divorced; Foreign born: 1.1%; Speak English only: 97.7%; With disability: 10.1%; Veterans: 7.1%; Ancestry: 27.0% German, 15.4% Irish, 12.7% English, 11.0% American, 7.6% Scottish
Employment: 25.2% management, business, and financial, 7.6% computer, engineering, and science, 6.8% education, legal, community service, arts, and media, 6.3% healthcare practitioners, 10.6% service, 21.2% sales and office, 14.3% natural resources, construction, and maintenance, 7.9% production, transportation, and material moving
Income: Per capita: $38,616; Median household: $63,721; Average household: $90,862; Households with income of $100,000 or more: 25.2%; Poverty rate: 5.8%
Educational Attainment: High school diploma or higher: 91.4%; Bachelor's degree or higher: 34.7%; Graduate/professional degree or higher: 13.1%
Housing: Homeownership rate: 80.4%; Median home value: $123,600; Median year structure built: 1981; Homeowner vacancy rate: 4.6%; Median gross rent: $739 per month; Rental vacancy rate: 19.7%
Health Insurance: 88.6% have insurance; 79.0% have private insurance; 20.2% have public insurance; 11.4% do not have insurance; 10.8% of children under 18 do not have insurance
Transportation: Commute: 98.0% car, 1.4% public transportation, 0.0% walk, 0.5% work from home; Median travel time to work: 23.1 minutes

STINESVILLE (town). Covers a land area of 0.108 square miles and a water area of 0 square miles. Located at 39.30° N. Lat; 86.65° W. Long. Elevation is 581 feet.
History: Old limestone quarries. Laid out 1855.
Population: 198; Growth (since 2000): 2.1%; Density: 1,826.6 persons per square mile; Race: 97.5% White, 0.0% Black/African American, 0.0% Asian, 0.0% American Indian/Alaska Native, 0.5% Native Hawaiian/Other Pacific Islander, 1.0% Two or more races, 2.0% Hispanic of any race; Average household size: 2.08; Median age: 45.8; Age under 18: 18.2%; Age 65 and over: 19.7%; Males per 100 females: 98.0
School District(s)
Richland-Bean Blossom C S C (PK-12)
    2012-13 Enrollment: 2,665 . . . . (812) 876-7100
Housing: Homeownership rate: 62.1%; Homeowner vacancy rate: 1.7%; Rental vacancy rate: 7.7%

UNIONVILLE (unincorporated postal area)
ZCTA: 47468
    Covers a land area of 26.325 square miles and a water area of 2.417 square miles. Located at 39.27° N. Lat; 86.39° W. Long. Elevation is 879 feet.
Population: 1,250; Growth (since 2000): 2.9%; Density: 47.5 persons per square mile; Race: 96.9% White, 0.4% Black/African American, 0.6% Asian, 0.4% American Indian/Alaska Native, 0.2% Native Hawaiian/Other Pacific Islander, 1.3% Two or more races, 0.8% Hispanic of any race; Average household size: 2.25; Median age: 49.0; Age under 18: 17.0%; Age 65 and over: 16.7%; Males per 100 females: 107.0
School District(s)
Monroe County Com Sch Corp (PK-12)
    2012-13 Enrollment: 10,810 . . . . (812) 330-7700
Housing: Homeownership rate: 85.9%; Homeownership vacancy rate: 3.8%; Rental vacancy rate: 12.2%

Montgomery County

Located in west central Indiana; drained by Sugar and Raccoon Creeks. Covers a land area of 504.613 square miles, a water area of 0.832 square miles, and is located in the Eastern Time Zone at 40.04° N. Lat., 86.89° W. Long. The county was founded in 1823. County seat is Crawfordsville.

Montgomery County is part of the Crawfordsville, IN Micropolitan Statistical Area. The entire metro area includes: Montgomery County, IN

Weather Station: Crawfordsville 5 S   Elevation: 762 feet

	Jan	Feb	Mar	Apr	May	Jun	Jul	Aug	Sep	Oct	Nov	Dec
High	35	39	50	62	72	82	84	83	78	65	51	38
Low	17	20	28	38	48	58	61	59	50	40	31	20
Precip	2.5	2.5	2.9	4.0	4.7	4.5	4.4	3.7	3.2	3.3	4.2	3.1
Snow	na	5.4	2.7	0.2	tr	0.0	0.0	0.0	0.0	tr	0.6	4.7

High and Low temperatures in degrees Fahrenheit; Precipitation and Snow in inches

Population: 38,124; Growth (since 2000): 1.3%; Density: 75.6 persons per square mile; Race: 95.2% White, 0.9% Black/African American, 0.6% Asian, 0.3% American Indian/Alaska Native, 0.0% Native Hawaiian/Other Pacific Islander, 1.2% two or more races, 4.6% Hispanic of any race; Average household size: 2.47; Median age: 39.4; Age under 18: 24.0%; Age 65 and over: 15.5%; Males per 100 females: 101.5; Marriage status: 23.7% never married, 57.6% now married, 1.0% separated, 5.9% widowed, 12.8% divorced; Foreign born: 2.6%; Speak English only: 95.4%; With disability: 14.1%; Veterans: 9.5%; Ancestry: 22.7% German, 19.0% American, 13.4% Irish, 12.4% English, 2.2% French
Religion: Six largest groups: 17.6% Baptist, 7.5% Non-denominational Protestant, 6.7% Catholicism, 5.5% Methodist/Pietist, 1.1% Holiness, 1.0% Lutheran
Economy: Unemployment rate: 5.1%; Leading industries: 14.4% retail trade; 13.8% other services (except public administration); 10.4% accommodation and food services; Farms: 732 totaling 286,949 acres; Company size: 1 employs 1,000 or more persons, 3 employ 500 to 999 persons, 16 employ 100 to 499 persons, 858 employ less than 100 persons; Business ownership: 637 women-owned, n/a Black-owned, n/a Hispanic-owned, 29 Asian-owned
Employment: 10.2% management, business, and financial, 3.3% computer, engineering, and science, 9.3% education, legal, community service, arts, and media, 3.3% healthcare practitioners, 16.1% service, 22.4% sales and office, 8.9% natural resources, construction, and maintenance, 26.4% production, transportation, and material moving
Income: Per capita: $22,679; Median household: $46,797; Average household: $57,199; Households with income of $100,000 or more: 13.0%; Poverty rate: 16.8%
Educational Attainment: High school diploma or higher: 87.8%; Bachelor's degree or higher: 17.8%; Graduate/professional degree or higher: 6.6%
Housing: Homeownership rate: 72.8%; Median home value: $108,300; Median year structure built: 1963; Homeowner vacancy rate: 2.8%; Median gross rent: $667 per month; Rental vacancy rate: 9.7%
Vital Statistics: Birth rate: 121.8 per 10,000 population; Death rate: 97.2 per 10,000 population; Age-adjusted cancer mortality rate: 190.3 deaths per 10,000 population
Health Insurance: 87.0% have insurance; 67.6% have private insurance; 32.9% have public insurance; 13.0% do not have insurance; 5.4% of children under 18 do not have insurance
Health Care: Physicians: 8.6 per 10,000 population; Hospital beds: 19.8 per 10,000 population; Hospital admissions: 603.0 per 10,000 population
Transportation: Commute: 91.7% car, 0.1% public transportation, 3.5% walk, 3.9% work from home; Median travel time to work: 21.1 minutes
Presidential Election: 29.6% Obama, 68.1% Romney (2012)
Additional Information Contacts
Montgomery Government . . . . (765) 364-6430
   http://www.montgomeryco.net

Montgomery County Communities

ALAMO (town). Covers a land area of 0.067 square miles and a water area of 0 square miles. Located at 39.98° N. Lat; 87.06° W. Long. Elevation is 814 feet.
Population: 66; Growth (since 2000): -51.8%; Density: 980.8 persons per square mile; Race: 89.4% White, 0.0% Black/African American, 0.0% Asian, 3.0% American Indian/Alaska Native, 0.0% Native Hawaiian/Other Pacific Islander, 1.5% Two or more races, 6.1% Hispanic of any race;

Average household size: 2.54; Median age: 36.7; Age under 18: 24.2%; Age 65 and over: 10.6%; Males per 100 females: 83.3
Housing: Homeownership rate: 69.3%; Homeowner vacancy rate: 5.3%; Rental vacancy rate: 0.0%

CRAWFORDSVILLE (city). County seat. Covers a land area of 9.146 square miles and a water area of 0 square miles. Located at 40.04° N. Lat; 86.90° W. Long. Elevation is 794 feet.
History: Crawfordsville was laid out in 1823 by Major Ambrose Whitlock, and named for Colonel William Crawford of Virginia. A prominent resident of Crawfordsville was Civil War General Lew Wallace, better known as the author of the novel "Ben Hur."
Population: 15,915; Growth (since 2000): 4.4%; Density: 1,740.0 persons per square mile; Race: 92.1% White, 1.7% Black/African American, 0.9% Asian, 0.4% American Indian/Alaska Native, 0.0% Native Hawaiian/Other Pacific Islander, 1.6% Two or more races, 8.2% Hispanic of any race; Average household size: 2.31; Median age: 36.6; Age under 18: 22.3%; Age 65 and over: 16.9%; Males per 100 females: 100.4; Marriage status: 28.5% never married, 48.6% now married, 2.0% separated, 7.9% widowed, 15.0% divorced; Foreign born: 4.5%; Speak English only: 92.4%; With disability: 16.2%; Veterans: 8.1%; Ancestry: 21.7% German, 21.5% American, 12.9% Irish, 10.1% English, 2.8% French
Employment: 6.9% management, business, and financial, 2.0% computer, engineering, and science, 11.7% education, legal, community service, arts, and media, 2.9% healthcare practitioners, 18.4% service, 23.4% sales and office, 5.9% natural resources, construction, and maintenance, 28.9% production, transportation, and material moving
Income: Per capita: $18,199; Median household: $34,453; Average household: $44,354; Households with income of $100,000 or more: 7.1%; Poverty rate: 27.2%
Educational Attainment: High school diploma or higher: 82.3%; Bachelor's degree or higher: 14.9%; Graduate/professional degree or higher: 6.0%

School District(s)
Crawfordsville Com Schools (PK-12)
  2012-13 Enrollment: 2,307 . . . . (765) 362-2342
North Montgomery Com Sch Corp (PK-12)
  2012-13 Enrollment: 1,989 . . . . (765) 359-2112
South Montgomery Com Sch Corp (KG-12)
  2012-13 Enrollment: 1,759 . . . . (765) 866-0203

Four-year College(s)
Wabash College (Private, Not-for-profit)
  Fall 2013 Enrollment: 902 . . . . (765) 361-6100
  2013-14 Tuition: In-state $35,650; Out-of-state $35,650

Housing: Homeownership rate: 58.0%; Median home value: $91,600; Median year structure built: 1958; Homeowner vacancy rate: 3.5%; Median gross rent: $645 per month; Rental vacancy rate: 9.6%
Health Insurance: 83.7% have insurance; 56.5% have private insurance; 40.0% have public insurance; 16.3% do not have insurance; 6.1% of children under 18 do not have insurance
Hospitals: Franciscan Saint Elizabeth Health - Crawfordsville (120 beds)
Safety: Violent crime rate: 14.3 per 10,000 population; Property crime rate: 332.0 per 10,000 population
Newspapers: Journal Review (daily circulation 9500); The Weekly (weekly circulation 7000)
Transportation: Commute: 88.4% car, 0.3% public transportation, 6.7% walk, 3.6% work from home; Median travel time to work: 16.7 minutes; Amtrak: Train service available.
Airports: Crawfordsville Municipal (general aviation)
Additional Information Contacts
City of Crawfordsville . . . . (765) 364-5150
  http://www.crawfordsville.net

DARLINGTON (town). Covers a land area of 0.332 square miles and a water area of 0 square miles. Located at 40.11° N. Lat; 86.78° W. Long. Elevation is 761 feet.
Population: 843; Growth (since 2000): -1.3%; Density: 2,539.1 persons per square mile; Race: 98.9% White, 0.1% Black/African American, 0.1% Asian, 0.1% American Indian/Alaska Native, 0.0% Native Hawaiian/Other Pacific Islander, 0.7% Two or more races, 0.2% Hispanic of any race; Average household size: 2.58; Median age: 35.8; Age under 18: 28.9%; Age 65 and over: 11.0%; Males per 100 females: 102.2
Housing: Homeownership rate: 73.1%; Homeowner vacancy rate: 3.6%; Rental vacancy rate: 12.0%

LADOGA (town). Covers a land area of 0.542 square miles and a water area of 0 square miles. Located at 39.92° N. Lat; 86.80° W. Long. Elevation is 823 feet.
Population: 985; Growth (since 2000): -5.9%; Density: 1,818.9 persons per square mile; Race: 98.4% White, 0.1% Black/African American, 0.3% Asian, 0.0% American Indian/Alaska Native, 0.0% Native Hawaiian/Other Pacific Islander, 0.9% Two or more races, 1.0% Hispanic of any race; Average household size: 2.61; Median age: 36.1; Age under 18: 28.3%; Age 65 and over: 11.9%; Males per 100 females: 98.6

School District(s)
South Montgomery Com Sch Corp (KG-12)
  2012-13 Enrollment: 1,759 . . . . (765) 866-0203

Housing: Homeownership rate: 75.4%; Homeowner vacancy rate: 8.3%; Rental vacancy rate: 17.7%

LAKE HOLIDAY (CDP). Covers a land area of 2.577 square miles and a water area of 0.202 square miles. Located at 39.96° N. Lat; 86.96° W. Long. Elevation is 774 feet.
Population: 910; Growth (since 2000): n/a; Density: 353.2 persons per square mile; Race: 99.5% White, 0.2% Black/African American, 0.0% Asian, 0.0% American Indian/Alaska Native, 0.0% Native Hawaiian/Other Pacific Islander, 0.0% Two or more races, 0.4% Hispanic of any race; Average household size: 2.59; Median age: 44.0; Age under 18: 22.5%; Age 65 and over: 16.6%; Males per 100 females: 106.3
Housing: Homeownership rate: 94.3%; Homeowner vacancy rate: 2.6%; Rental vacancy rate: 9.1%

LINDEN (town). Covers a land area of 0.418 square miles and a water area of 0 square miles. Located at 40.19° N. Lat; 86.90° W. Long. Elevation is 797 feet.
Population: 759; Growth (since 2000): 8.4%; Density: 1,815.6 persons per square mile; Race: 97.1% White, 0.5% Black/African American, 0.0% Asian, 0.9% American Indian/Alaska Native, 0.0% Native Hawaiian/Other Pacific Islander, 1.3% Two or more races, 1.7% Hispanic of any race; Average household size: 2.52; Median age: 34.0; Age under 18: 29.2%; Age 65 and over: 12.6%; Males per 100 females: 104.0
Housing: Homeownership rate: 69.1%; Homeowner vacancy rate: 4.6%; Rental vacancy rate: 7.0%

NEW MARKET (town). Covers a land area of 0.275 square miles and a water area of 0 square miles. Located at 39.95° N. Lat; 86.92° W. Long. Elevation is 807 feet.
Population: 636; Growth (since 2000): -3.5%; Density: 2,315.8 persons per square mile; Race: 99.1% White, 0.0% Black/African American, 0.2% Asian, 0.0% American Indian/Alaska Native, 0.0% Native Hawaiian/Other Pacific Islander, 0.2% Two or more races, 0.9% Hispanic of any race; Average household size: 2.67; Median age: 36.5; Age under 18: 29.1%; Age 65 and over: 14.6%; Males per 100 females: 95.1

School District(s)
South Montgomery Com Sch Corp (KG-12)
  2012-13 Enrollment: 1,759 . . . . (765) 866-0203

Housing: Homeownership rate: 81.0%; Homeowner vacancy rate: 1.5%; Rental vacancy rate: 2.2%

NEW RICHMOND (town). Covers a land area of 0.198 square miles and a water area of 0 square miles. Located at 40.19° N. Lat; 86.98° W. Long. Elevation is 784 feet.
Population: 333; Growth (since 2000): -4.6%; Density: 1,685.4 persons per square mile; Race: 97.0% White, 0.0% Black/African American, 0.3% Asian, 0.0% American Indian/Alaska Native, 0.0% Native Hawaiian/Other Pacific Islander, 2.7% Two or more races, 0.6% Hispanic of any race; Average household size: 2.49; Median age: 37.8; Age under 18: 26.7%; Age 65 and over: 12.3%; Males per 100 females: 99.4
Housing: Homeownership rate: 82.8%; Homeowner vacancy rate: 1.7%; Rental vacancy rate: 0.0%

NEW ROSS (town). Covers a land area of 0.322 square miles and a water area of 0 square miles. Located at 39.96° N. Lat; 86.71° W. Long. Elevation is 886 feet.
History: New Ross grew as a trading center for surrounding farms.
Population: 347; Growth (since 2000): 3.9%; Density: 1,079.2 persons per square mile; Race: 96.8% White, 0.0% Black/African American, 0.0% Asian, 0.0% American Indian/Alaska Native, 0.0% Native Hawaiian/Other Pacific Islander, 2.6% Two or more races, 1.7% Hispanic of any race;

Average household size: 2.57; Median age: 35.5; Age under 18: 28.8%; Age 65 and over: 14.1%; Males per 100 females: 107.8

School District(s)

South Montgomery Com Sch Corp (KG-12)
    2012-13 Enrollment: 1,759 . . . . (765) 866-0203

Housing: Homeownership rate: 80.0%; Homeowner vacancy rate: 3.6%; Rental vacancy rate: 6.9%

WAVELAND (town).
Covers a land area of 0.318 square miles and a water area of 0 square miles. Located at 39.88° N. Lat; 87.05° W. Long. Elevation is 781 feet.

History: Laid out 1835.

Population: 420; Growth (since 2000): 1.0%; Density: 1,319.4 persons per square mile; Race: 98.1% White, 0.0% Black/African American, 0.0% Asian, 0.2% American Indian/Alaska Native, 0.0% Native Hawaiian/Other Pacific Islander, 1.7% Two or more races, 2.6% Hispanic of any race; Average household size: 2.49; Median age: 36.8; Age under 18: 27.1%; Age 65 and over: 19.3%; Males per 100 females: 92.7

School District(s)

South Montgomery Com Sch Corp (KG-12)
    2012-13 Enrollment: 1,759 . . . . (765) 866-0203

Housing: Homeownership rate: 75.7%; Homeowner vacancy rate: 5.8%; Rental vacancy rate: 18.0%

WAYNETOWN (town).
Covers a land area of 0.478 square miles and a water area of 0 square miles. Located at 40.09° N. Lat; 87.07° W. Long. Elevation is 764 feet.

History: Waynetown developed around the tile factories and brick kilns that made use of the clay in the area.

Population: 958; Growth (since 2000): 5.4%; Density: 2,004.8 persons per square mile; Race: 98.3% White, 0.2% Black/African American, 0.0% Asian, 0.0% American Indian/Alaska Native, 0.0% Native Hawaiian/Other Pacific Islander, 1.0% Two or more races, 2.0% Hispanic of any race; Average household size: 2.45; Median age: 37.1; Age under 18: 26.6%; Age 65 and over: 15.4%; Males per 100 females: 93.9

Housing: Homeownership rate: 75.7%; Homeowner vacancy rate: 2.9%; Rental vacancy rate: 16.9%

WINGATE (town).
Covers a land area of 0.215 square miles and a water area of 0 square miles. Located at 40.17° N. Lat; 87.07° W. Long. Elevation is 781 feet.

Population: 263; Growth (since 2000): -12.0%; Density: 1,223.4 persons per square mile; Race: 100.0% White, 0.0% Black/African American, 0.0% Asian, 0.0% American Indian/Alaska Native, 0.0% Native Hawaiian/Other Pacific Islander, 0.0% Two or more races, 0.0% Hispanic of any race; Average household size: 2.31; Median age: 44.4; Age under 18: 21.7%; Age 65 and over: 19.0%; Males per 100 females: 99.2

Housing: Homeownership rate: 75.5%; Homeowner vacancy rate: 2.1%; Rental vacancy rate: 9.7%

Morgan County

Located in central Indiana; drained by the West Fork of the White River, Whitelick River, and Camp Creek. Covers a land area of 403.969 square miles, a water area of 5.458 square miles, and is located in the Eastern Time Zone at 39.48° N. Lat., 86.45° W. Long. The county was founded in 1821. County seat is Martinsville.

Morgan County is part of the Indianapolis-Carmel-Anderson, IN Metropolitan Statistical Area. The entire metro area includes: Boone County, IN; Brown County, IN; Hamilton County, IN; Hancock County, IN; Hendricks County, IN; Johnson County, IN; Madison County, IN; Marion County, IN; Morgan County, IN; Putnam County, IN; Shelby County, IN

Weather Station: Martinsville 2 SW   Elevation: 609 feet

	Jan	Feb	Mar	Apr	May	Jun	Jul	Aug	Sep	Oct	Nov	Dec
High	37	41	52	63	73	81	85	84	78	66	53	40
Low	19	22	30	40	50	59	63	61	52	40	32	23
Precip	2.7	2.4	3.4	4.4	5.3	4.6	4.3	3.8	3.5	3.4	3.6	3.2
Snow	5.6	4.2	2.0	0.1	0.0	0.0	0.0	0.0	0.0	0.2	0.3	3.6

High and Low temperatures in degrees Fahrenheit; Precipitation and Snow in inches

Population: 68,894; Growth (since 2000): 3.3%; Density: 170.5 persons per square mile; Race: 97.7% White, 0.3% Black/African American, 0.4% Asian, 0.3% American Indian/Alaska Native, 0.0% Native Hawaiian/Other Pacific Islander, 1.0% two or more races, 1.2% Hispanic of any race; Average household size: 2.65; Median age: 39.9; Age under 18: 25.2%; Age 65 and over: 12.9%; Males per 100 females: 98.4; Marriage status: 22.7% never married, 59.6% now married, 1.1% separated, 5.3% widowed, 12.5% divorced; Foreign born: 1.4%; Speak English only: 97.8%; With disability: 14.0%; Veterans: 10.7%; Ancestry: 21.9% German, 15.0% American, 13.3% Irish, 12.0% English, 3.1% Italian

Religion: Six largest groups: 14.3% Baptist, 6.0% Non-denominational Protestant, 4.4% Catholicism, 3.4% Holiness, 3.2% Methodist/Pietist, 2.0% Pentecostal

Economy: Unemployment rate: 4.7%; Leading industries: 16.6% retail trade; 15.2% construction; 12.3% other services (except public administration); Farms: 583 totaling 137,189 acres; Company size: 0 employ 1,000 or more persons, 1 employs 500 to 999 persons, 15 employ 100 to 499 persons, 1,160 employ less than 100 persons; Business ownership: n/a women-owned, n/a Black-owned, n/a Hispanic-owned, 82 Asian-owned

Employment: 13.0% management, business, and financial, 3.8% computer, engineering, and science, 6.6% education, legal, community service, arts, and media, 4.9% healthcare practitioners, 16.4% service, 24.6% sales and office, 13.1% natural resources, construction, and maintenance, 17.6% production, transportation, and material moving

Income: Per capita: $25,781; Median household: $55,354; Average household: $68,595; Households with income of $100,000 or more: 20.4%; Poverty rate: 11.5%

Educational Attainment: High school diploma or higher: 87.4%; Bachelor's degree or higher: 16.1%; Graduate/professional degree or higher: 5.6%

Housing: Homeownership rate: 77.7%; Median home value: $141,200; Median year structure built: 1977; Homeowner vacancy rate: 2.0%; Median gross rent: $760 per month; Rental vacancy rate: 8.0%

Vital Statistics: Birth rate: 117.5 per 10,000 population; Death rate: 84.3 per 10,000 population; Age-adjusted cancer mortality rate: 193.4 deaths per 100,000 population

Health Insurance: 87.4% have insurance; 72.1% have private insurance; 27.5% have public insurance; 12.6% do not have insurance; 7.5% of children under 18 do not have insurance

Health Care: Physicians: 11.7 per 10,000 population; Hospital beds: 26.6 per 10,000 population; Hospital admissions: 787.5 per 10,000 population

Air Quality Index: 88.8% good, 10.7% moderate, 0.5% unhealthy for sensitive individuals, 0.0% unhealthy (percent of days)

Transportation: Commute: 94.1% car, 0.1% public transportation, 1.1% walk, 3.4% work from home; Median travel time to work: 29.2 minutes

Presidential Election: 28.2% Obama, 69.3% Romney (2012)

National and State Parks: Bradford Woods State Reservation; Morgan Monroe State Forest

Additional Information Contacts

Morgan Government . . . . (765) 342-8110
   http://www.morgancounty.in.gov

Morgan County Communities

BETHANY (town).
Covers a land area of 0.083 square miles and a water area of 0.012 square miles. Located at 39.53° N. Lat; 86.38° W. Long. Elevation is 656 feet.

Population: 81; Growth (since 2000): -13.8%; Density: 973.5 persons per square mile; Race: 95.1% White, 0.0% Black/African American, 0.0% Asian, 1.2% American Indian/Alaska Native, 0.0% Native Hawaiian/Other Pacific Islander, 3.7% Two or more races, 1.2% Hispanic of any race; Average household size: 2.61; Median age: 35.8; Age under 18: 19.8%; Age 65 and over: 11.1%; Males per 100 females: 113.2

Housing: Homeownership rate: 83.9%; Homeowner vacancy rate: 0.0%; Rental vacancy rate: 28.6%

BROOKLYN (town).
Covers a land area of 0.669 square miles and a water area of 0.013 square miles. Located at 39.54° N. Lat; 86.37° W. Long. Elevation is 669 feet.

History: A supply of clay near Brooklyn provided the material for the manufacture of drain tile and brick. A brief gold rush took place in the early 1900's at Gold Creek, near Brooklyn.

Population: 1,598; Growth (since 2000): 3.4%; Density: 2,387.5 persons per square mile; Race: 97.8% White, 0.2% Black/African American, 0.2% Asian, 0.4% American Indian/Alaska Native, 0.0% Native Hawaiian/Other Pacific Islander, 0.8% Two or more races, 1.8% Hispanic of any race; Average household size: 2.76; Median age: 34.7; Age under 18: 28.1%; Age 65 and over: 11.0%; Males per 100 females: 101.8

School District(s)
M S D Martinsville Schools (PK-12)
    2012-13 Enrollment: 5,075 . . . . (765) 342-6641
Housing: Homeownership rate: 75.2%; Homeowner vacancy rate: 1.8%; Rental vacancy rate: 7.5%

CAMBY (unincorporated postal area)
ZCTA: 46113
Covers a land area of 16.398 square miles and a water area of 0.108 square miles. Located at 39.64° N. Lat; 86.30° W. Long..
Population: 14,063; Growth (since 2000): 111.0%; Density: 857.6 persons per square mile; Race: 90.5% White, 4.6% Black/African American, 1.1% Asian, 0.2% American Indian/Alaska Native, 0.0% Native Hawaiian/Other Pacific Islander, 1.9% Two or more races, 4.6% Hispanic of any race; Average household size: 2.85; Median age: 32.3; Age under 18: 30.0%; Age 65 and over: 7.6%; Males per 100 females: 99.4; Marriage status: 23.1% never married, 59.6% now married, 1.1% separated, 3.8% widowed, 13.4% divorced; Foreign born: 3.0%; Speak English only: 94.7%; With disability: 8.3%; Veterans: 8.5%; Ancestry: 19.8% German, 12.2% American, 12.1% Irish, 9.6% English, 3.0% Italian
Employment: 13.5% management, business, and financial, 4.6% computer, engineering, and science, 8.9% education, legal, community service, arts, and media, 5.3% healthcare practitioners, 14.5% service, 24.5% sales and office, 9.6% natural resources, construction, and maintenance, 19.0% production, transportation, and material moving
Income: Per capita: $22,483; Median household: $63,480; Average household: $69,079; Households with income of $100,000 or more: 17.8%; Poverty rate: 6.8%
Educational Attainment: High school diploma or higher: 92.1%; Bachelor's degree or higher: 18.0%; Graduate/professional degree or higher: 4.5%
School District(s)
Mooresville Con School Corp (PK-12)
    2012-13 Enrollment: 4,522 . . . . (317) 831-0950
Housing: Homeownership rate: 76.4%; Median home value: $124,500; Median year structure built: 2001; Homeowner vacancy rate: 2.7%; Median gross rent: $926 per month; Rental vacancy rate: 6.0%
Health Insurance: 83.5% have insurance; 73.2% have private insurance; 17.7% have public insurance; 16.5% do not have insurance; 16.3% of children under 18 do not have insurance
Transportation: Commute: 96.3% car, 0.1% public transportation, 0.2% walk, 3.0% work from home; Median travel time to work: 24.2 minutes

EMINENCE (unincorporated postal area)
ZCTA: 46125
Covers a land area of 0.034 square miles and a water area of 0 square miles. Located at 39.52° N. Lat; 86.64° W. Long. Elevation is 791 feet.
Population: 51; Growth (since 2000): -8.9%; Density: 1,500.0 persons per square mile; Race: 100.0% White, 0.0% Black/African American, 0.0% Asian, 0.0% American Indian/Alaska Native, 0.0% Native Hawaiian/Other Pacific Islander, 0.0% Two or more races, 2.0% Hispanic of any race; Average household size: 2.22; Median age: 45.9; Age under 18: 21.6%; Age 65 and over: 11.8%; Males per 100 females: 121.7
School District(s)
Eminence Community School Corp (KG-12)
    2012-13 Enrollment: 443 . . . . (765) 528-2101
Housing: Homeownership rate: 69.6%; Homeowner vacancy rate: 0.0%; Rental vacancy rate: 0.0%

MARTINSVILLE (city). County seat. Covers a land area of 4.490 square miles and a water area of 0.018 square miles. Located at 39.42° N. Lat; 86.42° W. Long. Elevation is 604 feet.
History: Named for John Martin, a member of the board of commissioners who made this city the county seat. Prospectors drilling for gas in Martinsville discovered artesian wells of therapeutic waters, giving the town the nickname of Artesian City.
Population: 11,828; Growth (since 2000): 1.1%; Density: 2,634.5 persons per square mile; Race: 97.5% White, 0.2% Black/African American, 0.4% Asian, 0.3% American Indian/Alaska Native, 0.1% Native Hawaiian/Other Pacific Islander, 1.0% Two or more races, 1.3% Hispanic of any race; Average household size: 2.47; Median age: 36.6; Age under 18: 25.0%; Age 65 and over: 14.5%; Males per 100 females: 94.4; Marriage status: 28.9% never married, 48.8% now married, 3.2% separated, 7.4% widowed, 14.9% divorced; Foreign born: 1.2%; Speak English only: 97.7%; With disability: 18.9%; Veterans: 8.3%; Ancestry: 21.8% German, 13.8% American, 12.3% Irish, 12.2% English, 3.5% Italian
Employment: 10.6% management, business, and financial, 1.8% computer, engineering, and science, 7.0% education, legal, community service, arts, and media, 3.9% healthcare practitioners, 22.6% service, 27.8% sales and office, 10.6% natural resources, construction, and maintenance, 15.8% production, transportation, and material moving
Income: Per capita: $18,419; Median household: $34,706; Average household: $44,874; Households with income of $100,000 or more: 7.2%; Poverty rate: 20.3%
Educational Attainment: High school diploma or higher: 81.1%; Bachelor's degree or higher: 11.0%; Graduate/professional degree or higher: 3.9%
School District(s)
M S D Martinsville Schools (PK-12)
    2012-13 Enrollment: 5,075 . . . . (765) 342-6641
Mooresville Con School Corp (PK-12)
    2012-13 Enrollment: 4,522 . . . . (317) 831-0950
Housing: Homeownership rate: 55.4%; Median home value: $97,400; Median year structure built: 1961; Homeowner vacancy rate: 3.4%; Median gross rent: $675 per month; Rental vacancy rate: 8.0%
Health Insurance: 83.3% have insurance; 57.1% have private insurance; 39.1% have public insurance; 16.7% do not have insurance; 9.8% of children under 18 do not have insurance
Hospitals: Indiana University Health Morgan Hospital (106 beds)
Safety: Violent crime rate: 5.9 per 10,000 population; Property crime rate: 602.2 per 10,000 population
Newspapers: Reporter-Times (daily circulation 5500)
Transportation: Commute: 89.3% car, 0.0% public transportation, 2.1% walk, 5.8% work from home; Median travel time to work: 25.3 minutes
Additional Information Contacts
City of Martinsville . . . . (765) 342-2861
http://www.martinsville.in.gov

MONROVIA (town). Covers a land area of 1.772 square miles and a water area of <.001 square miles. Located at 39.58° N. Lat; 86.48° W. Long. Elevation is 804 feet.
History: Laid out 1834.
Population: 1,063; Growth (since 2000): 69.3%; Density: 599.9 persons per square mile; Race: 97.3% White, 1.4% Black/African American, 0.6% Asian, 0.1% American Indian/Alaska Native, 0.0% Native Hawaiian/Other Pacific Islander, 0.5% Two or more races, 1.2% Hispanic of any race; Average household size: 2.91; Median age: 31.2; Age under 18: 31.1%; Age 65 and over: 6.9%; Males per 100 females: 97.2
School District(s)
Monroe-Gregg SD (KG-12)
    2012-13 Enrollment: 1,515 . . . . (317) 996-3720
Housing: Homeownership rate: 79.4%; Homeowner vacancy rate: 2.0%; Rental vacancy rate: 7.4%

MOORESVILLE (town). Covers a land area of 6.285 square miles and a water area of 0.057 square miles. Located at 39.60° N. Lat; 86.37° W. Long. Elevation is 718 feet.
History: Laid out 1824.
Population: 9,326; Growth (since 2000): 0.6%; Density: 1,483.9 persons per square mile; Race: 97.5% White, 0.3% Black/African American, 0.5% Asian, 0.2% American Indian/Alaska Native, 0.0% Native Hawaiian/Other Pacific Islander, 1.2% Two or more races, 1.1% Hispanic of any race; Average household size: 2.49; Median age: 38.6; Age under 18: 25.4%; Age 65 and over: 14.3%; Males per 100 females: 89.1; Marriage status: 23.7% never married, 53.6% now married, 0.9% separated, 6.8% widowed, 15.9% divorced; Foreign born: 1.6%; Speak English only: 98.1%; With disability: 14.0%; Veterans: 12.7%; Ancestry: 21.6% German, 15.0% American, 12.1% Irish, 11.3% English, 3.3% French
Employment: 11.4% management, business, and financial, 2.5% computer, engineering, and science, 7.7% education, legal, community service, arts, and media, 4.7% healthcare practitioners, 15.7% service, 28.5% sales and office, 8.6% natural resources, construction, and maintenance, 21.0% production, transportation, and material moving
Income: Per capita: $24,917; Median household: $53,658; Average household: $61,254; Households with income of $100,000 or more: 13.1%; Poverty rate: 11.9%

Educational Attainment: High school diploma or higher: 87.9%; Bachelor's degree or higher: 13.7%; Graduate/professional degree or higher: 2.3%

School District(s)
Mooresville Con School Corp (PK-12)
    2012-13 Enrollment: 4,522 . . . . (317) 831-0950
Housing: Homeownership rate: 67.0%; Median home value: $125,100; Median year structure built: 1974; Homeowner vacancy rate: 1.5%; Median gross rent: $738 per month; Rental vacancy rate: 6.8%
Health Insurance: 87.0% have insurance; 71.6% have private insurance; 28.1% have public insurance; 13.0% do not have insurance; 7.0% of children under 18 do not have insurance
Hospitals: Franciscan Saint Francis Health - Mooresville (64 beds)
Safety: Violent crime rate: 7.4 per 10,000 population; Property crime rate: 322.4 per 10,000 population
Transportation: Commute: 95.9% car, 0.0% public transportation, 1.6% walk, 1.5% work from home; Median travel time to work: 22.8 minutes
Additional Information Contacts
Town of Mooresville . . . . (317) 831-1608
   http://www.mooresville.org

MORGANTOWN (town).
Covers a land area of 0.378 square miles and a water area of 0 square miles. Located at 39.37° N. Lat; 86.26° W. Long. Elevation is 679 feet.
History: Laid out 1831.
Population: 986; Growth (since 2000): 2.3%; Density: 2,609.7 persons per square mile; Race: 98.5% White, 0.1% Black/African American, 0.2% Asian, 0.4% American Indian/Alaska Native, 0.0% Native Hawaiian/Other Pacific Islander, 0.5% Two or more races, 0.4% Hispanic of any race; Average household size: 2.54; Median age: 37.9; Age under 18: 26.5%; Age 65 and over: 16.1%; Males per 100 females: 90.7

School District(s)
Brown County School Corporation (KG-12)
    2012-13 Enrollment: 2,036 . . . . (812) 988-6601
Housing: Homeownership rate: 57.5%; Homeowner vacancy rate: 3.6%; Rental vacancy rate: 8.6%

PAINTED HILLS (CDP).
Covers a land area of 1.730 square miles and a water area of 0.222 square miles. Located at 39.40° N. Lat; 86.35° W. Long. Elevation is 722 feet.
Population: 677; Growth (since 2000): n/a; Density: 391.4 persons per square mile; Race: 98.4% White, 0.1% Black/African American, 0.1% Asian, 0.0% American Indian/Alaska Native, 0.0% Native Hawaiian/Other Pacific Islander, 0.4% Two or more races, 1.6% Hispanic of any race; Average household size: 2.37; Median age: 51.4; Age under 18: 16.7%; Age 65 and over: 19.4%; Males per 100 females: 96.2
Housing: Homeownership rate: 94.8%; Homeowner vacancy rate: 1.4%; Rental vacancy rate: 0.0%

PARAGON (town).
Covers a land area of 0.344 square miles and a water area of <.001 square miles. Located at 39.39° N. Lat; 86.56° W. Long. Elevation is 581 feet.
Population: 659; Growth (since 2000): -0.6%; Density: 1,918.0 persons per square mile; Race: 97.4% White, 0.2% Black/African American, 0.0% Asian, 0.0% American Indian/Alaska Native, 0.0% Native Hawaiian/Other Pacific Islander, 2.0% Two or more races, 0.9% Hispanic of any race; Average household size: 2.83; Median age: 33.3; Age under 18: 30.2%; Age 65 and over: 10.6%; Males per 100 females: 93.8

School District(s)
M S D Martinsville Schools (PK-12)
    2012-13 Enrollment: 5,075 . . . . (765) 342-6641
Housing: Homeownership rate: 59.2%; Homeowner vacancy rate: 3.5%; Rental vacancy rate: 6.9%

Newton County

Located in northwestern Indiana; bounded on the west by Illinois, and on the north by the Kankakee River; also drained by the Iroquois River. Covers a land area of 401.759 square miles, a water area of 1.679 square miles, and is located in the Central Time Zone at 40.96° N. Lat., 87.40° W. Long. The county was founded in 1857. County seat is Kentland.

Newton County is part of the Chicago-Naperville-Elgin, IL-IN-WI Metropolitan Statistical Area. The entire metro area includes: Chicago-Naperville-Arlington Heights, IL Metropolitan Division (Cook County, IL; DuPage County, IL; Grundy County, IL; Kendall County, IL; McHenry County, IL; Will County, IL); Elgin, IL Metropolitan Division (DeKalb County, IL; Kane County, IL); Gary, IN Metropolitan Division (Jasper County, IN; Lake County, IN; Newton County, IN; Porter County, IN); Lake County-Kenosha County, IL-WI Metropolitan Division (Lake County, IL; Kenosha County, WI)

Population: 14,244; Growth (since 2000): -2.2%; Density: 35.5 persons per square mile; Race: 96.2% White, 0.4% Black/African American, 0.3% Asian, 0.3% American Indian/Alaska Native, 0.0% Native Hawaiian/Other Pacific Islander, 1.1% two or more races, 5.0% Hispanic of any race; Average household size: 2.56; Median age: 42.4; Age under 18: 23.0%; Age 65 and over: 16.6%; Males per 100 females: 102.0; Marriage status: 22.2% never married, 58.1% now married, 1.0% separated, 6.7% widowed, 13.0% divorced; Foreign born: 2.0%; Speak English only: 97.0%; With disability: 15.9%; Veterans: 9.0%; Ancestry: 27.6% German, 14.2% Irish, 9.9% English, 8.9% Polish, 5.6% American
Religion: Six largest groups: 14.0% Catholicism, 9.1% Baptist, 5.8% Methodist/Pietist, 4.8% Presbyterian-Reformed, 1.1% Non-denominational Protestant, 0.7% Pentecostal
Economy: Unemployment rate: 5.3%; Leading industries: 15.2% retail trade; 13.3% construction; 11.5% other services (except public administration); Farms: 348 totaling 192,030 acres; Company size: 0 employ 1,000 or more persons, 0 employ 500 to 999 persons, 5 employ 100 to 499 persons, 265 employ less than 100 persons; Business ownership: n/a women-owned, n/a Black-owned, n/a Hispanic-owned, n/a Asian-owned
Employment: 9.0% management, business, and financial, 2.0% computer, engineering, and science, 4.9% education, legal, community service, arts, and media, 4.7% healthcare practitioners, 18.2% service, 21.0% sales and office, 12.8% natural resources, construction, and maintenance, 27.4% production, transportation, and material moving
Income: Per capita: $25,594; Median household: $50,262; Average household: $63,557; Households with income of $100,000 or more: 14.7%; Poverty rate: 11.2%
Educational Attainment: High school diploma or higher: 85.4%; Bachelor's degree or higher: 8.5%; Graduate/professional degree or higher: 2.7%
Housing: Homeownership rate: 81.1%; Median home value: $112,000; Median year structure built: 1968; Homeowner vacancy rate: 2.2%; Median gross rent: $717 per month; Rental vacancy rate: 8.6%
Vital Statistics: Birth rate: 105.8 per 10,000 population; Death rate: 94.4 per 10,000 population; Age-adjusted cancer mortality rate: 230.8 deaths per 100,000 population
Health Insurance: 85.8% have insurance; 65.6% have private insurance; 33.1% have public insurance; 14.2% do not have insurance; 5.1% of children under 18 do not have insurance
Health Care: Physicians: 1.4 per 10,000 population; Hospital beds: 0.0 per 10,000 population; Hospital admissions: 0.0 per 10,000 population
Transportation: Commute: 93.4% car, 1.3% public transportation, 1.1% walk, 3.6% work from home; Median travel time to work: 30.5 minutes
Presidential Election: 39.1% Obama, 58.2% Romney (2012)
National and State Parks: Kankakee River State Park; Willow Slough State Game Preserve
Additional Information Contacts
Newton Government . . . . (219) 474-6081
   http://www.newtoncountyin.com

Newton County Communities

BROOK (town).
Covers a land area of 0.663 square miles and a water area of 0.009 square miles. Located at 40.87° N. Lat; 87.37° W. Long. Elevation is 653 feet.
History: An early industry in Brook was the Hess Manufacturing Company, whose cosmetics line started when a local druggist concocted witch hazel lotion in a copper clothes boiler.
Population: 997; Growth (since 2000): -6.1%; Density: 1,504.4 persons per square mile; Race: 92.1% White, 0.1% Black/African American, 0.2% Asian, 0.7% American Indian/Alaska Native, 0.2% Native Hawaiian/Other Pacific Islander, 0.8% Two or more races, 10.0% Hispanic of any race; Average household size: 2.60; Median age: 40.5; Age under 18: 24.8%; Age 65 and over: 17.2%; Males per 100 females: 94.0
Housing: Homeownership rate: 73.9%; Homeowner vacancy rate: 2.4%; Rental vacancy rate: 4.8%

GOODLAND (town). Covers a land area of 0.782 square miles and a water area of 0 square miles. Located at 40.76° N. Lat; 87.30° W. Long. Elevation is 725 feet.
Population: 1,043; Growth (since 2000): -4.8%; Density: 1,333.0 persons per square mile; Race: 97.5% White, 0.7% Black/African American, 0.0% Asian, 0.4% American Indian/Alaska Native, 0.0% Native Hawaiian/Other Pacific Islander, 1.0% Two or more races, 2.1% Hispanic of any race; Average household size: 2.45; Median age: 42.3; Age under 18: 22.7%; Age 65 and over: 16.1%; Males per 100 females: 101.0
Housing: Homeownership rate: 74.1%; Homeowner vacancy rate: 1.5%; Rental vacancy rate: 8.3%

KENTLAND (town). County seat. Covers a land area of 1.530 square miles and a water area of 0 square miles. Located at 40.77° N. Lat; 87.45° W. Long. Elevation is 682 feet.
History: Kentland was the birthplace in 1866 of George Ade, Hoosier author, humorist, and playwright. An early industry here was the Whole Milk Cheese Factory.
Population: 1,748; Growth (since 2000): -4.1%; Density: 1,142.5 persons per square mile; Race: 94.2% White, 0.8% Black/African American, 0.5% Asian, 0.1% American Indian/Alaska Native, 0.0% Native Hawaiian/Other Pacific Islander, 1.8% Two or more races, 8.0% Hispanic of any race; Average household size: 2.46; Median age: 40.9; Age under 18: 24.7%; Age 65 and over: 15.8%; Males per 100 females: 96.2
School District(s)
South Newton School Corp (PK-12)
    2012-13 Enrollment: 873 . . . . (219) 474-5184
Housing: Homeownership rate: 71.7%; Homeowner vacancy rate: 4.9%; Rental vacancy rate: 10.4%
Newspapers: Community Media Group (weekly circulation 4000)

LAKE VILLAGE (CDP). Covers a land area of 3.944 square miles and a water area of 0 square miles. Located at 41.13° N. Lat; 87.44° W. Long. Elevation is 659 feet.
History: Lake Village was located on land that had been reclaimed from a swamp. It grew as the center of a farming and goat-raising area.
Population: 765; Growth (since 2000): -10.5%; Density: 194.0 persons per square mile; Race: 96.9% White, 0.8% Black/African American, 0.4% Asian, 0.5% American Indian/Alaska Native, 0.0% Native Hawaiian/Other Pacific Islander, 0.1% Two or more races, 2.6% Hispanic of any race; Average household size: 2.72; Median age: 38.2; Age under 18: 26.0%; Age 65 and over: 15.7%; Males per 100 females: 95.2
School District(s)
North Newton School Corp (KG-12)
    2012-13 Enrollment: 1,478 . . . . (219) 285-2228
Housing: Homeownership rate: 82.6%; Homeowner vacancy rate: 1.7%; Rental vacancy rate: 12.3%

MOROCCO (town). Covers a land area of 1.133 square miles and a water area of 0 square miles. Located at 40.94° N. Lat; 87.45° W. Long. Elevation is 699 feet.
History: The area in which Morocco was sited was once known as Beaver Prairie for the abundance of beaver in the streams.
Population: 1,129; Growth (since 2000): 0.2%; Density: 996.7 persons per square mile; Race: 99.1% White, 0.1% Black/African American, 0.2% Asian, 0.1% American Indian/Alaska Native, 0.0% Native Hawaiian/Other Pacific Islander, 0.4% Two or more races, 2.2% Hispanic of any race; Average household size: 2.44; Median age: 40.5; Age under 18: 23.3%; Age 65 and over: 18.2%; Males per 100 females: 102.0
School District(s)
North Newton School Corp (KG-12)
    2012-13 Enrollment: 1,478 . . . . (219) 285-2228
Housing: Homeownership rate: 73.6%; Homeowner vacancy rate: 2.3%; Rental vacancy rate: 12.2%

MOUNT AYR (town). Covers a land area of 0.149 square miles and a water area of 0 square miles. Located at 40.95° N. Lat; 87.30° W. Long. Elevation is 709 feet.
Population: 122; Growth (since 2000): -17.0%; Density: 817.6 persons per square mile; Race: 97.5% White, 0.0% Black/African American, 0.0% Asian, 0.0% American Indian/Alaska Native, 0.0% Native Hawaiian/Other Pacific Islander, 2.5% Two or more races, 5.7% Hispanic of any race; Average household size: 2.39; Median age: 47.5; Age under 18: 17.2%; Age 65 and over: 20.5%; Males per 100 females: 114.0

Housing: Homeownership rate: 86.3%; Homeowner vacancy rate: 2.2%; Rental vacancy rate: 22.2%

ROSELAWN (CDP). Covers a land area of 8.070 square miles and a water area of 0.012 square miles. Located at 41.16° N. Lat; 87.29° W. Long. Elevation is 682 feet.
Population: 4,131; Growth (since 2000): 5.0%; Density: 511.9 persons per square mile; Race: 94.2% White, 0.3% Black/African American, 0.7% Asian, 0.1% American Indian/Alaska Native, 0.0% Native Hawaiian/Other Pacific Islander, 0.7% Two or more races, 9.2% Hispanic of any race; Average household size: 2.84; Median age: 38.1; Age under 18: 26.5%; Age 65 and over: 12.6%; Males per 100 females: 102.9; Marriage status: 27.3% never married, 56.2% now married, 0.5% separated, 6.4% widowed, 10.0% divorced; Foreign born: 5.4%; Speak English only: 90.5%; With disability: 9.5%; Veterans: 7.0%; Ancestry: 23.2% German, 18.4% Irish, 13.4% Polish, 8.6% English, 6.6% Dutch
Employment: 5.1% management, business, and financial, 3.6% computer, engineering, and science, 5.7% education, legal, community service, arts, and media, 4.2% healthcare practitioners, 25.1% service, 20.9% sales and office, 11.1% natural resources, construction, and maintenance, 24.2% production, transportation, and material moving
Income: Per capita: $22,767; Median household: $58,038; Average household: $64,450; Households with income of $100,000 or more: 16.9%; Poverty rate: 8.9%
Educational Attainment: High school diploma or higher: 82.8%; Bachelor's degree or higher: 9.4%; Graduate/professional degree or higher: 3.2%
Housing: Homeownership rate: 86.8%; Median home value: $121,000; Median year structure built: 1982; Homeowner vacancy rate: 1.7%; Median gross rent: $867 per month; Rental vacancy rate: 5.0%
Health Insurance: 77.7% have insurance; 67.0% have private insurance; 21.0% have public insurance; 22.3% do not have insurance; 11.5% of children under 18 do not have insurance
Transportation: Commute: 95.3% car, 0.9% public transportation, 2.4% walk, 0.9% work from home; Median travel time to work: 30.2 minutes

SUMAVA RESORTS (unincorporated postal area)
ZCTA: 46379
    Covers a land area of 0.463 square miles and a water area of 0 square miles. Located at 41.17° N. Lat; 87.44° W. Long. Elevation is 633 feet.
    Population: 202; Growth (since 2000): -5.2%; Density: 436.2 persons per square mile; Race: 97.5% White, 0.0% Black/African American, 0.0% Asian, 0.0% American Indian/Alaska Native, 0.0% Native Hawaiian/Other Pacific Islander, 1.0% Two or more races, 4.5% Hispanic of any race; Average household size: 2.32; Median age: 41.7; Age under 18: 22.3%; Age 65 and over: 12.9%; Males per 100 females: 134.9
    Housing: Homeownership rate: 75.8%; Homeowner vacancy rate: 6.9%; Rental vacancy rate: 0.0%

THAYER (unincorporated postal area)
ZCTA: 46381
    Covers a land area of 0.909 square miles and a water area of 0 square miles. Located at 41.17° N. Lat; 87.32° W. Long. Elevation is 643 feet.
    Population: 235; Growth (since 2000): 46.9%; Density: 258.5 persons per square mile; Race: 98.3% White, 0.0% Black/African American, 0.0% Asian, 0.0% American Indian/Alaska Native, 0.0% Native Hawaiian/Other Pacific Islander, 0.9% Two or more races, 4.7% Hispanic of any race; Average household size: 2.55; Median age: 43.5; Age under 18: 23.0%; Age 65 and over: 18.7%; Males per 100 females: 95.8
    Housing: Homeownership rate: 88.0%; Homeowner vacancy rate: 0.0%; Rental vacancy rate: 7.7%

Noble County

Located in northeastern Indiana; drained by the Elkhart River; includes many small lakes. Covers a land area of 410.843 square miles, a water area of 6.590 square miles, and is located in the Eastern Time Zone at 41.40° N. Lat., 85.42° W. Long. The county was founded in 1835. County seat is Albion.

Noble County is part of the Kendallville, IN Micropolitan Statistical Area. The entire metro area includes: Noble County, IN

Population: 47,536; Growth (since 2000): 2.7%; Density: 115.7 persons per square mile; Race: 92.5% White, 0.4% Black/African American, 0.4% Asian, 0.2% American Indian/Alaska Native, 0.0% Native Hawaiian/Other Pacific Islander, 1.3% two or more races, 9.6% Hispanic of any race; Average household size: 2.69; Median age: 37.1; Age under 18: 27.0%; Age 65 and over: 12.5%; Males per 100 females: 100.1; Marriage status: 24.6% never married, 57.4% now married, 1.7% separated, 5.9% widowed, 12.1% divorced; Foreign born: 4.9%; Speak English only: 88.0%; With disability: 13.8%; Veterans: 9.6%; Ancestry: 29.0% German, 11.4% American, 10.0% Irish, 8.1% English, 2.9% French
Religion: Six largest groups: 6.1% Catholicism, 5.9% Lutheran, 5.7% Methodist/Pietist, 4.0% Non-denominational Protestant, 2.2% European Free-Church, 1.6% Holiness
Economy: Unemployment rate: 4.9%; Leading industries: 15.7% retail trade; 14.2% other services (except public administration); 13.9% manufacturing; Farms: 1,163 totaling 181,491 acres; Company size: 0 employ 1,000 or more persons, 3 employ 500 to 999 persons, 28 employ 100 to 499 persons, 858 employ less than 100 persons; Business ownership: 839 women-owned, n/a Black-owned, 61 Hispanic-owned, n/a Asian-owned
Employment: 10.0% management, business, and financial, 2.4% computer, engineering, and science, 6.2% education, legal, community service, arts, and media, 4.9% healthcare practitioners, 13.5% service, 19.0% sales and office, 11.5% natural resources, construction, and maintenance, 32.6% production, transportation, and material moving
Income: Per capita: $21,889; Median household: $47,117; Average household: $57,759; Households with income of $100,000 or more: 11.8%; Poverty rate: 14.2%
Educational Attainment: High school diploma or higher: 83.3%; Bachelor's degree or higher: 13.2%; Graduate/professional degree or higher: 4.7%
Housing: Homeownership rate: 77.6%; Median home value: $112,700; Median year structure built: 1972; Homeowner vacancy rate: 2.7%; Median gross rent: $613 per month; Rental vacancy rate: 12.7%
Vital Statistics: Birth rate: 119.6 per 10,000 population; Death rate: 88.7 per 10,000 population; Age-adjusted cancer mortality rate: 215.5 deaths per 100,000 population
Health Insurance: 84.2% have insurance; 67.2% have private insurance; 28.8% have public insurance; 15.8% do not have insurance; 11.4% of children under 18 do not have insurance
Health Care: Physicians: 4.6 per 10,000 population; Hospital beds: 6.5 per 10,000 population; Hospital admissions: 391.9 per 10,000 population
Transportation: Commute: 92.0% car, 0.1% public transportation, 2.2% walk, 3.3% work from home; Median travel time to work: 23.5 minutes
Presidential Election: 32.2% Obama, 65.7% Romney (2012)
National and State Parks: Chain O'Lakes State Park; Gene Stratton Porter State Memorial
Additional Information Contacts
Noble Government . . . . (260) 636-2658
http://www.nobleco.org

Noble County Communities

ALBION (town). County seat. Covers a land area of 1.908 square miles and a water area of 0 square miles. Located at 41.40° N. Lat; 85.42° W. Long. Elevation is 955 feet.
History: Albion was first called The Center. The name was changed to Albion about 1845, when the town was successful in its bid to become the new seat of Noble County. Albion was a station on the Underground Railroad, helping slaves to escape to freedom.
Population: 2,349; Growth (since 2000): 2.8%; Density: 1,231.1 persons per square mile; Race: 97.4% White, 0.4% Black/African American, 0.4% Asian, 0.2% American Indian/Alaska Native, 0.0% Native Hawaiian/Other Pacific Islander, 1.1% Two or more races, 3.2% Hispanic of any race; Average household size: 2.46; Median age: 35.3; Age under 18: 24.8%; Age 65 and over: 14.2%; Males per 100 females: 104.6
School District(s)
Central Noble Com School Corp (KG-12)
    2012-13 Enrollment: 1,313 . . . . (260) 636-2175
Housing: Homeownership rate: 63.7%; Homeowner vacancy rate: 2.9%; Rental vacancy rate: 11.2%
Safety: Violent crime rate: 0.0 per 10,000 population; Property crime rate: 0.0 per 10,000 population
Newspapers: New Era (weekly circulation 2000)
Additional Information Contacts
Town of Albion. . . . . (260) 636-2246
http://www.albion-in.org

AVILLA (town). Covers a land area of 1.481 square miles and a water area of 0 square miles. Located at 41.36° N. Lat; 85.23° W. Long. Elevation is 968 feet.
Population: 2,401; Growth (since 2000): 17.2%; Density: 1,621.3 persons per square mile; Race: 98.3% White, 0.7% Black/African American, 0.2% Asian, 0.0% American Indian/Alaska Native, 0.0% Native Hawaiian/Other Pacific Islander, 0.6% Two or more races, 1.5% Hispanic of any race; Average household size: 2.46; Median age: 36.2; Age under 18: 27.0%; Age 65 and over: 17.3%; Males per 100 females: 87.0
School District(s)
East Noble School Corp (KG-12)
    2012-13 Enrollment: 3,761 . . . . (260) 347-2502
Housing: Homeownership rate: 67.7%; Homeowner vacancy rate: 3.6%; Rental vacancy rate: 12.2%
Additional Information Contacts
Town of Avilla . . . . (260) 897-3627
http://www.avillachamber.com

CROMWELL (town). Covers a land area of 0.297 square miles and a water area of 0 square miles. Located at 41.40° N. Lat; 85.61° W. Long. Elevation is 958 feet.
Population: 512; Growth (since 2000): 13.3%; Density: 1,725.1 persons per square mile; Race: 92.6% White, 0.0% Black/African American, 0.0% Asian, 0.2% American Indian/Alaska Native, 0.0% Native Hawaiian/Other Pacific Islander, 1.2% Two or more races, 12.9% Hispanic of any race; Average household size: 2.80; Median age: 30.6; Age under 18: 30.1%; Age 65 and over: 7.6%; Males per 100 females: 86.9
Housing: Homeownership rate: 62.8%; Homeowner vacancy rate: 1.7%; Rental vacancy rate: 25.5%

KENDALLVILLE (city). Covers a land area of 6.045 square miles and a water area of 0.224 square miles. Located at 41.44° N. Lat; 85.26° W. Long. Elevation is 988 feet.
History: Kendallville was settled in 1833 when David Bundle opened a tavern to serve the many travelers that passed this way. When the New York Central Railroad came through in 1857, the village grew. The Flint & Walling Manufacturing Plant was founded here in 1865 as a machine shop, and became a producer of windmills and pumps.
Population: 9,862; Growth (since 2000): 2.6%; Density: 1,631.5 persons per square mile; Race: 94.1% White, 0.5% Black/African American, 0.5% Asian, 0.2% American Indian/Alaska Native, 0.0% Native Hawaiian/Other Pacific Islander, 1.8% Two or more races, 5.1% Hispanic of any race; Average household size: 2.46; Median age: 34.6; Age under 18: 27.4%; Age 65 and over: 12.9%; Males per 100 females: 93.0; Marriage status: 30.4% never married, 43.5% now married, 4.0% separated, 8.2% widowed, 17.9% divorced; Foreign born: 2.5%; Speak English only: 94.0%; With disability: 18.5%; Veterans: 10.0%; Ancestry: 24.1% German, 15.3% American, 12.3% Irish, 8.9% English, 1.7% Dutch
Employment: 10.4% management, business, and financial, 1.8% computer, engineering, and science, 5.0% education, legal, community service, arts, and media, 4.2% healthcare practitioners, 15.4% service, 20.4% sales and office, 9.1% natural resources, construction, and maintenance, 33.6% production, transportation, and material moving
Income: Per capita: $18,654; Median household: $38,802; Average household: $45,245; Households with income of $100,000 or more: 6.3%; Poverty rate: 23.6%
Educational Attainment: High school diploma or higher: 86.8%; Bachelor's degree or higher: 13.4%; Graduate/professional degree or higher: 3.7%
School District(s)
Dekalb County Eastern Com SD (KG-12)
    2012-13 Enrollment: 1,364 . . . . (260) 868-2125
East Noble School Corp (KG-12)
    2012-13 Enrollment: 3,761 . . . . (260) 347-2502
Housing: Homeownership rate: 61.7%; Median home value: $82,900; Median year structure built: 1966; Homeowner vacancy rate: 3.7%; Median gross rent: $617 per month; Rental vacancy rate: 12.2%
Health Insurance: 83.1% have insurance; 57.2% have private insurance; 40.1% have public insurance; 16.9% do not have insurance; 6.2% of children under 18 do not have insurance
Hospitals: Parkview Noble Hospital (66 beds)

Newspapers: Advance Leader (weekly circulation 3000); News-Sun (daily circulation 8600)
Transportation: Commute: 92.2% car, 0.0% public transportation, 4.5% walk, 1.6% work from home; Median travel time to work: 22.3 minutes
Airports: Kendallville Municipal (general aviation)
Additional Information Contacts
City of Kendallville . . . . (260) 347-2452
http://www.kendallville-in.org

KIMMELL (CDP).
Covers a land area of 0.960 square miles and a water area of 0.031 square miles. Located at 41.39° N. Lat; 85.55° W. Long. Elevation is 915 feet.
Population: 422; Growth (since 2000): n/a; Density: 439.8 persons per square mile; Race: 94.5% White, 0.5% Black/African American, 0.2% Asian, 0.0% American Indian/Alaska Native, 0.0% Native Hawaiian/Other Pacific Islander, 0.0% Two or more races, 13.7% Hispanic of any race; Average household size: 2.71; Median age: 35.3; Age under 18: 26.8%; Age 65 and over: 11.6%; Males per 100 females: 100.0
Housing: Homeownership rate: 81.4%; Homeowner vacancy rate: 5.8%; Rental vacancy rate: 21.6%

LAOTTO (unincorporated postal area)
ZCTA: 46763
Covers a land area of 22.431 square miles and a water area of 0.016 square miles. Located at 41.30° N. Lat; 85.23° W. Long. Elevation is 873 feet.
Population: 1,631; Growth (since 2000): -3.1%; Density: 72.7 persons per square mile; Race: 98.1% White, 0.1% Black/African American, 0.2% Asian, 0.1% American Indian/Alaska Native, 0.0% Native Hawaiian/Other Pacific Islander, 1.3% Two or more races, 0.9% Hispanic of any race; Average household size: 2.54; Median age: 42.5; Age under 18: 21.8%; Age 65 and over: 13.0%; Males per 100 females: 100.9
Housing: Homeownership rate: 88.3%; Homeowner vacancy rate: 1.2%; Rental vacancy rate: 3.7%

LIGONIER (city).
Covers a land area of 2.310 square miles and a water area of <.001 square miles. Located at 41.46° N. Lat; 85.59° W. Long. Elevation is 876 feet.
History: Ligonier was settled along the Elkhart River. Many of the early residents were Jewish.
Population: 4,405; Growth (since 2000): 1.1%; Density: 1,907.3 persons per square mile; Race: 69.6% White, 0.4% Black/African American, 0.5% Asian, 0.2% American Indian/Alaska Native, 0.0% Native Hawaiian/Other Pacific Islander, 2.7% Two or more races, 51.5% Hispanic of any race; Average household size: 3.26; Median age: 28.5; Age under 18: 34.7%; Age 65 and over: 8.0%; Males per 100 females: 99.1; Marriage status: 32.4% never married, 54.9% now married, 1.8% separated, 4.8% widowed, 7.9% divorced; Foreign born: 31.3%; Speak English only: 44.2%; With disability: 8.8%; Veterans: 5.7%; Ancestry: 9.5% German, 6.3% Irish, 5.3% American, 4.4% English, 2.8% French
Employment: 3.8% management, business, and financial, 0.0% computer, engineering, and science, 1.7% education, legal, community service, arts, and media, 1.1% healthcare practitioners, 9.1% service, 10.4% sales and office, 20.7% natural resources, construction, and maintenance, 53.1% production, transportation, and material moving
Income: Per capita: $16,007; Median household: $36,863; Average household: $49,380; Households with income of $100,000 or more: 5.6%; Poverty rate: 25.7%
Educational Attainment: High school diploma or higher: 53.3%; Bachelor's degree or higher: 4.4%; Graduate/professional degree or higher: 0.9%

School District(s)
West Noble School Corporation (KG-12)
2012-13 Enrollment: 2,465 . . . . (260) 894-3191
Housing: Homeownership rate: 65.5%; Median home value: $84,400; Median year structure built: 1949; Homeowner vacancy rate: 3.3%; Median gross rent: $555 per month; Rental vacancy rate: 18.0%
Health Insurance: 74.2% have insurance; 46.5% have private insurance; 37.2% have public insurance; 25.8% do not have insurance; 10.2% of children under 18 do not have insurance
Safety: Violent crime rate: 0.0 per 10,000 population; Property crime rate: 41.0 per 10,000 population
Transportation: Commute: 89.1% car, 0.0% public transportation, 4.1% walk, 4.2% work from home; Median travel time to work: 20.6 minutes

Additional Information Contacts
City of Ligonier . . . . (260) 894-4113
http://www.ligonier-in.org

ROME CITY (town).
Covers a land area of 1.157 square miles and a water area of 0.991 square miles. Located at 41.49° N. Lat; 85.36° W. Long. Elevation is 935 feet.
History: Rome City developed when a dam was built across a tributary of the Elkhart River, forming Sylvan Lake. The settlement, which became a resort community, was platted in 1839 and named by the Irish construction workers.
Population: 1,361; Growth (since 2000): -15.7%; Density: 1,176.7 persons per square mile; Race: 98.8% White, 0.4% Black/African American, 0.1% Asian, 0.2% American Indian/Alaska Native, 0.0% Native Hawaiian/Other Pacific Islander, 0.2% Two or more races, 1.1% Hispanic of any race; Average household size: 2.42; Median age: 44.4; Age under 18: 22.6%; Age 65 and over: 16.8%; Males per 100 females: 98.4

School District(s)
East Noble School Corp (KG-12)
2012-13 Enrollment: 3,761 . . . . (260) 347-2502
Housing: Homeownership rate: 74.0%; Homeowner vacancy rate: 4.9%; Rental vacancy rate: 10.9%

WAWAKA (unincorporated postal area)
ZCTA: 46794
Covers a land area of 25.732 square miles and a water area of 0.218 square miles. Located at 41.46° N. Lat; 85.46° W. Long. Elevation is 899 feet.
Population: 1,587; Growth (since 2000): -3.2%; Density: 61.7 persons per square mile; Race: 95.8% White, 0.3% Black/African American, 0.1% Asian, 0.2% American Indian/Alaska Native, 0.1% Native Hawaiian/Other Pacific Islander, 1.3% Two or more races, 3.9% Hispanic of any race; Average household size: 2.77; Median age: 38.4; Age under 18: 27.7%; Age 65 and over: 12.5%; Males per 100 females: 103.2
Housing: Homeownership rate: 84.4%; Homeowner vacancy rate: 2.4%; Rental vacancy rate: 9.2%

WOLCOTTVILLE (town).
Covers a land area of 1.015 square miles and a water area of 0 square miles. Located at 41.53° N. Lat; 85.37° W. Long. Elevation is 942 feet.
History: Wolcottville grew around a gristmill, sawmill, and distillery established by George Wolcott from Connecticut. The number of nearby lakes made Wolcottville a vacation center as well.
Population: 998; Growth (since 2000): 7.0%; Density: 983.0 persons per square mile; Race: 96.0% White, 0.5% Black/African American, 0.8% Asian, 0.7% American Indian/Alaska Native, 0.0% Native Hawaiian/Other Pacific Islander, 0.5% Two or more races, 1.8% Hispanic of any race; Average household size: 2.70; Median age: 33.8; Age under 18: 29.3%; Age 65 and over: 10.3%; Males per 100 females: 93.4

School District(s)
Lakeland School Corporation (KG-12)
2012-13 Enrollment: 2,178 . . . . (260) 499-2400
Housing: Homeownership rate: 58.2%; Homeowner vacancy rate: 6.1%; Rental vacancy rate: 19.3%

Ohio County

Located in southeastern Indiana; bounded on the east by the Ohio River and the Kentucky border. Covers a land area of 86.140 square miles, a water area of 1.294 square miles, and is located in the Eastern Time Zone at 38.94° N. Lat., 84.96° W. Long. The county was founded in 1844. County seat is Rising Sun.

Ohio County is part of the Cincinnati, OH-KY-IN Metropolitan Statistical Area. The entire metro area includes: Dearborn County, IN; Ohio County, IN; Union County, IN; Boone County, KY; Bracken County, KY; Campbell County, KY; Gallatin County, KY; Grant County, KY; Kenton County, KY; Pendleton County, KY; Brown County, OH; Butler County, OH; Clermont County, OH; Hamilton County, OH; Warren County, OH

Population: 6,128; Growth (since 2000): 9.0%; Density: 71.1 persons per square mile; Race: 98.1% White, 0.4% Black/African American, 0.3% Asian, 0.2% American Indian/Alaska Native, 0.0% Native Hawaiian/Other Pacific Islander, 0.7% two or more races, 1.1% Hispanic of any race;

Average household size: 2.45; Median age: 43.7; Age under 18: 21.2%; Age 65 and over: 16.6%; Males per 100 females: 98.0; Marriage status: 23.6% never married, 56.4% now married, 0.9% separated, 8.2% widowed, 11.8% divorced; Foreign born: 0.2%; Speak English only: 98.5%; With disability: 12.8%; Veterans: 11.4%; Ancestry: 32.7% German, 15.9% Irish, 12.2% American, 9.1% English, 6.0% Italian
Religion: Six largest groups: 20.1% Baptist, 3.3% Methodist/Pietist, 2.4% Non-denominational Protestant, 1.6% Presbyterian-Reformed, 1.3% Holiness, 0.0% Other Groups
Economy: Unemployment rate: 5.2%; Leading industries: 15.1% construction; 14.0% retail trade; 12.9% other services (except public administration); Farms: 171 totaling 21,461 acres; Company size: 0 employ 1,000 or more persons, 1 employs 500 to 999 persons, 0 employ 100 to 499 persons, 92 employ less than 100 persons; Business ownership: n/a women-owned, n/a Black-owned, n/a Hispanic-owned, n/a Asian-owned
Employment: 9.0% management, business, and financial, 2.8% computer, engineering, and science, 5.9% education, legal, community service, arts, and media, 4.5% healthcare practitioners, 20.0% service, 22.7% sales and office, 10.4% natural resources, construction, and maintenance, 24.8% production, transportation, and material moving
Income: Per capita: $25,443; Median household: $50,377; Average household: $61,382; Households with income of $100,000 or more: 18.1%; Poverty rate: 8.3%
Educational Attainment: High school diploma or higher: 85.4%; Bachelor's degree or higher: 13.1%; Graduate/professional degree or higher: 3.1%
Housing: Homeownership rate: 75.3%; Median home value: $137,900; Median year structure built: 1976; Homeowner vacancy rate: 2.6%; Median gross rent: $698 per month; Rental vacancy rate: 10.1%
Vital Statistics: Birth rate: 71.7 per 10,000 population; Death rate: 106.8 per 10,000 population; Age-adjusted cancer mortality rate: Unreliable deaths per 100,000 population
Health Insurance: 85.3% have insurance; 72.0% have private insurance; 28.6% have public insurance; 14.7% do not have insurance; 9.2% of children under 18 do not have insurance
Health Care: Physicians: 0.0 per 10,000 population; Hospital beds: 0.0 per 10,000 population; Hospital admissions: 0.0 per 10,000 population
Transportation: Commute: 93.8% car, 0.0% public transportation, 2.5% walk, 2.6% work from home; Median travel time to work: 32.4 minutes
Presidential Election: 35.2% Obama, 62.4% Romney (2012)
Additional Information Contacts
Ohio Government . . . . (812) 438-2062

Ohio County Communities

RISING SUN (city). County seat. Covers a land area of 1.449 square miles and a water area of 0.119 square miles. Located at 38.95° N. Lat; 84.85° W. Long. Elevation is 502 feet.
History: Rising Sun was platted in 1814 along the Ohio River, and grew as a shipping center.
Population: 2,304; Growth (since 2000): -6.7%; Density: 1,590.0 persons per square mile; Race: 97.8% White, 0.7% Black/African American, 0.4% Asian, 0.1% American Indian/Alaska Native, 0.0% Native Hawaiian/Other Pacific Islander, 0.6% Two or more races, 1.8% Hispanic of any race; Average household size: 2.24; Median age: 43.9; Age under 18: 19.6%; Age 65 and over: 19.8%; Males per 100 females: 91.2
School District(s)
Rising Sun-Ohio County Com (KG-12)
    2012-13 Enrollment: 850 . . . . (812) 438-2655
Housing: Homeownership rate: 57.5%; Homeowner vacancy rate: 3.8%; Rental vacancy rate: 9.7%
Newspapers: News Sun Recorder (weekly circulation 2000)
Additional Information Contacts
City of Rising Sun . . . . (812) 438-2475
    http://www.cityofrisingsun.com

Orange County

Located in southern Indiana; drained by the Lick, Lost, and Potoka Rivers. Covers a land area of 398.387 square miles, a water area of 9.805 square miles, and is located in the Eastern Time Zone at 38.55° N. Lat., 86.49° W. Long. The county was founded in 1815. County seat is Paoli.

Weather Station: Paoli   Elevation: 560 feet

	Jan	Feb	Mar	Apr	May	Jun	Jul	Aug	Sep	Oct	Nov	Dec
High	40	45	55	66	76	84	87	87	80	68	56	43
Low	21	24	32	41	51	60	64	62	54	42	34	24
Precip	3.3	3.1	4.4	5.0	5.4	4.1	4.2	3.4	3.8	3.4	4.0	3.7
Snow	3.3	3.2	1.1	tr	0.0	0.0	0.0	0.0	0.0	0.0	tr	3.6

High and Low temperatures in degrees Fahrenheit; Precipitation and Snow in inches

Population: 19,840; Growth (since 2000): 2.8%; Density: 49.8 persons per square mile; Race: 97.0% White, 0.9% Black/African American, 0.3% Asian, 0.3% American Indian/Alaska Native, 0.0% Native Hawaiian/Other Pacific Islander, 1.2% two or more races, 1.0% Hispanic of any race; Average household size: 2.49; Median age: 40.8; Age under 18: 24.6%; Age 65 and over: 15.8%; Males per 100 females: 98.8; Marriage status: 23.4% never married, 55.1% now married, 1.4% separated, 7.9% widowed, 13.6% divorced; Foreign born: 0.4%; Speak English only: 98.4%; With disability: 18.0%; Veterans: 9.5%; Ancestry: 22.3% German, 14.3% American, 13.0% Irish, 9.5% English, 1.9% Dutch
Religion: Six largest groups: 23.6% Baptist, 6.8% Methodist/Pietist, 4.5% European Free-Church, 3.5% Holiness, 1.9% Catholicism, 1.5% Non-denominational Protestant
Economy: Unemployment rate: 5.7%; Leading industries: 15.3% retail trade; 14.5% other services (except public administration); 12.0% construction; Farms: 478 totaling 98,251 acres; Company size: 1 employs 1,000 or more persons, 1 employs 500 to 999 persons, 12 employ 100 to 499 persons, 385 employ less than 100 persons; Business ownership: n/a women-owned, n/a Black-owned, n/a Hispanic-owned, n/a Asian-owned
Employment: 10.2% management, business, and financial, 1.6% computer, engineering, and science, 7.4% education, legal, community service, arts, and media, 5.0% healthcare practitioners, 21.7% service, 19.0% sales and office, 13.2% natural resources, construction, and maintenance, 21.9% production, transportation, and material moving
Income: Per capita: $18,576; Median household: $38,826; Average household: $46,360; Households with income of $100,000 or more: 7.6%; Poverty rate: 17.9%
Educational Attainment: High school diploma or higher: 80.4%; Bachelor's degree or higher: 12.6%; Graduate/professional degree or higher: 4.2%
Housing: Homeownership rate: 75.0%; Median home value: $88,100; Median year structure built: 1975; Homeowner vacancy rate: 2.9%; Median gross rent: $592 per month; Rental vacancy rate: 9.6%
Vital Statistics: Birth rate: 111.3 per 10,000 population; Death rate: 99.6 per 10,000 population; Age-adjusted cancer mortality rate: 229.6 deaths per 100,000 population
Health Insurance: 84.4% have insurance; 62.0% have private insurance; 34.9% have public insurance; 15.6% do not have insurance; 9.7% of children under 18 do not have insurance
Health Care: Physicians: 6.6 per 10,000 population; Hospital beds: 12.1 per 10,000 population; Hospital admissions: 280.7 per 10,000 population
Transportation: Commute: 94.0% car, 0.1% public transportation, 1.6% walk, 3.0% work from home; Median travel time to work: 26.7 minutes
Presidential Election: 37.9% Obama, 59.5% Romney (2012)
National and State Parks: Hoosier National Forest; Jackson State Recreation Area; Newton-Stewart State Recreation Area; Pioneer Mothers State Wayside Park; Springs Valley State Fish and Wildlife Area; Tillery Hill State Recreation Area
Additional Information Contacts
Orange Government . . . . (812) 723-2649
    http://www.co.orange.in.us

Orange County Communities

FRENCH LICK (town). Covers a land area of 1.766 square miles and a water area of 0.001 square miles. Located at 38.55° N. Lat; 86.62° W. Long. Elevation is 499 feet.
History: French Lick was founded in 1811 on the site of mineral springs where a trading post had been operated by the French in the early 1700's. The French Lick Springs Hotel was opened in 1840 by Dr. William A. Bowles, who not only entertained visitors to the medicinal springs, but marketed the spring water by boiling and bottling it as Pluto Water.
Population: 1,807; Growth (since 2000): -6.9%; Density: 1,023.1 persons per square mile; Race: 88.8% White, 5.8% Black/African American, 1.2% Asian, 0.3% American Indian/Alaska Native, 0.0% Native Hawaiian/Other Pacific Islander, 2.9% Two or more races, 2.1% Hispanic of any race;

Average household size: 2.27; Median age: 39.2; Age under 18: 24.0%; Age 65 and over: 18.4%; Males per 100 females: 88.4

School District(s)

Springs Valley Com School Corp (KG-12)
   2012-13 Enrollment: 934........................ (812) 936-4474
Housing: Homeownership rate: 55.1%; Homeowner vacancy rate: 8.1%; Rental vacancy rate: 16.8%
Newspapers: Springs Valley Herald (weekly circulation 2200)
Airports: French Lick Municipal (general aviation)

ORLEANS (town). Covers a land area of 1.709 square miles and a water area of <.001 square miles. Located at 38.66° N. Lat; 86.45° W. Long. Elevation is 633 feet.
History: Orleans was founded in 1815 shortly after General Jackson's victory at New Orleans, and the town was named for that event. Orleans developed as an orchard and dairy center.
Population: 2,142; Growth (since 2000): -5.8%; Density: 1,253.2 persons per square mile; Race: 98.6% White, 0.1% Black/African American, 0.4% Asian, 0.3% American Indian/Alaska Native, 0.0% Native Hawaiian/Other Pacific Islander, 0.7% Two or more races, 0.6% Hispanic of any race; Average household size: 2.37; Median age: 40.3; Age under 18: 24.5%; Age 65 and over: 17.8%; Males per 100 females: 89.4

School District(s)

Orleans Community Schools (KG-12)
   2012-13 Enrollment: 833........................ (812) 865-2688
Housing: Homeownership rate: 62.5%; Homeowner vacancy rate: 2.1%; Rental vacancy rate: 5.5%
Newspapers: Progress-Examiner (weekly circulation 2100)
Additional Information Contacts
Town of Orleans.................................... (812) 865-2539
   http://www.town.orleans.in.us

PAOLI (town). County seat. Covers a land area of 3.743 square miles and a water area of 0.014 square miles. Located at 38.56° N. Lat; 86.47° W. Long. Elevation is 623 feet.
History: The Orange County Courthouse was constructed in 1850 in Paoli, the county seat.
Population: 3,677; Growth (since 2000): -4.3%; Density: 982.3 persons per square mile; Race: 97.7% White, 0.3% Black/African American, 0.3% Asian, 0.2% American Indian/Alaska Native, 0.0% Native Hawaiian/Other Pacific Islander, 1.0% Two or more races, 1.3% Hispanic of any race; Average household size: 2.35; Median age: 39.7; Age under 18: 23.8%; Age 65 and over: 17.5%; Males per 100 females: 93.3; Marriage status: 28.0% never married, 47.6% now married, 1.6% separated, 8.3% widowed, 16.1% divorced; Foreign born: 0.3%; Speak English only: 99.1%; With disability: 15.8%; Veterans: 9.0%; Ancestry: 25.5% German, 15.4% Irish, 11.6% American, 9.8% English, 4.0% French
Employment: 8.8% management, business, and financial, 1.1% computer, engineering, and science, 11.6% education, legal, community service, arts, and media, 2.7% healthcare practitioners, 26.8% service, 18.5% sales and office, 10.5% natural resources, construction, and maintenance, 20.0% production, transportation, and material moving
Income: Per capita: $16,252; Median household: $37,188; Average household: $41,000; Households with income of $100,000 or more: 3.7%; Poverty rate: 13.7%
Educational Attainment: High school diploma or higher: 80.7%; Bachelor's degree or higher: 10.5%; Graduate/professional degree or higher: 4.5%

School District(s)

Lost River Career Cooperative (09-12)
   2012-13 Enrollment: n/a........................ (812) 723-4818
Paoli Community School Corp (KG-12)
   2012-13 Enrollment: 1,641...................... (812) 723-4717
South Central Area Special Ed (KG-12)
   2012-13 Enrollment: n/a........................ (812) 723-2089
Housing: Homeownership rate: 65.5%; Median home value: $75,100; Median year structure built: 1969; Homeowner vacancy rate: 2.7%; Median gross rent: $567 per month; Rental vacancy rate: 7.9%
Health Insurance: 84.0% have insurance; 57.1% have private insurance; 39.8% have public insurance; 16.0% do not have insurance; 2.6% of children under 18 do not have insurance
Hospitals: Indiana University Health Paoli Hospital
Newspapers: Orange Co. Publishing (weekly circulation 19000)
Transportation: Commute: 94.9% car, 0.3% public transportation, 1.3% walk, 3.0% work from home; Median travel time to work: 22.5 minutes

Additional Information Contacts
Town of Paoli...................................... (812) 723-4769
   http://www.paolichamber.com

WEST BADEN SPRINGS (town). Covers a land area of 1.089 square miles and a water area of 0.008 square miles. Located at 38.57° N. Lat; 86.61° W. Long. Elevation is 479 feet.
Population: 574; Growth (since 2000): -7.1%; Density: 527.2 persons per square mile; Race: 93.4% White, 3.1% Black/African American, 0.3% Asian, 0.5% American Indian/Alaska Native, 0.0% Native Hawaiian/Other Pacific Islander, 1.9% Two or more races, 1.4% Hispanic of any race; Average household size: 2.29; Median age: 40.4; Age under 18: 24.0%; Age 65 and over: 17.8%; Males per 100 females: 100.7
Housing: Homeownership rate: 62.2%; Homeowner vacancy rate: 6.5%; Rental vacancy rate: 11.2%

Owen County

Located in southwest central Indiana; drained by the West Fork of the White River and Mill Creek. Covers a land area of 385.288 square miles, a water area of 2.537 square miles, and is located in the Eastern Time Zone at 39.32° N. Lat., 86.84° W. Long. The county was founded in 1818. County seat is Spencer.

Owen County is part of the Bloomington, IN Metropolitan Statistical Area. The entire metro area includes: Monroe County, IN; Owen County, IN

Weather Station: Spencer   Elevation: 549 feet

	Jan	Feb	Mar	Apr	May	Jun	Jul	Aug	Sep	Oct	Nov	Dec
High	36	41	52	63	73	81	85	84	78	66	53	40
Low	19	21	29	39	49	59	63	61	52	40	32	22
Precip	2.9	2.7	3.7	4.7	5.4	5.0	4.9	4.0	3.6	3.7	4.0	3.5
Snow	5.7	4.5	1.4	tr	0.0	0.0	0.0	0.0	0.0	0.1	0.3	3.2

High and Low temperatures in degrees Fahrenheit; Precipitation and Snow in inches

Population: 21,575; Growth (since 2000): -1.0%; Density: 56.0 persons per square mile; Race: 97.9% White, 0.3% Black/African American, 0.3% Asian, 0.3% American Indian/Alaska Native, 0.0% Native Hawaiian/Other Pacific Islander, 0.9% two or more races, 0.9% Hispanic of any race; Average household size: 2.52; Median age: 42.4; Age under 18: 23.2%; Age 65 and over: 14.8%; Males per 100 females: 100.6; Marriage status: 21.5% never married, 59.1% now married, 1.0% separated, 6.3% widowed, 13.1% divorced; Foreign born: 1.1%; Speak English only: 97.5%; With disability: 16.4%; Veterans: 12.3%; Ancestry: 23.7% German, 15.4% Irish, 12.7% American, 9.7% English, 2.2% French
Religion: Six largest groups: 9.7% Baptist, 4.6% Non-denominational Protestant, 3.9% Methodist/Pietist, 1.8% Holiness, 1.3% Catholicism, 1.0% Pentecostal
Economy: Unemployment rate: 6.1%; Leading industries: 16.3% construction; 13.9% other services (except public administration); 12.9% retail trade; Farms: 549 totaling 95,527 acres; Company size: 0 employ 1,000 or more persons, 1 employs 500 to 999 persons, 2 employ 100 to 499 persons, 291 employs less than 100 persons; Business ownership: 335 women-owned, n/a Black-owned, n/a Hispanic-owned, n/a Asian-owned
Employment: 10.3% management, business, and financial, 2.9% computer, engineering, and science, 7.5% education, legal, community service, arts, and media, 3.7% healthcare practitioners, 15.2% service, 20.7% sales and office, 14.9% natural resources, construction, and maintenance, 24.9% production, transportation, and material moving
Income: Per capita: $21,318; Median household: $43,950; Average household: $53,213; Households with income of $100,000 or more: 10.6%; Poverty rate: 14.0%
Educational Attainment: High school diploma or higher: 83.2%; Bachelor's degree or higher: 11.0%; Graduate/professional degree or higher: 4.1%
Housing: Homeownership rate: 79.9%; Median home value: $101,900; Median year structure built: 1979; Homeowner vacancy rate: 2.7%; Median gross rent: $679 per month; Rental vacancy rate: 9.4%
Vital Statistics: Birth rate: 104.2 per 10,000 population; Death rate: 105.2 per 10,000 population; Age-adjusted cancer mortality rate: 215.9 deaths per 100,000 population
Health Insurance: 82.1% have insurance; 62.9% have private insurance; 33.9% have public insurance; 17.9% do not have insurance; 13.7% of children under 18 do not have insurance

Health Care: Physicians: 3.3 per 10,000 population; Hospital beds: 0.0 per 10,000 population; Hospital admissions: 0.0 per 10,000 population
Transportation: Commute: 91.6% car, 1.5% public transportation, 2.5% walk, 2.8% work from home; Median travel time to work: 32.5 minutes
Presidential Election: 34.8% Obama, 62.4% Romney (2012)
National and State Parks: McCormicks Creek State Park
Additional Information Contacts
Owen Government . . . . (812) 829-5015
http://www.owencounty.in.gov

Owen County Communities

BOWLING GREEN (unincorporated postal area)
ZCTA: 47833
Covers a land area of 37.149 square miles and a water area of 0.007 square miles. Located at 39.36° N. Lat; 86.98° W. Long..
Population: 1,010; Growth (since 2000): 6.0%; Density: 27.2 persons per square mile; Race: 97.6% White, 0.2% Black/African American, 0.0% Asian, 0.7% American Indian/Alaska Native, 0.0% Native Hawaiian/Other Pacific Islander, 1.2% Two or more races, 0.7% Hispanic of any race; Average household size: 2.54; Median age: 41.9; Age under 18: 23.3%; Age 65 and over: 12.0%; Males per 100 females: 97.3
Housing: Homeownership rate: 82.2%; Homeowner vacancy rate: 0.6%; Rental vacancy rate: 5.3%

COAL CITY (unincorporated postal area)
ZCTA: 47427
Covers a land area of 53.257 square miles and a water area of 0.287 square miles. Located at 39.23° N. Lat; 87.02° W. Long. Elevation is 653 feet.
Population: 1,093; Growth (since 2000): 0.2%; Density: 20.5 persons per square mile; Race: 97.1% White, 0.0% Black/African American, 0.1% Asian, 1.5% American Indian/Alaska Native, 0.0% Native Hawaiian/Other Pacific Islander, 1.3% Two or more races, 0.3% Hispanic of any race; Average household size: 2.71; Median age: 40.3; Age under 18: 28.3%; Age 65 and over: 13.6%; Males per 100 females: 103.2
Housing: Homeownership rate: 87.2%; Homeowner vacancy rate: 2.2%; Rental vacancy rate: 13.3%

FREEDOM (unincorporated postal area)
ZCTA: 47431
Covers a land area of 36.963 square miles and a water area of 0.029 square miles. Located at 39.24° N. Lat; 86.90° W. Long. Elevation is 538 feet.
Population: 1,366; Growth (since 2000): 6.8%; Density: 37.0 persons per square mile; Race: 97.7% White, 0.4% Black/African American, 0.5% Asian, 0.4% American Indian/Alaska Native, 0.0% Native Hawaiian/Other Pacific Islander, 1.0% Two or more races, 1.0% Hispanic of any race; Average household size: 2.66; Median age: 41.6; Age under 18: 25.2%; Age 65 and over: 15.4%; Males per 100 females: 107.6
Housing: Homeownership rate: 86.7%; Homeowner vacancy rate: 4.1%; Rental vacancy rate: 9.2%

GOSPORT (town).
Covers a land area of 0.385 square miles and a water area of 0 square miles. Located at 39.35° N. Lat; 86.67° W. Long. Elevation is 696 feet.
History: Gosport was laid out in 1829 as a shipping point for trade on the White River.
Population: 826; Growth (since 2000): 15.5%; Density: 2,144.9 persons per square mile; Race: 98.5% White, 0.7% Black/African American, 0.1% Asian, 0.0% American Indian/Alaska Native, 0.0% Native Hawaiian/Other Pacific Islander, 0.6% Two or more races, 1.0% Hispanic of any race; Average household size: 2.42; Median age: 38.2; Age under 18: 25.8%; Age 65 and over: 16.8%; Males per 100 females: 85.2
School District(s)
Spencer-Owen Community Schools (PK-12)
    2012-13 Enrollment: 2,728 . . . . (812) 829-2233
Housing: Homeownership rate: 53.5%; Homeowner vacancy rate: 2.8%; Rental vacancy rate: 14.1%

PATRICKSBURG (unincorporated postal area)
ZCTA: 47455
Covers a land area of 0.562 square miles and a water area of 0 square miles. Located at 39.32° N. Lat; 86.96° W. Long. Elevation is 715 feet.
Population: 124; Growth (since 2000): -53.0%; Density: 220.8 persons per square mile; Race: 96.0% White, 0.8% Black/African American, 0.0% Asian, 0.8% American Indian/Alaska Native, 0.0% Native Hawaiian/Other Pacific Islander, 0.8% Two or more races, 1.6% Hispanic of any race; Average household size: 2.64; Median age: 31.5; Age under 18: 26.6%; Age 65 and over: 8.1%; Males per 100 females: 103.3
School District(s)
Spencer-Owen Community Schools (PK-12)
    2012-13 Enrollment: 2,728 . . . . (812) 829-2233
Housing: Homeownership rate: 59.5%; Homeowner vacancy rate: 0.0%; Rental vacancy rate: 26.9%

POLAND (unincorporated postal area)
ZCTA: 47868
Covers a land area of 58.105 square miles and a water area of 1.644 square miles. Located at 39.41° N. Lat; 86.90° W. Long..
Population: 2,937; Growth (since 2000): -8.6%; Density: 50.5 persons per square mile; Race: 98.0% White, 0.3% Black/African American, 0.1% Asian, 0.6% American Indian/Alaska Native, 0.0% Native Hawaiian/Other Pacific Islander, 0.8% Two or more races, 0.5% Hispanic of any race; Average household size: 2.51; Median age: 45.1; Age under 18: 21.4%; Age 65 and over: 13.9%; Males per 100 females: 103.1; Marriage status: 23.0% never married, 66.5% now married, 1.3% separated, 2.0% widowed, 8.5% divorced; Foreign born: 0.4%; Speak English only: 99.0%; With disability: 21.2%; Veterans: 13.7%; Ancestry: 30.2% German, 20.0% Irish, 12.1% American, 6.5% English, 3.3% Scottish
Employment: 10.1% management, business, and financial, 3.1% computer, engineering, and science, 6.9% education, legal, community service, arts, and media, 5.4% healthcare practitioners, 9.7% service, 12.5% sales and office, 21.3% natural resources, construction, and maintenance, 31.0% production, transportation, and material moving
Income: Per capita: $24,608; Median household: $57,708; Average household: $64,165; Households with income of $100,000 or more: 22.1%; Poverty rate: 14.8%
Educational Attainment: High school diploma or higher: 86.4%; Bachelor's degree or higher: 8.2%; Graduate/professional degree or higher: 2.3%
Housing: Homeownership rate: 83.4%; Median home value: $108,300; Median year structure built: 1980; Homeowner vacancy rate: 3.8%; Median gross rent: $723 per month; Rental vacancy rate: 8.4%
Health Insurance: 80.5% have insurance; 62.1% have private insurance; 28.8% have public insurance; 19.5% do not have insurance; 5.6% of children under 18 do not have insurance
Transportation: Commute: 95.0% car, 2.8% public transportation, 1.3% walk, 0.0% work from home; Median travel time to work: 45.5 minutes

QUINCY (unincorporated postal area)
ZCTA: 47456
Covers a land area of 26.271 square miles and a water area of 0.154 square miles. Located at 39.47° N. Lat; 86.69° W. Long. Elevation is 738 feet.
Population: 1,200; Growth (since 2000): 50.2%; Density: 45.7 persons per square mile; Race: 98.7% White, 0.0% Black/African American, 0.0% Asian, 0.3% American Indian/Alaska Native, 0.0% Native Hawaiian/Other Pacific Islander, 0.7% Two or more races, 0.4% Hispanic of any race; Average household size: 2.55; Median age: 43.4; Age under 18: 21.6%; Age 65 and over: 14.4%; Males per 100 females: 112.8
Housing: Homeownership rate: 85.4%; Homeowner vacancy rate: 2.2%; Rental vacancy rate: 12.7%

SPENCER (town). County seat.
Covers a land area of 1.261 square miles and a water area of 0 square miles. Located at 39.29° N. Lat; 86.77° W. Long. Elevation is 564 feet.
History: Spencer was a farming, coal mining, and quarrying center named for Captain Spencer of Kentucky, who was killed at the Battle of Tippecanoe. Spencer was the hometown of poets William Herschell (1873-1939) and William Vaughn Moody (1869-1910).
Population: 2,217; Growth (since 2000): -11.6%; Density: 1,758.5 persons per square mile; Race: 98.1% White, 0.1% Black/African American, 0.5% Asian, 0.2% American Indian/Alaska Native, 0.0% Native Hawaiian/Other

Pacific Islander, 0.9% Two or more races, 2.1% Hispanic of any race; Average household size: 2.12; Median age: 41.8; Age under 18: 20.1%; Age 65 and over: 19.8%; Males per 100 females: 89.5

School District(s)
Spencer-Owen Community Schools (PK-12)
  2012-13 Enrollment: 2,728 . . . . (812) 829-2233
Housing: Homeownership rate: 60.0%; Homeowner vacancy rate: 3.0%; Rental vacancy rate: 11.0%
Newspapers: Owen Leader (weekly circulation 400); Spencer Evening World (daily circulation 3600)
Additional Information Contacts
Town of Spencer . . . . (812) 829-3213
  http://www.spencer.in.gov

Parke County

Located in western Indiana; bounded on the west by the Wabash River; drained by Sugar and Raccoon Creeks. Covers a land area of 444.663 square miles, a water area of 5.316 square miles, and is located in the Eastern Time Zone at 39.77° N. Lat., 87.20° W. Long. The county was founded in 1821. County seat is Rockville.

Weather Station: Rockville   Elevation: 689 feet

	Jan	Feb	Mar	Apr	May	Jun	Jul	Aug	Sep	Oct	Nov	Dec
High	37	42	54	66	76	84	87	85	79	67	54	40
Low	21	24	33	43	52	61	65	64	55	44	35	25
Precip	2.8	2.5	3.4	4.1	5.4	4.5	5.1	4.0	3.3	3.8	4.2	3.6
Snow	5.1	2.9	1.7	0.1	tr	0.0	0.0	0.0	0.0	tr	0.1	3.9

High and Low temperatures in degrees Fahrenheit; Precipitation and Snow in inches

Population: 17,339; Growth (since 2000): 0.6%; Density: 39.0 persons per square mile; Race: 96.1% White, 2.3% Black/African American, 0.2% Asian, 0.4% American Indian/Alaska Native, 0.0% Native Hawaiian/Other Pacific Islander, 0.6% two or more races, 1.2% Hispanic of any race; Average household size: 2.51; Median age: 41.3; Age under 18: 21.4%; Age 65 and over: 15.6%; Males per 100 females: 88.1; Marriage status: 25.3% never married, 52.1% now married, 1.0% separated, 6.4% widowed, 16.1% divorced; Foreign born: 1.2%; Speak English only: 93.7%; With disability: 14.6%; Veterans: 10.3%; Ancestry: 27.1% American, 19.8% German, 11.5% English, 10.4% Irish, 3.4% Dutch
Religion: Six largest groups: 12.6% Baptist, 8.7% European Free-Church, 6.3% Non-denominational Protestant, 3.6% Methodist/Pietist, 1.3% Catholicism, 1.2% Pentecostal
Economy: Unemployment rate: 5.8%; Leading industries: 17.4% other services (except public administration); 16.7% retail trade; 9.3% accommodation and food services; Farms: 574 totaling 176,571 acres; Company size: 0 employ 1,000 or more persons, 0 employ 500 to 999 persons, 1 employs 100 to 499 persons, 257 employ less than 100 persons; Business ownership: n/a women-owned, n/a Black-owned, n/a Hispanic-owned, n/a Asian-owned
Employment: 10.0% management, business, and financial, 2.0% computer, engineering, and science, 6.2% education, legal, community service, arts, and media, 5.0% healthcare practitioners, 17.2% service, 21.6% sales and office, 13.7% natural resources, construction, and maintenance, 24.4% production, transportation, and material moving
Income: Per capita: $20,534; Median household: $43,870; Average household: $56,460; Households with income of $100,000 or more: 9.7%; Poverty rate: 13.3%
Educational Attainment: High school diploma or higher: 82.8%; Bachelor's degree or higher: 13.7%; Graduate/professional degree or higher: 4.4%
Housing: Homeownership rate: 79.2%; Median home value: $87,600; Median year structure built: 1972; Homeowner vacancy rate: 2.2%; Median gross rent: $590 per month; Rental vacancy rate: 10.9%
Vital Statistics: Birth rate: 109.3 per 10,000 population; Death rate: 94.8 per 10,000 population; Age-adjusted cancer mortality rate: 185.6 deaths per 100,000 population
Health Insurance: 81.3% have insurance; 61.9% have private insurance; 33.6% have public insurance; 18.7% do not have insurance; 18.0% of children under 18 do not have insurance
Health Care: Physicians: 4.7 per 10,000 population; Hospital beds: 0.0 per 10,000 population; Hospital admissions: 0.0 per 10,000 population
Transportation: Commute: 89.7% car, 0.9% public transportation, 2.7% walk, 5.0% work from home; Median travel time to work: 25.9 minutes
Presidential Election: 32.4% Obama, 65.0% Romney (2012)

National and State Parks: Raccoon Lake State Recreation Area; Turkey Run State Park
Additional Information Contacts
Parke Government . . . . (765) 569-5132
  http://www.parkecounty-in.gov

Parke County Communities

BLOOMINGDALE (town). Covers a land area of 0.582 square miles and a water area of 0 square miles. Located at 39.83° N. Lat; 87.25° W. Long. Elevation is 643 feet.
Population: 335; Growth (since 2000): 5.0%; Density: 576.0 persons per square mile; Race: 97.6% White, 0.3% Black/African American, 0.0% Asian, 0.0% American Indian/Alaska Native, 0.0% Native Hawaiian/Other Pacific Islander, 2.1% Two or more races, 0.3% Hispanic of any race; Average household size: 2.60; Median age: 38.5; Age under 18: 23.6%; Age 65 and over: 12.8%; Males per 100 females: 101.8
Housing: Homeownership rate: 87.6%; Homeowner vacancy rate: 1.7%; Rental vacancy rate: 0.0%

BRIDGETON (unincorporated postal area)
ZCTA: 47836
  Covers a land area of 0.197 square miles and a water area of 0 square miles. Located at 39.65° N. Lat; 87.18° W. Long. Elevation is 564 feet.
Population: 47; Growth (since 2000): -62.7%; Density: 238.9 persons per square mile; Race: 97.9% White, 0.0% Black/African American, 2.1% Asian, 0.0% American Indian/Alaska Native, 0.0% Native Hawaiian/Other Pacific Islander, 0.0% Two or more races, 0.0% Hispanic of any race; Average household size: 2.35; Median age: 43.5; Age under 18: 25.5%; Age 65 and over: 17.0%; Males per 100 females: 80.8
Housing: Homeownership rate: 90.0%; Homeowner vacancy rate: 0.0%; Rental vacancy rate: 0.0%

MARSHALL (town). Covers a land area of 0.256 square miles and a water area of 0 square miles. Located at 39.85° N. Lat; 87.19° W. Long. Elevation is 702 feet.
History: Covered bridges in area. Laid out 1878.
Population: 324; Growth (since 2000): -10.0%; Density: 1,266.0 persons per square mile; Race: 98.5% White, 0.0% Black/African American, 0.0% Asian, 1.2% American Indian/Alaska Native, 0.0% Native Hawaiian/Other Pacific Islander, 0.0% Two or more races, 1.2% Hispanic of any race; Average household size: 2.68; Median age: 39.6; Age under 18: 23.8%; Age 65 and over: 12.7%; Males per 100 females: 88.4
School District(s)
Turkey Run Community Sch Corp (KG-12)
  2012-13 Enrollment: 510 . . . . (765) 597-2750
Housing: Homeownership rate: 81.0%; Homeowner vacancy rate: 2.9%; Rental vacancy rate: 8.0%

MECCA (town). Covers a land area of 0.393 square miles and a water area of 0 square miles. Located at 39.73° N. Lat; 87.33° W. Long. Elevation is 512 feet.
History: Covered bridges in area. Laid out 1890.
Population: 335; Growth (since 2000): -5.6%; Density: 852.8 persons per square mile; Race: 97.6% White, 0.0% Black/African American, 0.3% Asian, 0.0% American Indian/Alaska Native, 0.0% Native Hawaiian/Other Pacific Islander, 1.2% Two or more races, 0.9% Hispanic of any race; Average household size: 2.70; Median age: 35.5; Age under 18: 30.1%; Age 65 and over: 15.5%; Males per 100 females: 113.4
Housing: Homeownership rate: 77.4%; Homeowner vacancy rate: 0.0%; Rental vacancy rate: 15.2%

MONTEZUMA (town). Covers a land area of 0.600 square miles and a water area of 0 square miles. Located at 39.79° N. Lat; 87.37° W. Long. Elevation is 505 feet.
History: When the Wabash & Erie Canal was completed in 1848, Montezuma became a commercial center on the Wabash River. Montezuma was settled by Samuel Hill in 1821, and named for the Aztec emperor of Mexico.
Population: 1,022; Growth (since 2000): -13.3%; Density: 1,702.0 persons per square mile; Race: 96.1% White, 0.2% Black/African American, 0.5% Asian, 0.4% American Indian/Alaska Native, 0.0% Native Hawaiian/Other Pacific Islander, 1.3% Two or more races, 4.3% Hispanic of any race;

Average household size: 2.45; Median age: 38.5; Age under 18: 26.8%; Age 65 and over: 15.0%; Males per 100 females: 102.0
School District(s)
Southwest Parke Com Sch Corp (KG-12)
    2012-13 Enrollment: 967 . . . . (765) 569-2073
Housing: Homeownership rate: 68.1%; Homeowner vacancy rate: 2.0%; Rental vacancy rate: 20.7%

ROCKVILLE (town). County seat. Covers a land area of 1.492 square miles and a water area of 0 square miles. Located at 39.77° N. Lat; 87.23° W. Long. Elevation is 712 feet.
History: Joseph A. Wright, a governor of Indiana, began his law practice in Rockville.
Population: 2,607; Growth (since 2000): -5.7%; Density: 1,746.8 persons per square mile; Race: 98.7% White, 0.1% Black/African American, 0.2% Asian, 0.5% American Indian/Alaska Native, 0.0% Native Hawaiian/Other Pacific Islander, 0.5% Two or more races, 0.7% Hispanic of any race; Average household size: 2.14; Median age: 44.8; Age under 18: 20.9%; Age 65 and over: 22.3%; Males per 100 females: 87.8; Marriage status: 30.3% never married, 38.8% now married, 2.3% separated, 9.4% widowed, 21.6% divorced; Foreign born: 2.2%; Speak English only: 96.8%; With disability: 22.2%; Veterans: 12.5%; Ancestry: 21.9% German, 18.7% American, 17.4% Irish, 15.0% English, 4.4% French
Employment: 6.3% management, business, and financial, 1.3% computer, engineering, and science, 6.5% education, legal, community service, arts, and media, 3.8% healthcare practitioners, 19.0% service, 26.3% sales and office, 6.8% natural resources, construction, and maintenance, 30.0% production, transportation, and material moving
Income: Per capita: $15,397; Median household: $30,000; Average household: $44,279; Households with income of $100,000 or more: 4.2%; Poverty rate: 16.4%
Educational Attainment: High school diploma or higher: 79.8%; Bachelor's degree or higher: 11.2%; Graduate/professional degree or higher: 4.2%
School District(s)
Rockville Community School Corp (KG-12)
    2012-13 Enrollment: 795 . . . . (765) 569-5582
Housing: Homeownership rate: 61.2%; Median home value: $82,200; Median year structure built: 1957; Homeowner vacancy rate: 3.9%; Median gross rent: $463 per month; Rental vacancy rate: 8.4%
Health Insurance: 81.3% have insurance; 58.4% have private insurance; 41.6% have public insurance; 18.7% do not have insurance; 10.9% of children under 18 do not have insurance
Newspapers: Parke County Sentinel (weekly circulation 4500)
Transportation: Commute: 94.8% car, 0.0% public transportation, 2.0% walk, 2.5% work from home; Median travel time to work: 19.5 minutes
Additional Information Contacts
Town of Rockville . . . . (765) 569-5226
http://www.new.rockvilleindiana.org

ROSEDALE (town). Covers a land area of 0.395 square miles and a water area of 0 square miles. Located at 39.62° N. Lat; 87.28° W. Long. Elevation is 538 feet.
History: Settled c.1819.
Population: 725; Growth (since 2000): -3.3%; Density: 1,836.4 persons per square mile; Race: 98.2% White, 0.0% Black/African American, 0.0% Asian, 0.1% American Indian/Alaska Native, 0.0% Native Hawaiian/Other Pacific Islander, 1.5% Two or more races, 1.1% Hispanic of any race; Average household size: 2.53; Median age: 36.4; Age under 18: 27.2%; Age 65 and over: 12.8%; Males per 100 females: 86.4
School District(s)
Southwest Parke Com Sch Corp (KG-12)
    2012-13 Enrollment: 967 . . . . (765) 569-2073
Housing: Homeownership rate: 76.3%; Homeowner vacancy rate: 4.4%; Rental vacancy rate: 8.1%

Perry County

Located in southern Indiana; bounded on the south and partly on the east by the Ohio River and the Kentucky border; drained by the Anderson River. Covers a land area of 381.727 square miles, a water area of 4.563 square miles, and is located in the Central Time Zone at 38.08° N. Lat., 86.63° W. Long. The county was founded in 1814. County seat is Cannelton.

Weather Station: Tell City   Elevation: 399 feet

	Jan	Feb	Mar	Apr	May	Jun	Jul	Aug	Sep	Oct	Nov	Dec
High	42	46	56	67	76	84	87	87	81	70	57	45
Low	26	28	36	45	55	64	68	67	59	47	39	29
Precip	3.3	3.2	4.3	4.3	5.8	4.4	4.5	3.4	3.6	3.4	3.8	4.1
Snow	1.8	2.2	0.4	tr	0.0	0.0	0.0	0.0	0.0	0.0	0.1	0.8

High and Low temperatures in degrees Fahrenheit; Precipitation and Snow in inches

Population: 19,338; Growth (since 2000): 2.3%; Density: 50.7 persons per square mile; Race: 96.0% White, 2.4% Black/African American, 0.4% Asian, 0.2% American Indian/Alaska Native, 0.0% Native Hawaiian/Other Pacific Islander, 0.8% two or more races, 1.0% Hispanic of any race; Average household size: 2.38; Median age: 40.4; Age under 18: 21.4%; Age 65 and over: 15.2%; Males per 100 females: 112.8; Marriage status: 24.7% never married, 54.8% now married, 0.7% separated, 6.6% widowed, 14.0% divorced; Foreign born: 0.4%; Speak English only: 97.8%; With disability: 14.9%; Veterans: 9.2%; Ancestry: 33.6% German, 12.6% American, 11.0% Irish, 8.3% English, 7.7% French
Religion: Six largest groups: 30.8% Catholicism, 6.3% Baptist, 2.9% Methodist/Pietist, 2.6% Presbyterian-Reformed, 1.6% Latter-day Saints, 1.3% Lutheran
Economy: Unemployment rate: 4.8%; Leading industries: 17.7% retail trade; 11.4% other services (except public administration); 10.9% accommodation and food services; Farms: 413 totaling 66,275 acres; Company size: 0 employ 1,000 or more persons, 1 employs 500 to 999 persons, 6 employ 100 to 499 persons, 360 employ less than 100 persons; Business ownership: 353 women-owned, n/a Black-owned, n/a Hispanic-owned, n/a Asian-owned
Employment: 7.9% management, business, and financial, 2.1% computer, engineering, and science, 5.0% education, legal, community service, arts, and media, 5.0% healthcare practitioners, 18.3% service, 18.0% sales and office, 11.7% natural resources, construction, and maintenance, 32.0% production, transportation, and material moving
Income: Per capita: $20,934; Median household: $47,596; Average household: $54,398; Households with income of $100,000 or more: 11.8%; Poverty rate: 10.9%
Educational Attainment: High school diploma or higher: 84.0%; Bachelor's degree or higher: 10.9%; Graduate/professional degree or higher: 4.9%
Housing: Homeownership rate: 76.5%; Median home value: $97,300; Median year structure built: 1969; Homeowner vacancy rate: 2.9%; Median gross rent: $568 per month; Rental vacancy rate: 8.0%
Vital Statistics: Birth rate: 114.5 per 10,000 population; Death rate: 89.5 per 10,000 population; Age-adjusted cancer mortality rate: 208.2 deaths per 100,000 population
Health Insurance: 89.4% have insurance; 72.9% have private insurance; 30.9% have public insurance; 10.6% do not have insurance; 4.8% of children under 18 do not have insurance
Health Care: Physicians: 6.2 per 10,000 population; Hospital beds: 12.8 per 10,000 population; Hospital admissions: 702.0 per 10,000 population
Air Quality Index: 91.8% good, 8.2% moderate, 0.0% unhealthy for sensitive individuals, 0.0% unhealthy (percent of days)
Transportation: Commute: 96.1% car, 0.1% public transportation, 1.1% walk, 1.7% work from home; Median travel time to work: 22.6 minutes
Presidential Election: 54.8% Obama, 43.2% Romney (2012)
National and State Parks: Ferdinand State Forest; Harrison-Crawford State Forest
Additional Information Contacts
Perry Government . . . . (812) 547-6427
http://www.perrycounty.in.gov

Perry County Communities

BRANCHVILLE (unincorporated postal area)
ZCTA: 47514
    Covers a land area of 4.398 square miles and a water area of 0 square miles. Located at 38.16° N. Lat; 86.59° W. Long. Elevation is 433 feet.
    Population: 1,559; Growth (since 2000): 516.2%; Density: 354.4 persons per square mile; Race: 71.1% White, 28.0% Black/African American, 0.3% Asian, 0.0% American Indian/Alaska Native, 0.0% Native Hawaiian/Other Pacific Islander, 0.1% Two or more races, 1.7% Hispanic of any race; Average household size: 2.66; Median age: 32.4; Age under 18: 3.8%; Age 65 and over: 1.9%; Males per 100 females: ***.*

Housing: Homeownership rate: 87.6%; Homeowner vacancy rate: 0.0%; Rental vacancy rate: 8.3%

BRISTOW (unincorporated postal area)
ZCTA: 47515

Covers a land area of 55.762 square miles and a water area of 0.235 square miles. Located at 38.18° N. Lat; 86.70° W. Long. Elevation is 410 feet.

Population: 965; Growth (since 2000): -13.1%; Density: 17.3 persons per square mile; Race: 98.8% White, 0.0% Black/African American, 0.0% Asian, 0.2% American Indian/Alaska Native, 0.1% Native Hawaiian/Other Pacific Islander, 0.5% Two or more races, 0.8% Hispanic of any race; Average household size: 2.59; Median age: 40.2; Age under 18: 23.4%; Age 65 and over: 13.0%; Males per 100 females: 102.7

Housing: Homeownership rate: 88.4%; Homeowner vacancy rate: 1.5%; Rental vacancy rate: 8.5%

CANNELTON (city).
County seat. Covers a land area of 1.482 square miles and a water area of 0.102 square miles. Located at 37.91° N. Lat; 86.74° W. Long. Elevation is 410 feet.

History: Cannelton was founded in 1837 as a coal-mining town and shipping port on the Ohio River.

Population: 1,563; Growth (since 2000): 29.3%; Density: 1,054.8 persons per square mile; Race: 97.4% White, 0.1% Black/African American, 0.1% Asian, 0.6% American Indian/Alaska Native, 0.0% Native Hawaiian/Other Pacific Islander, 1.3% Two or more races, 0.8% Hispanic of any race; Average household size: 2.23; Median age: 38.5; Age under 18: 25.3%; Age 65 and over: 14.8%; Males per 100 females: 95.1

School District(s)
Cannelton City Schools (PK-12)
    2012-13 Enrollment: 242 . . . . (812) 547-2637

Housing: Homeownership rate: 49.9%; Homeowner vacancy rate: 5.0%; Rental vacancy rate: 10.1%

DERBY (unincorporated postal area)
ZCTA: 47525

Covers a land area of 28.878 square miles and a water area of 0.452 square miles. Located at 38.03° N. Lat; 86.56° W. Long. Elevation is 453 feet.

Population: 382; Growth (since 2000): -8.6%; Density: 13.2 persons per square mile; Race: 99.2% White, 0.0% Black/African American, 0.0% Asian, 0.0% American Indian/Alaska Native, 0.0% Native Hawaiian/Other Pacific Islander, 0.8% Two or more races, 0.5% Hispanic of any race; Average household size: 2.45; Median age: 47.5; Age under 18: 17.3%; Age 65 and over: 19.9%; Males per 100 females: 103.2

Housing: Homeownership rate: 88.5%; Homeowner vacancy rate: 2.1%; Rental vacancy rate: 0.0%

LEOPOLD (unincorporated postal area)
ZCTA: 47551

Covers a land area of 32.182 square miles and a water area of 0.011 square miles. Located at 38.11° N. Lat; 86.57° W. Long. Elevation is 725 feet.

Population: 649; Growth (since 2000): 14.3%; Density: 20.2 persons per square mile; Race: 98.9% White, 0.0% Black/African American, 0.0% Asian, 0.0% American Indian/Alaska Native, 0.0% Native Hawaiian/Other Pacific Islander, 1.1% Two or more races, 0.3% Hispanic of any race; Average household size: 2.79; Median age: 36.7; Age under 18: 29.9%; Age 65 and over: 12.0%; Males per 100 females: 107.3

School District(s)
Perry Central Com Schools Corp (PK-12)
    2012-13 Enrollment: 1,190 . . . . (812) 843-5576

Housing: Homeownership rate: 96.1%; Homeowner vacancy rate: 1.3%; Rental vacancy rate: 18.2%

ROME (unincorporated postal area)
ZCTA: 47574

Covers a land area of 14.548 square miles and a water area of 0.493 square miles. Located at 37.95° N. Lat; 86.56° W. Long. Elevation is 410 feet.

Population: 148; Growth (since 2000): -11.4%; Density: 10.2 persons per square mile; Race: 99.3% White, 0.7% Black/African American, 0.0% Asian, 0.0% American Indian/Alaska Native, 0.0% Native Hawaiian/Other Pacific Islander, 0.0% Two or more races, 0.0% Hispanic of any race; Average household size: 2.69; Median age: 47.0; Age under 18: 27.0%; Age 65 and over: 21.6%; Males per 100 females: 102.7

Housing: Homeownership rate: 83.6%; Homeowner vacancy rate: 4.2%; Rental vacancy rate: 0.0%

SAINT CROIX (unincorporated postal area)
ZCTA: 47576

Covers a land area of 21.766 square miles and a water area of 0.209 square miles. Located at 38.18° N. Lat; 86.62° W. Long. Elevation is 725 feet.

Population: 388; Growth (since 2000): -16.0%; Density: 17.8 persons per square mile; Race: 98.7% White, 0.0% Black/African American, 0.0% Asian, 0.0% American Indian/Alaska Native, 0.0% Native Hawaiian/Other Pacific Islander, 1.3% Two or more races, 0.0% Hispanic of any race; Average household size: 2.52; Median age: 41.7; Age under 18: 24.0%; Age 65 and over: 10.6%; Males per 100 females: 112.0

Housing: Homeownership rate: 84.4%; Homeowner vacancy rate: 0.7%; Rental vacancy rate: 0.0%

TELL CITY (city).
Covers a land area of 4.534 square miles and a water area of 0.105 square miles. Located at 37.95° N. Lat; 86.76° W. Long. Elevation is 420 feet.

History: Tell City was settled in 1857 by a group of Swiss immigrants, and named for the legendary Swiss hero William Tell. An early industry was furniture making.

Population: 7,272; Growth (since 2000): -7.3%; Density: 1,603.9 persons per square mile; Race: 97.5% White, 0.3% Black/African American, 0.7% Asian, 0.3% American Indian/Alaska Native, 0.0% Native Hawaiian/Other Pacific Islander, 0.9% Two or more races, 1.0% Hispanic of any race; Average household size: 2.23; Median age: 42.0; Age under 18: 22.0%; Age 65 and over: 19.3%; Males per 100 females: 90.3; Marriage status: 23.1% never married, 52.9% now married, 0.9% separated, 8.9% widowed, 15.1% divorced; Foreign born: 0.3%; Speak English only: 99.5%; With disability: 17.1%; Veterans: 8.7%; Ancestry: 35.5% German, 13.9% Irish, 12.1% American, 8.8% English, 6.8% French

Employment: 6.8% management, business, and financial, 2.4% computer, engineering, and science, 4.9% education, legal, community service, arts, and media, 5.4% healthcare practitioners, 19.8% service, 19.4% sales and office, 10.1% natural resources, construction, and maintenance, 31.1% production, transportation, and material moving

Income: Per capita: $23,264; Median household: $45,123; Average household: $52,784; Households with income of $100,000 or more: 10.1%; Poverty rate: 11.2%

Educational Attainment: High school diploma or higher: 84.6%; Bachelor's degree or higher: 13.5%; Graduate/professional degree or higher: 6.4%

School District(s)
Tell City-Troy Twp School Corp (KG-12)
    2012-13 Enrollment: 1,507 . . . . (812) 547-3300

Housing: Homeownership rate: 69.1%; Median home value: $90,200; Median year structure built: 1962; Homeowner vacancy rate: 4.2%; Median gross rent: $605 per month; Rental vacancy rate: 7.3%

Health Insurance: 89.8% have insurance; 71.4% have private insurance; 33.8% have public insurance; 10.2% do not have insurance; 1.3% of children under 18 do not have insurance

Hospitals: Perry County Memorial Hospital (38 beds)

Safety: Violent crime rate: 5.5 per 10,000 population; Property crime rate: 189.5 per 10,000 population

Newspapers: The Perry County News (weekly circulation 7400)

Transportation: Commute: 96.6% car, 0.0% public transportation, 1.9% walk, 0.9% work from home; Median travel time to work: 18.5 minutes

Additional Information Contacts
City of Tell City . . . . (812) 547-2349
    http://www.tellcityindiana.com

TROY (town).
Covers a land area of 0.318 square miles and a water area of 0 square miles. Located at 38.00° N. Lat; 86.80° W. Long. Elevation is 472 feet.

History: Troy was founded by families from Virginia. It served as the seat of Perry County until 1818.

Population: 385; Growth (since 2000): -1.8%; Density: 1,209.2 persons per square mile; Race: 98.4% White, 0.0% Black/African American, 0.0% Asian, 0.0% American Indian/Alaska Native, 0.0% Native Hawaiian/Other Pacific Islander, 1.6% Two or more races, 1.3% Hispanic of any race; Average household size: 2.36; Median age: 38.8; Age under 18: 23.4%; Age 65 and over: 14.5%; Males per 100 females: 86.0
Housing: Homeownership rate: 69.3%; Homeowner vacancy rate: 5.8%; Rental vacancy rate: 16.7%

Pike County

Located in southwestern Indiana; bounded on the north by the White River; drained by the Patoka River. Covers a land area of 334.238 square miles, a water area of 6.856 square miles, and is located in the Eastern Time Zone at 38.40° N. Lat., 87.23° W. Long. The county was founded in 1816. County seat is Petersburg.

Pike County is part of the Jasper, IN Micropolitan Statistical Area. The entire metro area includes: Dubois County, IN; Pike County, IN

Population: 12,845; Growth (since 2000): 0.1%; Density: 38.4 persons per square mile; Race: 98.2% White, 0.3% Black/African American, 0.2% Asian, 0.2% American Indian/Alaska Native, 0.0% Native Hawaiian/Other Pacific Islander, 0.8% two or more races, 0.9% Hispanic of any race; Average household size: 2.44; Median age: 42.8; Age under 18: 22.4%; Age 65 and over: 16.9%; Males per 100 females: 99.9; Marriage status: 20.2% never married, 60.0% now married, 1.4% separated, 7.3% widowed, 12.5% divorced; Foreign born: 0.4%; Speak English only: 99.1%; With disability: 17.5%; Veterans: 10.7%; Ancestry: 25.0% American, 23.0% German, 12.3% Irish, 11.0% English, 2.6% French
Religion: Six largest groups: 7.6% Methodist/Pietist, 7.3% Baptist, 4.2% Holiness, 2.9% Catholicism, 2.1% Lutheran, 1.0% Pentecostal
Economy: Unemployment rate: 4.9%; Leading industries: 18.2% other services (except public administration); 15.3% retail trade; 8.4% health care and social assistance; Farms: 321 totaling 80,016 acres; Company size: 0 employ 1,000 or more persons, 0 employ 500 to 999 persons, 4 employ 100 to 499 persons, 199 employ less than 100 persons; Business ownership: n/a women-owned, n/a Black-owned, n/a Hispanic-owned, n/a Asian-owned
Employment: 10.5% management, business, and financial, 2.3% computer, engineering, and science, 7.4% education, legal, community service, arts, and media, 2.9% healthcare practitioners, 11.4% service, 20.3% sales and office, 12.4% natural resources, construction, and maintenance, 32.7% production, transportation, and material moving
Income: Per capita: $22,245; Median household: $40,680; Average household: $54,064; Households with income of $100,000 or more: 10.7%; Poverty rate: 12.7%
Educational Attainment: High school diploma or higher: 85.8%; Bachelor's degree or higher: 11.2%; Graduate/professional degree or higher: 4.1%
Housing: Homeownership rate: 82.4%; Median home value: $85,800; Median year structure built: 1970; Homeowner vacancy rate: 1.9%; Median gross rent: $596 per month; Rental vacancy rate: 7.4%
Vital Statistics: Birth rate: 116.7 per 10,000 population; Death rate: 112.7 per 10,000 population; Age-adjusted cancer mortality rate: 200.2 deaths per 100,000 population
Health Insurance: 87.0% have insurance; 67.1% have private insurance; 35.5% have public insurance; 13.0% do not have insurance; 5.7% of children under 18 do not have insurance
Health Care: Physicians: 1.6 per 10,000 population; Hospital beds: 0.0 per 10,000 population; Hospital admissions: 0.0 per 10,000 population
Air Quality Index: 87.7% good, 6.8% moderate, 4.9% unhealthy for sensitive individuals, 0.5% unhealthy (percent of days)
Transportation: Commute: 94.9% car, 0.3% public transportation, 1.6% walk, 2.2% work from home; Median travel time to work: 25.2 minutes
Presidential Election: 35.9% Obama, 61.2% Romney (2012)
National and State Parks: Patoka State Fish and Wildlife Area; Pike State Forest
Additional Information Contacts
Pike Government . . . . (812) 354-8448

Pike County Communities

OTWELL (CDP). Covers a land area of 1.785 square miles and a water area of 0.004 square miles. Located at 38.46° N. Lat; 87.10° W. Long. Elevation is 499 feet.
Population: 434; Growth (since 2000): n/a; Density: 243.2 persons per square mile; Race: 97.7% White, 0.7% Black/African American, 0.2% Asian, 0.0% American Indian/Alaska Native, 0.0% Native Hawaiian/Other Pacific Islander, 0.9% Two or more races, 2.1% Hispanic of any race; Average household size: 1.99; Median age: 46.9; Age under 18: 17.7%; Age 65 and over: 21.0%; Males per 100 females: 87.9
School District(s)
Pike County School Corp (PK-12)
    2012-13 Enrollment: 1,981 . . . . (812) 354-8731
Housing: Homeownership rate: 66.5%; Homeowner vacancy rate: 2.0%; Rental vacancy rate: 3.8%

PETERSBURG (city). County seat. Covers a land area of 1.466 square miles and a water area of 0.004 square miles. Located at 38.49° N. Lat; 87.28° W. Long. Elevation is 482 feet.
History: Laid out 1817, incorporated 1924.
Population: 2,383; Growth (since 2000): -7.3%; Density: 1,625.5 persons per square mile; Race: 97.7% White, 0.5% Black/African American, 0.5% Asian, 0.3% American Indian/Alaska Native, 0.0% Native Hawaiian/Other Pacific Islander, 0.8% Two or more races, 0.9% Hispanic of any race; Average household size: 2.18; Median age: 43.8; Age under 18: 20.0%; Age 65 and over: 21.1%; Males per 100 females: 94.5
School District(s)
Pike County School Corp (PK-12)
    2012-13 Enrollment: 1,981 . . . . (812) 354-8731
Housing: Homeownership rate: 65.6%; Homeowner vacancy rate: 3.1%; Rental vacancy rate: 3.3%
Newspapers: Press Dispatch (weekly circulation 5700)
Additional Information Contacts
City of Petersburg . . . . (812) 354-8511
http://www.petersburg.in.gov

SPURGEON (town). Covers a land area of 0.175 square miles and a water area of <.001 square miles. Located at 38.26° N. Lat; 87.26° W. Long. Elevation is 502 feet.
History: Laid out 1860.
Population: 207; Growth (since 2000): -8.8%; Density: 1,180.3 persons per square mile; Race: 95.7% White, 0.0% Black/African American, 0.0% Asian, 0.0% American Indian/Alaska Native, 0.0% Native Hawaiian/Other Pacific Islander, 0.5% Two or more races, 3.4% Hispanic of any race; Average household size: 2.65; Median age: 40.4; Age under 18: 25.1%; Age 65 and over: 10.1%; Males per 100 females: 105.0
Housing: Homeownership rate: 80.7%; Homeowner vacancy rate: 1.5%; Rental vacancy rate: 16.7%

STENDAL (unincorporated postal area)
ZCTA: 47585
    Covers a land area of 35.405 square miles and a water area of 0.635 square miles. Located at 38.27° N. Lat; 87.16° W. Long. Elevation is 610 feet.
    Population: 592; Growth (since 2000): 25.2%; Density: 16.7 persons per square mile; Race: 97.1% White, 0.8% Black/African American, 0.2% Asian, 0.0% American Indian/Alaska Native, 0.0% Native Hawaiian/Other Pacific Islander, 1.7% Two or more races, 1.2% Hispanic of any race; Average household size: 2.36; Median age: 46.1; Age under 18: 19.9%; Age 65 and over: 19.4%; Males per 100 females: 98.7
    Housing: Homeownership rate: 86.1%; Homeowner vacancy rate: 1.8%; Rental vacancy rate: 5.4%

VELPEN (unincorporated postal area)
ZCTA: 47590
    Covers a land area of 39.432 square miles and a water area of 0.494 square miles. Located at 38.36° N. Lat; 87.10° W. Long. Elevation is 492 feet.
    Population: 713; Growth (since 2000): -4.6%; Density: 18.1 persons per square mile; Race: 98.3% White, 0.1% Black/African American, 0.1% Asian, 0.0% American Indian/Alaska Native, 0.0% Native Hawaiian/Other Pacific Islander, 1.3% Two or more races, 1.0%

Hispanic of any race; Average household size: 2.64; Median age: 38.1; Age under 18: 26.5%; Age 65 and over: 11.2%; Males per 100 females: 114.8
Housing: Homeownership rate: 91.1%; Homeowner vacancy rate: 2.0%; Rental vacancy rate: 7.4%

WINSLOW (town). Covers a land area of 0.634 square miles and a water area of 0.009 square miles. Located at 38.38° N. Lat; 87.21° W. Long. Elevation is 443 feet.
History: Winslow developed as a coal-mining town
Population: 864; Growth (since 2000): -1.9%; Density: 1,363.8 persons per square mile; Race: 97.8% White, 0.1% Black/African American, 0.1% Asian, 0.6% American Indian/Alaska Native, 0.0% Native Hawaiian/Other Pacific Islander, 1.3% Two or more races, 2.1% Hispanic of any race; Average household size: 2.57; Median age: 38.6; Age under 18: 26.5%; Age 65 and over: 15.9%; Males per 100 females: 88.2

School District(s)
Pike County School Corp (PK-12)
    2012-13 Enrollment: 1,981 . . . . (812) 354-8731
Housing: Homeownership rate: 72.9%; Homeowner vacancy rate: 5.8%; Rental vacancy rate: 13.3%

Porter County

Located in northwestern Indiana; bounded on the north by Lake Michigan, and on the south by the Kankakee River; drained by the Little Calumet and Grand Calumet Rivers. Covers a land area of 418.153 square miles, a water area of 103.628 square miles, and is located in the Central Time Zone at 41.51° N. Lat., 87.07° W. Long. The county was founded in 1835. County seat is Valparaiso.

Porter County is part of the Chicago-Naperville-Elgin, IL-IN-WI Metropolitan Statistical Area. The entire metro area includes: Chicago-Naperville-Arlington Heights, IL Metropolitan Division (Cook County, IL; DuPage County, IL; Grundy County, IL; Kendall County, IL; McHenry County, IL; Will County, IL); Elgin, IL Metropolitan Division (DeKalb County, IL; Kane County, IL); Gary, IN Metropolitan Division (Jasper County, IN; Lake County, IN; Newton County, IN; Porter County, IN); Lake County-Kenosha County, IL-WI Metropolitan Division (Lake County, IL; Kenosha County, WI)

Weather Station: Valparaiso Waterworks   Elevation: 799 feet

	Jan	Feb	Mar	Apr	May	Jun	Jul	Aug	Sep	Oct	Nov	Dec
High	32	37	47	60	71	80	83	81	75	63	49	36
Low	17	21	29	39	49	58	63	62	54	43	34	23
Precip	2.2	1.9	2.6	3.5	4.1	4.5	4.2	3.9	3.3	3.2	3.8	2.6
Snow	12.7	8.1	6.0	1.1	tr	0.0	0.0	0.0	0.0	0.2	2.2	9.5

High and Low temperatures in degrees Fahrenheit; Precipitation and Snow in inches

Weather Station: Wanatah 2 WNW   Elevation: 734 feet

	Jan	Feb	Mar	Apr	May	Jun	Jul	Aug	Sep	Oct	Nov	Dec
High	32	36	47	60	71	80	83	82	76	63	49	36
Low	15	18	27	37	47	57	61	59	50	40	31	20
Precip	1.9	1.7	2.5	3.3	3.8	4.1	4.2	4.3	3.4	3.5	3.4	2.3
Snow	11.9	9.5	4.9	0.8	tr	0.0	0.0	0.0	0.3	1.8	9.0

High and Low temperatures in degrees Fahrenheit; Precipitation and Snow in inches

Population: 164,343; Growth (since 2000): 12.0%; Density: 393.0 persons per square mile; Race: 91.3% White, 3.0% Black/African American, 1.2% Asian, 0.3% American Indian/Alaska Native, 0.0% Native Hawaiian/Other Pacific Islander, 1.9% two or more races, 8.5% Hispanic of any race; Average household size: 2.60; Median age: 38.4; Age under 18: 24.3%; Age 65 and over: 12.4%; Males per 100 females: 96.6; Marriage status: 28.3% never married, 54.9% now married, 1.3% separated, 5.6% widowed, 11.3% divorced; Foreign born: 3.7%; Speak English only: 93.4%; With disability: 10.9%; Veterans: 9.5%; Ancestry: 28.2% German, 18.0% Irish, 10.3% Polish, 8.6% English, 5.9% Italian
Religion: Six largest groups: 18.0% Catholicism, 4.7% Lutheran, 4.3% Methodist/Pietist, 3.9% Non-denominational Protestant, 2.9% Holiness, 2.4% Baptist
Economy: Unemployment rate: 5.5%; Leading industries: 12.9% retail trade; 11.4% other services (except public administration); 11.0% health care and social assistance; Farms: 481 totaling 120,554 acres; Company size: 4 employ 1,000 or more persons, 1 employs 500 to 999 persons, 61 employs 100 to 499 persons, 3,394 employ less than 100 persons; Business ownership: 3,621 women-owned, 179 Black-owned, 381 Hispanic-owned, 182 Asian-owned
Employment: 12.3% management, business, and financial, 3.9% computer, engineering, and science, 10.0% education, legal, community service, arts, and media, 7.1% healthcare practitioners, 17.1% service, 23.3% sales and office, 11.1% natural resources, construction, and maintenance, 15.2% production, transportation, and material moving
Income: Per capita: $28,669; Median household: $62,794; Average household: $75,404; Households with income of $100,000 or more: 26.3%; Poverty rate: 10.4%
Educational Attainment: High school diploma or higher: 91.4%; Bachelor's degree or higher: 25.4%; Graduate/professional degree or higher: 9.1%
Housing: Homeownership rate: 76.3%; Median home value: $165,700; Median year structure built: 1978; Homeowner vacancy rate: 1.7%; Median gross rent: $857 per month; Rental vacancy rate: 7.6%
Vital Statistics: Birth rate: 103.9 per 10,000 population; Death rate: 86.7 per 10,000 population; Age-adjusted cancer mortality rate: 182.8 deaths per 100,000 population
Health Insurance: 88.6% have insurance; 77.3% have private insurance; 23.3% have public insurance; 11.4% do not have insurance; 4.4% of children under 18 do not have insurance
Health Care: Physicians: 18.1 per 10,000 population; Hospital beds: 16.7 per 10,000 population; Hospital admissions: 813.4 per 10,000 population
Air Quality Index: 66.6% good, 32.9% moderate, 0.3% unhealthy for sensitive individuals, 0.3% unhealthy (percent of days)
Transportation: Commute: 93.2% car, 1.2% public transportation, 1.4% walk, 3.4% work from home; Median travel time to work: 26.8 minutes
Presidential Election: 51.0% Obama, 47.2% Romney (2012)
National and State Parks: Indiana Dunes National Lakeshore; Indiana Dunes State Park
Additional Information Contacts
Porter Government . . . . (219) 926-2255
    http://www.porterco.org

Porter County Communities

ABERDEEN (CDP). Covers a land area of 1.257 square miles and a water area of 0 square miles. Located at 41.44° N. Lat; 87.12° W. Long. Elevation is 725 feet.
Population: 1,875; Growth (since 2000): n/a; Density: 1,491.2 persons per square mile; Race: 91.1% White, 3.3% Black/African American, 2.6% Asian, 0.0% American Indian/Alaska Native, 0.0% Native Hawaiian/Other Pacific Islander, 2.0% Two or more races, 5.4% Hispanic of any race; Average household size: 2.53; Median age: 39.0; Age under 18: 27.1%; Age 65 and over: 11.2%; Males per 100 females: 95.5
Housing: Homeownership rate: 75.1%; Homeowner vacancy rate: 2.6%; Rental vacancy rate: 10.1%

BEVERLY SHORES (town). Covers a land area of 3.583 square miles and a water area of 2.245 square miles. Located at 41.69° N. Lat; 86.98° W. Long. Elevation is 620 feet.
Population: 613; Growth (since 2000): -13.4%; Density: 171.1 persons per square mile; Race: 96.6% White, 1.3% Black/African American, 0.3% Asian, 0.0% American Indian/Alaska Native, 0.0% Native Hawaiian/Other Pacific Islander, 1.0% Two or more races, 2.8% Hispanic of any race; Average household size: 1.96; Median age: 59.0; Age under 18: 9.8%; Age 65 and over: 34.1%; Males per 100 females: 101.0
Housing: Homeownership rate: 87.2%; Homeowner vacancy rate: 2.9%; Rental vacancy rate: 12.2%

BURNS HARBOR (town). Covers a land area of 6.665 square miles and a water area of 0.119 square miles. Located at 41.62° N. Lat; 87.12° W. Long. Elevation is 610 feet.
Population: 1,156; Growth (since 2000): 50.9%; Density: 173.4 persons per square mile; Race: 95.4% White, 1.8% Black/African American, 0.3% Asian, 0.3% American Indian/Alaska Native, 0.0% Native Hawaiian/Other Pacific Islander, 1.1% Two or more races, 5.8% Hispanic of any race; Average household size: 2.54; Median age: 34.6; Age under 18: 26.2%; Age 65 and over: 10.6%; Males per 100 females: 103.2
Housing: Homeownership rate: 84.4%; Homeowner vacancy rate: 1.8%; Rental vacancy rate: 15.5%

CHESTERTON (town). Covers a land area of 9.332 square miles and a water area of 0.113 square miles. Located at 41.60° N. Lat; 87.05° W. Long. Elevation is 640 feet.
History: Chesterton was first incorporated on October 5, 1869, ending the use of the former name, Calumet.
Population: 13,068; Growth (since 2000): 24.6%; Density: 1,400.3 persons per square mile; Race: 92.7% White, 1.4% Black/African American, 2.1% Asian, 0.3% American Indian/Alaska Native, 0.0% Native Hawaiian/Other Pacific Islander, 1.7% Two or more races, 6.9% Hispanic of any race; Average household size: 2.58; Median age: 37.8; Age under 18: 26.5%; Age 65 and over: 11.3%; Males per 100 females: 94.8; Marriage status: 28.2% never married, 57.3% now married, 1.5% separated, 3.0% widowed, 11.6% divorced; Foreign born: 3.6%; Speak English only: 94.0%; With disability: 8.6%; Veterans: 9.4%; Ancestry: 32.2% German, 17.5% Irish, 9.8% Polish, 7.7% Italian, 7.7% English
Employment: 14.2% management, business, and financial, 3.6% computer, engineering, and science, 9.4% education, legal, community service, arts, and media, 7.3% healthcare practitioners, 12.8% service, 25.0% sales and office, 8.8% natural resources, construction, and maintenance, 19.0% production, transportation, and material moving
Income: Per capita: $31,877; Median household: $68,673; Average household: $85,575; Households with income of $100,000 or more: 30.5%; Poverty rate: 9.6%
Educational Attainment: High school diploma or higher: 91.8%; Bachelor's degree or higher: 30.5%; Graduate/professional degree or higher: 12.2%

School District(s)
Duneland School Corporation (KG-12)
    2012-13 Enrollment: 5,957 . . . . (219) 983-3600
Housing: Homeownership rate: 70.7%; Median home value: $168,900; Median year structure built: 1980; Homeowner vacancy rate: 2.1%; Median gross rent: $890 per month; Rental vacancy rate: 7.8%
Health Insurance: 92.1% have insurance; 84.3% have private insurance; 19.7% have public insurance; 7.9% do not have insurance; 2.4% of children under 18 do not have insurance
Newspapers: Chesterton Tribune (daily circulation 5100)
Transportation: Commute: 93.5% car, 2.4% public transportation, 0.7% walk, 3.4% work from home; Median travel time to work: 25.5 minutes
Additional Information Contacts
Town of Chesterton . . . . (219) 926-1641
    http://www.chestertonin.org

DUNE ACRES (town). Covers a land area of 2.172 square miles and a water area of 1.266 square miles. Located at 41.65° N. Lat; 87.10° W. Long. Elevation is 627 feet.
Population: 182; Growth (since 2000): -14.6%; Density: 83.8 persons per square mile; Race: 95.1% White, 1.1% Black/African American, 2.2% Asian, 0.0% American Indian/Alaska Native, 0.0% Native Hawaiian/Other Pacific Islander, 1.1% Two or more races, 1.6% Hispanic of any race; Average household size: 1.94; Median age: 63.4; Age under 18: 8.8%; Age 65 and over: 46.7%; Males per 100 females: 109.2
Housing: Homeownership rate: 93.6%; Homeowner vacancy rate: 3.3%; Rental vacancy rate: 0.0%

HEBRON (town). Covers a land area of 1.976 square miles and a water area of 0 square miles. Located at 41.32° N. Lat; 87.20° W. Long. Elevation is 709 feet.
Population: 3,724; Growth (since 2000): 3.6%; Density: 1,884.8 persons per square mile; Race: 95.9% White, 1.1% Black/African American, 0.4% Asian, 0.2% American Indian/Alaska Native, 0.0% Native Hawaiian/Other Pacific Islander, 1.6% Two or more races, 6.1% Hispanic of any race; Average household size: 2.57; Median age: 33.6; Age under 18: 27.4%; Age 65 and over: 10.7%; Males per 100 females: 93.5; Marriage status: 27.0% never married, 54.8% now married, 3.2% separated, 6.6% widowed, 11.6% divorced; Foreign born: 3.3%; Speak English only: 91.6%; With disability: 10.3%; Veterans: 5.8%; Ancestry: 23.0% German, 17.4% Irish, 8.8% Polish, 6.8% American, 5.6% Yugoslavian
Employment: 10.1% management, business, and financial, 0.0% computer, engineering, and science, 6.8% education, legal, community service, arts, and media, 8.2% healthcare practitioners, 23.0% service, 17.9% sales and office, 16.2% natural resources, construction, and maintenance, 17.9% production, transportation, and material moving
Income: Per capita: $22,824; Median household: $54,050; Average household: $57,281; Households with income of $100,000 or more: 10.8%; Poverty rate: 17.8%
Educational Attainment: High school diploma or higher: 87.6%; Bachelor's degree or higher: 10.7%; Graduate/professional degree or higher: 3.2%

School District(s)
M S D Boone Township (KG-12)
    2012-13 Enrollment: 1,155 . . . . (219) 996-4771
Porter Township School Corp (KG-12)
    2012-13 Enrollment: 1,519 . . . . (219) 477-4933
Housing: Homeownership rate: 70.4%; Median home value: $131,600; Median year structure built: 1983; Homeowner vacancy rate: 1.9%; Median gross rent: $775 per month; Rental vacancy rate: 6.3%
Health Insurance: 83.8% have insurance; 70.7% have private insurance; 22.2% have public insurance; 16.2% do not have insurance; 17.8% of children under 18 do not have insurance
Transportation: Commute: 96.2% car, 0.0% public transportation, 1.3% walk, 2.5% work from home; Median travel time to work: 30.8 minutes
Additional Information Contacts
Town of Hebron . . . . (219) 996-4641
    http://www.visithebron.org

KOUTS (town). Covers a land area of 1.118 square miles and a water area of 0 square miles. Located at 41.32° N. Lat; 87.03° W. Long. Elevation is 682 feet.
History: Laid out 1864.
Population: 1,879; Growth (since 2000): 10.7%; Density: 1,680.9 persons per square mile; Race: 97.6% White, 0.3% Black/African American, 0.6% Asian, 0.3% American Indian/Alaska Native, 0.0% Native Hawaiian/Other Pacific Islander, 1.0% Two or more races, 5.1% Hispanic of any race; Average household size: 2.61; Median age: 35.5; Age under 18: 27.8%; Age 65 and over: 13.6%; Males per 100 females: 92.9

School District(s)
East Porter County School Corp (KG-12)
    2012-13 Enrollment: 2,452 . . . . (219) 766-2214
Housing: Homeownership rate: 81.9%; Homeowner vacancy rate: 1.8%; Rental vacancy rate: 2.3%
Additional Information Contacts
Town of Kouts . . . . (219) 766-2244
    http://www.kouts.info

OGDEN DUNES (town). Covers a land area of 0.736 square miles and a water area of 0.722 square miles. Located at 41.63° N. Lat; 87.19° W. Long. Elevation is 610 feet.
History: In 1916, on the site that became Ogden Dunes, a woman was found living alone and avoiding contact with other people. The newspapers called her Diana of the Dunes, and many stories were told about her.
Population: 1,110; Growth (since 2000): -15.5%; Density: 1,507.7 persons per square mile; Race: 96.1% White, 1.1% Black/African American, 1.3% Asian, 0.1% American Indian/Alaska Native, 0.0% Native Hawaiian/Other Pacific Islander, 1.4% Two or more races, 3.2% Hispanic of any race; Average household size: 2.19; Median age: 55.1; Age under 18: 15.7%; Age 65 and over: 25.3%; Males per 100 females: 98.9
Housing: Homeownership rate: 93.1%; Homeowner vacancy rate: 2.5%; Rental vacancy rate: 2.8%

PORTAGE (city). Covers a land area of 25.628 square miles and a water area of 1.984 square miles. Located at 41.59° N. Lat; 87.18° W. Long. Elevation is 636 feet.
History: Named for Portage, Ohio. A new port, accommodating ocean vessels, began operating here in the early 1970s (Burns International Harbor). Incorporated 1959.
Population: 36,828; Growth (since 2000): 9.9%; Density: 1,437.0 persons per square mile; Race: 83.6% White, 7.3% Black/African American, 0.9% Asian, 0.4% American Indian/Alaska Native, 0.0% Native Hawaiian/Other Pacific Islander, 2.6% Two or more races, 16.4% Hispanic of any race; Average household size: 2.61; Median age: 36.4; Age under 18: 25.7%; Age 65 and over: 12.1%; Males per 100 females: 93.7; Marriage status: 30.2% never married, 48.6% now married, 1.9% separated, 7.2% widowed, 14.0% divorced; Foreign born: 4.0%; Speak English only: 90.5%; With disability: 13.2%; Veterans: 9.8%; Ancestry: 21.6% German, 17.3% Irish, 9.8% Polish, 6.5% English, 5.3% Italian
Employment: 9.6% management, business, and financial, 3.5% computer, engineering, and science, 7.1% education, legal, community service, arts, and media, 5.7% healthcare practitioners, 22.3% service, 23.2% sales and office, 12.6% natural resources, construction, and maintenance, 16.1% production, transportation, and material moving

Income: Per capita: $23,918; Median household: $53,969; Average household: $61,667; Households with income of $100,000 or more: 18.3%; Poverty rate: 13.4%
Educational Attainment: High school diploma or higher: 88.2%; Bachelor's degree or higher: 15.0%; Graduate/professional degree or higher: 4.4%

School District(s)
Portage Township Schools (KG-12)
    2012-13 Enrollment: 8,096 . . . . (219) 762-6511
Housing: Homeownership rate: 71.0%; Median home value: $140,100; Median year structure built: 1978; Homeowner vacancy rate: 1.6%; Median gross rent: $818 per month; Rental vacancy rate: 7.8%
Health Insurance: 85.4% have insurance; 69.8% have private insurance; 27.5% have public insurance; 14.6% do not have insurance; 5.1% of children under 18 do not have insurance
Safety: Violent crime rate: 19.0 per 10,000 population; Property crime rate: 234.9 per 10,000 population
Transportation: Commute: 94.0% car, 1.0% public transportation, 2.1% walk, 1.8% work from home; Median travel time to work: 26.4 minutes
Additional Information Contacts
City of Portage. . . . . (219) 762-7784
http://www.ci.portage.in.us

PORTER (town).
Covers a land area of 6.200 square miles and a water area of 0.284 square miles. Located at 41.63° N. Lat; 87.08° W. Long. Elevation is 640 feet.
History: Laid out 1855.
Population: 4,858; Growth (since 2000): -2.3%; Density: 783.6 persons per square mile; Race: 94.3% White, 1.1% Black/African American, 0.9% Asian, 0.3% American Indian/Alaska Native, 0.0% Native Hawaiian/Other Pacific Islander, 1.7% Two or more races, 6.6% Hispanic of any race; Average household size: 2.65; Median age: 39.1; Age under 18: 25.6%; Age 65 and over: 10.7%; Males per 100 females: 98.1; Marriage status: 31.1% never married, 49.7% now married, 0.3% separated, 3.0% widowed, 16.1% divorced; Foreign born: 1.9%; Speak English only: 96.3%; With disability: 6.6%; Veterans: 12.9%; Ancestry: 29.7% German, 21.1% Irish, 13.4% Polish, 10.7% English, 7.1% American
Employment: 13.2% management, business, and financial, 3.5% computer, engineering, and science, 5.9% education, legal, community service, arts, and media, 5.0% healthcare practitioners, 16.1% service, 22.7% sales and office, 12.4% natural resources, construction, and maintenance, 21.2% production, transportation, and material moving
Income: Per capita: $32,223; Median household: $63,325; Average household: $80,777; Households with income of $100,000 or more: 32.4%; Poverty rate: 14.7%
Educational Attainment: High school diploma or higher: 89.8%; Bachelor's degree or higher: 29.3%; Graduate/professional degree or higher: 15.8%

School District(s)
Discovery Charter School (KG-07)
    2012-13 Enrollment: 455. . . . . (317) 695-2998
Duneland School Corporation (KG-12)
    2012-13 Enrollment: 5,957 . . . . (219) 983-3600
Housing: Homeownership rate: 79.2%; Median home value: $160,500; Median year structure built: 1978; Homeowner vacancy rate: 1.4%; Median gross rent: $872 per month; Rental vacancy rate: 5.0%
Health Insurance: 87.4% have insurance; 72.1% have private insurance; 23.9% have public insurance; 12.6% do not have insurance; 0.0% of children under 18 do not have insurance
Safety: Violent crime rate: 2.0 per 10,000 population; Property crime rate: 176.1 per 10,000 population
Transportation: Commute: 95.0% car, 2.1% public transportation, 1.0% walk, 1.9% work from home; Median travel time to work: 26.4 minutes
Additional Information Contacts
Town of Porter. . . . . (219) 926-2771
http://www.townofporter.com

SALT CREEK COMMONS (CDP).
Covers a land area of 0.370 square miles and a water area of 0 square miles. Located at 41.51° N. Lat; 87.14° W. Long.
Population: 2,117; Growth (since 2000): n/a; Density: 5,715.7 persons per square mile; Race: 94.2% White, 1.0% Black/African American, 1.6% Asian, 0.5% American Indian/Alaska Native, 0.0% Native Hawaiian/Other Pacific Islander, 1.6% Two or more races, 8.3% Hispanic of any race; Average household size: 3.10; Median age: 32.4; Age under 18: 31.2%; Age 65 and over: 3.7%; Males per 100 females: 101.0
Housing: Homeownership rate: 90.1%; Homeowner vacancy rate: 1.6%; Rental vacancy rate: 0.0%

SHOREWOOD FOREST (CDP).
Covers a land area of 1.899 square miles and a water area of 0.338 square miles. Located at 41.46° N. Lat; 87.15° W. Long. Elevation is 722 feet.
Population: 2,708; Growth (since 2000): n/a; Density: 1,426.3 persons per square mile; Race: 89.4% White, 3.8% Black/African American, 4.0% Asian, 0.0% American Indian/Alaska Native, 0.0% Native Hawaiian/Other Pacific Islander, 1.9% Two or more races, 3.7% Hispanic of any race; Average household size: 2.86; Median age: 47.0; Age under 18: 23.7%; Age 65 and over: 16.6%; Males per 100 females: 94.7; Marriage status: 27.6% never married, 63.4% now married, 0.0% separated, 2.9% widowed, 6.1% divorced; Foreign born: 5.1%; Speak English only: 93.1%; With disability: 5.2%; Veterans: 9.7%; Ancestry: 22.8% German, 20.0% Irish, 19.2% Polish, 14.1% Greek, 13.1% Italian
Employment: 14.4% management, business, and financial, 4.3% computer, engineering, and science, 14.8% education, legal, community service, arts, and media, 12.9% healthcare practitioners, 9.9% service, 24.2% sales and office, 12.4% natural resources, construction, and maintenance, 7.1% production, transportation, and material moving
Income: Per capita: $48,423; Median household: $106,926; Average household: $135,952; Households with income of $100,000 or more: 57.0%; Poverty rate: 3.1%
Educational Attainment: High school diploma or higher: 95.1%; Bachelor's degree or higher: 48.3%; Graduate/professional degree or higher: 20.2%
Housing: Homeownership rate: 95.9%; Median home value: $335,500; Median year structure built: 1984; Homeowner vacancy rate: 1.6%; Median gross rent: $1,837 per month; Rental vacancy rate: 2.5%
Health Insurance: 88.1% have insurance; 81.4% have private insurance; 20.5% have public insurance; 11.9% do not have insurance; 14.2% of children under 18 do not have insurance
Transportation: Commute: 97.1% car, 0.0% public transportation, 0.0% walk, 2.9% work from home; Median travel time to work: 28.5 minutes

SOUTH HAVEN (CDP).
Covers a land area of 1.243 square miles and a water area of 0 square miles. Located at 41.54° N. Lat; 87.14° W. Long. Elevation is 653 feet.
Population: 5,282; Growth (since 2000): -6.0%; Density: 4,250.2 persons per square mile; Race: 91.3% White, 3.0% Black/African American, 0.3% Asian, 0.2% American Indian/Alaska Native, 0.0% Native Hawaiian/Other Pacific Islander, 2.2% Two or more races, 9.8% Hispanic of any race; Average household size: 2.89; Median age: 35.0; Age under 18: 27.3%; Age 65 and over: 10.7%; Males per 100 females: 96.3; Marriage status: 27.8% never married, 53.0% now married, 1.2% separated, 6.1% widowed, 13.1% divorced; Foreign born: 1.2%; Speak English only: 97.3%; With disability: 13.2%; Veterans: 12.4%; Ancestry: 27.0% German, 23.9% Irish, 9.1% Polish, 7.3% English, 6.2% American
Employment: 8.5% management, business, and financial, 1.2% computer, engineering, and science, 5.9% education, legal, community service, arts, and media, 5.4% healthcare practitioners, 23.0% service, 20.3% sales and office, 12.9% natural resources, construction, and maintenance, 22.8% production, transportation, and material moving
Income: Per capita: $21,364; Median household: $48,264; Average household: $58,878; Households with income of $100,000 or more: 14.9%; Poverty rate: 11.2%
Educational Attainment: High school diploma or higher: 87.6%; Bachelor's degree or higher: 8.5%; Graduate/professional degree or higher: 1.9%
Housing: Homeownership rate: 78.8%; Median home value: $109,700; Median year structure built: 1967; Homeowner vacancy rate: 1.4%; Median gross rent: $943 per month; Rental vacancy rate: 16.4%
Health Insurance: 85.7% have insurance; 72.5% have private insurance; 25.7% have public insurance; 14.3% do not have insurance; 6.8% of children under 18 do not have insurance
Transportation: Commute: 95.7% car, 1.4% public transportation, 0.6% walk, 1.2% work from home; Median travel time to work: 26.2 minutes

TOWN OF PINES (town). Covers a land area of 2.255 square miles and a water area of 0 square miles. Located at 41.69° N. Lat; 86.95° W. Long. Elevation is 627 feet.
Population: 708; Growth (since 2000): -11.3%; Density: 314.0 persons per square mile; Race: 93.9% White, 2.3% Black/African American, 0.3% Asian, 0.4% American Indian/Alaska Native, 0.0% Native Hawaiian/Other Pacific Islander, 3.0% Two or more races, 3.1% Hispanic of any race; Average household size: 2.34; Median age: 45.3; Age under 18: 18.8%; Age 65 and over: 14.5%; Males per 100 females: 101.7
Housing: Homeownership rate: 75.5%; Homeowner vacancy rate: 3.0%; Rental vacancy rate: 16.7%

VALPARAISO (city). County seat. Covers a land area of 15.530 square miles and a water area of 0.048 square miles. Located at 41.48° N. Lat; 87.05° W. Long. Elevation is 794 feet.
History: Named for the city in Chile, near which Captain David Porter fought in the War of 1812. Valparaiso was sited on the Old Sauk Trail. In 1859 the Valparaiso Male and Female College was founded here by the Methodist Church. The College, purchased by the Lutheran Church in 1925, became Valparaiso University.
Population: 31,730; Growth (since 2000): 15.7%; Density: 2,043.1 persons per square mile; Race: 89.9% White, 3.3% Black/African American, 2.1% Asian, 0.3% American Indian/Alaska Native, 0.1% Native Hawaiian/Other Pacific Islander, 2.1% Two or more races, 7.1% Hispanic of any race; Average household size: 2.28; Median age: 33.4; Age under 18: 21.3%; Age 65 and over: 13.1%; Males per 100 females: 94.7; Marriage status: 37.0% never married, 44.3% now married, 1.3% separated, 6.7% widowed, 11.9% divorced; Foreign born: 5.5%; Speak English only: 92.3%; With disability: 10.0%; Veterans: 8.3%; Ancestry: 29.4% German, 16.5% Irish, 8.6% Polish, 8.4% English, 5.5% Italian
Employment: 11.5% management, business, and financial, 5.4% computer, engineering, and science, 14.3% education, legal, community service, arts, and media, 6.6% healthcare practitioners, 18.5% service, 24.8% sales and office, 6.2% natural resources, construction, and maintenance, 12.7% production, transportation, and material moving
Income: Per capita: $24,239; Median household: $48,703; Average household: $60,979; Households with income of $100,000 or more: 17.9%; Poverty rate: 14.4%
Educational Attainment: High school diploma or higher: 91.5%; Bachelor's degree or higher: 33.9%; Graduate/professional degree or higher: 11.5%

School District(s)
Duneland School Corporation (KG-12)
    2012-13 Enrollment: 5,957 . . . . (219) 983-3600
East Porter County School Corp (KG-12)
    2012-13 Enrollment: 2,452 . . . . (219) 766-2214
Portage Township Schools (KG-12)
    2012-13 Enrollment: 8,096 . . . . (219) 762-6511
Porter County Education Services (KG-12)
    2012-13 Enrollment: n/a . . . . (219) 464-9607
Porter Township School Corp (KG-12)
    2012-13 Enrollment: 1,519 . . . . (219) 477-4933
Union Township School Corp (KG-12)
    2012-13 Enrollment: 1,559 . . . . (219) 759-2531
Valparaiso Community Schools (KG-12)
    2012-13 Enrollment: 6,423 . . . . (219) 531-3000

Four-year College(s)
Valparaiso University (Private, Not-for-profit, Lutheran Church in America)
    Fall 2013 Enrollment: 4,508 . . . . (219) 464-5000
    2013-14 Tuition: In-state $33,480; Out-of-state $33,480

Vocational/Technical School(s)
Don Roberts Beauty School (Private, For-profit)
    Fall 2013 Enrollment: 77 . . . . (219) 462-5189
    2013-14 Tuition: $16,100

Housing: Homeownership rate: 55.4%; Median home value: $162,800; Median year structure built: 1976; Homeowner vacancy rate: 2.3%; Median gross rent: $836 per month; Rental vacancy rate: 7.2%
Health Insurance: 85.6% have insurance; 73.8% have private insurance; 22.4% have public insurance; 14.4% do not have insurance; 4.5% of children under 18 do not have insurance
Hospitals: Porter Regional Hospital (402 beds)
Safety: Violent crime rate: 10.3 per 10,000 population; Property crime rate: 207.2 per 10,000 population
Transportation: Commute: 88.7% car, 1.8% public transportation, 3.0% walk, 4.1% work from home; Median travel time to work: 22.3 minutes

Airports: Porter County Regional (general aviation)
Additional Information Contacts
City of Valparaiso . . . . (219) 462-1161
    http://www.ci.valparaiso.in.us

WHEELER (CDP). Covers a land area of 2.656 square miles and a water area of 0 square miles. Located at 41.51° N. Lat; 87.17° W. Long. Elevation is 666 feet.
Population: 443; Growth (since 2000): n/a; Density: 166.8 persons per square mile; Race: 94.1% White, 0.9% Black/African American, 0.2% Asian, 1.8% American Indian/Alaska Native, 0.2% Native Hawaiian/Other Pacific Islander, 2.5% Two or more races, 4.5% Hispanic of any race; Average household size: 2.65; Median age: 37.5; Age under 18: 25.3%; Age 65 and over: 13.5%; Males per 100 females: 92.6
Housing: Homeownership rate: 80.8%; Homeowner vacancy rate: 4.9%; Rental vacancy rate: 3.0%

Posey County

Located in southwestern Indiana; bounded on the west by the Wabash River and the Illinois border, and on the south by the Ohio River and the Kentucky border; drained by Big Creek. Covers a land area of 409.571 square miles, a water area of 9.754 square miles, and is located in the Central Time Zone at 38.03° N. Lat., 87.87° W. Long. The county was founded in 1814. County seat is Mount Vernon.

Posey County is part of the Evansville, IN-KY Metropolitan Statistical Area. The entire metro area includes: Posey County, IN; Vanderburgh County, IN; Warrick County, IN; Henderson County, KY

Weather Station: Mount Vernon   Elevation: 419 feet

	Jan	Feb	Mar	Apr	May	Jun	Jul	Aug	Sep	Oct	Nov	Dec
High	41	45	55	66	76	85	88	87	81	69	57	44
Low	24	27	35	45	56	65	68	66	58	47	38	28
Precip	3.5	3.1	4.3	4.4	5.7	3.9	3.8	2.9	3.0	3.4	4.0	3.9
Snow	2.3	3.2	1.3	0.1	0.0	0.0	0.0	0.0	0.0	0.1	0.1	1.8

High and Low temperatures in degrees Fahrenheit; Precipitation and Snow in inches

Population: 25,910; Growth (since 2000): -4.3%; Density: 63.3 persons per square mile; Race: 97.2% White, 0.9% Black/African American, 0.3% Asian, 0.2% American Indian/Alaska Native, 0.0% Native Hawaiian/Other Pacific Islander, 1.1% two or more races, 1.0% Hispanic of any race; Average household size: 2.52; Median age: 41.6; Age under 18: 23.7%; Age 65 and over: 14.4%; Males per 100 females: 99.0; Marriage status: 23.1% never married, 60.7% now married, 0.6% separated, 6.2% widowed, 10.0% divorced; Foreign born: 1.1%; Speak English only: 97.2%; With disability: 12.1%; Veterans: 9.7%; Ancestry: 40.9% German, 12.6% Irish, 11.7% American, 11.7% English, 1.9% Italian
Religion: Six largest groups: 22.7% Catholicism, 7.8% Methodist/Pietist, 6.9% Baptist, 5.3% Presbyterian-Reformed, 3.3% Non-denominational Protestant, 1.8% Pentecostal
Economy: Unemployment rate: 4.5%; Leading industries: 16.3% construction; 13.6% retail trade; 12.2% other services (except public administration); Farms: 408 totaling 228,748 acres; Company size: 1 employs 1,000 or more persons, 2 employ 500 to 999 persons, 12 employ 100 to 499 persons, 476 employ less than 100 persons; Business ownership: 490 women-owned, n/a Black-owned, n/a Hispanic-owned, n/a Asian-owned
Employment: 12.1% management, business, and financial, 3.8% computer, engineering, and science, 7.7% education, legal, community service, arts, and media, 5.4% healthcare practitioners, 13.6% service, 23.5% sales and office, 12.1% natural resources, construction, and maintenance, 21.7% production, transportation, and material moving
Income: Per capita: $29,187; Median household: $58,750; Average household: $73,218; Households with income of $100,000 or more: 21.7%; Poverty rate: 9.9%
Educational Attainment: High school diploma or higher: 92.1%; Bachelor's degree or higher: 20.5%; Graduate/professional degree or higher: 7.3%
Housing: Homeownership rate: 81.9%; Median home value: $127,900; Median year structure built: 1972; Homeowner vacancy rate: 2.0%; Median gross rent: $605 per month; Rental vacancy rate: 12.6%
Vital Statistics: Birth rate: 105.9 per 10,000 population; Death rate: 91.4 per 10,000 population; Age-adjusted cancer mortality rate: 158.0 deaths per 100,000 population

Health Insurance: 92.0% have insurance; 80.2% have private insurance; 24.7% have public insurance; 8.0% do not have insurance; 2.7% of children under 18 do not have insurance
Health Care: Physicians: 4.7 per 10,000 population; Hospital beds: 0.0 per 10,000 population; Hospital admissions: 0.0 per 10,000 population
Air Quality Index: 96.2% good, 3.8% moderate, 0.0% unhealthy for sensitive individuals, 0.0% unhealthy (percent of days)
Transportation: Commute: 95.9% car, 0.0% public transportation, 1.0% walk, 2.6% work from home; Median travel time to work: 23.2 minutes
Presidential Election: 37.1% Obama, 60.8% Romney (2012)
National and State Parks: Harmonie State Park; New Harmony State Memorial; The Labyrinth State Memorial
Additional Information Contacts
Posey Government . . . . (812) 838-3317
  http://www.poseycountygov.org

Posey County Communities

CYNTHIANA (town). Covers a land area of 0.399 square miles and a water area of 0 square miles. Located at 38.19° N. Lat; 87.71° W. Long. Elevation is 472 feet.
Population: 545; Growth (since 2000): -21.4%; Density: 1,366.6 persons per square mile; Race: 96.5% White, 0.2% Black/African American, 0.2% Asian, 0.2% American Indian/Alaska Native, 0.0% Native Hawaiian/Other Pacific Islander, 2.6% Two or more races, 0.6% Hispanic of any race; Average household size: 2.31; Median age: 42.5; Age under 18: 22.6%; Age 65 and over: 14.9%; Males per 100 females: 98.9
Housing: Homeownership rate: 79.7%; Homeowner vacancy rate: 2.5%; Rental vacancy rate: 10.7%

GRIFFIN (town). Covers a land area of 0.068 square miles and a water area of 0 square miles. Located at 38.20° N. Lat; 87.91° W. Long. Elevation is 387 feet.
History: Laid out 1881.
Population: 172; Growth (since 2000): 7.5%; Density: 2,515.8 persons per square mile; Race: 98.8% White, 0.6% Black/African American, 0.0% Asian, 0.0% American Indian/Alaska Native, 0.0% Native Hawaiian/Other Pacific Islander, 0.6% Two or more races, 0.0% Hispanic of any race; Average household size: 2.49; Median age: 37.3; Age under 18: 26.2%; Age 65 and over: 15.1%; Males per 100 females: 75.5
Housing: Homeownership rate: 84.0%; Homeowner vacancy rate: 1.7%; Rental vacancy rate: 0.0%

MOUNT VERNON (city). County seat. Covers a land area of 2.808 square miles and a water area of 0.050 square miles. Located at 37.94° N. Lat; 87.90° W. Long. Elevation is 400 feet.
History: Mount Vernon, founded in 1805 by Irish trader Andrew McFadden, was first called McFadden's Landing. The name was changed in 1816.
Population: 6,687; Growth (since 2000): -10.6%; Density: 2,381.7 persons per square mile; Race: 93.4% White, 2.8% Black/African American, 0.4% Asian, 0.3% American Indian/Alaska Native, 0.0% Native Hawaiian/Other Pacific Islander, 2.4% Two or more races, 1.7% Hispanic of any race; Average household size: 2.40; Median age: 40.2; Age under 18: 24.5%; Age 65 and over: 16.8%; Males per 100 females: 91.4; Marriage status: 26.7% never married, 52.8% now married, 1.2% separated, 6.6% widowed, 13.9% divorced; Foreign born: 2.9%; Speak English only: 94.0%; With disability: 14.9%; Veterans: 9.2%; Ancestry: 28.3% German, 13.8% English, 11.6% Irish, 10.0% American, 2.0% Dutch
Employment: 11.7% management, business, and financial, 4.3% computer, engineering, and science, 7.0% education, legal, community service, arts, and media, 4.5% healthcare practitioners, 15.2% service, 22.0% sales and office, 11.5% natural resources, construction, and maintenance, 23.9% production, transportation, and material moving
Income: Per capita: $26,466; Median household: $46,909; Average household: $64,866; Households with income of $100,000 or more: 16.6%; Poverty rate: 16.9%
Educational Attainment: High school diploma or higher: 88.5%; Bachelor's degree or higher: 20.1%; Graduate/professional degree or higher: 7.5%
School District(s)
M S D Mount Vernon (PK-12)
  2012-13 Enrollment: 2,199 . . . . (812) 838-4471
Housing: Homeownership rate: 67.2%; Median home value: $94,800; Median year structure built: 1966; Homeowner vacancy rate: 3.8%; Median gross rent: $576 per month; Rental vacancy rate: 11.5%
Health Insurance: 87.7% have insurance; 68.7% have private insurance; 31.9% have public insurance; 12.3% do not have insurance; 3.3% of children under 18 do not have insurance
Safety: Violent crime rate: 18.2 per 10,000 population; Property crime rate: 526.9 per 10,000 population
Newspapers: Mt. Vernon Democrat (weekly circulation 3900)
Transportation: Commute: 95.8% car, 0.0% public transportation, 1.8% walk, 1.9% work from home; Median travel time to work: 17.5 minutes
Additional Information Contacts
City of Mount Vernon. . . . . (812) 838-3317
  http://www.mountvernon.in.gov

NEW HARMONY (town). Covers a land area of 0.636 square miles and a water area of 0.009 square miles. Located at 38.13° N. Lat; 87.93° W. Long. Elevation is 381 feet.
History: New Harmony was the site of two social experiments. In 1815 the Rappites, a religious group of Germans from Pennsylvania, founded the village of Harmonie, trying to create a society based on cooperative living. After ten years their hard work had created a prosperous town out of the wildnerness, but also created discontent. They sold the village to Robert Owen, a Welsh philanthropist and social reformer whose dream was to found a communal society. Owen called his community New Harmony. The experiment as Owen envisioned it was a failure within two years, but New Harmony continued to be an intellectual center.
Population: 789; Growth (since 2000): -13.9%; Density: 1,241.4 persons per square mile; Race: 99.0% White, 0.0% Black/African American, 0.1% Asian, 0.3% American Indian/Alaska Native, 0.0% Native Hawaiian/Other Pacific Islander, 0.6% Two or more races, 0.0% Hispanic of any race; Average household size: 1.93; Median age: 55.1; Age under 18: 13.1%; Age 65 and over: 33.5%; Males per 100 females: 76.1
Housing: Homeownership rate: 67.8%; Homeowner vacancy rate: 7.3%; Rental vacancy rate: 15.6%
Newspapers: Posey County News (weekly circulation 4800)

PARKERS SETTLEMENT (CDP). Covers a land area of 1.752 square miles and a water area of 0 square miles. Located at 38.04° N. Lat; 87.71° W. Long. Elevation is 446 feet.
Population: 711; Growth (since 2000): n/a; Density: 405.9 persons per square mile; Race: 98.6% White, 0.4% Black/African American, 0.8% Asian, 0.0% American Indian/Alaska Native, 0.0% Native Hawaiian/Other Pacific Islander, 0.1% Two or more races, 0.3% Hispanic of any race; Average household size: 2.64; Median age: 41.7; Age under 18: 24.2%; Age 65 and over: 12.0%; Males per 100 females: 100.8
Housing: Homeownership rate: 91.8%; Homeowner vacancy rate: 1.2%; Rental vacancy rate: 23.3%

POSEYVILLE (town). Covers a land area of 0.645 square miles and a water area of 0 square miles. Located at 38.17° N. Lat; 87.78° W. Long. Elevation is 440 feet.
Population: 1,045; Growth (since 2000): -12.0%; Density: 1,619.7 persons per square mile; Race: 98.9% White, 0.0% Black/African American, 0.2% Asian, 0.3% American Indian/Alaska Native, 0.0% Native Hawaiian/Other Pacific Islander, 0.6% Two or more races, 0.2% Hispanic of any race; Average household size: 2.30; Median age: 44.1; Age under 18: 23.0%; Age 65 and over: 18.6%; Males per 100 females: 93.9
School District(s)
M S D North Posey County Schools (KG-12)
  2012-13 Enrollment: 1,450 . . . . (812) 874-2243
Housing: Homeownership rate: 80.6%; Homeowner vacancy rate: 1.6%; Rental vacancy rate: 11.0%

WADESVILLE (unincorporated postal area)
ZCTA: 47638
  Covers a land area of 49.196 square miles and a water area of 0.021 square miles. Located at 38.07° N. Lat; 87.78° W. Long. Elevation is 479 feet.
  Population: 3,577; Growth (since 2000): 3.9%; Density: 72.7 persons per square mile; Race: 98.8% White, 0.2% Black/African American, 0.2% Asian, 0.1% American Indian/Alaska Native, 0.0% Native Hawaiian/Other Pacific Islander, 0.5% Two or more races, 0.5% Hispanic of any race; Average household size: 2.66; Median age: 39.5; Age under 18: 25.0%; Age 65 and over: 11.4%; Males per 100 females:

99.6; Marriage status: 20.0% never married, 63.5% now married, 0.0% separated, 7.6% widowed, 8.9% divorced; Foreign born: 0.7%; Speak English only: 99.0%; With disability: 8.0%; Veterans: 7.4%; Ancestry: 46.5% German, 15.4% American, 14.3% English, 6.7% Irish, 3.6% Dutch
Employment: 7.6% management, business, and financial, 4.9% computer, engineering, and science, 9.6% education, legal, community service, arts, and media, 2.3% healthcare practitioners, 14.7% service, 25.3% sales and office, 13.4% natural resources, construction, and maintenance, 22.1% production, transportation, and material moving
Income: Per capita: $28,253; Median household: $61,175; Average household: $67,755; Households with income of $100,000 or more: 18.7%; Poverty rate: 3.4%
Educational Attainment: High school diploma or higher: 95.6%; Bachelor's degree or higher: 19.0%; Graduate/professional degree or higher: 5.7%

School District(s)
M S D North Posey County Schools (KG-12)
    2012-13 Enrollment: 1,450 . . . . (812) 874-2243
Housing: Homeownership rate: 87.9%; Median home value: $144,200; Median year structure built: 1976; Homeowner vacancy rate: 0.8%; Median gross rent: $656 per month; Rental vacancy rate: 7.8%
Health Insurance: 97.1% have insurance; 91.8% have private insurance; 17.1% have public insurance; 2.9% do not have insurance; 0.0% of children under 18 do not have insurance
Transportation: Commute: 98.1% car, 0.0% public transportation, 0.0% walk, 1.9% work from home; Median travel time to work: 27.4 minutes

Pulaski County

Located in northwestern Indiana; drained by the Tippecanoe River. Covers a land area of 433.649 square miles, a water area of 0.885 square miles, and is located in the Eastern Time Zone at 41.05° N. Lat., 86.69° W. Long. The county was founded in 1835. County seat is Winamac.

Weather Station: Winamac 2 SSE   Elevation: 689 feet

	Jan	Feb	Mar	Apr	May	Jun	Jul	Aug	Sep	Oct	Nov	Dec
High	32	36	48	61	72	80	83	82	76	63	50	36
Low	16	19	28	39	50	59	63	61	53	41	32	21
Precip	2.1	1.9	2.5	3.3	4.0	3.9	4.6	4.1	3.2	3.4	3.1	2.5
Snow	8.0	5.5	3.2	0.7	0.0	0.0	0.0	0.0	0.0	0.1	0.9	5.9

High and Low temperatures in degrees Fahrenheit; Precipitation and Snow in inches

Population: 13,402; Growth (since 2000): -2.6%; Density: 30.9 persons per square mile; Race: 97.2% White, 0.7% Black/African American, 0.2% Asian, 0.3% American Indian/Alaska Native, 0.0% Native Hawaiian/Other Pacific Islander, 1.0% two or more races, 2.4% Hispanic of any race; Average household size: 2.50; Median age: 41.7; Age under 18: 23.9%; Age 65 and over: 16.7%; Males per 100 females: 102.0; Marriage status: 23.4% never married, 57.6% now married, 0.9% separated, 6.8% widowed, 12.2% divorced; Foreign born: 0.8%; Speak English only: 98.0%; With disability: 17.0%; Veterans: 8.8%; Ancestry: 29.1% German, 12.0% Irish, 8.8% American, 7.6% English, 4.2% Polish
Religion: Six largest groups: 9.0% Baptist, 9.0% Catholicism, 6.1% Methodist/Pietist, 5.8% Non-denominational Protestant, 2.7% European Free-Church, 2.7% Lutheran
Economy: Unemployment rate: 4.2%; Leading industries: 18.6% retail trade; 12.1% other services (except public administration); 9.6% construction; Farms: 536 totaling 216,503 acres; Company size: 0 employ 1,000 or more persons, 0 employs 500 to 999 persons, 2 employ 100 to 499 persons, 320 employ less than 100 persons; Business ownership: 210 women-owned, n/a Black-owned, n/a Hispanic-owned, n/a Asian-owned
Employment: 10.5% management, business, and financial, 2.2% computer, engineering, and science, 8.1% education, legal, community service, arts, and media, 6.8% healthcare practitioners, 14.8% service, 19.6% sales and office, 10.3% natural resources, construction, and maintenance, 27.7% production, transportation, and material moving
Income: Per capita: $21,641; Median household: $44,764; Average household: $54,813; Households with income of $100,000 or more: 10.6%; Poverty rate: 14.0%
Educational Attainment: High school diploma or higher: 85.3%; Bachelor's degree or higher: 13.1%; Graduate/professional degree or higher: 3.6%

Housing: Homeownership rate: 78.9%; Median home value: $94,900; Median year structure built: 1966; Homeowner vacancy rate: 1.8%; Median gross rent: $607 per month; Rental vacancy rate: 9.5%
Vital Statistics: Birth rate: 91.5 per 10,000 population; Death rate: 103.8 per 10,000 population; Age-adjusted cancer mortality rate: 194.9 deaths per 100,000 population
Health Insurance: 85.9% have insurance; 66.5% have private insurance; 33.4% have public insurance; 14.1% do not have insurance; 9.6% of children under 18 do not have insurance
Health Care: Physicians: 4.6 per 10,000 population; Hospital beds: 18.8 per 10,000 population; Hospital admissions: 461.2 per 10,000 population
Transportation: Commute: 90.7% car, 0.3% public transportation, 1.0% walk, 6.3% work from home; Median travel time to work: 23.9 minutes
Presidential Election: 35.2% Obama, 62.3% Romney (2012)
National and State Parks: Winamac State Fish and Wildlife Area
Additional Information Contacts
Pulaski Government . . . . (574) 946-3313
    http://www.pulaskionline.org

Pulaski County Communities

FRANCESVILLE (town). Covers a land area of 0.304 square miles and a water area of 0 square miles. Located at 40.99° N. Lat; 86.88° W. Long. Elevation is 679 feet.
Population: 879; Growth (since 2000): -2.9%; Density: 2,895.4 persons per square mile; Race: 97.0% White, 0.2% Black/African American, 0.1% Asian, 0.7% American Indian/Alaska Native, 0.0% Native Hawaiian/Other Pacific Islander, 1.6% Two or more races, 3.6% Hispanic of any race; Average household size: 2.49; Median age: 39.6; Age under 18: 26.1%; Age 65 and over: 16.4%; Males per 100 females: 97.1

School District(s)
West Central School Corp (KG-12)
    2012-13 Enrollment: 849 . . . . (219) 567-9161
Housing: Homeownership rate: 77.6%; Homeowner vacancy rate: 3.5%; Rental vacancy rate: 9.1%
Newspapers: Francesville Tribune (weekly circulation 900)

MEDARYVILLE (town). Covers a land area of 0.459 square miles and a water area of 0 square miles. Located at 41.08° N. Lat; 86.89° W. Long. Elevation is 689 feet.
Population: 614; Growth (since 2000): 8.7%; Density: 1,337.9 persons per square mile; Race: 94.8% White, 0.0% Black/African American, 0.0% Asian, 0.2% American Indian/Alaska Native, 0.0% Native Hawaiian/Other Pacific Islander, 1.6% Two or more races, 6.4% Hispanic of any race; Average household size: 2.69; Median age: 35.2; Age under 18: 25.9%; Age 65 and over: 14.3%; Males per 100 females: 95.5
Housing: Homeownership rate: 67.6%; Homeowner vacancy rate: 4.9%; Rental vacancy rate: 10.8%

MONTEREY (town). Covers a land area of 0.183 square miles and a water area of 0 square miles. Located at 41.16° N. Lat; 86.48° W. Long. Elevation is 725 feet.
History: Laid out 1849.
Population: 218; Growth (since 2000): -5.6%; Density: 1,191.0 persons per square mile; Race: 97.7% White, 0.5% Black/African American, 0.0% Asian, 0.5% American Indian/Alaska Native, 0.0% Native Hawaiian/Other Pacific Islander, 1.4% Two or more races, 9.6% Hispanic of any race; Average household size: 2.56; Median age: 35.0; Age under 18: 31.7%; Age 65 and over: 14.7%; Males per 100 females: 109.6
Housing: Homeownership rate: 76.4%; Homeowner vacancy rate: 3.0%; Rental vacancy rate: 0.0%

STAR CITY (CDP). Covers a land area of 1.036 square miles and a water area of 0 square miles. Located at 40.97° N. Lat; 86.56° W. Long. Elevation is 715 feet.
History: Laid out 1859.
Population: 344; Growth (since 2000): -8.8%; Density: 332.0 persons per square mile; Race: 99.7% White, 0.0% Black/African American, 0.0% Asian, 0.0% American Indian/Alaska Native, 0.0% Native Hawaiian/Other Pacific Islander, 0.3% Two or more races, 0.3% Hispanic of any race; Average household size: 2.77; Median age: 34.4; Age under 18: 27.9%; Age 65 and over: 14.8%; Males per 100 females: 106.0
Housing: Homeownership rate: 86.3%; Homeowner vacancy rate: 0.9%; Rental vacancy rate: 5.6%

WINAMAC (town). County seat. Covers a land area of 1.361 square miles and a water area of 0 square miles. Located at 41.05° N. Lat; 86.60° W. Long. Elevation is 705 feet.
History: Winamac was founded in 1835 along the Tippecanoe River, and was named for Potawatomi Chief Winamac.
Population: 2,490; Growth (since 2000): 3.0%; Density: 1,829.0 persons per square mile; Race: 97.2% White, 0.5% Black/African American, 0.4% Asian, 0.3% American Indian/Alaska Native, 0.0% Native Hawaiian/Other Pacific Islander, 1.2% Two or more races, 2.3% Hispanic of any race; Average household size: 2.29; Median age: 38.8; Age under 18: 23.7%; Age 65 and over: 16.3%; Males per 100 females: 95.3

School District(s)
Eastern Pulaski Com Sch Corp (KG-12)
    2012-13 Enrollment: 1,234 . . . . (574) 946-4010
Housing: Homeownership rate: 65.6%; Homeowner vacancy rate: 2.7%; Rental vacancy rate: 12.4%
Hospitals: Pulaski Memorial Hospital
Newspapers: Pulaski County Journal (weekly circulation 3700)
Additional Information Contacts
Town of Winamac . . . . (574) 946-3451
  http://www.townofwinamac.com

Putnam County

Located in central Indiana; drained by the Eel River. Covers a land area of 480.528 square miles, a water area of 2.164 square miles, and is located in the Eastern Time Zone at 39.67° N. Lat., 86.85° W. Long. The county was founded in 1821. County seat is Greencastle.

Putnam County is part of the Indianapolis-Carmel-Anderson, IN Metropolitan Statistical Area. The entire metro area includes: Boone County, IN; Brown County, IN; Hamilton County, IN; Hancock County, IN; Hendricks County, IN; Johnson County, IN; Madison County, IN; Marion County, IN; Morgan County, IN; Putnam County, IN; Shelby County, IN

Weather Station: Greencastle 1 SE   Elevation: 859 feet

	Jan	Feb	Mar	Apr	May	Jun	Jul	Aug	Sep	Oct	Nov	Dec
High	35	40	50	63	73	82	85	84	78	65	52	39
Low	19	22	30	41	51	61	64	62	55	43	34	23
Precip	2.6	2.5	3.5	4.0	5.3	4.5	5.2	3.6	3.9	3.6	3.9	3.2
Snow	7.8	5.9	2.3	0.3	tr	0.0	0.0	0.0	0.0	0.0	0.9	5.1

High and Low temperatures in degrees Fahrenheit; Precipitation and Snow in inches

Population: 37,963; Growth (since 2000): 5.4%; Density: 79.0 persons per square mile; Race: 93.4% White, 4.0% Black/African American, 0.7% Asian, 0.3% American Indian/Alaska Native, 0.0% Native Hawaiian/Other Pacific Islander, 1.1% two or more races, 1.5% Hispanic of any race; Average household size: 2.52; Median age: 37.9; Age under 18: 21.1%; Age 65 and over: 13.5%; Males per 100 females: 111.9; Marriage status: 32.9% never married, 50.5% now married, 1.5% separated, 5.7% widowed, 10.9% divorced; Foreign born: 1.8%; Speak English only: 96.4%; With disability: 13.6%; Veterans: 9.2%; Ancestry: 24.2% German, 14.8% American, 14.7% Irish, 10.4% English, 3.0% Italian
Religion: Six largest groups: 17.3% Baptist, 4.3% Non-denominational Protestant, 2.8% Methodist/Pietist, 2.8% Catholicism, 2.0% Presbyterian-Reformed, 1.3% Pentecostal
Economy: Unemployment rate: 5.3%; Leading industries: 15.2% retail trade; 14.4% other services (except public administration); 11.0% construction; Farms: 847 totaling 197,619 acres; Company size: 1 employs 1,000 or more persons, 1 employs 500 to 999 persons, 15 employ 100 to 499 persons, 672 employ less than 100 persons; Business ownership: n/a women-owned, n/a Black-owned, n/a Hispanic-owned, n/a Asian-owned
Employment: 11.6% management, business, and financial, 3.2% computer, engineering, and science, 10.6% education, legal, community service, arts, and media, 4.7% healthcare practitioners, 18.3% service, 20.5% sales and office, 12.2% natural resources, construction, and maintenance, 18.9% production, transportation, and material moving
Income: Per capita: $21,520; Median household: $50,821; Average household: $62,845; Households with income of $100,000 or more: 15.5%; Poverty rate: 9.7%
Educational Attainment: High school diploma or higher: 85.9%; Bachelor's degree or higher: 16.2%; Graduate/professional degree or higher: 7.3%

Housing: Homeownership rate: 76.3%; Median home value: $125,800; Median year structure built: 1976; Homeowner vacancy rate: 2.5%; Median gross rent: $653 per month; Rental vacancy rate: 9.1%
Vital Statistics: Birth rate: 93.3 per 10,000 population; Death rate: 81.3 per 10,000 population; Age-adjusted cancer mortality rate: 208.0 deaths per 100,000 population
Health Insurance: 86.6% have insurance; 72.7% have private insurance; 25.7% have public insurance; 13.4% do not have insurance; 9.7% of children under 18 do not have insurance
Health Care: Physicians: 7.4 per 10,000 population; Hospital beds: 6.6 per 10,000 population; Hospital admissions: 304.0 per 10,000 population
Transportation: Commute: 88.7% car, 0.1% public transportation, 6.2% walk, 3.5% work from home; Median travel time to work: 28.5 minutes
Presidential Election: 32.6% Obama, 65.1% Romney (2012)
National and State Parks: Owen-Putnam State Forest; Richard Lieber State Park
Additional Information Contacts
Putnam Government . . . . (765) 653-2648
  http://www.co.putnam.in.us

Putnam County Communities

BAINBRIDGE (town). Covers a land area of 0.401 square miles and a water area of 0 square miles. Located at 39.76° N. Lat; 86.81° W. Long. Elevation is 932 feet.
Population: 746; Growth (since 2000): 0.4%; Density: 1,862.4 persons per square mile; Race: 98.1% White, 0.0% Black/African American, 0.4% Asian, 0.1% American Indian/Alaska Native, 0.0% Native Hawaiian/Other Pacific Islander, 1.1% Two or more races, 0.1% Hispanic of any race; Average household size: 2.58; Median age: 37.5; Age under 18: 28.7%; Age 65 and over: 11.7%; Males per 100 females: 97.9

School District(s)
North Putnam Community Schools (PK-12)
    2012-13 Enrollment: 1,626 . . . . (765) 522-6218
Housing: Homeownership rate: 64.0%; Homeowner vacancy rate: 3.1%; Rental vacancy rate: 9.6%

CLOVERDALE (town). Covers a land area of 3.458 square miles and a water area of 0.064 square miles. Located at 39.52° N. Lat; 86.80° W. Long. Elevation is 820 feet.
Population: 2,172; Growth (since 2000): -3.2%; Density: 628.0 persons per square mile; Race: 97.4% White, 0.6% Black/African American, 0.3% Asian, 0.3% American Indian/Alaska Native, 0.0% Native Hawaiian/Other Pacific Islander, 1.2% Two or more races, 0.9% Hispanic of any race; Average household size: 2.41; Median age: 42.2; Age under 18: 22.8%; Age 65 and over: 16.5%; Males per 100 females: 93.2

School District(s)
Cloverdale Community Schools (PK-12)
    2012-13 Enrollment: 1,290 . . . . (765) 795-4664
Housing: Homeownership rate: 65.9%; Homeowner vacancy rate: 4.4%; Rental vacancy rate: 8.2%
Newspapers: Hoosier Topics (weekly circulation 20000)
Additional Information Contacts
Town of Cloverdale . . . . (765) 653-2648
  http://www.co.putnam.in.us

FILLMORE (town). Covers a land area of 1.948 square miles and a water area of 0 square miles. Located at 39.67° N. Lat; 86.75° W. Long. Elevation is 837 feet.
History: Laid out 1837.
Population: 533; Growth (since 2000): -2.2%; Density: 273.5 persons per square mile; Race: 97.0% White, 0.6% Black/African American, 0.6% Asian, 0.2% American Indian/Alaska Native, 0.0% Native Hawaiian/Other Pacific Islander, 1.1% Two or more races, 5.3% Hispanic of any race; Average household size: 2.75; Median age: 35.9; Age under 18: 27.6%; Age 65 and over: 10.3%; Males per 100 females: 94.5

School District(s)
South Putnam Community Schools (KG-12)
    2012-13 Enrollment: 1,183 . . . . (765) 653-3119
Housing: Homeownership rate: 79.4%; Homeowner vacancy rate: 1.3%; Rental vacancy rate: 2.4%

GREENCASTLE (city)

County seat. Covers a land area of 5.242 square miles and a water area of 0.051 square miles. Located at 39.64° N. Lat; 86.85° W. Long. Elevation is 843 feet.

History: Indiana Asbury University, which later became DePauw University, was founded in 1837 in Greencastle by the Methodist Episcopal Church.

Population: 10,326; Growth (since 2000): 4.5%; Density: 1,969.8 persons per square mile; Race: 92.4% White, 2.7% Black/African American, 1.9% Asian, 0.3% American Indian/Alaska Native, 0.0% Native Hawaiian/Other Pacific Islander, 1.8% Two or more races, 2.5% Hispanic of any race; Average household size: 2.27; Median age: 27.4; Age under 18: 19.0%; Age 65 and over: 14.2%; Males per 100 females: 87.5; Marriage status: 46.6% never married, 36.6% now married, 1.6% separated, 6.8% widowed, 10.0% divorced; Foreign born: 4.1%; Speak English only: 94.1%; With disability: 13.9%; Veterans: 5.6%; Ancestry: 27.6% German, 18.4% Irish, 13.5% American, 7.0% English, 4.2% Polish

Employment: 10.8% management, business, and financial, 4.8% computer, engineering, and science, 17.5% education, legal, community service, arts, and media, 2.0% healthcare practitioners, 22.7% service, 18.2% sales and office, 5.1% natural resources, construction, and maintenance, 18.8% production, transportation, and material moving

Income: Per capita: $17,837; Median household: $40,949; Average household: $57,170; Households with income of $100,000 or more: 14.8%; Poverty rate: 14.0%

Educational Attainment: High school diploma or higher: 85.4%; Bachelor's degree or higher: 24.3%; Graduate/professional degree or higher: 12.2%

School District(s)
Area 30 Career Center Edu Inter (09-12)
    2012-13 Enrollment: n/a . . . . (765) 653-3515
Greencastle Community Sch Corp (PK-12)
    2012-13 Enrollment: 2,020 . . . . (765) 653-9771
Old National Trail Spec Serv Coop (PK-12)
    2012-13 Enrollment: n/a . . . . (765) 653-2781
South Putnam Community Schools (KG-12)
    2012-13 Enrollment: 1,183 . . . . (765) 653-3119

Four-year College(s)
DePauw University (Private, Not-for-profit, United Methodist)
    Fall 2013 Enrollment: 2,304 . . . . (765) 658-4800
    2013-14 Tuition: In-state $40,640; Out-of-state $40,640

Housing: Homeownership rate: 55.6%; Median home value: $115,400; Median year structure built: 1964; Homeowner vacancy rate: 3.8%; Median gross rent: $627 per month; Rental vacancy rate: 10.0%

Health Insurance: 90.1% have insurance; 75.3% have private insurance; 25.0% have public insurance; 9.9% do not have insurance; 7.8% of children under 18 do not have insurance

Hospitals: Putnam County Hospital (85 beds)

Newspapers: Banner-Graphic (daily circulation 6600)

Transportation: Commute: 74.1% car, 0.0% public transportation, 19.3% walk, 2.9% work from home; Median travel time to work: 17.2 minutes

Airports: Putnam County (general aviation)

Additional Information Contacts
City of Greencastle . . . . (765) 653-3100
http://www.cityofgreencastle.com

HERITAGE LAKE (CDP)

Covers a land area of 3.012 square miles and a water area of 0.469 square miles. Located at 39.73° N. Lat; 86.71° W. Long. Elevation is 860 feet.

Population: 2,880; Growth (since 2000): n/a; Density: 956.0 persons per square mile; Race: 97.3% White, 0.9% Black/African American, 0.2% Asian, 0.4% American Indian/Alaska Native, 0.0% Native Hawaiian/Other Pacific Islander, 0.7% Two or more races, 1.9% Hispanic of any race; Average household size: 2.69; Median age: 39.3; Age under 18: 26.1%; Age 65 and over: 12.1%; Males per 100 females: 102.7; Marriage status: 27.4% never married, 59.8% now married, 1.6% separated, 2.4% widowed, 10.4% divorced; Foreign born: 0.6%; Speak English only: 92.1%; With disability: 9.1%; Veterans: 10.4%; Ancestry: 33.3% German, 17.8% Irish, 17.2% English, 12.6% American, 7.5% Italian

Employment: 10.5% management, business, and financial, 0.0% computer, engineering, and science, 9.7% education, legal, community service, arts, and media, 4.1% healthcare practitioners, 12.3% service, 33.1% sales and office, 14.2% natural resources, construction, and maintenance, 16.1% production, transportation, and material moving

Income: Per capita: $28,242; Median household: $65,426; Average household: $79,161; Households with income of $100,000 or more: 16.4%; Poverty rate: 13.9%

Educational Attainment: High school diploma or higher: 90.5%; Bachelor's degree or higher: 13.2%; Graduate/professional degree or higher: 3.7%

Housing: Homeownership rate: 90.7%; Median home value: $139,600; Median year structure built: 1995; Homeowner vacancy rate: 3.6%; Median gross rent: $1,149 per month; Rental vacancy rate: 7.5%

Health Insurance: 82.1% have insurance; 66.5% have private insurance; 25.1% have public insurance; 17.9% do not have insurance; 13.4% of children under 18 do not have insurance

Transportation: Commute: 90.3% car, 0.0% public transportation, 0.0% walk, 9.7% work from home; Median travel time to work: 46.4 minutes

REELSVILLE (unincorporated postal area)

ZCTA: 46171

Covers a land area of 36.343 square miles and a water area of 0.067 square miles. Located at 39.53° N. Lat; 86.96° W. Long. Elevation is 702 feet.

Population: 1,695; Growth (since 2000): 1.0%; Density: 46.6 persons per square mile; Race: 97.1% White, 0.5% Black/African American, 0.2% Asian, 0.5% American Indian/Alaska Native, 0.0% Native Hawaiian/Other Pacific Islander, 1.3% Two or more races, 0.7% Hispanic of any race; Average household size: 2.60; Median age: 43.6; Age under 18: 22.3%; Age 65 and over: 14.6%; Males per 100 females: 99.6

School District(s)
South Putnam Community Schools (KG-12)
    2012-13 Enrollment: 1,183 . . . . (765) 653-3119

Housing: Homeownership rate: 89.0%; Homeowner vacancy rate: 2.5%; Rental vacancy rate: 7.7%

ROACHDALE (town)

Covers a land area of 0.507 square miles and a water area of 0 square miles. Located at 39.85° N. Lat; 86.80° W. Long. Elevation is 843 feet.

History: Laid out 1879.

Population: 926; Growth (since 2000): -5.0%; Density: 1,827.5 persons per square mile; Race: 99.2% White, 0.0% Black/African American, 0.0% Asian, 0.0% American Indian/Alaska Native, 0.0% Native Hawaiian/Other Pacific Islander, 0.8% Two or more races, 0.4% Hispanic of any race; Average household size: 2.60; Median age: 35.6; Age under 18: 29.3%; Age 65 and over: 13.3%; Males per 100 females: 98.7

School District(s)
North Putnam Community Schools (PK-12)
    2012-13 Enrollment: 1,626 . . . . (765) 522-6218

Housing: Homeownership rate: 67.5%; Homeowner vacancy rate: 2.4%; Rental vacancy rate: 13.1%

RUSSELLVILLE (town)

Covers a land area of 0.201 square miles and a water area of 0 square miles. Located at 39.86° N. Lat; 86.98° W. Long. Elevation is 820 feet.

History: Laid out 1828.

Population: 358; Growth (since 2000): 5.3%; Density: 1,776.9 persons per square mile; Race: 97.5% White, 0.0% Black/African American, 0.0% Asian, 1.1% American Indian/Alaska Native, 0.8% Native Hawaiian/Other Pacific Islander, 0.6% Two or more races, 0.3% Hispanic of any race; Average household size: 2.47; Median age: 42.6; Age under 18: 22.3%; Age 65 and over: 13.4%; Males per 100 females: 100.0

Housing: Homeownership rate: 78.0%; Homeowner vacancy rate: 3.4%; Rental vacancy rate: 3.0%

VAN BIBBER LAKE (CDP)

Covers a land area of 0.258 square miles and a water area of 0.097 square miles. Located at 39.73° N. Lat; 86.93° W. Long. Elevation is 804 feet.

Population: 485; Growth (since 2000): n/a; Density: 1,878.5 persons per square mile; Race: 98.8% White, 0.0% Black/African American, 0.6% Asian, 0.2% American Indian/Alaska Native, 0.0% Native Hawaiian/Other Pacific Islander, 0.0% Two or more races, 0.6% Hispanic of any race; Average household size: 2.29; Median age: 47.3; Age under 18: 19.8%; Age 65 and over: 20.0%; Males per 100 females: 106.4

Housing: Homeownership rate: 81.2%; Homeowner vacancy rate: 4.9%; Rental vacancy rate: 7.0%

Randolph County

Located in eastern Indiana; bounded on the east by Ohio; drained by the Mississinewa and Whitewater Rivers and the West Fork of the White River; includes the highest point in Indiana (1,240 ft). Covers a land area of 452.379 square miles, a water area of 0.935 square miles, and is located in the Eastern Time Zone at 40.16° N. Lat., 85.01° W. Long. The county was founded in 1818. County seat is Winchester.

Weather Station: Farmland 5 NNW   Elevation: 964 feet

	Jan	Feb	Mar	Apr	May	Jun	Jul	Aug	Sep	Oct	Nov	Dec
High	34	38	48	61	72	81	84	83	77	64	51	38
Low	17	19	28	38	49	59	62	60	52	40	32	22
Precip	2.1	1.9	2.8	3.7	4.3	4.2	4.8	3.6	3.0	3.0	3.3	2.6
Snow	7.1	5.9	3.1	0.4	tr	0.0	0.0	0.0	0.0	0.3	1.0	4.8

High and Low temperatures in degrees Fahrenheit; Precipitation and Snow in inches

Weather Station: Winchester Airport 3E   Elevation: 1,109 feet

	Jan	Feb	Mar	Apr	May	Jun	Jul	Aug	Sep	Oct	Nov	Dec
High	33	37	47	60	71	80	83	82	76	63	50	37
Low	18	20	29	40	51	60	63	61	54	43	33	22
Precip	2.1	1.7	2.7	3.7	4.4	4.5	4.4	3.5	2.9	3.0	3.3	2.8
Snow	5.9	5.4	2.5	0.3	0.0	0.0	0.0	0.0	0.0	0.1	0.5	3.9

High and Low temperatures in degrees Fahrenheit; Precipitation and Snow in inches

Population: 26,171; Growth (since 2000): -4.5%; Density: 57.9 persons per square mile; Race: 96.1% White, 0.4% Black/African American, 0.2% Asian, 0.3% American Indian/Alaska Native, 0.0% Native Hawaiian/Other Pacific Islander, 1.1% two or more races, 3.0% Hispanic of any race; Average household size: 2.47; Median age: 40.8; Age under 18: 24.4%; Age 65 and over: 17.1%; Males per 100 females: 97.4; Marriage status: 21.6% never married, 57.2% now married, 1.6% separated, 8.3% widowed, 12.9% divorced; Foreign born: 0.9%; Speak English only: 97.3%; With disability: 16.1%; Veterans: 10.0%; Ancestry: 22.7% German, 13.1% American, 10.8% Irish, 10.7% English, 2.3% French
Religion: Six largest groups: 9.2% Baptist, 7.1% Methodist/Pietist, 3.9% European Free-Church, 3.2% Holiness, 2.7% Catholicism, 2.3% Presbyterian-Reformed
Economy: Unemployment rate: 5.4%; Leading industries: 15.1% other services (except public administration); 14.1% retail trade; 9.7% manufacturing; Farms: 772 totaling 241,074 acres; Company size: 0 employ 1,000 or more persons, 0 employ 500 to 999 persons, 10 employ 100 to 499 persons, 486 employ less than 100 persons; Business ownership: 604 women-owned, n/a Black-owned, n/a Hispanic-owned, n/a Asian-owned
Employment: 10.1% management, business, and financial, 2.6% computer, engineering, and science, 8.8% education, legal, community service, arts, and media, 5.3% healthcare practitioners, 15.8% service, 19.9% sales and office, 12.6% natural resources, construction, and maintenance, 24.8% production, transportation, and material moving
Income: Per capita: $21,592; Median household: $40,904; Average household: $53,152; Households with income of $100,000 or more: 9.3%; Poverty rate: 17.4%
Educational Attainment: High school diploma or higher: 85.2%; Bachelor's degree or higher: 12.4%; Graduate/professional degree or higher: 4.5%
Housing: Homeownership rate: 73.3%; Median home value: $76,200; Median year structure built: 1956; Homeowner vacancy rate: 2.2%; Median gross rent: $606 per month; Rental vacancy rate: 10.1%
Vital Statistics: Birth rate: 114.3 per 10,000 population; Death rate: 101.5 per 10,000 population; Age-adjusted cancer mortality rate: 180.8 deaths per 100,000 population
Health Insurance: 85.5% have insurance; 63.6% have private insurance; 36.2% have public insurance; 14.5% do not have insurance; 10.0% of children under 18 do not have insurance
Health Care: Physicians: 5.0 per 10,000 population; Hospital beds: 9.6 per 10,000 population; Hospital admissions: 474.7 per 10,000 population
Transportation: Commute: 93.4% car, 0.3% public transportation, 2.0% walk, 3.1% work from home; Median travel time to work: 22.5 minutes
Presidential Election: 37.0% Obama, 61.0% Romney (2012)
Additional Information Contacts
Randolph Government .... (800) 905-0514
   http://www.randolphcounty.us

Randolph County Communities

FARMLAND (town). Covers a land area of 0.531 square miles and a water area of 0 square miles. Located at 40.19° N. Lat; 85.13° W. Long. Elevation is 1,040 feet.
History: Farmland was settled as a trading town for the surrounding farming area.
Population: 1,333; Growth (since 2000): -8.4%; Density: 2,510.9 persons per square mile; Race: 97.3% White, 0.2% Black/African American, 0.1% Asian, 1.4% American Indian/Alaska Native, 0.0% Native Hawaiian/Other Pacific Islander, 1.0% Two or more races, 1.1% Hispanic of any race; Average household size: 2.45; Median age: 39.3; Age under 18: 24.4%; Age 65 and over: 15.8%; Males per 100 females: 92.4
Housing: Homeownership rate: 72.1%; Homeowner vacancy rate: 4.6%; Rental vacancy rate: 12.7%

LOSANTVILLE (town). Covers a land area of 0.189 square miles and a water area of 0 square miles. Located at 40.02° N. Lat; 85.18° W. Long. Elevation is 1,132 feet.
History: Also called Bronson.
Population: 237; Growth (since 2000): -15.4%; Density: 1,256.5 persons per square mile; Race: 97.0% White, 0.0% Black/African American, 0.0% Asian, 0.4% American Indian/Alaska Native, 0.0% Native Hawaiian/Other Pacific Islander, 2.5% Two or more races, 0.0% Hispanic of any race; Average household size: 2.26; Median age: 37.4; Age under 18: 23.2%; Age 65 and over: 16.5%; Males per 100 females: 99.2
Housing: Homeownership rate: 71.4%; Homeowner vacancy rate: 8.5%; Rental vacancy rate: 23.1%

LYNN (town). Covers a land area of 0.565 square miles and a water area of 0 square miles. Located at 40.05° N. Lat; 84.94° W. Long. Elevation is 1,181 feet.
History: Lynn was established in 1847. The arrival of the railroad in 1852 brought a period of prosperity.
Population: 1,097; Growth (since 2000): -4.0%; Density: 1,942.2 persons per square mile; Race: 97.7% White, 0.5% Black/African American, 0.7% Asian, 0.1% American Indian/Alaska Native, 0.0% Native Hawaiian/Other Pacific Islander, 0.8% Two or more races, 1.9% Hispanic of any race; Average household size: 2.50; Median age: 37.9; Age under 18: 25.7%; Age 65 and over: 17.9%; Males per 100 females: 93.5
School District(s)
Randolph Southern School Corp (KG-12)
   2012-13 Enrollment: 535........................ (765) 874-1181
Housing: Homeownership rate: 68.8%; Homeowner vacancy rate: 1.6%; Rental vacancy rate: 13.8%

MODOC (town). Covers a land area of 0.103 square miles and a water area of 0 square miles. Located at 40.05° N. Lat; 85.13° W. Long. Elevation is 1,175 feet.
Population: 196; Growth (since 2000): -12.9%; Density: 1,896.9 persons per square mile; Race: 94.9% White, 0.5% Black/African American, 0.0% Asian, 0.0% American Indian/Alaska Native, 2.0% Native Hawaiian/Other Pacific Islander, 2.0% Two or more races, 1.5% Hispanic of any race; Average household size: 2.72; Median age: 33.0; Age under 18: 30.1%; Age 65 and over: 14.3%; Males per 100 females: 117.8
School District(s)
Union School Corporation (KG-12)
   2012-13 Enrollment: 392........................ (765) 853-5464
Housing: Homeownership rate: 65.3%; Homeowner vacancy rate: 6.0%; Rental vacancy rate: 3.8%

PARKER CITY (town). Covers a land area of 0.566 square miles and a water area of 0 square miles. Located at 40.19° N. Lat; 85.20° W. Long. Elevation is 1,024 feet.
History: Parker City was settled as a center for trading for the nearby farming communities.
Population: 1,419; Growth (since 2000): 0.2%; Density: 2,505.0 persons per square mile; Race: 97.7% White, 0.5% Black/African American, 0.0% Asian, 0.4% American Indian/Alaska Native, 0.0% Native Hawaiian/Other Pacific Islander, 1.4% Two or more races, 0.4% Hispanic of any race; Average household size: 2.46; Median age: 40.5; Age under 18: 25.3%; Age 65 and over: 19.4%; Males per 100 females: 86.5

School District(s)
Monroe Central School Corp (KG-12)
    2012-13 Enrollment: 977........................ (765) 468-6868
Housing: Homeownership rate: 72.1%; Homeowner vacancy rate: 3.4%; Rental vacancy rate: 3.8%

RIDGEVILLE
RIDGEVILLE (town). Covers a land area of 0.555 square miles and a water area of 0.001 square miles. Located at 40.29° N. Lat; 85.03° W. Long. Elevation is 997 feet.
History: Settled 1817, laid out 1837, incorporated 1868.
Population: 803; Growth (since 2000): -4.7%; Density: 1,447.9 persons per square mile; Race: 97.4% White, 0.0% Black/African American, 0.4% Asian, 0.4% American Indian/Alaska Native, 0.0% Native Hawaiian/Other Pacific Islander, 1.6% Two or more races, 0.6% Hispanic of any race; Average household size: 2.49; Median age: 35.1; Age under 18: 28.1%; Age 65 and over: 14.3%; Males per 100 females: 103.3
School District(s)
Randolph Central School Corp (KG-12)
    2012-13 Enrollment: 1,550 .... (765) 584-1401
Housing: Homeownership rate: 69.6%; Homeowner vacancy rate: 2.9%; Rental vacancy rate: 2.0%

SARATOGA
SARATOGA (town). Covers a land area of 0.265 square miles and a water area of 0 square miles. Located at 40.24° N. Lat; 84.92° W. Long. Elevation is 1,050 feet.
History: Laid out 1875.
Population: 254; Growth (since 2000): -11.8%; Density: 959.6 persons per square mile; Race: 98.8% White, 0.0% Black/African American, 0.0% Asian, 0.0% American Indian/Alaska Native, 0.0% Native Hawaiian/Other Pacific Islander, 0.4% Two or more races, 2.0% Hispanic of any race; Average household size: 2.49; Median age: 36.5; Age under 18: 28.7%; Age 65 and over: 14.6%; Males per 100 females: 84.1
Housing: Homeownership rate: 62.8%; Homeowner vacancy rate: 5.9%; Rental vacancy rate: 0.0%

UNION CITY
UNION CITY (city). Covers a land area of 2.200 square miles and a water area of 0.009 square miles. Located at 40.20° N. Lat; 84.82° W. Long. Elevation is 1,122 feet.
History: Union City was formed straddling the state line with Ohio. Isaac Pusey Gray, governor of Indiana from 1885-1889, lived here.
Population: 3,584; Growth (since 2000): -1.0%; Density: 1,628.9 persons per square mile; Race: 87.6% White, 1.1% Black/African American, 0.1% Asian, 0.1% American Indian/Alaska Native, 0.0% Native Hawaiian/Other Pacific Islander, 1.9% Two or more races, 12.8% Hispanic of any race; Average household size: 2.43; Median age: 35.4; Age under 18: 28.3%; Age 65 and over: 16.5%; Males per 100 females: 94.7; Marriage status: 24.7% never married, 49.4% now married, 3.0% separated, 6.2% widowed, 19.6% divorced; Foreign born: 2.7%; Speak English only: 93.2%; With disability: 16.9%; Veterans: 9.2%; Ancestry: 12.9% German, 12.4% Irish, 8.1% American, 7.1% English, 2.5% Dutch
Employment: 6.5% management, business, and financial, 4.6% computer, engineering, and science, 8.2% education, legal, community service, arts, and media, 5.8% healthcare practitioners, 15.5% service, 18.7% sales and office, 17.9% natural resources, construction, and maintenance, 22.9% production, transportation, and material moving
Income: Per capita: $15,359; Median household: $31,667; Average household: $38,505; Households with income of $100,000 or more: 4.5%; Poverty rate: 31.4%
Educational Attainment: High school diploma or higher: 80.0%; Bachelor's degree or higher: 7.9%; Graduate/professional degree or higher: 1.5%
School District(s)
Randolph Eastern School Corp (KG-12)
    2012-13 Enrollment: 903........................ (765) 964-4994
Housing: Homeownership rate: 58.6%; Median home value: $53,700; Median year structure built: 1955; Homeowner vacancy rate: 2.2%; Median gross rent: $586 per month; Rental vacancy rate: 16.2%
Health Insurance: 81.3% have insurance; 51.3% have private insurance; 46.0% have public insurance; 18.7% do not have insurance; 10.7% of children under 18 do not have insurance
Transportation: Commute: 92.2% car, 0.6% public transportation, 6.1% walk, 0.0% work from home; Median travel time to work: 22.5 minutes
Additional Information Contacts
City of Union City.. (765) 964-6534
   http://www.myunioncity.com

WINCHESTER
WINCHESTER (city). County seat. Covers a land area of 3.328 square miles and a water area of 0.013 square miles. Located at 40.17° N. Lat; 84.98° W. Long. Elevation is 1,093 feet.
History: Winchester developed as a grain and livestock shipping center, and as the seat of Randolph County.
Population: 4,935; Growth (since 2000): -2.0%; Density: 1,482.8 persons per square mile; Race: 96.1% White, 0.5% Black/African American, 0.5% Asian, 0.5% American Indian/Alaska Native, 0.0% Native Hawaiian/Other Pacific Islander, 1.1% Two or more races, 2.6% Hispanic of any race; Average household size: 2.32; Median age: 40.2; Age under 18: 23.6%; Age 65 and over: 18.9%; Males per 100 females: 91.0; Marriage status: 22.9% never married, 47.7% now married, 2.0% separated, 12.8% widowed, 16.5% divorced; Foreign born: 0.3%; Speak English only: 98.7%; With disability: 24.4%; Veterans: 9.6%; Ancestry: 24.7% German, 13.7% Irish, 13.5% American, 10.8% English, 4.6% French
Employment: 9.4% management, business, and financial, 3.1% computer, engineering, and science, 5.0% education, legal, community service, arts, and media, 5.5% healthcare practitioners, 19.5% service, 22.7% sales and office, 9.3% natural resources, construction, and maintenance, 25.5% production, transportation, and material moving
Income: Per capita: $23,839; Median household: $32,056; Average household: $56,502; Households with income of $100,000 or more: 9.4%; Poverty rate: 22.0%
Educational Attainment: High school diploma or higher: 79.1%; Bachelor's degree or higher: 7.9%; Graduate/professional degree or higher: 2.6%
School District(s)
Randolph Central School Corp (KG-12)
    2012-13 Enrollment: 1,550 .... (765) 584-1401
Housing: Homeownership rate: 60.7%; Median home value: $66,800; Median year structure built: 1954; Homeowner vacancy rate: 3.5%; Median gross rent: $623 per month; Rental vacancy rate: 9.9%
Health Insurance: 84.7% have insurance; 49.1% have private insurance; 48.6% have public insurance; 15.3% do not have insurance; 6.7% of children under 18 do not have insurance
Hospitals: Saint Vincent Randolph Hospital (25 beds)
Safety: Violent crime rate: 2.1 per 10,000 population; Property crime rate: 495.3 per 10,000 population
Newspapers: News-Gazette (daily circulation 3700)
Transportation: Commute: 92.4% car, 0.0% public transportation, 1.7% walk, 3.5% work from home; Median travel time to work: 19.2 minutes
Additional Information Contacts
City of Winchester....................................... (765) 584-1351
   http://www.winchester-in.gov

Ripley County

Located in southeastern Indiana; drained by Laughery and Graham Creeks. Covers a land area of 446.425 square miles, a water area of 1.636 square miles, and is located in the Eastern Time Zone at 39.10° N. Lat., 85.26° W. Long. The county was founded in 1816. County seat is Versailles.
Population: 28,818; Growth (since 2000): 8.7%; Density: 64.6 persons per square mile; Race: 97.6% White, 0.2% Black/African American, 0.5% Asian, 0.2% American Indian/Alaska Native, 0.0% Native Hawaiian/Other Pacific Islander, 0.9% two or more races, 1.5% Hispanic of any race; Average household size: 2.63; Median age: 39.2; Age under 18: 26.3%; Age 65 and over: 14.9%; Males per 100 females: 97.3; Marriage status: 22.5% never married, 59.3% now married, 1.2% separated, 6.5% widowed, 11.8% divorced; Foreign born: 1.4%; Speak English only: 97.5%; With disability: 13.8%; Veterans: 11.1%; Ancestry: 39.6% German, 12.8% Irish, 10.3% American, 8.6% English, 2.3% Italian
Religion: Six largest groups: 27.2% Catholicism, 14.8% Baptist, 6.3% Lutheran, 4.8% Methodist/Pietist, 2.2% Non-denominational Protestant, 1.4% Latter-day Saints
Economy: Unemployment rate: 5.9%; Leading industries: 16.3% retail trade; 13.0% other services (except public administration); 11.9% construction; Farms: 876 totaling 166,711 acres; Company size: 0 employ 1,000 or more persons, 6 employ 500 to 999 persons, 8 employ 100 to 499 persons, 624 employ less than 100 persons; Business ownership: n/a women-owned, n/a Black-owned, n/a Hispanic-owned, n/a Asian-owned
Employment: 10.5% management, business, and financial, 4.1% computer, engineering, and science, 6.7% education, legal, community service, arts, and media, 5.0% healthcare practitioners, 16.6% service,

24.4% sales and office, 12.6% natural resources, construction, and maintenance, 20.1% production, transportation, and material moving
Income: Per capita: $22,059; Median household: $47,537; Average household: $58,138; Households with income of $100,000 or more: 13.8%; Poverty rate: 9.4%
Educational Attainment: High school diploma or higher: 86.3%; Bachelor's degree or higher: 15.9%; Graduate/professional degree or higher: 4.3%
Housing: Homeownership rate: 76.1%; Median home value: $132,000; Median year structure built: 1973; Homeowner vacancy rate: 1.7%; Median gross rent: $653 per month; Rental vacancy rate: 10.9%
Vital Statistics: Birth rate: 109.1 per 10,000 population; Death rate: 98.5 per 10,000 population; Age-adjusted cancer mortality rate: 215.6 deaths per 100,000 population
Health Insurance: 88.3% have insurance; 73.0% have private insurance; 27.5% have public insurance; 11.7% do not have insurance; 5.5% of children under 18 do not have insurance
Health Care: Physicians: 12.6 per 10,000 population; Hospital beds: 8.7 per 10,000 population; Hospital admissions: 684.0 per 10,000 population
Transportation: Commute: 92.6% car, 0.4% public transportation, 1.7% walk, 3.7% work from home; Median travel time to work: 26.3 minutes
Presidential Election: 29.5% Obama, 68.1% Romney (2012)
National and State Parks: Versailles State Park
Additional Information Contacts
Ripley Government . . . . (812) 689-6115
  http://www.ripleycounty.com

Ripley County Communities

BATESVILLE (city). Covers a land area of 6.087 square miles and a water area of 0.066 square miles. Located at 39.30° N. Lat; 85.21° W. Long. Elevation is 971 feet.
History: Batesville was settled by German immigrants, and developed as a furniture manufacturing center.
Population: 6,520; Growth (since 2000): 8.1%; Density: 1,071.1 persons per square mile; Race: 95.1% White, 0.3% Black/African American, 1.7% Asian, 0.2% American Indian/Alaska Native, 0.1% Native Hawaiian/Other Pacific Islander, 1.0% Two or more races, 3.3% Hispanic of any race; Average household size: 2.55; Median age: 38.2; Age under 18: 28.6%; Age 65 and over: 15.9%; Males per 100 females: 91.3; Marriage status: 23.9% never married, 59.9% now married, 0.4% separated, 6.5% widowed, 9.7% divorced; Foreign born: 2.1%; Speak English only: 96.7%; With disability: 9.0%; Veterans: 8.4%; Ancestry: 47.7% German, 10.4% American, 10.4% Irish, 8.7% English, 2.6% Italian
Employment: 17.7% management, business, and financial, 6.1% computer, engineering, and science, 9.3% education, legal, community service, arts, and media, 3.9% healthcare practitioners, 14.2% service, 29.2% sales and office, 4.5% natural resources, construction, and maintenance, 15.0% production, transportation, and material moving
Income: Per capita: $30,852; Median household: $59,728; Average household: $81,004; Households with income of $100,000 or more: 25.4%; Poverty rate: 4.8%
Educational Attainment: High school diploma or higher: 92.4%; Bachelor's degree or higher: 31.4%; Graduate/professional degree or higher: 9.9%
School District(s)
Batesville Community Sch Corp (PK-12)
  2012-13 Enrollment: 2,146 . . . . (812) 934-2194
Housing: Homeownership rate: 66.5%; Median home value: $181,000; Median year structure built: 1977; Homeowner vacancy rate: 1.7%; Median gross rent: $734 per month; Rental vacancy rate: 10.3%
Health Insurance: 90.9% have insurance; 80.6% have private insurance; 22.5% have public insurance; 9.1% do not have insurance; 4.6% of children under 18 do not have insurance
Hospitals: Margaret Mary Community Hospital (79 beds)
Safety: Violent crime rate: 40.1 per 10,000 population; Property crime rate: 171.1 per 10,000 population
Newspapers: The Herald-Tribune (weekly circulation 4000)
Transportation: Commute: 93.1% car, 0.6% public transportation, 1.0% walk, 4.1% work from home; Median travel time to work: 17.8 minutes
Airports: Batesville (general aviation)
Additional Information Contacts
City of Batesville . . . . (812) 933-6101
  http://www.batesvilleindiana.us

CROSS PLAINS (unincorporated postal area)
ZCTA: 47017
  Covers a land area of 15.410 square miles and a water area of 0.080 square miles. Located at 38.94° N. Lat; 85.19° W. Long. Elevation is 961 feet.
Population: 507; Growth (since 2000): 4.8%; Density: 32.9 persons per square mile; Race: 98.4% White, 0.0% Black/African American, 0.0% Asian, 0.0% American Indian/Alaska Native, 0.0% Native Hawaiian/Other Pacific Islander, 1.6% Two or more races, 0.2% Hispanic of any race; Average household size: 2.57; Median age: 40.8; Age under 18: 24.1%; Age 65 and over: 15.0%; Males per 100 females: 103.6
Housing: Homeownership rate: 85.3%; Homeowner vacancy rate: 1.7%; Rental vacancy rate: 6.5%

HOLTON (town). Covers a land area of 1.807 square miles and a water area of 0 square miles. Located at 39.08° N. Lat; 85.38° W. Long. Elevation is 909 feet.
Population: 480; Growth (since 2000): 17.9%; Density: 265.6 persons per square mile; Race: 96.3% White, 1.5% Black/African American, 0.0% Asian, 0.2% American Indian/Alaska Native, 0.0% Native Hawaiian/Other Pacific Islander, 1.7% Two or more races, 0.4% Hispanic of any race; Average household size: 2.81; Median age: 32.5; Age under 18: 30.4%; Age 65 and over: 11.7%; Males per 100 females: 99.2
Housing: Homeownership rate: 71.4%; Homeowner vacancy rate: 2.4%; Rental vacancy rate: 15.5%

MILAN (town). Covers a land area of 1.950 square miles and a water area of 0.034 square miles. Located at 39.12° N. Lat; 85.13° W. Long. Elevation is 991 feet.
History: Laid out 1854.
Population: 1,899; Growth (since 2000): 4.6%; Density: 973.8 persons per square mile; Race: 97.7% White, 0.3% Black/African American, 0.1% Asian, 0.2% American Indian/Alaska Native, 0.0% Native Hawaiian/Other Pacific Islander, 1.4% Two or more races, 0.8% Hispanic of any race; Average household size: 2.53; Median age: 36.7; Age under 18: 28.1%; Age 65 and over: 17.9%; Males per 100 females: 87.3
School District(s)
Milan Community Schools (KG-12)
  2012-13 Enrollment: 1,200 . . . . (812) 654-2365
Housing: Homeownership rate: 61.5%; Homeowner vacancy rate: 2.7%; Rental vacancy rate: 10.5%

NAPOLEON (town). Covers a land area of 0.198 square miles and a water area of 0 square miles. Located at 39.20° N. Lat; 85.33° W. Long. Elevation is 965 feet.
History: Laid out 1820.
Population: 234; Growth (since 2000): -1.7%; Density: 1,180.9 persons per square mile; Race: 100.0% White, 0.0% Black/African American, 0.0% Asian, 0.0% American Indian/Alaska Native, 0.0% Native Hawaiian/Other Pacific Islander, 0.0% Two or more races, 1.3% Hispanic of any race; Average household size: 2.11; Median age: 45.3; Age under 18: 17.5%; Age 65 and over: 16.7%; Males per 100 females: 103.5
Housing: Homeownership rate: 66.6%; Homeowner vacancy rate: 5.1%; Rental vacancy rate: 17.8%

OSGOOD (town). Covers a land area of 1.451 square miles and a water area of 0.034 square miles. Located at 39.13° N. Lat; 85.29° W. Long. Elevation is 984 feet.
History: Laid out 1857.
Population: 1,624; Growth (since 2000): -2.7%; Density: 1,119.2 persons per square mile; Race: 98.2% White, 0.1% Black/African American, 0.0% Asian, 0.2% American Indian/Alaska Native, 0.0% Native Hawaiian/Other Pacific Islander, 1.5% Two or more races, 1.3% Hispanic of any race; Average household size: 2.45; Median age: 36.0; Age under 18: 26.9%; Age 65 and over: 16.4%; Males per 100 females: 90.4
School District(s)
Jac-Cen-Del Community Sch Corp (KG-12)
  2012-13 Enrollment: 874 . . . . (812) 689-4114
Housing: Homeownership rate: 61.1%; Homeowner vacancy rate: 3.2%; Rental vacancy rate: 11.1%

SUNMAN (town). Covers a land area of 1.171 square miles and a water area of 0 square miles. Located at 39.24° N. Lat; 85.09° W. Long. Elevation is 1,020 feet.
History: Laid out 1856.
Population: 1,049; Growth (since 2000): 30.3%; Density: 896.0 persons per square mile; Race: 95.1% White, 0.6% Black/African American, 0.2% Asian, 0.0% American Indian/Alaska Native, 0.0% Native Hawaiian/Other Pacific Islander, 1.4% Two or more races, 7.9% Hispanic of any race; Average household size: 2.83; Median age: 32.0; Age under 18: 30.0%; Age 65 and over: 11.9%; Males per 100 females: 104.9
School District(s)
Sunman-Dearborn Com Sch Corp (KG-12)
   2012-13 Enrollment: 4,133 . . . . (812) 623-2291
Housing: Homeownership rate: 59.5%; Homeowner vacancy rate: 1.8%; Rental vacancy rate: 18.0%

VERSAILLES (town). County seat. Covers a land area of 1.514 square miles and a water area of 0 square miles. Located at 39.06° N. Lat; 85.26° W. Long. Elevation is 965 feet.
History: Versailles was founded in 1818 as a farming center. General John Morgan and his men came to Versailles in 1863 and looted the office of the county treasurer.
Population: 2,113; Growth (since 2000): 18.4%; Density: 1,395.5 persons per square mile; Race: 98.2% White, 0.2% Black/African American, 0.3% Asian, 0.0% American Indian/Alaska Native, 0.0% Native Hawaiian/Other Pacific Islander, 1.2% Two or more races, 0.4% Hispanic of any race; Average household size: 2.32; Median age: 37.9; Age under 18: 23.6%; Age 65 and over: 15.9%; Males per 100 females: 90.5
School District(s)
South Ripley Com Sch Corp (KG-12)
   2012-13 Enrollment: 1,134 . . . . (812) 689-6282
Southeastern Career Center (09-12)
   2012-13 Enrollment: n/a . . . . (812) 689-5253
Housing: Homeownership rate: 57.6%; Homeowner vacancy rate: 4.7%; Rental vacancy rate: 13.9%
Newspapers: Osgood Journal (weekly circulation 5300); Versailles Republican (weekly circulation 5000)

Rush County

Located in east central Indiana; drained by the Big Blue River and Flatrock Creek. Covers a land area of 408.124 square miles, a water area of 0.337 square miles, and is located in the Eastern Time Zone at 39.62° N. Lat., 85.47° W. Long. The county was founded in 1821. County seat is Rushville.

Weather Station: Rushville Sewage Plant   Elevation: 959 feet

	Jan	Feb	Mar	Apr	May	Jun	Jul	Aug	Sep	Oct	Nov	Dec
High	35	39	50	62	73	81	84	83	77	65	52	39
Low	19	21	29	40	51	60	64	61	53	42	33	23
Precip	2.9	2.5	3.3	4.6	5.5	4.3	4.6	3.4	3.0	3.1	3.5	3.3
Snow	4.6	4.1	1.7	0.1	tr	0.0	0.0	0.0	0.0	0.3	0.2	3.7

High and Low temperatures in degrees Fahrenheit; Precipitation and Snow in inches

Population: 17,392; Growth (since 2000): -4.8%; Density: 42.6 persons per square mile; Race: 97.4% White, 0.8% Black/African American, 0.3% Asian, 0.2% American Indian/Alaska Native, 0.0% Native Hawaiian/Other Pacific Islander, 0.8% two or more races, 1.1% Hispanic of any race; Average household size: 2.54; Median age: 40.6; Age under 18: 24.8%; Age 65 and over: 15.8%; Males per 100 females: 97.3; Marriage status: 21.1% never married, 59.0% now married, 0.7% separated, 7.6% widowed, 12.3% divorced; Foreign born: 0.5%; Speak English only: 97.8%; With disability: 14.9%; Veterans: 10.7%; Ancestry: 21.5% German, 14.5% American, 12.3% English, 10.7% Irish, 1.9% French
Religion: Six largest groups: 24.6% Baptist, 9.4% Catholicism, 5.9% Methodist/Pietist, 2.9% Non-denominational Protestant, 2.1% Holiness, 2.0% European Free-Church
Economy: Unemployment rate: 4.6%; Leading industries: 14.7% other services (except public administration); 13.6% retail trade; 9.4% professional, scientific, and technical services; Farms: 601 totaling 207,572 acres; Company size: 0 employ 1,000 or more persons, 0 employ 500 to 999 persons, 5 employ 100 to 499 persons, 355 employ less than 100 persons; Business ownership: 394 women-owned, n/a Black-owned, n/a Hispanic-owned, n/a Asian-owned
Employment: 14.4% management, business, and financial, 2.9% computer, engineering, and science, 7.2% education, legal, community service, arts, and media, 5.5% healthcare practitioners, 14.4% service, 20.3% sales and office, 10.2% natural resources, construction, and maintenance, 25.0% production, transportation, and material moving
Income: Per capita: $23,396; Median household: $47,401; Average household: $58,363; Households with income of $100,000 or more: 14.6%; Poverty rate: 15.4%
Educational Attainment: High school diploma or higher: 87.1%; Bachelor's degree or higher: 15.1%; Graduate/professional degree or higher: 5.5%
Housing: Homeownership rate: 73.1%; Median home value: $104,700; Median year structure built: 1953; Homeowner vacancy rate: 2.3%; Median gross rent: $607 per month; Rental vacancy rate: 8.9%
Vital Statistics: Birth rate: 99.4 per 10,000 population; Death rate: 108.8 per 10,000 population; Age-adjusted cancer mortality rate: 244.5 deaths per 100,000 population
Health Insurance: 86.8% have insurance; 67.0% have private insurance; 32.9% have public insurance; 13.2% do not have insurance; 8.7% of children under 18 do not have insurance
Health Care: Physicians: 5.8 per 10,000 population; Hospital beds: 14.4 per 10,000 population; Hospital admissions: 276.4 per 10,000 population
Transportation: Commute: 91.7% car, 0.5% public transportation, 1.7% walk, 6.0% work from home; Median travel time to work: 26.3 minutes
Presidential Election: 31.6% Obama, 65.9% Romney (2012)
Additional Information Contacts
Rush Government . . . . (765) 932-5451
   http://www.rushcounty.in.gov

Rush County Communities

ARLINGTON (CDP). Covers a land area of 1.465 square miles and a water area of 0.018 square miles. Located at 39.65° N. Lat; 85.58° W. Long. Elevation is 922 feet.
Population: 433; Growth (since 2000): n/a; Density: 295.5 persons per square mile; Race: 97.7% White, 0.5% Black/African American, 0.7% Asian, 0.2% American Indian/Alaska Native, 0.2% Native Hawaiian/Other Pacific Islander, 0.7% Two or more races, 0.5% Hispanic of any race; Average household size: 2.64; Median age: 39.9; Age under 18: 24.7%; Age 65 and over: 14.8%; Males per 100 females: 104.2
School District(s)
Rush County Schools (PK-12)
   2012-13 Enrollment: 2,490 . . . . (765) 932-4186
Housing: Homeownership rate: 84.2%; Homeowner vacancy rate: 2.1%; Rental vacancy rate: 10.3%

CARTHAGE (town). Covers a land area of 0.582 square miles and a water area of 0 square miles. Located at 39.74° N. Lat; 85.57° W. Long. Elevation is 876 feet.
Population: 927; Growth (since 2000): -0.1%; Density: 1,593.8 persons per square mile; Race: 98.6% White, 0.0% Black/African American, 0.2% Asian, 0.2% American Indian/Alaska Native, 0.0% Native Hawaiian/Other Pacific Islander, 1.0% Two or more races, 0.3% Hispanic of any race; Average household size: 2.64; Median age: 37.3; Age under 18: 28.2%; Age 65 and over: 11.8%; Males per 100 females: 99.8
School District(s)
C A Beard Memorial School Corp (KG-12)
   2012-13 Enrollment: 1,318 . . . . (765) 345-5101
Housing: Homeownership rate: 66.1%; Homeowner vacancy rate: 4.1%; Rental vacancy rate: 18.5%

FALMOUTH (unincorporated postal area)
ZCTA: 46127
   Covers a land area of 23.642 square miles and a water area of 0 square miles. Located at 39.71° N. Lat; 85.31° W. Long. Elevation is 1,047 feet.
Population: 416; Growth (since 2000): 11.2%; Density: 17.6 persons per square mile; Race: 98.1% White, 0.7% Black/African American, 0.0% Asian, 0.0% American Indian/Alaska Native, 0.5% Native Hawaiian/Other Pacific Islander, 0.5% Two or more races, 0.2% Hispanic of any race; Average household size: 2.70; Median age: 39.8; Age under 18: 26.2%; Age 65 and over: 13.9%; Males per 100 females: 89.1
Housing: Homeownership rate: 81.8%; Homeowner vacancy rate: 2.3%; Rental vacancy rate: 9.7%

GLENWOOD (town). Covers a land area of 0.176 square miles and a water area of 0 square miles. Located at 39.63° N. Lat; 85.30° W. Long. Elevation is 1,086 feet.
Population: 250; Growth (since 2000): -21.4%; Density: 1,418.6 persons per square mile; Race: 100.0% White, 0.0% Black/African American, 0.0% Asian, 0.0% American Indian/Alaska Native, 0.0% Native Hawaiian/Other Pacific Islander, 0.0% Two or more races, 0.4% Hispanic of any race; Average household size: 2.29; Median age: 45.5; Age under 18: 22.4%; Age 65 and over: 20.4%; Males per 100 females: 83.8
Housing: Homeownership rate: 78.9%; Homeowner vacancy rate: 2.2%; Rental vacancy rate: 16.7%

HOMER (unincorporated postal area)
ZCTA: 46146
Covers a land area of 0.778 square miles and a water area of 0 square miles. Located at 39.59° N. Lat; 85.57° W. Long. Elevation is 906 feet.
Population: 117; Growth (since 2000): n/a; Density: 150.4 persons per square mile; Race: 98.3% White, 0.9% Black/African American, 0.0% Asian, 0.9% American Indian/Alaska Native, 0.0% Native Hawaiian/Other Pacific Islander, 0.0% Two or more races, 0.9% Hispanic of any race; Average household size: 2.25; Median age: 42.2; Age under 18: 23.1%; Age 65 and over: 18.8%; Males per 100 females: 116.7
Housing: Homeownership rate: 73.1%; Homeowner vacancy rate: 0.0%; Rental vacancy rate: 0.0%

MANILLA (CDP). Covers a land area of 0.226 square miles and a water area of 0 square miles. Located at 39.57° N. Lat; 85.62° W. Long. Elevation is 892 feet.
Population: 267; Growth (since 2000): n/a; Density: 1,184.0 persons per square mile; Race: 96.3% White, 0.0% Black/African American, 1.1% Asian, 0.4% American Indian/Alaska Native, 0.0% Native Hawaiian/Other Pacific Islander, 0.4% Two or more races, 2.6% Hispanic of any race; Average household size: 2.43; Median age: 44.3; Age under 18: 21.3%; Age 65 and over: 13.5%; Males per 100 females: 107.0
Housing: Homeownership rate: 81.8%; Homeowner vacancy rate: 1.1%; Rental vacancy rate: 4.8%

MAYS (unincorporated postal area)
ZCTA: 46155
Covers a land area of 0.023 square miles and a water area of 0 square miles. Located at 39.74° N. Lat; 85.43° W. Long. Elevation is 1,010 feet.
Population: 103; Growth (since 2000): -37.2%; Density: 4,509.0 persons per square mile; Race: 99.0% White, 1.0% Black/African American, 0.0% Asian, 0.0% American Indian/Alaska Native, 0.0% Native Hawaiian/Other Pacific Islander, 0.0% Two or more races, 1.0% Hispanic of any race; Average household size: 2.71; Median age: 32.2; Age under 18: 33.0%; Age 65 and over: 6.8%; Males per 100 females: 102.0
School District(s)
Rush County Schools (PK-12)
    2012-13 Enrollment: 2,490 . . . . (765) 932-4186
Housing: Homeownership rate: 84.2%; Homeowner vacancy rate: 0.0%; Rental vacancy rate: 0.0%

MILROY (CDP). Covers a land area of 0.662 square miles and a water area of 0 square miles. Located at 39.50° N. Lat; 85.47° W. Long. Elevation is 965 feet.
Population: 604; Growth (since 2000): n/a; Density: 912.0 persons per square mile; Race: 96.9% White, 0.2% Black/African American, 0.2% Asian, 1.2% American Indian/Alaska Native, 0.0% Native Hawaiian/Other Pacific Islander, 1.3% Two or more races, 1.8% Hispanic of any race; Average household size: 2.73; Median age: 38.7; Age under 18: 28.1%; Age 65 and over: 13.9%; Males per 100 females: 93.0
School District(s)
Rush County Schools (PK-12)
    2012-13 Enrollment: 2,490 . . . . (765) 932-4186
Housing: Homeownership rate: 75.6%; Homeowner vacancy rate: 3.4%; Rental vacancy rate: 18.2%

RUSHVILLE (city). County seat. Covers a land area of 3.091 square miles and a water area of 0 square miles. Located at 39.62° N. Lat; 85.45° W. Long. Elevation is 958 feet.
History: Rushville was founded in 1822 and named for Benjamin F. Rush, a Revolutionary War soldier and a signer of the Declaration of Independence.
Population: 6,341; Growth (since 2000): 5.8%; Density: 2,051.6 persons per square mile; Race: 95.8% White, 1.5% Black/African American, 0.6% Asian, 0.1% American Indian/Alaska Native, 0.0% Native Hawaiian/Other Pacific Islander, 1.2% Two or more races, 1.2% Hispanic of any race; Average household size: 2.36; Median age: 39.3; Age under 18: 24.0%; Age 65 and over: 17.5%; Males per 100 females: 90.5; Marriage status: 22.0% never married, 51.3% now married, 1.2% separated, 11.2% widowed, 15.6% divorced; Foreign born: 0.3%; Speak English only: 96.4%; With disability: 18.0%; Veterans: 12.1%; Ancestry: 20.7% German, 15.4% American, 12.1% Irish, 10.9% English, 2.6% French
Employment: 7.7% management, business, and financial, 4.2% computer, engineering, and science, 5.7% education, legal, community service, arts, and media, 5.4% healthcare practitioners, 18.5% service, 25.6% sales and office, 4.0% natural resources, construction, and maintenance, 29.0% production, transportation, and material moving
Income: Per capita: $18,347; Median household: $35,111; Average household: $41,767; Households with income of $100,000 or more: 5.3%; Poverty rate: 21.2%
Educational Attainment: High school diploma or higher: 84.1%; Bachelor's degree or higher: 11.9%; Graduate/professional degree or higher: 4.5%
School District(s)
Rush County Schools (PK-12)
    2012-13 Enrollment: 2,490 . . . . (765) 932-4186
Housing: Homeownership rate: 59.2%; Median home value: $82,000; Median year structure built: 1951; Homeowner vacancy rate: 3.9%; Median gross rent: $555 per month; Rental vacancy rate: 8.4%
Health Insurance: 83.0% have insurance; 58.6% have private insurance; 38.5% have public insurance; 17.0% do not have insurance; 6.5% of children under 18 do not have insurance
Hospitals: Rush Memorial Hospital (25 beds)
Safety: Violent crime rate: 16.1 per 10,000 population; Property crime rate: 467.4 per 10,000 population
Newspapers: Rushville Republican (daily circulation 2700)
Transportation: Commute: 94.0% car, 0.5% public transportation, 3.0% walk, 2.5% work from home; Median travel time to work: 22.0 minutes
Additional Information Contacts
City of Rushville. . . . . (765) 932-2672
    http://www.cityofrushville.in.gov

Saint Joseph County

Located in northern Indiana; bounded on the north by Michigan; drained by the Saint Joseph, Yellow, and Kankakee Rivers. Covers a land area of 457.850 square miles, a water area of 3.535 square miles, and is located in the Eastern Time Zone at 41.62° N. Lat., 86.29° W. Long. The county was founded in 1830. County seat is South Bend.

Saint Joseph County is part of the South Bend-Mishawaka, IN-MI Metropolitan Statistical Area. The entire metro area includes: Saint Joseph County, IN; Cass County, MI

Weather Station: South Bend Michiana Regional   Elevation: 772 feet

	Jan	Feb	Mar	Apr	May	Jun	Jul	Aug	Sep	Oct	Nov	Dec
High	32	36	47	60	70	80	83	81	74	62	49	36
Low	18	21	29	39	49	59	63	62	54	43	34	23
Precip	2.3	2.0	2.5	3.3	3.7	3.8	4.0	4.0	3.7	3.4	3.2	2.7
Snow	20.3	15.1	7.4	1.5	tr	tr	tr	tr	tr	0.5	5.0	17.5

High and Low temperatures in degrees Fahrenheit; Precipitation and Snow in inches

Population: 266,931; Growth (since 2000): 0.5%; Density: 583.0 persons per square mile; Race: 78.7% White, 12.7% Black/African American, 1.9% Asian, 0.4% American Indian/Alaska Native, 0.1% Native Hawaiian/Other Pacific Islander, 2.9% two or more races, 7.3% Hispanic of any race; Average household size: 2.48; Median age: 36.2; Age under 18: 24.7%; Age 65 and over: 13.3%; Males per 100 females: 94.1; Marriage status: 33.8% never married, 48.2% now married, 1.5% separated, 6.2% widowed, 11.8% divorced; Foreign born: 5.7%; Speak English only: 90.4%;

With disability: 12.9%; Veterans: 8.9%; Ancestry: 23.3% German, 14.6% Irish, 10.9% Polish, 7.4% English, 4.9% American
Religion: Six largest groups: 29.7% Methodist/Pietist, 19.7% Catholicism, 3.5% Non-denominational Protestant, 2.5% Baptist, 1.9% Lutheran, 1.7% Pentecostal
Economy: Unemployment rate: 6.0%; Leading industries: 15.6% retail trade; 11.5% other services (except public administration); 11.0% health care and social assistance; Farms: 691 totaling 151,975 acres; Company size: 4 employ 1,000 or more persons, 9 employ 500 to 999 persons, 154 employ 100 to 499 persons, 5,693 employ less than 100 persons; Business ownership: 5,452 women-owned, 1,335 Black-owned, 394 Hispanic-owned, 346 Asian-owned
Employment: 12.3% management, business, and financial, 3.9% computer, engineering, and science, 12.2% education, legal, community service, arts, and media, 5.8% healthcare practitioners, 17.9% service, 25.6% sales and office, 7.1% natural resources, construction, and maintenance, 15.3% production, transportation, and material moving
Income: Per capita: $23,509; Median household: $44,582; Average household: $60,014; Households with income of $100,000 or more: 15.7%; Poverty rate: 17.7%
Educational Attainment: High school diploma or higher: 87.8%; Bachelor's degree or higher: 26.5%; Graduate/professional degree or higher: 10.5%
Housing: Homeownership rate: 69.3%; Median home value: $115,100; Median year structure built: 1964; Homeowner vacancy rate: 2.8%; Median gross rent: $711 per month; Rental vacancy rate: 11.9%
Vital Statistics: Birth rate: 130.7 per 10,000 population; Death rate: 89.8 per 10,000 population; Age-adjusted cancer mortality rate: 188.1 deaths per 100,000 population
Health Insurance: 86.2% have insurance; 68.5% have private insurance; 28.7% have public insurance; 13.8% do not have insurance; 6.7% of children under 18 do not have insurance
Health Care: Physicians: 26.8 per 10,000 population; Hospital beds: 34.8 per 10,000 population; Hospital admissions: 1,492.9 per 10,000 population
Air Quality Index: 48.5% good, 51.0% moderate, 0.3% unhealthy for sensitive individuals, 0.3% unhealthy (percent of days)
Transportation: Commute: 90.4% car, 1.4% public transportation, 3.5% walk, 3.2% work from home; Median travel time to work: 20.2 minutes
Presidential Election: 51.0% Obama, 47.5% Romney (2012)
National and State Parks: Potato Creek State Park
Additional Information Contacts
Saint Joseph Government........................ (574) 235-9635
  http://www.stjosephcountyindiana.com

Saint Joseph County Communities

GRANGER (CDP). Covers a land area of 25.567 square miles and a water area of 0.001 square miles. Located at 41.74° N. Lat; 86.14° W. Long. Elevation is 801 feet.
Population: 30,465; Growth (since 2000): 7.7%; Density: 1,191.6 persons per square mile; Race: 90.3% White, 2.5% Black/African American, 4.6% Asian, 0.1% American Indian/Alaska Native, 0.1% Native Hawaiian/Other Pacific Islander, 1.6% Two or more races, 2.4% Hispanic of any race; Average household size: 2.93; Median age: 40.8; Age under 18: 29.6%; Age 65 and over: 10.9%; Males per 100 females: 98.2; Marriage status: 21.5% never married, 68.4% now married, 0.6% separated, 4.1% widowed, 6.1% divorced; Foreign born: 5.8%; Speak English only: 92.1%; With disability: 7.2%; Veterans: 8.7%; Ancestry: 27.8% German, 15.3% Irish, 12.3% English, 9.0% Polish, 6.4% Italian
Employment: 20.7% management, business, and financial, 5.3% computer, engineering, and science, 16.7% education, legal, community service, arts, and media, 9.3% healthcare practitioners, 9.1% service, 26.8% sales and office, 4.1% natural resources, construction, and maintenance, 8.0% production, transportation, and material moving
Income: Per capita: $39,598; Median household: $91,952; Average household: $114,518; Households with income of $100,000 or more: 45.7%; Poverty rate: 3.0%
Educational Attainment: High school diploma or higher: 96.3%; Bachelor's degree or higher: 51.9%; Graduate/professional degree or higher: 21.7%

School District(s)
Penn-Harris-Madison Sch Corp (KG-12)
  2012-13 Enrollment: 10,420 .... (574) 259-7941

Vocational/Technical School(s)
Ross Medical Education Center-Granger (Private, For-profit)
  Fall 2013 Enrollment: 174 .... (574) 273-4479
  2013-14 Tuition: $15,680
Housing: Homeownership rate: 96.8%; Median home value: $193,200; Median year structure built: 1987; Homeowner vacancy rate: 1.5%; Median gross rent: $1,195 per month; Rental vacancy rate: 6.1%
Health Insurance: 95.0% have insurance; 88.8% have private insurance; 16.7% have public insurance; 5.0% do not have insurance; 2.4% of children under 18 do not have insurance
Transportation: Commute: 94.1% car, 0.2% public transportation, 0.3% walk, 4.4% work from home; Median travel time to work: 22.2 minutes

INDIAN VILLAGE (town). Covers a land area of 0.089 square miles and a water area of 0 square miles. Located at 41.71° N. Lat; 86.23° W. Long. Elevation is 728 feet.
Population: 133; Growth (since 2000): -7.6%; Density: 1,496.5 persons per square mile; Race: 91.0% White, 4.5% Black/African American, 1.5% Asian, 0.0% American Indian/Alaska Native, 0.0% Native Hawaiian/Other Pacific Islander, 3.0% Two or more races, 0.0% Hispanic of any race; Average household size: 2.22; Median age: 51.3; Age under 18: 14.3%; Age 65 and over: 18.8%; Males per 100 females: 114.5
Housing: Homeownership rate: 93.4%; Homeowner vacancy rate: 0.0%; Rental vacancy rate: 0.0%

LAKEVILLE (town). Covers a land area of 0.607 square miles and a water area of 0.003 square miles. Located at 41.53° N. Lat; 86.28° W. Long. Elevation is 843 feet.
Population: 786; Growth (since 2000): 38.6%; Density: 1,294.0 persons per square mile; Race: 97.5% White, 0.1% Black/African American, 0.0% Asian, 0.4% American Indian/Alaska Native, 0.0% Native Hawaiian/Other Pacific Islander, 1.5% Two or more races, 3.2% Hispanic of any race; Average household size: 2.14; Median age: 36.5; Age under 18: 24.7%; Age 65 and over: 13.9%; Males per 100 females: 96.0

School District(s)
Union-North United School Corp (KG-12)
  2012-13 Enrollment: 1,200 .... (574) 784-8141
Housing: Homeownership rate: 51.2%; Homeowner vacancy rate: 7.4%; Rental vacancy rate: 20.4%

MISHAWAKA (city). Covers a land area of 16.997 square miles and a water area of 0.348 square miles. Located at 41.67° N. Lat; 86.17° W. Long. Elevation is 722 feet.
History: Mishawaka, situated along the St. Joseph River, developed around the Mishawaka Woolen and Rubber Manufacturing Company plant where felt, rubberboots, and raincoats were produced. Mishawaka was named for the daughter of Shawnee Chief Elkhart.
Population: 48,252; Growth (since 2000): 3.6%; Density: 2,838.8 persons per square mile; Race: 86.1% White, 6.9% Black/African American, 1.9% Asian, 0.4% American Indian/Alaska Native, 0.1% Native Hawaiian/Other Pacific Islander, 2.9% Two or more races, 4.5% Hispanic of any race; Average household size: 2.21; Median age: 34.7; Age under 18: 23.1%; Age 65 and over: 13.6%; Males per 100 females: 88.9; Marriage status: 34.0% never married, 41.5% now married, 2.0% separated, 7.3% widowed, 17.2% divorced; Foreign born: 6.0%; Speak English only: 91.8%; With disability: 14.3%; Veterans: 9.6%; Ancestry: 24.5% German, 15.5% Irish, 9.0% Polish, 7.5% English, 5.4% American
Employment: 10.2% management, business, and financial, 3.2% computer, engineering, and science, 9.9% education, legal, community service, arts, and media, 5.9% healthcare practitioners, 18.0% service, 27.4% sales and office, 7.7% natural resources, construction, and maintenance, 17.8% production, transportation, and material moving
Income: Per capita: $20,912; Median household: $36,590; Average household: $46,992; Households with income of $100,000 or more: 9.0%; Poverty rate: 21.7%
Educational Attainment: High school diploma or higher: 86.5%; Bachelor's degree or higher: 23.4%; Graduate/professional degree or higher: 8.8%

School District(s)
Penn-Harris-Madison Sch Corp (KG-12)
  2012-13 Enrollment: 10,420 .... (574) 259-7941
School City of Mishawaka (PK-12)
  2012-13 Enrollment: 5,071 .... (574) 254-4537

Four-year College(s)
Bethel College-Indiana (Private, Not-for-profit, Missionary Church Inc)
 Fall 2013 Enrollment: 1,804 . . . . (574) 807-7000
 2013-14 Tuition: In-state $24,970; Out-of-state $24,970
Vocational/Technical School(s)
Regency Beauty Institute-South Bend (Private, For-profit)
 Fall 2013 Enrollment: 102 . . . . (800) 787-6456
 2013-14 Tuition: $16,200
Housing: Homeownership rate: 52.3%; Median home value: $93,900; Median year structure built: 1971; Homeowner vacancy rate: 4.0%; Median gross rent: $693 per month; Rental vacancy rate: 13.7%
Health Insurance: 81.5% have insurance; 62.4% have private insurance; 30.4% have public insurance; 18.5% do not have insurance; 9.1% of children under 18 do not have insurance
Hospitals: Saint Joseph Regional Medical Center (125 beds); Unity Medical & Surgical Hospital
Safety: Violent crime rate: 28.4 per 10,000 population; Property crime rate: 563.7 per 10,000 population
Newspapers: The Enterprise (weekly circulation 1800)
Transportation: Commute: 92.0% car, 1.6% public transportation, 1.8% walk, 3.1% work from home; Median travel time to work: 20.5 minutes
Additional Information Contacts
City of Mishawaka . . . . (574) 258-1616
 http://www.mishawakacity.com

NEW CARLISLE (town).
Covers a land area of 2.085 square miles and a water area of 0 square miles. Located at 41.71° N. Lat; 86.51° W. Long. Elevation is 814 feet.
History: New Carlisle was founded in 1835 and named for its founder, Richard R. Carlisle, who was an adventurer. The town became a trading center for the surrounding farm lands.
Population: 1,861; Growth (since 2000): 23.7%; Density: 892.6 persons per square mile; Race: 96.0% White, 0.8% Black/African American, 0.4% Asian, 0.6% American Indian/Alaska Native, 0.0% Native Hawaiian/Other Pacific Islander, 2.0% Two or more races, 1.3% Hispanic of any race; Average household size: 2.59; Median age: 36.1; Age under 18: 28.2%; Age 65 and over: 11.9%; Males per 100 females: 91.9
School District(s)
New Prairie United School Corp (KG-12)
 2012-13 Enrollment: 2,844 . . . . (574) 654-7273
Housing: Homeownership rate: 71.2%; Homeowner vacancy rate: 3.6%; Rental vacancy rate: 13.7%

NORTH LIBERTY (town).
Covers a land area of 0.980 square miles and a water area of 0 square miles. Located at 41.53° N. Lat; 86.43° W. Long. Elevation is 732 feet.
History: Laid out 1836.
Population: 1,896; Growth (since 2000): 35.2%; Density: 1,933.7 persons per square mile; Race: 96.2% White, 0.5% Black/African American, 0.4% Asian, 0.4% American Indian/Alaska Native, 0.0% Native Hawaiian/Other Pacific Islander, 2.4% Two or more races, 2.5% Hispanic of any race; Average household size: 2.66; Median age: 30.6; Age under 18: 32.8%; Age 65 and over: 10.9%; Males per 100 females: 87.5
School District(s)
John Glenn School Corporation (KG-12)
 2012-13 Enrollment: 1,894 . . . . (574) 586-3129
Housing: Homeownership rate: 64.9%; Homeowner vacancy rate: 2.9%; Rental vacancy rate: 6.7%
Safety: Violent crime rate: 0.0 per 10,000 population; Property crime rate: 52.9 per 10,000 population

NOTRE DAME (CDP).
Covers a land area of 1.208 square miles and a water area of 0.066 square miles. Located at 41.70° N. Lat; 86.24° W. Long.
History: Notre Dame is located north of South Bend in St. Joseph County, Indiana, and it includes the campuses of three colleges: University of Notre Dame, Saint Mary's College, and Holy Cross College.
Population: 5,973; Growth (since 2000): n/a; Density: 4,944.3 persons per square mile; Race: 84.0% White, 2.8% Black/African American, 7.4% Asian, 0.2% American Indian/Alaska Native, 0.1% Native Hawaiian/Other Pacific Islander, 4.1% Two or more races, 9.9% Hispanic of any race; Average household size: 2.18; Median age: 20.4; Age under 18: 0.6%; Age 65 and over: 2.3%; Males per 100 females: 111.5; Marriage status: 98.6% never married, 0.5% now married, 0.0% separated, 0.4% widowed, 0.4% divorced; Foreign born: 6.4%; Speak English only: 86.6%; With disability: 3.9%; Veterans: 0.2%; Ancestry: 39.6% Irish, 27.7% German, 17.7% Italian, 9.7% Polish, 7.2% English
Employment: 6.3% management, business, and financial, 8.4% computer, engineering, and science, 23.3% education, legal, community service, arts, and media, 0.3% healthcare practitioners, 29.6% service, 28.6% sales and office, 1.5% natural resources, construction, and maintenance, 2.0% production, transportation, and material moving
Income: Per capita: $3,690; Median household: $10,313; Average household: $19,452; Households with income of $100,000 or more: n/a; Poverty rate: 74.5%
Educational Attainment: High school diploma or higher: 94.5%; Bachelor's degree or higher: 73.9%; Graduate/professional degree or higher: 37.6%
Four-year College(s)
Holy Cross College (Private, Not-for-profit, Roman Catholic)
 Fall 2013 Enrollment: 524 . . . . (574) 239-8377
 2013-14 Tuition: In-state $25,450; Out-of-state $25,450
Saint Mary's College (Private, Not-for-profit, Roman Catholic)
 Fall 2013 Enrollment: 1,479 . . . . (574) 284-4000
 2013-14 Tuition: In-state $34,600; Out-of-state $34,600
University of Notre Dame (Private, Not-for-profit, Roman Catholic)
 Fall 2013 Enrollment: 12,124 . . . . (574) 631-5000
 2013-14 Tuition: In-state $44,605; Out-of-state $44,605
Housing: Homeownership rate: 6.1%; Median home value: n/a; Median year structure built: 1992; Homeowner vacancy rate: 0.0%; Median gross rent: $642 per month; Rental vacancy rate: 3.6%
Health Insurance: 94.2% have insurance; 92.4% have private insurance; 3.9% have public insurance; 5.8% do not have insurance; 0.0% of children under 18 do not have insurance
Transportation: Commute: 8.7% car, 0.0% public transportation, 75.1% walk, 10.4% work from home; Median travel time to work: 8.6 minutes

OSCEOLA (town).
Covers a land area of 1.357 square miles and a water area of 0.007 square miles. Located at 41.66° N. Lat; 86.08° W. Long. Elevation is 738 feet.
Population: 2,463; Growth (since 2000): 32.5%; Density: 1,815.5 persons per square mile; Race: 95.5% White, 1.4% Black/African American, 0.7% Asian, 0.2% American Indian/Alaska Native, 0.2% Native Hawaiian/Other Pacific Islander, 1.7% Two or more races, 2.1% Hispanic of any race; Average household size: 2.72; Median age: 35.7; Age under 18: 27.4%; Age 65 and over: 10.9%; Males per 100 females: 102.4
School District(s)
Penn-Harris-Madison Sch Corp (KG-12)
 2012-13 Enrollment: 10,420 . . . . (574) 259-7941
Housing: Homeownership rate: 85.3%; Homeowner vacancy rate: 2.7%; Rental vacancy rate: 4.9%

ROSELAND (town).
Covers a land area of 0.383 square miles and a water area of 0 square miles. Located at 41.72° N. Lat; 86.25° W. Long. Elevation is 728 feet.
History: Wild roses that grew in the countryside were the inspiration for the name of Roseland. In 1855 St. Mary's College was founded here by the Roman Catholic Church as a sister institution to Notre Dame University.
Population: 630; Growth (since 2000): -65.2%; Density: 1,645.8 persons per square mile; Race: 87.5% White, 2.7% Black/African American, 4.6% Asian, 1.0% American Indian/Alaska Native, 0.2% Native Hawaiian/Other Pacific Islander, 2.2% Two or more races, 5.1% Hispanic of any race; Average household size: 2.20; Median age: 35.2; Age under 18: 14.3%; Age 65 and over: 13.2%; Males per 100 females: 95.7
Housing: Homeownership rate: 63.4%; Homeowner vacancy rate: 6.1%; Rental vacancy rate: 11.7%

SOUTH BEND (city).
County seat. Covers a land area of 41.458 square miles and a water area of 0.417 square miles. Located at 41.68° N. Lat; 86.27° W. Long. Elevation is 692 feet.
History: South Bend was founded in 1823 by Alexis Coquillard, who called it Big St. Joseph Station. The location at a bend of the St. Joseph River caused settlers to refer to their community as The Bend, and in 1830 the Post Office officially named it South Bend. Early industries in South Bend were the Studebaker blacksmith and wagon shop which later became an automobile manufacturer, and the Oliver Chilled Plow Works, which used a process for chilling and hardening steel to increase its uses.
Population: 101,168; Growth (since 2000): -6.1%; Density: 2,440.3 persons per square mile; Race: 60.5% White, 26.6% Black/African

American, 1.3% Asian, 0.5% American Indian/Alaska Native, 0.1% Native Hawaiian/Other Pacific Islander, 4.2% Two or more races, 13.0% Hispanic of any race; Average household size: 2.48; Median age: 33.3; Age under 18: 27.3%; Age 65 and over: 12.5%; Males per 100 females: 93.9; Marriage status: 39.9% never married, 40.2% now married, 2.1% separated, 6.7% widowed, 13.1% divorced; Foreign born: 7.4%; Speak English only: 86.6%; With disability: 14.9%; Veterans: 8.5%; Ancestry: 16.6% German, 11.7% Irish, 9.2% Polish, 5.6% English, 3.8% American
Employment: 9.7% management, business, and financial, 3.3% computer, engineering, and science, 13.0% education, legal, community service, arts, and media, 5.1% healthcare practitioners, 21.4% service, 25.2% sales and office, 6.0% natural resources, construction, and maintenance, 16.3% production, transportation, and material moving
Income: Per capita: $19,181; Median household: $34,502; Average household: $47,150; Households with income of $100,000 or more: 8.8%; Poverty rate: 27.8%
Educational Attainment: High school diploma or higher: 83.9%; Bachelor's degree or higher: 22.9%; Graduate/professional degree or higher: 9.5%

School District(s)
Career Academy At South Bend (07-09)
    2012-13 Enrollment: 340 . . . . (574) 299-9800
In Department of Correction (06-12)
    2012-13 Enrollment: 484 . . . . (317) 233-3111
South Bend Community Sch Corp (PK-12)
    2012-13 Enrollment: 19,476 . . . . (574) 283-8000
Veritas Academy (KG-08)
    2012-13 Enrollment: 128 . . . . (574) 287-3230
Xavier School of Excellence (KG-07)
    2012-13 Enrollment: 368 . . . . (574) 231-6600

Four-year College(s)
Brown Mackie College-South Bend (Private, For-profit)
    Fall 2013 Enrollment: 423 . . . . (574) 237-0774
    2013-14 Tuition: In-state $12,114; Out-of-state $12,114
ITT Technical Institute-South Bend (Private, For-profit)
    Fall 2013 Enrollment: 330 . . . . (574) 247-8300
    2013-14 Tuition: In-state $18,048; Out-of-state $18,048
Indiana University-South Bend (Public)
    Fall 2013 Enrollment: 8,073 . . . . (574) 520-4872
    2013-14 Tuition: In-state $6,816; Out-of-state $17,778

Housing: Homeownership rate: 59.9%; Median home value: $85,100; Median year structure built: 1954; Homeowner vacancy rate: 3.9%; Median gross rent: $706 per month; Rental vacancy rate: 11.9%
Health Insurance: 82.5% have insurance; 56.2% have private insurance; 36.4% have public insurance; 17.5% do not have insurance; 7.2% of children under 18 do not have insurance
Hospitals: Memorial Hospital of South Bend (526 beds)
Safety: Violent crime rate: 65.9 per 10,000 population; Property crime rate: 485.5 per 10,000 population
Newspapers: South Bend Tribune (daily circulation 69600); Tri County News (weekly circulation 1000)
Transportation: Commute: 90.0% car, 2.8% public transportation, 3.2% walk, 2.1% work from home; Median travel time to work: 18.8 minutes; Amtrak: Train service available.
Airports: South Bend International (primary service/non-hub)
Additional Information Contacts
City of South Bend . . . . (574) 235-9221
    http://www.ci.south-bend.in.us

WALKERTON (town). Covers a land area of 1.961 square miles and a water area of 0 square miles. Located at 41.47° N. Lat; 86.48° W. Long. Elevation is 725 feet.
History: Walkerton was known as one of the largest peppermint-growing centers in the country.
Population: 2,144; Growth (since 2000): -5.7%; Density: 1,093.5 persons per square mile; Race: 95.0% White, 0.4% Black/African American, 0.3% Asian, 0.7% American Indian/Alaska Native, 0.0% Native Hawaiian/Other Pacific Islander, 1.5% Two or more races, 5.0% Hispanic of any race; Average household size: 2.70; Median age: 37.2; Age under 18: 26.5%; Age 65 and over: 14.4%; Males per 100 females: 88.4

School District(s)
John Glenn School Corporation (KG-12)
    2012-13 Enrollment: 1,894 . . . . (574) 586-3129
Housing: Homeownership rate: 70.4%; Homeowner vacancy rate: 2.0%; Rental vacancy rate: 12.4%
Safety: Violent crime rate: 4.4 per 10,000 population; Property crime rate: 192.6 per 10,000 population
Additional Information Contacts
Town of Walkerton . . . . (574) 586-3100
    http://www.walkerton.org

WYATT (unincorporated postal area)
ZCTA: 46595
    Covers a land area of 0.228 square miles and a water area of 0 square miles. Located at 41.53° N. Lat; 86.17° W. Long. Elevation is 830 feet.
Population: 163; Growth (since 2000): 39.3%; Density: 714.5 persons per square mile; Race: 100.0% White, 0.0% Black/African American, 0.0% Asian, 0.0% American Indian/Alaska Native, 0.0% Native Hawaiian/Other Pacific Islander, 0.0% Two or more races, 0.0% Hispanic of any race; Average household size: 2.72; Median age: 36.2; Age under 18: 30.1%; Age 65 and over: 9.8%; Males per 100 females: 89.5
Housing: Homeownership rate: 80.0%; Homeowner vacancy rate: 2.0%; Rental vacancy rate: 7.7%

Scott County

Located in southeastern Indiana; bounded on the north by the Muscatatuck River, and drained by its tributaries. Covers a land area of 190.397 square miles, a water area of 2.351 square miles, and is located in the Eastern Time Zone at 38.68° N. Lat., 85.75° W. Long. The county was founded in 1820. County seat is Scottsburg.

Scott County is part of the Louisville/Jefferson County, KY-IN Metropolitan Statistical Area. The entire metro area includes: Clark County, IN; Floyd County, IN; Harrison County, IN; Scott County, IN; Washington County, IN; Bullitt County, KY; Henry County, KY; Jefferson County, KY; Oldham County, KY; Shelby County, KY; Spencer County, KY; Trimble County, KY

Weather Station: Scottsburg   Elevation: 549 feet

	Jan	Feb	Mar	Apr	May	Jun	Jul	Aug	Sep	Oct	Nov	Dec
High	40	44	55	66	75	84	87	87	80	68	55	43
Low	22	24	32	42	53	61	65	63	54	42	34	25
Precip	3.2	2.9	4.3	4.5	5.2	4.2	4.3	4.3	3.1	3.1	3.7	3.5
Snow	3.3	4.1	2.5	0.1	0.0	0.0	0.0	0.0	0.0	0.2	0.1	2.5

High and Low temperatures in degrees Fahrenheit; Precipitation and Snow in inches

Population: 24,181; Growth (since 2000): 5.3%; Density: 127.0 persons per square mile; Race: 97.9% White, 0.2% Black/African American, 0.4% Asian, 0.2% American Indian/Alaska Native, 0.1% Native Hawaiian/Other Pacific Islander, 0.7% two or more races, 1.5% Hispanic of any race; Average household size: 2.54; Median age: 39.3; Age under 18: 24.0%; Age 65 and over: 13.4%; Males per 100 females: 97.7; Marriage status: 25.5% never married, 53.4% now married, 2.2% separated, 6.8% widowed, 14.4% divorced; Foreign born: 1.2%; Speak English only: 98.0%; With disability: 18.5%; Veterans: 8.9%; Ancestry: 18.9% American, 14.5% German, 11.1% Irish, 9.3% English, 2.9% Scottish
Religion: Six largest groups: 25.8% Baptist, 4.1% Non-denominational Protestant, 3.7% Pentecostal, 2.9% Methodist/Pietist, 1.7% Catholicism, 1.0% Latter-day Saints
Economy: Unemployment rate: 5.4%; Leading industries: 19.3% retail trade; 13.1% health care and social assistance; 11.1% other services (except public administration); Farms: 321 totaling 51,472 acres; Company size: 0 employ 1,000 or more persons, 1 employs 500 to 999 persons, 10 employ 100 to 499 persons, 394 employ less than 100 persons; Business ownership: 213 women-owned, n/a Black-owned, n/a Hispanic-owned, n/a Asian-owned
Employment: 7.5% management, business, and financial, 2.9% computer, engineering, and science, 7.4% education, legal, community service, arts, and media, 4.4% healthcare practitioners, 17.6% service, 21.6% sales and office, 9.6% natural resources, construction, and maintenance, 29.0% production, transportation, and material moving
Income: Per capita: $20,481; Median household: $42,898; Average household: $52,814; Households with income of $100,000 or more: 10.1%; Poverty rate: 19.0%
Educational Attainment: High school diploma or higher: 78.7%; Bachelor's degree or higher: 11.5%; Graduate/professional degree or higher: 3.5%
Housing: Homeownership rate: 71.5%; Median home value: $101,400; Median year structure built: 1977; Homeowner vacancy rate: 2.5%; Median gross rent: $716 per month; Rental vacancy rate: 9.5%

Vital Statistics: Birth rate: 121.0 per 10,000 population; Death rate: 116.8 per 10,000 population; Age-adjusted cancer mortality rate: 198.5 deaths per 100,000 population
Health Insurance: 86.7% have insurance; 63.8% have private insurance; 35.6% have public insurance; 13.3% do not have insurance; 4.4% of children under 18 do not have insurance
Health Care: Physicians: 5.9 per 10,000 population; Hospital beds: 10.4 per 10,000 population; Hospital admissions: 456.2 per 10,000 population
Transportation: Commute: 96.1% car, 0.2% public transportation, 1.3% walk, 1.4% work from home; Median travel time to work: 26.7 minutes
Presidential Election: 45.9% Obama, 52.1% Romney (2012)
Additional Information Contacts
Scott Government . . . . (812) 752-8420

Scott County Communities

AUSTIN (city). Covers a land area of 2.577 square miles and a water area of 0 square miles. Located at 38.74° N. Lat; 85.81° W. Long. Elevation is 558 feet.
History: The Morgan Packing Company plant established the community of Austin as a canning center.
Population: 4,295; Growth (since 2000): -9.1%; Density: 1,666.7 persons per square mile; Race: 97.1% White, 0.3% Black/African American, 0.2% Asian, 0.3% American Indian/Alaska Native, 0.0% Native Hawaiian/Other Pacific Islander, 1.2% Two or more races, 2.1% Hispanic of any race; Average household size: 2.56; Median age: 36.7; Age under 18: 25.9%; Age 65 and over: 12.3%; Males per 100 females: 94.7; Marriage status: 28.6% never married, 51.3% now married, 6.7% separated, 7.5% widowed, 12.6% divorced; Foreign born: 1.5%; Speak English only: 97.9%; With disability: 18.5%; Veterans: 4.3%; Ancestry: 18.5% American, 10.5% German, 9.3% Irish, 7.2% English, 1.9% Polish
Employment: 2.2% management, business, and financial, 4.2% computer, engineering, and science, 4.8% education, legal, community service, arts, and media, 3.7% healthcare practitioners, 17.7% service, 18.1% sales and office, 8.9% natural resources, construction, and maintenance, 40.4% production, transportation, and material moving
Income: Per capita: $15,170; Median household: $33,109; Average household: $40,597; Households with income of $100,000 or more: 4.6%; Poverty rate: 25.8%
Educational Attainment: High school diploma or higher: 71.3%; Bachelor's degree or higher: 4.7%; Graduate/professional degree or higher: 0.7%

School District(s)
Scott County SD 1 (KG-12)
  2012-13 Enrollment: 1,316 . . . . (812) 794-8750
Housing: Homeownership rate: 56.9%; Median home value: $74,500; Median year structure built: 1968; Homeowner vacancy rate: 3.3%; Median gross rent: $692 per month; Rental vacancy rate: 10.0%
Health Insurance: 84.9% have insurance; 47.1% have private insurance; 47.1% have public insurance; 15.1% do not have insurance; 1.9% of children under 18 do not have insurance
Transportation: Commute: 88.6% car, 0.0% public transportation, 4.3% walk, 2.3% work from home; Median travel time to work: 23.0 minutes
Additional Information Contacts
Town of Austin. . . . . (812) 752-4080
  http://www.greatscottindiana.com

SCOTTSBURG (city). County seat. Covers a land area of 5.053 square miles and a water area of 0.019 square miles. Located at 38.69° N. Lat; 85.78° W. Long. Elevation is 564 feet.
History: Laid out 1871.
Population: 6,747; Growth (since 2000): 11.7%; Density: 1,335.3 persons per square mile; Race: 97.2% White, 0.3% Black/African American, 0.9% Asian, 0.2% American Indian/Alaska Native, 0.0% Native Hawaiian/Other Pacific Islander, 0.6% Two or more races, 1.8% Hispanic of any race; Average household size: 2.34; Median age: 37.5; Age under 18: 23.3%; Age 65 and over: 15.9%; Males per 100 females: 90.4; Marriage status: 29.2% never married, 45.3% now married, 1.6% separated, 7.6% widowed, 17.9% divorced; Foreign born: 2.2%; Speak English only: 95.0%; With disability: 20.7%; Veterans: 8.4%; Ancestry: 19.0% American, 18.4% German, 10.6% Irish, 8.3% English, 4.8% Scotch-Irish
Employment: 5.4% management, business, and financial, 2.5% computer, engineering, and science, 10.0% education, legal, community service, arts, and media, 2.5% healthcare practitioners, 18.5% service, 28.8% sales and office, 8.3% natural resources, construction, and maintenance, 24.1% production, transportation, and material moving
Income: Per capita: $17,323; Median household: $38,483; Average household: $42,218; Households with income of $100,000 or more: 5.8%; Poverty rate: 24.3%
Educational Attainment: High school diploma or higher: 76.6%; Bachelor's degree or higher: 14.1%; Graduate/professional degree or higher: 4.5%

School District(s)
Scott County SD 2 (PK-12)
  2012-13 Enrollment: 2,808 . . . . (812) 752-8946
Housing: Homeownership rate: 58.0%; Median home value: $99,300; Median year structure built: 1973; Homeowner vacancy rate: 3.7%; Median gross rent: $688 per month; Rental vacancy rate: 11.6%
Health Insurance: 85.7% have insurance; 62.8% have private insurance; 37.4% have public insurance; 14.3% do not have insurance; 3.0% of children under 18 do not have insurance
Hospitals: Scott Memorial Hospital (90 beds)
Safety: Violent crime rate: 42.3 per 10,000 population; Property crime rate: 453.6 per 10,000 population
Transportation: Commute: 98.5% car, 0.0% public transportation, 0.9% walk, 0.2% work from home; Median travel time to work: 27.7 minutes
Additional Information Contacts
City of Scottsburg . . . . (812) 752-4343
  http://www.cityofscottsburg.com

UNDERWOOD (unincorporated postal area)
ZCTA: 47177
  Covers a land area of 16.667 square miles and a water area of 0.119 square miles. Located at 38.59° N. Lat; 85.79° W. Long..
Population: 1,221; Growth (since 2000): 96.9%; Density: 73.3 persons per square mile; Race: 97.8% White, 0.2% Black/African American, 0.0% Asian, 0.1% American Indian/Alaska Native, 0.0% Native Hawaiian/Other Pacific Islander, 2.0% Two or more races, 0.4% Hispanic of any race; Average household size: 2.58; Median age: 43.6; Age under 18: 21.7%; Age 65 and over: 14.1%; Males per 100 females: 102.8
Housing: Homeownership rate: 85.6%; Homeowner vacancy rate: 1.2%; Rental vacancy rate: 4.2%

Shelby County

Located in central Indiana; drained by the Big Blue River. Covers a land area of 411.147 square miles, a water area of 1.609 square miles, and is located in the Eastern Time Zone at 39.52° N. Lat., 85.79° W. Long. The county was founded in 1821. County seat is Shelbyville.

Shelby County is part of the Indianapolis-Carmel-Anderson, IN Metropolitan Statistical Area. The entire metro area includes: Boone County, IN; Brown County, IN; Hamilton County, IN; Hancock County, IN; Hendricks County, IN; Johnson County, IN; Madison County, IN; Marion County, IN; Morgan County, IN; Putnam County, IN; Shelby County, IN

Weather Station: Shelbyville Sewage Plant   Elevation: 750 feet

	Jan	Feb	Mar	Apr	May	Jun	Jul	Aug	Sep	Oct	Nov	Dec
High	36	40	51	63	73	82	85	84	78	66	53	39
Low	20	22	31	42	52	61	64	62	54	43	34	23
Precip	2.8	2.4	3.3	4.2	5.0	4.1	4.0	3.3	3.0	2.9	3.2	3.0
Snow	2.4	1.7	0.9	tr	0.0	0.0	0.0	0.0	0.0	tr	tr	0.8

High and Low temperatures in degrees Fahrenheit; Precipitation and Snow in inches

Population: 44,436; Growth (since 2000): 2.3%; Density: 108.1 persons per square mile; Race: 95.4% White, 1.0% Black/African American, 0.5% Asian, 0.2% American Indian/Alaska Native, 0.0% Native Hawaiian/Other Pacific Islander, 1.2% two or more races, 3.7% Hispanic of any race; Average household size: 2.53; Median age: 39.9; Age under 18: 24.4%; Age 65 and over: 13.9%; Males per 100 females: 98.2; Marriage status: 24.9% never married, 53.9% now married, 1.6% separated, 7.5% widowed, 13.7% divorced; Foreign born: 2.4%; Speak English only: 95.6%; With disability: 13.2%; Veterans: 10.3%; Ancestry: 24.5% German, 16.7% American, 12.6% Irish, 9.2% English, 2.2% French
Religion: Six largest groups: 10.8% Baptist, 8.1% Catholicism, 5.7% Methodist/Pietist, 4.9% Non-denominational Protestant, 2.1% Presbyterian-Reformed, 1.8% Holiness
Economy: Unemployment rate: 4.9%; Leading industries: 13.2% retail trade; 12.1% construction; 11.5% other services (except public

administration); Farms: 569 totaling 233,059 acres; Company size: 0 employ 1,000 or more persons, 4 employ 500 to 999 persons, 23 employ 100 to 499 persons, 877 employ less than 100 persons; Business ownership: 870 women-owned, n/a Black-owned, n/a Hispanic-owned, n/a Asian-owned
Employment: 11.7% management, business, and financial, 3.1% computer, engineering, and science, 6.4% education, legal, community service, arts, and media, 5.5% healthcare practitioners, 16.9% service, 21.0% sales and office, 11.5% natural resources, construction, and maintenance, 23.9% production, transportation, and material moving
Income: Per capita: $24,459; Median household: $51,440; Average household: $61,580; Households with income of $100,000 or more: 16.4%; Poverty rate: 12.9%
Educational Attainment: High school diploma or higher: 85.6%; Bachelor's degree or higher: 14.8%; Graduate/professional degree or higher: 4.4%
Housing: Homeownership rate: 71.6%; Median home value: $125,000; Median year structure built: 1967; Homeowner vacancy rate: 2.7%; Median gross rent: $697 per month; Rental vacancy rate: 10.4%
Vital Statistics: Birth rate: 123.9 per 10,000 population; Death rate: 89.7 per 10,000 population; Age-adjusted cancer mortality rate: 186.9 deaths per 100,000 population
Health Insurance: 85.2% have insurance; 67.9% have private insurance; 29.5% have public insurance; 14.8% do not have insurance; 8.5% of children under 18 do not have insurance
Health Care: Physicians: 5.6 per 10,000 population; Hospital beds: 16.4 per 10,000 population; Hospital admissions: 600.4 per 10,000 population
Air Quality Index: 91.8% good, 8.2% moderate, 0.0% unhealthy for sensitive individuals, 0.0% unhealthy (percent of days)
Transportation: Commute: 94.6% car, 0.2% public transportation, 0.9% walk, 3.1% work from home; Median travel time to work: 24.0 minutes
Presidential Election: 32.0% Obama, 65.5% Romney (2012)
Additional Information Contacts
Shelby Government . . . . (317) 392-6330
http://www.co.shelby.in.us

Shelby County Communities

BOGGSTOWN (unincorporated postal area)
ZCTA: 46110
Covers a land area of 14.544 square miles and a water area of 0.092 square miles. Located at 39.56° N. Lat; 85.92° W. Long. Elevation is 748 feet.
Population: 500; Growth (since 2000): -0.2%; Density: 34.4 persons per square mile; Race: 98.0% White, 0.0% Black/African American, 0.2% Asian, 0.0% American Indian/Alaska Native, 0.0% Native Hawaiian/Other Pacific Islander, 0.8% Two or more races, 1.8% Hispanic of any race; Average household size: 2.76; Median age: 44.4; Age under 18: 23.4%; Age 65 and over: 15.4%; Males per 100 females: 106.6
Housing: Homeownership rate: 86.7%; Homeowner vacancy rate: 0.0%; Rental vacancy rate: 7.1%

FAIRLAND (town).
Covers a land area of 0.164 square miles and a water area of <.001 square miles. Located at 39.59° N. Lat; 85.86° W. Long. Elevation is 774 feet.
Population: 315; Growth (since 2000): -75.3%; Density: 1,920.8 persons per square mile; Race: 98.1% White, 0.0% Black/African American, 0.0% Asian, 0.0% American Indian/Alaska Native, 0.0% Native Hawaiian/Other Pacific Islander, 0.3% Two or more races, 3.5% Hispanic of any race; Average household size: 2.60; Median age: 37.5; Age under 18: 27.9%; Age 65 and over: 13.0%; Males per 100 females: 93.3
School District(s)
Northwestern Con School Corp (KG-12)
2012-13 Enrollment: 1,399 . . . . (317) 835-7461
Housing: Homeownership rate: 76.9%; Homeowner vacancy rate: 1.1%; Rental vacancy rate: 9.7%

FLAT ROCK (unincorporated postal area)
ZCTA: 47234
Covers a land area of 33.039 square miles and a water area of 0 square miles. Located at 39.38° N. Lat; 85.77° W. Long. Elevation is 689 feet.
Population: 1,379; Growth (since 2000): -4.3%; Density: 41.7 persons per square mile; Race: 98.4% White, 0.0% Black/African American, 0.1% Asian, 0.4% American Indian/Alaska Native, 0.0% Native Hawaiian/Other Pacific Islander, 0.3% Two or more races, 1.6% Hispanic of any race; Average household size: 2.56; Median age: 39.7; Age under 18: 23.8%; Age 65 and over: 11.6%; Males per 100 females: 106.7
Housing: Homeownership rate: 84.4%; Homeowner vacancy rate: 0.9%; Rental vacancy rate: 3.4%

FOUNTAINTOWN (unincorporated postal area)
ZCTA: 46130
Covers a land area of 29.775 square miles and a water area of 0.036 square miles. Located at 39.67° N. Lat; 85.84° W. Long. Elevation is 850 feet.
Population: 2,508; Growth (since 2000): 13.0%; Density: 84.2 persons per square mile; Race: 99.2% White, 0.3% Black/African American, 0.0% Asian, 0.1% American Indian/Alaska Native, 0.0% Native Hawaiian/Other Pacific Islander, 0.3% Two or more races, 1.0% Hispanic of any race; Average household size: 2.63; Median age: 43.0; Age under 18: 23.8%; Age 65 and over: 13.2%; Males per 100 females: 102.1; Marriage status: 20.7% never married, 61.5% now married, 0.3% separated, 4.0% widowed, 13.7% divorced; Foreign born: 0.0%; Speak English only: 98.2%; With disability: 16.4%; Veterans: 15.7%; Ancestry: 29.7% German, 13.6% Irish, 11.0% English, 5.3% Scottish, 5.1% American
Employment: 7.8% management, business, and financial, 6.6% computer, engineering, and science, 9.6% education, legal, community service, arts, and media, 9.7% healthcare practitioners, 11.4% service, 26.3% sales and office, 9.4% natural resources, construction, and maintenance, 19.3% production, transportation, and material moving
Income: Per capita: $24,782; Median household: $52,460; Average household: $63,918; Households with income of $100,000 or more: 20.7%; Poverty rate: 16.1%
Educational Attainment: High school diploma or higher: 92.2%; Bachelor's degree or higher: 21.4%; Graduate/professional degree or higher: 6.0%
Housing: Homeownership rate: 84.9%; Median home value: $161,000; Median year structure built: 1973; Homeowner vacancy rate: 1.8%; Median gross rent: $497 per month; Rental vacancy rate: 10.8%
Health Insurance: 89.1% have insurance; 75.5% have private insurance; 28.2% have public insurance; 10.9% do not have insurance; 2.1% of children under 18 do not have insurance
Transportation: Commute: 94.3% car, 0.0% public transportation, 0.0% walk, 4.8% work from home; Median travel time to work: 25.1 minutes

GWYNNEVILLE (unincorporated postal area)
ZCTA: 46144
Covers a land area of 0.519 square miles and a water area of 0 square miles. Located at 39.66° N. Lat; 85.65° W. Long. Elevation is 909 feet.
Population: 211; Growth (since 2000): 9.9%; Density: 406.9 persons per square mile; Race: 98.1% White, 0.0% Black/African American, 0.0% Asian, 0.5% American Indian/Alaska Native, 0.5% Native Hawaiian/Other Pacific Islander, 0.9% Two or more races, 0.0% Hispanic of any race; Average household size: 2.71; Median age: 37.8; Age under 18: 27.0%; Age 65 and over: 12.3%; Males per 100 females: 102.9
Housing: Homeownership rate: 66.7%; Homeowner vacancy rate: 0.0%; Rental vacancy rate: 10.3%

MORRISTOWN (town).
Covers a land area of 2.348 square miles and a water area of 0.018 square miles. Located at 39.67° N. Lat; 85.70° W. Long. Elevation is 833 feet.
History: Laid out 1828.
Population: 1,218; Growth (since 2000): 7.5%; Density: 518.8 persons per square mile; Race: 98.6% White, 0.1% Black/African American, 0.1% Asian, 0.7% American Indian/Alaska Native, 0.0% Native Hawaiian/Other Pacific Islander, 0.6% Two or more races, 1.3% Hispanic of any race; Average household size: 2.41; Median age: 38.0; Age under 18: 24.7%; Age 65 and over: 20.9%; Males per 100 females: 83.2
School District(s)
Shelby Eastern Schools (PK-12)
2012-13 Enrollment: 1,346 . . . . (765) 544-2246
Housing: Homeownership rate: 68.3%; Homeowner vacancy rate: 2.4%; Rental vacancy rate: 13.9%

SHELBYVILLE (city). County seat. Covers a land area of 11.564 square miles and a water area of 0.285 square miles. Located at 39.53° N. Lat; 85.77° W. Long. Elevation is 764 feet.
History: Shelbyville was laid out in 1822 and named for the first governor of Kentucky. Shelbyville was the home of Vice President Thomas A. Hendricks (1819-1885).
Population: 19,191; Growth (since 2000): 6.9%; Density: 1,659.6 persons per square mile; Race: 91.9% White, 1.9% Black/African American, 1.0% Asian, 0.2% American Indian/Alaska Native, 0.0% Native Hawaiian/Other Pacific Islander, 1.7% Two or more races, 7.1% Hispanic of any race; Average household size: 2.43; Median age: 35.9; Age under 18: 25.5%; Age 65 and over: 13.0%; Males per 100 females: 95.2; Marriage status: 29.5% never married, 44.4% now married, 2.4% separated, 9.9% widowed, 16.2% divorced; Foreign born: 4.7%; Speak English only: 92.7%; With disability: 14.9%; Veterans: 9.0%; Ancestry: 22.0% German, 16.5% American, 12.0% Irish, 8.0% English, 3.2% French
Employment: 8.9% management, business, and financial, 2.7% computer, engineering, and science, 6.1% education, legal, community service, arts, and media, 4.9% healthcare practitioners, 19.4% service, 20.3% sales and office, 9.1% natural resources, construction, and maintenance, 28.5% production, transportation, and material moving
Income: Per capita: $21,057; Median household: $38,578; Average household: $50,218; Households with income of $100,000 or more: 10.3%; Poverty rate: 18.1%
Educational Attainment: High school diploma or higher: 82.2%; Bachelor's degree or higher: 12.3%; Graduate/professional degree or higher: 3.3%

School District(s)
Blue River Career Programs (09-12)
    2012-13 Enrollment: n/a . . . . (317) 392-4191
Shelbyville Central Schools (PK-12)
    2012-13 Enrollment: 3,857 . . . . (317) 392-2505
Southwestern Con Sch Shelby County (KG-12)
    2012-13 Enrollment: 658. . . . . (317) 729-5746

Housing: Homeownership rate: 56.1%; Median home value: $98,500; Median year structure built: 1969; Homeowner vacancy rate: 4.5%; Median gross rent: $700 per month; Rental vacancy rate: 11.0%
Health Insurance: 81.2% have insurance; 58.2% have private insurance; 33.9% have public insurance; 18.8% do not have insurance; 10.1% of children under 18 do not have insurance
Hospitals: Major Hospital (89 beds)
Safety: Violent crime rate: n/a per 10,000 population; Property crime rate: 233.8 per 10,000 population
Newspapers: Shelbyville News (daily circulation 8300)
Transportation: Commute: 94.8% car, 0.0% public transportation, 1.2% walk, 1.5% work from home; Median travel time to work: 19.9 minutes
Airports: Shelbyville Municipal (general aviation)
Additional Information Contacts
City of Shelbyville . . . . (317) 392-5103
   http://www.cityofshelbyvillein.com

WALDRON (CDP). Covers a land area of 1.256 square miles and a water area of 0 square miles. Located at 39.45° N. Lat; 85.66° W. Long. Elevation is 823 feet.
Population: 804; Growth (since 2000): n/a; Density: 640.1 persons per square mile; Race: 98.1% White, 0.0% Black/African American, 0.1% Asian, 0.0% American Indian/Alaska Native, 0.0% Native Hawaiian/Other Pacific Islander, 1.0% Two or more races, 1.5% Hispanic of any race; Average household size: 2.55; Median age: 43.4; Age under 18: 22.8%; Age 65 and over: 20.0%; Males per 100 females: 88.7

School District(s)
Shelby Eastern Schools (PK-12)
    2012-13 Enrollment: 1,346 . . . . (765) 544-2246

Housing: Homeownership rate: 76.3%; Homeowner vacancy rate: 2.2%; Rental vacancy rate: 4.1%

Spencer County

Located in southwestern Indiana; bounded on the south by the Ohio River and the Kentucky border; drained by the Anderson River and Little Pigeon Creek. Covers a land area of 396.744 square miles, a water area of 4.682 square miles, and is located in the Central Time Zone at 38.01° N. Lat., 87.01° W. Long. The county was founded in 1818. County seat is Rockport.

Weather Station: Saint Meinrad   Elevation: 509 feet

	Jan	Feb	Mar	Apr	May	Jun	Jul	Aug	Sep	Oct	Nov	Dec
High	42	47	57	68	76	84	87	87	80	70	57	45
Low	25	28	36	45	54	63	66	65	58	46	38	28
Precip	3.4	3.3	4.4	4.4	5.3	4.1	4.4	3.1	3.7	3.4	4.0	3.8
Snow	2.5	2.1	1.2	tr	0.0	0.0	0.0	0.0	0.0	tr	tr	1.4

High and Low temperatures in degrees Fahrenheit; Precipitation and Snow in inches

Population: 20,952; Growth (since 2000): 2.8%; Density: 52.8 persons per square mile; Race: 96.9% White, 0.5% Black/African American, 0.3% Asian, 0.2% American Indian/Alaska Native, 0.0% Native Hawaiian/Other Pacific Islander, 0.8% two or more races, 2.5% Hispanic of any race; Average household size: 2.55; Median age: 41.9; Age under 18: 24.2%; Age 65 and over: 15.0%; Males per 100 females: 101.3; Marriage status: 21.9% never married, 60.5% now married, 0.6% separated, 6.5% widowed, 11.1% divorced; Foreign born: 2.0%; Speak English only: 96.2%; With disability: 12.9%; Veterans: 11.7%; Ancestry: 40.5% German, 13.7% Irish, 10.3% English, 9.4% American, 4.3% French
Religion: Six largest groups: 20.6% Catholicism, 12.6% Methodist/Pietist, 5.9% Baptist, 2.5% Lutheran, 2.4% Presbyterian-Reformed, 1.5% Holiness
Economy: Unemployment rate: 4.8%; Leading industries: 16.3% retail trade; 13.4% other services (except public administration); 11.1% construction; Farms: 597 totaling 170,406 acres; Company size: 0 employ 1,000 or more persons, 0 employ 500 to 999 persons, 10 employ 100 to 499 persons, 394 employ less than 100 persons; Business ownership: 280 women-owned, n/a Black-owned, n/a Hispanic-owned, n/a Asian-owned
Employment: 12.1% management, business, and financial, 3.2% computer, engineering, and science, 6.9% education, legal, community service, arts, and media, 5.0% healthcare practitioners, 15.1% service, 21.0% sales and office, 13.8% natural resources, construction, and maintenance, 22.9% production, transportation, and material moving
Income: Per capita: $23,641; Median household: $52,991; Average household: $60,498; Households with income of $100,000 or more: 14.3%; Poverty rate: 12.6%
Educational Attainment: High school diploma or higher: 86.5%; Bachelor's degree or higher: 15.5%; Graduate/professional degree or higher: 6.9%
Housing: Homeownership rate: 81.8%; Median home value: $113,300; Median year structure built: 1976; Homeowner vacancy rate: 2.1%; Median gross rent: $566 per month; Rental vacancy rate: 8.7%
Vital Statistics: Birth rate: 117.9 per 10,000 population; Death rate: 102.7 per 10,000 population; Age-adjusted cancer mortality rate: 173.9 deaths per 100,000 population
Health Insurance: 89.1% have insurance; 74.7% have private insurance; 29.1% have public insurance; 10.9% do not have insurance; 5.9% of children under 18 do not have insurance
Health Care: Physicians: 2.4 per 10,000 population; Hospital beds: 0.0 per 10,000 population; Hospital admissions: 0.0 per 10,000 population
Air Quality Index: 70.3% good, 29.7% moderate, 0.0% unhealthy for sensitive individuals, 0.0% unhealthy (percent of days)
Transportation: Commute: 93.6% car, 0.0% public transportation, 1.3% walk, 4.3% work from home; Median travel time to work: 26.8 minutes
Presidential Election: 41.4% Obama, 56.7% Romney (2012)
National and State Parks: Lincoln Boyhood National Memorial; Lincoln State Park; Nancy Hanks Lincoln State Memorial; Spencer County State Forest
Additional Information Contacts
Spencer Government . . . . (812) 649-2242
   http://spencercounty.in.gov

Spencer County Communities

CHRISNEY (town). Covers a land area of 0.706 square miles and a water area of 0.029 square miles. Located at 38.01° N. Lat; 87.03° W. Long. Elevation is 469 feet.
Population: 481; Growth (since 2000): -11.6%; Density: 681.6 persons per square mile; Race: 98.3% White, 0.0% Black/African American, 0.4% Asian, 0.0% American Indian/Alaska Native, 0.0% Native Hawaiian/Other Pacific Islander, 0.0% Two or more races, 0.6% Hispanic of any race; Average household size: 2.41; Median age: 41.4; Age under 18: 22.9%; Age 65 and over: 16.2%; Males per 100 females: 89.4

School District(s)
North Spencer County Sch Corp (PK-12)
    2012-13 Enrollment: 1,940 . . . . (812) 937-2400

Housing: Homeownership rate: 72.0%; Homeowner vacancy rate: 7.5%; Rental vacancy rate: 15.2%

DALE (town).
Covers a land area of 1.546 square miles and a water area of 0.010 square miles. Located at 38.17° N. Lat; 86.99° W. Long. Elevation is 466 feet.
History: Dale was named for Robert Dale Owen, who founded the colony at New Harmony.
Population: 1,593; Growth (since 2000): 1.6%; Density: 1,030.2 persons per square mile; Race: 84.6% White, 0.4% Black/African American, 0.6% Asian, 0.1% American Indian/Alaska Native, 0.0% Native Hawaiian/Other Pacific Islander, 1.8% Two or more races, 18.1% Hispanic of any race; Average household size: 2.50; Median age: 37.9; Age under 18: 24.9%; Age 65 and over: 15.8%; Males per 100 females: 101.6
School District(s)
North Spencer County Sch Corp (PK-12)
    2012-13 Enrollment: 1,940 . . . . (812) 937-2400
Housing: Homeownership rate: 67.3%; Homeowner vacancy rate: 2.6%; Rental vacancy rate: 6.6%
Newspapers: Spencer County Leader (weekly circulation 2000)

EVANSTON (unincorporated postal area)
ZCTA: 47531
Covers a land area of 36.936 square miles and a water area of 0.506 square miles. Located at 38.04° N. Lat; 86.85° W. Long. Elevation is 413 feet.
Population: 1,004; Growth (since 2000): 40.4%; Density: 27.2 persons per square mile; Race: 98.9% White, 0.3% Black/African American, 0.1% Asian, 0.1% American Indian/Alaska Native, 0.0% Native Hawaiian/Other Pacific Islander, 0.6% Two or more races, 1.0% Hispanic of any race; Average household size: 2.51; Median age: 43.6; Age under 18: 20.0%; Age 65 and over: 15.0%; Males per 100 females: 114.5
Housing: Homeownership rate: 91.3%; Homeowner vacancy rate: 1.4%; Rental vacancy rate: 2.8%

GENTRYVILLE (town).
Covers a land area of 0.394 square miles and a water area of 0.001 square miles. Located at 38.11° N. Lat; 87.03° W. Long. Elevation is 410 feet.
History: Abraham Lincoln was a clerk in the store of James Gentry, one of the first merchants in Gentryville and the man for whom the town was named.
Population: 268; Growth (since 2000): 2.3%; Density: 680.0 persons per square mile; Race: 95.9% White, 1.1% Black/African American, 0.0% Asian, 1.9% American Indian/Alaska Native, 0.0% Native Hawaiian/Other Pacific Islander, 0.4% Two or more races, 1.1% Hispanic of any race; Average household size: 2.44; Median age: 44.4; Age under 18: 19.0%; Age 65 and over: 16.4%; Males per 100 females: 91.4
Housing: Homeownership rate: 83.6%; Homeowner vacancy rate: 1.1%; Rental vacancy rate: 5.3%

GRANDVIEW (town).
Covers a land area of 0.959 square miles and a water area of 0.002 square miles. Located at 37.94° N. Lat; 86.98° W. Long. Elevation is 394 feet.
History: Grandview was named for its location on a bluff which afforded a view for five miles up and down the river.
Population: 749; Growth (since 2000): 7.6%; Density: 781.1 persons per square mile; Race: 96.1% White, 1.5% Black/African American, 0.0% Asian, 0.3% American Indian/Alaska Native, 0.0% Native Hawaiian/Other Pacific Islander, 2.0% Two or more races, 1.1% Hispanic of any race; Average household size: 2.60; Median age: 37.3; Age under 18: 27.9%; Age 65 and over: 12.3%; Males per 100 females: 84.5
Housing: Homeownership rate: 70.8%; Homeowner vacancy rate: 2.9%; Rental vacancy rate: 5.6%

HATFIELD (CDP).
Covers a land area of 1.172 square miles and a water area of <.001 square miles. Located at 37.90° N. Lat; 87.22° W. Long. Elevation is 387 feet.
Population: 813; Growth (since 2000): n/a; Density: 693.9 persons per square mile; Race: 98.0% White, 0.0% Black/African American, 0.1% Asian, 0.2% American Indian/Alaska Native, 0.0% Native Hawaiian/Other Pacific Islander, 0.9% Two or more races, 0.9% Hispanic of any race; Average household size: 2.55; Median age: 41.2; Age under 18: 23.6%; Age 65 and over: 14.0%; Males per 100 females: 100.7

Housing: Homeownership rate: 85.3%; Homeowner vacancy rate: 2.4%; Rental vacancy rate: 13.0%

LAMAR (unincorporated postal area)
ZCTA: 47550
Covers a land area of 35.126 square miles and a water area of 0.276 square miles. Located at 38.07° N. Lat; 86.92° W. Long. Elevation is 413 feet.
Population: 854; Growth (since 2000): 10.6%; Density: 24.3 persons per square mile; Race: 98.7% White, 0.1% Black/African American, 0.5% Asian, 0.1% American Indian/Alaska Native, 0.0% Native Hawaiian/Other Pacific Islander, 0.4% Two or more races, 0.2% Hispanic of any race; Average household size: 2.77; Median age: 38.9; Age under 18: 26.0%; Age 65 and over: 8.8%; Males per 100 females: 102.9
School District(s)
North Spencer County Sch Corp (PK-12)
    2012-13 Enrollment: 1,940 . . . . (812) 937-2400
Housing: Homeownership rate: 90.0%; Homeowner vacancy rate: 1.7%; Rental vacancy rate: 3.1%

LINCOLN CITY (unincorporated postal area)
ZCTA: 47552
Covers a land area of 5.162 square miles and a water area of 0.126 square miles. Located at 38.11° N. Lat; 87.00° W. Long. Elevation is 436 feet.
Population: 182; Growth (since 2000): 2.8%; Density: 35.3 persons per square mile; Race: 100.0% White, 0.0% Black/African American, 0.0% Asian, 0.0% American Indian/Alaska Native, 0.0% Native Hawaiian/Other Pacific Islander, 0.0% Two or more races, 0.0% Hispanic of any race; Average household size: 2.68; Median age: 43.0; Age under 18: 27.5%; Age 65 and over: 10.4%; Males per 100 females: 97.8
School District(s)
North Spencer County Sch Corp (PK-12)
    2012-13 Enrollment: 1,940 . . . . (812) 937-2400
Housing: Homeownership rate: 91.2%; Homeowner vacancy rate: 0.0%; Rental vacancy rate: 0.0%

RICHLAND (town).
Covers a land area of 0.515 square miles and a water area of <.001 square miles. Located at 37.95° N. Lat; 87.17° W. Long. Elevation is 390 feet.
Population: 425; Growth (since 2000): n/a; Density: 825.4 persons per square mile; Race: 98.6% White, 0.2% Black/African American, 0.0% Asian, 0.5% American Indian/Alaska Native, 0.0% Native Hawaiian/Other Pacific Islander, 0.7% Two or more races, 1.2% Hispanic of any race; Average household size: 2.50; Median age: 35.2; Age under 18: 28.0%; Age 65 and over: 12.0%; Males per 100 females: 100.5
School District(s)
South Spencer County Sch Corp (PK-12)
    2012-13 Enrollment: 1,413 . . . . (812) 649-2591
Housing: Homeownership rate: 86.4%; Homeowner vacancy rate: 2.6%; Rental vacancy rate: 17.9%

ROCKPORT (city).
County seat. Covers a land area of 1.571 square miles and a water area of 0.034 square miles. Located at 37.89° N. Lat; 87.05° W. Long. Elevation is 440 feet.
History: Rockport was first settled by Daniel Grass in 1807. The Lincoln family, and especially Abraham Lincoln, were visitors in Rockport when they lived 16 miles north. John Pitcher, a Rockport attorney, was a friend of Abe's who allowed him to use his extensive library of law, history, and fiction.
Population: 2,270; Growth (since 2000): 5.1%; Density: 1,444.8 persons per square mile; Race: 95.9% White, 1.8% Black/African American, 0.3% Asian, 0.2% American Indian/Alaska Native, 0.0% Native Hawaiian/Other Pacific Islander, 1.4% Two or more races, 2.6% Hispanic of any race; Average household size: 2.37; Median age: 39.1; Age under 18: 25.5%; Age 65 and over: 17.3%; Males per 100 females: 94.0
School District(s)
South Spencer County Sch Corp (PK-12)
    2012-13 Enrollment: 1,413 . . . . (812) 649-2591
Housing: Homeownership rate: 59.0%; Homeowner vacancy rate: 4.4%; Rental vacancy rate: 9.9%
Newspapers: Spencer County Journal Democrat (weekly circulation 6000)

SAINT MEINRAD (CDP). Covers a land area of 1.644 square miles and a water area of 0.023 square miles. Located at 38.17° N. Lat; 86.83° W. Long. Elevation is 443 feet.
Population: 706; Growth (since 2000): n/a; Density: 429.5 persons per square mile; Race: 97.0% White, 0.3% Black/African American, 0.7% Asian, 0.6% American Indian/Alaska Native, 0.0% Native Hawaiian/Other Pacific Islander, 1.0% Two or more races, 0.6% Hispanic of any race; Average household size: 2.40; Median age: 47.7; Age under 18: 18.6%; Age 65 and over: 25.8%; Males per 100 females: 166.4
Four-year College(s)
Saint Meinrad School of Theology (Private, Not-for-profit, Roman Catholic)
    Fall 2013 Enrollment: 246 . . . . (812) 357-6611
Housing: Homeownership rate: 77.7%; Homeowner vacancy rate: 1.1%; Rental vacancy rate: 12.3%

SANTA CLAUS (town). Covers a land area of 6.443 square miles and a water area of 0.421 square miles. Located at 38.12° N. Lat; 86.93° W. Long. Elevation is 472 feet.
History: Santa Claus was laid out in 1846. The suggested name of Santa Fe was rejected by the post office, and Santa Claus was suggested as a joke, since it was near Christmas. The name served to bring hundreds of letters through the Santa Claus post office each December, where Jim Martin, postmaster from 1897 to 1935, played Santa Claus.
Population: 2,481; Growth (since 2000): 21.6%; Density: 385.1 persons per square mile; Race: 98.1% White, 0.3% Black/African American, 0.5% Asian, 0.1% American Indian/Alaska Native, 0.0% Native Hawaiian/Other Pacific Islander, 0.4% Two or more races, 1.3% Hispanic of any race; Average household size: 2.65; Median age: 39.8; Age under 18: 27.7%; Age 65 and over: 15.0%; Males per 100 females: 91.9
Housing: Homeownership rate: 88.1%; Homeowner vacancy rate: 3.3%; Rental vacancy rate: 8.1%
Additional Information Contacts
Town of Santa Claus . . . . (812) 937-2551
   http://www.townofsantaclaus.com

Starke County

Located in northwestern Indiana; bounded on the northwest by the Kankakee River; drained by the Yellow River. Covers a land area of 309.134 square miles, a water area of 3.072 square miles, and is located in the Central Time Zone at 41.28° N. Lat., 86.65° W. Long. The county was founded in 1835. County seat is Knox.
Population: 23,363; Growth (since 2000): -0.8%; Density: 75.6 persons per square mile; Race: 97.1% White, 0.3% Black/African American, 0.2% Asian, 0.3% American Indian/Alaska Native, 0.0% Native Hawaiian/Other Pacific Islander, 1.3% two or more races, 3.3% Hispanic of any race; Average household size: 2.58; Median age: 40.4; Age under 18: 24.4%; Age 65 and over: 15.3%; Males per 100 females: 97.5; Marriage status: 23.7% never married, 56.6% now married, 1.8% separated, 7.3% widowed, 12.4% divorced; Foreign born: 1.8%; Speak English only: 96.8%; With disability: 17.8%; Veterans: 10.3%; Ancestry: 24.0% German, 13.5% Irish, 8.9% English, 8.3% Polish, 8.0% American
Religion: Six largest groups: 9.8% Catholicism, 5.1% Lutheran, 4.1% Methodist/Pietist, 2.4% Baptist, 2.3% Non-denominational Protestant, 1.6% Pentecostal
Economy: Unemployment rate: 6.1%; Leading industries: 18.8% retail trade; 15.3% other services (except public administration); 9.6% accommodation and food services; Farms: 511 totaling 133,459 acres; Company size: 0 employ 1,000 or more persons, 0 employ 500 to 999 persons, 3 employ 100 to 499 persons, 310 employ less than 100 persons; Business ownership: 437 women-owned, n/a Black-owned, n/a Hispanic-owned, n/a Asian-owned
Employment: 8.7% management, business, and financial, 2.3% computer, engineering, and science, 7.6% education, legal, community service, arts, and media, 5.1% healthcare practitioners, 18.3% service, 20.6% sales and office, 13.3% natural resources, construction, and maintenance, 24.0% production, transportation, and material moving
Income: Per capita: $19,773; Median household: $40,126; Average household: $50,681; Households with income of $100,000 or more: 8.1%; Poverty rate: 16.9%
Educational Attainment: High school diploma or higher: 82.2%; Bachelor's degree or higher: 12.3%; Graduate/professional degree or higher: 4.3%

Housing: Homeownership rate: 79.4%; Median home value: $96,900; Median year structure built: 1972; Homeowner vacancy rate: 2.6%; Median gross rent: $666 per month; Rental vacancy rate: 5.7%
Vital Statistics: Birth rate: 112.9 per 10,000 population; Death rate: 113.8 per 10,000 population; Age-adjusted cancer mortality rate: 202.8 deaths per 100,000 population
Health Insurance: 86.7% have insurance; 61.9% have private insurance; 38.5% have public insurance; 13.3% do not have insurance; 4.5% of children under 18 do not have insurance
Health Care: Physicians: 4.3 per 10,000 population; Hospital beds: 8.6 per 10,000 population; Hospital admissions: 367.3 per 10,000 population
Transportation: Commute: 94.6% car, 0.4% public transportation, 1.8% walk, 2.7% work from home; Median travel time to work: 28.9 minutes
Presidential Election: 43.5% Obama, 54.1% Romney (2012)
National and State Parks: Bass Lake State Beach; Kaukakee State Fish and Wildlife Area
Additional Information Contacts
Starke Government . . . . (574) 772-9107
   http://co.starke.in.us

Starke County Communities

BASS LAKE (CDP). Covers a land area of 9.088 square miles and a water area of 2.191 square miles. Located at 41.22° N. Lat; 86.59° W. Long. Elevation is 718 feet.
Population: 1,195; Growth (since 2000): -4.3%; Density: 131.5 persons per square mile; Race: 97.2% White, 0.3% Black/African American, 0.2% Asian, 0.5% American Indian/Alaska Native, 0.0% Native Hawaiian/Other Pacific Islander, 1.3% Two or more races, 3.3% Hispanic of any race; Average household size: 2.29; Median age: 47.9; Age under 18: 20.3%; Age 65 and over: 21.9%; Males per 100 females: 94.0
Housing: Homeownership rate: 83.3%; Homeowner vacancy rate: 6.0%; Rental vacancy rate: 6.3%

GROVERTOWN (unincorporated postal area)
ZCTA: 46531
   Covers a land area of 21.421 square miles and a water area of 0.010 square miles. Located at 41.36° N. Lat; 86.52° W. Long. Elevation is 728 feet.
Population: 1,458; Growth (since 2000): 9.2%; Density: 68.1 persons per square mile; Race: 97.6% White, 0.1% Black/African American, 0.1% Asian, 0.1% American Indian/Alaska Native, 0.0% Native Hawaiian/Other Pacific Islander, 1.1% Two or more races, 2.2% Hispanic of any race; Average household size: 2.75; Median age: 41.0; Age under 18: 24.0%; Age 65 and over: 14.1%; Males per 100 females: 104.8
Housing: Homeownership rate: 85.0%; Homeowner vacancy rate: 0.9%; Rental vacancy rate: 3.6%

HAMLET (town). Covers a land area of 0.965 square miles and a water area of 0.010 square miles. Located at 41.38° N. Lat; 86.58° W. Long. Elevation is 705 feet.
History: Hamlet was sited at the crossing of the Pennsylvania and New York Central Railroads. It was platted in 1863 by John Hamlet, for whom it was named, and soon became a shipping center.
Population: 800; Growth (since 2000): -2.4%; Density: 828.9 persons per square mile; Race: 96.6% White, 0.0% Black/African American, 0.1% Asian, 1.0% American Indian/Alaska Native, 0.0% Native Hawaiian/Other Pacific Islander, 1.6% Two or more races, 2.6% Hispanic of any race; Average household size: 2.68; Median age: 35.0; Age under 18: 27.6%; Age 65 and over: 12.6%; Males per 100 females: 98.0
School District(s)
Oregon-Davis School Corp (KG-12)
    2012-13 Enrollment: 589 . . . . (574) 867-2111
Housing: Homeownership rate: 70.6%; Homeowner vacancy rate: 5.4%; Rental vacancy rate: 2.2%

KNOX (city). County seat. Covers a land area of 3.920 square miles and a water area of 0 square miles. Located at 41.29° N. Lat; 86.62° W. Long. Elevation is 712 feet.
History: Knox developed as a trading center for the surrounding farmlands.
Population: 3,704; Growth (since 2000): -0.5%; Density: 944.8 persons per square mile; Race: 96.3% White, 0.4% Black/African American, 0.3% Asian, 0.2% American Indian/Alaska Native, 0.0% Native Hawaiian/Other

Pacific Islander, 1.7% Two or more races, 2.9% Hispanic of any race; Average household size: 2.53; Median age: 36.2; Age under 18: 26.0%; Age 65 and over: 13.5%; Males per 100 females: 86.2; Marriage status: 28.9% never married, 48.0% now married, 0.9% separated, 8.9% widowed, 14.3% divorced; Foreign born: 0.5%; Speak English only: 98.8%; With disability: 18.6%; Veterans: 8.9%; Ancestry: 19.8% German, 18.6% Irish, 10.6% English, 7.8% Polish, 5.7% American
Employment: 6.9% management, business, and financial, 1.3% computer, engineering, and science, 7.6% education, legal, community service, arts, and media, 2.5% healthcare practitioners, 28.0% service, 22.7% sales and office, 11.1% natural resources, construction, and maintenance, 19.9% production, transportation, and material moving
Income: Per capita: $16,311; Median household: $30,300; Average household: $42,018; Households with income of $100,000 or more: 4.0%; Poverty rate: 25.6%
Educational Attainment: High school diploma or higher: 76.6%; Bachelor's degree or higher: 5.5%; Graduate/professional degree or higher: 1.5%

School District(s)
Knox Community School Corp (KG-12)
    2012-13 Enrollment: 1,958 . . . . (574) 772-1600
Vocational/Technical School(s)
Knox Beauty College (Private, For-profit)
    Fall 2013 Enrollment: 39 . . . . (574) 772-5500
    2013-14 Tuition: $4,990

Housing: Homeownership rate: 61.5%; Median home value: $79,600; Median year structure built: 1957; Homeowner vacancy rate: 3.7%; Median gross rent: $650 per month; Rental vacancy rate: 4.1%
Health Insurance: 80.3% have insurance; 49.7% have private insurance; 41.8% have public insurance; 19.7% do not have insurance; 3.2% of children under 18 do not have insurance
Hospitals: Indiana University Health Starke Hospital (53 beds)
Safety: Violent crime rate: 16.4 per 10,000 population; Property crime rate: 120.3 per 10,000 population
Newspapers: The Leader (weekly circulation 2500)
Transportation: Commute: 93.4% car, 0.0% public transportation, 6.6% walk, 0.0% work from home; Median travel time to work: 22.1 minutes
Additional Information Contacts
City of Knox . . . . (574) 772-3032
    http://www.cityofknox.net

KOONTZ LAKE
(CDP). Covers a land area of 3.370 square miles and a water area of 0.522 square miles. Located at 41.41° N. Lat; 86.48° W. Long. Elevation is 732 feet.
Population: 1,557; Growth (since 2000): 0.2%; Density: 462.0 persons per square mile; Race: 97.2% White, 0.1% Black/African American, 0.1% Asian, 0.1% American Indian/Alaska Native, 0.0% Native Hawaiian/Other Pacific Islander, 1.7% Two or more races, 2.2% Hispanic of any race; Average household size: 2.34; Median age: 45.3; Age under 18: 20.2%; Age 65 and over: 19.5%; Males per 100 females: 102.7
Housing: Homeownership rate: 80.3%; Homeowner vacancy rate: 4.7%; Rental vacancy rate: 8.4%

NORTH JUDSON
(town). Covers a land area of 1.104 square miles and a water area of 0 square miles. Located at 41.22° N. Lat; 86.78° W. Long. Elevation is 712 feet.
History: Laid out 1861.
Population: 1,772; Growth (since 2000): 5.8%; Density: 1,604.4 persons per square mile; Race: 96.7% White, 0.1% Black/African American, 0.2% Asian, 0.3% American Indian/Alaska Native, 0.0% Native Hawaiian/Other Pacific Islander, 1.5% Two or more races, 7.3% Hispanic of any race; Average household size: 2.51; Median age: 37.7; Age under 18: 27.0%; Age 65 and over: 15.5%; Males per 100 females: 92.4
School District(s)
North Judson-San Pierre Sch Corp (KG-12)
    2012-13 Enrollment: 1,244 . . . . (574) 896-2155
Housing: Homeownership rate: 67.4%; Homeowner vacancy rate: 4.6%; Rental vacancy rate: 9.8%
Safety: Violent crime rate: 34.1 per 10,000 population; Property crime rate: 261.5 per 10,000 population

ORA
(unincorporated postal area)
ZCTA: 46968
    Covers a land area of 0.365 square miles and a water area of 0 square miles. Located at 41.18° N. Lat; 86.55° W. Long. Elevation is 718 feet.

Population: 73; Growth (since 2000): -16.1%; Density: 200.0 persons per square mile; Race: 100.0% White, 0.0% Black/African American, 0.0% Asian, 0.0% American Indian/Alaska Native, 0.0% Native Hawaiian/Other Pacific Islander, 0.0% Two or more races, 0.0% Hispanic of any race; Average household size: 3.04; Median age: 35.5; Age under 18: 31.5%; Age 65 and over: 11.0%; Males per 100 females: 102.8
Housing: Homeownership rate: 83.3%; Homeowner vacancy rate: 4.8%; Rental vacancy rate: 0.0%

SAN PIERRE
(CDP). Covers a land area of 0.141 square miles and a water area of 0 square miles. Located at 41.20° N. Lat; 86.89° W. Long. Elevation is 696 feet.
Population: 144; Growth (since 2000): -7.7%; Density: 1,023.2 persons per square mile; Race: 97.2% White, 0.0% Black/African American, 0.0% Asian, 0.7% American Indian/Alaska Native, 0.0% Native Hawaiian/Other Pacific Islander, 2.1% Two or more races, 0.0% Hispanic of any race; Average household size: 2.25; Median age: 42.5; Age under 18: 20.1%; Age 65 and over: 19.4%; Males per 100 females: 100.0
Housing: Homeownership rate: 82.8%; Homeowner vacancy rate: 5.4%; Rental vacancy rate: 8.3%

Steuben County

Located in northeastern Indiana; bounded on the north by Michigan, and on the east by Ohio; drained by Pigeon Creek; includes several lakes. Covers a land area of 308.939 square miles, a water area of 13.527 square miles, and is located in the Eastern Time Zone at 41.64° N. Lat., 85.00° W. Long. The county was founded in 1835. County seat is Angola.

Steuben County is part of the Angola, IN Micropolitan Statistical Area. The entire metro area includes: Steuben County, IN

Weather Station: Angola   Elevation: 1,009 feet

	Jan	Feb	Mar	Apr	May	Jun	Jul	Aug	Sep	Oct	Nov	Dec
High	30	34	44	58	69	78	82	80	73	60	47	34
Low	15	16	24	36	47	57	61	59	50	39	30	20
Precip	2.3	2.1	2.7	3.4	4.3	3.8	4.1	4.2	3.3	3.0	3.1	2.8
Snow	10.6	8.4	4.8	1.0	tr	0.0	0.0	0.0	0.0	0.0	0.3	2.1	9.2

High and Low temperatures in degrees Fahrenheit; Precipitation and Snow in inches

Population: 34,185; Growth (since 2000): 2.9%; Density: 110.7 persons per square mile; Race: 96.8% White, 0.5% Black/African American, 0.5% Asian, 0.3% American Indian/Alaska Native, 0.0% Native Hawaiian/Other Pacific Islander, 0.9% two or more races, 2.9% Hispanic of any race; Average household size: 2.47; Median age: 40.2; Age under 18: 22.9%; Age 65 and over: 14.9%; Males per 100 females: 101.9; Marriage status: 25.8% never married, 58.1% now married, 1.2% separated, 4.7% widowed, 11.5% divorced; Foreign born: 2.0%; Speak English only: 96.3%; With disability: 12.8%; Veterans: 10.0%; Ancestry: 34.7% German, 12.8% Irish, 11.8% English, 9.1% American, 3.2% Italian
Religion: Six largest groups: 9.8% Catholicism, 4.7% Methodist/Pietist, 4.5% Holiness, 4.2% Lutheran, 2.6% Baptist, 1.7% Non-denominational Protestant
Economy: Unemployment rate: 5.1%; Leading industries: 19.1% retail trade; 11.8% other services (except public administration); 9.7% manufacturing; Farms: 562 totaling 104,570 acres; Company size: 0 employ 1,000 or more persons, 1 employs 500 to 999 persons, 22 employ 100 to 499 persons, 951 employs less than 100 persons; Business ownership: 640 women-owned, n/a Black-owned, 27 Hispanic-owned, 31 Asian-owned
Employment: 9.4% management, business, and financial, 3.6% computer, engineering, and science, 9.9% education, legal, community service, arts, and media, 3.3% healthcare practitioners, 16.0% service, 25.4% sales and office, 9.3% natural resources, construction, and maintenance, 23.0% production, transportation, and material moving
Income: Per capita: $23,975; Median household: $48,080; Average household: $60,411; Households with income of $100,000 or more: 14.4%; Poverty rate: 11.5%
Educational Attainment: High school diploma or higher: 88.7%; Bachelor's degree or higher: 19.4%; Graduate/professional degree or higher: 6.6%
Housing: Homeownership rate: 76.2%; Median home value: $123,000; Median year structure built: 1975; Homeowner vacancy rate: 4.0%; Median gross rent: $656 per month; Rental vacancy rate: 12.8%

Vital Statistics: Birth rate: 110.6 per 10,000 population; Death rate: 85.6 per 10,000 population; Age-adjusted cancer mortality rate: 179.4 deaths per 100,000 population
Health Insurance: 87.0% have insurance; 70.0% have private insurance; 30.2% have public insurance; 13.0% do not have insurance; 7.1% of children under 18 do not have insurance
Health Care: Physicians: 6.4 per 10,000 population; Hospital beds: 7.3 per 10,000 population; Hospital admissions: 272.0 per 10,000 population
Transportation: Commute: 94.3% car, 0.2% public transportation, 1.6% walk, 2.5% work from home; Median travel time to work: 22.5 minutes
Presidential Election: 35.4% Obama, 62.5% Romney (2012)
National and State Parks: Cedar Lake Marsh State Fish and Wildlife Area; Marsh Lake Wetlands State Fish and Wildlife Area; Pokagon State Park
Additional Information Contacts
Steuben Government . . . . (260) 668-1000
http://www.co.steuben.in.us

Steuben County Communities

ANGOLA (city). County seat. Covers a land area of 6.344 square miles and a water area of 0.047 square miles. Located at 41.64° N. Lat; 85.00° W. Long. Elevation is 1,063 feet.
Population: 8,612; Growth (since 2000): 17.3%; Density: 1,357.6 persons per square mile; Race: 93.6% White, 1.4% Black/African American, 0.8% Asian, 0.3% American Indian/Alaska Native, 0.1% Native Hawaiian/Other Pacific Islander, 1.7% Two or more races, 6.3% Hispanic of any race; Average household size: 2.35; Median age: 30.3; Age under 18: 22.1%; Age 65 and over: 13.0%; Males per 100 females: 102.4; Marriage status: 38.1% never married, 44.5% now married, 2.7% separated, 6.2% widowed, 11.2% divorced; Foreign born: 3.1%; Speak English only: 95.1%; With disability: 15.7%; Veterans: 8.1%; Ancestry: 29.9% German, 15.1% Irish, 13.3% English, 6.7% American, 3.6% Scottish
Employment: 5.7% management, business, and financial, 3.3% computer, engineering, and science, 13.2% education, legal, community service, arts, and media, 4.9% healthcare practitioners, 18.8% service, 28.4% sales and office, 6.5% natural resources, construction, and maintenance, 19.2% production, transportation, and material moving
Income: Per capita: $19,175; Median household: $40,756; Average household: $49,561; Households with income of $100,000 or more: 10.2%; Poverty rate: 16.5%
Educational Attainment: High school diploma or higher: 84.6%; Bachelor's degree or higher: 19.4%; Graduate/professional degree or higher: 8.1%
School District(s)
M S D Steuben County (KG-12)
    2012-13 Enrollment: 3,057 . . . . (260) 665-2854
Four-year College(s)
Trine University (Private, Not-for-profit)
    Fall 2013 Enrollment: 1,875 . . . . (260) 665-4100
    2013-14 Tuition: In-state $28,850; Out-of-state $28,850
Housing: Homeownership rate: 50.6%; Median home value: $109,100; Median year structure built: 1976; Homeowner vacancy rate: 4.4%; Median gross rent: $600 per month; Rental vacancy rate: 9.9%
Health Insurance: 87.2% have insurance; 69.0% have private insurance; 30.8% have public insurance; 12.8% do not have insurance; 5.4% of children under 18 do not have insurance
Hospitals: Cameron Memorial Community Hospital (25 beds)
Safety: Violent crime rate: 7.0 per 10,000 population; Property crime rate: 450.7 per 10,000 population
Newspapers: Herald-Republican (daily circulation 4700)
Transportation: Commute: 88.7% car, 0.0% public transportation, 5.3% walk, 3.9% work from home; Median travel time to work: 15.5 minutes
Additional Information Contacts
City of Angola . . . . (260) 665-2514
http://www.angolain.org

CLEAR LAKE (town). Covers a land area of 1.040 square miles and a water area of 1.336 square miles. Located at 41.73° N. Lat; 84.84° W. Long. Elevation is 1,040 feet.
Population: 339; Growth (since 2000): 38.9%; Density: 326.0 persons per square mile; Race: 98.8% White, 0.0% Black/African American, 0.9% Asian, 0.0% American Indian/Alaska Native, 0.0% Native Hawaiian/Other Pacific Islander, 0.3% Two or more races, 0.6% Hispanic of any race; Average household size: 2.01; Median age: 58.9; Age under 18: 9.1%; Age 65 and over: 36.6%; Males per 100 females: 105.5
Housing: Homeownership rate: 92.9%; Homeowner vacancy rate: 5.4%; Rental vacancy rate: 35.0%

FREMONT (town). Covers a land area of 2.215 square miles and a water area of 0.006 square miles. Located at 41.73° N. Lat; 84.93° W. Long. Elevation is 1,053 feet.
Population: 2,138; Growth (since 2000): 26.1%; Density: 965.3 persons per square mile; Race: 98.6% White, 0.2% Black/African American, 0.3% Asian, 0.2% American Indian/Alaska Native, 0.0% Native Hawaiian/Other Pacific Islander, 0.3% Two or more races, 1.8% Hispanic of any race; Average household size: 2.62; Median age: 33.1; Age under 18: 29.1%; Age 65 and over: 10.5%; Males per 100 females: 93.7
School District(s)
Fremont Community Schools (KG-12)
    2012-13 Enrollment: 1,048 . . . . (260) 495-5005
Housing: Homeownership rate: 72.2%; Homeowner vacancy rate: 3.0%; Rental vacancy rate: 8.1%

HAMILTON (town). Covers a land area of 2.393 square miles and a water area of 0.758 square miles. Located at 41.54° N. Lat; 84.92° W. Long. Elevation is 902 feet.
History: Hamilton was called Enterprise when it was founded in 1836 at a site that provided water power. The town was incorporated in 1914.
Population: 1,532; Growth (since 2000): n/a; Density: 640.2 persons per square mile; Race: 98.4% White, 0.3% Black/African American, 0.3% Asian, 0.2% American Indian/Alaska Native, 0.0% Native Hawaiian/Other Pacific Islander, 0.8% Two or more races, 1.1% Hispanic of any race; Average household size: 2.24; Median age: 47.2; Age under 18: 19.8%; Age 65 and over: 19.3%; Males per 100 females: 96.2
School District(s)
Hamilton Community Schools (KG-12)
    2012-13 Enrollment: 430 . . . . (260) 488-2513
Housing: Homeownership rate: 74.3%; Homeowner vacancy rate: 6.0%; Rental vacancy rate: 10.2%
Newspapers: Hamilton News (weekly circulation 1000)

HUDSON (town). Covers a land area of 0.692 square miles and a water area of 0 square miles. Located at 41.53° N. Lat; 85.08° W. Long. Elevation is 991 feet.
Population: 518; Growth (since 2000): -13.1%; Density: 748.2 persons per square mile; Race: 98.1% White, 0.0% Black/African American, 0.6% Asian, 0.2% American Indian/Alaska Native, 0.2% Native Hawaiian/Other Pacific Islander, 0.4% Two or more races, 1.9% Hispanic of any race; Average household size: 2.80; Median age: 34.5; Age under 18: 31.3%; Age 65 and over: 10.0%; Males per 100 females: 102.3
Housing: Homeownership rate: 77.3%; Homeowner vacancy rate: 7.1%; Rental vacancy rate: 10.4%

ORLAND (town). Covers a land area of 0.663 square miles and a water area of 0 square miles. Located at 41.73° N. Lat; 85.17° W. Long. Elevation is 961 feet.
History: Laid out 1838.
Population: 434; Growth (since 2000): 27.3%; Density: 655.0 persons per square mile; Race: 96.3% White, 1.2% Black/African American, 0.0% Asian, 0.0% American Indian/Alaska Native, 0.0% Native Hawaiian/Other Pacific Islander, 0.9% Two or more races, 9.0% Hispanic of any race; Average household size: 2.58; Median age: 40.2; Age under 18: 24.0%; Age 65 and over: 16.1%; Males per 100 females: 100.0
Housing: Homeownership rate: 75.0%; Homeowner vacancy rate: 1.5%; Rental vacancy rate: 26.3%

PLEASANT LAKE (unincorporated postal area)
ZCTA: 46779
    Covers a land area of 35.411 square miles and a water area of 0.653 square miles. Located at 41.58° N. Lat; 85.04° W. Long. Elevation is 978 feet.
    Population: 2,166; Growth (since 2000): -1.1%; Density: 61.2 persons per square mile; Race: 97.6% White, 0.1% Black/African American, 0.3% Asian, 0.3% American Indian/Alaska Native, 0.0% Native Hawaiian/Other Pacific Islander, 1.1% Two or more races, 1.2% Hispanic of any race; Average household size: 2.54; Median age: 42.6; Age under 18: 23.8%; Age 65 and over: 14.8%; Males per 100 females: 101.5

School District(s)
M S D Steuben County (KG-12)
  2012-13 Enrollment: 3,057 . . . . (260) 665-2854
  Housing: Homeownership rate: 85.4%; Homeowner vacancy rate: 3.4%; Rental vacancy rate: 7.2%

Sullivan County

Located in southwestern Indiana; bounded on the west by the Wabash River and the Illinois border; drained by Busseron and Maria Creeks. Covers a land area of 447.142 square miles, a water area of 6.974 square miles, and is located in the Eastern Time Zone at 39.09° N. Lat., 87.42° W. Long. The county was founded in 1816. County seat is Sullivan.

Sullivan County is part of the Terre Haute, IN Metropolitan Statistical Area. The entire metro area includes: Clay County, IN; Sullivan County, IN; Vermillion County, IN; Vigo County, IN

Population: 21,475; Growth (since 2000): -1.3%; Density: 48.0 persons per square mile; Race: 93.7% White, 4.5% Black/African American, 0.2% Asian, 0.3% American Indian/Alaska Native, 0.0% Native Hawaiian/Other Pacific Islander, 1.0% two or more races, 1.4% Hispanic of any race; Average household size: 2.45; Median age: 39.8; Age under 18: 21.4%; Age 65 and over: 14.8%; Males per 100 females: 119.0; Marriage status: 27.7% never married, 52.0% now married, 0.9% separated, 6.5% widowed, 13.8% divorced; Foreign born: 1.0%; Speak English only: 98.2%; With disability: 18.1%; Veterans: 8.6%; Ancestry: 19.2% American, 17.0% German, 10.2% Irish, 9.2% English, 2.1% Scottish
Religion: Six largest groups: 18.5% Baptist, 6.1% Methodist/Pietist, 4.2% Non-denominational Protestant, 2.3% Catholicism, 2.2% Presbyterian-Reformed, 2.1% Pentecostal
Economy: Unemployment rate: 7.2%; Leading industries: 16.0% retail trade; 11.5% other services (except public administration); 10.9% construction; Farms: 433 totaling 170,245 acres; Company size: 0 employ 1,000 or more persons, 1 employs 500 to 999 persons, 5 employ 100 to 499 persons, 332 employ less than 100 persons; Business ownership: 365 women-owned, n/a Black-owned, n/a Hispanic-owned, n/a Asian-owned
Employment: 8.0% management, business, and financial, 3.1% computer, engineering, and science, 7.5% education, legal, community service, arts, and media, 8.1% healthcare practitioners, 20.1% service, 20.0% sales and office, 12.2% natural resources, construction, and maintenance, 21.0% production, transportation, and material moving
Income: Per capita: $19,821; Median household: $43,510; Average household: $53,678; Households with income of $100,000 or more: 11.4%; Poverty rate: 17.9%
Educational Attainment: High school diploma or higher: 85.3%; Bachelor's degree or higher: 13.2%; Graduate/professional degree or higher: 4.2%
Housing: Homeownership rate: 77.0%; Median home value: $77,600; Median year structure built: 1968; Homeowner vacancy rate: 2.6%; Median gross rent: $611 per month; Rental vacancy rate: 9.3%
Vital Statistics: Birth rate: 112.1 per 10,000 population; Death rate: 92.8 per 10,000 population; Age-adjusted cancer mortality rate: 230.7 deaths per 100,000 population
Health Insurance: 83.6% have insurance; 63.8% have private insurance; 34.4% have public insurance; 16.4% do not have insurance; 9.3% of children under 18 do not have insurance
Health Care: Physicians: 6.1 per 10,000 population; Hospital beds: 11.8 per 10,000 population; Hospital admissions: 464.5 per 10,000 population
Transportation: Commute: 94.4% car, 0.1% public transportation, 1.0% walk, 2.9% work from home; Median travel time to work: 23.8 minutes
Presidential Election: 38.5% Obama, 59.1% Romney (2012)
National and State Parks: Greene-Sullivan State Forest
Additional Information Contacts
Sullivan Government . . . . (812) 398-4924

Sullivan County Communities

CARLISLE (town). Covers a land area of 0.518 square miles and a water area of 0 square miles. Located at 38.96° N. Lat; 87.40° W. Long. Elevation is 482 feet.
History: Carlisle was settled in 1803 on land granted to Samuel Ledgerwood for services to the U.S. government. Its early industry was coal mining.
Population: 692; Growth (since 2000): -74.0%; Density: 1,335.2 persons per square mile; Race: 97.1% White, 0.0% Black/African American, 0.0% Asian, 0.6% American Indian/Alaska Native, 0.0% Native Hawaiian/Other Pacific Islander, 0.4% Two or more races, 2.7% Hispanic of any race; Average household size: 2.55; Median age: 38.2; Age under 18: 25.9%; Age 65 and over: 18.2%; Males per 100 females: 98.3
School District(s)
Southwest School Corp (PK-12)
  2012-13 Enrollment: 1,711 . . . . (812) 268-6311
Housing: Homeownership rate: 76.1%; Homeowner vacancy rate: 1.9%; Rental vacancy rate: 14.5%
Additional Information Contacts
Town of Carlisle . . . . (812) 847-4846
http://www.lintonchamber.org

DUGGER (town). Covers a land area of 0.586 square miles and a water area of 0 square miles. Located at 39.07° N. Lat; 87.26° W. Long. Elevation is 577 feet.
Population: 920; Growth (since 2000): -3.7%; Density: 1,570.5 persons per square mile; Race: 99.7% White, 0.0% Black/African American, 0.0% Asian, 0.0% American Indian/Alaska Native, 0.0% Native Hawaiian/Other Pacific Islander, 0.3% Two or more races, 0.4% Hispanic of any race; Average household size: 2.40; Median age: 38.8; Age under 18: 24.3%; Age 65 and over: 17.5%; Males per 100 females: 97.0
School District(s)
Northeast School Corp (PK-12)
  2012-13 Enrollment: 1,352 . . . . (812) 383-5761
Housing: Homeownership rate: 74.2%; Homeowner vacancy rate: 1.7%; Rental vacancy rate: 9.2%

FAIRBANKS (unincorporated postal area)
ZCTA: 47849
  Covers a land area of 26.057 square miles and a water area of 0.499 square miles. Located at 39.20° N. Lat; 87.56° W. Long. Elevation is 551 feet.
  Population: 496; Growth (since 2000): 19.5%; Density: 19.0 persons per square mile; Race: 98.0% White, 0.0% Black/African American, 0.0% Asian, 0.4% American Indian/Alaska Native, 0.0% Native Hawaiian/Other Pacific Islander, 1.6% Two or more races, 1.0% Hispanic of any race; Average household size: 2.43; Median age: 43.9; Age under 18: 21.6%; Age 65 and over: 17.5%; Males per 100 females: 113.8
  Housing: Homeownership rate: 88.8%; Homeowner vacancy rate: 0.5%; Rental vacancy rate: 7.7%

FARMERSBURG (town). Covers a land area of 0.743 square miles and a water area of 0 square miles. Located at 39.25° N. Lat; 87.38° W. Long. Elevation is 561 feet.
History: Farmersburg developed as a supply center for the surrounding farming community.
Population: 1,118; Growth (since 2000): -5.3%; Density: 1,504.8 persons per square mile; Race: 97.9% White, 0.6% Black/African American, 0.3% Asian, 0.4% American Indian/Alaska Native, 0.0% Native Hawaiian/Other Pacific Islander, 0.7% Two or more races, 1.3% Hispanic of any race; Average household size: 2.40; Median age: 38.7; Age under 18: 25.1%; Age 65 and over: 15.7%; Males per 100 females: 92.4
School District(s)
Northeast School Corp (PK-12)
  2012-13 Enrollment: 1,352 . . . . (812) 383-5761
Housing: Homeownership rate: 71.7%; Homeowner vacancy rate: 5.3%; Rental vacancy rate: 13.8%

HYMERA (town). Covers a land area of 0.712 square miles and a water area of 0 square miles. Located at 39.19° N. Lat; 87.30° W. Long. Elevation is 525 feet.
History: Hymera was platted in 1870 and named Pittsburg, after coal was discovered nearby. Postmaster John Badders changed the name to High Mary, referring to his daughter, and the name was later shortened to Hymera.
Population: 801; Growth (since 2000): -3.8%; Density: 1,124.7 persons per square mile; Race: 99.0% White, 0.0% Black/African American, 0.0% Asian, 0.2% American Indian/Alaska Native, 0.0% Native Hawaiian/Other Pacific Islander, 0.7% Two or more races, 0.1% Hispanic of any race; Average household size: 2.62; Median age: 37.5; Age under 18: 28.0%; Age 65 and over: 12.7%; Males per 100 females: 98.8

School District(s)
Northeast School Corp (PK-12)
   2012-13 Enrollment: 1,352 . . . . (812) 383-5761
Housing: Homeownership rate: 78.1%; Homeowner vacancy rate: 1.2%; Rental vacancy rate: 13.0%

MEROM (town). Covers a land area of 0.355 square miles and a water area of 0 square miles. Located at 39.06° N. Lat; 87.57° W. Long. Elevation is 548 feet.
History: From 1817 to 1842 Merom was the seat of Sullivan County and a shipping center. The name, which means "high ground along the waters," reflects Merom's location on a bluff of the Wabash River.
Population: 228; Growth (since 2000): -22.4%; Density: 641.4 persons per square mile; Race: 100.0% White, 0.0% Black/African American, 0.0% Asian, 0.0% American Indian/Alaska Native, 0.0% Native Hawaiian/Other Pacific Islander, 0.0% Two or more races, 0.4% Hispanic of any race; Average household size: 2.30; Median age: 39.4; Age under 18: 30.3%; Age 65 and over: 16.2%; Males per 100 females: 101.8
Housing: Homeownership rate: 86.9%; Homeowner vacancy rate: 3.4%; Rental vacancy rate: 6.7%

PAXTON (unincorporated postal area)
ZCTA: 47865
Covers a land area of 0.136 square miles and a water area of 0 square miles. Located at 39.02° N. Lat; 87.39° W. Long. Elevation is 522 feet.
Population: 79; Growth (since 2000): 11.3%; Density: 580.7 persons per square mile; Race: 100.0% White, 0.0% Black/African American, 0.0% Asian, 0.0% American Indian/Alaska Native, 0.0% Native Hawaiian/Other Pacific Islander, 0.0% Two or more races, 0.0% Hispanic of any race; Average household size: 2.14; Median age: 54.5; Age under 18: 11.4%; Age 65 and over: 27.8%; Males per 100 females: 61.2
Housing: Homeownership rate: 94.5%; Homeowner vacancy rate: 0.0%; Rental vacancy rate: 0.0%

SHELBURN (town). Covers a land area of 0.686 square miles and a water area of 0 square miles. Located at 39.18° N. Lat; 87.40° W. Long. Elevation is 541 feet.
History: Shelburn was founded in 1818. Growth was seen when the first coal mine was established in 1868.
Population: 1,252; Growth (since 2000): -1.3%; Density: 1,825.2 persons per square mile; Race: 96.2% White, 0.0% Black/African American, 0.6% Asian, 0.5% American Indian/Alaska Native, 0.0% Native Hawaiian/Other Pacific Islander, 2.2% Two or more races, 1.2% Hispanic of any race; Average household size: 2.58; Median age: 37.1; Age under 18: 26.8%; Age 65 and over: 12.5%; Males per 100 females: 94.1
School District(s)
Northeast School Corp (PK-12)
   2012-13 Enrollment: 1,352 . . . . (812) 383-5761
Housing: Homeownership rate: 67.8%; Homeowner vacancy rate: 3.4%; Rental vacancy rate: 6.0%

SULLIVAN (city). County seat. Covers a land area of 1.876 square miles and a water area of 0 square miles. Located at 39.10° N. Lat; 87.41° W. Long. Elevation is 528 feet.
History: Sullivan was laid out in 1842 as the seat of Sullivan County, which was moved from Merom to the more central location. The early economy of Sullivan was based on coal mining.
Population: 4,249; Growth (since 2000): -8.0%; Density: 2,265.2 persons per square mile; Race: 97.7% White, 0.1% Black/African American, 0.2% Asian, 0.4% American Indian/Alaska Native, 0.0% Native Hawaiian/Other Pacific Islander, 1.2% Two or more races, 1.4% Hispanic of any race; Average household size: 2.27; Median age: 39.8; Age under 18: 23.8%; Age 65 and over: 18.5%; Males per 100 females: 86.3; Marriage status: 29.9% never married, 44.4% now married, 0.7% separated, 9.5% widowed, 16.2% divorced; Foreign born: 0.6%; Speak English only: 98.0%; With disability: 24.5%; Veterans: 6.8%; Ancestry: 21.9% American, 20.7% German, 11.1% English, 7.4% Irish, 6.4% Scottish
Employment: 3.7% management, business, and financial, 0.6% computer, engineering, and science, 2.2% education, legal, community service, arts, and media, 5.1% healthcare practitioners, 28.5% service, 29.9% sales and office, 13.2% natural resources, construction, and maintenance, 16.8% production, transportation, and material moving
Income: Per capita: $16,147; Median household: $23,670; Average household: $34,842; Households with income of $100,000 or more: 4.7%; Poverty rate: 33.0%
Educational Attainment: High school diploma or higher: 83.2%; Bachelor's degree or higher: 8.7%; Graduate/professional degree or higher: 1.6%
School District(s)
Rural Community Schools Inc (KG-08)
   2012-13 Enrollment: 135. . . . . (812) 382-4500
Southwest School Corp (PK-12)
   2012-13 Enrollment: 1,711 . . . . (812) 268-6311
Housing: Homeownership rate: 59.4%; Median home value: $70,100; Median year structure built: 1958; Homeowner vacancy rate: 5.9%; Median gross rent: $618 per month; Rental vacancy rate: 9.7%
Health Insurance: 74.9% have insurance; 49.1% have private insurance; 43.3% have public insurance; 25.1% do not have insurance; 9.9% of children under 18 do not have insurance
Hospitals: Sullivan County Community Hospital (34 beds)
Newspapers: Sullivan Daily Times (daily circulation 4100)
Transportation: Commute: 91.7% car, 0.0% public transportation, 1.7% walk, 3.2% work from home; Median travel time to work: 16.9 minutes
Additional Information Contacts
City of Sullivan. . . . . (812) 268-6077
http://sullivancountyindiana.us

Switzerland County

Located in southeastern Indiana; bounded on the east and south by the Ohio River and the Kentucky border. Covers a land area of 220.633 square miles, a water area of 2.806 square miles, and is located in the Eastern Time Zone at 38.83° N. Lat., 85.03° W. Long. The county was founded in 1814. County seat is Vevay.

Weather Station: Vevay   Elevation: 470 feet

	Jan	Feb	Mar	Apr	May	Jun	Jul	Aug	Sep	Oct	Nov	Dec
High	41	47	56	68	77	85	89	87	81	69	56	44
Low	25	27	34	43	53	62	66	65	57	46	37	28
Precip	3.3	2.9	3.9	4.1	5.2	4.3	3.8	3.9	2.8	3.4	3.7	3.8
Snow	5.1	5.3	2.5	0.2	tr	0.0	0.0	0.0	0.0	0.3	0.4	4.9

High and Low temperatures in degrees Fahrenheit; Precipitation and Snow in inches

Population: 10,613; Growth (since 2000): 17.1%; Density: 48.1 persons per square mile; Race: 97.8% White, 0.3% Black/African American, 0.2% Asian, 0.2% American Indian/Alaska Native, 0.0% Native Hawaiian/Other Pacific Islander, 0.8% two or more races, 1.4% Hispanic of any race; Average household size: 2.60; Median age: 39.1; Age under 18: 25.6%; Age 65 and over: 14.6%; Males per 100 females: 104.1; Marriage status: 22.9% never married, 57.8% now married, 0.6% separated, 6.2% widowed, 13.2% divorced; Foreign born: 1.8%; Speak English only: 95.0%; With disability: 13.3%; Veterans: 11.2%; Ancestry: 26.7% German, 16.3% Irish, 12.8% American, 10.8% English, 2.8% Italian
Religion: Six largest groups: 14.5% Baptist, 4.4% European Free-Church, 2.7% Methodist/Pietist, 1.0% Non-denominational Protestant, 0.8% Catholicism, 0.1% Presbyterian-Reformed
Economy: Unemployment rate: 4.6%; Leading industries: 13.4% other services (except public administration); 12.6% construction; 12.6% accommodation and food services; Farms: 383 totaling 50,519 acres; Company size: 1 employs 1,000 or more persons, 0 employ 500 to 999 persons, 0 employ 100 to 499 persons, 126 employ less than 100 persons; Business ownership: n/a women-owned, n/a Black-owned, n/a Hispanic-owned, n/a Asian-owned
Employment: 7.6% management, business, and financial, 3.0% computer, engineering, and science, 3.6% education, legal, community service, arts, and media, 2.4% healthcare practitioners, 27.8% service, 19.6% sales and office, 12.9% natural resources, construction, and maintenance, 23.2% production, transportation, and material moving
Income: Per capita: $20,019; Median household: $44,143; Average household: $50,404; Households with income of $100,000 or more: 9.0%; Poverty rate: 22.2%
Educational Attainment: High school diploma or higher: 82.5%; Bachelor's degree or higher: 9.9%; Graduate/professional degree or higher: 3.1%
Housing: Homeownership rate: 75.6%; Median home value: $110,800; Median year structure built: 1980; Homeowner vacancy rate: 2.9%; Median gross rent: $740 per month; Rental vacancy rate: 9.1%

Vital Statistics: Birth rate: 107.4 per 10,000 population; Death rate: 97.9 per 10,000 population; Age-adjusted cancer mortality rate: 261.4 deaths per 100,000 population
Health Insurance: 81.4% have insurance; 58.8% have private insurance; 34.3% have public insurance; 18.6% do not have insurance; 14.2% of children under 18 do not have insurance
Health Care: Physicians: 1.9 per 10,000 population; Hospital beds: 0.0 per 10,000 population; Hospital admissions: 0.0 per 10,000 population
Transportation: Commute: 91.7% car, 0.6% public transportation, 1.2% walk, 5.0% work from home; Median travel time to work: 32.4 minutes
Presidential Election: 42.3% Obama, 55.1% Romney (2012)
Additional Information Contacts
Switzerland Government . . . . (800) 435-5688
   http://www.switzerland-county.com

Switzerland County Communities

BENNINGTON (unincorporated postal area)
ZCTA: 47011
   Covers a land area of 35.717 square miles and a water area of 0.070 square miles. Located at 38.88° N. Lat; 85.08° W. Long. Elevation is 889 feet.
   Population: 1,277; Growth (since 2000): 89.5%; Density: 35.8 persons per square mile; Race: 98.0% White, 0.4% Black/African American, 0.0% Asian, 0.2% American Indian/Alaska Native, 0.0% Native Hawaiian/Other Pacific Islander, 1.0% Two or more races, 0.6% Hispanic of any race; Average household size: 2.88; Median age: 36.3; Age under 18: 30.1%; Age 65 and over: 13.2%; Males per 100 females: 108.7
   Housing: Homeownership rate: 88.7%; Homeowner vacancy rate: 4.3%; Rental vacancy rate: 5.7%

EAST ENTERPRISE (CDP). Covers a land area of 0.519 square miles and a water area of 0 square miles. Located at 38.87° N. Lat; 84.99° W. Long. Elevation is 879 feet.
Population: 148; Growth (since 2000): n/a; Density: 285.2 persons per square mile; Race: 97.3% White, 0.7% Black/African American, 0.0% Asian, 0.7% American Indian/Alaska Native, 0.0% Native Hawaiian/Other Pacific Islander, 1.4% Two or more races, 0.0% Hispanic of any race; Average household size: 2.64; Median age: 39.5; Age under 18: 24.3%; Age 65 and over: 12.8%; Males per 100 females: 92.2
School District(s)
Switzerland County School Corp (PK-12)
   2012-13 Enrollment: 1,469 . . . . (812) 427-2611
Housing: Homeownership rate: 76.8%; Homeowner vacancy rate: 0.0%; Rental vacancy rate: 18.8%

FLORENCE (CDP). Covers a land area of 0.135 square miles and a water area of 0.017 square miles. Located at 38.78° N. Lat; 84.92° W. Long. Elevation is 476 feet.
Population: 80; Growth (since 2000): n/a; Density: 592.9 persons per square mile; Race: 100.0% White, 0.0% Black/African American, 0.0% Asian, 0.0% American Indian/Alaska Native, 0.0% Native Hawaiian/Other Pacific Islander, 0.0% Two or more races, 0.0% Hispanic of any race; Average household size: 2.29; Median age: 46.0; Age under 18: 16.2%; Age 65 and over: 22.5%; Males per 100 females: 90.5
Housing: Homeownership rate: 74.3%; Homeowner vacancy rate: 0.0%; Rental vacancy rate: 10.0%

PATRIOT (town). Covers a land area of 0.219 square miles and a water area of 0.041 square miles. Located at 38.84° N. Lat; 84.83° W. Long. Elevation is 472 feet.
History: Suffered during flood of 1937. Laid out 1820.
Population: 209; Growth (since 2000): 3.5%; Density: 955.5 persons per square mile; Race: 98.1% White, 0.0% Black/African American, 0.5% Asian, 0.5% American Indian/Alaska Native, 0.0% Native Hawaiian/Other Pacific Islander, 0.5% Two or more races, 1.4% Hispanic of any race; Average household size: 2.75; Median age: 42.1; Age under 18: 23.0%; Age 65 and over: 11.5%; Males per 100 females: 117.7
Housing: Homeownership rate: 60.5%; Homeowner vacancy rate: 4.1%; Rental vacancy rate: 9.1%

VEVAY (town). County seat. Covers a land area of 1.451 square miles and a water area of 0.097 square miles. Located at 38.74° N. Lat; 85.08° W. Long. Elevation is 482 feet.
History: Vevay was founded in 1801 by Swiss immigrants, who planted vineyards and became known for their fine wines. Vevay was the birthplace of Edward Eggleston, author of "The Hoosier Schoolmaster."
Population: 1,683; Growth (since 2000): -3.0%; Density: 1,159.6 persons per square mile; Race: 97.1% White, 0.5% Black/African American, 0.5% Asian, 0.0% American Indian/Alaska Native, 0.0% Native Hawaiian/Other Pacific Islander, 1.2% Two or more races, 1.1% Hispanic of any race; Average household size: 2.18; Median age: 40.8; Age under 18: 20.3%; Age 65 and over: 17.6%; Males per 100 females: 95.2
School District(s)
Switzerland County School Corp (PK-12)
   2012-13 Enrollment: 1,469 . . . . (812) 427-2611
Housing: Homeownership rate: 54.6%; Homeowner vacancy rate: 4.3%; Rental vacancy rate: 10.6%
Newspapers: Reveille-Enterprise (weekly circulation 2900); Switzerland Democrat (weekly circulation 600)
Additional Information Contacts
Town of Vevay. . . . . (812) 265-3135
   http://www.madisonchamber.org

Tippecanoe County

Located in west central Indiana; crossed by the Wabash River; drained by the Tippecanoe River. Covers a land area of 499.806 square miles, a water area of 3.437 square miles, and is located in the Eastern Time Zone at 40.39° N. Lat., 86.89° W. Long. The county was founded in 1826. County seat is Lafayette.

Tippecanoe County is part of the Lafayette-West Lafayette, IN Metropolitan Statistical Area. The entire metro area includes: Benton County, IN; Carroll County, IN; Tippecanoe County, IN

Weather Station: Lafayette 8 S   Elevation: 732 feet

	Jan	Feb	Mar	Apr	May	Jun	Jul	Aug	Sep	Oct	Nov	Dec
High	33	38	49	62	72	82	84	83	78	65	51	37
Low	17	20	29	40	51	60	63	62	54	42	33	21
Precip	2.1	2.0	2.7	3.4	4.6	4.4	4.1	3.8	2.8	2.8	3.2	2.6
Snow	6.9	5.3	2.4	0.6	tr	0.0	0.0	0.0	0.0	0.5	0.5	5.1

High and Low temperatures in degrees Fahrenheit; Precipitation and Snow in inches

Weather Station: West Lafayette 6 NW   Elevation: 705 feet

	Jan	Feb	Mar	Apr	May	Jun	Jul	Aug	Sep	Oct	Nov	Dec
High	33	37	48	61	72	81	84	83	77	65	51	37
Low	17	20	29	40	50	60	63	61	53	42	33	21
Precip	1.9	1.9	2.6	3.6	4.6	3.9	4.2	3.6	2.8	3.1	3.2	2.5
Snow	6.4	5.4	2.3	0.5	0.0	0.0	0.0	0.0	0.0	0.2	0.6	4.7

High and Low temperatures in degrees Fahrenheit; Precipitation and Snow in inches

Population: 172,780; Growth (since 2000): 16.0%; Density: 345.7 persons per square mile; Race: 84.0% White, 4.0% Black/African American, 6.2% Asian, 0.3% American Indian/Alaska Native, 0.0% Native Hawaiian/Other Pacific Islander, 2.2% two or more races, 7.5% Hispanic of any race; Average household size: 2.42; Median age: 27.7; Age under 18: 20.7%; Age 65 and over: 9.5%; Males per 100 females: 103.9; Marriage status: 43.0% never married, 43.4% now married, 0.9% separated, 4.3% widowed, 9.3% divorced; Foreign born: 10.4%; Speak English only: 85.6%; With disability: 9.5%; Veterans: 6.8%; Ancestry: 27.2% German, 13.7% Irish, 9.6% English, 7.3% American, 3.4% Polish
Religion: Six largest groups: 11.6% Catholicism, 4.8% Methodist/Pietist, 3.4% Baptist, 2.8% Presbyterian-Reformed, 2.8% Lutheran, 2.3% Non-denominational Protestant
Economy: Unemployment rate: 4.8%; Leading industries: 15.8% retail trade; 12.1% accommodation and food services; 11.7% health care and social assistance; Farms: 702 totaling 220,199 acres; Company size: 8 employ 1,000 or more persons, 5 employ 500 to 999 persons, 87 employ 100 to 499 persons, 3,232 employ less than 100 persons; Business ownership: 2,867 women-owned, n/a Black-owned, 320 Hispanic-owned, 411 Asian-owned
Employment: 11.3% management, business, and financial, 6.0% computer, engineering, and science, 16.0% education, legal, community service, arts, and media, 5.6% healthcare practitioners, 18.9% service, 21.1% sales and office, 6.9% natural resources, construction, and maintenance, 14.2% production, transportation, and material moving

Income: Per capita: $23,691; Median household: $44,246; Average household: $60,870; Households with income of $100,000 or more: 16.5%; Poverty rate: 21.6%
Educational Attainment: High school diploma or higher: 90.7%; Bachelor's degree or higher: 35.7%; Graduate/professional degree or higher: 15.9%
Housing: Homeownership rate: 55.0%; Median home value: $130,900; Median year structure built: 1978; Homeowner vacancy rate: 3.1%; Median gross rent: $788 per month; Rental vacancy rate: 8.1%
Vital Statistics: Birth rate: 123.6 per 10,000 population; Death rate: 58.9 per 10,000 population; Age-adjusted cancer mortality rate: 185.9 deaths per 100,000 population
Health Insurance: 87.6% have insurance; 75.6% have private insurance; 20.8% have public insurance; 12.4% do not have insurance; 5.2% of children under 18 do not have insurance
Health Care: Physicians: 21.4 per 10,000 population; Hospital beds: 27.9 per 10,000 population; Hospital admissions: 1,223.6 per 10,000 population
Air Quality Index: 46.3% good, 53.7% moderate, 0.0% unhealthy for sensitive individuals, 0.0% unhealthy (percent of days)
Transportation: Commute: 85.4% car, 3.1% public transportation, 5.8% walk, 3.4% work from home; Median travel time to work: 17.6 minutes
Presidential Election: 47.0% Obama, 50.6% Romney (2012)
Additional Information Contacts
Tippecanoe Government . . . . (765) 423-9326
  http://www.tippecanoe.in.gov

Tippecanoe County Communities

AMERICUS (CDP). Covers a land area of 1.263 square miles and a water area of 0.029 square miles. Located at 40.52° N. Lat; 86.75° W. Long. Elevation is 558 feet.
Population: 423; Growth (since 2000): n/a; Density: 334.8 persons per square mile; Race: 99.1% White, 0.2% Black/African American, 0.2% Asian, 0.2% American Indian/Alaska Native, 0.0% Native Hawaiian/Other Pacific Islander, 0.2% Two or more races, 0.9% Hispanic of any race; Average household size: 2.55; Median age: 43.7; Age under 18: 21.7%; Age 65 and over: 13.7%; Males per 100 females: 115.8
Housing: Homeownership rate: 85.6%; Homeowner vacancy rate: 0.0%; Rental vacancy rate: 11.1%

BATTLE GROUND (town). Covers a land area of 0.865 square miles and a water area of 0 square miles. Located at 40.51° N. Lat; 86.85° W. Long. Elevation is 587 feet.
History: A memorial park marks scene of the Battle of Tippecanoe (1811) between Native Americans and U.S. soldiers under Gen. W. H. Harrison.
Population: 1,334; Growth (since 2000): 0.8%; Density: 1,542.9 persons per square mile; Race: 98.2% White, 0.2% Black/African American, 0.2% Asian, 0.1% American Indian/Alaska Native, 0.0% Native Hawaiian/Other Pacific Islander, 0.4% Two or more races, 2.1% Hispanic of any race; Average household size: 2.67; Median age: 38.1; Age under 18: 27.3%; Age 65 and over: 9.3%; Males per 100 females: 93.6
School District(s)
Tippecanoe School Corp (KG-12)
  2012-13 Enrollment: 12,193 . . . . (765) 474-2481
Housing: Homeownership rate: 87.0%; Homeowner vacancy rate: 0.5%; Rental vacancy rate: 18.8%
Additional Information Contacts
Town of Battle Ground . . . . (765) 567-2603
  http://battleground.in.gov

BUCK CREEK (CDP). Covers a land area of 0.116 square miles and a water area of 0 square miles. Located at 40.49° N. Lat; 86.76° W. Long. Elevation is 659 feet.
Population: 207; Growth (since 2000): n/a; Density: 1,784.0 persons per square mile; Race: 100.0% White, 0.0% Black/African American, 0.0% Asian, 0.0% American Indian/Alaska Native, 0.0% Native Hawaiian/Other Pacific Islander, 0.0% Two or more races, 0.0% Hispanic of any race; Average household size: 2.62; Median age: 40.5; Age under 18: 27.1%; Age 65 and over: 8.7%; Males per 100 females: 95.3
Housing: Homeownership rate: 89.9%; Homeowner vacancy rate: 1.4%; Rental vacancy rate: 11.1%

CLARKS HILL (town). Covers a land area of 0.272 square miles and a water area of 0 square miles. Located at 40.25° N. Lat; 86.72° W. Long. Elevation is 827 feet.
Population: 611; Growth (since 2000): -10.1%; Density: 2,242.6 persons per square mile; Race: 97.9% White, 0.2% Black/African American, 0.0% Asian, 0.3% American Indian/Alaska Native, 0.0% Native Hawaiian/Other Pacific Islander, 1.6% Two or more races, 1.1% Hispanic of any race; Average household size: 2.66; Median age: 36.2; Age under 18: 29.3%; Age 65 and over: 10.0%; Males per 100 females: 102.3
Housing: Homeownership rate: 71.7%; Homeowner vacancy rate: 4.0%; Rental vacancy rate: 16.7%

COLBURN (CDP). Covers a land area of 0.096 square miles and a water area of 0 square miles. Located at 40.52° N. Lat; 86.71° W. Long. Elevation is 663 feet.
Population: 193; Growth (since 2000): n/a; Density: 2,018.7 persons per square mile; Race: 97.9% White, 0.5% Black/African American, 0.0% Asian, 0.5% American Indian/Alaska Native, 0.0% Native Hawaiian/Other Pacific Islander, 1.0% Two or more races, 0.0% Hispanic of any race; Average household size: 2.92; Median age: 31.8; Age under 18: 30.1%; Age 65 and over: 13.5%; Males per 100 females: 107.5
Housing: Homeownership rate: 75.7%; Homeowner vacancy rate: 3.8%; Rental vacancy rate: 5.9%

DAYTON (town). Covers a land area of 1.064 square miles and a water area of 0 square miles. Located at 40.38° N. Lat; 86.77° W. Long. Elevation is 676 feet.
Population: 1,420; Growth (since 2000): 26.8%; Density: 1,334.6 persons per square mile; Race: 95.4% White, 0.9% Black/African American, 0.2% Asian, 0.6% American Indian/Alaska Native, 0.0% Native Hawaiian/Other Pacific Islander, 1.8% Two or more races, 3.6% Hispanic of any race; Average household size: 2.65; Median age: 32.0; Age under 18: 29.2%; Age 65 and over: 8.1%; Males per 100 females: 98.9
School District(s)
Tippecanoe School Corp (KG-12)
  2012-13 Enrollment: 12,193 . . . . (765) 474-2481
Housing: Homeownership rate: 73.5%; Homeowner vacancy rate: 1.5%; Rental vacancy rate: 5.9%

LAFAYETTE (city). County seat. Covers a land area of 27.742 square miles and a water area of 0 square miles. Located at 40.40° N. Lat; 86.86° W. Long. Elevation is 702 feet.
History: Lafayette was founded in 1824 by William Digby, and named for the Marquis de Lafayette. Lafayette was an early shipping center along the Wabash River. It was from Lafayette that the balloon carrying the first airmail in the U.S. was launched. The flight failed to reach its destination and the mail continued on by train.
Population: 67,140; Growth (since 2000): 19.0%; Density: 2,420.1 persons per square mile; Race: 83.6% White, 6.2% Black/African American, 1.4% Asian, 0.4% American Indian/Alaska Native, 0.0% Native Hawaiian/Other Pacific Islander, 2.7% Two or more races, 12.1% Hispanic of any race; Average household size: 2.30; Median age: 31.9; Age under 18: 23.8%; Age 65 and over: 11.3%; Males per 100 females: 94.9; Marriage status: 35.5% never married, 45.5% now married, 1.3% separated, 5.7% widowed, 13.2% divorced; Foreign born: 7.5%; Speak English only: 87.0%; With disability: 13.0%; Veterans: 8.5%; Ancestry: 26.4% German, 14.1% Irish, 9.0% English, 7.5% American, 2.8% Polish
Employment: 10.3% management, business, and financial, 5.5% computer, engineering, and science, 11.8% education, legal, community service, arts, and media, 6.0% healthcare practitioners, 19.7% service, 21.4% sales and office, 6.8% natural resources, construction, and maintenance, 18.6% production, transportation, and material moving
Income: Per capita: $21,646; Median household: $39,345; Average household: $50,086; Households with income of $100,000 or more: 9.8%; Poverty rate: 19.6%
Educational Attainment: High school diploma or higher: 86.4%; Bachelor's degree or higher: 26.7%; Graduate/professional degree or higher: 9.5%
School District(s)
Lafayette School Corporation (KG-12)
  2012-13 Enrollment: 7,121 . . . . (765) 771-6000
New Community School (KG-08)
  2012-13 Enrollment: 213 . . . . (765) 420-9617
Tippecanoe School Corp (KG-12)
  2012-13 Enrollment: 12,193 . . . . (765) 474-2481

Two-year College(s)
Saint Elizabeth School of Nursing (Private, Not-for-profit, Roman Catholic)
Fall 2013 Enrollment: 269..........................(765) 423-6400
2013-14 Tuition: In-state $18,090; Out-of-state $18,090
Vocational/Technical School(s)
Lafayette Beauty Academy (Private, For-profit)
Fall 2013 Enrollment: 82..........................(765) 742-0068
2013-14 Tuition: $14,100

Housing: Homeownership rate: 51.3%; Median home value: $102,200; Median year structure built: 1970; Homeowner vacancy rate: 2.8%; Median gross rent: $744 per month; Rental vacancy rate: 9.1%

Health Insurance: 81.9% have insurance; 61.7% have private insurance; 29.8% have public insurance; 18.1% do not have insurance; 5.5% of children under 18 do not have insurance

Hospitals: Franciscan Saint Elizabeth Health - Lafayette Central (375 beds); Franciscan Saint Elizabeth Health - Lafayette East (263 beds); Indiana University Health Arnett Hospital

Safety: Violent crime rate: 57.1 per 10,000 population; Property crime rate: 501.1 per 10,000 population

Newspapers: Journal & Courier (daily circulation 35900); Lafayette Leader (weekly circulation 2000)

Transportation: Commute: 91.0% car, 2.7% public transportation, 2.2% walk, 2.1% work from home; Median travel time to work: 15.9 minutes; Amtrak: Train service available.

Airports: Purdue University (general aviation)

Additional Information Contacts
City of Lafayette..................................(765) 807-1021
http://www.lafayette.in.gov

MONTMORENCI (CDP).
Covers a land area of 1.358 square miles and a water area of 0 square miles. Located at 40.47° N. Lat; 87.04° W. Long. Elevation is 699 feet.

Population: 243; Growth (since 2000): n/a; Density: 179.0 persons per square mile; Race: 98.8% White, 0.0% Black/African American, 0.4% Asian, 0.4% American Indian/Alaska Native, 0.0% Native Hawaiian/Other Pacific Islander, 0.4% Two or more races, 0.4% Hispanic of any race; Average household size: 2.41; Median age: 44.1; Age under 18: 20.6%; Age 65 and over: 9.5%; Males per 100 females: 109.5

Housing: Homeownership rate: 91.1%; Homeowner vacancy rate: 4.1%; Rental vacancy rate: 0.0%

PURDUE UNIVERSITY (CDP).
Covers a land area of 1.298 square miles and a water area of 0 square miles. Located at 40.43° N. Lat; 86.92° W. Long.

History: Purdue University, established May 6, 1869 located in West Lafayette, Indiana, was named after its principal benefactor, John Purdue and is a primary institution in Tippecanoe County.

Population: 12,183; Growth (since 2000): n/a; Density: 9,389.0 persons per square mile; Race: 69.9% White, 3.7% Black/African American, 23.0% Asian, 0.1% American Indian/Alaska Native, 0.0% Native Hawaiian/Other Pacific Islander, 2.2% Two or more races, 3.6% Hispanic of any race; Average household size: 2.24; Median age: 19.9; Age under 18: 2.8%; Age 65 and over: 0.0%; Males per 100 females: 131.0; Marriage status: 89.9% never married, 9.2% now married, 0.3% separated, 0.0% widowed, 0.8% divorced; Foreign born: 22.1%; Speak English only: 74.5%; With disability: 2.6%; Veterans: 0.6%; Ancestry: 26.8% German, 13.5% Irish, 6.5% Italian, 6.3% Polish, 4.7% English

Employment: 3.9% management, business, and financial, 7.0% computer, engineering, and science, 26.5% education, legal, community service, arts, and media, 1.8% healthcare practitioners, 33.7% service, 22.2% sales and office, 1.8% natural resources, construction, and maintenance, 3.2% production, transportation, and material moving

Income: Per capita: $4,655; Median household: $19,263; Average household: $19,767; Households with income of $100,000 or more: n/a; Poverty rate: 52.2%

Educational Attainment: High school diploma or higher: 92.2%; Bachelor's degree or higher: 74.5%; Graduate/professional degree or higher: 49.8%

Housing: Homeownership rate: 0.3%; Median home value: n/a; Median year structure built: 1959; Homeowner vacancy rate: 0.0%; Median gross rent: $751 per month; Rental vacancy rate: 6.5%

Health Insurance: 95.4% have insurance; 92.9% have private insurance; 4.1% have public insurance; 4.6% do not have insurance; 2.5% of children under 18 do not have insurance

Transportation: Commute: 26.2% car, 9.9% public transportation, 43.3% walk, 15.1% work from home; Median travel time to work: 13.9 minutes

ROMNEY (unincorporated postal area)
ZCTA: 47981

Covers a land area of 36.371 square miles and a water area of 0 square miles. Located at 40.25° N. Lat; 86.93° W. Long. Elevation is 735 feet.

Population: 849; Growth (since 2000): 8.0%; Density: 23.3 persons per square mile; Race: 96.9% White, 0.0% Black/African American, 0.2% Asian, 0.0% American Indian/Alaska Native, 0.0% Native Hawaiian/Other Pacific Islander, 1.9% Two or more races, 1.9% Hispanic of any race; Average household size: 2.74; Median age: 38.8; Age under 18: 27.0%; Age 65 and over: 11.0%; Males per 100 females: 100.2

Housing: Homeownership rate: 81.6%; Homeowner vacancy rate: 3.1%; Rental vacancy rate: 3.3%

SHADELAND (town).
Covers a land area of 27.104 square miles and a water area of 0.232 square miles. Located at 40.34° N. Lat; 86.96° W. Long. Elevation is 620 feet.

History: Laid out 1824.

Population: 1,610; Growth (since 2000): -4.3%; Density: 59.4 persons per square mile; Race: 96.0% White, 0.4% Black/African American, 0.5% Asian, 0.6% American Indian/Alaska Native, 0.1% Native Hawaiian/Other Pacific Islander, 1.0% Two or more races, 3.3% Hispanic of any race; Average household size: 2.61; Median age: 43.2; Age under 18: 21.8%; Age 65 and over: 13.8%; Males per 100 females: 96.8

Housing: Homeownership rate: 82.3%; Homeowner vacancy rate: 5.2%; Rental vacancy rate: 4.4%

STOCKWELL (CDP).
Covers a land area of 2.613 square miles and a water area of 0 square miles. Located at 40.28° N. Lat; 86.77° W. Long. Elevation is 771 feet.

Population: 545; Growth (since 2000): n/a; Density: 208.6 persons per square mile; Race: 96.3% White, 0.2% Black/African American, 0.7% Asian, 0.2% American Indian/Alaska Native, 0.0% Native Hawaiian/Other Pacific Islander, 1.1% Two or more races, 2.6% Hispanic of any race; Average household size: 2.84; Median age: 35.9; Age under 18: 26.4%; Age 65 and over: 12.3%; Males per 100 females: 106.4

Housing: Homeownership rate: 87.0%; Homeowner vacancy rate: 1.8%; Rental vacancy rate: 3.8%

WEST LAFAYETTE (city).
Covers a land area of 7.615 square miles and a water area of 0.010 square miles. Located at 40.46° N. Lat; 86.91° W. Long. Elevation is 610 feet.

History: Purdue University was founded in 1874 in West Lafayette.

Population: 29,596; Growth (since 2000): 2.8%; Density: 3,886.4 persons per square mile; Race: 76.8% White, 2.7% Black/African American, 17.3% Asian, 0.1% American Indian/Alaska Native, 0.0% Native Hawaiian/Other Pacific Islander, 2.1% Two or more races, 3.6% Hispanic of any race; Average household size: 2.22; Median age: 22.8; Age under 18: 11.8%; Age 65 and over: 8.7%; Males per 100 females: 118.3; Marriage status: 65.3% never married, 26.5% now married, 0.5% separated, 3.9% widowed, 4.3% divorced; Foreign born: 22.5%; Speak English only: 74.9%; With disability: 5.8%; Veterans: 3.7%; Ancestry: 23.4% German, 13.0% Irish, 9.9% English, 4.3% Italian, 4.1% American

Employment: 12.1% management, business, and financial, 9.4% computer, engineering, and science, 31.6% education, legal, community service, arts, and media, 4.1% healthcare practitioners, 18.6% service, 18.4% sales and office, 2.0% natural resources, construction, and maintenance, 3.8% production, transportation, and material moving

Income: Per capita: $22,649; Median household: $29,936; Average household: $54,136; Households with income of $100,000 or more: 15.9%; Poverty rate: 38.5%

Educational Attainment: High school diploma or higher: 96.7%; Bachelor's degree or higher: 71.4%; Graduate/professional degree or higher: 42.5%

School District(s)
Beacon Academy (07-12)
2012-13 Enrollment: 33..........................(765) 838-2045
Tippecanoe School Corp (KG-12)
2012-13 Enrollment: 12,193......................(765) 474-2481
West Lafayette Com School Corp (KG-12)
2012-13 Enrollment: 2,204.......................(765) 746-1602

Four-year College(s)
Purdue University-Main Campus (Public)
 Fall 2013 Enrollment: 39,794 . . . . (765) 494-4600
 2013-14 Tuition: In-state $9,992; Out-of-state $28,794
Housing: Homeownership rate: 32.4%; Median home value: $174,500; Median year structure built: 1979; Homeowner vacancy rate: 2.6%; Median gross rent: $849 per month; Rental vacancy rate: 4.5%
Health Insurance: 93.0% have insurance; 89.9% have private insurance; 11.1% have public insurance; 7.0% do not have insurance; 2.3% of children under 18 do not have insurance
Safety: Violent crime rate: 12.1 per 10,000 population; Property crime rate: 174.7 per 10,000 population
Transportation: Commute: 66.1% car, 7.6% public transportation, 17.5% walk, 4.1% work from home; Median travel time to work: 15.5 minutes
Additional Information Contacts
City of West Lafayette . . . . (765) 775-5150
 http://www.westlafayette.in.gov

WEST POINT (CDP). Covers a land area of 4.856 square miles and a water area of 0 square miles. Located at 40.34° N. Lat; 87.04° W. Long.
Population: 594; Growth (since 2000): n/a; Density: 122.3 persons per square mile; Race: 98.8% White, 0.2% Black/African American, 0.0% Asian, 0.0% American Indian/Alaska Native, 0.0% Native Hawaiian/Other Pacific Islander, 1.0% Two or more races, 2.5% Hispanic of any race; Average household size: 2.76; Median age: 38.5; Age under 18: 24.7%; Age 65 and over: 11.6%; Males per 100 females: 105.5
Housing: Homeownership rate: 85.1%; Homeowner vacancy rate: 1.1%; Rental vacancy rate: 3.0%

WESTPOINT (unincorporated postal area)
ZCTA: 47992
 Covers a land area of 36.444 square miles and a water area of 0.263 square miles. Located at 40.32° N. Lat; 87.05° W. Long. Elevation is 673 feet.
Population: 1,465; Growth (since 2000): 10.3%; Density: 40.2 persons per square mile; Race: 98.8% White, 0.3% Black/African American, 0.1% Asian, 0.1% American Indian/Alaska Native, 0.0% Native Hawaiian/Other Pacific Islander, 0.8% Two or more races, 1.6% Hispanic of any race; Average household size: 2.75; Median age: 39.8; Age under 18: 25.9%; Age 65 and over: 11.4%; Males per 100 females: 106.3
Housing: Homeownership rate: 86.5%; Homeowner vacancy rate: 1.7%; Rental vacancy rate: 2.7%

Tipton County

Located in central Indiana; drained by Cicero and Turkey Creeks. Covers a land area of 260.541 square miles, a water area of 0.026 square miles, and is located in the Eastern Time Zone at 40.31° N. Lat., 86.06° W. Long. The county was founded in 1844. County seat is Tipton.
Population: 15,936; Growth (since 2000): -3.9%; Density: 61.2 persons per square mile; Race: 97.6% White, 0.2% Black/African American, 0.4% Asian, 0.1% American Indian/Alaska Native, 0.0% Native Hawaiian/Other Pacific Islander, 1.0% two or more races, 2.2% Hispanic of any race; Average household size: 2.47; Median age: 42.6; Age under 18: 23.2%; Age 65 and over: 17.2%; Males per 100 females: 97.0; Marriage status: 19.2% never married, 62.7% now married, 0.7% separated, 7.3% widowed, 10.7% divorced; Foreign born: 1.8%; Speak English only: 96.8%; With disability: 16.9%; Veterans: 12.4%; Ancestry: 24.5% German, 14.9% American, 11.8% Irish, 11.0% English, 2.4% French
Religion: Six largest groups: 13.1% Baptist, 6.9% Catholicism, 5.7% Non-denominational Protestant, 3.6% Methodist/Pietist, 3.1% Lutheran, 2.8% Holiness
Economy: Unemployment rate: 4.8%; Leading industries: 19.5% retail trade; 13.7% construction; 13.0% other services (except public administration); Farms: 377 totaling 145,181 acres; Company size: 0 employ 1,000 or more persons, 0 employ 500 to 999 persons, 5 employ 100 to 499 persons, 288 employ less than 100 persons; Business ownership: 291 women-owned, n/a Black-owned, n/a Hispanic-owned, n/a Asian-owned
Employment: 13.3% management, business, and financial, 2.9% computer, engineering, and science, 5.1% education, legal, community service, arts, and media, 6.3% healthcare practitioners, 16.1% service, 21.0% sales and office, 15.3% natural resources, construction, and maintenance, 20.0% production, transportation, and material moving

Income: Per capita: $25,093; Median household: $52,686; Average household: $61,392; Households with income of $100,000 or more: 14.1%; Poverty rate: 9.4%
Educational Attainment: High school diploma or higher: 88.7%; Bachelor's degree or higher: 16.4%; Graduate/professional degree or higher: 5.6%
Housing: Homeownership rate: 79.5%; Median home value: $108,300; Median year structure built: 1958; Homeowner vacancy rate: 1.9%; Median gross rent: $661 per month; Rental vacancy rate: 9.0%
Vital Statistics: Birth rate: 96.5 per 10,000 population; Death rate: 99.7 per 10,000 population; Age-adjusted cancer mortality rate: 175.7 deaths per 100,000 population
Health Insurance: 85.3% have insurance; 72.4% have private insurance; 29.1% have public insurance; 14.7% do not have insurance; 10.6% of children under 18 do not have insurance
Health Care: Physicians: 7.0 per 10,000 population; Hospital beds: 15.8 per 10,000 population; Hospital admissions: 866.6 per 10,000 population
Transportation: Commute: 93.1% car, 0.0% public transportation, 1.8% walk, 3.0% work from home; Median travel time to work: 24.4 minutes
Presidential Election: 33.0% Obama, 64.8% Romney (2012)
Additional Information Contacts
Tipton Government . . . . (765) 675-4165
 http://www.tiptoncounty.in.gov

Tipton County Communities

GOLDSMITH (unincorporated postal area)
ZCTA: 46045
 Covers a land area of 0.034 square miles and a water area of 0 square miles. Located at 40.29° N. Lat; 86.15° W. Long. Elevation is 912 feet.
Population: 93; Growth (since 2000): 69.1%; Density: 2,731.3 persons per square mile; Race: 97.8% White, 0.0% Black/African American, 0.0% Asian, 1.1% American Indian/Alaska Native, 0.0% Native Hawaiian/Other Pacific Islander, 1.1% Two or more races, 2.2% Hispanic of any race; Average household size: 2.51; Median age: 37.3; Age under 18: 33.3%; Age 65 and over: 10.8%; Males per 100 females: 138.5
Housing: Homeownership rate: 91.9%; Homeowner vacancy rate: 0.0%; Rental vacancy rate: 40.0%

HOBBS (unincorporated postal area)
ZCTA: 46047
 Covers a land area of 0.013 square miles and a water area of 0 square miles. Located at 40.28° N. Lat; 85.95° W. Long. Elevation is 869 feet.
Population: 43; Growth (since 2000): -42.7%; Density: 3,244.1 persons per square mile; Race: 100.0% White, 0.0% Black/African American, 0.0% Asian, 0.0% American Indian/Alaska Native, 0.0% Native Hawaiian/Other Pacific Islander, 0.0% Two or more races, 7.0% Hispanic of any race; Average household size: 2.87; Median age: 28.5; Age under 18: 37.2%; Age 65 and over: 2.3%; Males per 100 females: 87.0
Housing: Homeownership rate: 60.0%; Homeowner vacancy rate: 10.0%; Rental vacancy rate: 25.0%

KEMPTON (town). Covers a land area of 0.165 square miles and a water area of 0 square miles. Located at 40.29° N. Lat; 86.23° W. Long. Elevation is 928 feet.
Population: 335; Growth (since 2000): -11.8%; Density: 2,031.6 persons per square mile; Race: 98.8% White, 0.0% Black/African American, 0.3% Asian, 0.0% American Indian/Alaska Native, 0.0% Native Hawaiian/Other Pacific Islander, 0.9% Two or more races, 0.9% Hispanic of any race; Average household size: 2.60; Median age: 39.1; Age under 18: 23.6%; Age 65 and over: 16.7%; Males per 100 females: 113.4
Housing: Homeownership rate: 88.3%; Homeowner vacancy rate: 3.4%; Rental vacancy rate: 21.1%

SHARPSVILLE (town). Covers a land area of 0.239 square miles and a water area of 0 square miles. Located at 40.38° N. Lat; 86.09° W. Long. Elevation is 879 feet.
History: Laid out 1850.
Population: 607; Growth (since 2000): -1.8%; Density: 2,536.6 persons per square mile; Race: 97.5% White, 0.2% Black/African American, 0.0% Asian, 0.0% American Indian/Alaska Native, 0.0% Native Hawaiian/Other Pacific Islander, 1.6% Two or more races, 2.0% Hispanic of any race;

Average household size: 2.67; Median age: 38.2; Age under 18: 28.0%; Age 65 and over: 9.7%; Males per 100 females: 97.7

School District(s)
Tri-Central Community Schools (KG-12)
    2012-13 Enrollment: 887 . . . . (765) 963-2585
Housing: Homeownership rate: 77.5%; Homeowner vacancy rate: 3.8%; Rental vacancy rate: 3.8%

TIPTON (city). County seat. Covers a land area of 2.504 square miles and a water area of 0 square miles. Located at 40.28° N. Lat; 86.04° W. Long. Elevation is 869 feet.
History: Laid out 1839.
Population: 5,106; Growth (since 2000): -2.8%; Density: 2,039.3 persons per square mile; Race: 97.1% White, 0.1% Black/African American, 0.6% Asian, 0.2% American Indian/Alaska Native, 0.0% Native Hawaiian/Other Pacific Islander, 1.3% Two or more races, 2.7% Hispanic of any race; Average household size: 2.28; Median age: 39.9; Age under 18: 24.2%; Age 65 and over: 17.5%; Males per 100 females: 88.4; Marriage status: 21.1% never married, 57.8% now married, 1.2% separated, 7.8% widowed, 13.3% divorced; Foreign born: 1.6%; Speak English only: 97.0%; With disability: 20.8%; Veterans: 9.0%; Ancestry: 21.1% German, 16.0% American, 12.6% Irish, 9.8% English, 3.8% French
Employment: 10.6% management, business, and financial, 2.7% computer, engineering, and science, 3.8% education, legal, community service, arts, and media, 5.2% healthcare practitioners, 24.8% service, 20.8% sales and office, 13.8% natural resources, construction, and maintenance, 18.4% production, transportation, and material moving
Income: Per capita: $17,965; Median household: $39,592; Average household: $42,818; Households with income of $100,000 or more: 3.9%; Poverty rate: 17.0%
Educational Attainment: High school diploma or higher: 83.8%; Bachelor's degree or higher: 12.2%; Graduate/professional degree or higher: 4.2%

School District(s)
Tipton Community School Corp (KG-12)
    2012-13 Enrollment: 1,734 . . . . (765) 675-2147
Housing: Homeownership rate: 66.6%; Median home value: $86,700; Median year structure built: 1953; Homeowner vacancy rate: 2.7%; Median gross rent: $669 per month; Rental vacancy rate: 10.5%
Health Insurance: 85.3% have insurance; 67.0% have private insurance; 36.2% have public insurance; 14.7% do not have insurance; 9.1% of children under 18 do not have insurance
Hospitals: Indiana University Health Tipton Hospital (102 beds)
Safety: Violent crime rate: 28.1 per 10,000 population; Property crime rate: 287.0 per 10,000 population
Newspapers: Tipton Co. Tribune (daily circulation 2500)
Transportation: Commute: 91.6% car, 0.0% public transportation, 2.5% walk, 3.9% work from home; Median travel time to work: 22.7 minutes
Additional Information Contacts
City of Tipton . . . . (765) 675-4165
    http://www.tiptonguide.com

WINDFALL CITY (town). Covers a land area of 0.293 square miles and a water area of 0 square miles. Located at 40.36° N. Lat; 85.96° W. Long. Elevation is 863 feet.
Population: 708; Growth (since 2000): -0.6%; Density: 2,412.8 persons per square mile; Race: 97.2% White, 0.3% Black/African American, 0.3% Asian, 0.3% American Indian/Alaska Native, 0.0% Native Hawaiian/Other Pacific Islander, 0.8% Two or more races, 5.4% Hispanic of any race; Average household size: 2.54; Median age: 38.8; Age under 18: 25.4%; Age 65 and over: 15.5%; Males per 100 females: 97.8
Housing: Homeownership rate: 73.5%; Homeowner vacancy rate: 4.2%; Rental vacancy rate: 13.8%

Union County

Located in eastern Indiana; bounded on the east by Ohio; drained by the East Fork of the Whitewater River. Covers a land area of 161.224 square miles, a water area of 3.953 square miles, and is located in the Eastern Time Zone at 39.62° N. Lat., 84.93° W. Long. The county was founded in 1821. County seat is Liberty.

Union County is part of the Cincinnati, OH-KY-IN Metropolitan Statistical Area. The entire metro area includes: Dearborn County, IN; Ohio County, IN; Union County, IN; Boone County, KY; Bracken County, KY; Campbell County, KY; Gallatin County, KY; Grant County, KY; Kenton County, KY; Pendleton County, KY; Brown County, OH; Butler County, OH; Clermont County, OH; Hamilton County, OH; Warren County, OH

Population: 7,516; Growth (since 2000): 2.3%; Density: 46.6 persons per square mile; Race: 97.5% White, 0.4% Black/African American, 0.3% Asian, 0.3% American Indian/Alaska Native, 0.1% Native Hawaiian/Other Pacific Islander, 1.1% two or more races, 1.1% Hispanic of any race; Average household size: 2.54; Median age: 40.3; Age under 18: 25.1%; Age 65 and over: 14.5%; Males per 100 females: 97.7; Marriage status: 24.5% never married, 58.2% now married, 1.1% separated, 5.5% widowed, 11.8% divorced; Foreign born: 0.8%; Speak English only: 98.2%; With disability: 14.8%; Veterans: 10.4%; Ancestry: 28.6% German, 12.2% Irish, 11.8% English, 10.6% American, 4.0% Italian
Religion: Six largest groups: 11.4% Methodist/Pietist, 7.0% Catholicism, 6.8% Baptist, 5.1% Non-denominational Protestant, 1.9% Holiness, 1.1% Presbyterian-Reformed
Economy: Unemployment rate: 5.3%; Leading industries: 18.3% retail trade; 15.7% other services (except public administration); 11.3% construction; Farms: 242 totaling 74,491 acres; Company size: 0 employ 1,000 or more persons, 0 employ 500 to 999 persons, 1 employs 100 to 499 persons, 114 employ less than 100 persons; Business ownership: 182 women-owned, n/a Black-owned, n/a Hispanic-owned, n/a Asian-owned
Employment: 13.0% management, business, and financial, 2.4% computer, engineering, and science, 7.4% education, legal, community service, arts, and media, 7.4% healthcare practitioners, 17.4% service, 28.1% sales and office, 10.2% natural resources, construction, and maintenance, 14.1% production, transportation, and material moving
Income: Per capita: $20,883; Median household: $44,161; Average household: $51,464; Households with income of $100,000 or more: 10.0%; Poverty rate: 12.7%
Educational Attainment: High school diploma or higher: 85.4%; Bachelor's degree or higher: 18.4%; Graduate/professional degree or higher: 6.9%
Housing: Homeownership rate: 72.5%; Median home value: $103,200; Median year structure built: 1970; Homeowner vacancy rate: 1.8%; Median gross rent: $605 per month; Rental vacancy rate: 8.9%
Vital Statistics: Birth rate: 104.4 per 10,000 population; Death rate: 87.9 per 10,000 population; Age-adjusted cancer mortality rate: Unreliable deaths per 100,000 population
Health Insurance: 83.0% have insurance; 64.7% have private insurance; 29.2% have public insurance; 17.0% do not have insurance; 13.4% of children under 18 do not have insurance
Health Care: Physicians: 8.2 per 10,000 population; Hospital beds: 0.0 per 10,000 population; Hospital admissions: 0.0 per 10,000 population
Transportation: Commute: 95.8% car, 0.1% public transportation, 1.1% walk, 3.0% work from home; Median travel time to work: 23.8 minutes
Presidential Election: 32.8% Obama, 65.2% Romney (2012)
National and State Parks: Whitewater State Park
Additional Information Contacts
Union Government . . . . (765) 458-5464

Union County Communities

BROWNSVILLE (unincorporated postal area)
ZCTA: 47325
    Covers a land area of 20.348 square miles and a water area of 0.122 square miles. Located at 39.69° N. Lat; 85.02° W. Long. Elevation is 794 feet.
    Population: 667; Growth (since 2000): -13.9%; Density: 32.8 persons per square mile; Race: 97.5% White, 0.7% Black/African American, 0.6% Asian, 0.0% American Indian/Alaska Native, 0.1% Native Hawaiian/Other Pacific Islander, 0.7% Two or more races, 1.9% Hispanic of any race; Average household size: 2.63; Median age: 44.2; Age under 18: 20.5%; Age 65 and over: 14.1%; Males per 100 females: 109.7
    Housing: Homeownership rate: 81.1%; Homeowner vacancy rate: 1.0%; Rental vacancy rate: 2.0%

LIBERTY (town). County seat. Covers a land area of 0.857 square miles and a water area of 0.002 square miles. Located at 39.64° N. Lat; 84.93° W. Long. Elevation is 984 feet.
History: Liberty was the home from 1824 to 1843 of Ambrose Burnside who achieved military distinction during the Civil War, and later served as governor of Rhode Island and as a U.S. senator.

Population: 2,133; Growth (since 2000): 3.5%; Density: 2,487.8 persons per square mile; Race: 96.8% White, 0.8% Black/African American, 0.4% Asian, 0.3% American Indian/Alaska Native, 0.1% Native Hawaiian/Other Pacific Islander, 0.9% Two or more races, 1.5% Hispanic of any race; Average household size: 2.49; Median age: 34.7; Age under 18: 28.6%; Age 65 and over: 14.6%; Males per 100 females: 87.4

School District(s)
Union Co/clg Corner Joint SD (KG-12)
2012-13 Enrollment: 1,494 . . . . (765) 458-7471

Housing: Homeownership rate: 61.9%; Homeowner vacancy rate: 3.7%; Rental vacancy rate: 10.9%

Newspapers: Liberty Herald (weekly circulation 2600); Union County Review (weekly circulation 4600)

WEST COLLEGE CORNER (town). Covers a land area of 0.267 square miles and a water area of 0 square miles. Located at 39.57° N. Lat; 84.82° W. Long. Elevation is 988 feet.

Population: 676; Growth (since 2000): 6.6%; Density: 2,532.7 persons per square mile; Race: 97.5% White, 0.3% Black/African American, 0.0% Asian, 0.3% American Indian/Alaska Native, 0.1% Native Hawaiian/Other Pacific Islander, 1.2% Two or more races, 0.6% Hispanic of any race; Average household size: 2.47; Median age: 36.0; Age under 18: 29.1%; Age 65 and over: 10.7%; Males per 100 females: 91.0

Housing: Homeownership rate: 52.2%; Homeowner vacancy rate: 0.7%; Rental vacancy rate: 10.9%

Vanderburgh County

Located in southwestern Indiana; bounded on the south by the Ohio River and the Kentucky border; drained by Pigeon Creek. Covers a land area of 233.475 square miles, a water area of 2.855 square miles, and is located in the Central Time Zone at 38.02° N. Lat., 87.59° W. Long. The county was founded in 1818. County seat is Evansville.

Vanderburgh County is part of the Evansville, IN-KY Metropolitan Statistical Area. The entire metro area includes: Posey County, IN; Vanderburgh County, IN; Warrick County, IN; Henderson County, KY

Weather Station: Evansville Dress Regional Arpt   Elevation: 380 feet

	Jan	Feb	Mar	Apr	May	Jun	Jul	Aug	Sep	Oct	Nov	Dec
High	41	46	56	67	77	85	88	88	81	69	56	44
Low	25	28	36	45	55	64	68	66	57	46	37	28
Precip	3.1	3.2	4.3	4.4	5.4	3.9	4.0	3.0	3.1	3.3	4.1	3.7
Snow	3.4	3.8	1.3	0.2	tr	tr	0.0	0.0	tr	0.2	0.1	2.5

High and Low temperatures in degrees Fahrenheit; Precipitation and Snow in inches

Weather Station: Evansville Museum   Elevation: 379 feet

	Jan	Feb	Mar	Apr	May	Jun	Jul	Aug	Sep	Oct	Nov	Dec
High	43	48	59	70	79	87	90	90	83	72	59	46
Low	27	29	38	48	57	66	70	69	61	49	41	30
Precip	3.0	3.4	4.5	4.3	5.0	3.6	4.3	3.3	3.6	3.6	4.2	3.8
Snow	3.1	2.9	1.5	0.1	tr	0.0	0.0	0.0	0.0	tr	0.1	3.3

High and Low temperatures in degrees Fahrenheit; Precipitation and Snow in inches

Population: 179,703; Growth (since 2000): 4.5%; Density: 769.7 persons per square mile; Race: 86.2% White, 9.1% Black/African American, 1.1% Asian, 0.2% American Indian/Alaska Native, 0.1% Native Hawaiian/Other Pacific Islander, 2.3% two or more races, 2.2% Hispanic of any race; Average household size: 2.31; Median age: 37.5; Age under 18: 22.2%; Age 65 and over: 14.4%; Males per 100 females: 93.2; Marriage status: 31.6% never married, 47.2% now married, 0.9% separated, 6.7% widowed, 14.5% divorced; Foreign born: 2.5%; Speak English only: 96.0%; With disability: 13.5%; Veterans: 9.5%; Ancestry: 29.7% German, 18.4% American, 10.1% Irish, 8.9% English, 2.3% French

Religion: Six largest groups: 16.2% Catholicism, 15.1% Baptist, 7.2% Non-denominational Protestant, 4.7% Methodist/Pietist, 3.6% Presbyterian-Reformed, 2.5% Lutheran

Economy: Unemployment rate: 4.8%; Leading industries: 15.9% retail trade; 11.2% health care and social assistance; 11.2% other services (except public administration); Farms: 275 totaling 76,554 acres; Company size: 9 employ 1,000 or more persons, 8 employ 500 to 999 persons, 137 employ 100 to 499 persons, 4,820 employ less than 100 persons; Business ownership: 3,224 women-owned, 362 Black-owned, 156 Hispanic-owned, 192 Asian-owned

Employment: 11.1% management, business, and financial, 3.8% computer, engineering, and science, 8.7% education, legal, community service, arts, and media, 6.1% healthcare practitioners, 19.1% service, 26.4% sales and office, 8.6% natural resources, construction, and maintenance, 16.2% production, transportation, and material moving

Income: Per capita: $24,378; Median household: $43,540; Average household: $58,048; Households with income of $100,000 or more: 13.8%; Poverty rate: 15.9%

Educational Attainment: High school diploma or higher: 89.2%; Bachelor's degree or higher: 22.6%; Graduate/professional degree or higher: 7.3%

Housing: Homeownership rate: 64.5%; Median home value: $112,900; Median year structure built: 1963; Homeowner vacancy rate: 2.8%; Median gross rent: $709 per month; Rental vacancy rate: 11.4%

Vital Statistics: Birth rate: 125.2 per 10,000 population; Death rate: 99.8 per 10,000 population; Age-adjusted cancer mortality rate: 184.6 deaths per 100,000 population

Health Insurance: 87.1% have insurance; 69.6% have private insurance; 29.7% have public insurance; 12.9% do not have insurance; 6.5% of children under 18 do not have insurance

Health Care: Physicians: 28.5 per 10,000 population; Hospital beds: 72.5 per 10,000 population; Hospital admissions: 2,543.1 per 10,000 population

Air Quality Index: 61.4% good, 38.6% moderate, 0.0% unhealthy for sensitive individuals, 0.0% unhealthy (percent of days)

Transportation: Commute: 92.2% car, 1.7% public transportation, 2.0% walk, 2.7% work from home; Median travel time to work: 18.9 minutes

Presidential Election: 43.8% Obama, 54.4% Romney (2012)

National and State Parks: Angel Mounds State Memorial

Additional Information Contacts
Vanderburgh Government . . . . (812) 435-5160
http://www.vanderburghgov.org

Vanderburgh County Communities

DARMSTADT (town). Covers a land area of 4.516 square miles and a water area of 0.059 square miles. Located at 38.09° N. Lat; 87.58° W. Long. Elevation is 479 feet.

History: Established 1860.

Population: 1,407; Growth (since 2000): 7.2%; Density: 311.5 persons per square mile; Race: 97.5% White, 0.6% Black/African American, 0.8% Asian, 0.0% American Indian/Alaska Native, 0.1% Native Hawaiian/Other Pacific Islander, 0.8% Two or more races, 0.6% Hispanic of any race; Average household size: 2.59; Median age: 47.1; Age under 18: 21.3%; Age 65 and over: 17.0%; Males per 100 females: 106.3

Housing: Homeownership rate: 93.6%; Homeowner vacancy rate: 1.2%; Rental vacancy rate: 7.9%

EVANSVILLE (city). County seat. Covers a land area of 44.153 square miles and a water area of 0.472 square miles. Located at 37.99° N. Lat; 87.53° W. Long. Elevation is 387 feet.

History: Colonel Hugh McGary established a ferry at this spot on the Ohio River in 1812, and a village called McGary's Ferry grew up around it. McGary sold part of his holdings to General Robert Evans in 1818. When the community was designated as the seat of the new Vanderburgh County, it was named Evansville. The town had a good inland harbor, and soon became a transportation hub. It was chartered as a city in 1848.

Population: 117,429; Growth (since 2000): -3.4%; Density: 2,659.6 persons per square mile; Race: 82.0% White, 12.6% Black/African American, 1.0% Asian, 0.3% American Indian/Alaska Native, 0.1% Native Hawaiian/Other Pacific Islander, 2.8% Two or more races, 2.6% Hispanic of any race; Average household size: 2.23; Median age: 36.5; Age under 18: 22.1%; Age 65 and over: 14.4%; Males per 100 females: 92.7; Marriage status: 34.0% never married, 41.6% now married, 1.0% separated, 7.4% widowed, 17.0% divorced; Foreign born: 2.3%; Speak English only: 96.2%; With disability: 15.3%; Veterans: 9.3%; Ancestry: 26.4% German, 19.1% American, 9.9% Irish, 8.2% English, 2.2% French

Employment: 8.6% management, business, and financial, 2.7% computer, engineering, and science, 7.8% education, legal, community service, arts, and media, 5.7% healthcare practitioners, 22.2% service, 26.3% sales and office, 8.9% natural resources, construction, and maintenance, 17.6% production, transportation, and material moving

Income: Per capita: $20,984; Median household: $35,839; Average household: $47,612; Households with income of $100,000 or more: 8.5%; Poverty rate: 20.1%

Educational Attainment: High school diploma or higher: 86.8%; Bachelor's degree or higher: 18.0%; Graduate/professional degree or higher: 5.8%

School District(s)
Evansville Vanderburgh Sch Corp (PK-12)
  2012-13 Enrollment: 23,020 . . . . (812) 435-8477
Joshua Academy (KG-05)
  2012-13 Enrollment: 242. . . . . (812) 401-6300
Signature School Inc (09-12)
  2012-13 Enrollment: 337. . . . . (812) 421-1820

Four-year College(s)
University of Evansville (Private, Not-for-profit, United Methodist)
  Fall 2013 Enrollment: 2,630 . . . . (812) 488-2000
  2013-14 Tuition: In-state $30,596; Out-of-state $30,596
University of Southern Indiana (Public)
  Fall 2013 Enrollment: 9,902 . . . . (812) 464-8600
  2013-14 Tuition: In-state $6,698; Out-of-state $15,553

Vocational/Technical School(s)
Regency Beauty Institute-Evansville (Private, For-profit)
  Fall 2013 Enrollment: 65 . . . . (800) 787-6456
  2013-14 Tuition: $16,200
Rogers Academy of Hair Design (Private, For-profit)
  Fall 2013 Enrollment: 51 . . . . (812) 429-0110
  2013-14 Tuition: $11,700
The Salon Professional Academy-Evansville (Private, For-profit)
  Fall 2013 Enrollment: 105 . . . . (812) 437-8772
  2013-14 Tuition: $13,890

Housing: Homeownership rate: 56.0%; Median home value: $90,000; Median year structure built: 1956; Homeowner vacancy rate: 3.7%; Median gross rent: $692 per month; Rental vacancy rate: 11.8%
Health Insurance: 83.8% have insurance; 61.3% have private insurance; 34.0% have public insurance; 16.2% do not have insurance; 7.8% of children under 18 do not have insurance
Hospitals: Deaconess Hospital (400 beds); Saint Mary's Medical Center of Evansville (508 beds)
Safety: Violent crime rate: 46.9 per 10,000 population; Property crime rate: 487.1 per 10,000 population
Newspapers: Evansville Courier & Press (daily circulation 66200)
Transportation: Commute: 91.0% car, 2.5% public transportation, 2.6% walk, 2.4% work from home; Median travel time to work: 18.0 minutes
Airports: Evansville Regional (primary service/non-hub)
Additional Information Contacts
City of Evansville. . . . . (812) 436-4992
  http://www.evansvillegov.org

HIGHLAND
(CDP). Covers a land area of 2.267 square miles and a water area of 0.013 square miles. Located at 38.05° N. Lat; 87.56° W. Long. Elevation is 482 feet.
History: The area of Highland was almost entirely under water before it was first settled in 1848. Only a high sand ridge stood above the water. People referred to this area as 'Highlands.'.
Population: 4,489; Growth (since 2000): 9.3%; Density: 1,980.0 persons per square mile; Race: 96.1% White, 1.3% Black/African American, 1.2% Asian, 0.0% American Indian/Alaska Native, 0.0% Native Hawaiian/Other Pacific Islander, 1.1% Two or more races, 0.8% Hispanic of any race; Average household size: 2.57; Median age: 43.5; Age under 18: 23.8%; Age 65 and over: 15.6%; Males per 100 females: 95.9; Marriage status: 21.3% never married, 62.3% now married, 0.0% separated, 6.0% widowed, 10.4% divorced; Foreign born: 4.3%; Speak English only: 94.7%; With disability: 9.0%; Veterans: 8.1%; Ancestry: 37.8% German, 15.7% English, 15.3% Irish, 11.6% American, 3.1% Italian
Employment: 20.1% management, business, and financial; 5.7% computer, engineering, and science, 11.8% education, legal, community service, arts, and media, 8.9% healthcare practitioners, 9.2% service, 27.2% sales and office, 9.2% natural resources, construction, and maintenance, 7.9% production, transportation, and material moving
Income: Per capita: $34,625; Median household: $71,506; Average household: $85,211; Households with income of $100,000 or more: 29.1%; Poverty rate: 2.2%
Educational Attainment: High school diploma or higher: 93.8%; Bachelor's degree or higher: 37.4%; Graduate/professional degree or higher: 14.1%
Housing: Homeownership rate: 92.6%; Median home value: $154,100; Median year structure built: 1982; Homeowner vacancy rate: 1.1%; Median gross rent: $890 per month; Rental vacancy rate: 3.7%
Health Insurance: 92.3% have insurance; 87.5% have private insurance; 18.4% have public insurance; 7.7% do not have insurance; 5.8% of children under 18 do not have insurance
Transportation: Commute: 96.3% car, 0.0% public transportation, 0.4% walk, 2.6% work from home; Median travel time to work: 20.1 minutes

MELODY HILL
(CDP). Covers a land area of 1.361 square miles and a water area of 0.016 square miles. Located at 38.02° N. Lat; 87.51° W. Long. Elevation is 427 feet.
Population: 3,628; Growth (since 2000): 18.3%; Density: 2,666.3 persons per square mile; Race: 93.9% White, 3.4% Black/African American, 1.2% Asian, 0.1% American Indian/Alaska Native, 0.0% Native Hawaiian/Other Pacific Islander, 1.2% Two or more races, 1.5% Hispanic of any race; Average household size: 2.61; Median age: 40.9; Age under 18: 24.7%; Age 65 and over: 14.6%; Males per 100 females: 95.8; Marriage status: 24.2% never married, 64.9% now married, 0.0% separated, 2.7% widowed, 8.2% divorced; Foreign born: 4.3%; Speak English only: 93.4%; With disability: 9.2%; Veterans: 14.8%; Ancestry: 28.8% German, 14.7% American, 11.3% Irish, 11.0% English, 3.0% Ukrainian
Employment: 15.2% management, business, and financial, 6.0% computer, engineering, and science, 10.5% education, legal, community service, arts, and media, 9.0% healthcare practitioners, 15.4% service, 21.3% sales and office, 5.6% natural resources, construction, and maintenance, 17.1% production, transportation, and material moving
Income: Per capita: $32,728; Median household: $74,118; Average household: $87,834; Households with income of $100,000 or more: 28.4%; Poverty rate: 2.6%
Educational Attainment: High school diploma or higher: 96.3%; Bachelor's degree or higher: 27.9%; Graduate/professional degree or higher: 11.0%
Housing: Homeownership rate: 93.4%; Median home value: $150,600; Median year structure built: 1972; Homeowner vacancy rate: 1.7%; Median gross rent: n/a per month; Rental vacancy rate: 7.7%
Health Insurance: 90.2% have insurance; 82.7% have private insurance; 24.5% have public insurance; 9.8% do not have insurance; 11.4% of children under 18 do not have insurance
Transportation: Commute: 98.3% car, 0.0% public transportation, 0.0% walk, 1.7% work from home; Median travel time to work: 16.5 minutes

Vermillion County

Located in western Indiana; bounded on the west by Illinois, and on the east by the Wabash River; drained by the Vermilion River. Covers a land area of 256.878 square miles, a water area of 3.052 square miles, and is located in the Eastern Time Zone at 39.85° N. Lat., 87.46° W. Long. The county was founded in 1824. County seat is Newport.

Vermillion County is part of the Terre Haute, IN Metropolitan Statistical Area. The entire metro area includes: Clay County, IN; Sullivan County, IN; Vermillion County, IN; Vigo County, IN

Weather Station: Perrysville 4 WNW   Elevation: 620 feet

	Jan	Feb	Mar	Apr	May	Jun	Jul	Aug	Sep	Oct	Nov	Dec
High	34	39	50	63	74	83	85	84	79	66	52	38
Low	17	21	30	40	51	60	63	61	53	42	33	22
Precip	2.2	2.1	2.7	3.6	4.5	4.4	4.4	3.4	2.8	3.3	3.5	2.7
Snow	5.5	3.8	2.5	0.3	tr	0.0	0.0	0.0	0.0	0.0	1.1	4.5

High and Low temperatures in degrees Fahrenheit; Precipitation and Snow in inches

Population: 16,212; Growth (since 2000): -3.4%; Density: 63.1 persons per square mile; Race: 98.3% White, 0.1% Black/African American, 0.2% Asian, 0.2% American Indian/Alaska Native, 0.0% Native Hawaiian/Other Pacific Islander, 0.8% two or more races, 0.8% Hispanic of any race; Average household size: 2.42; Median age: 41.9; Age under 18: 23.1%; Age 65 and over: 16.9%; Males per 100 females: 97.9; Marriage status: 21.3% never married, 52.9% now married, 0.8% separated, 9.0% widowed, 16.8% divorced; Foreign born: 0.3%; Speak English only: 97.8%; With disability: 15.9%; Veterans: 12.5%; Ancestry: 21.0% American, 19.3% German, 14.9% Irish, 10.9% English, 9.1% Italian
Religion: Six largest groups: 14.2% Baptist, 6.9% Methodist/Pietist, 6.2% Catholicism, 3.5% Latter-day Saints, 2.5% Pentecostal, 2.0% Non-denominational Protestant
Economy: Unemployment rate: 6.9%; Leading industries: 19.0% retail trade; 13.9% other services (except public administration); 12.5% accommodation and food services; Farms: 270 totaling 118,394 acres; Company size: 0 employ 1,000 or more persons, 0 employ 500 to 999 persons, 8 employ 100 to 499 persons, 265 employ less than 100 persons; Business ownership: 254 women-owned, n/a Black-owned, n/a Hispanic-owned, 40 Asian-owned

Employment: 9.9% management, business, and financial, 1.6% computer, engineering, and science, 5.8% education, legal, community service, arts, and media, 5.4% healthcare practitioners, 20.1% service, 22.9% sales and office, 9.6% natural resources, construction, and maintenance, 24.7% production, transportation, and material moving
Income: Per capita: $22,875; Median household: $42,524; Average household: $54,591; Households with income of $100,000 or more: 9.9%; Poverty rate: 15.8%
Educational Attainment: High school diploma or higher: 89.1%; Bachelor's degree or higher: 13.0%; Graduate/professional degree or higher: 3.6%
Housing: Homeownership rate: 77.0%; Median home value: $75,100; Median year structure built: 1952; Homeowner vacancy rate: 2.2%; Median gross rent: $570 per month; Rental vacancy rate: 10.3%
Vital Statistics: Birth rate: 98.2 per 10,000 population; Death rate: 120.9 per 10,000 population; Age-adjusted cancer mortality rate: 264.3 deaths per 100,000 population
Health Insurance: 85.6% have insurance; 66.7% have private insurance; 33.9% have public insurance; 14.4% do not have insurance; 6.4% of children under 18 do not have insurance
Health Care: Physicians: 4.4 per 10,000 population; Hospital beds: 15.5 per 10,000 population; Hospital admissions: 832.8 per 10,000 population
Transportation: Commute: 94.9% car, 0.2% public transportation, 2.1% walk, 2.6% work from home; Median travel time to work: 24.4 minutes
Presidential Election: 45.3% Obama, 52.1% Romney (2012)
Additional Information Contacts
Vermillion Government . . . . (765) 492-5300
http://www.vermilliongov.us

Employment: 9.5% management, business, and financial, 1.4% computer, engineering, and science, 3.3% education, legal, community service, arts, and media, 3.1% healthcare practitioners, 23.8% service, 27.5% sales and office, 6.1% natural resources, construction, and maintenance, 25.3% production, transportation, and material moving
Income: Per capita: $20,331; Median household: $33,362; Average household: $50,769; Households with income of $100,000 or more: 6.6%; Poverty rate: 28.1%
Educational Attainment: High school diploma or higher: 84.1%; Bachelor's degree or higher: 12.8%; Graduate/professional degree or higher: 2.8%
School District(s)
South Vermillion Com Sch Corp (PK-12)
   2012-13 Enrollment: 1,858 . . . . (765) 832-2426
Housing: Homeownership rate: 64.0%; Median home value: $66,000; Median year structure built: 1942; Homeowner vacancy rate: 4.5%; Median gross rent: $532 per month; Rental vacancy rate: 9.4%
Health Insurance: 83.5% have insurance; 56.0% have private insurance; 38.9% have public insurance; 16.5% do not have insurance; 5.0% of children under 18 do not have insurance
Hospitals: Union Hospital Clinton
Safety: Violent crime rate: 33.3 per 10,000 population; Property crime rate: 170.5 per 10,000 population
Newspapers: Daily Clintonian (daily circulation 5100)
Transportation: Commute: 94.8% car, 0.1% public transportation, 5.1% walk, 0.0% work from home; Median travel time to work: 19.7 minutes
Additional Information Contacts
City of Clinton . . . . (765) 832-3844
http://greaterclintonchamber.org

Vermillion County Communities

BLANFORD (CDP).
Covers a land area of 0.734 square miles and a water area of 0 square miles. Located at 39.67° N. Lat; 87.52° W. Long. Elevation is 574 feet.
Population: 342; Growth (since 2000): n/a; Density: 465.9 persons per square mile; Race: 100.0% White, 0.0% Black/African American, 0.0% Asian, 0.0% American Indian/Alaska Native, 0.0% Native Hawaiian/Other Pacific Islander, 0.0% Two or more races, 0.0% Hispanic of any race; Average household size: 2.71; Median age: 39.0; Age under 18: 26.3%; Age 65 and over: 14.0%; Males per 100 females: 120.6
Housing: Homeownership rate: 85.8%; Homeowner vacancy rate: 2.7%; Rental vacancy rate: 10.0%

CAYUGA (town).
Covers a land area of 1.013 square miles and a water area of 0 square miles. Located at 39.95° N. Lat; 87.46° W. Long. Elevation is 509 feet.
Population: 1,162; Growth (since 2000): 4.8%; Density: 1,146.6 persons per square mile; Race: 97.8% White, 0.2% Black/African American, 0.1% Asian, 0.5% American Indian/Alaska Native, 0.0% Native Hawaiian/Other Pacific Islander, 1.2% Two or more races, 0.5% Hispanic of any race; Average household size: 2.45; Median age: 43.2; Age under 18: 22.5%; Age 65 and over: 17.6%; Males per 100 females: 93.0
School District(s)
North Vermillion Com Sch Corp (KG-12)
   2012-13 Enrollment: 727 . . . . (765) 492-4033
Housing: Homeownership rate: 72.2%; Homeowner vacancy rate: 1.4%; Rental vacancy rate: 10.2%
Newspapers: Cayuga Herald News (weekly circulation 800)

CLINTON (city).
Covers a land area of 2.238 square miles and a water area of 0.019 square miles. Located at 39.66° N. Lat; 87.40° W. Long. Elevation is 499 feet.
History: Clinton was laid out along the Wabash River in 1829, and named for DeWitt Clinton (1769-1828), governor of New York. Clinton developed as a coal-mining town.
Population: 4,893; Growth (since 2000): -4.5%; Density: 2,186.4 persons per square mile; Race: 97.5% White, 0.2% Black/African American, 0.2% Asian, 0.3% American Indian/Alaska Native, 0.0% Native Hawaiian/Other Pacific Islander, 1.5% Two or more races, 1.0% Hispanic of any race; Average household size: 2.36; Median age: 38.8; Age under 18: 24.7%; Age 65 and over: 17.7%; Males per 100 females: 90.6; Marriage status: 23.7% never married, 42.9% now married, 0.7% separated, 11.5% widowed, 21.9% divorced; Foreign born: 0.4%; Speak English only: 96.0%; With disability: 15.0%; Veterans: 10.4%; Ancestry: 21.7% German, 17.7% American, 13.6% Italian, 13.3% Irish, 8.5% English

DANA (town).
Covers a land area of 0.292 square miles and a water area of 0 square miles. Located at 39.81° N. Lat; 87.49° W. Long. Elevation is 640 feet.
History: Ernie Pyle State Memorial.
Population: 608; Growth (since 2000): -8.2%; Density: 2,082.3 persons per square mile; Race: 97.5% White, 0.2% Black/African American, 0.2% Asian, 0.5% American Indian/Alaska Native, 0.0% Native Hawaiian/Other Pacific Islander, 1.0% Two or more races, 1.3% Hispanic of any race; Average household size: 2.52; Median age: 40.7; Age under 18: 24.2%; Age 65 and over: 18.6%; Males per 100 females: 85.9
Housing: Homeownership rate: 80.5%; Homeowner vacancy rate: 4.4%; Rental vacancy rate: 7.8%

FAIRVIEW PARK (town).
Covers a land area of 0.880 square miles and a water area of 0 square miles. Located at 39.68° N. Lat; 87.41° W. Long. Elevation is 518 feet.
History: Laid out 1902.
Population: 1,386; Growth (since 2000): -7.4%; Density: 1,574.6 persons per square mile; Race: 98.2% White, 0.1% Black/African American, 0.2% Asian, 0.1% American Indian/Alaska Native, 0.1% Native Hawaiian/Other Pacific Islander, 0.5% Two or more races, 0.8% Hispanic of any race; Average household size: 2.28; Median age: 41.9; Age under 18: 20.9%; Age 65 and over: 16.9%; Males per 100 females: 102.9
Housing: Homeownership rate: 72.8%; Homeowner vacancy rate: 2.0%; Rental vacancy rate: 11.7%

HILLSDALE (unincorporated postal area)
ZCTA: 47854
   Covers a land area of 28.654 square miles and a water area of 0.525 square miles. Located at 39.80° N. Lat; 87.40° W. Long. Elevation is 623 feet.
Population: 849; Growth (since 2000): -11.7%; Density: 29.6 persons per square mile; Race: 98.9% White, 0.1% Black/African American, 0.2% Asian, 0.1% American Indian/Alaska Native, 0.0% Native Hawaiian/Other Pacific Islander, 0.5% Two or more races, 0.5% Hispanic of any race; Average household size: 2.56; Median age: 42.5; Age under 18: 25.0%; Age 65 and over: 15.7%; Males per 100 females: 103.1
Housing: Homeownership rate: 90.3%; Homeowner vacancy rate: 0.3%; Rental vacancy rate: 23.8%

NEWPORT (town). County seat. Covers a land area of 0.868 square miles and a water area of 0 square miles. Located at 39.88° N. Lat; 87.41° W. Long. Elevation is 528 feet.
Population: 515; Growth (since 2000): -10.9%; Density: 593.4 persons per square mile; Race: 99.8% White, 0.0% Black/African American, 0.0% Asian, 0.0% American Indian/Alaska Native, 0.0% Native Hawaiian/Other Pacific Islander, 0.2% Two or more races, 0.0% Hispanic of any race; Average household size: 2.44; Median age: 42.1; Age under 18: 23.3%; Age 65 and over: 17.7%; Males per 100 females: 97.3
Housing: Homeownership rate: 82.4%; Homeowner vacancy rate: 0.6%; Rental vacancy rate: 9.8%

PERRYSVILLE (town). Covers a land area of 0.255 square miles and a water area of 0 square miles. Located at 40.05° N. Lat; 87.44° W. Long. Elevation is 538 feet.
Population: 456; Growth (since 2000): -9.2%; Density: 1,787.5 persons per square mile; Race: 98.2% White, 0.4% Black/African American, 0.2% Asian, 0.0% American Indian/Alaska Native, 0.0% Native Hawaiian/Other Pacific Islander, 1.1% Two or more races, 0.2% Hispanic of any race; Average household size: 2.48; Median age: 40.2; Age under 18: 25.0%; Age 65 and over: 16.4%; Males per 100 females: 83.9
Housing: Homeownership rate: 82.6%; Homeowner vacancy rate: 1.9%; Rental vacancy rate: 23.8%

SAINT BERNICE (CDP). Covers a land area of 1.788 square miles and a water area of 0 square miles. Located at 39.71° N. Lat; 87.52° W. Long. Elevation is 577 feet.
Population: 646; Growth (since 2000): n/a; Density: 361.3 persons per square mile; Race: 98.8% White, 0.0% Black/African American, 0.0% Asian, 0.5% American Indian/Alaska Native, 0.2% Native Hawaiian/Other Pacific Islander, 0.5% Two or more races, 0.3% Hispanic of any race; Average household size: 2.56; Median age: 38.3; Age under 18: 25.4%; Age 65 and over: 14.2%; Males per 100 females: 98.8
Housing: Homeownership rate: 86.9%; Homeowner vacancy rate: 2.6%; Rental vacancy rate: 2.9%

UNIVERSAL (town). Covers a land area of 0.362 square miles and a water area of 0 square miles. Located at 39.62° N. Lat; 87.46° W. Long. Elevation is 584 feet.
History: Laid out 1911.
Population: 362; Growth (since 2000): -13.6%; Density: 999.5 persons per square mile; Race: 99.4% White, 0.3% Black/African American, 0.0% Asian, 0.0% American Indian/Alaska Native, 0.0% Native Hawaiian/Other Pacific Islander, 0.3% Two or more races, 1.7% Hispanic of any race; Average household size: 2.40; Median age: 38.8; Age under 18: 27.1%; Age 65 and over: 15.2%; Males per 100 females: 90.5
Housing: Homeownership rate: 78.8%; Homeowner vacancy rate: 0.8%; Rental vacancy rate: 5.9%

Vigo County

Located in western Indiana; bounded on the west by Illinois; crossed by the Wabash River; drained by Honey Creek. Covers a land area of 403.313 square miles, a water area of 7.138 square miles, and is located in the Eastern Time Zone at 39.43° N. Lat., 87.39° W. Long. The county was founded in 1818. County seat is Terre Haute.

Vigo County is part of the Terre Haute, IN Metropolitan Statistical Area. The entire metro area includes: Clay County, IN; Sullivan County, IN; Vermillion County, IN; Vigo County, IN

Weather Station: Terre Haute Indiana State   Elevation: 506 feet

	Jan	Feb	Mar	Apr	May	Jun	Jul	Aug	Sep	Oct	Nov	Dec
High	38	42	53	65	76	84	88	87	81	68	54	41
Low	19	22	32	43	52	61	66	63	55	43	33	23
Precip	2.6	2.5	3.5	4.5	5.0	4.5	4.4	3.4	3.5	3.7	3.6	3.1
Snow	3.9	3.3	1.0	0.1	0.0	0.0	0.0	0.0	0.0	0.0	0.3	2.9

High and Low temperatures in degrees Fahrenheit; Precipitation and Snow in inches

Population: 107,848; Growth (since 2000): 1.9%; Density: 267.4 persons per square mile; Race: 88.3% White, 6.9% Black/African American, 1.7% Asian, 0.3% American Indian/Alaska Native, 0.0% Native Hawaiian/Other Pacific Islander, 2.2% two or more races, 2.3% Hispanic of any race; Average household size: 2.38; Median age: 36.1; Age under 18: 21.4%; Age 65 and over: 13.5%; Males per 100 females: 102.3; Marriage status: 34.9% never married, 44.6% now married, 1.6% separated, 6.5% widowed, 14.1% divorced; Foreign born: 3.3%; Speak English only: 94.4%; With disability: 16.4%; Veterans: 9.4%; Ancestry: 25.0% American, 19.3% German, 10.1% Irish, 8.3% English, 3.4% French
Religion: Six largest groups: 7.3% Baptist, 7.0% Catholicism, 6.5% Non-denominational Protestant, 3.9% Methodist/Pietist, 2.5% Pentecostal, 1.9% Holiness
Economy: Unemployment rate: 6.7%; Leading industries: 17.6% retail trade; 14.4% health care and social assistance; 11.6% other services (except public administration); Farms: 450 totaling 117,530 acres; Company size: 3 employ 1,000 or more persons, 6 employ 500 to 999 persons, 64 employ 100 to 499 persons, 2,465 employ less than 100 persons; Business ownership: 1,615 women-owned, 337 Black-owned, 43 Hispanic-owned, 224 Asian-owned
Employment: 9.8% management, business, and financial, 3.5% computer, engineering, and science, 12.0% education, legal, community service, arts, and media, 6.5% healthcare practitioners, 19.3% service, 24.3% sales and office, 8.7% natural resources, construction, and maintenance, 16.0% production, transportation, and material moving
Income: Per capita: $21,192; Median household: $40,692; Average household: $54,562; Households with income of $100,000 or more: 12.8%; Poverty rate: 20.0%
Educational Attainment: High school diploma or higher: 86.6%; Bachelor's degree or higher: 21.2%; Graduate/professional degree or higher: 8.6%
Housing: Homeownership rate: 63.7%; Median home value: $91,600; Median year structure built: 1961; Homeowner vacancy rate: 2.4%; Median gross rent: $673 per month; Rental vacancy rate: 10.9%
Vital Statistics: Birth rate: 119.5 per 10,000 population; Death rate: 103.8 per 10,000 population; Age-adjusted cancer mortality rate: 186.9 deaths per 100,000 population
Health Insurance: 84.3% have insurance; 64.1% have private insurance; 31.8% have public insurance; 15.7% do not have insurance; 7.3% of children under 18 do not have insurance
Health Care: Physicians: 26.6 per 10,000 population; Hospital beds: 52.2 per 10,000 population; Hospital admissions: 2,299.9 per 10,000 population
Air Quality Index: 51.0% good, 44.9% moderate, 4.1% unhealthy for sensitive individuals, 0.0% unhealthy (percent of days)
Transportation: Commute: 91.8% car, 0.7% public transportation, 3.9% walk, 2.0% work from home; Median travel time to work: 19.9 minutes
Presidential Election: 49.5% Obama, 48.6% Romney (2012)
Additional Information Contacts
Vigo Government . . . . (812) 462-3211
   http://www.vigocounty.in.gov

Vigo County Communities

DRESSER (CDP). Covers a land area of 0.151 square miles and a water area of 0 square miles. Located at 39.46° N. Lat; 87.42° W. Long. Elevation is 469 feet.
Population: 104; Growth (since 2000): n/a; Density: 689.3 persons per square mile; Race: 100.0% White, 0.0% Black/African American, 0.0% Asian, 0.0% American Indian/Alaska Native, 0.0% Native Hawaiian/Other Pacific Islander, 0.0% Two or more races, 3.8% Hispanic of any race; Average household size: 3.25; Median age: 38.0; Age under 18: 22.1%; Age 65 and over: 12.5%; Males per 100 females: 103.9
Housing: Homeownership rate: 75.1%; Homeowner vacancy rate: 4.0%; Rental vacancy rate: 0.0%

FONTANET (CDP). Covers a land area of 3.854 square miles and a water area of 0.029 square miles. Located at 39.58° N. Lat; 87.23° W. Long. Elevation is 600 feet.
Population: 423; Growth (since 2000): n/a; Density: 109.8 persons per square mile; Race: 97.9% White, 1.4% Black/African American, 0.0% Asian, 0.2% American Indian/Alaska Native, 0.0% Native Hawaiian/Other Pacific Islander, 0.2% Two or more races, 1.2% Hispanic of any race; Average household size: 2.53; Median age: 42.3; Age under 18: 23.2%; Age 65 and over: 15.1%; Males per 100 females: 96.7
Housing: Homeownership rate: 85.0%; Homeowner vacancy rate: 0.7%; Rental vacancy rate: 10.7%

LEWIS (unincorporated postal area)
ZCTA: 47858

Covers a land area of 31.868 square miles and a water area of 0.039 square miles. Located at 39.26° N. Lat; 87.22° W. Long. Elevation is 610 feet.
Population: 698; Growth (since 2000): 0.6%; Density: 21.9 persons per square mile; Race: 97.9% White, 0.1% Black/African American, 0.0% Asian, 0.0% American Indian/Alaska Native, 0.0% Native Hawaiian/Other Pacific Islander, 0.3% Two or more races, 2.3% Hispanic of any race; Average household size: 2.72; Median age: 41.8; Age under 18: 23.5%; Age 65 and over: 14.0%; Males per 100 females: 96.1
Housing: Homeownership rate: 89.1%; Homeowner vacancy rate: 0.9%; Rental vacancy rate: 11.8%

NEW GOSHEN (CDP). Covers a land area of 3.310 square miles and a water area of 0.026 square miles. Located at 39.59° N. Lat; 87.47° W. Long. Elevation is 646 feet.
Population: 390; Growth (since 2000): n/a; Density: 117.8 persons per square mile; Race: 98.5% White, 0.0% Black/African American, 0.0% Asian, 0.0% American Indian/Alaska Native, 0.5% Native Hawaiian/Other Pacific Islander, 1.0% Two or more races, 0.0% Hispanic of any race; Average household size: 2.39; Median age: 42.0; Age under 18: 20.8%; Age 65 and over: 13.6%; Males per 100 females: 99.0
Housing: Homeownership rate: 85.3%; Homeowner vacancy rate: 0.7%; Rental vacancy rate: 17.2%

NORTH TERRE HAUTE (CDP). Covers a land area of 3.568 square miles and a water area of 0 square miles. Located at 39.54° N. Lat; 87.37° W. Long. Elevation is 495 feet.
History: The Markle Mill was built in 1816 on the banks of Otter Creek, near the site of North Terre Haute, and the town developed around it.
Population: 4,305; Growth (since 2000): -6.5%; Density: 1,206.7 persons per square mile; Race: 95.0% White, 1.9% Black/African American, 0.5% Asian, 0.2% American Indian/Alaska Native, 0.1% Native Hawaiian/Other Pacific Islander, 2.1% Two or more races, 1.2% Hispanic of any race; Average household size: 2.42; Median age: 39.9; Age under 18: 24.0%; Age 65 and over: 14.5%; Males per 100 females: 96.9; Marriage status: 24.7% never married, 55.0% now married, 0.5% separated, 7.2% widowed, 13.1% divorced; Foreign born: 0.0%; Speak English only: 98.0%; With disability: 17.0%; Veterans: 10.0%; Ancestry: 37.4% American, 10.1% German, 9.0% Irish, 5.8% English, 3.1% Italian
Employment: 6.4% management, business, and financial, 1.3% computer, engineering, and science, 10.4% education, legal, community service, arts, and media, 8.8% healthcare practitioners, 21.6% service, 25.2% sales and office, 6.0% natural resources, construction, and maintenance, 20.2% production, transportation, and material moving
Income: Per capita: $21,172; Median household: $44,330; Average household: $54,905; Households with income of $100,000 or more: 11.8%; Poverty rate: 13.0%
Educational Attainment: High school diploma or higher: 87.9%; Bachelor's degree or higher: 14.1%; Graduate/professional degree or higher: 3.2%
Housing: Homeownership rate: 68.7%; Median home value: $89,100; Median year structure built: 1966; Homeowner vacancy rate: 2.2%; Median gross rent: $667 per month; Rental vacancy rate: 8.0%
Health Insurance: 87.6% have insurance; 69.8% have private insurance; 31.4% have public insurance; 12.4% do not have insurance; 11.5% of children under 18 do not have insurance
Transportation: Commute: 95.0% car, 0.0% public transportation, 0.0% walk, 3.4% work from home; Median travel time to work: 23.7 minutes

PIMENTO (unincorporated postal area)
ZCTA: 47866
Covers a land area of 17.801 square miles and a water area of 0.093 square miles. Located at 39.29° N. Lat; 87.32° W. Long. Elevation is 600 feet.
Population: 347; Growth (since 2000): -15.8%; Density: 19.5 persons per square mile; Race: 99.1% White, 0.0% Black/African American, 0.0% Asian, 0.0% American Indian/Alaska Native, 0.0% Native Hawaiian/Other Pacific Islander, 0.6% Two or more races, 0.3% Hispanic of any race; Average household size: 2.46; Median age: 47.6; Age under 18: 21.6%; Age 65 and over: 19.6%; Males per 100 females: 104.1
Housing: Homeownership rate: 80.9%; Homeowner vacancy rate: 3.4%; Rental vacancy rate: 0.0%

PRAIRIE CREEK (unincorporated postal area)
ZCTA: 47869
Covers a land area of 0.109 square miles and a water area of 0 square miles. Located at 39.27° N. Lat; 87.50° W. Long. Elevation is 531 feet.
Population: 137; Growth (since 2000): n/a; Density: 1,262.5 persons per square mile; Race: 92.7% White, 0.7% Black/African American, 0.7% Asian, 0.7% American Indian/Alaska Native, 0.0% Native Hawaiian/Other Pacific Islander, 3.6% Two or more races, 4.4% Hispanic of any race; Average household size: 2.74; Median age: 35.2; Age under 18: 24.1%; Age 65 and over: 9.5%; Males per 100 females: 117.5
Housing: Homeownership rate: 76.0%; Homeowner vacancy rate: 0.0%; Rental vacancy rate: 14.3%

RILEY (town). Covers a land area of 0.090 square miles and a water area of 0 square miles. Located at 39.39° N. Lat; 87.30° W. Long. Elevation is 564 feet.
History: Riley, first known as Lockport, developed around a coal mine.
Population: 221; Growth (since 2000): 38.1%; Density: 2,465.9 persons per square mile; Race: 97.7% White, 0.5% Black/African American, 0.0% Asian, 0.5% American Indian/Alaska Native, 0.0% Native Hawaiian/Other Pacific Islander, 1.4% Two or more races, 0.5% Hispanic of any race; Average household size: 2.38; Median age: 32.8; Age under 18: 27.1%; Age 65 and over: 14.9%; Males per 100 females: 102.8
School District(s)
Vigo County School Corp (KG-12)
  2012-13 Enrollment: 15,404 . . . . (812) 462-4216
Housing: Homeownership rate: 69.9%; Homeowner vacancy rate: 4.4%; Rental vacancy rate: 0.0%

SAINT MARY OF THE WOODS (CDP). Covers a land area of 1.277 square miles and a water area of 0.019 square miles. Located at 39.51° N. Lat; 87.46° W. Long.
Population: 797; Growth (since 2000): n/a; Density: 624.3 persons per square mile; Race: 94.6% White, 1.4% Black/African American, 2.6% Asian, 0.3% American Indian/Alaska Native, 0.0% Native Hawaiian/Other Pacific Islander, 0.8% Two or more races, 1.4% Hispanic of any race; Average household size: 1.73; Median age: 55.3; Age under 18: 5.1%; Age 65 and over: 39.3%; Males per 100 females: 26.3
Four-year College(s)
Saint Mary-of-the-Woods College (Private, Not-for-profit, Roman Catholic)
  Fall 2013 Enrollment: 887 . . . . (812) 535-5151
  2013-14 Tuition: In-state $27,672; Out-of-state $27,672
Housing: Homeownership rate: 38.5%; Homeowner vacancy rate: 1.1%; Rental vacancy rate: 11.6%

SEELYVILLE (town). Covers a land area of 0.888 square miles and a water area of 0.020 square miles. Located at 39.49° N. Lat; 87.27° W. Long. Elevation is 584 feet.
History: Seelyville was established as a mining center.
Population: 1,029; Growth (since 2000): -12.9%; Density: 1,159.1 persons per square mile; Race: 97.8% White, 0.4% Black/African American, 0.2% Asian, 0.2% American Indian/Alaska Native, 0.0% Native Hawaiian/Other Pacific Islander, 1.3% Two or more races, 0.9% Hispanic of any race; Average household size: 2.40; Median age: 36.2; Age under 18: 23.2%; Age 65 and over: 11.4%; Males per 100 females: 99.8
Housing: Homeownership rate: 70.1%; Homeowner vacancy rate: 1.6%; Rental vacancy rate: 15.2%

SHEPARDSVILLE (CDP). Covers a land area of 0.919 square miles and a water area of 0.003 square miles. Located at 39.60° N. Lat; 87.42° W. Long. Elevation is 502 feet.
Population: 237; Growth (since 2000): n/a; Density: 257.8 persons per square mile; Race: 99.6% White, 0.4% Black/African American, 0.0% Asian, 0.0% American Indian/Alaska Native, 0.0% Native Hawaiian/Other Pacific Islander, 0.0% Two or more races, 0.0% Hispanic of any race; Average household size: 2.86; Median age: 37.8; Age under 18: 29.5%; Age 65 and over: 14.8%; Males per 100 females: 95.9
Housing: Homeownership rate: 86.7%; Homeowner vacancy rate: 0.0%; Rental vacancy rate: 26.7%

TECUMSEH (CDP). Covers a land area of 2.520 square miles and a water area of 0.079 square miles. Located at 39.57° N. Lat; 87.43° W. Long. Elevation is 554 feet.
Population: 658; Growth (since 2000): n/a; Density: 261.1 persons per square mile; Race: 97.3% White, 0.0% Black/African American, 1.5% Asian, 0.2% American Indian/Alaska Native, 0.0% Native Hawaiian/Other Pacific Islander, 1.1% Two or more races, 1.1% Hispanic of any race; Average household size: 2.56; Median age: 46.9; Age under 18: 22.0%; Age 65 and over: 16.7%; Males per 100 females: 94.7
Housing: Homeownership rate: 91.4%; Homeowner vacancy rate: 2.5%; Rental vacancy rate: 12.0%

TERRE HAUTE (city). County seat. Covers a land area of 34.536 square miles and a water area of 0.732 square miles. Located at 39.47° N. Lat; 87.38° W. Long. Elevation is 502 feet.
History: Terre Haute's name, meaning "high land," was given to it by French traders in the early 1700's. The city itself was established in 1816 by the Terre Haute Town Company, a group of Indiana and Kentucky businessmen. It was soon selected as the seat of Vigo County, and was incorporated as a town in 1832. Coal mining was the major industry in Terre Haute after 1875. It's reputation as a "union town" was influenced in part by Eugene V. Debs who lived and worked here.
Population: 60,785; Growth (since 2000): 2.0%; Density: 1,760.0 persons per square mile; Race: 83.5% White, 10.9% Black/African American, 1.4% Asian, 0.4% American Indian/Alaska Native, 0.0% Native Hawaiian/Other Pacific Islander, 2.9% Two or more races, 3.1% Hispanic of any race; Average household size: 2.29; Median age: 32.7; Age under 18: 20.0%; Age 65 and over: 12.6%; Males per 100 females: 106.8; Marriage status: 43.3% never married, 35.8% now married, 1.8% separated, 7.0% widowed, 14.0% divorced; Foreign born: 3.6%; Speak English only: 93.6%; With disability: 17.5%; Veterans: 8.3%; Ancestry: 23.6% American, 19.7% German, 10.3% Irish, 7.6% English, 2.8% French
Employment: 8.3% management, business, and financial, 3.3% computer, engineering, and science, 11.9% education, legal, community service, arts, and media, 5.2% healthcare practitioners, 21.8% service, 25.3% sales and office, 7.9% natural resources, construction, and maintenance, 16.2% production, transportation, and material moving
Income: Per capita: $17,589; Median household: $32,446; Average household: $44,993; Households with income of $100,000 or more: 8.3%; Poverty rate: 25.8%
Educational Attainment: High school diploma or higher: 84.3%; Bachelor's degree or higher: 19.6%; Graduate/professional degree or higher: 8.0%
School District(s)
Covered Bridge Spec Ed Dist (KG-12)
    2012-13 Enrollment: n/a . . . . (812) 462-4030
Vigo County School Corp (KG-12)
    2012-13 Enrollment: 15,404 . . . . (812) 462-4216
Four-year College(s)
Indiana State University (Public)
    Fall 2013 Enrollment: 12,448 . . . . (812) 237-6311
    2013-14 Tuition: In-state $8,256; Out-of-state $17,992
Rose-Hulman Institute of Technology (Private, Not-for-profit)
    Fall 2013 Enrollment: 2,302 . . . . (812) 877-1511
    2013-14 Tuition: In-state $42,654; Out-of-state $42,654
Vocational/Technical School(s)
J Michael Harrold Beauty Academy (Private, For-profit)
    Fall 2013 Enrollment: 86. . . . . (812) 232-8334
    2013-14 Tuition: $12,350
Housing: Homeownership rate: 55.5%; Median home value: $76,800; Median year structure built: 1949; Homeowner vacancy rate: 3.2%; Median gross rent: $655 per month; Rental vacancy rate: 11.1%
Health Insurance: 80.9% have insurance; 57.7% have private insurance; 33.7% have public insurance; 19.1% do not have insurance; 7.6% of children under 18 do not have insurance
Hospitals: Terre Haute Regional Hospital (278 beds); Union Hospital
Safety: Violent crime rate: 28.9 per 10,000 population; Property crime rate: 532.7 per 10,000 population
Newspapers: Tribune-Star (daily circulation 24600)
Transportation: Commute: 88.6% car, 0.8% public transportation, 6.3% walk, 2.1% work from home; Median travel time to work: 17.7 minutes
Airports: Terre Haute International-Hulman Field (general aviation)
Additional Information Contacts
City of Terre Haute . . . . (812) 232-3375
    http://www.terrehaute.in.gov

TOAD HOP (CDP). Covers a land area of 0.221 square miles and a water area of 0 square miles. Located at 39.46° N. Lat; 87.46° W. Long. Elevation is 469 feet.
Population: 108; Growth (since 2000): n/a; Density: 489.0 persons per square mile; Race: 99.1% White, 0.0% Black/African American, 0.0% Asian, 0.0% American Indian/Alaska Native, 0.0% Native Hawaiian/Other Pacific Islander, 0.9% Two or more races, 0.9% Hispanic of any race; Average household size: 2.92; Median age: 40.0; Age under 18: 25.9%; Age 65 and over: 12.0%; Males per 100 females: 77.0
Housing: Homeownership rate: 91.9%; Homeowner vacancy rate: 0.0%; Rental vacancy rate: 0.0%

WEST TERRE HAUTE (town). Covers a land area of 0.753 square miles and a water area of 0 square miles. Located at 39.46° N. Lat; 87.45° W. Long. Elevation is 469 feet.
History: West Terre Haute began as a coal-mining town.
Population: 2,236; Growth (since 2000): -4.0%; Density: 2,970.4 persons per square mile; Race: 97.3% White, 0.5% Black/African American, 0.0% Asian, 0.6% American Indian/Alaska Native, 0.0% Native Hawaiian/Other Pacific Islander, 1.2% Two or more races, 1.3% Hispanic of any race; Average household size: 2.67; Median age: 35.5; Age under 18: 26.0%; Age 65 and over: 12.6%; Males per 100 females: 93.9
School District(s)
Vigo County School Corp (KG-12)
    2012-13 Enrollment: 15,404 . . . . (812) 462-4216
Housing: Homeownership rate: 66.6%; Homeowner vacancy rate: 2.3%; Rental vacancy rate: 11.7%
Additional Information Contacts
Town of West Terre Haute . . . . (812) 232-3375
    http://www.terrehaute.in.gov

Wabash County

Located in northeast central Indiana; drained by the Wabash, Eel, Salamonie, and Mississinewa Rivers. Covers a land area of 412.434 square miles, a water area of 8.541 square miles, and is located in the Eastern Time Zone at 40.84° N. Lat., 85.80° W. Long. The county was founded in 1832. County seat is Wabash.

Wabash County is part of the Wabash, IN Micropolitan Statistical Area. The entire metro area includes: Wabash County, IN

Weather Station: Wabash   Elevation: 729 feet

	Jan	Feb	Mar	Apr	May	Jun	Jul	Aug	Sep	Oct	Nov	Dec
High	33	38	48	61	72	81	84	82	76	64	50	36
Low	16	19	27	38	48	58	61	60	51	40	32	21
Precip	2.5	2.3	2.7	3.4	4.5	4.2	4.3	4.1	3.1	3.1	3.2	2.5
Snow	7.0	5.3	3.0	0.7	0.0	0.0	0.0	0.0	0.0	0.2	0.9	5.9

High and Low temperatures in degrees Fahrenheit; Precipitation and Snow in inches

Population: 32,888; Growth (since 2000): -5.9%; Density: 79.7 persons per square mile; Race: 96.6% White, 0.5% Black/African American, 0.4% Asian, 0.7% American Indian/Alaska Native, 0.0% Native Hawaiian/Other Pacific Islander, 1.1% two or more races, 2.1% Hispanic of any race; Average household size: 2.43; Median age: 41.2; Age under 18: 22.7%; Age 65 and over: 18.1%; Males per 100 females: 94.4; Marriage status: 26.5% never married, 56.6% now married, 1.3% separated, 8.3% widowed, 8.6% divorced; Foreign born: 1.6%; Speak English only: 96.6%; With disability: 15.6%; Veterans: 9.9%; Ancestry: 27.7% German, 22.9% American, 10.3% Irish, 9.4% English, 2.5% Dutch
Religion: Six largest groups: 10.1% Baptist, 9.0% Methodist/Pietist, 7.3% European Free-Church, 4.4% Presbyterian-Reformed, 3.3% Catholicism, 2.5% Lutheran
Economy: Unemployment rate: 4.9%; Leading industries: 17.1% retail trade; 14.0% other services (except public administration); 10.5% construction; Farms: 745 totaling 197,588 acres; Company size: 0 employ 1,000 or more persons, 2 employ 500 to 999 persons, 18 employ 100 to 499 persons, 735 employ less than 100 persons; Business ownership: 790 women-owned, n/a Black-owned, n/a Hispanic-owned, n/a Asian-owned
Employment: 9.9% management, business, and financial, 2.9% computer, engineering, and science, 10.5% education, legal, community service, arts, and media, 5.1% healthcare practitioners, 17.4% service, 22.4% sales and office, 8.6% natural resources, construction, and maintenance, 23.1% production, transportation, and material moving

Income: Per capita: $21,201; Median household: $45,286; Average household: $53,170; Households with income of $100,000 or more: 9.6%; Poverty rate: 15.1%
Educational Attainment: High school diploma or higher: 86.1%; Bachelor's degree or higher: 17.0%; Graduate/professional degree or higher: 7.0%
Housing: Homeownership rate: 74.7%; Median home value: $95,000; Median year structure built: 1956; Homeowner vacancy rate: 3.5%; Median gross rent: $599 per month; Rental vacancy rate: 11.9%
Vital Statistics: Birth rate: 108.8 per 10,000 population; Death rate: 122.1 per 10,000 population; Age-adjusted cancer mortality rate: 213.0 deaths per 100,000 population
Health Insurance: 88.0% have insurance; 67.4% have private insurance; 34.5% have public insurance; 12.0% do not have insurance; 7.6% of children under 18 do not have insurance
Health Care: Physicians: 6.8 per 10,000 population; Hospital beds: 15.3 per 10,000 population; Hospital admissions: 254.4 per 10,000 population
Air Quality Index: 95.8% good, 4.2% moderate, 0.0% unhealthy for sensitive individuals, 0.0% unhealthy (percent of days)
Transportation: Commute: 92.2% car, 0.4% public transportation, 3.6% walk, 3.1% work from home; Median travel time to work: 19.2 minutes
Presidential Election: 30.9% Obama, 67.1% Romney (2012)
National and State Parks: Dora New Holland State Recreation Area; Frances Slocum State Recreation Area; Hogback Ridge State Recreation Area; Lost Bridge State Recreation Area; Miami State Recreation Area; Mount Hope State Recreation Area; Pearson Mill State Recreation Area; Red Bridge State Recreation Area; Salamonie River State Forest
Additional Information Contacts
Wabash Government . . . . (260) 563-0661
http://www.wabashcounty.in.gov

Wabash County Communities

LA FONTAINE (town). Covers a land area of 0.601 square miles and a water area of 0.011 square miles. Located at 40.67° N. Lat; 85.72° W. Long. Elevation is 804 feet.
Population: 875; Growth (since 2000): -2.8%; Density: 1,456.8 persons per square mile; Race: 98.5% White, 0.1% Black/African American, 0.0% Asian, 0.2% American Indian/Alaska Native, 0.0% Native Hawaiian/Other Pacific Islander, 0.9% Two or more races, 1.1% Hispanic of any race; Average household size: 2.39; Median age: 41.9; Age under 18: 23.2%; Age 65 and over: 24.6%; Males per 100 females: 83.8
School District(s)
M S D Wabash County Schools (PK-12)
  2012-13 Enrollment: 2,209 . . . . (260) 563-8050
Housing: Homeownership rate: 73.1%; Homeowner vacancy rate: 4.4%; Rental vacancy rate: 16.0%

LAGRO (town). Covers a land area of 0.593 square miles and a water area of 0.014 square miles. Located at 40.84° N. Lat; 85.73° W. Long. Elevation is 705 feet.
History: The Wabash & Erie Canal was the impetus for the settlement of Lagro, named for an Indian chief, Les Gros.
Population: 415; Growth (since 2000): -8.6%; Density: 699.5 persons per square mile; Race: 96.9% White, 0.0% Black/African American, 0.5% Asian, 1.7% American Indian/Alaska Native, 0.0% Native Hawaiian/Other Pacific Islander, 1.0% Two or more races, 0.0% Hispanic of any race; Average household size: 2.66; Median age: 36.6; Age under 18: 26.0%; Age 65 and over: 11.3%; Males per 100 females: 118.4
Housing: Homeownership rate: 82.7%; Homeowner vacancy rate: 1.5%; Rental vacancy rate: 17.6%

LAKETON (CDP). Covers a land area of 1.051 square miles and a water area of 0.140 square miles. Located at 40.98° N. Lat; 85.84° W. Long. Elevation is 755 feet.
Population: 623; Growth (since 2000): n/a; Density: 592.6 persons per square mile; Race: 96.0% White, 1.4% Black/African American, 0.0% Asian, 1.1% American Indian/Alaska Native, 0.0% Native Hawaiian/Other Pacific Islander, 1.0% Two or more races, 1.9% Hispanic of any race; Average household size: 2.51; Median age: 40.6; Age under 18: 25.8%; Age 65 and over: 15.9%; Males per 100 females: 94.7
School District(s)
Manchester Community Schools (KG-12)
  2012-13 Enrollment: 1,611 . . . . (260) 982-7518
Housing: Homeownership rate: 81.0%; Homeowner vacancy rate: 5.1%; Rental vacancy rate: 20.3%

LIBERTY MILLS (unincorporated postal area)
ZCTA: 46946
  Covers a land area of 0.325 square miles and a water area of 0.027 square miles. Located at 41.04° N. Lat; 85.73° W. Long. Elevation is 778 feet.
  Population: 136; Growth (since 2000): -2.2%; Density: 418.1 persons per square mile; Race: 94.9% White, 0.7% Black/African American, 0.0% Asian, 0.7% American Indian/Alaska Native, 0.0% Native Hawaiian/Other Pacific Islander, 2.9% Two or more races, 2.9% Hispanic of any race; Average household size: 2.89; Median age: 35.7; Age under 18: 27.9%; Age 65 and over: 14.7%; Males per 100 females: 119.4
  Housing: Homeownership rate: 78.8%; Homeowner vacancy rate: 2.6%; Rental vacancy rate: 16.7%

NORTH MANCHESTER (town). Covers a land area of 3.534 square miles and a water area of 0.079 square miles. Located at 41.00° N. Lat; 85.78° W. Long. Elevation is 774 feet.
History: Among the early residents in North Manchester was a group of Dunkers, members of a religious sect founded in Germany in 1708. Thomas R. Marshall, Vice President of the United States under Woodrow Wilson, was born in North Manchester.
Population: 6,112; Growth (since 2000): -2.4%; Density: 1,729.3 persons per square mile; Race: 95.2% White, 1.1% Black/African American, 0.8% Asian, 0.3% American Indian/Alaska Native, 0.0% Native Hawaiian/Other Pacific Islander, 1.3% Two or more races, 3.8% Hispanic of any race; Average household size: 2.25; Median age: 36.5; Age under 18: 18.1%; Age 65 and over: 22.1%; Males per 100 females: 84.6; Marriage status: 35.8% never married, 44.5% now married, 0.3% separated, 11.8% widowed, 7.9% divorced; Foreign born: 3.1%; Speak English only: 93.4%; With disability: 15.5%; Veterans: 5.2%; Ancestry: 33.0% German, 21.8% American, 7.7% English, 7.5% Irish, 2.4% Dutch
Employment: 9.3% management, business, and financial, 3.9% computer, engineering, and science, 18.3% education, legal, community service, arts, and media, 6.2% healthcare practitioners, 23.3% service, 19.3% sales and office, 4.6% natural resources, construction, and maintenance, 15.3% production, transportation, and material moving
Income: Per capita: $18,308; Median household: $43,627; Average household: $49,094; Households with income of $100,000 or more: 7.8%; Poverty rate: 21.5%
Educational Attainment: High school diploma or higher: 88.0%; Bachelor's degree or higher: 26.8%; Graduate/professional degree or higher: 13.6%
School District(s)
Manchester Community Schools (KG-12)
  2012-13 Enrollment: 1,611 . . . . (260) 982-7518
Four-year College(s)
Manchester University (Private, Not-for-profit, Church of Brethren)
  Fall 2013 Enrollment: 1,349 . . . . (260) 982-5000
  2013-14 Tuition: In-state $27,920; Out-of-state $27,920
Housing: Homeownership rate: 62.0%; Median home value: $94,700; Median year structure built: 1959; Homeowner vacancy rate: 4.2%; Median gross rent: $568 per month; Rental vacancy rate: 13.8%
Health Insurance: 88.8% have insurance; 66.3% have private insurance; 35.7% have public insurance; 11.2% do not have insurance; 10.2% of children under 18 do not have insurance
Safety: Violent crime rate: 18.4 per 10,000 population; Property crime rate: 180.4 per 10,000 population
Newspapers: The Manchester Monitor (weekly circulation 1100); The News-Journal (weekly circulation 1800)
Transportation: Commute: 83.0% car, 0.0% public transportation, 12.0% walk, 3.9% work from home; Median travel time to work: 19.1 minutes
Additional Information Contacts
Town of North Manchester . . . . (260) 982-9800
http://www.nmanchester.org

ROANN (town). Covers a land area of 0.228 square miles and a water area of 0 square miles. Located at 40.91° N. Lat; 85.92° W. Long. Elevation is 755 feet.
History: Laid out 1853.
Population: 479; Growth (since 2000): 19.8%; Density: 2,105.2 persons per square mile; Race: 98.5% White, 0.0% Black/African American, 0.4%

Asian, 0.6% American Indian/Alaska Native, 0.0% Native Hawaiian/Other Pacific Islander, 0.4% Two or more races, 0.0% Hispanic of any race; Average household size: 2.58; Median age: 35.6; Age under 18: 28.0%; Age 65 and over: 16.5%; Males per 100 females: 84.9
Housing: Homeownership rate: 73.6%; Homeowner vacancy rate: 1.4%; Rental vacancy rate: 12.5%

SOMERSET (CDP).
Covers a land area of 0.663 square miles and a water area of 0.138 square miles. Located at 40.67° N. Lat; 85.83° W. Long. Elevation is 810 feet.
Population: 401; Growth (since 2000): n/a; Density: 604.7 persons per square mile; Race: 98.5% White, 0.0% Black/African American, 0.2% Asian, 0.0% American Indian/Alaska Native, 0.0% Native Hawaiian/Other Pacific Islander, 1.0% Two or more races, 0.7% Hispanic of any race; Average household size: 2.23; Median age: 49.8; Age under 18: 19.0%; Age 65 and over: 20.4%; Males per 100 females: 107.8
Housing: Homeownership rate: 83.3%; Homeowner vacancy rate: 3.8%; Rental vacancy rate: 16.7%

URBANA (unincorporated postal area)
ZCTA: 46990
Covers a land area of 30.118 square miles and a water area of 0.037 square miles. Located at 40.90° N. Lat; 85.73° W. Long. Elevation is 797 feet.
Population: 801; Growth (since 2000): -5.9%; Density: 26.6 persons per square mile; Race: 99.0% White, 0.1% Black/African American, 0.2% Asian, 0.1% American Indian/Alaska Native, 0.0% Native Hawaiian/Other Pacific Islander, 0.5% Two or more races, 1.2% Hispanic of any race; Average household size: 2.62; Median age: 41.3; Age under 18: 24.0%; Age 65 and over: 18.0%; Males per 100 females: 107.5
Housing: Homeownership rate: 87.3%; Homeowner vacancy rate: 3.2%; Rental vacancy rate: 2.5%

WABASH (city).
County seat. Covers a land area of 8.886 square miles and a water area of 0.238 square miles. Located at 40.80° N. Lat; 85.83° W. Long. Elevation is 712 feet.
History: Its location along the Wabash River gave the town of Wabash its name, which comes from the Indian "oubache," meaning "water over white stones." The Wabash & Erie Canal was completed through this area in 1835, bringing Irish immigrants as canal workers.
Population: 10,666; Growth (since 2000): -9.2%; Density: 1,200.4 persons per square mile; Race: 96.3% White, 0.4% Black/African American, 0.5% Asian, 1.0% American Indian/Alaska Native, 0.0% Native Hawaiian/Other Pacific Islander, 1.2% Two or more races, 2.0% Hispanic of any race; Average household size: 2.31; Median age: 41.3; Age under 18: 22.5%; Age 65 and over: 18.8%; Males per 100 females: 89.2; Marriage status: 26.8% never married, 52.1% now married, 2.3% separated, 9.7% widowed, 11.3% divorced; Foreign born: 0.8%; Speak English only: 98.5%; With disability: 19.4%; Veterans: 10.7%; Ancestry: 23.8% American, 23.4% German, 12.4% Irish, 11.2% English, 1.9% French
Employment: 8.0% management, business, and financial, 3.2% computer, engineering, and science, 7.1% education, legal, community service, arts, and media, 6.2% healthcare practitioners, 17.4% service, 25.2% sales and office, 5.4% natural resources, construction, and maintenance, 27.5% production, transportation, and material moving
Income: Per capita: $20,106; Median household: $39,320; Average household: $46,873; Households with income of $100,000 or more: 5.5%; Poverty rate: 17.5%
Educational Attainment: High school diploma or higher: 83.6%; Bachelor's degree or higher: 11.5%; Graduate/professional degree or higher: 3.9%

School District(s)
Heartland Career Center (09-12)
    2012-13 Enrollment: n/a . . . . (260) 563-7481
M S D Wabash County Schools (PK-12)
    2012-13 Enrollment: 2,209 . . . . (260) 563-8050
Wabash City Schools (KG-12)
    2012-13 Enrollment: 1,467 . . . . (260) 563-2151
Housing: Homeownership rate: 65.9%; Median home value: $77,800; Median year structure built: 1953; Homeowner vacancy rate: 5.1%; Median gross rent: $569 per month; Rental vacancy rate: 12.0%
Health Insurance: 86.8% have insurance; 60.1% have private insurance; 40.6% have public insurance; 13.2% do not have insurance; 4.0% of children under 18 do not have insurance

Hospitals: Wabash County Hospital (25 beds)
Newspapers: Paper of Wabash County (weekly circulation 16000); Wabash Plain Dealer (daily circulation 6600)
Transportation: Commute: 92.7% car, 1.2% public transportation, 3.8% walk, 2.0% work from home; Median travel time to work: 15.0 minutes
Airports: Wabash Municipal (general aviation)
Additional Information Contacts
City of Wabash . . . . (260) 563-4171
   http://www.cityofwabash.com

Warren County

Located in western Indiana; bounded on the west by Illinois, and on the southeast by the Wabash River. Covers a land area of 364.681 square miles, a water area of 1.724 square miles, and is located in the Eastern Time Zone at 40.35° N. Lat., 87.38° W. Long. The county was founded in 1827. County seat is Williamsport.
Population: 8,508; Growth (since 2000): 1.1%; Density: 23.3 persons per square mile; Race: 98.3% White, 0.1% Black/African American, 0.4% Asian, 0.2% American Indian/Alaska Native, 0.1% Native Hawaiian/Other Pacific Islander, 0.7% two or more races, 0.8% Hispanic of any race; Average household size: 2.52; Median age: 42.4; Age under 18: 23.5%; Age 65 and over: 16.6%; Males per 100 females: 100.7; Marriage status: 21.4% never married, 61.1% now married, 0.7% separated, 7.7% widowed, 9.9% divorced; Foreign born: 1.1%; Speak English only: 98.4%; With disability: 17.3%; Veterans: 10.3%; Ancestry: 25.1% German, 14.1% American, 12.7% Irish, 8.6% English, 3.4% Dutch
Religion: Six largest groups: 12.5% Baptist, 10.8% Methodist/Pietist, 1.7% Presbyterian-Reformed, 1.4% Latter-day Saints, 1.2% Non-denominational Protestant, 1.1% Holiness
Economy: Unemployment rate: 4.7%; Leading industries: 12.9% construction; 12.1% retail trade; 12.1% other services (except public administration); Farms: 413 totaling 175,961 acres; Company size: 0 employ 1,000 or more persons, 0 employ 500 to 999 persons, 3 employ 100 to 499 persons, 113 employ less than 100 persons; Business ownership: 195 women-owned, n/a Black-owned, n/a Hispanic-owned, n/a Asian-owned
Employment: 12.0% management, business, and financial, 1.1% computer, engineering, and science, 6.6% education, legal, community service, arts, and media, 5.2% healthcare practitioners, 15.2% service, 21.7% sales and office, 11.9% natural resources, construction, and maintenance, 26.4% production, transportation, and material moving
Income: Per capita: $27,390; Median household: $52,317; Average household: $68,952; Households with income of $100,000 or more: 16.3%; Poverty rate: 7.1%
Educational Attainment: High school diploma or higher: 82.5%; Bachelor's degree or higher: 16.0%; Graduate/professional degree or higher: 4.7%
Housing: Homeownership rate: 80.3%; Median home value: $99,500; Median year structure built: 1968; Homeowner vacancy rate: 1.2%; Median gross rent: $709 per month; Rental vacancy rate: 7.1%
Vital Statistics: Birth rate: 126.0 per 10,000 population; Death rate: 89.1 per 10,000 population; Age-adjusted cancer mortality rate: Unreliable deaths per 100,000 population
Health Insurance: 90.8% have insurance; 74.4% have private insurance; 31.4% have public insurance; 9.2% do not have insurance; 5.9% of children under 18 do not have insurance
Health Care: Physicians: 4.8 per 10,000 population; Hospital beds: 18.9 per 10,000 population; Hospital admissions: 1,017.0 per 10,000 population
Transportation: Commute: 95.5% car, 0.5% public transportation, 0.9% walk, 2.8% work from home; Median travel time to work: 26.7 minutes
Presidential Election: 34.8% Obama, 62.6% Romney (2012)
Additional Information Contacts
Warren Government . . . . (765) 762-3510

Warren County Communities

PINE VILLAGE (town).
Covers a land area of 0.120 square miles and a water area of 0 square miles. Located at 40.45° N. Lat; 87.25° W. Long. Elevation is 692 feet.
Population: 217; Growth (since 2000): -14.9%; Density: 1,802.9 persons per square mile; Race: 99.1% White, 0.0% Black/African American, 0.9% Asian, 0.0% American Indian/Alaska Native, 0.0% Native Hawaiian/Other Pacific Islander, 0.0% Two or more races, 0.5% Hispanic of any race;

Average household size: 2.09; Median age: 41.4; Age under 18: 20.7%; Age 65 and over: 18.9%; Males per 100 females: 95.5

School District(s)
M S D Warren County (KG-12)
   2012-13 Enrollment: 1,157 . . . . (765) 762-3364
Housing: Homeownership rate: 73.1%; Homeowner vacancy rate: 1.3%; Rental vacancy rate: 12.5%

STATE LINE CITY (town).
Covers a land area of 0.139 square miles and a water area of 0 square miles. Located at 40.20° N. Lat; 87.53° W. Long. Elevation is 725 feet.
Population: 143; Growth (since 2000): 1.4%; Density: 1,027.6 persons per square mile; Race: 98.6% White, 0.7% Black/African American, 0.0% Asian, 0.0% American Indian/Alaska Native, 0.0% Native Hawaiian/Other Pacific Islander, 0.7% Two or more races, 0.7% Hispanic of any race; Average household size: 2.38; Median age: 46.1; Age under 18: 21.0%; Age 65 and over: 19.6%; Males per 100 females: 88.2
Housing: Homeownership rate: 88.3%; Homeowner vacancy rate: 0.0%; Rental vacancy rate: 12.5%

WEST LEBANON (town).
Covers a land area of 0.615 square miles and a water area of 0 square miles. Located at 40.27° N. Lat; 87.39° W. Long. Elevation is 718 feet.
History: Laid out 1830.
Population: 723; Growth (since 2000): -8.8%; Density: 1,174.7 persons per square mile; Race: 99.2% White, 0.0% Black/African American, 0.3% Asian, 0.1% American Indian/Alaska Native, 0.0% Native Hawaiian/Other Pacific Islander, 0.3% Two or more races, 0.1% Hispanic of any race; Average household size: 2.52; Median age: 37.4; Age under 18: 27.5%; Age 65 and over: 17.2%; Males per 100 females: 100.3

School District(s)
M S D Warren County (KG-12)
   2012-13 Enrollment: 1,157 . . . . (765) 762-3364
Housing: Homeownership rate: 66.5%; Homeowner vacancy rate: 2.5%; Rental vacancy rate: 9.3%

WILLIAMSPORT (town).
County seat. Covers a land area of 1.302 square miles and a water area of 0 square miles. Located at 40.29° N. Lat; 87.29° W. Long. Elevation is 633 feet.
History: The land on which Williamsport was founded was owned by General William Henry Harrison. A spur of the Wabash & Erie Canal was built to Williamsport, giving an early boost to commerce and bringing the nickname of Side Cut City.
Population: 1,898; Growth (since 2000): -1.9%; Density: 1,457.6 persons per square mile; Race: 98.3% White, 0.3% Black/African American, 0.5% Asian, 0.1% American Indian/Alaska Native, 0.2% Native Hawaiian/Other Pacific Islander, 0.4% Two or more races, 1.0% Hispanic of any race; Average household size: 2.37; Median age: 42.5; Age under 18: 22.4%; Age 65 and over: 20.9%; Males per 100 females: 90.4

School District(s)
M S D Warren County (KG-12)
   2012-13 Enrollment: 1,157 . . . . (765) 762-3364
Housing: Homeownership rate: 68.9%; Homeowner vacancy rate: 1.5%; Rental vacancy rate: 7.3%
Hospitals: Saint Vincent Williamsport Hospital (16 beds)
Newspapers: The Review-Republican (weekly circulation 3500)

Warrick County

Located in southwestern Indiana; bounded on the south by the Ohio River and the Kentucky border. Covers a land area of 384.815 square miles, a water area of 6.238 square miles, and is located in the Central Time Zone at 38.10° N. Lat., 87.27° W. Long. The county was founded in 1813. County seat is Boonville.

Warrick County is part of the Evansville, IN-KY Metropolitan Statistical Area. The entire metro area includes: Posey County, IN; Vanderburgh County, IN; Warrick County, IN; Henderson County, KY

Population: 59,689; Growth (since 2000): 13.9%; Density: 155.1 persons per square mile; Race: 95.0% White, 1.3% Black/African American, 1.6% Asian, 0.2% American Indian/Alaska Native, 0.0% Native Hawaiian/Other Pacific Islander, 1.3% two or more races, 1.6% Hispanic of any race; Average household size: 2.62; Median age: 39.7; Age under 18: 25.9%; Age 65 and over: 13.3%; Males per 100 females: 97.1; Marriage status: 19.7% never married, 64.1% now married, 0.6% separated, 5.3% widowed, 10.9% divorced; Foreign born: 2.5%; Speak English only: 96.4%; With disability: 10.7%; Veterans: 10.4%; Ancestry: 31.3% German, 14.8% Irish, 12.8% English, 12.3% American, 2.7% French
Religion: Six largest groups: 14.8% Baptist, 11.4% Catholicism, 8.7% Non-denominational Protestant, 4.3% Methodist/Pietist, 3.2% Presbyterian-Reformed, 1.2% Latter-day Saints
Economy: Unemployment rate: 4.3%; Leading industries: 17.5% construction; 12.5% other services (except public administration); 11.4% retail trade; Farms: 379 totaling 99,651 acres; Company size: 1 employs 1,000 or more persons, 2 employ 500 to 999 persons, 12 employ 100 to 499 persons, 1,086 employ less than 100 persons; Business ownership: 1,523 women-owned, n/a Black-owned, n/a Hispanic-owned, n/a Asian-owned
Employment: 13.3% management, business, and financial, 4.1% computer, engineering, and science, 9.3% education, legal, community service, arts, and media, 7.6% healthcare practitioners, 16.2% service, 26.7% sales and office, 9.5% natural resources, construction, and maintenance, 13.2% production, transportation, and material moving
Income: Per capita: $29,927; Median household: $62,351; Average household: $79,483; Households with income of $100,000 or more: 24.1%; Poverty rate: 9.0%
Educational Attainment: High school diploma or higher: 92.4%; Bachelor's degree or higher: 27.2%; Graduate/professional degree or higher: 9.5%
Housing: Homeownership rate: 81.0%; Median home value: $146,300; Median year structure built: 1980; Homeowner vacancy rate: 1.7%; Median gross rent: $766 per month; Rental vacancy rate: 12.5%
Vital Statistics: Birth rate: 102.0 per 10,000 population; Death rate: 88.5 per 10,000 population; Age-adjusted cancer mortality rate: 178.0 deaths per 100,000 population
Health Insurance: 90.4% have insurance; 78.9% have private insurance; 24.6% have public insurance; 9.6% do not have insurance; 4.9% of children under 18 do not have insurance
Health Care: Physicians: 39.5 per 10,000 population; Hospital beds: 22.1 per 10,000 population; Hospital admissions: 969.9 per 10,000 population
Air Quality Index: 91.3% good, 8.7% moderate, 0.0% unhealthy for sensitive individuals, 0.0% unhealthy (percent of days)
Transportation: Commute: 95.5% car, 0.2% public transportation, 0.7% walk, 2.8% work from home; Median travel time to work: 23.1 minutes
Presidential Election: 35.7% Obama, 62.3% Romney (2012)
Additional Information Contacts
Warrick Government . . . . (812) 897-6160
   http://www.warrickcounty.gov

Warrick County Communities

BOONVILLE (city).
County seat. Covers a land area of 3.001 square miles and a water area of 0.013 square miles. Located at 38.05° N. Lat; 87.27° W. Long. Elevation is 423 feet.
History: Boonville was laid out in 1818 as a coal-mining and farming center at a place where several wagon trails crossed. It was named for Jesse Boon, the father of Ratliff Boon who was the first treasurer of Warrick County, the first state representative from Warrick County in 1816, and a representative in Congress from 1825-1839.
Population: 6,246; Growth (since 2000): -8.6%; Density: 2,081.2 persons per square mile; Race: 97.7% White, 0.5% Black/African American, 0.1% Asian, 0.2% American Indian/Alaska Native, 0.0% Native Hawaiian/Other Pacific Islander, 1.1% Two or more races, 1.2% Hispanic of any race; Average household size: 2.39; Median age: 39.4; Age under 18: 23.3%; Age 65 and over: 18.0%; Males per 100 females: 86.3; Marriage status: 16.6% never married, 63.8% now married, 1.0% separated, 9.8% widowed, 9.8% divorced; Foreign born: 0.2%; Speak English only: 99.7%; With disability: 16.3%; Veterans: 10.9%; Ancestry: 22.9% German, 22.3% Irish, 14.2% American, 9.8% English, 3.4% French
Employment: 4.8% management, business, and financial, 0.0% computer, engineering, and science, 11.0% education, legal, community service, arts, and media, 3.3% healthcare practitioners, 19.2% service, 31.5% sales and office, 11.9% natural resources, construction, and maintenance, 18.3% production, transportation, and material moving
Income: Per capita: $23,876; Median household: $47,938; Average household: $57,251; Households with income of $100,000 or more: 9.8%; Poverty rate: 14.3%

Educational Attainment: High school diploma or higher: 85.7%; Bachelor's degree or higher: 15.4%; Graduate/professional degree or higher: 4.8%

School District(s)
Warrick County School Corp (PK-12)
   2012-13 Enrollment: 9,965 . . . . (812) 897-0400
Housing: Homeownership rate: 68.9%; Median home value: $90,600; Median year structure built: 1964; Homeowner vacancy rate: 3.3%; Median gross rent: $600 per month; Rental vacancy rate: 11.0%
Health Insurance: 86.3% have insurance; 69.4% have private insurance; 35.0% have public insurance; 13.7% do not have insurance; 5.3% of children under 18 do not have insurance
Hospitals: Saint Mary's Warrick Hospital (25 beds)
Safety: Violent crime rate: 32.3 per 10,000 population; Property crime rate: 317.9 per 10,000 population
Newspapers: Boonville Standard & Newburgh Register (weekly circulation 4500)
Transportation: Commute: 96.1% car, 0.0% public transportation, 2.1% walk, 0.4% work from home; Median travel time to work: 21.4 minutes
Additional Information Contacts
City of Boonville. . . . . (812) 897-6543
   http://www.cityofboonevilleindiana.com

CHANDLER (town).
Covers a land area of 2.033 square miles and a water area of 0 square miles. Located at 38.04° N. Lat; 87.37° W. Long. Elevation is 413 feet.
Population: 2,887; Growth (since 2000): -6.7%; Density: 1,419.9 persons per square mile; Race: 97.9% White, 0.3% Black/African American, 0.1% Asian, 0.1% American Indian/Alaska Native, 0.0% Native Hawaiian/Other Pacific Islander, 1.1% Two or more races, 1.3% Hispanic of any race; Average household size: 2.62; Median age: 36.0; Age under 18: 27.2%; Age 65 and over: 11.6%; Males per 100 females: 95.2; Marriage status: 24.1% never married, 59.7% now married, 1.0% separated, 4.3% widowed, 11.8% divorced; Foreign born: 0.0%; Speak English only: 99.6%; With disability: 17.3%; Veterans: 8.3%; Ancestry: 37.4% German, 14.2% Irish, 8.9% American, 8.8% English, 4.3% French
Employment: 8.1% management, business, and financial, 3.0% computer, engineering, and science, 4.3% education, legal, community service, arts, and media, 2.2% healthcare practitioners, 14.0% service, 35.6% sales and office, 8.2% natural resources, construction, and maintenance, 24.6% production, transportation, and material moving
Income: Per capita: $16,239; Median household: $41,164; Average household: $47,429; Households with income of $100,000 or more: 5.7%; Poverty rate: 24.3%
Educational Attainment: High school diploma or higher: 88.4%; Bachelor's degree or higher: 6.8%; Graduate/professional degree or higher: 2.5%

School District(s)
Warrick County School Corp (PK-12)
   2012-13 Enrollment: 9,965 . . . . (812) 897-0400
Housing: Homeownership rate: 72.3%; Median home value: $85,300; Median year structure built: 1975; Homeowner vacancy rate: 2.4%; Median gross rent: $827 per month; Rental vacancy rate: 28.3%
Health Insurance: 79.9% have insurance; 52.3% have private insurance; 41.4% have public insurance; 20.1% do not have insurance; 12.9% of children under 18 do not have insurance
Transportation: Commute: 97.4% car, 0.4% public transportation, 0.8% walk, 1.1% work from home; Median travel time to work: 20.8 minutes
Additional Information Contacts
Town of Chandler . . . . (812) 925-6882
   http://www.townofchandler.org

ELBERFELD (town).
Covers a land area of 0.306 square miles and a water area of 0 square miles. Located at 38.16° N. Lat; 87.45° W. Long. Elevation is 453 feet.
Population: 625; Growth (since 2000): -1.7%; Density: 2,043.0 persons per square mile; Race: 97.3% White, 0.2% Black/African American, 0.0% Asian, 1.0% American Indian/Alaska Native, 0.0% Native Hawaiian/Other Pacific Islander, 1.6% Two or more races, 1.3% Hispanic of any race; Average household size: 2.49; Median age: 38.3; Age under 18: 25.1%; Age 65 and over: 15.2%; Males per 100 females: 100.3

School District(s)
Warrick County School Corp (PK-12)
   2012-13 Enrollment: 9,965 . . . . (812) 897-0400
Housing: Homeownership rate: 85.3%; Homeowner vacancy rate: 0.9%; Rental vacancy rate: 17.8%

LYNNVILLE (town).
Covers a land area of 1.742 square miles and a water area of 0.236 square miles. Located at 38.20° N. Lat; 87.32° W. Long. Elevation is 463 feet.
Population: 888; Growth (since 2000): 13.7%; Density: 509.7 persons per square mile; Race: 98.9% White, 0.1% Black/African American, 0.0% Asian, 0.2% American Indian/Alaska Native, 0.0% Native Hawaiian/Other Pacific Islander, 0.8% Two or more races, 0.8% Hispanic of any race; Average household size: 2.50; Median age: 38.9; Age under 18: 24.5%; Age 65 and over: 13.2%; Males per 100 females: 108.5

School District(s)
Warrick County School Corp (PK-12)
   2012-13 Enrollment: 9,965 . . . . (812) 897-0400
Housing: Homeownership rate: 78.4%; Homeowner vacancy rate: 2.1%; Rental vacancy rate: 10.3%

NEWBURGH (town).
Covers a land area of 1.406 square miles and a water area of 0.001 square miles. Located at 37.95° N. Lat; 87.40° W. Long. Elevation is 394 feet.
History: Settled 1803, laid out 1818.
Population: 3,325; Growth (since 2000): 7.7%; Density: 2,364.5 persons per square mile; Race: 94.2% White, 1.4% Black/African American, 2.0% Asian, 0.1% American Indian/Alaska Native, 0.0% Native Hawaiian/Other Pacific Islander, 1.4% Two or more races, 2.0% Hispanic of any race; Average household size: 2.28; Median age: 42.1; Age under 18: 22.4%; Age 65 and over: 14.4%; Males per 100 females: 92.9; Marriage status: 21.6% never married, 59.6% now married, 1.5% separated, 3.9% widowed, 14.9% divorced; Foreign born: 4.4%; Speak English only: 94.8%; With disability: 12.8%; Veterans: 8.3%; Ancestry: 35.8% German, 14.0% Irish, 12.9% English, 11.4% American, 4.4% Polish
Employment: 9.3% management, business, and financial, 4.1% computer, engineering, and science, 9.6% education, legal, community service, arts, and media, 6.5% healthcare practitioners, 21.5% service, 20.8% sales and office, 8.4% natural resources, construction, and maintenance, 19.9% production, transportation, and material moving
Income: Per capita: $31,341; Median household: $45,481; Average household: $74,620; Households with income of $100,000 or more: 17.1%; Poverty rate: 8.9%
Educational Attainment: High school diploma or higher: 93.4%; Bachelor's degree or higher: 29.2%; Graduate/professional degree or higher: 10.5%

School District(s)
Warrick County School Corp (PK-12)
   2012-13 Enrollment: 9,965 . . . . (812) 897-0400

Four-year College(s)
ITT Technical Institute-Newburgh (Private, For-profit)
   Fall 2013 Enrollment: 295 . . . . (812) 858-1600
   2013-14 Tuition: In-state $18,048; Out-of-state $18,048
Housing: Homeownership rate: 74.3%; Median home value: $141,100; Median year structure built: 1972; Homeowner vacancy rate: 1.6%; Median gross rent: $557 per month; Rental vacancy rate: 12.8%
Health Insurance: 87.0% have insurance; 77.3% have private insurance; 20.4% have public insurance; 13.0% do not have insurance; 11.2% of children under 18 do not have insurance
Hospitals: The Heart Hospital at Deaconess Gateway (145 beds); The Women's Hospital
Transportation: Commute: 96.7% car, 0.0% public transportation, 0.0% walk, 0.0% work from home; Median travel time to work: 20.9 minutes
Additional Information Contacts
Town of Newburgh . . . . (812) 853-7111
   http://www.newburgh-in.gov

TENNYSON (town).
Covers a land area of 0.234 square miles and a water area of 0 square miles. Located at 38.08° N. Lat; 87.12° W. Long. Elevation is 407 feet.
Population: 279; Growth (since 2000): -3.8%; Density: 1,193.2 persons per square mile; Race: 99.3% White, 0.4% Black/African American, 0.0% Asian, 0.0% American Indian/Alaska Native, 0.0% Native Hawaiian/Other Pacific Islander, 0.0% Two or more races, 2.2% Hispanic of any race; Average household size: 2.63; Median age: 40.1; Age under 18: 24.4%; Age 65 and over: 12.9%; Males per 100 females: 102.2

School District(s)
Warrick County School Corp (PK-12)
  2012-13 Enrollment: 9,965 . . . . (812) 897-0400
Housing: Homeownership rate: 70.8%; Homeowner vacancy rate: 0.0%; Rental vacancy rate: 0.0%

Washington County

Located in southern Indiana; bounded on the north by the Muscatatuck River and the East Fork of the White River; drained by the Blue and Lost Rivers. Covers a land area of 513.725 square miles, a water area of 2.874 square miles, and is located in the Eastern Time Zone at 38.60° N. Lat., 86.10° W. Long. The county was founded in 1813. County seat is Salem.

Washington County is part of the Louisville/Jefferson County, KY-IN Metropolitan Statistical Area. The entire metro area includes: Clark County, IN; Floyd County, IN; Harrison County, IN; Scott County, IN; Washington County, IN; Bullitt County, KY; Henry County, KY; Jefferson County, KY; Oldham County, KY; Shelby County, KY; Spencer County, KY; Trimble County, KY

Weather Station: Salem   Elevation: 799 feet

	Jan	Feb	Mar	Apr	May	Jun	Jul	Aug	Sep	Oct	Nov	Dec
High	40	46	56	67	76	84	87	86	80	69	56	43
Low	23	26	34	43	52	61	65	63	55	44	36	27
Precip	3.2	2.9	4.3	4.4	5.3	3.9	3.9	3.4	3.3	3.2	3.7	3.7
Snow	4.7	4.1	2.4	0.2	0.0	0.0	0.0	0.0	0.0	0.2	0.2	2.8

High and Low temperatures in degrees Fahrenheit; Precipitation and Snow in inches

Population: 28,262; Growth (since 2000): 3.8%; Density: 55.0 persons per square mile; Race: 98.1% White, 0.2% Black/African American, 0.3% Asian, 0.2% American Indian/Alaska Native, 0.0% Native Hawaiian/Other Pacific Islander, 0.9% two or more races, 1.1% Hispanic of any race; Average household size: 2.58; Median age: 39.2; Age under 18: 25.2%; Age 65 and over: 13.5%; Males per 100 females: 99.7; Marriage status: 22.6% never married, 55.7% now married, 1.8% separated, 7.1% widowed, 14.6% divorced; Foreign born: 0.7%; Speak English only: 97.7%; With disability: 17.0%; Veterans: 9.7%; Ancestry: 24.0% American, 20.4% German, 12.1% Irish, 7.3% English, 2.2% Scottish
Religion: Six largest groups: 30.8% Baptist, 2.9% Methodist/Pietist, 2.1% European Free-Church, 1.1% Holiness, 0.9% Pentecostal, 0.9% Non-denominational Protestant
Economy: Unemployment rate: 5.1%; Leading industries: 18.6% retail trade; 14.9% construction; 10.5% health care and social assistance; Farms: 831 totaling 199,529 acres; Company size: 0 employ 1,000 or more persons, 0 employ 500 to 999 persons, 9 employ 100 to 499 persons, 420 employ less than 100 persons; Business ownership: 628 women-owned, n/a Black-owned, n/a Hispanic-owned, n/a Asian-owned
Employment: 8.4% management, business, and financial, 2.7% computer, engineering, and science, 6.7% education, legal, community service, arts, and media, 6.0% healthcare practitioners, 18.0% service, 19.0% sales and office, 13.0% natural resources, construction, and maintenance, 26.2% production, transportation, and material moving
Income: Per capita: $21,370; Median household: $41,986; Average household: $54,575; Households with income of $100,000 or more: 10.5%; Poverty rate: 15.1%
Educational Attainment: High school diploma or higher: 80.1%; Bachelor's degree or higher: 11.9%; Graduate/professional degree or higher: 5.5%
Housing: Homeownership rate: 78.2%; Median home value: $101,500; Median year structure built: 1978; Homeowner vacancy rate: 2.6%; Median gross rent: $631 per month; Rental vacancy rate: 11.3%
Vital Statistics: Birth rate: 99.7 per 10,000 population; Death rate: 99.7 per 10,000 population; Age-adjusted cancer mortality rate: 218.8 deaths per 100,000 population
Health Insurance: 85.5% have insurance; 64.8% have private insurance; 32.9% have public insurance; 14.5% do not have insurance; 7.6% of children under 18 do not have insurance
Health Care: Physicians: 6.1 per 10,000 population; Hospital beds: 8.9 per 10,000 population; Hospital admissions: 155.7 per 10,000 population
Transportation: Commute: 93.1% car, 0.1% public transportation, 1.2% walk, 4.4% work from home; Median travel time to work: 29.6 minutes
Presidential Election: 36.4% Obama, 60.9% Romney (2012)
National and State Parks: Clark State Forest; Jackson-Washington State Forest
Additional Information Contacts
Washington Government . . . . (812) 883-5748
http://www.washingtoncountyindiana.com

Washington County Communities

CAMPBELLSBURG (town). Covers a land area of 0.992 square miles and a water area of 0.002 square miles. Located at 38.65° N. Lat; 86.26° W. Long. Elevation is 837 feet.
Population: 585; Growth (since 2000): 1.2%; Density: 589.8 persons per square mile; Race: 98.5% White, 0.2% Black/African American, 0.3% Asian, 0.0% American Indian/Alaska Native, 0.0% Native Hawaiian/Other Pacific Islander, 1.0% Two or more races, 1.0% Hispanic of any race; Average household size: 2.57; Median age: 34.4; Age under 18: 30.1%; Age 65 and over: 12.1%; Males per 100 females: 96.3
School District(s)
West Washington School Corp (KG-12)
  2012-13 Enrollment: 859 . . . . (812) 755-4872
Housing: Homeownership rate: 63.6%; Homeowner vacancy rate: 3.9%; Rental vacancy rate: 22.2%

FREDERICKSBURG (town). Covers a land area of 0.993 square miles and a water area of 0.020 square miles. Located at 38.43° N. Lat; 86.19° W. Long. Elevation is 614 feet.
History: Fredericksburg was settled in 1805 and became a toll station on the plank road between New Albany and Vincennes. Many of the settlers here were Quakers who built the Lick Creek Friends Church in 1815.
Population: 85; Growth (since 2000): -7.6%; Density: 85.6 persons per square mile; Race: 92.9% White, 0.0% Black/African American, 0.0% Asian, 2.4% American Indian/Alaska Native, 0.0% Native Hawaiian/Other Pacific Islander, 4.7% Two or more races, 5.9% Hispanic of any race; Average household size: 2.43; Median age: 33.3; Age under 18: 29.4%; Age 65 and over: 16.5%; Males per 100 females: 123.7
Housing: Homeownership rate: 77.2%; Homeowner vacancy rate: 6.9%; Rental vacancy rate: 20.0%

HARDINSBURG (town). Covers a land area of 2.035 square miles and a water area of 0.003 square miles. Located at 38.47° N. Lat; 86.28° W. Long. Elevation is 689 feet.
History: Laid out 1838.
Population: 248; Growth (since 2000): 1.6%; Density: 121.9 persons per square mile; Race: 100.0% White, 0.0% Black/African American, 0.0% Asian, 0.0% American Indian/Alaska Native, 0.0% Native Hawaiian/Other Pacific Islander, 0.0% Two or more races, 0.4% Hispanic of any race; Average household size: 2.58; Median age: 37.0; Age under 18: 26.6%; Age 65 and over: 11.3%; Males per 100 females: 100.0
Housing: Homeownership rate: 77.1%; Homeowner vacancy rate: 3.8%; Rental vacancy rate: 20.7%

LITTLE YORK (town). Covers a land area of 0.979 square miles and a water area of 0 square miles. Located at 38.70° N. Lat; 85.90° W. Long. Elevation is 548 feet.
History: Laid out 1831.
Population: 192; Growth (since 2000): 3.8%; Density: 196.1 persons per square mile; Race: 97.9% White, 0.0% Black/African American, 0.0% Asian, 0.0% American Indian/Alaska Native, 0.0% Native Hawaiian/Other Pacific Islander, 2.1% Two or more races, 1.6% Hispanic of any race; Average household size: 2.43; Median age: 42.3; Age under 18: 21.9%; Age 65 and over: 14.6%; Males per 100 females: 104.3
Housing: Homeownership rate: 77.2%; Homeowner vacancy rate: 1.6%; Rental vacancy rate: 5.0%

LIVONIA (town). Covers a land area of 1.037 square miles and a water area of 0.002 square miles. Located at 38.55° N. Lat; 86.28° W. Long. Elevation is 787 feet.
History: Laid out 1819.
Population: 128; Growth (since 2000): 14.3%; Density: 123.5 persons per square mile; Race: 99.2% White, 0.0% Black/African American, 0.0% Asian, 0.0% American Indian/Alaska Native, 0.0% Native Hawaiian/Other Pacific Islander, 0.8% Two or more races, 0.0% Hispanic of any race; Average household size: 2.84; Median age: 41.0; Age under 18: 29.7%; Age 65 and over: 18.8%; Males per 100 females: 96.9
Housing: Homeownership rate: 86.7%; Homeowner vacancy rate: 0.0%; Rental vacancy rate: 0.0%

NEW PEKIN (town). Covers a land area of 2.370 square miles and a water area of 0.034 square miles. Located at 38.50° N. Lat; 86.01° W. Long. Elevation is 712 feet.
Population: 1,401; Growth (since 2000): 5.0%; Density: 591.1 persons per square mile; Race: 97.1% White, 0.6% Black/African American, 0.1% Asian, 0.2% American Indian/Alaska Native, 0.1% Native Hawaiian/Other Pacific Islander, 1.1% Two or more races, 2.4% Hispanic of any race; Average household size: 2.49; Median age: 36.8; Age under 18: 25.3%; Age 65 and over: 11.9%; Males per 100 females: 95.4
Housing: Homeownership rate: 59.5%; Homeowner vacancy rate: 2.2%; Rental vacancy rate: 5.8%

PEKIN (unincorporated postal area)
ZCTA: 47165
Covers a land area of 82.396 square miles and a water area of 0.325 square miles. Located at 38.50° N. Lat; 86.01° W. Long..
Population: 6,438; Growth (since 2000): 10.5%; Density: 78.1 persons per square mile; Race: 97.9% White, 0.2% Black/African American, 0.2% Asian, 0.2% American Indian/Alaska Native, 0.0% Native Hawaiian/Other Pacific Islander, 1.0% Two or more races, 1.4% Hispanic of any race; Average household size: 2.68; Median age: 37.9; Age under 18: 26.5%; Age 65 and over: 10.2%; Males per 100 females: 102.8; Marriage status: 19.6% never married, 61.8% now married, 0.7% separated, 5.1% widowed, 13.4% divorced; Foreign born: 0.4%; Speak English only: 98.3%; With disability: 19.3%; Veterans: 11.6%; Ancestry: 26.9% American, 20.8% German, 14.3% Irish, 7.5% English, 2.8% Scotch-Irish
Employment: 5.3% management, business, and financial, 2.8% computer, engineering, and science, 9.8% education, legal, community service, arts, and media, 3.2% healthcare practitioners, 19.2% service, 18.7% sales and office, 12.5% natural resources, construction, and maintenance, 28.5% production, transportation, and material moving
Income: Per capita: $21,163; Median household: $42,998; Average household: $54,538; Households with income of $100,000 or more: 12.9%; Poverty rate: 13.8%
Educational Attainment: High school diploma or higher: 80.4%; Bachelor's degree or higher: 13.5%; Graduate/professional degree or higher: 6.8%
School District(s)
East Washington School Corp (KG-12)
    2012-13 Enrollment: 1,517 . . . . (812) 967-3926
Housing: Homeownership rate: 80.3%; Median home value: $111,600; Median year structure built: 1985; Homeowner vacancy rate: 2.4%; Median gross rent: $659 per month; Rental vacancy rate: 8.4%
Health Insurance: 89.8% have insurance; 74.7% have private insurance; 28.1% have public insurance; 10.2% do not have insurance; 5.4% of children under 18 do not have insurance
Newspapers: Green Banner Publications (weekly circulation 66000)
Transportation: Commute: 90.3% car, 0.4% public transportation, 1.0% walk, 6.1% work from home; Median travel time to work: 32.7 minutes

SALEM (city). County seat. Covers a land area of 4.000 square miles and a water area of 0.018 square miles. Located at 38.60° N. Lat; 86.10° W. Long. Elevation is 751 feet.
History: Salem was founded in 1814 and named for Salem, North Carolina, the former home of the wife of the county surveyor. John Hay, statesman, diplomat, poet, and historian, was born in 1838 in Salem. In 1863 Salem was burned and looted by General Morgan and his raiders.
Population: 6,319; Growth (since 2000): 2.4%; Density: 1,579.8 persons per square mile; Race: 97.5% White, 0.4% Black/African American, 0.6% Asian, 0.3% American Indian/Alaska Native, 0.0% Native Hawaiian/Other Pacific Islander, 0.9% Two or more races, 1.0% Hispanic of any race; Average household size: 2.31; Median age: 38.3; Age under 18: 24.0%; Age 65 and over: 17.6%; Males per 100 females: 86.9; Marriage status: 25.2% never married, 43.6% now married, 2.4% separated, 11.7% widowed, 19.4% divorced; Foreign born: 0.2%; Speak English only: 98.6%; With disability: 17.7%; Veterans: 8.0%; Ancestry: 25.2% American, 19.5% German, 10.4% Irish, 6.6% English, 3.9% Scottish
Employment: 8.1% management, business, and financial, 0.4% computer, engineering, and science, 5.5% education, legal, community service, arts, and media, 8.3% healthcare practitioners, 17.6% service, 22.6% sales and office, 12.3% natural resources, construction, and maintenance, 25.2% production, transportation, and material moving
Income: Per capita: $18,613; Median household: $32,144; Average household: $44,419; Households with income of $100,000 or more: 5.4%; Poverty rate: 20.3%
Educational Attainment: High school diploma or higher: 77.8%; Bachelor's degree or higher: 13.4%; Graduate/professional degree or higher: 5.7%
School District(s)
Salem Community Schools (KG-12)
    2012-13 Enrollment: 1,955 . . . . (812) 883-4437
Housing: Homeownership rate: 63.0%; Median home value: $80,700; Median year structure built: 1965; Homeowner vacancy rate: 3.3%; Median gross rent: $585 per month; Rental vacancy rate: 12.3%
Health Insurance: 84.1% have insurance; 54.2% have private insurance; 42.9% have public insurance; 15.9% do not have insurance; 8.9% of children under 18 do not have insurance
Hospitals: Saint Vincent Salem Hospital (70 beds)
Newspapers: Salem Democrat (weekly circulation 6100); Salem Leader (weekly circulation 6100)
Transportation: Commute: 92.1% car, 0.0% public transportation, 4.0% walk, 2.5% work from home; Median travel time to work: 24.5 minutes
Additional Information Contacts
City of Salem. . . . . (812) 883-4264
    http://www.cityofsalemin.com

SALTILLO (town). Covers a land area of 1.151 square miles and a water area of 0.002 square miles. Located at 38.67° N. Lat; 86.30° W. Long. Elevation is 807 feet.
Population: 92; Growth (since 2000): -14.0%; Density: 79.9 persons per square mile; Race: 98.9% White, 0.0% Black/African American, 0.0% Asian, 0.0% American Indian/Alaska Native, 0.0% Native Hawaiian/Other Pacific Islander, 0.0% Two or more races, 1.1% Hispanic of any race; Average household size: 2.19; Median age: 48.3; Age under 18: 15.2%; Age 65 and over: 21.7%; Males per 100 females: 100.0
Housing: Homeownership rate: 85.7%; Homeowner vacancy rate: 5.3%; Rental vacancy rate: 45.5%

Wayne County

Located in eastern Indiana; bounded on the east by Ohio; drained by the Whitewater River and its East Fork. Covers a land area of 401.740 square miles, a water area of 2.601 square miles, and is located in the Eastern Time Zone at 39.86° N. Lat., 85.01° W. Long. The county was founded in 1810. County seat is Richmond.

Wayne County is part of the Richmond, IN Micropolitan Statistical Area. The entire metro area includes: Wayne County, IN

Weather Station: Richmond Water Works   Elevation: 1,015 feet

	Jan	Feb	Mar	Apr	May	Jun	Jul	Aug	Sep	Oct	Nov	Dec
High	36	40	50	63	73	81	85	83	77	64	52	39
Low	19	22	30	40	50	59	63	61	53	42	33	23
Precip	2.7	2.3	3.2	3.8	4.7	4.3	4.0	3.5	2.8	3.2	3.4	2.9
Snow	5.9	3.6	1.6	0.2	tr	0.0	0.0	0.0	0.0	0.2	0.4	3.8

High and Low temperatures in degrees Fahrenheit; Precipitation and Snow in inches

Population: 68,917; Growth (since 2000): -3.1%; Density: 171.5 persons per square mile; Race: 90.2% White, 5.0% Black/African American, 0.8% Asian, 0.2% American Indian/Alaska Native, 0.1% Native Hawaiian/Other Pacific Islander, 2.7% two or more races, 2.6% Hispanic of any race; Average household size: 2.41; Median age: 40.2; Age under 18: 23.0%; Age 65 and over: 16.4%; Males per 100 females: 94.4; Marriage status: 26.4% never married, 52.0% now married, 1.9% separated, 6.9% widowed, 14.7% divorced; Foreign born: 2.0%; Speak English only: 95.0%; With disability: 17.3%; Veterans: 10.9%; Ancestry: 21.9% German, 12.6% Irish, 10.1% English, 10.1% American, 2.9% Italian
Religion: Six largest groups: 12.3% Baptist, 7.0% Catholicism, 4.7% Methodist/Pietist, 4.0% Non-denominational Protestant, 3.9% Pentecostal, 3.7% Holiness
Economy: Unemployment rate: 6.1%; Leading industries: 17.3% retail trade; 13.1% health care and social assistance; 12.5% other services (except public administration); Farms: 805 totaling 155,931 acres; Company size: 2 employ 1,000 or more persons, 0 employ 500 to 999 persons, 34 employ 100 to 499 persons, 1,522 employ less than 100 persons; Business ownership: 801 women-owned, 103 Black-owned, n/a Hispanic-owned, 41 Asian-owned

Employment: 11.7% management, business, and financial, 2.4% computer, engineering, and science, 9.6% education, legal, community service, arts, and media, 6.7% healthcare practitioners, 20.0% service, 22.1% sales and office, 8.8% natural resources, construction, and maintenance, 18.8% production, transportation, and material moving
Income: Per capita: $21,114; Median household: $38,350; Average household: $50,745; Households with income of $100,000 or more: 10.2%; Poverty rate: 21.8%
Educational Attainment: High school diploma or higher: 83.4%; Bachelor's degree or higher: 17.4%; Graduate/professional degree or higher: 7.3%
Housing: Homeownership rate: 67.2%; Median home value: $94,100; Median year structure built: 1958; Homeowner vacancy rate: 3.5%; Median gross rent: $636 per month; Rental vacancy rate: 11.6%
Vital Statistics: Birth rate: 118.3 per 10,000 population; Death rate: 125.2 per 10,000 population; Age-adjusted cancer mortality rate: 190.2 deaths per 100,000 population
Health Insurance: 81.8% have insurance; 60.2% have private insurance; 35.3% have public insurance; 18.2% do not have insurance; 12.5% of children under 18 do not have insurance
Health Care: Physicians: 21.5 per 10,000 population; Hospital beds: 64.1 per 10,000 population; Hospital admissions: 1,720.7 per 10,000 population
Air Quality Index: 100.0% good, 0.0% moderate, 0.0% unhealthy for sensitive individuals, 0.0% unhealthy (percent of days)
Transportation: Commute: 93.2% car, 0.7% public transportation, 2.2% walk, 2.3% work from home; Median travel time to work: 19.6 minutes
Presidential Election: 41.6% Obama, 56.2% Romney (2012)
Additional Information Contacts
Wayne Government . . . . (765) 973-9220
http://www.co.wayne.in.us

Wayne County Communities

BOSTON (town). Covers a land area of 0.211 square miles and a water area of 0 square miles. Located at 39.74° N. Lat; 84.85° W. Long. Elevation is 1,132 feet.
Population: 138; Growth (since 2000): -22.0%; Density: 654.9 persons per square mile; Race: 97.8% White, 0.0% Black/African American, 1.4% Asian, 0.7% American Indian/Alaska Native, 0.0% Native Hawaiian/Other Pacific Islander, 0.0% Two or more races, 0.0% Hispanic of any race; Average household size: 2.30; Median age: 42.0; Age under 18: 22.5%; Age 65 and over: 19.6%; Males per 100 females: 109.1
Housing: Homeownership rate: 78.4%; Homeowner vacancy rate: 0.0%; Rental vacancy rate: 0.0%

CAMBRIDGE CITY (town). Covers a land area of 1.012 square miles and a water area of 0.007 square miles. Located at 39.81° N. Lat; 85.17° W. Long. Elevation is 935 feet.
History: Founded in 1836 as a depot on the Whitewater Canal, Cambridge City was a shipping center for Indianapolis merchants for a time.
Population: 1,870; Growth (since 2000): -11.8%; Density: 1,847.5 persons per square mile; Race: 98.5% White, 0.2% Black/African American, 0.3% Asian, 0.5% American Indian/Alaska Native, 0.0% Native Hawaiian/Other Pacific Islander, 0.5% Two or more races, 0.9% Hispanic of any race; Average household size: 2.38; Median age: 39.8; Age under 18: 24.5%; Age 65 and over: 17.0%; Males per 100 females: 95.4
School District(s)
Western Wayne Schools (KG-12)
    2012-13 Enrollment: 1,089 . . . . (765) 478-5375
Housing: Homeownership rate: 64.7%; Homeowner vacancy rate: 1.7%; Rental vacancy rate: 8.2%
Newspapers: Nettle Creek Gazette (weekly circulation 1000); Western Wayne News (weekly circulation 2700)
Additional Information Contacts
Town of Cambridge City . . . . (765) 478-4689
http://www.cambridgecityindiana.org

CENTERVILLE (town). Covers a land area of 2.404 square miles and a water area of <.001 square miles. Located at 39.83° N. Lat; 84.99° W. Long. Elevation is 1,014 feet.
History: Centerville was once the seat of Wayne County. It reluctantly gave up the county records to Richmond on August 14, 1873, when shots were fired into the jail where the Centerville citizens had barricaded themselves and the records.
Population: 2,552; Growth (since 2000): 5.2%; Density: 1,061.5 persons per square mile; Race: 96.1% White, 0.6% Black/African American, 0.6% Asian, 0.1% American Indian/Alaska Native, 0.0% Native Hawaiian/Other Pacific Islander, 1.2% Two or more races, 2.5% Hispanic of any race; Average household size: 2.46; Median age: 37.1; Age under 18: 27.4%; Age 65 and over: 13.5%; Males per 100 females: 90.4; Marriage status: 24.5% never married, 52.5% now married, 1.0% separated, 6.0% widowed, 17.0% divorced; Foreign born: 1.0%; Speak English only: 96.2%; With disability: 15.6%; Veterans: 12.7%; Ancestry: 21.7% German, 13.4% Irish, 10.5% American, 9.7% English, 2.6% Dutch
Employment: 14.6% management, business, and financial, 1.7% computer, engineering, and science, 6.0% education, legal, community service, arts, and media, 11.0% healthcare practitioners, 11.4% service, 27.8% sales and office, 7.8% natural resources, construction, and maintenance, 19.6% production, transportation, and material moving
Income: Per capita: $21,876; Median household: $40,417; Average household: $53,031; Households with income of $100,000 or more: 7.4%; Poverty rate: 16.8%
Educational Attainment: High school diploma or higher: 87.8%; Bachelor's degree or higher: 12.1%; Graduate/professional degree or higher: 6.2%
School District(s)
Centerville-Abington Com Schs (PK-12)
    2012-13 Enrollment: 1,681 . . . . (765) 855-3475
Housing: Homeownership rate: 69.7%; Median home value: $94,800; Median year structure built: 1956; Homeowner vacancy rate: 4.7%; Median gross rent: $708 per month; Rental vacancy rate: 8.2%
Health Insurance: 83.5% have insurance; 63.1% have private insurance; 35.1% have public insurance; 16.5% do not have insurance; 6.7% of children under 18 do not have insurance
Transportation: Commute: 96.8% car, 0.0% public transportation, 0.5% walk, 2.3% work from home; Median travel time to work: 22.7 minutes
Additional Information Contacts
Town of Centerville . . . . (765) 855-5515
http://www.town.centerville.in.us/index.php

DUBLIN (town). Covers a land area of 0.532 square miles and a water area of 0.011 square miles. Located at 39.81° N. Lat; 85.21° W. Long. Elevation is 1,053 feet.
History: Located on the Old National Road, Dublin was the site of The Maples, a tavern built in 1825.
Population: 790; Growth (since 2000): 13.3%; Density: 1,484.4 persons per square mile; Race: 98.0% White, 0.3% Black/African American, 0.5% Asian, 0.0% American Indian/Alaska Native, 0.0% Native Hawaiian/Other Pacific Islander, 1.3% Two or more races, 0.9% Hispanic of any race; Average household size: 2.43; Median age: 42.1; Age under 18: 22.9%; Age 65 and over: 18.7%; Males per 100 females: 89.4
Housing: Homeownership rate: 75.6%; Homeowner vacancy rate: 0.4%; Rental vacancy rate: 12.2%

EAST GERMANTOWN (town). Covers a land area of 0.128 square miles and a water area of 0 square miles. Located at 39.81° N. Lat; 85.14° W. Long. Elevation is 951 feet.
Population: 410; Growth (since 2000): 68.7%; Density: 3,204.7 persons per square mile; Race: 97.8% White, 0.2% Black/African American, 0.2% Asian, 0.2% American Indian/Alaska Native, 0.0% Native Hawaiian/Other Pacific Islander, 0.7% Two or more races, 0.7% Hispanic of any race; Average household size: 2.65; Median age: 39.4; Age under 18: 23.4%; Age 65 and over: 15.6%; Males per 100 females: 94.3
Housing: Homeownership rate: 79.3%; Homeowner vacancy rate: 3.1%; Rental vacancy rate: 11.1%

ECONOMY (town). Covers a land area of 0.098 square miles and a water area of 0 square miles. Located at 39.98° N. Lat; 85.09° W. Long. Elevation is 1,155 feet.
History: Economy was the site in 1936 of Dr. James R. King's experiment in cooperative medical care, the Economy Mutual Health Association.
Population: 187; Growth (since 2000): -6.5%; Density: 1,903.2 persons per square mile; Race: 98.4% White, 0.0% Black/African American, 0.0% Asian, 0.0% American Indian/Alaska Native, 0.0% Native Hawaiian/Other Pacific Islander, 1.6% Two or more races, 2.1% Hispanic of any race; Average household size: 2.56; Median age: 38.6; Age under 18: 25.1%; Age 65 and over: 12.8%; Males per 100 females: 92.8
Housing: Homeownership rate: 84.9%; Homeowner vacancy rate: 3.1%; Rental vacancy rate: 8.3%

FOUNTAIN CITY (town). Covers a land area of 0.263 square miles and a water area of 0 square miles. Located at 39.95° N. Lat; 84.92° W. Long. Elevation is 1,106 feet.
History: Fountain was incorporated as Newport in 1834, but the name was changed to Fountain City when water from an underground lake was found to rise to the surface when pipes were sunk to it. Fountain City was a major station on the Underground Railroad of freedom for fugitive slaves.
Population: 796; Growth (since 2000): 8.3%; Density: 3,026.3 persons per square mile; Race: 97.2% White, 0.9% Black/African American, 0.1% Asian, 0.0% American Indian/Alaska Native, 0.0% Native Hawaiian/Other Pacific Islander, 1.8% Two or more races, 0.1% Hispanic of any race; Average household size: 2.56; Median age: 37.6; Age under 18: 27.6%; Age 65 and over: 14.6%; Males per 100 females: 88.6
School District(s)
Northeastern Wayne Schools (PK-12)
 2012-13 Enrollment: 1,219 . . . . (765) 847-2821
Housing: Homeownership rate: 69.4%; Homeowner vacancy rate: 2.2%; Rental vacancy rate: 10.4%

GREENS FORK (town). Covers a land area of 0.160 square miles and a water area of 0.003 square miles. Located at 39.89° N. Lat; 85.04° W. Long. Elevation is 1,010 feet.
History: Laid out 1818.
Population: 423; Growth (since 2000): 14.0%; Density: 2,651.9 persons per square mile; Race: 99.3% White, 0.0% Black/African American, 0.2% Asian, 0.2% American Indian/Alaska Native, 0.0% Native Hawaiian/Other Pacific Islander, 0.2% Two or more races, 0.0% Hispanic of any race; Average household size: 2.88; Median age: 37.2; Age under 18: 27.2%; Age 65 and over: 13.9%; Males per 100 females: 88.0
Housing: Homeownership rate: 76.8%; Homeowner vacancy rate: 0.9%; Rental vacancy rate: 5.6%

HAGERSTOWN (town). Covers a land area of 1.340 square miles and a water area of 0.003 square miles. Located at 39.91° N. Lat; 85.15° W. Long. Elevation is 1,007 feet.
Population: 1,787; Growth (since 2000): 1.1%; Density: 1,334.0 persons per square mile; Race: 97.7% White, 0.6% Black/African American, 0.3% Asian, 0.2% American Indian/Alaska Native, 0.0% Native Hawaiian/Other Pacific Islander, 1.2% Two or more races, 0.8% Hispanic of any race; Average household size: 2.38; Median age: 37.9; Age under 18: 25.6%; Age 65 and over: 17.9%; Males per 100 females: 93.8
School District(s)
Nettle Creek School Corp (PK-12)
 2012-13 Enrollment: 1,144 . . . . (765) 489-4543
Housing: Homeownership rate: 72.7%; Homeowner vacancy rate: 2.1%; Rental vacancy rate: 11.9%
Safety: Violent crime rate: 17.0 per 10,000 population; Property crime rate: 192.7 per 10,000 population

MILTON (town). Covers a land area of 0.267 square miles and a water area of 0.003 square miles. Located at 39.79° N. Lat; 85.16° W. Long. Elevation is 932 feet.
Population: 490; Growth (since 2000): -19.8%; Density: 1,832.2 persons per square mile; Race: 98.4% White, 0.2% Black/African American, 0.0% Asian, 1.2% American Indian/Alaska Native, 0.0% Native Hawaiian/Other Pacific Islander, 0.2% Two or more races, 0.8% Hispanic of any race; Average household size: 2.49; Median age: 40.2; Age under 18: 22.0%; Age 65 and over: 14.1%; Males per 100 females: 101.6
Housing: Homeownership rate: 77.7%; Homeowner vacancy rate: 2.5%; Rental vacancy rate: 8.3%

MOUNT AUBURN (town). Covers a land area of 0.215 square miles and a water area of 0.016 square miles. Located at 39.81° N. Lat; 85.19° W. Long. Elevation is 991 feet.
Population: 117; Growth (since 2000): 56.0%; Density: 544.4 persons per square mile; Race: 98.3% White, 0.0% Black/African American, 0.9% Asian, 0.0% American Indian/Alaska Native, 0.0% Native Hawaiian/Other Pacific Islander, 0.9% Two or more races, 0.0% Hispanic of any race; Average household size: 2.39; Median age: 37.5; Age under 18: 25.6%; Age 65 and over: 19.7%; Males per 100 females: 95.0
Housing: Homeownership rate: 81.6%; Homeowner vacancy rate: 0.0%; Rental vacancy rate: 10.0%

RICHMOND (city). County seat. Covers a land area of 23.915 square miles and a water area of 0.157 square miles. Located at 39.83° N. Lat; 84.89° W. Long. Elevation is 981 feet.
History: Richmond was founded in 1805 by soldiers who had been with George Rogers Clark at the capture of Fort Sackville. They were joined by other settlers, many of them Quakers who founded Earlham College in 1847. Richmond was known for its greenhouses and rose cultivation, including the Richmond Rose hybrid developed in 1905.
Population: 36,812; Growth (since 2000): -5.9%; Density: 1,539.3 persons per square mile; Race: 83.9% White, 8.6% Black/African American, 1.1% Asian, 0.3% American Indian/Alaska Native, 0.1% Native Hawaiian/Other Pacific Islander, 4.0% Two or more races, 4.1% Hispanic of any race; Average household size: 2.29; Median age: 38.4; Age under 18: 22.1%; Age 65 and over: 16.5%; Males per 100 females: 91.8; Marriage status: 32.9% never married, 43.7% now married, 2.4% separated, 7.1% widowed, 16.3% divorced; Foreign born: 3.3%; Speak English only: 94.0%; With disability: 20.1%; Veterans: 10.8%; Ancestry: 19.4% German, 12.6% Irish, 10.4% English, 8.3% American, 3.7% Italian
Employment: 9.3% management, business, and financial, 2.8% computer, engineering, and science, 10.1% education, legal, community service, arts, and media, 6.1% healthcare practitioners, 25.0% service, 22.1% sales and office, 6.6% natural resources, construction, and maintenance, 17.9% production, transportation, and material moving
Income: Per capita: $18,796; Median household: $30,096; Average household: $43,936; Households with income of $100,000 or more: 8.1%; Poverty rate: 29.6%
Educational Attainment: High school diploma or higher: 80.5%; Bachelor's degree or higher: 17.8%; Graduate/professional degree or higher: 7.8%
School District(s)
Kenneth A Christmon Stemm Academy (KG-08)
 2012-13 Enrollment: 203 . . . . (765) 983-3709
Richmond Community Schools (PK-12)
 2012-13 Enrollment: 5,172 . . . . (765) 973-3300
Four-year College(s)
Bethany Theological Seminary (Private, Not-for-profit, Church of Brethren)
 Fall 2013 Enrollment: 60 . . . . (765) 983-1800
Earlham College (Private, Not-for-profit, Friends)
 Fall 2013 Enrollment: 1,159 . . . . (765) 983-1200
 2013-14 Tuition: In-state $41,450; Out-of-state $41,450
Indiana University-East (Public)
 Fall 2013 Enrollment: 4,456 . . . . (765) 973-8200
 2013-14 Tuition: In-state $6,639; Out-of-state $17,778
Vocational/Technical School(s)
PJ's College of Cosmetology-Richmond (Private, For-profit)
 Fall 2013 Enrollment: 37 . . . . (317) 846-8999
 2013-14 Tuition: $15,100
Housing: Homeownership rate: 56.2%; Median home value: $81,300; Median year structure built: 1954; Homeowner vacancy rate: 5.5%; Median gross rent: $614 per month; Rental vacancy rate: 12.4%
Health Insurance: 79.7% have insurance; 52.6% have private insurance; 39.5% have public insurance; 20.3% do not have insurance; 11.6% of children under 18 do not have insurance
Hospitals: Reid Hospital & Health Care Services (233 beds)
Newspapers: Palladium-Item (daily circulation 16800)
Transportation: Commute: 92.7% car, 0.7% public transportation, 3.0% walk, 2.1% work from home; Median travel time to work: 16.2 minutes
Airports: Richmond Municipal (general aviation)
Additional Information Contacts
City of Richmond . . . . (765) 983-7200
 http://www.richmondindiana.gov

SPRING GROVE (town). Covers a land area of 0.317 square miles and a water area of 0.001 square miles. Located at 39.85° N. Lat; 84.89° W. Long. Elevation is 984 feet.
Population: 344; Growth (since 2000): -10.9%; Density: 1,085.6 persons per square mile; Race: 89.2% White, 5.5% Black/African American, 1.2% Asian, 0.0% American Indian/Alaska Native, 0.0% Native Hawaiian/Other Pacific Islander, 4.1% Two or more races, 0.9% Hispanic of any race; Average household size: 2.17; Median age: 58.4; Age under 18: 15.4%; Age 65 and over: 40.7%; Males per 100 females: 73.7
Housing: Homeownership rate: 77.8%; Homeowner vacancy rate: 1.1%; Rental vacancy rate: 10.3%

WHITEWATER (town). Covers a land area of 0.080 square miles and a water area of 0 square miles. Located at 39.94° N. Lat; 84.83° W. Long. Elevation is 1,129 feet.
Population: 83; Growth (since 2000): 6.4%; Density: 1,039.9 persons per square mile; Race: 100.0% White, 0.0% Black/African American, 0.0% Asian, 0.0% American Indian/Alaska Native, 0.0% Native Hawaiian/Other Pacific Islander, 0.0% Two or more races, 0.0% Hispanic of any race; Average household size: 2.37; Median age: 38.5; Age under 18: 25.3%; Age 65 and over: 19.3%; Males per 100 females: 124.3
Housing: Homeownership rate: 80.0%; Homeowner vacancy rate: 0.0%; Rental vacancy rate: 0.0%

WILLIAMSBURG (unincorporated postal area)
ZCTA: 47393
Covers a land area of 37.210 square miles and a water area of 0.079 square miles. Located at 39.96° N. Lat; 85.00° W. Long. Elevation is 1,066 feet.
Population: 1,704; Growth (since 2000): 9.1%; Density: 45.8 persons per square mile; Race: 98.5% White, 0.5% Black/African American, 0.2% Asian, 0.1% American Indian/Alaska Native, 0.0% Native Hawaiian/Other Pacific Islander, 0.7% Two or more races, 0.5% Hispanic of any race; Average household size: 2.85; Median age: 39.0; Age under 18: 29.2%; Age 65 and over: 12.5%; Males per 100 females: 102.9
Housing: Homeownership rate: 83.3%; Homeowner vacancy rate: 1.2%; Rental vacancy rate: 6.5%

Wells County

Located in eastern Indiana; drained by the Wabash and Salamonie Rivers. Covers a land area of 368.087 square miles, a water area of 2.161 square miles, and is located in the Eastern Time Zone at 40.74° N. Lat., 85.21° W. Long. The county was founded in 1835. County seat is Bluffton.

Wells County is part of the Fort Wayne, IN Metropolitan Statistical Area. The entire metro area includes: Allen County, IN; Wells County, IN; Whitley County, IN

Weather Station: Bluffton 1 N — Elevation: 825 feet

	Jan	Feb	Mar	Apr	May	Jun	Jul	Aug	Sep	Oct	Nov	Dec
High	32	35	47	60	71	80	84	82	76	63	49	37
Low	17	19	28	39	50	60	63	61	53	41	32	22
Precip	2.1	2.1	2.5	3.4	4.5	4.0	4.3	3.6	3.0	2.8	3.1	2.7
Snow	7.3	6.7	3.3	0.7	0.0	0.0	tr	0.0	0.0	0.1	1.0	5.1

High and Low temperatures in degrees Fahrenheit; Precipitation and Snow in inches

Population: 27,636; Growth (since 2000): 0.1%; Density: 75.1 persons per square mile; Race: 97.3% White, 0.3% Black/African American, 0.4% Asian, 0.3% American Indian/Alaska Native, 0.0% Native Hawaiian/Other Pacific Islander, 0.9% two or more races, 2.0% Hispanic of any race; Average household size: 2.52; Median age: 40.2; Age under 18: 25.0%; Age 65 and over: 15.7%; Males per 100 females: 96.9; Marriage status: 21.5% never married, 58.8% now married, 1.6% separated, 7.5% widowed, 12.2% divorced; Foreign born: 1.2%; Speak English only: 96.8%; With disability: 12.3%; Veterans: 8.8%; Ancestry: 36.4% German, 12.6% American, 10.3% Irish, 9.7% English, 4.7% Swiss
Religion: Six largest groups: 8.0% Holiness, 7.1% European Free-Church, 7.0% Methodist/Pietist, 6.9% Baptist, 5.4% Non-denominational Protestant, 4.3% Lutheran
Economy: Unemployment rate: 4.1%; Leading industries: 16.5% other services (except public administration); 13.3% retail trade; 10.5% construction; Farms: 636 totaling 200,334 acres; Company size: 0 employ 1,000 or more persons, 1 employs 500 to 999 persons, 22 employ 100 to 499 persons, 607 employ less than 100 persons; Business ownership: n/a women-owned, n/a Black-owned, n/a Hispanic-owned, n/a Asian-owned
Employment: 11.5% management, business, and financial, 3.3% computer, engineering, and science, 7.8% education, legal, community service, arts, and media, 4.2% healthcare practitioners, 16.0% service, 23.3% sales and office, 11.3% natural resources, construction, and maintenance, 22.6% production, transportation, and material moving
Income: Per capita: $24,269; Median household: $48,136; Average household: $60,243; Households with income of $100,000 or more: 14.2%; Poverty rate: 10.7%
Educational Attainment: High school diploma or higher: 90.7%; Bachelor's degree or higher: 15.7%; Graduate/professional degree or higher: 5.3%
Housing: Homeownership rate: 78.8%; Median home value: $112,500; Median year structure built: 1968; Homeowner vacancy rate: 1.9%; Median gross rent: $577 per month; Rental vacancy rate: 9.5%
Vital Statistics: Birth rate: 131.2 per 10,000 population; Death rate: 83.8 per 10,000 population; Age-adjusted cancer mortality rate: 155.4 deaths per 100,000 population
Health Insurance: 88.5% have insurance; 72.5% have private insurance; 30.1% have public insurance; 11.5% do not have insurance; 6.5% of children under 18 do not have insurance
Health Care: Physicians: 10.5 per 10,000 population; Hospital beds: 28.5 per 10,000 population; Hospital admissions: 817.7 per 10,000 population
Transportation: Commute: 93.0% car, 0.1% public transportation, 1.6% walk, 3.3% work from home; Median travel time to work: 21.4 minutes
Presidential Election: 26.6% Obama, 71.6% Romney (2012)
National and State Parks: Ouabache State Park
Additional Information Contacts
Wells Government............................. (260) 824-6479
http://www.wellscounty.org

Wells County Communities

BLUFFTON (city). County seat. Covers a land area of 8.232 square miles and a water area of 0.129 square miles. Located at 40.74° N. Lat; 85.17° W. Long. Elevation is 827 feet.
History: Established in the mid-1800's, Bluffton was built on the bluffs overlooking the Wabash River.
Population: 9,897; Growth (since 2000): 3.8%; Density: 1,202.3 persons per square mile; Race: 96.0% White, 0.7% Black/African American, 0.5% Asian, 0.4% American Indian/Alaska Native, 0.0% Native Hawaiian/Other Pacific Islander, 1.1% Two or more races, 3.3% Hispanic of any race; Average household size: 2.34; Median age: 38.3; Age under 18: 24.6%; Age 65 and over: 16.9%; Males per 100 females: 92.3; Marriage status: 23.9% never married, 51.7% now married, 1.5% separated, 7.9% widowed, 16.4% divorced; Foreign born: 0.9%; Speak English only: 96.1%; With disability: 15.0%; Veterans: 9.0%; Ancestry: 29.4% German, 15.9% American, 9.0% Irish, 8.0% English, 4.5% Swiss
Employment: 10.1% management, business, and financial, 3.6% computer, engineering, and science, 9.2% education, legal, community service, arts, and media, 3.1% healthcare practitioners, 18.3% service, 21.9% sales and office, 10.4% natural resources, construction, and maintenance, 23.5% production, transportation, and material moving
Income: Per capita: $20,611; Median household: $39,245; Average household: $46,928; Households with income of $100,000 or more: 8.7%; Poverty rate: 16.7%
Educational Attainment: High school diploma or higher: 87.0%; Bachelor's degree or higher: 15.4%; Graduate/professional degree or higher: 5.9%

School District(s)
M S D Bluffton-Harrison (KG-12)
    2012-13 Enrollment: 1,473 .... (260) 824-2620
Northern Wells Com Schools (PK-12)
    2012-13 Enrollment: 2,394 .... (260) 622-4125
Housing: Homeownership rate: 67.8%; Median home value: $94,000; Median year structure built: 1967; Homeowner vacancy rate: 2.9%; Median gross rent: $532 per month; Rental vacancy rate: 10.3%
Health Insurance: 85.7% have insurance; 66.1% have private insurance; 36.2% have public insurance; 14.3% do not have insurance; 8.4% of children under 18 do not have insurance
Hospitals: Bluffton Regional Medical Center (79 beds)
Newspapers: News-Banner (daily circulation 4700)
Transportation: Commute: 92.7% car, 0.0% public transportation, 2.4% walk, 1.7% work from home; Median travel time to work: 18.4 minutes
Additional Information Contacts
City of Bluffton................................. (260) 824-1520
http://www.ci.bluffton.in.us

CRAIGVILLE (unincorporated postal area)
ZCTA: 46731
Covers a land area of 15.909 square miles and a water area of 0.029 square miles. Located at 40.79° N. Lat; 85.10° W. Long. Elevation is 850 feet.

Population: 559; Growth (since 2000): -14.1%; Density: 35.1 persons per square mile; Race: 98.7% White, 0.0% Black/African American, 0.0% Asian, 0.2% American Indian/Alaska Native, 0.0% Native Hawaiian/Other Pacific Islander, 0.5% Two or more races, 1.4% Hispanic of any race; Average household size: 2.78; Median age: 39.3; Age under 18: 27.5%; Age 65 and over: 12.0%; Males per 100 females: 104.0
Housing: Homeownership rate: 92.6%; Homeowner vacancy rate: 1.6%; Rental vacancy rate: 5.9%

KEYSTONE (unincorporated postal area)
ZCTA: 46759
Covers a land area of 29.605 square miles and a water area of 0.022 square miles. Located at 40.60° N. Lat; 85.18° W. Long. Elevation is 860 feet.
Population: 652; Growth (since 2000): -14.8%; Density: 22.0 persons per square mile; Race: 98.0% White, 0.0% Black/African American, 0.2% Asian, 0.9% American Indian/Alaska Native, 0.0% Native Hawaiian/Other Pacific Islander, 0.2% Two or more races, 0.9% Hispanic of any race; Average household size: 2.69; Median age: 40.4; Age under 18: 25.0%; Age 65 and over: 14.4%; Males per 100 females: 92.9
Housing: Homeownership rate: 88.0%; Homeowner vacancy rate: 0.0%; Rental vacancy rate: 0.0%

LIBERTY CENTER (unincorporated postal area)
ZCTA: 46766
Covers a land area of 20.262 square miles and a water area of 0.062 square miles. Located at 40.71° N. Lat; 85.28° W. Long. Elevation is 853 feet.
Population: 685; Growth (since 2000): 8.6%; Density: 33.8 persons per square mile; Race: 98.4% White, 0.0% Black/African American, 0.1% Asian, 0.3% American Indian/Alaska Native, 0.0% Native Hawaiian/Other Pacific Islander, 1.0% Two or more races, 1.2% Hispanic of any race; Average household size: 2.66; Median age: 37.8; Age under 18: 26.6%; Age 65 and over: 13.3%; Males per 100 females: 110.8
Housing: Homeownership rate: 87.3%; Homeowner vacancy rate: 1.3%; Rental vacancy rate: 2.8%

OSSIAN (town).
Covers a land area of 1.429 square miles and a water area of 0.008 square miles. Located at 40.88° N. Lat; 85.17° W. Long. Elevation is 840 feet.
History: Laid out 1850.
Population: 3,289; Growth (since 2000): 11.8%; Density: 2,301.8 persons per square mile; Race: 97.4% White, 0.2% Black/African American, 0.5% Asian, 0.1% American Indian/Alaska Native, 0.0% Native Hawaiian/Other Pacific Islander, 1.1% Two or more races, 1.4% Hispanic of any race; Average household size: 2.49; Median age: 37.4; Age under 18: 26.0%; Age 65 and over: 15.2%; Males per 100 females: 90.7; Marriage status: 24.4% never married, 53.4% now married, 0.7% separated, 10.0% widowed, 12.2% divorced; Foreign born: 0.6%; Speak English only: 98.0%; With disability: 11.9%; Veterans: 4.8%; Ancestry: 47.1% German, 14.6% Irish, 11.0% English, 10.1% American, 3.5% Swiss
Employment: 10.5% management, business, and financial, 1.8% computer, engineering, and science, 17.4% education, legal, community service, arts, and media, 1.1% healthcare practitioners, 24.8% service, 27.9% sales and office, 3.8% natural resources, construction, and maintenance, 12.7% production, transportation, and material moving
Income: Per capita: $20,443; Median household: $45,076; Average household: $51,802; Households with income of $100,000 or more: 10.2%; Poverty rate: 9.0%
Educational Attainment: High school diploma or higher: 92.6%; Bachelor's degree or higher: 19.9%; Graduate/professional degree or higher: 4.3%
School District(s)
Northern Wells Com Schools (PK-12)
    2012-13 Enrollment: 2,394 . . . . (260) 622-4125
Housing: Homeownership rate: 73.4%; Median home value: $109,500; Median year structure built: 1978; Homeowner vacancy rate: 2.1%; Median gross rent: $634 per month; Rental vacancy rate: 11.1%
Health Insurance: 87.5% have insurance; 73.3% have private insurance; 25.7% have public insurance; 12.5% do not have insurance; 9.4% of children under 18 do not have insurance
Newspapers: Ossian Journal (weekly circulation 700)

Transportation: Commute: 92.5% car, 0.0% public transportation, 0.8% walk, 1.0% work from home; Median travel time to work: 19.9 minutes
Additional Information Contacts
Town of Ossian . . . . (260) 622-4251
    http://www.ossianin.com

PONETO (town).
Covers a land area of 0.115 square miles and a water area of 0.001 square miles. Located at 40.66° N. Lat; 85.22° W. Long. Elevation is 850 feet.
Population: 166; Growth (since 2000): -30.8%; Density: 1,447.0 persons per square mile; Race: 99.4% White, 0.0% Black/African American, 0.0% Asian, 0.6% American Indian/Alaska Native, 0.0% Native Hawaiian/Other Pacific Islander, 0.0% Two or more races, 1.8% Hispanic of any race; Average household size: 2.41; Median age: 41.6; Age under 18: 20.5%; Age 65 and over: 13.9%; Males per 100 females: 93.0
School District(s)
Southern Wells Com Schools (KG-12)
    2012-13 Enrollment: 864 . . . . (765) 728-5537
Housing: Homeownership rate: 88.4%; Homeowner vacancy rate: 0.0%; Rental vacancy rate: 0.0%

UNIONDALE (town).
Covers a land area of 0.210 square miles and a water area of 0.002 square miles. Located at 40.83° N. Lat; 85.24° W. Long. Elevation is 814 feet.
History: Laid out 1883.
Population: 310; Growth (since 2000): 11.9%; Density: 1,477.1 persons per square mile; Race: 96.8% White, 0.3% Black/African American, 1.9% Asian, 0.3% American Indian/Alaska Native, 0.0% Native Hawaiian/Other Pacific Islander, 0.6% Two or more races, 1.0% Hispanic of any race; Average household size: 2.61; Median age: 37.4; Age under 18: 25.2%; Age 65 and over: 12.3%; Males per 100 females: 96.2
Housing: Homeownership rate: 88.2%; Homeowner vacancy rate: 1.9%; Rental vacancy rate: 0.0%

VERA CRUZ (town).
Covers a land area of 0.101 square miles and a water area of <.001 square miles. Located at 40.70° N. Lat; 85.08° W. Long. Elevation is 827 feet.
History: Laid out 1848.
Population: 80; Growth (since 2000): 45.5%; Density: 788.6 persons per square mile; Race: 93.8% White, 0.0% Black/African American, 0.0% Asian, 0.0% American Indian/Alaska Native, 0.0% Native Hawaiian/Other Pacific Islander, 1.3% Two or more races, 5.0% Hispanic of any race; Average household size: 2.58; Median age: 28.0; Age under 18: 27.5%; Age 65 and over: 10.0%; Males per 100 females: 100.0
Housing: Homeownership rate: 61.3%; Homeowner vacancy rate: 5.0%; Rental vacancy rate: 0.0%

ZANESVILLE (town).
Covers a land area of 0.821 square miles and a water area of 0.010 square miles. Located at 40.92° N. Lat; 85.28° W. Long. Elevation is 814 feet.
Population: 600; Growth (since 2000): -0.3%; Density: 730.6 persons per square mile; Race: 98.5% White, 0.2% Black/African American, 0.0% Asian, 0.2% American Indian/Alaska Native, 0.0% Native Hawaiian/Other Pacific Islander, 1.0% Two or more races, 1.5% Hispanic of any race; Average household size: 2.62; Median age: 38.3; Age under 18: 27.2%; Age 65 and over: 12.8%; Males per 100 females: 98.7
Housing: Homeownership rate: 86.0%; Homeowner vacancy rate: 2.0%; Rental vacancy rate: 3.0%

White County

Located in northwestern Indiana; bounded on the east by the Tippecanoe River; drained by the Tippecanoe River. Covers a land area of 505.125 square miles, a water area of 3.555 square miles, and is located in the Eastern Time Zone at 40.75° N. Lat., 86.86° W. Long. The county was founded in 1834. County seat is Monticello.
Population: 24,643; Growth (since 2000): -2.5%; Density: 48.8 persons per square mile; Race: 93.9% White, 0.3% Black/African American, 0.4% Asian, 0.3% American Indian/Alaska Native, 0.0% Native Hawaiian/Other Pacific Islander, 1.4% two or more races, 7.1% Hispanic of any race; Average household size: 2.50; Median age: 41.9; Age under 18: 24.2%; Age 65 and over: 17.2%; Males per 100 females: 96.8; Marriage status: 20.1% never married, 61.7% now married, 1.2% separated, 7.2% widowed, 11.0% divorced; Foreign born: 3.5%; Speak English only: 94.0%;

With disability: 15.2%; Veterans: 11.1%; Ancestry: 26.9% German, 11.6% Irish, 10.2% English, 8.5% American, 4.1% Dutch
Religion: Six largest groups: 12.1% Baptist, 10.0% Catholicism, 7.7% Methodist/Pietist, 4.2% Non-denominational Protestant, 3.4% Presbyterian-Reformed, 3.4% Lutheran
Economy: Unemployment rate: 4.9%; Leading industries: 16.0% retail trade; 11.2% construction; 10.4% accommodation and food services; Farms: 631 totaling 288,195 acres; Company size: 0 employ 1,000 or more persons, 1 employs 500 to 999 persons, 14 employ 100 to 499 persons, 592 employ less than 100 persons; Business ownership: 549 women-owned, n/a Black-owned, n/a Hispanic-owned, n/a Asian-owned
Employment: 10.9% management, business, and financial, 2.5% computer, engineering, and science, 7.7% education, legal, community service, arts, and media, 5.1% healthcare practitioners, 16.0% service, 24.7% sales and office, 11.5% natural resources, construction, and maintenance, 21.5% production, transportation, and material moving
Income: Per capita: $23,666; Median household: $51,444; Average household: $60,695; Households with income of $100,000 or more: 13.0%; Poverty rate: 10.8%
Educational Attainment: High school diploma or higher: 89.2%; Bachelor's degree or higher: 15.4%; Graduate/professional degree or higher: 5.6%
Housing: Homeownership rate: 76.3%; Median home value: $109,800; Median year structure built: 1968; Homeowner vacancy rate: 3.4%; Median gross rent: $687 per month; Rental vacancy rate: 10.9%
Vital Statistics: Birth rate: 120.6 per 10,000 population; Death rate: 111.6 per 10,000 population; Age-adjusted cancer mortality rate: 208.4 deaths per 100,000 population
Health Insurance: 87.9% have insurance; 72.1% have private insurance; 30.0% have public insurance; 12.1% do not have insurance; 11.8% of children under 18 do not have insurance
Health Care: Physicians: 6.5 per 10,000 population; Hospital beds: 10.2 per 10,000 population; Hospital admissions: 484.6 per 10,000 population
Transportation: Commute: 93.0% car, 0.2% public transportation, 2.0% walk, 3.7% work from home; Median travel time to work: 23.3 minutes
Presidential Election: 36.7% Obama, 60.3% Romney (2012)
Additional Information Contacts
White Government . . . . (574) 583-7755
http://www.whitecountyindiana.us

White County Communities

BROOKSTON (town). Covers a land area of 0.655 square miles and a water area of 0 square miles. Located at 40.60° N. Lat; 86.87° W. Long. Elevation is 682 feet.
Population: 1,554; Growth (since 2000): -9.5%; Density: 2,371.4 persons per square mile; Race: 98.0% White, 0.0% Black/African American, 0.2% Asian, 0.1% American Indian/Alaska Native, 0.1% Native Hawaiian/Other Pacific Islander, 1.2% Two or more races, 2.6% Hispanic of any race; Average household size: 2.49; Median age: 37.6; Age under 18: 26.6%; Age 65 and over: 11.9%; Males per 100 females: 86.6
School District(s)
Frontier School Corporation (KG-12)
    2012-13 Enrollment: 751 . . . . (219) 984-5009
Housing: Homeownership rate: 73.7%; Homeowner vacancy rate: 3.6%; Rental vacancy rate: 11.2%

BUFFALO (CDP). Covers a land area of 2.372 square miles and a water area of 0.165 square miles. Located at 40.89° N. Lat; 86.74° W. Long. Elevation is 666 feet.
Population: 692; Growth (since 2000): 3.0%; Density: 291.8 persons per square mile; Race: 96.4% White, 0.0% Black/African American, 0.0% Asian, 0.3% American Indian/Alaska Native, 0.0% Native Hawaiian/Other Pacific Islander, 1.3% Two or more races, 4.9% Hispanic of any race; Average household size: 2.42; Median age: 47.4; Age under 18: 18.9%; Age 65 and over: 17.9%; Males per 100 females: 103.5
Housing: Homeownership rate: 82.6%; Homeowner vacancy rate: 4.4%; Rental vacancy rate: 19.4%

BURNETTSVILLE (town). Covers a land area of 0.748 square miles and a water area of 0 square miles. Located at 40.76° N. Lat; 86.59° W. Long. Elevation is 712 feet.
Population: 346; Growth (since 2000): -7.2%; Density: 462.5 persons per square mile; Race: 98.3% White, 0.3% Black/African American, 0.3% Asian, 0.0% American Indian/Alaska Native, 0.0% Native Hawaiian/Other Pacific Islander, 1.2% Two or more races, 0.0% Hispanic of any race; Average household size: 2.26; Median age: 42.8; Age under 18: 21.4%; Age 65 and over: 17.1%; Males per 100 females: 87.0
School District(s)
Twin Lakes School Corp (PK-12)
    2012-13 Enrollment: 2,473 . . . . (574) 583-7211
Housing: Homeownership rate: 79.1%; Homeowner vacancy rate: 3.9%; Rental vacancy rate: 5.9%

CHALMERS (town). Covers a land area of 0.249 square miles and a water area of 0 square miles. Located at 40.66° N. Lat; 86.87° W. Long. Elevation is 712 feet.
Population: 508; Growth (since 2000): -1.0%; Density: 2,043.3 persons per square mile; Race: 97.0% White, 0.0% Black/African American, 0.2% Asian, 0.0% American Indian/Alaska Native, 0.0% Native Hawaiian/Other Pacific Islander, 1.0% Two or more races, 2.2% Hispanic of any race; Average household size: 2.50; Median age: 40.1; Age under 18: 25.0%; Age 65 and over: 13.2%; Males per 100 females: 96.1
School District(s)
Frontier School Corporation (KG-12)
    2012-13 Enrollment: 751 . . . . (219) 984-5009
Housing: Homeownership rate: 81.3%; Homeowner vacancy rate: 2.4%; Rental vacancy rate: 7.3%

IDAVILLE (CDP). Covers a land area of 5.836 square miles and a water area of 0 square miles. Located at 40.76° N. Lat; 86.65° W. Long. Elevation is 715 feet.
Population: 461; Growth (since 2000): n/a; Density: 79.0 persons per square mile; Race: 98.7% White, 0.2% Black/African American, 0.0% Asian, 0.0% American Indian/Alaska Native, 0.0% Native Hawaiian/Other Pacific Islander, 1.1% Two or more races, 4.8% Hispanic of any race; Average household size: 2.56; Median age: 40.6; Age under 18: 23.9%; Age 65 and over: 15.4%; Males per 100 females: 97.0
Housing: Homeownership rate: 80.0%; Homeowner vacancy rate: 2.0%; Rental vacancy rate: 2.6%

MONON (town). Covers a land area of 0.564 square miles and a water area of 0 square miles. Located at 40.86° N. Lat; 86.88° W. Long. Elevation is 679 feet.
History: Laid out 1853, incorporated 1879.
Population: 1,777; Growth (since 2000): 2.5%; Density: 3,150.8 persons per square mile; Race: 77.2% White, 0.6% Black/African American, 0.2% Asian, 0.4% American Indian/Alaska Native, 0.0% Native Hawaiian/Other Pacific Islander, 2.9% Two or more races, 28.4% Hispanic of any race; Average household size: 2.96; Median age: 31.8; Age under 18: 32.9%; Age 65 and over: 12.3%; Males per 100 females: 98.1
School District(s)
North White School Corp (PK-12)
    2012-13 Enrollment: 893 . . . . (219) 253-6618
Housing: Homeownership rate: 66.7%; Homeowner vacancy rate: 3.4%; Rental vacancy rate: 15.8%
Newspapers: The News & Review (weekly circulation 1300)

MONTICELLO (city). County seat. Covers a land area of 3.470 square miles and a water area of 0.216 square miles. Located at 40.75° N. Lat; 86.77° W. Long. Elevation is 676 feet.
History: Monticello was established as a resort town on the Tippecanoe River. When the Indiana Hydroelectric Power Company built dams across the river in 1923 and 1925, several lakes were formed which provided recreation sites.
Population: 5,378; Growth (since 2000): -6.0%; Density: 1,550.1 persons per square mile; Race: 90.8% White, 0.4% Black/African American, 0.8% Asian, 0.4% American Indian/Alaska Native, 0.0% Native Hawaiian/Other Pacific Islander, 2.1% Two or more races, 12.5% Hispanic of any race; Average household size: 2.33; Median age: 40.4; Age under 18: 24.0%; Age 65 and over: 21.1%; Males per 100 females: 89.9; Marriage status: 21.4% never married, 54.4% now married, 1.8% separated, 12.8% widowed, 11.4% divorced; Foreign born: 3.9%; Speak English only: 92.4%; With disability: 17.9%; Veterans: 11.1%; Ancestry: 28.5% German, 17.8% English, 12.2% Irish, 8.5% American, 4.1% French
Employment: 9.7% management, business, and financial, 3.0% computer, engineering, and science, 9.2% education, legal, community service, arts, and media, 5.7% healthcare practitioners, 17.6% service, 25.1% sales and office, 8.4% natural resources, construction, and maintenance, 21.3% production, transportation, and material moving

Income: Per capita: $21,736; Median household: $44,350; Average household: $52,395; Households with income of $100,000 or more: 9.3%; Poverty rate: 9.6%
Educational Attainment: High school diploma or higher: 86.8%; Bachelor's degree or higher: 18.7%; Graduate/professional degree or higher: 7.7%

School District(s)
Twin Lakes School Corp (PK-12)
    2012-13 Enrollment: 2,473 . . . . (574) 583-7211
Housing: Homeownership rate: 59.9%; Median home value: $96,300; Median year structure built: 1960; Homeowner vacancy rate: 3.9%; Median gross rent: $677 per month; Rental vacancy rate: 9.4%
Health Insurance: 87.4% have insurance; 69.8% have private insurance; 31.2% have public insurance; 12.6% do not have insurance; 14.3% of children under 18 do not have insurance
Hospitals: Indiana University Health White Memorial Hospital (25 beds)
Newspapers: Herald Journal (daily circulation 5100)
Transportation: Commute: 92.7% car, 0.4% public transportation, 2.0% walk, 2.8% work from home; Median travel time to work: 18.9 minutes
Additional Information Contacts
City of Monticello . . . . (574) 583-5712
    http://www.monticelloin.gov

NORWAY
NORWAY (CDP). Covers a land area of 0.894 square miles and a water area of 0.064 square miles. Located at 40.77° N. Lat; 86.77° W. Long. Elevation is 633 feet.
Population: 386; Growth (since 2000): -11.7%; Density: 431.9 persons per square mile; Race: 97.9% White, 0.0% Black/African American, 0.8% Asian, 0.3% American Indian/Alaska Native, 0.0% Native Hawaiian/Other Pacific Islander, 0.3% Two or more races, 3.1% Hispanic of any race; Average household size: 2.30; Median age: 45.5; Age under 18: 22.5%; Age 65 and over: 18.9%; Males per 100 females: 96.9
Housing: Homeownership rate: 69.7%; Homeowner vacancy rate: 10.0%; Rental vacancy rate: 12.1%

REYNOLDS
REYNOLDS (town). Covers a land area of 0.553 square miles and a water area of 0 square miles. Located at 40.75° N. Lat; 86.87° W. Long. Elevation is 699 feet.
Population: 533; Growth (since 2000): -2.6%; Density: 963.0 persons per square mile; Race: 91.4% White, 0.2% Black/African American, 0.0% Asian, 2.1% American Indian/Alaska Native, 0.0% Native Hawaiian/Other Pacific Islander, 1.1% Two or more races, 9.9% Hispanic of any race; Average household size: 2.48; Median age: 38.8; Age under 18: 24.4%; Age 65 and over: 16.1%; Males per 100 females: 89.7
Housing: Homeownership rate: 73.9%; Homeowner vacancy rate: 2.5%; Rental vacancy rate: 21.1%

WOLCOTT
WOLCOTT (town). Covers a land area of 0.592 square miles and a water area of 0 square miles. Located at 40.76° N. Lat; 87.04° W. Long. Elevation is 718 feet.
History: Laid out 1861.
Population: 1,001; Growth (since 2000): 1.2%; Density: 1,690.3 persons per square mile; Race: 95.3% White, 0.3% Black/African American, 0.3% Asian, 0.1% American Indian/Alaska Native, 0.0% Native Hawaiian/Other Pacific Islander, 2.9% Two or more races, 2.6% Hispanic of any race; Average household size: 2.60; Median age: 39.4; Age under 18: 26.2%; Age 65 and over: 17.4%; Males per 100 females: 98.6

School District(s)
Tri-County School Corp (KG-12)
    2012-13 Enrollment: 762 . . . . (219) 279-2418
Housing: Homeownership rate: 73.0%; Homeowner vacancy rate: 3.4%; Rental vacancy rate: 11.8%
Newspapers: The New Wolcott Enterprise (weekly circulation 700)

Whitley County

Located in northeastern Indiana; drained by the Eel River. Covers a land area of 335.569 square miles, a water area of 2.345 square miles, and is located in the Eastern Time Zone at 41.14° N. Lat., 85.50° W. Long. The county was founded in 1835. County seat is Columbia City.

Whitley County is part of the Fort Wayne, IN Metropolitan Statistical Area. The entire metro area includes: Allen County, IN; Wells County, IN; Whitley County, IN

Weather Station: Columbia City										Elevation: 850 feet		
	Jan	Feb	Mar	Apr	May	Jun	Jul	Aug	Sep	Oct	Nov	Dec
High	32	35	46	59	70	79	83	81	75	62	49	36
Low	16	18	27	37	48	58	61	60	52	40	31	21
Precip	2.3	1.9	2.8	3.5	4.1	4.4	4.0	3.9	3.3	3.1	3.3	2.9
Snow	8.8	6.7	3.5	0.7	0.0	0.0	0.0	0.0	0.0	0.2	1.2	6.4

High and Low temperatures in degrees Fahrenheit; Precipitation and Snow in inches

Population: 33,292; Growth (since 2000): 8.4%; Density: 99.2 persons per square mile; Race: 97.6% White, 0.3% Black/African American, 0.3% Asian, 0.3% American Indian/Alaska Native, 0.0% Native Hawaiian/Other Pacific Islander, 1.1% two or more races, 1.5% Hispanic of any race; Average household size: 2.53; Median age: 40.1; Age under 18: 24.6%; Age 65 and over: 14.0%; Males per 100 females: 98.9; Marriage status: 23.3% never married, 57.8% now married, 1.1% separated, 5.8% widowed, 13.1% divorced; Foreign born: 1.0%; Speak English only: 97.8%; With disability: 13.0%; Veterans: 10.4%; Ancestry: 33.0% German, 13.0% Irish, 10.8% American, 10.0% English, 3.3% French
Religion: Six largest groups: 8.0% Methodist/Pietist, 6.4% Catholicism, 5.8% Presbyterian-Reformed, 5.0% Lutheran, 4.4% Holiness, 3.0% Non-denominational Protestant
Economy: Unemployment rate: 4.4%; Leading industries: 15.9% retail trade; 14.3% other services (except public administration); 10.1% manufacturing; Farms: 710 totaling 140,099 acres; Company size: 0 employ 1,000 or more persons, 1 employs 500 to 999 persons, 17 employ 100 to 499 persons, 666 employ less than 100 persons; Business ownership: n/a women-owned, n/a Black-owned, n/a Hispanic-owned, n/a Asian-owned
Employment: 9.6% management, business, and financial, 3.6% computer, engineering, and science, 6.8% education, legal, community service, arts, and media, 4.2% healthcare practitioners, 14.8% service, 23.5% sales and office, 9.0% natural resources, construction, and maintenance, 28.4% production, transportation, and material moving
Income: Per capita: $24,613; Median household: $51,914; Average household: $61,532; Households with income of $100,000 or more: 14.7%; Poverty rate: 8.2%
Educational Attainment: High school diploma or higher: 90.4%; Bachelor's degree or higher: 16.7%; Graduate/professional degree or higher: 6.3%
Housing: Homeownership rate: 82.3%; Median home value: $126,300; Median year structure built: 1973; Homeowner vacancy rate: 2.0%; Median gross rent: $631 per month; Rental vacancy rate: 9.5%
Vital Statistics: Birth rate: 108.4 per 10,000 population; Death rate: 83.5 per 10,000 population; Age-adjusted cancer mortality rate: 216.7 deaths per 100,000 population
Health Insurance: 89.9% have insurance; 74.7% have private insurance; 27.2% have public insurance; 10.1% do not have insurance; 4.2% of children under 18 do not have insurance
Health Care: Physicians: 6.9 per 10,000 population; Hospital beds: 29.1 per 10,000 population; Hospital admissions: 482.0 per 10,000 population
Air Quality Index: 64.9% good, 34.8% moderate, 0.3% unhealthy for sensitive individuals, 0.0% unhealthy (percent of days)
Transportation: Commute: 94.0% car, 0.3% public transportation, 1.3% walk, 3.6% work from home; Median travel time to work: 24.0 minutes
Presidential Election: 29.5% Obama, 68.4% Romney (2012)
Additional Information Contacts
Whitley Government . . . . (260) 248-3140
    http://www.whitleygov.com

Whitley County Communities

CHURUBUSCO (town). Covers a land area of 0.902 square miles and a water area of 0 square miles. Located at 41.23° N. Lat; 85.32° W. Long. Elevation is 896 feet.
History: Churubusco got its name from a Mexican town where American forces won a battle during the war with Mexico.
Population: 1,796; Growth (since 2000): 7.8%; Density: 1,990.8 persons per square mile; Race: 97.8% White, 0.1% Black/African American, 0.2% Asian, 0.3% American Indian/Alaska Native, 0.0% Native Hawaiian/Other Pacific Islander, 1.2% Two or more races, 2.1% Hispanic of any race; Average household size: 2.54; Median age: 33.9; Age under 18: 27.1%; Age 65 and over: 11.7%; Males per 100 females: 93.3

School District(s)
Smith-Green Community Schools (KG-12)
    2012-13 Enrollment: 1,207 . . . . (260) 693-2007

Housing: Homeownership rate: 79.3%; Homeowner vacancy rate: 2.6%; Rental vacancy rate: 5.8%
Newspapers: The News (weekly circulation 2200)

COLUMBIA CITY (city). County seat. Covers a land area of 5.582 square miles and a water area of 0.021 square miles. Located at 41.16° N. Lat; 85.48° W. Long. Elevation is 860 feet.
History: Columbia City was the home of Thomas Riley Marshall (1854-1925), Vice-President under Woodrow Wilson, governor of Indiana from 1909-1913, and author of the statement, "What this country really needs is a good five-cent cigar." Also from Columbia City was historical novelist Lloyd C. Douglas, who was born here in 1877.
Population: 8,750; Growth (since 2000): 23.6%; Density: 1,567.6 persons per square mile; Race: 96.7% White, 0.5% Black/African American, 0.5% Asian, 0.3% American Indian/Alaska Native, 0.0% Native Hawaiian/Other Pacific Islander, 1.4% Two or more races, 2.2% Hispanic of any race; Average household size: 2.32; Median age: 36.1; Age under 18: 24.9%; Age 65 and over: 15.3%; Males per 100 females: 90.8; Marriage status: 27.5% never married, 46.6% now married, 1.2% separated, 8.2% widowed, 17.7% divorced; Foreign born: 1.3%; Speak English only: 97.8%; With disability: 18.0%; Veterans: 10.0%; Ancestry: 28.6% German, 12.7% Irish, 10.7% American, 8.7% English, 3.3% Italian
Employment: 5.4% management, business, and financial, 2.7% computer, engineering, and science, 4.5% education, legal, community service, arts, and media, 6.3% healthcare practitioners, 19.3% service, 26.0% sales and office, 5.4% natural resources, construction, and maintenance, 30.3% production, transportation, and material moving
Income: Per capita: $21,251; Median household: $39,916; Average household: $48,771; Households with income of $100,000 or more: 8.7%; Poverty rate: 14.4%
Educational Attainment: High school diploma or higher: 83.9%; Bachelor's degree or higher: 15.4%; Graduate/professional degree or higher: 6.7%

School District(s)
Whitley County Cons Schools (PK-12)
    2012-13 Enrollment: 3,574 . . . . (260) 244-5771
Housing: Homeownership rate: 67.2%; Median home value: $94,700; Median year structure built: 1974; Homeowner vacancy rate: 2.8%; Median gross rent: $631 per month; Rental vacancy rate: 9.0%
Health Insurance: 86.7% have insurance; 62.6% have private insurance; 39.2% have public insurance; 13.3% do not have insurance; 4.4% of children under 18 do not have insurance
Hospitals: Parkview Whitley Hospital (45 beds)
Safety: Violent crime rate: 4.5 per 10,000 population; Property crime rate: 159.3 per 10,000 population
Newspapers: Post & Mail (daily circulation 4100)
Transportation: Commute: 94.0% car, 0.5% public transportation, 2.7% walk, 1.6% work from home; Median travel time to work: 20.7 minutes
Additional Information Contacts

City of Columbia City. . . . . (260) 248-5100
http://www.columbiacity.net

LARWILL (town). Covers a land area of 0.223 square miles and a water area of 0 square miles. Located at 41.18° N. Lat; 85.62° W. Long. Elevation is 965 feet.
History: Laid out 1854.
Population: 283; Growth (since 2000): 0.4%; Density: 1,267.4 persons per square mile; Race: 98.9% White, 0.0% Black/African American, 0.0% Asian, 0.0% American Indian/Alaska Native, 0.0% Native Hawaiian/Other Pacific Islander, 1.1% Two or more races, 0.0% Hispanic of any race; Average household size: 2.83; Median age: 35.5; Age under 18: 26.1%; Age 65 and over: 11.0%; Males per 100 females: 96.5

School District(s)
Whitko Community School Corp (PK-12)
    2012-13 Enrollment: 1,714 . . . . (574) 594-2658
Housing: Homeownership rate: 82.0%; Homeowner vacancy rate: 5.6%; Rental vacancy rate: 41.9%

SOUTH WHITLEY (town). Covers a land area of 0.912 square miles and a water area of 0 square miles. Located at 41.08° N. Lat; 85.63° W. Long. Elevation is 804 feet.
History: Laid out 1837.
Population: 1,751; Growth (since 2000): -1.7%; Density: 1,920.8 persons per square mile; Race: 98.0% White, 0.2% Black/African American, 0.2% Asian, 0.1% American Indian/Alaska Native, 0.0% Native Hawaiian/Other Pacific Islander, 1.1% Two or more races, 1.9% Hispanic of any race; Average household size: 2.39; Median age: 37.6; Age under 18: 25.0%; Age 65 and over: 14.9%; Males per 100 females: 93.3

School District(s)
Whitko Community School Corp (PK-12)
    2012-13 Enrollment: 1,714 . . . . (574) 594-2658
Housing: Homeownership rate: 74.4%; Homeowner vacancy rate: 4.1%; Rental vacancy rate: 13.3%
Safety: Violent crime rate: 5.8 per 10,000 population; Property crime rate: 185.2 per 10,000 population
Newspapers: Tribune-News (weekly circulation 1500)

TRI-LAKES (CDP). Covers a land area of 3.417 square miles and a water area of 0.604 square miles. Located at 41.25° N. Lat; 85.45° W. Long. Elevation is 938 feet.
Population: 1,421; Growth (since 2000): -63.8%; Density: 415.8 persons per square mile; Race: 97.8% White, 0.1% Black/African American, 0.1% Asian, 0.2% American Indian/Alaska Native, 0.0% Native Hawaiian/Other Pacific Islander, 1.5% Two or more races, 1.1% Hispanic of any race; Average household size: 2.29; Median age: 48.6; Age under 18: 19.4%; Age 65 and over: 15.8%; Males per 100 females: 111.5
Housing: Homeownership rate: 88.5%; Homeowner vacancy rate: 2.6%; Rental vacancy rate: 3.8%

Aberdeen (CDP) Porter County, 160
Adams County, 44
Advance (town) Boone County, 52
Akron (town) Fulton County, 83
Alamo (town) Montgomery County, 145
Albany (town) Delaware County, 71
Albion (town) Noble County, 151
Alexandria (city) Madison County, 132
Alfordsville (town) Daviess County, 64
Allen County, 45
Alton (town) Crawford County, 63
Altona (town) DeKalb County, 69
Ambia (town) Benton County, 50
Amboy (town) Miami County, 142
Americus (CDP) Tippecanoe County, 186
Amo (town) Hendricks County, 97
Anderson (city) Madison County, 132
Andrews (town) Huntington County, 103
Angola (city) Steuben County, 182
Arcadia (town) Hamilton County, 90
Arcola (unincorporated) Allen County, 45
Argos (town) Marshall County, 139
Arlington (CDP) Rush County, 171
Ashley (town) DeKalb County, 69
Atlanta (town) Hamilton County, 91
Attica (city) Fountain County, 80
Atwood (unincorporated) Kosciusko County, 117
Auburn (city) DeKalb County, 70
Aurora (city) Dearborn County, 66
Austin (city) Scott County, 176
Avilla (town) Noble County, 151
Avoca (CDP) Lawrence County, 130
Avon (town) Hendricks County, 97
Bainbridge (town) Putnam County, 166
Bargersville (town) Johnson County, 112
Bartholomew County, 48
Bass Lake (CDP) Starke County, 180
Batesville (city) Ripley County, 170
Bath (unincorporated) Franklin County, 81
Battle Ground (town) Tippecanoe County, 186
Bedford (city) Lawrence County, 130
Beech Grove (city) Marion County, 135
Bennington (unincorporated) Switzerland County, 185
Benton County, 49
Berne (city) Adams County, 44
Bethany (town) Morgan County, 147
Beverly Shores (town) Porter County, 160
Bicknell (city) Knox County, 115
Birdseye (town) Dubois County, 73
Blackford County, 50
Blanford (CDP) Vermillion County, 192
Bloomfield (town) Greene County, 89
Bloomingdale (town) Parke County, 156
Bloomington (city) Monroe County, 144
Blountsville (town) Henry County, 99
Bluffton (city) Wells County, 204
Boggstown (unincorporated) Shelby County, 177
Boone County, 51
Boonville (city) Warrick County, 198
Borden (town) Clark County, 57
Boston (town) Wayne County, 202
Boswell (town) Benton County, 50

Bourbon (town) Marshall County, 139
Bowling Green (unincorporated) Owen County, 155
Branchville (unincorporated) Perry County, 157
Brazil (city) Clay County, 60
Bremen (town) Marshall County, 140
Bridgeton (unincorporated) Parke County, 156
Bright (CDP) Dearborn County, 66
Bringhurst (unincorporated) Carroll County, 54
Bristol (town) Elkhart County, 75
Bristow (unincorporated) Perry County, 158
Brook (town) Newton County, 149
Brooklyn (town) Morgan County, 147
Brooksburg (town) Jefferson County, 108
Brookston (town) White County, 206
Brookville (town) Franklin County, 82
Brown County, 53
Brownsburg (town) Hendricks County, 97
Brownstown (town) Jackson County, 104
Brownsville (unincorporated) Union County, 189
Bruceville (town) Knox County, 115
Bryant (town) Jay County, 107
Buck Creek (CDP) Tippecanoe County, 186
Buffalo (CDP) White County, 206
Bunker Hill (town) Miami County, 142
Burket (town) Kosciusko County, 117
Burlington (town) Carroll County, 55
Burnettsville (town) White County, 206
Burns City (CDP) Martin County, 141
Burns Harbor (town) Porter County, 160
Butler (city) DeKalb County, 70
Butlerville (CDP) Jennings County, 110
Cadiz (town) Henry County, 100
Cambridge City (town) Wayne County, 202
Camby (unincorporated) Morgan County, 148
Camden (town) Carroll County, 55
Campbellsburg (town) Washington County, 200
Canaan (CDP) Jefferson County, 109
Cannelburg (town) Daviess County, 64
Cannelton (city) Perry County, 158
Carbon (town) Clay County, 60
Carlisle (town) Sullivan County, 183
Carmel (city) Hamilton County, 91
Carroll County, 54
Carthage (town) Rush County, 171
Cass County, 55
Cayuga (town) Vermillion County, 192
Cedar Grove (town) Franklin County, 82
Cedar Lake (town) Lake County, 120
Celestine (unincorporated) Dubois County, 73
Center Point (town) Clay County, 60
Centerpoint (unincorporated) Clay County, 60
Centerville (town) Wayne County, 202
Central (unincorporated) Harrison County, 95
Chalmers (town) White County, 206
Chandler (town) Warrick County, 199
Charlestown (city) Clark County, 57
Charlottesville (unincorporated) Hancock County, 93
Chesterfield (town) Madison County, 133
Chesterton (town) Porter County, 161

Chrisney (town) Spencer County, 178
Churubusco (town) Whitley County, 207
Cicero (town) Hamilton County, 91
Clark County, 57
Clarks Hill (town) Tippecanoe County, 186
Clarksburg (CDP) Decatur County, 68
Clarksville (town) Clark County, 58
Clay City (town) Clay County, 60
Clay County, 59
Claypool (town) Kosciusko County, 117
Clayton (town) Hendricks County, 98
Clear Lake (town) Steuben County, 182
Clermont (town) Marion County, 135
Clifford (town) Bartholomew County, 48
Clinton (city) Vermillion County, 192
Clinton County, 61
Cloverdale (town) Putnam County, 166
Coal City (unincorporated) Owen County, 155
Coalmont (CDP) Clay County, 61
Coatesville (town) Hendricks County, 98
Colburn (CDP) Tippecanoe County, 186
Colfax (town) Clinton County, 61
Collegeville (CDP) Jasper County, 106
Columbia City (city) Whitley County, 208
Columbus (city) Bartholomew County, 48
Commiskey (unincorporated) Jennings County, 110
Connersville (city) Fayette County, 78
Converse (town) Miami County, 142
Cordry Sweetwater Lakes (CDP) Brown County, 53
Corunna (town) DeKalb County, 70
Cory (unincorporated) Clay County, 61
Corydon (town) Harrison County, 95
Country Club Heights (town) Madison County, 133
Country Squire Lakes (CDP) Jennings County, 111
Covington (city) Fountain County, 80
Craigville (unincorporated) Wells County, 204
Crandall (town) Harrison County, 95
Crane (town) Martin County, 141
Crawford County, 62
Crawfordsville (city) Montgomery County, 146
Cromwell (town) Noble County, 151
Cross Plains (unincorporated) Ripley County, 170
Crothersville (town) Jackson County, 104
Crown Point (city) Lake County, 121
Crows Nest (town) Marion County, 135
Culver (town) Marshall County, 140
Cumberland (town) Marion County, 136
Cutler (unincorporated) Carroll County, 55
Cynthiana (town) Posey County, 164
Dale (town) Spencer County, 179
Daleville (town) Delaware County, 71
Dana (town) Vermillion County, 192
Danville (town) Hendricks County, 98
Darlington (town) Montgomery County, 146
Darmstadt (town) Vanderburgh County, 190
Daviess County, 64
Dayton (town) Tippecanoe County, 186
De Motte (town) Jasper County, 106
Dearborn County, 65
Decatur (city) Adams County, 44

CDP = Census Designated Place

Place Name Index

Decatur County, 68
Decker (town) Knox County, 115
DeKalb County, 69
Delaware County, 71
Delphi (city) Carroll County, 55
Denver (town) Miami County, 142
Depauw (unincorporated) Harrison County, 95
Deputy (CDP) Jefferson County, 109
Derby (unincorporated) Perry County, 158
Dillsboro (town) Dearborn County, 66
Dover Hill (CDP) Martin County, 141
Dresser (CDP) Vigo County, 193
Dublin (town) Wayne County, 202
Dubois (CDP) Dubois County, 73
Dubois County, 73
Dugger (town) Sullivan County, 183
Dune Acres (town) Porter County, 161
Dunkirk (city) Jay County, 107
Dunlap (CDP) Elkhart County, 75
Dunreith (town) Henry County, 100
Dupont (town) Jefferson County, 109
Dyer (town) Lake County, 121
Earl Park (town) Benton County, 50
East Chicago (city) Lake County, 121
East Enterprise (CDP) Switzerland County, 185
East Germantown (town) Wayne County, 202
Eaton (town) Delaware County, 71
Eckerty (unincorporated) Crawford County, 63
Economy (town) Wayne County, 202
Edgewood (town) Madison County, 133
Edinburgh (town) Johnson County, 112
Edwardsport (town) Knox County, 115
Elberfeld (town) Warrick County, 199
Elizabeth (town) Harrison County, 96
Elizabethtown (town) Bartholomew County, 49
Elkhart (city) Elkhart County, 75
Elkhart County, 74
Ellettsville (town) Monroe County, 144
Elnora (town) Daviess County, 64
Elwood (city) Madison County, 133
Eminence (unincorporated) Morgan County, 148
Emison (CDP) Knox County, 115
English (town) Crawford County, 63
Etna Green (town) Kosciusko County, 117
Evanston (unincorporated) Spencer County, 179
Evansville (city) Vanderburgh County, 190
Fair Oaks (unincorporated) Jasper County, 106
Fairbanks (unincorporated) Sullivan County, 183
Fairland (town) Shelby County, 177
Fairmount (town) Grant County, 86
Fairview Park (town) Vermillion County, 192
Falmouth (unincorporated) Rush County, 171
Farmersburg (town) Sullivan County, 183
Farmland (town) Randolph County, 168
Fayette County, 77
Ferdinand (town) Dubois County, 73
Fillmore (town) Putnam County, 166
Fish Lake (CDP) LaPorte County, 127
Fishers (town) Hamilton County, 91

Flat Rock (unincorporated) Shelby County, 177
Flora (town) Carroll County, 55
Florence (CDP) Switzerland County, 185
Floyd County, 78
Floyds Knobs (unincorporated) Floyd County, 78
Fontanet (CDP) Vigo County, 193
Forest (unincorporated) Clinton County, 61
Fort Branch (town) Gibson County, 84
Fort Wayne (city) Allen County, 45
Fortville (town) Hancock County, 93
Fountain City (town) Wayne County, 203
Fountain County, 79
Fountaintown (unincorporated) Shelby County, 177
Fowler (town) Benton County, 50
Fowlerton (town) Grant County, 86
Francesville (town) Pulaski County, 165
Francisco (town) Gibson County, 84
Frankfort (city) Clinton County, 62
Franklin (city) Johnson County, 112
Franklin County, 81
Frankton (town) Madison County, 133
Fredericksburg (town) Washington County, 200
Freedom (unincorporated) Owen County, 155
Freelandville (CDP) Knox County, 115
Freetown (CDP) Jackson County, 105
Fremont (town) Steuben County, 182
French Lick (town) Orange County, 153
Fulton (town) Fulton County, 83
Fulton County, 82
Galena (CDP) Floyd County, 79
Galveston (town) Cass County, 56
Garrett (city) DeKalb County, 70
Gary (city) Lake County, 122
Gas City (city) Grant County, 86
Gaston (town) Delaware County, 72
Geneva (town) Adams County, 45
Gentryville (town) Spencer County, 179
Georgetown (town) Floyd County, 79
Gibson County, 83
Glenwood (town) Rush County, 172
Goldsmith (unincorporated) Tipton County, 188
Goodland (town) Newton County, 150
Goshen (city) Elkhart County, 76
Gosport (town) Owen County, 155
Grabill (town) Allen County, 46
Grandview (town) Spencer County, 179
Granger (CDP) Saint Joseph County, 173
Grant County, 85
Grantsburg (unincorporated) Crawford County, 63
Greencastle (city) Putnam County, 167
Greendale (city) Dearborn County, 66
Greene County, 88
Greenfield (city) Hancock County, 93
Greens Fork (town) Wayne County, 203
Greensboro (town) Henry County, 100
Greensburg (city) Decatur County, 68
Greentown (town) Howard County, 102
Greenville (town) Floyd County, 79
Greenwood (city) Johnson County, 113
Griffin (town) Posey County, 164

Griffith (town) Lake County, 122
Grissom AFB (CDP) Miami County, 142
Grovertown (unincorporated) Starke County, 180
Guilford (unincorporated) Dearborn County, 66
Gwynneville (unincorporated) Shelby County, 177
Hagerstown (town) Wayne County, 203
Hamilton (town) Steuben County, 182
Hamilton County, 90
Hamlet (town) Starke County, 180
Hammond (city) Lake County, 123
Hancock County, 92
Hanna (CDP) LaPorte County, 127
Hanover (town) Jefferson County, 109
Hardinsburg (town) Washington County, 200
Harlan (CDP) Allen County, 46
Harmony (town) Clay County, 61
Harrison County, 94
Harrodsburg (CDP) Monroe County, 144
Hartford City (city) Blackford County, 51
Hartsville (town) Bartholomew County, 49
Hatfield (CDP) Spencer County, 179
Haubstadt (town) Gibson County, 84
Hayden (CDP) Jennings County, 111
Hazleton (town) Gibson County, 84
Hebron (town) Porter County, 161
Heltonville (unincorporated) Lawrence County, 130
Hendricks County, 96
Henry County, 99
Henryville (CDP) Clark County, 58
Herbst (CDP) Grant County, 87
Heritage Lake (CDP) Putnam County, 167
Hidden Valley (CDP) Dearborn County, 67
Highland (town) Lake County, 123
Highland (CDP) Vanderburgh County, 191
Hillsboro (town) Fountain County, 80
Hillsdale (unincorporated) Vermillion County, 192
Hoagland (CDP) Allen County, 46
Hobart (city) Lake County, 123
Hobbs (unincorporated) Tipton County, 188
Holland (town) Dubois County, 74
Holton (town) Ripley County, 170
Homecroft (town) Marion County, 136
Homer (unincorporated) Rush County, 172
Hope (town) Bartholomew County, 49
Howard County, 101
Howe (CDP) LaGrange County, 119
Hudson (town) Steuben County, 182
Hudson Lake (CDP) LaPorte County, 127
Huntertown (town) Allen County, 46
Huntingburg (city) Dubois County, 74
Huntington (city) Huntington County, 103
Huntington County, 102
Hymera (town) Sullivan County, 183
Idaville (CDP) White County, 206
Indian Village (town) Saint Joseph County, 173
Indianapolis (city) Marion County, 136
Ingalls (town) Madison County, 134
Jackson County, 104
Jalapa (CDP) Grant County, 87
Jamestown (town) Boone County, 52

CDP = Census Designated Place

Jasonville (city) Greene County, 89
Jasper (city) Dubois County, 74
Jasper County, 105
Jay County, 107
Jefferson County, 108
Jeffersonville (city) Clark County, 58
Jennings County, 110
Johnson County, 111
Jonesboro (city) Grant County, 87
Jonesville (town) Bartholomew County, 49
Kempton (town) Tipton County, 188
Kendallville (city) Noble County, 151
Kennard (town) Henry County, 100
Kent (CDP) Jefferson County, 109
Kentland (town) Newton County, 150
Kewanna (town) Fulton County, 83
Keystone (unincorporated) Wells County, 205
Kimmell (CDP) Noble County, 152
Kingman (town) Fountain County, 81
Kingsbury (town) LaPorte County, 127
Kingsford Heights (town) LaPorte County, 128
Kirklin (town) Clinton County, 62
Knightstown (town) Henry County, 100
Knightsville (town) Clay County, 61
Knox (city) Starke County, 180
Knox County, 114
Kokomo (city) Howard County, 102
Koontz Lake (CDP) Starke County, 181
Kosciusko County, 116
Kouts (town) Porter County, 161
La Crosse (town) LaPorte County, 128
La Fontaine (town) Wabash County, 196
La Paz (town) Marshall County, 140
La Porte (city) LaPorte County, 128
Laconia (town) Harrison County, 96
Ladoga (town) Montgomery County, 146
Lafayette (city) Tippecanoe County, 186
Lagrange (town) LaGrange County, 119
LaGrange County, 119
Lagro (town) Wabash County, 196
Lake County, 120
Lake Dalecarlia (CDP) Lake County, 124
Lake Holiday (CDP) Montgomery County, 146
Lake Santee (CDP) Decatur County, 69
Lake Station (city) Lake County, 124
Lake Village (CDP) Newton County, 150
Lakes of the Four Seasons (CDP) Lake County, 124
Laketon (CDP) Wabash County, 196
Lakeville (town) Saint Joseph County, 173
Lamar (unincorporated) Spencer County, 179
Landess (CDP) Grant County, 87
Lanesville (town) Harrison County, 96
Laotto (unincorporated) Noble County, 152
Lapel (town) Madison County, 134
LaPorte County, 127
Larwill (town) Whitley County, 208
Laurel (town) Franklin County, 82
Lawrence (city) Marion County, 138
Lawrence County, 130
Lawrenceburg (city) Dearborn County, 67
Leavenworth (town) Crawford County, 63
Lebanon (city) Boone County, 52
Leesburg (town) Kosciusko County, 117

Leo-Cedarville (town) Allen County, 47
Leopold (unincorporated) Perry County, 158
Lewis (unincorporated) Vigo County, 193
Lewisville (town) Henry County, 100
Lexington (unincorporated) Jefferson County, 109
Liberty (town) Union County, 189
Liberty Center (unincorporated) Wells County, 205
Liberty Mills (unincorporated) Wabash County, 196
Ligonier (city) Noble County, 152
Lincoln City (unincorporated) Spencer County, 179
Linden (town) Montgomery County, 146
Linton (city) Greene County, 89
Little York (town) Washington County, 200
Livonia (town) Washington County, 200
Lizton (town) Hendricks County, 98
Logansport (city) Cass County, 56
Long Beach (town) LaPorte County, 128
Loogootee (city) Martin County, 141
Losantville (town) Randolph County, 168
Lowell (town) Lake County, 124
Lucerne (unincorporated) Cass County, 56
Lynn (town) Randolph County, 168
Lynnville (town) Warrick County, 199
Lyons (town) Greene County, 89
Mackey (town) Gibson County, 85
Macy (town) Miami County, 143
Madison (city) Jefferson County, 110
Madison County, 131
Manilla (CDP) Rush County, 172
Marengo (town) Crawford County, 63
Marion (city) Grant County, 87
Marion County, 134
Markle (town) Huntington County, 103
Markleville (town) Madison County, 134
Marshall (town) Parke County, 156
Marshall County, 139
Martin County, 141
Martinsville (city) Morgan County, 148
Marysville (unincorporated) Clark County, 59
Matthews (town) Grant County, 87
Mauckport (town) Harrison County, 96
Mays (unincorporated) Rush County, 172
McCordsville (town) Hancock County, 94
Mecca (town) Parke County, 156
Medaryville (town) Pulaski County, 165
Medora (town) Jackson County, 105
Mellott (town) Fountain County, 81
Melody Hill (CDP) Vanderburgh County, 191
Memphis (CDP) Clark County, 59
Mentone (town) Kosciusko County, 117
Meridian Hills (town) Marion County, 138
Merom (town) Sullivan County, 184
Merrillville (town) Lake County, 125
Metamora (CDP) Franklin County, 82
Mexico (CDP) Miami County, 143
Miami (unincorporated) Miami County, 143
Miami County, 142
Michiana Shores (town) LaPorte County, 128
Michigan City (city) LaPorte County, 128
Michigantown (town) Clinton County, 62
Middlebury (town) Elkhart County, 76
Middletown (town) Henry County, 100

Mier (CDP) Grant County, 87
Milan (town) Ripley County, 170
Milford (town) Kosciusko County, 117
Mill Creek (unincorporated) LaPorte County, 129
Millersburg (town) Elkhart County, 76
Millhousen (town) Decatur County, 69
Milltown (town) Crawford County, 63
Milroy (CDP) Rush County, 172
Milton (town) Wayne County, 203
Mishawaka (city) Saint Joseph County, 173
Mitchell (city) Lawrence County, 131
Modoc (town) Randolph County, 168
Monon (town) White County, 206
Monroe (town) Adams County, 45
Monroe City (town) Knox County, 115
Monroe County, 143
Monroeville (town) Allen County, 47
Monrovia (town) Morgan County, 148
Monterey (town) Pulaski County, 165
Montezuma (town) Parke County, 156
Montgomery (town) Daviess County, 64
Montgomery County, 145
Monticello (city) White County, 206
Montmorenci (CDP) Tippecanoe County, 187
Montpelier (city) Blackford County, 51
Mooreland (town) Henry County, 100
Moores Hill (town) Dearborn County, 67
Mooresville (town) Morgan County, 148
Morgan County, 147
Morgantown (town) Morgan County, 149
Morocco (town) Newton County, 150
Morristown (town) Shelby County, 177
Mount Auburn (town) Wayne County, 203
Mount Ayr (town) Newton County, 150
Mount Carmel (town) Franklin County, 82
Mount Etna (town) Huntington County, 103
Mount Summit (town) Henry County, 100
Mount Vernon (city) Posey County, 164
Mulberry (town) Clinton County, 62
Muncie (city) Delaware County, 72
Munster (town) Lake County, 125
Nabb (unincorporated) Clark County, 59
Napoleon (town) Ripley County, 170
Nappanee (city) Elkhart County, 76
Nashville (town) Brown County, 54
Needham (unincorporated) Johnson County, 113
New Albany (city) Floyd County, 79
New Amsterdam (town) Harrison County, 96
New Carlisle (town) Saint Joseph County, 174
New Castle (city) Henry County, 100
New Chicago (town) Lake County, 125
New Goshen (CDP) Vigo County, 194
New Harmony (town) Posey County, 164
New Haven (city) Allen County, 47
New Market (town) Montgomery County, 146
New Middletown (town) Harrison County, 96
New Palestine (town) Hancock County, 94
New Paris (CDP) Elkhart County, 77
New Pekin (town) Washington County, 201
New Point (town) Decatur County, 69
New Richmond (town) Montgomery County, 146
New Ross (town) Montgomery County, 146

CDP = Census Designated Place

New Salisbury (CDP) Harrison County, 96
New Trenton (CDP) Franklin County, 82
New Washington (CDP) Clark County, 59
New Waverly (unincorporated) Cass County, 56
New Whiteland (town) Johnson County, 113
Newberry (town) Greene County, 89
Newburgh (town) Warrick County, 199
Newport (town) Vermillion County, 193
Newton County, 149
Newtown (town) Fountain County, 81
Nineveh (unincorporated) Brown County, 54
Noble County, 150
Noblesville (city) Hamilton County, 92
Norman (unincorporated) Jackson County, 105
North Crows Nest (town) Marion County, 138
North Judson (town) Starke County, 181
North Liberty (town) Saint Joseph County, 174
North Manchester (town) Wabash County, 196
North Salem (town) Hendricks County, 98
North Terre Haute (CDP) Vigo County, 194
North Vernon (city) Jennings County, 111
North Webster (town) Kosciusko County, 117
Norway (CDP) White County, 207
Notre Dame (CDP) Saint Joseph County, 174
Oakland City (city) Gibson County, 85
Oaktown (town) Knox County, 115
Oakville (unincorporated) Delaware County, 72
Odon (town) Daviess County, 65
Ogden Dunes (town) Porter County, 161
Ohio County, 152
Oldenburg (town) Franklin County, 82
Onward (town) Cass County, 56
Oolitic (town) Lawrence County, 131
Ora (unincorporated) Starke County, 181
Orange County, 153
Orestes (town) Madison County, 134
Orland (town) Steuben County, 182
Orleans (town) Orange County, 154
Osceola (town) Saint Joseph County, 174
Osgood (town) Ripley County, 170
Ossian (town) Wells County, 205
Otisco (unincorporated) Clark County, 59
Otterbein (town) Benton County, 50
Otwell (CDP) Pike County, 159
Owen County, 154
Owensburg (CDP) Greene County, 89
Owensville (town) Gibson County, 85
Oxford (town) Benton County, 50
Painted Hills (CDP) Morgan County, 149
Palmyra (town) Harrison County, 96
Paoli (town) Orange County, 154
Paragon (town) Morgan County, 149
Paris Crossing (unincorporated) Jennings County, 111
Parke County, 156
Parker City (town) Randolph County, 168
Parkers Settlement (CDP) Posey County, 164
Patoka (town) Gibson County, 85
Patricksburg (unincorporated) Owen County, 155

Patriot (town) Switzerland County, 185
Paxton (unincorporated) Sullivan County, 184
Pekin (unincorporated) Washington County, 201
Pendleton (town) Madison County, 134
Pennville (town) Jay County, 107
Perry County, 157
Perrysville (town) Vermillion County, 193
Peru (city) Miami County, 143
Petersburg (city) Pike County, 159
Pierceton (town) Kosciusko County, 118
Pike County, 159
Pimento (unincorporated) Vigo County, 194
Pine Village (town) Warren County, 197
Pittsboro (town) Hendricks County, 98
Plainfield (town) Hendricks County, 99
Plainville (town) Daviess County, 65
Pleasant Lake (unincorporated) Steuben County, 182
Plymouth (city) Marshall County, 140
Point Isabel (CDP) Grant County, 87
Poland (unincorporated) Owen County, 155
Poneto (town) Wells County, 205
Portage (city) Porter County, 161
Porter (town) Porter County, 162
Porter County, 160
Portland (city) Jay County, 108
Posey County, 163
Poseyville (town) Posey County, 164
Pottawattamie Park (town) LaPorte County, 129
Prairie Creek (unincorporated) Vigo County, 194
Princes Lakes (town) Johnson County, 114
Princeton (city) Gibson County, 85
Pulaski County, 165
Purdue University (CDP) Tippecanoe County, 187
Putnam County, 166
Quincy (unincorporated) Owen County, 155
Raglesville (CDP) Daviess County, 65
Ragsdale (CDP) Knox County, 116
Ramsey (unincorporated) Harrison County, 96
Randolph County, 168
Redkey (town) Jay County, 108
Reelsville (unincorporated) Putnam County, 167
Remington (town) Jasper County, 106
Rensselaer (city) Jasper County, 106
Reynolds (town) White County, 207
Richland (town) Spencer County, 179
Richmond (city) Wayne County, 203
Ridgeville (town) Randolph County, 169
Riley (town) Vigo County, 194
Ripley County, 169
Rising Sun (city) Ohio County, 153
River Forest (town) Madison County, 134
Roachdale (town) Putnam County, 167
Roann (town) Wabash County, 196
Roanoke (town) Huntington County, 103
Rochester (city) Fulton County, 83
Rockport (city) Spencer County, 179
Rockville (town) Parke County, 157
Rocky Ripple (town) Marion County, 138
Rolling Prairie (CDP) LaPorte County, 129
Rome (unincorporated) Perry County, 158

Rome City (town) Noble County, 152
Romney (unincorporated) Tippecanoe County, 187
Rosedale (town) Parke County, 157
Roseland (town) Saint Joseph County, 174
Roselawn (CDP) Newton County, 150
Rossville (town) Clinton County, 62
Royal Center (town) Cass County, 56
Rush County, 171
Rushville (city) Rush County, 172
Russellville (town) Putnam County, 167
Russiaville (town) Howard County, 102
Saint Anthony (unincorporated) Dubois County, 74
Saint Bernice (CDP) Vermillion County, 193
Saint Croix (unincorporated) Perry County, 158
Saint Joe (town) DeKalb County, 71
Saint John (town) Lake County, 125
Saint Joseph County, 172
Saint Leon (town) Dearborn County, 67
Saint Mary of the Woods (CDP) Vigo County, 194
Saint Meinrad (CDP) Spencer County, 180
Saint Paul (town) Decatur County, 69
Salamonia (town) Jay County, 108
Salem (city) Washington County, 201
Salt Creek Commons (CDP) Porter County, 162
Saltillo (town) Washington County, 201
San Pierre (CDP) Starke County, 181
Sandborn (town) Knox County, 116
Santa Claus (town) Spencer County, 180
Saratoga (town) Randolph County, 169
Schererville (town) Lake County, 126
Schneider (town) Lake County, 126
Schnellville (unincorporated) Dubois County, 74
Scipio (CDP) Jennings County, 111
Scotland (CDP) Greene County, 89
Scott County, 175
Scottsburg (city) Scott County, 176
Seelyville (town) Vigo County, 194
Sellersburg (town) Clark County, 59
Selma (town) Delaware County, 72
Seymour (city) Jackson County, 105
Shadeland (town) Tippecanoe County, 187
Shamrock Lakes (town) Blackford County, 51
Sharpsville (town) Tipton County, 188
Shelburn (town) Sullivan County, 184
Shelby (CDP) Lake County, 126
Shelby County, 176
Shelbyville (city) Shelby County, 178
Shepardsville (CDP) Vigo County, 194
Sheridan (town) Hamilton County, 92
Shipshewana (town) LaGrange County, 120
Shirley (town) Hancock County, 94
Shoals (town) Martin County, 142
Shorewood Forest (CDP) Porter County, 162
Sidney (town) Kosciusko County, 118
Silver Lake (town) Kosciusko County, 118
Simonton Lake (CDP) Elkhart County, 77
Sims (CDP) Grant County, 88
Smithville-Sanders (CDP) Monroe County, 145

CDP = Census Designated Place

Solsberry (unincorporated) Greene County, 90
Somerset (CDP) Wabash County, 197
Somerville (town) Gibson County, 85
South Bend (city) Saint Joseph County, 174
South Haven (CDP) Porter County, 162
South Milford (unincorporated) LaGrange County, 120
South Whitley (town) Whitley County, 208
Southport (city) Marion County, 138
Speedway (town) Marion County, 138
Spencer (town) Owen County, 155
Spencer County, 178
Spencerville (unincorporated) Allen County, 47
Spiceland (town) Henry County, 101
Spring Grove (town) Wayne County, 203
Spring Hill (town) Marion County, 138
Spring Lake (town) Hancock County, 94
Springport (town) Henry County, 101
Springville (unincorporated) Lawrence County, 131
Spurgeon (town) Pike County, 159
Star City (CDP) Pulaski County, 165
Starke County, 180
State Line City (town) Warren County, 198
Staunton (town) Clay County, 61
Stendal (unincorporated) Pike County, 159
Steuben County, 181
Stilesville (town) Hendricks County, 99
Stinesville (town) Monroe County, 145
Stockwell (CDP) Tippecanoe County, 187
Straughn (town) Henry County, 101
Sullivan (city) Sullivan County, 184
Sullivan County, 183
Sulphur Springs (town) Henry County, 101
Sumava Resorts (unincorporated) Newton County, 150
Summitville (town) Madison County, 134
Sunman (town) Ripley County, 171
Swayzee (town) Grant County, 88
Sweetser (town) Grant County, 88
Switz City (town) Greene County, 90
Switzerland County, 184
Syracuse (town) Kosciusko County, 118
Taswell (unincorporated) Crawford County, 64
Taylorsville (CDP) Bartholomew County, 49
Tecumseh (CDP) Vigo County, 195
Tell City (city) Perry County, 158
Tennyson (town) Warrick County, 199
Terre Haute (city) Vigo County, 195
Thayer (unincorporated) Newton County, 150
Thorntown (town) Boone County, 52
Tippecanoe (unincorporated) Marshall County, 140
Tippecanoe County, 185
Tipton (city) Tipton County, 189
Tipton County, 188
Toad Hop (CDP) Vigo County, 195

Topeka (town) LaGrange County, 120
Town of Pines (town) Porter County, 163
Trafalgar (town) Johnson County, 114
Trail Creek (town) LaPorte County, 129
Tri-Lakes (CDP) Whitley County, 208
Troy (town) Perry County, 158
Tunnelton (unincorporated) Lawrence County, 131
Twelve Mile (unincorporated) Cass County, 57
Ulen (town) Boone County, 52
Underwood (unincorporated) Scott County, 176
Union City (city) Randolph County, 169
Union County, 189
Union Mills (unincorporated) LaPorte County, 129
Uniondale (town) Wells County, 205
Unionville (unincorporated) Monroe County, 145
Universal (town) Vermillion County, 193
Upland (town) Grant County, 88
Urbana (unincorporated) Wabash County, 197
Utica (town) Clark County, 59
Vallonia (CDP) Jackson County, 105
Valparaiso (city) Porter County, 163
Van Bibber Lake (CDP) Putnam County, 167
Van Buren (town) Grant County, 88
Vanderburgh County, 190
Veedersburg (town) Fountain County, 81
Velpen (unincorporated) Pike County, 159
Vera Cruz (town) Wells County, 205
Vermillion County, 191
Vernon (town) Jennings County, 111
Versailles (town) Ripley County, 171
Vevay (town) Switzerland County, 185
Vigo County, 193
Vincennes (city) Knox County, 116
Wabash (city) Wabash County, 197
Wabash County, 195
Wadesville (unincorporated) Posey County, 164
Wakarusa (town) Elkhart County, 77
Waldron (CDP) Shelby County, 178
Walkerton (town) Saint Joseph County, 175
Wallace (town) Fountain County, 81
Walton (town) Cass County, 57
Wanatah (town) LaPorte County, 129
Warren (town) Huntington County, 104
Warren County, 197
Warren Park (town) Marion County, 139
Warrick County, 198
Warsaw (city) Kosciusko County, 118
Washington (city) Daviess County, 65
Washington County, 200
Waterloo (town) DeKalb County, 71
Waveland (town) Montgomery County, 147
Wawaka (unincorporated) Noble County, 152
Wayne County, 201

Waynetown (town) Montgomery County, 147
Wells County, 204
West Baden Springs (town) Orange County, 154
West College Corner (town) Union County, 190
West Harrison (town) Dearborn County, 68
West Lafayette (city) Tippecanoe County, 187
West Lebanon (town) Warren County, 198
West Newton (unincorporated) Marion County, 139
West Point (CDP) Tippecanoe County, 188
West Terre Haute (town) Vigo County, 195
Westfield (city) Hamilton County, 92
Westphalia (CDP) Knox County, 116
Westpoint (unincorporated) Tippecanoe County, 188
Westport (town) Decatur County, 69
Westville (town) LaPorte County, 129
Wheatfield (town) Jasper County, 107
Wheatland (town) Knox County, 116
Wheeler (CDP) Porter County, 163
White County, 205
Whiteland (town) Johnson County, 114
Whitestown (town) Boone County, 52
Whitewater (town) Wayne County, 204
Whiting (city) Lake County, 126
Whitley County, 207
Wilkinson (town) Hancock County, 94
Williams (CDP) Lawrence County, 131
Williams Creek (town) Marion County, 139
Williamsburg (unincorporated) Wayne County, 204
Williamsport (town) Warren County, 198
Winamac (town) Pulaski County, 166
Winchester (city) Randolph County, 169
Windfall City (town) Tipton County, 189
Winfield (town) Lake County, 126
Wingate (town) Montgomery County, 147
Winona Lake (town) Kosciusko County, 118
Winslow (town) Pike County, 160
Wolcott (town) White County, 207
Wolcottville (town) Noble County, 152
Woodburn (city) Allen County, 48
Woodlawn Heights (town) Madison County, 134
Worthington (town) Greene County, 90
Wyatt (unincorporated) Saint Joseph County, 175
Wynnedale (town) Marion County, 139
Yeoman (town) Carroll County, 55
Yoder (unincorporated) Allen County, 48
Yorktown (town) Delaware County, 72
Young America (unincorporated) Cass County, 57
Zanesville (town) Wells County, 205
Zionsville (town) Boone County, 53

CDP = Census Designated Place

Comparative Statistics

This section compares the 100 largest cities by population in the state, by the following data points:

Population 216

Physical Characteristics 218

Population by Race/Hispanic Origin 220

Average Household Size, Age, and Male/Female Ratio 222

Foreign Born, Language Spoken, Disabled Persons, and Veterans 224

Five Largest Ancestry Groups 226

Marriage Status 228

Employment by Occupation 230

Educational Attainment 232

Health Insurance 234

Income and Poverty 236

Housing 238

Commute to Work 240

Crime 242

Population

Place	2000 Census	2010 Census	Growth 2000–2010 (%)
Anderson city *Madison Co.*	59,734	56,129	-6.0
Angola city *Steuben Co.*	7,344	8,612	17.2
Auburn city *DeKalb Co.*	12,074	12,731	5.4
Avon town *Hendricks Co.*	6,248	12,446	99.2
Batesville city *Ripley Co.*	6,033	6,520	8.0
Bedford city *Lawrence Co.*	13,768	13,413	-2.5
Beech Grove city *Marion Co.*	14,880	14,192	-4.6
Bloomington city *Monroe Co.*	69,291	80,405	16.0
Bluffton city *Wells Co.*	9,536	9,897	3.7
Brazil city *Clay Co.*	8,188	7,912	-3.3
Brownsburg town *Hendricks Co.*	14,520	21,285	46.5
Carmel city *Hamilton Co.*	37,733	79,191	109.8
Cedar Lake town *Lake Co.*	9,279	11,560	24.5
Charlestown city *Clark Co.*	5,993	7,585	26.5
Chesterton town *Porter Co.*	10,488	13,068	24.6
Clarksville town *Clark Co.*	21,400	21,724	1.5
Columbia City city *Whitley Co.*	7,077	8,750	23.6
Columbus city *Bartholomew Co.*	39,059	44,061	12.8
Connersville city *Fayette Co.*	15,411	13,481	-12.5
Crawfordsville city *Montgomery Co.*	15,243	15,915	4.4
Crown Point city *Lake Co.*	19,806	27,317	37.9
Danville town *Hendricks Co.*	6,418	9,001	40.2
Decatur city *Adams Co.*	9,528	9,405	-1.2
Dyer town *Lake Co.*	13,895	16,390	17.9
East Chicago city *Lake Co.*	32,414	29,698	-8.3
Elkhart city *Elkhart Co.*	51,874	50,949	-1.7
Ellettsville town *Monroe Co.*	5,078	6,378	25.6
Elwood city *Madison Co.*	9,737	8,614	-11.5
Evansville city *Vanderburgh Co.*	121,582	117,429	-3.4
Fishers town *Hamilton Co.*	37,835	76,794	102.9
Fort Wayne city *Allen Co.*	205,727	253,691	23.3
Frankfort city *Clinton Co.*	16,662	16,422	-1.4
Franklin city *Johnson Co.*	19,463	23,712	21.8
Gary city *Lake Co.*	102,746	80,294	-21.8
Goshen city *Elkhart Co.*	29,383	31,719	7.9
Granger cdp *Saint Joseph Co.*	28,284	30,465	7.7
Greencastle city *Putnam Co.*	9,880	10,326	4.5
Greenfield city *Hancock Co.*	14,600	20,602	41.1
Greensburg city *Decatur Co.*	10,260	11,492	12.0
Greenwood city *Johnson Co.*	36,037	49,791	38.1
Griffith town *Lake Co.*	17,334	16,893	-2.5
Hammond city *Lake Co.*	83,048	80,830	-2.6
Highland town *Lake Co.*	23,546	23,727	0.7
Hobart city *Lake Co.*	25,363	29,059	14.5
Huntington city *Huntington Co.*	17,450	17,391	-0.3
Indianapolis city *Marion Co.*	781,870	820,445	4.9
Jasper city *Dubois Co.*	12,100	15,038	24.2
Jeffersonville city *Clark Co.*	27,362	44,953	64.2
Kendallville city *Noble Co.*	9,616	9,862	2.5
Kokomo city *Howard Co.*	46,113	45,468	-1.4

Place	2000 Census	2010 Census	Growth 2000–2010 (%)
La Porte city *LaPorte Co.*	21,621	22,053	2.0
Lafayette city *Tippecanoe Co.*	56,397	67,140	19.0
Lake Station city *Lake Co.*	13,948	12,572	-9.8
Lakes of the Four Seasons cdp *Lake Co.*	7,291	7,033	-3.5
Lawrence city *Marion Co.*	38,915	46,001	18.2
Lebanon city *Boone Co.*	14,222	15,792	11.0
Logansport city *Cass Co.*	19,684	18,396	-6.5
Lowell town *Lake Co.*	7,505	9,276	23.6
Madison city *Jefferson Co.*	12,004	11,967	-0.3
Marion city *Grant Co.*	31,320	29,948	-4.3
Martinsville city *Morgan Co.*	11,698	11,828	1.1
Merrillville town *Lake Co.*	30,560	35,246	15.3
Michigan City city *LaPorte Co.*	32,900	31,479	-4.3
Mishawaka city *Saint Joseph Co.*	46,557	48,252	3.6
Mooresville town *Morgan Co.*	9,273	9,326	0.5
Mount Vernon city *Posey Co.*	7,478	6,687	-10.5
Muncie city *Delaware Co.*	67,430	70,085	3.9
Munster town *Lake Co.*	21,511	23,603	9.7
Nappanee city *Elkhart Co.*	6,710	6,648	-0.9
New Albany city *Floyd Co.*	37,603	36,372	-3.2
New Castle city *Henry Co.*	17,780	18,114	1.8
New Haven city *Allen Co.*	12,406	14,794	19.2
Noblesville city *Hamilton Co.*	28,590	51,969	81.7
North Vernon city *Jennings Co.*	6,515	6,728	3.2
Peru city *Miami Co.*	12,994	11,417	-12.1
Plainfield town *Hendricks Co.*	18,396	27,631	50.2
Plymouth city *Marshall Co.*	9,840	10,033	1.9
Portage city *Porter Co.*	33,496	36,828	9.9
Princeton city *Gibson Co.*	8,175	8,644	5.7
Purdue University cdp *Tippecanoe Co.*	n/a	12,183	n/a
Richmond city *Wayne Co.*	39,124	36,812	-5.9
Rushville city *Rush Co.*	5,995	6,341	5.7
Saint John town *Lake Co.*	8,382	14,850	77.1
Schererville town *Lake Co.*	24,851	29,243	17.6
Scottsburg city *Scott Co.*	6,040	6,747	11.7
Seymour city *Jackson Co.*	18,101	17,503	-3.3
Shelbyville city *Shelby Co.*	17,951	19,191	6.9
South Bend city *Saint Joseph Co.*	107,789	101,168	-6.1
Speedway town *Marion Co.*	12,881	11,812	-8.3
Tell City city *Perry Co.*	7,845	7,272	-7.3
Terre Haute city *Vigo Co.*	59,614	60,785	1.9
Valparaiso city *Porter Co.*	27,428	31,730	15.6
Vincennes city *Knox Co.*	18,701	18,423	-1.4
Wabash city *Wabash Co.*	11,743	10,666	-9.1
Warsaw city *Kosciusko Co.*	12,415	13,559	9.2
Washington city *Daviess Co.*	11,380	11,509	1.1
West Lafayette city *Tippecanoe Co.*	28,778	29,596	2.8
Westfield city *Hamilton Co.*	9,293	30,068	223.5
Yorktown town *Delaware Co.*	4,785	9,405	96.5
Zionsville town *Boone Co.*	8,775	14,160	61.3

SOURCE: U.S. Census Bureau, Census 2010, Census 2000

Physical Characteristics

Place	Density (persons per square mile)	Land Area (square miles)	Water Area (square miles)	Elevation (feet)
Anderson city *Madison Co.*	1,356.7	41.37	0.11	879
Angola city *Steuben Co.*	1,357.6	6.34	0.05	1,063
Auburn city *DeKalb Co.*	1,792.0	7.10	0.00	866
Avon town *Hendricks Co.*	874.0	14.24	0.10	833
Batesville city *Ripley Co.*	1,071.1	6.09	0.07	971
Bedford city *Lawrence Co.*	1,102.9	12.16	0.00	686
Beech Grove city *Marion Co.*	3,229.4	4.39	0.00	804
Bloomington city *Monroe Co.*	3,472.0	23.16	0.20	771
Bluffton city *Wells Co.*	1,202.3	8.23	0.13	827
Brazil city *Clay Co.*	2,613.8	3.03	0.03	653
Brownsburg town *Hendricks Co.*	1,921.7	11.08	0.08	883
Carmel city *Hamilton Co.*	1,668.5	47.46	1.08	853
Cedar Lake town *Lake Co.*	1,406.5	8.22	1.39	709
Charlestown city *Clark Co.*	662.7	11.45	0.04	591
Chesterton town *Porter Co.*	1,400.3	9.33	0.11	640
Clarksville town *Clark Co.*	2,178.2	9.97	0.20	456
Columbia City city *Whitley Co.*	1,567.6	5.58	0.02	860
Columbus city *Bartholomew Co.*	1,602.4	27.50	0.39	627
Connersville city *Fayette Co.*	1,740.7	7.74	0.02	823
Crawfordsville city *Montgomery Co.*	1,740.0	9.15	0.00	794
Crown Point city *Lake Co.*	1,542.2	17.71	0.02	732
Danville town *Hendricks Co.*	1,298.8	6.93	0.05	955
Decatur city *Adams Co.*	1,627.9	5.78	0.01	801
Dyer town *Lake Co.*	2,685.1	6.10	0.00	640
East Chicago city *Lake Co.*	2,108.1	14.09	2.06	591
Elkhart city *Elkhart Co.*	2,172.4	23.45	0.97	751
Ellettsville town *Monroe Co.*	1,504.3	4.24	0.00	696
Elwood city *Madison Co.*	2,282.5	3.77	0.00	863
Evansville city *Vanderburgh Co.*	2,659.6	44.15	0.47	387
Fishers town *Hamilton Co.*	2,286.5	33.59	2.25	817
Fort Wayne city *Allen Co.*	2,293.4	110.62	0.21	810
Frankfort city *Clinton Co.*	2,602.0	6.31	0.00	850
Franklin city *Johnson Co.*	1,823.1	13.01	0.00	725
Gary city *Lake Co.*	1,610.2	49.87	7.31	600
Goshen city *Elkhart Co.*	1,954.4	16.23	0.36	801
Granger cdp *Saint Joseph Co.*	1,191.6	25.57	0.00	801
Greencastle city *Putnam Co.*	1,969.8	5.24	0.05	843
Greenfield city *Hancock Co.*	1,641.5	12.55	0.11	883
Greensburg city *Decatur Co.*	1,239.8	9.27	0.05	958
Greenwood city *Johnson Co.*	2,345.3	21.23	0.00	804
Griffith town *Lake Co.*	2,184.6	7.73	0.00	630
Hammond city *Lake Co.*	3,549.0	22.78	2.11	600
Highland town *Lake Co.*	3,421.0	6.94	0.02	623
Hobart city *Lake Co.*	1,103.6	26.33	0.38	623
Huntington city *Huntington Co.*	1,997.3	8.71	0.13	748
Indianapolis city *Marion Co.*	2,270.0	361.43	6.59	718
Jasper city *Dubois Co.*	1,147.5	13.10	0.09	466
Jeffersonville city *Clark Co.*	1,319.7	34.06	0.29	446
Kendallville city *Noble Co.*	1,631.5	6.04	0.22	988
Kokomo city *Howard Co.*	2,458.1	18.50	0.06	810

Place	Density (persons per square mile)	Land Area (square miles)	Water Area (square miles)	Elevation (feet)
La Porte city *LaPorte Co.*	1,891.3	11.66	0.71	814
Lafayette city *Tippecanoe Co.*	2,420.1	27.74	0.00	702
Lake Station city *Lake Co.*	1,515.4	8.30	0.13	620
Lakes of the Four Seasons cdp *Lake Co.*	2,623.6	2.68	0.42	764
Lawrence city *Marion Co.*	2,285.0	20.13	0.11	873
Lebanon city *Boone Co.*	1,015.3	15.55	0.02	942
Logansport city *Cass Co.*	2,103.0	8.75	0.22	640
Lowell town *Lake Co.*	1,790.8	5.18	0.09	669
Madison city *Jefferson Co.*	1,395.6	8.57	0.27	489
Marion city *Grant Co.*	1,906.2	15.71	0.08	814
Martinsville city *Morgan Co.*	2,634.5	4.49	0.02	604
Merrillville town *Lake Co.*	1,061.1	33.22	0.04	656
Michigan City city *LaPorte Co.*	1,607.1	19.59	3.27	627
Mishawaka city *Saint Joseph Co.*	2,838.8	17.00	0.35	722
Mooresville town *Morgan Co.*	1,483.9	6.28	0.06	718
Mount Vernon city *Posey Co.*	2,381.7	2.81	0.05	400
Muncie city *Delaware Co.*	2,577.0	27.20	0.19	951
Munster town *Lake Co.*	3,117.9	7.57	0.08	610
Nappanee city *Elkhart Co.*	1,602.5	4.15	0.00	876
New Albany city *Floyd Co.*	2,434.8	14.94	0.17	449
New Castle city *Henry Co.*	2,483.2	7.29	0.02	1,063
New Haven city *Allen Co.*	1,499.3	9.87	0.01	758
Noblesville city *Hamilton Co.*	1,656.4	31.37	1.42	764
North Vernon city *Jennings Co.*	1,016.5	6.62	0.01	718
Peru city *Miami Co.*	2,236.5	5.10	0.07	653
Plainfield town *Hendricks Co.*	1,240.5	22.27	0.11	732
Plymouth city *Marshall Co.*	1,331.7	7.53	0.04	797
Portage city *Porter Co.*	1,437.0	25.63	1.98	636
Princeton city *Gibson Co.*	1,704.9	5.07	0.01	499
Purdue University cdp *Tippecanoe Co.*	9,389.0	1.30	0.00	n/a
Richmond city *Wayne Co.*	1,539.3	23.91	0.16	981
Rushville city *Rush Co.*	2,051.6	3.09	0.00	958
Saint John town *Lake Co.*	1,304.1	11.39	0.09	725
Schererville town *Lake Co.*	1,987.7	14.71	0.05	669
Scottsburg city *Scott Co.*	1,335.3	5.05	0.02	564
Seymour city *Jackson Co.*	1,532.4	11.42	0.00	600
Shelbyville city *Shelby Co.*	1,659.6	11.56	0.28	764
South Bend city *Saint Joseph Co.*	2,440.3	41.46	0.42	692
Speedway town *Marion Co.*	2,482.4	4.76	0.01	748
Tell City city *Perry Co.*	1,603.9	4.53	0.11	420
Terre Haute city *Vigo Co.*	1,760.0	34.54	0.73	502
Valparaiso city *Porter Co.*	2,043.1	15.53	0.05	794
Vincennes city *Knox Co.*	2,485.7	7.41	0.07	420
Wabash city *Wabash Co.*	1,200.4	8.89	0.24	712
Warsaw city *Kosciusko Co.*	1,171.3	11.58	1.34	827
Washington city *Daviess Co.*	2,432.9	4.73	0.04	502
West Lafayette city *Tippecanoe Co.*	3,886.4	7.62	0.01	610
Westfield city *Hamilton Co.*	1,120.3	26.84	0.24	886
Yorktown town *Delaware Co.*	1,071.3	8.78	0.08	915
Zionsville town *Boone Co.*	1,380.5	10.26	0.04	843

SOURCE: U.S. Census Bureau, Census 2010

Population by Race/Hispanic Origin

Place	White[1] (%)	Black[1] (%)	Asian[1] (%)	AIAN[1,2] (%)	NHOPI[1,3] (%)	Two or More Races (%)	Hispanic[4] (%)
Anderson city *Madison Co.*	78.8	15.2	0.5	0.3	0.0	2.6	4.8
Angola city *Steuben Co.*	93.6	1.4	0.8	0.3	0.1	1.7	6.3
Auburn city *DeKalb Co.*	96.9	0.4	0.7	0.2	0.0	1.0	2.6
Avon town *Hendricks Co.*	86.7	5.9	3.3	0.3	0.1	2.2	4.3
Batesville city *Ripley Co.*	95.1	0.3	1.7	0.2	0.1	1.0	3.3
Bedford city *Lawrence Co.*	96.2	0.8	0.9	0.3	0.0	1.3	1.8
Beech Grove city *Marion Co.*	91.5	3.2	0.7	0.3	0.0	2.1	4.2
Bloomington city *Monroe Co.*	83.0	4.6	8.0	0.3	0.1	3.0	3.5
Bluffton city *Wells Co.*	96.0	0.7	0.5	0.4	0.0	1.1	3.3
Brazil city *Clay Co.*	97.1	0.6	0.5	0.1	0.0	1.0	1.6
Brownsburg town *Hendricks Co.*	93.4	2.2	1.6	0.1	0.1	1.4	3.0
Carmel city *Hamilton Co.*	85.4	3.0	8.9	0.2	0.0	1.8	2.5
Cedar Lake town *Lake Co.*	94.9	0.5	0.4	0.3	0.0	1.7	6.5
Charlestown city *Clark Co.*	89.9	2.1	0.3	0.3	0.0	2.1	8.3
Chesterton town *Porter Co.*	92.7	1.4	2.1	0.3	0.0	1.7	6.9
Clarksville town *Clark Co.*	85.1	5.6	0.7	0.3	0.0	2.5	9.5
Columbia City city *Whitley Co.*	96.7	0.5	0.5	0.3	0.0	1.4	2.2
Columbus city *Bartholomew Co.*	86.9	2.7	5.6	0.2	0.1	2.0	5.8
Connersville city *Fayette Co.*	95.7	2.1	0.3	0.2	0.0	1.3	1.0
Crawfordsville city *Montgomery Co.*	92.1	1.7	0.9	0.4	0.0	1.6	8.2
Crown Point city *Lake Co.*	88.2	6.3	1.8	0.2	0.0	1.6	8.1
Danville town *Hendricks Co.*	96.8	0.8	0.4	0.2	0.0	1.4	1.8
Decatur city *Adams Co.*	94.7	0.5	0.4	0.4	0.0	1.4	8.4
Dyer town *Lake Co.*	90.1	2.5	2.9	0.2	0.0	1.8	9.3
East Chicago city *Lake Co.*	35.5	42.9	0.1	0.6	0.0	2.8	50.9
Elkhart city *Elkhart Co.*	66.1	15.4	0.9	0.6	0.1	4.1	22.5
Ellettsville town *Monroe Co.*	95.5	1.0	0.6	0.2	0.0	1.9	1.6
Elwood city *Madison Co.*	96.7	0.2	0.3	0.2	0.0	1.5	3.3
Evansville city *Vanderburgh Co.*	82.0	12.6	1.0	0.3	0.1	2.8	2.6
Fishers town *Hamilton Co.*	85.6	5.6	5.5	0.2	0.0	2.1	3.4
Fort Wayne city *Allen Co.*	73.6	15.4	3.3	0.4	0.1	3.5	8.0
Frankfort city *Clinton Co.*	83.9	0.6	0.2	0.3	0.0	1.8	25.0
Franklin city *Johnson Co.*	94.9	1.4	0.8	0.3	0.0	1.6	2.5
Gary city *Lake Co.*	10.7	84.8	0.2	0.3	0.0	2.1	5.1
Goshen city *Elkhart Co.*	78.2	2.6	1.2	0.5	0.0	2.7	28.1
Granger cdp *Saint Joseph Co.*	90.3	2.5	4.6	0.1	0.1	1.6	2.4
Greencastle city *Putnam Co.*	92.4	2.7	1.9	0.3	0.0	1.8	2.5
Greenfield city *Hancock Co.*	96.6	0.6	0.8	0.3	0.0	1.3	1.8
Greensburg city *Decatur Co.*	96.1	0.4	1.3	0.2	0.0	0.9	2.4
Greenwood city *Johnson Co.*	90.1	1.7	3.7	0.3	0.1	2.1	5.0
Griffith town *Lake Co.*	75.8	16.9	0.8	0.3	0.0	2.4	13.3
Hammond city *Lake Co.*	59.4	22.5	1.0	0.5	0.0	3.3	34.1
Highland town *Lake Co.*	88.6	4.2	1.6	0.2	0.0	2.0	12.8
Hobart city *Lake Co.*	85.3	7.0	1.0	0.4	0.0	2.4	13.9
Huntington city *Huntington Co.*	96.4	0.6	0.5	0.4	0.0	1.4	2.4
Indianapolis city *Marion Co.*	61.8	27.5	2.1	0.3	0.0	2.8	9.4
Jasper city *Dubois Co.*	93.6	0.4	0.9	0.2	0.0	0.9	7.7
Jeffersonville city *Clark Co.*	80.4	13.2	1.1	0.3	0.0	3.0	4.1
Kendallville city *Noble Co.*	94.1	0.5	0.5	0.2	0.0	1.8	5.1
Kokomo city *Howard Co.*	83.5	10.7	1.0	0.4	0.0	3.3	3.3

Place	White[1] (%)	Black[1] (%)	Asian[1] (%)	AIAN[1,2] (%)	NHOPI[1,3] (%)	Two or More Races (%)	Hispanic[4] (%)
La Porte city *LaPorte Co.*	88.6	3.0	0.5	0.3	0.0	2.6	11.2
Lafayette city *Tippecanoe Co.*	83.6	6.2	1.4	0.4	0.0	2.7	12.1
Lake Station city *Lake Co.*	79.7	3.6	0.3	0.5	0.0	4.1	28.0
Lakes of the Four Seasons cdp *Lake Co.*	93.4	1.2	1.0	0.2	0.1	1.9	8.5
Lawrence city *Marion Co.*	63.2	25.8	1.4	0.4	0.1	3.5	11.2
Lebanon city *Boone Co.*	96.1	0.5	0.6	0.2	0.0	1.5	3.1
Logansport city *Cass Co.*	80.7	2.3	1.7	0.8	0.1	2.2	21.6
Lowell town *Lake Co.*	95.9	0.5	0.3	0.4	0.1	1.2	6.9
Madison city *Jefferson Co.*	93.5	2.8	1.2	0.2	0.0	1.6	1.7
Marion city *Grant Co.*	78.1	14.7	0.7	0.4	0.0	3.6	5.5
Martinsville city *Morgan Co.*	97.5	0.2	0.4	0.3	0.1	1.0	1.3
Merrillville town *Lake Co.*	46.4	44.5	1.2	0.2	0.0	3.2	12.9
Michigan City city *LaPorte Co.*	64.9	28.1	0.7	0.4	0.0	3.7	5.9
Mishawaka city *Saint Joseph Co.*	86.1	6.9	1.9	0.4	0.1	2.9	4.5
Mooresville town *Morgan Co.*	97.5	0.3	0.5	0.2	0.0	1.2	1.1
Mount Vernon city *Posey Co.*	93.4	2.8	0.4	0.3	0.0	2.4	1.7
Muncie city *Delaware Co.*	84.0	10.9	1.2	0.3	0.1	2.8	2.3
Munster town *Lake Co.*	85.6	3.5	5.8	0.2	0.0	1.8	10.2
Nappanee city *Elkhart Co.*	94.8	0.7	0.2	0.3	0.1	1.5	6.2
New Albany city *Floyd Co.*	85.8	8.7	0.7	0.2	0.0	2.9	3.7
New Castle city *Henry Co.*	95.1	1.9	0.4	0.2	0.0	1.8	1.7
New Haven city *Allen Co.*	93.2	3.3	0.4	0.4	0.1	1.7	3.1
Noblesville city *Hamilton Co.*	91.1	3.6	1.7	0.2	0.1	1.8	4.3
North Vernon city *Jennings Co.*	95.0	1.5	0.4	0.2	0.0	1.7	2.4
Peru city *Miami Co.*	93.1	2.5	0.4	1.3	0.0	2.3	2.4
Plainfield town *Hendricks Co.*	85.2	7.9	3.3	0.2	0.0	1.8	4.0
Plymouth city *Marshall Co.*	87.2	0.9	0.5	0.6	0.0	2.5	20.0
Portage city *Porter Co.*	83.6	7.3	0.9	0.4	0.0	2.6	16.4
Princeton city *Gibson Co.*	90.4	4.6	0.7	0.2	0.0	3.0	2.5
Purdue University cdp *Tippecanoe Co.*	69.9	3.7	23.0	0.1	0.0	2.2	3.6
Richmond city *Wayne Co.*	83.9	8.6	1.1	0.3	0.1	4.0	4.1
Rushville city *Rush Co.*	95.8	1.5	0.6	0.1	0.0	1.2	1.2
Saint John town *Lake Co.*	93.5	1.3	1.3	0.1	0.1	1.2	8.2
Schererville town *Lake Co.*	86.8	5.4	2.8	0.2	0.0	1.8	10.6
Scottsburg city *Scott Co.*	97.2	0.3	0.9	0.2	0.0	0.6	1.8
Seymour city *Jackson Co.*	90.3	1.3	1.2	0.2	0.1	1.8	11.5
Shelbyville city *Shelby Co.*	91.9	1.9	1.0	0.2	0.0	1.7	7.1
South Bend city *Saint Joseph Co.*	60.5	26.6	1.3	0.5	0.1	4.2	13.0
Speedway town *Marion Co.*	74.2	16.7	2.0	0.3	0.0	2.3	7.6
Tell City city *Perry Co.*	97.5	0.3	0.7	0.3	0.0	0.9	1.0
Terre Haute city *Vigo Co.*	83.5	10.9	1.4	0.4	0.0	2.9	3.1
Valparaiso city *Porter Co.*	89.9	3.3	2.1	0.3	0.1	2.1	7.1
Vincennes city *Knox Co.*	91.9	4.7	0.7	0.3	0.0	1.7	1.9
Wabash city *Wabash Co.*	96.3	0.4	0.5	1.0	0.0	1.2	2.0
Warsaw city *Kosciusko Co.*	89.5	1.6	2.2	0.5	0.0	2.0	10.4
Washington city *Daviess Co.*	89.2	1.1	1.1	0.3	0.1	1.9	9.6
West Lafayette city *Tippecanoe Co.*	76.8	2.7	17.3	0.1	0.0	2.1	3.6
Westfield city *Hamilton Co.*	90.9	2.2	2.5	0.2	0.0	1.6	5.8
Yorktown town *Delaware Co.*	95.3	1.6	1.5	0.2	0.0	1.0	1.3
Zionsville town *Boone Co.*	94.0	1.2	2.7	0.1	0.0	1.4	2.1

NOTE: (1) Exclude multiple race combinations; (2) American Indian/Alaska Native; (3) Native Hawaiian/Other Pacific Islander; (4) May be of any race
SOURCE: U.S. Census Bureau, Census 2010

Average Household Size, Age, and Male/Female Ratio

Place	Average Household Size (persons)	Median Age (years)	Age Under 18 (%)	Age 65 and Over (%)	Males per 100 Females
Anderson city *Madison Co.*	2.28	37.8	22.4	16.3	91.9
Angola city *Steuben Co.*	2.35	30.3	22.1	13.0	102.4
Auburn city *DeKalb Co.*	2.38	37.9	25.3	15.6	92.8
Avon town *Hendricks Co.*	2.77	33.9	30.2	8.0	93.4
Batesville city *Ripley Co.*	2.55	38.2	28.6	15.9	91.3
Bedford city *Lawrence Co.*	2.22	41.5	22.3	20.1	89.8
Beech Grove city *Marion Co.*	2.36	37.7	24.6	14.9	86.8
Bloomington city *Monroe Co.*	2.09	23.3	11.4	7.9	101.1
Bluffton city *Wells Co.*	2.34	38.3	24.6	16.9	92.3
Brazil city *Clay Co.*	2.46	36.2	26.0	14.4	92.3
Brownsburg town *Hendricks Co.*	2.64	36.0	28.4	12.0	92.2
Carmel city *Hamilton Co.*	2.71	39.2	29.4	10.4	95.1
Cedar Lake town *Lake Co.*	2.75	34.9	26.6	8.6	102.8
Charlestown city *Clark Co.*	2.63	35.2	28.4	11.2	90.5
Chesterton town *Porter Co.*	2.58	37.8	26.5	11.3	94.8
Clarksville town *Clark Co.*	2.34	37.3	22.9	15.2	92.4
Columbia City city *Whitley Co.*	2.32	36.1	24.9	15.3	90.8
Columbus city *Bartholomew Co.*	2.43	37.1	25.2	14.4	93.9
Connersville city *Fayette Co.*	2.37	39.4	24.2	17.7	91.0
Crawfordsville city *Montgomery Co.*	2.31	36.6	22.3	16.9	100.4
Crown Point city *Lake Co.*	2.45	39.6	21.2	16.1	100.0
Danville town *Hendricks Co.*	2.66	34.3	29.3	11.6	94.1
Decatur city *Adams Co.*	2.32	37.2	24.7	14.6	93.8
Dyer town *Lake Co.*	2.68	42.9	23.1	15.5	93.8
East Chicago city *Lake Co.*	2.75	30.9	31.4	11.3	88.1
Elkhart city *Elkhart Co.*	2.60	32.7	29.1	11.5	93.0
Ellettsville town *Monroe Co.*	2.43	34.5	26.5	12.1	87.5
Elwood city *Madison Co.*	2.49	38.6	25.2	14.1	94.9
Evansville city *Vanderburgh Co.*	2.23	36.5	22.1	14.4	92.7
Fishers town *Hamilton Co.*	2.82	33.2	33.0	5.5	94.5
Fort Wayne city *Allen Co.*	2.44	34.5	26.4	12.0	93.8
Frankfort city *Clinton Co.*	2.71	33.5	28.2	13.8	97.1
Franklin city *Johnson Co.*	2.54	34.6	26.3	14.6	91.3
Gary city *Lake Co.*	2.54	36.7	28.1	14.5	85.1
Goshen city *Elkhart Co.*	2.67	32.4	27.4	14.9	95.5
Granger cdp *Saint Joseph Co.*	2.93	40.8	29.6	10.9	98.2
Greencastle city *Putnam Co.*	2.27	27.4	19.0	14.2	87.5
Greenfield city *Hancock Co.*	2.51	35.6	26.4	14.0	92.7
Greensburg city *Decatur Co.*	2.38	37.0	25.0	15.6	91.9
Greenwood city *Johnson Co.*	2.51	34.0	26.6	11.6	93.9
Griffith town *Lake Co.*	2.53	36.1	24.3	11.2	90.9
Hammond city *Lake Co.*	2.67	33.3	27.6	10.7	96.2
Highland town *Lake Co.*	2.39	41.5	20.9	17.3	92.3
Hobart city *Lake Co.*	2.48	38.0	23.1	14.4	94.2
Huntington city *Huntington Co.*	2.48	33.4	24.8	13.5	91.3
Indianapolis city *Marion Co.*	2.42	33.7	25.0	10.5	93.5
Jasper city *Dubois Co.*	2.41	39.3	24.9	15.6	96.7
Jeffersonville city *Clark Co.*	2.37	37.3	23.2	11.9	95.4
Kendallville city *Noble Co.*	2.46	34.6	27.4	12.9	93.0
Kokomo city *Howard Co.*	2.25	38.2	24.0	15.8	88.0

Place	Average Household Size (persons)	Median Age (years)	Age Under 18 (%)	Age 65 and Over (%)	Males per 100 Females
La Porte city *LaPorte Co.*	2.39	36.2	24.5	15.3	93.2
Lafayette city *Tippecanoe Co.*	2.30	31.9	23.8	11.3	94.9
Lake Station city *Lake Co.*	2.72	35.4	26.4	10.7	99.9
Lakes of the Four Seasons cdp *Lake Co.*	2.76	42.3	23.3	14.5	96.0
Lawrence city *Marion Co.*	2.56	34.2	28.2	9.6	90.5
Lebanon city *Boone Co.*	2.38	37.5	24.5	14.7	92.2
Logansport city *Cass Co.*	2.57	34.2	27.8	13.9	97.2
Lowell town *Lake Co.*	2.71	35.7	26.6	11.7	96.9
Madison city *Jefferson Co.*	2.18	42.2	21.0	17.2	81.2
Marion city *Grant Co.*	2.25	36.2	21.1	16.0	88.8
Martinsville city *Morgan Co.*	2.47	36.6	25.0	14.5	94.4
Merrillville town *Lake Co.*	2.54	36.7	25.5	13.7	88.6
Michigan City city *LaPorte Co.*	2.37	37.1	23.5	13.5	105.8
Mishawaka city *Saint Joseph Co.*	2.21	34.7	23.1	13.6	88.9
Mooresville town *Morgan Co.*	2.49	38.6	25.4	14.3	89.1
Mount Vernon city *Posey Co.*	2.40	40.2	24.5	16.8	91.4
Muncie city *Delaware Co.*	2.22	28.1	17.8	13.0	90.6
Munster town *Lake Co.*	2.59	44.8	23.4	18.7	92.5
Nappanee city *Elkhart Co.*	2.60	34.8	27.9	12.5	95.5
New Albany city *Floyd Co.*	2.27	37.1	22.9	13.9	90.5
New Castle city *Henry Co.*	2.29	39.5	23.4	16.7	87.6
New Haven city *Allen Co.*	2.52	37.5	26.2	13.9	92.7
Noblesville city *Hamilton Co.*	2.69	33.0	30.2	8.7	93.8
North Vernon city *Jennings Co.*	2.43	35.6	26.5	14.1	91.7
Peru city *Miami Co.*	2.36	39.0	24.5	15.6	90.4
Plainfield town *Hendricks Co.*	2.57	35.5	24.5	11.3	111.7
Plymouth city *Marshall Co.*	2.49	34.3	27.9	15.2	91.9
Portage city *Porter Co.*	2.61	36.4	25.7	12.1	93.7
Princeton city *Gibson Co.*	2.34	37.2	25.0	16.1	91.1
Purdue University cdp *Tippecanoe Co.*	2.24	19.9	2.8	0.0	131.0
Richmond city *Wayne Co.*	2.29	38.4	22.1	16.5	91.8
Rushville city *Rush Co.*	2.36	39.3	24.0	17.5	90.5
Saint John town *Lake Co.*	2.94	40.2	27.3	11.3	99.6
Schererville town *Lake Co.*	2.45	40.9	22.1	14.0	94.2
Scottsburg city *Scott Co.*	2.34	37.5	23.3	15.9	90.4
Seymour city *Jackson Co.*	2.49	35.5	25.3	13.4	95.1
Shelbyville city *Shelby Co.*	2.43	35.9	25.5	13.0	95.2
South Bend city *Saint Joseph Co.*	2.48	33.3	27.3	12.5	93.9
Speedway town *Marion Co.*	2.13	37.8	21.7	14.8	93.6
Tell City city *Perry Co.*	2.23	42.0	22.0	19.3	90.3
Terre Haute city *Vigo Co.*	2.29	32.7	20.0	12.6	106.8
Valparaiso city *Porter Co.*	2.28	33.4	21.3	13.1	94.7
Vincennes city *Knox Co.*	2.19	33.0	19.2	15.0	101.1
Wabash city *Wabash Co.*	2.31	41.3	22.5	18.8	89.2
Warsaw city *Kosciusko Co.*	2.38	34.8	25.2	13.4	96.4
Washington city *Daviess Co.*	2.43	37.3	25.5	15.9	92.9
West Lafayette city *Tippecanoe Co.*	2.22	22.8	11.8	8.7	118.3
Westfield city *Hamilton Co.*	2.85	33.7	31.9	6.8	95.7
Yorktown town *Delaware Co.*	2.55	41.2	25.7	17.0	90.5
Zionsville town *Boone Co.*	2.75	39.6	31.6	10.9	94.9

SOURCE: U.S. Census Bureau, Census 2010

Foreign Born, Language Spoken, Disabled Persons, and Veterans

Place	Foreign Born (%)	Speak English Only at Home (%)	With a Disability (%)	Veterans (%)
Anderson city *Madison Co.*	3.10	95.7	20.1	10.0
Angola city *Steuben Co.*	3.10	95.1	15.7	8.1
Auburn city *DeKalb Co.*	1.00	97.9	17.0	8.1
Avon town *Hendricks Co.*	6.90	91.2	4.9	11.0
Batesville city *Ripley Co.*	2.10	96.7	9.0	8.4
Bedford city *Lawrence Co.*	2.70	95.8	20.1	10.4
Beech Grove city *Marion Co.*	2.10	95.7	13.6	9.2
Bloomington city *Monroe Co.*	11.80	85.6	8.7	4.0
Bluffton city *Wells Co.*	0.90	96.1	15.0	9.0
Brazil city *Clay Co.*	0.60	98.8	17.8	9.0
Brownsburg town *Hendricks Co.*	3.70	95.0	9.0	9.1
Carmel city *Hamilton Co.*	11.80	86.0	6.3	7.3
Cedar Lake town *Lake Co.*	2.30	95.3	12.9	7.8
Charlestown city *Clark Co.*	4.90	92.6	14.2	8.4
Chesterton town *Porter Co.*	3.60	94.0	8.6	9.4
Clarksville town *Clark Co.*	6.30	90.9	14.4	9.6
Columbia City city *Whitley Co.*	1.30	97.8	18.0	10.0
Columbus city *Bartholomew Co.*	10.00	89.3	12.4	8.7
Connersville city *Fayette Co.*	1.10	96.5	20.5	12.3
Crawfordsville city *Montgomery Co.*	4.50	92.4	16.2	8.1
Crown Point city *Lake Co.*	8.00	87.6	10.3	9.0
Danville town *Hendricks Co.*	0.50	97.7	10.2	8.0
Decatur city *Adams Co.*	1.00	93.5	16.0	7.0
Dyer town *Lake Co.*	5.90	91.7	10.4	8.8
East Chicago city *Lake Co.*	15.10	62.2	15.1	6.0
Elkhart city *Elkhart Co.*	13.90	76.8	14.6	8.6
Ellettsville town *Monroe Co.*	1.80	96.8	16.2	7.7
Elwood city *Madison Co.*	1.80	95.9	20.6	9.0
Evansville city *Vanderburgh Co.*	2.30	96.2	15.3	9.3
Fishers town *Hamilton Co.*	7.60	90.0	5.0	6.9
Fort Wayne city *Allen Co.*	7.60	89.0	11.7	8.9
Frankfort city *Clinton Co.*	12.00	77.0	13.3	8.2
Franklin city *Johnson Co.*	1.90	96.1	13.4	11.1
Gary city *Lake Co.*	1.60	95.0	18.6	9.8
Goshen city *Elkhart Co.*	15.80	72.7	12.5	6.7
Granger cdp *Saint Joseph Co.*	5.80	92.1	7.2	8.7
Greencastle city *Putnam Co.*	4.10	94.1	13.9	5.6
Greenfield city *Hancock Co.*	1.10	97.5	12.9	9.5
Greensburg city *Decatur Co.*	3.20	96.7	16.0	8.4
Greenwood city *Johnson Co.*	7.40	90.5	9.7	9.6
Griffith town *Lake Co.*	4.70	89.1	12.1	9.1
Hammond city *Lake Co.*	12.00	73.0	14.4	7.6
Highland town *Lake Co.*	5.10	87.7	11.7	9.1
Hobart city *Lake Co.*	4.60	90.2	12.2	11.9
Huntington city *Huntington Co.*	1.90	97.0	14.8	8.4
Indianapolis city *Marion Co.*	8.70	87.4	12.9	8.1
Jasper city *Dubois Co.*	4.20	89.3	7.6	10.3
Jeffersonville city *Clark Co.*	3.60	95.1	16.4	10.4
Kendallville city *Noble Co.*	2.50	94.0	18.5	10.0
Kokomo city *Howard Co.*	2.30	95.5	17.6	12.3

Place	Foreign Born (%)	Speak English Only at Home (%)	With a Disability (%)	Veterans (%)
La Porte city *LaPorte Co.*	5.90	90.1	15.6	11.3
Lafayette city *Tippecanoe Co.*	7.50	87.0	13.0	8.5
Lake Station city *Lake Co.*	4.30	83.3	19.8	8.8
Lakes of the Four Seasons cdp *Lake Co.*	5.00	92.9	9.4	12.5
Lawrence city *Marion Co.*	7.40	87.8	11.0	11.5
Lebanon city *Boone Co.*	3.20	95.6	12.8	8.7
Logansport city *Cass Co.*	14.80	78.4	15.6	9.3
Lowell town *Lake Co.*	1.80	96.5	12.2	10.2
Madison city *Jefferson Co.*	1.40	96.7	16.1	8.8
Marion city *Grant Co.*	1.80	96.4	19.6	9.5
Martinsville city *Morgan Co.*	1.20	97.7	18.9	8.3
Merrillville town *Lake Co.*	5.90	88.4	14.9	10.3
Michigan City city *LaPorte Co.*	3.80	94.2	18.0	9.0
Mishawaka city *Saint Joseph Co.*	6.00	91.8	14.3	9.6
Mooresville town *Morgan Co.*	1.60	98.1	14.0	12.7
Mount Vernon city *Posey Co.*	2.90	94.0	14.9	9.2
Muncie city *Delaware Co.*	2.80	96.2	18.4	7.9
Munster town *Lake Co.*	10.80	81.3	10.7	8.5
Nappanee city *Elkhart Co.*	1.60	91.6	9.9	6.9
New Albany city *Floyd Co.*	2.30	95.6	17.4	10.7
New Castle city *Henry Co.*	1.20	96.6	19.1	12.1
New Haven city *Allen Co.*	1.80	94.9	10.9	10.4
Noblesville city *Hamilton Co.*	4.10	93.4	7.6	8.8
North Vernon city *Jennings Co.*	0.60	98.2	17.7	8.3
Peru city *Miami Co.*	0.90	97.8	20.3	11.6
Plainfield town *Hendricks Co.*	6.80	89.3	12.5	10.7
Plymouth city *Marshall Co.*	13.30	76.8	15.0	9.2
Portage city *Porter Co.*	4.00	90.5	13.2	9.8
Princeton city *Gibson Co.*	2.00	96.8	16.5	11.2
Purdue University cdp *Tippecanoe Co.*	22.10	74.5	2.6	0.6
Richmond city *Wayne Co.*	3.30	94.0	20.1	10.8
Rushville city *Rush Co.*	0.30	96.4	18.0	12.1
Saint John town *Lake Co.*	5.10	89.4	7.8	8.1
Schererville town *Lake Co.*	9.60	83.7	9.7	8.1
Scottsburg city *Scott Co.*	2.20	95.0	20.7	8.4
Seymour city *Jackson Co.*	10.60	86.4	14.4	8.9
Shelbyville city *Shelby Co.*	4.70	92.7	14.9	9.0
South Bend city *Saint Joseph Co.*	7.40	86.6	14.9	8.5
Speedway town *Marion Co.*	8.90	88.5	15.6	10.0
Tell City city *Perry Co.*	0.30	99.5	17.1	8.7
Terre Haute city *Vigo Co.*	3.60	93.6	17.5	8.3
Valparaiso city *Porter Co.*	5.50	92.3	10.0	8.3
Vincennes city *Knox Co.*	1.00	98.2	14.6	7.3
Wabash city *Wabash Co.*	0.80	98.5	19.4	10.7
Warsaw city *Kosciusko Co.*	8.20	85.3	11.5	8.4
Washington city *Daviess Co.*	5.30	91.0	18.5	10.4
West Lafayette city *Tippecanoe Co.*	22.50	74.9	5.8	3.7
Westfield city *Hamilton Co.*	5.10	93.1	6.7	7.4
Yorktown town *Delaware Co.*	1.40	98.2	14.3	12.4
Zionsville town *Boone Co.*	5.40	94.2	4.1	6.2

SOURCE: U.S. Census Bureau, American Community Survey, 2009-2013 Five-Year Estimates

Five Largest Ancestry Groups

Place	Group 1	Group 2	Group 3	Group 4	Group 5
Anderson city *Madison Co.*	German (16.8%)	American (11.6%)	Irish (11.1%)	English (7.9%)	French (1.8%)
Angola city *Steuben Co.*	German (29.9%)	Irish (15.1%)	English (13.3%)	American (6.7%)	Scottish (3.6%)
Auburn city *DeKalb Co.*	German (38.2%)	Irish (15.4%)	American (10.6%)	English (9.1%)	Scottish (3.2%)
Avon town *Hendricks Co.*	German (26.6%)	English (19.6%)	Irish (14.8%)	American (6.7%)	African (3.0%)
Batesville city *Ripley Co.*	German (47.7%)	American (10.4%)	Irish (10.4%)	English (8.7%)	Italian (2.6%)
Bedford city *Lawrence Co.*	German (16.2%)	Irish (13.6%)	American (13.3%)	English (8.3%)	Italian (2.6%)
Beech Grove city *Marion Co.*	German (23.8%)	Irish (16.0%)	American (11.0%)	English (7.8%)	Italian (3.9%)
Bloomington city *Monroe Co.*	German (23.7%)	Irish (14.4%)	English (10.3%)	Italian (4.5%)	Polish (4.3%)
Bluffton city *Wells Co.*	German (29.4%)	American (15.9%)	Irish (9.0%)	English (8.0%)	Swiss (4.5%)
Brazil city *Clay Co.*	American (22.8%)	German (19.7%)	Irish (11.7%)	English (7.4%)	French (5.4%)
Brownsburg town *Hendricks Co.*	German (22.4%)	English (18.7%)	Irish (15.9%)	American (9.3%)	Polish (2.9%)
Carmel city *Hamilton Co.*	German (25.6%)	Irish (12.8%)	English (11.7%)	American (7.5%)	Italian (4.5%)
Cedar Lake town *Lake Co.*	German (27.5%)	Polish (15.9%)	Irish (15.0%)	American (10.0%)	English (9.6%)
Charlestown city *Clark Co.*	German (23.4%)	Irish (15.6%)	American (13.9%)	English (9.7%)	Dutch (3.5%)
Chesterton town *Porter Co.*	German (32.2%)	Irish (17.5%)	Polish (9.8%)	Italian (7.7%)	English (7.7%)
Clarksville town *Clark Co.*	German (20.0%)	Irish (12.6%)	American (10.7%)	English (6.9%)	French (2.3%)
Columbia City city *Whitley Co.*	German (28.6%)	Irish (12.7%)	American (10.7%)	English (8.7%)	Italian (3.3%)
Columbus city *Bartholomew Co.*	German (24.1%)	American (17.0%)	English (12.3%)	Irish (10.5%)	Scottish (2.5%)
Connersville city *Fayette Co.*	German (16.8%)	American (13.0%)	Irish (10.3%)	English (7.7%)	French (1.5%)
Crawfordsville city *Montgomery Co.*	German (21.7%)	American (21.5%)	Irish (12.9%)	English (10.1%)	French (2.8%)
Crown Point city *Lake Co.*	German (25.2%)	Irish (12.6%)	Polish (10.5%)	English (7.1%)	American (6.8%)
Danville town *Hendricks Co.*	German (26.7%)	Irish (22.3%)	English (14.7%)	American (10.0%)	Dutch (3.9%)
Decatur city *Adams Co.*	German (37.6%)	American (12.8%)	Irish (10.9%)	English (7.5%)	Swiss (2.5%)
Dyer town *Lake Co.*	German (20.0%)	Polish (18.4%)	Irish (16.6%)	English (10.4%)	Italian (10.2%)
East Chicago city *Lake Co.*	Polish (2.2%)	Irish (1.8%)	American (1.1%)	German (1.1%)	Hungarian (0.6%)
Elkhart city *Elkhart Co.*	German (17.8%)	American (9.3%)	Irish (8.1%)	English (5.3%)	Italian (3.4%)
Ellettsville town *Monroe Co.*	German (34.6%)	Irish (16.9%)	American (10.6%)	English (9.9%)	French (4.1%)
Elwood city *Madison Co.*	German (23.4%)	American (15.6%)	Irish (14.7%)	English (6.7%)	Italian (1.9%)
Evansville city *Vanderburgh Co.*	German (26.4%)	American (19.1%)	Irish (9.9%)	English (8.2%)	French (2.2%)
Fishers town *Hamilton Co.*	German (26.1%)	Irish (15.1%)	English (10.4%)	American (7.1%)	French (3.9%)
Fort Wayne city *Allen Co.*	German (27.1%)	American (11.9%)	Irish (9.6%)	English (6.9%)	African (3.7%)
Frankfort city *Clinton Co.*	German (19.6%)	American (9.4%)	Irish (8.9%)	English (7.9%)	Italian (1.6%)
Franklin city *Johnson Co.*	German (24.6%)	American (13.0%)	Irish (11.9%)	English (9.7%)	Scottish (1.9%)
Gary city *Lake Co.*	Irish (2.8%)	German (2.6%)	English (1.8%)	American (1.6%)	African (1.5%)
Goshen city *Elkhart Co.*	German (23.2%)	American (9.6%)	Irish (7.9%)	English (5.6%)	Swiss (3.8%)
Granger cdp *Saint Joseph Co.*	German (27.8%)	Irish (15.3%)	English (12.3%)	Polish (9.0%)	Italian (6.4%)
Greencastle city *Putnam Co.*	German (27.6%)	Irish (18.4%)	American (13.5%)	English (7.0%)	Polish (4.2%)
Greenfield city *Hancock Co.*	German (22.9%)	Irish (13.0%)	American (11.6%)	English (10.7%)	European (1.8%)
Greensburg city *Decatur Co.*	German (30.4%)	American (19.1%)	Irish (11.6%)	English (6.9%)	French (2.5%)
Greenwood city *Johnson Co.*	German (25.8%)	Irish (12.2%)	English (11.1%)	American (9.8%)	Italian (3.5%)
Griffith town *Lake Co.*	German (20.6%)	Irish (15.5%)	Polish (9.4%)	English (8.0%)	Italian (4.6%)
Hammond city *Lake Co.*	Irish (9.5%)	German (9.3%)	Polish (8.2%)	English (3.6%)	American (3.0%)
Highland town *Lake Co.*	German (19.5%)	Polish (16.1%)	Irish (14.3%)	Dutch (6.5%)	American (5.9%)
Hobart city *Lake Co.*	German (19.7%)	Irish (16.4%)	Polish (9.4%)	English (6.6%)	Italian (5.0%)
Huntington city *Huntington Co.*	German (31.7%)	Irish (14.9%)	American (14.1%)	English (9.5%)	French (3.1%)
Indianapolis city *Marion Co.*	German (17.0%)	Irish (10.4%)	English (7.1%)	American (7.0%)	African (3.5%)
Jasper city *Dubois Co.*	German (48.4%)	Irish (9.9%)	American (9.9%)	English (6.3%)	Italian (2.6%)
Jeffersonville city *Clark Co.*	German (22.5%)	Irish (13.8%)	American (12.0%)	English (8.1%)	French (2.1%)
Kendallville city *Noble Co.*	German (24.1%)	American (15.3%)	Irish (12.3%)	English (8.9%)	Dutch (1.7%)
Kokomo city *Howard Co.*	German (20.1%)	American (18.6%)	Irish (11.1%)	English (9.5%)	Italian (2.4%)

Place	Group 1	Group 2	Group 3	Group 4	Group 5
La Porte city *LaPorte Co.*	German (26.9%)	Irish (16.4%)	Polish (9.8%)	English (8.1%)	American (6.6%)
Lafayette city *Tippecanoe Co.*	German (26.4%)	Irish (14.1%)	English (9.0%)	American (7.5%)	Polish (2.8%)
Lake Station city *Lake Co.*	German (18.2%)	Irish (14.9%)	Polish (7.0%)	American (5.9%)	Italian (5.4%)
Lakes of the Four Seasons cdp *Lake Co.*	German (27.9%)	Irish (20.1%)	Polish (16.4%)	Italian (10.9%)	English (8.9%)
Lawrence city *Marion Co.*	German (15.8%)	Irish (12.3%)	English (7.4%)	American (6.6%)	Italian (3.4%)
Lebanon city *Boone Co.*	German (25.4%)	English (22.6%)	Irish (13.2%)	American (7.4%)	Scottish (3.7%)
Logansport city *Cass Co.*	German (18.1%)	American (16.1%)	Irish (9.9%)	English (7.9%)	Italian (3.3%)
Lowell town *Lake Co.*	German (34.2%)	Irish (19.8%)	Polish (9.4%)	English (9.4%)	American (8.8%)
Madison city *Jefferson Co.*	German (20.0%)	English (11.6%)	Irish (11.1%)	American (10.8%)	Scottish (3.4%)
Marion city *Grant Co.*	German (19.2%)	American (9.8%)	Irish (8.5%)	English (7.8%)	Dutch (2.1%)
Martinsville city *Morgan Co.*	German (21.8%)	American (13.8%)	Irish (12.3%)	English (12.2%)	Italian (3.5%)
Merrillville town *Lake Co.*	German (10.5%)	Irish (7.2%)	Polish (5.1%)	English (4.0%)	American (3.5%)
Michigan City city *LaPorte Co.*	German (18.9%)	Irish (13.0%)	Polish (9.6%)	English (4.9%)	American (4.9%)
Mishawaka city *Saint Joseph Co.*	German (24.5%)	Irish (15.5%)	Polish (9.0%)	English (7.5%)	American (5.4%)
Mooresville town *Morgan Co.*	German (21.6%)	American (15.0%)	Irish (12.1%)	English (11.3%)	French (3.3%)
Mount Vernon city *Posey Co.*	German (28.3%)	English (13.8%)	Irish (11.6%)	American (10.0%)	Dutch (2.0%)
Muncie city *Delaware Co.*	German (20.0%)	Irish (13.0%)	English (9.2%)	American (9.0%)	Italian (2.7%)
Munster town *Lake Co.*	German (19.5%)	Polish (16.2%)	Irish (14.3%)	English (7.6%)	Italian (6.4%)
Nappanee city *Elkhart Co.*	German (39.7%)	American (11.4%)	Irish (10.6%)	English (5.8%)	French (4.0%)
New Albany city *Floyd Co.*	German (22.3%)	American (15.4%)	Irish (11.4%)	English (9.5%)	French (3.1%)
New Castle city *Henry Co.*	German (16.0%)	American (13.9%)	Irish (12.5%)	English (7.2%)	Scottish (1.9%)
New Haven city *Allen Co.*	German (33.9%)	American (16.1%)	Irish (9.7%)	English (9.2%)	French (5.5%)
Noblesville city *Hamilton Co.*	German (27.2%)	Irish (12.5%)	English (12.1%)	American (7.8%)	Italian (4.1%)
North Vernon city *Jennings Co.*	German (20.2%)	American (16.6%)	Irish (8.6%)	English (8.0%)	French (3.8%)
Peru city *Miami Co.*	American (27.2%)	German (19.2%)	Irish (12.6%)	English (7.3%)	Dutch (2.1%)
Plainfield town *Hendricks Co.*	German (22.5%)	English (14.2%)	Irish (13.0%)	American (11.2%)	Scottish (3.6%)
Plymouth city *Marshall Co.*	German (22.4%)	Irish (8.2%)	American (6.7%)	English (6.6%)	Polish (6.6%)
Portage city *Porter Co.*	German (21.6%)	Irish (17.3%)	Polish (9.8%)	English (6.5%)	Italian (5.3%)
Princeton city *Gibson Co.*	German (18.6%)	American (15.5%)	Irish (13.5%)	English (11.3%)	French (2.7%)
Purdue University cdp *Tippecanoe Co.*	German (26.8%)	Irish (13.5%)	Italian (6.5%)	Polish (6.3%)	English (4.7%)
Richmond city *Wayne Co.*	German (19.4%)	Irish (12.6%)	English (10.4%)	American (8.3%)	Italian (3.7%)
Rushville city *Rush Co.*	German (20.7%)	American (15.4%)	Irish (12.1%)	English (10.9%)	French (2.6%)
Saint John town *Lake Co.*	German (25.2%)	Polish (19.4%)	Irish (17.5%)	Italian (11.2%)	Dutch (6.8%)
Schererville town *Lake Co.*	German (21.8%)	Polish (16.7%)	Irish (13.9%)	English (6.9%)	American (5.6%)
Scottsburg city *Scott Co.*	American (19.0%)	German (18.4%)	Irish (10.6%)	English (8.3%)	Scotch-Irish (4.8%)
Seymour city *Jackson Co.*	German (22.9%)	American (21.4%)	Irish (11.3%)	English (8.2%)	Italian (1.4%)
Shelbyville city *Shelby Co.*	German (22.0%)	American (16.5%)	Irish (12.0%)	English (8.0%)	French (3.2%)
South Bend city *Saint Joseph Co.*	German (16.6%)	Irish (11.7%)	Polish (9.2%)	English (5.6%)	American (3.8%)
Speedway town *Marion Co.*	German (20.3%)	Irish (12.9%)	English (12.2%)	American (11.0%)	Italian (2.5%)
Tell City city *Perry Co.*	German (35.5%)	Irish (13.9%)	American (12.1%)	English (8.8%)	French (6.8%)
Terre Haute city *Vigo Co.*	American (23.6%)	German (19.7%)	Irish (10.3%)	English (7.6%)	French (2.8%)
Valparaiso city *Porter Co.*	German (29.4%)	Irish (16.5%)	Polish (8.6%)	English (8.4%)	Italian (5.5%)
Vincennes city *Knox Co.*	American (19.7%)	German (18.7%)	Irish (12.2%)	English (7.4%)	French (5.6%)
Wabash city *Wabash Co.*	American (23.8%)	German (23.4%)	Irish (12.4%)	English (11.2%)	French (1.9%)
Warsaw city *Kosciusko Co.*	German (20.0%)	Irish (13.4%)	American (11.0%)	English (7.8%)	Dutch (3.4%)
Washington city *Daviess Co.*	German (22.3%)	American (15.5%)	Irish (13.2%)	English (7.5%)	French (1.8%)
West Lafayette city *Tippecanoe Co.*	German (23.4%)	Irish (13.0%)	English (9.9%)	Italian (4.3%)	American (4.1%)
Westfield city *Hamilton Co.*	German (27.5%)	Irish (14.5%)	English (10.6%)	American (8.9%)	Italian (6.3%)
Yorktown town *Delaware Co.*	German (31.7%)	Irish (18.9%)	English (14.2%)	American (12.8%)	Dutch (2.6%)
Zionsville town *Boone Co.*	German (29.1%)	English (17.5%)	Irish (14.1%)	American (7.9%)	Italian (5.0%)

NOTE: "French" excludes Basque; Please refer to the User Guide for more information.
SOURCE: U.S. Census Bureau, American Community Survey, 2009-2013 Five-Year Estimates

Marriage Status

Place	Never Married (%)	Now Married[1] (%)	Separated (%)	Widowed (%)	Divorced (%)
Anderson city Madison Co.	33.0	40.9	1.7	8.2	17.9
Angola city Steuben Co.	38.1	44.5	2.7	6.2	11.2
Auburn city DeKalb Co.	28.2	51.6	0.9	7.9	12.3
Avon town Hendricks Co.	25.4	57.4	0.3	2.8	14.4
Batesville city Ripley Co.	23.9	59.9	0.4	6.5	9.7
Bedford city Lawrence Co.	22.6	49.2	1.5	10.5	17.7
Beech Grove city Marion Co.	30.9	47.9	1.4	7.4	13.7
Bloomington city Monroe Co.	64.2	24.6	0.9	3.2	8.0
Bluffton city Wells Co.	23.9	51.7	1.5	7.9	16.4
Brazil city Clay Co.	27.8	46.3	1.3	6.9	18.9
Brownsburg town Hendricks Co.	21.4	59.7	0.6	6.9	12.1
Carmel city Hamilton Co.	21.8	67.5	0.7	3.5	7.2
Cedar Lake town Lake Co.	28.3	52.2	1.7	6.6	13.0
Charlestown city Clark Co.	32.6	44.8	1.7	6.2	16.4
Chesterton town Porter Co.	28.2	57.3	1.5	3.0	11.6
Clarksville town Clark Co.	29.5	45.9	1.6	9.3	15.3
Columbia City city Whitley Co.	27.5	46.6	1.2	8.2	17.7
Columbus city Bartholomew Co.	26.7	52.7	1.6	6.9	13.8
Connersville city Fayette Co.	23.4	47.7	3.2	9.2	19.6
Crawfordsville city Montgomery Co.	28.5	48.6	2.0	7.9	15.0
Crown Point city Lake Co.	28.4	54.4	1.6	7.1	10.1
Danville town Hendricks Co.	21.6	57.0	0.9	5.8	15.6
Decatur city Adams Co.	25.0	54.7	1.3	7.9	12.3
Dyer town Lake Co.	26.8	59.6	0.8	7.0	6.5
East Chicago city Lake Co.	47.3	33.8	3.5	7.4	11.5
Elkhart city Elkhart Co.	36.1	43.1	2.4	6.2	14.6
Ellettsville town Monroe Co.	25.7	50.2	0.5	7.3	16.8
Elwood city Madison Co.	24.7	53.5	2.6	6.5	15.2
Evansville city Vanderburgh Co.	34.0	41.6	1.0	7.4	17.0
Fishers town Hamilton Co.	24.4	63.8	0.9	2.2	9.5
Fort Wayne city Allen Co.	33.6	47.3	1.6	6.1	12.9
Frankfort city Clinton Co.	28.5	47.9	2.2	8.2	15.4
Franklin city Johnson Co.	26.9	51.5	2.0	7.1	14.4
Gary city Lake Co.	45.1	30.3	3.3	9.6	15.0
Goshen city Elkhart Co.	28.6	52.3	1.9	7.1	12.0
Granger cdp Saint Joseph Co.	21.5	68.4	0.6	4.1	6.1
Greencastle city Putnam Co.	46.6	36.6	1.6	6.8	10.0
Greenfield city Hancock Co.	27.6	49.3	2.4	6.1	17.0
Greensburg city Decatur Co.	27.5	48.7	1.5	8.1	15.7
Greenwood city Johnson Co.	26.4	53.9	0.9	5.9	13.9
Griffith town Lake Co.	33.4	48.3	0.7	4.7	13.6
Hammond city Lake Co.	39.1	43.3	3.0	6.3	11.3
Highland town Lake Co.	29.2	52.2	1.0	7.3	11.3
Hobart city Lake Co.	28.3	53.5	1.5	6.8	11.5
Huntington city Huntington Co.	31.9	45.8	1.3	8.0	14.3
Indianapolis city Marion Co.	38.7	42.4	2.5	5.5	13.4
Jasper city Dubois Co.	25.3	55.1	1.5	7.0	12.7
Jeffersonville city Clark Co.	30.9	47.4	1.8	6.3	15.4
Kendallville city Noble Co.	30.4	43.5	4.0	8.2	17.9
Kokomo city Howard Co.	26.0	49.3	1.5	7.6	17.1

Place	Never Married (%)	Now Married[1] (%)	Separated (%)	Widowed (%)	Divorced (%)
La Porte city *LaPorte Co.*	28.7	49.3	1.5	7.7	14.2
Lafayette city *Tippecanoe Co.*	35.5	45.5	1.3	5.7	13.2
Lake Station city *Lake Co.*	30.7	47.7	2.4	6.3	15.3
Lakes of the Four Seasons cdp *Lake Co.*	21.4	66.0	0.3	4.2	8.5
Lawrence city *Marion Co.*	31.6	49.8	2.3	5.3	13.3
Lebanon city *Boone Co.*	22.6	50.3	1.4	8.4	18.7
Logansport city *Cass Co.*	32.4	45.3	2.6	7.5	14.7
Lowell town *Lake Co.*	32.8	54.9	1.6	4.7	7.6
Madison city *Jefferson Co.*	27.9	47.1	1.1	9.5	15.4
Marion city *Grant Co.*	37.6	37.5	1.9	9.1	15.8
Martinsville city *Morgan Co.*	28.9	48.8	3.2	7.4	14.9
Merrillville town *Lake Co.*	35.1	44.0	2.1	7.1	13.8
Michigan City city *LaPorte Co.*	37.9	38.7	2.5	7.3	16.2
Mishawaka city *Saint Joseph Co.*	34.0	41.5	2.0	7.3	17.2
Mooresville town *Morgan Co.*	23.7	53.6	0.9	6.8	15.9
Mount Vernon city *Posey Co.*	26.7	52.8	1.2	6.6	13.9
Muncie city *Delaware Co.*	48.2	32.8	1.5	6.0	13.1
Munster town *Lake Co.*	26.1	56.3	1.6	10.3	7.3
Nappanee city *Elkhart Co.*	21.1	64.3	1.8	4.6	10.0
New Albany city *Floyd Co.*	32.7	42.4	2.5	8.4	16.5
New Castle city *Henry Co.*	27.9	44.0	2.1	7.7	20.3
New Haven city *Allen Co.*	25.2	55.0	1.2	6.1	13.7
Noblesville city *Hamilton Co.*	22.7	60.9	1.0	5.1	11.3
North Vernon city *Jennings Co.*	26.4	46.6	2.0	8.1	18.9
Peru city *Miami Co.*	31.5	43.3	1.9	7.3	17.8
Plainfield town *Hendricks Co.*	29.2	51.3	1.9	5.4	14.1
Plymouth city *Marshall Co.*	27.7	49.6	2.7	7.9	14.8
Portage city *Porter Co.*	30.2	48.6	1.9	7.2	14.0
Princeton city *Gibson Co.*	27.9	50.7	1.9	6.6	14.9
Purdue University cdp *Tippecanoe Co.*	89.9	9.2	0.3	0.0	0.8
Richmond city *Wayne Co.*	32.9	43.7	2.4	7.1	16.3
Rushville city *Rush Co.*	22.0	51.3	1.2	11.2	15.6
Saint John town *Lake Co.*	21.7	67.2	0.4	5.1	6.0
Schererville town *Lake Co.*	27.8	56.4	0.9	6.2	9.5
Scottsburg city *Scott Co.*	29.2	45.3	1.6	7.6	17.9
Seymour city *Jackson Co.*	24.1	52.1	1.6	7.5	16.2
Shelbyville city *Shelby Co.*	29.5	44.4	2.4	9.9	16.2
South Bend city *Saint Joseph Co.*	39.9	40.2	2.1	6.7	13.1
Speedway town *Marion Co.*	34.6	43.1	2.1	7.3	15.0
Tell City city *Perry Co.*	23.1	52.9	0.9	8.9	15.1
Terre Haute city *Vigo Co.*	43.3	35.8	1.8	7.0	14.0
Valparaiso city *Porter Co.*	37.0	44.3	1.3	6.7	11.9
Vincennes city *Knox Co.*	36.8	41.3	1.2	8.0	13.9
Wabash city *Wabash Co.*	26.8	52.1	2.3	9.7	11.3
Warsaw city *Kosciusko Co.*	30.2	50.2	1.2	8.2	11.4
Washington city *Daviess Co.*	23.7	48.5	2.0	9.7	18.1
West Lafayette city *Tippecanoe Co.*	65.3	26.5	0.5	3.9	4.3
Westfield city *Hamilton Co.*	22.4	65.7	0.7	2.5	9.4
Yorktown town *Delaware Co.*	18.4	64.7	0.9	6.9	10.0
Zionsville town *Boone Co.*	19.2	68.4	0.9	4.5	7.9

NOTE: (1) Includes separated.
SOURCE: U.S. Census Bureau, American Community Survey, 2009-2013 Five-Year Estimates

Employment by Occupation

Place	MBF[1] (%)	CES[2] (%)	ELCAM[3] (%)	HPT[4] (%)	S[5] (%)	SO[6] (%)	NRCM[7] (%)	PTMM[8] (%)
Anderson city *Madison Co.*	9.0	2.8	7.1	5.3	24.6	26.3	9.1	15.7
Angola city *Steuben Co.*	5.7	3.3	13.2	4.9	18.8	28.4	6.5	19.2
Auburn city *DeKalb Co.*	11.3	5.8	11.0	4.9	15.6	23.1	3.9	24.5
Avon town *Hendricks Co.*	20.4	5.9	8.8	8.6	10.9	27.5	8.5	9.5
Batesville city *Ripley Co.*	17.7	6.1	9.3	3.9	14.2	29.2	4.5	15.0
Bedford city *Lawrence Co.*	10.0	2.8	6.2	6.6	23.5	23.4	10.3	17.1
Beech Grove city *Marion Co.*	9.4	3.0	7.3	4.3	17.8	29.4	9.3	19.5
Bloomington city *Monroe Co.*	11.4	5.7	25.7	3.3	22.3	20.2	3.1	8.3
Bluffton city *Wells Co.*	10.1	3.6	9.2	3.1	18.3	21.9	10.4	23.5
Brazil city *Clay Co.*	12.0	2.9	6.2	6.9	22.7	21.6	5.7	22.1
Brownsburg town *Hendricks Co.*	16.6	6.2	9.3	8.4	14.3	27.2	6.4	11.7
Carmel city *Hamilton Co.*	24.3	12.1	14.1	9.3	8.8	24.6	2.8	4.2
Cedar Lake town *Lake Co.*	12.3	2.2	6.7	5.3	16.4	23.9	20.5	12.6
Charlestown city *Clark Co.*	9.8	2.2	4.5	5.2	15.9	31.2	7.0	24.2
Chesterton town *Porter Co.*	14.2	3.6	9.4	7.3	12.8	25.0	8.8	19.0
Clarksville town *Clark Co.*	13.9	2.9	6.4	5.7	20.5	26.5	6.4	17.8
Columbia City city *Whitley Co.*	5.4	2.7	4.5	6.3	19.3	26.0	5.4	30.3
Columbus city *Bartholomew Co.*	17.0	10.8	9.3	6.6	15.0	19.9	5.1	16.4
Connersville city *Fayette Co.*	6.7	1.5	5.3	7.6	23.5	24.6	6.6	24.1
Crawfordsville city *Montgomery Co.*	6.9	2.0	11.7	2.9	18.4	23.4	5.9	28.9
Crown Point city *Lake Co.*	13.3	5.1	10.8	11.4	14.4	21.4	8.9	14.9
Danville town *Hendricks Co.*	12.4	3.6	10.6	6.3	17.8	26.6	11.1	11.6
Decatur city *Adams Co.*	6.7	2.5	7.4	5.4	18.9	25.6	8.7	24.8
Dyer town *Lake Co.*	14.4	2.9	9.8	7.1	15.1	26.9	8.9	14.9
East Chicago city *Lake Co.*	5.8	0.6	5.1	4.8	30.6	22.5	8.5	22.2
Elkhart city *Elkhart Co.*	7.4	2.7	6.3	2.9	17.7	18.6	5.3	39.1
Ellettsville town *Monroe Co.*	12.8	3.2	11.0	5.6	18.9	23.8	6.7	17.9
Elwood city *Madison Co.*	9.5	2.3	7.9	2.1	21.1	20.9	5.7	30.5
Evansville city *Vanderburgh Co.*	8.6	2.7	7.8	5.7	22.2	26.3	8.9	17.6
Fishers town *Hamilton Co.*	23.7	10.0	12.2	9.3	10.7	27.2	3.3	3.7
Fort Wayne city *Allen Co.*	11.8	5.1	10.7	5.7	18.0	25.5	6.3	16.8
Frankfort city *Clinton Co.*	4.0	1.3	5.5	3.6	15.9	19.2	9.0	41.4
Franklin city *Johnson Co.*	10.1	2.9	10.6	4.9	18.1	26.6	8.6	18.2
Gary city *Lake Co.*	7.3	1.6	11.1	4.5	27.9	22.3	5.9	19.5
Goshen city *Elkhart Co.*	8.2	2.5	9.7	3.8	16.0	20.4	10.9	28.5
Granger cdp *Saint Joseph Co.*	20.7	5.3	16.7	9.3	9.1	26.8	4.1	8.0
Greencastle city *Putnam Co.*	10.8	4.8	17.5	2.0	22.7	18.2	5.1	18.8
Greenfield city *Hancock Co.*	13.2	4.5	8.8	5.1	17.3	25.9	8.7	16.5
Greensburg city *Decatur Co.*	9.6	5.5	7.3	5.3	17.5	20.4	7.0	27.4
Greenwood city *Johnson Co.*	13.5	6.2	7.5	7.1	14.9	27.1	9.8	14.0
Griffith town *Lake Co.*	9.2	3.9	8.0	3.9	21.8	25.5	11.8	15.9
Hammond city *Lake Co.*	6.9	2.2	8.3	3.8	22.7	24.5	9.6	22.1
Highland town *Lake Co.*	13.3	3.3	11.0	6.4	16.3	25.1	10.1	14.4
Hobart city *Lake Co.*	10.6	3.0	6.9	5.4	19.9	25.6	12.3	16.3
Huntington city *Huntington Co.*	8.5	2.7	8.5	3.5	20.2	19.0	8.2	29.3
Indianapolis city *Marion Co.*	13.6	4.7	9.8	5.9	18.8	25.9	7.3	14.1
Jasper city *Dubois Co.*	11.9	3.2	9.0	4.6	11.9	29.4	5.3	24.5
Jeffersonville city *Clark Co.*	11.3	3.9	6.9	6.4	18.9	27.6	7.4	17.4
Kendallville city *Noble Co.*	10.4	1.8	5.0	4.2	15.4	20.4	9.1	33.6
Kokomo city *Howard Co.*	9.1	3.2	8.3	5.2	23.1	24.1	7.3	19.7

Place	MBF[1] (%)	CES[2] (%)	ELCAM[3] (%)	HPT[4] (%)	S[5] (%)	SO[6] (%)	NRCM[7] (%)	PTMM[8] (%)
La Porte city *LaPorte Co.*	7.3	2.2	8.9	3.4	22.2	26.7	7.6	21.7
Lafayette city *Tippecanoe Co.*	10.3	5.5	11.8	6.0	19.7	21.4	6.8	18.6
Lake Station city *Lake Co.*	6.0	1.3	6.6	4.7	23.1	20.3	16.5	21.4
Lakes of the Four Seasons cdp *Lake Co.*	9.6	6.1	13.8	10.2	14.1	28.5	8.4	9.3
Lawrence city *Marion Co.*	17.7	4.6	8.8	4.6	19.1	27.1	7.0	11.2
Lebanon city *Boone Co.*	11.3	4.5	5.3	6.0	19.1	24.6	13.0	16.2
Logansport city *Cass Co.*	6.2	0.4	8.5	4.5	18.9	18.9	8.1	34.5
Lowell town *Lake Co.*	8.8	3.7	10.0	8.3	14.4	20.3	15.9	18.7
Madison city *Jefferson Co.*	8.5	3.1	12.6	7.7	19.5	24.0	8.8	15.7
Marion city *Grant Co.*	11.4	2.0	8.5	5.9	21.5	27.8	5.3	17.6
Martinsville city *Morgan Co.*	10.6	1.8	7.0	3.9	22.6	27.8	10.6	15.8
Merrillville town *Lake Co.*	8.1	1.8	8.8	7.3	21.2	25.4	7.3	20.1
Michigan City city *LaPorte Co.*	10.7	1.8	7.8	2.9	23.6	24.8	7.4	21.1
Mishawaka city *Saint Joseph Co.*	10.2	3.2	9.9	5.9	18.0	27.4	7.7	17.8
Mooresville town *Morgan Co.*	11.4	2.5	7.7	4.7	15.7	28.5	8.6	21.0
Mount Vernon city *Posey Co.*	11.7	4.3	7.0	4.5	15.2	22.0	11.5	23.9
Muncie city *Delaware Co.*	9.3	2.3	13.6	4.9	26.4	24.4	5.1	14.0
Munster town *Lake Co.*	17.8	5.8	12.6	9.7	12.0	24.6	7.3	10.3
Nappanee city *Elkhart Co.*	8.9	2.1	6.3	2.4	14.9	29.3	7.3	28.8
New Albany city *Floyd Co.*	9.8	3.3	9.1	4.0	21.6	27.4	7.1	17.6
New Castle city *Henry Co.*	8.7	1.8	9.9	4.7	20.0	24.5	8.1	22.3
New Haven city *Allen Co.*	12.2	4.2	9.8	4.3	16.3	25.0	8.7	19.5
Noblesville city *Hamilton Co.*	19.5	5.7	12.6	7.5	14.8	27.6	4.3	8.0
North Vernon city *Jennings Co.*	4.5	2.1	6.2	7.9	26.6	19.6	7.0	26.1
Peru city *Miami Co.*	5.3	1.5	9.5	6.1	24.6	18.7	10.4	23.8
Plainfield town *Hendricks Co.*	16.1	5.6	9.9	5.1	14.5	26.9	8.1	13.9
Plymouth city *Marshall Co.*	4.2	2.1	6.9	4.0	18.0	26.6	8.5	29.6
Portage city *Porter Co.*	9.6	3.5	7.1	5.7	22.3	23.2	12.6	16.1
Princeton city *Gibson Co.*	10.0	1.5	7.0	2.6	20.6	17.4	9.9	31.1
Purdue University cdp *Tippecanoe Co.*	3.9	7.0	26.5	1.8	33.7	22.2	1.8	3.2
Richmond city *Wayne Co.*	9.3	2.8	10.1	6.1	25.0	22.1	6.6	17.9
Rushville city *Rush Co.*	7.7	4.2	5.7	5.4	18.5	25.6	4.0	29.0
Saint John town *Lake Co.*	21.7	4.2	13.5	7.3	12.3	22.2	8.8	9.9
Schererville town *Lake Co.*	19.1	4.5	10.5	9.4	12.4	22.2	7.5	14.4
Scottsburg city *Scott Co.*	5.4	2.5	10.0	2.5	18.5	28.8	8.3	24.1
Seymour city *Jackson Co.*	8.6	4.0	5.0	5.2	18.0	22.2	9.1	27.9
Shelbyville city *Shelby Co.*	8.9	2.7	6.1	4.9	19.4	20.3	9.1	28.5
South Bend city *Saint Joseph Co.*	9.7	3.3	13.0	5.1	21.4	25.2	6.0	16.3
Speedway town *Marion Co.*	12.8	5.1	10.0	5.5	18.6	21.6	8.9	17.4
Tell City city *Perry Co.*	6.8	2.4	4.9	5.4	19.8	19.4	10.1	31.1
Terre Haute city *Vigo Co.*	8.3	3.3	11.9	5.2	21.8	25.3	7.9	16.2
Valparaiso city *Porter Co.*	11.5	5.4	14.3	6.6	18.5	24.8	6.2	12.7
Vincennes city *Knox Co.*	10.4	2.4	9.1	4.0	23.4	23.0	7.6	20.0
Wabash city *Wabash Co.*	8.0	3.2	7.1	6.2	17.4	25.2	5.4	27.5
Warsaw city *Kosciusko Co.*	9.9	3.7	10.5	3.6	14.1	22.0	4.4	31.8
Washington city *Daviess Co.*	8.7	0.8	6.2	5.1	21.9	18.2	12.6	26.4
West Lafayette city *Tippecanoe Co.*	12.1	9.4	31.6	4.1	18.6	18.4	2.0	3.8
Westfield city *Hamilton Co.*	24.4	9.1	10.6	9.0	11.6	23.8	3.6	7.8
Yorktown town *Delaware Co.*	15.8	4.6	12.3	8.5	15.3	27.1	6.2	10.1
Zionsville town *Boone Co.*	25.6	7.6	15.7	12.3	8.7	21.2	3.4	5.7

NOTES: (1) Management, business, and financial occupations; (2) Computer, engineering, and science occupations; (3) Education, legal, community service, arts, and media occupations; (4) Healthcare practitioners and technical occupations; (5) Service occupations; (6) Sales and office occupations; (7) Natural resources, construction, and maintenance occupations; (8) Production, transportation, and material moving occupations
SOURCE: U.S. Census Bureau, American Community Survey, 2009-2013 Five-Year Estimates

Educational Attainment

Place	High School Diploma or Higher[1]	Bachelor's Degree or Higher	Graduate/Professional Degree
Anderson city *Madison Co.*	83.4	14.5	4.8
Angola city *Steuben Co.*	84.6	19.4	8.1
Auburn city *DeKalb Co.*	89.2	22.4	8.6
Avon town *Hendricks Co.*	95.8	32.0	8.7
Batesville city *Ripley Co.*	92.4	31.4	9.9
Bedford city *Lawrence Co.*	81.2	11.9	3.8
Beech Grove city *Marion Co.*	86.4	15.5	5.0
Bloomington city *Monroe Co.*	92.9	56.6	31.0
Bluffton city *Wells Co.*	87.0	15.4	5.9
Brazil city *Clay Co.*	76.6	9.5	3.6
Brownsburg town *Hendricks Co.*	94.0	37.0	9.7
Carmel city *Hamilton Co.*	98.3	68.1	30.2
Cedar Lake town *Lake Co.*	88.0	13.4	3.5
Charlestown city *Clark Co.*	85.8	13.3	4.9
Chesterton town *Porter Co.*	91.8	30.5	12.2
Clarksville town *Clark Co.*	84.6	19.4	5.1
Columbia City city *Whitley Co.*	83.9	15.4	6.7
Columbus city *Bartholomew Co.*	90.1	31.9	13.9
Connersville city *Fayette Co.*	75.4	6.9	2.5
Crawfordsville city *Montgomery Co.*	82.3	14.9	6.0
Crown Point city *Lake Co.*	92.4	30.2	9.4
Danville town *Hendricks Co.*	91.2	26.1	6.2
Decatur city *Adams Co.*	86.4	13.9	4.5
Dyer town *Lake Co.*	92.0	28.9	8.5
East Chicago city *Lake Co.*	71.7	7.0	2.1
Elkhart city *Elkhart Co.*	75.5	14.0	4.6
Ellettsville town *Monroe Co.*	85.9	23.8	7.2
Elwood city *Madison Co.*	83.8	9.6	1.8
Evansville city *Vanderburgh Co.*	86.8	18.0	5.8
Fishers town *Hamilton Co.*	97.9	59.7	19.1
Fort Wayne city *Allen Co.*	87.9	25.6	8.5
Frankfort city *Clinton Co.*	77.4	10.5	3.7
Franklin city *Johnson Co.*	88.5	20.9	7.9
Gary city *Lake Co.*	82.9	12.3	4.2
Goshen city *Elkhart Co.*	77.2	21.1	7.8
Granger cdp *Saint Joseph Co.*	96.3	51.9	21.7
Greencastle city *Putnam Co.*	85.4	24.3	12.2
Greenfield city *Hancock Co.*	88.2	19.7	8.1
Greensburg city *Decatur Co.*	87.2	14.6	5.0
Greenwood city *Johnson Co.*	89.6	26.4	8.3
Griffith town *Lake Co.*	90.5	16.7	4.5
Hammond city *Lake Co.*	79.3	12.9	4.0
Highland town *Lake Co.*	91.9	26.5	8.2
Hobart city *Lake Co.*	88.7	15.4	4.7
Huntington city *Huntington Co.*	85.1	15.2	5.3
Indianapolis city *Marion Co.*	84.3	27.3	9.4
Jasper city *Dubois Co.*	87.1	21.7	6.7
Jeffersonville city *Clark Co.*	87.1	20.8	7.3
Kendallville city *Noble Co.*	86.8	13.4	3.7
Kokomo city *Howard Co.*	87.3	17.3	6.3

Place	High School Diploma or Higher[1]	Bachelor's Degree or Higher	Graduate/Professional Degree
La Porte city *LaPorte Co.*	85.2	14.6	4.6
Lafayette city *Tippecanoe Co.*	86.4	26.7	9.5
Lake Station city *Lake Co.*	79.1	5.6	1.0
Lakes of the Four Seasons cdp *Lake Co.*	94.3	29.7	8.9
Lawrence city *Marion Co.*	87.1	31.6	9.3
Lebanon city *Boone Co.*	87.2	18.4	5.6
Logansport city *Cass Co.*	75.7	11.9	3.1
Lowell town *Lake Co.*	94.1	18.1	6.4
Madison city *Jefferson Co.*	83.4	22.6	11.3
Marion city *Grant Co.*	81.1	14.9	5.9
Martinsville city *Morgan Co.*	81.1	11.0	3.9
Merrillville town *Lake Co.*	90.0	20.9	7.8
Michigan City city *LaPorte Co.*	83.4	15.6	5.7
Mishawaka city *Saint Joseph Co.*	86.5	23.4	8.8
Mooresville town *Morgan Co.*	87.9	13.7	2.3
Mount Vernon city *Posey Co.*	88.5	20.1	7.5
Muncie city *Delaware Co.*	83.5	22.4	10.8
Munster town *Lake Co.*	94.2	40.6	16.7
Nappanee city *Elkhart Co.*	83.6	16.7	4.7
New Albany city *Floyd Co.*	83.2	16.1	4.6
New Castle city *Henry Co.*	81.9	13.2	5.1
New Haven city *Allen Co.*	88.6	19.1	5.3
Noblesville city *Hamilton Co.*	94.7	47.2	14.6
North Vernon city *Jennings Co.*	82.3	11.3	5.7
Peru city *Miami Co.*	78.0	8.4	3.4
Plainfield town *Hendricks Co.*	90.3	26.9	8.1
Plymouth city *Marshall Co.*	76.7	13.0	3.3
Portage city *Porter Co.*	88.2	15.0	4.4
Princeton city *Gibson Co.*	88.3	13.6	2.1
Purdue University cdp *Tippecanoe Co.*	92.2	74.5	49.8
Richmond city *Wayne Co.*	80.5	17.8	7.8
Rushville city *Rush Co.*	84.1	11.9	4.5
Saint John town *Lake Co.*	96.6	36.7	11.6
Schererville town *Lake Co.*	93.0	32.4	13.9
Scottsburg city *Scott Co.*	76.6	14.1	4.5
Seymour city *Jackson Co.*	83.2	16.1	5.1
Shelbyville city *Shelby Co.*	82.2	12.3	3.3
South Bend city *Saint Joseph Co.*	83.9	22.9	9.5
Speedway town *Marion Co.*	88.6	24.5	8.0
Tell City city *Perry Co.*	84.6	13.5	6.4
Terre Haute city *Vigo Co.*	84.3	19.6	8.0
Valparaiso city *Porter Co.*	91.5	33.9	11.5
Vincennes city *Knox Co.*	83.6	14.1	5.1
Wabash city *Wabash Co.*	83.6	11.5	3.9
Warsaw city *Kosciusko Co.*	84.3	22.5	9.7
Washington city *Daviess Co.*	82.3	14.0	6.0
West Lafayette city *Tippecanoe Co.*	96.7	71.4	42.5
Westfield city *Hamilton Co.*	95.9	56.6	16.6
Yorktown town *Delaware Co.*	94.7	33.1	13.0
Zionsville town *Boone Co.*	97.6	66.9	31.7

Percent of Population 25 Years and Over with:

NOTE: (1) Includes General Equivalency Diploma (GED)
SOURCE: U.S. Census Bureau, American Community Survey, 2009-2013 Five-Year Estimates

Health Insurance

Place	Any Insurance	Private Insurance	Public Insurance	No Insurance	Percent of Population[1] Under Age 18 without Health Insurance
Anderson city *Madison Co.*	79.3	53.0	40.9	20.7	13.2
Angola city *Steuben Co.*	87.2	69.0	30.8	12.8	5.4
Auburn city *DeKalb Co.*	85.7	72.3	27.6	14.3	9.8
Avon town *Hendricks Co.*	90.3	82.9	15.1	9.7	8.2
Batesville city *Ripley Co.*	90.9	80.6	22.5	9.1	4.6
Bedford city *Lawrence Co.*	82.5	57.0	41.2	17.5	9.2
Beech Grove city *Marion Co.*	87.5	64.4	35.9	12.5	4.0
Bloomington city *Monroe Co.*	87.7	77.5	16.9	12.3	4.3
Bluffton city *Wells Co.*	85.7	66.1	36.2	14.3	8.4
Brazil city *Clay Co.*	80.4	49.9	41.4	19.6	9.3
Brownsburg town *Hendricks Co.*	90.6	84.7	16.1	9.4	7.9
Carmel city *Hamilton Co.*	95.5	91.1	13.0	4.5	2.7
Cedar Lake town *Lake Co.*	85.8	70.3	24.9	14.2	11.5
Charlestown city *Clark Co.*	84.2	64.3	30.5	15.8	6.0
Chesterton town *Porter Co.*	92.1	84.3	19.7	7.9	2.4
Clarksville town *Clark Co.*	81.5	62.7	29.7	18.5	12.7
Columbia City city *Whitley Co.*	86.7	62.6	39.2	13.3	4.4
Columbus city *Bartholomew Co.*	87.9	75.2	25.1	12.1	9.6
Connersville city *Fayette Co.*	79.8	47.1	47.3	20.2	6.4
Crawfordsville city *Montgomery Co.*	83.7	56.5	40.0	16.3	6.1
Crown Point city *Lake Co.*	89.2	79.4	23.4	10.8	4.4
Danville town *Hendricks Co.*	90.4	77.7	22.7	9.6	2.6
Decatur city *Adams Co.*	86.7	69.6	28.0	13.3	9.8
Dyer town *Lake Co.*	92.4	84.4	21.0	7.6	2.1
East Chicago city *Lake Co.*	79.1	39.2	48.1	20.9	9.3
Elkhart city *Elkhart Co.*	75.7	47.1	39.0	24.3	12.6
Ellettsville town *Monroe Co.*	84.6	69.9	28.0	15.4	6.4
Elwood city *Madison Co.*	85.0	57.7	38.0	15.0	12.4
Evansville city *Vanderburgh Co.*	83.8	61.3	34.0	16.2	7.8
Fishers town *Hamilton Co.*	92.7	88.1	9.1	7.3	3.2
Fort Wayne city *Allen Co.*	83.7	62.6	30.7	16.3	9.3
Frankfort city *Clinton Co.*	79.4	56.6	34.4	20.6	7.0
Franklin city *Johnson Co.*	89.6	72.6	29.0	10.4	4.0
Gary city *Lake Co.*	81.1	41.0	52.1	18.9	4.7
Goshen city *Elkhart Co.*	78.5	56.8	33.9	21.5	13.5
Granger cdp *Saint Joseph Co.*	95.0	88.8	16.7	5.0	2.4
Greencastle city *Putnam Co.*	90.1	75.3	25.0	9.9	7.8
Greenfield city *Hancock Co.*	87.1	71.8	28.2	12.9	7.2
Greensburg city *Decatur Co.*	84.4	62.4	33.5	15.6	9.0
Greenwood city *Johnson Co.*	84.8	69.2	26.3	15.2	9.4
Griffith town *Lake Co.*	88.2	74.4	25.9	11.8	6.0
Hammond city *Lake Co.*	79.3	53.4	34.9	20.7	8.7
Highland town *Lake Co.*	90.1	77.8	25.9	9.9	7.1
Hobart city *Lake Co.*	88.0	75.0	26.3	12.0	6.3
Huntington city *Huntington Co.*	82.6	60.3	33.8	17.4	6.0
Indianapolis city *Marion Co.*	82.6	59.4	32.6	17.4	9.2
Jasper city *Dubois Co.*	92.5	82.2	24.1	7.5	5.0
Jeffersonville city *Clark Co.*	86.3	71.1	28.3	13.7	7.7
Kendallville city *Noble Co.*	83.1	57.2	40.1	16.9	6.2
Kokomo city *Howard Co.*	84.5	62.7	37.4	15.5	8.6

	Percent of Total Population with:				Percent of Population[1] Under Age 18 without Health Insurance
Place	Any Insurance	Private Insurance	Public Insurance	No Insurance	
La Porte city *LaPorte Co.*	82.3	58.4	35.9	17.7	8.3
Lafayette city *Tippecanoe Co.*	81.9	61.7	29.8	18.1	5.5
Lake Station city *Lake Co.*	75.8	52.9	33.8	24.2	14.4
Lakes of the Four Seasons cdp *Lake Co.*	91.4	86.0	19.6	8.6	5.9
Lawrence city *Marion Co.*	84.9	65.6	28.9	15.1	5.5
Lebanon city *Boone Co.*	83.0	67.2	27.0	17.0	8.8
Logansport city *Cass Co.*	77.9	55.5	34.1	22.1	11.3
Lowell town *Lake Co.*	86.3	75.4	20.2	13.7	12.4
Madison city *Jefferson Co.*	85.7	68.9	32.7	14.3	11.2
Marion city *Grant Co.*	83.5	55.4	42.7	16.5	6.9
Martinsville city *Morgan Co.*	83.3	57.1	39.1	16.7	9.8
Merrillville town *Lake Co.*	85.5	65.3	33.3	14.5	6.3
Michigan City city *LaPorte Co.*	83.2	53.4	41.7	16.8	5.8
Mishawaka city *Saint Joseph Co.*	81.5	62.4	30.4	18.5	9.1
Mooresville town *Morgan Co.*	87.0	71.6	28.1	13.0	7.0
Mount Vernon city *Posey Co.*	87.7	68.7	31.9	12.3	3.3
Muncie city *Delaware Co.*	83.5	62.8	32.1	16.5	7.7
Munster town *Lake Co.*	92.5	82.7	22.7	7.5	1.6
Nappanee city *Elkhart Co.*	83.6	66.1	29.2	16.4	9.4
New Albany city *Floyd Co.*	83.3	61.9	34.5	16.7	10.5
New Castle city *Henry Co.*	81.2	56.1	40.4	18.8	9.3
New Haven city *Allen Co.*	85.3	69.5	27.8	14.7	7.4
Noblesville city *Hamilton Co.*	90.7	82.5	17.0	9.3	6.4
North Vernon city *Jennings Co.*	79.0	52.1	40.6	21.0	12.5
Peru city *Miami Co.*	82.5	51.4	43.5	17.5	5.4
Plainfield town *Hendricks Co.*	88.0	75.2	24.5	12.0	6.9
Plymouth city *Marshall Co.*	80.6	51.8	38.5	19.4	9.7
Portage city *Porter Co.*	85.4	69.8	27.5	14.6	5.1
Princeton city *Gibson Co.*	86.4	65.1	37.5	13.6	5.8
Purdue University cdp *Tippecanoe Co.*	95.4	92.9	4.1	4.6	2.5
Richmond city *Wayne Co.*	79.7	52.6	39.5	20.3	11.6
Rushville city *Rush Co.*	83.0	58.6	38.5	17.0	6.5
Saint John town *Lake Co.*	93.4	88.3	14.2	6.6	4.1
Schererville town *Lake Co.*	90.3	82.2	20.7	9.7	2.9
Scottsburg city *Scott Co.*	85.7	62.8	37.4	14.3	3.0
Seymour city *Jackson Co.*	82.9	65.3	27.9	17.1	12.4
Shelbyville city *Shelby Co.*	81.2	58.2	33.9	18.8	10.1
South Bend city *Saint Joseph Co.*	82.5	56.2	36.4	17.5	7.2
Speedway town *Marion Co.*	81.5	58.6	33.3	18.5	10.7
Tell City city *Perry Co.*	89.8	71.4	33.8	10.2	1.3
Terre Haute city *Vigo Co.*	80.9	57.7	33.7	19.1	7.6
Valparaiso city *Porter Co.*	85.6	73.8	22.4	14.4	4.5
Vincennes city *Knox Co.*	83.8	64.5	31.9	16.2	9.0
Wabash city *Wabash Co.*	86.8	60.1	40.6	13.2	4.0
Warsaw city *Kosciusko Co.*	84.2	66.5	30.3	15.8	7.1
Washington city *Daviess Co.*	86.3	60.7	36.5	13.7	3.1
West Lafayette city *Tippecanoe Co.*	93.0	89.9	11.1	7.0	2.3
Westfield city *Hamilton Co.*	93.6	87.4	12.5	6.4	3.0
Yorktown town *Delaware Co.*	93.5	78.0	32.5	6.5	2.1
Zionsville town *Boone Co.*	96.3	92.2	11.8	3.7	0.5

NOTE: (1) Civilian noninstitutionalized population.
SOURCE: U.S. Census Bureau, American Community Survey, 2009-2013 Five-Year Estimates

Income and Poverty

Place	Average Household Income ($)	Median Household Income ($)	Per Capita Income ($)	Households w/$100,000+ Income (%)	Poverty Rate (%)
Anderson city *Madison Co.*	41,963	33,574	18,216	6.0	25.8
Angola city *Steuben Co.*	49,561	40,756	19,175	10.2	16.5
Auburn city *DeKalb Co.*	57,496	42,855	23,963	14.8	13.5
Avon town *Hendricks Co.*	86,635	75,425	29,362	37.0	3.7
Batesville city *Ripley Co.*	81,004	59,728	30,852	25.4	4.8
Bedford city *Lawrence Co.*	44,051	34,706	19,348	7.9	21.4
Beech Grove city *Marion Co.*	49,189	39,444	20,095	8.8	19.5
Bloomington city *Monroe Co.*	47,606	27,395	18,987	11.6	39.2
Bluffton city *Wells Co.*	46,928	39,245	20,611	8.7	16.7
Brazil city *Clay Co.*	41,019	29,981	16,194	5.8	28.7
Brownsburg town *Hendricks Co.*	82,255	65,340	31,829	24.7	4.6
Carmel city *Hamilton Co.*	139,859	106,121	51,767	53.3	3.6
Cedar Lake town *Lake Co.*	66,505	58,401	24,893	15.3	7.5
Charlestown city *Clark Co.*	51,301	40,034	19,981	11.8	19.8
Chesterton town *Porter Co.*	85,575	68,673	31,877	30.5	9.6
Clarksville town *Clark Co.*	51,922	43,715	21,662	10.6	14.2
Columbia City city *Whitley Co.*	48,771	39,916	21,251	8.7	14.4
Columbus city *Bartholomew Co.*	69,804	53,045	28,739	22.1	11.6
Connersville city *Fayette Co.*	40,044	30,952	16,825	4.8	27.9
Crawfordsville city *Montgomery Co.*	44,354	34,453	18,199	7.1	27.2
Crown Point city *Lake Co.*	78,090	63,121	31,177	25.5	7.0
Danville town *Hendricks Co.*	72,462	58,907	27,095	21.9	8.4
Decatur city *Adams Co.*	50,891	41,949	20,909	10.5	17.0
Dyer town *Lake Co.*	102,104	76,457	36,269	34.1	2.6
East Chicago city *Lake Co.*	37,716	27,583	13,497	5.4	35.7
Elkhart city *Elkhart Co.*	43,008	34,443	16,770	5.5	28.5
Ellettsville town *Monroe Co.*	49,849	47,674	20,532	9.3	8.3
Elwood city *Madison Co.*	46,897	35,625	18,402	9.5	18.2
Evansville city *Vanderburgh Co.*	47,612	35,839	20,984	8.5	20.1
Fishers town *Hamilton Co.*	110,390	90,437	38,577	44.1	3.3
Fort Wayne city *Allen Co.*	57,768	43,969	23,400	13.5	18.7
Frankfort city *Clinton Co.*	48,045	40,368	17,641	7.9	18.1
Franklin city *Johnson Co.*	62,447	48,415	23,537	17.7	15.0
Gary city *Lake Co.*	38,600	26,885	15,931	6.4	38.1
Goshen city *Elkhart Co.*	50,917	41,579	19,369	9.0	20.8
Granger cdp *Saint Joseph Co.*	114,518	91,952	39,598	45.7	3.0
Greencastle city *Putnam Co.*	57,170	40,949	17,837	14.8	14.0
Greenfield city *Hancock Co.*	58,482	49,940	23,112	13.7	11.1
Greensburg city *Decatur Co.*	49,865	42,840	20,677	9.8	18.5
Greenwood city *Johnson Co.*	66,335	52,252	26,646	19.4	14.2
Griffith town *Lake Co.*	64,871	53,552	25,247	17.5	11.7
Hammond city *Lake Co.*	47,709	38,365	17,920	8.7	22.9
Highland town *Lake Co.*	70,886	61,353	29,560	21.3	5.7
Hobart city *Lake Co.*	61,955	55,617	25,392	14.9	10.2
Huntington city *Huntington Co.*	45,949	37,043	18,789	5.7	16.7
Indianapolis city *Marion Co.*	58,562	41,962	24,012	14.5	20.9
Jasper city *Dubois Co.*	68,905	53,968	28,540	16.1	7.6
Jeffersonville city *Clark Co.*	60,227	50,020	24,781	15.1	12.3
Kendallville city *Noble Co.*	45,245	38,802	18,654	6.3	23.6
Kokomo city *Howard Co.*	49,616	37,215	22,006	10.6	20.6

Place	Average Household Income ($)	Median Household Income ($)	Per Capita Income ($)	Households w/$100,000+ Income (%)	Poverty Rate (%)
La Porte city *LaPorte Co.*	45,732	34,597	19,025	7.0	21.9
Lafayette city *Tippecanoe Co.*	50,086	39,345	21,646	9.8	19.6
Lake Station city *Lake Co.*	44,380	38,537	16,970	7.4	21.5
Lakes of the Four Seasons cdp *Lake Co.*	94,008	87,929	34,342	37.6	2.5
Lawrence city *Marion Co.*	63,507	51,384	24,726	17.4	15.1
Lebanon city *Boone Co.*	56,213	43,154	23,673	10.8	14.9
Logansport city *Cass Co.*	44,124	32,838	17,207	4.9	22.1
Lowell town *Lake Co.*	69,914	61,660	23,592	19.2	7.5
Madison city *Jefferson Co.*	56,838	45,882	24,256	12.6	10.2
Marion city *Grant Co.*	41,914	31,391	17,808	6.5	26.0
Martinsville city *Morgan Co.*	44,874	34,706	18,419	7.2	20.3
Merrillville town *Lake Co.*	58,756	51,389	22,989	13.6	16.7
Michigan City city *LaPorte Co.*	46,249	35,601	19,027	7.6	26.3
Mishawaka city *Saint Joseph Co.*	46,992	36,590	20,912	9.0	21.7
Mooresville town *Morgan Co.*	61,254	53,658	24,917	13.1	11.9
Mount Vernon city *Posey Co.*	64,866	46,909	26,466	16.6	16.9
Muncie city *Delaware Co.*	40,856	29,287	17,066	6.6	33.4
Munster town *Lake Co.*	96,848	72,583	37,099	36.1	6.6
Nappanee city *Elkhart Co.*	53,935	45,813	19,498	9.9	13.7
New Albany city *Floyd Co.*	48,539	39,607	21,183	8.4	22.2
New Castle city *Henry Co.*	39,638	32,859	17,126	4.5	25.0
New Haven city *Allen Co.*	57,895	47,931	23,192	13.0	14.2
Noblesville city *Hamilton Co.*	81,877	66,644	31,261	27.3	7.4
North Vernon city *Jennings Co.*	44,507	35,106	17,792	5.7	28.3
Peru city *Miami Co.*	44,303	32,947	18,035	5.6	19.6
Plainfield town *Hendricks Co.*	70,523	59,036	25,978	20.0	8.1
Plymouth city *Marshall Co.*	41,507	32,486	15,596	5.9	31.6
Portage city *Porter Co.*	61,667	53,969	23,918	18.3	13.4
Princeton city *Gibson Co.*	51,524	41,099	20,981	10.3	16.4
Purdue University cdp *Tippecanoe Co.*	19,767	19,263	4,655	0.0	52.2
Richmond city *Wayne Co.*	43,936	30,096	18,796	8.1	29.6
Rushville city *Rush Co.*	41,767	35,111	18,347	5.3	21.2
Saint John town *Lake Co.*	106,902	94,526	37,513	47.1	3.9
Schererville town *Lake Co.*	82,777	66,449	33,969	30.0	6.6
Scottsburg city *Scott Co.*	42,218	38,483	17,323	5.8	24.3
Seymour city *Jackson Co.*	52,727	42,044	21,508	9.3	16.3
Shelbyville city *Shelby Co.*	50,218	38,578	21,057	10.3	18.1
South Bend city *Saint Joseph Co.*	47,150	34,502	19,181	8.8	27.8
Speedway town *Marion Co.*	49,903	38,896	25,181	10.8	15.2
Tell City city *Perry Co.*	52,784	45,123	23,264	10.1	11.2
Terre Haute city *Vigo Co.*	44,993	32,446	17,589	8.3	25.8
Valparaiso city *Porter Co.*	60,979	48,703	24,239	17.9	14.4
Vincennes city *Knox Co.*	44,297	35,165	17,896	6.7	20.5
Wabash city *Wabash Co.*	46,873	39,320	20,106	5.5	17.5
Warsaw city *Kosciusko Co.*	54,517	42,648	23,167	10.9	15.0
Washington city *Daviess Co.*	54,332	42,287	21,352	9.1	19.0
West Lafayette city *Tippecanoe Co.*	54,136	29,936	22,649	15.9	38.5
Westfield city *Hamilton Co.*	101,700	87,435	36,068	42.8	6.1
Yorktown town *Delaware Co.*	73,736	58,880	28,405	22.8	6.0
Zionsville town *Boone Co.*	150,719	106,071	52,793	53.9	2.6

SOURCE: U.S. Census Bureau, American Community Survey, 2009-2013 Five-Year Estimates

Housing

Place	Homeownership Rate (%)	Median Home Value ($)	Median Year Structure Built	Homeowner Vacancy Rate (%)	Median Gross Rent ($/month)	Rental Vacancy Rate (%)
Anderson city *Madison Co.*	58.4	$73,600	1959	4.5	$672	15.9
Angola city *Steuben Co.*	50.6	$109,100	1976	4.4	$600	9.9
Auburn city *DeKalb Co.*	72.2	$104,800	1975	4.0	$613	9.7
Avon town *Hendricks Co.*	79.7	$164,900	2001	3.4	$878	6.7
Batesville city *Ripley Co.*	66.5	$181,000	1977	1.7	$734	10.3
Bedford city *Lawrence Co.*	61.6	$88,600	1954	4.8	$611	9.0
Beech Grove city *Marion Co.*	55.7	$93,600	1960	3.2	$730	10.3
Bloomington city *Monroe Co.*	33.1	$171,900	1978	2.0	$782	4.4
Bluffton city *Wells Co.*	67.8	$94,000	1967	2.9	$532	10.3
Brazil city *Clay Co.*	57.2	$72,500	1957	3.8	$641	7.3
Brownsburg town *Hendricks Co.*	78.4	$144,100	1995	1.8	$896	7.6
Carmel city *Hamilton Co.*	80.5	$297,300	1993	1.7	$1,077	10.8
Cedar Lake town *Lake Co.*	77.1	$153,900	1973	3.4	$856	8.2
Charlestown city *Clark Co.*	61.4	$110,600	1970	3.5	$618	8.3
Chesterton town *Porter Co.*	70.7	$168,900	1980	2.1	$890	7.8
Clarksville town *Clark Co.*	59.8	$114,200	1970	2.7	$755	7.3
Columbia City city *Whitley Co.*	67.2	$94,700	1974	2.8	$631	9.0
Columbus city *Bartholomew Co.*	62.6	$140,900	1972	2.9	$794	14.2
Connersville city *Fayette Co.*	60.4	$68,900	1950	3.3	$630	13.7
Crawfordsville city *Montgomery Co.*	58.0	$91,600	1958	3.5	$645	9.6
Crown Point city *Lake Co.*	78.9	$172,500	1981	2.0	$914	7.6
Danville town *Hendricks Co.*	67.9	$150,200	1993	1.8	$757	9.7
Decatur city *Adams Co.*	64.8	$93,800	1959	3.8	$541	10.8
Dyer town *Lake Co.*	91.2	$191,100	1980	0.8	$921	4.0
East Chicago city *Lake Co.*	41.5	$82,900	1940	3.6	$670	10.2
Elkhart city *Elkhart Co.*	50.8	$85,900	1960	3.9	$671	15.8
Ellettsville town *Monroe Co.*	70.8	$119,400	1983	3.1	$733	5.3
Elwood city *Madison Co.*	67.3	$73,200	1945	5.3	$665	12.6
Evansville city *Vanderburgh Co.*	56.0	$90,000	1956	3.7	$692	11.8
Fishers town *Hamilton Co.*	82.3	$209,700	1998	1.6	$1,058	8.4
Fort Wayne city *Allen Co.*	63.3	$99,900	1968	2.9	$656	12.5
Frankfort city *Clinton Co.*	60.3	$82,300	1950	3.4	$650	12.4
Franklin city *Johnson Co.*	65.8	$115,700	1990	2.7	$835	11.1
Gary city *Lake Co.*	52.7	$65,400	1955	3.6	$711	14.5
Goshen city *Elkhart Co.*	58.6	$107,800	1978	3.7	$734	11.6
Granger cdp *Saint Joseph Co.*	96.8	$193,200	1987	1.5	$1,195	6.1
Greencastle city *Putnam Co.*	55.6	$115,400	1964	3.8	$627	10.0
Greenfield city *Hancock Co.*	66.1	$118,100	1989	3.4	$814	12.1
Greensburg city *Decatur Co.*	58.5	$103,300	1970	3.3	$712	11.6
Greenwood city *Johnson Co.*	62.3	$131,900	1991	2.5	$811	10.9
Griffith town *Lake Co.*	66.1	$140,900	1968	1.3	$830	9.0
Hammond city *Lake Co.*	61.3	$92,400	1949	2.6	$802	6.9
Highland town *Lake Co.*	78.7	$153,900	1966	1.1	$946	4.7
Hobart city *Lake Co.*	73.3	$132,800	1967	1.9	$838	8.1
Huntington city *Huntington Co.*	66.3	$75,000	1950	4.7	$636	12.5
Indianapolis city *Marion Co.*	55.8	$118,000	1969	3.4	$770	12.3
Jasper city *Dubois Co.*	67.3	$128,600	1978	2.6	$638	6.2
Jeffersonville city *Clark Co.*	66.9	$126,300	1976	2.3	$730	8.7
Kendallville city *Noble Co.*	61.7	$82,900	1966	3.7	$617	12.2
Kokomo city *Howard Co.*	59.3	$84,000	1963	4.4	$637	12.6

Place	Homeownership Rate (%)	Median Home Value ($)	Median Year Structure Built	Homeowner Vacancy Rate (%)	Median Gross Rent ($/month)	Rental Vacancy Rate (%)
La Porte city *LaPorte Co.*	59.0	$91,600	1954	3.1	$652	10.1
Lafayette city *Tippecanoe Co.*	51.3	$102,200	1970	2.8	$744	9.1
Lake Station city *Lake Co.*	72.2	$81,200	1955	3.7	$768	8.6
Lakes of the Four Seasons cdp *Lake Co.*	95.0	$179,700	1979	1.7	n/a	0.7
Lawrence city *Marion Co.*	69.5	$125,500	1990	3.2	$804	12.9
Lebanon city *Boone Co.*	64.6	$112,700	1973	3.3	$667	10.8
Logansport city *Cass Co.*	60.4	$65,100	1941	4.5	$606	9.8
Lowell town *Lake Co.*	77.9	$145,600	1977	2.3	$883	9.2
Madison city *Jefferson Co.*	62.6	$117,800	1964	3.9	$604	11.2
Marion city *Grant Co.*	56.6	$65,200	1957	3.7	$579	13.7
Martinsville city *Morgan Co.*	55.4	$97,400	1961	3.4	$675	8.0
Merrillville town *Lake Co.*	66.4	$130,400	1973	3.2	$931	10.1
Michigan City city *LaPorte Co.*	58.8	$93,100	1959	3.0	$690	12.8
Mishawaka city *Saint Joseph Co.*	52.3	$93,900	1971	4.0	$693	13.7
Mooresville town *Morgan Co.*	67.0	$125,100	1974	1.5	$738	6.8
Mount Vernon city *Posey Co.*	67.2	$94,800	1966	3.8	$576	11.5
Muncie city *Delaware Co.*	51.4	$73,200	1959	3.8	$670	10.1
Munster town *Lake Co.*	86.8	$196,400	1971	1.4	$962	5.9
Nappanee city *Elkhart Co.*	64.0	$129,900	1976	3.5	$630	15.4
New Albany city *Floyd Co.*	56.1	$110,100	1959	3.9	$697	9.4
New Castle city *Henry Co.*	59.7	$67,400	1956	4.0	$618	13.0
New Haven city *Allen Co.*	75.4	$92,200	1970	1.9	$700	10.8
Noblesville city *Hamilton Co.*	74.6	$168,500	1997	2.6	$889	15.6
North Vernon city *Jennings Co.*	56.7	$78,400	1965	3.5	$642	11.0
Peru city *Miami Co.*	67.4	$57,000	1940	3.7	$596	11.0
Plainfield town *Hendricks Co.*	69.0	$147,900	1990	2.0	$898	7.0
Plymouth city *Marshall Co.*	56.2	$85,700	1975	5.8	$626	12.0
Portage city *Porter Co.*	71.0	$140,100	1978	1.6	$818	7.8
Princeton city *Gibson Co.*	58.9	$82,400	1961	4.4	$643	9.2
Purdue University cdp *Tippecanoe Co.*	0.3	n/a	1959	0.0	$751	6.5
Richmond city *Wayne Co.*	56.2	$81,300	1954	5.5	$614	12.4
Rushville city *Rush Co.*	59.2	$82,000	1951	3.9	$555	8.4
Saint John town *Lake Co.*	97.0	$250,300	1996	2.0	$1,031	3.3
Schererville town *Lake Co.*	78.1	$207,800	1987	1.3	$832	7.0
Scottsburg city *Scott Co.*	58.0	$99,300	1973	3.7	$688	11.6
Seymour city *Jackson Co.*	61.4	$101,200	1973	3.4	$720	13.1
Shelbyville city *Shelby Co.*	56.1	$98,500	1969	4.5	$700	11.0
South Bend city *Saint Joseph Co.*	59.9	$85,100	1954	3.9	$706	11.9
Speedway town *Marion Co.*	48.5	$117,500	1961	1.6	$721	22.2
Tell City city *Perry Co.*	69.1	$90,200	1962	4.2	$605	7.3
Terre Haute city *Vigo Co.*	55.5	$76,800	1949	3.2	$655	11.1
Valparaiso city *Porter Co.*	55.4	$162,800	1976	2.3	$836	7.2
Vincennes city *Knox Co.*	53.5	$74,000	1952	3.1	$606	8.4
Wabash city *Wabash Co.*	65.9	$77,800	1953	5.1	$569	12.0
Warsaw city *Kosciusko Co.*	57.5	$115,900	1972	3.2	$644	10.3
Washington city *Daviess Co.*	60.5	$76,700	1954	3.5	$568	7.8
West Lafayette city *Tippecanoe Co.*	32.4	$174,500	1979	2.6	$849	4.5
Westfield city *Hamilton Co.*	82.4	$217,400	2001	2.5	$876	12.2
Yorktown town *Delaware Co.*	80.8	$125,000	1971	3.2	$710	8.8
Zionsville town *Boone Co.*	77.5	$336,700	1992	2.1	$1,155	16.0

SOURCE: *U.S. Census Bureau, Census 2010; U.S. Census Bureau, American Community Survey, 2009-2013 Five-Year Estimates*

Commute to Work

Place	Automobile (%)	Public Transportation (%)	Walk (%)	Work from Home (%)	Median Travel Time to Work (minutes)
Anderson city *Madison Co.*	90.5	0.9	4.4	2.6	22.8
Angola city *Steuben Co.*	88.7	0.0	5.3	3.9	15.5
Auburn city *DeKalb Co.*	92.8	0.0	0.9	3.9	18.2
Avon town *Hendricks Co.*	95.0	0.0	0.0	3.9	28.2
Batesville city *Ripley Co.*	93.1	0.6	1.0	4.1	17.8
Bedford city *Lawrence Co.*	91.2	1.3	2.3	4.2	19.8
Beech Grove city *Marion Co.*	95.7	0.3	1.2	2.2	21.1
Bloomington city *Monroe Co.*	69.7	7.0	13.8	4.6	15.3
Bluffton city *Wells Co.*	92.7	0.0	2.4	1.7	18.4
Brazil city *Clay Co.*	96.7	0.0	1.8	1.0	22.5
Brownsburg town *Hendricks Co.*	95.4	0.0	0.6	2.9	26.0
Carmel city *Hamilton Co.*	91.1	0.4	1.0	6.6	24.8
Cedar Lake town *Lake Co.*	95.9	0.6	0.2	2.4	32.8
Charlestown city *Clark Co.*	95.8	0.6	0.4	1.6	25.0
Chesterton town *Porter Co.*	93.5	2.4	0.7	3.4	25.5
Clarksville town *Clark Co.*	96.0	0.6	0.7	1.7	21.5
Columbia City city *Whitley Co.*	94.0	0.5	2.7	1.6	20.7
Columbus city *Bartholomew Co.*	93.8	0.7	1.1	2.7	17.2
Connersville city *Fayette Co.*	92.9	0.6	1.8	2.0	25.3
Crawfordsville city *Montgomery Co.*	88.4	0.3	6.7	3.6	16.7
Crown Point city *Lake Co.*	92.7	1.6	1.5	2.9	27.6
Danville town *Hendricks Co.*	95.6	0.4	1.2	2.0	25.5
Decatur city *Adams Co.*	95.7	0.0	1.4	1.6	18.4
Dyer town *Lake Co.*	93.0	5.1	0.3	1.4	29.8
East Chicago city *Lake Co.*	88.2	4.9	5.4	0.8	21.7
Elkhart city *Elkhart Co.*	91.9	1.4	1.9	0.7	19.7
Ellettsville town *Monroe Co.*	92.5	0.0	3.6	3.6	20.6
Elwood city *Madison Co.*	92.3	0.0	1.9	2.9	30.6
Evansville city *Vanderburgh Co.*	91.0	2.5	2.6	2.4	18.0
Fishers town *Hamilton Co.*	92.2	0.2	0.4	6.4	27.4
Fort Wayne city *Allen Co.*	93.2	0.9	1.4	3.3	19.7
Frankfort city *Clinton Co.*	94.4	0.0	0.5	1.0	19.3
Franklin city *Johnson Co.*	91.4	1.2	2.7	2.8	23.8
Gary city *Lake Co.*	89.9	3.7	3.2	1.9	24.7
Goshen city *Elkhart Co.*	90.2	0.9	4.3	2.0	17.4
Granger cdp *Saint Joseph Co.*	94.1	0.2	0.3	4.4	22.2
Greencastle city *Putnam Co.*	74.1	0.0	19.3	2.9	17.2
Greenfield city *Hancock Co.*	94.9	0.0	1.8	2.5	24.5
Greensburg city *Decatur Co.*	94.6	0.4	2.5	1.5	19.5
Greenwood city *Johnson Co.*	95.8	0.4	0.5	2.8	25.8
Griffith town *Lake Co.*	93.9	3.4	0.5	0.4	25.7
Hammond city *Lake Co.*	91.7	3.9	2.2	1.4	27.0
Highland town *Lake Co.*	94.6	2.5	1.0	1.6	25.6
Hobart city *Lake Co.*	95.6	1.7	0.3	2.0	26.7
Huntington city *Huntington Co.*	90.8	0.3	4.1	3.3	18.5
Indianapolis city *Marion Co.*	91.8	2.1	2.0	2.9	22.6
Jasper city *Dubois Co.*	93.5	0.0	1.8	3.9	16.5
Jeffersonville city *Clark Co.*	94.5	0.3	1.8	2.3	21.5
Kendallville city *Noble Co.*	92.2	0.0	4.5	1.6	22.3
Kokomo city *Howard Co.*	93.3	0.6	2.0	2.4	19.6

Place	Automobile (%)	Public Transportation (%)	Walk (%)	Work from Home (%)	Median Travel Time to Work (minutes)
La Porte city *LaPorte Co.*	95.3	0.7	2.1	1.0	18.6
Lafayette city *Tippecanoe Co.*	91.0	2.7	2.2	2.1	15.9
Lake Station city *Lake Co.*	95.8	0.5	0.1	2.4	24.9
Lakes of the Four Seasons cdp *Lake Co.*	96.4	2.3	0.0	1.3	38.5
Lawrence city *Marion Co.*	94.5	0.1	1.5	3.8	24.8
Lebanon city *Boone Co.*	94.3	0.0	0.9	2.2	21.8
Logansport city *Cass Co.*	92.8	1.6	1.4	1.5	18.7
Lowell town *Lake Co.*	96.2	0.2	0.8	1.7	35.1
Madison city *Jefferson Co.*	92.1	0.5	2.1	3.7	18.7
Marion city *Grant Co.*	84.6	0.2	5.7	7.8	16.5
Martinsville city *Morgan Co.*	89.3	0.0	2.1	5.8	25.3
Merrillville town *Lake Co.*	93.8	1.6	0.7	1.8	27.2
Michigan City city *LaPorte Co.*	91.5	2.5	2.2	3.2	19.2
Mishawaka city *Saint Joseph Co.*	92.0	1.6	1.8	3.1	20.5
Mooresville town *Morgan Co.*	95.9	0.0	1.6	1.5	22.8
Mount Vernon city *Posey Co.*	95.8	0.0	1.8	1.9	17.5
Muncie city *Delaware Co.*	85.4	2.6	7.9	2.1	17.7
Munster town *Lake Co.*	89.2	5.0	0.7	4.5	27.8
Nappanee city *Elkhart Co.*	95.9	0.0	2.1	1.5	21.3
New Albany city *Floyd Co.*	94.0	1.2	1.7	2.0	20.1
New Castle city *Henry Co.*	94.7	0.5	1.9	1.8	22.6
New Haven city *Allen Co.*	93.0	0.1	2.6	3.1	19.3
Noblesville city *Hamilton Co.*	92.5	0.1	1.2	5.5	27.5
North Vernon city *Jennings Co.*	92.2	0.0	2.2	3.3	21.5
Peru city *Miami Co.*	90.3	0.4	3.5	1.8	19.2
Plainfield town *Hendricks Co.*	95.0	0.2	0.8	2.0	23.5
Plymouth city *Marshall Co.*	92.1	0.0	3.3	2.5	16.7
Portage city *Porter Co.*	94.0	1.0	2.1	1.8	26.4
Princeton city *Gibson Co.*	93.2	0.5	4.7	1.5	15.6
Purdue University cdp *Tippecanoe Co.*	26.2	9.9	43.3	15.1	13.9
Richmond city *Wayne Co.*	92.7	0.7	3.0	2.1	16.2
Rushville city *Rush Co.*	94.0	0.5	3.0	2.5	22.0
Saint John town *Lake Co.*	92.6	2.4	0.0	3.6	32.9
Schererville town *Lake Co.*	94.5	2.0	0.5	1.7	29.8
Scottsburg city *Scott Co.*	98.5	0.0	0.9	0.2	27.7
Seymour city *Jackson Co.*	92.0	0.2	1.2	1.3	16.0
Shelbyville city *Shelby Co.*	94.8	0.0	1.2	1.5	19.9
South Bend city *Saint Joseph Co.*	90.0	2.8	3.2	2.1	18.8
Speedway town *Marion Co.*	91.3	3.0	0.9	3.6	23.5
Tell City city *Perry Co.*	96.6	0.0	1.9	0.9	18.5
Terre Haute city *Vigo Co.*	88.6	0.8	6.3	2.1	17.7
Valparaiso city *Porter Co.*	88.7	1.8	3.0	4.1	22.3
Vincennes city *Knox Co.*	91.6	0.5	4.4	1.2	16.0
Wabash city *Wabash Co.*	92.7	1.2	3.8	2.0	15.0
Warsaw city *Kosciusko Co.*	92.3	0.5	3.1	2.0	15.7
Washington city *Daviess Co.*	95.2	0.5	2.0	1.0	16.0
West Lafayette city *Tippecanoe Co.*	66.1	7.6	17.5	4.1	15.5
Westfield city *Hamilton Co.*	93.4	0.3	0.9	3.2	26.1
Yorktown town *Delaware Co.*	94.6	0.0	0.5	3.6	19.5
Zionsville town *Boone Co.*	91.1	0.2	0.4	7.0	23.8

SOURCE: U.S. Census Bureau, American Community Survey, 2009-2013 Five-Year Estimates

Crime

Place	Violent Crime Rate (crimes per 10,000 population)	Property Crime Rate (crimes per 10,000 population)
Anderson city *Madison Co.*	36.1	481.2
Angola city *Steuben Co.*	7.0	450.7
Auburn city *DeKalb Co.*	8.6	194.5
Avon town *Hendricks Co.*	n/a	n/a
Batesville city *Ripley Co.*	40.1	171.1
Bedford city *Lawrence Co.*	52.2	337.3
Beech Grove city *Marion Co.*	22.9	374.7
Bloomington city *Monroe Co.*	33.4	316.2
Bluffton city *Wells Co.*	n/a	n/a
Brazil city *Clay Co.*	n/a	n/a
Brownsburg town *Hendricks Co.*	14.4	168.1
Carmel city *Hamilton Co.*	2.4	87.7
Cedar Lake town *Lake Co.*	11.1	212.2
Charlestown city *Clark Co.*	n/a	n/a
Chesterton town *Porter Co.*	n/a	n/a
Clarksville town *Clark Co.*	55.8	699.3
Columbia City city *Whitley Co.*	4.5	159.3
Columbus city *Bartholomew Co.*	17.9	463.0
Connersville city *Fayette Co.*	n/a	n/a
Crawfordsville city *Montgomery Co.*	14.3	332.0
Crown Point city *Lake Co.*	n/a	n/a
Danville town *Hendricks Co.*	32.8	97.3
Decatur city *Adams Co.*	10.7	199.0
Dyer town *Lake Co.*	6.7	120.3
East Chicago city *Lake Co.*	66.7	497.3
Elkhart city *Elkhart Co.*	n/a	n/a
Ellettsville town *Monroe Co.*	38.0	115.4
Elwood city *Madison Co.*	8.2	335.6
Evansville city *Vanderburgh Co.*	46.9	487.1
Fishers town *Hamilton Co.*	1.9	99.1
Fort Wayne city *Allen Co.*	37.2	384.9
Frankfort city *Clinton Co.*	n/a	n/a
Franklin city *Johnson Co.*	28.7	381.1
Gary city *Lake Co.*	112.0	598.7
Goshen city *Elkhart Co.*	9.3	341.0
Granger cdp *Saint Joseph Co.*	n/a	n/a
Greencastle city *Putnam Co.*	n/a	n/a
Greenfield city *Hancock Co.*	5.7	192.2
Greensburg city *Decatur Co.*	27.4	50.5
Greenwood city *Johnson Co.*	37.6	358.6
Griffith town *Lake Co.*	18.0	338.9
Hammond city *Lake Co.*	82.4	407.8
Highland town *Lake Co.*	3.9	324.3
Hobart city *Lake Co.*	21.3	536.8
Huntington city *Huntington Co.*	15.6	216.0
Indianapolis city *Marion Co.*	123.3	524.6
Jasper city *Dubois Co.*	31.6	88.8
Jeffersonville city *Clark Co.*	76.1	366.0
Kendallville city *Noble Co.*	n/a	n/a
Kokomo city *Howard Co.*	32.5	388.6

Place	Violent Crime Rate (crimes per 10,000 population)	Property Crime Rate (crimes per 10,000 population)
La Porte city *LaPorte Co.*	19.9	393.0
Lafayette city *Tippecanoe Co.*	57.1	501.1
Lake Station city *Lake Co.*	40.5	471.0
Lakes of the Four Seasons cdp *Lake Co.*	n/a	n/a
Lawrence city *Marion Co.*	n/a	n/a
Lebanon city *Boone Co.*	n/a	n/a
Logansport city *Cass Co.*	n/a	n/a
Lowell town *Lake Co.*	19.2	112.3
Madison city *Jefferson Co.*	n/a	n/a
Marion city *Grant Co.*	27.1	388.5
Martinsville city *Morgan Co.*	5.9	602.2
Merrillville town *Lake Co.*	27.7	373.9
Michigan City city *LaPorte Co.*	n/a	n/a
Mishawaka city *Saint Joseph Co.*	28.4	563.7
Mooresville town *Morgan Co.*	7.4	322.4
Mount Vernon city *Posey Co.*	18.2	526.9
Muncie city *Delaware Co.*	41.1	429.2
Munster town *Lake Co.*	n/a	n/a
Nappanee city *Elkhart Co.*	4.5	168.8
New Albany city *Floyd Co.*	23.8	548.6
New Castle city *Henry Co.*	n/a	n/a
New Haven city *Allen Co.*	15.4	341.6
Noblesville city *Hamilton Co.*	n/a	n/a
North Vernon city *Jennings Co.*	33.1	590.4
Peru city *Miami Co.*	18.7	118.5
Plainfield town *Hendricks Co.*	16.9	298.9
Plymouth city *Marshall Co.*	7.0	314.9
Portage city *Porter Co.*	19.0	234.9
Princeton city *Gibson Co.*	n/a	n/a
Purdue University cdp *Tippecanoe Co.*	n/a	n/a
Richmond city *Wayne Co.*	n/a	n/a
Rushville city *Rush Co.*	16.1	467.4
Saint John town *Lake Co.*	n/a	n/a
Schererville town *Lake Co.*	7.1	240.3
Scottsburg city *Scott Co.*	42.3	453.6
Seymour city *Jackson Co.*	53.6	643.8
Shelbyville city *Shelby Co.*	n/a	233.8
South Bend city *Saint Joseph Co.*	65.9	485.5
Speedway town *Marion Co.*	24.2	524.8
Tell City city *Perry Co.*	5.5	189.5
Terre Haute city *Vigo Co.*	28.9	532.7
Valparaiso city *Porter Co.*	10.3	207.2
Vincennes city *Knox Co.*	n/a	n/a
Wabash city *Wabash Co.*	n/a	n/a
Warsaw city *Kosciusko Co.*	76.3	321.7
Washington city *Daviess Co.*	36.4	639.1
West Lafayette city *Tippecanoe Co.*	12.1	174.7
Westfield city *Hamilton Co.*	6.4	149.2
Yorktown town *Delaware Co.*	n/a	n/a
Zionsville town *Boone Co.*	0.8	25.8

NOTE: n/a not available.
SOURCE: Federal Bureau of Investigation, Uniform Crime Reports, 2013

Community Rankings

This section ranks incorporated places and CDPs (Census Designated Places) with populations of 2,500 or more. Unincorporated postal areas were not considered. For each topic below, you will find two tables, one in Descending Order—highest to lowest, and one in Ascending Order—lowest to highest. Four topics are exceptions to this rule, and only include Descending Order—Water Area, Ancestry (five tables), Native Hawaiian/Other Pacific Islander, and Commute to Work: Public Transportation. This is because there are an extraordinarily large number of places that place at the bottom of these topics with zero numbers.

Land Area	247
Water Area	249
Elevation	250
Population	252
Population Growth	254
Population Density	256
White Population	258
Black/African American Population	260
Asian Population	262
American Indian/Alaska Native Population	264
Native Hawaiian/Other Pacific Islander Population	266
Two or More Races	267
Hispanic Population	269
Average Household Size	271
Median Age	273
Population Under Age 18	275
Population Age 65 and Over	277
Males per 100 Females	279
Marriage Status: Never Married	281
Marriage Status: Now Married	283
Marriage Status: Separated	285
Marriage Status: Widowed	287
Marriage Status: Divorced	289
Foreign Born	291
Speak English Only at Home	293
Individuals with a Disability	295
Veterans	297
Ancestry: German	299
Ancestry: English	300
Ancestry: American	301
Ancestry: Irish	302
Ancestry: Italian	303
Employment: Management, Business, and Financial Occupations	304
Employment: Computer, Engineering, and Science Occupations	306
Employment: Education, Legal, Community Service, Arts, and Media Occupations	308
Employment: Healthcare Practitioners	310
Employment: Service Occupations	312
Employment: Sales and Office Occupations	314
Employment: Natural Resources, Construction, and Maintenance Occupations	316

Employment: Production, Transportation, and Material Moving Occupations 318
Per Capita Income 320
Median Household Income 322
Average Household Income. 324
Households with Income of $100,000 or More 326
Poverty Rate 328
Educational Attainment: High School Diploma or Higher 330
Educational Attainment: Bachelor's Degree or Higher 332
Educational Attainment: Graduate/Professional Degree or Higher 334
Homeownership Rate 336
Median Home Value. 338
Median Year Structure Built 340
Homeowner Vacancy Rate 342
Median Gross Rent 344
Rental Vacancy Rate 346
Population with Health Insurance 348
Population with Private Health Insurance 350
Population with Public Health Insurance 352
Population with No Health Insurance 354
Population Under 18 Years Old with No Health Insurance 356
Commute to Work: Car 358
Commute to Work: Public Transportation 360
Commute to Work: Walk 361
Commute to Work: Work from Home 363
Median Travel Time to Work 365
Violent Crime Rate per 10,000 Population 367
Property Crime Rate per 10,000 Population. 369

Land Area
Top 150 Places Ranked in *Descending* Order

State Rank	Sq. Miles	Place
1	361.433	**Indianapolis** (city) Marion County
2	110.618	**Fort Wayne** (city) Allen County
3	49.865	**Gary** (city) Lake County
4	47.463	**Carmel** (city) Hamilton County
5	44.153	**Evansville** (city) Vanderburgh County
6	41.458	**South Bend** (city) Saint Joseph County
7	41.371	**Anderson** (city) Madison County
8	34.536	**Terre Haute** (city) Vigo County
9	34.064	**Jeffersonville** (city) Clark County
10	33.585	**Fishers** (town) Hamilton County
11	33.216	**Merrillville** (town) Lake County
12	31.374	**Noblesville** (city) Hamilton County
13	27.742	**Lafayette** (city) Tippecanoe County
14	27.497	**Columbus** (city) Bartholomew County
15	27.196	**Muncie** (city) Delaware County
16	26.838	**Westfield** (city) Hamilton County
17	26.331	**Hobart** (city) Lake County
18	25.628	**Portage** (city) Porter County
19	25.567	**Granger** (CDP) Saint Joseph County
20	23.915	**Richmond** (city) Wayne County
21	23.453	**Elkhart** (city) Elkhart County
22	23.158	**Bloomington** (city) Monroe County
23	22.776	**Hammond** (city) Lake County
24	22.274	**Plainfield** (town) Hendricks County
25	21.230	**Greenwood** (city) Johnson County
26	20.132	**Lawrence** (city) Marion County
27	19.588	**Michigan City** (city) LaPorte County
28	18.497	**Kokomo** (city) Howard County
29	17.713	**Crown Point** (city) Lake County
30	16.997	**Mishawaka** (city) Saint Joseph County
31	16.229	**Goshen** (city) Elkhart County
32	15.711	**Marion** (city) Grant County
33	15.555	**Lebanon** (city) Boone County
34	15.530	**Valparaiso** (city) Porter County
35	14.939	**New Albany** (city) Floyd County
36	14.712	**Schererville** (town) Lake County
37	14.241	**Avon** (town) Hendricks County
38	14.088	**East Chicago** (city) Lake County
39	13.105	**Jasper** (city) Dubois County
40	13.006	**Franklin** (city) Johnson County
41	12.551	**Greenfield** (city) Hancock County
42	12.548	**Bright** (CDP) Dearborn County
43	12.161	**Bedford** (city) Lawrence County
44	11.975	**Winfield** (town) Lake County
45	11.660	**La Porte** (city) LaPorte County
46	11.576	**Warsaw** (city) Kosciusko County
47	11.564	**Shelbyville** (city) Shelby County
48	11.446	**Charlestown** (city) Clark County
49	11.422	**Seymour** (city) Jackson County
50	11.387	**Saint John** (town) Lake County
51	11.166	**Pendleton** (town) Madison County
52	11.076	**Brownsburg** (town) Hendricks County
53	10.720	**Smithville-Sanders** (CDP) Monroe County
54	10.458	**Whitestown** (town) Boone County
55	10.257	**Zionsville** (town) Boone County
56	9.973	**Clarksville** (town) Clark County
57	9.867	**New Haven** (city) Allen County
58	9.332	**Chesterton** (town) Porter County
59	9.270	**Greensburg** (city) Decatur County
60	9.146	**Crawfordsville** (city) Montgomery County
61	8.886	**Wabash** (city) Wabash County
62	8.779	**Yorktown** (town) Delaware County
63	8.748	**Logansport** (city) Cass County
64	8.707	**Huntington** (city) Huntington County
65	8.575	**Madison** (city) Jefferson County
66	8.296	**Lake Station** (city) Lake County
67	8.232	**Bluffton** (city) Wells County
68	8.219	**Cedar Lake** (town) Lake County
69	8.070	**Roselawn** (CDP) Newton County
70	7.745	**Connersville** (city) Fayette County
71	7.733	**Griffith** (town) Lake County
72	7.615	**West Lafayette** (city) Tippecanoe County
73	7.570	**Munster** (town) Lake County
74	7.534	**Plymouth** (city) Marshall County
75	7.412	**Vincennes** (city) Knox County
76	7.295	**New Castle** (city) Henry County
77	7.104	**Auburn** (city) DeKalb County
78	6.936	**Highland** (town) Lake County
79	6.930	**Danville** (town) Hendricks County
80	6.619	**North Vernon** (city) Jennings County
81	6.344	**Angola** (city) Steuben County
82	6.311	**Frankfort** (city) Clinton County
83	6.285	**Mooresville** (town) Morgan County
84	6.200	**Porter** (town) Porter County
85	6.104	**Dyer** (town) Lake County
86	6.087	**Batesville** (city) Ripley County
87	6.045	**Kendallville** (city) Noble County
88	5.777	**Decatur** (city) Adams County
89	5.712	**Greendale** (city) Dearborn County
90	5.582	**Columbia City** (city) Whitley County
91	5.242	**Greencastle** (city) Putnam County
92	5.180	**Lowell** (town) Lake County
93	5.105	**Peru** (city) Miami County
94	5.070	**Princeton** (city) Gibson County
95	5.061	**Huntingburg** (city) Dubois County
96	5.053	**Scottsburg** (city) Scott County
97	4.992	**Grissom AFB** (CDP) Miami County
98	4.941	**Lawrenceburg** (city) Dearborn County
99	4.926	**Bargersville** (town) Johnson County
100	4.900	**Dunlap** (CDP) Elkhart County
101	4.758	**Speedway** (town) Marion County
102	4.731	**Washington** (city) Daviess County
103	4.701	**McCordsville** (town) Hancock County
104	4.691	**Rochester** (city) Fulton County
105	4.651	**Portland** (city) Jay County
106	4.556	**Gas City** (city) Grant County
107	4.534	**Tell City** (city) Perry County
108	4.490	**Martinsville** (city) Morgan County
109	4.395	**Beech Grove** (city) Marion County
110	4.240	**Ellettsville** (town) Monroe County
111	4.149	**Nappanee** (city) Elkhart County
112	4.138	**Hidden Valley** (CDP) Dearborn County
113	4.000	**Salem** (city) Washington County
114	3.943	**Sellersburg** (town) Clark County
115	3.920	**Knox** (city) Starke County
116	3.875	**Hartford City** (city) Blackford County
117	3.851	**Garrett** (city) DeKalb County
118	3.802	**Huntertown** (town) Allen County
119	3.800	**Rensselaer** (city) Jasper County
120	3.774	**Elwood** (city) Madison County
121	3.755	**Middlebury** (town) Elkhart County
122	3.743	**Paoli** (town) Orange County
123	3.713	**Leo-Cedarville** (town) Allen County
124	3.609	**De Motte** (town) Jasper County
125	3.568	**North Terre Haute** (CDP) Vigo County
126	3.564	**Simonton Lake** (CDP) Elkhart County
127	3.534	**North Manchester** (town) Wabash County
128	3.470	**Monticello** (city) White County
129	3.328	**Winchester** (city) Randolph County
130	3.276	**Mitchell** (city) Lawrence County
131	3.219	**Whiteland** (town) Johnson County
132	3.138	**Upland** (town) Grant County
133	3.109	**Edinburgh** (town) Johnson County
134	3.091	**Rushville** (city) Rush County
135	3.088	**Westville** (town) LaPorte County
136	3.027	**Brazil** (city) Clay County
137	3.022	**Linton** (city) Greene County
138	3.012	**Heritage Lake** (CDP) Putnam County
139	3.001	**Boonville** (city) Warrick County
140	2.976	**Fortville** (town) Hancock County
141	2.951	**Pittsboro** (town) Hendricks County
142	2.808	**Mount Vernon** (city) Posey County
143	2.763	**Winona Lake** (town) Kosciusko County
144	2.761	**Aurora** (city) Dearborn County
145	2.726	**Delphi** (city) Carroll County
146	2.715	**Bremen** (town) Marshall County
147	2.681	**Lakes of the Four Seasons** (CDP) Lake County
148	2.627	**Alexandria** (city) Madison County
149	2.577	**Austin** (city) Scott County
150	2.562	**Country Squire Lakes** (CDP) Jennings County

Note: *This section ranks incorporated places and CDPs (Census Designated Places) with populations of 2,500 or more. Unincorporated postal areas were not considered. Please refer to the User Guide for additional information.*

Land Area
Top 150 Places Ranked in *Ascending* Order

State Rank	Sq. Miles	Place
1	1.097	**Fort Branch** (town) Gibson County
2	1.176	**Covington** (city) Fountain County
3	1.208	**Notre Dame** (CDP) Saint Joseph County
4	1.243	**South Haven** (CDP) Porter County
5	1.298	**Purdue University** (CDP) Tippecanoe County
6	1.323	**Chesterfield** (town) Madison County
7	1.346	**Bicknell** (city) Knox County
8	1.361	**Melody Hill** (CDP) Vanderburgh County
9	1.406	**Newburgh** (town) Warrick County
10	1.429	**Ossian** (town) Wells County
11	1.461	**New Whiteland** (town) Johnson County
12	1.492	**Rockville** (town) Parke County
13	1.498	**Brookville** (town) Franklin County
14	1.567	**Loogootee** (city) Martin County
15	1.583	**Fairmount** (town) Grant County
16	1.588	**Brownstown** (town) Jackson County
17	1.600	**Attica** (city) Fountain County
18	1.649	**Corydon** (town) Harrison County
19	1.704	**Lagrange** (town) LaGrange County
20	1.708	**Cicero** (town) Hamilton County
21	1.787	**Syracuse** (town) Kosciusko County
22	1.798	**Whiting** (city) Lake County
23	1.876	**Sullivan** (city) Sullivan County
24	1.899	**Shorewood Forest** (CDP) Porter County
25	1.976	**Hebron** (town) Porter County
26	2.033	**Chandler** (town) Warrick County
27	2.049	**Georgetown** (town) Floyd County
28	2.058	**Cumberland** (town) Marion County
29	2.078	**Berne** (city) Adams County
30	2.093	**Butler** (city) DeKalb County
31	2.137	**Sheridan** (town) Hamilton County
32	2.200	**Union City** (city) Randolph County
33	2.238	**Clinton** (city) Vermillion County
34	2.267	**Highland** (CDP) Vanderburgh County
35	2.308	**Hanover** (town) Jefferson County
36	2.310	**Ligonier** (city) Noble County
37	2.404	**Centerville** (town) Wayne County
38	2.504	**Tipton** (city) Tipton County
39	2.562	**Country Squire Lakes** (CDP) Jennings County
40	2.577	**Austin** (city) Scott County
41	2.627	**Alexandria** (city) Madison County
42	2.681	**Lakes of the Four Seasons** (CDP) Lake County
43	2.715	**Bremen** (town) Marshall County
44	2.726	**Delphi** (city) Carroll County
45	2.761	**Aurora** (city) Dearborn County
46	2.763	**Winona Lake** (town) Kosciusko County
47	2.808	**Mount Vernon** (city) Posey County
48	2.951	**Pittsboro** (town) Hendricks County
49	2.976	**Fortville** (town) Hancock County
50	3.001	**Boonville** (city) Warrick County
51	3.012	**Heritage Lake** (CDP) Putnam County
52	3.022	**Linton** (city) Greene County
53	3.027	**Brazil** (city) Clay County
54	3.088	**Westville** (town) LaPorte County
55	3.091	**Rushville** (city) Rush County
56	3.109	**Edinburgh** (town) Johnson County
57	3.138	**Upland** (town) Grant County
58	3.219	**Whiteland** (town) Johnson County
59	3.276	**Mitchell** (city) Lawrence County
60	3.328	**Winchester** (city) Randolph County
61	3.470	**Monticello** (city) White County
62	3.534	**North Manchester** (town) Wabash County
63	3.564	**Simonton Lake** (CDP) Elkhart County
64	3.568	**North Terre Haute** (CDP) Vigo County
65	3.609	**De Motte** (town) Jasper County
66	3.713	**Leo-Cedarville** (town) Allen County
67	3.743	**Paoli** (town) Orange County
68	3.755	**Middlebury** (town) Elkhart County
69	3.774	**Elwood** (city) Madison County
70	3.800	**Rensselaer** (city) Jasper County
71	3.802	**Huntertown** (town) Allen County
72	3.851	**Garrett** (city) DeKalb County
73	3.875	**Hartford City** (city) Blackford County
74	3.920	**Knox** (city) Starke County
75	3.943	**Sellersburg** (town) Clark County
76	4.000	**Salem** (city) Washington County
77	4.138	**Hidden Valley** (CDP) Dearborn County
78	4.149	**Nappanee** (city) Elkhart County
79	4.240	**Ellettsville** (town) Monroe County
80	4.395	**Beech Grove** (city) Marion County
81	4.490	**Martinsville** (city) Morgan County
82	4.534	**Tell City** (city) Perry County
83	4.556	**Gas City** (city) Grant County
84	4.651	**Portland** (city) Jay County
85	4.691	**Rochester** (city) Fulton County
86	4.701	**McCordsville** (town) Hancock County
87	4.731	**Washington** (city) Daviess County
88	4.758	**Speedway** (town) Marion County
89	4.900	**Dunlap** (CDP) Elkhart County
90	4.926	**Bargersville** (town) Johnson County
91	4.941	**Lawrenceburg** (city) Dearborn County
92	4.992	**Grissom AFB** (CDP) Miami County
93	5.053	**Scottsburg** (city) Scott County
94	5.061	**Huntingburg** (city) Dubois County
95	5.070	**Princeton** (city) Gibson County
96	5.105	**Peru** (city) Miami County
97	5.180	**Lowell** (town) Lake County
98	5.242	**Greencastle** (city) Putnam County
99	5.582	**Columbia City** (city) Whitley County
100	5.712	**Greendale** (city) Dearborn County
101	5.777	**Decatur** (city) Adams County
102	6.045	**Kendallville** (city) Noble County
103	6.087	**Batesville** (city) Ripley County
104	6.104	**Dyer** (town) Lake County
105	6.200	**Porter** (town) Porter County
106	6.285	**Mooresville** (town) Morgan County
107	6.311	**Frankfort** (city) Clinton County
108	6.344	**Angola** (city) Steuben County
109	6.619	**North Vernon** (city) Jennings County
110	6.930	**Danville** (town) Hendricks County
111	6.936	**Highland** (town) Lake County
112	7.104	**Auburn** (city) DeKalb County
113	7.295	**New Castle** (city) Henry County
114	7.412	**Vincennes** (city) Knox County
115	7.534	**Plymouth** (city) Marshall County
116	7.570	**Munster** (town) Lake County
117	7.615	**West Lafayette** (city) Tippecanoe County
118	7.733	**Griffith** (town) Lake County
119	7.745	**Connersville** (city) Fayette County
120	8.070	**Roselawn** (CDP) Newton County
121	8.219	**Cedar Lake** (town) Lake County
122	8.232	**Bluffton** (city) Wells County
123	8.296	**Lake Station** (city) Lake County
124	8.575	**Madison** (city) Jefferson County
125	8.707	**Huntington** (city) Huntington County
126	8.748	**Logansport** (city) Cass County
127	8.779	**Yorktown** (town) Delaware County
128	8.886	**Wabash** (city) Wabash County
129	9.146	**Crawfordsville** (city) Montgomery County
130	9.270	**Greensburg** (city) Decatur County
131	9.332	**Chesterton** (town) Porter County
132	9.867	**New Haven** (city) Allen County
133	9.973	**Clarksville** (town) Clark County
134	10.257	**Zionsville** (town) Boone County
135	10.458	**Whitestown** (town) Boone County
136	10.720	**Smithville-Sanders** (CDP) Monroe County
137	11.076	**Brownsburg** (town) Hendricks County
138	11.166	**Pendleton** (town) Madison County
139	11.387	**Saint John** (town) Lake County
140	11.422	**Seymour** (city) Jackson County
141	11.446	**Charlestown** (city) Clark County
142	11.564	**Shelbyville** (city) Shelby County
143	11.576	**Warsaw** (city) Kosciusko County
144	11.660	**La Porte** (city) LaPorte County
145	11.975	**Winfield** (town) Lake County
146	12.161	**Bedford** (city) Lawrence County
147	12.548	**Bright** (CDP) Dearborn County
148	12.551	**Greenfield** (city) Hancock County
149	13.006	**Franklin** (city) Johnson County
150	13.105	**Jasper** (city) Dubois County

Note: This section ranks incorporated places and CDPs (Census Designated Places) with populations of 2,500 or more. Unincorporated postal areas were not considered. Please refer to the User Guide for additional information.

Water Area
Top 150 Places Ranked in *Descending* Order

State Rank	Sq. Miles	Place
1	7.310	**Gary** (city) Lake County
2	6.592	**Indianapolis** (city) Marion County
3	3.265	**Michigan City** (city) LaPorte County
4	2.249	**Fishers** (town) Hamilton County
5	2.106	**Hammond** (city) Lake County
6	2.065	**East Chicago** (city) Lake County
7	1.984	**Portage** (city) Porter County
8	1.429	**Whiting** (city) Lake County
9	1.415	**Noblesville** (city) Hamilton County
10	1.387	**Cedar Lake** (town) Lake County
11	1.338	**Warsaw** (city) Kosciusko County
12	1.111	**Rochester** (city) Fulton County
13	1.085	**Carmel** (city) Hamilton County
14	0.967	**Elkhart** (city) Elkhart County
15	0.732	**Terre Haute** (city) Vigo County
16	0.710	**La Porte** (city) LaPorte County
17	0.490	**Winona Lake** (town) Kosciusko County
18	0.472	**Evansville** (city) Vanderburgh County
19	0.471	**Simonton Lake** (CDP) Elkhart County
20	0.469	**Heritage Lake** (CDP) Putnam County
21	0.417	**South Bend** (city) Saint Joseph County
22	0.416	**Lakes of the Four Seasons** (CDP) Lake County
23	0.412	**Cicero** (town) Hamilton County
24	0.386	**Columbus** (city) Bartholomew County
25	0.375	**Hobart** (city) Lake County
26	0.366	**Syracuse** (town) Kosciusko County
27	0.355	**Goshen** (city) Elkhart County
28	0.348	**Mishawaka** (city) Saint Joseph County
29	0.338	**Shorewood Forest** (CDP) Porter County
30	0.327	**Aurora** (city) Dearborn County
31	0.294	**Jeffersonville** (city) Clark County
32	0.285	**Shelbyville** (city) Shelby County
33	0.284	**Porter** (town) Porter County
34	0.272	**Madison** (city) Jefferson County
35	0.270	**Lawrenceburg** (city) Dearborn County
36	0.270	**Hidden Valley** (CDP) Dearborn County
37	0.241	**Westfield** (city) Hamilton County
38	0.238	**Wabash** (city) Wabash County
39	0.224	**Kendallville** (city) Noble County
40	0.222	**Logansport** (city) Cass County
41	0.216	**Monticello** (city) White County
42	0.214	**Fort Wayne** (city) Allen County
43	0.213	**Huntingburg** (city) Dubois County
44	0.203	**Clarksville** (town) Clark County
45	0.199	**Bloomington** (city) Monroe County
46	0.192	**Muncie** (city) Delaware County
47	0.171	**New Albany** (city) Floyd County
48	0.157	**Richmond** (city) Wayne County
49	0.139	**Country Squire Lakes** (CDP) Jennings County
50	0.136	**Leo-Cedarville** (town) Allen County
51	0.134	**Huntington** (city) Huntington County
52	0.131	**Lake Station** (city) Lake County
53	0.129	**Bluffton** (city) Wells County
54	0.113	**Chesterton** (town) Porter County
55	0.112	**Greenfield** (city) Hancock County
56	0.110	**Lawrence** (city) Marion County
57	0.109	**Anderson** (city) Madison County
58	0.109	**Plainfield** (town) Hendricks County
59	0.105	**Tell City** (city) Perry County
60	0.102	**Avon** (town) Hendricks County
61	0.091	**Jasper** (city) Dubois County
62	0.091	**Saint John** (town) Lake County
63	0.086	**Lowell** (town) Lake County
64	0.084	**Marion** (city) Grant County
65	0.083	**Yorktown** (town) Delaware County
66	0.081	**Munster** (town) Lake County
67	0.079	**North Manchester** (town) Wabash County
68	0.076	**Brownsburg** (town) Hendricks County
69	0.075	**Greendale** (city) Dearborn County
70	0.073	**Peru** (city) Miami County
71	0.068	**Vincennes** (city) Knox County
72	0.067	**Pendleton** (town) Madison County
73	0.066	**Winfield** (town) Lake County
74	0.066	**Notre Dame** (CDP) Saint Joseph County
75	0.066	**Batesville** (city) Ripley County
76	0.060	**Rensselaer** (city) Jasper County
77	0.059	**Kokomo** (city) Howard County
78	0.057	**Mooresville** (town) Morgan County
79	0.053	**Schererville** (town) Lake County
80	0.051	**Greencastle** (city) Putnam County
81	0.050	**Mount Vernon** (city) Posey County
82	0.048	**Valparaiso** (city) Porter County
83	0.047	**Angola** (city) Steuben County
84	0.046	**Danville** (town) Hendricks County
85	0.045	**Greensburg** (city) Decatur County
86	0.043	**Brookville** (town) Franklin County
87	0.040	**Plymouth** (city) Marshall County
88	0.039	**Charlestown** (city) Clark County
89	0.038	**Zionsville** (town) Boone County
90	0.037	**Washington** (city) Daviess County
91	0.035	**Merrillville** (town) Lake County
92	0.030	**Sellersburg** (town) Clark County
93	0.028	**Brazil** (city) Clay County
94	0.023	**Highland** (town) Lake County
95	0.022	**Middlebury** (town) Elkhart County
96	0.021	**Columbia City** (city) Whitley County
97	0.021	**New Castle** (city) Henry County
98	0.021	**Hartford City** (city) Blackford County
99	0.019	**Scottsburg** (city) Scott County
100	0.019	**Clinton** (city) Vermillion County
101	0.018	**Martinsville** (city) Morgan County
102	0.018	**Bright** (CDP) Dearborn County
103	0.018	**Georgetown** (town) Floyd County
104	0.018	**Salem** (city) Washington County
105	0.016	**Melody Hill** (CDP) Vanderburgh County
106	0.016	**Lebanon** (city) Boone County
107	0.015	**Crown Point** (city) Lake County
108	0.015	**Connersville** (city) Fayette County
109	0.014	**Paoli** (town) Orange County
110	0.013	**Boonville** (city) Warrick County
111	0.013	**Winchester** (city) Randolph County
112	0.013	**Highland** (CDP) Vanderburgh County
113	0.012	**Roselawn** (CDP) Newton County
114	0.012	**Upland** (town) Grant County
115	0.011	**Fort Branch** (town) Gibson County
116	0.010	**Huntertown** (town) Allen County
117	0.010	**North Vernon** (city) Jennings County
118	0.010	**West Lafayette** (city) Tippecanoe County
119	0.010	**Dunlap** (CDP) Elkhart County
120	0.010	**Cumberland** (town) Marion County
121	0.009	**Union City** (city) Randolph County
122	0.009	**McCordsville** (town) Hancock County
123	0.008	**Ossian** (town) Wells County
124	0.008	**Speedway** (town) Marion County
125	0.007	**Fortville** (town) Hancock County
126	0.006	**Decatur** (city) Adams County
127	0.006	**Brownstown** (town) Jackson County
128	0.005	**Mitchell** (city) Lawrence County
129	0.005	**Princeton** (city) Gibson County
130	0.005	**New Haven** (city) Allen County
131	0.005	**Seymour** (city) Jackson County
132	0.004	**Bremen** (town) Marshall County
133	0.004	**Hanover** (town) Jefferson County
134	0.004	**Sheridan** (town) Hamilton County
135	0.004	**Loogootee** (city) Martin County
136	0.003	**Grissom AFB** (CDP) Miami County
137	0.003	**Portland** (city) Jay County
138	0.003	**De Motte** (town) Jasper County
139	0.001	**Granger** (CDP) Saint Joseph County
140	0.001	**Newburgh** (town) Warrick County
141	0.001	**Greenwood** (city) Johnson County
142	0.001	**Centerville** (town) Wayne County
143	0.000	**Berne** (city) Adams County
144	0.000	**Ligonier** (city) Noble County
145	0.000	**Alexandria** (city) Madison County
145	0.000	**Attica** (city) Fountain County
145	0.000	**Auburn** (city) DeKalb County
145	0.000	**Austin** (city) Scott County
145	0.000	**Bargersville** (town) Johnson County
145	0.000	**Bedford** (city) Lawrence County

Note: This section ranks incorporated places and CDPs (Census Designated Places) with populations of 2,500 or more. Unincorporated postal areas were not considered. Please refer to the User Guide for additional information.

Elevation
Top 150 Places Ranked in *Descending* Order

State Rank	Feet	Place
1	1,122	Union City (city) Randolph County
2	1,093	Winchester (city) Randolph County
3	1,063	Angola (city) Steuben County
3	1,063	New Castle (city) Henry County
5	1,014	Centerville (town) Wayne County
6	988	Kendallville (city) Noble County
7	981	Richmond (city) Wayne County
8	971	Batesville (city) Ripley County
9	958	Greensburg (city) Decatur County
9	958	Rushville (city) Rush County
11	955	Danville (town) Hendricks County
12	951	Muncie (city) Delaware County
13	948	Sheridan (town) Hamilton County
14	942	Lebanon (city) Boone County
14	942	Pittsboro (town) Hendricks County
16	938	Whitestown (town) Boone County
17	935	Upland (town) Grant County
18	932	Lagrange (town) LaGrange County
19	922	Bright (CDP) Dearborn County
20	919	Hartford City (city) Blackford County
21	915	Yorktown (town) Delaware County
22	909	Chesterfield (town) Madison County
23	906	Portland (city) Jay County
24	886	Westfield (city) Hamilton County
25	883	Brownsburg (town) Hendricks County
25	883	Garrett (city) DeKalb County
25	883	Greenfield (city) Hancock County
28	879	Anderson (city) Madison County
28	879	Syracuse (town) Kosciusko County
30	876	Ligonier (city) Noble County
30	876	Nappanee (city) Elkhart County
32	873	Fairmount (town) Grant County
32	873	Lawrence (city) Marion County
34	869	Alexandria (city) Madison County
34	869	Tipton (city) Tipton County
36	866	Auburn (city) DeKalb County
36	866	Butler (city) DeKalb County
38	863	Elwood (city) Madison County
39	860	Columbia City (city) Whitley County
39	860	Heritage Lake (CDP) Putnam County
41	856	Fortville (town) Hancock County
41	856	Gas City (city) Grant County
43	853	Bremen (town) Marshall County
43	853	Carmel (city) Hamilton County
43	853	Cumberland (town) Marion County
46	850	Frankfort (city) Clinton County
46	850	McCordsville (town) Hancock County
48	846	Berne (city) Adams County
48	846	Pendleton (town) Madison County
50	843	Greencastle (city) Putnam County
50	843	Zionsville (town) Boone County
52	840	Ossian (town) Wells County
53	837	Middlebury (town) Elkhart County
54	833	Avon (town) Hendricks County
54	833	Cicero (town) Hamilton County
54	833	Huntertown (town) Allen County
57	827	Bluffton (city) Wells County
57	827	Warsaw (city) Kosciusko County
59	823	Connersville (city) Fayette County
60	820	Bargersville (town) Johnson County
61	817	Fishers (town) Hamilton County
61	817	Winona Lake (town) Kosciusko County
63	814	La Porte (city) LaPorte County
63	814	Marion (city) Grant County
65	810	Fort Wayne (city) Allen County
65	810	Kokomo (city) Howard County
67	807	New Whiteland (town) Johnson County
68	804	Beech Grove (city) Marion County
68	804	Greenwood (city) Johnson County
70	801	Decatur (city) Adams County
70	801	Goshen (city) Elkhart County
70	801	Granger (CDP) Saint Joseph County
73	797	Leo-Cedarville (town) Allen County
73	797	Plymouth (city) Marshall County
75	794	Crawfordsville (city) Montgomery County
75	794	Valparaiso (city) Porter County
75	794	Westville (town) LaPorte County
75	794	Whiteland (town) Johnson County
79	784	Hanover (town) Jefferson County
79	784	Simonton Lake (CDP) Elkhart County
81	781	Rochester (city) Fulton County
82	778	Dunlap (CDP) Elkhart County
83	774	North Manchester (town) Wabash County
84	771	Bloomington (city) Monroe County
85	764	Lakes of the Four Seasons (CDP) Lake County
85	764	Noblesville (city) Hamilton County
85	764	Shelbyville (city) Shelby County
88	758	New Haven (city) Allen County
89	751	Elkhart (city) Elkhart County
89	751	Salem (city) Washington County
91	748	Huntington (city) Huntington County
91	748	Speedway (town) Marion County
93	732	Crown Point (city) Lake County
93	732	Plainfield (town) Hendricks County
95	725	Franklin (city) Johnson County
95	725	Saint John (town) Lake County
97	722	Georgetown (town) Floyd County
97	722	Mishawaka (city) Saint Joseph County
97	722	Shorewood Forest (CDP) Porter County
100	718	Indianapolis (city) Marion County
100	718	Mooresville (town) Morgan County
100	718	North Vernon (city) Jennings County
103	712	Knox (city) Starke County
103	712	Rockville (town) Parke County
103	712	Wabash (city) Wabash County
106	709	Cedar Lake (town) Lake County
106	709	Hebron (town) Porter County
106	709	Winfield (town) Lake County
109	702	Country Squire Lakes (CDP) Jennings County
109	702	Lafayette (city) Tippecanoe County
111	696	Ellettsville (town) Monroe County
112	692	South Bend (city) Saint Joseph County
113	686	Bedford (city) Lawrence County
114	682	Mitchell (city) Lawrence County
114	682	Roselawn (CDP) Newton County
116	676	Monticello (city) White County
117	673	Edinburgh (town) Johnson County
118	669	De Motte (town) Jasper County
118	669	Lowell (town) Lake County
118	669	Schererville (town) Lake County
121	666	Brookville (town) Franklin County
122	663	Rensselaer (city) Jasper County
123	656	Merrillville (town) Lake County
124	653	Brazil (city) Clay County
124	653	Peru (city) Miami County
124	653	South Haven (CDP) Porter County
127	640	Chesterton (town) Porter County
127	640	Dyer (town) Lake County
127	640	Logansport (city) Cass County
127	640	Porter (town) Porter County
131	636	Portage (city) Porter County
132	630	Griffith (town) Lake County
133	627	Columbus (city) Bartholomew County
133	627	Michigan City (city) LaPorte County
135	623	Brownstown (town) Jackson County
135	623	Highland (town) Lake County
135	623	Hobart (city) Lake County
135	623	Paoli (town) Orange County
139	620	Lake Station (city) Lake County
140	610	Munster (town) Lake County
140	610	West Lafayette (city) Tippecanoe County
142	604	Martinsville (city) Morgan County
143	600	Gary (city) Lake County
143	600	Hammond (city) Lake County
143	600	Seymour (city) Jackson County
146	591	Charlestown (city) Clark County
146	591	East Chicago (city) Lake County
148	587	Corydon (town) Harrison County
148	587	Whiting (city) Lake County
150	568	Delphi (city) Carroll County

Note: This section ranks incorporated places and CDPs (Census Designated Places) with populations of 2,500 or more. Unincorporated postal areas were not considered. Please refer to the User Guide for additional information.

Elevation

Top 150 Places Ranked in *Ascending* Order

State Rank	Feet	Place
1	387	**Evansville** (city) Vanderburgh County
2	394	**Newburgh** (town) Warrick County
3	400	**Mount Vernon** (city) Posey County
4	413	**Chandler** (town) Warrick County
5	420	**Tell City** (city) Perry County
5	420	**Vincennes** (city) Knox County
7	423	**Boonville** (city) Warrick County
8	427	**Melody Hill** (CDP) Vanderburgh County
9	446	**Jeffersonville** (city) Clark County
10	449	**Fort Branch** (town) Gibson County
10	449	**New Albany** (city) Floyd County
12	456	**Clarksville** (town) Clark County
13	466	**Jasper** (city) Dubois County
14	479	**Lawrenceburg** (city) Dearborn County
15	482	**Highland** (CDP) Vanderburgh County
16	486	**Aurora** (city) Dearborn County
16	486	**Sellersburg** (town) Clark County
18	489	**Huntingburg** (city) Dubois County
18	489	**Madison** (city) Jefferson County
20	495	**North Terre Haute** (CDP) Vigo County
21	499	**Clinton** (city) Vermillion County
21	499	**Princeton** (city) Gibson County
23	502	**Terre Haute** (city) Vigo County
23	502	**Washington** (city) Daviess County
25	515	**Bicknell** (city) Knox County
26	528	**Greendale** (city) Dearborn County
26	528	**Sullivan** (city) Sullivan County
28	531	**Linton** (city) Greene County
29	538	**Loogootee** (city) Martin County
30	541	**Attica** (city) Fountain County
31	548	**Hidden Valley** (CDP) Dearborn County
32	558	**Austin** (city) Scott County
33	564	**Covington** (city) Fountain County
33	564	**Scottsburg** (city) Scott County
35	568	**Delphi** (city) Carroll County
36	587	**Corydon** (town) Harrison County
36	587	**Whiting** (city) Lake County
38	591	**Charlestown** (city) Clark County
38	591	**East Chicago** (city) Lake County
40	600	**Gary** (city) Lake County
40	600	**Hammond** (city) Lake County
40	600	**Seymour** (city) Jackson County
43	604	**Martinsville** (city) Morgan County
44	610	**Munster** (town) Lake County
44	610	**West Lafayette** (city) Tippecanoe County
46	620	**Lake Station** (city) Lake County
47	623	**Brownstown** (town) Jackson County
47	623	**Highland** (town) Lake County
47	623	**Hobart** (city) Lake County
47	623	**Paoli** (town) Orange County
51	627	**Columbus** (city) Bartholomew County
51	627	**Michigan City** (city) LaPorte County
53	630	**Griffith** (town) Lake County
54	636	**Portage** (city) Porter County
55	640	**Chesterton** (town) Porter County
55	640	**Dyer** (town) Lake County
55	640	**Logansport** (city) Cass County
55	640	**Porter** (town) Porter County
59	653	**Brazil** (city) Clay County
59	653	**Peru** (city) Miami County
59	653	**South Haven** (CDP) Porter County
62	656	**Merrillville** (town) Lake County
63	663	**Rensselaer** (city) Jasper County
64	666	**Brookville** (town) Franklin County
65	669	**De Motte** (town) Jasper County
65	669	**Lowell** (town) Lake County
65	669	**Schererville** (town) Lake County
68	673	**Edinburgh** (town) Johnson County
69	676	**Monticello** (city) White County
70	682	**Mitchell** (city) Lawrence County
70	682	**Roselawn** (CDP) Newton County
72	686	**Bedford** (city) Lawrence County
73	692	**South Bend** (city) Saint Joseph County
74	696	**Ellettsville** (town) Monroe County
75	702	**Country Squire Lakes** (CDP) Jennings County
75	702	**Lafayette** (city) Tippecanoe County
77	709	**Cedar Lake** (town) Lake County
77	709	**Hebron** (town) Porter County
77	709	**Winfield** (town) Lake County
80	712	**Knox** (city) Starke County
80	712	**Rockville** (town) Parke County
80	712	**Wabash** (city) Wabash County
83	718	**Indianapolis** (city) Marion County
83	718	**Mooresville** (town) Morgan County
83	718	**North Vernon** (city) Jennings County
86	722	**Georgetown** (town) Floyd County
86	722	**Mishawaka** (city) Saint Joseph County
86	722	**Shorewood Forest** (CDP) Porter County
89	725	**Franklin** (city) Johnson County
89	725	**Saint John** (town) Lake County
91	732	**Crown Point** (city) Lake County
91	732	**Plainfield** (town) Hendricks County
93	748	**Huntington** (city) Huntington County
93	748	**Speedway** (town) Marion County
95	751	**Elkhart** (city) Elkhart County
95	751	**Salem** (city) Washington County
97	758	**New Haven** (city) Allen County
98	764	**Lakes of the Four Seasons** (CDP) Lake County
98	764	**Noblesville** (city) Hamilton County
98	764	**Shelbyville** (city) Shelby County
101	771	**Bloomington** (city) Monroe County
102	774	**North Manchester** (town) Wabash County
103	778	**Dunlap** (CDP) Elkhart County
104	781	**Rochester** (city) Fulton County
105	784	**Hanover** (town) Jefferson County
105	784	**Simonton Lake** (CDP) Elkhart County
107	794	**Crawfordsville** (city) Montgomery County
107	794	**Valparaiso** (city) Porter County
107	794	**Westville** (town) LaPorte County
107	794	**Whiteland** (town) Johnson County
111	797	**Leo-Cedarville** (town) Allen County
111	797	**Plymouth** (city) Marshall County
113	801	**Decatur** (city) Adams County
113	801	**Goshen** (city) Elkhart County
113	801	**Granger** (CDP) Saint Joseph County
116	804	**Beech Grove** (city) Marion County
116	804	**Greenwood** (city) Johnson County
118	807	**New Whiteland** (town) Johnson County
119	810	**Fort Wayne** (city) Allen County
119	810	**Kokomo** (city) Howard County
121	814	**La Porte** (city) LaPorte County
121	814	**Marion** (city) Grant County
123	817	**Fishers** (town) Hamilton County
123	817	**Winona Lake** (town) Kosciusko County
125	820	**Bargersville** (town) Johnson County
126	823	**Connersville** (city) Fayette County
127	827	**Bluffton** (city) Wells County
127	827	**Warsaw** (city) Kosciusko County
129	833	**Avon** (town) Hendricks County
129	833	**Cicero** (town) Hamilton County
129	833	**Huntertown** (town) Allen County
132	837	**Middlebury** (town) Elkhart County
133	840	**Ossian** (town) Wells County
134	843	**Greencastle** (city) Putnam County
134	843	**Zionsville** (town) Boone County
136	846	**Berne** (city) Adams County
136	846	**Pendleton** (town) Madison County
138	850	**Frankfort** (city) Clinton County
138	850	**McCordsville** (town) Hancock County
140	853	**Bremen** (town) Marshall County
140	853	**Carmel** (city) Hamilton County
140	853	**Cumberland** (town) Marion County
143	856	**Fortville** (town) Hancock County
143	856	**Gas City** (city) Grant County
145	860	**Columbia City** (city) Whitley County
145	860	**Heritage Lake** (CDP) Putnam County
147	863	**Elwood** (city) Madison County
148	866	**Auburn** (city) DeKalb County
148	866	**Butler** (city) DeKalb County
150	869	**Alexandria** (city) Madison County

Note: This section ranks incorporated places and CDPs (Census Designated Places) with populations of 2,500 or more. Unincorporated postal areas were not considered. Please refer to the User Guide for additional information.

Population

Top 150 Places Ranked in *Descending* Order

State Rank	Number	Place
1	820,445	**Indianapolis** (city) Marion County
2	253,691	**Fort Wayne** (city) Allen County
3	117,429	**Evansville** (city) Vanderburgh County
4	101,168	**South Bend** (city) Saint Joseph County
5	80,830	**Hammond** (city) Lake County
6	80,405	**Bloomington** (city) Monroe County
7	80,294	**Gary** (city) Lake County
8	79,191	**Carmel** (city) Hamilton County
9	76,794	**Fishers** (town) Hamilton County
10	70,085	**Muncie** (city) Delaware County
11	67,140	**Lafayette** (city) Tippecanoe County
12	60,785	**Terre Haute** (city) Vigo County
13	56,129	**Anderson** (city) Madison County
14	51,969	**Noblesville** (city) Hamilton County
15	50,949	**Elkhart** (city) Elkhart County
16	49,791	**Greenwood** (city) Johnson County
17	48,252	**Mishawaka** (city) Saint Joseph County
18	46,001	**Lawrence** (city) Marion County
19	45,468	**Kokomo** (city) Howard County
20	44,953	**Jeffersonville** (city) Clark County
21	44,061	**Columbus** (city) Bartholomew County
22	36,828	**Portage** (city) Porter County
23	36,812	**Richmond** (city) Wayne County
24	36,372	**New Albany** (city) Floyd County
25	35,246	**Merrillville** (town) Lake County
26	31,730	**Valparaiso** (city) Porter County
27	31,719	**Goshen** (city) Elkhart County
28	31,479	**Michigan City** (city) LaPorte County
29	30,465	**Granger** (CDP) Saint Joseph County
30	30,068	**Westfield** (city) Hamilton County
31	29,948	**Marion** (city) Grant County
32	29,698	**East Chicago** (city) Lake County
33	29,596	**West Lafayette** (city) Tippecanoe County
34	29,243	**Schererville** (town) Lake County
35	29,059	**Hobart** (city) Lake County
36	27,631	**Plainfield** (town) Hendricks County
37	27,317	**Crown Point** (city) Lake County
38	23,727	**Highland** (town) Lake County
39	23,712	**Franklin** (city) Johnson County
40	23,603	**Munster** (town) Lake County
41	22,053	**La Porte** (city) LaPorte County
42	21,724	**Clarksville** (town) Clark County
43	21,285	**Brownsburg** (town) Hendricks County
44	20,602	**Greenfield** (city) Hancock County
45	19,191	**Shelbyville** (city) Shelby County
46	18,423	**Vincennes** (city) Knox County
47	18,396	**Logansport** (city) Cass County
48	18,114	**New Castle** (city) Henry County
49	17,503	**Seymour** (city) Jackson County
50	17,391	**Huntington** (city) Huntington County
51	16,893	**Griffith** (town) Lake County
52	16,422	**Frankfort** (city) Clinton County
53	16,390	**Dyer** (town) Lake County
54	15,915	**Crawfordsville** (city) Montgomery County
55	15,792	**Lebanon** (city) Boone County
56	15,038	**Jasper** (city) Dubois County
57	14,850	**Saint John** (town) Lake County
58	14,794	**New Haven** (city) Allen County
59	14,192	**Beech Grove** (city) Marion County
60	14,160	**Zionsville** (town) Boone County
61	13,559	**Warsaw** (city) Kosciusko County
62	13,481	**Connersville** (city) Fayette County
63	13,413	**Bedford** (city) Lawrence County
64	13,068	**Chesterton** (town) Porter County
65	12,731	**Auburn** (city) DeKalb County
66	12,572	**Lake Station** (city) Lake County
67	12,446	**Avon** (town) Hendricks County
68	12,183	**Purdue University** (CDP) Tippecanoe County
69	11,967	**Madison** (city) Jefferson County
70	11,828	**Martinsville** (city) Morgan County
71	11,812	**Speedway** (town) Marion County
72	11,560	**Cedar Lake** (town) Lake County
73	11,509	**Washington** (city) Daviess County
74	11,492	**Greensburg** (city) Decatur County
75	11,417	**Peru** (city) Miami County
76	10,666	**Wabash** (city) Wabash County
77	10,326	**Greencastle** (city) Putnam County
78	10,033	**Plymouth** (city) Marshall County
79	9,897	**Bluffton** (city) Wells County
80	9,862	**Kendallville** (city) Noble County
81	9,405	**Decatur** (city) Adams County
81	9,405	**Yorktown** (town) Delaware County
83	9,326	**Mooresville** (town) Morgan County
84	9,276	**Lowell** (town) Lake County
85	9,001	**Danville** (town) Hendricks County
86	8,750	**Columbia City** (city) Whitley County
87	8,644	**Princeton** (city) Gibson County
88	8,614	**Elwood** (city) Madison County
89	8,612	**Angola** (city) Steuben County
90	7,912	**Brazil** (city) Clay County
91	7,585	**Charlestown** (city) Clark County
92	7,272	**Tell City** (city) Perry County
93	7,033	**Lakes of the Four Seasons** (CDP) Lake County
94	6,747	**Scottsburg** (city) Scott County
95	6,728	**North Vernon** (city) Jennings County
96	6,687	**Mount Vernon** (city) Posey County
97	6,648	**Nappanee** (city) Elkhart County
98	6,520	**Batesville** (city) Ripley County
99	6,378	**Ellettsville** (town) Monroe County
100	6,341	**Rushville** (city) Rush County
101	6,319	**Salem** (city) Washington County
102	6,286	**Garrett** (city) DeKalb County
103	6,246	**Boonville** (city) Warrick County
104	6,235	**Dunlap** (CDP) Elkhart County
105	6,223	**Portland** (city) Jay County
106	6,220	**Hartford City** (city) Blackford County
107	6,218	**Rochester** (city) Fulton County
108	6,128	**Sellersburg** (town) Clark County
109	6,112	**North Manchester** (town) Wabash County
110	6,057	**Huntingburg** (city) Dubois County
111	5,973	**Notre Dame** (CDP) Saint Joseph County
112	5,965	**Gas City** (city) Grant County
113	5,859	**Rensselaer** (city) Jasper County
114	5,853	**Westville** (town) LaPorte County
115	5,693	**Bright** (CDP) Dearborn County
116	5,537	**Grissom AFB** (CDP) Miami County
117	5,472	**New Whiteland** (town) Johnson County
118	5,413	**Linton** (city) Greene County
119	5,387	**Hidden Valley** (CDP) Dearborn County
120	5,378	**Monticello** (city) White County
121	5,282	**South Haven** (CDP) Porter County
122	5,169	**Cumberland** (town) Marion County
123	5,145	**Alexandria** (city) Madison County
124	5,106	**Tipton** (city) Tipton County
125	5,042	**Lawrenceburg** (city) Dearborn County
126	4,997	**Whiting** (city) Lake County
127	4,935	**Winchester** (city) Randolph County
128	4,908	**Winona Lake** (town) Kosciusko County
129	4,893	**Clinton** (city) Vermillion County
130	4,858	**Porter** (town) Porter County
131	4,812	**Cicero** (town) Hamilton County
132	4,810	**Huntertown** (town) Allen County
133	4,797	**McCordsville** (town) Hancock County
134	4,678	**Simonton Lake** (CDP) Elkhart County
135	4,588	**Bremen** (town) Marshall County
136	4,520	**Greendale** (city) Dearborn County
137	4,489	**Highland** (CDP) Vanderburgh County
138	4,480	**Edinburgh** (town) Johnson County
139	4,405	**Ligonier** (city) Noble County
140	4,383	**Winfield** (town) Lake County
141	4,350	**Mitchell** (city) Lawrence County
142	4,305	**North Terre Haute** (CDP) Vigo County
143	4,295	**Austin** (city) Scott County
144	4,253	**Pendleton** (town) Madison County
145	4,249	**Sullivan** (city) Sullivan County
146	4,169	**Whiteland** (town) Johnson County
147	4,131	**Roselawn** (CDP) Newton County
148	4,013	**Bargersville** (town) Johnson County
149	3,999	**Berne** (city) Adams County
150	3,929	**Fortville** (town) Hancock County

Note: This section ranks incorporated places and CDPs (Census Designated Places) with populations of 2,500 or more. Unincorporated postal areas were not considered. Please refer to the User Guide for additional information.

Population
Top 150 Places Ranked in *Ascending* Order

State Rank	Number	Place
1	2,547	**Chesterfield** (town) Madison County
2	2,552	**Centerville** (town) Wayne County
3	2,596	**Brookville** (town) Franklin County
4	2,607	**Rockville** (town) Parke County
5	2,625	**Lagrange** (town) LaGrange County
6	2,645	**Covington** (city) Fountain County
7	2,665	**Sheridan** (town) Hamilton County
8	2,684	**Butler** (city) DeKalb County
9	2,708	**Shorewood Forest** (CDP) Porter County
10	2,751	**Loogootee** (city) Martin County
11	2,771	**Fort Branch** (town) Gibson County
12	2,810	**Syracuse** (town) Kosciusko County
13	2,867	**Whitestown** (town) Boone County
14	2,876	**Georgetown** (town) Floyd County
15	2,880	**Heritage Lake** (CDP) Putnam County
16	2,887	**Chandler** (town) Warrick County
17	2,893	**Delphi** (city) Carroll County
18	2,915	**Bicknell** (city) Knox County
19	2,928	**Pittsboro** (town) Hendricks County
20	2,947	**Brownstown** (town) Jackson County
21	2,954	**Fairmount** (town) Grant County
22	3,122	**Corydon** (town) Harrison County
23	3,184	**Smithville-Sanders** (CDP) Monroe County
24	3,245	**Attica** (city) Fountain County
25	3,289	**Ossian** (town) Wells County
26	3,325	**Newburgh** (town) Warrick County
27	3,420	**Middlebury** (town) Elkhart County
28	3,546	**Hanover** (town) Jefferson County
29	3,571	**Country Squire Lakes** (CDP) Jennings County
30	3,584	**Union City** (city) Randolph County
31	3,603	**Leo-Cedarville** (town) Allen County
32	3,628	**Melody Hill** (CDP) Vanderburgh County
33	3,677	**Paoli** (town) Orange County
34	3,704	**Knox** (city) Starke County
35	3,724	**Hebron** (town) Porter County
36	3,750	**Aurora** (city) Dearborn County
37	3,814	**De Motte** (town) Jasper County
38	3,845	**Upland** (town) Grant County
39	3,929	**Fortville** (town) Hancock County
40	3,999	**Berne** (city) Adams County
41	4,013	**Bargersville** (town) Johnson County
42	4,131	**Roselawn** (CDP) Newton County
43	4,169	**Whiteland** (town) Johnson County
44	4,249	**Sullivan** (city) Sullivan County
45	4,253	**Pendleton** (town) Madison County
46	4,295	**Austin** (city) Scott County
47	4,305	**North Terre Haute** (CDP) Vigo County
48	4,350	**Mitchell** (city) Lawrence County
49	4,383	**Winfield** (town) Lake County
50	4,405	**Ligonier** (city) Noble County
51	4,480	**Edinburgh** (town) Johnson County
52	4,489	**Highland** (CDP) Vanderburgh County
53	4,520	**Greendale** (city) Dearborn County
54	4,588	**Bremen** (town) Marshall County
55	4,678	**Simonton Lake** (CDP) Elkhart County
56	4,797	**McCordsville** (town) Hancock County
57	4,810	**Huntertown** (town) Allen County
58	4,812	**Cicero** (town) Hamilton County
59	4,858	**Porter** (town) Porter County
60	4,893	**Clinton** (city) Vermillion County
61	4,908	**Winona Lake** (town) Kosciusko County
62	4,935	**Winchester** (city) Randolph County
63	4,997	**Whiting** (city) Lake County
64	5,042	**Lawrenceburg** (city) Dearborn County
65	5,106	**Tipton** (city) Tipton County
66	5,145	**Alexandria** (city) Madison County
67	5,169	**Cumberland** (town) Marion County
68	5,282	**South Haven** (CDP) Porter County
69	5,378	**Monticello** (city) White County
70	5,387	**Hidden Valley** (CDP) Dearborn County
71	5,413	**Linton** (city) Greene County
72	5,472	**New Whiteland** (town) Johnson County
73	5,537	**Grissom AFB** (CDP) Miami County
74	5,693	**Bright** (CDP) Dearborn County
75	5,853	**Westville** (town) LaPorte County
76	5,859	**Rensselaer** (city) Jasper County
77	5,965	**Gas City** (city) Grant County
78	5,973	**Notre Dame** (CDP) Saint Joseph County
79	6,057	**Huntingburg** (city) Dubois County
80	6,112	**North Manchester** (town) Wabash County
81	6,128	**Sellersburg** (town) Clark County
82	6,218	**Rochester** (city) Fulton County
83	6,220	**Hartford City** (city) Blackford County
84	6,223	**Portland** (city) Jay County
85	6,235	**Dunlap** (CDP) Elkhart County
86	6,246	**Boonville** (city) Warrick County
87	6,286	**Garrett** (city) DeKalb County
88	6,319	**Salem** (city) Washington County
89	6,341	**Rushville** (city) Rush County
90	6,378	**Ellettsville** (town) Monroe County
91	6,520	**Batesville** (city) Ripley County
92	6,648	**Nappanee** (city) Elkhart County
93	6,687	**Mount Vernon** (city) Posey County
94	6,728	**North Vernon** (city) Jennings County
95	6,747	**Scottsburg** (city) Scott County
96	7,033	**Lakes of the Four Seasons** (CDP) Lake County
97	7,272	**Tell City** (city) Perry County
98	7,585	**Charlestown** (city) Clark County
99	7,912	**Brazil** (city) Clay County
100	8,612	**Angola** (city) Steuben County
101	8,614	**Elwood** (city) Madison County
102	8,644	**Princeton** (city) Gibson County
103	8,750	**Columbia City** (city) Whitley County
104	9,001	**Danville** (town) Hendricks County
105	9,276	**Lowell** (town) Lake County
106	9,326	**Mooresville** (town) Morgan County
107	9,405	**Decatur** (city) Adams County
107	9,405	**Yorktown** (town) Delaware County
109	9,862	**Kendallville** (city) Noble County
110	9,897	**Bluffton** (city) Wells County
111	10,033	**Plymouth** (city) Marshall County
112	10,326	**Greencastle** (city) Putnam County
113	10,666	**Wabash** (city) Wabash County
114	11,417	**Peru** (city) Miami County
115	11,492	**Greensburg** (city) Decatur County
116	11,509	**Washington** (city) Daviess County
117	11,560	**Cedar Lake** (town) Lake County
118	11,812	**Speedway** (town) Marion County
119	11,828	**Martinsville** (city) Morgan County
120	11,967	**Madison** (city) Jefferson County
121	12,183	**Purdue University** (CDP) Tippecanoe County
122	12,446	**Avon** (town) Hendricks County
123	12,572	**Lake Station** (city) Lake County
124	12,731	**Auburn** (city) DeKalb County
125	13,068	**Chesterton** (town) Porter County
126	13,413	**Bedford** (city) Lawrence County
127	13,481	**Connersville** (city) Fayette County
128	13,559	**Warsaw** (city) Kosciusko County
129	14,160	**Zionsville** (town) Boone County
130	14,192	**Beech Grove** (city) Marion County
131	14,794	**New Haven** (city) Allen County
132	14,850	**Saint John** (town) Lake County
133	15,038	**Jasper** (city) Dubois County
134	15,792	**Lebanon** (city) Boone County
135	15,915	**Crawfordsville** (city) Montgomery County
136	16,390	**Dyer** (town) Lake County
137	16,422	**Frankfort** (city) Clinton County
138	16,893	**Griffith** (town) Lake County
139	17,391	**Huntington** (city) Huntington County
140	17,503	**Seymour** (city) Jackson County
141	18,114	**New Castle** (city) Henry County
142	18,396	**Logansport** (city) Cass County
143	18,423	**Vincennes** (city) Knox County
144	19,191	**Shelbyville** (city) Shelby County
145	20,602	**Greenfield** (city) Hancock County
146	21,285	**Brownsburg** (town) Hendricks County
147	21,724	**Clarksville** (town) Clark County
148	22,053	**La Porte** (city) LaPorte County
149	23,603	**Munster** (town) Lake County
150	23,712	**Franklin** (city) Johnson County

Note: *This section ranks incorporated places and CDPs (Census Designated Places) with populations of 2,500 or more. Unincorporated postal areas were not considered. Please refer to the User Guide for additional information.*

Population Growth

Top 150 Places Ranked in *Descending* Order

State Rank	Percent	Place
1	508.7	**Whitestown** (town) Boone County
2	323.0	**McCordsville** (town) Hancock County
3	235.2	**Grissom AFB** (CDP) Miami County
4	223.6	**Westfield** (city) Hamilton County
5	176.6	**Westville** (town) LaPorte County
6	171.6	**Huntertown** (town) Allen County
7	109.9	**Carmel** (city) Hamilton County
8	103.0	**Fishers** (town) Hamilton County
9	99.2	**Avon** (town) Hendricks County
10	96.6	**Yorktown** (town) Delaware County
11	90.7	**Winfield** (town) Lake County
12	89.3	**Bargersville** (town) Johnson County
13	84.4	**Pittsboro** (town) Hendricks County
14	81.8	**Noblesville** (city) Hamilton County
15	77.2	**Saint John** (town) Lake County
16	64.3	**Jeffersonville** (city) Clark County
17	61.4	**Zionsville** (town) Boone County
18	50.2	**Plainfield** (town) Hendricks County
19	46.6	**Brownsburg** (town) Hendricks County
20	41.1	**Greenfield** (city) Hancock County
21	40.2	**Danville** (town) Hendricks County
22	38.2	**Greenwood** (city) Johnson County
23	37.9	**Crown Point** (city) Lake County
24	29.5	**Leo-Cedarville** (town) Allen County
25	29.1	**Georgetown** (town) Floyd County
26	26.6	**Charlestown** (city) Clark County
27	25.6	**Ellettsville** (town) Monroe County
28	25.1	**Hanover** (town) Jefferson County
29	24.6	**Cedar Lake** (town) Lake County
29	24.6	**Chesterton** (town) Porter County
31	24.3	**Jasper** (city) Dubois County
32	23.6	**Columbia City** (city) Whitley County
32	23.6	**Lowell** (town) Lake County
34	23.3	**Fort Wayne** (city) Allen County
35	23.1	**Winona Lake** (town) Kosciusko County
36	22.0	**Hidden Valley** (CDP) Dearborn County
37	21.8	**Franklin** (city) Johnson County
38	19.5	**New Whiteland** (town) Johnson County
39	19.4	**Fort Branch** (town) Gibson County
40	19.2	**New Haven** (city) Allen County
41	19.0	**Lafayette** (city) Tippecanoe County
42	18.3	**Melody Hill** (CDP) Vanderburgh County
43	18.2	**Lawrence** (city) Marion County
44	18.0	**Dyer** (town) Lake County
45	17.9	**De Motte** (town) Jasper County
46	17.7	**Schererville** (town) Lake County
47	17.3	**Angola** (city) Steuben County
48	16.0	**Bloomington** (city) Monroe County
49	15.7	**Middlebury** (town) Elkhart County
49	15.7	**Valparaiso** (city) Porter County
51	15.4	**Simonton Lake** (CDP) Elkhart County
52	15.3	**Merrillville** (town) Lake County
53	15.0	**Corydon** (town) Harrison County
54	14.6	**Hobart** (city) Lake County
55	14.1	**Fortville** (town) Hancock County
56	12.8	**Columbus** (city) Bartholomew County
57	12.0	**Greensburg** (city) Decatur County
58	11.8	**Cicero** (town) Hamilton County
58	11.8	**Ossian** (town) Wells County
60	11.7	**Scottsburg** (city) Scott County
61	11.0	**Lebanon** (city) Boone County
62	10.7	**Rensselaer** (city) Jasper County
63	9.9	**Portage** (city) Porter County
64	9.8	**Pendleton** (town) Madison County
65	9.7	**Munster** (town) Lake County
66	9.3	**Highland** (CDP) Vanderburgh County
67	9.2	**Warsaw** (city) Kosciusko County
68	8.3	**Garrett** (city) DeKalb County
69	8.2	**Huntingburg** (city) Dubois County
70	8.1	**Batesville** (city) Ripley County
71	8.0	**Goshen** (city) Elkhart County
72	7.7	**Granger** (CDP) Saint Joseph County
72	7.7	**Newburgh** (town) Warrick County
74	7.6	**Lawrenceburg** (city) Dearborn County
75	6.9	**Shelbyville** (city) Shelby County
76	5.9	**Dunlap** (CDP) Elkhart County
77	5.8	**Rushville** (city) Rush County
77	5.8	**Sheridan** (town) Hamilton County
79	5.7	**Princeton** (city) Gibson County
80	5.4	**Auburn** (city) DeKalb County
81	5.3	**Bright** (CDP) Dearborn County
81	5.3	**Whiteland** (town) Johnson County
83	5.2	**Centerville** (town) Wayne County
83	5.2	**Greendale** (city) Dearborn County
85	5.0	**Roselawn** (CDP) Newton County
86	4.9	**Indianapolis** (city) Marion County
87	4.5	**Greencastle** (city) Putnam County
88	4.4	**Crawfordsville** (city) Montgomery County
89	3.9	**Muncie** (city) Delaware County
90	3.8	**Bluffton** (city) Wells County
91	3.6	**Hebron** (town) Porter County
91	3.6	**Mishawaka** (city) Saint Joseph County
93	3.3	**North Vernon** (city) Jennings County
94	3.1	**Covington** (city) Fountain County
95	2.8	**West Lafayette** (city) Tippecanoe County
96	2.6	**Kendallville** (city) Noble County
97	2.4	**Salem** (city) Washington County
98	2.3	**Bremen** (town) Marshall County
99	2.0	**La Porte** (city) LaPorte County
99	2.0	**Plymouth** (city) Marshall County
99	2.0	**Terre Haute** (city) Vigo County
102	1.9	**New Castle** (city) Henry County
103	1.5	**Clarksville** (town) Clark County
104	1.1	**Ligonier** (city) Noble County
104	1.1	**Martinsville** (city) Morgan County
104	1.1	**Upland** (town) Grant County
104	1.1	**Washington** (city) Daviess County
108	0.9	**Sellersburg** (town) Clark County
109	0.8	**Highland** (town) Lake County
110	0.6	**Mooresville** (town) Morgan County
111	0.4	**Gas City** (city) Grant County
111	0.4	**Loogootee** (city) Martin County
113	-0.3	**Huntington** (city) Huntington County
113	-0.3	**Madison** (city) Jefferson County
115	-0.5	**Knox** (city) Starke County
116	-0.6	**Edinburgh** (town) Johnson County
117	-0.9	**Nappanee** (city) Elkhart County
118	-1.0	**Brownstown** (town) Jackson County
118	-1.0	**Country Squire Lakes** (CDP) Jennings County
118	-1.0	**Heritage Lake** (CDP) Putnam County
118	-1.0	**Notre Dame** (CDP) Saint Joseph County
118	-1.0	**Purdue University** (CDP) Tippecanoe County
118	-1.0	**Shorewood Forest** (CDP) Porter County
118	-1.0	**Smithville-Sanders** (CDP) Monroe County
118	-1.0	**Union City** (city) Randolph County
126	-1.3	**Decatur** (city) Adams County
126	-1.3	**Fairmount** (town) Grant County
128	-1.4	**Frankfort** (city) Clinton County
128	-1.4	**Kokomo** (city) Howard County
130	-1.5	**Butler** (city) DeKalb County
130	-1.5	**Vincennes** (city) Knox County
132	-1.8	**Elkhart** (city) Elkhart County
133	-2.0	**Winchester** (city) Randolph County
134	-2.1	**Brookville** (town) Franklin County
135	-2.3	**Porter** (town) Porter County
136	-2.4	**North Manchester** (town) Wabash County
137	-2.5	**Griffith** (town) Lake County
138	-2.6	**Bedford** (city) Lawrence County
139	-2.7	**Hammond** (city) Lake County
139	-2.7	**Whiting** (city) Lake County
141	-2.8	**Tipton** (city) Tipton County
142	-3.1	**Rochester** (city) Fulton County
143	-3.3	**New Albany** (city) Floyd County
143	-3.3	**Portland** (city) Jay County
143	-3.3	**Seymour** (city) Jackson County
146	-3.4	**Brazil** (city) Clay County
146	-3.4	**Evansville** (city) Vanderburgh County
148	-3.5	**Lakes of the Four Seasons** (CDP) Lake County
149	-3.6	**Berne** (city) Adams County
150	-4.0	**Delphi** (city) Carroll County

Note: This section ranks incorporated places and CDPs (Census Designated Places) with populations of 2,500 or more. Unincorporated postal areas were not considered. Please refer to the User Guide for additional information.

Population Growth

Top 150 Places Ranked in *Ascending* Order

State Rank	Percent	Place
1	-21.9	**Gary** (city) Lake County
2	-17.8	**Alexandria** (city) Madison County
3	-14.2	**Chesterfield** (town) Madison County
4	-13.7	**Bicknell** (city) Knox County
5	-12.5	**Connersville** (city) Fayette County
6	-12.1	**Peru** (city) Miami County
7	-11.5	**Elwood** (city) Madison County
8	-10.6	**Mount Vernon** (city) Posey County
9	-10.2	**Hartford City** (city) Blackford County
10	-10.1	**Lagrange** (town) LaGrange County
11	-9.9	**Lake Station** (city) Lake County
12	-9.2	**Wabash** (city) Wabash County
13	-9.1	**Austin** (city) Scott County
14	-8.6	**Boonville** (city) Warrick County
15	-8.4	**East Chicago** (city) Lake County
16	-8.3	**Speedway** (town) Marion County
17	-8.0	**Sullivan** (city) Sullivan County
18	-7.5	**Syracuse** (town) Kosciusko County
19	-7.3	**Tell City** (city) Perry County
20	-7.0	**Attica** (city) Fountain County
21	-6.7	**Chandler** (town) Warrick County
22	-6.5	**Logansport** (city) Cass County
22	-6.5	**North Terre Haute** (CDP) Vigo County
24	-6.3	**Linton** (city) Greene County
25	-6.1	**South Bend** (city) Saint Joseph County
26	-6.0	**Anderson** (city) Madison County
26	-6.0	**Cumberland** (town) Marion County
26	-6.0	**Monticello** (city) White County
26	-6.0	**South Haven** (CDP) Porter County
30	-5.9	**Richmond** (city) Wayne County
31	-5.7	**Rockville** (town) Parke County
32	-5.4	**Aurora** (city) Dearborn County
33	-4.8	**Mitchell** (city) Lawrence County
34	-4.6	**Beech Grove** (city) Marion County
35	-4.5	**Clinton** (city) Vermillion County
36	-4.4	**Marion** (city) Grant County
37	-4.3	**Michigan City** (city) LaPorte County
37	-4.3	**Paoli** (town) Orange County
39	-4.0	**Delphi** (city) Carroll County
40	-3.6	**Berne** (city) Adams County
41	-3.5	**Lakes of the Four Seasons** (CDP) Lake County
42	-3.4	**Brazil** (city) Clay County
42	-3.4	**Evansville** (city) Vanderburgh County
44	-3.3	**New Albany** (city) Floyd County
44	-3.3	**Portland** (city) Jay County
44	-3.3	**Seymour** (city) Jackson County
47	-3.1	**Rochester** (city) Fulton County
48	-2.8	**Tipton** (city) Tipton County
49	-2.7	**Hammond** (city) Lake County
49	-2.7	**Whiting** (city) Lake County
51	-2.6	**Bedford** (city) Lawrence County
52	-2.5	**Griffith** (town) Lake County
53	-2.4	**North Manchester** (town) Wabash County
54	-2.3	**Porter** (town) Porter County
55	-2.1	**Brookville** (town) Franklin County
56	-2.0	**Winchester** (city) Randolph County
57	-1.8	**Elkhart** (city) Elkhart County
58	-1.5	**Butler** (city) DeKalb County
58	-1.5	**Vincennes** (city) Knox County
60	-1.4	**Frankfort** (city) Clinton County
60	-1.4	**Kokomo** (city) Howard County
62	-1.3	**Decatur** (city) Adams County
62	-1.3	**Fairmount** (town) Grant County
64	-1.0	**Brownstown** (town) Jackson County
64	-1.0	**Union City** (city) Randolph County
66	-0.9	**Nappanee** (city) Elkhart County
67	-0.6	**Edinburgh** (town) Johnson County
68	-0.5	**Knox** (city) Starke County
69	-0.3	**Huntington** (city) Huntington County
69	-0.3	**Madison** (city) Jefferson County
71	0.4	**Gas City** (city) Grant County
71	0.4	**Loogootee** (city) Martin County
73	0.6	**Mooresville** (town) Morgan County
74	0.8	**Highland** (town) Lake County
75	0.9	**Sellersburg** (town) Clark County
76	1.1	**Ligonier** (city) Noble County
76	1.1	**Martinsville** (city) Morgan County
76	1.1	**Upland** (town) Grant County
76	1.1	**Washington** (city) Daviess County
80	1.5	**Clarksville** (town) Clark County
81	1.9	**New Castle** (city) Henry County
82	2.0	**La Porte** (city) LaPorte County
82	2.0	**Plymouth** (city) Marshall County
82	2.0	**Terre Haute** (city) Vigo County
85	2.3	**Bremen** (town) Marshall County
86	2.4	**Salem** (city) Washington County
87	2.6	**Kendallville** (city) Noble County
88	2.8	**West Lafayette** (city) Tippecanoe County
89	3.1	**Covington** (city) Fountain County
90	3.3	**North Vernon** (city) Jennings County
91	3.6	**Hebron** (town) Porter County
91	3.6	**Mishawaka** (city) Saint Joseph County
93	3.8	**Bluffton** (city) Wells County
94	3.9	**Muncie** (city) Delaware County
95	4.4	**Crawfordsville** (city) Montgomery County
96	4.5	**Greencastle** (city) Putnam County
97	4.9	**Indianapolis** (city) Marion County
98	5.0	**Roselawn** (CDP) Newton County
99	5.2	**Centerville** (town) Wayne County
99	5.2	**Greendale** (city) Dearborn County
101	5.3	**Bright** (CDP) Dearborn County
101	5.3	**Whiteland** (town) Johnson County
103	5.4	**Auburn** (city) DeKalb County
104	5.7	**Princeton** (city) Gibson County
105	5.8	**Rushville** (city) Rush County
105	5.8	**Sheridan** (town) Hamilton County
107	5.9	**Dunlap** (CDP) Elkhart County
108	6.9	**Shelbyville** (city) Shelby County
109	7.6	**Lawrenceburg** (city) Dearborn County
110	7.7	**Granger** (CDP) Saint Joseph County
110	7.7	**Newburgh** (town) Warrick County
112	8.0	**Goshen** (city) Elkhart County
113	8.1	**Batesville** (city) Ripley County
114	8.2	**Huntingburg** (city) Dubois County
115	8.3	**Garrett** (city) DeKalb County
116	9.2	**Warsaw** (city) Kosciusko County
117	9.3	**Highland** (CDP) Vanderburgh County
118	9.7	**Munster** (town) Lake County
119	9.8	**Pendleton** (town) Madison County
120	9.9	**Portage** (city) Porter County
121	10.7	**Rensselaer** (city) Jasper County
122	11.0	**Lebanon** (city) Boone County
123	11.7	**Scottsburg** (city) Scott County
124	11.8	**Cicero** (town) Hamilton County
124	11.8	**Ossian** (town) Wells County
126	12.0	**Greensburg** (city) Decatur County
127	12.8	**Columbus** (city) Bartholomew County
128	14.1	**Fortville** (town) Hancock County
129	14.6	**Hobart** (city) Lake County
130	15.0	**Corydon** (town) Harrison County
131	15.3	**Merrillville** (town) Lake County
132	15.4	**Simonton Lake** (CDP) Elkhart County
133	15.7	**Middlebury** (town) Elkhart County
133	15.7	**Valparaiso** (city) Porter County
135	16.0	**Bloomington** (city) Monroe County
136	17.3	**Angola** (city) Steuben County
137	17.7	**Schererville** (town) Lake County
138	17.9	**De Motte** (town) Jasper County
139	18.0	**Dyer** (town) Lake County
140	18.2	**Lawrence** (city) Marion County
141	18.3	**Melody Hill** (CDP) Vanderburgh County
142	19.0	**Lafayette** (city) Tippecanoe County
143	19.2	**New Haven** (city) Allen County
144	19.4	**Fort Branch** (town) Gibson County
145	19.5	**New Whiteland** (town) Johnson County
146	21.8	**Franklin** (city) Johnson County
147	22.0	**Hidden Valley** (CDP) Dearborn County
148	23.1	**Winona Lake** (town) Kosciusko County
149	23.3	**Fort Wayne** (city) Allen County
150	23.6	**Columbia City** (city) Whitley County

Note: This section ranks incorporated places and CDPs (Census Designated Places) with populations of 2,500 or more. Unincorporated postal areas were not considered. Please refer to the User Guide for additional information.

Population Density

Top 150 Places Ranked in *Descending* Order

State Rank	Pop./Sq. Mi.	Place
1	9,389.0	**Purdue University** (CDP) Tippecanoe County
2	4,944.3	**Notre Dame** (CDP) Saint Joseph County
3	4,250.2	**South Haven** (CDP) Porter County
4	3,886.4	**West Lafayette** (city) Tippecanoe County
5	3,744.4	**New Whiteland** (town) Johnson County
6	3,549.0	**Hammond** (city) Lake County
7	3,472.0	**Bloomington** (city) Monroe County
8	3,421.0	**Highland** (town) Lake County
9	3,229.4	**Beech Grove** (city) Marion County
10	3,117.9	**Munster** (town) Lake County
11	2,838.8	**Mishawaka** (city) Saint Joseph County
12	2,817.3	**Cicero** (town) Hamilton County
13	2,779.8	**Whiting** (city) Lake County
14	2,685.1	**Dyer** (town) Lake County
15	2,666.3	**Melody Hill** (CDP) Vanderburgh County
16	2,659.6	**Evansville** (city) Vanderburgh County
17	2,634.5	**Martinsville** (city) Morgan County
18	2,623.6	**Lakes of the Four Seasons** (CDP) Lake County
19	2,613.8	**Brazil** (city) Clay County
20	2,602.0	**Frankfort** (city) Clinton County
21	2,577.0	**Muncie** (city) Delaware County
22	2,526.0	**Fort Branch** (town) Gibson County
23	2,511.3	**Cumberland** (town) Marion County
24	2,485.7	**Vincennes** (city) Knox County
25	2,483.2	**New Castle** (city) Henry County
26	2,482.4	**Speedway** (town) Marion County
27	2,458.1	**Kokomo** (city) Howard County
28	2,440.3	**South Bend** (city) Saint Joseph County
29	2,434.8	**New Albany** (city) Floyd County
30	2,432.9	**Washington** (city) Daviess County
31	2,420.1	**Lafayette** (city) Tippecanoe County
32	2,381.2	**Mount Vernon** (city) Posey County
33	2,364.5	**Newburgh** (town) Warrick County
34	2,345.3	**Greenwood** (city) Johnson County
35	2,301.8	**Ossian** (town) Wells County
36	2,293.4	**Fort Wayne** (city) Allen County
37	2,286.5	**Fishers** (town) Hamilton County
38	2,285.0	**Lawrence** (city) Marion County
39	2,282.5	**Elwood** (city) Madison County
40	2,270.0	**Indianapolis** (city) Marion County
41	2,265.2	**Sullivan** (city) Sullivan County
42	2,249.3	**Covington** (city) Fountain County
43	2,236.5	**Peru** (city) Miami County
44	2,186.4	**Clinton** (city) Vermillion County
45	2,184.6	**Griffith** (town) Lake County
46	2,178.2	**Clarksville** (city) Clark County
47	2,172.4	**Elkhart** (city) Elkhart County
48	2,165.4	**Bicknell** (city) Knox County
49	2,108.1	**East Chicago** (city) Lake County
50	2,103.0	**Logansport** (city) Cass County
51	2,081.2	**Boonville** (city) Warrick County
52	2,051.6	**Rushville** (city) Rush County
53	2,043.1	**Valparaiso** (city) Porter County
54	2,039.3	**Tipton** (city) Tipton County
55	2,028.3	**Attica** (city) Fountain County
56	1,997.3	**Huntington** (city) Huntington County
57	1,987.7	**Schererville** (town) Lake County
58	1,980.0	**Highland** (CDP) Vanderburgh County
59	1,969.8	**Greencastle** (city) Putnam County
60	1,958.3	**Alexandria** (city) Madison County
61	1,954.4	**Goshen** (city) Elkhart County
62	1,925.8	**Chesterfield** (town) Madison County
63	1,924.7	**Berne** (city) Adams County
64	1,921.7	**Brownsburg** (town) Hendricks County
65	1,907.3	**Ligonier** (city) Noble County
66	1,906.2	**Marion** (city) Grant County
67	1,895.5	**Westville** (town) LaPorte County
68	1,892.8	**Corydon** (town) Harrison County
69	1,891.3	**La Porte** (city) LaPorte County
70	1,884.6	**Hebron** (town) Porter County
71	1,866.4	**Fairmount** (town) Grant County
72	1,855.7	**Brownstown** (town) Jackson County
73	1,823.1	**Franklin** (city) Johnson County
74	1,792.0	**Auburn** (city) DeKalb County
75	1,791.5	**Linton** (city) Greene County
76	1,790.8	**Lowell** (town) Lake County
77	1,776.5	**Winona Lake** (town) Kosciusko County
78	1,760.0	**Terre Haute** (city) Vigo County
79	1,755.5	**Loogootee** (city) Martin County
80	1,746.8	**Rockville** (town) Parke County
81	1,740.7	**Connersville** (city) Fayette County
82	1,740.0	**Crawfordsville** (city) Montgomery County
83	1,732.5	**Brookville** (town) Franklin County
84	1,729.3	**North Manchester** (town) Wabash County
85	1,704.9	**Princeton** (city) Gibson County
86	1,689.6	**Bremen** (town) Marshall County
87	1,668.5	**Carmel** (city) Hamilton County
88	1,666.7	**Austin** (city) Scott County
89	1,659.6	**Shelbyville** (city) Shelby County
90	1,656.4	**Noblesville** (city) Hamilton County
91	1,641.5	**Greenfield** (city) Hancock County
92	1,632.5	**Garrett** (city) DeKalb County
93	1,631.5	**Kendallville** (city) Noble County
94	1,628.9	**Union City** (city) Randolph County
95	1,627.9	**Decatur** (city) Adams County
96	1,610.2	**Gary** (city) Lake County
97	1,607.1	**Michigan City** (city) LaPorte County
98	1,605.0	**Hartford City** (city) Blackford County
99	1,603.9	**Tell City** (city) Perry County
100	1,602.5	**Nappanee** (city) Elkhart County
101	1,602.4	**Columbus** (city) Bartholomew County
102	1,579.8	**Salem** (city) Washington County
103	1,572.4	**Syracuse** (town) Kosciusko County
104	1,567.6	**Columbia City** (city) Whitley County
105	1,554.3	**Sellersburg** (town) Clark County
106	1,550.1	**Monticello** (city) White County
107	1,542.2	**Crown Point** (city) Lake County
108	1,541.8	**Rensselaer** (city) Jasper County
109	1,540.7	**Lagrange** (town) LaGrange County
110	1,539.3	**Richmond** (city) Wayne County
111	1,536.5	**Hanover** (town) Jefferson County
112	1,532.4	**Seymour** (city) Jackson County
113	1,515.4	**Lake Station** (city) Lake County
114	1,504.3	**Ellettsville** (town) Monroe County
115	1,499.3	**New Haven** (city) Allen County
116	1,483.9	**Mooresville** (town) Morgan County
117	1,482.8	**Winchester** (city) Randolph County
118	1,440.8	**Edinburgh** (town) Johnson County
119	1,437.0	**Portage** (city) Porter County
120	1,426.3	**Shorewood Forest** (CDP) Porter County
121	1,419.9	**Chandler** (town) Warrick County
122	1,406.5	**Cedar Lake** (town) Lake County
123	1,403.5	**Georgetown** (town) Floyd County
124	1,400.3	**Chesterton** (town) Porter County
125	1,395.6	**Madison** (city) Jefferson County
126	1,393.7	**Country Squire Lakes** (CDP) Jennings County
127	1,380.5	**Zionsville** (town) Boone County
128	1,358.4	**Aurora** (city) Dearborn County
129	1,357.6	**Angola** (city) Steuben County
130	1,356.7	**Anderson** (city) Madison County
131	1,338.0	**Portland** (city) Jay County
132	1,335.3	**Scottsburg** (city) Scott County
133	1,331.7	**Plymouth** (city) Marshall County
134	1,327.8	**Mitchell** (city) Lawrence County
135	1,325.6	**Rochester** (city) Fulton County
136	1,320.0	**Fortville** (town) Hancock County
137	1,319.7	**Jeffersonville** (city) Clark County
138	1,312.7	**Simonton Lake** (CDP) Elkhart County
139	1,309.1	**Gas City** (city) Grant County
140	1,304.1	**Saint John** (town) Lake County
141	1,301.8	**Hidden Valley** (CDP) Dearborn County
142	1,298.8	**Danville** (town) Hendricks County
143	1,294.9	**Whiteland** (town) Johnson County
144	1,282.3	**Butler** (city) DeKalb County
145	1,272.3	**Dunlap** (CDP) Elkhart County
146	1,265.0	**Huntertown** (town) Allen County
147	1,247.0	**Sheridan** (town) Hamilton County
148	1,240.5	**Plainfield** (town) Hendricks County
149	1,239.8	**Greensburg** (city) Decatur County
150	1,225.2	**Upland** (town) Grant County

Note: This section ranks incorporated places and CDPs (Census Designated Places) with populations of 2,500 or more. Unincorporated postal areas were not considered. Please refer to the User Guide for additional information.

Population Density

Top 150 Places Ranked in *Ascending* Order

State Rank	Pop./Sq. Mi.	Place
1	274.1	**Whitestown** (town) Boone County
2	297.0	**Smithville-Sanders** (CDP) Monroe County
3	366.0	**Winfield** (town) Lake County
4	380.9	**Pendleton** (town) Madison County
5	453.7	**Bright** (CDP) Dearborn County
6	511.9	**Roselawn** (CDP) Newton County
7	662.7	**Charlestown** (city) Clark County
8	783.6	**Porter** (town) Porter County
9	791.3	**Greendale** (city) Dearborn County
10	814.7	**Bargersville** (town) Johnson County
11	874.0	**Avon** (town) Hendricks County
12	910.7	**Middlebury** (town) Elkhart County
13	944.8	**Knox** (city) Starke County
14	956.0	**Heritage Lake** (CDP) Putnam County
15	970.3	**Leo-Cedarville** (town) Allen County
16	982.3	**Paoli** (town) Orange County
17	992.2	**Pittsboro** (town) Hendricks County
18	1,015.3	**Lebanon** (city) Boone County
19	1,016.5	**North Vernon** (city) Jennings County
20	1,020.4	**Lawrenceburg** (city) Dearborn County
20	1,020.4	**McCordsville** (town) Hancock County
22	1,056.8	**De Motte** (town) Jasper County
23	1,061.1	**Merrillville** (town) Lake County
24	1,061.3	**Delphi** (city) Carroll County
25	1,061.5	**Centerville** (town) Wayne County
26	1,071.1	**Batesville** (city) Ripley County
27	1,071.3	**Yorktown** (town) Delaware County
28	1,102.9	**Bedford** (city) Lawrence County
29	1,103.6	**Hobart** (city) Lake County
30	1,109.3	**Grissom AFB** (CDP) Miami County
31	1,120.3	**Westfield** (city) Hamilton County
32	1,147.5	**Jasper** (city) Dubois County
33	1,171.3	**Warsaw** (city) Kosciusko County
34	1,191.6	**Granger** (CDP) Saint Joseph County
35	1,196.7	**Huntingburg** (city) Dubois County
36	1,200.4	**Wabash** (city) Wabash County
37	1,202.3	**Bluffton** (city) Wells County
38	1,206.7	**North Terre Haute** (CDP) Vigo County
39	1,225.2	**Upland** (town) Grant County
40	1,239.8	**Greensburg** (city) Decatur County
41	1,240.5	**Plainfield** (town) Hendricks County
42	1,247.0	**Sheridan** (town) Hamilton County
43	1,265.0	**Huntertown** (town) Allen County
44	1,272.3	**Dunlap** (CDP) Elkhart County
45	1,282.3	**Butler** (city) DeKalb County
46	1,294.9	**Whiteland** (town) Johnson County
47	1,298.5	**Danville** (town) Hendricks County
48	1,301.8	**Hidden Valley** (CDP) Dearborn County
49	1,304.1	**Saint John** (town) Lake County
50	1,309.1	**Gas City** (city) Grant County
51	1,312.7	**Simonton Lake** (CDP) Elkhart County
52	1,319.7	**Jeffersonville** (city) Clark County
53	1,320.0	**Fortville** (town) Hancock County
54	1,325.6	**Rochester** (city) Fulton County
55	1,327.8	**Mitchell** (city) Lawrence County
56	1,331.9	**Plymouth** (city) Marshall County
57	1,335.3	**Scottsburg** (city) Scott County
58	1,338.0	**Portland** (city) Jay County
59	1,356.7	**Anderson** (city) Madison County
60	1,357.6	**Angola** (city) Steuben County
61	1,358.4	**Aurora** (city) Dearborn County
62	1,380.5	**Zionsville** (town) Boone County
63	1,393.7	**Country Squire Lakes** (CDP) Jennings County
64	1,395.6	**Madison** (city) Jefferson County
65	1,400.3	**Chesterton** (town) Porter County
66	1,403.5	**Georgetown** (town) Floyd County
67	1,406.5	**Cedar Lake** (town) Lake County
68	1,419.9	**Chandler** (town) Warrick County
69	1,426.3	**Shorewood Forest** (CDP) Porter County
70	1,437.0	**Portage** (city) Porter County
71	1,440.5	**Edinburgh** (town) Johnson County
72	1,482.8	**Winchester** (city) Randolph County
73	1,483.9	**Mooresville** (town) Morgan County
74	1,499.3	**New Haven** (city) Allen County
75	1,504.3	**Ellettsville** (town) Monroe County
76	1,515.4	**Lake Station** (city) Lake County
77	1,532.4	**Seymour** (city) Jackson County
78	1,536.5	**Hanover** (town) Jefferson County
79	1,539.3	**Richmond** (city) Wayne County
80	1,540.7	**Lagrange** (town) LaGrange County
81	1,541.8	**Rensselaer** (city) Jasper County
82	1,542.2	**Crown Point** (city) Lake County
83	1,550.1	**Monticello** (city) White County
84	1,554.3	**Sellersburg** (town) Clark County
85	1,567.6	**Columbia City** (city) Whitley County
86	1,572.4	**Syracuse** (town) Kosciusko County
87	1,579.8	**Salem** (city) Washington County
88	1,602.4	**Columbus** (city) Bartholomew County
89	1,602.5	**Nappanee** (city) Elkhart County
90	1,603.9	**Tell City** (city) Perry County
91	1,605.0	**Hartford City** (city) Blackford County
92	1,607.1	**Michigan City** (city) LaPorte County
93	1,610.2	**Gary** (city) Lake County
94	1,627.9	**Decatur** (city) Adams County
95	1,628.9	**Union City** (city) Randolph County
96	1,631.5	**Kendallville** (city) Noble County
97	1,632.5	**Garrett** (city) DeKalb County
98	1,641.5	**Greenfield** (city) Hancock County
99	1,656.4	**Noblesville** (city) Hamilton County
100	1,659.6	**Shelbyville** (city) Shelby County
101	1,666.7	**Austin** (city) Scott County
102	1,668.5	**Carmel** (city) Hamilton County
103	1,689.6	**Bremen** (town) Marshall County
104	1,704.9	**Princeton** (city) Gibson County
105	1,729.3	**North Manchester** (town) Wabash County
106	1,732.5	**Brookville** (town) Franklin County
107	1,740.0	**Crawfordsville** (city) Montgomery County
108	1,740.7	**Connersville** (city) Fayette County
109	1,746.8	**Rockville** (town) Parke County
110	1,755.5	**Loogootee** (city) Martin County
111	1,760.0	**Terre Haute** (city) Vigo County
112	1,776.5	**Winona Lake** (town) Kosciusko County
113	1,790.8	**Lowell** (town) Lake County
114	1,791.5	**Linton** (city) Greene County
115	1,792.0	**Auburn** (city) DeKalb County
116	1,823.1	**Franklin** (city) Johnson County
117	1,855.7	**Brownstown** (town) Jackson County
118	1,866.4	**Fairmount** (town) Grant County
119	1,884.8	**Hebron** (town) Porter County
120	1,891.3	**La Porte** (city) LaPorte County
121	1,892.8	**Corydon** (town) Harrison County
122	1,895.5	**Westville** (town) LaPorte County
123	1,906.2	**Marion** (city) Grant County
124	1,907.3	**Ligonier** (city) Noble County
125	1,921.7	**Brownsburg** (town) Hendricks County
126	1,924.7	**Berne** (city) Adams County
127	1,925.8	**Chesterfield** (town) Madison County
128	1,954.4	**Goshen** (city) Elkhart County
129	1,958.3	**Alexandria** (city) Madison County
130	1,969.8	**Greencastle** (city) Putnam County
131	1,980.0	**Highland** (CDP) Vanderburgh County
132	1,987.7	**Schererville** (town) Lake County
133	1,997.3	**Huntington** (city) Huntington County
134	2,028.3	**Attica** (city) Fountain County
135	2,039.3	**Tipton** (city) Tipton County
136	2,043.1	**Valparaiso** (city) Porter County
137	2,051.6	**Rushville** (city) Rush County
138	2,081.2	**Boonville** (city) Warrick County
139	2,103.0	**Logansport** (city) Cass County
140	2,108.1	**East Chicago** (city) Lake County
141	2,165.4	**Bicknell** (city) Knox County
142	2,172.4	**Elkhart** (city) Elkhart County
143	2,178.2	**Clarksville** (town) Clark County
144	2,184.6	**Griffith** (town) Lake County
145	2,186.4	**Clinton** (city) Vermillion County
146	2,236.5	**Peru** (city) Miami County
147	2,249.3	**Covington** (city) Fountain County
148	2,265.2	**Sullivan** (city) Sullivan County
149	2,270.0	**Indianapolis** (city) Marion County
150	2,282.5	**Elwood** (city) Madison County

Note: *This section ranks incorporated places and CDPs (Census Designated Places) with populations of 2,500 or more. Unincorporated postal areas were not considered. Please refer to the User Guide for additional information.*

White Population
Top 150 Places Ranked in *Descending* Order

State Rank	Percent	Place
1	98.7	**Rockville** (town) Parke County
2	98.6	**Fairmount** (town) Grant County
3	98.3	**Bright** (CDP) Dearborn County
3	98.3	**Brownstown** (town) Jackson County
3	98.3	**Loogootee** (city) Martin County
6	97.9	**Chandler** (town) Warrick County
7	97.8	**Attica** (city) Fountain County
8	97.7	**Boonville** (city) Warrick County
8	97.7	**Linton** (city) Greene County
8	97.7	**Paoli** (town) Orange County
8	97.7	**Sullivan** (city) Sullivan County
12	97.6	**Bicknell** (city) Knox County
12	97.6	**Covington** (city) Fountain County
12	97.6	**Hidden Valley** (CDP) Dearborn County
12	97.6	**Mitchell** (city) Lawrence County
16	97.5	**Aurora** (city) Dearborn County
16	97.5	**Brookville** (town) Franklin County
16	97.5	**Clinton** (city) Vermillion County
16	97.5	**Martinsville** (city) Morgan County
16	97.5	**Mooresville** (town) Morgan County
16	97.5	**Salem** (city) Washington County
16	97.5	**Tell City** (city) Perry County
23	97.4	**Alexandria** (city) Madison County
23	97.4	**Chesterfield** (town) Madison County
23	97.4	**Ossian** (town) Wells County
26	97.3	**Georgetown** (town) Floyd County
26	97.3	**Hartford City** (city) Blackford County
26	97.3	**Heritage Lake** (CDP) Putnam County
29	97.2	**Scottsburg** (city) Scott County
30	97.1	**Austin** (city) Scott County
30	97.1	**Brazil** (city) Clay County
30	97.1	**Leo-Cedarville** (town) Allen County
30	97.1	**Tipton** (city) Tipton County
34	97.0	**Whiteland** (town) Johnson County
35	96.9	**Auburn** (city) DeKalb County
36	96.8	**Cicero** (town) Hamilton County
36	96.8	**Danville** (town) Hendricks County
36	96.8	**Fort Branch** (town) Gibson County
39	96.7	**Columbia City** (city) Whitley County
39	96.7	**Corydon** (town) Harrison County
39	96.7	**Elwood** (city) Madison County
39	96.7	**Pittsboro** (town) Hendricks County
43	96.6	**Greenfield** (city) Hancock County
43	96.6	**New Whiteland** (town) Johnson County
43	96.6	**Pendleton** (town) Madison County
46	96.5	**Berne** (city) Adams County
47	96.4	**Huntington** (city) Huntington County
48	96.3	**Knox** (city) Starke County
48	96.3	**Wabash** (city) Wabash County
50	96.2	**Bedford** (city) Lawrence County
50	96.2	**De Motte** (town) Jasper County
50	96.2	**Fortville** (town) Hancock County
50	96.2	**Gas City** (city) Grant County
54	96.1	**Centerville** (town) Wayne County
54	96.1	**Greensburg** (city) Decatur County
54	96.1	**Highland** (CDP) Vanderburgh County
54	96.1	**Lebanon** (city) Boone County
54	96.1	**Winchester** (city) Randolph County
59	96.0	**Bluffton** (city) Wells County
60	95.9	**Garrett** (city) DeKalb County
60	95.9	**Hebron** (town) Porter County
60	95.9	**Lowell** (town) Lake County
60	95.9	**Rochester** (city) Fulton County
60	95.9	**Smithville-Sanders** (CDP) Monroe County
65	95.8	**Rushville** (city) Rush County
66	95.7	**Connersville** (city) Fayette County
66	95.7	**Syracuse** (town) Kosciusko County
68	95.6	**Bargersville** (town) Johnson County
68	95.6	**Greendale** (city) Dearborn County
68	95.6	**Middlebury** (town) Elkhart County
71	95.5	**Ellettsville** (town) Monroe County
72	95.4	**Rensselaer** (city) Jasper County
73	95.3	**Sheridan** (town) Hamilton County
73	95.3	**Yorktown** (town) Delaware County
75	95.2	**Edinburgh** (town) Johnson County
75	95.2	**North Manchester** (town) Wabash County
77	95.1	**Batesville** (city) Ripley County
77	95.1	**New Castle** (city) Henry County
79	95.0	**North Terre Haute** (CDP) Vigo County
79	95.0	**North Vernon** (city) Jennings County
81	94.9	**Butler** (city) DeKalb County
81	94.9	**Cedar Lake** (town) Lake County
81	94.9	**Franklin** (city) Johnson County
81	94.9	**Hanover** (town) Jefferson County
85	94.8	**Nappanee** (city) Elkhart County
86	94.7	**Decatur** (city) Adams County
87	94.6	**Upland** (town) Grant County
88	94.5	**Portland** (city) Jay County
89	94.3	**Porter** (town) Porter County
90	94.2	**Newburgh** (town) Warrick County
90	94.2	**Roselawn** (CDP) Newton County
90	94.2	**Sellersburg** (town) Clark County
93	94.1	**Kendallville** (city) Noble County
94	94.0	**Zionsville** (town) Boone County
95	93.9	**Melody Hill** (CDP) Vanderburgh County
96	93.7	**Lagrange** (town) LaGrange County
97	93.6	**Angola** (city) Steuben County
97	93.6	**Huntertown** (town) Allen County
97	93.6	**Jasper** (city) Dubois County
100	93.5	**Lawrenceburg** (city) Dearborn County
100	93.5	**Madison** (city) Jefferson County
100	93.5	**Saint John** (town) Lake County
103	93.4	**Brownsburg** (town) Hendricks County
103	93.4	**Lakes of the Four Seasons** (CDP) Lake County
103	93.4	**Mount Vernon** (city) Posey County
106	93.2	**New Haven** (city) Allen County
107	93.1	**Peru** (city) Miami County
108	93.0	**Country Squire Lakes** (CDP) Jennings County
109	92.7	**Chesterton** (town) Porter County
110	92.4	**Greencastle** (city) Putnam County
111	92.2	**Winona Lake** (town) Kosciusko County
112	92.1	**Crawfordsville** (city) Montgomery County
113	91.9	**Shelbyville** (city) Shelby County
113	91.9	**Vincennes** (city) Knox County
115	91.7	**Delphi** (city) Carroll County
116	91.5	**Beech Grove** (city) Marion County
117	91.3	**South Haven** (CDP) Porter County
118	91.1	**Noblesville** (city) Hamilton County
119	90.9	**Westfield** (city) Hamilton County
119	90.9	**Whitestown** (town) Boone County
121	90.8	**Monticello** (city) White County
122	90.4	**Princeton** (city) Gibson County
123	90.3	**Granger** (CDP) Saint Joseph County
123	90.3	**Seymour** (city) Jackson County
125	90.1	**Dyer** (town) Lake County
125	90.1	**Greenwood** (city) Johnson County
127	89.9	**Charlestown** (city) Clark County
127	89.9	**Valparaiso** (city) Porter County
129	89.5	**Warsaw** (city) Kosciusko County
130	89.4	**Shorewood Forest** (CDP) Porter County
131	89.2	**Washington** (city) Daviess County
132	88.6	**Highland** (town) Lake County
132	88.6	**La Porte** (city) LaPorte County
134	88.5	**Winfield** (town) Lake County
135	88.2	**Crown Point** (city) Lake County
136	87.8	**Simonton Lake** (CDP) Elkhart County
137	87.6	**Union City** (city) Randolph County
138	87.3	**Huntingburg** (city) Dubois County
139	87.2	**Plymouth** (city) Marshall County
140	86.9	**Columbus** (city) Bartholomew County
141	86.8	**Schererville** (town) Lake County
142	86.7	**Avon** (town) Hendricks County
143	86.5	**Bremen** (town) Marshall County
144	86.3	**Dunlap** (CDP) Elkhart County
145	86.1	**Mishawaka** (city) Saint Joseph County
146	85.8	**New Albany** (city) Floyd County
147	85.6	**Fishers** (town) Hamilton County
147	85.6	**Munster** (town) Lake County
149	85.4	**Carmel** (city) Hamilton County
150	85.3	**Hobart** (city) Lake County

Note: This section ranks incorporated places and CDPs (Census Designated Places) with populations of 2,500 or more. Unincorporated postal areas were not considered. Please refer to the User Guide for additional information.

White Population
Top 150 Places Ranked in *Ascending* Order

State Rank	Percent	Place
1	10.7	**Gary** (city) Lake County
2	35.5	**East Chicago** (city) Lake County
3	46.4	**Merrillville** (town) Lake County
4	59.4	**Hammond** (city) Lake County
5	60.5	**South Bend** (city) Saint Joseph County
6	61.8	**Indianapolis** (city) Marion County
7	63.2	**Lawrence** (city) Marion County
8	64.9	**Michigan City** (city) LaPorte County
9	66.1	**Elkhart** (city) Elkhart County
10	69.6	**Ligonier** (city) Noble County
11	69.9	**Purdue University** (CDP) Tippecanoe County
12	72.1	**Westville** (town) LaPorte County
13	73.6	**Fort Wayne** (city) Allen County
14	74.2	**Speedway** (town) Marion County
15	74.4	**Grissom AFB** (CDP) Miami County
16	75.8	**Griffith** (town) Lake County
17	76.3	**Whiting** (city) Lake County
18	76.8	**West Lafayette** (city) Tippecanoe County
19	77.0	**Cumberland** (town) Marion County
20	78.1	**Marion** (city) Grant County
21	78.2	**Goshen** (city) Elkhart County
22	78.8	**Anderson** (city) Madison County
23	79.7	**Lake Station** (city) Lake County
24	80.4	**Jeffersonville** (city) Clark County
25	80.7	**Logansport** (city) Cass County
26	82.0	**Evansville** (city) Vanderburgh County
27	83.0	**Bloomington** (city) Monroe County
28	83.2	**McCordsville** (town) Hancock County
29	83.5	**Kokomo** (city) Howard County
29	83.5	**Terre Haute** (city) Vigo County
31	83.6	**Lafayette** (city) Tippecanoe County
31	83.6	**Portage** (city) Porter County
33	83.9	**Frankfort** (city) Clinton County
33	83.9	**Richmond** (city) Wayne County
35	84.0	**Muncie** (city) Delaware County
35	84.0	**Notre Dame** (CDP) Saint Joseph County
37	85.1	**Clarksville** (town) Clark County
38	85.2	**Plainfield** (town) Hendricks County
39	85.3	**Hobart** (city) Lake County
40	85.4	**Carmel** (city) Hamilton County
41	85.6	**Fishers** (town) Hamilton County
41	85.6	**Munster** (town) Lake County
43	85.8	**New Albany** (city) Floyd County
44	86.1	**Mishawaka** (city) Saint Joseph County
45	86.3	**Dunlap** (CDP) Elkhart County
46	86.5	**Bremen** (town) Marshall County
47	86.7	**Avon** (town) Hendricks County
48	86.8	**Schererville** (town) Lake County
49	86.9	**Columbus** (city) Bartholomew County
50	87.2	**Plymouth** (city) Marshall County
51	87.3	**Huntingburg** (city) Dubois County
52	87.6	**Union City** (city) Randolph County
53	87.8	**Simonton Lake** (CDP) Elkhart County
54	88.2	**Crown Point** (city) Lake County
55	88.5	**Winfield** (town) Lake County
56	88.6	**Highland** (town) Lake County
56	88.6	**La Porte** (city) LaPorte County
58	89.2	**Washington** (city) Daviess County
59	89.4	**Shorewood Forest** (CDP) Porter County
60	89.5	**Warsaw** (city) Kosciusko County
61	89.9	**Charlestown** (city) Clark County
61	89.9	**Valparaiso** (city) Porter County
63	90.1	**Dyer** (town) Lake County
63	90.1	**Greenwood** (city) Johnson County
65	90.3	**Granger** (CDP) Saint Joseph County
65	90.3	**Seymour** (city) Jackson County
67	90.4	**Princeton** (city) Gibson County
68	90.8	**Monticello** (city) White County
69	90.9	**Westfield** (city) Hamilton County
69	90.9	**Whitestown** (town) Boone County
71	91.1	**Noblesville** (city) Hamilton County
72	91.3	**South Haven** (CDP) Porter County
73	91.5	**Beech Grove** (city) Marion County
74	91.7	**Delphi** (city) Carroll County
75	91.9	**Shelbyville** (city) Shelby County
75	91.9	**Vincennes** (city) Knox County
77	92.1	**Crawfordsville** (city) Montgomery County
78	92.2	**Winona Lake** (town) Kosciusko County
79	92.4	**Greencastle** (city) Putnam County
80	92.7	**Chesterton** (town) Porter County
81	93.0	**Country Squire Lakes** (CDP) Jennings County
82	93.1	**Peru** (city) Miami County
83	93.2	**New Haven** (city) Allen County
84	93.4	**Brownsburg** (town) Hendricks County
84	93.4	**Lakes of the Four Seasons** (CDP) Lake County
84	93.4	**Mount Vernon** (city) Posey County
87	93.5	**Lawrenceburg** (city) Dearborn County
87	93.5	**Madison** (city) Jefferson County
87	93.5	**Saint John** (town) Lake County
90	93.6	**Angola** (city) Steuben County
90	93.6	**Huntertown** (town) Allen County
90	93.6	**Jasper** (city) Dubois County
93	93.7	**Lagrange** (town) LaGrange County
94	93.9	**Melody Hill** (CDP) Vanderburgh County
95	94.0	**Zionsville** (town) Boone County
96	94.1	**Kendallville** (city) Noble County
97	94.2	**Newburgh** (town) Warrick County
97	94.2	**Roselawn** (CDP) Newton County
97	94.2	**Sellersburg** (town) Clark County
100	94.3	**Porter** (town) Porter County
101	94.5	**Portland** (city) Jay County
102	94.6	**Upland** (town) Grant County
103	94.7	**Decatur** (city) Adams County
104	94.8	**Nappanee** (city) Elkhart County
105	94.9	**Butler** (city) DeKalb County
105	94.9	**Cedar Lake** (town) Lake County
105	94.9	**Franklin** (city) Johnson County
105	94.9	**Hanover** (town) Jefferson County
109	95.0	**North Terre Haute** (CDP) Vigo County
109	95.0	**North Vernon** (city) Jennings County
111	95.1	**Batesville** (city) Ripley County
111	95.1	**New Castle** (city) Henry County
113	95.2	**Edinburgh** (town) Johnson County
113	95.2	**North Manchester** (town) Wabash County
115	95.3	**Sheridan** (town) Hamilton County
115	95.3	**Yorktown** (town) Delaware County
117	95.4	**Rensselaer** (city) Jasper County
118	95.5	**Ellettsville** (town) Monroe County
119	95.6	**Bargersville** (town) Johnson County
119	95.6	**Greendale** (city) Dearborn County
119	95.6	**Middlebury** (town) Elkhart County
122	95.7	**Connersville** (city) Fayette County
122	95.7	**Syracuse** (town) Kosciusko County
124	95.8	**Rushville** (city) Rush County
125	95.9	**Garrett** (city) DeKalb County
125	95.9	**Hebron** (town) Porter County
125	95.9	**Lowell** (town) Lake County
125	95.9	**Rochester** (city) Fulton County
125	95.9	**Smithville-Sanders** (CDP) Monroe County
130	96.0	**Bluffton** (city) Wells County
131	96.1	**Centerville** (town) Wayne County
131	96.1	**Greensburg** (city) Decatur County
131	96.1	**Highland** (CDP) Vanderburgh County
131	96.1	**Lebanon** (city) Boone County
131	96.1	**Winchester** (city) Randolph County
136	96.2	**Bedford** (city) Lawrence County
136	96.2	**De Motte** (town) Jasper County
136	96.2	**Fortville** (town) Hancock County
136	96.2	**Gas City** (city) Grant County
140	96.3	**Knox** (city) Starke County
140	96.3	**Wabash** (city) Wabash County
142	96.4	**Huntington** (city) Huntington County
143	96.5	**Berne** (city) Adams County
144	96.6	**Greenfield** (city) Hancock County
144	96.6	**New Whiteland** (town) Johnson County
144	96.6	**Pendleton** (town) Madison County
147	96.7	**Columbia City** (city) Whitley County
147	96.7	**Corydon** (town) Harrison County
147	96.7	**Elwood** (city) Madison County
147	96.7	**Pittsboro** (town) Hendricks County

Note: This section ranks incorporated places and CDPs (Census Designated Places) with populations of 2,500 or more. Unincorporated postal areas were not considered. Please refer to the User Guide for additional information.

Black/African American Population
Top 150 Places Ranked in *Descending* Order

State Rank	Percent	Place
1	84.8	Gary (city) Lake County
2	44.5	Merrillville (town) Lake County
3	42.9	East Chicago (city) Lake County
4	28.1	Michigan City (city) LaPorte County
5	27.5	Indianapolis (city) Marion County
6	26.6	South Bend (city) Saint Joseph County
7	25.8	Lawrence (city) Marion County
8	25.1	Westville (town) LaPorte County
9	22.5	Grissom AFB (CDP) Miami County
9	22.5	Hammond (city) Lake County
11	16.9	Griffith (town) Lake County
12	16.8	Cumberland (town) Marion County
13	16.7	Speedway (town) Marion County
14	15.4	Elkhart (city) Elkhart County
14	15.4	Fort Wayne (city) Allen County
16	15.2	Anderson (city) Madison County
17	14.7	Marion (city) Grant County
18	13.2	Jeffersonville (city) Clark County
19	12.6	Evansville (city) Vanderburgh County
20	10.9	Muncie (city) Delaware County
20	10.9	Terre Haute (city) Vigo County
22	10.7	Kokomo (city) Howard County
23	10.3	McCordsville (town) Hancock County
24	8.7	New Albany (city) Floyd County
25	8.6	Richmond (city) Wayne County
26	7.9	Plainfield (town) Hendricks County
27	7.3	Portage (city) Porter County
28	7.0	Hobart (city) Lake County
29	6.9	Mishawaka (city) Saint Joseph County
30	6.3	Crown Point (city) Lake County
31	6.2	Lafayette (city) Tippecanoe County
32	5.9	Avon (town) Hendricks County
33	5.6	Clarksville (town) Clark County
33	5.6	Fishers (town) Hamilton County
35	5.4	Schererville (town) Lake County
36	4.9	Simonton Lake (CDP) Elkhart County
37	4.7	Vincennes (city) Knox County
38	4.6	Bloomington (city) Monroe County
38	4.6	Princeton (city) Gibson County
40	4.2	Highland (town) Lake County
41	4.0	Dunlap (CDP) Elkhart County
42	3.8	Shorewood Forest (CDP) Porter County
43	3.7	Purdue University (CDP) Tippecanoe County
43	3.7	Winfield (town) Lake County
45	3.6	Lake Station (city) Lake County
45	3.6	Noblesville (city) Hamilton County
47	3.5	Munster (town) Lake County
47	3.5	Whiting (city) Lake County
49	3.4	Melody Hill (CDP) Vanderburgh County
50	3.3	New Haven (city) Allen County
50	3.3	Valparaiso (city) Porter County
52	3.2	Beech Grove (city) Marion County
53	3.0	Carmel (city) Hamilton County
53	3.0	La Porte (city) LaPorte County
53	3.0	Lawrenceburg (city) Dearborn County
53	3.0	South Haven (CDP) Porter County
57	2.8	Madison (city) Jefferson County
57	2.8	Mount Vernon (city) Posey County
57	2.8	Notre Dame (CDP) Saint Joseph County
57	2.8	Whitestown (town) Boone County
61	2.7	Columbus (city) Bartholomew County
61	2.7	Greencastle (city) Putnam County
61	2.7	West Lafayette (city) Tippecanoe County
64	2.6	Goshen (city) Elkhart County
65	2.5	Dyer (town) Lake County
65	2.5	Granger (CDP) Saint Joseph County
65	2.5	Peru (city) Miami County
68	2.3	Hanover (town) Jefferson County
68	2.3	Logansport (city) Cass County
70	2.2	Brownsburg (town) Hendricks County
70	2.2	Westfield (town) Hamilton County
72	2.1	Charlestown (city) Clark County
72	2.1	Connersville (city) Fayette County
74	1.9	New Castle (city) Henry County
74	1.9	North Terre Haute (CDP) Vigo County
74	1.9	Shelbyville (city) Shelby County
77	1.7	Crawfordsville (city) Montgomery County
77	1.7	Greenwood (city) Johnson County
79	1.6	Upland (town) Grant County
79	1.6	Warsaw (city) Kosciusko County
79	1.6	Yorktown (town) Delaware County
82	1.5	North Vernon (city) Jennings County
82	1.5	Rushville (city) Rush County
82	1.5	Winona Lake (town) Kosciusko County
85	1.4	Angola (city) Steuben County
85	1.4	Chesterton (town) Porter County
85	1.4	Franklin (city) Johnson County
85	1.4	Huntertown (town) Allen County
85	1.4	Newburgh (town) Warrick County
90	1.3	Fortville (town) Hancock County
90	1.3	Highland (CDP) Vanderburgh County
90	1.3	Saint John (town) Lake County
90	1.3	Seymour (city) Jackson County
94	1.2	Country Squire Lakes (CDP) Jennings County
94	1.2	Lakes of the Four Seasons (CDP) Lake County
94	1.2	Zionsville (town) Boone County
97	1.1	Bargersville (town) Johnson County
97	1.1	Hebron (town) Porter County
97	1.1	North Manchester (town) Wabash County
97	1.1	Porter (town) Porter County
97	1.1	Union City (city) Randolph County
97	1.1	Washington (city) Daviess County
103	1.0	Ellettsville (town) Monroe County
103	1.0	Greendale (city) Dearborn County
103	1.0	Pendleton (town) Madison County
103	1.0	Smithville-Sanders (CDP) Monroe County
107	0.9	Gas City (city) Grant County
107	0.9	Heritage Lake (CDP) Putnam County
107	0.9	Plymouth (city) Marshall County
110	0.8	Bedford (city) Lawrence County
110	0.8	Danville (town) Hendricks County
110	0.8	Sellersburg (town) Clark County
110	0.8	Sheridan (town) Hamilton County
114	0.7	Bluffton (city) Wells County
114	0.7	Corydon (town) Harrison County
114	0.7	Nappanee (city) Elkhart County
114	0.7	Rensselaer (city) Jasper County
118	0.6	Brazil (city) Clay County
118	0.6	Centerville (town) Wayne County
118	0.6	Cicero (town) Hamilton County
118	0.6	Frankfort (city) Clinton County
118	0.6	Greenfield (city) Hancock County
118	0.6	Huntington (city) Huntington County
118	0.6	Lagrange (town) LaGrange County
118	0.6	Middlebury (town) Elkhart County
118	0.6	Rochester (city) Fulton County
118	0.6	Syracuse (town) Kosciusko County
128	0.5	Aurora (city) Dearborn County
128	0.5	Berne (city) Adams County
128	0.5	Bicknell (city) Knox County
128	0.5	Boonville (city) Warrick County
128	0.5	Butler (city) DeKalb County
128	0.5	Cedar Lake (town) Lake County
128	0.5	Columbia City (city) Whitley County
128	0.5	Decatur (city) Adams County
128	0.5	Huntingburg (city) Dubois County
128	0.5	Kendallville (city) Noble County
128	0.5	Lebanon (city) Boone County
128	0.5	Lowell (town) Lake County
128	0.5	Winchester (city) Randolph County
141	0.4	Auburn (city) DeKalb County
141	0.4	Bremen (town) Marshall County
141	0.4	Chesterfield (town) Madison County
141	0.4	De Motte (town) Jasper County
141	0.4	Delphi (city) Carroll County
141	0.4	Garrett (city) DeKalb County
141	0.4	Greensburg (city) Decatur County
141	0.4	Jasper (city) Dubois County
141	0.4	Knox (city) Starke County
141	0.4	Ligonier (city) Noble County

Note: This section ranks incorporated places and CDPs (Census Designated Places) with populations of 2,500 or more. Unincorporated postal areas were not considered. Please refer to the User Guide for additional information.

Black/African American Population
Top 150 Places Ranked in *Ascending* Order

State Rank	Percent	Place
1	0.1	**Attica** (city) Fountain County
1	0.1	**Brownstown** (town) Jackson County
1	0.1	**Fairmount** (town) Grant County
1	0.1	**Leo-Cedarville** (town) Allen County
1	0.1	**Linton** (city) Greene County
1	0.1	**Loogootee** (city) Martin County
1	0.1	**Rockville** (town) Parke County
1	0.1	**Sullivan** (city) Sullivan County
1	0.1	**Tipton** (city) Tipton County
10	0.2	**Clinton** (city) Vermillion County
10	0.2	**Covington** (city) Fountain County
10	0.2	**Elwood** (city) Madison County
10	0.2	**Hidden Valley** (CDP) Dearborn County
10	0.2	**Martinsville** (city) Morgan County
10	0.2	**Ossian** (town) Wells County
16	0.3	**Alexandria** (city) Madison County
16	0.3	**Austin** (city) Scott County
16	0.3	**Batesville** (city) Ripley County
16	0.3	**Bright** (CDP) Dearborn County
16	0.3	**Brookville** (town) Franklin County
16	0.3	**Chandler** (town) Warrick County
16	0.3	**Edinburgh** (town) Johnson County
16	0.3	**Fort Branch** (town) Gibson County
16	0.3	**Georgetown** (town) Floyd County
16	0.3	**Hartford City** (city) Blackford County
16	0.3	**Mooresville** (town) Morgan County
16	0.3	**Paoli** (town) Orange County
16	0.3	**Roselawn** (CDP) Newton County
16	0.3	**Scottsburg** (city) Scott County
16	0.3	**Tell City** (city) Perry County
31	0.4	**Auburn** (city) DeKalb County
31	0.4	**Bremen** (town) Marshall County
31	0.4	**Chesterfield** (town) Madison County
31	0.4	**De Motte** (town) Jasper County
31	0.4	**Delphi** (city) Carroll County
31	0.4	**Garrett** (city) DeKalb County
31	0.4	**Greensburg** (city) Decatur County
31	0.4	**Jasper** (city) Dubois County
31	0.4	**Knox** (city) Starke County
31	0.4	**Ligonier** (city) Noble County
31	0.4	**Mitchell** (city) Lawrence County
31	0.4	**Monticello** (city) White County
31	0.4	**New Whiteland** (town) Johnson County
31	0.4	**Pittsboro** (town) Hendricks County
31	0.4	**Portland** (city) Jay County
31	0.4	**Salem** (city) Washington County
31	0.4	**Wabash** (city) Wabash County
31	0.4	**Whiteland** (town) Johnson County
49	0.5	**Aurora** (city) Dearborn County
49	0.5	**Berne** (city) Adams County
49	0.5	**Bicknell** (city) Knox County
49	0.5	**Boonville** (city) Warrick County
49	0.5	**Butler** (city) DeKalb County
49	0.5	**Cedar Lake** (town) Lake County
49	0.5	**Columbia City** (city) Whitley County
49	0.5	**Decatur** (city) Adams County
49	0.5	**Huntingburg** (city) Dubois County
49	0.5	**Kendallville** (city) Noble County
49	0.5	**Lebanon** (city) Boone County
49	0.5	**Lowell** (town) Lake County
49	0.5	**Winchester** (city) Randolph County
62	0.6	**Brazil** (city) Clay County
62	0.6	**Centerville** (town) Wayne County
62	0.6	**Cicero** (town) Hamilton County
62	0.6	**Frankfort** (city) Clinton County
62	0.6	**Greenfield** (city) Hancock County
62	0.6	**Huntington** (city) Huntington County
62	0.6	**Lagrange** (town) LaGrange County
62	0.6	**Middlebury** (town) Elkhart County
62	0.6	**Rochester** (city) Fulton County
62	0.6	**Syracuse** (town) Kosciusko County
72	0.7	**Bluffton** (city) Wells County
72	0.7	**Corydon** (town) Harrison County
72	0.7	**Nappanee** (city) Elkhart County
72	0.7	**Rensselaer** (city) Jasper County
76	0.8	**Bedford** (city) Lawrence County
76	0.8	**Danville** (town) Hendricks County
76	0.8	**Sellersburg** (town) Clark County
76	0.8	**Sheridan** (town) Hamilton County
80	0.9	**Gas City** (city) Grant County
80	0.9	**Heritage Lake** (CDP) Putnam County
80	0.9	**Plymouth** (city) Marshall County
83	1.0	**Ellettsville** (town) Monroe County
83	1.0	**Greendale** (city) Dearborn County
83	1.0	**Pendleton** (town) Madison County
83	1.0	**Smithville-Sanders** (CDP) Monroe County
87	1.1	**Bargersville** (town) Johnson County
87	1.1	**Hebron** (town) Porter County
87	1.1	**North Manchester** (town) Wabash County
87	1.1	**Porter** (town) Porter County
87	1.1	**Union City** (city) Randolph County
87	1.1	**Washington** (city) Daviess County
93	1.2	**Country Squire Lakes** (CDP) Jennings County
93	1.2	**Lakes of the Four Seasons** (CDP) Lake County
93	1.2	**Zionsville** (town) Boone County
96	1.3	**Fortville** (town) Hancock County
96	1.3	**Highland** (CDP) Vanderburgh County
96	1.3	**Saint John** (town) Lake County
96	1.3	**Seymour** (city) Jackson County
100	1.4	**Angola** (city) Steuben County
100	1.4	**Chesterton** (town) Porter County
100	1.4	**Franklin** (city) Johnson County
100	1.4	**Huntertown** (town) Allen County
100	1.4	**Newburgh** (town) Warrick County
105	1.5	**North Vernon** (city) Jennings County
105	1.5	**Rushville** (city) Rush County
105	1.5	**Winona Lake** (town) Kosciusko County
108	1.6	**Upland** (town) Grant County
108	1.6	**Warsaw** (city) Kosciusko County
108	1.6	**Yorktown** (town) Delaware County
111	1.7	**Crawfordsville** (city) Montgomery County
111	1.7	**Greenwood** (city) Johnson County
113	1.9	**New Castle** (city) Henry County
113	1.9	**North Terre Haute** (CDP) Vigo County
113	1.9	**Shelbyville** (city) Shelby County
116	2.1	**Charlestown** (city) Clark County
116	2.1	**Connersville** (city) Fayette County
118	2.2	**Brownsburg** (town) Hendricks County
118	2.2	**Westfield** (city) Hamilton County
120	2.3	**Hanover** (town) Jefferson County
120	2.3	**Logansport** (city) Cass County
122	2.5	**Dyer** (town) Lake County
122	2.5	**Granger** (CDP) Saint Joseph County
122	2.5	**Peru** (city) Miami County
125	2.6	**Goshen** (city) Elkhart County
126	2.7	**Columbus** (city) Bartholomew County
126	2.7	**Greencastle** (city) Putnam County
126	2.7	**West Lafayette** (city) Tippecanoe County
129	2.8	**Madison** (city) Jefferson County
129	2.8	**Mount Vernon** (city) Posey County
129	2.8	**Notre Dame** (CDP) Saint Joseph County
129	2.8	**Whitestown** (town) Boone County
133	3.0	**Carmel** (city) Hamilton County
133	3.0	**La Porte** (city) LaPorte County
133	3.0	**Lawrenceburg** (city) Dearborn County
133	3.0	**South Haven** (CDP) Porter County
137	3.2	**Beech Grove** (city) Marion County
138	3.3	**New Haven** (city) Allen County
138	3.3	**Valparaiso** (city) Porter County
140	3.4	**Melody Hill** (CDP) Vanderburgh County
141	3.5	**Munster** (town) Lake County
141	3.5	**Whiting** (city) Lake County
143	3.6	**Lake Station** (city) Lake County
143	3.6	**Noblesville** (city) Hamilton County
145	3.7	**Purdue University** (CDP) Tippecanoe County
145	3.7	**Winfield** (town) Lake County
147	3.8	**Shorewood Forest** (CDP) Porter County
148	4.0	**Dunlap** (CDP) Elkhart County
149	4.2	**Highland** (town) Lake County
150	4.6	**Bloomington** (city) Monroe County

Note: This section ranks incorporated places and CDPs (Census Designated Places) with populations of 2,500 or more. Unincorporated postal areas were not considered. Please refer to the User Guide for additional information.

Asian Population
Top 150 Places Ranked in *Descending* Order

State Rank	Percent	Place
1	23.0	Purdue University (CDP) Tippecanoe County
2	17.3	West Lafayette (city) Tippecanoe County
3	8.9	Carmel (city) Hamilton County
4	8.0	Bloomington (city) Monroe County
5	7.4	Notre Dame (CDP) Saint Joseph County
6	5.8	Munster (town) Lake County
7	5.6	Columbus (city) Bartholomew County
8	5.5	Fishers (town) Hamilton County
9	4.6	Granger (CDP) Saint Joseph County
10	4.0	Shorewood Forest (CDP) Porter County
11	3.7	Greenwood (city) Johnson County
12	3.5	Winfield (town) Lake County
13	3.3	Avon (town) Hendricks County
13	3.3	Fort Wayne (city) Allen County
13	3.3	Plainfield (town) Hendricks County
16	2.9	Dyer (town) Lake County
16	2.9	Whitestown (town) Boone County
18	2.8	Schererville (town) Lake County
18	2.8	Simonton Lake (CDP) Elkhart County
20	2.7	Zionsville (town) Boone County
21	2.5	Westfield (city) Hamilton County
22	2.3	McCordsville (town) Hancock County
23	2.2	Warsaw (city) Kosciusko County
24	2.1	Chesterton (town) Porter County
24	2.1	Indianapolis (city) Marion County
24	2.1	Valparaiso (city) Porter County
27	2.0	Huntertown (town) Allen County
27	2.0	Newburgh (town) Warrick County
27	2.0	Speedway (town) Marion County
30	1.9	Greencastle (city) Putnam County
30	1.9	Mishawaka (city) Saint Joseph County
32	1.8	Crown Point (city) Lake County
33	1.7	Batesville (city) Ripley County
33	1.7	Logansport (city) Cass County
33	1.7	Noblesville (city) Hamilton County
36	1.6	Brownsburg (town) Hendricks County
36	1.6	Highland (town) Lake County
38	1.5	Yorktown (town) Delaware County
39	1.4	Lafayette (city) Tippecanoe County
39	1.4	Lawrence (city) Marion County
39	1.4	Terre Haute (city) Vigo County
42	1.3	Dunlap (CDP) Elkhart County
42	1.3	Greensburg (city) Decatur County
42	1.3	Saint John (town) Lake County
42	1.3	South Bend (city) Saint Joseph County
46	1.2	Fort Branch (town) Gibson County
46	1.2	Goshen (city) Elkhart County
46	1.2	Highland (CDP) Vanderburgh County
46	1.2	Madison (city) Jefferson County
46	1.2	Melody Hill (CDP) Vanderburgh County
46	1.2	Merrillville (town) Lake County
46	1.2	Middlebury (town) Elkhart County
46	1.2	Muncie (city) Delaware County
46	1.2	Seymour (city) Jackson County
46	1.2	Upland (town) Grant County
56	1.1	Jeffersonville (city) Clark County
56	1.1	Richmond (city) Wayne County
56	1.1	Smithville-Sanders (CDP) Monroe County
56	1.1	Washington (city) Daviess County
60	1.0	Bargersville (town) Johnson County
60	1.0	Evansville (city) Vanderburgh County
60	1.0	Hammond (city) Lake County
60	1.0	Hobart (city) Lake County
60	1.0	Kokomo (city) Howard County
60	1.0	Lakes of the Four Seasons (CDP) Lake County
60	1.0	New Whiteland (town) Johnson County
60	1.0	Shelbyville (city) Shelby County
60	1.0	Winona Lake (town) Kosciusko County
69	0.9	Bedford (city) Lawrence County
69	0.9	Crawfordsville (city) Montgomery County
69	0.9	Cumberland (town) Marion County
69	0.9	Elkhart (city) Elkhart County
69	0.9	Jasper (city) Dubois County
69	0.9	Portage (city) Porter County
69	0.9	Porter (town) Porter County
69	0.9	Rochester (city) Fulton County
69	0.9	Scottsburg (city) Scott County
78	0.8	Angola (city) Steuben County
78	0.8	Franklin (city) Johnson County
78	0.8	Greendale (city) Dearborn County
78	0.8	Greenfield (city) Hancock County
78	0.8	Griffith (town) Lake County
78	0.8	Hanover (town) Jefferson County
78	0.8	Lawrenceburg (city) Dearborn County
78	0.8	Leo-Cedarville (town) Allen County
78	0.8	Monticello (city) White County
78	0.8	North Manchester (town) Wabash County
78	0.8	Pendleton (town) Madison County
89	0.7	Auburn (city) DeKalb County
89	0.7	Beech Grove (city) Marion County
89	0.7	Chesterfield (town) Madison County
89	0.7	Clarksville (town) Clark County
89	0.7	Marion (city) Grant County
89	0.7	Michigan City (city) LaPorte County
89	0.7	New Albany (city) Floyd County
89	0.7	Pittsboro (town) Hendricks County
89	0.7	Princeton (city) Gibson County
89	0.7	Roselawn (CDP) Newton County
89	0.7	Syracuse (town) Kosciusko County
89	0.7	Tell City (city) Perry County
89	0.7	Vincennes (city) Knox County
89	0.7	Whiteland (town) Johnson County
89	0.7	Whiting (city) Lake County
104	0.6	Berne (city) Adams County
104	0.6	Centerville (town) Wayne County
104	0.6	Ellettsville (town) Monroe County
104	0.6	Georgetown (town) Floyd County
104	0.6	Lebanon (city) Boone County
104	0.6	Rushville (city) Rush County
104	0.6	Salem (city) Washington County
104	0.6	Tipton (city) Tipton County
112	0.5	Anderson (city) Madison County
112	0.5	Bluffton (city) Wells County
112	0.5	Brazil (city) Clay County
112	0.5	Cicero (town) Hamilton County
112	0.5	Columbia City (city) Whitley County
112	0.5	Hidden Valley (CDP) Dearborn County
112	0.5	Huntington (city) Huntington County
112	0.5	Kendallville (city) Noble County
112	0.5	La Porte (city) LaPorte County
112	0.5	Ligonier (city) Noble County
112	0.5	Mooresville (town) Morgan County
112	0.5	North Terre Haute (CDP) Vigo County
112	0.5	Ossian (town) Wells County
112	0.5	Plymouth (city) Marshall County
112	0.5	Portland (city) Jay County
112	0.5	Wabash (city) Wabash County
112	0.5	Winchester (city) Randolph County
129	0.4	Cedar Lake (town) Lake County
129	0.4	Danville (town) Hendricks County
129	0.4	De Motte (town) Jasper County
129	0.4	Decatur (city) Adams County
129	0.4	Garrett (city) DeKalb County
129	0.4	Gas City (city) Grant County
129	0.4	Hebron (town) Porter County
129	0.4	Lagrange (town) LaGrange County
129	0.4	Linton (city) Greene County
129	0.4	Martinsville (city) Morgan County
129	0.4	Mount Vernon (city) Posey County
129	0.4	New Castle (city) Henry County
129	0.4	New Haven (city) Allen County
129	0.4	North Vernon (city) Jennings County
129	0.4	Peru (city) Miami County
129	0.4	Rensselaer (city) Jasper County
129	0.4	Sheridan (town) Hamilton County
146	0.3	Attica (city) Fountain County
146	0.3	Aurora (city) Dearborn County
146	0.3	Bremen (town) Marshall County
146	0.3	Bright (CDP) Dearborn County
146	0.3	Charlestown (city) Clark County

Note: This section ranks incorporated places and CDPs (Census Designated Places) with populations of 2,500 or more. Unincorporated postal areas were not considered. Please refer to the User Guide for additional information.

Asian Population
Top 150 Places Ranked in *Ascending* Order

State Rank	Percent	Place
1	0.1	**Boonville** (city) Warrick County
1	0.1	**Chandler** (town) Warrick County
1	0.1	**East Chicago** (city) Lake County
1	0.1	**Edinburgh** (town) Johnson County
1	0.1	**Fortville** (town) Hancock County
1	0.1	**Hartford City** (city) Blackford County
1	0.1	**Union City** (city) Randolph County
8	0.2	**Alexandria** (city) Madison County
8	0.2	**Austin** (city) Scott County
8	0.2	**Bicknell** (city) Knox County
8	0.2	**Brookville** (town) Franklin County
8	0.2	**Brownstown** (town) Jackson County
8	0.2	**Butler** (city) DeKalb County
8	0.2	**Clinton** (city) Vermillion County
8	0.2	**Corydon** (town) Harrison County
8	0.2	**Country Squire Lakes** (CDP) Jennings County
8	0.2	**Delphi** (city) Carroll County
8	0.2	**Fairmount** (town) Grant County
8	0.2	**Frankfort** (city) Clinton County
8	0.2	**Gary** (city) Lake County
8	0.2	**Grissom AFB** (CDP) Miami County
8	0.2	**Heritage Lake** (CDP) Putnam County
8	0.2	**Nappanee** (city) Elkhart County
8	0.2	**Rockville** (town) Parke County
8	0.2	**Sullivan** (city) Sullivan County
26	0.3	**Attica** (city) Fountain County
26	0.3	**Aurora** (city) Dearborn County
26	0.3	**Bremen** (town) Marshall County
26	0.3	**Bright** (CDP) Dearborn County
26	0.3	**Charlestown** (city) Clark County
26	0.3	**Connersville** (city) Fayette County
26	0.3	**Covington** (city) Fountain County
26	0.3	**Elwood** (city) Madison County
26	0.3	**Huntingburg** (city) Dubois County
26	0.3	**Knox** (city) Starke County
26	0.3	**Lake Station** (city) Lake County
26	0.3	**Loogootee** (city) Martin County
26	0.3	**Lowell** (town) Lake County
26	0.3	**Mitchell** (city) Lawrence County
26	0.3	**Paoli** (town) Orange County
26	0.3	**Sellersburg** (town) Clark County
26	0.3	**South Haven** (CDP) Porter County
26	0.3	**Westville** (town) LaPorte County
44	0.4	**Cedar Lake** (town) Lake County
44	0.4	**Danville** (town) Hendricks County
44	0.4	**De Motte** (town) Jasper County
44	0.4	**Decatur** (city) Adams County
44	0.4	**Garrett** (city) DeKalb County
44	0.4	**Gas City** (city) Grant County
44	0.4	**Hebron** (town) Porter County
44	0.4	**Lagrange** (town) LaGrange County
44	0.4	**Linton** (city) Greene County
44	0.4	**Martinsville** (city) Morgan County
44	0.4	**Mount Vernon** (city) Posey County
44	0.4	**New Castle** (city) Henry County
44	0.4	**New Haven** (city) Allen County
44	0.4	**North Vernon** (city) Jennings County
44	0.4	**Peru** (city) Miami County
44	0.4	**Rensselaer** (city) Jasper County
44	0.4	**Sheridan** (town) Hamilton County
61	0.5	**Anderson** (city) Madison County
61	0.5	**Bluffton** (city) Wells County
61	0.5	**Brazil** (city) Clay County
61	0.5	**Cicero** (town) Hamilton County
61	0.5	**Columbia City** (city) Whitley County
61	0.5	**Hidden Valley** (CDP) Dearborn County
61	0.5	**Huntington** (city) Huntington County
61	0.5	**Kendallville** (city) Noble County
61	0.5	**La Porte** (city) LaPorte County
61	0.5	**Ligonier** (city) Noble County
61	0.5	**Mooresville** (town) Morgan County
61	0.5	**North Terre Haute** (CDP) Vigo County
61	0.5	**Ossian** (town) Wells County
61	0.5	**Plymouth** (city) Marshall County
61	0.5	**Portland** (city) Jay County
61	0.5	**Wabash** (city) Wabash County
61	0.5	**Winchester** (city) Randolph County
78	0.6	**Berne** (city) Adams County
78	0.6	**Centerville** (town) Wayne County
78	0.6	**Ellettsville** (town) Monroe County
78	0.6	**Georgetown** (town) Floyd County
78	0.6	**Lebanon** (city) Boone County
78	0.6	**Rushville** (city) Rush County
78	0.6	**Salem** (city) Washington County
78	0.6	**Tipton** (city) Tipton County
86	0.7	**Auburn** (city) DeKalb County
86	0.7	**Beech Grove** (city) Marion County
86	0.7	**Chesterfield** (town) Madison County
86	0.7	**Clarksville** (town) Clark County
86	0.7	**Marion** (city) Grant County
86	0.7	**Michigan City** (city) LaPorte County
86	0.7	**New Albany** (city) Floyd County
86	0.7	**Pittsboro** (town) Hendricks County
86	0.7	**Princeton** (city) Gibson County
86	0.7	**Roselawn** (CDP) Newton County
86	0.7	**Syracuse** (town) Kosciusko County
86	0.7	**Tell City** (city) Perry County
86	0.7	**Vincennes** (city) Knox County
86	0.7	**Whiteland** (town) Johnson County
86	0.7	**Whiting** (city) Lake County
101	0.8	**Angola** (city) Steuben County
101	0.8	**Franklin** (city) Johnson County
101	0.8	**Greendale** (city) Dearborn County
101	0.8	**Greenfield** (city) Hancock County
101	0.8	**Griffith** (town) Lake County
101	0.8	**Hanover** (town) Jefferson County
101	0.8	**Lawrenceburg** (city) Dearborn County
101	0.8	**Leo-Cedarville** (town) Allen County
101	0.8	**Monticello** (city) White County
101	0.8	**North Manchester** (town) Wabash County
101	0.8	**Pendleton** (town) Madison County
112	0.9	**Bedford** (city) Lawrence County
112	0.9	**Crawfordsville** (city) Montgomery County
112	0.9	**Cumberland** (town) Marion County
112	0.9	**Elkhart** (city) Elkhart County
112	0.9	**Jasper** (city) Dubois County
112	0.9	**Portage** (city) Porter County
112	0.9	**Porter** (town) Porter County
112	0.9	**Rochester** (city) Fulton County
112	0.9	**Scottsburg** (city) Scott County
121	1.0	**Bargersville** (town) Johnson County
121	1.0	**Evansville** (city) Vanderburgh County
121	1.0	**Hammond** (city) Lake County
121	1.0	**Hobart** (city) Lake County
121	1.0	**Kokomo** (city) Howard County
121	1.0	**Lakes of the Four Seasons** (CDP) Lake County
121	1.0	**New Whiteland** (town) Johnson County
121	1.0	**Shelbyville** (city) Shelby County
121	1.0	**Winona Lake** (town) Kosciusko County
130	1.1	**Jeffersonville** (city) Clark County
130	1.1	**Richmond** (city) Wayne County
130	1.1	**Smithville-Sanders** (CDP) Monroe County
130	1.1	**Washington** (city) Daviess County
134	1.2	**Fort Branch** (town) Gibson County
134	1.2	**Goshen** (city) Elkhart County
134	1.2	**Highland** (CDP) Vanderburgh County
134	1.2	**Madison** (city) Jefferson County
134	1.2	**Melody Hill** (CDP) Vanderburgh County
134	1.2	**Merrillville** (town) Lake County
134	1.2	**Middlebury** (town) Elkhart County
134	1.2	**Muncie** (city) Delaware County
134	1.2	**Seymour** (city) Jackson County
134	1.2	**Upland** (town) Grant County
144	1.3	**Dunlap** (CDP) Elkhart County
144	1.3	**Greensburg** (city) Decatur County
144	1.3	**Saint John** (town) Lake County
144	1.3	**South Bend** (city) Saint Joseph County
148	1.4	**Lafayette** (city) Tippecanoe County
148	1.4	**Lawrence** (city) Marion County
148	1.4	**Terre Haute** (city) Vigo County

Note: This section ranks incorporated places and CDPs (Census Designated Places) with populations of 2,500 or more. Unincorporated postal areas were not considered. Please refer to the User Guide for additional information.

American Indian/Alaska Native Population
Top 150 Places Ranked in *Descending* Order

State Rank	Percent	Place
1	1.3	**Peru** (city) Miami County
2	1.0	**Wabash** (city) Wabash County
3	0.8	**Logansport** (city) Cass County
4	0.7	**Whiting** (city) Lake County
5	0.6	**Cicero** (town) Hamilton County
5	0.6	**Cumberland** (town) Marion County
5	0.6	**East Chicago** (city) Lake County
5	0.6	**Elkhart** (city) Elkhart County
5	0.6	**Plymouth** (city) Marshall County
10	0.5	**Covington** (city) Fountain County
10	0.5	**Goshen** (city) Elkhart County
10	0.5	**Hammond** (city) Lake County
10	0.5	**Lake Station** (city) Lake County
10	0.5	**Rockville** (town) Parke County
10	0.5	**South Bend** (city) Saint Joseph County
10	0.5	**Warsaw** (city) Kosciusko County
10	0.5	**Winchester** (city) Randolph County
18	0.4	**Bluffton** (city) Wells County
18	0.4	**Butler** (city) DeKalb County
18	0.4	**Crawfordsville** (city) Montgomery County
18	0.4	**Decatur** (city) Adams County
18	0.4	**Fort Wayne** (city) Allen County
18	0.4	**Garrett** (city) DeKalb County
18	0.4	**Heritage Lake** (CDP) Putnam County
18	0.4	**Hobart** (city) Lake County
18	0.4	**Huntertown** (town) Allen County
18	0.4	**Huntington** (city) Huntington County
18	0.4	**Kokomo** (city) Howard County
18	0.4	**Lafayette** (city) Tippecanoe County
18	0.4	**Lagrange** (town) LaGrange County
18	0.4	**Lawrence** (city) Marion County
18	0.4	**Lowell** (town) Lake County
18	0.4	**Marion** (city) Grant County
18	0.4	**Michigan City** (city) LaPorte County
18	0.4	**Mishawaka** (city) Saint Joseph County
18	0.4	**Monticello** (city) White County
18	0.4	**New Haven** (city) Allen County
18	0.4	**Pittsboro** (town) Hendricks County
18	0.4	**Portage** (city) Porter County
18	0.4	**Rensselaer** (city) Jasper County
18	0.4	**Rochester** (city) Fulton County
18	0.4	**Sullivan** (city) Sullivan County
18	0.4	**Terre Haute** (city) Vigo County
18	0.4	**Winfield** (town) Lake County
45	0.3	**Anderson** (city) Madison County
45	0.3	**Angola** (city) Steuben County
45	0.3	**Aurora** (city) Dearborn County
45	0.3	**Austin** (city) Scott County
45	0.3	**Avon** (town) Hendricks County
45	0.3	**Bargersville** (town) Johnson County
45	0.3	**Bedford** (city) Lawrence County
45	0.3	**Beech Grove** (city) Marion County
45	0.3	**Bloomington** (city) Monroe County
45	0.3	**Brookville** (town) Franklin County
45	0.3	**Brownstown** (town) Jackson County
45	0.3	**Cedar Lake** (town) Lake County
45	0.3	**Charlestown** (city) Clark County
45	0.3	**Chesterton** (town) Porter County
45	0.3	**Clarksville** (town) Clark County
45	0.3	**Clinton** (city) Vermillion County
45	0.3	**Columbia City** (city) Whitley County
45	0.3	**De Motte** (town) Jasper County
45	0.3	**Evansville** (city) Vanderburgh County
45	0.3	**Fortville** (town) Hancock County
45	0.3	**Frankfort** (city) Clinton County
45	0.3	**Franklin** (city) Johnson County
45	0.3	**Gary** (city) Lake County
45	0.3	**Gas City** (city) Grant County
45	0.3	**Georgetown** (town) Floyd County
45	0.3	**Greencastle** (city) Putnam County
45	0.3	**Greenfield** (city) Hancock County
45	0.3	**Greenwood** (city) Johnson County
45	0.3	**Griffith** (town) Lake County
45	0.3	**Grissom AFB** (CDP) Miami County
45	0.3	**Indianapolis** (city) Marion County
45	0.3	**Jeffersonville** (city) Clark County
45	0.3	**La Porte** (city) LaPorte County
45	0.3	**Lawrenceburg** (city) Dearborn County
45	0.3	**Linton** (city) Greene County
45	0.3	**Martinsville** (city) Morgan County
45	0.3	**McCordsville** (town) Hancock County
45	0.3	**Mount Vernon** (city) Posey County
45	0.3	**Muncie** (city) Delaware County
45	0.3	**Nappanee** (city) Elkhart County
45	0.3	**North Manchester** (town) Wabash County
45	0.3	**Pendleton** (town) Madison County
45	0.3	**Porter** (town) Porter County
45	0.3	**Richmond** (city) Wayne County
45	0.3	**Salem** (city) Washington County
45	0.3	**Sellersburg** (town) Clark County
45	0.3	**Sheridan** (town) Hamilton County
45	0.3	**Simonton Lake** (CDP) Elkhart County
45	0.3	**Speedway** (town) Marion County
45	0.3	**Tell City** (city) Perry County
45	0.3	**Valparaiso** (city) Porter County
45	0.3	**Vincennes** (city) Knox County
45	0.3	**Washington** (city) Daviess County
98	0.2	**Attica** (city) Fountain County
98	0.2	**Auburn** (city) DeKalb County
98	0.2	**Batesville** (city) Ripley County
98	0.2	**Bicknell** (city) Knox County
98	0.2	**Boonville** (city) Warrick County
98	0.2	**Bremen** (town) Marshall County
98	0.2	**Carmel** (city) Hamilton County
98	0.2	**Chesterfield** (town) Madison County
98	0.2	**Columbus** (city) Bartholomew County
98	0.2	**Connersville** (city) Fayette County
98	0.2	**Corydon** (town) Harrison County
98	0.2	**Crown Point** (city) Lake County
98	0.2	**Danville** (town) Hendricks County
98	0.2	**Delphi** (city) Carroll County
98	0.2	**Dunlap** (CDP) Elkhart County
98	0.2	**Dyer** (town) Lake County
98	0.2	**Edinburgh** (town) Johnson County
98	0.2	**Ellettsville** (town) Monroe County
98	0.2	**Elwood** (city) Madison County
98	0.2	**Fairmount** (town) Grant County
98	0.2	**Fishers** (town) Hamilton County
98	0.2	**Greendale** (city) Dearborn County
98	0.2	**Greensburg** (city) Decatur County
98	0.2	**Hanover** (town) Jefferson County
98	0.2	**Hartford City** (city) Blackford County
98	0.2	**Hebron** (town) Porter County
98	0.2	**Highland** (town) Lake County
98	0.2	**Huntingburg** (city) Dubois County
98	0.2	**Jasper** (city) Dubois County
98	0.2	**Kendallville** (city) Noble County
98	0.2	**Knox** (city) Starke County
98	0.2	**Lakes of the Four Seasons** (CDP) Lake County
98	0.2	**Lebanon** (city) Boone County
98	0.2	**Leo-Cedarville** (town) Allen County
98	0.2	**Ligonier** (city) Noble County
98	0.2	**Loogootee** (city) Martin County
98	0.2	**Madison** (city) Jefferson County
98	0.2	**Merrillville** (town) Lake County
98	0.2	**Mitchell** (city) Lawrence County
98	0.2	**Mooresville** (town) Morgan County
98	0.2	**Munster** (town) Lake County
98	0.2	**New Albany** (city) Floyd County
98	0.2	**New Castle** (city) Henry County
98	0.2	**Noblesville** (city) Hamilton County
98	0.2	**North Terre Haute** (CDP) Vigo County
98	0.2	**North Vernon** (city) Jennings County
98	0.2	**Notre Dame** (CDP) Saint Joseph County
98	0.2	**Paoli** (town) Orange County
98	0.2	**Plainfield** (town) Hendricks County
98	0.2	**Princeton** (city) Gibson County
98	0.2	**Schererville** (town) Lake County
98	0.2	**Scottsburg** (city) Scott County
98	0.2	**Seymour** (city) Jackson County

Note: This section ranks incorporated places and CDPs (Census Designated Places) with populations of 2,500 or more. Unincorporated postal areas were not considered. Please refer to the User Guide for additional information.

American Indian/Alaska Native Population
Top 150 Places Ranked in *Ascending* Order

State Rank	Percent	Place
1	0.0	Highland (CDP) Vanderburgh County
1	0.0	Portland (city) Jay County
1	0.0	Shorewood Forest (CDP) Porter County
4	0.1	Alexandria (city) Madison County
4	0.1	Berne (city) Adams County
4	0.1	Brazil (city) Clay County
4	0.1	Bright (CDP) Dearborn County
4	0.1	Brownsburg (town) Hendricks County
4	0.1	Centerville (town) Wayne County
4	0.1	Chandler (town) Warrick County
4	0.1	Country Squire Lakes (CDP) Jennings County
4	0.1	Fort Branch (town) Gibson County
4	0.1	Granger (CDP) Saint Joseph County
4	0.1	Hidden Valley (CDP) Dearborn County
4	0.1	Melody Hill (CDP) Vanderburgh County
4	0.1	Middlebury (town) Elkhart County
4	0.1	New Whiteland (town) Johnson County
4	0.1	Newburgh (town) Warrick County
4	0.1	Ossian (town) Wells County
4	0.1	Purdue University (CDP) Tippecanoe County
4	0.1	Roselawn (CDP) Newton County
4	0.1	Rushville (city) Rush County
4	0.1	Saint John (town) Lake County
4	0.1	Smithville-Sanders (CDP) Monroe County
4	0.1	Syracuse (town) Kosciusko County
4	0.1	Union City (city) Randolph County
4	0.1	West Lafayette (city) Tippecanoe County
4	0.1	Whitestown (town) Boone County
4	0.1	Winona Lake (town) Kosciusko County
4	0.1	Zionsville (town) Boone County
31	0.2	Attica (city) Fountain County
31	0.2	Auburn (city) DeKalb County
31	0.2	Batesville (city) Ripley County
31	0.2	Bicknell (city) Knox County
31	0.2	Boonville (city) Warrick County
31	0.2	Bremen (town) Marshall County
31	0.2	Carmel (city) Hamilton County
31	0.2	Chesterfield (town) Madison County
31	0.2	Columbus (city) Bartholomew County
31	0.2	Connersville (city) Fayette County
31	0.2	Corydon (town) Harrison County
31	0.2	Crown Point (city) Lake County
31	0.2	Danville (town) Hendricks County
31	0.2	Delphi (city) Carroll County
31	0.2	Dunlap (CDP) Elkhart County
31	0.2	Dyer (town) Lake County
31	0.2	Edinburgh (town) Johnson County
31	0.2	Ellettsville (town) Monroe County
31	0.2	Elwood (city) Madison County
31	0.2	Fairmount (town) Grant County
31	0.2	Fishers (town) Hamilton County
31	0.2	Greendale (city) Dearborn County
31	0.2	Greensburg (city) Decatur County
31	0.2	Hanover (town) Jefferson County
31	0.2	Hartford City (city) Blackford County
31	0.2	Hebron (town) Porter County
31	0.2	Highland (town) Lake County
31	0.2	Huntingburg (city) Dubois County
31	0.2	Jasper (city) Dubois County
31	0.2	Kendallville (city) Noble County
31	0.2	Knox (city) Starke County
31	0.2	Lakes of the Four Seasons (CDP) Lake County
31	0.2	Lebanon (city) Boone County
31	0.2	Leo-Cedarville (town) Allen County
31	0.2	Ligonier (city) Noble County
31	0.2	Loogootee (city) Martin County
31	0.2	Madison (city) Jefferson County
31	0.2	Merrillville (town) Lake County
31	0.2	Mitchell (city) Lawrence County
31	0.2	Mooresville (town) Morgan County
31	0.2	Munster (town) Lake County
31	0.2	New Albany (city) Floyd County
31	0.2	New Castle (city) Henry County
31	0.2	Noblesville (city) Hamilton County
31	0.2	North Terre Haute (CDP) Vigo County
31	0.2	North Vernon (city) Jennings County
31	0.2	Notre Dame (CDP) Saint Joseph County
31	0.2	Paoli (town) Orange County
31	0.2	Plainfield (town) Hendricks County
31	0.2	Princeton (city) Gibson County
31	0.2	Schererville (town) Lake County
31	0.2	Scottsburg (city) Scott County
31	0.2	Seymour (city) Jackson County
31	0.2	Shelbyville (city) Shelby County
31	0.2	South Haven (CDP) Porter County
31	0.2	Tipton (city) Tipton County
31	0.2	Upland (town) Grant County
31	0.2	Westfield (city) Hamilton County
31	0.2	Westville (town) LaPorte County
31	0.2	Whiteland (town) Johnson County
31	0.2	Yorktown (town) Delaware County
92	0.3	Anderson (city) Madison County
92	0.3	Angola (city) Steuben County
92	0.3	Aurora (city) Dearborn County
92	0.3	Austin (city) Scott County
92	0.3	Avon (town) Hendricks County
92	0.3	Bargersville (town) Johnson County
92	0.3	Bedford (city) Lawrence County
92	0.3	Beech Grove (city) Marion County
92	0.3	Bloomington (city) Monroe County
92	0.3	Brookville (town) Franklin County
92	0.3	Brownstown (town) Jackson County
92	0.3	Cedar Lake (town) Lake County
92	0.3	Charlestown (city) Clark County
92	0.3	Chesterton (town) Porter County
92	0.3	Clarksville (town) Clark County
92	0.3	Clinton (city) Vermillion County
92	0.3	Columbia City (city) Whitley County
92	0.3	De Motte (town) Jasper County
92	0.3	Evansville (city) Vanderburgh County
92	0.3	Fortville (town) Hancock County
92	0.3	Frankfort (city) Clinton County
92	0.3	Franklin (city) Johnson County
92	0.3	Gary (city) Lake County
92	0.3	Gas City (city) Grant County
92	0.3	Georgetown (town) Floyd County
92	0.3	Greencastle (city) Putnam County
92	0.3	Greenfield (city) Hancock County
92	0.3	Greenwood (city) Johnson County
92	0.3	Griffith (town) Lake County
92	0.3	Grissom AFB (CDP) Miami County
92	0.3	Indianapolis (city) Marion County
92	0.3	Jeffersonville (city) Clark County
92	0.3	La Porte (city) LaPorte County
92	0.3	Lawrenceburg (city) Dearborn County
92	0.3	Linton (city) Greene County
92	0.3	Martinsville (city) Morgan County
92	0.3	McCordsville (town) Hancock County
92	0.3	Mount Vernon (city) Posey County
92	0.3	Muncie (city) Delaware County
92	0.3	Nappanee (city) Elkhart County
92	0.3	North Manchester (town) Wabash County
92	0.3	Pendleton (town) Madison County
92	0.3	Porter (town) Porter County
92	0.3	Richmond (city) Wayne County
92	0.3	Salem (city) Washington County
92	0.3	Sellersburg (town) Clark County
92	0.3	Sheridan (town) Hamilton County
92	0.3	Simonton Lake (CDP) Elkhart County
92	0.3	Speedway (town) Marion County
92	0.3	Tell City (city) Perry County
92	0.3	Valparaiso (city) Porter County
92	0.3	Vincennes (city) Knox County
92	0.3	Washington (city) Daviess County
145	0.4	Bluffton (city) Wells County
145	0.4	Butler (city) DeKalb County
145	0.4	Crawfordsville (city) Montgomery County
145	0.4	Decatur (city) Adams County
145	0.4	Fort Wayne (city) Allen County
145	0.4	Garrett (city) DeKalb County

Note: This section ranks incorporated places and CDPs (Census Designated Places) with populations of 2,500 or more. Unincorporated postal areas were not considered. Please refer to the User Guide for additional information.

Native Hawaiian/Other Pacific Islander Population
Top 150 Places Ranked in *Descending* Order

State Rank	Percent	Place
1	0.1	Angola (city) Steuben County
1	0.1	Avon (town) Hendricks County
1	0.1	Batesville (city) Ripley County
1	0.1	Bloomington (city) Monroe County
1	0.1	Brownsburg (town) Hendricks County
1	0.1	Brownstown (town) Jackson County
1	0.1	Columbus (city) Bartholomew County
1	0.1	Corydon (town) Harrison County
1	0.1	Cumberland (town) Marion County
1	0.1	Elkhart (city) Elkhart County
1	0.1	Evansville (city) Vanderburgh County
1	0.1	Fort Wayne (city) Allen County
1	0.1	Garrett (city) DeKalb County
1	0.1	Granger (CDP) Saint Joseph County
1	0.1	Greenwood (city) Johnson County
1	0.1	Hartford City (city) Blackford County
1	0.1	Lakes of the Four Seasons (CDP) Lake County
1	0.1	Lawrence (city) Marion County
1	0.1	Logansport (city) Cass County
1	0.1	Lowell (town) Lake County
1	0.1	Martinsville (city) Morgan County
1	0.1	Mishawaka (city) Saint Joseph County
1	0.1	Mitchell (city) Lawrence County
1	0.1	Muncie (city) Delaware County
1	0.1	Nappanee (city) Elkhart County
1	0.1	New Haven (city) Allen County
1	0.1	Noblesville (city) Hamilton County
1	0.1	North Terre Haute (CDP) Vigo County
1	0.1	Notre Dame (CDP) Saint Joseph County
1	0.1	Pendleton (town) Madison County
1	0.1	Rensselaer (city) Jasper County
1	0.1	Richmond (city) Wayne County
1	0.1	Saint John (town) Lake County
1	0.1	Seymour (city) Jackson County
1	0.1	South Bend (city) Saint Joseph County
1	0.1	Upland (town) Grant County
1	0.1	Valparaiso (city) Porter County
1	0.1	Washington (city) Daviess County
1	0.1	Whiteland (town) Johnson County
40	0.0	Alexandria (city) Madison County
40	0.0	Anderson (city) Madison County
40	0.0	Attica (city) Fountain County
40	0.0	Auburn (city) DeKalb County
40	0.0	Aurora (city) Dearborn County
40	0.0	Austin (city) Scott County
40	0.0	Bargersville (town) Johnson County
40	0.0	Bedford (city) Lawrence County
40	0.0	Beech Grove (city) Marion County
40	0.0	Berne (city) Adams County
40	0.0	Bicknell (city) Knox County
40	0.0	Bluffton (city) Wells County
40	0.0	Boonville (city) Warrick County
40	0.0	Brazil (city) Clay County
40	0.0	Bremen (town) Marshall County
40	0.0	Bright (CDP) Dearborn County
40	0.0	Brookville (town) Franklin County
40	0.0	Butler (city) DeKalb County
40	0.0	Carmel (city) Hamilton County
40	0.0	Cedar Lake (town) Lake County
40	0.0	Centerville (town) Wayne County
40	0.0	Chandler (town) Warrick County
40	0.0	Charlestown (city) Clark County
40	0.0	Chesterfield (town) Madison County
40	0.0	Chesterton (town) Porter County
40	0.0	Cicero (town) Hamilton County
40	0.0	Clarksville (town) Clark County
40	0.0	Clinton (city) Vermillion County
40	0.0	Columbia City (city) Whitley County
40	0.0	Connersville (city) Fayette County
40	0.0	Country Squire Lakes (CDP) Jennings County
40	0.0	Covington (city) Fountain County
40	0.0	Crawfordsville (city) Montgomery County
40	0.0	Crown Point (city) Lake County
40	0.0	Danville (town) Hendricks County
40	0.0	De Motte (town) Jasper County
40	0.0	Decatur (city) Adams County
40	0.0	Delphi (city) Carroll County
40	0.0	Dunlap (CDP) Elkhart County
40	0.0	Dyer (town) Lake County
40	0.0	East Chicago (city) Lake County
40	0.0	Edinburgh (town) Johnson County
40	0.0	Ellettsville (town) Monroe County
40	0.0	Elwood (city) Madison County
40	0.0	Fairmount (town) Grant County
40	0.0	Fishers (town) Hamilton County
40	0.0	Fort Branch (town) Gibson County
40	0.0	Fortville (town) Hancock County
40	0.0	Frankfort (city) Clinton County
40	0.0	Franklin (city) Johnson County
40	0.0	Gary (city) Lake County
40	0.0	Gas City (city) Grant County
40	0.0	Georgetown (town) Floyd County
40	0.0	Goshen (city) Elkhart County
40	0.0	Greencastle (city) Putnam County
40	0.0	Greendale (city) Dearborn County
40	0.0	Greenfield (city) Hancock County
40	0.0	Greensburg (city) Decatur County
40	0.0	Griffith (town) Lake County
40	0.0	Grissom AFB (CDP) Miami County
40	0.0	Hammond (city) Lake County
40	0.0	Hanover (town) Jefferson County
40	0.0	Hebron (town) Porter County
40	0.0	Heritage Lake (CDP) Putnam County
40	0.0	Hidden Valley (CDP) Dearborn County
40	0.0	Highland (CDP) Vanderburgh County
40	0.0	Highland (town) Lake County
40	0.0	Hobart (city) Lake County
40	0.0	Huntertown (town) Allen County
40	0.0	Huntingburg (city) Dubois County
40	0.0	Huntington (city) Huntington County
40	0.0	Indianapolis (city) Marion County
40	0.0	Jasper (city) Dubois County
40	0.0	Jeffersonville (city) Clark County
40	0.0	Kendallville (city) Noble County
40	0.0	Knox (city) Starke County
40	0.0	Kokomo (city) Howard County
40	0.0	La Porte (city) LaPorte County
40	0.0	Lafayette (city) Tippecanoe County
40	0.0	Lagrange (town) LaGrange County
40	0.0	Lake Station (city) Lake County
40	0.0	Lawrenceburg (city) Dearborn County
40	0.0	Lebanon (city) Boone County
40	0.0	Leo-Cedarville (town) Allen County
40	0.0	Ligonier (city) Noble County
40	0.0	Linton (city) Greene County
40	0.0	Loogootee (city) Martin County
40	0.0	Madison (city) Jefferson County
40	0.0	Marion (city) Grant County
40	0.0	McCordsville (town) Hancock County
40	0.0	Melody Hill (CDP) Vanderburgh County
40	0.0	Merrillville (town) Lake County
40	0.0	Michigan City (city) LaPorte County
40	0.0	Middlebury (town) Elkhart County
40	0.0	Monticello (city) White County
40	0.0	Mooresville (town) Morgan County
40	0.0	Mount Vernon (city) Posey County
40	0.0	Munster (town) Lake County
40	0.0	New Albany (city) Floyd County
40	0.0	New Castle (city) Henry County
40	0.0	New Whiteland (town) Johnson County
40	0.0	Newburgh (town) Warrick County
40	0.0	North Manchester (town) Wabash County
40	0.0	North Vernon (city) Jennings County
40	0.0	Ossian (town) Wells County
40	0.0	Paoli (town) Orange County
40	0.0	Peru (city) Miami County
40	0.0	Pittsboro (town) Hendricks County
40	0.0	Plainfield (town) Hendricks County
40	0.0	Plymouth (city) Marshall County
40	0.0	Portage (city) Porter County

Note: This section ranks incorporated places and CDPs (Census Designated Places) with populations of 2,500 or more. Unincorporated postal areas were not considered. Please refer to the User Guide for additional information.

Two or More Races

Top 150 Places Ranked in *Descending* Order

State Rank	Percent	Place
1	4.2	**South Bend** (city) Saint Joseph County
2	4.1	**Elkhart** (city) Elkhart County
2	4.1	**Lake Station** (city) Lake County
2	4.1	**Notre Dame** (CDP) Saint Joseph County
5	4.0	**Richmond** (city) Wayne County
6	3.7	**Michigan City** (city) LaPorte County
7	3.6	**Marion** (city) Grant County
8	3.5	**Fort Wayne** (city) Allen County
8	3.5	**Lawrence** (city) Marion County
10	3.3	**Hammond** (city) Lake County
10	3.3	**Kokomo** (city) Howard County
12	3.2	**Merrillville** (town) Lake County
12	3.2	**Whiting** (city) Lake County
14	3.0	**Bloomington** (city) Monroe County
14	3.0	**Jeffersonville** (city) Clark County
14	3.0	**Princeton** (city) Gibson County
17	2.9	**Mishawaka** (city) Saint Joseph County
17	2.9	**New Albany** (city) Floyd County
17	2.9	**Terre Haute** (city) Vigo County
20	2.8	**East Chicago** (city) Lake County
20	2.8	**Evansville** (city) Vanderburgh County
20	2.8	**Indianapolis** (city) Marion County
20	2.8	**Muncie** (city) Delaware County
24	2.7	**Goshen** (city) Elkhart County
24	2.7	**Lafayette** (city) Tippecanoe County
24	2.7	**Ligonier** (city) Noble County
27	2.6	**Anderson** (city) Madison County
27	2.6	**La Porte** (city) LaPorte County
27	2.6	**McCordsville** (town) Hancock County
27	2.6	**Portage** (city) Porter County
27	2.6	**Simonton Lake** (CDP) Elkhart County
32	2.5	**Clarksville** (town) Clark County
32	2.5	**Plymouth** (city) Marshall County
34	2.4	**Griffith** (town) Lake County
34	2.4	**Hobart** (city) Lake County
34	2.4	**Mount Vernon** (city) Posey County
37	2.3	**Cumberland** (town) Marion County
37	2.3	**Peru** (city) Miami County
37	2.3	**Speedway** (town) Marion County
40	2.2	**Avon** (town) Hendricks County
40	2.2	**Country Squire Lakes** (CDP) Jennings County
40	2.2	**Lawrenceburg** (city) Dearborn County
40	2.2	**Logansport** (city) Cass County
40	2.2	**Purdue University** (CDP) Tippecanoe County
40	2.2	**South Haven** (CDP) Porter County
40	2.2	**Whitestown** (town) Boone County
47	2.1	**Beech Grove** (city) Marion County
47	2.1	**Charlestown** (city) Clark County
47	2.1	**Dunlap** (CDP) Elkhart County
47	2.1	**Fishers** (town) Hamilton County
47	2.1	**Gary** (city) Lake County
47	2.1	**Greenwood** (city) Johnson County
47	2.1	**Monticello** (city) White County
47	2.1	**North Terre Haute** (CDP) Vigo County
47	2.1	**Valparaiso** (city) Porter County
47	2.1	**West Lafayette** (city) Tippecanoe County
57	2.0	**Columbus** (city) Bartholomew County
57	2.0	**Highland** (town) Lake County
57	2.0	**Warsaw** (city) Kosciusko County
60	1.9	**Delphi** (city) Carroll County
60	1.9	**Ellettsville** (town) Monroe County
60	1.9	**Huntertown** (town) Allen County
60	1.9	**Lakes of the Four Seasons** (CDP) Lake County
60	1.9	**Shorewood Forest** (CDP) Porter County
60	1.9	**Union City** (city) Randolph County
60	1.9	**Washington** (city) Daviess County
67	1.8	**Butler** (city) DeKalb County
67	1.8	**Carmel** (city) Hamilton County
67	1.8	**Dyer** (town) Lake County
67	1.8	**Frankfort** (city) Clinton County
67	1.8	**Greencastle** (city) Putnam County
67	1.8	**Greendale** (city) Dearborn County
67	1.8	**Huntingburg** (city) Dubois County
67	1.8	**Kendallville** (city) Noble County
67	1.8	**Munster** (town) Lake County
67	1.8	**New Castle** (city) Henry County
67	1.8	**Noblesville** (city) Hamilton County
67	1.8	**Plainfield** (town) Hendricks County
67	1.8	**Schererville** (town) Lake County
67	1.8	**Seymour** (city) Jackson County
81	1.7	**Angola** (city) Steuben County
81	1.7	**Cedar Lake** (town) Lake County
81	1.7	**Chesterton** (town) Porter County
81	1.7	**Gas City** (city) Grant County
81	1.7	**Hartford City** (city) Blackford County
81	1.7	**Knox** (city) Starke County
81	1.7	**New Haven** (city) Allen County
81	1.7	**North Vernon** (city) Jennings County
81	1.7	**Pittsboro** (town) Hendricks County
81	1.7	**Porter** (town) Porter County
81	1.7	**Shelbyville** (city) Shelby County
81	1.7	**Sheridan** (town) Hamilton County
81	1.7	**Smithville-Sanders** (CDP) Monroe County
81	1.7	**Vincennes** (city) Knox County
95	1.6	**Bargersville** (town) Johnson County
95	1.6	**Crawfordsville** (city) Montgomery County
95	1.6	**Crown Point** (city) Lake County
95	1.6	**Franklin** (city) Johnson County
95	1.6	**Granger** (CDP) Saint Joseph County
95	1.6	**Hebron** (town) Porter County
95	1.6	**Madison** (city) Jefferson County
95	1.6	**Sellersburg** (town) Clark County
95	1.6	**Westfield** (city) Hamilton County
104	1.5	**Bremen** (town) Marshall County
104	1.5	**Clinton** (city) Vermillion County
104	1.5	**Elwood** (city) Madison County
104	1.5	**Garrett** (city) DeKalb County
104	1.5	**Grissom AFB** (CDP) Miami County
104	1.5	**Lebanon** (city) Boone County
104	1.5	**Middlebury** (town) Elkhart County
104	1.5	**Nappanee** (city) Elkhart County
104	1.5	**Portland** (city) Jay County
104	1.5	**Upland** (town) Grant County
114	1.4	**Brownsburg** (town) Hendricks County
114	1.4	**Columbia City** (city) Whitley County
114	1.4	**Danville** (town) Hendricks County
114	1.4	**Decatur** (city) Adams County
114	1.4	**Huntington** (city) Huntington County
114	1.4	**New Whiteland** (town) Johnson County
114	1.4	**Newburgh** (town) Warrick County
114	1.4	**Zionsville** (town) Boone County
122	1.3	**Bedford** (city) Lawrence County
122	1.3	**Chesterfield** (town) Madison County
122	1.3	**Connersville** (city) Fayette County
122	1.3	**De Motte** (town) Jasper County
122	1.3	**Fortville** (town) Hancock County
122	1.3	**Greenfield** (city) Hancock County
122	1.3	**Hanover** (town) Jefferson County
122	1.3	**North Manchester** (town) Wabash County
122	1.3	**Rensselaer** (city) Jasper County
122	1.3	**Syracuse** (town) Kosciusko County
122	1.3	**Tipton** (city) Tipton County
122	1.3	**Winfield** (town) Lake County
134	1.2	**Austin** (city) Scott County
134	1.2	**Centerville** (town) Wayne County
134	1.2	**Corydon** (town) Harrison County
134	1.2	**Leo-Cedarville** (town) Allen County
134	1.2	**Linton** (city) Greene County
134	1.2	**Lowell** (town) Lake County
134	1.2	**Melody Hill** (CDP) Vanderburgh County
134	1.2	**Mooresville** (town) Morgan County
134	1.2	**Rochester** (city) Fulton County
134	1.2	**Rushville** (city) Rush County
134	1.2	**Saint John** (town) Lake County
134	1.2	**Sullivan** (city) Sullivan County
134	1.2	**Wabash** (city) Wabash County
134	1.2	**Winona Lake** (town) Kosciusko County
148	1.1	**Alexandria** (city) Madison County
148	1.1	**Bluffton** (city) Wells County
148	1.1	**Boonville** (city) Warrick County

Note: This section ranks incorporated places and CDPs (Census Designated Places) with populations of 2,500 or more. Unincorporated postal areas were not considered. Please refer to the User Guide for additional information.

Two or More Races
Top 150 Places Ranked in *Ascending* Order

State Rank	Percent	Place
1	0.5	**Loogootee** (city) Martin County
1	0.5	**Rockville** (town) Parke County
3	0.6	**Bright** (CDP) Dearborn County
3	0.6	**Scottsburg** (city) Scott County
5	0.7	**Aurora** (city) Dearborn County
5	0.7	**Fairmount** (town) Grant County
5	0.7	**Heritage Lake** (CDP) Putnam County
5	0.7	**Lagrange** (town) LaGrange County
5	0.7	**Roselawn** (CDP) Newton County
5	0.7	**Westville** (town) LaPorte County
11	0.8	**Brownstown** (town) Jackson County
11	0.8	**Mitchell** (city) Lawrence County
13	0.9	**Brookville** (town) Franklin County
13	0.9	**Fort Branch** (town) Gibson County
13	0.9	**Greensburg** (city) Decatur County
13	0.9	**Jasper** (city) Dubois County
13	0.9	**Pendleton** (town) Madison County
13	0.9	**Salem** (city) Washington County
13	0.9	**Tell City** (city) Perry County
20	1.0	**Attica** (city) Fountain County
20	1.0	**Auburn** (city) DeKalb County
20	1.0	**Batesville** (city) Ripley County
20	1.0	**Berne** (city) Adams County
20	1.0	**Bicknell** (city) Knox County
20	1.0	**Brazil** (city) Clay County
20	1.0	**Hidden Valley** (CDP) Dearborn County
20	1.0	**Martinsville** (city) Morgan County
20	1.0	**Paoli** (town) Orange County
20	1.0	**Yorktown** (town) Delaware County
30	1.1	**Alexandria** (city) Madison County
30	1.1	**Bluffton** (city) Wells County
30	1.1	**Boonville** (city) Warrick County
30	1.1	**Chandler** (town) Warrick County
30	1.1	**Cicero** (town) Hamilton County
30	1.1	**Covington** (city) Fountain County
30	1.1	**Edinburgh** (town) Johnson County
30	1.1	**Georgetown** (town) Floyd County
30	1.1	**Highland** (CDP) Vanderburgh County
30	1.1	**Ossian** (town) Wells County
30	1.1	**Whiteland** (town) Johnson County
30	1.1	**Winchester** (city) Randolph County
42	1.2	**Austin** (city) Scott County
42	1.2	**Centerville** (town) Wayne County
42	1.2	**Corydon** (town) Harrison County
42	1.2	**Leo-Cedarville** (town) Allen County
42	1.2	**Linton** (city) Greene County
42	1.2	**Lowell** (town) Lake County
42	1.2	**Melody Hill** (CDP) Vanderburgh County
42	1.2	**Mooresville** (town) Morgan County
42	1.2	**Rochester** (city) Fulton County
42	1.2	**Rushville** (city) Rush County
42	1.2	**Saint John** (town) Lake County
42	1.2	**Sullivan** (city) Sullivan County
42	1.2	**Wabash** (city) Wabash County
42	1.2	**Winona Lake** (town) Kosciusko County
56	1.3	**Bedford** (city) Lawrence County
56	1.3	**Chesterfield** (town) Madison County
56	1.3	**Connersville** (city) Fayette County
56	1.3	**De Motte** (town) Jasper County
56	1.3	**Fortville** (town) Hancock County
56	1.3	**Greenfield** (city) Hancock County
56	1.3	**Hanover** (town) Jefferson County
56	1.3	**North Manchester** (town) Wabash County
56	1.3	**Rensselaer** (city) Jasper County
56	1.3	**Syracuse** (town) Kosciusko County
56	1.3	**Tipton** (city) Tipton County
56	1.3	**Winfield** (town) Lake County
68	1.4	**Brownsburg** (town) Hendricks County
68	1.4	**Columbia City** (city) Whitley County
68	1.4	**Danville** (town) Hendricks County
68	1.4	**Decatur** (city) Adams County
68	1.4	**Huntington** (city) Huntington County
68	1.4	**New Whiteland** (town) Johnson County
68	1.4	**Newburgh** (town) Warrick County
68	1.4	**Zionsville** (town) Boone County
76	1.5	**Bremen** (town) Marshall County
76	1.5	**Clinton** (city) Vermillion County
76	1.5	**Elwood** (city) Madison County
76	1.5	**Garrett** (city) DeKalb County
76	1.5	**Grissom AFB** (CDP) Miami County
76	1.5	**Lebanon** (city) Boone County
76	1.5	**Middlebury** (town) Elkhart County
76	1.5	**Nappanee** (city) Elkhart County
76	1.5	**Portland** (city) Jay County
76	1.5	**Upland** (town) Grant County
86	1.6	**Bargersville** (town) Johnson County
86	1.6	**Crawfordsville** (city) Montgomery County
86	1.6	**Crown Point** (city) Lake County
86	1.6	**Franklin** (city) Johnson County
86	1.6	**Granger** (CDP) Saint Joseph County
86	1.6	**Hebron** (town) Porter County
86	1.6	**Madison** (city) Jefferson County
86	1.6	**Sellersburg** (town) Clark County
86	1.6	**Westfield** (city) Hamilton County
95	1.7	**Angola** (city) Steuben County
95	1.7	**Cedar Lake** (town) Lake County
95	1.7	**Chesterton** (town) Porter County
95	1.7	**Gas City** (city) Grant County
95	1.7	**Hartford City** (city) Blackford County
95	1.7	**Knox** (city) Starke County
95	1.7	**New Haven** (city) Allen County
95	1.7	**North Vernon** (city) Jennings County
95	1.7	**Pittsboro** (town) Hendricks County
95	1.7	**Porter** (town) Porter County
95	1.7	**Shelbyville** (city) Shelby County
95	1.7	**Sheridan** (town) Hamilton County
95	1.7	**Smithville-Sanders** (CDP) Monroe County
95	1.7	**Vincennes** (city) Knox County
109	1.8	**Butler** (city) DeKalb County
109	1.8	**Carmel** (city) Hamilton County
109	1.8	**Dyer** (town) Lake County
109	1.8	**Frankfort** (city) Clinton County
109	1.8	**Greencastle** (city) Putnam County
109	1.8	**Greendale** (city) Dearborn County
109	1.8	**Huntingburg** (city) Dubois County
109	1.8	**Kendallville** (city) Noble County
109	1.8	**Munster** (town) Lake County
109	1.8	**New Castle** (city) Henry County
109	1.8	**Noblesville** (city) Hamilton County
109	1.8	**Plainfield** (town) Hendricks County
109	1.8	**Schererville** (town) Lake County
109	1.8	**Seymour** (city) Jackson County
123	1.9	**Delphi** (city) Carroll County
123	1.9	**Ellettsville** (town) Monroe County
123	1.9	**Huntertown** (town) Allen County
123	1.9	**Lakes of the Four Seasons** (CDP) Lake County
123	1.9	**Shorewood Forest** (CDP) Porter County
123	1.9	**Union City** (city) Randolph County
123	1.9	**Washington** (city) Daviess County
130	2.0	**Columbus** (city) Bartholomew County
130	2.0	**Highland** (town) Lake County
130	2.0	**Warsaw** (city) Kosciusko County
133	2.1	**Beech Grove** (city) Marion County
133	2.1	**Charlestown** (city) Clark County
133	2.1	**Dunlap** (CDP) Elkhart County
133	2.1	**Fishers** (town) Hamilton County
133	2.1	**Gary** (city) Lake County
133	2.1	**Greenwood** (city) Johnson County
133	2.1	**Monticello** (city) White County
133	2.1	**North Terre Haute** (CDP) Vigo County
133	2.1	**Valparaiso** (city) Porter County
133	2.1	**West Lafayette** (city) Tippecanoe County
143	2.2	**Avon** (town) Hendricks County
143	2.2	**Country Squire Lakes** (CDP) Jennings County
143	2.2	**Lawrenceburg** (city) Dearborn County
143	2.2	**Logansport** (city) Cass County
143	2.2	**Purdue University** (CDP) Tippecanoe County
143	2.2	**South Haven** (CDP) Porter County
143	2.2	**Whitestown** (town) Boone County
150	2.3	**Cumberland** (town) Marion County

Note: This section ranks incorporated places and CDPs (Census Designated Places) with populations of 2,500 or more. Unincorporated postal areas were not considered. Please refer to the User Guide for additional information.

Hispanic Population

Top 150 Places Ranked in *Descending* Order

State Rank	Percent	Place
1	51.5	**Ligonier** (city) Noble County
2	50.9	**East Chicago** (city) Lake County
3	40.7	**Whiting** (city) Lake County
4	34.1	**Hammond** (city) Lake County
5	28.1	**Goshen** (city) Elkhart County
6	28.0	**Lake Station** (city) Lake County
7	25.0	**Frankfort** (city) Clinton County
8	22.5	**Elkhart** (city) Elkhart County
9	21.6	**Logansport** (city) Cass County
10	20.0	**Plymouth** (city) Marshall County
11	18.5	**Huntingburg** (city) Dubois County
12	18.0	**Bremen** (town) Marshall County
13	16.4	**Portage** (city) Porter County
14	13.9	**Hobart** (city) Lake County
15	13.3	**Griffith** (town) Lake County
16	13.0	**South Bend** (city) Saint Joseph County
17	12.9	**Merrillville** (town) Lake County
18	12.8	**Highland** (town) Lake County
18	12.8	**Union City** (city) Randolph County
20	12.5	**Monticello** (city) White County
21	12.1	**Lafayette** (city) Tippecanoe County
22	11.5	**Seymour** (city) Jackson County
23	11.3	**Delphi** (city) Carroll County
24	11.2	**La Porte** (city) LaPorte County
24	11.2	**Lawrence** (city) Marion County
26	10.6	**Dunlap** (CDP) Elkhart County
26	10.6	**Schererville** (town) Lake County
28	10.4	**Warsaw** (city) Kosciusko County
29	10.2	**Munster** (town) Lake County
30	9.9	**Notre Dame** (CDP) Saint Joseph County
31	9.8	**South Haven** (CDP) Porter County
32	9.6	**Washington** (city) Daviess County
33	9.5	**Clarksville** (town) Clark County
33	9.5	**Lagrange** (town) LaGrange County
35	9.4	**Indianapolis** (city) Marion County
36	9.3	**Dyer** (town) Lake County
37	9.2	**Roselawn** (CDP) Newton County
38	8.9	**Winfield** (town) Lake County
39	8.5	**Lakes of the Four Seasons** (CDP) Lake County
40	8.4	**Decatur** (city) Adams County
41	8.3	**Charlestown** (city) Clark County
42	8.2	**Crawfordsville** (city) Montgomery County
42	8.2	**Saint John** (town) Lake County
44	8.1	**Crown Point** (city) Lake County
45	8.0	**Fort Wayne** (city) Allen County
46	7.7	**Jasper** (city) Dubois County
47	7.6	**Speedway** (town) Marion County
48	7.4	**Winona Lake** (town) Kosciusko County
49	7.1	**Shelbyville** (city) Shelby County
49	7.1	**Valparaiso** (city) Porter County
51	6.9	**Chesterton** (town) Porter County
51	6.9	**Lowell** (town) Lake County
53	6.6	**Porter** (town) Porter County
54	6.5	**Cedar Lake** (town) Lake County
55	6.3	**Angola** (city) Steuben County
55	6.3	**Westville** (town) LaPorte County
57	6.2	**Nappanee** (city) Elkhart County
58	6.1	**Hebron** (town) Porter County
59	5.9	**Michigan City** (city) LaPorte County
60	5.8	**Columbus** (city) Bartholomew County
60	5.8	**Portland** (city) Jay County
60	5.8	**Westfield** (city) Hamilton County
63	5.5	**Edinburgh** (town) Johnson County
63	5.5	**Marion** (city) Grant County
63	5.5	**Sellersburg** (town) Clark County
66	5.4	**Country Squire Lakes** (CDP) Jennings County
66	5.4	**Rensselaer** (city) Jasper County
68	5.3	**Cumberland** (town) Marion County
69	5.2	**Syracuse** (town) Kosciusko County
70	5.1	**Gary** (city) Lake County
70	5.1	**Kendallville** (city) Noble County
72	5.0	**Greenwood** (city) Johnson County
73	4.8	**Anderson** (city) Madison County
74	4.7	**De Motte** (town) Jasper County
74	4.7	**Simonton Lake** (CDP) Elkhart County
76	4.6	**Grissom AFB** (CDP) Miami County
77	4.5	**Mishawaka** (city) Saint Joseph County
78	4.4	**McCordsville** (town) Hancock County
79	4.3	**Avon** (town) Hendricks County
79	4.3	**Butler** (city) DeKalb County
79	4.3	**Noblesville** (city) Hamilton County
82	4.2	**Beech Grove** (city) Marion County
83	4.1	**Jeffersonville** (city) Clark County
83	4.1	**Richmond** (city) Wayne County
85	4.0	**Berne** (city) Adams County
85	4.0	**Plainfield** (town) Hendricks County
87	3.8	**North Manchester** (town) Wabash County
88	3.7	**New Albany** (city) Floyd County
88	3.7	**Shorewood Forest** (CDP) Porter County
90	3.6	**Purdue University** (CDP) Tippecanoe County
90	3.6	**West Lafayette** (city) Tippecanoe County
92	3.5	**Bloomington** (city) Monroe County
92	3.5	**Garrett** (city) DeKalb County
92	3.5	**Whitestown** (town) Boone County
95	3.4	**Fishers** (town) Hamilton County
95	3.4	**Rochester** (city) Fulton County
97	3.3	**Batesville** (city) Ripley County
97	3.3	**Bluffton** (city) Wells County
97	3.3	**Elwood** (city) Madison County
97	3.3	**Kokomo** (city) Howard County
97	3.3	**Sheridan** (town) Hamilton County
102	3.2	**Middlebury** (town) Elkhart County
103	3.1	**Lebanon** (city) Boone County
103	3.1	**New Haven** (city) Allen County
103	3.1	**Terre Haute** (city) Vigo County
106	3.0	**Brownsburg** (town) Hendricks County
107	2.9	**Knox** (city) Starke County
108	2.7	**Tipton** (city) Tipton County
109	2.6	**Auburn** (city) DeKalb County
109	2.6	**Corydon** (town) Harrison County
109	2.6	**Evansville** (city) Vanderburgh County
109	2.6	**Winchester** (city) Randolph County
113	2.5	**Carmel** (city) Hamilton County
113	2.5	**Centerville** (town) Wayne County
113	2.5	**Franklin** (city) Johnson County
113	2.5	**Greencastle** (city) Putnam County
113	2.5	**Princeton** (city) Gibson County
118	2.4	**Attica** (city) Fountain County
118	2.4	**Gas City** (city) Grant County
118	2.4	**Granger** (CDP) Saint Joseph County
118	2.4	**Greensburg** (city) Decatur County
118	2.4	**Hanover** (town) Jefferson County
118	2.4	**Huntington** (city) Huntington County
118	2.4	**North Vernon** (city) Jennings County
118	2.4	**Peru** (city) Miami County
126	2.3	**Fortville** (town) Hancock County
126	2.3	**Huntertown** (town) Allen County
126	2.3	**Muncie** (city) Delaware County
126	2.3	**Upland** (town) Grant County
130	2.2	**Columbia City** (city) Whitley County
131	2.1	**Austin** (city) Scott County
131	2.1	**Bargersville** (town) Johnson County
131	2.1	**Zionsville** (town) Boone County
134	2.0	**New Whiteland** (town) Johnson County
134	2.0	**Newburgh** (town) Warrick County
134	2.0	**Wabash** (city) Wabash County
137	1.9	**Bicknell** (city) Knox County
137	1.9	**Georgetown** (town) Floyd County
137	1.9	**Heritage Lake** (CDP) Putnam County
137	1.9	**Vincennes** (city) Knox County
141	1.8	**Bedford** (city) Lawrence County
141	1.8	**Danville** (town) Hendricks County
141	1.8	**Greenfield** (city) Hancock County
141	1.8	**Scottsburg** (city) Scott County
141	1.8	**Whiteland** (town) Johnson County
146	1.7	**Alexandria** (city) Madison County
146	1.7	**Madison** (city) Jefferson County
146	1.7	**Mount Vernon** (city) Posey County
146	1.7	**New Castle** (city) Henry County
150	1.6	**Brazil** (city) Clay County

Note: This section ranks incorporated places and CDPs (Census Designated Places) with populations of 2,500 or more. Unincorporated postal areas were not considered. Please refer to the User Guide for additional information.

Hispanic Population
Top 150 Places Ranked in *Ascending* Order

State Rank	Percent	Place
1	0.7	**Bright** (CDP) Dearborn County
1	0.7	**Rockville** (town) Parke County
3	0.8	**Highland** (CDP) Vanderburgh County
3	0.8	**Loogootee** (city) Martin County
5	0.9	**Fairmount** (town) Grant County
5	0.9	**Fort Branch** (town) Gibson County
7	1.0	**Brownstown** (town) Jackson County
7	1.0	**Clinton** (city) Vermillion County
7	1.0	**Connersville** (city) Fayette County
7	1.0	**Pendleton** (town) Madison County
7	1.0	**Salem** (city) Washington County
7	1.0	**Tell City** (city) Perry County
13	1.1	**Chesterfield** (town) Madison County
13	1.1	**Covington** (city) Fountain County
13	1.1	**Mooresville** (town) Morgan County
16	1.2	**Boonville** (city) Warrick County
16	1.2	**Hartford City** (city) Blackford County
16	1.2	**Lawrenceburg** (city) Dearborn County
16	1.2	**Linton** (city) Greene County
16	1.2	**North Terre Haute** (CDP) Vigo County
16	1.2	**Rushville** (city) Rush County
22	1.3	**Chandler** (town) Warrick County
22	1.3	**Martinsville** (city) Morgan County
22	1.3	**Paoli** (town) Orange County
22	1.3	**Smithville-Sanders** (CDP) Monroe County
22	1.3	**Yorktown** (town) Delaware County
27	1.4	**Hidden Valley** (CDP) Dearborn County
27	1.4	**Mitchell** (city) Lawrence County
27	1.4	**Ossian** (town) Wells County
27	1.4	**Pittsboro** (town) Hendricks County
27	1.4	**Sullivan** (city) Sullivan County
32	1.5	**Aurora** (city) Dearborn County
32	1.5	**Cicero** (town) Hamilton County
32	1.5	**Melody Hill** (CDP) Vanderburgh County
35	1.6	**Brazil** (city) Clay County
35	1.6	**Brookville** (town) Franklin County
35	1.6	**Ellettsville** (town) Monroe County
35	1.6	**Greendale** (city) Dearborn County
35	1.6	**Leo-Cedarville** (town) Allen County
40	1.7	**Alexandria** (city) Madison County
40	1.7	**Madison** (city) Jefferson County
40	1.7	**Mount Vernon** (city) Posey County
40	1.7	**New Castle** (city) Henry County
44	1.8	**Bedford** (city) Lawrence County
44	1.8	**Danville** (town) Hendricks County
44	1.8	**Greenfield** (city) Hancock County
44	1.8	**Scottsburg** (city) Scott County
44	1.8	**Whiteland** (town) Johnson County
49	1.9	**Bicknell** (city) Knox County
49	1.9	**Georgetown** (town) Floyd County
49	1.9	**Heritage Lake** (CDP) Putnam County
49	1.9	**Vincennes** (city) Knox County
53	2.0	**New Whiteland** (town) Johnson County
53	2.0	**Newburgh** (town) Warrick County
53	2.0	**Wabash** (city) Wabash County
56	2.1	**Austin** (city) Scott County
56	2.1	**Bargersville** (town) Johnson County
56	2.1	**Zionsville** (town) Boone County
59	2.2	**Columbia City** (city) Whitley County
60	2.3	**Fortville** (town) Hancock County
60	2.3	**Huntertown** (town) Allen County
60	2.3	**Muncie** (city) Delaware County
60	2.3	**Upland** (town) Grant County
64	2.4	**Attica** (city) Fountain County
64	2.4	**Gas City** (city) Grant County
64	2.4	**Granger** (CDP) Saint Joseph County
64	2.4	**Greensburg** (city) Decatur County
64	2.4	**Hanover** (town) Jefferson County
64	2.4	**Huntington** (city) Huntington County
64	2.4	**North Vernon** (city) Jennings County
64	2.4	**Peru** (city) Miami County
72	2.5	**Carmel** (city) Hamilton County
72	2.5	**Centerville** (town) Wayne County
72	2.5	**Franklin** (city) Johnson County
72	2.5	**Greencastle** (city) Putnam County
72	2.5	**Princeton** (city) Gibson County
77	2.6	**Auburn** (city) DeKalb County
77	2.6	**Corydon** (town) Harrison County
77	2.6	**Evansville** (city) Vanderburgh County
77	2.6	**Winchester** (city) Randolph County
81	2.7	**Tipton** (city) Tipton County
82	2.9	**Knox** (city) Starke County
83	3.0	**Brownsburg** (town) Hendricks County
84	3.1	**Lebanon** (city) Boone County
84	3.1	**New Haven** (city) Allen County
84	3.1	**Terre Haute** (city) Vigo County
87	3.2	**Middlebury** (town) Elkhart County
88	3.3	**Batesville** (city) Ripley County
88	3.3	**Bluffton** (city) Wells County
88	3.3	**Elwood** (city) Madison County
88	3.3	**Kokomo** (city) Howard County
88	3.3	**Sheridan** (town) Hamilton County
93	3.4	**Fishers** (town) Hamilton County
93	3.4	**Rochester** (city) Fulton County
95	3.5	**Bloomington** (city) Monroe County
95	3.5	**Garrett** (city) DeKalb County
95	3.5	**Whitestown** (town) Boone County
98	3.6	**Purdue University** (CDP) Tippecanoe County
98	3.6	**West Lafayette** (city) Tippecanoe County
100	3.7	**New Albany** (city) Floyd County
100	3.7	**Shorewood Forest** (CDP) Porter County
102	3.8	**North Manchester** (town) Wabash County
103	4.0	**Berne** (city) Adams County
103	4.0	**Plainfield** (town) Hendricks County
105	4.1	**Jeffersonville** (city) Clark County
105	4.1	**Richmond** (city) Wayne County
107	4.2	**Beech Grove** (city) Marion County
108	4.3	**Avon** (town) Hendricks County
108	4.3	**Butler** (city) DeKalb County
108	4.3	**Noblesville** (city) Hamilton County
111	4.4	**McCordsville** (town) Hancock County
112	4.5	**Mishawaka** (city) Saint Joseph County
113	4.6	**Grissom AFB** (CDP) Miami County
114	4.7	**De Motte** (town) Jasper County
114	4.7	**Simonton Lake** (CDP) Elkhart County
116	4.8	**Anderson** (city) Madison County
117	5.0	**Greenwood** (city) Johnson County
118	5.1	**Gary** (city) Lake County
118	5.1	**Kendallville** (city) Noble County
120	5.2	**Syracuse** (town) Kosciusko County
121	5.3	**Cumberland** (town) Marion County
122	5.4	**Country Squire Lakes** (CDP) Jennings County
122	5.4	**Rensselaer** (city) Jasper County
124	5.5	**Edinburgh** (town) Johnson County
124	5.5	**Marion** (city) Grant County
124	5.5	**Sellersburg** (town) Clark County
127	5.8	**Columbus** (city) Bartholomew County
127	5.8	**Portland** (city) Jay County
127	5.8	**Westfield** (city) Hamilton County
130	5.9	**Michigan City** (city) LaPorte County
131	6.1	**Hebron** (town) Porter County
132	6.2	**Nappanee** (city) Elkhart County
133	6.3	**Angola** (city) Steuben County
133	6.3	**Westville** (town) LaPorte County
135	6.5	**Cedar Lake** (town) Lake County
136	6.6	**Porter** (town) Porter County
137	6.9	**Chesterton** (town) Porter County
137	6.9	**Lowell** (town) Lake County
139	7.1	**Shelbyville** (city) Shelby County
139	7.1	**Valparaiso** (city) Porter County
141	7.4	**Winona Lake** (town) Kosciusko County
142	7.6	**Speedway** (town) Marion County
143	7.7	**Jasper** (city) Dubois County
144	8.0	**Fort Wayne** (city) Allen County
145	8.1	**Crown Point** (city) Lake County
146	8.2	**Crawfordsville** (city) Montgomery County
146	8.2	**Saint John** (town) Lake County
148	8.3	**Charlestown** (city) Clark County
149	8.4	**Decatur** (city) Adams County
150	8.5	**Lakes of the Four Seasons** (CDP) Lake County

Note: This section ranks incorporated places and CDPs (Census Designated Places) with populations of 2,500 or more. Unincorporated postal areas were not considered. Please refer to the User Guide for additional information.

Average Household Size
Top 150 Places Ranked in *Descending* Order

State Rank	Persons	Place
1	3.2	**Ligonier** (city) Noble County
2	3.0	**Leo-Cedarville** (town) Allen County
3	3.0	**Winfield** (town) Lake County
4	2.9	**Saint John** (town) Lake County
5	2.9	**Granger** (CDP) Saint Joseph County
6	2.9	**McCordsville** (town) Hancock County
7	2.8	**South Haven** (CDP) Porter County
8	2.8	**New Whiteland** (town) Johnson County
9	2.8	**Dunlap** (CDP) Elkhart County
9	2.8	**Shorewood Forest** (CDP) Porter County
11	2.8	**Westfield** (city) Hamilton County
12	2.8	**Roselawn** (CDP) Newton County
12	2.8	**Whiteland** (town) Johnson County
14	2.8	**Fishers** (town) Hamilton County
14	2.8	**Hidden Valley** (CDP) Dearborn County
16	2.8	**Grissom AFB** (CDP) Miami County
17	2.7	**Huntertown** (town) Allen County
18	2.7	**Avon** (town) Hendricks County
18	2.7	**Bright** (CDP) Dearborn County
20	2.7	**Lakes of the Four Seasons** (CDP) Lake County
21	2.7	**Cedar Lake** (town) Lake County
21	2.7	**East Chicago** (city) Lake County
21	2.7	**Zionsville** (town) Boone County
24	2.7	**Country Squire Lakes** (CDP) Jennings County
24	2.7	**Pittsboro** (town) Hendricks County
26	2.7	**Lake Station** (city) Lake County
26	2.7	**Whitestown** (town) Boone County
28	2.7	**Butler** (city) DeKalb County
28	2.7	**Carmel** (city) Hamilton County
28	2.7	**Frankfort** (city) Clinton County
28	2.7	**Lowell** (town) Lake County
32	2.7	**Middlebury** (town) Elkhart County
33	2.6	**Bargersville** (town) Johnson County
33	2.6	**Heritage Lake** (CDP) Putnam County
33	2.6	**Noblesville** (city) Hamilton County
36	2.6	**Dyer** (town) Lake County
37	2.6	**Garrett** (city) DeKalb County
37	2.6	**Goshen** (city) Elkhart County
37	2.6	**Hammond** (city) Lake County
40	2.6	**Danville** (town) Hendricks County
41	2.6	**Porter** (town) Porter County
42	2.6	**Brownsburg** (town) Hendricks County
42	2.6	**Georgetown** (town) Floyd County
44	2.6	**Charlestown** (city) Clark County
44	2.6	**Whiting** (city) Lake County
46	2.6	**Chandler** (town) Warrick County
46	2.6	**Sheridan** (town) Hamilton County
46	2.6	**Winona Lake** (town) Kosciusko County
49	2.6	**Cumberland** (town) Marion County
49	2.6	**Melody Hill** (CDP) Vanderburgh County
49	2.6	**Portage** (city) Porter County
52	2.6	**Elkhart** (city) Elkhart County
52	2.6	**Nappanee** (city) Elkhart County
52	2.6	**Upland** (town) Grant County
55	2.5	**Munster** (town) Lake County
56	2.5	**Bremen** (town) Marshall County
56	2.5	**Chesterton** (town) Porter County
58	2.5	**Hebron** (town) Porter County
58	2.5	**Highland** (CDP) Vanderburgh County
58	2.5	**Logansport** (city) Cass County
58	2.5	**Plainfield** (town) Hendricks County
62	2.5	**Austin** (city) Scott County
62	2.5	**Lawrence** (city) Marion County
64	2.5	**Aurora** (city) Dearborn County
64	2.5	**Batesville** (city) Ripley County
64	2.5	**Edinburgh** (town) Johnson County
64	2.5	**Huntingburg** (city) Dubois County
64	2.5	**Yorktown** (town) Delaware County
69	2.5	**Franklin** (city) Johnson County
69	2.5	**Gary** (city) Lake County
69	2.5	**Merrillville** (town) Lake County
72	2.5	**Fortville** (town) Hancock County
72	2.5	**Griffith** (town) Lake County
72	2.5	**Knox** (city) Starke County
75	2.5	**New Haven** (city) Allen County
75	2.5	**Simonton Lake** (CDP) Elkhart County
77	2.5	**Greenfield** (city) Hancock County
77	2.5	**Greenwood** (city) Johnson County
79	2.5	**Greendale** (city) Dearborn County
80	2.4	**Elwood** (city) Madison County
80	2.4	**Mooresville** (town) Morgan County
80	2.4	**Ossian** (town) Wells County
80	2.4	**Plymouth** (city) Marshall County
80	2.4	**Seymour** (city) Jackson County
85	2.4	**Hobart** (city) Lake County
85	2.4	**Huntington** (city) Huntington County
85	2.4	**Sellersburg** (town) Clark County
85	2.4	**South Bend** (city) Saint Joseph County
89	2.4	**Cicero** (town) Hamilton County
89	2.4	**Martinsville** (city) Morgan County
91	2.4	**Brazil** (city) Clay County
91	2.4	**Centerville** (town) Wayne County
91	2.4	**Delphi** (city) Carroll County
91	2.4	**Kendallville** (city) Noble County
95	2.4	**Attica** (city) Fountain County
95	2.4	**Bicknell** (city) Knox County
95	2.4	**Crown Point** (city) Lake County
95	2.4	**Gas City** (city) Grant County
95	2.4	**Schererville** (town) Lake County
95	2.4	**Westville** (town) LaPorte County
101	2.4	**Fort Wayne** (city) Allen County
102	2.4	**Columbus** (city) Bartholomew County
102	2.4	**Ellettsville** (town) Monroe County
102	2.4	**Hanover** (town) Jefferson County
102	2.4	**Lagrange** (town) LaGrange County
102	2.4	**North Vernon** (city) Jennings County
102	2.4	**Shelbyville** (city) Shelby County
102	2.4	**Syracuse** (town) Kosciusko County
102	2.4	**Union City** (city) Randolph County
102	2.4	**Washington** (city) Daviess County
111	2.4	**Brownstown** (town) Jackson County
111	2.4	**De Motte** (town) Jasper County
111	2.4	**Indianapolis** (city) Marion County
111	2.4	**North Terre Haute** (CDP) Vigo County
111	2.4	**Rensselaer** (city) Jasper County
116	2.4	**Alexandria** (city) Madison County
116	2.4	**Jasper** (city) Dubois County
118	2.4	**Mount Vernon** (city) Posey County
119	2.3	**Boonville** (city) Warrick County
119	2.3	**Highland** (town) Lake County
119	2.3	**La Porte** (city) LaPorte County
122	2.3	**Auburn** (city) DeKalb County
122	2.3	**Fairmount** (town) Grant County
122	2.3	**Fort Branch** (town) Gibson County
122	2.3	**Greensburg** (city) Decatur County
122	2.3	**Lebanon** (city) Boone County
122	2.3	**Mitchell** (city) Lawrence County
122	2.3	**Warsaw** (city) Kosciusko County
129	2.3	**Connersville** (city) Fayette County
129	2.3	**Jeffersonville** (city) Clark County
129	2.3	**Michigan City** (city) LaPorte County
129	2.3	**Pendleton** (town) Madison County
133	2.3	**Beech Grove** (city) Marion County
133	2.3	**Clinton** (city) Vermillion County
133	2.3	**Peru** (city) Miami County
133	2.3	**Rushville** (city) Rush County
137	2.3	**Angola** (city) Steuben County
137	2.3	**Berne** (city) Adams County
137	2.3	**Paoli** (town) Orange County
137	2.3	**Smithville-Sanders** (CDP) Monroe County
141	2.3	**Bluffton** (city) Wells County
141	2.3	**Clarksville** (town) Clark County
141	2.3	**Princeton** (city) Gibson County
141	2.3	**Scottsburg** (city) Scott County
145	2.3	**Monticello** (city) White County
146	2.3	**Columbia City** (city) Whitley County
146	2.3	**Decatur** (city) Adams County
146	2.3	**Hartford City** (city) Blackford County
146	2.3	**Portland** (city) Jay County
146	2.3	**Winchester** (city) Randolph County

Note: This section ranks incorporated places and CDPs (Census Designated Places) with populations of 2,500 or more. Unincorporated postal areas were not considered. Please refer to the User Guide for additional information.

Average Household Size
Top 150 Places Ranked in *Ascending* Order

State Rank	Persons	Place
1	2.0	Bloomington (city) Monroe County
2	2.1	Speedway (town) Marion County
3	2.1	Corydon (town) Harrison County
3	2.1	Rockville (town) Parke County
5	2.1	Madison (city) Jefferson County
5	2.1	Notre Dame (CDP) Saint Joseph County
7	2.1	Vincennes (city) Knox County
8	2.2	Mishawaka (city) Saint Joseph County
9	2.2	Bedford (city) Lawrence County
9	2.2	Muncie (city) Delaware County
9	2.2	West Lafayette (city) Tippecanoe County
12	2.2	Evansville (city) Vanderburgh County
12	2.2	Tell City (city) Perry County
14	2.2	Brookville (town) Franklin County
14	2.2	Purdue University (CDP) Tippecanoe County
16	2.2	Covington (city) Fountain County
16	2.2	Kokomo (city) Howard County
16	2.2	Loogootee (city) Martin County
16	2.2	Marion (city) Grant County
16	2.2	North Manchester (town) Wabash County
21	2.2	Lawrenceburg (city) Dearborn County
21	2.2	Rochester (city) Fulton County
23	2.2	Greencastle (city) Putnam County
23	2.2	New Albany (city) Floyd County
23	2.2	Sullivan (city) Sullivan County
26	2.2	Anderson (city) Madison County
26	2.2	Chesterfield (town) Madison County
26	2.2	Newburgh (town) Warrick County
26	2.2	Tipton (city) Tipton County
26	2.2	Valparaiso (city) Porter County
31	2.2	New Castle (city) Henry County
31	2.2	Richmond (city) Wayne County
31	2.2	Terre Haute (city) Vigo County
34	2.3	Lafayette (city) Tippecanoe County
34	2.3	Linton (city) Greene County
36	2.3	Crawfordsville (city) Montgomery County
36	2.3	Salem (city) Washington County
36	2.3	Wabash (city) Wabash County
39	2.3	Columbia City (city) Whitley County
39	2.3	Decatur (city) Adams County
39	2.3	Hartford City (city) Blackford County
39	2.3	Portland (city) Jay County
39	2.3	Winchester (city) Randolph County
44	2.3	Monticello (city) White County
45	2.3	Bluffton (city) Wells County
45	2.3	Clarksville (town) Clark County
45	2.3	Princeton (city) Gibson County
45	2.3	Scottsburg (city) Scott County
49	2.3	Angola (city) Steuben County
49	2.3	Berne (city) Adams County
49	2.3	Paoli (town) Orange County
49	2.3	Smithville-Sanders (CDP) Monroe County
53	2.3	Beech Grove (city) Marion County
53	2.3	Clinton (city) Vermillion County
53	2.3	Peru (city) Miami County
53	2.3	Rushville (city) Rush County
57	2.3	Connersville (city) Fayette County
57	2.3	Jeffersonville (city) Clark County
57	2.3	Michigan City (city) LaPorte County
57	2.3	Pendleton (town) Madison County
61	2.3	Auburn (city) DeKalb County
61	2.3	Fairmount (city) Grant County
61	2.3	Fort Branch (town) Gibson County
61	2.3	Greensburg (city) Decatur County
61	2.3	Lebanon (city) Boone County
61	2.3	Mitchell (city) Lawrence County
61	2.3	Warsaw (city) Kosciusko County
68	2.3	Boonville (city) Warrick County
68	2.3	Highland (town) Lake County
68	2.3	La Porte (city) LaPorte County
71	2.4	Mount Vernon (city) Posey County
72	2.4	Alexandria (city) Madison County
72	2.4	Jasper (city) Dubois County
74	2.4	Brownstown (town) Jackson County
74	2.4	De Motte (town) Jasper County
74	2.4	Indianapolis (city) Marion County
74	2.4	North Terre Haute (CDP) Vigo County
74	2.4	Rensselaer (city) Jasper County
79	2.4	Columbus (city) Bartholomew County
79	2.4	Ellettsville (town) Monroe County
79	2.4	Hanover (town) Jefferson County
79	2.4	Lagrange (town) LaGrange County
79	2.4	North Vernon (city) Jennings County
79	2.4	Shelbyville (city) Shelby County
79	2.4	Syracuse (town) Kosciusko County
79	2.4	Union City (city) Randolph County
79	2.4	Washington (city) Daviess County
88	2.4	Fort Wayne (city) Allen County
89	2.4	Attica (city) Fountain County
89	2.4	Bicknell (city) Knox County
89	2.4	Crown Point (city) Lake County
89	2.4	Gas City (city) Grant County
89	2.4	Schererville (town) Lake County
89	2.4	Westville (town) LaPorte County
95	2.4	Brazil (city) Clay County
95	2.4	Centerville (town) Wayne County
95	2.4	Delphi (city) Carroll County
95	2.4	Kendallville (city) Noble County
99	2.4	Cicero (town) Hamilton County
99	2.4	Martinsville (city) Morgan County
101	2.4	Hobart (city) Lake County
101	2.4	Huntington (city) Huntington County
101	2.4	Sellersburg (town) Clark County
101	2.4	South Bend (city) Saint Joseph County
105	2.4	Elwood (city) Madison County
105	2.4	Mooresville (town) Morgan County
105	2.4	Ossian (town) Wells County
105	2.4	Plymouth (city) Marshall County
105	2.4	Seymour (city) Jackson County
110	2.5	Greendale (city) Dearborn County
111	2.5	Greenfield (city) Hancock County
111	2.5	Greenwood (city) Johnson County
113	2.5	New Haven (city) Allen County
113	2.5	Simonton Lake (CDP) Elkhart County
115	2.5	Fortville (town) Hancock County
115	2.5	Griffith (town) Lake County
115	2.5	Knox (city) Starke County
118	2.5	Franklin (city) Johnson County
118	2.5	Gary (city) Lake County
118	2.5	Merrillville (town) Lake County
121	2.5	Aurora (city) Dearborn County
121	2.5	Batesville (city) Ripley County
121	2.5	Edinburgh (town) Johnson County
121	2.5	Huntingburg (city) Dubois County
121	2.5	Yorktown (town) Delaware County
126	2.5	Austin (city) Scott County
126	2.5	Lawrence (city) Marion County
128	2.5	Hebron (town) Porter County
128	2.5	Highland (CDP) Vanderburgh County
128	2.5	Logansport (city) Cass County
128	2.5	Plainfield (town) Hendricks County
132	2.5	Bremen (town) Marshall County
132	2.5	Chesterton (town) Porter County
134	2.5	Munster (town) Lake County
135	2.6	Elkhart (city) Elkhart County
135	2.6	Nappanee (city) Elkhart County
135	2.6	Upland (town) Grant County
138	2.6	Cumberland (town) Marion County
138	2.6	Melody Hill (CDP) Vanderburgh County
138	2.6	Portage (city) Porter County
141	2.6	Chandler (town) Warrick County
141	2.6	Sheridan (town) Hamilton County
141	2.6	Winona Lake (town) Kosciusko County
144	2.6	Charlestown (city) Clark County
144	2.6	Whiting (city) Lake County
146	2.6	Brownsburg (town) Hendricks County
146	2.6	Georgetown (town) Floyd County
148	2.6	Porter (town) Porter County
149	2.6	Danville (town) Hendricks County
150	2.6	Garrett (city) DeKalb County

Note: This section ranks incorporated places and CDPs (Census Designated Places) with populations of 2,500 or more. Unincorporated postal areas were not considered. Please refer to the User Guide for additional information.

Median Age

Top 150 Places Ranked in *Descending* Order

State Rank	Years	Place
1	47.0	**Shorewood Forest** (CDP) Porter County
2	44.8	**Munster** (town) Lake County
2	44.8	**Rockville** (town) Parke County
4	44.0	**Covington** (city) Fountain County
5	43.5	**Highland** (CDP) Vanderburgh County
6	42.9	**Dyer** (town) Lake County
7	42.3	**Lakes of the Four Seasons** (CDP) Lake County
8	42.2	**Madison** (city) Jefferson County
9	42.1	**Newburgh** (town) Warrick County
10	42.0	**Berne** (city) Adams County
10	42.0	**Tell City** (city) Perry County
12	41.8	**Smithville-Sanders** (CDP) Monroe County
13	41.6	**Rochester** (city) Fulton County
14	41.5	**Bedford** (city) Lawrence County
14	41.5	**Highland** (town) Lake County
16	41.3	**Hartford City** (city) Blackford County
16	41.3	**Wabash** (city) Wabash County
18	41.2	**Yorktown** (town) Delaware County
19	41.1	**Simonton Lake** (CDP) Elkhart County
20	40.9	**Melody Hill** (CDP) Vanderburgh County
20	40.9	**Schererville** (town) Lake County
22	40.8	**Corydon** (town) Harrison County
22	40.8	**Granger** (CDP) Saint Joseph County
24	40.4	**Loogootee** (city) Martin County
24	40.4	**Monticello** (city) White County
26	40.3	**Fairmount** (town) Grant County
27	40.2	**Mount Vernon** (city) Posey County
27	40.2	**Saint John** (town) Lake County
27	40.2	**Winchester** (city) Randolph County
30	40.1	**Greendale** (city) Dearborn County
31	39.9	**Hidden Valley** (CDP) Dearborn County
31	39.9	**North Terre Haute** (CDP) Vigo County
31	39.9	**Tipton** (city) Tipton County
34	39.8	**Cicero** (town) Hamilton County
34	39.8	**Linton** (city) Greene County
34	39.8	**Sullivan** (city) Sullivan County
37	39.7	**Paoli** (town) Orange County
38	39.6	**Brookville** (town) Franklin County
38	39.6	**Crown Point** (city) Lake County
38	39.6	**Zionsville** (town) Boone County
41	39.5	**Chesterfield** (town) Madison County
41	39.5	**New Castle** (city) Henry County
43	39.4	**Boonville** (city) Warrick County
43	39.4	**Connersville** (city) Fayette County
43	39.4	**De Motte** (town) Jasper County
43	39.4	**Gas City** (city) Grant County
43	39.4	**Portland** (city) Jay County
48	39.3	**Heritage Lake** (CDP) Putnam County
48	39.3	**Jasper** (city) Dubois County
48	39.3	**Rushville** (city) Rush County
51	39.2	**Carmel** (city) Hamilton County
51	39.2	**Mitchell** (city) Lawrence County
53	39.1	**Porter** (town) Porter County
54	39.0	**Bright** (CDP) Dearborn County
54	39.0	**Peru** (city) Miami County
56	38.9	**Attica** (city) Fountain County
57	38.8	**Clinton** (city) Vermillion County
58	38.7	**Bicknell** (city) Knox County
58	38.7	**Brownstown** (town) Jackson County
58	38.7	**Winfield** (town) Lake County
61	38.6	**Elwood** (city) Madison County
61	38.6	**Mooresville** (town) Morgan County
63	38.4	**Cumberland** (town) Marion County
63	38.4	**Dunlap** (CDP) Elkhart County
63	38.4	**Richmond** (city) Wayne County
66	38.3	**Bluffton** (city) Wells County
66	38.3	**Edinburgh** (town) Johnson County
66	38.3	**Salem** (city) Washington County
69	38.2	**Alexandria** (city) Madison County
69	38.2	**Batesville** (city) Ripley County
69	38.2	**Kokomo** (city) Howard County
72	38.1	**Leo-Cedarville** (town) Allen County
72	38.1	**Roselawn** (CDP) Newton County
74	38.0	**Fort Branch** (town) Gibson County
74	38.0	**Hobart** (city) Lake County
74	38.0	**Sellersburg** (town) Clark County
77	37.9	**Auburn** (city) DeKalb County
78	37.8	**Anderson** (city) Madison County
78	37.8	**Chesterton** (town) Porter County
78	37.8	**Speedway** (town) Marion County
81	37.7	**Beech Grove** (city) Marion County
81	37.7	**Lagrange** (town) LaGrange County
83	37.6	**Pendleton** (town) Madison County
84	37.5	**Delphi** (city) Carroll County
84	37.5	**Lebanon** (city) Boone County
84	37.5	**New Haven** (city) Allen County
84	37.5	**Scottsburg** (city) Scott County
88	37.4	**Ossian** (town) Wells County
88	37.4	**Syracuse** (town) Kosciusko County
90	37.3	**Clarksville** (town) Clark County
90	37.3	**Jeffersonville** (city) Clark County
90	37.3	**Washington** (city) Daviess County
90	37.3	**Whiteland** (town) Johnson County
94	37.2	**Decatur** (city) Adams County
94	37.2	**Princeton** (city) Gibson County
96	37.1	**Centerville** (town) Wayne County
96	37.1	**Columbus** (city) Bartholomew County
96	37.1	**Michigan City** (city) LaPorte County
96	37.1	**New Albany** (city) Floyd County
100	37.0	**Greensburg** (city) Decatur County
101	36.7	**Austin** (city) Scott County
101	36.7	**Gary** (city) Lake County
101	36.7	**Merrillville** (town) Lake County
101	36.7	**Middlebury** (town) Elkhart County
105	36.6	**Bremen** (town) Marshall County
105	36.6	**Crawfordsville** (city) Montgomery County
105	36.6	**Martinsville** (city) Morgan County
105	36.6	**Rensselaer** (city) Jasper County
109	36.5	**Evansville** (city) Vanderburgh County
109	36.5	**North Manchester** (town) Wabash County
111	36.4	**Portage** (city) Porter County
112	36.3	**Pittsboro** (town) Hendricks County
113	36.2	**Aurora** (city) Dearborn County
113	36.2	**Brazil** (city) Clay County
113	36.2	**Knox** (city) Starke County
113	36.2	**La Porte** (city) LaPorte County
113	36.2	**Marion** (city) Grant County
118	36.1	**Columbia City** (city) Whitley County
118	36.1	**Griffith** (town) Lake County
120	36.0	**Brownsburg** (town) Hendricks County
120	36.0	**Chandler** (town) Warrick County
122	35.9	**Shelbyville** (city) Shelby County
123	35.7	**Fortville** (town) Hancock County
123	35.7	**Lowell** (town) Lake County
125	35.6	**Greenfield** (city) Hancock County
125	35.6	**North Vernon** (city) Jennings County
127	35.5	**Lawrenceburg** (city) Dearborn County
127	35.5	**Plainfield** (town) Hendricks County
127	35.5	**Seymour** (city) Jackson County
130	35.4	**Georgetown** (town) Floyd County
130	35.4	**Lake Station** (city) Lake County
130	35.4	**Union City** (city) Randolph County
133	35.2	**Charlestown** (city) Clark County
133	35.2	**Country Squire Lakes** (CDP) Jennings County
135	35.1	**Huntingburg** (city) Dubois County
136	35.0	**South Haven** (CDP) Porter County
137	34.9	**Cedar Lake** (town) Lake County
138	34.8	**Nappanee** (city) Elkhart County
138	34.8	**Warsaw** (city) Kosciusko County
140	34.7	**Mishawaka** (city) Saint Joseph County
141	34.6	**Franklin** (city) Johnson County
141	34.6	**Kendallville** (city) Noble County
143	34.5	**Ellettsville** (town) Monroe County
143	34.5	**Fort Wayne** (city) Allen County
145	34.4	**Whiting** (city) Lake County
146	34.3	**Danville** (town) Hendricks County
146	34.3	**Plymouth** (city) Marshall County
148	34.2	**Grissom AFB** (CDP) Miami County
148	34.2	**Lawrence** (city) Marion County
148	34.2	**Logansport** (city) Cass County

Note: This section ranks incorporated places and CDPs (Census Designated Places) with populations of 2,500 or more. Unincorporated postal areas were not considered. Please refer to the User Guide for additional information.

Median Age
Top 150 Places Ranked in *Ascending* Order

State Rank	Years	Place
1	19.9	**Purdue University** (CDP) Tippecanoe County
2	20.4	**Notre Dame** (CDP) Saint Joseph County
3	21.8	**Upland** (town) Grant County
4	22.8	**West Lafayette** (city) Tippecanoe County
5	23.3	**Bloomington** (city) Monroe County
6	26.2	**Hanover** (town) Jefferson County
7	27.4	**Greencastle** (city) Putnam County
8	28.1	**Muncie** (city) Delaware County
9	28.3	**Winona Lake** (town) Kosciusko County
10	28.5	**Ligonier** (city) Noble County
11	30.0	**Whitestown** (town) Boone County
12	30.3	**Angola** (city) Steuben County
13	30.9	**East Chicago** (city) Lake County
14	31.5	**Huntertown** (town) Allen County
15	31.9	**Lafayette** (city) Tippecanoe County
16	32.4	**Goshen** (city) Elkhart County
17	32.7	**Elkhart** (city) Elkhart County
17	32.7	**McCordsville** (town) Hancock County
17	32.7	**Terre Haute** (city) Vigo County
20	33.0	**Noblesville** (city) Hamilton County
20	33.0	**Vincennes** (city) Knox County
22	33.1	**Westville** (town) LaPorte County
23	33.2	**Bargersville** (town) Johnson County
23	33.2	**Fishers** (town) Hamilton County
25	33.3	**Hammond** (city) Lake County
25	33.3	**South Bend** (city) Saint Joseph County
27	33.4	**Huntington** (city) Huntington County
27	33.4	**Valparaiso** (city) Porter County
29	33.5	**Frankfort** (city) Clinton County
30	33.6	**Hebron** (town) Porter County
31	33.7	**Butler** (city) DeKalb County
31	33.7	**Garrett** (city) DeKalb County
31	33.7	**Indianapolis** (city) Marion County
31	33.7	**New Whiteland** (town) Johnson County
31	33.7	**Westfield** (city) Hamilton County
36	33.8	**Sheridan** (town) Hamilton County
37	33.9	**Avon** (town) Hendricks County
38	34.0	**Greenwood** (city) Johnson County
39	34.2	**Grissom AFB** (CDP) Miami County
39	34.2	**Lawrence** (city) Marion County
39	34.2	**Logansport** (city) Cass County
42	34.3	**Danville** (town) Hendricks County
42	34.3	**Plymouth** (city) Marshall County
44	34.4	**Whiting** (city) Lake County
45	34.5	**Ellettsville** (town) Monroe County
45	34.5	**Fort Wayne** (city) Allen County
47	34.6	**Franklin** (city) Johnson County
47	34.6	**Kendallville** (city) Noble County
49	34.7	**Mishawaka** (city) Saint Joseph County
50	34.8	**Nappanee** (city) Elkhart County
50	34.8	**Warsaw** (city) Kosciusko County
52	34.9	**Cedar Lake** (town) Lake County
53	35.0	**South Haven** (CDP) Porter County
54	35.1	**Huntingburg** (city) Dubois County
55	35.2	**Charlestown** (city) Clark County
55	35.2	**Country Squire Lakes** (CDP) Jennings County
57	35.4	**Georgetown** (town) Floyd County
57	35.4	**Lake Station** (city) Lake County
57	35.4	**Union City** (city) Randolph County
60	35.5	**Lawrenceburg** (city) Dearborn County
60	35.5	**Plainfield** (town) Hendricks County
60	35.5	**Seymour** (city) Jackson County
63	35.6	**Greenfield** (city) Hancock County
63	35.6	**North Vernon** (city) Jennings County
65	35.7	**Fortville** (town) Hancock County
65	35.7	**Lowell** (town) Lake County
67	35.9	**Shelbyville** (city) Shelby County
68	36.0	**Brownsburg** (town) Hendricks County
68	36.0	**Chandler** (town) Warrick County
70	36.1	**Columbia City** (city) Whitley County
70	36.1	**Griffith** (town) Lake County
72	36.2	**Aurora** (city) Dearborn County
72	36.2	**Brazil** (city) Clay County
72	36.2	**Knox** (city) Starke County
72	36.2	**La Porte** (city) LaPorte County
72	36.2	**Marion** (city) Grant County
77	36.3	**Pittsboro** (town) Hendricks County
78	36.4	**Portage** (city) Porter County
79	36.5	**Evansville** (city) Vanderburgh County
79	36.5	**North Manchester** (town) Wabash County
81	36.6	**Bremen** (town) Marshall County
81	36.6	**Crawfordsville** (city) Montgomery County
81	36.6	**Martinsville** (city) Morgan County
81	36.6	**Rensselaer** (city) Jasper County
85	36.7	**Austin** (city) Scott County
85	36.7	**Gary** (city) Lake County
85	36.7	**Merrillville** (town) Lake County
85	36.7	**Middlebury** (town) Elkhart County
89	37.0	**Greensburg** (city) Decatur County
90	37.1	**Centerville** (town) Wayne County
90	37.1	**Columbus** (city) Bartholomew County
90	37.1	**Michigan City** (city) LaPorte County
90	37.1	**New Albany** (city) Floyd County
94	37.2	**Decatur** (city) Adams County
94	37.2	**Princeton** (city) Gibson County
96	37.3	**Clarksville** (town) Clark County
96	37.3	**Jeffersonville** (city) Clark County
96	37.3	**Washington** (city) Daviess County
96	37.3	**Whiteland** (town) Johnson County
100	37.4	**Ossian** (town) Wells County
100	37.4	**Syracuse** (town) Kosciusko County
102	37.5	**Delphi** (city) Carroll County
102	37.5	**Lebanon** (city) Boone County
102	37.5	**New Haven** (city) Allen County
102	37.5	**Scottsburg** (city) Scott County
106	37.6	**Pendleton** (town) Madison County
107	37.7	**Beech Grove** (city) Marion County
107	37.7	**Lagrange** (town) LaGrange County
109	37.8	**Anderson** (city) Madison County
109	37.8	**Chesterton** (town) Porter County
109	37.8	**Speedway** (town) Marion County
112	37.9	**Auburn** (city) DeKalb County
113	38.0	**Fort Branch** (town) Gibson County
113	38.0	**Hobart** (city) Lake County
113	38.0	**Sellersburg** (town) Clark County
116	38.1	**Leo-Cedarville** (town) Allen County
116	38.1	**Roselawn** (CDP) Newton County
118	38.2	**Alexandria** (city) Madison County
118	38.2	**Batesville** (city) Ripley County
118	38.2	**Kokomo** (city) Howard County
121	38.3	**Bluffton** (city) Wells County
121	38.3	**Edinburgh** (town) Johnson County
121	38.3	**Salem** (city) Washington County
124	38.4	**Cumberland** (town) Marion County
124	38.4	**Dunlap** (CDP) Elkhart County
124	38.4	**Richmond** (city) Wayne County
127	38.6	**Elwood** (city) Madison County
127	38.6	**Mooresville** (town) Morgan County
129	38.7	**Bicknell** (city) Knox County
129	38.7	**Brownstown** (town) Jackson County
129	38.7	**Winfield** (town) Lake County
132	38.8	**Clinton** (city) Vermillion County
133	38.9	**Attica** (city) Fountain County
134	39.0	**Bright** (CDP) Dearborn County
134	39.0	**Peru** (city) Miami County
136	39.1	**Porter** (town) Porter County
137	39.2	**Carmel** (city) Hamilton County
137	39.2	**Mitchell** (city) Lawrence County
139	39.3	**Heritage Lake** (CDP) Putnam County
139	39.3	**Jasper** (city) Dubois County
139	39.3	**Rushville** (city) Rush County
142	39.4	**Boonville** (city) Warrick County
142	39.4	**Connersville** (city) Fayette County
142	39.4	**De Motte** (town) Jasper County
142	39.4	**Gas City** (city) Grant County
142	39.4	**Portland** (city) Jay County
147	39.5	**Chesterfield** (town) Madison County
147	39.5	**New Castle** (city) Henry County
149	39.6	**Brookville** (town) Franklin County
149	39.6	**Crown Point** (city) Lake County

Note: *This section ranks incorporated places and CDPs (Census Designated Places) with populations of 2,500 or more. Unincorporated postal areas were not considered. Please refer to the User Guide for additional information.*

Population Under Age 18
Top 150 Places Ranked in *Descending* Order

State Rank	Percent	Place
1	34.7	**Ligonier** (city) Noble County
2	33.0	**Fishers** (town) Hamilton County
3	32.4	**McCordsville** (town) Hancock County
4	32.3	**Leo-Cedarville** (town) Allen County
5	31.9	**Huntertown** (town) Allen County
5	31.9	**Westfield** (city) Hamilton County
7	31.6	**Zionsville** (town) Boone County
8	31.4	**East Chicago** (city) Lake County
9	30.8	**Pittsboro** (town) Hendricks County
10	30.6	**Whitestown** (town) Boone County
11	30.2	**Avon** (town) Hendricks County
11	30.2	**Noblesville** (city) Hamilton County
13	29.8	**New Whiteland** (town) Johnson County
14	29.6	**Granger** (CDP) Saint Joseph County
15	29.4	**Carmel** (city) Hamilton County
16	29.3	**Butler** (city) DeKalb County
16	29.3	**Danville** (town) Hendricks County
16	29.3	**Sheridan** (town) Hamilton County
19	29.2	**Bargersville** (town) Johnson County
19	29.2	**Country Squire Lakes** (CDP) Jennings County
19	29.2	**Garrett** (city) DeKalb County
22	29.1	**Elkhart** (city) Elkhart County
23	29.0	**Middlebury** (town) Elkhart County
23	29.0	**Winfield** (town) Lake County
25	28.6	**Batesville** (city) Ripley County
26	28.4	**Brownsburg** (town) Hendricks County
26	28.4	**Charlestown** (city) Clark County
28	28.3	**Fortville** (town) Hancock County
28	28.3	**Union City** (city) Randolph County
30	28.2	**Frankfort** (city) Clinton County
30	28.2	**Lawrence** (city) Marion County
32	28.1	**Gary** (city) Lake County
33	27.9	**Huntingburg** (city) Dubois County
33	27.9	**Nappanee** (city) Elkhart County
33	27.9	**Plymouth** (city) Marshall County
36	27.8	**Logansport** (city) Cass County
37	27.7	**Dunlap** (CDP) Elkhart County
37	27.7	**Georgetown** (town) Floyd County
39	27.6	**Bremen** (town) Marshall County
39	27.6	**Hammond** (city) Lake County
39	27.6	**Whiteland** (town) Johnson County
42	27.4	**Centerville** (town) Wayne County
42	27.4	**Cumberland** (town) Marion County
42	27.4	**Goshen** (city) Elkhart County
42	27.4	**Hebron** (town) Porter County
42	27.4	**Kendallville** (city) Noble County
47	27.3	**Saint John** (town) Lake County
47	27.3	**South Bend** (city) Saint Joseph County
47	27.3	**South Haven** (CDP) Porter County
50	27.2	**Chandler** (town) Warrick County
51	27.0	**Lagrange** (town) LaGrange County
52	26.9	**Whiting** (city) Lake County
53	26.6	**Aurora** (city) Dearborn County
53	26.6	**Cedar Lake** (town) Lake County
53	26.6	**Greenwood** (city) Johnson County
53	26.6	**Lowell** (town) Lake County
57	26.5	**Bright** (CDP) Dearborn County
57	26.5	**Chesterton** (town) Porter County
57	26.5	**Ellettsville** (town) Monroe County
57	26.5	**North Vernon** (city) Jennings County
57	26.5	**Roselawn** (CDP) Newton County
62	26.4	**Fort Wayne** (city) Allen County
62	26.4	**Greenfield** (city) Hancock County
62	26.4	**Hidden Valley** (CDP) Dearborn County
62	26.4	**Lake Station** (city) Lake County
62	26.4	**Pendleton** (town) Madison County
67	26.3	**Franklin** (city) Johnson County
68	26.2	**New Haven** (city) Allen County
69	26.1	**Heritage Lake** (CDP) Putnam County
70	26.0	**Brazil** (city) Clay County
70	26.0	**Knox** (city) Starke County
70	26.0	**Ossian** (town) Wells County
73	25.9	**Austin** (city) Scott County
73	25.9	**Delphi** (city) Carroll County
75	25.7	**Brownstown** (town) Jackson County
75	25.7	**Portage** (city) Porter County
75	25.7	**Yorktown** (town) Delaware County
78	25.6	**Alexandria** (city) Madison County
78	25.6	**Porter** (town) Porter County
80	25.5	**Merrillville** (town) Lake County
80	25.5	**Rensselaer** (city) Jasper County
80	25.5	**Shelbyville** (city) Shelby County
80	25.5	**Washington** (city) Daviess County
84	25.4	**Mooresville** (town) Morgan County
85	25.3	**Auburn** (city) DeKalb County
85	25.3	**Seymour** (city) Jackson County
87	25.2	**Attica** (city) Fountain County
87	25.2	**Cicero** (town) Hamilton County
87	25.2	**Columbus** (city) Bartholomew County
87	25.2	**Elwood** (city) Madison County
87	25.2	**Warsaw** (city) Kosciusko County
92	25.1	**Bicknell** (city) Knox County
92	25.1	**Syracuse** (town) Kosciusko County
94	25.0	**Greensburg** (city) Decatur County
94	25.0	**Indianapolis** (city) Marion County
94	25.0	**Martinsville** (city) Morgan County
94	25.0	**Princeton** (city) Gibson County
98	24.9	**Columbia City** (city) Whitley County
98	24.9	**Jasper** (city) Dubois County
98	24.9	**Mitchell** (city) Lawrence County
101	24.8	**Huntington** (city) Huntington County
102	24.7	**Clinton** (city) Vermillion County
102	24.7	**Decatur** (city) Adams County
102	24.7	**Melody Hill** (CDP) Vanderburgh County
105	24.6	**Beech Grove** (city) Marion County
105	24.6	**Bluffton** (city) Wells County
105	24.6	**Gas City** (city) Grant County
105	24.6	**Sellersburg** (town) Clark County
109	24.5	**Edinburgh** (town) Johnson County
109	24.5	**La Porte** (city) LaPorte County
109	24.5	**Lebanon** (city) Boone County
109	24.5	**Mount Vernon** (city) Posey County
109	24.5	**Peru** (city) Miami County
109	24.5	**Plainfield** (town) Hendricks County
115	24.4	**De Motte** (town) Jasper County
115	24.4	**Fort Branch** (town) Gibson County
115	24.4	**Greendale** (city) Dearborn County
118	24.3	**Griffith** (town) Lake County
119	24.2	**Connersville** (city) Fayette County
119	24.2	**Tipton** (city) Tipton County
121	24.1	**Berne** (city) Adams County
121	24.1	**Brookville** (town) Franklin County
121	24.1	**Lawrenceburg** (city) Dearborn County
124	24.0	**Kokomo** (city) Howard County
124	24.0	**Monticello** (city) White County
124	24.0	**North Terre Haute** (CDP) Vigo County
124	24.0	**Rushville** (city) Rush County
124	24.0	**Salem** (city) Washington County
129	23.9	**Fairmount** (town) Grant County
130	23.8	**Highland** (CDP) Vanderburgh County
130	23.8	**Lafayette** (city) Tippecanoe County
130	23.8	**Paoli** (town) Orange County
130	23.8	**Sullivan** (city) Sullivan County
134	23.7	**Portland** (city) Jay County
134	23.7	**Shorewood Forest** (CDP) Porter County
134	23.7	**Winona Lake** (town) Kosciusko County
137	23.6	**Winchester** (city) Randolph County
138	23.5	**Michigan City** (city) LaPorte County
138	23.5	**Simonton Lake** (CDP) Elkhart County
140	23.4	**Linton** (city) Greene County
140	23.4	**Loogootee** (city) Martin County
140	23.4	**Munster** (town) Lake County
140	23.4	**New Castle** (city) Henry County
144	23.3	**Boonville** (city) Warrick County
144	23.3	**Lakes of the Four Seasons** (CDP) Lake County
144	23.3	**Scottsburg** (city) Scott County
147	23.2	**Jeffersonville** (city) Clark County
148	23.1	**Dyer** (town) Lake County
148	23.1	**Hartford City** (city) Blackford County
148	23.1	**Hobart** (city) Lake County

Note: This section ranks incorporated places and CDPs (Census Designated Places) with populations of 2,500 or more. Unincorporated postal areas were not considered. Please refer to the User Guide for additional information.

Population Under Age 18
Top 150 Places Ranked in *Ascending* Order

State Rank	Percent	Place
1	0.6	**Notre Dame** (CDP) Saint Joseph County
2	2.8	**Purdue University** (CDP) Tippecanoe County
3	11.4	**Bloomington** (city) Monroe County
4	11.8	**West Lafayette** (city) Tippecanoe County
5	12.0	**Westville** (town) LaPorte County
6	14.1	**Upland** (town) Grant County
7	14.8	**Grissom AFB** (CDP) Miami County
8	17.8	**Muncie** (city) Delaware County
9	18.1	**North Manchester** (town) Wabash County
10	18.6	**Hanover** (town) Jefferson County
11	19.0	**Greencastle** (city) Putnam County
12	19.2	**Vincennes** (city) Knox County
13	20.0	**Terre Haute** (city) Vigo County
14	20.5	**Corydon** (town) Harrison County
15	20.9	**Highland** (town) Lake County
15	20.9	**Rockville** (town) Parke County
17	21.0	**Madison** (city) Jefferson County
18	21.1	**Marion** (city) Grant County
19	21.2	**Crown Point** (city) Lake County
20	21.3	**Valparaiso** (city) Porter County
21	21.7	**Speedway** (town) Marion County
22	22.0	**Tell City** (city) Perry County
23	22.1	**Angola** (city) Steuben County
23	22.1	**Evansville** (city) Vanderburgh County
23	22.1	**Richmond** (city) Wayne County
23	22.1	**Schererville** (town) Lake County
27	22.3	**Bedford** (city) Lawrence County
27	22.3	**Crawfordsville** (city) Montgomery County
29	22.4	**Anderson** (city) Madison County
29	22.4	**Covington** (city) Fountain County
29	22.4	**Newburgh** (town) Warrick County
32	22.5	**Rochester** (city) Fulton County
32	22.5	**Wabash** (city) Wabash County
34	22.8	**Chesterfield** (town) Madison County
35	22.9	**Clarksville** (town) Clark County
35	22.9	**New Albany** (city) Floyd County
37	23.1	**Dyer** (town) Lake County
37	23.1	**Hartford City** (city) Blackford County
37	23.1	**Hobart** (city) Lake County
37	23.1	**Mishawaka** (city) Saint Joseph County
37	23.1	**Smithville-Sanders** (CDP) Monroe County
42	23.2	**Jeffersonville** (city) Clark County
43	23.3	**Boonville** (city) Warrick County
43	23.3	**Lakes of the Four Seasons** (CDP) Lake County
43	23.3	**Scottsburg** (city) Scott County
46	23.4	**Linton** (city) Greene County
46	23.4	**Loogootee** (city) Martin County
46	23.4	**Munster** (town) Lake County
46	23.4	**New Castle** (city) Henry County
50	23.5	**Michigan City** (city) LaPorte County
50	23.5	**Simonton Lake** (CDP) Elkhart County
52	23.6	**Winchester** (city) Randolph County
53	23.7	**Portland** (city) Jay County
53	23.7	**Shorewood Forest** (CDP) Porter County
53	23.7	**Winona Lake** (town) Kosciusko County
56	23.8	**Highland** (CDP) Vanderburgh County
56	23.8	**Lafayette** (city) Tippecanoe County
56	23.8	**Paoli** (town) Orange County
56	23.8	**Sullivan** (city) Sullivan County
60	23.9	**Fairmount** (town) Grant County
61	24.0	**Kokomo** (city) Howard County
61	24.0	**Monticello** (city) White County
61	24.0	**North Terre Haute** (CDP) Vigo County
61	24.0	**Rushville** (city) Rush County
61	24.0	**Salem** (city) Washington County
66	24.1	**Berne** (city) Adams County
66	24.1	**Brookville** (town) Franklin County
66	24.1	**Lawrenceburg** (city) Dearborn County
69	24.2	**Connersville** (city) Fayette County
69	24.2	**Tipton** (city) Tipton County
71	24.3	**Griffith** (town) Lake County
72	24.4	**De Motte** (town) Jasper County
72	24.4	**Fort Branch** (town) Gibson County
72	24.4	**Greendale** (city) Dearborn County
75	24.5	**Edinburgh** (town) Johnson County
75	24.5	**La Porte** (city) LaPorte County
75	24.5	**Lebanon** (city) Boone County
75	24.5	**Mount Vernon** (city) Posey County
75	24.5	**Peru** (city) Miami County
75	24.5	**Plainfield** (town) Hendricks County
81	24.6	**Beech Grove** (city) Marion County
81	24.6	**Bluffton** (city) Wells County
81	24.6	**Gas City** (city) Grant County
81	24.6	**Sellersburg** (town) Clark County
85	24.7	**Clinton** (city) Vermillion County
85	24.7	**Decatur** (city) Adams County
85	24.7	**Melody Hill** (CDP) Vanderburgh County
88	24.8	**Huntington** (city) Huntington County
89	24.9	**Columbia City** (city) Whitley County
89	24.9	**Jasper** (city) Dubois County
89	24.9	**Mitchell** (city) Lawrence County
92	25.0	**Greensburg** (city) Decatur County
92	25.0	**Indianapolis** (city) Marion County
92	25.0	**Martinsville** (city) Morgan County
92	25.0	**Princeton** (city) Gibson County
96	25.1	**Bicknell** (city) Knox County
96	25.1	**Syracuse** (town) Kosciusko County
98	25.2	**Attica** (city) Fountain County
98	25.2	**Cicero** (town) Hamilton County
98	25.2	**Columbus** (city) Bartholomew County
98	25.2	**Elwood** (city) Madison County
98	25.2	**Warsaw** (city) Kosciusko County
103	25.3	**Auburn** (city) DeKalb County
103	25.3	**Seymour** (city) Jackson County
105	25.4	**Mooresville** (town) Morgan County
106	25.5	**Merrillville** (town) Lake County
106	25.5	**Rensselaer** (city) Jasper County
106	25.5	**Shelbyville** (city) Shelby County
106	25.5	**Washington** (city) Daviess County
110	25.6	**Alexandria** (city) Madison County
110	25.6	**Porter** (town) Porter County
112	25.7	**Brownstown** (town) Jackson County
112	25.7	**Portage** (city) Porter County
112	25.7	**Yorktown** (town) Delaware County
115	25.9	**Austin** (city) Scott County
115	25.9	**Delphi** (city) Carroll County
117	26.0	**Brazil** (city) Clay County
117	26.0	**Knox** (city) Starke County
117	26.0	**Ossian** (town) Wells County
120	26.1	**Heritage Lake** (CDP) Putnam County
121	26.2	**New Haven** (city) Allen County
122	26.3	**Franklin** (city) Johnson County
123	26.4	**Fort Wayne** (city) Allen County
123	26.4	**Greenfield** (city) Hancock County
123	26.4	**Hidden Valley** (CDP) Dearborn County
123	26.4	**Lake Station** (city) Lake County
123	26.4	**Pendleton** (town) Madison County
128	26.5	**Bright** (CDP) Dearborn County
128	26.5	**Chesterton** (town) Porter County
128	26.5	**Ellettsville** (town) Monroe County
128	26.5	**North Vernon** (city) Jennings County
128	26.5	**Roselawn** (CDP) Newton County
133	26.6	**Aurora** (city) Dearborn County
133	26.6	**Cedar Lake** (town) Lake County
133	26.6	**Greenwood** (city) Johnson County
133	26.6	**Lowell** (town) Lake County
137	26.9	**Whiting** (city) Lake County
138	27.0	**Lagrange** (town) LaGrange County
139	27.2	**Chandler** (town) Warrick County
140	27.3	**Saint John** (town) Lake County
140	27.3	**South Bend** (city) Saint Joseph County
140	27.3	**South Haven** (CDP) Porter County
143	27.4	**Centerville** (town) Wayne County
143	27.4	**Cumberland** (town) Marion County
143	27.4	**Goshen** (city) Elkhart County
143	27.4	**Hebron** (town) Porter County
143	27.4	**Kendallville** (city) Noble County
148	27.6	**Bremen** (town) Marshall County
148	27.6	**Hammond** (city) Lake County
148	27.6	**Whiteland** (town) Johnson County

Note: This section ranks incorporated places and CDPs (Census Designated Places) with populations of 2,500 or more. Unincorporated postal areas were not considered. Please refer to the User Guide for additional information.

Population Age 65 and Over
Top 150 Places Ranked in *Descending* Order

State Rank	Percent	Place
1	24.0	**Berne** (city) Adams County
2	23.6	**Covington** (city) Fountain County
3	23.4	**Corydon** (town) Harrison County
4	22.3	**Rockville** (town) Parke County
5	22.1	**North Manchester** (town) Wabash County
6	21.1	**Monticello** (city) White County
7	20.7	**De Motte** (town) Jasper County
8	20.2	**Brookville** (town) Franklin County
9	20.1	**Bedford** (city) Lawrence County
10	19.5	**Rochester** (city) Fulton County
11	19.3	**Tell City** (city) Perry County
12	19.2	**Linton** (city) Greene County
13	18.9	**Winchester** (city) Randolph County
14	18.8	**Wabash** (city) Wabash County
15	18.7	**Munster** (town) Lake County
16	18.6	**Brownstown** (town) Jackson County
17	18.5	**Sullivan** (city) Sullivan County
18	18.4	**Hartford City** (city) Blackford County
19	18.0	**Boonville** (city) Warrick County
19	18.0	**Delphi** (city) Carroll County
21	17.9	**Portland** (city) Jay County
22	17.8	**Lagrange** (town) LaGrange County
23	17.7	**Clinton** (city) Vermillion County
23	17.7	**Connersville** (city) Fayette County
25	17.6	**Salem** (city) Washington County
26	17.5	**Paoli** (town) Orange County
26	17.5	**Rushville** (city) Rush County
26	17.5	**Tipton** (city) Tipton County
29	17.3	**Chesterfield** (town) Madison County
29	17.3	**Highland** (town) Lake County
31	17.2	**Attica** (city) Fountain County
31	17.2	**Madison** (city) Jefferson County
33	17.1	**Loogootee** (city) Martin County
33	17.1	**Mitchell** (city) Lawrence County
35	17.0	**Yorktown** (town) Delaware County
36	16.9	**Bluffton** (city) Wells County
36	16.9	**Crawfordsville** (city) Montgomery County
38	16.8	**Mount Vernon** (city) Posey County
39	16.7	**New Castle** (city) Henry County
40	16.6	**Shorewood Forest** (CDP) Porter County
41	16.5	**Fairmount** (town) Grant County
41	16.5	**Richmond** (city) Wayne County
41	16.5	**Union City** (city) Randolph County
44	16.4	**Bicknell** (city) Knox County
44	16.4	**Rensselaer** (city) Jasper County
46	16.3	**Anderson** (city) Madison County
47	16.1	**Crown Point** (city) Lake County
47	16.1	**Princeton** (city) Gibson County
49	16.0	**Bremen** (town) Marshall County
49	16.0	**Marion** (city) Grant County
51	15.9	**Batesville** (city) Ripley County
51	15.9	**Scottsburg** (city) Scott County
51	15.9	**Washington** (city) Daviess County
54	15.8	**Kokomo** (city) Howard County
55	15.6	**Alexandria** (city) Madison County
55	15.6	**Auburn** (city) DeKalb County
55	15.6	**Greensburg** (city) Decatur County
55	15.6	**Highland** (CDP) Vanderburgh County
55	15.6	**Jasper** (city) Dubois County
55	15.6	**Peru** (city) Miami County
61	15.5	**Dyer** (town) Lake County
62	15.4	**Gas City** (city) Grant County
63	15.3	**Columbia City** (city) Whitley County
63	15.3	**Greendale** (city) Dearborn County
63	15.3	**La Porte** (city) LaPorte County
66	15.2	**Clarksville** (town) Clark County
66	15.2	**Ossian** (town) Wells County
66	15.2	**Plymouth** (city) Marshall County
69	15.0	**Pendleton** (town) Madison County
69	15.0	**Vincennes** (city) Knox County
71	14.9	**Beech Grove** (city) Marion County
71	14.9	**Goshen** (city) Elkhart County
73	14.8	**Speedway** (town) Marion County
74	14.7	**Lawrenceburg** (city) Dearborn County
74	14.7	**Lebanon** (city) Boone County
74	14.7	**Sellersburg** (town) Clark County
77	14.6	**Decatur** (city) Adams County
77	14.6	**Franklin** (city) Johnson County
77	14.6	**Melody Hill** (CDP) Vanderburgh County
80	14.5	**Gary** (city) Lake County
80	14.5	**Lakes of the Four Seasons** (CDP) Lake County
80	14.5	**Martinsville** (city) Morgan County
80	14.5	**North Terre Haute** (CDP) Vigo County
84	14.4	**Brazil** (city) Clay County
84	14.4	**Columbus** (city) Bartholomew County
84	14.4	**Evansville** (city) Vanderburgh County
84	14.4	**Fort Branch** (town) Gibson County
84	14.4	**Hobart** (city) Lake County
84	14.4	**Newburgh** (town) Warrick County
84	14.4	**Simonton Lake** (CDP) Elkhart County
91	14.3	**Mooresville** (town) Morgan County
92	14.2	**Greencastle** (city) Putnam County
93	14.1	**Elwood** (city) Madison County
93	14.1	**North Vernon** (city) Jennings County
95	14.0	**Greenfield** (city) Hancock County
95	14.0	**Schererville** (town) Lake County
97	13.9	**Logansport** (city) Cass County
97	13.9	**New Albany** (city) Floyd County
97	13.9	**New Haven** (city) Allen County
100	13.8	**Frankfort** (city) Clinton County
101	13.7	**Merrillville** (town) Lake County
102	13.6	**Mishawaka** (city) Saint Joseph County
103	13.5	**Centerville** (town) Wayne County
103	13.5	**Huntingburg** (city) Dubois County
103	13.5	**Huntington** (city) Huntington County
103	13.5	**Knox** (city) Starke County
103	13.5	**Michigan City** (city) LaPorte County
103	13.5	**Middlebury** (town) Elkhart County
109	13.4	**Seymour** (city) Jackson County
109	13.4	**Warsaw** (city) Kosciusko County
111	13.1	**Syracuse** (town) Kosciusko County
111	13.1	**Valparaiso** (city) Porter County
113	13.0	**Angola** (city) Steuben County
113	13.0	**Dunlap** (CDP) Elkhart County
113	13.0	**Muncie** (city) Delaware County
113	13.0	**Shelbyville** (city) Shelby County
113	13.0	**Winfield** (town) Lake County
118	12.9	**Aurora** (city) Dearborn County
118	12.9	**Kendallville** (city) Noble County
120	12.7	**Winona Lake** (town) Kosciusko County
121	12.6	**Roselawn** (CDP) Newton County
121	12.6	**Terre Haute** (city) Vigo County
123	12.5	**Nappanee** (city) Elkhart County
123	12.5	**South Bend** (city) Saint Joseph County
125	12.3	**Austin** (city) Scott County
126	12.1	**Ellettsville** (town) Monroe County
126	12.1	**Heritage Lake** (CDP) Putnam County
126	12.1	**Portage** (city) Porter County
129	12.0	**Brownsburg** (town) Hendricks County
129	12.0	**Edinburgh** (town) Johnson County
129	12.0	**Fort Wayne** (city) Allen County
129	12.0	**Hanover** (town) Jefferson County
133	11.9	**Butler** (city) DeKalb County
133	11.9	**Jeffersonville** (city) Clark County
135	11.7	**Lowell** (town) Lake County
136	11.6	**Chandler** (town) Warrick County
136	11.6	**Cicero** (town) Hamilton County
136	11.6	**Danville** (town) Hendricks County
136	11.6	**Fortville** (town) Hancock County
136	11.6	**Greenwood** (city) Johnson County
136	11.6	**Whiting** (city) Lake County
142	11.5	**Cumberland** (town) Marion County
142	11.5	**Elkhart** (city) Elkhart County
142	11.5	**Smithville-Sanders** (CDP) Monroe County
145	11.3	**Bright** (CDP) Dearborn County
145	11.3	**Chesterton** (town) Porter County
145	11.3	**East Chicago** (city) Lake County
145	11.3	**Lafayette** (city) Tippecanoe County
145	11.3	**Plainfield** (town) Hendricks County
145	11.3	**Saint John** (town) Lake County

Note: *This section ranks incorporated places and CDPs (Census Designated Places) with populations of 2,500 or more. Unincorporated postal areas were not considered. Please refer to the User Guide for additional information.*

Population Age 65 and Over
Top 150 Places Ranked in *Ascending* Order

State Rank	Percent	Place
1	0.0	**Purdue University** (CDP) Tippecanoe County
2	2.3	**Notre Dame** (CDP) Saint Joseph County
3	4.3	**Grissom AFB** (CDP) Miami County
3	4.3	**Whitestown** (town) Boone County
5	5.0	**McCordsville** (town) Hancock County
6	5.5	**Fishers** (town) Hamilton County
6	5.5	**Westville** (town) LaPorte County
8	6.4	**Huntertown** (town) Allen County
9	6.8	**Westfield** (city) Hamilton County
10	7.7	**Bargersville** (town) Johnson County
11	7.9	**Bloomington** (city) Monroe County
12	8.0	**Avon** (town) Hendricks County
12	8.0	**Ligonier** (city) Noble County
14	8.5	**Whiteland** (town) Johnson County
15	8.6	**Cedar Lake** (town) Lake County
16	8.7	**Noblesville** (city) Hamilton County
16	8.7	**West Lafayette** (city) Tippecanoe County
18	9.0	**Georgetown** (town) Floyd County
19	9.4	**Leo-Cedarville** (town) Allen County
20	9.5	**Upland** (town) Grant County
21	9.6	**Lawrence** (city) Marion County
22	10.4	**Carmel** (city) Hamilton County
22	10.4	**New Whiteland** (town) Johnson County
24	10.5	**Indianapolis** (city) Marion County
25	10.7	**Hammond** (city) Lake County
25	10.7	**Hebron** (town) Porter County
25	10.7	**Lake Station** (city) Lake County
25	10.7	**Porter** (town) Porter County
25	10.7	**South Haven** (CDP) Porter County
30	10.9	**Granger** (CDP) Saint Joseph County
30	10.9	**Pittsboro** (town) Hendricks County
30	10.9	**Zionsville** (town) Boone County
33	11.0	**Sheridan** (town) Hamilton County
34	11.2	**Charlestown** (city) Clark County
34	11.2	**Country Squire Lakes** (CDP) Jennings County
34	11.2	**Garrett** (city) DeKalb County
34	11.2	**Griffith** (town) Lake County
34	11.2	**Hidden Valley** (CDP) Dearborn County
39	11.3	**Bright** (CDP) Dearborn County
39	11.3	**Chesterton** (town) Porter County
39	11.3	**East Chicago** (city) Lake County
39	11.3	**Lafayette** (city) Tippecanoe County
39	11.3	**Plainfield** (town) Hendricks County
39	11.3	**Saint John** (town) Lake County
45	11.5	**Cumberland** (town) Marion County
45	11.5	**Elkhart** (city) Elkhart County
45	11.5	**Smithville-Sanders** (CDP) Monroe County
48	11.6	**Chandler** (town) Warrick County
48	11.6	**Cicero** (town) Hamilton County
48	11.6	**Danville** (town) Hendricks County
48	11.6	**Fortville** (town) Hancock County
48	11.6	**Greenwood** (city) Johnson County
48	11.6	**Whiting** (city) Lake County
54	11.7	**Lowell** (town) Lake County
55	11.9	**Butler** (city) DeKalb County
55	11.9	**Jeffersonville** (city) Clark County
57	12.0	**Brownsburg** (town) Hendricks County
57	12.0	**Edinburgh** (town) Johnson County
57	12.0	**Fort Wayne** (city) Allen County
57	12.0	**Hanover** (town) Jefferson County
61	12.1	**Ellettsville** (town) Monroe County
61	12.1	**Heritage Lake** (CDP) Putnam County
61	12.1	**Portage** (city) Porter County
64	12.3	**Austin** (city) Scott County
65	12.5	**Nappanee** (city) Elkhart County
65	12.5	**South Bend** (city) Saint Joseph County
67	12.6	**Roselawn** (CDP) Newton County
67	12.6	**Terre Haute** (city) Vigo County
69	12.7	**Winona Lake** (town) Kosciusko County
70	12.9	**Aurora** (city) Dearborn County
70	12.9	**Kendallville** (city) Noble County
72	13.0	**Angola** (city) Steuben County
72	13.0	**Dunlap** (CDP) Elkhart County
72	13.0	**Muncie** (city) Delaware County
72	13.0	**Shelbyville** (city) Shelby County
72	13.0	**Winfield** (town) Lake County
77	13.1	**Syracuse** (town) Kosciusko County
77	13.1	**Valparaiso** (city) Porter County
79	13.4	**Seymour** (city) Jackson County
79	13.4	**Warsaw** (city) Kosciusko County
81	13.5	**Centerville** (town) Wayne County
81	13.5	**Huntingburg** (city) Dubois County
81	13.5	**Huntington** (city) Huntington County
81	13.5	**Knox** (city) Starke County
81	13.5	**Michigan City** (city) LaPorte County
81	13.5	**Middlebury** (town) Elkhart County
87	13.6	**Mishawaka** (city) Saint Joseph County
88	13.7	**Merrillville** (town) Lake County
89	13.8	**Frankfort** (city) Clinton County
90	13.9	**Logansport** (city) Cass County
90	13.9	**New Albany** (city) Floyd County
90	13.9	**New Haven** (city) Allen County
93	14.0	**Greenfield** (city) Hancock County
93	14.0	**Schererville** (town) Lake County
95	14.1	**Elwood** (city) Madison County
95	14.1	**North Vernon** (city) Jennings County
97	14.2	**Greencastle** (city) Putnam County
98	14.3	**Mooresville** (town) Morgan County
99	14.4	**Brazil** (city) Clay County
99	14.4	**Columbus** (city) Bartholomew County
99	14.4	**Evansville** (city) Vanderburgh County
99	14.4	**Fort Branch** (town) Gibson County
99	14.4	**Hobart** (city) Lake County
99	14.4	**Newburgh** (town) Warrick County
99	14.4	**Simonton Lake** (CDP) Elkhart County
106	14.5	**Gary** (city) Lake County
106	14.5	**Lakes of the Four Seasons** (CDP) Lake County
106	14.5	**Martinsville** (city) Morgan County
106	14.5	**North Terre Haute** (CDP) Vigo County
110	14.6	**Decatur** (city) Adams County
110	14.6	**Franklin** (city) Johnson County
110	14.6	**Melody Hill** (CDP) Vanderburgh County
113	14.7	**Lawrenceburg** (city) Dearborn County
113	14.7	**Lebanon** (city) Boone County
113	14.7	**Sellersburg** (town) Clark County
116	14.8	**Speedway** (town) Marion County
117	14.9	**Beech Grove** (city) Marion County
117	14.9	**Goshen** (city) Elkhart County
119	15.0	**Pendleton** (town) Madison County
119	15.0	**Vincennes** (city) Knox County
121	15.2	**Clarksville** (town) Clark County
121	15.2	**Ossian** (town) Wells County
121	15.2	**Plymouth** (city) Marshall County
124	15.3	**Columbia City** (city) Whitley County
124	15.3	**Greendale** (city) Dearborn County
124	15.3	**La Porte** (city) LaPorte County
127	15.4	**Gas City** (city) Grant County
128	15.5	**Dyer** (town) Lake County
129	15.6	**Alexandria** (city) Madison County
129	15.6	**Auburn** (city) DeKalb County
129	15.6	**Greensburg** (city) Decatur County
129	15.6	**Highland** (CDP) Vanderburgh County
129	15.6	**Jasper** (city) Dubois County
129	15.6	**Peru** (city) Miami County
135	15.8	**Kokomo** (city) Howard County
136	15.9	**Batesville** (city) Ripley County
136	15.9	**Scottsburg** (city) Scott County
136	15.9	**Washington** (city) Daviess County
139	16.0	**Bremen** (town) Marshall County
139	16.0	**Marion** (city) Grant County
141	16.1	**Crown Point** (city) Lake County
141	16.1	**Princeton** (city) Gibson County
143	16.3	**Anderson** (city) Madison County
144	16.4	**Bicknell** (city) Knox County
144	16.4	**Rensselaer** (city) Jasper County
146	16.5	**Fairmount** (town) Grant County
146	16.5	**Richmond** (city) Wayne County
146	16.5	**Union City** (city) Randolph County
149	16.6	**Shorewood Forest** (CDP) Porter County
150	16.7	**New Castle** (city) Henry County

Note: This section ranks incorporated places and CDPs (Census Designated Places) with populations of 2,500 or more. Unincorporated postal areas were not considered. Please refer to the User Guide for additional information.

Males per 100 Females
Top 150 Places Ranked in *Descending* Order

State Rank	Ratio	Place
1	338.1	**Grissom AFB** (CDP) Miami County
2	333.2	**Westville** (town) LaPorte County
3	131.0	**Purdue University** (CDP) Tippecanoe County
4	118.3	**West Lafayette** (city) Tippecanoe County
5	111.7	**Plainfield** (town) Hendricks County
6	111.5	**Notre Dame** (CDP) Saint Joseph County
7	106.8	**Terre Haute** (city) Vigo County
8	105.8	**Michigan City** (city) LaPorte County
9	104.8	**Bargersville** (town) Johnson County
10	102.9	**Roselawn** (CDP) Newton County
11	102.8	**Cedar Lake** (town) Lake County
12	102.7	**Heritage Lake** (CDP) Putnam County
13	102.4	**Angola** (city) Steuben County
14	102.3	**Country Squire Lakes** (CDP) Jennings County
15	101.9	**Whitestown** (town) Boone County
16	101.6	**Smithville-Sanders** (CDP) Monroe County
17	101.4	**Hidden Valley** (CDP) Dearborn County
17	101.4	**Syracuse** (town) Kosciusko County
19	101.1	**Bloomington** (city) Monroe County
19	101.1	**Vincennes** (city) Knox County
21	100.4	**Crawfordsville** (city) Montgomery County
22	100.2	**Sheridan** (town) Hamilton County
23	100.0	**Crown Point** (city) Lake County
24	99.9	**Lake Station** (city) Lake County
25	99.6	**Edinburgh** (town) Johnson County
25	99.6	**Saint John** (town) Lake County
27	99.4	**Butler** (city) DeKalb County
27	99.4	**Fort Branch** (town) Gibson County
27	99.4	**Leo-Cedarville** (town) Allen County
30	99.1	**Ligonier** (city) Noble County
31	98.3	**Bright** (CDP) Dearborn County
32	98.2	**Granger** (CDP) Saint Joseph County
33	98.1	**Porter** (town) Porter County
34	97.4	**Aurora** (city) Dearborn County
35	97.2	**Logansport** (city) Cass County
36	97.1	**Dunlap** (CDP) Elkhart County
36	97.1	**Frankfort** (city) Clinton County
38	97.0	**Cicero** (town) Hamilton County
39	96.9	**Lowell** (town) Lake County
39	96.9	**North Terre Haute** (CDP) Vigo County
41	96.7	**Huntertown** (town) Allen County
41	96.7	**Jasper** (city) Dubois County
41	96.7	**Simonton Lake** (CDP) Elkhart County
44	96.6	**Whiting** (city) Lake County
45	96.4	**Warsaw** (city) Kosciusko County
45	96.4	**Whiteland** (town) Johnson County
47	96.3	**Lawrenceburg** (city) Dearborn County
47	96.3	**South Haven** (CDP) Porter County
49	96.2	**Hammond** (city) Lake County
50	96.0	**Lakes of the Four Seasons** (CDP) Lake County
51	95.9	**Highland** (CDP) Vanderburgh County
52	95.8	**Melody Hill** (CDP) Vanderburgh County
53	95.7	**Attica** (city) Fountain County
53	95.7	**Westfield** (city) Hamilton County
55	95.5	**Goshen** (city) Elkhart County
55	95.5	**Nappanee** (city) Elkhart County
57	95.4	**Jeffersonville** (city) Clark County
58	95.2	**Chandler** (town) Warrick County
58	95.2	**Shelbyville** (city) Shelby County
60	95.1	**Carmel** (city) Hamilton County
60	95.1	**Seymour** (city) Jackson County
62	95.0	**Winfield** (town) Lake County
63	94.9	**Bicknell** (city) Knox County
63	94.9	**Elwood** (city) Madison County
63	94.9	**Lafayette** (city) Tippecanoe County
63	94.9	**Zionsville** (town) Boone County
67	94.8	**Chesterton** (town) Porter County
68	94.7	**Austin** (city) Scott County
68	94.7	**Shorewood Forest** (CDP) Porter County
68	94.7	**Union City** (city) Randolph County
68	94.7	**Valparaiso** (city) Porter County
72	94.6	**Middlebury** (town) Elkhart County
72	94.6	**New Whiteland** (town) Johnson County
74	94.5	**Fishers** (town) Hamilton County
74	94.5	**Fortville** (town) Hancock County
76	94.4	**Martinsville** (city) Morgan County
76	94.4	**Sellersburg** (town) Clark County
78	94.3	**Chesterfield** (town) Madison County
78	94.3	**Fairmount** (town) Grant County
80	94.2	**Hobart** (city) Lake County
80	94.2	**Schererville** (town) Lake County
82	94.1	**Danville** (town) Hendricks County
83	93.9	**Columbus** (city) Bartholomew County
83	93.9	**Greenwood** (city) Johnson County
83	93.9	**Pittsboro** (town) Hendricks County
83	93.9	**South Bend** (city) Saint Joseph County
87	93.8	**Decatur** (city) Adams County
87	93.8	**Dyer** (town) Lake County
87	93.8	**Fort Wayne** (city) Allen County
87	93.8	**McCordsville** (town) Hancock County
87	93.8	**Noblesville** (city) Hamilton County
92	93.7	**Portage** (city) Porter County
93	93.6	**Speedway** (town) Marion County
94	93.5	**Hebron** (town) Porter County
94	93.5	**Indianapolis** (city) Marion County
96	93.4	**Avon** (town) Hendricks County
96	93.4	**Georgetown** (town) Floyd County
98	93.3	**Paoli** (town) Orange County
99	93.2	**La Porte** (city) LaPorte County
100	93.1	**Brownstown** (town) Jackson County
101	93.0	**Elkhart** (city) Elkhart County
101	93.0	**Gas City** (city) Grant County
101	93.0	**Kendallville** (city) Noble County
104	92.9	**Newburgh** (town) Warrick County
104	92.9	**Washington** (city) Daviess County
106	92.8	**Auburn** (city) DeKalb County
107	92.7	**Evansville** (city) Vanderburgh County
107	92.7	**Greenfield** (city) Hancock County
107	92.7	**New Haven** (city) Allen County
110	92.6	**Cumberland** (town) Marion County
111	92.5	**Munster** (town) Lake County
112	92.4	**Clarksville** (town) Clark County
113	92.3	**Bluffton** (city) Wells County
113	92.3	**Brazil** (city) Clay County
113	92.3	**Highland** (town) Lake County
116	92.2	**Brownsburg** (town) Hendricks County
116	92.2	**Lebanon** (city) Boone County
116	92.2	**Rensselaer** (city) Jasper County
119	92.1	**Garrett** (city) DeKalb County
120	91.9	**Anderson** (city) Madison County
120	91.9	**Greensburg** (city) Decatur County
120	91.9	**Plymouth** (city) Marshall County
120	91.9	**Rochester** (city) Fulton County
124	91.8	**Delphi** (city) Carroll County
124	91.8	**Richmond** (city) Wayne County
126	91.7	**North Vernon** (city) Jennings County
127	91.6	**Alexandria** (city) Madison County
127	91.6	**Greendale** (city) Dearborn County
129	91.5	**Bremen** (town) Marshall County
130	91.4	**Mount Vernon** (city) Posey County
131	91.3	**Batesville** (city) Ripley County
131	91.3	**Franklin** (city) Johnson County
131	91.3	**Huntington** (city) Huntington County
131	91.3	**Loogootee** (city) Martin County
135	91.2	**Huntingburg** (city) Dubois County
135	91.2	**Upland** (town) Grant County
137	91.1	**Linton** (city) Greene County
137	91.1	**Princeton** (city) Gibson County
139	91.0	**Connersville** (city) Fayette County
139	91.0	**Winchester** (city) Randolph County
141	90.9	**Griffith** (town) Lake County
142	90.8	**Columbia City** (city) Whitley County
143	90.7	**Hanover** (town) Jefferson County
143	90.7	**Hartford City** (city) Blackford County
143	90.7	**Ossian** (town) Wells County
146	90.6	**Clinton** (city) Vermillion County
146	90.6	**Muncie** (city) Delaware County
148	90.5	**Charlestown** (city) Clark County
148	90.5	**Lawrence** (city) Marion County
148	90.5	**New Albany** (city) Floyd County

Note: *This section ranks incorporated places and CDPs (Census Designated Places) with populations of 2,500 or more. Unincorporated postal areas were not considered. Please refer to the User Guide for additional information.*

Males per 100 Females
Top 150 Places Ranked in *Ascending* Order

State Rank	Ratio	Place
1	81.2	**Madison** (city) Jefferson County
2	84.0	**Corydon** (town) Harrison County
3	84.6	**North Manchester** (town) Wabash County
4	85.1	**Gary** (city) Lake County
5	85.6	**Berne** (city) Adams County
6	86.2	**Knox** (city) Starke County
7	86.3	**Boonville** (city) Warrick County
7	86.3	**Sullivan** (city) Sullivan County
9	86.8	**Beech Grove** (city) Marion County
10	86.9	**Mitchell** (city) Lawrence County
10	86.9	**Salem** (city) Washington County
12	87.1	**De Motte** (town) Jasper County
13	87.3	**Winona Lake** (town) Kosciusko County
14	87.5	**Ellettsville** (town) Monroe County
14	87.5	**Greencastle** (city) Putnam County
16	87.6	**New Castle** (city) Henry County
17	87.8	**Brookville** (town) Franklin County
17	87.8	**Lagrange** (town) LaGrange County
17	87.8	**Portland** (city) Jay County
17	87.8	**Rockville** (town) Parke County
21	88.0	**Kokomo** (city) Howard County
22	88.1	**Covington** (city) Fountain County
22	88.1	**East Chicago** (city) Lake County
24	88.4	**Tipton** (city) Tipton County
25	88.6	**Merrillville** (town) Lake County
26	88.8	**Marion** (city) Grant County
27	88.9	**Mishawaka** (city) Saint Joseph County
28	89.1	**Mooresville** (town) Morgan County
29	89.2	**Wabash** (city) Wabash County
30	89.7	**Pendleton** (town) Madison County
31	89.8	**Bedford** (city) Lawrence County
32	89.9	**Monticello** (city) White County
33	90.3	**Tell City** (city) Perry County
34	90.4	**Centerville** (town) Wayne County
34	90.4	**Peru** (city) Miami County
34	90.4	**Scottsburg** (city) Scott County
37	90.5	**Charlestown** (city) Clark County
37	90.5	**Lawrence** (city) Marion County
37	90.5	**New Albany** (city) Floyd County
37	90.5	**Rushville** (city) Rush County
37	90.5	**Yorktown** (town) Delaware County
42	90.6	**Clinton** (city) Vermillion County
42	90.6	**Muncie** (city) Delaware County
44	90.7	**Hanover** (town) Jefferson County
44	90.7	**Hartford City** (city) Blackford County
44	90.7	**Ossian** (town) Wells County
47	90.8	**Columbia City** (city) Whitley County
48	90.9	**Griffith** (town) Lake County
49	91.0	**Connersville** (city) Fayette County
49	91.0	**Winchester** (city) Randolph County
51	91.1	**Linton** (city) Greene County
51	91.1	**Princeton** (city) Gibson County
53	91.2	**Huntingburg** (city) Dubois County
53	91.2	**Upland** (town) Grant County
55	91.3	**Batesville** (city) Ripley County
55	91.3	**Franklin** (city) Johnson County
55	91.3	**Huntington** (city) Huntington County
55	91.3	**Loogootee** (city) Martin County
59	91.4	**Mount Vernon** (city) Posey County
60	91.5	**Bremen** (town) Marshall County
61	91.6	**Alexandria** (city) Madison County
61	91.6	**Greendale** (city) Dearborn County
63	91.7	**North Vernon** (city) Jennings County
64	91.8	**Delphi** (city) Carroll County
64	91.8	**Richmond** (city) Wayne County
66	91.9	**Anderson** (city) Madison County
66	91.9	**Greensburg** (city) Decatur County
66	91.9	**Plymouth** (city) Marshall County
66	91.9	**Rochester** (city) Fulton County
70	92.1	**Garrett** (city) DeKalb County
71	92.2	**Brownsburg** (town) Hendricks County
71	92.2	**Lebanon** (city) Boone County
71	92.2	**Rensselaer** (city) Jasper County
74	92.3	**Bluffton** (city) Wells County
74	92.3	**Brazil** (city) Clay County
74	92.3	**Highland** (town) Lake County
77	92.4	**Clarksville** (town) Clark County
78	92.5	**Munster** (town) Lake County
79	92.6	**Cumberland** (town) Marion County
80	92.7	**Evansville** (city) Vanderburgh County
80	92.7	**Greenfield** (city) Hancock County
80	92.7	**New Haven** (city) Allen County
83	92.8	**Auburn** (city) DeKalb County
84	92.9	**Newburgh** (town) Warrick County
84	92.9	**Washington** (city) Daviess County
86	93.0	**Elkhart** (city) Elkhart County
86	93.0	**Gas City** (city) Grant County
86	93.0	**Kendallville** (city) Noble County
89	93.1	**Brownstown** (town) Jackson County
90	93.2	**La Porte** (city) LaPorte County
91	93.3	**Paoli** (town) Orange County
92	93.4	**Avon** (town) Hendricks County
92	93.4	**Georgetown** (town) Floyd County
94	93.5	**Hebron** (town) Porter County
94	93.5	**Indianapolis** (city) Marion County
96	93.6	**Speedway** (town) Marion County
97	93.7	**Portage** (city) Porter County
98	93.8	**Decatur** (city) Adams County
98	93.8	**Dyer** (town) Lake County
98	93.8	**Fort Wayne** (city) Allen County
98	93.8	**McCordsville** (town) Hancock County
98	93.8	**Noblesville** (city) Hamilton County
103	93.9	**Columbus** (city) Bartholomew County
103	93.9	**Greenwood** (city) Johnson County
103	93.9	**Pittsboro** (town) Hendricks County
103	93.9	**South Bend** (city) Saint Joseph County
107	94.1	**Danville** (town) Hendricks County
108	94.2	**Hobart** (city) Lake County
108	94.2	**Schererville** (town) Lake County
110	94.3	**Chesterfield** (town) Madison County
110	94.3	**Fairmount** (town) Grant County
112	94.4	**Martinsville** (city) Morgan County
112	94.4	**Sellersburg** (town) Clark County
114	94.5	**Fishers** (town) Hamilton County
114	94.5	**Fortville** (town) Hancock County
116	94.6	**Middlebury** (town) Elkhart County
116	94.6	**New Whiteland** (town) Johnson County
118	94.7	**Austin** (city) Scott County
118	94.7	**Shorewood Forest** (CDP) Porter County
118	94.7	**Union City** (city) Randolph County
118	94.7	**Valparaiso** (city) Porter County
122	94.8	**Chesterton** (town) Porter County
123	94.9	**Bicknell** (city) Knox County
123	94.9	**Elwood** (city) Madison County
123	94.9	**Lafayette** (city) Tippecanoe County
123	94.9	**Zionsville** (town) Boone County
127	95.0	**Winfield** (town) Lake County
128	95.1	**Carmel** (city) Hamilton County
128	95.1	**Seymour** (city) Jackson County
130	95.2	**Chandler** (town) Warrick County
130	95.2	**Shelbyville** (city) Shelby County
132	95.4	**Jeffersonville** (city) Clark County
133	95.5	**Goshen** (city) Elkhart County
133	95.5	**Nappanee** (city) Elkhart County
135	95.7	**Attica** (city) Fountain County
135	95.7	**Westfield** (city) Hamilton County
137	95.8	**Melody Hill** (CDP) Vanderburgh County
138	95.9	**Highland** (CDP) Vanderburgh County
139	96.0	**Lakes of the Four Seasons** (CDP) Lake County
140	96.2	**Hammond** (city) Lake County
141	96.3	**Lawrenceburg** (city) Dearborn County
141	96.3	**South Haven** (CDP) Porter County
143	96.4	**Warsaw** (city) Kosciusko County
143	96.4	**Whiteland** (town) Johnson County
145	96.6	**Whiting** (city) Lake County
146	96.7	**Huntertown** (town) Allen County
146	96.7	**Jasper** (city) Dubois County
146	96.7	**Simonton Lake** (CDP) Elkhart County
149	96.9	**Lowell** (town) Lake County
149	96.9	**North Terre Haute** (CDP) Vigo County

Note: This section ranks incorporated places and CDPs (Census Designated Places) with populations of 2,500 or more. Unincorporated postal areas were not considered. Please refer to the User Guide for additional information.

Marriage Status: Never Married
Top 150 Places Ranked in *Descending* Order

State Rank	Percent	Place
1	98.6	**Notre Dame** (CDP) Saint Joseph County
2	89.9	**Purdue University** (CDP) Tippecanoe County
3	65.3	**West Lafayette** (city) Tippecanoe County
4	64.2	**Bloomington** (city) Monroe County
5	56.8	**Westville** (town) LaPorte County
6	55.7	**Upland** (town) Grant County
7	48.6	**Hanover** (town) Jefferson County
8	48.2	**Muncie** (city) Delaware County
9	47.3	**East Chicago** (city) Lake County
10	46.6	**Greencastle** (city) Putnam County
11	45.1	**Gary** (city) Lake County
12	43.3	**Terre Haute** (city) Vigo County
13	39.9	**South Bend** (city) Saint Joseph County
14	39.1	**Hammond** (city) Lake County
15	38.7	**Indianapolis** (city) Marion County
16	38.1	**Angola** (city) Steuben County
17	37.9	**Michigan City** (city) LaPorte County
18	37.6	**Marion** (city) Grant County
19	37.0	**Valparaiso** (city) Porter County
20	36.8	**Vincennes** (city) Knox County
21	36.4	**Whiting** (city) Lake County
22	36.1	**Elkhart** (city) Elkhart County
23	35.8	**North Manchester** (town) Wabash County
24	35.5	**Lafayette** (city) Tippecanoe County
25	35.1	**Merrillville** (town) Lake County
26	34.6	**Speedway** (town) Marion County
27	34.0	**Evansville** (city) Vanderburgh County
27	34.0	**Mishawaka** (city) Saint Joseph County
29	33.6	**Fort Wayne** (city) Allen County
30	33.4	**Griffith** (town) Lake County
31	33.0	**Anderson** (city) Madison County
32	32.9	**Richmond** (city) Wayne County
33	32.8	**Lowell** (town) Lake County
34	32.7	**New Albany** (city) Floyd County
35	32.6	**Charlestown** (city) Clark County
36	32.4	**Ligonier** (city) Noble County
36	32.4	**Logansport** (city) Cass County
38	31.9	**Huntington** (city) Huntington County
39	31.7	**Butler** (city) DeKalb County
40	31.6	**Grissom AFB** (CDP) Miami County
40	31.6	**Lawrence** (city) Marion County
42	31.5	**Peru** (city) Miami County
43	31.2	**Cumberland** (town) Marion County
44	31.1	**Porter** (town) Porter County
45	30.9	**Beech Grove** (city) Marion County
45	30.9	**Jeffersonville** (city) Clark County
47	30.8	**Greendale** (city) Dearborn County
48	30.7	**Lake Station** (city) Lake County
49	30.5	**Aurora** (city) Dearborn County
50	30.4	**Kendallville** (city) Noble County
51	30.3	**Rockville** (town) Parke County
52	30.2	**Portage** (city) Porter County
52	30.2	**Warsaw** (city) Kosciusko County
54	30.1	**Country Squire Lakes** (CDP) Jennings County
54	30.1	**Winona Lake** (town) Kosciusko County
56	29.9	**Sullivan** (city) Sullivan County
57	29.7	**Bremen** (town) Marshall County
58	29.5	**Clarksville** (town) Clark County
58	29.5	**Shelbyville** (city) Shelby County
60	29.2	**Highland** (town) Lake County
60	29.2	**Plainfield** (town) Hendricks County
60	29.2	**Scottsburg** (city) Scott County
63	29.1	**Sheridan** (town) Hamilton County
64	28.9	**Knox** (city) Starke County
64	28.9	**Martinsville** (city) Morgan County
66	28.8	**Chesterfield** (town) Madison County
67	28.7	**Delphi** (city) Carroll County
67	28.7	**La Porte** (city) LaPorte County
69	28.6	**Austin** (city) Scott County
69	28.6	**Goshen** (city) Elkhart County
71	28.5	**Crawfordsville** (city) Montgomery County
71	28.5	**Frankfort** (city) Clinton County
73	28.4	**Crown Point** (city) Lake County
73	28.4	**Simonton Lake** (CDP) Elkhart County
75	28.3	**Cedar Lake** (town) Lake County
75	28.3	**Hobart** (city) Lake County
77	28.2	**Auburn** (city) DeKalb County
77	28.2	**Chesterton** (town) Porter County
77	28.2	**Rensselaer** (city) Jasper County
80	28.1	**McCordsville** (town) Hancock County
81	28.0	**Paoli** (town) Orange County
82	27.9	**Madison** (city) Jefferson County
82	27.9	**New Castle** (city) Henry County
82	27.9	**Princeton** (city) Gibson County
85	27.8	**Brazil** (city) Clay County
85	27.8	**Schererville** (town) Lake County
85	27.8	**South Haven** (CDP) Porter County
88	27.7	**Plymouth** (city) Marshall County
89	27.6	**Greenfield** (city) Hancock County
89	27.6	**Shorewood Forest** (CDP) Porter County
91	27.5	**Columbia City** (city) Whitley County
91	27.5	**Greensburg** (city) Decatur County
93	27.4	**Heritage Lake** (CDP) Putnam County
93	27.4	**Portland** (city) Jay County
95	27.3	**Lawrenceburg** (city) Dearborn County
95	27.3	**Roselawn** (CDP) Newton County
97	27.0	**Hebron** (town) Porter County
98	26.9	**Franklin** (city) Johnson County
99	26.8	**Dyer** (town) Lake County
99	26.8	**Wabash** (city) Wabash County
101	26.7	**Columbus** (city) Bartholomew County
101	26.7	**Mount Vernon** (city) Posey County
103	26.5	**Fortville** (town) Hancock County
104	26.4	**Greenwood** (city) Johnson County
104	26.4	**North Vernon** (city) Jennings County
106	26.2	**Brookville** (town) Franklin County
107	26.1	**Munster** (town) Lake County
108	26.0	**Kokomo** (city) Howard County
109	25.9	**Bicknell** (city) Knox County
109	25.9	**Corydon** (town) Harrison County
111	25.7	**Ellettsville** (town) Monroe County
112	25.6	**Gas City** (city) Grant County
113	25.5	**Whitestown** (town) Boone County
114	25.4	**Avon** (town) Hendricks County
115	25.3	**Jasper** (city) Dubois County
116	25.2	**Attica** (city) Fountain County
116	25.2	**Huntingburg** (city) Dubois County
116	25.2	**New Haven** (city) Allen County
116	25.2	**Salem** (city) Washington County
120	25.0	**Decatur** (city) Adams County
121	24.7	**Elwood** (city) Madison County
121	24.7	**North Terre Haute** (CDP) Vigo County
121	24.7	**Union City** (city) Randolph County
124	24.5	**Centerville** (town) Wayne County
125	24.4	**Fishers** (town) Hamilton County
125	24.4	**Ossian** (town) Wells County
125	24.4	**Pendleton** (town) Madison County
128	24.2	**Loogootee** (city) Martin County
128	24.2	**Melody Hill** (CDP) Vanderburgh County
130	24.1	**Chandler** (town) Warrick County
130	24.1	**Seymour** (city) Jackson County
132	24.0	**Berne** (city) Adams County
133	23.9	**Batesville** (city) Ripley County
133	23.9	**Bluffton** (city) Wells County
135	23.7	**Clinton** (city) Vermillion County
135	23.7	**Mooresville** (town) Morgan County
135	23.7	**Washington** (city) Daviess County
138	23.6	**Bright** (CDP) Dearborn County
138	23.6	**Hartford City** (city) Blackford County
140	23.5	**Fairmount** (town) Grant County
140	23.5	**Mitchell** (city) Lawrence County
142	23.4	**Brownstown** (town) Jackson County
142	23.4	**Connersville** (city) Fayette County
144	23.3	**Dunlap** (CDP) Elkhart County
145	23.1	**Tell City** (city) Perry County
146	22.9	**Garrett** (city) DeKalb County
146	22.9	**Winchester** (city) Randolph County
148	22.8	**Fort Branch** (town) Gibson County
149	22.7	**Noblesville** (city) Hamilton County
150	22.6	**Bedford** (city) Lawrence County

Note: This section ranks incorporated places and CDPs (Census Designated Places) with populations of 2,500 or more. Unincorporated postal areas were not considered. Please refer to the User Guide for additional information.

Marriage Status: Never Married
Top 150 Places Ranked in *Ascending* Order

State Rank	Percent	Place
1	15.6	**Bargersville** (town) Johnson County
2	16.6	**Boonville** (city) Warrick County
3	17.6	**Whiteland** (town) Johnson County
4	18.4	**Yorktown** (town) Delaware County
5	18.5	**Sellersburg** (town) Clark County
6	19.2	**Hidden Valley** (CDP) Dearborn County
6	19.2	**Zionsville** (town) Boone County
8	19.5	**Smithville-Sanders** (CDP) Monroe County
9	19.6	**Linton** (city) Greene County
10	20.5	**Cicero** (town) Hamilton County
10	20.5	**Covington** (city) Fountain County
10	20.5	**Winfield** (town) Lake County
13	20.9	**De Motte** (town) Jasper County
14	21.1	**Nappanee** (city) Elkhart County
14	21.1	**Tipton** (city) Tipton County
16	21.2	**Huntertown** (town) Allen County
17	21.3	**Highland** (CDP) Vanderburgh County
18	21.4	**Brownsburg** (town) Hendricks County
18	21.4	**Lakes of the Four Seasons** (CDP) Lake County
18	21.4	**Middlebury** (town) Elkhart County
18	21.4	**Monticello** (city) White County
22	21.5	**Granger** (CDP) Saint Joseph County
23	21.6	**Danville** (town) Hendricks County
23	21.6	**Georgetown** (town) Floyd County
23	21.6	**Newburgh** (town) Warrick County
23	21.6	**Syracuse** (town) Kosciusko County
27	21.7	**Saint John** (town) Lake County
28	21.8	**Carmel** (city) Hamilton County
29	22.0	**Edinburgh** (town) Johnson County
29	22.0	**Rushville** (city) Rush County
31	22.1	**Leo-Cedarville** (town) Allen County
32	22.2	**Alexandria** (city) Madison County
33	22.4	**Lagrange** (town) LaGrange County
33	22.4	**Westfield** (city) Hamilton County
35	22.5	**New Whiteland** (town) Johnson County
36	22.6	**Bedford** (city) Lawrence County
36	22.6	**Lebanon** (city) Boone County
36	22.6	**Pittsboro** (town) Hendricks County
36	22.6	**Rochester** (city) Fulton County
40	22.7	**Noblesville** (city) Hamilton County
41	22.8	**Fort Branch** (town) Gibson County
42	22.9	**Garrett** (city) DeKalb County
42	22.9	**Winchester** (city) Randolph County
44	23.1	**Tell City** (city) Perry County
45	23.3	**Dunlap** (CDP) Elkhart County
46	23.4	**Brownstown** (town) Jackson County
46	23.4	**Connersville** (city) Fayette County
48	23.5	**Fairmount** (town) Grant County
48	23.5	**Mitchell** (city) Lawrence County
50	23.6	**Bright** (CDP) Dearborn County
50	23.6	**Hartford City** (city) Blackford County
52	23.7	**Clinton** (city) Vermillion County
52	23.7	**Mooresville** (town) Morgan County
52	23.7	**Washington** (city) Daviess County
55	23.9	**Batesville** (city) Ripley County
55	23.9	**Bluffton** (city) Wells County
57	24.0	**Berne** (city) Adams County
58	24.1	**Chandler** (town) Warrick County
58	24.1	**Seymour** (city) Jackson County
60	24.2	**Loogootee** (city) Martin County
60	24.2	**Melody Hill** (CDP) Vanderburgh County
62	24.4	**Fishers** (town) Hamilton County
62	24.4	**Ossian** (town) Wells County
62	24.4	**Pendleton** (town) Madison County
65	24.5	**Centerville** (town) Wayne County
66	24.7	**Elwood** (city) Madison County
66	24.7	**North Terre Haute** (CDP) Vigo County
66	24.7	**Union City** (city) Randolph County
69	25.0	**Decatur** (city) Adams County
70	25.2	**Attica** (city) Fountain County
70	25.2	**Huntingburg** (city) Dubois County
70	25.2	**New Haven** (city) Allen County
70	25.2	**Salem** (city) Washington County
74	25.3	**Jasper** (city) Dubois County
75	25.4	**Avon** (town) Hendricks County
76	25.5	**Whitestown** (town) Boone County
77	25.6	**Gas City** (city) Grant County
78	25.7	**Ellettsville** (town) Monroe County
79	25.9	**Bicknell** (city) Knox County
79	25.9	**Corydon** (town) Harrison County
81	26.0	**Kokomo** (city) Howard County
82	26.1	**Munster** (town) Lake County
83	26.2	**Brookville** (town) Franklin County
84	26.4	**Greenwood** (city) Johnson County
84	26.4	**North Vernon** (city) Jennings County
86	26.5	**Fortville** (town) Hancock County
87	26.7	**Columbus** (city) Bartholomew County
87	26.7	**Mount Vernon** (city) Posey County
89	26.8	**Dyer** (town) Lake County
89	26.8	**Wabash** (city) Wabash County
91	26.9	**Franklin** (city) Johnson County
92	27.0	**Hebron** (town) Porter County
93	27.3	**Lawrenceburg** (city) Dearborn County
93	27.3	**Roselawn** (CDP) Newton County
95	27.4	**Heritage Lake** (CDP) Putnam County
95	27.4	**Portland** (city) Jay County
97	27.5	**Columbia City** (city) Whitley County
97	27.5	**Greensburg** (city) Decatur County
99	27.6	**Greenfield** (city) Hancock County
99	27.6	**Shorewood Forest** (CDP) Porter County
101	27.7	**Plymouth** (city) Marshall County
102	27.8	**Brazil** (city) Clay County
102	27.8	**Schererville** (town) Lake County
102	27.8	**South Haven** (CDP) Porter County
105	27.9	**Madison** (city) Jefferson County
105	27.9	**New Castle** (city) Henry County
105	27.9	**Princeton** (city) Gibson County
108	28.0	**Paoli** (town) Orange County
109	28.1	**McCordsville** (town) Hancock County
110	28.2	**Auburn** (city) DeKalb County
110	28.2	**Chesterton** (town) Porter County
110	28.2	**Rensselaer** (city) Jasper County
113	28.3	**Cedar Lake** (town) Lake County
113	28.3	**Hobart** (city) Lake County
115	28.4	**Crown Point** (city) Lake County
115	28.4	**Simonton Lake** (CDP) Elkhart County
117	28.5	**Crawfordsville** (city) Montgomery County
117	28.5	**Frankfort** (city) Clinton County
119	28.6	**Austin** (city) Scott County
119	28.6	**Goshen** (city) Elkhart County
121	28.7	**Delphi** (city) Carroll County
121	28.7	**La Porte** (city) LaPorte County
123	28.8	**Chesterfield** (town) Madison County
124	28.9	**Knox** (city) Starke County
124	28.9	**Martinsville** (city) Morgan County
126	29.1	**Sheridan** (town) Hamilton County
127	29.2	**Highland** (town) Lake County
127	29.2	**Plainfield** (town) Hendricks County
127	29.2	**Scottsburg** (city) Scott County
130	29.5	**Clarksville** (town) Clark County
130	29.5	**Shelbyville** (city) Shelby County
132	29.7	**Bremen** (town) Marshall County
133	29.9	**Sullivan** (city) Sullivan County
134	30.1	**Country Squire Lakes** (CDP) Jennings County
134	30.1	**Winona Lake** (town) Kosciusko County
136	30.2	**Portage** (city) Porter County
136	30.2	**Warsaw** (city) Kosciusko County
138	30.3	**Rockville** (town) Parke County
139	30.4	**Kendallville** (city) Noble County
140	30.5	**Aurora** (city) Dearborn County
141	30.7	**Lake Station** (city) Lake County
142	30.8	**Greendale** (city) Dearborn County
143	30.9	**Beech Grove** (city) Marion County
143	30.9	**Jeffersonville** (city) Clark County
145	31.1	**Porter** (town) Porter County
146	31.2	**Cumberland** (town) Marion County
147	31.5	**Peru** (city) Miami County
148	31.6	**Grissom AFB** (CDP) Miami County
148	31.6	**Lawrence** (city) Marion County
150	31.7	**Butler** (city) DeKalb County

Note: This section ranks incorporated places and CDPs (Census Designated Places) with populations of 2,500 or more. Unincorporated postal areas were not considered. Please refer to the User Guide for additional information.

Marriage Status: Now Married
Top 150 Places Ranked in *Descending* Order

State Rank	Percent	Place
1	69.0	**Hidden Valley** (CDP) Dearborn County
2	68.8	**Bargersville** (town) Johnson County
3	68.4	**Granger** (CDP) Saint Joseph County
3	68.4	**Zionsville** (town) Boone County
5	67.5	**Carmel** (city) Hamilton County
6	67.4	**Leo-Cedarville** (town) Allen County
7	67.2	**Saint John** (town) Lake County
8	66.0	**Lakes of the Four Seasons** (CDP) Lake County
9	65.7	**Westfield** (city) Hamilton County
10	64.9	**Melody Hill** (CDP) Vanderburgh County
11	64.7	**Yorktown** (town) Delaware County
12	64.5	**Dunlap** (CDP) Elkhart County
13	64.4	**Middlebury** (town) Elkhart County
14	64.3	**Nappanee** (city) Elkhart County
14	64.3	**Whitestown** (town) Boone County
16	63.8	**Boonville** (city) Warrick County
16	63.8	**Fishers** (town) Hamilton County
16	63.8	**Winfield** (town) Lake County
19	63.5	**Pittsboro** (town) Hendricks County
20	63.4	**Shorewood Forest** (CDP) Porter County
21	63.2	**Whiteland** (town) Johnson County
22	62.3	**Highland** (CDP) Vanderburgh County
23	61.7	**Huntertown** (town) Allen County
24	61.4	**Covington** (city) Fountain County
25	60.9	**Noblesville** (city) Hamilton County
26	60.7	**New Whiteland** (town) Johnson County
27	59.9	**Batesville** (city) Ripley County
28	59.8	**Heritage Lake** (CDP) Putnam County
29	59.7	**Brownsburg** (town) Hendricks County
29	59.7	**Chandler** (town) Warrick County
31	59.6	**Dyer** (town) Lake County
31	59.6	**Newburgh** (town) Warrick County
33	59.5	**De Motte** (town) Jasper County
34	58.0	**Bright** (CDP) Dearborn County
35	57.8	**Tipton** (city) Tipton County
36	57.7	**Fort Branch** (town) Gibson County
37	57.5	**Huntingburg** (city) Dubois County
38	57.4	**Avon** (town) Hendricks County
39	57.3	**Chesterton** (town) Porter County
40	57.0	**Danville** (town) Hendricks County
40	57.0	**Smithville-Sanders** (CDP) Monroe County
42	56.4	**Schererville** (town) Lake County
43	56.3	**Munster** (town) Lake County
44	56.2	**Georgetown** (town) Floyd County
44	56.2	**McCordsville** (town) Hancock County
44	56.2	**Roselawn** (CDP) Newton County
47	55.9	**Fairmount** (town) Grant County
48	55.7	**Winona Lake** (town) Kosciusko County
49	55.3	**Garrett** (city) DeKalb County
50	55.1	**Jasper** (city) Dubois County
50	55.1	**Sellersburg** (town) Clark County
52	55.0	**New Haven** (city) Allen County
52	55.0	**North Terre Haute** (CDP) Vigo County
54	54.9	**Ligonier** (city) Noble County
54	54.9	**Lowell** (town) Lake County
54	54.9	**Syracuse** (town) Kosciusko County
57	54.8	**Hebron** (town) Porter County
58	54.7	**Cicero** (town) Hamilton County
58	54.7	**Decatur** (city) Adams County
60	54.4	**Crown Point** (city) Lake County
60	54.4	**Monticello** (city) White County
62	54.2	**Cumberland** (town) Marion County
63	53.9	**Greenwood** (city) Johnson County
64	53.6	**Mooresville** (town) Morgan County
65	53.5	**Elwood** (city) Madison County
65	53.5	**Hobart** (city) Lake County
67	53.4	**Ossian** (town) Wells County
68	53.0	**South Haven** (CDP) Porter County
69	52.9	**Tell City** (city) Perry County
70	52.8	**Fortville** (town) Hancock County
70	52.8	**Hartford City** (city) Blackford County
70	52.8	**Mount Vernon** (city) Posey County
73	52.7	**Columbus** (city) Bartholomew County
74	52.6	**Edinburgh** (town) Johnson County
75	52.5	**Centerville** (town) Wayne County
76	52.3	**Goshen** (city) Elkhart County
77	52.2	**Cedar Lake** (town) Lake County
77	52.2	**Highland** (town) Lake County
79	52.1	**Seymour** (city) Jackson County
79	52.1	**Wabash** (city) Wabash County
81	52.0	**Linton** (city) Greene County
82	51.8	**Rensselaer** (city) Jasper County
83	51.7	**Berne** (city) Adams County
83	51.7	**Bluffton** (city) Wells County
85	51.6	**Auburn** (city) DeKalb County
85	51.6	**Rochester** (city) Fulton County
87	51.5	**Franklin** (city) Johnson County
88	51.3	**Austin** (city) Scott County
88	51.3	**Greendale** (city) Dearborn County
88	51.3	**Plainfield** (town) Hendricks County
88	51.3	**Rushville** (city) Rush County
92	51.2	**Sheridan** (town) Hamilton County
93	50.7	**Princeton** (city) Gibson County
94	50.3	**Gas City** (city) Grant County
94	50.3	**Lebanon** (city) Boone County
96	50.2	**Brownstown** (town) Jackson County
96	50.2	**Ellettsville** (town) Monroe County
96	50.2	**Warsaw** (city) Kosciusko County
99	49.8	**Lawrence** (city) Marion County
100	49.7	**Porter** (town) Porter County
101	49.6	**Pendleton** (town) Madison County
101	49.6	**Plymouth** (city) Marshall County
103	49.5	**Aurora** (city) Dearborn County
103	49.5	**Simonton Lake** (CDP) Elkhart County
105	49.4	**Union City** (city) Randolph County
106	49.3	**Greenfield** (city) Hancock County
106	49.3	**Kokomo** (city) Howard County
106	49.3	**La Porte** (city) LaPorte County
109	49.2	**Alexandria** (city) Madison County
109	49.2	**Bedford** (city) Lawrence County
111	48.9	**Brookville** (town) Franklin County
112	48.8	**Martinsville** (city) Morgan County
113	48.7	**Greensburg** (city) Decatur County
114	48.6	**Crawfordsville** (city) Montgomery County
114	48.6	**Portage** (city) Porter County
116	48.5	**Washington** (city) Daviess County
117	48.3	**Griffith** (town) Lake County
118	48.0	**Knox** (city) Starke County
118	48.0	**Mitchell** (city) Lawrence County
120	47.9	**Beech Grove** (city) Marion County
120	47.9	**Frankfort** (city) Clinton County
122	47.7	**Connersville** (city) Fayette County
122	47.7	**Lake Station** (city) Lake County
122	47.7	**Winchester** (city) Randolph County
125	47.6	**Bremen** (town) Marshall County
125	47.6	**Paoli** (town) Orange County
127	47.5	**Portland** (city) Jay County
128	47.4	**Jeffersonville** (city) Clark County
129	47.3	**Fort Wayne** (city) Allen County
130	47.1	**Madison** (city) Jefferson County
131	47.0	**Bicknell** (city) Knox County
132	46.8	**Whiting** (city) Lake County
133	46.7	**Chesterfield** (town) Madison County
134	46.6	**Columbia City** (city) Whitley County
134	46.6	**North Vernon** (city) Jennings County
136	46.3	**Brazil** (city) Clay County
137	45.9	**Butler** (city) DeKalb County
137	45.9	**Clarksville** (town) Clark County
139	45.8	**Huntington** (city) Huntington County
140	45.5	**Lafayette** (city) Tippecanoe County
141	45.3	**Logansport** (city) Cass County
141	45.3	**Scottsburg** (city) Scott County
143	45.1	**Lawrenceburg** (city) Dearborn County
144	44.8	**Charlestown** (city) Clark County
145	44.5	**Angola** (city) Steuben County
145	44.5	**North Manchester** (town) Wabash County
147	44.4	**Shelbyville** (city) Shelby County
147	44.4	**Sullivan** (city) Sullivan County
149	44.3	**Valparaiso** (city) Porter County
150	44.2	**Country Squire Lakes** (CDP) Jennings County

Note: This section ranks incorporated places and CDPs (Census Designated Places) with populations of 2,500 or more. Unincorporated postal areas were not considered. Please refer to the User Guide for additional information.

Marriage Status: Now Married
Top 150 Places Ranked in *Ascending* Order

State Rank	Percent	Place
1	0.5	Notre Dame (CDP) Saint Joseph County
2	9.2	Purdue University (CDP) Tippecanoe County
3	21.5	Westville (town) LaPorte County
4	24.6	Bloomington (city) Monroe County
5	26.5	West Lafayette (city) Tippecanoe County
6	30.3	Gary (city) Lake County
7	31.5	Hanover (town) Jefferson County
8	32.8	Muncie (city) Delaware County
9	33.8	East Chicago (city) Lake County
10	34.0	Upland (town) Grant County
11	35.4	Corydon (town) Harrison County
12	35.8	Terre Haute (city) Vigo County
13	36.6	Greencastle (city) Putnam County
14	37.5	Marion (city) Grant County
15	38.7	Grissom AFB (CDP) Miami County
15	38.7	Michigan City (city) LaPorte County
17	38.8	Rockville (town) Parke County
18	38.9	Lagrange (town) LaGrange County
19	40.2	South Bend (city) Saint Joseph County
20	40.9	Anderson (city) Madison County
21	41.3	Vincennes (city) Knox County
22	41.4	Attica (city) Fountain County
23	41.5	Mishawaka (city) Saint Joseph County
24	41.6	Evansville (city) Vanderburgh County
25	42.4	Indianapolis (city) Marion County
25	42.4	New Albany (city) Floyd County
27	42.9	Clinton (city) Vermillion County
28	43.1	Elkhart (city) Elkhart County
28	43.1	Speedway (town) Marion County
30	43.3	Hammond (city) Lake County
30	43.3	Peru (city) Miami County
32	43.5	Kendallville (city) Noble County
32	43.5	Loogootee (city) Martin County
34	43.6	Salem (city) Washington County
35	43.7	Richmond (city) Wayne County
36	43.8	Delphi (city) Carroll County
37	44.0	Merrillville (town) Lake County
37	44.0	New Castle (city) Henry County
39	44.2	Country Squire Lakes (CDP) Jennings County
40	44.3	Valparaiso (city) Porter County
41	44.4	Shelbyville (city) Shelby County
41	44.4	Sullivan (city) Sullivan County
43	44.5	Angola (city) Steuben County
43	44.5	North Manchester (town) Wabash County
45	44.8	Charlestown (city) Clark County
46	45.1	Lawrenceburg (city) Dearborn County
47	45.3	Logansport (city) Cass County
47	45.3	Scottsburg (city) Scott County
49	45.5	Lafayette (city) Tippecanoe County
50	45.8	Huntington (city) Huntington County
51	45.9	Butler (city) DeKalb County
51	45.9	Clarksville (town) Clark County
53	46.3	Brazil (city) Clay County
54	46.6	Columbia City (city) Whitley County
54	46.6	North Vernon (city) Jennings County
56	46.7	Chesterfield (town) Madison County
57	46.8	Whiting (city) Lake County
58	47.0	Bicknell (city) Knox County
59	47.1	Madison (city) Jefferson County
60	47.3	Fort Wayne (city) Allen County
61	47.4	Jeffersonville (city) Clark County
62	47.5	Portland (city) Jay County
63	47.6	Bremen (town) Marshall County
63	47.6	Paoli (town) Orange County
65	47.7	Connersville (city) Fayette County
65	47.7	Lake Station (city) Lake County
65	47.7	Winchester (city) Randolph County
68	47.9	Beech Grove (city) Marion County
68	47.9	Frankfort (city) Clinton County
70	48.0	Knox (city) Starke County
70	48.0	Mitchell (city) Lawrence County
72	48.3	Griffith (town) Lake County
73	48.5	Washington (city) Daviess County
74	48.6	Crawfordsville (city) Montgomery County
74	48.6	Portage (city) Porter County
76	48.7	Greensburg (city) Decatur County
77	48.8	Martinsville (city) Morgan County
78	48.9	Brookville (town) Franklin County
79	49.2	Alexandria (city) Madison County
79	49.2	Bedford (city) Lawrence County
81	49.3	Greenfield (city) Hancock County
81	49.3	Kokomo (city) Howard County
81	49.3	La Porte (city) LaPorte County
84	49.4	Union City (city) Randolph County
85	49.5	Aurora (city) Dearborn County
85	49.5	Simonton Lake (CDP) Elkhart County
87	49.6	Pendleton (town) Madison County
87	49.6	Plymouth (city) Marshall County
89	49.7	Porter (town) Porter County
90	49.8	Lawrence (city) Marion County
91	50.2	Brownstown (town) Jackson County
91	50.2	Ellettsville (town) Monroe County
91	50.2	Warsaw (city) Kosciusko County
94	50.3	Gas City (city) Grant County
94	50.3	Lebanon (city) Boone County
96	50.7	Princeton (city) Gibson County
97	51.2	Sheridan (town) Hamilton County
98	51.3	Austin (city) Scott County
98	51.3	Greendale (city) Dearborn County
98	51.3	Plainfield (town) Hendricks County
98	51.3	Rushville (city) Rush County
102	51.5	Franklin (city) Johnson County
103	51.6	Auburn (city) DeKalb County
103	51.6	Rochester (city) Fulton County
105	51.7	Berne (city) Adams County
105	51.7	Bluffton (city) Wells County
107	51.8	Rensselaer (city) Jasper County
108	52.0	Linton (city) Greene County
109	52.1	Seymour (city) Jackson County
109	52.1	Wabash (city) Wabash County
111	52.2	Cedar Lake (town) Lake County
111	52.2	Highland (town) Lake County
113	52.3	Goshen (city) Elkhart County
114	52.5	Centerville (town) Wayne County
115	52.6	Edinburgh (town) Johnson County
116	52.7	Columbus (city) Bartholomew County
117	52.8	Fortville (town) Hancock County
117	52.8	Hartford City (city) Blackford County
117	52.8	Mount Vernon (city) Posey County
120	52.9	Tell City (city) Perry County
121	53.0	South Haven (CDP) Porter County
122	53.4	Ossian (town) Wells County
123	53.5	Elwood (city) Madison County
123	53.5	Hobart (city) Lake County
125	53.6	Mooresville (town) Morgan County
126	53.9	Greenwood (city) Johnson County
127	54.2	Cumberland (town) Marion County
128	54.4	Crown Point (city) Lake County
128	54.4	Monticello (city) White County
130	54.7	Cicero (town) Hamilton County
130	54.7	Decatur (city) Adams County
132	54.8	Hebron (town) Porter County
133	54.9	Ligonier (city) Noble County
133	54.9	Lowell (town) Lake County
133	54.9	Syracuse (town) Kosciusko County
136	55.0	New Haven (city) Allen County
136	55.0	North Terre Haute (CDP) Vigo County
138	55.1	Jasper (city) Dubois County
138	55.1	Sellersburg (town) Clark County
140	55.3	Garrett (city) DeKalb County
141	55.7	Winona Lake (town) Kosciusko County
142	55.9	Fairmount (town) Grant County
143	56.2	Georgetown (town) Floyd County
143	56.2	McCordsville (town) Hancock County
143	56.2	Roselawn (CDP) Newton County
146	56.3	Munster (town) Lake County
147	56.4	Schererville (town) Lake County
148	57.0	Danville (town) Hendricks County
148	57.0	Smithville-Sanders (CDP) Monroe County
150	57.3	Chesterton (town) Porter County

Note: This section ranks incorporated places and CDPs (Census Designated Places) with populations of 2,500 or more. Unincorporated postal areas were not considered. Please refer to the User Guide for additional information.

Marriage Status: Separated
Top 150 Places Ranked in *Descending* Order

State Rank	Percent	Place
1	6.7	Austin (city) Scott County
2	4.5	Sheridan (town) Hamilton County
3	4.3	Cumberland (town) Marion County
4	4.0	Kendallville (city) Noble County
5	3.5	Aurora (city) Dearborn County
5	3.5	East Chicago (city) Lake County
7	3.4	Grissom AFB (CDP) Miami County
7	3.4	Lawrenceburg (city) Dearborn County
9	3.3	Gary (city) Lake County
10	3.2	Connersville (city) Fayette County
10	3.2	Hebron (town) Porter County
10	3.2	Martinsville (city) Morgan County
13	3.1	Butler (city) DeKalb County
14	3.0	Hammond (city) Lake County
14	3.0	Union City (city) Randolph County
14	3.0	Westville (town) LaPorte County
17	2.7	Angola (city) Steuben County
17	2.7	Plymouth (city) Marshall County
19	2.6	Edinburgh (town) Johnson County
19	2.6	Elwood (city) Madison County
19	2.6	Logansport (city) Cass County
22	2.5	Bremen (town) Marshall County
22	2.5	Indianapolis (city) Marion County
22	2.5	Michigan City (city) LaPorte County
22	2.5	New Albany (city) Floyd County
26	2.4	Elkhart (city) Elkhart County
26	2.4	Fairmount (town) Grant County
26	2.4	Georgetown (town) Floyd County
26	2.4	Greenfield (city) Hancock County
26	2.4	Huntingburg (city) Dubois County
26	2.4	Lake Station (city) Lake County
26	2.4	Richmond (city) Wayne County
26	2.4	Salem (city) Washington County
26	2.4	Shelbyville (city) Shelby County
35	2.3	Lawrence (city) Marion County
35	2.3	Rockville (town) Parke County
35	2.3	Wabash (city) Wabash County
38	2.2	Dunlap (CDP) Elkhart County
38	2.2	Frankfort (city) Clinton County
40	2.1	Merrillville (town) Lake County
40	2.1	Mitchell (city) Lawrence County
40	2.1	New Castle (city) Henry County
40	2.1	South Bend (city) Saint Joseph County
40	2.1	Speedway (town) Marion County
45	2.0	Bargersville (town) Johnson County
45	2.0	Country Squire Lakes (CDP) Jennings County
45	2.0	Crawfordsville (city) Montgomery County
45	2.0	Franklin (city) Johnson County
45	2.0	Mishawaka (city) Saint Joseph County
45	2.0	North Vernon (city) Jennings County
45	2.0	Washington (city) Daviess County
45	2.0	Whiting (city) Lake County
45	2.0	Winchester (city) Randolph County
54	1.9	Corydon (town) Harrison County
54	1.9	Goshen (city) Elkhart County
54	1.9	Marion (city) Grant County
54	1.9	Peru (city) Miami County
54	1.9	Pittsboro (town) Hendricks County
54	1.9	Plainfield (town) Hendricks County
54	1.9	Portage (city) Porter County
54	1.9	Princeton (city) Gibson County
62	1.8	Brownstown (town) Jackson County
62	1.8	Gas City (city) Grant County
62	1.8	Jeffersonville (city) Clark County
62	1.8	Ligonier (city) Noble County
62	1.8	McCordsville (town) Hancock County
62	1.8	Monticello (city) White County
62	1.8	Nappanee (city) Elkhart County
62	1.8	Terre Haute (city) Vigo County
70	1.7	Anderson (city) Madison County
70	1.7	Cedar Lake (town) Lake County
70	1.7	Charlestown (city) Clark County
70	1.7	Portland (city) Jay County
70	1.7	Rensselaer (city) Jasper County
75	1.6	Bicknell (city) Knox County
75	1.6	Clarksville (town) Clark County
75	1.6	Columbus (city) Bartholomew County
75	1.6	Crown Point (city) Lake County
75	1.6	Fort Wayne (city) Allen County
75	1.6	Garrett (city) DeKalb County
75	1.6	Greencastle (city) Putnam County
75	1.6	Heritage Lake (CDP) Putnam County
75	1.6	Lagrange (town) LaGrange County
75	1.6	Lowell (town) Lake County
75	1.6	Munster (town) Lake County
75	1.6	Paoli (town) Orange County
75	1.6	Scottsburg (city) Scott County
75	1.6	Seymour (city) Jackson County
89	1.5	Bedford (city) Lawrence County
89	1.5	Bluffton (city) Wells County
89	1.5	Chesterton (town) Porter County
89	1.5	Greensburg (city) Decatur County
89	1.5	Hanover (town) Jefferson County
89	1.5	Hobart (city) Lake County
89	1.5	Jasper (city) Dubois County
89	1.5	Kokomo (city) Howard County
89	1.5	La Porte (city) LaPorte County
89	1.5	Muncie (city) Delaware County
89	1.5	Newburgh (town) Warrick County
89	1.5	Rochester (city) Fulton County
101	1.4	Beech Grove (city) Marion County
101	1.4	Lebanon (city) Boone County
101	1.4	Whiteland (town) Johnson County
104	1.3	Brazil (city) Clay County
104	1.3	Decatur (city) Adams County
104	1.3	Huntington (city) Huntington County
104	1.3	Lafayette (city) Tippecanoe County
104	1.3	Valparaiso (city) Porter County
109	1.2	Columbia City (city) Whitley County
109	1.2	Covington (city) Fountain County
109	1.2	Mount Vernon (city) Posey County
109	1.2	New Haven (city) Allen County
109	1.2	Rushville (city) Rush County
109	1.2	South Haven (CDP) Porter County
109	1.2	Tipton (city) Tipton County
109	1.2	Vincennes (city) Knox County
109	1.2	Warsaw (city) Kosciusko County
109	1.2	Winona Lake (town) Kosciusko County
119	1.1	Bright (CDP) Dearborn County
119	1.1	Greendale (city) Dearborn County
119	1.1	Hartford City (city) Blackford County
119	1.1	Madison (city) Jefferson County
123	1.0	Alexandria (city) Madison County
123	1.0	Boonville (city) Warrick County
123	1.0	Centerville (town) Wayne County
123	1.0	Chandler (town) Warrick County
123	1.0	Evansville (city) Vanderburgh County
123	1.0	Highland (town) Lake County
123	1.0	Noblesville (city) Hamilton County
123	1.0	Pendleton (town) Madison County
131	0.9	Auburn (city) DeKalb County
131	0.9	Bloomington (city) Monroe County
131	0.9	Brookville (town) Franklin County
131	0.9	Chesterfield (town) Madison County
131	0.9	Danville (town) Hendricks County
131	0.9	De Motte (town) Jasper County
131	0.9	Fishers (town) Hamilton County
131	0.9	Greenwood (city) Johnson County
131	0.9	Knox (city) Starke County
131	0.9	Mooresville (town) Morgan County
131	0.9	Schererville (town) Lake County
131	0.9	Tell City (city) Perry County
131	0.9	Whitestown (town) Boone County
131	0.9	Yorktown (town) Delaware County
131	0.9	Zionsville (town) Boone County
146	0.8	Berne (city) Adams County
146	0.8	Dyer (town) Lake County
146	0.8	Linton (city) Greene County
146	0.8	Loogootee (city) Martin County
150	0.7	Carmel (city) Hamilton County

Note: This section ranks incorporated places and CDPs (Census Designated Places) with populations of 2,500 or more. Unincorporated postal areas were not considered. Please refer to the User Guide for additional information.

Marriage Status: Separated
Top 150 Places Ranked in *Ascending* Order

State Rank	Percent	Place
1	0.0	**Highland** (CDP) Vanderburgh County
1	0.0	**Huntertown** (town) Allen County
1	0.0	**Melody Hill** (CDP) Vanderburgh County
1	0.0	**New Whiteland** (town) Johnson County
1	0.0	**Notre Dame** (CDP) Saint Joseph County
1	0.0	**Shorewood Forest** (CDP) Porter County
7	0.2	**Attica** (city) Fountain County
7	0.2	**Syracuse** (town) Kosciusko County
9	0.3	**Avon** (town) Hendricks County
9	0.3	**Delphi** (city) Carroll County
9	0.3	**Lakes of the Four Seasons** (CDP) Lake County
9	0.3	**North Manchester** (town) Wabash County
9	0.3	**Porter** (town) Porter County
9	0.3	**Purdue University** (CDP) Tippecanoe County
15	0.4	**Batesville** (city) Ripley County
15	0.4	**Cicero** (town) Hamilton County
15	0.4	**Fortville** (town) Hancock County
15	0.4	**Leo-Cedarville** (town) Allen County
15	0.4	**Saint John** (town) Lake County
15	0.4	**Simonton Lake** (CDP) Elkhart County
21	0.5	**Ellettsville** (town) Monroe County
21	0.5	**Fort Branch** (town) Gibson County
21	0.5	**North Terre Haute** (CDP) Vigo County
21	0.5	**Roselawn** (CDP) Newton County
21	0.5	**Smithville-Sanders** (CDP) Monroe County
21	0.5	**West Lafayette** (city) Tippecanoe County
27	0.6	**Brownsburg** (town) Hendricks County
27	0.6	**Granger** (CDP) Saint Joseph County
27	0.6	**Hidden Valley** (CDP) Dearborn County
27	0.6	**Upland** (town) Grant County
27	0.6	**Winfield** (town) Lake County
32	0.7	**Carmel** (city) Hamilton County
32	0.7	**Clinton** (city) Vermillion County
32	0.7	**Griffith** (town) Lake County
32	0.7	**Middlebury** (town) Elkhart County
32	0.7	**Ossian** (town) Wells County
32	0.7	**Sellersburg** (town) Clark County
32	0.7	**Sullivan** (city) Sullivan County
32	0.7	**Westfield** (city) Hamilton County
40	0.8	**Berne** (city) Adams County
40	0.8	**Dyer** (town) Lake County
40	0.8	**Linton** (city) Greene County
40	0.8	**Loogootee** (city) Martin County
44	0.9	**Auburn** (city) DeKalb County
44	0.9	**Bloomington** (city) Monroe County
44	0.9	**Brookville** (town) Franklin County
44	0.9	**Chesterfield** (town) Madison County
44	0.9	**Danville** (town) Hendricks County
44	0.9	**De Motte** (town) Jasper County
44	0.9	**Fishers** (town) Hamilton County
44	0.9	**Greenwood** (city) Johnson County
44	0.9	**Knox** (city) Starke County
44	0.9	**Mooresville** (town) Morgan County
44	0.9	**Schererville** (town) Lake County
44	0.9	**Tell City** (city) Perry County
44	0.9	**Whitestown** (town) Boone County
44	0.9	**Yorktown** (town) Delaware County
44	0.9	**Zionsville** (town) Boone County
59	1.0	**Alexandria** (city) Madison County
59	1.0	**Boonville** (city) Warrick County
59	1.0	**Centerville** (town) Wayne County
59	1.0	**Chandler** (town) Warrick County
59	1.0	**Evansville** (city) Vanderburgh County
59	1.0	**Highland** (town) Lake County
59	1.0	**Noblesville** (city) Hamilton County
59	1.0	**Pendleton** (town) Madison County
67	1.1	**Bright** (CDP) Dearborn County
67	1.1	**Greendale** (city) Dearborn County
67	1.1	**Hartford City** (city) Blackford County
67	1.1	**Madison** (city) Jefferson County
71	1.2	**Columbia City** (city) Whitley County
71	1.2	**Covington** (city) Fountain County
71	1.2	**Mount Vernon** (city) Posey County
71	1.2	**New Haven** (city) Allen County
71	1.2	**Rushville** (city) Rush County
71	1.2	**South Haven** (CDP) Porter County
71	1.2	**Tipton** (city) Tipton County
71	1.2	**Vincennes** (city) Knox County
71	1.2	**Warsaw** (city) Kosciusko County
71	1.2	**Winona Lake** (town) Kosciusko County
81	1.3	**Brazil** (city) Clay County
81	1.3	**Decatur** (city) Adams County
81	1.3	**Huntington** (city) Huntington County
81	1.3	**Lafayette** (city) Tippecanoe County
81	1.3	**Valparaiso** (city) Porter County
86	1.4	**Beech Grove** (city) Marion County
86	1.4	**Lebanon** (city) Boone County
86	1.4	**Whiteland** (town) Johnson County
89	1.5	**Bedford** (city) Lawrence County
89	1.5	**Bluffton** (city) Wells County
89	1.5	**Chesterton** (town) Porter County
89	1.5	**Greensburg** (city) Decatur County
89	1.5	**Hanover** (town) Jefferson County
89	1.5	**Hobart** (city) Lake County
89	1.5	**Jasper** (city) Dubois County
89	1.5	**Kokomo** (city) Howard County
89	1.5	**La Porte** (city) LaPorte County
89	1.5	**Muncie** (city) Delaware County
89	1.5	**Newburgh** (town) Warrick County
89	1.5	**Rochester** (city) Fulton County
101	1.6	**Bicknell** (city) Knox County
101	1.6	**Clarksville** (town) Clark County
101	1.6	**Columbus** (city) Bartholomew County
101	1.6	**Crown Point** (city) Lake County
101	1.6	**Fort Wayne** (city) Allen County
101	1.6	**Garrett** (city) DeKalb County
101	1.6	**Greencastle** (city) Putnam County
101	1.6	**Heritage Lake** (CDP) Putnam County
101	1.6	**Lagrange** (town) LaGrange County
101	1.6	**Lowell** (town) Lake County
101	1.6	**Munster** (town) Lake County
101	1.6	**Paoli** (town) Orange County
101	1.6	**Scottsburg** (city) Scott County
101	1.6	**Seymour** (city) Jackson County
115	1.7	**Anderson** (city) Madison County
115	1.7	**Cedar Lake** (town) Lake County
115	1.7	**Charlestown** (city) Clark County
115	1.7	**Portland** (city) Jay County
115	1.7	**Rensselaer** (city) Jasper County
120	1.8	**Brownstown** (town) Jackson County
120	1.8	**Gas City** (city) Grant County
120	1.8	**Jeffersonville** (city) Clark County
120	1.8	**Ligonier** (city) Noble County
120	1.8	**McCordsville** (town) Hancock County
120	1.8	**Monticello** (city) White County
120	1.8	**Nappanee** (city) Elkhart County
120	1.8	**Terre Haute** (city) Vigo County
128	1.9	**Corydon** (town) Harrison County
128	1.9	**Goshen** (city) Elkhart County
128	1.9	**Marion** (city) Grant County
128	1.9	**Peru** (city) Miami County
128	1.9	**Pittsboro** (town) Hendricks County
128	1.9	**Plainfield** (town) Hendricks County
128	1.9	**Portage** (city) Porter County
128	1.9	**Princeton** (city) Gibson County
136	2.0	**Bargersville** (town) Johnson County
136	2.0	**Country Squire Lakes** (CDP) Jennings County
136	2.0	**Crawfordsville** (city) Montgomery County
136	2.0	**Franklin** (city) Johnson County
136	2.0	**Mishawaka** (city) Saint Joseph County
136	2.0	**North Vernon** (city) Jennings County
136	2.0	**Washington** (city) Daviess County
136	2.0	**Whiting** (city) Lake County
136	2.0	**Winchester** (city) Randolph County
145	2.1	**Merrillville** (town) Lake County
145	2.1	**Mitchell** (city) Lawrence County
145	2.1	**New Castle** (city) Henry County
145	2.1	**South Bend** (city) Saint Joseph County
145	2.1	**Speedway** (town) Marion County
150	2.2	**Dunlap** (CDP) Elkhart County

Note: This section ranks incorporated places and CDPs (Census Designated Places) with populations of 2,500 or more. Unincorporated postal areas were not considered. Please refer to the User Guide for additional information.

Marriage Status: Widowed
Top 150 Places Ranked in *Descending* Order

State Rank	Percent	Place
1	14.0	**Lagrange** (town) LaGrange County
2	13.5	**Attica** (city) Fountain County
2	13.5	**Corydon** (town) Harrison County
4	13.3	**Berne** (city) Adams County
5	12.8	**Monticello** (city) White County
5	12.8	**Winchester** (city) Randolph County
7	12.0	**Brownstown** (town) Jackson County
8	11.8	**North Manchester** (town) Wabash County
9	11.7	**Linton** (city) Greene County
9	11.7	**Salem** (city) Washington County
11	11.5	**Clinton** (city) Vermillion County
12	11.2	**Rushville** (city) Rush County
13	10.8	**Rochester** (city) Fulton County
14	10.7	**Alexandria** (city) Madison County
15	10.5	**Bedford** (city) Lawrence County
16	10.3	**Munster** (town) Lake County
16	10.3	**Portland** (city) Jay County
18	10.2	**Rensselaer** (city) Jasper County
19	10.0	**Ossian** (town) Wells County
20	9.9	**Edinburgh** (town) Johnson County
20	9.9	**Shelbyville** (city) Shelby County
22	9.8	**Boonville** (city) Warrick County
23	9.7	**Wabash** (city) Wabash County
23	9.7	**Washington** (city) Daviess County
25	9.6	**Gary** (city) Lake County
25	9.6	**Winfield** (town) Lake County
27	9.5	**Madison** (city) Jefferson County
27	9.5	**Sullivan** (city) Sullivan County
29	9.4	**Bicknell** (city) Knox County
29	9.4	**Rockville** (town) Parke County
31	9.3	**Clarksville** (town) Clark County
32	9.2	**Connersville** (city) Fayette County
33	9.1	**Brookville** (town) Franklin County
33	9.1	**Marion** (city) Grant County
35	8.9	**Knox** (city) Starke County
35	8.9	**Tell City** (city) Perry County
37	8.8	**Simonton Lake** (CDP) Elkhart County
38	8.7	**Loogootee** (city) Martin County
39	8.6	**Fairmount** (town) Grant County
40	8.5	**De Motte** (town) Jasper County
40	8.5	**Sellersburg** (town) Clark County
42	8.4	**Lebanon** (city) Boone County
42	8.4	**New Albany** (city) Floyd County
44	8.3	**Covington** (city) Fountain County
44	8.3	**Paoli** (town) Orange County
46	8.2	**Anderson** (city) Madison County
46	8.2	**Columbia City** (city) Whitley County
46	8.2	**Delphi** (city) Carroll County
46	8.2	**Frankfort** (city) Clinton County
46	8.2	**Kendallville** (city) Noble County
46	8.2	**Warsaw** (city) Kosciusko County
52	8.1	**Greensburg** (city) Decatur County
52	8.1	**Mitchell** (city) Lawrence County
52	8.1	**North Vernon** (city) Jennings County
52	8.1	**Winona Lake** (town) Kosciusko County
56	8.0	**Huntington** (city) Huntington County
56	8.0	**Vincennes** (city) Knox County
58	7.9	**Auburn** (city) DeKalb County
58	7.9	**Bluffton** (city) Wells County
58	7.9	**Crawfordsville** (city) Montgomery County
58	7.9	**Decatur** (city) Adams County
58	7.9	**Plymouth** (city) Marshall County
63	7.8	**Hanover** (town) Jefferson County
63	7.8	**Tipton** (city) Tipton County
65	7.7	**La Porte** (city) LaPorte County
65	7.7	**New Castle** (city) Henry County
67	7.6	**Huntingburg** (city) Dubois County
67	7.6	**Kokomo** (city) Howard County
67	7.6	**Pendleton** (town) Madison County
67	7.6	**Scottsburg** (city) Scott County
71	7.5	**Austin** (city) Scott County
71	7.5	**Logansport** (city) Cass County
71	7.5	**Seymour** (city) Jackson County
74	7.4	**Beech Grove** (city) Marion County
74	7.4	**East Chicago** (city) Lake County
74	7.4	**Evansville** (city) Vanderburgh County
74	7.4	**Martinsville** (city) Morgan County
74	7.4	**Syracuse** (town) Kosciusko County
79	7.3	**Cicero** (town) Hamilton County
79	7.3	**Ellettsville** (town) Monroe County
79	7.3	**Highland** (town) Lake County
79	7.3	**Michigan City** (city) LaPorte County
79	7.3	**Mishawaka** (city) Saint Joseph County
79	7.3	**Peru** (city) Miami County
79	7.3	**Speedway** (town) Marion County
79	7.3	**Whiting** (city) Lake County
87	7.2	**North Terre Haute** (CDP) Vigo County
87	7.2	**Portage** (city) Porter County
89	7.1	**Crown Point** (city) Lake County
89	7.1	**Franklin** (city) Johnson County
89	7.1	**Goshen** (city) Elkhart County
89	7.1	**Hartford City** (city) Blackford County
89	7.1	**Merrillville** (town) Lake County
89	7.1	**Richmond** (city) Wayne County
95	7.0	**Dyer** (town) Lake County
95	7.0	**Jasper** (city) Dubois County
95	7.0	**Terre Haute** (city) Vigo County
98	6.9	**Brazil** (city) Clay County
98	6.9	**Bremen** (town) Marshall County
98	6.9	**Bright** (CDP) Dearborn County
98	6.9	**Brownsburg** (town) Hendricks County
98	6.9	**Columbus** (city) Bartholomew County
98	6.9	**Smithville-Sanders** (CDP) Monroe County
98	6.9	**Yorktown** (town) Delaware County
105	6.8	**Greencastle** (city) Putnam County
105	6.8	**Hobart** (city) Lake County
105	6.8	**Lawrenceburg** (city) Dearborn County
105	6.8	**Mooresville** (town) Morgan County
109	6.7	**South Bend** (city) Saint Joseph County
109	6.7	**Valparaiso** (city) Porter County
111	6.6	**Cedar Lake** (town) Lake County
111	6.6	**Hebron** (town) Porter County
111	6.6	**Mount Vernon** (city) Posey County
111	6.6	**Princeton** (city) Gibson County
115	6.5	**Batesville** (city) Ripley County
115	6.5	**Butler** (city) DeKalb County
115	6.5	**Elwood** (city) Madison County
118	6.4	**Country Squire Lakes** (CDP) Jennings County
118	6.4	**Greendale** (city) Dearborn County
118	6.4	**Roselawn** (CDP) Newton County
121	6.3	**Chesterfield** (town) Madison County
121	6.3	**Hammond** (city) Lake County
121	6.3	**Jeffersonville** (city) Clark County
121	6.3	**Lake Station** (city) Lake County
121	6.3	**Sheridan** (town) Hamilton County
126	6.2	**Angola** (city) Steuben County
126	6.2	**Charlestown** (city) Clark County
126	6.2	**Elkhart** (city) Elkhart County
126	6.2	**Fort Branch** (town) Gibson County
126	6.2	**Schererville** (town) Lake County
126	6.2	**Union City** (city) Randolph County
132	6.1	**Aurora** (city) Dearborn County
132	6.1	**Fort Wayne** (city) Allen County
132	6.1	**Garrett** (city) DeKalb County
132	6.1	**Georgetown** (town) Floyd County
132	6.1	**Greenfield** (city) Hancock County
132	6.1	**New Haven** (city) Allen County
132	6.1	**South Haven** (CDP) Porter County
139	6.0	**Centerville** (town) Wayne County
139	6.0	**Gas City** (city) Grant County
139	6.0	**Highland** (CDP) Vanderburgh County
139	6.0	**Muncie** (city) Delaware County
143	5.9	**Greenwood** (city) Johnson County
144	5.8	**Danville** (town) Hendricks County
145	5.7	**Lafayette** (city) Tippecanoe County
146	5.5	**Indianapolis** (city) Marion County
146	5.5	**Whiteland** (town) Johnson County
148	5.4	**New Whiteland** (town) Johnson County
148	5.4	**Plainfield** (town) Hendricks County
150	5.3	**Lawrence** (city) Marion County

Note: *This section ranks incorporated places and CDPs (Census Designated Places) with populations of 2,500 or more. Unincorporated postal areas were not considered. Please refer to the User Guide for additional information.*

Marriage Status: Widowed
Top 150 Places Ranked in *Ascending* Order

State Rank	Percent	Place
1	0.0	**Purdue University** (CDP) Tippecanoe County
2	0.4	**Notre Dame** (CDP) Saint Joseph County
3	1.1	**Westville** (town) LaPorte County
4	1.4	**Whitestown** (town) Boone County
5	2.0	**McCordsville** (town) Hancock County
6	2.2	**Fishers** (town) Hamilton County
7	2.4	**Heritage Lake** (CDP) Putnam County
8	2.5	**Westfield** (city) Hamilton County
9	2.6	**Cumberland** (town) Marion County
9	2.6	**Leo-Cedarville** (town) Allen County
11	2.7	**Melody Hill** (CDP) Vanderburgh County
12	2.8	**Avon** (town) Hendricks County
13	2.9	**Shorewood Forest** (CDP) Porter County
14	3.0	**Chesterton** (town) Porter County
14	3.0	**Porter** (town) Porter County
16	3.2	**Bloomington** (city) Monroe County
17	3.3	**Upland** (town) Grant County
18	3.5	**Carmel** (city) Hamilton County
19	3.7	**Fortville** (town) Hancock County
20	3.8	**Hidden Valley** (CDP) Dearborn County
21	3.9	**Newburgh** (town) Warrick County
21	3.9	**West Lafayette** (city) Tippecanoe County
23	4.0	**Dunlap** (CDP) Elkhart County
24	4.1	**Granger** (CDP) Saint Joseph County
24	4.1	**Pittsboro** (town) Hendricks County
26	4.2	**Lakes of the Four Seasons** (CDP) Lake County
27	4.3	**Chandler** (town) Warrick County
28	4.5	**Huntertown** (town) Allen County
28	4.5	**Zionsville** (town) Boone County
30	4.6	**Grissom AFB** (CDP) Miami County
30	4.6	**Nappanee** (city) Elkhart County
32	4.7	**Bargersville** (town) Johnson County
32	4.7	**Griffith** (town) Lake County
32	4.7	**Lowell** (town) Lake County
35	4.8	**Ligonier** (city) Noble County
36	5.0	**Middlebury** (town) Elkhart County
37	5.1	**Noblesville** (city) Hamilton County
37	5.1	**Saint John** (town) Lake County
39	5.3	**Lawrence** (city) Marion County
40	5.4	**New Whiteland** (town) Johnson County
40	5.4	**Plainfield** (town) Hendricks County
42	5.5	**Indianapolis** (city) Marion County
42	5.5	**Whiteland** (town) Johnson County
44	5.7	**Lafayette** (city) Tippecanoe County
45	5.8	**Danville** (town) Hendricks County
46	5.9	**Greenwood** (city) Johnson County
47	6.0	**Centerville** (town) Wayne County
47	6.0	**Gas City** (city) Grant County
47	6.0	**Highland** (CDP) Vanderburgh County
47	6.0	**Muncie** (city) Delaware County
51	6.1	**Aurora** (city) Dearborn County
51	6.1	**Fort Wayne** (city) Allen County
51	6.1	**Garrett** (city) DeKalb County
51	6.1	**Georgetown** (town) Floyd County
51	6.1	**Greenfield** (city) Hancock County
51	6.1	**New Haven** (city) Allen County
51	6.1	**South Haven** (CDP) Porter County
58	6.2	**Angola** (city) Steuben County
58	6.2	**Charlestown** (city) Clark County
58	6.2	**Elkhart** (city) Elkhart County
58	6.2	**Fort Branch** (town) Gibson County
58	6.2	**Schererville** (town) Lake County
58	6.2	**Union City** (city) Randolph County
64	6.3	**Chesterfield** (town) Madison County
64	6.3	**Hammond** (city) Lake County
64	6.3	**Jeffersonville** (city) Clark County
64	6.3	**Lake Station** (city) Lake County
64	6.3	**Sheridan** (town) Hamilton County
69	6.4	**Country Squire Lakes** (CDP) Jennings County
69	6.4	**Greendale** (city) Dearborn County
69	6.4	**Roselawn** (CDP) Newton County
72	6.5	**Batesville** (city) Ripley County
72	6.5	**Butler** (city) DeKalb County
72	6.5	**Elwood** (city) Madison County
75	6.6	**Cedar Lake** (town) Lake County
75	6.6	**Hebron** (town) Porter County
75	6.6	**Mount Vernon** (city) Posey County
75	6.6	**Princeton** (city) Gibson County
79	6.7	**South Bend** (city) Saint Joseph County
79	6.7	**Valparaiso** (city) Porter County
81	6.8	**Greencastle** (city) Putnam County
81	6.8	**Hobart** (city) Lake County
81	6.8	**Lawrenceburg** (city) Dearborn County
81	6.8	**Mooresville** (town) Morgan County
85	6.9	**Brazil** (city) Clay County
85	6.9	**Bremen** (town) Marshall County
85	6.9	**Bright** (CDP) Dearborn County
85	6.9	**Brownsburg** (town) Hendricks County
85	6.9	**Columbus** (city) Bartholomew County
85	6.9	**Smithville-Sanders** (CDP) Monroe County
85	6.9	**Yorktown** (town) Delaware County
92	7.0	**Dyer** (town) Lake County
92	7.0	**Jasper** (city) Dubois County
92	7.0	**Terre Haute** (city) Vigo County
95	7.1	**Crown Point** (city) Lake County
95	7.1	**Franklin** (city) Johnson County
95	7.1	**Goshen** (city) Elkhart County
95	7.1	**Hartford City** (city) Blackford County
95	7.1	**Merrillville** (town) Lake County
95	7.1	**Richmond** (city) Wayne County
101	7.2	**North Terre Haute** (CDP) Vigo County
101	7.2	**Portage** (city) Porter County
103	7.3	**Cicero** (town) Hamilton County
103	7.3	**Ellettsville** (town) Monroe County
103	7.3	**Highland** (town) Lake County
103	7.3	**Michigan City** (city) LaPorte County
103	7.3	**Mishawaka** (city) Saint Joseph County
103	7.3	**Peru** (city) Miami County
103	7.3	**Speedway** (town) Marion County
103	7.3	**Whiting** (city) Lake County
111	7.4	**Beech Grove** (city) Marion County
111	7.4	**East Chicago** (city) Lake County
111	7.4	**Evansville** (city) Vanderburgh County
111	7.4	**Martinsville** (city) Morgan County
111	7.4	**Syracuse** (town) Kosciusko County
116	7.5	**Austin** (city) Scott County
116	7.5	**Logansport** (city) Cass County
116	7.5	**Seymour** (city) Jackson County
119	7.6	**Huntingburg** (city) Dubois County
119	7.6	**Kokomo** (city) Howard County
119	7.6	**Pendleton** (town) Madison County
119	7.6	**Scottsburg** (city) Scott County
123	7.7	**La Porte** (city) LaPorte County
123	7.7	**New Castle** (city) Henry County
125	7.8	**Hanover** (town) Jefferson County
125	7.8	**Tipton** (city) Tipton County
127	7.9	**Auburn** (city) DeKalb County
127	7.9	**Bluffton** (city) Wells County
127	7.9	**Crawfordsville** (city) Montgomery County
127	7.9	**Decatur** (city) Adams County
127	7.9	**Plymouth** (city) Marshall County
132	8.0	**Huntington** (city) Huntington County
132	8.0	**Vincennes** (city) Knox County
134	8.1	**Greensburg** (city) Decatur County
134	8.1	**Mitchell** (city) Lawrence County
134	8.1	**North Vernon** (city) Jennings County
134	8.1	**Winona Lake** (town) Kosciusko County
138	8.2	**Anderson** (city) Madison County
138	8.2	**Columbia City** (city) Whitley County
138	8.2	**Delphi** (city) Carroll County
138	8.2	**Frankfort** (city) Clinton County
138	8.2	**Kendallville** (city) Noble County
138	8.2	**Warsaw** (city) Kosciusko County
144	8.3	**Covington** (city) Fountain County
144	8.3	**Paoli** (town) Orange County
146	8.4	**Lebanon** (city) Boone County
146	8.4	**New Albany** (city) Floyd County
148	8.5	**De Motte** (town) Jasper County
148	8.5	**Sellersburg** (town) Clark County
150	8.6	**Fairmount** (town) Grant County

Note: This section ranks incorporated places and CDPs (Census Designated Places) with populations of 2,500 or more. Unincorporated postal areas were not considered. Please refer to the User Guide for additional information.

Marriage Status: Divorced
Top 150 Places Ranked in *Descending* Order

State Rank	Percent	Place
1	25.2	**Corydon** (town) Harrison County
1	25.2	**Grissom AFB** (CDP) Miami County
3	24.7	**Lagrange** (town) LaGrange County
4	23.6	**Loogootee** (city) Martin County
5	21.9	**Clinton** (city) Vermillion County
6	21.6	**Rockville** (town) Parke County
7	20.9	**Lawrenceburg** (city) Dearborn County
8	20.6	**Westville** (town) LaPorte County
9	20.5	**Mitchell** (city) Lawrence County
10	20.3	**New Castle** (city) Henry County
11	20.0	**Attica** (city) Fountain County
12	19.6	**Connersville** (city) Fayette County
12	19.6	**Union City** (city) Randolph County
14	19.4	**Delphi** (city) Carroll County
14	19.4	**Salem** (city) Washington County
16	19.2	**Country Squire Lakes** (CDP) Jennings County
17	18.9	**Brazil** (city) Clay County
17	18.9	**North Vernon** (city) Jennings County
19	18.7	**Lebanon** (city) Boone County
20	18.4	**Pendleton** (town) Madison County
21	18.1	**Chesterfield** (town) Madison County
21	18.1	**Gas City** (city) Grant County
21	18.1	**Washington** (city) Daviess County
24	17.9	**Alexandria** (city) Madison County
24	17.9	**Anderson** (city) Madison County
24	17.9	**Kendallville** (city) Noble County
24	17.9	**Scottsburg** (city) Scott County
28	17.8	**Peru** (city) Miami County
28	17.8	**Sellersburg** (town) Clark County
30	17.7	**Bedford** (city) Lawrence County
30	17.7	**Columbia City** (city) Whitley County
32	17.6	**Bicknell** (city) Knox County
33	17.4	**Cicero** (town) Hamilton County
34	17.2	**Mishawaka** (city) Saint Joseph County
35	17.1	**Kokomo** (city) Howard County
36	17.0	**Centerville** (town) Wayne County
36	17.0	**Evansville** (city) Vanderburgh County
36	17.0	**Greenfield** (city) Hancock County
39	16.9	**Fortville** (town) Hancock County
40	16.8	**Ellettsville** (town) Monroe County
41	16.7	**Linton** (city) Greene County
42	16.6	**Smithville-Sanders** (CDP) Monroe County
43	16.5	**New Albany** (city) Floyd County
43	16.5	**Winchester** (city) Randolph County
45	16.4	**Bluffton** (city) Wells County
45	16.4	**Charlestown** (city) Clark County
45	16.4	**Hartford City** (city) Blackford County
48	16.3	**Richmond** (city) Wayne County
49	16.2	**Michigan City** (city) LaPorte County
49	16.2	**Seymour** (city) Jackson County
49	16.2	**Shelbyville** (city) Shelby County
49	16.2	**Sullivan** (city) Sullivan County
53	16.1	**Paoli** (town) Orange County
53	16.1	**Porter** (town) Porter County
53	16.1	**Syracuse** (town) Kosciusko County
56	16.0	**Georgetown** (town) Floyd County
57	15.9	**Bremen** (town) Marshall County
57	15.9	**Mooresville** (town) Morgan County
59	15.8	**Brookville** (town) Franklin County
59	15.8	**Butler** (city) DeKalb County
59	15.8	**Marion** (city) Grant County
62	15.7	**Garrett** (city) DeKalb County
62	15.7	**Greensburg** (city) Decatur County
64	15.6	**Danville** (town) Hendricks County
64	15.6	**Rushville** (city) Rush County
66	15.4	**Edinburgh** (town) Johnson County
66	15.4	**Frankfort** (city) Clinton County
66	15.4	**Jeffersonville** (city) Clark County
66	15.4	**Madison** (city) Jefferson County
70	15.3	**Clarksville** (town) Clark County
70	15.3	**Lake Station** (city) Lake County
72	15.2	**Elwood** (city) Madison County
73	15.1	**Tell City** (city) Perry County
74	15.0	**Crawfordsville** (city) Montgomery County
74	15.0	**Gary** (city) Lake County
74	15.0	**Rochester** (city) Fulton County
74	15.0	**Speedway** (town) Marion County
78	14.9	**Martinsville** (city) Morgan County
78	14.9	**Newburgh** (town) Warrick County
78	14.9	**Princeton** (city) Gibson County
81	14.8	**Plymouth** (city) Marshall County
81	14.8	**Portland** (city) Jay County
83	14.7	**Logansport** (city) Cass County
84	14.6	**Elkhart** (city) Elkhart County
85	14.5	**Brownstown** (town) Jackson County
86	14.4	**Avon** (town) Hendricks County
86	14.4	**Franklin** (city) Johnson County
88	14.3	**Huntington** (city) Huntington County
88	14.3	**Knox** (city) Starke County
90	14.2	**La Porte** (city) LaPorte County
91	14.1	**Plainfield** (town) Hendricks County
92	14.0	**Portage** (city) Porter County
92	14.0	**Terre Haute** (city) Vigo County
94	13.9	**Aurora** (city) Dearborn County
94	13.9	**Greenwood** (city) Johnson County
94	13.9	**Mount Vernon** (city) Posey County
94	13.9	**Vincennes** (city) Knox County
98	13.8	**Columbus** (city) Bartholomew County
98	13.8	**McCordsville** (town) Hancock County
98	13.8	**Merrillville** (town) Lake County
101	13.7	**Beech Grove** (city) Marion County
101	13.7	**New Haven** (city) Allen County
101	13.7	**Whiteland** (town) Johnson County
104	13.6	**Griffith** (town) Lake County
105	13.4	**Indianapolis** (city) Marion County
105	13.4	**Sheridan** (town) Hamilton County
107	13.3	**Lawrence** (city) Marion County
107	13.3	**Simonton Lake** (CDP) Elkhart County
107	13.3	**Tipton** (city) Tipton County
110	13.2	**Fort Branch** (town) Gibson County
110	13.2	**Lafayette** (city) Tippecanoe County
112	13.1	**Muncie** (city) Delaware County
112	13.1	**North Terre Haute** (CDP) Vigo County
112	13.1	**South Bend** (city) Saint Joseph County
112	13.1	**South Haven** (CDP) Porter County
116	13.0	**Cedar Lake** (town) Lake County
117	12.9	**Fort Wayne** (city) Allen County
118	12.7	**Jasper** (city) Dubois County
119	12.6	**Austin** (city) Scott County
119	12.6	**Huntertown** (town) Allen County
121	12.3	**Auburn** (city) DeKalb County
121	12.3	**Decatur** (city) Adams County
123	12.2	**Ossian** (town) Wells County
124	12.1	**Brownsburg** (town) Hendricks County
124	12.1	**Fairmount** (town) Grant County
124	12.1	**Hanover** (town) Jefferson County
127	12.0	**Cumberland** (town) Marion County
127	12.0	**Goshen** (city) Elkhart County
129	11.9	**Valparaiso** (city) Porter County
130	11.8	**Chandler** (town) Warrick County
131	11.6	**Bright** (CDP) Dearborn County
131	11.6	**Chesterton** (town) Porter County
131	11.6	**Hebron** (town) Porter County
134	11.5	**East Chicago** (city) Lake County
134	11.5	**Hobart** (city) Lake County
134	11.5	**New Whiteland** (town) Johnson County
137	11.4	**Greendale** (city) Dearborn County
137	11.4	**Monticello** (city) White County
137	11.4	**Warsaw** (city) Kosciusko County
140	11.3	**Hammond** (city) Lake County
140	11.3	**Highland** (town) Lake County
140	11.3	**Noblesville** (city) Hamilton County
140	11.3	**Wabash** (city) Wabash County
144	11.2	**Angola** (city) Steuben County
145	11.1	**Berne** (city) Adams County
146	11.0	**De Motte** (town) Jasper County
147	10.9	**Bargersville** (town) Johnson County
148	10.4	**Heritage Lake** (CDP) Putnam County
148	10.4	**Highland** (CDP) Vanderburgh County
150	10.1	**Crown Point** (city) Lake County

Note: This section ranks incorporated places and CDPs (Census Designated Places) with populations of 2,500 or more. Unincorporated postal areas were not considered. Please refer to the User Guide for additional information.

Marriage Status: Divorced
Top 150 Places Ranked in *Ascending* Order

State Rank	Percent	Place
1	0.4	**Notre Dame** (CDP) Saint Joseph County
2	0.8	**Purdue University** (CDP) Tippecanoe County
3	4.3	**West Lafayette** (city) Tippecanoe County
4	6.0	**Saint John** (town) Lake County
5	6.1	**Granger** (CDP) Saint Joseph County
5	6.1	**Shorewood Forest** (CDP) Porter County
5	6.1	**Winfield** (town) Lake County
5	6.1	**Winona Lake** (town) Kosciusko County
9	6.5	**Dyer** (town) Lake County
10	7.0	**Upland** (town) Grant County
11	7.2	**Carmel** (city) Hamilton County
12	7.3	**Munster** (town) Lake County
13	7.6	**Lowell** (town) Lake County
14	7.9	**Leo-Cedarville** (town) Allen County
14	7.9	**Ligonier** (city) Noble County
14	7.9	**North Manchester** (town) Wabash County
14	7.9	**Zionsville** (town) Boone County
18	8.0	**Bloomington** (city) Monroe County
19	8.1	**Hidden Valley** (CDP) Dearborn County
20	8.2	**Dunlap** (CDP) Elkhart County
20	8.2	**Melody Hill** (CDP) Vanderburgh County
22	8.5	**Lakes of the Four Seasons** (CDP) Lake County
23	8.8	**Whitestown** (town) Boone County
24	9.2	**Middlebury** (town) Elkhart County
25	9.4	**Westfield** (city) Hamilton County
26	9.5	**Fishers** (town) Hamilton County
26	9.5	**Schererville** (town) Lake County
26	9.5	**Whiting** (city) Lake County
29	9.7	**Batesville** (city) Ripley County
29	9.7	**Huntingburg** (city) Dubois County
31	9.8	**Boonville** (city) Warrick County
31	9.8	**Covington** (city) Fountain County
31	9.8	**Pittsboro** (town) Hendricks County
31	9.8	**Rensselaer** (city) Jasper County
35	10.0	**Greencastle** (city) Putnam County
35	10.0	**Nappanee** (city) Elkhart County
35	10.0	**Roselawn** (CDP) Newton County
35	10.0	**Yorktown** (town) Delaware County
39	10.1	**Crown Point** (city) Lake County
40	10.4	**Heritage Lake** (CDP) Putnam County
40	10.4	**Highland** (CDP) Vanderburgh County
42	10.9	**Bargersville** (town) Johnson County
43	11.0	**De Motte** (town) Jasper County
44	11.1	**Berne** (city) Adams County
45	11.2	**Angola** (city) Steuben County
46	11.3	**Hammond** (city) Lake County
46	11.3	**Highland** (town) Lake County
46	11.3	**Noblesville** (city) Hamilton County
46	11.3	**Wabash** (city) Wabash County
50	11.4	**Greendale** (city) Dearborn County
50	11.4	**Monticello** (city) White County
50	11.4	**Warsaw** (city) Kosciusko County
53	11.5	**East Chicago** (city) Lake County
53	11.5	**Hobart** (city) Lake County
53	11.5	**New Whiteland** (town) Johnson County
56	11.6	**Bright** (CDP) Dearborn County
56	11.6	**Chesterton** (town) Porter County
56	11.6	**Hebron** (town) Porter County
59	11.8	**Chandler** (town) Warrick County
60	11.9	**Valparaiso** (city) Porter County
61	12.0	**Cumberland** (town) Marion County
61	12.0	**Goshen** (city) Elkhart County
63	12.1	**Brownsburg** (town) Hendricks County
63	12.1	**Fairmount** (town) Grant County
63	12.1	**Hanover** (town) Jefferson County
66	12.2	**Ossian** (town) Wells County
67	12.3	**Auburn** (city) DeKalb County
67	12.3	**Decatur** (city) Adams County
69	12.6	**Austin** (city) Scott County
69	12.6	**Huntertown** (town) Allen County
71	12.7	**Jasper** (city) Dubois County
72	12.9	**Fort Wayne** (city) Allen County
73	13.0	**Cedar Lake** (town) Lake County
74	13.1	**Muncie** (city) Delaware County
74	13.1	**North Terre Haute** (CDP) Vigo County
74	13.1	**South Bend** (city) Saint Joseph County
74	13.1	**South Haven** (CDP) Porter County
78	13.2	**Fort Branch** (town) Gibson County
78	13.2	**Lafayette** (city) Tippecanoe County
80	13.3	**Lawrence** (city) Marion County
80	13.3	**Simonton Lake** (CDP) Elkhart County
80	13.3	**Tipton** (city) Tipton County
83	13.4	**Indianapolis** (city) Marion County
83	13.4	**Sheridan** (town) Hamilton County
85	13.6	**Griffith** (town) Lake County
86	13.7	**Beech Grove** (city) Marion County
86	13.7	**New Haven** (city) Allen County
86	13.7	**Whiteland** (town) Johnson County
89	13.8	**Columbus** (city) Bartholomew County
89	13.8	**McCordsville** (town) Hancock County
89	13.8	**Merrillville** (town) Lake County
92	13.9	**Aurora** (city) Dearborn County
92	13.9	**Greenwood** (city) Johnson County
92	13.9	**Mount Vernon** (city) Posey County
92	13.9	**Vincennes** (city) Knox County
96	14.0	**Portage** (city) Porter County
96	14.0	**Terre Haute** (city) Vigo County
98	14.1	**Plainfield** (town) Hendricks County
99	14.2	**La Porte** (city) LaPorte County
100	14.3	**Huntington** (city) Huntington County
100	14.3	**Knox** (city) Starke County
102	14.4	**Avon** (town) Hendricks County
102	14.4	**Franklin** (city) Johnson County
104	14.5	**Brownstown** (town) Jackson County
105	14.6	**Elkhart** (city) Elkhart County
106	14.7	**Logansport** (city) Cass County
107	14.8	**Plymouth** (city) Marshall County
107	14.8	**Portland** (city) Jay County
109	14.9	**Martinsville** (city) Morgan County
109	14.9	**Newburgh** (town) Warrick County
109	14.9	**Princeton** (city) Gibson County
112	15.0	**Crawfordsville** (city) Montgomery County
112	15.0	**Gary** (city) Lake County
112	15.0	**Rochester** (city) Fulton County
112	15.0	**Speedway** (town) Marion County
116	15.1	**Tell City** (city) Perry County
117	15.2	**Elwood** (city) Madison County
118	15.3	**Clarksville** (town) Clark County
118	15.3	**Lake Station** (city) Lake County
120	15.4	**Edinburgh** (town) Johnson County
120	15.4	**Frankfort** (city) Clinton County
120	15.4	**Jeffersonville** (city) Clark County
120	15.4	**Madison** (city) Jefferson County
124	15.6	**Danville** (town) Hendricks County
124	15.6	**Rushville** (city) Rush County
126	15.7	**Garrett** (city) DeKalb County
126	15.7	**Greensburg** (city) Decatur County
128	15.8	**Brookville** (town) Franklin County
128	15.8	**Butler** (city) DeKalb County
128	15.8	**Marion** (city) Grant County
131	15.9	**Bremen** (town) Marshall County
131	15.9	**Mooresville** (town) Morgan County
133	16.0	**Georgetown** (town) Floyd County
134	16.1	**Paoli** (town) Orange County
134	16.1	**Porter** (town) Porter County
134	16.1	**Syracuse** (town) Kosciusko County
137	16.2	**Michigan City** (city) LaPorte County
137	16.2	**Seymour** (city) Jackson County
137	16.2	**Shelbyville** (city) Shelby County
137	16.2	**Sullivan** (city) Sullivan County
141	16.3	**Richmond** (city) Wayne County
142	16.4	**Bluffton** (city) Wells County
142	16.4	**Charlestown** (city) Clark County
142	16.4	**Hartford City** (city) Blackford County
145	16.5	**New Albany** (city) Floyd County
145	16.5	**Winchester** (city) Randolph County
147	16.6	**Smithville-Sanders** (CDP) Monroe County
148	16.7	**Linton** (city) Greene County
149	16.8	**Ellettsville** (town) Monroe County
150	16.9	**Fortville** (town) Hancock County

Note: This section ranks incorporated places and CDPs (Census Designated Places) with populations of 2,500 or more. Unincorporated postal areas were not considered. Please refer to the User Guide for additional information.

Foreign Born
Top 150 Places Ranked in *Descending* Order

State Rank	Percent	Place
1	31.3	**Ligonier** (city) Noble County
2	22.5	**West Lafayette** (city) Tippecanoe County
3	22.1	**Purdue University** (CDP) Tippecanoe County
4	15.8	**Goshen** (city) Elkhart County
5	15.1	**East Chicago** (city) Lake County
6	14.8	**Logansport** (city) Cass County
7	13.9	**Elkhart** (city) Elkhart County
8	13.4	**Huntingburg** (city) Dubois County
9	13.3	**Plymouth** (city) Marshall County
10	12.0	**Frankfort** (city) Clinton County
10	12.0	**Hammond** (city) Lake County
12	11.8	**Bloomington** (city) Monroe County
12	11.8	**Carmel** (city) Hamilton County
14	10.8	**Munster** (town) Lake County
15	10.6	**Seymour** (city) Jackson County
16	10.0	**Columbus** (city) Bartholomew County
17	9.6	**Schererville** (town) Lake County
18	8.9	**Speedway** (town) Marion County
19	8.7	**Indianapolis** (city) Marion County
20	8.2	**Warsaw** (city) Kosciusko County
21	8.0	**Crown Point** (city) Lake County
21	8.0	**Winfield** (town) Lake County
23	7.6	**Fishers** (town) Hamilton County
23	7.6	**Fort Wayne** (city) Allen County
23	7.6	**Whiting** (city) Lake County
26	7.5	**Lafayette** (city) Tippecanoe County
27	7.4	**Greenwood** (city) Johnson County
27	7.4	**Lawrence** (city) Marion County
27	7.4	**South Bend** (city) Saint Joseph County
30	6.9	**Avon** (town) Hendricks County
31	6.8	**Delphi** (city) Carroll County
31	6.8	**Plainfield** (town) Hendricks County
33	6.4	**Notre Dame** (CDP) Saint Joseph County
34	6.3	**Clarksville** (town) Clark County
35	6.0	**Mishawaka** (city) Saint Joseph County
36	5.9	**Dunlap** (CDP) Elkhart County
36	5.9	**Dyer** (town) Lake County
36	5.9	**La Porte** (city) LaPorte County
36	5.9	**Merrillville** (town) Lake County
40	5.8	**Granger** (CDP) Saint Joseph County
41	5.5	**Valparaiso** (city) Porter County
42	5.4	**Roselawn** (CDP) Newton County
42	5.4	**Winona Lake** (town) Kosciusko County
42	5.4	**Zionsville** (town) Boone County
45	5.3	**Washington** (city) Daviess County
46	5.1	**Highland** (town) Lake County
46	5.1	**Saint John** (town) Lake County
46	5.1	**Shorewood Forest** (CDP) Porter County
46	5.1	**Westfield** (city) Hamilton County
50	5.0	**Lakes of the Four Seasons** (CDP) Lake County
51	4.9	**Charlestown** (city) Clark County
52	4.8	**Bremen** (town) Marshall County
53	4.7	**Griffith** (town) Lake County
53	4.7	**Shelbyville** (city) Shelby County
55	4.6	**Hobart** (city) Lake County
56	4.5	**Crawfordsville** (city) Montgomery County
57	4.4	**Newburgh** (town) Warrick County
58	4.3	**Country Squire Lakes** (CDP) Jennings County
58	4.3	**Highland** (CDP) Vanderburgh County
58	4.3	**Lake Station** (city) Lake County
58	4.3	**Melody Hill** (CDP) Vanderburgh County
62	4.2	**Jasper** (city) Dubois County
63	4.1	**Greencastle** (city) Putnam County
63	4.1	**Noblesville** (city) Hamilton County
65	4.0	**Portage** (city) Porter County
66	3.9	**Lagrange** (town) LaGrange County
66	3.9	**Monticello** (city) White County
66	3.9	**Pittsboro** (town) Hendricks County
66	3.9	**Syracuse** (town) Kosciusko County
70	3.8	**Michigan City** (city) LaPorte County
71	3.7	**Brownsburg** (town) Hendricks County
72	3.6	**Chesterton** (town) Porter County
72	3.6	**Jeffersonville** (city) Clark County
72	3.6	**Terre Haute** (city) Vigo County
75	3.4	**McCordsville** (town) Hancock County
75	3.4	**Sellersburg** (town) Clark County
77	3.3	**Hebron** (town) Porter County
77	3.3	**Richmond** (city) Wayne County
79	3.2	**Greensburg** (city) Decatur County
79	3.2	**Lebanon** (city) Boone County
81	3.1	**Anderson** (city) Madison County
81	3.1	**Angola** (city) Steuben County
81	3.1	**De Motte** (town) Jasper County
81	3.1	**North Manchester** (town) Wabash County
85	3.0	**Bargersville** (town) Johnson County
86	2.9	**Mount Vernon** (city) Posey County
87	2.8	**Muncie** (city) Delaware County
88	2.7	**Bedford** (city) Lawrence County
88	2.7	**Simonton Lake** (CDP) Elkhart County
88	2.7	**Union City** (city) Randolph County
88	2.7	**Upland** (town) Grant County
92	2.6	**Cumberland** (town) Marion County
92	2.6	**Whitestown** (town) Boone County
94	2.5	**Huntertown** (town) Allen County
94	2.5	**Kendallville** (city) Noble County
96	2.4	**Portland** (city) Jay County
97	2.3	**Cedar Lake** (town) Lake County
97	2.3	**Evansville** (city) Vanderburgh County
97	2.3	**Hanover** (town) Jefferson County
97	2.3	**Kokomo** (city) Howard County
97	2.3	**New Albany** (city) Floyd County
102	2.2	**Rockville** (town) Parke County
102	2.2	**Scottsburg** (city) Scott County
102	2.2	**Westville** (town) LaPorte County
105	2.1	**Batesville** (city) Ripley County
105	2.1	**Beech Grove** (city) Marion County
105	2.1	**Loogootee** (city) Martin County
108	2.0	**Brownstown** (town) Jackson County
108	2.0	**Edinburgh** (town) Johnson County
108	2.0	**Princeton** (city) Gibson County
108	2.0	**Rochester** (city) Fulton County
112	1.9	**Franklin** (city) Johnson County
112	1.9	**Huntington** (city) Huntington County
112	1.9	**Porter** (town) Porter County
115	1.8	**Ellettsville** (town) Monroe County
115	1.8	**Elwood** (city) Madison County
115	1.8	**Hidden Valley** (CDP) Dearborn County
115	1.8	**Lowell** (town) Lake County
115	1.8	**Marion** (city) Grant County
115	1.8	**New Haven** (city) Allen County
121	1.7	**Attica** (city) Fountain County
122	1.6	**Gary** (city) Lake County
122	1.6	**Grissom AFB** (CDP) Miami County
122	1.6	**Mooresville** (town) Morgan County
122	1.6	**Nappanee** (city) Elkhart County
122	1.6	**Tipton** (city) Tipton County
127	1.5	**Austin** (city) Scott County
127	1.5	**Bright** (CDP) Dearborn County
127	1.5	**Whiteland** (town) Johnson County
130	1.4	**Chesterfield** (town) Madison County
130	1.4	**Madison** (city) Jefferson County
130	1.4	**Yorktown** (town) Delaware County
133	1.3	**Columbia City** (city) Whitley County
133	1.3	**Greendale** (city) Dearborn County
133	1.3	**Leo-Cedarville** (town) Allen County
136	1.2	**Aurora** (city) Dearborn County
136	1.2	**Martinsville** (city) Morgan County
136	1.2	**New Castle** (city) Henry County
136	1.2	**South Haven** (CDP) Porter County
140	1.1	**Cicero** (town) Hamilton County
140	1.1	**Connersville** (city) Fayette County
140	1.1	**Fortville** (town) Hancock County
140	1.1	**Greenfield** (city) Hancock County
140	1.1	**New Whiteland** (town) Johnson County
140	1.1	**Rensselaer** (city) Jasper County
140	1.1	**Smithville-Sanders** (CDP) Monroe County
147	1.0	**Auburn** (city) DeKalb County
147	1.0	**Centerville** (town) Wayne County
147	1.0	**Decatur** (city) Adams County
147	1.0	**Vincennes** (city) Knox County

Note: This section ranks incorporated places and CDPs (Census Designated Places) with populations of 2,500 or more. Unincorporated postal areas were not considered. Please refer to the User Guide for additional information.

Foreign Born
Top 150 Places Ranked in *Ascending* Order

State Rank	Percent	Place
1	0.0	**Chandler** (town) Warrick County
1	0.0	**Corydon** (town) Harrison County
1	0.0	**Fairmount** (town) Grant County
1	0.0	**North Terre Haute** (CDP) Vigo County
5	0.2	**Boonville** (city) Warrick County
5	0.2	**Salem** (city) Washington County
7	0.3	**Paoli** (town) Orange County
7	0.3	**Rushville** (city) Rush County
7	0.3	**Tell City** (city) Perry County
7	0.3	**Winchester** (city) Randolph County
11	0.4	**Alexandria** (city) Madison County
11	0.4	**Berne** (city) Adams County
11	0.4	**Bicknell** (city) Knox County
11	0.4	**Butler** (city) DeKalb County
11	0.4	**Clinton** (city) Vermillion County
16	0.5	**Covington** (city) Fountain County
16	0.5	**Danville** (town) Hendricks County
16	0.5	**Garrett** (city) DeKalb County
16	0.5	**Hartford City** (city) Blackford County
16	0.5	**Knox** (city) Starke County
16	0.5	**Lawrenceburg** (city) Dearborn County
16	0.5	**Mitchell** (city) Lawrence County
23	0.6	**Brazil** (city) Clay County
23	0.6	**Heritage Lake** (CDP) Putnam County
23	0.6	**North Vernon** (city) Jennings County
23	0.6	**Ossian** (town) Wells County
23	0.6	**Sheridan** (town) Hamilton County
23	0.6	**Sullivan** (city) Sullivan County
29	0.7	**Brookville** (town) Franklin County
29	0.7	**Middlebury** (town) Elkhart County
31	0.8	**Gas City** (city) Grant County
31	0.8	**Georgetown** (town) Floyd County
31	0.8	**Linton** (city) Greene County
31	0.8	**Wabash** (city) Wabash County
35	0.9	**Bluffton** (city) Wells County
35	0.9	**Fort Branch** (town) Gibson County
35	0.9	**Pendleton** (town) Madison County
35	0.9	**Peru** (city) Miami County
39	1.0	**Auburn** (city) DeKalb County
39	1.0	**Centerville** (town) Wayne County
39	1.0	**Decatur** (city) Adams County
39	1.0	**Vincennes** (city) Knox County
43	1.1	**Cicero** (town) Hamilton County
43	1.1	**Connersville** (city) Fayette County
43	1.1	**Fortville** (town) Hancock County
43	1.1	**Greenfield** (city) Hancock County
43	1.1	**New Whiteland** (town) Johnson County
43	1.1	**Rensselaer** (city) Jasper County
43	1.1	**Smithville-Sanders** (CDP) Monroe County
50	1.2	**Aurora** (city) Dearborn County
50	1.2	**Martinsville** (city) Morgan County
50	1.2	**New Castle** (city) Henry County
50	1.2	**South Haven** (CDP) Porter County
54	1.3	**Columbia City** (city) Whitley County
54	1.3	**Greendale** (city) Dearborn County
54	1.3	**Leo-Cedarville** (town) Allen County
57	1.4	**Chesterfield** (town) Madison County
57	1.4	**Madison** (city) Jefferson County
57	1.4	**Yorktown** (town) Delaware County
60	1.5	**Austin** (city) Scott County
60	1.5	**Bright** (CDP) Dearborn County
60	1.5	**Whiteland** (town) Johnson County
63	1.6	**Gary** (city) Lake County
63	1.6	**Grissom AFB** (CDP) Miami County
63	1.6	**Mooresville** (town) Morgan County
63	1.6	**Nappanee** (city) Elkhart County
63	1.6	**Tipton** (city) Tipton County
68	1.7	**Attica** (city) Fountain County
69	1.8	**Ellettsville** (town) Monroe County
69	1.8	**Elwood** (city) Madison County
69	1.8	**Hidden Valley** (CDP) Dearborn County
69	1.8	**Lowell** (town) Lake County
69	1.8	**Marion** (city) Grant County
69	1.8	**New Haven** (city) Allen County
75	1.9	**Franklin** (city) Johnson County
75	1.9	**Huntington** (city) Huntington County
75	1.9	**Porter** (town) Porter County
78	2.0	**Brownstown** (town) Jackson County
78	2.0	**Edinburgh** (town) Johnson County
78	2.0	**Princeton** (city) Gibson County
78	2.0	**Rochester** (city) Fulton County
82	2.1	**Batesville** (city) Ripley County
82	2.1	**Beech Grove** (city) Marion County
82	2.1	**Loogootee** (city) Martin County
85	2.2	**Rockville** (town) Parke County
85	2.2	**Scottsburg** (city) Scott County
85	2.2	**Westville** (town) LaPorte County
88	2.3	**Cedar Lake** (town) Lake County
88	2.3	**Evansville** (city) Vanderburgh County
88	2.3	**Hanover** (town) Jefferson County
88	2.3	**Kokomo** (city) Howard County
88	2.3	**New Albany** (city) Floyd County
93	2.4	**Portland** (city) Jay County
94	2.5	**Huntertown** (town) Allen County
94	2.5	**Kendallville** (city) Noble County
96	2.6	**Cumberland** (town) Marion County
96	2.6	**Whitestown** (town) Boone County
98	2.7	**Bedford** (city) Lawrence County
98	2.7	**Simonton Lake** (CDP) Elkhart County
98	2.7	**Union City** (city) Randolph County
98	2.7	**Upland** (town) Grant County
102	2.8	**Muncie** (city) Delaware County
103	2.9	**Mount Vernon** (city) Posey County
104	3.0	**Bargersville** (town) Johnson County
105	3.1	**Anderson** (city) Madison County
105	3.1	**Angola** (city) Steuben County
105	3.1	**De Motte** (town) Jasper County
105	3.1	**North Manchester** (town) Wabash County
109	3.2	**Greensburg** (city) Decatur County
109	3.2	**Lebanon** (city) Boone County
111	3.3	**Hebron** (town) Porter County
111	3.3	**Richmond** (city) Wayne County
113	3.4	**McCordsville** (town) Hancock County
113	3.4	**Sellersburg** (town) Clark County
115	3.6	**Chesterton** (town) Porter County
115	3.6	**Jeffersonville** (city) Clark County
115	3.6	**Terre Haute** (city) Vigo County
118	3.7	**Brownsburg** (town) Hendricks County
119	3.8	**Michigan City** (city) LaPorte County
120	3.9	**Lagrange** (town) LaGrange County
120	3.9	**Monticello** (city) White County
120	3.9	**Pittsboro** (town) Hendricks County
120	3.9	**Syracuse** (town) Kosciusko County
124	4.0	**Portage** (city) Porter County
125	4.1	**Greencastle** (city) Putnam County
125	4.1	**Noblesville** (city) Hamilton County
127	4.2	**Jasper** (city) Dubois County
128	4.3	**Country Squire Lakes** (CDP) Jennings County
128	4.3	**Highland** (CDP) Vanderburgh County
128	4.3	**Lake Station** (city) Lake County
128	4.3	**Melody Hill** (CDP) Vanderburgh County
132	4.4	**Newburgh** (town) Warrick County
133	4.5	**Crawfordsville** (city) Montgomery County
134	4.6	**Hobart** (city) Lake County
135	4.7	**Griffith** (town) Lake County
135	4.7	**Shelbyville** (city) Shelby County
137	4.8	**Bremen** (town) Marshall County
138	4.9	**Charlestown** (city) Clark County
139	5.0	**Lakes of the Four Seasons** (CDP) Lake County
140	5.1	**Highland** (town) Lake County
140	5.1	**Saint John** (town) Lake County
140	5.1	**Shorewood Forest** (CDP) Porter County
140	5.1	**Westfield** (city) Hamilton County
144	5.3	**Washington** (city) Daviess County
145	5.4	**Roselawn** (CDP) Newton County
145	5.4	**Winona Lake** (town) Kosciusko County
145	5.4	**Zionsville** (town) Boone County
148	5.5	**Valparaiso** (city) Porter County
149	5.8	**Granger** (CDP) Saint Joseph County
150	5.9	**Dunlap** (CDP) Elkhart County

Note: This section ranks incorporated places and CDPs (Census Designated Places) with populations of 2,500 or more. Unincorporated postal areas were not considered. Please refer to the User Guide for additional information.

Speak English Only at Home
Top 150 Places Ranked in *Descending* Order

State Rank	Percent	Place
1	99.7	**Boonville** (city) Warrick County
2	99.6	**Chandler** (town) Warrick County
3	99.5	**Bicknell** (city) Knox County
3	99.5	**Fortville** (town) Hancock County
3	99.5	**Tell City** (city) Perry County
6	99.1	**Paoli** (town) Orange County
7	99.0	**Fairmount** (town) Grant County
7	99.0	**Linton** (city) Greene County
9	98.9	**Brookville** (town) Franklin County
9	98.9	**Butler** (city) DeKalb County
9	98.9	**Hartford City** (city) Blackford County
9	98.9	**Whiteland** (town) Johnson County
13	98.8	**Brazil** (city) Clay County
13	98.8	**Gas City** (city) Grant County
13	98.8	**Knox** (city) Starke County
16	98.7	**Chesterfield** (town) Madison County
16	98.7	**Pendleton** (town) Madison County
16	98.7	**Winchester** (city) Randolph County
19	98.6	**Covington** (city) Fountain County
19	98.6	**Salem** (city) Washington County
21	98.5	**Wabash** (city) Wabash County
22	98.3	**Lawrenceburg** (city) Dearborn County
22	98.3	**New Whiteland** (town) Johnson County
22	98.3	**Rensselaer** (city) Jasper County
25	98.2	**Alexandria** (city) Madison County
25	98.2	**North Vernon** (city) Jennings County
25	98.2	**Vincennes** (city) Knox County
25	98.2	**Yorktown** (town) Delaware County
29	98.1	**Mooresville** (town) Morgan County
30	98.0	**North Terre Haute** (CDP) Vigo County
30	98.0	**Ossian** (town) Wells County
30	98.0	**Sullivan** (city) Sullivan County
33	97.9	**Auburn** (city) DeKalb County
33	97.9	**Austin** (city) Scott County
33	97.9	**Leo-Cedarville** (town) Allen County
36	97.8	**Columbia City** (city) Whitley County
36	97.8	**Corydon** (town) Harrison County
36	97.8	**Fort Branch** (town) Gibson County
36	97.8	**Peru** (city) Miami County
40	97.7	**Danville** (town) Hendricks County
40	97.7	**Hanover** (town) Jefferson County
40	97.7	**Loogootee** (city) Martin County
40	97.7	**Martinsville** (city) Morgan County
40	97.7	**Smithville-Sanders** (CDP) Monroe County
45	97.6	**Aurora** (city) Dearborn County
45	97.6	**Mitchell** (city) Lawrence County
47	97.5	**Bright** (CDP) Dearborn County
47	97.5	**Greenfield** (city) Hancock County
49	97.4	**Brownstown** (town) Jackson County
49	97.4	**Georgetown** (town) Floyd County
51	97.3	**Berne** (city) Adams County
51	97.3	**South Haven** (CDP) Porter County
53	97.0	**Huntington** (city) Huntington County
53	97.0	**Tipton** (city) Tipton County
55	96.8	**Ellettsville** (town) Monroe County
55	96.8	**Princeton** (city) Gibson County
55	96.8	**Rockville** (town) Parke County
58	96.7	**Batesville** (city) Ripley County
58	96.7	**Greendale** (city) Dearborn County
58	96.7	**Greensburg** (city) Decatur County
58	96.7	**Madison** (city) Jefferson County
62	96.6	**New Castle** (city) Henry County
62	96.6	**Sheridan** (town) Hamilton County
64	96.5	**Connersville** (city) Fayette County
64	96.5	**Hidden Valley** (CDP) Dearborn County
64	96.5	**Lowell** (town) Lake County
67	96.4	**Marion** (city) Grant County
67	96.4	**Rushville** (city) Rush County
69	96.3	**Porter** (town) Porter County
70	96.2	**Centerville** (town) Wayne County
70	96.2	**Evansville** (city) Vanderburgh County
70	96.2	**Muncie** (city) Delaware County
73	96.1	**Bluffton** (city) Wells County
73	96.1	**Franklin** (city) Johnson County
73	96.1	**Upland** (town) Grant County
76	96.0	**Clinton** (city) Vermillion County
77	95.9	**Elwood** (city) Madison County
78	95.8	**Bedford** (city) Lawrence County
78	95.8	**Cicero** (town) Hamilton County
78	95.8	**Garrett** (city) DeKalb County
81	95.7	**Anderson** (city) Madison County
81	95.7	**Beech Grove** (city) Marion County
83	95.6	**Lebanon** (city) Boone County
83	95.6	**New Albany** (city) Floyd County
83	95.6	**Westville** (town) LaPorte County
86	95.5	**Kokomo** (city) Howard County
86	95.5	**Sellersburg** (town) Clark County
88	95.3	**Cedar Lake** (town) Lake County
89	95.2	**Attica** (city) Fountain County
89	95.2	**Edinburgh** (town) Johnson County
89	95.2	**Rochester** (city) Fulton County
92	95.1	**Angola** (city) Steuben County
92	95.1	**Jeffersonville** (city) Clark County
94	95.0	**Brownsburg** (town) Hendricks County
94	95.0	**Gary** (city) Lake County
94	95.0	**Scottsburg** (city) Scott County
97	94.9	**Cumberland** (town) Marion County
97	94.9	**Huntertown** (town) Allen County
97	94.9	**McCordsville** (town) Hancock County
97	94.9	**New Haven** (city) Allen County
97	94.9	**Pittsboro** (town) Hendricks County
102	94.8	**Newburgh** (town) Warrick County
102	94.8	**Whitestown** (town) Boone County
104	94.7	**Highland** (CDP) Vanderburgh County
105	94.2	**Michigan City** (city) LaPorte County
105	94.2	**Zionsville** (town) Boone County
107	94.1	**Greencastle** (city) Putnam County
108	94.0	**Chesterton** (town) Porter County
108	94.0	**Kendallville** (city) Noble County
108	94.0	**Mount Vernon** (city) Posey County
108	94.0	**Richmond** (city) Wayne County
112	93.6	**Terre Haute** (city) Vigo County
113	93.5	**Decatur** (city) Adams County
114	93.4	**Melody Hill** (CDP) Vanderburgh County
114	93.4	**Noblesville** (city) Hamilton County
114	93.4	**North Manchester** (town) Wabash County
117	93.3	**De Motte** (town) Jasper County
118	93.2	**Middlebury** (town) Elkhart County
118	93.2	**Portland** (city) Jay County
118	93.2	**Union City** (city) Randolph County
121	93.1	**Bargersville** (town) Johnson County
121	93.1	**Shorewood Forest** (CDP) Porter County
121	93.1	**Westfield** (city) Hamilton County
121	93.1	**Winona Lake** (town) Kosciusko County
125	92.9	**Lakes of the Four Seasons** (CDP) Lake County
125	92.9	**Simonton Lake** (CDP) Elkhart County
127	92.7	**Shelbyville** (city) Shelby County
128	92.6	**Charlestown** (city) Clark County
129	92.4	**Crawfordsville** (city) Montgomery County
129	92.4	**Grissom AFB** (CDP) Miami County
129	92.4	**Monticello** (city) White County
132	92.3	**Valparaiso** (city) Porter County
133	92.1	**Granger** (CDP) Saint Joseph County
133	92.1	**Heritage Lake** (CDP) Putnam County
135	91.8	**Mishawaka** (city) Saint Joseph County
136	91.7	**Dyer** (town) Lake County
137	91.6	**Hebron** (town) Porter County
137	91.6	**Nappanee** (city) Elkhart County
139	91.4	**Bremen** (town) Marshall County
140	91.2	**Avon** (town) Hendricks County
141	91.0	**Washington** (city) Daviess County
142	90.9	**Clarksville** (town) Clark County
143	90.6	**Syracuse** (town) Kosciusko County
144	90.5	**Greenwood** (city) Johnson County
144	90.5	**Portage** (city) Porter County
144	90.5	**Roselawn** (CDP) Newton County
147	90.3	**Country Squire Lakes** (CDP) Jennings County
148	90.2	**Hobart** (city) Lake County
149	90.1	**Dunlap** (CDP) Elkhart County
149	90.1	**La Porte** (city) LaPorte County

Note: This section ranks incorporated places and CDPs (Census Designated Places) with populations of 2,500 or more. Unincorporated postal areas were not considered. Please refer to the User Guide for additional information.

Speak English Only at Home
Top 150 Places Ranked in *Ascending* Order

State Rank	Percent	Place
1	44.2	**Ligonier** (city) Noble County
2	62.2	**East Chicago** (city) Lake County
3	72.7	**Goshen** (city) Elkhart County
4	73.0	**Hammond** (city) Lake County
5	74.5	**Purdue University** (CDP) Tippecanoe County
6	74.9	**West Lafayette** (city) Tippecanoe County
7	75.1	**Whiting** (city) Lake County
8	76.8	**Elkhart** (city) Elkhart County
8	76.8	**Plymouth** (city) Marshall County
10	77.0	**Frankfort** (city) Clinton County
11	78.4	**Logansport** (city) Cass County
12	81.3	**Huntingburg** (city) Dubois County
12	81.3	**Munster** (town) Lake County
14	83.3	**Lake Station** (city) Lake County
15	83.7	**Schererville** (town) Lake County
16	85.3	**Warsaw** (city) Kosciusko County
17	85.6	**Bloomington** (city) Monroe County
18	85.7	**Winfield** (town) Lake County
19	86.0	**Carmel** (city) Hamilton County
20	86.4	**Seymour** (city) Jackson County
21	86.6	**Notre Dame** (CDP) Saint Joseph County
21	86.6	**South Bend** (city) Saint Joseph County
23	87.0	**Lafayette** (city) Tippecanoe County
24	87.4	**Indianapolis** (city) Marion County
25	87.5	**Lagrange** (town) LaGrange County
26	87.6	**Crown Point** (city) Lake County
27	87.7	**Delphi** (city) Carroll County
27	87.7	**Highland** (town) Lake County
29	87.8	**Lawrence** (city) Marion County
30	88.4	**Merrillville** (town) Lake County
31	88.5	**Speedway** (town) Marion County
32	89.0	**Fort Wayne** (city) Allen County
33	89.1	**Griffith** (town) Lake County
34	89.3	**Columbus** (city) Bartholomew County
34	89.3	**Jasper** (city) Dubois County
34	89.3	**Plainfield** (town) Hendricks County
37	89.4	**Saint John** (town) Lake County
38	90.0	**Fishers** (town) Hamilton County
39	90.1	**Dunlap** (CDP) Elkhart County
39	90.1	**La Porte** (city) LaPorte County
41	90.2	**Hobart** (city) Lake County
42	90.3	**Country Squire Lakes** (CDP) Jennings County
43	90.5	**Greenwood** (city) Johnson County
43	90.5	**Portage** (city) Porter County
43	90.5	**Roselawn** (CDP) Newton County
46	90.6	**Syracuse** (town) Kosciusko County
47	90.9	**Clarksville** (town) Clark County
48	91.0	**Washington** (city) Daviess County
49	91.2	**Avon** (town) Hendricks County
50	91.4	**Bremen** (town) Marshall County
51	91.6	**Hebron** (town) Porter County
51	91.6	**Nappanee** (city) Elkhart County
53	91.7	**Dyer** (town) Lake County
54	91.8	**Mishawaka** (city) Saint Joseph County
55	92.1	**Granger** (CDP) Saint Joseph County
55	92.1	**Heritage Lake** (CDP) Putnam County
57	92.3	**Valparaiso** (city) Porter County
58	92.4	**Crawfordsville** (city) Montgomery County
58	92.4	**Grissom AFB** (CDP) Miami County
58	92.4	**Monticello** (city) White County
61	92.6	**Charlestown** (city) Clark County
62	92.7	**Shelbyville** (city) Shelby County
63	92.9	**Lakes of the Four Seasons** (CDP) Lake County
63	92.9	**Simonton Lake** (CDP) Elkhart County
65	93.1	**Bargersville** (town) Johnson County
65	93.1	**Shorewood Forest** (CDP) Porter County
65	93.1	**Westfield** (city) Hamilton County
65	93.1	**Winona Lake** (town) Kosciusko County
69	93.2	**Middlebury** (town) Elkhart County
69	93.2	**Portland** (city) Jay County
69	93.2	**Union City** (city) Randolph County
72	93.3	**De Motte** (town) Jasper County
73	93.4	**Melody Hill** (CDP) Vanderburgh County
73	93.4	**Noblesville** (city) Hamilton County
73	93.4	**North Manchester** (town) Wabash County
76	93.5	**Decatur** (city) Adams County
77	93.6	**Terre Haute** (city) Vigo County
78	94.0	**Chesterton** (town) Porter County
78	94.0	**Kendallville** (city) Noble County
78	94.0	**Mount Vernon** (city) Posey County
78	94.0	**Richmond** (city) Wayne County
82	94.1	**Greencastle** (city) Putnam County
83	94.2	**Michigan City** (city) LaPorte County
83	94.2	**Zionsville** (town) Boone County
85	94.7	**Highland** (CDP) Vanderburgh County
86	94.8	**Newburgh** (town) Warrick County
86	94.8	**Whitestown** (town) Boone County
88	94.9	**Cumberland** (town) Marion County
88	94.9	**Huntertown** (town) Allen County
88	94.9	**McCordsville** (town) Hancock County
88	94.9	**New Haven** (city) Allen County
88	94.9	**Pittsboro** (town) Hendricks County
93	95.0	**Brownsburg** (town) Hendricks County
93	95.0	**Gary** (city) Lake County
93	95.0	**Scottsburg** (city) Scott County
96	95.1	**Angola** (city) Steuben County
96	95.1	**Jeffersonville** (city) Clark County
98	95.2	**Attica** (city) Fountain County
98	95.2	**Edinburgh** (town) Johnson County
98	95.2	**Rochester** (city) Fulton County
101	95.3	**Cedar Lake** (town) Lake County
102	95.5	**Kokomo** (city) Howard County
102	95.5	**Sellersburg** (town) Clark County
104	95.6	**Lebanon** (city) Boone County
104	95.6	**New Albany** (city) Floyd County
104	95.6	**Westville** (town) LaPorte County
107	95.7	**Anderson** (city) Madison County
107	95.7	**Beech Grove** (city) Marion County
109	95.8	**Bedford** (city) Lawrence County
109	95.8	**Cicero** (town) Hamilton County
109	95.8	**Garrett** (city) DeKalb County
112	95.9	**Elwood** (city) Madison County
113	96.0	**Clinton** (city) Vermillion County
114	96.1	**Bluffton** (city) Wells County
114	96.1	**Franklin** (city) Johnson County
114	96.1	**Upland** (town) Grant County
117	96.2	**Centerville** (town) Wayne County
117	96.2	**Evansville** (city) Vanderburgh County
117	96.2	**Muncie** (city) Delaware County
120	96.3	**Porter** (town) Porter County
121	96.4	**Marion** (city) Grant County
121	96.4	**Rushville** (city) Rush County
123	96.5	**Connersville** (city) Fayette County
123	96.5	**Hidden Valley** (CDP) Dearborn County
123	96.5	**Lowell** (town) Lake County
126	96.6	**New Castle** (city) Henry County
126	96.6	**Sheridan** (town) Hamilton County
128	96.7	**Batesville** (city) Ripley County
128	96.7	**Greendale** (city) Dearborn County
128	96.7	**Greensburg** (city) Decatur County
128	96.7	**Madison** (city) Jefferson County
132	96.8	**Ellettsville** (town) Monroe County
132	96.8	**Princeton** (city) Gibson County
132	96.8	**Rockville** (town) Parke County
135	97.0	**Huntington** (city) Huntington County
135	97.0	**Tipton** (city) Tipton County
137	97.3	**Berne** (city) Adams County
137	97.3	**South Haven** (CDP) Porter County
139	97.4	**Brownstown** (town) Jackson County
139	97.4	**Georgetown** (town) Floyd County
141	97.5	**Bright** (CDP) Dearborn County
141	97.5	**Greenfield** (city) Hancock County
143	97.6	**Aurora** (city) Dearborn County
143	97.6	**Mitchell** (city) Lawrence County
145	97.7	**Danville** (town) Hendricks County
145	97.7	**Hanover** (town) Jefferson County
145	97.7	**Loogootee** (city) Martin County
145	97.7	**Martinsville** (city) Morgan County
145	97.7	**Smithville-Sanders** (CDP) Monroe County
150	97.8	**Columbia City** (city) Whitley County

Note: This section ranks incorporated places and CDPs (Census Designated Places) with populations of 2,500 or more. Unincorporated postal areas were not considered. Please refer to the User Guide for additional information.

Individuals with a Disability
Top 150 Places Ranked in *Descending* Order

State Rank	Percent	Place
1	25.4	**Linton** (city) Greene County
2	24.6	**Mitchell** (city) Lawrence County
3	24.5	**Sullivan** (city) Sullivan County
4	24.4	**Winchester** (city) Randolph County
5	23.0	**Country Squire Lakes** (CDP) Jennings County
6	22.9	**Hartford City** (city) Blackford County
7	22.6	**Rochester** (city) Fulton County
8	22.2	**Rockville** (town) Parke County
9	21.8	**Bicknell** (city) Knox County
10	21.6	**Lagrange** (town) LaGrange County
11	21.2	**Chesterfield** (town) Madison County
12	20.9	**Edinburgh** (town) Johnson County
13	20.8	**Tipton** (city) Tipton County
14	20.7	**Scottsburg** (city) Scott County
15	20.6	**Elwood** (city) Madison County
16	20.5	**Connersville** (city) Fayette County
17	20.3	**Peru** (city) Miami County
18	20.1	**Anderson** (city) Madison County
18	20.1	**Attica** (city) Fountain County
18	20.1	**Aurora** (city) Dearborn County
18	20.1	**Bedford** (city) Lawrence County
18	20.1	**Richmond** (city) Wayne County
23	19.8	**Lake Station** (city) Lake County
24	19.6	**Marion** (city) Grant County
25	19.5	**Brookville** (town) Franklin County
26	19.4	**Wabash** (city) Wabash County
27	19.1	**Lawrenceburg** (city) Dearborn County
27	19.1	**New Castle** (city) Henry County
29	19.0	**Fairmount** (town) Grant County
30	18.9	**Martinsville** (city) Morgan County
31	18.8	**Rensselaer** (city) Jasper County
32	18.6	**Gary** (city) Lake County
32	18.6	**Knox** (city) Starke County
34	18.5	**Austin** (city) Scott County
34	18.5	**Kendallville** (city) Noble County
34	18.5	**Washington** (city) Daviess County
37	18.4	**Muncie** (city) Delaware County
38	18.0	**Columbia City** (city) Whitley County
38	18.0	**Michigan City** (city) LaPorte County
38	18.0	**Rushville** (city) Rush County
41	17.9	**Monticello** (city) White County
42	17.8	**Brazil** (city) Clay County
42	17.8	**Corydon** (town) Harrison County
44	17.7	**North Vernon** (city) Jennings County
44	17.7	**Portland** (city) Jay County
44	17.7	**Salem** (city) Washington County
47	17.6	**Kokomo** (city) Howard County
48	17.5	**Alexandria** (city) Madison County
48	17.5	**Fortville** (town) Hancock County
48	17.5	**Terre Haute** (city) Vigo County
51	17.4	**New Albany** (city) Floyd County
52	17.3	**Chandler** (town) Warrick County
53	17.1	**Tell City** (city) Perry County
54	17.0	**Auburn** (city) DeKalb County
54	17.0	**North Terre Haute** (CDP) Vigo County
56	16.9	**Simonton Lake** (CDP) Elkhart County
56	16.9	**Union City** (city) Randolph County
58	16.6	**Gas City** (city) Grant County
59	16.5	**Princeton** (city) Gibson County
60	16.4	**Jeffersonville** (city) Clark County
61	16.3	**Boonville** (city) Warrick County
62	16.2	**Butler** (city) DeKalb County
62	16.2	**Crawfordsville** (city) Montgomery County
62	16.2	**Ellettsville** (town) Monroe County
65	16.1	**Madison** (city) Jefferson County
66	16.0	**Decatur** (city) Adams County
66	16.0	**Greensburg** (city) Decatur County
68	15.8	**Paoli** (town) Orange County
69	15.7	**Angola** (city) Steuben County
70	15.6	**Centerville** (town) Wayne County
70	15.6	**La Porte** (city) LaPorte County
70	15.6	**Logansport** (city) Cass County
70	15.6	**Speedway** (town) Marion County
74	15.5	**North Manchester** (town) Wabash County
75	15.4	**Garrett** (city) DeKalb County
76	15.3	**Delphi** (city) Carroll County
76	15.3	**Evansville** (city) Vanderburgh County
76	15.3	**Grissom AFB** (CDP) Miami County
79	15.1	**East Chicago** (city) Lake County
79	15.1	**Pendleton** (town) Madison County
81	15.0	**Bluffton** (city) Wells County
81	15.0	**Clinton** (city) Vermillion County
81	15.0	**Plymouth** (city) Marshall County
84	14.9	**Merrillville** (town) Lake County
84	14.9	**Mount Vernon** (city) Posey County
84	14.9	**Shelbyville** (city) Shelby County
84	14.9	**South Bend** (city) Saint Joseph County
88	14.8	**Huntington** (city) Huntington County
88	14.8	**Whiting** (city) Lake County
90	14.7	**Berne** (city) Adams County
91	14.6	**Elkhart** (city) Elkhart County
91	14.6	**Vincennes** (city) Knox County
93	14.4	**Clarksville** (town) Clark County
93	14.4	**Hammond** (city) Lake County
93	14.4	**Seymour** (city) Jackson County
96	14.3	**Mishawaka** (city) Saint Joseph County
96	14.3	**Winona Lake** (town) Kosciusko County
96	14.3	**Yorktown** (town) Delaware County
99	14.2	**Charlestown** (city) Clark County
100	14.0	**Mooresville** (town) Morgan County
101	13.9	**Greencastle** (city) Putnam County
102	13.6	**Beech Grove** (city) Marion County
103	13.5	**Sheridan** (town) Hamilton County
104	13.4	**Franklin** (city) Johnson County
105	13.3	**Frankfort** (city) Clinton County
106	13.2	**Portage** (city) Porter County
106	13.2	**South Haven** (CDP) Porter County
106	13.2	**Whiteland** (town) Johnson County
109	13.0	**Lafayette** (city) Tippecanoe County
110	12.9	**Cedar Lake** (town) Lake County
110	12.9	**Greenfield** (city) Hancock County
110	12.9	**Indianapolis** (city) Marion County
113	12.8	**Lebanon** (city) Boone County
113	12.8	**Newburgh** (town) Warrick County
115	12.7	**De Motte** (town) Jasper County
115	12.7	**Fort Branch** (town) Gibson County
115	12.7	**Greendale** (city) Dearborn County
115	12.7	**Huntingburg** (city) Dubois County
119	12.6	**Cumberland** (town) Marion County
120	12.5	**Goshen** (city) Elkhart County
120	12.5	**Plainfield** (town) Hendricks County
122	12.4	**Columbus** (city) Bartholomew County
123	12.3	**Sellersburg** (town) Clark County
124	12.2	**Hobart** (city) Lake County
124	12.2	**Loogootee** (city) Martin County
124	12.2	**Lowell** (town) Lake County
127	12.1	**Griffith** (town) Lake County
127	12.1	**Syracuse** (town) Kosciusko County
129	11.9	**Ossian** (town) Wells County
130	11.8	**Brownstown** (town) Jackson County
131	11.7	**Fort Wayne** (city) Allen County
131	11.7	**Highland** (town) Lake County
133	11.6	**Covington** (city) Fountain County
134	11.5	**Bremen** (town) Marshall County
134	11.5	**Warsaw** (city) Kosciusko County
136	11.1	**Cicero** (town) Hamilton County
137	11.0	**Lawrence** (city) Marion County
138	10.9	**New Haven** (city) Allen County
139	10.8	**Winfield** (town) Lake County
140	10.7	**Dunlap** (CDP) Elkhart County
140	10.7	**Munster** (town) Lake County
142	10.6	**Westville** (town) LaPorte County
143	10.4	**Dyer** (town) Lake County
144	10.3	**Crown Point** (city) Lake County
144	10.3	**Hebron** (town) Porter County
146	10.2	**Danville** (town) Hendricks County
147	10.1	**Smithville-Sanders** (CDP) Monroe County
148	10.0	**Middlebury** (town) Elkhart County
148	10.0	**Valparaiso** (city) Porter County
150	9.9	**Nappanee** (city) Elkhart County

Note: This section ranks incorporated places and CDPs (Census Designated Places) with populations of 2,500 or more. Unincorporated postal areas were not considered. Please refer to the User Guide for additional information.

Individuals with a Disability
Top 150 Places Ranked in *Ascending* Order

State Rank	Percent	Place
1	2.6	**Purdue University** (CDP) Tippecanoe County
2	3.9	**Notre Dame** (CDP) Saint Joseph County
3	4.1	**Zionsville** (town) Boone County
4	4.2	**Whitestown** (town) Boone County
5	4.9	**Avon** (town) Hendricks County
6	5.0	**Fishers** (town) Hamilton County
7	5.2	**Shorewood Forest** (CDP) Porter County
8	5.7	**McCordsville** (town) Hancock County
9	5.8	**West Lafayette** (city) Tippecanoe County
10	6.3	**Carmel** (city) Hamilton County
11	6.6	**Porter** (town) Porter County
12	6.7	**Westfield** (city) Hamilton County
13	7.0	**Bargersville** (town) Johnson County
13	7.0	**Upland** (town) Grant County
15	7.2	**Granger** (CDP) Saint Joseph County
16	7.4	**Huntertown** (town) Allen County
17	7.6	**Jasper** (city) Dubois County
17	7.6	**Noblesville** (city) Hamilton County
19	7.8	**Saint John** (town) Lake County
20	8.1	**New Whiteland** (town) Johnson County
21	8.4	**Leo-Cedarville** (town) Allen County
22	8.5	**Pittsboro** (town) Hendricks County
23	8.6	**Chesterton** (town) Porter County
24	8.7	**Bloomington** (city) Monroe County
24	8.7	**Georgetown** (town) Floyd County
26	8.8	**Ligonier** (city) Noble County
27	8.9	**Bright** (CDP) Dearborn County
28	9.0	**Batesville** (city) Ripley County
28	9.0	**Brownsburg** (town) Hendricks County
28	9.0	**Highland** (CDP) Vanderburgh County
31	9.1	**Heritage Lake** (CDP) Putnam County
32	9.2	**Melody Hill** (CDP) Vanderburgh County
33	9.4	**Hanover** (town) Jefferson County
33	9.4	**Lakes of the Four Seasons** (CDP) Lake County
35	9.5	**Hidden Valley** (CDP) Dearborn County
35	9.5	**Roselawn** (CDP) Newton County
37	9.7	**Greenwood** (city) Johnson County
37	9.7	**Schererville** (town) Lake County
39	9.9	**Nappanee** (city) Elkhart County
40	10.0	**Middlebury** (town) Elkhart County
40	10.0	**Valparaiso** (city) Porter County
42	10.1	**Smithville-Sanders** (CDP) Monroe County
43	10.2	**Danville** (town) Hendricks County
44	10.3	**Crown Point** (city) Lake County
44	10.3	**Hebron** (town) Porter County
46	10.4	**Dyer** (town) Lake County
47	10.6	**Westville** (town) LaPorte County
48	10.7	**Dunlap** (CDP) Elkhart County
48	10.7	**Munster** (town) Lake County
50	10.8	**Winfield** (town) Lake County
51	10.9	**New Haven** (city) Allen County
52	11.0	**Lawrence** (city) Marion County
53	11.1	**Cicero** (town) Hamilton County
54	11.5	**Bremen** (town) Marshall County
54	11.5	**Warsaw** (city) Kosciusko County
56	11.6	**Covington** (city) Fountain County
57	11.7	**Fort Wayne** (city) Allen County
57	11.7	**Highland** (town) Lake County
59	11.8	**Brownstown** (town) Jackson County
60	11.9	**Ossian** (town) Wells County
61	12.1	**Griffith** (town) Lake County
61	12.1	**Syracuse** (town) Kosciusko County
63	12.2	**Hobart** (city) Lake County
63	12.2	**Loogootee** (city) Martin County
63	12.2	**Lowell** (town) Lake County
66	12.3	**Sellersburg** (town) Clark County
67	12.4	**Columbus** (city) Bartholomew County
68	12.5	**Goshen** (city) Elkhart County
68	12.5	**Plainfield** (town) Hendricks County
70	12.6	**Cumberland** (town) Marion County
71	12.7	**De Motte** (town) Jasper County
71	12.7	**Fort Branch** (town) Gibson County
71	12.7	**Greendale** (city) Dearborn County
71	12.7	**Huntingburg** (city) Dubois County
75	12.8	**Lebanon** (city) Boone County
75	12.8	**Newburgh** (town) Warrick County
77	12.9	**Cedar Lake** (town) Lake County
77	12.9	**Greenfield** (city) Hancock County
77	12.9	**Indianapolis** (city) Marion County
80	13.0	**Lafayette** (city) Tippecanoe County
81	13.2	**Portage** (city) Porter County
81	13.2	**South Haven** (CDP) Porter County
81	13.2	**Whiteland** (town) Johnson County
84	13.3	**Frankfort** (city) Clinton County
85	13.4	**Franklin** (city) Johnson County
86	13.5	**Sheridan** (town) Hamilton County
87	13.6	**Beech Grove** (city) Marion County
88	13.9	**Greencastle** (city) Putnam County
89	14.0	**Mooresville** (town) Morgan County
90	14.2	**Charlestown** (city) Clark County
91	14.3	**Mishawaka** (city) Saint Joseph County
91	14.3	**Winona Lake** (town) Kosciusko County
91	14.3	**Yorktown** (town) Delaware County
94	14.4	**Clarksville** (town) Clark County
94	14.4	**Hammond** (city) Lake County
94	14.4	**Seymour** (city) Jackson County
97	14.6	**Elkhart** (city) Elkhart County
97	14.6	**Vincennes** (city) Knox County
99	14.7	**Berne** (city) Adams County
100	14.8	**Huntington** (city) Huntington County
100	14.8	**Whiting** (city) Lake County
102	14.9	**Merrillville** (town) Lake County
102	14.9	**Mount Vernon** (city) Posey County
102	14.9	**Shelbyville** (city) Shelby County
102	14.9	**South Bend** (city) Saint Joseph County
106	15.0	**Bluffton** (city) Wells County
106	15.0	**Clinton** (city) Vermillion County
106	15.0	**Plymouth** (city) Marshall County
109	15.1	**East Chicago** (city) Lake County
109	15.1	**Pendleton** (town) Madison County
111	15.3	**Delphi** (city) Carroll County
111	15.3	**Evansville** (city) Vanderburgh County
111	15.3	**Grissom AFB** (CDP) Miami County
114	15.4	**Garrett** (city) DeKalb County
115	15.5	**North Manchester** (town) Wabash County
116	15.6	**Centerville** (town) Wayne County
116	15.6	**La Porte** (city) LaPorte County
116	15.6	**Logansport** (city) Cass County
116	15.6	**Speedway** (town) Marion County
120	15.7	**Angola** (city) Steuben County
121	15.8	**Paoli** (town) Orange County
122	16.0	**Decatur** (city) Adams County
122	16.0	**Greensburg** (city) Decatur County
124	16.1	**Madison** (city) Jefferson County
125	16.2	**Butler** (city) DeKalb County
125	16.2	**Crawfordsville** (city) Montgomery County
125	16.2	**Ellettsville** (town) Monroe County
128	16.3	**Boonville** (city) Warrick County
129	16.4	**Jeffersonville** (city) Clark County
130	16.5	**Princeton** (city) Gibson County
131	16.6	**Gas City** (city) Grant County
132	16.9	**Simonton Lake** (CDP) Elkhart County
132	16.9	**Union City** (city) Randolph County
134	17.0	**Auburn** (city) DeKalb County
134	17.0	**North Terre Haute** (CDP) Vigo County
136	17.1	**Tell City** (city) Perry County
137	17.3	**Chandler** (town) Warrick County
138	17.4	**New Albany** (city) Floyd County
139	17.5	**Alexandria** (city) Madison County
139	17.5	**Fortville** (town) Hancock County
139	17.5	**Terre Haute** (city) Vigo County
142	17.6	**Kokomo** (city) Howard County
143	17.7	**North Vernon** (city) Jennings County
143	17.7	**Portland** (city) Jay County
143	17.7	**Salem** (city) Washington County
146	17.8	**Brazil** (city) Clay County
146	17.8	**Corydon** (town) Harrison County
148	17.9	**Monticello** (city) White County
149	18.0	**Columbia City** (city) Whitley County
149	18.0	**Michigan City** (city) LaPorte County

Note: This section ranks incorporated places and CDPs (Census Designated Places) with populations of 2,500 or more. Unincorporated postal areas were not considered. Please refer to the User Guide for additional information.

Veterans

Top 150 Places Ranked in *Descending* Order

State Rank	Percent	Place
1	15.3	**Corydon** (town) Harrison County
2	14.8	**Melody Hill** (CDP) Vanderburgh County
3	14.7	**Bicknell** (city) Knox County
4	14.4	**Country Squire Lakes** (CDP) Jennings County
5	14.0	**Chesterfield** (town) Madison County
6	13.6	**Cicero** (town) Hamilton County
7	13.5	**Pendleton** (town) Madison County
8	13.4	**Lagrange** (town) LaGrange County
9	13.3	**Gas City** (city) Grant County
10	13.2	**De Motte** (town) Jasper County
11	13.1	**Aurora** (city) Dearborn County
12	12.9	**Porter** (town) Porter County
13	12.8	**Covington** (city) Fountain County
13	12.8	**Hidden Valley** (CDP) Dearborn County
15	12.7	**Centerville** (town) Wayne County
15	12.7	**Mooresville** (town) Morgan County
17	12.6	**Loogootee** (city) Martin County
18	12.5	**Lakes of the Four Seasons** (CDP) Lake County
18	12.5	**Rockville** (town) Parke County
20	12.4	**Grissom AFB** (CDP) Miami County
20	12.4	**South Haven** (CDP) Porter County
20	12.4	**Yorktown** (town) Delaware County
23	12.3	**Connersville** (city) Fayette County
23	12.3	**Kokomo** (city) Howard County
25	12.2	**Hartford City** (city) Blackford County
26	12.1	**New Castle** (city) Henry County
26	12.1	**Rushville** (city) Rush County
28	12.0	**Linton** (city) Greene County
29	11.9	**Hobart** (city) Lake County
30	11.6	**Peru** (city) Miami County
30	11.6	**Sheridan** (town) Hamilton County
32	11.5	**Lawrence** (city) Marion County
33	11.3	**La Porte** (city) LaPorte County
34	11.2	**Princeton** (city) Gibson County
35	11.1	**Franklin** (city) Johnson County
35	11.1	**Monticello** (city) White County
37	11.0	**Avon** (town) Hendricks County
37	11.0	**Bargersville** (town) Johnson County
37	11.0	**Delphi** (city) Carroll County
40	10.9	**Boonville** (city) Warrick County
40	10.9	**Cumberland** (town) Marion County
40	10.9	**Lawrenceburg** (city) Dearborn County
40	10.9	**Mitchell** (city) Lawrence County
44	10.8	**Richmond** (city) Wayne County
45	10.7	**Huntertown** (town) Allen County
45	10.7	**New Albany** (city) Floyd County
45	10.7	**Plainfield** (town) Hendricks County
45	10.7	**Wabash** (city) Wabash County
49	10.6	**Fort Branch** (town) Gibson County
49	10.6	**Fortville** (town) Hancock County
51	10.5	**Sellersburg** (town) Clark County
52	10.4	**Bedford** (city) Lawrence County
52	10.4	**Clinton** (city) Vermillion County
52	10.4	**Heritage Lake** (CDP) Putnam County
52	10.4	**Huntingburg** (city) Dubois County
52	10.4	**Jeffersonville** (city) Clark County
52	10.4	**McCordsville** (town) Hancock County
52	10.4	**New Haven** (city) Allen County
52	10.4	**Washington** (city) Daviess County
60	10.3	**Jasper** (city) Dubois County
60	10.3	**Merrillville** (town) Lake County
62	10.2	**Lowell** (town) Lake County
62	10.2	**Rochester** (city) Fulton County
64	10.0	**Anderson** (city) Madison County
64	10.0	**Columbia City** (city) Whitley County
64	10.0	**Georgetown** (town) Floyd County
64	10.0	**Kendallville** (city) Noble County
64	10.0	**North Terre Haute** (CDP) Vigo County
64	10.0	**Speedway** (town) Marion County
70	9.9	**Butler** (city) DeKalb County
71	9.8	**Garrett** (city) DeKalb County
71	9.8	**Gary** (city) Lake County
71	9.8	**Portage** (city) Porter County
71	9.8	**Simonton Lake** (CDP) Elkhart County
75	9.7	**Shorewood Forest** (CDP) Porter County
75	9.7	**Syracuse** (town) Kosciusko County
77	9.6	**Clarksville** (town) Clark County
77	9.6	**Greenwood** (city) Johnson County
77	9.6	**Mishawaka** (city) Saint Joseph County
77	9.6	**Winchester** (city) Randolph County
81	9.5	**Greenfield** (city) Hancock County
81	9.5	**Marion** (city) Grant County
81	9.5	**Rensselaer** (city) Jasper County
81	9.5	**Whiting** (city) Lake County
85	9.4	**Brookville** (town) Franklin County
85	9.4	**Chesterton** (town) Porter County
87	9.3	**Evansville** (city) Vanderburgh County
87	9.3	**Logansport** (city) Cass County
89	9.2	**Beech Grove** (city) Marion County
89	9.2	**Brownstown** (town) Jackson County
89	9.2	**Mount Vernon** (city) Posey County
89	9.2	**Plymouth** (city) Marshall County
89	9.2	**Union City** (city) Randolph County
94	9.1	**Brownsburg** (town) Hendricks County
94	9.1	**Fairmount** (town) Grant County
94	9.1	**Griffith** (town) Lake County
94	9.1	**Highland** (town) Lake County
98	9.0	**Bluffton** (city) Wells County
98	9.0	**Brazil** (city) Clay County
98	9.0	**Crown Point** (city) Lake County
98	9.0	**Dunlap** (CDP) Elkhart County
98	9.0	**Elwood** (city) Madison County
98	9.0	**Michigan City** (city) LaPorte County
98	9.0	**Paoli** (town) Orange County
98	9.0	**Shelbyville** (city) Shelby County
98	9.0	**Tipton** (city) Tipton County
107	8.9	**Alexandria** (city) Madison County
107	8.9	**Fort Wayne** (city) Allen County
107	8.9	**Knox** (city) Starke County
107	8.9	**Seymour** (city) Jackson County
111	8.8	**Dyer** (town) Lake County
111	8.8	**Edinburgh** (town) Johnson County
111	8.8	**Lake Station** (city) Lake County
111	8.8	**Madison** (city) Jefferson County
111	8.8	**Noblesville** (city) Hamilton County
116	8.7	**Columbus** (city) Bartholomew County
116	8.7	**Granger** (CDP) Saint Joseph County
116	8.7	**Lebanon** (city) Boone County
116	8.7	**Tell City** (city) Perry County
120	8.6	**Elkhart** (city) Elkhart County
120	8.6	**Winfield** (town) Lake County
122	8.5	**Lafayette** (city) Tippecanoe County
122	8.5	**Munster** (town) Lake County
122	8.5	**South Bend** (city) Saint Joseph County
125	8.4	**Batesville** (city) Ripley County
125	8.4	**Bright** (CDP) Dearborn County
125	8.4	**Charlestown** (city) Clark County
125	8.4	**Greensburg** (city) Decatur County
125	8.4	**Huntington** (city) Huntington County
125	8.4	**Scottsburg** (city) Scott County
125	8.4	**Warsaw** (city) Kosciusko County
132	8.3	**Chandler** (town) Warrick County
132	8.3	**Martinsville** (city) Morgan County
132	8.3	**Newburgh** (town) Warrick County
132	8.3	**North Vernon** (city) Jennings County
132	8.3	**Terre Haute** (city) Vigo County
132	8.3	**Valparaiso** (city) Porter County
138	8.2	**Frankfort** (city) Clinton County
138	8.2	**Portland** (city) Jay County
140	8.1	**Angola** (city) Steuben County
140	8.1	**Attica** (city) Fountain County
140	8.1	**Auburn** (city) DeKalb County
140	8.1	**Crawfordsville** (city) Montgomery County
140	8.1	**Highland** (CDP) Vanderburgh County
140	8.1	**Indianapolis** (city) Marion County
140	8.1	**Leo-Cedarville** (town) Allen County
140	8.1	**Saint John** (town) Lake County
140	8.1	**Schererville** (town) Lake County
149	8.0	**Danville** (town) Hendricks County
149	8.0	**Greendale** (city) Dearborn County

Note: This section ranks incorporated places and CDPs (Census Designated Places) with populations of 2,500 or more. Unincorporated postal areas were not considered. Please refer to the User Guide for additional information.

Veterans
Top 150 Places Ranked in *Ascending* Order

State Rank	Percent	Place
1	0.2	**Notre Dame** (CDP) Saint Joseph County
2	0.6	**Purdue University** (CDP) Tippecanoe County
3	3.5	**Middlebury** (town) Elkhart County
4	3.7	**West Lafayette** (city) Tippecanoe County
5	4.0	**Bloomington** (city) Monroe County
6	4.3	**Austin** (city) Scott County
7	4.4	**Whitestown** (town) Boone County
8	4.8	**Ossian** (town) Wells County
9	5.0	**Berne** (city) Adams County
10	5.2	**North Manchester** (town) Wabash County
11	5.6	**Greencastle** (city) Putnam County
11	5.6	**Upland** (town) Grant County
13	5.7	**Ligonier** (city) Noble County
14	5.8	**Hebron** (town) Porter County
15	5.9	**Whiteland** (town) Johnson County
16	6.0	**East Chicago** (city) Lake County
17	6.2	**Zionsville** (town) Boone County
18	6.7	**Goshen** (city) Elkhart County
19	6.8	**Sullivan** (city) Sullivan County
20	6.9	**Fishers** (town) Hamilton County
20	6.9	**Nappanee** (city) Elkhart County
20	6.9	**Westville** (town) LaPorte County
23	7.0	**Decatur** (city) Adams County
23	7.0	**Roselawn** (CDP) Newton County
25	7.1	**Smithville-Sanders** (CDP) Monroe County
26	7.3	**Carmel** (city) Hamilton County
26	7.3	**Vincennes** (city) Knox County
28	7.4	**Hanover** (town) Jefferson County
28	7.4	**Westfield** (city) Hamilton County
30	7.5	**Bremen** (town) Marshall County
31	7.6	**Hammond** (city) Lake County
31	7.6	**Pittsboro** (town) Hendricks County
33	7.7	**Ellettsville** (town) Monroe County
33	7.7	**New Whiteland** (town) Johnson County
35	7.8	**Cedar Lake** (town) Lake County
35	7.8	**Winona Lake** (town) Kosciusko County
37	7.9	**Muncie** (city) Delaware County
38	8.0	**Danville** (town) Hendricks County
38	8.0	**Greendale** (city) Dearborn County
38	8.0	**Salem** (city) Washington County
41	8.1	**Angola** (city) Steuben County
41	8.1	**Attica** (city) Fountain County
41	8.1	**Auburn** (city) DeKalb County
41	8.1	**Crawfordsville** (city) Montgomery County
41	8.1	**Highland** (CDP) Vanderburgh County
41	8.1	**Indianapolis** (city) Marion County
41	8.1	**Leo-Cedarville** (town) Allen County
41	8.1	**Saint John** (town) Lake County
41	8.1	**Schererville** (town) Lake County
50	8.2	**Frankfort** (city) Clinton County
50	8.2	**Portland** (city) Jay County
52	8.3	**Chandler** (town) Warrick County
52	8.3	**Martinsville** (city) Morgan County
52	8.3	**Newburgh** (town) Warrick County
52	8.3	**North Vernon** (city) Jennings County
52	8.3	**Terre Haute** (city) Vigo County
52	8.3	**Valparaiso** (city) Porter County
58	8.4	**Batesville** (city) Ripley County
58	8.4	**Bright** (CDP) Dearborn County
58	8.4	**Charlestown** (city) Clark County
58	8.4	**Greensburg** (city) Decatur County
58	8.4	**Huntington** (city) Huntington County
58	8.4	**Scottsburg** (city) Scott County
58	8.4	**Warsaw** (city) Kosciusko County
65	8.5	**Lafayette** (city) Tippecanoe County
65	8.5	**Munster** (town) Lake County
65	8.5	**South Bend** (city) Saint Joseph County
68	8.6	**Elkhart** (city) Elkhart County
68	8.6	**Winfield** (town) Lake County
70	8.7	**Columbus** (city) Bartholomew County
70	8.7	**Granger** (CDP) Saint Joseph County
70	8.7	**Lebanon** (city) Boone County
70	8.7	**Tell City** (city) Perry County
74	8.8	**Dyer** (town) Lake County
74	8.8	**Edinburgh** (town) Johnson County
74	8.8	**Lake Station** (city) Lake County
74	8.8	**Madison** (city) Jefferson County
74	8.8	**Noblesville** (city) Hamilton County
79	8.9	**Alexandria** (city) Madison County
79	8.9	**Fort Wayne** (city) Allen County
79	8.9	**Knox** (city) Starke County
79	8.9	**Seymour** (city) Jackson County
83	9.0	**Bluffton** (city) Wells County
83	9.0	**Brazil** (city) Clay County
83	9.0	**Crown Point** (city) Lake County
83	9.0	**Dunlap** (CDP) Elkhart County
83	9.0	**Elwood** (city) Madison County
83	9.0	**Michigan City** (city) LaPorte County
83	9.0	**Paoli** (town) Orange County
83	9.0	**Shelbyville** (city) Shelby County
83	9.0	**Tipton** (city) Tipton County
92	9.1	**Brownsburg** (town) Hendricks County
92	9.1	**Fairmount** (town) Grant County
92	9.1	**Griffith** (town) Lake County
92	9.1	**Highland** (town) Lake County
96	9.2	**Beech Grove** (city) Marion County
96	9.2	**Brownstown** (town) Jackson County
96	9.2	**Mount Vernon** (city) Posey County
96	9.2	**Plymouth** (city) Marshall County
96	9.2	**Union City** (city) Randolph County
101	9.3	**Evansville** (city) Vanderburgh County
101	9.3	**Logansport** (city) Cass County
103	9.4	**Brookville** (town) Franklin County
103	9.4	**Chesterton** (town) Porter County
105	9.5	**Greenfield** (city) Hancock County
105	9.5	**Marion** (city) Grant County
105	9.5	**Rensselaer** (city) Jasper County
105	9.5	**Whiting** (city) Lake County
109	9.6	**Clarksville** (town) Clark County
109	9.6	**Greenwood** (city) Johnson County
109	9.6	**Mishawaka** (city) Saint Joseph County
109	9.6	**Winchester** (city) Randolph County
113	9.7	**Shorewood Forest** (CDP) Porter County
113	9.7	**Syracuse** (town) Kosciusko County
115	9.8	**Garrett** (city) DeKalb County
115	9.8	**Gary** (city) Lake County
115	9.8	**Portage** (city) Porter County
115	9.8	**Simonton Lake** (CDP) Elkhart County
119	9.9	**Butler** (city) DeKalb County
120	10.0	**Anderson** (city) Madison County
120	10.0	**Columbia City** (city) Whitley County
120	10.0	**Georgetown** (town) Floyd County
120	10.0	**Kendallville** (city) Noble County
120	10.0	**North Terre Haute** (CDP) Vigo County
120	10.0	**Speedway** (town) Marion County
126	10.2	**Lowell** (town) Lake County
126	10.2	**Rochester** (city) Fulton County
128	10.3	**Jasper** (city) Dubois County
128	10.3	**Merrillville** (town) Lake County
130	10.4	**Bedford** (city) Lawrence County
130	10.4	**Clinton** (city) Vermillion County
130	10.4	**Heritage Lake** (CDP) Putnam County
130	10.4	**Huntingburg** (city) Dubois County
130	10.4	**Jeffersonville** (city) Clark County
130	10.4	**McCordsville** (town) Hancock County
130	10.4	**New Haven** (city) Allen County
130	10.4	**Washington** (city) Daviess County
138	10.5	**Sellersburg** (town) Clark County
139	10.6	**Fort Branch** (town) Gibson County
139	10.6	**Fortville** (town) Hancock County
141	10.7	**Huntertown** (town) Allen County
141	10.7	**New Albany** (city) Floyd County
141	10.7	**Plainfield** (town) Hendricks County
141	10.7	**Wabash** (city) Wabash County
145	10.8	**Richmond** (city) Wayne County
146	10.9	**Boonville** (city) Warrick County
146	10.9	**Cumberland** (town) Marion County
146	10.9	**Lawrenceburg** (city) Dearborn County
146	10.9	**Mitchell** (city) Lawrence County
150	11.0	**Avon** (town) Hendricks County

Note: This section ranks incorporated places and CDPs (Census Designated Places) with populations of 2,500 or more. Unincorporated postal areas were not considered. Please refer to the User Guide for additional information.

Ancestry: German
Top 150 Places Ranked in *Descending* Order

State Rank	Percent	Place
1	76.8	**Chilton** (city) Calumet County
2	73.3	**Barton** (town) Washington County
3	73.0	**Addison** (town) Washington County
4	72.6	**Dyersville** (city) Dubuque County
5	70.9	**Jackson** (town) Washington County
6	70.5	**Howards Grove** (village) Sheboygan County
7	70.3	**Mayville** (city) Dodge County
8	69.9	**Minster** (village) Auglaize County
9	69.1	**Hartford** (town) Washington County
9	69.1	**Polk** (town) Washington County
11	68.4	**Medford** (town) Taylor County
12	68.1	**Brillion** (city) Calumet County
13	67.8	**Kiel** (city) Manitowoc County
14	67.7	**Hortonville** (village) Outagamie County
15	66.9	**Wakefield** (township) Stearns County
16	66.1	**Center** (town) Outagamie County
17	66.0	**Plymouth** (town) Sheboygan County
17	66.0	**Sheboygan** (town) Sheboygan County
17	66.0	**Trenton** (town) Washington County
20	65.8	**Fayette** (township) Juniata County
20	65.8	**Wheatland** (town) Kenosha County
22	65.5	**Kewaskum** (village) Washington County
23	65.4	**Springfield** (town) Dane County
24	65.2	**Empire** (town) Fond du Lac County
25	64.8	**Mukwa** (town) Waupaca County
26	64.2	**Albany** (city) Stearns County
27	64.0	**Jackson** (village) Washington County
28	63.9	**New Bremen** (village) Auglaize County
29	63.8	**New Ulm** (city) Brown County
30	63.0	**Coldwater** (village) Mercer County
30	63.0	**West Bend** (town) Washington County
32	62.3	**Breese** (city) Clinton County
33	61.9	**Taycheedah** (town) Fond du Lac County
34	61.4	**Merrill** (town) Lincoln County
34	61.4	**New Holstein** (city) Calumet County
36	60.9	**Beaver Dam** (town) Dodge County
36	60.9	**Friendship** (town) Fond du Lac County
36	60.9	**Mandan** (city) Morton County
39	60.8	**Miami Heights** (CDP) Hamilton County
40	60.6	**Plymouth** (city) Sheboygan County
40	60.6	**Sheboygan Falls** (city) Sheboygan County
42	60.4	**Medford** (city) Taylor County
43	60.3	**Merrill** (city) Lincoln County
43	60.3	**Saint Marys** (city) Elk County
45	60.2	**Elizabeth** (township) Lancaster County
46	59.7	**Stettin** (town) Marathon County
47	59.6	**Merton** (village) Waukesha County
48	59.5	**Wales** (village) Waukesha County
49	59.4	**Dale** (town) Outagamie County
49	59.4	**Germantown** (village) Washington County
49	59.4	**Grundy Center** (city) Grundy County
49	59.4	**Saint Augusta** (city) Stearns County
53	59.3	**Columbus** (city) Columbia County
53	59.3	**Farmington** (town) Washington County
55	59.2	**Fond du Lac** (town) Fond du Lac County
55	59.2	**Wayne** (city) Wayne County
57	59.1	**Caledonia** (city) Houston County
58	58.9	**Ixonia** (town) Jefferson County
58	58.9	**Lodi** (town) Columbia County
60	58.3	**Horicon** (city) Dodge County
61	58.2	**Johnson Creek** (village) Jefferson County
62	58.0	**Oakland** (town) Jefferson County
62	58.0	**Sauk Centre** (city) Stearns County
64	57.8	**Richfield** (village) Washington County
65	57.7	**Harrison** (town) Calumet County
65	57.7	**Sebewaing** (township) Huron County
67	57.6	**Fox** (township) Elk County
67	57.6	**West Bend** (city) Washington County
69	57.4	**Grafton** (town) Ozaukee County
69	57.4	**Ripon** (city) Fond du Lac County
71	57.3	**Harrison** (city) Hamilton County
72	57.2	**Carroll** (city) Carroll County
72	57.2	**Washington** (township) Schuylkill County
74	57.1	**Kronenwetter** (village) Marathon County
75	56.9	**Ellington** (town) Outagamie County
76	56.8	**Norwood Young America** (city) Carver County
76	56.8	**Saukville** (village) Ozaukee County
78	56.5	**Sherwood** (village) Calumet County
78	56.5	**Slinger** (village) Washington County
80	56.4	**Delphos** (city) Allen County
80	56.4	**Oregon** (town) Dane County
80	56.4	**Shelby** (town) La Crosse County
83	56.3	**Lisbon** (town) Waukesha County
83	56.3	**Sussex** (village) Waukesha County
85	56.2	**Bismarck** (city) Burleigh County
85	56.2	**Poynette** (village) Columbia County
87	56.0	**Alsace** (township) Berks County
87	56.0	**Jordan** (city) Scott County
89	55.9	**Eagle** (town) Waukesha County
90	55.8	**Waukesha** (town) Waukesha County
91	55.7	**Clayton** (town) Winnebago County
91	55.7	**Pine Grove** (township) Schuylkill County
93	55.6	**Ashippun** (town) Dodge County
93	55.6	**Rockland** (township) Berks County
95	55.5	**Clintonville** (city) Waupaca County
95	55.5	**Pewaukee** (city) Waukesha County
95	55.5	**Sevastopol** (town) Door County
98	55.3	**Lake Crystal** (city) Blue Earth County
98	55.3	**Plainview** (city) Wabasha County
98	55.3	**Rock Rapids** (city) Lyon County
101	55.2	**De Witt** (city) Clinton County
101	55.2	**Merton** (town) Waukesha County
101	55.2	**Watertown** (city) Jefferson County
104	55.1	**Hartford** (city) Washington County
105	55.0	**Upper Augusta** (township) Northumberland County
106	54.9	**Delhi Hills** (CDP) Hamilton County
107	54.8	**Aberdeen** (city) Brown County
107	54.8	**Delafield** (city) Waukesha County
109	54.7	**Jamestown** (city) Stutsman County
110	54.6	**Cottage Grove** (town) Dane County
110	54.6	**Hallam** (borough) York County
110	54.6	**Vernon** (town) Waukesha County
113	54.5	**Monticello** (city) Jones County
113	54.5	**Mukwonago** (town) Waukesha County
115	54.4	**Milbank** (city) Grant County
116	54.3	**Beulah** (city) Mercer County
116	54.3	**Cross Plains** (village) Dane County
116	54.3	**Lima** (town) Sheboygan County
119	54.2	**Algoma** (city) Kewaunee County
119	54.2	**Cold Spring** (city) Stearns County
119	54.2	**Lodi** (city) Columbia County
119	54.2	**Monfort Heights** (CDP) Hamilton County
123	54.1	**Mack** (CDP) Hamilton County
123	54.1	**North Mankato** (city) Nicollet County
125	54.0	**Menasha** (town) Winnebago County
125	54.0	**Rome** (town) Adams County
127	53.9	**Hays** (city) Ellis County
128	53.8	**Brockway** (township) Stearns County
128	53.8	**Dent** (CDP) Hamilton County
128	53.8	**Lake Wazeecha** (CDP) Wood County
128	53.8	**Sleepy Eye** (city) Brown County
132	53.7	**Zumbrota** (city) Goodhue County
133	53.6	**Dickinson** (city) Stark County
134	53.5	**Beaver Dam** (city) Dodge County
134	53.5	**Fond du Lac** (city) Fond du Lac County
134	53.5	**Wescott** (town) Shawano County
137	53.4	**Eagle Point** (town) Chippewa County
137	53.4	**Grafton** (village) Ozaukee County
139	53.3	**Freeburg** (village) Saint Clair County
140	53.2	**Lake Wisconsin** (CDP) Columbia County
140	53.2	**Marshfield** (city) Wood County
142	53.1	**Dell Rapids** (city) Minnehaha County
142	53.1	**Lake Mills** (city) Jefferson County
142	53.1	**Muskego** (city) Waukesha County
142	53.1	**Oregon** (village) Dane County
142	53.1	**Portage** (city) Columbia County
147	53.0	**Hereford** (township) Berks County
147	53.0	**Marysville** (city) Marshall County
147	53.0	**North Fond du Lac** (village) Fond du Lac County
150	52.9	**Blackhawk** (CDP) Meade County

Note: This section ranks incorporated places and CDPs (Census Designated Places) with populations of 2,500 or more. Unincorporated postal areas were not considered. Please refer to the User Guide for additional information.

Ancestry: English
Top 150 Places Ranked in *Descending* Order

State Rank	Percent	Place
1	84.4	**Hildale** (city) Washington County
2	66.2	**Colorado City** (town) Mohave County
3	42.2	**Alpine** (city) Utah County
4	41.5	**Fruit Heights** (city) Davis County
4	41.5	**Manti** (city) Sanpete County
6	40.8	**Highland** (city) Utah County
7	40.5	**Mapleton** (city) Utah County
8	39.1	**Beaver** (city) Beaver County
9	38.4	**Centerville** (city) Davis County
10	38.2	**Hooper** (city) Weber County
10	38.2	**Hopkinton** (town) Merrimack County
12	37.8	**Sheridan** (city) Grant County
13	36.9	**Santa Clara** (city) Washington County
14	36.0	**Saint George** (town) Knox County
15	35.9	**Farmingdale** (town) Kennebec County
16	35.7	**Bountiful** (city) Davis County
17	35.6	**Rockport** (town) Knox County
18	35.4	**Kanab** (city) Kane County
18	35.4	**McCall** (city) Valley County
20	35.0	**Wolfeboro** (CDP) Carroll County
21	34.8	**Farr West** (city) Weber County
21	34.8	**Providence** (city) Cache County
23	34.6	**Bristol** (town) Lincoln County
23	34.6	**Rexburg** (city) Madison County
25	34.5	**North Logan** (city) Cache County
26	34.3	**Boothbay** (town) Lincoln County
26	34.3	**Parowan** (city) Iron County
28	34.2	**Pleasant View** (city) Weber County
29	33.8	**Wellsville** (city) Cache County
30	33.6	**Monmouth** (town) Kennebec County
31	33.5	**Holladay** (city) Salt Lake County
32	33.4	**Hyde Park** (city) Cache County
32	33.4	**Trent Woods** (town) Craven County
34	33.0	**Salem** (city) Utah County
35	32.9	**Delta** (city) Millard County
36	32.8	**Freeport** (town) Cumberland County
36	32.8	**Midway** (city) Wasatch County
36	32.8	**West Bountiful** (city) Davis County
39	32.6	**Farmington** (city) Davis County
39	32.6	**Kaysville** (city) Davis County
41	32.5	**Kennebunkport** (town) York County
42	32.4	**Wolfeboro** (town) Carroll County
43	32.2	**Woodstock** (town) Windsor County
44	32.0	**Santaquin** (city) Utah County
45	31.9	**Chichester** (town) Merrimack County
46	31.8	**American Fork** (city) Utah County
46	31.8	**Anson** (town) Somerset County
46	31.8	**Camden** (town) Knox County
46	31.8	**Hyrum** (city) Cache County
50	31.6	**Spring Arbor** (township) Jackson County
51	31.5	**Poland** (town) Androscoggin County
52	31.4	**Herriman** (city) Salt Lake County
53	31.3	**Morgan** (city) Morgan County
54	31.1	**Alamo** (town) Wheeler County
54	31.1	**Charlestown** (town) Sullivan County
56	31.0	**Spanish Fork** (city) Utah County
56	31.0	**Waldoboro** (town) Lincoln County
58	30.9	**Ivins** (city) Washington County
59	30.8	**Yarmouth** (town) Cumberland County
60	30.7	**Cedar Hills** (city) Utah County
61	30.6	**Bethel** (town) Oxford County
61	30.6	**Bridgton** (town) Cumberland County
61	30.6	**Lake San Marcos** (CDP) San Diego County
61	30.6	**Rockland** (city) Knox County
61	30.6	**Saint George** (city) Washington County
61	30.6	**Woods Cross** (city) Davis County
67	30.5	**Cedar City** (city) Iron County
68	30.3	**North Salt Lake** (city) Davis County
68	30.3	**South Jordan** (city) Salt Lake County
70	30.2	**Eagle Mountain** (city) Utah County
71	30.1	**Preston** (city) Franklin County
72	29.9	**Camden** (CDP) Knox County
73	29.8	**South Beach** (CDP) Indian River County
74	29.7	**Harpswell** (town) Cumberland County
74	29.7	**Indian River Shores** (town) Indian River County
76	29.5	**Helena** (city) Telfair County
76	29.5	**Manchester** (town) Kennebec County
76	29.5	**Nephi** (city) Juab County
76	29.5	**Washington Terrace** (city) Weber County
80	29.4	**Yarmouth** (CDP) Cumberland County
81	29.3	**Springville** (city) Utah County
82	29.2	**Clinton** (town) Kennebec County
82	29.2	**Grantsville** (city) Tooele County
84	29.1	**Little Compton** (town) Newport County
84	29.1	**Plain City** (city) Weber County
86	29.0	**Cottonwood Heights** (city) Salt Lake County
86	29.0	**Warren** (town) Knox County
88	28.9	**Madison** (town) Carroll County
88	28.9	**Washington** (city) Washington County
90	28.8	**Lindon** (city) Utah County
90	28.8	**Livermore Falls** (town) Androscoggin County
90	28.8	**Nibley** (city) Cache County
93	28.7	**Orem** (city) Utah County
93	28.7	**Woolwich** (town) Sagadahoc County
95	28.6	**Pleasant Grove** (city) Utah County
96	28.5	**Arundel** (town) York County
96	28.5	**China** (town) Kennebec County
98	28.4	**Lehi** (city) Utah County
98	28.4	**Tamworth** (town) Carroll County
100	28.3	**Bradford** (town) Orange County
100	28.3	**Enoch** (city) Iron County
102	28.2	**Oneida** (town) Scott County
102	28.2	**Oxford** (town) Oxford County
102	28.2	**South Weber** (city) Davis County
105	28.1	**Maeser** (CDP) Uintah County
105	28.1	**Walpole** (town) Cheshire County
107	28.0	**Hampden** (CDP) Penobscot County
107	28.0	**Sandy** (city) Salt Lake County
109	27.9	**Northfield** (town) Franklin County
109	27.9	**Perry** (city) Box Elder County
111	27.8	**Limerick** (town) York County
111	27.8	**Orleans** (town) Barnstable County
111	27.8	**Riverton** (city) Salt Lake County
114	27.7	**Draper** (city) Salt Lake County
114	27.7	**Hartland** (town) Windsor County
114	27.7	**Otisco** (town) Onondaga County
114	27.7	**Saratoga Springs** (city) Utah County
114	27.7	**Smithfield** (city) Cache County
119	27.6	**Bluffdale** (city) Salt Lake County
119	27.6	**Bowdoin** (town) Sagadahoc County
119	27.6	**East Bloomfield** (town) Ontario County
119	27.6	**North Yarmouth** (town) Cumberland County
119	27.6	**Syracuse** (city) Davis County
124	27.5	**Harrison** (town) Cumberland County
124	27.5	**Highland Park** (town) Dallas County
124	27.5	**South Eliot** (CDP) York County
127	27.4	**Hampden** (town) Penobscot County
127	27.4	**Montpelier** (city) Bear Lake County
127	27.4	**Winston** (city) Douglas County
130	27.3	**Buxton** (town) York County
130	27.3	**North Ogden** (city) Weber County
130	27.3	**White Hall** (city) Jefferson County
133	27.2	**Thetford** (town) Orange County
134	27.1	**Greene** (town) Chenango County
134	27.1	**Wakefield** (town) Carroll County
136	26.9	**New Durham** (town) Strafford County
136	26.9	**Stansbury Park** (CDP) Tooele County
136	26.9	**Surfside Beach** (town) Horry County
139	26.8	**Stratham** (town) Rockingham County
140	26.6	**Concord** (township) Jackson County
140	26.6	**Millcreek** (CDP) Salt Lake County
140	26.6	**Peterborough** (CDP) Hillsborough County
140	26.6	**Turner** (town) Androscoggin County
144	26.5	**Foster** (town) Providence County
144	26.5	**Hope** (township) Barry County
144	26.5	**Norwich** (town) Windsor County
147	26.4	**Belle Meade** (city) Davidson County
148	26.3	**Belfast** (city) Waldo County
149	26.2	**Richfield** (city) Sevier County
149	26.2	**South Duxbury** (CDP) Plymouth County

Note: This section ranks incorporated places and CDPs (Census Designated Places) with populations of 2,500 or more. Unincorporated postal areas were not considered. Please refer to the User Guide for additional information.

Ancestry: American
Top 150 Places Ranked in *Descending* Order

State Rank	Percent	Place
1	66.4	**La Follette** (city) Campbell County
2	60.0	**Gloverville** (CDP) Aiken County
3	54.6	**Clearwater** (CDP) Aiken County
4	54.4	**Treasure Lake** (CDP) Clearfield County
5	51.7	**Healdton** (city) Carter County
6	45.9	**Bonifay** (city) Holmes County
7	45.8	**Harlem** (CDP) Hendry County
8	45.5	**Bean Station** (city) Grainger County
8	45.5	**Stanford** (city) Lincoln County
10	44.5	**Pell City** (city) Saint Clair County
11	44.3	**New Tazewell** (town) Claiborne County
12	43.9	**Dresden** (town) Weakley County
13	43.6	**Hartford** (city) Ohio County
14	43.2	**Blue Hill** (town) Hancock County
15	43.1	**Eaton** (town) Madison County
16	43.0	**Church Hill** (city) Hawkins County
17	42.6	**Middlesborough** (city) Bell County
18	42.1	**Temple** (city) Carroll County
19	41.1	**Georgetown** (city) Vermilion County
20	40.9	**Grantville** (city) Coweta County
20	40.9	**Summerville** (city) Chattooga County
22	40.6	**Morehead** (city) Rowan County
23	40.5	**Bayou Vista** (CDP) Saint Mary Parish
24	40.4	**Lone Grove** (city) Carter County
24	40.4	**Wilkesboro** (town) Wilkes County
26	39.9	**Chincoteague** (town) Accomack County
27	39.8	**Bremen** (city) Haralson County
28	39.7	**Cullowhee** (CDP) Jackson County
29	39.4	**Nassau Village-Ratliff** (CDP) Nassau County
30	38.8	**Crab Orchard** (CDP) Raleigh County
31	38.7	**Stanton** (city) Powell County
32	38.4	**Rogersville** (town) Hawkins County
33	38.2	**Cookeville** (city) Putnam County
34	38.0	**Livingston** (town) Overton County
35	37.6	**Gray Summit** (CDP) Franklin County
35	37.6	**Harrogate** (city) Claiborne County
37	37.4	**North Terre Haute** (CDP) Vigo County
38	37.3	**Mount Carmel** (CDP) Clermont County
39	36.9	**Atkins** (city) Pope County
39	36.9	**Burnettown** (town) Aiken County
39	36.9	**De Funiak Springs** (city) Walton County
42	36.8	**Lake of the Woods** (CDP) Champaign County
42	36.8	**Suncoast Estates** (CDP) Lee County
44	36.7	**Lancaster** (city) Garrard County
44	36.7	**Sandy** (township) Clearfield County
46	36.6	**Donalsonville** (city) Seminole County
47	36.3	**Bradford** (township) Clearfield County
47	36.3	**Broadway** (town) Rockingham County
47	36.3	**Jena** (town) La Salle Parish
50	36.2	**Algood** (city) Putnam County
50	36.2	**Sylva** (town) Jackson County
52	36.0	**Unicoi** (town) Unicoi County
53	35.6	**Bloomingdale** (CDP) Sullivan County
53	35.6	**Somerset** (city) Pulaski County
53	35.6	**Timberville** (town) Rockingham County
56	35.5	**Beaver Dam** (city) Ohio County
56	35.5	**Oliver Springs** (town) Anderson County
58	35.4	**Bucksport** (CDP) Hancock County
59	35.1	**England** (city) Lonoke County
59	35.1	**Fairview** (CDP) Walker County
59	35.1	**LaFayette** (city) Walker County
62	34.9	**Bucksport** (town) Hancock County
62	34.9	**Mountain City** (town) Johnson County
62	34.9	**Shepherdsville** (city) Bullitt County
65	34.8	**Blennerhassett** (CDP) Wood County
66	34.7	**South Lebanon** (village) Warren County
67	34.5	**Mount Carmel** (town) Hawkins County
68	34.3	**Hannahs Mill** (CDP) Upson County
69	34.2	**Mills** (town) Natrona County
69	34.2	**Rockwood** (city) Roane County
71	33.5	**North Wilkesboro** (town) Wilkes County
71	33.5	**Odenville** (town) Saint Clair County
73	33.3	**Ward** (city) Lonoke County
74	33.2	**Bawcomville** (CDP) Ouachita Parish
75	33.1	**Bethel** (village) Clermont County
75	33.1	**Grottoes** (town) Rockingham County
77	33.0	**Shelbyville** (city) Bedford County
78	32.7	**Dawson Springs** (city) Hopkins County
78	32.7	**Galena** (city) Cherokee County
78	32.7	**Pike Road** (town) Montgomery County
81	32.6	**Erwin** (town) Unicoi County
81	32.6	**Honea Path** (town) Anderson County
83	32.5	**West Tisbury** (town) Dukes County
84	32.3	**Pearisburg** (town) Giles County
85	32.2	**Evansville** (town) Natrona County
86	32.0	**Moody** (city) Saint Clair County
86	32.0	**Pittsburg** (city) Crawford County
88	31.9	**Woodbury** (town) Cannon County
89	31.8	**Dandridge** (town) Jefferson County
90	31.7	**Withamsville** (CDP) Clermont County
91	31.5	**Margaret** (town) Saint Clair County
92	31.4	**Pigeon Forge** (city) Sevier County
93	31.3	**Alva** (CDP) Lee County
94	31.1	**Hilliard** (town) Nassau County
95	30.8	**Monterey** (town) Putnam County
96	30.7	**Icard** (CDP) Burke County
97	30.5	**Flemingsburg** (city) Fleming County
97	30.5	**Shady Spring** (CDP) Raleigh County
99	30.4	**Irvine** (city) Estill County
100	30.3	**Cloverdale** (CDP) Botetourt County
100	30.3	**Hamilton** (town) Madison County
100	30.3	**Sylacauga** (city) Talladega County
100	30.3	**Underwood-Petersville** (CDP) Lauderdale County
104	30.2	**Central City** (city) Muhlenberg County
104	30.2	**Harriman** (city) Roane County
104	30.2	**Prestonsburg** (city) Floyd County
107	30.1	**Stuarts Draft** (CDP) Augusta County
108	30.0	**Madison** (town) Madison County
108	30.0	**Verona** (CDP) Augusta County
108	30.0	**Waynesville** (town) Haywood County
111	29.8	**Granville** (town) Washington County
111	29.8	**Paris** (city) Bourbon County
111	29.8	**Winchester** (city) Clark County
114	29.7	**Byron** (city) Peach County
114	29.7	**Emmett** (city) Gem County
114	29.7	**Hillview** (city) Bullitt County
114	29.7	**Oak Grove** (CDP) Washington County
114	29.7	**Sunnyvale** (town) Dallas County
114	29.7	**Wickenburg** (town) Maricopa County
120	29.6	**Jefferson City** (city) Jefferson County
121	29.5	**Ball** (town) Rapides Parish
121	29.5	**Corinth** (town) Penobscot County
121	29.5	**Lincoln** (city) Talladega County
124	29.4	**Manchester** (city) Coffee County
124	29.4	**Owensboro** (city) Daviess County
126	29.3	**Kings Mountain** (city) Cleveland County
127	29.2	**Buckner** (CDP) Oldham County
127	29.2	**Malabar** (town) Brevard County
129	29.1	**Baxter Springs** (city) Cherokee County
130	28.9	**Kingston** (city) Roane County
130	28.9	**Morristown** (city) Hamblen County
132	28.8	**Bayshore** (CDP) New Hanover County
132	28.8	**Buena Vista** (independent city)
134	28.7	**Grissom AFB** (CDP) Miami County
134	28.7	**Hodgenville** (city) Larue County
136	28.5	**Claiborne** (CDP) Ouachita Parish
136	28.5	**Inwood** (CDP) Polk County
136	28.5	**Moyock** (CDP) Currituck County
136	28.5	**Richlands** (town) Tazewell County
136	28.5	**Tabor City** (town) Columbus County
141	28.4	**Dundee** (town) Polk County
141	28.4	**Jan Phyl Village** (CDP) Polk County
141	28.4	**Morgan** (city) Morgan County
144	28.3	**West Liberty** (city) Morgan County
145	28.2	**Bicknell** (city) Knox County
145	28.2	**Fort Scott** (city) Bourbon County
145	28.2	**Putney** (CDP) Dougherty County
148	28.1	**Berwick** (town) Saint Mary Parish
148	28.1	**Corinth** (town) Saratoga County
148	28.1	**Middleton** (city) Canyon County

Note: This section ranks incorporated places and CDPs (Census Designated Places) with populations of 2,500 or more. Unincorporated postal areas were not considered. Please refer to the User Guide for additional information.

Ancestry: Irish
Top 150 Places Ranked in *Descending* Order

State Rank	Percent	Place
1	52.0	Pearl River (CDP) Rockland County
2	51.7	Ocean Bluff-Brant Rock (CDP) Plymouth County
3	50.6	Green Harbor-Cedar Crest (CDP) Plymouth County
4	49.4	Rockledge (borough) Montgomery County
5	48.3	Walpole (CDP) Norfolk County
6	47.4	North Scituate (CDP) Plymouth County
7	47.0	Scituate (CDP) Plymouth County
8	46.9	Marshfield (town) Plymouth County
9	46.2	Scituate (town) Plymouth County
10	45.8	Ridley Park (borough) Delaware County
11	45.5	Spring Lake Heights (borough) Monmouth County
12	45.3	Oak Valley (CDP) Gloucester County
13	45.2	Hanover (town) Plymouth County
14	44.7	Norwell (town) Plymouth County
15	44.2	Glenside (CDP) Montgomery County
15	44.2	Manasquan (borough) Monmouth County
17	43.8	Norwood (borough) Delaware County
18	42.9	Walpole (town) Norfolk County
18	42.9	Wynantskill (CDP) Rensselaer County
20	42.8	Springfield (township) Delaware County
21	42.6	Folsom (CDP) Delaware County
21	42.6	Glenolden (borough) Delaware County
21	42.6	Highlands (borough) Monmouth County
24	42.2	Marshfield (CDP) Plymouth County
25	41.7	North Middletown (CDP) Monmouth County
26	41.6	Braintree Town (city) Norfolk County
27	41.4	Weymouth Town (city) Norfolk County
28	41.1	Littleton Common (CDP) Middlesex County
28	41.1	North Wildwood (city) Cape May County
30	41.0	Bridgewater (CDP) Plymouth County
31	40.9	Abington (cdp/town) Plymouth County
31	40.9	Nahant (cdp/town) Essex County
31	40.9	Spring Lake (borough) Monmouth County
34	40.6	Whitman (town) Plymouth County
35	40.5	Cohasset (town) Norfolk County
35	40.5	Hopedale (CDP) Worcester County
35	40.5	Sayville (CDP) Suffolk County
38	40.4	Brielle (borough) Monmouth County
39	40.3	Hull (cdp/town) Plymouth County
40	40.2	Gloucester City (city) Camden County
41	39.9	Churchville (CDP) Bucks County
42	39.7	Haddon Heights (borough) Camden County
43	39.6	Notre Dame (CDP) Saint Joseph County
44	39.5	Ashland (borough) Schuylkill County
44	39.5	Hingham (town) Plymouth County
46	39.4	Avon (town) Norfolk County
47	39.3	Garden City (village) Nassau County
47	39.3	Tinicum (township) Delaware County
49	39.2	Milton (cdp/town) Norfolk County
49	39.2	Ramtown (CDP) Monmouth County
51	39.1	Ridley (township) Delaware County
52	38.8	Bridgewater (town) Plymouth County
53	38.5	Hanson (town) Plymouth County
53	38.5	North Reading (town) Middlesex County
53	38.5	Prospect Park (borough) Delaware County
53	38.5	Rockland (town) Plymouth County
57	38.4	Hingham (CDP) Plymouth County
58	38.3	Foxborough (town) Norfolk County
59	38.1	Foxborough (CDP) Norfolk County
60	38.0	Barrington (borough) Camden County
61	37.9	Aldan (borough) Delaware County
61	37.9	Mansfield Center (CDP) Bristol County
61	37.9	National Park (borough) Gloucester County
64	37.8	East Sandwich (CDP) Barnstable County
65	37.6	Haverford (township) Delaware County
65	37.6	West Brandywine (township) Chester County
67	37.5	East Bridgewater (town) Plymouth County
68	37.4	Buzzards Bay (CDP) Barnstable County
69	37.3	Blauvelt (CDP) Rockland County
69	37.3	East Quogue (CDP) Suffolk County
71	37.2	Canton (town) Norfolk County
71	37.2	North Falmouth (CDP) Barnstable County
73	37.1	Pembroke (town) Plymouth County
73	37.1	Upton (CDP) Worcester County
73	37.1	Woodbury Heights (borough) Gloucester County
76	36.9	Fair Haven (borough) Monmouth County
77	36.8	Clementon (borough) Camden County
77	36.8	Duxbury (town) Plymouth County
79	36.7	Fairview (CDP) Monmouth County
79	36.7	Folcroft (borough) Delaware County
79	36.7	Newtown (township) Delaware County
82	36.6	Rockville Centre (village) Nassau County
83	36.5	Oceanport (borough) Monmouth County
83	36.5	West Bridgewater (town) Plymouth County
85	36.2	Audubon (borough) Camden County
85	36.2	Campo (CDP) San Diego County
87	36.0	Orleans (town) Jefferson County
87	36.0	Shark River Hills (CDP) Monmouth County
89	35.8	Drexel Hill (CDP) Delaware County
89	35.8	Trappe (borough) Montgomery County
89	35.8	West Sayville (CDP) Suffolk County
92	35.5	Leonardo (CDP) Monmouth County
92	35.5	Little Silver (borough) Monmouth County
94	35.3	Bethlehem (township) Hunterdon County
95	35.2	East Islip (CDP) Suffolk County
95	35.2	Kingston (town) Plymouth County
97	35.1	Dedham (cdp/town) Norfolk County
97	35.1	Hopedale (town) Worcester County
97	35.1	Wilmington (cdp/town) Middlesex County
100	35.0	Green Island (town/village) Albany County
100	35.0	Medford Lakes (borough) Burlington County
102	34.9	Holbrook (cdp/town) Norfolk County
102	34.9	Mansfield (town) Bristol County
104	34.8	LaFayette (town) Onondaga County
104	34.8	North Plymouth (CDP) Plymouth County
104	34.8	Norton (town) Bristol County
104	34.8	Tuckerton (borough) Ocean County
104	34.8	Wakefield (cdp/town) Middlesex County
109	34.7	Cape Neddick (CDP) York County
109	34.7	Tewksbury (town) Middlesex County
109	34.7	Woodlyn (CDP) Delaware County
109	34.7	Woolwich (township) Gloucester County
113	34.6	Wanamassa (CDP) Monmouth County
114	34.5	East Shoreham (CDP) Suffolk County
114	34.5	Horsham (CDP) Montgomery County
114	34.5	Skippack (CDP) Montgomery County
117	34.4	Plymouth (town) Plymouth County
117	34.4	Western Springs (village) Cook County
119	34.3	Bethel (township) Delaware County
119	34.3	Melrose (city) Middlesex County
119	34.3	Point Pleasant (borough) Ocean County
122	34.2	Aston (township) Delaware County
122	34.2	North Seekonk (CDP) Bristol County
122	34.2	Wanakah (CDP) Erie County
122	34.2	Westvale (CDP) Onondaga County
126	34.1	Reading (cdp/town) Middlesex County
126	34.1	Winthrop Town (city) Suffolk County
128	34.0	Atkinson (town) Rockingham County
128	34.0	Bella Vista (CDP) Shasta County
128	34.0	Hopkinton (CDP) Middlesex County
128	34.0	Plymouth (CDP) Plymouth County
128	34.0	Washington (town) Dutchess County
128	34.0	Williston Park (village) Nassau County
134	33.9	Norwood (cdp/town) Norfolk County
135	33.8	Clinton (town) Worcester County
135	33.8	Halifax (town) Plymouth County
135	33.8	Mystic Island (CDP) Ocean County
135	33.8	Wall (township) Monmouth County
139	33.7	Massapequa Park (village) Nassau County
140	33.6	Cold Spring Harbor (CDP) Suffolk County
140	33.6	Dalton (town) Berkshire County
142	33.5	Colonie (village) Albany County
142	33.5	Middletown (township) Monmouth County
142	33.5	Seabrook (town) Rockingham County
142	33.5	Waterford (township) Camden County
146	33.4	Medfield (CDP) Norfolk County
146	33.4	Montgomery (village) Orange County
146	33.4	Mount Ephraim (borough) Camden County
149	33.3	Dover (town) Dutchess County
149	33.3	Fort Salonga (CDP) Suffolk County

Note: This section ranks incorporated places and CDPs (Census Designated Places) with populations of 2,500 or more. Unincorporated postal areas were not considered. Please refer to the User Guide for additional information.

Ancestry: Italian
Top 150 Places Ranked in *Descending* Order

State Rank	Percent	Place
1	51.2	**Johnston** (town) Providence County
2	50.9	**Fairfield** (township) Essex County
3	49.0	**North Massapequa** (CDP) Nassau County
4	47.7	**East Haven** (cdp/town) New Haven County
5	47.3	**Watertown** (CDP) Litchfield County
6	46.3	**Massapequa** (CDP) Nassau County
7	45.4	**Eastchester** (CDP) Westchester County
8	45.3	**Thornwood** (CDP) Westchester County
9	44.4	**Glendora** (CDP) Camden County
10	44.0	**Frankfort** (village) Herkimer County
11	43.5	**Hawthorne** (CDP) Westchester County
12	43.4	**Hammonton** (town) Atlantic County
13	43.3	**North Branford** (town) New Haven County
13	43.3	**Turnersville** (CDP) Gloucester County
15	42.8	**West Islip** (CDP) Suffolk County
16	42.6	**Massapequa Park** (village) Nassau County
17	42.1	**Franklin Square** (CDP) Nassau County
18	41.9	**Islip Terrace** (CDP) Suffolk County
19	41.6	**Watertown** (town) Litchfield County
20	41.4	**Nesconset** (CDP) Suffolk County
21	41.1	**Lake Grove** (village) Suffolk County
22	40.4	**North Haven** (cdp/town) New Haven County
23	40.3	**Gibbstown** (CDP) Gloucester County
24	40.2	**Saint James** (CDP) Suffolk County
24	40.2	**Seaford** (CDP) Nassau County
26	40.1	**East Hanover** (township) Morris County
26	40.1	**Saugus** (cdp/town) Essex County
28	39.9	**Marlboro** (cdp) Ulster County
29	39.7	**Beach Haven West** (CDP) Ocean County
30	39.5	**East Islip** (CDP) Suffolk County
30	39.5	**Smithtown** (CDP) Suffolk County
32	39.3	**Jefferson Valley-Yorktown** (CDP) Westchester County
33	39.2	**Jessup** (borough) Lackawanna County
33	39.2	**Monmouth Beach** (borough) Monmouth County
35	39.0	**Brightwaters** (village) Suffolk County
36	38.7	**South Farmingdale** (CDP) Nassau County
37	38.1	**Frankfort** (town) Herkimer County
37	38.1	**Richwood** (CDP) Gloucester County
39	38.0	**Bayville** (village) Nassau County
39	38.0	**Malverne** (village) Nassau County
39	38.0	**North Providence** (town) Providence County
42	37.9	**Cedar Grove** (township) Essex County
43	37.8	**Plainedge** (CDP) Nassau County
44	37.7	**Holtsville** (CDP) Suffolk County
44	37.7	**Oakville** (CDP) Litchfield County
46	37.6	**Blackwood** (CDP) Camden County
46	37.6	**Holbrook** (CDP) Suffolk County
48	37.4	**Center Moriches** (CDP) Suffolk County
48	37.4	**Dunmore** (borough) Lackawanna County
48	37.4	**Smithtown** (town) Suffolk County
51	37.2	**North Great River** (CDP) Suffolk County
52	37.1	**Blue Point** (CDP) Suffolk County
52	37.1	**East Norwich** (CDP) Nassau County
52	37.1	**Ronkonkoma** (CDP) Suffolk County
52	37.1	**West Pittston** (borough) Luzerne County
56	36.9	**Hauppauge** (CDP) Suffolk County
57	36.8	**Bohemia** (CDP) Suffolk County
57	36.8	**Farmingville** (CDP) Suffolk County
57	36.8	**Old Forge** (borough) Lackawanna County
57	36.8	**Pemberwick** (CDP) Fairfield County
61	36.7	**Mechanicville** (city) Saratoga County
61	36.7	**Miller Place** (CDP) Suffolk County
61	36.7	**Nutley** (township) Essex County
61	36.7	**Selden** (CDP) Suffolk County
61	36.7	**Wood-Ridge** (borough) Bergen County
66	36.6	**Glen Head** (CDP) Nassau County
67	36.5	**Pittston** (city) Luzerne County
68	36.4	**Centerport** (CDP) Suffolk County
69	36.2	**Barnegat** (CDP) Ocean County
70	36.1	**Mahopac** (CDP) Putnam County
70	36.1	**Ocean Acres** (CDP) Ocean County
72	36.0	**Lindenhurst** (village) Suffolk County
72	36.0	**Lyncourt** (CDP) Onondaga County
72	36.0	**Union Vale** (town) Dutchess County
72	36.0	**Washington** (township) Gloucester County
76	35.9	**Eastchester** (town) Westchester County
77	35.8	**Garden City South** (CDP) Nassau County
77	35.8	**Greenwich** (township) Gloucester County
77	35.8	**Manorville** (cdp) Suffolk County
80	35.7	**Lake Pocotopaug** (CDP) Middlesex County
80	35.7	**Moonachie** (borough) Bergen County
80	35.7	**Oyster Bay** (CDP) Nassau County
83	35.6	**East Freehold** (CDP) Monmouth County
83	35.6	**Oakdale** (CDP) Suffolk County
83	35.6	**Ramtown** (CDP) Monmouth County
86	35.5	**Kensington** (CDP) Hartford County
86	35.5	**Pelham Manor** (village) Westchester County
88	35.4	**Holiday City-Berkeley** (CDP) Ocean County
88	35.4	**Yaphank** (CDP) Suffolk County
90	35.2	**Carmel** (town) Putnam County
91	35.1	**Commack** (CDP) Suffolk County
92	34.9	**Hazlet** (township) Monmouth County
92	34.9	**Somers** (town) Westchester County
94	34.5	**Bethpage** (CDP) Nassau County
94	34.5	**Middle Island** (CDP) Suffolk County
94	34.5	**Port Jefferson Station** (CDP) Suffolk County
97	34.4	**Lynnfield** (cdp/town) Essex County
98	34.3	**Kings Park** (CDP) Suffolk County
98	34.3	**North Babylon** (CDP) Suffolk County
98	34.3	**West Babylon** (CDP) Suffolk County
101	34.2	**Totowa** (borough) Passaic County
102	34.1	**Ellwood City** (borough) Lawrence County
102	34.1	**Stoneham** (cdp/town) Middlesex County
104	34.0	**Cranston** (city) Providence County
104	34.0	**Shirley** (CDP) Suffolk County
106	33.9	**Pequannock** (township) Morris County
106	33.9	**Pine Lake Park** (CDP) Ocean County
108	33.8	**East Fishkill** (town) Dutchess County
108	33.8	**Montrose** (CDP) Westchester County
110	33.7	**Locust Valley** (CDP) Nassau County
110	33.7	**Neshannock** (township) Lawrence County
110	33.7	**West Bay Shore** (CDP) Suffolk County
110	33.7	**Yorktown** (town) Westchester County
114	33.6	**Holiday City South** (CDP) Ocean County
114	33.6	**Kenmore** (village) Erie County
114	33.6	**Lacey** (township) Ocean County
114	33.6	**Prospect** (town) New Haven County
114	33.6	**Roseland** (borough) Essex County
114	33.6	**Wantagh** (CDP) Nassau County
120	33.5	**Waldwick** (borough) Bergen County
120	33.5	**Wolcott** (town) New Haven County
122	33.4	**East Shoreham** (CDP) Suffolk County
122	33.4	**South Huntington** (CDP) Suffolk County
122	33.4	**West Sayville** (CDP) Suffolk County
125	33.3	**Exeter** (borough) Luzerne County
125	33.3	**Toms River** (township) Ocean County
127	33.2	**East Williston** (village) Nassau County
127	33.2	**Lyndhurst** (township) Bergen County
129	33.1	**Lake Ronkonkoma** (CDP) Suffolk County
129	33.1	**Toms River** (CDP) Ocean County
129	33.1	**Westerly** (CDP) Washington County
132	33.0	**Cold Spring Harbor** (CDP) Suffolk County
132	33.0	**Mount Sinai** (CDP) Suffolk County
134	32.9	**Hasbrouck Heights** (borough) Bergen County
134	32.9	**Stafford** (township) Ocean County
136	32.8	**Berlin** (town) Hartford County
136	32.8	**Galeville** (CDP) Onondaga County
136	32.8	**West Caldwell** (township) Essex County
139	32.7	**Putnam Valley** (town) Putnam County
139	32.7	**Sound Beach** (CDP) Suffolk County
141	32.6	**Babylon** (village) Suffolk County
141	32.6	**Centereach** (CDP) Suffolk County
141	32.6	**Elwood** (CDP) Suffolk County
141	32.6	**Middletown** (township) Monmouth County
141	32.6	**North Patchogue** (CDP) Suffolk County
146	32.5	**Lincroft** (CDP) Monmouth County
147	32.4	**Barnegat** (township) Ocean County
147	32.4	**Caldwell** (borough) Essex County
147	32.4	**Levittown** (CDP) Nassau County
147	32.4	**Oceanport** (borough) Monmouth County

Note: This section ranks incorporated places and CDPs (Census Designated Places) with populations of 2,500 or more. Unincorporated postal areas were not considered. Please refer to the User Guide for additional information.

Employment: Management, Business, and Financial Occupations
Top 150 Places Ranked in *Descending* Order

State Rank	Percent	Place
1	25.6	**Zionsville** (town) Boone County
2	25.2	**Smithville-Sanders** (CDP) Monroe County
3	24.4	**Westfield** (city) Hamilton County
4	24.3	**Carmel** (city) Hamilton County
5	24.2	**Winfield** (town) Lake County
6	23.7	**Fishers** (town) Hamilton County
7	22.5	**Huntertown** (town) Allen County
8	21.8	**Winona Lake** (town) Kosciusko County
9	21.7	**Saint John** (town) Lake County
10	20.7	**Granger** (CDP) Saint Joseph County
11	20.4	**Avon** (town) Hendricks County
12	20.2	**McCordsville** (town) Hancock County
13	20.1	**Highland** (CDP) Vanderburgh County
14	19.5	**Noblesville** (city) Hamilton County
15	19.3	**Pittsboro** (town) Hendricks County
15	19.3	**Whitestown** (town) Boone County
17	19.1	**Fortville** (town) Hancock County
17	19.1	**Schererville** (town) Lake County
19	18.7	**Georgetown** (town) Floyd County
20	17.8	**Munster** (town) Lake County
21	17.7	**Batesville** (city) Ripley County
21	17.7	**Lawrence** (city) Marion County
23	17.0	**Columbus** (city) Bartholomew County
24	16.8	**Bargersville** (town) Johnson County
25	16.6	**Brownsburg** (town) Hendricks County
25	16.6	**Whiteland** (town) Johnson County
27	16.1	**Plainfield** (town) Hendricks County
28	15.8	**Yorktown** (town) Delaware County
29	15.2	**Melody Hill** (CDP) Vanderburgh County
30	14.9	**Leo-Cedarville** (town) Allen County
30	14.9	**Simonton Lake** (CDP) Elkhart County
32	14.6	**Centerville** (town) Wayne County
33	14.4	**Dyer** (town) Lake County
33	14.4	**Shorewood Forest** (CDP) Porter County
35	14.3	**Greendale** (city) Dearborn County
36	14.2	**Chesterton** (town) Porter County
37	13.9	**Clarksville** (town) Clark County
38	13.6	**Indianapolis** (city) Marion County
39	13.5	**Bright** (CDP) Dearborn County
39	13.5	**Dunlap** (CDP) Elkhart County
39	13.5	**Greenwood** (city) Johnson County
42	13.3	**Crown Point** (city) Lake County
42	13.3	**Highland** (town) Lake County
44	13.2	**Greenfield** (city) Hancock County
44	13.2	**Porter** (town) Porter County
46	12.8	**Ellettsville** (town) Monroe County
46	12.8	**Speedway** (town) Marion County
48	12.4	**Danville** (town) Hendricks County
49	12.3	**Cedar Lake** (town) Lake County
49	12.3	**Cicero** (town) Hamilton County
49	12.3	**Cumberland** (town) Marion County
52	12.2	**New Haven** (city) Allen County
53	12.1	**Bremen** (town) Marshall County
53	12.1	**Rensselaer** (city) Jasper County
53	12.1	**West Lafayette** (city) Tippecanoe County
56	12.0	**Brazil** (city) Clay County
57	11.9	**Jasper** (city) Dubois County
58	11.8	**Fort Wayne** (city) Allen County
59	11.7	**Mount Vernon** (city) Posey County
60	11.5	**Valparaiso** (city) Porter County
61	11.4	**Bloomington** (city) Monroe County
61	11.4	**Loogootee** (city) Martin County
61	11.4	**Marion** (city) Grant County
61	11.4	**Mooresville** (town) Morgan County
65	11.3	**Auburn** (city) DeKalb County
65	11.3	**Jeffersonville** (city) Clark County
65	11.3	**Lebanon** (city) Boone County
65	11.3	**Pendleton** (town) Madison County
69	11.1	**Brookville** (town) Franklin County
69	11.1	**Sellersburg** (town) Clark County
71	11.0	**New Whiteland** (town) Johnson County
72	10.8	**Greencastle** (city) Putnam County
72	10.8	**Linton** (city) Greene County
74	10.7	**Michigan City** (city) LaPorte County
74	10.7	**Westville** (town) LaPorte County
76	10.6	**Hobart** (city) Lake County
76	10.6	**Martinsville** (city) Morgan County
76	10.6	**Tipton** (city) Tipton County
79	10.5	**Heritage Lake** (CDP) Putnam County
79	10.5	**Ossian** (town) Wells County
81	10.4	**Kendallville** (city) Noble County
81	10.4	**Vincennes** (city) Knox County
83	10.3	**Hartford City** (city) Blackford County
83	10.3	**Hidden Valley** (CDP) Dearborn County
83	10.3	**Lafayette** (city) Tippecanoe County
86	10.2	**Mishawaka** (city) Saint Joseph County
86	10.2	**Rochester** (city) Fulton County
86	10.2	**Sheridan** (town) Hamilton County
89	10.1	**Alexandria** (city) Madison County
89	10.1	**Bluffton** (city) Wells County
89	10.1	**Franklin** (city) Johnson County
89	10.1	**Hebron** (town) Porter County
93	10.0	**Bedford** (city) Lawrence County
93	10.0	**Princeton** (city) Gibson County
95	9.9	**Warsaw** (city) Kosciusko County
96	9.8	**Charlestown** (city) Clark County
96	9.8	**Middlebury** (town) Elkhart County
96	9.8	**New Albany** (city) Floyd County
99	9.7	**Monticello** (city) White County
99	9.7	**South Bend** (city) Saint Joseph County
101	9.6	**Greensburg** (city) Decatur County
101	9.6	**Lakes of the Four Seasons** (CDP) Lake County
101	9.6	**Portage** (city) Porter County
104	9.5	**Clinton** (city) Vermillion County
104	9.5	**Elwood** (city) Madison County
106	9.4	**Beech Grove** (city) Marion County
106	9.4	**Huntingburg** (city) Dubois County
106	9.4	**Winchester** (city) Randolph County
109	9.3	**Corydon** (town) Harrison County
109	9.3	**Muncie** (city) Delaware County
109	9.3	**Newburgh** (town) Warrick County
109	9.3	**North Manchester** (town) Wabash County
109	9.3	**Richmond** (city) Wayne County
114	9.2	**Griffith** (town) Lake County
115	9.1	**Kokomo** (city) Howard County
115	9.1	**Upland** (town) Grant County
117	9.0	**Anderson** (city) Madison County
117	9.0	**Brownstown** (town) Jackson County
119	8.9	**Fairmount** (town) Grant County
119	8.9	**Nappanee** (city) Elkhart County
119	8.9	**Shelbyville** (city) Shelby County
122	8.8	**Lowell** (town) Lake County
122	8.8	**Paoli** (town) Orange County
124	8.7	**Covington** (city) Fountain County
124	8.7	**New Castle** (city) Henry County
124	8.7	**Washington** (city) Daviess County
127	8.6	**Evansville** (city) Vanderburgh County
127	8.6	**Seymour** (city) Jackson County
129	8.5	**Huntington** (city) Huntington County
129	8.5	**Madison** (city) Jefferson County
129	8.5	**South Haven** (CDP) Porter County
129	8.5	**Whiting** (city) Lake County
133	8.3	**Berne** (city) Adams County
133	8.3	**Terre Haute** (city) Vigo County
135	8.2	**Attica** (city) Fountain County
135	8.2	**Aurora** (city) Dearborn County
135	8.2	**Goshen** (city) Elkhart County
138	8.1	**Chandler** (town) Warrick County
138	8.1	**Merrillville** (town) Lake County
138	8.1	**Salem** (city) Washington County
141	8.0	**Garrett** (city) DeKalb County
141	8.0	**Wabash** (city) Wabash County
143	7.7	**De Motte** (town) Jasper County
143	7.7	**Rushville** (city) Rush County
145	7.4	**Elkhart** (city) Elkhart County
146	7.3	**Fort Branch** (town) Gibson County
146	7.3	**Gary** (city) Lake County
146	7.3	**La Porte** (city) LaPorte County
149	6.9	**Crawfordsville** (city) Montgomery County
149	6.9	**Hammond** (city) Lake County

Note: This section ranks incorporated places and CDPs (Census Designated Places) with populations of 2,500 or more. Unincorporated postal areas were not considered. Please refer to the User Guide for additional information.

Employment: Management, Business, and Financial Occupations
Top 150 Places Ranked in *Ascending* Order

State Rank	Percent	Place
1	2.2	**Austin** (city) Scott County
2	2.5	**Bicknell** (city) Knox County
3	2.6	**Grissom AFB** (CDP) Miami County
4	3.0	**Lagrange** (town) LaGrange County
5	3.7	**Sullivan** (city) Sullivan County
6	3.8	**Ligonier** (city) Noble County
7	3.9	**Butler** (city) DeKalb County
7	3.9	**Purdue University** (CDP) Tippecanoe County
9	4.0	**Frankfort** (city) Clinton County
10	4.1	**Country Squire Lakes** (CDP) Jennings County
11	4.2	**Gas City** (city) Grant County
11	4.2	**Plymouth** (city) Marshall County
13	4.5	**North Vernon** (city) Jennings County
14	4.8	**Boonville** (city) Warrick County
14	4.8	**Lawrenceburg** (city) Dearborn County
16	4.9	**Delphi** (city) Carroll County
17	5.1	**Roselawn** (CDP) Newton County
18	5.3	**Peru** (city) Miami County
19	5.4	**Columbia City** (city) Whitley County
19	5.4	**Scottsburg** (city) Scott County
21	5.7	**Angola** (city) Steuben County
22	5.8	**Chesterfield** (town) Madison County
22	5.8	**East Chicago** (city) Lake County
24	6.0	**Lake Station** (city) Lake County
24	6.0	**Mitchell** (city) Lawrence County
26	6.2	**Logansport** (city) Cass County
27	6.3	**Notre Dame** (CDP) Saint Joseph County
27	6.3	**Rockville** (town) Parke County
29	6.4	**Edinburgh** (town) Johnson County
29	6.4	**Hanover** (town) Jefferson County
29	6.4	**North Terre Haute** (CDP) Vigo County
32	6.5	**Union City** (city) Randolph County
33	6.6	**Portland** (city) Jay County
34	6.7	**Connersville** (city) Fayette County
34	6.7	**Decatur** (city) Adams County
36	6.8	**Tell City** (city) Perry County
37	6.9	**Crawfordsville** (city) Montgomery County
37	6.9	**Hammond** (city) Lake County
37	6.9	**Knox** (city) Starke County
37	6.9	**Syracuse** (town) Kosciusko County
41	7.3	**Fort Branch** (town) Gibson County
41	7.3	**Gary** (city) Lake County
41	7.3	**La Porte** (city) LaPorte County
44	7.4	**Elkhart** (city) Elkhart County
45	7.7	**De Motte** (town) Jasper County
45	7.7	**Rushville** (city) Rush County
47	8.0	**Garrett** (city) DeKalb County
47	8.0	**Wabash** (city) Wabash County
49	8.1	**Chandler** (town) Warrick County
49	8.1	**Merrillville** (town) Lake County
49	8.1	**Salem** (city) Washington County
52	8.2	**Attica** (city) Fountain County
52	8.2	**Aurora** (city) Dearborn County
52	8.2	**Goshen** (city) Elkhart County
55	8.3	**Berne** (city) Adams County
55	8.3	**Terre Haute** (city) Vigo County
57	8.5	**Huntington** (city) Huntington County
57	8.5	**Madison** (city) Jefferson County
57	8.5	**South Haven** (CDP) Porter County
57	8.5	**Whiting** (city) Lake County
61	8.6	**Evansville** (city) Vanderburgh County
61	8.6	**Seymour** (city) Jackson County
63	8.7	**Covington** (city) Fountain County
63	8.7	**New Castle** (city) Henry County
63	8.7	**Washington** (city) Daviess County
66	8.8	**Lowell** (town) Lake County
66	8.8	**Paoli** (town) Orange County
68	8.9	**Fairmount** (town) Grant County
68	8.9	**Nappanee** (city) Elkhart County
68	8.9	**Shelbyville** (city) Shelby County
71	9.0	**Anderson** (city) Madison County
71	9.0	**Brownstown** (town) Jackson County
73	9.1	**Kokomo** (city) Howard County
73	9.1	**Upland** (town) Grant County
75	9.2	**Griffith** (town) Lake County
76	9.3	**Corydon** (town) Harrison County
76	9.3	**Muncie** (city) Delaware County
76	9.3	**Newburgh** (town) Warrick County
76	9.3	**North Manchester** (town) Wabash County
76	9.3	**Richmond** (city) Wayne County
81	9.4	**Beech Grove** (city) Marion County
81	9.4	**Huntingburg** (city) Dubois County
81	9.4	**Winchester** (city) Randolph County
84	9.5	**Clinton** (city) Vermillion County
84	9.5	**Elwood** (city) Madison County
86	9.6	**Greensburg** (city) Decatur County
86	9.6	**Lakes of the Four Seasons** (CDP) Lake County
86	9.6	**Portage** (city) Porter County
89	9.7	**Monticello** (city) White County
89	9.7	**South Bend** (city) Saint Joseph County
91	9.8	**Charlestown** (city) Clark County
91	9.8	**Middlebury** (town) Elkhart County
91	9.8	**New Albany** (city) Floyd County
94	9.9	**Warsaw** (city) Kosciusko County
95	10.0	**Bedford** (city) Lawrence County
95	10.0	**Princeton** (city) Gibson County
97	10.1	**Alexandria** (city) Madison County
97	10.1	**Bluffton** (city) Wells County
97	10.1	**Franklin** (city) Johnson County
97	10.1	**Hebron** (town) Porter County
101	10.2	**Mishawaka** (city) Saint Joseph County
101	10.2	**Rochester** (city) Fulton County
101	10.2	**Sheridan** (town) Hamilton County
104	10.3	**Hartford City** (city) Blackford County
104	10.3	**Hidden Valley** (CDP) Dearborn County
104	10.3	**Lafayette** (city) Tippecanoe County
107	10.4	**Kendallville** (city) Noble County
107	10.4	**Vincennes** (city) Knox County
109	10.5	**Heritage Lake** (CDP) Putnam County
109	10.5	**Ossian** (town) Wells County
111	10.6	**Hobart** (city) Lake County
111	10.6	**Martinsville** (city) Morgan County
111	10.6	**Tipton** (city) Tipton County
114	10.7	**Michigan City** (city) LaPorte County
114	10.7	**Westville** (town) LaPorte County
116	10.8	**Greencastle** (city) Putnam County
116	10.8	**Linton** (city) Greene County
118	11.0	**New Whiteland** (town) Johnson County
119	11.1	**Brookville** (town) Franklin County
119	11.1	**Sellersburg** (town) Clark County
121	11.3	**Auburn** (city) DeKalb County
121	11.3	**Jeffersonville** (city) Clark County
121	11.3	**Lebanon** (city) Boone County
121	11.3	**Pendleton** (town) Madison County
125	11.4	**Bloomington** (city) Monroe County
125	11.4	**Loogootee** (city) Martin County
125	11.4	**Marion** (city) Grant County
125	11.4	**Mooresville** (town) Morgan County
129	11.5	**Valparaiso** (city) Porter County
130	11.7	**Mount Vernon** (city) Posey County
131	11.8	**Fort Wayne** (city) Allen County
132	11.9	**Jasper** (city) Dubois County
133	12.0	**Brazil** (city) Clay County
134	12.1	**Bremen** (town) Marshall County
134	12.1	**Rensselaer** (city) Jasper County
134	12.1	**West Lafayette** (city) Tippecanoe County
137	12.2	**New Haven** (city) Allen County
138	12.3	**Cedar Lake** (town) Lake County
138	12.3	**Cicero** (town) Hamilton County
138	12.3	**Cumberland** (town) Marion County
141	12.4	**Danville** (town) Hendricks County
142	12.8	**Ellettsville** (town) Monroe County
142	12.8	**Speedway** (town) Marion County
144	13.2	**Greenfield** (city) Hancock County
144	13.2	**Porter** (town) Porter County
146	13.3	**Crown Point** (city) Lake County
146	13.3	**Highland** (town) Lake County
148	13.5	**Bright** (CDP) Dearborn County
148	13.5	**Dunlap** (CDP) Elkhart County
148	13.5	**Greenwood** (city) Johnson County

Note: This section ranks incorporated places and CDPs (Census Designated Places) with populations of 2,500 or more. Unincorporated postal areas were not considered. Please refer to the User Guide for additional information.

Employment: Computer, Engineering, and Science Occupations
Top 150 Places Ranked in *Descending* Order

State Rank	Percent	Place
1	12.1	**Carmel** (city) Hamilton County
2	11.1	**Whitestown** (town) Boone County
3	10.8	**Columbus** (city) Bartholomew County
4	10.5	**McCordsville** (town) Hancock County
5	10.0	**Fishers** (town) Hamilton County
6	9.4	**West Lafayette** (city) Tippecanoe County
7	9.1	**Westfield** (city) Hamilton County
8	8.4	**Notre Dame** (CDP) Saint Joseph County
9	7.8	**Huntertown** (town) Allen County
10	7.6	**Smithville-Sanders** (CDP) Monroe County
10	7.6	**Zionsville** (town) Boone County
12	7.0	**Purdue University** (CDP) Tippecanoe County
13	6.2	**Brownsburg** (town) Hendricks County
13	6.2	**Greenwood** (city) Johnson County
15	6.1	**Batesville** (city) Ripley County
15	6.1	**Georgetown** (town) Floyd County
15	6.1	**Lakes of the Four Seasons** (CDP) Lake County
18	6.0	**Hidden Valley** (CDP) Dearborn County
18	6.0	**Melody Hill** (CDP) Vanderburgh County
20	5.9	**Avon** (town) Hendricks County
21	5.8	**Auburn** (city) DeKalb County
21	5.8	**Munster** (town) Lake County
23	5.7	**Bloomington** (city) Monroe County
23	5.7	**Highland** (CDP) Vanderburgh County
23	5.7	**Noblesville** (city) Hamilton County
26	5.6	**Plainfield** (town) Hendricks County
27	5.5	**Greensburg** (city) Decatur County
27	5.5	**Lafayette** (city) Tippecanoe County
29	5.4	**Valparaiso** (city) Porter County
30	5.3	**Granger** (CDP) Saint Joseph County
30	5.3	**Upland** (town) Grant County
32	5.1	**Crown Point** (city) Lake County
32	5.1	**Fort Wayne** (city) Allen County
32	5.1	**Speedway** (town) Marion County
35	4.8	**Greencastle** (city) Putnam County
36	4.7	**De Motte** (town) Jasper County
36	4.7	**Indianapolis** (city) Marion County
38	4.6	**Lawrence** (city) Marion County
38	4.6	**Leo-Cedarville** (town) Allen County
38	4.6	**Pittsboro** (town) Hendricks County
38	4.6	**Union City** (city) Randolph County
38	4.6	**Yorktown** (town) Delaware County
43	4.5	**Greenfield** (city) Hancock County
43	4.5	**Lebanon** (city) Boone County
43	4.5	**Schererville** (town) Lake County
43	4.5	**Sheridan** (town) Hamilton County
43	4.5	**Winfield** (town) Lake County
48	4.4	**Cumberland** (town) Marion County
49	4.3	**Bright** (CDP) Dearborn County
49	4.3	**Chesterfield** (town) Madison County
49	4.3	**Mount Vernon** (city) Posey County
49	4.3	**Shorewood Forest** (CDP) Porter County
53	4.2	**Austin** (city) Scott County
53	4.2	**New Haven** (city) Allen County
53	4.2	**Rushville** (city) Rush County
53	4.2	**Saint John** (town) Lake County
57	4.1	**Aurora** (city) Dearborn County
57	4.1	**Dunlap** (CDP) Elkhart County
57	4.1	**Newburgh** (town) Warrick County
60	4.0	**Cicero** (town) Hamilton County
60	4.0	**Seymour** (city) Jackson County
62	3.9	**Bicknell** (city) Knox County
62	3.9	**Griffith** (town) Lake County
62	3.9	**Jeffersonville** (city) Clark County
62	3.9	**North Manchester** (town) Wabash County
66	3.8	**Loogootee** (city) Martin County
67	3.7	**Lowell** (town) Lake County
67	3.7	**Warsaw** (city) Kosciusko County
69	3.6	**Bluffton** (city) Wells County
69	3.6	**Chesterton** (town) Porter County
69	3.6	**Danville** (town) Hendricks County
69	3.6	**Roselawn** (CDP) Newton County
73	3.5	**Country Squire Lakes** (CDP) Jennings County
73	3.5	**Garrett** (city) DeKalb County
73	3.5	**Huntingburg** (city) Dubois County
73	3.5	**Pendleton** (town) Madison County
73	3.5	**Portage** (city) Porter County
73	3.5	**Porter** (town) Porter County
73	3.5	**Westville** (town) LaPorte County
73	3.5	**Winona Lake** (town) Kosciusko County
81	3.4	**Attica** (city) Fountain County
81	3.4	**Bargersville** (town) Johnson County
83	3.3	**Angola** (city) Steuben County
83	3.3	**Fort Branch** (town) Gibson County
83	3.3	**Highland** (town) Lake County
83	3.3	**New Albany** (city) Floyd County
83	3.3	**South Bend** (city) Saint Joseph County
83	3.3	**Terre Haute** (city) Vigo County
83	3.3	**Whiteland** (town) Johnson County
90	3.2	**Alexandria** (city) Madison County
90	3.2	**Ellettsville** (town) Monroe County
90	3.2	**Jasper** (city) Dubois County
90	3.2	**Kokomo** (city) Howard County
90	3.2	**Mishawaka** (city) Saint Joseph County
90	3.2	**Wabash** (city) Wabash County
96	3.1	**Linton** (city) Greene County
96	3.1	**Madison** (city) Jefferson County
96	3.1	**Winchester** (city) Randolph County
99	3.0	**Beech Grove** (city) Marion County
99	3.0	**Chandler** (town) Warrick County
99	3.0	**Hobart** (city) Lake County
99	3.0	**Monticello** (city) White County
103	2.9	**Brazil** (city) Clay County
103	2.9	**Clarksville** (town) Clark County
103	2.9	**Dyer** (town) Lake County
103	2.9	**Franklin** (city) Johnson County
103	2.9	**Whiting** (city) Lake County
108	2.8	**Anderson** (city) Madison County
108	2.8	**Bedford** (city) Lawrence County
108	2.8	**Brookville** (town) Franklin County
108	2.8	**Richmond** (city) Wayne County
112	2.7	**Columbia City** (city) Whitley County
112	2.7	**Elkhart** (city) Elkhart County
112	2.7	**Evansville** (city) Vanderburgh County
112	2.7	**Huntington** (city) Huntington County
112	2.7	**Middlebury** (town) Elkhart County
112	2.7	**Shelbyville** (city) Shelby County
112	2.7	**Tipton** (city) Tipton County
119	2.6	**Fortville** (town) Hancock County
119	2.6	**Greendale** (city) Dearborn County
119	2.6	**New Whiteland** (town) Johnson County
119	2.6	**Simonton Lake** (CDP) Elkhart County
123	2.5	**Brownstown** (town) Jackson County
123	2.5	**Decatur** (city) Adams County
123	2.5	**Goshen** (city) Elkhart County
123	2.5	**Mooresville** (town) Morgan County
123	2.5	**Rochester** (city) Fulton County
123	2.5	**Scottsburg** (city) Scott County
123	2.5	**Sellersburg** (town) Clark County
130	2.4	**Tell City** (city) Perry County
130	2.4	**Vincennes** (city) Knox County
132	2.3	**Elwood** (city) Madison County
132	2.3	**Muncie** (city) Delaware County
134	2.2	**Cedar Lake** (town) Lake County
134	2.2	**Charlestown** (city) Clark County
134	2.2	**Hammond** (city) Lake County
134	2.2	**La Porte** (city) LaPorte County
134	2.2	**Mitchell** (city) Lawrence County
139	2.1	**Nappanee** (city) Elkhart County
139	2.1	**North Vernon** (city) Jennings County
139	2.1	**Plymouth** (city) Marshall County
139	2.1	**Syracuse** (town) Kosciusko County
143	2.0	**Berne** (city) Adams County
143	2.0	**Crawfordsville** (city) Montgomery County
143	2.0	**Marion** (city) Grant County
146	1.8	**Corydon** (town) Harrison County
146	1.8	**Kendallville** (city) Noble County
146	1.8	**Martinsville** (city) Morgan County
146	1.8	**Merrillville** (town) Lake County
146	1.8	**Michigan City** (city) LaPorte County

Note: This section ranks incorporated places and CDPs (Census Designated Places) with populations of 2,500 or more. Unincorporated postal areas were not considered. Please refer to the User Guide for additional information.

Employment: Computer, Engineering, and Science Occupations
Top 150 Places Ranked in *Ascending* Order

State Rank	Percent	Place
1	0.0	**Boonville** (city) Warrick County
1	0.0	**Delphi** (city) Carroll County
1	0.0	**Grissom AFB** (CDP) Miami County
1	0.0	**Hartford City** (city) Blackford County
1	0.0	**Hebron** (town) Porter County
1	0.0	**Heritage Lake** (CDP) Putnam County
1	0.0	**Ligonier** (city) Noble County
8	0.4	**Lagrange** (town) LaGrange County
8	0.4	**Logansport** (city) Cass County
8	0.4	**Salem** (city) Washington County
11	0.5	**Gas City** (city) Grant County
12	0.6	**East Chicago** (city) Lake County
12	0.6	**Sullivan** (city) Sullivan County
14	0.7	**Covington** (city) Fountain County
15	0.8	**Washington** (city) Daviess County
16	0.9	**Butler** (city) DeKalb County
16	0.9	**Hanover** (town) Jefferson County
18	1.0	**Edinburgh** (town) Johnson County
19	1.1	**Paoli** (town) Orange County
19	1.1	**Rensselaer** (city) Jasper County
21	1.2	**Bremen** (town) Marshall County
21	1.2	**Lawrenceburg** (city) Dearborn County
21	1.2	**South Haven** (CDP) Porter County
24	1.3	**Frankfort** (city) Clinton County
24	1.3	**Knox** (city) Starke County
24	1.3	**Lake Station** (city) Lake County
24	1.3	**North Terre Haute** (CDP) Vigo County
24	1.3	**Rockville** (town) Parke County
29	1.4	**Clinton** (city) Vermillion County
29	1.4	**Fairmount** (town) Grant County
31	1.5	**Connersville** (city) Fayette County
31	1.5	**Peru** (city) Miami County
31	1.5	**Princeton** (city) Gibson County
34	1.6	**Gary** (city) Lake County
35	1.7	**Centerville** (town) Wayne County
35	1.7	**Portland** (city) Jay County
37	1.8	**Corydon** (town) Harrison County
37	1.8	**Kendallville** (city) Noble County
37	1.8	**Martinsville** (city) Morgan County
37	1.8	**Merrillville** (town) Lake County
37	1.8	**Michigan City** (city) LaPorte County
37	1.8	**New Castle** (city) Henry County
37	1.8	**Ossian** (town) Wells County
44	2.0	**Berne** (city) Adams County
44	2.0	**Crawfordsville** (city) Montgomery County
44	2.0	**Marion** (city) Grant County
47	2.1	**Nappanee** (city) Elkhart County
47	2.1	**North Vernon** (city) Jennings County
47	2.1	**Plymouth** (city) Marshall County
47	2.1	**Syracuse** (town) Kosciusko County
51	2.2	**Cedar Lake** (town) Lake County
51	2.2	**Charlestown** (city) Clark County
51	2.2	**Hammond** (city) Lake County
51	2.2	**La Porte** (city) LaPorte County
51	2.2	**Mitchell** (city) Lawrence County
56	2.3	**Elwood** (city) Madison County
56	2.3	**Muncie** (city) Delaware County
58	2.4	**Tell City** (city) Perry County
58	2.4	**Vincennes** (city) Knox County
60	2.5	**Brownstown** (town) Jackson County
60	2.5	**Decatur** (city) Adams County
60	2.5	**Goshen** (city) Elkhart County
60	2.5	**Mooresville** (town) Morgan County
60	2.5	**Rochester** (city) Fulton County
60	2.5	**Scottsburg** (city) Scott County
60	2.5	**Sellersburg** (town) Clark County
67	2.6	**Fortville** (town) Hancock County
67	2.6	**Greendale** (city) Dearborn County
67	2.6	**New Whiteland** (town) Johnson County
67	2.6	**Simonton Lake** (CDP) Elkhart County
71	2.7	**Columbia City** (city) Whitley County
71	2.7	**Elkhart** (city) Elkhart County
71	2.7	**Evansville** (city) Vanderburgh County
71	2.7	**Huntington** (city) Huntington County
71	2.7	**Middlebury** (town) Elkhart County
71	2.7	**Shelbyville** (city) Shelby County
71	2.7	**Tipton** (city) Tipton County
78	2.8	**Anderson** (city) Madison County
78	2.8	**Bedford** (city) Lawrence County
78	2.8	**Brookville** (town) Franklin County
78	2.8	**Richmond** (city) Wayne County
82	2.9	**Brazil** (city) Clay County
82	2.9	**Clarksville** (town) Clark County
82	2.9	**Dyer** (town) Lake County
82	2.9	**Franklin** (city) Johnson County
82	2.9	**Whiting** (city) Lake County
87	3.0	**Beech Grove** (city) Marion County
87	3.0	**Chandler** (town) Warrick County
87	3.0	**Hobart** (city) Lake County
87	3.0	**Monticello** (city) White County
91	3.1	**Linton** (city) Greene County
91	3.1	**Madison** (city) Jefferson County
91	3.1	**Winchester** (city) Randolph County
94	3.2	**Alexandria** (city) Madison County
94	3.2	**Ellettsville** (town) Monroe County
94	3.2	**Jasper** (city) Dubois County
94	3.2	**Kokomo** (city) Howard County
94	3.2	**Mishawaka** (city) Saint Joseph County
94	3.2	**Wabash** (city) Wabash County
100	3.3	**Angola** (city) Steuben County
100	3.3	**Fort Branch** (town) Gibson County
100	3.3	**Highland** (town) Lake County
100	3.3	**New Albany** (city) Floyd County
100	3.3	**South Bend** (city) Saint Joseph County
100	3.3	**Terre Haute** (city) Vigo County
100	3.3	**Whiteland** (town) Johnson County
107	3.4	**Attica** (city) Fountain County
107	3.4	**Bargersville** (town) Johnson County
109	3.5	**Country Squire Lakes** (CDP) Jennings County
109	3.5	**Garrett** (city) DeKalb County
109	3.5	**Huntingburg** (city) Dubois County
109	3.5	**Pendleton** (town) Madison County
109	3.5	**Portage** (city) Porter County
109	3.5	**Porter** (town) Porter County
109	3.5	**Westville** (town) LaPorte County
109	3.5	**Winona Lake** (town) Kosciusko County
117	3.6	**Bluffton** (city) Wells County
117	3.6	**Chesterton** (town) Porter County
117	3.6	**Danville** (town) Hendricks County
117	3.6	**Roselawn** (CDP) Newton County
121	3.7	**Lowell** (town) Lake County
121	3.7	**Warsaw** (city) Kosciusko County
123	3.8	**Loogootee** (city) Martin County
124	3.9	**Bicknell** (city) Knox County
124	3.9	**Griffith** (town) Lake County
124	3.9	**Jeffersonville** (city) Clark County
124	3.9	**North Manchester** (town) Wabash County
128	4.0	**Cicero** (town) Hamilton County
128	4.0	**Seymour** (city) Jackson County
130	4.1	**Aurora** (city) Dearborn County
130	4.1	**Dunlap** (CDP) Elkhart County
130	4.1	**Newburgh** (town) Warrick County
133	4.2	**Austin** (city) Scott County
133	4.2	**New Haven** (city) Allen County
133	4.2	**Rushville** (city) Rush County
133	4.2	**Saint John** (town) Lake County
137	4.3	**Bright** (CDP) Dearborn County
137	4.3	**Chesterfield** (town) Madison County
137	4.3	**Mount Vernon** (city) Posey County
137	4.3	**Shorewood Forest** (CDP) Porter County
141	4.4	**Cumberland** (town) Marion County
142	4.5	**Greenfield** (city) Hancock County
142	4.5	**Lebanon** (city) Boone County
142	4.5	**Schererville** (town) Lake County
142	4.5	**Sheridan** (town) Hamilton County
142	4.5	**Winfield** (town) Lake County
147	4.6	**Lawrence** (city) Marion County
147	4.6	**Leo-Cedarville** (town) Allen County
147	4.6	**Pittsboro** (town) Hendricks County
147	4.6	**Union City** (city) Randolph County

Note: This section ranks incorporated places and CDPs (Census Designated Places) with populations of 2,500 or more. Unincorporated postal areas were not considered. Please refer to the User Guide for additional information.

Employment: Education, Legal, Community Service, Arts, and Media Occupations
Top 150 Places Ranked in *Descending* Order

State Rank	Percent	Place
1	31.6	**West Lafayette** (city) Tippecanoe County
2	26.5	**Purdue University** (CDP) Tippecanoe County
3	25.7	**Bloomington** (city) Monroe County
4	23.3	**Notre Dame** (CDP) Saint Joseph County
5	23.2	**Upland** (town) Grant County
6	19.5	**Winona Lake** (town) Kosciusko County
7	18.3	**North Manchester** (town) Wabash County
8	17.5	**Greencastle** (city) Putnam County
9	17.4	**Ossian** (town) Wells County
10	16.7	**Granger** (CDP) Saint Joseph County
11	15.7	**Zionsville** (town) Boone County
12	14.8	**Shorewood Forest** (CDP) Porter County
13	14.3	**Valparaiso** (city) Porter County
14	14.1	**Carmel** (city) Hamilton County
15	13.8	**Lakes of the Four Seasons** (CDP) Lake County
16	13.6	**Muncie** (city) Delaware County
17	13.5	**Middlebury** (town) Elkhart County
17	13.5	**Saint John** (town) Lake County
19	13.2	**Angola** (city) Steuben County
20	13.0	**South Bend** (city) Saint Joseph County
21	12.7	**Covington** (city) Fountain County
22	12.6	**Madison** (city) Jefferson County
22	12.6	**Munster** (town) Lake County
22	12.6	**Noblesville** (city) Hamilton County
22	12.6	**Pendleton** (town) Madison County
26	12.3	**Fortville** (town) Hancock County
26	12.3	**Yorktown** (town) Delaware County
28	12.2	**Fishers** (town) Hamilton County
29	12.0	**Georgetown** (town) Floyd County
29	12.0	**McCordsville** (town) Hancock County
31	11.9	**Terre Haute** (city) Vigo County
32	11.8	**Highland** (CDP) Vanderburgh County
32	11.8	**Lafayette** (city) Tippecanoe County
34	11.7	**Crawfordsville** (city) Montgomery County
35	11.6	**Paoli** (town) Orange County
36	11.2	**Gas City** (city) Grant County
37	11.1	**Berne** (city) Adams County
37	11.1	**Gary** (city) Lake County
39	11.0	**Auburn** (city) DeKalb County
39	11.0	**Boonville** (city) Warrick County
39	11.0	**Ellettsville** (town) Monroe County
39	11.0	**Highland** (town) Lake County
43	10.8	**Crown Point** (city) Lake County
44	10.7	**Corydon** (town) Harrison County
44	10.7	**Fort Wayne** (city) Allen County
46	10.6	**Danville** (town) Hendricks County
46	10.6	**Franklin** (city) Johnson County
46	10.6	**Westfield** (town) Hamilton County
49	10.5	**Bright** (CDP) Dearborn County
49	10.5	**Melody Hill** (CDP) Vanderburgh County
49	10.5	**Schererville** (town) Lake County
49	10.5	**Warsaw** (city) Kosciusko County
53	10.4	**North Terre Haute** (CDP) Vigo County
54	10.3	**Winfield** (town) Lake County
55	10.2	**Attica** (city) Fountain County
55	10.2	**Delphi** (city) Carroll County
55	10.2	**Leo-Cedarville** (town) Allen County
58	10.1	**Richmond** (city) Wayne County
59	10.0	**Lowell** (town) Lake County
59	10.0	**Rochester** (city) Fulton County
59	10.0	**Scottsburg** (city) Scott County
59	10.0	**Speedway** (town) Marion County
63	9.9	**Greendale** (city) Dearborn County
63	9.9	**Hanover** (town) Jefferson County
63	9.9	**Mishawaka** (city) Saint Joseph County
63	9.9	**New Castle** (city) Henry County
63	9.9	**Plainfield** (town) Hendricks County
68	9.8	**Dyer** (town) Lake County
68	9.8	**Indianapolis** (city) Marion County
68	9.8	**New Haven** (city) Allen County
68	9.8	**Whitestown** (town) Boone County
72	9.7	**Goshen** (city) Elkhart County
72	9.7	**Heritage Lake** (CDP) Putnam County
72	9.7	**Linton** (city) Greene County
75	9.6	**Newburgh** (town) Warrick County
76	9.5	**Cumberland** (town) Marion County
76	9.5	**Peru** (city) Miami County
78	9.4	**Chesterton** (town) Porter County
79	9.3	**Batesville** (city) Ripley County
79	9.3	**Brownsburg** (town) Hendricks County
79	9.3	**Columbus** (city) Bartholomew County
79	9.3	**Whiteland** (town) Johnson County
83	9.2	**Bluffton** (city) Wells County
83	9.2	**Monticello** (city) White County
85	9.1	**New Albany** (city) Floyd County
85	9.1	**Vincennes** (city) Knox County
87	9.0	**Huntertown** (town) Allen County
87	9.0	**Jasper** (city) Dubois County
89	8.9	**La Porte** (city) LaPorte County
90	8.8	**Avon** (town) Hendricks County
90	8.8	**Greenfield** (city) Hancock County
90	8.8	**Lawrence** (city) Marion County
90	8.8	**Merrillville** (town) Lake County
94	8.6	**Hidden Valley** (CDP) Dearborn County
95	8.5	**Huntington** (city) Huntington County
95	8.5	**Lagrange** (town) LaGrange County
95	8.5	**Logansport** (city) Cass County
95	8.5	**Marion** (city) Grant County
99	8.4	**Fort Branch** (town) Gibson County
100	8.3	**Hammond** (city) Lake County
100	8.3	**Kokomo** (city) Howard County
102	8.2	**Rensselaer** (city) Jasper County
102	8.2	**Union City** (city) Randolph County
104	8.0	**Dunlap** (CDP) Elkhart County
104	8.0	**Griffith** (town) Lake County
104	8.0	**Westville** (town) LaPorte County
104	8.0	**Whiting** (city) Lake County
108	7.9	**Elwood** (city) Madison County
108	7.9	**Garrett** (city) DeKalb County
110	7.8	**Evansville** (city) Vanderburgh County
110	7.8	**Michigan City** (city) LaPorte County
112	7.7	**Mooresville** (town) Morgan County
113	7.6	**Knox** (city) Starke County
114	7.5	**Greenwood** (city) Johnson County
115	7.4	**Decatur** (city) Adams County
116	7.3	**Beech Grove** (city) Marion County
116	7.3	**Brookville** (town) Franklin County
116	7.3	**Greensburg** (city) Decatur County
116	7.3	**Simonton Lake** (CDP) Elkhart County
120	7.2	**Bremen** (town) Marshall County
121	7.1	**Anderson** (city) Madison County
121	7.1	**Portage** (city) Porter County
121	7.1	**Wabash** (city) Wabash County
124	7.0	**Martinsville** (city) Morgan County
124	7.0	**Mount Vernon** (city) Posey County
124	7.0	**Princeton** (city) Gibson County
127	6.9	**Hobart** (city) Lake County
127	6.9	**Jeffersonville** (city) Clark County
127	6.9	**Plymouth** (city) Marshall County
130	6.8	**Hebron** (town) Porter County
130	6.8	**Smithville-Sanders** (CDP) Monroe County
132	6.7	**Cedar Lake** (town) Lake County
133	6.6	**Lake Station** (city) Lake County
133	6.6	**Pittsboro** (town) Hendricks County
135	6.5	**De Motte** (town) Jasper County
135	6.5	**Rockville** (town) Parke County
137	6.4	**Clarksville** (town) Clark County
138	6.3	**Bargersville** (town) Johnson County
138	6.3	**Elkhart** (city) Elkhart County
138	6.3	**Nappanee** (city) Elkhart County
141	6.2	**Bedford** (city) Lawrence County
141	6.2	**Brazil** (city) Clay County
141	6.2	**North Vernon** (city) Jennings County
141	6.2	**Washington** (city) Daviess County
145	6.1	**Shelbyville** (city) Shelby County
146	6.0	**Centerville** (town) Wayne County
147	5.9	**Alexandria** (city) Madison County
147	5.9	**Country Squire Lakes** (CDP) Jennings County
147	5.9	**Edinburgh** (town) Johnson County
147	5.9	**Porter** (town) Porter County

Note: This section ranks incorporated places and CDPs (Census Designated Places) with populations of 2,500 or more. Unincorporated postal areas were not considered. Please refer to the User Guide for additional information.

Employment: Education, Legal, Community Service, Arts, and Media Occupations

Top 150 Places Ranked in *Ascending* Order

State Rank	Percent	Place
1	1.6	New Whiteland (town) Johnson County
2	1.7	Ligonier (city) Noble County
3	2.0	Cicero (town) Hamilton County
4	2.2	Aurora (city) Dearborn County
4	2.2	Sullivan (city) Sullivan County
6	3.3	Clinton (city) Vermillion County
7	3.8	Tipton (city) Tipton County
8	3.9	Chesterfield (town) Madison County
9	4.0	Syracuse (town) Kosciusko County
10	4.1	Butler (city) DeKalb County
10	4.1	Loogootee (city) Martin County
12	4.3	Chandler (town) Warrick County
13	4.5	Charlestown (city) Clark County
13	4.5	Columbia City (city) Whitley County
15	4.6	Huntingburg (city) Dubois County
15	4.6	Lawrenceburg (city) Dearborn County
17	4.8	Austin (city) Scott County
17	4.8	Grissom AFB (CDP) Miami County
17	4.8	Hartford City (city) Blackford County
17	4.8	Sellersburg (town) Clark County
21	4.9	Tell City (city) Perry County
22	5.0	Kendallville (city) Noble County
22	5.0	Seymour (city) Jackson County
22	5.0	Winchester (city) Randolph County
25	5.1	East Chicago (city) Lake County
26	5.2	Brownstown (town) Jackson County
26	5.2	Fairmount (town) Grant County
28	5.3	Connersville (city) Fayette County
28	5.3	Lebanon (city) Boone County
28	5.3	Mitchell (city) Lawrence County
31	5.5	Frankfort (city) Clinton County
31	5.5	Salem (city) Washington County
33	5.6	Bicknell (city) Knox County
34	5.7	Roselawn (CDP) Newton County
34	5.7	Rushville (city) Rush County
36	5.9	Alexandria (city) Madison County
36	5.9	Country Squire Lakes (CDP) Jennings County
36	5.9	Edinburgh (town) Johnson County
36	5.9	Porter (town) Porter County
36	5.9	Portland (city) Jay County
36	5.9	Sheridan (town) Hamilton County
36	5.9	South Haven (CDP) Porter County
43	6.0	Centerville (town) Wayne County
44	6.1	Shelbyville (city) Shelby County
45	6.2	Bedford (city) Lawrence County
45	6.2	Brazil (city) Clay County
45	6.2	North Vernon (city) Jennings County
45	6.2	Washington (city) Daviess County
49	6.3	Bargersville (town) Johnson County
49	6.3	Elkhart (city) Elkhart County
49	6.3	Nappanee (city) Elkhart County
52	6.4	Clarksville (town) Clark County
53	6.5	De Motte (town) Jasper County
53	6.5	Rockville (town) Parke County
55	6.6	Lake Station (city) Lake County
55	6.6	Pittsboro (town) Hendricks County
57	6.7	Cedar Lake (town) Lake County
58	6.8	Hebron (town) Porter County
58	6.8	Smithville-Sanders (CDP) Monroe County
60	6.9	Hobart (city) Lake County
60	6.9	Jeffersonville (city) Clark County
60	6.9	Plymouth (city) Marshall County
63	7.0	Martinsville (city) Morgan County
63	7.0	Mount Vernon (city) Posey County
63	7.0	Princeton (city) Gibson County
66	7.1	Anderson (city) Madison County
66	7.1	Portage (city) Porter County
66	7.1	Wabash (city) Wabash County
69	7.2	Bremen (town) Marshall County
70	7.3	Beech Grove (city) Marion County
70	7.3	Brookville (town) Franklin County
70	7.3	Greensburg (city) Decatur County
70	7.3	Simonton Lake (CDP) Elkhart County
74	7.4	Decatur (city) Adams County
75	7.5	Greenwood (city) Johnson County
76	7.6	Knox (city) Starke County
77	7.7	Mooresville (town) Morgan County
78	7.8	Evansville (city) Vanderburgh County
78	7.8	Michigan City (city) LaPorte County
80	7.9	Elwood (city) Madison County
80	7.9	Garrett (city) DeKalb County
82	8.0	Dunlap (CDP) Elkhart County
82	8.0	Griffith (town) Lake County
82	8.0	Westville (town) LaPorte County
82	8.0	Whiting (city) Lake County
86	8.2	Rensselaer (city) Jasper County
86	8.2	Union City (city) Randolph County
88	8.3	Hammond (city) Lake County
88	8.3	Kokomo (city) Howard County
90	8.4	Fort Branch (town) Gibson County
91	8.5	Huntington (city) Huntington County
91	8.5	Lagrange (town) LaGrange County
91	8.5	Logansport (city) Cass County
91	8.5	Marion (city) Grant County
95	8.6	Hidden Valley (CDP) Dearborn County
96	8.8	Avon (town) Hendricks County
96	8.8	Greenfield (city) Hancock County
96	8.8	Lawrence (city) Marion County
96	8.8	Merrillville (town) Lake County
100	8.9	La Porte (city) LaPorte County
101	9.0	Huntertown (town) Allen County
101	9.0	Jasper (city) Dubois County
103	9.1	New Albany (city) Floyd County
103	9.1	Vincennes (city) Knox County
105	9.2	Bluffton (city) Wells County
105	9.2	Monticello (city) White County
107	9.3	Batesville (city) Ripley County
107	9.3	Brownsburg (town) Hendricks County
107	9.3	Columbus (city) Bartholomew County
107	9.3	Whiteland (town) Johnson County
111	9.4	Chesterton (town) Porter County
112	9.5	Cumberland (town) Marion County
112	9.5	Peru (city) Miami County
114	9.6	Newburgh (town) Warrick County
115	9.7	Goshen (city) Elkhart County
115	9.7	Heritage Lake (CDP) Putnam County
115	9.7	Linton (city) Greene County
118	9.8	Dyer (town) Lake County
118	9.8	Indianapolis (city) Marion County
118	9.8	New Haven (city) Allen County
118	9.8	Whitestown (town) Boone County
122	9.9	Greendale (city) Dearborn County
122	9.9	Hanover (town) Jefferson County
122	9.9	Mishawaka (city) Saint Joseph County
122	9.9	New Castle (city) Henry County
122	9.9	Plainfield (town) Hendricks County
127	10.0	Lowell (town) Lake County
127	10.0	Rochester (city) Fulton County
127	10.0	Scottsburg (city) Scott County
127	10.0	Speedway (town) Marion County
131	10.1	Richmond (city) Wayne County
132	10.2	Attica (city) Fountain County
132	10.2	Delphi (city) Carroll County
132	10.2	Leo-Cedarville (town) Allen County
135	10.3	Winfield (town) Lake County
136	10.4	North Terre Haute (CDP) Vigo County
137	10.5	Bright (CDP) Dearborn County
137	10.5	Melody Hill (CDP) Vanderburgh County
137	10.5	Schererville (town) Lake County
137	10.5	Warsaw (city) Kosciusko County
141	10.6	Danville (town) Hendricks County
141	10.6	Franklin (city) Johnson County
141	10.6	Westfield (city) Hamilton County
144	10.7	Corydon (town) Harrison County
144	10.7	Fort Wayne (city) Allen County
146	10.8	Crown Point (city) Lake County
147	11.0	Auburn (city) DeKalb County
147	11.0	Boonville (city) Warrick County
147	11.0	Ellettsville (town) Monroe County
147	11.0	Highland (town) Lake County

Note: This section ranks incorporated places and CDPs (Census Designated Places) with populations of 2,500 or more. Unincorporated postal areas were not considered. Please refer to the User Guide for additional information.

Employment: Healthcare Practitioners
Top 150 Places Ranked in *Descending* Order

State Rank	Percent	Place
1	12.9	Shorewood Forest (CDP) Porter County
2	12.3	Zionsville (town) Boone County
3	11.8	Whitestown (town) Boone County
4	11.4	Crown Point (city) Lake County
5	11.0	Centerville (town) Wayne County
6	10.9	McCordsville (town) Hancock County
7	10.2	Lakes of the Four Seasons (CDP) Lake County
8	9.7	Munster (town) Lake County
9	9.4	Schererville (town) Lake County
10	9.3	Carmel (city) Hamilton County
10	9.3	Fishers (town) Hamilton County
10	9.3	Granger (CDP) Saint Joseph County
10	9.3	Leo-Cedarville (town) Allen County
14	9.2	Brookville (town) Franklin County
14	9.2	Brownstown (town) Jackson County
16	9.0	Melody Hill (CDP) Vanderburgh County
16	9.0	Westfield (city) Hamilton County
18	8.9	Highland (CDP) Vanderburgh County
19	8.8	North Terre Haute (CDP) Vigo County
20	8.7	Greendale (city) Dearborn County
21	8.6	Avon (town) Hendricks County
21	8.6	Pendleton (town) Madison County
23	8.5	Yorktown (town) Delaware County
24	8.4	Brownsburg (town) Hendricks County
24	8.4	Cicero (town) Hamilton County
26	8.3	Lowell (town) Lake County
26	8.3	Salem (city) Washington County
28	8.2	Hebron (town) Porter County
28	8.2	Huntingburg (city) Dubois County
30	7.9	Grissom AFB (CDP) Miami County
30	7.9	North Vernon (city) Jennings County
32	7.7	Madison (city) Jefferson County
32	7.7	Pittsboro (town) Hendricks County
32	7.7	Portland (city) Jay County
35	7.6	Connersville (city) Fayette County
36	7.5	Noblesville (city) Hamilton County
37	7.3	Chesterton (town) Porter County
37	7.3	Merrillville (town) Lake County
37	7.3	Saint John (town) Lake County
40	7.2	Alexandria (city) Madison County
41	7.1	Dyer (town) Lake County
41	7.1	Greenwood (city) Johnson County
43	6.9	Brazil (city) Clay County
43	6.9	Huntertown (town) Allen County
45	6.8	Loogootee (city) Martin County
46	6.6	Bedford (city) Lawrence County
46	6.6	Columbus (city) Bartholomew County
46	6.6	Georgetown (town) Floyd County
46	6.6	Valparaiso (city) Porter County
50	6.5	Newburgh (town) Warrick County
50	6.5	Simonton Lake (CDP) Elkhart County
50	6.5	Winfield (town) Lake County
53	6.4	Berne (city) Adams County
53	6.4	Gas City (city) Grant County
53	6.4	Highland (town) Lake County
53	6.4	Jeffersonville (city) Clark County
57	6.3	Columbia City (city) Whitley County
57	6.3	Cumberland (town) Marion County
57	6.3	Danville (town) Hendricks County
57	6.3	Smithville-Sanders (CDP) Monroe County
61	6.2	Mitchell (city) Lawrence County
61	6.2	North Manchester (town) Wabash County
61	6.2	Syracuse (town) Kosciusko County
61	6.2	Wabash (city) Wabash County
65	6.1	Peru (city) Miami County
65	6.1	Richmond (city) Wayne County
67	6.0	Lafayette (city) Tippecanoe County
67	6.0	Lebanon (city) Boone County
69	5.9	Indianapolis (city) Marion County
69	5.9	Marion (city) Grant County
69	5.9	Mishawaka (city) Saint Joseph County
72	5.8	Union City (city) Randolph County
72	5.8	Westville (town) LaPorte County
74	5.7	Clarksville (town) Clark County
74	5.7	Evansville (city) Vanderburgh County
74	5.7	Fort Wayne (city) Allen County
74	5.7	Hidden Valley (CDP) Dearborn County
74	5.7	Monticello (city) White County
74	5.7	Portage (city) Porter County
80	5.6	Ellettsville (town) Monroe County
81	5.5	Attica (city) Fountain County
81	5.5	Speedway (town) Marion County
81	5.5	Winchester (city) Randolph County
84	5.4	Aurora (city) Dearborn County
84	5.4	Decatur (city) Adams County
84	5.4	Hobart (city) Lake County
84	5.4	Linton (city) Greene County
84	5.4	Rushville (city) Rush County
84	5.4	South Haven (CDP) Porter County
84	5.4	Tell City (city) Perry County
91	5.3	Anderson (city) Madison County
91	5.3	Cedar Lake (town) Lake County
91	5.3	Dunlap (CDP) Elkhart County
91	5.3	Fort Branch (town) Gibson County
91	5.3	Greensburg (city) Decatur County
91	5.3	New Whiteland (town) Johnson County
97	5.2	Charlestown (city) Clark County
97	5.2	Kokomo (city) Howard County
97	5.2	Seymour (city) Jackson County
97	5.2	Terre Haute (city) Vigo County
97	5.2	Tipton (city) Tipton County
102	5.1	Greenfield (city) Hancock County
102	5.1	Plainfield (town) Hendricks County
102	5.1	South Bend (city) Saint Joseph County
102	5.1	Sullivan (city) Sullivan County
102	5.1	Washington (city) Daviess County
107	5.0	Bright (CDP) Dearborn County
107	5.0	Hartford City (city) Blackford County
107	5.0	Porter (town) Porter County
110	4.9	Angola (city) Steuben County
110	4.9	Auburn (city) DeKalb County
110	4.9	Bargersville (town) Johnson County
110	4.9	Franklin (city) Johnson County
110	4.9	Muncie (city) Delaware County
110	4.9	Shelbyville (city) Shelby County
116	4.8	East Chicago (city) Lake County
116	4.8	Rensselaer (city) Jasper County
118	4.7	Lake Station (city) Lake County
118	4.7	Mooresville (town) Morgan County
118	4.7	New Castle (city) Henry County
121	4.6	Corydon (town) Harrison County
121	4.6	Covington (city) Fountain County
121	4.6	Jasper (city) Dubois County
121	4.6	Lawrence (city) Marion County
125	4.5	Gary (city) Lake County
125	4.5	Logansport (city) Cass County
125	4.5	Mount Vernon (city) Posey County
128	4.3	Beech Grove (city) Marion County
128	4.3	New Haven (city) Allen County
130	4.2	Chesterfield (town) Madison County
130	4.2	Kendallville (city) Noble County
130	4.2	Roselawn (CDP) Newton County
133	4.1	Fortville (town) Hancock County
133	4.1	Heritage Lake (CDP) Putnam County
133	4.1	West Lafayette (city) Tippecanoe County
136	4.0	Garrett (city) DeKalb County
136	4.0	New Albany (city) Floyd County
136	4.0	Plymouth (city) Marshall County
136	4.0	Vincennes (city) Knox County
136	4.0	Winona Lake (town) Kosciusko County
141	3.9	Batesville (city) Ripley County
141	3.9	Griffith (town) Lake County
141	3.9	Martinsville (city) Morgan County
144	3.8	Goshen (city) Elkhart County
144	3.8	Hammond (city) Lake County
144	3.8	Lagrange (town) LaGrange County
144	3.8	Rockville (town) Parke County
148	3.7	Austin (city) Scott County
148	3.7	Hanover (town) Jefferson County
150	3.6	Bremen (town) Marshall County

Note: This section ranks incorporated places and CDPs (Census Designated Places) with populations of 2,500 or more. Unincorporated postal areas were not considered. Please refer to the User Guide for additional information.

Employment: Healthcare Practitioners
Top 150 Places Ranked in *Ascending* Order

State Rank	Percent	Place
1	0.3	**Middlebury** (town) Elkhart County
1	0.3	**Notre Dame** (CDP) Saint Joseph County
3	1.1	**Ligonier** (city) Noble County
3	1.1	**Ossian** (town) Wells County
5	1.2	**Whiting** (city) Lake County
6	1.8	**Purdue University** (CDP) Tippecanoe County
7	1.9	**Country Squire Lakes** (CDP) Jennings County
8	2.0	**Fairmount** (town) Grant County
8	2.0	**Greencastle** (city) Putnam County
10	2.1	**Delphi** (city) Carroll County
10	2.1	**Elwood** (city) Madison County
12	2.2	**Chandler** (town) Warrick County
13	2.4	**Edinburgh** (town) Johnson County
13	2.4	**Nappanee** (city) Elkhart County
15	2.5	**Knox** (city) Starke County
15	2.5	**Scottsburg** (city) Scott County
17	2.6	**Princeton** (city) Gibson County
18	2.7	**Butler** (city) DeKalb County
18	2.7	**Paoli** (town) Orange County
20	2.8	**De Motte** (town) Jasper County
20	2.8	**Sellersburg** (town) Clark County
22	2.9	**Crawfordsville** (city) Montgomery County
22	2.9	**Elkhart** (city) Elkhart County
22	2.9	**Michigan City** (city) LaPorte County
22	2.9	**Whiteland** (town) Johnson County
26	3.1	**Bluffton** (city) Wells County
26	3.1	**Clinton** (city) Vermillion County
28	3.3	**Bloomington** (city) Monroe County
28	3.3	**Boonville** (city) Warrick County
28	3.3	**Rochester** (city) Fulton County
31	3.4	**La Porte** (city) LaPorte County
31	3.4	**Lawrenceburg** (city) Dearborn County
31	3.4	**Sheridan** (town) Hamilton County
34	3.5	**Bicknell** (city) Knox County
34	3.5	**Huntington** (city) Huntington County
34	3.5	**Upland** (town) Grant County
37	3.6	**Bremen** (town) Marshall County
37	3.6	**Frankfort** (city) Clinton County
37	3.6	**Warsaw** (city) Kosciusko County
40	3.7	**Austin** (city) Scott County
40	3.7	**Hanover** (town) Jefferson County
42	3.8	**Goshen** (city) Elkhart County
42	3.8	**Hammond** (city) Lake County
42	3.8	**Lagrange** (town) LaGrange County
42	3.8	**Rockville** (town) Parke County
46	3.9	**Batesville** (city) Ripley County
46	3.9	**Griffith** (town) Lake County
46	3.9	**Martinsville** (city) Morgan County
49	4.0	**Garrett** (city) DeKalb County
49	4.0	**New Albany** (city) Floyd County
49	4.0	**Plymouth** (city) Marshall County
49	4.0	**Vincennes** (city) Knox County
49	4.0	**Winona Lake** (town) Kosciusko County
54	4.1	**Fortville** (town) Hancock County
54	4.1	**Heritage Lake** (CDP) Putnam County
54	4.1	**West Lafayette** (city) Tippecanoe County
57	4.2	**Chesterfield** (town) Madison County
57	4.2	**Kendallville** (city) Noble County
57	4.2	**Roselawn** (CDP) Newton County
60	4.3	**Beech Grove** (city) Marion County
60	4.3	**New Haven** (city) Allen County
62	4.5	**Gary** (city) Lake County
62	4.5	**Logansport** (city) Cass County
62	4.5	**Mount Vernon** (city) Posey County
65	4.6	**Corydon** (town) Harrison County
65	4.6	**Covington** (city) Fountain County
65	4.6	**Jasper** (city) Dubois County
65	4.6	**Lawrence** (city) Marion County
69	4.7	**Lake Station** (city) Lake County
69	4.7	**Mooresville** (town) Morgan County
69	4.7	**New Castle** (city) Henry County
72	4.8	**East Chicago** (city) Lake County
72	4.8	**Rensselaer** (city) Jasper County
74	4.9	**Angola** (city) Steuben County
74	4.9	**Auburn** (city) DeKalb County
74	4.9	**Bargersville** (town) Johnson County
74	4.9	**Franklin** (city) Johnson County
74	4.9	**Muncie** (city) Delaware County
74	4.9	**Shelbyville** (city) Shelby County
80	5.0	**Bright** (CDP) Dearborn County
80	5.0	**Hartford City** (city) Blackford County
80	5.0	**Porter** (town) Porter County
83	5.1	**Greenfield** (city) Hancock County
83	5.1	**Plainfield** (town) Hendricks County
83	5.1	**South Bend** (city) Saint Joseph County
83	5.1	**Sullivan** (city) Sullivan County
83	5.1	**Washington** (city) Daviess County
88	5.2	**Charlestown** (city) Clark County
88	5.2	**Kokomo** (city) Howard County
88	5.2	**Seymour** (city) Jackson County
88	5.2	**Terre Haute** (city) Vigo County
88	5.2	**Tipton** (city) Tipton County
93	5.3	**Anderson** (city) Madison County
93	5.3	**Cedar Lake** (town) Lake County
93	5.3	**Dunlap** (CDP) Elkhart County
93	5.3	**Fort Branch** (town) Gibson County
93	5.3	**Greensburg** (city) Decatur County
93	5.3	**New Whiteland** (town) Johnson County
99	5.4	**Aurora** (city) Dearborn County
99	5.4	**Decatur** (city) Adams County
99	5.4	**Hobart** (city) Lake County
99	5.4	**Linton** (city) Greene County
99	5.4	**Rushville** (city) Rush County
99	5.4	**South Haven** (CDP) Porter County
99	5.4	**Tell City** (city) Perry County
106	5.5	**Attica** (city) Fountain County
106	5.5	**Speedway** (town) Marion County
106	5.5	**Winchester** (city) Randolph County
109	5.6	**Ellettsville** (town) Monroe County
110	5.7	**Clarksville** (town) Clark County
110	5.7	**Evansville** (city) Vanderburgh County
110	5.7	**Fort Wayne** (city) Allen County
110	5.7	**Hidden Valley** (CDP) Dearborn County
110	5.7	**Monticello** (city) White County
110	5.7	**Portage** (city) Porter County
116	5.8	**Union City** (city) Randolph County
116	5.8	**Westville** (town) LaPorte County
118	5.9	**Indianapolis** (city) Marion County
118	5.9	**Marion** (city) Grant County
118	5.9	**Mishawaka** (city) Saint Joseph County
121	6.0	**Lafayette** (city) Tippecanoe County
121	6.0	**Lebanon** (city) Boone County
123	6.1	**Peru** (city) Miami County
123	6.1	**Richmond** (city) Wayne County
125	6.2	**Mitchell** (city) Lawrence County
125	6.2	**North Manchester** (town) Wabash County
125	6.2	**Syracuse** (town) Kosciusko County
125	6.2	**Wabash** (city) Wabash County
129	6.3	**Columbia City** (city) Whitley County
129	6.3	**Cumberland** (town) Marion County
129	6.3	**Danville** (town) Hendricks County
129	6.3	**Smithville-Sanders** (CDP) Monroe County
133	6.4	**Berne** (city) Adams County
133	6.4	**Gas City** (city) Grant County
133	6.4	**Highland** (town) Lake County
133	6.4	**Jeffersonville** (city) Clark County
137	6.5	**Newburgh** (town) Warrick County
137	6.5	**Simonton Lake** (CDP) Elkhart County
137	6.5	**Winfield** (town) Lake County
140	6.6	**Bedford** (city) Lawrence County
140	6.6	**Columbus** (city) Bartholomew County
140	6.6	**Georgetown** (town) Floyd County
140	6.6	**Valparaiso** (city) Porter County
144	6.8	**Loogootee** (city) Martin County
145	6.9	**Brazil** (city) Clay County
145	6.9	**Huntertown** (town) Allen County
147	7.1	**Dyer** (town) Lake County
147	7.1	**Greenwood** (city) Johnson County
149	7.2	**Alexandria** (city) Madison County
150	7.3	**Chesterton** (town) Porter County

Note: This section ranks incorporated places and CDPs (Census Designated Places) with populations of 2,500 or more. Unincorporated postal areas were not considered. Please refer to the User Guide for additional information.

Employment: Service Occupations
Top 150 Places Ranked in *Descending* Order

State Rank	Percent	Place
1	33.7	Purdue University (CDP) Tippecanoe County
2	30.6	East Chicago (city) Lake County
3	30.3	Fairmount (town) Grant County
4	29.6	Notre Dame (CDP) Saint Joseph County
5	28.7	Mitchell (city) Lawrence County
6	28.5	Sullivan (city) Sullivan County
7	28.4	Aurora (city) Dearborn County
8	28.0	Knox (city) Starke County
9	27.9	Chesterfield (town) Madison County
9	27.9	Gary (city) Lake County
11	27.1	Sheridan (town) Hamilton County
12	27.0	Linton (city) Greene County
13	26.8	Paoli (town) Orange County
14	26.6	North Vernon (city) Jennings County
15	26.4	Muncie (city) Delaware County
16	26.3	Rensselaer (city) Jasper County
17	25.6	Bicknell (city) Knox County
17	25.6	Fort Branch (town) Gibson County
19	25.1	Roselawn (CDP) Newton County
20	25.0	Richmond (city) Wayne County
21	24.9	Hanover (town) Jefferson County
22	24.8	Ossian (town) Wells County
22	24.8	Tipton (city) Tipton County
24	24.6	Anderson (city) Madison County
24	24.6	Peru (city) Miami County
26	24.5	Country Squire Lakes (CDP) Jennings County
27	24.1	Hartford City (city) Blackford County
28	23.8	Clinton (city) Vermillion County
29	23.6	Michigan City (city) LaPorte County
30	23.5	Bedford (city) Lawrence County
30	23.5	Connersville (city) Fayette County
32	23.4	Butler (city) DeKalb County
32	23.4	Vincennes (city) Knox County
34	23.3	North Manchester (town) Wabash County
35	23.1	Kokomo (city) Howard County
35	23.1	Lake Station (city) Lake County
37	23.0	Hebron (town) Porter County
37	23.0	South Haven (CDP) Porter County
39	22.7	Brazil (city) Clay County
39	22.7	Greencastle (city) Putnam County
39	22.7	Hammond (city) Lake County
42	22.6	Martinsville (city) Morgan County
43	22.3	Bloomington (city) Monroe County
43	22.3	Portage (city) Porter County
45	22.2	Evansville (city) Vanderburgh County
45	22.2	La Porte (city) LaPorte County
47	22.0	Lawrenceburg (city) Dearborn County
48	21.9	Washington (city) Daviess County
49	21.8	Griffith (town) Lake County
49	21.8	Terre Haute (city) Vigo County
51	21.6	New Albany (city) Floyd County
51	21.6	North Terre Haute (CDP) Vigo County
53	21.5	Marion (city) Grant County
53	21.5	Newburgh (town) Warrick County
55	21.4	South Bend (city) Saint Joseph County
56	21.2	Merrillville (town) Lake County
56	21.2	Pendleton (town) Madison County
58	21.1	Covington (city) Fountain County
58	21.1	Elwood (city) Madison County
60	21.0	Brownstown (town) Jackson County
61	20.6	Princeton (city) Gibson County
62	20.5	Clarksville (town) Clark County
63	20.2	Huntington (city) Huntington County
64	20.0	Cicero (town) Hamilton County
64	20.0	New Castle (city) Henry County
66	19.9	Berne (city) Adams County
66	19.9	Hobart (city) Lake County
68	19.8	Tell City (city) Perry County
69	19.7	Lafayette (city) Tippecanoe County
70	19.6	Upland (town) Grant County
71	19.5	Madison (city) Jefferson County
71	19.5	Winchester (city) Randolph County
73	19.4	Delphi (city) Carroll County
73	19.4	Shelbyville (city) Shelby County
73	19.4	Whiting (city) Lake County
76	19.3	Columbia City (city) Whitley County
76	19.3	Corydon (town) Harrison County
78	19.2	Boonville (city) Warrick County
78	19.2	New Whiteland (town) Johnson County
80	19.1	Lawrence (city) Marion County
80	19.1	Lebanon (city) Boone County
82	19.0	Rockville (town) Parke County
83	18.9	Decatur (city) Adams County
83	18.9	Ellettsville (town) Monroe County
83	18.9	Jeffersonville (city) Clark County
83	18.9	Logansport (city) Cass County
83	18.9	Loogootee (city) Martin County
88	18.8	Angola (city) Steuben County
88	18.8	De Motte (town) Jasper County
88	18.8	Garrett (city) DeKalb County
88	18.8	Indianapolis (city) Marion County
92	18.6	Speedway (town) Marion County
92	18.6	West Lafayette (city) Tippecanoe County
94	18.5	Rushville (city) Rush County
94	18.5	Scottsburg (city) Scott County
94	18.5	Valparaiso (city) Porter County
97	18.4	Alexandria (city) Madison County
97	18.4	Crawfordsville (city) Montgomery County
97	18.4	Lagrange (town) LaGrange County
100	18.3	Bluffton (city) Wells County
101	18.1	Franklin (city) Johnson County
102	18.0	Fort Wayne (city) Allen County
102	18.0	Mishawaka (city) Saint Joseph County
102	18.0	Plymouth (city) Marshall County
102	18.0	Seymour (city) Jackson County
106	17.8	Bargersville (town) Johnson County
106	17.8	Beech Grove (city) Marion County
106	17.8	Danville (town) Hendricks County
109	17.7	Austin (city) Scott County
109	17.7	Elkhart (city) Elkhart County
111	17.6	Monticello (city) White County
111	17.6	Salem (city) Washington County
113	17.5	Greensburg (city) Decatur County
114	17.4	Wabash (city) Wabash County
115	17.3	Greenfield (city) Hancock County
116	17.2	Syracuse (town) Kosciusko County
117	16.7	Fortville (town) Hancock County
118	16.4	Cedar Lake (town) Lake County
119	16.3	Highland (town) Lake County
119	16.3	New Haven (city) Allen County
119	16.3	Whiteland (town) Johnson County
122	16.1	Leo-Cedarville (town) Allen County
122	16.1	Porter (town) Porter County
124	16.0	Goshen (city) Elkhart County
125	15.9	Charlestown (city) Clark County
125	15.9	Frankfort (city) Clinton County
127	15.7	Mooresville (town) Morgan County
127	15.7	Simonton Lake (CDP) Elkhart County
129	15.6	Auburn (city) DeKalb County
129	15.6	Huntingburg (city) Dubois County
129	15.6	Pittsboro (town) Hendricks County
132	15.5	Union City (city) Randolph County
133	15.4	Kendallville (city) Noble County
133	15.4	Melody Hill (CDP) Vanderburgh County
135	15.3	Yorktown (town) Delaware County
136	15.2	Mount Vernon (city) Posey County
137	15.1	Dyer (town) Lake County
137	15.1	Gas City (city) Grant County
139	15.0	Columbus (city) Bartholomew County
139	15.0	Greendale (city) Dearborn County
141	14.9	Greenwood (city) Johnson County
141	14.9	Nappanee (city) Elkhart County
141	14.9	Westville (town) LaPorte County
144	14.8	Noblesville (city) Hamilton County
145	14.6	Rochester (city) Fulton County
146	14.5	Plainfield (town) Hendricks County
147	14.4	Bright (CDP) Dearborn County
147	14.4	Crown Point (city) Lake County
147	14.4	Lowell (town) Lake County
150	14.3	Brownsburg (town) Hendricks County

Note: This section ranks incorporated places and CDPs (Census Designated Places) with populations of 2,500 or more. Unincorporated postal areas were not considered. Please refer to the User Guide for additional information.

Employment: Service Occupations
Top 150 Places Ranked in *Ascending* Order

State Rank	Percent	Place
1	8.7	**Georgetown** (town) Floyd County
1	8.7	**Zionsville** (town) Boone County
3	8.8	**Carmel** (city) Hamilton County
4	9.1	**Granger** (CDP) Saint Joseph County
4	9.1	**Ligonier** (city) Noble County
6	9.2	**Highland** (CDP) Vanderburgh County
7	9.9	**Shorewood Forest** (CDP) Porter County
8	10.6	**Smithville-Sanders** (CDP) Monroe County
9	10.7	**Fishers** (town) Hamilton County
10	10.8	**McCordsville** (town) Hancock County
11	10.9	**Avon** (town) Hendricks County
12	11.2	**Winfield** (town) Lake County
13	11.3	**Dunlap** (CDP) Elkhart County
14	11.4	**Centerville** (town) Wayne County
15	11.6	**Westfield** (city) Hamilton County
16	11.8	**Cumberland** (town) Marion County
17	11.9	**Jasper** (city) Dubois County
17	11.9	**Sellersburg** (town) Clark County
19	12.0	**Munster** (town) Lake County
20	12.1	**Winona Lake** (town) Kosciusko County
21	12.3	**Heritage Lake** (CDP) Putnam County
21	12.3	**Saint John** (town) Lake County
23	12.4	**Schererville** (town) Lake County
24	12.8	**Chesterton** (town) Porter County
25	13.1	**Grissom AFB** (CDP) Miami County
26	13.2	**Whitestown** (town) Boone County
27	13.4	**Bremen** (town) Marshall County
28	13.5	**Brookville** (town) Franklin County
28	13.5	**Hidden Valley** (CDP) Dearborn County
30	13.6	**Attica** (city) Fountain County
30	13.6	**Portland** (city) Jay County
32	13.8	**Edinburgh** (town) Johnson County
32	13.8	**Huntertown** (town) Allen County
34	14.0	**Chandler** (town) Warrick County
35	14.1	**Lakes of the Four Seasons** (CDP) Lake County
35	14.1	**Middlebury** (town) Elkhart County
35	14.1	**Warsaw** (city) Kosciusko County
38	14.2	**Batesville** (city) Ripley County
39	14.3	**Brownsburg** (town) Hendricks County
40	14.4	**Bright** (CDP) Dearborn County
40	14.4	**Crown Point** (city) Lake County
40	14.4	**Lowell** (town) Lake County
43	14.5	**Plainfield** (town) Hendricks County
44	14.6	**Rochester** (city) Fulton County
45	14.8	**Noblesville** (city) Hamilton County
46	14.9	**Greenwood** (city) Johnson County
46	14.9	**Nappanee** (city) Elkhart County
46	14.9	**Westville** (town) LaPorte County
49	15.0	**Columbus** (city) Bartholomew County
49	15.0	**Greendale** (city) Dearborn County
51	15.1	**Dyer** (town) Lake County
51	15.1	**Gas City** (city) Grant County
53	15.2	**Mount Vernon** (city) Posey County
54	15.3	**Yorktown** (town) Delaware County
55	15.4	**Kendallville** (city) Noble County
55	15.4	**Melody Hill** (CDP) Vanderburgh County
57	15.5	**Union City** (city) Randolph County
58	15.6	**Auburn** (city) DeKalb County
58	15.6	**Huntingburg** (city) Dubois County
58	15.6	**Pittsboro** (town) Hendricks County
61	15.7	**Mooresville** (town) Morgan County
61	15.7	**Simonton Lake** (CDP) Elkhart County
63	15.9	**Charlestown** (city) Clark County
63	15.9	**Frankfort** (city) Clinton County
65	16.0	**Goshen** (city) Elkhart County
66	16.1	**Leo-Cedarville** (town) Allen County
66	16.1	**Porter** (town) Porter County
68	16.3	**Highland** (town) Lake County
68	16.3	**New Haven** (city) Allen County
68	16.3	**Whiteland** (town) Johnson County
71	16.4	**Cedar Lake** (town) Lake County
72	16.7	**Fortville** (town) Hancock County
73	17.2	**Syracuse** (town) Kosciusko County
74	17.3	**Greenfield** (city) Hancock County
75	17.4	**Wabash** (city) Wabash County
76	17.5	**Greensburg** (city) Decatur County
77	17.6	**Monticello** (city) White County
77	17.6	**Salem** (city) Washington County
79	17.7	**Austin** (city) Scott County
79	17.7	**Elkhart** (city) Elkhart County
81	17.8	**Bargersville** (town) Johnson County
81	17.8	**Beech Grove** (city) Marion County
81	17.8	**Danville** (town) Hendricks County
84	18.0	**Fort Wayne** (city) Allen County
84	18.0	**Mishawaka** (city) Saint Joseph County
84	18.0	**Plymouth** (city) Marshall County
84	18.0	**Seymour** (city) Jackson County
88	18.1	**Franklin** (city) Johnson County
89	18.3	**Bluffton** (city) Wells County
90	18.4	**Alexandria** (city) Madison County
90	18.4	**Crawfordsville** (city) Montgomery County
90	18.4	**Lagrange** (town) LaGrange County
93	18.5	**Rushville** (city) Rush County
93	18.5	**Scottsburg** (city) Scott County
93	18.5	**Valparaiso** (city) Porter County
96	18.6	**Speedway** (town) Marion County
96	18.6	**West Lafayette** (city) Tippecanoe County
98	18.8	**Angola** (city) Steuben County
98	18.8	**De Motte** (town) Jasper County
98	18.8	**Garrett** (city) DeKalb County
98	18.8	**Indianapolis** (city) Marion County
102	18.9	**Decatur** (city) Adams County
102	18.9	**Ellettsville** (town) Monroe County
102	18.9	**Jeffersonville** (city) Clark County
102	18.9	**Logansport** (city) Cass County
102	18.9	**Loogootee** (city) Martin County
107	19.0	**Rockville** (town) Parke County
108	19.1	**Lawrence** (city) Marion County
108	19.1	**Lebanon** (city) Boone County
110	19.2	**Boonville** (city) Warrick County
110	19.2	**New Whiteland** (town) Johnson County
112	19.3	**Columbia City** (city) Whitley County
112	19.3	**Corydon** (town) Harrison County
114	19.4	**Delphi** (city) Carroll County
114	19.4	**Shelbyville** (city) Shelby County
114	19.4	**Whiting** (city) Lake County
117	19.5	**Madison** (city) Jefferson County
117	19.5	**Winchester** (city) Randolph County
119	19.6	**Upland** (town) Grant County
120	19.7	**Lafayette** (city) Tippecanoe County
121	19.8	**Tell City** (city) Perry County
122	19.9	**Berne** (city) Adams County
122	19.9	**Hobart** (city) Lake County
124	20.0	**Cicero** (town) Hamilton County
124	20.0	**New Castle** (city) Henry County
126	20.2	**Huntington** (city) Huntington County
127	20.5	**Clarksville** (town) Clark County
128	20.6	**Princeton** (city) Gibson County
129	21.0	**Brownstown** (town) Jackson County
130	21.1	**Covington** (city) Fountain County
130	21.1	**Elwood** (city) Madison County
132	21.2	**Merrillville** (town) Lake County
132	21.2	**Pendleton** (town) Madison County
134	21.4	**South Bend** (city) Saint Joseph County
135	21.5	**Marion** (city) Grant County
135	21.5	**Newburgh** (town) Warrick County
137	21.6	**New Albany** (city) Floyd County
137	21.6	**North Terre Haute** (CDP) Vigo County
139	21.8	**Griffith** (town) Lake County
139	21.8	**Terre Haute** (city) Vigo County
141	21.9	**Washington** (city) Daviess County
142	22.0	**Lawrenceburg** (city) Dearborn County
143	22.2	**Evansville** (city) Vanderburgh County
143	22.2	**La Porte** (city) LaPorte County
145	22.3	**Bloomington** (city) Monroe County
145	22.3	**Portage** (city) Porter County
147	22.6	**Martinsville** (city) Morgan County
148	22.7	**Brazil** (city) Clay County
148	22.7	**Greencastle** (city) Putnam County
148	22.7	**Hammond** (city) Lake County

Note: This section ranks incorporated places and CDPs (Census Designated Places) with populations of 2,500 or more. Unincorporated postal areas were not considered. Please refer to the User Guide for additional information.

Employment: Sales and Office Occupations
Top 150 Places Ranked in *Descending* Order

State Rank	Percent	Place
1	35.6	**Chandler** (town) Warrick County
2	33.4	**Chesterfield** (town) Madison County
3	33.1	**Heritage Lake** (CDP) Putnam County
4	32.7	**Whiteland** (town) Johnson County
5	32.5	**Sellersburg** (town) Clark County
6	31.7	**Cumberland** (town) Marion County
7	31.5	**Boonville** (city) Warrick County
8	31.2	**Charlestown** (city) Clark County
9	30.8	**Gas City** (city) Grant County
9	30.8	**Hidden Valley** (CDP) Dearborn County
11	30.1	**Greendale** (city) Dearborn County
12	29.9	**Sullivan** (city) Sullivan County
13	29.4	**Beech Grove** (city) Marion County
13	29.4	**Jasper** (city) Dubois County
15	29.3	**Bargersville** (town) Johnson County
15	29.3	**Nappanee** (city) Elkhart County
17	29.2	**Batesville** (city) Ripley County
18	28.9	**Loogootee** (city) Martin County
19	28.8	**Scottsburg** (city) Scott County
20	28.6	**Notre Dame** (CDP) Saint Joseph County
20	28.6	**Upland** (town) Grant County
22	28.5	**Lakes of the Four Seasons** (CDP) Lake County
22	28.5	**Mooresville** (town) Morgan County
24	28.4	**Angola** (city) Steuben County
24	28.4	**De Motte** (town) Jasper County
26	28.1	**Fairmount** (town) Grant County
27	28.0	**Brookville** (town) Franklin County
28	27.9	**Ossian** (town) Wells County
29	27.8	**Centerville** (town) Wayne County
29	27.8	**Leo-Cedarville** (town) Allen County
29	27.8	**Marion** (city) Grant County
29	27.8	**Martinsville** (city) Morgan County
33	27.7	**Middlebury** (town) Elkhart County
34	27.6	**Jeffersonville** (city) Clark County
34	27.6	**Noblesville** (city) Hamilton County
36	27.5	**Avon** (town) Hendricks County
36	27.5	**Clinton** (city) Vermillion County
38	27.4	**Mishawaka** (city) Saint Joseph County
38	27.4	**New Albany** (city) Floyd County
40	27.3	**Cicero** (town) Hamilton County
41	27.2	**Brownsburg** (town) Hendricks County
41	27.2	**Fishers** (town) Hamilton County
41	27.2	**Highland** (CDP) Vanderburgh County
44	27.1	**Greenwood** (city) Johnson County
44	27.1	**Lawrence** (city) Marion County
44	27.1	**Yorktown** (town) Delaware County
47	27.0	**McCordsville** (town) Hancock County
48	26.9	**Dyer** (town) Lake County
48	26.9	**Plainfield** (town) Hendricks County
50	26.8	**Granger** (CDP) Saint Joseph County
51	26.7	**La Porte** (city) LaPorte County
52	26.6	**Danville** (town) Hendricks County
52	26.6	**Franklin** (city) Johnson County
52	26.6	**Plymouth** (city) Marshall County
55	26.5	**Clarksville** (town) Clark County
55	26.5	**New Whiteland** (town) Johnson County
57	26.3	**Anderson** (city) Madison County
57	26.3	**Evansville** (city) Vanderburgh County
57	26.3	**Rockville** (town) Parke County
60	26.0	**Columbia City** (city) Whitley County
61	25.9	**Greenfield** (city) Hancock County
61	25.9	**Indianapolis** (city) Marion County
61	25.9	**Simonton Lake** (CDP) Elkhart County
64	25.8	**Pendleton** (town) Madison County
65	25.6	**Decatur** (city) Adams County
65	25.6	**Hobart** (city) Lake County
65	25.6	**Rushville** (city) Rush County
68	25.5	**Fort Wayne** (city) Allen County
68	25.5	**Georgetown** (town) Floyd County
68	25.5	**Griffith** (town) Lake County
68	25.5	**Westville** (town) LaPorte County
68	25.5	**Whiting** (city) Lake County
73	25.4	**Merrillville** (town) Lake County
74	25.3	**Terre Haute** (city) Vigo County
75	25.2	**North Terre Haute** (CDP) Vigo County
75	25.2	**South Bend** (city) Saint Joseph County
75	25.2	**Wabash** (city) Wabash County
78	25.1	**Highland** (town) Lake County
78	25.1	**Monticello** (city) White County
80	25.0	**Chesterton** (town) Porter County
80	25.0	**New Haven** (city) Allen County
82	24.8	**Michigan City** (city) LaPorte County
82	24.8	**Valparaiso** (city) Porter County
84	24.7	**Lawrenceburg** (city) Dearborn County
85	24.6	**Berne** (city) Adams County
85	24.6	**Bright** (CDP) Dearborn County
85	24.6	**Carmel** (city) Hamilton County
85	24.6	**Connersville** (city) Fayette County
85	24.6	**Lebanon** (city) Boone County
85	24.6	**Munster** (town) Lake County
91	24.5	**Hammond** (city) Lake County
91	24.5	**New Castle** (city) Henry County
93	24.4	**Covington** (city) Fountain County
93	24.4	**Muncie** (city) Delaware County
95	24.3	**Grissom AFB** (CDP) Miami County
96	24.2	**Shorewood Forest** (CDP) Porter County
97	24.1	**Kokomo** (city) Howard County
98	24.0	**Madison** (city) Jefferson County
99	23.9	**Cedar Lake** (town) Lake County
100	23.8	**Ellettsville** (town) Monroe County
100	23.8	**Westfield** (city) Hamilton County
102	23.4	**Bedford** (city) Lawrence County
102	23.4	**Crawfordsville** (city) Montgomery County
104	23.3	**Dunlap** (CDP) Elkhart County
105	23.2	**Edinburgh** (town) Johnson County
105	23.2	**Portage** (city) Porter County
105	23.2	**Sheridan** (town) Hamilton County
108	23.1	**Alexandria** (city) Madison County
108	23.1	**Auburn** (city) DeKalb County
108	23.1	**Aurora** (city) Dearborn County
111	23.0	**Vincennes** (city) Knox County
112	22.7	**Corydon** (town) Harrison County
112	22.7	**Knox** (city) Starke County
112	22.7	**Porter** (town) Porter County
112	22.7	**Winchester** (city) Randolph County
116	22.6	**Salem** (city) Washington County
117	22.5	**Delphi** (city) Carroll County
117	22.5	**East Chicago** (city) Lake County
119	22.3	**Gary** (city) Lake County
120	22.2	**Purdue University** (CDP) Tippecanoe County
120	22.2	**Saint John** (town) Lake County
120	22.2	**Schererville** (town) Lake County
120	22.2	**Seymour** (city) Jackson County
124	22.1	**Hanover** (town) Jefferson County
124	22.1	**Richmond** (city) Wayne County
126	22.0	**Mount Vernon** (city) Posey County
126	22.0	**Warsaw** (city) Kosciusko County
128	21.9	**Bluffton** (city) Wells County
129	21.6	**Brazil** (city) Clay County
129	21.6	**Hartford City** (city) Blackford County
129	21.6	**Speedway** (town) Marion County
132	21.4	**Crown Point** (city) Lake County
132	21.4	**Lafayette** (city) Tippecanoe County
134	21.3	**Melody Hill** (CDP) Vanderburgh County
134	21.3	**Pittsboro** (town) Hendricks County
134	21.3	**Whitestown** (town) Boone County
137	21.2	**Smithville-Sanders** (CDP) Monroe County
137	21.2	**Zionsville** (town) Boone County
139	20.9	**Elwood** (city) Madison County
139	20.9	**Roselawn** (CDP) Newton County
141	20.8	**Fortville** (town) Hancock County
141	20.8	**Newburgh** (town) Warrick County
141	20.8	**Tipton** (city) Tipton County
144	20.4	**Goshen** (city) Elkhart County
144	20.4	**Greensburg** (city) Decatur County
144	20.4	**Huntertown** (town) Allen County
144	20.4	**Kendallville** (city) Noble County
148	20.3	**Lagrange** (town) LaGrange County
148	20.3	**Lake Station** (city) Lake County
148	20.3	**Lowell** (town) Lake County

Note: This section ranks incorporated places and CDPs (Census Designated Places) with populations of 2,500 or more. Unincorporated postal areas were not considered. Please refer to the User Guide for additional information.

Employment: Sales and Office Occupations
Top 150 Places Ranked in *Ascending* Order

State Rank	Percent	Place
1	10.4	**Ligonier** (city) Noble County
2	10.9	**Bicknell** (city) Knox County
3	14.7	**Attica** (city) Fountain County
4	15.6	**Butler** (city) DeKalb County
5	15.8	**Country Squire Lakes** (CDP) Jennings County
6	16.3	**Rochester** (city) Fulton County
7	16.8	**Garrett** (city) DeKalb County
7	16.8	**Linton** (city) Greene County
9	17.1	**Bremen** (town) Marshall County
9	17.1	**Fort Branch** (town) Gibson County
11	17.4	**Princeton** (city) Gibson County
12	17.9	**Hebron** (town) Porter County
13	18.1	**Austin** (city) Scott County
14	18.2	**Greencastle** (city) Putnam County
14	18.2	**Washington** (city) Daviess County
16	18.3	**Rensselaer** (city) Jasper County
17	18.4	**West Lafayette** (city) Tippecanoe County
18	18.5	**Huntingburg** (city) Dubois County
18	18.5	**Paoli** (town) Orange County
18	18.5	**Portland** (city) Jay County
21	18.6	**Elkhart** (city) Elkhart County
22	18.7	**Mitchell** (city) Lawrence County
22	18.7	**Peru** (city) Miami County
22	18.7	**Union City** (city) Randolph County
25	18.9	**Logansport** (city) Cass County
26	19.0	**Huntington** (city) Huntington County
27	19.1	**Brownstown** (town) Jackson County
28	19.2	**Frankfort** (city) Clinton County
28	19.2	**Syracuse** (town) Kosciusko County
30	19.3	**North Manchester** (town) Wabash County
31	19.4	**Tell City** (city) Perry County
32	19.6	**North Vernon** (city) Jennings County
32	19.6	**Winfield** (town) Lake County
34	19.9	**Columbus** (city) Bartholomew County
35	20.0	**Winona Lake** (town) Kosciusko County
36	20.2	**Bloomington** (city) Monroe County
37	20.3	**Lagrange** (town) LaGrange County
37	20.3	**Lake Station** (city) Lake County
37	20.3	**Lowell** (town) Lake County
37	20.3	**Shelbyville** (city) Shelby County
37	20.3	**South Haven** (CDP) Porter County
42	20.4	**Goshen** (city) Elkhart County
42	20.4	**Greensburg** (city) Decatur County
42	20.4	**Huntertown** (town) Allen County
42	20.4	**Kendallville** (city) Noble County
46	20.8	**Fortville** (town) Hancock County
46	20.8	**Newburgh** (town) Warrick County
46	20.8	**Tipton** (city) Tipton County
49	20.9	**Elwood** (city) Madison County
49	20.9	**Roselawn** (CDP) Newton County
51	21.2	**Smithville-Sanders** (CDP) Monroe County
51	21.2	**Zionsville** (town) Boone County
53	21.3	**Melody Hill** (CDP) Vanderburgh County
53	21.3	**Pittsboro** (town) Hendricks County
53	21.3	**Whitestown** (town) Boone County
56	21.4	**Crown Point** (city) Lake County
56	21.4	**Lafayette** (city) Tippecanoe County
58	21.6	**Brazil** (city) Clay County
58	21.6	**Hartford City** (city) Blackford County
58	21.6	**Speedway** (town) Marion County
61	21.9	**Bluffton** (city) Wells County
62	22.0	**Mount Vernon** (city) Posey County
62	22.0	**Warsaw** (city) Kosciusko County
64	22.1	**Hanover** (town) Jefferson County
64	22.1	**Richmond** (city) Wayne County
66	22.2	**Purdue University** (CDP) Tippecanoe County
66	22.2	**Saint John** (town) Lake County
66	22.2	**Schererville** (town) Lake County
66	22.2	**Seymour** (city) Jackson County
70	22.3	**Gary** (city) Lake County
71	22.5	**Delphi** (city) Carroll County
71	22.5	**East Chicago** (city) Lake County
73	22.6	**Salem** (city) Washington County
74	22.7	**Corydon** (town) Harrison County
74	22.7	**Knox** (city) Starke County
74	22.7	**Porter** (town) Porter County
74	22.7	**Winchester** (city) Randolph County
78	23.0	**Vincennes** (city) Knox County
79	23.1	**Alexandria** (city) Madison County
79	23.1	**Auburn** (city) DeKalb County
79	23.1	**Aurora** (city) Dearborn County
82	23.2	**Edinburgh** (town) Johnson County
82	23.2	**Portage** (city) Porter County
82	23.2	**Sheridan** (town) Hamilton County
85	23.3	**Dunlap** (CDP) Elkhart County
86	23.4	**Bedford** (city) Lawrence County
86	23.4	**Crawfordsville** (city) Montgomery County
88	23.8	**Ellettsville** (town) Monroe County
88	23.8	**Westfield** (city) Hamilton County
90	23.9	**Cedar Lake** (town) Lake County
91	24.0	**Madison** (city) Jefferson County
92	24.1	**Kokomo** (city) Howard County
93	24.2	**Shorewood Forest** (CDP) Porter County
94	24.3	**Grissom AFB** (CDP) Miami County
95	24.4	**Covington** (city) Fountain County
95	24.4	**Muncie** (city) Delaware County
97	24.5	**Hammond** (city) Lake County
97	24.5	**New Castle** (city) Henry County
99	24.6	**Berne** (city) Adams County
99	24.6	**Bright** (CDP) Dearborn County
99	24.6	**Carmel** (city) Hamilton County
99	24.6	**Connersville** (city) Fayette County
99	24.6	**Lebanon** (city) Boone County
99	24.6	**Munster** (town) Lake County
105	24.7	**Lawrenceburg** (city) Dearborn County
106	24.8	**Michigan City** (city) LaPorte County
106	24.8	**Valparaiso** (city) Porter County
108	25.0	**Chesterton** (town) Porter County
108	25.0	**New Haven** (city) Allen County
110	25.1	**Highland** (town) Lake County
110	25.1	**Monticello** (city) White County
112	25.2	**North Terre Haute** (CDP) Vigo County
112	25.2	**South Bend** (city) Saint Joseph County
112	25.2	**Wabash** (city) Wabash County
115	25.3	**Terre Haute** (city) Vigo County
116	25.4	**Merrillville** (town) Lake County
117	25.5	**Fort Wayne** (city) Allen County
117	25.5	**Georgetown** (town) Floyd County
117	25.5	**Griffith** (town) Lake County
117	25.5	**Westville** (town) LaPorte County
117	25.5	**Whiting** (city) Lake County
122	25.6	**Decatur** (city) Adams County
122	25.6	**Hobart** (city) Lake County
122	25.6	**Rushville** (city) Rush County
125	25.8	**Pendleton** (town) Madison County
126	25.9	**Greenfield** (city) Hancock County
126	25.9	**Indianapolis** (city) Marion County
126	25.9	**Simonton Lake** (CDP) Elkhart County
129	26.0	**Columbia City** (city) Whitley County
130	26.3	**Anderson** (city) Madison County
130	26.3	**Evansville** (city) Vanderburgh County
130	26.3	**Rockville** (town) Parke County
133	26.5	**Clarksville** (town) Clark County
133	26.5	**New Whiteland** (town) Johnson County
135	26.6	**Danville** (town) Hendricks County
135	26.6	**Franklin** (city) Johnson County
135	26.6	**Plymouth** (city) Marshall County
138	26.7	**La Porte** (city) LaPorte County
139	26.8	**Granger** (CDP) Saint Joseph County
140	26.9	**Dyer** (town) Lake County
140	26.9	**Plainfield** (town) Hendricks County
142	27.0	**McCordsville** (town) Hancock County
143	27.1	**Greenwood** (city) Johnson County
143	27.1	**Lawrence** (city) Marion County
143	27.1	**Yorktown** (town) Delaware County
146	27.2	**Brownsburg** (town) Hendricks County
146	27.2	**Fishers** (town) Hamilton County
146	27.2	**Highland** (CDP) Vanderburgh County
149	27.3	**Cicero** (town) Hamilton County
150	27.4	**Mishawaka** (city) Saint Joseph County

Note: *This section ranks incorporated places and CDPs (Census Designated Places) with populations of 2,500 or more. Unincorporated postal areas were not considered. Please refer to the User Guide for additional information.*

Employment: Natural Resources, Construction, and Maintenance Occupations
Top 150 Places Ranked in *Descending* Order

State Rank	Percent	Place
1	25.3	De Motte (town) Jasper County
2	20.7	Ligonier (city) Noble County
3	20.5	Cedar Lake (town) Lake County
4	18.2	Delphi (city) Carroll County
5	17.9	Cumberland (town) Marion County
5	17.9	Union City (city) Randolph County
7	16.5	Lake Station (city) Lake County
8	16.2	Hebron (town) Porter County
9	15.9	Lowell (town) Lake County
10	15.6	Bicknell (city) Knox County
11	15.1	Aurora (city) Dearborn County
12	14.7	Pittsboro (town) Hendricks County
13	14.5	Grissom AFB (CDP) Miami County
14	14.3	Smithville-Sanders (CDP) Monroe County
15	14.2	Heritage Lake (CDP) Putnam County
16	13.9	Lagrange (town) LaGrange County
17	13.8	Tipton (city) Tipton County
18	13.2	Sullivan (city) Sullivan County
19	13.0	Lebanon (city) Boone County
20	12.9	South Haven (CDP) Porter County
21	12.6	Portage (city) Porter County
21	12.6	Washington (city) Daviess County
23	12.4	Porter (town) Porter County
23	12.4	Shorewood Forest (CDP) Porter County
25	12.3	Hobart (city) Lake County
25	12.3	Salem (city) Washington County
27	12.2	Covington (city) Fountain County
27	12.2	Hidden Valley (CDP) Dearborn County
29	12.1	Sellersburg (town) Clark County
30	12.0	Fort Branch (town) Gibson County
31	11.9	Boonville (city) Warrick County
32	11.8	Griffith (town) Lake County
32	11.8	Rensselaer (city) Jasper County
34	11.6	Bright (CDP) Dearborn County
35	11.5	Garrett (city) DeKalb County
35	11.5	Mount Vernon (city) Posey County
37	11.2	Sheridan (town) Hamilton County
38	11.1	Danville (town) Hendricks County
38	11.1	Knox (city) Starke County
38	11.1	Roselawn (CDP) Newton County
41	10.9	Goshen (city) Elkhart County
42	10.6	Hanover (town) Jefferson County
42	10.6	Martinsville (city) Morgan County
44	10.5	Paoli (town) Orange County
45	10.4	Bluffton (city) Wells County
45	10.4	Peru (city) Miami County
47	10.3	Bedford (city) Lawrence County
47	10.3	Fairmount (town) Grant County
49	10.1	Alexandria (city) Madison County
49	10.1	Highland (town) Lake County
49	10.1	Tell City (city) Perry County
52	10.0	Edinburgh (town) Johnson County
52	10.0	New Whiteland (town) Johnson County
54	9.9	Linton (city) Greene County
54	9.9	Princeton (city) Gibson County
56	9.8	Greenwood (city) Johnson County
56	9.8	Lawrenceburg (city) Dearborn County
58	9.7	Cicero (town) Hamilton County
58	9.7	Pendleton (town) Madison County
60	9.6	Hammond (city) Lake County
61	9.5	Winfield (town) Lake County
62	9.4	Brownstown (town) Jackson County
63	9.3	Beech Grove (city) Marion County
63	9.3	Fortville (town) Hancock County
63	9.3	Winchester (city) Randolph County
66	9.2	Highland (CDP) Vanderburgh County
67	9.1	Anderson (city) Madison County
67	9.1	Kendallville (city) Noble County
67	9.1	Seymour (city) Jackson County
67	9.1	Shelbyville (city) Shelby County
71	9.0	Frankfort (city) Clinton County
71	9.0	Westville (town) LaPorte County
73	8.9	Austin (city) Scott County
73	8.9	Country Squire Lakes (CDP) Jennings County
73	8.9	Crown Point (city) Lake County
73	8.9	Dyer (town) Lake County
73	8.9	Evansville (city) Vanderburgh County
73	8.9	Speedway (town) Marion County
79	8.8	Chesterton (town) Porter County
79	8.8	Madison (city) Jefferson County
79	8.8	Saint John (town) Lake County
82	8.7	Decatur (city) Adams County
82	8.7	Greenfield (city) Hancock County
82	8.7	New Haven (city) Allen County
82	8.7	Rochester (city) Fulton County
86	8.6	Franklin (city) Johnson County
86	8.6	Mooresville (town) Morgan County
88	8.5	Avon (town) Hendricks County
88	8.5	East Chicago (city) Lake County
88	8.5	Plymouth (city) Marshall County
91	8.4	Lakes of the Four Seasons (CDP) Lake County
91	8.4	Monticello (city) White County
91	8.4	Newburgh (town) Warrick County
91	8.4	Syracuse (town) Kosciusko County
95	8.3	Scottsburg (city) Scott County
96	8.2	Chandler (town) Warrick County
96	8.2	Huntington (city) Huntington County
96	8.2	Middlebury (town) Elkhart County
99	8.1	Logansport (city) Cass County
99	8.1	New Castle (city) Henry County
99	8.1	Plainfield (town) Hendricks County
102	7.9	Terre Haute (city) Vigo County
103	7.8	Centerville (town) Wayne County
103	7.8	Gas City (city) Grant County
105	7.7	Mishawaka (city) Saint Joseph County
106	7.6	Attica (city) Fountain County
106	7.6	La Porte (city) LaPorte County
106	7.6	Vincennes (city) Knox County
106	7.6	Whitestown (town) Boone County
110	7.5	Schererville (town) Lake County
111	7.4	Jeffersonville (city) Clark County
111	7.4	Michigan City (city) LaPorte County
113	7.3	Bargersville (town) Johnson County
113	7.3	Huntingburg (city) Dubois County
113	7.3	Indianapolis (city) Marion County
113	7.3	Kokomo (city) Howard County
113	7.3	Merrillville (town) Lake County
113	7.3	Munster (town) Lake County
113	7.3	Nappanee (city) Elkhart County
120	7.1	New Albany (city) Floyd County
121	7.0	Charlestown (city) Clark County
121	7.0	Greensburg (city) Decatur County
121	7.0	Lawrence (city) Marion County
121	7.0	North Vernon (city) Jennings County
121	7.0	Portland (city) Jay County
126	6.9	Huntertown (town) Allen County
127	6.8	Lafayette (city) Tippecanoe County
127	6.8	Rockville (town) Parke County
129	6.7	Bremen (town) Marshall County
129	6.7	Dunlap (CDP) Elkhart County
129	6.7	Ellettsville (town) Monroe County
132	6.6	Connersville (city) Fayette County
132	6.6	Richmond (city) Wayne County
132	6.6	Whiteland (town) Johnson County
135	6.5	Angola (city) Steuben County
135	6.5	Chesterfield (town) Madison County
137	6.4	Brownsburg (town) Hendricks County
137	6.4	Clarksville (town) Clark County
139	6.3	Fort Wayne (city) Allen County
139	6.3	McCordsville (town) Hancock County
139	6.3	Whiting (city) Lake County
142	6.2	Valparaiso (city) Porter County
142	6.2	Yorktown (town) Delaware County
144	6.1	Clinton (city) Vermillion County
145	6.0	Berne (city) Adams County
145	6.0	North Terre Haute (CDP) Vigo County
145	6.0	South Bend (city) Saint Joseph County
148	5.9	Crawfordsville (city) Montgomery County
148	5.9	Gary (city) Lake County
148	5.9	Simonton Lake (CDP) Elkhart County

Note: This section ranks incorporated places and CDPs (Census Designated Places) with populations of 2,500 or more. Unincorporated postal areas were not considered. Please refer to the User Guide for additional information.

Employment: Natural Resources, Construction, and Maintenance Occupations
Top 150 Places Ranked in *Ascending* Order

State Rank	Percent	Place
1	1.5	**Notre Dame** (CDP) Saint Joseph County
2	1.8	**Purdue University** (CDP) Tippecanoe County
3	2.0	**West Lafayette** (city) Tippecanoe County
4	2.8	**Carmel** (city) Hamilton County
5	3.1	**Bloomington** (city) Monroe County
6	3.3	**Fishers** (town) Hamilton County
7	3.4	**Zionsville** (town) Boone County
8	3.5	**Brookville** (town) Franklin County
9	3.6	**Upland** (town) Grant County
9	3.6	**Westfield** (city) Hamilton County
11	3.8	**Ossian** (town) Wells County
12	3.9	**Auburn** (city) DeKalb County
13	4.0	**Hartford City** (city) Blackford County
13	4.0	**Rushville** (city) Rush County
15	4.1	**Granger** (CDP) Saint Joseph County
16	4.3	**Noblesville** (city) Hamilton County
17	4.4	**Leo-Cedarville** (town) Allen County
17	4.4	**Warsaw** (city) Kosciusko County
19	4.5	**Batesville** (city) Ripley County
20	4.6	**North Manchester** (town) Wabash County
21	4.8	**Corydon** (town) Harrison County
22	5.1	**Columbus** (city) Bartholomew County
22	5.1	**Georgetown** (town) Floyd County
22	5.1	**Greencastle** (city) Putnam County
22	5.1	**Muncie** (city) Delaware County
26	5.3	**Elkhart** (city) Elkhart County
26	5.3	**Jasper** (city) Dubois County
26	5.3	**Marion** (city) Grant County
29	5.4	**Butler** (city) DeKalb County
29	5.4	**Columbia City** (city) Whitley County
29	5.4	**Greendale** (city) Dearborn County
29	5.4	**Loogootee** (city) Martin County
29	5.4	**Wabash** (city) Wabash County
34	5.6	**Melody Hill** (CDP) Vanderburgh County
34	5.6	**Winona Lake** (town) Kosciusko County
36	5.7	**Brazil** (city) Clay County
36	5.7	**Elwood** (city) Madison County
38	5.8	**Mitchell** (city) Lawrence County
39	5.9	**Crawfordsville** (city) Montgomery County
39	5.9	**Gary** (city) Lake County
39	5.9	**Simonton Lake** (CDP) Elkhart County
42	6.0	**Berne** (city) Adams County
42	6.0	**North Terre Haute** (CDP) Vigo County
42	6.0	**South Bend** (city) Saint Joseph County
45	6.1	**Clinton** (city) Vermillion County
46	6.2	**Valparaiso** (city) Porter County
46	6.2	**Yorktown** (town) Delaware County
48	6.3	**Fort Wayne** (city) Allen County
48	6.3	**McCordsville** (town) Hancock County
48	6.3	**Whiting** (city) Lake County
51	6.4	**Brownsburg** (town) Hendricks County
51	6.4	**Clarksville** (town) Clark County
53	6.5	**Angola** (city) Steuben County
53	6.5	**Chesterfield** (town) Madison County
55	6.6	**Connersville** (city) Fayette County
55	6.6	**Richmond** (city) Wayne County
55	6.6	**Whiteland** (town) Johnson County
58	6.7	**Bremen** (town) Marshall County
58	6.7	**Dunlap** (CDP) Elkhart County
58	6.7	**Ellettsville** (town) Monroe County
61	6.8	**Lafayette** (city) Tippecanoe County
61	6.8	**Rockville** (town) Parke County
63	6.9	**Huntertown** (town) Allen County
64	7.0	**Charlestown** (city) Clark County
64	7.0	**Greensburg** (city) Decatur County
64	7.0	**Lawrence** (city) Marion County
64	7.0	**North Vernon** (city) Jennings County
64	7.0	**Portland** (city) Jay County
69	7.1	**New Albany** (city) Floyd County
70	7.3	**Bargersville** (town) Johnson County
70	7.3	**Huntingburg** (city) Dubois County
70	7.3	**Indianapolis** (city) Marion County
70	7.3	**Kokomo** (city) Howard County
70	7.3	**Merrillville** (town) Lake County
70	7.3	**Munster** (town) Lake County
70	7.3	**Nappanee** (city) Elkhart County
77	7.4	**Jeffersonville** (city) Clark County
77	7.4	**Michigan City** (city) LaPorte County
79	7.5	**Schererville** (town) Lake County
80	7.6	**Attica** (city) Fountain County
80	7.6	**La Porte** (city) LaPorte County
80	7.6	**Vincennes** (city) Knox County
80	7.6	**Whitestown** (town) Boone County
84	7.7	**Mishawaka** (city) Saint Joseph County
85	7.8	**Centerville** (town) Wayne County
85	7.8	**Gas City** (city) Grant County
87	7.9	**Terre Haute** (city) Vigo County
88	8.1	**Logansport** (city) Cass County
88	8.1	**New Castle** (city) Henry County
88	8.1	**Plainfield** (town) Hendricks County
91	8.2	**Chandler** (town) Warrick County
91	8.2	**Huntington** (city) Huntington County
91	8.2	**Middlebury** (town) Elkhart County
94	8.3	**Scottsburg** (city) Scott County
95	8.4	**Lakes of the Four Seasons** (CDP) Lake County
95	8.4	**Monticello** (city) White County
95	8.4	**Newburgh** (town) Warrick County
95	8.4	**Syracuse** (town) Kosciusko County
99	8.5	**Avon** (town) Hendricks County
99	8.5	**East Chicago** (city) Lake County
99	8.5	**Plymouth** (city) Marshall County
102	8.6	**Franklin** (city) Johnson County
102	8.6	**Mooresville** (town) Morgan County
104	8.7	**Decatur** (city) Adams County
104	8.7	**Greenfield** (city) Hancock County
104	8.7	**New Haven** (city) Allen County
104	8.7	**Rochester** (city) Fulton County
108	8.8	**Chesterton** (town) Porter County
108	8.8	**Madison** (city) Jefferson County
108	8.8	**Saint John** (town) Lake County
111	8.9	**Austin** (city) Scott County
111	8.9	**Country Squire Lakes** (CDP) Jennings County
111	8.9	**Crown Point** (city) Lake County
111	8.9	**Dyer** (town) Lake County
111	8.9	**Evansville** (city) Vanderburgh County
111	8.9	**Speedway** (town) Marion County
117	9.0	**Frankfort** (city) Clinton County
117	9.0	**Westville** (town) LaPorte County
119	9.1	**Anderson** (city) Madison County
119	9.1	**Kendallville** (city) Noble County
119	9.1	**Seymour** (city) Jackson County
119	9.1	**Shelbyville** (city) Shelby County
123	9.2	**Highland** (CDP) Vanderburgh County
124	9.3	**Beech Grove** (city) Marion County
124	9.3	**Fortville** (town) Hancock County
124	9.3	**Winchester** (city) Randolph County
127	9.4	**Brownstown** (town) Jackson County
128	9.5	**Winfield** (town) Lake County
129	9.6	**Hammond** (city) Lake County
130	9.7	**Cicero** (town) Hamilton County
130	9.7	**Pendleton** (town) Madison County
132	9.8	**Greenwood** (city) Johnson County
132	9.8	**Lawrenceburg** (city) Dearborn County
134	9.9	**Linton** (city) Greene County
134	9.9	**Princeton** (city) Gibson County
136	10.0	**Edinburgh** (town) Johnson County
136	10.0	**New Whiteland** (town) Johnson County
138	10.1	**Alexandria** (city) Madison County
138	10.1	**Highland** (town) Lake County
138	10.1	**Tell City** (city) Perry County
141	10.3	**Bedford** (city) Lawrence County
141	10.3	**Fairmount** (town) Grant County
143	10.4	**Bluffton** (city) Wells County
143	10.4	**Peru** (city) Miami County
145	10.5	**Paoli** (town) Orange County
146	10.6	**Hanover** (town) Jefferson County
146	10.6	**Martinsville** (city) Morgan County
148	10.9	**Goshen** (city) Elkhart County
149	11.1	**Danville** (town) Hendricks County
149	11.1	**Knox** (city) Starke County

Note: This section ranks incorporated places and CDPs (Census Designated Places) with populations of 2,500 or more. Unincorporated postal areas were not considered. Please refer to the User Guide for additional information.

Employment: Production, Transportation, and Material Moving Occupations
Top 150 Places Ranked in *Descending* Order

State Rank	Percent	Place
1	53.1	**Ligonier** (city) Noble County
2	44.0	**Butler** (city) DeKalb County
3	41.4	**Frankfort** (city) Clinton County
4	40.4	**Austin** (city) Scott County
5	39.1	**Elkhart** (city) Elkhart County
6	38.9	**Portland** (city) Jay County
7	38.5	**Bremen** (town) Marshall County
8	37.3	**Edinburgh** (town) Johnson County
9	36.8	**Attica** (city) Fountain County
10	36.0	**Syracuse** (town) Kosciusko County
11	35.5	**Country Squire Lakes** (CDP) Jennings County
12	34.5	**Logansport** (city) Cass County
12	34.5	**Rochester** (city) Fulton County
14	33.6	**Kendallville** (city) Noble County
15	32.9	**Huntingburg** (city) Dubois County
16	32.7	**Grissom AFB** (CDP) Miami County
17	32.3	**Bicknell** (city) Knox County
18	31.8	**Warsaw** (city) Kosciusko County
19	31.7	**Lagrange** (town) LaGrange County
20	31.1	**Princeton** (city) Gibson County
20	31.1	**Tell City** (city) Perry County
22	30.5	**Elwood** (city) Madison County
23	30.3	**Columbia City** (city) Whitley County
24	30.2	**Hartford City** (city) Blackford County
25	30.0	**Rockville** (town) Parke County
26	29.6	**Garrett** (city) DeKalb County
26	29.6	**Plymouth** (city) Marshall County
28	29.5	**Lawrenceburg** (city) Dearborn County
29	29.3	**Huntington** (city) Huntington County
30	29.0	**Rushville** (city) Rush County
31	28.9	**Crawfordsville** (city) Montgomery County
32	28.8	**Nappanee** (city) Elkhart County
33	28.5	**Goshen** (city) Elkhart County
33	28.5	**Shelbyville** (city) Shelby County
35	28.3	**Whiting** (city) Lake County
36	27.9	**Seymour** (city) Jackson County
37	27.8	**Dunlap** (CDP) Elkhart County
38	27.5	**Wabash** (city) Wabash County
39	27.4	**Greensburg** (city) Decatur County
40	27.1	**Mitchell** (city) Lawrence County
41	26.8	**Corydon** (town) Harrison County
42	26.4	**Washington** (city) Daviess County
43	26.1	**North Vernon** (city) Jennings County
44	25.5	**Winchester** (city) Randolph County
45	25.3	**Clinton** (city) Vermillion County
46	25.2	**Salem** (city) Washington County
47	24.8	**Decatur** (city) Adams County
48	24.7	**Brookville** (town) Franklin County
49	24.6	**Brownstown** (town) Jackson County
49	24.6	**Chandler** (town) Warrick County
51	24.5	**Auburn** (city) DeKalb County
51	24.5	**Jasper** (city) Dubois County
53	24.2	**Charlestown** (city) Clark County
53	24.2	**Roselawn** (CDP) Newton County
55	24.1	**Connersville** (city) Fayette County
55	24.1	**Gas City** (city) Grant County
55	24.1	**Scottsburg** (city) Scott County
58	23.9	**Mount Vernon** (city) Posey County
59	23.8	**Peru** (city) Miami County
60	23.7	**New Whiteland** (town) Johnson County
61	23.6	**Middlebury** (town) Elkhart County
62	23.5	**Bluffton** (city) Wells County
63	22.9	**Union City** (city) Randolph County
64	22.8	**South Haven** (CDP) Porter County
65	22.6	**Delphi** (city) Carroll County
66	22.5	**Westville** (town) LaPorte County
67	22.3	**New Castle** (city) Henry County
68	22.2	**East Chicago** (city) Lake County
68	22.2	**Sellersburg** (town) Clark County
70	22.1	**Brazil** (city) Clay County
70	22.1	**Hammond** (city) Lake County
72	21.9	**Alexandria** (city) Madison County
73	21.7	**La Porte** (city) LaPorte County
74	21.6	**Berne** (city) Adams County
74	21.6	**Hanover** (town) Jefferson County

State Rank	Percent	Place
76	21.4	**Lake Station** (city) Lake County
77	21.3	**Monticello** (city) White County
78	21.2	**Porter** (town) Porter County
78	21.2	**Simonton Lake** (CDP) Elkhart County
80	21.1	**Michigan City** (city) LaPorte County
81	21.0	**Fort Branch** (town) Gibson County
81	21.0	**Mooresville** (town) Morgan County
83	20.6	**Loogootee** (city) Martin County
84	20.2	**North Terre Haute** (CDP) Vigo County
85	20.1	**Merrillville** (town) Lake County
86	20.0	**Paoli** (town) Orange County
86	20.0	**Vincennes** (city) Knox County
88	19.9	**Knox** (city) Starke County
88	19.9	**Newburgh** (town) Warrick County
90	19.7	**Kokomo** (city) Howard County
91	19.6	**Centerville** (town) Wayne County
92	19.5	**Beech Grove** (city) Marion County
92	19.5	**Gary** (city) Lake County
92	19.5	**New Haven** (city) Allen County
95	19.2	**Angola** (city) Steuben County
96	19.0	**Chesterton** (town) Porter County
97	18.8	**Greencastle** (city) Putnam County
98	18.7	**Lowell** (town) Lake County
99	18.6	**Lafayette** (city) Tippecanoe County
100	18.4	**Tipton** (city) Tipton County
101	18.3	**Boonville** (city) Warrick County
102	18.2	**Franklin** (city) Johnson County
103	17.9	**Ellettsville** (town) Monroe County
103	17.9	**Hebron** (town) Porter County
103	17.9	**Richmond** (city) Wayne County
106	17.8	**Clarksville** (town) Clark County
106	17.8	**Mishawaka** (city) Saint Joseph County
108	17.6	**Evansville** (city) Vanderburgh County
108	17.6	**Georgetown** (town) Floyd County
108	17.6	**Marion** (city) Grant County
108	17.6	**New Albany** (city) Floyd County
112	17.5	**Linton** (city) Greene County
113	17.4	**Jeffersonville** (city) Clark County
113	17.4	**Rensselaer** (city) Jasper County
113	17.4	**Speedway** (town) Marion County
116	17.1	**Bedford** (city) Lawrence County
116	17.1	**Melody Hill** (CDP) Vanderburgh County
118	16.8	**Fort Wayne** (city) Allen County
118	16.8	**Sullivan** (city) Sullivan County
120	16.5	**Greenfield** (city) Hancock County
121	16.4	**Cicero** (town) Hamilton County
121	16.4	**Columbus** (city) Bartholomew County
123	16.3	**Hobart** (city) Lake County
123	16.3	**South Bend** (city) Saint Joseph County
125	16.2	**Lebanon** (city) Boone County
125	16.2	**Terre Haute** (city) Vigo County
127	16.1	**Heritage Lake** (CDP) Putnam County
127	16.1	**Portage** (city) Porter County
129	16.0	**Bright** (CDP) Dearborn County
130	15.9	**Griffith** (town) Lake County
131	15.8	**Martinsville** (city) Morgan County
132	15.7	**Anderson** (city) Madison County
132	15.7	**Madison** (city) Jefferson County
134	15.6	**Covington** (city) Fountain County
135	15.3	**North Manchester** (town) Wabash County
136	15.1	**Fortville** (town) Hancock County
137	15.0	**Batesville** (city) Ripley County
138	14.9	**Crown Point** (city) Lake County
138	14.9	**Dyer** (town) Lake County
140	14.5	**Sheridan** (town) Hamilton County
141	14.4	**Highland** (town) Lake County
141	14.4	**Schererville** (town) Lake County
143	14.2	**Bargersville** (town) Johnson County
143	14.2	**Winfield** (town) Lake County
145	14.1	**Chesterfield** (town) Madison County
145	14.1	**Greendale** (city) Dearborn County
145	14.1	**Indianapolis** (city) Marion County
148	14.0	**Greenwood** (city) Johnson County
148	14.0	**Muncie** (city) Delaware County
150	13.9	**Plainfield** (town) Hendricks County

Note: This section ranks incorporated places and CDPs (Census Designated Places) with populations of 2,500 or more. Unincorporated postal areas were not considered. Please refer to the User Guide for additional information.

Employment: Production, Transportation, and Material Moving Occupations
Top 150 Places Ranked in *Ascending* Order

State Rank	Percent	Place
1	2.0	**Notre Dame** (CDP) Saint Joseph County
2	2.3	**McCordsville** (town) Hancock County
3	3.2	**Purdue University** (CDP) Tippecanoe County
4	3.7	**Fishers** (town) Hamilton County
5	3.8	**West Lafayette** (city) Tippecanoe County
6	4.2	**Carmel** (city) Hamilton County
7	5.7	**De Motte** (town) Jasper County
7	5.7	**Zionsville** (town) Boone County
9	5.9	**Whitestown** (town) Boone County
10	6.2	**Cumberland** (town) Marion County
11	7.1	**Shorewood Forest** (CDP) Porter County
11	7.1	**Upland** (town) Grant County
13	7.2	**Pendleton** (town) Madison County
14	7.8	**Westfield** (city) Hamilton County
15	7.9	**Highland** (CDP) Vanderburgh County
15	7.9	**Smithville-Sanders** (CDP) Monroe County
17	8.0	**Granger** (CDP) Saint Joseph County
17	8.0	**Noblesville** (city) Hamilton County
19	8.3	**Bloomington** (city) Monroe County
20	9.3	**Lakes of the Four Seasons** (CDP) Lake County
21	9.5	**Avon** (town) Hendricks County
22	9.9	**Saint John** (town) Lake County
23	10.1	**Yorktown** (town) Delaware County
24	10.2	**Pittsboro** (town) Hendricks County
25	10.3	**Munster** (town) Lake County
26	11.2	**Lawrence** (city) Marion County
27	11.6	**Danville** (town) Hendricks County
28	11.7	**Brownsburg** (town) Hendricks County
29	12.3	**Whiteland** (town) Johnson County
30	12.6	**Cedar Lake** (town) Lake County
30	12.6	**Leo-Cedarville** (town) Allen County
32	12.7	**Ossian** (town) Wells County
32	12.7	**Valparaiso** (city) Porter County
34	12.8	**Huntertown** (town) Allen County
35	12.9	**Hidden Valley** (CDP) Dearborn County
36	13.5	**Aurora** (city) Dearborn County
36	13.5	**Winona Lake** (town) Kosciusko County
38	13.6	**Fairmount** (town) Grant County
39	13.9	**Plainfield** (town) Hendricks County
40	14.0	**Greenwood** (city) Johnson County
40	14.0	**Muncie** (city) Delaware County
42	14.1	**Chesterfield** (town) Madison County
42	14.1	**Greendale** (city) Dearborn County
42	14.1	**Indianapolis** (city) Marion County
45	14.2	**Bargersville** (town) Johnson County
45	14.2	**Winfield** (town) Lake County
47	14.4	**Highland** (town) Lake County
47	14.4	**Schererville** (town) Lake County
49	14.5	**Sheridan** (town) Hamilton County
50	14.9	**Crown Point** (city) Lake County
50	14.9	**Dyer** (town) Lake County
52	15.0	**Batesville** (city) Ripley County
53	15.1	**Fortville** (town) Hancock County
54	15.3	**North Manchester** (town) Wabash County
55	15.6	**Covington** (city) Fountain County
56	15.7	**Anderson** (city) Madison County
56	15.7	**Madison** (city) Jefferson County
58	15.8	**Martinsville** (city) Morgan County
59	15.9	**Griffith** (town) Lake County
60	16.0	**Bright** (CDP) Dearborn County
61	16.1	**Heritage Lake** (CDP) Putnam County
61	16.1	**Portage** (city) Porter County
63	16.2	**Lebanon** (city) Boone County
63	16.2	**Terre Haute** (city) Vigo County
65	16.3	**Hobart** (city) Lake County
65	16.3	**South Bend** (city) Saint Joseph County
67	16.4	**Cicero** (town) Hamilton County
67	16.4	**Columbus** (city) Bartholomew County
69	16.5	**Greenfield** (city) Hancock County
70	16.8	**Fort Wayne** (city) Allen County
70	16.8	**Sullivan** (city) Sullivan County
72	17.1	**Bedford** (city) Lawrence County
72	17.1	**Melody Hill** (CDP) Vanderburgh County
74	17.4	**Jeffersonville** (city) Clark County
74	17.4	**Rensselaer** (city) Jasper County
74	17.4	**Speedway** (town) Marion County
77	17.5	**Linton** (city) Greene County
78	17.6	**Evansville** (city) Vanderburgh County
78	17.6	**Georgetown** (town) Floyd County
78	17.6	**Marion** (city) Grant County
78	17.6	**New Albany** (city) Floyd County
82	17.8	**Clarksville** (town) Clark County
82	17.8	**Mishawaka** (city) Saint Joseph County
84	17.9	**Ellettsville** (town) Monroe County
84	17.9	**Hebron** (town) Porter County
84	17.9	**Richmond** (city) Wayne County
87	18.2	**Franklin** (city) Johnson County
88	18.3	**Boonville** (city) Warrick County
89	18.4	**Tipton** (city) Tipton County
90	18.6	**Lafayette** (city) Tippecanoe County
91	18.7	**Lowell** (town) Lake County
92	18.8	**Greencastle** (city) Putnam County
93	19.0	**Chesterton** (town) Porter County
94	19.2	**Angola** (city) Steuben County
95	19.5	**Beech Grove** (city) Marion County
95	19.5	**Gary** (city) Lake County
95	19.5	**New Haven** (city) Allen County
98	19.6	**Centerville** (town) Wayne County
99	19.7	**Kokomo** (city) Howard County
100	19.9	**Knox** (city) Starke County
100	19.9	**Newburgh** (town) Warrick County
102	20.0	**Paoli** (town) Orange County
102	20.0	**Vincennes** (city) Knox County
104	20.1	**Merrillville** (town) Lake County
105	20.2	**North Terre Haute** (CDP) Vigo County
106	20.6	**Loogootee** (city) Martin County
107	21.0	**Fort Branch** (town) Gibson County
107	21.0	**Mooresville** (town) Morgan County
109	21.1	**Michigan City** (city) LaPorte County
110	21.2	**Porter** (town) Porter County
110	21.2	**Simonton Lake** (CDP) Elkhart County
112	21.3	**Monticello** (city) White County
113	21.4	**Lake Station** (city) Lake County
114	21.6	**Berne** (city) Adams County
114	21.6	**Hanover** (town) Jefferson County
116	21.7	**La Porte** (city) LaPorte County
117	21.9	**Alexandria** (city) Madison County
118	22.1	**Brazil** (city) Clay County
118	22.1	**Hammond** (city) Lake County
120	22.2	**East Chicago** (city) Lake County
120	22.2	**Sellersburg** (town) Clark County
122	22.3	**New Castle** (city) Henry County
123	22.5	**Westville** (town) LaPorte County
124	22.6	**Delphi** (city) Carroll County
125	22.8	**South Haven** (CDP) Porter County
126	22.9	**Union City** (city) Randolph County
127	23.5	**Bluffton** (city) Wells County
128	23.6	**Middlebury** (town) Elkhart County
129	23.7	**New Whiteland** (town) Johnson County
130	23.8	**Peru** (city) Miami County
131	23.9	**Mount Vernon** (city) Posey County
132	24.1	**Connersville** (city) Fayette County
132	24.1	**Gas City** (city) Grant County
132	24.1	**Scottsburg** (city) Scott County
135	24.2	**Charlestown** (city) Clark County
135	24.2	**Roselawn** (CDP) Newton County
137	24.5	**Auburn** (city) DeKalb County
137	24.5	**Jasper** (city) Dubois County
139	24.6	**Brownstown** (town) Jackson County
139	24.6	**Chandler** (town) Warrick County
141	24.7	**Brookville** (town) Franklin County
142	24.8	**Decatur** (city) Adams County
143	25.2	**Salem** (city) Washington County
144	25.3	**Clinton** (city) Vermillion County
145	25.5	**Winchester** (city) Randolph County
146	26.1	**North Vernon** (city) Jennings County
147	26.4	**Washington** (city) Daviess County
148	26.8	**Corydon** (town) Harrison County
149	27.1	**Mitchell** (city) Lawrence County
150	27.4	**Greensburg** (city) Decatur County

Note: *This section ranks incorporated places and CDPs (Census Designated Places) with populations of 2,500 or more. Unincorporated postal areas were not considered. Please refer to the User Guide for additional information.*

Per Capita Income
Top 150 Places Ranked in *Descending* Order

State Rank	Dollars	Place
1	52,793	**Zionsville** (town) Boone County
2	51,767	**Carmel** (city) Hamilton County
3	48,423	**Shorewood Forest** (CDP) Porter County
4	43,419	**Hidden Valley** (CDP) Dearborn County
5	39,598	**Granger** (CDP) Saint Joseph County
6	38,616	**Smithville-Sanders** (CDP) Monroe County
7	38,577	**Fishers** (town) Hamilton County
8	38,349	**McCordsville** (town) Hancock County
9	37,513	**Saint John** (town) Lake County
10	37,099	**Munster** (town) Lake County
11	36,269	**Dyer** (town) Lake County
12	36,068	**Westfield** (city) Hamilton County
13	34,625	**Highland** (CDP) Vanderburgh County
14	34,342	**Lakes of the Four Seasons** (CDP) Lake County
15	33,969	**Schererville** (town) Lake County
16	33,428	**Whitestown** (town) Boone County
17	32,728	**Melody Hill** (CDP) Vanderburgh County
18	32,688	**Bargersville** (town) Johnson County
19	32,223	**Porter** (town) Porter County
20	32,148	**Georgetown** (town) Floyd County
21	31,877	**Chesterton** (town) Porter County
22	31,829	**Brownsburg** (town) Hendricks County
23	31,535	**Winfield** (town) Lake County
24	31,341	**Newburgh** (town) Warrick County
25	31,261	**Noblesville** (city) Hamilton County
26	31,177	**Crown Point** (city) Lake County
27	30,852	**Batesville** (city) Ripley County
28	30,720	**Bright** (CDP) Dearborn County
29	29,560	**Highland** (town) Lake County
30	29,362	**Avon** (town) Hendricks County
31	28,739	**Columbus** (city) Bartholomew County
32	28,595	**Huntertown** (town) Allen County
33	28,540	**Jasper** (city) Dubois County
34	28,405	**Yorktown** (town) Delaware County
35	28,242	**Heritage Lake** (CDP) Putnam County
36	28,231	**Middlebury** (town) Elkhart County
37	28,215	**Pendleton** (town) Madison County
38	27,874	**Winona Lake** (town) Kosciusko County
39	27,843	**Cicero** (town) Hamilton County
40	27,653	**Pittsboro** (town) Hendricks County
41	27,095	**Danville** (town) Hendricks County
42	26,646	**Greenwood** (city) Johnson County
43	26,466	**Mount Vernon** (city) Posey County
44	26,400	**Whiteland** (town) Johnson County
45	26,305	**Greendale** (city) Dearborn County
46	26,069	**Berne** (city) Adams County
47	25,978	**Plainfield** (town) Hendricks County
48	25,767	**Covington** (city) Fountain County
49	25,697	**Rensselaer** (city) Jasper County
50	25,618	**Simonton Lake** (CDP) Elkhart County
51	25,392	**Hobart** (city) Lake County
52	25,247	**Griffith** (town) Lake County
53	25,181	**Speedway** (town) Marion County
54	24,917	**Mooresville** (town) Morgan County
55	24,893	**Cedar Lake** (town) Lake County
56	24,781	**Jeffersonville** (city) Clark County
57	24,726	**Lawrence** (city) Marion County
58	24,256	**Madison** (city) Jefferson County
59	24,239	**Valparaiso** (city) Porter County
60	24,012	**Indianapolis** (city) Marion County
61	23,963	**Auburn** (city) DeKalb County
62	23,918	**Portage** (city) Porter County
63	23,876	**Boonville** (city) Warrick County
64	23,839	**Winchester** (city) Randolph County
65	23,673	**Lebanon** (city) Boone County
66	23,639	**Leo-Cedarville** (town) Allen County
67	23,592	**Lowell** (town) Lake County
68	23,537	**Franklin** (city) Johnson County
69	23,400	**Fort Wayne** (city) Allen County
70	23,286	**Whiting** (city) Lake County
71	23,264	**Tell City** (city) Perry County
72	23,204	**Sellersburg** (town) Clark County
73	23,192	**New Haven** (city) Allen County
74	23,167	**Warsaw** (city) Kosciusko County
75	23,112	**Greenfield** (city) Hancock County
76	23,002	**Fort Branch** (town) Gibson County
77	22,989	**Merrillville** (town) Lake County
78	22,914	**Dunlap** (CDP) Elkhart County
79	22,824	**Hebron** (town) Porter County
80	22,795	**Rochester** (city) Fulton County
81	22,767	**Roselawn** (CDP) Newton County
82	22,649	**West Lafayette** (city) Tippecanoe County
83	22,616	**De Motte** (town) Jasper County
84	22,006	**Kokomo** (city) Howard County
85	21,876	**Centerville** (town) Wayne County
86	21,736	**Monticello** (city) White County
87	21,691	**Brookville** (town) Franklin County
88	21,662	**Clarksville** (town) Clark County
89	21,646	**Lafayette** (city) Tippecanoe County
90	21,549	**Cumberland** (town) Marion County
91	21,508	**Seymour** (city) Jackson County
92	21,438	**Brownstown** (town) Jackson County
93	21,364	**South Haven** (CDP) Porter County
94	21,352	**Washington** (city) Daviess County
95	21,251	**Columbia City** (city) Whitley County
96	21,183	**New Albany** (city) Floyd County
97	21,172	**North Terre Haute** (CDP) Vigo County
98	21,057	**Shelbyville** (city) Shelby County
99	20,984	**Evansville** (city) Vanderburgh County
100	20,981	**Princeton** (city) Gibson County
101	20,967	**Fortville** (town) Hancock County
102	20,912	**Mishawaka** (city) Saint Joseph County
103	20,909	**Decatur** (city) Adams County
104	20,864	**Attica** (city) Fountain County
105	20,677	**Greensburg** (city) Decatur County
106	20,611	**Bluffton** (city) Wells County
107	20,532	**Ellettsville** (town) Monroe County
108	20,443	**Ossian** (town) Wells County
109	20,431	**New Whiteland** (town) Johnson County
110	20,398	**Syracuse** (town) Kosciusko County
111	20,331	**Clinton** (city) Vermillion County
112	20,295	**Gas City** (city) Grant County
113	20,203	**Sheridan** (town) Hamilton County
114	20,106	**Wabash** (city) Wabash County
115	20,095	**Beech Grove** (city) Marion County
116	19,981	**Charlestown** (city) Clark County
117	19,761	**Loogootee** (city) Martin County
118	19,720	**Aurora** (city) Dearborn County
119	19,697	**Chesterfield** (town) Madison County
120	19,614	**Alexandria** (city) Madison County
121	19,498	**Nappanee** (city) Elkhart County
122	19,369	**Goshen** (city) Elkhart County
123	19,348	**Bedford** (city) Lawrence County
124	19,181	**South Bend** (city) Saint Joseph County
125	19,175	**Angola** (city) Steuben County
126	19,164	**Linton** (city) Greene County
127	19,027	**Michigan City** (city) LaPorte County
128	19,025	**La Porte** (city) LaPorte County
129	18,987	**Bloomington** (city) Monroe County
130	18,942	**Fairmount** (town) Grant County
131	18,902	**Hartford City** (city) Blackford County
132	18,813	**Huntingburg** (city) Dubois County
133	18,796	**Delphi** (city) Carroll County
133	18,796	**Richmond** (city) Wayne County
135	18,789	**Huntington** (city) Huntington County
136	18,786	**Bremen** (town) Marshall County
137	18,715	**Corydon** (town) Harrison County
138	18,654	**Kendallville** (city) Noble County
139	18,613	**Salem** (city) Washington County
140	18,419	**Martinsville** (city) Morgan County
141	18,402	**Elwood** (city) Madison County
142	18,359	**Garrett** (city) DeKalb County
143	18,347	**Rushville** (city) Rush County
144	18,308	**North Manchester** (town) Wabash County
145	18,216	**Anderson** (city) Madison County
146	18,199	**Crawfordsville** (city) Montgomery County
147	18,170	**Portland** (city) Jay County
148	18,035	**Peru** (city) Miami County
149	17,965	**Tipton** (city) Tipton County
150	17,920	**Hammond** (city) Lake County

Note: This section ranks incorporated places and CDPs (Census Designated Places) with populations of 2,500 or more. Unincorporated postal areas were not considered. Please refer to the User Guide for additional information.

Per Capita Income
Top 150 Places Ranked in *Ascending* Order

State Rank	Dollars	Place
1	3,690	**Notre Dame** (CDP) Saint Joseph County
2	4,655	**Purdue University** (CDP) Tippecanoe County
3	7,153	**Westville** (town) LaPorte County
4	13,252	**Hanover** (town) Jefferson County
5	13,497	**East Chicago** (city) Lake County
6	13,779	**Country Squire Lakes** (CDP) Jennings County
7	14,149	**Upland** (town) Grant County
8	15,170	**Austin** (city) Scott County
9	15,359	**Union City** (city) Randolph County
10	15,397	**Rockville** (town) Parke County
11	15,476	**Grissom AFB** (CDP) Miami County
12	15,596	**Plymouth** (city) Marshall County
13	15,931	**Gary** (city) Lake County
14	16,007	**Ligonier** (city) Noble County
15	16,123	**Lawrenceburg** (city) Dearborn County
16	16,147	**Sullivan** (city) Sullivan County
17	16,194	**Brazil** (city) Clay County
18	16,239	**Chandler** (town) Warrick County
19	16,250	**Butler** (city) DeKalb County
20	16,252	**Paoli** (town) Orange County
21	16,311	**Knox** (city) Starke County
22	16,596	**Lagrange** (town) LaGrange County
23	16,770	**Elkhart** (city) Elkhart County
24	16,825	**Connersville** (city) Fayette County
25	16,878	**Edinburgh** (town) Johnson County
26	16,970	**Lake Station** (city) Lake County
27	17,066	**Muncie** (city) Delaware County
28	17,126	**New Castle** (city) Henry County
29	17,207	**Logansport** (city) Cass County
30	17,323	**Scottsburg** (city) Scott County
31	17,589	**Terre Haute** (city) Vigo County
32	17,618	**Mitchell** (city) Lawrence County
33	17,641	**Frankfort** (city) Clinton County
34	17,792	**North Vernon** (city) Jennings County
35	17,808	**Marion** (city) Grant County
36	17,837	**Greencastle** (city) Putnam County
37	17,856	**Bicknell** (city) Knox County
38	17,896	**Vincennes** (city) Knox County
39	17,920	**Hammond** (city) Lake County
40	17,965	**Tipton** (city) Tipton County
41	18,035	**Peru** (city) Miami County
42	18,170	**Portland** (city) Jay County
43	18,199	**Crawfordsville** (city) Montgomery County
44	18,216	**Anderson** (city) Madison County
45	18,308	**North Manchester** (town) Wabash County
46	18,347	**Rushville** (city) Rush County
47	18,359	**Garrett** (city) DeKalb County
48	18,402	**Elwood** (city) Madison County
49	18,419	**Martinsville** (city) Morgan County
50	18,613	**Salem** (city) Washington County
51	18,654	**Kendallville** (city) Noble County
52	18,715	**Corydon** (town) Harrison County
53	18,786	**Bremen** (town) Marshall County
54	18,789	**Huntington** (city) Huntington County
55	18,796	**Delphi** (city) Carroll County
55	18,796	**Richmond** (city) Wayne County
57	18,813	**Huntingburg** (city) Dubois County
58	18,902	**Hartford City** (city) Blackford County
59	18,942	**Fairmount** (town) Grant County
60	18,987	**Bloomington** (city) Monroe County
61	19,025	**La Porte** (city) LaPorte County
62	19,027	**Michigan City** (city) LaPorte County
63	19,164	**Linton** (city) Greene County
64	19,175	**Angola** (city) Steuben County
65	19,181	**South Bend** (city) Saint Joseph County
66	19,348	**Bedford** (city) Lawrence County
67	19,369	**Goshen** (city) Elkhart County
68	19,498	**Nappanee** (city) Elkhart County
69	19,614	**Alexandria** (city) Madison County
70	19,697	**Chesterfield** (town) Madison County
71	19,720	**Aurora** (city) Dearborn County
72	19,761	**Loogootee** (city) Martin County
73	19,981	**Charlestown** (city) Clark County
74	20,095	**Beech Grove** (city) Marion County
75	20,106	**Wabash** (city) Wabash County
76	20,203	**Sheridan** (town) Hamilton County
77	20,295	**Gas City** (city) Grant County
78	20,331	**Clinton** (city) Vermillion County
79	20,398	**Syracuse** (town) Kosciusko County
80	20,431	**New Whiteland** (town) Johnson County
81	20,443	**Ossian** (town) Wells County
82	20,532	**Ellettsville** (town) Monroe County
83	20,611	**Bluffton** (city) Wells County
84	20,677	**Greensburg** (city) Decatur County
85	20,864	**Attica** (city) Fountain County
86	20,909	**Decatur** (city) Adams County
87	20,912	**Mishawaka** (city) Saint Joseph County
88	20,967	**Fortville** (town) Hancock County
89	20,981	**Princeton** (city) Gibson County
90	20,984	**Evansville** (city) Vanderburgh County
91	21,057	**Shelbyville** (city) Shelby County
92	21,172	**North Terre Haute** (CDP) Vigo County
93	21,183	**New Albany** (city) Floyd County
94	21,251	**Columbia City** (city) Whitley County
95	21,352	**Washington** (city) Daviess County
96	21,364	**South Haven** (CDP) Porter County
97	21,438	**Brownstown** (town) Jackson County
98	21,508	**Seymour** (city) Jackson County
99	21,549	**Cumberland** (town) Marion County
100	21,646	**Lafayette** (city) Tippecanoe County
101	21,662	**Clarksville** (town) Clark County
102	21,691	**Brookville** (town) Franklin County
103	21,736	**Monticello** (city) White County
104	21,876	**Centerville** (town) Wayne County
105	22,006	**Kokomo** (city) Howard County
106	22,616	**De Motte** (town) Jasper County
107	22,649	**West Lafayette** (city) Tippecanoe County
108	22,767	**Roselawn** (CDP) Newton County
109	22,795	**Rochester** (city) Fulton County
110	22,824	**Hebron** (town) Porter County
111	22,914	**Dunlap** (CDP) Elkhart County
112	22,989	**Merrillville** (town) Lake County
113	23,002	**Fort Branch** (town) Gibson County
114	23,112	**Greenfield** (city) Hancock County
115	23,167	**Warsaw** (city) Kosciusko County
116	23,192	**New Haven** (city) Allen County
117	23,204	**Sellersburg** (town) Clark County
118	23,264	**Tell City** (city) Perry County
119	23,286	**Whiting** (city) Lake County
120	23,400	**Fort Wayne** (city) Allen County
121	23,537	**Franklin** (city) Johnson County
122	23,592	**Lowell** (town) Lake County
123	23,639	**Leo-Cedarville** (town) Allen County
124	23,673	**Lebanon** (city) Boone County
125	23,839	**Winchester** (city) Randolph County
126	23,876	**Boonville** (city) Warrick County
127	23,918	**Portage** (city) Porter County
128	23,963	**Auburn** (city) DeKalb County
129	24,012	**Indianapolis** (city) Marion County
130	24,239	**Valparaiso** (city) Porter County
131	24,256	**Madison** (city) Jefferson County
132	24,726	**Lawrence** (city) Marion County
133	24,781	**Jeffersonville** (city) Clark County
134	24,893	**Cedar Lake** (town) Lake County
135	24,917	**Mooresville** (town) Morgan County
136	25,181	**Speedway** (town) Marion County
137	25,247	**Griffith** (town) Lake County
138	25,392	**Hobart** (city) Lake County
139	25,618	**Simonton Lake** (CDP) Elkhart County
140	25,697	**Rensselaer** (city) Jasper County
141	25,767	**Covington** (city) Fountain County
142	25,978	**Plainfield** (town) Hendricks County
143	26,069	**Berne** (city) Adams County
144	26,305	**Greendale** (city) Dearborn County
145	26,400	**Whiteland** (town) Johnson County
146	26,466	**Mount Vernon** (city) Posey County
147	26,646	**Greenwood** (city) Johnson County
148	27,095	**Danville** (town) Hendricks County
149	27,653	**Pittsboro** (town) Hendricks County
150	27,843	**Cicero** (town) Hamilton County

Note: This section ranks incorporated places and CDPs (Census Designated Places) with populations of 2,500 or more. Unincorporated postal areas were not considered. Please refer to the User Guide for additional information.

Median Household Income
Top 150 Places Ranked in *Descending* Order

State Rank	Dollars	Place
1	106,926	**Shorewood Forest** (CDP) Porter County
2	106,121	**Carmel** (city) Hamilton County
3	106,071	**Zionsville** (town) Boone County
4	94,526	**Saint John** (town) Lake County
5	91,952	**Granger** (CDP) Saint Joseph County
6	90,437	**Fishers** (town) Hamilton County
7	87,929	**Lakes of the Four Seasons** (CDP) Lake County
8	87,435	**Westfield** (town) Hamilton County
9	80,417	**McCordsville** (town) Hancock County
10	79,896	**Hidden Valley** (CDP) Dearborn County
11	78,348	**Pittsboro** (town) Hendricks County
12	76,457	**Dyer** (town) Lake County
13	76,123	**Winfield** (town) Lake County
14	75,425	**Avon** (town) Hendricks County
15	74,638	**Whitestown** (town) Boone County
16	74,118	**Melody Hill** (CDP) Vanderburgh County
17	73,636	**Huntertown** (town) Allen County
18	73,205	**Bargersville** (town) Johnson County
19	72,583	**Munster** (town) Lake County
20	71,506	**Highland** (CDP) Vanderburgh County
21	71,146	**Whiteland** (town) Johnson County
22	68,673	**Chesterton** (town) Porter County
23	67,898	**Georgetown** (town) Floyd County
24	66,644	**Noblesville** (city) Hamilton County
25	66,449	**Schererville** (town) Lake County
26	65,900	**Bright** (CDP) Dearborn County
27	65,426	**Heritage Lake** (CDP) Putnam County
28	65,340	**Brownsburg** (town) Hendricks County
29	63,721	**Smithville-Sanders** (CDP) Monroe County
30	63,325	**Porter** (town) Porter County
31	63,121	**Crown Point** (city) Lake County
32	62,865	**Leo-Cedarville** (town) Allen County
33	61,660	**Lowell** (town) Lake County
34	61,353	**Highland** (town) Lake County
35	59,728	**Batesville** (city) Ripley County
36	59,036	**Plainfield** (town) Hendricks County
37	58,907	**Danville** (town) Hendricks County
38	58,880	**Yorktown** (town) Delaware County
39	58,401	**Cedar Lake** (town) Lake County
40	58,038	**Roselawn** (CDP) Newton County
41	57,033	**New Whiteland** (town) Johnson County
42	56,301	**Dunlap** (CDP) Elkhart County
43	55,617	**Hobart** (city) Lake County
44	55,118	**Middlebury** (town) Elkhart County
45	54,750	**Winona Lake** (town) Kosciusko County
46	54,050	**Hebron** (town) Porter County
47	53,969	**Portage** (city) Porter County
48	53,968	**Jasper** (city) Dubois County
49	53,658	**Mooresville** (town) Morgan County
50	53,552	**Griffith** (town) Lake County
51	53,048	**Cicero** (town) Hamilton County
52	53,045	**Columbus** (city) Bartholomew County
53	52,259	**Sellersburg** (town) Clark County
54	52,252	**Greenwood** (city) Johnson County
55	52,188	**Greendale** (city) Dearborn County
56	52,098	**De Motte** (town) Jasper County
57	51,892	**Westville** (town) LaPorte County
58	51,742	**Covington** (city) Fountain County
59	51,481	**Pendleton** (town) Madison County
60	51,389	**Merrillville** (town) Lake County
61	51,384	**Lawrence** (city) Marion County
62	50,020	**Jeffersonville** (city) Clark County
63	49,940	**Greenfield** (city) Hancock County
64	49,583	**Simonton Lake** (CDP) Elkhart County
65	49,563	**Whiting** (city) Lake County
66	48,703	**Valparaiso** (city) Porter County
67	48,415	**Franklin** (city) Johnson County
68	48,333	**Upland** (town) Grant County
69	48,264	**South Haven** (CDP) Porter County
70	47,938	**Boonville** (city) Warrick County
71	47,931	**New Haven** (city) Allen County
72	47,674	**Ellettsville** (town) Monroe County
73	46,909	**Mount Vernon** (city) Posey County
74	46,821	**Fort Branch** (town) Gibson County
75	45,882	**Madison** (city) Jefferson County
76	45,813	**Nappanee** (city) Elkhart County
77	45,625	**Syracuse** (town) Kosciusko County
78	45,481	**Newburgh** (town) Warrick County
79	45,123	**Tell City** (city) Perry County
80	45,076	**Ossian** (town) Wells County
81	44,974	**Sheridan** (town) Hamilton County
82	44,637	**Cumberland** (town) Marion County
83	44,350	**Monticello** (city) White County
84	44,330	**North Terre Haute** (CDP) Vigo County
85	44,178	**Rensselaer** (city) Jasper County
86	43,969	**Fort Wayne** (city) Allen County
87	43,715	**Clarksville** (town) Clark County
88	43,627	**North Manchester** (town) Wabash County
89	43,154	**Lebanon** (city) Boone County
90	43,080	**Fairmount** (town) Grant County
91	42,903	**Huntingburg** (city) Dubois County
92	42,855	**Auburn** (city) DeKalb County
93	42,840	**Greensburg** (city) Decatur County
94	42,719	**Garrett** (city) DeKalb County
95	42,648	**Warsaw** (city) Kosciusko County
96	42,287	**Washington** (city) Daviess County
97	42,100	**Gas City** (city) Grant County
98	42,044	**Seymour** (city) Jackson County
99	41,962	**Indianapolis** (city) Marion County
100	41,949	**Decatur** (city) Adams County
101	41,579	**Goshen** (city) Elkhart County
102	41,164	**Chandler** (town) Warrick County
103	41,099	**Princeton** (city) Gibson County
104	41,090	**Aurora** (city) Dearborn County
105	41,005	**Fortville** (town) Hancock County
106	40,949	**Greencastle** (city) Putnam County
107	40,756	**Angola** (city) Steuben County
108	40,417	**Centerville** (town) Wayne County
109	40,368	**Frankfort** (city) Clinton County
110	40,034	**Charlestown** (city) Clark County
111	39,916	**Columbia City** (city) Whitley County
112	39,725	**Grissom AFB** (CDP) Miami County
113	39,621	**Delphi** (city) Carroll County
114	39,607	**New Albany** (city) Floyd County
115	39,592	**Tipton** (city) Tipton County
116	39,444	**Beech Grove** (city) Marion County
117	39,345	**Lafayette** (city) Tippecanoe County
118	39,344	**Hartford City** (city) Blackford County
119	39,320	**Wabash** (city) Wabash County
120	39,245	**Bluffton** (city) Wells County
121	38,896	**Speedway** (town) Marion County
122	38,819	**Brownstown** (town) Jackson County
123	38,802	**Kendallville** (city) Noble County
124	38,671	**Berne** (city) Adams County
125	38,578	**Shelbyville** (city) Shelby County
126	38,537	**Lake Station** (city) Lake County
127	38,536	**Hanover** (town) Jefferson County
128	38,483	**Scottsburg** (city) Scott County
129	38,365	**Hammond** (city) Lake County
130	38,208	**Loogootee** (city) Martin County
131	37,500	**Edinburgh** (town) Johnson County
132	37,215	**Kokomo** (city) Howard County
133	37,188	**Paoli** (town) Orange County
134	37,043	**Huntington** (city) Huntington County
135	36,863	**Ligonier** (city) Noble County
136	36,745	**Alexandria** (city) Madison County
137	36,590	**Mishawaka** (city) Saint Joseph County
138	36,391	**Linton** (city) Greene County
139	36,250	**Attica** (city) Fountain County
140	35,839	**Evansville** (city) Vanderburgh County
141	35,625	**Elwood** (city) Madison County
142	35,613	**Bremen** (town) Marshall County
143	35,601	**Michigan City** (city) LaPorte County
144	35,469	**Butler** (city) DeKalb County
145	35,165	**Vincennes** (city) Knox County
146	35,111	**Rushville** (city) Rush County
147	35,106	**North Vernon** (city) Jennings County
148	34,944	**Portland** (city) Jay County
149	34,706	**Bedford** (city) Lawrence County
149	34,706	**Martinsville** (city) Morgan County

Note: This section ranks incorporated places and CDPs (Census Designated Places) with populations of 2,500 or more. Unincorporated postal areas were not considered. Please refer to the User Guide for additional information.

Median Household Income

Top 150 Places Ranked in *Ascending* Order

State Rank	Dollars	Place
1	10,313	Notre Dame (CDP) Saint Joseph County
2	19,263	Purdue University (CDP) Tippecanoe County
3	23,670	Sullivan (city) Sullivan County
4	26,885	Gary (city) Lake County
5	26,901	Bicknell (city) Knox County
6	27,395	Bloomington (city) Monroe County
7	27,583	East Chicago (city) Lake County
8	29,111	Mitchell (city) Lawrence County
9	29,287	Muncie (city) Delaware County
10	29,731	Rochester (city) Fulton County
11	29,936	West Lafayette (city) Tippecanoe County
12	29,981	Brazil (city) Clay County
13	30,000	Rockville (town) Parke County
14	30,096	Richmond (city) Wayne County
15	30,300	Knox (city) Starke County
16	30,833	Brookville (town) Franklin County
17	30,952	Connersville (city) Fayette County
18	31,375	Country Squire Lakes (CDP) Jennings County
19	31,391	Marion (city) Grant County
20	31,667	Union City (city) Randolph County
21	32,056	Winchester (city) Randolph County
22	32,120	Corydon (town) Harrison County
23	32,144	Salem (city) Washington County
24	32,446	Terre Haute (city) Vigo County
25	32,486	Plymouth (city) Marshall County
26	32,838	Logansport (city) Cass County
27	32,859	New Castle (city) Henry County
28	32,947	Peru (city) Miami County
29	33,109	Austin (city) Scott County
30	33,362	Clinton (city) Vermillion County
31	33,574	Anderson (city) Madison County
32	34,270	Lawrenceburg (city) Dearborn County
33	34,279	Lagrange (town) LaGrange County
34	34,423	Chesterfield (town) Madison County
35	34,443	Elkhart (city) Elkhart County
36	34,453	Crawfordsville (city) Montgomery County
37	34,502	South Bend (city) Saint Joseph County
38	34,597	La Porte (city) LaPorte County
39	34,706	Bedford (city) Lawrence County
39	34,706	Martinsville (city) Morgan County
41	34,944	Portland (city) Jay County
42	35,106	North Vernon (city) Jennings County
43	35,111	Rushville (city) Rush County
44	35,165	Vincennes (city) Knox County
45	35,469	Butler (city) DeKalb County
46	35,601	Michigan City (city) LaPorte County
47	35,613	Bremen (town) Marshall County
48	35,625	Elwood (city) Madison County
49	35,839	Evansville (city) Vanderburgh County
50	36,250	Attica (city) Fountain County
51	36,391	Linton (city) Greene County
52	36,590	Mishawaka (city) Saint Joseph County
53	36,745	Alexandria (city) Madison County
54	36,863	Ligonier (city) Noble County
55	37,043	Huntington (city) Huntington County
56	37,188	Paoli (town) Orange County
57	37,215	Kokomo (city) Howard County
58	37,500	Edinburgh (town) Johnson County
59	38,208	Loogootee (city) Martin County
60	38,365	Hammond (city) Lake County
61	38,483	Scottsburg (city) Scott County
62	38,536	Hanover (town) Jefferson County
63	38,537	Lake Station (city) Lake County
64	38,578	Shelbyville (city) Shelby County
65	38,671	Berne (city) Adams County
66	38,802	Kendallville (city) Noble County
67	38,819	Brownstown (town) Jackson County
68	38,896	Speedway (town) Marion County
69	39,245	Bluffton (city) Wells County
70	39,320	Wabash (city) Wabash County
71	39,344	Hartford City (city) Blackford County
72	39,345	Lafayette (city) Tippecanoe County
73	39,444	Beech Grove (city) Marion County
74	39,592	Tipton (city) Tipton County
75	39,607	New Albany (city) Floyd County
76	39,621	Delphi (city) Carroll County
77	39,725	Grissom AFB (CDP) Miami County
78	39,916	Columbia City (city) Whitley County
79	40,034	Charlestown (city) Clark County
80	40,368	Frankfort (city) Clinton County
81	40,417	Centerville (town) Wayne County
82	40,756	Angola (city) Steuben County
83	40,949	Greencastle (city) Putnam County
84	41,005	Fortville (town) Hancock County
85	41,090	Aurora (city) Dearborn County
86	41,099	Princeton (city) Gibson County
87	41,164	Chandler (town) Warrick County
88	41,579	Goshen (city) Elkhart County
89	41,949	Decatur (city) Adams County
90	41,962	Indianapolis (city) Marion County
91	42,044	Seymour (city) Jackson County
92	42,100	Gas City (city) Grant County
93	42,287	Washington (city) Daviess County
94	42,648	Warsaw (city) Kosciusko County
95	42,719	Garrett (city) DeKalb County
96	42,840	Greensburg (city) Decatur County
97	42,855	Auburn (city) DeKalb County
98	42,903	Huntingburg (city) Dubois County
99	43,080	Fairmount (town) Grant County
100	43,154	Lebanon (city) Boone County
101	43,627	North Manchester (town) Wabash County
102	43,715	Clarksville (town) Clark County
103	43,969	Fort Wayne (city) Allen County
104	44,178	Rensselaer (city) Jasper County
105	44,330	North Terre Haute (CDP) Vigo County
106	44,350	Monticello (city) White County
107	44,637	Cumberland (town) Marion County
108	44,974	Sheridan (town) Hamilton County
109	45,076	Ossian (town) Wells County
110	45,123	Tell City (city) Perry County
111	45,481	Newburgh (town) Warrick County
112	45,625	Syracuse (town) Kosciusko County
113	45,813	Nappanee (city) Elkhart County
114	45,882	Madison (city) Jefferson County
115	46,821	Fort Branch (town) Gibson County
116	46,909	Mount Vernon (city) Posey County
117	47,674	Ellettsville (town) Monroe County
118	47,931	New Haven (city) Allen County
119	47,938	Boonville (city) Warrick County
120	48,264	South Haven (CDP) Porter County
121	48,333	Upland (town) Grant County
122	48,415	Franklin (city) Johnson County
123	48,703	Valparaiso (city) Porter County
124	49,563	Whiting (city) Lake County
125	49,583	Simonton Lake (CDP) Elkhart County
126	49,940	Greenfield (city) Hancock County
127	50,020	Jeffersonville (city) Clark County
128	51,384	Lawrence (city) Marion County
129	51,389	Merrillville (town) Lake County
130	51,481	Pendleton (town) Madison County
131	51,742	Covington (city) Fountain County
132	51,892	Westville (town) LaPorte County
133	52,098	De Motte (town) Jasper County
134	52,188	Greendale (city) Dearborn County
135	52,252	Greenwood (city) Johnson County
136	52,259	Sellersburg (town) Clark County
137	53,045	Columbus (city) Bartholomew County
138	53,048	Cicero (town) Hamilton County
139	53,552	Griffith (town) Lake County
140	53,658	Mooresville (town) Morgan County
141	53,968	Jasper (city) Dubois County
142	53,969	Portage (city) Porter County
143	54,050	Hebron (town) Porter County
144	54,750	Winona Lake (town) Kosciusko County
145	55,118	Middlebury (town) Elkhart County
146	55,617	Hobart (city) Lake County
147	56,301	Dunlap (CDP) Elkhart County
148	57,033	New Whiteland (town) Johnson County
149	58,038	Roselawn (CDP) Newton County
150	58,401	Cedar Lake (town) Lake County

Note: *This section ranks incorporated places and CDPs (Census Designated Places) with populations of 2,500 or more. Unincorporated postal areas were not considered. Please refer to the User Guide for additional information.*

Average Household Income
Top 150 Places Ranked in *Descending* Order

State Rank	Dollars	Place
1	150,719	**Zionsville** (town) Boone County
2	139,859	**Carmel** (city) Hamilton County
3	135,952	**Shorewood Forest** (CDP) Porter County
4	121,052	**Hidden Valley** (CDP) Dearborn County
5	114,518	**Granger** (CDP) Saint Joseph County
6	110,390	**Fishers** (town) Hamilton County
7	106,902	**Saint John** (town) Lake County
8	102,104	**Dyer** (town) Lake County
9	101,700	**Westfield** (city) Hamilton County
10	101,292	**McCordsville** (town) Hancock County
11	96,848	**Munster** (town) Lake County
12	94,008	**Lakes of the Four Seasons** (CDP) Lake County
13	91,625	**Whitestown** (town) Boone County
14	90,862	**Smithville-Sanders** (CDP) Monroe County
15	90,229	**Winfield** (town) Lake County
16	88,451	**Bargersville** (town) Johnson County
17	87,834	**Melody Hill** (CDP) Vanderburgh County
18	86,663	**Huntertown** (town) Allen County
19	86,635	**Avon** (town) Hendricks County
20	85,575	**Chesterton** (town) Porter County
21	85,211	**Highland** (CDP) Vanderburgh County
22	83,141	**Georgetown** (town) Floyd County
23	82,777	**Schererville** (town) Lake County
24	82,255	**Brownsburg** (town) Hendricks County
25	82,199	**Bright** (CDP) Dearborn County
26	81,877	**Noblesville** (city) Hamilton County
27	81,004	**Batesville** (city) Ripley County
28	80,777	**Porter** (town) Porter County
29	79,161	**Heritage Lake** (CDP) Putnam County
30	78,291	**Middlebury** (town) Elkhart County
31	78,090	**Crown Point** (city) Lake County
32	77,840	**Pittsboro** (town) Hendricks County
33	77,226	**Winona Lake** (town) Kosciusko County
34	74,620	**Newburgh** (town) Warrick County
35	73,736	**Yorktown** (town) Delaware County
36	73,218	**Leo-Cedarville** (town) Allen County
37	72,462	**Danville** (town) Hendricks County
38	72,336	**Whiteland** (town) Johnson County
39	71,531	**Pendleton** (town) Madison County
40	70,886	**Highland** (town) Lake County
41	70,523	**Plainfield** (town) Hendricks County
42	69,914	**Lowell** (town) Lake County
43	69,804	**Columbus** (city) Bartholomew County
44	68,905	**Jasper** (city) Dubois County
45	66,581	**Dunlap** (CDP) Elkhart County
46	66,505	**Cedar Lake** (town) Lake County
47	66,335	**Greenwood** (city) Johnson County
48	64,871	**Griffith** (town) Lake County
49	64,866	**Mount Vernon** (city) Posey County
50	64,704	**Greendale** (city) Dearborn County
51	64,450	**Roselawn** (CDP) Newton County
52	64,395	**Cicero** (town) Hamilton County
53	63,507	**Lawrence** (city) Marion County
54	62,817	**Berne** (city) Adams County
55	62,447	**Franklin** (city) Johnson County
56	62,131	**Covington** (city) Fountain County
57	61,955	**Hobart** (city) Lake County
58	61,667	**Portage** (city) Porter County
59	61,254	**Mooresville** (town) Morgan County
60	61,246	**Whiting** (city) Lake County
61	60,979	**Valparaiso** (city) Porter County
62	60,902	**Simonton Lake** (CDP) Elkhart County
63	60,227	**Jeffersonville** (city) Clark County
64	59,135	**Sellersburg** (town) Clark County
65	58,966	**Rensselaer** (city) Jasper County
66	58,878	**South Haven** (CDP) Porter County
67	58,756	**Merrillville** (town) Lake County
68	58,562	**Indianapolis** (city) Marion County
69	58,482	**Greenfield** (city) Hancock County
70	58,028	**New Whiteland** (town) Johnson County
71	57,895	**New Haven** (city) Allen County
72	57,768	**Fort Wayne** (city) Allen County
73	57,496	**Auburn** (city) DeKalb County
74	57,281	**Hebron** (town) Porter County
75	57,251	**Boonville** (city) Warrick County
76	57,170	**Greencastle** (city) Putnam County
77	57,029	**Westville** (town) LaPorte County
78	56,838	**Madison** (city) Jefferson County
79	56,502	**Winchester** (city) Randolph County
80	56,223	**Fort Branch** (town) Gibson County
81	56,213	**Lebanon** (city) Boone County
82	54,905	**North Terre Haute** (CDP) Vigo County
83	54,880	**Fortville** (town) Hancock County
84	54,535	**De Motte** (town) Jasper County
85	54,517	**Warsaw** (city) Kosciusko County
86	54,332	**Washington** (city) Daviess County
87	54,211	**Syracuse** (town) Kosciusko County
88	54,136	**West Lafayette** (city) Tippecanoe County
89	54,021	**Cumberland** (town) Marion County
90	53,935	**Nappanee** (city) Elkhart County
91	53,424	**Sheridan** (town) Hamilton County
92	53,407	**Upland** (town) Grant County
93	53,031	**Centerville** (town) Wayne County
94	52,784	**Tell City** (city) Perry County
95	52,727	**Seymour** (city) Jackson County
96	52,395	**Monticello** (city) White County
97	51,922	**Clarksville** (town) Clark County
98	51,802	**Ossian** (town) Wells County
99	51,524	**Princeton** (city) Gibson County
100	51,301	**Charlestown** (city) Clark County
101	51,236	**Huntingburg** (city) Dubois County
102	51,077	**Gas City** (city) Grant County
103	50,917	**Goshen** (city) Elkhart County
104	50,891	**Decatur** (city) Adams County
105	50,769	**Clinton** (city) Vermillion County
106	50,218	**Shelbyville** (city) Shelby County
107	50,086	**Lafayette** (city) Tippecanoe County
108	49,903	**Speedway** (town) Marion County
109	49,865	**Greensburg** (city) Decatur County
110	49,849	**Ellettsville** (town) Monroe County
111	49,656	**Fairmount** (town) Grant County
112	49,616	**Kokomo** (city) Howard County
113	49,561	**Angola** (city) Steuben County
114	49,380	**Ligonier** (city) Noble County
115	49,189	**Beech Grove** (city) Marion County
116	49,094	**North Manchester** (town) Wabash County
117	49,092	**Attica** (city) Fountain County
118	49,076	**Rochester** (city) Fulton County
119	48,771	**Columbia City** (city) Whitley County
120	48,539	**New Albany** (city) Floyd County
121	48,436	**Garrett** (city) DeKalb County
122	48,162	**Brownstown** (town) Jackson County
123	48,045	**Frankfort** (city) Clinton County
124	47,709	**Hammond** (city) Lake County
125	47,658	**Aurora** (city) Dearborn County
126	47,612	**Evansville** (city) Vanderburgh County
127	47,606	**Bloomington** (city) Monroe County
128	47,599	**Bremen** (town) Marshall County
129	47,429	**Chandler** (town) Warrick County
130	47,150	**South Bend** (city) Saint Joseph County
131	46,992	**Mishawaka** (city) Saint Joseph County
132	46,928	**Bluffton** (city) Wells County
133	46,897	**Elwood** (city) Madison County
134	46,881	**Delphi** (city) Carroll County
135	46,873	**Wabash** (city) Wabash County
136	46,369	**Loogootee** (city) Martin County
137	46,249	**Michigan City** (city) LaPorte County
138	46,154	**Grissom AFB** (CDP) Miami County
139	46,042	**Hartford City** (city) Blackford County
140	45,949	**Huntington** (city) Huntington County
141	45,732	**La Porte** (city) LaPorte County
142	45,704	**Brookville** (town) Franklin County
143	45,245	**Kendallville** (city) Noble County
144	44,993	**Terre Haute** (city) Vigo County
145	44,874	**Martinsville** (city) Morgan County
146	44,621	**Linton** (city) Greene County
147	44,507	**North Vernon** (city) Jennings County
148	44,429	**Alexandria** (city) Madison County
149	44,419	**Salem** (city) Washington County
150	44,380	**Lake Station** (city) Lake County

Note: This section ranks incorporated places and CDPs (Census Designated Places) with populations of 2,500 or more. Unincorporated postal areas were not considered. Please refer to the User Guide for additional information.

Average Household Income
Top 150 Places Ranked in *Ascending* Order

State Rank	Dollars	Place
1	19,452	**Notre Dame** (CDP) Saint Joseph County
2	19,767	**Purdue University** (CDP) Tippecanoe County
3	34,842	**Sullivan** (city) Sullivan County
4	35,009	**Country Squire Lakes** (CDP) Jennings County
5	37,716	**East Chicago** (city) Lake County
6	38,505	**Union City** (city) Randolph County
7	38,600	**Gary** (city) Lake County
8	38,989	**Lagrange** (town) LaGrange County
9	39,148	**Lawrenceburg** (city) Dearborn County
10	39,638	**New Castle** (city) Henry County
11	39,792	**Mitchell** (city) Lawrence County
12	40,044	**Connersville** (city) Fayette County
13	40,597	**Austin** (city) Scott County
14	40,856	**Muncie** (city) Delaware County
15	41,000	**Paoli** (town) Orange County
16	41,019	**Brazil** (city) Clay County
17	41,316	**Corydon** (town) Harrison County
18	41,494	**Chesterfield** (town) Madison County
19	41,507	**Plymouth** (city) Marshall County
20	41,767	**Rushville** (city) Rush County
21	41,783	**Bicknell** (city) Knox County
22	41,875	**Portland** (city) Jay County
23	41,914	**Marion** (city) Grant County
24	41,963	**Anderson** (city) Madison County
25	42,018	**Knox** (city) Starke County
26	42,218	**Scottsburg** (city) Scott County
27	42,669	**Hanover** (town) Jefferson County
28	42,818	**Tipton** (city) Tipton County
29	43,008	**Elkhart** (city) Elkhart County
30	43,572	**Butler** (city) DeKalb County
31	43,936	**Richmond** (city) Wayne County
32	44,051	**Bedford** (city) Lawrence County
33	44,124	**Logansport** (city) Cass County
34	44,251	**Edinburgh** (town) Johnson County
35	44,279	**Rockville** (town) Parke County
36	44,297	**Vincennes** (city) Knox County
37	44,303	**Peru** (city) Miami County
38	44,354	**Crawfordsville** (city) Montgomery County
39	44,380	**Lake Station** (city) Lake County
40	44,419	**Salem** (city) Washington County
41	44,429	**Alexandria** (city) Madison County
42	44,507	**North Vernon** (city) Jennings County
43	44,621	**Linton** (city) Greene County
44	44,874	**Martinsville** (city) Morgan County
45	44,993	**Terre Haute** (city) Vigo County
46	45,245	**Kendallville** (city) Noble County
47	45,704	**Brookville** (town) Franklin County
48	45,732	**La Porte** (city) LaPorte County
49	45,949	**Huntington** (city) Huntington County
50	46,042	**Hartford City** (city) Blackford County
51	46,154	**Grissom AFB** (CDP) Miami County
52	46,249	**Michigan City** (city) LaPorte County
53	46,369	**Loogootee** (city) Martin County
54	46,873	**Wabash** (city) Wabash County
55	46,881	**Delphi** (city) Carroll County
56	46,897	**Elwood** (city) Madison County
57	46,928	**Bluffton** (city) Wells County
58	46,992	**Mishawaka** (city) Saint Joseph County
59	47,150	**South Bend** (city) Saint Joseph County
60	47,429	**Chandler** (town) Warrick County
61	47,599	**Bremen** (town) Marshall County
62	47,606	**Bloomington** (city) Monroe County
63	47,612	**Evansville** (city) Vanderburgh County
64	47,658	**Aurora** (city) Dearborn County
65	47,709	**Hammond** (city) Lake County
66	48,045	**Frankfort** (city) Clinton County
67	48,162	**Brownstown** (town) Jackson County
68	48,436	**Garrett** (city) DeKalb County
69	48,539	**New Albany** (city) Floyd County
70	48,771	**Columbia City** (city) Whitley County
71	49,076	**Rochester** (city) Fulton County
72	49,092	**Attica** (city) Fountain County
73	49,094	**North Manchester** (town) Wabash County
74	49,189	**Beech Grove** (city) Marion County
75	49,380	**Ligonier** (city) Noble County
76	49,561	**Angola** (city) Steuben County
77	49,616	**Kokomo** (city) Howard County
78	49,656	**Fairmount** (town) Grant County
79	49,849	**Ellettsville** (town) Monroe County
80	49,865	**Greensburg** (city) Decatur County
81	49,903	**Speedway** (town) Marion County
82	50,086	**Lafayette** (city) Tippecanoe County
83	50,218	**Shelbyville** (city) Shelby County
84	50,769	**Clinton** (city) Vermillion County
85	50,891	**Decatur** (city) Adams County
86	50,917	**Goshen** (city) Elkhart County
87	51,077	**Gas City** (city) Grant County
88	51,236	**Huntingburg** (city) Dubois County
89	51,301	**Charlestown** (city) Clark County
90	51,524	**Princeton** (city) Gibson County
91	51,802	**Ossian** (town) Wells County
92	51,922	**Clarksville** (town) Clark County
93	52,395	**Monticello** (city) White County
94	52,727	**Seymour** (city) Jackson County
95	52,784	**Tell City** (city) Perry County
96	53,031	**Centerville** (town) Wayne County
97	53,407	**Upland** (town) Grant County
98	53,424	**Sheridan** (town) Hamilton County
99	53,935	**Nappanee** (city) Elkhart County
100	54,021	**Cumberland** (town) Marion County
101	54,136	**West Lafayette** (city) Tippecanoe County
102	54,211	**Syracuse** (town) Kosciusko County
103	54,332	**Washington** (city) Daviess County
104	54,517	**Warsaw** (city) Kosciusko County
105	54,535	**De Motte** (town) Jasper County
106	54,880	**Fortville** (town) Hancock County
107	54,905	**North Terre Haute** (CDP) Vigo County
108	56,213	**Lebanon** (city) Boone County
109	56,223	**Fort Branch** (town) Gibson County
110	56,502	**Winchester** (city) Randolph County
111	56,838	**Madison** (city) Jefferson County
112	57,029	**Westville** (town) LaPorte County
113	57,170	**Greencastle** (city) Putnam County
114	57,251	**Boonville** (city) Warrick County
115	57,281	**Hebron** (town) Porter County
116	57,496	**Auburn** (city) DeKalb County
117	57,768	**Fort Wayne** (city) Allen County
118	57,895	**New Haven** (city) Allen County
119	58,028	**New Whiteland** (town) Johnson County
120	58,482	**Greenfield** (city) Hancock County
121	58,562	**Indianapolis** (city) Marion County
122	58,756	**Merrillville** (town) Lake County
123	58,878	**South Haven** (CDP) Porter County
124	58,966	**Rensselaer** (city) Jasper County
125	59,135	**Sellersburg** (town) Clark County
126	60,227	**Jeffersonville** (city) Clark County
127	60,902	**Simonton Lake** (CDP) Elkhart County
128	60,979	**Valparaiso** (city) Porter County
129	61,246	**Whiting** (city) Lake County
130	61,254	**Mooresville** (town) Morgan County
131	61,667	**Portage** (city) Porter County
132	61,955	**Hobart** (city) Lake County
133	62,131	**Covington** (city) Fountain County
134	62,447	**Franklin** (city) Johnson County
135	62,817	**Berne** (city) Adams County
136	63,507	**Lawrence** (city) Marion County
137	64,395	**Cicero** (town) Hamilton County
138	64,450	**Roselawn** (CDP) Newton County
139	64,704	**Greendale** (city) Dearborn County
140	64,866	**Mount Vernon** (city) Posey County
141	64,871	**Griffith** (town) Lake County
142	66,335	**Greenwood** (city) Johnson County
143	66,505	**Cedar Lake** (town) Lake County
144	66,581	**Dunlap** (CDP) Elkhart County
145	68,905	**Jasper** (city) Dubois County
146	69,804	**Columbus** (city) Bartholomew County
147	69,914	**Lowell** (town) Lake County
148	70,523	**Plainfield** (town) Hendricks County
149	70,886	**Highland** (town) Lake County
150	71,531	**Pendleton** (town) Madison County

Note: This section ranks incorporated places and CDPs (Census Designated Places) with populations of 2,500 or more. Unincorporated postal areas were not considered. Please refer to the User Guide for additional information.

Households with Income of $100,000 or More
Top 150 Places Ranked in *Descending* Order

State Rank	Percent	Place
1	57.0	**Shorewood Forest** (CDP) Porter County
2	53.9	**Zionsville** (town) Boone County
3	53.3	**Carmel** (city) Hamilton County
4	47.1	**Saint John** (town) Lake County
5	45.7	**Granger** (CDP) Saint Joseph County
6	44.1	**Fishers** (town) Hamilton County
7	42.8	**Westfield** (city) Hamilton County
8	37.6	**Lakes of the Four Seasons** (CDP) Lake County
9	37.0	**Avon** (town) Hendricks County
10	36.1	**Munster** (town) Lake County
11	35.2	**Hidden Valley** (CDP) Dearborn County
12	34.1	**Dyer** (town) Lake County
13	32.4	**Porter** (town) Porter County
14	31.4	**Whitestown** (town) Boone County
15	30.8	**McCordsville** (town) Hancock County
16	30.5	**Chesterton** (town) Porter County
17	30.1	**Winfield** (town) Lake County
18	30.0	**Schererville** (town) Lake County
19	29.1	**Highland** (CDP) Vanderburgh County
20	28.9	**Winona Lake** (town) Kosciusko County
21	28.4	**Melody Hill** (CDP) Vanderburgh County
21	28.4	**Pittsboro** (town) Hendricks County
23	27.6	**Bargersville** (town) Johnson County
24	27.3	**Noblesville** (city) Hamilton County
25	26.0	**Bright** (CDP) Dearborn County
26	25.5	**Crown Point** (city) Lake County
27	25.4	**Batesville** (city) Ripley County
28	25.2	**Smithville-Sanders** (CDP) Monroe County
29	24.7	**Brownsburg** (town) Hendricks County
30	22.9	**Huntertown** (town) Allen County
31	22.8	**Yorktown** (town) Delaware County
32	22.6	**Leo-Cedarville** (town) Allen County
33	22.2	**Cicero** (town) Hamilton County
34	22.1	**Columbus** (city) Bartholomew County
35	21.9	**Danville** (town) Hendricks County
35	21.9	**Georgetown** (town) Floyd County
35	21.9	**Greendale** (city) Dearborn County
38	21.3	**Highland** (town) Lake County
38	21.3	**Whiteland** (town) Johnson County
40	21.2	**Pendleton** (town) Madison County
41	20.0	**Plainfield** (town) Hendricks County
42	19.4	**Greenwood** (city) Johnson County
43	19.2	**Lowell** (town) Lake County
44	18.6	**Dunlap** (CDP) Elkhart County
45	18.4	**Whiting** (city) Lake County
46	18.3	**Portage** (city) Porter County
47	17.9	**Valparaiso** (city) Porter County
48	17.7	**Franklin** (city) Johnson County
49	17.5	**Griffith** (town) Lake County
50	17.4	**Lawrence** (city) Marion County
51	17.1	**Newburgh** (town) Warrick County
52	16.9	**Roselawn** (CDP) Newton County
53	16.6	**Mount Vernon** (city) Posey County
54	16.4	**Heritage Lake** (CDP) Putnam County
55	16.1	**Jasper** (city) Dubois County
56	15.9	**West Lafayette** (city) Tippecanoe County
57	15.3	**Cedar Lake** (town) Lake County
58	15.1	**Covington** (city) Fountain County
58	15.1	**Jeffersonville** (city) Clark County
60	15.0	**Fort Branch** (town) Gibson County
60	15.0	**Middlebury** (town) Elkhart County
62	14.9	**Hobart** (city) Lake County
62	14.9	**South Haven** (CDP) Porter County
64	14.8	**Auburn** (city) DeKalb County
64	14.8	**Berne** (city) Adams County
64	14.8	**Greencastle** (city) Putnam County
67	14.5	**Indianapolis** (city) Marion County
68	13.8	**Simonton Lake** (CDP) Elkhart County
69	13.7	**Greenfield** (city) Hancock County
70	13.6	**Merrillville** (town) Lake County
71	13.5	**Fort Wayne** (city) Allen County
72	13.1	**Mooresville** (town) Morgan County
73	13.0	**New Haven** (city) Allen County
74	12.8	**Syracuse** (town) Kosciusko County
75	12.6	**Madison** (city) Jefferson County
76	12.5	**Fortville** (town) Hancock County
77	12.3	**Rensselaer** (city) Jasper County
78	11.8	**Charlestown** (city) Clark County
78	11.8	**North Terre Haute** (CDP) Vigo County
78	11.8	**Upland** (town) Grant County
81	11.6	**Bloomington** (city) Monroe County
82	11.1	**Westville** (town) LaPorte County
83	10.9	**Warsaw** (city) Kosciusko County
84	10.8	**Attica** (city) Fountain County
84	10.8	**Hebron** (town) Porter County
84	10.8	**Lebanon** (city) Boone County
84	10.8	**Speedway** (town) Marion County
88	10.6	**Clarksville** (town) Clark County
88	10.6	**Kokomo** (city) Howard County
90	10.5	**Decatur** (city) Adams County
91	10.4	**Delphi** (city) Carroll County
91	10.4	**Rochester** (city) Fulton County
93	10.3	**Princeton** (city) Gibson County
93	10.3	**Shelbyville** (city) Shelby County
95	10.2	**Angola** (city) Steuben County
95	10.2	**Ossian** (town) Wells County
95	10.2	**Sellersburg** (town) Clark County
98	10.1	**Tell City** (city) Perry County
99	10.0	**Alexandria** (city) Madison County
99	10.0	**Corydon** (town) Harrison County
101	9.9	**Nappanee** (city) Elkhart County
102	9.8	**Boonville** (city) Warrick County
102	9.8	**Greensburg** (city) Decatur County
102	9.8	**Lafayette** (city) Tippecanoe County
105	9.6	**Huntingburg** (city) Dubois County
106	9.5	**Cumberland** (town) Marion County
106	9.5	**Elwood** (city) Madison County
108	9.4	**Winchester** (city) Randolph County
109	9.3	**Ellettsville** (town) Monroe County
109	9.3	**Monticello** (city) White County
109	9.3	**Seymour** (city) Jackson County
112	9.1	**Washington** (city) Daviess County
113	9.0	**Goshen** (city) Elkhart County
113	9.0	**Mishawaka** (city) Saint Joseph County
115	8.8	**Beech Grove** (city) Marion County
115	8.8	**South Bend** (city) Saint Joseph County
117	8.7	**Bluffton** (city) Wells County
117	8.7	**Bremen** (town) Marshall County
117	8.7	**Columbia City** (city) Whitley County
117	8.7	**Grissom AFB** (CDP) Miami County
117	8.7	**Hammond** (city) Lake County
122	8.6	**Butler** (city) DeKalb County
123	8.5	**Evansville** (city) Vanderburgh County
124	8.4	**New Albany** (city) Floyd County
125	8.3	**Gas City** (city) Grant County
125	8.3	**Terre Haute** (city) Vigo County
127	8.1	**Richmond** (city) Wayne County
128	8.0	**Fairmount** (town) Grant County
128	8.0	**Linton** (city) Greene County
128	8.0	**New Whiteland** (town) Johnson County
131	7.9	**Bedford** (city) Lawrence County
131	7.9	**Brookville** (town) Franklin County
131	7.9	**De Motte** (town) Jasper County
131	7.9	**Frankfort** (city) Clinton County
135	7.8	**North Manchester** (town) Wabash County
136	7.6	**Michigan City** (city) LaPorte County
137	7.4	**Centerville** (town) Wayne County
137	7.4	**Lake Station** (city) Lake County
139	7.2	**Bicknell** (city) Knox County
139	7.2	**Martinsville** (city) Morgan County
141	7.1	**Crawfordsville** (city) Montgomery County
141	7.1	**Garrett** (city) DeKalb County
143	7.0	**La Porte** (city) LaPorte County
143	7.0	**Sheridan** (town) Hamilton County
145	6.7	**Vincennes** (city) Knox County
146	6.6	**Clinton** (city) Vermillion County
146	6.6	**Muncie** (city) Delaware County
148	6.5	**Aurora** (city) Dearborn County
148	6.5	**Marion** (city) Grant County
150	6.4	**Gary** (city) Lake County

Note: *This section ranks incorporated places and CDPs (Census Designated Places) with populations of 2,500 or more. Unincorporated postal areas were not considered. Please refer to the User Guide for additional information.*

Households with Income of $100,000 or More
Top 150 Places Ranked in *Ascending* Order

State Rank	Percent	Place
1	0.0	**Notre Dame** (CDP) Saint Joseph County
1	0.0	**Purdue University** (CDP) Tippecanoe County
3	0.9	**Country Squire Lakes** (CDP) Jennings County
4	3.7	**Paoli** (town) Orange County
5	3.9	**Chesterfield** (town) Madison County
5	3.9	**Tipton** (city) Tipton County
7	4.0	**Knox** (city) Starke County
8	4.2	**Rockville** (town) Parke County
9	4.4	**Brownstown** (town) Jackson County
10	4.5	**New Castle** (city) Henry County
10	4.5	**Union City** (city) Randolph County
12	4.6	**Austin** (city) Scott County
12	4.6	**Hanover** (town) Jefferson County
14	4.7	**Sullivan** (city) Sullivan County
15	4.8	**Connersville** (city) Fayette County
16	4.9	**Lagrange** (town) LaGrange County
16	4.9	**Logansport** (city) Cass County
18	5.0	**Hartford City** (city) Blackford County
19	5.2	**Lawrenceburg** (city) Dearborn County
20	5.3	**Portland** (city) Jay County
20	5.3	**Rushville** (city) Rush County
22	5.4	**East Chicago** (city) Lake County
22	5.4	**Mitchell** (city) Lawrence County
22	5.4	**Salem** (city) Washington County
25	5.5	**Elkhart** (city) Elkhart County
25	5.5	**Wabash** (city) Wabash County
27	5.6	**Ligonier** (city) Noble County
27	5.6	**Peru** (city) Miami County
29	5.7	**Chandler** (town) Warrick County
29	5.7	**Huntington** (city) Huntington County
29	5.7	**North Vernon** (city) Jennings County
32	5.8	**Brazil** (city) Clay County
32	5.8	**Scottsburg** (city) Scott County
34	5.9	**Plymouth** (city) Marshall County
35	6.0	**Anderson** (city) Madison County
36	6.1	**Edinburgh** (town) Johnson County
37	6.3	**Kendallville** (city) Noble County
38	6.4	**Gary** (city) Lake County
38	6.4	**Loogootee** (city) Martin County
40	6.5	**Aurora** (city) Dearborn County
40	6.5	**Marion** (city) Grant County
42	6.6	**Clinton** (city) Vermillion County
42	6.6	**Muncie** (city) Delaware County
44	6.7	**Vincennes** (city) Knox County
45	7.0	**La Porte** (city) LaPorte County
45	7.0	**Sheridan** (town) Hamilton County
47	7.1	**Crawfordsville** (city) Montgomery County
47	7.1	**Garrett** (city) DeKalb County
49	7.2	**Bicknell** (city) Knox County
49	7.2	**Martinsville** (city) Morgan County
51	7.4	**Centerville** (town) Wayne County
51	7.4	**Lake Station** (city) Lake County
53	7.6	**Michigan City** (city) LaPorte County
54	7.8	**North Manchester** (town) Wabash County
55	7.9	**Bedford** (city) Lawrence County
55	7.9	**Brookville** (town) Franklin County
55	7.9	**De Motte** (town) Jasper County
55	7.9	**Frankfort** (city) Clinton County
59	8.0	**Fairmount** (town) Grant County
59	8.0	**Linton** (city) Greene County
59	8.0	**New Whiteland** (town) Johnson County
62	8.1	**Richmond** (city) Wayne County
63	8.3	**Gas City** (city) Grant County
63	8.3	**Terre Haute** (city) Vigo County
65	8.4	**New Albany** (city) Floyd County
66	8.5	**Evansville** (city) Vanderburgh County
67	8.6	**Butler** (city) DeKalb County
68	8.7	**Bluffton** (city) Wells County
68	8.7	**Bremen** (town) Marshall County
68	8.7	**Columbia City** (city) Whitley County
68	8.7	**Grissom AFB** (CDP) Miami County
68	8.7	**Hammond** (city) Lake County
73	8.8	**Beech Grove** (city) Marion County
73	8.8	**South Bend** (city) Saint Joseph County
75	9.0	**Goshen** (city) Elkhart County
75	9.0	**Mishawaka** (city) Saint Joseph County
77	9.1	**Washington** (city) Daviess County
78	9.3	**Ellettsville** (town) Monroe County
78	9.3	**Monticello** (city) White County
78	9.3	**Seymour** (city) Jackson County
81	9.4	**Winchester** (city) Randolph County
82	9.5	**Cumberland** (town) Marion County
82	9.5	**Elwood** (city) Madison County
84	9.6	**Huntingburg** (city) Dubois County
85	9.8	**Boonville** (city) Warrick County
85	9.8	**Greensburg** (city) Decatur County
85	9.8	**Lafayette** (city) Tippecanoe County
88	9.9	**Nappanee** (city) Elkhart County
89	10.0	**Alexandria** (city) Madison County
89	10.0	**Corydon** (town) Harrison County
91	10.1	**Tell City** (city) Perry County
92	10.2	**Angola** (city) Steuben County
92	10.2	**Ossian** (town) Wells County
92	10.2	**Sellersburg** (town) Clark County
95	10.3	**Princeton** (city) Gibson County
95	10.3	**Shelbyville** (city) Shelby County
97	10.4	**Delphi** (city) Carroll County
97	10.4	**Rochester** (city) Fulton County
99	10.5	**Decatur** (city) Adams County
100	10.6	**Clarksville** (town) Clark County
100	10.6	**Kokomo** (city) Howard County
102	10.8	**Attica** (city) Fountain County
102	10.8	**Hebron** (town) Porter County
102	10.8	**Lebanon** (city) Boone County
102	10.8	**Speedway** (town) Marion County
106	10.9	**Warsaw** (city) Kosciusko County
107	11.1	**Westville** (town) LaPorte County
108	11.6	**Bloomington** (city) Monroe County
109	11.8	**Charlestown** (city) Clark County
109	11.8	**North Terre Haute** (CDP) Vigo County
109	11.8	**Upland** (town) Grant County
112	12.3	**Rensselaer** (city) Jasper County
113	12.5	**Fortville** (town) Hancock County
114	12.6	**Madison** (city) Jefferson County
115	12.8	**Syracuse** (town) Kosciusko County
116	13.0	**New Haven** (city) Allen County
117	13.1	**Mooresville** (town) Morgan County
118	13.5	**Fort Wayne** (city) Allen County
119	13.6	**Merrillville** (town) Lake County
120	13.7	**Greenfield** (city) Hancock County
121	13.8	**Simonton Lake** (CDP) Elkhart County
122	14.5	**Indianapolis** (city) Marion County
123	14.8	**Auburn** (city) DeKalb County
123	14.8	**Berne** (city) Adams County
123	14.8	**Greencastle** (city) Putnam County
126	14.9	**Hobart** (city) Lake County
126	14.9	**South Haven** (CDP) Porter County
128	15.0	**Fort Branch** (town) Gibson County
128	15.0	**Middlebury** (town) Elkhart County
130	15.1	**Covington** (city) Fountain County
130	15.1	**Jeffersonville** (city) Clark County
132	15.3	**Cedar Lake** (town) Lake County
133	15.9	**West Lafayette** (city) Tippecanoe County
134	16.1	**Jasper** (city) Dubois County
135	16.4	**Heritage Lake** (CDP) Putnam County
136	16.6	**Mount Vernon** (city) Posey County
137	16.9	**Roselawn** (CDP) Newton County
138	17.1	**Newburgh** (town) Warrick County
139	17.4	**Lawrence** (city) Marion County
140	17.5	**Griffith** (town) Lake County
141	17.7	**Franklin** (city) Johnson County
142	17.9	**Valparaiso** (city) Porter County
143	18.3	**Portage** (city) Porter County
144	18.4	**Whiting** (city) Lake County
145	18.6	**Dunlap** (CDP) Elkhart County
146	19.2	**Lowell** (town) Lake County
147	19.4	**Greenwood** (city) Johnson County
148	20.0	**Plainfield** (town) Hendricks County
149	21.2	**Pendleton** (town) Madison County
150	21.3	**Highland** (town) Lake County

Note: *This section ranks incorporated places and CDPs (Census Designated Places) with populations of 2,500 or more. Unincorporated postal areas were not considered. Please refer to the User Guide for additional information.*

Poverty Rate
Top 150 Places Ranked in *Descending* Order

State Rank	Percent	Place
1	74.5	Notre Dame (CDP) Saint Joseph County
2	52.2	Purdue University (CDP) Tippecanoe County
3	39.2	Bloomington (city) Monroe County
4	38.5	West Lafayette (city) Tippecanoe County
5	38.1	Gary (city) Lake County
6	35.7	East Chicago (city) Lake County
7	34.1	Corydon (town) Harrison County
8	33.4	Muncie (city) Delaware County
9	33.0	Sullivan (city) Sullivan County
10	32.1	Country Squire Lakes (CDP) Jennings County
11	31.6	Plymouth (city) Marshall County
12	31.4	Union City (city) Randolph County
13	29.6	Richmond (city) Wayne County
14	28.7	Brazil (city) Clay County
15	28.5	Elkhart (city) Elkhart County
16	28.3	North Vernon (city) Jennings County
17	28.1	Clinton (city) Vermillion County
18	27.9	Connersville (city) Fayette County
19	27.8	South Bend (city) Saint Joseph County
20	27.2	Crawfordsville (city) Montgomery County
21	26.3	Michigan City (city) LaPorte County
22	26.0	Marion (city) Grant County
23	25.8	Anderson (city) Madison County
23	25.8	Austin (city) Scott County
23	25.8	Terre Haute (city) Vigo County
26	25.7	Ligonier (city) Noble County
27	25.6	Knox (city) Starke County
28	25.4	Hanover (town) Jefferson County
29	25.0	New Castle (city) Henry County
30	24.9	Mitchell (city) Lawrence County
31	24.6	Lagrange (town) LaGrange County
32	24.3	Chandler (town) Warrick County
32	24.3	Scottsburg (city) Scott County
34	23.7	Edinburgh (town) Johnson County
35	23.6	Kendallville (city) Noble County
35	23.6	Loogootee (city) Martin County
37	22.9	Hammond (city) Lake County
38	22.8	Butler (city) DeKalb County
39	22.7	Grissom AFB (CDP) Miami County
40	22.3	Gas City (city) Grant County
41	22.2	New Albany (city) Floyd County
42	22.1	Logansport (city) Cass County
43	22.0	Winchester (city) Randolph County
44	21.9	La Porte (city) LaPorte County
45	21.7	Mishawaka (city) Saint Joseph County
46	21.6	Huntingburg (city) Dubois County
47	21.5	Lake Station (city) Lake County
47	21.5	North Manchester (town) Wabash County
49	21.4	Bedford (city) Lawrence County
50	21.2	Rushville (city) Rush County
51	20.9	Fortville (town) Hancock County
51	20.9	Indianapolis (city) Marion County
53	20.8	Goshen (city) Elkhart County
54	20.7	Rochester (city) Fulton County
55	20.6	Kokomo (city) Howard County
56	20.5	Vincennes (city) Knox County
57	20.3	Martinsville (city) Morgan County
57	20.3	Salem (city) Washington County
59	20.1	Bicknell (city) Knox County
59	20.1	Evansville (city) Vanderburgh County
61	19.8	Charlestown (city) Clark County
62	19.6	Lafayette (city) Tippecanoe County
62	19.6	Peru (city) Miami County
64	19.5	Beech Grove (city) Marion County
65	19.4	Brookville (town) Franklin County
66	19.0	Washington (city) Daviess County
67	18.7	Fort Wayne (city) Allen County
68	18.5	Greensburg (city) Decatur County
69	18.2	Elwood (city) Madison County
70	18.1	Frankfort (city) Clinton County
70	18.1	Shelbyville (city) Shelby County
72	17.8	Hebron (town) Porter County
73	17.6	Linton (city) Greene County
74	17.5	Wabash (city) Wabash County
75	17.3	Alexandria (city) Madison County
76	17.0	Decatur (city) Adams County
76	17.0	Tipton (city) Tipton County
78	16.9	Hartford City (city) Blackford County
78	16.9	Lawrenceburg (city) Dearborn County
78	16.9	Mount Vernon (city) Posey County
81	16.8	Centerville (town) Wayne County
82	16.7	Bluffton (city) Wells County
82	16.7	Huntington (city) Huntington County
82	16.7	Merrillville (town) Lake County
85	16.6	Fairmount (town) Grant County
86	16.5	Angola (city) Steuben County
87	16.4	Princeton (city) Gibson County
87	16.4	Rockville (town) Parke County
89	16.3	Seymour (city) Jackson County
90	15.7	Sheridan (town) Hamilton County
91	15.6	Westville (town) LaPorte County
92	15.2	Speedway (town) Marion County
93	15.1	Lawrence (city) Marion County
94	15.0	Franklin (city) Johnson County
94	15.0	Warsaw (city) Kosciusko County
96	14.9	Lebanon (city) Boone County
97	14.7	Cumberland (town) Marion County
97	14.7	Porter (town) Porter County
99	14.5	Delphi (city) Carroll County
100	14.4	Columbia City (city) Whitley County
100	14.4	Valparaiso (city) Porter County
102	14.3	Berne (city) Adams County
102	14.3	Boonville (city) Warrick County
102	14.3	Portland (city) Jay County
105	14.2	Clarksville (town) Clark County
105	14.2	Greenwood (city) Johnson County
105	14.2	New Haven (city) Allen County
108	14.1	Aurora (city) Dearborn County
108	14.1	Greendale (city) Dearborn County
110	14.0	Attica (city) Fountain County
110	14.0	Greencastle (city) Putnam County
112	13.9	Heritage Lake (CDP) Putnam County
112	13.9	Upland (town) Grant County
114	13.7	Nappanee (city) Elkhart County
114	13.7	Paoli (town) Orange County
116	13.5	Auburn (city) DeKalb County
117	13.4	Portage (city) Porter County
118	13.2	Dunlap (CDP) Elkhart County
118	13.2	Simonton Lake (CDP) Elkhart County
120	13.0	North Terre Haute (CDP) Vigo County
121	12.9	Whiting (city) Lake County
122	12.3	Jeffersonville (city) Clark County
122	12.3	Rensselaer (city) Jasper County
124	12.2	Garrett (city) DeKalb County
125	11.9	Mooresville (town) Morgan County
125	11.9	Syracuse (town) Kosciusko County
127	11.7	Griffith (town) Lake County
128	11.6	Bargersville (town) Johnson County
128	11.6	Columbus (city) Bartholomew County
128	11.6	Winona Lake (town) Kosciusko County
131	11.5	Cicero (town) Hamilton County
132	11.3	Chesterfield (town) Madison County
133	11.2	South Haven (CDP) Porter County
133	11.2	Tell City (city) Perry County
135	11.1	Greenfield (city) Hancock County
136	10.3	Pendleton (town) Madison County
136	10.3	Sellersburg (town) Clark County
138	10.2	Hobart (city) Lake County
138	10.2	Madison (city) Jefferson County
140	9.8	Whitestown (town) Boone County
141	9.7	Middlebury (town) Elkhart County
142	9.6	Bremen (town) Marshall County
142	9.6	Chesterton (town) Porter County
142	9.6	Monticello (city) White County
145	9.4	De Motte (town) Jasper County
146	9.0	Ossian (town) Wells County
147	8.9	Brownstown (town) Jackson County
147	8.9	Newburgh (town) Warrick County
147	8.9	Roselawn (CDP) Newton County
150	8.4	Danville (town) Hendricks County

Note: This section ranks incorporated places and CDPs (Census Designated Places) with populations of 2,500 or more. Unincorporated postal areas were not considered. Please refer to the User Guide for additional information.

Poverty Rate
Top 150 Places Ranked in *Ascending* Order

State Rank	Percent	Place
1	2.2	**Highland** (CDP) Vanderburgh County
2	2.5	**Lakes of the Four Seasons** (CDP) Lake County
3	2.6	**Dyer** (town) Lake County
3	2.6	**Melody Hill** (CDP) Vanderburgh County
3	2.6	**Zionsville** (town) Boone County
6	2.9	**Bright** (CDP) Dearborn County
6	2.9	**Huntertown** (town) Allen County
8	3.0	**Granger** (CDP) Saint Joseph County
9	3.1	**Shorewood Forest** (CDP) Porter County
10	3.3	**Fishers** (town) Hamilton County
11	3.6	**Carmel** (city) Hamilton County
12	3.7	**Avon** (town) Hendricks County
13	3.9	**Saint John** (town) Lake County
14	4.3	**Leo-Cedarville** (town) Allen County
15	4.6	**Brownsburg** (town) Hendricks County
15	4.6	**Georgetown** (town) Floyd County
15	4.6	**Winfield** (town) Lake County
18	4.8	**Batesville** (city) Ripley County
19	5.6	**Whiteland** (town) Johnson County
20	5.7	**Highland** (town) Lake County
21	5.8	**Hidden Valley** (CDP) Dearborn County
21	5.8	**Smithville-Sanders** (CDP) Monroe County
23	6.0	**Yorktown** (town) Delaware County
24	6.1	**Westfield** (city) Hamilton County
25	6.5	**New Whiteland** (town) Johnson County
26	6.6	**Munster** (town) Lake County
26	6.6	**Schererville** (town) Lake County
28	7.0	**Crown Point** (city) Lake County
29	7.2	**Pittsboro** (town) Hendricks County
30	7.4	**Noblesville** (city) Hamilton County
31	7.5	**Cedar Lake** (town) Lake County
31	7.5	**Covington** (city) Fountain County
31	7.5	**Lowell** (town) Lake County
31	7.5	**McCordsville** (town) Hancock County
35	7.6	**Jasper** (city) Dubois County
36	7.9	**Fort Branch** (town) Gibson County
37	8.1	**Plainfield** (town) Hendricks County
38	8.3	**Ellettsville** (town) Monroe County
39	8.4	**Danville** (town) Hendricks County
40	8.9	**Brownstown** (town) Jackson County
40	8.9	**Newburgh** (town) Warrick County
40	8.9	**Roselawn** (CDP) Newton County
43	9.0	**Ossian** (town) Wells County
44	9.4	**De Motte** (town) Jasper County
45	9.6	**Bremen** (town) Marshall County
45	9.6	**Chesterton** (town) Porter County
45	9.6	**Monticello** (city) White County
48	9.7	**Middlebury** (town) Elkhart County
49	9.8	**Whitestown** (town) Boone County
50	10.2	**Hobart** (city) Lake County
50	10.2	**Madison** (city) Jefferson County
52	10.3	**Pendleton** (town) Madison County
52	10.3	**Sellersburg** (town) Clark County
54	11.1	**Greenfield** (city) Hancock County
55	11.2	**South Haven** (CDP) Porter County
55	11.2	**Tell City** (city) Perry County
57	11.3	**Chesterfield** (town) Madison County
58	11.5	**Cicero** (town) Hamilton County
59	11.6	**Bargersville** (town) Johnson County
59	11.6	**Columbus** (city) Bartholomew County
59	11.6	**Winona Lake** (town) Kosciusko County
62	11.7	**Griffith** (town) Lake County
63	11.9	**Mooresville** (town) Morgan County
63	11.9	**Syracuse** (town) Kosciusko County
65	12.2	**Garrett** (city) DeKalb County
66	12.3	**Jeffersonville** (city) Clark County
66	12.3	**Rensselaer** (city) Jasper County
68	12.9	**Whiting** (city) Lake County
69	13.0	**North Terre Haute** (CDP) Vigo County
70	13.2	**Dunlap** (CDP) Elkhart County
70	13.2	**Simonton Lake** (CDP) Elkhart County
72	13.4	**Portage** (city) Porter County
73	13.5	**Auburn** (city) DeKalb County
74	13.7	**Nappanee** (city) Elkhart County
74	13.7	**Paoli** (town) Orange County
76	13.9	**Heritage Lake** (CDP) Putnam County
76	13.9	**Upland** (town) Grant County
78	14.0	**Attica** (city) Fountain County
78	14.0	**Greencastle** (city) Putnam County
80	14.1	**Aurora** (city) Dearborn County
80	14.1	**Greendale** (city) Dearborn County
82	14.2	**Clarksville** (town) Clark County
82	14.2	**Greenwood** (city) Johnson County
82	14.2	**New Haven** (city) Allen County
85	14.3	**Berne** (city) Adams County
85	14.3	**Boonville** (city) Warrick County
85	14.3	**Portland** (city) Jay County
88	14.4	**Columbia City** (city) Whitley County
88	14.4	**Valparaiso** (city) Porter County
90	14.5	**Delphi** (city) Carroll County
91	14.7	**Cumberland** (town) Marion County
91	14.7	**Porter** (town) Porter County
93	14.9	**Lebanon** (city) Boone County
94	15.0	**Franklin** (city) Johnson County
94	15.0	**Warsaw** (city) Kosciusko County
96	15.1	**Lawrence** (city) Marion County
97	15.2	**Speedway** (town) Marion County
98	15.6	**Westville** (town) LaPorte County
99	15.7	**Sheridan** (town) Hamilton County
100	16.3	**Seymour** (city) Jackson County
101	16.4	**Princeton** (city) Gibson County
101	16.4	**Rockville** (town) Parke County
103	16.5	**Angola** (city) Steuben County
104	16.6	**Fairmount** (town) Grant County
105	16.7	**Bluffton** (city) Wells County
105	16.7	**Huntington** (city) Huntington County
105	16.7	**Merrillville** (town) Lake County
108	16.8	**Centerville** (town) Wayne County
109	16.9	**Hartford City** (city) Blackford County
109	16.9	**Lawrenceburg** (city) Dearborn County
109	16.9	**Mount Vernon** (city) Posey County
112	17.0	**Decatur** (city) Adams County
112	17.0	**Tipton** (city) Tipton County
114	17.3	**Alexandria** (city) Madison County
115	17.5	**Wabash** (city) Wabash County
116	17.6	**Linton** (city) Greene County
117	17.8	**Hebron** (town) Porter County
118	18.1	**Frankfort** (city) Clinton County
118	18.1	**Shelbyville** (city) Shelby County
120	18.2	**Elwood** (city) Madison County
121	18.5	**Greensburg** (city) Decatur County
122	18.7	**Fort Wayne** (city) Allen County
123	19.0	**Washington** (city) Daviess County
124	19.4	**Brookville** (town) Franklin County
125	19.5	**Beech Grove** (city) Marion County
126	19.6	**Lafayette** (city) Tippecanoe County
126	19.6	**Peru** (city) Miami County
128	19.8	**Charlestown** (city) Clark County
129	20.1	**Bicknell** (city) Knox County
129	20.1	**Evansville** (city) Vanderburgh County
131	20.3	**Martinsville** (city) Morgan County
131	20.3	**Salem** (city) Washington County
133	20.5	**Vincennes** (city) Knox County
134	20.6	**Kokomo** (city) Howard County
135	20.7	**Rochester** (city) Fulton County
136	20.8	**Goshen** (city) Elkhart County
137	20.9	**Fortville** (town) Hancock County
137	20.9	**Indianapolis** (city) Marion County
139	21.2	**Rushville** (city) Rush County
140	21.4	**Bedford** (city) Lawrence County
141	21.5	**Lake Station** (city) Lake County
141	21.5	**North Manchester** (town) Wabash County
143	21.6	**Huntingburg** (city) Dubois County
144	21.7	**Mishawaka** (city) Saint Joseph County
145	21.9	**La Porte** (city) LaPorte County
146	22.0	**Winchester** (city) Randolph County
147	22.1	**Logansport** (city) Cass County
148	22.2	**New Albany** (city) Floyd County
149	22.3	**Gas City** (city) Grant County
150	22.7	**Grissom AFB** (CDP) Miami County

Note: This section ranks incorporated places and CDPs (Census Designated Places) with populations of 2,500 or more. Unincorporated postal areas were not considered. Please refer to the User Guide for additional information.

Educational Attainment: High School Diploma or Higher
Top 150 Places Ranked in *Descending* Order

State Rank	Percent	Place
1	98.6	**Bright** (CDP) Dearborn County
2	98.3	**Carmel** (city) Hamilton County
3	97.9	**Fishers** (town) Hamilton County
4	97.7	**McCordsville** (town) Hancock County
5	97.6	**Zionsville** (town) Boone County
6	96.7	**Leo-Cedarville** (town) Allen County
6	96.7	**West Lafayette** (city) Tippecanoe County
8	96.6	**Saint John** (town) Lake County
9	96.3	**Granger** (CDP) Saint Joseph County
9	96.3	**Huntertown** (town) Allen County
9	96.3	**Melody Hill** (CDP) Vanderburgh County
12	95.9	**Westfield** (city) Hamilton County
13	95.8	**Avon** (town) Hendricks County
13	95.8	**Upland** (town) Grant County
15	95.6	**Whitestown** (town) Boone County
16	95.1	**Shorewood Forest** (CDP) Porter County
17	94.7	**Noblesville** (city) Hamilton County
17	94.7	**Yorktown** (town) Delaware County
19	94.6	**Hidden Valley** (CDP) Dearborn County
20	94.5	**Notre Dame** (CDP) Saint Joseph County
21	94.3	**Bargersville** (town) Johnson County
21	94.3	**Lakes of the Four Seasons** (CDP) Lake County
23	94.2	**Munster** (town) Lake County
24	94.1	**Lowell** (town) Lake County
25	94.0	**Brownsburg** (town) Hendricks County
26	93.8	**Highland** (CDP) Vanderburgh County
27	93.6	**Fort Branch** (town) Gibson County
28	93.4	**Newburgh** (town) Warrick County
29	93.2	**Georgetown** (town) Floyd County
30	93.0	**Schererville** (town) Lake County
31	92.9	**Bloomington** (city) Monroe County
32	92.8	**Winfield** (town) Lake County
33	92.6	**Ossian** (town) Wells County
34	92.4	**Batesville** (city) Ripley County
34	92.4	**Crown Point** (city) Lake County
36	92.2	**Purdue University** (CDP) Tippecanoe County
37	92.0	**Dyer** (town) Lake County
38	91.9	**Highland** (town) Lake County
38	91.9	**New Whiteland** (town) Johnson County
40	91.8	**Chesterton** (town) Porter County
40	91.8	**Simonton Lake** (CDP) Elkhart County
42	91.7	**Pendleton** (town) Madison County
42	91.7	**Pittsboro** (town) Hendricks County
44	91.5	**Valparaiso** (city) Porter County
45	91.4	**Smithville-Sanders** (CDP) Monroe County
46	91.2	**Danville** (town) Hendricks County
46	91.2	**Winona Lake** (town) Kosciusko County
48	91.0	**Covington** (city) Fountain County
49	90.8	**Greendale** (city) Dearborn County
50	90.6	**Berne** (city) Adams County
50	90.6	**Cicero** (town) Hamilton County
50	90.6	**De Motte** (town) Jasper County
53	90.5	**Griffith** (town) Lake County
53	90.5	**Heritage Lake** (CDP) Putnam County
55	90.3	**Plainfield** (town) Hendricks County
55	90.3	**Whiteland** (town) Johnson County
57	90.1	**Columbus** (city) Bartholomew County
57	90.1	**Fortville** (town) Hancock County
59	90.0	**Merrillville** (town) Lake County
60	89.8	**Porter** (town) Porter County
61	89.7	**Chesterfield** (town) Madison County
62	89.6	**Greenwood** (city) Johnson County
63	89.3	**Brownstown** (town) Jackson County
64	89.2	**Auburn** (city) DeKalb County
65	88.7	**Hobart** (city) Lake County
66	88.6	**New Haven** (city) Allen County
66	88.6	**Speedway** (town) Marion County
66	88.6	**Whiting** (city) Lake County
69	88.5	**Corydon** (town) Harrison County
69	88.5	**Franklin** (city) Johnson County
69	88.5	**Mount Vernon** (city) Posey County
72	88.4	**Chandler** (town) Warrick County
73	88.3	**Princeton** (city) Gibson County
74	88.2	**Greenfield** (city) Hancock County
74	88.2	**Middlebury** (town) Elkhart County
74	88.2	**Portage** (city) Porter County
77	88.0	**Cedar Lake** (town) Lake County
77	88.0	**North Manchester** (town) Wabash County
79	87.9	**Fort Wayne** (city) Allen County
79	87.9	**Mooresville** (town) Morgan County
79	87.9	**North Terre Haute** (CDP) Vigo County
82	87.8	**Centerville** (town) Wayne County
83	87.6	**Hebron** (town) Porter County
83	87.6	**South Haven** (CDP) Porter County
85	87.3	**Kokomo** (city) Howard County
86	87.2	**Greensburg** (city) Decatur County
86	87.2	**Lebanon** (city) Boone County
88	87.1	**Jasper** (city) Dubois County
88	87.1	**Jeffersonville** (city) Clark County
88	87.1	**Lawrence** (city) Marion County
88	87.1	**Sellersburg** (town) Clark County
92	87.0	**Bluffton** (city) Wells County
93	86.8	**Evansville** (city) Vanderburgh County
93	86.8	**Kendallville** (city) Noble County
93	86.8	**Monticello** (city) White County
96	86.5	**Mishawaka** (city) Saint Joseph County
97	86.4	**Beech Grove** (city) Marion County
97	86.4	**Decatur** (city) Adams County
97	86.4	**Hartford City** (city) Blackford County
97	86.4	**Lafayette** (city) Tippecanoe County
97	86.4	**Sheridan** (town) Hamilton County
102	86.1	**Gas City** (city) Grant County
103	86.0	**Cumberland** (town) Marion County
104	85.9	**Ellettsville** (town) Monroe County
105	85.8	**Charlestown** (city) Clark County
106	85.7	**Boonville** (city) Warrick County
107	85.6	**Syracuse** (town) Kosciusko County
108	85.4	**Greencastle** (city) Putnam County
109	85.2	**Brookville** (town) Franklin County
109	85.2	**La Porte** (city) LaPorte County
111	85.1	**Huntington** (city) Huntington County
112	84.6	**Angola** (city) Steuben County
112	84.6	**Clarksville** (town) Clark County
112	84.6	**Tell City** (city) Perry County
115	84.5	**Rensselaer** (city) Jasper County
116	84.4	**Dunlap** (CDP) Elkhart County
116	84.4	**Fairmount** (town) Grant County
116	84.4	**Garrett** (city) DeKalb County
116	84.4	**Rochester** (city) Fulton County
120	84.3	**Indianapolis** (city) Marion County
120	84.3	**Terre Haute** (city) Vigo County
120	84.3	**Warsaw** (city) Kosciusko County
123	84.1	**Clinton** (city) Vermillion County
123	84.1	**Rushville** (city) Rush County
125	83.9	**Columbia City** (city) Whitley County
125	83.9	**South Bend** (city) Saint Joseph County
127	83.8	**Elwood** (city) Madison County
127	83.8	**Tipton** (city) Tipton County
129	83.6	**Nappanee** (city) Elkhart County
129	83.6	**Vincennes** (city) Knox County
129	83.6	**Wabash** (city) Wabash County
132	83.5	**Muncie** (city) Delaware County
133	83.4	**Anderson** (city) Madison County
133	83.4	**Madison** (city) Jefferson County
133	83.4	**Michigan City** (city) LaPorte County
136	83.2	**Attica** (city) Fountain County
136	83.2	**New Albany** (city) Floyd County
136	83.2	**Seymour** (city) Jackson County
136	83.2	**Sullivan** (city) Sullivan County
140	82.9	**Gary** (city) Lake County
141	82.8	**Roselawn** (CDP) Newton County
142	82.6	**Portland** (city) Jay County
143	82.5	**Alexandria** (city) Madison County
143	82.5	**Lagrange** (town) LaGrange County
145	82.4	**Bremen** (town) Marshall County
146	82.3	**Crawfordsville** (city) Montgomery County
146	82.3	**North Vernon** (city) Jennings County
146	82.3	**Washington** (city) Daviess County
149	82.2	**Shelbyville** (city) Shelby County
150	81.9	**New Castle** (city) Henry County

Note: This section ranks incorporated places and CDPs (Census Designated Places) with populations of 2,500 or more. Unincorporated postal areas were not considered. Please refer to the User Guide for additional information.

Educational Attainment: High School Diploma or Higher
Top 150 Places Ranked in *Ascending* Order

State Rank	Percent	Place
1	53.3	**Ligonier** (city) Noble County
2	69.2	**Westville** (town) LaPorte County
3	69.9	**Country Squire Lakes** (CDP) Jennings County
4	71.3	**Austin** (city) Scott County
5	71.7	**East Chicago** (city) Lake County
6	73.3	**Huntingburg** (city) Dubois County
7	74.7	**Lawrenceburg** (city) Dearborn County
8	75.2	**Mitchell** (city) Lawrence County
9	75.4	**Connersville** (city) Fayette County
10	75.5	**Elkhart** (city) Elkhart County
11	75.7	**Logansport** (city) Cass County
12	76.6	**Brazil** (city) Clay County
12	76.6	**Knox** (city) Starke County
12	76.6	**Scottsburg** (city) Scott County
15	76.7	**Plymouth** (city) Marshall County
16	77.2	**Goshen** (city) Elkhart County
17	77.4	**Frankfort** (city) Clinton County
18	77.6	**Grissom AFB** (CDP) Miami County
19	77.8	**Salem** (city) Washington County
20	78.0	**Peru** (city) Miami County
21	79.1	**Lake Station** (city) Lake County
21	79.1	**Winchester** (city) Randolph County
23	79.3	**Hammond** (city) Lake County
24	79.4	**Loogootee** (city) Martin County
25	79.5	**Delphi** (city) Carroll County
26	79.8	**Rockville** (town) Parke County
27	80.0	**Union City** (city) Randolph County
28	80.1	**Butler** (city) DeKalb County
29	80.5	**Richmond** (city) Wayne County
30	80.6	**Edinburgh** (town) Johnson County
31	80.7	**Linton** (city) Greene County
31	80.7	**Paoli** (town) Orange County
33	81.0	**Aurora** (city) Dearborn County
33	81.0	**Hanover** (town) Jefferson County
35	81.1	**Marion** (city) Grant County
35	81.1	**Martinsville** (city) Morgan County
37	81.2	**Bedford** (city) Lawrence County
38	81.5	**Bicknell** (city) Knox County
39	81.9	**New Castle** (city) Henry County
40	82.2	**Shelbyville** (city) Shelby County
41	82.3	**Crawfordsville** (city) Montgomery County
41	82.3	**North Vernon** (city) Jennings County
41	82.3	**Washington** (city) Daviess County
44	82.4	**Bremen** (town) Marshall County
45	82.5	**Alexandria** (city) Madison County
45	82.5	**Lagrange** (town) LaGrange County
47	82.6	**Portland** (city) Jay County
48	82.8	**Roselawn** (CDP) Newton County
49	82.9	**Gary** (city) Lake County
50	83.2	**Attica** (city) Fountain County
50	83.2	**New Albany** (city) Floyd County
50	83.2	**Seymour** (city) Jackson County
50	83.2	**Sullivan** (city) Sullivan County
54	83.4	**Anderson** (city) Madison County
54	83.4	**Madison** (city) Jefferson County
54	83.4	**Michigan City** (city) LaPorte County
57	83.5	**Muncie** (city) Delaware County
58	83.6	**Nappanee** (city) Elkhart County
58	83.6	**Vincennes** (city) Knox County
58	83.6	**Wabash** (city) Wabash County
61	83.8	**Elwood** (city) Madison County
61	83.8	**Tipton** (city) Tipton County
63	83.9	**Columbia City** (city) Whitley County
63	83.9	**South Bend** (city) Saint Joseph County
65	84.1	**Clinton** (city) Vermillion County
65	84.1	**Rushville** (city) Rush County
67	84.3	**Indianapolis** (city) Marion County
67	84.3	**Terre Haute** (city) Vigo County
67	84.3	**Warsaw** (city) Kosciusko County
70	84.4	**Dunlap** (CDP) Elkhart County
70	84.4	**Fairmount** (town) Grant County
70	84.4	**Garrett** (city) DeKalb County
70	84.4	**Rochester** (city) Fulton County
74	84.5	**Rensselaer** (city) Jasper County
75	84.6	**Angola** (city) Steuben County
75	84.6	**Clarksville** (town) Clark County
75	84.6	**Tell City** (city) Perry County
78	85.1	**Huntington** (city) Huntington County
79	85.2	**Brookville** (town) Franklin County
79	85.2	**La Porte** (city) LaPorte County
81	85.4	**Greencastle** (city) Putnam County
82	85.6	**Syracuse** (town) Kosciusko County
83	85.7	**Boonville** (city) Warrick County
84	85.8	**Charlestown** (city) Clark County
85	85.9	**Ellettsville** (town) Monroe County
86	86.0	**Cumberland** (town) Marion County
87	86.1	**Gas City** (city) Grant County
88	86.4	**Beech Grove** (city) Marion County
88	86.4	**Decatur** (city) Adams County
88	86.4	**Hartford City** (city) Blackford County
88	86.4	**Lafayette** (city) Tippecanoe County
88	86.4	**Sheridan** (town) Hamilton County
93	86.5	**Mishawaka** (city) Saint Joseph County
94	86.8	**Evansville** (city) Vanderburgh County
94	86.8	**Kendallville** (city) Noble County
94	86.8	**Monticello** (city) White County
97	87.0	**Bluffton** (city) Wells County
98	87.1	**Jasper** (city) Dubois County
98	87.1	**Jeffersonville** (city) Clark County
98	87.1	**Lawrence** (city) Marion County
98	87.1	**Sellersburg** (town) Clark County
102	87.2	**Greensburg** (city) Decatur County
102	87.2	**Lebanon** (city) Boone County
104	87.3	**Kokomo** (city) Howard County
105	87.6	**Hebron** (town) Porter County
105	87.6	**South Haven** (CDP) Porter County
107	87.8	**Centerville** (town) Wayne County
108	87.9	**Fort Wayne** (city) Allen County
108	87.9	**Mooresville** (town) Morgan County
108	87.9	**North Terre Haute** (CDP) Vigo County
111	88.0	**Cedar Lake** (town) Lake County
111	88.0	**North Manchester** (town) Wabash County
113	88.2	**Greenfield** (city) Hancock County
113	88.2	**Middlebury** (town) Elkhart County
113	88.2	**Portage** (city) Porter County
116	88.3	**Princeton** (city) Gibson County
117	88.4	**Chandler** (town) Warrick County
118	88.5	**Corydon** (town) Harrison County
118	88.5	**Franklin** (city) Johnson County
118	88.5	**Mount Vernon** (city) Posey County
121	88.6	**New Haven** (city) Allen County
121	88.6	**Speedway** (town) Marion County
121	88.6	**Whiting** (city) Lake County
124	88.7	**Hobart** (city) Lake County
125	89.2	**Auburn** (city) DeKalb County
126	89.3	**Brownstown** (town) Jackson County
127	89.6	**Greenwood** (city) Johnson County
128	89.7	**Chesterfield** (town) Madison County
129	89.8	**Porter** (town) Porter County
130	90.0	**Merrillville** (town) Lake County
131	90.1	**Columbus** (city) Bartholomew County
131	90.1	**Fortville** (town) Hancock County
133	90.3	**Plainfield** (town) Hendricks County
133	90.3	**Whiteland** (town) Johnson County
135	90.5	**Griffith** (town) Lake County
135	90.5	**Heritage Lake** (CDP) Putnam County
137	90.6	**Berne** (city) Adams County
137	90.6	**Cicero** (town) Hamilton County
137	90.6	**De Motte** (town) Jasper County
140	90.8	**Greendale** (city) Dearborn County
141	91.0	**Covington** (city) Fountain County
142	91.2	**Danville** (town) Hendricks County
142	91.2	**Winona Lake** (town) Kosciusko County
144	91.4	**Smithville-Sanders** (CDP) Monroe County
145	91.5	**Valparaiso** (city) Porter County
146	91.7	**Pendleton** (town) Madison County
146	91.7	**Pittsboro** (town) Hendricks County
148	91.8	**Chesterton** (town) Porter County
148	91.8	**Simonton Lake** (CDP) Elkhart County
150	91.9	**Highland** (town) Lake County

Note: This section ranks incorporated places and CDPs (Census Designated Places) with populations of 2,500 or more. Unincorporated postal areas were not considered. Please refer to the User Guide for additional information.

Educational Attainment: Bachelor's Degree or Higher
Top 150 Places Ranked in *Descending* Order

State Rank	Percent	Place
1	74.5	Purdue University (CDP) Tippecanoe County
2	73.9	Notre Dame (CDP) Saint Joseph County
3	71.4	West Lafayette (city) Tippecanoe County
4	68.1	Carmel (city) Hamilton County
5	66.9	Zionsville (town) Boone County
6	59.7	Fishers (town) Hamilton County
7	56.6	Bloomington (city) Monroe County
7	56.6	Westfield (city) Hamilton County
9	51.9	Granger (CDP) Saint Joseph County
10	51.5	Whitestown (town) Boone County
11	48.3	Shorewood Forest (CDP) Porter County
12	47.6	McCordsville (town) Hancock County
13	47.2	Noblesville (city) Hamilton County
14	46.9	Winona Lake (town) Kosciusko County
15	45.8	Upland (town) Grant County
16	40.6	Munster (town) Lake County
17	37.4	Highland (CDP) Vanderburgh County
18	37.0	Brownsburg (town) Hendricks County
19	36.7	Saint John (town) Lake County
20	34.7	Smithville-Sanders (CDP) Monroe County
21	34.3	Georgetown (town) Floyd County
22	33.9	Valparaiso (city) Porter County
23	33.1	Yorktown (town) Delaware County
24	32.4	Schererville (town) Lake County
25	32.0	Avon (town) Hendricks County
25	32.0	Winfield (town) Lake County
27	31.9	Columbus (city) Bartholomew County
28	31.8	Leo-Cedarville (town) Allen County
29	31.7	Bargersville (town) Johnson County
30	31.6	Lawrence (city) Marion County
31	31.4	Batesville (city) Ripley County
32	30.5	Chesterton (town) Porter County
32	30.5	Huntertown (town) Allen County
34	30.2	Crown Point (city) Lake County
35	29.7	Lakes of the Four Seasons (CDP) Lake County
36	29.3	Porter (town) Porter County
37	29.2	Newburgh (town) Warrick County
38	28.9	Dyer (town) Lake County
39	27.9	Melody Hill (CDP) Vanderburgh County
40	27.3	Indianapolis (city) Marion County
41	26.9	Plainfield (town) Hendricks County
42	26.8	North Manchester (town) Wabash County
43	26.7	Lafayette (city) Tippecanoe County
44	26.6	Greendale (city) Dearborn County
45	26.5	Highland (town) Lake County
46	26.4	Greenwood (city) Johnson County
47	26.1	Danville (town) Hendricks County
48	25.9	Pendleton (town) Madison County
49	25.8	Pittsboro (town) Hendricks County
50	25.7	Hidden Valley (CDP) Dearborn County
51	25.6	Fort Wayne (city) Allen County
52	24.5	Speedway (town) Marion County
53	24.3	Greencastle (city) Putnam County
54	24.2	Berne (city) Adams County
54	24.2	Cicero (town) Hamilton County
56	23.8	Ellettsville (town) Monroe County
57	23.4	Mishawaka (city) Saint Joseph County
58	23.1	Bright (CDP) Dearborn County
58	23.1	Simonton Lake (CDP) Elkhart County
60	22.9	South Bend (city) Saint Joseph County
61	22.6	Madison (city) Jefferson County
62	22.5	Warsaw (city) Kosciusko County
63	22.4	Auburn (city) DeKalb County
63	22.4	Muncie (city) Delaware County
65	21.8	Fortville (town) Hancock County
66	21.7	Jasper (city) Dubois County
67	21.1	Dunlap (CDP) Elkhart County
67	21.1	Goshen (city) Elkhart County
69	21.0	Whiteland (town) Johnson County
70	20.9	Franklin (city) Johnson County
70	20.9	Merrillville (town) Lake County
72	20.8	Jeffersonville (city) Clark County
73	20.4	Middlebury (town) Elkhart County
74	20.1	Mount Vernon (city) Posey County
75	19.9	Ossian (town) Wells County
76	19.7	Greenfield (city) Hancock County
77	19.6	Terre Haute (city) Vigo County
78	19.4	Angola (city) Steuben County
78	19.4	Clarksville (town) Clark County
80	19.1	New Haven (city) Allen County
80	19.1	Whiting (city) Lake County
82	18.8	Brookville (town) Franklin County
83	18.7	Monticello (city) White County
84	18.6	Cumberland (town) Marion County
85	18.4	Lebanon (city) Boone County
86	18.1	Lowell (town) Lake County
86	18.1	Rochester (city) Fulton County
88	18.0	Evansville (city) Vanderburgh County
89	17.8	Richmond (city) Wayne County
90	17.3	Kokomo (city) Howard County
90	17.3	Rensselaer (city) Jasper County
92	16.7	Covington (city) Fountain County
92	16.7	Griffith (town) Lake County
92	16.7	Nappanee (city) Elkhart County
95	16.5	Fort Branch (town) Gibson County
96	16.1	New Albany (city) Floyd County
96	16.1	Seymour (city) Jackson County
98	15.6	Michigan City (city) LaPorte County
99	15.5	Beech Grove (city) Marion County
100	15.4	Bluffton (city) Wells County
100	15.4	Boonville (city) Warrick County
100	15.4	Columbia City (city) Whitley County
100	15.4	Hobart (city) Lake County
104	15.2	Huntington (city) Huntington County
105	15.0	Portage (city) Porter County
106	14.9	Crawfordsville (city) Montgomery County
106	14.9	Marion (city) Grant County
108	14.6	Greensburg (city) Decatur County
108	14.6	La Porte (city) LaPorte County
110	14.5	Anderson (city) Madison County
110	14.5	Corydon (town) Harrison County
112	14.1	Huntingburg (city) Dubois County
112	14.1	North Terre Haute (CDP) Vigo County
112	14.1	Scottsburg (city) Scott County
112	14.1	Vincennes (city) Knox County
116	14.0	Elkhart (city) Elkhart County
116	14.0	Fairmount (town) Grant County
116	14.0	Washington (city) Daviess County
119	13.9	Decatur (city) Adams County
120	13.7	Mooresville (town) Morgan County
121	13.6	Princeton (city) Gibson County
122	13.5	Tell City (city) Perry County
123	13.4	Cedar Lake (town) Lake County
123	13.4	Kendallville (city) Noble County
123	13.4	Salem (city) Washington County
126	13.3	Charlestown (city) Clark County
127	13.2	Bremen (town) Marshall County
127	13.2	Heritage Lake (CDP) Putnam County
127	13.2	New Castle (city) Henry County
127	13.2	Sellersburg (town) Clark County
131	13.0	Plymouth (city) Marshall County
132	12.9	Hammond (city) Lake County
133	12.8	Clinton (city) Vermillion County
133	12.8	Sheridan (town) Hamilton County
135	12.7	Attica (city) Fountain County
136	12.5	Delphi (city) Carroll County
137	12.4	Syracuse (town) Kosciusko County
138	12.3	Gary (city) Lake County
138	12.3	Shelbyville (city) Shelby County
140	12.2	Tipton (city) Tipton County
141	12.1	Centerville (town) Wayne County
142	11.9	Bedford (city) Lawrence County
142	11.9	Hanover (town) Jefferson County
142	11.9	Logansport (city) Cass County
142	11.9	Rushville (city) Rush County
146	11.5	Gas City (city) Grant County
146	11.5	Wabash (city) Wabash County
148	11.4	Garrett (city) DeKalb County
149	11.3	North Vernon (city) Jennings County
150	11.2	Linton (city) Greene County

Note: This section ranks incorporated places and CDPs (Census Designated Places) with populations of 2,500 or more. Unincorporated postal areas were not considered. Please refer to the User Guide for additional information.

Educational Attainment: Bachelor's Degree or Higher
Top 150 Places Ranked in *Ascending* Order

State Rank	Percent	Place
1	2.7	Country Squire Lakes (CDP) Jennings County
2	4.4	Ligonier (city) Noble County
3	4.7	Austin (city) Scott County
4	5.5	Knox (city) Starke County
5	5.6	Lake Station (city) Lake County
6	5.8	Grissom AFB (CDP) Miami County
7	6.1	Bicknell (city) Knox County
8	6.3	Westville (town) LaPorte County
9	6.4	Butler (city) DeKalb County
10	6.8	Chandler (town) Warrick County
10	6.8	Lagrange (town) LaGrange County
12	6.9	Connersville (city) Fayette County
13	7.0	East Chicago (city) Lake County
14	7.4	Lawrenceburg (city) Dearborn County
15	7.7	De Motte (town) Jasper County
15	7.7	Edinburgh (town) Johnson County
17	7.9	Union City (city) Randolph County
17	7.9	Winchester (city) Randolph County
19	8.4	Peru (city) Miami County
20	8.5	South Haven (CDP) Porter County
21	8.7	Hartford City (city) Blackford County
21	8.7	Sullivan (city) Sullivan County
23	8.8	New Whiteland (town) Johnson County
24	8.9	Aurora (city) Dearborn County
24	8.9	Loogootee (city) Martin County
26	9.4	Roselawn (CDP) Newton County
27	9.5	Brazil (city) Clay County
28	9.6	Elwood (city) Madison County
29	9.7	Portland (city) Jay County
30	10.2	Brownstown (town) Jackson County
31	10.4	Mitchell (city) Lawrence County
32	10.5	Frankfort (city) Clinton County
32	10.5	Paoli (town) Orange County
34	10.7	Alexandria (city) Madison County
34	10.7	Hebron (town) Porter County
36	10.8	Chesterfield (town) Madison County
37	11.0	Martinsville (city) Morgan County
38	11.2	Linton (city) Greene County
38	11.2	Rockville (town) Parke County
40	11.3	North Vernon (city) Jennings County
41	11.4	Garrett (city) DeKalb County
42	11.5	Gas City (city) Grant County
42	11.5	Wabash (city) Wabash County
44	11.9	Bedford (city) Lawrence County
44	11.9	Hanover (town) Jefferson County
44	11.9	Logansport (city) Cass County
44	11.9	Rushville (city) Rush County
48	12.1	Centerville (town) Wayne County
49	12.2	Tipton (city) Tipton County
50	12.3	Gary (city) Lake County
50	12.3	Shelbyville (city) Shelby County
52	12.4	Syracuse (town) Kosciusko County
53	12.5	Delphi (city) Carroll County
54	12.7	Attica (city) Fountain County
55	12.8	Clinton (city) Vermillion County
55	12.8	Sheridan (town) Hamilton County
57	12.9	Hammond (city) Lake County
58	13.0	Plymouth (city) Marshall County
59	13.2	Bremen (town) Marshall County
59	13.2	Heritage Lake (CDP) Putnam County
59	13.2	New Castle (city) Henry County
59	13.2	Sellersburg (town) Clark County
63	13.3	Charlestown (city) Clark County
64	13.4	Cedar Lake (town) Lake County
64	13.4	Kendallville (city) Noble County
64	13.4	Salem (city) Washington County
67	13.5	Tell City (city) Perry County
68	13.6	Princeton (city) Gibson County
69	13.7	Mooresville (town) Morgan County
70	13.9	Decatur (city) Adams County
71	14.0	Elkhart (city) Elkhart County
71	14.0	Fairmount (town) Grant County
71	14.0	Washington (city) Daviess County
74	14.1	Huntingburg (city) Dubois County
74	14.1	North Terre Haute (CDP) Vigo County
74	14.1	Scottsburg (city) Scott County
74	14.1	Vincennes (city) Knox County
78	14.5	Anderson (city) Madison County
78	14.5	Corydon (town) Harrison County
80	14.6	Greensburg (city) Decatur County
80	14.6	La Porte (city) LaPorte County
82	14.9	Crawfordsville (city) Montgomery County
82	14.9	Marion (city) Grant County
84	15.0	Portage (city) Porter County
85	15.2	Huntington (city) Huntington County
86	15.4	Bluffton (city) Wells County
86	15.4	Boonville (city) Warrick County
86	15.4	Columbia City (city) Whitley County
86	15.4	Hobart (city) Lake County
90	15.5	Beech Grove (city) Marion County
91	15.6	Michigan City (city) LaPorte County
92	16.1	New Albany (city) Floyd County
92	16.1	Seymour (city) Jackson County
94	16.5	Fort Branch (town) Gibson County
95	16.7	Covington (city) Fountain County
95	16.7	Griffith (town) Lake County
95	16.7	Nappanee (city) Elkhart County
98	17.3	Kokomo (city) Howard County
98	17.3	Rensselaer (city) Jasper County
100	17.8	Richmond (city) Wayne County
101	18.0	Evansville (city) Vanderburgh County
102	18.1	Lowell (town) Lake County
102	18.1	Rochester (city) Fulton County
104	18.4	Lebanon (city) Boone County
105	18.6	Cumberland (town) Marion County
106	18.7	Monticello (city) White County
107	18.8	Brookville (town) Franklin County
108	19.1	New Haven (city) Allen County
108	19.1	Whiting (city) Lake County
110	19.4	Angola (city) Steuben County
110	19.4	Clarksville (town) Clark County
112	19.6	Terre Haute (city) Vigo County
113	19.7	Greenfield (city) Hancock County
114	19.9	Ossian (town) Wells County
115	20.1	Mount Vernon (city) Posey County
116	20.4	Middlebury (town) Elkhart County
117	20.8	Jeffersonville (city) Clark County
118	20.9	Franklin (city) Johnson County
118	20.9	Merrillville (town) Lake County
120	21.0	Whiteland (town) Johnson County
121	21.1	Dunlap (CDP) Elkhart County
121	21.1	Goshen (city) Elkhart County
123	21.7	Jasper (city) Dubois County
124	21.8	Fortville (town) Hancock County
125	22.4	Auburn (city) DeKalb County
125	22.4	Muncie (city) Delaware County
127	22.5	Warsaw (city) Kosciusko County
128	22.6	Madison (city) Jefferson County
129	22.9	South Bend (city) Saint Joseph County
130	23.1	Bright (CDP) Dearborn County
130	23.1	Simonton Lake (CDP) Elkhart County
132	23.4	Mishawaka (city) Saint Joseph County
133	23.8	Ellettsville (town) Monroe County
134	24.2	Berne (city) Adams County
134	24.2	Cicero (town) Hamilton County
136	24.3	Greencastle (city) Putnam County
137	24.5	Speedway (town) Marion County
138	25.6	Fort Wayne (city) Allen County
139	25.7	Hidden Valley (CDP) Dearborn County
140	25.8	Pittsboro (town) Hendricks County
141	25.9	Pendleton (town) Madison County
142	26.1	Danville (town) Hendricks County
143	26.4	Greenwood (city) Johnson County
144	26.5	Highland (town) Lake County
145	26.6	Greendale (city) Dearborn County
146	26.7	Lafayette (city) Tippecanoe County
147	26.8	North Manchester (town) Wabash County
148	26.9	Plainfield (town) Hendricks County
149	27.3	Indianapolis (city) Marion County
150	27.9	Melody Hill (CDP) Vanderburgh County

Note: This section ranks incorporated places and CDPs (Census Designated Places) with populations of 2,500 or more. Unincorporated postal areas were not considered. Please refer to the User Guide for additional information.

Educational Attainment: Graduate/Professional Degree or Higher
Top 150 Places Ranked in *Descending* Order

State Rank	Percent	Place
1	49.8	Purdue University (CDP) Tippecanoe County
2	42.5	West Lafayette (city) Tippecanoe County
3	37.6	Notre Dame (CDP) Saint Joseph County
4	31.7	Zionsville (town) Boone County
5	31.0	Bloomington (city) Monroe County
6	30.2	Carmel (city) Hamilton County
7	21.7	Granger (CDP) Saint Joseph County
8	20.4	Upland (town) Grant County
9	20.2	Shorewood Forest (CDP) Porter County
10	19.1	Fishers (town) Hamilton County
11	17.6	Winona Lake (town) Kosciusko County
12	16.7	Munster (town) Lake County
13	16.6	Westfield (city) Hamilton County
14	16.1	Whitestown (town) Boone County
15	15.8	Porter (town) Porter County
16	14.6	Noblesville (city) Hamilton County
17	14.1	Highland (CDP) Vanderburgh County
18	13.9	Columbus (city) Bartholomew County
18	13.9	Schererville (town) Lake County
20	13.6	North Manchester (town) Wabash County
21	13.1	Smithville-Sanders (CDP) Monroe County
22	13.0	Yorktown (town) Delaware County
23	12.2	Chesterton (town) Porter County
23	12.2	Greencastle (city) Putnam County
25	11.6	Saint John (town) Lake County
26	11.5	Valparaiso (city) Porter County
27	11.3	Madison (city) Jefferson County
27	11.3	McCordsville (town) Hancock County
29	11.0	Melody Hill (CDP) Vanderburgh County
30	10.9	Winfield (town) Lake County
31	10.8	Muncie (city) Delaware County
32	10.5	Newburgh (town) Warrick County
33	9.9	Batesville (city) Ripley County
33	9.9	Huntertown (town) Allen County
35	9.8	Georgetown (town) Floyd County
36	9.7	Brownsburg (town) Hendricks County
36	9.7	Hidden Valley (CDP) Dearborn County
36	9.7	Warsaw (city) Kosciusko County
39	9.5	Lafayette (city) Tippecanoe County
39	9.5	South Bend (city) Saint Joseph County
41	9.4	Crown Point (city) Lake County
41	9.4	Indianapolis (city) Marion County
43	9.3	Lawrence (city) Marion County
44	9.0	Bargersville (town) Johnson County
45	8.9	Lakes of the Four Seasons (CDP) Lake County
46	8.8	Middlebury (town) Elkhart County
46	8.8	Mishawaka (city) Saint Joseph County
48	8.7	Avon (town) Hendricks County
48	8.7	Berne (city) Adams County
50	8.6	Auburn (city) DeKalb County
51	8.5	Dyer (town) Lake County
51	8.5	Fort Wayne (city) Allen County
51	8.5	Greendale (city) Dearborn County
54	8.3	Greenwood (city) Johnson County
55	8.2	Highland (town) Lake County
56	8.1	Angola (city) Steuben County
56	8.1	Dunlap (CDP) Elkhart County
56	8.1	Greenfield (city) Hancock County
56	8.1	Plainfield (town) Hendricks County
60	8.0	Speedway (town) Marion County
60	8.0	Terre Haute (city) Vigo County
62	7.9	Franklin (city) Johnson County
63	7.8	Goshen (city) Elkhart County
63	7.8	Merrillville (town) Lake County
63	7.8	Richmond (city) Wayne County
66	7.7	Leo-Cedarville (town) Allen County
66	7.7	Monticello (city) White County
66	7.7	Pendleton (town) Madison County
69	7.5	Mount Vernon (city) Posey County
69	7.5	Rochester (city) Fulton County
71	7.3	Jeffersonville (city) Clark County
72	7.2	Bright (CDP) Dearborn County
72	7.2	Ellettsville (town) Monroe County
74	7.0	Fairmount (town) Grant County
74	7.0	Pittsboro (town) Hendricks County
76	6.7	Columbia City (city) Whitley County
76	6.7	Jasper (city) Dubois County
76	6.7	Rensselaer (city) Jasper County
79	6.6	Cumberland (town) Marion County
80	6.4	Delphi (city) Carroll County
80	6.4	Fortville (town) Hancock County
80	6.4	Lowell (town) Lake County
80	6.4	Tell City (city) Perry County
80	6.4	Whiting (city) Lake County
85	6.3	Kokomo (city) Howard County
85	6.3	Simonton Lake (CDP) Elkhart County
87	6.2	Centerville (town) Wayne County
87	6.2	Danville (town) Hendricks County
89	6.0	Crawfordsville (city) Montgomery County
89	6.0	Washington (city) Daviess County
91	5.9	Bluffton (city) Wells County
91	5.9	Covington (city) Fountain County
91	5.9	Marion (city) Grant County
94	5.8	Evansville (city) Vanderburgh County
95	5.7	Attica (city) Fountain County
95	5.7	Michigan City (city) LaPorte County
95	5.7	North Vernon (city) Jennings County
95	5.7	Salem (city) Washington County
95	5.7	Sellersburg (town) Clark County
100	5.6	Fort Branch (town) Gibson County
100	5.6	Lebanon (city) Boone County
102	5.4	Corydon (town) Harrison County
103	5.3	Huntington (city) Huntington County
103	5.3	New Haven (city) Allen County
105	5.1	Clarksville (town) Clark County
105	5.1	New Castle (city) Henry County
105	5.1	Seymour (city) Jackson County
105	5.1	Vincennes (city) Knox County
109	5.0	Beech Grove (city) Marion County
109	5.0	Brookville (town) Franklin County
109	5.0	Greensburg (city) Decatur County
112	4.9	Charlestown (city) Clark County
112	4.9	Cicero (town) Hamilton County
114	4.8	Anderson (city) Madison County
114	4.8	Boonville (city) Warrick County
116	4.7	Hanover (town) Jefferson County
116	4.7	Hobart (city) Lake County
116	4.7	Nappanee (city) Elkhart County
116	4.7	Whiteland (town) Johnson County
120	4.6	Elkhart (city) Elkhart County
120	4.6	La Porte (city) LaPorte County
120	4.6	New Albany (city) Floyd County
120	4.6	Syracuse (town) Kosciusko County
124	4.5	Decatur (city) Adams County
124	4.5	Griffith (town) Lake County
124	4.5	Paoli (town) Orange County
124	4.5	Rushville (city) Rush County
124	4.5	Scottsburg (city) Scott County
129	4.4	Portage (city) Porter County
130	4.3	Bremen (town) Marshall County
130	4.3	Ossian (town) Wells County
132	4.2	Aurora (city) Dearborn County
132	4.2	Gary (city) Lake County
132	4.2	Huntingburg (city) Dubois County
132	4.2	Rockville (town) Parke County
132	4.2	Tipton (city) Tipton County
137	4.1	Linton (city) Greene County
138	4.0	Hammond (city) Lake County
138	4.0	Portland (city) Jay County
140	3.9	Lagrange (town) LaGrange County
140	3.9	Martinsville (city) Morgan County
140	3.9	Mitchell (city) Lawrence County
140	3.9	Sheridan (town) Hamilton County
140	3.9	Wabash (city) Wabash County
145	3.8	Bedford (city) Lawrence County
146	3.7	Chesterfield (town) Madison County
146	3.7	Frankfort (city) Clinton County
146	3.7	Heritage Lake (CDP) Putnam County
146	3.7	Kendallville (city) Noble County
150	3.6	Brazil (city) Clay County

Note: This section ranks incorporated places and CDPs (Census Designated Places) with populations of 2,500 or more. Unincorporated postal areas were not considered. Please refer to the User Guide for additional information.

Educational Attainment: Graduate/Professional Degree or Higher

Top 150 Places Ranked in *Ascending* Order

State Rank	Percent	Place
1	0.0	**Country Squire Lakes** (CDP) Jennings County
2	0.3	**New Whiteland** (town) Johnson County
3	0.7	**Austin** (city) Scott County
4	0.9	**Ligonier** (city) Noble County
5	1.0	**Lake Station** (city) Lake County
6	1.5	**Knox** (city) Starke County
6	1.5	**Union City** (city) Randolph County
8	1.6	**Sullivan** (city) Sullivan County
9	1.7	**Westville** (town) LaPorte County
10	1.8	**Elwood** (city) Madison County
11	1.9	**Grissom AFB** (CDP) Miami County
11	1.9	**South Haven** (CDP) Porter County
13	2.1	**East Chicago** (city) Lake County
13	2.1	**Princeton** (city) Gibson County
15	2.3	**Edinburgh** (town) Johnson County
15	2.3	**Mooresville** (town) Morgan County
17	2.4	**Bicknell** (city) Knox County
17	2.4	**Garrett** (city) DeKalb County
17	2.4	**Lawrenceburg** (city) Dearborn County
20	2.5	**Chandler** (town) Warrick County
20	2.5	**Connersville** (city) Fayette County
22	2.6	**Winchester** (city) Randolph County
23	2.8	**Clinton** (city) Vermillion County
24	2.9	**Gas City** (city) Grant County
25	3.1	**Brownstown** (town) Jackson County
25	3.1	**Hartford City** (city) Blackford County
25	3.1	**Logansport** (city) Cass County
25	3.1	**Loogootee** (city) Martin County
29	3.2	**Hebron** (town) Porter County
29	3.2	**North Terre Haute** (CDP) Vigo County
29	3.2	**Roselawn** (CDP) Newton County
32	3.3	**De Motte** (town) Jasper County
32	3.3	**Plymouth** (city) Marshall County
32	3.3	**Shelbyville** (city) Shelby County
35	3.4	**Butler** (city) DeKalb County
35	3.4	**Peru** (city) Miami County
37	3.5	**Alexandria** (city) Madison County
37	3.5	**Cedar Lake** (town) Lake County
39	3.6	**Brazil** (city) Clay County
40	3.7	**Chesterfield** (town) Madison County
40	3.7	**Frankfort** (city) Clinton County
40	3.7	**Heritage Lake** (CDP) Putnam County
40	3.7	**Kendallville** (city) Noble County
44	3.8	**Bedford** (city) Lawrence County
45	3.9	**Lagrange** (town) LaGrange County
45	3.9	**Martinsville** (city) Morgan County
45	3.9	**Mitchell** (city) Lawrence County
45	3.9	**Sheridan** (town) Hamilton County
45	3.9	**Wabash** (city) Wabash County
50	4.0	**Hammond** (city) Lake County
50	4.0	**Portland** (city) Jay County
52	4.1	**Linton** (city) Greene County
53	4.2	**Aurora** (city) Dearborn County
53	4.2	**Gary** (city) Lake County
53	4.2	**Huntingburg** (city) Dubois County
53	4.2	**Rockville** (town) Parke County
53	4.2	**Tipton** (city) Tipton County
58	4.3	**Bremen** (town) Marshall County
58	4.3	**Ossian** (town) Wells County
60	4.4	**Portage** (city) Porter County
61	4.5	**Decatur** (city) Adams County
61	4.5	**Griffith** (town) Lake County
61	4.5	**Paoli** (town) Orange County
61	4.5	**Rushville** (city) Rush County
61	4.5	**Scottsburg** (city) Scott County
66	4.6	**Elkhart** (city) Elkhart County
66	4.6	**La Porte** (city) LaPorte County
66	4.6	**New Albany** (city) Floyd County
66	4.6	**Syracuse** (town) Kosciusko County
70	4.7	**Hanover** (town) Jefferson County
70	4.7	**Hobart** (city) Lake County
70	4.7	**Nappanee** (city) Elkhart County
70	4.7	**Whiteland** (town) Johnson County
74	4.8	**Anderson** (city) Madison County
74	4.8	**Boonville** (city) Warrick County
76	4.9	**Charlestown** (city) Clark County
76	4.9	**Cicero** (town) Hamilton County
78	5.0	**Beech Grove** (city) Marion County
78	5.0	**Brookville** (town) Franklin County
78	5.0	**Greensburg** (city) Decatur County
81	5.1	**Clarksville** (town) Clark County
81	5.1	**New Castle** (city) Henry County
81	5.1	**Seymour** (city) Jackson County
81	5.1	**Vincennes** (city) Knox County
85	5.3	**Huntington** (city) Huntington County
85	5.3	**New Haven** (city) Allen County
87	5.4	**Corydon** (town) Harrison County
88	5.6	**Fort Branch** (town) Gibson County
88	5.6	**Lebanon** (city) Boone County
90	5.7	**Attica** (city) Fountain County
90	5.7	**Michigan City** (city) LaPorte County
90	5.7	**North Vernon** (city) Jennings County
90	5.7	**Salem** (city) Washington County
90	5.7	**Sellersburg** (town) Clark County
95	5.8	**Evansville** (city) Vanderburgh County
96	5.9	**Bluffton** (city) Wells County
96	5.9	**Covington** (city) Fountain County
96	5.9	**Marion** (city) Grant County
99	6.0	**Crawfordsville** (city) Montgomery County
99	6.0	**Washington** (city) Daviess County
101	6.2	**Centerville** (town) Wayne County
101	6.2	**Danville** (town) Hendricks County
103	6.3	**Kokomo** (city) Howard County
103	6.3	**Simonton Lake** (CDP) Elkhart County
105	6.4	**Delphi** (city) Carroll County
105	6.4	**Fortville** (town) Hancock County
105	6.4	**Lowell** (town) Lake County
105	6.4	**Tell City** (city) Perry County
105	6.4	**Whiting** (city) Lake County
110	6.6	**Cumberland** (town) Marion County
111	6.7	**Columbia City** (city) Whitley County
111	6.7	**Jasper** (city) Dubois County
111	6.7	**Rensselaer** (city) Jasper County
114	7.0	**Fairmount** (town) Grant County
114	7.0	**Pittsboro** (town) Hendricks County
116	7.2	**Bright** (CDP) Dearborn County
116	7.2	**Ellettsville** (town) Monroe County
118	7.3	**Jeffersonville** (city) Clark County
119	7.5	**Mount Vernon** (city) Posey County
119	7.5	**Rochester** (city) Fulton County
121	7.7	**Leo-Cedarville** (town) Allen County
121	7.7	**Monticello** (city) White County
121	7.7	**Pendleton** (town) Madison County
124	7.8	**Goshen** (city) Elkhart County
124	7.8	**Merrillville** (town) Lake County
124	7.8	**Richmond** (city) Wayne County
127	7.9	**Franklin** (city) Johnson County
128	8.0	**Speedway** (town) Marion County
128	8.0	**Terre Haute** (city) Vigo County
130	8.1	**Angola** (city) Steuben County
130	8.1	**Dunlap** (CDP) Elkhart County
130	8.1	**Greenfield** (city) Hancock County
130	8.1	**Plainfield** (town) Hendricks County
134	8.2	**Highland** (town) Lake County
135	8.3	**Greenwood** (city) Johnson County
136	8.5	**Dyer** (town) Lake County
136	8.5	**Fort Wayne** (city) Allen County
136	8.5	**Greendale** (city) Dearborn County
139	8.6	**Auburn** (city) DeKalb County
140	8.7	**Avon** (town) Hendricks County
140	8.7	**Berne** (city) Adams County
142	8.8	**Middlebury** (town) Elkhart County
142	8.8	**Mishawaka** (city) Saint Joseph County
144	8.9	**Lakes of the Four Seasons** (CDP) Lake County
145	9.0	**Bargersville** (town) Johnson County
146	9.3	**Lawrence** (city) Marion County
147	9.4	**Crown Point** (city) Lake County
147	9.4	**Indianapolis** (city) Marion County
149	9.5	**Lafayette** (city) Tippecanoe County
149	9.5	**South Bend** (city) Saint Joseph County

Note: This section ranks incorporated places and CDPs (Census Designated Places) with populations of 2,500 or more. Unincorporated postal areas were not considered. Please refer to the User Guide for additional information.

Homeownership Rate

Top 150 Places Ranked in *Descending* Order

State Rank	Percent	Place
1	97.0	**Saint John** (town) Lake County
2	96.8	**Granger** (CDP) Saint Joseph County
3	95.9	**Shorewood Forest** (CDP) Porter County
4	95.0	**Lakes of the Four Seasons** (CDP) Lake County
5	93.9	**Hidden Valley** (CDP) Dearborn County
6	93.4	**Melody Hill** (CDP) Vanderburgh County
7	92.6	**Highland** (CDP) Vanderburgh County
8	91.2	**Dyer** (town) Lake County
9	90.7	**Heritage Lake** (CDP) Putnam County
10	90.6	**Leo-Cedarville** (town) Allen County
11	90.4	**Winfield** (town) Lake County
12	89.8	**Dunlap** (CDP) Elkhart County
13	87.5	**Huntertown** (town) Allen County
14	86.8	**Munster** (town) Lake County
14	86.8	**Roselawn** (CDP) Newton County
16	85.3	**Whiteland** (town) Johnson County
16	85.3	**Whitestown** (town) Boone County
18	85.0	**Bright** (CDP) Dearborn County
18	85.0	**McCordsville** (town) Hancock County
20	84.4	**New Whiteland** (town) Johnson County
21	82.5	**Pittsboro** (town) Hendricks County
22	82.4	**Westfield** (city) Hamilton County
23	82.3	**Fishers** (town) Hamilton County
24	81.9	**Georgetown** (town) Floyd County
25	80.8	**Yorktown** (town) Delaware County
26	80.5	**Carmel** (city) Hamilton County
27	80.4	**Smithville-Sanders** (CDP) Monroe County
28	79.7	**Avon** (town) Hendricks County
29	79.2	**Porter** (town) Porter County
30	78.9	**Crown Point** (city) Lake County
31	78.8	**South Haven** (CDP) Porter County
31	78.8	**Westville** (town) LaPorte County
33	78.7	**Highland** (town) Lake County
34	78.4	**Brownsburg** (town) Hendricks County
35	78.3	**Cicero** (town) Hamilton County
36	78.1	**Schererville** (town) Lake County
37	77.9	**Lowell** (town) Lake County
38	77.5	**Zionsville** (town) Boone County
39	77.1	**Cedar Lake** (town) Lake County
40	77.0	**Country Squire Lakes** (CDP) Jennings County
41	76.7	**Sellersburg** (town) Clark County
42	76.5	**Greendale** (city) Dearborn County
43	76.1	**Fort Branch** (town) Gibson County
44	75.5	**Simonton Lake** (CDP) Elkhart County
45	75.4	**Fairmount** (town) Grant County
45	75.4	**New Haven** (city) Allen County
47	74.6	**Noblesville** (city) Hamilton County
48	74.3	**Newburgh** (town) Warrick County
49	73.5	**Garrett** (city) DeKalb County
50	73.4	**Ossian** (town) Wells County
51	73.3	**Hobart** (city) Lake County
52	72.6	**Chesterfield** (town) Madison County
53	72.3	**Chandler** (town) Warrick County
54	72.2	**Auburn** (city) DeKalb County
54	72.2	**Lake Station** (city) Lake County
54	72.2	**Sheridan** (town) Hamilton County
57	71.5	**Gas City** (city) Grant County
58	71.0	**Portage** (city) Porter County
59	70.9	**Covington** (city) Fountain County
59	70.9	**Middlebury** (town) Elkhart County
61	70.8	**Ellettsville** (town) Monroe County
62	70.7	**Chesterton** (town) Porter County
63	70.4	**Bargersville** (town) Johnson County
63	70.4	**Hebron** (town) Porter County
65	69.7	**Centerville** (town) Wayne County
66	69.6	**Hartford City** (city) Blackford County
67	69.5	**Lawrence** (city) Marion County
68	69.3	**Loogootee** (city) Martin County
69	69.1	**Tell City** (city) Perry County
70	69.0	**Plainfield** (town) Hendricks County
71	68.9	**Boonville** (city) Warrick County
72	68.7	**North Terre Haute** (CDP) Vigo County
73	68.6	**Cumberland** (town) Marion County
73	68.6	**De Motte** (town) Jasper County
75	67.9	**Danville** (town) Hendricks County
76	67.8	**Bluffton** (city) Wells County
77	67.7	**Upland** (town) Grant County
77	67.7	**Winona Lake** (town) Kosciusko County
79	67.6	**Bremen** (town) Marshall County
80	67.4	**Brownstown** (town) Jackson County
80	67.4	**Peru** (city) Miami County
82	67.3	**Elwood** (city) Madison County
82	67.3	**Jasper** (city) Dubois County
84	67.2	**Columbia City** (city) Whitley County
84	67.2	**Mount Vernon** (city) Posey County
86	67.1	**Syracuse** (town) Kosciusko County
87	67.0	**Mooresville** (town) Morgan County
88	66.9	**Jeffersonville** (city) Clark County
88	66.9	**Linton** (city) Greene County
90	66.6	**Tipton** (city) Tipton County
91	66.5	**Batesville** (city) Ripley County
91	66.5	**Pendleton** (town) Madison County
93	66.4	**Merrillville** (town) Lake County
94	66.3	**Attica** (city) Fountain County
94	66.3	**Huntington** (city) Huntington County
96	66.1	**Greenfield** (city) Hancock County
96	66.1	**Griffith** (town) Lake County
98	65.9	**Huntingburg** (city) Dubois County
98	65.9	**Wabash** (city) Wabash County
100	65.8	**Berne** (city) Adams County
100	65.8	**Butler** (city) DeKalb County
100	65.8	**Franklin** (city) Johnson County
103	65.5	**Ligonier** (city) Noble County
103	65.5	**Paoli** (town) Orange County
105	65.4	**Mitchell** (city) Lawrence County
106	64.8	**Decatur** (city) Adams County
107	64.6	**Lebanon** (city) Boone County
108	64.2	**Alexandria** (city) Madison County
109	64.1	**Portland** (city) Jay County
110	64.0	**Clinton** (city) Vermillion County
110	64.0	**Nappanee** (city) Elkhart County
112	63.9	**Fortville** (town) Hancock County
113	63.8	**Bicknell** (city) Knox County
114	63.3	**Fort Wayne** (city) Allen County
115	63.0	**Salem** (city) Washington County
116	62.6	**Columbus** (city) Bartholomew County
116	62.6	**Madison** (city) Jefferson County
118	62.4	**Rochester** (city) Fulton County
119	62.3	**Greenwood** (city) Johnson County
120	62.0	**North Manchester** (town) Wabash County
121	61.7	**Kendallville** (city) Noble County
122	61.6	**Bedford** (city) Lawrence County
123	61.5	**Knox** (city) Starke County
124	61.4	**Charlestown** (city) Clark County
124	61.4	**Seymour** (city) Jackson County
126	61.3	**Edinburgh** (town) Johnson County
126	61.3	**Hammond** (city) Lake County
128	61.2	**Rockville** (town) Parke County
129	61.0	**Delphi** (city) Carroll County
130	60.7	**Winchester** (city) Randolph County
131	60.5	**Washington** (city) Daviess County
132	60.4	**Connersville** (city) Fayette County
132	60.4	**Logansport** (city) Cass County
134	60.3	**Frankfort** (city) Clinton County
135	59.9	**Monticello** (city) White County
135	59.9	**Rensselaer** (city) Jasper County
135	59.9	**South Bend** (city) Saint Joseph County
138	59.8	**Clarksville** (town) Clark County
139	59.7	**New Castle** (city) Henry County
140	59.4	**Sullivan** (city) Sullivan County
141	59.3	**Kokomo** (city) Howard County
142	59.2	**Rushville** (city) Rush County
143	59.0	**La Porte** (city) LaPorte County
144	58.9	**Princeton** (city) Gibson County
145	58.8	**Michigan City** (city) LaPorte County
146	58.7	**Hanover** (town) Jefferson County
147	58.6	**Goshen** (city) Elkhart County
147	58.6	**Union City** (city) Randolph County
149	58.5	**Greensburg** (city) Decatur County
150	58.4	**Anderson** (city) Madison County

Note: This section ranks incorporated places and CDPs (Census Designated Places) with populations of 2,500 or more. Unincorporated postal areas were not considered. Please refer to the User Guide for additional information.

Homeownership Rate
Top 150 Places Ranked in *Ascending* Order

State Rank	Percent	Place
1	0.3	**Purdue University** (CDP) Tippecanoe County
2	6.1	**Notre Dame** (CDP) Saint Joseph County
3	29.6	**Grissom AFB** (CDP) Miami County
4	32.4	**West Lafayette** (city) Tippecanoe County
5	33.1	**Bloomington** (city) Monroe County
6	39.7	**Lawrenceburg** (city) Dearborn County
7	41.5	**East Chicago** (city) Lake County
8	48.5	**Speedway** (town) Marion County
9	50.6	**Angola** (city) Steuben County
10	50.8	**Elkhart** (city) Elkhart County
11	51.3	**Lafayette** (city) Tippecanoe County
12	51.4	**Muncie** (city) Delaware County
13	52.3	**Mishawaka** (city) Saint Joseph County
14	52.7	**Gary** (city) Lake County
15	53.5	**Vincennes** (city) Knox County
16	54.8	**Corydon** (town) Harrison County
17	55.4	**Martinsville** (city) Morgan County
17	55.4	**Valparaiso** (city) Porter County
19	55.5	**Terre Haute** (city) Vigo County
19	55.5	**Whiting** (city) Lake County
21	55.6	**Greencastle** (city) Putnam County
22	55.7	**Beech Grove** (city) Marion County
23	55.8	**Indianapolis** (city) Marion County
24	56.0	**Evansville** (city) Vanderburgh County
25	56.1	**New Albany** (city) Floyd County
25	56.1	**Shelbyville** (city) Shelby County
27	56.2	**Plymouth** (city) Marshall County
27	56.2	**Richmond** (city) Wayne County
29	56.3	**Brookville** (town) Franklin County
30	56.4	**Aurora** (city) Dearborn County
31	56.6	**Marion** (city) Grant County
32	56.7	**North Vernon** (city) Jennings County
33	56.9	**Austin** (city) Scott County
34	57.2	**Brazil** (city) Clay County
35	57.5	**Warsaw** (city) Kosciusko County
36	57.7	**Lagrange** (town) LaGrange County
37	58.0	**Crawfordsville** (city) Montgomery County
37	58.0	**Scottsburg** (city) Scott County
39	58.4	**Anderson** (city) Madison County
40	58.5	**Greensburg** (city) Decatur County
41	58.6	**Goshen** (city) Elkhart County
41	58.6	**Union City** (city) Randolph County
43	58.7	**Hanover** (town) Jefferson County
44	58.8	**Michigan City** (city) LaPorte County
45	58.9	**Princeton** (city) Gibson County
46	59.0	**La Porte** (city) LaPorte County
47	59.2	**Rushville** (city) Rush County
48	59.3	**Kokomo** (city) Howard County
49	59.4	**Sullivan** (city) Sullivan County
50	59.7	**New Castle** (city) Henry County
51	59.8	**Clarksville** (town) Clark County
52	59.9	**Monticello** (city) White County
52	59.9	**Rensselaer** (city) Jasper County
52	59.9	**South Bend** (city) Saint Joseph County
55	60.3	**Frankfort** (city) Clinton County
56	60.4	**Connersville** (city) Fayette County
56	60.4	**Logansport** (city) Cass County
58	60.5	**Washington** (city) Daviess County
59	60.7	**Winchester** (city) Randolph County
60	61.0	**Delphi** (city) Carroll County
61	61.2	**Rockville** (town) Parke County
62	61.3	**Edinburgh** (town) Johnson County
62	61.3	**Hammond** (city) Lake County
64	61.4	**Charlestown** (city) Clark County
64	61.4	**Seymour** (city) Jackson County
66	61.5	**Knox** (city) Starke County
67	61.6	**Bedford** (city) Lawrence County
68	61.7	**Kendallville** (city) Noble County
69	62.0	**North Manchester** (town) Wabash County
70	62.3	**Greenwood** (city) Johnson County
71	62.4	**Rochester** (city) Fulton County
72	62.6	**Columbus** (city) Bartholomew County
72	62.6	**Madison** (city) Jefferson County
74	63.0	**Salem** (city) Washington County
75	63.3	**Fort Wayne** (city) Allen County
76	63.8	**Bicknell** (city) Knox County
77	63.9	**Fortville** (town) Hancock County
78	64.0	**Clinton** (city) Vermillion County
78	64.0	**Nappanee** (city) Elkhart County
80	64.1	**Portland** (city) Jay County
81	64.2	**Alexandria** (city) Madison County
82	64.6	**Lebanon** (city) Boone County
83	64.8	**Decatur** (city) Adams County
84	65.4	**Mitchell** (city) Lawrence County
85	65.5	**Ligonier** (city) Noble County
85	65.5	**Paoli** (town) Orange County
87	65.8	**Berne** (city) Adams County
87	65.8	**Butler** (city) DeKalb County
87	65.8	**Franklin** (city) Johnson County
90	65.9	**Huntingburg** (city) Dubois County
90	65.9	**Wabash** (city) Wabash County
92	66.1	**Greenfield** (city) Hancock County
92	66.1	**Griffith** (town) Lake County
94	66.3	**Attica** (city) Fountain County
94	66.3	**Huntington** (city) Huntington County
96	66.4	**Merrillville** (town) Lake County
97	66.5	**Batesville** (city) Ripley County
97	66.5	**Pendleton** (town) Madison County
99	66.6	**Tipton** (city) Tipton County
100	66.9	**Jeffersonville** (city) Clark County
100	66.9	**Linton** (city) Greene County
102	67.0	**Mooresville** (town) Morgan County
103	67.1	**Syracuse** (town) Kosciusko County
104	67.2	**Columbia City** (city) Whitley County
104	67.2	**Mount Vernon** (city) Posey County
106	67.3	**Elwood** (city) Madison County
106	67.3	**Jasper** (city) Dubois County
108	67.4	**Brownstown** (town) Jackson County
108	67.4	**Peru** (city) Miami County
110	67.6	**Bremen** (town) Marshall County
111	67.7	**Upland** (town) Grant County
111	67.7	**Winona Lake** (town) Kosciusko County
113	67.8	**Bluffton** (city) Wells County
114	67.9	**Danville** (town) Hendricks County
115	68.6	**Cumberland** (town) Marion County
115	68.6	**De Motte** (town) Jasper County
117	68.7	**North Terre Haute** (CDP) Vigo County
118	68.9	**Boonville** (city) Warrick County
119	69.0	**Plainfield** (town) Hendricks County
120	69.1	**Tell City** (city) Perry County
121	69.3	**Loogootee** (city) Martin County
122	69.5	**Lawrence** (city) Marion County
123	69.6	**Hartford City** (city) Blackford County
124	69.7	**Centerville** (town) Wayne County
125	70.4	**Bargersville** (town) Johnson County
125	70.4	**Hebron** (town) Porter County
127	70.7	**Chesterton** (town) Porter County
128	70.8	**Ellettsville** (town) Monroe County
129	70.9	**Covington** (city) Fountain County
129	70.9	**Middlebury** (town) Elkhart County
131	71.0	**Portage** (city) Porter County
132	71.5	**Gas City** (city) Grant County
133	72.2	**Auburn** (city) DeKalb County
133	72.2	**Lake Station** (city) Lake County
133	72.2	**Sheridan** (town) Hamilton County
136	72.3	**Chandler** (town) Warrick County
137	72.6	**Chesterfield** (town) Madison County
138	73.3	**Hobart** (city) Lake County
139	73.4	**Ossian** (town) Wells County
140	73.5	**Garrett** (city) DeKalb County
141	74.3	**Newburgh** (town) Warrick County
142	74.6	**Noblesville** (city) Hamilton County
143	75.4	**Fairmount** (town) Grant County
143	75.4	**New Haven** (city) Allen County
145	75.5	**Simonton Lake** (CDP) Elkhart County
146	76.1	**Fort Branch** (town) Gibson County
147	76.5	**Greendale** (city) Dearborn County
148	76.7	**Sellersburg** (town) Clark County
149	77.0	**Country Squire Lakes** (CDP) Jennings County
150	77.1	**Cedar Lake** (town) Lake County

Note: *This section ranks incorporated places and CDPs (Census Designated Places) with populations of 2,500 or more. Unincorporated postal areas were not considered. Please refer to the User Guide for additional information.*

Median Home Value
Top 150 Places Ranked in *Descending* Order

State Rank	Dollars	Place
1	336,700	Zionsville (town) Boone County
2	335,500	Shorewood Forest (CDP) Porter County
3	297,300	Carmel (city) Hamilton County
4	250,300	Saint John (town) Lake County
5	226,700	Winfield (town) Lake County
6	217,400	Westfield (city) Hamilton County
7	209,700	Fishers (town) Hamilton County
8	207,800	Schererville (town) Lake County
9	196,400	Munster (town) Lake County
10	193,200	Granger (CDP) Saint Joseph County
11	191,100	Dyer (town) Lake County
12	188,100	Hidden Valley (CDP) Dearborn County
13	182,500	McCordsville (town) Hancock County
14	181,000	Batesville (city) Ripley County
15	179,700	Lakes of the Four Seasons (CDP) Lake County
16	174,500	West Lafayette (city) Tippecanoe County
17	172,500	Crown Point (city) Lake County
18	171,900	Bloomington (city) Monroe County
19	170,900	Bright (CDP) Dearborn County
20	169,700	Bargersville (town) Johnson County
21	168,900	Chesterton (town) Porter County
22	168,500	Noblesville (city) Hamilton County
23	166,100	Winona Lake (town) Kosciusko County
24	164,900	Avon (town) Hendricks County
25	163,100	Whitestown (town) Boone County
26	162,800	Valparaiso (city) Porter County
27	160,500	Porter (town) Porter County
28	159,600	Leo-Cedarville (town) Allen County
29	154,500	Pittsboro (town) Hendricks County
30	154,100	Highland (CDP) Vanderburgh County
31	153,900	Cedar Lake (town) Lake County
31	153,900	Georgetown (town) Floyd County
31	153,900	Highland (town) Lake County
34	151,000	De Motte (town) Jasper County
35	150,800	Cicero (town) Hamilton County
36	150,600	Melody Hill (CDP) Vanderburgh County
37	150,200	Danville (town) Hendricks County
38	147,900	Plainfield (town) Hendricks County
39	145,600	Lowell (town) Lake County
40	144,100	Brownsburg (town) Hendricks County
41	141,600	Simonton Lake (CDP) Elkhart County
42	141,100	Newburgh (town) Warrick County
43	140,900	Columbus (city) Bartholomew County
43	140,900	Griffith (town) Lake County
45	140,100	Portage (city) Porter County
46	139,600	Heritage Lake (CDP) Putnam County
47	138,500	Cumberland (town) Marion County
48	136,400	Pendleton (town) Madison County
49	136,300	Greendale (city) Dearborn County
50	134,200	Huntertown (town) Allen County
51	132,800	Hobart (city) Lake County
52	131,900	Greenwood (city) Johnson County
53	131,600	Hebron (town) Porter County
54	130,400	Merrillville (town) Lake County
55	129,900	Nappanee (city) Elkhart County
56	128,600	Jasper (city) Dubois County
57	126,300	Jeffersonville (city) Clark County
57	126,300	Whiteland (town) Johnson County
59	125,500	Lawrence (city) Marion County
60	125,100	Mooresville (town) Morgan County
61	125,000	Dunlap (CDP) Elkhart County
61	125,000	Middlebury (town) Elkhart County
61	125,000	Yorktown (town) Delaware County
64	123,600	Lawrenceburg (city) Dearborn County
64	123,600	Smithville-Sanders (CDP) Monroe County
66	121,100	Upland (town) Grant County
67	121,000	Roselawn (CDP) Newton County
68	119,400	Ellettsville (town) Monroe County
69	118,900	Fortville (town) Hancock County
70	118,100	Greenfield (city) Hancock County
71	118,000	Indianapolis (city) Marion County
72	117,800	Madison (city) Jefferson County
73	117,500	Speedway (town) Marion County
74	115,900	Warsaw (city) Kosciusko County
75	115,700	Franklin (city) Johnson County
76	115,400	Greencastle (city) Putnam County
77	115,200	Brownstown (town) Jackson County
78	114,800	Aurora (city) Dearborn County
79	114,200	Clarksville (town) Clark County
80	113,000	Brookville (town) Franklin County
81	112,700	Lebanon (city) Boone County
82	112,100	Whiting (city) Lake County
83	111,600	Rensselaer (city) Jasper County
84	110,600	Charlestown (city) Clark County
85	110,100	Bremen (town) Marshall County
85	110,100	New Albany (city) Floyd County
87	109,700	South Haven (CDP) Porter County
88	109,500	Ossian (town) Wells County
89	109,300	Sellersburg (town) Clark County
90	109,100	Angola (city) Steuben County
91	108,200	Westville (town) LaPorte County
92	107,900	Huntingburg (city) Dubois County
93	107,800	Goshen (city) Elkhart County
94	107,600	Syracuse (town) Kosciusko County
95	106,200	Fort Branch (town) Gibson County
96	104,800	Auburn (city) DeKalb County
97	103,300	Greensburg (city) Decatur County
98	102,200	Lafayette (city) Tippecanoe County
99	101,500	Sheridan (town) Hamilton County
100	101,200	Seymour (city) Jackson County
101	99,900	Fort Wayne (city) Allen County
102	99,300	Scottsburg (city) Scott County
103	98,500	Shelbyville (city) Shelby County
104	97,400	Martinsville (city) Morgan County
105	96,300	Monticello (city) White County
106	96,000	Covington (city) Fountain County
107	95,300	New Whiteland (town) Johnson County
108	94,800	Centerville (town) Wayne County
108	94,800	Mount Vernon (city) Posey County
110	94,700	Columbia City (city) Whitley County
110	94,700	North Manchester (town) Wabash County
112	94,000	Bluffton (city) Wells County
113	93,900	Mishawaka (city) Saint Joseph County
114	93,800	Decatur (city) Adams County
115	93,600	Beech Grove (city) Marion County
116	93,300	Lagrange (town) LaGrange County
117	93,100	Michigan City (city) LaPorte County
118	92,400	Hammond (city) Lake County
119	92,200	New Haven (city) Allen County
120	91,900	Berne (city) Adams County
121	91,600	Crawfordsville (city) Montgomery County
121	91,600	La Porte (city) LaPorte County
123	90,600	Boonville (city) Warrick County
124	90,200	Tell City (city) Perry County
125	90,000	Evansville (city) Vanderburgh County
126	89,500	Rochester (city) Fulton County
127	89,100	North Terre Haute (CDP) Vigo County
128	88,600	Bedford (city) Lawrence County
129	87,800	Corydon (town) Harrison County
130	86,700	Tipton (city) Tipton County
131	85,900	Elkhart (city) Elkhart County
132	85,700	Plymouth (city) Marshall County
133	85,300	Chandler (town) Warrick County
134	85,100	South Bend (city) Saint Joseph County
135	84,400	Ligonier (city) Noble County
136	84,300	Edinburgh (town) Johnson County
137	84,000	Kokomo (city) Howard County
138	83,900	Attica (city) Fountain County
139	82,900	Delphi (city) Carroll County
139	82,900	East Chicago (city) Lake County
139	82,900	Kendallville (city) Noble County
142	82,400	Princeton (city) Gibson County
143	82,300	Frankfort (city) Clinton County
143	82,300	Garrett (city) DeKalb County
145	82,200	Rockville (town) Parke County
146	82,000	Rushville (city) Rush County
147	81,700	Loogootee (city) Martin County
148	81,300	Richmond (city) Wayne County
149	81,200	Lake Station (city) Lake County
150	80,700	Grissom AFB (CDP) Miami County

Note: This section ranks incorporated places and CDPs (Census Designated Places) with populations of 2,500 or more. Unincorporated postal areas were not considered. Please refer to the User Guide for additional information.

Median Home Value

Top 150 Places Ranked in *Ascending* Order

State Rank	Dollars	Place
1	28,800	**Country Squire Lakes** (CDP) Jennings County
2	53,100	**Bicknell** (city) Knox County
3	53,700	**Union City** (city) Randolph County
4	57,000	**Peru** (city) Miami County
5	60,700	**Hartford City** (city) Blackford County
6	65,000	**Linton** (city) Greene County
7	65,100	**Logansport** (city) Cass County
8	65,200	**Marion** (city) Grant County
9	65,400	**Gary** (city) Lake County
10	66,000	**Clinton** (city) Vermillion County
11	66,400	**Chesterfield** (town) Madison County
12	66,800	**Winchester** (city) Randolph County
13	67,000	**Alexandria** (city) Madison County
14	67,400	**New Castle** (city) Henry County
15	68,400	**Portland** (city) Jay County
16	68,600	**Butler** (city) DeKalb County
17	68,900	**Connersville** (city) Fayette County
18	70,100	**Sullivan** (city) Sullivan County
19	72,500	**Brazil** (city) Clay County
20	73,200	**Elwood** (city) Madison County
20	73,200	**Muncie** (city) Delaware County
22	73,600	**Anderson** (city) Madison County
23	74,000	**Vincennes** (city) Knox County
24	74,300	**Fairmount** (town) Grant County
25	74,500	**Austin** (city) Scott County
26	75,000	**Huntington** (city) Huntington County
27	75,100	**Paoli** (town) Orange County
28	75,500	**Hanover** (town) Jefferson County
29	75,800	**Mitchell** (city) Lawrence County
30	76,700	**Washington** (city) Daviess County
31	76,800	**Terre Haute** (city) Vigo County
32	77,800	**Wabash** (city) Wabash County
33	78,000	**Gas City** (city) Grant County
34	78,400	**North Vernon** (city) Jennings County
35	79,600	**Knox** (city) Starke County
36	80,700	**Grissom AFB** (CDP) Miami County
36	80,700	**Salem** (city) Washington County
38	81,200	**Lake Station** (city) Lake County
39	81,300	**Richmond** (city) Wayne County
40	81,700	**Loogootee** (city) Martin County
41	82,000	**Rushville** (city) Rush County
42	82,200	**Rockville** (town) Parke County
43	82,300	**Frankfort** (city) Clinton County
43	82,300	**Garrett** (city) DeKalb County
45	82,400	**Princeton** (city) Gibson County
46	82,900	**Delphi** (city) Carroll County
46	82,900	**East Chicago** (city) Lake County
46	82,900	**Kendallville** (city) Noble County
49	83,900	**Attica** (city) Fountain County
50	84,000	**Kokomo** (city) Howard County
51	84,300	**Edinburgh** (town) Johnson County
52	84,400	**Ligonier** (city) Noble County
53	85,100	**South Bend** (city) Saint Joseph County
54	85,300	**Chandler** (town) Warrick County
55	85,700	**Plymouth** (city) Marshall County
56	85,900	**Elkhart** (city) Elkhart County
57	86,700	**Tipton** (city) Tipton County
58	87,800	**Corydon** (town) Harrison County
59	88,600	**Bedford** (city) Lawrence County
60	89,100	**North Terre Haute** (CDP) Vigo County
61	89,500	**Rochester** (city) Fulton County
62	90,000	**Evansville** (city) Vanderburgh County
63	90,200	**Tell City** (city) Perry County
64	90,600	**Boonville** (city) Warrick County
65	91,600	**Crawfordsville** (city) Montgomery County
65	91,600	**La Porte** (city) LaPorte County
67	91,900	**Berne** (city) Adams County
68	92,200	**New Haven** (city) Allen County
69	92,400	**Hammond** (city) Lake County
70	93,100	**Michigan City** (city) LaPorte County
71	93,300	**Lagrange** (town) LaGrange County
72	93,600	**Beech Grove** (city) Marion County
73	93,800	**Decatur** (city) Adams County
74	93,900	**Mishawaka** (city) Saint Joseph County
75	94,000	**Bluffton** (city) Wells County
76	94,700	**Columbia City** (city) Whitley County
76	94,700	**North Manchester** (town) Wabash County
78	94,800	**Centerville** (town) Wayne County
78	94,800	**Mount Vernon** (city) Posey County
80	95,300	**New Whiteland** (town) Johnson County
81	96,000	**Covington** (city) Fountain County
82	96,300	**Monticello** (city) White County
83	97,400	**Martinsville** (city) Morgan County
84	98,500	**Shelbyville** (city) Shelby County
85	99,300	**Scottsburg** (city) Scott County
86	99,900	**Fort Wayne** (city) Allen County
87	101,200	**Seymour** (city) Jackson County
88	101,500	**Sheridan** (town) Hamilton County
89	102,200	**Lafayette** (city) Tippecanoe County
90	103,300	**Greensburg** (city) Decatur County
91	104,800	**Auburn** (city) DeKalb County
92	106,200	**Fort Branch** (town) Gibson County
93	107,600	**Syracuse** (town) Kosciusko County
94	107,800	**Goshen** (city) Elkhart County
95	107,900	**Huntingburg** (city) Dubois County
96	108,200	**Westville** (town) LaPorte County
97	109,100	**Angola** (city) Steuben County
98	109,300	**Sellersburg** (town) Clark County
99	109,500	**Ossian** (town) Wells County
100	109,700	**South Haven** (CDP) Porter County
101	110,100	**Bremen** (town) Marshall County
101	110,100	**New Albany** (city) Floyd County
103	110,600	**Charlestown** (city) Clark County
104	111,600	**Rensselaer** (city) Jasper County
105	112,100	**Whiting** (city) Lake County
106	112,700	**Lebanon** (city) Boone County
107	113,000	**Brookville** (town) Franklin County
108	114,200	**Clarksville** (town) Clark County
109	114,800	**Aurora** (city) Dearborn County
110	115,200	**Brownstown** (town) Jackson County
111	115,400	**Greencastle** (city) Putnam County
112	115,700	**Franklin** (city) Johnson County
113	115,900	**Warsaw** (city) Kosciusko County
114	117,500	**Speedway** (town) Marion County
115	117,800	**Madison** (city) Jefferson County
116	118,000	**Indianapolis** (city) Marion County
117	118,100	**Greenfield** (city) Hancock County
118	118,900	**Fortville** (town) Hancock County
119	119,400	**Ellettsville** (town) Monroe County
120	121,000	**Roselawn** (CDP) Newton County
121	121,100	**Upland** (town) Grant County
122	123,600	**Lawrenceburg** (city) Dearborn County
122	123,600	**Smithville-Sanders** (CDP) Monroe County
124	125,000	**Dunlap** (CDP) Elkhart County
124	125,000	**Middlebury** (town) Elkhart County
124	125,000	**Yorktown** (town) Delaware County
127	125,100	**Mooresville** (town) Morgan County
128	125,500	**Lawrence** (city) Marion County
129	126,300	**Jeffersonville** (city) Clark County
129	126,300	**Whiteland** (town) Johnson County
131	128,600	**Jasper** (city) Dubois County
132	129,900	**Nappanee** (city) Elkhart County
133	130,400	**Merrillville** (town) Lake County
134	131,600	**Hebron** (town) Porter County
135	131,900	**Greenwood** (city) Johnson County
136	132,900	**Hobart** (city) Lake County
137	134,200	**Huntertown** (town) Allen County
138	136,300	**Greendale** (city) Dearborn County
139	136,400	**Pendleton** (town) Madison County
140	138,500	**Cumberland** (town) Marion County
141	139,600	**Heritage Lake** (CDP) Putnam County
142	140,100	**Portage** (city) Porter County
143	140,900	**Columbus** (city) Bartholomew County
143	140,900	**Griffith** (town) Lake County
145	141,100	**Newburgh** (town) Warrick County
146	141,600	**Simonton Lake** (CDP) Elkhart County
147	144,100	**Brownsburg** (town) Hendricks County
148	145,600	**Lowell** (town) Lake County
149	147,900	**Plainfield** (town) Hendricks County
150	150,200	**Danville** (town) Hendricks County

Note: This section ranks incorporated places and CDPs (Census Designated Places) with populations of 2,500 or more. Unincorporated postal areas were not considered. Please refer to the User Guide for additional information.

Median Year Structure Built
Top 150 Places Ranked in *Descending* Order

State Rank	Year	Place
1	2005	**Whitestown** (town) Boone County
2	2003	**McCordsville** (town) Hancock County
3	2001	**Avon** (town) Hendricks County
3	2001	**Westfield** (city) Hamilton County
3	2001	**Winfield** (town) Lake County
6	2000	**Huntertown** (town) Allen County
7	1998	**Fishers** (town) Hamilton County
7	1998	**Pittsboro** (town) Hendricks County
9	1997	**Noblesville** (city) Hamilton County
10	1996	**Bargersville** (town) Johnson County
10	1996	**Saint John** (town) Lake County
12	1995	**Brownsburg** (town) Hendricks County
12	1995	**Heritage Lake** (CDP) Putnam County
14	1994	**Hidden Valley** (CDP) Dearborn County
15	1993	**Carmel** (city) Hamilton County
15	1993	**Danville** (town) Hendricks County
17	1992	**De Motte** (town) Jasper County
17	1992	**Notre Dame** (CDP) Saint Joseph County
17	1992	**Zionsville** (town) Boone County
20	1991	**Greenwood** (city) Johnson County
20	1991	**Leo-Cedarville** (town) Allen County
22	1990	**Franklin** (city) Johnson County
22	1990	**Lawrence** (city) Marion County
22	1990	**Middlebury** (town) Elkhart County
22	1990	**Plainfield** (town) Hendricks County
26	1989	**Greenfield** (city) Hancock County
26	1989	**Whiteland** (town) Johnson County
28	1987	**Granger** (CDP) Saint Joseph County
28	1987	**Schererville** (town) Lake County
28	1987	**Westville** (town) LaPorte County
31	1985	**Country Squire Lakes** (CDP) Jennings County
32	1984	**Bright** (CDP) Dearborn County
32	1984	**Fortville** (town) Hancock County
32	1984	**Shorewood Forest** (CDP) Porter County
35	1983	**Ellettsville** (town) Monroe County
35	1983	**Hebron** (town) Porter County
35	1983	**Winona Lake** (town) Kosciusko County
38	1982	**Highland** (CDP) Vanderburgh County
38	1982	**Roselawn** (CDP) Newton County
40	1981	**Crown Point** (city) Lake County
40	1981	**Smithville-Sanders** (CDP) Monroe County
42	1980	**Chesterton** (town) Porter County
42	1980	**Dyer** (town) Lake County
44	1979	**Cicero** (town) Hamilton County
44	1979	**Georgetown** (town) Floyd County
44	1979	**Lakes of the Four Seasons** (CDP) Lake County
44	1979	**West Lafayette** (city) Tippecanoe County
48	1978	**Bloomington** (city) Monroe County
48	1978	**Goshen** (city) Elkhart County
48	1978	**Jasper** (city) Dubois County
48	1978	**Ossian** (town) Wells County
48	1978	**Portage** (city) Porter County
48	1978	**Porter** (town) Porter County
54	1977	**Batesville** (city) Ripley County
54	1977	**Lowell** (town) Lake County
54	1977	**Simonton Lake** (CDP) Elkhart County
57	1976	**Angola** (city) Steuben County
57	1976	**Cumberland** (town) Marion County
57	1976	**Dunlap** (CDP) Elkhart County
57	1976	**Jeffersonville** (city) Clark County
57	1976	**Nappanee** (city) Elkhart County
57	1976	**Valparaiso** (city) Porter County
63	1975	**Auburn** (city) DeKalb County
63	1975	**Chandler** (town) Warrick County
63	1975	**Plymouth** (city) Marshall County
66	1974	**Columbia City** (city) Whitley County
66	1974	**Mooresville** (town) Morgan County
68	1973	**Cedar Lake** (town) Lake County
68	1973	**Hanover** (town) Jefferson County
68	1973	**Lebanon** (city) Boone County
68	1973	**Merrillville** (town) Lake County
68	1973	**Scottsburg** (city) Scott County
68	1973	**Seymour** (city) Jackson County
74	1972	**Columbus** (city) Bartholomew County
74	1972	**Melody Hill** (CDP) Vanderburgh County
74	1972	**Newburgh** (town) Warrick County
74	1972	**Upland** (town) Grant County
74	1972	**Warsaw** (city) Kosciusko County
79	1971	**Brownstown** (town) Jackson County
79	1971	**Mishawaka** (city) Saint Joseph County
79	1971	**Munster** (town) Lake County
79	1971	**New Whiteland** (town) Johnson County
79	1971	**Sheridan** (town) Hamilton County
79	1971	**Yorktown** (town) Delaware County
85	1970	**Berne** (city) Adams County
85	1970	**Charlestown** (city) Clark County
85	1970	**Clarksville** (town) Clark County
85	1970	**Garrett** (city) DeKalb County
85	1970	**Greensburg** (city) Decatur County
85	1970	**Lafayette** (city) Tippecanoe County
85	1970	**New Haven** (city) Allen County
85	1970	**Sellersburg** (town) Clark County
85	1970	**Syracuse** (town) Kosciusko County
94	1969	**Indianapolis** (city) Marion County
94	1969	**Lawrenceburg** (city) Dearborn County
94	1969	**Paoli** (town) Orange County
94	1969	**Shelbyville** (city) Shelby County
98	1968	**Austin** (city) Scott County
98	1968	**Fort Wayne** (city) Allen County
98	1968	**Griffith** (town) Lake County
98	1968	**Pendleton** (town) Madison County
102	1967	**Bluffton** (city) Wells County
102	1967	**Gas City** (city) Grant County
102	1967	**Hobart** (city) Lake County
102	1967	**South Haven** (CDP) Porter County
106	1966	**Highland** (town) Lake County
106	1966	**Kendallville** (city) Noble County
106	1966	**Mount Vernon** (city) Posey County
106	1966	**North Terre Haute** (CDP) Vigo County
110	1965	**Edinburgh** (town) Johnson County
110	1965	**North Vernon** (city) Jennings County
110	1965	**Rochester** (city) Fulton County
110	1965	**Salem** (city) Washington County
114	1964	**Boonville** (city) Warrick County
114	1964	**Greencastle** (city) Putnam County
114	1964	**Linton** (city) Greene County
114	1964	**Madison** (city) Jefferson County
114	1964	**Mitchell** (city) Lawrence County
119	1963	**Kokomo** (city) Howard County
119	1963	**Lagrange** (town) LaGrange County
121	1962	**Covington** (city) Fountain County
121	1962	**Fort Branch** (town) Gibson County
121	1962	**Huntingburg** (city) Dubois County
121	1962	**Tell City** (city) Perry County
125	1961	**Chesterfield** (town) Madison County
125	1961	**Loogootee** (city) Martin County
125	1961	**Martinsville** (city) Morgan County
125	1961	**Princeton** (city) Gibson County
125	1961	**Speedway** (town) Marion County
130	1960	**Beech Grove** (city) Marion County
130	1960	**Bremen** (town) Marshall County
130	1960	**Butler** (city) DeKalb County
130	1960	**Elkhart** (city) Elkhart County
130	1960	**Fairmount** (town) Grant County
130	1960	**Hartford City** (city) Blackford County
130	1960	**Monticello** (city) White County
137	1959	**Anderson** (city) Madison County
137	1959	**Decatur** (city) Adams County
137	1959	**Greendale** (city) Dearborn County
137	1959	**Grissom AFB** (CDP) Miami County
137	1959	**Michigan City** (city) LaPorte County
137	1959	**Muncie** (city) Delaware County
137	1959	**New Albany** (city) Floyd County
137	1959	**North Manchester** (town) Wabash County
137	1959	**Purdue University** (CDP) Tippecanoe County
146	1958	**Brookville** (town) Franklin County
146	1958	**Crawfordsville** (city) Montgomery County
146	1958	**Sullivan** (city) Sullivan County
149	1957	**Brazil** (city) Clay County
149	1957	**Knox** (city) Starke County

Note: This section ranks incorporated places and CDPs (Census Designated Places) with populations of 2,500 or more. Unincorporated postal areas were not considered. Please refer to the User Guide for additional information.

Median Year Structure Built
Top 150 Places Ranked in *Ascending* Order

State Rank	Year	Place
1	<1940	**Bicknell** (city) Knox County
1	<1940	**Whiting** (city) Lake County
3	1940	**East Chicago** (city) Lake County
3	1940	**Peru** (city) Miami County
5	1941	**Logansport** (city) Cass County
6	1942	**Clinton** (city) Vermillion County
7	1945	**Elwood** (city) Madison County
8	1947	**Aurora** (city) Dearborn County
9	1949	**Hammond** (city) Lake County
9	1949	**Ligonier** (city) Noble County
9	1949	**Terre Haute** (city) Vigo County
12	1950	**Connersville** (city) Fayette County
12	1950	**Frankfort** (city) Clinton County
12	1950	**Huntington** (city) Huntington County
15	1951	**Rushville** (city) Rush County
16	1952	**Vincennes** (city) Knox County
17	1953	**Delphi** (city) Carroll County
17	1953	**Portland** (city) Jay County
17	1953	**Tipton** (city) Tipton County
17	1953	**Wabash** (city) Wabash County
21	1954	**Alexandria** (city) Madison County
21	1954	**Attica** (city) Fountain County
21	1954	**Bedford** (city) Lawrence County
21	1954	**La Porte** (city) LaPorte County
21	1954	**Richmond** (city) Wayne County
21	1954	**South Bend** (city) Saint Joseph County
21	1954	**Washington** (city) Daviess County
21	1954	**Winchester** (city) Randolph County
29	1955	**Corydon** (town) Harrison County
29	1955	**Gary** (city) Lake County
29	1955	**Lake Station** (city) Lake County
29	1955	**Union City** (city) Randolph County
33	1956	**Centerville** (town) Wayne County
33	1956	**Evansville** (city) Vanderburgh County
33	1956	**New Castle** (city) Henry County
36	1957	**Brazil** (city) Clay County
36	1957	**Knox** (city) Starke County
36	1957	**Marion** (city) Grant County
36	1957	**Rensselaer** (city) Jasper County
36	1957	**Rockville** (town) Parke County
41	1958	**Brookville** (town) Franklin County
41	1958	**Crawfordsville** (city) Montgomery County
41	1958	**Sullivan** (city) Sullivan County
44	1959	**Anderson** (city) Madison County
44	1959	**Decatur** (city) Adams County
44	1959	**Greendale** (city) Dearborn County
44	1959	**Grissom AFB** (CDP) Miami County
44	1959	**Michigan City** (city) LaPorte County
44	1959	**Muncie** (city) Delaware County
44	1959	**New Albany** (city) Floyd County
44	1959	**North Manchester** (town) Wabash County
44	1959	**Purdue University** (CDP) Tippecanoe County
53	1960	**Beech Grove** (city) Marion County
53	1960	**Bremen** (town) Marshall County
53	1960	**Butler** (city) DeKalb County
53	1960	**Elkhart** (city) Elkhart County
53	1960	**Fairmount** (town) Grant County
53	1960	**Hartford City** (city) Blackford County
53	1960	**Monticello** (city) White County
60	1961	**Chesterfield** (town) Madison County
60	1961	**Loogootee** (city) Martin County
60	1961	**Martinsville** (city) Morgan County
60	1961	**Princeton** (city) Gibson County
60	1961	**Speedway** (town) Marion County
65	1962	**Covington** (city) Fountain County
65	1962	**Fort Branch** (town) Gibson County
65	1962	**Huntingburg** (city) Dubois County
65	1962	**Tell City** (city) Perry County
69	1963	**Kokomo** (city) Howard County
69	1963	**Lagrange** (town) LaGrange County
71	1964	**Boonville** (city) Warrick County
71	1964	**Greencastle** (city) Putnam County
71	1964	**Linton** (city) Greene County
71	1964	**Madison** (city) Jefferson County
71	1964	**Mitchell** (city) Lawrence County
76	1965	**Edinburgh** (town) Johnson County
76	1965	**North Vernon** (city) Jennings County
76	1965	**Rochester** (city) Fulton County
76	1965	**Salem** (city) Washington County
80	1966	**Highland** (town) Lake County
80	1966	**Kendallville** (city) Noble County
80	1966	**Mount Vernon** (city) Posey County
80	1966	**North Terre Haute** (CDP) Vigo County
84	1967	**Bluffton** (city) Wells County
84	1967	**Gas City** (city) Grant County
84	1967	**Hobart** (city) Lake County
84	1967	**South Haven** (CDP) Porter County
88	1968	**Austin** (city) Scott County
88	1968	**Fort Wayne** (city) Allen County
88	1968	**Griffith** (town) Lake County
88	1968	**Pendleton** (town) Madison County
92	1969	**Indianapolis** (city) Marion County
92	1969	**Lawrenceburg** (city) Dearborn County
92	1969	**Paoli** (town) Orange County
92	1969	**Shelbyville** (city) Shelby County
96	1970	**Berne** (city) Adams County
96	1970	**Charlestown** (city) Clark County
96	1970	**Clarksville** (town) Clark County
96	1970	**Garrett** (city) DeKalb County
96	1970	**Greensburg** (city) Decatur County
96	1970	**Lafayette** (city) Tippecanoe County
96	1970	**New Haven** (city) Allen County
96	1970	**Sellersburg** (town) Clark County
96	1970	**Syracuse** (town) Kosciusko County
105	1971	**Brownstown** (town) Jackson County
105	1971	**Mishawaka** (city) Saint Joseph County
105	1971	**Munster** (town) Lake County
105	1971	**New Whiteland** (town) Johnson County
105	1971	**Sheridan** (town) Hamilton County
105	1971	**Yorktown** (town) Delaware County
111	1972	**Columbus** (city) Bartholomew County
111	1972	**Melody Hill** (CDP) Vanderburgh County
111	1972	**Newburgh** (town) Warrick County
111	1972	**Upland** (town) Grant County
111	1972	**Warsaw** (city) Kosciusko County
116	1973	**Cedar Lake** (town) Lake County
116	1973	**Hanover** (town) Jefferson County
116	1973	**Lebanon** (city) Boone County
116	1973	**Merrillville** (town) Lake County
116	1973	**Scottsburg** (city) Scott County
116	1973	**Seymour** (city) Jackson County
122	1974	**Columbia City** (city) Whitley County
122	1974	**Mooresville** (town) Morgan County
124	1975	**Auburn** (city) DeKalb County
124	1975	**Chandler** (town) Warrick County
124	1975	**Plymouth** (city) Marshall County
127	1976	**Angola** (city) Steuben County
127	1976	**Cumberland** (town) Marion County
127	1976	**Dunlap** (CDP) Elkhart County
127	1976	**Jeffersonville** (city) Clark County
127	1976	**Nappanee** (city) Elkhart County
127	1976	**Valparaiso** (city) Porter County
133	1977	**Batesville** (city) Ripley County
133	1977	**Lowell** (town) Lake County
133	1977	**Simonton Lake** (CDP) Elkhart County
136	1978	**Bloomington** (city) Monroe County
136	1978	**Goshen** (city) Elkhart County
136	1978	**Jasper** (city) Dubois County
136	1978	**Ossian** (town) Wells County
136	1978	**Portage** (city) Porter County
136	1978	**Porter** (town) Porter County
142	1979	**Cicero** (town) Hamilton County
142	1979	**Georgetown** (town) Floyd County
142	1979	**Lakes of the Four Seasons** (CDP) Lake County
142	1979	**West Lafayette** (city) Tippecanoe County
146	1980	**Chesterton** (town) Porter County
146	1980	**Dyer** (town) Lake County
148	1981	**Crown Point** (city) Lake County
148	1981	**Smithville-Sanders** (CDP) Monroe County
150	1982	**Highland** (CDP) Vanderburgh County

Note: *This section ranks incorporated places and CDPs (Census Designated Places) with populations of 2,500 or more. Unincorporated postal areas were not considered. Please refer to the User Guide for additional information.*

Homeowner Vacancy Rate

Top 150 Places Ranked in *Descending* Order

State Rank	Percent	Place
1	7.4	**Lawrenceburg** (city) Dearborn County
2	5.9	**Sullivan** (city) Sullivan County
3	5.8	**Plymouth** (city) Marshall County
4	5.7	**Alexandria** (city) Madison County
4	5.7	**Butler** (city) DeKalb County
6	5.5	**Richmond** (city) Wayne County
7	5.3	**Elwood** (city) Madison County
8	5.2	**Hartford City** (city) Blackford County
9	5.1	**Wabash** (city) Wabash County
10	4.9	**Grissom AFB** (CDP) Miami County
11	4.8	**Bedford** (city) Lawrence County
12	4.7	**Centerville** (town) Wayne County
12	4.7	**Huntington** (city) Huntington County
12	4.7	**Lagrange** (town) LaGrange County
15	4.6	**Country Squire Lakes** (CDP) Jennings County
15	4.6	**Smithville-Sanders** (CDP) Monroe County
17	4.5	**Anderson** (city) Madison County
17	4.5	**Chesterfield** (town) Madison County
17	4.5	**Clinton** (city) Vermillion County
17	4.5	**Logansport** (city) Cass County
17	4.5	**Shelbyville** (city) Shelby County
17	4.5	**Sheridan** (town) Hamilton County
23	4.4	**Angola** (city) Steuben County
23	4.4	**Kokomo** (city) Howard County
23	4.4	**Middlebury** (town) Elkhart County
23	4.4	**Princeton** (city) Gibson County
23	4.4	**Rensselaer** (city) Jasper County
28	4.2	**North Manchester** (town) Wabash County
28	4.2	**Tell City** (city) Perry County
30	4.1	**Brookville** (town) Franklin County
31	4.0	**Auburn** (city) DeKalb County
31	4.0	**Aurora** (city) Dearborn County
31	4.0	**Mishawaka** (city) Saint Joseph County
31	4.0	**New Castle** (city) Henry County
35	3.9	**Elkhart** (city) Elkhart County
35	3.9	**Madison** (city) Jefferson County
35	3.9	**Monticello** (city) White County
35	3.9	**New Albany** (city) Floyd County
35	3.9	**Rockville** (town) Parke County
35	3.9	**Rushville** (city) Rush County
35	3.9	**South Bend** (city) Saint Joseph County
42	3.8	**Bicknell** (city) Knox County
42	3.8	**Brazil** (city) Clay County
42	3.8	**Decatur** (city) Adams County
42	3.8	**Greencastle** (city) Putnam County
42	3.8	**Mount Vernon** (city) Posey County
42	3.8	**Muncie** (city) Delaware County
48	3.7	**Evansville** (city) Vanderburgh County
48	3.7	**Goshen** (city) Elkhart County
48	3.7	**Kendallville** (city) Noble County
48	3.7	**Knox** (city) Starke County
48	3.7	**Lake Station** (city) Lake County
48	3.7	**Marion** (city) Grant County
48	3.7	**Peru** (city) Miami County
48	3.7	**Scottsburg** (city) Scott County
56	3.6	**Berne** (city) Adams County
56	3.6	**East Chicago** (city) Lake County
56	3.6	**Gary** (city) Lake County
56	3.6	**Heritage Lake** (CDP) Putnam County
56	3.6	**Portland** (city) Jay County
56	3.6	**Syracuse** (town) Kosciusko County
56	3.6	**Whiting** (city) Lake County
63	3.5	**Charlestown** (city) Clark County
63	3.5	**Crawfordsville** (city) Montgomery County
63	3.5	**Delphi** (city) Carroll County
63	3.5	**Nappanee** (city) Elkhart County
63	3.5	**North Vernon** (city) Jennings County
63	3.5	**Washington** (city) Daviess County
63	3.5	**Winchester** (city) Randolph County
70	3.4	**Avon** (town) Hendricks County
70	3.4	**Cedar Lake** (town) Lake County
70	3.4	**Frankfort** (city) Clinton County
70	3.4	**Garrett** (city) DeKalb County
70	3.4	**Greenfield** (city) Hancock County
70	3.4	**Indianapolis** (city) Marion County
70	3.4	**Martinsville** (city) Morgan County
70	3.4	**Rochester** (city) Fulton County
70	3.4	**Seymour** (city) Jackson County
79	3.3	**Austin** (city) Scott County
79	3.3	**Boonville** (city) Warrick County
79	3.3	**Cicero** (town) Hamilton County
79	3.3	**Connersville** (city) Fayette County
79	3.3	**Edinburgh** (town) Johnson County
79	3.3	**Greensburg** (city) Decatur County
79	3.3	**Lebanon** (city) Boone County
79	3.3	**Ligonier** (city) Noble County
79	3.3	**Salem** (city) Washington County
79	3.3	**Winfield** (town) Lake County
89	3.2	**Beech Grove** (city) Marion County
89	3.2	**Brownstown** (town) Jackson County
89	3.2	**Hanover** (town) Jefferson County
89	3.2	**Lawrence** (city) Marion County
89	3.2	**Merrillville** (town) Lake County
89	3.2	**Terre Haute** (city) Vigo County
89	3.2	**Warsaw** (city) Kosciusko County
89	3.2	**Yorktown** (town) Delaware County
97	3.1	**Ellettsville** (town) Monroe County
97	3.1	**La Porte** (city) LaPorte County
97	3.1	**Vincennes** (city) Knox County
100	3.0	**Linton** (city) Greene County
100	3.0	**Michigan City** (city) LaPorte County
102	2.9	**Bargersville** (town) Johnson County
102	2.9	**Bluffton** (city) Wells County
102	2.9	**Bremen** (town) Marshall County
102	2.9	**Columbus** (city) Bartholomew County
102	2.9	**Fort Wayne** (city) Allen County
102	2.9	**Georgetown** (town) Floyd County
108	2.8	**Attica** (city) Fountain County
108	2.8	**Columbia City** (city) Whitley County
108	2.8	**Huntertown** (town) Allen County
108	2.8	**Lafayette** (city) Tippecanoe County
108	2.8	**Whitestown** (town) Boone County
113	2.7	**Clarksville** (town) Clark County
113	2.7	**Cumberland** (town) Marion County
113	2.7	**Franklin** (city) Johnson County
113	2.7	**Mitchell** (city) Lawrence County
113	2.7	**Paoli** (town) Orange County
113	2.7	**Tipton** (city) Tipton County
119	2.6	**Hammond** (city) Lake County
119	2.6	**Huntingburg** (city) Dubois County
119	2.6	**Jasper** (city) Dubois County
119	2.6	**Noblesville** (city) Hamilton County
119	2.6	**West Lafayette** (city) Tippecanoe County
124	2.5	**Fortville** (town) Hancock County
124	2.5	**Greendale** (city) Dearborn County
124	2.5	**Greenwood** (city) Johnson County
124	2.5	**New Whiteland** (town) Johnson County
124	2.5	**Simonton Lake** (CDP) Elkhart County
124	2.5	**Westfield** (city) Hamilton County
130	2.4	**Chandler** (town) Warrick County
130	2.4	**Corydon** (town) Harrison County
130	2.4	**De Motte** (town) Jasper County
130	2.4	**Fort Branch** (town) Gibson County
130	2.4	**Gas City** (city) Grant County
130	2.4	**Sellersburg** (town) Clark County
136	2.3	**Jeffersonville** (city) Clark County
136	2.3	**Lowell** (town) Lake County
136	2.3	**Valparaiso** (city) Porter County
136	2.3	**Winona Lake** (town) Kosciusko County
140	2.2	**North Terre Haute** (CDP) Vigo County
140	2.2	**Union City** (city) Randolph County
142	2.1	**Chesterton** (town) Porter County
142	2.1	**Hidden Valley** (CDP) Dearborn County
142	2.1	**Ossian** (town) Wells County
142	2.1	**Zionsville** (town) Boone County
146	2.0	**Bloomington** (city) Monroe County
146	2.0	**Crown Point** (city) Lake County
146	2.0	**Pittsboro** (town) Hendricks County
146	2.0	**Plainfield** (town) Hendricks County
146	2.0	**Saint John** (town) Lake County

Note: *This section ranks incorporated places and CDPs (Census Designated Places) with populations of 2,500 or more. Unincorporated postal areas were not considered. Please refer to the User Guide for additional information.*

Homeowner Vacancy Rate
Top 150 Places Ranked in *Ascending* Order

State Rank	Percent	Place
1	0.0	**Notre Dame** (CDP) Saint Joseph County
1	0.0	**Purdue University** (CDP) Tippecanoe County
3	0.8	**Dyer** (town) Lake County
3	0.8	**Leo-Cedarville** (town) Allen County
5	1.1	**Highland** (CDP) Vanderburgh County
5	1.1	**Highland** (town) Lake County
7	1.2	**Bright** (CDP) Dearborn County
8	1.3	**Fairmount** (town) Grant County
8	1.3	**Griffith** (town) Lake County
8	1.3	**Schererville** (town) Lake County
11	1.4	**Munster** (town) Lake County
11	1.4	**Porter** (town) Porter County
11	1.4	**South Haven** (CDP) Porter County
11	1.4	**Whiteland** (town) Johnson County
15	1.5	**Granger** (CDP) Saint Joseph County
15	1.5	**Loogootee** (city) Martin County
15	1.5	**Mooresville** (town) Morgan County
18	1.6	**Fishers** (town) Hamilton County
18	1.6	**Newburgh** (town) Warrick County
18	1.6	**Portage** (city) Porter County
18	1.6	**Shorewood Forest** (CDP) Porter County
18	1.6	**Speedway** (town) Marion County
23	1.7	**Batesville** (city) Ripley County
23	1.7	**Carmel** (city) Hamilton County
23	1.7	**Covington** (city) Fountain County
23	1.7	**Lakes of the Four Seasons** (CDP) Lake County
23	1.7	**McCordsville** (town) Hancock County
23	1.7	**Melody Hill** (CDP) Vanderburgh County
23	1.7	**Roselawn** (CDP) Newton County
30	1.8	**Brownsburg** (town) Hendricks County
30	1.8	**Danville** (town) Hendricks County
30	1.8	**Pendleton** (town) Madison County
30	1.8	**Upland** (town) Grant County
30	1.8	**Westville** (town) LaPorte County
35	1.9	**Dunlap** (CDP) Elkhart County
35	1.9	**Hebron** (town) Porter County
35	1.9	**Hobart** (city) Lake County
35	1.9	**New Haven** (city) Allen County
39	2.0	**Bloomington** (city) Monroe County
39	2.0	**Crown Point** (city) Lake County
39	2.0	**Pittsboro** (town) Hendricks County
39	2.0	**Plainfield** (town) Hendricks County
39	2.0	**Saint John** (town) Lake County
44	2.1	**Chesterton** (town) Porter County
44	2.1	**Hidden Valley** (CDP) Dearborn County
44	2.1	**Ossian** (town) Wells County
44	2.1	**Zionsville** (town) Boone County
48	2.2	**North Terre Haute** (CDP) Vigo County
48	2.2	**Union City** (city) Randolph County
50	2.3	**Jeffersonville** (city) Clark County
50	2.3	**Lowell** (town) Lake County
50	2.3	**Valparaiso** (city) Porter County
50	2.3	**Winona Lake** (town) Kosciusko County
54	2.4	**Chandler** (town) Warrick County
54	2.4	**Corydon** (town) Harrison County
54	2.4	**De Motte** (town) Jasper County
54	2.4	**Fort Branch** (town) Gibson County
54	2.4	**Gas City** (city) Grant County
54	2.4	**Sellersburg** (town) Clark County
60	2.5	**Fortville** (town) Hancock County
60	2.5	**Greendale** (city) Dearborn County
60	2.5	**Greenwood** (city) Johnson County
60	2.5	**New Whiteland** (town) Johnson County
60	2.5	**Simonton Lake** (CDP) Elkhart County
60	2.5	**Westfield** (city) Hamilton County
66	2.6	**Hammond** (city) Lake County
66	2.6	**Huntingburg** (city) Dubois County
66	2.6	**Jasper** (city) Dubois County
66	2.6	**Noblesville** (city) Hamilton County
66	2.6	**West Lafayette** (city) Tippecanoe County
71	2.7	**Clarksville** (town) Clark County
71	2.7	**Cumberland** (town) Marion County
71	2.7	**Franklin** (city) Johnson County
71	2.7	**Mitchell** (city) Lawrence County
71	2.7	**Paoli** (town) Orange County
71	2.7	**Tipton** (city) Tipton County
77	2.8	**Attica** (city) Fountain County
77	2.8	**Columbia City** (city) Whitley County
77	2.8	**Huntertown** (town) Allen County
77	2.8	**Lafayette** (city) Tippecanoe County
77	2.8	**Whitestown** (town) Boone County
82	2.9	**Bargersville** (town) Johnson County
82	2.9	**Bluffton** (city) Wells County
82	2.9	**Bremen** (town) Marshall County
82	2.9	**Columbus** (city) Bartholomew County
82	2.9	**Fort Wayne** (city) Allen County
82	2.9	**Georgetown** (town) Floyd County
88	3.0	**Linton** (city) Greene County
88	3.0	**Michigan City** (city) LaPorte County
90	3.1	**Ellettsville** (town) Monroe County
90	3.1	**La Porte** (city) LaPorte County
90	3.1	**Vincennes** (city) Knox County
93	3.2	**Beech Grove** (city) Marion County
93	3.2	**Brownstown** (town) Jackson County
93	3.2	**Hanover** (town) Jefferson County
93	3.2	**Lawrence** (city) Marion County
93	3.2	**Merrillville** (town) Lake County
93	3.2	**Terre Haute** (city) Vigo County
93	3.2	**Warsaw** (city) Kosciusko County
93	3.2	**Yorktown** (town) Delaware County
101	3.3	**Austin** (city) Scott County
101	3.3	**Boonville** (city) Warrick County
101	3.3	**Cicero** (town) Hamilton County
101	3.3	**Connersville** (city) Fayette County
101	3.3	**Edinburgh** (town) Johnson County
101	3.3	**Greensburg** (city) Decatur County
101	3.3	**Lebanon** (city) Boone County
101	3.3	**Ligonier** (city) Noble County
101	3.3	**Salem** (city) Washington County
101	3.3	**Winfield** (town) Lake County
111	3.4	**Avon** (town) Hendricks County
111	3.4	**Cedar Lake** (town) Lake County
111	3.4	**Frankfort** (city) Clinton County
111	3.4	**Garrett** (city) DeKalb County
111	3.4	**Greenfield** (city) Hancock County
111	3.4	**Indianapolis** (city) Marion County
111	3.4	**Martinsville** (city) Morgan County
111	3.4	**Rochester** (city) Fulton County
111	3.4	**Seymour** (city) Jackson County
120	3.5	**Charlestown** (city) Clark County
120	3.5	**Crawfordsville** (city) Montgomery County
120	3.5	**Delphi** (city) Carroll County
120	3.5	**Nappanee** (city) Elkhart County
120	3.5	**North Vernon** (city) Jennings County
120	3.5	**Washington** (city) Daviess County
120	3.5	**Winchester** (city) Randolph County
127	3.6	**Berne** (city) Adams County
127	3.6	**East Chicago** (city) Lake County
127	3.6	**Gary** (city) Lake County
127	3.6	**Heritage Lake** (CDP) Putnam County
127	3.6	**Portland** (city) Jay County
127	3.6	**Syracuse** (town) Kosciusko County
127	3.6	**Whiting** (city) Lake County
134	3.7	**Evansville** (city) Vanderburgh County
134	3.7	**Goshen** (city) Elkhart County
134	3.7	**Kendallville** (city) Noble County
134	3.7	**Knox** (city) Starke County
134	3.7	**Lake Station** (city) Lake County
134	3.7	**Marion** (city) Grant County
134	3.7	**Peru** (city) Miami County
134	3.7	**Scottsburg** (city) Scott County
142	3.8	**Bicknell** (city) Knox County
142	3.8	**Brazil** (city) Clay County
142	3.8	**Decatur** (city) Adams County
142	3.8	**Greencastle** (city) Putnam County
142	3.8	**Mount Vernon** (city) Posey County
142	3.8	**Muncie** (city) Delaware County
148	3.9	**Elkhart** (city) Elkhart County
148	3.9	**Madison** (city) Jefferson County
148	3.9	**Monticello** (city) White County

Note: *This section ranks incorporated places and CDPs (Census Designated Places) with populations of 2,500 or more. Unincorporated postal areas were not considered. Please refer to the User Guide for additional information.*

Median Gross Rent
Top 150 Places Ranked in *Descending* Order

State Rank	Dollars	Place
1	1,837	**Shorewood Forest** (CDP) Porter County
2	1,385	**Hidden Valley** (CDP) Dearborn County
3	1,284	**Pittsboro** (town) Hendricks County
4	1,221	**Whitestown** (town) Boone County
5	1,209	**New Whiteland** (town) Johnson County
6	1,195	**Granger** (CDP) Saint Joseph County
7	1,174	**McCordsville** (town) Hancock County
8	1,155	**Zionsville** (town) Boone County
9	1,149	**Heritage Lake** (CDP) Putnam County
10	1,077	**Carmel** (city) Hamilton County
11	1,058	**Fishers** (town) Hamilton County
12	1,031	**Saint John** (town) Lake County
13	975	**Sellersburg** (town) Clark County
14	962	**Munster** (town) Lake County
15	946	**Dunlap** (CDP) Elkhart County
15	946	**Highland** (town) Lake County
17	943	**South Haven** (CDP) Porter County
18	935	**Whiteland** (town) Johnson County
19	931	**Merrillville** (town) Lake County
20	930	**Leo-Cedarville** (town) Allen County
21	921	**Dyer** (town) Lake County
22	914	**Crown Point** (city) Lake County
23	898	**Plainfield** (town) Hendricks County
24	896	**Brownsburg** (town) Hendricks County
25	890	**Chesterton** (town) Porter County
25	890	**Highland** (CDP) Vanderburgh County
27	889	**Noblesville** (city) Hamilton County
28	883	**Lowell** (town) Lake County
29	878	**Avon** (town) Hendricks County
30	876	**Westfield** (city) Hamilton County
31	872	**Porter** (town) Porter County
32	867	**Roselawn** (CDP) Newton County
33	856	**Cedar Lake** (town) Lake County
34	849	**West Lafayette** (city) Tippecanoe County
35	841	**Pendleton** (town) Madison County
36	838	**Hobart** (city) Lake County
37	836	**Valparaiso** (city) Porter County
38	835	**Franklin** (city) Johnson County
39	832	**Schererville** (town) Lake County
40	830	**Griffith** (town) Lake County
41	827	**Chandler** (town) Warrick County
42	825	**Huntertown** (town) Allen County
43	823	**Middlebury** (town) Elkhart County
44	818	**Portage** (city) Porter County
45	814	**Greenfield** (city) Hancock County
46	811	**Bargersville** (town) Johnson County
46	811	**Greenwood** (city) Johnson County
48	804	**Lawrence** (city) Marion County
49	802	**Hammond** (city) Lake County
50	794	**Columbus** (city) Bartholomew County
51	785	**Sheridan** (town) Hamilton County
52	783	**Cicero** (town) Hamilton County
53	782	**Bloomington** (city) Monroe County
54	777	**Georgetown** (town) Floyd County
55	775	**Hebron** (town) Porter County
56	770	**Indianapolis** (city) Marion County
57	768	**Lake Station** (city) Lake County
58	757	**Danville** (town) Hendricks County
59	756	**Fortville** (town) Hancock County
60	755	**Clarksville** (town) Clark County
61	753	**Aurora** (city) Dearborn County
62	751	**Purdue University** (CDP) Tippecanoe County
63	746	**Winfield** (town) Lake County
64	744	**Lafayette** (city) Tippecanoe County
65	739	**Smithville-Sanders** (CDP) Monroe County
66	738	**Mooresville** (town) Morgan County
67	734	**Batesville** (city) Ripley County
67	734	**Cumberland** (town) Marion County
67	734	**Goshen** (city) Elkhart County
70	733	**Ellettsville** (town) Monroe County
71	730	**Beech Grove** (city) Marion County
71	730	**Jeffersonville** (city) Clark County
73	727	**Whiting** (city) Lake County
74	721	**Speedway** (town) Marion County
75	720	**Seymour** (city) Jackson County
76	712	**Greensburg** (city) Decatur County
77	711	**Gary** (city) Lake County
78	710	**Yorktown** (town) Delaware County
79	708	**Centerville** (town) Wayne County
80	706	**South Bend** (city) Saint Joseph County
81	704	**Country Squire Lakes** (CDP) Jennings County
82	703	**Edinburgh** (town) Johnson County
82	703	**Simonton Lake** (CDP) Elkhart County
84	702	**Berne** (city) Adams County
85	701	**Grissom AFB** (CDP) Miami County
86	700	**New Haven** (city) Allen County
86	700	**Shelbyville** (city) Shelby County
88	697	**New Albany** (city) Floyd County
89	693	**Mishawaka** (city) Saint Joseph County
90	692	**Austin** (city) Scott County
90	692	**Corydon** (town) Harrison County
90	692	**Evansville** (city) Vanderburgh County
93	690	**Michigan City** (city) LaPorte County
94	688	**Scottsburg** (city) Scott County
95	686	**De Motte** (town) Jasper County
96	680	**Hanover** (town) Jefferson County
97	677	**Monticello** (city) White County
98	675	**Martinsville** (city) Morgan County
99	674	**Greendale** (city) Dearborn County
99	674	**Winona Lake** (town) Kosciusko County
101	672	**Anderson** (city) Madison County
101	672	**Lagrange** (town) LaGrange County
103	671	**Elkhart** (city) Elkhart County
103	671	**Gas City** (city) Grant County
105	670	**East Chicago** (city) Lake County
105	670	**Muncie** (city) Delaware County
107	669	**Tipton** (city) Tipton County
108	667	**Lawrenceburg** (city) Dearborn County
108	667	**Lebanon** (city) Boone County
108	667	**North Terre Haute** (CDP) Vigo County
111	665	**Elwood** (city) Madison County
112	658	**Westville** (town) LaPorte County
113	656	**Fort Wayne** (city) Allen County
114	655	**Terre Haute** (city) Vigo County
115	653	**Fairmount** (town) Grant County
116	652	**La Porte** (city) LaPorte County
117	650	**Frankfort** (city) Clinton County
117	650	**Knox** (city) Starke County
119	645	**Crawfordsville** (city) Montgomery County
120	644	**Warsaw** (city) Kosciusko County
121	643	**Princeton** (city) Gibson County
122	642	**North Vernon** (city) Jennings County
122	642	**Notre Dame** (CDP) Saint Joseph County
124	641	**Brazil** (city) Clay County
125	639	**Butler** (city) DeKalb County
126	638	**Jasper** (city) Dubois County
127	637	**Kokomo** (city) Howard County
128	636	**Garrett** (city) DeKalb County
128	636	**Huntington** (city) Huntington County
130	634	**Ossian** (town) Wells County
131	631	**Columbia City** (city) Whitley County
132	630	**Brownstown** (town) Jackson County
132	630	**Connersville** (city) Fayette County
132	630	**Nappanee** (city) Elkhart County
135	627	**Greencastle** (city) Putnam County
136	626	**Plymouth** (city) Marshall County
137	623	**Rochester** (city) Fulton County
137	623	**Winchester** (city) Randolph County
139	620	**Delphi** (city) Carroll County
140	618	**Charlestown** (city) Clark County
140	618	**Covington** (city) Fountain County
140	618	**New Castle** (city) Henry County
140	618	**Sullivan** (city) Sullivan County
144	617	**Bright** (CDP) Dearborn County
144	617	**Kendallville** (city) Noble County
146	614	**Richmond** (city) Wayne County
147	613	**Auburn** (city) DeKalb County
148	611	**Bedford** (city) Lawrence County
148	611	**Rensselaer** (city) Jasper County
150	610	**Chesterfield** (town) Madison County

Note: This section ranks incorporated places and CDPs (Census Designated Places) with populations of 2,500 or more. Unincorporated postal areas were not considered. Please refer to the User Guide for additional information.

Median Gross Rent

Top 150 Places Ranked in *Ascending* Order

State Rank	Dollars	Place
1	463	**Rockville** (town) Parke County
2	508	**Fort Branch** (town) Gibson County
3	513	**Bicknell** (city) Knox County
4	526	**Portland** (city) Jay County
5	532	**Bluffton** (city) Wells County
5	532	**Clinton** (city) Vermillion County
7	541	**Decatur** (city) Adams County
8	548	**Syracuse** (town) Kosciusko County
9	550	**Loogootee** (city) Martin County
10	551	**Mitchell** (city) Lawrence County
11	554	**Brookville** (town) Franklin County
12	555	**Ligonier** (city) Noble County
12	555	**Rushville** (city) Rush County
14	557	**Newburgh** (town) Warrick County
15	567	**Paoli** (town) Orange County
16	568	**North Manchester** (town) Wabash County
16	568	**Washington** (city) Daviess County
18	569	**Wabash** (city) Wabash County
19	573	**Upland** (town) Grant County
20	576	**Linton** (city) Greene County
20	576	**Mount Vernon** (city) Posey County
22	579	**Marion** (city) Grant County
23	585	**Salem** (city) Washington County
24	586	**Union City** (city) Randolph County
25	589	**Huntingburg** (city) Dubois County
26	591	**Attica** (city) Fountain County
27	596	**Peru** (city) Miami County
28	598	**Hartford City** (city) Blackford County
29	599	**Alexandria** (city) Madison County
30	600	**Angola** (city) Steuben County
30	600	**Boonville** (city) Warrick County
30	600	**Bremen** (town) Marshall County
33	604	**Madison** (city) Jefferson County
34	605	**Tell City** (city) Perry County
35	606	**Logansport** (city) Cass County
35	606	**Vincennes** (city) Knox County
37	610	**Chesterfield** (town) Madison County
38	611	**Bedford** (city) Lawrence County
38	611	**Rensselaer** (city) Jasper County
40	613	**Auburn** (city) DeKalb County
41	614	**Richmond** (city) Wayne County
42	617	**Bright** (CDP) Dearborn County
42	617	**Kendallville** (city) Noble County
44	618	**Charlestown** (city) Clark County
44	618	**Covington** (city) Fountain County
44	618	**New Castle** (city) Henry County
44	618	**Sullivan** (city) Sullivan County
48	620	**Delphi** (city) Carroll County
49	623	**Rochester** (city) Fulton County
49	623	**Winchester** (city) Randolph County
51	626	**Plymouth** (city) Marshall County
52	627	**Greencastle** (city) Putnam County
53	630	**Brownstown** (town) Jackson County
53	630	**Connersville** (city) Fayette County
53	630	**Nappanee** (city) Elkhart County
56	631	**Columbia City** (city) Whitley County
57	634	**Ossian** (town) Wells County
58	636	**Garrett** (city) DeKalb County
58	636	**Huntington** (city) Huntington County
60	637	**Kokomo** (city) Howard County
61	638	**Jasper** (city) Dubois County
62	639	**Butler** (city) DeKalb County
63	641	**Brazil** (city) Clay County
64	642	**North Vernon** (city) Jennings County
64	642	**Notre Dame** (CDP) Saint Joseph County
66	643	**Princeton** (city) Gibson County
67	644	**Warsaw** (city) Kosciusko County
68	645	**Crawfordsville** (city) Montgomery County
69	650	**Frankfort** (city) Clinton County
69	650	**Knox** (city) Starke County
71	652	**La Porte** (city) LaPorte County
72	653	**Fairmount** (town) Grant County
73	655	**Terre Haute** (city) Vigo County
74	656	**Fort Wayne** (city) Allen County
75	658	**Westville** (town) LaPorte County
76	665	**Elwood** (city) Madison County
77	667	**Lawrenceburg** (city) Dearborn County
77	667	**Lebanon** (city) Boone County
77	667	**North Terre Haute** (CDP) Vigo County
80	669	**Tipton** (city) Tipton County
81	670	**East Chicago** (city) Lake County
81	670	**Muncie** (city) Delaware County
83	671	**Elkhart** (city) Elkhart County
83	671	**Gas City** (city) Grant County
85	672	**Anderson** (city) Madison County
85	672	**Lagrange** (town) LaGrange County
87	674	**Greendale** (city) Dearborn County
87	674	**Winona Lake** (town) Kosciusko County
89	675	**Martinsville** (city) Morgan County
90	677	**Monticello** (city) White County
91	680	**Hanover** (town) Jefferson County
92	686	**De Motte** (town) Jasper County
93	688	**Scottsburg** (city) Scott County
94	690	**Michigan City** (city) LaPorte County
95	692	**Austin** (city) Scott County
95	692	**Corydon** (town) Harrison County
95	692	**Evansville** (city) Vanderburgh County
98	693	**Mishawaka** (city) Saint Joseph County
99	697	**New Albany** (city) Floyd County
100	700	**New Haven** (city) Allen County
100	700	**Shelbyville** (city) Shelby County
102	701	**Grissom AFB** (CDP) Miami County
103	702	**Berne** (city) Adams County
104	703	**Edinburgh** (town) Johnson County
104	703	**Simonton Lake** (CDP) Elkhart County
106	704	**Country Squire Lakes** (CDP) Jennings County
107	706	**South Bend** (city) Saint Joseph County
108	708	**Centerville** (town) Wayne County
109	710	**Yorktown** (town) Delaware County
110	711	**Gary** (city) Lake County
111	712	**Greensburg** (city) Decatur County
112	720	**Seymour** (city) Jackson County
113	721	**Speedway** (town) Marion County
114	727	**Whiting** (city) Lake County
115	730	**Beech Grove** (city) Marion County
115	730	**Jeffersonville** (city) Clark County
117	733	**Ellettsville** (town) Monroe County
118	734	**Batesville** (city) Ripley County
118	734	**Cumberland** (town) Marion County
118	734	**Goshen** (city) Elkhart County
121	738	**Mooresville** (town) Morgan County
122	739	**Smithville-Sanders** (CDP) Monroe County
123	744	**Lafayette** (city) Tippecanoe County
124	746	**Winfield** (town) Lake County
125	751	**Purdue University** (CDP) Tippecanoe County
126	753	**Aurora** (city) Dearborn County
127	755	**Clarksville** (town) Clark County
128	756	**Fortville** (town) Hancock County
129	757	**Danville** (town) Hendricks County
130	768	**Lake Station** (city) Lake County
131	770	**Indianapolis** (city) Marion County
132	775	**Hebron** (town) Porter County
133	777	**Georgetown** (town) Floyd County
134	782	**Bloomington** (city) Monroe County
135	783	**Cicero** (town) Hamilton County
136	785	**Sheridan** (town) Hamilton County
137	794	**Columbus** (city) Bartholomew County
138	802	**Hammond** (city) Lake County
139	804	**Lawrence** (city) Marion County
140	811	**Bargersville** (town) Johnson County
140	811	**Greenwood** (city) Johnson County
142	814	**Greenfield** (city) Hancock County
143	818	**Portage** (city) Porter County
144	823	**Middlebury** (town) Elkhart County
145	825	**Huntertown** (town) Allen County
146	827	**Chandler** (town) Warrick County
147	830	**Griffith** (town) Lake County
148	832	**Schererville** (town) Lake County
149	835	**Franklin** (city) Johnson County
150	836	**Valparaiso** (city) Porter County

Note: This section ranks incorporated places and CDPs (Census Designated Places) with populations of 2,500 or more. Unincorporated postal areas were not considered. Please refer to the User Guide for additional information.

Rental Vacancy Rate
Top 150 Places Ranked in *Descending* Order

State Rank	Percent	Place
1	29.1	**Grissom AFB** (CDP) Miami County
2	28.3	**Chandler** (town) Warrick County
3	23.1	**Syracuse** (town) Kosciusko County
4	22.2	**Speedway** (town) Marion County
5	22.0	**Cumberland** (town) Marion County
6	20.9	**Bargersville** (town) Johnson County
7	20.2	**Chesterfield** (town) Madison County
8	19.7	**Smithville-Sanders** (CDP) Monroe County
9	19.1	**Country Squire Lakes** (CDP) Jennings County
10	18.0	**Ligonier** (city) Noble County
11	17.4	**Butler** (city) DeKalb County
12	17.3	**Bicknell** (city) Knox County
13	17.2	**Westville** (town) LaPorte County
14	16.8	**Lagrange** (town) LaGrange County
15	16.4	**South Haven** (CDP) Porter County
16	16.2	**Union City** (city) Randolph County
17	16.0	**Zionsville** (town) Boone County
18	15.9	**Anderson** (city) Madison County
19	15.8	**Elkhart** (city) Elkhart County
20	15.6	**Noblesville** (city) Hamilton County
21	15.4	**Berne** (city) Adams County
21	15.4	**Nappanee** (city) Elkhart County
23	15.3	**Sheridan** (town) Hamilton County
24	15.2	**Alexandria** (city) Madison County
25	14.5	**Gary** (city) Lake County
26	14.2	**Columbus** (city) Bartholomew County
27	13.9	**Hanover** (town) Jefferson County
28	13.8	**North Manchester** (town) Wabash County
29	13.7	**Connersville** (city) Fayette County
29	13.7	**Marion** (city) Grant County
29	13.7	**Mishawaka** (city) Saint Joseph County
29	13.7	**Whitestown** (town) Boone County
33	13.6	**Portland** (city) Jay County
34	13.1	**Seymour** (city) Jackson County
35	13.0	**New Castle** (city) Henry County
36	12.9	**Lawrence** (city) Marion County
37	12.8	**Bremen** (town) Marshall County
37	12.8	**Michigan City** (city) LaPorte County
37	12.8	**Newburgh** (town) Warrick County
40	12.6	**Elwood** (city) Madison County
40	12.6	**Kokomo** (city) Howard County
42	12.5	**Fort Wayne** (city) Allen County
42	12.5	**Huntington** (city) Huntington County
44	12.4	**Frankfort** (city) Clinton County
44	12.4	**Richmond** (city) Wayne County
46	12.3	**Indianapolis** (city) Marion County
46	12.3	**Salem** (city) Washington County
48	12.2	**Kendallville** (city) Noble County
48	12.2	**Westfield** (city) Hamilton County
50	12.1	**Greenfield** (city) Hancock County
50	12.1	**Winona Lake** (town) Kosciusko County
52	12.0	**Plymouth** (city) Marshall County
52	12.0	**Wabash** (city) Wabash County
54	11.9	**South Bend** (city) Saint Joseph County
55	11.8	**Evansville** (city) Vanderburgh County
56	11.6	**Goshen** (city) Elkhart County
56	11.6	**Greensburg** (city) Decatur County
56	11.6	**Scottsburg** (city) Scott County
59	11.5	**Mount Vernon** (city) Posey County
60	11.4	**Attica** (city) Fountain County
61	11.2	**Madison** (city) Jefferson County
62	11.1	**Franklin** (city) Johnson County
62	11.1	**Ossian** (town) Wells County
62	11.1	**Terre Haute** (city) Vigo County
65	11.0	**Aurora** (city) Dearborn County
65	11.0	**Boonville** (city) Warrick County
65	11.0	**North Vernon** (city) Jennings County
65	11.0	**Peru** (city) Miami County
65	11.0	**Shelbyville** (city) Shelby County
70	10.9	**Greenwood** (city) Johnson County
71	10.8	**Carmel** (city) Hamilton County
71	10.8	**Decatur** (city) Adams County
71	10.8	**Lebanon** (city) Boone County
71	10.8	**New Haven** (city) Allen County
75	10.6	**Hartford City** (city) Blackford County
76	10.5	**Tipton** (city) Tipton County
77	10.3	**Batesville** (city) Ripley County
77	10.3	**Beech Grove** (city) Marion County
77	10.3	**Bluffton** (city) Wells County
77	10.3	**Warsaw** (city) Kosciusko County
81	10.2	**East Chicago** (city) Lake County
82	10.1	**La Porte** (city) LaPorte County
82	10.1	**Merrillville** (town) Lake County
82	10.1	**Muncie** (city) Delaware County
85	10.0	**Austin** (city) Scott County
85	10.0	**Greencastle** (city) Putnam County
87	9.9	**Angola** (city) Steuben County
87	9.9	**Rochester** (city) Fulton County
87	9.9	**Winchester** (city) Randolph County
90	9.8	**Logansport** (city) Cass County
91	9.7	**Auburn** (city) DeKalb County
91	9.7	**Danville** (town) Hendricks County
91	9.7	**Fairmount** (town) Grant County
91	9.7	**Sullivan** (city) Sullivan County
95	9.6	**Crawfordsville** (city) Montgomery County
95	9.6	**Linton** (city) Greene County
97	9.5	**Fortville** (town) Hancock County
98	9.4	**Clinton** (city) Vermillion County
98	9.4	**Monticello** (city) White County
98	9.4	**New Albany** (city) Floyd County
101	9.3	**Upland** (town) Grant County
102	9.2	**Loogootee** (city) Martin County
102	9.2	**Lowell** (town) Lake County
102	9.2	**Princeton** (city) Gibson County
105	9.1	**Lafayette** (city) Tippecanoe County
106	9.0	**Bedford** (city) Lawrence County
106	9.0	**Columbia City** (city) Whitley County
106	9.0	**Griffith** (town) Lake County
109	8.9	**Fort Branch** (town) Gibson County
109	8.9	**Pendleton** (town) Madison County
111	8.8	**Yorktown** (town) Delaware County
112	8.7	**Garrett** (city) DeKalb County
112	8.7	**Jeffersonville** (city) Clark County
114	8.6	**Lake Station** (city) Lake County
115	8.5	**Corydon** (town) Harrison County
116	8.4	**Fishers** (town) Hamilton County
116	8.4	**Rockville** (town) Parke County
116	8.4	**Rushville** (city) Rush County
116	8.4	**Vincennes** (city) Knox County
120	8.3	**Charlestown** (city) Clark County
121	8.2	**Cedar Lake** (town) Lake County
121	8.2	**Centerville** (town) Wayne County
121	8.2	**Cicero** (town) Hamilton County
121	8.2	**Delphi** (city) Carroll County
125	8.1	**Hobart** (city) Lake County
126	8.0	**Martinsville** (city) Morgan County
126	8.0	**North Terre Haute** (CDP) Vigo County
128	7.9	**Brownstown** (town) Jackson County
128	7.9	**Covington** (city) Fountain County
128	7.9	**Paoli** (town) Orange County
131	7.8	**Chesterton** (town) Porter County
131	7.8	**Portage** (city) Porter County
131	7.8	**Washington** (city) Daviess County
134	7.7	**De Motte** (town) Jasper County
134	7.7	**Melody Hill** (CDP) Vanderburgh County
136	7.6	**Brownsburg** (town) Hendricks County
136	7.6	**Crown Point** (city) Lake County
138	7.5	**Brookville** (town) Franklin County
138	7.5	**Heritage Lake** (CDP) Putnam County
140	7.4	**Bright** (CDP) Dearborn County
140	7.4	**Winfield** (town) Lake County
142	7.3	**Brazil** (city) Clay County
142	7.3	**Clarksville** (town) Clark County
142	7.3	**Tell City** (city) Perry County
145	7.2	**Gas City** (city) Grant County
145	7.2	**Valparaiso** (city) Porter County
147	7.0	**Plainfield** (town) Hendricks County
147	7.0	**Schererville** (town) Lake County
149	6.9	**Hammond** (city) Lake County
149	6.9	**Huntertown** (town) Allen County

Note: This section ranks incorporated places and CDPs (Census Designated Places) with populations of 2,500 or more. Unincorporated postal areas were not considered. Please refer to the User Guide for additional information.

Rental Vacancy Rate
Top 150 Places Ranked in *Ascending* Order

State Rank	Percent	Place
1	0.7	**Lakes of the Four Seasons** (CDP) Lake County
2	2.5	**Shorewood Forest** (CDP) Porter County
3	2.7	**Whiteland** (town) Johnson County
4	3.0	**Pittsboro** (town) Hendricks County
5	3.3	**Saint John** (town) Lake County
6	3.6	**Notre Dame** (CDP) Saint Joseph County
7	3.7	**Highland** (CDP) Vanderburgh County
8	3.9	**New Whiteland** (town) Johnson County
9	4.0	**Dyer** (town) Lake County
10	4.1	**Knox** (city) Starke County
11	4.2	**McCordsville** (town) Hancock County
11	4.2	**Middlebury** (town) Elkhart County
11	4.2	**Simonton Lake** (CDP) Elkhart County
14	4.4	**Bloomington** (city) Monroe County
15	4.5	**West Lafayette** (city) Tippecanoe County
16	4.7	**Highland** (town) Lake County
17	4.8	**Whiting** (city) Lake County
18	5.0	**Porter** (town) Porter County
18	5.0	**Roselawn** (CDP) Newton County
20	5.3	**Ellettsville** (town) Monroe County
21	5.7	**Huntingburg** (city) Dubois County
22	5.9	**Munster** (town) Lake County
23	6.1	**Granger** (CDP) Saint Joseph County
23	6.1	**Lawrenceburg** (city) Dearborn County
25	6.2	**Jasper** (city) Dubois County
25	6.2	**Rensselaer** (city) Jasper County
27	6.3	**Dunlap** (CDP) Elkhart County
27	6.3	**Hebron** (town) Porter County
27	6.3	**Hidden Valley** (CDP) Dearborn County
30	6.4	**Greendale** (city) Dearborn County
31	6.5	**Mitchell** (city) Lawrence County
31	6.5	**Purdue University** (CDP) Tippecanoe County
33	6.6	**Georgetown** (town) Floyd County
34	6.7	**Avon** (town) Hendricks County
34	6.7	**Leo-Cedarville** (town) Allen County
34	6.7	**Sellersburg** (town) Clark County
37	6.8	**Edinburgh** (town) Johnson County
37	6.8	**Mooresville** (town) Morgan County
39	6.9	**Hammond** (city) Lake County
39	6.9	**Huntertown** (town) Allen County
41	7.0	**Plainfield** (town) Hendricks County
41	7.0	**Schererville** (town) Lake County
43	7.2	**Gas City** (city) Grant County
43	7.2	**Valparaiso** (city) Porter County
45	7.3	**Brazil** (city) Clay County
45	7.3	**Clarksville** (town) Clark County
45	7.3	**Tell City** (city) Perry County
48	7.4	**Bright** (CDP) Dearborn County
48	7.4	**Winfield** (town) Lake County
50	7.5	**Brookville** (town) Franklin County
50	7.5	**Heritage Lake** (CDP) Putnam County
52	7.6	**Brownsburg** (town) Hendricks County
52	7.6	**Crown Point** (city) Lake County
54	7.7	**De Motte** (town) Jasper County
54	7.7	**Melody Hill** (CDP) Vanderburgh County
56	7.8	**Chesterton** (town) Porter County
56	7.8	**Portage** (city) Porter County
56	7.8	**Washington** (city) Daviess County
59	7.9	**Brownstown** (town) Jackson County
59	7.9	**Covington** (city) Fountain County
59	7.9	**Paoli** (town) Orange County
62	8.0	**Martinsville** (city) Morgan County
62	8.0	**North Terre Haute** (CDP) Vigo County
64	8.1	**Hobart** (city) Lake County
65	8.2	**Cedar Lake** (town) Lake County
65	8.2	**Centerville** (town) Wayne County
65	8.2	**Cicero** (town) Hamilton County
65	8.2	**Delphi** (city) Carroll County
69	8.3	**Charlestown** (city) Clark County
70	8.4	**Fishers** (town) Hamilton County
70	8.4	**Rockville** (town) Parke County
70	8.4	**Rushville** (city) Rush County
70	8.4	**Vincennes** (city) Knox County
74	8.5	**Corydon** (town) Harrison County
75	8.6	**Lake Station** (city) Lake County
76	8.7	**Garrett** (city) DeKalb County
76	8.7	**Jeffersonville** (city) Clark County
78	8.8	**Yorktown** (town) Delaware County
79	8.9	**Fort Branch** (town) Gibson County
79	8.9	**Pendleton** (town) Madison County
81	9.0	**Bedford** (city) Lawrence County
81	9.0	**Columbia City** (city) Whitley County
81	9.0	**Griffith** (town) Lake County
84	9.1	**Lafayette** (city) Tippecanoe County
85	9.2	**Loogootee** (city) Martin County
85	9.2	**Lowell** (town) Lake County
85	9.2	**Princeton** (city) Gibson County
88	9.3	**Upland** (town) Grant County
89	9.4	**Clinton** (city) Vermillion County
89	9.4	**Monticello** (city) White County
89	9.4	**New Albany** (city) Floyd County
92	9.5	**Fortville** (town) Hancock County
93	9.6	**Crawfordsville** (city) Montgomery County
93	9.6	**Linton** (city) Greene County
95	9.7	**Auburn** (city) DeKalb County
95	9.7	**Danville** (town) Hendricks County
95	9.7	**Fairmount** (town) Grant County
95	9.7	**Sullivan** (city) Sullivan County
99	9.8	**Logansport** (city) Cass County
100	9.9	**Angola** (city) Steuben County
100	9.9	**Rochester** (city) Fulton County
100	9.9	**Winchester** (city) Randolph County
103	10.0	**Austin** (city) Scott County
103	10.0	**Greencastle** (city) Putnam County
105	10.1	**La Porte** (city) LaPorte County
105	10.1	**Merrillville** (town) Lake County
105	10.1	**Muncie** (city) Delaware County
108	10.2	**East Chicago** (city) Lake County
109	10.3	**Batesville** (city) Ripley County
109	10.3	**Beech Grove** (city) Marion County
109	10.3	**Bluffton** (city) Wells County
109	10.3	**Warsaw** (city) Kosciusko County
113	10.5	**Tipton** (city) Tipton County
114	10.6	**Hartford City** (city) Blackford County
115	10.8	**Carmel** (city) Hamilton County
115	10.8	**Decatur** (city) Adams County
115	10.8	**Lebanon** (city) Boone County
115	10.8	**New Haven** (city) Allen County
119	10.9	**Greenwood** (city) Johnson County
120	11.0	**Aurora** (city) Dearborn County
120	11.0	**Boonville** (city) Warrick County
120	11.0	**North Vernon** (city) Jennings County
120	11.0	**Peru** (city) Miami County
120	11.0	**Shelbyville** (city) Shelby County
125	11.1	**Franklin** (city) Johnson County
125	11.1	**Ossian** (town) Wells County
125	11.1	**Terre Haute** (city) Vigo County
128	11.2	**Madison** (city) Jefferson County
129	11.4	**Attica** (city) Fountain County
130	11.5	**Mount Vernon** (city) Posey County
131	11.6	**Goshen** (city) Elkhart County
131	11.6	**Greensburg** (city) Decatur County
131	11.6	**Scottsburg** (city) Scott County
134	11.8	**Evansville** (city) Vanderburgh County
135	11.9	**South Bend** (city) Saint Joseph County
136	12.0	**Plymouth** (city) Marshall County
136	12.0	**Wabash** (city) Wabash County
138	12.1	**Greenfield** (city) Hancock County
138	12.1	**Winona Lake** (town) Kosciusko County
140	12.2	**Kendallville** (city) Noble County
140	12.2	**Westfield** (city) Hamilton County
142	12.3	**Indianapolis** (city) Marion County
142	12.3	**Salem** (city) Washington County
144	12.4	**Frankfort** (city) Clinton County
144	12.4	**Richmond** (city) Wayne County
146	12.5	**Fort Wayne** (city) Allen County
146	12.5	**Huntington** (city) Huntington County
148	12.6	**Elwood** (city) Madison County
148	12.6	**Kokomo** (city) Howard County
150	12.8	**Bremen** (town) Marshall County

Note: *This section ranks incorporated places and CDPs (Census Designated Places) with populations of 2,500 or more. Unincorporated postal areas were not considered. Please refer to the User Guide for additional information.*

Population with Health Insurance
Top 150 Places Ranked in *Descending* Order

State Rank	Percent	Place
1	96.3	**Zionsville** (town) Boone County
2	95.5	**Carmel** (city) Hamilton County
3	95.4	**Purdue University** (CDP) Tippecanoe County
4	95.0	**Granger** (CDP) Saint Joseph County
4	95.0	**Winfield** (town) Lake County
6	94.8	**Leo-Cedarville** (town) Allen County
7	94.6	**Huntertown** (town) Allen County
8	94.4	**Georgetown** (town) Floyd County
9	94.2	**Hidden Valley** (CDP) Dearborn County
9	94.2	**Notre Dame** (CDP) Saint Joseph County
11	94.1	**Bright** (CDP) Dearborn County
12	93.6	**Westfield** (city) Hamilton County
13	93.5	**Yorktown** (town) Delaware County
14	93.4	**Saint John** (town) Lake County
15	93.2	**Bargersville** (town) Johnson County
16	93.0	**West Lafayette** (city) Tippecanoe County
17	92.8	**Whiteland** (town) Johnson County
18	92.7	**Fishers** (town) Hamilton County
19	92.5	**Jasper** (city) Dubois County
19	92.5	**Munster** (town) Lake County
21	92.4	**Dyer** (town) Lake County
22	92.3	**Highland** (CDP) Vanderburgh County
23	92.1	**Chesterton** (town) Porter County
24	91.9	**Whitestown** (town) Boone County
25	91.8	**Fort Branch** (town) Gibson County
26	91.4	**Lakes of the Four Seasons** (CDP) Lake County
27	91.2	**Covington** (city) Fountain County
28	91.1	**Cumberland** (town) Marion County
28	91.1	**Upland** (town) Grant County
30	90.9	**Batesville** (city) Ripley County
31	90.7	**Noblesville** (city) Hamilton County
32	90.6	**Brownsburg** (town) Hendricks County
33	90.4	**Danville** (town) Hendricks County
34	90.3	**Avon** (town) Hendricks County
34	90.3	**Schererville** (town) Lake County
36	90.2	**Melody Hill** (CDP) Vanderburgh County
36	90.2	**Middlebury** (town) Elkhart County
38	90.1	**Berne** (city) Adams County
38	90.1	**Greencastle** (city) Putnam County
38	90.1	**Highland** (town) Lake County
41	89.8	**Tell City** (city) Perry County
42	89.6	**Franklin** (city) Johnson County
43	89.2	**Crown Point** (city) Lake County
43	89.2	**Winona Lake** (town) Kosciusko County
45	89.1	**Garrett** (city) DeKalb County
46	88.9	**Rensselaer** (city) Jasper County
47	88.8	**North Manchester** (town) Wabash County
48	88.7	**Loogootee** (city) Martin County
49	88.6	**Smithville-Sanders** (CDP) Monroe County
50	88.4	**Pittsboro** (town) Hendricks County
51	88.3	**De Motte** (town) Jasper County
52	88.2	**Griffith** (town) Lake County
53	88.1	**Shorewood Forest** (CDP) Porter County
54	88.0	**Hobart** (city) Lake County
54	88.0	**Plainfield** (town) Hendricks County
56	87.9	**Columbus** (city) Bartholomew County
57	87.8	**Greendale** (city) Dearborn County
58	87.7	**Bloomington** (city) Monroe County
58	87.7	**Fortville** (town) Hancock County
58	87.7	**Mount Vernon** (city) Posey County
61	87.6	**North Terre Haute** (CDP) Vigo County
61	87.6	**Pendleton** (town) Madison County
63	87.5	**Beech Grove** (city) Marion County
63	87.5	**Ossian** (town) Wells County
65	87.4	**Monticello** (city) White County
65	87.4	**Porter** (town) Porter County
67	87.3	**Attica** (city) Fountain County
67	87.3	**New Whiteland** (town) Johnson County
69	87.2	**Angola** (city) Steuben County
70	87.1	**Brookville** (town) Franklin County
70	87.1	**Greenfield** (city) Hancock County
70	87.1	**Lawrenceburg** (city) Dearborn County
70	87.1	**Westville** (town) LaPorte County
74	87.0	**Mooresville** (town) Morgan County
74	87.0	**Newburgh** (town) Warrick County
76	86.9	**Fairmount** (town) Grant County
77	86.8	**Wabash** (city) Wabash County
78	86.7	**Columbia City** (city) Whitley County
78	86.7	**Decatur** (city) Adams County
78	86.7	**Hanover** (town) Jefferson County
81	86.6	**Whiting** (city) Lake County
82	86.4	**Princeton** (city) Gibson County
83	86.3	**Boonville** (city) Warrick County
83	86.3	**Jeffersonville** (city) Clark County
83	86.3	**Lowell** (town) Lake County
83	86.3	**Washington** (city) Daviess County
87	86.2	**Bremen** (town) Marshall County
88	85.8	**Cedar Lake** (town) Lake County
89	85.7	**Auburn** (city) DeKalb County
89	85.7	**Bluffton** (city) Wells County
89	85.7	**Madison** (city) Jefferson County
89	85.7	**Scottsburg** (city) Scott County
89	85.7	**South Haven** (CDP) Porter County
94	85.6	**Valparaiso** (city) Porter County
95	85.5	**Grissom AFB** (CDP) Miami County
95	85.5	**Merrillville** (town) Lake County
95	85.5	**Rochester** (city) Fulton County
98	85.4	**Brownstown** (town) Jackson County
98	85.4	**Portage** (city) Porter County
100	85.3	**New Haven** (city) Allen County
100	85.3	**Simonton Lake** (CDP) Elkhart County
100	85.3	**Tipton** (city) Tipton County
103	85.1	**Linton** (city) Greene County
104	85.0	**Elwood** (city) Madison County
104	85.0	**Sheridan** (town) Hamilton County
106	84.9	**Austin** (city) Scott County
106	84.9	**Lawrence** (city) Marion County
108	84.8	**Alexandria** (city) Madison County
108	84.8	**Aurora** (city) Dearborn County
108	84.8	**Greenwood** (city) Johnson County
108	84.8	**Portland** (city) Jay County
112	84.7	**Delphi** (city) Carroll County
112	84.7	**Winchester** (city) Randolph County
114	84.6	**Ellettsville** (town) Monroe County
115	84.5	**Kokomo** (city) Howard County
116	84.4	**Corydon** (town) Harrison County
116	84.4	**Greensburg** (city) Decatur County
118	84.2	**Charlestown** (city) Clark County
118	84.2	**Warsaw** (city) Kosciusko County
120	84.1	**Salem** (city) Washington County
121	84.0	**Paoli** (town) Orange County
122	83.8	**Evansville** (city) Vanderburgh County
122	83.8	**Hebron** (town) Porter County
122	83.8	**Vincennes** (city) Knox County
125	83.7	**Crawfordsville** (city) Montgomery County
125	83.7	**Fort Wayne** (city) Allen County
127	83.6	**Nappanee** (city) Elkhart County
128	83.5	**Centerville** (town) Wayne County
128	83.5	**Clinton** (city) Vermillion County
128	83.5	**Edinburgh** (town) Johnson County
128	83.5	**Marion** (city) Grant County
128	83.5	**Muncie** (city) Delaware County
133	83.3	**Martinsville** (city) Morgan County
133	83.3	**New Albany** (city) Floyd County
135	83.2	**Michigan City** (city) LaPorte County
136	83.1	**Kendallville** (city) Noble County
137	83.0	**Lebanon** (city) Boone County
137	83.0	**Rushville** (city) Rush County
139	82.9	**Chesterfield** (town) Madison County
139	82.9	**Seymour** (city) Jackson County
141	82.7	**Sellersburg** (town) Clark County
142	82.6	**Huntington** (city) Huntington County
142	82.6	**Indianapolis** (city) Marion County
144	82.5	**Bedford** (city) Lawrence County
144	82.5	**Bicknell** (city) Knox County
144	82.5	**Peru** (city) Miami County
144	82.5	**South Bend** (city) Saint Joseph County
148	82.3	**La Porte** (city) LaPorte County
148	82.3	**McCordsville** (town) Hancock County
150	82.1	**Heritage Lake** (CDP) Putnam County

Note: This section ranks incorporated places and CDPs (Census Designated Places) with populations of 2,500 or more. Unincorporated postal areas were not considered. Please refer to the User Guide for additional information.

Population with Health Insurance
Top 150 Places Ranked in *Ascending* Order

State Rank	Percent	Place
1	73.1	**Country Squire Lakes** (CDP) Jennings County
2	73.2	**Mitchell** (city) Lawrence County
3	73.3	**Lagrange** (town) LaGrange County
4	74.2	**Ligonier** (city) Noble County
5	74.9	**Sullivan** (city) Sullivan County
6	75.2	**Cicero** (town) Hamilton County
7	75.7	**Elkhart** (city) Elkhart County
8	75.8	**Lake Station** (city) Lake County
9	77.7	**Roselawn** (CDP) Newton County
9	77.7	**Syracuse** (town) Kosciusko County
11	77.9	**Logansport** (city) Cass County
12	78.5	**Goshen** (city) Elkhart County
13	78.6	**Hartford City** (city) Blackford County
14	78.8	**Butler** (city) DeKalb County
15	79.0	**North Vernon** (city) Jennings County
16	79.1	**East Chicago** (city) Lake County
17	79.3	**Anderson** (city) Madison County
17	79.3	**Hammond** (city) Lake County
19	79.4	**Frankfort** (city) Clinton County
19	79.4	**Huntingburg** (city) Dubois County
21	79.7	**Richmond** (city) Wayne County
22	79.8	**Connersville** (city) Fayette County
23	79.9	**Chandler** (town) Warrick County
24	80.3	**Knox** (city) Starke County
25	80.4	**Brazil** (city) Clay County
25	80.4	**Dunlap** (CDP) Elkhart County
27	80.6	**Plymouth** (city) Marshall County
28	80.9	**Terre Haute** (city) Vigo County
29	81.1	**Gary** (city) Lake County
30	81.2	**New Castle** (city) Henry County
30	81.2	**Shelbyville** (city) Shelby County
32	81.3	**Rockville** (town) Parke County
32	81.3	**Union City** (city) Randolph County
34	81.4	**Gas City** (city) Grant County
35	81.5	**Clarksville** (town) Clark County
35	81.5	**Mishawaka** (city) Saint Joseph County
35	81.5	**Speedway** (town) Marion County
38	81.9	**Lafayette** (city) Tippecanoe County
39	82.1	**Heritage Lake** (CDP) Putnam County
40	82.3	**La Porte** (city) LaPorte County
40	82.3	**McCordsville** (town) Hancock County
42	82.5	**Bedford** (city) Lawrence County
42	82.5	**Bicknell** (city) Knox County
42	82.5	**Peru** (city) Miami County
42	82.5	**South Bend** (city) Saint Joseph County
46	82.6	**Huntington** (city) Huntington County
46	82.6	**Indianapolis** (city) Marion County
48	82.7	**Sellersburg** (town) Clark County
49	82.9	**Chesterfield** (town) Madison County
49	82.9	**Seymour** (city) Jackson County
51	83.0	**Lebanon** (city) Boone County
51	83.0	**Rushville** (city) Rush County
53	83.1	**Kendallville** (city) Noble County
54	83.2	**Michigan City** (city) LaPorte County
55	83.3	**Martinsville** (city) Morgan County
55	83.3	**New Albany** (city) Floyd County
57	83.5	**Centerville** (town) Wayne County
57	83.5	**Clinton** (city) Vermillion County
57	83.5	**Edinburgh** (town) Johnson County
57	83.5	**Marion** (city) Grant County
57	83.5	**Muncie** (city) Delaware County
62	83.6	**Nappanee** (city) Elkhart County
63	83.7	**Crawfordsville** (city) Montgomery County
63	83.7	**Fort Wayne** (city) Allen County
65	83.8	**Evansville** (city) Vanderburgh County
65	83.8	**Hebron** (town) Porter County
65	83.8	**Vincennes** (city) Knox County
68	84.0	**Paoli** (town) Orange County
69	84.1	**Salem** (city) Washington County
70	84.2	**Charlestown** (city) Clark County
70	84.2	**Warsaw** (city) Kosciusko County
72	84.4	**Corydon** (town) Harrison County
72	84.4	**Greensburg** (city) Decatur County
74	84.5	**Kokomo** (city) Howard County
75	84.6	**Ellettsville** (town) Monroe County
76	84.7	**Delphi** (city) Carroll County
76	84.7	**Winchester** (city) Randolph County
78	84.8	**Alexandria** (city) Madison County
78	84.8	**Aurora** (city) Dearborn County
78	84.8	**Greenwood** (city) Johnson County
78	84.8	**Portland** (city) Jay County
82	84.9	**Austin** (city) Scott County
82	84.9	**Lawrence** (city) Marion County
84	85.0	**Elwood** (city) Madison County
84	85.0	**Sheridan** (town) Hamilton County
86	85.1	**Linton** (city) Greene County
87	85.3	**New Haven** (city) Allen County
87	85.3	**Simonton Lake** (CDP) Elkhart County
87	85.3	**Tipton** (city) Tipton County
90	85.4	**Brownstown** (town) Jackson County
90	85.4	**Portage** (city) Porter County
92	85.5	**Grissom AFB** (CDP) Miami County
92	85.5	**Merrillville** (town) Lake County
92	85.5	**Rochester** (city) Fulton County
95	85.6	**Valparaiso** (city) Porter County
96	85.7	**Auburn** (city) DeKalb County
96	85.7	**Bluffton** (city) Wells County
96	85.7	**Madison** (city) Jefferson County
96	85.7	**Scottsburg** (city) Scott County
96	85.7	**South Haven** (CDP) Porter County
101	85.8	**Cedar Lake** (town) Lake County
102	86.2	**Bremen** (town) Marshall County
103	86.3	**Boonville** (city) Warrick County
103	86.3	**Jeffersonville** (city) Clark County
103	86.3	**Lowell** (town) Lake County
103	86.3	**Washington** (city) Daviess County
107	86.4	**Princeton** (city) Gibson County
108	86.6	**Whiting** (city) Lake County
109	86.7	**Columbia City** (city) Whitley County
109	86.7	**Decatur** (city) Adams County
109	86.7	**Hanover** (town) Jefferson County
112	86.8	**Wabash** (city) Wabash County
113	86.9	**Fairmount** (town) Grant County
114	87.0	**Mooresville** (town) Morgan County
114	87.0	**Newburgh** (town) Warrick County
116	87.1	**Brookville** (town) Franklin County
116	87.1	**Greenfield** (city) Hancock County
116	87.1	**Lawrenceburg** (city) Dearborn County
116	87.1	**Westville** (town) LaPorte County
120	87.2	**Angola** (city) Steuben County
121	87.3	**Attica** (city) Fountain County
121	87.3	**New Whiteland** (town) Johnson County
123	87.4	**Monticello** (city) White County
123	87.4	**Porter** (town) Porter County
125	87.5	**Beech Grove** (city) Marion County
125	87.5	**Ossian** (town) Wells County
127	87.6	**North Terre Haute** (CDP) Vigo County
127	87.6	**Pendleton** (town) Madison County
129	87.7	**Bloomington** (city) Monroe County
129	87.7	**Fortville** (town) Hancock County
129	87.7	**Mount Vernon** (city) Posey County
132	87.8	**Greendale** (city) Dearborn County
133	87.9	**Columbus** (city) Bartholomew County
134	88.0	**Hobart** (city) Lake County
134	88.0	**Plainfield** (town) Hendricks County
136	88.1	**Shorewood Forest** (CDP) Porter County
137	88.2	**Griffith** (town) Lake County
138	88.3	**De Motte** (town) Jasper County
139	88.4	**Pittsboro** (town) Hendricks County
140	88.6	**Smithville-Sanders** (CDP) Monroe County
141	88.7	**Loogootee** (city) Martin County
142	88.8	**North Manchester** (town) Wabash County
143	88.9	**Rensselaer** (city) Jasper County
144	89.1	**Garrett** (city) DeKalb County
145	89.2	**Crown Point** (city) Lake County
145	89.2	**Winona Lake** (town) Kosciusko County
147	89.6	**Franklin** (city) Johnson County
148	89.8	**Tell City** (city) Perry County
149	90.1	**Berne** (city) Adams County
149	90.1	**Greencastle** (city) Putnam County

Note: *This section ranks incorporated places and CDPs (Census Designated Places) with populations of 2,500 or more. Unincorporated postal areas were not considered. Please refer to the User Guide for additional information.*

Population with Private Health Insurance
Top 150 Places Ranked in *Descending* Order

State Rank	Percent	Place
1	92.9	**Purdue University** (CDP) Tippecanoe County
2	92.4	**Notre Dame** (CDP) Saint Joseph County
3	92.2	**Zionsville** (town) Boone County
4	91.1	**Carmel** (city) Hamilton County
5	89.9	**West Lafayette** (city) Tippecanoe County
6	89.7	**Huntertown** (town) Allen County
7	88.8	**Granger** (CDP) Saint Joseph County
8	88.3	**Saint John** (town) Lake County
9	88.1	**Fishers** (town) Hamilton County
10	87.5	**Highland** (CDP) Vanderburgh County
11	87.4	**Westfield** (city) Hamilton County
12	86.0	**Lakes of the Four Seasons** (CDP) Lake County
13	85.6	**Georgetown** (town) Floyd County
14	85.4	**Bargersville** (town) Johnson County
15	84.8	**Hidden Valley** (CDP) Dearborn County
16	84.7	**Brownsburg** (town) Hendricks County
17	84.6	**Winfield** (town) Lake County
18	84.4	**Dyer** (town) Lake County
19	84.3	**Chesterton** (town) Porter County
20	84.1	**Upland** (town) Grant County
21	83.3	**Whitestown** (town) Boone County
22	82.9	**Avon** (town) Hendricks County
22	82.9	**Bright** (CDP) Dearborn County
24	82.7	**Melody Hill** (CDP) Vanderburgh County
24	82.7	**Munster** (town) Lake County
26	82.5	**Noblesville** (city) Hamilton County
27	82.4	**Leo-Cedarville** (town) Allen County
28	82.3	**Whiteland** (town) Johnson County
29	82.2	**Jasper** (city) Dubois County
29	82.2	**Schererville** (town) Lake County
31	81.4	**Shorewood Forest** (CDP) Porter County
32	80.7	**McCordsville** (town) Hancock County
33	80.6	**Batesville** (city) Ripley County
34	80.3	**Winona Lake** (town) Kosciusko County
35	79.4	**Crown Point** (city) Lake County
36	79.0	**Smithville-Sanders** (CDP) Monroe County
37	78.9	**Pittsboro** (town) Hendricks County
38	78.1	**Fort Branch** (town) Gibson County
38	78.1	**Middlebury** (town) Elkhart County
40	78.0	**Yorktown** (town) Delaware County
41	77.8	**Highland** (town) Lake County
42	77.7	**Danville** (town) Hendricks County
43	77.5	**Bloomington** (city) Monroe County
44	77.3	**Newburgh** (town) Warrick County
45	76.7	**De Motte** (town) Jasper County
46	76.4	**Covington** (city) Fountain County
47	75.4	**Lowell** (town) Lake County
48	75.3	**Greencastle** (city) Putnam County
49	75.2	**Columbus** (city) Bartholomew County
49	75.2	**Plainfield** (town) Hendricks County
51	75.1	**Rensselaer** (city) Jasper County
52	75.0	**Hobart** (city) Lake County
53	74.4	**Griffith** (town) Lake County
54	73.8	**Valparaiso** (city) Porter County
55	73.3	**Ossian** (town) Wells County
56	72.7	**Simonton Lake** (CDP) Elkhart County
57	72.6	**Brownstown** (town) Jackson County
57	72.6	**Franklin** (city) Johnson County
57	72.6	**New Whiteland** (town) Johnson County
60	72.5	**South Haven** (CDP) Porter County
61	72.3	**Auburn** (city) DeKalb County
62	72.1	**Porter** (town) Porter County
63	72.0	**Berne** (city) Adams County
64	71.8	**Greenfield** (city) Hancock County
65	71.6	**Mooresville** (town) Morgan County
66	71.4	**Tell City** (city) Perry County
67	71.2	**Greendale** (city) Dearborn County
68	71.1	**Jeffersonville** (city) Clark County
69	70.8	**Sellersburg** (town) Clark County
70	70.7	**Hebron** (town) Porter County
71	70.3	**Cedar Lake** (town) Lake County
72	69.9	**Ellettsville** (town) Monroe County
72	69.9	**Hanover** (town) Jefferson County
74	69.8	**Monticello** (city) White County
74	69.8	**North Terre Haute** (CDP) Vigo County
74	69.8	**Portage** (city) Porter County
77	69.6	**Decatur** (city) Adams County
78	69.5	**New Haven** (city) Allen County
79	69.4	**Boonville** (city) Warrick County
80	69.2	**Greenwood** (city) Johnson County
81	69.0	**Angola** (city) Steuben County
82	68.9	**Madison** (city) Jefferson County
83	68.7	**Mount Vernon** (city) Posey County
84	68.4	**Fairmount** (town) Grant County
85	67.9	**Cicero** (town) Hamilton County
86	67.8	**Bremen** (town) Marshall County
86	67.8	**Garrett** (city) DeKalb County
88	67.5	**Delphi** (city) Carroll County
88	67.5	**Whiting** (city) Lake County
90	67.3	**Pendleton** (town) Madison County
91	67.2	**Lebanon** (city) Boone County
92	67.0	**Attica** (city) Fountain County
92	67.0	**Roselawn** (CDP) Newton County
92	67.0	**Tipton** (city) Tipton County
95	66.7	**Dunlap** (CDP) Elkhart County
96	66.6	**Sheridan** (town) Hamilton County
97	66.5	**Heritage Lake** (CDP) Putnam County
97	66.5	**Warsaw** (city) Kosciusko County
99	66.4	**Alexandria** (city) Madison County
100	66.3	**North Manchester** (town) Wabash County
101	66.1	**Bluffton** (city) Wells County
101	66.1	**Fortville** (town) Hancock County
101	66.1	**Nappanee** (city) Elkhart County
104	65.6	**Lawrence** (city) Marion County
105	65.5	**Portland** (city) Jay County
106	65.3	**Merrillville** (town) Lake County
106	65.3	**Seymour** (city) Jackson County
108	65.1	**Princeton** (city) Gibson County
109	64.5	**Vincennes** (city) Knox County
110	64.4	**Beech Grove** (city) Marion County
111	64.3	**Charlestown** (city) Clark County
112	63.9	**Brookville** (town) Franklin County
113	63.4	**Lawrenceburg** (city) Dearborn County
114	63.1	**Centerville** (town) Wayne County
115	62.8	**Muncie** (city) Delaware County
115	62.8	**Scottsburg** (city) Scott County
117	62.7	**Clarksville** (town) Clark County
117	62.7	**Kokomo** (city) Howard County
119	62.6	**Columbia City** (city) Whitley County
119	62.6	**Fort Wayne** (city) Allen County
121	62.4	**Greensburg** (city) Decatur County
121	62.4	**Mishawaka** (city) Saint Joseph County
123	62.0	**Syracuse** (town) Kosciusko County
124	61.9	**New Albany** (city) Floyd County
125	61.8	**Aurora** (city) Dearborn County
126	61.7	**Lafayette** (city) Tippecanoe County
127	61.3	**Evansville** (city) Vanderburgh County
128	60.8	**Grissom AFB** (CDP) Miami County
129	60.7	**Washington** (city) Daviess County
130	60.5	**Cumberland** (town) Marion County
131	60.3	**Huntington** (city) Huntington County
132	60.1	**Wabash** (city) Wabash County
133	59.8	**Loogootee** (city) Martin County
134	59.4	**Indianapolis** (city) Marion County
135	58.9	**Linton** (city) Greene County
136	58.6	**Rushville** (city) Rush County
136	58.6	**Speedway** (town) Marion County
138	58.4	**La Porte** (city) LaPorte County
138	58.4	**Rockville** (town) Parke County
140	58.3	**Westville** (town) LaPorte County
141	58.2	**Shelbyville** (city) Shelby County
142	58.0	**Hartford City** (city) Blackford County
143	57.7	**Elwood** (city) Madison County
143	57.7	**Terre Haute** (city) Vigo County
145	57.4	**Chesterfield** (town) Madison County
146	57.2	**Kendallville** (city) Noble County
147	57.1	**Martinsville** (city) Morgan County
147	57.1	**Paoli** (town) Orange County
149	57.0	**Bedford** (city) Lawrence County
150	56.8	**Goshen** (city) Elkhart County

Note: This section ranks incorporated places and CDPs (Census Designated Places) with populations of 2,500 or more. Unincorporated postal areas were not considered. Please refer to the User Guide for additional information.

Population with Private Health Insurance
Top 150 Places Ranked in *Ascending* Order

State Rank	Percent	Place
1	37.3	**Country Squire Lakes** (CDP) Jennings County
2	39.2	**East Chicago** (city) Lake County
3	41.0	**Gary** (city) Lake County
4	46.5	**Ligonier** (city) Noble County
5	47.1	**Austin** (city) Scott County
5	47.1	**Connersville** (city) Fayette County
5	47.1	**Elkhart** (city) Elkhart County
8	47.3	**Mitchell** (city) Lawrence County
9	48.2	**Lagrange** (town) LaGrange County
10	49.1	**Sullivan** (city) Sullivan County
10	49.1	**Winchester** (city) Randolph County
12	49.2	**Butler** (city) DeKalb County
13	49.7	**Knox** (city) Starke County
14	49.9	**Brazil** (city) Clay County
15	51.3	**Union City** (city) Randolph County
16	51.4	**Peru** (city) Miami County
17	51.8	**Plymouth** (city) Marshall County
18	52.1	**North Vernon** (city) Jennings County
19	52.2	**Bicknell** (city) Knox County
20	52.3	**Chandler** (town) Warrick County
21	52.6	**Richmond** (city) Wayne County
22	52.9	**Lake Station** (city) Lake County
23	53.0	**Anderson** (city) Madison County
24	53.4	**Hammond** (city) Lake County
24	53.4	**Michigan City** (city) LaPorte County
26	53.7	**Edinburgh** (town) Johnson County
27	54.2	**Salem** (city) Washington County
28	54.6	**Rochester** (city) Fulton County
29	55.4	**Marion** (city) Grant County
30	55.5	**Huntingburg** (city) Dubois County
30	55.5	**Logansport** (city) Cass County
32	55.9	**Corydon** (town) Harrison County
33	56.0	**Clinton** (city) Vermillion County
34	56.1	**New Castle** (city) Henry County
35	56.2	**South Bend** (city) Saint Joseph County
36	56.5	**Crawfordsville** (city) Montgomery County
37	56.6	**Frankfort** (city) Clinton County
38	56.7	**Gas City** (city) Grant County
39	56.8	**Goshen** (city) Elkhart County
40	57.0	**Bedford** (city) Lawrence County
41	57.1	**Martinsville** (city) Morgan County
41	57.1	**Paoli** (town) Orange County
43	57.2	**Kendallville** (city) Noble County
44	57.4	**Chesterfield** (town) Madison County
45	57.7	**Elwood** (city) Madison County
45	57.7	**Terre Haute** (city) Vigo County
47	58.0	**Hartford City** (city) Blackford County
48	58.2	**Shelbyville** (city) Shelby County
49	58.3	**Westville** (town) LaPorte County
50	58.4	**La Porte** (city) LaPorte County
50	58.4	**Rockville** (town) Parke County
52	58.6	**Rushville** (city) Rush County
52	58.6	**Speedway** (town) Marion County
54	58.9	**Linton** (city) Greene County
55	59.4	**Indianapolis** (city) Marion County
56	59.8	**Loogootee** (city) Martin County
57	60.1	**Wabash** (city) Wabash County
58	60.3	**Huntington** (city) Huntington County
59	60.5	**Cumberland** (town) Marion County
60	60.7	**Washington** (city) Daviess County
61	60.8	**Grissom AFB** (CDP) Miami County
62	61.3	**Evansville** (city) Vanderburgh County
63	61.7	**Lafayette** (city) Tippecanoe County
64	61.8	**Aurora** (city) Dearborn County
65	61.9	**New Albany** (city) Floyd County
66	62.0	**Syracuse** (town) Kosciusko County
67	62.4	**Greensburg** (city) Decatur County
67	62.4	**Mishawaka** (city) Saint Joseph County
69	62.6	**Columbia City** (city) Whitley County
69	62.6	**Fort Wayne** (city) Allen County
71	62.7	**Clarksville** (town) Clark County
71	62.7	**Kokomo** (city) Howard County
73	62.8	**Muncie** (city) Delaware County
73	62.8	**Scottsburg** (city) Scott County
75	63.1	**Centerville** (town) Wayne County
76	63.4	**Lawrenceburg** (city) Dearborn County
77	63.9	**Brookville** (town) Franklin County
78	64.3	**Charlestown** (city) Clark County
79	64.4	**Beech Grove** (city) Marion County
80	64.5	**Vincennes** (city) Knox County
81	65.1	**Princeton** (city) Gibson County
82	65.3	**Merrillville** (town) Lake County
82	65.3	**Seymour** (city) Jackson County
84	65.5	**Portland** (city) Jay County
85	65.6	**Lawrence** (city) Marion County
86	66.1	**Bluffton** (city) Wells County
86	66.1	**Fortville** (town) Hancock County
86	66.1	**Nappanee** (city) Elkhart County
89	66.3	**North Manchester** (town) Wabash County
90	66.4	**Alexandria** (city) Madison County
91	66.5	**Heritage Lake** (CDP) Putnam County
91	66.5	**Warsaw** (city) Kosciusko County
93	66.6	**Sheridan** (town) Hamilton County
94	66.7	**Dunlap** (CDP) Elkhart County
95	67.0	**Attica** (city) Fountain County
95	67.0	**Roselawn** (CDP) Newton County
95	67.0	**Tipton** (city) Tipton County
98	67.2	**Lebanon** (city) Boone County
99	67.3	**Pendleton** (town) Madison County
100	67.5	**Delphi** (city) Carroll County
100	67.5	**Whiting** (city) Lake County
102	67.8	**Bremen** (town) Marshall County
102	67.8	**Garrett** (city) DeKalb County
104	67.9	**Cicero** (town) Hamilton County
105	68.4	**Fairmount** (town) Grant County
106	68.7	**Mount Vernon** (city) Posey County
107	68.9	**Madison** (city) Jefferson County
108	69.0	**Angola** (city) Steuben County
109	69.2	**Greenwood** (city) Johnson County
110	69.4	**Boonville** (city) Warrick County
111	69.5	**New Haven** (city) Allen County
112	69.6	**Decatur** (city) Adams County
113	69.8	**Monticello** (city) White County
113	69.8	**North Terre Haute** (CDP) Vigo County
113	69.8	**Portage** (city) Porter County
116	69.9	**Ellettsville** (town) Monroe County
116	69.9	**Hanover** (town) Jefferson County
118	70.3	**Cedar Lake** (town) Lake County
119	70.7	**Hebron** (town) Porter County
120	70.8	**Sellersburg** (town) Clark County
121	71.1	**Jeffersonville** (city) Clark County
122	71.2	**Greendale** (city) Dearborn County
123	71.4	**Tell City** (city) Perry County
124	71.6	**Mooresville** (town) Morgan County
125	71.8	**Greenfield** (city) Hancock County
126	72.0	**Berne** (city) Adams County
127	72.1	**Porter** (town) Porter County
128	72.3	**Auburn** (city) DeKalb County
129	72.5	**South Haven** (CDP) Porter County
130	72.6	**Brownstown** (town) Jackson County
130	72.6	**Franklin** (city) Johnson County
130	72.6	**New Whiteland** (town) Johnson County
133	72.7	**Simonton Lake** (CDP) Elkhart County
134	73.3	**Ossian** (town) Wells County
135	73.8	**Valparaiso** (city) Porter County
136	74.4	**Griffith** (town) Lake County
137	75.0	**Hobart** (city) Lake County
138	75.1	**Rensselaer** (city) Jasper County
139	75.2	**Columbus** (city) Bartholomew County
139	75.2	**Plainfield** (town) Hendricks County
141	75.3	**Greencastle** (city) Putnam County
142	75.4	**Lowell** (town) Lake County
143	76.4	**Covington** (city) Fountain County
144	76.7	**De Motte** (town) Jasper County
145	77.3	**Newburgh** (town) Warrick County
146	77.5	**Bloomington** (town) Monroe County
147	77.7	**Danville** (town) Hendricks County
148	77.8	**Highland** (town) Lake County
149	78.0	**Yorktown** (town) Delaware County
150	78.1	**Fort Branch** (town) Gibson County

Note: This section ranks incorporated places and CDPs (Census Designated Places) with populations of 2,500 or more. Unincorporated postal areas were not considered. Please refer to the User Guide for additional information.

Population with Public Health Insurance
Top 150 Places Ranked in *Descending* Order

State Rank	Percent	Place
1	52.1	**Gary** (city) Lake County
2	50.2	**Country Squire Lakes** (CDP) Jennings County
3	48.6	**Winchester** (city) Randolph County
4	48.1	**East Chicago** (city) Lake County
5	47.3	**Connersville** (city) Fayette County
6	47.1	**Austin** (city) Scott County
7	46.1	**Loogootee** (city) Martin County
7	46.1	**Rochester** (city) Fulton County
9	46.0	**Union City** (city) Randolph County
10	44.8	**Brookville** (town) Franklin County
11	43.9	**Edinburgh** (town) Johnson County
12	43.5	**Peru** (city) Miami County
13	43.3	**Sullivan** (city) Sullivan County
14	42.9	**Linton** (city) Greene County
14	42.9	**Salem** (city) Washington County
16	42.7	**Marion** (city) Grant County
17	42.6	**Bicknell** (city) Knox County
18	42.4	**Corydon** (town) Harrison County
19	42.1	**Chesterfield** (town) Madison County
20	41.8	**Knox** (city) Starke County
21	41.7	**Michigan City** (city) LaPorte County
22	41.6	**Rockville** (town) Parke County
23	41.4	**Brazil** (city) Clay County
23	41.4	**Chandler** (town) Warrick County
25	41.2	**Bedford** (city) Lawrence County
26	40.9	**Anderson** (city) Madison County
27	40.6	**North Vernon** (city) Jennings County
27	40.6	**Wabash** (city) Wabash County
29	40.4	**Lagrange** (town) LaGrange County
29	40.4	**New Castle** (city) Henry County
31	40.1	**Kendallville** (city) Noble County
32	40.0	**Crawfordsville** (city) Montgomery County
33	39.9	**Lawrenceburg** (city) Dearborn County
34	39.8	**Paoli** (town) Orange County
35	39.5	**Butler** (city) DeKalb County
35	39.5	**Richmond** (city) Wayne County
37	39.2	**Columbia City** (city) Whitley County
38	39.1	**Martinsville** (city) Morgan County
39	39.0	**Berne** (city) Adams County
39	39.0	**Elkhart** (city) Elkhart County
41	38.9	**Clinton** (city) Vermillion County
41	38.9	**Hartford City** (city) Blackford County
43	38.5	**Mitchell** (city) Lawrence County
43	38.5	**Plymouth** (city) Marshall County
43	38.5	**Rushville** (city) Rush County
46	38.2	**Cumberland** (town) Marion County
47	38.0	**Elwood** (city) Madison County
48	37.5	**Princeton** (city) Gibson County
49	37.4	**Kokomo** (city) Howard County
49	37.4	**Scottsburg** (city) Scott County
51	37.2	**Ligonier** (city) Noble County
52	37.1	**Pendleton** (town) Madison County
53	37.0	**Grissom AFB** (CDP) Miami County
54	36.9	**Gas City** (city) Grant County
55	36.6	**Middlebury** (town) Elkhart County
56	36.5	**Attica** (city) Fountain County
56	36.5	**Washington** (city) Daviess County
58	36.4	**Aurora** (city) Dearborn County
58	36.4	**South Bend** (city) Saint Joseph County
60	36.2	**Bluffton** (city) Wells County
60	36.2	**Tipton** (city) Tipton County
62	36.1	**Alexandria** (city) Madison County
63	35.9	**Beech Grove** (city) Marion County
63	35.9	**La Porte** (city) LaPorte County
65	35.7	**North Manchester** (town) Wabash County
66	35.3	**Fortville** (town) Hancock County
67	35.1	**Centerville** (town) Wayne County
68	35.0	**Boonville** (city) Warrick County
69	34.9	**Hammond** (city) Lake County
70	34.8	**Westville** (town) LaPorte County
71	34.5	**New Albany** (city) Floyd County
72	34.4	**Frankfort** (city) Clinton County
73	34.2	**Covington** (city) Fountain County
74	34.1	**Logansport** (city) Cass County
75	34.0	**Evansville** (city) Vanderburgh County
75	34.0	**Huntingburg** (city) Dubois County
77	33.9	**Goshen** (city) Elkhart County
77	33.9	**Shelbyville** (city) Shelby County
79	33.8	**Huntington** (city) Huntington County
79	33.8	**Lake Station** (city) Lake County
79	33.8	**Tell City** (city) Perry County
82	33.7	**Terre Haute** (city) Vigo County
83	33.5	**Greensburg** (city) Decatur County
84	33.4	**Portland** (city) Jay County
85	33.3	**Merrillville** (town) Lake County
85	33.3	**Speedway** (town) Marion County
87	33.0	**Brownstown** (town) Jackson County
88	32.7	**Madison** (city) Jefferson County
89	32.6	**Indianapolis** (city) Marion County
90	32.5	**Simonton Lake** (CDP) Elkhart County
90	32.5	**Yorktown** (town) Delaware County
92	32.4	**Delphi** (city) Carroll County
93	32.1	**Muncie** (city) Delaware County
94	31.9	**Garrett** (city) DeKalb County
94	31.9	**Mount Vernon** (city) Posey County
94	31.9	**Vincennes** (city) Knox County
97	31.4	**North Terre Haute** (CDP) Vigo County
98	31.2	**Monticello** (city) White County
99	31.0	**Fairmount** (town) Grant County
100	30.8	**Angola** (city) Steuben County
101	30.7	**Fort Wayne** (city) Allen County
102	30.5	**Charlestown** (city) Clark County
103	30.4	**Mishawaka** (city) Saint Joseph County
104	30.3	**Warsaw** (city) Kosciusko County
105	30.1	**Bremen** (town) Marshall County
106	29.8	**Lafayette** (city) Tippecanoe County
107	29.7	**Clarksville** (town) Clark County
108	29.6	**Rensselaer** (city) Jasper County
109	29.2	**Nappanee** (city) Elkhart County
110	29.0	**Franklin** (city) Johnson County
111	28.9	**Lawrence** (city) Marion County
112	28.8	**De Motte** (town) Jasper County
113	28.4	**Greendale** (city) Dearborn County
114	28.3	**Jeffersonville** (city) Clark County
115	28.2	**Greenfield** (city) Hancock County
116	28.1	**Mooresville** (town) Morgan County
117	28.0	**Decatur** (city) Adams County
117	28.0	**Ellettsville** (town) Monroe County
117	28.0	**Whiting** (city) Lake County
120	27.9	**Seymour** (city) Jackson County
121	27.8	**New Haven** (city) Allen County
122	27.6	**Auburn** (city) DeKalb County
123	27.5	**Portage** (city) Porter County
124	27.0	**Fort Branch** (town) Gibson County
124	27.0	**Lebanon** (city) Boone County
124	27.0	**Sheridan** (town) Hamilton County
127	26.6	**Syracuse** (town) Kosciusko County
128	26.3	**Greenwood** (city) Johnson County
128	26.3	**Hobart** (city) Lake County
130	26.0	**Hanover** (town) Jefferson County
131	25.9	**Griffith** (town) Lake County
131	25.9	**Highland** (town) Lake County
133	25.7	**Ossian** (town) Wells County
133	25.7	**South Haven** (CDP) Porter County
135	25.1	**Columbus** (city) Bartholomew County
135	25.1	**Heritage Lake** (CDP) Putnam County
137	25.0	**Greencastle** (city) Putnam County
138	24.9	**Cedar Lake** (town) Lake County
139	24.8	**Dunlap** (CDP) Elkhart County
140	24.5	**Melody Hill** (CDP) Vanderburgh County
140	24.5	**Plainfield** (town) Hendricks County
142	24.1	**Jasper** (city) Dubois County
143	23.9	**Porter** (town) Porter County
144	23.4	**Crown Point** (city) Lake County
144	23.4	**New Whiteland** (town) Johnson County
146	22.7	**Danville** (town) Hendricks County
146	22.7	**Munster** (town) Lake County
148	22.5	**Batesville** (city) Ripley County
149	22.4	**Sellersburg** (town) Clark County
149	22.4	**Valparaiso** (city) Porter County

Note: This section ranks incorporated places and CDPs (Census Designated Places) with populations of 2,500 or more. Unincorporated postal areas were not considered. Please refer to the User Guide for additional information.

Population with Public Health Insurance

Top 150 Places Ranked in *Ascending* Order

State Rank	Percent	Place
1	3.9	**Notre Dame** (CDP) Saint Joseph County
2	4.0	**McCordsville** (town) Hancock County
3	4.1	**Purdue University** (CDP) Tippecanoe County
4	9.1	**Fishers** (town) Hamilton County
5	11.1	**West Lafayette** (city) Tippecanoe County
6	11.8	**Zionsville** (town) Boone County
7	12.5	**Westfield** (city) Hamilton County
8	13.0	**Carmel** (city) Hamilton County
8	13.0	**Whitestown** (town) Boone County
10	13.6	**Huntertown** (town) Allen County
11	14.2	**Saint John** (town) Lake County
12	15.1	**Avon** (town) Hendricks County
13	15.9	**Bargersville** (town) Johnson County
14	16.1	**Brownsburg** (town) Hendricks County
15	16.4	**Pittsboro** (town) Hendricks County
16	16.6	**Upland** (town) Grant County
17	16.7	**Granger** (CDP) Saint Joseph County
18	16.9	**Bloomington** (city) Monroe County
19	17.0	**Noblesville** (city) Hamilton County
20	18.1	**Georgetown** (town) Floyd County
21	18.4	**Highland** (CDP) Vanderburgh County
22	18.7	**Leo-Cedarville** (town) Allen County
23	18.9	**Winona Lake** (town) Kosciusko County
24	19.4	**Whiteland** (town) Johnson County
25	19.6	**Lakes of the Four Seasons** (CDP) Lake County
26	19.7	**Chesterton** (town) Porter County
27	20.2	**Lowell** (town) Lake County
27	20.2	**Smithville-Sanders** (CDP) Monroe County
29	20.4	**Newburgh** (town) Warrick County
30	20.5	**Shorewood Forest** (CDP) Porter County
31	20.7	**Schererville** (town) Lake County
32	21.0	**Dyer** (town) Lake County
32	21.0	**Roselawn** (CDP) Newton County
34	21.6	**Cicero** (town) Hamilton County
34	21.6	**Winfield** (town) Lake County
36	21.8	**Bright** (CDP) Dearborn County
37	21.9	**Hidden Valley** (CDP) Dearborn County
38	22.2	**Hebron** (town) Porter County
39	22.4	**Sellersburg** (town) Clark County
39	22.4	**Valparaiso** (city) Porter County
41	22.5	**Batesville** (city) Ripley County
42	22.7	**Danville** (town) Hendricks County
42	22.7	**Munster** (town) Lake County
44	23.4	**Crown Point** (city) Lake County
44	23.4	**New Whiteland** (town) Johnson County
46	23.9	**Porter** (town) Porter County
47	24.1	**Jasper** (city) Dubois County
48	24.5	**Melody Hill** (CDP) Vanderburgh County
48	24.5	**Plainfield** (town) Hendricks County
50	24.8	**Dunlap** (CDP) Elkhart County
51	24.9	**Cedar Lake** (town) Lake County
52	25.0	**Greencastle** (city) Putnam County
53	25.1	**Columbus** (city) Bartholomew County
53	25.1	**Heritage Lake** (CDP) Putnam County
55	25.7	**Ossian** (town) Wells County
55	25.7	**South Haven** (CDP) Porter County
57	25.9	**Griffith** (town) Lake County
57	25.9	**Highland** (town) Lake County
59	26.0	**Hanover** (town) Jefferson County
60	26.3	**Greenwood** (city) Johnson County
60	26.3	**Hobart** (city) Lake County
62	26.6	**Syracuse** (town) Kosciusko County
63	27.0	**Fort Branch** (town) Gibson County
63	27.0	**Lebanon** (city) Boone County
63	27.0	**Sheridan** (town) Hamilton County
66	27.5	**Portage** (city) Porter County
67	27.6	**Auburn** (city) DeKalb County
68	27.8	**New Haven** (city) Allen County
69	27.9	**Seymour** (city) Jackson County
70	28.0	**Decatur** (city) Adams County
70	28.0	**Ellettsville** (town) Monroe County
70	28.0	**Whiting** (city) Lake County
73	28.1	**Mooresville** (town) Morgan County
74	28.2	**Greenfield** (city) Hancock County
75	28.3	**Jeffersonville** (city) Clark County
76	28.4	**Greendale** (city) Dearborn County
77	28.8	**De Motte** (town) Jasper County
78	28.9	**Lawrence** (city) Marion County
79	29.0	**Franklin** (city) Johnson County
80	29.2	**Nappanee** (city) Elkhart County
81	29.6	**Rensselaer** (city) Jasper County
82	29.7	**Clarksville** (town) Clark County
83	29.8	**Lafayette** (city) Tippecanoe County
84	30.1	**Bremen** (town) Marshall County
85	30.3	**Warsaw** (city) Kosciusko County
86	30.4	**Mishawaka** (city) Saint Joseph County
87	30.5	**Charlestown** (city) Clark County
88	30.7	**Fort Wayne** (city) Allen County
89	30.8	**Angola** (city) Steuben County
90	31.0	**Fairmount** (town) Grant County
91	31.2	**Monticello** (city) White County
92	31.4	**North Terre Haute** (CDP) Vigo County
93	31.9	**Garrett** (city) DeKalb County
93	31.9	**Mount Vernon** (city) Posey County
93	31.9	**Vincennes** (city) Knox County
96	32.1	**Muncie** (city) Delaware County
97	32.4	**Delphi** (city) Carroll County
98	32.5	**Simonton Lake** (CDP) Elkhart County
98	32.5	**Yorktown** (town) Delaware County
100	32.6	**Indianapolis** (city) Marion County
101	32.7	**Madison** (city) Jefferson County
102	33.0	**Brownstown** (town) Jackson County
103	33.3	**Merrillville** (town) Lake County
103	33.3	**Speedway** (town) Marion County
105	33.4	**Portland** (city) Jay County
106	33.5	**Greensburg** (city) Decatur County
107	33.7	**Terre Haute** (city) Vigo County
108	33.8	**Huntington** (city) Huntington County
108	33.8	**Lake Station** (city) Lake County
108	33.8	**Tell City** (city) Perry County
111	33.9	**Goshen** (city) Elkhart County
111	33.9	**Shelbyville** (city) Shelby County
113	34.0	**Evansville** (city) Vanderburgh County
113	34.0	**Huntingburg** (city) Dubois County
115	34.1	**Logansport** (city) Cass County
116	34.2	**Covington** (city) Fountain County
117	34.4	**Frankfort** (city) Clinton County
118	34.5	**New Albany** (city) Floyd County
119	34.8	**Westville** (town) LaPorte County
120	34.9	**Hammond** (city) Lake County
121	35.0	**Boonville** (city) Warrick County
122	35.1	**Centerville** (town) Wayne County
123	35.3	**Fortville** (town) Hancock County
124	35.7	**North Manchester** (town) Wabash County
125	35.9	**Beech Grove** (city) Marion County
125	35.9	**La Porte** (city) LaPorte County
127	36.1	**Alexandria** (city) Madison County
128	36.2	**Bluffton** (city) Wells County
128	36.2	**Tipton** (city) Tipton County
130	36.4	**Aurora** (city) Dearborn County
130	36.4	**South Bend** (city) Saint Joseph County
132	36.5	**Attica** (city) Fountain County
132	36.5	**Washington** (city) Daviess County
134	36.6	**Middlebury** (town) Elkhart County
135	36.9	**Gas City** (city) Grant County
136	37.0	**Grissom AFB** (CDP) Miami County
137	37.1	**Pendleton** (town) Madison County
138	37.2	**Ligonier** (city) Noble County
139	37.4	**Kokomo** (city) Howard County
139	37.4	**Scottsburg** (city) Scott County
141	37.5	**Princeton** (city) Gibson County
142	38.0	**Elwood** (city) Madison County
143	38.2	**Cumberland** (town) Marion County
144	38.5	**Mitchell** (city) Lawrence County
144	38.5	**Plymouth** (city) Marshall County
144	38.5	**Rushville** (city) Rush County
147	38.9	**Clinton** (city) Vermillion County
147	38.9	**Hartford City** (city) Blackford County
149	39.0	**Berne** (city) Adams County
149	39.0	**Elkhart** (city) Elkhart County

Note: This section ranks incorporated places and CDPs (Census Designated Places) with populations of 2,500 or more. Unincorporated postal areas were not considered. Please refer to the User Guide for additional information.

Population with No Health Insurance

Top 150 Places Ranked in *Descending* Order

State Rank	Percent	Place
1	26.9	Country Squire Lakes (CDP) Jennings County
2	26.8	Mitchell (city) Lawrence County
3	26.7	Lagrange (town) LaGrange County
4	25.8	Ligonier (city) Noble County
5	25.1	Sullivan (city) Sullivan County
6	24.8	Cicero (town) Hamilton County
7	24.3	Elkhart (city) Elkhart County
8	24.2	Lake Station (city) Lake County
9	22.3	Roselawn (CDP) Newton County
9	22.3	Syracuse (town) Kosciusko County
11	22.1	Logansport (city) Cass County
12	21.5	Goshen (city) Elkhart County
13	21.4	Hartford City (city) Blackford County
14	21.2	Butler (city) DeKalb County
15	21.0	North Vernon (city) Jennings County
16	20.9	East Chicago (city) Lake County
17	20.7	Anderson (city) Madison County
17	20.7	Hammond (city) Lake County
19	20.6	Frankfort (city) Clinton County
19	20.6	Huntingburg (city) Dubois County
21	20.3	Richmond (city) Wayne County
22	20.2	Connersville (city) Fayette County
23	20.1	Chandler (town) Warrick County
24	19.7	Knox (city) Starke County
25	19.6	Brazil (city) Clay County
25	19.6	Dunlap (CDP) Elkhart County
27	19.4	Plymouth (city) Marshall County
28	19.1	Terre Haute (city) Vigo County
29	18.9	Gary (city) Lake County
30	18.8	New Castle (city) Henry County
30	18.8	Shelbyville (city) Shelby County
32	18.7	Rockville (town) Parke County
32	18.7	Union City (city) Randolph County
34	18.6	Gas City (city) Grant County
35	18.5	Clarksville (town) Clark County
35	18.5	Mishawaka (city) Saint Joseph County
35	18.5	Speedway (town) Marion County
38	18.1	Lafayette (city) Tippecanoe County
39	17.9	Heritage Lake (CDP) Putnam County
40	17.7	La Porte (city) LaPorte County
40	17.7	McCordsville (town) Hancock County
42	17.5	Bedford (city) Lawrence County
42	17.5	Bicknell (city) Knox County
42	17.5	Peru (city) Miami County
42	17.5	South Bend (city) Saint Joseph County
46	17.4	Huntington (city) Huntington County
46	17.4	Indianapolis (city) Marion County
48	17.3	Sellersburg (town) Clark County
49	17.1	Chesterfield (town) Madison County
49	17.1	Seymour (city) Jackson County
51	17.0	Lebanon (city) Boone County
51	17.0	Rushville (city) Rush County
53	16.9	Kendallville (city) Noble County
54	16.8	Michigan City (city) LaPorte County
55	16.7	Martinsville (city) Morgan County
55	16.7	New Albany (city) Floyd County
57	16.5	Centerville (town) Wayne County
57	16.5	Clinton (city) Vermillion County
57	16.5	Edinburgh (town) Johnson County
57	16.5	Marion (city) Grant County
57	16.5	Muncie (city) Delaware County
62	16.4	Nappanee (city) Elkhart County
63	16.3	Crawfordsville (city) Montgomery County
63	16.3	Fort Wayne (city) Allen County
65	16.2	Evansville (city) Vanderburgh County
65	16.2	Hebron (town) Porter County
65	16.2	Vincennes (city) Knox County
68	16.0	Paoli (town) Orange County
69	15.9	Salem (city) Washington County
70	15.8	Charlestown (city) Clark County
70	15.8	Warsaw (city) Kosciusko County
72	15.6	Corydon (town) Harrison County
72	15.6	Greensburg (city) Decatur County
74	15.5	Kokomo (city) Howard County
75	15.4	Ellettsville (town) Monroe County
76	15.3	Delphi (city) Carroll County
76	15.3	Winchester (city) Randolph County
78	15.2	Alexandria (city) Madison County
78	15.2	Aurora (city) Dearborn County
78	15.2	Greenwood (city) Johnson County
78	15.2	Portland (city) Jay County
82	15.1	Austin (city) Scott County
82	15.1	Lawrence (city) Marion County
84	15.0	Elwood (city) Madison County
84	15.0	Sheridan (town) Hamilton County
86	14.9	Linton (city) Greene County
87	14.7	New Haven (city) Allen County
87	14.7	Simonton Lake (CDP) Elkhart County
87	14.7	Tipton (city) Tipton County
90	14.6	Brownstown (town) Jackson County
90	14.6	Portage (city) Porter County
92	14.5	Grissom AFB (CDP) Miami County
92	14.5	Merrillville (town) Lake County
92	14.5	Rochester (city) Fulton County
95	14.4	Valparaiso (city) Porter County
96	14.3	Auburn (city) DeKalb County
96	14.3	Bluffton (city) Wells County
96	14.3	Madison (city) Jefferson County
96	14.3	Scottsburg (city) Scott County
96	14.3	South Haven (CDP) Porter County
101	14.2	Cedar Lake (town) Lake County
102	13.8	Bremen (town) Marshall County
103	13.7	Boonville (city) Warrick County
103	13.7	Jeffersonville (city) Clark County
103	13.7	Lowell (town) Lake County
103	13.7	Washington (city) Daviess County
107	13.6	Princeton (city) Gibson County
108	13.4	Whiting (city) Lake County
109	13.3	Columbia City (city) Whitley County
109	13.3	Decatur (city) Adams County
109	13.3	Hanover (town) Jefferson County
112	13.2	Wabash (city) Wabash County
113	13.1	Fairmount (town) Grant County
114	13.0	Mooresville (town) Morgan County
114	13.0	Newburgh (town) Warrick County
116	12.9	Brookville (town) Franklin County
116	12.9	Greenfield (city) Hancock County
116	12.9	Lawrenceburg (city) Dearborn County
116	12.9	Westville (town) LaPorte County
120	12.8	Angola (city) Steuben County
121	12.7	Attica (city) Fountain County
121	12.7	New Whiteland (town) Johnson County
123	12.6	Monticello (city) White County
123	12.6	Porter (town) Porter County
125	12.5	Beech Grove (city) Marion County
125	12.5	Ossian (town) Wells County
127	12.4	North Terre Haute (CDP) Vigo County
127	12.4	Pendleton (town) Madison County
129	12.3	Bloomington (city) Monroe County
129	12.3	Fortville (town) Hancock County
129	12.3	Mount Vernon (city) Posey County
132	12.2	Greendale (city) Dearborn County
133	12.1	Columbus (city) Bartholomew County
134	12.0	Hobart (city) Lake County
134	12.0	Plainfield (town) Hendricks County
136	11.9	Shorewood Forest (CDP) Porter County
137	11.8	Griffith (town) Lake County
138	11.7	De Motte (town) Jasper County
139	11.6	Pittsboro (town) Hendricks County
140	11.4	Smithville-Sanders (CDP) Monroe County
141	11.3	Loogootee (city) Martin County
142	11.2	North Manchester (town) Wabash County
143	11.1	Rensselaer (city) Jasper County
144	10.9	Garrett (city) DeKalb County
145	10.8	Crown Point (city) Lake County
145	10.8	Winona Lake (town) Kosciusko County
147	10.4	Franklin (city) Johnson County
148	10.2	Tell City (city) Perry County
149	9.9	Berne (city) Adams County
149	9.9	Greencastle (city) Putnam County

Note: *This section ranks incorporated places and CDPs (Census Designated Places) with populations of 2,500 or more. Unincorporated postal areas were not considered. Please refer to the User Guide for additional information.*

Population with No Health Insurance
Top 150 Places Ranked in *Ascending* Order

State Rank	Percent	Place
1	3.7	**Zionsville** (town) Boone County
2	4.5	**Carmel** (city) Hamilton County
3	4.6	**Purdue University** (CDP) Tippecanoe County
4	5.0	**Granger** (CDP) Saint Joseph County
4	5.0	**Winfield** (town) Lake County
6	5.2	**Leo-Cedarville** (town) Allen County
7	5.4	**Huntertown** (town) Allen County
8	5.6	**Georgetown** (town) Floyd County
9	5.8	**Hidden Valley** (CDP) Dearborn County
9	5.8	**Notre Dame** (CDP) Saint Joseph County
11	5.9	**Bright** (CDP) Dearborn County
12	6.4	**Westfield** (city) Hamilton County
13	6.5	**Yorktown** (town) Delaware County
14	6.6	**Saint John** (town) Lake County
15	6.8	**Bargersville** (town) Johnson County
16	7.0	**West Lafayette** (city) Tippecanoe County
17	7.2	**Whiteland** (town) Johnson County
18	7.3	**Fishers** (town) Hamilton County
19	7.5	**Jasper** (city) Dubois County
19	7.5	**Munster** (town) Lake County
21	7.6	**Dyer** (town) Lake County
22	7.7	**Highland** (CDP) Vanderburgh County
23	7.9	**Chesterton** (town) Porter County
24	8.1	**Whitestown** (town) Boone County
25	8.2	**Fort Branch** (town) Gibson County
26	8.6	**Lakes of the Four Seasons** (CDP) Lake County
27	8.8	**Covington** (city) Fountain County
28	8.9	**Cumberland** (town) Marion County
28	8.9	**Upland** (town) Grant County
30	9.1	**Batesville** (city) Ripley County
31	9.3	**Noblesville** (city) Hamilton County
32	9.4	**Brownsburg** (town) Hendricks County
33	9.6	**Danville** (town) Hendricks County
34	9.7	**Avon** (town) Hendricks County
34	9.7	**Schererville** (town) Lake County
36	9.8	**Melody Hill** (CDP) Vanderburgh County
36	9.8	**Middlebury** (town) Elkhart County
38	9.9	**Berne** (city) Adams County
38	9.9	**Greencastle** (city) Putnam County
38	9.9	**Highland** (town) Lake County
41	10.2	**Tell City** (city) Perry County
42	10.4	**Franklin** (city) Johnson County
43	10.8	**Crown Point** (city) Lake County
43	10.8	**Winona Lake** (town) Kosciusko County
45	10.9	**Garrett** (city) DeKalb County
46	11.1	**Rensselaer** (city) Jasper County
47	11.2	**North Manchester** (town) Wabash County
48	11.3	**Loogootee** (city) Martin County
49	11.4	**Smithville-Sanders** (CDP) Monroe County
50	11.6	**Pittsboro** (town) Hendricks County
51	11.7	**De Motte** (town) Jasper County
52	11.8	**Griffith** (town) Lake County
53	11.9	**Shorewood Forest** (CDP) Porter County
54	12.0	**Hobart** (city) Lake County
54	12.0	**Plainfield** (town) Hendricks County
56	12.1	**Columbus** (city) Bartholomew County
57	12.2	**Greendale** (city) Dearborn County
58	12.3	**Bloomington** (city) Monroe County
58	12.3	**Fortville** (town) Hancock County
58	12.3	**Mount Vernon** (city) Posey County
61	12.4	**North Terre Haute** (CDP) Vigo County
61	12.4	**Pendleton** (town) Madison County
63	12.5	**Beech Grove** (city) Marion County
63	12.5	**Ossian** (town) Wells County
65	12.6	**Monticello** (city) White County
65	12.6	**Porter** (town) Porter County
67	12.7	**Attica** (city) Fountain County
67	12.7	**New Whiteland** (town) Johnson County
69	12.8	**Angola** (city) Steuben County
70	12.9	**Brookville** (town) Franklin County
70	12.9	**Greenfield** (city) Hancock County
70	12.9	**Lawrenceburg** (city) Dearborn County
70	12.9	**Westville** (town) LaPorte County
74	13.0	**Mooresville** (town) Morgan County
74	13.0	**Newburgh** (town) Warrick County
76	13.1	**Fairmount** (town) Grant County
77	13.2	**Wabash** (city) Wabash County
78	13.3	**Columbia City** (city) Whitley County
78	13.3	**Decatur** (city) Adams County
78	13.3	**Hanover** (town) Jefferson County
81	13.4	**Whiting** (city) Lake County
82	13.6	**Princeton** (city) Gibson County
83	13.7	**Boonville** (city) Warrick County
83	13.7	**Jeffersonville** (city) Clark County
83	13.7	**Lowell** (town) Lake County
83	13.7	**Washington** (city) Daviess County
87	13.8	**Bremen** (town) Marshall County
88	14.2	**Cedar Lake** (town) Lake County
89	14.3	**Auburn** (city) DeKalb County
89	14.3	**Bluffton** (city) Wells County
89	14.3	**Madison** (city) Jefferson County
89	14.3	**Scottsburg** (city) Scott County
89	14.3	**South Haven** (CDP) Porter County
94	14.4	**Valparaiso** (city) Porter County
95	14.5	**Grissom AFB** (CDP) Miami County
95	14.5	**Merrillville** (town) Lake County
95	14.5	**Rochester** (city) Fulton County
98	14.6	**Brownstown** (town) Jackson County
98	14.6	**Portage** (city) Porter County
100	14.7	**New Haven** (city) Allen County
100	14.7	**Simonton Lake** (CDP) Elkhart County
100	14.7	**Tipton** (city) Tipton County
103	14.9	**Linton** (city) Greene County
104	15.0	**Elwood** (city) Madison County
104	15.0	**Sheridan** (town) Hamilton County
106	15.1	**Austin** (city) Scott County
106	15.1	**Lawrence** (city) Marion County
108	15.2	**Alexandria** (city) Madison County
108	15.2	**Aurora** (city) Dearborn County
108	15.2	**Greenwood** (city) Johnson County
108	15.2	**Portland** (city) Jay County
112	15.3	**Delphi** (city) Carroll County
112	15.3	**Winchester** (city) Randolph County
114	15.4	**Ellettsville** (town) Monroe County
115	15.5	**Kokomo** (city) Howard County
116	15.6	**Corydon** (town) Harrison County
116	15.6	**Greensburg** (city) Decatur County
118	15.8	**Charlestown** (city) Clark County
118	15.8	**Warsaw** (city) Kosciusko County
120	15.9	**Salem** (city) Washington County
121	16.0	**Paoli** (town) Orange County
122	16.2	**Evansville** (city) Vanderburgh County
122	16.2	**Hebron** (town) Porter County
122	16.2	**Vincennes** (city) Knox County
125	16.3	**Crawfordsville** (city) Montgomery County
125	16.3	**Fort Wayne** (city) Allen County
127	16.4	**Nappanee** (city) Elkhart County
128	16.5	**Centerville** (town) Wayne County
128	16.5	**Clinton** (city) Vermillion County
128	16.5	**Edinburgh** (town) Johnson County
128	16.5	**Marion** (city) Grant County
128	16.5	**Muncie** (city) Delaware County
133	16.7	**Martinsville** (city) Morgan County
133	16.7	**New Albany** (city) Floyd County
135	16.8	**Michigan City** (city) LaPorte County
136	16.9	**Kendallville** (city) Noble County
137	17.0	**Lebanon** (city) Boone County
137	17.0	**Rushville** (city) Rush County
139	17.1	**Chesterfield** (town) Madison County
139	17.1	**Seymour** (city) Jackson County
141	17.3	**Sellersburg** (town) Clark County
142	17.4	**Huntington** (city) Huntington County
142	17.4	**Indianapolis** (city) Marion County
144	17.5	**Bedford** (city) Lawrence County
144	17.5	**Bicknell** (city) Knox County
144	17.5	**Peru** (city) Miami County
144	17.5	**South Bend** (city) Saint Joseph County
148	17.7	**La Porte** (city) LaPorte County
148	17.7	**McCordsville** (town) Hancock County
150	17.9	**Heritage Lake** (CDP) Putnam County

Note: This section ranks incorporated places and CDPs (Census Designated Places) with populations of 2,500 or more. Unincorporated postal areas were not considered. Please refer to the User Guide for additional information.

Population Under 18 Years Old with No Health Insurance
Top 150 Places Ranked in *Descending* Order

State Rank	Percent	Place
1	36.5	**Cicero** (town) Hamilton County
2	24.0	**Mitchell** (city) Lawrence County
3	22.5	**Lagrange** (town) LaGrange County
4	19.2	**Syracuse** (town) Kosciusko County
5	19.0	**Gas City** (city) Grant County
6	17.8	**Hebron** (town) Porter County
7	15.8	**Sellersburg** (town) Clark County
8	14.8	**Dunlap** (CDP) Elkhart County
8	14.8	**Hartford City** (city) Blackford County
10	14.5	**Middlebury** (town) Elkhart County
11	14.4	**Lake Station** (city) Lake County
12	14.3	**Monticello** (city) White County
13	14.2	**Shorewood Forest** (CDP) Porter County
14	13.5	**Goshen** (city) Elkhart County
15	13.4	**Heritage Lake** (CDP) Putnam County
16	13.2	**Anderson** (city) Madison County
17	13.0	**Country Squire Lakes** (CDP) Jennings County
18	12.9	**Bremen** (town) Marshall County
18	12.9	**Chandler** (town) Warrick County
20	12.7	**Clarksville** (town) Clark County
21	12.6	**Elkhart** (city) Elkhart County
22	12.5	**North Vernon** (city) Jennings County
23	12.4	**Elwood** (city) Madison County
23	12.4	**Lowell** (town) Lake County
23	12.4	**Seymour** (city) Jackson County
23	12.4	**Simonton Lake** (CDP) Elkhart County
27	12.3	**Rochester** (city) Fulton County
28	12.1	**Huntingburg** (city) Dubois County
29	12.0	**Aurora** (city) Dearborn County
30	11.6	**Richmond** (city) Wayne County
31	11.5	**Cedar Lake** (town) Lake County
31	11.5	**North Terre Haute** (CDP) Vigo County
31	11.5	**Roselawn** (CDP) Newton County
34	11.4	**McCordsville** (town) Hancock County
34	11.4	**Melody Hill** (CDP) Vanderburgh County
36	11.3	**Logansport** (city) Cass County
37	11.2	**Madison** (city) Jefferson County
37	11.2	**Newburgh** (town) Warrick County
39	11.0	**Sheridan** (town) Hamilton County
40	10.9	**Rockville** (town) Parke County
41	10.8	**Smithville-Sanders** (CDP) Monroe County
42	10.7	**Speedway** (town) Marion County
42	10.7	**Union City** (city) Randolph County
44	10.6	**Alexandria** (city) Madison County
45	10.5	**Berne** (city) Adams County
45	10.5	**New Albany** (city) Floyd County
47	10.2	**Ligonier** (city) Noble County
47	10.2	**North Manchester** (town) Wabash County
49	10.1	**Shelbyville** (city) Shelby County
50	9.9	**Sullivan** (city) Sullivan County
51	9.8	**Auburn** (city) DeKalb County
51	9.8	**Brownstown** (town) Jackson County
51	9.8	**Decatur** (city) Adams County
51	9.8	**Martinsville** (city) Morgan County
55	9.7	**Plymouth** (city) Marshall County
56	9.6	**Columbus** (city) Bartholomew County
57	9.4	**Greenwood** (city) Johnson County
57	9.4	**Nappanee** (city) Elkhart County
57	9.4	**Ossian** (town) Wells County
60	9.3	**Brazil** (city) Clay County
60	9.3	**East Chicago** (city) Lake County
60	9.3	**Fort Wayne** (city) Allen County
60	9.3	**New Castle** (city) Henry County
64	9.2	**Bedford** (city) Lawrence County
64	9.2	**Indianapolis** (city) Marion County
66	9.1	**Mishawaka** (city) Saint Joseph County
66	9.1	**Tipton** (city) Tipton County
68	9.0	**Greensburg** (city) Decatur County
68	9.0	**Vincennes** (city) Knox County
70	8.9	**Salem** (city) Washington County
71	8.8	**Lebanon** (city) Boone County
72	8.7	**Hammond** (city) Lake County
72	8.7	**Winona Lake** (town) Kosciusko County
74	8.6	**Kokomo** (city) Howard County
75	8.5	**Loogootee** (city) Martin County
76	8.4	**Bluffton** (city) Wells County
77	8.3	**La Porte** (city) LaPorte County
77	8.3	**Upland** (town) Grant County
79	8.2	**Avon** (town) Hendricks County
80	7.9	**Brownsburg** (town) Hendricks County
80	7.9	**Rensselaer** (city) Jasper County
82	7.8	**Evansville** (city) Vanderburgh County
82	7.8	**Fairmount** (town) Grant County
82	7.8	**Greencastle** (city) Putnam County
85	7.7	**Jeffersonville** (city) Clark County
85	7.7	**Muncie** (city) Delaware County
87	7.6	**Terre Haute** (city) Vigo County
88	7.4	**New Haven** (city) Allen County
89	7.3	**Pittsboro** (town) Hendricks County
89	7.3	**Portland** (city) Jay County
91	7.2	**Greenfield** (city) Hancock County
91	7.2	**South Bend** (city) Saint Joseph County
93	7.1	**Highland** (town) Lake County
93	7.1	**Warsaw** (city) Kosciusko County
95	7.0	**Frankfort** (city) Clinton County
95	7.0	**Mooresville** (town) Morgan County
97	6.9	**Marion** (city) Grant County
97	6.9	**Plainfield** (town) Hendricks County
99	6.8	**South Haven** (CDP) Porter County
100	6.7	**Centerville** (town) Wayne County
100	6.7	**Edinburgh** (town) Johnson County
100	6.7	**Winchester** (city) Randolph County
103	6.5	**Corydon** (town) Harrison County
103	6.5	**Rushville** (city) Rush County
105	6.4	**Connersville** (city) Fayette County
105	6.4	**Ellettsville** (town) Monroe County
105	6.4	**Noblesville** (city) Hamilton County
105	6.4	**Whiting** (city) Lake County
109	6.3	**Hanover** (town) Jefferson County
109	6.3	**Hobart** (city) Lake County
109	6.3	**Merrillville** (town) Lake County
112	6.2	**Kendallville** (city) Noble County
113	6.1	**Crawfordsville** (city) Montgomery County
114	6.0	**Brookville** (town) Franklin County
114	6.0	**Charlestown** (city) Clark County
114	6.0	**Griffith** (town) Lake County
114	6.0	**Huntington** (city) Huntington County
118	5.9	**Lakes of the Four Seasons** (CDP) Lake County
119	5.8	**Highland** (CDP) Vanderburgh County
119	5.8	**Michigan City** (city) LaPorte County
119	5.8	**Princeton** (city) Gibson County
122	5.7	**Hidden Valley** (CDP) Dearborn County
123	5.5	**Lafayette** (city) Tippecanoe County
123	5.5	**Lawrence** (city) Marion County
125	5.4	**Angola** (city) Steuben County
125	5.4	**Butler** (city) DeKalb County
125	5.4	**Peru** (city) Miami County
128	5.3	**Boonville** (city) Warrick County
128	5.3	**Pendleton** (town) Madison County
130	5.2	**Linton** (city) Greene County
131	5.1	**Portage** (city) Porter County
132	5.0	**Attica** (city) Fountain County
132	5.0	**Clinton** (city) Vermillion County
132	5.0	**Jasper** (city) Dubois County
135	4.7	**Gary** (city) Lake County
136	4.6	**Batesville** (city) Ripley County
137	4.5	**Valparaiso** (city) Porter County
138	4.4	**Columbia City** (city) Whitley County
138	4.4	**Crown Point** (city) Lake County
138	4.4	**Grissom AFB** (CDP) Miami County
141	4.3	**Bicknell** (city) Knox County
141	4.3	**Bloomington** (city) Monroe County
143	4.1	**Saint John** (town) Lake County
144	4.0	**Beech Grove** (city) Marion County
144	4.0	**Franklin** (city) Johnson County
144	4.0	**Wabash** (city) Wabash County
147	3.7	**Fort Branch** (town) Gibson County
147	3.7	**Whitestown** (town) Boone County
149	3.3	**Mount Vernon** (city) Posey County
150	3.2	**Fishers** (town) Hamilton County

Note: This section ranks incorporated places and CDPs (Census Designated Places) with populations of 2,500 or more. Unincorporated postal areas were not considered. Please refer to the User Guide for additional information.

Population Under 18 Years Old with No Health Insurance

Top 150 Places Ranked in *Ascending* Order

State Rank	Percent	Place
1	0.0	**Delphi** (city) Carroll County
1	0.0	**Notre Dame** (CDP) Saint Joseph County
1	0.0	**Porter** (town) Porter County
1	0.0	**Westville** (town) LaPorte County
5	0.5	**Bargersville** (town) Johnson County
5	0.5	**Zionsville** (town) Boone County
7	0.7	**Fortville** (town) Hancock County
8	1.0	**Garrett** (city) DeKalb County
9	1.3	**Georgetown** (town) Floyd County
9	1.3	**Tell City** (city) Perry County
11	1.5	**New Whiteland** (town) Johnson County
12	1.6	**Munster** (town) Lake County
13	1.9	**Austin** (city) Scott County
13	1.9	**Chesterfield** (town) Madison County
15	2.0	**Winfield** (town) Lake County
16	2.1	**Bright** (CDP) Dearborn County
16	2.1	**Dyer** (town) Lake County
16	2.1	**Yorktown** (town) Delaware County
19	2.3	**Covington** (city) Fountain County
19	2.3	**West Lafayette** (city) Tippecanoe County
19	2.3	**Whiteland** (town) Johnson County
22	2.4	**Chesterton** (town) Porter County
22	2.4	**Granger** (CDP) Saint Joseph County
24	2.5	**Purdue University** (CDP) Tippecanoe County
25	2.6	**Cumberland** (town) Marion County
25	2.6	**Danville** (town) Hendricks County
25	2.6	**De Motte** (town) Jasper County
25	2.6	**Leo-Cedarville** (town) Allen County
25	2.6	**Paoli** (town) Orange County
30	2.7	**Carmel** (city) Hamilton County
31	2.9	**Lawrenceburg** (city) Dearborn County
31	2.9	**Schererville** (town) Lake County
33	3.0	**Greendale** (city) Dearborn County
33	3.0	**Scottsburg** (city) Scott County
33	3.0	**Westfield** (city) Hamilton County
36	3.1	**Washington** (city) Daviess County
37	3.2	**Fishers** (town) Hamilton County
37	3.2	**Huntertown** (town) Allen County
37	3.2	**Knox** (city) Starke County
40	3.3	**Mount Vernon** (city) Posey County
41	3.7	**Fort Branch** (town) Gibson County
41	3.7	**Whitestown** (town) Boone County
43	4.0	**Beech Grove** (city) Marion County
43	4.0	**Franklin** (city) Johnson County
43	4.0	**Wabash** (city) Wabash County
46	4.1	**Saint John** (town) Lake County
47	4.3	**Bicknell** (city) Knox County
47	4.3	**Bloomington** (city) Monroe County
49	4.4	**Columbia City** (city) Whitley County
49	4.4	**Crown Point** (city) Lake County
49	4.4	**Grissom AFB** (CDP) Miami County
52	4.5	**Valparaiso** (city) Porter County
53	4.6	**Batesville** (city) Ripley County
54	4.7	**Gary** (city) Lake County
55	5.0	**Attica** (city) Fountain County
55	5.0	**Clinton** (city) Vermillion County
55	5.0	**Jasper** (city) Dubois County
58	5.1	**Portage** (city) Porter County
59	5.2	**Linton** (city) Greene County
60	5.3	**Boonville** (city) Warrick County
60	5.3	**Pendleton** (town) Madison County
62	5.4	**Angola** (city) Steuben County
62	5.4	**Butler** (city) DeKalb County
62	5.4	**Peru** (city) Miami County
65	5.5	**Lafayette** (city) Tippecanoe County
65	5.5	**Lawrence** (city) Marion County
67	5.7	**Hidden Valley** (CDP) Dearborn County
68	5.8	**Highland** (CDP) Vanderburgh County
68	5.8	**Michigan City** (city) LaPorte County
68	5.8	**Princeton** (city) Gibson County
71	5.9	**Lakes of the Four Seasons** (CDP) Lake County
72	6.0	**Brookville** (town) Franklin County
72	6.0	**Charlestown** (city) Clark County
72	6.0	**Griffith** (town) Lake County
72	6.0	**Huntington** (city) Huntington County
76	6.1	**Crawfordsville** (city) Montgomery County
77	6.2	**Kendallville** (city) Noble County
78	6.3	**Hanover** (town) Jefferson County
78	6.3	**Hobart** (city) Lake County
78	6.3	**Merrillville** (town) Lake County
81	6.4	**Connersville** (city) Fayette County
81	6.4	**Ellettsville** (town) Monroe County
81	6.4	**Noblesville** (city) Hamilton County
81	6.4	**Whiting** (city) Lake County
85	6.5	**Corydon** (town) Harrison County
85	6.5	**Rushville** (city) Rush County
87	6.7	**Centerville** (town) Wayne County
87	6.7	**Edinburgh** (town) Johnson County
87	6.7	**Winchester** (city) Randolph County
90	6.8	**South Haven** (CDP) Porter County
91	6.9	**Marion** (city) Grant County
91	6.9	**Plainfield** (town) Hendricks County
93	7.0	**Frankfort** (city) Clinton County
93	7.0	**Mooresville** (town) Morgan County
95	7.1	**Highland** (town) Lake County
95	7.1	**Warsaw** (city) Kosciusko County
97	7.2	**Greenfield** (city) Hancock County
97	7.2	**South Bend** (city) Saint Joseph County
99	7.3	**Pittsboro** (town) Hendricks County
99	7.3	**Portland** (city) Jay County
101	7.4	**New Haven** (city) Allen County
102	7.6	**Terre Haute** (city) Vigo County
103	7.7	**Jeffersonville** (city) Clark County
103	7.7	**Muncie** (city) Delaware County
105	7.8	**Evansville** (city) Vanderburgh County
105	7.8	**Fairmount** (town) Grant County
105	7.8	**Greencastle** (city) Putnam County
108	7.9	**Brownsburg** (town) Hendricks County
108	7.9	**Rensselaer** (city) Jasper County
110	8.2	**Avon** (town) Hendricks County
111	8.3	**La Porte** (city) LaPorte County
111	8.3	**Upland** (town) Grant County
113	8.4	**Bluffton** (city) Wells County
114	8.5	**Loogootee** (city) Martin County
115	8.6	**Kokomo** (city) Howard County
116	8.7	**Hammond** (city) Lake County
116	8.7	**Winona Lake** (town) Kosciusko County
118	8.8	**Lebanon** (city) Boone County
119	8.9	**Salem** (city) Washington County
120	9.0	**Greensburg** (city) Decatur County
120	9.0	**Vincennes** (city) Knox County
122	9.1	**Mishawaka** (city) Saint Joseph County
122	9.1	**Tipton** (city) Tipton County
124	9.2	**Bedford** (city) Lawrence County
124	9.2	**Indianapolis** (city) Marion County
126	9.3	**Brazil** (city) Clay County
126	9.3	**East Chicago** (city) Lake County
126	9.3	**Fort Wayne** (city) Allen County
126	9.3	**New Castle** (city) Henry County
130	9.4	**Greenwood** (city) Johnson County
130	9.4	**Nappanee** (city) Elkhart County
130	9.4	**Ossian** (town) Wells County
133	9.6	**Columbus** (city) Bartholomew County
134	9.7	**Plymouth** (city) Marshall County
135	9.8	**Auburn** (city) DeKalb County
135	9.8	**Brownstown** (town) Jackson County
135	9.8	**Decatur** (city) Adams County
135	9.8	**Martinsville** (city) Morgan County
139	9.9	**Sullivan** (city) Sullivan County
140	10.1	**Shelbyville** (city) Shelby County
141	10.2	**Ligonier** (city) Noble County
141	10.2	**North Manchester** (town) Wabash County
143	10.5	**Berne** (city) Adams County
143	10.5	**New Albany** (city) Floyd County
145	10.6	**Alexandria** (city) Madison County
146	10.7	**Speedway** (town) Marion County
146	10.7	**Union City** (city) Randolph County
148	10.8	**Smithville-Sanders** (CDP) Monroe County
149	10.9	**Rockville** (town) Parke County
150	11.0	**Sheridan** (town) Hamilton County

Note: *This section ranks incorporated places and CDPs (Census Designated Places) with populations of 2,500 or more. Unincorporated postal areas were not considered. Please refer to the User Guide for additional information.*

Commute to Work: Car
Top 150 Places Ranked in *Descending* Order

State Rank	Percent	Place
1	99.1	**Simonton Lake** (CDP) Elkhart County
2	98.7	**Huntertown** (town) Allen County
3	98.5	**New Whiteland** (town) Johnson County
3	98.5	**Scottsburg** (city) Scott County
5	98.3	**Melody Hill** (CDP) Vanderburgh County
6	98.1	**Bicknell** (city) Knox County
7	98.0	**Dunlap** (CDP) Elkhart County
7	98.0	**Smithville-Sanders** (CDP) Monroe County
9	97.8	**Greendale** (city) Dearborn County
10	97.4	**Chandler** (town) Warrick County
11	97.3	**Pendleton** (town) Madison County
12	97.1	**Garrett** (city) DeKalb County
12	97.1	**Shorewood Forest** (CDP) Porter County
14	97.0	**Loogootee** (city) Martin County
15	96.8	**Alexandria** (city) Madison County
15	96.8	**Centerville** (town) Wayne County
17	96.7	**Brazil** (city) Clay County
17	96.7	**Georgetown** (town) Floyd County
17	96.7	**Newburgh** (town) Warrick County
20	96.6	**Pittsboro** (town) Hendricks County
20	96.6	**Tell City** (city) Perry County
22	96.4	**Lakes of the Four Seasons** (CDP) Lake County
22	96.4	**Sellersburg** (town) Clark County
22	96.4	**Whiteland** (town) Johnson County
25	96.3	**Highland** (CDP) Vanderburgh County
25	96.3	**Sheridan** (town) Hamilton County
27	96.2	**Hebron** (town) Porter County
27	96.2	**Lowell** (town) Lake County
29	96.1	**Boonville** (city) Warrick County
30	96.0	**Clarksville** (town) Clark County
31	95.9	**Cedar Lake** (town) Lake County
31	95.9	**Fort Branch** (town) Gibson County
31	95.9	**Mooresville** (town) Morgan County
31	95.9	**Nappanee** (city) Elkhart County
35	95.8	**Charlestown** (city) Clark County
35	95.8	**Greenwood** (city) Johnson County
35	95.8	**Lake Station** (city) Lake County
35	95.8	**Mount Vernon** (city) Posey County
39	95.7	**Beech Grove** (city) Marion County
39	95.7	**Decatur** (city) Adams County
39	95.7	**Leo-Cedarville** (town) Allen County
39	95.7	**South Haven** (CDP) Porter County
39	95.7	**Whitestown** (town) Boone County
44	95.6	**Bright** (CDP) Dearborn County
44	95.6	**Danville** (town) Hendricks County
44	95.6	**Hobart** (city) Lake County
47	95.5	**Grissom AFB** (CDP) Miami County
48	95.4	**Brownsburg** (town) Hendricks County
49	95.3	**De Motte** (town) Jasper County
49	95.3	**La Porte** (city) LaPorte County
49	95.3	**Roselawn** (CDP) Newton County
52	95.2	**Washington** (city) Daviess County
53	95.0	**Avon** (town) Hendricks County
53	95.0	**North Terre Haute** (CDP) Vigo County
53	95.0	**Plainfield** (town) Hendricks County
53	95.0	**Porter** (town) Porter County
57	94.9	**Greenfield** (city) Hancock County
57	94.9	**Paoli** (town) Orange County
59	94.8	**Aurora** (city) Dearborn County
59	94.8	**Clinton** (city) Vermillion County
59	94.8	**Hidden Valley** (CDP) Dearborn County
59	94.8	**Rockville** (town) Parke County
59	94.8	**Shelbyville** (city) Shelby County
64	94.7	**New Castle** (city) Henry County
65	94.6	**Greensburg** (city) Decatur County
65	94.6	**Highland** (town) Lake County
65	94.6	**Yorktown** (town) Delaware County
68	94.5	**Jeffersonville** (city) Clark County
68	94.5	**Lawrence** (city) Marion County
68	94.5	**Schererville** (town) Lake County
71	94.4	**Fortville** (town) Hancock County
71	94.4	**Frankfort** (city) Clinton County
73	94.3	**Lebanon** (city) Boone County
74	94.1	**Granger** (CDP) Saint Joseph County
75	94.0	**Berne** (city) Adams County
75	94.0	**Columbia City** (city) Whitley County
75	94.0	**Hartford City** (city) Blackford County
75	94.0	**Linton** (city) Greene County
75	94.0	**New Albany** (city) Floyd County
75	94.0	**Portage** (city) Porter County
75	94.0	**Rushville** (city) Rush County
82	93.9	**Griffith** (town) Lake County
83	93.8	**Columbus** (city) Bartholomew County
83	93.8	**Merrillville** (town) Lake County
83	93.8	**Middlebury** (town) Elkhart County
86	93.7	**Mitchell** (city) Lawrence County
87	93.6	**Fairmount** (town) Grant County
87	93.6	**Westville** (town) LaPorte County
89	93.5	**Chesterton** (town) Porter County
89	93.5	**Jasper** (city) Dubois County
91	93.4	**Butler** (city) DeKalb County
91	93.4	**Knox** (city) Starke County
91	93.4	**Westfield** (city) Hamilton County
94	93.3	**Kokomo** (city) Howard County
95	93.2	**Fort Wayne** (city) Allen County
95	93.2	**Princeton** (city) Gibson County
97	93.1	**Batesville** (city) Ripley County
98	93.0	**Dyer** (town) Lake County
98	93.0	**New Haven** (city) Allen County
100	92.9	**Connersville** (city) Fayette County
101	92.8	**Auburn** (city) DeKalb County
101	92.8	**Chesterfield** (town) Madison County
101	92.8	**Gas City** (city) Grant County
101	92.8	**Logansport** (city) Cass County
101	92.8	**Winfield** (town) Lake County
106	92.7	**Bluffton** (city) Wells County
106	92.7	**Crown Point** (city) Lake County
106	92.7	**Monticello** (city) White County
106	92.7	**Richmond** (city) Wayne County
106	92.7	**Wabash** (city) Wabash County
111	92.6	**Cumberland** (town) Marion County
111	92.6	**McCordsville** (town) Hancock County
111	92.6	**Saint John** (town) Lake County
114	92.5	**Ellettsville** (town) Monroe County
114	92.5	**Noblesville** (city) Hamilton County
114	92.5	**Ossian** (town) Wells County
114	92.5	**Portland** (city) Jay County
118	92.4	**Winchester** (city) Randolph County
119	92.3	**Elwood** (city) Madison County
119	92.3	**Warsaw** (city) Kosciusko County
121	92.2	**Fishers** (town) Hamilton County
121	92.2	**Kendallville** (city) Noble County
121	92.2	**North Vernon** (city) Jennings County
121	92.2	**Union City** (city) Randolph County
125	92.1	**Madison** (city) Jefferson County
125	92.1	**Plymouth** (city) Marshall County
125	92.1	**Salem** (city) Washington County
125	92.1	**Syracuse** (town) Kosciusko County
129	92.0	**Brownstown** (town) Jackson County
129	92.0	**Cicero** (town) Hamilton County
129	92.0	**Mishawaka** (city) Saint Joseph County
129	92.0	**Seymour** (city) Jackson County
133	91.9	**Elkhart** (city) Elkhart County
134	91.8	**Indianapolis** (city) Marion County
135	91.7	**Brookville** (town) Franklin County
135	91.7	**Hammond** (city) Lake County
135	91.7	**Sullivan** (city) Sullivan County
138	91.6	**Attica** (city) Fountain County
138	91.6	**Tipton** (city) Tipton County
138	91.6	**Vincennes** (city) Knox County
141	91.5	**Michigan City** (city) LaPorte County
142	91.4	**Country Squire Lakes** (CDP) Jennings County
142	91.4	**Franklin** (city) Johnson County
144	91.3	**Speedway** (town) Marion County
145	91.2	**Bedford** (city) Lawrence County
146	91.1	**Carmel** (city) Hamilton County
146	91.1	**Zionsville** (town) Boone County
148	91.0	**Evansville** (city) Vanderburgh County
148	91.0	**Lafayette** (city) Tippecanoe County
150	90.8	**Edinburgh** (town) Johnson County

Note: This section ranks incorporated places and CDPs (Census Designated Places) with populations of 2,500 or more. Unincorporated postal areas were not considered. Please refer to the User Guide for additional information.

Commute to Work: Car
Top 150 Places Ranked in *Ascending* Order

State Rank	Percent	Place
1	8.7	**Notre Dame** (CDP) Saint Joseph County
2	26.2	**Purdue University** (CDP) Tippecanoe County
3	57.8	**Upland** (town) Grant County
4	66.1	**West Lafayette** (city) Tippecanoe County
5	69.7	**Bloomington** (city) Monroe County
6	74.1	**Greencastle** (city) Putnam County
7	80.5	**Hanover** (town) Jefferson County
8	82.5	**Winona Lake** (town) Kosciusko County
9	83.0	**North Manchester** (town) Wabash County
10	84.6	**Marion** (city) Grant County
11	85.3	**Covington** (city) Fountain County
12	85.4	**Muncie** (city) Delaware County
13	86.7	**Lagrange** (town) LaGrange County
14	86.8	**Delphi** (city) Carroll County
15	87.1	**Rochester** (city) Fulton County
16	88.2	**East Chicago** (city) Lake County
17	88.4	**Crawfordsville** (city) Montgomery County
17	88.4	**Whiting** (city) Lake County
19	88.6	**Austin** (city) Scott County
19	88.6	**Terre Haute** (city) Vigo County
21	88.7	**Angola** (city) Steuben County
21	88.7	**Lawrenceburg** (city) Dearborn County
21	88.7	**Valparaiso** (city) Porter County
24	89.0	**Bargersville** (town) Johnson County
25	89.1	**Corydon** (town) Harrison County
25	89.1	**Ligonier** (city) Noble County
27	89.2	**Munster** (town) Lake County
28	89.3	**Martinsville** (city) Morgan County
29	89.9	**Gary** (city) Lake County
30	90.0	**Bremen** (town) Marshall County
30	90.0	**South Bend** (city) Saint Joseph County
32	90.2	**Goshen** (city) Elkhart County
33	90.3	**Heritage Lake** (CDP) Putnam County
33	90.3	**Peru** (city) Miami County
35	90.5	**Anderson** (city) Madison County
36	90.6	**Rensselaer** (city) Jasper County
37	90.8	**Edinburgh** (town) Johnson County
37	90.8	**Huntingburg** (city) Dubois County
37	90.8	**Huntington** (city) Huntington County
40	91.0	**Evansville** (city) Vanderburgh County
40	91.0	**Lafayette** (city) Tippecanoe County
42	91.1	**Carmel** (city) Hamilton County
42	91.1	**Zionsville** (town) Boone County
44	91.2	**Bedford** (city) Lawrence County
45	91.3	**Speedway** (town) Marion County
46	91.4	**Country Squire Lakes** (CDP) Jennings County
46	91.4	**Franklin** (city) Johnson County
48	91.5	**Michigan City** (city) LaPorte County
49	91.6	**Attica** (city) Fountain County
49	91.6	**Tipton** (city) Tipton County
49	91.6	**Vincennes** (city) Knox County
52	91.7	**Brookville** (town) Franklin County
52	91.7	**Hammond** (city) Lake County
52	91.7	**Sullivan** (city) Sullivan County
55	91.8	**Indianapolis** (city) Marion County
56	91.9	**Elkhart** (city) Elkhart County
57	92.0	**Brownstown** (town) Jackson County
57	92.0	**Cicero** (town) Hamilton County
57	92.0	**Mishawaka** (city) Saint Joseph County
57	92.0	**Seymour** (city) Jackson County
61	92.1	**Madison** (city) Jefferson County
61	92.1	**Plymouth** (city) Marshall County
61	92.1	**Salem** (city) Washington County
61	92.1	**Syracuse** (town) Kosciusko County
65	92.2	**Fishers** (town) Hamilton County
65	92.2	**Kendallville** (city) Noble County
65	92.2	**North Vernon** (city) Jennings County
65	92.2	**Union City** (city) Randolph County
69	92.3	**Elwood** (city) Madison County
69	92.3	**Warsaw** (city) Kosciusko County
71	92.4	**Winchester** (city) Randolph County
72	92.5	**Ellettsville** (town) Monroe County
72	92.5	**Noblesville** (city) Hamilton County
72	92.5	**Ossian** (town) Wells County
72	92.5	**Portland** (city) Jay County
76	92.6	**Cumberland** (town) Marion County
76	92.6	**McCordsville** (town) Hancock County
76	92.6	**Saint John** (town) Lake County
79	92.7	**Bluffton** (city) Wells County
79	92.7	**Crown Point** (city) Lake County
79	92.7	**Monticello** (city) White County
79	92.7	**Richmond** (city) Wayne County
79	92.7	**Wabash** (city) Wabash County
84	92.8	**Auburn** (city) DeKalb County
84	92.8	**Chesterfield** (town) Madison County
84	92.8	**Gas City** (city) Grant County
84	92.8	**Logansport** (city) Cass County
84	92.8	**Winfield** (town) Lake County
89	92.9	**Connersville** (city) Fayette County
90	93.0	**Dyer** (town) Lake County
90	93.0	**New Haven** (city) Allen County
92	93.1	**Batesville** (city) Ripley County
93	93.2	**Fort Wayne** (city) Allen County
93	93.2	**Princeton** (city) Gibson County
95	93.3	**Kokomo** (city) Howard County
96	93.4	**Butler** (city) DeKalb County
96	93.4	**Knox** (city) Starke County
96	93.4	**Westfield** (town) Hamilton County
99	93.5	**Chesterton** (town) Porter County
99	93.5	**Jasper** (city) Dubois County
101	93.6	**Fairmount** (town) Grant County
101	93.6	**Westville** (town) LaPorte County
103	93.7	**Mitchell** (city) Lawrence County
104	93.8	**Columbus** (city) Bartholomew County
104	93.8	**Merrillville** (town) Lake County
104	93.8	**Middlebury** (town) Elkhart County
107	93.9	**Griffith** (town) Lake County
108	94.0	**Berne** (city) Adams County
108	94.0	**Columbia City** (city) Whitley County
108	94.0	**Hartford City** (city) Blackford County
108	94.0	**Linton** (city) Greene County
108	94.0	**New Albany** (city) Floyd County
108	94.0	**Portage** (city) Porter County
108	94.0	**Rushville** (city) Rush County
115	94.1	**Granger** (CDP) Saint Joseph County
116	94.3	**Lebanon** (city) Boone County
117	94.4	**Fortville** (town) Hancock County
117	94.4	**Frankfort** (city) Clinton County
119	94.5	**Jeffersonville** (city) Clark County
119	94.5	**Lawrence** (city) Marion County
119	94.5	**Schererville** (town) Lake County
122	94.6	**Greensburg** (city) Decatur County
122	94.6	**Highland** (town) Lake County
122	94.6	**Yorktown** (town) Delaware County
125	94.7	**New Castle** (city) Henry County
126	94.8	**Aurora** (city) Dearborn County
126	94.8	**Clinton** (city) Vermillion County
126	94.8	**Hidden Valley** (CDP) Dearborn County
126	94.8	**Rockville** (town) Parke County
126	94.8	**Shelbyville** (city) Shelby County
131	94.9	**Greenfield** (city) Hancock County
131	94.9	**Paoli** (town) Orange County
133	95.0	**Avon** (town) Hendricks County
133	95.0	**North Terre Haute** (CDP) Vigo County
133	95.0	**Plainfield** (town) Hendricks County
133	95.0	**Porter** (town) Porter County
137	95.2	**Washington** (city) Daviess County
138	95.3	**De Motte** (town) Jasper County
138	95.3	**La Porte** (city) LaPorte County
138	95.3	**Roselawn** (CDP) Newton County
141	95.4	**Brownsburg** (town) Hendricks County
142	95.5	**Grissom AFB** (CDP) Miami County
143	95.6	**Bright** (CDP) Dearborn County
143	95.6	**Danville** (town) Hendricks County
143	95.6	**Hobart** (city) Lake County
146	95.7	**Beech Grove** (city) Marion County
146	95.7	**Decatur** (city) Adams County
146	95.7	**Leo-Cedarville** (town) Allen County
146	95.7	**South Haven** (CDP) Porter County
146	95.7	**Whitestown** (town) Boone County

Note: This section ranks incorporated places and CDPs (Census Designated Places) with populations of 2,500 or more. Unincorporated postal areas were not considered. Please refer to the User Guide for additional information.

Commute to Work: Public Transportation
Top 150 Places Ranked in *Descending* Order

State Rank	Percent	Place
1	9.9	**Purdue University** (CDP) Tippecanoe County
2	7.6	**West Lafayette** (city) Tippecanoe County
3	7.0	**Bloomington** (city) Monroe County
4	5.1	**Dyer** (town) Lake County
5	5.0	**Munster** (town) Lake County
6	4.9	**East Chicago** (city) Lake County
7	3.9	**Hammond** (city) Lake County
8	3.7	**Gary** (city) Lake County
9	3.4	**Griffith** (town) Lake County
10	3.0	**Speedway** (town) Marion County
11	2.8	**South Bend** (city) Saint Joseph County
12	2.7	**Lafayette** (city) Tippecanoe County
13	2.6	**Muncie** (city) Delaware County
14	2.5	**Evansville** (city) Vanderburgh County
14	2.5	**Highland** (town) Lake County
14	2.5	**Michigan City** (city) LaPorte County
17	2.4	**Chesterton** (town) Porter County
17	2.4	**Saint John** (town) Lake County
19	2.3	**Lakes of the Four Seasons** (CDP) Lake County
20	2.1	**Indianapolis** (city) Marion County
20	2.1	**Porter** (town) Porter County
22	2.0	**Schererville** (town) Lake County
23	1.8	**Valparaiso** (city) Porter County
24	1.7	**Hobart** (city) Lake County
25	1.6	**Crown Point** (city) Lake County
25	1.6	**Logansport** (city) Cass County
25	1.6	**Merrillville** (town) Lake County
25	1.6	**Mishawaka** (city) Saint Joseph County
29	1.4	**Elkhart** (city) Elkhart County
29	1.4	**Smithville-Sanders** (CDP) Monroe County
29	1.4	**South Haven** (CDP) Porter County
29	1.4	**Whiting** (city) Lake County
33	1.3	**Bedford** (city) Lawrence County
34	1.2	**Franklin** (city) Johnson County
34	1.2	**Huntingburg** (city) Dubois County
34	1.2	**New Albany** (city) Floyd County
34	1.2	**Wabash** (city) Wabash County
38	1.1	**Lagrange** (town) LaGrange County
38	1.1	**Linton** (city) Greene County
40	1.0	**Portage** (city) Porter County
40	1.0	**Westville** (town) LaPorte County
42	0.9	**Anderson** (city) Madison County
42	0.9	**Fort Wayne** (city) Allen County
42	0.9	**Gas City** (city) Grant County
42	0.9	**Goshen** (city) Elkhart County
42	0.9	**Roselawn** (CDP) Newton County
47	0.8	**Terre Haute** (city) Vigo County
47	0.8	**Winfield** (town) Lake County
49	0.7	**Columbus** (city) Bartholomew County
49	0.7	**La Porte** (city) LaPorte County
49	0.7	**Richmond** (city) Wayne County
49	0.7	**Sellersburg** (town) Clark County
53	0.6	**Batesville** (city) Ripley County
53	0.6	**Cedar Lake** (town) Lake County
53	0.6	**Charlestown** (city) Clark County
53	0.6	**Clarksville** (town) Clark County
53	0.6	**Connersville** (city) Fayette County
53	0.6	**Kokomo** (city) Howard County
53	0.6	**Mitchell** (city) Lawrence County
53	0.6	**Union City** (city) Randolph County
53	0.6	**Whitestown** (town) Boone County
62	0.5	**Butler** (city) DeKalb County
62	0.5	**Columbia City** (city) Whitley County
62	0.5	**Cumberland** (town) Marion County
62	0.5	**Lake Station** (city) Lake County
62	0.5	**Madison** (city) Jefferson County
62	0.5	**New Castle** (city) Henry County
62	0.5	**Princeton** (city) Gibson County
62	0.5	**Rushville** (city) Rush County
62	0.5	**Vincennes** (city) Knox County
62	0.5	**Warsaw** (city) Kosciusko County
62	0.5	**Washington** (city) Daviess County
73	0.4	**Aurora** (city) Dearborn County
73	0.4	**Carmel** (city) Hamilton County
73	0.4	**Chandler** (town) Warrick County
73	0.4	**Danville** (town) Hendricks County
73	0.4	**Greensburg** (city) Decatur County
73	0.4	**Greenwood** (city) Johnson County
73	0.4	**Loogootee** (city) Martin County
73	0.4	**Monticello** (city) White County
73	0.4	**Peru** (city) Miami County
82	0.3	**Beech Grove** (city) Marion County
82	0.3	**Crawfordsville** (city) Montgomery County
82	0.3	**Huntington** (city) Huntington County
82	0.3	**Jeffersonville** (city) Clark County
82	0.3	**Paoli** (town) Orange County
82	0.3	**Westfield** (city) Hamilton County
88	0.2	**Fishers** (town) Hamilton County
88	0.2	**Granger** (CDP) Saint Joseph County
88	0.2	**Lowell** (town) Lake County
88	0.2	**Marion** (city) Grant County
88	0.2	**Plainfield** (town) Hendricks County
88	0.2	**Seymour** (city) Jackson County
88	0.2	**Sheridan** (town) Hamilton County
88	0.2	**Zionsville** (town) Boone County
96	0.1	**Clinton** (city) Vermillion County
96	0.1	**Fortville** (town) Hancock County
96	0.1	**Lawrence** (city) Marion County
96	0.1	**New Haven** (city) Allen County
96	0.1	**Noblesville** (city) Hamilton County
96	0.1	**Rochester** (city) Fulton County
96	0.1	**Upland** (town) Grant County
103	0.0	**Alexandria** (city) Madison County
103	0.0	**Angola** (city) Steuben County
103	0.0	**Attica** (city) Fountain County
103	0.0	**Auburn** (city) DeKalb County
103	0.0	**Austin** (city) Scott County
103	0.0	**Avon** (town) Hendricks County
103	0.0	**Bargersville** (town) Johnson County
103	0.0	**Berne** (city) Adams County
103	0.0	**Bicknell** (city) Knox County
103	0.0	**Bluffton** (city) Wells County
103	0.0	**Boonville** (city) Warrick County
103	0.0	**Brazil** (city) Clay County
103	0.0	**Bremen** (town) Marshall County
103	0.0	**Bright** (CDP) Dearborn County
103	0.0	**Brookville** (town) Franklin County
103	0.0	**Brownsburg** (town) Hendricks County
103	0.0	**Brownstown** (town) Jackson County
103	0.0	**Centerville** (town) Wayne County
103	0.0	**Chesterfield** (town) Madison County
103	0.0	**Cicero** (town) Hamilton County
103	0.0	**Corydon** (town) Harrison County
103	0.0	**Country Squire Lakes** (CDP) Jennings County
103	0.0	**Covington** (city) Fountain County
103	0.0	**De Motte** (town) Jasper County
103	0.0	**Decatur** (city) Adams County
103	0.0	**Delphi** (city) Carroll County
103	0.0	**Dunlap** (CDP) Elkhart County
103	0.0	**Edinburgh** (town) Johnson County
103	0.0	**Ellettsville** (town) Monroe County
103	0.0	**Elwood** (city) Madison County
103	0.0	**Fairmount** (town) Grant County
103	0.0	**Fort Branch** (town) Gibson County
103	0.0	**Frankfort** (city) Clinton County
103	0.0	**Garrett** (city) DeKalb County
103	0.0	**Georgetown** (town) Floyd County
103	0.0	**Greencastle** (city) Putnam County
103	0.0	**Greendale** (city) Dearborn County
103	0.0	**Greenfield** (city) Hancock County
103	0.0	**Grissom AFB** (CDP) Miami County
103	0.0	**Hanover** (town) Jefferson County
103	0.0	**Hartford City** (city) Blackford County
103	0.0	**Hebron** (town) Porter County
103	0.0	**Heritage Lake** (CDP) Putnam County
103	0.0	**Hidden Valley** (CDP) Dearborn County
103	0.0	**Highland** (CDP) Vanderburgh County
103	0.0	**Huntertown** (town) Allen County
103	0.0	**Jasper** (city) Dubois County
103	0.0	**Kendallville** (city) Noble County

Note: This section ranks incorporated places and CDPs (Census Designated Places) with populations of 2,500 or more. Unincorporated postal areas were not considered. Please refer to the User Guide for additional information.

Commute to Work: Walk
Top 150 Places Ranked in *Descending* Order

State Rank	Percent	Place
1	75.1	**Notre Dame** (CDP) Saint Joseph County
2	43.3	**Purdue University** (CDP) Tippecanoe County
3	19.3	**Greencastle** (city) Putnam County
4	17.5	**West Lafayette** (city) Tippecanoe County
5	14.3	**Hanover** (town) Jefferson County
6	13.8	**Bloomington** (city) Monroe County
7	12.9	**Upland** (town) Grant County
8	12.0	**North Manchester** (town) Wabash County
9	9.7	**Winona Lake** (town) Kosciusko County
10	9.6	**Delphi** (city) Carroll County
11	7.9	**Muncie** (city) Delaware County
12	7.8	**Covington** (city) Fountain County
13	7.7	**Lawrenceburg** (city) Dearborn County
14	6.8	**Syracuse** (town) Kosciusko County
14	6.8	**Whiting** (city) Lake County
16	6.7	**Crawfordsville** (city) Montgomery County
17	6.6	**Knox** (city) Starke County
18	6.4	**Bremen** (town) Marshall County
19	6.3	**Terre Haute** (city) Vigo County
20	6.2	**Rensselaer** (city) Jasper County
21	6.1	**Union City** (city) Randolph County
22	5.7	**Marion** (city) Grant County
23	5.4	**East Chicago** (city) Lake County
24	5.3	**Angola** (city) Steuben County
25	5.2	**Butler** (city) DeKalb County
26	5.1	**Clinton** (city) Vermillion County
27	5.0	**Attica** (city) Fountain County
28	4.9	**Edinburgh** (town) Johnson County
29	4.8	**Corydon** (town) Harrison County
30	4.7	**Princeton** (city) Gibson County
31	4.5	**Kendallville** (city) Noble County
32	4.4	**Anderson** (city) Madison County
32	4.4	**Vincennes** (city) Knox County
34	4.3	**Austin** (city) Scott County
34	4.3	**Goshen** (city) Elkhart County
36	4.1	**Huntington** (city) Huntington County
36	4.1	**Ligonier** (city) Noble County
38	4.0	**Rochester** (city) Fulton County
38	4.0	**Salem** (city) Washington County
40	3.9	**Chesterfield** (town) Madison County
40	3.9	**Lagrange** (town) LaGrange County
42	3.8	**Wabash** (city) Wabash County
43	3.7	**Gas City** (city) Grant County
44	3.6	**Ellettsville** (town) Monroe County
45	3.5	**Peru** (city) Miami County
46	3.3	**Brookville** (town) Franklin County
46	3.3	**Middlebury** (town) Elkhart County
46	3.3	**Plymouth** (city) Marshall County
49	3.2	**Gary** (city) Lake County
49	3.2	**Hartford City** (city) Blackford County
49	3.2	**South Bend** (city) Saint Joseph County
52	3.1	**Brownstown** (town) Jackson County
52	3.1	**Linton** (city) Greene County
52	3.1	**Warsaw** (city) Kosciusko County
55	3.0	**Richmond** (city) Wayne County
55	3.0	**Rushville** (city) Rush County
55	3.0	**Valparaiso** (city) Porter County
58	2.7	**Columbia City** (city) Whitley County
58	2.7	**Franklin** (city) Johnson County
60	2.6	**Berne** (city) Adams County
60	2.6	**Cicero** (town) Hamilton County
60	2.6	**Evansville** (city) Vanderburgh County
60	2.6	**New Haven** (city) Allen County
64	2.5	**Garrett** (city) DeKalb County
64	2.5	**Greensburg** (city) Decatur County
64	2.5	**Tipton** (city) Tipton County
67	2.4	**Aurora** (city) Dearborn County
67	2.4	**Bluffton** (city) Wells County
67	2.4	**Roselawn** (CDP) Newton County
70	2.3	**Bedford** (city) Lawrence County
71	2.2	**De Motte** (town) Jasper County
71	2.2	**Hammond** (city) Lake County
71	2.2	**Lafayette** (city) Tippecanoe County
71	2.2	**Michigan City** (city) LaPorte County
71	2.2	**North Vernon** (city) Jennings County
71	2.2	**Portland** (city) Jay County
77	2.1	**Boonville** (city) Warrick County
77	2.1	**La Porte** (city) LaPorte County
77	2.1	**Madison** (city) Jefferson County
77	2.1	**Martinsville** (city) Morgan County
77	2.1	**Nappanee** (city) Elkhart County
77	2.1	**Portage** (city) Porter County
83	2.0	**Fortville** (town) Hancock County
83	2.0	**Huntingburg** (city) Dubois County
83	2.0	**Indianapolis** (city) Marion County
83	2.0	**Kokomo** (city) Howard County
83	2.0	**Monticello** (city) White County
83	2.0	**Rockville** (town) Parke County
83	2.0	**Washington** (city) Daviess County
90	1.9	**Bicknell** (city) Knox County
90	1.9	**Elkhart** (city) Elkhart County
90	1.9	**Elwood** (city) Madison County
90	1.9	**Mitchell** (city) Lawrence County
90	1.9	**New Castle** (city) Henry County
90	1.9	**Tell City** (city) Perry County
96	1.8	**Brazil** (city) Clay County
96	1.8	**Connersville** (city) Fayette County
96	1.8	**Greenfield** (city) Hancock County
96	1.8	**Jasper** (city) Dubois County
96	1.8	**Jeffersonville** (city) Clark County
96	1.8	**Mishawaka** (city) Saint Joseph County
96	1.8	**Mount Vernon** (city) Posey County
103	1.7	**New Albany** (city) Floyd County
103	1.7	**Sullivan** (city) Sullivan County
103	1.7	**Westville** (town) LaPorte County
103	1.7	**Winchester** (city) Randolph County
103	1.7	**Winfield** (town) Lake County
108	1.6	**Fort Branch** (town) Gibson County
108	1.6	**Mooresville** (town) Morgan County
110	1.5	**Alexandria** (city) Madison County
110	1.5	**Bright** (CDP) Dearborn County
110	1.5	**Crown Point** (city) Lake County
110	1.5	**Lawrence** (city) Marion County
114	1.4	**Cumberland** (town) Marion County
114	1.4	**Decatur** (city) Adams County
114	1.4	**Fort Wayne** (city) Allen County
114	1.4	**Logansport** (city) Cass County
118	1.3	**Hebron** (town) Porter County
118	1.3	**Paoli** (town) Orange County
120	1.2	**Beech Grove** (city) Marion County
120	1.2	**Country Squire Lakes** (CDP) Jennings County
120	1.2	**Danville** (town) Hendricks County
120	1.2	**Noblesville** (city) Hamilton County
120	1.2	**Seymour** (city) Jackson County
120	1.2	**Shelbyville** (city) Shelby County
126	1.1	**Columbus** (city) Bartholomew County
126	1.1	**Pittsboro** (town) Hendricks County
128	1.0	**Batesville** (city) Ripley County
128	1.0	**Carmel** (city) Hamilton County
128	1.0	**Highland** (town) Lake County
128	1.0	**Porter** (town) Porter County
132	0.9	**Auburn** (city) DeKalb County
132	0.9	**Bargersville** (town) Johnson County
132	0.9	**Lebanon** (city) Boone County
132	0.9	**Scottsburg** (city) Scott County
132	0.9	**Speedway** (town) Marion County
132	0.9	**Westfield** (city) Hamilton County
138	0.8	**Chandler** (town) Warrick County
138	0.8	**Lowell** (town) Lake County
138	0.8	**Ossian** (town) Wells County
138	0.8	**Plainfield** (town) Hendricks County
138	0.8	**Sheridan** (town) Hamilton County
143	0.7	**Chesterton** (town) Porter County
143	0.7	**Clarksville** (town) Clark County
143	0.7	**Greendale** (city) Dearborn County
143	0.7	**Loogootee** (city) Martin County
143	0.7	**McCordsville** (town) Hancock County
143	0.7	**Merrillville** (town) Lake County
143	0.7	**Munster** (town) Lake County
143	0.7	**Whiteland** (town) Johnson County

Note: This section ranks incorporated places and CDPs (Census Designated Places) with populations of 2,500 or more. Unincorporated postal areas were not considered. Please refer to the User Guide for additional information.

Commute to Work: Walk
Top 150 Places Ranked in *Ascending* Order

State Rank	Percent	Place
1	0.0	Avon (town) Hendricks County
1	0.0	Fairmount (town) Grant County
1	0.0	Grissom AFB (CDP) Miami County
1	0.0	Heritage Lake (CDP) Putnam County
1	0.0	Hidden Valley (CDP) Dearborn County
1	0.0	Lakes of the Four Seasons (CDP) Lake County
1	0.0	Melody Hill (CDP) Vanderburgh County
1	0.0	New Whiteland (town) Johnson County
1	0.0	Newburgh (town) Warrick County
1	0.0	North Terre Haute (CDP) Vigo County
1	0.0	Pendleton (town) Madison County
1	0.0	Saint John (town) Lake County
1	0.0	Shorewood Forest (CDP) Porter County
1	0.0	Simonton Lake (CDP) Elkhart County
1	0.0	Smithville-Sanders (CDP) Monroe County
16	0.1	Lake Station (city) Lake County
17	0.2	Cedar Lake (town) Lake County
17	0.2	Huntertown (town) Allen County
19	0.3	Dyer (town) Lake County
19	0.3	Granger (CDP) Saint Joseph County
19	0.3	Hobart (city) Lake County
19	0.3	Leo-Cedarville (town) Allen County
19	0.3	Whitestown (town) Boone County
24	0.4	Charlestown (city) Clark County
24	0.4	Dunlap (CDP) Elkhart County
24	0.4	Fishers (town) Hamilton County
24	0.4	Highland (CDP) Vanderburgh County
24	0.4	Sellersburg (town) Clark County
24	0.4	Zionsville (town) Boone County
30	0.5	Centerville (town) Wayne County
30	0.5	Frankfort (city) Clinton County
30	0.5	Greenwood (city) Johnson County
30	0.5	Griffith (town) Lake County
30	0.5	Schererville (town) Lake County
30	0.5	Yorktown (town) Delaware County
36	0.6	Brownsburg (town) Hendricks County
36	0.6	Georgetown (town) Floyd County
36	0.6	South Haven (CDP) Porter County
39	0.7	Chesterton (town) Porter County
39	0.7	Clarksville (town) Clark County
39	0.7	Greendale (city) Dearborn County
39	0.7	Loogootee (city) Martin County
39	0.7	McCordsville (town) Hancock County
39	0.7	Merrillville (town) Lake County
39	0.7	Munster (town) Lake County
39	0.7	Whiteland (town) Johnson County
47	0.8	Chandler (town) Warrick County
47	0.8	Lowell (town) Lake County
47	0.8	Ossian (town) Wells County
47	0.8	Plainfield (town) Hendricks County
47	0.8	Sheridan (town) Hamilton County
52	0.9	Auburn (city) DeKalb County
52	0.9	Bargersville (town) Johnson County
52	0.9	Lebanon (city) Boone County
52	0.9	Scottsburg (city) Scott County
52	0.9	Speedway (town) Marion County
52	0.9	Westfield (city) Hamilton County
58	1.0	Batesville (city) Ripley County
58	1.0	Carmel (city) Hamilton County
58	1.0	Highland (town) Lake County
58	1.0	Porter (town) Porter County
62	1.1	Columbus (city) Bartholomew County
62	1.1	Pittsboro (town) Hendricks County
64	1.2	Beech Grove (city) Marion County
64	1.2	Country Squire Lakes (CDP) Jennings County
64	1.2	Danville (town) Hendricks County
64	1.2	Noblesville (city) Hamilton County
64	1.2	Seymour (city) Jackson County
64	1.2	Shelbyville (city) Shelby County
70	1.3	Hebron (town) Porter County
70	1.3	Paoli (town) Orange County
72	1.4	Cumberland (town) Marion County
72	1.4	Decatur (city) Adams County
72	1.4	Fort Wayne (city) Allen County
72	1.4	Logansport (city) Cass County
76	1.5	Alexandria (city) Madison County
76	1.5	Bright (CDP) Dearborn County
76	1.5	Crown Point (city) Lake County
76	1.5	Lawrence (city) Marion County
80	1.6	Fort Branch (town) Gibson County
80	1.6	Mooresville (town) Morgan County
82	1.7	New Albany (city) Floyd County
82	1.7	Sullivan (city) Sullivan County
82	1.7	Westville (town) LaPorte County
82	1.7	Winchester (city) Randolph County
82	1.7	Winfield (town) Lake County
87	1.8	Brazil (city) Clay County
87	1.8	Connersville (city) Fayette County
87	1.8	Greenfield (city) Hancock County
87	1.8	Jasper (city) Dubois County
87	1.8	Jeffersonville (city) Clark County
87	1.8	Mishawaka (city) Saint Joseph County
87	1.8	Mount Vernon (city) Posey County
94	1.9	Bicknell (city) Knox County
94	1.9	Elkhart (city) Elkhart County
94	1.9	Elwood (city) Madison County
94	1.9	Mitchell (city) Lawrence County
94	1.9	New Castle (city) Henry County
94	1.9	Tell City (city) Perry County
100	2.0	Fortville (town) Hancock County
100	2.0	Huntingburg (city) Dubois County
100	2.0	Indianapolis (city) Marion County
100	2.0	Kokomo (city) Howard County
100	2.0	Monticello (city) White County
100	2.0	Rockville (town) Parke County
100	2.0	Washington (city) Daviess County
107	2.1	Boonville (city) Warrick County
107	2.1	La Porte (city) LaPorte County
107	2.1	Madison (city) Jefferson County
107	2.1	Martinsville (city) Morgan County
107	2.1	Nappanee (city) Elkhart County
107	2.1	Portage (city) Porter County
113	2.2	De Motte (town) Jasper County
113	2.2	Hammond (city) Lake County
113	2.2	Lafayette (city) Tippecanoe County
113	2.2	Michigan City (city) LaPorte County
113	2.2	North Vernon (city) Jennings County
113	2.2	Portland (city) Jay County
119	2.3	Bedford (city) Lawrence County
120	2.4	Aurora (city) Dearborn County
120	2.4	Bluffton (city) Wells County
120	2.4	Roselawn (CDP) Newton County
123	2.5	Garrett (city) DeKalb County
123	2.5	Greensburg (city) Decatur County
123	2.5	Tipton (city) Tipton County
126	2.6	Berne (city) Adams County
126	2.6	Cicero (town) Hamilton County
126	2.6	Evansville (city) Vanderburgh County
126	2.6	New Haven (city) Allen County
130	2.7	Columbia City (city) Whitley County
130	2.7	Franklin (city) Johnson County
132	3.0	Richmond (city) Wayne County
132	3.0	Rushville (city) Rush County
132	3.0	Valparaiso (city) Porter County
135	3.1	Brownstown (town) Jackson County
135	3.1	Linton (city) Greene County
135	3.1	Warsaw (city) Kosciusko County
138	3.2	Gary (city) Lake County
138	3.2	Hartford City (city) Blackford County
138	3.2	South Bend (city) Saint Joseph County
141	3.3	Brookville (town) Franklin County
141	3.3	Middlebury (town) Elkhart County
141	3.3	Plymouth (city) Marshall County
144	3.5	Peru (city) Miami County
145	3.6	Ellettsville (town) Monroe County
146	3.7	Gas City (city) Grant County
147	3.8	Wabash (city) Wabash County
148	3.9	Chesterfield (town) Madison County
148	3.9	Lagrange (town) LaGrange County
150	4.0	Rochester (city) Fulton County

Note: This section ranks incorporated places and CDPs (Census Designated Places) with populations of 2,500 or more. Unincorporated postal areas were not considered. Please refer to the User Guide for additional information.

Commute to Work: Work from Home
Top 150 Places Ranked in *Descending* Order

State Rank	Percent	Place
1	27.0	**Upland** (town) Grant County
2	15.1	**Purdue University** (CDP) Tippecanoe County
3	10.4	**Notre Dame** (CDP) Saint Joseph County
4	9.7	**Heritage Lake** (CDP) Putnam County
5	8.5	**Bargersville** (town) Johnson County
6	7.8	**Marion** (city) Grant County
6	7.8	**Winona Lake** (town) Kosciusko County
8	7.0	**Lagrange** (town) LaGrange County
8	7.0	**Zionsville** (town) Boone County
10	6.9	**Rochester** (city) Fulton County
11	6.7	**McCordsville** (town) Hancock County
12	6.6	**Carmel** (city) Hamilton County
13	6.4	**Fishers** (town) Hamilton County
14	5.8	**Martinsville** (city) Morgan County
15	5.5	**Noblesville** (city) Hamilton County
16	5.4	**Cicero** (town) Hamilton County
16	5.4	**Covington** (city) Fountain County
16	5.4	**Huntingburg** (city) Dubois County
19	5.2	**Hanover** (town) Jefferson County
20	5.1	**Corydon** (town) Harrison County
21	4.8	**Winfield** (town) Lake County
22	4.6	**Bloomington** (city) Monroe County
23	4.5	**Munster** (town) Lake County
24	4.4	**Fairmount** (town) Grant County
24	4.4	**Granger** (CDP) Saint Joseph County
26	4.2	**Bedford** (city) Lawrence County
26	4.2	**Hidden Valley** (CDP) Dearborn County
26	4.2	**Ligonier** (city) Noble County
29	4.1	**Batesville** (city) Ripley County
29	4.1	**Valparaiso** (city) Porter County
29	4.1	**West Lafayette** (city) Tippecanoe County
32	3.9	**Angola** (city) Steuben County
32	3.9	**Auburn** (city) DeKalb County
32	3.9	**Avon** (town) Hendricks County
32	3.9	**Jasper** (city) Dubois County
32	3.9	**North Manchester** (town) Wabash County
32	3.9	**Tipton** (city) Tipton County
38	3.8	**Lawrence** (city) Marion County
39	3.7	**Leo-Cedarville** (town) Allen County
39	3.7	**Madison** (city) Jefferson County
41	3.6	**Brookville** (town) Franklin County
41	3.6	**Country Squire Lakes** (CDP) Jennings County
41	3.6	**Crawfordsville** (city) Montgomery County
41	3.6	**Ellettsville** (town) Monroe County
41	3.6	**Lawrenceburg** (city) Dearborn County
41	3.6	**Saint John** (town) Lake County
41	3.6	**Speedway** (town) Marion County
41	3.6	**Yorktown** (town) Delaware County
49	3.5	**Winchester** (city) Randolph County
50	3.4	**Chesterton** (town) Porter County
50	3.4	**North Terre Haute** (CDP) Vigo County
50	3.4	**Whitestown** (town) Boone County
53	3.3	**Fort Wayne** (city) Allen County
53	3.3	**Huntington** (city) Huntington County
53	3.3	**North Vernon** (city) Jennings County
56	3.2	**Delphi** (city) Carroll County
56	3.2	**Michigan City** (city) LaPorte County
56	3.2	**Mitchell** (city) Lawrence County
56	3.2	**Sullivan** (city) Sullivan County
56	3.2	**Westfield** (city) Hamilton County
61	3.1	**Mishawaka** (city) Saint Joseph County
61	3.1	**New Haven** (city) Allen County
63	3.0	**Cumberland** (town) Marion County
63	3.0	**Paoli** (town) Orange County
63	3.0	**Whiteland** (town) Johnson County
66	2.9	**Brownsburg** (town) Hendricks County
66	2.9	**Crown Point** (city) Lake County
66	2.9	**Elwood** (city) Madison County
66	2.9	**Greencastle** (city) Putnam County
66	2.9	**Indianapolis** (city) Marion County
66	2.9	**Shorewood Forest** (CDP) Porter County
72	2.8	**Franklin** (city) Johnson County
72	2.8	**Greenwood** (city) Johnson County
72	2.8	**Monticello** (city) White County
75	2.7	**Columbus** (city) Bartholomew County
75	2.7	**Rensselaer** (city) Jasper County
75	2.7	**Sheridan** (town) Hamilton County
78	2.6	**Anderson** (city) Madison County
78	2.6	**Bremen** (town) Marshall County
78	2.6	**Bright** (CDP) Dearborn County
78	2.6	**Highland** (CDP) Vanderburgh County
82	2.5	**Greenfield** (city) Hancock County
82	2.5	**Hebron** (town) Porter County
82	2.5	**Middlebury** (town) Elkhart County
82	2.5	**Plymouth** (city) Marshall County
82	2.5	**Rockville** (town) Parke County
82	2.5	**Rushville** (city) Rush County
82	2.5	**Salem** (city) Washington County
89	2.4	**Cedar Lake** (town) Lake County
89	2.4	**Evansville** (city) Vanderburgh County
89	2.4	**Kokomo** (city) Howard County
89	2.4	**Lake Station** (city) Lake County
93	2.3	**Austin** (city) Scott County
93	2.3	**Centerville** (town) Wayne County
93	2.3	**Fortville** (town) Hancock County
93	2.3	**Gas City** (city) Grant County
93	2.3	**Georgetown** (town) Floyd County
93	2.3	**Jeffersonville** (city) Clark County
99	2.2	**Beech Grove** (city) Marion County
99	2.2	**Lebanon** (city) Boone County
99	2.2	**Portland** (city) Jay County
99	2.2	**Sellersburg** (town) Clark County
99	2.2	**Westville** (town) LaPorte County
104	2.1	**Fort Branch** (town) Gibson County
104	2.1	**Lafayette** (city) Tippecanoe County
104	2.1	**Muncie** (city) Delaware County
104	2.1	**Pendleton** (town) Madison County
104	2.1	**Richmond** (city) Wayne County
104	2.1	**South Bend** (city) Saint Joseph County
104	2.1	**Terre Haute** (city) Vigo County
111	2.0	**Connersville** (city) Fayette County
111	2.0	**Danville** (town) Hendricks County
111	2.0	**Goshen** (city) Elkhart County
111	2.0	**Hobart** (city) Lake County
111	2.0	**New Albany** (city) Floyd County
111	2.0	**Plainfield** (town) Hendricks County
111	2.0	**Wabash** (city) Wabash County
111	2.0	**Warsaw** (city) Kosciusko County
119	1.9	**Attica** (city) Fountain County
119	1.9	**Gary** (city) Lake County
119	1.9	**Mount Vernon** (city) Posey County
119	1.9	**Porter** (town) Porter County
123	1.8	**Merrillville** (town) Lake County
123	1.8	**New Castle** (city) Henry County
123	1.8	**Peru** (city) Miami County
123	1.8	**Portage** (city) Porter County
127	1.7	**Alexandria** (city) Madison County
127	1.7	**Aurora** (city) Dearborn County
127	1.7	**Bluffton** (city) Wells County
127	1.7	**Clarksville** (town) Clark County
127	1.7	**De Motte** (town) Jasper County
127	1.7	**Lowell** (town) Lake County
127	1.7	**Melody Hill** (CDP) Vanderburgh County
127	1.7	**Schererville** (town) Lake County
135	1.6	**Charlestown** (city) Clark County
135	1.6	**Columbia City** (city) Whitley County
135	1.6	**Decatur** (city) Adams County
135	1.6	**Dunlap** (CDP) Elkhart County
135	1.6	**Highland** (town) Lake County
135	1.6	**Kendallville** (city) Noble County
141	1.5	**Brownstown** (town) Jackson County
141	1.5	**Greensburg** (city) Decatur County
141	1.5	**Logansport** (city) Cass County
141	1.5	**Mooresville** (town) Morgan County
141	1.5	**Nappanee** (city) Elkhart County
141	1.5	**New Whiteland** (town) Johnson County
141	1.5	**Princeton** (city) Gibson County
141	1.5	**Shelbyville** (city) Shelby County
149	1.4	**Chesterfield** (town) Madison County
149	1.4	**Dyer** (town) Lake County

Note: This section ranks incorporated places and CDPs (Census Designated Places) with populations of 2,500 or more. Unincorporated postal areas were not considered. Please refer to the User Guide for additional information.

Commute to Work: Work from Home
Top 150 Places Ranked in *Ascending* Order

State Rank	Percent	Place
1	0.0	**Berne** (city) Adams County
1	0.0	**Bicknell** (city) Knox County
1	0.0	**Clinton** (city) Vermillion County
1	0.0	**Knox** (city) Starke County
1	0.0	**Newburgh** (town) Warrick County
1	0.0	**Union City** (city) Randolph County
7	0.2	**Scottsburg** (city) Scott County
8	0.3	**Garrett** (city) DeKalb County
8	0.3	**Huntertown** (town) Allen County
10	0.4	**Boonville** (city) Warrick County
10	0.4	**Griffith** (town) Lake County
12	0.5	**Linton** (city) Greene County
12	0.5	**Smithville-Sanders** (CDP) Monroe County
14	0.7	**Elkhart** (city) Elkhart County
15	0.8	**East Chicago** (city) Lake County
15	0.8	**Loogootee** (city) Martin County
17	0.9	**Butler** (city) DeKalb County
17	0.9	**Greendale** (city) Dearborn County
17	0.9	**Roselawn** (CDP) Newton County
17	0.9	**Simonton Lake** (CDP) Elkhart County
17	0.9	**Tell City** (city) Perry County
17	0.9	**Whiting** (city) Lake County
23	1.0	**Brazil** (city) Clay County
23	1.0	**Frankfort** (city) Clinton County
23	1.0	**La Porte** (city) LaPorte County
23	1.0	**Ossian** (town) Wells County
23	1.0	**Washington** (city) Daviess County
28	1.1	**Chandler** (town) Warrick County
28	1.1	**Hartford City** (city) Blackford County
28	1.1	**Syracuse** (town) Kosciusko County
31	1.2	**Edinburgh** (town) Johnson County
31	1.2	**South Haven** (CDP) Porter County
31	1.2	**Vincennes** (city) Knox County
34	1.3	**Grissom AFB** (CDP) Miami County
34	1.3	**Lakes of the Four Seasons** (CDP) Lake County
34	1.3	**Pittsboro** (town) Hendricks County
34	1.3	**Seymour** (city) Jackson County
38	1.4	**Chesterfield** (town) Madison County
38	1.4	**Dyer** (town) Lake County
38	1.4	**Hammond** (city) Lake County
41	1.5	**Brownstown** (town) Jackson County
41	1.5	**Greensburg** (city) Decatur County
41	1.5	**Logansport** (city) Cass County
41	1.5	**Mooresville** (town) Morgan County
41	1.5	**Nappanee** (city) Elkhart County
41	1.5	**New Whiteland** (town) Johnson County
41	1.5	**Princeton** (city) Gibson County
41	1.5	**Shelbyville** (city) Shelby County
49	1.6	**Charlestown** (city) Clark County
49	1.6	**Columbia City** (city) Whitley County
49	1.6	**Decatur** (city) Adams County
49	1.6	**Dunlap** (CDP) Elkhart County
49	1.6	**Highland** (town) Lake County
49	1.6	**Kendallville** (city) Noble County
55	1.7	**Alexandria** (city) Madison County
55	1.7	**Aurora** (city) Dearborn County
55	1.7	**Bluffton** (city) Wells County
55	1.7	**Clarksville** (town) Clark County
55	1.7	**De Motte** (town) Jasper County
55	1.7	**Lowell** (town) Lake County
55	1.7	**Melody Hill** (CDP) Vanderburgh County
55	1.7	**Schererville** (town) Lake County
63	1.8	**Merrillville** (town) Lake County
63	1.8	**New Castle** (city) Henry County
63	1.8	**Peru** (city) Miami County
63	1.8	**Portage** (city) Porter County
67	1.9	**Attica** (city) Fountain County
67	1.9	**Gary** (city) Lake County
67	1.9	**Mount Vernon** (city) Posey County
67	1.9	**Porter** (town) Porter County
71	2.0	**Connersville** (city) Fayette County
71	2.0	**Danville** (town) Hendricks County
71	2.0	**Goshen** (city) Elkhart County
71	2.0	**Hobart** (city) Lake County
71	2.0	**New Albany** (city) Floyd County
71	2.0	**Plainfield** (town) Hendricks County
71	2.0	**Wabash** (city) Wabash County
71	2.0	**Warsaw** (city) Kosciusko County
79	2.1	**Fort Branch** (town) Gibson County
79	2.1	**Lafayette** (city) Tippecanoe County
79	2.1	**Muncie** (city) Delaware County
79	2.1	**Pendleton** (town) Madison County
79	2.1	**Richmond** (city) Wayne County
79	2.1	**South Bend** (city) Saint Joseph County
79	2.1	**Terre Haute** (city) Vigo County
86	2.2	**Beech Grove** (city) Marion County
86	2.2	**Lebanon** (city) Boone County
86	2.2	**Portland** (city) Jay County
86	2.2	**Sellersburg** (town) Clark County
86	2.2	**Westville** (town) LaPorte County
91	2.3	**Austin** (city) Scott County
91	2.3	**Centerville** (town) Wayne County
91	2.3	**Fortville** (town) Hancock County
91	2.3	**Gas City** (city) Grant County
91	2.3	**Georgetown** (town) Floyd County
91	2.3	**Jeffersonville** (city) Clark County
97	2.4	**Cedar Lake** (town) Lake County
97	2.4	**Evansville** (city) Vanderburgh County
97	2.4	**Kokomo** (city) Howard County
97	2.4	**Lake Station** (city) Lake County
101	2.5	**Greenfield** (city) Hancock County
101	2.5	**Hebron** (town) Porter County
101	2.5	**Middlebury** (town) Elkhart County
101	2.5	**Plymouth** (city) Marshall County
101	2.5	**Rockville** (town) Parke County
101	2.5	**Rushville** (city) Rush County
101	2.5	**Salem** (city) Washington County
108	2.6	**Anderson** (city) Madison County
108	2.6	**Bremen** (town) Marshall County
108	2.6	**Bright** (CDP) Dearborn County
108	2.6	**Highland** (CDP) Vanderburgh County
112	2.7	**Columbus** (city) Bartholomew County
112	2.7	**Rensselaer** (city) Jasper County
112	2.7	**Sheridan** (town) Hamilton County
115	2.8	**Franklin** (city) Johnson County
115	2.8	**Greenwood** (city) Johnson County
115	2.8	**Monticello** (city) White County
118	2.9	**Brownsburg** (town) Hendricks County
118	2.9	**Crown Point** (city) Lake County
118	2.9	**Elwood** (city) Madison County
118	2.9	**Greencastle** (city) Putnam County
118	2.9	**Indianapolis** (city) Marion County
118	2.9	**Shorewood Forest** (CDP) Porter County
124	3.0	**Cumberland** (town) Marion County
124	3.0	**Paoli** (town) Orange County
124	3.0	**Whiteland** (town) Johnson County
127	3.1	**Mishawaka** (city) Saint Joseph County
127	3.1	**New Haven** (city) Allen County
129	3.2	**Delphi** (city) Carroll County
129	3.2	**Michigan City** (city) LaPorte County
129	3.2	**Mitchell** (city) Lawrence County
129	3.2	**Sullivan** (city) Sullivan County
129	3.2	**Westfield** (city) Hamilton County
134	3.3	**Fort Wayne** (city) Allen County
134	3.3	**Huntington** (city) Huntington County
134	3.3	**North Vernon** (city) Jennings County
137	3.4	**Chesterton** (town) Porter County
137	3.4	**North Terre Haute** (CDP) Vigo County
137	3.4	**Whitestown** (town) Boone County
140	3.5	**Winchester** (city) Randolph County
141	3.6	**Brookville** (town) Franklin County
141	3.6	**Country Squire Lakes** (CDP) Jennings County
141	3.6	**Crawfordsville** (city) Montgomery County
141	3.6	**Ellettsville** (town) Monroe County
141	3.6	**Lawrenceburg** (city) Dearborn County
141	3.6	**Saint John** (town) Lake County
141	3.6	**Speedway** (town) Marion County
141	3.6	**Yorktown** (town) Delaware County
149	3.7	**Leo-Cedarville** (town) Allen County
149	3.7	**Madison** (city) Jefferson County

Note: *This section ranks incorporated places and CDPs (Census Designated Places) with populations of 2,500 or more. Unincorporated postal areas were not considered. Please refer to the User Guide for additional information.*

Median Travel Time to Work
Top 150 Places Ranked in *Descending* Order

State Rank	Minutes	Place
1	46.4	**Heritage Lake** (CDP) Putnam County
2	38.5	**Lakes of the Four Seasons** (CDP) Lake County
3	35.1	**Lowell** (town) Lake County
4	33.8	**Hidden Valley** (CDP) Dearborn County
5	32.9	**Saint John** (town) Lake County
6	32.8	**Cedar Lake** (town) Lake County
7	30.8	**Hebron** (town) Porter County
8	30.7	**De Motte** (town) Jasper County
9	30.6	**Bargersville** (town) Johnson County
9	30.6	**Bright** (CDP) Dearborn County
9	30.6	**Elwood** (city) Madison County
12	30.3	**Cicero** (town) Hamilton County
13	30.2	**Roselawn** (CDP) Newton County
14	29.8	**Dyer** (town) Lake County
14	29.8	**Schererville** (town) Lake County
16	29.7	**Winfield** (town) Lake County
17	29.4	**Georgetown** (town) Floyd County
18	28.5	**Shorewood Forest** (CDP) Porter County
19	28.4	**Country Squire Lakes** (CDP) Jennings County
20	28.2	**Avon** (town) Hendricks County
21	27.8	**Munster** (town) Lake County
22	27.7	**Scottsburg** (city) Scott County
23	27.6	**Crown Point** (city) Lake County
23	27.6	**Cumberland** (town) Marion County
25	27.5	**Noblesville** (city) Hamilton County
26	27.4	**Fishers** (town) Hamilton County
27	27.3	**Corydon** (town) Harrison County
28	27.2	**Brookville** (town) Franklin County
28	27.2	**Merrillville** (town) Lake County
30	27.1	**Bicknell** (city) Knox County
30	27.1	**Pendleton** (town) Madison County
32	27.0	**Hammond** (city) Lake County
32	27.0	**Sheridan** (town) Hamilton County
34	26.9	**Whiteland** (town) Johnson County
35	26.7	**Hobart** (city) Lake County
36	26.6	**Whitestown** (town) Boone County
37	26.5	**New Whiteland** (town) Johnson County
38	26.4	**Portage** (city) Porter County
38	26.4	**Porter** (town) Porter County
40	26.2	**Pittsboro** (town) Hendricks County
40	26.2	**South Haven** (CDP) Porter County
42	26.1	**Westfield** (city) Hamilton County
43	26.0	**Brownsburg** (town) Hendricks County
44	25.9	**Mitchell** (city) Lawrence County
45	25.8	**Greenwood** (city) Johnson County
46	25.7	**Griffith** (town) Lake County
47	25.6	**Highland** (town) Lake County
48	25.5	**Alexandria** (city) Madison County
48	25.5	**Chesterton** (town) Porter County
48	25.5	**Danville** (town) Hendricks County
51	25.3	**Connersville** (city) Fayette County
51	25.3	**Martinsville** (city) Morgan County
51	25.3	**McCordsville** (town) Hancock County
54	25.0	**Charlestown** (city) Clark County
55	24.9	**Lake Station** (city) Lake County
56	24.8	**Aurora** (city) Dearborn County
56	24.8	**Carmel** (city) Hamilton County
56	24.8	**Lawrence** (city) Marion County
59	24.7	**Gary** (city) Lake County
60	24.5	**Greenfield** (city) Hancock County
60	24.5	**Salem** (city) Washington County
62	24.3	**Huntertown** (town) Allen County
63	23.8	**Franklin** (city) Johnson County
63	23.8	**Grissom AFB** (CDP) Miami County
63	23.8	**Westville** (town) LaPorte County
63	23.8	**Zionsville** (town) Boone County
67	23.7	**North Terre Haute** (CDP) Vigo County
68	23.6	**Greendale** (city) Dearborn County
69	23.5	**Plainfield** (town) Hendricks County
69	23.5	**Speedway** (town) Marion County
69	23.5	**Whiting** (city) Lake County
72	23.4	**Fortville** (town) Hancock County
73	23.1	**Smithville-Sanders** (CDP) Monroe County
74	23.0	**Austin** (city) Scott County
75	22.8	**Anderson** (city) Madison County
75	22.8	**Mooresville** (town) Morgan County
77	22.7	**Centerville** (town) Wayne County
77	22.7	**Tipton** (city) Tipton County
79	22.6	**Indianapolis** (city) Marion County
79	22.6	**New Castle** (city) Henry County
81	22.5	**Brazil** (city) Clay County
81	22.5	**Paoli** (town) Orange County
81	22.5	**Union City** (city) Randolph County
84	22.4	**Linton** (city) Greene County
85	22.3	**Kendallville** (city) Noble County
85	22.3	**Valparaiso** (city) Porter County
87	22.2	**Granger** (CDP) Saint Joseph County
87	22.2	**Huntingburg** (city) Dubois County
87	22.2	**Syracuse** (town) Kosciusko County
90	22.1	**Knox** (city) Starke County
91	22.0	**Lagrange** (town) LaGrange County
91	22.0	**Rushville** (city) Rush County
93	21.9	**Hartford City** (city) Blackford County
94	21.8	**Lebanon** (city) Boone County
95	21.7	**East Chicago** (city) Lake County
95	21.7	**Fairmount** (town) Grant County
97	21.6	**Delphi** (city) Carroll County
98	21.5	**Clarksville** (town) Clark County
98	21.5	**Jeffersonville** (city) Clark County
98	21.5	**North Vernon** (city) Jennings County
101	21.4	**Boonville** (city) Warrick County
101	21.4	**Leo-Cedarville** (town) Allen County
103	21.3	**Nappanee** (city) Elkhart County
103	21.3	**Sellersburg** (town) Clark County
105	21.2	**Attica** (city) Fountain County
106	21.1	**Beech Grove** (city) Marion County
107	21.0	**Covington** (city) Fountain County
108	20.9	**Newburgh** (town) Warrick County
109	20.8	**Chandler** (town) Warrick County
110	20.7	**Columbia City** (city) Whitley County
111	20.6	**Ellettsville** (town) Monroe County
111	20.6	**Garrett** (city) DeKalb County
111	20.6	**Ligonier** (city) Noble County
114	20.5	**Mishawaka** (city) Saint Joseph County
115	20.3	**Butler** (city) DeKalb County
115	20.3	**Lawrenceburg** (city) Dearborn County
117	20.1	**Highland** (CDP) Vanderburgh County
117	20.1	**New Albany** (city) Floyd County
119	20.0	**Chesterfield** (town) Madison County
120	19.9	**Ossian** (town) Wells County
120	19.9	**Shelbyville** (city) Shelby County
122	19.8	**Bedford** (city) Lawrence County
123	19.7	**Clinton** (city) Vermillion County
123	19.7	**Elkhart** (city) Elkhart County
123	19.7	**Fort Wayne** (city) Allen County
126	19.6	**Kokomo** (city) Howard County
126	19.6	**Simonton Lake** (CDP) Elkhart County
128	19.5	**Fort Branch** (town) Gibson County
128	19.5	**Greensburg** (city) Decatur County
128	19.5	**Rockville** (town) Parke County
128	19.5	**Yorktown** (town) Delaware County
132	19.4	**Rochester** (city) Fulton County
133	19.3	**Frankfort** (city) Clinton County
133	19.3	**New Haven** (city) Allen County
135	19.2	**Michigan City** (city) LaPorte County
135	19.2	**Peru** (city) Miami County
135	19.2	**Winchester** (city) Randolph County
138	19.1	**North Manchester** (town) Wabash County
139	18.9	**Brownstown** (town) Jackson County
139	18.9	**Monticello** (city) White County
139	18.9	**Winona Lake** (town) Kosciusko County
142	18.8	**South Bend** (city) Saint Joseph County
143	18.7	**Logansport** (city) Cass County
143	18.7	**Madison** (city) Jefferson County
145	18.6	**Dunlap** (CDP) Elkhart County
145	18.6	**La Porte** (city) LaPorte County
147	18.5	**Huntington** (city) Huntington County
147	18.5	**Tell City** (city) Perry County
149	18.4	**Bluffton** (city) Wells County
149	18.4	**Decatur** (city) Adams County

Note: This section ranks incorporated places and CDPs (Census Designated Places) with populations of 2,500 or more. Unincorporated postal areas were not considered. Please refer to the User Guide for additional information.

Median Travel Time to Work

Top 150 Places Ranked in *Ascending* Order

State Rank	Minutes	Place
1	8.6	Notre Dame (CDP) Saint Joseph County
2	13.9	Purdue University (CDP) Tippecanoe County
3	14.3	Berne (city) Adams County
4	15.0	Wabash (city) Wabash County
5	15.3	Bloomington (city) Monroe County
5	15.3	Portland (city) Jay County
7	15.4	Bremen (town) Marshall County
8	15.5	Angola (city) Steuben County
8	15.5	West Lafayette (city) Tippecanoe County
10	15.6	Princeton (city) Gibson County
11	15.7	Warsaw (city) Kosciusko County
12	15.9	Lafayette (city) Tippecanoe County
13	16.0	Seymour (city) Jackson County
13	16.0	Vincennes (city) Knox County
13	16.0	Washington (city) Daviess County
16	16.2	Richmond (city) Wayne County
17	16.5	Jasper (city) Dubois County
17	16.5	Marion (city) Grant County
17	16.5	Melody Hill (CDP) Vanderburgh County
17	16.5	Rensselaer (city) Jasper County
21	16.6	Middlebury (town) Elkhart County
22	16.7	Crawfordsville (city) Montgomery County
22	16.7	Plymouth (city) Marshall County
24	16.9	Sullivan (city) Sullivan County
25	17.2	Columbus (city) Bartholomew County
25	17.2	Greencastle (city) Putnam County
25	17.2	Hanover (town) Jefferson County
28	17.4	Goshen (city) Elkhart County
29	17.5	Mount Vernon (city) Posey County
30	17.7	Muncie (city) Delaware County
30	17.7	Terre Haute (city) Vigo County
32	17.8	Batesville (city) Ripley County
33	17.9	Edinburgh (town) Johnson County
34	18.0	Evansville (city) Vanderburgh County
34	18.0	Upland (town) Grant County
36	18.2	Auburn (city) DeKalb County
36	18.2	Loogootee (city) Martin County
38	18.3	Gas City (city) Grant County
39	18.4	Bluffton (city) Wells County
39	18.4	Decatur (city) Adams County
41	18.5	Huntington (city) Huntington County
41	18.5	Tell City (city) Perry County
43	18.6	Dunlap (CDP) Elkhart County
43	18.6	La Porte (city) LaPorte County
45	18.7	Logansport (city) Cass County
45	18.7	Madison (city) Jefferson County
47	18.8	South Bend (city) Saint Joseph County
48	18.9	Brownstown (town) Jackson County
48	18.9	Monticello (city) White County
48	18.9	Winona Lake (town) Kosciusko County
51	19.1	North Manchester (town) Wabash County
52	19.2	Michigan City (city) LaPorte County
52	19.2	Peru (city) Miami County
52	19.2	Winchester (city) Randolph County
55	19.3	Frankfort (city) Clinton County
55	19.3	New Haven (city) Allen County
57	19.4	Rochester (city) Fulton County
58	19.5	Fort Branch (town) Gibson County
58	19.5	Greensburg (city) Decatur County
58	19.5	Rockville (town) Parke County
58	19.5	Yorktown (town) Delaware County
62	19.6	Kokomo (city) Howard County
62	19.6	Simonton Lake (CDP) Elkhart County
64	19.7	Clinton (city) Vermillion County
64	19.7	Elkhart (city) Elkhart County
64	19.7	Fort Wayne (city) Allen County
67	19.8	Bedford (city) Lawrence County
68	19.9	Ossian (town) Wells County
68	19.9	Shelbyville (city) Shelby County
70	20.0	Chesterfield (town) Madison County
71	20.1	Highland (CDP) Vanderburgh County
71	20.1	New Albany (city) Floyd County
73	20.3	Butler (city) DeKalb County
73	20.3	Lawrenceburg (city) Dearborn County
75	20.5	Mishawaka (city) Saint Joseph County
76	20.6	Ellettsville (town) Monroe County
76	20.6	Garrett (city) DeKalb County
76	20.6	Ligonier (city) Noble County
79	20.7	Columbia City (city) Whitley County
80	20.8	Chandler (town) Warrick County
81	20.9	Newburgh (town) Warrick County
82	21.0	Covington (city) Fountain County
83	21.1	Beech Grove (city) Marion County
84	21.2	Attica (city) Fountain County
85	21.3	Nappanee (city) Elkhart County
85	21.3	Sellersburg (town) Clark County
87	21.4	Boonville (city) Warrick County
87	21.4	Leo-Cedarville (town) Allen County
89	21.5	Clarksville (town) Clark County
89	21.5	Jeffersonville (city) Clark County
89	21.5	North Vernon (city) Jennings County
92	21.6	Delphi (city) Carroll County
93	21.7	East Chicago (city) Lake County
93	21.7	Fairmount (town) Grant County
95	21.8	Lebanon (city) Boone County
96	21.9	Hartford City (city) Blackford County
97	22.0	Lagrange (town) LaGrange County
97	22.0	Rushville (city) Rush County
99	22.1	Knox (city) Starke County
100	22.2	Granger (CDP) Saint Joseph County
100	22.2	Huntingburg (city) Dubois County
100	22.2	Syracuse (town) Kosciusko County
103	22.3	Kendallville (city) Noble County
103	22.3	Valparaiso (city) Porter County
105	22.4	Linton (city) Greene County
106	22.5	Brazil (city) Clay County
106	22.5	Paoli (town) Orange County
106	22.5	Union City (city) Randolph County
109	22.6	Indianapolis (city) Marion County
109	22.6	New Castle (city) Henry County
111	22.7	Centerville (town) Wayne County
111	22.7	Tipton (city) Tipton County
113	22.8	Anderson (city) Madison County
113	22.8	Mooresville (town) Morgan County
115	23.0	Austin (city) Scott County
116	23.1	Smithville-Sanders (CDP) Monroe County
117	23.4	Fortville (town) Hancock County
118	23.5	Plainfield (town) Hendricks County
118	23.5	Speedway (town) Marion County
118	23.5	Whiting (city) Lake County
121	23.6	Greendale (city) Dearborn County
122	23.7	North Terre Haute (CDP) Vigo County
123	23.8	Franklin (city) Johnson County
123	23.8	Grissom AFB (CDP) Miami County
123	23.8	Westville (town) LaPorte County
123	23.8	Zionsville (town) Boone County
127	24.3	Huntertown (town) Allen County
128	24.5	Greenfield (city) Hancock County
128	24.5	Salem (city) Washington County
130	24.7	Gary (city) Lake County
131	24.8	Aurora (city) Dearborn County
131	24.8	Carmel (city) Hamilton County
131	24.8	Lawrence (city) Marion County
134	24.9	Lake Station (city) Lake County
135	25.0	Charlestown (city) Clark County
136	25.3	Connersville (city) Fayette County
136	25.3	Martinsville (city) Morgan County
136	25.3	McCordsville (town) Hancock County
139	25.5	Alexandria (city) Madison County
139	25.5	Chesterton (town) Porter County
139	25.5	Danville (town) Hendricks County
142	25.6	Highland (town) Lake County
143	25.7	Griffith (town) Lake County
144	25.8	Greenwood (city) Johnson County
145	25.9	Mitchell (city) Lawrence County
146	26.0	Brownsburg (town) Hendricks County
147	26.1	Westfield (city) Hamilton County
148	26.2	Pittsboro (town) Hendricks County
148	26.2	South Haven (CDP) Porter County
150	26.4	Portage (city) Porter County

Note: This section ranks incorporated places and CDPs (Census Designated Places) with populations of 2,500 or more. Unincorporated postal areas were not considered. Please refer to the User Guide for additional information.

Violent Crime Rate per 10,000 Population
Top 150 Places Ranked in *Descending* Order

State Rank	Rate	Place
1	123.3	**Indianapolis** (city) Marion County
2	112.0	**Gary** (city) Lake County
3	82.4	**Hammond** (city) Lake County
4	76.3	**Warsaw** (city) Kosciusko County
5	76.1	**Jeffersonville** (city) Clark County
6	66.7	**East Chicago** (city) Lake County
7	65.9	**South Bend** (city) Saint Joseph County
8	57.1	**Lafayette** (city) Tippecanoe County
9	55.8	**Clarksville** (town) Clark County
10	53.7	**Aurora** (city) Dearborn County
11	53.6	**Seymour** (city) Jackson County
12	52.2	**Bedford** (city) Lawrence County
13	50.3	**Whitestown** (town) Boone County
14	46.9	**Evansville** (city) Vanderburgh County
15	45.0	**Delphi** (city) Carroll County
16	44.0	**Rensselaer** (city) Jasper County
17	42.3	**Scottsburg** (city) Scott County
18	41.1	**Muncie** (city) Delaware County
19	40.5	**Lake Station** (city) Lake County
20	40.1	**Batesville** (city) Ripley County
21	38.3	**Cumberland** (town) Marion County
22	38.0	**Ellettsville** (town) Monroe County
23	37.6	**Greenwood** (city) Johnson County
24	37.2	**Fort Wayne** (city) Allen County
25	36.4	**Washington** (city) Daviess County
26	36.1	**Anderson** (city) Madison County
27	33.4	**Bloomington** (city) Monroe County
28	33.3	**Clinton** (city) Vermillion County
29	33.1	**North Vernon** (city) Jennings County
30	32.8	**Danville** (town) Hendricks County
31	32.6	**Bremen** (town) Marshall County
32	32.5	**Kokomo** (city) Howard County
33	32.3	**Boonville** (city) Warrick County
34	31.6	**Jasper** (city) Dubois County
35	31.0	**Edinburgh** (town) Johnson County
36	28.9	**Terre Haute** (city) Vigo County
37	28.7	**Franklin** (city) Johnson County
38	28.4	**Mishawaka** (city) Saint Joseph County
39	28.1	**Tipton** (city) Tipton County
40	27.7	**Merrillville** (town) Lake County
41	27.4	**Greensburg** (city) Decatur County
42	27.1	**Marion** (city) Grant County
43	24.3	**Winona Lake** (town) Kosciusko County
44	24.2	**Speedway** (town) Marion County
45	23.8	**New Albany** (city) Floyd County
46	22.9	**Beech Grove** (city) Marion County
47	21.3	**Hobart** (city) Lake County
48	19.9	**La Porte** (city) LaPorte County
49	19.2	**Lowell** (town) Lake County
50	19.0	**Portage** (city) Porter County
51	18.7	**Peru** (city) Miami County
52	18.4	**North Manchester** (town) Wabash County
53	18.2	**Mount Vernon** (city) Posey County
54	18.0	**Griffith** (town) Lake County
55	17.9	**Columbus** (city) Bartholomew County
56	16.9	**Plainfield** (town) Hendricks County
57	16.4	**Knox** (city) Starke County
58	16.1	**Rushville** (city) Rush County
59	16.0	**Lawrenceburg** (city) Dearborn County
60	15.6	**Huntington** (city) Huntington County
61	15.4	**New Haven** (city) Allen County
62	14.4	**Brownsburg** (town) Hendricks County
63	14.3	**Crawfordsville** (city) Montgomery County
64	13.8	**Fairmount** (town) Grant County
65	12.1	**West Lafayette** (city) Tippecanoe County
66	11.9	**Alexandria** (city) Madison County
67	11.1	**Cedar Lake** (town) Lake County
68	10.7	**Decatur** (city) Adams County
69	10.6	**New Whiteland** (town) Johnson County
70	10.3	**Valparaiso** (city) Porter County
71	9.9	**Hartford City** (city) Blackford County
72	9.3	**Goshen** (city) Elkhart County
73	8.6	**Auburn** (city) DeKalb County
74	8.2	**Elwood** (city) Madison County
75	8.1	**Whiting** (city) Lake County
76	7.4	**Mooresville** (town) Morgan County
77	7.1	**Schererville** (town) Lake County
78	7.0	**Angola** (city) Steuben County
78	7.0	**Plymouth** (city) Marshall County
80	6.7	**Dyer** (town) Lake County
81	6.4	**Westfield** (city) Hamilton County
82	5.9	**Martinsville** (city) Morgan County
83	5.7	**Greenfield** (city) Hancock County
84	5.5	**Tell City** (city) Perry County
85	4.5	**Columbia City** (city) Whitley County
85	4.5	**Nappanee** (city) Elkhart County
87	4.0	**Chesterfield** (town) Madison County
88	3.9	**Highland** (town) Lake County
89	3.2	**Garrett** (city) DeKalb County
90	2.5	**Berne** (city) Adams County
91	2.4	**Carmel** (city) Hamilton County
92	2.1	**Winchester** (city) Randolph County
93	2.0	**Porter** (town) Porter County
94	1.9	**Fishers** (town) Hamilton County
95	1.6	**Portland** (city) Jay County
96	0.8	**Zionsville** (town) Boone County
97	0.0	**Ligonier** (city) Noble County
97	0.0	**Linton** (city) Greene County
99	n/a	**Attica** (city) Fountain County
99	n/a	**Austin** (city) Scott County
99	n/a	**Avon** (town) Hendricks County
99	n/a	**Bargersville** (town) Johnson County
99	n/a	**Bicknell** (city) Knox County
99	n/a	**Bluffton** (city) Wells County
99	n/a	**Brazil** (city) Clay County
99	n/a	**Bright** (CDP) Dearborn County
99	n/a	**Brookville** (town) Franklin County
99	n/a	**Brownstown** (town) Jackson County
99	n/a	**Butler** (city) DeKalb County
99	n/a	**Centerville** (town) Wayne County
99	n/a	**Chandler** (town) Warrick County
99	n/a	**Charlestown** (city) Clark County
99	n/a	**Chesterton** (town) Porter County
99	n/a	**Cicero** (town) Hamilton County
99	n/a	**Connersville** (city) Fayette County
99	n/a	**Corydon** (town) Harrison County
99	n/a	**Country Squire Lakes** (CDP) Jennings County
99	n/a	**Covington** (city) Fountain County
99	n/a	**Crown Point** (city) Lake County
99	n/a	**De Motte** (town) Jasper County
99	n/a	**Dunlap** (CDP) Elkhart County
99	n/a	**Elkhart** (city) Elkhart County
99	n/a	**Fort Branch** (town) Gibson County
99	n/a	**Fortville** (town) Hancock County
99	n/a	**Frankfort** (city) Clinton County
99	n/a	**Gas City** (city) Grant County
99	n/a	**Georgetown** (town) Floyd County
99	n/a	**Granger** (CDP) Saint Joseph County
99	n/a	**Greencastle** (city) Putnam County
99	n/a	**Greendale** (city) Dearborn County
99	n/a	**Grissom AFB** (CDP) Miami County
99	n/a	**Hanover** (town) Jefferson County
99	n/a	**Hebron** (town) Porter County
99	n/a	**Heritage Lake** (CDP) Putnam County
99	n/a	**Hidden Valley** (CDP) Dearborn County
99	n/a	**Highland** (CDP) Vanderburgh County
99	n/a	**Huntertown** (town) Allen County
99	n/a	**Huntingburg** (city) Dubois County
99	n/a	**Kendallville** (city) Noble County
99	n/a	**Lagrange** (town) LaGrange County
99	n/a	**Lakes of the Four Seasons** (CDP) Lake County
99	n/a	**Lawrence** (city) Marion County
99	n/a	**Lebanon** (city) Boone County
99	n/a	**Leo-Cedarville** (town) Allen County
99	n/a	**Logansport** (city) Cass County
99	n/a	**Loogootee** (city) Martin County
99	n/a	**Madison** (city) Jefferson County
99	n/a	**McCordsville** (town) Hancock County
99	n/a	**Melody Hill** (CDP) Vanderburgh County
99	n/a	**Michigan City** (city) LaPorte County

Note: This section ranks incorporated places and CDPs (Census Designated Places) with populations of 2,500 or more. Unincorporated postal areas were not considered. Please refer to the User Guide for additional information.

Violent Crime Rate per 10,000 Population
Top 150 Places Ranked in *Ascending* Order

State Rank	Rate	Place
1	0.0	**Ligonier** (city) Noble County
1	0.0	**Linton** (city) Greene County
3	0.8	**Zionsville** (town) Boone County
4	1.6	**Portland** (city) Jay County
5	1.9	**Fishers** (town) Hamilton County
6	2.0	**Porter** (town) Porter County
7	2.1	**Winchester** (city) Randolph County
8	2.4	**Carmel** (city) Hamilton County
9	2.5	**Berne** (city) Adams County
10	3.2	**Garrett** (city) DeKalb County
11	3.9	**Highland** (town) Lake County
12	4.0	**Chesterfield** (town) Madison County
13	4.5	**Columbia City** (city) Whitley County
13	4.5	**Nappanee** (city) Elkhart County
15	5.5	**Tell City** (city) Perry County
16	5.7	**Greenfield** (city) Hancock County
17	5.9	**Martinsville** (city) Morgan County
18	6.4	**Westfield** (city) Hamilton County
19	6.7	**Dyer** (town) Lake County
20	7.0	**Angola** (city) Steuben County
20	7.0	**Plymouth** (city) Marshall County
22	7.1	**Schererville** (town) Lake County
23	7.4	**Mooresville** (town) Morgan County
24	8.1	**Whiting** (city) Lake County
25	8.2	**Elwood** (city) Madison County
26	8.6	**Auburn** (city) DeKalb County
27	9.3	**Goshen** (city) Elkhart County
28	9.9	**Hartford City** (city) Blackford County
29	10.3	**Valparaiso** (city) Porter County
30	10.6	**New Whiteland** (town) Johnson County
31	10.7	**Decatur** (city) Adams County
32	11.1	**Cedar Lake** (town) Lake County
33	11.9	**Alexandria** (city) Madison County
34	12.1	**West Lafayette** (city) Tippecanoe County
35	13.8	**Fairmount** (town) Grant County
36	14.3	**Crawfordsville** (city) Montgomery County
37	14.4	**Brownsburg** (town) Hendricks County
38	15.4	**New Haven** (city) Allen County
39	15.6	**Huntington** (city) Huntington County
40	16.0	**Lawrenceburg** (city) Dearborn County
41	16.1	**Rushville** (city) Rush County
42	16.4	**Knox** (city) Starke County
43	16.9	**Plainfield** (town) Hendricks County
44	17.9	**Columbus** (city) Bartholomew County
45	18.0	**Griffith** (town) Lake County
46	18.2	**Mount Vernon** (city) Posey County
47	18.4	**North Manchester** (town) Wabash County
48	18.7	**Peru** (city) Miami County
49	19.0	**Portage** (city) Porter County
50	19.2	**Lowell** (town) Lake County
51	19.9	**La Porte** (city) LaPorte County
52	21.3	**Hobart** (city) Lake County
53	22.9	**Beech Grove** (city) Marion County
54	23.8	**New Albany** (city) Floyd County
55	24.2	**Speedway** (town) Marion County
56	24.3	**Winona Lake** (town) Kosciusko County
57	27.1	**Marion** (city) Grant County
58	27.4	**Greensburg** (city) Decatur County
59	27.7	**Merrillville** (town) Lake County
60	28.1	**Tipton** (city) Tipton County
61	28.4	**Mishawaka** (city) Saint Joseph County
62	28.7	**Franklin** (city) Johnson County
63	28.9	**Terre Haute** (city) Vigo County
64	31.0	**Edinburgh** (town) Johnson County
65	31.6	**Jasper** (city) Dubois County
66	32.3	**Boonville** (city) Warrick County
67	32.5	**Kokomo** (city) Howard County
68	32.6	**Bremen** (town) Marshall County
69	32.8	**Danville** (town) Hendricks County
70	33.1	**North Vernon** (city) Jennings County
71	33.3	**Clinton** (city) Vermillion County
72	33.4	**Bloomington** (city) Monroe County
73	36.1	**Anderson** (city) Madison County
74	36.4	**Washington** (city) Daviess County
75	37.2	**Fort Wayne** (city) Allen County
76	37.6	**Greenwood** (city) Johnson County
77	38.0	**Ellettsville** (town) Monroe County
78	38.3	**Cumberland** (town) Marion County
79	40.1	**Batesville** (city) Ripley County
80	40.5	**Lake Station** (city) Lake County
81	41.1	**Muncie** (city) Delaware County
82	42.3	**Scottsburg** (city) Scott County
83	44.0	**Rensselaer** (city) Jasper County
84	45.0	**Delphi** (city) Carroll County
85	46.9	**Evansville** (city) Vanderburgh County
86	50.3	**Whitestown** (town) Boone County
87	52.2	**Bedford** (city) Lawrence County
88	53.6	**Seymour** (city) Jackson County
89	53.7	**Aurora** (city) Dearborn County
90	55.8	**Clarksville** (town) Clark County
91	57.1	**Lafayette** (city) Tippecanoe County
92	65.9	**South Bend** (city) Saint Joseph County
93	66.7	**East Chicago** (city) Lake County
94	76.1	**Jeffersonville** (city) Clark County
95	76.3	**Warsaw** (city) Kosciusko County
96	82.4	**Hammond** (city) Lake County
97	112.0	**Gary** (city) Lake County
98	123.3	**Indianapolis** (city) Marion County

Note: This section ranks incorporated places and CDPs (Census Designated Places) with populations of 2,500 or more. Unincorporated postal areas were not considered. Please refer to the User Guide for additional information.

Property Crime Rate per 10,000 Population

Top 150 Places Ranked in *Descending* Order

State Rank	Rate	Place
1	1,009.1	**Edinburgh** (town) Johnson County
2	699.3	**Clarksville** (town) Clark County
3	643.8	**Seymour** (city) Jackson County
4	639.1	**Washington** (city) Daviess County
5	602.2	**Martinsville** (city) Morgan County
6	598.7	**Gary** (city) Lake County
7	590.4	**North Vernon** (city) Jennings County
8	572.4	**Aurora** (city) Dearborn County
9	563.7	**Mishawaka** (city) Saint Joseph County
10	548.6	**New Albany** (city) Floyd County
11	536.8	**Hobart** (city) Lake County
12	532.7	**Terre Haute** (city) Vigo County
13	526.9	**Mount Vernon** (city) Posey County
14	524.8	**Speedway** (town) Marion County
15	524.6	**Indianapolis** (city) Marion County
16	501.1	**Lafayette** (city) Tippecanoe County
17	497.3	**East Chicago** (city) Lake County
18	495.3	**Winchester** (city) Randolph County
19	487.1	**Evansville** (city) Vanderburgh County
20	485.5	**South Bend** (city) Saint Joseph County
21	481.2	**Anderson** (city) Madison County
22	471.0	**Lake Station** (city) Lake County
23	467.4	**Rushville** (city) Rush County
24	463.0	**Columbus** (city) Bartholomew County
25	453.6	**Scottsburg** (city) Scott County
26	450.7	**Angola** (city) Steuben County
27	446.7	**Garrett** (city) DeKalb County
28	429.2	**Muncie** (city) Delaware County
29	408.1	**Hartford City** (city) Blackford County
30	407.8	**Hammond** (city) Lake County
31	393.0	**La Porte** (city) LaPorte County
32	388.7	**Portland** (city) Jay County
33	388.6	**Kokomo** (city) Howard County
34	388.5	**Marion** (city) Grant County
35	384.9	**Fort Wayne** (city) Allen County
36	381.1	**Franklin** (city) Johnson County
37	374.7	**Beech Grove** (city) Marion County
38	373.9	**Merrillville** (town) Lake County
39	369.2	**Rensselaer** (city) Jasper County
40	368.0	**Cumberland** (town) Marion County
41	366.0	**Jeffersonville** (city) Clark County
42	358.6	**Greenwood** (city) Johnson County
43	357.1	**Lawrenceburg** (city) Dearborn County
44	341.6	**New Haven** (city) Allen County
45	341.0	**Goshen** (city) Elkhart County
46	339.6	**Linton** (city) Greene County
47	338.9	**Griffith** (town) Lake County
48	337.3	**Bedford** (city) Lawrence County
49	335.6	**Elwood** (city) Madison County
50	332.0	**Crawfordsville** (city) Montgomery County
51	329.4	**Whiting** (city) Lake County
52	324.3	**Highland** (town) Lake County
53	322.4	**Mooresville** (town) Morgan County
54	321.7	**Warsaw** (city) Kosciusko County
55	317.9	**Boonville** (city) Warrick County
56	316.2	**Bloomington** (city) Monroe County
57	314.9	**Plymouth** (city) Marshall County
58	301.7	**Whitestown** (town) Boone County
59	298.9	**Plainfield** (town) Hendricks County
60	287.0	**Tipton** (city) Tipton County
61	240.3	**Schererville** (town) Lake County
62	239.1	**Alexandria** (city) Madison County
63	234.9	**Portage** (city) Porter County
64	233.8	**Shelbyville** (city) Shelby County
65	216.0	**Huntington** (city) Huntington County
66	214.8	**Delphi** (city) Carroll County
67	212.2	**Cedar Lake** (town) Lake County
68	207.2	**Valparaiso** (city) Porter County
69	203.3	**Chesterfield** (town) Madison County
70	199.0	**Decatur** (city) Adams County
71	194.5	**Auburn** (city) DeKalb County
72	192.2	**Greenfield** (city) Hancock County
73	189.5	**Tell City** (city) Perry County
74	180.4	**North Manchester** (town) Wabash County
75	177.2	**Sellersburg** (town) Clark County
76	176.1	**Porter** (town) Porter County
77	174.7	**West Lafayette** (city) Tippecanoe County
78	171.1	**Batesville** (city) Ripley County
79	170.5	**Clinton** (city) Vermillion County
80	168.8	**Nappanee** (city) Elkhart County
81	168.1	**Brownsburg** (town) Hendricks County
82	159.3	**Columbia City** (city) Whitley County
83	149.2	**Westfield** (city) Hamilton County
84	128.3	**Bremen** (town) Marshall County
85	120.3	**Dyer** (town) Lake County
85	120.3	**Knox** (city) Starke County
87	118.5	**Peru** (city) Miami County
88	115.4	**Ellettsville** (town) Monroe County
89	112.3	**Lowell** (town) Lake County
90	99.1	**Fishers** (town) Hamilton County
91	97.3	**Danville** (town) Hendricks County
92	88.8	**Jasper** (city) Dubois County
93	87.7	**Carmel** (city) Hamilton County
94	78.2	**Berne** (city) Adams County
95	54.7	**Winona Lake** (town) Kosciusko County
96	50.5	**Greensburg** (city) Decatur County
97	45.9	**New Whiteland** (town) Johnson County
98	41.0	**Ligonier** (city) Noble County
99	31.0	**Fairmount** (town) Grant County
100	25.8	**Zionsville** (town) Boone County
101	n/a	**Attica** (city) Fountain County
101	n/a	**Austin** (city) Scott County
101	n/a	**Avon** (town) Hendricks County
101	n/a	**Bargersville** (town) Johnson County
101	n/a	**Bicknell** (city) Knox County
101	n/a	**Bluffton** (city) Wells County
101	n/a	**Brazil** (city) Clay County
101	n/a	**Bright** (CDP) Dearborn County
101	n/a	**Brookville** (town) Franklin County
101	n/a	**Brownstown** (town) Jackson County
101	n/a	**Butler** (city) DeKalb County
101	n/a	**Centerville** (town) Wayne County
101	n/a	**Chandler** (town) Warrick County
101	n/a	**Charlestown** (city) Clark County
101	n/a	**Chesterton** (town) Porter County
101	n/a	**Cicero** (town) Hamilton County
101	n/a	**Connersville** (city) Fayette County
101	n/a	**Corydon** (town) Harrison County
101	n/a	**Country Squire Lakes** (CDP) Jennings County
101	n/a	**Covington** (city) Fountain County
101	n/a	**Crown Point** (city) Lake County
101	n/a	**De Motte** (town) Jasper County
101	n/a	**Dunlap** (CDP) Elkhart County
101	n/a	**Elkhart** (city) Elkhart County
101	n/a	**Fort Branch** (town) Gibson County
101	n/a	**Fortville** (town) Hancock County
101	n/a	**Frankfort** (city) Clinton County
101	n/a	**Gas City** (city) Grant County
101	n/a	**Georgetown** (town) Floyd County
101	n/a	**Granger** (CDP) Saint Joseph County
101	n/a	**Greencastle** (city) Putnam County
101	n/a	**Greendale** (city) Dearborn County
101	n/a	**Grissom AFB** (CDP) Miami County
101	n/a	**Hanover** (town) Jefferson County
101	n/a	**Hebron** (town) Porter County
101	n/a	**Heritage Lake** (CDP) Putnam County
101	n/a	**Hidden Valley** (CDP) Dearborn County
101	n/a	**Highland** (CDP) Vanderburgh County
101	n/a	**Huntertown** (town) Allen County
101	n/a	**Huntingburg** (city) Dubois County
101	n/a	**Kendallville** (city) Noble County
101	n/a	**Lagrange** (town) LaGrange County
101	n/a	**Lakes of the Four Seasons** (CDP) Lake County
101	n/a	**Lawrence** (city) Marion County
101	n/a	**Lebanon** (city) Boone County
101	n/a	**Leo-Cedarville** (town) Allen County
101	n/a	**Logansport** (city) Cass County
101	n/a	**Loogootee** (city) Martin County
101	n/a	**Madison** (city) Jefferson County
101	n/a	**McCordsville** (town) Hancock County

Note: This section ranks incorporated places and CDPs (Census Designated Places) with populations of 2,500 or more. Unincorporated postal areas were not considered. Please refer to the User Guide for additional information.

Property Crime Rate per 10,000 Population
Top 150 Places Ranked in *Ascending* Order

State Rank	Rate	Place
1	25.8	**Zionsville** (town) Boone County
2	31.0	**Fairmount** (town) Grant County
3	41.0	**Ligonier** (city) Noble County
4	45.9	**New Whiteland** (town) Johnson County
5	50.5	**Greensburg** (city) Decatur County
6	54.7	**Winona Lake** (town) Kosciusko County
7	78.2	**Berne** (city) Adams County
8	87.7	**Carmel** (city) Hamilton County
9	88.8	**Jasper** (city) Dubois County
10	97.3	**Danville** (town) Hendricks County
11	99.1	**Fishers** (town) Hamilton County
12	112.3	**Lowell** (town) Lake County
13	115.4	**Ellettsville** (town) Monroe County
14	118.5	**Peru** (city) Miami County
15	120.3	**Dyer** (town) Lake County
15	120.3	**Knox** (city) Starke County
17	128.3	**Bremen** (town) Marshall County
18	149.2	**Westfield** (city) Hamilton County
19	159.3	**Columbia City** (city) Whitley County
20	168.1	**Brownsburg** (town) Hendricks County
21	168.8	**Nappanee** (city) Elkhart County
22	170.5	**Clinton** (city) Vermillion County
23	171.1	**Batesville** (city) Ripley County
24	174.7	**West Lafayette** (city) Tippecanoe County
25	176.1	**Porter** (town) Porter County
26	177.2	**Sellersburg** (town) Clark County
27	180.4	**North Manchester** (town) Wabash County
28	189.5	**Tell City** (city) Perry County
29	192.2	**Greenfield** (city) Hancock County
30	194.5	**Auburn** (city) DeKalb County
31	199.0	**Decatur** (city) Adams County
32	203.3	**Chesterfield** (town) Madison County
33	207.2	**Valparaiso** (city) Porter County
34	212.2	**Cedar Lake** (town) Lake County
35	214.8	**Delphi** (city) Carroll County
36	216.0	**Huntington** (city) Huntington County
37	233.8	**Shelbyville** (city) Shelby County
38	234.9	**Portage** (city) Porter County
39	239.1	**Alexandria** (city) Madison County
40	240.3	**Schererville** (town) Lake County
41	287.0	**Tipton** (city) Tipton County
42	298.9	**Plainfield** (town) Hendricks County
43	301.7	**Whitestown** (town) Boone County
44	314.9	**Plymouth** (city) Marshall County
45	316.2	**Bloomington** (city) Monroe County
46	317.9	**Boonville** (city) Warrick County
47	321.7	**Warsaw** (city) Kosciusko County
48	322.4	**Mooresville** (town) Morgan County
49	324.3	**Highland** (town) Lake County
50	329.4	**Whiting** (city) Lake County
51	332.0	**Crawfordsville** (city) Montgomery County
52	335.6	**Elwood** (city) Madison County
53	337.3	**Bedford** (city) Lawrence County
54	338.9	**Griffith** (town) Lake County
55	339.6	**Linton** (city) Greene County
56	341.0	**Goshen** (city) Elkhart County
57	341.6	**New Haven** (city) Allen County
58	357.1	**Lawrenceburg** (city) Dearborn County
59	358.6	**Greenwood** (city) Johnson County
60	366.0	**Jeffersonville** (city) Clark County
61	368.0	**Cumberland** (town) Marion County
62	369.2	**Rensselaer** (city) Jasper County
63	373.9	**Merrillville** (town) Lake County
64	374.7	**Beech Grove** (city) Marion County
65	381.1	**Franklin** (city) Johnson County
66	384.9	**Fort Wayne** (city) Allen County
67	388.5	**Marion** (city) Grant County
68	388.6	**Kokomo** (city) Howard County
69	388.7	**Portland** (city) Jay County
70	393.0	**La Porte** (city) LaPorte County
71	407.8	**Hammond** (city) Lake County
72	408.1	**Hartford City** (city) Blackford County
73	429.2	**Muncie** (city) Delaware County
74	446.7	**Garrett** (city) DeKalb County
75	450.7	**Angola** (city) Steuben County
76	453.6	**Scottsburg** (city) Scott County
77	463.0	**Columbus** (city) Bartholomew County
78	467.4	**Rushville** (city) Rush County
79	471.0	**Lake Station** (city) Lake County
80	481.2	**Anderson** (city) Madison County
81	485.5	**South Bend** (city) Saint Joseph County
82	487.1	**Evansville** (city) Vanderburgh County
83	495.3	**Winchester** (city) Randolph County
84	497.3	**East Chicago** (city) Lake County
85	501.1	**Lafayette** (city) Tippecanoe County
86	524.6	**Indianapolis** (city) Marion County
87	524.8	**Speedway** (town) Marion County
88	526.9	**Mount Vernon** (city) Posey County
89	532.7	**Terre Haute** (city) Vigo County
90	536.8	**Hobart** (city) Lake County
91	548.6	**New Albany** (city) Floyd County
92	563.7	**Mishawaka** (city) Saint Joseph County
93	572.4	**Aurora** (city) Dearborn County
94	590.4	**North Vernon** (city) Jennings County
95	598.7	**Gary** (city) Lake County
96	602.2	**Martinsville** (city) Morgan County
97	639.1	**Washington** (city) Daviess County
98	643.8	**Seymour** (city) Jackson County
99	699.3	**Clarksville** (town) Clark County
100	1,009.1	**Edinburgh** (town) Johnson County

Note: This section ranks incorporated places and CDPs (Census Designated Places) with populations of 2,500 or more. Unincorporated postal areas were not considered. Please refer to the User Guide for additional information.

Education

Indiana Public School Educational Profile

Category	Value	Category	Value
Schools *(2011-2012)*	1,934	**Diploma Recipients** *(2009-2010)*	64,551
Instructional Level		White, Non-Hispanic	52,160
Primary	1,108	Black, Non-Hispanic	6,583
Middle	346	Asian/Pacific Islander, Non-Hispanic	900
High	365	American Indian/Alaskan Native, Non-Hispanic	182
Other/Not Reported	115	Hawaiian Native/Pacific Islander, Non-Hispanic	n/a
Curriculum		Two or More Races, Non-Hispanic	n/a
Regular	1,861	Hispanic of Any Race	3,168
Special Education	34	**Staff** *(2011-2012)*	
Vocational	28	Teachers (FTE)	61,769.0
Alternative	11	Salary[1] ($)	50,644
Type		Librarians/Media Specialists (FTE)	868.0
Magnet	33	Guidance Counselors (FTE)	1,946.0
Charter	65	**Ratios** *(2011-2012)*	
Title I Eligible	1,484	Number of Students per Teacher	16.8 to 1
School-wide Title I	1,144	Number of Students per Librarian	1,199.0 to 1
Students *(2011-2012)*	1,040,765	Number of Students per Guidance Counselor	534.8 to 1
Gender (%)		**Finances** *(2010-2011)*	
Male	51.2	Current Expenditures ($ per student)	
Female	48.8	Total	9,251
Race/Ethnicity (%)		Instruction	5,445
White, Non-Hispanic	72.5	Support Services	3,395
Black, Non-Hispanic	12.2	Other	411
Asian, Non-Hispanic	1.7	General Revenue ($ per student)	
American Indian/Alaskan Native, Non-Hisp.	0.3	Total	11,231
Hawaiian Native/Pacific Islander, Non-Hisp.	0.1	From Federal Sources	999
Two or More Races, Non-Hispanic	4.3	From State Sources	6,240
Hispanic of Any Race	9.0	From Local Sources	3,993
Special Programs (%)		Long-Term Debt Outstanding ($ per student)	
Individual Education Program (IEP)	15.8	At Beginning of Fiscal Year	11,706
English Language Learner (ELL)	4.9	Issued During Fiscal Year	702
Eligible for Free Lunch Program	39.8	Retired During Fiscal Year	853
Eligible for Reduced-Price Lunch Program	8.2	At End of Fiscal Year	11,554
Average Freshman Grad. Rate (%) *(2009-2010)*	77.2	**College Entrance Exam Scores**	
White, Non-Hispanic	79.1	SAT Reasoning Test™ *(2013)*	
Black, Non-Hispanic	61.6	Participation Rate (%)	70
Asian/Pacific Islander, Non-Hispanic	95.2	Mean Critical Reading Score	493
American Indian/Alaskan Native, Non-Hispanic	75.5	Mean Math Score	500
Hispanic of Any Race	71.8	Mean Writing Score	477
High School Drop-out Rate (%) *(2009-2010)*	1.6	ACT *(2013)*	
White, Non-Hispanic	1.3	Participation Rate (%)	38
Black, Non-Hispanic	3.1	Mean Composite Score	21.7
Asian/Pacific Islander, Non-Hispanic	1.1	Mean English Score	21.0
American Indian/Alaskan Native, Non-Hispanic	2.2	Mean Math Score	21.9
Hawaiian Native/Pacific Islander, Non-Hispanic	n/a	Mean Reading Score	22.1
Two or More Races, Non-Hispanic	n/a	Mean Science Score	21.4
Hispanic of Any Race	2.4		

Note: For an explanation of data, please refer to the User's Guide in the front of the book; (1) Average salary for classroom teachers in 2013-14

Number of Schools

Rank	Number	District Name	City
1	68	Indianapolis Public Schools	Indianapolis
2	51	Fort Wayne Community Schools	Fort Wayne
3	40	Evansville Vanderburgh Sch Corp	Evansville
4	39	South Bend Community Sch Corp	South Bend
5	29	Vigo County School Corp	Terre Haute
6	22	Monroe County Com Sch Corp	Bloomington
7	21	School City of Hammond	Hammond
8	20	Elkhart Community Schools	Elkhart
8	20	Gary Community School Corp	Gary
8	20	Greater Clark County Schools	Jeffersonville
8	20	Hamilton Southeastern Schools	Fishers
12	19	Tippecanoe School Corp	Lafayette
13	18	M S D Warren Township	Indianapolis
13	18	M S D Wayne Township	Indianapolis
15	17	Bartholomew Con School Corp	Columbus
15	17	Carmel Clay Schools	Carmel
15	17	East Allen County Schools	New Haven
15	17	M S D Lawrence Township	Indianapolis
15	17	M S D Perry Township	Indianapolis
15	17	Warrick County School Corp	Boonville
21	16	New Albany-Floyd County Con Sch	New Albany
21	16	North Lawrence Com Schools	Bedford
23	15	Muncie Community Schools	Muncie
23	15	Penn-Harris-Madison Sch Corp	Mishawaka
25	14	Michigan City Area Schools	Michigan City
25	14	Richmond Community Schools	Richmond
27	13	M S D Pike Township	Indianapolis
27	13	M S D Washington Twp	Indianapolis
29	12	Anderson Community School Corp	Anderson
29	12	Avon Community School Corp	Avon
29	12	Lafayette School Corporation	Lafayette
29	12	Valparaiso Community Schools	Valparaiso
33	11	Huntington County Com Sch Corp	Huntington
33	11	Lake Central School Corp	Saint John
33	11	Laporte Community School Corp	Laporte
33	11	M S D Martinsville Schools	Martinsville
33	11	Northwest Allen County Schools	Fort Wayne
33	11	Portage Township Schools	Portage
33	11	School City of Mishawaka	Mishawaka
33	11	Warsaw Community Schools	Warsaw
41	10	Clay Community Schools	Knightsville
41	10	Crown Point Community Sch Corp	Crown Point
41	10	Fayette County School Corp	Connersville
41	10	Goshen Community Schools	Goshen
41	10	Jay School Corp	Portland
41	10	Kokomo-Center Twp Con Sch Corp	Kokomo
41	10	Marion Community Schools	Marion
48	9	Brownsburg Community Sch Corp	Brownsburg
48	9	Duneland School Corporation	Chesterton
48	9	Franklin Township Com Sch Corp	Indianapolis
48	9	Jennings County Schools	North Vernon
48	9	Logansport Community Sch Corp	Logansport
48	9	M S D Decatur Township	Indianapolis
48	9	M S D Southwest Allen County	Fort Wayne
48	9	New Castle Community Sch Corp	New Castle
48	9	Noblesville Schools	Noblesville
48	9	South Harrison Com Schools	Corydon
48	9	Westfield-Washington Schools	Westfield
59	8	Center Grove Com Sch Corp	Greenwood
59	8	Clark-Pleasant Com School Corp	Whiteland
59	8	Franklin Community School Corp	Franklin
59	8	Greenfield-Central Com Schools	Greenfield
59	8	M S D Wabash County Schools	Wabash
59	8	Madison Consolidated Schools	Madison
59	8	Merrillville Community School	Merrillville
59	8	School City of East Chicago	East Chicago
59	8	West Clark Community Schools	Sellersburg
59	8	Zionsville Community Schools	Zionsville
69	7	Concord Community Schools	Elkhart
69	7	East Noble School Corp	Kendallville
69	7	Middlebury Community Schools	Middlebury
69	7	Mooresville Con School Corp	Mooresville
69	7	Plymouth Community School Corp	Plymouth
69	7	Richland-Bean Blossom C S C	Ellettsville
69	7	Rush County Schools	Rushville
69	7	Seymour Community Schools	Seymour
69	7	Sunman-Dearborn Com Sch Corp	Saint Leon
78	6	Brown County School Corporation	Nashville
78	6	Crawford County Com School Corp	Marengo
78	6	Dekalb County Ctl United SD	Waterloo
78	6	East Porter County School Corp	Kouts
78	6	Greater Jasper Con Schs	Jasper
78	6	Greenwood Community Sch Corp	Greenwood
78	6	Lebanon Community School Corp	Lebanon
78	6	M S D Steuben County	Angola
78	6	North Spencer County Sch Corp	Lincoln City
78	6	Plainfield Community Sch Corp	Plainfield
78	6	School City of Hobart	Hobart
78	6	School Town of Highland	Highland
78	6	School Town of Speedway	Speedway
78	6	Scott County SD 2	Scottsburg
78	6	Shelbyville Central Schools	Shelbyville
78	6	South Dearborn Com School Corp	Aurora
78	6	South Montgomery Com Sch Corp	New Market
78	6	Spencer-Owen Community Schools	Spencer
78	6	Twin Lakes School Corp	Monticello
78	6	Vincennes Community Sch Corp	Vincennes
78	6	Washington Com Schools	Washington
78	6	Whitley County Cons Schools	Columbia City
100	5	Beech Grove City Schools	Beech Grove
100	5	Blackford County Schools	Hartford City
100	5	Community Schools of Frankfort	Frankfort
100	5	Crawfordsville Com Schools	Crawfordsville
100	5	Delaware Community School Corp	Muncie
100	5	Eastbrook Community Sch Corp	Marion
100	5	Franklin County Com Sch Corp	Brookville
100	5	Frankton-Lapel Community Schs	Anderson
100	5	Greencastle Community Sch Corp	Greencastle
100	5	Griffith Public Schools	Griffith
100	5	Kankakee Valley School Corp	Wheatfield
100	5	Lake Ridge Schools	Gary
100	5	Lakeland School Corporation	Lagrange
100	5	M S D Mount Vernon	Mount Vernon
100	5	Mississinewa Community School Corp	Gas City
100	5	Mt Vernon Community Sch Corp	Fortville
100	5	New Prairie United School Corp	New Carlisle
100	5	North Montgomery Com Sch Corp	Crawfordsville
100	5	North West Hendricks Schools	Lizton
100	5	Oak Hill United School Corp	Converse
100	5	Peru Community Schools	Peru
100	5	Pike County School Corp	Petersburg
100	5	Randolph Central School Corp	Winchester
100	5	School Town of Munster	Munster
100	5	South Madison Com Sch Corp	Pendleton
100	5	South Vermillion Com Sch Corp	Clinton
100	5	Southern Hancock Co. Com Sch Corp	New Palestine
100	5	Tri-Creek School Corporation	Lowell
100	5	Wa-Nee Community Schools	Nappanee
100	5	Wawasee Community School Corp	Syracuse
100	5	Westview School Corporation	Topeka
131	4	Batesville Community Sch Corp	Batesville
131	4	Baugo Community Schools	Elkhart
131	4	Benton Community School Corp	Fowler
131	4	Brownstown Cnt Com Sch Corp	Brownstown
131	4	Centerville-Abington Com Schs	Centerville
131	4	Danville Community School Corp	Danville
131	4	Decatur County Com Schools	Greensburg
131	4	Elwood Community School Corp	Elwood
131	4	Fairfield Community Schools	Goshen
131	4	Hamilton Heights School Corp	Arcadia
131	4	Hanover Community School Corp	Cedar Lake
131	4	John Glenn School Corporation	Walkerton
131	4	Lawrenceburg Com School Corp	Lawrenceburg
131	4	Maconaquah School Corp	Bunker Hill
131	4	Mill Creek Community Sch Corp	Clayton
131	4	Mitchell Community Schools	Mitchell
131	4	Nineveh-Hensley-Jackson United	Trafalgar
131	4	North Adams Community Schools	Decatur
131	4	North Gibson School Corp	Princeton
131	4	North Harrison Com School Corp	Ramsey
131	4	North Putnam Community Schools	Bainbridge
131	4	Northern Wells Com Schools	Ossian
131	4	Northwestern School Corp	Kokomo
131	4	Porter Township School Corp	Valparaiso
131	4	Rensselaer Central School Corp	Rensselaer
131	4	River Forest Community Sch Corp	Hobart
131	4	Rochester Community Sch Corp	Rochester
131	4	Salem Community Schools	Salem
131	4	South Gibson School Corp	Fort Branch
131	4	Southwest Dubois County Sch Corp	Huntingburg
131	4	Southwest School Corp	Sullivan
131	4	Tippecanoe Valley School Corp	Akron
131	4	Union Co/clg Corner Joint SD	Liberty
131	4	Union Township School Corp	Valparaiso
131	4	West Noble School Corporation	Ligonier
131	4	Western School Corp	Russiaville
131	4	Whitko Community School Corp	Pierceton
131	4	Yorktown Community Schools	Yorktown
169	3	Alexandria Com School Corp	Alexandria
169	3	Delphi Community School Corp	Delphi
169	3	East Washington School Corp	Pekin
169	3	Garrett-Keyser-Butler Com	Garrett
169	3	Greensburg Community Schools	Greensburg
169	3	Knox Community School Corp	Knox
169	3	Manchester Community Schools	N Manchester
169	3	Southeastern School Corp	Walton
169	3	Tipton Community School Corp	Tipton
169	3	West Lafayette Com School Corp	West Lafayette
169	3	Western Boone County Com SD	Thorntown
180	2	Paoli Community School Corp	Paoli
180	2	Tell City-Troy Twp School Corp	Tell City
182	1	Hoosier Acad Virtual Charter	Indianapolis
182	1	In Connections Acad Virtual Pilot	Indianapolis
182	1	Thea Bowman Leadership Academy	Gary

Number of Teachers

Rank	Number	District Name	City
1	2,160.4	Indianapolis Public Schools	Indianapolis
2	1,818.0	Fort Wayne Community Schools	Fort Wayne
3	1,551.5	Evansville Vanderburgh Sch Corp	Evansville
4	1,169.9	South Bend Community Sch Corp	South Bend
5	1,012.3	Hamilton Southeastern Schools	Fishers
6	949.0	Carmel Clay Schools	Carmel
7	941.4	M S D Wayne Township	Indianapolis
8	937.1	Vigo County School Corp	Terre Haute
9	780.9	M S D Lawrence Township	Indianapolis
10	767.7	Elkhart Community Schools	Elkhart
11	766.5	M S D Perry Township	Indianapolis
12	766.4	School City of Hammond	Hammond
13	710.5	Monroe County Com Sch Corp	Bloomington
14	665.4	Tippecanoe School Corp	Lafayette
15	655.5	M S D Warren Township	Indianapolis
16	634.4	M S D Washington Twp	Indianapolis
17	613.5	Greater Clark County Schools	Jeffersonville
18	602.6	New Albany-Floyd County Con Sch	New Albany
19	597.9	Gary Community School Corp	Gary
20	597.2	Bartholomew Con School Corp	Columbus
21	595.0	Warrick County School Corp	Boonville
22	555.3	M S D Pike Township	Indianapolis
23	553.1	Lake Central School Corp	Saint John
24	544.4	East Allen County Schools	New Haven
25	517.0	Noblesville Schools	Noblesville
26	492.8	Penn-Harris-Madison Sch Corp	Mishawaka
27	483.9	Lafayette School Corporation	Lafayette
28	477.1	Muncie Community Schools	Muncie
29	451.9	Franklin Township Com Sch Corp	Indianapolis
30	442.0	Brownsburg Community Sch Corp	Brownsburg
31	440.6	Michigan City Area Schools	Michigan City
32	437.6	Warsaw Community Schools	Warsaw
33	433.3	Goshen Community Schools	Goshen
34	433.2	Crown Point Community Sch Corp	Crown Point
35	432.0	Avon Community School Corp	Avon
36	428.8	Portage Township Schools	Portage
37	422.2	M S D Southwest Allen County	Fort Wayne
38	421.1	Anderson Community School Corp	Anderson
39	417.9	Center Grove Com Sch Corp	Greenwood
40	408.0	Kokomo-Center Twp Con Sch Corp	Kokomo
41	390.4	Laporte Community School Corp	Laporte
42	387.2	Merrillville Community School	Merrillville
43	374.9	Huntington County Com Sch Corp	Huntington
44	373.9	Richmond Community Schools	Richmond
45	356.3	Logansport Community Sch Corp	Logansport
46	355.9	School City of East Chicago	East Chicago
47	355.2	Northwest Allen County Schools	Fort Wayne
48	348.6	Westfield-Washington Schools	Westfield
49	342.0	M S D Decatur Township	Indianapolis
50	338.7	Valparaiso Community Schools	Valparaiso
51	337.5	School City of Mishawaka	Mishawaka
52	317.7	M S D Martinsville Schools	Martinsville
53	304.4	Zionsville Community Schools	Zionsville
54	302.5	Concord Community Schools	Elkhart
55	296.9	Jennings County Schools	North Vernon
56	295.9	Duneland School Corporation	Chesterton
57	291.5	North Lawrence Com Schools	Bedford
58	279.3	Franklin Community School Corp	Franklin
59	277.1	Clay Community Schools	Knightsville
60	276.0	New Castle Community Sch Corp	New Castle
61	261.7	Middlebury Community Schools	Middlebury
61	261.7	Plainfield Community Sch Corp	Plainfield
63	258.4	Clark-Pleasant Com School Corp	Whiteland

Note: This section only includes districts with 1,500 or more students; All categories are ranked from high to low

64	256.2	West Clark Community Schools	Sellersburg
65	240.8	East Noble School Corp	Kendallville
66	238.7	Fayette County School Corp	Connersville
67	238.6	Jay School Corp	Portland
68	236.5	Marion Community Schools	Marion
69	234.3	Community Schools of Frankfort	Frankfort
70	232.1	Shelbyville Central Schools	Shelbyville
71	224.5	Greenwood Community Sch Corp	Greenwood
72	223.3	Whitley County Cons Schools	Columbia City
73	217.7	Greenfield-Central Com Schools	Greenfield
73	217.7	School Town of Munster	Munster
75	215.5	Mooresville Con School Corp	Mooresville
76	212.2	Seymour Community Schools	Seymour
76	212.2	South Madison Com Sch Corp	Pendleton
78	208.9	Dekalb County Ctl United SD	Waterloo
79	206.7	Sunman-Dearborn Com Sch Corp	Saint Leon
80	205.6	Lebanon Community School Corp	Lebanon
81	199.1	South Harrison Com Schools	Corydon
82	195.7	Kankakee Valley School Corp	Wheatfield
82	195.7	School City of Hobart	Hobart
84	193.5	Wawasee Community School Corp	Syracuse
85	191.4	Tri-Creek School Corporation	Lowell
86	190.3	Plymouth Community School Corp	Plymouth
87	185.9	Wa-Nee Community Schools	Nappanee
88	180.4	Madison Consolidated Schools	Madison
89	176.0	Richland-Bean Blossom C S C	Ellettsville
90	174.8	Mt Vernon Community Sch Corp	Fortville
91	172.7	Greater Jasper Con Schs	Jasper
92	171.6	M S D Steuben County	Angola
93	169.4	School Town of Highland	Highland
94	169.3	Rush County Schools	Rushville
95	168.3	Western School Corp	Russiaville
96	166.0	South Dearborn Com School Corp	Aurora
97	162.8	West Noble School Corporation	Ligonier
98	160.5	Delaware Community School Corp	Muncie
99	159.5	M S D Wabash County Schools	Wabash
100	159.4	Crawfordsville Com Schools	Crawfordsville
100	159.4	Vincennes Community Sch Corp	Vincennes
102	158.4	Beech Grove City Schools	Beech Grove
103	157.3	Scott County SD 2	Scottsburg
104	155.1	Franklin County Com Sch Corp	Brookville
105	152.9	Southern Hancock Co. Com Sch Corp	New Palestine
106	151.8	Frankton-Lapel Community Schs	Anderson
107	151.7	New Prairie United School Corp	New Carlisle
107	151.7	Pike County School Corp	Petersburg
109	150.7	Twin Lakes School Corp	Monticello
110	149.6	Brown County School Corporation	Nashville
111	149.5	Spencer-Owen Community Schools	Spencer
112	148.5	Decatur County Com Schools	Greensburg
113	147.3	Westview School Corporation	Topeka
114	146.3	East Porter County School Corp	Kouts
115	145.2	M S D Mount Vernon	Mount Vernon
116	141.9	Greensburg Community Schools	Greensburg
117	139.7	Danville Community School Corp	Danville
118	138.6	Mississinewa Community School Corp	Gas City
118	138.6	Washington Com Schools	Washington
120	135.3	North Gibson School Corp	Princeton
120	135.3	West Lafayette Com School Corp	West Lafayette
122	135.2	Lakeland School Corporation	Lagrange
123	134.2	Maconaquah School Corp	Bunker Hill
124	133.1	North Montgomery Com Sch Corp	Crawfordsville
125	133.0	Northern Wells Com Schools	Ossian
126	132.0	South Vermillion Com Sch Corp	Clinton
127	130.9	South Montgomery Com Sch Corp	New Market
128	128.7	Griffith Public Schools	Griffith
129	127.6	Hamilton Heights School Corp	Arcadia
129	127.6	North Spencer County Sch Corp	Lincoln City
129	127.6	Union Co/clg Corner Joint SD	Liberty
132	126.5	Greencastle Community Sch Corp	Greencastle
133	125.4	Batesville Community Sch Corp	Batesville
133	125.4	Nineveh-Hensley-Jackson United	Trafalgar
133	125.4	Yorktown Community Schools	Yorktown
136	123.2	Fairfield Community Schools	Goshen
136	123.2	North Adams Community Schools	Decatur
138	123.1	Peru Community Schools	Peru
139	121.0	Benton Community School Corp	Fowler
140	118.8	South Gibson School Corp	Fort Branch
141	117.7	Rensselaer Central School Corp	Rensselaer
142	115.5	John Glenn School Corporation	Walkerton
142	115.5	Knox Community School Corp	Knox
142	115.5	Randolph Central School Corp	Winchester
145	114.4	Lawrenceburg Com School Corp	Lawrenceburg
145	114.4	School Town of Speedway	Speedway
147	113.3	Tipton Community School Corp	Tipton
148	112.2	Garrett-Keyser-Butler Com	Garrett
149	112.1	Lake Ridge Schools	Gary
149	112.1	Mitchell Community Schools	Mitchell
151	111.1	Northwestern School Corp	Kokomo
151	111.1	Rochester Community Sch Corp	Rochester
153	110.0	Tippecanoe Valley School Corp	Akron
154	107.7	North Harrison Com School Corp	Ramsey
154	107.7	North Putnam Community Schools	Bainbridge
156	106.7	Blackford County Schools	Hartford City
156	106.7	Hanover Community School Corp	Cedar Lake
156	106.7	Southwest School Corp	Sullivan
159	105.6	Eastbrook Community Sch Corp	Marion
160	105.5	Whitko Community School Corp	Pierceton
161	104.5	North West Hendricks Schools	Lizton
162	102.3	Baugo Community Schools	Elkhart
162	102.3	Centerville-Abington Com Schs	Centerville
162	102.3	Paoli Community School Corp	Paoli
165	100.1	Crawford County Com School Corp	Marengo
166	99.0	Tell City-Troy Twp School Corp	Tell City
167	98.9	Western Boone County Com SD	Thorntown
168	95.7	East Washington School Corp	Pekin
169	94.6	Delphi Community School Corp	Delphi
169	94.6	Southeastern School Corp	Walton
169	94.6	Union Township School Corp	Valparaiso
172	93.5	Alexandria Com School Corp	Alexandria
172	93.5	Brownstown Cnt Com Sch Corp	Brownstown
172	93.5	Mill Creek Community Sch Corp	Clayton
172	93.5	Oak Hill United School Corp	Converse
176	88.0	Southwest Dubois County Sch Corp	Huntingburg
177	86.9	Manchester Community Schools	N Manchester
177	86.9	Thea Bowman Leadership Academy	Gary
179	84.7	Elwood Community School Corp	Elwood
180	81.4	Porter Township School Corp	Valparaiso
181	45.1	Hoosier Acad Virtual Charter	Indianapolis
181	45.1	In Connections Acad Virtual Pilot	Indianapolis
n/a	n/a	River Forest Community Sch Corp	Hobart
n/a	n/a	Salem Community Schools	Salem

Number of Students

Rank	Number	District Name	City
1	31,999	Indianapolis Public Schools	Indianapolis
2	30,821	Fort Wayne Community Schools	Fort Wayne
3	22,799	Evansville Vanderburgh Sch Corp	Evansville
4	20,077	South Bend Community Sch Corp	South Bend
5	19,053	Hamilton Southeastern Schools	Fishers
6	16,276	M S D Wayne Township	Indianapolis
7	15,750	Carmel Clay Schools	Carmel
8	15,601	Vigo County School Corp	Terre Haute
9	14,878	M S D Lawrence Township	Indianapolis
10	14,432	M S D Perry Township	Indianapolis
11	13,742	School City of Hammond	Hammond
12	12,536	Elkhart Community Schools	Elkhart
13	11,899	M S D Warren Township	Indianapolis
14	11,844	Tippecanoe School Corp	Lafayette
15	11,458	New Albany-Floyd County Con Sch	New Albany
16	11,394	Bartholomew Con School Corp	Columbus
17	11,223	M S D Washington Twp	Indianapolis
18	10,918	M S D Pike Township	Indianapolis
19	10,794	Monroe County Com Sch Corp	Bloomington
20	10,593	Greater Clark County Schools	Jeffersonville
21	10,451	Penn-Harris-Madison Sch Corp	Mishawaka
22	10,215	Gary Community School Corp	Gary
23	10,037	Lake Central School Corp	Saint John
24	9,924	Warrick County School Corp	Boonville
25	9,452	East Allen County Schools	New Haven
26	9,444	Noblesville Schools	Noblesville
27	8,521	Avon Community School Corp	Avon
28	8,478	Franklin Township Com Sch Corp	Indianapolis
29	8,065	Portage Township Schools	Portage
30	7,733	Crown Point Community Sch Corp	Crown Point
31	7,624	Brownsburg Community Sch Corp	Brownsburg
32	7,583	Center Grove Com Sch Corp	Greenwood
33	7,142	Anderson Community School Corp	Anderson
34	7,011	Lafayette School Corporation	Lafayette
35	6,948	Warsaw Community Schools	Warsaw
36	6,900	Merrillville Community School	Merrillville
37	6,873	M S D Southwest Allen County	Fort Wayne
38	6,871	Muncie Community Schools	Muncie
39	6,583	Michigan City Area Schools	Michigan City
40	6,517	Northwest Allen County Schools	Fort Wayne
41	6,450	Goshen Community Schools	Goshen
42	6,418	Valparaiso Community Schools	Valparaiso
43	6,402	Westfield-Washington Schools	Westfield
44	6,325	Laporte Community School Corp	Laporte
45	6,304	M S D Decatur Township	Indianapolis
46	6,265	Kokomo-Center Twp Con Sch Corp	Kokomo
47	5,913	Duneland School Corporation	Chesterton
48	5,891	Clark-Pleasant Com School Corp	Whiteland
49	5,883	Huntington County Com Sch Corp	Huntington
50	5,740	Zionsville Community Schools	Zionsville
51	5,461	School City of East Chicago	East Chicago
52	5,383	Richmond Community Schools	Richmond
53	5,345	North Lawrence Com Schools	Bedford
54	5,325	M S D Martinsville Schools	Martinsville
55	5,159	Franklin Community School Corp	Franklin
56	5,097	School City of Mishawaka	Mishawaka
57	4,950	Concord Community Schools	Elkhart
58	4,904	Plainfield Community Sch Corp	Plainfield
59	4,853	Jennings County Schools	North Vernon
60	4,740	Greenfield-Central Com Schools	Greenfield
61	4,511	Mooresville Con School Corp	Mooresville
62	4,500	South Madison Com Sch Corp	Pendleton
63	4,440	West Clark Community Schools	Sellersburg
64	4,400	Clay Community Schools	Knightsville
64	4,400	Middlebury Community Schools	Middlebury
66	4,255	Seymour Community Schools	Seymour
67	4,205	Logansport Community Sch Corp	Logansport
68	4,117	Sunman-Dearborn Com Sch Corp	Saint Leon
69	4,110	School Town of Munster	Munster
70	4,059	Fayette County School Corp	Connersville
71	4,017	Marion Community Schools	Marion
72	3,968	School City of Hobart	Hobart
73	3,943	Dekalb County Ctl United SD	Waterloo
74	3,927	Shelbyville Central Schools	Shelbyville
75	3,822	Greenwood Community Sch Corp	Greenwood
76	3,802	East Noble School Corp	Kendallville
77	3,653	New Castle Community Sch Corp	New Castle
78	3,640	Plymouth Community School Corp	Plymouth
79	3,604	Jay School Corp	Portland
80	3,593	Whitley County Cons Schools	Columbia City
81	3,591	Tri-Creek School Corporation	Lowell
82	3,547	Lebanon Community School Corp	Lebanon
83	3,519	Kankakee Valley School Corp	Wheatfield
84	3,513	Mt Vernon Community Sch Corp	Fortville
85	3,316	School Town of Highland	Highland
86	3,258	Greater Jasper Con Schs	Jasper
87	3,243	Southern Hancock Co. Com Sch Corp	New Palestine
88	3,230	Madison Consolidated Schools	Madison
89	3,195	Wawasee Community School Corp	Syracuse
90	3,188	Community Schools of Frankfort	Frankfort
91	3,135	Wa-Nee Community Schools	Nappanee
92	3,086	M S D Steuben County	Angola
93	3,077	South Harrison Com Schools	Corydon
94	2,883	Frankton-Lapel Community Schs	Anderson
95	2,869	Franklin County Com Sch Corp	Brookville
96	2,822	New Prairie United School Corp	New Carlisle
97	2,820	South Dearborn Com School Corp	Aurora
98	2,799	Scott County SD 2	Scottsburg
99	2,770	Richland-Bean Blossom C S C	Ellettsville
100	2,762	Spencer-Owen Community Schools	Spencer
101	2,734	Beech Grove City Schools	Beech Grove
102	2,673	Vincennes Community Sch Corp	Vincennes
103	2,620	Western School Corp	Russiaville
104	2,614	Danville Community School Corp	Danville
105	2,606	Delaware Community School Corp	Muncie
106	2,584	Griffith Public Schools	Griffith
107	2,549	Mississinewa Community School Corp	Gas City
108	2,542	Rush County Schools	Rushville
109	2,530	Northern Wells Com Schools	Ossian
110	2,504	Washington Com Schools	Washington
111	2,482	Twin Lakes School Corp	Monticello
112	2,478	West Noble School Corporation	Ligonier
113	2,426	Westview School Corporation	Topeka
114	2,399	East Porter County School Corp	Kouts
115	2,323	Yorktown Community Schools	Yorktown
116	2,317	Crawfordsville Com Schools	Crawfordsville
117	2,294	Greensburg Community Schools	Greensburg
118	2,289	Maconaquah School Corp	Bunker Hill
119	2,266	Hamilton Heights School Corp	Arcadia
120	2,250	North Harrison Com School Corp	Ramsey
121	2,247	M S D Wabash County Schools	Wabash
122	2,240	M S D Mount Vernon	Mount Vernon
123	2,220	Lakeland School Corporation	Lagrange
124	2,219	Peru Community Schools	Peru
125	2,148	North Gibson School Corp	Princeton
126	2,142	Decatur County Com Schools	Greensburg
127	2,137	West Lafayette Com School Corp	West Lafayette
128	2,099	Batesville Community Sch Corp	Batesville
129	2,083	Fairfield Community Schools	Goshen

Note: This section only includes districts with 1,500 or more students; All categories are ranked from high to low

130	2,064	Hanover Community School Corp	Cedar Lake
131	2,062	Greencastle Community Sch Corp	Greencastle
132	2,060	Brown County School Corporation	Nashville
133	2,050	North Montgomery Com Sch Corp	Crawfordsville
133	2,050	Tippecanoe Valley School Corp	Akron
135	2,012	Salem Community Schools	Salem
136	2,008	Knox Community School Corp	Knox
137	1,999	Pike County School Corp	Petersburg
138	1,983	Baugo Community Schools	Elkhart
139	1,952	North Spencer County Sch Corp	Lincoln City
139	1,952	South Gibson School Corp	Fort Branch
141	1,937	Lake Ridge Schools	Gary
142	1,932	Lawrenceburg Com School Corp	Lawrenceburg
143	1,921	South Vermillion Com Sch Corp	Clinton
144	1,910	Mitchell Community Schools	Mitchell
145	1,905	Rochester Community Sch Corp	Rochester
146	1,883	Blackford County Schools	Hartford City
147	1,880	Benton Community School Corp	Fowler
148	1,874	North West Hendricks Schools	Lizton
149	1,873	Nineveh-Hensley-Jackson United	Trafalgar
150	1,858	North Adams Community Schools	Decatur
151	1,854	John Glenn School Corporation	Walkerton
152	1,853	Hoosier Acad Virtual Charter	Indianapolis
153	1,809	Western Boone County Com SD	Thorntown
154	1,805	Whitko Community School Corp	Pierceton
155	1,801	South Montgomery Com Sch Corp	New Market
156	1,747	Southwest Dubois County Sch Corp	Huntingburg
157	1,742	Southwest School Corp	Sullivan
158	1,740	Rensselaer Central School Corp	Rensselaer
159	1,731	Garrett-Keyser-Butler Com	Garrett
160	1,730	Brownstown Cnt Com Sch Corp	Brownstown
161	1,720	North Putnam Community Schools	Bainbridge
162	1,700	Eastbrook Community Sch Corp	Marion
163	1,694	Tipton Community School Corp	Tipton
164	1,675	In Connections Acad Virtual Pilot	Indianapolis
164	1,675	Northwestern School Corp	Kokomo
166	1,668	Centerville-Abington Com Schs	Centerville
167	1,631	Union Township School Corp	Valparaiso
168	1,627	Crawford County Com School Corp	Marengo
169	1,624	School Town of Speedway	Speedway
170	1,620	Randolph Central School Corp	Winchester
171	1,618	Delphi Community School Corp	Delphi
171	1,618	Paoli Community School Corp	Paoli
173	1,612	Alexandria Com School Corp	Alexandria
174	1,596	Elwood Community School Corp	Elwood
175	1,573	Oak Hill United School Corp	Converse
176	1,567	East Washington School Corp	Pekin
177	1,563	Mill Creek Community Sch Corp	Clayton
178	1,552	River Forest Community Sch Corp	Hobart
179	1,521	Porter Township School Corp	Valparaiso
179	1,521	Union Co/clg Corner Joint SD	Liberty
181	1,517	Tell City-Troy Twp School Corp	Tell City
182	1,516	Manchester Community Schools	N Manchester
183	1,506	Southeastern School Corp	Walton
184	1,500	Thea Bowman Leadership Academy	Gary

Male Students

Rank	Percent	District Name	City
1	54.2	Brownstown Cnt Com Sch Corp	Brownstown
1	54.2	Southwest School Corp	Sullivan
3	54.1	School Town of Speedway	Speedway
4	53.6	Batesville Community Sch Corp	Batesville
5	53.3	Union Co/clg Corner Joint SD	Liberty
5	53.3	Wawasee Community School Corp	Syracuse
7	53.2	Blackford County Schools	Hartford City
7	53.2	North Gibson School Corp	Princeton
9	53.1	John Glenn School Corporation	Walkerton
9	53.1	Whitko Community School Corp	Pierceton
11	53.0	Greenfield-Central Com Schools	Greenfield
12	52.8	Delaware Community School Corp	Muncie
13	52.7	Decatur County Com Schools	Greensburg
13	52.7	Vincennes Community Sch Corp	Vincennes
15	52.6	Anderson Community School Corp	Anderson
15	52.6	Fairfield Community Schools	Goshen
17	52.5	Greencastle Community Sch Corp	Greencastle
17	52.5	Nineveh-Hensley-Jackson United	Trafalgar
17	52.5	Porter Township School Corp	Valparaiso
17	52.5	Rensselaer Central School Corp	Rensselaer
21	52.4	Dekalb County Ctl United SD	Waterloo
21	52.4	Mississinewa Community School Corp	Gas City
21	52.4	North Montgomery Com Sch Corp	Crawfordsville
24	52.3	Community Schools of Frankfort	Frankfort
24	52.3	Greater Clark County Schools	Jeffersonville
24	52.3	Mill Creek Community Sch Corp	Clayton
24	52.3	South Vermillion Com Sch Corp	Clinton
28	52.2	Rochester Community Sch Corp	Rochester
28	52.2	Tipton Community School Corp	Tipton
30	52.1	Crawford County Com School Corp	Marengo
30	52.1	Frankton-Lapel Community Schs	Anderson
30	52.1	Indianapolis Public Schools	Indianapolis
30	52.1	Mitchell Community Schools	Mitchell
30	52.1	Southeastern School Corp	Walton
35	52.0	Danville Community School Corp	Danville
35	52.0	North Lawrence Com Schools	Bedford
37	51.9	Center Grove Com Sch Corp	Greenwood
37	51.9	East Allen County Schools	New Haven
37	51.9	Goshen Community Schools	Goshen
37	51.9	M S D Martinsville Schools	Martinsville
37	51.9	M S D Wabash County Schools	Wabash
37	51.9	Michigan City Area Schools	Michigan City
37	51.9	Muncie Community Schools	Muncie
37	51.9	Paoli Community School Corp	Paoli
37	51.9	South Madison Com Sch Corp	Pendleton
37	51.9	Warrick County School Corp	Boonville
37	51.9	Washington Com Schools	Washington
48	51.8	Benton Community School Corp	Fowler
48	51.8	Fayette County School Corp	Connersville
48	51.8	Hamilton Heights School Corp	Arcadia
48	51.8	Jay School Corp	Portland
48	51.8	Lakeland School Corporation	Lagrange
48	51.8	M S D Perry Township	Indianapolis
48	51.8	M S D Wayne Township	Indianapolis
48	51.8	Portage Township Schools	Portage
48	51.8	Southern Hancock Co. Com Sch Corp	New Palestine
57	51.7	Brown County School Corporation	Nashville
57	51.7	Elwood Community School Corp	Elwood
57	51.7	Hanover Community School Corp	Cedar Lake
57	51.7	M S D Mount Vernon	Mount Vernon
57	51.7	Marion Community Schools	Marion
57	51.7	North Putnam Community Schools	Bainbridge
57	51.7	River Forest Community Sch Corp	Hobart
57	51.7	Zionsville Community Schools	Zionsville
65	51.6	Clark-Pleasant Com School Corp	Whiteland
65	51.6	New Albany-Floyd County Con Sch	New Albany
65	51.6	School City of East Chicago	East Chicago
65	51.6	Shelbyville Central Schools	Shelbyville
69	51.5	East Washington School Corp	Pekin
69	51.5	Kokomo-Center Twp Con Sch Corp	Kokomo
69	51.5	M S D Washington Twp	Indianapolis
69	51.5	Pike County School Corp	Petersburg
69	51.5	Valparaiso Community Schools	Valparaiso
69	51.5	Vigo County School Corp	Terre Haute
75	51.4	Greensburg Community Schools	Greensburg
75	51.4	Huntington County Com Sch Corp	Huntington
75	51.4	Plymouth Community School Corp	Plymouth
75	51.4	School City of Hammond	Hammond
75	51.4	South Bend Community Sch Corp	South Bend
75	51.4	Western Boone County Com SD	Thorntown
81	51.3	Crown Point Community Sch Corp	Crown Point
81	51.3	Franklin Township Com Sch Corp	Indianapolis
81	51.3	Jennings County Schools	North Vernon
81	51.3	North Adams Community Schools	Decatur
81	51.3	Northern Wells Com Schools	Ossian
81	51.3	Rush County Schools	Rushville
81	51.3	Spencer-Owen Community Schools	Spencer
81	51.3	Tri-Creek School Corporation	Lowell
81	51.3	Warsaw Community Schools	Warsaw
81	51.3	Western School Corp	Russiaville
91	51.2	Lake Central School Corp	Saint John
91	51.2	Laporte Community School Corp	Laporte
91	51.2	Madison Consolidated Schools	Madison
91	51.2	New Castle Community Sch Corp	New Castle
91	51.2	New Prairie United School Corp	New Carlisle
91	51.2	North Harrison Com School Corp	Ramsey
91	51.2	North West Hendricks Schools	Lizton
91	51.2	Peru Community Schools	Peru
91	51.2	Randolph Central School Corp	Winchester
91	51.2	Richmond Community Schools	Richmond
91	51.2	Scott County SD 2	Scottsburg
91	51.2	South Dearborn Com School Corp	Aurora
91	51.2	Tippecanoe School Corp	Lafayette
104	51.1	Brownsburg Community Sch Corp	Brownsburg
104	51.1	Fort Wayne Community Schools	Fort Wayne
104	51.1	Franklin County Com Sch Corp	Brookville
104	51.1	Lake Ridge Schools	Gary
104	51.1	M S D Steuben County	Angola
104	51.1	Manchester Community Schools	N Manchester
104	51.1	Monroe County Com Sch Corp	Bloomington
104	51.1	Noblesville Schools	Noblesville
104	51.1	School Town of Munster	Munster
104	51.1	Westfield-Washington Schools	Westfield
114	51.0	Duneland School Corporation	Chesterton
114	51.0	Lafayette School Corporation	Lafayette
114	51.0	Lebanon Community School Corp	Lebanon
117	50.9	Bartholomew Con School Corp	Columbus
117	50.9	East Porter County School Corp	Kouts
117	50.9	Evansville Vanderburgh Sch Corp	Evansville
117	50.9	Mooresville Con School Corp	Mooresville
117	50.9	Mt Vernon Community Sch Corp	Fortville
117	50.9	Richland-Bean Blossom C S C	Ellettsville
117	50.9	School City of Hobart	Hobart
117	50.9	School City of Mishawaka	Mishawaka
117	50.9	Wa-Nee Community Schools	Nappanee
117	50.9	Westview School Corporation	Topeka
117	50.9	Whitley County Cons Schools	Columbia City
128	50.8	Carmel Clay Schools	Carmel
128	50.8	Logansport Community Sch Corp	Logansport
128	50.8	M S D Lawrence Township	Indianapolis
128	50.8	Plainfield Community Sch Corp	Plainfield
128	50.8	School Town of Highland	Highland
128	50.8	Sunman-Dearborn Com Sch Corp	Saint Leon
128	50.8	Twin Lakes School Corp	Monticello
128	50.8	West Clark Community Schools	Sellersburg
136	50.7	Franklin Community School Corp	Franklin
136	50.7	M S D Warren Township	Indianapolis
136	50.7	Merrillville Community School	Merrillville
136	50.7	North Spencer County Sch Corp	Lincoln City
136	50.7	Penn-Harris-Madison Sch Corp	Mishawaka
136	50.7	South Montgomery Com Sch Corp	New Market
142	50.6	Greater Jasper Con Schs	Jasper
142	50.6	Lawrenceburg Com School Corp	Lawrenceburg
142	50.6	Salem Community Schools	Salem
142	50.6	Tell City-Troy Twp School Corp	Tell City
142	50.6	Union Township School Corp	Valparaiso
147	50.5	Concord Community Schools	Elkhart
147	50.5	Elkhart Community Schools	Elkhart
147	50.5	Kankakee Valley School Corp	Wheatfield
147	50.5	M S D Decatur Township	Indianapolis
151	50.4	Gary Community School Corp	Gary
151	50.4	Greenwood Community Sch Corp	Greenwood
151	50.4	Knox Community School Corp	Knox
151	50.4	M S D Pike Township	Indianapolis
151	50.4	Middlebury Community Schools	Middlebury
151	50.4	Northwest Allen County Schools	Fort Wayne
151	50.4	Seymour Community Schools	Seymour
151	50.4	Tippecanoe Valley School Corp	Akron
151	50.4	West Noble School Corporation	Ligonier
160	50.3	Avon Community School Corp	Avon
160	50.3	M S D Southwest Allen County	Fort Wayne
160	50.3	South Harrison Com Schools	Corydon
163	50.2	Hamilton Southeastern Schools	Fishers
163	50.2	West Lafayette Com School Corp	West Lafayette
165	50.1	Beech Grove City Schools	Beech Grove
166	50.0	Maconaquah School Corp	Bunker Hill
167	49.9	East Noble School Corp	Kendallville
168	49.8	Centerville-Abington Com Schs	Centerville
169	49.7	Alexandria Com School Corp	Alexandria
169	49.7	Oak Hill United School Corp	Converse
171	49.6	Delphi Community School Corp	Delphi
171	49.6	Eastbrook Community Sch Corp	Marion
173	49.5	Baugo Community Schools	Elkhart
173	49.5	Northwestern School Corp	Kokomo
175	49.4	Yorktown Community Schools	Yorktown
176	49.3	South Gibson School Corp	Fort Branch
177	49.2	Clay Community Schools	Knightsville
178	48.8	Garrett-Keyser-Butler Com	Garrett
179	48.6	Griffith Public Schools	Griffith
179	48.6	In Connections Acad Virtual Pilot	Indianapolis
181	48.5	Crawfordsville Com Schools	Crawfordsville
182	47.6	Southwest Dubois County Sch Corp	Huntingburg
183	47.4	Hoosier Acad Virtual Charter	Indianapolis
184	45.9	Thea Bowman Leadership Academy	Gary

Female Students

Rank	Percent	District Name	City
1	54.1	Thea Bowman Leadership Academy	Gary
2	52.6	Hoosier Acad Virtual Charter	Indianapolis
3	52.4	Southwest Dubois County Sch Corp	Huntingburg
4	51.5	Crawfordsville Com Schools	Crawfordsville
5	51.4	Griffith Public Schools	Griffith
5	51.4	In Connections Acad Virtual Pilot	Indianapolis

Note: This section only includes districts with 1,500 or more students; All categories are ranked from high to low

7	51.2	Garrett-Keyser-Butler Com	Garrett
8	50.8	Clay Community Schools	Knightsville
9	50.7	South Gibson School Corp	Fort Branch
10	50.6	Yorktown Community Schools	Yorktown
11	50.5	Baugo Community Schools	Elkhart
11	50.5	Northwestern School Corp	Kokomo
13	50.4	Delphi Community School Corp	Delphi
13	50.4	Eastbrook Community Sch Corp	Marion
15	50.3	Alexandria Com School Corp	Alexandria
15	50.3	Oak Hill United School Corp	Converse
17	50.2	Centerville-Abington Com Schs	Centerville
18	50.1	East Noble School Corp	Kendallville
19	50.0	Maconaquah School Corp	Bunker Hill
20	49.9	Beech Grove City Schools	Beech Grove
21	49.8	Hamilton Southeastern Schools	Fishers
21	49.8	West Lafayette Com School Corp	West Lafayette
23	49.7	Avon Community School Corp	Avon
23	49.7	M S D Southwest Allen County	Fort Wayne
23	49.7	South Harrison Com Schools	Corydon
26	49.6	Gary Community School Corp	Gary
26	49.6	Greenwood Community Sch Corp	Greenwood
26	49.6	Knox Community School Corp	Knox
26	49.6	M S D Pike Township	Indianapolis
26	49.6	Middlebury Community Schools	Middlebury
26	49.6	Northwest Allen County Schools	Fort Wayne
26	49.6	Seymour Community Schools	Seymour
26	49.6	Tippecanoe Valley School Corp	Akron
26	49.6	West Noble School Corporation	Ligonier
35	49.5	Concord Community Schools	Elkhart
35	49.5	Elkhart Community Schools	Elkhart
35	49.5	Kankakee Valley School Corp	Wheatfield
35	49.5	M S D Decatur Township	Indianapolis
39	49.4	Greater Jasper Con Schs	Jasper
39	49.4	Lawrenceburg Com School Corp	Lawrenceburg
39	49.4	Salem Community Schools	Salem
39	49.4	Tell City-Troy Twp School Corp	Tell City
39	49.4	Union Township School Corp	Valparaiso
44	49.3	Franklin Community School Corp	Franklin
44	49.3	M S D Warren Township	Indianapolis
44	49.3	Merrillville Community School	Merrillville
44	49.3	North Spencer County Sch Corp	Lincoln City
44	49.3	Penn-Harris-Madison Sch Corp	Mishawaka
44	49.3	South Montgomery Com Sch Corp	New Market
50	49.2	Carmel Clay Schools	Carmel
50	49.2	Logansport Community Sch Corp	Logansport
50	49.2	M S D Lawrence Township	Indianapolis
50	49.2	Plainfield Community Sch Corp	Plainfield
50	49.2	School Town of Highland	Highland
50	49.2	Sunman-Dearborn Com Sch Corp	Saint Leon
50	49.2	Twin Lakes School Corp	Monticello
50	49.2	West Clark Community Schools	Sellersburg
58	49.1	Bartholomew Con School Corp	Columbus
58	49.1	East Porter County School Corp	Kouts
58	49.1	Evansville Vanderburgh Sch Corp	Evansville
58	49.1	Mooresville Con School Corp	Mooresville
58	49.1	Mt Vernon Community Sch Corp	Fortville
58	49.1	Richland-Bean Blossom C S C	Ellettsville
58	49.1	School City of Hobart	Hobart
58	49.1	School City of Mishawaka	Mishawaka
58	49.1	Wa-Nee Community Schools	Nappanee
58	49.1	Westview School Corporation	Topeka
58	49.1	Whitley County Cons Schools	Columbia City
69	49.0	Duneland School Corporation	Chesterton
69	49.0	Lafayette School Corporation	Lafayette
69	49.0	Lebanon Community School Corp	Lebanon
72	48.9	Brownsburg Community Sch Corp	Brownsburg
72	48.9	Fort Wayne Community Schools	Fort Wayne
72	48.9	Franklin County Com Sch Corp	Brookville
72	48.9	Lake Ridge Schools	Gary
72	48.9	M S D Steuben County	Angola
72	48.9	Manchester Community Schools	N Manchester
72	48.9	Monroe County Com Sch Corp	Bloomington
72	48.9	Noblesville Schools	Noblesville
72	48.9	School Town of Munster	Munster
72	48.9	Westfield-Washington Schools	Westfield
82	48.8	Lake Central School Corp	Saint John
82	48.8	Laporte Community School Corp	Laporte
82	48.8	Madison Consolidated Schools	Madison
82	48.8	New Castle Community Sch Corp	New Castle
82	48.8	New Prairie United School Corp	New Carlisle
82	48.8	North Harrison Com School Corp	Ramsey
82	48.8	North West Hendricks Schools	Lizton
82	48.8	Peru Community Schools	Peru
82	48.8	Randolph Central School Corp	Winchester
82	48.8	Richmond Community Schools	Richmond
82	48.8	Scott County SD 2	Scottsburg
82	48.8	South Dearborn Com School Corp	Aurora
82	48.8	Tippecanoe School Corp	Lafayette
95	48.7	Crown Point Community Sch Corp	Crown Point
95	48.7	Franklin Township Com Sch Corp	Indianapolis
95	48.7	Jennings County Schools	North Vernon
95	48.7	North Adams Community Schools	Decatur
95	48.7	Northern Wells Com Schools	Ossian
95	48.7	Rush County Schools	Rushville
95	48.7	Spencer-Owen Community Schools	Spencer
95	48.7	Tri-Creek School Corporation	Lowell
95	48.7	Warsaw Community Schools	Warsaw
95	48.7	Western School Corp	Russiaville
105	48.6	Greensburg Community Schools	Greensburg
105	48.6	Huntington County Com Sch Corp	Huntington
105	48.6	Plymouth Community School Corp	Plymouth
105	48.6	School City of Hammond	Hammond
105	48.6	South Bend Community Sch Corp	South Bend
105	48.6	Western Boone County Com SD	Thorntown
111	48.5	East Washington School Corp	Pekin
111	48.5	Kokomo-Center Twp Con Sch Corp	Kokomo
111	48.5	M S D Washington Twp	Indianapolis
111	48.5	Pike County School Corp	Petersburg
111	48.5	Valparaiso Community Schools	Valparaiso
111	48.5	Vigo County School Corp	Terre Haute
117	48.4	Clark-Pleasant Com School Corp	Whiteland
117	48.4	New Albany-Floyd County Con Sch	New Albany
117	48.4	School City of East Chicago	East Chicago
117	48.4	Shelbyville Central Schools	Shelbyville
121	48.3	Brown County School Corporation	Nashville
121	48.3	Elwood Community School Corp	Elwood
121	48.3	Hanover Community School Corp	Cedar Lake
121	48.3	M S D Mount Vernon	Mount Vernon
121	48.3	Marion Community Schools	Marion
121	48.3	North Putnam Community Schools	Bainbridge
121	48.3	River Forest Community Sch Corp	Hobart
121	48.3	Zionsville Community Schools	Zionsville
129	48.2	Benton Community School Corp	Fowler
129	48.2	Fayette County School Corp	Connersville
129	48.2	Hamilton Heights School Corp	Arcadia
129	48.2	Jay School Corp	Portland
129	48.2	Lakeland School Corporation	Lagrange
129	48.2	M S D Perry Township	Indianapolis
129	48.2	M S D Wayne Township	Indianapolis
129	48.2	Portage Township Schools	Portage
129	48.2	Southern Hancock Co. Com Sch Corp	New Palestine
138	48.1	Center Grove Com Sch Corp	Greenwood
138	48.1	East Allen County Schools	New Haven
138	48.1	Goshen Community Schools	Goshen
138	48.1	M S D Martinsville Schools	Martinsville
138	48.1	M S D Wabash County Schools	Wabash
138	48.1	Michigan City Area Schools	Michigan City
138	48.1	Muncie Community Schools	Muncie
138	48.1	Paoli Community School Corp	Paoli
138	48.1	South Madison Com Sch Corp	Pendleton
138	48.1	Warrick County School Corp	Boonville
138	48.1	Washington Com Schools	Washington
149	48.0	Danville Community School Corp	Danville
149	48.0	North Lawrence Com Schools	Bedford
151	47.9	Crawford County Com School Corp	Marengo
151	47.9	Frankton-Lapel Community Schs	Anderson
151	47.9	Indianapolis Public Schools	Indianapolis
151	47.9	Mitchell Community Schools	Mitchell
151	47.9	Southeastern School Corp	Walton
156	47.8	Rochester Community Sch Corp	Rochester
156	47.8	Tipton Community School Corp	Tipton
158	47.7	Community Schools of Frankfort	Frankfort
158	47.7	Greater Clark County Schools	Jeffersonville
158	47.7	Mill Creek Community Sch Corp	Clayton
158	47.7	South Vermillion Com Sch Corp	Clinton
162	47.6	Dekalb County Ctl United SD	Waterloo
162	47.6	Mississinewa Community School Corp	Gas City
162	47.6	North Montgomery Com Sch Corp	Crawfordsville
165	47.5	Greencastle Community Sch Corp	Greencastle
165	47.5	Nineveh-Hensley-Jackson United	Trafalgar
165	47.5	Porter Township School Corp	Valparaiso
165	47.5	Rensselaer Central School Corp	Rensselaer
169	47.4	Anderson Community School Corp	Anderson
169	47.4	Fairfield Community Schools	Goshen
171	47.3	Decatur County Com Schools	Greensburg
171	47.3	Vincennes Community Sch Corp	Vincennes
173	47.2	Delaware Community School Corp	Muncie
174	47.0	Greenfield-Central Com Schools	Greenfield
175	46.9	John Glenn School Corporation	Walkerton
175	46.9	Whitko Community School Corp	Pierceton
177	46.8	Blackford County Schools	Hartford City
177	46.8	North Gibson School Corp	Princeton
179	46.7	Union Co/clg Corner Joint SD	Liberty
179	46.7	Wawasee Community School Corp	Syracuse
181	46.4	Batesville Community Sch Corp	Batesville
182	45.9	School Town of Speedway	Speedway
183	45.8	Brownstown Cnt Com Sch Corp	Brownstown
183	45.8	Southwest School Corp	Sullivan

Individual Education Program Students

Rank	Percent	District Name	City
1	27.9	Jay School Corp	Portland
2	26.0	North Gibson School Corp	Princeton
3	25.5	Benton Community School Corp	Fowler
4	24.1	M S D Mount Vernon	Mount Vernon
5	23.9	Anderson Community School Corp	Anderson
6	23.2	Vigo County School Corp	Terre Haute
7	23.1	Brown County School Corporation	Nashville
8	22.7	Jennings County Schools	North Vernon
9	22.3	Kokomo-Center Twp Con Sch Corp	Kokomo
10	22.1	Pike County School Corp	Petersburg
11	22.0	Muncie Community Schools	Muncie
12	21.8	Warrick County School Corp	Boonville
13	21.7	South Gibson School Corp	Fort Branch
14	21.6	Clay Community Schools	Knightsville
15	21.2	Richmond Community Schools	Richmond
16	21.1	South Bend Community Sch Corp	South Bend
17	21.0	Spencer-Owen Community Schools	Spencer
18	20.9	Indianapolis Public Schools	Indianapolis
19	20.8	Washington Com Schools	Washington
20	20.3	New Castle Community Sch Corp	New Castle
21	20.2	Greenfield-Central Com Schools	Greenfield
21	20.2	Salem Community Schools	Salem
23	20.1	Randolph Central School Corp	Winchester
24	19.9	Blackford County Schools	Hartford City
24	19.9	Lafayette School Corporation	Lafayette
24	19.9	Lebanon Community School Corp	Lebanon
27	19.8	North Putnam Community Schools	Bainbridge
27	19.8	South Montgomery Com Sch Corp	New Market
29	19.6	Mitchell Community Schools	Mitchell
30	19.1	North Harrison Com School Corp	Ramsey
31	19.0	Elwood Community School Corp	Elwood
31	19.0	Greencastle Community Sch Corp	Greencastle
33	18.9	South Dearborn Com School Corp	Aurora
33	18.9	South Madison Com Sch Corp	Pendleton
35	18.7	Michigan City Area Schools	Michigan City
36	18.6	Crawfordsville Com Schools	Crawfordsville
37	18.5	School Town of Speedway	Speedway
38	18.4	Evansville Vanderburgh Sch Corp	Evansville
39	18.3	Alexandria Com School Corp	Alexandria
39	18.3	Decatur County Com Schools	Greensburg
41	18.1	Richland-Bean Blossom C S C	Ellettsville
42	18.0	North Lawrence Com Schools	Bedford
43	17.9	Delaware Community School Corp	Muncie
43	17.9	Greater Clark County Schools	Jeffersonville
43	17.9	South Vermillion Com Sch Corp	Clinton
43	17.9	Tippecanoe Valley School Corp	Akron
47	17.7	M S D Martinsville Schools	Martinsville
47	17.7	New Albany-Floyd County Con Sch	New Albany
47	17.7	Shelbyville Central Schools	Shelbyville
50	17.6	Vincennes Community Sch Corp	Vincennes
51	17.5	East Washington School Corp	Pekin
51	17.5	Elkhart Community Schools	Elkhart
53	17.4	Marion Community Schools	Marion
53	17.4	Tipton Community School Corp	Tipton
55	17.2	Rensselaer Central School Corp	Rensselaer
55	17.2	Wawasee Community School Corp	Syracuse
57	17.1	Crawford County Com School Corp	Marengo
58	17.0	East Noble School Corp	Kendallville
58	17.0	North Adams Community Schools	Decatur
60	16.9	Scott County SD 2	Scottsburg
60	16.9	Union Co/clg Corner Joint SD	Liberty
62	16.8	Gary Community School Corp	Gary
62	16.8	Mill Creek Community Sch Corp	Clayton
64	16.7	School City of East Chicago	East Chicago
64	16.7	School City of Mishawaka	Mishawaka
64	16.7	South Harrison Com Schools	Corydon
67	16.6	Beech Grove City Schools	Beech Grove
67	16.6	Paoli Community School Corp	Paoli
67	16.6	Sunman-Dearborn Com Sch Corp	Saint Leon
70	16.5	Northern Wells Com Schools	Ossian
70	16.5	Union Township School Corp	Valparaiso
72	16.4	Monroe County Com Sch Corp	Bloomington

Note: This section only includes districts with 1,500 or more students; All categories are ranked from high to low

73	16.3	Lake Ridge Schools	Gary
73	16.3	Whitko Community School Corp	Pierceton
75	16.1	Brownstown Cnt Com Sch Corp	Brownstown
75	16.1	Lakeland School Corporation	Lagrange
75	16.1	M S D Warren Township	Indianapolis
75	16.1	Southern Hancock Co. Com Sch Corp	New Palestine
79	15.8	Franklin County Com Sch Corp	Brookville
79	15.8	Southwest Dubois County Sch Corp	Huntingburg
81	15.7	Franklin Township Com Sch Corp	Indianapolis
81	15.7	Garrett-Keyser-Butler Com	Garrett
81	15.7	Western Boone County Com SD	Thorntown
84	15.6	Fort Wayne Community Schools	Fort Wayne
84	15.6	Goshen Community Schools	Goshen
84	15.6	Warsaw Community Schools	Warsaw
87	15.4	Madison Consolidated Schools	Madison
87	15.4	North Montgomery Com Sch Corp	Crawfordsville
89	15.3	Community Schools of Frankfort	Frankfort
90	15.2	Duneland School Corporation	Chesterton
90	15.2	Tippecanoe School Corp	Lafayette
92	15.1	Westfield-Washington Schools	Westfield
93	15.0	Fayette County School Corp	Connersville
93	15.0	Mt Vernon Community Sch Corp	Fortville
95	14.9	Greensburg Community Schools	Greensburg
96	14.8	Franklin Community School Corp	Franklin
96	14.8	Laporte Community School Corp	Laporte
96	14.8	Lawrenceburg Com School Corp	Lawrenceburg
96	14.8	Portage Township Schools	Portage
96	14.8	Rochester Community Sch Corp	Rochester
101	14.7	School City of Hammond	Hammond
102	14.6	M S D Steuben County	Angola
102	14.6	Noblesville Schools	Noblesville
104	14.5	North Spencer County Sch Corp	Lincoln City
104	14.5	Peru Community Schools	Peru
104	14.5	Plainfield Community Sch Corp	Plainfield
107	14.4	Hamilton Heights School Corp	Arcadia
107	14.4	West Clark Community Schools	Sellersburg
109	14.3	Clark-Pleasant Com School Corp	Whiteland
110	14.2	Huntington County Com Sch Corp	Huntington
111	14.1	Maconaquah School Corp	Bunker Hill
111	14.1	Nineveh-Hensley-Jackson United	Trafalgar
113	14.0	Avon Community School Corp	Avon
113	14.0	New Prairie United School Corp	New Carlisle
113	14.0	Northwestern School Corp	Kokomo
113	14.0	Seymour Community Schools	Seymour
117	13.9	M S D Pike Township	Indianapolis
117	13.9	Valparaiso Community Schools	Valparaiso
119	13.8	East Porter County School Corp	Kouts
119	13.8	Eastbrook Community Sch Corp	Marion
119	13.8	Lake Central School Corp	Saint John
119	13.8	Penn-Harris-Madison Sch Corp	Mishawaka
119	13.8	Yorktown Community Schools	Yorktown
124	13.7	Center Grove Com Sch Corp	Greenwood
124	13.7	Kankakee Valley School Corp	Wheatfield
124	13.7	River Forest Community Sch Corp	Hobart
127	13.6	School Town of Munster	Munster
128	13.5	Dekalb County Ctl United SD	Waterloo
128	13.5	M S D Washington Twp	Indianapolis
128	13.5	Tell City-Troy Twp School Corp	Tell City
131	13.4	Concord Community Schools	Elkhart
131	13.4	Hoosier Acad Virtual Charter	Indianapolis
133	13.3	Greenwood Community Sch Corp	Greenwood
133	13.3	M S D Decatur Township	Indianapolis
133	13.3	Wa-Nee Community Schools	Nappanee
136	13.2	Western School Corp	Russiaville
137	13.1	Rush County Schools	Rushville
137	13.1	Zionsville Community Schools	Zionsville
139	13.0	Baugo Community Schools	Elkhart
139	13.0	Manchester Community Schools	N Manchester
139	13.0	Porter Township School Corp	Valparaiso
139	13.0	Southwest School Corp	Sullivan
143	12.9	Bartholomew Con School Corp	Columbus
144	12.7	M S D Perry Township	Indianapolis
144	12.7	Middlebury Community Schools	Middlebury
144	12.7	Westview School Corporation	Topeka
147	12.6	Northwest Allen County Schools	Fort Wayne
147	12.6	Twin Lakes School Corp	Monticello
149	12.2	M S D Lawrence Township	Indianapolis
149	12.2	Mooresville Con School Corp	Mooresville
149	12.2	Whitley County Cons Schools	Columbia City
152	12.1	Logansport Community Sch Corp	Logansport
152	12.1	M S D Wayne Township	Indianapolis
154	12.0	Fairfield Community Schools	Goshen
154	12.0	In Connections Acad Virtual Pilot	Indianapolis
154	12.0	Merrillville Community School	Merrillville
154	12.0	Oak Hill United School Corp	Converse
158	11.9	Batesville Community Sch Corp	Batesville
158	11.9	M S D Wabash County Schools	Wabash
160	11.7	Southeastern School Corp	Walton
161	11.5	Danville Community School Corp	Danville
161	11.5	Mississinewa Community School Corp	Gas City
163	11.4	Delphi Community School Corp	Delphi
163	11.4	Knox Community School Corp	Knox
163	11.4	North West Hendricks Schools	Lizton
163	11.4	School City of Hobart	Hobart
167	11.3	Griffith Public Schools	Griffith
168	11.2	Brownsburg Community Sch Corp	Brownsburg
169	11.1	Greater Jasper Con Schs	Jasper
170	11.0	Crown Point Community Sch Corp	Crown Point
170	11.0	East Allen County Schools	New Haven
172	10.9	Hamilton Southeastern Schools	Fishers
173	10.8	Hanover Community School Corp	Cedar Lake
174	10.7	Plymouth Community School Corp	Plymouth
174	10.7	West Noble School Corporation	Ligonier
176	10.6	John Glenn School Corporation	Walkerton
176	10.6	Tri-Creek School Corporation	Lowell
178	10.0	Carmel Clay Schools	Carmel
179	9.9	School Town of Highland	Highland
180	9.8	West Lafayette Com School Corp	West Lafayette
181	9.5	M S D Southwest Allen County	Fort Wayne
182	9.4	Frankton-Lapel Community Schs	Anderson
183	8.8	Centerville-Abington Com Schs	Centerville
184	6.3	Thea Bowman Leadership Academy	Gary

English Language Learner Students

Rank	Percent	District Name	City
1	30.8	West Noble School Corporation	Ligonier
2	29.6	Westview School Corporation	Topeka
3	28.1	Community Schools of Frankfort	Frankfort
4	27.7	Goshen Community Schools	Goshen
5	22.2	Logansport Community Sch Corp	Logansport
6	17.9	Elkhart Community Schools	Elkhart
7	17.0	Concord Community Schools	Elkhart
8	16.6	School City of Hammond	Hammond
9	16.5	M S D Pike Township	Indianapolis
10	16.4	River Forest Community Sch Corp	Hobart
11	15.1	Fairfield Community Schools	Goshen
11	15.1	M S D Perry Township	Indianapolis
13	14.1	M S D Washington Twp	Indianapolis
14	13.6	School City of East Chicago	East Chicago
15	13.2	M S D Wayne Township	Indianapolis
16	13.1	Lafayette School Corporation	Lafayette
17	12.6	Indianapolis Public Schools	Indianapolis
18	12.1	South Bend Community Sch Corp	South Bend
19	11.5	Lakeland School Corporation	Lagrange
20	11.4	Plymouth Community School Corp	Plymouth
21	10.9	Warsaw Community Schools	Warsaw
22	10.5	M S D Lawrence Township	Indianapolis
23	10.3	Southwest Dubois County Sch Corp	Huntingburg
24	9.5	School Town of Speedway	Speedway
25	8.7	Washington Com Schools	Washington
26	8.3	East Allen County Schools	New Haven
27	8.2	Crawfordsville Com Schools	Crawfordsville
28	8.0	Fort Wayne Community Schools	Fort Wayne
29	7.8	Middlebury Community Schools	Middlebury
30	7.3	Bartholomew Con School Corp	Columbus
31	6.6	Greater Jasper Con Schs	Jasper
32	6.5	Wa-Nee Community Schools	Nappanee
33	6.2	Twin Lakes School Corp	Monticello
34	6.1	M S D Warren Township	Indianapolis
35	6.0	Greenwood Community Sch Corp	Greenwood
35	6.0	Shelbyville Central Schools	Shelbyville
35	6.0	Tippecanoe School Corp	Lafayette
38	5.9	Seymour Community Schools	Seymour
39	5.6	Delphi Community School Corp	Delphi
40	5.4	Tippecanoe Valley School Corp	Akron
40	5.4	Wawasee Community School Corp	Syracuse
42	5.0	West Lafayette Com School Corp	West Lafayette
43	4.9	Greater Clark County Schools	Jeffersonville
44	4.7	Anderson Community School Corp	Anderson
44	4.7	Laporte Community School Corp	Laporte
46	4.4	Kankakee Valley School Corp	Wheatfield
47	4.1	Lake Ridge Schools	Gary
47	4.1	Westfield-Washington Schools	Westfield
49	4.0	Clark-Pleasant Com School Corp	Whiteland
49	4.0	M S D Decatur Township	Indianapolis
49	4.0	M S D Steuben County	Angola
52	3.9	Avon Community School Corp	Avon
52	3.9	Marion Community Schools	Marion
54	3.7	Southeastern School Corp	Walton
55	3.6	North Spencer County Sch Corp	Lincoln City
55	3.6	School Town of Munster	Munster
57	3.4	School Town of Highland	Highland
58	3.1	Franklin Township Com Sch Corp	Indianapolis
58	3.1	Monroe County Com Sch Corp	Bloomington
60	3.0	Carmel Clay Schools	Carmel
60	3.0	Merrillville Community School	Merrillville
60	3.0	School City of Hobart	Hobart
63	2.9	Elwood Community School Corp	Elwood
63	2.9	Jay School Corp	Portland
63	2.9	New Prairie United School Corp	New Carlisle
63	2.9	Penn-Harris-Madison Sch Corp	Mishawaka
67	2.8	Brownsburg Community Sch Corp	Brownsburg
67	2.8	East Noble School Corp	Kendallville
67	2.8	Noblesville Schools	Noblesville
70	2.7	Baugo Community Schools	Elkhart
70	2.7	Hamilton Southeastern Schools	Fishers
70	2.7	Richmond Community Schools	Richmond
73	2.6	Benton Community School Corp	Fowler
74	2.4	Rensselaer Central School Corp	Rensselaer
75	2.3	Beech Grove City Schools	Beech Grove
75	2.3	Crown Point Community Sch Corp	Crown Point
75	2.3	Lake Central School Corp	Saint John
75	2.3	Manchester Community Schools	N Manchester
75	2.3	Valparaiso Community Schools	Valparaiso
80	2.2	Batesville Community Sch Corp	Batesville
81	2.1	Hanover Community School Corp	Cedar Lake
82	2.0	Madison Consolidated Schools	Madison
82	2.0	West Clark Community Schools	Sellersburg
84	1.9	New Albany-Floyd County Con Sch	New Albany
84	1.9	Portage Township Schools	Portage
84	1.9	Tri-Creek School Corporation	Lowell
87	1.8	Garrett-Keyser-Butler Com	Garrett
87	1.8	Knox Community School Corp	Knox
87	1.8	Michigan City Area Schools	Michigan City
87	1.8	Plainfield Community Sch Corp	Plainfield
91	1.7	In Connections Acad Virtual Pilot	Indianapolis
91	1.7	Northwest Allen County Schools	Fort Wayne
93	1.6	Evansville Vanderburgh Sch Corp	Evansville
93	1.6	Franklin Community School Corp	Franklin
95	1.5	Kokomo-Center Twp Con Sch Corp	Kokomo
95	1.5	North Adams Community Schools	Decatur
97	1.4	Dekalb County Ctl United SD	Waterloo
97	1.4	M S D Southwest Allen County	Fort Wayne
97	1.4	Maconaquah School Corp	Bunker Hill
97	1.4	School City of Mishawaka	Mishawaka
101	1.3	Griffith Public Schools	Griffith
101	1.3	Yorktown Community Schools	Yorktown
103	1.2	Lebanon Community School Corp	Lebanon
103	1.2	South Harrison Com Schools	Corydon
103	1.2	Vigo County School Corp	Terre Haute
106	1.1	Jennings County Schools	North Vernon
106	1.1	Mill Creek Community Sch Corp	Clayton
106	1.1	Porter Township School Corp	Valparaiso
106	1.1	Warrick County School Corp	Boonville
110	1.0	Center Grove Com Sch Corp	Greenwood
110	1.0	Greensburg Community Schools	Greensburg
110	1.0	Muncie Community Schools	Muncie
110	1.0	North Montgomery Com Sch Corp	Crawfordsville
110	1.0	Zionsville Community Schools	Zionsville
115	0.9	Greencastle Community Sch Corp	Greencastle
115	0.9	John Glenn School Corporation	Walkerton
115	0.9	Mt Vernon Community Sch Corp	Fortville
115	0.9	Northern Wells Com Schools	Ossian
115	0.9	Rochester Community Sch Corp	Rochester
115	0.9	Union Township School Corp	Valparaiso
121	0.8	Lawrenceburg Com School Corp	Lawrenceburg
122	0.7	Alexandria Com School Corp	Alexandria
122	0.7	Duneland School Corporation	Chesterton
122	0.7	Frankton-Lapel Community Schs	Anderson
122	0.7	Northwestern School Corp	Kokomo
126	0.6	Danville Community School Corp	Danville
126	0.6	North Gibson School Corp	Princeton
126	0.6	Oak Hill United School Corp	Converse
126	0.6	Peru Community Schools	Peru
126	0.6	Rush County Schools	Rushville
126	0.6	Scott County SD 2	Scottsburg
126	0.6	Southern Hancock Co. Com Sch Corp	New Palestine
133	0.5	East Porter County School Corp	Kouts
133	0.5	Greenfield-Central Com Schools	Greenfield
133	0.5	Hamilton Heights School Corp	Arcadia
133	0.5	M S D Mount Vernon	Mount Vernon
133	0.5	Mississinewa Community School Corp	Gas City
133	0.5	Mooresville Con School Corp	Mooresville
133	0.5	New Castle Community Sch Corp	New Castle

Note: This section only includes districts with 1,500 or more students; All categories are ranked from high to low

133	0.5	Pike County School Corp	Petersburg
133	0.5	Randolph Central School Corp	Winchester
133	0.5	South Madison Com Sch Corp	Pendleton
133	0.5	Tell City-Troy Twp School Corp	Tell City
133	0.5	Western School Corp	Russiaville
133	0.5	Whitley County Cons Schools	Columbia City
146	0.4	Eastbrook Community Sch Corp	Marion
146	0.4	North West Hendricks Schools	Lizton
146	0.4	Richland-Bean Blossom C S C	Ellettsville
146	0.4	Sunman-Dearborn Com Sch Corp	Saint Leon
146	0.4	Vincennes Community Sch Corp	Vincennes
146	0.4	Whitko Community School Corp	Pierceton
152	0.3	Blackford County Schools	Hartford City
152	0.3	Brown County School Corporation	Nashville
152	0.3	Brownstown Cnt Com Sch Corp	Brownstown
152	0.3	Clay Community Schools	Knightsville
152	0.3	East Washington School Corp	Pekin
152	0.3	Hoosier Acad Virtual Charter	Indianapolis
152	0.3	Huntington County Com Sch Corp	Huntington
152	0.3	M S D Wabash County Schools	Wabash
152	0.3	North Harrison Com School Corp	Ramsey
152	0.3	South Gibson School Corp	Fort Branch
152	0.3	Tipton Community School Corp	Tipton
163	0.2	Centerville-Abington Com Schs	Centerville
163	0.2	Delaware Community School Corp	Muncie
163	0.2	Gary Community School Corp	Gary
163	0.2	M S D Martinsville Schools	Martinsville
163	0.2	Mitchell Community Schools	Mitchell
163	0.2	Salem Community Schools	Salem
163	0.2	South Dearborn Com School Corp	Aurora
163	0.2	Union Co/clg Corner Joint SD	Liberty
171	0.1	Decatur County Com Schools	Greensburg
171	0.1	Fayette County School Corp	Connersville
171	0.1	Nineveh-Hensley-Jackson United	Trafalgar
171	0.1	North Lawrence Com Schools	Bedford
171	0.1	North Putnam Community Schools	Bainbridge
171	0.1	South Montgomery Com Sch Corp	New Market
171	0.1	South Vermillion Com Sch Corp	Clinton
171	0.1	Southwest School Corp	Sullivan
171	0.1	Spencer-Owen Community Schools	Spencer
171	0.1	Western Boone County Com SD	Thorntown
181	0.0	Crawford County Com School Corp	Marengo
181	0.0	Franklin County Com Sch Corp	Brookville
181	0.0	Paoli Community School Corp	Paoli
181	0.0	Thea Bowman Leadership Academy	Gary

Students Eligible for Free Lunch

Rank	Percent	District Name	City
1	88.0	School City of East Chicago	East Chicago
2	77.9	Gary Community School Corp	Gary
3	75.6	Lake Ridge Schools	Gary
4	72.6	River Forest Community Sch Corp	Hobart
5	72.4	School City of Hammond	Hammond
6	70.6	Indianapolis Public Schools	Indianapolis
7	66.2	Anderson Community School Corp	Anderson
8	65.8	Muncie Community Schools	Muncie
9	64.0	Michigan City Area Schools	Michigan City
10	63.9	Marion Community Schools	Marion
11	62.1	Thea Bowman Leadership Academy	Gary
12	61.9	Richmond Community Schools	Richmond
13	61.3	South Bend Community Sch Corp	South Bend
14	61.1	M S D Wayne Township	Indianapolis
15	60.5	Elkhart Community Schools	Elkhart
16	59.9	Community Schools of Frankfort	Frankfort
17	59.5	Fort Wayne Community Schools	Fort Wayne
18	59.1	Kokomo-Center Twp Con Sch Corp	Kokomo
19	58.5	Lafayette School Corporation	Lafayette
20	58.0	Goshen Community Schools	Goshen
21	56.3	West Noble School Corporation	Ligonier
22	55.4	Fayette County School Corp	Connersville
23	55.2	M S D Warren Township	Indianapolis
24	54.4	M S D Decatur Township	Indianapolis
25	53.3	M S D Pike Township	Indianapolis
26	53.2	Crawfordsville Com Schools	Crawfordsville
27	53.1	Beech Grove City Schools	Beech Grove
28	52.6	Knox Community School Corp	Knox
29	50.6	Vincennes Community Sch Corp	Vincennes
30	50.3	School City of Mishawaka	Mishawaka
31	50.2	Logansport Community Sch Corp	Logansport
31	50.2	Peru Community Schools	Peru
33	50.0	New Castle Community Sch Corp	New Castle
34	49.9	Crawford County Com School Corp	Marengo
35	49.7	Washington Com Schools	Washington
36	49.3	M S D Perry Township	Indianapolis
37	48.3	Mississinewa Community School Corp	Gas City
38	48.1	M S D Washington Twp	Indianapolis
39	47.4	Concord Community Schools	Elkhart
39	47.4	Evansville Vanderburgh Sch Corp	Evansville
41	47.0	Paoli Community School Corp	Paoli
42	46.6	Merrillville Community School	Merrillville
43	46.5	M S D Lawrence Township	Indianapolis
44	46.3	Jennings County Schools	North Vernon
45	46.0	Randolph Central School Corp	Winchester
45	46.0	Vigo County School Corp	Terre Haute
47	45.9	Plymouth Community School Corp	Plymouth
48	45.7	Greater Clark County Schools	Jeffersonville
48	45.7	Tippecanoe Valley School Corp	Akron
50	44.8	School Town of Speedway	Speedway
51	43.9	Maconaquah School Corp	Bunker Hill
52	43.8	Shelbyville Central Schools	Shelbyville
53	43.5	Lakeland School Corporation	Lagrange
54	43.4	Salem Community Schools	Salem
55	43.3	Scott County SD 2	Scottsburg
56	43.2	Seymour Community Schools	Seymour
57	43.0	Mitchell Community Schools	Mitchell
58	42.6	Alexandria Com School Corp	Alexandria
59	42.5	Portage Township Schools	Portage
60	42.3	Jay School Corp	Portland
61	42.0	Madison Consolidated Schools	Madison
62	41.8	Blackford County Schools	Hartford City
63	41.6	Rochester Community Sch Corp	Rochester
64	41.1	Garrett-Keyser-Butler Com	Garrett
65	40.9	South Vermillion Com Sch Corp	Clinton
65	40.9	Spencer-Owen Community Schools	Spencer
67	40.8	Laporte Community School Corp	Laporte
68	40.7	East Washington School Corp	Pekin
69	40.5	Greensburg Community Schools	Greensburg
70	40.3	Delphi Community School Corp	Delphi
70	40.3	M S D Martinsville Schools	Martinsville
72	40.0	Clay Community Schools	Knightsville
73	39.7	North Gibson School Corp	Princeton
74	39.1	Warsaw Community Schools	Warsaw
75	39.0	Griffith Public Schools	Griffith
75	39.0	Twin Lakes School Corp	Monticello
77	38.7	Tell City-Troy Twp School Corp	Tell City
78	38.6	East Allen County Schools	New Haven
79	38.5	M S D Steuben County	Angola
80	38.3	Manchester Community Schools	N Manchester
81	37.9	New Albany-Floyd County Con Sch	New Albany
82	37.7	North Adams Community Schools	Decatur
83	37.5	North Lawrence Com Schools	Bedford
84	37.4	In Connections Acad Virtual Pilot	Indianapolis
85	37.3	Brown County School Corporation	Nashville
85	37.3	Greenwood Community Sch Corp	Greenwood
85	37.3	Southwest School Corp	Sullivan
88	37.2	East Noble School Corp	Kendallville
88	37.2	Rush County Schools	Rushville
90	37.1	Greencastle Community Sch Corp	Greencastle
91	37.0	Benton Community School Corp	Fowler
92	36.3	South Dearborn Com School Corp	Aurora
92	36.3	Wawasee Community School Corp	Syracuse
94	36.1	Franklin County Com Sch Corp	Brookville
95	36.0	Union Co/clg Corner Joint SD	Liberty
96	35.9	Southwest Dubois County Sch Corp	Huntingburg
97	35.4	Lawrenceburg Com School Corp	Lawrenceburg
98	35.2	North Harrison Com School Corp	Ramsey
99	35.1	South Harrison Com Schools	Corydon
100	35.0	Huntington County Com Sch Corp	Huntington
101	34.3	Bartholomew Con School Corp	Columbus
101	34.3	Rensselaer Central School Corp	Rensselaer
103	33.9	Decatur County Com Schools	Greensburg
104	33.8	Lebanon Community School Corp	Lebanon
105	33.2	School City of Hobart	Hobart
106	32.6	Clark-Pleasant Com School Corp	Whiteland
106	32.6	Franklin Community School Corp	Franklin
106	32.6	John Glenn School Corporation	Walkerton
109	32.4	M S D Wabash County Schools	Wabash
109	32.4	North Putnam Community Schools	Bainbridge
111	32.3	Baugo Community Schools	Elkhart
112	31.2	Monroe County Com Sch Corp	Bloomington
113	31.0	Brownstown Cnt Com Sch Corp	Brownstown
113	31.0	Pike County School Corp	Petersburg
115	30.2	M S D Mount Vernon	Mount Vernon
116	30.0	Centerville-Abington Com Schs	Centerville
117	29.9	Whitko Community School Corp	Pierceton
118	29.7	Dekalb County Ctl United SD	Waterloo
119	29.4	Delaware Community School Corp	Muncie
120	28.8	South Montgomery Com Sch Corp	New Market
121	28.6	Tippecanoe School Corp	Lafayette
122	28.2	Eastbrook Community Sch Corp	Marion
123	28.0	Southeastern School Corp	Walton
124	27.8	New Prairie United School Corp	New Carlisle
125	27.5	Kankakee Valley School Corp	Wheatfield
125	27.5	North Montgomery Com Sch Corp	Crawfordsville
127	27.3	Mooresville Con School Corp	Mooresville
128	26.8	West Clark Community Schools	Sellersburg
129	26.7	Franklin Township Com Sch Corp	Indianapolis
130	26.4	School Town of Highland	Highland
130	26.4	Western Boone County Com SD	Thorntown
132	26.3	Greenfield-Central Com Schools	Greenfield
132	26.3	Oak Hill United School Corp	Converse
134	25.6	Richland-Bean Blossom C S C	Ellettsville
135	25.4	Frankton-Lapel Community Schs	Anderson
136	25.3	Westview School Corporation	Topeka
137	25.2	Wa-Nee Community Schools	Nappanee
138	25.1	Tipton Community School Corp	Tipton
139	24.7	Nineveh-Hensley-Jackson United	Trafalgar
140	24.5	Hamilton Heights School Corp	Arcadia
141	24.4	Western School Corp	Russiaville
142	24.1	Northern Wells Com Schools	Ossian
142	24.1	South Madison Com Sch Corp	Pendleton
144	23.9	Whitley County Cons Schools	Columbia City
145	23.5	Yorktown Community Schools	Yorktown
146	23.3	Valparaiso Community Schools	Valparaiso
147	23.0	Middlebury Community Schools	Middlebury
148	22.9	Hanover Community School Corp	Cedar Lake
149	22.7	Mill Creek Community Sch Corp	Clayton
150	22.5	Warrick County School Corp	Boonville
151	22.2	Plainfield Community Sch Corp	Plainfield
152	21.5	Greater Jasper Con Schs	Jasper
153	21.4	Duneland School Corporation	Chesterton
154	21.2	Hoosier Acad Virtual Charter	Indianapolis
155	20.6	Penn-Harris-Madison Sch Corp	Mishawaka
156	19.8	North Spencer County Sch Corp	Lincoln City
157	19.7	Danville Community School Corp	Danville
158	19.4	Tri-Creek School Corporation	Lowell
159	19.1	Batesville Community Sch Corp	Batesville
160	18.0	Noblesville Schools	Noblesville
161	17.9	Northwestern School Corp	Kokomo
161	17.9	Sunman-Dearborn Com Sch Corp	Saint Leon
163	17.8	Crown Point Community Sch Corp	Crown Point
164	17.4	Fairfield Community Schools	Goshen
165	17.3	Mt Vernon Community Sch Corp	Fortville
166	16.9	South Gibson School Corp	Fort Branch
167	16.6	Porter Township School Corp	Valparaiso
168	16.4	Avon Community School Corp	Avon
168	16.4	Union Township School Corp	Valparaiso
170	16.2	Brownsburg Community Sch Corp	Brownsburg
171	15.7	North West Hendricks Schools	Lizton
172	14.3	Lake Central School Corp	Saint John
173	14.1	Center Grove Com Sch Corp	Greenwood
173	14.1	Westfield-Washington Schools	Westfield
175	13.8	Southern Hancock Co. Com Sch Corp	New Palestine
176	13.4	East Porter County School Corp	Kouts
177	12.4	School Town of Munster	Munster
178	10.7	Northwest Allen County Schools	Fort Wayne
179	10.5	M S D Southwest Allen County	Fort Wayne
180	10.2	West Lafayette Com School Corp	West Lafayette
181	8.9	Hamilton Southeastern Schools	Fishers
182	6.8	Carmel Clay Schools	Carmel
183	3.6	Zionsville Community Schools	Zionsville
n/a	n/a	Elwood Community School Corp	Elwood

Students Eligible for Reduced-Price Lunch

Rank	Percent	District Name	City
1	23.5	Westview School Corporation	Topeka
2	15.9	In Connections Acad Virtual Pilot	Indianapolis
3	15.7	Lakeland School Corporation	Lagrange
4	14.2	Brown County School Corporation	Nashville
5	13.9	Wa-Nee Community Schools	Nappanee
6	13.0	Whitko Community School Corp	Pierceton
7	12.7	School City of Mishawaka	Mishawaka
8	12.5	Clay Community Schools	Knightsville
9	12.1	Delphi Community School Corp	Delphi
9	12.1	Manchester Community Schools	N Manchester
11	12.0	Mississinewa Community School Corp	Gas City
12	11.8	Clark-Pleasant Com School Corp	Whiteland
12	11.8	Portage Township Schools	Portage
14	11.7	Crawford County Com School Corp	Marengo
15	11.5	Greater Clark County Schools	Jeffersonville
15	11.5	West Noble School Corporation	Ligonier

Note: This section only includes districts with 1,500 or more students; All categories are ranked from high to low

17	11.3	Griffith Public Schools	Griffith
17	11.3	Knox Community School Corp	Knox
17	11.3	M S D Warren Township	Indianapolis
20	11.2	Concord Community Schools	Elkhart
20	11.2	Jay School Corp	Portland
20	11.2	Rensselaer Central School Corp	Rensselaer
23	11.0	Fairfield Community Schools	Goshen
23	11.0	Peru Community Schools	Peru
25	10.9	Merrillville Community School	Merrillville
26	10.8	Jennings County Schools	North Vernon
26	10.8	Union Co/clg Corner Joint SD	Liberty
28	10.7	Tippecanoe Valley School Corp	Akron
28	10.7	Twin Lakes School Corp	Monticello
30	10.6	Decatur County Com Schools	Greensburg
30	10.6	Goshen Community Schools	Goshen
32	10.5	Beech Grove City Schools	Beech Grove
33	10.4	Wawasee Community School Corp	Syracuse
34	10.3	East Noble School Corp	Kendallville
34	10.3	M S D Steuben County	Angola
34	10.3	Warsaw Community Schools	Warsaw
37	10.2	Lake Ridge Schools	Gary
37	10.2	North Harrison Com School Corp	Ramsey
37	10.2	Plymouth Community School Corp	Plymouth
40	10.1	Greensburg Community Schools	Greensburg
40	10.1	Seymour Community Schools	Seymour
42	10.0	Garrett-Keyser-Butler Com	Garrett
42	10.0	Middlebury Community Schools	Middlebury
42	10.0	North Lawrence Com Schools	Bedford
45	9.9	Delaware Community School Corp	Muncie
46	9.8	Benton Community School Corp	Fowler
46	9.8	Franklin Community School Corp	Franklin
46	9.8	Franklin County Com Sch Corp	Brookville
46	9.8	North Putnam Community Schools	Bainbridge
50	9.7	Fort Wayne Community Schools	Fort Wayne
50	9.7	Pike County School Corp	Petersburg
52	9.6	Community Schools of Frankfort	Frankfort
52	9.6	M S D Wayne Township	Indianapolis
52	9.6	Madison Consolidated Schools	Madison
52	9.6	School City of Hobart	Hobart
52	9.6	School Town of Speedway	Speedway
52	9.6	Scott County SD 2	Scottsburg
52	9.6	Whitley County Cons Schools	Columbia City
59	9.5	Laporte Community School Corp	Laporte
59	9.5	Maconaquah School Corp	Bunker Hill
59	9.5	North Gibson School Corp	Princeton
62	9.4	Baugo Community Schools	Elkhart
62	9.4	Dekalb County Ctl United SD	Waterloo
62	9.4	Evansville Vanderburgh Sch Corp	Evansville
62	9.4	North Adams Community Schools	Decatur
62	9.4	Salem Community Schools	Salem
67	9.3	Spencer-Owen Community Schools	Spencer
68	9.2	Blackford County Schools	Hartford City
68	9.2	Huntington County Com Sch Corp	Huntington
70	9.1	M S D Pike Township	Indianapolis
70	9.1	Southwest School Corp	Sullivan
70	9.1	West Clark Community Schools	Sellersburg
73	9.0	East Washington School Corp	Pekin
73	9.0	Franklin Township Com Sch Corp	Indianapolis
73	9.0	South Madison Com Sch Corp	Pendleton
73	9.0	Tell City-Troy Twp School Corp	Tell City
77	8.9	Centerville-Abington Com Schs	Centerville
77	8.9	Frankton-Lapel Community Schs	Anderson
77	8.9	John Glenn School Corporation	Walkerton
77	8.9	M S D Lawrence Township	Indianapolis
77	8.9	M S D Martinsville Schools	Martinsville
77	8.9	Rochester Community Sch Corp	Rochester
83	8.8	Eastbrook Community Sch Corp	Marion
83	8.8	Kokomo-Center Twp Con Sch Corp	Kokomo
83	8.8	New Castle Community Sch Corp	New Castle
83	8.8	Paoli Community School Corp	Paoli
83	8.8	Shelbyville Central Schools	Shelbyville
88	8.7	Greencastle Community Sch Corp	Greencastle
88	8.7	Rush County Schools	Rushville
88	8.7	South Bend Community Sch Corp	South Bend
88	8.7	South Harrison Com Schools	Corydon
88	8.7	South Vermillion Com Sch Corp	Clinton
93	8.6	Elkhart Community Schools	Elkhart
94	8.5	Fayette County School Corp	Connersville
94	8.5	New Prairie United School Corp	New Carlisle
94	8.5	Richmond Community Schools	Richmond
94	8.5	South Montgomery Com Sch Corp	New Market
98	8.4	Greenwood Community Sch Corp	Greenwood
98	8.4	Lebanon Community School Corp	Lebanon
98	8.4	M S D Perry Township	Indianapolis
98	8.4	Washington Com Schools	Washington
102	8.3	Lafayette School Corporation	Lafayette
102	8.3	Logansport Community Sch Corp	Logansport
102	8.3	Northern Wells Com Schools	Ossian
102	8.3	Randolph Central School Corp	Winchester
102	8.3	Tipton Community School Corp	Tipton
107	8.2	East Allen County Schools	New Haven
107	8.2	Mooresville Con School Corp	Mooresville
109	8.0	North Montgomery Com Sch Corp	Crawfordsville
109	8.0	School City of Hammond	Hammond
111	7.9	Alexandria Com School Corp	Alexandria
111	7.9	Anderson Community School Corp	Anderson
111	7.9	Muncie Community Schools	Muncie
111	7.9	Richland-Bean Blossom C S C	Ellettsville
111	7.9	Vigo County School Corp	Terre Haute
116	7.8	Bartholomew Con School Corp	Columbus
116	7.8	Southwest Dubois County Sch Corp	Huntingburg
118	7.7	Kankakee Valley School Corp	Wheatfield
118	7.7	Michigan City Area Schools	Michigan City
118	7.7	Western Boone County Com SD	Thorntown
121	7.6	Brownstown Cnt Com Sch Corp	Brownstown
121	7.6	Warrick County School Corp	Boonville
123	7.4	North Spencer County Sch Corp	Lincoln City
123	7.4	Oak Hill United School Corp	Converse
123	7.4	Southeastern School Corp	Walton
126	7.3	Plainfield Community Sch Corp	Plainfield
127	7.2	Danville Community School Corp	Danville
128	7.1	M S D Washington Twp	Indianapolis
129	7.0	River Forest Community Sch Corp	Hobart
129	7.0	Vincennes Community Sch Corp	Vincennes
131	6.9	Crawfordsville Com Schools	Crawfordsville
132	6.8	Marion Community Schools	Marion
132	6.8	Northwestern School Corp	Kokomo
132	6.8	School Town of Highland	Highland
132	6.8	Yorktown Community Schools	Yorktown
136	6.7	East Porter County School Corp	Kouts
136	6.7	Mt Vernon Community Sch Corp	Fortville
138	6.6	Mill Creek Community Sch Corp	Clayton
139	6.5	Avon Community School Corp	Avon
139	6.5	Nineveh-Hensley-Jackson United	Trafalgar
141	6.4	Greenfield-Central Com Schools	Greenfield
141	6.4	M S D Wabash County Schools	Wabash
141	6.4	Monroe County Com Sch Corp	Bloomington
144	6.3	Tippecanoe School Corp	Lafayette
144	6.3	Western School Corp	Russiaville
146	6.2	New Albany-Floyd County Con Sch	New Albany
146	6.2	Penn-Harris-Madison Sch Corp	Mishawaka
146	6.2	Porter Township School Corp	Valparaiso
149	6.1	Lawrenceburg Com School Corp	Lawrenceburg
149	6.1	M S D Decatur Township	Indianapolis
149	6.1	Noblesville Schools	Noblesville
152	5.9	Brownsburg Community Sch Corp	Brownsburg
152	5.9	Mitchell Community Schools	Mitchell
152	5.9	North West Hendricks Schools	Lizton
155	5.7	Batesville Community Sch Corp	Batesville
155	5.7	Greater Jasper Con Schs	Jasper
155	5.7	South Dearborn Com School Corp	Aurora
158	5.6	Hamilton Heights School Corp	Arcadia
158	5.6	Sunman-Dearborn Com Sch Corp	Saint Leon
160	5.5	School Town of Munster	Munster
161	5.4	Crown Point Community Sch Corp	Crown Point
161	5.4	Duneland School Corporation	Chesterton
163	5.3	South Gibson School Corp	Fort Branch
164	5.2	M S D Mount Vernon	Mount Vernon
165	5.1	Valparaiso Community Schools	Valparaiso
166	5.0	Indianapolis Public Schools	Indianapolis
166	5.0	Northwest Allen County Schools	Fort Wayne
168	4.9	Hanover Community School Corp	Cedar Lake
168	4.9	Thea Bowman Leadership Academy	Gary
170	4.8	Hamilton Southeastern Schools	Fishers
171	4.7	Tri-Creek School Corporation	Lowell
172	4.6	Lake Central School Corp	Saint John
173	4.5	Hoosier Acad Virtual Charter	Indianapolis
173	4.5	School City of East Chicago	East Chicago
175	4.4	Southern Hancock Co. Com Sch Corp	New Palestine
176	4.2	Center Grove Com Sch Corp	Greenwood
177	4.0	Union Township School Corp	Valparaiso
178	3.8	Westfield-Washington Schools	Westfield
179	3.6	M S D Southwest Allen County	Fort Wayne
180	3.1	West Lafayette Com School Corp	West Lafayette
181	2.9	Carmel Clay Schools	Carmel
182	2.5	Gary Community School Corp	Gary
183	2.0	Zionsville Community Schools	Zionsville
n/a	n/a	Elwood Community School Corp	Elwood

Student/Teacher Ratio

(number of students per teacher)

Rank	Number	District Name	City
1	11.8	Logansport Community Sch Corp	Logansport
2	11.9	Union Co/clg Corner Joint SD	Liberty
3	13.2	New Castle Community Sch Corp	New Castle
3	13.2	Pike County School Corp	Petersburg
5	13.6	Community Schools of Frankfort	Frankfort
6	13.8	Brown County School Corporation	Nashville
6	13.8	South Montgomery Com Sch Corp	New Market
8	14.0	Randolph Central School Corp	Winchester
9	14.1	M S D Wabash County Schools	Wabash
10	14.2	School Town of Speedway	Speedway
11	14.4	Decatur County Com Schools	Greensburg
11	14.4	Muncie Community Schools	Muncie
11	14.4	Richmond Community Schools	Richmond
14	14.5	Crawfordsville Com Schools	Crawfordsville
14	14.5	Lafayette School Corporation	Lafayette
16	14.6	South Vermillion Com Sch Corp	Clinton
17	14.7	Evansville Vanderburgh Sch Corp	Evansville
18	14.8	Indianapolis Public Schools	Indianapolis
18	14.8	Rensselaer Central School Corp	Rensselaer
20	14.9	Goshen Community Schools	Goshen
20	14.9	Michigan City Area Schools	Michigan City
20	14.9	Nineveh-Hensley-Jackson United	Trafalgar
23	15.0	Rush County Schools	Rushville
23	15.0	Tipton Community School Corp	Tipton
25	15.1	Jay School Corp	Portland
25	15.1	North Adams Community Schools	Decatur
25	15.1	Northwestern School Corp	Kokomo
25	15.1	School City of Mishawaka	Mishawaka
29	15.2	Monroe County Com Sch Corp	Bloomington
29	15.2	West Noble School Corporation	Ligonier
31	15.3	North Spencer County Sch Corp	Lincoln City
31	15.3	School City of East Chicago	East Chicago
31	15.3	Tell City-Troy Twp School Corp	Tell City
34	15.4	Garrett-Keyser-Butler Com	Garrett
34	15.4	Kokomo-Center Twp Con Sch Corp	Kokomo
34	15.4	M S D Mount Vernon	Mount Vernon
34	15.4	North Montgomery Com Sch Corp	Crawfordsville
38	15.5	Benton Community School Corp	Fowler
38	15.5	South Harrison Com Schools	Corydon
40	15.6	Western School Corp	Russiaville
41	15.7	Huntington County Com Sch Corp	Huntington
41	15.7	Richland-Bean Blossom C S C	Ellettsville
43	15.8	East Noble School Corp	Kendallville
43	15.8	Paoli Community School Corp	Paoli
43	15.8	West Lafayette Com School Corp	West Lafayette
46	15.9	Clay Community Schools	Knightsville
46	15.9	North Gibson School Corp	Princeton
46	15.9	Southeastern School Corp	Walton
46	15.9	Warsaw Community Schools	Warsaw
50	16.0	North Putnam Community Schools	Bainbridge
51	16.1	Eastbrook Community Sch Corp	Marion
51	16.1	John Glenn School Corporation	Walkerton
51	16.1	Whitley County Cons Schools	Columbia City
54	16.2	Delaware Community School Corp	Muncie
54	16.2	Greensburg Community Schools	Greensburg
54	16.2	Laporte Community School Corp	Laporte
57	16.3	Centerville-Abington Com Schs	Centerville
57	16.3	Crawford County Com School Corp	Marengo
57	16.3	Elkhart Community Schools	Elkhart
57	16.3	Greencastle Community Sch Corp	Greencastle
57	16.3	Jennings County Schools	North Vernon
57	16.3	M S D Southwest Allen County	Fort Wayne
57	16.3	Southwest School Corp	Sullivan
64	16.4	Concord Community Schools	Elkhart
64	16.4	East Porter County School Corp	Kouts
64	16.4	East Washington School Corp	Pekin
64	16.4	Lakeland School Corporation	Lagrange
64	16.4	South Gibson School Corp	Fort Branch
69	16.5	Twin Lakes School Corp	Monticello
69	16.5	Wawasee Community School Corp	Syracuse
69	16.5	Westview School Corporation	Topeka
72	16.6	Carmel Clay Schools	Carmel
72	16.6	Vigo County School Corp	Terre Haute
74	16.7	Batesville Community Sch Corp	Batesville
74	16.7	Mill Creek Community Sch Corp	Clayton
74	16.7	Warrick County School Corp	Boonville
77	16.8	M S D Martinsville Schools	Martinsville
77	16.8	Middlebury Community Schools	Middlebury
77	16.8	Oak Hill United School Corp	Converse
77	16.8	Vincennes Community Sch Corp	Vincennes

Note: This section only includes districts with 1,500 or more students; All categories are ranked from high to low

81	16.9	Fairfield Community Schools	Goshen
81	16.9	Lawrenceburg Com School Corp	Lawrenceburg
81	16.9	Shelbyville Central Schools	Shelbyville
81	16.9	Wa-Nee Community Schools	Nappanee
85	17.0	Anderson Community School Corp	Anderson
85	17.0	Fayette County School Corp	Connersville
85	17.0	Fort Wayne Community Schools	Fort Wayne
85	17.0	Greenwood Community Sch Corp	Greenwood
85	17.0	Marion Community Schools	Marion
85	17.0	Mitchell Community Schools	Mitchell
85	17.0	South Dearborn Com School Corp	Aurora
92	17.1	Delphi Community School Corp	Delphi
92	17.1	Gary Community School Corp	Gary
92	17.1	Maconaquah School Corp	Bunker Hill
92	17.1	Rochester Community Sch Corp	Rochester
92	17.1	Whitko Community School Corp	Pierceton
97	17.2	Alexandria Com School Corp	Alexandria
97	17.2	Brownsburg Community Sch Corp	Brownsburg
97	17.2	South Bend Community Sch Corp	South Bend
97	17.2	Union Township School Corp	Valparaiso
101	17.3	Beech Grove City Schools	Beech Grove
101	17.3	Greater Clark County Schools	Jeffersonville
101	17.3	Lake Ridge Schools	Gary
101	17.3	Lebanon Community School Corp	Lebanon
101	17.3	M S D Wayne Township	Indianapolis
101	17.3	Thea Bowman Leadership Academy	Gary
101	17.3	West Clark Community Schools	Sellersburg
108	17.4	East Allen County Schools	New Haven
108	17.4	Knox Community School Corp	Knox
108	17.4	Manchester Community Schools	N Manchester
111	17.7	Blackford County Schools	Hartford City
111	17.7	M S D Washington Twp	Indianapolis
113	17.8	Hamilton Heights School Corp	Arcadia
113	17.8	Merrillville Community School	Merrillville
113	17.8	Scott County SD 2	Scottsburg
113	17.8	Tippecanoe School Corp	Lafayette
117	17.9	Crown Point Community Sch Corp	Crown Point
117	17.9	Madison Consolidated Schools	Madison
117	17.9	North West Hendricks Schools	Lizton
117	17.9	School City of Hammond	Hammond
121	18.0	Kankakee Valley School Corp	Wheatfield
121	18.0	M S D Steuben County	Angola
121	18.0	Peru Community Schools	Peru
124	18.1	Center Grove Com Sch Corp	Greenwood
124	18.1	Lake Central School Corp	Saint John
124	18.1	Washington Com Schools	Washington
127	18.2	M S D Warren Township	Indianapolis
128	18.3	Noblesville Schools	Noblesville
128	18.3	North Lawrence Com Schools	Bedford
128	18.3	Northwest Allen County Schools	Fort Wayne
128	18.3	Western Boone County Com SD	Thorntown
132	18.4	M S D Decatur Township	Indianapolis
132	18.4	Mississinewa Community School Corp	Gas City
132	18.4	Westfield-Washington Schools	Westfield
135	18.5	Brownstown Cnt Com Sch Corp	Brownstown
135	18.5	Franklin Community School Corp	Franklin
135	18.5	Franklin County Com Sch Corp	Brookville
135	18.5	Spencer-Owen Community Schools	Spencer
135	18.5	Yorktown Community Schools	Yorktown
140	18.6	New Prairie United School Corp	New Carlisle
140	18.6	Tippecanoe Valley School Corp	Akron
142	18.7	Danville Community School Corp	Danville
142	18.7	Plainfield Community Sch Corp	Plainfield
142	18.7	Porter Township School Corp	Valparaiso
145	18.8	Elwood Community School Corp	Elwood
145	18.8	Franklin Township Com Sch Corp	Indianapolis
145	18.8	Hamilton Southeastern Schools	Fishers
145	18.8	M S D Perry Township	Indianapolis
145	18.8	Portage Township Schools	Portage
145	18.8	Tri-Creek School Corporation	Lowell
151	18.9	Dekalb County Ctl United SD	Waterloo
151	18.9	Greater Jasper Con Schs	Jasper
151	18.9	School Town of Munster	Munster
151	18.9	Valparaiso Community Schools	Valparaiso
151	18.9	Zionsville Community Schools	Zionsville
156	19.0	Frankton-Lapel Community Schs	Anderson
156	19.0	New Albany-Floyd County Con Sch	New Albany
156	19.0	Northern Wells Com Schools	Ossian
159	19.1	Bartholomew Con School Corp	Columbus
159	19.1	M S D Lawrence Township	Indianapolis
159	19.1	Plymouth Community School Corp	Plymouth
162	19.3	Hanover Community School Corp	Cedar Lake
163	19.4	Baugo Community Schools	Elkhart
164	19.6	School Town of Highland	Highland
165	19.7	Avon Community School Corp	Avon
165	19.7	M S D Pike Township	Indianapolis
167	19.9	Southwest Dubois County Sch Corp	Huntingburg
167	19.9	Sunman-Dearborn Com Sch Corp	Saint Leon
169	20.0	Duneland School Corporation	Chesterton
170	20.1	Griffith Public Schools	Griffith
170	20.1	Mt Vernon Community Sch Corp	Fortville
170	20.1	Seymour Community Schools	Seymour
173	20.3	School City of Hobart	Hobart
174	20.9	Mooresville Con School Corp	Mooresville
174	20.9	North Harrison Com School Corp	Ramsey
176	21.2	Penn-Harris-Madison Sch Corp	Mishawaka
176	21.2	South Madison Com Sch Corp	Pendleton
176	21.2	Southern Hancock Co. Com Sch Corp	New Palestine
179	21.8	Greenfield-Central Com Schools	Greenfield
180	22.8	Clark-Pleasant Com School Corp	Whiteland
181	37.1	In Connections Acad Virtual Pilot	Indianapolis
182	41.1	Hoosier Acad Virtual Charter	Indianapolis
n/a	n/a	River Forest Community Sch Corp	Hobart
n/a	n/a	Salem Community Schools	Salem

Student/Librarian Ratio

(number of students per librarian)

Rank	Number	District Name	City
1	324.0	Randolph Central School Corp	Winchester
2	325.3	North Spencer County Sch Corp	Lincoln City
3	363.1	Rush County Schools	Rushville
4	412.4	Greencastle Community Sch Corp	Greencastle
5	419.8	Batesville Community Sch Corp	Batesville
6	432.8	Garrett-Keyser-Butler Com	Garrett
7	448.0	M S D Mount Vernon	Mount Vernon
8	448.6	Richmond Community Schools	Richmond
9	463.4	Crawfordsville Com Schools	Crawfordsville
10	464.5	North Adams Community Schools	Decatur
11	500.8	Washington Com Schools	Washington
12	503.0	Salem Community Schools	Salem
13	512.5	Tippecanoe Valley School Corp	Akron
14	528.5	Muncie Community Schools	Muncie
15	532.0	Elwood Community School Corp	Elwood
16	537.6	Gary Community School Corp	Gary
17	548.6	Michigan City Area Schools	Michigan City
18	551.7	Indianapolis Public Schools	Indianapolis
19	564.7	Tipton Community School Corp	Tipton
20	566.5	Hamilton Heights School Corp	Arcadia
21	573.5	Greensburg Community Schools	Greensburg
22	582.3	Southwest Dubois County Sch Corp	Huntingburg
23	591.3	Duneland School Corporation	Chesterton
24	603.0	Western Boone County Com SD	Thorntown
25	619.5	West Noble School Corporation	Ligonier
26	624.3	Nineveh-Hensley-Jackson United	Trafalgar
27	624.7	North West Hendricks Schools	Lizton
28	636.7	Mitchell Community Schools	Mitchell
29	674.6	Monroe County Com Sch Corp	Bloomington
30	678.3	Vigo County School Corp	Terre Haute
31	692.5	Richland-Bean Blossom C S C	Ellettsville
32	696.1	Kokomo-Center Twp Con Sch Corp	Kokomo
33	700.6	Plainfield Community Sch Corp	Plainfield
34	705.0	South Dearborn Com School Corp	Aurora
35	711.3	Westfield-Washington Schools	Westfield
36	712.3	West Lafayette Com School Corp	West Lafayette
37	727.9	M S D Pike Township	Indianapolis
38	750.0	North Harrison Com School Corp	Ramsey
39	763.4	School City of Hammond	Hammond
40	770.7	Franklin Township Com Sch Corp	Indianapolis
41	783.5	East Washington School Corp	Pekin
42	809.0	Delphi Community School Corp	Delphi
42	809.0	Paoli Community School Corp	Paoli
44	812.0	School Town of Speedway	Speedway
45	834.0	Centerville-Abington Com Schs	Centerville
46	836.5	South Bend Community Sch Corp	South Bend
47	841.0	Logansport Community Sch Corp	Logansport
48	847.1	Brownsburg Community Sch Corp	Brownsburg
49	865.0	Brownstown Cnt Com Sch Corp	Brownstown
50	886.8	Lebanon Community School Corp	Lebanon
51	888.0	West Clark Community Schools	Sellersburg
52	900.6	M S D Decatur Township	Indianapolis
53	935.3	M S D Washington Twp	Indianapolis
54	952.7	Hamilton Southeastern Schools	Fishers
55	956.3	Franklin County Com Sch Corp	Brookville
56	966.0	Lawrenceburg Com School Corp	Lawrenceburg
57	1,001.6	Lafayette School Corporation	Lafayette
58	1,004.0	Knox Community School Corp	Knox
59	1,017.3	M S D Wayne Township	Indianapolis
60	1,020.3	Anderson Community School Corp	Anderson
61	1,025.0	North Montgomery Com Sch Corp	Crawfordsville
62	1,030.0	Brown County School Corporation	Nashville
63	1,049.3	Noblesville Schools	Noblesville
64	1,050.0	Carmel Clay Schools	Carmel
65	1,062.7	Community Schools of Frankfort	Frankfort
66	1,074.0	North Gibson School Corp	Princeton
67	1,109.5	Peru Community Schools	Peru
68	1,123.5	M S D Wabash County Schools	Wabash
69	1,144.5	Maconaquah School Corp	Bunker Hill
70	1,201.3	Jay School Corp	Portland
71	1,217.3	Avon Community School Corp	Avon
72	1,241.0	Twin Lakes School Corp	Monticello
73	1,303.0	Delaware Community School Corp	Muncie
74	1,307.0	Danville Community School Corp	Danville
75	1,331.3	M S D Martinsville Schools	Martinsville
76	1,336.5	Vincennes Community Sch Corp	Vincennes
77	1,380.0	Merrillville Community School	Merrillville
78	1,399.5	Scott County SD 2	Scottsburg
79	1,417.7	Warrick County School Corp	Boonville
80	1,500.0	Thea Bowman Leadership Academy	Gary
81	1,506.0	Southeastern School Corp	Walton
82	1,516.0	Manchester Community Schools	N Manchester
83	1,517.0	Tell City-Troy Twp School Corp	Tell City
84	1,521.0	Porter Township School Corp	Valparaiso
84	1,521.0	Union Co/clg Corner Joint SD	Liberty
86	1,552.0	River Forest Community Sch Corp	Hobart
87	1,563.0	Mill Creek Community Sch Corp	Clayton
88	1,581.3	Laporte Community School Corp	Laporte
89	1,612.0	Alexandria Com School Corp	Alexandria
90	1,627.7	Bartholomew Con School Corp	Columbus
91	1,631.0	Union Township School Corp	Valparaiso
92	1,653.1	M S D Lawrence Township	Indianapolis
93	1,658.0	School Town of Highland	Highland
94	1,675.0	Northwestern School Corp	Kokomo
95	1,700.0	Eastbrook Community Sch Corp	Marion
96	1,720.0	North Putnam Community Schools	Bainbridge
97	1,737.0	Warsaw Community Schools	Warsaw
98	1,740.0	Rensselaer Central School Corp	Rensselaer
99	1,742.0	Southwest School Corp	Sullivan
100	1,756.5	Mt Vernon Community Sch Corp	Fortville
101	1,765.5	Greater Clark County Schools	Jeffersonville
102	1,781.7	North Lawrence Com Schools	Bedford
103	1,801.0	South Montgomery Com Sch Corp	New Market
104	1,804.0	M S D Perry Township	Indianapolis
105	1,805.0	Whitko Community School Corp	Pierceton
106	1,854.0	John Glenn School Corporation	Walkerton
107	1,880.0	Benton Community School Corp	Fowler
108	1,883.0	Blackford County Schools	Hartford City
109	1,905.0	Rochester Community Sch Corp	Rochester
110	1,921.0	South Vermillion Com Sch Corp	Clinton
111	1,926.3	Fort Wayne Community Schools	Fort Wayne
112	1,937.0	Lake Ridge Schools	Gary
113	1,963.5	Shelbyville Central Schools	Shelbyville
114	1,983.0	Baugo Community Schools	Elkhart
115	1,983.2	M S D Warren Township	Indianapolis
116	1,999.0	Pike County School Corp	Petersburg
117	2,016.3	Portage Township Schools	Portage
118	2,029.5	Fayette County School Corp	Connersville
119	2,055.0	School Town of Munster	Munster
120	2,083.0	Fairfield Community Schools	Goshen
121	2,089.3	Elkhart Community Schools	Elkhart
122	2,139.3	Valparaiso Community Schools	Valparaiso
123	2,142.0	Decatur County Com Schools	Greensburg
124	2,220.0	Lakeland School Corporation	Lagrange
125	2,250.0	South Madison Com Sch Corp	Pendleton
126	2,291.0	M S D Southwest Allen County	Fort Wayne
127	2,291.6	New Albany-Floyd County Con Sch	New Albany
128	2,323.0	Yorktown Community Schools	Yorktown
129	2,363.0	East Allen County Schools	New Haven
130	2,399.0	East Porter County School Corp	Kouts
131	2,426.0	Westview School Corporation	Topeka
132	2,475.0	Concord Community Schools	Elkhart
133	2,530.0	Northern Wells Com Schools	Ossian
134	2,548.5	School City of Mishawaka	Mishawaka
135	2,549.0	Mississinewa Community School Corp	Gas City
136	2,620.0	Western School Corp	Russiaville
137	2,734.0	Beech Grove City Schools	Beech Grove
138	2,822.0	New Prairie United School Corp	New Carlisle
139	2,870.0	Zionsville Community Schools	Zionsville
140	2,941.5	Huntington County Com Sch Corp	Huntington
141	2,945.5	Clark-Pleasant Com School Corp	Whiteland
142	3,077.0	South Harrison Com Schools	Corydon
143	3,086.0	M S D Steuben County	Angola
144	3,135.0	Wa-Nee Community Schools	Nappanee
145	3,195.0	Wawasee Community School Corp	Syracuse

Note: This section only includes districts with 1,500 or more students; All categories are ranked from high to low

146	3,225.0	Goshen Community Schools	Goshen
147	3,230.0	Madison Consolidated Schools	Madison
148	3,243.0	Southern Hancock Co. Com Sch Corp	New Palestine
149	3,258.0	Greater Jasper Con Schs	Jasper
150	3,258.5	Northwest Allen County Schools	Fort Wayne
151	3,519.0	Kankakee Valley School Corp	Wheatfield
152	3,591.0	Tri-Creek School Corporation	Lowell
153	3,593.0	Whitley County Cons Schools	Columbia City
154	3,640.0	Plymouth Community School Corp	Plymouth
155	3,653.0	New Castle Community Sch Corp	New Castle
156	3,791.5	Center Grove Com Sch Corp	Greenwood
157	3,802.0	East Noble School Corp	Kendallville
158	3,866.5	Crown Point Community Sch Corp	Crown Point
159	3,943.0	Dekalb County Ctl United SD	Waterloo
160	3,948.0	Tippecanoe School Corp	Lafayette
161	3,968.0	School City of Hobart	Hobart
162	4,017.0	Marion Community Schools	Marion
163	4,117.0	Sunman-Dearborn Com Sch Corp	Saint Leon
164	4,400.0	Clay Community Schools	Knightsville
164	4,400.0	Middlebury Community Schools	Middlebury
166	4,511.0	Mooresville Con School Corp	Mooresville
167	4,559.8	Evansville Vanderburgh Sch Corp	Evansville
168	4,853.0	Jennings County Schools	North Vernon
169	5,159.0	Franklin Community School Corp	Franklin
170	5,461.0	School City of East Chicago	East Chicago
171	10,037.0	Lake Central School Corp	Saint John
172	10,451.0	Penn-Harris-Madison Sch Corp	Mishawaka
n/a	n/a	Crawford County Com School Corp	Marengo
n/a	n/a	Frankton-Lapel Community Schs	Anderson
n/a	n/a	Greenfield-Central Com Schools	Greenfield
n/a	n/a	Greenwood Community Sch Corp	Greenwood
n/a	n/a	Griffith Public Schools	Griffith
n/a	n/a	Hanover Community School Corp	Cedar Lake
n/a	n/a	Hoosier Acad Virtual Charter	Indianapolis
n/a	n/a	In Connections Acad Virtual Pilot	Indianapolis
n/a	n/a	Oak Hill United School Corp	Converse
n/a	n/a	Seymour Community Schools	Seymour
n/a	n/a	South Gibson School Corp	Fort Branch
n/a	n/a	Spencer-Owen Community Schools	Spencer

Student/Counselor Ratio

(number of students per counselor)

Rank	Number	District Name	City
1	203.4	Crawford County Com School Corp	Marengo
2	206.4	North Adams Community Schools	Decatur
3	233.3	Scott County SD 2	Scottsburg
4	249.7	M S D Wabash County Schools	Wabash
5	257.3	South Montgomery Com Sch Corp	New Market
6	261.2	East Washington School Corp	Pekin
7	270.0	Randolph Central School Corp	Winchester
8	286.2	Michigan City Area Schools	Michigan City
9	301.5	School Town of Highland	Highland
10	303.3	Dekalb County Ctl United SD	Waterloo
11	309.8	West Noble School Corporation	Ligonier
12	310.3	Twin Lakes School Corp	Monticello
13	312.2	Nineveh-Hensley-Jackson United	Trafalgar
14	320.2	South Vermillion Com Sch Corp	Clinton
15	322.8	Lake Ridge Schools	Gary
16	329.5	Gary Community School Corp	Gary
17	335.3	Salem Community Schools	Salem
18	338.3	Fayette County School Corp	Connersville
19	340.0	Eastbrook Community Sch Corp	Marion
20	341.7	North Montgomery Com Sch Corp	Crawfordsville
21	341.9	South Harrison Com Schools	Corydon
22	343.7	Greencastle Community Sch Corp	Greencastle
23	344.0	North Putnam Community Schools	Bainbridge
24	346.2	Garrett-Keyser-Butler Com	Garrett
25	347.2	Fairfield Community Schools	Goshen
26	354.2	Community Schools of Frankfort	Frankfort
27	357.0	Decatur County Com Schools	Greensburg
28	358.1	New Albany-Floyd County Con Sch	New Albany
29	361.0	Whitko Community School Corp	Pierceton
30	361.7	M S D Southwest Allen County	Fort Wayne
31	370.0	Lakeland School Corporation	Lagrange
32	370.8	John Glenn School Corporation	Walkerton
33	373.3	Jennings County Schools	North Vernon
34	375.0	North Harrison Com School Corp	Ramsey
35	376.6	Blackford County Schools	Hartford City
36	381.7	Muncie Community Schools	Muncie
37	382.0	Mitchell Community Schools	Mitchell
38	382.3	Greensburg Community Schools	Greensburg
39	383.4	Northwest Allen County Schools	Fort Wayne
40	391.9	Wa-Nee Community Schools	Nappanee
41	392.2	Huntington County Com Sch Corp	Huntington
42	394.1	Lebanon Community School Corp	Lebanon
43	395.3	Laporte Community School Corp	Laporte
44	396.6	Baugo Community Schools	Elkhart
45	396.8	Franklin Community School Corp	Franklin
46	399.2	Whitley County Cons Schools	Columbia City
47	399.8	Pike County School Corp	Petersburg
48	400.0	Middlebury Community Schools	Middlebury
49	404.5	Delphi Community School Corp	Delphi
50	405.8	Avon Community School Corp	Avon
51	406.0	School Town of Speedway	Speedway
52	410.0	Tippecanoe Valley School Corp	Akron
53	418.8	In Connections Acad Virtual Pilot	Indianapolis
53	418.8	Northwestern School Corp	Kokomo
55	419.8	Batesville Community Sch Corp	Batesville
56	421.7	Northern Wells Com Schools	Ossian
57	422.2	Evansville Vanderburgh Sch Corp	Evansville
58	422.4	Duneland School Corporation	Chesterton
59	426.8	Westfield-Washington Schools	Westfield
60	430.0	Goshen Community Schools	Goshen
61	435.0	Rensselaer Central School Corp	Rensselaer
62	438.3	Indianapolis Public Schools	Indianapolis
63	441.5	Zionsville Community Schools	Zionsville
64	450.0	Concord Community Schools	Elkhart
65	450.5	Jay School Corp	Portland
66	453.2	Clark-Pleasant Com School Corp	Whiteland
67	461.7	Richland-Bean Blossom C S C	Ellettsville
68	463.4	Crawfordsville Com Schools	Crawfordsville
69	467.4	Lafayette School Corporation	Lafayette
70	470.3	New Prairie United School Corp	New Carlisle
71	474.8	Bartholomew Con School Corp	Columbus
72	476.3	Rochester Community Sch Corp	Rochester
73	478.0	Lake Central School Corp	Saint John
74	487.5	Vigo County School Corp	Terre Haute
75	488.0	North Spencer County Sch Corp	Lincoln City
76	493.7	Valparaiso Community Schools	Valparaiso
77	501.4	Hamilton Southeastern Schools	Fishers
78	502.0	Knox Community School Corp	Knox
79	502.7	Kankakee Valley School Corp	Wheatfield
80	505.7	Tell City-Troy Twp School Corp	Tell City
81	508.3	Brownsburg Community Sch Corp	Brownsburg
82	514.3	M S D Steuben County	Angola
83	514.6	Sunman-Dearborn Com Sch Corp	Saint Leon
84	515.0	Brown County School Corporation	Nashville
85	521.0	Mill Creek Community Sch Corp	Clayton
86	521.2	Delaware Community School Corp	Muncie
87	522.8	Danville Community School Corp	Danville
88	524.3	Oak Hill United School Corp	Converse
89	525.1	East Allen County Schools	New Haven
90	529.9	Franklin Township Com Sch Corp	Indianapolis
91	532.0	Elwood Community School Corp	Elwood
92	534.4	M S D Washington Twp	Indianapolis
93	538.3	Madison Consolidated Schools	Madison
94	539.3	Paoli Community School Corp	Paoli
95	541.6	Center Grove Com Sch Corp	Greenwood
96	550.0	Clay Community Schools	Knightsville
97	554.8	Peru Community Schools	Peru
98	555.0	West Clark Community Schools	Sellersburg
99	555.5	Noblesville Schools	Noblesville
100	556.0	Centerville-Abington Com Schs	Centerville
101	566.5	Hamilton Heights School Corp	Arcadia
102	572.3	Maconaquah School Corp	Bunker Hill
103	575.0	Merrillville Community School	Merrillville
104	576.7	Brownstown Cnt Com Sch Corp	Brownstown
105	580.8	Yorktown Community Schools	Yorktown
106	582.3	Southwest Dubois County Sch Corp	Huntingburg
107	585.5	Mt Vernon Community Sch Corp	Fortville
108	591.7	M S D Martinsville Schools	Martinsville
109	599.7	Monroe County Com Sch Corp	Bloomington
110	603.0	Western Boone County Com SD	Thorntown
111	608.8	New Castle Community Sch Corp	New Castle
112	623.1	Greater Clark County Schools	Jeffersonville
113	623.4	Tippecanoe School Corp	Lafayette
114	626.5	Kokomo-Center Twp Con Sch Corp	Kokomo
115	626.7	Benton Community School Corp	Fowler
116	633.7	East Noble School Corp	Kendallville
117	635.5	Rush County Schools	Rushville
118	639.0	Wawasee Community School Corp	Syracuse
119	642.2	M S D Pike Township	Indianapolis
120	646.0	Griffith Public Schools	Griffith
121	650.7	South Gibson School Corp	Fort Branch
122	655.0	Western School Corp	Russiaville
123	656.3	Carmel Clay Schools	Carmel
124	661.3	School City of Hobart	Hobart
125	668.1	North Lawrence Com Schools	Bedford
126	677.1	Greenfield-Central Com Schools	Greenfield
127	685.0	School Town of Munster	Munster
128	687.1	School City of Hammond	Hammond
129	696.4	Elkhart Community Schools	Elkhart
130	696.7	Penn-Harris-Madison Sch Corp	Mishawaka
131	700.8	Logansport Community Sch Corp	Logansport
132	708.5	M S D Lawrence Township	Indianapolis
133	712.3	West Lafayette Com School Corp	West Lafayette
134	716.0	North Gibson School Corp	Princeton
135	717.3	Franklin County Com Sch Corp	Brookville
136	718.2	Tri-Creek School Corporation	Lowell
137	720.8	Frankton-Lapel Community Schs	Anderson
138	728.1	School City of Mishawaka	Mishawaka
139	739.8	M S D Wayne Township	Indianapolis
140	743.7	M S D Warren Township	Indianapolis
141	746.7	M S D Mount Vernon	Mount Vernon
142	753.0	Southeastern School Corp	Walton
143	758.0	Manchester Community Schools	N Manchester
144	760.5	Porter Township School Corp	Valparaiso
144	760.5	Union Co/clg Corner Joint SD	Liberty
146	763.4	Warrick County School Corp	Boonville
147	764.4	Greenwood Community Sch Corp	Greenwood
148	769.0	Richmond Community Schools	Richmond
149	772.2	South Bend Community Sch Corp	South Bend
150	776.0	River Forest Community Sch Corp	Hobart
151	785.4	Shelbyville Central Schools	Shelbyville
152	803.4	Marion Community Schools	Marion
153	806.0	Alexandria Com School Corp	Alexandria
154	810.8	Southern Hancock Co. Com Sch Corp	New Palestine
155	815.5	Union Township School Corp	Valparaiso
156	834.7	Washington Com Schools	Washington
157	847.0	Tipton Community School Corp	Tipton
158	848.9	M S D Perry Township	Indianapolis
159	891.0	Vincennes Community Sch Corp	Vincennes
160	896.1	Portage Township Schools	Portage
161	900.0	South Madison Com Sch Corp	Pendleton
162	902.2	Mooresville Con School Corp	Mooresville
163	911.3	Beech Grove City Schools	Beech Grove
164	934.0	Fort Wayne Community Schools	Fort Wayne
165	937.0	North West Hendricks Schools	Lizton
166	940.0	South Dearborn Com School Corp	Aurora
167	966.0	Lawrenceburg Com School Corp	Lawrenceburg
168	966.6	Crown Point Community Sch Corp	Crown Point
169	980.8	Plainfield Community Sch Corp	Plainfield
170	992.6	Warsaw Community Schools	Warsaw
171	1,020.3	Anderson Community School Corp	Anderson
172	1,032.0	Hanover Community School Corp	Cedar Lake
173	1,050.7	M S D Decatur Township	Indianapolis
174	1,086.0	Greater Jasper Con Schs	Jasper
175	1,092.2	School City of East Chicago	East Chicago
176	1,213.0	Westview School Corporation	Topeka
177	1,213.3	Plymouth Community School Corp	Plymouth
178	1,274.5	Mississinewa Community School Corp	Gas City
179	1,381.0	Spencer-Owen Community Schools	Spencer
180	1,853.0	Hoosier Acad Virtual Charter	Indianapolis
181	2,127.5	Seymour Community Schools	Seymour
n/a	n/a	East Porter County School Corp	Kouts
n/a	n/a	Southwest School Corp	Sullivan
n/a	n/a	Thea Bowman Leadership Academy	Gary

Current Expenditures per Student

Rank	Dollars	District Name	City
1	14,284	Gary Community School Corp	Gary
2	13,908	Indianapolis Public Schools	Indianapolis
3	12,586	School City of East Chicago	East Chicago
4	12,209	School City of Mishawaka	Mishawaka
5	11,861	South Bend Community Sch Corp	South Bend
6	11,582	Marion Community Schools	Marion
7	11,575	Muncie Community Schools	Muncie
8	11,535	Lafayette School Corporation	Lafayette
9	11,192	M S D Mount Vernon	Mount Vernon
10	11,114	M S D Wayne Township	Indianapolis
11	11,094	Lake Ridge Schools	Gary
12	11,093	Kokomo-Center Twp Con Sch Corp	Kokomo
13	10,983	Logansport Community Sch Corp	Logansport
14	10,969	Garrett-Keyser-Butler Com	Garrett
15	10,924	Greater Jasper Con Schs	Jasper
16	10,607	New Castle Community Sch Corp	New Castle
17	10,596	Bartholomew Con School Corp	Columbus
18	10,513	Jennings County Schools	North Vernon
19	10,501	School Town of Speedway	Speedway
20	10,373	Brown County School Corporation	Nashville
21	10,363	Crawford County Com School Corp	Marengo

Note: This section only includes districts with 1,500 or more students; All categories are ranked from high to low

22	10,264	Goshen Community Schools	Goshen
23	10,257	M S D Wabash County Schools	Wabash
24	10,255	Benton Community School Corp	Fowler
25	10,241	School City of Hammond	Hammond
26	10,239	Union Co/clg Corner Joint SD	Liberty
27	10,233	Maconaquah School Corp	Bunker Hill
28	10,207	Fayette County School Corp	Connersville
29	10,089	M S D Washington Twp	Indianapolis
30	10,039	Pike County School Corp	Petersburg
31	10,037	Crawfordsville Com Schools	Crawfordsville
32	10,030	Jay School Corp	Portland
33	10,010	Greater Clark County Schools	Jeffersonville
34	10,005	Richmond Community Schools	Richmond
35	9,985	Elkhart Community Schools	Elkhart
36	9,942	Southwest School Corp	Sullivan
37	9,904	Anderson Community School Corp	Anderson
38	9,885	Greenfield-Central Com Schools	Greenfield
39	9,883	Evansville Vanderburgh Sch Corp	Evansville
39	9,883	North Harrison Com School Corp	Ramsey
41	9,799	Fort Wayne Community Schools	Fort Wayne
42	9,795	M S D Pike Township	Indianapolis
43	9,659	M S D Warren Township	Indianapolis
44	9,638	Lake Central School Corp	Saint John
45	9,632	Carmel Clay Schools	Carmel
46	9,609	Vincennes Community Sch Corp	Vincennes
47	9,580	M S D Perry Township	Indianapolis
48	9,560	Michigan City Area Schools	Michigan City
49	9,517	Southwest Dubois County Sch Corp	Huntingburg
50	9,461	Randolph Central School Corp	Winchester
51	9,389	Dekalb County Ctl United SD	Waterloo
52	9,372	New Albany-Floyd County Con Sch	New Albany
53	9,325	M S D Lawrence Township	Indianapolis
54	9,202	Blackford County Schools	Hartford City
55	9,183	Richland-Bean Blossom C S C	Ellettsville
56	9,168	Community Schools of Frankfort	Frankfort
57	9,135	River Forest Community Sch Corp	Hobart
58	9,124	North Lawrence Com Schools	Bedford
59	9,072	Monroe County Com Sch Corp	Bloomington
60	9,066	North Gibson School Corp	Princeton
61	9,057	Madison Consolidated Schools	Madison
62	9,055	Laporte Community School Corp	Laporte
63	9,052	Westfield-Washington Schools	Westfield
64	9,033	West Noble School Corporation	Ligonier
65	9,024	South Montgomery Com Sch Corp	New Market
66	8,997	Elwood Community School Corp	Elwood
67	8,985	Clay Community Schools	Knightsville
68	8,981	Spencer-Owen Community Schools	Spencer
69	8,955	M S D Martinsville Schools	Martinsville
70	8,953	Delphi Community School Corp	Delphi
71	8,942	Paoli Community School Corp	Paoli
72	8,917	M S D Decatur Township	Indianapolis
73	8,906	Northwestern School Corp	Kokomo
74	8,875	Greencastle Community Sch Corp	Greencastle
75	8,861	Warsaw Community Schools	Warsaw
76	8,831	Rush County Schools	Rushville
77	8,828	Avon Community School Corp	Avon
78	8,827	South Harrison Com Schools	Corydon
79	8,824	Westview School Corporation	Topeka
80	8,808	Vigo County School Corp	Terre Haute
81	8,766	Huntington County Com Sch Corp	Huntington
82	8,728	West Lafayette Com School Corp	West Lafayette
83	8,674	Lakeland School Corporation	Lagrange
84	8,671	Zionsville Community Schools	Zionsville
85	8,654	South Dearborn Com School Corp	Aurora
86	8,624	Alexandria Com School Corp	Alexandria
86	8,624	Sunman-Dearborn Com Sch Corp	Saint Leon
88	8,600	M S D Steuben County	Angola
89	8,598	Penn-Harris-Madison Sch Corp	Mishawaka
90	8,591	Wawasee Community School Corp	Syracuse
91	8,575	Scott County SD 2	Scottsburg
92	8,566	Clark-Pleasant Com School Corp	Whiteland
92	8,566	Greensburg Community Schools	Greensburg
94	8,556	Tell City-Troy Twp School Corp	Tell City
95	8,536	South Vermillion Com Sch Corp	Clinton
96	8,523	Tippecanoe Valley School Corp	Akron
97	8,504	East Washington School Corp	Pekin
98	8,494	East Allen County Schools	New Haven
99	8,479	Lawrenceburg Com School Corp	Lawrenceburg
100	8,465	Lebanon Community School Corp	Lebanon
101	8,457	North Adams Community Schools	Decatur
102	8,456	Whitley County Cons Schools	Columbia City
103	8,445	Middlebury Community Schools	Middlebury
104	8,443	Knox Community School Corp	Knox
105	8,369	North Montgomery Com Sch Corp	Crawfordsville
106	8,358	North Spencer County Sch Corp	Lincoln City
107	8,352	Mt Vernon Community Sch Corp	Fortville
108	8,336	Mitchell Community Schools	Mitchell
109	8,319	M S D Southwest Allen County	Fort Wayne
110	8,268	Valparaiso Community Schools	Valparaiso
111	8,235	Washington Com Schools	Washington
112	8,225	Brownstown Cnt Com Sch Corp	Brownstown
113	8,220	School Town of Munster	Munster
114	8,218	Twin Lakes School Corp	Monticello
115	8,214	Salem Community Schools	Salem
116	8,203	Shelbyville Central Schools	Shelbyville
117	8,166	Manchester Community Schools	N Manchester
118	8,159	Western Boone County Com SD	Thorntown
119	8,150	Whitko Community School Corp	Pierceton
120	8,113	Mooresville Con School Corp	Mooresville
121	8,112	Thea Bowman Leadership Academy	Gary
122	8,090	East Noble School Corp	Kendallville
123	8,083	Hamilton Heights School Corp	Arcadia
124	8,058	Seymour Community Schools	Seymour
125	8,024	Beech Grove City Schools	Beech Grove
126	8,014	Concord Community Schools	Elkhart
127	7,951	Delaware Community School Corp	Muncie
128	7,943	Greenwood Community Sch Corp	Greenwood
129	7,937	Oak Hill United School Corp	Converse
130	7,900	Tipton Community School Corp	Tipton
131	7,814	Danville Community School Corp	Danville
132	7,797	Wa-Nee Community Schools	Nappanee
133	7,796	Rensselaer Central School Corp	Rensselaer
134	7,790	Franklin County Com Sch Corp	Brookville
135	7,785	Fairfield Community Schools	Goshen
136	7,778	Peru Community Schools	Peru
137	7,769	West Clark Community Schools	Sellersburg
138	7,765	Rochester Community Sch Corp	Rochester
139	7,758	Duneland School Corporation	Chesterton
140	7,756	Decatur County Com Schools	Greensburg
141	7,754	Mississinewa Community School Corp	Gas City
142	7,746	North West Hendricks Schools	Lizton
143	7,742	Merrillville Community School	Merrillville
144	7,740	North Putnam Community Schools	Bainbridge
145	7,705	Southeastern School Corp	Walton
146	7,686	Franklin Community School Corp	Franklin
147	7,672	Centerville-Abington Com Schs	Centerville
148	7,652	Batesville Community Sch Corp	Batesville
148	7,652	Eastbrook Community Sch Corp	Marion
150	7,647	Union Township School Corp	Valparaiso
151	7,631	Crown Point Community Sch Corp	Crown Point
152	7,599	Baugo Community Schools	Elkhart
153	7,582	School City of Hobart	Hobart
154	7,572	Brownsburg Community Sch Corp	Brownsburg
155	7,557	Plymouth Community School Corp	Plymouth
156	7,548	Franklin Township Com Sch Corp	Indianapolis
157	7,547	Tippecanoe School Corp	Lafayette
158	7,534	Nineveh-Hensley-Jackson United	Trafalgar
159	7,521	Warrick County School Corp	Boonville
160	7,501	John Glenn School Corporation	Walkerton
161	7,474	Plainfield Community Sch Corp	Plainfield
162	7,473	School Town of Highland	Highland
163	7,467	Tri-Creek School Corporation	Lowell
164	7,418	Frankton-Lapel Community Schs	Anderson
165	7,398	Kankakee Valley School Corp	Wheatfield
166	7,386	Portage Township Schools	Portage
167	7,374	Hamilton Southeastern Schools	Fishers
167	7,374	South Gibson School Corp	Fort Branch
169	7,340	Porter Township School Corp	Valparaiso
170	7,310	New Prairie United School Corp	New Carlisle
171	7,268	Western School Corp	Russiaville
172	7,238	Center Grove Com Sch Corp	Greenwood
173	7,226	Northwest Allen County Schools	Fort Wayne
174	7,225	Griffith Public Schools	Griffith
175	7,165	Yorktown Community Schools	Yorktown
176	7,154	Mill Creek Community Sch Corp	Clayton
177	7,136	East Porter County School Corp	Kouts
178	7,129	Hanover Community School Corp	Cedar Lake
179	6,860	Noblesville Schools	Noblesville
180	6,819	Northern Wells Com Schools	Ossian
181	6,795	Southern Hancock Co. Com Sch Corp	New Palestine
182	5,978	South Madison Com Sch Corp	Pendleton
183	3,992	In Connections Acad Virtual Pilot	Indianapolis
184	2,319	Hoosier Acad Virtual Charter	Indianapolis

Total General Revenue per Student

Rank	Dollars	District Name	City
1	16,246	School City of Mishawaka	Mishawaka
2	16,222	Anderson Community School Corp	Anderson
3	15,906	Indianapolis Public Schools	Indianapolis
4	15,540	South Bend Community Sch Corp	South Bend
5	14,921	Muncie Community Schools	Muncie
6	14,651	Lafayette School Corporation	Lafayette
7	14,640	Greater Jasper Con Schs	Jasper
8	14,445	M S D Mount Vernon	Mount Vernon
9	14,033	School City of East Chicago	East Chicago
10	13,948	Goshen Community Schools	Goshen
11	13,873	Logansport Community Sch Corp	Logansport
12	13,725	Lake Ridge Schools	Gary
13	13,705	Southwest Dubois County Sch Corp	Huntingburg
14	13,704	M S D Wayne Township	Indianapolis
15	13,630	Gary Community School Corp	Gary
16	13,580	New Albany-Floyd County Con Sch	New Albany
17	13,467	Greenfield-Central Com Schools	Greenfield
18	13,328	Crawfordsville Com Schools	Crawfordsville
19	13,235	Elkhart Community Schools	Elkhart
20	13,200	Garrett-Keyser-Butler Com	Garrett
21	13,156	Kokomo-Center Twp Con Sch Corp	Kokomo
22	13,092	Marion Community Schools	Marion
23	12,990	Community Schools of Frankfort	Frankfort
24	12,955	North Adams Community Schools	Decatur
25	12,824	Union Co/clg Corner Joint SD	Liberty
26	12,804	New Castle Community Sch Corp	New Castle
27	12,790	Benton Community School Corp	Fowler
28	12,764	Sunman-Dearborn Com Sch Corp	Saint Leon
29	12,742	Westfield-Washington Schools	Westfield
30	12,682	Carmel Clay Schools	Carmel
31	12,632	M S D Wabash County Schools	Wabash
32	12,586	M S D Lawrence Township	Indianapolis
33	12,545	Southwest School Corp	Sullivan
34	12,528	West Lafayette Com School Corp	West Lafayette
35	12,408	South Montgomery Com Sch Corp	New Market
36	12,331	Brown County School Corporation	Nashville
37	12,150	M S D Pike Township	Indianapolis
38	12,137	Clark-Pleasant Com School Corp	Whiteland
39	12,132	Crawford County Com School Corp	Marengo
40	12,103	Tippecanoe Valley School Corp	Akron
41	12,092	Zionsville Community Schools	Zionsville
42	12,085	Wawasee Community School Corp	Syracuse
43	12,074	North Montgomery Com Sch Corp	Crawfordsville
44	12,039	North Gibson School Corp	Princeton
45	12,033	Vincennes Community Sch Corp	Vincennes
46	12,032	Jennings County Schools	North Vernon
47	12,000	Madison Consolidated Schools	Madison
48	11,993	M S D Warren Township	Indianapolis
49	11,952	M S D Perry Township	Indianapolis
50	11,941	Elwood Community School Corp	Elwood
51	11,937	Avon Community School Corp	Avon
52	11,909	Greater Clark County Schools	Jeffersonville
53	11,904	Twin Lakes School Corp	Monticello
54	11,849	Bartholomew Con School Corp	Columbus
55	11,848	Lake Central School Corp	Saint John
56	11,791	M S D Decatur Township	Indianapolis
57	11,739	Pike County School Corp	Petersburg
58	11,703	Greencastle Community Sch Corp	Greencastle
59	11,696	M S D Washington Twp	Indianapolis
60	11,635	Monroe County Com Sch Corp	Bloomington
61	11,519	School Town of Speedway	Speedway
62	11,510	Dekalb County Ctl United SD	Waterloo
63	11,487	South Harrison Com Schools	Corydon
64	11,473	Middlebury Community Schools	Middlebury
65	11,470	Lebanon Community School Corp	Lebanon
66	11,436	Maconaquah School Corp	Bunker Hill
67	11,429	Northwestern School Corp	Kokomo
68	11,395	School City of Hammond	Hammond
69	11,394	North Lawrence Com Schools	Bedford
70	11,393	Beech Grove City Schools	Beech Grove
71	11,376	Jay School Corp	Portland
72	11,372	Spencer-Owen Community Schools	Spencer
73	11,343	Fayette County School Corp	Connersville
74	11,341	Delphi Community School Corp	Delphi
75	11,335	Warsaw Community Schools	Warsaw
76	11,322	Merrillville Community School	Merrillville
77	11,279	School Town of Munster	Munster
78	11,277	Whitko Community School Corp	Pierceton
79	11,269	Michigan City Area Schools	Michigan City
80	11,267	Tell City-Troy Twp School Corp	Tell City
81	11,254	Delaware Community School Corp	Muncie
82	11,217	Westview School Corporation	Topeka
83	11,203	East Porter County School Corp	Kouts
84	11,175	Duneland School Corporation	Chesterton
85	11,143	Penn-Harris-Madison Sch Corp	Mishawaka
86	11,131	Shelbyville Central Schools	Shelbyville
87	11,122	Concord Community Schools	Elkhart

Note: This section only includes districts with 1,500 or more students; All categories are ranked from high to low

88	11,115	North West Hendricks Schools	Lizton
89	11,109	Fort Wayne Community Schools	Fort Wayne
90	11,103	Franklin Community School Corp	Franklin
91	11,091	Franklin Township Com Sch Corp	Indianapolis
92	11,075	South Gibson School Corp	Fort Branch
93	11,058	Yorktown Community Schools	Yorktown
94	11,051	Hamilton Heights School Corp	Arcadia
95	11,034	M S D Steuben County	Angola
96	11,027	South Madison Com Sch Corp	Pendleton
97	11,005	Lawrenceburg Com School Corp	Lawrenceburg
98	11,003	Evansville Vanderburgh Sch Corp	Evansville
99	10,999	Richmond Community Schools	Richmond
100	10,980	Brownsburg Community Sch Corp	Brownsburg
101	10,968	Plainfield Community Sch Corp	Plainfield
102	10,961	Tippecanoe School Corp	Lafayette
103	10,960	West Noble School Corporation	Ligonier
104	10,954	Blackford County Schools	Hartford City
105	10,946	Western Boone County Com SD	Thorntown
106	10,931	Lakeland School Corporation	Lagrange
107	10,915	North Harrison Com School Corp	Ramsey
108	10,870	Mt Vernon Community Sch Corp	Fortville
109	10,863	River Forest Community Sch Corp	Hobart
110	10,850	Richland-Bean Blossom C S C	Ellettsville
111	10,813	Wa-Nee Community Schools	Nappanee
112	10,780	South Dearborn Com School Corp	Aurora
113	10,764	North Putnam Community Schools	Bainbridge
114	10,747	South Vermillion Com Sch Corp	Clinton
115	10,730	Danville Community School Corp	Danville
116	10,722	Manchester Community Schools	N Manchester
117	10,714	North Spencer County Sch Corp	Lincoln City
118	10,693	East Washington School Corp	Pekin
119	10,677	Paoli Community School Corp	Paoli
120	10,675	Porter Township School Corp	Valparaiso
121	10,665	Knox Community School Corp	Knox
122	10,626	Union Township School Corp	Valparaiso
123	10,616	Laporte Community School Corp	Laporte
124	10,605	Washington Com Schools	Washington
125	10,535	East Noble School Corp	Kendallville
126	10,486	M S D Southwest Allen County	Fort Wayne
127	10,465	Frankton-Lapel Community Schs	Anderson
128	10,453	Baugo Community Schools	Elkhart
129	10,448	Tri-Creek School Corporation	Lowell
130	10,446	Salem Community Schools	Salem
131	10,441	Greensburg Community Schools	Greensburg
132	10,363	Rush County Schools	Rushville
133	10,346	Oak Hill United School Corp	Converse
134	10,335	Center Grove Com Sch Corp	Greenwood
135	10,334	Whitley County Cons Schools	Columbia City
136	10,313	Mill Creek Community Sch Corp	Clayton
137	10,308	Randolph Central School Corp	Winchester
138	10,290	Portage Township Schools	Portage
139	10,279	Vigo County School Corp	Terre Haute
140	10,268	Clay Community Schools	Knightsville
141	10,254	Brownstown Cnt Com Sch Corp	Brownstown
142	10,237	Rochester Community Sch Corp	Rochester
143	10,228	Fairfield Community Schools	Goshen
144	10,189	Plymouth Community School Corp	Plymouth
145	10,144	Seymour Community Schools	Seymour
146	10,142	Alexandria Com School Corp	Alexandria
147	10,129	Mitchell Community Schools	Mitchell
148	10,115	Hamilton Southeastern Schools	Fishers
149	10,112	Noblesville Schools	Noblesville
150	10,099	Kankakee Valley School Corp	Wheatfield
151	10,072	Scott County SD 2	Scottsburg
152	10,068	Northwest Allen County Schools	Fort Wayne
153	10,053	West Clark Community Schools	Sellersburg
154	10,008	Batesville Community Sch Corp	Batesville
154	10,008	Huntington County Com Sch Corp	Huntington
154	10,008	Rensselaer Central School Corp	Rensselaer
157	10,006	M S D Martinsville Schools	Martinsville
158	10,004	Greenwood Community Sch Corp	Greenwood
159	9,928	Centerville-Abington Com Schs	Centerville
159	9,928	Tipton Community School Corp	Tipton
161	9,912	Southern Hancock Co. Com Sch Corp	New Palestine
162	9,881	Mississinewa Community School Corp	Gas City
163	9,858	Valparaiso Community Schools	Valparaiso
164	9,812	New Prairie United School Corp	New Carlisle
165	9,788	Peru Community Schools	Peru
166	9,786	Decatur County Com Schools	Greensburg
167	9,742	East Allen County Schools	New Haven
168	9,711	Southeastern School Corp	Walton
169	9,656	Warrick County School Corp	Boonville
170	9,629	Eastbrook Community Sch Corp	Marion
171	9,548	Nineveh-Hensley-Jackson United	Trafalgar
172	9,465	School Town of Highland	Highland
173	9,464	Franklin County Com Sch Corp	Brookville
174	9,451	Thea Bowman Leadership Academy	Gary
175	9,428	Griffith Public Schools	Griffith
176	9,417	Hanover Community School Corp	Cedar Lake
177	9,387	Northern Wells Com Schools	Ossian
178	9,361	Western School Corp	Russiaville
179	9,286	School City of Hobart	Hobart
180	9,260	Crown Point Community Sch Corp	Crown Point
181	9,129	John Glenn School Corporation	Walkerton
182	8,799	Mooresville Con School Corp	Mooresville
183	3,368	Hoosier Acad Virtual Charter	Indianapolis
184	2,395	In Connections Acad Virtual Pilot	Indianapolis

Long-Term Debt per Student (end of FY)

Rank	Dollars	District Name	City
1	38,261	Zionsville Community Schools	Zionsville
2	35,447	Hanover Community School Corp	Cedar Lake
3	35,205	North West Hendricks Schools	Lizton
4	34,653	Mt Vernon Community Sch Corp	Fortville
5	31,565	Westfield-Washington Schools	Westfield
6	30,788	Avon Community School Corp	Avon
7	29,396	Franklin Community School Corp	Franklin
8	28,042	Franklin Township Com Sch Corp	Indianapolis
9	27,192	Plainfield Community Sch Corp	Plainfield
10	25,004	Clark-Pleasant Com School Corp	Whiteland
11	24,875	Brownsburg Community Sch Corp	Brownsburg
12	24,236	M S D Decatur Township	Indianapolis
13	24,157	Tri-Creek School Corporation	Lowell
14	23,948	Danville Community School Corp	Danville
15	23,723	School Town of Munster	Munster
16	23,229	North Gibson School Corp	Princeton
17	23,165	Greenfield-Central Com Schools	Greenfield
18	22,209	Northwest Allen County Schools	Fort Wayne
19	22,099	Frankton-Lapel Community Schs	Anderson
20	21,879	Western Boone County Com SD	Thorntown
21	20,998	Merrillville Community School	Merrillville
22	20,917	Indianapolis Public Schools	Indianapolis
23	20,267	Crown Point Community Sch Corp	Crown Point
24	19,829	School City of Hobart	Hobart
25	19,656	East Porter County School Corp	Kouts
25	19,656	Middlebury Community Schools	Middlebury
27	18,620	Sunman-Dearborn Com Sch Corp	Saint Leon
28	18,500	Lebanon Community School Corp	Lebanon
29	18,334	South Gibson School Corp	Fort Branch
30	18,147	Concord Community Schools	Elkhart
31	18,119	Kankakee Valley School Corp	Wheatfield
32	18,099	West Clark Community Schools	Sellersburg
33	18,044	Noblesville Schools	Noblesville
34	17,558	South Madison Com Sch Corp	Pendleton
35	17,429	M S D Wayne Township	Indianapolis
36	17,306	Southwest Dubois County Sch Corp	Huntingburg
37	17,078	Griffith Public Schools	Griffith
38	16,862	Anderson Community School Corp	Anderson
39	16,800	Southern Hancock Co. Com Sch Corp	New Palestine
40	16,780	Southwest School Corp	Sullivan
41	16,723	Tell City-Troy Twp School Corp	Tell City
42	16,195	Lake Ridge Schools	Gary
43	16,107	South Harrison Com Schools	Corydon
44	15,909	Hamilton Southeastern Schools	Fishers
45	15,655	Thea Bowman Leadership Academy	Gary
46	15,631	Richland-Bean Blossom C S C	Ellettsville
47	15,571	Garrett-Keyser-Butler Com	Garrett
48	15,381	Baugo Community Schools	Elkhart
49	15,349	Mill Creek Community Sch Corp	Clayton
50	15,233	New Prairie United School Corp	New Carlisle
51	14,248	Beech Grove City Schools	Beech Grove
52	14,168	Warsaw Community Schools	Warsaw
53	14,133	Vincennes Community Sch Corp	Vincennes
54	14,024	School City of Hammond	Hammond
55	13,925	Wawasee Community School Corp	Syracuse
56	13,665	Jay School Corp	Portland
57	13,660	South Dearborn Com School Corp	Aurora
58	13,507	Shelbyville Central Schools	Shelbyville
59	13,453	Community Schools of Frankfort	Frankfort
60	13,357	Greater Jasper Con Schs	Jasper
61	13,209	New Albany-Floyd County Con Sch	New Albany
62	13,201	South Montgomery Com Sch Corp	New Market
63	12,767	Bartholomew Con School Corp	Columbus
64	12,761	Fairfield Community Schools	Goshen
65	12,739	Benton Community School Corp	Fowler
66	12,683	Mitchell Community Schools	Mitchell
67	12,618	Michigan City Area Schools	Michigan City
68	12,286	North Harrison Com School Corp	Ramsey
69	12,198	M S D Lawrence Township	Indianapolis
70	11,851	Carmel Clay Schools	Carmel
71	11,706	North Adams Community Schools	Decatur
72	11,567	M S D Steuben County	Angola
73	11,553	Duneland School Corporation	Chesterton
74	11,464	Union Township School Corp	Valparaiso
75	11,416	Northwestern School Corp	Kokomo
76	11,397	Washington Com Schools	Washington
77	11,330	Goshen Community Schools	Goshen
78	11,246	Western School Corp	Russiaville
79	11,159	Whitley County Cons Schools	Columbia City
80	10,849	Spencer-Owen Community Schools	Spencer
81	10,835	Monroe County Com Sch Corp	Bloomington
82	10,814	Center Grove Com Sch Corp	Greenwood
83	10,801	Greencastle Community Sch Corp	Greencastle
84	10,753	School Town of Highland	Highland
85	10,732	River Forest Community Sch Corp	Hobart
86	10,671	West Lafayette Com School Corp	West Lafayette
87	10,611	Greater Clark County Schools	Jeffersonville
88	10,514	School City of Mishawaka	Mishawaka
89	10,400	Whitko Community School Corp	Pierceton
90	10,239	North Lawrence Com Schools	Bedford
91	10,127	Pike County School Corp	Petersburg
92	10,056	Crawford County Com School Corp	Marengo
93	10,052	South Bend Community Sch Corp	South Bend
94	10,016	East Washington School Corp	Pekin
95	9,904	Tippecanoe Valley School Corp	Akron
96	9,881	Westview School Corporation	Topeka
97	9,578	Union Co/clg Corner Joint SD	Liberty
98	9,572	Rush County Schools	Rushville
99	9,466	Plymouth Community School Corp	Plymouth
100	9,455	Lawrenceburg Com School Corp	Lawrenceburg
101	9,349	John Glenn School Corporation	Walkerton
102	9,302	Tippecanoe School Corp	Lafayette
103	9,131	Muncie Community Schools	Muncie
104	9,082	Lafayette School Corporation	Lafayette
105	9,007	Elkhart Community Schools	Elkhart
106	8,998	M S D Warren Township	Indianapolis
107	8,996	Hamilton Heights School Corp	Arcadia
108	8,991	Knox Community School Corp	Knox
109	8,967	West Noble School Corporation	Ligonier
110	8,965	Rochester Community Sch Corp	Rochester
111	8,938	Nineveh-Hensley-Jackson United	Trafalgar
112	8,875	Greensburg Community Schools	Greensburg
113	8,869	Porter Township School Corp	Valparaiso
114	8,804	M S D Southwest Allen County	Fort Wayne
115	8,670	Valparaiso Community Schools	Valparaiso
116	8,574	School City of East Chicago	East Chicago
117	8,512	Evansville Vanderburgh Sch Corp	Evansville
118	8,362	Salem Community Schools	Salem
119	8,248	East Noble School Corp	Kendallville
120	8,243	Portage Township Schools	Portage
121	8,177	Northern Wells Com Schools	Ossian
122	8,165	Centerville-Abington Com Schs	Centerville
123	8,072	Blackford County Schools	Hartford City
124	8,007	M S D Mount Vernon	Mount Vernon
125	7,944	M S D Perry Township	Indianapolis
126	7,911	Tipton Community School Corp	Tipton
127	7,828	Oak Hill United School Corp	Converse
128	7,766	Peru Community Schools	Peru
129	7,567	Logansport Community Sch Corp	Logansport
130	7,431	Lake Central School Corp	Saint John
131	7,248	Decatur County Com Schools	Greensburg
132	7,163	Crawfordsville Com Schools	Crawfordsville
133	7,106	North Montgomery Com Sch Corp	Crawfordsville
134	7,020	North Spencer County Sch Corp	Lincoln City
135	7,009	Huntington County Com Sch Corp	Huntington
136	6,837	Seymour Community Schools	Seymour
137	6,829	Elwood Community School Corp	Elwood
138	6,820	Wa-Nee Community Schools	Nappanee
139	6,794	Marion Community Schools	Marion
140	6,671	Penn-Harris-Madison Sch Corp	Mishawaka
141	6,342	Madison Consolidated Schools	Madison
142	6,108	Eastbrook Community Sch Corp	Marion
143	6,037	Delaware Community School Corp	Muncie
144	5,803	Southeastern School Corp	Walton
145	5,683	Scott County SD 2	Scottsburg
146	5,642	Brown County School Corporation	Nashville
147	5,300	Kokomo-Center Twp Con Sch Corp	Kokomo
148	5,286	Greenwood Community Sch Corp	Greenwood
149	5,143	South Vermillion Com Sch Corp	Clinton
150	5,073	Mississinewa Community School Corp	Gas City
151	5,069	Delphi Community School Corp	Delphi
152	5,011	Clay Community Schools	Knightsville
153	4,865	Jennings County Schools	North Vernon

Note: This section only includes districts with 1,500 or more students; All categories are ranked from high to low

154	4,752	M S D Washington Twp	Indianapolis
155	4,750	Dekalb County Ctl United SD	Waterloo
156	4,625	Fayette County School Corp	Connersville
157	4,603	Laporte Community School Corp	Laporte
158	4,545	Yorktown Community Schools	Yorktown
159	4,509	Mooresville Con School Corp	Mooresville
160	4,495	Brownstown Cnt Com Sch Corp	Brownstown
161	4,380	Warrick County School Corp	Boonville
162	4,338	North Putnam Community Schools	Bainbridge
163	4,310	Gary Community School Corp	Gary
164	4,287	Vigo County School Corp	Terre Haute
165	4,267	Randolph Central School Corp	Winchester
166	4,199	Manchester Community Schools	N Manchester
167	4,042	East Allen County Schools	New Haven
168	3,530	New Castle Community Sch Corp	New Castle
169	3,416	Franklin County Com Sch Corp	Brookville
170	3,212	Maconaquah School Corp	Bunker Hill
171	3,188	Alexandria Com School Corp	Alexandria
172	3,186	Paoli Community School Corp	Paoli
173	3,058	M S D Pike Township	Indianapolis
174	3,036	Batesville Community Sch Corp	Batesville
175	2,920	Twin Lakes School Corp	Monticello
176	2,866	M S D Wabash County Schools	Wabash
177	2,823	Fort Wayne Community Schools	Fort Wayne
178	2,748	Richmond Community Schools	Richmond
179	2,619	Rensselaer Central School Corp	Rensselaer
180	2,264	Lakeland School Corporation	Lagrange
181	1,960	M S D Martinsville Schools	Martinsville
182	0	Hoosier Acad Virtual Charter	Indianapolis
182	0	In Connections Acad Virtual Pilot	Indianapolis
182	0	School Town of Speedway	Speedway

Number of Diploma Recipients

Rank	Number	District Name	City
1	1,898	Fort Wayne Community Schools	Fort Wayne
2	1,416	Evansville Vanderburgh Sch Corp	Evansville
3	1,159	Indianapolis Public Schools	Indianapolis
4	1,109	South Bend Community Sch Corp	South Bend
5	1,079	M S D Lawrence Township	Indianapolis
6	952	Vigo County School Corp	Terre Haute
7	916	Carmel Clay Schools	Carmel
8	863	Hamilton Southeastern Schools	Fishers
9	797	New Albany-Floyd County Con Sch	New Albany
10	786	M S D Wayne Township	Indianapolis
11	736	Tippecanoe School Corp	Lafayette
12	719	Penn-Harris-Madison Sch Corp	Mishawaka
13	713	East Allen County Schools	New Haven
14	707	Monroe County Com Sch Corp	Bloomington
15	705	Lake Central School Corp	Saint John
16	704	M S D Warren Township	Indianapolis
17	680	M S D Perry Township	Indianapolis
18	677	Bartholomew Con School Corp	Columbus
19	670	Warrick County School Corp	Boonville
20	645	M S D Washington Twp	Indianapolis
21	644	School City of Hammond	Hammond
22	638	Elkhart Community Schools	Elkhart
23	633	M S D Pike Township	Indianapolis
24	588	Greater Clark County Schools	Jeffersonville
25	573	Gary Community School Corp	Gary
26	540	Crown Point Community Sch Corp	Crown Point
27	535	Center Grove Com Sch Corp	Greenwood
28	514	Avon Community School Corp	Avon
29	502	Merrillville Community School	Merrillville
30	494	Portage Township Schools	Portage
31	479	Noblesville Schools	Noblesville
32	471	Valparaiso Community Schools	Valparaiso
33	466	M S D Southwest Allen County	Fort Wayne
34	461	Franklin Township Com Sch Corp	Indianapolis
35	453	Anderson Community School Corp	Anderson
36	450	Lafayette School Corporation	Lafayette
37	432	Brownsburg Community Sch Corp	Brownsburg
38	426	Duneland School Corporation	Chesterton
39	399	Huntington County Com Sch Corp	Huntington
40	398	Warsaw Community Schools	Warsaw
41	397	School Town of Munster	Munster
42	396	Muncie Community Schools	Muncie
43	395	Northwest Allen County Schools	Fort Wayne
44	387	Laporte Community School Corp	Laporte
45	378	Kokomo-Center Twp Con Sch Corp	Kokomo
46	365	Zionsville Community Schools	Zionsville
47	357	Michigan City Area Schools	Michigan City
48	344	School City of Mishawaka	Mishawaka
49	342	Westfield-Washington Schools	Westfield
50	341	Clark-Pleasant Com School Corp	Whiteland
51	325	M S D Decatur Township	Indianapolis
52	324	M S D Martinsville Schools	Martinsville
53	323	Richmond Community Schools	Richmond
54	322	North Lawrence Com Schools	Bedford
55	321	Goshen Community Schools	Goshen
56	312	Jennings County Schools	North Vernon
57	310	Sunman-Dearborn Com Sch Corp	Saint Leon
58	309	Mooresville Con School Corp	Mooresville
59	300	Franklin Community School Corp	Franklin
60	299	Concord Community Schools	Elkhart
61	291	Plainfield Community Sch Corp	Plainfield
62	286	Middlebury Community Schools	Middlebury
63	279	Marion Community Schools	Marion
63	279	School City of Hobart	Hobart
65	276	Dekalb County Ctl United SD	Waterloo
66	269	Clay Community Schools	Knightsville
66	269	East Noble School Corp	Kendallville
68	268	Tri-Creek School Corporation	Lowell
69	262	Seymour Community Schools	Seymour
70	261	Jay School Corp	Portland
70	261	Logansport Community Sch Corp	Logansport
72	255	West Clark Community Schools	Sellersburg
73	248	Whitley County Cons Schools	Columbia City
74	245	South Madison Com Sch Corp	Pendleton
75	244	School Town of Highland	Highland
76	242	Greenfield-Central Com Schools	Greenfield
77	235	Southern Hancock Co. Com Sch Corp	New Palestine
78	234	Wawasee Community School Corp	Syracuse
79	225	Fayette County School Corp	Connersville
79	225	Greater Jasper Con Schs	Jasper
81	222	Lebanon Community School Corp	Lebanon
82	221	Greenwood Community Sch Corp	Greenwood
82	221	Wa-Nee Community Schools	Nappanee
84	219	Mt Vernon Community Sch Corp	Fortville
85	218	New Castle Community Sch Corp	New Castle
86	214	North Adams Community Schools	Decatur
87	212	Madison Consolidated Schools	Madison
88	208	Shelbyville Central Schools	Shelbyville
88	208	South Dearborn Com School Corp	Aurora
90	206	Plymouth Community School Corp	Plymouth
91	204	Frankton-Lapel Community Schs	Anderson
92	201	M S D Steuben County	Angola
93	200	South Harrison Com Schools	Corydon
94	198	M S D Mount Vernon	Mount Vernon
94	198	Richland-Bean Blossom C S C	Ellettsville
96	197	Kankakee Valley School Corp	Wheatfield
97	192	Northern Wells Com Schools	Ossian
98	189	School City of East Chicago	East Chicago
99	183	Griffith Public Schools	Griffith
100	182	Danville Community School Corp	Danville
101	180	Spencer-Owen Community Schools	Spencer
102	177	Community Schools of Frankfort	Frankfort
102	177	Delaware Community School Corp	Muncie
104	175	New Prairie United School Corp	New Carlisle
104	175	Yorktown Community Schools	Yorktown
106	174	North Montgomery Com Sch Corp	Crawfordsville
107	171	Western School Corp	Russiaville
108	164	Brown County School Corporation	Nashville
109	163	Tippecanoe Valley School Corp	Akron
110	162	Blackford County Schools	Hartford City
110	162	Franklin County Com Sch Corp	Brookville
112	160	M S D Wabash County Schools	Wabash
113	159	Batesville Community Sch Corp	Batesville
114	157	Crawfordsville Com Schools	Crawfordsville
114	157	Twin Lakes School Corp	Monticello
116	156	Decatur County Com Schools	Greensburg
116	156	West Lafayette Com School Corp	West Lafayette
118	155	Eastbrook Community Sch Corp	Marion
119	154	East Porter County School Corp	Kouts
120	153	Hamilton Heights School Corp	Arcadia
121	152	Mississinewa Community School Corp	Gas City
121	152	North Harrison Com School Corp	Ramsey
121	152	Scott County SD 2	Scottsburg
124	147	Rush County Schools	Rushville
124	147	South Gibson School Corp	Fort Branch
126	145	North Spencer County Sch Corp	Lincoln City
127	144	Vincennes Community Sch Corp	Vincennes
128	143	Lakeland School Corporation	Lagrange
128	143	Pike County School Corp	Petersburg
130	142	Northwestern School Corp	Kokomo
131	141	Western Boone County Com SD	Thorntown
132	140	Crawford County Com School Corp	Marengo
133	139	Benton Community School Corp	Fowler
133	139	Southwest Dubois County Sch Corp	Huntingburg
133	139	Washington Com Schools	Washington
136	137	Fairfield Community Schools	Goshen
136	137	Hanover Community School Corp	Cedar Lake
136	137	Peru Community Schools	Peru
139	136	Greensburg Community Schools	Greensburg
139	136	John Glenn School Corporation	Walkerton
139	136	Knox Community School Corp	Knox
139	136	Maconaquah School Corp	Bunker Hill
139	136	South Montgomery Com Sch Corp	New Market
144	135	Lake Ridge Schools	Gary
144	135	Southwest School Corp	Sullivan
146	132	Lawrenceburg Com School Corp	Lawrenceburg
146	132	Union Township School Corp	Valparaiso
148	131	Garrett-Keyser-Butler Com	Garrett
148	131	Nineveh-Hensley-Jackson United	Trafalgar
150	130	West Noble School Corporation	Ligonier
151	127	Brownstown Cnt Com Sch Corp	Brownstown
151	127	Delphi Community School Corp	Delphi
153	126	Baugo Community Schools	Elkhart
154	125	Beech Grove City Schools	Beech Grove
154	125	Rochester Community Sch Corp	Rochester
154	125	South Vermillion Com Sch Corp	Clinton
157	124	North Gibson School Corp	Princeton
158	123	Rensselaer Central School Corp	Rensselaer
159	120	North West Hendricks Schools	Lizton
159	120	Salem Community Schools	Salem
161	119	Whitko Community School Corp	Pierceton
162	118	School Town of Speedway	Speedway
163	117	Greencastle Community Sch Corp	Greencastle
164	116	Southeastern School Corp	Walton
165	115	Elwood Community School Corp	Elwood
165	115	Oak Hill United School Corp	Converse
167	114	Tipton Community School Corp	Tipton
168	113	Alexandria Com School Corp	Alexandria
168	113	North Putnam Community Schools	Bainbridge
168	113	Porter Township School Corp	Valparaiso
171	108	Mill Creek Community Sch Corp	Clayton
172	106	East Washington School Corp	Pekin
173	104	Mitchell Community Schools	Mitchell
174	103	Union Co/clg Corner Joint SD	Liberty
175	101	Paoli Community School Corp	Paoli
176	100	Centerville-Abington Com Schs	Centerville
177	95	Randolph Central School Corp	Winchester
178	94	Tell City-Troy Twp School Corp	Tell City
179	90	Manchester Community Schools	N Manchester
180	84	Westview School Corporation	Topeka
181	72	River Forest Community Sch Corp	Hobart
n/a	n/a	Hoosier Acad Virtual Charter	Indianapolis
n/a	n/a	In Connections Acad Virtual Pilot	Indianapolis
n/a	n/a	Thea Bowman Leadership Academy	Gary

High School Drop-out Rate

Rank	Percent	District Name	City
1	5.8	Michigan City Area Schools	Michigan City
2	5.7	Tippecanoe Valley School Corp	Akron
3	5.1	Indianapolis Public Schools	Indianapolis
3	5.1	New Castle Community Sch Corp	New Castle
5	5.0	Marion Community Schools	Marion
6	4.8	Lake Ridge Schools	Gary
7	4.7	Madison Consolidated Schools	Madison
7	4.7	West Noble School Corporation	Ligonier
9	4.3	Baugo Community Schools	Elkhart
10	4.2	River Forest Community Sch Corp	Hobart
11	3.9	School City of East Chicago	East Chicago
12	3.8	Community Schools of Frankfort	Frankfort
12	3.8	Mitchell Community Schools	Mitchell
14	3.7	Franklin Township Com Sch Corp	Indianapolis
14	3.7	Tell City-Troy Twp School Corp	Tell City
16	3.4	Bartholomew Con School Corp	Columbus
16	3.4	Franklin Community School Corp	Franklin
18	3.3	Fayette County School Corp	Connersville
19	3.2	South Bend Community Sch Corp	South Bend
20	3.1	Greencastle Community Sch Corp	Greencastle
20	3.1	Monroe County Com Sch Corp	Bloomington
22	3.0	Greater Clark County Schools	Jeffersonville
22	3.0	Lafayette School Corporation	Lafayette
22	3.0	M S D Martinsville Schools	Martinsville
22	3.0	M S D Wabash County Schools	Wabash
22	3.0	School Town of Highland	Highland
27	2.9	Anderson Community School Corp	Anderson
27	2.9	Crawford County Com School Corp	Marengo
27	2.9	Logansport Community Sch Corp	Logansport
27	2.9	Richmond Community Schools	Richmond

Note: This section only includes districts with 1,500 or more students; All categories are ranked from high to low

31	2.6	North West Hendricks Schools	Lizton
32	2.5	M S D Perry Township	Indianapolis
32	2.5	North Harrison Com School Corp	Ramsey
32	2.5	Scott County SD 2	Scottsburg
35	2.4	Beech Grove City Schools	Beech Grove
35	2.4	Elkhart Community Schools	Elkhart
35	2.4	M S D Wayne Township	Indianapolis
35	2.4	Plymouth Community School Corp	Plymouth
35	2.4	Wawasee Community School Corp	Syracuse
40	2.3	Randolph Central School Corp	Winchester
40	2.3	Rensselaer Central School Corp	Rensselaer
42	2.2	Eastbrook Community Sch Corp	Marion
42	2.2	North Gibson School Corp	Princeton
42	2.2	School City of Hammond	Hammond
42	2.2	School City of Mishawaka	Mishawaka
42	2.2	Wa-Nee Community Schools	Nappanee
42	2.2	Western Boone County Com SD	Thorntown
42	2.2	Whitko Community School Corp	Pierceton
49	2.1	Goshen Community Schools	Goshen
49	2.1	Southeastern School Corp	Walton
49	2.1	Southwest Dubois County Sch Corp	Huntingburg
49	2.1	Vincennes Community Sch Corp	Vincennes
49	2.1	Westview School Corporation	Topeka
54	2.0	South Vermillion Com Sch Corp	Clinton
54	2.0	Southwest School Corp	Sullivan
56	1.9	Northern Wells Com Schools	Ossian
56	1.9	Shelbyville Central Schools	Shelbyville
56	1.9	Sunman-Dearborn Com Sch Corp	Saint Leon
56	1.9	Twin Lakes School Corp	Monticello
60	1.8	Delphi Community School Corp	Delphi
60	1.8	East Allen County Schools	New Haven
60	1.8	Evansville Vanderburgh Sch Corp	Evansville
60	1.8	M S D Decatur Township	Indianapolis
60	1.8	M S D Mount Vernon	Mount Vernon
60	1.8	M S D Pike Township	Indianapolis
60	1.8	North Putnam Community Schools	Bainbridge
60	1.8	Porter Township School Corp	Valparaiso
60	1.8	Rochester Community Sch Corp	Rochester
60	1.8	South Dearborn Com School Corp	Aurora
60	1.8	Whitley County Cons Schools	Columbia City
71	1.7	East Noble School Corp	Kendallville
71	1.7	Lakeland School Corporation	Lagrange
71	1.7	Seymour Community Schools	Seymour
71	1.7	South Harrison Com Schools	Corydon
75	1.6	Blackford County Schools	Hartford City
75	1.6	Jay School Corp	Portland
75	1.6	M S D Lawrence Township	Indianapolis
75	1.6	M S D Washington Twp	Indianapolis
75	1.6	Penn-Harris-Madison Sch Corp	Mishawaka
75	1.6	Peru Community Schools	Peru
81	1.5	Greenfield-Central Com Schools	Greenfield
81	1.5	Hamilton Heights School Corp	Arcadia
81	1.5	Northwestern School Corp	Kokomo
81	1.5	Spencer-Owen Community Schools	Spencer
85	1.4	Delaware Community School Corp	Muncie
85	1.4	Kankakee Valley School Corp	Wheatfield
85	1.4	M S D Warren Township	Indianapolis
85	1.4	Oak Hill United School Corp	Converse
89	1.3	Elwood Community School Corp	Elwood
89	1.3	Frankton-Lapel Community Schs	Anderson
89	1.3	Mt Vernon Community Sch Corp	Fortville
89	1.3	New Prairie United School Corp	New Carlisle
89	1.3	Tipton Community School Corp	Tipton
89	1.3	Valparaiso Community Schools	Valparaiso
95	1.2	Clay Community Schools	Knightsville
95	1.2	Crown Point Community Sch Corp	Crown Point
95	1.2	Mississinewa Community School Corp	Gas City
95	1.2	Nineveh-Hensley-Jackson United	Trafalgar
95	1.2	Richland-Bean Blossom C S C	Ellettsville
95	1.2	South Madison Com Sch Corp	Pendleton
101	1.1	Gary Community School Corp	Gary
101	1.1	Jennings County Schools	North Vernon
101	1.1	Lawrenceburg Com School Corp	Lawrenceburg
101	1.1	M S D Steuben County	Angola
101	1.1	Manchester Community Schools	N Manchester
101	1.1	North Spencer County Sch Corp	Lincoln City
101	1.1	Northwest Allen County Schools	Fort Wayne
101	1.1	Portage Township Schools	Portage
101	1.1	Union Township School Corp	Valparaiso
101	1.1	West Clark Community Schools	Sellersburg
111	1.0	Centerville-Abington Com Schs	Centerville
111	1.0	East Porter County School Corp	Kouts
111	1.0	Yorktown Community Schools	Yorktown
114	0.9	Brown County School Corporation	Nashville
114	0.9	Tippecanoe School Corp	Lafayette
114	0.9	Washington Com Schools	Washington
114	0.9	West Lafayette Com School Corp	West Lafayette
114	0.9	Westfield-Washington Schools	Westfield
119	0.8	Concord Community Schools	Elkhart
119	0.8	Crawfordsville Com Schools	Crawfordsville
119	0.8	Danville Community School Corp	Danville
119	0.8	Fort Wayne Community Schools	Fort Wayne
119	0.8	Mooresville Con School Corp	Mooresville
119	0.8	New Albany-Floyd County Con Sch	New Albany
119	0.8	North Lawrence Com Schools	Bedford
119	0.8	Salem Community Schools	Salem
119	0.8	School Town of Munster	Munster
119	0.8	Warrick County School Corp	Boonville
129	0.7	Avon Community School Corp	Avon
129	0.7	Brownsburg Community Sch Corp	Brownsburg
129	0.7	Center Grove Com Sch Corp	Greenwood
129	0.7	Kokomo-Center Twp Con Sch Corp	Kokomo
129	0.7	Merrillville Community School	Merrillville
134	0.6	Griffith Public Schools	Griffith
134	0.6	Huntington County Com Sch Corp	Huntington
134	0.6	Knox Community School Corp	Knox
134	0.6	Lake Central School Corp	Saint John
134	0.6	Maconaquah School Corp	Bunker Hill
134	0.6	Middlebury Community Schools	Middlebury
134	0.6	North Adams Community Schools	Decatur
141	0.5	Carmel Clay Schools	Carmel
141	0.5	Dekalb County Ctl United SD	Waterloo
141	0.5	Hamilton Southeastern Schools	Fishers
141	0.5	Muncie Community Schools	Muncie
141	0.5	Warsaw Community Schools	Warsaw
146	0.4	Franklin County Com Sch Corp	Brookville
146	0.4	Greater Jasper Con Schs	Jasper
146	0.4	Laporte Community School Corp	Laporte
146	0.4	M S D Southwest Allen County	Fort Wayne
146	0.4	School City of Hobart	Hobart
146	0.4	Tri-Creek School Corporation	Lowell
152	0.3	Zionsville Community Schools	Zionsville
153	0.1	Vigo County School Corp	Terre Haute
n/a	n/a	Benton Community School Corp	Fowler
n/a	n/a	Duneland School Corporation	Chesterton
n/a	n/a	Greensburg Community Schools	Greensburg
n/a	n/a	Hoosier Acad Virtual Charter	Indianapolis
n/a	n/a	In Connections Acad Virtual Pilot	Indianapolis
n/a	n/a	Mill Creek Community Sch Corp	Clayton
n/a	n/a	North Montgomery Com Sch Corp	Crawfordsville
n/a	n/a	Paoli Community School Corp	Paoli
n/a	n/a	School Town of Speedway	Speedway
n/a	n/a	Union Co/clg Corner Joint SD	Liberty
n/a	n/a	Thea Bowman Leadership Academy	Gary
n/a	n/a	Alexandria Com School Corp	Alexandria
n/a	n/a	Batesville Community Sch Corp	Batesville
n/a	n/a	Brownstown Cnt Com Sch Corp	Brownstown
n/a	n/a	Clark-Pleasant Com School Corp	Whiteland
n/a	n/a	Decatur County Com Schools	Greensburg
n/a	n/a	East Washington School Corp	Pekin
n/a	n/a	Fairfield Community Schools	Goshen
n/a	n/a	Garrett-Keyser-Butler Com	Garrett
n/a	n/a	Greenwood Community Sch Corp	Greenwood
n/a	n/a	Hanover Community School Corp	Cedar Lake
n/a	n/a	John Glenn School Corporation	Walkerton
n/a	n/a	Lebanon Community School Corp	Lebanon
n/a	n/a	Noblesville Schools	Noblesville
n/a	n/a	Pike County School Corp	Petersburg
n/a	n/a	Plainfield Community Sch Corp	Plainfield
n/a	n/a	Rush County Schools	Rushville
n/a	n/a	South Gibson School Corp	Fort Branch
n/a	n/a	South Montgomery Com Sch Corp	New Market
n/a	n/a	Southern Hancock Co. Com Sch Corp	New Palestine
n/a	n/a	Western School Corp	Russiaville

Average Freshman Graduation Rate

Rank	Percent	District Name	City
1	100.0	Garrett-Keyser-Butler Com	Garrett
1	100.0	School Town of Munster	Munster
3	99.2	Union Township School Corp	Valparaiso
4	98.0	Crown Point Community Sch Corp	Crown Point
5	97.2	Clark-Pleasant Com School Corp	Whiteland
6	94.9	Frankton-Lapel Community Schs	Anderson
7	94.6	Hamilton Southeastern Schools	Fishers
7	94.6	Zionsville Community Schools	Zionsville
9	94.5	Hanover Community School Corp	Cedar Lake
10	94.1	Batesville Community Sch Corp	Batesville
10	94.1	Middlebury Community Schools	Middlebury
12	93.7	Westfield-Washington Schools	Westfield
13	93.6	M S D Southwest Allen County	Fort Wayne
14	92.8	Northwestern School Corp	Kokomo
15	92.6	North Adams Community Schools	Decatur
16	91.8	Valparaiso Community Schools	Valparaiso
17	91.3	Center Grove Com Sch Corp	Greenwood
18	91.1	East Porter County School Corp	Kouts
19	90.9	Carmel Clay Schools	Carmel
20	90.7	Greater Jasper Con Schs	Jasper
20	90.7	West Lafayette Com School Corp	West Lafayette
22	90.0	Southern Hancock Co. Com Sch Corp	New Palestine
23	89.1	Avon Community School Corp	Avon
24	89.0	Penn-Harris-Madison Sch Corp	Mishawaka
25	88.5	Mill Creek Community Sch Corp	Clayton
26	88.3	Danville Community School Corp	Danville
27	88.2	West Clark Community Schools	Sellersburg
28	88.1	Eastbrook Community Sch Corp	Marion
29	87.8	Brownsburg Community Sch Corp	Brownsburg
30	87.6	Western Boone County Com SD	Thorntown
31	87.4	Mississinewa Community School Corp	Gas City
31	87.4	North Montgomery Com Sch Corp	Crawfordsville
33	87.2	John Glenn School Corporation	Walkerton
33	87.2	Richland-Bean Blossom C S C	Ellettsville
35	87.1	Oak Hill United School Corp	Converse
36	87.0	North West Hendricks Schools	Lizton
36	87.0	South Gibson School Corp	Fort Branch
38	86.8	North Spencer County Sch Corp	Lincoln City
39	86.7	Whitley County Cons Schools	Columbia City
40	86.6	Noblesville Schools	Noblesville
41	86.5	Southwest School Corp	Sullivan
42	86.4	Western School Corp	Russiaville
43	86.3	Porter Township School Corp	Valparaiso
44	86.2	Plymouth Community School Corp	Plymouth
45	86.1	M S D Mount Vernon	Mount Vernon
46	86.0	Tippecanoe School Corp	Lafayette
47	85.9	Lake Central School Corp	Saint John
48	85.8	Delphi Community School Corp	Delphi
48	85.8	Plainfield Community Sch Corp	Plainfield
50	85.5	Merrillville Community School	Merrillville
51	85.3	Southwest Dubois County Sch Corp	Huntingburg
52	85.1	Fairfield Community Schools	Goshen
52	85.1	Northwest Allen County Schools	Fort Wayne
54	85.0	Yorktown Community Schools	Yorktown
55	84.7	Sunman-Dearborn Com Sch Corp	Saint Leon
56	84.6	Lawrenceburg Com School Corp	Lawrenceburg
56	84.6	South Dearborn Com School Corp	Aurora
58	84.5	Tri-Creek School Corporation	Lowell
59	84.4	Wa-Nee Community Schools	Nappanee
59	84.4	West Noble School Corporation	Ligonier
61	84.3	School City of Hobart	Hobart
62	84.2	Mt Vernon Community Sch Corp	Fortville
63	84.0	Baugo Community Schools	Elkhart
63	84.0	Duneland School Corporation	Chesterton
65	83.7	New Prairie United School Corp	New Carlisle
66	83.3	Mooresville Con School Corp	Mooresville
67	83.1	School Town of Speedway	Speedway
68	82.6	Warrick County School Corp	Boonville
69	82.5	Brownstown Cnt Com Sch Corp	Brownstown
70	82.2	Benton Community School Corp	Fowler
71	82.1	Dekalb County Ctl United SD	Waterloo
71	82.1	Northern Wells Com Schools	Ossian
73	82.0	East Noble School Corp	Kendallville
74	81.9	South Montgomery Com Sch Corp	New Market
75	81.4	Seymour Community Schools	Seymour
76	81.3	Decatur County Com Schools	Greensburg
76	81.3	Pike County School Corp	Petersburg
76	81.3	School Town of Highland	Highland
79	80.9	South Madison Com Sch Corp	Pendleton
80	80.3	Tipton Community School Corp	Tipton
81	80.1	East Allen County Schools	New Haven
82	80.0	Brown County School Corporation	Nashville
82	80.0	Centerville-Abington Com Schs	Centerville
82	80.0	Crawford County Com School Corp	Marengo
85	79.7	Monroe County Com Sch Corp	Bloomington
86	79.5	Paoli Community School Corp	Paoli
86	79.5	Southeastern School Corp	Walton
88	79.4	New Albany-Floyd County Con Sch	New Albany
89	79.2	Franklin Community School Corp	Franklin
90	79.1	Kankakee Valley School Corp	Wheatfield
90	79.1	M S D Steuben County	Angola
90	79.1	South Harrison Com Schools	Corydon
93	78.9	Griffith Public Schools	Griffith
94	78.8	M S D Pike Township	Indianapolis
95	78.5	Crawfordsville Com Schools	Crawfordsville
95	78.5	Twin Lakes School Corp	Monticello
97	78.3	Blackford County Schools	Hartford City

Note: This section only includes districts with 1,500 or more students; All categories are ranked from high to low

Rank	Score	District	City	Rank	Score	District	City	Rank	Score	District	City
98	78.1	Jay School Corp	Portland	128	73.4	Alexandria Com School Corp	Alexandria	158	67.4	Jennings County Schools	North Vernon
99	78.0	Nineveh-Hensley-Jackson United	Trafalgar	128	73.4	North Gibson School Corp	Princeton	158	67.4	Kokomo-Center Twp Con Sch Corp	Kokomo
100	77.9	East Washington School Corp	Pekin	128	73.4	Warsaw Community Schools	Warsaw	160	67.2	Goshen Community Schools	Goshen
100	77.9	Lebanon Community School Corp	Lebanon	131	73.1	Knox Community School Corp	Knox	161	66.5	New Castle Community Sch Corp	New Castle
100	77.9	Salem Community Schools	Salem	131	73.1	Madison Consolidated Schools	Madison	162	66.4	Vincennes Community Sch Corp	Vincennes
103	77.7	Hamilton Heights School Corp	Arcadia	131	73.1	Portage Township Schools	Portage	163	66.3	South Bend Community Sch Corp	South Bend
104	77.6	M S D Lawrence Township	Indianapolis	134	72.9	Peru Community Schools	Peru	164	65.4	M S D Warren Township	Indianapolis
105	77.5	Greencastle Community Sch Corp	Greencastle	135	72.3	Richmond Community Schools	Richmond	165	65.2	Scott County SD 2	Scottsburg
106	77.4	Rensselaer Central School Corp	Rensselaer	136	72.0	North Lawrence Com Schools	Bedford	165	65.2	Spencer-Owen Community Schools	Spencer
107	77.1	Concord Community Schools	Elkhart	136	72.0	North Putnam Community Schools	Bainbridge	167	64.6	Marion Community Schools	Marion
108	77.0	Delaware Community School Corp	Muncie	138	71.9	Lakeland School Corporation	Lagrange	168	64.1	Michigan City Area Schools	Michigan City
109	76.9	Union Co/clg Corner Joint SD	Liberty	139	71.8	Tell City-Troy Twp School Corp	Tell City	169	63.9	Rush County Schools	Rushville
110	76.8	Greensburg Community Schools	Greensburg	140	71.7	Shelbyville Central Schools	Shelbyville	170	63.7	Fayette County School Corp	Connersville
111	76.4	Lafayette School Corporation	Lafayette	141	71.6	Greenfield-Central Com Schools	Greenfield	171	63.6	Westview School Corporation	Topeka
112	76.3	Logansport Community Sch Corp	Logansport	141	71.6	Vigo County School Corp	Terre Haute	172	62.0	Muncie Community Schools	Muncie
113	76.0	Randolph Central School Corp	Winchester	143	71.5	Franklin Township Com Sch Corp	Indianapolis	173	61.8	M S D Perry Township	Indianapolis
114	75.9	Huntington County Com Sch Corp	Huntington	144	71.3	Greenwood Community Sch Corp	Greenwood	174	61.6	Elkhart Community Schools	Elkhart
115	75.8	Tippecanoe Valley School Corp	Akron	145	71.2	Mitchell Community Schools	Mitchell	175	60.5	River Forest Community Sch Corp	Hobart
116	75.7	Evansville Vanderburgh Sch Corp	Evansville	146	71.1	Laporte Community School Corp	Laporte	176	58.1	Beech Grove City Schools	Beech Grove
117	75.5	Bartholomew Con School Corp	Columbus	147	70.8	Fort Wayne Community Schools	Fort Wayne	177	56.3	School City of Hammond	Hammond
118	75.3	Rochester Community Sch Corp	Rochester	148	70.7	Lake Ridge Schools	Gary	178	52.9	Anderson Community School Corp	Anderson
119	75.2	Elwood Community School Corp	Elwood	148	70.7	M S D Decatur Township	Indianapolis	179	43.1	Gary Community School Corp	Gary
120	75.1	M S D Washington Twp	Indianapolis	150	70.2	Greater Clark County Schools	Jeffersonville	180	42.0	School City of East Chicago	East Chicago
121	75.0	Manchester Community Schools	N Manchester	151	70.1	Franklin County Com Sch Corp	Brookville	181	35.0	Indianapolis Public Schools	Indianapolis
122	74.8	M S D Wabash County Schools	Wabash	152	70.0	Community Schools of Frankfort	Frankfort	n/a	n/a	Hoosier Acad Virtual Charter	Indianapolis
123	74.4	Whitko Community School Corp	Pierceton	153	69.7	M S D Martinsville Schools	Martinsville	n/a	n/a	In Connections Acad Virtual Pilot	Indianapolis
124	74.3	Washington Com Schools	Washington	154	69.2	School City of Mishawaka	Mishawaka	n/a	n/a	Thea Bowman Leadership Academy	Gary
125	74.0	South Vermillion Com Sch Corp	Clinton	155	67.9	Clay Community Schools	Knightsville				
126	73.8	North Harrison Com School Corp	Ramsey	156	67.7	Maconaquah School Corp	Bunker Hill				
127	73.6	Wawasee Community School Corp	Syracuse	157	67.6	M S D Wayne Township	Indianapolis				

Note: This section only includes districts with 1,500 or more students; All categories are ranked from high to low

Profiles of Indiana — National Assessment of Educational Progress (NAEP) — 387

The Nation's Report Card

2015 Mathematics State Snapshot Report
Indiana • Grade 4 • Public Schools

Overall Results

- In 2015, the average score of fourth-grade students in Indiana was 248. This was higher than the average score of 240 for public school students in the nation.
- The average score for students in Indiana in 2015 (248) was not significantly different from their average score in 2013 (249) and was higher than their average score in 2000 (233).
- The percentage of students in Indiana who performed at or above the NAEP *Proficient* level was 50 percent in 2015. This percentage was not significantly different from that in 2013 (52 percent) and was greater than that in 2000 (30 percent).
- The percentage of students in Indiana who performed at or above the NAEP *Basic* level was 89 percent in 2015. This percentage was not significantly different from that in 2013 (90 percent) and was greater than that in 2000 (77 percent).

Achievement-Level Percentages and Average Score Results

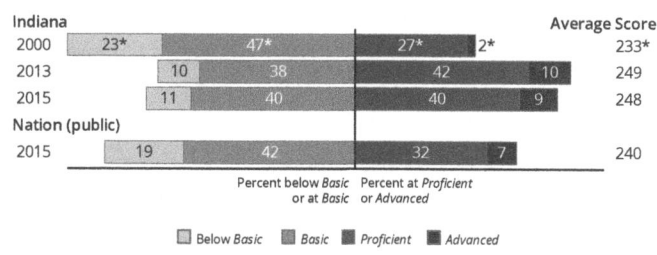

Indiana	Below Basic	Basic	Proficient	Advanced	Average Score
2000	23*	47*	27*	2*	233*
2013	10	38	42	10	249
2015	11	40	40	9	248
Nation (public) 2015	19	42	32	7	240

Percent below *Basic* or at *Basic* — Percent at *Proficient* or *Advanced*

* Significantly different (*p* < .05) from state's results in 2015. Significance tests were performed using unrounded numbers.
NOTE: Detail may not sum to totals because of rounding.

Compare the Average Score in 2015 to Other States/Jurisdictions

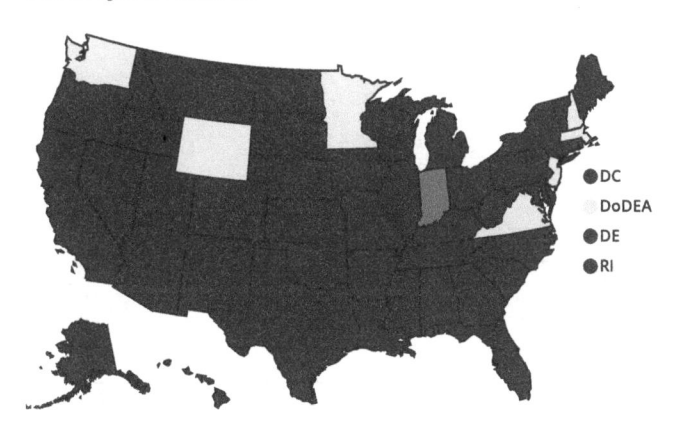

In 2015, the average score in Indiana (248) was
- lower than those in 0 states/jurisdictions
- higher than those in 43 states/jurisdictions
- not significantly different from those in 8 states/jurisdictions

DoDEA = Department of Defense Education Activity (overseas and domestic schools)

Average Scores for State/Jurisdiction and Nation (public)

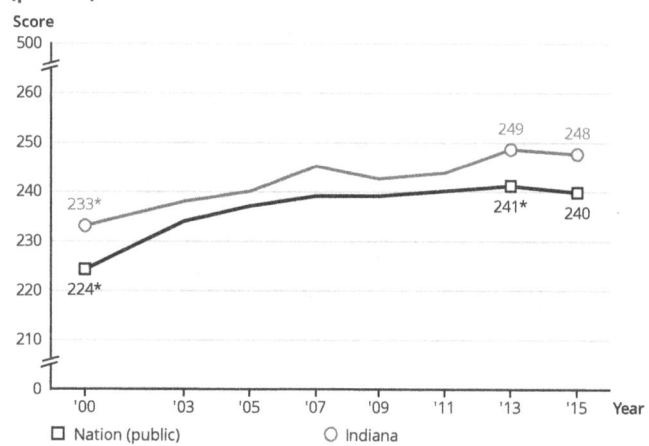

Indiana: 224* ('00) → 233* → ... → 249 ('13) → 248 ('15)
Nation (public): 233* ('00) → ... → 241* → 240 ('15)

* Significantly different (*p* < .05) from 2015. Significance tests were performed using unrounded numbers.

Results for Student Groups in 2015

Reporting Groups	Percentage of students	Avg. score	Percentage at or above Basic	Percentage at or above Proficient	Percentage at Advanced
Race/Ethnicity					
White	69	252	93	57	11
Black	12	229	74	22	2
Hispanic	11	240	86	35	5
Asian	2	‡	‡	‡	‡
American Indian/Alaska Native	#	‡	‡	‡	‡
Native Hawaiian/Pacific Islander	#	‡	‡	‡	‡
Two or more races	5	244	88	45	5
Gender					
Male	50	248	89	51	11
Female	50	247	90	48	8
National School Lunch Program					
Eligible	52	239	84	36	4
Not eligible	47	258	95	65	16

Rounds to zero.
‡ Reporting standards not met.
NOTE: Detail may not sum to totals because of rounding, and because the "Information not available" category for the National School Lunch Program, which provides free/reduced-price lunches, is not displayed. Black includes African American and Hispanic includes Latino. Race categories exclude Hispanic origin.

Score Gaps for Student Groups

- In 2015, Black students had an average score that was 22 points lower than that for White students. This performance gap was not significantly different from that in 2000 (25 points).
- In 2015, Hispanic students had an average score that was 12 points lower than that for White students. Data are not reported for Hispanic students in 2000, because reporting standards were not met.
- In 2015, male students in Indiana had an average score that was not significantly different from that for female students.
- In 2015, students who were eligible for free/reduced-price school lunch, an indicator of low family income, had an average score that was 18 points lower than that for students who were not eligible. This performance gap was not significantly different from that in 2000 (20 points).

ies NATIONAL CENTER FOR EDUCATION STATISTICS
Institute of Education Sciences

NOTE: Statistical comparisons are calculated on the basis of unrounded scale scores or percentages.
SOURCE: U.S. Department of Education, Institute of Education Sciences, National Center for Education Statistics, National Assessment of Educational Progress (NAEP), various years, 2000-2015 Mathematics Assessments.

The Nation's Report Card

2015 Mathematics State Snapshot Report
Indiana • Grade 8 • Public Schools

Overall Results

- In 2015, the average score of eighth-grade students in Indiana was 287. This was higher than the average score of 281 for public school students in the nation.
- The average score for students in Indiana in 2015 (287) was not significantly different from their average score in 2013 (288) and was higher than their average score in 2000 (281).
- The percentage of students in Indiana who performed at or above the NAEP *Proficient* level was 39 percent in 2015. This percentage was not significantly different from that in 2013 (38 percent) and was greater than that in 2000 (29 percent).
- The percentage of students in Indiana who performed at or above the NAEP *Basic* level was 77 percent in 2015. This percentage was not significantly different from that in 2013 (77 percent) and in 2000 (74 percent).

Achievement-Level Percentages and Average Score Results

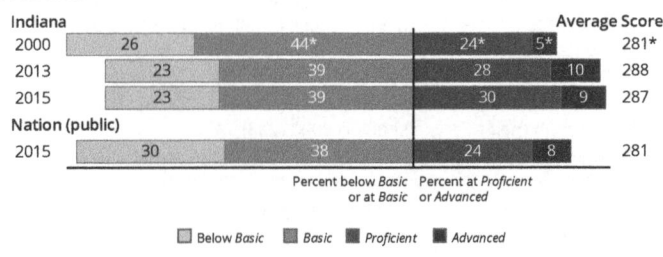

Indiana	Below Basic	Basic	Proficient	Advanced	Average Score
2000	26	44*	24*	5*	281*
2013	23	39	28	10	288
2015	23	39	30	9	287
Nation (public) 2015	30	38	24	8	281

* Significantly different (*p* < .05) from state's results in 2015. Significance tests were performed using unrounded numbers.
NOTE: Detail may not sum to totals because of rounding.

Compare the Average Score in 2015 to Other States/Jurisdictions

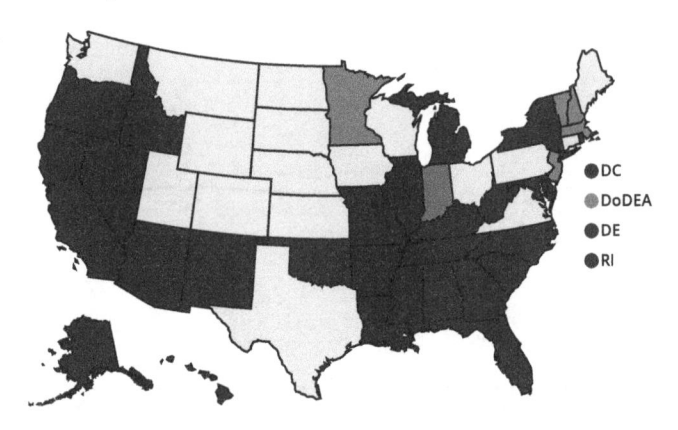

In 2015, the average score in Indiana (287) was
- lower than those in 6 states/jurisdictions
- higher than those in 28 states/jurisdictions
- not significantly different from those in 17 states/jurisdictions

DoDEA = Department of Defense Education Activity (overseas and domestic schools)

Average Scores for State/Jurisdiction and Nation (public)

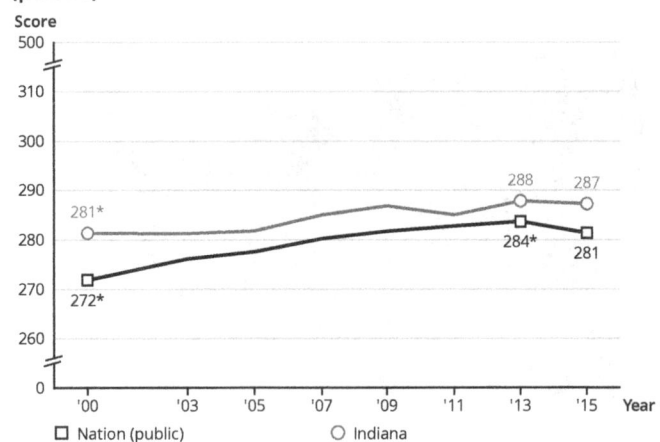

Indiana: 281* ('00), 288 ('13), 287 ('15)
Nation (public): 272* ('00), 284* ('13), 281 ('15)

* Significantly different (*p* < .05) from 2015. Significance tests were performed using unrounded numbers.

Results for Student Groups in 2015

Reporting Groups	Percentage of students	Avg. score	Percentage at or above Basic	Percentage at or above Proficient	Percentage at Advanced
Race/Ethnicity					
White	73	294	84	45	11
Black	11	257	44	10	1
Hispanic	10	271	64	23	2
Asian	2	‡	‡	‡	‡
American Indian/Alaska Native	#	‡	‡	‡	‡
Native Hawaiian/Pacific Islander	#	‡	‡	‡	‡
Two or more races	4	281	72	27	9
Gender					
Male	51	288	78	39	10
Female	49	287	77	38	8
National School Lunch Program					
Eligible	46	274	66	24	3
Not eligible	54	298	86	51	14

\# Rounds to zero.
‡ Reporting standards not met.
NOTE: Detail may not sum to totals because of rounding, and because the "Information not available" category for the National School Lunch Program, which provides free/reduced-price lunches, is not displayed. Black includes African American and Hispanic includes Latino. Race categories exclude Hispanic origin.

Score Gaps for Student Groups

- In 2015, Black students had an average score that was 37 points lower than that for White students. This performance gap was not significantly different from that in 2000 (29 points).
- In 2015, Hispanic students had an average score that was 23 points lower than that for White students. Data are not reported for Hispanic students in 2000, because reporting standards were not met.
- In 2015, male students in Indiana had an average score that was not significantly different from that for female students.
- In 2015, students who were eligible for free/reduced-price school lunch, an indicator of low family income, had an average score that was 24 points lower than that for students who were not eligible. This performance gap was wider than that in 2000 (17 points).

NOTE: Statistical comparisons are calculated on the basis of unrounded scale scores or percentages.
SOURCE: U.S. Department of Education, Institute of Education Sciences, National Center for Education Statistics, National Assessment of Educational Progress (NAEP), various years, 2000-2015 Mathematics Assessments.

The Nation's Report Card

2015 Reading State Snapshot Report
Indiana • Grade 4 • Public Schools

Overall Results

- In 2015, the average score of fourth-grade students in Indiana was 227. This was higher than the average score of 221 for public school students in the nation.
- The average score for students in Indiana in 2015 (227) was not significantly different from their average score in 2013 (225) and was higher than their average score in 2002 (222).
- The percentage of students in Indiana who performed at or above the NAEP *Proficient* level was 40 percent in 2015. This percentage was not significantly different from that in 2013 (38 percent) and was greater than that in 2002 (33 percent).
- The percentage of students in Indiana who performed at or above the NAEP *Basic* level was 75 percent in 2015. This percentage was not significantly different from that in 2013 (73 percent) and was greater than that in 2002 (68 percent).

Achievement-Level Percentages and Average Score Results

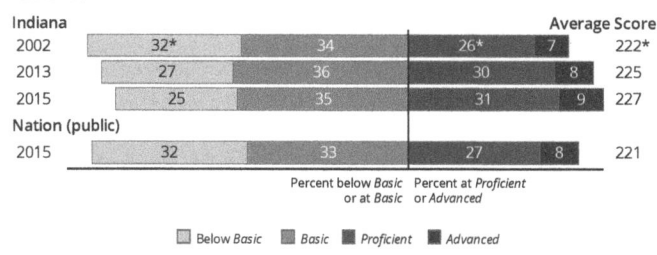

Indiana	Below Basic	Basic	Proficient	Advanced	Average Score
2002	32*	34	26*	7	222*
2013	27	36	30	8	225
2015	25	35	31	9	227
Nation (public) 2015	32	33	27	8	221

* Significantly different (*p* < .05) from state's results in 2015. Significance tests were performed using unrounded numbers.
NOTE: Detail may not sum to totals because of rounding.

Compare the Average Score in 2015 to Other States/Jurisdictions

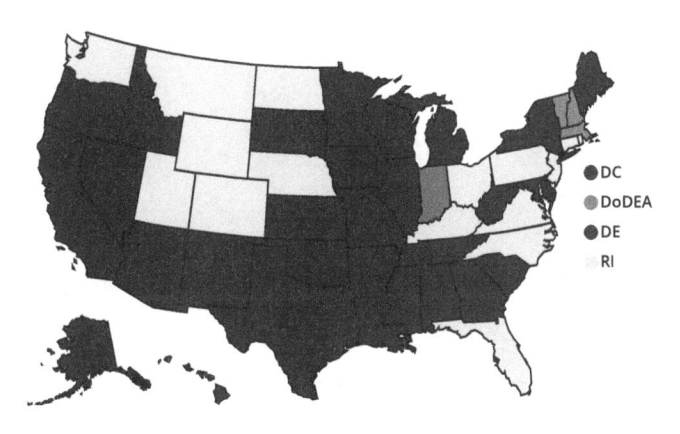

In 2015, the average score in Indiana (227) was
- lower than those in 4 states/jurisdictions
- higher than those in 31 states/jurisdictions
- not significantly different from those in 16 states/jurisdictions

DoDEA = Department of Defense Education Activity (overseas and domestic schools)

Average Scores for State/Jurisdiction and Nation (public)

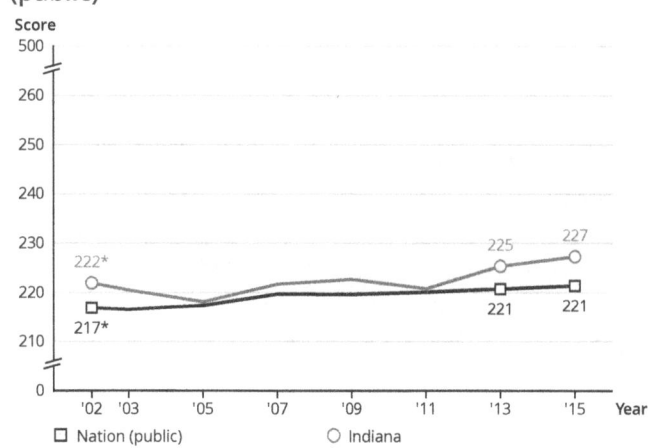

Indiana: 222* ('02), 225 ('13), 227 ('15)
Nation (public): 217* ('02), 221 ('13), 221 ('15)

* Significantly different (*p* < .05) from 2015. Significance tests were performed using unrounded numbers.

Results for Student Groups in 2015

Reporting Groups	Percentage of students	Avg. score	Percentage at or above Basic	Percentage at or above Proficient	Percentage at Advanced
Race/Ethnicity					
White	69	231	80	44	10
Black	12	212	56	22	3
Hispanic	11	216	63	29	5
Asian	2	‡	‡	‡	‡
American Indian/Alaska Native	#	‡	‡	‡	‡
Native Hawaiian/Pacific Islander	#	‡	‡	‡	‡
Two or more races	5	228	74	40	8
Gender					
Male	50	224	71	37	8
Female	50	230	78	43	10
National School Lunch Program					
Eligible	50	217	64	28	5
Not eligible	49	238	86	52	14

\# Rounds to zero.
‡ Reporting standards not met.
NOTE: Detail may not sum to totals because of rounding, and because the "Information not available" category for the National School Lunch Program, which provides free/reduced-price lunches, is not displayed. Black includes African American and Hispanic includes Latino. Race categories exclude Hispanic origin.

Score Gaps for Student Groups

- In 2015, Black students had an average score that was 20 points lower than that for White students. This performance gap was not significantly different from that in 2002 (23 points).
- In 2015, Hispanic students had an average score that was 16 points lower than that for White students. This performance gap was not significantly different from that in 2002 (9 points).
- In 2015, female students in Indiana had an average score that was higher than that for male students by 6 points.
- In 2015, students who were eligible for free/reduced-price school lunch, an indicator of low family income, had an average score that was 21 points lower than that for students who were not eligible. This performance gap was not significantly different from that in 2002 (23 points).

NOTE: Statistical comparisons are calculated on the basis of unrounded scale scores or percentages.
SOURCE: U.S. Department of Education, Institute of Education Sciences, National Center for Education Statistics, National Assessment of Educational Progress (NAEP), various years, 2002-2015 Reading Assessments.

The Nation's Report Card

2015 Reading State Snapshot Report
Indiana • Grade 8 • Public Schools

Overall Results

- In 2015, the average score of eighth-grade students in Indiana was 268. This was higher than the average score of 264 for public school students in the nation.
- The average score for students in Indiana in 2015 (268) was not significantly different from their average score in 2013 (267) and in 2002 (265).
- The percentage of students in Indiana who performed at or above the NAEP *Proficient* level was 37 percent in 2015. This percentage was not significantly different from that in 2013 (35 percent) and was greater than that in 2002 (32 percent).
- The percentage of students in Indiana who performed at or above the NAEP *Basic* level was 80 percent in 2015. This percentage was not significantly different from that in 2013 (79 percent) and in 2002 (77 percent).

Achievement-Level Percentages and Average Score Results

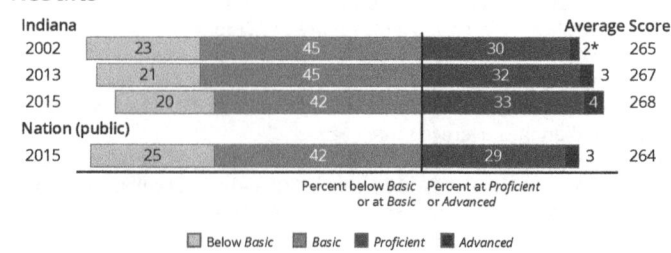

Indiana	Below Basic	Basic	Proficient	Advanced	Average Score
2002	23	45	30	2*	265
2013	21	45	32	3	267
2015	20	42	33	4	268
Nation (public) 2015	25	42	29	3	264

* Significantly different (p < .05) from state's results in 2015. Significance tests were performed using unrounded numbers.
NOTE: Detail may not sum to totals because of rounding.

Compare the Average Score in 2015 to Other States/Jurisdictions

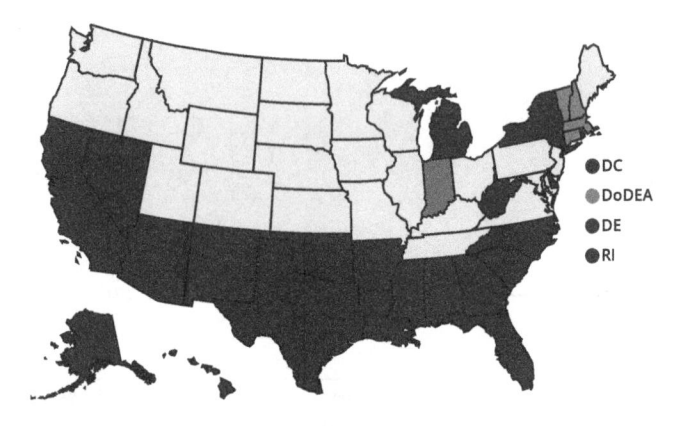

In 2015, the average score in Indiana (268) was
- lower than those in 5 states/jurisdictions
- higher than those in 22 states/jurisdictions
- not significantly different from those in 24 states/jurisdictions

DoDEA = Department of Defense Education Activity (overseas and domestic schools)

Average Scores for State/Jurisdiction and Nation (public)

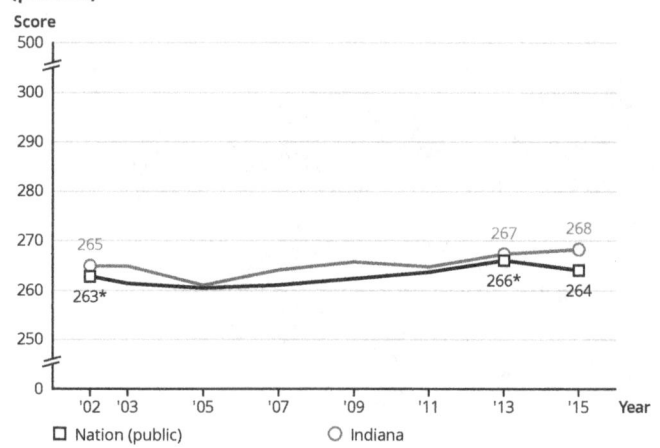

* Significantly different (p < .05) from 2015. Significance tests were performed using unrounded numbers.

Results for Student Groups in 2015

Reporting Groups	Percentage of students	Avg. score	Percentage at or above Basic	Percentage at or above Proficient	Percentage at Advanced
Race/Ethnicity					
White	73	272	84	42	4
Black	11	252	63	19	1
Hispanic	10	257	70	25	1
Asian	2	‡	‡	‡	‡
American Indian/Alaska Native	#	‡	‡	‡	‡
Native Hawaiian/Pacific Islander	#	‡	‡	‡	‡
Two or more races	4	260	68	27	2
Gender					
Male	51	264	76	32	3
Female	49	273	83	42	5
National School Lunch Program					
Eligible	49	257	70	23	1
Not eligible	50	280	89	51	6

Rounds to zero.
‡ Reporting standards not met.
NOTE: Detail may not sum to totals because of rounding, and because the "Information not available" category for the National School Lunch Program, which provides free/reduced-price lunches, is not displayed. Black includes African American and Hispanic includes Latino. Race categories exclude Hispanic origin.

Score Gaps for Student Groups

- In 2015, Black students had an average score that was 20 points lower than that for White students. This performance gap was not significantly different from that in 2002 (20 points).
- In 2015, Hispanic students had an average score that was 15 points lower than that for White students. Data are not reported for Hispanic students in 2002, because reporting standards were not met.
- In 2015, female students in Indiana had an average score that was higher than that for male students by 10 points.
- In 2015, students who were eligible for free/reduced-price school lunch, an indicator of low family income, had an average score that was 23 points lower than that for students who were not eligible. This performance gap was not significantly different from that in 2002 (16 points).

NOTE: Statistical comparisons are calculated on the basis of unrounded scale scores or percentages.
SOURCE: U.S. Department of Education, Institute of Education Sciences, National Center for Education Statistics, National Assessment of Educational Progress (NAEP), various years, 2002-2015 Reading Assessments.

The Nation's Report Card — Science 2009 State Snapshot Report

Indiana — Grade 4 — Public Schools

2009 Science Assessment Content

Guided by a new framework, the NAEP science assessment was updated in 2009 to keep the content current with key developments in science, curriculum standards, assessments, and research. The 2009 framework organizes science content into three broad content areas.

Physical science includes concepts related to properties and changes of matter, forms of energy, energy transfer and conservation, position and motion of objects, and forces affecting motion.

Life science includes concepts related to organization and development, matter and energy transformations, interdependence, heredity and reproduction, and evolution and diversity.

Earth and space sciences includes concepts related to objects in the universe, the history of the Earth, properties of Earth materials, tectonics, energy in Earth systems, climate and weather, and biogeochemical cycles.

The 2009 science assessment was composed of 143 questions at grade 4, 162 at grade 8, and 179 at grade 12. Students responded to only a portion of the questions, which included both multiple-choice questions and questions that required a written response.

Compare the Average Score in 2009 to Other States/Jurisdictions

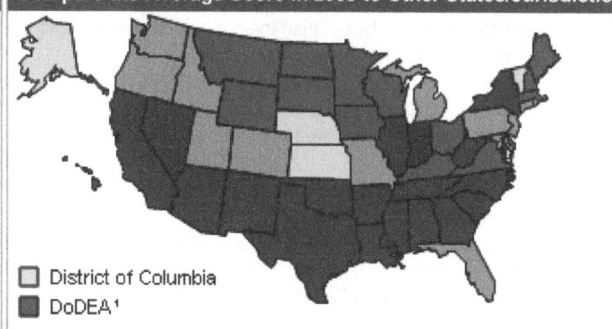

[1] Department of Defense Education Activity (overseas and domestic schools).

In 2009, the average score in **Indiana** was
- lower than those in 14 states/jurisdictions
- higher than those in 18 states/jurisdictions
- not significantly different from those in 14 states/jurisdictions
- 5 states/jurisdictions did not participate

Overall Results

- In 2009, the average score of fourth-grade students in Indiana was 153. This was higher than the average score of 149 for public school students in the nation.
- The percentage of students in Indiana who performed at or above the NAEP *Proficient* level was 35 percent in 2009. This percentage was not significantly different from the nation (32 percent).
- The percentage of students in Indiana who performed at or above the NAEP *Basic* level was 78 percent in 2009. This percentage was greater than the nation (71 percent).

Achievement-Level Percentages and Average Score Results

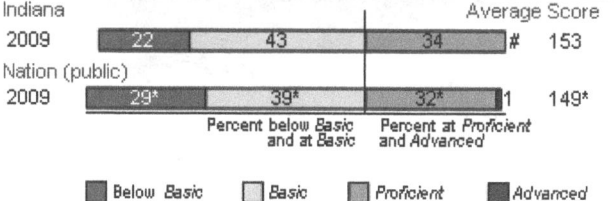

	Below Basic	Basic	Proficient	Advanced	Average Score
Indiana 2009	22	43	34	#	153
Nation (public) 2009	29*	39*	32*	1	149*

* Significantly different (p < .05) from Indiana. Significance tests were performed using unrounded numbers.
# Rounds to zero.

NOTE: Detail may not sum to totals because of rounding.

Results for Student Groups in 2009

Reporting Groups	Percent of students	Avg. score	Percentages at or above Basic	Percentages at or above Proficient	Percent at Advanced
Gender					
Male	51	153	78	36	1
Female	49	152	77	34	#
Race/Ethnicity					
White	77	158	84	41	1
Black	11	129	50	9	#
Hispanic	6	136	59	15	#
Asian/Pacific Islander	2	‡	‡	‡	‡
American Indian/Alaska Native	#	‡	‡	‡	‡
National School Lunch Program					
Eligible	45	141	66	21	#
Not eligible	55	162	87	46	1

Rounds to zero. ‡ Reporting standards not met.

NOTE: Detail may not sum to totals because of rounding, and because the "Information not available" category for the National School Lunch Program, which provides free/reduced-price lunches, and the "Unclassified" category for race/ethnicity are not displayed.

Score Gaps for Student Groups

- In 2009, male students in Indiana had an average score that was not significantly different from female students.
- In 2009, Black students had an average score that was 29 points lower than White students. This performance gap was narrower than the nation (35 points).
- In 2009, Hispanic students had an average score that was 23 points lower than White students. This performance gap was narrower than the nation (32 points).
- In 2009, students who were eligible for free/reduced-price school lunch, an indicator of low family income, had an average score that was 21 points lower than students who were not eligible for free/reduced-price school lunch. This performance gap was narrower than the nation (29 points).

NOTE: Statistical comparisons are calculated on the basis of unrounded scale scores or percentages.
SOURCE: U.S. Department of Education, Institute of Education Sciences, National Center for Education Statistics, National Assessment of Educational Progress (NAEP), 2009 Science Assessment.

The Nation's Report Card
Science 2011 State Snapshot Report

**Indiana
Grade 8
Public Schools**

Overall Results

- In 2011, the average score of eighth-grade students in Indiana was 153. This was higher than the average score of 151 for public school students in the nation.
- The average score for students in Indiana in 2011 (153) was not significantly different from their average score in 2009 (152).
- In 2011, the score gap between students in Indiana at the 75th percentile and students at the 25th percentile was 43 points. This performance gap was not significantly different from that of 2009 (43 points).
- The percentage of students in Indiana who performed at or above the NAEP *Proficient* level was 33 percent in 2011. This percentage was not significantly different from that in 2009 (32 percent).
- The percentage of students in Indiana who performed at or above the NAEP *Basic* level was 67 percent in 2011. This percentage was not significantly different from that in 2009 (67 percent).

Achievement-Level Percentages and Average Score Results

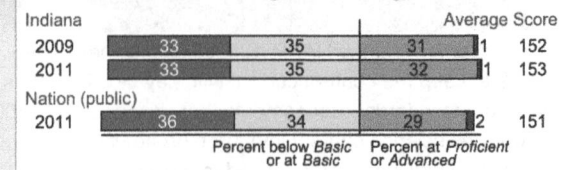

	Below *Basic*	*Basic*	*Proficient*	*Advanced*	Average Score
Indiana 2009	33	35	31	1	152
Indiana 2011	33	35	32	1	153
Nation (public) 2011	36	34	29	2	151

NOTE: Detail may not sum to totals because of rounding.

Compare the Average Score in 2011 to Other States/Jurisdictions

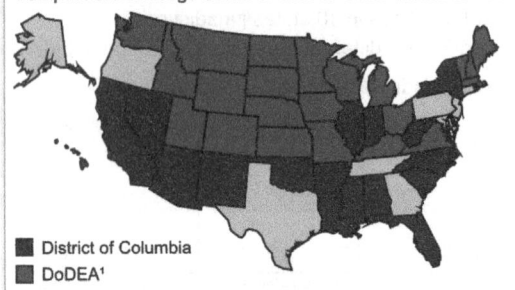

In 2011, the average score in Indiana (153) was
- lower than those in 23 states/jurisdictions
- higher than those in 19 states/jurisdictions
- not significantly different from those in 9 states/jurisdictions

Average Scores for State/Jurisdiction and Nation (public)

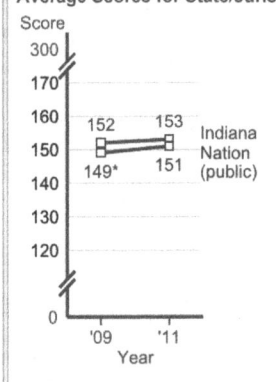

Year	Indiana	Nation (public)
'09	152	149*
'11	153	151

* Significantly different (*p* < .05) from 2011. Significance tests were performed using unrounded numbers.

Results for Student Groups in 2011

Reporting Groups	Percent of students	Avg. score	Percentages at or above *Basic*	Percentages at or above *Proficient*	Percent at *Advanced*
Race/Ethnicity					
White	73	160	77	40	1
Black	14	125	29	8	#
Hispanic	8	136	45	14	#
Asian	1	‡	‡	‡	‡
American Indian/Alaska Native	#	‡	‡	‡	‡
Native Hawaiian/Pacific Islander	#	‡	‡	‡	‡
Two or more races	4	148	61	26	#
Gender					
Male	50	157	71	38	2
Female	50	149	63	27	#
National School Lunch Program					
Eligible	44	139	50	18	#
Not eligible	56	164	81	44	2

Rounds to zero. ‡ Reporting standards not met.

NOTE: Detail may not sum to totals because of rounding, and because the "Information not available" category for the National School Lunch Program, which provides free/reduced-price lunches, is not displayed. Black includes African American and Hispanic includes Latino. Race categories exclude Hispanic origin.

Score Gaps for Student Groups

- In 2011, Black students had an average score that was 36 points lower than White students. This performance gap was not significantly different from that in 2009 (33 points).
- In 2011, Hispanic students had an average score that was 25 points lower than White students. This performance gap was not significantly different from that in 2009 (24 points).
- In 2011, male students in Indiana had an average score that was higher than female students by 7 points.
- In 2011, students who were eligible for free/reduced-price school lunch, an indicator of low family income, had an average score that was 25 points lower than students who were not eligible for free/reduced-price school lunch. This performance gap was not significantly different from that in 2009 (26 points).

NOTE: Statistical comparisons are calculated on the basis of unrounded scale scores or percentages.
SOURCE: U.S. Department of Education, Institute of Education Sciences, National Center for Education Statistics, National Assessment of Educational Progress (NAEP), 2009 and 2011 Science Assessments.

The Nation's Report Card

State Writing 2002 — Snapshot Report

Indiana — Grade 4 — Public School

NCES 2003-532IN4

The writing assessment of the National Assessment of Educational Progress (NAEP) measures narrative, informative, and persuasive writing–three purposes identified in the NAEP framework. The NAEP writing scale ranges from 0 to 300.

Overall Writing Results for Indiana

- The average scale score for fourth-grade students in Indiana was 154.
- Indiana's average score (154) was not found to be significantly different[1] from that of the nation's public schools (153).
- Students' average scale scores in Indiana were higher than those in 24 jurisdictions[2], not significantly different from those in 16 jurisdictions, and lower than those in 7 jurisdictions.
- The percentage of students who performed at or above the NAEP *Proficient* level was 26 percent. The percentage of students who performed at or above the *Basic* level was 88 percent.

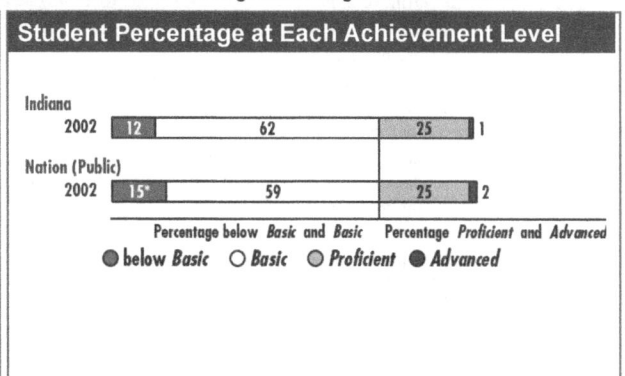

Student Percentage at Each Achievement Level

Indiana 2002: 12 | 62 | 25 | 1
Nation (Public) 2002: 15* | 59 | 25 | 2

Percentage below *Basic* and *Basic* — Percentage *Proficient* and *Advanced*
● below *Basic*   ○ *Basic*   ○ *Proficient*   ● *Advanced*

Performance of NAEP Reporting Groups in Indiana

Reporting groups	Percentage of students	Average Score	Below *Basic*	*Basic*	*Proficient*	*Advanced*
Male	50	144	18	65	16	#
Female	50	163	7 ↓	58	33	3
White	80	157 ↓	11	61 ↑	27	2 ↓
Black	13	138	22	66	11	#
Hispanic	4	144	21	62	17	#
Asian/Pacific Islander	1	---	---	---	---	---
American Indian/Alaska Native	1	---	---	---	---	---
Free/reduced-priced school lunch						
Eligible	33	141	21	65	14	#
Not eligible	60	160 ↓	9	60 ↑	29 ↓	2 ↓
Information not available	7	167 ↑	6 ↓	55	37	2

Average Score Gaps Between Selected Groups

- Female students in Indiana had an average score that was higher than that of male students (19 points). This performance gap was not significantly different from that of the Nation (18 points).
- White students had an average score that was higher than that of Black students (18 points). This performance gap was not significantly different from that of the Nation (20 points).
- White students had an average score that was higher than that of Hispanic students (13 points). This performance gap was not significantly different from that of the Nation (19 points).
- Students who were not eligible for free/reduced-price school lunch had an average score that was higher than that of students who were eligible (18 points). This performance gap was not significantly different from that of the Nation (22 points).

Writing Scale Scores at Selected Percentiles

Scale Score Distribution

	25th Percentile	50th Percentile	75th Percentile
Indiana	131 ↑	154	177
Nation (Public)	128	153	178

An examination of scores at different percentiles on the 0-300 NAEP writing scale at each grade indicates how well students at lower, middle, and higher levels of the distribution performed. For example, the data above shows that 75 percent of students in public schools nationally scored below *178*, while 75 percent of students in Indiana scored below *177*.

\# Percentage rounds to zero.   --- Reporting standards not met; sample size insufficient to permit a reliable estimate.
* Significantly different from Indiana.   ↑ Significantly higher than, ↓ lower than appropriate subgroup in the nation (public).
[1] Comparisons (higher/lower/not different) are based on statistical tests. The .05 level was used for testing statistical significance.
[2] "Jurisdictions" includes participating states and other jurisdictions (such as Guam or the District of Columbia).
NOTE: Detail may not sum to totals because of rounding. Score gaps are calculated based on differences between unrounded average scale scores.
Visit http://nces.ed.gov/nationsreportcard/states/ for additional results and detailed information.
SOURCE: U.S. Department of Education, Institute of Education Sciences, National Center for Education Statistics, National Assessment of Educational Progress (NAEP), 2002 Writing Assessment.

Writing 2007 State Snapshot Report

Indiana
Grade 8
Public Schools

NCES 2008-470IN8

The National Assessment of Educational Progress (NAEP) assesses writing for three purposes identified in the NAEP framework: narrative, informative, and persuasive. The NAEP writing scale ranges from 0 to 300.

Overall Writing Results for Indiana

- In 2007, the average scale score for eighth-grade students in Indiana was 155. This was higher than their average score in 2002 (150).[1]
- Indiana's average score (155) in 2007 was not significantly different from that of the nation's public schools (154).
- Of the 45 states and one other jurisdiction that participated in the 2007 eighth-grade assessment, students' average scale score in Indiana was higher than those in 13 jurisdictions, not significantly different from those in 21 jurisdictions, and lower than those in 11 jurisdictions.[2]
- The percentage of students in Indiana who performed at or above the NAEP *Proficient* level was 30 percent in 2007. This percentage was not significantly different from that in 2002 (26 percent).
- The percentage of students in Indiana who performed at or above the NAEP *Basic* level was 89 percent in 2007. This percentage was greater than that in 2002 (85 percent).

Percentages at NAEP Achievement Levels and Average Score

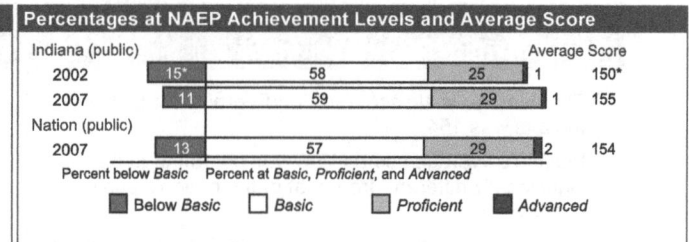

Indiana (public)
- 2002: 15* | 58 | 25 | 1 — Average Score 150*
- 2007: 11 | 59 | 29 | 1 — 155

Nation (public)
- 2007: 13 | 57 | 29 | 2 — 154

Percent below *Basic* | Percent at *Basic*, *Proficient*, and *Advanced*

■ Below *Basic* □ *Basic* ▨ *Proficient* ■ *Advanced*

NOTE: The NAEP grade 8 writing achievement levels correspond to the following scale points: Below *Basic*, 113 or lower; *Basic*, 114–172; *Proficient*, 173–223; *Advanced*, 224 or above.

Performance of NAEP Reporting Groups in Indiana: 2007

Reporting groups	Percent of students	Average score	Percent below *Basic*	Percent of students at or above *Basic*	Percent of students at or above *Proficient*	Percent *Advanced*
Male	50	144↑	16↓	84↑	17	#
Female	50	165	5	95	42	1
White	78↓	158↑	9↓	91↑	33	1
Black	12	140↑	18↓	82↑	12	#
Hispanic	6↑	139	22	78	18	#
Asian/Pacific Islander	1	‡	‡	‡	‡	‡
American Indian/Alaska Native	#	‡	‡	‡	‡	‡
Eligible for National School Lunch Program	35↑	142	18	82	17	#
Not eligible for National School Lunch Program	65	161↑	7↓	93↑	37	1

Average Score Gaps Between Selected Groups

- In 2007, male students in Indiana had an average score that was lower than that of female students by 22 points. This performance gap was not significantly different from that of 2002 (24 points).
- In 2007, Black students had an average score that was lower than that of White students by 18 points. This performance gap was not significantly different from that of 2002 (27 points).
- In 2007, Hispanic students had an average score that was lower than that of White students by 19 points. Data are not reported for Hispanic students in 2002, because reporting standards were not met. Therefore, the performance gap results are not reported.
- In 2007, students who were eligible for free/reduced-price school lunch, an indicator of poverty, had an average score that was lower than that of students who were not eligible for free/reduced-price school lunch by 19 points. This performance gap was not significantly different from that of 2002 (17 points).
- In 2007, the score gap between students at the 75th percentile and students at the 25th percentile was 42 points. This performance gap was not significantly different from that of 2002 (47 points).

Writing Scores at Selected Percentiles in Indiana

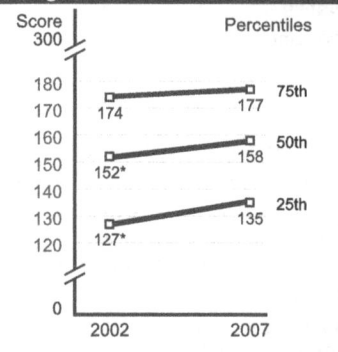

Percentile	2002	2007
75th	174	177
50th	152*	158
25th	127*	135

NOTE: Scores at selected percentiles on the NAEP writing scale indicate how well students at lower, middle, and higher levels performed.

\# Rounds to zero.
‡ Reporting standards not met.
* Significantly different from 2007.
↑ Significantly higher than 2002. ↓ Significantly lower than 2002.

[1] Comparisons (higher/lower/narrower/wider/not different) are based on statistical tests. The .05 level with appropriate adjustments for multiple comparisons was used for testing statistical significance. Statistical comparisons are calculated on the basis of unrounded scale scores or percentages. Comparisons across jurisdictions and comparisons with the nation or within a jurisdiction across years may be affected by differences in exclusion rates for students with disabilities (SD) and English language learners (ELL). The exclusion rates for SD and ELL in Indiana were 3 percent and 1 percent in 2007, respectively. For more information on NAEP significance testing, see http://nces.ed.gov/nationsreportcard/writing/interpret-results.asp#statistical.
[2] "Jurisdiction" refers to states, the District of Columbia, and the Department of Defense Education Activity schools.

NOTE: Detail may not sum to totals because of rounding and because the "Information not available" category for the National School Lunch Program, which provides free and reduced-price lunches, and the "Unclassified" category for race/ethnicity are not displayed. Visit http://nces.ed.gov/nationsreportcard/states/ for additional results and detailed information.

SOURCE: U.S. Department of Education, Institute of Education Sciences, National Center for Education Statistics, National Assessment of Educational Progress (NAEP), 2002 and 2007 Writing Assessments.

ISTEP+ Historical Statewide Results
English/Language Arts

Statewide	2013-14 ELA Pass N	2013-14 ELA Pass %	2012-13 ELA Pass N	2012-13 ELA Pass %	2011-12 ELA Pass N	2011-12 ELA Pass %	2010-11 ELA Pass N	2010-11 ELA Pass %
Grade 3	68130	83.6%	70375	85.2%	68818	86.2%	68375	84.2%
Grade 4	69649	86.5%	65569	84.4%	65795	82.4%	69345	82.7%
Grade 5	63982	81.5%	63280	79.3%	64963	78.4%	62049	76.3%
Grade 6	63162	78.7%	64492	77.8%	63647	78.7%	61571	76.7%
Grade 7	65065	77.8%	60314	74.2%	60772	76.3%	62657	78.1%
Grade 8	62335	76.4%	60945	76.3%	58927	74.2%	58871	73.6%
Grand Total	392323	80.7%	384975	79.5%	382922	79.4%	382868	78.7%

Public	2013-14 ELA Pass N	2013-14 ELA Pass %	2012-13 ELA Pass N	2012-13 ELA Pass %	2011-12 ELA Pass N	2011-12 ELA Pass %	2010-11 ELA Pass N	2010-11 ELA Pass %
Grade 3	61990	83.0%	64378	84.7%	63129	85.5%	63060	83.5%
Grade 4	63464	86.0%	59947	83.9%	60235	81.6%	64100	82.0%
Grade 5	58306	80.9%	57776	78.6%	59542	77.5%	57149	75.3%
Grade 6	57716	78.0%	59117	77.1%	58484	77.8%	56895	75.8%
Grade 7	59617	76.9%	55308	73.3%	56044	75.3%	58115	77.2%
Grade 8	57283	75.5%	56112	75.4%	54228	73.1%	54323	72.4%
Grand Total	358376	80.0%	352638	78.8%	351662	78.5%	353642	77.7%

Non-Public	2013-14 ELA Pass N	2013-14 ELA Pass %	2012-13 ELA Pass N	2012-13 ELA Pass %	2011-12 ELA Pass N	2011-12 ELA Pass %	2010-11 ELA Pass N	2010-11 ELA Pass %
Grade 3	6140	89.6%	5996	92.0%	5688	94.3%	5315	94.2%
Grade 4	6180	91.2%	5622	89.8%	5560	92.0%	5244	92.6%
Grade 5	5674	88.1%	5504	87.3%	5421	89.5%	4900	89.9%
Grade 6	5444	87.0%	5375	86.5%	5162	90.5%	4676	91.2%
Grade 7	5447	89.1%	5006	86.7%	4727	90.8%	4541	93.0%
Grade 8	5052	87.8%	4832	88.9%	4697	89.8%	4548	91.6%
Grand Total	33937	88.8%	32335	88.6%	31255	91.2%	29224	92.1%

Source: Indiana Department of Education

ISTEP+ Historical Statewide Results
Mathematics

Statewide	2013-14 Math Pass N	2013-14 Math Pass %	2012-13 Math Pass N	2012-13 Math Pass %	2011-12 Math Pass N	2011-12 Math Pass %	2010-11 Math Pass N	2010-11 Math Pass %
Grade 3	66224	80.8%	66455	80.2%	63959	79.6%	64748	79.4%
Grade 4	67195	83.0%	65378	83.9%	63490	79.1%	66731	79.3%
Grade 5	70478	89.3%	69644	87.0%	71792	86.2%	70729	86.6%
Grade 6	69197	85.8%	70118	84.2%	67536	83.0%	65470	81.1%
Grade 7	67763	80.5%	66273	81.2%	63315	79.0%	60972	76.1%
Grade 8	67209	81.9%	65187	81.3%	63922	80.1%	62407	77.8%
Grand Total	408066	83.5%	403055	83.0%	394014	81.2%	391057	80.1%

Public	2013-14 Math Pass N	2013-14 Math Pass %	2012-13 Math Pass N	2012-13 Math Pass %	2011-12 Math Pass N	2011-12 Math Pass %	2010-11 Math Pass N	2010-11 Math Pass %
Grade 3	60297	80.3%	60797	79.7%	58690	78.9%	59616	78.5%
Grade 4	61309	82.7%	59899	83.6%	58308	78.5%	61725	78.6%
Grade 5	64554	89.1%	63870	86.7%	66221	85.8%	65636	86.1%
Grade 6	63458	85.3%	64560	83.8%	62306	82.4%	60757	80.3%
Grade 7	62397	80.0%	61167	80.7%	58635	78.3%	56560	75.2%
Grade 8	62101	81.4%	60374	80.8%	59240	79.4%	57913	77.0%
Grand Total	374116	83.1%	370667	82.5%	363400	80.6%	362207	79.3%

Non-Public	2013-14 Math Pass N	2013-14 Math Pass %	2012-13 Math Pass N	2012-13 Math Pass %	2011-12 Math Pass N	2011-12 Math Pass %	2010-11 Math Pass N	2010-11 Math Pass %
Grade 3	5927	86.2%	5658	86.6%	5268	87.1%	5132	90.8%
Grade 4	5883	86.8%	5479	87.4%	5182	85.6%	5004	88.3%
Grade 5	5922	91.9%	5774	91.3%	5571	91.8%	5093	93.3%
Grade 6	5738	91.7%	5557	89.6%	5229	91.5%	4713	91.7%
Grade 7	5365	87.6%	5106	88.4%	4679	89.7%	4411	90.1%
Grade 8	5108	88.5%	4813	88.9%	4681	89.3%	4494	90.6%
Grand Total	33943	88.7%	32387	88.7%	30610	89.1%	28847	90.8%

Source: Indiana Department of Education

ISTEP+ Historical Statewide Results
Science

Statewide	2013-14 Science Pass N	2013-14 Science Pass %	2012-13 Science Pass N	2012-13 Science Pass %	2011-12 Science Pass N	2011-12 Science Pass %	2010-11 Science Pass N	2010-11 Science Pass %
Grade 4	60614	74.9%	57420	73.6%	63320	78.9%	65111	77.3%
Grade 6	55487	68.9%	56826	68.3%	52979	65.2%	50858	63.0%
Grand Total	116101	71.9%	114246	70.8%	116299	72.0%	115969	70.3%

Public	2013-14 Science Pass N	2013-14 Science Pass %	2012-13 Science Pass N	2012-13 Science Pass %	2011-12 Science Pass N	2011-12 Science Pass %	2010-11 Science Pass N	2010-11 Science Pass %
Grade 4	54953	74.1%	52288	72.9%	57883	78.1%	59972	76.4%
Grade 6	50612	68.2%	52028	67.6%	48386	64.1%	46645	61.7%
Grand Total	105565	71.2%	104316	70.1%	106269	71.0%	106617	69.2%

Non-Public	2013-14 Science Pass N	2013-14 Science Pass %	2012-13 Science Pass N	2012-13 Science Pass %	2011-12 Science Pass N	2011-12 Science Pass %	2010-11 Science Pass N	2010-11 Science Pass %
Grade 4	5660	83.5%	5132	81.7%	5437	89.7%	5138	90.7%
Grade 6	4874	77.7%	4798	77.2%	4593	80.4%	4213	82.0%
Grand Total	10534	80.7%	9930	79.5%	10030	85.2%	9351	86.5%

Source: Indiana Department of Education

ISTEP+ Historical Statewide Results
Social Studies

Statewide	2013-14 Social Studies Pass N	2013-14 Social Studies Pass %	2012-13 Social Studies Pass N	2012-13 Social Studies Pass %	2011-12 Social Studies Pass N	2011-12 Social Studies Pass %	2010-11 Social Studies Pass N	2010-11 Social Studies Pass %
Grade 5	56227	71.4%	57229	71.5%	56958	68.5%	55772	68.3%
Grade 7	61420	73.2%	59330	72.8%	57520	72.1%	55300	69.0%
Grand Total	117647	72.4%	116559	72.1%	114478	70.3%	111072	68.6%

Public	2013-14 Social Studies Pass N	2013-14 Social Studies Pass %	2012-13 Social Studies Pass N	2012-13 Social Studies Pass %	2011-12 Social Studies Pass N	2011-12 Social Studies Pass %	2010-11 Social Studies Pass N	2010-11 Social Studies Pass %
Grade 5	50811	70.3%	51854	70.3%	51751	67.1%	51003	67.0%
Grade 7	56204	72.3%	54435	71.9%	53012	71.1%	51007	67.8%
Grand Total	107015	71.3%	106289	71.1%	104763	69.1%	102010	67.4%

Non-Public	2013-14 Social Studies Pass N	2013-14 Social Studies Pass %	2012-13 Social Studies Pass N	2012-13 Social Studies Pass %	2011-12 Social Studies Pass N	2011-12 Social Studies Pass %	2010-11 Social Studies Pass N	2010-11 Social Studies Pass %
Grade 5	5416	84.0%	5375	85.1%	5207	85.8%	4769	87.3%
Grade 7	5216	85.2%	4895	84.7%	4507	86.5%	4292	87.6%
Grand Total	10632	84.6%	10270	84.9%	9714	86.1%	9061	87.5%

Source: Indiana Department of Education

Ancestry and Ethnicity

State Profile

Population: 6,483,802

Ancestry	Population	%
Afghan (242)	261	<0.01
African, Sub-Saharan (65,151)	79,021	1.23
African (56,028)	68,814	1.07
Cape Verdean (9)	28	<0.01
Ethiopian (1,265)	1,431	0.02
Ghanaian (303)	322	0.01
Kenyan (647)	663	0.01
Liberian (732)	771	0.01
Nigerian (3,000)	3,311	0.05
Senegalese (179)	193	0.01
Sierra Leonean (0)	41	<0.01
Somalian (586)	626	0.01
South African (376)	600	0.01
Sudanese (422)	433	0.01
Ugandan (69)	109	<0.01
Zimbabwean (149)	162	<0.01
Other Sub-Saharan African (1,386)	1,517	0.02
Albanian (458)	703	0.01
Alsatian (82)	300	<0.01
American (644,285)	644,285	10.04
Arab (10,118)	15,838	0.25
Arab (2,653)	3,625	0.06
Egyptian (1,080)	1,376	0.02
Iraqi (304)	594	0.01
Jordanian (521)	596	0.01
Lebanese (2,109)	4,417	0.07
Moroccan (406)	571	0.01
Palestinian (774)	885	0.01
Syrian (839)	2,104	0.03
Other Arab (1,432)	1,670	0.03
Armenian (479)	1,080	0.02
Assyrian/Chaldean/Syriac (199)	453	0.01
Australian (687)	1,313	0.02
Austrian (2,431)	9,059	0.14
Basque (3)	81	<0.01
Belgian (4,026)	13,481	0.21
Brazilian (1,192)	1,706	0.03
British (10,920)	23,647	0.37
Bulgarian (676)	1,359	0.02
Cajun (301)	666	0.01
Canadian (4,537)	9,085	0.14
Carpatho Rusyn (24)	62	<0.01
Celtic (252)	636	0.01
Croatian (4,180)	13,306	0.21
Cypriot (88)	88	<0.01
Czech (4,832)	18,523	0.29
Czechoslovakian (2,305)	5,115	0.08
Danish (3,532)	13,281	0.21
Dutch (37,596)	144,391	2.25
Eastern European (2,179)	2,605	0.04
English (248,297)	623,154	9.71
Estonian (51)	365	0.01
European (51,753)	58,511	0.91
Finnish (1,411)	5,241	0.08
French, ex. Basque (34,177)	167,332	2.61
French Canadian (6,999)	17,621	0.27
German (740,501)	1,692,418	26.37
German Russian (34)	194	<0.01
Greek (11,608)	23,572	0.37
Guyanese (81)	158	<0.01
Hungarian (12,566)	38,908	0.61
Icelander (146)	292	<0.01
Iranian (1,687)	2,332	0.04
Irish (234,713)	827,853	12.90
Israeli (343)	483	0.01
Italian (64,626)	185,128	2.88
Latvian (814)	1,490	0.02
Lithuanian (4,371)	11,699	0.18
Luxemburger (94)	591	0.01
Macedonian (3,873)	5,064	0.08
Maltese (43)	197	<0.01
New Zealander (221)	318	<0.01
Northern European (3,042)	3,363	0.05
Norwegian (10,599)	36,566	0.57
Pennsylvania German (10,066)	13,018	0.20
Polish (76,354)	210,729	3.28
Portuguese (1,567)	4,720	0.07
Romanian (4,190)	8,644	0.13
Russian (9,274)	25,824	0.40
Scandinavian (2,637)	6,406	0.10
Scotch-Irish (38,900)	95,439	1.49
Scottish (42,470)	123,773	1.93
Serbian (6,179)	11,326	0.18
Slavic (922)	2,352	0.04
Slovak (7,358)	21,051	0.33
Slovene (996)	2,873	0.04
Soviet Union (0)	0	<0.01
Swedish (16,589)	65,409	1.02
Swiss (14,649)	44,777	0.70
Turkish (1,124)	1,592	0.02
Ukrainian (4,411)	9,005	0.14
Welsh (9,294)	38,925	0.61
West Indian, ex. Hispanic (3,921)	6,151	0.10
Bahamian (68)	109	<0.01
Barbadian (41)	97	<0.01
Belizean (79)	147	<0.01
Bermudan (42)	42	<0.01
British West Indian (212)	347	0.01
Dutch West Indian (51)	294	<0.01
Haitian (1,290)	1,721	0.03
Jamaican (1,605)	2,228	0.03
Trinidadian/Tobagonian (156)	233	<0.01
U.S. Virgin Islander (8)	8	<0.01
West Indian (290)	804	0.01
Other West Indian (79)	121	<0.01
Yugoslavian (4,274)	6,328	0.10

Hispanic Origin	Population	%
Hispanic or Latino (of any race)	389,707	6.01
Central American, ex. Mexican	22,093	0.34
Costa Rican	592	0.01
Guatemalan	5,933	0.09
Honduran	5,345	0.08
Nicaraguan	1,431	0.02
Panamanian	1,218	0.02
Salvadoran	7,401	0.11
Other Central American	173	<0.01
Cuban	4,042	0.06
Dominican Republic	2,340	0.04
Mexican	295,373	4.56
Puerto Rican	30,304	0.47
South American	10,032	0.15
Argentinean	1,027	0.02
Bolivian	425	0.01
Chilean	647	0.01
Colombian	2,854	0.04
Ecuadorian	1,092	0.02
Paraguayan	88	<0.01
Peruvian	2,225	0.03
Uruguayan	150	<0.01
Venezuelan	1,440	0.02
Other South American	84	<0.01
Other Hispanic or Latino	25,523	0.39

Race*	Population	%
African-American/Black (591,397)	654,415	10.09
Not Hispanic (582,140)	638,353	9.85
Hispanic (9,257)	16,062	0.25
American Indian/Alaska Native (18,462)	49,738	0.77
Not Hispanic (14,165)	41,469	0.64
Hispanic (4,297)	8,269	0.13
Alaska Athabascan (Ala. Nat.) (23)	36	<0.01
Aleut (Alaska Native) (40)	55	<0.01
Apache (277)	824	0.01
Arapaho (20)	43	<0.01
Blackfeet (375)	2,065	0.03
Canadian/French Am. Ind. (101)	248	<0.01
Central American Ind. (87)	152	<0.01
Cherokee (3,036)	12,583	0.19
Cheyenne (43)	157	<0.01
Chickasaw (83)	195	<0.01
Chippewa (618)	1,208	0.02
Choctaw (323)	852	0.01
Colville (11)	14	<0.01
Comanche (64)	142	<0.01
Cree (38)	115	<0.01
Creek (186)	375	0.01
Crow (36)	122	<0.01
Delaware (77)	196	<0.01
Hopi (20)	60	<0.01
Houma (29)	43	<0.01
Inupiat (Alaska Native) (42)	95	<0.01
Iroquois (255)	640	0.01
Kiowa (24)	35	<0.01
Lumbee (101)	189	<0.01
Menominee (40)	71	<0.01
Mexican American Ind. (938)	1,441	0.02
Navajo (230)	547	0.01
Osage (39)	114	<0.01
Ottawa (82)	164	<0.01
Paiute (18)	36	<0.01
Pima (12)	24	<0.01
Potawatomi (368)	724	0.01
Pueblo (62)	132	<0.01
Puget Sound Salish (13)	19	<0.01
Seminole (27)	149	<0.01
Shoshone (26)	75	<0.01
Sioux (508)	1,340	0.02
South American Ind. (99)	257	<0.01
Spanish American Ind. (91)	137	<0.01
Tlingit-Haida (Alaska Native) (43)	65	<0.01
Tohono O'Odham (11)	26	<0.01
Tsimshian (Alaska Native) (3)	5	<0.01
Ute (33)	56	<0.01
Yakama (5)	7	<0.01
Yaqui (22)	50	<0.01
Yuman (8)	13	<0.01
Yup'ik (Alaska Native) (21)	29	<0.01
Asian (102,474)	126,750	1.95
Not Hispanic (101,444)	123,750	1.91
Hispanic (1,030)	3,000	0.05
Bangladeshi (480)	539	0.01
Bhutanese (1)	3	<0.01
Burmese (7,523)	7,868	0.12
Cambodian (816)	1,019	0.02
Chinese, ex. Taiwanese (21,100)	24,468	0.38
Filipino (10,652)	16,988	0.26
Hmong (175)	218	<0.01
Indian (27,598)	30,947	0.48
Indonesian (547)	823	0.01
Japanese (4,896)	8,437	0.13
Korean (10,322)	13,685	0.21
Laotian (1,129)	1,466	0.02
Malaysian (332)	471	0.01
Nepalese (253)	278	<0.01
Pakistani (2,685)	3,098	0.05
Sri Lankan (331)	372	0.01
Taiwanese (1,387)	1,646	0.03
Thai (1,432)	2,176	0.03
Vietnamese (6,845)	8,175	0.13
Hawaii Native/Pacific Islander (2,348)	6,385	0.10
Not Hispanic (1,853)	5,116	0.08
Hispanic (495)	1,269	0.02
Fijian (15)	35	<0.01
Guamanian/Chamorro (636)	1,113	0.02
Marshallese (71)	82	<0.01
Native Hawaiian (728)	2,223	0.03
Samoan (326)	830	0.01
Tongan (60)	114	<0.01
White (5,467,906)	5,583,367	86.11
Not Hispanic (5,286,453)	5,377,916	82.94
Hispanic (181,453)	205,451	3.17

Notes: † The Census 2010 population figure is used to calculate the percentages in the Hispanic Origin and Race categories. Ancestry percentages are based on the 2006-2010 American Community Survey population (not shown); ‡ Numbers in parentheses indicate the number of people reporting a single ancestry; * Numbers in parentheses indicate the number of persons reporting this race alone, not in combination with any other race; Please refer to the Explanation of Data for more information.

County Profiles

Adams County
Population: 34,387

Ancestry	Population	%
Afghan (0)	0	<0.01
African, Sub-Saharan (0)	2	0.01
African (0)	2	0.01
Cape Verdean (0)	0	<0.01
Ethiopian (0)	0	<0.01
Ghanaian (0)	0	<0.01
Kenyan (0)	0	<0.01
Liberian (0)	0	<0.01
Nigerian (0)	0	<0.01
Senegalese (0)	0	<0.01
Sierra Leonean (0)	0	<0.01
Somalian (0)	0	<0.01
South African (0)	0	<0.01
Sudanese (0)	0	<0.01
Ugandan (0)	0	<0.01
Zimbabwean (0)	0	<0.01
Other Sub-Saharan African (0)	0	<0.01
Albanian (0)	0	<0.01
Alsatian (0)	0	<0.01
American (2,706)	2,706	7.92
Arab (67)	67	0.20
Arab (40)	40	0.12
Egyptian (0)	0	<0.01
Iraqi (0)	0	<0.01
Jordanian (0)	0	<0.01
Lebanese (0)	0	<0.01
Moroccan (0)	0	<0.01
Palestinian (0)	0	<0.01
Syrian (0)	0	<0.01
Other Arab (27)	27	0.08
Armenian (0)	0	<0.01
Assyrian/Chaldean/Syriac (0)	0	<0.01
Australian (0)	0	<0.01
Austrian (0)	0	<0.01
Basque (0)	0	<0.01
Belgian (0)	6	0.02
Brazilian (0)	0	<0.01
British (30)	120	0.35
Bulgarian (0)	0	<0.01
Cajun (0)	0	<0.01
Canadian (0)	0	<0.01
Carpatho Rusyn (0)	0	<0.01
Celtic (0)	0	<0.01
Croatian (0)	0	<0.01
Cypriot (0)	0	<0.01
Czech (22)	85	0.25
Czechoslovakian (0)	0	<0.01
Danish (9)	13	0.04
Dutch (124)	414	1.21
Eastern European (0)	0	<0.01
English (876)	2,362	6.91
Estonian (0)	0	<0.01
European (151)	179	0.52
Finnish (0)	0	<0.01
French, ex. Basque (151)	869	2.54
French Canadian (8)	15	0.04
German (8,189)	14,656	42.90
German Russian (0)	0	<0.01
Greek (0)	0	<0.01
Guyanese (0)	0	<0.01
Hungarian (0)	112	0.33
Icelander (0)	0	<0.01
Iranian (0)	0	<0.01
Irish (747)	2,818	8.25
Israeli (0)	0	<0.01
Italian (97)	295	0.86
Latvian (0)	0	<0.01
Lithuanian (0)	21	0.06
Luxemburger (0)	0	<0.01
Macedonian (0)	0	<0.01
Maltese (0)	0	<0.01
New Zealander (0)	0	<0.01
Northern European (0)	0	<0.01
Norwegian (17)	132	0.39
Pennsylvania German (355)	422	1.24
Polish (153)	288	0.84
Portuguese (0)	19	0.06
Romanian (0)	13	0.04
Russian (11)	19	0.06
Scandinavian (12)	12	0.04
Scotch-Irish (95)	297	0.87
Scottish (177)	298	0.87
Serbian (0)	4	0.01
Slavic (0)	0	<0.01
Slovak (0)	0	<0.01
Slovene (0)	0	<0.01
Soviet Union (0)	0	<0.01
Swedish (73)	184	0.54
Swiss (2,133)	4,826	14.13
Turkish (0)	0	<0.01
Ukrainian (0)	0	<0.01
Welsh (5)	32	0.09
West Indian, ex. Hispanic (0)	0	<0.01
Bahamian (0)	0	<0.01
Barbadian (0)	0	<0.01
Belizean (0)	0	<0.01
Bermudan (0)	0	<0.01
British West Indian (0)	0	<0.01
Dutch West Indian (0)	0	<0.01
Haitian (0)	0	<0.01
Jamaican (0)	0	<0.01
Trinidadian/Tobagonian (0)	0	<0.01
U.S. Virgin Islander (0)	0	<0.01
West Indian (0)	0	<0.01
Other West Indian (0)	0	<0.01
Yugoslavian (0)	19	0.06

Hispanic Origin	Population	%
Hispanic or Latino (of any race)	1,412	4.11
Central American, ex. Mexican	27	0.08
Costa Rican	2	0.01
Guatemalan	8	0.02
Honduran	7	0.02
Nicaraguan	3	0.01
Panamanian	0	<0.01
Salvadoran	7	0.02
Other Central American	0	<0.01
Cuban	1	<0.01
Dominican Republic	1	<0.01
Mexican	1,229	3.57
Puerto Rican	36	0.10
South American	5	0.01
Argentinean	0	<0.01
Bolivian	0	<0.01
Chilean	0	<0.01
Colombian	2	0.01
Ecuadorian	1	<0.01
Paraguayan	0	<0.01
Peruvian	2	0.01
Uruguayan	0	<0.01
Venezuelan	0	<0.01
Other South American	0	<0.01
Other Hispanic or Latino	113	0.33

Race*	Population	%
African-American/Black (107)	190	0.55
Not Hispanic (102)	171	0.50
Hispanic (5)	19	0.06
American Indian/Alaska Native (71)	160	0.47
Not Hispanic (60)	139	0.40
Hispanic (11)	21	0.06
Alaska Athabascan (Ala. Nat.) (0)	0	<0.01
Aleut (Alaska Native) (0)	0	<0.01
Apache (1)	1	<0.01
Arapaho (0)	0	<0.01
Blackfeet (1)	11	0.03
Canadian/French Am. Ind. (0)	0	<0.01
Central American Ind. (0)	0	<0.01
Cherokee (13)	38	0.11
Cheyenne (0)	2	0.01
Chickasaw (0)	0	<0.01
Chippewa (0)	1	<0.01
Choctaw (0)	0	<0.01
Colville (0)	0	<0.01
Comanche (0)	0	<0.01
Cree (0)	0	<0.01
Creek (1)	2	0.01
Crow (0)	0	<0.01
Delaware (0)	0	<0.01
Hopi (0)	0	<0.01
Houma (0)	0	<0.01
Inupiat (Alaska Native) (0)	0	<0.01
Iroquois (0)	0	<0.01
Kiowa (0)	0	<0.01
Lumbee (1)	4	0.01
Menominee (1)	1	<0.01
Mexican American Ind. (2)	5	0.01
Navajo (0)	1	<0.01
Osage (0)	0	<0.01
Ottawa (6)	8	0.02
Paiute (0)	0	<0.01
Pima (0)	0	<0.01
Potawatomi (0)	0	<0.01
Pueblo (0)	0	<0.01
Puget Sound Salish (0)	0	<0.01
Seminole (0)	0	<0.01
Shoshone (0)	0	<0.01
Sioux (0)	2	0.01
South American Ind. (0)	0	<0.01
Spanish American Ind. (0)	0	<0.01
Tlingit-Haida (Alaska Native) (1)	1	<0.01
Tohono O'Odham (0)	0	<0.01
Tsimshian (Alaska Native) (0)	0	<0.01
Ute (0)	0	<0.01
Yakama (0)	0	<0.01
Yaqui (0)	0	<0.01
Yuman (0)	0	<0.01
Yup'ik (Alaska Native) (0)	0	<0.01
Asian (78)	119	0.35
Not Hispanic (78)	118	0.34
Hispanic (0)	1	<0.01
Bangladeshi (0)	0	<0.01
Bhutanese (0)	0	<0.01
Burmese (0)	0	<0.01
Cambodian (2)	2	0.01
Chinese, ex. Taiwanese (33)	37	0.11
Filipino (8)	11	0.03
Hmong (0)	0	<0.01
Indian (11)	15	0.04
Indonesian (0)	0	<0.01
Japanese (10)	20	0.06
Korean (12)	25	0.07
Laotian (0)	1	<0.01
Malaysian (0)	0	<0.01
Nepalese (0)	0	<0.01
Pakistani (0)	1	<0.01
Sri Lankan (0)	0	<0.01
Taiwanese (0)	0	<0.01
Thai (1)	1	<0.01
Vietnamese (0)	1	<0.01
Hawaii Native/Pacific Islander (7)	16	0.05
Not Hispanic (7)	14	0.04
Hispanic (0)	2	0.01
Fijian (0)	0	<0.01
Guamanian/Chamorro (4)	7	0.02
Marshallese (0)	0	<0.01
Native Hawaiian (2)	3	0.01
Samoan (1)	1	<0.01
Tongan (0)	0	<0.01
White (33,349)	33,642	97.83
Not Hispanic (32,521)	32,712	95.13
Hispanic (828)	930	2.70

Notes: † The Census 2010 population figure is used to calculate the percentages in the Hispanic Origin and Race categories. Ancestry percentages are based on the 2006-2010 American Community Survey population (not shown); ‡ Numbers in parentheses indicate the number of people reporting a single ancestry; * Numbers in parentheses indicate the number of persons reporting this race alone, not in combination with any other race; Please refer to the Explanation of Data for more information.

Allen County
Population: 355,329

Ancestry	Population	%
Afghan (20)	20	0.01
African, Sub-Saharan (13,880)	14,109	4.02
African (13,341)	13,561	3.86
Cape Verdean (0)	0	<0.01
Ethiopian (47)	47	0.01
Ghanaian (0)	0	<0.01
Kenyan (38)	38	0.01
Liberian (0)	0	<0.01
Nigerian (179)	179	0.05
Senegalese (0)	0	<0.01
Sierra Leonean (0)	0	<0.01
Somalian (68)	68	0.02
South African (43)	52	0.01
Sudanese (0)	0	<0.01
Ugandan (0)	0	<0.01
Zimbabwean (0)	0	<0.01
Other Sub-Saharan African (164)	164	0.05
Albanian (33)	33	0.01
Alsatian (8)	8	<0.01
American (37,575)	37,575	10.70
Arab (572)	850	0.24
Arab (207)	222	0.06
Egyptian (25)	79	0.02
Iraqi (44)	54	0.02
Jordanian (10)	10	<0.01
Lebanese (168)	304	0.09
Moroccan (10)	10	<0.01
Palestinian (24)	24	0.01
Syrian (63)	126	0.04
Other Arab (21)	21	0.01
Armenian (81)	111	0.03
Assyrian/Chaldean/Syriac (10)	10	<0.01
Australian (27)	54	0.02
Austrian (180)	417	0.12
Basque (0)	0	<0.01
Belgian (54)	361	0.10
Brazilian (0)	21	0.01
British (497)	1,044	0.30
Bulgarian (204)	240	0.07
Cajun (0)	0	<0.01
Canadian (374)	823	0.23
Carpatho Rusyn (0)	0	<0.01
Celtic (8)	39	0.01
Croatian (161)	285	0.08
Cypriot (0)	0	<0.01
Czech (323)	1,167	0.33
Czechoslovakian (77)	163	0.05
Danish (231)	818	0.23
Dutch (1,406)	5,546	1.58
Eastern European (119)	128	0.04
English (9,653)	28,287	8.05
Estonian (0)	12	<0.01
European (2,248)	2,447	0.70
Finnish (44)	387	0.11
French, ex. Basque (2,975)	14,701	4.18
French Canadian (406)	1,101	0.31
German (58,425)	117,343	33.40
German Russian (0)	0	<0.01
Greek (490)	980	0.28
Guyanese (0)	0	<0.01
Hungarian (461)	1,535	0.44
Icelander (0)	16	<0.01
Iranian (32)	32	0.01
Irish (11,114)	40,071	11.41
Israeli (34)	34	0.01
Italian (3,789)	10,076	2.87
Latvian (70)	86	0.02
Lithuanian (74)	368	0.10
Luxemburger (0)	36	0.01
Macedonian (393)	718	0.20
Maltese (0)	16	<0.01
New Zealander (0)	11	<0.01
Northern European (136)	136	0.04
Norwegian (639)	2,413	0.69
Pennsylvania German (592)	702	0.20
Polish (2,538)	8,297	2.36
Portuguese (175)	337	0.10
Romanian (267)	564	0.16
Russian (555)	1,249	0.36
Scandinavian (227)	562	0.16
Scotch-Irish (1,495)	4,257	1.21
Scottish (1,887)	6,619	1.88
Serbian (0)	93	0.03
Slavic (59)	104	0.03
Slovak (208)	604	0.17
Slovene (34)	71	0.02
Soviet Union (0)	0	<0.01
Swedish (613)	3,110	0.89
Swiss (953)	3,644	1.04
Turkish (46)	46	0.01
Ukrainian (257)	583	0.17
Welsh (366)	1,757	0.50
West Indian, ex. Hispanic (573)	671	0.19
Bahamian (0)	0	<0.01
Barbadian (0)	0	<0.01
Belizean (0)	0	<0.01
Bermudan (0)	0	<0.01
British West Indian (74)	74	0.02
Dutch West Indian (0)	0	<0.01
Haitian (346)	377	0.11
Jamaican (147)	196	0.06
Trinidadian/Tobagonian (0)	0	<0.01
U.S. Virgin Islander (0)	0	<0.01
West Indian (6)	24	0.01
Other West Indian (0)	0	<0.01
Yugoslavian (1,518)	1,589	0.45

Hispanic Origin	Population	%
Hispanic or Latino (of any race)	23,093	6.50
Central American, ex. Mexican	1,489	0.42
Costa Rican	39	0.01
Guatemalan	809	0.23
Honduran	148	0.04
Nicaraguan	42	0.01
Panamanian	56	0.02
Salvadoran	385	0.11
Other Central American	10	<0.01
Cuban	226	0.06
Dominican Republic	86	0.02
Mexican	17,596	4.95
Puerto Rican	1,119	0.31
South American	785	0.22
Argentinean	46	0.01
Bolivian	25	0.01
Chilean	19	0.01
Colombian	299	0.08
Ecuadorian	172	0.05
Paraguayan	6	<0.01
Peruvian	149	0.04
Uruguayan	11	<0.01
Venezuelan	57	0.02
Other South American	1	<0.01
Other Hispanic or Latino	1,792	0.50

Race*	Population	%
African-American/Black (41,618)	47,666	13.41
Not Hispanic (40,998)	46,357	13.05
Hispanic (620)	1,309	0.37
American Indian/Alaska Native (1,246)	3,335	0.94
Not Hispanic (987)	2,735	0.77
Hispanic (259)	600	0.17
Alaska Athabascan (Ala. Nat.) (4)	4	<0.01
Aleut (Alaska Native) (1)	1	<0.01
Apache (19)	51	0.01
Arapaho (2)	3	<0.01
Blackfeet (26)	133	0.04
Canadian/French Am. Ind. (2)	6	<0.01
Central American Ind. (5)	12	<0.01
Cherokee (164)	615	0.17
Cheyenne (2)	8	<0.01
Chickasaw (5)	13	<0.01
Chippewa (46)	87	0.02
Choctaw (22)	68	0.02
Colville (0)	0	<0.01
Comanche (3)	10	<0.01
Cree (1)	9	<0.01
Creek (12)	30	0.01
Crow (1)	12	<0.01
Delaware (1)	12	<0.01
Hopi (2)	7	<0.01
Houma (0)	3	<0.01
Inupiat (Alaska Native) (3)	3	<0.01
Iroquois (32)	61	0.02
Kiowa (3)	3	<0.01
Lumbee (1)	4	<0.01
Menominee (0)	1	<0.01
Mexican American Ind. (59)	88	0.02
Navajo (12)	32	0.01
Osage (3)	6	<0.01
Ottawa (11)	17	<0.01
Paiute (0)	1	<0.01
Pima (4)	7	<0.01
Potawatomi (11)	30	0.01
Pueblo (2)	7	<0.01
Puget Sound Salish (0)	0	<0.01
Seminole (1)	12	<0.01
Shoshone (0)	0	<0.01
Sioux (23)	77	0.02
South American Ind. (4)	10	<0.01
Spanish American Ind. (2)	3	<0.01
Tlingit-Haida (Alaska Native) (2)	5	<0.01
Tohono O'Odham (0)	0	<0.01
Tsimshian (Alaska Native) (0)	0	<0.01
Ute (1)	2	<0.01
Yakama (0)	0	<0.01
Yaqui (4)	7	<0.01
Yuman (0)	0	<0.01
Yup'ik (Alaska Native) (1)	2	<0.01
Asian (9,721)	11,438	3.22
Not Hispanic (9,611)	11,184	3.15
Hispanic (110)	254	0.07
Bangladeshi (45)	48	0.01
Bhutanese (0)	0	<0.01
Burmese (3,676)	3,846	1.08
Cambodian (45)	60	0.02
Chinese, ex. Taiwanese (686)	877	0.25
Filipino (679)	1,066	0.30
Hmong (0)	0	<0.01
Indian (1,560)	1,862	0.52
Indonesian (24)	36	0.01
Japanese (183)	346	0.10
Korean (397)	603	0.17
Laotian (347)	439	0.12
Malaysian (19)	44	0.01
Nepalese (10)	11	<0.01
Pakistani (174)	243	0.07
Sri Lankan (31)	37	0.01
Taiwanese (41)	57	0.02
Thai (154)	235	0.07
Vietnamese (1,014)	1,156	0.33
Hawaii Native/Pacific Islander (189)	454	0.13
Not Hispanic (119)	334	0.09
Hispanic (70)	120	0.03
Fijian (2)	2	<0.01
Guamanian/Chamorro (71)	112	0.03
Marshallese (2)	2	<0.01
Native Hawaiian (61)	162	0.05
Samoan (15)	50	0.01
Tongan (0)	1	<0.01
White (281,653)	291,063	81.91
Not Hispanic (271,789)	279,219	78.58
Hispanic (9,864)	11,844	3.33

Notes: † The Census 2010 population figure is used to calculate the percentages in the Hispanic Origin and Race categories. Ancestry percentages are based on the 2006-2010 American Community Survey population (not shown); ‡ Numbers in parentheses indicate the number of people reporting a single ancestry; * Numbers in parentheses indicate the number of persons reporting this race alone, not in combination with any other race; Please refer to the Explanation of Data for more information.

Bartholomew County
Population: 76,794

Ancestry	Population	%
Afghan (0)	0	<0.01
African, Sub-Saharan (33)	132	0.17
African (5)	34	0.04
Cape Verdean (0)	0	<0.01
Ethiopian (0)	0	<0.01
Ghanaian (10)	10	0.01
Kenyan (0)	0	<0.01
Liberian (0)	0	<0.01
Nigerian (18)	88	0.12
Senegalese (0)	0	<0.01
Sierra Leonean (0)	0	<0.01
Somalian (0)	0	<0.01
South African (0)	0	<0.01
Sudanese (0)	0	<0.01
Ugandan (0)	0	<0.01
Zimbabwean (0)	0	<0.01
Other Sub-Saharan African (0)	0	<0.01
Albanian (0)	0	<0.01
Alsatian (0)	0	<0.01
American (8,145)	8,145	10.74
Arab (59)	109	0.14
Arab (0)	11	0.01
Egyptian (20)	39	0.05
Iraqi (0)	0	<0.01
Jordanian (0)	0	<0.01
Lebanese (0)	20	0.03
Moroccan (39)	39	0.05
Palestinian (0)	0	<0.01
Syrian (0)	0	<0.01
Other Arab (0)	0	<0.01
Armenian (20)	28	0.04
Assyrian/Chaldean/Syriac (0)	0	<0.01
Australian (0)	0	<0.01
Austrian (0)	26	0.03
Basque (0)	0	<0.01
Belgian (9)	20	0.03
Brazilian (23)	23	0.03
British (336)	620	0.82
Bulgarian (0)	8	0.01
Cajun (36)	36	0.05
Canadian (28)	101	0.13
Carpatho Rusyn (0)	0	<0.01
Celtic (0)	0	<0.01
Croatian (86)	124	0.16
Cypriot (0)	0	<0.01
Czech (50)	270	0.36
Czechoslovakian (16)	116	0.15
Danish (81)	313	0.41
Dutch (422)	1,313	1.73
Eastern European (0)	0	<0.01
English (3,715)	9,397	12.39
Estonian (0)	0	<0.01
European (675)	793	1.05
Finnish (30)	61	0.08
French, ex. Basque (511)	1,903	2.51
French Canadian (110)	179	0.24
German (10,414)	21,608	28.49
German Russian (0)	0	<0.01
Greek (73)	129	0.17
Guyanese (0)	0	<0.01
Hungarian (91)	181	0.24
Icelander (0)	0	<0.01
Iranian (0)	0	<0.01
Irish (2,883)	9,281	12.24
Israeli (0)	0	<0.01
Italian (655)	1,675	2.21
Latvian (0)	0	<0.01
Lithuanian (0)	33	0.04
Luxemburger (0)	0	<0.01
Macedonian (0)	8	0.01
Maltese (0)	0	<0.01
New Zealander (0)	0	<0.01
Northern European (17)	17	0.02
Norwegian (138)	656	0.86
Pennsylvania German (42)	54	0.07
Polish (362)	1,523	2.01
Portuguese (13)	13	0.02
Romanian (189)	189	0.25
Russian (43)	221	0.29
Scandinavian (108)	247	0.33
Scotch-Irish (676)	1,789	2.36
Scottish (727)	2,450	3.23
Serbian (0)	11	0.01
Slavic (0)	0	<0.01
Slovak (11)	52	0.07
Slovene (8)	21	0.03
Soviet Union (0)	0	<0.01
Swedish (127)	467	0.62
Swiss (130)	420	0.55
Turkish (0)	0	<0.01
Ukrainian (13)	44	0.06
Welsh (91)	638	0.84
West Indian, ex. Hispanic (42)	53	0.07
Bahamian (0)	0	<0.01
Barbadian (0)	0	<0.01
Belizean (0)	0	<0.01
Bermudan (0)	0	<0.01
British West Indian (0)	0	<0.01
Dutch West Indian (0)	0	<0.01
Haitian (24)	24	0.03
Jamaican (0)	11	0.01
Trinidadian/Tobagonian (0)	0	<0.01
U.S. Virgin Islander (0)	0	<0.01
West Indian (10)	10	0.01
Other West Indian (8)	8	0.01
Yugoslavian (42)	45	0.06

Hispanic Origin	Population	%
Hispanic or Latino (of any race)	4,762	6.20
Central American, ex. Mexican	202	0.26
Costa Rican	5	0.01
Guatemalan	111	0.14
Honduran	32	0.04
Nicaraguan	2	<0.01
Panamanian	5	0.01
Salvadoran	41	0.05
Other Central American	6	0.01
Cuban	21	0.03
Dominican Republic	9	0.01
Mexican	3,985	5.19
Puerto Rican	198	0.26
South American	92	0.12
Argentinean	18	0.02
Bolivian	2	<0.01
Chilean	10	0.01
Colombian	22	0.03
Ecuadorian	10	0.01
Paraguayan	0	<0.01
Peruvian	12	0.02
Uruguayan	3	<0.01
Venezuelan	15	0.02
Other South American	0	<0.01
Other Hispanic or Latino	255	0.33

Race*	Population	%
African-American/Black (1,420)	1,937	2.52
Not Hispanic (1,360)	1,841	2.40
Hispanic (60)	96	0.13
American Indian/Alaska Native (209)	522	0.68
Not Hispanic (145)	417	0.54
Hispanic (64)	105	0.14
Alaska Athabascan (Ala. Nat.) (0)	0	<0.01
Aleut (Alaska Native) (0)	0	<0.01
Apache (2)	9	0.01
Arapaho (1)	1	<0.01
Blackfeet (2)	25	0.03
Canadian/French Am. Ind. (0)	1	<0.01
Central American Ind. (5)	8	0.01
Cherokee (24)	146	0.19
Cheyenne (0)	3	<0.01
Chickasaw (0)	1	<0.01
Chippewa (5)	5	0.01
Choctaw (3)	7	0.01
Colville (0)	0	<0.01
Comanche (0)	0	<0.01
Cree (0)	0	<0.01
Creek (0)	0	<0.01
Crow (0)	1	<0.01
Delaware (0)	1	<0.01
Hopi (1)	1	<0.01
Houma (0)	0	<0.01
Inupiat (Alaska Native) (1)	1	<0.01
Iroquois (2)	4	0.01
Kiowa (0)	0	<0.01
Lumbee (0)	0	<0.01
Menominee (0)	1	<0.01
Mexican American Ind. (10)	19	0.02
Navajo (11)	22	0.03
Osage (0)	0	<0.01
Ottawa (2)	3	<0.01
Paiute (0)	0	<0.01
Pima (0)	0	<0.01
Potawatomi (5)	5	0.01
Pueblo (1)	1	<0.01
Puget Sound Salish (0)	0	<0.01
Seminole (1)	1	<0.01
Shoshone (0)	0	<0.01
Sioux (5)	10	0.01
South American Ind. (0)	1	<0.01
Spanish American Ind. (0)	0	<0.01
Tlingit-Haida (Alaska Native) (0)	0	<0.01
Tohono O'Odham (0)	0	<0.01
Tsimshian (Alaska Native) (0)	0	<0.01
Ute (6)	6	0.01
Yakama (0)	0	<0.01
Yaqui (0)	1	<0.01
Yuman (0)	0	<0.01
Yup'ik (Alaska Native) (0)	0	<0.01
Asian (2,632)	2,846	3.71
Not Hispanic (2,622)	2,814	3.66
Hispanic (10)	32	0.04
Bangladeshi (16)	17	0.02
Bhutanese (0)	0	<0.01
Burmese (0)	0	<0.01
Cambodian (0)	0	<0.01
Chinese, ex. Taiwanese (414)	460	0.60
Filipino (71)	117	0.15
Hmong (4)	4	0.01
Indian (1,379)	1,425	1.86
Indonesian (12)	16	0.02
Japanese (391)	437	0.57
Korean (70)	101	0.13
Laotian (12)	15	0.02
Malaysian (6)	11	0.01
Nepalese (3)	3	<0.01
Pakistani (15)	17	0.02
Sri Lankan (4)	4	0.01
Taiwanese (28)	32	0.04
Thai (15)	28	0.04
Vietnamese (131)	146	0.19
Hawaii Native/Pacific Islander (48)	128	0.17
Not Hispanic (37)	106	0.14
Hispanic (11)	22	0.03
Fijian (0)	0	<0.01
Guamanian/Chamorro (13)	30	0.04
Marshallese (0)	0	<0.01
Native Hawaiian (21)	62	0.08
Samoan (7)	9	0.01
Tongan (1)	2	<0.01
White (68,824)	69,950	91.09
Not Hispanic (66,817)	67,711	88.17
Hispanic (2,007)	2,239	2.92

Notes: † The Census 2010 population figure is used to calculate the percentages in the Hispanic Origin and Race categories. Ancestry percentages are based on the 2006-2010 American Community Survey population (not shown); ‡ Numbers in parentheses indicate the number of people reporting a single ancestry; * Numbers in parentheses indicate the number of persons reporting this race alone, not in combination with any other race; Please refer to the Explanation of Data for more information.

Benton County
Population: 8,854

Ancestry	Population	%
Afghan (0)	0	<0.01
African, Sub-Saharan (7)	7	0.08
African (0)	0	<0.01
Cape Verdean (0)	0	<0.01
Ethiopian (0)	0	<0.01
Ghanaian (0)	0	<0.01
Kenyan (0)	0	<0.01
Liberian (0)	0	<0.01
Nigerian (0)	0	<0.01
Senegalese (0)	0	<0.01
Sierra Leonean (0)	0	<0.01
Somalian (0)	0	<0.01
South African (7)	7	0.08
Sudanese (0)	0	<0.01
Ugandan (0)	0	<0.01
Zimbabwean (0)	0	<0.01
Other Sub-Saharan African (0)	0	<0.01
Albanian (0)	0	<0.01
Alsatian (0)	0	<0.01
American (999)	999	11.33
Arab (0)	0	<0.01
Arab (0)	0	<0.01
Egyptian (0)	0	<0.01
Iraqi (0)	0	<0.01
Jordanian (0)	0	<0.01
Lebanese (0)	0	<0.01
Moroccan (0)	0	<0.01
Palestinian (0)	0	<0.01
Syrian (0)	0	<0.01
Other Arab (0)	0	<0.01
Armenian (0)	0	<0.01
Assyrian/Chaldean/Syriac (0)	0	<0.01
Australian (0)	0	<0.01
Austrian (13)	45	0.51
Basque (0)	0	<0.01
Belgian (0)	4	0.05
Brazilian (0)	0	<0.01
British (7)	22	0.25
Bulgarian (0)	0	<0.01
Cajun (0)	0	<0.01
Canadian (1)	1	0.01
Carpatho Rusyn (0)	0	<0.01
Celtic (0)	0	<0.01
Croatian (0)	0	<0.01
Cypriot (0)	0	<0.01
Czech (0)	9	0.10
Czechoslovakian (0)	0	<0.01
Danish (0)	9	0.10
Dutch (74)	261	2.96
Eastern European (0)	0	<0.01
English (314)	763	8.65
Estonian (0)	0	<0.01
European (44)	62	0.70
Finnish (0)	38	0.43
French, ex. Basque (73)	429	4.86
French Canadian (21)	30	0.34
German (1,188)	2,854	32.36
German Russian (0)	0	<0.01
Greek (16)	16	0.18
Guyanese (0)	0	<0.01
Hungarian (3)	3	0.03
Icelander (0)	0	<0.01
Iranian (0)	0	<0.01
Irish (370)	1,495	16.95
Israeli (0)	0	<0.01
Italian (31)	102	1.16
Latvian (0)	0	<0.01
Lithuanian (5)	8	0.09
Luxemburger (0)	0	<0.01
Macedonian (0)	0	<0.01
Maltese (0)	0	<0.01
New Zealander (0)	0	<0.01
Northern European (0)	0	<0.01
Norwegian (24)	71	0.80
Pennsylvania German (0)	0	<0.01
Polish (67)	189	2.14
Portuguese (0)	0	<0.01
Romanian (0)	0	<0.01
Russian (0)	8	0.09
Scandinavian (22)	34	0.39
Scotch-Irish (41)	158	1.79
Scottish (76)	140	1.59
Serbian (0)	0	<0.01
Slavic (0)	0	<0.01
Slovak (0)	0	<0.01
Slovene (0)	0	<0.01
Soviet Union (0)	0	<0.01
Swedish (70)	149	1.69
Swiss (0)	17	0.19
Turkish (0)	0	<0.01
Ukrainian (0)	0	<0.01
Welsh (0)	15	0.17
West Indian, ex. Hispanic (0)	0	<0.01
Bahamian (0)	0	<0.01
Barbadian (0)	0	<0.01
Belizean (0)	0	<0.01
Bermudan (0)	0	<0.01
British West Indian (0)	0	<0.01
Dutch West Indian (0)	0	<0.01
Haitian (0)	0	<0.01
Jamaican (0)	0	<0.01
Trinidadian/Tobagonian (0)	0	<0.01
U.S. Virgin Islander (0)	0	<0.01
West Indian (0)	0	<0.01
Other West Indian (0)	0	<0.01
Yugoslavian (0)	0	<0.01

Hispanic Origin	Population	%
Hispanic or Latino (of any race)	431	4.87
Central American, ex. Mexican	6	0.07
Costa Rican	0	<0.01
Guatemalan	0	<0.01
Honduran	0	<0.01
Nicaraguan	0	<0.01
Panamanian	0	<0.01
Salvadoran	2	0.02
Other Central American	4	0.05
Cuban	9	0.10
Dominican Republic	0	<0.01
Mexican	378	4.27
Puerto Rican	7	0.08
South American	5	0.06
Argentinean	0	<0.01
Bolivian	0	<0.01
Chilean	4	0.05
Colombian	1	0.01
Ecuadorian	0	<0.01
Paraguayan	0	<0.01
Peruvian	0	<0.01
Uruguayan	0	<0.01
Venezuelan	0	<0.01
Other South American	0	<0.01
Other Hispanic or Latino	26	0.29

Race*	Population	%
African-American/Black (42)	78	0.88
Not Hispanic (36)	64	0.72
Hispanic (6)	14	0.16
American Indian/Alaska Native (11)	38	0.43
Not Hispanic (11)	36	0.41
Hispanic (0)	2	0.02
Alaska Athabascan (Ala. Nat.) (0)	0	<0.01
Aleut (Alaska Native) (0)	0	<0.01
Apache (0)	0	<0.01
Arapaho (0)	0	<0.01
Blackfeet (0)	1	0.01
Canadian/French Am. Ind. (0)	0	<0.01
Central American Ind. (0)	0	<0.01
Cherokee (10)	18	0.20
Cheyenne (0)	0	<0.01
Chickasaw (0)	0	<0.01
Chippewa (0)	0	<0.01
Choctaw (0)	0	<0.01
Colville (0)	0	<0.01
Comanche (0)	0	<0.01
Cree (0)	1	0.01
Creek (0)	0	<0.01
Crow (0)	0	<0.01
Delaware (0)	0	<0.01
Hopi (0)	0	<0.01
Houma (0)	0	<0.01
Inupiat (Alaska Native) (0)	0	<0.01
Iroquois (1)	1	0.01
Kiowa (0)	0	<0.01
Lumbee (0)	0	<0.01
Menominee (0)	0	<0.01
Mexican American Ind. (0)	1	0.01
Navajo (0)	0	<0.01
Osage (0)	0	<0.01
Ottawa (0)	0	<0.01
Paiute (0)	0	<0.01
Pima (0)	0	<0.01
Potawatomi (0)	0	<0.01
Pueblo (0)	0	<0.01
Puget Sound Salish (0)	0	<0.01
Seminole (0)	1	0.01
Shoshone (0)	0	<0.01
Sioux (0)	2	0.02
South American Ind. (0)	0	<0.01
Spanish American Ind. (0)	0	<0.01
Tlingit-Haida (Alaska Native) (0)	0	<0.01
Tohono O'Odham (0)	0	<0.01
Tsimshian (Alaska Native) (0)	0	<0.01
Ute (0)	0	<0.01
Yakama (0)	0	<0.01
Yaqui (0)	0	<0.01
Yuman (0)	0	<0.01
Yup'ik (Alaska Native) (0)	0	<0.01
Asian (15)	22	0.25
Not Hispanic (15)	22	0.25
Hispanic (0)	0	<0.01
Bangladeshi (0)	0	<0.01
Bhutanese (0)	0	<0.01
Burmese (0)	0	<0.01
Cambodian (0)	0	<0.01
Chinese, ex. Taiwanese (7)	7	0.08
Filipino (2)	3	0.03
Hmong (0)	0	<0.01
Indian (4)	9	0.10
Indonesian (0)	0	<0.01
Japanese (0)	0	<0.01
Korean (1)	2	0.02
Laotian (0)	0	<0.01
Malaysian (0)	0	<0.01
Nepalese (0)	0	<0.01
Pakistani (0)	0	<0.01
Sri Lankan (0)	0	<0.01
Taiwanese (0)	0	<0.01
Thai (0)	0	<0.01
Vietnamese (0)	0	<0.01
Hawaii Native/Pacific Islander (3)	3	0.03
Not Hispanic (3)	3	0.03
Hispanic (0)	0	<0.01
Fijian (0)	0	<0.01
Guamanian/Chamorro (2)	2	0.02
Marshallese (0)	0	<0.01
Native Hawaiian (0)	0	<0.01
Samoan (0)	1	0.01
Tongan (0)	0	<0.01
White (8,489)	8,586	96.97
Not Hispanic (8,298)	8,355	94.36
Hispanic (191)	231	2.61

Notes: † The Census 2010 population figure is used to calculate the percentages in the Hispanic Origin and Race categories. Ancestry percentages are based on the 2006-2010 American Community Survey population (not shown); ‡ Numbers in parentheses indicate the number of people reporting a single ancestry; * Numbers in parentheses indicate the number of persons reporting this race alone, not in combination with any other race; Please refer to the Explanation of Data for more information.

Blackford County
Population: 12,766

Ancestry	Population	%
Afghan (0)	0	<0.01
African, Sub-Saharan (0)	0	<0.01
African (0)	0	<0.01
Cape Verdean (0)	0	<0.01
Ethiopian (0)	0	<0.01
Ghanaian (0)	0	<0.01
Kenyan (0)	0	<0.01
Liberian (0)	0	<0.01
Nigerian (0)	0	<0.01
Senegalese (0)	0	<0.01
Sierra Leonean (0)	0	<0.01
Somalian (0)	0	<0.01
South African (0)	0	<0.01
Sudanese (0)	0	<0.01
Ugandan (0)	0	<0.01
Zimbabwean (0)	0	<0.01
Other Sub-Saharan African (0)	0	<0.01
Albanian (0)	0	<0.01
Alsatian (0)	0	<0.01
American (1,514)	1,514	11.68
Arab (0)	0	<0.01
Arab (0)	0	<0.01
Egyptian (0)	0	<0.01
Iraqi (0)	0	<0.01
Jordanian (0)	0	<0.01
Lebanese (0)	0	<0.01
Moroccan (0)	0	<0.01
Palestinian (0)	0	<0.01
Syrian (0)	0	<0.01
Other Arab (0)	0	<0.01
Armenian (0)	0	<0.01
Assyrian/Chaldean/Syriac (0)	0	<0.01
Australian (0)	0	<0.01
Austrian (0)	0	<0.01
Basque (0)	0	<0.01
Belgian (0)	0	<0.01
Brazilian (0)	0	<0.01
British (30)	112	0.86
Bulgarian (0)	0	<0.01
Cajun (0)	0	<0.01
Canadian (0)	28	0.22
Carpatho Rusyn (0)	0	<0.01
Celtic (0)	0	<0.01
Croatian (0)	0	<0.01
Cypriot (0)	0	<0.01
Czech (0)	35	0.27
Czechoslovakian (0)	0	<0.01
Danish (0)	0	<0.01
Dutch (189)	534	4.12
Eastern European (0)	0	<0.01
English (917)	1,760	13.58
Estonian (0)	0	<0.01
European (104)	115	0.89
Finnish (6)	13	0.10
French, ex. Basque (31)	252	1.94
French Canadian (29)	129	1.00
German (2,153)	3,992	30.80
German Russian (0)	0	<0.01
Greek (0)	10	0.08
Guyanese (0)	0	<0.01
Hungarian (22)	22	0.17
Icelander (0)	0	<0.01
Iranian (0)	0	<0.01
Irish (483)	2,170	16.74
Israeli (0)	0	<0.01
Italian (39)	183	1.41
Latvian (0)	0	<0.01
Lithuanian (0)	0	<0.01
Luxemburger (0)	0	<0.01
Macedonian (0)	0	<0.01
Maltese (0)	0	<0.01
New Zealander (0)	0	<0.01
Northern European (0)	0	<0.01
Norwegian (19)	19	0.15
Pennsylvania German (16)	16	0.12
Polish (31)	104	0.80
Portuguese (0)	0	<0.01
Romanian (0)	0	<0.01
Russian (2)	2	0.02
Scandinavian (0)	0	<0.01
Scotch-Irish (79)	183	1.41
Scottish (39)	132	1.02
Serbian (0)	0	<0.01
Slavic (0)	0	<0.01
Slovak (0)	12	0.09
Slovene (0)	0	<0.01
Soviet Union (0)	0	<0.01
Swedish (9)	48	0.37
Swiss (11)	78	0.60
Turkish (0)	0	<0.01
Ukrainian (0)	19	0.15
Welsh (6)	162	1.25
West Indian, ex. Hispanic (0)	0	<0.01
Bahamian (0)	0	<0.01
Barbadian (0)	0	<0.01
Belizean (0)	0	<0.01
Bermudan (0)	0	<0.01
British West Indian (0)	0	<0.01
Dutch West Indian (0)	0	<0.01
Haitian (0)	0	<0.01
Jamaican (0)	0	<0.01
Trinidadian/Tobagonian (0)	0	<0.01
U.S. Virgin Islander (0)	0	<0.01
West Indian (0)	0	<0.01
Other West Indian (0)	0	<0.01
Yugoslavian (0)	0	<0.01

Hispanic Origin	Population	%
Hispanic or Latino (of any race)	117	0.92
Central American, ex. Mexican	2	0.02
Costa Rican	0	<0.01
Guatemalan	2	0.02
Honduran	0	<0.01
Nicaraguan	0	<0.01
Panamanian	0	<0.01
Salvadoran	0	<0.01
Other Central American	0	<0.01
Cuban	1	0.01
Dominican Republic	0	<0.01
Mexican	90	0.70
Puerto Rican	8	0.06
South American	0	<0.01
Argentinean	0	<0.01
Bolivian	0	<0.01
Chilean	0	<0.01
Colombian	0	<0.01
Ecuadorian	0	<0.01
Paraguayan	0	<0.01
Peruvian	0	<0.01
Uruguayan	0	<0.01
Venezuelan	0	<0.01
Other South American	0	<0.01
Other Hispanic or Latino	16	0.13

Race*	Population	%
African-American/Black (49)	95	0.74
Not Hispanic (48)	93	0.73
Hispanic (1)	2	0.02
American Indian/Alaska Native (22)	100	0.78
Not Hispanic (22)	96	0.75
Hispanic (0)	4	0.03
Alaska Athabascan (Ala. Nat.) (0)	0	<0.01
Aleut (Alaska Native) (0)	0	<0.01
Apache (1)	1	0.01
Arapaho (0)	0	<0.01
Blackfeet (0)	5	0.04
Canadian/French Am. Ind. (0)	0	<0.01
Central American Ind. (0)	0	<0.01
Cherokee (1)	20	0.16
Cheyenne (0)	1	0.01
Chickasaw (0)	0	<0.01
Chippewa (0)	0	<0.01
Choctaw (0)	0	<0.01
Colville (0)	0	<0.01
Comanche (0)	0	<0.01
Cree (0)	1	0.01
Creek (0)	0	<0.01
Crow (0)	0	<0.01
Delaware (0)	0	<0.01
Hopi (0)	0	<0.01
Houma (0)	0	<0.01
Inupiat (Alaska Native) (0)	1	0.01
Iroquois (1)	5	0.04
Kiowa (0)	0	<0.01
Lumbee (2)	2	0.02
Menominee (1)	1	0.01
Mexican American Ind. (0)	0	<0.01
Navajo (0)	0	<0.01
Osage (0)	0	<0.01
Ottawa (1)	2	0.02
Paiute (0)	0	<0.01
Pima (0)	0	<0.01
Potawatomi (0)	0	<0.01
Pueblo (0)	2	0.02
Puget Sound Salish (0)	0	<0.01
Seminole (0)	0	<0.01
Shoshone (2)	2	0.02
Sioux (1)	5	0.04
South American Ind. (0)	0	<0.01
Spanish American Ind. (0)	0	<0.01
Tlingit-Haida (Alaska Native) (0)	0	<0.01
Tohono O'Odham (0)	0	<0.01
Tsimshian (Alaska Native) (0)	0	<0.01
Ute (0)	0	<0.01
Yakama (0)	0	<0.01
Yaqui (0)	0	<0.01
Yuman (0)	0	<0.01
Yup'ik (Alaska Native) (0)	0	<0.01
Asian (19)	39	0.31
Not Hispanic (19)	39	0.31
Hispanic (0)	0	<0.01
Bangladeshi (0)	0	<0.01
Bhutanese (0)	0	<0.01
Burmese (0)	0	<0.01
Cambodian (0)	0	<0.01
Chinese, ex. Taiwanese (4)	4	0.03
Filipino (4)	15	0.12
Hmong (0)	0	<0.01
Indian (2)	6	0.05
Indonesian (0)	0	<0.01
Japanese (1)	2	0.02
Korean (4)	8	0.06
Laotian (0)	0	<0.01
Malaysian (0)	0	<0.01
Nepalese (0)	0	<0.01
Pakistani (0)	0	<0.01
Sri Lankan (0)	0	<0.01
Taiwanese (0)	0	<0.01
Thai (0)	0	<0.01
Vietnamese (2)	2	0.02
Hawaii Native/Pacific Islander (4)	13	0.10
Not Hispanic (4)	12	0.09
Hispanic (0)	1	0.01
Fijian (0)	0	<0.01
Guamanian/Chamorro (0)	0	<0.01
Marshallese (0)	0	<0.01
Native Hawaiian (3)	9	0.07
Samoan (1)	4	0.03
Tongan (0)	0	<0.01
White (12,470)	12,629	98.93
Not Hispanic (12,403)	12,545	98.27
Hispanic (67)	84	0.66

Notes: † The Census 2010 population figure is used to calculate the percentages in the Hispanic Origin and Race categories. Ancestry percentages are based on the 2006-2010 American Community Survey population (not shown); ‡ Numbers in parentheses indicate the number of people reporting a single ancestry; * Numbers in parentheses indicate the number of persons reporting this race alone, not in combination with any other race; Please refer to the Explanation of Data for more information.

Boone County
Population: 56,640

Ancestry	Population	%
Afghan (0)	0	<0.01
African, Sub-Saharan (81)	113	0.21
African (0)	32	0.06
Cape Verdean (0)	0	<0.01
Ethiopian (12)	12	0.02
Ghanaian (0)	0	<0.01
Kenyan (0)	0	<0.01
Liberian (0)	0	<0.01
Nigerian (0)	0	<0.01
Senegalese (0)	0	<0.01
Sierra Leonean (0)	0	<0.01
Somalian (69)	69	0.13
South African (0)	0	<0.01
Sudanese (0)	0	<0.01
Ugandan (0)	0	<0.01
Zimbabwean (0)	0	<0.01
Other Sub-Saharan African (0)	0	<0.01
Albanian (13)	13	0.02
Alsatian (0)	0	<0.01
American (4,933)	4,933	9.00
Arab (53)	174	0.32
Arab (0)	0	<0.01
Egyptian (27)	38	0.07
Iraqi (0)	0	<0.01
Jordanian (0)	0	<0.01
Lebanese (0)	45	0.08
Moroccan (0)	0	<0.01
Palestinian (0)	0	<0.01
Syrian (0)	65	0.12
Other Arab (26)	26	0.05
Armenian (0)	0	<0.01
Assyrian/Chaldean/Syriac (0)	0	<0.01
Australian (0)	0	<0.01
Austrian (10)	74	0.14
Basque (0)	10	0.02
Belgian (59)	102	0.19
Brazilian (0)	0	<0.01
British (243)	329	0.60
Bulgarian (0)	54	0.10
Cajun (0)	0	<0.01
Canadian (108)	169	0.31
Carpatho Rusyn (0)	0	<0.01
Celtic (0)	17	0.03
Croatian (9)	95	0.17
Cypriot (0)	0	<0.01
Czech (41)	194	0.35
Czechoslovakian (99)	99	0.18
Danish (46)	173	0.32
Dutch (328)	1,300	2.37
Eastern European (33)	71	0.13
English (5,917)	10,595	19.34
Estonian (0)	0	<0.01
European (877)	976	1.78
Finnish (41)	104	0.19
French, ex. Basque (310)	1,843	3.36
French Canadian (87)	178	0.32
German (6,755)	15,863	28.95
German Russian (0)	0	<0.01
Greek (144)	217	0.40
Guyanese (0)	0	<0.01
Hungarian (48)	262	0.48
Icelander (0)	0	<0.01
Iranian (52)	66	0.12
Irish (2,326)	7,740	14.13
Israeli (0)	0	<0.01
Italian (718)	2,000	3.65
Latvian (0)	0	<0.01
Lithuanian (12)	104	0.19
Luxemburger (0)	11	0.02
Macedonian (2)	10	0.02
Maltese (0)	0	<0.01
New Zealander (13)	13	0.02
Northern European (58)	58	0.11
Norwegian (104)	294	0.54
Pennsylvania German (21)	42	0.08
Polish (486)	1,107	2.02
Portuguese (62)	62	0.11
Romanian (20)	83	0.15
Russian (77)	344	0.63
Scandinavian (0)	10	0.02
Scotch-Irish (527)	923	1.68
Scottish (756)	1,623	2.96
Serbian (0)	42	0.08
Slavic (105)	119	0.22
Slovak (144)	286	0.52
Slovene (18)	63	0.11
Soviet Union (0)	0	<0.01
Swedish (164)	464	0.85
Swiss (30)	182	0.33
Turkish (0)	0	<0.01
Ukrainian (97)	206	0.38
Welsh (75)	250	0.46
West Indian, ex. Hispanic (0)	14	0.03
Bahamian (0)	0	<0.01
Barbadian (0)	0	<0.01
Belizean (0)	0	<0.01
Bermudan (0)	0	<0.01
British West Indian (0)	0	<0.01
Dutch West Indian (0)	14	0.03
Haitian (0)	0	<0.01
Jamaican (0)	0	<0.01
Trinidadian/Tobagonian (0)	0	<0.01
U.S. Virgin Islander (0)	0	<0.01
West Indian (0)	0	<0.01
Other West Indian (0)	0	<0.01
Yugoslavian (55)	55	0.10

Hispanic Origin	Population	%
Hispanic or Latino (of any race)	1,270	2.24
Central American, ex. Mexican	107	0.19
Costa Rican	5	0.01
Guatemalan	40	0.07
Honduran	27	0.05
Nicaraguan	6	0.01
Panamanian	14	0.02
Salvadoran	14	0.02
Other Central American	1	<0.01
Cuban	35	0.06
Dominican Republic	16	0.03
Mexican	741	1.31
Puerto Rican	135	0.24
South American	120	0.21
Argentinean	19	0.03
Bolivian	7	0.01
Chilean	6	0.01
Colombian	52	0.09
Ecuadorian	14	0.02
Paraguayan	1	<0.01
Peruvian	10	0.02
Uruguayan	1	<0.01
Venezuelan	10	0.02
Other South American	0	<0.01
Other Hispanic or Latino	116	0.20

Race*	Population	%
African-American/Black (495)	741	1.31
Not Hispanic (484)	706	1.25
Hispanic (11)	35	0.06
American Indian/Alaska Native (103)	305	0.54
Not Hispanic (91)	283	0.50
Hispanic (12)	22	0.04
Alaska Athabascan (Ala. Nat.) (0)	0	<0.01
Aleut (Alaska Native) (0)	0	<0.01
Apache (0)	3	0.01
Arapaho (0)	0	<0.01
Blackfeet (4)	10	0.02
Canadian/French Am. Ind. (0)	1	<0.01
Central American Ind. (0)	0	<0.01
Cherokee (19)	76	0.13
Cheyenne (1)	2	<0.01
Chickasaw (1)	2	<0.01
Chippewa (0)	4	0.01
Choctaw (5)	7	0.01
Colville (0)	0	<0.01
Comanche (0)	1	<0.01
Cree (0)	0	<0.01
Creek (0)	1	<0.01
Crow (0)	1	<0.01
Delaware (3)	3	0.01
Hopi (0)	0	<0.01
Houma (0)	0	<0.01
Inupiat (Alaska Native) (0)	2	<0.01
Iroquois (3)	7	0.01
Kiowa (4)	4	0.01
Lumbee (2)	4	0.01
Menominee (0)	0	<0.01
Mexican American Ind. (0)	1	<0.01
Navajo (3)	5	0.01
Osage (0)	1	<0.01
Ottawa (0)	1	<0.01
Paiute (2)	4	0.01
Pima (0)	0	<0.01
Potawatomi (0)	3	0.01
Pueblo (3)	3	0.01
Puget Sound Salish (0)	0	<0.01
Seminole (0)	1	<0.01
Shoshone (0)	0	<0.01
Sioux (4)	9	0.02
South American Ind. (0)	5	0.01
Spanish American Ind. (0)	0	<0.01
Tlingit-Haida (Alaska Native) (0)	0	<0.01
Tohono O'Odham (0)	0	<0.01
Tsimshian (Alaska Native) (0)	0	<0.01
Ute (0)	0	<0.01
Yakama (0)	0	<0.01
Yaqui (0)	0	<0.01
Yuman (0)	0	<0.01
Yup'ik (Alaska Native) (0)	0	<0.01
Asian (942)	1,214	2.14
Not Hispanic (941)	1,201	2.12
Hispanic (1)	13	0.02
Bangladeshi (2)	5	0.01
Bhutanese (0)	0	<0.01
Burmese (0)	1	<0.01
Cambodian (1)	1	<0.01
Chinese, ex. Taiwanese (329)	362	0.64
Filipino (73)	140	0.25
Hmong (8)	12	0.02
Indian (216)	257	0.45
Indonesian (1)	5	0.01
Japanese (38)	82	0.14
Korean (71)	122	0.22
Laotian (3)	3	0.01
Malaysian (1)	1	<0.01
Nepalese (0)	0	<0.01
Pakistani (50)	54	0.10
Sri Lankan (3)	3	0.01
Taiwanese (21)	24	0.04
Thai (11)	14	0.02
Vietnamese (68)	80	0.14
Hawaii Native/Pacific Islander (11)	30	0.05
Not Hispanic (10)	28	0.05
Hispanic (1)	2	<0.01
Fijian (0)	0	<0.01
Guamanian/Chamorro (1)	3	0.01
Marshallese (0)	0	<0.01
Native Hawaiian (1)	6	0.01
Samoan (1)	3	0.01
Tongan (0)	0	<0.01
White (53,953)	54,685	96.55
Not Hispanic (53,151)	53,789	94.97
Hispanic (802)	896	1.58

Notes: † The Census 2010 population figure is used to calculate the percentages in the Hispanic Origin and Race categories. Ancestry percentages are based on the 2006-2010 American Community Survey population (not shown); ‡ Numbers in parentheses indicate the number of people reporting a single ancestry; * Numbers in parentheses indicate the number of persons reporting this race alone, not in combination with any other race; Please refer to the Explanation of Data for more information.

Brown County
Population: 15,242

Ancestry	Population	%
Afghan (0)	0	<0.01
African, Sub-Saharan (0)	23	0.15
African (0)	23	0.15
Cape Verdean (0)	0	<0.01
Ethiopian (0)	0	<0.01
Ghanaian (0)	0	<0.01
Kenyan (0)	0	<0.01
Liberian (0)	0	<0.01
Nigerian (0)	0	<0.01
Senegalese (0)	0	<0.01
Sierra Leonean (0)	0	<0.01
Somalian (0)	0	<0.01
South African (0)	0	<0.01
Sudanese (0)	0	<0.01
Ugandan (0)	0	<0.01
Zimbabwean (0)	0	<0.01
Other Sub-Saharan African (0)	0	<0.01
Albanian (0)	0	<0.01
Alsatian (0)	0	<0.01
American (1,719)	1,719	11.26
Arab (0)	0	<0.01
Arab (0)	0	<0.01
Egyptian (0)	0	<0.01
Iraqi (0)	0	<0.01
Jordanian (0)	0	<0.01
Lebanese (0)	0	<0.01
Moroccan (0)	0	<0.01
Palestinian (0)	0	<0.01
Syrian (0)	0	<0.01
Other Arab (0)	0	<0.01
Armenian (0)	0	<0.01
Assyrian/Chaldean/Syriac (0)	0	<0.01
Australian (0)	0	<0.01
Austrian (0)	3	0.02
Basque (0)	0	<0.01
Belgian (0)	58	0.38
Brazilian (0)	0	<0.01
British (73)	148	0.97
Bulgarian (0)	0	<0.01
Cajun (0)	0	<0.01
Canadian (11)	31	0.20
Carpatho Rusyn (0)	0	<0.01
Celtic (0)	0	<0.01
Croatian (0)	0	<0.01
Cypriot (0)	0	<0.01
Czech (9)	9	0.06
Czechoslovakian (5)	5	0.03
Danish (0)	12	0.08
Dutch (40)	396	2.59
Eastern European (18)	18	0.12
English (758)	1,764	11.55
Estonian (0)	0	<0.01
European (234)	283	1.85
Finnish (0)	0	<0.01
French, ex. Basque (114)	330	2.16
French Canadian (28)	40	0.26
German (1,793)	4,159	27.23
German Russian (0)	0	<0.01
Greek (25)	136	0.89
Guyanese (0)	0	<0.01
Hungarian (13)	95	0.62
Icelander (0)	0	<0.01
Iranian (0)	0	<0.01
Irish (520)	2,000	13.10
Israeli (0)	0	<0.01
Italian (186)	358	2.34
Latvian (0)	0	<0.01
Lithuanian (0)	0	<0.01
Luxemburger (0)	0	<0.01
Macedonian (0)	0	<0.01
Maltese (0)	0	<0.01
New Zealander (0)	0	<0.01
Northern European (0)	23	0.15
Norwegian (27)	78	0.51
Pennsylvania German (0)	0	<0.01
Polish (109)	347	2.27
Portuguese (0)	0	<0.01
Romanian (13)	47	0.31
Russian (0)	62	0.41
Scandinavian (0)	0	<0.01
Scotch-Irish (102)	291	1.91
Scottish (266)	474	3.10
Serbian (0)	0	<0.01
Slavic (0)	0	<0.01
Slovak (18)	67	0.44
Slovene (0)	0	<0.01
Soviet Union (0)	0	<0.01
Swedish (12)	93	0.61
Swiss (9)	9	0.06
Turkish (0)	0	<0.01
Ukrainian (0)	0	<0.01
Welsh (11)	112	0.73
West Indian, ex. Hispanic (0)	0	<0.01
Bahamian (0)	0	<0.01
Barbadian (0)	0	<0.01
Belizean (0)	0	<0.01
Bermudan (0)	0	<0.01
British West Indian (0)	0	<0.01
Dutch West Indian (0)	0	<0.01
Haitian (0)	0	<0.01
Jamaican (0)	0	<0.01
Trinidadian/Tobagonian (0)	0	<0.01
U.S. Virgin Islander (0)	0	<0.01
West Indian (0)	0	<0.01
Other West Indian (0)	0	<0.01
Yugoslavian (0)	41	0.27

Hispanic Origin	Population	%
Hispanic or Latino (of any race)	178	1.17
Central American, ex. Mexican	12	0.08
Costa Rican	0	<0.01
Guatemalan	6	0.04
Honduran	5	0.03
Nicaraguan	0	<0.01
Panamanian	1	0.01
Salvadoran	0	<0.01
Other Central American	0	<0.01
Cuban	8	0.05
Dominican Republic	0	<0.01
Mexican	129	0.85
Puerto Rican	6	0.04
South American	4	0.03
Argentinean	1	0.01
Bolivian	0	<0.01
Chilean	0	<0.01
Colombian	1	0.01
Ecuadorian	0	<0.01
Paraguayan	1	0.01
Peruvian	0	<0.01
Uruguayan	0	<0.01
Venezuelan	1	0.01
Other South American	0	<0.01
Other Hispanic or Latino	19	0.12

Race*	Population	%
African-American/Black (53)	85	0.56
Not Hispanic (53)	85	0.56
Hispanic (0)	0	<0.01
American Indian/Alaska Native (50)	147	0.96
Not Hispanic (47)	128	0.84
Hispanic (3)	19	0.12
Alaska Athabascan (Ala. Nat.) (0)	0	<0.01
Aleut (Alaska Native) (0)	0	<0.01
Apache (0)	4	0.03
Arapaho (0)	0	<0.01
Blackfeet (0)	8	0.05
Canadian/French Am. Ind. (0)	0	<0.01
Central American Ind. (0)	0	<0.01
Cherokee (3)	38	0.25
Cheyenne (0)	0	<0.01
Chickasaw (0)	0	<0.01
Chippewa (2)	4	0.03
Choctaw (0)	1	0.01
Colville (0)	0	<0.01
Comanche (0)	0	<0.01
Cree (0)	0	<0.01
Creek (0)	0	<0.01
Crow (0)	0	<0.01
Delaware (0)	0	<0.01
Hopi (0)	0	<0.01
Houma (0)	0	<0.01
Inupiat (Alaska Native) (0)	0	<0.01
Iroquois (0)	0	<0.01
Kiowa (0)	0	<0.01
Lumbee (0)	0	<0.01
Menominee (0)	0	<0.01
Mexican American Ind. (0)	0	<0.01
Navajo (0)	0	<0.01
Osage (0)	0	<0.01
Ottawa (0)	0	<0.01
Paiute (0)	0	<0.01
Pima (0)	0	<0.01
Potawatomi (1)	1	0.01
Pueblo (2)	2	0.01
Puget Sound Salish (0)	0	<0.01
Seminole (0)	0	<0.01
Shoshone (0)	0	<0.01
Sioux (5)	11	0.07
South American Ind. (0)	0	<0.01
Spanish American Ind. (0)	0	<0.01
Tlingit-Haida (Alaska Native) (0)	0	<0.01
Tohono O'Odham (1)	1	0.01
Tsimshian (Alaska Native) (0)	0	<0.01
Ute (0)	7	0.05
Yakama (0)	0	<0.01
Yaqui (0)	0	<0.01
Yuman (0)	0	<0.01
Yup'ik (Alaska Native) (0)	0	<0.01
Asian (44)	78	0.51
Not Hispanic (44)	77	0.51
Hispanic (0)	1	0.01
Bangladeshi (0)	0	<0.01
Bhutanese (0)	0	<0.01
Burmese (0)	0	<0.01
Cambodian (0)	0	<0.01
Chinese, ex. Taiwanese (11)	12	0.08
Filipino (17)	29	0.19
Hmong (0)	0	<0.01
Indian (1)	5	0.03
Indonesian (0)	0	<0.01
Japanese (1)	7	0.05
Korean (4)	9	0.06
Laotian (0)	0	<0.01
Malaysian (1)	1	0.01
Nepalese (0)	0	<0.01
Pakistani (0)	0	<0.01
Sri Lankan (0)	0	<0.01
Taiwanese (1)	1	0.01
Thai (4)	6	0.04
Vietnamese (0)	3	0.02
Hawaii Native/Pacific Islander (1)	8	0.05
Not Hispanic (1)	8	0.05
Hispanic (0)	0	<0.01
Fijian (0)	0	<0.01
Guamanian/Chamorro (1)	2	0.01
Marshallese (0)	0	<0.01
Native Hawaiian (0)	1	0.01
Samoan (0)	0	<0.01
Tongan (0)	0	<0.01
White (14,874)	15,040	98.67
Not Hispanic (14,761)	14,900	97.76
Hispanic (113)	140	0.92

*Notes: † The Census 2010 population figure is used to calculate the percentages in the Hispanic Origin and Race categories. Ancestry percentages are based on the 2006-2010 American Community Survey population (not shown); ‡ Numbers in parentheses indicate the number of people reporting a single ancestry; * Numbers in parentheses indicate the number of persons reporting this race alone, not in combination with any other race; Please refer to the Explanation of Data for more information.*

Carroll County
Population: 20,155

Ancestry	Population	%
Afghan (0)	0	<0.01
African, Sub-Saharan (0)	0	<0.01
African (0)	0	<0.01
Cape Verdean (0)	0	<0.01
Ethiopian (0)	0	<0.01
Ghanaian (0)	0	<0.01
Kenyan (0)	0	<0.01
Liberian (0)	0	<0.01
Nigerian (0)	0	<0.01
Senegalese (0)	0	<0.01
Sierra Leonean (0)	0	<0.01
Somalian (0)	0	<0.01
South African (0)	0	<0.01
Sudanese (0)	0	<0.01
Ugandan (0)	0	<0.01
Zimbabwean (0)	0	<0.01
Other Sub-Saharan African (0)	0	<0.01
Albanian (0)	0	<0.01
Alsatian (0)	0	<0.01
American (2,964)	2,964	14.72
Arab (31)	90	0.45
Arab (31)	90	0.45
Egyptian (0)	0	<0.01
Iraqi (0)	0	<0.01
Jordanian (0)	0	<0.01
Lebanese (0)	0	<0.01
Moroccan (0)	0	<0.01
Palestinian (0)	0	<0.01
Syrian (0)	0	<0.01
Other Arab (0)	0	<0.01
Armenian (0)	0	<0.01
Assyrian/Chaldean/Syriac (0)	0	<0.01
Australian (8)	8	0.04
Austrian (0)	0	<0.01
Basque (0)	0	<0.01
Belgian (0)	25	0.12
Brazilian (0)	0	<0.01
British (20)	40	0.20
Bulgarian (0)	18	0.09
Cajun (0)	0	<0.01
Canadian (0)	0	<0.01
Carpatho Rusyn (0)	0	<0.01
Celtic (23)	23	0.11
Croatian (0)	8	0.04
Cypriot (0)	0	<0.01
Czech (15)	30	0.15
Czechoslovakian (29)	64	0.32
Danish (14)	26	0.13
Dutch (100)	555	2.76
Eastern European (21)	21	0.10
English (799)	1,779	8.84
Estonian (0)	0	<0.01
European (46)	46	0.23
Finnish (0)	0	<0.01
French, ex. Basque (107)	401	1.99
French Canadian (12)	32	0.16
German (2,761)	5,987	29.73
German Russian (0)	0	<0.01
Greek (27)	27	0.13
Guyanese (0)	0	<0.01
Hungarian (13)	52	0.26
Icelander (0)	0	<0.01
Iranian (0)	0	<0.01
Irish (770)	2,543	12.63
Israeli (0)	0	<0.01
Italian (149)	480	2.38
Latvian (0)	0	<0.01
Lithuanian (9)	36	0.18
Luxemburger (0)	0	<0.01
Macedonian (0)	0	<0.01
Maltese (0)	0	<0.01
New Zealander (0)	0	<0.01
Northern European (0)	0	<0.01
Norwegian (49)	122	0.61
Pennsylvania German (61)	72	0.36
Polish (150)	383	1.90
Portuguese (30)	63	0.31
Romanian (10)	10	0.05
Russian (0)	13	0.06
Scandinavian (12)	12	0.06
Scotch-Irish (161)	267	1.33
Scottish (183)	578	2.87
Serbian (0)	0	<0.01
Slavic (0)	0	<0.01
Slovak (19)	32	0.16
Slovene (6)	6	0.03
Soviet Union (0)	0	<0.01
Swedish (131)	382	1.90
Swiss (6)	64	0.32
Turkish (0)	0	<0.01
Ukrainian (11)	11	0.05
Welsh (7)	85	0.42
West Indian, ex. Hispanic (0)	0	<0.01
Bahamian (0)	0	<0.01
Barbadian (0)	0	<0.01
Belizean (0)	0	<0.01
Bermudan (0)	0	<0.01
British West Indian (0)	0	<0.01
Dutch West Indian (0)	0	<0.01
Haitian (0)	0	<0.01
Jamaican (0)	0	<0.01
Trinidadian/Tobagonian (0)	0	<0.01
U.S. Virgin Islander (0)	0	<0.01
West Indian (0)	0	<0.01
Other West Indian (0)	0	<0.01
Yugoslavian (0)	0	<0.01

Hispanic Origin	Population	%
Hispanic or Latino (of any race)	711	3.53
Central American, ex. Mexican	80	0.40
Costa Rican	1	<0.01
Guatemalan	35	0.17
Honduran	6	0.03
Nicaraguan	0	<0.01
Panamanian	0	<0.01
Salvadoran	38	0.19
Other Central American	0	<0.01
Cuban	17	0.08
Dominican Republic	0	<0.01
Mexican	546	2.71
Puerto Rican	21	0.10
South American	6	0.03
Argentinean	0	<0.01
Bolivian	0	<0.01
Chilean	0	<0.01
Colombian	3	0.01
Ecuadorian	0	<0.01
Paraguayan	0	<0.01
Peruvian	1	<0.01
Uruguayan	2	0.01
Venezuelan	0	<0.01
Other South American	0	<0.01
Other Hispanic or Latino	41	0.20

Race*	Population	%
African-American/Black (48)	111	0.55
Not Hispanic (42)	101	0.50
Hispanic (6)	10	0.05
American Indian/Alaska Native (38)	112	0.56
Not Hispanic (33)	85	0.42
Hispanic (5)	27	0.13
Alaska Athabascan (Ala. Nat.) (0)	0	<0.01
Aleut (Alaska Native) (0)	0	<0.01
Apache (2)	4	0.02
Arapaho (0)	0	<0.01
Blackfeet (0)	1	<0.01
Canadian/French Am. Ind. (1)	8	0.04
Central American Ind. (0)	0	<0.01
Cherokee (12)	32	0.16
Cheyenne (0)	0	<0.01
Chickasaw (0)	0	<0.01
Chippewa (0)	1	<0.01
Choctaw (2)	2	0.01
Colville (0)	0	<0.01
Comanche (0)	0	<0.01
Cree (0)	0	<0.01
Creek (0)	0	<0.01
Crow (0)	2	0.01
Delaware (0)	0	<0.01
Hopi (0)	0	<0.01
Houma (0)	0	<0.01
Inupiat (Alaska Native) (0)	0	<0.01
Iroquois (0)	1	<0.01
Kiowa (0)	0	<0.01
Lumbee (0)	0	<0.01
Menominee (0)	0	<0.01
Mexican American Ind. (1)	11	0.05
Navajo (0)	0	<0.01
Osage (0)	0	<0.01
Ottawa (1)	1	<0.01
Paiute (0)	0	<0.01
Pima (0)	0	<0.01
Potawatomi (1)	2	0.01
Pueblo (0)	0	<0.01
Puget Sound Salish (0)	0	<0.01
Seminole (0)	0	<0.01
Shoshone (0)	0	<0.01
Sioux (1)	6	0.03
South American Ind. (0)	0	<0.01
Spanish American Ind. (0)	0	<0.01
Tlingit-Haida (Alaska Native) (0)	0	<0.01
Tohono O'Odham (0)	0	<0.01
Tsimshian (Alaska Native) (0)	0	<0.01
Ute (0)	0	<0.01
Yakama (0)	0	<0.01
Yaqui (0)	0	<0.01
Yuman (0)	0	<0.01
Yup'ik (Alaska Native) (0)	0	<0.01
Asian (21)	52	0.26
Not Hispanic (20)	51	0.25
Hispanic (1)	1	<0.01
Bangladeshi (0)	0	<0.01
Bhutanese (0)	0	<0.01
Burmese (0)	0	<0.01
Cambodian (0)	0	<0.01
Chinese, ex. Taiwanese (8)	12	0.06
Filipino (6)	17	0.08
Hmong (0)	0	<0.01
Indian (1)	4	0.02
Indonesian (0)	1	<0.01
Japanese (1)	8	0.04
Korean (1)	6	0.03
Laotian (1)	1	<0.01
Malaysian (0)	0	<0.01
Nepalese (0)	0	<0.01
Pakistani (0)	0	<0.01
Sri Lankan (0)	0	<0.01
Taiwanese (0)	1	<0.01
Thai (1)	1	<0.01
Vietnamese (0)	1	<0.01
Hawaii Native/Pacific Islander (1)	8	0.04
Not Hispanic (1)	6	0.03
Hispanic (0)	2	0.01
Fijian (0)	0	<0.01
Guamanian/Chamorro (0)	1	<0.01
Marshallese (0)	0	<0.01
Native Hawaiian (0)	5	0.02
Samoan (0)	1	<0.01
Tongan (0)	0	<0.01
White (19,500)	19,687	97.68
Not Hispanic (19,188)	19,332	95.92
Hispanic (312)	355	1.76

Notes: † The Census 2010 population figure is used to calculate the percentages in the Hispanic Origin and Race categories. Ancestry percentages are based on the 2006-2010 American Community Survey population (not shown); ‡ Numbers in parentheses indicate the number of people reporting a single ancestry; * Numbers in parentheses indicate the number of persons reporting this race alone, not in combination with any other race; Please refer to the Explanation of Data for more information.

Cass County
Population: 38,966

Ancestry	Population	%
Afghan (0)	0	<0.01
African, Sub-Saharan (66)	70	0.18
African (66)	70	0.18
Cape Verdean (0)	0	<0.01
Ethiopian (0)	0	<0.01
Ghanaian (0)	0	<0.01
Kenyan (0)	0	<0.01
Liberian (0)	0	<0.01
Nigerian (0)	0	<0.01
Senegalese (0)	0	<0.01
Sierra Leonean (0)	0	<0.01
Somalian (0)	0	<0.01
South African (0)	0	<0.01
Sudanese (0)	0	<0.01
Ugandan (0)	0	<0.01
Zimbabwean (0)	0	<0.01
Other Sub-Saharan African (0)	0	<0.01
Albanian (0)	0	<0.01
Alsatian (0)	0	<0.01
American (5,862)	5,862	15.01
Arab (0)	0	<0.01
Arab (0)	0	<0.01
Egyptian (0)	0	<0.01
Iraqi (0)	0	<0.01
Jordanian (0)	0	<0.01
Lebanese (0)	0	<0.01
Moroccan (0)	0	<0.01
Palestinian (0)	0	<0.01
Syrian (0)	0	<0.01
Other Arab (0)	0	<0.01
Armenian (0)	0	<0.01
Assyrian/Chaldean/Syriac (0)	0	<0.01
Australian (0)	12	0.03
Austrian (0)	13	0.03
Basque (0)	0	<0.01
Belgian (0)	22	0.06
Brazilian (0)	0	<0.01
British (4)	38	0.10
Bulgarian (0)	0	<0.01
Cajun (0)	0	<0.01
Canadian (11)	63	0.16
Carpatho Rusyn (0)	0	<0.01
Celtic (0)	0	<0.01
Croatian (0)	9	0.02
Cypriot (0)	0	<0.01
Czech (18)	89	0.23
Czechoslovakian (26)	26	0.07
Danish (19)	144	0.37
Dutch (148)	839	2.15
Eastern European (0)	11	0.03
English (1,315)	3,523	9.02
Estonian (0)	0	<0.01
European (145)	157	0.40
Finnish (16)	16	0.04
French, ex. Basque (135)	823	2.11
French Canadian (12)	61	0.16
German (4,131)	9,358	23.96
German Russian (0)	0	<0.01
Greek (33)	64	0.16
Guyanese (0)	0	<0.01
Hungarian (14)	93	0.24
Icelander (0)	0	<0.01
Iranian (0)	0	<0.01
Irish (1,310)	4,619	11.83
Israeli (0)	0	<0.01
Italian (613)	1,328	3.40
Latvian (0)	0	<0.01
Lithuanian (14)	17	0.04
Luxemburger (0)	0	<0.01
Macedonian (0)	0	<0.01
Maltese (0)	0	<0.01
New Zealander (0)	0	<0.01
Northern European (13)	13	0.03
Norwegian (35)	79	0.20
Pennsylvania German (9)	23	0.06
Polish (301)	842	2.16
Portuguese (0)	0	<0.01
Romanian (0)	0	<0.01
Russian (19)	33	0.08
Scandinavian (32)	40	0.10
Scotch-Irish (159)	278	0.71
Scottish (79)	303	0.78
Serbian (52)	52	0.13
Slavic (0)	0	<0.01
Slovak (26)	31	0.08
Slovene (0)	0	<0.01
Soviet Union (0)	0	<0.01
Swedish (132)	423	1.08
Swiss (40)	105	0.27
Turkish (0)	0	<0.01
Ukrainian (14)	31	0.08
Welsh (72)	216	0.55
West Indian, ex. Hispanic (0)	0	<0.01
Bahamian (0)	0	<0.01
Barbadian (0)	0	<0.01
Belizean (0)	0	<0.01
Bermudan (0)	0	<0.01
British West Indian (0)	0	<0.01
Dutch West Indian (0)	0	<0.01
Haitian (0)	0	<0.01
Jamaican (0)	0	<0.01
Trinidadian/Tobagonian (0)	0	<0.01
U.S. Virgin Islander (0)	0	<0.01
West Indian (0)	0	<0.01
Other West Indian (0)	0	<0.01
Yugoslavian (0)	0	<0.01

Hispanic Origin	Population	%
Hispanic or Latino (of any race)	4,897	12.57
Central American, ex. Mexican	699	1.79
Costa Rican	0	<0.01
Guatemalan	430	1.10
Honduran	75	0.19
Nicaraguan	12	0.03
Panamanian	2	0.01
Salvadoran	180	0.46
Other Central American	0	<0.01
Cuban	66	0.17
Dominican Republic	50	0.13
Mexican	3,571	9.16
Puerto Rican	90	0.23
South American	73	0.19
Argentinean	4	0.01
Bolivian	0	<0.01
Chilean	0	<0.01
Colombian	7	0.02
Ecuadorian	13	0.03
Paraguayan	0	<0.01
Peruvian	47	0.12
Uruguayan	0	<0.01
Venezuelan	2	0.01
Other South American	0	<0.01
Other Hispanic or Latino	348	0.89

Race*	Population	%
African-American/Black (578)	787	2.02
Not Hispanic (519)	703	1.80
Hispanic (59)	84	0.22
American Indian/Alaska Native (199)	351	0.90
Not Hispanic (100)	227	0.58
Hispanic (99)	124	0.32
Alaska Athabascan (Ala. Nat.) (0)	0	<0.01
Aleut (Alaska Native) (1)	1	<0.01
Apache (6)	6	0.02
Arapaho (0)	1	<0.01
Blackfeet (0)	0	<0.01
Canadian/French Am. Ind. (1)	3	0.01
Central American Ind. (30)	30	0.08
Cherokee (15)	52	0.13
Cheyenne (0)	4	0.01
Chickasaw (0)	0	<0.01
Chippewa (5)	6	0.02
Choctaw (3)	4	0.01
Colville (0)	0	<0.01
Comanche (0)	0	<0.01
Cree (3)	3	0.01
Creek (0)	1	<0.01
Crow (0)	6	0.02
Delaware (0)	0	<0.01
Hopi (0)	0	<0.01
Houma (0)	0	<0.01
Inupiat (Alaska Native) (0)	0	<0.01
Iroquois (2)	5	0.01
Kiowa (0)	0	<0.01
Lumbee (0)	0	<0.01
Menominee (0)	0	<0.01
Mexican American Ind. (20)	32	0.08
Navajo (1)	1	<0.01
Osage (0)	4	0.01
Ottawa (0)	0	<0.01
Paiute (0)	0	<0.01
Pima (0)	0	<0.01
Potawatomi (0)	3	0.01
Pueblo (0)	0	<0.01
Puget Sound Salish (0)	0	<0.01
Seminole (0)	0	<0.01
Shoshone (0)	0	<0.01
Sioux (7)	15	0.04
South American Ind. (0)	0	<0.01
Spanish American Ind. (0)	0	<0.01
Tlingit-Haida (Alaska Native) (1)	2	0.01
Tohono O'Odham (0)	0	<0.01
Tsimshian (Alaska Native) (0)	0	<0.01
Ute (0)	0	<0.01
Yakama (0)	0	<0.01
Yaqui (0)	0	<0.01
Yuman (0)	0	<0.01
Yup'ik (Alaska Native) (0)	0	<0.01
Asian (419)	497	1.28
Not Hispanic (407)	465	1.19
Hispanic (12)	32	0.08
Bangladeshi (0)	0	<0.01
Bhutanese (0)	0	<0.01
Burmese (142)	144	0.37
Cambodian (0)	0	<0.01
Chinese, ex. Taiwanese (38)	46	0.12
Filipino (53)	74	0.19
Hmong (0)	0	<0.01
Indian (27)	35	0.09
Indonesian (1)	1	<0.01
Japanese (10)	21	0.05
Korean (3)	8	0.02
Laotian (55)	64	0.16
Malaysian (0)	0	<0.01
Nepalese (0)	0	<0.01
Pakistani (0)	3	0.01
Sri Lankan (0)	0	<0.01
Taiwanese (2)	3	0.01
Thai (13)	14	0.04
Vietnamese (39)	40	0.10
Hawaii Native/Pacific Islander (30)	45	0.12
Not Hispanic (3)	10	0.03
Hispanic (27)	35	0.09
Fijian (0)	0	<0.01
Guamanian/Chamorro (19)	22	0.06
Marshallese (0)	0	<0.01
Native Hawaiian (7)	11	0.03
Samoan (0)	0	<0.01
Tongan (0)	5	0.01
White (34,385)	34,942	89.67
Not Hispanic (32,624)	32,974	84.62
Hispanic (1,761)	1,968	5.05

Notes: † The Census 2010 population figure is used to calculate the percentages in the Hispanic Origin and Race categories. Ancestry percentages are based on the 2006-2010 American Community Survey population (not shown); ‡ Numbers in parentheses indicate the number of people reporting a single ancestry; * Numbers in parentheses indicate the number of persons reporting this race alone, not in combination with any other race; Please refer to the Explanation of Data for more information.

Clark County
Population: 110,232

Ancestry	Population	%
Afghan (0)	0	<0.01
African, Sub-Saharan (121)	166	0.15
African (73)	106	0.10
Cape Verdean (0)	0	<0.01
Ethiopian (0)	0	<0.01
Ghanaian (0)	0	<0.01
Kenyan (0)	0	<0.01
Liberian (0)	0	<0.01
Nigerian (0)	0	<0.01
Senegalese (0)	0	<0.01
Sierra Leonean (0)	0	<0.01
Somalian (0)	0	<0.01
South African (48)	60	0.06
Sudanese (0)	0	<0.01
Ugandan (0)	0	<0.01
Zimbabwean (0)	0	<0.01
Other Sub-Saharan African (0)	0	<0.01
Albanian (0)	0	<0.01
Alsatian (0)	0	<0.01
American (13,939)	13,939	12.98
Arab (31)	54	0.05
Arab (0)	0	<0.01
Egyptian (0)	0	<0.01
Iraqi (0)	0	<0.01
Jordanian (0)	0	<0.01
Lebanese (19)	42	0.04
Moroccan (12)	12	0.01
Palestinian (0)	0	<0.01
Syrian (0)	0	<0.01
Other Arab (0)	0	<0.01
Armenian (0)	0	<0.01
Assyrian/Chaldean/Syriac (0)	0	<0.01
Australian (14)	14	0.01
Austrian (0)	20	0.02
Basque (0)	0	<0.01
Belgian (42)	91	0.08
Brazilian (95)	95	0.09
British (218)	329	0.31
Bulgarian (0)	0	<0.01
Cajun (20)	84	0.08
Canadian (17)	73	0.07
Carpatho Rusyn (0)	0	<0.01
Celtic (8)	25	0.02
Croatian (236)	264	0.25
Cypriot (0)	0	<0.01
Czech (43)	143	0.13
Czechoslovakian (30)	41	0.04
Danish (14)	147	0.14
Dutch (294)	1,774	1.65
Eastern European (0)	0	<0.01
English (4,820)	10,538	9.81
Estonian (0)	0	<0.01
European (601)	668	0.62
Finnish (2)	5	<0.01
French, ex. Basque (569)	2,795	2.60
French Canadian (183)	293	0.27
German (11,509)	26,105	24.31
German Russian (0)	0	<0.01
Greek (35)	99	0.09
Guyanese (0)	0	<0.01
Hungarian (106)	227	0.21
Icelander (17)	25	0.02
Iranian (0)	19	0.02
Irish (5,085)	16,094	14.99
Israeli (0)	0	<0.01
Italian (865)	2,483	2.31
Latvian (0)	0	<0.01
Lithuanian (19)	35	0.03
Luxemburger (0)	0	<0.01
Macedonian (0)	0	<0.01
Maltese (0)	0	<0.01
New Zealander (0)	33	0.03
Northern European (0)	0	<0.01
Norwegian (61)	255	0.24
Pennsylvania German (0)	50	0.05
Polish (420)	1,122	1.04
Portuguese (26)	130	0.12
Romanian (85)	96	0.09
Russian (38)	261	0.24
Scandinavian (39)	64	0.06
Scotch-Irish (719)	1,670	1.56
Scottish (896)	2,140	1.99
Serbian (40)	40	0.04
Slavic (0)	0	<0.01
Slovak (48)	99	0.09
Slovene (11)	37	0.03
Soviet Union (0)	0	<0.01
Swedish (121)	371	0.35
Swiss (49)	315	0.29
Turkish (0)	0	<0.01
Ukrainian (0)	12	0.01
Welsh (57)	439	0.41
West Indian, ex. Hispanic (18)	37	0.03
Bahamian (0)	0	<0.01
Barbadian (0)	0	<0.01
Belizean (0)	0	<0.01
Bermudan (0)	0	<0.01
British West Indian (0)	0	<0.01
Dutch West Indian (0)	0	<0.01
Haitian (13)	32	0.03
Jamaican (5)	5	<0.01
Trinidadian/Tobagonian (0)	0	<0.01
U.S. Virgin Islander (0)	0	<0.01
West Indian (0)	0	<0.01
Other West Indian (0)	0	<0.01
Yugoslavian (17)	29	0.03

Hispanic Origin	Population	%
Hispanic or Latino (of any race)	5,350	4.85
Central American, ex. Mexican	362	0.33
Costa Rican	14	0.01
Guatemalan	64	0.06
Honduran	116	0.11
Nicaraguan	14	0.01
Panamanian	23	0.02
Salvadoran	131	0.12
Other Central American	0	<0.01
Cuban	127	0.12
Dominican Republic	15	0.01
Mexican	3,970	3.60
Puerto Rican	361	0.33
South American	115	0.10
Argentinean	17	0.02
Bolivian	9	0.01
Chilean	2	<0.01
Colombian	23	0.02
Ecuadorian	26	0.02
Paraguayan	0	<0.01
Peruvian	21	0.02
Uruguayan	0	<0.01
Venezuelan	17	0.02
Other South American	0	<0.01
Other Hispanic or Latino	400	0.36

Race*	Population	%
African-American/Black (7,661)	9,134	8.29
Not Hispanic (7,541)	8,927	8.10
Hispanic (120)	207	0.19
American Indian/Alaska Native (303)	844	0.77
Not Hispanic (255)	745	0.68
Hispanic (48)	99	0.09
Alaska Athabascan (Ala. Nat.) (0)	0	<0.01
Aleut (Alaska Native) (0)	0	<0.01
Apache (7)	14	0.01
Arapaho (0)	0	<0.01
Blackfeet (11)	23	0.02
Canadian/French Am. Ind. (4)	5	<0.01
Central American Ind. (0)	0	<0.01
Cherokee (67)	277	0.25
Cheyenne (0)	1	<0.01
Chickasaw (2)	9	0.01
Chippewa (5)	12	0.01
Choctaw (11)	30	0.03
Colville (0)	0	<0.01
Comanche (1)	2	<0.01
Cree (0)	0	<0.01
Creek (8)	12	0.01
Crow (0)	0	<0.01
Delaware (1)	4	<0.01
Hopi (0)	0	<0.01
Houma (4)	4	<0.01
Inupiat (Alaska Native) (4)	4	<0.01
Iroquois (4)	12	0.01
Kiowa (0)	0	<0.01
Lumbee (3)	3	<0.01
Menominee (0)	1	<0.01
Mexican American Ind. (23)	26	0.02
Navajo (6)	8	0.01
Osage (1)	2	<0.01
Ottawa (0)	4	<0.01
Paiute (0)	0	<0.01
Pima (3)	3	<0.01
Potawatomi (3)	5	<0.01
Pueblo (0)	0	<0.01
Puget Sound Salish (0)	0	<0.01
Seminole (3)	3	<0.01
Shoshone (0)	2	<0.01
Sioux (8)	20	0.02
South American Ind. (0)	1	<0.01
Spanish American Ind. (0)	0	<0.01
Tlingit-Haida (Alaska Native) (0)	0	<0.01
Tohono O'Odham (0)	0	<0.01
Tsimshian (Alaska Native) (0)	0	<0.01
Ute (0)	0	<0.01
Yakama (0)	0	<0.01
Yaqui (0)	0	<0.01
Yuman (0)	0	<0.01
Yup'ik (Alaska Native) (0)	0	<0.01
Asian (875)	1,228	1.11
Not Hispanic (858)	1,186	1.08
Hispanic (17)	42	0.04
Bangladeshi (0)	1	<0.01
Bhutanese (0)	0	<0.01
Burmese (6)	6	0.01
Cambodian (16)	17	0.02
Chinese, ex. Taiwanese (117)	151	0.14
Filipino (182)	290	0.26
Hmong (0)	0	<0.01
Indian (171)	220	0.20
Indonesian (2)	7	0.01
Japanese (62)	104	0.09
Korean (93)	156	0.14
Laotian (6)	10	0.01
Malaysian (1)	1	<0.01
Nepalese (0)	0	<0.01
Pakistani (24)	27	0.02
Sri Lankan (5)	5	<0.01
Taiwanese (23)	26	0.02
Thai (19)	33	0.03
Vietnamese (57)	69	0.06
Hawaii Native/Pacific Islander (53)	154	0.14
Not Hispanic (43)	141	0.13
Hispanic (10)	13	0.01
Fijian (0)	0	<0.01
Guamanian/Chamorro (27)	47	0.04
Marshallese (0)	0	<0.01
Native Hawaiian (14)	56	0.05
Samoan (5)	11	0.01
Tongan (0)	0	<0.01
White (95,961)	98,242	89.12
Not Hispanic (93,887)	95,860	86.96
Hispanic (2,074)	2,382	2.16

Notes: † The Census 2010 population figure is used to calculate the percentages in the Hispanic Origin and Race categories. Ancestry percentages are based on the 2006-2010 American Community Survey population (not shown); ‡ Numbers in parentheses indicate the number of people reporting a single ancestry; * Numbers in parentheses indicate the number of persons reporting this race alone, not in combination with any other race; Please refer to the Explanation of Data for more information.

Clay County
Population: 26,890

Ancestry	Population	%
Afghan (0)	0	<0.01
African, Sub-Saharan (0)	41	0.15
African (0)	41	0.15
Cape Verdean (0)	0	<0.01
Ethiopian (0)	0	<0.01
Ghanaian (0)	0	<0.01
Kenyan (0)	0	<0.01
Liberian (0)	0	<0.01
Nigerian (0)	0	<0.01
Senegalese (0)	0	<0.01
Sierra Leonean (0)	0	<0.01
Somalian (0)	0	<0.01
South African (0)	0	<0.01
Sudanese (0)	0	<0.01
Ugandan (0)	0	<0.01
Zimbabwean (0)	0	<0.01
Other Sub-Saharan African (0)	0	<0.01
Albanian (0)	0	<0.01
Alsatian (0)	0	<0.01
American (5,442)	5,442	20.17
Arab (4)	17	0.06
Arab (0)	0	<0.01
Egyptian (4)	4	0.01
Iraqi (0)	0	<0.01
Jordanian (0)	0	<0.01
Lebanese (0)	0	<0.01
Moroccan (0)	0	<0.01
Palestinian (0)	0	<0.01
Syrian (0)	13	0.05
Other Arab (0)	0	<0.01
Armenian (0)	0	<0.01
Assyrian/Chaldean/Syriac (0)	0	<0.01
Australian (0)	0	<0.01
Austrian (10)	62	0.23
Basque (0)	0	<0.01
Belgian (2)	55	0.20
Brazilian (0)	0	<0.01
British (47)	219	0.81
Bulgarian (0)	14	0.05
Cajun (0)	0	<0.01
Canadian (55)	71	0.26
Carpatho Rusyn (0)	0	<0.01
Celtic (0)	0	<0.01
Croatian (4)	20	0.07
Cypriot (0)	0	<0.01
Czech (0)	7	0.03
Czechoslovakian (0)	0	<0.01
Danish (2)	15	0.06
Dutch (63)	670	2.48
Eastern European (0)	0	<0.01
English (1,207)	2,980	11.04
Estonian (0)	0	<0.01
European (208)	208	0.77
Finnish (26)	43	0.16
French, ex. Basque (158)	1,070	3.97
French Canadian (0)	44	0.16
German (2,902)	7,877	29.19
German Russian (0)	0	<0.01
Greek (0)	0	<0.01
Guyanese (0)	0	<0.01
Hungarian (0)	27	0.10
Icelander (0)	0	<0.01
Iranian (0)	0	<0.01
Irish (787)	3,444	12.76
Israeli (0)	0	<0.01
Italian (135)	561	2.08
Latvian (11)	11	0.04
Lithuanian (11)	14	0.05
Luxemburger (0)	0	<0.01
Macedonian (0)	0	<0.01
Maltese (0)	0	<0.01
New Zealander (0)	0	<0.01
Northern European (0)	0	<0.01
Norwegian (6)	41	0.15
Pennsylvania German (0)	0	<0.01
Polish (118)	358	1.33
Portuguese (25)	25	0.09
Romanian (0)	0	<0.01
Russian (29)	75	0.28
Scandinavian (18)	18	0.07
Scotch-Irish (200)	441	1.63
Scottish (133)	545	2.02
Serbian (0)	23	0.09
Slavic (0)	24	0.09
Slovak (9)	37	0.14
Slovene (0)	0	<0.01
Soviet Union (0)	0	<0.01
Swedish (7)	78	0.29
Swiss (12)	112	0.42
Turkish (19)	39	0.14
Ukrainian (0)	0	<0.01
Welsh (56)	350	1.30
West Indian, ex. Hispanic (0)	0	<0.01
Bahamian (0)	0	<0.01
Barbadian (0)	0	<0.01
Belizean (0)	0	<0.01
Bermudan (0)	0	<0.01
British West Indian (0)	0	<0.01
Dutch West Indian (0)	0	<0.01
Haitian (0)	0	<0.01
Jamaican (0)	0	<0.01
Trinidadian/Tobagonian (0)	0	<0.01
U.S. Virgin Islander (0)	0	<0.01
West Indian (0)	0	<0.01
Other West Indian (0)	0	<0.01
Yugoslavian (0)	23	0.09

Hispanic Origin	Population	%
Hispanic or Latino (of any race)	307	1.14
Central American, ex. Mexican	9	0.03
Costa Rican	1	<0.01
Guatemalan	5	0.02
Honduran	1	<0.01
Nicaraguan	0	<0.01
Panamanian	2	0.01
Salvadoran	0	<0.01
Other Central American	0	<0.01
Cuban	5	0.02
Dominican Republic	0	<0.01
Mexican	214	0.80
Puerto Rican	21	0.08
South American	9	0.03
Argentinean	0	<0.01
Bolivian	0	<0.01
Chilean	0	<0.01
Colombian	9	0.03
Ecuadorian	0	<0.01
Paraguayan	0	<0.01
Peruvian	0	<0.01
Uruguayan	0	<0.01
Venezuelan	0	<0.01
Other South American	0	<0.01
Other Hispanic or Latino	49	0.18

Race*	Population	%
African-American/Black (87)	183	0.68
Not Hispanic (85)	177	0.66
Hispanic (2)	6	0.02
American Indian/Alaska Native (59)	156	0.58
Not Hispanic (57)	151	0.56
Hispanic (2)	5	0.02
Alaska Athabascan (Ala. Nat.) (0)	0	<0.01
Aleut (Alaska Native) (0)	0	<0.01
Apache (0)	0	<0.01
Arapaho (0)	0	<0.01
Blackfeet (0)	12	0.04
Canadian/French Am. Ind. (0)	0	<0.01
Central American Ind. (0)	0	<0.01
Cherokee (15)	53	0.20
Cheyenne (0)	6	0.02
Chickasaw (0)	1	<0.01
Chippewa (0)	0	<0.01
Choctaw (0)	1	<0.01
Colville (0)	0	<0.01
Comanche (0)	0	<0.01
Cree (1)	1	<0.01
Creek (0)	1	<0.01
Crow (1)	3	0.01
Delaware (0)	0	<0.01
Hopi (0)	0	<0.01
Houma (0)	0	<0.01
Inupiat (Alaska Native) (1)	2	0.01
Iroquois (0)	0	<0.01
Kiowa (0)	0	<0.01
Lumbee (0)	2	0.01
Menominee (0)	0	<0.01
Mexican American Ind. (1)	1	<0.01
Navajo (5)	8	0.03
Osage (0)	0	<0.01
Ottawa (0)	0	<0.01
Paiute (0)	0	<0.01
Pima (0)	0	<0.01
Potawatomi (0)	0	<0.01
Pueblo (0)	0	<0.01
Puget Sound Salish (0)	0	<0.01
Seminole (0)	0	<0.01
Shoshone (0)	0	<0.01
Sioux (2)	8	0.03
South American Ind. (0)	0	<0.01
Spanish American Ind. (0)	0	<0.01
Tlingit-Haida (Alaska Native) (0)	0	<0.01
Tohono O'Odham (0)	0	<0.01
Tsimshian (Alaska Native) (0)	0	<0.01
Ute (0)	0	<0.01
Yakama (0)	0	<0.01
Yaqui (0)	0	<0.01
Yuman (0)	0	<0.01
Yup'ik (Alaska Native) (0)	0	<0.01
Asian (60)	85	0.32
Not Hispanic (60)	85	0.32
Hispanic (0)	0	<0.01
Bangladeshi (0)	0	<0.01
Bhutanese (0)	0	<0.01
Burmese (0)	0	<0.01
Cambodian (0)	0	<0.01
Chinese, ex. Taiwanese (12)	13	0.05
Filipino (9)	13	0.05
Hmong (0)	0	<0.01
Indian (20)	27	0.10
Indonesian (0)	0	<0.01
Japanese (1)	4	0.01
Korean (6)	9	0.03
Laotian (0)	0	<0.01
Malaysian (0)	0	<0.01
Nepalese (0)	0	<0.01
Pakistani (0)	0	<0.01
Sri Lankan (0)	0	<0.01
Taiwanese (0)	0	<0.01
Thai (3)	4	0.01
Vietnamese (6)	6	0.02
Hawaii Native/Pacific Islander (8)	15	0.06
Not Hispanic (8)	15	0.06
Hispanic (0)	0	<0.01
Fijian (0)	0	<0.01
Guamanian/Chamorro (0)	0	<0.01
Marshallese (0)	0	<0.01
Native Hawaiian (7)	13	0.05
Samoan (0)	2	0.01
Tongan (0)	0	<0.01
White (26,303)	26,539	98.69
Not Hispanic (26,146)	26,362	98.04
Hispanic (157)	177	0.66

Notes: † The Census 2010 population figure is used to calculate the percentages in the Hispanic Origin and Race categories. Ancestry percentages are based on the 2006-2010 American Community Survey population (not shown); ‡ Numbers in parentheses indicate the number of people reporting a single ancestry; * Numbers in parentheses indicate the number of persons reporting this race alone, not in combination with any other race; Please refer to the Explanation of Data for more information.

Clinton County
Population: 33,224

Ancestry	Population	%
Afghan (0)	0	<0.01
African, Sub-Saharan (12)	12	0.04
African (12)	12	0.04
Cape Verdean (0)	0	<0.01
Ethiopian (0)	0	<0.01
Ghanaian (0)	0	<0.01
Kenyan (0)	0	<0.01
Liberian (0)	0	<0.01
Nigerian (0)	0	<0.01
Senegalese (0)	0	<0.01
Sierra Leonean (0)	0	<0.01
Somalian (0)	0	<0.01
South African (0)	0	<0.01
Sudanese (0)	0	<0.01
Ugandan (0)	0	<0.01
Zimbabwean (0)	0	<0.01
Other Sub-Saharan African (0)	0	<0.01
Albanian (0)	3	0.01
Alsatian (0)	0	<0.01
American (3,678)	3,678	11.06
Arab (9)	39	0.12
Arab (0)	0	<0.01
Egyptian (0)	0	<0.01
Iraqi (0)	0	<0.01
Jordanian (0)	0	<0.01
Lebanese (0)	0	<0.01
Moroccan (0)	0	<0.01
Palestinian (0)	0	<0.01
Syrian (9)	39	0.12
Other Arab (0)	0	<0.01
Armenian (0)	0	<0.01
Assyrian/Chaldean/Syriac (0)	0	<0.01
Australian (0)	0	<0.01
Austrian (0)	17	0.05
Basque (0)	0	<0.01
Belgian (27)	104	0.31
Brazilian (0)	0	<0.01
British (12)	45	0.14
Bulgarian (0)	0	<0.01
Cajun (0)	0	<0.01
Canadian (16)	16	0.05
Carpatho Rusyn (0)	0	<0.01
Celtic (0)	0	<0.01
Croatian (11)	66	0.20
Cypriot (0)	0	<0.01
Czech (26)	30	0.09
Czechoslovakian (0)	0	<0.01
Danish (17)	80	0.24
Dutch (201)	848	2.55
Eastern European (0)	0	<0.01
English (1,469)	3,188	9.58
Estonian (0)	0	<0.01
European (243)	312	0.94
Finnish (0)	12	0.04
French, ex. Basque (204)	684	2.06
French Canadian (17)	17	0.05
German (3,236)	7,465	22.44
German Russian (0)	0	<0.01
Greek (0)	109	0.33
Guyanese (0)	0	<0.01
Hungarian (24)	84	0.25
Icelander (0)	0	<0.01
Iranian (0)	0	<0.01
Irish (1,057)	3,413	10.26
Israeli (0)	0	<0.01
Italian (158)	460	1.38
Latvian (0)	0	<0.01
Lithuanian (9)	13	0.04
Luxemburger (0)	0	<0.01
Macedonian (0)	0	<0.01
Maltese (0)	0	<0.01
New Zealander (22)	22	0.07
Northern European (3)	3	0.01
Norwegian (39)	154	0.46
Pennsylvania German (38)	50	0.15
Polish (215)	450	1.35
Portuguese (0)	0	<0.01
Romanian (10)	18	0.05
Russian (0)	0	<0.01
Scandinavian (38)	38	0.11
Scotch-Irish (129)	324	0.97
Scottish (551)	899	2.70
Serbian (63)	162	0.49
Slavic (0)	0	<0.01
Slovak (0)	3	0.01
Slovene (0)	0	<0.01
Soviet Union (0)	0	<0.01
Swedish (72)	392	1.18
Swiss (5)	73	0.22
Turkish (0)	0	<0.01
Ukrainian (26)	26	0.08
Welsh (57)	222	0.67
West Indian, ex. Hispanic (0)	0	<0.01
Bahamian (0)	0	<0.01
Barbadian (0)	0	<0.01
Belizean (0)	0	<0.01
Bermudan (0)	0	<0.01
British West Indian (0)	0	<0.01
Dutch West Indian (0)	0	<0.01
Haitian (0)	0	<0.01
Jamaican (0)	0	<0.01
Trinidadian/Tobagonian (0)	0	<0.01
U.S. Virgin Islander (0)	0	<0.01
West Indian (0)	0	<0.01
Other West Indian (0)	0	<0.01
Yugoslavian (30)	30	0.09

Hispanic Origin	Population	%
Hispanic or Latino (of any race)	4,395	13.23
Central American, ex. Mexican	121	0.36
Costa Rican	1	<0.01
Guatemalan	55	0.17
Honduran	9	0.03
Nicaraguan	9	0.03
Panamanian	2	0.01
Salvadoran	45	0.14
Other Central American	0	<0.01
Cuban	4	0.01
Dominican Republic	0	<0.01
Mexican	3,958	11.91
Puerto Rican	53	0.16
South American	14	0.04
Argentinean	4	0.01
Bolivian	0	<0.01
Chilean	0	<0.01
Colombian	9	0.03
Ecuadorian	0	<0.01
Paraguayan	0	<0.01
Peruvian	1	<0.01
Uruguayan	0	<0.01
Venezuelan	0	<0.01
Other South American	0	<0.01
Other Hispanic or Latino	245	0.74

Race*	Population	%
African-American/Black (142)	229	0.69
Not Hispanic (138)	205	0.62
Hispanic (4)	24	0.07
American Indian/Alaska Native (83)	212	0.64
Not Hispanic (44)	143	0.43
Hispanic (39)	69	0.21
Alaska Athabascan (Ala. Nat.) (0)	0	<0.01
Aleut (Alaska Native) (0)	0	<0.01
Apache (2)	2	0.01
Arapaho (0)	0	<0.01
Blackfeet (2)	7	0.02
Canadian/French Am. Ind. (0)	0	<0.01
Central American Ind. (0)	0	<0.01
Cherokee (13)	59	0.18
Cheyenne (0)	1	<0.01
Chickasaw (1)	1	<0.01
Chippewa (2)	5	0.02
Choctaw (3)	4	0.01
Colville (0)	0	<0.01
Comanche (0)	0	<0.01
Cree (1)	1	<0.01
Creek (0)	0	<0.01
Crow (0)	0	<0.01
Delaware (0)	0	<0.01
Hopi (0)	0	<0.01
Houma (0)	0	<0.01
Inupiat (Alaska Native) (3)	4	0.01
Iroquois (0)	3	0.01
Kiowa (0)	0	<0.01
Lumbee (0)	0	<0.01
Menominee (0)	0	<0.01
Mexican American Ind. (6)	10	0.03
Navajo (0)	0	<0.01
Osage (0)	0	<0.01
Ottawa (1)	1	<0.01
Paiute (1)	1	<0.01
Pima (0)	0	<0.01
Potawatomi (0)	1	<0.01
Pueblo (0)	0	<0.01
Puget Sound Salish (0)	0	<0.01
Seminole (0)	0	<0.01
Shoshone (0)	0	<0.01
Sioux (1)	1	<0.01
South American Ind. (0)	1	<0.01
Spanish American Ind. (2)	2	0.01
Tlingit-Haida (Alaska Native) (0)	0	<0.01
Tohono O'Odham (0)	0	<0.01
Tsimshian (Alaska Native) (0)	0	<0.01
Ute (0)	0	<0.01
Yakama (0)	0	<0.01
Yaqui (0)	0	<0.01
Yuman (0)	0	<0.01
Yup'ik (Alaska Native) (0)	0	<0.01
Asian (72)	124	0.37
Not Hispanic (65)	95	0.29
Hispanic (7)	29	0.09
Bangladeshi (0)	0	<0.01
Bhutanese (0)	0	<0.01
Burmese (0)	0	<0.01
Cambodian (0)	0	<0.01
Chinese, ex. Taiwanese (12)	15	0.05
Filipino (23)	42	0.13
Hmong (0)	0	<0.01
Indian (10)	13	0.04
Indonesian (1)	1	<0.01
Japanese (6)	13	0.04
Korean (13)	16	0.05
Laotian (0)	1	<0.01
Malaysian (0)	0	<0.01
Nepalese (0)	0	<0.01
Pakistani (0)	0	<0.01
Sri Lankan (0)	0	<0.01
Taiwanese (0)	0	<0.01
Thai (1)	5	0.02
Vietnamese (2)	4	0.01
Hawaii Native/Pacific Islander (3)	25	0.08
Not Hispanic (3)	13	0.04
Hispanic (0)	12	0.04
Fijian (0)	0	<0.01
Guamanian/Chamorro (0)	1	<0.01
Marshallese (0)	0	<0.01
Native Hawaiian (2)	8	0.02
Samoan (1)	3	0.01
Tongan (0)	0	<0.01
White (30,232)	30,625	92.18
Not Hispanic (28,349)	28,552	85.94
Hispanic (1,883)	2,073	6.24

Notes: † The Census 2010 population figure is used to calculate the percentages in the Hispanic Origin and Race categories. Ancestry percentages are based on the 2006-2010 American Community Survey population (not shown); ‡ Numbers in parentheses indicate the number of people reporting a single ancestry; * Numbers in parentheses indicate the number of persons reporting this race alone, not in combination with any other race; Please refer to the Explanation of Data for more information.

Crawford County

Population: 10,713

Ancestry	Population	%
Afghan (0)	0	<0.01
African, Sub-Saharan (0)	0	<0.01
African (0)	0	<0.01
Cape Verdean (0)	0	<0.01
Ethiopian (0)	0	<0.01
Ghanaian (0)	0	<0.01
Kenyan (0)	0	<0.01
Liberian (0)	0	<0.01
Nigerian (0)	0	<0.01
Senegalese (0)	0	<0.01
Sierra Leonean (0)	0	<0.01
Somalian (0)	0	<0.01
South African (0)	0	<0.01
Sudanese (0)	0	<0.01
Ugandan (0)	0	<0.01
Zimbabwean (0)	0	<0.01
Other Sub-Saharan African (0)	0	<0.01
Albanian (0)	0	<0.01
Alsatian (0)	0	<0.01
American (1,454)	1,454	13.43
Arab (0)	0	<0.01
Arab (0)	0	<0.01
Egyptian (0)	0	<0.01
Iraqi (0)	0	<0.01
Jordanian (0)	0	<0.01
Lebanese (0)	0	<0.01
Moroccan (0)	0	<0.01
Palestinian (0)	0	<0.01
Syrian (0)	0	<0.01
Other Arab (0)	0	<0.01
Armenian (0)	0	<0.01
Assyrian/Chaldean/Syriac (0)	0	<0.01
Australian (0)	0	<0.01
Austrian (3)	25	0.23
Basque (0)	0	<0.01
Belgian (0)	0	<0.01
Brazilian (0)	0	<0.01
British (5)	17	0.16
Bulgarian (0)	0	<0.01
Cajun (0)	0	<0.01
Canadian (0)	0	<0.01
Carpatho Rusyn (0)	0	<0.01
Celtic (0)	0	<0.01
Croatian (0)	3	0.03
Cypriot (0)	0	<0.01
Czech (0)	0	<0.01
Czechoslovakian (0)	0	<0.01
Danish (72)	72	0.67
Dutch (29)	283	2.61
Eastern European (0)	0	<0.01
English (449)	940	8.68
Estonian (0)	0	<0.01
European (198)	228	2.11
Finnish (0)	0	<0.01
French, ex. Basque (58)	251	2.32
French Canadian (33)	80	0.74
German (965)	2,577	23.81
German Russian (0)	0	<0.01
Greek (24)	62	0.57
Guyanese (0)	0	<0.01
Hungarian (0)	26	0.24
Icelander (0)	0	<0.01
Iranian (0)	0	<0.01
Irish (564)	1,881	17.38
Israeli (0)	0	<0.01
Italian (20)	70	0.65
Latvian (0)	0	<0.01
Lithuanian (0)	0	<0.01
Luxemburger (0)	0	<0.01
Macedonian (0)	0	<0.01
Maltese (0)	0	<0.01
New Zealander (0)	0	<0.01
Northern European (0)	0	<0.01
Norwegian (8)	8	0.07
Pennsylvania German (0)	0	<0.01
Polish (22)	70	0.65
Portuguese (10)	12	0.11
Romanian (0)	0	<0.01
Russian (85)	88	0.81
Scandinavian (0)	0	<0.01
Scotch-Irish (88)	176	1.63
Scottish (48)	326	3.01
Serbian (0)	0	<0.01
Slavic (0)	0	<0.01
Slovak (0)	6	0.06
Slovene (0)	0	<0.01
Soviet Union (0)	0	<0.01
Swedish (22)	198	1.83
Swiss (16)	44	0.41
Turkish (0)	0	<0.01
Ukrainian (0)	0	<0.01
Welsh (8)	40	0.37
West Indian, ex. Hispanic (0)	0	<0.01
Bahamian (0)	0	<0.01
Barbadian (0)	0	<0.01
Belizean (0)	0	<0.01
Bermudan (0)	0	<0.01
British West Indian (0)	0	<0.01
Dutch West Indian (0)	0	<0.01
Haitian (0)	0	<0.01
Jamaican (0)	0	<0.01
Trinidadian/Tobagonian (0)	0	<0.01
U.S. Virgin Islander (0)	0	<0.01
West Indian (0)	0	<0.01
Other West Indian (0)	0	<0.01
Yugoslavian (0)	0	<0.01

Hispanic Origin	Population	%
Hispanic or Latino (of any race)	126	1.18
Central American, ex. Mexican	10	0.09
Costa Rican	0	<0.01
Guatemalan	4	0.04
Honduran	4	0.04
Nicaraguan	0	<0.01
Panamanian	2	0.02
Salvadoran	0	<0.01
Other Central American	0	<0.01
Cuban	0	<0.01
Dominican Republic	0	<0.01
Mexican	70	0.65
Puerto Rican	18	0.17
South American	3	0.03
Argentinean	0	<0.01
Bolivian	0	<0.01
Chilean	0	<0.01
Colombian	0	<0.01
Ecuadorian	1	0.01
Paraguayan	0	<0.01
Peruvian	2	0.02
Uruguayan	0	<0.01
Venezuelan	0	<0.01
Other South American	0	<0.01
Other Hispanic or Latino	25	0.23

Race*	Population	%
African-American/Black (24)	47	0.44
Not Hispanic (21)	42	0.39
Hispanic (3)	5	0.05
American Indian/Alaska Native (43)	103	0.96
Not Hispanic (40)	99	0.92
Hispanic (3)	4	0.04
Alaska Athabascan (Ala. Nat.) (0)	0	<0.01
Aleut (Alaska Native) (0)	0	<0.01
Apache (0)	3	0.03
Arapaho (0)	0	<0.01
Blackfeet (0)	1	0.01
Canadian/French Am. Ind. (1)	1	0.01
Central American Ind. (0)	0	<0.01
Cherokee (9)	42	0.39
Cheyenne (0)	0	<0.01
Chickasaw (0)	1	0.01
Chippewa (1)	2	0.02
Choctaw (0)	0	<0.01
Colville (0)	0	<0.01
Comanche (0)	0	<0.01
Cree (0)	0	<0.01
Creek (0)	1	0.01
Crow (0)	0	<0.01
Delaware (0)	0	<0.01
Hopi (0)	0	<0.01
Houma (0)	0	<0.01
Inupiat (Alaska Native) (0)	0	<0.01
Iroquois (1)	1	0.01
Kiowa (0)	0	<0.01
Lumbee (0)	0	<0.01
Menominee (1)	1	0.01
Mexican American Ind. (0)	0	<0.01
Navajo (0)	3	0.03
Osage (0)	5	0.05
Ottawa (0)	0	<0.01
Paiute (0)	0	<0.01
Pima (0)	0	<0.01
Potawatomi (0)	0	<0.01
Pueblo (0)	3	0.03
Puget Sound Salish (0)	0	<0.01
Seminole (1)	5	0.05
Shoshone (0)	0	<0.01
Sioux (0)	2	0.02
South American Ind. (0)	0	<0.01
Spanish American Ind. (0)	0	<0.01
Tlingit-Haida (Alaska Native) (0)	0	<0.01
Tohono O'Odham (0)	0	<0.01
Tsimshian (Alaska Native) (0)	0	<0.01
Ute (0)	0	<0.01
Yakama (0)	0	<0.01
Yaqui (0)	0	<0.01
Yuman (0)	0	<0.01
Yup'ik (Alaska Native) (0)	0	<0.01
Asian (20)	36	0.34
Not Hispanic (20)	36	0.34
Hispanic (0)	0	<0.01
Bangladeshi (0)	0	<0.01
Bhutanese (0)	0	<0.01
Burmese (0)	0	<0.01
Cambodian (0)	0	<0.01
Chinese, ex. Taiwanese (3)	5	0.05
Filipino (11)	14	0.13
Hmong (0)	0	<0.01
Indian (2)	5	0.05
Indonesian (0)	0	<0.01
Japanese (1)	4	0.04
Korean (0)	0	<0.01
Laotian (0)	0	<0.01
Malaysian (0)	0	<0.01
Nepalese (0)	0	<0.01
Pakistani (0)	0	<0.01
Sri Lankan (0)	0	<0.01
Taiwanese (0)	0	<0.01
Thai (0)	8	0.07
Vietnamese (1)	1	0.01
Hawaii Native/Pacific Islander (9)	13	0.12
Not Hispanic (9)	12	0.11
Hispanic (0)	1	0.01
Fijian (0)	0	<0.01
Guamanian/Chamorro (0)	2	0.02
Marshallese (0)	0	<0.01
Native Hawaiian (8)	8	0.07
Samoan (0)	0	<0.01
Tongan (0)	0	<0.01
White (10,438)	10,556	98.53
Not Hispanic (10,390)	10,492	97.94
Hispanic (48)	64	0.60

Notes: † The Census 2010 population figure is used to calculate the percentages in the Hispanic Origin and Race categories. Ancestry percentages are based on the 2006-2010 American Community Survey population (not shown); ‡ Numbers in parentheses indicate the number of people reporting a single ancestry; * Numbers in parentheses indicate the number of persons reporting this race alone, not in combination with any other race; Please refer to the Explanation of Data for more information.

Daviess County
Population: 31,648

Ancestry	Population	%
Afghan (0)	0	<0.01
African, Sub-Saharan (0)	0	<0.01
African (0)	0	<0.01
Cape Verdean (0)	0	<0.01
Ethiopian (0)	0	<0.01
Ghanaian (0)	0	<0.01
Kenyan (0)	0	<0.01
Liberian (0)	0	<0.01
Nigerian (0)	0	<0.01
Senegalese (0)	0	<0.01
Sierra Leonean (0)	0	<0.01
Somalian (0)	0	<0.01
South African (0)	0	<0.01
Sudanese (0)	0	<0.01
Ugandan (0)	0	<0.01
Zimbabwean (0)	0	<0.01
Other Sub-Saharan African (0)	0	<0.01
Albanian (0)	0	<0.01
Alsatian (0)	0	<0.01
American (3,345)	3,345	10.77
Arab (0)	0	<0.01
Arab (0)	0	<0.01
Egyptian (0)	0	<0.01
Iraqi (0)	0	<0.01
Jordanian (0)	0	<0.01
Lebanese (0)	0	<0.01
Moroccan (0)	0	<0.01
Palestinian (0)	0	<0.01
Syrian (0)	0	<0.01
Other Arab (0)	0	<0.01
Armenian (0)	0	<0.01
Assyrian/Chaldean/Syriac (0)	0	<0.01
Australian (0)	0	<0.01
Austrian (56)	71	0.23
Basque (0)	0	<0.01
Belgian (0)	0	<0.01
Brazilian (0)	0	<0.01
British (25)	67	0.22
Bulgarian (0)	0	<0.01
Cajun (0)	0	<0.01
Canadian (28)	28	0.09
Carpatho Rusyn (0)	0	<0.01
Celtic (0)	0	<0.01
Croatian (0)	0	<0.01
Cypriot (0)	0	<0.01
Czech (9)	27	0.09
Czechoslovakian (0)	0	<0.01
Danish (0)	107	0.34
Dutch (137)	465	1.50
Eastern European (0)	0	<0.01
English (1,595)	3,282	10.57
Estonian (0)	0	<0.01
European (126)	126	0.41
Finnish (0)	0	<0.01
French, ex. Basque (193)	1,010	3.25
French Canadian (118)	120	0.39
German (6,043)	9,761	31.44
German Russian (0)	0	<0.01
Greek (9)	19	0.06
Guyanese (0)	0	<0.01
Hungarian (0)	31	0.10
Icelander (0)	0	<0.01
Iranian (0)	0	<0.01
Irish (1,363)	4,056	13.06
Israeli (0)	0	<0.01
Italian (188)	335	1.08
Latvian (0)	0	<0.01
Lithuanian (0)	0	<0.01
Luxemburger (0)	0	<0.01
Macedonian (0)	0	<0.01
Maltese (0)	0	<0.01
New Zealander (0)	0	<0.01
Northern European (34)	34	0.11
Norwegian (11)	117	0.38
Pennsylvania German (545)	545	1.76
Polish (76)	190	0.61
Portuguese (0)	0	<0.01
Romanian (0)	6	0.02
Russian (0)	0	<0.01
Scandinavian (0)	0	<0.01
Scotch-Irish (551)	776	2.50
Scottish (63)	307	0.99
Serbian (0)	11	0.04
Slavic (0)	15	0.05
Slovak (0)	0	<0.01
Slovene (0)	0	<0.01
Soviet Union (0)	0	<0.01
Swedish (178)	607	1.96
Swiss (238)	359	1.16
Turkish (0)	0	<0.01
Ukrainian (0)	0	<0.01
Welsh (64)	105	0.34
West Indian, ex. Hispanic (0)	63	0.20
Bahamian (0)	0	<0.01
Barbadian (0)	0	<0.01
Belizean (0)	0	<0.01
Bermudan (0)	0	<0.01
British West Indian (0)	0	<0.01
Dutch West Indian (0)	0	<0.01
Haitian (0)	0	<0.01
Jamaican (0)	63	0.20
Trinidadian/Tobagonian (0)	0	<0.01
U.S. Virgin Islander (0)	0	<0.01
West Indian (0)	0	<0.01
Other West Indian (0)	0	<0.01
Yugoslavian (0)	0	<0.01

Hispanic Origin	Population	%
Hispanic or Latino (of any race)	1,314	4.15
Central American, ex. Mexican	265	0.84
Costa Rican	1	<0.01
Guatemalan	75	0.24
Honduran	14	0.04
Nicaraguan	4	0.01
Panamanian	1	<0.01
Salvadoran	169	0.53
Other Central American	1	<0.01
Cuban	9	0.03
Dominican Republic	6	0.02
Mexican	917	2.90
Puerto Rican	42	0.13
South American	15	0.05
Argentinean	0	<0.01
Bolivian	0	<0.01
Chilean	0	<0.01
Colombian	3	0.01
Ecuadorian	1	<0.01
Paraguayan	0	<0.01
Peruvian	11	0.03
Uruguayan	0	<0.01
Venezuelan	0	<0.01
Other South American	0	<0.01
Other Hispanic or Latino	60	0.19

Race*	Population	%
African-American/Black (172)	311	0.98
Not Hispanic (165)	292	0.92
Hispanic (7)	19	0.06
American Indian/Alaska Native (71)	142	0.45
Not Hispanic (62)	117	0.37
Hispanic (9)	25	0.08
Alaska Athabascan (Ala. Nat.) (0)	0	<0.01
Aleut (Alaska Native) (0)	0	<0.01
Apache (4)	5	0.02
Arapaho (0)	0	<0.01
Blackfeet (0)	0	<0.01
Canadian/French Am. Ind. (0)	0	<0.01
Central American Ind. (0)	0	<0.01
Cherokee (15)	36	0.11
Cheyenne (0)	0	<0.01
Chickasaw (0)	0	<0.01
Chippewa (1)	2	0.01
Choctaw (3)	9	0.03
Colville (0)	0	<0.01
Comanche (0)	1	<0.01
Cree (0)	0	<0.01
Creek (0)	0	<0.01
Crow (0)	0	<0.01
Delaware (0)	0	<0.01
Hopi (0)	0	<0.01
Houma (0)	0	<0.01
Inupiat (Alaska Native) (0)	0	<0.01
Iroquois (1)	2	0.01
Kiowa (0)	0	<0.01
Lumbee (1)	2	0.01
Menominee (0)	0	<0.01
Mexican American Ind. (2)	3	0.01
Navajo (6)	6	0.02
Osage (0)	0	<0.01
Ottawa (0)	0	<0.01
Paiute (0)	0	<0.01
Pima (0)	0	<0.01
Potawatomi (0)	0	<0.01
Pueblo (0)	0	<0.01
Puget Sound Salish (0)	0	<0.01
Seminole (0)	0	<0.01
Shoshone (0)	0	<0.01
Sioux (5)	5	0.02
South American Ind. (1)	1	<0.01
Spanish American Ind. (0)	0	<0.01
Tlingit-Haida (Alaska Native) (0)	0	<0.01
Tohono O'Odham (0)	0	<0.01
Tsimshian (Alaska Native) (0)	0	<0.01
Ute (0)	0	<0.01
Yakama (0)	0	<0.01
Yaqui (0)	0	<0.01
Yuman (0)	0	<0.01
Yup'ik (Alaska Native) (3)	3	0.01
Asian (161)	195	0.62
Not Hispanic (161)	195	0.62
Hispanic (0)	0	<0.01
Bangladeshi (0)	0	<0.01
Bhutanese (0)	0	<0.01
Burmese (79)	80	0.25
Cambodian (0)	0	<0.01
Chinese, ex. Taiwanese (15)	17	0.05
Filipino (21)	35	0.11
Hmong (0)	0	<0.01
Indian (10)	13	0.04
Indonesian (0)	0	<0.01
Japanese (7)	18	0.06
Korean (9)	13	0.04
Laotian (0)	0	<0.01
Malaysian (0)	1	<0.01
Nepalese (0)	0	<0.01
Pakistani (9)	9	0.03
Sri Lankan (0)	0	<0.01
Taiwanese (1)	1	<0.01
Thai (2)	2	0.01
Vietnamese (4)	4	0.01
Hawaii Native/Pacific Islander (8)	21	0.07
Not Hispanic (6)	18	0.06
Hispanic (2)	3	0.01
Fijian (0)	0	<0.01
Guamanian/Chamorro (1)	1	<0.01
Marshallese (0)	0	<0.01
Native Hawaiian (5)	13	0.04
Samoan (0)	0	<0.01
Tongan (0)	0	<0.01
White (30,077)	30,395	96.04
Not Hispanic (29,696)	29,921	94.54
Hispanic (381)	474	1.50

Notes: † The Census 2010 population figure is used to calculate the percentages in the Hispanic Origin and Race categories. Ancestry percentages are based on the 2006-2010 American Community Survey population (not shown); ‡ Numbers in parentheses indicate the number of people reporting a single ancestry; * Numbers in parentheses indicate the number of persons reporting this race alone, not in combination with any other race; Please refer to the Explanation of Data for more information.

DeKalb County
Population: 42,223

Ancestry	Population	%
Afghan (0)	0	<0.01
African, Sub-Saharan (0)	0	<0.01
African (0)	0	<0.01
Cape Verdean (0)	0	<0.01
Ethiopian (0)	0	<0.01
Ghanaian (0)	0	<0.01
Kenyan (0)	0	<0.01
Liberian (0)	0	<0.01
Nigerian (0)	0	<0.01
Senegalese (0)	0	<0.01
Sierra Leonean (0)	0	<0.01
Somalian (0)	0	<0.01
South African (0)	0	<0.01
Sudanese (0)	0	<0.01
Ugandan (0)	0	<0.01
Zimbabwean (0)	0	<0.01
Other Sub-Saharan African (0)	0	<0.01
Albanian (0)	0	<0.01
Alsatian (0)	12	0.03
American (4,559)	4,559	10.86
Arab (0)	16	0.04
Arab (0)	0	<0.01
Egyptian (0)	0	<0.01
Iraqi (0)	0	<0.01
Jordanian (0)	0	<0.01
Lebanese (0)	16	0.04
Moroccan (0)	0	<0.01
Palestinian (0)	0	<0.01
Syrian (0)	0	<0.01
Other Arab (0)	0	<0.01
Armenian (0)	0	<0.01
Assyrian/Chaldean/Syriac (0)	0	<0.01
Australian (10)	41	0.10
Austrian (0)	0	<0.01
Basque (0)	0	<0.01
Belgian (46)	233	0.56
Brazilian (0)	0	<0.01
British (36)	83	0.20
Bulgarian (0)	0	<0.01
Cajun (0)	0	<0.01
Canadian (16)	20	0.05
Carpatho Rusyn (0)	0	<0.01
Celtic (0)	0	<0.01
Croatian (9)	23	0.05
Cypriot (0)	0	<0.01
Czech (21)	45	0.11
Czechoslovakian (15)	44	0.10
Danish (2)	33	0.08
Dutch (208)	1,078	2.57
Eastern European (0)	0	<0.01
English (1,250)	3,814	9.09
Estonian (0)	0	<0.01
European (276)	315	0.75
Finnish (9)	19	0.05
French, ex. Basque (191)	1,666	3.97
French Canadian (44)	113	0.27
German (7,441)	15,242	36.32
German Russian (0)	0	<0.01
Greek (25)	32	0.08
Guyanese (0)	0	<0.01
Hungarian (13)	116	0.28
Icelander (0)	0	<0.01
Iranian (0)	0	<0.01
Irish (1,085)	4,517	10.76
Israeli (0)	0	<0.01
Italian (389)	1,155	2.75
Latvian (0)	0	<0.01
Lithuanian (0)	0	<0.01
Luxemburger (0)	0	<0.01
Macedonian (0)	0	<0.01
Maltese (0)	0	<0.01
New Zealander (0)	0	<0.01
Northern European (0)	0	<0.01
Norwegian (20)	219	0.52
Pennsylvania German (66)	190	0.45
Polish (548)	1,695	4.04
Portuguese (9)	20	0.05
Romanian (22)	32	0.08
Russian (38)	86	0.20
Scandinavian (12)	12	0.03
Scotch-Irish (162)	495	1.18
Scottish (238)	929	2.21
Serbian (0)	0	<0.01
Slavic (0)	0	<0.01
Slovak (43)	138	0.33
Slovene (0)	12	0.03
Soviet Union (0)	0	<0.01
Swedish (65)	446	1.06
Swiss (154)	662	1.58
Turkish (0)	0	<0.01
Ukrainian (57)	145	0.35
Welsh (27)	206	0.49
West Indian, ex. Hispanic (0)	0	<0.01
Bahamian (0)	0	<0.01
Barbadian (0)	0	<0.01
Belizean (0)	0	<0.01
Bermudan (0)	0	<0.01
British West Indian (0)	0	<0.01
Dutch West Indian (0)	0	<0.01
Haitian (0)	0	<0.01
Jamaican (0)	0	<0.01
Trinidadian/Tobagonian (0)	0	<0.01
U.S. Virgin Islander (0)	0	<0.01
West Indian (0)	0	<0.01
Other West Indian (0)	0	<0.01
Yugoslavian (0)	17	0.04

Hispanic Origin	Population	%
Hispanic or Latino (of any race)	1,031	2.44
Central American, ex. Mexican	34	0.08
Costa Rican	2	<0.01
Guatemalan	16	0.04
Honduran	7	0.02
Nicaraguan	2	<0.01
Panamanian	0	<0.01
Salvadoran	7	0.02
Other Central American	0	<0.01
Cuban	8	0.02
Dominican Republic	1	<0.01
Mexican	838	1.98
Puerto Rican	51	0.12
South American	19	0.04
Argentinean	0	<0.01
Bolivian	1	<0.01
Chilean	3	0.01
Colombian	5	0.01
Ecuadorian	2	<0.01
Paraguayan	0	<0.01
Peruvian	1	<0.01
Uruguayan	6	0.01
Venezuelan	1	<0.01
Other South American	0	<0.01
Other Hispanic or Latino	80	0.19

Race*	Population	%
African-American/Black (148)	298	0.71
Not Hispanic (141)	275	0.65
Hispanic (7)	23	0.05
American Indian/Alaska Native (99)	258	0.61
Not Hispanic (84)	221	0.52
Hispanic (15)	37	0.09
Alaska Athabascan (Ala. Nat.) (0)	0	<0.01
Aleut (Alaska Native) (1)	1	<0.01
Apache (0)	10	0.02
Arapaho (0)	0	<0.01
Blackfeet (5)	15	0.04
Canadian/French Am. Ind. (0)	0	<0.01
Central American Ind. (1)	1	<0.01
Cherokee (26)	62	0.15
Cheyenne (1)	1	<0.01
Chickasaw (0)	0	<0.01
Chippewa (7)	10	0.02
Choctaw (3)	5	0.01
Colville (0)	0	<0.01
Comanche (0)	0	<0.01
Cree (0)	0	<0.01
Creek (0)	0	<0.01
Crow (0)	0	<0.01
Delaware (0)	0	<0.01
Hopi (0)	0	<0.01
Houma (0)	0	<0.01
Inupiat (Alaska Native) (0)	0	<0.01
Iroquois (4)	7	0.02
Kiowa (0)	0	<0.01
Lumbee (1)	1	<0.01
Menominee (0)	0	<0.01
Mexican American Ind. (2)	5	0.01
Navajo (0)	3	0.01
Osage (0)	0	<0.01
Ottawa (1)	1	<0.01
Paiute (0)	0	<0.01
Pima (0)	0	<0.01
Potawatomi (4)	6	0.01
Pueblo (0)	0	<0.01
Puget Sound Salish (0)	0	<0.01
Seminole (0)	0	<0.01
Shoshone (0)	1	<0.01
Sioux (1)	6	0.01
South American Ind. (0)	0	<0.01
Spanish American Ind. (0)	0	<0.01
Tlingit-Haida (Alaska Native) (0)	0	<0.01
Tohono O'Odham (0)	0	<0.01
Tsimshian (Alaska Native) (0)	0	<0.01
Ute (0)	0	<0.01
Yakama (0)	0	<0.01
Yaqui (0)	0	<0.01
Yuman (0)	0	<0.01
Yup'ik (Alaska Native) (0)	0	<0.01
Asian (192)	264	0.63
Not Hispanic (186)	245	0.58
Hispanic (6)	19	0.04
Bangladeshi (0)	0	<0.01
Bhutanese (0)	0	<0.01
Burmese (0)	0	<0.01
Cambodian (10)	13	0.03
Chinese, ex. Taiwanese (29)	34	0.08
Filipino (45)	64	0.15
Hmong (0)	0	<0.01
Indian (35)	35	0.08
Indonesian (1)	1	<0.01
Japanese (9)	19	0.04
Korean (13)	17	0.04
Laotian (1)	1	<0.01
Malaysian (0)	0	<0.01
Nepalese (0)	0	<0.01
Pakistani (3)	10	0.02
Sri Lankan (0)	0	<0.01
Taiwanese (0)	0	<0.01
Thai (8)	8	0.02
Vietnamese (27)	45	0.11
Hawaii Native/Pacific Islander (17)	39	0.09
Not Hispanic (17)	34	0.08
Hispanic (0)	5	0.01
Fijian (0)	0	<0.01
Guamanian/Chamorro (8)	18	0.04
Marshallese (0)	0	<0.01
Native Hawaiian (2)	13	0.03
Samoan (0)	0	<0.01
Tongan (0)	0	<0.01
White (40,931)	41,392	98.03
Not Hispanic (40,406)	40,737	96.48
Hispanic (525)	655	1.55

Notes: † The Census 2010 population figure is used to calculate the percentages in the Hispanic Origin and Race categories. Ancestry percentages are based on the 2006-2010 American Community Survey population (not shown); ‡ Numbers in parentheses indicate the number of people reporting a single ancestry; * Numbers in parentheses indicate the number of persons reporting this race alone, not in combination with any other race; Please refer to the Explanation of Data for more information.

Dearborn County
Population: 50,047

Ancestry	Population	%
Afghan (0)	0	<0.01
African, Sub-Saharan (0)	37	0.07
African (0)	37	0.07
Cape Verdean (0)	0	<0.01
Ethiopian (0)	0	<0.01
Ghanaian (0)	0	<0.01
Kenyan (0)	0	<0.01
Liberian (0)	0	<0.01
Nigerian (0)	0	<0.01
Senegalese (0)	0	<0.01
Sierra Leonean (0)	0	<0.01
Somalian (0)	0	<0.01
South African (0)	0	<0.01
Sudanese (0)	0	<0.01
Ugandan (0)	0	<0.01
Zimbabwean (0)	0	<0.01
Other Sub-Saharan African (0)	0	<0.01
Albanian (0)	0	<0.01
Alsatian (0)	53	0.11
American (3,843)	3,843	7.75
Arab (31)	60	0.12
Arab (0)	0	<0.01
Egyptian (0)	0	<0.01
Iraqi (0)	0	<0.01
Jordanian (0)	0	<0.01
Lebanese (17)	46	0.09
Moroccan (14)	14	0.03
Palestinian (0)	0	<0.01
Syrian (0)	0	<0.01
Other Arab (0)	0	<0.01
Armenian (0)	0	<0.01
Assyrian/Chaldean/Syriac (0)	0	<0.01
Australian (0)	0	<0.01
Austrian (26)	160	0.32
Basque (0)	0	<0.01
Belgian (0)	13	0.03
Brazilian (0)	0	<0.01
British (46)	70	0.14
Bulgarian (0)	0	<0.01
Cajun (22)	22	0.04
Canadian (17)	34	0.07
Carpatho Rusyn (0)	0	<0.01
Celtic (0)	0	<0.01
Croatian (0)	10	0.02
Cypriot (0)	0	<0.01
Czech (12)	57	0.11
Czechoslovakian (23)	31	0.06
Danish (13)	123	0.25
Dutch (84)	1,060	2.14
Eastern European (0)	0	<0.01
English (1,503)	5,667	11.43
Estonian (0)	0	<0.01
European (625)	636	1.28
Finnish (15)	182	0.37
French, ex. Basque (257)	1,528	3.08
French Canadian (35)	89	0.18
German (10,530)	23,046	46.48
German Russian (0)	0	<0.01
Greek (22)	201	0.41
Guyanese (0)	0	<0.01
Hungarian (25)	144	0.29
Icelander (0)	0	<0.01
Iranian (0)	0	<0.01
Irish (2,500)	9,509	19.18
Israeli (0)	0	<0.01
Italian (577)	1,814	3.66
Latvian (0)	0	<0.01
Lithuanian (44)	54	0.11
Luxemburger (0)	0	<0.01
Macedonian (0)	0	<0.01
Maltese (0)	0	<0.01
New Zealander (0)	0	<0.01
Northern European (0)	0	<0.01
Norwegian (14)	131	0.26
Pennsylvania German (11)	11	0.02
Polish (109)	641	1.29
Portuguese (0)	30	0.06
Romanian (10)	110	0.22
Russian (111)	268	0.54
Scandinavian (22)	33	0.07
Scotch-Irish (304)	716	1.44
Scottish (283)	675	1.36
Serbian (0)	0	<0.01
Slavic (0)	9	0.02
Slovak (0)	0	<0.01
Slovene (0)	42	0.08
Soviet Union (0)	0	<0.01
Swedish (37)	162	0.33
Swiss (32)	112	0.23
Turkish (0)	0	<0.01
Ukrainian (18)	35	0.07
Welsh (60)	255	0.51
West Indian, ex. Hispanic (0)	0	<0.01
Bahamian (0)	0	<0.01
Barbadian (0)	0	<0.01
Belizean (0)	0	<0.01
Bermudan (0)	0	<0.01
British West Indian (0)	0	<0.01
Dutch West Indian (0)	0	<0.01
Haitian (0)	0	<0.01
Jamaican (0)	0	<0.01
Trinidadian/Tobagonian (0)	0	<0.01
U.S. Virgin Islander (0)	0	<0.01
West Indian (0)	0	<0.01
Other West Indian (0)	0	<0.01
Yugoslavian (13)	13	0.03

Hispanic Origin	Population	%
Hispanic or Latino (of any race)	502	1.00
Central American, ex. Mexican	39	0.08
Costa Rican	4	0.01
Guatemalan	19	0.04
Honduran	10	0.02
Nicaraguan	0	<0.01
Panamanian	1	<0.01
Salvadoran	5	0.01
Other Central American	0	<0.01
Cuban	9	0.02
Dominican Republic	15	0.03
Mexican	292	0.58
Puerto Rican	49	0.10
South American	35	0.07
Argentinean	2	<0.01
Bolivian	0	<0.01
Chilean	4	0.01
Colombian	11	0.02
Ecuadorian	1	<0.01
Paraguayan	4	0.01
Peruvian	4	0.01
Uruguayan	0	<0.01
Venezuelan	6	0.01
Other South American	3	0.01
Other Hispanic or Latino	63	0.13

Race*	Population	%
African-American/Black (300)	492	0.98
Not Hispanic (291)	481	0.96
Hispanic (9)	11	0.02
American Indian/Alaska Native (87)	249	0.50
Not Hispanic (79)	225	0.45
Hispanic (8)	24	0.05
Alaska Athabascan (Ala. Nat.) (0)	0	<0.01
Aleut (Alaska Native) (0)	0	<0.01
Apache (1)	6	0.01
Arapaho (0)	0	<0.01
Blackfeet (5)	14	0.03
Canadian/French Am. Ind. (0)	1	<0.01
Central American Ind. (0)	0	<0.01
Cherokee (19)	75	0.15
Cheyenne (0)	0	<0.01
Chickasaw (0)	0	<0.01
Chippewa (5)	5	0.01
Choctaw (2)	6	0.01
Colville (0)	0	<0.01
Comanche (1)	1	<0.01
Cree (1)	1	<0.01
Creek (2)	2	<0.01
Crow (0)	0	<0.01
Delaware (0)	0	<0.01
Hopi (0)	0	<0.01
Houma (0)	0	<0.01
Inupiat (Alaska Native) (2)	2	<0.01
Iroquois (0)	1	<0.01
Kiowa (0)	0	<0.01
Lumbee (1)	1	<0.01
Menominee (0)	0	<0.01
Mexican American Ind. (4)	4	0.01
Navajo (0)	3	0.01
Osage (0)	0	<0.01
Ottawa (0)	0	<0.01
Paiute (0)	0	<0.01
Pima (2)	2	<0.01
Potawatomi (0)	1	<0.01
Pueblo (0)	0	<0.01
Puget Sound Salish (0)	0	<0.01
Seminole (0)	0	<0.01
Shoshone (0)	0	<0.01
Sioux (1)	8	0.02
South American Ind. (0)	0	<0.01
Spanish American Ind. (1)	1	<0.01
Tlingit-Haida (Alaska Native) (1)	3	0.01
Tohono O'Odham (0)	0	<0.01
Tsimshian (Alaska Native) (0)	0	<0.01
Ute (0)	0	<0.01
Yakama (0)	0	<0.01
Yaqui (0)	0	<0.01
Yuman (0)	0	<0.01
Yup'ik (Alaska Native) (0)	0	<0.01
Asian (189)	286	0.57
Not Hispanic (187)	282	0.56
Hispanic (2)	4	0.01
Bangladeshi (0)	0	<0.01
Bhutanese (0)	0	<0.01
Burmese (0)	0	<0.01
Cambodian (1)	1	<0.01
Chinese, ex. Taiwanese (29)	35	0.07
Filipino (50)	92	0.18
Hmong (0)	0	<0.01
Indian (25)	32	0.06
Indonesian (0)	0	<0.01
Japanese (18)	28	0.06
Korean (18)	32	0.06
Laotian (0)	0	<0.01
Malaysian (0)	0	<0.01
Nepalese (0)	0	<0.01
Pakistani (1)	1	<0.01
Sri Lankan (0)	0	<0.01
Taiwanese (2)	2	<0.01
Thai (4)	7	0.01
Vietnamese (33)	42	0.08
Hawaii Native/Pacific Islander (26)	44	0.09
Not Hispanic (24)	40	0.08
Hispanic (2)	4	0.01
Fijian (0)	0	<0.01
Guamanian/Chamorro (5)	7	0.01
Marshallese (1)	1	<0.01
Native Hawaiian (6)	13	0.03
Samoan (6)	7	0.01
Tongan (0)	0	<0.01
White (48,780)	49,247	98.40
Not Hispanic (48,486)	48,894	97.70
Hispanic (294)	353	0.71

Notes: † The Census 2010 population figure is used to calculate the percentages in the Hispanic Origin and Race categories. Ancestry percentages are based on the 2006-2010 American Community Survey population (not shown); ‡ Numbers in parentheses indicate the number of people reporting a single ancestry; * Numbers in parentheses indicate the number of persons reporting this race alone, not in combination with any other race; Please refer to the Explanation of Data for more information.

Decatur County
Population: 25,740

Ancestry	Population	%
Afghan (0)	0	<0.01
African, Sub-Saharan (0)	0	<0.01
African (0)	0	<0.01
Cape Verdean (0)	0	<0.01
Ethiopian (0)	0	<0.01
Ghanaian (0)	0	<0.01
Kenyan (0)	0	<0.01
Liberian (0)	0	<0.01
Nigerian (0)	0	<0.01
Senegalese (0)	0	<0.01
Sierra Leonean (0)	0	<0.01
Somalian (0)	0	<0.01
South African (0)	0	<0.01
Sudanese (0)	0	<0.01
Ugandan (0)	0	<0.01
Zimbabwean (0)	0	<0.01
Other Sub-Saharan African (0)	0	<0.01
Albanian (0)	0	<0.01
Alsatian (0)	0	<0.01
American (4,383)	4,383	17.13
Arab (16)	64	0.25
Arab (0)	0	<0.01
Egyptian (0)	0	<0.01
Iraqi (0)	0	<0.01
Jordanian (0)	0	<0.01
Lebanese (16)	64	0.25
Moroccan (0)	0	<0.01
Palestinian (0)	0	<0.01
Syrian (0)	0	<0.01
Other Arab (0)	0	<0.01
Armenian (0)	0	<0.01
Assyrian/Chaldean/Syriac (0)	0	<0.01
Australian (0)	0	<0.01
Austrian (0)	0	<0.01
Basque (0)	0	<0.01
Belgian (0)	0	<0.01
Brazilian (0)	0	<0.01
British (49)	208	0.81
Bulgarian (0)	0	<0.01
Cajun (0)	0	<0.01
Canadian (8)	8	0.03
Carpatho Rusyn (0)	0	<0.01
Celtic (0)	0	<0.01
Croatian (0)	61	0.24
Cypriot (0)	0	<0.01
Czech (0)	33	0.13
Czechoslovakian (0)	0	<0.01
Danish (0)	15	0.06
Dutch (96)	459	1.79
Eastern European (0)	0	<0.01
English (1,148)	2,400	9.38
Estonian (0)	0	<0.01
European (86)	95	0.37
Finnish (0)	30	0.12
French, ex. Basque (42)	497	1.94
French Canadian (3)	21	0.08
German (4,867)	7,607	29.73
German Russian (0)	0	<0.01
Greek (20)	20	0.08
Guyanese (0)	0	<0.01
Hungarian (15)	15	0.06
Icelander (0)	0	<0.01
Iranian (0)	0	<0.01
Irish (1,094)	2,596	10.15
Israeli (0)	0	<0.01
Italian (191)	408	1.59
Latvian (0)	0	<0.01
Lithuanian (0)	0	<0.01
Luxemburger (0)	0	<0.01
Macedonian (0)	0	<0.01
Maltese (0)	0	<0.01
New Zealander (0)	0	<0.01
Northern European (38)	38	0.15
Norwegian (75)	138	0.54
Pennsylvania German (9)	9	0.04
Polish (60)	135	0.53
Portuguese (0)	0	<0.01
Romanian (0)	8	0.03
Russian (13)	32	0.13
Scandinavian (0)	0	<0.01
Scotch-Irish (106)	388	1.52
Scottish (57)	248	0.97
Serbian (0)	0	<0.01
Slavic (0)	0	<0.01
Slovak (5)	5	0.02
Slovene (0)	0	<0.01
Soviet Union (0)	0	<0.01
Swedish (31)	114	0.45
Swiss (4)	18	0.07
Turkish (0)	0	<0.01
Ukrainian (0)	0	<0.01
Welsh (53)	125	0.49
West Indian, ex. Hispanic (0)	0	<0.01
Bahamian (0)	0	<0.01
Barbadian (0)	0	<0.01
Belizean (0)	0	<0.01
Bermudan (0)	0	<0.01
British West Indian (0)	0	<0.01
Dutch West Indian (0)	0	<0.01
Haitian (0)	0	<0.01
Jamaican (0)	0	<0.01
Trinidadian/Tobagonian (0)	0	<0.01
U.S. Virgin Islander (0)	0	<0.01
West Indian (0)	0	<0.01
Other West Indian (0)	0	<0.01
Yugoslavian (0)	0	<0.01

Hispanic Origin	Population	%
Hispanic or Latino (of any race)	426	1.66
Central American, ex. Mexican	17	0.07
Costa Rican	0	<0.01
Guatemalan	12	0.05
Honduran	2	0.01
Nicaraguan	0	<0.01
Panamanian	3	0.01
Salvadoran	0	<0.01
Other Central American	0	<0.01
Cuban	6	0.02
Dominican Republic	6	0.02
Mexican	304	1.18
Puerto Rican	20	0.08
South American	13	0.05
Argentinean	0	<0.01
Bolivian	0	<0.01
Chilean	0	<0.01
Colombian	10	0.04
Ecuadorian	0	<0.01
Paraguayan	0	<0.01
Peruvian	1	<0.01
Uruguayan	0	<0.01
Venezuelan	2	0.01
Other South American	0	<0.01
Other Hispanic or Latino	60	0.23

Race*	Population	%
African-American/Black (82)	139	0.54
Not Hispanic (76)	128	0.50
Hispanic (6)	11	0.04
American Indian/Alaska Native (39)	140	0.54
Not Hispanic (36)	130	0.51
Hispanic (3)	10	0.04
Alaska Athabascan (Ala. Nat.) (0)	0	<0.01
Aleut (Alaska Native) (0)	0	<0.01
Apache (2)	5	0.02
Arapaho (0)	0	<0.01
Blackfeet (5)	16	0.06
Canadian/French Am. Ind. (0)	0	<0.01
Central American Ind. (0)	0	<0.01
Cherokee (12)	51	0.20
Cheyenne (0)	0	<0.01
Chickasaw (1)	1	<0.01
Chippewa (0)	1	<0.01
Choctaw (0)	0	<0.01
Colville (0)	0	<0.01
Comanche (0)	0	<0.01
Cree (0)	0	<0.01
Creek (0)	0	<0.01
Crow (0)	0	<0.01
Delaware (0)	0	<0.01
Hopi (0)	0	<0.01
Houma (0)	0	<0.01
Inupiat (Alaska Native) (0)	0	<0.01
Iroquois (1)	6	0.02
Kiowa (1)	1	<0.01
Lumbee (0)	0	<0.01
Menominee (0)	0	<0.01
Mexican American Ind. (0)	2	0.01
Navajo (0)	0	<0.01
Osage (0)	0	<0.01
Ottawa (0)	0	<0.01
Paiute (0)	0	<0.01
Pima (0)	0	<0.01
Potawatomi (2)	2	0.01
Pueblo (0)	0	<0.01
Puget Sound Salish (0)	0	<0.01
Seminole (0)	0	<0.01
Shoshone (0)	0	<0.01
Sioux (1)	1	<0.01
South American Ind. (0)	0	<0.01
Spanish American Ind. (0)	0	<0.01
Tlingit-Haida (Alaska Native) (0)	0	<0.01
Tohono O'Odham (0)	0	<0.01
Tsimshian (Alaska Native) (0)	0	<0.01
Ute (0)	0	<0.01
Yakama (0)	0	<0.01
Yaqui (1)	1	<0.01
Yuman (0)	0	<0.01
Yup'ik (Alaska Native) (0)	0	<0.01
Asian (186)	228	0.89
Not Hispanic (178)	217	0.84
Hispanic (8)	11	0.04
Bangladeshi (0)	0	<0.01
Bhutanese (0)	0	<0.01
Burmese (0)	0	<0.01
Cambodian (0)	0	<0.01
Chinese, ex. Taiwanese (21)	35	0.14
Filipino (44)	62	0.24
Hmong (0)	0	<0.01
Indian (37)	42	0.16
Indonesian (3)	3	0.01
Japanese (46)	52	0.20
Korean (12)	23	0.09
Laotian (0)	0	<0.01
Malaysian (0)	0	<0.01
Nepalese (0)	0	<0.01
Pakistani (0)	0	<0.01
Sri Lankan (0)	0	<0.01
Taiwanese (0)	0	<0.01
Thai (1)	3	0.01
Vietnamese (12)	14	0.05
Hawaii Native/Pacific Islander (7)	15	0.06
Not Hispanic (7)	15	0.06
Hispanic (0)	0	<0.01
Fijian (0)	0	<0.01
Guamanian/Chamorro (0)	5	0.02
Marshallese (0)	0	<0.01
Native Hawaiian (7)	7	0.03
Samoan (0)	0	<0.01
Tongan (0)	0	<0.01
White (25,053)	25,270	98.17
Not Hispanic (24,796)	24,987	97.07
Hispanic (257)	283	1.10

Notes: † The Census 2010 population figure is used to calculate the percentages in the Hispanic Origin and Race categories. Ancestry percentages are based on the 2006-2010 American Community Survey population (not shown); ‡ Numbers in parentheses indicate the number of people reporting a single ancestry; * Numbers in parentheses indicate the number of persons reporting this race alone, not in combination with any other race; Please refer to the Explanation of Data for more information.

Delaware County
Population: 117,671

Ancestry	Population	%
Afghan (57)	57	0.05
African, Sub-Saharan (681)	888	0.76
African (559)	750	0.64
Cape Verdean (0)	0	<0.01
Ethiopian (0)	0	<0.01
Ghanaian (0)	0	<0.01
Kenyan (14)	14	0.01
Liberian (0)	0	<0.01
Nigerian (0)	0	<0.01
Senegalese (0)	0	<0.01
Sierra Leonean (0)	0	<0.01
Somalian (0)	0	<0.01
South African (0)	16	0.01
Sudanese (0)	0	<0.01
Ugandan (0)	0	<0.01
Zimbabwean (0)	0	<0.01
Other Sub-Saharan African (108)	108	0.09
Albanian (57)	57	0.05
Alsatian (0)	22	0.02
American (12,465)	12,465	10.62
Arab (20)	308	0.26
Arab (0)	84	0.07
Egyptian (0)	14	0.01
Iraqi (0)	14	0.01
Jordanian (0)	0	<0.01
Lebanese (0)	0	<0.01
Moroccan (0)	13	0.01
Palestinian (20)	20	0.02
Syrian (0)	145	0.12
Other Arab (0)	18	0.02
Armenian (0)	0	<0.01
Assyrian/Chaldean/Syriac (0)	0	<0.01
Australian (14)	42	0.04
Austrian (27)	97	0.08
Basque (0)	0	<0.01
Belgian (0)	120	0.10
Brazilian (0)	0	<0.01
British (280)	528	0.45
Bulgarian (9)	27	0.02
Cajun (0)	0	<0.01
Canadian (151)	236	0.20
Carpatho Rusyn (0)	0	<0.01
Celtic (10)	10	0.01
Croatian (0)	103	0.09
Cypriot (0)	0	<0.01
Czech (110)	134	0.11
Czechoslovakian (0)	0	<0.01
Danish (66)	176	0.15
Dutch (573)	2,448	2.09
Eastern European (0)	14	0.01
English (4,920)	12,070	10.29
Estonian (0)	0	<0.01
European (1,015)	1,091	0.93
Finnish (26)	59	0.05
French, ex. Basque (507)	2,992	2.55
French Canadian (34)	94	0.08
German (11,023)	26,947	22.96
German Russian (0)	0	<0.01
Greek (193)	317	0.27
Guyanese (0)	0	<0.01
Hungarian (114)	260	0.22
Icelander (0)	0	<0.01
Iranian (72)	78	0.07
Irish (4,908)	16,641	14.18
Israeli (24)	35	0.03
Italian (1,127)	2,615	2.23
Latvian (0)	9	0.01
Lithuanian (77)	99	0.08
Luxemburger (0)	32	0.03
Macedonian (12)	33	0.03
Maltese (0)	0	<0.01
New Zealander (0)	18	0.02
Northern European (17)	17	0.01
Norwegian (120)	575	0.49
Pennsylvania German (34)	73	0.06
Polish (560)	1,704	1.45
Portuguese (0)	19	0.02
Romanian (52)	157	0.13
Russian (96)	284	0.24
Scandinavian (0)	74	0.06
Scotch-Irish (707)	1,477	1.26
Scottish (789)	2,382	2.03
Serbian (0)	15	0.01
Slavic (22)	22	0.02
Slovak (30)	118	0.10
Slovene (0)	0	<0.01
Soviet Union (0)	0	<0.01
Swedish (297)	860	0.73
Swiss (146)	495	0.42
Turkish (34)	34	0.03
Ukrainian (18)	48	0.04
Welsh (207)	744	0.63
West Indian, ex. Hispanic (41)	41	0.03
Bahamian (0)	0	<0.01
Barbadian (28)	28	0.02
Belizean (0)	0	<0.01
Bermudan (0)	0	<0.01
British West Indian (0)	0	<0.01
Dutch West Indian (0)	0	<0.01
Haitian (0)	0	<0.01
Jamaican (13)	13	0.01
Trinidadian/Tobagonian (0)	0	<0.01
U.S. Virgin Islander (0)	0	<0.01
West Indian (0)	0	<0.01
Other West Indian (0)	0	<0.01
Yugoslavian (12)	27	0.02

Hispanic Origin	Population	%
Hispanic or Latino (of any race)	2,088	1.77
Central American, ex. Mexican	86	0.07
Costa Rican	5	<0.01
Guatemalan	20	0.02
Honduran	15	0.01
Nicaraguan	7	0.01
Panamanian	25	0.02
Salvadoran	11	0.01
Other Central American	3	<0.01
Cuban	47	0.04
Dominican Republic	28	0.02
Mexican	1,409	1.20
Puerto Rican	166	0.14
South American	87	0.07
Argentinean	12	0.01
Bolivian	9	0.01
Chilean	14	0.01
Colombian	12	0.01
Ecuadorian	2	<0.01
Paraguayan	1	<0.01
Peruvian	18	0.02
Uruguayan	2	<0.01
Venezuelan	13	0.01
Other South American	4	<0.01
Other Hispanic or Latino	265	0.23

Race*	Population	%
African-American/Black (8,146)	9,525	8.09
Not Hispanic (8,051)	9,346	7.94
Hispanic (95)	179	0.15
American Indian/Alaska Native (302)	921	0.78
Not Hispanic (255)	822	0.70
Hispanic (47)	99	0.08
Alaska Athabascan (Ala. Nat.) (0)	2	<0.01
Aleut (Alaska Native) (0)	0	<0.01
Apache (4)	19	0.02
Arapaho (0)	1	<0.01
Blackfeet (7)	50	0.04
Canadian/French Am. Ind. (3)	3	<0.01
Central American Ind. (1)	1	<0.01
Cherokee (80)	296	0.25
Cheyenne (0)	0	<0.01
Chickasaw (1)	1	<0.01
Chippewa (2)	8	0.01
Choctaw (1)	3	<0.01
Colville (0)	0	<0.01
Comanche (0)	0	<0.01
Cree (1)	5	<0.01
Creek (0)	3	<0.01
Crow (4)	4	<0.01
Delaware (0)	7	0.01
Hopi (0)	0	<0.01
Houma (0)	0	<0.01
Inupiat (Alaska Native) (0)	0	<0.01
Iroquois (6)	8	0.01
Kiowa (0)	0	<0.01
Lumbee (3)	3	<0.01
Menominee (1)	1	<0.01
Mexican American Ind. (16)	18	0.02
Navajo (4)	8	0.01
Osage (0)	1	<0.01
Ottawa (0)	1	<0.01
Paiute (0)	0	<0.01
Pima (0)	0	<0.01
Potawatomi (5)	5	<0.01
Pueblo (0)	1	<0.01
Puget Sound Salish (1)	1	<0.01
Seminole (1)	2	<0.01
Shoshone (0)	6	0.01
Sioux (8)	20	0.02
South American Ind. (2)	4	<0.01
Spanish American Ind. (3)	3	<0.01
Tlingit-Haida (Alaska Native) (5)	7	0.01
Tohono O'Odham (0)	0	<0.01
Tsimshian (Alaska Native) (0)	0	<0.01
Ute (0)	0	<0.01
Yakama (0)	0	<0.01
Yaqui (0)	0	<0.01
Yuman (0)	0	<0.01
Yup'ik (Alaska Native) (0)	0	<0.01
Asian (1,144)	1,577	1.34
Not Hispanic (1,128)	1,541	1.31
Hispanic (16)	36	0.03
Bangladeshi (23)	25	0.02
Bhutanese (0)	0	<0.01
Burmese (2)	2	<0.01
Cambodian (0)	0	<0.01
Chinese, ex. Taiwanese (301)	343	0.29
Filipino (132)	226	0.19
Hmong (2)	2	<0.01
Indian (289)	347	0.29
Indonesian (2)	3	<0.01
Japanese (64)	128	0.11
Korean (142)	195	0.17
Laotian (2)	6	0.01
Malaysian (3)	5	<0.01
Nepalese (10)	13	0.01
Pakistani (22)	25	0.02
Sri Lankan (4)	4	<0.01
Taiwanese (23)	26	0.02
Thai (14)	26	0.02
Vietnamese (68)	81	0.07
Hawaii Native/Pacific Islander (60)	188	0.16
Not Hispanic (56)	175	0.15
Hispanic (4)	13	0.01
Fijian (0)	1	<0.01
Guamanian/Chamorro (7)	17	0.01
Marshallese (0)	0	<0.01
Native Hawaiian (22)	69	0.06
Samoan (13)	31	0.03
Tongan (1)	3	<0.01
White (104,872)	107,158	91.07
Not Hispanic (103,721)	105,750	89.87
Hispanic (1,151)	1,408	1.20

Notes: † The Census 2010 population figure is used to calculate the percentages in the Hispanic Origin and Race categories. Ancestry percentages are based on the 2006-2010 American Community Survey population (not shown); ‡ Numbers in parentheses indicate the number of people reporting a single ancestry; * Numbers in parentheses indicate the number of persons reporting this race alone, not in combination with any other race; Please refer to the Explanation of Data for more information.

Dubois County
Population: 41,889

Ancestry	Population	%
Afghan (0)	0	<0.01
African, Sub-Saharan (15)	48	0.11
African (15)	48	0.11
Cape Verdean (0)	0	<0.01
Ethiopian (0)	0	<0.01
Ghanaian (0)	0	<0.01
Kenyan (0)	0	<0.01
Liberian (0)	0	<0.01
Nigerian (0)	0	<0.01
Senegalese (0)	0	<0.01
Sierra Leonean (0)	0	<0.01
Somalian (0)	0	<0.01
South African (0)	0	<0.01
Sudanese (0)	0	<0.01
Ugandan (0)	0	<0.01
Zimbabwean (0)	0	<0.01
Other Sub-Saharan African (0)	0	<0.01
Albanian (0)	0	<0.01
Alsatian (0)	0	<0.01
American (3,742)	3,742	8.95
Arab (43)	43	0.10
Arab (0)	0	<0.01
Egyptian (0)	0	<0.01
Iraqi (0)	0	<0.01
Jordanian (0)	0	<0.01
Lebanese (0)	0	<0.01
Moroccan (0)	0	<0.01
Palestinian (0)	0	<0.01
Syrian (0)	0	<0.01
Other Arab (43)	43	0.10
Armenian (0)	0	<0.01
Assyrian/Chaldean/Syriac (0)	0	<0.01
Australian (0)	0	<0.01
Austrian (0)	8	0.02
Basque (0)	0	<0.01
Belgian (0)	17	0.04
Brazilian (0)	0	<0.01
British (16)	45	0.11
Bulgarian (0)	0	<0.01
Cajun (0)	11	0.03
Canadian (28)	28	0.07
Carpatho Rusyn (0)	0	<0.01
Celtic (0)	0	<0.01
Croatian (42)	42	0.10
Cypriot (0)	0	<0.01
Czech (0)	0	<0.01
Czechoslovakian (7)	19	0.05
Danish (0)	21	0.05
Dutch (102)	597	1.43
Eastern European (14)	14	0.03
English (1,346)	2,809	6.72
Estonian (0)	0	<0.01
European (281)	315	0.75
Finnish (0)	0	<0.01
French, ex. Basque (208)	904	2.16
French Canadian (0)	110	0.26
German (19,473)	24,267	58.04
German Russian (0)	0	<0.01
Greek (51)	59	0.14
Guyanese (0)	0	<0.01
Hungarian (23)	28	0.07
Icelander (0)	0	<0.01
Iranian (0)	0	<0.01
Irish (1,006)	3,394	8.12
Israeli (0)	0	<0.01
Italian (156)	419	1.00
Latvian (0)	0	<0.01
Lithuanian (0)	0	<0.01
Luxemburger (0)	0	<0.01
Macedonian (0)	0	<0.01
Maltese (0)	9	0.02
New Zealander (0)	0	<0.01
Northern European (49)	49	0.12
Norwegian (24)	137	0.33
Pennsylvania German (0)	0	<0.01
Polish (36)	205	0.49
Portuguese (0)	28	0.07
Romanian (0)	0	<0.01
Russian (16)	80	0.19
Scandinavian (0)	0	<0.01
Scotch-Irish (183)	426	1.02
Scottish (62)	330	0.79
Serbian (17)	17	0.04
Slavic (0)	0	<0.01
Slovak (0)	17	0.04
Slovene (0)	0	<0.01
Soviet Union (0)	0	<0.01
Swedish (56)	272	0.65
Swiss (100)	327	0.78
Turkish (0)	0	<0.01
Ukrainian (0)	0	<0.01
Welsh (13)	55	0.13
West Indian, ex. Hispanic (36)	47	0.11
Bahamian (0)	0	<0.01
Barbadian (0)	0	<0.01
Belizean (0)	0	<0.01
Bermudan (0)	0	<0.01
British West Indian (0)	0	<0.01
Dutch West Indian (0)	0	<0.01
Haitian (0)	0	<0.01
Jamaican (36)	47	0.11
Trinidadian/Tobagonian (0)	0	<0.01
U.S. Virgin Islander (0)	0	<0.01
West Indian (0)	0	<0.01
Other West Indian (0)	0	<0.01
Yugoslavian (0)	0	<0.01

Hispanic Origin	Population	%
Hispanic or Latino (of any race)	2,521	6.02
Central American, ex. Mexican	932	2.22
Costa Rican	0	<0.01
Guatemalan	62	0.15
Honduran	44	0.11
Nicaraguan	0	<0.01
Panamanian	4	0.01
Salvadoran	822	1.96
Other Central American	0	<0.01
Cuban	24	0.06
Dominican Republic	1	<0.01
Mexican	1,212	2.89
Puerto Rican	50	0.12
South American	36	0.09
Argentinean	1	<0.01
Bolivian	1	<0.01
Chilean	2	<0.01
Colombian	12	0.03
Ecuadorian	3	0.01
Paraguayan	0	<0.01
Peruvian	16	0.04
Uruguayan	0	<0.01
Venezuelan	1	<0.01
Other South American	0	<0.01
Other Hispanic or Latino	266	0.64

Race*	Population	%
African-American/Black (122)	216	0.52
Not Hispanic (109)	177	0.42
Hispanic (13)	39	0.09
American Indian/Alaska Native (66)	147	0.35
Not Hispanic (51)	128	0.31
Hispanic (15)	19	0.05
Alaska Athabascan (Ala. Nat.) (0)	0	<0.01
Aleut (Alaska Native) (0)	0	<0.01
Apache (0)	0	<0.01
Arapaho (3)	3	0.01
Blackfeet (0)	2	<0.01
Canadian/French Am. Ind. (0)	0	<0.01
Central American Ind. (1)	1	<0.01
Cherokee (4)	33	0.08
Cheyenne (0)	0	<0.01
Chickasaw (1)	1	<0.01
Chippewa (1)	1	<0.01
Choctaw (5)	5	0.01
Colville (0)	0	<0.01
Comanche (0)	1	<0.01
Cree (0)	0	<0.01
Creek (3)	8	0.02
Crow (0)	0	<0.01
Delaware (0)	0	<0.01
Hopi (0)	0	<0.01
Houma (0)	0	<0.01
Inupiat (Alaska Native) (1)	1	<0.01
Iroquois (1)	1	<0.01
Kiowa (0)	0	<0.01
Lumbee (0)	0	<0.01
Menominee (0)	0	<0.01
Mexican American Ind. (2)	2	<0.01
Navajo (1)	2	<0.01
Osage (0)	0	<0.01
Ottawa (0)	0	<0.01
Paiute (0)	0	<0.01
Pima (0)	0	<0.01
Potawatomi (0)	0	<0.01
Pueblo (0)	0	<0.01
Puget Sound Salish (0)	0	<0.01
Seminole (0)	0	<0.01
Shoshone (0)	0	<0.01
Sioux (1)	8	0.02
South American Ind. (0)	0	<0.01
Spanish American Ind. (0)	0	<0.01
Tlingit-Haida (Alaska Native) (0)	0	<0.01
Tohono O'Odham (0)	0	<0.01
Tsimshian (Alaska Native) (0)	0	<0.01
Ute (0)	0	<0.01
Yakama (0)	0	<0.01
Yaqui (0)	0	<0.01
Yuman (0)	0	<0.01
Yup'ik (Alaska Native) (0)	0	<0.01
Asian (189)	246	0.59
Not Hispanic (189)	241	0.58
Hispanic (0)	5	0.01
Bangladeshi (0)	0	<0.01
Bhutanese (0)	0	<0.01
Burmese (0)	0	<0.01
Cambodian (0)	0	<0.01
Chinese, ex. Taiwanese (42)	46	0.11
Filipino (26)	57	0.14
Hmong (0)	0	<0.01
Indian (72)	83	0.20
Indonesian (1)	1	<0.01
Japanese (5)	11	0.03
Korean (8)	8	0.02
Laotian (0)	0	<0.01
Malaysian (1)	1	<0.01
Nepalese (0)	0	<0.01
Pakistani (0)	0	<0.01
Sri Lankan (0)	0	<0.01
Taiwanese (0)	1	<0.01
Thai (2)	2	<0.01
Vietnamese (25)	25	0.06
Hawaii Native/Pacific Islander (11)	32	0.08
Not Hispanic (5)	13	0.03
Hispanic (6)	19	0.05
Fijian (0)	0	<0.01
Guamanian/Chamorro (5)	6	0.01
Marshallese (0)	0	<0.01
Native Hawaiian (5)	8	0.02
Samoan (0)	0	<0.01
Tongan (0)	0	<0.01
White (39,839)	40,176	95.91
Not Hispanic (38,791)	38,991	93.08
Hispanic (1,048)	1,185	2.83

Notes: † The Census 2010 population figure is used to calculate the percentages in the Hispanic Origin and Race categories. Ancestry percentages are based on the 2006-2010 American Community Survey population (not shown); ‡ Numbers in parentheses indicate the number of people reporting a single ancestry; * Numbers in parentheses indicate the number of persons reporting this race alone, not in combination with any other race; Please refer to the Explanation of Data for more information.

Elkhart County
Population: 197,559

Ancestry	Population	%
Afghan (0)	0	<0.01
African, Sub-Saharan (433)	555	0.28
African (310)	380	0.19
Cape Verdean (0)	0	<0.01
Ethiopian (7)	7	<0.01
Ghanaian (0)	0	<0.01
Kenyan (100)	100	0.05
Liberian (0)	0	<0.01
Nigerian (0)	0	<0.01
Senegalese (16)	16	0.01
Sierra Leonean (0)	9	<0.01
Somalian (0)	0	<0.01
South African (0)	0	<0.01
Sudanese (0)	0	<0.01
Ugandan (0)	0	<0.01
Zimbabwean (0)	13	0.01
Other Sub-Saharan African (0)	30	0.02
Albanian (0)	0	<0.01
Alsatian (0)	24	0.01
American (14,962)	14,962	7.60
Arab (202)	259	0.13
Arab (23)	23	0.01
Egyptian (0)	0	<0.01
Iraqi (11)	11	0.01
Jordanian (0)	0	<0.01
Lebanese (9)	51	0.03
Moroccan (16)	16	0.01
Palestinian (0)	0	<0.01
Syrian (40)	55	0.03
Other Arab (103)	103	0.05
Armenian (0)	0	<0.01
Assyrian/Chaldean/Syriac (0)	0	<0.01
Australian (0)	0	<0.01
Austrian (15)	263	0.13
Basque (0)	0	<0.01
Belgian (219)	547	0.28
Brazilian (89)	151	0.08
British (212)	414	0.21
Bulgarian (0)	0	<0.01
Cajun (64)	64	0.03
Canadian (119)	319	0.16
Carpatho Rusyn (0)	0	<0.01
Celtic (0)	0	<0.01
Croatian (12)	43	0.02
Cypriot (0)	0	<0.01
Czech (295)	911	0.46
Czechoslovakian (55)	55	0.03
Danish (112)	406	0.21
Dutch (2,047)	6,429	3.27
Eastern European (35)	35	0.02
English (5,739)	14,886	7.56
Estonian (0)	0	<0.01
European (1,759)	1,842	0.94
Finnish (50)	174	0.09
French, ex. Basque (588)	4,474	2.27
French Canadian (269)	780	0.40
German (24,238)	55,836	28.36
German Russian (0)	47	0.02
Greek (91)	381	0.19
Guyanese (10)	10	0.01
Hungarian (281)	1,307	0.66
Icelander (0)	0	<0.01
Iranian (0)	0	<0.01
Irish (5,104)	20,060	10.19
Israeli (0)	0	<0.01
Italian (2,143)	5,372	2.73
Latvian (17)	17	0.01
Lithuanian (82)	132	0.07
Luxemburger (0)	0	<0.01
Macedonian (0)	0	<0.01
Maltese (0)	0	<0.01
New Zealander (0)	0	<0.01
Northern European (54)	54	0.03
Norwegian (263)	1,166	0.59
Pennsylvania German (2,244)	2,673	1.36
Polish (1,563)	5,788	2.94
Portuguese (85)	111	0.06
Romanian (38)	114	0.06
Russian (371)	873	0.44
Scandinavian (119)	150	0.08
Scotch-Irish (1,010)	2,457	1.25
Scottish (862)	2,628	1.33
Serbian (24)	24	0.01
Slavic (16)	26	0.01
Slovak (22)	75	0.04
Slovene (30)	71	0.04
Soviet Union (0)	0	<0.01
Swedish (980)	2,441	1.24
Swiss (1,495)	6,590	3.35
Turkish (0)	10	0.01
Ukrainian (556)	764	0.39
Welsh (208)	1,017	0.52
West Indian, ex. Hispanic (278)	278	0.14
Bahamian (0)	0	<0.01
Barbadian (0)	0	<0.01
Belizean (0)	0	<0.01
Bermudan (0)	0	<0.01
British West Indian (0)	0	<0.01
Dutch West Indian (14)	14	0.01
Haitian (93)	93	0.05
Jamaican (171)	171	0.09
Trinidadian/Tobagonian (0)	0	<0.01
U.S. Virgin Islander (0)	0	<0.01
West Indian (0)	0	<0.01
Other West Indian (0)	0	<0.01
Yugoslavian (12)	50	0.03

Hispanic Origin	Population	%
Hispanic or Latino (of any race)	27,886	14.12
Central American, ex. Mexican	1,736	0.88
Costa Rican	21	0.01
Guatemalan	270	0.14
Honduran	699	0.35
Nicaraguan	36	0.02
Panamanian	30	0.02
Salvadoran	665	0.34
Other Central American	15	0.01
Cuban	105	0.05
Dominican Republic	57	0.03
Mexican	22,867	11.57
Puerto Rican	1,176	0.60
South American	407	0.21
Argentinean	23	0.01
Bolivian	74	0.04
Chilean	21	0.01
Colombian	82	0.04
Ecuadorian	50	0.03
Paraguayan	7	<0.01
Peruvian	45	0.02
Uruguayan	20	0.01
Venezuelan	79	0.04
Other South American	6	<0.01
Other Hispanic or Latino	1,538	0.78

Race*	Population	%
African-American/Black (11,307)	13,745	6.96
Not Hispanic (10,989)	13,153	6.66
Hispanic (318)	592	0.30
American Indian/Alaska Native (747)	1,830	0.93
Not Hispanic (434)	1,299	0.66
Hispanic (313)	531	0.27
Alaska Athabascan (Ala. Nat.) (0)	0	<0.01
Aleut (Alaska Native) (1)	1	<0.01
Apache (6)	22	0.01
Arapaho (0)	2	<0.01
Blackfeet (13)	77	0.04
Canadian/French Am. Ind. (1)	9	<0.01
Central American Ind. (1)	4	<0.01
Cherokee (88)	351	0.18
Cheyenne (1)	5	<0.01
Chickasaw (4)	9	<0.01
Chippewa (19)	52	0.03
Choctaw (15)	31	0.02
Colville (0)	0	<0.01
Comanche (7)	12	0.01
Cree (1)	6	<0.01
Creek (0)	4	<0.01
Crow (1)	7	<0.01
Delaware (0)	5	<0.01
Hopi (0)	0	<0.01
Houma (0)	0	<0.01
Inupiat (Alaska Native) (0)	0	<0.01
Iroquois (9)	19	0.01
Kiowa (0)	0	<0.01
Lumbee (7)	8	<0.01
Menominee (1)	1	<0.01
Mexican American Ind. (83)	134	0.07
Navajo (11)	20	0.01
Osage (0)	2	<0.01
Ottawa (7)	13	0.01
Paiute (0)	4	<0.01
Pima (0)	0	<0.01
Potawatomi (31)	69	0.03
Pueblo (1)	6	<0.01
Puget Sound Salish (0)	0	<0.01
Seminole (3)	9	<0.01
Shoshone (0)	2	<0.01
Sioux (18)	54	0.03
South American Ind. (4)	11	0.01
Spanish American Ind. (7)	8	<0.01
Tlingit-Haida (Alaska Native) (1)	1	<0.01
Tohono O'Odham (0)	1	<0.01
Tsimshian (Alaska Native) (1)	1	<0.01
Ute (0)	0	<0.01
Yakama (0)	0	<0.01
Yaqui (0)	3	<0.01
Yuman (0)	0	<0.01
Yup'ik (Alaska Native) (3)	3	<0.01
Asian (1,915)	2,597	1.31
Not Hispanic (1,879)	2,496	1.26
Hispanic (36)	101	0.05
Bangladeshi (15)	16	0.01
Bhutanese (0)	0	<0.01
Burmese (1)	6	<0.01
Cambodian (214)	263	0.13
Chinese, ex. Taiwanese (239)	317	0.16
Filipino (178)	307	0.16
Hmong (1)	4	<0.01
Indian (371)	468	0.24
Indonesian (11)	43	0.02
Japanese (56)	130	0.07
Korean (156)	250	0.13
Laotian (292)	355	0.18
Malaysian (3)	7	<0.01
Nepalese (11)	13	0.01
Pakistani (27)	41	0.02
Sri Lankan (17)	17	0.01
Taiwanese (9)	9	<0.01
Thai (27)	47	0.02
Vietnamese (153)	214	0.11
Hawaii Native/Pacific Islander (81)	208	0.11
Not Hispanic (60)	148	0.07
Hispanic (21)	60	0.03
Fijian (1)	2	<0.01
Guamanian/Chamorro (22)	45	0.02
Marshallese (5)	8	<0.01
Native Hawaiian (13)	53	0.03
Samoan (10)	24	0.01
Tongan (6)	6	<0.01
White (163,792)	168,311	85.20
Not Hispanic (152,555)	155,820	78.87
Hispanic (11,237)	12,491	6.32

Notes: † The Census 2010 population figure is used to calculate the percentages in the Hispanic Origin and Race categories. Ancestry percentages are based on the 2006-2010 American Community Survey population (not shown); ‡ Numbers in parentheses indicate the number of people reporting a single ancestry; * Numbers in parentheses indicate the number of persons reporting this race alone, not in combination with any other race; Please refer to the Explanation of Data for more information.

Fayette County
Population: 24,277

Ancestry	Population	%
Afghan (0)	0	<0.01
African, Sub-Saharan (25)	25	0.10
African (25)	25	0.10
Cape Verdean (0)	0	<0.01
Ethiopian (0)	0	<0.01
Ghanaian (0)	0	<0.01
Kenyan (0)	0	<0.01
Liberian (0)	0	<0.01
Nigerian (0)	0	<0.01
Senegalese (0)	0	<0.01
Sierra Leonean (0)	0	<0.01
Somalian (0)	0	<0.01
South African (0)	0	<0.01
Sudanese (0)	0	<0.01
Ugandan (0)	0	<0.01
Zimbabwean (0)	0	<0.01
Other Sub-Saharan African (0)	0	<0.01
Albanian (0)	0	<0.01
Alsatian (0)	0	<0.01
American (3,695)	3,695	15.16
Arab (7)	7	0.03
Arab (0)	0	<0.01
Egyptian (0)	0	<0.01
Iraqi (0)	0	<0.01
Jordanian (0)	0	<0.01
Lebanese (7)	7	0.03
Moroccan (0)	0	<0.01
Palestinian (0)	0	<0.01
Syrian (0)	0	<0.01
Other Arab (0)	0	<0.01
Armenian (0)	0	<0.01
Assyrian/Chaldean/Syriac (0)	0	<0.01
Australian (0)	0	<0.01
Austrian (0)	0	<0.01
Basque (0)	0	<0.01
Belgian (0)	0	<0.01
Brazilian (0)	0	<0.01
British (50)	73	0.30
Bulgarian (0)	0	<0.01
Cajun (0)	0	<0.01
Canadian (16)	16	0.07
Carpatho Rusyn (0)	0	<0.01
Celtic (0)	0	<0.01
Croatian (0)	0	<0.01
Cypriot (0)	0	<0.01
Czech (6)	6	0.02
Czechoslovakian (0)	0	<0.01
Danish (0)	0	<0.01
Dutch (54)	298	1.22
Eastern European (0)	0	<0.01
English (1,152)	1,989	8.16
Estonian (0)	0	<0.01
European (66)	100	0.41
Finnish (0)	19	0.08
French, ex. Basque (118)	358	1.47
French Canadian (0)	0	<0.01
German (2,516)	4,991	20.48
German Russian (0)	0	<0.01
Greek (32)	32	0.13
Guyanese (0)	0	<0.01
Hungarian (27)	50	0.21
Icelander (0)	0	<0.01
Iranian (0)	0	<0.01
Irish (1,030)	2,887	11.85
Israeli (0)	0	<0.01
Italian (105)	248	1.02
Latvian (0)	0	<0.01
Lithuanian (26)	26	0.11
Luxemburger (0)	0	<0.01
Macedonian (0)	0	<0.01
Maltese (0)	0	<0.01
New Zealander (0)	0	<0.01
Northern European (0)	0	<0.01
Norwegian (11)	57	0.23
Pennsylvania German (11)	19	0.08
Polish (59)	150	0.62
Portuguese (0)	0	<0.01
Romanian (0)	0	<0.01
Russian (0)	0	<0.01
Scandinavian (0)	18	0.07
Scotch-Irish (185)	393	1.61
Scottish (252)	351	1.44
Serbian (0)	0	<0.01
Slavic (0)	0	<0.01
Slovak (8)	52	0.21
Slovene (0)	0	<0.01
Soviet Union (0)	0	<0.01
Swedish (7)	49	0.20
Swiss (7)	7	0.03
Turkish (0)	0	<0.01
Ukrainian (0)	0	<0.01
Welsh (21)	62	0.25
West Indian, ex. Hispanic (0)	11	0.05
Bahamian (0)	0	<0.01
Barbadian (0)	0	<0.01
Belizean (0)	0	<0.01
Bermudan (0)	0	<0.01
British West Indian (0)	0	<0.01
Dutch West Indian (0)	11	0.05
Haitian (0)	0	<0.01
Jamaican (0)	0	<0.01
Trinidadian/Tobagonian (0)	0	<0.01
U.S. Virgin Islander (0)	0	<0.01
West Indian (0)	0	<0.01
Other West Indian (0)	0	<0.01
Yugoslavian (0)	0	<0.01

Hispanic Origin	Population	%
Hispanic or Latino (of any race)	223	0.92
Central American, ex. Mexican	14	0.06
Costa Rican	0	<0.01
Guatemalan	7	0.03
Honduran	3	0.01
Nicaraguan	0	<0.01
Panamanian	3	0.01
Salvadoran	1	<0.01
Other Central American	0	<0.01
Cuban	6	0.02
Dominican Republic	0	<0.01
Mexican	127	0.52
Puerto Rican	23	0.09
South American	16	0.07
Argentinean	5	0.02
Bolivian	0	<0.01
Chilean	0	<0.01
Colombian	0	<0.01
Ecuadorian	0	<0.01
Paraguayan	0	<0.01
Peruvian	4	0.02
Uruguayan	0	<0.01
Venezuelan	7	0.03
Other South American	0	<0.01
Other Hispanic or Latino	37	0.15

Race*	Population	%
African-American/Black (322)	428	1.76
Not Hispanic (318)	423	1.74
Hispanic (4)	5	0.02
American Indian/Alaska Native (32)	126	0.52
Not Hispanic (30)	124	0.51
Hispanic (2)	2	0.01
Alaska Athabascan (Ala. Nat.) (0)	0	<0.01
Aleut (Alaska Native) (0)	0	<0.01
Apache (0)	1	<0.01
Arapaho (0)	0	<0.01
Blackfeet (0)	0	<0.01
Canadian/French Am. Ind. (0)	0	<0.01
Central American Ind. (0)	0	<0.01
Cherokee (6)	41	0.17
Cheyenne (0)	0	<0.01
Chickasaw (0)	0	<0.01
Chippewa (0)	1	<0.01
Choctaw (0)	0	<0.01
Colville (0)	0	<0.01
Comanche (0)	0	<0.01
Cree (0)	0	<0.01
Creek (0)	3	0.01
Crow (0)	0	<0.01
Delaware (2)	2	0.01
Hopi (0)	0	<0.01
Houma (0)	0	<0.01
Inupiat (Alaska Native) (0)	0	<0.01
Iroquois (0)	3	0.01
Kiowa (0)	0	<0.01
Lumbee (0)	0	<0.01
Menominee (0)	0	<0.01
Mexican American Ind. (2)	2	0.01
Navajo (1)	1	<0.01
Osage (0)	0	<0.01
Ottawa (0)	0	<0.01
Paiute (0)	0	<0.01
Pima (0)	0	<0.01
Potawatomi (0)	0	<0.01
Pueblo (0)	0	<0.01
Puget Sound Salish (0)	0	<0.01
Seminole (0)	0	<0.01
Shoshone (1)	1	<0.01
Sioux (0)	5	0.02
South American Ind. (0)	0	<0.01
Spanish American Ind. (0)	0	<0.01
Tlingit-Haida (Alaska Native) (0)	0	<0.01
Tohono O'Odham (0)	0	<0.01
Tsimshian (Alaska Native) (0)	0	<0.01
Ute (0)	0	<0.01
Yakama (0)	0	<0.01
Yaqui (0)	0	<0.01
Yuman (0)	0	<0.01
Yup'ik (Alaska Native) (0)	0	<0.01
Asian (81)	101	0.42
Not Hispanic (79)	98	0.40
Hispanic (2)	3	0.01
Bangladeshi (0)	0	<0.01
Bhutanese (0)	0	<0.01
Burmese (0)	0	<0.01
Cambodian (1)	1	<0.01
Chinese, ex. Taiwanese (15)	16	0.07
Filipino (20)	23	0.09
Hmong (0)	0	<0.01
Indian (20)	22	0.09
Indonesian (4)	4	0.02
Japanese (3)	5	0.02
Korean (7)	12	0.05
Laotian (0)	0	<0.01
Malaysian (0)	0	<0.01
Nepalese (0)	0	<0.01
Pakistani (1)	1	<0.01
Sri Lankan (0)	0	<0.01
Taiwanese (0)	0	<0.01
Thai (0)	0	<0.01
Vietnamese (8)	10	0.04
Hawaii Native/Pacific Islander (0)	7	0.03
Not Hispanic (0)	7	0.03
Hispanic (0)	0	<0.01
Fijian (0)	0	<0.01
Guamanian/Chamorro (0)	0	<0.01
Marshallese (0)	0	<0.01
Native Hawaiian (0)	5	0.02
Samoan (0)	0	<0.01
Tongan (0)	0	<0.01
White (23,532)	23,765	97.89
Not Hispanic (23,392)	23,609	97.25
Hispanic (140)	156	0.64

Notes: † The Census 2010 population figure is used to calculate the percentages in the Hispanic Origin and Race categories. Ancestry percentages are based on the 2006-2010 American Community Survey population (not shown); ‡ Numbers in parentheses indicate the number of people reporting a single ancestry; * Numbers in parentheses indicate the number of persons reporting this race alone, not in combination with any other race; Please refer to the Explanation of Data for more information.

Floyd County
Population: 74,578

Ancestry	Population	%
Afghan (0)	0	<0.01
African, Sub-Saharan (40)	61	0.08
African (40)	61	0.08
Cape Verdean (0)	0	<0.01
Ethiopian (0)	0	<0.01
Ghanaian (0)	0	<0.01
Kenyan (0)	0	<0.01
Liberian (0)	0	<0.01
Nigerian (0)	0	<0.01
Senegalese (0)	0	<0.01
Sierra Leonean (0)	0	<0.01
Somalian (0)	0	<0.01
South African (0)	0	<0.01
Sudanese (0)	0	<0.01
Ugandan (0)	0	<0.01
Zimbabwean (0)	0	<0.01
Other Sub-Saharan African (0)	0	<0.01
Albanian (0)	0	<0.01
Alsatian (4)	4	0.01
American (7,820)	7,820	10.63
Arab (34)	66	0.09
Arab (0)	0	<0.01
Egyptian (0)	0	<0.01
Iraqi (10)	10	0.01
Jordanian (0)	0	<0.01
Lebanese (11)	43	0.06
Moroccan (0)	0	<0.01
Palestinian (13)	13	0.02
Syrian (0)	0	<0.01
Other Arab (0)	0	<0.01
Armenian (0)	8	0.01
Assyrian/Chaldean/Syriac (0)	0	<0.01
Australian (0)	0	<0.01
Austrian (34)	45	0.06
Basque (0)	17	0.02
Belgian (16)	65	0.09
Brazilian (0)	0	<0.01
British (109)	295	0.40
Bulgarian (0)	7	0.01
Cajun (0)	0	<0.01
Canadian (51)	79	0.11
Carpatho Rusyn (0)	0	<0.01
Celtic (0)	14	0.02
Croatian (33)	66	0.09
Cypriot (0)	0	<0.01
Czech (25)	44	0.06
Czechoslovakian (0)	8	0.01
Danish (18)	58	0.08
Dutch (253)	1,193	1.62
Eastern European (0)	0	<0.01
English (3,186)	8,122	11.04
Estonian (0)	0	<0.01
European (872)	951	1.29
Finnish (9)	76	0.10
French, ex. Basque (529)	2,728	3.71
French Canadian (68)	119	0.16
German (9,945)	21,642	29.41
German Russian (0)	0	<0.01
Greek (54)	141	0.19
Guyanese (0)	0	<0.01
Hungarian (14)	134	0.18
Icelander (0)	0	<0.01
Iranian (0)	0	<0.01
Irish (3,515)	11,068	15.04
Israeli (0)	0	<0.01
Italian (542)	1,490	2.02
Latvian (14)	39	0.05
Lithuanian (23)	57	0.08
Luxemburger (0)	0	<0.01
Macedonian (0)	0	<0.01
Maltese (0)	0	<0.01
New Zealander (0)	0	<0.01
Northern European (8)	8	0.01
Norwegian (136)	361	0.49
Pennsylvania German (11)	11	0.01
Polish (138)	570	0.77
Portuguese (0)	81	0.11
Romanian (0)	60	0.08
Russian (55)	148	0.20
Scandinavian (19)	19	0.03
Scotch-Irish (471)	1,332	1.81
Scottish (598)	1,651	2.24
Serbian (0)	0	<0.01
Slavic (0)	11	0.01
Slovak (18)	122	0.17
Slovene (15)	53	0.07
Soviet Union (0)	0	<0.01
Swedish (86)	279	0.38
Swiss (96)	452	0.61
Turkish (0)	0	<0.01
Ukrainian (0)	28	0.04
Welsh (203)	556	0.76
West Indian, ex. Hispanic (0)	0	<0.01
Bahamian (0)	0	<0.01
Barbadian (0)	0	<0.01
Belizean (0)	0	<0.01
Bermudan (0)	0	<0.01
British West Indian (0)	0	<0.01
Dutch West Indian (0)	0	<0.01
Haitian (0)	0	<0.01
Jamaican (0)	0	<0.01
Trinidadian/Tobagonian (0)	0	<0.01
U.S. Virgin Islander (0)	0	<0.01
West Indian (0)	0	<0.01
Other West Indian (0)	0	<0.01
Yugoslavian (0)	0	<0.01

Hispanic Origin	Population	%
Hispanic or Latino (of any race)	1,972	2.64
Central American, ex. Mexican	137	0.18
Costa Rican	2	<0.01
Guatemalan	50	0.07
Honduran	37	0.05
Nicaraguan	2	<0.01
Panamanian	24	0.03
Salvadoran	21	0.03
Other Central American	1	<0.01
Cuban	47	0.06
Dominican Republic	5	0.01
Mexican	1,372	1.84
Puerto Rican	167	0.22
South American	75	0.10
Argentinean	2	<0.01
Bolivian	3	<0.01
Chilean	4	0.01
Colombian	27	0.04
Ecuadorian	22	0.03
Paraguayan	1	<0.01
Peruvian	10	0.01
Uruguayan	0	<0.01
Venezuelan	6	0.01
Other South American	0	<0.01
Other Hispanic or Latino	169	0.23

Race*	Population	%
African-American/Black (3,873)	4,753	6.37
Not Hispanic (3,822)	4,660	6.25
Hispanic (51)	93	0.12
American Indian/Alaska Native (168)	531	0.71
Not Hispanic (146)	478	0.64
Hispanic (22)	53	0.07
Alaska Athabascan (Ala. Nat.) (0)	1	<0.01
Aleut (Alaska Native) (5)	6	0.01
Apache (4)	7	0.01
Arapaho (0)	0	<0.01
Blackfeet (2)	16	0.02
Canadian/French Am. Ind. (0)	0	<0.01
Central American Ind. (3)	4	0.01
Cherokee (47)	208	0.28
Cheyenne (0)	1	<0.01
Chickasaw (2)	4	0.01
Chippewa (8)	12	0.02
Choctaw (10)	17	0.02
Colville (0)	0	<0.01
Comanche (0)	0	<0.01
Cree (0)	0	<0.01
Creek (1)	4	0.01
Crow (0)	0	<0.01
Delaware (0)	0	<0.01
Hopi (0)	0	<0.01
Houma (0)	0	<0.01
Inupiat (Alaska Native) (0)	0	<0.01
Iroquois (0)	5	0.01
Kiowa (0)	0	<0.01
Lumbee (2)	2	<0.01
Menominee (0)	0	<0.01
Mexican American Ind. (6)	7	0.01
Navajo (0)	4	0.01
Osage (0)	0	<0.01
Ottawa (3)	3	<0.01
Paiute (0)	0	<0.01
Pima (0)	1	<0.01
Potawatomi (1)	2	<0.01
Pueblo (0)	0	<0.01
Puget Sound Salish (0)	0	<0.01
Seminole (0)	3	<0.01
Shoshone (1)	1	<0.01
Sioux (4)	12	0.02
South American Ind. (1)	1	<0.01
Spanish American Ind. (0)	0	<0.01
Tlingit-Haida (Alaska Native) (0)	1	<0.01
Tohono O'Odham (0)	0	<0.01
Tsimshian (Alaska Native) (0)	0	<0.01
Ute (1)	1	<0.01
Yakama (0)	0	<0.01
Yaqui (0)	0	<0.01
Yuman (0)	0	<0.01
Yup'ik (Alaska Native) (0)	0	<0.01
Asian (704)	965	1.29
Not Hispanic (694)	947	1.27
Hispanic (10)	18	0.02
Bangladeshi (0)	0	<0.01
Bhutanese (0)	0	<0.01
Burmese (0)	0	<0.01
Cambodian (34)	44	0.06
Chinese, ex. Taiwanese (127)	160	0.21
Filipino (127)	198	0.27
Hmong (1)	4	0.01
Indian (143)	167	0.22
Indonesian (0)	2	<0.01
Japanese (72)	117	0.16
Korean (67)	114	0.15
Laotian (3)	4	0.01
Malaysian (0)	0	<0.01
Nepalese (0)	0	<0.01
Pakistani (43)	43	0.06
Sri Lankan (1)	3	<0.01
Taiwanese (7)	9	0.01
Thai (8)	15	0.02
Vietnamese (31)	39	0.05
Hawaii Native/Pacific Islander (16)	55	0.07
Not Hispanic (16)	48	0.06
Hispanic (0)	7	0.01
Fijian (0)	0	<0.01
Guamanian/Chamorro (2)	8	0.01
Marshallese (0)	0	<0.01
Native Hawaiian (8)	21	0.03
Samoan (1)	8	0.01
Tongan (0)	0	<0.01
White (67,408)	68,838	92.30
Not Hispanic (66,505)	67,736	90.83
Hispanic (903)	1,102	1.48

Notes: † The Census 2010 population figure is used to calculate the percentages in the Hispanic Origin and Race categories. Ancestry percentages are based on the 2006-2010 American Community Survey population (not shown); ‡ Numbers in parentheses indicate the number of people reporting a single ancestry; * Numbers in parentheses indicate the number of persons reporting this race alone, not in combination with any other race; Please refer to the Explanation of Data for more information.

Fountain County
Population: 17,240

Ancestry	Population	%
Afghan (0)	0	<0.01
African, Sub-Saharan (20)	20	0.12
African (0)	0	<0.01
Cape Verdean (0)	0	<0.01
Ethiopian (20)	20	0.12
Ghanaian (0)	0	<0.01
Kenyan (0)	0	<0.01
Liberian (0)	0	<0.01
Nigerian (0)	0	<0.01
Senegalese (0)	0	<0.01
Sierra Leonean (0)	0	<0.01
Somalian (0)	0	<0.01
South African (0)	0	<0.01
Sudanese (0)	0	<0.01
Ugandan (0)	0	<0.01
Zimbabwean (0)	0	<0.01
Other Sub-Saharan African (0)	0	<0.01
Albanian (0)	0	<0.01
Alsatian (0)	0	<0.01
American (2,482)	2,482	14.32
Arab (6)	15	0.09
Arab (0)	0	<0.01
Egyptian (0)	0	<0.01
Iraqi (0)	0	<0.01
Jordanian (0)	0	<0.01
Lebanese (0)	0	<0.01
Moroccan (0)	9	0.05
Palestinian (0)	0	<0.01
Syrian (6)	6	0.03
Other Arab (0)	0	<0.01
Armenian (0)	0	<0.01
Assyrian/Chaldean/Syriac (0)	0	<0.01
Australian (0)	0	<0.01
Austrian (8)	8	0.05
Basque (0)	0	<0.01
Belgian (13)	72	0.42
Brazilian (0)	0	<0.01
British (33)	71	0.41
Bulgarian (0)	0	<0.01
Cajun (0)	0	<0.01
Canadian (0)	5	0.03
Carpatho Rusyn (0)	0	<0.01
Celtic (0)	0	<0.01
Croatian (0)	0	<0.01
Cypriot (0)	0	<0.01
Czech (0)	40	0.23
Czechoslovakian (4)	4	0.02
Danish (8)	15	0.09
Dutch (127)	582	3.36
Eastern European (0)	0	<0.01
English (943)	2,168	12.51
Estonian (0)	0	<0.01
European (186)	212	1.22
Finnish (0)	0	<0.01
French, ex. Basque (175)	436	2.52
French Canadian (40)	82	0.47
German (1,147)	3,742	21.59
German Russian (0)	0	<0.01
Greek (0)	0	<0.01
Guyanese (0)	0	<0.01
Hungarian (0)	64	0.37
Icelander (0)	0	<0.01
Iranian (0)	0	<0.01
Irish (626)	2,497	14.41
Israeli (0)	0	<0.01
Italian (86)	240	1.38
Latvian (12)	12	0.07
Lithuanian (36)	50	0.29
Luxemburger (0)	0	<0.01
Macedonian (0)	0	<0.01
Maltese (0)	0	<0.01
New Zealander (0)	0	<0.01
Northern European (0)	0	<0.01
Norwegian (7)	26	0.15
Pennsylvania German (8)	16	0.09
Polish (47)	214	1.23
Portuguese (0)	0	<0.01
Romanian (0)	0	<0.01
Russian (0)	13	0.08
Scandinavian (3)	3	0.02
Scotch-Irish (138)	443	2.56
Scottish (169)	326	1.88
Serbian (0)	0	<0.01
Slavic (0)	0	<0.01
Slovak (0)	7	0.04
Slovene (0)	0	<0.01
Soviet Union (0)	0	<0.01
Swedish (64)	306	1.77
Swiss (0)	22	0.13
Turkish (0)	0	<0.01
Ukrainian (20)	20	0.12
Welsh (12)	126	0.73
West Indian, ex. Hispanic (0)	13	0.08
Bahamian (0)	0	<0.01
Barbadian (0)	0	<0.01
Belizean (0)	0	<0.01
Bermudan (0)	0	<0.01
British West Indian (0)	0	<0.01
Dutch West Indian (0)	13	0.08
Haitian (0)	0	<0.01
Jamaican (0)	0	<0.01
Trinidadian/Tobagonian (0)	0	<0.01
U.S. Virgin Islander (0)	0	<0.01
West Indian (0)	0	<0.01
Other West Indian (0)	0	<0.01
Yugoslavian (0)	0	<0.01

Hispanic Origin	Population	%
Hispanic or Latino (of any race)	373	2.16
Central American, ex. Mexican	15	0.09
Costa Rican	0	<0.01
Guatemalan	2	0.01
Honduran	11	0.06
Nicaraguan	0	<0.01
Panamanian	2	0.01
Salvadoran	0	<0.01
Other Central American	0	<0.01
Cuban	1	0.01
Dominican Republic	0	<0.01
Mexican	314	1.82
Puerto Rican	12	0.07
South American	6	0.03
Argentinean	0	<0.01
Bolivian	0	<0.01
Chilean	0	<0.01
Colombian	2	0.01
Ecuadorian	0	<0.01
Paraguayan	0	<0.01
Peruvian	4	0.02
Uruguayan	0	<0.01
Venezuelan	0	<0.01
Other South American	0	<0.01
Other Hispanic or Latino	25	0.15

Race*	Population	%
African-American/Black (28)	67	0.39
Not Hispanic (26)	62	0.36
Hispanic (2)	5	0.03
American Indian/Alaska Native (54)	132	0.77
Not Hispanic (48)	125	0.73
Hispanic (6)	7	0.04
Alaska Athabascan (Ala. Nat.) (0)	0	<0.01
Aleut (Alaska Native) (0)	0	<0.01
Apache (0)	2	0.01
Arapaho (0)	0	<0.01
Blackfeet (0)	6	0.03
Canadian/French Am. Ind. (0)	0	<0.01
Central American Ind. (1)	1	0.01
Cherokee (19)	61	0.35
Cheyenne (0)	0	<0.01
Chickasaw (1)	1	0.01
Chippewa (9)	11	0.06
Choctaw (4)	6	0.03
Colville (0)	0	<0.01
Comanche (0)	0	<0.01
Cree (0)	0	<0.01
Creek (0)	0	<0.01
Crow (0)	0	<0.01
Delaware (0)	0	<0.01
Hopi (0)	0	<0.01
Houma (0)	0	<0.01
Inupiat (Alaska Native) (3)	3	0.02
Iroquois (1)	1	0.01
Kiowa (0)	0	<0.01
Lumbee (0)	0	<0.01
Menominee (0)	0	<0.01
Mexican American Ind. (0)	2	0.01
Navajo (0)	0	<0.01
Osage (0)	0	<0.01
Ottawa (2)	2	0.01
Paiute (0)	0	<0.01
Pima (0)	0	<0.01
Potawatomi (3)	3	0.02
Pueblo (0)	0	<0.01
Puget Sound Salish (0)	0	<0.01
Seminole (0)	0	<0.01
Shoshone (0)	0	<0.01
Sioux (0)	1	0.01
South American Ind. (1)	1	0.01
Spanish American Ind. (0)	0	<0.01
Tlingit-Haida (Alaska Native) (0)	0	<0.01
Tohono O'Odham (0)	0	<0.01
Tsimshian (Alaska Native) (0)	0	<0.01
Ute (0)	0	<0.01
Yakama (0)	0	<0.01
Yaqui (0)	0	<0.01
Yuman (0)	0	<0.01
Yup'ik (Alaska Native) (0)	0	<0.01
Asian (35)	70	0.41
Not Hispanic (35)	69	0.40
Hispanic (0)	1	0.01
Bangladeshi (0)	0	<0.01
Bhutanese (0)	0	<0.01
Burmese (0)	0	<0.01
Cambodian (0)	0	<0.01
Chinese, ex. Taiwanese (10)	14	0.08
Filipino (10)	25	0.15
Hmong (0)	0	<0.01
Indian (4)	7	0.04
Indonesian (0)	0	<0.01
Japanese (4)	15	0.09
Korean (3)	12	0.07
Laotian (1)	1	0.01
Malaysian (0)	0	<0.01
Nepalese (0)	0	<0.01
Pakistani (0)	0	<0.01
Sri Lankan (0)	0	<0.01
Taiwanese (0)	0	<0.01
Thai (1)	1	0.01
Vietnamese (0)	0	<0.01
Hawaii Native/Pacific Islander (1)	8	0.05
Not Hispanic (1)	7	0.04
Hispanic (0)	1	0.01
Fijian (0)	0	<0.01
Guamanian/Chamorro (0)	1	0.01
Marshallese (0)	0	<0.01
Native Hawaiian (1)	4	0.02
Samoan (0)	0	<0.01
Tongan (0)	0	<0.01
White (16,802)	16,973	98.45
Not Hispanic (16,598)	16,748	97.15
Hispanic (204)	225	1.31

Notes: † The Census 2010 population figure is used to calculate the percentages in the Hispanic Origin and Race categories. Ancestry percentages are based on the 2006-2010 American Community Survey population (not shown); ‡ Numbers in parentheses indicate the number of people reporting a single ancestry; * Numbers in parentheses indicate the number of persons reporting this race alone, not in combination with any other race; Please refer to the Explanation of Data for more information.

Franklin County
Population: 23,087

Ancestry	Population	%
Afghan (0)	0	<0.01
African, Sub-Saharan (0)	0	<0.01
African (0)	0	<0.01
Cape Verdean (0)	0	<0.01
Ethiopian (0)	0	<0.01
Ghanaian (0)	0	<0.01
Kenyan (0)	0	<0.01
Liberian (0)	0	<0.01
Nigerian (0)	0	<0.01
Senegalese (0)	0	<0.01
Sierra Leonean (0)	0	<0.01
Somalian (0)	0	<0.01
South African (0)	0	<0.01
Sudanese (0)	0	<0.01
Ugandan (0)	0	<0.01
Zimbabwean (0)	0	<0.01
Other Sub-Saharan African (0)	0	<0.01
Albanian (0)	0	<0.01
Alsatian (0)	15	0.06
American (3,410)	3,410	14.70
Arab (0)	31	0.13
Arab (0)	0	<0.01
Egyptian (0)	0	<0.01
Iraqi (0)	0	<0.01
Jordanian (0)	0	<0.01
Lebanese (0)	0	<0.01
Moroccan (0)	0	<0.01
Palestinian (0)	0	<0.01
Syrian (0)	31	0.13
Other Arab (0)	0	<0.01
Armenian (0)	0	<0.01
Assyrian/Chaldean/Syriac (0)	0	<0.01
Australian (0)	0	<0.01
Austrian (28)	53	0.23
Basque (0)	0	<0.01
Belgian (11)	11	0.05
Brazilian (14)	14	0.06
British (12)	59	0.25
Bulgarian (0)	0	<0.01
Cajun (0)	0	<0.01
Canadian (16)	29	0.13
Carpatho Rusyn (0)	0	<0.01
Celtic (0)	0	<0.01
Croatian (10)	31	0.13
Cypriot (0)	0	<0.01
Czech (0)	0	<0.01
Czechoslovakian (0)	0	<0.01
Danish (0)	62	0.27
Dutch (18)	253	1.09
Eastern European (2)	2	0.01
English (832)	2,208	9.52
Estonian (0)	0	<0.01
European (98)	98	0.42
Finnish (24)	27	0.12
French, ex. Basque (90)	461	1.99
French Canadian (12)	21	0.09
German (6,045)	9,354	40.33
German Russian (0)	0	<0.01
Greek (0)	0	<0.01
Guyanese (0)	0	<0.01
Hungarian (87)	127	0.55
Icelander (0)	0	<0.01
Iranian (0)	0	<0.01
Irish (787)	3,045	13.13
Israeli (0)	0	<0.01
Italian (110)	400	1.72
Latvian (0)	0	<0.01
Lithuanian (8)	8	0.03
Luxemburger (0)	10	0.04
Macedonian (0)	0	<0.01
Maltese (0)	0	<0.01
New Zealander (0)	0	<0.01
Northern European (19)	19	0.08
Norwegian (7)	53	0.23
Pennsylvania German (8)	8	0.03
Polish (41)	202	0.87
Portuguese (0)	0	<0.01
Romanian (0)	19	0.08
Russian (86)	189	0.81
Scandinavian (0)	0	<0.01
Scotch-Irish (107)	198	0.85
Scottish (230)	387	1.67
Serbian (0)	0	<0.01
Slavic (0)	0	<0.01
Slovak (0)	0	<0.01
Slovene (0)	8	0.03
Soviet Union (0)	0	<0.01
Swedish (12)	210	0.91
Swiss (19)	57	0.25
Turkish (0)	0	<0.01
Ukrainian (11)	22	0.09
Welsh (8)	99	0.43
West Indian, ex. Hispanic (0)	0	<0.01
Bahamian (0)	0	<0.01
Barbadian (0)	0	<0.01
Belizean (0)	0	<0.01
Bermudan (0)	0	<0.01
British West Indian (0)	0	<0.01
Dutch West Indian (0)	0	<0.01
Haitian (0)	0	<0.01
Jamaican (0)	0	<0.01
Trinidadian/Tobagonian (0)	0	<0.01
U.S. Virgin Islander (0)	0	<0.01
West Indian (0)	0	<0.01
Other West Indian (0)	0	<0.01
Yugoslavian (9)	9	0.04

Hispanic Origin	Population	%
Hispanic or Latino (of any race)	210	0.91
Central American, ex. Mexican	26	0.11
Costa Rican	2	0.01
Guatemalan	7	0.03
Honduran	7	0.03
Nicaraguan	0	<0.01
Panamanian	2	0.01
Salvadoran	8	0.03
Other Central American	0	<0.01
Cuban	4	0.02
Dominican Republic	3	0.01
Mexican	140	0.61
Puerto Rican	18	0.08
South American	5	0.02
Argentinean	0	<0.01
Bolivian	0	<0.01
Chilean	0	<0.01
Colombian	0	<0.01
Ecuadorian	1	<0.01
Paraguayan	0	<0.01
Peruvian	4	0.02
Uruguayan	0	<0.01
Venezuelan	0	<0.01
Other South American	0	<0.01
Other Hispanic or Latino	14	0.06

Race*	Population	%
African-American/Black (37)	79	0.34
Not Hispanic (34)	69	0.30
Hispanic (3)	10	0.04
American Indian/Alaska Native (34)	129	0.56
Not Hispanic (27)	115	0.50
Hispanic (7)	14	0.06
Alaska Athabascan (Ala. Nat.) (0)	0	<0.01
Aleut (Alaska Native) (0)	0	<0.01
Apache (0)	0	<0.01
Arapaho (0)	0	<0.01
Blackfeet (1)	7	0.03
Canadian/French Am. Ind. (0)	0	<0.01
Central American Ind. (0)	0	<0.01
Cherokee (12)	55	0.24
Cheyenne (0)	0	<0.01
Chickasaw (0)	0	<0.01
Chippewa (1)	1	<0.01
Choctaw (0)	1	<0.01
Colville (0)	0	<0.01
Comanche (0)	0	<0.01
Cree (0)	0	<0.01
Creek (0)	0	<0.01
Crow (0)	0	<0.01
Delaware (0)	0	<0.01
Hopi (0)	0	<0.01
Houma (0)	0	<0.01
Inupiat (Alaska Native) (0)	0	<0.01
Iroquois (4)	7	0.03
Kiowa (1)	1	<0.01
Lumbee (0)	0	<0.01
Menominee (0)	0	<0.01
Mexican American Ind. (2)	2	0.01
Navajo (2)	2	0.01
Osage (0)	0	<0.01
Ottawa (0)	0	<0.01
Paiute (0)	0	<0.01
Pima (1)	2	0.01
Potawatomi (0)	0	<0.01
Pueblo (0)	0	<0.01
Puget Sound Salish (0)	0	<0.01
Seminole (0)	0	<0.01
Shoshone (0)	1	<0.01
Sioux (0)	0	<0.01
South American Ind. (0)	0	<0.01
Spanish American Ind. (1)	1	<0.01
Tlingit-Haida (Alaska Native) (0)	0	<0.01
Tohono O'Odham (0)	0	<0.01
Tsimshian (Alaska Native) (0)	0	<0.01
Ute (0)	0	<0.01
Yakama (0)	0	<0.01
Yaqui (0)	0	<0.01
Yuman (0)	0	<0.01
Yup'ik (Alaska Native) (0)	0	<0.01
Asian (55)	82	0.36
Not Hispanic (55)	82	0.36
Hispanic (0)	0	<0.01
Bangladeshi (0)	0	<0.01
Bhutanese (0)	0	<0.01
Burmese (0)	0	<0.01
Cambodian (1)	3	0.01
Chinese, ex. Taiwanese (19)	29	0.13
Filipino (19)	32	0.14
Hmong (0)	0	<0.01
Indian (5)	7	0.03
Indonesian (0)	0	<0.01
Japanese (2)	2	0.01
Korean (5)	5	0.02
Laotian (0)	0	<0.01
Malaysian (0)	1	<0.01
Nepalese (0)	0	<0.01
Pakistani (0)	0	<0.01
Sri Lankan (0)	0	<0.01
Taiwanese (0)	0	<0.01
Thai (0)	0	<0.01
Vietnamese (4)	4	0.02
Hawaii Native/Pacific Islander (2)	14	0.06
Not Hispanic (2)	14	0.06
Hispanic (0)	0	<0.01
Fijian (0)	0	<0.01
Guamanian/Chamorro (1)	1	<0.01
Marshallese (0)	0	<0.01
Native Hawaiian (1)	6	0.03
Samoan (0)	1	<0.01
Tongan (0)	0	<0.01
White (22,703)	22,877	99.09
Not Hispanic (22,600)	22,748	98.53
Hispanic (103)	129	0.56

Notes: † The Census 2010 population figure is used to calculate the percentages in the Hispanic Origin and Race categories. Ancestry percentages are based on the 2006-2010 American Community Survey population (not shown); ‡ Numbers in parentheses indicate the number of people reporting a single ancestry; * Numbers in parentheses indicate the number of persons reporting this race alone, not in combination with any other race; Please refer to the Explanation of Data for more information.

Fulton County
Population: 20,836

Ancestry	Population	%
Afghan (0)	0	<0.01
African, Sub-Saharan (0)	25	0.12
African (0)	9	0.04
Cape Verdean (0)	0	<0.01
Ethiopian (0)	0	<0.01
Ghanaian (0)	0	<0.01
Kenyan (0)	0	<0.01
Liberian (0)	0	<0.01
Nigerian (0)	0	<0.01
Senegalese (0)	0	<0.01
Sierra Leonean (0)	0	<0.01
Somalian (0)	0	<0.01
South African (0)	16	0.08
Sudanese (0)	0	<0.01
Ugandan (0)	0	<0.01
Zimbabwean (0)	0	<0.01
Other Sub-Saharan African (0)	0	<0.01
Albanian (40)	40	0.19
Alsatian (0)	0	<0.01
American (3,922)	3,922	18.96
Arab (0)	0	<0.01
Arab (0)	0	<0.01
Egyptian (0)	0	<0.01
Iraqi (0)	0	<0.01
Jordanian (0)	0	<0.01
Lebanese (0)	0	<0.01
Moroccan (0)	0	<0.01
Palestinian (0)	0	<0.01
Syrian (0)	0	<0.01
Other Arab (0)	0	<0.01
Armenian (0)	0	<0.01
Assyrian/Chaldean/Syriac (0)	0	<0.01
Australian (0)	0	<0.01
Austrian (0)	14	0.07
Basque (0)	0	<0.01
Belgian (8)	8	0.04
Brazilian (0)	0	<0.01
British (26)	42	0.20
Bulgarian (0)	0	<0.01
Cajun (0)	0	<0.01
Canadian (4)	7	0.03
Carpatho Rusyn (0)	0	<0.01
Celtic (0)	0	<0.01
Croatian (11)	66	0.32
Cypriot (0)	0	<0.01
Czech (0)	69	0.33
Czechoslovakian (30)	30	0.15
Danish (8)	19	0.09
Dutch (122)	545	2.63
Eastern European (0)	0	<0.01
English (950)	2,061	9.96
Estonian (0)	0	<0.01
European (108)	108	0.52
Finnish (0)	0	<0.01
French, ex. Basque (79)	400	1.93
French Canadian (34)	41	0.20
German (3,052)	5,940	28.72
German Russian (0)	0	<0.01
Greek (0)	26	0.13
Guyanese (0)	0	<0.01
Hungarian (26)	55	0.27
Icelander (0)	0	<0.01
Iranian (0)	0	<0.01
Irish (665)	2,250	10.88
Israeli (0)	0	<0.01
Italian (87)	485	2.34
Latvian (3)	3	0.01
Lithuanian (28)	68	0.33
Luxemburger (0)	0	<0.01
Macedonian (0)	0	<0.01
Maltese (0)	0	<0.01
New Zealander (0)	0	<0.01
Northern European (0)	0	<0.01
Norwegian (109)	183	0.88
Pennsylvania German (100)	143	0.69
Polish (120)	347	1.68
Portuguese (10)	17	0.08
Romanian (0)	11	0.05
Russian (31)	42	0.20
Scandinavian (9)	18	0.09
Scotch-Irish (104)	273	1.32
Scottish (111)	297	1.44
Serbian (13)	13	0.06
Slavic (0)	0	<0.01
Slovak (0)	0	<0.01
Slovene (0)	76	0.37
Soviet Union (0)	0	<0.01
Swedish (55)	158	0.76
Swiss (0)	7	0.03
Turkish (0)	0	<0.01
Ukrainian (0)	0	<0.01
Welsh (6)	119	0.58
West Indian, ex. Hispanic (0)	0	<0.01
Bahamian (0)	0	<0.01
Barbadian (0)	0	<0.01
Belizean (0)	0	<0.01
Bermudan (0)	0	<0.01
British West Indian (0)	0	<0.01
Dutch West Indian (0)	0	<0.01
Haitian (0)	0	<0.01
Jamaican (0)	0	<0.01
Trinidadian/Tobagonian (0)	0	<0.01
U.S. Virgin Islander (0)	0	<0.01
West Indian (0)	0	<0.01
Other West Indian (0)	0	<0.01
Yugoslavian (24)	39	0.19

Hispanic Origin	Population	%
Hispanic or Latino (of any race)	882	4.23
Central American, ex. Mexican	10	0.05
Costa Rican	1	<0.01
Guatemalan	1	<0.01
Honduran	1	<0.01
Nicaraguan	2	0.01
Panamanian	5	0.02
Salvadoran	0	<0.01
Other Central American	0	<0.01
Cuban	5	0.02
Dominican Republic	4	0.02
Mexican	763	3.66
Puerto Rican	41	0.20
South American	10	0.05
Argentinean	0	<0.01
Bolivian	0	<0.01
Chilean	0	<0.01
Colombian	0	<0.01
Ecuadorian	2	0.01
Paraguayan	0	<0.01
Peruvian	8	0.04
Uruguayan	0	<0.01
Venezuelan	0	<0.01
Other South American	0	<0.01
Other Hispanic or Latino	49	0.24

Race*	Population	%
African-American/Black (150)	244	1.17
Not Hispanic (144)	231	1.11
Hispanic (6)	13	0.06
American Indian/Alaska Native (96)	181	0.87
Not Hispanic (73)	153	0.73
Hispanic (23)	28	0.13
Alaska Athabascan (Ala. Nat.) (1)	1	<0.01
Aleut (Alaska Native) (0)	0	<0.01
Apache (1)	1	<0.01
Arapaho (0)	0	<0.01
Blackfeet (2)	11	0.05
Canadian/French Am. Ind. (0)	2	0.01
Central American Ind. (0)	0	<0.01
Cherokee (16)	42	0.20
Cheyenne (2)	2	0.01
Chickasaw (0)	0	<0.01
Chippewa (4)	4	0.02
Choctaw (2)	2	0.01
Colville (0)	0	<0.01
Comanche (0)	0	<0.01
Cree (0)	0	<0.01
Creek (0)	0	<0.01
Crow (0)	0	<0.01
Delaware (0)	0	<0.01
Hopi (0)	0	<0.01
Houma (0)	0	<0.01
Inupiat (Alaska Native) (1)	1	<0.01
Iroquois (2)	2	0.01
Kiowa (2)	2	0.01
Lumbee (0)	0	<0.01
Menominee (0)	0	<0.01
Mexican American Ind. (0)	0	<0.01
Navajo (0)	0	<0.01
Osage (0)	0	<0.01
Ottawa (0)	0	<0.01
Paiute (0)	0	<0.01
Pima (0)	0	<0.01
Potawatomi (0)	3	0.01
Pueblo (0)	0	<0.01
Puget Sound Salish (0)	0	<0.01
Seminole (0)	0	<0.01
Shoshone (0)	0	<0.01
Sioux (1)	2	0.01
South American Ind. (0)	0	<0.01
Spanish American Ind. (0)	0	<0.01
Tlingit-Haida (Alaska Native) (0)	0	<0.01
Tohono O'Odham (0)	0	<0.01
Tsimshian (Alaska Native) (0)	0	<0.01
Ute (0)	0	<0.01
Yakama (0)	0	<0.01
Yaqui (0)	0	<0.01
Yuman (0)	0	<0.01
Yup'ik (Alaska Native) (0)	0	<0.01
Asian (101)	129	0.62
Not Hispanic (101)	125	0.60
Hispanic (0)	4	0.02
Bangladeshi (0)	0	<0.01
Bhutanese (0)	0	<0.01
Burmese (0)	0	<0.01
Cambodian (0)	0	<0.01
Chinese, ex. Taiwanese (38)	42	0.20
Filipino (25)	39	0.19
Hmong (0)	0	<0.01
Indian (12)	15	0.07
Indonesian (1)	1	<0.01
Japanese (2)	3	0.01
Korean (12)	14	0.07
Laotian (2)	4	0.02
Malaysian (0)	0	<0.01
Nepalese (0)	0	<0.01
Pakistani (4)	4	0.02
Sri Lankan (0)	0	<0.01
Taiwanese (1)	1	<0.01
Thai (0)	0	<0.01
Vietnamese (1)	3	0.01
Hawaii Native/Pacific Islander (5)	9	0.04
Not Hispanic (5)	9	0.04
Hispanic (0)	0	<0.01
Fijian (0)	0	<0.01
Guamanian/Chamorro (0)	0	<0.01
Marshallese (0)	0	<0.01
Native Hawaiian (2)	6	0.03
Samoan (0)	0	<0.01
Tongan (0)	0	<0.01
White (19,800)	20,019	96.08
Not Hispanic (19,438)	19,616	94.14
Hispanic (362)	403	1.93

Notes: † The Census 2010 population figure is used to calculate the percentages in the Hispanic Origin and Race categories. Ancestry percentages are based on the 2006-2010 American Community Survey population (not shown); ‡ Numbers in parentheses indicate the number of people reporting a single ancestry; * Numbers in parentheses indicate the number of persons reporting this race alone, not in combination with any other race; Please refer to the Explanation of Data for more information.

Gibson County
Population: 33,503

Ancestry	Population	%
Afghan (0)	0	<0.01
African, Sub-Saharan (16)	47	0.14
African (0)	31	0.09
Cape Verdean (0)	0	<0.01
Ethiopian (16)	16	0.05
Ghanaian (0)	0	<0.01
Kenyan (0)	0	<0.01
Liberian (0)	0	<0.01
Nigerian (0)	0	<0.01
Senegalese (0)	0	<0.01
Sierra Leonean (0)	0	<0.01
Somalian (0)	0	<0.01
South African (0)	0	<0.01
Sudanese (0)	0	<0.01
Ugandan (0)	0	<0.01
Zimbabwean (0)	0	<0.01
Other Sub-Saharan African (0)	0	<0.01
Albanian (0)	0	<0.01
Alsatian (0)	0	<0.01
American (8,119)	8,119	24.32
Arab (19)	19	0.06
Arab (19)	19	0.06
Egyptian (0)	0	<0.01
Iraqi (0)	0	<0.01
Jordanian (0)	0	<0.01
Lebanese (0)	0	<0.01
Moroccan (0)	0	<0.01
Palestinian (0)	0	<0.01
Syrian (0)	0	<0.01
Other Arab (0)	0	<0.01
Armenian (0)	0	<0.01
Assyrian/Chaldean/Syriac (0)	0	<0.01
Australian (0)	124	0.37
Austrian (26)	26	0.08
Basque (0)	0	<0.01
Belgian (0)	27	0.08
Brazilian (0)	0	<0.01
British (53)	89	0.27
Bulgarian (0)	0	<0.01
Cajun (0)	0	<0.01
Canadian (0)	6	0.02
Carpatho Rusyn (0)	0	<0.01
Celtic (0)	0	<0.01
Croatian (5)	5	0.01
Cypriot (0)	0	<0.01
Czech (3)	50	0.15
Czechoslovakian (0)	0	<0.01
Danish (44)	46	0.14
Dutch (145)	645	1.93
Eastern European (0)	4	0.01
English (1,984)	3,899	11.68
Estonian (0)	0	<0.01
European (132)	132	0.40
Finnish (0)	0	<0.01
French, ex. Basque (421)	1,217	3.65
French Canadian (41)	57	0.17
German (4,779)	9,440	28.28
German Russian (0)	0	<0.01
Greek (0)	104	0.31
Guyanese (0)	0	<0.01
Hungarian (12)	18	0.05
Icelander (0)	0	<0.01
Iranian (0)	0	<0.01
Irish (1,282)	4,383	13.13
Israeli (0)	0	<0.01
Italian (216)	688	2.06
Latvian (0)	0	<0.01
Lithuanian (0)	0	<0.01
Luxemburger (0)	0	<0.01
Macedonian (0)	0	<0.01
Maltese (0)	0	<0.01
New Zealander (0)	35	0.10
Northern European (0)	0	<0.01
Norwegian (13)	79	0.24
Pennsylvania German (0)	9	0.03
Polish (147)	379	1.14
Portuguese (0)	100	0.30
Romanian (5)	5	0.01
Russian (0)	33	0.10
Scandinavian (18)	36	0.11
Scotch-Irish (244)	886	2.65
Scottish (100)	314	0.94
Serbian (0)	0	<0.01
Slavic (0)	0	<0.01
Slovak (0)	0	<0.01
Slovene (0)	0	<0.01
Soviet Union (0)	0	<0.01
Swedish (78)	339	1.02
Swiss (0)	36	0.11
Turkish (0)	0	<0.01
Ukrainian (0)	100	0.30
Welsh (72)	124	0.37
West Indian, ex. Hispanic (6)	6	0.02
Bahamian (0)	0	<0.01
Barbadian (0)	0	<0.01
Belizean (0)	0	<0.01
Bermudan (0)	0	<0.01
British West Indian (0)	0	<0.01
Dutch West Indian (0)	0	<0.01
Haitian (0)	0	<0.01
Jamaican (6)	6	0.02
Trinidadian/Tobagonian (0)	0	<0.01
U.S. Virgin Islander (0)	0	<0.01
West Indian (0)	0	<0.01
Other West Indian (0)	0	<0.01
Yugoslavian (0)	0	<0.01

Hispanic Origin	Population	%
Hispanic or Latino (of any race)	441	1.32
Central American, ex. Mexican	38	0.11
Costa Rican	2	0.01
Guatemalan	9	0.03
Honduran	0	<0.01
Nicaraguan	2	0.01
Panamanian	10	0.03
Salvadoran	15	0.04
Other Central American	0	<0.01
Cuban	9	0.03
Dominican Republic	5	0.01
Mexican	277	0.83
Puerto Rican	39	0.12
South American	32	0.10
Argentinean	3	0.01
Bolivian	0	<0.01
Chilean	0	<0.01
Colombian	8	0.02
Ecuadorian	1	<0.01
Paraguayan	0	<0.01
Peruvian	3	0.01
Uruguayan	0	<0.01
Venezuelan	17	0.05
Other South American	0	<0.01
Other Hispanic or Latino	41	0.12

Race*	Population	%
African-American/Black (597)	913	2.73
Not Hispanic (589)	892	2.66
Hispanic (8)	21	0.06
American Indian/Alaska Native (72)	239	0.71
Not Hispanic (59)	208	0.62
Hispanic (13)	31	0.09
Alaska Athabascan (Ala. Nat.) (0)	0	<0.01
Aleut (Alaska Native) (0)	0	<0.01
Apache (1)	5	0.01
Arapaho (0)	0	<0.01
Blackfeet (2)	22	0.07
Canadian/French Am. Ind. (0)	4	0.01
Central American Ind. (0)	0	<0.01
Cherokee (14)	79	0.24
Cheyenne (0)	0	<0.01
Chickasaw (6)	6	0.02
Chippewa (2)	3	0.01
Choctaw (2)	4	0.01
Colville (0)	0	<0.01
Comanche (1)	1	<0.01
Cree (0)	0	<0.01
Creek (0)	1	<0.01
Crow (0)	1	<0.01
Delaware (1)	2	0.01
Hopi (0)	0	<0.01
Houma (0)	0	<0.01
Inupiat (Alaska Native) (0)	0	<0.01
Iroquois (0)	0	<0.01
Kiowa (0)	0	<0.01
Lumbee (0)	0	<0.01
Menominee (0)	0	<0.01
Mexican American Ind. (3)	5	0.01
Navajo (2)	7	0.02
Osage (0)	0	<0.01
Ottawa (0)	0	<0.01
Paiute (0)	0	<0.01
Pima (0)	0	<0.01
Potawatomi (0)	1	<0.01
Pueblo (0)	0	<0.01
Puget Sound Salish (0)	0	<0.01
Seminole (0)	0	<0.01
Shoshone (0)	0	<0.01
Sioux (3)	6	0.02
South American Ind. (0)	0	<0.01
Spanish American Ind. (0)	0	<0.01
Tlingit-Haida (Alaska Native) (0)	0	<0.01
Tohono O'Odham (0)	0	<0.01
Tsimshian (Alaska Native) (0)	0	<0.01
Ute (0)	0	<0.01
Yakama (0)	0	<0.01
Yaqui (0)	0	<0.01
Yuman (0)	0	<0.01
Yup'ik (Alaska Native) (0)	0	<0.01
Asian (156)	211	0.63
Not Hispanic (155)	209	0.62
Hispanic (1)	2	0.01
Bangladeshi (0)	0	<0.01
Bhutanese (0)	0	<0.01
Burmese (0)	0	<0.01
Cambodian (0)	0	<0.01
Chinese, ex. Taiwanese (21)	22	0.07
Filipino (30)	47	0.14
Hmong (14)	14	0.04
Indian (50)	51	0.15
Indonesian (0)	0	<0.01
Japanese (14)	27	0.08
Korean (6)	17	0.05
Laotian (0)	0	<0.01
Malaysian (0)	0	<0.01
Nepalese (2)	3	0.01
Pakistani (0)	0	<0.01
Sri Lankan (0)	0	<0.01
Taiwanese (0)	2	0.01
Thai (6)	8	0.02
Vietnamese (11)	15	0.04
Hawaii Native/Pacific Islander (3)	9	0.03
Not Hispanic (2)	7	0.02
Hispanic (1)	2	0.01
Fijian (1)	2	0.01
Guamanian/Chamorro (1)	1	<0.01
Marshallese (0)	0	<0.01
Native Hawaiian (1)	1	<0.01
Samoan (0)	0	<0.01
Tongan (0)	0	<0.01
White (31,986)	32,500	97.01
Not Hispanic (31,752)	32,210	96.14
Hispanic (234)	290	0.87

Notes: † The Census 2010 population figure is used to calculate the percentages in the Hispanic Origin and Race categories. Ancestry percentages are based on the 2006-2010 American Community Survey population (not shown); ‡ Numbers in parentheses indicate the number of people reporting a single ancestry; * Numbers in parentheses indicate the number of persons reporting this race alone, not in combination with any other race; Please refer to the Explanation of Data for more information.

Grant County
Population: 70,061

Ancestry	Population	%
Afghan (0)	0	<0.01
African, Sub-Saharan (111)	153	0.22
African (111)	153	0.22
Cape Verdean (0)	0	<0.01
Ethiopian (0)	0	<0.01
Ghanaian (0)	0	<0.01
Kenyan (0)	0	<0.01
Liberian (0)	0	<0.01
Nigerian (0)	0	<0.01
Senegalese (0)	0	<0.01
Sierra Leonean (0)	0	<0.01
Somalian (0)	0	<0.01
South African (0)	0	<0.01
Sudanese (0)	0	<0.01
Ugandan (0)	0	<0.01
Zimbabwean (0)	0	<0.01
Other Sub-Saharan African (0)	0	<0.01
Albanian (0)	0	<0.01
Alsatian (0)	0	<0.01
American (8,708)	8,708	12.41
Arab (34)	58	0.08
Arab (0)	0	<0.01
Egyptian (0)	0	<0.01
Iraqi (0)	0	<0.01
Jordanian (0)	0	<0.01
Lebanese (0)	16	0.02
Moroccan (12)	12	0.02
Palestinian (0)	0	<0.01
Syrian (22)	30	0.04
Other Arab (0)	0	<0.01
Armenian (0)	0	<0.01
Assyrian/Chaldean/Syriac (0)	2	<0.01
Australian (0)	14	0.02
Austrian (42)	45	0.06
Basque (0)	0	<0.01
Belgian (41)	123	0.18
Brazilian (0)	0	<0.01
British (200)	293	0.42
Bulgarian (0)	0	<0.01
Cajun (0)	0	<0.01
Canadian (33)	81	0.12
Carpatho Rusyn (0)	0	<0.01
Celtic (0)	0	<0.01
Croatian (0)	13	0.02
Cypriot (0)	0	<0.01
Czech (24)	50	0.07
Czechoslovakian (0)	27	0.04
Danish (9)	35	0.05
Dutch (226)	1,352	1.93
Eastern European (14)	37	0.05
English (3,162)	6,288	8.96
Estonian (0)	0	<0.01
European (384)	444	0.63
Finnish (4)	27	0.04
French, ex. Basque (315)	1,293	1.84
French Canadian (40)	61	0.09
German (6,141)	13,704	19.53
German Russian (8)	8	0.01
Greek (102)	155	0.22
Guyanese (0)	0	<0.01
Hungarian (17)	110	0.16
Icelander (13)	13	0.02
Iranian (41)	41	0.06
Irish (2,378)	7,039	10.03
Israeli (0)	0	<0.01
Italian (579)	1,186	1.69
Latvian (0)	13	0.02
Lithuanian (9)	16	0.02
Luxemburger (0)	0	<0.01
Macedonian (0)	0	<0.01
Maltese (0)	0	<0.01
New Zealander (0)	0	<0.01
Northern European (26)	26	0.04
Norwegian (122)	258	0.37
Pennsylvania German (18)	49	0.07
Polish (211)	749	1.07
Portuguese (41)	41	0.06
Romanian (12)	15	0.02
Russian (22)	61	0.09
Scandinavian (28)	54	0.08
Scotch-Irish (578)	892	1.27
Scottish (529)	1,245	1.77
Serbian (0)	0	<0.01
Slavic (0)	0	<0.01
Slovak (64)	141	0.20
Slovene (0)	0	<0.01
Soviet Union (0)	0	<0.01
Swedish (223)	641	0.91
Swiss (34)	189	0.27
Turkish (0)	0	<0.01
Ukrainian (12)	12	0.02
Welsh (154)	520	0.74
West Indian, ex. Hispanic (21)	72	0.10
Bahamian (0)	0	<0.01
Barbadian (0)	0	<0.01
Belizean (0)	0	<0.01
Bermudan (0)	0	<0.01
British West Indian (0)	0	<0.01
Dutch West Indian (0)	51	0.07
Haitian (0)	0	<0.01
Jamaican (0)	0	<0.01
Trinidadian/Tobagonian (0)	0	<0.01
U.S. Virgin Islander (0)	0	<0.01
West Indian (0)	0	<0.01
Other West Indian (21)	21	0.03
Yugoslavian (48)	48	0.07

Hispanic Origin	Population	%
Hispanic or Latino (of any race)	2,517	3.59
Central American, ex. Mexican	50	0.07
Costa Rican	4	0.01
Guatemalan	14	0.02
Honduran	11	0.02
Nicaraguan	7	0.01
Panamanian	6	0.01
Salvadoran	8	0.01
Other Central American	0	<0.01
Cuban	41	0.06
Dominican Republic	4	0.01
Mexican	1,962	2.80
Puerto Rican	145	0.21
South American	52	0.07
Argentinean	2	<0.01
Bolivian	5	0.01
Chilean	4	0.01
Colombian	9	0.01
Ecuadorian	10	0.01
Paraguayan	0	<0.01
Peruvian	8	0.01
Uruguayan	1	<0.01
Venezuelan	11	0.02
Other South American	2	<0.01
Other Hispanic or Latino	263	0.38

Race*	Population	%
African-American/Black (4,888)	5,917	8.45
Not Hispanic (4,805)	5,747	8.20
Hispanic (83)	170	0.24
American Indian/Alaska Native (234)	580	0.83
Not Hispanic (218)	528	0.75
Hispanic (16)	52	0.07
Alaska Athabascan (Ala. Nat.) (0)	0	<0.01
Aleut (Alaska Native) (0)	0	<0.01
Apache (2)	19	0.03
Arapaho (0)	0	<0.01
Blackfeet (1)	25	0.04
Canadian/French Am. Ind. (2)	2	<0.01
Central American Ind. (1)	3	<0.01
Cherokee (49)	158	0.23
Cheyenne (1)	2	<0.01
Chickasaw (1)	4	0.01
Chippewa (7)	14	0.02
Choctaw (10)	18	0.03
Colville (0)	0	<0.01
Comanche (1)	1	<0.01
Cree (0)	0	<0.01
Creek (0)	1	<0.01
Crow (1)	4	0.01
Delaware (0)	4	0.01
Hopi (1)	1	<0.01
Houma (0)	0	<0.01
Inupiat (Alaska Native) (0)	0	<0.01
Iroquois (0)	3	<0.01
Kiowa (0)	0	<0.01
Lumbee (1)	6	0.01
Menominee (0)	0	<0.01
Mexican American Ind. (5)	5	0.01
Navajo (4)	5	0.01
Osage (0)	1	<0.01
Ottawa (0)	0	<0.01
Paiute (0)	0	<0.01
Pima (0)	0	<0.01
Potawatomi (4)	4	0.01
Pueblo (1)	1	<0.01
Puget Sound Salish (0)	0	<0.01
Seminole (0)	0	<0.01
Shoshone (0)	0	<0.01
Sioux (1)	11	0.02
South American Ind. (0)	0	<0.01
Spanish American Ind. (1)	1	<0.01
Tlingit-Haida (Alaska Native) (0)	0	<0.01
Tohono O'Odham (0)	0	<0.01
Tsimshian (Alaska Native) (0)	0	<0.01
Ute (0)	0	<0.01
Yakama (0)	0	<0.01
Yaqui (0)	0	<0.01
Yuman (0)	0	<0.01
Yup'ik (Alaska Native) (0)	0	<0.01
Asian (411)	615	0.88
Not Hispanic (408)	594	0.85
Hispanic (3)	21	0.03
Bangladeshi (0)	0	<0.01
Bhutanese (0)	0	<0.01
Burmese (0)	0	<0.01
Cambodian (7)	7	0.01
Chinese, ex. Taiwanese (69)	106	0.15
Filipino (105)	148	0.21
Hmong (0)	0	<0.01
Indian (93)	105	0.15
Indonesian (0)	2	<0.01
Japanese (14)	56	0.08
Korean (55)	98	0.14
Laotian (0)	0	<0.01
Malaysian (0)	0	<0.01
Nepalese (0)	0	<0.01
Pakistani (7)	8	0.01
Sri Lankan (4)	6	0.01
Taiwanese (0)	1	<0.01
Thai (6)	11	0.02
Vietnamese (39)	50	0.07
Hawaii Native/Pacific Islander (17)	61	0.09
Not Hispanic (14)	48	0.07
Hispanic (3)	13	0.02
Fijian (0)	7	0.01
Guamanian/Chamorro (1)	4	0.01
Marshallese (0)	0	<0.01
Native Hawaiian (5)	20	0.03
Samoan (6)	15	0.02
Tongan (0)	0	<0.01
White (61,811)	63,396	90.49
Not Hispanic (60,633)	61,954	88.43
Hispanic (1,178)	1,442	2.06

Notes: † The Census 2010 population figure is used to calculate the percentages in the Hispanic Origin and Race categories. Ancestry percentages are based on the 2006-2010 American Community Survey population (not shown); ‡ Numbers in parentheses indicate the number of people reporting a single ancestry; * Numbers in parentheses indicate the number of persons reporting this race alone, not in combination with any other race; Please refer to the Explanation of Data for more information.

Greene County
Population: 33,165

Ancestry	Population	%
Afghan (0)	0	<0.01
African, Sub-Saharan (0)	53	0.16
African (0)	53	0.16
Cape Verdean (0)	0	<0.01
Ethiopian (0)	0	<0.01
Ghanaian (0)	0	<0.01
Kenyan (0)	0	<0.01
Liberian (0)	0	<0.01
Nigerian (0)	0	<0.01
Senegalese (0)	0	<0.01
Sierra Leonean (0)	0	<0.01
Somalian (0)	0	<0.01
South African (0)	0	<0.01
Sudanese (0)	0	<0.01
Ugandan (0)	0	<0.01
Zimbabwean (0)	0	<0.01
Other Sub-Saharan African (0)	0	<0.01
Albanian (0)	0	<0.01
Alsatian (0)	0	<0.01
American (4,269)	4,269	12.90
Arab (18)	18	0.05
Arab (0)	0	<0.01
Egyptian (0)	0	<0.01
Iraqi (0)	0	<0.01
Jordanian (0)	0	<0.01
Lebanese (18)	18	0.05
Moroccan (0)	0	<0.01
Palestinian (0)	0	<0.01
Syrian (0)	0	<0.01
Other Arab (0)	0	<0.01
Armenian (0)	0	<0.01
Assyrian/Chaldean/Syriac (0)	0	<0.01
Australian (0)	0	<0.01
Austrian (0)	51	0.15
Basque (0)	0	<0.01
Belgian (9)	31	0.09
Brazilian (0)	0	<0.01
British (43)	289	0.87
Bulgarian (0)	0	<0.01
Cajun (0)	0	<0.01
Canadian (10)	18	0.05
Carpatho Rusyn (0)	0	<0.01
Celtic (0)	10	0.03
Croatian (0)	16	0.05
Cypriot (12)	12	0.04
Czech (33)	44	0.13
Czechoslovakian (6)	6	0.02
Danish (48)	116	0.35
Dutch (168)	1,040	3.14
Eastern European (0)	0	<0.01
English (1,524)	3,696	11.17
Estonian (0)	0	<0.01
European (37)	143	0.43
Finnish (17)	30	0.09
French, ex. Basque (213)	1,195	3.61
French Canadian (22)	49	0.15
German (2,525)	8,429	25.48
German Russian (0)	0	<0.01
Greek (59)	86	0.26
Guyanese (0)	0	<0.01
Hungarian (0)	64	0.19
Icelander (0)	0	<0.01
Iranian (0)	0	<0.01
Irish (1,146)	5,543	16.75
Israeli (0)	0	<0.01
Italian (123)	461	1.39
Latvian (0)	0	<0.01
Lithuanian (10)	15	0.05
Luxemburger (0)	0	<0.01
Macedonian (0)	0	<0.01
Maltese (0)	0	<0.01
New Zealander (0)	0	<0.01
Northern European (22)	22	0.07
Norwegian (34)	133	0.40
Pennsylvania German (68)	73	0.22
Polish (78)	285	0.86
Portuguese (11)	263	0.79
Romanian (0)	0	<0.01
Russian (33)	106	0.32
Scandinavian (0)	19	0.06
Scotch-Irish (181)	492	1.49
Scottish (349)	671	2.03
Serbian (0)	0	<0.01
Slavic (0)	0	<0.01
Slovak (10)	31	0.09
Slovene (0)	8	0.02
Soviet Union (0)	0	<0.01
Swedish (177)	432	1.31
Swiss (58)	162	0.49
Turkish (0)	7	0.02
Ukrainian (0)	0	<0.01
Welsh (98)	389	1.18
West Indian, ex. Hispanic (0)	5	0.02
Bahamian (0)	0	<0.01
Barbadian (0)	0	<0.01
Belizean (0)	0	<0.01
Bermudan (0)	0	<0.01
British West Indian (0)	0	<0.01
Dutch West Indian (0)	0	<0.01
Haitian (0)	0	<0.01
Jamaican (0)	0	<0.01
Trinidadian/Tobagonian (0)	0	<0.01
U.S. Virgin Islander (0)	0	<0.01
West Indian (0)	5	0.02
Other West Indian (0)	0	<0.01
Yugoslavian (0)	0	<0.01

Hispanic Origin	Population	%
Hispanic or Latino (of any race)	322	0.97
Central American, ex. Mexican	11	0.03
Costa Rican	1	<0.01
Guatemalan	3	0.01
Honduran	4	0.01
Nicaraguan	0	<0.01
Panamanian	2	0.01
Salvadoran	1	<0.01
Other Central American	0	<0.01
Cuban	15	0.05
Dominican Republic	0	<0.01
Mexican	206	0.62
Puerto Rican	41	0.12
South American	19	0.06
Argentinean	4	0.01
Bolivian	0	<0.01
Chilean	4	0.01
Colombian	8	0.02
Ecuadorian	0	<0.01
Paraguayan	0	<0.01
Peruvian	2	0.01
Uruguayan	0	<0.01
Venezuelan	1	<0.01
Other South American	0	<0.01
Other Hispanic or Latino	30	0.09

Race*	Population	%
African-American/Black (49)	111	0.33
Not Hispanic (49)	104	0.31
Hispanic (0)	7	0.02
American Indian/Alaska Native (93)	232	0.70
Not Hispanic (82)	214	0.65
Hispanic (11)	18	0.05
Alaska Athabascan (Ala. Nat.) (0)	0	<0.01
Aleut (Alaska Native) (0)	0	<0.01
Apache (3)	3	0.01
Arapaho (0)	0	<0.01
Blackfeet (0)	5	0.02
Canadian/French Am. Ind. (0)	0	<0.01
Central American Ind. (0)	0	<0.01
Cherokee (20)	75	0.23
Cheyenne (0)	0	<0.01
Chickasaw (0)	0	<0.01
Chippewa (1)	6	0.02
Choctaw (2)	4	0.01
Colville (0)	0	<0.01
Comanche (0)	0	<0.01
Cree (0)	0	<0.01
Creek (11)	11	0.03
Crow (0)	0	<0.01
Delaware (0)	0	<0.01
Hopi (0)	0	<0.01
Houma (0)	0	<0.01
Inupiat (Alaska Native) (0)	0	<0.01
Iroquois (2)	5	0.02
Kiowa (0)	0	<0.01
Lumbee (1)	1	<0.01
Menominee (0)	0	<0.01
Mexican American Ind. (0)	1	<0.01
Navajo (6)	9	0.03
Osage (2)	4	0.01
Ottawa (1)	1	<0.01
Paiute (0)	0	<0.01
Pima (1)	1	<0.01
Potawatomi (1)	1	<0.01
Pueblo (0)	0	<0.01
Puget Sound Salish (0)	0	<0.01
Seminole (0)	3	0.01
Shoshone (0)	0	<0.01
Sioux (5)	10	0.03
South American Ind. (0)	1	<0.01
Spanish American Ind. (0)	0	<0.01
Tlingit-Haida (Alaska Native) (0)	0	<0.01
Tohono O'Odham (0)	0	<0.01
Tsimshian (Alaska Native) (0)	0	<0.01
Ute (0)	0	<0.01
Yakama (0)	0	<0.01
Yaqui (0)	0	<0.01
Yuman (0)	0	<0.01
Yup'ik (Alaska Native) (0)	0	<0.01
Asian (96)	148	0.45
Not Hispanic (96)	147	0.44
Hispanic (0)	1	<0.01
Bangladeshi (0)	0	<0.01
Bhutanese (0)	0	<0.01
Burmese (0)	0	<0.01
Cambodian (0)	0	<0.01
Chinese, ex. Taiwanese (25)	29	0.09
Filipino (26)	49	0.15
Hmong (0)	0	<0.01
Indian (14)	23	0.07
Indonesian (2)	2	0.01
Japanese (5)	7	0.02
Korean (7)	9	0.03
Laotian (0)	0	<0.01
Malaysian (0)	0	<0.01
Nepalese (0)	0	<0.01
Pakistani (0)	0	<0.01
Sri Lankan (0)	0	<0.01
Taiwanese (0)	1	<0.01
Thai (9)	11	0.03
Vietnamese (7)	8	0.02
Hawaii Native/Pacific Islander (4)	15	0.05
Not Hispanic (4)	14	0.04
Hispanic (0)	1	<0.01
Fijian (0)	0	<0.01
Guamanian/Chamorro (2)	2	0.01
Marshallese (0)	0	<0.01
Native Hawaiian (1)	3	0.01
Samoan (1)	2	0.01
Tongan (0)	0	<0.01
White (32,548)	32,819	98.96
Not Hispanic (32,343)	32,581	98.24
Hispanic (205)	238	0.72

Notes: † The Census 2010 population figure is used to calculate the percentages in the Hispanic Origin and Race categories. Ancestry percentages are based on the 2006-2010 American Community Survey population (not shown); ‡ Numbers in parentheses indicate the number of people reporting a single ancestry; * Numbers in parentheses indicate the number of persons reporting this race alone, not in combination with any other race; Please refer to the Explanation of Data for more information.

Hamilton County
Population: 274,569

Ancestry	Population	%
Afghan (33)	52	0.02
African, Sub-Saharan (512)	865	0.33
African (292)	491	0.19
Cape Verdean (0)	0	<0.01
Ethiopian (12)	12	<0.01
Ghanaian (0)	0	<0.01
Kenyan (57)	57	0.02
Liberian (0)	0	<0.01
Nigerian (79)	79	0.03
Senegalese (13)	13	<0.01
Sierra Leonean (0)	0	<0.01
Somalian (0)	0	<0.01
South African (13)	147	0.06
Sudanese (0)	11	<0.01
Ugandan (0)	0	<0.01
Zimbabwean (0)	0	<0.01
Other Sub-Saharan African (46)	55	0.02
Albanian (40)	50	0.02
Alsatian (0)	0	<0.01
American (20,130)	20,130	7.71
Arab (929)	1,516	0.58
Arab (293)	472	0.18
Egyptian (313)	342	0.13
Iraqi (0)	14	0.01
Jordanian (33)	45	0.02
Lebanese (126)	351	0.13
Moroccan (25)	48	0.02
Palestinian (24)	24	0.01
Syrian (43)	105	0.04
Other Arab (72)	115	0.04
Armenian (10)	31	0.01
Assyrian/Chaldean/Syriac (0)	0	<0.01
Australian (45)	92	0.04
Austrian (132)	463	0.18
Basque (0)	0	<0.01
Belgian (188)	853	0.33
Brazilian (88)	113	0.04
British (949)	1,717	0.66
Bulgarian (29)	68	0.03
Cajun (0)	22	0.01
Canadian (254)	569	0.22
Carpatho Rusyn (0)	16	0.01
Celtic (39)	54	0.02
Croatian (59)	420	0.16
Cypriot (0)	0	<0.01
Czech (244)	1,135	0.43
Czechoslovakian (222)	345	0.13
Danish (351)	1,114	0.43
Dutch (1,397)	6,141	2.35
Eastern European (375)	436	0.17
English (11,345)	34,092	13.05
Estonian (0)	13	<0.01
European (4,212)	4,815	1.84
Finnish (125)	304	0.12
French, ex. Basque (1,492)	8,233	3.15
French Canadian (420)	997	0.38
German (28,858)	75,694	28.97
German Russian (0)	0	<0.01
Greek (609)	1,579	0.60
Guyanese (0)	0	<0.01
Hungarian (313)	1,807	0.69
Icelander (0)	12	<0.01
Iranian (420)	565	0.22
Irish (10,366)	38,147	14.60
Israeli (21)	21	0.01
Italian (4,036)	12,040	4.61
Latvian (313)	439	0.17
Lithuanian (147)	488	0.19
Luxemburger (0)	22	0.01
Macedonian (67)	139	0.05
Maltese (0)	0	<0.01
New Zealander (14)	14	0.01
Northern European (153)	153	0.06
Norwegian (870)	3,017	1.15
Pennsylvania German (109)	189	0.07
Polish (2,509)	9,200	3.52
Portuguese (124)	368	0.14
Romanian (295)	476	0.18
Russian (1,243)	2,517	0.96
Scandinavian (237)	459	0.18
Scotch-Irish (1,543)	4,467	1.71
Scottish (2,503)	8,076	3.09
Serbian (74)	250	0.10
Slavic (12)	50	0.02
Slovak (234)	698	0.27
Slovene (89)	259	0.10
Soviet Union (0)	0	<0.01
Swedish (792)	4,394	1.68
Swiss (356)	1,505	0.58
Turkish (95)	121	0.05
Ukrainian (424)	901	0.34
Welsh (751)	2,739	1.05
West Indian, ex. Hispanic (150)	231	0.09
Bahamian (0)	0	<0.01
Barbadian (0)	0	<0.01
Belizean (11)	31	0.01
Bermudan (19)	19	0.01
British West Indian (13)	13	<0.01
Dutch West Indian (0)	0	<0.01
Haitian (12)	28	0.01
Jamaican (70)	115	0.04
Trinidadian/Tobagonian (13)	13	<0.01
U.S. Virgin Islander (0)	0	<0.01
West Indian (12)	12	<0.01
Other West Indian (0)	0	<0.01
Yugoslavian (273)	338	0.13

Hispanic Origin	Population	%
Hispanic or Latino (of any race)	9,426	3.43
Central American, ex. Mexican	796	0.29
Costa Rican	40	0.01
Guatemalan	269	0.10
Honduran	94	0.03
Nicaraguan	60	0.02
Panamanian	98	0.04
Salvadoran	220	0.08
Other Central American	15	0.01
Cuban	272	0.10
Dominican Republic	147	0.05
Mexican	5,449	1.98
Puerto Rican	885	0.32
South American	1,071	0.39
Argentinean	99	0.04
Bolivian	36	0.01
Chilean	59	0.02
Colombian	362	0.13
Ecuadorian	33	0.01
Paraguayan	9	<0.01
Peruvian	178	0.06
Uruguayan	12	<0.01
Venezuelan	273	0.10
Other South American	10	<0.01
Other Hispanic or Latino	806	0.29

Race*	Population	%
African-American/Black (9,603)	11,401	4.15
Not Hispanic (9,395)	11,044	4.02
Hispanic (208)	357	0.13
American Indian/Alaska Native (529)	1,309	0.48
Not Hispanic (437)	1,130	0.41
Hispanic (92)	179	0.07
Alaska Athabascan (Ala. Nat.) (0)	0	<0.01
Aleut (Alaska Native) (1)	1	<0.01
Apache (24)	35	0.01
Arapaho (0)	0	<0.01
Blackfeet (17)	50	0.02
Canadian/French Am. Ind. (1)	1	<0.01
Central American Ind. (1)	4	<0.01
Cherokee (80)	256	0.09
Cheyenne (0)	0	<0.01
Chickasaw (0)	1	<0.01
Chippewa (26)	45	0.02
Choctaw (7)	26	0.01
Colville (0)	0	<0.01
Comanche (0)	3	<0.01
Cree (3)	4	<0.01
Creek (5)	11	<0.01
Crow (2)	2	<0.01
Delaware (0)	3	<0.01
Hopi (2)	4	<0.01
Houma (0)	0	<0.01
Inupiat (Alaska Native) (2)	3	<0.01
Iroquois (5)	15	0.01
Kiowa (2)	2	<0.01
Lumbee (7)	8	<0.01
Menominee (1)	2	<0.01
Mexican American Ind. (42)	55	0.02
Navajo (12)	17	0.01
Osage (4)	10	<0.01
Ottawa (2)	6	<0.01
Paiute (2)	3	<0.01
Pima (0)	0	<0.01
Potawatomi (12)	23	0.01
Pueblo (0)	1	<0.01
Puget Sound Salish (0)	0	<0.01
Seminole (0)	3	<0.01
Shoshone (0)	1	<0.01
Sioux (17)	26	0.01
South American Ind. (2)	13	<0.01
Spanish American Ind. (2)	5	<0.01
Tlingit-Haida (Alaska Native) (1)	1	<0.01
Tohono O'Odham (0)	0	<0.01
Tsimshian (Alaska Native) (0)	2	<0.01
Ute (2)	3	<0.01
Yakama (0)	0	<0.01
Yaqui (2)	3	<0.01
Yuman (0)	0	<0.01
Yup'ik (Alaska Native) (0)	1	<0.01
Asian (13,175)	15,326	5.58
Not Hispanic (13,122)	15,185	5.53
Hispanic (53)	141	0.05
Bangladeshi (77)	83	0.03
Bhutanese (1)	3	<0.01
Burmese (4)	16	0.01
Cambodian (103)	120	0.04
Chinese, ex. Taiwanese (3,567)	3,954	1.44
Filipino (734)	1,189	0.43
Hmong (102)	113	0.04
Indian (4,541)	4,889	1.78
Indonesian (102)	126	0.05
Japanese (650)	938	0.34
Korean (1,248)	1,565	0.57
Laotian (36)	51	0.02
Malaysian (21)	33	0.01
Nepalese (35)	35	0.01
Pakistani (413)	457	0.17
Sri Lankan (52)	58	0.02
Taiwanese (200)	237	0.09
Thai (72)	137	0.05
Vietnamese (839)	974	0.35
Hawaii Native/Pacific Islander (97)	264	0.10
Not Hispanic (72)	215	0.08
Hispanic (25)	49	0.02
Fijian (0)	0	<0.01
Guamanian/Chamorro (14)	33	0.01
Marshallese (1)	1	<0.01
Native Hawaiian (48)	113	0.04
Samoan (14)	41	0.01
Tongan (4)	7	<0.01
White (242,985)	247,416	90.11
Not Hispanic (237,317)	241,153	87.83
Hispanic (5,668)	6,263	2.28

Notes: † The Census 2010 population figure is used to calculate the percentages in the Hispanic Origin and Race categories. Ancestry percentages are based on the 2006-2010 American Community Survey population (not shown); ‡ Numbers in parentheses indicate the number of people reporting a single ancestry; * Numbers in parentheses indicate the number of persons reporting this race alone, not in combination with any other race; Please refer to the Explanation of Data for more information.

Hancock County
Population: 70,002

Ancestry	Population	%
Afghan (0)	0	<0.01
African, Sub-Saharan (11)	110	0.16
African (0)	6	0.01
Cape Verdean (0)	0	<0.01
Ethiopian (0)	93	0.14
Ghanaian (0)	0	<0.01
Kenyan (11)	11	0.02
Liberian (0)	0	<0.01
Nigerian (0)	0	<0.01
Senegalese (0)	0	<0.01
Sierra Leonean (0)	0	<0.01
Somalian (0)	0	<0.01
South African (0)	0	<0.01
Sudanese (0)	0	<0.01
Ugandan (0)	0	<0.01
Zimbabwean (0)	0	<0.01
Other Sub-Saharan African (0)	0	<0.01
Albanian (0)	0	<0.01
Alsatian (0)	3	<0.01
American (8,011)	8,011	11.78
Arab (25)	50	0.07
Arab (6)	6	0.01
Egyptian (17)	17	0.02
Iraqi (0)	0	<0.01
Jordanian (0)	0	<0.01
Lebanese (0)	25	0.04
Moroccan (0)	0	<0.01
Palestinian (2)	2	<0.01
Syrian (0)	0	<0.01
Other Arab (0)	0	<0.01
Armenian (0)	0	<0.01
Assyrian/Chaldean/Syriac (0)	0	<0.01
Australian (34)	34	0.05
Austrian (0)	104	0.15
Basque (0)	0	<0.01
Belgian (0)	17	0.02
Brazilian (0)	0	<0.01
British (145)	421	0.62
Bulgarian (12)	12	0.02
Cajun (0)	0	<0.01
Canadian (63)	184	0.27
Carpatho Rusyn (0)	0	<0.01
Celtic (0)	12	0.02
Croatian (10)	12	0.02
Cypriot (0)	0	<0.01
Czech (34)	71	0.10
Czechoslovakian (17)	59	0.09
Danish (0)	72	0.11
Dutch (525)	1,448	2.13
Eastern European (41)	41	0.06
English (3,875)	8,036	11.82
Estonian (0)	0	<0.01
European (574)	583	0.86
Finnish (6)	46	0.07
French, ex. Basque (378)	1,556	2.29
French Canadian (153)	229	0.34
German (8,009)	17,832	26.22
German Russian (0)	0	<0.01
Greek (76)	120	0.18
Guyanese (0)	0	<0.01
Hungarian (35)	201	0.30
Icelander (0)	0	<0.01
Iranian (0)	25	0.04
Irish (3,413)	9,434	13.87
Israeli (0)	0	<0.01
Italian (456)	1,510	2.22
Latvian (0)	0	<0.01
Lithuanian (14)	67	0.10
Luxemburger (0)	11	0.02
Macedonian (0)	0	<0.01
Maltese (0)	12	0.02
New Zealander (0)	0	<0.01
Northern European (89)	89	0.13
Norwegian (58)	284	0.42
Pennsylvania German (15)	17	0.02
Polish (309)	950	1.40
Portuguese (30)	91	0.13
Romanian (78)	100	0.15
Russian (112)	264	0.39
Scandinavian (19)	56	0.08
Scotch-Irish (516)	985	1.45
Scottish (647)	1,351	1.99
Serbian (0)	2	<0.01
Slavic (7)	20	0.03
Slovak (0)	38	0.06
Slovene (0)	12	0.02
Soviet Union (0)	0	<0.01
Swedish (138)	385	0.57
Swiss (10)	185	0.27
Turkish (119)	119	0.17
Ukrainian (86)	166	0.24
Welsh (95)	565	0.83
West Indian, ex. Hispanic (14)	14	0.02
Bahamian (0)	0	<0.01
Barbadian (0)	0	<0.01
Belizean (0)	0	<0.01
Bermudan (14)	14	0.02
British West Indian (0)	0	<0.01
Dutch West Indian (0)	0	<0.01
Haitian (0)	0	<0.01
Jamaican (0)	0	<0.01
Trinidadian/Tobagonian (0)	0	<0.01
U.S. Virgin Islander (0)	0	<0.01
West Indian (0)	0	<0.01
Other West Indian (0)	0	<0.01
Yugoslavian (28)	28	0.04

Hispanic Origin	Population	%
Hispanic or Latino (of any race)	1,216	1.74
Central American, ex. Mexican	60	0.09
Costa Rican	7	0.01
Guatemalan	16	0.02
Honduran	9	0.01
Nicaraguan	2	<0.01
Panamanian	10	0.01
Salvadoran	16	0.02
Other Central American	0	<0.01
Cuban	41	0.06
Dominican Republic	21	0.03
Mexican	768	1.10
Puerto Rican	155	0.22
South American	60	0.09
Argentinean	5	0.01
Bolivian	7	0.01
Chilean	3	<0.01
Colombian	7	0.01
Ecuadorian	3	<0.01
Paraguayan	0	<0.01
Peruvian	15	0.02
Uruguayan	0	<0.01
Venezuelan	20	0.03
Other South American	0	<0.01
Other Hispanic or Latino	111	0.16

Race*	Population	%
African-American/Black (1,452)	1,758	2.51
Not Hispanic (1,420)	1,702	2.43
Hispanic (32)	56	0.08
American Indian/Alaska Native (154)	443	0.63
Not Hispanic (136)	392	0.56
Hispanic (18)	51	0.07
Alaska Athabascan (Ala. Nat.) (0)	0	<0.01
Aleut (Alaska Native) (2)	7	0.01
Apache (4)	8	0.01
Arapaho (2)	4	0.01
Blackfeet (5)	19	0.03
Canadian/French Am. Ind. (0)	0	<0.01
Central American Ind. (0)	0	<0.01
Cherokee (16)	112	0.16
Cheyenne (0)	1	<0.01
Chickasaw (1)	1	<0.01
Chippewa (4)	6	0.01
Choctaw (7)	14	0.02
Colville (0)	0	<0.01
Comanche (0)	1	<0.01
Cree (0)	0	<0.01
Creek (2)	2	<0.01
Crow (5)	5	0.01
Delaware (3)	6	0.01
Hopi (0)	1	<0.01
Houma (1)	1	<0.01
Inupiat (Alaska Native) (0)	0	<0.01
Iroquois (2)	8	0.01
Kiowa (0)	0	<0.01
Lumbee (3)	3	<0.01
Menominee (0)	0	<0.01
Mexican American Ind. (6)	6	0.01
Navajo (0)	0	<0.01
Osage (0)	0	<0.01
Ottawa (0)	0	<0.01
Paiute (0)	0	<0.01
Pima (0)	1	<0.01
Potawatomi (3)	4	0.01
Pueblo (0)	0	<0.01
Puget Sound Salish (0)	0	<0.01
Seminole (0)	0	<0.01
Shoshone (0)	0	<0.01
Sioux (6)	18	0.03
South American Ind. (0)	3	<0.01
Spanish American Ind. (0)	0	<0.01
Tlingit-Haida (Alaska Native) (0)	0	<0.01
Tohono O'Odham (0)	0	<0.01
Tsimshian (Alaska Native) (0)	0	<0.01
Ute (1)	1	<0.01
Yakama (0)	0	<0.01
Yaqui (1)	2	<0.01
Yuman (0)	0	<0.01
Yup'ik (Alaska Native) (0)	0	<0.01
Asian (558)	796	1.14
Not Hispanic (554)	787	1.12
Hispanic (4)	9	0.01
Bangladeshi (0)	2	<0.01
Bhutanese (0)	0	<0.01
Burmese (0)	0	<0.01
Cambodian (1)	6	0.01
Chinese, ex. Taiwanese (79)	102	0.15
Filipino (106)	183	0.26
Hmong (0)	0	<0.01
Indian (114)	147	0.21
Indonesian (2)	2	<0.01
Japanese (42)	81	0.12
Korean (89)	134	0.19
Laotian (7)	8	0.01
Malaysian (0)	0	<0.01
Nepalese (0)	0	<0.01
Pakistani (6)	11	0.02
Sri Lankan (0)	0	<0.01
Taiwanese (6)	6	0.01
Thai (13)	19	0.03
Vietnamese (54)	63	0.09
Hawaii Native/Pacific Islander (20)	35	0.05
Not Hispanic (14)	26	0.04
Hispanic (6)	9	0.01
Fijian (0)	0	<0.01
Guamanian/Chamorro (11)	11	0.02
Marshallese (1)	1	<0.01
Native Hawaiian (4)	11	0.02
Samoan (3)	3	<0.01
Tongan (0)	0	<0.01
White (66,644)	67,458	96.37
Not Hispanic (65,859)	66,557	95.08
Hispanic (785)	901	1.29

Notes: † The Census 2010 population figure is used to calculate the percentages in the Hispanic Origin and Race categories. Ancestry percentages are based on the 2006-2010 American Community Survey population (not shown); ‡ Numbers in parentheses indicate the number of people reporting a single ancestry; * Numbers in parentheses indicate the number of persons reporting this race alone, not in combination with any other race; Please refer to the Explanation of Data for more information.

Harrison County
Population: 39,364

Ancestry	Population	%
Afghan (0)	0	<0.01
African, Sub-Saharan (0)	5	0.01
African (0)	5	0.01
Cape Verdean (0)	0	<0.01
Ethiopian (0)	0	<0.01
Ghanaian (0)	0	<0.01
Kenyan (0)	0	<0.01
Liberian (0)	0	<0.01
Nigerian (0)	0	<0.01
Senegalese (0)	0	<0.01
Sierra Leonean (0)	0	<0.01
Somalian (0)	0	<0.01
South African (0)	0	<0.01
Sudanese (0)	0	<0.01
Ugandan (0)	0	<0.01
Zimbabwean (0)	0	<0.01
Other Sub-Saharan African (0)	0	<0.01
Albanian (0)	0	<0.01
Alsatian (0)	0	<0.01
American (6,364)	6,364	16.48
Arab (0)	0	<0.01
Arab (0)	0	<0.01
Egyptian (0)	0	<0.01
Iraqi (0)	0	<0.01
Jordanian (0)	0	<0.01
Lebanese (0)	0	<0.01
Moroccan (0)	0	<0.01
Palestinian (0)	0	<0.01
Syrian (0)	0	<0.01
Other Arab (0)	0	<0.01
Armenian (0)	0	<0.01
Assyrian/Chaldean/Syriac (0)	0	<0.01
Australian (0)	0	<0.01
Austrian (0)	22	0.06
Basque (0)	0	<0.01
Belgian (0)	15	0.04
Brazilian (0)	0	<0.01
British (28)	150	0.39
Bulgarian (0)	0	<0.01
Cajun (15)	15	0.04
Canadian (3)	14	0.04
Carpatho Rusyn (0)	0	<0.01
Celtic (0)	0	<0.01
Croatian (0)	0	<0.01
Cypriot (0)	0	<0.01
Czech (0)	26	0.07
Czechoslovakian (0)	0	<0.01
Danish (70)	101	0.26
Dutch (58)	331	0.86
Eastern European (0)	10	0.03
English (2,195)	4,943	12.80
Estonian (0)	0	<0.01
European (433)	441	1.14
Finnish (0)	42	0.11
French, ex. Basque (194)	1,332	3.45
French Canadian (16)	38	0.10
German (5,776)	12,024	31.14
German Russian (0)	0	<0.01
Greek (16)	95	0.25
Guyanese (0)	0	<0.01
Hungarian (79)	156	0.40
Icelander (0)	0	<0.01
Iranian (0)	0	<0.01
Irish (1,678)	4,952	12.82
Israeli (0)	0	<0.01
Italian (140)	643	1.67
Latvian (0)	0	<0.01
Lithuanian (28)	28	0.07
Luxemburger (0)	0	<0.01
Macedonian (0)	0	<0.01
Maltese (0)	0	<0.01
New Zealander (0)	0	<0.01
Northern European (0)	0	<0.01
Norwegian (42)	207	0.54
Pennsylvania German (0)	0	<0.01
Polish (71)	410	1.06
Portuguese (0)	30	0.08
Romanian (0)	0	<0.01
Russian (0)	12	0.03
Scandinavian (13)	54	0.14
Scotch-Irish (204)	572	1.48
Scottish (325)	890	2.30
Serbian (0)	0	<0.01
Slavic (11)	11	0.03
Slovak (0)	37	0.10
Slovene (0)	0	<0.01
Soviet Union (0)	0	<0.01
Swedish (17)	271	0.70
Swiss (0)	145	0.38
Turkish (0)	0	<0.01
Ukrainian (0)	15	0.04
Welsh (86)	190	0.49
West Indian, ex. Hispanic (0)	0	<0.01
Bahamian (0)	0	<0.01
Barbadian (0)	0	<0.01
Belizean (0)	0	<0.01
Bermudan (0)	0	<0.01
British West Indian (0)	0	<0.01
Dutch West Indian (0)	0	<0.01
Haitian (0)	0	<0.01
Jamaican (0)	0	<0.01
Trinidadian/Tobagonian (0)	0	<0.01
U.S. Virgin Islander (0)	0	<0.01
West Indian (0)	0	<0.01
Other West Indian (0)	0	<0.01
Yugoslavian (0)	0	<0.01

Hispanic Origin	Population	%
Hispanic or Latino (of any race)	581	1.48
Central American, ex. Mexican	24	0.06
Costa Rican	0	<0.01
Guatemalan	15	0.04
Honduran	4	0.01
Nicaraguan	1	<0.01
Panamanian	3	0.01
Salvadoran	1	<0.01
Other Central American	0	<0.01
Cuban	17	0.04
Dominican Republic	3	0.01
Mexican	412	1.05
Puerto Rican	34	0.09
South American	18	0.05
Argentinean	0	<0.01
Bolivian	0	<0.01
Chilean	0	<0.01
Colombian	3	0.01
Ecuadorian	4	0.01
Paraguayan	0	<0.01
Peruvian	8	0.02
Uruguayan	0	<0.01
Venezuelan	3	0.01
Other South American	0	<0.01
Other Hispanic or Latino	73	0.19

Race*	Population	%
African-American/Black (178)	299	0.76
Not Hispanic (167)	284	0.72
Hispanic (11)	15	0.04
American Indian/Alaska Native (88)	251	0.64
Not Hispanic (84)	243	0.62
Hispanic (4)	8	0.02
Alaska Athabascan (Ala. Nat.) (0)	0	<0.01
Aleut (Alaska Native) (0)	0	<0.01
Apache (0)	2	0.01
Arapaho (0)	0	<0.01
Blackfeet (2)	7	0.02
Canadian/French Am. Ind. (0)	0	<0.01
Central American Ind. (0)	0	<0.01
Cherokee (23)	84	0.21
Cheyenne (0)	0	<0.01
Chickasaw (1)	2	0.01
Chippewa (9)	11	0.03
Choctaw (2)	6	0.02
Colville (0)	0	<0.01
Comanche (0)	0	<0.01
Cree (0)	5	0.01
Creek (1)	1	<0.01
Crow (0)	0	<0.01
Delaware (0)	0	<0.01
Hopi (0)	0	<0.01
Houma (0)	1	<0.01
Inupiat (Alaska Native) (0)	1	<0.01
Iroquois (1)	8	0.02
Kiowa (0)	0	<0.01
Lumbee (0)	0	<0.01
Menominee (0)	0	<0.01
Mexican American Ind. (0)	1	<0.01
Navajo (3)	5	0.01
Osage (3)	3	0.01
Ottawa (0)	0	<0.01
Paiute (0)	0	<0.01
Pima (0)	1	<0.01
Potawatomi (0)	0	<0.01
Pueblo (0)	0	<0.01
Puget Sound Salish (0)	0	<0.01
Seminole (0)	0	<0.01
Shoshone (0)	2	0.01
Sioux (2)	5	0.01
South American Ind. (0)	0	<0.01
Spanish American Ind. (0)	0	<0.01
Tlingit-Haida (Alaska Native) (0)	0	<0.01
Tohono O'Odham (0)	0	<0.01
Tsimshian (Alaska Native) (0)	0	<0.01
Ute (0)	0	<0.01
Yakama (0)	0	<0.01
Yaqui (0)	0	<0.01
Yuman (0)	0	<0.01
Yup'ik (Alaska Native) (0)	0	<0.01
Asian (155)	228	0.58
Not Hispanic (153)	222	0.56
Hispanic (2)	6	0.02
Bangladeshi (0)	0	<0.01
Bhutanese (0)	0	<0.01
Burmese (0)	0	<0.01
Cambodian (13)	13	0.03
Chinese, ex. Taiwanese (23)	30	0.08
Filipino (42)	61	0.15
Hmong (0)	0	<0.01
Indian (24)	37	0.09
Indonesian (2)	4	0.01
Japanese (13)	30	0.08
Korean (16)	27	0.07
Laotian (1)	1	<0.01
Malaysian (2)	4	0.01
Nepalese (0)	0	<0.01
Pakistani (0)	0	<0.01
Sri Lankan (0)	0	<0.01
Taiwanese (0)	0	<0.01
Thai (3)	4	0.01
Vietnamese (3)	6	0.02
Hawaii Native/Pacific Islander (11)	35	0.09
Not Hispanic (9)	31	0.08
Hispanic (2)	4	0.01
Fijian (0)	0	<0.01
Guamanian/Chamorro (2)	3	0.01
Marshallese (1)	1	<0.01
Native Hawaiian (4)	18	0.05
Samoan (1)	7	0.02
Tongan (0)	0	<0.01
White (38,341)	38,711	98.34
Not Hispanic (37,984)	38,330	97.37
Hispanic (357)	381	0.97

Notes: † The Census 2010 population figure is used to calculate the percentages in the Hispanic Origin and Race categories. Ancestry percentages are based on the 2006-2010 American Community Survey population (not shown); ‡ Numbers in parentheses indicate the number of people reporting a single ancestry; * Numbers in parentheses indicate the number of persons reporting this race alone, not in combination with any other race; Please refer to the Explanation of Data for more information.

Hendricks County
Population: 145,448

Ancestry	Population	%
Afghan (0)	0	<0.01
African, Sub-Saharan (771)	852	0.61
African (342)	414	0.30
Cape Verdean (0)	0	<0.01
Ethiopian (222)	227	0.16
Ghanaian (0)	0	<0.01
Kenyan (9)	9	0.01
Liberian (0)	0	<0.01
Nigerian (178)	178	0.13
Senegalese (0)	0	<0.01
Sierra Leonean (0)	0	<0.01
Somalian (0)	0	<0.01
South African (0)	0	<0.01
Sudanese (0)	0	<0.01
Ugandan (0)	0	<0.01
Zimbabwean (0)	0	<0.01
Other Sub-Saharan African (20)	24	0.02
Albanian (0)	0	<0.01
Alsatian (0)	0	<0.01
American (13,161)	13,161	9.40
Arab (278)	493	0.35
Arab (105)	105	0.07
Egyptian (0)	8	0.01
Iraqi (0)	0	<0.01
Jordanian (11)	34	0.02
Lebanese (14)	114	0.08
Moroccan (9)	9	0.01
Palestinian (0)	0	<0.01
Syrian (118)	202	0.14
Other Arab (21)	21	0.01
Armenian (0)	41	0.03
Assyrian/Chaldean/Syriac (0)	0	<0.01
Australian (37)	46	0.03
Austrian (52)	187	0.13
Basque (0)	0	<0.01
Belgian (78)	276	0.20
Brazilian (149)	178	0.13
British (301)	641	0.46
Bulgarian (10)	21	0.01
Cajun (13)	23	0.02
Canadian (86)	97	0.07
Carpatho Rusyn (0)	0	<0.01
Celtic (15)	36	0.03
Croatian (81)	94	0.07
Cypriot (0)	0	<0.01
Czech (62)	434	0.31
Czechoslovakian (35)	94	0.07
Danish (144)	406	0.29
Dutch (651)	2,584	1.85
Eastern European (0)	0	<0.01
English (12,097)	22,690	16.20
Estonian (0)	0	<0.01
European (1,380)	1,495	1.07
Finnish (25)	189	0.13
French, ex. Basque (970)	3,793	2.71
French Canadian (233)	668	0.48
German (16,426)	39,646	28.31
German Russian (0)	0	<0.01
Greek (261)	550	0.39
Guyanese (13)	18	0.01
Hungarian (228)	392	0.28
Icelander (10)	31	0.02
Iranian (38)	38	0.03
Irish (7,226)	21,306	15.22
Israeli (0)	0	<0.01
Italian (1,531)	4,460	3.19
Latvian (40)	126	0.09
Lithuanian (99)	336	0.24
Luxemburger (0)	0	<0.01
Macedonian (50)	71	0.05
Maltese (0)	11	0.01
New Zealander (0)	0	<0.01
Northern European (122)	148	0.11
Norwegian (425)	1,048	0.75
Pennsylvania German (83)	91	0.06
Polish (880)	2,693	1.92
Portuguese (89)	219	0.16
Romanian (131)	285	0.20
Russian (243)	750	0.54
Scandinavian (49)	240	0.17
Scotch-Irish (1,537)	2,756	1.97
Scottish (1,356)	4,228	3.02
Serbian (103)	156	0.11
Slavic (68)	137	0.10
Slovak (189)	404	0.29
Slovene (33)	129	0.09
Soviet Union (0)	0	<0.01
Swedish (238)	1,343	0.96
Swiss (161)	403	0.29
Turkish (0)	11	0.01
Ukrainian (41)	86	0.06
Welsh (171)	987	0.70
West Indian, ex. Hispanic (159)	314	0.22
Bahamian (13)	13	0.01
Barbadian (0)	0	<0.01
Belizean (0)	0	<0.01
Bermudan (0)	0	<0.01
British West Indian (100)	150	0.11
Dutch West Indian (0)	0	<0.01
Haitian (32)	46	0.03
Jamaican (0)	0	<0.01
Trinidadian/Tobagonian (14)	14	0.01
U.S. Virgin Islander (0)	0	<0.01
West Indian (0)	91	0.06
Other West Indian (0)	0	<0.01
Yugoslavian (125)	178	0.13

Hispanic Origin	Population	%
Hispanic or Latino (of any race)	4,379	3.01
Central American, ex. Mexican	483	0.33
Costa Rican	33	0.02
Guatemalan	101	0.07
Honduran	103	0.07
Nicaraguan	38	0.03
Panamanian	38	0.03
Salvadoran	165	0.11
Other Central American	5	<0.01
Cuban	84	0.06
Dominican Republic	120	0.08
Mexican	2,479	1.70
Puerto Rican	422	0.29
South American	417	0.29
Argentinean	23	0.02
Bolivian	8	0.01
Chilean	39	0.03
Colombian	79	0.05
Ecuadorian	47	0.03
Paraguayan	0	<0.01
Peruvian	168	0.12
Uruguayan	3	<0.01
Venezuelan	49	0.03
Other South American	1	<0.01
Other Hispanic or Latino	374	0.26

Race*	Population	%
African-American/Black (7,084)	8,091	5.56
Not Hispanic (6,988)	7,929	5.45
Hispanic (96)	162	0.11
American Indian/Alaska Native (293)	777	0.53
Not Hispanic (231)	667	0.46
Hispanic (62)	110	0.08
Alaska Athabascan (Ala. Nat.) (0)	2	<0.01
Aleut (Alaska Native) (0)	0	<0.01
Apache (3)	10	0.01
Arapaho (0)	0	<0.01
Blackfeet (4)	26	0.02
Canadian/French Am. Ind. (4)	4	<0.01
Central American Ind. (4)	8	0.01
Cherokee (46)	186	0.13
Cheyenne (2)	2	<0.01
Chickasaw (7)	9	0.01
Chippewa (6)	14	0.01
Choctaw (5)	15	0.01
Colville (0)	0	<0.01
Comanche (0)	0	<0.01
Cree (2)	4	<0.01
Creek (0)	2	<0.01
Crow (0)	0	<0.01
Delaware (3)	9	0.01
Hopi (0)	4	<0.01
Houma (0)	2	<0.01
Inupiat (Alaska Native) (0)	0	<0.01
Iroquois (6)	12	0.01
Kiowa (1)	1	<0.01
Lumbee (1)	1	<0.01
Menominee (0)	0	<0.01
Mexican American Ind. (13)	20	0.01
Navajo (2)	6	<0.01
Osage (0)	0	<0.01
Ottawa (0)	0	<0.01
Paiute (0)	0	<0.01
Pima (0)	0	<0.01
Potawatomi (4)	11	0.01
Pueblo (2)	4	<0.01
Puget Sound Salish (0)	0	<0.01
Seminole (0)	2	<0.01
Shoshone (0)	0	<0.01
Sioux (11)	22	0.02
South American Ind. (6)	7	<0.01
Spanish American Ind. (3)	3	<0.01
Tlingit-Haida (Alaska Native) (0)	0	<0.01
Tohono O'Odham (0)	0	<0.01
Tsimshian (Alaska Native) (0)	0	<0.01
Ute (1)	3	<0.01
Yakama (1)	1	<0.01
Yaqui (1)	1	<0.01
Yuman (2)	2	<0.01
Yup'ik (Alaska Native) (0)	0	<0.01
Asian (3,028)	3,757	2.58
Not Hispanic (2,984)	3,657	2.51
Hispanic (44)	100	0.07
Bangladeshi (17)	17	0.01
Bhutanese (0)	0	<0.01
Burmese (6)	6	<0.01
Cambodian (16)	16	0.01
Chinese, ex. Taiwanese (317)	391	0.27
Filipino (442)	680	0.47
Hmong (0)	0	<0.01
Indian (1,205)	1,325	0.91
Indonesian (19)	37	0.03
Japanese (113)	203	0.14
Korean (152)	267	0.18
Laotian (12)	22	0.02
Malaysian (6)	9	0.01
Nepalese (4)	4	<0.01
Pakistani (217)	240	0.17
Sri Lankan (2)	2	<0.01
Taiwanese (34)	40	0.03
Thai (28)	52	0.04
Vietnamese (316)	351	0.24
Hawaii Native/Pacific Islander (59)	170	0.12
Not Hispanic (47)	141	0.10
Hispanic (12)	29	0.02
Fijian (1)	1	<0.01
Guamanian/Chamorro (21)	29	0.02
Marshallese (0)	0	<0.01
Native Hawaiian (22)	72	0.05
Samoan (10)	19	0.01
Tongan (0)	0	<0.01
White (131,117)	133,198	91.58
Not Hispanic (128,664)	130,451	89.69
Hispanic (2,453)	2,747	1.89

Notes: † The Census 2010 population figure is used to calculate the percentages in the Hispanic Origin and Race categories. Ancestry percentages are based on the 2006-2010 American Community Survey population (not shown); ‡ Numbers in parentheses indicate the number of people reporting a single ancestry; * Numbers in parentheses indicate the number of persons reporting this race alone, not in combination with any other race; Please refer to the Explanation of Data for more information.

Henry County
Population: 49,462

Ancestry	Population	%
Afghan (0)	0	<0.01
African, Sub-Saharan (169)	186	0.38
African (169)	186	0.38
Cape Verdean (0)	0	<0.01
Ethiopian (0)	0	<0.01
Ghanaian (0)	0	<0.01
Kenyan (0)	0	<0.01
Liberian (0)	0	<0.01
Nigerian (0)	0	<0.01
Senegalese (0)	0	<0.01
Sierra Leonean (0)	0	<0.01
Somalian (0)	0	<0.01
South African (0)	0	<0.01
Sudanese (0)	0	<0.01
Ugandan (0)	0	<0.01
Zimbabwean (0)	0	<0.01
Other Sub-Saharan African (0)	0	<0.01
Albanian (0)	0	<0.01
Alsatian (0)	0	<0.01
American (6,509)	6,509	13.31
Arab (16)	34	0.07
Arab (16)	16	0.03
Egyptian (0)	0	<0.01
Iraqi (0)	0	<0.01
Jordanian (0)	0	<0.01
Lebanese (0)	0	<0.01
Moroccan (0)	18	0.04
Palestinian (0)	0	<0.01
Syrian (0)	0	<0.01
Other Arab (0)	0	<0.01
Armenian (0)	0	<0.01
Assyrian/Chaldean/Syriac (0)	0	<0.01
Australian (0)	0	<0.01
Austrian (0)	111	0.23
Basque (0)	0	<0.01
Belgian (0)	16	0.03
Brazilian (0)	0	<0.01
British (113)	134	0.27
Bulgarian (0)	0	<0.01
Cajun (0)	0	<0.01
Canadian (25)	39	0.08
Carpatho Rusyn (0)	0	<0.01
Celtic (0)	0	<0.01
Croatian (17)	63	0.13
Cypriot (0)	0	<0.01
Czech (0)	48	0.10
Czechoslovakian (50)	63	0.13
Danish (17)	88	0.18
Dutch (261)	997	2.04
Eastern European (0)	0	<0.01
English (2,484)	4,466	9.13
Estonian (0)	0	<0.01
European (365)	378	0.77
Finnish (0)	16	0.03
French, ex. Basque (361)	1,123	2.30
French Canadian (41)	42	0.09
German (4,692)	9,750	19.93
German Russian (0)	0	<0.01
Greek (154)	171	0.35
Guyanese (0)	0	<0.01
Hungarian (55)	102	0.21
Icelander (0)	0	<0.01
Iranian (0)	0	<0.01
Irish (2,011)	5,789	11.83
Israeli (0)	0	<0.01
Italian (255)	583	1.19
Latvian (0)	0	<0.01
Lithuanian (0)	2	<0.01
Luxemburger (0)	0	<0.01
Macedonian (0)	0	<0.01
Maltese (0)	0	<0.01
New Zealander (0)	0	<0.01
Northern European (88)	88	0.18
Norwegian (27)	155	0.32
Pennsylvania German (55)	55	0.11
Polish (145)	326	0.67
Portuguese (35)	44	0.09
Romanian (0)	10	0.02
Russian (8)	38	0.08
Scandinavian (18)	96	0.20
Scotch-Irish (356)	542	1.11
Scottish (384)	884	1.81
Serbian (0)	0	<0.01
Slavic (0)	0	<0.01
Slovak (0)	19	0.04
Slovene (0)	0	<0.01
Soviet Union (0)	0	<0.01
Swedish (60)	119	0.24
Swiss (57)	128	0.26
Turkish (0)	0	<0.01
Ukrainian (0)	0	<0.01
Welsh (28)	141	0.29
West Indian, ex. Hispanic (18)	29	0.06
Bahamian (0)	0	<0.01
Barbadian (0)	0	<0.01
Belizean (0)	0	<0.01
Bermudan (0)	0	<0.01
British West Indian (0)	0	<0.01
Dutch West Indian (0)	11	0.02
Haitian (0)	0	<0.01
Jamaican (0)	0	<0.01
Trinidadian/Tobagonian (0)	0	<0.01
U.S. Virgin Islander (0)	0	<0.01
West Indian (18)	18	0.04
Other West Indian (0)	0	<0.01
Yugoslavian (4)	4	0.01

Hispanic Origin	Population	%
Hispanic or Latino (of any race)	691	1.40
Central American, ex. Mexican	24	0.05
Costa Rican	0	<0.01
Guatemalan	5	0.01
Honduran	6	0.01
Nicaraguan	1	<0.01
Panamanian	2	<0.01
Salvadoran	10	0.02
Other Central American	0	<0.01
Cuban	39	0.08
Dominican Republic	2	<0.01
Mexican	474	0.96
Puerto Rican	45	0.09
South American	14	0.03
Argentinean	0	<0.01
Bolivian	0	<0.01
Chilean	1	<0.01
Colombian	6	0.01
Ecuadorian	0	<0.01
Paraguayan	0	<0.01
Peruvian	4	0.01
Uruguayan	0	<0.01
Venezuelan	3	0.01
Other South American	0	<0.01
Other Hispanic or Latino	93	0.19

Race*	Population	%
African-American/Black (1,070)	1,326	2.68
Not Hispanic (1,064)	1,295	2.62
Hispanic (6)	31	0.06
American Indian/Alaska Native (72)	310	0.63
Not Hispanic (63)	285	0.58
Hispanic (9)	25	0.05
Alaska Athabascan (Ala. Nat.) (0)	0	<0.01
Aleut (Alaska Native) (0)	0	<0.01
Apache (0)	4	0.01
Arapaho (0)	0	<0.01
Blackfeet (6)	19	0.04
Canadian/French Am. Ind. (1)	2	<0.01
Central American Ind. (0)	0	<0.01
Cherokee (12)	89	0.18
Cheyenne (0)	0	<0.01
Chickasaw (0)	0	<0.01
Chippewa (2)	5	0.01
Choctaw (1)	4	0.01
Colville (0)	0	<0.01
Comanche (0)	0	<0.01
Cree (0)	0	<0.01
Creek (2)	2	<0.01
Crow (0)	0	<0.01
Delaware (0)	0	<0.01
Hopi (1)	2	<0.01
Houma (0)	0	<0.01
Inupiat (Alaska Native) (0)	0	<0.01
Iroquois (0)	0	<0.01
Kiowa (0)	0	<0.01
Lumbee (0)	0	<0.01
Menominee (0)	0	<0.01
Mexican American Ind. (2)	2	<0.01
Navajo (1)	1	<0.01
Osage (0)	0	<0.01
Ottawa (0)	1	<0.01
Paiute (0)	0	<0.01
Pima (0)	0	<0.01
Potawatomi (0)	0	<0.01
Pueblo (0)	0	<0.01
Puget Sound Salish (0)	0	<0.01
Seminole (0)	2	<0.01
Shoshone (0)	0	<0.01
Sioux (2)	6	0.01
South American Ind. (1)	1	<0.01
Spanish American Ind. (0)	0	<0.01
Tlingit-Haida (Alaska Native) (0)	0	<0.01
Tohono O'Odham (0)	0	<0.01
Tsimshian (Alaska Native) (0)	0	<0.01
Ute (1)	1	<0.01
Yakama (0)	0	<0.01
Yaqui (0)	0	<0.01
Yuman (0)	0	<0.01
Yup'ik (Alaska Native) (0)	0	<0.01
Asian (156)	255	0.52
Not Hispanic (154)	248	0.50
Hispanic (2)	7	0.01
Bangladeshi (0)	0	<0.01
Bhutanese (0)	0	<0.01
Burmese (0)	0	<0.01
Cambodian (0)	0	<0.01
Chinese, ex. Taiwanese (31)	50	0.10
Filipino (18)	53	0.11
Hmong (0)	0	<0.01
Indian (42)	53	0.11
Indonesian (3)	3	0.01
Japanese (15)	31	0.06
Korean (13)	22	0.04
Laotian (0)	1	<0.01
Malaysian (2)	5	0.01
Nepalese (0)	0	<0.01
Pakistani (3)	3	0.01
Sri Lankan (0)	0	<0.01
Taiwanese (0)	0	<0.01
Thai (4)	4	0.01
Vietnamese (18)	22	0.04
Hawaii Native/Pacific Islander (5)	26	0.05
Not Hispanic (5)	24	0.05
Hispanic (0)	2	<0.01
Fijian (0)	0	<0.01
Guamanian/Chamorro (1)	1	<0.01
Marshallese (0)	0	<0.01
Native Hawaiian (3)	18	0.04
Samoan (0)	6	0.01
Tongan (0)	0	<0.01
White (47,351)	47,916	96.87
Not Hispanic (46,933)	47,429	95.89
Hispanic (418)	487	0.98

Notes: † The Census 2010 population figure is used to calculate the percentages in the Hispanic Origin and Race categories. Ancestry percentages are based on the 2006-2010 American Community Survey population (not shown); ‡ Numbers in parentheses indicate the number of people reporting a single ancestry; * Numbers in parentheses indicate the number of persons reporting this race alone, not in combination with any other race; Please refer to the Explanation of Data for more information.

Howard County
Population: 82,752

Ancestry	Population	%
Afghan (0)	0	<0.01
African, Sub-Saharan (90)	326	0.39
African (90)	326	0.39
Cape Verdean (0)	0	<0.01
Ethiopian (0)	0	<0.01
Ghanaian (0)	0	<0.01
Kenyan (0)	0	<0.01
Liberian (0)	0	<0.01
Nigerian (0)	0	<0.01
Senegalese (0)	0	<0.01
Sierra Leonean (0)	0	<0.01
Somalian (0)	0	<0.01
South African (0)	0	<0.01
Sudanese (0)	0	<0.01
Ugandan (0)	0	<0.01
Zimbabwean (0)	0	<0.01
Other Sub-Saharan African (0)	0	<0.01
Albanian (0)	11	0.01
Alsatian (5)	5	0.01
American (12,747)	12,747	15.30
Arab (36)	98	0.12
Arab (0)	25	0.03
Egyptian (0)	0	<0.01
Iraqi (0)	0	<0.01
Jordanian (0)	0	<0.01
Lebanese (24)	52	0.06
Moroccan (0)	0	<0.01
Palestinian (12)	12	0.01
Syrian (0)	9	0.01
Other Arab (0)	0	<0.01
Armenian (0)	0	<0.01
Assyrian/Chaldean/Syriac (0)	0	<0.01
Australian (10)	17	0.02
Austrian (15)	65	0.08
Basque (0)	0	<0.01
Belgian (0)	73	0.09
Brazilian (9)	9	0.01
British (189)	335	0.40
Bulgarian (0)	0	<0.01
Cajun (0)	18	0.02
Canadian (24)	74	0.09
Carpatho Rusyn (0)	0	<0.01
Celtic (0)	0	<0.01
Croatian (0)	7	0.01
Cypriot (0)	0	<0.01
Czech (57)	123	0.15
Czechoslovakian (13)	47	0.06
Danish (13)	58	0.07
Dutch (268)	1,877	2.25
Eastern European (0)	0	<0.01
English (4,070)	8,975	10.77
Estonian (0)	0	<0.01
European (529)	663	0.80
Finnish (0)	59	0.07
French, ex. Basque (360)	1,675	2.01
French Canadian (116)	442	0.53
German (7,665)	18,627	22.35
German Russian (0)	0	<0.01
Greek (210)	328	0.39
Guyanese (37)	37	0.04
Hungarian (114)	273	0.33
Icelander (0)	13	0.02
Iranian (0)	0	<0.01
Irish (2,507)	8,466	10.16
Israeli (0)	0	<0.01
Italian (733)	1,872	2.25
Latvian (0)	0	<0.01
Lithuanian (45)	74	0.09
Luxemburger (0)	0	<0.01
Macedonian (0)	0	<0.01
Maltese (0)	0	<0.01
New Zealander (0)	0	<0.01
Northern European (34)	34	0.04
Norwegian (288)	608	0.73
Pennsylvania German (68)	99	0.12
Polish (623)	1,589	1.91
Portuguese (22)	75	0.09
Romanian (122)	224	0.27
Russian (64)	92	0.11
Scandinavian (7)	42	0.05
Scotch-Irish (555)	1,130	1.36
Scottish (392)	1,270	1.52
Serbian (0)	21	0.03
Slavic (0)	0	<0.01
Slovak (40)	115	0.14
Slovene (8)	8	0.01
Soviet Union (0)	0	<0.01
Swedish (210)	793	0.95
Swiss (76)	293	0.35
Turkish (0)	0	<0.01
Ukrainian (47)	70	0.08
Welsh (72)	459	0.55
West Indian, ex. Hispanic (10)	21	0.03
Bahamian (0)	0	<0.01
Barbadian (0)	0	<0.01
Belizean (0)	0	<0.01
Bermudan (0)	0	<0.01
British West Indian (10)	10	0.01
Dutch West Indian (0)	0	<0.01
Haitian (0)	0	<0.01
Jamaican (0)	11	0.01
Trinidadian/Tobagonian (0)	0	<0.01
U.S. Virgin Islander (0)	0	<0.01
West Indian (0)	0	<0.01
Other West Indian (0)	0	<0.01
Yugoslavian (40)	40	0.05

Hispanic Origin	Population	%
Hispanic or Latino (of any race)	2,203	2.66
Central American, ex. Mexican	66	0.08
Costa Rican	4	<0.01
Guatemalan	21	0.03
Honduran	17	0.02
Nicaraguan	2	<0.01
Panamanian	8	0.01
Salvadoran	14	0.02
Other Central American	0	<0.01
Cuban	31	0.04
Dominican Republic	2	<0.01
Mexican	1,552	1.88
Puerto Rican	212	0.26
South American	53	0.06
Argentinean	0	<0.01
Bolivian	3	<0.01
Chilean	14	0.02
Colombian	20	0.02
Ecuadorian	1	<0.01
Paraguayan	0	<0.01
Peruvian	5	0.01
Uruguayan	0	<0.01
Venezuelan	9	0.01
Other South American	1	<0.01
Other Hispanic or Latino	287	0.35

Race*	Population	%
African-American/Black (5,680)	6,891	8.33
Not Hispanic (5,585)	6,701	8.10
Hispanic (95)	190	0.23
American Indian/Alaska Native (286)	782	0.94
Not Hispanic (246)	692	0.84
Hispanic (40)	90	0.11
Alaska Athabascan (Ala. Nat.) (0)	0	<0.01
Aleut (Alaska Native) (0)	0	<0.01
Apache (2)	8	0.01
Arapaho (1)	1	<0.01
Blackfeet (10)	24	0.03
Canadian/French Am. Ind. (0)	1	<0.01
Central American Ind. (0)	0	<0.01
Cherokee (55)	227	0.27
Cheyenne (0)	0	<0.01
Chickasaw (0)	0	<0.01
Chippewa (16)	30	0.04
Choctaw (9)	17	0.02
Colville (2)	2	<0.01
Comanche (0)	2	<0.01
Cree (0)	7	0.01
Creek (4)	6	0.01
Crow (1)	1	<0.01
Delaware (0)	0	<0.01
Hopi (1)	2	<0.01
Houma (0)	0	<0.01
Inupiat (Alaska Native) (0)	3	<0.01
Iroquois (4)	8	0.01
Kiowa (0)	0	<0.01
Lumbee (0)	3	<0.01
Menominee (0)	0	<0.01
Mexican American Ind. (8)	18	0.02
Navajo (1)	5	0.01
Osage (1)	4	<0.01
Ottawa (0)	0	<0.01
Paiute (1)	1	<0.01
Pima (0)	0	<0.01
Potawatomi (1)	3	<0.01
Pueblo (0)	2	<0.01
Puget Sound Salish (0)	0	<0.01
Seminole (0)	3	<0.01
Shoshone (4)	4	<0.01
Sioux (10)	26	0.03
South American Ind. (2)	2	<0.01
Spanish American Ind. (2)	2	<0.01
Tlingit-Haida (Alaska Native) (1)	1	<0.01
Tohono O'Odham (0)	0	<0.01
Tsimshian (Alaska Native) (0)	0	<0.01
Ute (0)	1	<0.01
Yakama (0)	0	<0.01
Yaqui (0)	0	<0.01
Yuman (0)	0	<0.01
Yup'ik (Alaska Native) (0)	0	<0.01
Asian (740)	1,020	1.23
Not Hispanic (737)	992	1.20
Hispanic (3)	28	0.03
Bangladeshi (5)	5	0.01
Bhutanese (0)	0	<0.01
Burmese (0)	0	<0.01
Cambodian (0)	0	<0.01
Chinese, ex. Taiwanese (176)	217	0.26
Filipino (149)	205	0.25
Hmong (5)	5	0.01
Indian (156)	196	0.24
Indonesian (0)	3	<0.01
Japanese (22)	78	0.09
Korean (51)	103	0.12
Laotian (0)	0	<0.01
Malaysian (1)	4	<0.01
Nepalese (1)	1	<0.01
Pakistani (16)	17	0.02
Sri Lankan (8)	8	0.01
Taiwanese (7)	14	0.02
Thai (11)	19	0.02
Vietnamese (105)	123	0.15
Hawaii Native/Pacific Islander (20)	70	0.08
Not Hispanic (13)	59	0.07
Hispanic (7)	11	0.01
Fijian (0)	0	<0.01
Guamanian/Chamorro (8)	10	0.01
Marshallese (0)	0	<0.01
Native Hawaiian (6)	29	0.04
Samoan (5)	18	0.02
Tongan (0)	0	<0.01
White (73,284)	75,188	90.86
Not Hispanic (72,091)	73,744	89.11
Hispanic (1,193)	1,444	1.74

Notes: † The Census 2010 population figure is used to calculate the percentages in the Hispanic Origin and Race categories. Ancestry percentages are based on the 2006-2010 American Community Survey population (not shown); ‡ Numbers in parentheses indicate the number of people reporting a single ancestry; * Numbers in parentheses indicate the number of persons reporting this race alone, not in combination with any other race; Please refer to the Explanation of Data for more information.

Huntington County
Population: 37,124

Ancestry	Population	%
Afghan (0)	0	<0.01
African, Sub-Saharan (0)	0	<0.01
African (0)	0	<0.01
Cape Verdean (0)	0	<0.01
Ethiopian (0)	0	<0.01
Ghanaian (0)	0	<0.01
Kenyan (0)	0	<0.01
Liberian (0)	0	<0.01
Nigerian (0)	0	<0.01
Senegalese (0)	0	<0.01
Sierra Leonean (0)	0	<0.01
Somalian (0)	0	<0.01
South African (0)	0	<0.01
Sudanese (0)	0	<0.01
Ugandan (0)	0	<0.01
Zimbabwean (0)	0	<0.01
Other Sub-Saharan African (0)	0	<0.01
Albanian (0)	0	<0.01
Alsatian (0)	0	<0.01
American (4,815)	4,815	12.90
Arab (20)	20	0.05
Arab (0)	0	<0.01
Egyptian (11)	11	0.03
Iraqi (0)	0	<0.01
Jordanian (0)	0	<0.01
Lebanese (9)	9	0.02
Moroccan (0)	0	<0.01
Palestinian (0)	0	<0.01
Syrian (0)	0	<0.01
Other Arab (0)	0	<0.01
Armenian (0)	0	<0.01
Assyrian/Chaldean/Syriac (0)	0	<0.01
Australian (0)	0	<0.01
Austrian (3)	19	0.05
Basque (0)	0	<0.01
Belgian (102)	126	0.34
Brazilian (0)	0	<0.01
British (38)	109	0.29
Bulgarian (0)	0	<0.01
Cajun (0)	0	<0.01
Canadian (45)	50	0.13
Carpatho Rusyn (0)	0	<0.01
Celtic (0)	0	<0.01
Croatian (15)	25	0.07
Cypriot (0)	0	<0.01
Czech (25)	105	0.28
Czechoslovakian (11)	41	0.11
Danish (11)	86	0.23
Dutch (272)	936	2.51
Eastern European (0)	0	<0.01
English (1,986)	4,525	12.12
Estonian (0)	0	<0.01
European (310)	316	0.85
Finnish (0)	8	0.02
French, ex. Basque (272)	1,299	3.48
French Canadian (55)	153	0.41
German (6,921)	14,143	37.90
German Russian (0)	0	<0.01
Greek (32)	53	0.14
Guyanese (0)	0	<0.01
Hungarian (3)	42	0.11
Icelander (0)	0	<0.01
Iranian (0)	0	<0.01
Irish (1,416)	5,560	14.90
Israeli (0)	0	<0.01
Italian (250)	745	2.00
Latvian (0)	0	<0.01
Lithuanian (11)	93	0.25
Luxemburger (0)	0	<0.01
Macedonian (0)	0	<0.01
Maltese (0)	8	0.02
New Zealander (0)	0	<0.01
Northern European (0)	0	<0.01
Norwegian (121)	298	0.80
Pennsylvania German (13)	23	0.06
Polish (158)	664	1.78
Portuguese (0)	0	<0.01
Romanian (0)	13	0.03
Russian (9)	72	0.19
Scandinavian (29)	33	0.09
Scotch-Irish (150)	395	1.06
Scottish (221)	646	1.73
Serbian (0)	0	<0.01
Slavic (0)	0	<0.01
Slovak (8)	27	0.07
Slovene (0)	0	<0.01
Soviet Union (0)	0	<0.01
Swedish (134)	376	1.01
Swiss (64)	238	0.64
Turkish (0)	13	0.03
Ukrainian (31)	62	0.17
Welsh (50)	192	0.51
West Indian, ex. Hispanic (0)	0	<0.01
Bahamian (0)	0	<0.01
Barbadian (0)	0	<0.01
Belizean (0)	0	<0.01
Bermudan (0)	0	<0.01
British West Indian (0)	0	<0.01
Dutch West Indian (0)	0	<0.01
Haitian (0)	0	<0.01
Jamaican (0)	0	<0.01
Trinidadian/Tobagonian (0)	0	<0.01
U.S. Virgin Islander (0)	0	<0.01
West Indian (0)	0	<0.01
Other West Indian (0)	0	<0.01
Yugoslavian (5)	5	0.01

Hispanic Origin	Population	%
Hispanic or Latino (of any race)	631	1.70
Central American, ex. Mexican	30	0.08
Costa Rican	0	<0.01
Guatemalan	19	0.05
Honduran	5	0.01
Nicaraguan	0	<0.01
Panamanian	1	<0.01
Salvadoran	5	0.01
Other Central American	0	<0.01
Cuban	7	0.02
Dominican Republic	1	<0.01
Mexican	455	1.23
Puerto Rican	46	0.12
South American	13	0.04
Argentinean	1	<0.01
Bolivian	0	<0.01
Chilean	4	0.01
Colombian	2	0.01
Ecuadorian	3	0.01
Paraguayan	0	<0.01
Peruvian	2	0.01
Uruguayan	0	<0.01
Venezuelan	1	<0.01
Other South American	0	<0.01
Other Hispanic or Latino	79	0.21

Race*	Population	%
African-American/Black (160)	295	0.79
Not Hispanic (155)	286	0.77
Hispanic (5)	9	0.02
American Indian/Alaska Native (140)	291	0.78
Not Hispanic (124)	257	0.69
Hispanic (16)	34	0.09
Alaska Athabascan (Ala. Nat.) (0)	0	<0.01
Aleut (Alaska Native) (0)	0	<0.01
Apache (3)	5	0.01
Arapaho (0)	0	<0.01
Blackfeet (1)	8	0.02
Canadian/French Am. Ind. (0)	0	<0.01
Central American Ind. (1)	1	<0.01
Cherokee (30)	64	0.17
Cheyenne (0)	0	<0.01
Chickasaw (0)	0	<0.01
Chippewa (1)	2	0.01
Choctaw (0)	0	<0.01
Colville (0)	0	<0.01
Comanche (0)	0	<0.01
Cree (0)	0	<0.01
Creek (1)	1	<0.01
Crow (0)	1	<0.01
Delaware (3)	3	0.01
Hopi (0)	0	<0.01
Houma (0)	0	<0.01
Inupiat (Alaska Native) (0)	0	<0.01
Iroquois (0)	1	<0.01
Kiowa (0)	0	<0.01
Lumbee (0)	1	<0.01
Menominee (0)	0	<0.01
Mexican American Ind. (5)	5	0.01
Navajo (0)	1	<0.01
Osage (0)	3	0.01
Ottawa (4)	6	0.02
Paiute (0)	0	<0.01
Pima (0)	0	<0.01
Potawatomi (1)	1	<0.01
Pueblo (5)	5	0.01
Puget Sound Salish (3)	3	0.01
Seminole (0)	0	<0.01
Shoshone (0)	0	<0.01
Sioux (2)	4	0.01
South American Ind. (0)	0	<0.01
Spanish American Ind. (0)	1	<0.01
Tlingit-Haida (Alaska Native) (0)	0	<0.01
Tohono O'Odham (0)	0	<0.01
Tsimshian (Alaska Native) (0)	0	<0.01
Ute (0)	0	<0.01
Yakama (0)	0	<0.01
Yaqui (0)	0	<0.01
Yuman (0)	0	<0.01
Yup'ik (Alaska Native) (0)	0	<0.01
Asian (167)	243	0.65
Not Hispanic (167)	234	0.63
Hispanic (0)	9	0.02
Bangladeshi (0)	0	<0.01
Bhutanese (0)	0	<0.01
Burmese (2)	2	0.01
Cambodian (9)	9	0.02
Chinese, ex. Taiwanese (40)	51	0.14
Filipino (19)	36	0.10
Hmong (0)	0	<0.01
Indian (43)	49	0.13
Indonesian (0)	0	<0.01
Japanese (16)	31	0.08
Korean (21)	43	0.12
Laotian (0)	0	<0.01
Malaysian (1)	2	0.01
Nepalese (0)	0	<0.01
Pakistani (0)	1	<0.01
Sri Lankan (0)	0	<0.01
Taiwanese (1)	3	0.01
Thai (1)	5	0.01
Vietnamese (3)	6	0.02
Hawaii Native/Pacific Islander (8)	18	0.05
Not Hispanic (6)	15	0.04
Hispanic (2)	3	0.01
Fijian (0)	0	<0.01
Guamanian/Chamorro (4)	6	0.02
Marshallese (0)	0	<0.01
Native Hawaiian (1)	6	0.02
Samoan (1)	2	0.01
Tongan (0)	0	<0.01
White (36,062)	36,463	98.22
Not Hispanic (35,692)	36,016	97.02
Hispanic (370)	447	1.20

Notes: † The Census 2010 population figure is used to calculate the percentages in the Hispanic Origin and Race categories. Ancestry percentages are based on the 2006-2010 American Community Survey population (not shown); ‡ Numbers in parentheses indicate the number of people reporting a single ancestry; * Numbers in parentheses indicate the number of persons reporting this race alone, not in combination with any other race; Please refer to the Explanation of Data for more information.

Jackson County
Population: 42,376

Ancestry	Population	%
Afghan (0)	0	<0.01
African, Sub-Saharan (0)	0	<0.01
African (0)	0	<0.01
Cape Verdean (0)	0	<0.01
Ethiopian (0)	0	<0.01
Ghanaian (0)	0	<0.01
Kenyan (0)	0	<0.01
Liberian (0)	0	<0.01
Nigerian (0)	0	<0.01
Senegalese (0)	0	<0.01
Sierra Leonean (0)	0	<0.01
Somalian (0)	0	<0.01
South African (0)	0	<0.01
Sudanese (0)	0	<0.01
Ugandan (0)	0	<0.01
Zimbabwean (0)	0	<0.01
Other Sub-Saharan African (0)	0	<0.01
Albanian (0)	0	<0.01
Alsatian (0)	0	<0.01
American (5,488)	5,488	13.10
Arab (0)	47	0.11
Arab (0)	0	<0.01
Egyptian (0)	42	0.10
Iraqi (0)	0	<0.01
Jordanian (0)	0	<0.01
Lebanese (0)	5	0.01
Moroccan (0)	0	<0.01
Palestinian (0)	0	<0.01
Syrian (0)	0	<0.01
Other Arab (0)	0	<0.01
Armenian (3)	3	0.01
Assyrian/Chaldean/Syriac (0)	0	<0.01
Australian (0)	9	0.02
Austrian (0)	11	0.03
Basque (0)	0	<0.01
Belgian (0)	4	0.01
Brazilian (0)	0	<0.01
British (19)	75	0.18
Bulgarian (0)	0	<0.01
Cajun (15)	15	0.04
Canadian (0)	0	<0.01
Carpatho Rusyn (0)	0	<0.01
Celtic (0)	0	<0.01
Croatian (0)	0	<0.01
Cypriot (0)	0	<0.01
Czech (0)	0	<0.01
Czechoslovakian (78)	78	0.19
Danish (141)	141	0.34
Dutch (96)	923	2.20
Eastern European (0)	3	0.01
English (1,647)	3,842	9.17
Estonian (0)	0	<0.01
European (180)	186	0.44
Finnish (0)	19	0.05
French, ex. Basque (206)	946	2.26
French Canadian (62)	131	0.31
German (6,586)	12,053	28.76
German Russian (0)	0	<0.01
Greek (69)	91	0.22
Guyanese (0)	0	<0.01
Hungarian (9)	21	0.05
Icelander (0)	0	<0.01
Iranian (0)	0	<0.01
Irish (1,075)	5,351	12.77
Israeli (0)	0	<0.01
Italian (224)	507	1.21
Latvian (0)	0	<0.01
Lithuanian (0)	0	<0.01
Luxemburger (0)	0	<0.01
Macedonian (0)	0	<0.01
Maltese (0)	0	<0.01
New Zealander (0)	0	<0.01
Northern European (0)	0	<0.01
Norwegian (18)	95	0.23
Pennsylvania German (0)	0	<0.01
Polish (34)	205	0.49
Portuguese (0)	66	0.16
Romanian (0)	0	<0.01
Russian (0)	11	0.03
Scandinavian (0)	23	0.05
Scotch-Irish (192)	551	1.31
Scottish (551)	959	2.29
Serbian (0)	9	0.02
Slavic (0)	0	<0.01
Slovak (0)	26	0.06
Slovene (0)	0	<0.01
Soviet Union (0)	0	<0.01
Swedish (76)	122	0.29
Swiss (12)	17	0.04
Turkish (33)	62	0.15
Ukrainian (0)	26	0.06
Welsh (47)	245	0.58
West Indian, ex. Hispanic (0)	0	<0.01
Bahamian (0)	0	<0.01
Barbadian (0)	0	<0.01
Belizean (0)	0	<0.01
Bermudan (0)	0	<0.01
British West Indian (0)	0	<0.01
Dutch West Indian (0)	0	<0.01
Haitian (0)	0	<0.01
Jamaican (0)	0	<0.01
Trinidadian/Tobagonian (0)	0	<0.01
U.S. Virgin Islander (0)	0	<0.01
West Indian (0)	0	<0.01
Other West Indian (0)	0	<0.01
Yugoslavian (0)	6	0.01

Hispanic Origin	Population	%
Hispanic or Latino (of any race)	2,410	5.69
Central American, ex. Mexican	127	0.30
Costa Rican	2	<0.01
Guatemalan	41	0.10
Honduran	52	0.12
Nicaraguan	6	0.01
Panamanian	18	0.04
Salvadoran	8	0.02
Other Central American	0	<0.01
Cuban	7	0.02
Dominican Republic	3	0.01
Mexican	1,942	4.58
Puerto Rican	79	0.19
South American	11	0.03
Argentinean	0	<0.01
Bolivian	0	<0.01
Chilean	2	<0.01
Colombian	1	<0.01
Ecuadorian	5	0.01
Paraguayan	0	<0.01
Peruvian	1	<0.01
Uruguayan	0	<0.01
Venezuelan	2	<0.01
Other South American	0	<0.01
Other Hispanic or Latino	241	0.57

Race*	Population	%
African-American/Black (282)	439	1.04
Not Hispanic (265)	410	0.97
Hispanic (17)	29	0.07
American Indian/Alaska Native (89)	295	0.70
Not Hispanic (82)	265	0.63
Hispanic (7)	30	0.07
Alaska Athabascan (Ala. Nat.) (0)	0	<0.01
Aleut (Alaska Native) (0)	0	<0.01
Apache (1)	2	<0.01
Arapaho (0)	0	<0.01
Blackfeet (5)	11	0.03
Canadian/French Am. Ind. (0)	0	<0.01
Central American Ind. (1)	4	0.01
Cherokee (27)	118	0.28
Cheyenne (1)	1	<0.01
Chickasaw (0)	0	<0.01
Chippewa (2)	3	0.01
Choctaw (3)	9	0.02
Colville (0)	0	<0.01
Comanche (0)	1	<0.01
Cree (0)	0	<0.01
Creek (1)	1	<0.01
Crow (0)	1	<0.01
Delaware (0)	0	<0.01
Hopi (0)	0	<0.01
Houma (0)	0	<0.01
Inupiat (Alaska Native) (0)	4	0.01
Iroquois (1)	2	<0.01
Kiowa (0)	1	<0.01
Lumbee (0)	0	<0.01
Menominee (0)	0	<0.01
Mexican American Ind. (0)	1	<0.01
Navajo (0)	0	<0.01
Osage (0)	0	<0.01
Ottawa (0)	0	<0.01
Paiute (0)	0	<0.01
Pima (0)	0	<0.01
Potawatomi (1)	1	<0.01
Pueblo (0)	0	<0.01
Puget Sound Salish (0)	0	<0.01
Seminole (0)	0	<0.01
Shoshone (0)	0	<0.01
Sioux (4)	7	0.02
South American Ind. (0)	0	<0.01
Spanish American Ind. (0)	0	<0.01
Tlingit-Haida (Alaska Native) (0)	0	<0.01
Tohono O'Odham (0)	0	<0.01
Tsimshian (Alaska Native) (0)	0	<0.01
Ute (0)	0	<0.01
Yakama (0)	0	<0.01
Yaqui (0)	0	<0.01
Yuman (0)	0	<0.01
Yup'ik (Alaska Native) (0)	0	<0.01
Asian (359)	427	1.01
Not Hispanic (356)	420	0.99
Hispanic (3)	7	0.02
Bangladeshi (0)	0	<0.01
Bhutanese (0)	0	<0.01
Burmese (0)	0	<0.01
Cambodian (0)	0	<0.01
Chinese, ex. Taiwanese (33)	36	0.08
Filipino (52)	81	0.19
Hmong (1)	3	0.01
Indian (50)	58	0.14
Indonesian (3)	8	0.02
Japanese (145)	158	0.37
Korean (16)	23	0.05
Laotian (0)	0	<0.01
Malaysian (1)	1	<0.01
Nepalese (1)	1	<0.01
Pakistani (10)	11	0.03
Sri Lankan (0)	0	<0.01
Taiwanese (0)	0	<0.01
Thai (6)	6	0.01
Vietnamese (35)	40	0.09
Hawaii Native/Pacific Islander (27)	47	0.11
Not Hispanic (18)	35	0.08
Hispanic (9)	12	0.03
Fijian (0)	0	<0.01
Guamanian/Chamorro (16)	20	0.05
Marshallese (0)	0	<0.01
Native Hawaiian (11)	21	0.05
Samoan (0)	1	<0.01
Tongan (0)	0	<0.01
White (40,044)	40,573	95.75
Not Hispanic (38,826)	39,210	92.53
Hispanic (1,218)	1,363	3.22

Notes: † The Census 2010 population figure is used to calculate the percentages in the Hispanic Origin and Race categories. Ancestry percentages are based on the 2006-2010 American Community Survey population (not shown); ‡ Numbers in parentheses indicate the number of people reporting a single ancestry; * Numbers in parentheses indicate the number of persons reporting this race alone, not in combination with any other race; Please refer to the Explanation of Data for more information.

Jasper County
Population: 33,478

Ancestry	Population	%
Afghan (0)	0	<0.01
African, Sub-Saharan (16)	16	0.05
African (16)	16	0.05
Cape Verdean (0)	0	<0.01
Ethiopian (0)	0	<0.01
Ghanaian (0)	0	<0.01
Kenyan (0)	0	<0.01
Liberian (0)	0	<0.01
Nigerian (0)	0	<0.01
Senegalese (0)	0	<0.01
Sierra Leonean (0)	0	<0.01
Somalian (0)	0	<0.01
South African (0)	0	<0.01
Sudanese (0)	0	<0.01
Ugandan (0)	0	<0.01
Zimbabwean (0)	0	<0.01
Other Sub-Saharan African (0)	0	<0.01
Albanian (0)	0	<0.01
Alsatian (0)	0	<0.01
American (2,281)	2,281	6.90
Arab (0)	0	<0.01
Arab (0)	0	<0.01
Egyptian (0)	0	<0.01
Iraqi (0)	0	<0.01
Jordanian (0)	0	<0.01
Lebanese (0)	0	<0.01
Moroccan (0)	0	<0.01
Palestinian (0)	0	<0.01
Syrian (0)	0	<0.01
Other Arab (0)	0	<0.01
Armenian (0)	0	<0.01
Assyrian/Chaldean/Syriac (0)	7	0.02
Australian (0)	0	<0.01
Austrian (21)	40	0.12
Basque (0)	0	<0.01
Belgian (0)	16	0.05
Brazilian (0)	0	<0.01
British (28)	50	0.15
Bulgarian (0)	0	<0.01
Cajun (0)	0	<0.01
Canadian (9)	9	0.03
Carpatho Rusyn (0)	0	<0.01
Celtic (0)	0	<0.01
Croatian (36)	171	0.52
Cypriot (0)	0	<0.01
Czech (103)	225	0.68
Czechoslovakian (0)	77	0.23
Danish (0)	48	0.15
Dutch (1,680)	3,174	9.60
Eastern European (11)	11	0.03
English (799)	3,076	9.31
Estonian (0)	0	<0.01
European (208)	305	0.92
Finnish (0)	70	0.21
French, ex. Basque (187)	916	2.77
French Canadian (35)	132	0.40
German (2,624)	9,110	27.56
German Russian (0)	0	<0.01
Greek (100)	151	0.46
Guyanese (0)	0	<0.01
Hungarian (97)	365	1.10
Icelander (0)	0	<0.01
Iranian (0)	0	<0.01
Irish (1,233)	5,461	16.52
Israeli (0)	0	<0.01
Italian (156)	813	2.46
Latvian (0)	0	<0.01
Lithuanian (43)	120	0.36
Luxemburger (0)	0	<0.01
Macedonian (5)	5	0.02
Maltese (0)	0	<0.01
New Zealander (0)	0	<0.01
Northern European (0)	0	<0.01
Norwegian (74)	247	0.75
Pennsylvania German (13)	34	0.10
Polish (774)	1,994	6.03
Portuguese (0)	14	0.04
Romanian (23)	98	0.30
Russian (27)	108	0.33
Scandinavian (23)	50	0.15
Scotch-Irish (197)	538	1.63
Scottish (233)	731	2.21
Serbian (94)	260	0.79
Slavic (0)	10	0.03
Slovak (46)	255	0.77
Slovene (0)	16	0.05
Soviet Union (0)	0	<0.01
Swedish (108)	618	1.87
Swiss (4)	68	0.21
Turkish (0)	0	<0.01
Ukrainian (49)	62	0.19
Welsh (20)	191	0.58
West Indian, ex. Hispanic (0)	0	<0.01
Bahamian (0)	0	<0.01
Barbadian (0)	0	<0.01
Belizean (0)	0	<0.01
Bermudan (0)	0	<0.01
British West Indian (0)	0	<0.01
Dutch West Indian (0)	0	<0.01
Haitian (0)	0	<0.01
Jamaican (0)	0	<0.01
Trinidadian/Tobagonian (0)	0	<0.01
U.S. Virgin Islander (0)	0	<0.01
West Indian (0)	0	<0.01
Other West Indian (0)	0	<0.01
Yugoslavian (0)	0	<0.01

Hispanic Origin	Population	%
Hispanic or Latino (of any race)	1,823	5.45
Central American, ex. Mexican	60	0.18
Costa Rican	4	0.01
Guatemalan	15	0.04
Honduran	36	0.11
Nicaraguan	2	0.01
Panamanian	0	<0.01
Salvadoran	3	0.01
Other Central American	0	<0.01
Cuban	20	0.06
Dominican Republic	0	<0.01
Mexican	1,517	4.53
Puerto Rican	99	0.30
South American	14	0.04
Argentinean	2	0.01
Bolivian	2	0.01
Chilean	1	<0.01
Colombian	2	0.01
Ecuadorian	1	<0.01
Paraguayan	0	<0.01
Peruvian	6	0.02
Uruguayan	0	<0.01
Venezuelan	0	<0.01
Other South American	0	<0.01
Other Hispanic or Latino	113	0.34

Race*	Population	%
African-American/Black (212)	310	0.93
Not Hispanic (208)	298	0.89
Hispanic (4)	12	0.04
American Indian/Alaska Native (68)	191	0.57
Not Hispanic (53)	157	0.47
Hispanic (15)	34	0.10
Alaska Athabascan (Ala. Nat.) (0)	0	<0.01
Aleut (Alaska Native) (0)	0	<0.01
Apache (3)	9	0.03
Arapaho (0)	0	<0.01
Blackfeet (3)	6	0.02
Canadian/French Am. Ind. (0)	0	<0.01
Central American Ind. (0)	0	<0.01
Cherokee (13)	49	0.15
Cheyenne (0)	0	<0.01
Chickasaw (0)	0	<0.01
Chippewa (2)	4	0.01
Choctaw (3)	9	0.03
Colville (0)	0	<0.01
Comanche (0)	1	<0.01
Cree (0)	0	<0.01
Creek (1)	1	<0.01
Crow (0)	0	<0.01
Delaware (0)	0	<0.01
Hopi (0)	0	<0.01
Houma (0)	0	<0.01
Inupiat (Alaska Native) (0)	0	<0.01
Iroquois (0)	1	<0.01
Kiowa (0)	0	<0.01
Lumbee (0)	0	<0.01
Menominee (0)	0	<0.01
Mexican American Ind. (1)	2	0.01
Navajo (0)	1	<0.01
Osage (0)	0	<0.01
Ottawa (0)	0	<0.01
Paiute (0)	0	<0.01
Pima (0)	0	<0.01
Potawatomi (1)	1	<0.01
Pueblo (0)	1	<0.01
Puget Sound Salish (0)	0	<0.01
Seminole (0)	1	<0.01
Shoshone (0)	0	<0.01
Sioux (0)	5	0.01
South American Ind. (2)	2	0.01
Spanish American Ind. (0)	0	<0.01
Tlingit-Haida (Alaska Native) (0)	0	<0.01
Tohono O'Odham (0)	0	<0.01
Tsimshian (Alaska Native) (0)	0	<0.01
Ute (0)	0	<0.01
Yakama (0)	0	<0.01
Yaqui (0)	0	<0.01
Yuman (0)	0	<0.01
Yup'ik (Alaska Native) (0)	0	<0.01
Asian (133)	194	0.58
Not Hispanic (123)	179	0.53
Hispanic (10)	15	0.04
Bangladeshi (0)	0	<0.01
Bhutanese (0)	0	<0.01
Burmese (0)	0	<0.01
Cambodian (0)	0	<0.01
Chinese, ex. Taiwanese (23)	32	0.10
Filipino (49)	68	0.20
Hmong (0)	0	<0.01
Indian (27)	35	0.10
Indonesian (1)	3	0.01
Japanese (4)	23	0.07
Korean (12)	14	0.04
Laotian (0)	0	<0.01
Malaysian (0)	0	<0.01
Nepalese (0)	0	<0.01
Pakistani (0)	2	0.01
Sri Lankan (0)	0	<0.01
Taiwanese (0)	0	<0.01
Thai (4)	4	0.01
Vietnamese (2)	5	0.01
Hawaii Native/Pacific Islander (11)	29	0.09
Not Hispanic (9)	27	0.08
Hispanic (2)	2	0.01
Fijian (0)	0	<0.01
Guamanian/Chamorro (6)	6	0.02
Marshallese (0)	0	<0.01
Native Hawaiian (1)	12	0.04
Samoan (0)	3	0.01
Tongan (3)	4	0.01
White (32,056)	32,375	96.71
Not Hispanic (30,988)	31,235	93.30
Hispanic (1,068)	1,140	3.41

Notes: † The Census 2010 population figure is used to calculate the percentages in the Hispanic Origin and Race categories. Ancestry percentages are based on the 2006-2010 American Community Survey population (not shown); ‡ Numbers in parentheses indicate the number of people reporting a single ancestry; * Numbers in parentheses indicate the number of persons reporting this race alone, not in combination with any other race; Please refer to the Explanation of Data for more information.

Jay County
Population: 21,253

Ancestry	Population	%
Afghan (0)	0	<0.01
African, Sub-Saharan (0)	0	<0.01
African (0)	0	<0.01
Cape Verdean (0)	0	<0.01
Ethiopian (0)	0	<0.01
Ghanaian (0)	0	<0.01
Kenyan (0)	0	<0.01
Liberian (0)	0	<0.01
Nigerian (0)	0	<0.01
Senegalese (0)	0	<0.01
Sierra Leonean (0)	0	<0.01
Somalian (0)	0	<0.01
South African (0)	0	<0.01
Sudanese (0)	0	<0.01
Ugandan (0)	0	<0.01
Zimbabwean (0)	0	<0.01
Other Sub-Saharan African (0)	0	<0.01
Albanian (0)	0	<0.01
Alsatian (17)	17	0.08
American (2,803)	2,803	13.07
Arab (0)	0	<0.01
Arab (0)	0	<0.01
Egyptian (0)	0	<0.01
Iraqi (0)	0	<0.01
Jordanian (0)	0	<0.01
Lebanese (0)	0	<0.01
Moroccan (0)	0	<0.01
Palestinian (0)	0	<0.01
Syrian (0)	0	<0.01
Other Arab (0)	0	<0.01
Armenian (0)	0	<0.01
Assyrian/Chaldean/Syriac (0)	0	<0.01
Australian (0)	0	<0.01
Austrian (0)	0	<0.01
Basque (0)	0	<0.01
Belgian (18)	133	0.62
Brazilian (0)	0	<0.01
British (3)	69	0.32
Bulgarian (0)	24	0.11
Cajun (0)	0	<0.01
Canadian (0)	0	<0.01
Carpatho Rusyn (0)	0	<0.01
Celtic (0)	0	<0.01
Croatian (0)	0	<0.01
Cypriot (0)	0	<0.01
Czech (0)	0	<0.01
Czechoslovakian (5)	5	0.02
Danish (12)	47	0.22
Dutch (68)	357	1.67
Eastern European (0)	0	<0.01
English (1,384)	2,503	11.67
Estonian (0)	0	<0.01
European (45)	49	0.23
Finnish (13)	13	0.06
French, ex. Basque (36)	289	1.35
French Canadian (92)	127	0.59
German (4,242)	7,321	34.14
German Russian (0)	0	<0.01
Greek (0)	17	0.08
Guyanese (0)	0	<0.01
Hungarian (8)	37	0.17
Icelander (0)	0	<0.01
Iranian (0)	0	<0.01
Irish (615)	2,486	11.59
Israeli (0)	0	<0.01
Italian (110)	260	1.21
Latvian (9)	9	0.04
Lithuanian (0)	0	<0.01
Luxemburger (0)	0	<0.01
Macedonian (0)	0	<0.01
Maltese (0)	0	<0.01
New Zealander (0)	0	<0.01
Northern European (0)	0	<0.01
Norwegian (22)	51	0.24
Pennsylvania German (41)	66	0.31
Polish (30)	80	0.37
Portuguese (72)	72	0.34
Romanian (0)	0	<0.01
Russian (0)	4	0.02
Scandinavian (0)	0	<0.01
Scotch-Irish (109)	156	0.73
Scottish (87)	269	1.25
Serbian (0)	0	<0.01
Slavic (0)	0	<0.01
Slovak (0)	0	<0.01
Slovene (0)	0	<0.01
Soviet Union (0)	0	<0.01
Swedish (44)	117	0.55
Swiss (152)	405	1.89
Turkish (0)	0	<0.01
Ukrainian (0)	0	<0.01
Welsh (45)	293	1.37
West Indian, ex. Hispanic (0)	0	<0.01
Bahamian (0)	0	<0.01
Barbadian (0)	0	<0.01
Belizean (0)	0	<0.01
Bermudan (0)	0	<0.01
British West Indian (0)	0	<0.01
Dutch West Indian (0)	0	<0.01
Haitian (0)	0	<0.01
Jamaican (0)	0	<0.01
Trinidadian/Tobagonian (0)	0	<0.01
U.S. Virgin Islander (0)	0	<0.01
West Indian (0)	0	<0.01
Other West Indian (0)	0	<0.01
Yugoslavian (0)	0	<0.01

Hispanic Origin	Population	%
Hispanic or Latino (of any race)	577	2.71
Central American, ex. Mexican	12	0.06
Costa Rican	1	<0.01
Guatemalan	4	0.02
Honduran	4	0.02
Nicaraguan	0	<0.01
Panamanian	2	0.01
Salvadoran	1	<0.01
Other Central American	0	<0.01
Cuban	2	0.01
Dominican Republic	0	<0.01
Mexican	503	2.37
Puerto Rican	7	0.03
South American	3	0.01
Argentinean	0	<0.01
Bolivian	0	<0.01
Chilean	0	<0.01
Colombian	2	0.01
Ecuadorian	0	<0.01
Paraguayan	1	<0.01
Peruvian	0	<0.01
Uruguayan	0	<0.01
Venezuelan	0	<0.01
Other South American	0	<0.01
Other Hispanic or Latino	50	0.24

Race*	Population	%
African-American/Black (60)	102	0.48
Not Hispanic (58)	98	0.46
Hispanic (2)	4	0.02
American Indian/Alaska Native (23)	98	0.46
Not Hispanic (21)	95	0.45
Hispanic (2)	3	0.01
Alaska Athabascan (Ala. Nat.) (0)	0	<0.01
Aleut (Alaska Native) (0)	0	<0.01
Apache (0)	0	<0.01
Arapaho (0)	0	<0.01
Blackfeet (0)	1	<0.01
Canadian/French Am. Ind. (0)	1	<0.01
Central American Ind. (2)	2	0.01
Cherokee (7)	35	0.16
Cheyenne (0)	0	<0.01
Chickasaw (0)	1	<0.01
Chippewa (0)	0	<0.01
Choctaw (1)	1	<0.01
Colville (0)	0	<0.01
Comanche (0)	0	<0.01
Cree (0)	0	<0.01
Creek (2)	2	0.01
Crow (0)	1	<0.01
Delaware (0)	0	<0.01
Hopi (0)	0	<0.01
Houma (0)	0	<0.01
Inupiat (Alaska Native) (0)	0	<0.01
Iroquois (0)	1	<0.01
Kiowa (0)	0	<0.01
Lumbee (0)	0	<0.01
Menominee (0)	0	<0.01
Mexican American Ind. (0)	1	<0.01
Navajo (0)	0	<0.01
Osage (0)	0	<0.01
Ottawa (0)	0	<0.01
Paiute (0)	0	<0.01
Pima (0)	0	<0.01
Potawatomi (0)	0	<0.01
Pueblo (0)	0	<0.01
Puget Sound Salish (0)	0	<0.01
Seminole (1)	1	<0.01
Shoshone (0)	0	<0.01
Sioux (1)	1	<0.01
South American Ind. (0)	1	<0.01
Spanish American Ind. (0)	0	<0.01
Tlingit-Haida (Alaska Native) (0)	0	<0.01
Tohono O'Odham (0)	0	<0.01
Tsimshian (Alaska Native) (0)	0	<0.01
Ute (0)	0	<0.01
Yakama (0)	0	<0.01
Yaqui (0)	0	<0.01
Yuman (0)	0	<0.01
Yup'ik (Alaska Native) (0)	0	<0.01
Asian (78)	122	0.57
Not Hispanic (77)	118	0.56
Hispanic (1)	4	0.02
Bangladeshi (0)	0	<0.01
Bhutanese (0)	0	<0.01
Burmese (0)	0	<0.01
Cambodian (4)	4	0.02
Chinese, ex. Taiwanese (5)	6	0.03
Filipino (22)	37	0.17
Hmong (0)	0	<0.01
Indian (12)	14	0.07
Indonesian (0)	0	<0.01
Japanese (27)	46	0.22
Korean (2)	6	0.03
Laotian (0)	0	<0.01
Malaysian (0)	0	<0.01
Nepalese (0)	0	<0.01
Pakistani (0)	0	<0.01
Sri Lankan (0)	0	<0.01
Taiwanese (0)	0	<0.01
Thai (2)	2	0.01
Vietnamese (3)	3	0.01
Hawaii Native/Pacific Islander (0)	8	0.04
Not Hispanic (0)	7	0.03
Hispanic (0)	1	<0.01
Fijian (0)	0	<0.01
Guamanian/Chamorro (0)	2	0.01
Marshallese (0)	0	<0.01
Native Hawaiian (0)	2	0.01
Samoan (0)	1	<0.01
Tongan (0)	0	<0.01
White (20,619)	20,804	97.89
Not Hispanic (20,356)	20,502	96.47
Hispanic (263)	302	1.42

Notes: † The Census 2010 population figure is used to calculate the percentages in the Hispanic Origin and Race categories. Ancestry percentages are based on the 2006-2010 American Community Survey population (not shown); ‡ Numbers in parentheses indicate the number of people reporting a single ancestry; * Numbers in parentheses indicate the number of persons reporting this race alone, not in combination with any other race; Please refer to the Explanation of Data for more information.

Jefferson County
Population: 32,428

Ancestry	Population	%
Afghan (12)	12	0.04
African, Sub-Saharan (0)	43	0.13
African (0)	43	0.13
Cape Verdean (0)	0	<0.01
Ethiopian (0)	0	<0.01
Ghanaian (0)	0	<0.01
Kenyan (0)	0	<0.01
Liberian (0)	0	<0.01
Nigerian (0)	0	<0.01
Senegalese (0)	0	<0.01
Sierra Leonean (0)	0	<0.01
Somalian (0)	0	<0.01
South African (0)	0	<0.01
Sudanese (0)	0	<0.01
Ugandan (0)	0	<0.01
Zimbabwean (0)	0	<0.01
Other Sub-Saharan African (0)	0	<0.01
Albanian (0)	0	<0.01
Alsatian (0)	0	<0.01
American (4,982)	4,982	15.38
Arab (25)	25	0.08
Arab (10)	10	0.03
Egyptian (0)	0	<0.01
Iraqi (0)	0	<0.01
Jordanian (0)	0	<0.01
Lebanese (0)	0	<0.01
Moroccan (0)	0	<0.01
Palestinian (0)	0	<0.01
Syrian (15)	15	0.05
Other Arab (0)	0	<0.01
Armenian (15)	15	0.05
Assyrian/Chaldean/Syriac (0)	0	<0.01
Australian (0)	0	<0.01
Austrian (0)	27	0.08
Basque (0)	0	<0.01
Belgian (45)	61	0.19
Brazilian (0)	0	<0.01
British (20)	123	0.38
Bulgarian (0)	0	<0.01
Cajun (0)	0	<0.01
Canadian (8)	8	0.02
Carpatho Rusyn (0)	0	<0.01
Celtic (44)	71	0.22
Croatian (7)	65	0.20
Cypriot (0)	0	<0.01
Czech (0)	11	0.03
Czechoslovakian (0)	0	<0.01
Danish (0)	92	0.28
Dutch (77)	531	1.64
Eastern European (0)	0	<0.01
English (1,900)	3,641	11.24
Estonian (0)	0	<0.01
European (259)	274	0.85
Finnish (0)	0	<0.01
French, ex. Basque (222)	871	2.69
French Canadian (57)	119	0.37
German (3,292)	7,622	23.53
German Russian (0)	0	<0.01
Greek (24)	86	0.27
Guyanese (0)	0	<0.01
Hungarian (31)	194	0.60
Icelander (0)	0	<0.01
Iranian (0)	0	<0.01
Irish (1,254)	4,191	12.94
Israeli (0)	0	<0.01
Italian (195)	621	1.92
Latvian (0)	0	<0.01
Lithuanian (18)	18	0.06
Luxemburger (0)	0	<0.01
Macedonian (25)	25	0.08
Maltese (0)	0	<0.01
New Zealander (0)	0	<0.01
Northern European (12)	28	0.09
Norwegian (59)	100	0.31
Pennsylvania German (23)	23	0.07
Polish (67)	457	1.41
Portuguese (0)	17	0.05
Romanian (0)	0	<0.01
Russian (0)	75	0.23
Scandinavian (18)	28	0.09
Scotch-Irish (445)	886	2.74
Scottish (356)	788	2.43
Serbian (0)	19	0.06
Slavic (0)	12	0.04
Slovak (0)	95	0.29
Slovene (0)	0	<0.01
Soviet Union (0)	0	<0.01
Swedish (80)	204	0.63
Swiss (39)	252	0.78
Turkish (0)	0	<0.01
Ukrainian (17)	34	0.10
Welsh (71)	273	0.84
West Indian, ex. Hispanic (0)	0	<0.01
Bahamian (0)	0	<0.01
Barbadian (0)	0	<0.01
Belizean (0)	0	<0.01
Bermudan (0)	0	<0.01
British West Indian (0)	0	<0.01
Dutch West Indian (0)	0	<0.01
Haitian (0)	0	<0.01
Jamaican (0)	0	<0.01
Trinidadian/Tobagonian (0)	0	<0.01
U.S. Virgin Islander (0)	0	<0.01
West Indian (0)	0	<0.01
Other West Indian (0)	0	<0.01
Yugoslavian (34)	34	0.10

Hispanic Origin	Population	%
Hispanic or Latino (of any race)	755	2.33
Central American, ex. Mexican	55	0.17
Costa Rican	0	<0.01
Guatemalan	5	0.02
Honduran	44	0.14
Nicaraguan	0	<0.01
Panamanian	2	0.01
Salvadoran	4	0.01
Other Central American	0	<0.01
Cuban	12	0.04
Dominican Republic	0	<0.01
Mexican	564	1.74
Puerto Rican	50	0.15
South American	25	0.08
Argentinean	2	0.01
Bolivian	3	0.01
Chilean	2	0.01
Colombian	8	0.02
Ecuadorian	5	0.02
Paraguayan	0	<0.01
Peruvian	2	0.01
Uruguayan	0	<0.01
Venezuelan	3	0.01
Other South American	0	<0.01
Other Hispanic or Latino	49	0.15

Race*	Population	%
African-American/Black (542)	743	2.29
Not Hispanic (530)	725	2.24
Hispanic (12)	18	0.06
American Indian/Alaska Native (69)	195	0.60
Not Hispanic (59)	179	0.55
Hispanic (10)	16	0.05
Alaska Athabascan (Ala. Nat.) (0)	0	<0.01
Aleut (Alaska Native) (0)	0	<0.01
Apache (0)	4	0.01
Arapaho (0)	0	<0.01
Blackfeet (4)	12	0.04
Canadian/French Am. Ind. (0)	1	<0.01
Central American Ind. (0)	0	<0.01
Cherokee (21)	63	0.19
Cheyenne (0)	0	<0.01
Chickasaw (1)	1	<0.01
Chippewa (5)	5	0.02
Choctaw (2)	2	0.01
Colville (0)	0	<0.01
Comanche (0)	0	<0.01
Cree (0)	0	<0.01
Creek (0)	2	0.01
Crow (0)	0	<0.01
Delaware (0)	1	<0.01
Hopi (0)	0	<0.01
Houma (0)	0	<0.01
Inupiat (Alaska Native) (1)	3	0.01
Iroquois (1)	5	0.02
Kiowa (0)	0	<0.01
Lumbee (0)	0	<0.01
Menominee (0)	0	<0.01
Mexican American Ind. (1)	1	<0.01
Navajo (1)	1	<0.01
Osage (0)	0	<0.01
Ottawa (0)	0	<0.01
Paiute (0)	1	<0.01
Pima (0)	0	<0.01
Potawatomi (2)	2	0.01
Pueblo (0)	0	<0.01
Puget Sound Salish (0)	1	<0.01
Seminole (0)	0	<0.01
Shoshone (0)	0	<0.01
Sioux (1)	11	0.03
South American Ind. (0)	0	<0.01
Spanish American Ind. (0)	0	<0.01
Tlingit-Haida (Alaska Native) (0)	0	<0.01
Tohono O'Odham (0)	0	<0.01
Tsimshian (Alaska Native) (0)	0	<0.01
Ute (0)	0	<0.01
Yakama (0)	0	<0.01
Yaqui (0)	0	<0.01
Yuman (0)	0	<0.01
Yup'ik (Alaska Native) (0)	0	<0.01
Asian (211)	279	0.86
Not Hispanic (211)	276	0.85
Hispanic (0)	3	0.01
Bangladeshi (0)	0	<0.01
Bhutanese (0)	0	<0.01
Burmese (0)	0	<0.01
Cambodian (0)	0	<0.01
Chinese, ex. Taiwanese (64)	69	0.21
Filipino (42)	72	0.22
Hmong (0)	2	0.01
Indian (33)	43	0.13
Indonesian (4)	4	0.01
Japanese (39)	47	0.14
Korean (12)	20	0.06
Laotian (0)	0	<0.01
Malaysian (0)	0	<0.01
Nepalese (0)	0	<0.01
Pakistani (3)	3	0.01
Sri Lankan (0)	0	<0.01
Taiwanese (0)	0	<0.01
Thai (2)	3	0.01
Vietnamese (6)	9	0.03
Hawaii Native/Pacific Islander (6)	19	0.06
Not Hispanic (5)	16	0.05
Hispanic (1)	3	0.01
Fijian (0)	0	<0.01
Guamanian/Chamorro (1)	4	0.01
Marshallese (0)	0	<0.01
Native Hawaiian (3)	7	0.02
Samoan (1)	2	0.01
Tongan (0)	0	<0.01
White (30,876)	31,283	96.47
Not Hispanic (30,463)	30,829	95.07
Hispanic (413)	454	1.40

Notes: † The Census 2010 population figure is used to calculate the percentages in the Hispanic Origin and Race categories. Ancestry percentages are based on the 2006-2010 American Community Survey population (not shown); ‡ Numbers in parentheses indicate the number of people reporting a single ancestry; * Numbers in parentheses indicate the number of persons reporting this race alone, not in combination with any other race; Please refer to the Explanation of Data for more information.

Jennings County
Population: 28,525

Ancestry	Population	%
Afghan (0)	0	<0.01
African, Sub-Saharan (51)	51	0.18
African (51)	51	0.18
Cape Verdean (0)	0	<0.01
Ethiopian (0)	0	<0.01
Ghanaian (0)	0	<0.01
Kenyan (0)	0	<0.01
Liberian (0)	0	<0.01
Nigerian (0)	0	<0.01
Senegalese (0)	0	<0.01
Sierra Leonean (0)	0	<0.01
Somalian (0)	0	<0.01
South African (0)	0	<0.01
Sudanese (0)	0	<0.01
Ugandan (0)	0	<0.01
Zimbabwean (0)	0	<0.01
Other Sub-Saharan African (0)	0	<0.01
Albanian (0)	0	<0.01
Alsatian (0)	0	<0.01
American (4,191)	4,191	14.72
Arab (91)	110	0.39
Arab (84)	84	0.30
Egyptian (0)	0	<0.01
Iraqi (0)	0	<0.01
Jordanian (0)	0	<0.01
Lebanese (7)	26	0.09
Moroccan (0)	0	<0.01
Palestinian (0)	0	<0.01
Syrian (0)	0	<0.01
Other Arab (0)	0	<0.01
Armenian (0)	0	<0.01
Assyrian/Chaldean/Syriac (0)	0	<0.01
Australian (0)	109	0.38
Austrian (11)	29	0.10
Basque (0)	0	<0.01
Belgian (0)	25	0.09
Brazilian (0)	0	<0.01
British (13)	49	0.17
Bulgarian (0)	0	<0.01
Cajun (0)	0	<0.01
Canadian (84)	138	0.48
Carpatho Rusyn (0)	0	<0.01
Celtic (0)	0	<0.01
Croatian (0)	0	<0.01
Cypriot (0)	0	<0.01
Czech (0)	16	0.06
Czechoslovakian (9)	21	0.07
Danish (0)	0	<0.01
Dutch (43)	399	1.40
Eastern European (0)	0	<0.01
English (1,050)	2,036	7.15
Estonian (0)	0	<0.01
European (163)	163	0.57
Finnish (0)	21	0.07
French, ex. Basque (93)	479	1.68
French Canadian (0)	0	<0.01
German (3,063)	7,449	26.16
German Russian (0)	0	<0.01
Greek (0)	0	<0.01
Guyanese (0)	0	<0.01
Hungarian (29)	47	0.17
Icelander (0)	0	<0.01
Iranian (0)	0	<0.01
Irish (1,240)	4,631	16.27
Israeli (0)	0	<0.01
Italian (47)	301	1.06
Latvian (0)	0	<0.01
Lithuanian (0)	0	<0.01
Luxemburger (0)	0	<0.01
Macedonian (0)	0	<0.01
Maltese (0)	0	<0.01
New Zealander (0)	0	<0.01
Northern European (0)	0	<0.01
Norwegian (33)	347	1.22
Pennsylvania German (0)	65	0.23
Polish (9)	65	0.23
Portuguese (0)	22	0.08
Romanian (9)	9	0.03
Russian (0)	35	0.12
Scandinavian (0)	0	<0.01
Scotch-Irish (133)	452	1.59
Scottish (236)	343	1.20
Serbian (0)	0	<0.01
Slavic (0)	0	<0.01
Slovak (0)	0	<0.01
Slovene (0)	0	<0.01
Soviet Union (0)	0	<0.01
Swedish (24)	119	0.42
Swiss (12)	23	0.08
Turkish (0)	0	<0.01
Ukrainian (0)	0	<0.01
Welsh (21)	47	0.17
West Indian, ex. Hispanic (10)	19	0.07
Bahamian (0)	0	<0.01
Barbadian (0)	0	<0.01
Belizean (0)	0	<0.01
Bermudan (0)	0	<0.01
British West Indian (0)	0	<0.01
Dutch West Indian (0)	0	<0.01
Haitian (0)	0	<0.01
Jamaican (0)	9	0.03
Trinidadian/Tobagonian (0)	0	<0.01
U.S. Virgin Islander (0)	0	<0.01
West Indian (10)	10	0.04
Other West Indian (0)	0	<0.01
Yugoslavian (0)	0	<0.01

Hispanic Origin	Population	%
Hispanic or Latino (of any race)	571	2.00
Central American, ex. Mexican	27	0.09
Costa Rican	1	<0.01
Guatemalan	6	0.02
Honduran	6	0.02
Nicaraguan	5	0.02
Panamanian	3	0.01
Salvadoran	6	0.02
Other Central American	0	<0.01
Cuban	6	0.02
Dominican Republic	1	<0.01
Mexican	464	1.63
Puerto Rican	17	0.06
South American	9	0.03
Argentinean	0	<0.01
Bolivian	0	<0.01
Chilean	1	<0.01
Colombian	7	0.02
Ecuadorian	0	<0.01
Paraguayan	0	<0.01
Peruvian	1	<0.01
Uruguayan	0	<0.01
Venezuelan	0	<0.01
Other South American	0	<0.01
Other Hispanic or Latino	47	0.16

Race*	Population	%
African-American/Black (216)	327	1.15
Not Hispanic (206)	314	1.10
Hispanic (10)	13	0.05
American Indian/Alaska Native (30)	166	0.58
Not Hispanic (30)	162	0.57
Hispanic (0)	4	0.01
Alaska Athabascan (Ala. Nat.) (3)	3	0.01
Aleut (Alaska Native) (0)	0	<0.01
Apache (0)	2	0.01
Arapaho (0)	1	<0.01
Blackfeet (0)	14	0.05
Canadian/French Am. Ind. (1)	1	<0.01
Central American Ind. (0)	0	<0.01
Cherokee (7)	76	0.27
Cheyenne (1)	1	<0.01
Chickasaw (0)	1	<0.01
Chippewa (2)	2	0.01
Choctaw (0)	2	0.01
Colville (0)	0	<0.01
Comanche (0)	0	<0.01
Cree (0)	6	0.02
Creek (0)	1	<0.01
Crow (0)	0	<0.01
Delaware (0)	2	0.01
Hopi (0)	0	<0.01
Houma (0)	0	<0.01
Inupiat (Alaska Native) (0)	0	<0.01
Iroquois (0)	0	<0.01
Kiowa (0)	0	<0.01
Lumbee (0)	0	<0.01
Menominee (0)	0	<0.01
Mexican American Ind. (0)	0	<0.01
Navajo (0)	6	0.02
Osage (0)	0	<0.01
Ottawa (0)	0	<0.01
Paiute (0)	0	<0.01
Pima (0)	0	<0.01
Potawatomi (0)	1	<0.01
Pueblo (0)	0	<0.01
Puget Sound Salish (0)	0	<0.01
Seminole (0)	0	<0.01
Shoshone (0)	0	<0.01
Sioux (4)	6	0.02
South American Ind. (0)	0	<0.01
Spanish American Ind. (0)	0	<0.01
Tlingit-Haida (Alaska Native) (0)	0	<0.01
Tohono O'Odham (0)	0	<0.01
Tsimshian (Alaska Native) (0)	0	<0.01
Ute (0)	0	<0.01
Yakama (0)	0	<0.01
Yaqui (0)	0	<0.01
Yuman (0)	0	<0.01
Yup'ik (Alaska Native) (0)	0	<0.01
Asian (62)	107	0.38
Not Hispanic (62)	107	0.38
Hispanic (0)	0	<0.01
Bangladeshi (0)	0	<0.01
Bhutanese (0)	0	<0.01
Burmese (0)	0	<0.01
Cambodian (3)	3	0.01
Chinese, ex. Taiwanese (6)	10	0.04
Filipino (10)	19	0.07
Hmong (0)	0	<0.01
Indian (9)	16	0.06
Indonesian (0)	0	<0.01
Japanese (16)	29	0.10
Korean (8)	17	0.06
Laotian (0)	0	<0.01
Malaysian (0)	0	<0.01
Nepalese (0)	0	<0.01
Pakistani (1)	1	<0.01
Sri Lankan (0)	0	<0.01
Taiwanese (0)	0	<0.01
Thai (3)	3	0.01
Vietnamese (5)	5	0.02
Hawaii Native/Pacific Islander (0)	5	0.02
Not Hispanic (0)	3	0.01
Hispanic (0)	2	0.01
Fijian (0)	0	<0.01
Guamanian/Chamorro (0)	1	<0.01
Marshallese (0)	0	<0.01
Native Hawaiian (0)	2	0.01
Samoan (0)	0	<0.01
Tongan (0)	0	<0.01
White (27,611)	27,929	97.91
Not Hispanic (27,361)	27,630	96.86
Hispanic (250)	299	1.05

Notes: † The Census 2010 population figure is used to calculate the percentages in the Hispanic Origin and Race categories. Ancestry percentages are based on the 2006-2010 American Community Survey population (not shown); ‡ Numbers in parentheses indicate the number of people reporting a single ancestry; * Numbers in parentheses indicate the number of persons reporting this race alone, not in combination with any other race; Please refer to the Explanation of Data for more information.

Johnson County
Population: 139,654

Ancestry	Population	%
Afghan (0)	0	<0.01
African, Sub-Saharan (105)	105	0.08
African (33)	33	0.02
Cape Verdean (0)	0	<0.01
Ethiopian (0)	0	<0.01
Ghanaian (46)	46	0.03
Kenyan (26)	26	0.02
Liberian (0)	0	<0.01
Nigerian (0)	0	<0.01
Senegalese (0)	0	<0.01
Sierra Leonean (0)	0	<0.01
Somalian (0)	0	<0.01
South African (0)	0	<0.01
Sudanese (0)	0	<0.01
Ugandan (0)	0	<0.01
Zimbabwean (0)	0	<0.01
Other Sub-Saharan African (0)	0	<0.01
Albanian (14)	37	0.03
Alsatian (0)	0	<0.01
American (13,982)	13,982	10.28
Arab (262)	345	0.25
Arab (65)	83	0.06
Egyptian (0)	0	<0.01
Iraqi (0)	0	<0.01
Jordanian (101)	101	0.07
Lebanese (30)	77	0.06
Moroccan (24)	24	0.02
Palestinian (0)	0	<0.01
Syrian (0)	0	<0.01
Other Arab (42)	60	0.04
Armenian (0)	0	<0.01
Assyrian/Chaldean/Syriac (0)	0	<0.01
Australian (3)	3	<0.01
Austrian (18)	123	0.09
Basque (0)	0	<0.01
Belgian (21)	85	0.06
Brazilian (0)	0	<0.01
British (391)	1,089	0.80
Bulgarian (49)	49	0.04
Cajun (0)	83	0.06
Canadian (77)	287	0.21
Carpatho Rusyn (0)	0	<0.01
Celtic (0)	20	0.01
Croatian (58)	220	0.16
Cypriot (0)	0	<0.01
Czech (60)	210	0.15
Czechoslovakian (28)	40	0.03
Danish (79)	239	0.18
Dutch (978)	3,206	2.36
Eastern European (66)	66	0.05
English (6,193)	15,677	11.53
Estonian (0)	17	0.01
European (1,400)	1,600	1.18
Finnish (77)	244	0.18
French, ex. Basque (813)	3,000	2.21
French Canadian (290)	564	0.41
German (16,159)	38,193	28.08
German Russian (0)	9	0.01
Greek (90)	390	0.29
Guyanese (0)	0	<0.01
Hungarian (179)	694	0.51
Icelander (0)	0	<0.01
Iranian (79)	110	0.08
Irish (6,701)	21,347	15.70
Israeli (0)	0	<0.01
Italian (1,629)	4,981	3.66
Latvian (10)	10	0.01
Lithuanian (0)	61	0.04
Luxemburger (0)	0	<0.01
Macedonian (65)	65	0.05
Maltese (0)	0	<0.01
New Zealander (24)	24	0.02
Northern European (93)	114	0.08
Norwegian (353)	903	0.66
Pennsylvania German (70)	80	0.06
Polish (828)	2,800	2.06
Portuguese (17)	121	0.09
Romanian (76)	189	0.14
Russian (192)	477	0.35
Scandinavian (43)	70	0.05
Scotch-Irish (941)	2,434	1.79
Scottish (1,328)	3,328	2.45
Serbian (15)	32	0.02
Slavic (15)	33	0.02
Slovak (99)	191	0.14
Slovene (64)	118	0.09
Soviet Union (0)	0	<0.01
Swedish (222)	1,194	0.88
Swiss (265)	584	0.43
Turkish (36)	36	0.03
Ukrainian (56)	98	0.07
Welsh (163)	849	0.62
West Indian, ex. Hispanic (27)	36	0.03
Bahamian (0)	0	<0.01
Barbadian (0)	0	<0.01
Belizean (0)	0	<0.01
Bermudan (0)	0	<0.01
British West Indian (0)	0	<0.01
Dutch West Indian (0)	0	<0.01
Haitian (0)	0	<0.01
Jamaican (27)	36	0.03
Trinidadian/Tobagonian (0)	0	<0.01
U.S. Virgin Islander (0)	0	<0.01
West Indian (0)	0	<0.01
Other West Indian (0)	0	<0.01
Yugoslavian (36)	40	0.03

Hispanic Origin	Population	%
Hispanic or Latino (of any race)	4,270	3.06
Central American, ex. Mexican	201	0.14
Costa Rican	10	0.01
Guatemalan	48	0.03
Honduran	61	0.04
Nicaraguan	13	0.01
Panamanian	29	0.02
Salvadoran	37	0.03
Other Central American	3	<0.01
Cuban	56	0.04
Dominican Republic	32	0.02
Mexican	3,168	2.27
Puerto Rican	354	0.25
South American	185	0.13
Argentinean	16	0.01
Bolivian	9	0.01
Chilean	9	0.01
Colombian	47	0.03
Ecuadorian	6	<0.01
Paraguayan	4	<0.01
Peruvian	57	0.04
Uruguayan	0	<0.01
Venezuelan	36	0.03
Other South American	1	<0.01
Other Hispanic or Latino	274	0.20

Race*	Population	%
African-American/Black (1,578)	2,365	1.69
Not Hispanic (1,536)	2,260	1.62
Hispanic (42)	105	0.08
American Indian/Alaska Native (315)	878	0.63
Not Hispanic (252)	756	0.54
Hispanic (63)	122	0.09
Alaska Athabascan (Ala. Nat.) (0)	1	<0.01
Aleut (Alaska Native) (0)	2	<0.01
Apache (6)	17	0.01
Arapaho (0)	0	<0.01
Blackfeet (10)	35	0.03
Canadian/French Am. Ind. (0)	0	<0.01
Central American Ind. (0)	1	<0.01
Cherokee (61)	258	0.18
Cheyenne (1)	3	<0.01
Chickasaw (1)	5	<0.01
Chippewa (2)	20	0.01
Choctaw (13)	25	0.02
Colville (0)	1	<0.01
Comanche (0)	3	<0.01
Cree (0)	0	<0.01
Creek (5)	12	0.01
Crow (3)	10	0.01
Delaware (0)	0	<0.01
Hopi (0)	1	<0.01
Houma (0)	0	<0.01
Inupiat (Alaska Native) (0)	0	<0.01
Iroquois (4)	8	0.01
Kiowa (0)	0	<0.01
Lumbee (0)	4	<0.01
Menominee (0)	0	<0.01
Mexican American Ind. (13)	24	0.02
Navajo (5)	8	0.01
Osage (0)	0	<0.01
Ottawa (0)	6	<0.01
Paiute (0)	0	<0.01
Pima (0)	0	<0.01
Potawatomi (5)	5	<0.01
Pueblo (3)	6	<0.01
Puget Sound Salish (0)	0	<0.01
Seminole (0)	0	<0.01
Shoshone (0)	1	<0.01
Sioux (11)	24	0.02
South American Ind. (1)	1	<0.01
Spanish American Ind. (0)	0	<0.01
Tlingit-Haida (Alaska Native) (0)	0	<0.01
Tohono O'Odham (0)	6	<0.01
Tsimshian (Alaska Native) (0)	0	<0.01
Ute (0)	0	<0.01
Yakama (0)	0	<0.01
Yaqui (1)	1	<0.01
Yuman (0)	0	<0.01
Yup'ik (Alaska Native) (1)	1	<0.01
Asian (2,744)	3,360	2.41
Not Hispanic (2,716)	3,303	2.37
Hispanic (28)	57	0.04
Bangladeshi (1)	2	<0.01
Bhutanese (0)	0	<0.01
Burmese (5)	5	<0.01
Cambodian (6)	10	0.01
Chinese, ex. Taiwanese (310)	368	0.26
Filipino (235)	435	0.31
Hmong (3)	3	<0.01
Indian (1,613)	1,738	1.24
Indonesian (10)	15	0.01
Japanese (163)	267	0.19
Korean (124)	182	0.13
Laotian (1)	2	<0.01
Malaysian (2)	2	<0.01
Nepalese (9)	9	0.01
Pakistani (24)	28	0.02
Sri Lankan (5)	5	<0.01
Taiwanese (13)	15	0.01
Thai (18)	32	0.02
Vietnamese (133)	161	0.12
Hawaii Native/Pacific Islander (46)	140	0.10
Not Hispanic (46)	119	0.09
Hispanic (0)	21	0.02
Fijian (0)	0	<0.01
Guamanian/Chamorro (3)	16	0.01
Marshallese (0)	0	<0.01
Native Hawaiian (14)	48	0.03
Samoan (7)	15	0.01
Tongan (0)	0	<0.01
White (131,140)	133,110	95.31
Not Hispanic (128,903)	130,545	93.48
Hispanic (2,237)	2,565	1.84

Notes: † The Census 2010 population figure is used to calculate the percentages in the Hispanic Origin and Race categories. Ancestry percentages are based on the 2006-2010 American Community Survey population (not shown); ‡ Numbers in parentheses indicate the number of people reporting a single ancestry; * Numbers in parentheses indicate the number of persons reporting this race alone, not in combination with any other race; Please refer to the Explanation of Data for more information.

Knox County
Population: 38,440

Ancestry	Population	%
Afghan (0)	0	<0.01
African, Sub-Saharan (0)	4	0.01
African (0)	4	0.01
Cape Verdean (0)	0	<0.01
Ethiopian (0)	0	<0.01
Ghanaian (0)	0	<0.01
Kenyan (0)	0	<0.01
Liberian (0)	0	<0.01
Nigerian (0)	0	<0.01
Senegalese (0)	0	<0.01
Sierra Leonean (0)	0	<0.01
Somalian (0)	0	<0.01
South African (0)	0	<0.01
Sudanese (0)	0	<0.01
Ugandan (0)	0	<0.01
Zimbabwean (0)	0	<0.01
Other Sub-Saharan African (0)	0	<0.01
Albanian (0)	0	<0.01
Alsatian (0)	0	<0.01
American (7,662)	7,662	19.94
Arab (12)	12	0.03
Arab (0)	0	<0.01
Egyptian (0)	0	<0.01
Iraqi (0)	0	<0.01
Jordanian (0)	0	<0.01
Lebanese (0)	0	<0.01
Moroccan (0)	0	<0.01
Palestinian (0)	0	<0.01
Syrian (12)	12	0.03
Other Arab (0)	0	<0.01
Armenian (0)	0	<0.01
Assyrian/Chaldean/Syriac (0)	0	<0.01
Australian (0)	0	<0.01
Austrian (0)	54	0.14
Basque (0)	0	<0.01
Belgian (57)	105	0.27
Brazilian (0)	0	<0.01
British (68)	113	0.29
Bulgarian (0)	0	<0.01
Cajun (0)	0	<0.01
Canadian (18)	54	0.14
Carpatho Rusyn (0)	0	<0.01
Celtic (0)	0	<0.01
Croatian (0)	14	0.04
Cypriot (0)	0	<0.01
Czech (0)	35	0.09
Czechoslovakian (0)	49	0.13
Danish (14)	73	0.19
Dutch (62)	467	1.22
Eastern European (0)	0	<0.01
English (1,791)	3,502	9.11
Estonian (0)	0	<0.01
European (130)	169	0.44
Finnish (0)	6	0.02
French, ex. Basque (640)	2,181	5.68
French Canadian (10)	58	0.15
German (4,962)	10,340	26.91
German Russian (0)	0	<0.01
Greek (78)	118	0.31
Guyanese (0)	0	<0.01
Hungarian (36)	128	0.33
Icelander (0)	0	<0.01
Iranian (0)	0	<0.01
Irish (1,408)	4,980	12.96
Israeli (0)	0	<0.01
Italian (249)	825	2.15
Latvian (0)	0	<0.01
Lithuanian (0)	65	0.17
Luxemburger (0)	0	<0.01
Macedonian (0)	0	<0.01
Maltese (0)	0	<0.01
New Zealander (0)	0	<0.01
Northern European (0)	0	<0.01
Norwegian (73)	191	0.50
Pennsylvania German (0)	21	0.05
Polish (249)	347	0.90
Portuguese (0)	0	<0.01
Romanian (0)	0	<0.01
Russian (45)	55	0.14
Scandinavian (12)	12	0.03
Scotch-Irish (305)	581	1.51
Scottish (251)	572	1.49
Serbian (34)	34	0.09
Slavic (0)	0	<0.01
Slovak (0)	0	<0.01
Slovene (0)	0	<0.01
Soviet Union (0)	0	<0.01
Swedish (16)	98	0.26
Swiss (39)	60	0.16
Turkish (0)	0	<0.01
Ukrainian (0)	14	0.04
Welsh (30)	223	0.58
West Indian, ex. Hispanic (34)	34	0.09
Bahamian (34)	34	0.09
Barbadian (0)	0	<0.01
Belizean (0)	0	<0.01
Bermudan (0)	0	<0.01
British West Indian (0)	0	<0.01
Dutch West Indian (0)	0	<0.01
Haitian (0)	0	<0.01
Jamaican (0)	0	<0.01
Trinidadian/Tobagonian (0)	0	<0.01
U.S. Virgin Islander (0)	0	<0.01
West Indian (0)	0	<0.01
Other West Indian (0)	0	<0.01
Yugoslavian (0)	0	<0.01

Hispanic Origin	Population	%
Hispanic or Latino (of any race)	590	1.53
Central American, ex. Mexican	30	0.08
Costa Rican	8	0.02
Guatemalan	11	0.03
Honduran	7	0.02
Nicaraguan	1	<0.01
Panamanian	0	<0.01
Salvadoran	3	0.01
Other Central American	0	<0.01
Cuban	8	0.02
Dominican Republic	0	<0.01
Mexican	421	1.10
Puerto Rican	55	0.14
South American	21	0.05
Argentinean	1	<0.01
Bolivian	1	<0.01
Chilean	0	<0.01
Colombian	7	0.02
Ecuadorian	5	0.01
Paraguayan	0	<0.01
Peruvian	1	<0.01
Uruguayan	1	<0.01
Venezuelan	4	0.01
Other South American	1	<0.01
Other Hispanic or Latino	55	0.14

Race*	Population	%
African-American/Black (1,009)	1,220	3.17
Not Hispanic (994)	1,191	3.10
Hispanic (15)	29	0.08
American Indian/Alaska Native (73)	222	0.58
Not Hispanic (64)	207	0.54
Hispanic (9)	15	0.04
Alaska Athabascan (Ala. Nat.) (0)	0	<0.01
Aleut (Alaska Native) (0)	0	<0.01
Apache (0)	1	<0.01
Arapaho (0)	2	0.01
Blackfeet (2)	12	0.03
Canadian/French Am. Ind. (0)	5	0.01
Central American Ind. (0)	0	<0.01
Cherokee (18)	67	0.17
Cheyenne (4)	6	0.02
Chickasaw (0)	1	<0.01
Chippewa (3)	7	0.02
Choctaw (2)	2	0.01
Colville (0)	0	<0.01
Comanche (0)	0	<0.01
Cree (0)	0	<0.01
Creek (2)	2	0.01
Crow (0)	1	<0.01
Delaware (0)	0	<0.01
Hopi (0)	0	<0.01
Houma (0)	0	<0.01
Inupiat (Alaska Native) (0)	0	<0.01
Iroquois (0)	1	<0.01
Kiowa (0)	0	<0.01
Lumbee (0)	0	<0.01
Menominee (1)	1	<0.01
Mexican American Ind. (4)	5	0.01
Navajo (0)	4	0.01
Osage (1)	3	0.01
Ottawa (0)	0	<0.01
Paiute (0)	0	<0.01
Pima (0)	0	<0.01
Potawatomi (0)	1	<0.01
Pueblo (0)	0	<0.01
Puget Sound Salish (0)	0	<0.01
Seminole (0)	0	<0.01
Shoshone (0)	0	<0.01
Sioux (1)	5	0.01
South American Ind. (1)	1	<0.01
Spanish American Ind. (0)	0	<0.01
Tlingit-Haida (Alaska Native) (0)	0	<0.01
Tohono O'Odham (0)	1	<0.01
Tsimshian (Alaska Native) (0)	0	<0.01
Ute (0)	0	<0.01
Yakama (0)	0	<0.01
Yaqui (0)	0	<0.01
Yuman (0)	0	<0.01
Yup'ik (Alaska Native) (0)	0	<0.01
Asian (215)	281	0.73
Not Hispanic (214)	277	0.72
Hispanic (1)	4	0.01
Bangladeshi (0)	0	<0.01
Bhutanese (0)	0	<0.01
Burmese (10)	10	0.03
Cambodian (1)	3	0.01
Chinese, ex. Taiwanese (31)	41	0.11
Filipino (49)	67	0.17
Hmong (0)	0	<0.01
Indian (30)	34	0.09
Indonesian (0)	0	<0.01
Japanese (21)	36	0.09
Korean (44)	54	0.14
Laotian (0)	0	<0.01
Malaysian (2)	2	0.01
Nepalese (0)	0	<0.01
Pakistani (1)	1	<0.01
Sri Lankan (0)	0	<0.01
Taiwanese (3)	3	0.01
Thai (5)	7	0.02
Vietnamese (12)	14	0.04
Hawaii Native/Pacific Islander (11)	24	0.06
Not Hispanic (11)	24	0.06
Hispanic (0)	0	<0.01
Fijian (0)	0	<0.01
Guamanian/Chamorro (1)	3	0.01
Marshallese (0)	0	<0.01
Native Hawaiian (8)	15	0.04
Samoan (0)	2	0.01
Tongan (0)	0	<0.01
White (36,475)	36,919	96.04
Not Hispanic (36,154)	36,531	95.03
Hispanic (321)	388	1.01

Notes: † The Census 2010 population figure is used to calculate the percentages in the Hispanic Origin and Race categories. Ancestry percentages are based on the 2006-2010 American Community Survey population (not shown); ‡ Numbers in parentheses indicate the number of people reporting a single ancestry; * Numbers in parentheses indicate the number of persons reporting this race alone, not in combination with any other race; Please refer to the Explanation of Data for more information.

Kosciusko County
Population: 77,358

Ancestry	Population	%
Afghan (0)	0	<0.01
African, Sub-Saharan (74)	121	0.16
African (15)	62	0.08
Cape Verdean (0)	0	<0.01
Ethiopian (0)	0	<0.01
Ghanaian (0)	0	<0.01
Kenyan (0)	0	<0.01
Liberian (0)	0	<0.01
Nigerian (0)	0	<0.01
Senegalese (0)	0	<0.01
Sierra Leonean (0)	0	<0.01
Somalian (0)	0	<0.01
South African (59)	59	0.08
Sudanese (0)	0	<0.01
Ugandan (0)	0	<0.01
Zimbabwean (0)	0	<0.01
Other Sub-Saharan African (0)	0	<0.01
Albanian (0)	0	<0.01
Alsatian (0)	0	<0.01
American (6,279)	6,279	8.16
Arab (52)	81	0.11
Arab (0)	0	<0.01
Egyptian (0)	0	<0.01
Iraqi (0)	0	<0.01
Jordanian (21)	21	0.03
Lebanese (31)	49	0.06
Moroccan (0)	0	<0.01
Palestinian (0)	0	<0.01
Syrian (0)	0	<0.01
Other Arab (0)	11	0.01
Armenian (0)	15	0.02
Assyrian/Chaldean/Syriac (0)	0	<0.01
Australian (0)	8	0.01
Austrian (59)	90	0.12
Basque (0)	0	<0.01
Belgian (36)	188	0.24
Brazilian (0)	0	<0.01
British (98)	109	0.14
Bulgarian (11)	11	0.01
Cajun (0)	0	<0.01
Canadian (38)	74	0.10
Carpatho Rusyn (0)	13	0.02
Celtic (0)	0	<0.01
Croatian (0)	24	0.03
Cypriot (0)	0	<0.01
Czech (12)	31	0.04
Czechoslovakian (19)	19	0.02
Danish (15)	83	0.11
Dutch (660)	2,983	3.87
Eastern European (30)	30	0.04
English (3,275)	8,348	10.84
Estonian (0)	0	<0.01
European (592)	612	0.79
Finnish (12)	33	0.04
French, ex. Basque (297)	2,131	2.77
French Canadian (127)	248	0.32
German (11,595)	25,753	33.45
German Russian (0)	0	<0.01
Greek (175)	439	0.57
Guyanese (0)	0	<0.01
Hungarian (135)	364	0.47
Icelander (9)	9	0.01
Iranian (0)	0	<0.01
Irish (2,722)	8,867	11.52
Israeli (0)	0	<0.01
Italian (796)	1,855	2.41
Latvian (0)	8	0.01
Lithuanian (91)	114	0.15
Luxemburger (0)	0	<0.01
Macedonian (0)	0	<0.01
Maltese (0)	0	<0.01
New Zealander (0)	0	<0.01
Northern European (12)	12	0.02
Norwegian (145)	485	0.63
Pennsylvania German (336)	445	0.58
Polish (494)	1,845	2.40
Portuguese (23)	69	0.09
Romanian (0)	15	0.02
Russian (12)	119	0.15
Scandinavian (0)	49	0.06
Scotch-Irish (242)	784	1.02
Scottish (478)	1,343	1.74
Serbian (2)	41	0.05
Slavic (0)	0	<0.01
Slovak (3)	44	0.06
Slovene (11)	11	0.01
Soviet Union (0)	0	<0.01
Swedish (130)	547	0.71
Swiss (386)	1,393	1.81
Turkish (0)	0	<0.01
Ukrainian (18)	45	0.06
Welsh (248)	864	1.12
West Indian, ex. Hispanic (0)	0	<0.01
Bahamian (0)	0	<0.01
Barbadian (0)	0	<0.01
Belizean (0)	0	<0.01
Bermudan (0)	0	<0.01
British West Indian (0)	0	<0.01
Dutch West Indian (0)	0	<0.01
Haitian (0)	0	<0.01
Jamaican (0)	0	<0.01
Trinidadian/Tobagonian (0)	0	<0.01
U.S. Virgin Islander (0)	0	<0.01
West Indian (0)	0	<0.01
Other West Indian (0)	0	<0.01
Yugoslavian (10)	23	0.03

Hispanic Origin	Population	%
Hispanic or Latino (of any race)	5,634	7.28
Central American, ex. Mexican	137	0.18
Costa Rican	5	0.01
Guatemalan	55	0.07
Honduran	47	0.06
Nicaraguan	5	0.01
Panamanian	13	0.02
Salvadoran	12	0.02
Other Central American	0	<0.01
Cuban	16	0.02
Dominican Republic	7	0.01
Mexican	4,942	6.39
Puerto Rican	118	0.15
South American	106	0.14
Argentinean	30	0.04
Bolivian	0	<0.01
Chilean	4	0.01
Colombian	37	0.05
Ecuadorian	10	0.01
Paraguayan	0	<0.01
Peruvian	18	0.02
Uruguayan	0	<0.01
Venezuelan	3	<0.01
Other South American	4	0.01
Other Hispanic or Latino	308	0.40

Race*	Population	%
African-American/Black (572)	871	1.13
Not Hispanic (542)	816	1.05
Hispanic (30)	55	0.07
American Indian/Alaska Native (232)	525	0.68
Not Hispanic (178)	450	0.58
Hispanic (54)	75	0.10
Alaska Athabascan (Ala. Nat.) (0)	0	<0.01
Aleut (Alaska Native) (1)	1	<0.01
Apache (6)	10	0.01
Arapaho (0)	0	<0.01
Blackfeet (5)	27	0.03
Canadian/French Am. Ind. (0)	0	<0.01
Central American Ind. (0)	0	<0.01
Cherokee (41)	119	0.15
Cheyenne (0)	0	<0.01
Chickasaw (0)	2	<0.01
Chippewa (12)	22	0.03
Choctaw (9)	15	0.02
Colville (0)	0	<0.01
Comanche (2)	2	<0.01
Cree (0)	0	<0.01
Creek (3)	6	0.01
Crow (0)	2	<0.01
Delaware (0)	0	<0.01
Hopi (0)	0	<0.01
Houma (0)	0	<0.01
Inupiat (Alaska Native) (1)	1	<0.01
Iroquois (0)	6	0.01
Kiowa (0)	0	<0.01
Lumbee (0)	0	<0.01
Menominee (1)	3	<0.01
Mexican American Ind. (14)	14	0.02
Navajo (6)	8	0.01
Osage (0)	0	<0.01
Ottawa (1)	1	<0.01
Paiute (1)	1	<0.01
Pima (0)	0	<0.01
Potawatomi (7)	12	0.02
Pueblo (1)	1	<0.01
Puget Sound Salish (0)	0	<0.01
Seminole (0)	1	<0.01
Shoshone (0)	0	<0.01
Sioux (3)	9	0.01
South American Ind. (2)	6	0.01
Spanish American Ind. (2)	2	<0.01
Tlingit-Haida (Alaska Native) (0)	0	<0.01
Tohono O'Odham (0)	0	<0.01
Tsimshian (Alaska Native) (0)	0	<0.01
Ute (0)	0	<0.01
Yakama (1)	2	<0.01
Yaqui (0)	0	<0.01
Yuman (0)	0	<0.01
Yup'ik (Alaska Native) (0)	0	<0.01
Asian (650)	832	1.08
Not Hispanic (642)	815	1.05
Hispanic (8)	17	0.02
Bangladeshi (0)	0	<0.01
Bhutanese (0)	0	<0.01
Burmese (0)	1	<0.01
Cambodian (25)	33	0.04
Chinese, ex. Taiwanese (149)	180	0.23
Filipino (87)	132	0.17
Hmong (0)	0	<0.01
Indian (224)	236	0.31
Indonesian (1)	1	<0.01
Japanese (19)	50	0.06
Korean (52)	82	0.11
Laotian (20)	24	0.03
Malaysian (0)	0	<0.01
Nepalese (4)	4	0.01
Pakistani (7)	9	0.01
Sri Lankan (0)	0	<0.01
Taiwanese (0)	0	<0.01
Thai (18)	21	0.03
Vietnamese (35)	53	0.07
Hawaii Native/Pacific Islander (19)	55	0.07
Not Hispanic (19)	48	0.06
Hispanic (0)	7	0.01
Fijian (0)	0	<0.01
Guamanian/Chamorro (4)	14	0.02
Marshallese (0)	0	<0.01
Native Hawaiian (5)	24	0.03
Samoan (5)	5	0.01
Tongan (0)	0	<0.01
White (72,188)	73,202	94.63
Not Hispanic (69,531)	70,242	90.80
Hispanic (2,657)	2,960	3.83

Notes: † The Census 2010 population figure is used to calculate the percentages in the Hispanic Origin and Race categories. Ancestry percentages are based on the 2006-2010 American Community Survey population (not shown); ‡ Numbers in parentheses indicate the number of people reporting a single ancestry; * Numbers in parentheses indicate the number of persons reporting this race alone, not in combination with any other race; Please refer to the Explanation of Data for more information.

LaGrange County
Population: 37,128

Ancestry	Population	%
Afghan (0)	0	<0.01
African, Sub-Saharan (3)	3	0.01
African (0)	0	<0.01
Cape Verdean (0)	0	<0.01
Ethiopian (3)	3	0.01
Ghanaian (0)	0	<0.01
Kenyan (0)	0	<0.01
Liberian (0)	0	<0.01
Nigerian (0)	0	<0.01
Senegalese (0)	0	<0.01
Sierra Leonean (0)	0	<0.01
Somalian (0)	0	<0.01
South African (0)	0	<0.01
Sudanese (0)	0	<0.01
Ugandan (0)	0	<0.01
Zimbabwean (0)	0	<0.01
Other Sub-Saharan African (0)	0	<0.01
Albanian (0)	0	<0.01
Alsatian (0)	0	<0.01
American (4,915)	4,915	13.29
Arab (38)	38	0.10
Arab (0)	0	<0.01
Egyptian (0)	0	<0.01
Iraqi (0)	0	<0.01
Jordanian (0)	0	<0.01
Lebanese (0)	0	<0.01
Moroccan (0)	0	<0.01
Palestinian (0)	0	<0.01
Syrian (0)	0	<0.01
Other Arab (38)	38	0.10
Armenian (0)	0	<0.01
Assyrian/Chaldean/Syriac (0)	0	<0.01
Australian (0)	0	<0.01
Austrian (0)	9	0.02
Basque (0)	0	<0.01
Belgian (0)	0	<0.01
Brazilian (0)	0	<0.01
British (0)	0	<0.01
Bulgarian (0)	0	<0.01
Cajun (0)	0	<0.01
Canadian (0)	9	0.02
Carpatho Rusyn (0)	0	<0.01
Celtic (0)	0	<0.01
Croatian (0)	0	<0.01
Cypriot (0)	0	<0.01
Czech (12)	12	0.03
Czechoslovakian (0)	9	0.02
Danish (9)	53	0.14
Dutch (383)	850	2.30
Eastern European (0)	0	<0.01
English (1,188)	2,364	6.39
Estonian (0)	0	<0.01
European (348)	377	1.02
Finnish (27)	50	0.14
French, ex. Basque (92)	734	1.98
French Canadian (8)	115	0.31
German (7,663)	13,346	36.07
German Russian (0)	0	<0.01
Greek (36)	50	0.14
Guyanese (0)	0	<0.01
Hungarian (44)	76	0.21
Icelander (0)	0	<0.01
Iranian (0)	0	<0.01
Irish (478)	2,377	6.43
Israeli (0)	0	<0.01
Italian (252)	409	1.11
Latvian (0)	0	<0.01
Lithuanian (0)	7	0.02
Luxemburger (0)	0	<0.01
Macedonian (0)	0	<0.01
Maltese (0)	0	<0.01
New Zealander (0)	0	<0.01
Northern European (0)	0	<0.01
Norwegian (0)	46	0.12
Pennsylvania German (1,342)	1,373	3.71
Polish (174)	553	1.49
Portuguese (0)	0	<0.01
Romanian (0)	13	0.04
Russian (10)	10	0.03
Scandinavian (5)	14	0.04
Scotch-Irish (173)	365	0.99
Scottish (109)	393	1.06
Serbian (0)	0	<0.01
Slavic (0)	22	0.06
Slovak (0)	20	0.05
Slovene (0)	0	<0.01
Soviet Union (0)	0	<0.01
Swedish (190)	397	1.07
Swiss (2,569)	4,215	11.39
Turkish (0)	0	<0.01
Ukrainian (8)	8	0.02
Welsh (10)	82	0.22
West Indian, ex. Hispanic (0)	0	<0.01
Bahamian (0)	0	<0.01
Barbadian (0)	0	<0.01
Belizean (0)	0	<0.01
Bermudan (0)	0	<0.01
British West Indian (0)	0	<0.01
Dutch West Indian (0)	0	<0.01
Haitian (0)	0	<0.01
Jamaican (0)	0	<0.01
Trinidadian/Tobagonian (0)	0	<0.01
U.S. Virgin Islander (0)	0	<0.01
West Indian (0)	0	<0.01
Other West Indian (0)	0	<0.01
Yugoslavian (0)	0	<0.01

Hispanic Origin	Population	%
Hispanic or Latino (of any race)	1,317	3.55
Central American, ex. Mexican	28	0.08
Costa Rican	0	<0.01
Guatemalan	2	0.01
Honduran	1	<0.01
Nicaraguan	0	<0.01
Panamanian	3	0.01
Salvadoran	21	0.06
Other Central American	1	<0.01
Cuban	5	0.01
Dominican Republic	0	<0.01
Mexican	1,197	3.22
Puerto Rican	27	0.07
South American	12	0.03
Argentinean	0	<0.01
Bolivian	5	0.01
Chilean	0	<0.01
Colombian	0	<0.01
Ecuadorian	3	0.01
Paraguayan	3	0.01
Peruvian	1	<0.01
Uruguayan	0	<0.01
Venezuelan	0	<0.01
Other South American	0	<0.01
Other Hispanic or Latino	48	0.13

Race*	Population	%
African-American/Black (117)	182	0.49
Not Hispanic (109)	161	0.43
Hispanic (8)	21	0.06
American Indian/Alaska Native (71)	176	0.47
Not Hispanic (65)	165	0.44
Hispanic (6)	11	0.03
Alaska Athabascan (Ala. Nat.) (0)	0	<0.01
Aleut (Alaska Native) (1)	1	<0.01
Apache (0)	0	<0.01
Arapaho (0)	0	<0.01
Blackfeet (1)	2	0.01
Canadian/French Am. Ind. (0)	1	<0.01
Central American Ind. (0)	0	<0.01
Cherokee (19)	51	0.14
Cheyenne (0)	0	<0.01
Chickasaw (0)	0	<0.01
Chippewa (9)	13	0.04
Choctaw (0)	0	<0.01
Colville (0)	0	<0.01
Comanche (0)	0	<0.01
Cree (0)	1	<0.01
Creek (0)	0	<0.01
Crow (0)	0	<0.01
Delaware (0)	0	<0.01
Hopi (0)	0	<0.01
Houma (0)	0	<0.01
Inupiat (Alaska Native) (0)	0	<0.01
Iroquois (0)	1	<0.01
Kiowa (0)	0	<0.01
Lumbee (0)	0	<0.01
Menominee (0)	0	<0.01
Mexican American Ind. (0)	0	<0.01
Navajo (1)	7	0.02
Osage (0)	0	<0.01
Ottawa (1)	3	0.01
Paiute (0)	0	<0.01
Pima (0)	0	<0.01
Potawatomi (6)	10	0.03
Pueblo (1)	1	<0.01
Puget Sound Salish (0)	0	<0.01
Seminole (0)	1	<0.01
Shoshone (0)	0	<0.01
Sioux (2)	6	0.02
South American Ind. (0)	0	<0.01
Spanish American Ind. (0)	0	<0.01
Tlingit-Haida (Alaska Native) (0)	0	<0.01
Tohono O'Odham (0)	1	<0.01
Tsimshian (Alaska Native) (0)	0	<0.01
Ute (0)	0	<0.01
Yakama (0)	0	<0.01
Yaqui (0)	0	<0.01
Yuman (0)	0	<0.01
Yup'ik (Alaska Native) (0)	0	<0.01
Asian (118)	196	0.53
Not Hispanic (118)	186	0.50
Hispanic (0)	10	0.03
Bangladeshi (0)	0	<0.01
Bhutanese (0)	0	<0.01
Burmese (7)	7	0.02
Cambodian (0)	0	<0.01
Chinese, ex. Taiwanese (42)	51	0.14
Filipino (20)	24	0.06
Hmong (0)	0	<0.01
Indian (10)	26	0.07
Indonesian (0)	0	<0.01
Japanese (3)	9	0.02
Korean (12)	20	0.05
Laotian (0)	1	<0.01
Malaysian (0)	0	<0.01
Nepalese (0)	0	<0.01
Pakistani (0)	0	<0.01
Sri Lankan (0)	0	<0.01
Taiwanese (0)	2	0.01
Thai (4)	4	0.01
Vietnamese (12)	22	0.06
Hawaii Native/Pacific Islander (2)	10	0.03
Not Hispanic (1)	7	0.02
Hispanic (1)	3	0.01
Fijian (0)	0	<0.01
Guamanian/Chamorro (2)	3	0.01
Marshallese (0)	0	<0.01
Native Hawaiian (0)	5	0.01
Samoan (0)	0	<0.01
Tongan (0)	0	<0.01
White (35,874)	36,168	97.41
Not Hispanic (35,290)	35,507	95.63
Hispanic (584)	661	1.78

Notes: † The Census 2010 population figure is used to calculate the percentages in the Hispanic Origin and Race categories. Ancestry percentages are based on the 2006-2010 American Community Survey population (not shown); ‡ Numbers in parentheses indicate the number of people reporting a single ancestry; * Numbers in parentheses indicate the number of persons reporting this race alone, not in combination with any other race; Please refer to the Explanation of Data for more information.

LaPorte County
Population: 111,467

Ancestry	Population	%
Afghan (0)	0	<0.01
African, Sub-Saharan (1,031)	1,164	1.05
African (1,015)	1,148	1.03
Cape Verdean (0)	0	<0.01
Ethiopian (8)	8	0.01
Ghanaian (0)	0	<0.01
Kenyan (0)	0	<0.01
Liberian (0)	0	<0.01
Nigerian (8)	8	0.01
Senegalese (0)	0	<0.01
Sierra Leonean (0)	0	<0.01
Somalian (0)	0	<0.01
South African (0)	0	<0.01
Sudanese (0)	0	<0.01
Ugandan (0)	0	<0.01
Zimbabwean (0)	0	<0.01
Other Sub-Saharan African (0)	0	<0.01
Albanian (26)	42	0.04
Alsatian (0)	0	<0.01
American (6,496)	6,496	5.86
Arab (388)	627	0.57
Arab (8)	30	0.03
Egyptian (0)	0	<0.01
Iraqi (0)	0	<0.01
Jordanian (0)	0	<0.01
Lebanese (348)	555	0.50
Moroccan (15)	15	0.01
Palestinian (7)	7	0.01
Syrian (10)	20	0.02
Other Arab (0)	0	<0.01
Armenian (21)	36	0.03
Assyrian/Chaldean/Syriac (0)	18	0.02
Australian (5)	5	<0.01
Austrian (46)	222	0.20
Basque (0)	0	<0.01
Belgian (73)	225	0.20
Brazilian (0)	0	<0.01
British (137)	336	0.30
Bulgarian (0)	0	<0.01
Cajun (0)	0	<0.01
Canadian (74)	129	0.12
Carpatho Rusyn (0)	0	<0.01
Celtic (11)	14	0.01
Croatian (39)	136	0.12
Cypriot (0)	0	<0.01
Czech (132)	940	0.85
Czechoslovakian (101)	152	0.14
Danish (51)	325	0.29
Dutch (662)	2,757	2.49
Eastern European (23)	23	0.02
English (2,406)	9,237	8.33
Estonian (0)	0	<0.01
European (947)	1,001	0.90
Finnish (33)	115	0.10
French, ex. Basque (422)	2,330	2.10
French Canadian (190)	412	0.37
German (12,739)	34,098	30.74
German Russian (0)	0	<0.01
Greek (160)	366	0.33
Guyanese (0)	0	<0.01
Hungarian (301)	1,270	1.14
Icelander (0)	5	<0.01
Iranian (60)	60	0.05
Irish (4,123)	17,004	15.33
Israeli (0)	0	<0.01
Italian (920)	3,794	3.42
Latvian (0)	17	0.02
Lithuanian (197)	606	0.55
Luxemburger (10)	10	0.01
Macedonian (0)	0	<0.01
Maltese (0)	0	<0.01
New Zealander (0)	0	<0.01
Northern European (24)	24	0.02
Norwegian (257)	691	0.62
Pennsylvania German (36)	87	0.08
Polish (5,037)	12,809	11.55
Portuguese (7)	69	0.06
Romanian (33)	159	0.14
Russian (149)	490	0.44
Scandinavian (71)	201	0.18
Scotch-Irish (327)	1,160	1.05
Scottish (486)	1,879	1.69
Serbian (45)	155	0.14
Slavic (42)	134	0.12
Slovak (127)	338	0.30
Slovene (53)	99	0.09
Soviet Union (0)	0	<0.01
Swedish (804)	2,892	2.61
Swiss (93)	401	0.36
Turkish (0)	0	<0.01
Ukrainian (88)	135	0.12
Welsh (90)	436	0.39
West Indian, ex. Hispanic (68)	76	0.07
Bahamian (0)	0	<0.01
Barbadian (0)	0	<0.01
Belizean (0)	0	<0.01
Bermudan (9)	9	0.01
British West Indian (0)	0	<0.01
Dutch West Indian (0)	0	<0.01
Haitian (28)	28	0.03
Jamaican (31)	39	0.04
Trinidadian/Tobagonian (0)	0	<0.01
U.S. Virgin Islander (0)	0	<0.01
West Indian (0)	0	<0.01
Other West Indian (0)	0	<0.01
Yugoslavian (3)	42	0.04

Hispanic Origin	Population	%
Hispanic or Latino (of any race)	6,093	5.47
Central American, ex. Mexican	109	0.10
Costa Rican	3	<0.01
Guatemalan	33	0.03
Honduran	10	0.01
Nicaraguan	20	0.02
Panamanian	24	0.02
Salvadoran	19	0.02
Other Central American	0	<0.01
Cuban	65	0.06
Dominican Republic	6	0.01
Mexican	4,997	4.48
Puerto Rican	498	0.45
South American	65	0.06
Argentinean	5	<0.01
Bolivian	2	<0.01
Chilean	1	<0.01
Colombian	24	0.02
Ecuadorian	3	<0.01
Paraguayan	0	<0.01
Peruvian	23	0.02
Uruguayan	2	<0.01
Venezuelan	2	<0.01
Other South American	3	<0.01
Other Hispanic or Latino	353	0.32

Race*	Population	%
African-American/Black (12,001)	13,400	12.02
Not Hispanic (11,835)	13,082	11.74
Hispanic (166)	318	0.29
American Indian/Alaska Native (306)	886	0.79
Not Hispanic (246)	750	0.67
Hispanic (60)	136	0.12
Alaska Athabascan (Ala. Nat.) (1)	1	<0.01
Aleut (Alaska Native) (1)	1	<0.01
Apache (6)	28	0.03
Arapaho (0)	0	<0.01
Blackfeet (5)	66	0.06
Canadian/French Am. Ind. (1)	4	<0.01
Central American Ind. (0)	0	<0.01
Cherokee (51)	245	0.22
Cheyenne (0)	3	<0.01
Chickasaw (3)	9	0.01
Chippewa (19)	38	0.03
Choctaw (3)	7	0.01
Colville (1)	1	<0.01
Comanche (1)	1	<0.01
Cree (0)	0	<0.01
Creek (4)	5	<0.01
Crow (0)	2	<0.01
Delaware (0)	1	<0.01
Hopi (0)	1	<0.01
Houma (0)	0	<0.01
Inupiat (Alaska Native) (0)	0	<0.01
Iroquois (1)	12	0.01
Kiowa (0)	0	<0.01
Lumbee (0)	0	<0.01
Menominee (3)	4	<0.01
Mexican American Ind. (15)	23	0.02
Navajo (5)	15	0.01
Osage (0)	0	<0.01
Ottawa (1)	1	<0.01
Paiute (0)	0	<0.01
Pima (0)	0	<0.01
Potawatomi (7)	17	0.02
Pueblo (0)	0	<0.01
Puget Sound Salish (0)	0	<0.01
Seminole (0)	0	<0.01
Shoshone (0)	2	<0.01
Sioux (9)	31	0.03
South American Ind. (1)	2	<0.01
Spanish American Ind. (1)	1	<0.01
Tlingit-Haida (Alaska Native) (0)	0	<0.01
Tohono O'Odham (1)	1	<0.01
Tsimshian (Alaska Native) (0)	0	<0.01
Ute (0)	0	<0.01
Yakama (0)	0	<0.01
Yaqui (0)	0	<0.01
Yuman (0)	0	<0.01
Yup'ik (Alaska Native) (0)	0	<0.01
Asian (583)	883	0.79
Not Hispanic (570)	828	0.74
Hispanic (13)	55	0.05
Bangladeshi (0)	0	<0.01
Bhutanese (0)	0	<0.01
Burmese (0)	0	<0.01
Cambodian (3)	3	<0.01
Chinese, ex. Taiwanese (114)	137	0.12
Filipino (119)	203	0.18
Hmong (0)	0	<0.01
Indian (161)	203	0.18
Indonesian (2)	5	<0.01
Japanese (30)	84	0.08
Korean (57)	88	0.08
Laotian (1)	1	<0.01
Malaysian (0)	0	<0.01
Nepalese (0)	0	<0.01
Pakistani (15)	20	0.02
Sri Lankan (4)	5	<0.01
Taiwanese (5)	7	0.01
Thai (11)	16	0.01
Vietnamese (42)	52	0.05
Hawaii Native/Pacific Islander (21)	77	0.07
Not Hispanic (13)	55	0.05
Hispanic (8)	22	0.02
Fijian (0)	0	<0.01
Guamanian/Chamorro (3)	5	<0.01
Marshallese (0)	0	<0.01
Native Hawaiian (7)	31	0.03
Samoan (6)	14	0.01
Tongan (0)	2	<0.01
White (93,787)	96,128	86.24
Not Hispanic (90,695)	92,503	82.99
Hispanic (3,092)	3,625	3.25

Notes: † The Census 2010 population figure is used to calculate the percentages in the Hispanic Origin and Race categories. Ancestry percentages are based on the 2006-2010 American Community Survey population (not shown); ‡ Numbers in parentheses indicate the number of people reporting a single ancestry; * Numbers in parentheses indicate the number of persons reporting this race alone, not in combination with any other race; Please refer to the Explanation of Data for more information.

Lake County
Population: 496,005

Ancestry	Population	%
Afghan (3)	3	<0.01
African, Sub-Saharan (4,161)	4,695	0.95
African (3,731)	4,119	0.83
Cape Verdean (9)	28	0.01
Ethiopian (171)	171	0.03
Ghanaian (28)	40	0.01
Kenyan (0)	0	<0.01
Liberian (0)	11	<0.01
Nigerian (179)	270	0.05
Senegalese (0)	0	<0.01
Sierra Leonean (0)	0	<0.01
Somalian (0)	0	<0.01
South African (43)	43	0.01
Sudanese (0)	0	<0.01
Ugandan (0)	0	<0.01
Zimbabwean (0)	0	<0.01
Other Sub-Saharan African (0)	13	<0.01
Albanian (31)	113	0.02
Alsatian (0)	18	<0.01
American (18,230)	18,230	3.69
Arab (1,852)	2,164	0.44
Arab (643)	753	0.15
Egyptian (294)	294	0.06
Iraqi (0)	0	<0.01
Jordanian (104)	104	0.02
Lebanese (105)	170	0.03
Moroccan (27)	57	0.01
Palestinian (475)	545	0.11
Syrian (142)	162	0.03
Other Arab (62)	79	0.02
Armenian (67)	104	0.02
Assyrian/Chaldean/Syriac (89)	99	0.02
Australian (39)	56	0.01
Austrian (154)	761	0.15
Basque (0)	0	<0.01
Belgian (121)	529	0.11
Brazilian (58)	80	0.02
British (271)	596	0.12
Bulgarian (134)	204	0.04
Cajun (0)	0	<0.01
Canadian (121)	447	0.09
Carpatho Rusyn (24)	33	0.01
Celtic (0)	7	<0.01
Croatian (1,920)	6,296	1.27
Cypriot (0)	0	<0.01
Czech (699)	2,416	0.49
Czechoslovakian (330)	845	0.17
Danish (179)	1,008	0.20
Dutch (5,546)	14,612	2.96
Eastern European (369)	412	0.08
English (7,382)	26,727	5.41
Estonian (0)	51	0.01
European (1,875)	2,139	0.43
Finnish (81)	403	0.08
French, ex. Basque (1,095)	8,687	1.76
French Canadian (266)	1,263	0.26
German (22,632)	79,686	16.12
German Russian (0)	0	<0.01
Greek (3,437)	5,765	1.17
Guyanese (14)	14	<0.01
Hungarian (2,159)	6,256	1.27
Icelander (14)	28	0.01
Iranian (0)	9	<0.01
Irish (12,098)	54,906	11.11
Israeli (0)	0	<0.01
Italian (7,796)	23,510	4.76
Latvian (0)	118	0.02
Lithuanian (1,156)	3,170	0.64
Luxemburger (0)	19	<0.01
Macedonian (2,383)	2,623	0.53
Maltese (10)	58	0.01
New Zealander (0)	0	<0.01
Northern European (225)	243	0.05
Norwegian (628)	2,635	0.53
Pennsylvania German (63)	281	0.06
Polish (18,732)	47,271	9.56
Portuguese (41)	191	0.04
Romanian (684)	1,504	0.30
Russian (956)	2,898	0.59
Scandinavian (37)	306	0.06
Scotch-Irish (1,452)	4,669	0.94
Scottish (1,170)	5,537	1.12
Serbian (3,318)	5,406	1.09
Slavic (164)	312	0.06
Slovak (3,772)	9,890	2.00
Slovene (123)	262	0.05
Soviet Union (0)	0	<0.01
Swedish (1,440)	7,763	1.57
Swiss (123)	755	0.15
Turkish (141)	176	0.04
Ukrainian (616)	1,355	0.27
Welsh (438)	1,892	0.38
West Indian, ex. Hispanic (377)	710	0.14
Bahamian (0)	14	<0.01
Barbadian (0)	0	<0.01
Belizean (31)	31	0.01
Bermudan (0)	0	<0.01
British West Indian (0)	64	0.01
Dutch West Indian (0)	0	<0.01
Haitian (42)	100	0.02
Jamaican (254)	353	0.07
Trinidadian/Tobagonian (18)	18	<0.01
U.S. Virgin Islander (0)	0	<0.01
West Indian (7)	105	0.02
Other West Indian (25)	25	0.01
Yugoslavian (404)	753	0.15

Hispanic Origin	Population	%
Hispanic or Latino (of any race)	82,663	16.67
Central American, ex. Mexican	1,194	0.24
Costa Rican	34	0.01
Guatemalan	390	0.08
Honduran	265	0.05
Nicaraguan	92	0.02
Panamanian	78	0.02
Salvadoran	325	0.07
Other Central American	10	<0.01
Cuban	467	0.09
Dominican Republic	125	0.03
Mexican	64,912	13.09
Puerto Rican	11,991	2.42
South American	719	0.14
Argentinean	103	0.02
Bolivian	24	<0.01
Chilean	36	0.01
Colombian	185	0.04
Ecuadorian	143	0.03
Paraguayan	4	<0.01
Peruvian	170	0.03
Uruguayan	19	<0.01
Venezuelan	33	0.01
Other South American	2	<0.01
Other Hispanic or Latino	3,255	0.66

Race*	Population	%
African-American/Black (128,263)	133,434	26.90
Not Hispanic (125,506)	129,279	26.06
Hispanic (2,757)	4,155	0.84
American Indian/Alaska Native (1,628)	4,217	0.85
Not Hispanic (913)	2,839	0.57
Hispanic (715)	1,378	0.28
Alaska Athabascan (Ala. Nat.) (3)	8	<0.01
Aleut (Alaska Native) (1)	1	<0.01
Apache (32)	87	0.02
Arapaho (1)	8	<0.01
Blackfeet (26)	155	0.03
Canadian/French Am. Ind. (10)	24	<0.01
Central American Ind. (5)	10	<0.01
Cherokee (158)	872	0.18
Cheyenne (1)	9	<0.01
Chickasaw (4)	13	<0.01
Chippewa (50)	113	0.02
Choctaw (13)	72	0.01
Colville (0)	0	<0.01
Comanche (3)	8	<0.01
Cree (4)	11	<0.01
Creek (25)	56	0.01
Crow (2)	8	<0.01
Delaware (2)	12	<0.01
Hopi (1)	2	<0.01
Houma (5)	6	<0.01
Inupiat (Alaska Native) (2)	11	<0.01
Iroquois (21)	52	0.01
Kiowa (2)	3	<0.01
Lumbee (8)	13	<0.01
Menominee (4)	20	<0.01
Mexican American Ind. (124)	203	0.04
Navajo (12)	39	0.01
Osage (3)	5	<0.01
Ottawa (2)	10	<0.01
Paiute (3)	4	<0.01
Pima (1)	3	<0.01
Potawatomi (12)	29	0.01
Pueblo (4)	6	<0.01
Puget Sound Salish (0)	2	<0.01
Seminole (0)	19	<0.01
Shoshone (8)	11	<0.01
Sioux (41)	105	0.02
South American Ind. (15)	51	0.01
Spanish American Ind. (5)	9	<0.01
Tlingit-Haida (Alaska Native) (10)	13	<0.01
Tohono O'Odham (1)	1	<0.01
Tsimshian (Alaska Native) (1)	1	<0.01
Ute (6)	7	<0.01
Yakama (0)	0	<0.01
Yaqui (4)	6	<0.01
Yuman (0)	0	<0.01
Yup'ik (Alaska Native) (0)	2	<0.01
Asian (6,142)	7,952	1.60
Not Hispanic (5,981)	7,441	1.50
Hispanic (161)	511	0.10
Bangladeshi (34)	39	0.01
Bhutanese (0)	0	<0.01
Burmese (5)	5	<0.01
Cambodian (25)	30	0.01
Chinese, ex. Taiwanese (1,038)	1,278	0.26
Filipino (1,464)	2,054	0.41
Hmong (4)	5	<0.01
Indian (1,899)	2,115	0.43
Indonesian (23)	41	0.01
Japanese (123)	335	0.07
Korean (514)	704	0.14
Laotian (17)	20	<0.01
Malaysian (5)	13	<0.01
Nepalese (14)	15	<0.01
Pakistani (320)	364	0.07
Sri Lankan (4)	4	<0.01
Taiwanese (36)	44	0.01
Thai (126)	194	0.04
Vietnamese (280)	367	0.07
Hawaii Native/Pacific Islander (108)	408	0.08
Not Hispanic (63)	256	0.05
Hispanic (45)	152	0.03
Fijian (1)	5	<0.01
Guamanian/Chamorro (15)	55	0.01
Marshallese (0)	0	<0.01
Native Hawaiian (47)	112	0.02
Samoan (18)	71	0.01
Tongan (0)	0	<0.01
White (319,412)	329,031	66.34
Not Hispanic (274,162)	279,401	56.33
Hispanic (45,250)	49,630	10.01

Notes: † The Census 2010 population figure is used to calculate the percentages in the Hispanic Origin and Race categories. Ancestry percentages are based on the 2006-2010 American Community Survey population (not shown); ‡ Numbers in parentheses indicate the number of people reporting a single ancestry; * Numbers in parentheses indicate the number of persons reporting this race alone, not in combination with any other race; Please refer to the Explanation of Data for more information.

Lawrence County
Population: 46,134

Ancestry	Population	%
Afghan (0)	0	<0.01
African, Sub-Saharan (0)	0	<0.01
African (0)	0	<0.01
Cape Verdean (0)	0	<0.01
Ethiopian (0)	0	<0.01
Ghanaian (0)	0	<0.01
Kenyan (0)	0	<0.01
Liberian (0)	0	<0.01
Nigerian (0)	0	<0.01
Senegalese (0)	0	<0.01
Sierra Leonean (0)	0	<0.01
Somalian (0)	0	<0.01
South African (0)	0	<0.01
Sudanese (0)	0	<0.01
Ugandan (0)	0	<0.01
Zimbabwean (0)	0	<0.01
Other Sub-Saharan African (0)	0	<0.01
Albanian (0)	0	<0.01
Alsatian (0)	0	<0.01
American (6,069)	6,069	13.14
Arab (11)	11	0.02
Arab (1)	1	<0.01
Egyptian (10)	10	0.02
Iraqi (0)	0	<0.01
Jordanian (0)	0	<0.01
Lebanese (0)	0	<0.01
Moroccan (0)	0	<0.01
Palestinian (0)	0	<0.01
Syrian (0)	0	<0.01
Other Arab (0)	0	<0.01
Armenian (0)	0	<0.01
Assyrian/Chaldean/Syriac (0)	0	<0.01
Australian (0)	0	<0.01
Austrian (21)	67	0.15
Basque (0)	0	<0.01
Belgian (11)	11	0.02
Brazilian (10)	10	0.02
British (33)	64	0.14
Bulgarian (0)	0	<0.01
Cajun (0)	0	<0.01
Canadian (49)	67	0.15
Carpatho Rusyn (0)	0	<0.01
Celtic (3)	3	0.01
Croatian (0)	36	0.08
Cypriot (0)	0	<0.01
Czech (0)	37	0.08
Czechoslovakian (0)	0	<0.01
Danish (58)	105	0.23
Dutch (163)	593	1.28
Eastern European (9)	9	0.02
English (2,075)	4,826	10.45
Estonian (0)	0	<0.01
European (302)	403	0.87
Finnish (0)	57	0.12
French, ex. Basque (300)	1,128	2.44
French Canadian (158)	202	0.44
German (3,506)	8,521	18.45
German Russian (0)	0	<0.01
Greek (16)	57	0.12
Guyanese (0)	0	<0.01
Hungarian (59)	112	0.24
Icelander (0)	0	<0.01
Iranian (0)	0	<0.01
Irish (2,296)	6,726	14.56
Israeli (0)	0	<0.01
Italian (457)	1,098	2.38
Latvian (0)	0	<0.01
Lithuanian (28)	37	0.08
Luxemburger (0)	0	<0.01
Macedonian (0)	0	<0.01
Maltese (0)	0	<0.01
New Zealander (0)	0	<0.01
Northern European (0)	0	<0.01
Norwegian (56)	133	0.29
Pennsylvania German (103)	103	0.22
Polish (135)	325	0.70
Portuguese (0)	0	<0.01
Romanian (51)	100	0.22
Russian (28)	83	0.18
Scandinavian (4)	75	0.16
Scotch-Irish (441)	946	2.05
Scottish (395)	1,344	2.91
Serbian (0)	0	<0.01
Slavic (0)	0	<0.01
Slovak (10)	38	0.08
Slovene (0)	0	<0.01
Soviet Union (0)	0	<0.01
Swedish (44)	249	0.54
Swiss (0)	6	0.01
Turkish (0)	0	<0.01
Ukrainian (0)	0	<0.01
Welsh (153)	291	0.63
West Indian, ex. Hispanic (11)	73	0.16
Bahamian (0)	0	<0.01
Barbadian (0)	0	<0.01
Belizean (0)	0	<0.01
Bermudan (0)	0	<0.01
British West Indian (0)	0	<0.01
Dutch West Indian (11)	58	0.13
Haitian (0)	15	0.03
Jamaican (0)	0	<0.01
Trinidadian/Tobagonian (0)	0	<0.01
U.S. Virgin Islander (0)	0	<0.01
West Indian (0)	0	<0.01
Other West Indian (0)	0	<0.01
Yugoslavian (9)	9	0.02

Hispanic Origin	Population	%
Hispanic or Latino (of any race)	545	1.18
Central American, ex. Mexican	20	0.04
Costa Rican	10	0.02
Guatemalan	3	0.01
Honduran	1	<0.01
Nicaraguan	2	<0.01
Panamanian	1	<0.01
Salvadoran	3	0.01
Other Central American	0	<0.01
Cuban	18	0.04
Dominican Republic	3	0.01
Mexican	364	0.79
Puerto Rican	45	0.10
South American	21	0.05
Argentinean	0	<0.01
Bolivian	3	0.01
Chilean	0	<0.01
Colombian	11	0.02
Ecuadorian	0	<0.01
Paraguayan	0	<0.01
Peruvian	4	0.01
Uruguayan	0	<0.01
Venezuelan	2	<0.01
Other South American	1	<0.01
Other Hispanic or Latino	74	0.16

Race*	Population	%
African-American/Black (186)	301	0.65
Not Hispanic (181)	293	0.64
Hispanic (5)	8	0.02
American Indian/Alaska Native (158)	418	0.91
Not Hispanic (148)	393	0.85
Hispanic (10)	25	0.05
Alaska Athabascan (Ala. Nat.) (0)	0	<0.01
Aleut (Alaska Native) (0)	0	<0.01
Apache (0)	4	0.01
Arapaho (0)	0	<0.01
Blackfeet (1)	7	0.02
Canadian/French Am. Ind. (1)	3	0.01
Central American Ind. (0)	1	<0.01
Cherokee (48)	147	0.32
Cheyenne (1)	1	<0.01
Chickasaw (1)	1	<0.01
Chippewa (9)	11	0.02
Choctaw (2)	9	0.02
Colville (0)	0	<0.01
Comanche (0)	0	<0.01
Cree (0)	0	<0.01
Creek (1)	2	<0.01
Crow (0)	0	<0.01
Delaware (1)	1	<0.01
Hopi (0)	0	<0.01
Houma (0)	0	<0.01
Inupiat (Alaska Native) (0)	0	<0.01
Iroquois (6)	8	0.02
Kiowa (0)	0	<0.01
Lumbee (6)	11	0.02
Menominee (0)	0	<0.01
Mexican American Ind. (3)	3	0.01
Navajo (1)	7	0.02
Osage (0)	0	<0.01
Ottawa (0)	0	<0.01
Paiute (0)	0	<0.01
Pima (0)	0	<0.01
Potawatomi (1)	1	<0.01
Pueblo (0)	0	<0.01
Puget Sound Salish (0)	1	<0.01
Seminole (0)	0	<0.01
Shoshone (0)	0	<0.01
Sioux (7)	18	0.04
South American Ind. (1)	1	<0.01
Spanish American Ind. (3)	3	0.01
Tlingit-Haida (Alaska Native) (0)	0	<0.01
Tohono O'Odham (0)	0	<0.01
Tsimshian (Alaska Native) (0)	0	<0.01
Ute (1)	1	<0.01
Yakama (0)	0	<0.01
Yaqui (0)	0	<0.01
Yuman (0)	0	<0.01
Yup'ik (Alaska Native) (0)	0	<0.01
Asian (224)	315	0.68
Not Hispanic (224)	300	0.65
Hispanic (0)	15	0.03
Bangladeshi (0)	0	<0.01
Bhutanese (0)	0	<0.01
Burmese (0)	0	<0.01
Cambodian (0)	0	<0.01
Chinese, ex. Taiwanese (51)	63	0.14
Filipino (57)	108	0.23
Hmong (0)	0	<0.01
Indian (58)	66	0.14
Indonesian (0)	0	<0.01
Japanese (9)	21	0.05
Korean (15)	19	0.04
Laotian (0)	0	<0.01
Malaysian (0)	0	<0.01
Nepalese (0)	0	<0.01
Pakistani (0)	0	<0.01
Sri Lankan (0)	0	<0.01
Taiwanese (1)	4	0.01
Thai (3)	5	0.01
Vietnamese (24)	27	0.06
Hawaii Native/Pacific Islander (14)	32	0.07
Not Hispanic (9)	25	0.05
Hispanic (5)	7	0.02
Fijian (0)	0	<0.01
Guamanian/Chamorro (9)	13	0.03
Marshallese (0)	0	<0.01
Native Hawaiian (3)	5	0.01
Samoan (0)	2	<0.01
Tongan (0)	0	<0.01
White (44,905)	45,406	98.42
Not Hispanic (44,562)	45,003	97.55
Hispanic (343)	403	0.87

Notes: † The Census 2010 population figure is used to calculate the percentages in the Hispanic Origin and Race categories. Ancestry percentages are based on the 2006-2010 American Community Survey population (not shown); ‡ Numbers in parentheses indicate the number of people reporting a single ancestry; * Numbers in parentheses indicate the number of persons reporting this race alone, not in combination with any other race; Please refer to the Explanation of Data for more information.

Madison County
Population: 131,636

Ancestry	Population	%
Afghan (0)	0	<0.01
African, Sub-Saharan (735)	768	0.58
African (630)	663	0.50
Cape Verdean (0)	0	<0.01
Ethiopian (18)	18	0.01
Ghanaian (0)	0	<0.01
Kenyan (43)	43	0.03
Liberian (0)	0	<0.01
Nigerian (0)	0	<0.01
Senegalese (0)	0	<0.01
Sierra Leonean (0)	0	<0.01
Somalian (0)	0	<0.01
South African (0)	0	<0.01
Sudanese (18)	18	0.01
Ugandan (0)	0	<0.01
Zimbabwean (0)	0	<0.01
Other Sub-Saharan African (26)	26	0.02
Albanian (0)	0	<0.01
Alsatian (0)	0	<0.01
American (16,493)	16,493	12.55
Arab (30)	71	0.05
Arab (0)	0	<0.01
Egyptian (0)	0	<0.01
Iraqi (0)	0	<0.01
Jordanian (0)	0	<0.01
Lebanese (12)	41	0.03
Moroccan (18)	30	0.02
Palestinian (0)	0	<0.01
Syrian (0)	0	<0.01
Other Arab (0)	0	<0.01
Armenian (0)	0	<0.01
Assyrian/Chaldean/Syriac (0)	0	<0.01
Australian (12)	12	0.01
Austrian (85)	230	0.17
Basque (0)	0	<0.01
Belgian (5)	60	0.05
Brazilian (0)	0	<0.01
British (224)	469	0.36
Bulgarian (24)	24	0.02
Cajun (31)	44	0.03
Canadian (96)	125	0.10
Carpatho Rusyn (0)	0	<0.01
Celtic (0)	12	0.01
Croatian (9)	133	0.10
Cypriot (0)	0	<0.01
Czech (57)	196	0.15
Czechoslovakian (13)	56	0.04
Danish (28)	148	0.11
Dutch (753)	3,039	2.31
Eastern European (51)	51	0.04
English (6,450)	13,634	10.37
Estonian (0)	0	<0.01
European (947)	1,060	0.81
Finnish (13)	121	0.09
French, ex. Basque (1,072)	3,068	2.33
French Canadian (158)	266	0.20
German (12,897)	28,231	21.48
German Russian (0)	0	<0.01
Greek (221)	300	0.23
Guyanese (0)	0	<0.01
Hungarian (65)	197	0.15
Icelander (0)	0	<0.01
Iranian (11)	11	0.01
Irish (4,927)	15,124	11.51
Israeli (0)	0	<0.01
Italian (921)	2,169	1.65
Latvian (8)	8	0.01
Lithuanian (6)	17	0.01
Luxemburger (0)	6	<0.01
Macedonian (15)	15	0.01
Maltese (0)	0	<0.01
New Zealander (0)	0	<0.01
Northern European (90)	107	0.08
Norwegian (114)	353	0.27
Pennsylvania German (28)	40	0.03
Polish (618)	1,642	1.25
Portuguese (36)	136	0.10
Romanian (84)	108	0.08
Russian (76)	194	0.15
Scandinavian (15)	162	0.12
Scotch-Irish (729)	1,856	1.41
Scottish (1,189)	2,721	2.07
Serbian (78)	90	0.07
Slavic (13)	26	0.02
Slovak (39)	69	0.05
Slovene (0)	23	0.02
Soviet Union (0)	0	<0.01
Swedish (364)	903	0.69
Swiss (79)	401	0.31
Turkish (35)	113	0.09
Ukrainian (9)	84	0.06
Welsh (314)	923	0.70
West Indian, ex. Hispanic (42)	56	0.04
Bahamian (0)	0	<0.01
Barbadian (0)	0	<0.01
Belizean (0)	0	<0.01
Bermudan (0)	0	<0.01
British West Indian (0)	0	<0.01
Dutch West Indian (0)	0	<0.01
Haitian (0)	0	<0.01
Jamaican (29)	29	0.02
Trinidadian/Tobagonian (0)	0	<0.01
U.S. Virgin Islander (0)	0	<0.01
West Indian (0)	0	<0.01
Other West Indian (13)	27	0.02
Yugoslavian (8)	40	0.03

Hispanic Origin	Population	%
Hispanic or Latino (of any race)	4,189	3.18
Central American, ex. Mexican	175	0.13
Costa Rican	1	<0.01
Guatemalan	81	0.06
Honduran	30	0.02
Nicaraguan	19	0.01
Panamanian	6	<0.01
Salvadoran	38	0.03
Other Central American	0	<0.01
Cuban	48	0.04
Dominican Republic	23	0.02
Mexican	3,302	2.51
Puerto Rican	202	0.15
South American	73	0.06
Argentinean	12	0.01
Bolivian	3	<0.01
Chilean	7	0.01
Colombian	30	0.02
Ecuadorian	8	0.01
Paraguayan	0	<0.01
Peruvian	7	0.01
Uruguayan	0	<0.01
Venezuelan	5	<0.01
Other South American	1	<0.01
Other Hispanic or Latino	366	0.28

Race*	Population	%
African-American/Black (10,963)	12,333	9.37
Not Hispanic (10,887)	12,168	9.24
Hispanic (76)	165	0.13
American Indian/Alaska Native (320)	907	0.69
Not Hispanic (253)	784	0.60
Hispanic (67)	123	0.09
Alaska Athabascan (Ala. Nat.) (0)	0	<0.01
Aleut (Alaska Native) (0)	0	<0.01
Apache (11)	16	0.01
Arapaho (0)	0	<0.01
Blackfeet (2)	41	0.03
Canadian/French Am. Ind. (5)	7	0.01
Central American Ind. (0)	7	0.01
Cherokee (78)	249	0.19
Cheyenne (2)	9	0.01
Chickasaw (0)	1	<0.01
Chippewa (6)	9	0.01
Choctaw (8)	19	0.01
Colville (0)	0	<0.01
Comanche (0)	0	<0.01
Cree (0)	0	<0.01
Creek (2)	4	<0.01
Crow (0)	0	<0.01
Delaware (0)	9	0.01
Hopi (0)	1	<0.01
Houma (0)	0	<0.01
Inupiat (Alaska Native) (2)	6	<0.01
Iroquois (0)	8	0.01
Kiowa (1)	1	<0.01
Lumbee (1)	1	<0.01
Menominee (0)	2	<0.01
Mexican American Ind. (21)	35	0.03
Navajo (2)	11	0.01
Osage (2)	3	<0.01
Ottawa (0)	0	<0.01
Paiute (0)	0	<0.01
Pima (0)	0	<0.01
Potawatomi (3)	7	0.01
Pueblo (0)	0	<0.01
Puget Sound Salish (0)	0	<0.01
Seminole (0)	3	<0.01
Shoshone (0)	1	<0.01
Sioux (10)	22	0.02
South American Ind. (0)	6	<0.01
Spanish American Ind. (2)	4	<0.01
Tlingit-Haida (Alaska Native) (0)	0	<0.01
Tohono O'Odham (0)	0	<0.01
Tsimshian (Alaska Native) (0)	0	<0.01
Ute (4)	4	<0.01
Yakama (0)	0	<0.01
Yaqui (0)	0	<0.01
Yuman (0)	0	<0.01
Yup'ik (Alaska Native) (0)	0	<0.01
Asian (553)	851	0.65
Not Hispanic (547)	815	0.62
Hispanic (6)	36	0.03
Bangladeshi (5)	5	<0.01
Bhutanese (0)	0	<0.01
Burmese (0)	0	<0.01
Cambodian (0)	0	<0.01
Chinese, ex. Taiwanese (122)	153	0.12
Filipino (98)	180	0.14
Hmong (0)	0	<0.01
Indian (84)	108	0.08
Indonesian (7)	7	0.01
Japanese (53)	123	0.09
Korean (58)	112	0.09
Laotian (1)	5	<0.01
Malaysian (0)	1	<0.01
Nepalese (0)	0	<0.01
Pakistani (7)	7	0.01
Sri Lankan (0)	0	<0.01
Taiwanese (1)	4	<0.01
Thai (18)	25	0.02
Vietnamese (48)	71	0.05
Hawaii Native/Pacific Islander (45)	106	0.08
Not Hispanic (41)	85	0.06
Hispanic (4)	21	0.02
Fijian (0)	0	<0.01
Guamanian/Chamorro (7)	16	0.01
Marshallese (0)	0	<0.01
Native Hawaiian (13)	47	0.04
Samoan (12)	17	0.01
Tongan (2)	5	<0.01
White (115,452)	117,627	89.36
Not Hispanic (113,577)	115,443	87.70
Hispanic (1,875)	2,184	1.66

Notes: † The Census 2010 population figure is used to calculate the percentages in the Hispanic Origin and Race categories. Ancestry percentages are based on the 2006-2010 American Community Survey population (not shown); ‡ Numbers in parentheses indicate the number of people reporting a single ancestry; * Numbers in parentheses indicate the number of persons reporting this race alone, not in combination with any other race; Please refer to the Explanation of Data for more information.

Marion County
Population: 903,393

Ancestry	Population	%
Afghan (29)	29	<0.01
African, Sub-Saharan (36,354)	46,331	5.20
African (31,078)	40,758	4.57
Cape Verdean (0)	0	<0.01
Ethiopian (469)	489	0.05
Ghanaian (154)	154	0.02
Kenyan (85)	85	0.01
Liberian (687)	687	0.08
Nigerian (1,976)	2,117	0.24
Senegalese (150)	150	0.02
Sierra Leonean (0)	0	<0.01
Somalian (432)	464	0.05
South African (20)	43	<0.01
Sudanese (376)	376	0.04
Ugandan (14)	54	0.01
Zimbabwean (149)	149	0.02
Other Sub-Saharan African (764)	805	0.09
Albanian (51)	108	0.01
Alsatian (0)	12	<0.01
American (58,784)	58,784	6.60
Arab (1,866)	2,962	0.33
Arab (445)	610	0.07
Egyptian (147)	158	0.02
Iraqi (132)	192	0.02
Jordanian (152)	182	0.02
Lebanese (444)	892	0.10
Moroccan (96)	141	0.02
Palestinian (12)	45	0.01
Syrian (79)	274	0.03
Other Arab (359)	468	0.05
Armenian (34)	162	0.02
Assyrian/Chaldean/Syriac (44)	54	0.01
Australian (198)	269	0.03
Austrian (359)	1,206	0.14
Basque (0)	0	<0.01
Belgian (291)	896	0.10
Brazilian (158)	303	0.03
British (1,883)	3,902	0.44
Bulgarian (18)	80	0.01
Cajun (29)	52	0.01
Canadian (749)	1,489	0.17
Carpatho Rusyn (0)	0	<0.01
Celtic (15)	23	<0.01
Croatian (130)	477	0.05
Cypriot (0)	0	<0.01
Czech (427)	1,642	0.18
Czechoslovakian (229)	479	0.05
Danish (528)	1,777	0.20
Dutch (3,129)	13,035	1.46
Eastern European (312)	348	0.04
English (27,379)	75,268	8.45
Estonian (27)	113	0.01
European (8,667)	10,318	1.16
Finnish (213)	505	0.06
French, ex. Basque (3,707)	17,752	1.99
French Canadian (652)	1,747	0.20
German (64,968)	168,045	18.86
German Russian (22)	22	<0.01
Greek (1,310)	2,786	0.31
Guyanese (0)	0	<0.01
Hungarian (967)	3,106	0.35
Icelander (0)	0	<0.01
Iranian (349)	515	0.06
Irish (32,321)	105,245	11.81
Israeli (55)	107	0.01
Italian (8,233)	23,155	2.60
Latvian (158)	291	0.03
Lithuanian (325)	1,236	0.14
Luxemburger (34)	110	0.01
Macedonian (199)	381	0.04
Maltese (22)	56	0.01
New Zealander (54)	54	0.01
Northern European (657)	688	0.08
Norwegian (1,065)	4,086	0.46
Pennsylvania German (339)	438	0.05
Polish (4,171)	13,696	1.54
Portuguese (159)	545	0.06
Romanian (659)	1,037	0.12
Russian (1,431)	3,445	0.39
Scandinavian (609)	1,225	0.14
Scotch-Irish (5,607)	12,209	1.37
Scottish (5,392)	15,696	1.76
Serbian (259)	778	0.09
Slavic (134)	489	0.05
Slovak (397)	1,138	0.13
Slovene (221)	549	0.06
Soviet Union (0)	0	<0.01
Swedish (1,561)	6,274	0.70
Swiss (582)	2,601	0.29
Turkish (160)	263	0.03
Ukrainian (482)	914	0.10
Welsh (1,418)	5,354	0.60
West Indian, ex. Hispanic (1,343)	2,084	0.23
Bahamian (8)	8	<0.01
Barbadian (13)	55	0.01
Belizean (28)	76	0.01
Bermudan (0)	0	<0.01
British West Indian (0)	13	<0.01
Dutch West Indian (0)	38	<0.01
Haitian (569)	810	0.09
Jamaican (545)	627	0.07
Trinidadian/Tobagonian (72)	110	0.01
U.S. Virgin Islander (0)	0	<0.01
West Indian (96)	335	0.04
Other West Indian (12)	12	<0.01
Yugoslavian (356)	567	0.06

Hispanic Origin	Population	%
Hispanic or Latino (of any race)	84,466	9.35
Central American, ex. Mexican	8,394	0.93
Costa Rican	131	0.01
Guatemalan	1,787	0.20
Honduran	2,530	0.28
Nicaraguan	739	0.08
Panamanian	324	0.04
Salvadoran	2,814	0.31
Other Central American	69	0.01
Cuban	829	0.09
Dominican Republic	1,189	0.13
Mexican	61,972	6.86
Puerto Rican	3,880	0.43
South American	2,298	0.25
Argentinean	217	0.02
Bolivian	51	0.01
Chilean	90	0.01
Colombian	643	0.07
Ecuadorian	187	0.02
Paraguayan	13	<0.01
Peruvian	684	0.08
Uruguayan	32	<0.01
Venezuelan	359	0.04
Other South American	22	<0.01
Other Hispanic or Latino	5,904	0.65

Race*	Population	%
African-American/Black (240,975)	256,418	28.38
Not Hispanic (238,454)	252,235	27.92
Hispanic (2,521)	4,183	0.46
American Indian/Alaska Native (2,901)	8,132	0.90
Not Hispanic (1,954)	6,488	0.72
Hispanic (947)	1,644	0.18
Alaska Athabascan (Ala. Nat.) (2)	3	<0.01
Aleut (Alaska Native) (12)	14	<0.01
Apache (46)	115	0.01
Arapaho (5)	5	<0.01
Blackfeet (67)	387	0.04
Canadian/French Am. Ind. (10)	27	<0.01
Central American Ind. (8)	13	<0.01
Cherokee (421)	1,851	0.20
Cheyenne (1)	20	<0.01
Chickasaw (6)	12	<0.01
Chippewa (80)	154	0.02
Choctaw (28)	112	0.01
Colville (4)	4	<0.01
Comanche (11)	31	<0.01
Cree (0)	14	<0.01
Creek (19)	36	<0.01
Crow (1)	11	<0.01
Delaware (15)	34	<0.01
Hopi (4)	13	<0.01
Houma (3)	3	<0.01
Inupiat (Alaska Native) (9)	20	<0.01
Iroquois (40)	107	0.01
Kiowa (3)	6	<0.01
Lumbee (12)	23	<0.01
Menominee (4)	5	<0.01
Mexican American Ind. (199)	284	0.03
Navajo (42)	104	0.01
Osage (4)	15	<0.01
Ottawa (3)	15	<0.01
Paiute (0)	5	<0.01
Pima (0)	1	<0.01
Potawatomi (58)	95	0.01
Pueblo (11)	31	<0.01
Puget Sound Salish (0)	0	<0.01
Seminole (2)	17	<0.01
Shoshone (2)	12	<0.01
Sioux (65)	225	0.02
South American Ind. (15)	41	<0.01
Spanish American Ind. (31)	38	<0.01
Tlingit-Haida (Alaska Native) (4)	6	<0.01
Tohono O'Odham (1)	2	<0.01
Tsimshian (Alaska Native) (1)	1	<0.01
Ute (2)	5	<0.01
Yakama (0)	1	<0.01
Yaqui (3)	5	<0.01
Yuman (2)	4	<0.01
Yup'ik (Alaska Native) (0)	2	<0.01
Asian (18,314)	22,872	2.53
Not Hispanic (18,119)	22,304	2.47
Hispanic (195)	568	0.06
Bangladeshi (125)	138	0.02
Bhutanese (0)	0	<0.01
Burmese (3,525)	3,671	0.41
Cambodian (102)	139	0.02
Chinese, ex. Taiwanese (2,851)	3,455	0.38
Filipino (1,826)	2,930	0.32
Hmong (15)	24	<0.01
Indian (4,901)	5,565	0.62
Indonesian (80)	149	0.02
Japanese (567)	1,234	0.14
Korean (1,255)	1,903	0.21
Laotian (120)	147	0.02
Malaysian (29)	46	0.01
Nepalese (54)	56	0.01
Pakistani (574)	655	0.07
Sri Lankan (37)	45	<0.01
Taiwanese (154)	178	0.02
Thai (258)	394	0.04
Vietnamese (1,210)	1,438	0.16
Hawaii Native/Pacific Islander (458)	1,258	0.14
Not Hispanic (333)	924	0.10
Hispanic (125)	334	0.04
Fijian (3)	7	<0.01
Guamanian/Chamorro (154)	252	0.03
Marshallese (1)	1	<0.01
Native Hawaiian (137)	401	0.04
Samoan (84)	164	0.02
Tongan (5)	10	<0.01
White (566,853)	588,637	65.16
Not Hispanic (537,905)	555,252	61.46
Hispanic (28,948)	33,385	3.70

Notes: † The Census 2010 population figure is used to calculate the percentages in the Hispanic Origin and Race categories. Ancestry percentages are based on the 2006-2010 American Community Survey population (not shown); ‡ Numbers in parentheses indicate the number of people reporting a single ancestry; * Numbers in parentheses indicate the number of persons reporting this race alone, not in combination with any other race; Please refer to the Explanation of Data for more information.

Marshall County
Population: 47,051

Ancestry	Population	%
Afghan (0)	0	<0.01
African, Sub-Saharan (29)	29	0.06
African (0)	0	<0.01
Cape Verdean (0)	0	<0.01
Ethiopian (0)	0	<0.01
Ghanaian (0)	0	<0.01
Kenyan (0)	0	<0.01
Liberian (0)	0	<0.01
Nigerian (29)	29	0.06
Senegalese (0)	0	<0.01
Sierra Leonean (0)	0	<0.01
Somalian (0)	0	<0.01
South African (0)	0	<0.01
Sudanese (0)	0	<0.01
Ugandan (0)	0	<0.01
Zimbabwean (0)	0	<0.01
Other Sub-Saharan African (0)	0	<0.01
Albanian (0)	0	<0.01
Alsatian (0)	4	0.01
American (4,404)	4,404	9.38
Arab (3)	124	0.26
Arab (0)	0	<0.01
Egyptian (0)	12	0.03
Iraqi (0)	0	<0.01
Jordanian (0)	0	<0.01
Lebanese (3)	3	0.01
Moroccan (0)	0	<0.01
Palestinian (0)	0	<0.01
Syrian (0)	109	0.23
Other Arab (0)	0	<0.01
Armenian (0)	0	<0.01
Assyrian/Chaldean/Syriac (0)	29	0.06
Australian (0)	0	<0.01
Austrian (69)	69	0.15
Basque (0)	0	<0.01
Belgian (52)	181	0.39
Brazilian (0)	0	<0.01
British (56)	83	0.18
Bulgarian (0)	14	0.03
Cajun (0)	0	<0.01
Canadian (11)	38	0.08
Carpatho Rusyn (0)	0	<0.01
Celtic (0)	0	<0.01
Croatian (23)	62	0.13
Cypriot (0)	0	<0.01
Czech (104)	369	0.79
Czechoslovakian (23)	79	0.17
Danish (35)	70	0.15
Dutch (218)	1,220	2.60
Eastern European (20)	20	0.04
English (1,198)	4,012	8.54
Estonian (0)	7	0.01
European (541)	566	1.20
Finnish (0)	3	0.01
French, ex. Basque (206)	981	2.09
French Canadian (9)	89	0.19
German (8,027)	16,645	35.43
German Russian (0)	0	<0.01
Greek (75)	232	0.49
Guyanese (0)	0	<0.01
Hungarian (118)	293	0.62
Icelander (0)	0	<0.01
Iranian (19)	30	0.06
Irish (1,370)	5,238	11.15
Israeli (0)	0	<0.01
Italian (332)	1,265	2.69
Latvian (4)	4	0.01
Lithuanian (75)	111	0.24
Luxemburger (10)	10	0.02
Macedonian (0)	0	<0.01
Maltese (0)	0	<0.01
New Zealander (0)	0	<0.01
Northern European (16)	16	0.03
Norwegian (39)	197	0.42
Pennsylvania German (398)	476	1.01
Polish (746)	2,260	4.81
Portuguese (23)	93	0.20
Romanian (114)	225	0.48
Russian (17)	130	0.28
Scandinavian (10)	67	0.14
Scotch-Irish (161)	653	1.39
Scottish (343)	735	1.56
Serbian (331)	347	0.74
Slavic (0)	26	0.06
Slovak (14)	21	0.04
Slovene (4)	4	0.01
Soviet Union (0)	0	<0.01
Swedish (195)	680	1.45
Swiss (151)	689	1.47
Turkish (16)	16	0.03
Ukrainian (55)	80	0.17
Welsh (0)	119	0.25
West Indian, ex. Hispanic (24)	24	0.05
Bahamian (0)	0	<0.01
Barbadian (0)	0	<0.01
Belizean (0)	0	<0.01
Bermudan (0)	0	<0.01
British West Indian (0)	0	<0.01
Dutch West Indian (0)	0	<0.01
Haitian (16)	16	0.03
Jamaican (8)	8	0.02
Trinidadian/Tobagonian (0)	0	<0.01
U.S. Virgin Islander (0)	0	<0.01
West Indian (0)	0	<0.01
Other West Indian (0)	0	<0.01
Yugoslavian (27)	27	0.06

Hispanic Origin	Population	%
Hispanic or Latino (of any race)	3,971	8.44
Central American, ex. Mexican	320	0.68
Costa Rican	1	<0.01
Guatemalan	26	0.06
Honduran	284	0.60
Nicaraguan	1	<0.01
Panamanian	1	<0.01
Salvadoran	7	0.01
Other Central American	0	<0.01
Cuban	16	0.03
Dominican Republic	11	0.02
Mexican	3,078	6.54
Puerto Rican	97	0.21
South American	37	0.08
Argentinean	0	<0.01
Bolivian	3	0.01
Chilean	6	0.01
Colombian	9	0.02
Ecuadorian	1	<0.01
Paraguayan	1	<0.01
Peruvian	12	0.03
Uruguayan	0	<0.01
Venezuelan	0	<0.01
Other South American	5	0.01
Other Hispanic or Latino	412	0.88

Race*	Population	%
African-American/Black (220)	446	0.95
Not Hispanic (196)	391	0.83
Hispanic (24)	55	0.12
American Indian/Alaska Native (116)	352	0.75
Not Hispanic (80)	296	0.63
Hispanic (36)	56	0.12
Alaska Athabascan (Ala. Nat.) (0)	0	<0.01
Aleut (Alaska Native) (1)	1	<0.01
Apache (0)	3	0.01
Arapaho (0)	0	<0.01
Blackfeet (2)	18	0.04
Canadian/French Am. Ind. (6)	14	0.03
Central American Ind. (0)	3	0.01
Cherokee (18)	86	0.18
Cheyenne (0)	2	<0.01
Chickasaw (0)	0	<0.01
Chippewa (4)	6	0.01
Choctaw (0)	2	<0.01
Colville (0)	0	<0.01
Comanche (0)	0	<0.01
Cree (0)	3	0.01
Creek (0)	2	<0.01
Crow (0)	1	<0.01
Delaware (2)	2	<0.01
Hopi (0)	0	<0.01
Houma (0)	0	<0.01
Inupiat (Alaska Native) (0)	0	<0.01
Iroquois (2)	5	0.01
Kiowa (0)	0	<0.01
Lumbee (0)	0	<0.01
Menominee (0)	0	<0.01
Mexican American Ind. (4)	11	0.02
Navajo (1)	4	0.01
Osage (0)	1	<0.01
Ottawa (0)	0	<0.01
Paiute (0)	0	<0.01
Pima (0)	0	<0.01
Potawatomi (2)	10	0.02
Pueblo (2)	2	<0.01
Puget Sound Salish (0)	0	<0.01
Seminole (0)	1	<0.01
Shoshone (3)	3	0.01
Sioux (1)	5	0.01
South American Ind. (0)	0	<0.01
Spanish American Ind. (0)	0	<0.01
Tlingit-Haida (Alaska Native) (0)	0	<0.01
Tohono O'Odham (0)	0	<0.01
Tsimshian (Alaska Native) (0)	0	<0.01
Ute (0)	0	<0.01
Yakama (0)	0	<0.01
Yaqui (0)	1	<0.01
Yuman (0)	0	<0.01
Yup'ik (Alaska Native) (0)	0	<0.01
Asian (215)	306	0.65
Not Hispanic (210)	291	0.62
Hispanic (5)	15	0.03
Bangladeshi (0)	0	<0.01
Bhutanese (0)	0	<0.01
Burmese (0)	0	<0.01
Cambodian (1)	1	<0.01
Chinese, ex. Taiwanese (46)	48	0.10
Filipino (43)	69	0.15
Hmong (0)	0	<0.01
Indian (17)	29	0.06
Indonesian (3)	5	0.01
Japanese (5)	29	0.06
Korean (21)	42	0.09
Laotian (14)	21	0.04
Malaysian (0)	0	<0.01
Nepalese (0)	0	<0.01
Pakistani (7)	7	0.01
Sri Lankan (1)	1	<0.01
Taiwanese (2)	2	<0.01
Thai (15)	23	0.05
Vietnamese (29)	32	0.07
Hawaii Native/Pacific Islander (7)	12	0.03
Not Hispanic (2)	7	0.01
Hispanic (5)	5	0.01
Fijian (0)	1	<0.01
Guamanian/Chamorro (2)	2	<0.01
Marshallese (0)	0	<0.01
Native Hawaiian (2)	5	0.01
Samoan (0)	0	<0.01
Tongan (0)	0	<0.01
White (44,000)	44,694	94.99
Not Hispanic (42,098)	42,569	90.47
Hispanic (1,902)	2,125	4.52

*Notes: † The Census 2010 population figure is used to calculate the percentages in the Hispanic Origin and Race categories. Ancestry percentages are based on the 2006-2010 American Community Survey population (not shown); ‡ Numbers in parentheses indicate the number of people reporting a single ancestry; * Numbers in parentheses indicate the number of persons reporting this race alone, not in combination with any other race; Please refer to the Explanation of Data for more information.*

Martin County

Population: 10,334

Ancestry	Population	%
Afghan (0)	0	<0.01
African, Sub-Saharan (0)	0	<0.01
African (0)	0	<0.01
Cape Verdean (0)	0	<0.01
Ethiopian (0)	0	<0.01
Ghanaian (0)	0	<0.01
Kenyan (0)	0	<0.01
Liberian (0)	0	<0.01
Nigerian (0)	0	<0.01
Senegalese (0)	0	<0.01
Sierra Leonean (0)	0	<0.01
Somalian (0)	0	<0.01
South African (0)	0	<0.01
Sudanese (0)	0	<0.01
Ugandan (0)	0	<0.01
Zimbabwean (0)	0	<0.01
Other Sub-Saharan African (0)	0	<0.01
Albanian (0)	0	<0.01
Alsatian (0)	0	<0.01
American (1,307)	1,307	12.66
Arab (0)	0	<0.01
Arab (0)	0	<0.01
Egyptian (0)	0	<0.01
Iraqi (0)	0	<0.01
Jordanian (0)	0	<0.01
Lebanese (0)	0	<0.01
Moroccan (0)	0	<0.01
Palestinian (0)	0	<0.01
Syrian (0)	0	<0.01
Other Arab (0)	0	<0.01
Armenian (0)	0	<0.01
Assyrian/Chaldean/Syriac (0)	0	<0.01
Australian (0)	0	<0.01
Austrian (0)	0	<0.01
Basque (0)	0	<0.01
Belgian (0)	8	0.08
Brazilian (0)	0	<0.01
British (33)	33	0.32
Bulgarian (0)	0	<0.01
Cajun (0)	0	<0.01
Canadian (0)	0	<0.01
Carpatho Rusyn (0)	0	<0.01
Celtic (0)	0	<0.01
Croatian (0)	0	<0.01
Cypriot (0)	0	<0.01
Czech (0)	0	<0.01
Czechoslovakian (0)	0	<0.01
Danish (0)	0	<0.01
Dutch (2)	56	0.54
Eastern European (0)	0	<0.01
English (907)	1,539	14.91
Estonian (0)	0	<0.01
European (0)	0	<0.01
Finnish (0)	0	<0.01
French, ex. Basque (32)	208	2.01
French Canadian (0)	0	<0.01
German (1,657)	2,873	27.83
German Russian (0)	0	<0.01
Greek (0)	0	<0.01
Guyanese (0)	0	<0.01
Hungarian (0)	16	0.15
Icelander (0)	0	<0.01
Iranian (0)	0	<0.01
Irish (757)	1,982	19.20
Israeli (0)	0	<0.01
Italian (0)	18	0.17
Latvian (0)	0	<0.01
Lithuanian (0)	0	<0.01
Luxemburger (0)	0	<0.01
Macedonian (0)	0	<0.01
Maltese (0)	0	<0.01
New Zealander (0)	0	<0.01
Northern European (0)	0	<0.01
Norwegian (0)	41	0.40
Pennsylvania German (63)	63	0.61
Polish (50)	65	0.63
Portuguese (0)	0	<0.01
Romanian (0)	0	<0.01
Russian (10)	37	0.36
Scandinavian (0)	0	<0.01
Scotch-Irish (55)	137	1.33
Scottish (35)	66	0.64
Serbian (0)	0	<0.01
Slavic (0)	9	0.09
Slovak (0)	0	<0.01
Slovene (0)	0	<0.01
Soviet Union (0)	0	<0.01
Swedish (0)	6	0.06
Swiss (0)	21	0.20
Turkish (0)	0	<0.01
Ukrainian (0)	0	<0.01
Welsh (0)	0	<0.01
West Indian, ex. Hispanic (0)	0	<0.01
Bahamian (0)	0	<0.01
Barbadian (0)	0	<0.01
Belizean (0)	0	<0.01
Bermudan (0)	0	<0.01
British West Indian (0)	0	<0.01
Dutch West Indian (0)	0	<0.01
Haitian (0)	0	<0.01
Jamaican (0)	0	<0.01
Trinidadian/Tobagonian (0)	0	<0.01
U.S. Virgin Islander (0)	0	<0.01
West Indian (0)	0	<0.01
Other West Indian (0)	0	<0.01
Yugoslavian (0)	0	<0.01

Hispanic Origin	Population	%
Hispanic or Latino (of any race)	70	0.68
Central American, ex. Mexican	3	0.03
Costa Rican	0	<0.01
Guatemalan	3	0.03
Honduran	0	<0.01
Nicaraguan	0	<0.01
Panamanian	0	<0.01
Salvadoran	0	<0.01
Other Central American	0	<0.01
Cuban	3	0.03
Dominican Republic	0	<0.01
Mexican	55	0.53
Puerto Rican	2	0.02
South American	1	0.01
Argentinean	0	<0.01
Bolivian	0	<0.01
Chilean	0	<0.01
Colombian	1	0.01
Ecuadorian	0	<0.01
Paraguayan	0	<0.01
Peruvian	0	<0.01
Uruguayan	0	<0.01
Venezuelan	0	<0.01
Other South American	0	<0.01
Other Hispanic or Latino	6	0.06

Race*	Population	%
African-American/Black (10)	40	0.39
Not Hispanic (10)	36	0.35
Hispanic (0)	4	0.04
American Indian/Alaska Native (30)	63	0.61
Not Hispanic (26)	56	0.54
Hispanic (4)	7	0.07
Alaska Athabascan (Ala. Nat.) (0)	0	<0.01
Aleut (Alaska Native) (0)	0	<0.01
Apache (0)	1	0.01
Arapaho (0)	0	<0.01
Blackfeet (1)	2	0.02
Canadian/French Am. Ind. (0)	1	0.01
Central American Ind. (0)	0	<0.01
Cherokee (12)	26	0.25
Cheyenne (0)	0	<0.01
Chickasaw (0)	0	<0.01
Chippewa (0)	0	<0.01
Choctaw (0)	0	<0.01
Colville (0)	0	<0.01
Comanche (0)	0	<0.01
Cree (0)	0	<0.01
Creek (0)	0	<0.01
Crow (0)	0	<0.01
Delaware (0)	0	<0.01
Hopi (0)	1	0.01
Houma (0)	0	<0.01
Inupiat (Alaska Native) (0)	0	<0.01
Iroquois (0)	2	0.02
Kiowa (0)	0	<0.01
Lumbee (0)	0	<0.01
Menominee (0)	0	<0.01
Mexican American Ind. (3)	3	0.03
Navajo (0)	0	<0.01
Osage (0)	0	<0.01
Ottawa (0)	0	<0.01
Paiute (0)	0	<0.01
Pima (0)	0	<0.01
Potawatomi (0)	1	0.01
Pueblo (0)	0	<0.01
Puget Sound Salish (0)	0	<0.01
Seminole (0)	0	<0.01
Shoshone (0)	0	<0.01
Sioux (2)	2	0.02
South American Ind. (0)	0	<0.01
Spanish American Ind. (0)	0	<0.01
Tlingit-Haida (Alaska Native) (0)	0	<0.01
Tohono O'Odham (0)	0	<0.01
Tsimshian (Alaska Native) (0)	0	<0.01
Ute (0)	0	<0.01
Yakama (0)	0	<0.01
Yaqui (0)	1	0.01
Yuman (0)	0	<0.01
Yup'ik (Alaska Native) (0)	0	<0.01
Asian (29)	41	0.40
Not Hispanic (29)	41	0.40
Hispanic (0)	0	<0.01
Bangladeshi (0)	0	<0.01
Bhutanese (0)	0	<0.01
Burmese (0)	0	<0.01
Cambodian (0)	0	<0.01
Chinese, ex. Taiwanese (9)	9	0.09
Filipino (10)	15	0.15
Hmong (0)	0	<0.01
Indian (0)	4	0.04
Indonesian (0)	0	<0.01
Japanese (4)	4	0.04
Korean (3)	6	0.06
Laotian (0)	0	<0.01
Malaysian (0)	0	<0.01
Nepalese (0)	0	<0.01
Pakistani (0)	0	<0.01
Sri Lankan (0)	0	<0.01
Taiwanese (0)	0	<0.01
Thai (1)	1	0.01
Vietnamese (0)	0	<0.01
Hawaii Native/Pacific Islander (0)	2	0.02
Not Hispanic (0)	2	0.02
Hispanic (0)	0	<0.01
Fijian (0)	0	<0.01
Guamanian/Chamorro (0)	0	<0.01
Marshallese (0)	0	<0.01
Native Hawaiian (0)	0	<0.01
Samoan (0)	0	<0.01
Tongan (0)	0	<0.01
White (10,164)	10,237	99.06
Not Hispanic (10,125)	10,193	98.64
Hispanic (39)	44	0.43

Notes: † The Census 2010 population figure is used to calculate the percentages in the Hispanic Origin and Race categories. Ancestry percentages are based on the 2006-2010 American Community Survey population (not shown); ‡ Numbers in parentheses indicate the number of people reporting a single ancestry; * Numbers in parentheses indicate the number of persons reporting this race alone, not in combination with any other race; Please refer to the Explanation of Data for more information.

Miami County
Population: 36,903

Ancestry	Population	%
Afghan (0)	0	<0.01
African, Sub-Saharan (77)	77	0.21
African (69)	69	0.18
Cape Verdean (0)	0	<0.01
Ethiopian (0)	0	<0.01
Ghanaian (0)	0	<0.01
Kenyan (0)	0	<0.01
Liberian (0)	0	<0.01
Nigerian (0)	0	<0.01
Senegalese (0)	0	<0.01
Sierra Leonean (0)	0	<0.01
Somalian (0)	0	<0.01
South African (8)	8	0.02
Sudanese (0)	0	<0.01
Ugandan (0)	0	<0.01
Zimbabwean (0)	0	<0.01
Other Sub-Saharan African (0)	0	<0.01
Albanian (0)	0	<0.01
Alsatian (0)	0	<0.01
American (6,467)	6,467	17.33
Arab (36)	36	0.10
Arab (0)	0	<0.01
Egyptian (0)	0	<0.01
Iraqi (0)	0	<0.01
Jordanian (0)	0	<0.01
Lebanese (27)	27	0.07
Moroccan (0)	0	<0.01
Palestinian (0)	0	<0.01
Syrian (9)	9	0.02
Other Arab (0)	0	<0.01
Armenian (11)	11	0.03
Assyrian/Chaldean/Syriac (0)	0	<0.01
Australian (6)	6	0.02
Austrian (13)	24	0.06
Basque (0)	0	<0.01
Belgian (0)	20	0.05
Brazilian (0)	0	<0.01
British (17)	49	0.13
Bulgarian (0)	4	0.01
Cajun (0)	0	<0.01
Canadian (25)	60	0.16
Carpatho Rusyn (0)	0	<0.01
Celtic (0)	0	<0.01
Croatian (21)	32	0.09
Cypriot (0)	0	<0.01
Czech (19)	148	0.40
Czechoslovakian (0)	0	<0.01
Danish (0)	97	0.26
Dutch (248)	933	2.50
Eastern European (0)	0	<0.01
English (1,159)	3,121	8.37
Estonian (0)	0	<0.01
European (439)	508	1.36
Finnish (0)	77	0.21
French, ex. Basque (82)	626	1.68
French Canadian (109)	219	0.59
German (4,894)	10,153	27.21
German Russian (4)	4	0.01
Greek (4)	69	0.18
Guyanese (0)	0	<0.01
Hungarian (58)	136	0.36
Icelander (0)	0	<0.01
Iranian (0)	0	<0.01
Irish (1,271)	4,473	11.99
Israeli (0)	0	<0.01
Italian (620)	951	2.55
Latvian (0)	0	<0.01
Lithuanian (18)	63	0.17
Luxemburger (0)	0	<0.01
Macedonian (0)	0	<0.01
Maltese (0)	0	<0.01
New Zealander (0)	0	<0.01
Northern European (8)	8	0.02
Norwegian (35)	94	0.25
Pennsylvania German (99)	139	0.37
Polish (148)	668	1.79
Portuguese (0)	19	0.05
Romanian (0)	26	0.07
Russian (0)	80	0.21
Scandinavian (0)	7	0.02
Scotch-Irish (95)	360	0.96
Scottish (241)	642	1.72
Serbian (0)	0	<0.01
Slavic (0)	0	<0.01
Slovak (34)	74	0.20
Slovene (0)	0	<0.01
Soviet Union (0)	0	<0.01
Swedish (140)	324	0.87
Swiss (146)	221	0.59
Turkish (0)	0	<0.01
Ukrainian (44)	53	0.14
Welsh (53)	173	0.46
West Indian, ex. Hispanic (9)	9	0.02
Bahamian (0)	0	<0.01
Barbadian (0)	0	<0.01
Belizean (0)	0	<0.01
Bermudan (0)	0	<0.01
British West Indian (0)	0	<0.01
Dutch West Indian (0)	0	<0.01
Haitian (0)	0	<0.01
Jamaican (9)	9	0.02
Trinidadian/Tobagonian (0)	0	<0.01
U.S. Virgin Islander (0)	0	<0.01
West Indian (0)	0	<0.01
Other West Indian (0)	0	<0.01
Yugoslavian (0)	5	0.01

Hispanic Origin	Population	%
Hispanic or Latino (of any race)	906	2.46
Central American, ex. Mexican	35	0.09
Costa Rican	0	<0.01
Guatemalan	7	0.02
Honduran	17	0.05
Nicaraguan	2	0.01
Panamanian	2	0.01
Salvadoran	7	0.02
Other Central American	0	<0.01
Cuban	18	0.05
Dominican Republic	0	<0.01
Mexican	695	1.88
Puerto Rican	89	0.24
South American	10	0.03
Argentinean	1	<0.01
Bolivian	1	<0.01
Chilean	0	<0.01
Colombian	1	<0.01
Ecuadorian	0	<0.01
Paraguayan	0	<0.01
Peruvian	3	0.01
Uruguayan	1	<0.01
Venezuelan	3	0.01
Other South American	0	<0.01
Other Hispanic or Latino	59	0.16

Race*	Population	%
African-American/Black (1,673)	1,941	5.26
Not Hispanic (1,649)	1,893	5.13
Hispanic (24)	48	0.13
American Indian/Alaska Native (335)	592	1.60
Not Hispanic (309)	551	1.49
Hispanic (26)	41	0.11
Alaska Athabascan *(Ala. Nat.)* (0)	0	<0.01
Aleut *(Alaska Native)* (0)	0	<0.01
Apache (0)	3	0.01
Arapaho (0)	0	<0.01
Blackfeet (5)	14	0.04
Canadian/French Am. Ind. (0)	1	<0.01
Central American Ind. (0)	0	<0.01
Cherokee (23)	72	0.20
Cheyenne (1)	1	<0.01
Chickasaw (3)	3	0.01
Chippewa (10)	18	0.05
Choctaw (8)	9	0.02
Colville (0)	0	<0.01
Comanche (3)	3	0.01
Cree (1)	1	<0.01
Creek (0)	0	<0.01
Crow (0)	0	<0.01
Delaware (0)	0	<0.01
Hopi (0)	0	<0.01
Houma (0)	0	<0.01
Inupiat *(Alaska Native)* (0)	0	<0.01
Iroquois (5)	8	0.02
Kiowa (0)	0	<0.01
Lumbee (0)	0	<0.01
Menominee (0)	0	<0.01
Mexican American Ind. (5)	6	0.02
Navajo (5)	6	0.02
Osage (0)	0	<0.01
Ottawa (0)	0	<0.01
Paiute (0)	0	<0.01
Pima (0)	0	<0.01
Potawatomi (3)	6	0.02
Pueblo (0)	1	<0.01
Puget Sound Salish (0)	0	<0.01
Seminole (0)	1	<0.01
Shoshone (0)	0	<0.01
Sioux (0)	4	0.01
South American Ind. (3)	4	0.01
Spanish American Ind. (0)	0	<0.01
Tlingit-Haida *(Alaska Native)* (0)	0	<0.01
Tohono O'Odham (0)	0	<0.01
Tsimshian *(Alaska Native)* (0)	0	<0.01
Ute (1)	2	0.01
Yakama (0)	0	<0.01
Yaqui (0)	0	<0.01
Yuman (0)	0	<0.01
Yup'ik *(Alaska Native)* (0)	0	<0.01
Asian (129)	219	0.59
Not Hispanic (128)	215	0.58
Hispanic (1)	4	0.01
Bangladeshi (0)	0	<0.01
Bhutanese (0)	0	<0.01
Burmese (0)	0	<0.01
Cambodian (1)	1	<0.01
Chinese, ex. Taiwanese (39)	46	0.12
Filipino (28)	57	0.15
Hmong (0)	0	<0.01
Indian (10)	17	0.05
Indonesian (2)	3	0.01
Japanese (13)	28	0.08
Korean (14)	42	0.11
Laotian (0)	0	<0.01
Malaysian (0)	0	<0.01
Nepalese (0)	0	<0.01
Pakistani (0)	0	<0.01
Sri Lankan (0)	0	<0.01
Taiwanese (1)	2	0.01
Thai (9)	13	0.04
Vietnamese (2)	7	0.02
Hawaii Native/Pacific Islander (8)	30	0.08
Not Hispanic (8)	23	0.06
Hispanic (0)	7	0.02
Fijian (0)	0	<0.01
Guamanian/Chamorro (0)	2	0.01
Marshallese (1)	1	<0.01
Native Hawaiian (6)	23	0.06
Samoan (1)	1	<0.01
Tongan (0)	0	<0.01
White (33,876)	34,512	93.52
Not Hispanic (33,307)	33,868	91.78
Hispanic (569)	644	1.75

*Notes: † The Census 2010 population figure is used to calculate the percentages in the Hispanic Origin and Race categories. Ancestry percentages are based on the 2006-2010 American Community Survey population (not shown); ‡ Numbers in parentheses indicate the number of people reporting a single ancestry; * Numbers in parentheses indicate the number of persons reporting this race alone, not in combination with any other race; Please refer to the Explanation of Data for more information.*

Monroe County
Population: 137,974

Ancestry	Population	%
Afghan (59)	59	0.04
African, Sub-Saharan (554)	680	0.51
African (445)	567	0.42
Cape Verdean (0)	0	<0.01
Ethiopian (32)	33	0.02
Ghanaian (0)	0	<0.01
Kenyan (0)	0	<0.01
Liberian (0)	0	<0.01
Nigerian (14)	14	0.01
Senegalese (0)	0	<0.01
Sierra Leonean (0)	0	<0.01
Somalian (0)	0	<0.01
South African (63)	63	0.05
Sudanese (0)	0	<0.01
Ugandan (0)	0	<0.01
Zimbabwean (0)	0	<0.01
Other Sub-Saharan African (0)	3	<0.01
Albanian (20)	20	0.01
Alsatian (0)	19	0.01
American (10,838)	10,838	8.06
Arab (408)	623	0.46
Arab (187)	196	0.15
Egyptian (8)	21	0.02
Iraqi (30)	30	0.02
Jordanian (0)	10	0.01
Lebanese (67)	180	0.13
Moroccan (27)	27	0.02
Palestinian (0)	8	0.01
Syrian (13)	75	0.06
Other Arab (76)	76	0.06
Armenian (14)	37	0.03
Assyrian/Chaldean/Syriac (0)	0	<0.01
Australian (25)	53	0.04
Austrian (115)	577	0.43
Basque (0)	49	0.04
Belgian (53)	285	0.21
Brazilian (103)	132	0.10
British (278)	1,053	0.78
Bulgarian (29)	29	0.02
Cajun (16)	32	0.02
Canadian (145)	266	0.20
Carpatho Rusyn (0)	0	<0.01
Celtic (0)	0	<0.01
Croatian (48)	185	0.14
Cypriot (0)	0	<0.01
Czech (173)	852	0.63
Czechoslovakian (21)	186	0.14
Danish (155)	464	0.35
Dutch (1,078)	3,442	2.56
Eastern European (296)	354	0.26
English (5,578)	15,851	11.79
Estonian (0)	27	0.02
European (2,220)	2,518	1.87
Finnish (12)	66	0.05
French, ex. Basque (921)	4,080	3.03
French Canadian (185)	477	0.35
German (10,605)	33,322	24.79
German Russian (0)	0	<0.01
Greek (265)	656	0.49
Guyanese (0)	0	<0.01
Hungarian (228)	977	0.73
Icelander (21)	41	0.03
Iranian (187)	209	0.16
Irish (5,191)	18,106	13.47
Israeli (91)	168	0.12
Italian (1,545)	5,397	4.01
Latvian (10)	10	0.01
Lithuanian (105)	406	0.30
Luxemburger (0)	66	0.05
Macedonian (48)	62	0.05
Maltese (0)	0	<0.01
New Zealander (0)	0	<0.01
Northern European (118)	154	0.11
Norwegian (459)	1,703	1.27
Pennsylvania German (71)	123	0.09
Polish (1,312)	4,992	3.71
Portuguese (18)	87	0.06
Romanian (110)	320	0.24
Russian (573)	1,627	1.21
Scandinavian (88)	268	0.20
Scotch-Irish (1,432)	3,759	2.80
Scottish (1,032)	3,952	2.94
Serbian (61)	174	0.13
Slavic (0)	23	0.02
Slovak (55)	247	0.18
Slovene (19)	96	0.07
Soviet Union (0)	0	<0.01
Swedish (421)	1,891	1.41
Swiss (143)	663	0.49
Turkish (111)	111	0.08
Ukrainian (164)	350	0.26
Welsh (299)	1,280	0.95
West Indian, ex. Hispanic (85)	137	0.10
Bahamian (0)	0	<0.01
Barbadian (0)	0	<0.01
Belizean (0)	0	<0.01
Bermudan (0)	0	<0.01
British West Indian (0)	0	<0.01
Dutch West Indian (0)	36	0.03
Haitian (0)	0	<0.01
Jamaican (72)	72	0.05
Trinidadian/Tobagonian (0)	0	<0.01
U.S. Virgin Islander (0)	0	<0.01
West Indian (13)	29	0.02
Other West Indian (0)	0	<0.01
Yugoslavian (17)	50	0.04

Hispanic Origin	Population	%
Hispanic or Latino (of any race)	4,029	2.92
Central American, ex. Mexican	245	0.18
Costa Rican	43	0.03
Guatemalan	48	0.03
Honduran	38	0.03
Nicaraguan	34	0.02
Panamanian	34	0.02
Salvadoran	44	0.03
Other Central American	4	<0.01
Cuban	157	0.11
Dominican Republic	55	0.04
Mexican	2,249	1.63
Puerto Rican	449	0.33
South American	435	0.32
Argentinean	65	0.05
Bolivian	11	0.01
Chilean	51	0.04
Colombian	108	0.08
Ecuadorian	42	0.03
Paraguayan	6	<0.01
Peruvian	76	0.06
Uruguayan	7	0.01
Venezuelan	69	0.05
Other South American	0	<0.01
Other Hispanic or Latino	439	0.32

Race*	Population	%
African-American/Black (4,491)	5,857	4.25
Not Hispanic (4,363)	5,617	4.07
Hispanic (128)	240	0.17
American Indian/Alaska Native (353)	1,141	0.83
Not Hispanic (288)	955	0.69
Hispanic (65)	186	0.13
Alaska Athabascan (Ala. Nat.) (1)	1	<0.01
Aleut (Alaska Native) (0)	2	<0.01
Apache (5)	15	0.01
Arapaho (2)	2	<0.01
Blackfeet (0)	52	0.04
Canadian/French Am. Ind. (3)	6	<0.01
Central American Ind. (3)	7	0.01
Cherokee (61)	281	0.20
Cheyenne (0)	0	<0.01
Chickasaw (5)	5	<0.01
Chippewa (14)	35	0.03
Choctaw (9)	24	0.02
Colville (1)	1	<0.01
Comanche (0)	0	<0.01
Cree (0)	1	<0.01
Creek (7)	8	0.01
Crow (1)	2	<0.01
Delaware (7)	11	0.01
Hopi (1)	2	<0.01
Houma (0)	0	<0.01
Inupiat (Alaska Native) (0)	3	<0.01
Iroquois (8)	17	0.01
Kiowa (0)	0	<0.01
Lumbee (4)	9	0.01
Menominee (1)	2	<0.01
Mexican American Ind. (9)	23	0.02
Navajo (9)	15	0.01
Osage (0)	2	<0.01
Ottawa (1)	1	<0.01
Paiute (0)	0	<0.01
Pima (0)	0	<0.01
Potawatomi (3)	12	0.01
Pueblo (1)	4	<0.01
Puget Sound Salish (5)	5	<0.01
Seminole (2)	5	<0.01
Shoshone (0)	1	<0.01
Sioux (11)	28	0.02
South American Ind. (2)	7	0.01
Spanish American Ind. (3)	21	0.02
Tlingit-Haida (Alaska Native) (1)	2	<0.01
Tohono O'Odham (3)	8	0.01
Tsimshian (Alaska Native) (0)	0	<0.01
Ute (0)	0	<0.01
Yakama (3)	3	<0.01
Yaqui (0)	0	<0.01
Yuman (0)	0	<0.01
Yup'ik (Alaska Native) (0)	1	<0.01
Asian (7,214)	8,487	6.15
Not Hispanic (7,190)	8,402	6.09
Hispanic (24)	85	0.06
Bangladeshi (24)	33	0.02
Bhutanese (0)	0	<0.01
Burmese (23)	24	0.02
Cambodian (6)	10	0.01
Chinese, ex. Taiwanese (2,196)	2,472	1.79
Filipino (300)	548	0.40
Hmong (5)	6	<0.01
Indian (1,393)	1,553	1.13
Indonesian (80)	93	0.07
Japanese (288)	486	0.35
Korean (1,850)	2,001	1.45
Laotian (7)	11	0.01
Malaysian (50)	60	0.04
Nepalese (21)	21	0.02
Pakistani (96)	112	0.08
Sri Lankan (38)	40	0.03
Taiwanese (252)	282	0.20
Thai (96)	121	0.09
Vietnamese (204)	262	0.19
Hawaii Native/Pacific Islander (62)	167	0.12
Not Hispanic (56)	138	0.10
Hispanic (6)	29	0.02
Fijian (1)	1	<0.01
Guamanian/Chamorro (12)	26	0.02
Marshallese (0)	0	<0.01
Native Hawaiian (20)	54	0.04
Samoan (6)	21	0.02
Tongan (0)	0	<0.01
White (121,109)	124,277	90.07
Not Hispanic (118,837)	121,628	88.15
Hispanic (2,272)	2,649	1.92

Notes: † The Census 2010 population figure is used to calculate the percentages in the Hispanic Origin and Race categories. Ancestry percentages are based on the 2006-2010 American Community Survey population (not shown); ‡ Numbers in parentheses indicate the number of people reporting a single ancestry; * Numbers in parentheses indicate the number of persons reporting this race alone, not in combination with any other race; Please refer to the Explanation of Data for more information.

Montgomery County
Population: 38,124

Ancestry	Population	%
Afghan (0)	0	<0.01
African, Sub-Saharan (0)	0	<0.01
African (0)	0	<0.01
Cape Verdean (0)	0	<0.01
Ethiopian (0)	0	<0.01
Ghanaian (0)	0	<0.01
Kenyan (0)	0	<0.01
Liberian (0)	0	<0.01
Nigerian (0)	0	<0.01
Senegalese (0)	0	<0.01
Sierra Leonean (0)	0	<0.01
Somalian (0)	0	<0.01
South African (0)	0	<0.01
Sudanese (0)	0	<0.01
Ugandan (0)	0	<0.01
Zimbabwean (0)	0	<0.01
Other Sub-Saharan African (0)	0	<0.01
Albanian (34)	34	0.09
Alsatian (0)	0	<0.01
American (6,304)	6,304	16.53
Arab (3)	8	0.02
Arab (0)	0	<0.01
Egyptian (0)	0	<0.01
Iraqi (0)	0	<0.01
Jordanian (0)	0	<0.01
Lebanese (3)	8	0.02
Moroccan (0)	0	<0.01
Palestinian (0)	0	<0.01
Syrian (0)	0	<0.01
Other Arab (0)	0	<0.01
Armenian (0)	0	<0.01
Assyrian/Chaldean/Syriac (0)	0	<0.01
Australian (0)	0	<0.01
Austrian (0)	0	<0.01
Basque (0)	0	<0.01
Belgian (6)	6	0.02
Brazilian (0)	0	<0.01
British (30)	80	0.21
Bulgarian (0)	0	<0.01
Cajun (11)	11	0.03
Canadian (23)	34	0.09
Carpatho Rusyn (0)	0	<0.01
Celtic (0)	0	<0.01
Croatian (41)	95	0.25
Cypriot (0)	0	<0.01
Czech (4)	20	0.05
Czechoslovakian (37)	74	0.19
Danish (0)	17	0.04
Dutch (186)	1,044	2.74
Eastern European (0)	0	<0.01
English (2,222)	4,610	12.09
Estonian (0)	0	<0.01
European (175)	193	0.51
Finnish (0)	68	0.18
French, ex. Basque (189)	686	1.80
French Canadian (12)	88	0.23
German (3,226)	8,601	22.55
German Russian (0)	0	<0.01
Greek (25)	44	0.12
Guyanese (0)	0	<0.01
Hungarian (0)	0	<0.01
Icelander (0)	0	<0.01
Iranian (0)	0	<0.01
Irish (1,442)	5,508	14.44
Israeli (0)	0	<0.01
Italian (406)	854	2.24
Latvian (0)	13	0.03
Lithuanian (0)	50	0.13
Luxemburger (0)	0	<0.01
Macedonian (0)	0	<0.01
Maltese (0)	0	<0.01
New Zealander (0)	0	<0.01
Northern European (0)	0	<0.01
Norwegian (25)	159	0.42
Pennsylvania German (0)	4	0.01
Polish (85)	389	1.02
Portuguese (0)	8	0.02
Romanian (45)	91	0.24
Russian (0)	0	<0.01
Scandinavian (31)	48	0.13
Scotch-Irish (272)	678	1.78
Scottish (454)	959	2.51
Serbian (0)	0	<0.01
Slavic (0)	6	0.02
Slovak (22)	50	0.13
Slovene (0)	11	0.03
Soviet Union (0)	0	<0.01
Swedish (65)	348	0.91
Swiss (9)	152	0.40
Turkish (0)	0	<0.01
Ukrainian (48)	68	0.18
Welsh (105)	252	0.66
West Indian, ex. Hispanic (0)	0	<0.01
Bahamian (0)	0	<0.01
Barbadian (0)	0	<0.01
Belizean (0)	0	<0.01
Bermudan (0)	0	<0.01
British West Indian (0)	0	<0.01
Dutch West Indian (0)	0	<0.01
Haitian (0)	0	<0.01
Jamaican (0)	0	<0.01
Trinidadian/Tobagonian (0)	0	<0.01
U.S. Virgin Islander (0)	0	<0.01
West Indian (0)	0	<0.01
Other West Indian (0)	0	<0.01
Yugoslavian (0)	0	<0.01

Hispanic Origin	Population	%
Hispanic or Latino (of any race)	1,739	4.56
Central American, ex. Mexican	57	0.15
Costa Rican	1	<0.01
Guatemalan	45	0.12
Honduran	6	0.02
Nicaraguan	0	<0.01
Panamanian	0	<0.01
Salvadoran	5	0.01
Other Central American	0	<0.01
Cuban	11	0.03
Dominican Republic	0	<0.01
Mexican	1,523	3.99
Puerto Rican	36	0.09
South American	37	0.10
Argentinean	6	0.02
Bolivian	1	<0.01
Chilean	5	0.01
Colombian	15	0.04
Ecuadorian	1	<0.01
Paraguayan	0	<0.01
Peruvian	8	0.02
Uruguayan	0	<0.01
Venezuelan	1	<0.01
Other South American	0	<0.01
Other Hispanic or Latino	75	0.20

Race*	Population	%
African-American/Black (327)	496	1.30
Not Hispanic (307)	469	1.23
Hispanic (20)	27	0.07
American Indian/Alaska Native (98)	259	0.68
Not Hispanic (72)	213	0.56
Hispanic (26)	46	0.12
Alaska Athabascan (Ala. Nat.) (0)	0	<0.01
Aleut (Alaska Native) (0)	0	<0.01
Apache (0)	6	0.02
Arapaho (0)	0	<0.01
Blackfeet (3)	7	0.02
Canadian/French Am. Ind. (0)	0	<0.01
Central American Ind. (0)	0	<0.01
Cherokee (18)	73	0.19
Cheyenne (1)	1	<0.01
Chickasaw (0)	0	<0.01
Chippewa (0)	0	<0.01
Choctaw (5)	11	0.03
Colville (0)	0	<0.01
Comanche (0)	0	<0.01
Cree (0)	0	<0.01
Creek (0)	0	<0.01
Crow (1)	1	<0.01
Delaware (0)	0	<0.01
Hopi (0)	0	<0.01
Houma (0)	0	<0.01
Inupiat (Alaska Native) (0)	0	<0.01
Iroquois (3)	7	0.02
Kiowa (1)	2	0.01
Lumbee (0)	0	<0.01
Menominee (0)	0	<0.01
Mexican American Ind. (5)	8	0.02
Navajo (0)	3	0.01
Osage (0)	0	<0.01
Ottawa (1)	1	<0.01
Paiute (0)	0	<0.01
Pima (0)	0	<0.01
Potawatomi (0)	0	<0.01
Pueblo (4)	4	0.01
Puget Sound Salish (0)	0	<0.01
Seminole (2)	2	0.01
Shoshone (0)	0	<0.01
Sioux (4)	9	0.02
South American Ind. (0)	0	<0.01
Spanish American Ind. (1)	3	0.01
Tlingit-Haida (Alaska Native) (0)	0	<0.01
Tohono O'Odham (0)	0	<0.01
Tsimshian (Alaska Native) (0)	0	<0.01
Ute (2)	2	0.01
Yakama (0)	0	<0.01
Yaqui (0)	0	<0.01
Yuman (0)	0	<0.01
Yup'ik (Alaska Native) (0)	0	<0.01
Asian (213)	287	0.75
Not Hispanic (209)	281	0.74
Hispanic (4)	6	0.02
Bangladeshi (5)	5	0.01
Bhutanese (0)	0	<0.01
Burmese (0)	0	<0.01
Cambodian (0)	0	<0.01
Chinese, ex. Taiwanese (62)	71	0.19
Filipino (27)	59	0.15
Hmong (0)	0	<0.01
Indian (57)	59	0.15
Indonesian (0)	0	<0.01
Japanese (20)	36	0.09
Korean (20)	32	0.08
Laotian (0)	0	<0.01
Malaysian (0)	1	<0.01
Nepalese (1)	1	<0.01
Pakistani (1)	1	<0.01
Sri Lankan (0)	0	<0.01
Taiwanese (1)	1	<0.01
Thai (1)	1	<0.01
Vietnamese (14)	15	0.04
Hawaii Native/Pacific Islander (6)	25	0.07
Not Hispanic (6)	22	0.06
Hispanic (0)	3	0.01
Fijian (0)	0	<0.01
Guamanian/Chamorro (0)	3	0.01
Marshallese (0)	0	<0.01
Native Hawaiian (4)	8	0.02
Samoan (1)	5	0.01
Tongan (0)	0	<0.01
White (36,309)	36,764	96.43
Not Hispanic (35,374)	35,752	93.78
Hispanic (935)	1,012	2.65

Notes: † The Census 2010 population figure is used to calculate the percentages in the Hispanic Origin and Race categories. Ancestry percentages are based on the 2006-2010 American Community Survey population (not shown); ‡ Numbers in parentheses indicate the number of people reporting a single ancestry; * Numbers in parentheses indicate the number of persons reporting this race alone, not in combination with any other race; Please refer to the Explanation of Data for more information.

Morgan County
Population: 68,894

Ancestry	Population	%
Afghan (0)	0	<0.01
African, Sub-Saharan (25)	79	0.12
African (25)	79	0.12
Cape Verdean (0)	0	<0.01
Ethiopian (0)	0	<0.01
Ghanaian (0)	0	<0.01
Kenyan (0)	0	<0.01
Liberian (0)	0	<0.01
Nigerian (0)	0	<0.01
Senegalese (0)	0	<0.01
Sierra Leonean (0)	0	<0.01
Somalian (0)	0	<0.01
South African (0)	0	<0.01
Sudanese (0)	0	<0.01
Ugandan (0)	0	<0.01
Zimbabwean (0)	0	<0.01
Other Sub-Saharan African (0)	0	<0.01
Albanian (0)	0	<0.01
Alsatian (0)	0	<0.01
American (9,793)	9,793	14.26
Arab (34)	50	0.07
Arab (0)	0	<0.01
Egyptian (0)	0	<0.01
Iraqi (0)	0	<0.01
Jordanian (16)	16	0.02
Lebanese (18)	34	0.05
Moroccan (0)	0	<0.01
Palestinian (0)	0	<0.01
Syrian (0)	0	<0.01
Other Arab (0)	0	<0.01
Armenian (0)	0	<0.01
Assyrian/Chaldean/Syriac (0)	0	<0.01
Australian (0)	0	<0.01
Austrian (16)	26	0.04
Basque (0)	0	<0.01
Belgian (0)	41	0.06
Brazilian (0)	0	<0.01
British (112)	286	0.42
Bulgarian (0)	0	<0.01
Cajun (0)	0	<0.01
Canadian (16)	43	0.06
Carpatho Rusyn (0)	0	<0.01
Celtic (0)	0	<0.01
Croatian (0)	5	0.01
Cypriot (0)	0	<0.01
Czech (11)	119	0.17
Czechoslovakian (48)	91	0.13
Danish (10)	45	0.07
Dutch (304)	1,510	2.20
Eastern European (0)	0	<0.01
English (4,750)	9,130	13.30
Estonian (0)	0	<0.01
European (524)	663	0.97
Finnish (15)	66	0.10
French, ex. Basque (341)	1,662	2.42
French Canadian (103)	118	0.17
German (6,614)	17,306	25.21
German Russian (0)	0	<0.01
Greek (43)	218	0.32
Guyanese (0)	0	<0.01
Hungarian (107)	254	0.37
Icelander (0)	0	<0.01
Iranian (0)	0	<0.01
Irish (3,575)	10,663	15.53
Israeli (0)	0	<0.01
Italian (556)	1,340	1.95
Latvian (0)	0	<0.01
Lithuanian (3)	3	<0.01
Luxemburger (0)	0	<0.01
Macedonian (0)	0	<0.01
Maltese (0)	0	<0.01
New Zealander (0)	0	<0.01
Northern European (23)	35	0.05
Norwegian (52)	325	0.47
Pennsylvania German (0)	26	0.04
Polish (290)	880	1.28
Portuguese (17)	40	0.06
Romanian (29)	90	0.13
Russian (23)	61	0.09
Scandinavian (0)	102	0.15
Scotch-Irish (429)	1,276	1.86
Scottish (583)	2,018	2.94
Serbian (0)	0	<0.01
Slavic (0)	12	0.02
Slovak (21)	53	0.08
Slovene (36)	142	0.21
Soviet Union (0)	0	<0.01
Swedish (62)	431	0.63
Swiss (208)	307	0.45
Turkish (0)	0	<0.01
Ukrainian (9)	37	0.05
Welsh (111)	408	0.59
West Indian, ex. Hispanic (0)	0	<0.01
Bahamian (0)	0	<0.01
Barbadian (0)	0	<0.01
Belizean (0)	0	<0.01
Bermudan (0)	0	<0.01
British West Indian (0)	0	<0.01
Dutch West Indian (0)	0	<0.01
Haitian (0)	0	<0.01
Jamaican (0)	0	<0.01
Trinidadian/Tobagonian (0)	0	<0.01
U.S. Virgin Islander (0)	0	<0.01
West Indian (0)	0	<0.01
Other West Indian (0)	0	<0.01
Yugoslavian (0)	23	0.03

Hispanic Origin	Population	%
Hispanic or Latino (of any race)	820	1.19
Central American, ex. Mexican	51	0.07
Costa Rican	8	0.01
Guatemalan	19	0.03
Honduran	5	0.01
Nicaraguan	4	0.01
Panamanian	14	0.02
Salvadoran	1	<0.01
Other Central American	0	<0.01
Cuban	30	0.04
Dominican Republic	6	0.01
Mexican	529	0.77
Puerto Rican	71	0.10
South American	38	0.06
Argentinean	5	0.01
Bolivian	2	<0.01
Chilean	1	<0.01
Colombian	12	0.02
Ecuadorian	2	<0.01
Paraguayan	0	<0.01
Peruvian	14	0.02
Uruguayan	0	<0.01
Venezuelan	2	<0.01
Other South American	0	<0.01
Other Hispanic or Latino	95	0.14

Race*	Population	%
African-American/Black (176)	396	0.57
Not Hispanic (175)	388	0.56
Hispanic (1)	8	0.01
American Indian/Alaska Native (200)	506	0.73
Not Hispanic (177)	472	0.69
Hispanic (23)	34	0.05
Alaska Athabascan (Ala. Nat.) (0)	0	<0.01
Aleut (Alaska Native) (0)	0	<0.01
Apache (0)	3	<0.01
Arapaho (1)	1	<0.01
Blackfeet (2)	7	0.01
Canadian/French Am. Ind. (3)	3	<0.01
Central American Ind. (2)	2	<0.01
Cherokee (54)	186	0.27
Cheyenne (0)	0	<0.01
Chickasaw (3)	3	<0.01
Chippewa (4)	11	0.02
Choctaw (3)	10	0.01
Colville (0)	0	<0.01
Comanche (5)	6	0.01
Cree (0)	0	<0.01
Creek (4)	5	0.01
Crow (0)	2	<0.01
Delaware (2)	2	<0.01
Hopi (0)	1	<0.01
Houma (0)	3	<0.01
Inupiat (Alaska Native) (2)	2	<0.01
Iroquois (1)	1	<0.01
Kiowa (1)	1	<0.01
Lumbee (6)	6	0.01
Menominee (0)	0	<0.01
Mexican American Ind. (5)	6	0.01
Navajo (2)	4	0.01
Osage (0)	0	<0.01
Ottawa (1)	1	<0.01
Paiute (1)	2	<0.01
Pima (0)	0	<0.01
Potawatomi (0)	0	<0.01
Pueblo (0)	0	<0.01
Puget Sound Salish (0)	0	<0.01
Seminole (0)	0	<0.01
Shoshone (0)	1	<0.01
Sioux (6)	24	0.03
South American Ind. (0)	1	<0.01
Spanish American Ind. (0)	0	<0.01
Tlingit-Haida (Alaska Native) (0)	0	<0.01
Tohono O'Odham (0)	0	<0.01
Tsimshian (Alaska Native) (0)	0	<0.01
Ute (0)	0	<0.01
Yakama (0)	0	<0.01
Yaqui (0)	0	<0.01
Yuman (0)	0	<0.01
Yup'ik (Alaska Native) (0)	0	<0.01
Asian (248)	377	0.55
Not Hispanic (241)	369	0.54
Hispanic (7)	8	0.01
Bangladeshi (0)	0	<0.01
Bhutanese (0)	0	<0.01
Burmese (0)	0	<0.01
Cambodian (3)	3	<0.01
Chinese, ex. Taiwanese (69)	81	0.12
Filipino (61)	98	0.14
Hmong (0)	0	<0.01
Indian (30)	45	0.07
Indonesian (0)	0	<0.01
Japanese (13)	34	0.05
Korean (25)	43	0.06
Laotian (1)	4	0.01
Malaysian (1)	1	<0.01
Nepalese (0)	0	<0.01
Pakistani (0)	1	<0.01
Sri Lankan (0)	0	<0.01
Taiwanese (3)	11	0.02
Thai (6)	10	0.01
Vietnamese (17)	24	0.03
Hawaii Native/Pacific Islander (19)	44	0.06
Not Hispanic (19)	44	0.06
Hispanic (0)	0	<0.01
Fijian (0)	0	<0.01
Guamanian/Chamorro (1)	9	0.01
Marshallese (0)	0	<0.01
Native Hawaiian (2)	8	0.01
Samoan (0)	8	0.01
Tongan (0)	0	<0.01
White (67,307)	68,005	98.71
Not Hispanic (66,782)	67,418	97.86
Hispanic (525)	587	0.85

Notes: † The Census 2010 population figure is used to calculate the percentages in the Hispanic Origin and Race categories. Ancestry percentages are based on the 2006-2010 American Community Survey population (not shown); ‡ Numbers in parentheses indicate the number of people reporting a single ancestry; * Numbers in parentheses indicate the number of persons reporting this race alone, not in combination with any other race; Please refer to the Explanation of Data for more information.

Newton County
Population: 14,244

Ancestry	Population	%
Afghan (0)	0	<0.01
African, Sub-Saharan (33)	33	0.23
African (33)	33	0.23
Cape Verdean (0)	0	<0.01
Ethiopian (0)	0	<0.01
Ghanaian (0)	0	<0.01
Kenyan (0)	0	<0.01
Liberian (0)	0	<0.01
Nigerian (0)	0	<0.01
Senegalese (0)	0	<0.01
Sierra Leonean (0)	0	<0.01
Somalian (0)	0	<0.01
South African (0)	0	<0.01
Sudanese (0)	0	<0.01
Ugandan (0)	0	<0.01
Zimbabwean (0)	0	<0.01
Other Sub-Saharan African (0)	0	<0.01
Albanian (0)	0	<0.01
Alsatian (0)	0	<0.01
American (929)	929	6.50
Arab (8)	18	0.13
Arab (0)	0	<0.01
Egyptian (0)	0	<0.01
Iraqi (0)	0	<0.01
Jordanian (0)	0	<0.01
Lebanese (8)	8	0.06
Moroccan (0)	0	<0.01
Palestinian (0)	0	<0.01
Syrian (0)	10	0.07
Other Arab (0)	0	<0.01
Armenian (0)	0	<0.01
Assyrian/Chaldean/Syriac (0)	0	<0.01
Australian (4)	4	0.03
Austrian (25)	96	0.67
Basque (0)	0	<0.01
Belgian (0)	0	<0.01
Brazilian (0)	0	<0.01
British (0)	0	<0.01
Bulgarian (0)	3	0.02
Cajun (0)	0	<0.01
Canadian (3)	3	0.02
Carpatho Rusyn (0)	0	<0.01
Celtic (0)	0	<0.01
Croatian (28)	124	0.87
Cypriot (0)	0	<0.01
Czech (5)	149	1.04
Czechoslovakian (0)	13	0.09
Danish (23)	53	0.37
Dutch (273)	1,082	7.57
Eastern European (8)	8	0.06
English (598)	1,571	10.99
Estonian (0)	0	<0.01
European (141)	141	0.99
Finnish (24)	47	0.33
French, ex. Basque (112)	741	5.18
French Canadian (47)	118	0.83
German (1,384)	4,351	30.43
German Russian (0)	0	<0.01
Greek (16)	22	0.15
Guyanese (0)	0	<0.01
Hungarian (55)	86	0.60
Icelander (0)	0	<0.01
Iranian (0)	0	<0.01
Irish (452)	2,418	16.91
Israeli (0)	0	<0.01
Italian (144)	566	3.96
Latvian (0)	6	0.04
Lithuanian (4)	4	0.03
Luxemburger (0)	5	0.03
Macedonian (0)	0	<0.01
Maltese (0)	0	<0.01
New Zealander (0)	0	<0.01
Northern European (9)	9	0.06
Norwegian (4)	121	0.85
Pennsylvania German (6)	15	0.10
Polish (449)	1,152	8.06
Portuguese (3)	3	0.02
Romanian (41)	41	0.29
Russian (0)	90	0.63
Scandinavian (0)	0	<0.01
Scotch-Irish (107)	282	1.97
Scottish (72)	249	1.74
Serbian (13)	21	0.15
Slavic (0)	0	<0.01
Slovak (24)	71	0.50
Slovene (0)	0	<0.01
Soviet Union (0)	0	<0.01
Swedish (56)	284	1.99
Swiss (0)	13	0.09
Turkish (0)	0	<0.01
Ukrainian (0)	0	<0.01
Welsh (36)	82	0.57
West Indian, ex. Hispanic (0)	0	<0.01
Bahamian (0)	0	<0.01
Barbadian (0)	0	<0.01
Belizean (0)	0	<0.01
Bermudan (0)	0	<0.01
British West Indian (0)	0	<0.01
Dutch West Indian (0)	0	<0.01
Haitian (0)	0	<0.01
Jamaican (0)	0	<0.01
Trinidadian/Tobagonian (0)	0	<0.01
U.S. Virgin Islander (0)	0	<0.01
West Indian (0)	0	<0.01
Other West Indian (0)	0	<0.01
Yugoslavian (0)	0	<0.01

Hispanic Origin	Population	%
Hispanic or Latino (of any race)	717	5.03
Central American, ex. Mexican	70	0.49
Costa Rican	0	<0.01
Guatemalan	5	0.04
Honduran	1	0.01
Nicaraguan	0	<0.01
Panamanian	0	<0.01
Salvadoran	64	0.45
Other Central American	0	<0.01
Cuban	2	0.01
Dominican Republic	0	<0.01
Mexican	536	3.76
Puerto Rican	33	0.23
South American	5	0.04
Argentinean	0	<0.01
Bolivian	0	<0.01
Chilean	1	0.01
Colombian	0	<0.01
Ecuadorian	0	<0.01
Paraguayan	0	<0.01
Peruvian	0	<0.01
Uruguayan	0	<0.01
Venezuelan	4	0.03
Other South American	0	<0.01
Other Hispanic or Latino	71	0.50

Race*	Population	%
African-American/Black (56)	91	0.64
Not Hispanic (53)	82	0.58
Hispanic (3)	9	0.06
American Indian/Alaska Native (42)	102	0.72
Not Hispanic (33)	84	0.59
Hispanic (9)	18	0.13
Alaska Athabascan (Ala. Nat.) (0)	0	<0.01
Aleut (Alaska Native) (0)	0	<0.01
Apache (0)	2	0.01
Arapaho (0)	0	<0.01
Blackfeet (0)	2	0.01
Canadian/French Am. Ind. (0)	0	<0.01
Central American Ind. (0)	0	<0.01
Cherokee (4)	21	0.15
Cheyenne (0)	1	0.01
Chickasaw (0)	0	<0.01
Chippewa (5)	11	0.08
Choctaw (0)	0	<0.01
Colville (0)	0	<0.01
Comanche (0)	0	<0.01
Cree (0)	0	<0.01
Creek (0)	3	0.02
Crow (1)	1	0.01
Delaware (0)	0	<0.01
Hopi (0)	0	<0.01
Houma (0)	0	<0.01
Inupiat (Alaska Native) (0)	0	<0.01
Iroquois (0)	3	0.02
Kiowa (0)	0	<0.01
Lumbee (0)	0	<0.01
Menominee (0)	0	<0.01
Mexican American Ind. (0)	2	0.01
Navajo (0)	0	<0.01
Osage (0)	0	<0.01
Ottawa (0)	0	<0.01
Paiute (0)	0	<0.01
Pima (0)	0	<0.01
Potawatomi (0)	2	0.01
Pueblo (0)	0	<0.01
Puget Sound Salish (0)	0	<0.01
Seminole (0)	1	0.01
Shoshone (0)	0	<0.01
Sioux (0)	4	0.03
South American Ind. (0)	0	<0.01
Spanish American Ind. (0)	0	<0.01
Tlingit-Haida (Alaska Native) (0)	0	<0.01
Tohono O'Odham (0)	0	<0.01
Tsimshian (Alaska Native) (0)	0	<0.01
Ute (0)	0	<0.01
Yakama (0)	0	<0.01
Yaqui (0)	0	<0.01
Yuman (0)	0	<0.01
Yup'ik (Alaska Native) (0)	0	<0.01
Asian (38)	51	0.36
Not Hispanic (38)	50	0.35
Hispanic (0)	1	0.01
Bangladeshi (0)	0	<0.01
Bhutanese (0)	0	<0.01
Burmese (0)	0	<0.01
Cambodian (0)	0	<0.01
Chinese, ex. Taiwanese (10)	13	0.09
Filipino (13)	20	0.14
Hmong (0)	0	<0.01
Indian (4)	5	0.04
Indonesian (0)	0	<0.01
Japanese (1)	1	0.01
Korean (6)	8	0.06
Laotian (0)	0	<0.01
Malaysian (0)	0	<0.01
Nepalese (0)	0	<0.01
Pakistani (0)	0	<0.01
Sri Lankan (0)	0	<0.01
Taiwanese (0)	0	<0.01
Thai (1)	1	0.01
Vietnamese (3)	3	0.02
Hawaii Native/Pacific Islander (2)	5	0.04
Not Hispanic (2)	5	0.04
Hispanic (0)	0	<0.01
Fijian (0)	0	<0.01
Guamanian/Chamorro (0)	0	<0.01
Marshallese (0)	0	<0.01
Native Hawaiian (0)	0	<0.01
Samoan (0)	0	<0.01
Tongan (0)	0	<0.01
White (13,700)	13,846	97.21
Not Hispanic (13,296)	13,391	94.01
Hispanic (404)	455	3.19

*Notes: † The Census 2010 population figure is used to calculate the percentages in the Hispanic Origin and Race categories. Ancestry percentages are based on the 2006-2010 American Community Survey population (not shown); ‡ Numbers in parentheses indicate the number of people reporting a single ancestry; * Numbers in parentheses indicate the number of persons reporting this race alone, not in combination with any other race; Please refer to the Explanation of Data for more information.*

Noble County
Population: 47,536

Ancestry	Population	%
Afghan (0)	0	<0.01
African, Sub-Saharan (32)	40	0.08
African (0)	0	<0.01
Cape Verdean (0)	0	<0.01
Ethiopian (0)	0	<0.01
Ghanaian (0)	0	<0.01
Kenyan (0)	0	<0.01
Liberian (0)	0	<0.01
Nigerian (0)	0	<0.01
Senegalese (0)	0	<0.01
Sierra Leonean (0)	0	<0.01
Somalian (0)	0	<0.01
South African (32)	40	0.08
Sudanese (0)	0	<0.01
Ugandan (0)	0	<0.01
Zimbabwean (0)	0	<0.01
Other Sub-Saharan African (0)	0	<0.01
Albanian (0)	0	<0.01
Alsatian (0)	0	<0.01
American (5,294)	5,294	11.14
Arab (16)	35	0.07
Arab (0)	0	<0.01
Egyptian (0)	19	0.04
Iraqi (0)	0	<0.01
Jordanian (0)	0	<0.01
Lebanese (16)	16	0.03
Moroccan (0)	0	<0.01
Palestinian (0)	0	<0.01
Syrian (0)	0	<0.01
Other Arab (0)	0	<0.01
Armenian (0)	0	<0.01
Assyrian/Chaldean/Syriac (0)	0	<0.01
Australian (0)	0	<0.01
Austrian (9)	45	0.09
Basque (0)	0	<0.01
Belgian (17)	160	0.34
Brazilian (0)	0	<0.01
British (61)	133	0.28
Bulgarian (0)	0	<0.01
Cajun (0)	0	<0.01
Canadian (82)	110	0.23
Carpatho Rusyn (0)	0	<0.01
Celtic (0)	0	<0.01
Croatian (0)	0	<0.01
Cypriot (0)	0	<0.01
Czech (56)	89	0.19
Czechoslovakian (0)	0	<0.01
Danish (0)	104	0.22
Dutch (408)	1,136	2.39
Eastern European (2)	2	<0.01
English (1,450)	4,033	8.49
Estonian (0)	0	<0.01
European (282)	289	0.61
Finnish (0)	0	<0.01
French, ex. Basque (291)	1,493	3.14
French Canadian (70)	112	0.24
German (7,671)	15,283	32.17
German Russian (0)	88	0.19
Greek (16)	72	0.15
Guyanese (0)	0	<0.01
Hungarian (52)	118	0.25
Icelander (0)	0	<0.01
Iranian (0)	0	<0.01
Irish (1,419)	4,657	9.80
Israeli (0)	0	<0.01
Italian (175)	770	1.62
Latvian (0)	0	<0.01
Lithuanian (13)	24	0.05
Luxemburger (0)	0	<0.01
Macedonian (0)	0	<0.01
Maltese (0)	0	<0.01
New Zealander (0)	0	<0.01
Northern European (0)	0	<0.01
Norwegian (68)	265	0.56
Pennsylvania German (430)	490	1.03
Polish (495)	1,055	2.22
Portuguese (0)	0	<0.01
Romanian (7)	11	0.02
Russian (31)	31	0.07
Scandinavian (35)	35	0.07
Scotch-Irish (183)	619	1.30
Scottish (157)	889	1.87
Serbian (0)	0	<0.01
Slavic (0)	0	<0.01
Slovak (0)	82	0.17
Slovene (0)	0	<0.01
Soviet Union (0)	0	<0.01
Swedish (157)	526	1.11
Swiss (156)	293	0.62
Turkish (0)	0	<0.01
Ukrainian (0)	0	<0.01
Welsh (16)	148	0.31
West Indian, ex. Hispanic (0)	75	0.16
Bahamian (0)	0	<0.01
Barbadian (0)	0	<0.01
Belizean (0)	0	<0.01
Bermudan (0)	0	<0.01
British West Indian (0)	0	<0.01
Dutch West Indian (0)	0	<0.01
Haitian (0)	0	<0.01
Jamaican (0)	75	0.16
Trinidadian/Tobagonian (0)	0	<0.01
U.S. Virgin Islander (0)	0	<0.01
West Indian (0)	0	<0.01
Other West Indian (0)	0	<0.01
Yugoslavian (14)	59	0.12

Hispanic Origin	Population	%
Hispanic or Latino (of any race)	4,567	9.61
Central American, ex. Mexican	54	0.11
Costa Rican	0	<0.01
Guatemalan	20	0.04
Honduran	18	0.04
Nicaraguan	0	<0.01
Panamanian	0	<0.01
Salvadoran	16	0.03
Other Central American	0	<0.01
Cuban	5	0.01
Dominican Republic	3	0.01
Mexican	4,297	9.04
Puerto Rican	38	0.08
South American	13	0.03
Argentinean	0	<0.01
Bolivian	0	<0.01
Chilean	0	<0.01
Colombian	4	0.01
Ecuadorian	2	<0.01
Paraguayan	0	<0.01
Peruvian	6	0.01
Uruguayan	0	<0.01
Venezuelan	1	<0.01
Other South American	0	<0.01
Other Hispanic or Latino	157	0.33

Race*	Population	%
African-American/Black (185)	335	0.70
Not Hispanic (170)	309	0.65
Hispanic (15)	26	0.05
American Indian/Alaska Native (102)	290	0.61
Not Hispanic (90)	254	0.53
Hispanic (12)	36	0.08
Alaska Athabascan (Ala. Nat.) (0)	0	<0.01
Aleut (Alaska Native) (1)	1	<0.01
Apache (0)	2	<0.01
Arapaho (0)	0	<0.01
Blackfeet (2)	7	0.01
Canadian/French Am. Ind. (0)	2	<0.01
Central American Ind. (0)	0	<0.01
Cherokee (18)	83	0.17
Cheyenne (0)	0	<0.01
Chickasaw (0)	0	<0.01
Chippewa (8)	12	0.03
Choctaw (0)	1	<0.01
Colville (0)	0	<0.01
Comanche (0)	0	<0.01
Cree (0)	0	<0.01
Creek (0)	0	<0.01
Crow (5)	5	0.01
Delaware (0)	1	<0.01
Hopi (0)	0	<0.01
Houma (0)	0	<0.01
Inupiat (Alaska Native) (0)	0	<0.01
Iroquois (2)	6	0.01
Kiowa (0)	0	<0.01
Lumbee (0)	0	<0.01
Menominee (1)	1	<0.01
Mexican American Ind. (5)	10	0.02
Navajo (5)	6	0.01
Osage (0)	1	<0.01
Ottawa (0)	0	<0.01
Paiute (0)	0	<0.01
Pima (0)	0	<0.01
Potawatomi (0)	1	<0.01
Pueblo (0)	0	<0.01
Puget Sound Salish (0)	0	<0.01
Seminole (0)	0	<0.01
Shoshone (0)	0	<0.01
Sioux (10)	17	0.04
South American Ind. (1)	1	<0.01
Spanish American Ind. (0)	0	<0.01
Tlingit-Haida (Alaska Native) (2)	2	<0.01
Tohono O'Odham (0)	0	<0.01
Tsimshian (Alaska Native) (0)	0	<0.01
Ute (0)	0	<0.01
Yakama (0)	0	<0.01
Yaqui (0)	0	<0.01
Yuman (0)	0	<0.01
Yup'ik (Alaska Native) (0)	0	<0.01
Asian (176)	267	0.56
Not Hispanic (174)	258	0.54
Hispanic (2)	9	0.02
Bangladeshi (0)	0	<0.01
Bhutanese (0)	0	<0.01
Burmese (0)	0	<0.01
Cambodian (7)	7	0.01
Chinese, ex. Taiwanese (31)	36	0.08
Filipino (40)	78	0.16
Hmong (0)	0	<0.01
Indian (24)	33	0.07
Indonesian (0)	0	<0.01
Japanese (7)	13	0.03
Korean (14)	18	0.04
Laotian (11)	11	0.02
Malaysian (0)	0	<0.01
Nepalese (0)	0	<0.01
Pakistani (5)	5	0.01
Sri Lankan (1)	1	<0.01
Taiwanese (0)	0	<0.01
Thai (5)	6	0.01
Vietnamese (28)	47	0.10
Hawaii Native/Pacific Islander (6)	30	0.06
Not Hispanic (5)	24	0.05
Hispanic (1)	6	0.01
Fijian (0)	0	<0.01
Guamanian/Chamorro (2)	4	0.01
Marshallese (0)	0	<0.01
Native Hawaiian (2)	14	0.03
Samoan (0)	0	<0.01
Tongan (0)	0	<0.01
White (43,970)	44,565	93.75
Not Hispanic (42,104)	42,498	89.40
Hispanic (1,866)	2,067	4.35

Notes: † The Census 2010 population figure is used to calculate the percentages in the Hispanic Origin and Race categories. Ancestry percentages are based on the 2006-2010 American Community Survey population (not shown); ‡ Numbers in parentheses indicate the number of people reporting a single ancestry; * Numbers in parentheses indicate the number of persons reporting this race alone, not in combination with any other race; Please refer to the Explanation of Data for more information.

Ohio County
Population: 6,128

Ancestry	Population	%
Afghan (0)	0	<0.01
African, Sub-Saharan (0)	0	<0.01
African (0)	0	<0.01
Cape Verdean (0)	0	<0.01
Ethiopian (0)	0	<0.01
Ghanaian (0)	0	<0.01
Kenyan (0)	0	<0.01
Liberian (0)	0	<0.01
Nigerian (0)	0	<0.01
Senegalese (0)	0	<0.01
Sierra Leonean (0)	0	<0.01
Somalian (0)	0	<0.01
South African (0)	0	<0.01
Sudanese (0)	0	<0.01
Ugandan (0)	0	<0.01
Zimbabwean (0)	0	<0.01
Other Sub-Saharan African (0)	0	<0.01
Albanian (0)	0	<0.01
Alsatian (0)	0	<0.01
American (742)	742	12.23
Arab (0)	0	<0.01
Arab (0)	0	<0.01
Egyptian (0)	0	<0.01
Iraqi (0)	0	<0.01
Jordanian (0)	0	<0.01
Lebanese (0)	0	<0.01
Moroccan (0)	0	<0.01
Palestinian (0)	0	<0.01
Syrian (0)	0	<0.01
Other Arab (0)	0	<0.01
Armenian (0)	0	<0.01
Assyrian/Chaldean/Syriac (0)	0	<0.01
Australian (0)	0	<0.01
Austrian (0)	0	<0.01
Basque (0)	0	<0.01
Belgian (0)	26	0.43
Brazilian (0)	0	<0.01
British (18)	18	0.30
Bulgarian (0)	0	<0.01
Cajun (0)	0	<0.01
Canadian (0)	0	<0.01
Carpatho Rusyn (0)	0	<0.01
Celtic (0)	0	<0.01
Croatian (0)	0	<0.01
Cypriot (0)	0	<0.01
Czech (0)	0	<0.01
Czechoslovakian (0)	0	<0.01
Danish (0)	0	<0.01
Dutch (26)	60	0.99
Eastern European (0)	0	<0.01
English (221)	443	7.30
Estonian (0)	0	<0.01
European (62)	62	1.02
Finnish (0)	0	<0.01
French, ex. Basque (53)	137	2.26
French Canadian (6)	40	0.66
German (1,078)	2,031	33.48
German Russian (0)	0	<0.01
Greek (0)	0	<0.01
Guyanese (0)	0	<0.01
Hungarian (53)	82	1.35
Icelander (0)	0	<0.01
Iranian (0)	0	<0.01
Irish (268)	764	12.59
Israeli (0)	0	<0.01
Italian (93)	263	4.33
Latvian (0)	0	<0.01
Lithuanian (0)	0	<0.01
Luxemburger (0)	0	<0.01
Macedonian (0)	0	<0.01
Maltese (0)	0	<0.01
New Zealander (0)	0	<0.01
Northern European (0)	0	<0.01
Norwegian (0)	0	<0.01
Pennsylvania German (0)	0	<0.01
Polish (109)	118	1.94
Portuguese (0)	3	0.05
Romanian (0)	3	0.05
Russian (0)	0	<0.01
Scandinavian (0)	6	0.10
Scotch-Irish (16)	72	1.19
Scottish (53)	95	1.57
Serbian (0)	0	<0.01
Slavic (0)	0	<0.01
Slovak (5)	12	0.20
Slovene (0)	0	<0.01
Soviet Union (0)	0	<0.01
Swedish (0)	3	0.05
Swiss (0)	0	<0.01
Turkish (0)	0	<0.01
Ukrainian (0)	0	<0.01
Welsh (0)	0	<0.01
West Indian, ex. Hispanic (0)	0	<0.01
Bahamian (0)	0	<0.01
Barbadian (0)	0	<0.01
Belizean (0)	0	<0.01
Bermudan (0)	0	<0.01
British West Indian (0)	0	<0.01
Dutch West Indian (0)	0	<0.01
Haitian (0)	0	<0.01
Jamaican (0)	0	<0.01
Trinidadian/Tobagonian (0)	0	<0.01
U.S. Virgin Islander (0)	0	<0.01
West Indian (0)	0	<0.01
Other West Indian (0)	0	<0.01
Yugoslavian (0)	0	<0.01

Hispanic Origin	Population	%
Hispanic or Latino (of any race)	69	1.13
Central American, ex. Mexican	7	0.11
Costa Rican	0	<0.01
Guatemalan	5	0.08
Honduran	1	0.02
Nicaraguan	1	0.02
Panamanian	0	<0.01
Salvadoran	0	<0.01
Other Central American	0	<0.01
Cuban	1	0.02
Dominican Republic	0	<0.01
Mexican	48	0.78
Puerto Rican	2	0.03
South American	2	0.03
Argentinean	1	0.02
Bolivian	0	<0.01
Chilean	0	<0.01
Colombian	0	<0.01
Ecuadorian	0	<0.01
Paraguayan	0	<0.01
Peruvian	1	0.02
Uruguayan	0	<0.01
Venezuelan	0	<0.01
Other South American	0	<0.01
Other Hispanic or Latino	9	0.15

Race*	Population	%
African-American/Black (22)	31	0.51
Not Hispanic (21)	30	0.49
Hispanic (1)	1	0.02
American Indian/Alaska Native (12)	34	0.55
Not Hispanic (11)	33	0.54
Hispanic (1)	1	0.02
Alaska Athabascan (Ala. Nat.) (0)	0	<0.01
Aleut (Alaska Native) (0)	0	<0.01
Apache (0)	0	<0.01
Arapaho (0)	0	<0.01
Blackfeet (0)	0	<0.01
Canadian/French Am. Ind. (0)	0	<0.01
Central American Ind. (0)	0	<0.01
Cherokee (2)	14	0.23
Cheyenne (0)	0	<0.01
Chickasaw (0)	0	<0.01
Chippewa (0)	0	<0.01
Choctaw (0)	1	0.02
Colville (0)	0	<0.01
Comanche (0)	0	<0.01
Cree (0)	0	<0.01
Creek (0)	0	<0.01
Crow (0)	0	<0.01
Delaware (3)	7	0.11
Hopi (0)	0	<0.01
Houma (0)	0	<0.01
Inupiat (Alaska Native) (0)	0	<0.01
Iroquois (0)	0	<0.01
Kiowa (0)	0	<0.01
Lumbee (0)	0	<0.01
Menominee (0)	0	<0.01
Mexican American Ind. (0)	0	<0.01
Navajo (0)	0	<0.01
Osage (0)	0	<0.01
Ottawa (0)	0	<0.01
Paiute (0)	0	<0.01
Pima (0)	0	<0.01
Potawatomi (0)	0	<0.01
Pueblo (0)	0	<0.01
Puget Sound Salish (0)	0	<0.01
Seminole (0)	0	<0.01
Shoshone (0)	0	<0.01
Sioux (0)	0	<0.01
South American Ind. (0)	0	<0.01
Spanish American Ind. (0)	0	<0.01
Tlingit-Haida (Alaska Native) (0)	0	<0.01
Tohono O'Odham (0)	0	<0.01
Tsimshian (Alaska Native) (0)	0	<0.01
Ute (0)	0	<0.01
Yakama (0)	0	<0.01
Yaqui (0)	0	<0.01
Yuman (0)	0	<0.01
Yup'ik (Alaska Native) (0)	0	<0.01
Asian (19)	25	0.41
Not Hispanic (19)	25	0.41
Hispanic (0)	0	<0.01
Bangladeshi (0)	0	<0.01
Bhutanese (0)	0	<0.01
Burmese (0)	0	<0.01
Cambodian (0)	0	<0.01
Chinese, ex. Taiwanese (6)	6	0.10
Filipino (7)	7	0.11
Hmong (0)	0	<0.01
Indian (0)	0	<0.01
Indonesian (0)	0	<0.01
Japanese (1)	6	0.10
Korean (1)	1	0.02
Laotian (0)	0	<0.01
Malaysian (0)	0	<0.01
Nepalese (0)	0	<0.01
Pakistani (0)	0	<0.01
Sri Lankan (0)	0	<0.01
Taiwanese (0)	0	<0.01
Thai (1)	1	0.02
Vietnamese (3)	3	0.05
Hawaii Native/Pacific Islander (0)	0	<0.01
Not Hispanic (0)	0	<0.01
Hispanic (0)	0	<0.01
Fijian (0)	0	<0.01
Guamanian/Chamorro (0)	0	<0.01
Marshallese (0)	0	<0.01
Native Hawaiian (0)	0	<0.01
Samoan (0)	0	<0.01
Tongan (0)	0	<0.01
White (6,012)	6,056	98.83
Not Hispanic (5,967)	6,005	97.99
Hispanic (45)	51	0.83

Notes: † The Census 2010 population figure is used to calculate the percentages in the Hispanic Origin and Race categories. Ancestry percentages are based on the 2006-2010 American Community Survey population (not shown); ‡ Numbers in parentheses indicate the number of people reporting a single ancestry; * Numbers in parentheses indicate the number of persons reporting this race alone, not in combination with any other race; Please refer to the Explanation of Data for more information.

Orange County
Population: 19,840

Ancestry	Population	%
Afghan (0)	0	<0.01
African, Sub-Saharan (10)	10	0.05
African (10)	10	0.05
Cape Verdean (0)	0	<0.01
Ethiopian (0)	0	<0.01
Ghanaian (0)	0	<0.01
Kenyan (0)	0	<0.01
Liberian (0)	0	<0.01
Nigerian (0)	0	<0.01
Senegalese (0)	0	<0.01
Sierra Leonean (0)	0	<0.01
Somalian (0)	0	<0.01
South African (0)	0	<0.01
Sudanese (0)	0	<0.01
Ugandan (0)	0	<0.01
Zimbabwean (0)	0	<0.01
Other Sub-Saharan African (0)	0	<0.01
Albanian (0)	0	<0.01
Alsatian (0)	0	<0.01
American (2,390)	2,390	12.06
Arab (0)	0	<0.01
Arab (0)	0	<0.01
Egyptian (0)	0	<0.01
Iraqi (0)	0	<0.01
Jordanian (0)	0	<0.01
Lebanese (0)	0	<0.01
Moroccan (0)	0	<0.01
Palestinian (0)	0	<0.01
Syrian (0)	0	<0.01
Other Arab (0)	0	<0.01
Armenian (0)	0	<0.01
Assyrian/Chaldean/Syriac (0)	0	<0.01
Australian (0)	0	<0.01
Austrian (0)	0	<0.01
Basque (0)	0	<0.01
Belgian (0)	0	<0.01
Brazilian (0)	0	<0.01
British (41)	53	0.27
Bulgarian (0)	0	<0.01
Cajun (0)	34	0.17
Canadian (0)	0	<0.01
Carpatho Rusyn (0)	0	<0.01
Celtic (0)	5	0.03
Croatian (0)	0	<0.01
Cypriot (0)	0	<0.01
Czech (8)	18	0.09
Czechoslovakian (0)	0	<0.01
Danish (12)	12	0.06
Dutch (79)	341	1.72
Eastern European (0)	0	<0.01
English (1,068)	1,929	9.73
Estonian (0)	0	<0.01
European (148)	154	0.78
Finnish (0)	11	0.06
French, ex. Basque (70)	370	1.87
French Canadian (18)	18	0.09
German (1,681)	3,731	18.82
German Russian (0)	0	<0.01
Greek (0)	8	0.04
Guyanese (0)	0	<0.01
Hungarian (0)	51	0.26
Icelander (0)	0	<0.01
Iranian (0)	0	<0.01
Irish (919)	2,449	12.36
Israeli (0)	0	<0.01
Italian (70)	229	1.16
Latvian (0)	0	<0.01
Lithuanian (0)	0	<0.01
Luxemburger (0)	0	<0.01
Macedonian (0)	0	<0.01
Maltese (0)	0	<0.01
New Zealander (0)	0	<0.01
Northern European (0)	0	<0.01
Norwegian (37)	49	0.25
Pennsylvania German (856)	913	4.61
Polish (102)	142	0.72
Portuguese (0)	0	<0.01
Romanian (7)	28	0.14
Russian (0)	27	0.14
Scandinavian (0)	0	<0.01
Scotch-Irish (164)	338	1.71
Scottish (166)	304	1.53
Serbian (0)	0	<0.01
Slavic (0)	0	<0.01
Slovak (0)	32	0.16
Slovene (0)	0	<0.01
Soviet Union (0)	0	<0.01
Swedish (15)	76	0.38
Swiss (32)	109	0.55
Turkish (0)	0	<0.01
Ukrainian (0)	0	<0.01
Welsh (47)	107	0.54
West Indian, ex. Hispanic (37)	84	0.42
Bahamian (0)	0	<0.01
Barbadian (0)	0	<0.01
Belizean (0)	0	<0.01
Bermudan (0)	0	<0.01
British West Indian (0)	0	<0.01
Dutch West Indian (0)	0	<0.01
Haitian (0)	0	<0.01
Jamaican (37)	84	0.42
Trinidadian/Tobagonian (0)	0	<0.01
U.S. Virgin Islander (0)	0	<0.01
West Indian (0)	0	<0.01
Other West Indian (0)	0	<0.01
Yugoslavian (0)	0	<0.01

Hispanic Origin	Population	%
Hispanic or Latino (of any race)	194	0.98
Central American, ex. Mexican	8	0.04
Costa Rican	2	0.01
Guatemalan	3	0.02
Honduran	0	<0.01
Nicaraguan	1	0.01
Panamanian	2	0.01
Salvadoran	0	<0.01
Other Central American	0	<0.01
Cuban	3	0.02
Dominican Republic	1	0.01
Mexican	139	0.70
Puerto Rican	20	0.10
South American	7	0.04
Argentinean	0	<0.01
Bolivian	0	<0.01
Chilean	0	<0.01
Colombian	4	0.02
Ecuadorian	3	0.02
Paraguayan	0	<0.01
Peruvian	0	<0.01
Uruguayan	0	<0.01
Venezuelan	0	<0.01
Other South American	0	<0.01
Other Hispanic or Latino	16	0.08

Race*	Population	%
African-American/Black (170)	242	1.22
Not Hispanic (168)	237	1.19
Hispanic (2)	5	0.03
American Indian/Alaska Native (62)	187	0.94
Not Hispanic (52)	172	0.87
Hispanic (10)	15	0.08
Alaska Athabascan (Ala. Nat.) (0)	0	<0.01
Aleut (Alaska Native) (0)	0	<0.01
Apache (1)	2	0.01
Arapaho (0)	0	<0.01
Blackfeet (0)	3	0.02
Canadian/French Am. Ind. (1)	1	0.01
Central American Ind. (0)	0	<0.01
Cherokee (14)	72	0.36
Cheyenne (0)	0	<0.01
Chickasaw (0)	3	0.02
Chippewa (1)	5	0.03
Choctaw (1)	6	0.03
Colville (0)	0	<0.01
Comanche (0)	3	0.02
Cree (0)	0	<0.01
Creek (1)	1	0.01
Crow (0)	0	<0.01
Delaware (1)	1	0.01
Hopi (0)	0	<0.01
Houma (0)	0	<0.01
Inupiat (Alaska Native) (0)	0	<0.01
Iroquois (0)	0	<0.01
Kiowa (0)	0	<0.01
Lumbee (0)	1	0.01
Menominee (0)	0	<0.01
Mexican American Ind. (0)	1	0.01
Navajo (0)	0	<0.01
Osage (0)	0	<0.01
Ottawa (0)	1	0.01
Paiute (0)	0	<0.01
Pima (0)	0	<0.01
Potawatomi (0)	1	0.01
Pueblo (0)	0	<0.01
Puget Sound Salish (0)	0	<0.01
Seminole (0)	2	0.01
Shoshone (0)	0	<0.01
Sioux (0)	6	0.03
South American Ind. (0)	0	<0.01
Spanish American Ind. (0)	0	<0.01
Tlingit-Haida (Alaska Native) (1)	1	0.01
Tohono O'Odham (0)	0	<0.01
Tsimshian (Alaska Native) (0)	0	<0.01
Ute (0)	0	<0.01
Yakama (0)	0	<0.01
Yaqui (1)	3	0.02
Yuman (0)	0	<0.01
Yup'ik (Alaska Native) (0)	0	<0.01
Asian (62)	85	0.43
Not Hispanic (61)	84	0.42
Hispanic (1)	1	0.01
Bangladeshi (0)	0	<0.01
Bhutanese (0)	0	<0.01
Burmese (0)	0	<0.01
Cambodian (0)	0	<0.01
Chinese, ex. Taiwanese (11)	13	0.07
Filipino (33)	42	0.21
Hmong (0)	0	<0.01
Indian (12)	17	0.09
Indonesian (0)	1	0.01
Japanese (0)	3	0.02
Korean (2)	4	0.02
Laotian (0)	0	<0.01
Malaysian (0)	0	<0.01
Nepalese (0)	0	<0.01
Pakistani (2)	2	0.01
Sri Lankan (0)	0	<0.01
Taiwanese (0)	1	0.01
Thai (1)	1	0.01
Vietnamese (1)	1	0.01
Hawaii Native/Pacific Islander (2)	7	0.04
Not Hispanic (2)	7	0.04
Hispanic (0)	0	<0.01
Fijian (0)	0	<0.01
Guamanian/Chamorro (1)	1	0.01
Marshallese (0)	0	<0.01
Native Hawaiian (1)	4	0.02
Samoan (0)	1	0.01
Tongan (0)	0	<0.01
White (19,245)	19,476	98.17
Not Hispanic (19,144)	19,353	97.55
Hispanic (101)	123	0.62

Notes: † The Census 2010 population figure is used to calculate the percentages in the Hispanic Origin and Race categories. Ancestry percentages are based on the 2006-2010 American Community Survey population (not shown); ‡ Numbers in parentheses indicate the number of people reporting a single ancestry; * Numbers in parentheses indicate the number of persons reporting this race alone, not in combination with any other race; Please refer to the Explanation of Data for more information.

Owen County

Population: 21,575

Ancestry	Population	%
Afghan (0)	0	<0.01
African, Sub-Saharan (0)	0	<0.01
African (0)	0	<0.01
Cape Verdean (0)	0	<0.01
Ethiopian (0)	0	<0.01
Ghanaian (0)	0	<0.01
Kenyan (0)	0	<0.01
Liberian (0)	0	<0.01
Nigerian (0)	0	<0.01
Senegalese (0)	0	<0.01
Sierra Leonean (0)	0	<0.01
Somalian (0)	0	<0.01
South African (0)	0	<0.01
Sudanese (0)	0	<0.01
Ugandan (0)	0	<0.01
Zimbabwean (0)	0	<0.01
Other Sub-Saharan African (0)	0	<0.01
Albanian (0)	0	<0.01
Alsatian (0)	0	<0.01
American (1,817)	1,817	8.36
Arab (3)	16	0.07
Arab (0)	0	<0.01
Egyptian (0)	0	<0.01
Iraqi (0)	0	<0.01
Jordanian (0)	0	<0.01
Lebanese (0)	0	<0.01
Moroccan (3)	3	0.01
Palestinian (0)	0	<0.01
Syrian (0)	13	0.06
Other Arab (0)	0	<0.01
Armenian (0)	0	<0.01
Assyrian/Chaldean/Syriac (0)	0	<0.01
Australian (0)	0	<0.01
Austrian (0)	18	0.08
Basque (0)	0	<0.01
Belgian (0)	0	<0.01
Brazilian (0)	0	<0.01
British (32)	45	0.21
Bulgarian (0)	0	<0.01
Cajun (0)	7	0.03
Canadian (0)	0	<0.01
Carpatho Rusyn (0)	0	<0.01
Celtic (0)	0	<0.01
Croatian (0)	0	<0.01
Cypriot (0)	0	<0.01
Czech (0)	9	0.04
Czechoslovakian (0)	10	0.05
Danish (0)	16	0.07
Dutch (84)	448	2.06
Eastern European (0)	0	<0.01
English (602)	1,927	8.87
Estonian (0)	0	<0.01
European (120)	166	0.76
Finnish (0)	0	<0.01
French, ex. Basque (100)	414	1.90
French Canadian (14)	33	0.15
German (2,612)	6,233	28.67
German Russian (0)	0	<0.01
Greek (27)	67	0.31
Guyanese (0)	0	<0.01
Hungarian (46)	122	0.56
Icelander (0)	0	<0.01
Iranian (0)	0	<0.01
Irish (1,110)	4,506	20.73
Israeli (0)	0	<0.01
Italian (74)	241	1.11
Latvian (7)	7	0.03
Lithuanian (0)	19	0.09
Luxemburger (0)	0	<0.01
Macedonian (0)	0	<0.01
Maltese (0)	0	<0.01
New Zealander (0)	0	<0.01
Northern European (0)	0	<0.01
Norwegian (0)	6	0.03
Pennsylvania German (53)	53	0.24
Polish (108)	268	1.23
Portuguese (0)	11	0.05
Romanian (0)	3	0.01
Russian (29)	88	0.40
Scandinavian (0)	19	0.09
Scotch-Irish (124)	317	1.46
Scottish (157)	486	2.24
Serbian (0)	0	<0.01
Slavic (0)	7	0.03
Slovak (17)	17	0.08
Slovene (0)	0	<0.01
Soviet Union (0)	0	<0.01
Swedish (149)	202	0.93
Swiss (0)	58	0.27
Turkish (0)	0	<0.01
Ukrainian (0)	0	<0.01
Welsh (0)	61	0.28
West Indian, ex. Hispanic (0)	0	<0.01
Bahamian (0)	0	<0.01
Barbadian (0)	0	<0.01
Belizean (0)	0	<0.01
Bermudan (0)	0	<0.01
British West Indian (0)	0	<0.01
Dutch West Indian (0)	0	<0.01
Haitian (0)	0	<0.01
Jamaican (0)	0	<0.01
Trinidadian/Tobagonian (0)	0	<0.01
U.S. Virgin Islander (0)	0	<0.01
West Indian (0)	0	<0.01
Other West Indian (0)	0	<0.01
Yugoslavian (24)	38	0.17

Hispanic Origin	Population	%
Hispanic or Latino (of any race)	198	0.92
Central American, ex. Mexican	4	0.02
Costa Rican	0	<0.01
Guatemalan	2	0.01
Honduran	0	<0.01
Nicaraguan	1	<0.01
Panamanian	1	<0.01
Salvadoran	0	<0.01
Other Central American	0	<0.01
Cuban	3	0.01
Dominican Republic	0	<0.01
Mexican	133	0.62
Puerto Rican	18	0.08
South American	9	0.04
Argentinean	2	0.01
Bolivian	0	<0.01
Chilean	0	<0.01
Colombian	4	0.02
Ecuadorian	0	<0.01
Paraguayan	0	<0.01
Peruvian	0	<0.01
Uruguayan	0	<0.01
Venezuelan	3	0.01
Other South American	0	<0.01
Other Hispanic or Latino	31	0.14

Race*	Population	%
African-American/Black (65)	116	0.54
Not Hispanic (65)	116	0.54
Hispanic (0)	0	<0.01
American Indian/Alaska Native (75)	172	0.80
Not Hispanic (72)	167	0.77
Hispanic (3)	5	0.02
Alaska Athabascan (Ala. Nat.) (0)	0	<0.01
Aleut (Alaska Native) (0)	0	<0.01
Apache (0)	0	<0.01
Arapaho (0)	0	<0.01
Blackfeet (2)	15	0.07
Canadian/French Am. Ind. (0)	0	<0.01
Central American Ind. (0)	1	<0.01
Cherokee (21)	55	0.25
Cheyenne (0)	0	<0.01
Chickasaw (1)	3	0.01
Chippewa (7)	8	0.04
Choctaw (2)	4	0.02
Colville (0)	0	<0.01
Comanche (0)	0	<0.01
Cree (3)	5	0.02
Creek (4)	4	0.02
Crow (0)	4	0.02
Delaware (0)	1	<0.01
Hopi (0)	0	<0.01
Houma (0)	0	<0.01
Inupiat (Alaska Native) (0)	1	<0.01
Iroquois (0)	3	0.01
Kiowa (0)	0	<0.01
Lumbee (0)	1	<0.01
Menominee (0)	0	<0.01
Mexican American Ind. (1)	1	<0.01
Navajo (0)	0	<0.01
Osage (0)	1	<0.01
Ottawa (0)	0	<0.01
Paiute (0)	0	<0.01
Pima (0)	0	<0.01
Potawatomi (0)	0	<0.01
Pueblo (1)	1	<0.01
Puget Sound Salish (0)	0	<0.01
Seminole (0)	0	<0.01
Shoshone (0)	1	<0.01
Sioux (1)	7	0.03
South American Ind. (0)	0	<0.01
Spanish American Ind. (0)	0	<0.01
Tlingit-Haida (Alaska Native) (0)	0	<0.01
Tohono O'Odham (0)	0	<0.01
Tsimshian (Alaska Native) (0)	0	<0.01
Ute (0)	0	<0.01
Yakama (0)	0	<0.01
Yaqui (0)	0	<0.01
Yuman (0)	0	<0.01
Yup'ik (Alaska Native) (0)	0	<0.01
Asian (66)	108	0.50
Not Hispanic (65)	107	0.50
Hispanic (1)	1	<0.01
Bangladeshi (0)	0	<0.01
Bhutanese (0)	0	<0.01
Burmese (0)	0	<0.01
Cambodian (0)	0	<0.01
Chinese, ex. Taiwanese (13)	14	0.06
Filipino (21)	36	0.17
Hmong (0)	0	<0.01
Indian (9)	16	0.07
Indonesian (0)	0	<0.01
Japanese (6)	13	0.06
Korean (5)	14	0.06
Laotian (1)	1	<0.01
Malaysian (0)	0	<0.01
Nepalese (0)	0	<0.01
Pakistani (2)	2	0.01
Sri Lankan (0)	0	<0.01
Taiwanese (0)	3	0.01
Thai (2)	2	0.01
Vietnamese (2)	3	0.01
Hawaii Native/Pacific Islander (1)	6	0.03
Not Hispanic (1)	6	0.03
Hispanic (0)	0	<0.01
Fijian (0)	0	<0.01
Guamanian/Chamorro (0)	0	<0.01
Marshallese (0)	0	<0.01
Native Hawaiian (1)	5	0.02
Samoan (0)	0	<0.01
Tongan (0)	0	<0.01
White (21,129)	21,315	98.79
Not Hispanic (20,983)	21,157	98.06
Hispanic (146)	158	0.73

Notes: † The Census 2010 population figure is used to calculate the percentages in the Hispanic Origin and Race categories. Ancestry percentages are based on the 2006-2010 American Community Survey population (not shown); ‡ Numbers in parentheses indicate the number of people reporting a single ancestry; * Numbers in parentheses indicate the number of persons reporting this race alone, not in combination with any other race; Please refer to the Explanation of Data for more information.

Parke County
Population: 17,339

Ancestry	Population	%
Afghan (0)	0	<0.01
African, Sub-Saharan (12)	21	0.12
African (12)	21	0.12
Cape Verdean (0)	0	<0.01
Ethiopian (0)	0	<0.01
Ghanaian (0)	0	<0.01
Kenyan (0)	0	<0.01
Liberian (0)	0	<0.01
Nigerian (0)	0	<0.01
Senegalese (0)	0	<0.01
Sierra Leonean (0)	0	<0.01
Somalian (0)	0	<0.01
South African (0)	0	<0.01
Sudanese (0)	0	<0.01
Ugandan (0)	0	<0.01
Zimbabwean (0)	0	<0.01
Other Sub-Saharan African (0)	0	<0.01
Albanian (0)	0	<0.01
Alsatian (0)	0	<0.01
American (4,820)	4,820	27.71
Arab (56)	56	0.32
Arab (0)	0	<0.01
Egyptian (0)	0	<0.01
Iraqi (0)	0	<0.01
Jordanian (0)	0	<0.01
Lebanese (0)	0	<0.01
Moroccan (0)	0	<0.01
Palestinian (0)	0	<0.01
Syrian (56)	56	0.32
Other Arab (0)	0	<0.01
Armenian (0)	0	<0.01
Assyrian/Chaldean/Syriac (0)	0	<0.01
Australian (0)	0	<0.01
Austrian (0)	21	0.12
Basque (0)	0	<0.01
Belgian (0)	0	<0.01
Brazilian (0)	0	<0.01
British (4)	31	0.18
Bulgarian (0)	0	<0.01
Cajun (0)	0	<0.01
Canadian (46)	46	0.26
Carpatho Rusyn (0)	0	<0.01
Celtic (0)	13	0.07
Croatian (16)	16	0.09
Cypriot (0)	0	<0.01
Czech (5)	14	0.08
Czechoslovakian (0)	0	<0.01
Danish (25)	25	0.14
Dutch (116)	533	3.06
Eastern European (0)	0	<0.01
English (842)	1,749	10.06
Estonian (0)	0	<0.01
European (33)	33	0.19
Finnish (0)	0	<0.01
French, ex. Basque (74)	403	2.32
French Canadian (0)	0	<0.01
German (2,135)	4,115	23.66
German Russian (0)	0	<0.01
Greek (0)	27	0.16
Guyanese (0)	0	<0.01
Hungarian (71)	94	0.54
Icelander (0)	0	<0.01
Iranian (0)	0	<0.01
Irish (653)	1,859	10.69
Israeli (0)	0	<0.01
Italian (156)	262	1.51
Latvian (0)	0	<0.01
Lithuanian (14)	27	0.16
Luxemburger (0)	0	<0.01
Macedonian (0)	0	<0.01
Maltese (0)	0	<0.01
New Zealander (0)	0	<0.01
Northern European (38)	38	0.22
Norwegian (7)	61	0.35
Pennsylvania German (109)	109	0.63
Polish (68)	159	0.91
Portuguese (19)	19	0.11
Romanian (0)	39	0.22
Russian (9)	14	0.08
Scandinavian (8)	8	0.05
Scotch-Irish (89)	220	1.26
Scottish (132)	322	1.85
Serbian (9)	9	0.05
Slavic (0)	12	0.07
Slovak (0)	20	0.11
Slovene (0)	0	<0.01
Soviet Union (0)	0	<0.01
Swedish (27)	91	0.52
Swiss (225)	242	1.39
Turkish (13)	13	0.07
Ukrainian (14)	14	0.08
Welsh (173)	217	1.25
West Indian, ex. Hispanic (0)	0	<0.01
Bahamian (0)	0	<0.01
Barbadian (0)	0	<0.01
Belizean (0)	0	<0.01
Bermudan (0)	0	<0.01
British West Indian (0)	0	<0.01
Dutch West Indian (0)	0	<0.01
Haitian (0)	0	<0.01
Jamaican (0)	0	<0.01
Trinidadian/Tobagonian (0)	0	<0.01
U.S. Virgin Islander (0)	0	<0.01
West Indian (0)	0	<0.01
Other West Indian (0)	0	<0.01
Yugoslavian (0)	0	<0.01

Hispanic Origin	Population	%
Hispanic or Latino (of any race)	215	1.24
Central American, ex. Mexican	1	0.01
Costa Rican	0	<0.01
Guatemalan	0	<0.01
Honduran	1	0.01
Nicaraguan	0	<0.01
Panamanian	0	<0.01
Salvadoran	0	<0.01
Other Central American	0	<0.01
Cuban	1	0.01
Dominican Republic	0	<0.01
Mexican	184	1.06
Puerto Rican	11	0.06
South American	1	0.01
Argentinean	0	<0.01
Bolivian	0	<0.01
Chilean	0	<0.01
Colombian	0	<0.01
Ecuadorian	0	<0.01
Paraguayan	0	<0.01
Peruvian	0	<0.01
Uruguayan	0	<0.01
Venezuelan	1	0.01
Other South American	0	<0.01
Other Hispanic or Latino	17	0.10

Race*	Population	%
African-American/Black (397)	436	2.51
Not Hispanic (391)	429	2.47
Hispanic (6)	7	0.04
American Indian/Alaska Native (64)	108	0.62
Not Hispanic (53)	96	0.55
Hispanic (11)	12	0.07
Alaska Athabascan (Ala. Nat.) (0)	0	<0.01
Aleut (Alaska Native) (0)	1	0.01
Apache (1)	2	0.01
Arapaho (0)	0	<0.01
Blackfeet (2)	2	0.01
Canadian/French Am. Ind. (0)	1	0.01
Central American Ind. (0)	0	<0.01
Cherokee (14)	31	0.18
Cheyenne (0)	0	<0.01
Chickasaw (0)	0	<0.01
Chippewa (1)	1	0.01
Choctaw (0)	2	0.01
Colville (0)	0	<0.01
Comanche (0)	0	<0.01
Cree (0)	0	<0.01
Creek (0)	0	<0.01
Crow (0)	0	<0.01
Delaware (0)	0	<0.01
Hopi (0)	0	<0.01
Houma (0)	0	<0.01
Inupiat (Alaska Native) (0)	0	<0.01
Iroquois (0)	2	0.01
Kiowa (0)	0	<0.01
Lumbee (1)	1	0.01
Menominee (0)	0	<0.01
Mexican American Ind. (1)	2	0.01
Navajo (2)	2	0.01
Osage (0)	0	<0.01
Ottawa (0)	0	<0.01
Paiute (0)	0	<0.01
Pima (0)	0	<0.01
Potawatomi (4)	4	0.02
Pueblo (0)	0	<0.01
Puget Sound Salish (0)	0	<0.01
Seminole (0)	0	<0.01
Shoshone (0)	0	<0.01
Sioux (0)	0	<0.01
South American Ind. (0)	0	<0.01
Spanish American Ind. (1)	1	0.01
Tlingit-Haida (Alaska Native) (0)	0	<0.01
Tohono O'Odham (0)	0	<0.01
Tsimshian (Alaska Native) (0)	0	<0.01
Ute (0)	0	<0.01
Yakama (0)	0	<0.01
Yaqui (0)	0	<0.01
Yuman (0)	0	<0.01
Yup'ik (Alaska Native) (0)	0	<0.01
Asian (34)	44	0.25
Not Hispanic (33)	42	0.24
Hispanic (1)	2	0.01
Bangladeshi (0)	0	<0.01
Bhutanese (0)	0	<0.01
Burmese (0)	0	<0.01
Cambodian (0)	0	<0.01
Chinese, ex. Taiwanese (5)	6	0.03
Filipino (8)	11	0.06
Hmong (0)	0	<0.01
Indian (2)	2	0.01
Indonesian (0)	0	<0.01
Japanese (6)	10	0.06
Korean (8)	9	0.05
Laotian (0)	0	<0.01
Malaysian (0)	0	<0.01
Nepalese (0)	0	<0.01
Pakistani (0)	0	<0.01
Sri Lankan (0)	0	<0.01
Taiwanese (0)	0	<0.01
Thai (1)	1	0.01
Vietnamese (2)	3	0.02
Hawaii Native/Pacific Islander (4)	5	0.03
Not Hispanic (4)	5	0.03
Hispanic (0)	0	<0.01
Fijian (1)	1	0.01
Guamanian/Chamorro (0)	0	<0.01
Marshallese (0)	0	<0.01
Native Hawaiian (1)	1	0.01
Samoan (0)	0	<0.01
Tongan (0)	0	<0.01
White (16,671)	16,767	96.70
Not Hispanic (16,545)	16,635	95.94
Hispanic (126)	132	0.76

Notes: † The Census 2010 population figure is used to calculate the percentages in the Hispanic Origin and Race categories. Ancestry percentages are based on the 2006-2010 American Community Survey population (not shown); ‡ Numbers in parentheses indicate the number of people reporting a single ancestry; * Numbers in parentheses indicate the number of persons reporting this race alone, not in combination with any other race; Please refer to the Explanation of Data for more information.

Perry County

Population: 19,338

Ancestry	Population	%
Afghan (0)	0	<0.01
African, Sub-Saharan (0)	4	0.02
African (0)	4	0.02
Cape Verdean (0)	0	<0.01
Ethiopian (0)	0	<0.01
Ghanaian (0)	0	<0.01
Kenyan (0)	0	<0.01
Liberian (0)	0	<0.01
Nigerian (0)	0	<0.01
Senegalese (0)	0	<0.01
Sierra Leonean (0)	0	<0.01
Somalian (0)	0	<0.01
South African (0)	0	<0.01
Sudanese (0)	0	<0.01
Ugandan (0)	0	<0.01
Zimbabwean (0)	0	<0.01
Other Sub-Saharan African (0)	0	<0.01
Albanian (0)	0	<0.01
Alsatian (0)	0	<0.01
American (2,237)	2,237	11.58
Arab (0)	9	0.05
Arab (0)	0	<0.01
Egyptian (0)	0	<0.01
Iraqi (0)	0	<0.01
Jordanian (0)	0	<0.01
Lebanese (0)	0	<0.01
Moroccan (0)	0	<0.01
Palestinian (0)	0	<0.01
Syrian (0)	9	0.05
Other Arab (0)	0	<0.01
Armenian (0)	0	<0.01
Assyrian/Chaldean/Syriac (0)	0	<0.01
Australian (0)	0	<0.01
Austrian (0)	0	<0.01
Basque (0)	0	<0.01
Belgian (93)	360	1.86
Brazilian (0)	0	<0.01
British (13)	86	0.45
Bulgarian (0)	11	0.06
Cajun (0)	0	<0.01
Canadian (12)	12	0.06
Carpatho Rusyn (0)	0	<0.01
Celtic (2)	2	0.01
Croatian (0)	0	<0.01
Cypriot (0)	0	<0.01
Czech (0)	26	0.13
Czechoslovakian (0)	0	<0.01
Danish (0)	0	<0.01
Dutch (3)	247	1.28
Eastern European (0)	0	<0.01
English (831)	1,679	8.69
Estonian (0)	0	<0.01
European (109)	109	0.56
Finnish (0)	0	<0.01
French, ex. Basque (304)	1,216	6.30
French Canadian (0)	4	0.02
German (3,720)	7,309	37.84
German Russian (0)	0	<0.01
Greek (0)	0	<0.01
Guyanese (0)	0	<0.01
Hungarian (0)	0	<0.01
Icelander (0)	0	<0.01
Iranian (0)	0	<0.01
Irish (888)	2,779	14.39
Israeli (0)	0	<0.01
Italian (95)	220	1.14
Latvian (0)	0	<0.01
Lithuanian (0)	0	<0.01
Luxemburger (0)	0	<0.01
Macedonian (0)	0	<0.01
Maltese (0)	0	<0.01
New Zealander (0)	0	<0.01
Northern European (0)	0	<0.01
Norwegian (12)	12	0.06
Pennsylvania German (0)	10	0.05
Polish (99)	231	1.20
Portuguese (0)	0	<0.01
Romanian (0)	0	<0.01
Russian (8)	16	0.08
Scandinavian (0)	0	<0.01
Scotch-Irish (36)	198	1.03
Scottish (45)	254	1.31
Serbian (0)	0	<0.01
Slavic (0)	8	0.04
Slovak (0)	0	<0.01
Slovene (0)	0	<0.01
Soviet Union (0)	0	<0.01
Swedish (0)	77	0.40
Swiss (113)	320	1.66
Turkish (0)	0	<0.01
Ukrainian (0)	0	<0.01
Welsh (49)	135	0.70
West Indian, ex. Hispanic (5)	10	0.05
Bahamian (0)	0	<0.01
Barbadian (0)	0	<0.01
Belizean (0)	0	<0.01
Bermudan (0)	0	<0.01
British West Indian (0)	0	<0.01
Dutch West Indian (0)	0	<0.01
Haitian (0)	0	<0.01
Jamaican (0)	5	0.03
Trinidadian/Tobagonian (0)	0	<0.01
U.S. Virgin Islander (0)	0	<0.01
West Indian (5)	5	0.03
Other West Indian (0)	0	<0.01
Yugoslavian (0)	0	<0.01

Hispanic Origin	Population	%
Hispanic or Latino (of any race)	192	0.99
Central American, ex. Mexican	7	0.04
Costa Rican	0	<0.01
Guatemalan	0	<0.01
Honduran	2	0.01
Nicaraguan	0	<0.01
Panamanian	0	<0.01
Salvadoran	5	0.03
Other Central American	0	<0.01
Cuban	0	<0.01
Dominican Republic	0	<0.01
Mexican	142	0.73
Puerto Rican	17	0.09
South American	2	0.01
Argentinean	0	<0.01
Bolivian	1	0.01
Chilean	0	<0.01
Colombian	0	<0.01
Ecuadorian	0	<0.01
Paraguayan	0	<0.01
Peruvian	1	0.01
Uruguayan	0	<0.01
Venezuelan	0	<0.01
Other South American	0	<0.01
Other Hispanic or Latino	24	0.12

Race*	Population	%
African-American/Black (471)	515	2.66
Not Hispanic (469)	510	2.64
Hispanic (2)	5	0.03
American Indian/Alaska Native (36)	94	0.49
Not Hispanic (34)	90	0.47
Hispanic (2)	4	0.02
Alaska Athabascan (Ala. Nat.) (0)	0	<0.01
Aleut (Alaska Native) (2)	2	0.01
Apache (3)	3	0.02
Arapaho (0)	0	<0.01
Blackfeet (1)	2	0.01
Canadian/French Am. Ind. (0)	0	<0.01
Central American Ind. (0)	0	<0.01
Cherokee (3)	28	0.14
Cheyenne (0)	0	<0.01
Chickasaw (0)	0	<0.01
Chippewa (3)	6	0.03
Choctaw (1)	1	0.01
Colville (0)	0	<0.01
Comanche (0)	0	<0.01
Cree (0)	0	<0.01
Creek (3)	3	0.02
Crow (0)	1	0.01
Delaware (0)	0	<0.01
Hopi (0)	0	<0.01
Houma (0)	0	<0.01
Inupiat (Alaska Native) (0)	0	<0.01
Iroquois (2)	2	0.01
Kiowa (0)	0	<0.01
Lumbee (1)	1	0.01
Menominee (0)	0	<0.01
Mexican American Ind. (0)	0	<0.01
Navajo (0)	0	<0.01
Osage (0)	0	<0.01
Ottawa (0)	0	<0.01
Paiute (0)	0	<0.01
Pima (0)	0	<0.01
Potawatomi (1)	1	0.01
Pueblo (0)	0	<0.01
Puget Sound Salish (0)	0	<0.01
Seminole (0)	0	<0.01
Shoshone (4)	4	0.02
Sioux (0)	2	0.01
South American Ind. (1)	1	0.01
Spanish American Ind. (0)	0	<0.01
Tlingit-Haida (Alaska Native) (0)	0	<0.01
Tohono O'Odham (0)	0	<0.01
Tsimshian (Alaska Native) (0)	0	<0.01
Ute (0)	0	<0.01
Yakama (0)	0	<0.01
Yaqui (0)	0	<0.01
Yuman (0)	0	<0.01
Yup'ik (Alaska Native) (0)	0	<0.01
Asian (69)	95	0.49
Not Hispanic (69)	95	0.49
Hispanic (0)	0	<0.01
Bangladeshi (0)	0	<0.01
Bhutanese (0)	0	<0.01
Burmese (0)	0	<0.01
Cambodian (0)	0	<0.01
Chinese, ex. Taiwanese (16)	17	0.09
Filipino (12)	20	0.10
Hmong (0)	0	<0.01
Indian (11)	12	0.06
Indonesian (1)	2	0.01
Japanese (20)	24	0.12
Korean (5)	9	0.05
Laotian (0)	0	<0.01
Malaysian (0)	0	<0.01
Nepalese (0)	0	<0.01
Pakistani (3)	3	0.02
Sri Lankan (0)	0	<0.01
Taiwanese (0)	0	<0.01
Thai (1)	1	0.01
Vietnamese (0)	0	<0.01
Hawaii Native/Pacific Islander (4)	6	0.03
Not Hispanic (4)	6	0.03
Hispanic (0)	0	<0.01
Fijian (0)	0	<0.01
Guamanian/Chamorro (1)	1	0.01
Marshallese (0)	0	<0.01
Native Hawaiian (3)	3	0.02
Samoan (0)	1	0.01
Tongan (0)	0	<0.01
White (18,557)	18,700	96.70
Not Hispanic (18,428)	18,553	95.94
Hispanic (129)	147	0.76

Notes: † The Census 2010 population figure is used to calculate the percentages in the Hispanic Origin and Race categories. Ancestry percentages are based on the 2006-2010 American Community Survey population (not shown); ‡ Numbers in parentheses indicate the number of people reporting a single ancestry; * Numbers in parentheses indicate the number of persons reporting this race alone, not in combination with any other race; Please refer to the Explanation of Data for more information.

Pike County
Population: 12,845

Ancestry	Population	%
Afghan (0)	0	<0.01
African, Sub-Saharan (0)	0	<0.01
African (0)	0	<0.01
Cape Verdean (0)	0	<0.01
Ethiopian (0)	0	<0.01
Ghanaian (0)	0	<0.01
Kenyan (0)	0	<0.01
Liberian (0)	0	<0.01
Nigerian (0)	0	<0.01
Senegalese (0)	0	<0.01
Sierra Leonean (0)	0	<0.01
Somalian (0)	0	<0.01
South African (0)	0	<0.01
Sudanese (0)	0	<0.01
Ugandan (0)	0	<0.01
Zimbabwean (0)	0	<0.01
Other Sub-Saharan African (0)	0	<0.01
Albanian (0)	0	<0.01
Alsatian (0)	0	<0.01
American (3,325)	3,325	25.67
Arab (0)	0	<0.01
Arab (0)	0	<0.01
Egyptian (0)	0	<0.01
Iraqi (0)	0	<0.01
Jordanian (0)	0	<0.01
Lebanese (0)	0	<0.01
Moroccan (0)	0	<0.01
Palestinian (0)	0	<0.01
Syrian (0)	0	<0.01
Other Arab (0)	0	<0.01
Armenian (0)	0	<0.01
Assyrian/Chaldean/Syriac (0)	0	<0.01
Australian (0)	2	0.02
Austrian (0)	0	<0.01
Basque (0)	0	<0.01
Belgian (0)	0	<0.01
Brazilian (0)	0	<0.01
British (64)	99	0.76
Bulgarian (0)	0	<0.01
Cajun (0)	0	<0.01
Canadian (0)	0	<0.01
Carpatho Rusyn (0)	0	<0.01
Celtic (0)	0	<0.01
Croatian (0)	3	0.02
Cypriot (0)	0	<0.01
Czech (0)	3	0.02
Czechoslovakian (0)	0	<0.01
Danish (0)	35	0.27
Dutch (22)	119	0.92
Eastern European (9)	9	0.07
English (698)	1,473	11.37
Estonian (0)	0	<0.01
European (92)	151	1.17
Finnish (0)	0	<0.01
French, ex. Basque (62)	431	3.33
French Canadian (16)	23	0.18
German (1,781)	3,248	25.07
German Russian (0)	0	<0.01
Greek (0)	0	<0.01
Guyanese (0)	0	<0.01
Hungarian (0)	20	0.15
Icelander (0)	0	<0.01
Iranian (0)	0	<0.01
Irish (608)	2,052	15.84
Israeli (0)	0	<0.01
Italian (7)	75	0.58
Latvian (0)	0	<0.01
Lithuanian (0)	0	<0.01
Luxemburger (0)	0	<0.01
Macedonian (0)	0	<0.01
Maltese (0)	0	<0.01
New Zealander (0)	0	<0.01
Northern European (0)	0	<0.01
Norwegian (14)	14	0.11
Pennsylvania German (0)	0	<0.01
Polish (45)	112	0.86
Portuguese (25)	40	0.31
Romanian (0)	0	<0.01
Russian (25)	52	0.40
Scandinavian (0)	0	<0.01
Scotch-Irish (165)	220	1.70
Scottish (69)	162	1.25
Serbian (0)	0	<0.01
Slavic (0)	0	<0.01
Slovak (0)	0	<0.01
Slovene (0)	0	<0.01
Soviet Union (0)	0	<0.01
Swedish (19)	39	0.30
Swiss (0)	6	0.05
Turkish (0)	0	<0.01
Ukrainian (10)	10	0.08
Welsh (0)	84	0.65
West Indian, ex. Hispanic (0)	0	<0.01
Bahamian (0)	0	<0.01
Barbadian (0)	0	<0.01
Belizean (0)	0	<0.01
Bermudan (0)	0	<0.01
British West Indian (0)	0	<0.01
Dutch West Indian (0)	0	<0.01
Haitian (0)	0	<0.01
Jamaican (0)	0	<0.01
Trinidadian/Tobagonian (0)	0	<0.01
U.S. Virgin Islander (0)	0	<0.01
West Indian (0)	0	<0.01
Other West Indian (0)	0	<0.01
Yugoslavian (0)	0	<0.01

Hispanic Origin	Population	%
Hispanic or Latino (of any race)	120	0.93
Central American, ex. Mexican	12	0.09
Costa Rican	1	0.01
Guatemalan	6	0.05
Honduran	1	0.01
Nicaraguan	0	<0.01
Panamanian	0	<0.01
Salvadoran	4	0.03
Other Central American	0	<0.01
Cuban	2	0.02
Dominican Republic	1	0.01
Mexican	69	0.54
Puerto Rican	19	0.15
South American	3	0.02
Argentinean	0	<0.01
Bolivian	0	<0.01
Chilean	0	<0.01
Colombian	2	0.02
Ecuadorian	0	<0.01
Paraguayan	0	<0.01
Peruvian	1	0.01
Uruguayan	0	<0.01
Venezuelan	0	<0.01
Other South American	0	<0.01
Other Hispanic or Latino	14	0.11

Race*	Population	%
African-American/Black (39)	62	0.48
Not Hispanic (38)	60	0.47
Hispanic (1)	2	0.02
American Indian/Alaska Native (27)	69	0.54
Not Hispanic (25)	66	0.51
Hispanic (2)	3	0.02
Alaska Athabascan (Ala. Nat.) (0)	0	<0.01
Aleut (Alaska Native) (0)	0	<0.01
Apache (2)	2	0.02
Arapaho (0)	0	<0.01
Blackfeet (1)	8	0.06
Canadian/French Am. Ind. (0)	0	<0.01
Central American Ind. (0)	0	<0.01
Cherokee (3)	19	0.15
Cheyenne (0)	0	<0.01
Chickasaw (0)	0	<0.01
Chippewa (0)	0	<0.01
Choctaw (6)	7	0.05
Colville (0)	0	<0.01
Comanche (0)	0	<0.01
Cree (0)	0	<0.01
Creek (0)	0	<0.01
Crow (0)	0	<0.01
Delaware (0)	0	<0.01
Hopi (0)	0	<0.01
Houma (0)	0	<0.01
Inupiat (Alaska Native) (0)	0	<0.01
Iroquois (3)	3	0.02
Kiowa (0)	0	<0.01
Lumbee (0)	0	<0.01
Menominee (0)	0	<0.01
Mexican American Ind. (0)	0	<0.01
Navajo (1)	1	0.01
Osage (0)	0	<0.01
Ottawa (0)	0	<0.01
Paiute (0)	0	<0.01
Pima (0)	0	<0.01
Potawatomi (0)	0	<0.01
Pueblo (0)	0	<0.01
Puget Sound Salish (0)	0	<0.01
Seminole (0)	0	<0.01
Shoshone (0)	0	<0.01
Sioux (1)	2	0.02
South American Ind. (0)	0	<0.01
Spanish American Ind. (0)	0	<0.01
Tlingit-Haida (Alaska Native) (0)	0	<0.01
Tohono O'Odham (0)	0	<0.01
Tsimshian (Alaska Native) (0)	0	<0.01
Ute (0)	0	<0.01
Yakama (0)	0	<0.01
Yaqui (0)	0	<0.01
Yuman (0)	0	<0.01
Yup'ik (Alaska Native) (0)	0	<0.01
Asian (25)	43	0.33
Not Hispanic (25)	43	0.33
Hispanic (0)	0	<0.01
Bangladeshi (0)	0	<0.01
Bhutanese (0)	0	<0.01
Burmese (0)	0	<0.01
Cambodian (0)	0	<0.01
Chinese, ex. Taiwanese (7)	8	0.06
Filipino (9)	18	0.14
Hmong (0)	0	<0.01
Indian (4)	7	0.05
Indonesian (0)	0	<0.01
Japanese (1)	1	0.01
Korean (2)	2	0.02
Laotian (0)	0	<0.01
Malaysian (0)	0	<0.01
Nepalese (0)	0	<0.01
Pakistani (0)	0	<0.01
Sri Lankan (0)	0	<0.01
Taiwanese (0)	0	<0.01
Thai (1)	1	0.01
Vietnamese (1)	1	0.01
Hawaii Native/Pacific Islander (4)	8	0.06
Not Hispanic (3)	7	0.05
Hispanic (1)	1	0.01
Fijian (0)	0	<0.01
Guamanian/Chamorro (1)	1	0.01
Marshallese (0)	0	<0.01
Native Hawaiian (2)	4	0.03
Samoan (0)	0	<0.01
Tongan (0)	0	<0.01
White (12,610)	12,708	98.93
Not Hispanic (12,544)	12,622	98.26
Hispanic (66)	86	0.67

Notes: † The Census 2010 population figure is used to calculate the percentages in the Hispanic Origin and Race categories. Ancestry percentages are based on the 2006-2010 American Community Survey population (not shown); ‡ Numbers in parentheses indicate the number of people reporting a single ancestry; * Numbers in parentheses indicate the number of persons reporting this race alone, not in combination with any other race; Please refer to the Explanation of Data for more information.

Porter County
Population: 164,343

Ancestry	Population	%
Afghan (13)	13	0.01
African, Sub-Saharan (408)	525	0.32
African (389)	499	0.31
Cape Verdean (0)	0	<0.01
Ethiopian (0)	0	<0.01
Ghanaian (0)	7	<0.01
Kenyan (0)	0	<0.01
Liberian (0)	0	<0.01
Nigerian (0)	0	<0.01
Senegalese (0)	0	<0.01
Sierra Leonean (0)	0	<0.01
Somalian (0)	0	<0.01
South African (0)	0	<0.01
Sudanese (19)	19	0.01
Ugandan (0)	0	<0.01
Zimbabwean (0)	0	<0.01
Other Sub-Saharan African (0)	0	<0.01
Albanian (0)	21	0.01
Alsatian (48)	59	0.04
American (9,144)	9,144	5.64
Arab (266)	428	0.26
Arab (75)	120	0.07
Egyptian (0)	8	<0.01
Iraqi (0)	0	<0.01
Jordanian (28)	28	0.02
Lebanese (107)	178	0.11
Moroccan (0)	0	<0.01
Palestinian (0)	0	<0.01
Syrian (44)	80	0.05
Other Arab (12)	14	0.01
Armenian (61)	244	0.15
Assyrian/Chaldean/Syriac (48)	110	0.07
Australian (13)	24	0.01
Austrian (151)	524	0.32
Basque (3)	3	<0.01
Belgian (39)	152	0.09
Brazilian (38)	42	0.03
British (150)	376	0.23
Bulgarian (12)	26	0.02
Cajun (15)	25	0.02
Canadian (160)	420	0.26
Carpatho Rusyn (0)	0	<0.01
Celtic (0)	17	0.01
Croatian (723)	1,989	1.23
Cypriot (7)	7	<0.01
Czech (342)	1,147	0.71
Czechoslovakian (125)	403	0.25
Danish (152)	620	0.38
Dutch (1,229)	4,652	2.87
Eastern European (79)	91	0.06
English (3,833)	15,704	9.69
Estonian (0)	0	<0.01
European (1,356)	1,511	0.93
Finnish (51)	189	0.12
French, ex. Basque (745)	4,574	2.82
French Canadian (394)	961	0.59
German (15,720)	47,080	29.06
German Russian (0)	0	<0.01
Greek (1,225)	2,145	1.32
Guyanese (0)	0	<0.01
Hungarian (929)	2,850	1.76
Icelander (18)	18	0.01
Iranian (44)	143	0.09
Irish (7,617)	30,032	18.54
Israeli (5)	5	<0.01
Italian (2,981)	9,415	5.81
Latvian (0)	16	0.01
Lithuanian (862)	1,338	0.83
Luxemburger (3)	44	0.03
Macedonian (483)	668	0.41
Maltese (0)	0	<0.01
New Zealander (0)	0	<0.01
Northern European (138)	138	0.09
Norwegian (601)	1,823	1.13
Pennsylvania German (15)	106	0.07
Polish (5,895)	16,382	10.11
Portuguese (0)	0	<0.01
Romanian (225)	688	0.42
Russian (235)	1,703	1.05
Scandinavian (69)	126	0.08
Scotch-Irish (1,176)	2,783	1.72
Scottish (1,063)	3,644	2.25
Serbian (888)	1,781	1.10
Slavic (144)	328	0.20
Slovak (1,039)	3,403	2.10
Slovene (74)	342	0.21
Soviet Union (0)	0	<0.01
Swedish (1,022)	4,337	2.68
Swiss (73)	445	0.27
Turkish (0)	0	<0.01
Ukrainian (262)	645	0.40
Welsh (205)	1,320	0.81
West Indian, ex. Hispanic (30)	86	0.05
Bahamian (0)	0	<0.01
Barbadian (0)	0	<0.01
Belizean (0)	0	<0.01
Bermudan (0)	0	<0.01
British West Indian (0)	0	<0.01
Dutch West Indian (0)	6	<0.01
Haitian (0)	0	<0.01
Jamaican (10)	10	0.01
Trinidadian/Tobagonian (0)	13	0.01
U.S. Virgin Islander (0)	0	<0.01
West Indian (20)	57	0.04
Other West Indian (0)	0	<0.01
Yugoslavian (92)	200	0.12

Hispanic Origin	Population	%
Hispanic or Latino (of any race)	13,933	8.48
Central American, ex. Mexican	216	0.13
Costa Rican	12	0.01
Guatemalan	107	0.07
Honduran	24	0.01
Nicaraguan	10	0.01
Panamanian	34	0.02
Salvadoran	25	0.02
Other Central American	4	<0.01
Cuban	123	0.07
Dominican Republic	33	0.02
Mexican	9,521	5.79
Puerto Rican	2,893	1.76
South American	306	0.19
Argentinean	63	0.04
Bolivian	32	0.02
Chilean	48	0.03
Colombian	37	0.02
Ecuadorian	30	0.02
Paraguayan	3	<0.01
Peruvian	67	0.04
Uruguayan	1	<0.01
Venezuelan	22	0.01
Other South American	3	<0.01
Other Hispanic or Latino	841	0.51

Race*	Population	%
African-American/Black (4,894)	5,884	3.58
Not Hispanic (4,649)	5,438	3.31
Hispanic (245)	446	0.27
American Indian/Alaska Native (494)	1,340	0.82
Not Hispanic (349)	1,023	0.62
Hispanic (145)	317	0.19
Alaska Athabascan (Ala. Nat.) (1)	1	<0.01
Aleut (Alaska Native) (0)	0	<0.01
Apache (4)	22	0.01
Arapaho (0)	0	<0.01
Blackfeet (9)	69	0.04
Canadian/French Am. Ind. (5)	7	<0.01
Central American Ind. (2)	5	<0.01
Cherokee (76)	341	0.21
Cheyenne (0)	1	<0.01
Chickasaw (1)	2	<0.01
Chippewa (42)	81	0.05
Choctaw (4)	16	0.01
Colville (0)	0	<0.01
Comanche (1)	2	<0.01
Cree (2)	2	<0.01
Creek (6)	24	0.01
Crow (0)	0	<0.01
Delaware (1)	4	<0.01
Hopi (0)	2	<0.01
Houma (2)	2	<0.01
Inupiat (Alaska Native) (0)	0	<0.01
Iroquois (9)	24	0.01
Kiowa (0)	1	<0.01
Lumbee (0)	0	<0.01
Menominee (1)	5	<0.01
Mexican American Ind. (23)	46	0.03
Navajo (7)	25	0.02
Osage (0)	7	<0.01
Ottawa (2)	3	<0.01
Paiute (0)	0	<0.01
Pima (0)	0	<0.01
Potawatomi (8)	19	0.01
Pueblo (5)	6	<0.01
Puget Sound Salish (0)	0	<0.01
Seminole (1)	5	<0.01
Shoshone (0)	3	<0.01
Sioux (24)	52	0.03
South American Ind. (11)	18	0.01
Spanish American Ind. (1)	2	<0.01
Tlingit-Haida (Alaska Native) (1)	1	<0.01
Tohono O'Odham (4)	4	<0.01
Tsimshian (Alaska Native) (0)	0	<0.01
Ute (2)	2	<0.01
Yakama (0)	0	<0.01
Yaqui (1)	6	<0.01
Yuman (0)	0	<0.01
Yup'ik (Alaska Native) (2)	2	<0.01
Asian (1,994)	2,690	1.64
Not Hispanic (1,960)	2,562	1.56
Hispanic (34)	128	0.08
Bangladeshi (3)	3	<0.01
Bhutanese (0)	0	<0.01
Burmese (1)	1	<0.01
Cambodian (7)	8	<0.01
Chinese, ex. Taiwanese (474)	572	0.35
Filipino (382)	593	0.36
Hmong (0)	0	<0.01
Indian (487)	568	0.35
Indonesian (2)	3	<0.01
Japanese (77)	196	0.12
Korean (156)	254	0.15
Laotian (17)	22	0.01
Malaysian (0)	1	<0.01
Nepalese (0)	0	<0.01
Pakistani (85)	95	0.06
Sri Lankan (7)	11	0.01
Taiwanese (13)	21	0.01
Thai (57)	93	0.06
Vietnamese (150)	178	0.11
Hawaii Native/Pacific Islander (36)	127	0.08
Not Hispanic (31)	107	0.07
Hispanic (5)	20	0.01
Fijian (0)	0	<0.01
Guamanian/Chamorro (17)	23	0.01
Marshallese (1)	1	<0.01
Native Hawaiian (4)	34	0.02
Samoan (5)	10	0.01
Tongan (0)	4	<0.01
White (149,995)	152,894	93.03
Not Hispanic (141,243)	143,149	87.10
Hispanic (8,752)	9,745	5.93

Notes: † The Census 2010 population figure is used to calculate the percentages in the Hispanic Origin and Race categories. Ancestry percentages are based on the 2006-2010 American Community Survey population (not shown); ‡ Numbers in parentheses indicate the number of people reporting a single ancestry; * Numbers in parentheses indicate the number of persons reporting this race alone, not in combination with any other race; Please refer to the Explanation of Data for more information.

Posey County
Population: 25,910

Ancestry	Population	%
Afghan (0)	0	<0.01
African, Sub-Saharan (0)	0	<0.01
African (0)	0	<0.01
Cape Verdean (0)	0	<0.01
Ethiopian (0)	0	<0.01
Ghanaian (0)	0	<0.01
Kenyan (0)	0	<0.01
Liberian (0)	0	<0.01
Nigerian (0)	0	<0.01
Senegalese (0)	0	<0.01
Sierra Leonean (0)	0	<0.01
Somalian (0)	0	<0.01
South African (0)	0	<0.01
Sudanese (0)	0	<0.01
Ugandan (0)	0	<0.01
Zimbabwean (0)	0	<0.01
Other Sub-Saharan African (0)	0	<0.01
Albanian (0)	0	<0.01
Alsatian (0)	0	<0.01
American (3,553)	3,553	13.61
Arab (0)	0	<0.01
Arab (0)	0	<0.01
Egyptian (0)	0	<0.01
Iraqi (0)	0	<0.01
Jordanian (0)	0	<0.01
Lebanese (0)	0	<0.01
Moroccan (0)	0	<0.01
Palestinian (0)	0	<0.01
Syrian (0)	0	<0.01
Other Arab (0)	0	<0.01
Armenian (0)	0	<0.01
Assyrian/Chaldean/Syriac (0)	0	<0.01
Australian (0)	0	<0.01
Austrian (0)	0	<0.01
Basque (0)	0	<0.01
Belgian (0)	3	0.01
Brazilian (0)	0	<0.01
British (22)	38	0.15
Bulgarian (0)	0	<0.01
Cajun (0)	0	<0.01
Canadian (36)	46	0.18
Carpatho Rusyn (0)	0	<0.01
Celtic (0)	0	<0.01
Croatian (0)	0	<0.01
Cypriot (0)	0	<0.01
Czech (0)	168	0.64
Czechoslovakian (12)	12	0.05
Danish (0)	10	0.04
Dutch (63)	293	1.12
Eastern European (0)	0	<0.01
English (1,195)	2,921	11.19
Estonian (0)	0	<0.01
European (36)	77	0.30
Finnish (17)	67	0.26
French, ex. Basque (182)	606	2.32
French Canadian (0)	12	0.05
German (6,955)	11,392	43.65
German Russian (0)	0	<0.01
Greek (17)	72	0.28
Guyanese (0)	0	<0.01
Hungarian (0)	35	0.13
Icelander (0)	0	<0.01
Iranian (0)	0	<0.01
Irish (893)	3,028	11.60
Israeli (38)	38	0.15
Italian (58)	436	1.67
Latvian (0)	0	<0.01
Lithuanian (0)	5	0.02
Luxemburger (0)	0	<0.01
Macedonian (0)	0	<0.01
Maltese (0)	0	<0.01
New Zealander (0)	0	<0.01
Northern European (5)	5	0.02
Norwegian (7)	124	0.48
Pennsylvania German (0)	0	<0.01
Polish (64)	224	0.86
Portuguese (0)	0	<0.01
Romanian (0)	0	<0.01
Russian (112)	136	0.52
Scandinavian (0)	6	0.02
Scotch-Irish (141)	438	1.68
Scottish (83)	452	1.73
Serbian (0)	0	<0.01
Slavic (0)	8	0.03
Slovak (0)	13	0.05
Slovene (0)	0	<0.01
Soviet Union (0)	0	<0.01
Swedish (1)	29	0.11
Swiss (22)	139	0.53
Turkish (0)	0	<0.01
Ukrainian (21)	21	0.08
Welsh (63)	140	0.54
West Indian, ex. Hispanic (0)	0	<0.01
Bahamian (0)	0	<0.01
Barbadian (0)	0	<0.01
Belizean (0)	0	<0.01
Bermudan (0)	0	<0.01
British West Indian (0)	0	<0.01
Dutch West Indian (0)	0	<0.01
Haitian (0)	0	<0.01
Jamaican (0)	0	<0.01
Trinidadian/Tobagonian (0)	0	<0.01
U.S. Virgin Islander (0)	0	<0.01
West Indian (0)	0	<0.01
Other West Indian (0)	0	<0.01
Yugoslavian (0)	0	<0.01

Hispanic Origin	Population	%
Hispanic or Latino (of any race)	248	0.96
Central American, ex. Mexican	8	0.03
Costa Rican	1	<0.01
Guatemalan	5	0.02
Honduran	0	<0.01
Nicaraguan	0	<0.01
Panamanian	0	<0.01
Salvadoran	2	0.01
Other Central American	0	<0.01
Cuban	9	0.03
Dominican Republic	3	0.01
Mexican	143	0.55
Puerto Rican	39	0.15
South American	23	0.09
Argentinean	5	0.02
Bolivian	2	0.01
Chilean	2	0.01
Colombian	3	0.01
Ecuadorian	5	0.02
Paraguayan	0	<0.01
Peruvian	1	<0.01
Uruguayan	0	<0.01
Venezuelan	5	0.02
Other South American	0	<0.01
Other Hispanic or Latino	23	0.09

Race*	Population	%
African-American/Black (233)	388	1.50
Not Hispanic (230)	383	1.48
Hispanic (3)	5	0.02
American Indian/Alaska Native (48)	144	0.56
Not Hispanic (42)	138	0.53
Hispanic (6)	6	0.02
Alaska Athabascan (Ala. Nat.) (0)	0	<0.01
Aleut (Alaska Native) (0)	0	<0.01
Apache (1)	1	<0.01
Arapaho (0)	0	<0.01
Blackfeet (4)	4	0.02
Canadian/French Am. Ind. (2)	2	0.01
Central American Ind. (0)	0	<0.01
Cherokee (9)	46	0.18
Cheyenne (0)	0	<0.01
Chickasaw (1)	1	<0.01
Chippewa (2)	3	0.01
Choctaw (0)	0	<0.01
Colville (0)	0	<0.01
Comanche (0)	4	0.02
Cree (0)	0	<0.01
Creek (0)	1	<0.01
Crow (0)	0	<0.01
Delaware (6)	6	0.02
Hopi (0)	0	<0.01
Houma (0)	0	<0.01
Inupiat (Alaska Native) (0)	0	<0.01
Iroquois (0)	1	<0.01
Kiowa (0)	0	<0.01
Lumbee (2)	2	0.01
Menominee (0)	0	<0.01
Mexican American Ind. (3)	3	0.01
Navajo (1)	1	<0.01
Osage (0)	1	<0.01
Ottawa (0)	0	<0.01
Paiute (0)	0	<0.01
Pima (0)	0	<0.01
Potawatomi (1)	4	0.02
Pueblo (0)	0	<0.01
Puget Sound Salish (0)	0	<0.01
Seminole (0)	0	<0.01
Shoshone (0)	0	<0.01
Sioux (0)	1	<0.01
South American Ind. (0)	0	<0.01
Spanish American Ind. (1)	1	<0.01
Tlingit-Haida (Alaska Native) (0)	0	<0.01
Tohono O'Odham (0)	0	<0.01
Tsimshian (Alaska Native) (0)	0	<0.01
Ute (0)	0	<0.01
Yakama (0)	0	<0.01
Yaqui (0)	0	<0.01
Yuman (0)	0	<0.01
Yup'ik (Alaska Native) (0)	0	<0.01
Asian (70)	98	0.38
Not Hispanic (70)	96	0.37
Hispanic (0)	2	0.01
Bangladeshi (0)	0	<0.01
Bhutanese (0)	0	<0.01
Burmese (0)	0	<0.01
Cambodian (0)	0	<0.01
Chinese, ex. Taiwanese (25)	25	0.10
Filipino (6)	8	0.03
Hmong (0)	0	<0.01
Indian (17)	24	0.09
Indonesian (0)	0	<0.01
Japanese (3)	6	0.02
Korean (8)	17	0.07
Laotian (0)	0	<0.01
Malaysian (0)	0	<0.01
Nepalese (0)	0	<0.01
Pakistani (0)	0	<0.01
Sri Lankan (0)	0	<0.01
Taiwanese (1)	1	<0.01
Thai (4)	10	0.04
Vietnamese (6)	6	0.02
Hawaii Native/Pacific Islander (4)	8	0.03
Not Hispanic (4)	8	0.03
Hispanic (0)	0	<0.01
Fijian (0)	0	<0.01
Guamanian/Chamorro (3)	5	0.02
Marshallese (0)	0	<0.01
Native Hawaiian (0)	1	<0.01
Samoan (0)	0	<0.01
Tongan (0)	0	<0.01
White (25,185)	25,455	98.24
Not Hispanic (25,046)	25,294	97.62
Hispanic (139)	161	0.62

Notes: † The Census 2010 population figure is used to calculate the percentages in the Hispanic Origin and Race categories. Ancestry percentages are based on the 2006-2010 American Community Survey population (not shown); ‡ Numbers in parentheses indicate the number of people reporting a single ancestry; * Numbers in parentheses indicate the number of persons reporting this race alone, not in combination with any other race; Please refer to the Explanation of Data for more information.

Pulaski County
Population: 13,402

Ancestry	Population	%
Afghan (0)	0	<0.01
African, Sub-Saharan (0)	0	<0.01
African (0)	0	<0.01
Cape Verdean (0)	0	<0.01
Ethiopian (0)	0	<0.01
Ghanaian (0)	0	<0.01
Kenyan (0)	0	<0.01
Liberian (0)	0	<0.01
Nigerian (0)	0	<0.01
Senegalese (0)	0	<0.01
Sierra Leonean (0)	0	<0.01
Somalian (0)	0	<0.01
South African (0)	0	<0.01
Sudanese (0)	0	<0.01
Ugandan (0)	0	<0.01
Zimbabwean (0)	0	<0.01
Other Sub-Saharan African (0)	0	<0.01
Albanian (0)	0	<0.01
Alsatian (0)	0	<0.01
American (1,115)	1,115	8.20
Arab (0)	0	<0.01
Arab (0)	0	<0.01
Egyptian (0)	0	<0.01
Iraqi (0)	0	<0.01
Jordanian (0)	0	<0.01
Lebanese (0)	0	<0.01
Moroccan (0)	0	<0.01
Palestinian (0)	0	<0.01
Syrian (0)	0	<0.01
Other Arab (0)	0	<0.01
Armenian (0)	0	<0.01
Assyrian/Chaldean/Syriac (0)	0	<0.01
Australian (0)	0	<0.01
Austrian (4)	15	0.11
Basque (0)	0	<0.01
Belgian (0)	8	0.06
Brazilian (0)	0	<0.01
British (0)	25	0.18
Bulgarian (0)	0	<0.01
Cajun (0)	0	<0.01
Canadian (0)	0	<0.01
Carpatho Rusyn (0)	0	<0.01
Celtic (0)	0	<0.01
Croatian (16)	37	0.27
Cypriot (0)	0	<0.01
Czech (14)	103	0.76
Czechoslovakian (9)	34	0.25
Danish (24)	40	0.29
Dutch (72)	280	2.06
Eastern European (0)	0	<0.01
English (432)	1,173	8.63
Estonian (0)	0	<0.01
European (6)	83	0.61
Finnish (0)	8	0.06
French, ex. Basque (80)	302	2.22
French Canadian (0)	9	0.07
German (2,138)	4,404	32.39
German Russian (0)	0	<0.01
Greek (36)	50	0.37
Guyanese (0)	0	<0.01
Hungarian (27)	87	0.64
Icelander (0)	0	<0.01
Iranian (0)	0	<0.01
Irish (360)	1,656	12.18
Israeli (0)	0	<0.01
Italian (148)	261	1.92
Latvian (0)	0	<0.01
Lithuanian (96)	183	1.35
Luxemburger (0)	11	0.08
Macedonian (0)	0	<0.01
Maltese (0)	0	<0.01
New Zealander (0)	0	<0.01
Northern European (0)	0	<0.01
Norwegian (90)	176	1.29
Pennsylvania German (4)	4	0.03
Polish (203)	531	3.91
Portuguese (0)	0	<0.01
Romanian (0)	28	0.21
Russian (0)	60	0.44
Scandinavian (0)	0	<0.01
Scotch-Irish (103)	166	1.22
Scottish (24)	112	0.82
Serbian (8)	10	0.07
Slavic (0)	0	<0.01
Slovak (0)	11	0.08
Slovene (0)	0	<0.01
Soviet Union (0)	0	<0.01
Swedish (68)	165	1.21
Swiss (8)	211	1.55
Turkish (0)	0	<0.01
Ukrainian (0)	0	<0.01
Welsh (20)	117	0.86
West Indian, ex. Hispanic (0)	0	<0.01
Bahamian (0)	0	<0.01
Barbadian (0)	0	<0.01
Belizean (0)	0	<0.01
Bermudan (0)	0	<0.01
British West Indian (0)	0	<0.01
Dutch West Indian (0)	0	<0.01
Haitian (0)	0	<0.01
Jamaican (0)	0	<0.01
Trinidadian/Tobagonian (0)	0	<0.01
U.S. Virgin Islander (0)	0	<0.01
West Indian (0)	0	<0.01
Other West Indian (0)	0	<0.01
Yugoslavian (24)	24	0.18

Hispanic Origin	Population	%
Hispanic or Latino (of any race)	325	2.43
Central American, ex. Mexican	19	0.14
Costa Rican	0	<0.01
Guatemalan	0	<0.01
Honduran	0	<0.01
Nicaraguan	0	<0.01
Panamanian	0	<0.01
Salvadoran	19	0.14
Other Central American	0	<0.01
Cuban	2	0.01
Dominican Republic	0	<0.01
Mexican	261	1.95
Puerto Rican	19	0.14
South American	1	0.01
Argentinean	0	<0.01
Bolivian	0	<0.01
Chilean	0	<0.01
Colombian	0	<0.01
Ecuadorian	1	0.01
Paraguayan	0	<0.01
Peruvian	0	<0.01
Uruguayan	0	<0.01
Venezuelan	0	<0.01
Other South American	0	<0.01
Other Hispanic or Latino	23	0.17

Race*	Population	%
African-American/Black (88)	104	0.78
Not Hispanic (87)	102	0.76
Hispanic (1)	2	0.01
American Indian/Alaska Native (40)	109	0.81
Not Hispanic (38)	100	0.75
Hispanic (2)	9	0.07
Alaska Athabascan (Ala. Nat.) (0)	0	<0.01
Aleut (Alaska Native) (0)	0	<0.01
Apache (1)	4	0.03
Arapaho (0)	0	<0.01
Blackfeet (0)	4	0.03
Canadian/French Am. Ind. (0)	0	<0.01
Central American Ind. (0)	0	<0.01
Cherokee (12)	25	0.19
Cheyenne (0)	0	<0.01
Chickasaw (0)	0	<0.01
Chippewa (0)	8	0.06
Choctaw (0)	1	0.01
Colville (0)	0	<0.01
Comanche (2)	5	0.04
Cree (0)	0	<0.01
Creek (2)	2	0.01
Crow (0)	0	<0.01
Delaware (1)	1	0.01
Hopi (0)	0	<0.01
Houma (0)	0	<0.01
Inupiat (Alaska Native) (0)	0	<0.01
Iroquois (0)	0	<0.01
Kiowa (0)	0	<0.01
Lumbee (0)	0	<0.01
Menominee (0)	0	<0.01
Mexican American Ind. (1)	2	0.01
Navajo (1)	1	0.01
Osage (0)	3	0.02
Ottawa (0)	0	<0.01
Paiute (0)	0	<0.01
Pima (0)	0	<0.01
Potawatomi (0)	0	<0.01
Pueblo (0)	0	<0.01
Puget Sound Salish (0)	0	<0.01
Seminole (0)	0	<0.01
Shoshone (0)	0	<0.01
Sioux (0)	1	0.01
South American Ind. (0)	0	<0.01
Spanish American Ind. (0)	0	<0.01
Tlingit-Haida (Alaska Native) (0)	0	<0.01
Tohono O'Odham (0)	0	<0.01
Tsimshian (Alaska Native) (0)	0	<0.01
Ute (0)	4	0.03
Yakama (0)	0	<0.01
Yaqui (0)	0	<0.01
Yuman (0)	0	<0.01
Yup'ik (Alaska Native) (0)	0	<0.01
Asian (29)	50	0.37
Not Hispanic (27)	45	0.34
Hispanic (2)	5	0.04
Bangladeshi (0)	0	<0.01
Bhutanese (0)	0	<0.01
Burmese (0)	0	<0.01
Cambodian (0)	0	<0.01
Chinese, ex. Taiwanese (10)	10	0.07
Filipino (13)	26	0.19
Hmong (0)	0	<0.01
Indian (1)	5	0.04
Indonesian (0)	0	<0.01
Japanese (2)	3	0.02
Korean (1)	3	0.02
Laotian (0)	0	<0.01
Malaysian (0)	0	<0.01
Nepalese (0)	0	<0.01
Pakistani (0)	0	<0.01
Sri Lankan (0)	0	<0.01
Taiwanese (0)	0	<0.01
Thai (0)	1	0.01
Vietnamese (0)	0	<0.01
Hawaii Native/Pacific Islander (3)	4	0.03
Not Hispanic (3)	3	0.02
Hispanic (0)	1	0.01
Fijian (0)	0	<0.01
Guamanian/Chamorro (0)	0	<0.01
Marshallese (0)	0	<0.01
Native Hawaiian (1)	2	0.01
Samoan (0)	0	<0.01
Tongan (0)	0	<0.01
White (13,025)	13,159	98.19
Not Hispanic (12,823)	12,922	96.42
Hispanic (202)	237	1.77

Notes: † The Census 2010 population figure is used to calculate the percentages in the Hispanic Origin and Race categories. Ancestry percentages are based on the 2006-2010 American Community Survey population (not shown); ‡ Numbers in parentheses indicate the number of people reporting a single ancestry; * Numbers in parentheses indicate the number of persons reporting this race alone, not in combination with any other race; Please refer to the Explanation of Data for more information.

Putnam County
Population: 37,963

Ancestry	Population	%
Afghan (0)	0	<0.01
African, Sub-Saharan (167)	251	0.66
African (125)	195	0.51
Cape Verdean (0)	0	<0.01
Ethiopian (0)	0	<0.01
Ghanaian (14)	14	0.04
Kenyan (0)	0	<0.01
Liberian (0)	0	<0.01
Nigerian (14)	14	0.04
Senegalese (0)	14	0.04
Sierra Leonean (0)	0	<0.01
Somalian (0)	0	<0.01
South African (14)	14	0.04
Sudanese (0)	0	<0.01
Ugandan (0)	0	<0.01
Zimbabwean (0)	0	<0.01
Other Sub-Saharan African (0)	0	<0.01
Albanian (0)	0	<0.01
Alsatian (0)	0	<0.01
American (5,804)	5,804	15.25
Arab (86)	148	0.39
Arab (76)	110	0.29
Egyptian (0)	0	<0.01
Iraqi (0)	0	<0.01
Jordanian (0)	0	<0.01
Lebanese (10)	20	0.05
Moroccan (0)	0	<0.01
Palestinian (0)	0	<0.01
Syrian (0)	18	0.05
Other Arab (0)	0	<0.01
Armenian (0)	0	<0.01
Assyrian/Chaldean/Syriac (0)	0	<0.01
Australian (0)	43	0.11
Austrian (0)	49	0.13
Basque (0)	0	<0.01
Belgian (0)	26	0.07
Brazilian (0)	0	<0.01
British (38)	50	0.13
Bulgarian (0)	116	0.30
Cajun (0)	0	<0.01
Canadian (24)	89	0.23
Carpatho Rusyn (0)	0	<0.01
Celtic (15)	24	0.06
Croatian (0)	13	0.03
Cypriot (0)	0	<0.01
Czech (30)	163	0.43
Czechoslovakian (39)	91	0.24
Danish (0)	20	0.05
Dutch (140)	1,194	3.14
Eastern European (0)	0	<0.01
English (2,464)	4,786	12.58
Estonian (0)	0	<0.01
European (401)	401	1.05
Finnish (0)	0	<0.01
French, ex. Basque (150)	1,071	2.81
French Canadian (43)	117	0.31
German (3,897)	8,993	23.64
German Russian (0)	0	<0.01
Greek (13)	63	0.17
Guyanese (0)	0	<0.01
Hungarian (149)	158	0.42
Icelander (0)	0	<0.01
Iranian (0)	0	<0.01
Irish (1,213)	4,826	12.68
Israeli (19)	19	0.05
Italian (414)	972	2.55
Latvian (11)	11	0.03
Lithuanian (0)	0	<0.01
Luxemburger (0)	0	<0.01
Macedonian (8)	8	0.02
Maltese (0)	0	<0.01
New Zealander (0)	0	<0.01
Northern European (23)	78	0.21
Norwegian (74)	248	0.65
Pennsylvania German (16)	70	0.18
Polish (109)	581	1.53
Portuguese (25)	25	0.07
Romanian (0)	0	<0.01
Russian (14)	20	0.05
Scandinavian (31)	52	0.14
Scotch-Irish (489)	994	2.61
Scottish (448)	879	2.31
Serbian (0)	23	0.06
Slavic (12)	33	0.09
Slovak (53)	53	0.14
Slovene (25)	25	0.07
Soviet Union (0)	0	<0.01
Swedish (57)	307	0.81
Swiss (67)	185	0.49
Turkish (3)	3	0.01
Ukrainian (2)	29	0.08
Welsh (69)	350	0.92
West Indian, ex. Hispanic (9)	18	0.05
Bahamian (0)	0	<0.01
Barbadian (0)	0	<0.01
Belizean (0)	0	<0.01
Bermudan (0)	0	<0.01
British West Indian (0)	0	<0.01
Dutch West Indian (0)	0	<0.01
Haitian (9)	9	0.02
Jamaican (0)	9	0.02
Trinidadian/Tobagonian (0)	0	<0.01
U.S. Virgin Islander (0)	0	<0.01
West Indian (0)	0	<0.01
Other West Indian (0)	0	<0.01
Yugoslavian (2)	101	0.27

Hispanic Origin	Population	%
Hispanic or Latino (of any race)	587	1.55
Central American, ex. Mexican	40	0.11
Costa Rican	4	0.01
Guatemalan	8	0.02
Honduran	8	0.02
Nicaraguan	6	0.02
Panamanian	6	0.02
Salvadoran	8	0.02
Other Central American	0	<0.01
Cuban	9	0.02
Dominican Republic	1	<0.01
Mexican	394	1.04
Puerto Rican	68	0.18
South American	23	0.06
Argentinean	1	<0.01
Bolivian	0	<0.01
Chilean	4	0.01
Colombian	7	0.02
Ecuadorian	0	<0.01
Paraguayan	1	<0.01
Peruvian	7	0.02
Uruguayan	0	<0.01
Venezuelan	3	0.01
Other South American	0	<0.01
Other Hispanic or Latino	52	0.14

Race*	Population	%
African-American/Black (1,505)	1,648	4.34
Not Hispanic (1,485)	1,624	4.28
Hispanic (20)	24	0.06
American Indian/Alaska Native (98)	247	0.65
Not Hispanic (90)	219	0.58
Hispanic (8)	28	0.07
Alaska Athabascan (Ala. Nat.) (0)	0	<0.01
Aleut (Alaska Native) (0)	0	<0.01
Apache (3)	12	0.03
Arapaho (0)	1	<0.01
Blackfeet (6)	15	0.04
Canadian/French Am. Ind. (0)	0	<0.01
Central American Ind. (1)	1	<0.01
Cherokee (18)	69	0.18
Cheyenne (0)	0	<0.01
Chickasaw (2)	6	0.02
Chippewa (1)	1	<0.01
Choctaw (1)	3	0.01
Colville (0)	2	0.01
Comanche (0)	0	<0.01
Cree (0)	0	<0.01
Creek (3)	4	0.01
Crow (0)	2	0.01
Delaware (2)	3	0.01
Hopi (0)	0	<0.01
Houma (0)	0	<0.01
Inupiat (Alaska Native) (0)	0	<0.01
Iroquois (1)	2	0.01
Kiowa (0)	0	<0.01
Lumbee (0)	0	<0.01
Menominee (0)	0	<0.01
Mexican American Ind. (0)	0	<0.01
Navajo (1)	9	0.02
Osage (0)	1	<0.01
Ottawa (0)	0	<0.01
Paiute (0)	0	<0.01
Pima (0)	0	<0.01
Potawatomi (0)	0	<0.01
Pueblo (0)	0	<0.01
Puget Sound Salish (0)	0	<0.01
Seminole (0)	1	<0.01
Shoshone (0)	0	<0.01
Sioux (4)	6	0.02
South American Ind. (1)	1	<0.01
Spanish American Ind. (0)	0	<0.01
Tlingit-Haida (Alaska Native) (0)	0	<0.01
Tohono O'Odham (0)	0	<0.01
Tsimshian (Alaska Native) (0)	0	<0.01
Ute (0)	0	<0.01
Yakama (0)	0	<0.01
Yaqui (0)	0	<0.01
Yuman (0)	0	<0.01
Yup'ik (Alaska Native) (4)	4	0.01
Asian (279)	362	0.95
Not Hispanic (273)	347	0.91
Hispanic (6)	15	0.04
Bangladeshi (0)	0	<0.01
Bhutanese (0)	0	<0.01
Burmese (0)	0	<0.01
Cambodian (0)	0	<0.01
Chinese, ex. Taiwanese (72)	85	0.22
Filipino (29)	46	0.12
Hmong (0)	0	<0.01
Indian (30)	43	0.11
Indonesian (1)	3	0.01
Japanese (76)	93	0.24
Korean (23)	43	0.11
Laotian (3)	6	0.02
Malaysian (0)	1	<0.01
Nepalese (0)	0	<0.01
Pakistani (4)	4	0.01
Sri Lankan (0)	0	<0.01
Taiwanese (0)	0	<0.01
Thai (3)	5	0.01
Vietnamese (19)	28	0.07
Hawaii Native/Pacific Islander (14)	38	0.10
Not Hispanic (10)	30	0.08
Hispanic (4)	8	0.02
Fijian (0)	0	<0.01
Guamanian/Chamorro (0)	0	<0.01
Marshallese (0)	0	<0.01
Native Hawaiian (7)	21	0.06
Samoan (1)	5	0.01
Tongan (0)	0	<0.01
White (35,449)	35,844	94.42
Not Hispanic (35,128)	35,474	93.44
Hispanic (321)	370	0.97

Notes: † The Census 2010 population figure is used to calculate the percentages in the Hispanic Origin and Race categories. Ancestry percentages are based on the 2006-2010 American Community Survey population (not shown); ‡ Numbers in parentheses indicate the number of people reporting a single ancestry; * Numbers in parentheses indicate the number of persons reporting this race alone, not in combination with any other race; Please refer to the Explanation of Data for more information.

Randolph County
Population: 26,171

Ancestry	Population	%
Afghan (0)	0	<0.01
African, Sub-Saharan (26)	26	0.10
African (0)	0	<0.01
Cape Verdean (0)	0	<0.01
Ethiopian (0)	0	<0.01
Ghanaian (0)	0	<0.01
Kenyan (0)	0	<0.01
Liberian (0)	0	<0.01
Nigerian (0)	0	<0.01
Senegalese (0)	0	<0.01
Sierra Leonean (0)	0	<0.01
Somalian (0)	0	<0.01
South African (26)	26	0.10
Sudanese (0)	0	<0.01
Ugandan (0)	0	<0.01
Zimbabwean (0)	0	<0.01
Other Sub-Saharan African (0)	0	<0.01
Albanian (0)	0	<0.01
Alsatian (0)	0	<0.01
American (3,020)	3,020	11.50
Arab (0)	0	<0.01
Arab (0)	0	<0.01
Egyptian (0)	0	<0.01
Iraqi (0)	0	<0.01
Jordanian (0)	0	<0.01
Lebanese (0)	0	<0.01
Moroccan (0)	0	<0.01
Palestinian (0)	0	<0.01
Syrian (0)	0	<0.01
Other Arab (0)	0	<0.01
Armenian (0)	8	0.03
Assyrian/Chaldean/Syriac (0)	0	<0.01
Australian (0)	0	<0.01
Austrian (0)	0	<0.01
Basque (0)	0	<0.01
Belgian (3)	11	0.04
Brazilian (0)	0	<0.01
British (29)	36	0.14
Bulgarian (0)	0	<0.01
Cajun (0)	0	<0.01
Canadian (3)	8	0.03
Carpatho Rusyn (0)	0	<0.01
Celtic (0)	0	<0.01
Croatian (0)	0	<0.01
Cypriot (0)	0	<0.01
Czech (17)	17	0.06
Czechoslovakian (0)	27	0.10
Danish (22)	43	0.16
Dutch (127)	620	2.36
Eastern European (0)	0	<0.01
English (1,603)	2,985	11.37
Estonian (0)	0	<0.01
European (109)	109	0.42
Finnish (5)	11	0.04
French, ex. Basque (83)	536	2.04
French Canadian (7)	19	0.07
German (2,854)	6,229	23.72
German Russian (0)	0	<0.01
Greek (4)	4	0.02
Guyanese (0)	0	<0.01
Hungarian (0)	32	0.12
Icelander (0)	0	<0.01
Iranian (0)	0	<0.01
Irish (1,347)	3,656	13.92
Israeli (0)	0	<0.01
Italian (157)	512	1.95
Latvian (0)	0	<0.01
Lithuanian (0)	17	0.06
Luxemburger (0)	0	<0.01
Macedonian (5)	5	0.02
Maltese (0)	0	<0.01
New Zealander (0)	0	<0.01
Northern European (0)	0	<0.01
Norwegian (19)	39	0.15
Pennsylvania German (81)	133	0.51
Polish (107)	263	1.00
Portuguese (0)	9	0.03
Romanian (0)	8	0.03
Russian (5)	5	0.02
Scandinavian (0)	3	0.01
Scotch-Irish (160)	355	1.35
Scottish (239)	459	1.75
Serbian (0)	0	<0.01
Slavic (0)	0	<0.01
Slovak (16)	16	0.06
Slovene (0)	0	<0.01
Soviet Union (0)	0	<0.01
Swedish (23)	70	0.27
Swiss (28)	130	0.50
Turkish (0)	0	<0.01
Ukrainian (10)	42	0.16
Welsh (43)	84	0.32
West Indian, ex. Hispanic (0)	0	<0.01
Bahamian (0)	0	<0.01
Barbadian (0)	0	<0.01
Belizean (0)	0	<0.01
Bermudan (0)	0	<0.01
British West Indian (0)	0	<0.01
Dutch West Indian (0)	0	<0.01
Haitian (0)	0	<0.01
Jamaican (0)	0	<0.01
Trinidadian/Tobagonian (0)	0	<0.01
U.S. Virgin Islander (0)	0	<0.01
West Indian (0)	0	<0.01
Other West Indian (0)	0	<0.01
Yugoslavian (3)	12	0.05

Hispanic Origin	Population	%
Hispanic or Latino (of any race)	790	3.02
Central American, ex. Mexican	25	0.10
Costa Rican	0	<0.01
Guatemalan	19	0.07
Honduran	4	0.02
Nicaraguan	1	<0.01
Panamanian	1	<0.01
Salvadoran	0	<0.01
Other Central American	0	<0.01
Cuban	14	0.05
Dominican Republic	1	<0.01
Mexican	680	2.60
Puerto Rican	14	0.05
South American	3	0.01
Argentinean	0	<0.01
Bolivian	0	<0.01
Chilean	2	0.01
Colombian	1	<0.01
Ecuadorian	0	<0.01
Paraguayan	0	<0.01
Peruvian	0	<0.01
Uruguayan	0	<0.01
Venezuelan	0	<0.01
Other South American	0	<0.01
Other Hispanic or Latino	53	0.20

Race*	Population	%
African-American/Black (117)	221	0.84
Not Hispanic (114)	204	0.78
Hispanic (3)	17	0.06
American Indian/Alaska Native (89)	182	0.70
Not Hispanic (83)	169	0.65
Hispanic (6)	13	0.05
Alaska Athabascan (Ala. Nat.) (0)	0	<0.01
Aleut (Alaska Native) (0)	0	<0.01
Apache (0)	0	<0.01
Arapaho (0)	0	<0.01
Blackfeet (3)	8	0.03
Canadian/French Am. Ind. (0)	0	<0.01
Central American Ind. (0)	0	<0.01
Cherokee (30)	67	0.26
Cheyenne (0)	3	0.01
Chickasaw (1)	1	<0.01
Chippewa (5)	5	0.02
Choctaw (0)	0	<0.01
Colville (0)	0	<0.01
Comanche (0)	0	<0.01
Cree (1)	1	<0.01
Creek (1)	1	<0.01
Crow (0)	0	<0.01
Delaware (0)	1	<0.01
Hopi (0)	0	<0.01
Houma (0)	0	<0.01
Inupiat (Alaska Native) (0)	0	<0.01
Iroquois (0)	0	<0.01
Kiowa (0)	0	<0.01
Lumbee (2)	4	0.02
Menominee (0)	0	<0.01
Mexican American Ind. (1)	1	<0.01
Navajo (0)	0	<0.01
Osage (0)	1	<0.01
Ottawa (2)	2	0.01
Paiute (0)	0	<0.01
Pima (0)	0	<0.01
Potawatomi (2)	3	0.01
Pueblo (0)	0	<0.01
Puget Sound Salish (0)	0	<0.01
Seminole (0)	0	<0.01
Shoshone (0)	0	<0.01
Sioux (3)	3	0.01
South American Ind. (1)	1	<0.01
Spanish American Ind. (0)	0	<0.01
Tlingit-Haida (Alaska Native) (1)	1	<0.01
Tohono O'Odham (0)	0	<0.01
Tsimshian (Alaska Native) (0)	0	<0.01
Ute (0)	0	<0.01
Yakama (0)	0	<0.01
Yaqui (0)	0	<0.01
Yuman (0)	0	<0.01
Yup'ik (Alaska Native) (0)	0	<0.01
Asian (61)	108	0.41
Not Hispanic (57)	101	0.39
Hispanic (4)	7	0.03
Bangladeshi (0)	0	<0.01
Bhutanese (0)	0	<0.01
Burmese (0)	0	<0.01
Cambodian (0)	0	<0.01
Chinese, ex. Taiwanese (11)	12	0.05
Filipino (11)	24	0.09
Hmong (0)	0	<0.01
Indian (10)	19	0.07
Indonesian (0)	0	<0.01
Japanese (5)	14	0.05
Korean (6)	15	0.06
Laotian (0)	0	<0.01
Malaysian (0)	0	<0.01
Nepalese (0)	0	<0.01
Pakistani (3)	3	0.01
Sri Lankan (0)	0	<0.01
Taiwanese (0)	0	<0.01
Thai (7)	12	0.05
Vietnamese (2)	2	0.01
Hawaii Native/Pacific Islander (8)	19	0.07
Not Hispanic (8)	18	0.07
Hispanic (0)	1	<0.01
Fijian (0)	0	<0.01
Guamanian/Chamorro (4)	4	0.02
Marshallese (0)	0	<0.01
Native Hawaiian (0)	9	0.03
Samoan (0)	0	<0.01
Tongan (0)	0	<0.01
White (25,158)	25,422	97.14
Not Hispanic (24,895)	25,100	95.91
Hispanic (263)	322	1.23

Notes: † The Census 2010 population figure is used to calculate the percentages in the Hispanic Origin and Race categories. Ancestry percentages are based on the 2006-2010 American Community Survey population (not shown); ‡ Numbers in parentheses indicate the number of people reporting a single ancestry; * Numbers in parentheses indicate the number of persons reporting this race alone, not in combination with any other race; Please refer to the Explanation of Data for more information.

Ripley County
Population: 28,818

Ancestry	Population	%
Afghan (0)	0	<0.01
African, Sub-Saharan (0)	13	0.05
African (0)	5	0.02
Cape Verdean (0)	0	<0.01
Ethiopian (0)	0	<0.01
Ghanaian (0)	0	<0.01
Kenyan (0)	0	<0.01
Liberian (0)	0	<0.01
Nigerian (0)	0	<0.01
Senegalese (0)	0	<0.01
Sierra Leonean (0)	0	<0.01
Somalian (0)	8	0.03
South African (0)	0	<0.01
Sudanese (0)	0	<0.01
Ugandan (0)	0	<0.01
Zimbabwean (0)	0	<0.01
Other Sub-Saharan African (0)	0	<0.01
Albanian (0)	0	<0.01
Alsatian (0)	0	<0.01
American (4,046)	4,046	14.16
Arab (100)	103	0.36
Arab (0)	0	<0.01
Egyptian (62)	62	0.22
Iraqi (35)	35	0.12
Jordanian (0)	0	<0.01
Lebanese (3)	6	0.02
Moroccan (0)	0	<0.01
Palestinian (0)	0	<0.01
Syrian (0)	0	<0.01
Other Arab (0)	0	<0.01
Armenian (0)	0	<0.01
Assyrian/Chaldean/Syriac (0)	0	<0.01
Australian (0)	0	<0.01
Austrian (0)	31	0.11
Basque (0)	0	<0.01
Belgian (29)	57	0.20
Brazilian (0)	0	<0.01
British (27)	42	0.15
Bulgarian (0)	13	0.05
Cajun (0)	0	<0.01
Canadian (47)	77	0.27
Carpatho Rusyn (0)	0	<0.01
Celtic (0)	0	<0.01
Croatian (0)	8	0.03
Cypriot (0)	0	<0.01
Czech (14)	14	0.05
Czechoslovakian (0)	0	<0.01
Danish (7)	7	0.02
Dutch (98)	504	1.76
Eastern European (7)	7	0.02
English (990)	2,480	8.68
Estonian (0)	0	<0.01
European (115)	115	0.40
Finnish (0)	0	<0.01
French, ex. Basque (65)	534	1.87
French Canadian (11)	74	0.26
German (7,279)	12,391	43.37
German Russian (0)	0	<0.01
Greek (3)	9	0.03
Guyanese (0)	0	<0.01
Hungarian (13)	47	0.16
Icelander (0)	0	<0.01
Iranian (0)	0	<0.01
Irish (1,007)	3,984	13.94
Israeli (0)	0	<0.01
Italian (211)	823	2.88
Latvian (0)	0	<0.01
Lithuanian (0)	0	<0.01
Luxemburger (0)	18	0.06
Macedonian (0)	0	<0.01
Maltese (0)	0	<0.01
New Zealander (0)	0	<0.01
Northern European (0)	0	<0.01
Norwegian (67)	92	0.32
Pennsylvania German (0)	10	0.04
Polish (65)	201	0.70
Portuguese (0)	13	0.05
Romanian (14)	31	0.11
Russian (6)	24	0.08
Scandinavian (0)	0	<0.01
Scotch-Irish (210)	386	1.35
Scottish (84)	373	1.31
Serbian (70)	96	0.34
Slavic (0)	0	<0.01
Slovak (0)	13	0.05
Slovene (0)	0	<0.01
Soviet Union (0)	0	<0.01
Swedish (0)	94	0.33
Swiss (21)	96	0.34
Turkish (13)	13	0.05
Ukrainian (11)	11	0.04
Welsh (24)	101	0.35
West Indian, ex. Hispanic (0)	0	<0.01
Bahamian (0)	0	<0.01
Barbadian (0)	0	<0.01
Belizean (0)	0	<0.01
Bermudan (0)	0	<0.01
British West Indian (0)	0	<0.01
Dutch West Indian (0)	0	<0.01
Haitian (0)	0	<0.01
Jamaican (0)	0	<0.01
Trinidadian/Tobagonian (0)	0	<0.01
U.S. Virgin Islander (0)	0	<0.01
West Indian (0)	0	<0.01
Other West Indian (0)	0	<0.01
Yugoslavian (6)	6	0.02

Hispanic Origin	Population	%
Hispanic or Latino (of any race)	445	1.54
Central American, ex. Mexican	31	0.11
Costa Rican	0	<0.01
Guatemalan	14	0.05
Honduran	9	0.03
Nicaraguan	0	<0.01
Panamanian	0	<0.01
Salvadoran	8	0.03
Other Central American	0	<0.01
Cuban	3	0.01
Dominican Republic	2	0.01
Mexican	351	1.22
Puerto Rican	20	0.07
South American	7	0.02
Argentinean	0	<0.01
Bolivian	0	<0.01
Chilean	0	<0.01
Colombian	2	0.01
Ecuadorian	1	<0.01
Paraguayan	0	<0.01
Peruvian	1	<0.01
Uruguayan	1	<0.01
Venezuelan	2	0.01
Other South American	0	<0.01
Other Hispanic or Latino	31	0.11

Race*	Population	%
African-American/Black (69)	129	0.45
Not Hispanic (67)	118	0.41
Hispanic (2)	11	0.04
American Indian/Alaska Native (51)	199	0.69
Not Hispanic (37)	171	0.59
Hispanic (14)	28	0.10
Alaska Athabascan (Ala. Nat.) (0)	0	<0.01
Aleut (Alaska Native) (0)	0	<0.01
Apache (0)	2	0.01
Arapaho (0)	0	<0.01
Blackfeet (0)	4	0.01
Canadian/French Am. Ind. (0)	1	<0.01
Central American Ind. (0)	0	<0.01
Cherokee (3)	46	0.16
Cheyenne (0)	2	0.01
Chickasaw (0)	0	<0.01
Chippewa (1)	2	0.01
Choctaw (0)	0	<0.01
Colville (0)	0	<0.01
Comanche (0)	0	<0.01
Cree (0)	0	<0.01
Creek (0)	0	<0.01
Crow (0)	0	<0.01
Delaware (0)	0	<0.01
Hopi (0)	0	<0.01
Houma (0)	0	<0.01
Inupiat (Alaska Native) (0)	0	<0.01
Iroquois (5)	8	0.03
Kiowa (0)	0	<0.01
Lumbee (0)	0	<0.01
Menominee (0)	0	<0.01
Mexican American Ind. (5)	5	0.02
Navajo (0)	0	<0.01
Osage (0)	0	<0.01
Ottawa (0)	0	<0.01
Paiute (0)	0	<0.01
Pima (0)	0	<0.01
Potawatomi (4)	4	0.01
Pueblo (0)	0	<0.01
Puget Sound Salish (0)	1	<0.01
Seminole (0)	0	<0.01
Shoshone (0)	0	<0.01
Sioux (0)	1	<0.01
South American Ind. (0)	0	<0.01
Spanish American Ind. (0)	0	<0.01
Tlingit-Haida (Alaska Native) (1)	1	<0.01
Tohono O'Odham (0)	0	<0.01
Tsimshian (Alaska Native) (0)	0	<0.01
Ute (0)	0	<0.01
Yakama (0)	0	<0.01
Yaqui (0)	0	<0.01
Yuman (0)	0	<0.01
Yup'ik (Alaska Native) (0)	0	<0.01
Asian (146)	190	0.66
Not Hispanic (146)	183	0.64
Hispanic (0)	7	0.02
Bangladeshi (0)	0	<0.01
Bhutanese (0)	0	<0.01
Burmese (0)	0	<0.01
Cambodian (0)	0	<0.01
Chinese, ex. Taiwanese (24)	25	0.09
Filipino (19)	38	0.13
Hmong (0)	0	<0.01
Indian (86)	91	0.32
Indonesian (0)	0	<0.01
Japanese (8)	17	0.06
Korean (6)	8	0.03
Laotian (0)	0	<0.01
Malaysian (0)	0	<0.01
Nepalese (0)	0	<0.01
Pakistani (0)	1	<0.01
Sri Lankan (0)	0	<0.01
Taiwanese (2)	3	0.01
Thai (1)	1	<0.01
Vietnamese (0)	0	<0.01
Hawaii Native/Pacific Islander (4)	11	0.04
Not Hispanic (3)	9	0.03
Hispanic (1)	2	0.01
Fijian (0)	0	<0.01
Guamanian/Chamorro (1)	1	<0.01
Marshallese (0)	0	<0.01
Native Hawaiian (2)	3	0.01
Samoan (0)	4	0.01
Tongan (1)	1	<0.01
White (28,132)	28,386	98.50
Not Hispanic (27,879)	28,099	97.51
Hispanic (253)	287	1.00

*Notes: † The Census 2010 population figure is used to calculate the percentages in the Hispanic Origin and Race categories. Ancestry percentages are based on the 2006-2010 American Community Survey population (not shown); ‡ Numbers in parentheses indicate the number of people reporting a single ancestry; * Numbers in parentheses indicate the number of persons reporting this race alone, not in combination with any other race; Please refer to the Explanation of Data for more information.*

Rush County
Population: 17,392

Ancestry	Population	%
Afghan (0)	0	<0.01
African, Sub-Saharan (0)	0	<0.01
African (0)	0	<0.01
Cape Verdean (0)	0	<0.01
Ethiopian (0)	0	<0.01
Ghanaian (0)	0	<0.01
Kenyan (0)	0	<0.01
Liberian (0)	0	<0.01
Nigerian (0)	0	<0.01
Senegalese (0)	0	<0.01
Sierra Leonean (0)	0	<0.01
Somalian (0)	0	<0.01
South African (0)	0	<0.01
Sudanese (0)	0	<0.01
Ugandan (0)	0	<0.01
Zimbabwean (0)	0	<0.01
Other Sub-Saharan African (0)	0	<0.01
Albanian (0)	0	<0.01
Alsatian (0)	0	<0.01
American (2,956)	2,956	16.83
Arab (0)	0	<0.01
Arab (0)	0	<0.01
Egyptian (0)	0	<0.01
Iraqi (0)	0	<0.01
Jordanian (0)	0	<0.01
Lebanese (0)	0	<0.01
Moroccan (0)	0	<0.01
Palestinian (0)	0	<0.01
Syrian (0)	0	<0.01
Other Arab (0)	0	<0.01
Armenian (0)	0	<0.01
Assyrian/Chaldean/Syriac (0)	0	<0.01
Australian (0)	0	<0.01
Austrian (2)	2	0.01
Basque (0)	0	<0.01
Belgian (0)	29	0.17
Brazilian (0)	0	<0.01
British (0)	0	<0.01
Bulgarian (0)	0	<0.01
Cajun (3)	3	0.02
Canadian (0)	0	<0.01
Carpatho Rusyn (0)	0	<0.01
Celtic (0)	0	<0.01
Croatian (0)	0	<0.01
Cypriot (0)	0	<0.01
Czech (0)	8	0.05
Czechoslovakian (0)	0	<0.01
Danish (0)	0	<0.01
Dutch (148)	414	2.36
Eastern European (0)	0	<0.01
English (1,233)	2,089	11.89
Estonian (0)	0	<0.01
European (186)	194	1.10
Finnish (0)	0	<0.01
French, ex. Basque (81)	238	1.35
French Canadian (0)	0	<0.01
German (2,018)	4,105	23.37
German Russian (0)	0	<0.01
Greek (0)	33	0.19
Guyanese (0)	0	<0.01
Hungarian (8)	36	0.20
Icelander (0)	0	<0.01
Iranian (0)	0	<0.01
Irish (823)	2,106	11.99
Israeli (0)	0	<0.01
Italian (78)	104	0.59
Latvian (0)	0	<0.01
Lithuanian (12)	12	0.07
Luxemburger (0)	0	<0.01
Macedonian (0)	0	<0.01
Maltese (0)	0	<0.01
New Zealander (0)	0	<0.01
Northern European (0)	0	<0.01
Norwegian (14)	41	0.23
Pennsylvania German (0)	0	<0.01
Polish (72)	187	1.06
Portuguese (0)	0	<0.01
Romanian (0)	35	0.20
Russian (16)	26	0.15
Scandinavian (21)	21	0.12
Scotch-Irish (158)	233	1.33
Scottish (207)	354	2.02
Serbian (0)	0	<0.01
Slavic (0)	0	<0.01
Slovak (0)	0	<0.01
Slovene (0)	0	<0.01
Soviet Union (0)	0	<0.01
Swedish (0)	134	0.76
Swiss (67)	67	0.38
Turkish (0)	0	<0.01
Ukrainian (0)	0	<0.01
Welsh (3)	113	0.64
West Indian, ex. Hispanic (0)	0	<0.01
Bahamian (0)	0	<0.01
Barbadian (0)	0	<0.01
Belizean (0)	0	<0.01
Bermudan (0)	0	<0.01
British West Indian (0)	0	<0.01
Dutch West Indian (0)	0	<0.01
Haitian (0)	0	<0.01
Jamaican (0)	0	<0.01
Trinidadian/Tobagonian (0)	0	<0.01
U.S. Virgin Islander (0)	0	<0.01
West Indian (0)	0	<0.01
Other West Indian (0)	0	<0.01
Yugoslavian (0)	0	<0.01

Hispanic Origin	Population	%
Hispanic or Latino (of any race)	190	1.09
Central American, ex. Mexican	5	0.03
Costa Rican	0	<0.01
Guatemalan	4	0.02
Honduran	1	0.01
Nicaraguan	0	<0.01
Panamanian	0	<0.01
Salvadoran	0	<0.01
Other Central American	0	<0.01
Cuban	8	0.05
Dominican Republic	0	<0.01
Mexican	142	0.82
Puerto Rican	11	0.06
South American	2	0.01
Argentinean	0	<0.01
Bolivian	0	<0.01
Chilean	0	<0.01
Colombian	0	<0.01
Ecuadorian	1	0.01
Paraguayan	0	<0.01
Peruvian	0	<0.01
Uruguayan	0	<0.01
Venezuelan	1	0.01
Other South American	0	<0.01
Other Hispanic or Latino	22	0.13

Race*	Population	%
African-American/Black (132)	210	1.21
Not Hispanic (129)	204	1.17
Hispanic (3)	6	0.03
American Indian/Alaska Native (32)	82	0.47
Not Hispanic (32)	80	0.46
Hispanic (0)	2	0.01
Alaska Athabascan (Ala. Nat.) (0)	0	<0.01
Aleut (Alaska Native) (0)	0	<0.01
Apache (0)	0	<0.01
Arapaho (0)	0	<0.01
Blackfeet (0)	3	0.02
Canadian/French Am. Ind. (0)	0	<0.01
Central American Ind. (0)	0	<0.01
Cherokee (3)	24	0.14
Cheyenne (0)	0	<0.01
Chickasaw (0)	0	<0.01
Chippewa (0)	0	<0.01
Choctaw (0)	1	0.01
Colville (0)	0	<0.01
Comanche (0)	0	<0.01
Cree (0)	0	<0.01
Creek (0)	0	<0.01
Crow (0)	0	<0.01
Delaware (6)	6	0.03
Hopi (0)	0	<0.01
Houma (0)	0	<0.01
Inupiat (Alaska Native) (0)	0	<0.01
Iroquois (0)	0	<0.01
Kiowa (0)	0	<0.01
Lumbee (0)	0	<0.01
Menominee (0)	0	<0.01
Mexican American Ind. (0)	1	0.01
Navajo (0)	0	<0.01
Osage (0)	0	<0.01
Ottawa (0)	0	<0.01
Paiute (0)	0	<0.01
Pima (0)	0	<0.01
Potawatomi (1)	1	0.01
Pueblo (0)	0	<0.01
Puget Sound Salish (0)	0	<0.01
Seminole (0)	0	<0.01
Shoshone (0)	0	<0.01
Sioux (2)	2	0.01
South American Ind. (0)	0	<0.01
Spanish American Ind. (0)	0	<0.01
Tlingit-Haida (Alaska Native) (2)	2	0.01
Tohono O'Odham (0)	0	<0.01
Tsimshian (Alaska Native) (0)	0	<0.01
Ute (0)	0	<0.01
Yakama (0)	0	<0.01
Yaqui (0)	0	<0.01
Yuman (0)	0	<0.01
Yup'ik (Alaska Native) (1)	1	0.01
Asian (57)	66	0.38
Not Hispanic (57)	66	0.38
Hispanic (0)	0	<0.01
Bangladeshi (0)	0	<0.01
Bhutanese (0)	0	<0.01
Burmese (0)	0	<0.01
Cambodian (0)	1	0.01
Chinese, ex. Taiwanese (12)	12	0.07
Filipino (12)	13	0.07
Hmong (0)	0	<0.01
Indian (6)	7	0.04
Indonesian (0)	0	<0.01
Japanese (13)	16	0.09
Korean (12)	13	0.07
Laotian (0)	0	<0.01
Malaysian (0)	0	<0.01
Nepalese (0)	0	<0.01
Pakistani (1)	1	0.01
Sri Lankan (0)	0	<0.01
Taiwanese (0)	0	<0.01
Thai (0)	0	<0.01
Vietnamese (1)	2	0.01
Hawaii Native/Pacific Islander (4)	8	0.05
Not Hispanic (3)	6	0.03
Hispanic (1)	2	0.01
Fijian (0)	0	<0.01
Guamanian/Chamorro (1)	1	0.01
Marshallese (0)	0	<0.01
Native Hawaiian (0)	3	0.02
Samoan (1)	1	0.01
Tongan (0)	0	<0.01
White (16,945)	17,074	98.17
Not Hispanic (16,839)	16,954	97.48
Hispanic (106)	120	0.69

Notes: † The Census 2010 population figure is used to calculate the percentages in the Hispanic Origin and Race categories. Ancestry percentages are based on the 2006-2010 American Community Survey population (not shown); ‡ Numbers in parentheses indicate the number of people reporting a single ancestry; * Numbers in parentheses indicate the number of persons reporting this race alone, not in combination with any other race; Please refer to the Explanation of Data for more information.

Scott County
Population: 24,181

Ancestry	Population	%
Afghan (0)	0	<0.01
African, Sub-Saharan (15)	59	0.24
African (0)	44	0.18
Cape Verdean (0)	0	<0.01
Ethiopian (0)	0	<0.01
Ghanaian (0)	0	<0.01
Kenyan (0)	0	<0.01
Liberian (0)	0	<0.01
Nigerian (0)	0	<0.01
Senegalese (0)	0	<0.01
Sierra Leonean (0)	0	<0.01
Somalian (0)	0	<0.01
South African (0)	0	<0.01
Sudanese (0)	0	<0.01
Ugandan (0)	0	<0.01
Zimbabwean (0)	0	<0.01
Other Sub-Saharan African (15)	15	0.06
Albanian (0)	0	<0.01
Alsatian (0)	0	<0.01
American (4,841)	4,841	20.08
Arab (0)	0	<0.01
Arab (0)	0	<0.01
Egyptian (0)	0	<0.01
Iraqi (0)	0	<0.01
Jordanian (0)	0	<0.01
Lebanese (0)	0	<0.01
Moroccan (0)	0	<0.01
Palestinian (0)	0	<0.01
Syrian (0)	0	<0.01
Other Arab (0)	0	<0.01
Armenian (0)	0	<0.01
Assyrian/Chaldean/Syriac (0)	0	<0.01
Australian (0)	0	<0.01
Austrian (14)	42	0.17
Basque (0)	0	<0.01
Belgian (0)	0	<0.01
Brazilian (0)	0	<0.01
British (23)	23	0.10
Bulgarian (0)	0	<0.01
Cajun (0)	0	<0.01
Canadian (9)	9	0.04
Carpatho Rusyn (0)	0	<0.01
Celtic (0)	0	<0.01
Croatian (21)	67	0.28
Cypriot (0)	0	<0.01
Czech (28)	43	0.18
Czechoslovakian (11)	11	0.05
Danish (0)	15	0.06
Dutch (162)	331	1.37
Eastern European (0)	0	<0.01
English (1,519)	2,418	10.03
Estonian (0)	0	<0.01
European (15)	38	0.16
Finnish (0)	41	0.17
French, ex. Basque (173)	536	2.22
French Canadian (0)	9	0.04
German (1,824)	3,752	15.56
German Russian (0)	0	<0.01
Greek (0)	49	0.20
Guyanese (0)	0	<0.01
Hungarian (13)	13	0.05
Icelander (5)	5	0.02
Iranian (0)	0	<0.01
Irish (1,336)	2,862	11.87
Israeli (0)	0	<0.01
Italian (323)	531	2.20
Latvian (0)	0	<0.01
Lithuanian (0)	0	<0.01
Luxemburger (0)	0	<0.01
Macedonian (0)	0	<0.01
Maltese (0)	0	<0.01
New Zealander (0)	0	<0.01
Northern European (11)	11	0.05
Norwegian (85)	117	0.49
Pennsylvania German (0)	11	0.05
Polish (56)	206	0.85
Portuguese (0)	0	<0.01
Romanian (0)	0	<0.01
Russian (0)	0	<0.01
Scandinavian (0)	9	0.04
Scotch-Irish (319)	493	2.04
Scottish (307)	612	2.54
Serbian (0)	0	<0.01
Slavic (15)	38	0.16
Slovak (8)	8	0.03
Slovene (0)	0	<0.01
Soviet Union (0)	0	<0.01
Swedish (39)	204	0.85
Swiss (0)	0	<0.01
Turkish (0)	0	<0.01
Ukrainian (0)	0	<0.01
Welsh (72)	134	0.56
West Indian, ex. Hispanic (0)	0	<0.01
Bahamian (0)	0	<0.01
Barbadian (0)	0	<0.01
Belizean (0)	0	<0.01
Bermudan (0)	0	<0.01
British West Indian (0)	0	<0.01
Dutch West Indian (0)	0	<0.01
Haitian (0)	0	<0.01
Jamaican (0)	0	<0.01
Trinidadian/Tobagonian (0)	0	<0.01
U.S. Virgin Islander (0)	0	<0.01
West Indian (0)	0	<0.01
Other West Indian (0)	0	<0.01
Yugoslavian (0)	0	<0.01

Hispanic Origin	Population	%
Hispanic or Latino (of any race)	354	1.46
Central American, ex. Mexican	8	0.03
Costa Rican	0	<0.01
Guatemalan	0	<0.01
Honduran	2	0.01
Nicaraguan	0	<0.01
Panamanian	2	0.01
Salvadoran	4	0.02
Other Central American	0	<0.01
Cuban	1	<0.01
Dominican Republic	1	<0.01
Mexican	267	1.10
Puerto Rican	21	0.09
South American	6	0.02
Argentinean	0	<0.01
Bolivian	1	<0.01
Chilean	0	<0.01
Colombian	3	0.01
Ecuadorian	2	0.01
Paraguayan	0	<0.01
Peruvian	0	<0.01
Uruguayan	0	<0.01
Venezuelan	0	<0.01
Other South American	0	<0.01
Other Hispanic or Latino	50	0.21

Race*	Population	%
African-American/Black (57)	106	0.44
Not Hispanic (52)	98	0.41
Hispanic (5)	8	0.03
American Indian/Alaska Native (46)	112	0.46
Not Hispanic (43)	100	0.41
Hispanic (3)	12	0.05
Alaska Athabascan (Ala. Nat.) (0)	0	<0.01
Aleut (Alaska Native) (0)	0	<0.01
Apache (1)	4	0.02
Arapaho (0)	3	0.01
Blackfeet (5)	7	0.03
Canadian/French Am. Ind. (0)	0	<0.01
Central American Ind. (0)	0	<0.01
Cherokee (15)	45	0.19
Cheyenne (0)	4	0.02
Chickasaw (0)	0	<0.01
Chippewa (1)	1	<0.01
Choctaw (0)	0	<0.01
Colville (0)	0	<0.01
Comanche (1)	1	<0.01
Cree (0)	0	<0.01
Creek (0)	1	<0.01
Crow (1)	1	<0.01
Delaware (0)	0	<0.01
Hopi (0)	0	<0.01
Houma (0)	0	<0.01
Inupiat (Alaska Native) (0)	0	<0.01
Iroquois (0)	0	<0.01
Kiowa (0)	0	<0.01
Lumbee (0)	0	<0.01
Menominee (0)	0	<0.01
Mexican American Ind. (0)	0	<0.01
Navajo (0)	0	<0.01
Osage (0)	0	<0.01
Ottawa (0)	0	<0.01
Paiute (0)	0	<0.01
Pima (0)	0	<0.01
Potawatomi (4)	10	0.04
Pueblo (0)	0	<0.01
Puget Sound Salish (0)	0	<0.01
Seminole (0)	1	<0.01
Shoshone (0)	0	<0.01
Sioux (2)	2	0.01
South American Ind. (0)	0	<0.01
Spanish American Ind. (0)	0	<0.01
Tlingit-Haida (Alaska Native) (0)	0	<0.01
Tohono O'Odham (0)	0	<0.01
Tsimshian (Alaska Native) (0)	0	<0.01
Ute (0)	0	<0.01
Yakama (0)	0	<0.01
Yaqui (0)	0	<0.01
Yuman (0)	0	<0.01
Yup'ik (Alaska Native) (0)	0	<0.01
Asian (108)	140	0.58
Not Hispanic (104)	131	0.54
Hispanic (4)	9	0.04
Bangladeshi (0)	0	<0.01
Bhutanese (0)	0	<0.01
Burmese (0)	0	<0.01
Cambodian (0)	0	<0.01
Chinese, ex. Taiwanese (14)	16	0.07
Filipino (38)	41	0.17
Hmong (0)	2	0.01
Indian (20)	28	0.12
Indonesian (0)	2	0.01
Japanese (18)	20	0.08
Korean (15)	21	0.09
Laotian (0)	0	<0.01
Malaysian (0)	0	<0.01
Nepalese (0)	0	<0.01
Pakistani (0)	2	0.01
Sri Lankan (0)	0	<0.01
Taiwanese (0)	0	<0.01
Thai (1)	2	0.01
Vietnamese (1)	5	0.02
Hawaii Native/Pacific Islander (14)	21	0.09
Not Hispanic (14)	21	0.09
Hispanic (0)	0	<0.01
Fijian (0)	0	<0.01
Guamanian/Chamorro (6)	6	0.02
Marshallese (0)	0	<0.01
Native Hawaiian (5)	7	0.03
Samoan (3)	3	0.01
Tongan (0)	0	<0.01
White (23,667)	23,838	98.58
Not Hispanic (23,471)	23,603	97.61
Hispanic (196)	235	0.97

Notes: † The Census 2010 population figure is used to calculate the percentages in the Hispanic Origin and Race categories. Ancestry percentages are based on the 2006-2010 American Community Survey population (not shown); ‡ Numbers in parentheses indicate the number of people reporting a single ancestry; * Numbers in parentheses indicate the number of persons reporting this race alone, not in combination with any other race; Please refer to the Explanation of Data for more information.

Shelby County
Population: 44,436

Ancestry	Population	%
Afghan (0)	0	<0.01
African, Sub-Saharan (0)	0	<0.01
African (0)	0	<0.01
Cape Verdean (0)	0	<0.01
Ethiopian (0)	0	<0.01
Ghanaian (0)	0	<0.01
Kenyan (0)	0	<0.01
Liberian (0)	0	<0.01
Nigerian (0)	0	<0.01
Senegalese (0)	0	<0.01
Sierra Leonean (0)	0	<0.01
Somalian (0)	0	<0.01
South African (0)	0	<0.01
Sudanese (0)	0	<0.01
Ugandan (0)	0	<0.01
Zimbabwean (0)	0	<0.01
Other Sub-Saharan African (0)	0	<0.01
Albanian (0)	0	<0.01
Alsatian (0)	0	<0.01
American (5,789)	5,789	13.09
Arab (14)	47	0.11
Arab (0)	0	<0.01
Egyptian (0)	0	<0.01
Iraqi (0)	0	<0.01
Jordanian (0)	0	<0.01
Lebanese (0)	12	0.03
Moroccan (0)	0	<0.01
Palestinian (0)	0	<0.01
Syrian (14)	35	0.08
Other Arab (0)	0	<0.01
Armenian (11)	11	0.02
Assyrian/Chaldean/Syriac (0)	0	<0.01
Australian (13)	13	0.03
Austrian (10)	20	0.05
Basque (0)	0	<0.01
Belgian (0)	48	0.11
Brazilian (0)	0	<0.01
British (124)	246	0.56
Bulgarian (0)	0	<0.01
Cajun (0)	0	<0.01
Canadian (43)	69	0.16
Carpatho Rusyn (0)	0	<0.01
Celtic (0)	0	<0.01
Croatian (0)	0	<0.01
Cypriot (0)	0	<0.01
Czech (34)	34	0.08
Czechoslovakian (0)	0	<0.01
Danish (0)	23	0.05
Dutch (174)	899	2.03
Eastern European (0)	0	<0.01
English (2,010)	3,980	9.00
Estonian (0)	0	<0.01
European (237)	249	0.56
Finnish (0)	34	0.08
French, ex. Basque (317)	867	1.96
French Canadian (21)	58	0.13
German (6,717)	12,619	28.53
German Russian (0)	0	<0.01
Greek (0)	52	0.12
Guyanese (0)	0	<0.01
Hungarian (17)	33	0.07
Icelander (0)	0	<0.01
Iranian (0)	0	<0.01
Irish (1,991)	5,388	12.18
Israeli (35)	35	0.08
Italian (268)	599	1.35
Latvian (0)	11	0.02
Lithuanian (13)	13	0.03
Luxemburger (0)	0	<0.01
Macedonian (0)	0	<0.01
Maltese (0)	0	<0.01
New Zealander (0)	0	<0.01
Northern European (0)	0	<0.01
Norwegian (44)	44	0.10
Pennsylvania German (12)	40	0.09
Polish (130)	477	1.08
Portuguese (0)	0	<0.01
Romanian (0)	27	0.06
Russian (44)	100	0.23
Scandinavian (31)	48	0.11
Scotch-Irish (360)	642	1.45
Scottish (256)	823	1.86
Serbian (0)	17	0.04
Slavic (0)	0	<0.01
Slovak (9)	9	0.02
Slovene (0)	10	0.02
Soviet Union (0)	0	<0.01
Swedish (53)	347	0.78
Swiss (47)	159	0.36
Turkish (0)	0	<0.01
Ukrainian (14)	20	0.05
Welsh (100)	276	0.62
West Indian, ex. Hispanic (0)	0	<0.01
Bahamian (0)	0	<0.01
Barbadian (0)	0	<0.01
Belizean (0)	0	<0.01
Bermudan (0)	0	<0.01
British West Indian (0)	0	<0.01
Dutch West Indian (0)	0	<0.01
Haitian (0)	0	<0.01
Jamaican (0)	0	<0.01
Trinidadian/Tobagonian (0)	0	<0.01
U.S. Virgin Islander (0)	0	<0.01
West Indian (0)	0	<0.01
Other West Indian (0)	0	<0.01
Yugoslavian (0)	8	0.02

Hispanic Origin	Population	%
Hispanic or Latino (of any race)	1,647	3.71
Central American, ex. Mexican	49	0.11
Costa Rican	1	<0.01
Guatemalan	19	0.04
Honduran	14	0.03
Nicaraguan	6	0.01
Panamanian	3	0.01
Salvadoran	5	0.01
Other Central American	1	<0.01
Cuban	6	0.01
Dominican Republic	14	0.03
Mexican	1,413	3.18
Puerto Rican	45	0.10
South American	43	0.10
Argentinean	1	<0.01
Bolivian	2	<0.01
Chilean	2	<0.01
Colombian	6	0.01
Ecuadorian	1	<0.01
Paraguayan	0	<0.01
Peruvian	30	0.07
Uruguayan	0	<0.01
Venezuelan	1	<0.01
Other South American	0	<0.01
Other Hispanic or Latino	77	0.17

Race*	Population	%
African-American/Black (455)	646	1.45
Not Hispanic (428)	608	1.37
Hispanic (27)	38	0.09
American Indian/Alaska Native (95)	241	0.54
Not Hispanic (85)	208	0.47
Hispanic (10)	33	0.07
Alaska Athabascan (Ala. Nat.) (0)	0	<0.01
Aleut (Alaska Native) (0)	0	<0.01
Apache (3)	3	0.01
Arapaho (0)	0	<0.01
Blackfeet (1)	5	0.01
Canadian/French Am. Ind. (1)	1	<0.01
Central American Ind. (0)	0	<0.01
Cherokee (33)	88	0.20
Cheyenne (0)	1	<0.01
Chickasaw (0)	0	<0.01
Chippewa (5)	5	0.01
Choctaw (0)	3	0.01
Colville (0)	0	<0.01
Comanche (1)	1	<0.01
Cree (0)	0	<0.01
Creek (0)	0	<0.01
Crow (0)	0	<0.01
Delaware (1)	1	<0.01
Hopi (0)	0	<0.01
Houma (0)	0	<0.01
Inupiat (Alaska Native) (0)	0	<0.01
Iroquois (1)	1	<0.01
Kiowa (0)	0	<0.01
Lumbee (1)	1	<0.01
Menominee (0)	0	<0.01
Mexican American Ind. (3)	6	0.01
Navajo (0)	0	<0.01
Osage (0)	0	<0.01
Ottawa (0)	0	<0.01
Paiute (1)	1	<0.01
Pima (0)	0	<0.01
Potawatomi (2)	2	<0.01
Pueblo (0)	1	<0.01
Puget Sound Salish (0)	0	<0.01
Seminole (0)	3	0.01
Shoshone (0)	0	<0.01
Sioux (7)	12	0.03
South American Ind. (0)	1	<0.01
Spanish American Ind. (0)	0	<0.01
Tlingit-Haida (Alaska Native) (0)	0	<0.01
Tohono O'Odham (0)	0	<0.01
Tsimshian (Alaska Native) (0)	0	<0.01
Ute (0)	0	<0.01
Yakama (0)	0	<0.01
Yaqui (0)	0	<0.01
Yuman (0)	0	<0.01
Yup'ik (Alaska Native) (0)	0	<0.01
Asian (244)	336	0.76
Not Hispanic (242)	318	0.72
Hispanic (2)	18	0.04
Bangladeshi (0)	0	<0.01
Bhutanese (0)	0	<0.01
Burmese (0)	0	<0.01
Cambodian (4)	4	0.01
Chinese, ex. Taiwanese (42)	51	0.11
Filipino (33)	70	0.16
Hmong (1)	1	<0.01
Indian (18)	23	0.05
Indonesian (0)	0	<0.01
Japanese (102)	118	0.27
Korean (20)	38	0.09
Laotian (0)	0	<0.01
Malaysian (0)	2	<0.01
Nepalese (0)	0	<0.01
Pakistani (2)	2	<0.01
Sri Lankan (0)	0	<0.01
Taiwanese (0)	0	<0.01
Thai (4)	4	0.01
Vietnamese (1)	6	0.01
Hawaii Native/Pacific Islander (13)	34	0.08
Not Hispanic (7)	23	0.05
Hispanic (6)	11	0.02
Fijian (0)	1	<0.01
Guamanian/Chamorro (9)	11	0.02
Marshallese (0)	0	<0.01
Native Hawaiian (3)	10	0.02
Samoan (0)	2	<0.01
Tongan (1)	1	<0.01
White (42,402)	42,899	96.54
Not Hispanic (41,622)	42,004	94.53
Hispanic (780)	895	2.01

Notes: † The Census 2010 population figure is used to calculate the percentages in the Hispanic Origin and Race categories. Ancestry percentages are based on the 2006-2010 American Community Survey population (not shown); ‡ Numbers in parentheses indicate the number of people reporting a single ancestry; * Numbers in parentheses indicate the number of persons reporting this race alone, not in combination with any other race; Please refer to the Explanation of Data for more information.

Spencer County

Population: 20,952

Ancestry	Population	%
Afghan (0)	0	<0.01
African, Sub-Saharan (0)	0	<0.01
African (0)	0	<0.01
Cape Verdean (0)	0	<0.01
Ethiopian (0)	0	<0.01
Ghanaian (0)	0	<0.01
Kenyan (0)	0	<0.01
Liberian (0)	0	<0.01
Nigerian (0)	0	<0.01
Senegalese (0)	0	<0.01
Sierra Leonean (0)	0	<0.01
Somalian (0)	0	<0.01
South African (0)	0	<0.01
Sudanese (0)	0	<0.01
Ugandan (0)	0	<0.01
Zimbabwean (0)	0	<0.01
Other Sub-Saharan African (0)	0	<0.01
Albanian (0)	0	<0.01
Alsatian (0)	0	<0.01
American (2,337)	2,337	11.14
Arab (0)	0	<0.01
Arab (0)	0	<0.01
Egyptian (0)	0	<0.01
Iraqi (0)	0	<0.01
Jordanian (0)	0	<0.01
Lebanese (0)	0	<0.01
Moroccan (0)	0	<0.01
Palestinian (0)	0	<0.01
Syrian (0)	0	<0.01
Other Arab (0)	0	<0.01
Armenian (0)	0	<0.01
Assyrian/Chaldean/Syriac (0)	0	<0.01
Australian (0)	0	<0.01
Austrian (0)	5	0.02
Basque (0)	2	0.01
Belgian (20)	61	0.29
Brazilian (0)	0	<0.01
British (8)	35	0.17
Bulgarian (0)	0	<0.01
Cajun (0)	0	<0.01
Canadian (41)	41	0.20
Carpatho Rusyn (0)	0	<0.01
Celtic (0)	0	<0.01
Croatian (0)	0	<0.01
Cypriot (0)	0	<0.01
Czech (40)	104	0.50
Czechoslovakian (0)	7	0.03
Danish (0)	33	0.16
Dutch (58)	475	2.26
Eastern European (0)	0	<0.01
English (1,039)	2,633	12.55
Estonian (0)	0	<0.01
European (15)	26	0.12
Finnish (0)	0	<0.01
French, ex. Basque (192)	828	3.95
French Canadian (0)	8	0.04
German (5,956)	9,861	47.01
German Russian (0)	0	<0.01
Greek (0)	11	0.05
Guyanese (0)	0	<0.01
Hungarian (0)	8	0.04
Icelander (0)	0	<0.01
Iranian (0)	0	<0.01
Irish (945)	3,446	16.43
Israeli (0)	0	<0.01
Italian (39)	217	1.03
Latvian (0)	0	<0.01
Lithuanian (0)	0	<0.01
Luxemburger (0)	0	<0.01
Macedonian (0)	0	<0.01
Maltese (0)	5	0.02
New Zealander (0)	0	<0.01
Northern European (0)	0	<0.01
Norwegian (20)	56	0.27
Pennsylvania German (0)	8	0.04
Polish (27)	171	0.82
Portuguese (0)	7	0.03
Romanian (8)	22	0.10
Russian (19)	39	0.19
Scandinavian (0)	0	<0.01
Scotch-Irish (90)	343	1.64
Scottish (96)	367	1.75
Serbian (0)	0	<0.01
Slavic (0)	0	<0.01
Slovak (0)	0	<0.01
Slovene (0)	0	<0.01
Soviet Union (0)	0	<0.01
Swedish (0)	57	0.27
Swiss (40)	89	0.42
Turkish (0)	0	<0.01
Ukrainian (5)	11	0.05
Welsh (55)	137	0.65
West Indian, ex. Hispanic (0)	0	<0.01
Bahamian (0)	0	<0.01
Barbadian (0)	0	<0.01
Belizean (0)	0	<0.01
Bermudan (0)	0	<0.01
British West Indian (0)	0	<0.01
Dutch West Indian (0)	0	<0.01
Haitian (0)	0	<0.01
Jamaican (0)	0	<0.01
Trinidadian/Tobagonian (0)	0	<0.01
U.S. Virgin Islander (0)	0	<0.01
West Indian (0)	0	<0.01
Other West Indian (0)	0	<0.01
Yugoslavian (9)	12	0.06

Hispanic Origin	Population	%
Hispanic or Latino (of any race)	517	2.47
Central American, ex. Mexican	40	0.19
Costa Rican	0	<0.01
Guatemalan	23	0.11
Honduran	0	<0.01
Nicaraguan	0	<0.01
Panamanian	1	<0.01
Salvadoran	16	0.08
Other Central American	0	<0.01
Cuban	2	0.01
Dominican Republic	0	<0.01
Mexican	426	2.03
Puerto Rican	23	0.11
South American	3	0.01
Argentinean	0	<0.01
Bolivian	0	<0.01
Chilean	0	<0.01
Colombian	3	0.01
Ecuadorian	0	<0.01
Paraguayan	0	<0.01
Peruvian	0	<0.01
Uruguayan	0	<0.01
Venezuelan	0	<0.01
Other South American	0	<0.01
Other Hispanic or Latino	23	0.11

Race*	Population	%
African-American/Black (96)	166	0.79
Not Hispanic (96)	154	0.74
Hispanic (0)	12	0.06
American Indian/Alaska Native (41)	93	0.44
Not Hispanic (38)	85	0.41
Hispanic (3)	8	0.04
Alaska Athabascan (Ala. Nat.) (0)	0	<0.01
Aleut (Alaska Native) (0)	0	<0.01
Apache (1)	1	<0.01
Arapaho (0)	0	<0.01
Blackfeet (0)	4	0.02
Canadian/French Am. Ind. (0)	0	<0.01
Central American Ind. (0)	0	<0.01
Cherokee (8)	27	0.13
Cheyenne (0)	0	<0.01
Chickasaw (1)	1	<0.01
Chippewa (5)	7	0.03
Choctaw (0)	0	<0.01
Colville (0)	0	<0.01
Comanche (1)	1	<0.01
Cree (0)	0	<0.01
Creek (0)	3	0.01
Crow (0)	0	<0.01
Delaware (1)	1	<0.01
Hopi (0)	0	<0.01
Houma (0)	0	<0.01
Inupiat (Alaska Native) (0)	0	<0.01
Iroquois (1)	5	0.02
Kiowa (0)	0	<0.01
Lumbee (0)	2	0.01
Menominee (0)	0	<0.01
Mexican American Ind. (0)	3	0.01
Navajo (0)	0	<0.01
Osage (0)	0	<0.01
Ottawa (0)	0	<0.01
Paiute (0)	0	<0.01
Pima (0)	0	<0.01
Potawatomi (0)	1	<0.01
Pueblo (0)	0	<0.01
Puget Sound Salish (0)	0	<0.01
Seminole (0)	0	<0.01
Shoshone (0)	0	<0.01
Sioux (0)	1	<0.01
South American Ind. (0)	0	<0.01
Spanish American Ind. (0)	0	<0.01
Tlingit-Haida (Alaska Native) (0)	0	<0.01
Tohono O'Odham (0)	0	<0.01
Tsimshian (Alaska Native) (0)	0	<0.01
Ute (0)	0	<0.01
Yakama (0)	0	<0.01
Yaqui (0)	0	<0.01
Yuman (0)	0	<0.01
Yup'ik (Alaska Native) (0)	0	<0.01
Asian (72)	91	0.43
Not Hispanic (69)	83	0.40
Hispanic (3)	8	0.04
Bangladeshi (0)	0	<0.01
Bhutanese (0)	0	<0.01
Burmese (0)	0	<0.01
Cambodian (0)	0	<0.01
Chinese, ex. Taiwanese (14)	14	0.07
Filipino (23)	29	0.14
Hmong (0)	0	<0.01
Indian (10)	13	0.06
Indonesian (0)	0	<0.01
Japanese (4)	10	0.05
Korean (12)	16	0.08
Laotian (0)	0	<0.01
Malaysian (0)	0	<0.01
Nepalese (0)	0	<0.01
Pakistani (0)	0	<0.01
Sri Lankan (0)	0	<0.01
Taiwanese (0)	0	<0.01
Thai (4)	4	0.02
Vietnamese (2)	4	0.02
Hawaii Native/Pacific Islander (0)	2	0.01
Not Hispanic (0)	2	0.01
Hispanic (0)	0	<0.01
Fijian (0)	0	<0.01
Guamanian/Chamorro (0)	0	<0.01
Marshallese (0)	0	<0.01
Native Hawaiian (0)	1	<0.01
Samoan (0)	1	<0.01
Tongan (0)	0	<0.01
White (20,295)	20,452	97.61
Not Hispanic (20,101)	20,221	96.51
Hispanic (194)	231	1.10

Notes: † The Census 2010 population figure is used to calculate the percentages in the Hispanic Origin and Race categories. Ancestry percentages are based on the 2006-2010 American Community Survey population (not shown); ‡ Numbers in parentheses indicate the number of people reporting a single ancestry; * Numbers in parentheses indicate the number of persons reporting this race alone, not in combination with any other race; Please refer to the Explanation of Data for more information.

St. Joseph County
Population: 266,931

Ancestry	Population	%
Afghan (0)	0	<0.01
African, Sub-Saharan (1,951)	2,311	0.87
African (1,405)	1,676	0.63
Cape Verdean (0)	0	<0.01
Ethiopian (117)	130	0.05
Ghanaian (51)	51	0.02
Kenyan (202)	218	0.08
Liberian (13)	41	0.02
Nigerian (26)	26	0.01
Senegalese (0)	0	<0.01
Sierra Leonean (0)	32	0.01
Somalian (0)	0	<0.01
South African (0)	0	<0.01
Sudanese (0)	0	<0.01
Ugandan (8)	8	<0.01
Zimbabwean (0)	0	<0.01
Other Sub-Saharan African (129)	129	0.05
Albanian (9)	22	0.01
Alsatian (0)	12	<0.01
American (12,056)	12,056	4.52
Arab (727)	1,372	0.51
Arab (114)	177	0.07
Egyptian (15)	15	0.01
Iraqi (23)	213	0.08
Jordanian (0)	0	<0.01
Lebanese (225)	541	0.20
Moroccan (0)	6	<0.01
Palestinian (119)	119	0.04
Syrian (28)	98	0.04
Other Arab (203)	203	0.08
Armenian (8)	84	0.03
Assyrian/Chaldean/Syriac (0)	65	0.02
Australian (14)	21	0.01
Austrian (233)	1,075	0.40
Basque (0)	0	<0.01
Belgian (1,903)	5,196	1.95
Brazilian (94)	191	0.07
British (396)	1,048	0.39
Bulgarian (22)	60	0.02
Cajun (0)	21	0.01
Canadian (185)	432	0.16
Carpatho Rusyn (0)	0	<0.01
Celtic (42)	117	0.04
Croatian (83)	531	0.20
Cypriot (8)	8	<0.01
Czech (167)	992	0.37
Czechoslovakian (90)	221	0.08
Danish (161)	817	0.31
Dutch (1,193)	7,104	2.67
Eastern European (102)	155	0.06
English (6,156)	22,539	8.46
Estonian (16)	61	0.02
European (2,257)	2,495	0.94
Finnish (82)	344	0.13
French, ex. Basque (1,130)	7,792	2.92
French Canadian (298)	1,298	0.49
German (20,852)	67,432	25.30
German Russian (0)	10	<0.01
Greek (331)	1,145	0.43
Guyanese (0)	0	<0.01
Hungarian (3,146)	8,972	3.37
Icelander (13)	13	<0.01
Iranian (97)	146	0.05
Irish (9,304)	41,235	15.47
Israeli (0)	0	<0.01
Italian (3,413)	12,012	4.51
Latvian (10)	22	0.01
Lithuanian (148)	656	0.25
Luxemburger (16)	55	0.02
Macedonian (0)	96	0.04
Maltese (0)	0	<0.01
New Zealander (0)	0	<0.01
Northern European (204)	244	0.09
Norwegian (605)	2,350	0.88
Pennsylvania German (204)	499	0.19
Polish (14,234)	31,955	11.99
Portuguese (86)	405	0.15
Romanian (182)	265	0.10
Russian (448)	1,628	0.61
Scandinavian (152)	402	0.15
Scotch-Irish (1,280)	3,995	1.50
Scottish (1,023)	4,114	1.54
Serbian (201)	437	0.16
Slavic (23)	69	0.03
Slovak (104)	391	0.15
Slovene (37)	127	0.05
Soviet Union (0)	0	<0.01
Swedish (1,330)	5,105	1.92
Swiss (381)	1,502	0.56
Turkish (58)	135	0.05
Ukrainian (129)	424	0.16
Welsh (262)	1,380	0.52
West Indian, ex. Hispanic (202)	289	0.11
Bahamian (0)	9	<0.01
Barbadian (0)	0	<0.01
Belizean (0)	0	<0.01
Bermudan (0)	0	<0.01
British West Indian (15)	15	0.01
Dutch West Indian (11)	11	<0.01
Haitian (0)	0	<0.01
Jamaican (81)	136	0.05
Trinidadian/Tobagonian (39)	52	0.02
U.S. Virgin Islander (0)	0	<0.01
West Indian (56)	66	0.02
Other West Indian (0)	0	<0.01
Yugoslavian (816)	1,000	0.38

Hispanic Origin	Population	%
Hispanic or Latino (of any race)	19,395	7.27
Central American, ex. Mexican	626	0.23
Costa Rican	31	0.01
Guatemalan	142	0.05
Honduran	121	0.05
Nicaraguan	87	0.03
Panamanian	62	0.02
Salvadoran	176	0.07
Other Central American	7	<0.01
Cuban	259	0.10
Dominican Republic	80	0.03
Mexican	15,338	5.75
Puerto Rican	1,074	0.40
South American	632	0.24
Argentinean	57	0.02
Bolivian	15	0.01
Chilean	67	0.03
Colombian	148	0.06
Ecuadorian	94	0.04
Paraguayan	15	0.01
Peruvian	66	0.02
Uruguayan	14	0.01
Venezuelan	153	0.06
Other South American	3	<0.01
Other Hispanic or Latino	1,386	0.52

Race*	Population	%
African-American/Black (33,958)	38,255	14.33
Not Hispanic (33,407)	37,205	13.94
Hispanic (551)	1,050	0.39
American Indian/Alaska Native (1,030)	2,825	1.06
Not Hispanic (791)	2,345	0.88
Hispanic (239)	480	0.18
Alaska Athabascan (Ala. Nat.) (0)	0	<0.01
Aleut (Alaska Native) (2)	3	<0.01
Apache (9)	38	0.01
Arapaho (1)	2	<0.01
Blackfeet (19)	122	0.05
Canadian/French Am. Ind. (13)	35	0.01
Central American Ind. (3)	8	<0.01
Cherokee (125)	609	0.23
Cheyenne (2)	3	<0.01
Chickasaw (6)	19	0.01
Chippewa (31)	84	0.03
Choctaw (14)	49	0.02
Colville (1)	1	<0.01
Comanche (4)	5	<0.01
Cree (1)	6	<0.01
Creek (11)	21	0.01
Crow (2)	4	<0.01
Delaware (2)	11	<0.01
Hopi (1)	2	<0.01
Houma (2)	2	<0.01
Inupiat (Alaska Native) (0)	3	<0.01
Iroquois (5)	19	0.01
Kiowa (0)	0	<0.01
Lumbee (6)	16	0.01
Menominee (4)	4	<0.01
Mexican American Ind. (56)	88	0.03
Navajo (2)	12	<0.01
Osage (1)	2	<0.01
Ottawa (3)	13	<0.01
Paiute (3)	4	<0.01
Pima (0)	0	<0.01
Potawatomi (109)	212	0.08
Pueblo (1)	5	<0.01
Puget Sound Salish (1)	2	<0.01
Seminole (0)	7	<0.01
Shoshone (0)	1	<0.01
Sioux (16)	39	0.01
South American Ind. (7)	20	0.01
Spanish American Ind. (8)	11	<0.01
Tlingit-Haida (Alaska Native) (5)	6	<0.01
Tohono O'Odham (0)	0	<0.01
Tsimshian (Alaska Native) (0)	0	<0.01
Ute (0)	1	<0.01
Yakama (0)	0	<0.01
Yaqui (1)	2	<0.01
Yuman (0)	0	<0.01
Yup'ik (Alaska Native) (4)	4	<0.01
Asian (5,036)	6,342	2.38
Not Hispanic (4,985)	6,168	2.31
Hispanic (51)	174	0.07
Bangladeshi (10)	13	<0.01
Bhutanese (0)	0	<0.01
Burmese (5)	5	<0.01
Cambodian (115)	134	0.05
Chinese, ex. Taiwanese (1,272)	1,538	0.58
Filipino (507)	853	0.32
Hmong (2)	4	<0.01
Indian (1,127)	1,293	0.48
Indonesian (28)	36	0.01
Japanese (179)	350	0.13
Korean (631)	814	0.30
Laotian (81)	112	0.04
Malaysian (4)	5	<0.01
Nepalese (6)	7	<0.01
Pakistani (158)	172	0.06
Sri Lankan (27)	31	0.01
Taiwanese (59)	68	0.03
Thai (62)	94	0.04
Vietnamese (581)	652	0.24
Hawaii Native/Pacific Islander (194)	428	0.16
Not Hispanic (180)	381	0.14
Hispanic (14)	47	0.02
Fijian (0)	0	<0.01
Guamanian/Chamorro (26)	50	0.02
Marshallese (2)	2	<0.01
Native Hawaiian (39)	118	0.04
Samoan (43)	107	0.04
Tongan (34)	58	0.02
White (209,972)	216,802	81.22
Not Hispanic (201,701)	207,214	77.63
Hispanic (8,271)	9,588	3.59

Notes: † The Census 2010 population figure is used to calculate the percentages in the Hispanic Origin and Race categories. Ancestry percentages are based on the 2006-2010 American Community Survey population (not shown); ‡ Numbers in parentheses indicate the number of people reporting a single ancestry; * Numbers in parentheses indicate the number of persons reporting this race alone, not in combination with any other race; Please refer to the Explanation of Data for more information.

Starke County
Population: 23,363

Ancestry	Population	%
Afghan (0)	0	<0.01
African, Sub-Saharan (5)	5	0.02
African (5)	5	0.02
Cape Verdean (0)	0	<0.01
Ethiopian (0)	0	<0.01
Ghanaian (0)	0	<0.01
Kenyan (0)	0	<0.01
Liberian (0)	0	<0.01
Nigerian (0)	0	<0.01
Senegalese (0)	0	<0.01
Sierra Leonean (0)	0	<0.01
Somalian (0)	0	<0.01
South African (0)	0	<0.01
Sudanese (0)	0	<0.01
Ugandan (0)	0	<0.01
Zimbabwean (0)	0	<0.01
Other Sub-Saharan African (0)	0	<0.01
Albanian (0)	0	<0.01
Alsatian (0)	0	<0.01
American (2,038)	2,038	8.73
Arab (12)	18	0.08
Arab (12)	12	0.05
Egyptian (0)	0	<0.01
Iraqi (0)	0	<0.01
Jordanian (0)	0	<0.01
Lebanese (0)	6	0.03
Moroccan (0)	0	<0.01
Palestinian (0)	0	<0.01
Syrian (0)	0	<0.01
Other Arab (0)	0	<0.01
Armenian (19)	19	0.08
Assyrian/Chaldean/Syriac (0)	0	<0.01
Australian (0)	0	<0.01
Austrian (4)	15	0.06
Basque (0)	0	<0.01
Belgian (0)	17	0.07
Brazilian (0)	0	<0.01
British (18)	18	0.08
Bulgarian (20)	20	0.09
Cajun (0)	0	<0.01
Canadian (3)	12	0.05
Carpatho Rusyn (0)	0	<0.01
Celtic (0)	0	<0.01
Croatian (3)	20	0.09
Cypriot (0)	0	<0.01
Czech (136)	421	1.80
Czechoslovakian (36)	46	0.20
Danish (8)	73	0.31
Dutch (140)	633	2.71
Eastern European (0)	0	<0.01
English (808)	2,067	8.85
Estonian (0)	0	<0.01
European (166)	172	0.74
Finnish (0)	12	0.05
French, ex. Basque (119)	782	3.35
French Canadian (11)	77	0.33
German (2,476)	6,355	27.22
German Russian (0)	0	<0.01
Greek (70)	102	0.44
Guyanese (0)	0	<0.01
Hungarian (60)	178	0.76
Icelander (0)	0	<0.01
Iranian (0)	0	<0.01
Irish (977)	3,799	16.27
Israeli (0)	0	<0.01
Italian (392)	913	3.91
Latvian (0)	0	<0.01
Lithuanian (91)	178	0.76
Luxemburger (12)	14	0.06
Macedonian (0)	0	<0.01
Maltese (0)	0	<0.01
New Zealander (0)	0	<0.01
Northern European (2)	2	0.01
Norwegian (59)	270	1.16
Pennsylvania German (38)	96	0.41
Polish (912)	1,621	6.94
Portuguese (0)	0	<0.01
Romanian (0)	76	0.33
Russian (13)	107	0.46
Scandinavian (15)	33	0.14
Scotch-Irish (86)	338	1.45
Scottish (272)	629	2.69
Serbian (73)	128	0.55
Slavic (0)	35	0.15
Slovak (11)	108	0.46
Slovene (0)	0	<0.01
Soviet Union (0)	0	<0.01
Swedish (157)	436	1.87
Swiss (0)	16	0.07
Turkish (0)	0	<0.01
Ukrainian (7)	22	0.09
Welsh (0)	113	0.48
West Indian, ex. Hispanic (0)	0	<0.01
Bahamian (0)	0	<0.01
Barbadian (0)	0	<0.01
Belizean (0)	0	<0.01
Bermudan (0)	0	<0.01
British West Indian (0)	0	<0.01
Dutch West Indian (0)	0	<0.01
Haitian (0)	0	<0.01
Jamaican (0)	0	<0.01
Trinidadian/Tobagonian (0)	0	<0.01
U.S. Virgin Islander (0)	0	<0.01
West Indian (0)	0	<0.01
Other West Indian (0)	0	<0.01
Yugoslavian (0)	24	0.10

Hispanic Origin	Population	%
Hispanic or Latino (of any race)	766	3.28
Central American, ex. Mexican	9	0.04
Costa Rican	2	0.01
Guatemalan	6	0.03
Honduran	0	<0.01
Nicaraguan	0	<0.01
Panamanian	0	<0.01
Salvadoran	1	<0.01
Other Central American	0	<0.01
Cuban	7	0.03
Dominican Republic	1	<0.01
Mexican	544	2.33
Puerto Rican	106	0.45
South American	7	0.03
Argentinean	0	<0.01
Bolivian	0	<0.01
Chilean	4	0.02
Colombian	2	0.01
Ecuadorian	0	<0.01
Paraguayan	0	<0.01
Peruvian	1	<0.01
Uruguayan	0	<0.01
Venezuelan	0	<0.01
Other South American	0	<0.01
Other Hispanic or Latino	92	0.39

Race*	Population	%
African-American/Black (66)	132	0.56
Not Hispanic (63)	124	0.53
Hispanic (3)	8	0.03
American Indian/Alaska Native (76)	209	0.89
Not Hispanic (61)	181	0.77
Hispanic (15)	28	0.12
Alaska Athabascan (Ala. Nat.) (0)	0	<0.01
Aleut (Alaska Native) (0)	0	<0.01
Apache (2)	9	0.04
Arapaho (0)	0	<0.01
Blackfeet (2)	10	0.04
Canadian/French Am. Ind. (5)	12	0.05
Central American Ind. (0)	0	<0.01
Cherokee (8)	44	0.19
Cheyenne (3)	3	0.01
Chickasaw (0)	0	<0.01
Chippewa (4)	11	0.05
Choctaw (0)	0	<0.01
Colville (0)	0	<0.01
Comanche (0)	1	<0.01
Cree (2)	3	0.01
Creek (0)	0	<0.01
Crow (0)	0	<0.01
Delaware (0)	0	<0.01
Hopi (0)	0	<0.01
Houma (0)	0	<0.01
Inupiat (Alaska Native) (0)	0	<0.01
Iroquois (2)	2	0.01
Kiowa (0)	0	<0.01
Lumbee (0)	0	<0.01
Menominee (8)	8	0.03
Mexican American Ind. (0)	5	0.02
Navajo (0)	0	<0.01
Osage (2)	2	0.01
Ottawa (2)	7	0.03
Paiute (0)	0	<0.01
Pima (0)	0	<0.01
Potawatomi (4)	6	0.03
Pueblo (0)	0	<0.01
Puget Sound Salish (0)	0	<0.01
Seminole (0)	0	<0.01
Shoshone (0)	2	0.01
Sioux (1)	6	0.03
South American Ind. (0)	0	<0.01
Spanish American Ind. (0)	0	<0.01
Tlingit-Haida (Alaska Native) (0)	0	<0.01
Tohono O'Odham (0)	0	<0.01
Tsimshian (Alaska Native) (0)	0	<0.01
Ute (0)	0	<0.01
Yakama (0)	0	<0.01
Yaqui (0)	0	<0.01
Yuman (0)	0	<0.01
Yup'ik (Alaska Native) (0)	0	<0.01
Asian (41)	75	0.32
Not Hispanic (41)	72	0.31
Hispanic (0)	3	0.01
Bangladeshi (0)	0	<0.01
Bhutanese (0)	0	<0.01
Burmese (0)	0	<0.01
Cambodian (0)	0	<0.01
Chinese, ex. Taiwanese (8)	9	0.04
Filipino (12)	27	0.12
Hmong (0)	0	<0.01
Indian (6)	11	0.05
Indonesian (0)	0	<0.01
Japanese (5)	14	0.06
Korean (7)	13	0.06
Laotian (0)	0	<0.01
Malaysian (0)	0	<0.01
Nepalese (0)	0	<0.01
Pakistani (0)	1	<0.01
Sri Lankan (0)	0	<0.01
Taiwanese (0)	0	<0.01
Thai (1)	1	<0.01
Vietnamese (1)	1	<0.01
Hawaii Native/Pacific Islander (0)	2	0.01
Not Hispanic (0)	2	0.01
Hispanic (0)	0	<0.01
Fijian (0)	0	<0.01
Guamanian/Chamorro (0)	1	<0.01
Marshallese (0)	0	<0.01
Native Hawaiian (0)	1	<0.01
Samoan (0)	0	<0.01
Tongan (0)	0	<0.01
White (22,683)	22,970	98.32
Not Hispanic (22,212)	22,426	95.99
Hispanic (471)	544	2.33

Notes: † The Census 2010 population figure is used to calculate the percentages in the Hispanic Origin and Race categories. Ancestry percentages are based on the 2006-2010 American Community Survey population (not shown); ‡ Numbers in parentheses indicate the number of people reporting a single ancestry; * Numbers in parentheses indicate the number of persons reporting this race alone, not in combination with any other race; Please refer to the Explanation of Data for more information.

Steuben County
Population: 34,185

Ancestry	Population	%
Afghan (0)	0	<0.01
African, Sub-Saharan (11)	14	0.04
African (11)	11	0.03
Cape Verdean (0)	0	<0.01
Ethiopian (0)	0	<0.01
Ghanaian (0)	0	<0.01
Kenyan (0)	0	<0.01
Liberian (0)	0	<0.01
Nigerian (0)	0	<0.01
Senegalese (0)	0	<0.01
Sierra Leonean (0)	0	<0.01
Somalian (0)	0	<0.01
South African (0)	3	0.01
Sudanese (0)	0	<0.01
Ugandan (0)	0	<0.01
Zimbabwean (0)	0	<0.01
Other Sub-Saharan African (0)	0	<0.01
Albanian (0)	0	<0.01
Alsatian (0)	0	<0.01
American (2,789)	2,789	8.18
Arab (14)	18	0.05
Arab (0)	0	<0.01
Egyptian (0)	0	<0.01
Iraqi (3)	3	0.01
Jordanian (0)	0	<0.01
Lebanese (11)	11	0.03
Moroccan (0)	0	<0.01
Palestinian (0)	0	<0.01
Syrian (0)	4	0.01
Other Arab (0)	0	<0.01
Armenian (0)	0	<0.01
Assyrian/Chaldean/Syriac (0)	0	<0.01
Australian (0)	0	<0.01
Austrian (46)	82	0.24
Basque (0)	0	<0.01
Belgian (10)	19	0.06
Brazilian (0)	0	<0.01
British (33)	65	0.19
Bulgarian (0)	0	<0.01
Cajun (0)	0	<0.01
Canadian (105)	139	0.41
Carpatho Rusyn (0)	0	<0.01
Celtic (0)	0	<0.01
Croatian (0)	26	0.08
Cypriot (0)	0	<0.01
Czech (37)	246	0.72
Czechoslovakian (4)	80	0.23
Danish (8)	45	0.13
Dutch (258)	1,012	2.97
Eastern European (0)	0	<0.01
English (1,336)	4,294	12.60
Estonian (0)	0	<0.01
European (147)	149	0.44
Finnish (0)	3	0.01
French, ex. Basque (127)	1,173	3.44
French Canadian (54)	109	0.32
German (6,144)	12,899	37.84
German Russian (0)	0	<0.01
Greek (94)	162	0.48
Guyanese (0)	0	<0.01
Hungarian (50)	175	0.51
Icelander (0)	0	<0.01
Iranian (0)	0	<0.01
Irish (871)	3,573	10.48
Israeli (0)	0	<0.01
Italian (505)	1,449	4.25
Latvian (2)	2	0.01
Lithuanian (18)	26	0.08
Luxemburger (0)	12	0.04
Macedonian (11)	11	0.03
Maltese (0)	0	<0.01
New Zealander (0)	0	<0.01
Northern European (20)	20	0.06
Norwegian (59)	307	0.90
Pennsylvania German (33)	51	0.15
Polish (389)	1,207	3.54
Portuguese (11)	11	0.03
Romanian (37)	37	0.11
Russian (17)	94	0.28
Scandinavian (11)	22	0.06
Scotch-Irish (226)	571	1.67
Scottish (219)	562	1.65
Serbian (0)	0	<0.01
Slavic (0)	0	<0.01
Slovak (12)	49	0.14
Slovene (0)	10	0.03
Soviet Union (0)	0	<0.01
Swedish (93)	373	1.09
Swiss (81)	351	1.03
Turkish (0)	0	<0.01
Ukrainian (0)	25	0.07
Welsh (43)	309	0.91
West Indian, ex. Hispanic (0)	0	<0.01
Bahamian (0)	0	<0.01
Barbadian (0)	0	<0.01
Belizean (0)	0	<0.01
Bermudan (0)	0	<0.01
British West Indian (0)	0	<0.01
Dutch West Indian (0)	0	<0.01
Haitian (0)	0	<0.01
Jamaican (0)	0	<0.01
Trinidadian/Tobagonian (0)	0	<0.01
U.S. Virgin Islander (0)	0	<0.01
West Indian (0)	0	<0.01
Other West Indian (0)	0	<0.01
Yugoslavian (28)	130	0.38

Hispanic Origin	Population	%
Hispanic or Latino (of any race)	982	2.87
Central American, ex. Mexican	26	0.08
Costa Rican	3	0.01
Guatemalan	3	0.01
Honduran	1	<0.01
Nicaraguan	0	<0.01
Panamanian	1	<0.01
Salvadoran	18	0.05
Other Central American	0	<0.01
Cuban	4	0.01
Dominican Republic	0	<0.01
Mexican	774	2.26
Puerto Rican	83	0.24
South American	16	0.05
Argentinean	3	0.01
Bolivian	1	<0.01
Chilean	1	<0.01
Colombian	4	0.01
Ecuadorian	2	0.01
Paraguayan	0	<0.01
Peruvian	2	0.01
Uruguayan	1	<0.01
Venezuelan	2	0.01
Other South American	0	<0.01
Other Hispanic or Latino	79	0.23

Race*	Population	%
African-American/Black (179)	275	0.80
Not Hispanic (155)	243	0.71
Hispanic (24)	32	0.09
American Indian/Alaska Native (93)	206	0.60
Not Hispanic (81)	191	0.56
Hispanic (12)	15	0.04
Alaska Athabascan (Ala. Nat.) (0)	0	<0.01
Aleut (Alaska Native) (0)	0	<0.01
Apache (0)	1	<0.01
Arapaho (0)	0	<0.01
Blackfeet (0)	5	0.01
Canadian/French Am. Ind. (0)	1	<0.01
Central American Ind. (0)	0	<0.01
Cherokee (19)	46	0.13
Cheyenne (0)	3	0.01
Chickasaw (0)	1	<0.01
Chippewa (4)	9	0.03
Choctaw (1)	6	0.02
Colville (0)	0	<0.01
Comanche (0)	0	<0.01
Cree (0)	0	<0.01
Creek (0)	0	<0.01
Crow (1)	1	<0.01
Delaware (0)	0	<0.01
Hopi (0)	3	0.01
Houma (0)	0	<0.01
Inupiat (Alaska Native) (0)	0	<0.01
Iroquois (4)	7	0.02
Kiowa (0)	0	<0.01
Lumbee (0)	0	<0.01
Menominee (0)	0	<0.01
Mexican American Ind. (3)	3	0.01
Navajo (3)	6	0.02
Osage (0)	1	<0.01
Ottawa (3)	6	0.02
Paiute (0)	0	<0.01
Pima (0)	0	<0.01
Potawatomi (0)	2	0.01
Pueblo (0)	0	<0.01
Puget Sound Salish (0)	0	<0.01
Seminole (0)	0	<0.01
Shoshone (0)	1	<0.01
Sioux (0)	3	0.01
South American Ind. (1)	1	<0.01
Spanish American Ind. (0)	0	<0.01
Tlingit-Haida (Alaska Native) (0)	0	<0.01
Tohono O'Odham (0)	0	<0.01
Tsimshian (Alaska Native) (0)	0	<0.01
Ute (1)	1	<0.01
Yakama (0)	0	<0.01
Yaqui (0)	0	<0.01
Yuman (0)	0	<0.01
Yup'ik (Alaska Native) (0)	0	<0.01
Asian (167)	248	0.73
Not Hispanic (162)	241	0.70
Hispanic (5)	7	0.02
Bangladeshi (1)	1	<0.01
Bhutanese (0)	0	<0.01
Burmese (0)	0	<0.01
Cambodian (0)	0	<0.01
Chinese, ex. Taiwanese (29)	33	0.10
Filipino (31)	55	0.16
Hmong (0)	0	<0.01
Indian (33)	49	0.14
Indonesian (0)	0	<0.01
Japanese (8)	16	0.05
Korean (29)	41	0.12
Laotian (0)	0	<0.01
Malaysian (2)	3	0.01
Nepalese (4)	4	0.01
Pakistani (12)	13	0.04
Sri Lankan (0)	0	<0.01
Taiwanese (2)	3	0.01
Thai (10)	12	0.04
Vietnamese (2)	3	0.01
Hawaii Native/Pacific Islander (11)	18	0.05
Not Hispanic (6)	12	0.04
Hispanic (5)	6	0.02
Fijian (0)	0	<0.01
Guamanian/Chamorro (6)	7	0.02
Marshallese (0)	0	<0.01
Native Hawaiian (3)	7	0.02
Samoan (0)	0	<0.01
Tongan (0)	0	<0.01
White (33,098)	33,400	97.70
Not Hispanic (32,513)	32,778	95.88
Hispanic (585)	622	1.82

Notes: † The Census 2010 population figure is used to calculate the percentages in the Hispanic Origin and Race categories. Ancestry percentages are based on the 2006-2010 American Community Survey population (not shown); ‡ Numbers in parentheses indicate the number of people reporting a single ancestry; * Numbers in parentheses indicate the number of persons reporting this race alone, not in combination with any other race; Please refer to the Explanation of Data for more information.

Sullivan County
Population: 21,475

Ancestry	Population	%
Afghan (0)	0	<0.01
African, Sub-Saharan (158)	176	0.82
African (140)	158	0.73
Cape Verdean (0)	0	<0.01
Ethiopian (0)	0	<0.01
Ghanaian (0)	0	<0.01
Kenyan (0)	0	<0.01
Liberian (0)	0	<0.01
Nigerian (0)	0	<0.01
Senegalese (0)	0	<0.01
Sierra Leonean (0)	0	<0.01
Somalian (0)	0	<0.01
South African (0)	0	<0.01
Sudanese (0)	0	<0.01
Ugandan (0)	0	<0.01
Zimbabwean (0)	0	<0.01
Other Sub-Saharan African (18)	18	0.08
Albanian (0)	0	<0.01
Alsatian (0)	0	<0.01
American (4,259)	4,259	19.79
Arab (17)	35	0.16
Arab (0)	0	<0.01
Egyptian (0)	0	<0.01
Iraqi (0)	0	<0.01
Jordanian (0)	0	<0.01
Lebanese (0)	0	<0.01
Moroccan (17)	26	0.12
Palestinian (0)	0	<0.01
Syrian (0)	0	<0.01
Other Arab (0)	9	0.04
Armenian (0)	0	<0.01
Assyrian/Chaldean/Syriac (0)	0	<0.01
Australian (0)	0	<0.01
Austrian (0)	10	0.05
Basque (0)	0	<0.01
Belgian (28)	31	0.14
Brazilian (0)	0	<0.01
British (8)	16	0.07
Bulgarian (0)	0	<0.01
Cajun (0)	0	<0.01
Canadian (0)	0	<0.01
Carpatho Rusyn (0)	0	<0.01
Celtic (2)	7	0.03
Croatian (0)	0	<0.01
Cypriot (0)	0	<0.01
Czech (22)	137	0.64
Czechoslovakian (16)	16	0.07
Danish (0)	0	<0.01
Dutch (111)	473	2.20
Eastern European (0)	0	<0.01
English (1,135)	2,083	9.68
Estonian (0)	0	<0.01
European (101)	114	0.53
Finnish (0)	0	<0.01
French, ex. Basque (211)	537	2.50
French Canadian (14)	34	0.16
German (1,960)	4,475	20.79
German Russian (0)	0	<0.01
Greek (11)	18	0.08
Guyanese (0)	0	<0.01
Hungarian (20)	52	0.24
Icelander (0)	0	<0.01
Iranian (0)	0	<0.01
Irish (697)	2,223	10.33
Israeli (0)	0	<0.01
Italian (114)	316	1.47
Latvian (0)	0	<0.01
Lithuanian (14)	19	0.09
Luxemburger (0)	0	<0.01
Macedonian (0)	0	<0.01
Maltese (0)	0	<0.01
New Zealander (0)	0	<0.01
Northern European (0)	0	<0.01
Norwegian (21)	30	0.14
Pennsylvania German (15)	15	0.07
Polish (149)	420	1.95
Portuguese (0)	0	<0.01
Romanian (0)	0	<0.01
Russian (21)	34	0.16
Scandinavian (0)	0	<0.01
Scotch-Irish (146)	440	2.04
Scottish (58)	332	1.54
Serbian (0)	0	<0.01
Slavic (0)	0	<0.01
Slovak (2)	4	0.02
Slovene (0)	0	<0.01
Soviet Union (0)	0	<0.01
Swedish (4)	89	0.41
Swiss (0)	124	0.58
Turkish (0)	0	<0.01
Ukrainian (0)	6	0.03
Welsh (5)	122	0.57
West Indian, ex. Hispanic (0)	0	<0.01
Bahamian (0)	0	<0.01
Barbadian (0)	0	<0.01
Belizean (0)	0	<0.01
Bermudan (0)	0	<0.01
British West Indian (0)	0	<0.01
Dutch West Indian (0)	0	<0.01
Haitian (0)	0	<0.01
Jamaican (0)	0	<0.01
Trinidadian/Tobagonian (0)	0	<0.01
U.S. Virgin Islander (0)	0	<0.01
West Indian (0)	0	<0.01
Other West Indian (0)	0	<0.01
Yugoslavian (15)	15	0.07

Hispanic Origin	Population	%
Hispanic or Latino (of any race)	294	1.37
Central American, ex. Mexican	9	0.04
Costa Rican	0	<0.01
Guatemalan	3	0.01
Honduran	3	0.01
Nicaraguan	0	<0.01
Panamanian	2	0.01
Salvadoran	1	<0.01
Other Central American	0	<0.01
Cuban	10	0.05
Dominican Republic	1	<0.01
Mexican	205	0.95
Puerto Rican	21	0.10
South American	6	0.03
Argentinean	0	<0.01
Bolivian	0	<0.01
Chilean	2	0.01
Colombian	4	0.02
Ecuadorian	0	<0.01
Paraguayan	0	<0.01
Peruvian	0	<0.01
Uruguayan	0	<0.01
Venezuelan	0	<0.01
Other South American	0	<0.01
Other Hispanic or Latino	42	0.20

Race*	Population	%
African-American/Black (961)	1,024	4.77
Not Hispanic (946)	1,007	4.69
Hispanic (15)	17	0.08
American Indian/Alaska Native (58)	170	0.79
Not Hispanic (53)	159	0.74
Hispanic (5)	11	0.05
Alaska Athabascan (Ala. Nat.) (0)	0	<0.01
Aleut (Alaska Native) (0)	0	<0.01
Apache (1)	4	0.02
Arapaho (0)	1	<0.01
Blackfeet (4)	10	0.05
Canadian/French Am. Ind. (1)	1	<0.01
Central American Ind. (0)	0	<0.01
Cherokee (11)	47	0.22
Cheyenne (0)	0	<0.01
Chickasaw (0)	1	<0.01
Chippewa (1)	6	0.03
Choctaw (0)	0	<0.01
Colville (0)	0	<0.01
Comanche (0)	0	<0.01
Cree (0)	0	<0.01
Creek (4)	4	0.02
Crow (0)	0	<0.01
Delaware (0)	0	<0.01
Hopi (0)	0	<0.01
Houma (0)	0	<0.01
Inupiat (Alaska Native) (0)	0	<0.01
Iroquois (2)	6	0.03
Kiowa (0)	0	<0.01
Lumbee (1)	1	<0.01
Menominee (0)	0	<0.01
Mexican American Ind. (1)	2	<0.01
Navajo (2)	3	0.01
Osage (1)	1	<0.01
Ottawa (1)	1	<0.01
Paiute (0)	0	<0.01
Pima (0)	0	<0.01
Potawatomi (0)	1	<0.01
Pueblo (0)	1	<0.01
Puget Sound Salish (0)	0	<0.01
Seminole (0)	0	<0.01
Shoshone (0)	0	<0.01
Sioux (1)	1	<0.01
South American Ind. (0)	0	<0.01
Spanish American Ind. (1)	1	<0.01
Tlingit-Haida (Alaska Native) (0)	0	<0.01
Tohono O'Odham (0)	0	<0.01
Tsimshian (Alaska Native) (0)	0	<0.01
Ute (0)	0	<0.01
Yakama (0)	0	<0.01
Yaqui (0)	0	<0.01
Yuman (0)	0	<0.01
Yup'ik (Alaska Native) (1)	2	0.01
Asian (40)	76	0.35
Not Hispanic (39)	72	0.34
Hispanic (1)	4	0.02
Bangladeshi (0)	0	<0.01
Bhutanese (0)	0	<0.01
Burmese (0)	0	<0.01
Cambodian (0)	0	<0.01
Chinese, ex. Taiwanese (5)	5	0.02
Filipino (8)	16	0.07
Hmong (0)	0	<0.01
Indian (18)	27	0.13
Indonesian (0)	0	<0.01
Japanese (1)	11	0.05
Korean (2)	6	0.03
Laotian (1)	2	0.01
Malaysian (0)	0	<0.01
Nepalese (0)	0	<0.01
Pakistani (1)	3	0.01
Sri Lankan (0)	0	<0.01
Taiwanese (0)	0	<0.01
Thai (0)	2	0.01
Vietnamese (2)	3	0.01
Hawaii Native/Pacific Islander (1)	2	0.01
Not Hispanic (1)	2	0.01
Hispanic (0)	0	<0.01
Fijian (0)	0	<0.01
Guamanian/Chamorro (0)	0	<0.01
Marshallese (0)	0	<0.01
Native Hawaiian (1)	2	0.01
Samoan (0)	0	<0.01
Tongan (0)	0	<0.01
White (20,132)	20,347	94.75
Not Hispanic (19,930)	20,130	93.74
Hispanic (202)	217	1.01

Notes: † The Census 2010 population figure is used to calculate the percentages in the Hispanic Origin and Race categories. Ancestry percentages are based on the 2006-2010 American Community Survey population (not shown); ‡ Numbers in parentheses indicate the number of people reporting a single ancestry; * Numbers in parentheses indicate the number of persons reporting this race alone, not in combination with any other race; Please refer to the Explanation of Data for more information.

Switzerland County

Population: 10,613

Ancestry	Population	%
Afghan (0)	0	<0.01
African, Sub-Saharan (0)	0	<0.01
African (0)	0	<0.01
Cape Verdean (0)	0	<0.01
Ethiopian (0)	0	<0.01
Ghanaian (0)	0	<0.01
Kenyan (0)	0	<0.01
Liberian (0)	0	<0.01
Nigerian (0)	0	<0.01
Senegalese (0)	0	<0.01
Sierra Leonean (0)	0	<0.01
Somalian (0)	0	<0.01
South African (0)	0	<0.01
Sudanese (0)	0	<0.01
Ugandan (0)	0	<0.01
Zimbabwean (0)	0	<0.01
Other Sub-Saharan African (0)	0	<0.01
Albanian (0)	0	<0.01
Alsatian (0)	0	<0.01
American (1,670)	1,670	16.07
Arab (9)	12	0.12
Arab (0)	0	<0.01
Egyptian (9)	9	0.09
Iraqi (0)	0	<0.01
Jordanian (0)	0	<0.01
Lebanese (0)	3	0.03
Moroccan (0)	0	<0.01
Palestinian (0)	0	<0.01
Syrian (0)	0	<0.01
Other Arab (0)	0	<0.01
Armenian (0)	0	<0.01
Assyrian/Chaldean/Syriac (0)	0	<0.01
Australian (34)	34	0.33
Austrian (0)	16	0.15
Basque (0)	0	<0.01
Belgian (0)	0	<0.01
Brazilian (0)	0	<0.01
British (0)	0	<0.01
Bulgarian (0)	0	<0.01
Cajun (0)	0	<0.01
Canadian (0)	0	<0.01
Carpatho Rusyn (0)	0	<0.01
Celtic (0)	0	<0.01
Croatian (0)	0	<0.01
Cypriot (0)	0	<0.01
Czech (3)	58	0.56
Czechoslovakian (0)	0	<0.01
Danish (0)	23	0.22
Dutch (10)	135	1.30
Eastern European (0)	0	<0.01
English (447)	1,049	10.09
Estonian (0)	0	<0.01
European (0)	0	<0.01
Finnish (0)	0	<0.01
French, ex. Basque (24)	151	1.45
French Canadian (0)	20	0.19
German (940)	2,635	25.35
German Russian (0)	0	<0.01
Greek (12)	55	0.53
Guyanese (0)	0	<0.01
Hungarian (3)	8	0.08
Icelander (0)	0	<0.01
Iranian (0)	0	<0.01
Irish (509)	1,372	13.20
Israeli (0)	0	<0.01
Italian (16)	176	1.69
Latvian (0)	0	<0.01
Lithuanian (0)	0	<0.01
Luxemburger (0)	0	<0.01
Macedonian (0)	0	<0.01
Maltese (0)	0	<0.01
New Zealander (0)	0	<0.01
Northern European (51)	51	0.49
Norwegian (0)	52	0.50
Pennsylvania German (5)	5	0.05
Polish (20)	147	1.41
Portuguese (0)	0	<0.01
Romanian (0)	0	<0.01
Russian (0)	4	0.04
Scandinavian (0)	0	<0.01
Scotch-Irish (89)	348	3.35
Scottish (132)	278	2.67
Serbian (0)	0	<0.01
Slavic (0)	0	<0.01
Slovak (0)	4	0.04
Slovene (0)	0	<0.01
Soviet Union (0)	0	<0.01
Swedish (0)	37	0.36
Swiss (14)	120	1.15
Turkish (0)	0	<0.01
Ukrainian (0)	0	<0.01
Welsh (85)	100	0.96
West Indian, ex. Hispanic (3)	3	0.03
Bahamian (0)	0	<0.01
Barbadian (0)	0	<0.01
Belizean (0)	0	<0.01
Bermudan (0)	0	<0.01
British West Indian (0)	0	<0.01
Dutch West Indian (0)	0	<0.01
Haitian (0)	0	<0.01
Jamaican (3)	3	0.03
Trinidadian/Tobagonian (0)	0	<0.01
U.S. Virgin Islander (0)	0	<0.01
West Indian (0)	0	<0.01
Other West Indian (0)	0	<0.01
Yugoslavian (0)	121	1.16

Hispanic Origin	Population	%
Hispanic or Latino (of any race)	147	1.39
Central American, ex. Mexican	7	0.07
Costa Rican	0	<0.01
Guatemalan	4	0.04
Honduran	2	0.02
Nicaraguan	0	<0.01
Panamanian	1	0.01
Salvadoran	0	<0.01
Other Central American	0	<0.01
Cuban	5	0.05
Dominican Republic	0	<0.01
Mexican	113	1.06
Puerto Rican	9	0.08
South American	1	0.01
Argentinean	0	<0.01
Bolivian	0	<0.01
Chilean	0	<0.01
Colombian	0	<0.01
Ecuadorian	0	<0.01
Paraguayan	0	<0.01
Peruvian	1	0.01
Uruguayan	0	<0.01
Venezuelan	0	<0.01
Other South American	0	<0.01
Other Hispanic or Latino	12	0.11

Race*	Population	%
African-American/Black (32)	56	0.53
Not Hispanic (31)	54	0.51
Hispanic (1)	2	0.02
American Indian/Alaska Native (18)	62	0.58
Not Hispanic (16)	56	0.53
Hispanic (2)	6	0.06
Alaska Athabascan (Ala. Nat.) (0)	0	<0.01
Aleut (Alaska Native) (0)	0	<0.01
Apache (1)	1	0.01
Arapaho (0)	0	<0.01
Blackfeet (0)	5	0.05
Canadian/French Am. Ind. (0)	0	<0.01
Central American Ind. (0)	0	<0.01
Cherokee (4)	21	0.20
Cheyenne (0)	0	<0.01
Chickasaw (0)	1	0.01
Chippewa (1)	2	0.02
Choctaw (1)	1	0.01
Colville (0)	0	<0.01
Comanche (0)	0	<0.01
Cree (0)	0	<0.01
Creek (0)	0	<0.01
Crow (0)	0	<0.01
Delaware (0)	0	<0.01
Hopi (0)	0	<0.01
Houma (0)	0	<0.01
Inupiat (Alaska Native) (0)	0	<0.01
Iroquois (1)	1	0.01
Kiowa (0)	0	<0.01
Lumbee (0)	0	<0.01
Menominee (0)	0	<0.01
Mexican American Ind. (1)	1	0.01
Navajo (0)	0	<0.01
Osage (0)	0	<0.01
Ottawa (0)	0	<0.01
Paiute (0)	0	<0.01
Pima (0)	0	<0.01
Potawatomi (0)	0	<0.01
Pueblo (0)	0	<0.01
Puget Sound Salish (0)	0	<0.01
Seminole (1)	8	0.08
Shoshone (0)	0	<0.01
Sioux (0)	1	0.01
South American Ind. (0)	0	<0.01
Spanish American Ind. (0)	0	<0.01
Tlingit-Haida (Alaska Native) (0)	0	<0.01
Tohono O'Odham (0)	0	<0.01
Tsimshian (Alaska Native) (0)	0	<0.01
Ute (0)	0	<0.01
Yakama (0)	0	<0.01
Yaqui (0)	0	<0.01
Yuman (0)	0	<0.01
Yup'ik (Alaska Native) (0)	0	<0.01
Asian (18)	23	0.22
Not Hispanic (18)	23	0.22
Hispanic (0)	0	<0.01
Bangladeshi (0)	0	<0.01
Bhutanese (0)	0	<0.01
Burmese (0)	0	<0.01
Cambodian (1)	1	0.01
Chinese, ex. Taiwanese (0)	0	<0.01
Filipino (2)	2	0.02
Hmong (0)	0	<0.01
Indian (9)	13	0.12
Indonesian (0)	0	<0.01
Japanese (0)	0	<0.01
Korean (2)	2	0.02
Laotian (0)	0	<0.01
Malaysian (0)	0	<0.01
Nepalese (0)	0	<0.01
Pakistani (0)	0	<0.01
Sri Lankan (0)	0	<0.01
Taiwanese (1)	1	0.01
Thai (2)	3	0.03
Vietnamese (0)	0	<0.01
Hawaii Native/Pacific Islander (2)	5	0.05
Not Hispanic (2)	3	0.03
Hispanic (0)	2	0.02
Fijian (0)	0	<0.01
Guamanian/Chamorro (0)	0	<0.01
Marshallese (0)	0	<0.01
Native Hawaiian (2)	3	0.03
Samoan (0)	0	<0.01
Tongan (0)	0	<0.01
White (10,381)	10,460	98.56
Not Hispanic (10,318)	10,387	97.87
Hispanic (63)	73	0.69

Notes: † The Census 2010 population figure is used to calculate the percentages in the Hispanic Origin and Race categories. Ancestry percentages are based on the 2006-2010 American Community Survey population (not shown); ‡ Numbers in parentheses indicate the number of people reporting a single ancestry; * Numbers in parentheses indicate the number of persons reporting this race alone, not in combination with any other race; Please refer to the Explanation of Data for more information.

Tippecanoe County
Population: 172,780

Ancestry	Population	%
Afghan (16)	16	0.01
African, Sub-Saharan (614)	719	0.43
African (250)	324	0.19
Cape Verdean (0)	0	<0.01
Ethiopian (72)	72	0.04
Ghanaian (0)	0	<0.01
Kenyan (62)	62	0.04
Liberian (32)	32	0.02
Nigerian (101)	101	0.06
Senegalese (0)	0	<0.01
Sierra Leonean (0)	0	<0.01
Somalian (0)	0	<0.01
South African (0)	0	<0.01
Sudanese (9)	9	0.01
Ugandan (0)	0	<0.01
Zimbabwean (0)	0	<0.01
Other Sub-Saharan African (88)	119	0.07
Albanian (90)	90	0.05
Alsatian (0)	0	<0.01
American (10,255)	10,255	6.08
Arab (281)	478	0.28
Arab (46)	92	0.05
Egyptian (65)	103	0.06
Iraqi (0)	0	<0.01
Jordanian (24)	24	0.01
Lebanese (59)	140	0.08
Moroccan (42)	42	0.02
Palestinian (0)	0	<0.01
Syrian (0)	21	0.01
Other Arab (45)	56	0.03
Armenian (20)	20	0.01
Assyrian/Chaldean/Syriac (8)	59	0.03
Australian (80)	96	0.06
Austrian (85)	310	0.18
Basque (0)	0	<0.01
Belgian (72)	356	0.21
Brazilian (149)	183	0.11
British (487)	1,072	0.64
Bulgarian (26)	51	0.03
Cajun (11)	22	0.01
Canadian (80)	254	0.15
Carpatho Rusyn (0)	0	<0.01
Celtic (0)	23	0.01
Croatian (10)	261	0.15
Cypriot (61)	61	0.04
Czech (220)	597	0.35
Czechoslovakian (17)	70	0.04
Danish (99)	444	0.26
Dutch (1,714)	5,265	3.12
Eastern European (47)	77	0.05
English (6,797)	18,157	10.77
Estonian (8)	8	<0.01
European (1,712)	1,938	1.15
Finnish (93)	174	0.10
French, ex. Basque (1,102)	5,699	3.38
French Canadian (139)	398	0.24
German (16,261)	46,342	27.48
German Russian (0)	0	<0.01
Greek (289)	482	0.29
Guyanese (0)	0	<0.01
Hungarian (257)	842	0.50
Icelander (0)	18	0.01
Iranian (42)	47	0.03
Irish (6,393)	23,518	13.95
Israeli (0)	0	<0.01
Italian (2,306)	6,187	3.67
Latvian (15)	33	0.02
Lithuanian (28)	244	0.14
Luxemburger (0)	58	0.03
Macedonian (9)	9	0.01
Maltese (0)	0	<0.01
New Zealander (94)	94	0.06
Northern European (111)	111	0.07
Norwegian (289)	1,212	0.72
Pennsylvania German (52)	135	0.08
Polish (1,698)	5,824	3.45
Portuguese (27)	105	0.06
Romanian (117)	229	0.14
Russian (567)	1,438	0.85
Scandinavian (32)	122	0.07
Scotch-Irish (1,018)	2,944	1.75
Scottish (1,400)	3,847	2.28
Serbian (55)	135	0.08
Slavic (0)	38	0.02
Slovak (72)	205	0.12
Slovene (23)	36	0.02
Soviet Union (0)	0	<0.01
Swedish (468)	2,125	1.26
Swiss (340)	1,084	0.64
Turkish (164)	164	0.10
Ukrainian (45)	227	0.13
Welsh (249)	1,360	0.81
West Indian, ex. Hispanic (80)	147	0.09
Bahamian (13)	13	0.01
Barbadian (0)	0	<0.01
Belizean (0)	0	<0.01
Bermudan (0)	0	<0.01
British West Indian (0)	8	<0.01
Dutch West Indian (0)	8	<0.01
Haitian (7)	17	0.01
Jamaican (22)	36	0.02
Trinidadian/Tobagonian (0)	13	0.01
U.S. Virgin Islander (8)	8	<0.01
West Indian (30)	30	0.02
Other West Indian (0)	14	0.01
Yugoslavian (40)	95	0.06

Hispanic Origin	Population	%
Hispanic or Latino (of any race)	12,947	7.49
Central American, ex. Mexican	587	0.34
Costa Rican	39	0.02
Guatemalan	143	0.08
Honduran	50	0.03
Nicaraguan	55	0.03
Panamanian	92	0.05
Salvadoran	208	0.12
Other Central American	0	<0.01
Cuban	163	0.09
Dominican Republic	68	0.04
Mexican	10,271	5.94
Puerto Rican	581	0.34
South American	575	0.33
Argentinean	106	0.06
Bolivian	33	0.02
Chilean	40	0.02
Colombian	209	0.12
Ecuadorian	64	0.04
Paraguayan	2	<0.01
Peruvian	71	0.04
Uruguayan	8	<0.01
Venezuelan	39	0.02
Other South American	3	<0.01
Other Hispanic or Latino	702	0.41

Race*	Population	%
African-American/Black (6,913)	8,421	4.87
Not Hispanic (6,731)	8,044	4.66
Hispanic (182)	377	0.22
American Indian/Alaska Native (453)	1,261	0.73
Not Hispanic (349)	1,064	0.62
Hispanic (104)	197	0.11
Alaska Athabascan (Ala. Nat.) (5)	5	<0.01
Aleut (Alaska Native) (1)	2	<0.01
Apache (4)	19	0.01
Arapaho (0)	0	<0.01
Blackfeet (7)	39	0.02
Canadian/French Am. Ind. (2)	5	<0.01
Central American Ind. (1)	1	<0.01
Cherokee (72)	337	0.20
Cheyenne (2)	8	<0.01
Chickasaw (4)	7	<0.01
Chippewa (20)	28	0.02
Choctaw (8)	21	0.01
Colville (0)	0	<0.01
Comanche (2)	4	<0.01
Cree (2)	2	<0.01
Creek (4)	18	0.01
Crow (2)	3	<0.01
Delaware (1)	5	<0.01
Hopi (1)	1	<0.01
Houma (6)	6	<0.01
Inupiat (Alaska Native) (3)	8	<0.01
Iroquois (10)	20	0.01
Kiowa (0)	0	<0.01
Lumbee (7)	9	0.01
Menominee (1)	1	<0.01
Mexican American Ind. (30)	36	0.02
Navajo (0)	5	<0.01
Osage (2)	5	<0.01
Ottawa (11)	14	0.01
Paiute (1)	1	<0.01
Pima (0)	0	<0.01
Potawatomi (3)	16	0.01
Pueblo (1)	3	<0.01
Puget Sound Salish (1)	1	<0.01
Seminole (3)	8	<0.01
Shoshone (0)	0	<0.01
Sioux (15)	36	0.02
South American Ind. (2)	12	0.01
Spanish American Ind. (0)	0	<0.01
Tlingit-Haida (Alaska Native) (0)	5	<0.01
Tohono O'Odham (0)	0	<0.01
Tsimshian (Alaska Native) (0)	0	<0.01
Ute (0)	1	<0.01
Yakama (0)	0	<0.01
Yaqui (1)	1	<0.01
Yuman (0)	1	<0.01
Yup'ik (Alaska Native) (1)	1	<0.01
Asian (10,730)	11,876	6.87
Not Hispanic (10,679)	11,745	6.80
Hispanic (51)	131	0.08
Bangladeshi (53)	60	0.03
Bhutanese (0)	0	<0.01
Burmese (13)	17	0.01
Cambodian (6)	10	0.01
Chinese, ex. Taiwanese (3,657)	3,941	2.28
Filipino (363)	611	0.35
Hmong (1)	1	<0.01
Indian (2,713)	2,858	1.65
Indonesian (85)	99	0.06
Japanese (425)	578	0.33
Korean (1,918)	2,090	1.21
Laotian (16)	29	0.02
Malaysian (149)	169	0.10
Nepalese (21)	22	0.01
Pakistani (198)	220	0.13
Sri Lankan (72)	73	0.04
Taiwanese (353)	405	0.23
Thai (117)	152	0.09
Vietnamese (302)	363	0.21
Hawaii Native/Pacific Islander (50)	187	0.11
Not Hispanic (41)	157	0.09
Hispanic (9)	30	0.02
Fijian (3)	3	<0.01
Guamanian/Chamorro (21)	33	0.02
Marshallese (0)	0	<0.01
Native Hawaiian (14)	55	0.03
Samoan (3)	23	0.01
Tongan (2)	3	<0.01
White (145,190)	148,641	86.03
Not Hispanic (138,855)	141,569	81.94
Hispanic (6,335)	7,072	4.09

Notes: † The Census 2010 population figure is used to calculate the percentages in the Hispanic Origin and Race categories. Ancestry percentages are based on the 2006-2010 American Community Survey population (not shown); ‡ Numbers in parentheses indicate the number of people reporting a single ancestry; * Numbers in parentheses indicate the number of persons reporting this race alone, not in combination with any other race; Please refer to the Explanation of Data for more information.

Tipton County
Population: 15,936

Ancestry	Population	%
Afghan (0)	0	<0.01
African, Sub-Saharan (0)	3	0.02
African (0)	3	0.02
Cape Verdean (0)	0	<0.01
Ethiopian (0)	0	<0.01
Ghanaian (0)	0	<0.01
Kenyan (0)	0	<0.01
Liberian (0)	0	<0.01
Nigerian (0)	0	<0.01
Senegalese (0)	0	<0.01
Sierra Leonean (0)	0	<0.01
Somalian (0)	0	<0.01
South African (0)	0	<0.01
Sudanese (0)	0	<0.01
Ugandan (0)	0	<0.01
Zimbabwean (0)	0	<0.01
Other Sub-Saharan African (0)	0	<0.01
Albanian (0)	9	0.06
Alsatian (0)	0	<0.01
American (2,345)	2,345	14.54
Arab (0)	16	0.10
Arab (0)	0	<0.01
Egyptian (0)	0	<0.01
Iraqi (0)	0	<0.01
Jordanian (0)	0	<0.01
Lebanese (0)	16	0.10
Moroccan (0)	0	<0.01
Palestinian (0)	0	<0.01
Syrian (0)	0	<0.01
Other Arab (0)	0	<0.01
Armenian (0)	0	<0.01
Assyrian/Chaldean/Syriac (0)	0	<0.01
Australian (0)	0	<0.01
Austrian (23)	23	0.14
Basque (0)	0	<0.01
Belgian (0)	0	<0.01
Brazilian (0)	0	<0.01
British (37)	72	0.45
Bulgarian (0)	0	<0.01
Cajun (0)	0	<0.01
Canadian (0)	3	0.02
Carpatho Rusyn (0)	0	<0.01
Celtic (0)	0	<0.01
Croatian (0)	5	0.03
Cypriot (0)	0	<0.01
Czech (0)	16	0.10
Czechoslovakian (0)	0	<0.01
Danish (18)	43	0.27
Dutch (159)	384	2.38
Eastern European (0)	0	<0.01
English (859)	1,988	12.32
Estonian (0)	0	<0.01
European (69)	78	0.48
Finnish (0)	0	<0.01
French, ex. Basque (70)	352	2.18
French Canadian (14)	42	0.26
German (2,062)	4,602	28.53
German Russian (0)	0	<0.01
Greek (41)	41	0.25
Guyanese (0)	0	<0.01
Hungarian (19)	134	0.83
Icelander (0)	0	<0.01
Iranian (0)	0	<0.01
Irish (366)	1,551	9.61
Israeli (0)	0	<0.01
Italian (31)	231	1.43
Latvian (0)	0	<0.01
Lithuanian (0)	0	<0.01
Luxemburger (0)	0	<0.01
Macedonian (0)	0	<0.01
Maltese (0)	0	<0.01
New Zealander (0)	0	<0.01
Northern European (0)	0	<0.01
Norwegian (12)	115	0.71
Pennsylvania German (2)	2	0.01
Polish (58)	202	1.25
Portuguese (10)	10	0.06
Romanian (0)	0	<0.01
Russian (21)	27	0.17
Scandinavian (0)	2	0.01
Scotch-Irish (158)	360	2.23
Scottish (116)	477	2.96
Serbian (0)	0	<0.01
Slavic (0)	0	<0.01
Slovak (23)	23	0.14
Slovene (0)	0	<0.01
Soviet Union (0)	0	<0.01
Swedish (20)	94	0.58
Swiss (18)	44	0.27
Turkish (0)	0	<0.01
Ukrainian (6)	6	0.04
Welsh (10)	13	0.08
West Indian, ex. Hispanic (0)	0	<0.01
Bahamian (0)	0	<0.01
Barbadian (0)	0	<0.01
Belizean (0)	0	<0.01
Bermudan (0)	0	<0.01
British West Indian (0)	0	<0.01
Dutch West Indian (0)	0	<0.01
Haitian (0)	0	<0.01
Jamaican (0)	0	<0.01
Trinidadian/Tobagonian (0)	0	<0.01
U.S. Virgin Islander (0)	0	<0.01
West Indian (0)	0	<0.01
Other West Indian (0)	0	<0.01
Yugoslavian (12)	12	0.07

Hispanic Origin	Population	%
Hispanic or Latino (of any race)	346	2.17
Central American, ex. Mexican	6	0.04
Costa Rican	0	<0.01
Guatemalan	1	0.01
Honduran	0	<0.01
Nicaraguan	0	<0.01
Panamanian	1	0.01
Salvadoran	4	0.03
Other Central American	0	<0.01
Cuban	5	0.03
Dominican Republic	0	<0.01
Mexican	280	1.76
Puerto Rican	12	0.08
South American	6	0.04
Argentinean	0	<0.01
Bolivian	0	<0.01
Chilean	0	<0.01
Colombian	2	0.01
Ecuadorian	0	<0.01
Paraguayan	0	<0.01
Peruvian	0	<0.01
Uruguayan	0	<0.01
Venezuelan	4	0.03
Other South American	0	<0.01
Other Hispanic or Latino	37	0.23

Race*	Population	%
African-American/Black (29)	77	0.48
Not Hispanic (28)	74	0.46
Hispanic (1)	3	0.02
American Indian/Alaska Native (23)	66	0.41
Not Hispanic (20)	57	0.36
Hispanic (3)	9	0.06
Alaska Athabascan (Ala. Nat.) (0)	0	<0.01
Aleut (Alaska Native) (0)	0	<0.01
Apache (0)	0	<0.01
Arapaho (0)	0	<0.01
Blackfeet (3)	4	0.03
Canadian/French Am. Ind. (0)	0	<0.01
Central American Ind. (0)	0	<0.01
Cherokee (0)	18	0.11
Cheyenne (0)	0	<0.01
Chickasaw (0)	0	<0.01
Chippewa (0)	0	<0.01
Choctaw (0)	0	<0.01
Colville (1)	1	0.01
Comanche (3)	5	0.03
Cree (0)	0	<0.01
Creek (0)	0	<0.01
Crow (0)	0	<0.01
Delaware (0)	0	<0.01
Hopi (0)	0	<0.01
Houma (0)	0	<0.01
Inupiat (Alaska Native) (0)	0	<0.01
Iroquois (0)	0	<0.01
Kiowa (0)	0	<0.01
Lumbee (0)	0	<0.01
Menominee (0)	0	<0.01
Mexican American Ind. (0)	0	<0.01
Navajo (0)	0	<0.01
Osage (0)	0	<0.01
Ottawa (1)	3	0.02
Paiute (0)	0	<0.01
Pima (0)	0	<0.01
Potawatomi (0)	0	<0.01
Pueblo (0)	0	<0.01
Puget Sound Salish (0)	0	<0.01
Seminole (0)	0	<0.01
Shoshone (0)	0	<0.01
Sioux (3)	3	0.02
South American Ind. (0)	0	<0.01
Spanish American Ind. (0)	0	<0.01
Tlingit-Haida (Alaska Native) (0)	0	<0.01
Tohono O'Odham (0)	0	<0.01
Tsimshian (Alaska Native) (0)	0	<0.01
Ute (0)	0	<0.01
Yakama (0)	0	<0.01
Yaqui (0)	0	<0.01
Yuman (0)	0	<0.01
Yup'ik (Alaska Native) (0)	0	<0.01
Asian (65)	88	0.55
Not Hispanic (64)	83	0.52
Hispanic (1)	5	0.03
Bangladeshi (0)	0	<0.01
Bhutanese (0)	0	<0.01
Burmese (0)	0	<0.01
Cambodian (0)	0	<0.01
Chinese, ex. Taiwanese (9)	12	0.08
Filipino (7)	14	0.09
Hmong (0)	0	<0.01
Indian (17)	24	0.15
Indonesian (0)	0	<0.01
Japanese (4)	7	0.04
Korean (10)	13	0.08
Laotian (0)	0	<0.01
Malaysian (0)	0	<0.01
Nepalese (0)	0	<0.01
Pakistani (1)	1	0.01
Sri Lankan (0)	0	<0.01
Taiwanese (1)	1	0.01
Thai (1)	2	0.01
Vietnamese (9)	9	0.06
Hawaii Native/Pacific Islander (5)	15	0.09
Not Hispanic (5)	15	0.09
Hispanic (0)	0	<0.01
Fijian (0)	0	<0.01
Guamanian/Chamorro (0)	0	<0.01
Marshallese (0)	0	<0.01
Native Hawaiian (4)	11	0.07
Samoan (0)	1	0.01
Tongan (0)	0	<0.01
White (15,551)	15,705	98.55
Not Hispanic (15,355)	15,469	97.07
Hispanic (196)	236	1.48

Notes: † The Census 2010 population figure is used to calculate the percentages in the Hispanic Origin and Race categories. Ancestry percentages are based on the 2006-2010 American Community Survey population (not shown); ‡ Numbers in parentheses indicate the number of people reporting a single ancestry; * Numbers in parentheses indicate the number of persons reporting this race alone, not in combination with any other race; Please refer to the Explanation of Data for more information.

Union County
Population: 7,516

Ancestry	Population	%
Afghan (0)	0	<0.01
African, Sub-Saharan (0)	0	<0.01
African (0)	0	<0.01
Cape Verdean (0)	0	<0.01
Ethiopian (0)	0	<0.01
Ghanaian (0)	0	<0.01
Kenyan (0)	0	<0.01
Liberian (0)	0	<0.01
Nigerian (0)	0	<0.01
Senegalese (0)	0	<0.01
Sierra Leonean (0)	0	<0.01
Somalian (0)	0	<0.01
South African (0)	0	<0.01
Sudanese (0)	0	<0.01
Ugandan (0)	0	<0.01
Zimbabwean (0)	0	<0.01
Other Sub-Saharan African (0)	0	<0.01
Albanian (0)	0	<0.01
Alsatian (0)	0	<0.01
American (865)	865	11.59
Arab (0)	0	<0.01
Arab (0)	0	<0.01
Egyptian (0)	0	<0.01
Iraqi (0)	0	<0.01
Jordanian (0)	0	<0.01
Lebanese (0)	0	<0.01
Moroccan (0)	0	<0.01
Palestinian (0)	0	<0.01
Syrian (0)	0	<0.01
Other Arab (0)	0	<0.01
Armenian (0)	0	<0.01
Assyrian/Chaldean/Syriac (0)	0	<0.01
Australian (0)	0	<0.01
Austrian (0)	9	0.12
Basque (0)	0	<0.01
Belgian (0)	0	<0.01
Brazilian (0)	0	<0.01
British (0)	18	0.24
Bulgarian (0)	0	<0.01
Cajun (0)	0	<0.01
Canadian (0)	0	<0.01
Carpatho Rusyn (0)	0	<0.01
Celtic (0)	0	<0.01
Croatian (0)	0	<0.01
Cypriot (0)	0	<0.01
Czech (0)	0	<0.01
Czechoslovakian (0)	0	<0.01
Danish (0)	0	<0.01
Dutch (68)	197	2.64
Eastern European (0)	0	<0.01
English (400)	900	12.06
Estonian (0)	0	<0.01
European (25)	25	0.33
Finnish (0)	14	0.19
French, ex. Basque (4)	102	1.37
French Canadian (15)	19	0.25
German (917)	1,954	26.18
German Russian (0)	0	<0.01
Greek (0)	0	<0.01
Guyanese (0)	0	<0.01
Hungarian (0)	0	<0.01
Icelander (0)	0	<0.01
Iranian (0)	0	<0.01
Irish (391)	1,197	16.04
Israeli (0)	0	<0.01
Italian (63)	256	3.43
Latvian (0)	0	<0.01
Lithuanian (0)	0	<0.01
Luxemburger (0)	0	<0.01
Macedonian (0)	0	<0.01
Maltese (0)	0	<0.01
New Zealander (0)	0	<0.01
Northern European (0)	0	<0.01
Norwegian (3)	12	0.16
Pennsylvania German (0)	0	<0.01
Polish (37)	62	0.83
Portuguese (0)	0	<0.01
Romanian (0)	12	0.16
Russian (0)	18	0.24
Scandinavian (5)	9	0.12
Scotch-Irish (90)	137	1.84
Scottish (52)	173	2.32
Serbian (0)	0	<0.01
Slavic (0)	0	<0.01
Slovak (0)	13	0.17
Slovene (8)	8	0.11
Soviet Union (0)	0	<0.01
Swedish (0)	3	0.04
Swiss (12)	42	0.56
Turkish (0)	0	<0.01
Ukrainian (0)	0	<0.01
Welsh (33)	36	0.48
West Indian, ex. Hispanic (0)	0	<0.01
Bahamian (0)	0	<0.01
Barbadian (0)	0	<0.01
Belizean (0)	0	<0.01
Bermudan (0)	0	<0.01
British West Indian (0)	0	<0.01
Dutch West Indian (0)	0	<0.01
Haitian (0)	0	<0.01
Jamaican (0)	0	<0.01
Trinidadian/Tobagonian (0)	0	<0.01
U.S. Virgin Islander (0)	0	<0.01
West Indian (0)	0	<0.01
Other West Indian (0)	0	<0.01
Yugoslavian (0)	0	<0.01

Hispanic Origin	Population	%
Hispanic or Latino (of any race)	82	1.09
Central American, ex. Mexican	6	0.08
Costa Rican	0	<0.01
Guatemalan	5	0.07
Honduran	0	<0.01
Nicaraguan	0	<0.01
Panamanian	1	0.01
Salvadoran	0	<0.01
Other Central American	0	<0.01
Cuban	0	<0.01
Dominican Republic	6	0.08
Mexican	51	0.68
Puerto Rican	4	0.05
South American	1	0.01
Argentinean	0	<0.01
Bolivian	0	<0.01
Chilean	0	<0.01
Colombian	1	0.01
Ecuadorian	0	<0.01
Paraguayan	0	<0.01
Peruvian	0	<0.01
Uruguayan	0	<0.01
Venezuelan	0	<0.01
Other South American	0	<0.01
Other Hispanic or Latino	14	0.19

Race*	Population	%
African-American/Black (33)	47	0.63
Not Hispanic (33)	47	0.63
Hispanic (0)	0	<0.01
American Indian/Alaska Native (23)	59	0.78
Not Hispanic (19)	53	0.71
Hispanic (4)	6	0.08
Alaska Athabascan (Ala. Nat.) (0)	0	<0.01
Aleut (Alaska Native) (0)	0	<0.01
Apache (0)	1	0.01
Arapaho (0)	0	<0.01
Blackfeet (1)	4	0.05
Canadian/French Am. Ind. (0)	0	<0.01
Central American Ind. (0)	0	<0.01
Cherokee (3)	22	0.29
Cheyenne (0)	0	<0.01
Chickasaw (0)	0	<0.01
Chippewa (0)	0	<0.01
Choctaw (5)	7	0.09
Colville (0)	0	<0.01
Comanche (0)	1	0.01
Cree (0)	0	<0.01
Creek (0)	0	<0.01
Crow (0)	0	<0.01
Delaware (0)	1	0.01
Hopi (0)	0	<0.01
Houma (0)	0	<0.01
Inupiat (Alaska Native) (0)	0	<0.01
Iroquois (0)	0	<0.01
Kiowa (0)	0	<0.01
Lumbee (0)	0	<0.01
Menominee (0)	0	<0.01
Mexican American Ind. (1)	1	0.01
Navajo (3)	3	0.04
Osage (0)	0	<0.01
Ottawa (0)	0	<0.01
Paiute (0)	0	<0.01
Pima (0)	0	<0.01
Potawatomi (0)	0	<0.01
Pueblo (0)	0	<0.01
Puget Sound Salish (0)	0	<0.01
Seminole (0)	0	<0.01
Shoshone (0)	0	<0.01
Sioux (0)	1	0.01
South American Ind. (0)	0	<0.01
Spanish American Ind. (0)	0	<0.01
Tlingit-Haida (Alaska Native) (0)	0	<0.01
Tohono O'Odham (0)	0	<0.01
Tsimshian (Alaska Native) (0)	0	<0.01
Ute (0)	0	<0.01
Yakama (0)	0	<0.01
Yaqui (0)	1	0.01
Yuman (0)	0	<0.01
Yup'ik (Alaska Native) (0)	0	<0.01
Asian (19)	40	0.53
Not Hispanic (19)	40	0.53
Hispanic (0)	0	<0.01
Bangladeshi (0)	0	<0.01
Bhutanese (0)	0	<0.01
Burmese (0)	0	<0.01
Cambodian (0)	0	<0.01
Chinese, ex. Taiwanese (1)	2	0.03
Filipino (6)	22	0.29
Hmong (0)	0	<0.01
Indian (7)	9	0.12
Indonesian (0)	0	<0.01
Japanese (1)	3	0.04
Korean (2)	2	0.03
Laotian (0)	0	<0.01
Malaysian (0)	0	<0.01
Nepalese (0)	0	<0.01
Pakistani (0)	0	<0.01
Sri Lankan (0)	0	<0.01
Taiwanese (0)	0	<0.01
Thai (0)	0	<0.01
Vietnamese (0)	2	0.03
Hawaii Native/Pacific Islander (6)	13	0.17
Not Hispanic (6)	13	0.17
Hispanic (0)	0	<0.01
Fijian (0)	0	<0.01
Guamanian/Chamorro (0)	0	<0.01
Marshallese (0)	0	<0.01
Native Hawaiian (6)	12	0.16
Samoan (0)	0	<0.01
Tongan (0)	0	<0.01
White (7,331)	7,408	98.56
Not Hispanic (7,280)	7,352	97.82
Hispanic (51)	56	0.75

Notes: † The Census 2010 population figure is used to calculate the percentages in the Hispanic Origin and Race categories. Ancestry percentages are based on the 2006-2010 American Community Survey population (not shown); ‡ Numbers in parentheses indicate the number of people reporting a single ancestry; * Numbers in parentheses indicate the number of persons reporting this race alone, not in combination with any other race; Please refer to the Explanation of Data for more information.

Vanderburgh County
Population: 179,703

Ancestry	Population	%
Afghan (0)	0	<0.01
African, Sub-Saharan (169)	291	0.16
African (101)	180	0.10
Cape Verdean (0)	0	<0.01
Ethiopian (38)	72	0.04
Ghanaian (0)	0	<0.01
Kenyan (0)	0	<0.01
Liberian (0)	0	<0.01
Nigerian (8)	17	0.01
Senegalese (0)	0	<0.01
Sierra Leonean (0)	0	<0.01
Somalian (0)	0	<0.01
South African (0)	0	<0.01
Sudanese (0)	0	<0.01
Ugandan (14)	14	0.01
Zimbabwean (0)	0	<0.01
Other Sub-Saharan African (8)	8	<0.01
Albanian (0)	0	<0.01
Alsatian (0)	13	0.01
American (32,701)	32,701	18.34
Arab (116)	189	0.11
Arab (20)	55	0.03
Egyptian (0)	0	<0.01
Iraqi (16)	16	0.01
Jordanian (15)	15	0.01
Lebanese (24)	51	0.03
Moroccan (0)	0	<0.01
Palestinian (30)	30	0.02
Syrian (0)	11	0.01
Other Arab (11)	11	0.01
Armenian (70)	78	0.04
Assyrian/Chaldean/Syriac (0)	0	<0.01
Australian (39)	39	0.02
Austrian (15)	189	0.11
Basque (0)	0	<0.01
Belgian (0)	75	0.04
Brazilian (62)	62	0.03
British (377)	676	0.38
Bulgarian (12)	24	0.01
Cajun (0)	12	0.01
Canadian (150)	201	0.11
Carpatho Rusyn (0)	0	<0.01
Celtic (15)	38	0.02
Croatian (38)	95	0.05
Cypriot (0)	0	<0.01
Czech (55)	306	0.17
Czechoslovakian (84)	202	0.11
Danish (21)	217	0.12
Dutch (662)	2,816	1.58
Eastern European (13)	27	0.02
English (6,870)	16,696	9.36
Estonian (0)	3	<0.01
European (1,067)	1,215	0.68
Finnish (31)	93	0.05
French, ex. Basque (1,257)	4,630	2.60
French Canadian (174)	323	0.18
German (32,284)	57,653	32.34
German Russian (0)	0	<0.01
Greek (136)	296	0.17
Guyanese (0)	49	0.03
Hungarian (56)	284	0.16
Icelander (19)	19	0.01
Iranian (20)	20	0.01
Irish (5,702)	20,941	11.74
Israeli (0)	0	<0.01
Italian (928)	3,274	1.84
Latvian (12)	12	0.01
Lithuanian (23)	187	0.10
Luxemburger (0)	0	<0.01
Macedonian (0)	0	<0.01
Maltese (0)	0	<0.01
New Zealander (0)	0	<0.01
Northern European (40)	57	0.03
Norwegian (307)	903	0.51
Pennsylvania German (86)	111	0.06
Polish (868)	2,648	1.49
Portuguese (89)	121	0.07
Romanian (0)	10	0.01
Russian (347)	736	0.41
Scandinavian (19)	29	0.02
Scotch-Irish (971)	2,757	1.55
Scottish (1,164)	2,907	1.63
Serbian (27)	27	0.02
Slavic (0)	11	0.01
Slovak (63)	221	0.12
Slovene (0)	0	<0.01
Soviet Union (0)	0	<0.01
Swedish (324)	747	0.42
Swiss (44)	455	0.26
Turkish (11)	25	0.01
Ukrainian (215)	304	0.17
Welsh (142)	658	0.37
West Indian, ex. Hispanic (63)	111	0.06
Bahamian (0)	0	<0.01
Barbadian (0)	0	<0.01
Belizean (9)	9	0.01
Bermudan (0)	0	<0.01
British West Indian (0)	0	<0.01
Dutch West Indian (0)	0	<0.01
Haitian (31)	58	0.03
Jamaican (23)	44	0.02
Trinidadian/Tobagonian (0)	0	<0.01
U.S. Virgin Islander (0)	0	<0.01
West Indian (0)	0	<0.01
Other West Indian (0)	0	<0.01
Yugoslavian (0)	24	0.01

Hispanic Origin	Population	%
Hispanic or Latino (of any race)	3,873	2.16
Central American, ex. Mexican	299	0.17
Costa Rican	20	0.01
Guatemalan	66	0.04
Honduran	49	0.03
Nicaraguan	49	0.03
Panamanian	31	0.02
Salvadoran	76	0.04
Other Central American	8	<0.01
Cuban	99	0.06
Dominican Republic	29	0.02
Mexican	2,521	1.40
Puerto Rican	328	0.18
South American	173	0.10
Argentinean	9	0.01
Bolivian	18	0.01
Chilean	14	0.01
Colombian	42	0.02
Ecuadorian	10	0.01
Paraguayan	2	<0.01
Peruvian	47	0.03
Uruguayan	1	<0.01
Venezuelan	29	0.02
Other South American	1	<0.01
Other Hispanic or Latino	424	0.24

Race*	Population	%
African-American/Black (16,347)	19,012	10.58
Not Hispanic (16,228)	18,759	10.44
Hispanic (119)	253	0.14
American Indian/Alaska Native (399)	1,168	0.65
Not Hispanic (345)	1,060	0.59
Hispanic (54)	108	0.06
Alaska Athabascan (Ala. Nat.) (0)	1	<0.01
Aleut (Alaska Native) (0)	0	<0.01
Apache (6)	25	0.01
Arapaho (1)	1	<0.01
Blackfeet (8)	57	0.03
Canadian/French Am. Ind. (1)	2	<0.01
Central American Ind. (2)	2	<0.01
Cherokee (86)	364	0.20
Cheyenne (4)	11	0.01
Chickasaw (1)	4	<0.01
Chippewa (12)	22	0.01
Choctaw (7)	20	0.01
Colville (1)	1	<0.01
Comanche (0)	2	<0.01
Cree (0)	2	<0.01
Creek (1)	1	<0.01
Crow (0)	2	<0.01
Delaware (4)	6	<0.01
Hopi (0)	1	<0.01
Houma (2)	4	<0.01
Inupiat (Alaska Native) (0)	1	<0.01
Iroquois (4)	16	0.01
Kiowa (0)	1	<0.01
Lumbee (5)	16	0.01
Menominee (0)	0	<0.01
Mexican American Ind. (8)	10	0.01
Navajo (5)	13	0.01
Osage (2)	2	<0.01
Ottawa (0)	0	<0.01
Paiute (0)	0	<0.01
Pima (0)	0	<0.01
Potawatomi (0)	3	<0.01
Pueblo (1)	3	<0.01
Puget Sound Salish (0)	0	<0.01
Seminole (1)	3	<0.01
Shoshone (0)	6	<0.01
Sioux (33)	65	0.04
South American Ind. (3)	6	<0.01
Spanish American Ind. (1)	1	<0.01
Tlingit-Haida (Alaska Native) (1)	1	<0.01
Tohono O'Odham (0)	0	<0.01
Tsimshian (Alaska Native) (0)	0	<0.01
Ute (0)	0	<0.01
Yakama (0)	0	<0.01
Yaqui (0)	1	<0.01
Yuman (0)	0	<0.01
Yup'ik (Alaska Native) (0)	0	<0.01
Asian (2,003)	2,666	1.48
Not Hispanic (1,986)	2,616	1.46
Hispanic (17)	50	0.03
Bangladeshi (7)	7	<0.01
Bhutanese (0)	0	<0.01
Burmese (3)	5	<0.01
Cambodian (4)	9	0.01
Chinese, ex. Taiwanese (482)	573	0.32
Filipino (246)	396	0.22
Hmong (0)	0	<0.01
Indian (484)	566	0.31
Indonesian (8)	15	0.01
Japanese (171)	266	0.15
Korean (184)	290	0.16
Laotian (5)	13	0.01
Malaysian (15)	19	0.01
Nepalese (15)	26	0.01
Pakistani (5)	12	0.01
Sri Lankan (1)	3	<0.01
Taiwanese (8)	12	0.01
Thai (32)	62	0.03
Vietnamese (277)	330	0.18
Hawaii Native/Pacific Islander (104)	237	0.13
Not Hispanic (89)	201	0.11
Hispanic (15)	36	0.02
Fijian (0)	0	<0.01
Guamanian/Chamorro (24)	40	0.02
Marshallese (51)	56	0.03
Native Hawaiian (14)	71	0.04
Samoan (5)	24	0.01
Tongan (0)	0	<0.01
White (154,882)	158,732	88.33
Not Hispanic (153,080)	156,600	87.14
Hispanic (1,802)	2,132	1.19

Notes: † The Census 2010 population figure is used to calculate the percentages in the Hispanic Origin and Race categories. Ancestry percentages are based on the 2006-2010 American Community Survey population (not shown); ‡ Numbers in parentheses indicate the number of people reporting a single ancestry; * Numbers in parentheses indicate the number of persons reporting this race alone, not in combination with any other race; Please refer to the Explanation of Data for more information.

Vermillion County
Population: 16,212

Ancestry	Population	%
Afghan (0)	0	<0.01
African, Sub-Saharan (0)	0	<0.01
African (0)	0	<0.01
Cape Verdean (0)	0	<0.01
Ethiopian (0)	0	<0.01
Ghanaian (0)	0	<0.01
Kenyan (0)	0	<0.01
Liberian (0)	0	<0.01
Nigerian (0)	0	<0.01
Senegalese (0)	0	<0.01
Sierra Leonean (0)	0	<0.01
Somalian (0)	0	<0.01
South African (0)	0	<0.01
Sudanese (0)	0	<0.01
Ugandan (0)	0	<0.01
Zimbabwean (0)	0	<0.01
Other Sub-Saharan African (0)	0	<0.01
Albanian (0)	0	<0.01
Alsatian (0)	0	<0.01
American (4,058)	4,058	24.73
Arab (12)	58	0.35
Arab (0)	0	<0.01
Egyptian (0)	0	<0.01
Iraqi (0)	0	<0.01
Jordanian (0)	0	<0.01
Lebanese (0)	0	<0.01
Moroccan (0)	0	<0.01
Palestinian (0)	0	<0.01
Syrian (0)	46	0.28
Other Arab (12)	12	0.07
Armenian (0)	0	<0.01
Assyrian/Chaldean/Syriac (0)	0	<0.01
Australian (0)	0	<0.01
Austrian (2)	7	0.04
Basque (0)	0	<0.01
Belgian (17)	58	0.35
Brazilian (0)	0	<0.01
British (27)	66	0.40
Bulgarian (0)	0	<0.01
Cajun (0)	0	<0.01
Canadian (5)	5	0.03
Carpatho Rusyn (0)	0	<0.01
Celtic (0)	0	<0.01
Croatian (0)	0	<0.01
Cypriot (0)	0	<0.01
Czech (19)	82	0.50
Czechoslovakian (0)	25	0.15
Danish (3)	12	0.07
Dutch (21)	429	2.61
Eastern European (0)	0	<0.01
English (836)	1,604	9.77
Estonian (0)	0	<0.01
European (232)	240	1.46
Finnish (0)	12	0.07
French, ex. Basque (106)	456	2.78
French Canadian (9)	16	0.10
German (1,506)	3,203	19.52
German Russian (0)	0	<0.01
Greek (16)	53	0.32
Guyanese (0)	0	<0.01
Hungarian (70)	141	0.86
Icelander (0)	0	<0.01
Iranian (0)	0	<0.01
Irish (546)	1,802	10.98
Israeli (0)	0	<0.01
Italian (746)	1,301	7.93
Latvian (0)	0	<0.01
Lithuanian (25)	67	0.41
Luxemburger (0)	2	0.01
Macedonian (0)	0	<0.01
Maltese (0)	0	<0.01
New Zealander (0)	0	<0.01
Northern European (0)	0	<0.01
Norwegian (13)	45	0.27
Pennsylvania German (5)	8	0.05
Polish (61)	218	1.33
Portuguese (26)	37	0.23
Romanian (17)	21	0.13
Russian (0)	14	0.09
Scandinavian (11)	11	0.07
Scotch-Irish (122)	234	1.43
Scottish (105)	382	2.33
Serbian (27)	90	0.55
Slavic (10)	10	0.06
Slovak (2)	2	0.01
Slovene (3)	3	0.02
Soviet Union (0)	0	<0.01
Swedish (28)	187	1.14
Swiss (3)	20	0.12
Turkish (0)	16	0.10
Ukrainian (0)	0	<0.01
Welsh (27)	208	1.27
West Indian, ex. Hispanic (0)	0	<0.01
Bahamian (0)	0	<0.01
Barbadian (0)	0	<0.01
Belizean (0)	0	<0.01
Bermudan (0)	0	<0.01
British West Indian (0)	0	<0.01
Dutch West Indian (0)	0	<0.01
Haitian (0)	0	<0.01
Jamaican (0)	0	<0.01
Trinidadian/Tobagonian (0)	0	<0.01
U.S. Virgin Islander (0)	0	<0.01
West Indian (0)	0	<0.01
Other West Indian (0)	0	<0.01
Yugoslavian (0)	56	0.34

Hispanic Origin	Population	%
Hispanic or Latino (of any race)	130	0.80
Central American, ex. Mexican	3	0.02
Costa Rican	0	<0.01
Guatemalan	1	0.01
Honduran	0	<0.01
Nicaraguan	0	<0.01
Panamanian	2	0.01
Salvadoran	0	<0.01
Other Central American	0	<0.01
Cuban	3	0.02
Dominican Republic	0	<0.01
Mexican	83	0.51
Puerto Rican	19	0.12
South American	2	0.01
Argentinean	1	0.01
Bolivian	0	<0.01
Chilean	0	<0.01
Colombian	0	<0.01
Ecuadorian	0	<0.01
Paraguayan	0	<0.01
Peruvian	0	<0.01
Uruguayan	0	<0.01
Venezuelan	0	<0.01
Other South American	1	0.01
Other Hispanic or Latino	20	0.12

Race*	Population	%
African-American/Black (24)	68	0.42
Not Hispanic (21)	63	0.39
Hispanic (3)	5	0.03
American Indian/Alaska Native (37)	92	0.57
Not Hispanic (29)	82	0.51
Hispanic (8)	10	0.06
Alaska Athabascan (Ala. Nat.) (0)	0	<0.01
Aleut (Alaska Native) (0)	0	<0.01
Apache (1)	3	0.02
Arapaho (0)	0	<0.01
Blackfeet (0)	2	0.01
Canadian/French Am. Ind. (0)	0	<0.01
Central American Ind. (0)	0	<0.01
Cherokee (12)	35	0.22
Cheyenne (0)	1	0.01
Chickasaw (0)	0	<0.01
Chippewa (1)	2	0.01
Choctaw (0)	4	0.02
Colville (0)	0	<0.01
Comanche (0)	0	<0.01
Cree (0)	0	<0.01
Creek (0)	0	<0.01
Crow (0)	0	<0.01
Delaware (0)	0	<0.01
Hopi (0)	0	<0.01
Houma (0)	0	<0.01
Inupiat (Alaska Native) (0)	0	<0.01
Iroquois (0)	0	<0.01
Kiowa (0)	0	<0.01
Lumbee (0)	0	<0.01
Menominee (0)	0	<0.01
Mexican American Ind. (0)	0	<0.01
Navajo (2)	2	0.01
Osage (1)	1	0.01
Ottawa (0)	0	<0.01
Paiute (0)	0	<0.01
Pima (0)	0	<0.01
Potawatomi (0)	1	0.01
Pueblo (0)	0	<0.01
Puget Sound Salish (0)	0	<0.01
Seminole (0)	0	<0.01
Shoshone (0)	0	<0.01
Sioux (2)	3	0.02
South American Ind. (0)	0	<0.01
Spanish American Ind. (0)	0	<0.01
Tlingit-Haida (Alaska Native) (0)	0	<0.01
Tohono O'Odham (0)	0	<0.01
Tsimshian (Alaska Native) (0)	0	<0.01
Ute (0)	0	<0.01
Yakama (0)	0	<0.01
Yaqui (0)	0	<0.01
Yuman (0)	0	<0.01
Yup'ik (Alaska Native) (0)	0	<0.01
Asian (31)	57	0.35
Not Hispanic (31)	57	0.35
Hispanic (0)	0	<0.01
Bangladeshi (0)	0	<0.01
Bhutanese (0)	0	<0.01
Burmese (0)	0	<0.01
Cambodian (0)	0	<0.01
Chinese, ex. Taiwanese (10)	10	0.06
Filipino (5)	18	0.11
Hmong (0)	0	<0.01
Indian (2)	5	0.03
Indonesian (0)	0	<0.01
Japanese (2)	10	0.06
Korean (3)	8	0.05
Laotian (0)	0	<0.01
Malaysian (0)	0	<0.01
Nepalese (0)	0	<0.01
Pakistani (0)	0	<0.01
Sri Lankan (0)	0	<0.01
Taiwanese (0)	0	<0.01
Thai (4)	5	0.03
Vietnamese (2)	2	0.01
Hawaii Native/Pacific Islander (5)	16	0.10
Not Hispanic (5)	16	0.10
Hispanic (0)	0	<0.01
Fijian (0)	0	<0.01
Guamanian/Chamorro (1)	3	0.02
Marshallese (0)	0	<0.01
Native Hawaiian (2)	7	0.04
Samoan (1)	3	0.02
Tongan (0)	0	<0.01
White (15,932)	16,064	99.09
Not Hispanic (15,862)	15,985	98.60
Hispanic (70)	79	0.49

Notes: † The Census 2010 population figure is used to calculate the percentages in the Hispanic Origin and Race categories. Ancestry percentages are based on the 2006-2010 American Community Survey population (not shown); ‡ Numbers in parentheses indicate the number of people reporting a single ancestry; * Numbers in parentheses indicate the number of persons reporting this race alone, not in combination with any other race; Please refer to the Explanation of Data for more information.

Vigo County

Population: 107,848

Ancestry	Population	%
Afghan (0)	0	<0.01
African, Sub-Saharan (879)	1,024	0.96
African (757)	902	0.84
Cape Verdean (0)	0	<0.01
Ethiopian (0)	0	<0.01
Ghanaian (0)	0	<0.01
Kenyan (0)	0	<0.01
Liberian (0)	0	<0.01
Nigerian (100)	100	0.09
Senegalese (0)	0	<0.01
Sierra Leonean (0)	0	<0.01
Somalian (6)	6	0.01
South African (0)	0	<0.01
Sudanese (0)	0	<0.01
Ugandan (16)	16	0.01
Zimbabwean (0)	0	<0.01
Other Sub-Saharan African (0)	0	<0.01
Albanian (0)	0	<0.01
Alsatian (0)	0	<0.01
American (21,645)	21,645	20.20
Arab (560)	632	0.59
Arab (127)	136	0.13
Egyptian (0)	0	<0.01
Iraqi (0)	0	<0.01
Jordanian (6)	6	0.01
Lebanese (75)	75	0.07
Moroccan (0)	0	<0.01
Palestinian (0)	0	<0.01
Syrian (100)	163	0.15
Other Arab (252)	252	0.24
Armenian (0)	0	<0.01
Assyrian/Chaldean/Syriac (0)	0	<0.01
Australian (0)	0	<0.01
Austrian (36)	190	0.18
Basque (0)	0	<0.01
Belgian (35)	112	0.10
Brazilian (0)	0	<0.01
British (326)	551	0.51
Bulgarian (22)	64	0.06
Cajun (0)	0	<0.01
Canadian (71)	100	0.09
Carpatho Rusyn (0)	0	<0.01
Celtic (0)	0	<0.01
Croatian (51)	85	0.08
Cypriot (0)	0	<0.01
Czech (106)	382	0.36
Czechoslovakian (69)	89	0.08
Danish (41)	81	0.08
Dutch (544)	2,378	2.22
Eastern European (36)	36	0.03
English (4,354)	11,058	10.32
Estonian (0)	0	<0.01
European (935)	1,075	1.00
Finnish (32)	56	0.05
French, ex. Basque (963)	3,480	3.25
French Canadian (75)	160	0.15
German (9,794)	24,242	22.62
German Russian (0)	0	<0.01
Greek (40)	92	0.09
Guyanese (0)	0	<0.01
Hungarian (178)	708	0.66
Icelander (0)	13	0.01
Iranian (0)	2	<0.01
Irish (3,683)	13,045	12.17
Israeli (13)	13	0.01
Italian (1,585)	3,352	3.13
Latvian (69)	118	0.11
Lithuanian (59)	227	0.21
Luxemburger (0)	8	0.01
Macedonian (0)	0	<0.01
Maltese (0)	0	<0.01
New Zealander (0)	0	<0.01
Northern European (8)	11	0.01
Norwegian (218)	513	0.48
Pennsylvania German (14)	51	0.05
Polish (516)	1,905	1.78
Portuguese (0)	12	0.01
Romanian (235)	320	0.30
Russian (35)	301	0.28
Scandinavian (41)	50	0.05
Scotch-Irish (618)	1,739	1.62
Scottish (759)	2,295	2.14
Serbian (24)	98	0.09
Slavic (0)	43	0.04
Slovak (68)	247	0.23
Slovene (37)	37	0.03
Soviet Union (0)	0	<0.01
Swedish (232)	782	0.73
Swiss (65)	246	0.23
Turkish (8)	23	0.02
Ukrainian (133)	133	0.12
Welsh (220)	1,081	1.01
West Indian, ex. Hispanic (27)	32	0.03
Bahamian (0)	0	<0.01
Barbadian (0)	0	<0.01
Belizean (0)	0	<0.01
Bermudan (0)	0	<0.01
British West Indian (0)	0	<0.01
Dutch West Indian (0)	5	<0.01
Haitian (27)	27	0.03
Jamaican (0)	0	<0.01
Trinidadian/Tobagonian (0)	0	<0.01
U.S. Virgin Islander (0)	0	<0.01
West Indian (0)	0	<0.01
Other West Indian (0)	0	<0.01
Yugoslavian (27)	55	0.05

Hispanic Origin	Population	%
Hispanic or Latino (of any race)	2,469	2.29
Central American, ex. Mexican	79	0.07
Costa Rican	5	<0.01
Guatemalan	25	0.02
Honduran	23	0.02
Nicaraguan	2	<0.01
Panamanian	11	0.01
Salvadoran	13	0.01
Other Central American	0	<0.01
Cuban	58	0.05
Dominican Republic	16	0.01
Mexican	1,881	1.74
Puerto Rican	188	0.17
South American	92	0.09
Argentinean	15	0.01
Bolivian	6	0.01
Chilean	8	0.01
Colombian	33	0.03
Ecuadorian	6	0.01
Paraguayan	3	<0.01
Peruvian	8	0.01
Uruguayan	0	<0.01
Venezuelan	13	0.01
Other South American	0	<0.01
Other Hispanic or Latino	155	0.14

Race*	Population	%
African-American/Black (7,437)	8,887	8.24
Not Hispanic (7,371)	8,749	8.11
Hispanic (66)	138	0.13
American Indian/Alaska Native (364)	948	0.88
Not Hispanic (321)	866	0.80
Hispanic (43)	82	0.08
Alaska Athabascan (Ala. Nat.) (2)	2	<0.01
Aleut (Alaska Native) (0)	0	<0.01
Apache (3)	21	0.02
Arapaho (0)	0	<0.01
Blackfeet (3)	39	0.04
Canadian/French Am. Ind. (1)	2	<0.01
Central American Ind. (1)	1	<0.01
Cherokee (52)	233	0.22
Cheyenne (1)	7	0.01
Chickasaw (0)	4	<0.01
Chippewa (9)	14	0.01
Choctaw (3)	9	0.01
Colville (0)	0	<0.01
Comanche (1)	4	<0.01
Cree (8)	9	0.01
Creek (7)	8	0.01
Crow (0)	1	<0.01
Delaware (2)	3	<0.01
Hopi (2)	2	<0.01
Houma (2)	2	<0.01
Inupiat (Alaska Native) (0)	0	<0.01
Iroquois (2)	9	0.01
Kiowa (2)	2	<0.01
Lumbee (0)	2	<0.01
Menominee (2)	2	<0.01
Mexican American Ind. (17)	25	0.02
Navajo (1)	7	0.01
Osage (4)	4	<0.01
Ottawa (1)	1	<0.01
Paiute (0)	0	<0.01
Pima (0)	0	<0.01
Potawatomi (13)	15	0.01
Pueblo (0)	0	<0.01
Puget Sound Salish (0)	0	<0.01
Seminole (0)	2	<0.01
Shoshone (1)	2	<0.01
Sioux (18)	43	0.04
South American Ind. (1)	1	<0.01
Spanish American Ind. (0)	0	<0.01
Tlingit-Haida (Alaska Native) (0)	1	<0.01
Tohono O'Odham (0)	0	<0.01
Tsimshian (Alaska Native) (0)	0	<0.01
Ute (1)	1	<0.01
Yakama (0)	0	<0.01
Yaqui (0)	3	<0.01
Yuman (2)	2	<0.01
Yup'ik (Alaska Native) (0)	0	<0.01
Asian (1,781)	2,173	2.01
Not Hispanic (1,777)	2,159	2.00
Hispanic (4)	14	0.01
Bangladeshi (12)	12	0.01
Bhutanese (0)	0	<0.01
Burmese (0)	0	<0.01
Cambodian (1)	1	<0.01
Chinese, ex. Taiwanese (346)	395	0.37
Filipino (277)	368	0.34
Hmong (6)	8	0.01
Indian (553)	605	0.56
Indonesian (7)	10	0.01
Japanese (123)	204	0.19
Korean (182)	230	0.21
Laotian (0)	5	<0.01
Malaysian (3)	14	0.01
Nepalese (15)	15	0.01
Pakistani (17)	24	0.02
Sri Lankan (0)	1	<0.01
Taiwanese (57)	62	0.06
Thai (15)	17	0.02
Vietnamese (95)	113	0.10
Hawaii Native/Pacific Islander (36)	112	0.10
Not Hispanic (32)	106	0.10
Hispanic (4)	6	0.01
Fijian (0)	0	<0.01
Guamanian/Chamorro (9)	12	0.01
Marshallese (1)	4	<0.01
Native Hawaiian (15)	64	0.06
Samoan (5)	16	0.01
Tongan (0)	2	<0.01
White (95,207)	97,436	90.35
Not Hispanic (93,550)	95,591	88.63
Hispanic (1,657)	1,845	1.71

Notes: † The Census 2010 population figure is used to calculate the percentages in the Hispanic Origin and Race categories. Ancestry percentages are based on the 2006-2010 American Community Survey population (not shown); ‡ Numbers in parentheses indicate the number of people reporting a single ancestry; * Numbers in parentheses indicate the number of persons reporting this race alone, not in combination with any other race; Please refer to the Explanation of Data for more information.

Wabash County
Population: 32,888

Ancestry	Population	%
Afghan (0)	0	<0.01
African, Sub-Saharan (67)	73	0.22
African (39)	45	0.14
Cape Verdean (0)	0	<0.01
Ethiopian (0)	0	<0.01
Ghanaian (0)	0	<0.01
Kenyan (0)	0	<0.01
Liberian (0)	0	<0.01
Nigerian (0)	0	<0.01
Senegalese (0)	0	<0.01
Sierra Leonean (0)	0	<0.01
Somalian (11)	11	0.03
South African (0)	0	<0.01
Sudanese (0)	0	<0.01
Ugandan (17)	17	0.05
Zimbabwean (0)	0	<0.01
Other Sub-Saharan African (0)	0	<0.01
Albanian (0)	0	<0.01
Alsatian (0)	0	<0.01
American (6,017)	6,017	18.11
Arab (0)	0	<0.01
Arab (0)	0	<0.01
Egyptian (0)	0	<0.01
Iraqi (0)	0	<0.01
Jordanian (0)	0	<0.01
Lebanese (0)	0	<0.01
Moroccan (0)	0	<0.01
Palestinian (0)	0	<0.01
Syrian (0)	0	<0.01
Other Arab (0)	0	<0.01
Armenian (0)	0	<0.01
Assyrian/Chaldean/Syriac (0)	0	<0.01
Australian (0)	0	<0.01
Austrian (27)	41	0.12
Basque (0)	0	<0.01
Belgian (11)	41	0.12
Brazilian (0)	0	<0.01
British (30)	128	0.39
Bulgarian (18)	18	0.05
Cajun (0)	0	<0.01
Canadian (21)	29	0.09
Carpatho Rusyn (0)	0	<0.01
Celtic (0)	0	<0.01
Croatian (0)	13	0.04
Cypriot (0)	0	<0.01
Czech (53)	58	0.17
Czechoslovakian (40)	40	0.12
Danish (7)	18	0.05
Dutch (267)	928	2.79
Eastern European (0)	0	<0.01
English (1,313)	3,342	10.06
Estonian (0)	0	<0.01
European (187)	192	0.58
Finnish (0)	0	<0.01
French, ex. Basque (173)	712	2.14
French Canadian (24)	35	0.11
German (5,604)	10,394	31.28
German Russian (0)	0	<0.01
Greek (9)	20	0.06
Guyanese (0)	0	<0.01
Hungarian (27)	45	0.14
Icelander (0)	0	<0.01
Iranian (0)	0	<0.01
Irish (1,038)	3,323	10.00
Israeli (0)	0	<0.01
Italian (180)	450	1.35
Latvian (0)	0	<0.01
Lithuanian (0)	0	<0.01
Luxemburger (0)	0	<0.01
Macedonian (0)	0	<0.01
Maltese (0)	0	<0.01
New Zealander (0)	0	<0.01
Northern European (39)	39	0.12
Norwegian (76)	99	0.30
Pennsylvania German (63)	76	0.23
Polish (157)	344	1.04
Portuguese (0)	0	<0.01
Romanian (0)	0	<0.01
Russian (0)	7	0.02
Scandinavian (0)	37	0.11
Scotch-Irish (196)	451	1.36
Scottish (172)	574	1.73
Serbian (4)	12	0.04
Slavic (0)	0	<0.01
Slovak (9)	36	0.11
Slovene (0)	0	<0.01
Soviet Union (0)	0	<0.01
Swedish (66)	141	0.42
Swiss (66)	146	0.44
Turkish (0)	0	<0.01
Ukrainian (25)	25	0.08
Welsh (26)	206	0.62
West Indian, ex. Hispanic (32)	32	0.10
Bahamian (0)	0	<0.01
Barbadian (0)	0	<0.01
Belizean (0)	0	<0.01
Bermudan (0)	0	<0.01
British West Indian (0)	0	<0.01
Dutch West Indian (15)	15	0.05
Haitian (10)	10	0.03
Jamaican (0)	0	<0.01
Trinidadian/Tobagonian (0)	0	<0.01
U.S. Virgin Islander (0)	0	<0.01
West Indian (7)	7	0.02
Other West Indian (0)	0	<0.01
Yugoslavian (0)	0	<0.01

Hispanic Origin	Population	%
Hispanic or Latino (of any race)	697	2.12
Central American, ex. Mexican	13	0.04
Costa Rican	1	<0.01
Guatemalan	10	0.03
Honduran	1	<0.01
Nicaraguan	0	<0.01
Panamanian	0	<0.01
Salvadoran	1	<0.01
Other Central American	0	<0.01
Cuban	8	0.02
Dominican Republic	0	<0.01
Mexican	584	1.78
Puerto Rican	29	0.09
South American	15	0.05
Argentinean	0	<0.01
Bolivian	2	0.01
Chilean	0	<0.01
Colombian	8	0.02
Ecuadorian	0	<0.01
Paraguayan	0	<0.01
Peruvian	1	<0.01
Uruguayan	0	<0.01
Venezuelan	4	0.01
Other South American	0	<0.01
Other Hispanic or Latino	48	0.15

Race*	Population	%
African-American/Black (163)	272	0.83
Not Hispanic (155)	258	0.78
Hispanic (8)	14	0.04
American Indian/Alaska Native (217)	396	1.20
Not Hispanic (211)	377	1.15
Hispanic (6)	19	0.06
Alaska Athabascan (Ala. Nat.) (0)	0	<0.01
Aleut (Alaska Native) (0)	0	<0.01
Apache (3)	3	0.01
Arapaho (0)	0	<0.01
Blackfeet (1)	8	0.02
Canadian/French Am. Ind. (0)	1	<0.01
Central American Ind. (1)	1	<0.01
Cherokee (21)	69	0.21
Cheyenne (0)	0	<0.01
Chickasaw (0)	0	<0.01
Chippewa (2)	2	0.01
Choctaw (6)	7	0.02
Colville (0)	0	<0.01
Comanche (1)	1	<0.01
Cree (0)	0	<0.01
Creek (3)	3	0.01
Crow (0)	1	<0.01
Delaware (0)	0	<0.01
Hopi (0)	0	<0.01
Houma (1)	3	0.01
Inupiat (Alaska Native) (0)	0	<0.01
Iroquois (2)	4	0.01
Kiowa (0)	2	0.01
Lumbee (0)	0	<0.01
Menominee (1)	1	<0.01
Mexican American Ind. (2)	5	0.02
Navajo (1)	3	0.01
Osage (1)	2	0.01
Ottawa (0)	0	<0.01
Paiute (0)	0	<0.01
Pima (0)	0	<0.01
Potawatomi (0)	2	0.01
Pueblo (2)	2	0.01
Puget Sound Salish (0)	0	<0.01
Seminole (0)	0	<0.01
Shoshone (0)	0	<0.01
Sioux (4)	6	0.02
South American Ind. (0)	2	0.01
Spanish American Ind. (0)	0	<0.01
Tlingit-Haida (Alaska Native) (0)	0	<0.01
Tohono O'Odham (0)	0	<0.01
Tsimshian (Alaska Native) (0)	0	<0.01
Ute (0)	0	<0.01
Yakama (0)	0	<0.01
Yaqui (0)	0	<0.01
Yuman (0)	2	0.01
Yup'ik (Alaska Native) (0)	0	<0.01
Asian (138)	179	0.54
Not Hispanic (134)	172	0.52
Hispanic (4)	7	0.02
Bangladeshi (0)	0	<0.01
Bhutanese (0)	0	<0.01
Burmese (3)	3	0.01
Cambodian (7)	7	0.02
Chinese, ex. Taiwanese (18)	19	0.06
Filipino (23)	37	0.11
Hmong (0)	0	<0.01
Indian (32)	36	0.11
Indonesian (0)	0	<0.01
Japanese (12)	18	0.05
Korean (18)	22	0.07
Laotian (12)	15	0.05
Malaysian (0)	0	<0.01
Nepalese (0)	0	<0.01
Pakistani (0)	0	<0.01
Sri Lankan (1)	1	<0.01
Taiwanese (4)	4	0.01
Thai (4)	4	0.01
Vietnamese (3)	8	0.02
Hawaii Native/Pacific Islander (6)	17	0.05
Not Hispanic (6)	15	0.05
Hispanic (0)	2	0.01
Fijian (0)	0	<0.01
Guamanian/Chamorro (2)	4	0.01
Marshallese (1)	1	<0.01
Native Hawaiian (1)	2	0.01
Samoan (2)	5	0.02
Tongan (0)	0	<0.01
White (31,764)	32,112	97.64
Not Hispanic (31,369)	31,668	96.29
Hispanic (395)	444	1.35

Notes: † The Census 2010 population figure is used to calculate the percentages in the Hispanic Origin and Race categories. Ancestry percentages are based on the 2006-2010 American Community Survey population (not shown); ‡ Numbers in parentheses indicate the number of people reporting a single ancestry; * Numbers in parentheses indicate the number of persons reporting this race alone, not in combination with any other race; Please refer to the Explanation of Data for more information.

Warren County
Population: 8,508

Ancestry	Population	%
Afghan (0)	0	<0.01
African, Sub-Saharan (0)	0	<0.01
African (0)	0	<0.01
Cape Verdean (0)	0	<0.01
Ethiopian (0)	0	<0.01
Ghanaian (0)	0	<0.01
Kenyan (0)	0	<0.01
Liberian (0)	0	<0.01
Nigerian (0)	0	<0.01
Senegalese (0)	0	<0.01
Sierra Leonean (0)	0	<0.01
Somalian (0)	0	<0.01
South African (0)	0	<0.01
Sudanese (0)	0	<0.01
Ugandan (0)	0	<0.01
Zimbabwean (0)	0	<0.01
Other Sub-Saharan African (0)	0	<0.01
Albanian (0)	0	<0.01
Alsatian (0)	0	<0.01
American (789)	789	9.21
Arab (0)	0	<0.01
Arab (0)	0	<0.01
Egyptian (0)	0	<0.01
Iraqi (0)	0	<0.01
Jordanian (0)	0	<0.01
Lebanese (0)	0	<0.01
Moroccan (0)	0	<0.01
Palestinian (0)	0	<0.01
Syrian (0)	0	<0.01
Other Arab (0)	0	<0.01
Armenian (0)	0	<0.01
Assyrian/Chaldean/Syriac (0)	0	<0.01
Australian (3)	3	0.04
Austrian (0)	9	0.11
Basque (0)	0	<0.01
Belgian (0)	12	0.14
Brazilian (0)	0	<0.01
British (0)	14	0.16
Bulgarian (0)	0	<0.01
Cajun (0)	0	<0.01
Canadian (12)	15	0.18
Carpatho Rusyn (0)	0	<0.01
Celtic (0)	0	<0.01
Croatian (0)	0	<0.01
Cypriot (0)	0	<0.01
Czech (2)	4	0.05
Czechoslovakian (0)	0	<0.01
Danish (0)	48	0.56
Dutch (72)	398	4.65
Eastern European (0)	0	<0.01
English (471)	968	11.30
Estonian (0)	0	<0.01
European (27)	64	0.75
Finnish (0)	0	<0.01
French, ex. Basque (36)	202	2.36
French Canadian (7)	7	0.08
German (902)	2,368	27.65
German Russian (0)	0	<0.01
Greek (0)	0	<0.01
Guyanese (0)	0	<0.01
Hungarian (0)	0	<0.01
Icelander (0)	0	<0.01
Iranian (0)	0	<0.01
Irish (158)	934	10.91
Israeli (0)	0	<0.01
Italian (16)	85	0.99
Latvian (0)	0	<0.01
Lithuanian (3)	3	0.04
Luxemburger (0)	0	<0.01
Macedonian (0)	0	<0.01
Maltese (0)	0	<0.01
New Zealander (0)	0	<0.01
Northern European (9)	15	0.18
Norwegian (15)	36	0.42
Pennsylvania German (0)	0	<0.01
Polish (103)	177	2.07
Portuguese (26)	26	0.30
Romanian (0)	0	<0.01
Russian (0)	0	<0.01
Scandinavian (0)	0	<0.01
Scotch-Irish (99)	141	1.65
Scottish (141)	264	3.08
Serbian (0)	0	<0.01
Slavic (0)	0	<0.01
Slovak (0)	0	<0.01
Slovene (0)	0	<0.01
Soviet Union (0)	0	<0.01
Swedish (65)	202	2.36
Swiss (10)	11	0.13
Turkish (0)	0	<0.01
Ukrainian (0)	0	<0.01
Welsh (1)	54	0.63
West Indian, ex. Hispanic (0)	0	<0.01
Bahamian (0)	0	<0.01
Barbadian (0)	0	<0.01
Belizean (0)	0	<0.01
Bermudan (0)	0	<0.01
British West Indian (0)	0	<0.01
Dutch West Indian (0)	0	<0.01
Haitian (0)	0	<0.01
Jamaican (0)	0	<0.01
Trinidadian/Tobagonian (0)	0	<0.01
U.S. Virgin Islander (0)	0	<0.01
West Indian (0)	0	<0.01
Other West Indian (0)	0	<0.01
Yugoslavian (0)	0	<0.01

Hispanic Origin	Population	%
Hispanic or Latino (of any race)	70	0.82
Central American, ex. Mexican	0	<0.01
Costa Rican	0	<0.01
Guatemalan	0	<0.01
Honduran	0	<0.01
Nicaraguan	0	<0.01
Panamanian	0	<0.01
Salvadoran	0	<0.01
Other Central American	0	<0.01
Cuban	1	0.01
Dominican Republic	0	<0.01
Mexican	47	0.55
Puerto Rican	7	0.08
South American	5	0.06
Argentinean	0	<0.01
Bolivian	0	<0.01
Chilean	0	<0.01
Colombian	3	0.04
Ecuadorian	0	<0.01
Paraguayan	0	<0.01
Peruvian	0	<0.01
Uruguayan	0	<0.01
Venezuelan	0	<0.01
Other South American	2	0.02
Other Hispanic or Latino	10	0.12

Race*	Population	%
African-American/Black (11)	27	0.32
Not Hispanic (10)	26	0.31
Hispanic (1)	1	0.01
American Indian/Alaska Native (13)	35	0.41
Not Hispanic (13)	35	0.41
Hispanic (0)	0	<0.01
Alaska Athabascan (Ala. Nat.) (0)	0	<0.01
Aleut (Alaska Native) (4)	4	0.05
Apache (0)	0	<0.01
Arapaho (0)	0	<0.01
Blackfeet (0)	0	<0.01
Canadian/French Am. Ind. (0)	0	<0.01
Central American Ind. (0)	0	<0.01
Cherokee (5)	19	0.22
Cheyenne (0)	0	<0.01
Chickasaw (0)	0	<0.01
Chippewa (0)	0	<0.01
Choctaw (0)	0	<0.01
Colville (0)	0	<0.01
Comanche (0)	0	<0.01
Cree (0)	0	<0.01
Creek (0)	0	<0.01
Crow (0)	0	<0.01
Delaware (0)	0	<0.01
Hopi (0)	0	<0.01
Houma (0)	0	<0.01
Inupiat (Alaska Native) (1)	1	0.01
Iroquois (0)	0	<0.01
Kiowa (0)	0	<0.01
Lumbee (0)	0	<0.01
Menominee (0)	0	<0.01
Mexican American Ind. (0)	0	<0.01
Navajo (0)	0	<0.01
Osage (0)	2	0.02
Ottawa (0)	0	<0.01
Paiute (0)	0	<0.01
Pima (0)	0	<0.01
Potawatomi (0)	0	<0.01
Pueblo (0)	0	<0.01
Puget Sound Salish (0)	0	<0.01
Seminole (0)	0	<0.01
Shoshone (0)	0	<0.01
Sioux (0)	0	<0.01
South American Ind. (0)	0	<0.01
Spanish American Ind. (0)	0	<0.01
Tlingit-Haida (Alaska Native) (0)	0	<0.01
Tohono O'Odham (0)	0	<0.01
Tsimshian (Alaska Native) (0)	0	<0.01
Ute (0)	0	<0.01
Yakama (0)	0	<0.01
Yaqui (0)	0	<0.01
Yuman (0)	0	<0.01
Yup'ik (Alaska Native) (0)	0	<0.01
Asian (36)	48	0.56
Not Hispanic (36)	47	0.55
Hispanic (0)	1	0.01
Bangladeshi (0)	0	<0.01
Bhutanese (0)	0	<0.01
Burmese (0)	0	<0.01
Cambodian (0)	0	<0.01
Chinese, ex. Taiwanese (2)	2	0.02
Filipino (11)	15	0.18
Hmong (0)	0	<0.01
Indian (8)	10	0.12
Indonesian (0)	0	<0.01
Japanese (4)	5	0.06
Korean (0)	2	0.02
Laotian (0)	0	<0.01
Malaysian (0)	0	<0.01
Nepalese (0)	0	<0.01
Pakistani (0)	0	<0.01
Sri Lankan (0)	0	<0.01
Taiwanese (0)	0	<0.01
Thai (4)	5	0.06
Vietnamese (6)	6	0.07
Hawaii Native/Pacific Islander (6)	7	0.08
Not Hispanic (6)	7	0.08
Hispanic (0)	0	<0.01
Fijian (0)	0	<0.01
Guamanian/Chamorro (0)	0	<0.01
Marshallese (0)	0	<0.01
Native Hawaiian (2)	2	0.02
Samoan (4)	4	0.05
Tongan (0)	0	<0.01
White (8,363)	8,420	98.97
Not Hispanic (8,321)	8,369	98.37
Hispanic (42)	51	0.60

Notes: † The Census 2010 population figure is used to calculate the percentages in the Hispanic Origin and Race categories. Ancestry percentages are based on the 2006-2010 American Community Survey population (not shown); ‡ Numbers in parentheses indicate the number of people reporting a single ancestry; * Numbers in parentheses indicate the number of persons reporting this race alone, not in combination with any other race; Please refer to the Explanation of Data for more information.

Warrick County
Population: 59,689

Ancestry	Population	%
Afghan (0)	0	<0.01
African, Sub-Saharan (112)	130	0.22
African (21)	39	0.07
Cape Verdean (0)	0	<0.01
Ethiopian (0)	0	<0.01
Ghanaian (0)	0	<0.01
Kenyan (0)	0	<0.01
Liberian (0)	0	<0.01
Nigerian (91)	91	0.16
Senegalese (0)	0	<0.01
Sierra Leonean (0)	0	<0.01
Somalian (0)	0	<0.01
South African (0)	0	<0.01
Sudanese (0)	0	<0.01
Ugandan (0)	0	<0.01
Zimbabwean (0)	0	<0.01
Other Sub-Saharan African (0)	0	<0.01
Albanian (0)	0	<0.01
Alsatian (0)	0	<0.01
American (7,842)	7,842	13.43
Arab (80)	102	0.17
Arab (0)	0	<0.01
Egyptian (53)	53	0.09
Iraqi (0)	0	<0.01
Jordanian (0)	0	<0.01
Lebanese (17)	17	0.03
Moroccan (0)	0	<0.01
Palestinian (0)	0	<0.01
Syrian (10)	32	0.05
Other Arab (0)	0	<0.01
Armenian (0)	0	<0.01
Assyrian/Chaldean/Syriac (0)	0	<0.01
Australian (0)	0	<0.01
Austrian (37)	49	0.08
Basque (0)	0	<0.01
Belgian (13)	136	0.23
Brazilian (39)	85	0.15
British (82)	210	0.36
Bulgarian (15)	45	0.08
Cajun (0)	0	<0.01
Canadian (82)	91	0.16
Carpatho Rusyn (0)	0	<0.01
Celtic (0)	0	<0.01
Croatian (5)	5	0.01
Cypriot (0)	0	<0.01
Czech (35)	110	0.19
Czechoslovakian (9)	32	0.05
Danish (0)	141	0.24
Dutch (212)	1,030	1.76
Eastern European (0)	0	<0.01
English (2,828)	7,311	12.52
Estonian (0)	0	<0.01
European (436)	501	0.86
Finnish (23)	51	0.09
French, ex. Basque (385)	2,146	3.68
French Canadian (52)	109	0.19
German (10,375)	20,598	35.27
German Russian (0)	0	<0.01
Greek (27)	27	0.05
Guyanese (0)	0	<0.01
Hungarian (23)	160	0.27
Icelander (0)	0	<0.01
Iranian (20)	62	0.11
Irish (2,323)	9,014	15.44
Israeli (8)	8	0.01
Italian (283)	1,227	2.10
Latvian (0)	0	<0.01
Lithuanian (5)	31	0.05
Luxemburger (9)	9	0.02
Macedonian (0)	0	<0.01
Maltese (0)	0	<0.01
New Zealander (0)	0	<0.01
Northern European (0)	0	<0.01
Norwegian (50)	208	0.36
Pennsylvania German (0)	22	0.04
Polish (598)	1,145	1.96
Portuguese (0)	11	0.02
Romanian (12)	25	0.04
Russian (164)	211	0.36
Scandinavian (9)	59	0.10
Scotch-Irish (342)	843	1.44
Scottish (520)	1,857	3.18
Serbian (105)	105	0.18
Slavic (0)	0	<0.01
Slovak (0)	63	0.11
Slovene (0)	0	<0.01
Soviet Union (0)	0	<0.01
Swedish (81)	306	0.52
Swiss (50)	129	0.22
Turkish (0)	0	<0.01
Ukrainian (60)	184	0.32
Welsh (72)	370	0.63
West Indian, ex. Hispanic (0)	18	0.03
Bahamian (0)	18	0.03
Barbadian (0)	0	<0.01
Belizean (0)	0	<0.01
Bermudan (0)	0	<0.01
British West Indian (0)	0	<0.01
Dutch West Indian (0)	0	<0.01
Haitian (0)	0	<0.01
Jamaican (0)	0	<0.01
Trinidadian/Tobagonian (0)	0	<0.01
U.S. Virgin Islander (0)	0	<0.01
West Indian (0)	0	<0.01
Other West Indian (0)	0	<0.01
Yugoslavian (0)	0	<0.01

Hispanic Origin	Population	%
Hispanic or Latino (of any race)	946	1.58
Central American, ex. Mexican	60	0.10
Costa Rican	5	0.01
Guatemalan	23	0.04
Honduran	7	0.01
Nicaraguan	6	0.01
Panamanian	5	0.01
Salvadoran	14	0.02
Other Central American	0	<0.01
Cuban	28	0.05
Dominican Republic	6	0.01
Mexican	536	0.90
Puerto Rican	105	0.18
South American	86	0.14
Argentinean	3	0.01
Bolivian	0	<0.01
Chilean	11	0.02
Colombian	23	0.04
Ecuadorian	9	0.02
Paraguayan	0	<0.01
Peruvian	23	0.04
Uruguayan	0	<0.01
Venezuelan	17	0.03
Other South American	0	<0.01
Other Hispanic or Latino	125	0.21

Race*	Population	%
African-American/Black (803)	1,148	1.92
Not Hispanic (780)	1,102	1.85
Hispanic (23)	46	0.08
American Indian/Alaska Native (124)	361	0.60
Not Hispanic (98)	330	0.55
Hispanic (26)	31	0.05
Alaska Athabascan (Ala. Nat.) (0)	0	<0.01
Aleut (Alaska Native) (1)	1	<0.01
Apache (1)	3	0.01
Arapaho (0)	0	<0.01
Blackfeet (2)	9	0.02
Canadian/French Am. Ind. (2)	9	0.02
Central American Ind. (0)	2	<0.01
Cherokee (30)	128	0.21
Cheyenne (0)	1	<0.01
Chickasaw (3)	4	0.01
Chippewa (2)	6	0.01
Choctaw (9)	12	0.02
Colville (0)	0	<0.01
Comanche (1)	2	<0.01
Cree (0)	0	<0.01
Creek (1)	2	<0.01
Crow (0)	3	0.01
Delaware (0)	0	<0.01
Hopi (1)	2	<0.01
Houma (0)	0	<0.01
Inupiat (Alaska Native) (0)	0	<0.01
Iroquois (3)	6	0.01
Kiowa (0)	0	<0.01
Lumbee (0)	0	<0.01
Menominee (0)	0	<0.01
Mexican American Ind. (7)	8	0.01
Navajo (1)	5	0.01
Osage (0)	0	<0.01
Ottawa (0)	0	<0.01
Paiute (0)	0	<0.01
Pima (0)	0	<0.01
Potawatomi (5)	6	0.01
Pueblo (0)	3	0.01
Puget Sound Salish (0)	0	<0.01
Seminole (3)	4	0.01
Shoshone (0)	0	<0.01
Sioux (2)	2	<0.01
South American Ind. (0)	0	<0.01
Spanish American Ind. (0)	0	<0.01
Tlingit-Haida (Alaska Native) (1)	1	<0.01
Tohono O'Odham (0)	0	<0.01
Tsimshian (Alaska Native) (0)	0	<0.01
Ute (0)	0	<0.01
Yakama (0)	0	<0.01
Yaqui (1)	1	<0.01
Yuman (0)	0	<0.01
Yup'ik (Alaska Native) (0)	0	<0.01
Asian (960)	1,178	1.97
Not Hispanic (957)	1,169	1.96
Hispanic (3)	9	0.02
Bangladeshi (0)	2	<0.01
Bhutanese (0)	0	<0.01
Burmese (4)	4	0.01
Cambodian (1)	1	<0.01
Chinese, ex. Taiwanese (121)	145	0.24
Filipino (132)	212	0.36
Hmong (0)	0	<0.01
Indian (354)	383	0.64
Indonesian (2)	6	0.01
Japanese (67)	100	0.17
Korean (67)	89	0.15
Laotian (0)	0	<0.01
Malaysian (0)	0	<0.01
Nepalese (11)	12	0.02
Pakistani (64)	68	0.11
Sri Lankan (0)	1	<0.01
Taiwanese (3)	4	0.01
Thai (12)	17	0.03
Vietnamese (85)	99	0.17
Hawaii Native/Pacific Islander (18)	35	0.06
Not Hispanic (18)	33	0.06
Hispanic (0)	2	<0.01
Fijian (1)	1	<0.01
Guamanian/Chamorro (5)	8	0.01
Marshallese (2)	2	<0.01
Native Hawaiian (6)	15	0.03
Samoan (1)	2	<0.01
Tongan (0)	0	<0.01
White (56,700)	57,454	96.26
Not Hispanic (56,095)	56,799	95.16
Hispanic (605)	655	1.10

Notes: † The Census 2010 population figure is used to calculate the percentages in the Hispanic Origin and Race categories. Ancestry percentages are based on the 2006-2010 American Community Survey population (not shown); ‡ Numbers in parentheses indicate the number of people reporting a single ancestry; * Numbers in parentheses indicate the number of persons reporting this race alone, not in combination with any other race; Please refer to the Explanation of Data for more information.

Washington County
Population: 28,262

Ancestry	Population	%
Afghan (0)	0	<0.01
African, Sub-Saharan (0)	0	<0.01
African (0)	0	<0.01
Cape Verdean (0)	0	<0.01
Ethiopian (0)	0	<0.01
Ghanaian (0)	0	<0.01
Kenyan (0)	0	<0.01
Liberian (0)	0	<0.01
Nigerian (0)	0	<0.01
Senegalese (0)	0	<0.01
Sierra Leonean (0)	0	<0.01
Somalian (0)	0	<0.01
South African (0)	0	<0.01
Sudanese (0)	0	<0.01
Ugandan (0)	0	<0.01
Zimbabwean (0)	0	<0.01
Other Sub-Saharan African (0)	0	<0.01
Albanian (0)	0	<0.01
Alsatian (0)	0	<0.01
American (4,023)	4,023	14.25
Arab (0)	18	0.06
Arab (0)	0	<0.01
Egyptian (0)	18	0.06
Iraqi (0)	0	<0.01
Jordanian (0)	0	<0.01
Lebanese (0)	0	<0.01
Moroccan (0)	0	<0.01
Palestinian (0)	0	<0.01
Syrian (0)	0	<0.01
Other Arab (0)	0	<0.01
Armenian (0)	0	<0.01
Assyrian/Chaldean/Syriac (0)	0	<0.01
Australian (0)	0	<0.01
Austrian (0)	0	<0.01
Basque (0)	0	<0.01
Belgian (0)	2	0.01
Brazilian (0)	0	<0.01
British (40)	64	0.23
Bulgarian (0)	0	<0.01
Cajun (0)	10	0.04
Canadian (11)	11	0.04
Carpatho Rusyn (0)	0	<0.01
Celtic (0)	0	<0.01
Croatian (0)	0	<0.01
Cypriot (0)	0	<0.01
Czech (0)	0	<0.01
Czechoslovakian (5)	5	0.02
Danish (9)	16	0.06
Dutch (293)	577	2.04
Eastern European (7)	14	0.05
English (1,504)	2,714	9.62
Estonian (0)	0	<0.01
European (116)	116	0.41
Finnish (25)	25	0.09
French, ex. Basque (97)	637	2.26
French Canadian (0)	30	0.11
German (3,234)	7,109	25.19
German Russian (0)	0	<0.01
Greek (12)	20	0.07
Guyanese (0)	0	<0.01
Hungarian (10)	10	0.04
Icelander (0)	0	<0.01
Iranian (0)	0	<0.01
Irish (1,401)	3,854	13.65
Israeli (0)	0	<0.01
Italian (114)	290	1.03
Latvian (0)	0	<0.01
Lithuanian (0)	0	<0.01
Luxemburger (0)	0	<0.01
Macedonian (0)	0	<0.01
Maltese (0)	0	<0.01
New Zealander (0)	0	<0.01
Northern European (0)	0	<0.01
Norwegian (2)	4	0.01
Pennsylvania German (167)	167	0.59
Polish (37)	146	0.52
Portuguese (0)	0	<0.01
Romanian (0)	8	0.03
Russian (22)	111	0.39
Scandinavian (0)	38	0.13
Scotch-Irish (224)	581	2.06
Scottish (299)	572	2.03
Serbian (0)	0	<0.01
Slavic (0)	0	<0.01
Slovak (0)	0	<0.01
Slovene (0)	0	<0.01
Soviet Union (0)	0	<0.01
Swedish (32)	97	0.34
Swiss (36)	135	0.48
Turkish (0)	0	<0.01
Ukrainian (0)	0	<0.01
Welsh (16)	242	0.86
West Indian, ex. Hispanic (0)	0	<0.01
Bahamian (0)	0	<0.01
Barbadian (0)	0	<0.01
Belizean (0)	0	<0.01
Bermudan (0)	0	<0.01
British West Indian (0)	0	<0.01
Dutch West Indian (0)	0	<0.01
Haitian (0)	0	<0.01
Jamaican (0)	0	<0.01
Trinidadian/Tobagonian (0)	0	<0.01
U.S. Virgin Islander (0)	0	<0.01
West Indian (0)	0	<0.01
Other West Indian (0)	0	<0.01
Yugoslavian (0)	0	<0.01

Hispanic Origin	Population	%
Hispanic or Latino (of any race)	304	1.08
Central American, ex. Mexican	5	0.02
Costa Rican	0	<0.01
Guatemalan	1	<0.01
Honduran	0	<0.01
Nicaraguan	0	<0.01
Panamanian	0	<0.01
Salvadoran	3	0.01
Other Central American	1	<0.01
Cuban	8	0.03
Dominican Republic	0	<0.01
Mexican	215	0.76
Puerto Rican	39	0.14
South American	4	0.01
Argentinean	0	<0.01
Bolivian	0	<0.01
Chilean	0	<0.01
Colombian	0	<0.01
Ecuadorian	0	<0.01
Paraguayan	0	<0.01
Peruvian	4	0.01
Uruguayan	0	<0.01
Venezuelan	0	<0.01
Other South American	0	<0.01
Other Hispanic or Latino	33	0.12

Race*	Population	%
African-American/Black (64)	111	0.39
Not Hispanic (63)	106	0.38
Hispanic (1)	5	0.02
American Indian/Alaska Native (62)	188	0.67
Not Hispanic (45)	159	0.56
Hispanic (17)	29	0.10
Alaska Athabascan (Ala. Nat.) (0)	0	<0.01
Aleut (Alaska Native) (0)	0	<0.01
Apache (2)	12	0.04
Arapaho (0)	0	<0.01
Blackfeet (1)	3	0.01
Canadian/French Am. Ind. (2)	3	0.01
Central American Ind. (0)	0	<0.01
Cherokee (14)	72	0.25
Cheyenne (2)	3	0.01
Chickasaw (0)	5	0.02
Chippewa (0)	1	<0.01
Choctaw (1)	5	0.02
Colville (0)	0	<0.01
Comanche (2)	3	0.01
Cree (0)	0	<0.01
Creek (0)	0	<0.01
Crow (0)	0	<0.01
Delaware (0)	1	<0.01
Hopi (0)	0	<0.01
Houma (0)	0	<0.01
Inupiat (Alaska Native) (0)	0	<0.01
Iroquois (0)	1	<0.01
Kiowa (0)	1	<0.01
Lumbee (0)	0	<0.01
Menominee (0)	0	<0.01
Mexican American Ind. (0)	1	<0.01
Navajo (1)	1	<0.01
Osage (0)	1	<0.01
Ottawa (1)	1	<0.01
Paiute (0)	0	<0.01
Pima (0)	0	<0.01
Potawatomi (0)	0	<0.01
Pueblo (0)	0	<0.01
Puget Sound Salish (2)	2	0.01
Seminole (0)	0	<0.01
Shoshone (0)	0	<0.01
Sioux (4)	9	0.03
South American Ind. (0)	0	<0.01
Spanish American Ind. (0)	0	<0.01
Tlingit-Haida (Alaska Native) (0)	0	<0.01
Tohono O'Odham (0)	0	<0.01
Tsimshian (Alaska Native) (0)	0	<0.01
Ute (0)	0	<0.01
Yakama (0)	0	<0.01
Yaqui (0)	0	<0.01
Yuman (0)	0	<0.01
Yup'ik (Alaska Native) (0)	0	<0.01
Asian (86)	128	0.45
Not Hispanic (86)	125	0.44
Hispanic (0)	3	0.01
Bangladeshi (0)	0	<0.01
Bhutanese (0)	0	<0.01
Burmese (0)	0	<0.01
Cambodian (1)	2	0.01
Chinese, ex. Taiwanese (14)	17	0.06
Filipino (24)	51	0.18
Hmong (0)	0	<0.01
Indian (2)	5	0.02
Indonesian (0)	0	<0.01
Japanese (11)	16	0.06
Korean (4)	5	0.02
Laotian (0)	0	<0.01
Malaysian (0)	0	<0.01
Nepalese (0)	0	<0.01
Pakistani (0)	0	<0.01
Sri Lankan (0)	0	<0.01
Taiwanese (0)	0	<0.01
Thai (10)	16	0.06
Vietnamese (10)	11	0.04
Hawaii Native/Pacific Islander (2)	6	0.02
Not Hispanic (2)	6	0.02
Hispanic (0)	0	<0.01
Fijian (0)	0	<0.01
Guamanian/Chamorro (0)	0	<0.01
Marshallese (0)	0	<0.01
Native Hawaiian (1)	2	0.01
Samoan (0)	0	<0.01
Tongan (0)	0	<0.01
White (27,714)	27,954	98.91
Not Hispanic (27,539)	27,736	98.14
Hispanic (175)	218	0.77

Notes: † The Census 2010 population figure is used to calculate the percentages in the Hispanic Origin and Race categories. Ancestry percentages are based on the 2006-2010 American Community Survey population (not shown); ‡ Numbers in parentheses indicate the number of people reporting a single ancestry; * Numbers in parentheses indicate the number of persons reporting this race alone, not in combination with any other race; Please refer to the Explanation of Data for more information.

Wayne County

Population: 68,917

Ancestry	Population	%
Afghan (0)	0	<0.01
African, Sub-Saharan (172)	195	0.28
African (172)	192	0.28
Cape Verdean (0)	0	<0.01
Ethiopian (0)	0	<0.01
Ghanaian (0)	0	<0.01
Kenyan (0)	0	<0.01
Liberian (0)	0	<0.01
Nigerian (0)	0	<0.01
Senegalese (0)	0	<0.01
Sierra Leonean (0)	0	<0.01
Somalian (0)	0	<0.01
South African (0)	3	<0.01
Sudanese (0)	0	<0.01
Ugandan (0)	0	<0.01
Zimbabwean (0)	0	<0.01
Other Sub-Saharan African (0)	0	<0.01
Albanian (0)	0	<0.01
Alsatian (0)	0	<0.01
American (7,563)	7,563	10.93
Arab (33)	33	0.05
Arab (0)	0	<0.01
Egyptian (0)	0	<0.01
Iraqi (0)	0	<0.01
Jordanian (0)	0	<0.01
Lebanese (17)	17	0.02
Moroccan (0)	0	<0.01
Palestinian (9)	9	0.01
Syrian (0)	0	<0.01
Other Arab (7)	7	0.01
Armenian (14)	14	0.02
Assyrian/Chaldean/Syriac (0)	0	<0.01
Australian (0)	0	<0.01
Austrian (0)	11	0.02
Basque (0)	0	<0.01
Belgian (0)	40	0.06
Brazilian (0)	0	<0.01
British (114)	288	0.42
Bulgarian (0)	0	<0.01
Cajun (0)	0	<0.01
Canadian (106)	139	0.20
Carpatho Rusyn (0)	0	<0.01
Celtic (0)	0	<0.01
Croatian (15)	21	0.03
Cypriot (0)	0	<0.01
Czech (15)	64	0.09
Czechoslovakian (0)	6	0.01
Danish (28)	118	0.17
Dutch (414)	1,908	2.76
Eastern European (10)	10	0.01
English (3,421)	7,639	11.04
Estonian (0)	0	<0.01
European (741)	782	1.13
Finnish (0)	0	<0.01
French, ex. Basque (255)	1,119	1.62
French Canadian (16)	65	0.09
German (7,720)	16,908	24.44
German Russian (0)	6	0.01
Greek (90)	131	0.19
Guyanese (7)	30	0.04
Hungarian (108)	233	0.34
Icelander (0)	0	<0.01
Iranian (104)	104	0.15
Irish (2,655)	8,196	11.85
Israeli (0)	0	<0.01
Italian (993)	2,010	2.91
Latvian (9)	9	0.01
Lithuanian (16)	24	0.03
Luxemburger (0)	12	0.02
Macedonian (93)	93	0.13
Maltese (11)	22	0.03
New Zealander (0)	0	<0.01
Northern European (41)	41	0.06
Norwegian (43)	272	0.39
Pennsylvania German (79)	95	0.14
Polish (215)	760	1.10
Portuguese (10)	32	0.05
Romanian (0)	0	<0.01
Russian (93)	143	0.21
Scandinavian (19)	19	0.03
Scotch-Irish (532)	1,333	1.93
Scottish (456)	1,247	1.80
Serbian (19)	19	0.03
Slavic (16)	16	0.02
Slovak (16)	27	0.04
Slovene (6)	13	0.02
Soviet Union (0)	0	<0.01
Swedish (143)	297	0.43
Swiss (148)	278	0.40
Turkish (0)	13	0.02
Ukrainian (24)	30	0.04
Welsh (92)	372	0.54
West Indian, ex. Hispanic (18)	21	0.03
Bahamian (0)	0	<0.01
Barbadian (0)	0	<0.01
Belizean (0)	0	<0.01
Bermudan (0)	0	<0.01
British West Indian (0)	0	<0.01
Dutch West Indian (0)	3	<0.01
Haitian (12)	12	0.02
Jamaican (6)	6	0.01
Trinidadian/Tobagonian (0)	0	<0.01
U.S. Virgin Islander (0)	0	<0.01
West Indian (0)	0	<0.01
Other West Indian (0)	0	<0.01
Yugoslavian (0)	23	0.03

Hispanic Origin	Population	%
Hispanic or Latino (of any race)	1,804	2.62
Central American, ex. Mexican	64	0.09
Costa Rican	2	<0.01
Guatemalan	19	0.03
Honduran	14	0.02
Nicaraguan	2	<0.01
Panamanian	13	0.02
Salvadoran	10	0.01
Other Central American	4	0.01
Cuban	38	0.06
Dominican Republic	4	0.01
Mexican	1,278	1.85
Puerto Rican	182	0.26
South American	98	0.14
Argentinean	3	<0.01
Bolivian	1	<0.01
Chilean	8	0.01
Colombian	32	0.05
Ecuadorian	13	0.02
Paraguayan	0	<0.01
Peruvian	33	0.05
Uruguayan	1	<0.01
Venezuelan	6	0.01
Other South American	1	<0.01
Other Hispanic or Latino	140	0.20

Race*	Population	%
African-American/Black (3,418)	4,558	6.61
Not Hispanic (3,349)	4,451	6.46
Hispanic (69)	107	0.16
American Indian/Alaska Native (171)	629	0.91
Not Hispanic (140)	566	0.82
Hispanic (31)	63	0.09
Alaska Athabascan (Ala. Nat.) (0)	0	<0.01
Aleut (Alaska Native) (0)	0	<0.01
Apache (1)	9	0.01
Arapaho (0)	0	<0.01
Blackfeet (4)	29	0.04
Canadian/French Am. Ind. (0)	3	<0.01
Central American Ind. (0)	2	<0.01
Cherokee (43)	187	0.27
Cheyenne (0)	0	<0.01
Chickasaw (0)	6	0.01
Chippewa (7)	14	0.02
Choctaw (1)	4	0.01
Colville (0)	0	<0.01
Comanche (3)	3	<0.01
Cree (0)	0	<0.01
Creek (0)	2	<0.01
Crow (0)	1	<0.01
Delaware (0)	0	<0.01
Hopi (1)	3	<0.01
Houma (1)	1	<0.01
Inupiat (Alaska Native) (0)	0	<0.01
Iroquois (6)	10	0.01
Kiowa (0)	0	<0.01
Lumbee (1)	5	0.01
Menominee (2)	2	<0.01
Mexican American Ind. (11)	17	0.02
Navajo (2)	7	0.01
Osage (0)	0	<0.01
Ottawa (0)	0	<0.01
Paiute (2)	2	<0.01
Pima (2)	2	<0.01
Potawatomi (1)	4	0.01
Pueblo (1)	2	<0.01
Puget Sound Salish (0)	0	<0.01
Seminole (1)	2	<0.01
Shoshone (0)	0	<0.01
Sioux (1)	9	0.01
South American Ind. (3)	3	<0.01
Spanish American Ind. (5)	8	0.01
Tlingit-Haida (Alaska Native) (0)	0	<0.01
Tohono O'Odham (0)	0	<0.01
Tsimshian (Alaska Native) (0)	0	<0.01
Ute (0)	0	<0.01
Yakama (0)	0	<0.01
Yaqui (0)	0	<0.01
Yuman (0)	0	<0.01
Yup'ik (Alaska Native) (0)	0	<0.01
Asian (527)	734	1.07
Not Hispanic (522)	721	1.05
Hispanic (5)	13	0.02
Bangladeshi (0)	0	<0.01
Bhutanese (0)	0	<0.01
Burmese (0)	0	<0.01
Cambodian (4)	12	0.02
Chinese, ex. Taiwanese (78)	88	0.13
Filipino (104)	159	0.23
Hmong (0)	0	<0.01
Indian (130)	145	0.21
Indonesian (2)	5	0.01
Japanese (55)	81	0.12
Korean (31)	48	0.07
Laotian (18)	23	0.03
Malaysian (0)	0	<0.01
Nepalese (1)	2	<0.01
Pakistani (12)	12	0.02
Sri Lankan (1)	2	<0.01
Taiwanese (3)	4	0.01
Thai (6)	7	0.01
Vietnamese (36)	45	0.07
Hawaii Native/Pacific Islander (49)	138	0.20
Not Hispanic (44)	130	0.19
Hispanic (5)	8	0.01
Fijian (0)	0	<0.01
Guamanian/Chamorro (4)	4	0.01
Marshallese (0)	0	<0.01
Native Hawaiian (8)	28	0.04
Samoan (2)	3	<0.01
Tongan (0)	0	<0.01
White (62,140)	63,798	92.57
Not Hispanic (61,322)	62,805	91.13
Hispanic (818)	993	1.44

Notes: † The Census 2010 population figure is used to calculate the percentages in the Hispanic Origin and Race categories. Ancestry percentages are based on the 2006-2010 American Community Survey population (not shown); ‡ Numbers in parentheses indicate the number of people reporting a single ancestry; * Numbers in parentheses indicate the number of persons reporting this race alone, not in combination with any other race; Please refer to the Explanation of Data for more information.

Wells County
Population: 27,636

Ancestry	Population	%
Afghan (0)	0	<0.01
African, Sub-Saharan (0)	0	<0.01
African (0)	0	<0.01
Cape Verdean (0)	0	<0.01
Ethiopian (0)	0	<0.01
Ghanaian (0)	0	<0.01
Kenyan (0)	0	<0.01
Liberian (0)	0	<0.01
Nigerian (0)	0	<0.01
Senegalese (0)	0	<0.01
Sierra Leonean (0)	0	<0.01
Somalian (0)	0	<0.01
South African (0)	0	<0.01
Sudanese (0)	0	<0.01
Ugandan (0)	0	<0.01
Zimbabwean (0)	0	<0.01
Other Sub-Saharan African (0)	0	<0.01
Albanian (0)	0	<0.01
Alsatian (0)	0	<0.01
American (2,856)	2,856	10.29
Arab (0)	0	<0.01
Arab (0)	0	<0.01
Egyptian (0)	0	<0.01
Iraqi (0)	0	<0.01
Jordanian (0)	0	<0.01
Lebanese (0)	0	<0.01
Moroccan (0)	0	<0.01
Palestinian (0)	0	<0.01
Syrian (0)	0	<0.01
Other Arab (0)	0	<0.01
Armenian (0)	0	<0.01
Assyrian/Chaldean/Syriac (0)	0	<0.01
Australian (0)	0	<0.01
Austrian (28)	28	0.10
Basque (0)	0	<0.01
Belgian (8)	25	0.09
Brazilian (0)	0	<0.01
British (35)	71	0.26
Bulgarian (0)	0	<0.01
Cajun (0)	0	<0.01
Canadian (6)	6	0.02
Carpatho Rusyn (0)	0	<0.01
Celtic (0)	0	<0.01
Croatian (0)	0	<0.01
Cypriot (0)	0	<0.01
Czech (9)	9	0.03
Czechoslovakian (0)	0	<0.01
Danish (30)	58	0.21
Dutch (174)	726	2.62
Eastern European (0)	0	<0.01
English (1,819)	3,418	12.32
Estonian (0)	0	<0.01
European (130)	132	0.48
Finnish (47)	94	0.34
French, ex. Basque (151)	1,027	3.70
French Canadian (143)	225	0.81
German (5,702)	10,646	38.37
German Russian (0)	0	<0.01
Greek (14)	14	0.05
Guyanese (0)	0	<0.01
Hungarian (41)	66	0.24
Icelander (0)	0	<0.01
Iranian (0)	0	<0.01
Irish (821)	3,009	10.85
Israeli (0)	0	<0.01
Italian (160)	589	2.12
Latvian (0)	0	<0.01
Lithuanian (9)	9	0.03
Luxemburger (0)	0	<0.01
Macedonian (0)	0	<0.01
Maltese (0)	0	<0.01
New Zealander (0)	0	<0.01
Northern European (5)	5	0.02
Norwegian (24)	46	0.17
Pennsylvania German (37)	37	0.13
Polish (120)	439	1.58
Portuguese (0)	0	<0.01
Romanian (0)	0	<0.01
Russian (7)	31	0.11
Scandinavian (14)	30	0.11
Scotch-Irish (92)	159	0.57
Scottish (184)	423	1.52
Serbian (13)	13	0.05
Slavic (0)	0	<0.01
Slovak (9)	33	0.12
Slovene (0)	0	<0.01
Soviet Union (0)	0	<0.01
Swedish (21)	54	0.19
Swiss (864)	1,426	5.14
Turkish (0)	0	<0.01
Ukrainian (16)	23	0.08
Welsh (19)	152	0.55
West Indian, ex. Hispanic (0)	0	<0.01
Bahamian (0)	0	<0.01
Barbadian (0)	0	<0.01
Belizean (0)	0	<0.01
Bermudan (0)	0	<0.01
British West Indian (0)	0	<0.01
Dutch West Indian (0)	0	<0.01
Haitian (0)	0	<0.01
Jamaican (0)	0	<0.01
Trinidadian/Tobagonian (0)	0	<0.01
U.S. Virgin Islander (0)	0	<0.01
West Indian (0)	0	<0.01
Other West Indian (0)	0	<0.01
Yugoslavian (3)	6	0.02

Hispanic Origin	Population	%
Hispanic or Latino (of any race)	564	2.04
Central American, ex. Mexican	22	0.08
Costa Rican	2	0.01
Guatemalan	4	0.01
Honduran	2	0.01
Nicaraguan	0	<0.01
Panamanian	5	0.02
Salvadoran	9	0.03
Other Central American	0	<0.01
Cuban	2	0.01
Dominican Republic	0	<0.01
Mexican	424	1.53
Puerto Rican	46	0.17
South American	21	0.08
Argentinean	0	<0.01
Bolivian	0	<0.01
Chilean	0	<0.01
Colombian	17	0.06
Ecuadorian	3	0.01
Paraguayan	0	<0.01
Peruvian	1	<0.01
Uruguayan	0	<0.01
Venezuelan	0	<0.01
Other South American	0	<0.01
Other Hispanic or Latino	49	0.18

Race*	Population	%
African-American/Black (96)	187	0.68
Not Hispanic (89)	165	0.60
Hispanic (7)	22	0.08
American Indian/Alaska Native (76)	181	0.65
Not Hispanic (71)	161	0.58
Hispanic (5)	20	0.07
Alaska Athabascan (Ala. Nat.) (0)	0	<0.01
Aleut (Alaska Native) (0)	0	<0.01
Apache (0)	0	<0.01
Arapaho (0)	0	<0.01
Blackfeet (4)	8	0.03
Canadian/French Am. Ind. (0)	0	<0.01
Central American Ind. (0)	0	<0.01
Cherokee (21)	60	0.22
Cheyenne (1)	2	0.01
Chickasaw (0)	0	<0.01
Chippewa (1)	1	<0.01
Choctaw (0)	1	<0.01
Colville (0)	0	<0.01
Comanche (0)	0	<0.01
Cree (0)	0	<0.01
Creek (2)	8	0.03
Crow (0)	0	<0.01
Delaware (0)	0	<0.01
Hopi (0)	0	<0.01
Houma (0)	0	<0.01
Inupiat (Alaska Native) (0)	0	<0.01
Iroquois (1)	2	0.01
Kiowa (0)	0	<0.01
Lumbee (0)	0	<0.01
Menominee (0)	0	<0.01
Mexican American Ind. (2)	2	0.01
Navajo (0)	0	<0.01
Osage (0)	0	<0.01
Ottawa (2)	2	0.01
Paiute (0)	0	<0.01
Pima (0)	0	<0.01
Potawatomi (0)	0	<0.01
Pueblo (1)	1	<0.01
Puget Sound Salish (0)	0	<0.01
Seminole (0)	0	<0.01
Shoshone (0)	0	<0.01
Sioux (11)	13	0.05
South American Ind. (0)	1	<0.01
Spanish American Ind. (0)	0	<0.01
Tlingit-Haida (Alaska Native) (0)	0	<0.01
Tohono O'Odham (0)	0	<0.01
Tsimshian (Alaska Native) (0)	0	<0.01
Ute (0)	0	<0.01
Yakama (0)	0	<0.01
Yaqui (0)	0	<0.01
Yuman (2)	2	0.01
Yup'ik (Alaska Native) (0)	0	<0.01
Asian (107)	141	0.51
Not Hispanic (102)	136	0.49
Hispanic (5)	5	0.02
Bangladeshi (0)	0	<0.01
Bhutanese (0)	0	<0.01
Burmese (0)	0	<0.01
Cambodian (4)	6	0.02
Chinese, ex. Taiwanese (33)	33	0.12
Filipino (25)	33	0.12
Hmong (0)	1	<0.01
Indian (0)	5	0.02
Indonesian (0)	0	<0.01
Japanese (5)	5	0.02
Korean (20)	25	0.09
Laotian (0)	1	<0.01
Malaysian (0)	0	<0.01
Nepalese (0)	0	<0.01
Pakistani (0)	0	<0.01
Sri Lankan (0)	0	<0.01
Taiwanese (1)	1	<0.01
Thai (5)	7	0.03
Vietnamese (5)	5	0.02
Hawaii Native/Pacific Islander (3)	9	0.03
Not Hispanic (3)	9	0.03
Hispanic (0)	0	<0.01
Fijian (0)	0	<0.01
Guamanian/Chamorro (1)	2	0.01
Marshallese (0)	0	<0.01
Native Hawaiian (1)	1	<0.01
Samoan (0)	0	<0.01
Tongan (0)	0	<0.01
White (26,902)	27,132	98.18
Not Hispanic (26,604)	26,796	96.96
Hispanic (298)	336	1.22

Notes: † The Census 2010 population figure is used to calculate the percentages in the Hispanic Origin and Race categories. Ancestry percentages are based on the 2006-2010 American Community Survey population (not shown); ‡ Numbers in parentheses indicate the number of people reporting a single ancestry; * Numbers in parentheses indicate the number of persons reporting this race alone, not in combination with any other race; Please refer to the Explanation of Data for more information.

White County
Population: 24,643

Ancestry	Population	%
Afghan (0)	0	<0.01
African, Sub-Saharan (0)	0	<0.01
African (0)	0	<0.01
Cape Verdean (0)	0	<0.01
Ethiopian (0)	0	<0.01
Ghanaian (0)	0	<0.01
Kenyan (0)	0	<0.01
Liberian (0)	0	<0.01
Nigerian (0)	0	<0.01
Senegalese (0)	0	<0.01
Sierra Leonean (0)	0	<0.01
Somalian (0)	0	<0.01
South African (0)	0	<0.01
Sudanese (0)	0	<0.01
Ugandan (0)	0	<0.01
Zimbabwean (0)	0	<0.01
Other Sub-Saharan African (0)	0	<0.01
Albanian (0)	0	<0.01
Alsatian (0)	0	<0.01
American (2,068)	2,068	8.36
Arab (0)	5	0.02
Arab (0)	3	0.01
Egyptian (0)	0	<0.01
Iraqi (0)	0	<0.01
Jordanian (0)	0	<0.01
Lebanese (0)	2	0.01
Moroccan (0)	0	<0.01
Palestinian (0)	0	<0.01
Syrian (0)	0	<0.01
Other Arab (0)	0	<0.01
Armenian (0)	0	<0.01
Assyrian/Chaldean/Syriac (0)	0	<0.01
Australian (0)	0	<0.01
Austrian (13)	25	0.10
Basque (0)	0	<0.01
Belgian (0)	24	0.10
Brazilian (0)	0	<0.01
British (40)	45	0.18
Bulgarian (0)	0	<0.01
Cajun (0)	0	<0.01
Canadian (21)	107	0.43
Carpatho Rusyn (0)	0	<0.01
Celtic (0)	0	<0.01
Croatian (28)	59	0.24
Cypriot (0)	0	<0.01
Czech (36)	106	0.43
Czechoslovakian (14)	14	0.06
Danish (35)	121	0.49
Dutch (261)	985	3.98
Eastern European (0)	0	<0.01
English (839)	2,392	9.67
Estonian (0)	0	<0.01
European (61)	147	0.59
Finnish (0)	9	0.04
French, ex. Basque (247)	683	2.76
French Canadian (7)	84	0.34
German (2,961)	6,687	27.04
German Russian (0)	0	<0.01
Greek (9)	18	0.07
Guyanese (0)	0	<0.01
Hungarian (48)	83	0.34
Icelander (0)	0	<0.01
Iranian (0)	0	<0.01
Irish (923)	3,284	13.28
Israeli (0)	0	<0.01
Italian (133)	576	2.33
Latvian (0)	0	<0.01
Lithuanian (13)	29	0.12
Luxemburger (0)	0	<0.01
Macedonian (0)	8	0.03
Maltese (0)	0	<0.01
New Zealander (0)	0	<0.01
Northern European (30)	30	0.12
Norwegian (54)	98	0.40
Pennsylvania German (12)	18	0.07
Polish (343)	1,061	4.29
Portuguese (0)	8	0.03
Romanian (0)	0	<0.01
Russian (0)	86	0.35
Scandinavian (11)	11	0.04
Scotch-Irish (176)	401	1.62
Scottish (174)	488	1.97
Serbian (20)	24	0.10
Slavic (12)	12	0.05
Slovak (3)	43	0.17
Slovene (0)	9	0.04
Soviet Union (0)	0	<0.01
Swedish (129)	425	1.72
Swiss (18)	57	0.23
Turkish (9)	10	0.04
Ukrainian (0)	24	0.10
Welsh (81)	121	0.49
West Indian, ex. Hispanic (0)	0	<0.01
Bahamian (0)	0	<0.01
Barbadian (0)	0	<0.01
Belizean (0)	0	<0.01
Bermudan (0)	0	<0.01
British West Indian (0)	0	<0.01
Dutch West Indian (0)	0	<0.01
Haitian (0)	0	<0.01
Jamaican (0)	0	<0.01
Trinidadian/Tobagonian (0)	0	<0.01
U.S. Virgin Islander (0)	0	<0.01
West Indian (0)	0	<0.01
Other West Indian (0)	0	<0.01
Yugoslavian (0)	0	<0.01

Hispanic Origin	Population	%
Hispanic or Latino (of any race)	1,746	7.09
Central American, ex. Mexican	349	1.42
Costa Rican	0	<0.01
Guatemalan	12	0.05
Honduran	8	0.03
Nicaraguan	5	0.02
Panamanian	2	0.01
Salvadoran	322	1.31
Other Central American	0	<0.01
Cuban	6	0.02
Dominican Republic	0	<0.01
Mexican	1,225	4.97
Puerto Rican	48	0.19
South American	4	0.02
Argentinean	0	<0.01
Bolivian	0	<0.01
Chilean	0	<0.01
Colombian	2	0.01
Ecuadorian	0	<0.01
Paraguayan	0	<0.01
Peruvian	0	<0.01
Uruguayan	0	<0.01
Venezuelan	0	<0.01
Other South American	2	0.01
Other Hispanic or Latino	114	0.46

Race*	Population	%
African-American/Black (68)	126	0.51
Not Hispanic (51)	104	0.42
Hispanic (17)	22	0.09
American Indian/Alaska Native (71)	214	0.87
Not Hispanic (52)	172	0.70
Hispanic (19)	42	0.17
Alaska Athabascan (Ala. Nat.) (0)	0	<0.01
Aleut (Alaska Native) (0)	0	<0.01
Apache (1)	10	0.04
Arapaho (0)	0	<0.01
Blackfeet (2)	10	0.04
Canadian/French Am. Ind. (4)	5	0.02
Central American Ind. (0)	0	<0.01
Cherokee (7)	73	0.30
Cheyenne (4)	4	0.02
Chickasaw (0)	0	<0.01
Chippewa (3)	3	0.01
Choctaw (0)	2	0.01
Colville (0)	0	<0.01
Comanche (0)	0	<0.01
Cree (0)	0	<0.01
Creek (4)	6	0.02
Crow (0)	0	<0.01
Delaware (0)	0	<0.01
Hopi (0)	0	<0.01
Houma (0)	0	<0.01
Inupiat (Alaska Native) (0)	0	<0.01
Iroquois (1)	1	<0.01
Kiowa (0)	0	<0.01
Lumbee (0)	1	<0.01
Menominee (0)	0	<0.01
Mexican American Ind. (1)	1	<0.01
Navajo (0)	3	0.01
Osage (0)	0	<0.01
Ottawa (0)	0	<0.01
Paiute (0)	1	<0.01
Pima (0)	0	<0.01
Potawatomi (0)	1	<0.01
Pueblo (0)	0	<0.01
Puget Sound Salish (0)	0	<0.01
Seminole (0)	0	<0.01
Shoshone (0)	0	<0.01
Sioux (1)	5	0.02
South American Ind. (0)	0	<0.01
Spanish American Ind. (0)	0	<0.01
Tlingit-Haida (Alaska Native) (0)	0	<0.01
Tohono O'Odham (0)	0	<0.01
Tsimshian (Alaska Native) (0)	0	<0.01
Ute (0)	0	<0.01
Yakama (0)	0	<0.01
Yaqui (0)	0	<0.01
Yuman (0)	0	<0.01
Yup'ik (Alaska Native) (0)	0	<0.01
Asian (89)	140	0.57
Not Hispanic (83)	131	0.53
Hispanic (6)	9	0.04
Bangladeshi (0)	0	<0.01
Bhutanese (0)	0	<0.01
Burmese (0)	0	<0.01
Cambodian (0)	0	<0.01
Chinese, ex. Taiwanese (17)	24	0.10
Filipino (30)	47	0.19
Hmong (0)	0	<0.01
Indian (4)	5	0.02
Indonesian (1)	1	<0.01
Japanese (5)	24	0.10
Korean (6)	12	0.05
Laotian (0)	0	<0.01
Malaysian (0)	0	<0.01
Nepalese (0)	0	<0.01
Pakistani (8)	9	0.04
Sri Lankan (0)	0	<0.01
Taiwanese (0)	0	<0.01
Thai (2)	2	0.01
Vietnamese (11)	11	0.04
Hawaii Native/Pacific Islander (5)	18	0.07
Not Hispanic (4)	17	0.07
Hispanic (1)	1	<0.01
Fijian (0)	0	<0.01
Guamanian/Chamorro (1)	1	<0.01
Marshallese (0)	0	<0.01
Native Hawaiian (0)	8	0.03
Samoan (1)	2	0.01
Tongan (0)	0	<0.01
White (23,132)	23,471	95.24
Not Hispanic (22,470)	22,696	92.10
Hispanic (662)	775	3.14

*Notes: † The Census 2010 population figure is used to calculate the percentages in the Hispanic Origin and Race categories. Ancestry percentages are based on the 2006-2010 American Community Survey population (not shown); ‡ Numbers in parentheses indicate the number of people reporting a single ancestry; * Numbers in parentheses indicate the number of persons reporting this race alone, not in combination with any other race; Please refer to the Explanation of Data for more information.*

Whitley County
Population: 33,292

Ancestry	Population	%
Afghan (0)	0	<0.01
African, Sub-Saharan (1)	1	<0.01
African (0)	0	<0.01
Cape Verdean (0)	0	<0.01
Ethiopian (1)	1	<0.01
Ghanaian (0)	0	<0.01
Kenyan (0)	0	<0.01
Liberian (0)	0	<0.01
Nigerian (0)	0	<0.01
Senegalese (0)	0	<0.01
Sierra Leonean (0)	0	<0.01
Somalian (0)	0	<0.01
South African (0)	0	<0.01
Sudanese (0)	0	<0.01
Ugandan (0)	0	<0.01
Zimbabwean (0)	0	<0.01
Other Sub-Saharan African (0)	0	<0.01
Albanian (0)	0	<0.01
Alsatian (0)	0	<0.01
American (4,128)	4,128	12.51
Arab (37)	83	0.25
Arab (0)	40	0.12
Egyptian (0)	0	<0.01
Iraqi (0)	2	0.01
Jordanian (0)	0	<0.01
Lebanese (4)	8	0.02
Moroccan (0)	0	<0.01
Palestinian (27)	27	0.08
Syrian (6)	6	0.02
Other Arab (0)	0	<0.01
Armenian (0)	0	<0.01
Assyrian/Chaldean/Syriac (0)	0	<0.01
Australian (0)	6	0.02
Austrian (0)	23	0.07
Basque (0)	0	<0.01
Belgian (15)	26	0.08
Brazilian (14)	14	0.04
British (27)	45	0.14
Bulgarian (0)	0	<0.01
Cajun (0)	0	<0.01
Canadian (12)	17	0.05
Carpatho Rusyn (0)	0	<0.01
Celtic (0)	0	<0.01
Croatian (0)	3	0.01
Cypriot (0)	0	<0.01
Czech (4)	27	0.08
Czechoslovakian (14)	14	0.04
Danish (46)	139	0.42
Dutch (195)	763	2.31
Eastern European (0)	0	<0.01
English (1,248)	3,056	9.26
Estonian (0)	0	<0.01
European (291)	291	0.88
Finnish (10)	23	0.07
French, ex. Basque (284)	1,079	3.27
French Canadian (37)	55	0.17
German (6,903)	12,613	38.23
German Russian (0)	0	<0.01
Greek (39)	59	0.18
Guyanese (0)	0	<0.01
Hungarian (111)	187	0.57
Icelander (7)	13	0.04
Iranian (0)	0	<0.01
Irish (887)	4,141	12.55
Israeli (0)	0	<0.01
Italian (238)	575	1.74
Latvian (0)	0	<0.01
Lithuanian (0)	11	0.03
Luxemburger (0)	0	<0.01
Macedonian (0)	11	0.03
Maltese (0)	0	<0.01
New Zealander (0)	0	<0.01
Northern European (0)	0	<0.01
Norwegian (116)	252	0.76
Pennsylvania German (37)	37	0.11
Polish (193)	479	1.45
Portuguese (0)	45	0.14
Romanian (12)	28	0.08
Russian (7)	129	0.39
Scandinavian (27)	39	0.12
Scotch-Irish (245)	573	1.74
Scottish (279)	628	1.90
Serbian (0)	0	<0.01
Slavic (22)	22	0.07
Slovak (0)	0	<0.01
Slovene (0)	46	0.14
Soviet Union (0)	0	<0.01
Swedish (236)	334	1.01
Swiss (87)	514	1.56
Turkish (0)	0	<0.01
Ukrainian (0)	0	<0.01
Welsh (30)	134	0.41
West Indian, ex. Hispanic (19)	47	0.14
Bahamian (0)	0	<0.01
Barbadian (0)	14	0.04
Belizean (0)	0	<0.01
Bermudan (0)	0	<0.01
British West Indian (0)	0	<0.01
Dutch West Indian (0)	0	<0.01
Haitian (19)	19	0.06
Jamaican (0)	0	<0.01
Trinidadian/Tobagonian (0)	0	<0.01
U.S. Virgin Islander (0)	0	<0.01
West Indian (0)	0	<0.01
Other West Indian (0)	14	0.04
Yugoslavian (0)	61	0.18

Hispanic Origin	Population	%
Hispanic or Latino (of any race)	515	1.55
Central American, ex. Mexican	20	0.06
Costa Rican	1	<0.01
Guatemalan	14	0.04
Honduran	1	<0.01
Nicaraguan	0	<0.01
Panamanian	0	<0.01
Salvadoran	4	0.01
Other Central American	0	<0.01
Cuban	3	0.01
Dominican Republic	0	<0.01
Mexican	397	1.19
Puerto Rican	34	0.10
South American	5	0.02
Argentinean	1	<0.01
Bolivian	0	<0.01
Chilean	0	<0.01
Colombian	2	0.01
Ecuadorian	0	<0.01
Paraguayan	0	<0.01
Peruvian	0	<0.01
Uruguayan	0	<0.01
Venezuelan	2	0.01
Other South American	0	<0.01
Other Hispanic or Latino	56	0.17

Race*	Population	%
African-American/Black (99)	199	0.60
Not Hispanic (96)	189	0.57
Hispanic (3)	10	0.03
American Indian/Alaska Native (92)	259	0.78
Not Hispanic (76)	230	0.69
Hispanic (16)	29	0.09
Alaska Athabascan (Ala. Nat.) (0)	0	<0.01
Aleut (Alaska Native) (0)	0	<0.01
Apache (1)	2	0.01
Arapaho (0)	0	<0.01
Blackfeet (0)	7	0.02
Canadian/French Am. Ind. (0)	1	<0.01
Central American Ind. (0)	0	<0.01
Cherokee (7)	67	0.20
Cheyenne (0)	0	<0.01
Chickasaw (0)	0	<0.01
Chippewa (3)	5	0.02
Choctaw (1)	1	<0.01
Colville (0)	0	<0.01
Comanche (2)	2	0.01
Cree (0)	0	<0.01
Creek (0)	0	<0.01
Crow (0)	0	<0.01
Delaware (0)	0	<0.01
Hopi (0)	0	<0.01
Houma (0)	0	<0.01
Inupiat (Alaska Native) (0)	0	<0.01
Iroquois (0)	2	0.01
Kiowa (0)	0	<0.01
Lumbee (0)	0	<0.01
Menominee (0)	0	<0.01
Mexican American Ind. (4)	7	0.02
Navajo (3)	4	0.01
Osage (1)	1	<0.01
Ottawa (0)	0	<0.01
Paiute (0)	0	<0.01
Pima (0)	0	<0.01
Potawatomi (2)	2	0.01
Pueblo (5)	9	0.03
Puget Sound Salish (0)	0	<0.01
Seminole (0)	0	<0.01
Shoshone (0)	0	<0.01
Sioux (1)	5	0.02
South American Ind. (0)	1	<0.01
Spanish American Ind. (1)	1	<0.01
Tlingit-Haida (Alaska Native) (0)	0	<0.01
Tohono O'Odham (0)	0	<0.01
Tsimshian (Alaska Native) (0)	0	<0.01
Ute (0)	0	<0.01
Yakama (0)	0	<0.01
Yaqui (0)	0	<0.01
Yuman (0)	0	<0.01
Yup'ik (Alaska Native) (0)	0	<0.01
Asian (105)	184	0.55
Not Hispanic (105)	183	0.55
Hispanic (0)	1	<0.01
Bangladeshi (0)	0	<0.01
Bhutanese (0)	0	<0.01
Burmese (1)	1	<0.01
Cambodian (0)	0	<0.01
Chinese, ex. Taiwanese (34)	40	0.12
Filipino (25)	34	0.10
Hmong (0)	0	<0.01
Indian (21)	25	0.08
Indonesian (0)	2	0.01
Japanese (9)	28	0.08
Korean (5)	25	0.08
Laotian (1)	2	0.01
Malaysian (0)	0	<0.01
Nepalese (0)	0	<0.01
Pakistani (1)	5	0.02
Sri Lankan (1)	1	<0.01
Taiwanese (0)	0	<0.01
Thai (3)	7	0.02
Vietnamese (2)	5	0.02
Hawaii Native/Pacific Islander (7)	28	0.08
Not Hispanic (7)	27	0.08
Hispanic (0)	1	<0.01
Fijian (0)	0	<0.01
Guamanian/Chamorro (0)	0	<0.01
Marshallese (0)	0	<0.01
Native Hawaiian (1)	9	0.03
Samoan (6)	11	0.03
Tongan (0)	0	<0.01
White (32,479)	32,852	98.68
Not Hispanic (32,147)	32,466	97.52
Hispanic (332)	386	1.16

Notes: † The Census 2010 population figure is used to calculate the percentages in the Hispanic Origin and Race categories. Ancestry percentages are based on the 2006-2010 American Community Survey population (not shown); ‡ Numbers in parentheses indicate the number of people reporting a single ancestry; * Numbers in parentheses indicate the number of persons reporting this race alone, not in combination with any other race; Please refer to the Explanation of Data for more information.

Anderson

Place Type: City
County: Madison
Population: 56,129

Ancestry	Population	%
Afghan (0)	0	<0.01
African, Sub-Saharan (628)	648	1.14
African (523)	543	0.96
Cape Verdean (0)	0	<0.01
Ethiopian (18)	18	0.03
Ghanaian (0)	0	<0.01
Kenyan (43)	43	0.08
Liberian (0)	0	<0.01
Nigerian (0)	0	<0.01
Senegalese (0)	0	<0.01
Sierra Leonean (0)	0	<0.01
Somalian (0)	0	<0.01
South African (0)	0	<0.01
Sudanese (18)	18	0.03
Ugandan (0)	0	<0.01
Zimbabwean (0)	0	<0.01
Other Sub-Saharan African (26)	26	0.05
Albanian (0)	0	<0.01
Alsatian (0)	0	<0.01
American (5,914)	5,914	10.42
Arab (12)	24	0.04
Arab (0)	0	<0.01
Egyptian (0)	0	<0.01
Iraqi (0)	0	<0.01
Jordanian (0)	0	<0.01
Lebanese (0)	0	<0.01
Moroccan (12)	24	0.04
Palestinian (0)	0	<0.01
Syrian (0)	0	<0.01
Other Arab (0)	0	<0.01
Armenian (0)	0	<0.01
Assyrian/Chaldean/Syriac (0)	0	<0.01
Australian (12)	12	0.02
Austrian (44)	103	0.18
Basque (0)	0	<0.01
Belgian (0)	23	0.04
Brazilian (0)	0	<0.01
British (73)	153	0.27
Bulgarian (0)	0	<0.01
Cajun (0)	0	<0.01
Canadian (21)	50	0.09
Carpatho Rusyn (0)	0	<0.01
Celtic (0)	12	0.02
Croatian (9)	59	0.10
Cypriot (0)	0	<0.01
Czech (25)	45	0.08
Czechoslovakian (12)	12	0.02
Danish (0)	33	0.06
Dutch (429)	1,593	2.81
Eastern European (0)	0	<0.01
English (2,333)	4,934	8.69
Estonian (0)	0	<0.01
European (290)	313	0.55
Finnish (13)	35	0.06
French, ex. Basque (493)	1,268	2.23
French Canadian (18)	66	0.12
German (4,469)	10,377	18.28
German Russian (0)	0	<0.01
Greek (82)	126	0.22
Guyanese (0)	0	<0.01
Hungarian (41)	83	0.15
Icelander (0)	0	<0.01
Iranian (0)	0	<0.01
Irish (1,989)	6,464	11.39
Israeli (0)	0	<0.01
Italian (364)	869	1.53
Latvian (0)	0	<0.01
Lithuanian (0)	0	<0.01
Luxemburger (0)	6	0.01
Macedonian (0)	0	<0.01
Maltese (0)	0	<0.01
New Zealander (0)	0	<0.01
Northern European (0)	0	<0.01
Norwegian (62)	167	0.29
Pennsylvania German (0)	12	0.02
Polish (295)	917	1.62
Portuguese (21)	26	0.05
Romanian (17)	17	0.03
Russian (21)	61	0.11
Scandinavian (0)	75	0.13
Scotch-Irish (302)	792	1.40
Scottish (453)	861	1.52
Serbian (0)	12	0.02
Slavic (0)	13	0.02
Slovak (23)	23	0.04
Slovene (0)	9	0.02
Soviet Union (0)	0	<0.01
Swedish (160)	302	0.53
Swiss (30)	113	0.20
Turkish (10)	33	0.06
Ukrainian (0)	22	0.04
Welsh (94)	399	0.70
West Indian, ex. Hispanic (42)	56	0.10
Bahamian (0)	0	<0.01
Barbadian (0)	0	<0.01
Belizean (0)	0	<0.01
Bermudan (0)	0	<0.01
British West Indian (0)	0	<0.01
Dutch West Indian (0)	0	<0.01
Haitian (0)	0	<0.01
Jamaican (29)	29	0.05
Trinidadian/Tobagonian (0)	0	<0.01
U.S. Virgin Islander (0)	0	<0.01
West Indian (0)	0	<0.01
Other West Indian (13)	27	0.05
Yugoslavian (0)	12	0.02

Hispanic Origin	Population	%
Hispanic or Latino (of any race)	2,719	4.84
Central American, ex. Mexican	115	0.20
Costa Rican	1	<0.01
Guatemalan	59	0.11
Honduran	16	0.03
Nicaraguan	19	0.03
Panamanian	1	<0.01
Salvadoran	19	0.03
Other Central American	0	<0.01
Cuban	26	0.05
Dominican Republic	15	0.03
Mexican	2,199	3.92
Puerto Rican	118	0.21
South American	23	0.04
Argentinean	3	0.01
Bolivian	3	0.01
Chilean	3	0.01
Colombian	6	0.01
Ecuadorian	2	<0.01
Paraguayan	0	<0.01
Peruvian	3	0.01
Uruguayan	0	<0.01
Venezuelan	3	0.01
Other South American	0	<0.01
Other Hispanic or Latino	223	0.40

Race*	Population	%
African-American/Black (8,532)	9,500	16.93
Not Hispanic (8,470)	9,376	16.70
Hispanic (62)	124	0.22
American Indian/Alaska Native (185)	528	0.94
Not Hispanic (134)	432	0.77
Hispanic (51)	96	0.17
Alaska Athabascan (Ala. Nat.) (0)	0	<0.01
Aleut (Alaska Native) (0)	0	<0.01
Apache (7)	9	0.02
Arapaho (0)	0	<0.01
Blackfeet (1)	32	0.06
Canadian/French Am. Ind. (0)	1	<0.01
Central American Ind. (0)	7	0.01
Cherokee (44)	127	0.23
Cheyenne (1)	4	0.01
Chickasaw (0)	1	<0.01
Chippewa (3)	6	0.01
Choctaw (5)	10	0.02
Colville (0)	0	<0.01
Comanche (0)	0	<0.01
Cree (0)	0	<0.01
Creek (2)	3	0.01
Crow (0)	0	<0.01
Delaware (0)	6	0.01
Hopi (0)	1	<0.01
Houma (0)	0	<0.01
Inupiat (Alaska Native) (0)	1	<0.01
Iroquois (0)	7	0.01
Kiowa (1)	1	<0.01
Lumbee (0)	0	<0.01
Menominee (0)	0	<0.01
Mexican American Ind. (16)	30	0.05
Navajo (2)	11	0.02
Osage (2)	2	<0.01
Ottawa (0)	0	<0.01
Paiute (0)	0	<0.01
Pima (0)	0	<0.01
Potawatomi (3)	7	0.01
Pueblo (0)	0	<0.01
Puget Sound Salish (0)	0	<0.01
Seminole (0)	2	<0.01
Shoshone (0)	1	<0.01
Sioux (3)	11	0.02
South American Ind. (0)	0	<0.01
Spanish American Ind. (1)	2	<0.01
Tlingit-Haida (Alaska Native) (0)	0	<0.01
Tohono O'Odham (0)	0	<0.01
Tsimshian (Alaska Native) (0)	0	<0.01
Ute (4)	4	0.01
Yakama (0)	0	<0.01
Yaqui (0)	0	<0.01
Yuman (0)	0	<0.01
Yup'ik (Alaska Native) (0)	0	<0.01
Asian (265)	401	0.71
Not Hispanic (264)	383	0.68
Hispanic (1)	18	0.03
Bangladeshi (0)	0	<0.01
Bhutanese (0)	0	<0.01
Burmese (0)	0	<0.01
Cambodian (0)	0	<0.01
Chinese, ex. Taiwanese (46)	58	0.10
Filipino (50)	76	0.14
Hmong (0)	0	<0.01
Indian (39)	53	0.09
Indonesian (0)	0	<0.01
Japanese (19)	57	0.10
Korean (32)	58	0.10
Laotian (0)	2	<0.01
Malaysian (1)	1	<0.01
Nepalese (0)	0	<0.01
Pakistani (1)	1	<0.01
Sri Lankan (0)	0	<0.01
Taiwanese (0)	2	<0.01
Thai (7)	11	0.02
Vietnamese (37)	46	0.08
Hawaii Native/Pacific Islander (25)	54	0.10
Not Hispanic (22)	43	0.08
Hispanic (3)	11	0.02
Fijian (0)	0	<0.01
Guamanian/Chamorro (5)	8	0.01
Marshallese (0)	0	<0.01
Native Hawaiian (5)	22	0.04
Samoan (8)	11	0.02
Tongan (0)	0	<0.01
White (44,204)	45,548	81.15
Not Hispanic (43,181)	44,327	78.97
Hispanic (1,023)	1,221	2.18

Notes: † The Census 2010 population figure is used to calculate the percentages in the Hispanic Origin and Race categories. Ancestry percentages are based on the 2006-2010 American Community Survey population (not shown); ‡ Numbers in parentheses indicate the number of people reporting a single ancestry; * Numbers in parentheses indicate the number of persons reporting this race alone, not in combination with any other race; Please refer to the Explanation of Data for more information.

Bloomington

Place Type: City
County: Monroe
Population: 80,405

Ancestry	Population	%
Afghan (59)	59	0.08
African, Sub-Saharan (498)	593	0.76
African (417)	508	0.65
Cape Verdean (0)	0	<0.01
Ethiopian (4)	5	0.01
Ghanaian (0)	0	<0.01
Kenyan (0)	0	<0.01
Liberian (0)	0	<0.01
Nigerian (14)	14	0.02
Senegalese (0)	0	<0.01
Sierra Leonean (0)	0	<0.01
Somalian (0)	0	<0.01
South African (63)	63	0.08
Sudanese (0)	0	<0.01
Ugandan (0)	0	<0.01
Zimbabwean (0)	0	<0.01
Other Sub-Saharan African (0)	3	<0.01
Albanian (20)	20	0.03
Alsatian (0)	19	0.02
American (3,411)	3,411	4.35
Arab (363)	548	0.70
Arab (187)	187	0.24
Egyptian (8)	21	0.03
Iraqi (30)	30	0.04
Jordanian (0)	10	0.01
Lebanese (67)	167	0.21
Moroccan (27)	27	0.03
Palestinian (0)	0	<0.01
Syrian (13)	75	0.10
Other Arab (31)	31	0.04
Armenian (14)	37	0.05
Assyrian/Chaldean/Syriac (0)	0	<0.01
Australian (18)	46	0.06
Austrian (70)	439	0.56
Basque (0)	0	<0.01
Belgian (23)	155	0.20
Brazilian (40)	69	0.09
British (181)	729	0.93
Bulgarian (29)	29	0.04
Cajun (0)	0	<0.01
Canadian (71)	138	0.18
Carpatho Rusyn (0)	0	<0.01
Celtic (0)	0	<0.01
Croatian (48)	171	0.22
Cypriot (0)	0	<0.01
Czech (129)	478	0.61
Czechoslovakian (19)	85	0.11
Danish (127)	353	0.45
Dutch (483)	1,696	2.16
Eastern European (296)	354	0.45
English (2,870)	8,739	11.13
Estonian (0)	15	0.02
European (1,245)	1,404	1.79
Finnish (12)	42	0.05
French, ex. Basque (581)	2,654	3.38
French Canadian (73)	305	0.39
German (5,754)	19,499	24.84
German Russian (0)	0	<0.01
Greek (227)	551	0.70
Guyanese (0)	0	<0.01
Hungarian (165)	767	0.98
Icelander (21)	41	0.05
Iranian (187)	201	0.26
Irish (3,083)	10,941	13.94
Israeli (91)	168	0.21
Italian (1,043)	3,669	4.67
Latvian (10)	10	0.01
Lithuanian (82)	362	0.46
Luxemburger (0)	0	<0.01
Macedonian (48)	62	0.08
Maltese (0)	0	<0.01
New Zealander (0)	0	<0.01
Northern European (62)	98	0.12
Norwegian (240)	1,150	1.47
Pennsylvania German (21)	58	0.07
Polish (952)	3,792	4.83
Portuguese (9)	52	0.07
Romanian (110)	270	0.34
Russian (341)	1,268	1.62
Scandinavian (25)	161	0.21
Scotch-Irish (826)	2,163	2.76
Scottish (576)	2,274	2.90
Serbian (49)	155	0.20
Slavic (0)	23	0.03
Slovak (37)	194	0.25
Slovene (10)	65	0.08
Soviet Union (0)	0	<0.01
Swedish (305)	1,462	1.86
Swiss (98)	457	0.58
Turkish (111)	111	0.14
Ukrainian (122)	232	0.30
Welsh (171)	840	1.07
West Indian, ex. Hispanic (57)	96	0.12
Bahamian (0)	0	<0.01
Barbadian (0)	0	<0.01
Belizean (0)	0	<0.01
Bermudan (0)	0	<0.01
British West Indian (0)	0	<0.01
Dutch West Indian (0)	23	0.03
Haitian (0)	0	<0.01
Jamaican (57)	57	0.07
Trinidadian/Tobagonian (0)	0	<0.01
U.S. Virgin Islander (0)	0	<0.01
West Indian (0)	16	0.02
Other West Indian (0)	0	<0.01
Yugoslavian (17)	50	0.06

Hispanic Origin	Population	%
Hispanic or Latino (of any race)	2,823	3.51
Central American, ex. Mexican	165	0.21
Costa Rican	21	0.03
Guatemalan	38	0.05
Honduran	21	0.03
Nicaraguan	28	0.03
Panamanian	22	0.03
Salvadoran	31	0.04
Other Central American	4	<0.01
Cuban	126	0.16
Dominican Republic	43	0.05
Mexican	1,506	1.87
Puerto Rican	348	0.43
South American	349	0.43
Argentinean	57	0.07
Bolivian	11	0.01
Chilean	36	0.04
Colombian	85	0.11
Ecuadorian	30	0.04
Paraguayan	5	0.01
Peruvian	67	0.08
Uruguayan	5	0.01
Venezuelan	53	0.07
Other South American	0	<0.01
Other Hispanic or Latino	286	0.36

Race*	Population	%
African-American/Black (3,671)	4,618	5.74
Not Hispanic (3,562)	4,423	5.50
Hispanic (109)	195	0.24
American Indian/Alaska Native (214)	699	0.87
Not Hispanic (176)	591	0.74
Hispanic (38)	108	0.13
Alaska Athabascan (Ala. Nat.) (1)	1	<0.01
Aleut (Alaska Native) (0)	2	<0.01
Apache (4)	11	0.01
Arapaho (0)	0	<0.01
Blackfeet (0)	26	0.03
Canadian/French Am. Ind. (0)	1	<0.01
Central American Ind. (1)	2	<0.01
Cherokee (37)	161	0.20
Cheyenne (0)	0	<0.01
Chickasaw (2)	2	<0.01
Chippewa (10)	21	0.03
Choctaw (8)	19	0.02
Colville (0)	0	<0.01
Comanche (0)	0	<0.01
Cree (0)	1	<0.01
Creek (4)	5	0.01
Crow (0)	0	<0.01
Delaware (5)	8	0.01
Hopi (1)	2	<0.01
Houma (0)	0	<0.01
Inupiat (Alaska Native) (0)	3	<0.01
Iroquois (5)	9	0.01
Kiowa (0)	0	<0.01
Lumbee (4)	4	<0.01
Menominee (1)	2	<0.01
Mexican American Ind. (6)	14	0.02
Navajo (3)	9	0.01
Osage (0)	2	<0.01
Ottawa (1)	1	<0.01
Paiute (0)	0	<0.01
Pima (0)	0	<0.01
Potawatomi (3)	10	0.01
Pueblo (0)	3	<0.01
Puget Sound Salish (5)	5	0.01
Seminole (0)	3	<0.01
Shoshone (0)	1	<0.01
Sioux (9)	24	0.03
South American Ind. (2)	4	<0.01
Spanish American Ind. (3)	21	0.03
Tlingit-Haida (Alaska Native) (0)	1	<0.01
Tohono O'Odham (3)	8	0.01
Tsimshian (Alaska Native) (0)	0	<0.01
Ute (0)	0	<0.01
Yakama (3)	3	<0.01
Yaqui (0)	0	<0.01
Yuman (0)	0	<0.01
Yup'ik (Alaska Native) (0)	1	<0.01
Asian (6,399)	7,368	9.16
Not Hispanic (6,378)	7,298	9.08
Hispanic (21)	70	0.09
Bangladeshi (21)	27	0.03
Bhutanese (0)	0	<0.01
Burmese (17)	18	0.02
Cambodian (5)	9	0.01
Chinese, ex. Taiwanese (2,004)	2,230	2.77
Filipino (161)	312	0.39
Hmong (4)	5	0.01
Indian (1,263)	1,390	1.73
Indonesian (71)	78	0.10
Japanese (242)	395	0.49
Korean (1,696)	1,807	2.25
Laotian (6)	8	0.01
Malaysian (49)	59	0.07
Nepalese (19)	19	0.02
Pakistani (76)	87	0.11
Sri Lankan (38)	40	0.05
Taiwanese (235)	260	0.32
Thai (83)	103	0.13
Vietnamese (168)	203	0.25
Hawaii Native/Pacific Islander (42)	120	0.15
Not Hispanic (37)	95	0.12
Hispanic (5)	25	0.03
Fijian (1)	1	<0.01
Guamanian/Chamorro (11)	24	0.03
Marshallese (0)	0	<0.01
Native Hawaiian (11)	37	0.05
Samoan (6)	16	0.02
Tongan (0)	0	<0.01
White (66,751)	68,936	85.74
Not Hispanic (65,189)	67,128	83.49
Hispanic (1,562)	1,808	2.25

Notes: † The Census 2010 population figure is used to calculate the percentages in the Hispanic Origin and Race categories. Ancestry percentages are based on the 2006-2010 American Community Survey population (not shown); ‡ Numbers in parentheses indicate the number of people reporting a single ancestry; * Numbers in parentheses indicate the number of persons reporting this race alone, not in combination with any other race; Please refer to the Explanation of Data for more information.

Carmel

Place Type: City
County: Hamilton
Population: 79,191

Ancestry	Population	%
Afghan (18)	37	0.05
African, Sub-Saharan (83)	255	0.33
African (58)	95	0.12
Cape Verdean (0)	0	<0.01
Ethiopian (12)	12	0.02
Ghanaian (0)	0	<0.01
Kenyan (0)	0	<0.01
Liberian (0)	0	<0.01
Nigerian (0)	0	<0.01
Senegalese (0)	0	<0.01
Sierra Leonean (0)	0	<0.01
Somalian (0)	0	<0.01
South African (13)	137	0.18
Sudanese (0)	11	0.01
Ugandan (0)	0	<0.01
Zimbabwean (0)	0	<0.01
Other Sub-Saharan African (0)	0	<0.01
Albanian (0)	0	<0.01
Alsatian (0)	0	<0.01
American (4,712)	4,712	6.14
Arab (378)	563	0.73
Arab (86)	101	0.13
Egyptian (164)	164	0.21
Iraqi (0)	0	<0.01
Jordanian (8)	8	0.01
Lebanese (40)	160	0.21
Moroccan (13)	36	0.05
Palestinian (24)	24	0.03
Syrian (0)	0	<0.01
Other Arab (43)	70	0.09
Armenian (0)	21	0.03
Assyrian/Chaldean/Syriac (0)	0	<0.01
Australian (31)	42	0.05
Austrian (32)	161	0.21
Basque (0)	0	<0.01
Belgian (26)	352	0.46
Brazilian (0)	11	0.01
British (449)	626	0.82
Bulgarian (0)	16	0.02
Cajun (0)	0	<0.01
Canadian (77)	166	0.22
Carpatho Rusyn (0)	16	0.02
Celtic (14)	14	0.02
Croatian (23)	175	0.23
Cypriot (0)	0	<0.01
Czech (33)	336	0.44
Czechoslovakian (60)	115	0.15
Danish (161)	597	0.78
Dutch (320)	1,777	2.31
Eastern European (149)	164	0.21
English (3,161)	11,352	14.79
Estonian (0)	13	0.02
European (1,056)	1,241	1.62
Finnish (14)	70	0.09
French, ex. Basque (305)	2,214	2.88
French Canadian (128)	225	0.29
German (7,760)	21,955	28.60
German Russian (0)	0	<0.01
Greek (192)	485	0.63
Guyanese (0)	0	<0.01
Hungarian (86)	504	0.66
Icelander (0)	12	0.02
Iranian (203)	253	0.33
Irish (3,191)	12,211	15.91
Israeli (0)	0	<0.01
Italian (1,290)	3,728	4.86
Latvian (129)	129	0.17
Lithuanian (57)	120	0.16
Luxemburger (0)	22	0.03
Macedonian (55)	104	0.14
Maltese (0)	0	<0.01
New Zealander (0)	0	<0.01
Northern European (105)	105	0.14
Norwegian (335)	995	1.30
Pennsylvania German (15)	42	0.05
Polish (680)	3,117	4.06
Portuguese (22)	112	0.15
Romanian (112)	200	0.26
Russian (676)	1,522	1.98
Scandinavian (74)	90	0.12
Scotch-Irish (468)	1,430	1.86
Scottish (684)	2,632	3.43
Serbian (21)	40	0.05
Slavic (0)	0	<0.01
Slovak (103)	356	0.46
Slovene (17)	109	0.14
Soviet Union (0)	0	<0.01
Swedish (222)	1,414	1.84
Swiss (49)	431	0.56
Turkish (69)	69	0.09
Ukrainian (161)	271	0.35
Welsh (83)	628	0.82
West Indian, ex. Hispanic (39)	55	0.07
Bahamian (0)	0	<0.01
Barbadian (0)	0	<0.01
Belizean (0)	0	<0.01
Bermudan (0)	0	<0.01
British West Indian (0)	0	<0.01
Dutch West Indian (0)	0	<0.01
Haitian (0)	16	0.02
Jamaican (39)	39	0.05
Trinidadian/Tobagonian (0)	0	<0.01
U.S. Virgin Islander (0)	0	<0.01
West Indian (0)	0	<0.01
Other West Indian (0)	0	<0.01
Yugoslavian (51)	67	0.09

Hispanic Origin	Population	%
Hispanic or Latino (of any race)	2,009	2.54
Central American, ex. Mexican	181	0.23
Costa Rican	8	0.01
Guatemalan	87	0.11
Honduran	9	0.01
Nicaraguan	20	0.03
Panamanian	28	0.04
Salvadoran	28	0.04
Other Central American	1	<0.01
Cuban	101	0.13
Dominican Republic	40	0.05
Mexican	944	1.19
Puerto Rican	226	0.29
South American	310	0.39
Argentinean	38	0.05
Bolivian	12	0.02
Chilean	22	0.03
Colombian	125	0.16
Ecuadorian	17	0.02
Paraguayan	3	<0.01
Peruvian	49	0.06
Uruguayan	3	<0.01
Venezuelan	40	0.05
Other South American	1	<0.01
Other Hispanic or Latino	207	0.26

Race*	Population	%
African-American/Black (2,354)	2,767	3.49
Not Hispanic (2,299)	2,674	3.38
Hispanic (55)	93	0.12
American Indian/Alaska Native (130)	354	0.45
Not Hispanic (104)	304	0.38
Hispanic (26)	50	0.06
Alaska Athabascan (Ala. Nat.) (0)	0	<0.01
Aleut (Alaska Native) (0)	0	<0.01
Apache (6)	6	0.01
Arapaho (0)	0	<0.01
Blackfeet (4)	16	0.02
Canadian/French Am. Ind. (0)	0	<0.01
Central American Ind. (1)	2	<0.01
Cherokee (17)	57	0.07
Cheyenne (0)	0	<0.01
Chickasaw (0)	0	<0.01
Chippewa (4)	6	0.01
Choctaw (5)	11	0.01
Colville (0)	0	<0.01
Comanche (0)	3	<0.01
Cree (3)	3	<0.01
Creek (0)	1	<0.01
Crow (1)	1	<0.01
Delaware (0)	0	<0.01
Hopi (2)	4	0.01
Houma (0)	0	<0.01
Inupiat (Alaska Native) (1)	1	<0.01
Iroquois (1)	8	0.01
Kiowa (0)	0	<0.01
Lumbee (2)	2	<0.01
Menominee (0)	0	<0.01
Mexican American Ind. (16)	21	0.03
Navajo (1)	4	0.01
Osage (3)	3	<0.01
Ottawa (1)	5	0.01
Paiute (0)	0	<0.01
Pima (0)	0	<0.01
Potawatomi (3)	11	0.01
Pueblo (0)	0	<0.01
Puget Sound Salish (0)	0	<0.01
Seminole (0)	1	<0.01
Shoshone (0)	0	<0.01
Sioux (3)	5	0.01
South American Ind. (1)	1	<0.01
Spanish American Ind. (2)	2	<0.01
Tlingit-Haida (Alaska Native) (0)	0	<0.01
Tohono O'Odham (0)	0	<0.01
Tsimshian (Alaska Native) (0)	0	<0.01
Ute (0)	1	<0.01
Yakama (0)	0	<0.01
Yaqui (2)	2	<0.01
Yuman (0)	0	<0.01
Yup'ik (Alaska Native) (0)	1	<0.01
Asian (7,009)	7,838	9.90
Not Hispanic (6,988)	7,790	9.84
Hispanic (21)	48	0.06
Bangladeshi (34)	35	0.04
Bhutanese (0)	0	<0.01
Burmese (1)	8	0.01
Cambodian (17)	22	0.03
Chinese, ex. Taiwanese (2,557)	2,754	3.48
Filipino (265)	411	0.52
Hmong (27)	27	0.03
Indian (2,384)	2,526	3.19
Indonesian (32)	41	0.05
Japanese (320)	415	0.52
Korean (583)	684	0.86
Laotian (9)	9	0.01
Malaysian (7)	17	0.02
Nepalese (12)	12	0.02
Pakistani (186)	211	0.27
Sri Lankan (30)	35	0.04
Taiwanese (145)	177	0.22
Thai (24)	42	0.05
Vietnamese (236)	279	0.35
Hawaii Native/Pacific Islander (20)	87	0.11
Not Hispanic (17)	77	0.10
Hispanic (3)	10	0.01
Fijian (0)	0	<0.01
Guamanian/Chamorro (5)	11	0.01
Marshallese (0)	0	<0.01
Native Hawaiian (8)	33	0.04
Samoan (5)	16	0.02
Tongan (0)	0	<0.01
White (67,654)	68,938	87.05
Not Hispanic (66,295)	67,446	85.17
Hispanic (1,359)	1,492	1.88

Notes: † The Census 2010 population figure is used to calculate the percentages in the Hispanic Origin and Race categories. Ancestry percentages are based on the 2006-2010 American Community Survey population (not shown); ‡ Numbers in parentheses indicate the number of people reporting a single ancestry; * Numbers in parentheses indicate the number of persons reporting this race alone, not in combination with any other race; Please refer to the Explanation of Data for more information.

Elkhart

Place Type: City
County: Elkhart
Population: 50,949

Ancestry	Population	%
Afghan (0)	0	<0.01
African, Sub-Saharan (296)	409	0.79
African (235)	305	0.59
Cape Verdean (0)	0	<0.01
Ethiopian (0)	0	<0.01
Ghanaian (0)	0	<0.01
Kenyan (61)	61	0.12
Liberian (0)	0	<0.01
Nigerian (0)	0	<0.01
Senegalese (0)	0	<0.01
Sierra Leonean (0)	0	<0.01
Somalian (0)	0	<0.01
South African (0)	0	<0.01
Sudanese (0)	0	<0.01
Ugandan (0)	0	<0.01
Zimbabwean (0)	13	0.03
Other Sub-Saharan African (0)	30	0.06
Albanian (0)	0	<0.01
Alsatian (0)	0	<0.01
American (2,012)	2,012	3.88
Arab (109)	109	0.21
Arab (23)	23	0.04
Egyptian (0)	0	<0.01
Iraqi (0)	0	<0.01
Jordanian (0)	0	<0.01
Lebanese (9)	9	0.02
Moroccan (16)	16	0.03
Palestinian (0)	0	<0.01
Syrian (0)	0	<0.01
Other Arab (61)	61	0.12
Armenian (0)	0	<0.01
Assyrian/Chaldean/Syriac (0)	0	<0.01
Australian (0)	0	<0.01
Austrian (0)	38	0.07
Basque (0)	0	<0.01
Belgian (18)	123	0.24
Brazilian (30)	92	0.18
British (41)	111	0.21
Bulgarian (0)	0	<0.01
Cajun (0)	0	<0.01
Canadian (15)	79	0.15
Carpatho Rusyn (0)	0	<0.01
Celtic (0)	0	<0.01
Croatian (0)	17	0.03
Cypriot (0)	0	<0.01
Czech (106)	195	0.38
Czechoslovakian (14)	14	0.03
Danish (21)	53	0.10
Dutch (374)	1,346	2.60
Eastern European (9)	9	0.02
English (1,054)	3,278	6.32
Estonian (0)	0	<0.01
European (207)	207	0.40
Finnish (34)	48	0.09
French, ex. Basque (155)	1,022	1.97
French Canadian (35)	203	0.39
German (3,461)	9,960	19.21
German Russian (0)	0	<0.01
Greek (51)	82	0.16
Guyanese (0)	0	<0.01
Hungarian (111)	258	0.50
Icelander (0)	0	<0.01
Iranian (0)	0	<0.01
Irish (1,183)	5,091	9.82
Israeli (0)	0	<0.01
Italian (711)	1,611	3.11
Latvian (11)	11	0.02
Lithuanian (21)	21	0.04
Luxemburger (0)	0	<0.01
Macedonian (0)	0	<0.01
Maltese (0)	0	<0.01
New Zealander (0)	0	<0.01
Northern European (26)	26	0.05
Norwegian (55)	299	0.58
Pennsylvania German (226)	347	0.67
Polish (487)	1,234	2.38
Portuguese (42)	42	0.08
Romanian (11)	40	0.08
Russian (27)	162	0.31
Scandinavian (60)	60	0.12
Scotch-Irish (331)	647	1.25
Scottish (137)	679	1.31
Serbian (0)	0	<0.01
Slavic (0)	0	<0.01
Slovak (0)	11	0.02
Slovene (18)	18	0.03
Soviet Union (0)	0	<0.01
Swedish (105)	422	0.81
Swiss (64)	504	0.97
Turkish (0)	0	<0.01
Ukrainian (29)	39	0.08
Welsh (44)	213	0.41
West Indian, ex. Hispanic (121)	121	0.23
Bahamian (0)	0	<0.01
Barbadian (0)	0	<0.01
Belizean (0)	0	<0.01
Bermudan (0)	0	<0.01
British West Indian (0)	0	<0.01
Dutch West Indian (0)	0	<0.01
Haitian (0)	0	<0.01
Jamaican (121)	121	0.23
Trinidadian/Tobagonian (0)	0	<0.01
U.S. Virgin Islander (0)	0	<0.01
West Indian (0)	0	<0.01
Other West Indian (0)	0	<0.01
Yugoslavian (0)	0	<0.01

Hispanic Origin	Population	%
Hispanic or Latino (of any race)	11,451	22.48
Central American, ex. Mexican	912	1.79
Costa Rican	1	<0.01
Guatemalan	93	0.18
Honduran	390	0.77
Nicaraguan	14	0.03
Panamanian	2	<0.01
Salvadoran	400	0.79
Other Central American	12	0.02
Cuban	26	0.05
Dominican Republic	19	0.04
Mexican	9,313	18.28
Puerto Rican	392	0.77
South American	121	0.24
Argentinean	10	0.02
Bolivian	29	0.06
Chilean	6	0.01
Colombian	24	0.05
Ecuadorian	7	0.01
Paraguayan	2	<0.01
Peruvian	20	0.04
Uruguayan	1	<0.01
Venezuelan	22	0.04
Other South American	0	<0.01
Other Hispanic or Latino	668	1.31

Race*	Population	%
African-American/Black (7,862)	9,108	17.88
Not Hispanic (7,705)	8,843	17.36
Hispanic (157)	265	0.52
American Indian/Alaska Native (290)	706	1.39
Not Hispanic (154)	482	0.95
Hispanic (136)	224	0.44
Alaska Athabascan (Ala. Nat.) (0)	0	<0.01
Aleut (Alaska Native) (0)	0	<0.01
Apache (0)	5	0.01
Arapaho (0)	0	<0.01
Blackfeet (5)	31	0.06
Canadian/French Am. Ind. (0)	5	0.01
Central American Ind. (1)	4	0.01
Cherokee (28)	120	0.24
Cheyenne (0)	3	0.01
Chickasaw (2)	2	<0.01
Chippewa (4)	14	0.03
Choctaw (4)	12	0.02
Colville (0)	0	<0.01
Comanche (2)	2	<0.01
Cree (1)	4	0.01
Creek (0)	4	0.01
Crow (0)	4	0.01
Delaware (0)	0	<0.01
Hopi (0)	0	<0.01
Houma (0)	0	<0.01
Inupiat (Alaska Native) (0)	0	<0.01
Iroquois (3)	5	0.01
Kiowa (0)	0	<0.01
Lumbee (7)	8	0.02
Menominee (0)	0	<0.01
Mexican American Ind. (32)	55	0.11
Navajo (3)	7	0.01
Osage (0)	0	<0.01
Ottawa (4)	6	0.01
Paiute (0)	3	0.01
Pima (0)	0	<0.01
Potawatomi (14)	28	0.05
Pueblo (0)	0	<0.01
Puget Sound Salish (0)	0	<0.01
Seminole (0)	0	<0.01
Shoshone (0)	0	<0.01
Sioux (7)	21	0.04
South American Ind. (3)	4	0.01
Spanish American Ind. (2)	3	0.01
Tlingit-Haida (Alaska Native) (0)	0	<0.01
Tohono O'Odham (0)	0	<0.01
Tsimshian (Alaska Native) (0)	0	<0.01
Ute (0)	0	<0.01
Yakama (0)	0	<0.01
Yaqui (0)	0	<0.01
Yuman (0)	0	<0.01
Yup'ik (Alaska Native) (0)	0	<0.01
Asian (452)	660	1.30
Not Hispanic (430)	625	1.23
Hispanic (22)	35	0.07
Bangladeshi (3)	3	0.01
Bhutanese (0)	0	<0.01
Burmese (0)	0	<0.01
Cambodian (49)	66	0.13
Chinese, ex. Taiwanese (43)	77	0.15
Filipino (46)	76	0.15
Hmong (0)	0	<0.01
Indian (93)	115	0.23
Indonesian (1)	8	0.02
Japanese (10)	32	0.06
Korean (37)	60	0.12
Laotian (87)	115	0.23
Malaysian (0)	1	<0.01
Nepalese (0)	0	<0.01
Pakistani (9)	15	0.03
Sri Lankan (4)	4	0.01
Taiwanese (1)	1	<0.01
Thai (11)	22	0.04
Vietnamese (12)	24	0.05
Hawaii Native/Pacific Islander (33)	71	0.14
Not Hispanic (20)	44	0.09
Hispanic (13)	27	0.05
Fijian (0)	0	<0.01
Guamanian/Chamorro (11)	17	0.03
Marshallese (1)	1	<0.01
Native Hawaiian (6)	19	0.04
Samoan (5)	8	0.02
Tongan (6)	6	0.01
White (33,672)	35,539	69.75
Not Hispanic (29,565)	30,987	60.82
Hispanic (4,107)	4,552	8.93

Notes: † The Census 2010 population figure is used to calculate the percentages in the Hispanic Origin and Race categories. Ancestry percentages are based on the 2006-2010 American Community Survey population (not shown); ‡ Numbers in parentheses indicate the number of people reporting a single ancestry; * Numbers in parentheses indicate the number of persons reporting this race alone, not in combination with any other race; Please refer to the Explanation of Data for more information.

Evansville

Place Type: City
County: Vanderburgh
Population: 117,429

Ancestry	Population	%
Afghan (0)	0	<0.01
African, Sub-Saharan (120)	233	0.20
African (90)	160	0.14
Cape Verdean (0)	0	<0.01
Ethiopian (0)	34	0.03
Ghanaian (0)	0	<0.01
Kenyan (0)	0	<0.01
Liberian (0)	0	<0.01
Nigerian (8)	17	0.01
Senegalese (0)	0	<0.01
Sierra Leonean (0)	0	<0.01
Somalian (0)	0	<0.01
South African (0)	0	<0.01
Sudanese (0)	0	<0.01
Ugandan (14)	14	0.01
Zimbabwean (0)	0	<0.01
Other Sub-Saharan African (8)	8	0.01
Albanian (0)	0	<0.01
Alsatian (0)	0	<0.01
American (23,162)	23,162	19.60
Arab (79)	117	0.10
Arab (7)	7	0.01
Egyptian (0)	0	<0.01
Iraqi (16)	16	0.01
Jordanian (15)	15	0.01
Lebanese (0)	27	0.02
Moroccan (0)	0	<0.01
Palestinian (30)	30	0.03
Syrian (0)	11	0.01
Other Arab (11)	11	0.01
Armenian (70)	78	0.07
Assyrian/Chaldean/Syriac (0)	0	<0.01
Australian (39)	39	0.03
Austrian (9)	109	0.09
Basque (0)	0	<0.01
Belgian (0)	75	0.06
Brazilian (62)	62	0.05
British (257)	446	0.38
Bulgarian (0)	0	<0.01
Cajun (0)	12	0.01
Canadian (61)	71	0.06
Carpatho Rusyn (0)	0	<0.01
Celtic (0)	23	0.02
Croatian (0)	47	0.04
Cypriot (0)	0	<0.01
Czech (39)	152	0.13
Czechoslovakian (44)	73	0.06
Danish (8)	133	0.11
Dutch (466)	1,856	1.57
Eastern European (0)	14	0.01
English (4,204)	9,922	8.40
Estonian (0)	0	<0.01
European (672)	768	0.65
Finnish (18)	80	0.07
French, ex. Basque (892)	2,952	2.50
French Canadian (99)	110	0.09
German (18,318)	33,828	28.62
German Russian (0)	0	<0.01
Greek (52)	135	0.11
Guyanese (0)	49	0.04
Hungarian (56)	136	0.12
Icelander (0)	0	<0.01
Iranian (20)	20	0.02
Irish (3,732)	14,073	11.91
Israeli (0)	0	<0.01
Italian (622)	2,111	1.79
Latvian (12)	12	0.01
Lithuanian (0)	83	0.07
Luxemburger (0)	0	<0.01
Macedonian (0)	0	<0.01
Maltese (0)	0	<0.01
New Zealander (0)	0	<0.01
Northern European (17)	34	0.03
Norwegian (132)	375	0.32
Pennsylvania German (21)	33	0.03
Polish (462)	1,485	1.26
Portuguese (63)	95	0.08
Romanian (0)	10	0.01
Russian (177)	381	0.32
Scandinavian (17)	25	0.02
Scotch-Irish (666)	1,964	1.66
Scottish (823)	2,023	1.71
Serbian (13)	13	0.01
Slavic (0)	11	0.01
Slovak (55)	157	0.13
Slovene (0)	0	<0.01
Soviet Union (0)	0	<0.01
Swedish (203)	477	0.40
Swiss (11)	216	0.18
Turkish (11)	25	0.02
Ukrainian (129)	129	0.11
Welsh (82)	380	0.32
West Indian, ex. Hispanic (23)	55	0.05
Bahamian (0)	0	<0.01
Barbadian (0)	0	<0.01
Belizean (0)	0	<0.01
Bermudan (0)	0	<0.01
British West Indian (0)	0	<0.01
Dutch West Indian (0)	0	<0.01
Haitian (0)	11	0.01
Jamaican (23)	44	0.04
Trinidadian/Tobagonian (0)	0	<0.01
U.S. Virgin Islander (0)	0	<0.01
West Indian (0)	0	<0.01
Other West Indian (0)	0	<0.01
Yugoslavian (0)	0	<0.01

Hispanic Origin	Population	%
Hispanic or Latino (of any race)	3,014	2.57
Central American, ex. Mexican	178	0.15
Costa Rican	7	0.01
Guatemalan	31	0.03
Honduran	31	0.03
Nicaraguan	35	0.03
Panamanian	24	0.02
Salvadoran	45	0.04
Other Central American	5	<0.01
Cuban	64	0.05
Dominican Republic	24	0.02
Mexican	2,073	1.77
Puerto Rican	245	0.21
South American	118	0.10
Argentinean	9	0.01
Bolivian	4	<0.01
Chilean	4	<0.01
Colombian	32	0.03
Ecuadorian	9	0.01
Paraguayan	2	<0.01
Peruvian	33	0.03
Uruguayan	0	<0.01
Venezuelan	24	0.02
Other South American	1	<0.01
Other Hispanic or Latino	312	0.27

Race*	Population	%
African-American/Black (14,766)	17,089	14.55
Not Hispanic (14,672)	16,871	14.37
Hispanic (94)	218	0.19
American Indian/Alaska Native (312)	916	0.78
Not Hispanic (269)	831	0.71
Hispanic (43)	85	0.07
Alaska Athabascan *(Ala. Nat.)* (0)	1	<0.01
Aleut *(Alaska Native)* (0)	0	<0.01
Apache (6)	23	0.02
Arapaho (1)	1	<0.01
Blackfeet (5)	39	0.03
Canadian/French Am. Ind. (1)	2	<0.01
Central American Ind. (1)	1	<0.01
Cherokee (71)	283	0.24
Cheyenne (4)	11	0.01
Chickasaw (1)	3	<0.01
Chippewa (12)	18	0.02
Choctaw (5)	16	0.01
Colville (1)	1	<0.01
Comanche (0)	2	<0.01
Cree (0)	2	<0.01
Creek (0)	0	<0.01
Crow (0)	1	<0.01
Delaware (4)	6	0.01
Hopi (0)	1	<0.01
Houma (2)	4	<0.01
Inupiat *(Alaska Native)* (0)	1	<0.01
Iroquois (3)	14	0.01
Kiowa (0)	1	<0.01
Lumbee (1)	11	0.01
Menominee (0)	0	<0.01
Mexican American Ind. (5)	7	0.01
Navajo (3)	10	0.01
Osage (2)	2	<0.01
Ottawa (0)	0	<0.01
Paiute (0)	0	<0.01
Pima (0)	0	<0.01
Potawatomi (0)	1	<0.01
Pueblo (1)	3	<0.01
Puget Sound Salish (0)	0	<0.01
Seminole (1)	3	<0.01
Shoshone (0)	0	<0.01
Sioux (25)	52	0.04
South American Ind. (2)	4	<0.01
Spanish American Ind. (1)	1	<0.01
Tlingit-Haida *(Alaska Native)* (0)	0	<0.01
Tohono O'Odham (0)	0	<0.01
Tsimshian *(Alaska Native)* (0)	0	<0.01
Ute (0)	0	<0.01
Yakama (0)	0	<0.01
Yaqui (0)	1	<0.01
Yuman (0)	0	<0.01
Yup'ik *(Alaska Native)* (0)	0	<0.01
Asian (1,160)	1,578	1.34
Not Hispanic (1,149)	1,544	1.31
Hispanic (11)	34	0.03
Bangladeshi (6)	6	0.01
Bhutanese (0)	0	<0.01
Burmese (1)	1	<0.01
Cambodian (2)	3	<0.01
Chinese, ex. Taiwanese (254)	319	0.27
Filipino (161)	248	0.21
Hmong (0)	0	<0.01
Indian (307)	369	0.31
Indonesian (6)	12	0.01
Japanese (69)	135	0.11
Korean (102)	162	0.14
Laotian (2)	2	<0.01
Malaysian (13)	17	0.01
Nepalese (14)	23	0.02
Pakistani (5)	10	0.01
Sri Lankan (0)	0	<0.01
Taiwanese (6)	10	0.01
Thai (23)	40	0.03
Vietnamese (155)	194	0.17
Hawaii Native/Pacific Islander (84)	176	0.15
Not Hispanic (72)	150	0.13
Hispanic (12)	26	0.02
Fijian (0)	0	<0.01
Guamanian/Chamorro (18)	30	0.03
Marshallese (44)	49	0.04
Native Hawaiian (12)	49	0.04
Samoan (5)	20	0.02
Tongan (0)	0	<0.01
White (96,266)	99,372	84.62
Not Hispanic (94,961)	97,793	83.28
Hispanic (1,305)	1,579	1.34

Notes: † The Census 2010 population figure is used to calculate the percentages in the Hispanic Origin and Race categories. Ancestry percentages are based on the 2006-2010 American Community Survey population (not shown); ‡ Numbers in parentheses indicate the number of people reporting a single ancestry; * Numbers in parentheses indicate the number of persons reporting this race alone, not in combination with any other race; Please refer to the Explanation of Data for more information.

Fishers

Place Type: Town
County: Hamilton
Population: 76,794

Ancestry	Population	%
Afghan (15)	15	0.02
African, Sub-Saharan (240)	258	0.36
African (102)	111	0.15
Cape Verdean (0)	0	<0.01
Ethiopian (0)	0	<0.01
Ghanaian (0)	0	<0.01
Kenyan (0)	0	<0.01
Liberian (0)	0	<0.01
Nigerian (79)	79	0.11
Senegalese (13)	13	0.02
Sierra Leonean (0)	0	<0.01
Somalian (0)	0	<0.01
South African (0)	0	<0.01
Sudanese (0)	0	<0.01
Ugandan (0)	0	<0.01
Zimbabwean (0)	0	<0.01
Other Sub-Saharan African (46)	55	0.08
Albanian (0)	10	0.01
Alsatian (0)	0	<0.01
American (3,929)	3,929	5.48
Arab (450)	580	0.81
Arab (207)	235	0.33
Egyptian (113)	125	0.17
Iraqi (0)	0	<0.01
Jordanian (25)	37	0.05
Lebanese (73)	135	0.19
Moroccan (0)	0	<0.01
Palestinian (0)	0	<0.01
Syrian (32)	32	0.04
Other Arab (0)	16	0.02
Armenian (10)	10	0.01
Assyrian/Chaldean/Syriac (0)	0	<0.01
Australian (0)	36	0.05
Austrian (46)	233	0.32
Basque (0)	0	<0.01
Belgian (74)	165	0.23
Brazilian (10)	24	0.03
British (228)	451	0.63
Bulgarian (0)	0	<0.01
Cajun (0)	22	0.03
Canadian (95)	195	0.27
Carpatho Rusyn (0)	0	<0.01
Celtic (14)	14	0.02
Croatian (19)	84	0.12
Cypriot (0)	0	<0.01
Czech (105)	513	0.72
Czechoslovakian (27)	41	0.06
Danish (129)	282	0.39
Dutch (353)	1,512	2.11
Eastern European (75)	75	0.10
English (3,213)	9,173	12.79
Estonian (0)	0	<0.01
European (1,290)	1,428	1.99
Finnish (13)	83	0.12
French, ex. Basque (468)	2,611	3.64
French Canadian (108)	382	0.53
German (8,414)	20,883	29.11
German Russian (0)	0	<0.01
Greek (206)	637	0.89
Guyanese (0)	0	<0.01
Hungarian (127)	463	0.65
Icelander (0)	0	<0.01
Iranian (161)	181	0.25
Irish (3,090)	10,537	14.69
Israeli (21)	21	0.03
Italian (1,156)	3,343	4.66
Latvian (13)	13	0.02
Lithuanian (24)	166	0.23
Luxemburger (0)	0	<0.01
Macedonian (0)	10	0.01
Maltese (0)	0	<0.01
New Zealander (14)	14	0.02
Northern European (24)	24	0.03
Norwegian (335)	843	1.17
Pennsylvania German (12)	27	0.04
Polish (774)	2,912	4.06
Portuguese (59)	185	0.26
Romanian (85)	109	0.15
Russian (142)	350	0.49
Scandinavian (97)	183	0.26
Scotch-Irish (518)	1,293	1.80
Scottish (656)	2,188	3.05
Serbian (29)	47	0.07
Slavic (12)	50	0.07
Slovak (36)	63	0.09
Slovene (48)	54	0.08
Soviet Union (0)	0	<0.01
Swedish (283)	1,288	1.80
Swiss (143)	576	0.80
Turkish (0)	0	<0.01
Ukrainian (39)	97	0.14
Welsh (393)	930	1.30
West Indian, ex. Hispanic (13)	58	0.08
Bahamian (0)	0	<0.01
Barbadian (0)	0	<0.01
Belizean (0)	0	<0.01
Bermudan (0)	0	<0.01
British West Indian (13)	13	0.02
Dutch West Indian (0)	0	<0.01
Haitian (0)	0	<0.01
Jamaican (0)	45	0.06
Trinidadian/Tobagonian (0)	0	<0.01
U.S. Virgin Islander (0)	0	<0.01
West Indian (0)	0	<0.01
Other West Indian (0)	0	<0.01
Yugoslavian (90)	133	0.19

Hispanic Origin	Population	%
Hispanic or Latino (of any race)	2,638	3.44
Central American, ex. Mexican	162	0.21
Costa Rican	9	0.01
Guatemalan	54	0.07
Honduran	16	0.02
Nicaraguan	13	0.02
Panamanian	39	0.05
Salvadoran	28	0.04
Other Central American	3	<0.01
Cuban	90	0.12
Dominican Republic	46	0.06
Mexican	1,389	1.81
Puerto Rican	349	0.45
South American	359	0.47
Argentinean	29	0.04
Bolivian	5	0.01
Chilean	15	0.02
Colombian	127	0.17
Ecuadorian	9	0.01
Paraguayan	3	<0.01
Peruvian	62	0.08
Uruguayan	7	0.01
Venezuelan	93	0.12
Other South American	9	0.01
Other Hispanic or Latino	243	0.32

Race*	Population	%
African-American/Black (4,299)	4,958	6.46
Not Hispanic (4,228)	4,837	6.30
Hispanic (71)	121	0.16
American Indian/Alaska Native (126)	302	0.39
Not Hispanic (109)	267	0.35
Hispanic (17)	35	0.05
Alaska Athabascan (Ala. Nat.) (0)	0	<0.01
Aleut (Alaska Native) (0)	0	<0.01
Apache (4)	9	0.01
Arapaho (0)	0	<0.01
Blackfeet (2)	4	0.01
Canadian/French Am. Ind. (0)	0	<0.01
Central American Ind. (0)	1	<0.01
Cherokee (20)	61	0.08
Cheyenne (0)	0	<0.01
Chickasaw (0)	1	<0.01
Chippewa (5)	9	0.01
Choctaw (0)	6	0.01
Colville (0)	0	<0.01
Comanche (0)	0	<0.01
Cree (0)	1	<0.01
Creek (1)	1	<0.01
Crow (0)	0	<0.01
Delaware (0)	2	<0.01
Hopi (0)	0	<0.01
Houma (0)	0	<0.01
Inupiat (Alaska Native) (0)	0	<0.01
Iroquois (3)	6	0.01
Kiowa (1)	1	<0.01
Lumbee (5)	6	0.01
Menominee (1)	2	<0.01
Mexican American Ind. (3)	3	<0.01
Navajo (0)	2	<0.01
Osage (0)	0	<0.01
Ottawa (1)	1	<0.01
Paiute (2)	3	<0.01
Pima (0)	0	<0.01
Potawatomi (6)	7	0.01
Pueblo (0)	1	<0.01
Puget Sound Salish (0)	0	<0.01
Seminole (0)	0	<0.01
Shoshone (0)	0	<0.01
Sioux (7)	9	0.01
South American Ind. (0)	10	0.01
Spanish American Ind. (0)	0	<0.01
Tlingit-Haida (Alaska Native) (1)	1	<0.01
Tohono O'Odham (0)	0	<0.01
Tsimshian (Alaska Native) (0)	0	<0.01
Ute (0)	0	<0.01
Yakama (0)	0	<0.01
Yaqui (0)	0	<0.01
Yuman (0)	0	<0.01
Yup'ik (Alaska Native) (0)	0	<0.01
Asian (4,188)	4,930	6.42
Not Hispanic (4,174)	4,883	6.36
Hispanic (14)	47	0.06
Bangladeshi (31)	35	0.05
Bhutanese (1)	3	<0.01
Burmese (2)	6	0.01
Cambodian (9)	14	0.02
Chinese, ex. Taiwanese (703)	818	1.07
Filipino (241)	391	0.51
Hmong (11)	11	0.01
Indian (1,639)	1,785	2.32
Indonesian (46)	53	0.07
Japanese (220)	316	0.41
Korean (457)	575	0.75
Laotian (19)	25	0.03
Malaysian (8)	10	0.01
Nepalese (18)	18	0.02
Pakistani (177)	189	0.25
Sri Lankan (10)	11	0.01
Taiwanese (40)	45	0.06
Thai (24)	47	0.06
Vietnamese (383)	439	0.57
Hawaii Native/Pacific Islander (19)	58	0.08
Not Hispanic (14)	46	0.06
Hispanic (5)	12	0.02
Fijian (0)	0	<0.01
Guamanian/Chamorro (3)	6	0.01
Marshallese (0)	0	<0.01
Native Hawaiian (5)	16	0.02
Samoan (4)	11	0.01
Tongan (3)	6	0.01
White (65,754)	67,165	87.46
Not Hispanic (64,058)	65,289	85.02
Hispanic (1,696)	1,876	2.44

Notes: † The Census 2010 population figure is used to calculate the percentages in the Hispanic Origin and Race categories. Ancestry percentages are based on the 2006-2010 American Community Survey population (not shown); ‡ Numbers in parentheses indicate the number of people reporting a single ancestry; * Numbers in parentheses indicate the number of persons reporting this race alone, not in combination with any other race; Please refer to the Explanation of Data for more information.

Fort Wayne

Place Type: City
County: Allen
Population: 253,691

Ancestry	Population	%
Afghan (20)	20	0.01
African, Sub-Saharan (13,049)	13,249	5.22
African (12,562)	12,753	5.03
Cape Verdean (0)	0	<0.01
Ethiopian (47)	47	0.02
Ghanaian (0)	0	<0.01
Kenyan (27)	27	0.01
Liberian (0)	0	<0.01
Nigerian (138)	138	0.05
Senegalese (0)	0	<0.01
Sierra Leonean (0)	0	<0.01
Somalian (68)	68	0.03
South African (43)	52	0.02
Sudanese (0)	0	<0.01
Ugandan (0)	0	<0.01
Zimbabwean (0)	0	<0.01
Other Sub-Saharan African (164)	164	0.06
Albanian (33)	33	0.01
Alsatian (8)	8	<0.01
American (25,688)	25,688	10.12
Arab (475)	664	0.26
Arab (207)	222	0.09
Egyptian (8)	8	<0.01
Iraqi (44)	54	0.02
Jordanian (10)	10	<0.01
Lebanese (121)	235	0.09
Moroccan (10)	10	<0.01
Palestinian (0)	0	<0.01
Syrian (54)	104	0.04
Other Arab (21)	21	0.01
Armenian (81)	81	0.03
Assyrian/Chaldean/Syriac (10)	10	<0.01
Australian (27)	54	0.02
Austrian (105)	250	0.10
Basque (0)	0	<0.01
Belgian (27)	220	0.09
Brazilian (0)	21	0.01
British (375)	767	0.30
Bulgarian (126)	156	0.06
Cajun (0)	0	<0.01
Canadian (295)	681	0.27
Carpatho Rusyn (0)	0	<0.01
Celtic (8)	30	0.01
Croatian (150)	244	0.10
Cypriot (0)	0	<0.01
Czech (224)	837	0.33
Czechoslovakian (53)	130	0.05
Danish (182)	601	0.24
Dutch (872)	3,612	1.42
Eastern European (101)	110	0.04
English (6,224)	19,734	7.78
Estonian (0)	12	<0.01
European (1,501)	1,608	0.63
Finnish (18)	185	0.07
French, ex. Basque (1,952)	9,917	3.91
French Canadian (321)	813	0.32
German (36,666)	76,622	30.20
German Russian (0)	0	<0.01
Greek (380)	732	0.29
Guyanese (0)	0	<0.01
Hungarian (350)	1,122	0.44
Icelander (0)	9	<0.01
Iranian (8)	8	<0.01
Irish (8,309)	28,352	11.17
Israeli (34)	34	0.01
Italian (2,543)	6,703	2.64
Latvian (70)	70	0.03
Lithuanian (39)	278	0.11
Luxemburger (0)	36	0.01
Macedonian (328)	580	0.23
Maltese (0)	0	<0.01
New Zealander (0)	11	<0.01
Northern European (96)	96	0.04
Norwegian (393)	1,488	0.59
Pennsylvania German (190)	255	0.10
Polish (1,714)	5,438	2.14
Portuguese (175)	324	0.13
Romanian (184)	387	0.15
Russian (344)	913	0.36
Scandinavian (153)	269	0.11
Scotch-Irish (998)	3,125	1.23
Scottish (1,270)	4,615	1.82
Serbian (0)	75	0.03
Slavic (47)	92	0.04
Slovak (196)	468	0.18
Slovene (0)	37	0.01
Soviet Union (0)	0	<0.01
Swedish (460)	1,940	0.76
Swiss (615)	2,499	0.98
Turkish (46)	46	0.02
Ukrainian (155)	293	0.12
Welsh (248)	1,388	0.55
West Indian, ex. Hispanic (567)	665	0.26
Bahamian (0)	0	<0.01
Barbadian (0)	0	<0.01
Belizean (0)	0	<0.01
Bermudan (0)	0	<0.01
British West Indian (74)	74	0.03
Dutch West Indian (0)	0	<0.01
Haitian (346)	377	0.15
Jamaican (147)	196	0.08
Trinidadian/Tobagonian (0)	0	<0.01
U.S. Virgin Islander (0)	0	<0.01
West Indian (0)	18	0.01
Other West Indian (0)	0	<0.01
Yugoslavian (1,385)	1,443	0.57

Hispanic Origin	Population	%
Hispanic or Latino (of any race)	20,200	7.96
Central American, ex. Mexican	1,346	0.53
Costa Rican	38	0.01
Guatemalan	729	0.29
Honduran	129	0.05
Nicaraguan	37	0.01
Panamanian	38	0.01
Salvadoran	369	0.15
Other Central American	6	<0.01
Cuban	174	0.07
Dominican Republic	72	0.03
Mexican	15,545	6.13
Puerto Rican	939	0.37
South American	651	0.26
Argentinean	36	0.01
Bolivian	15	0.01
Chilean	18	0.01
Colombian	235	0.09
Ecuadorian	159	0.06
Paraguayan	4	<0.01
Peruvian	128	0.05
Uruguayan	10	<0.01
Venezuelan	45	0.02
Other South American	1	<0.01
Other Hispanic or Latino	1,473	0.58

Race*	Population	%
African-American/Black (39,085)	44,499	17.54
Not Hispanic (38,514)	43,301	17.07
Hispanic (571)	1,198	0.47
American Indian/Alaska Native (939)	2,669	1.05
Not Hispanic (730)	2,172	0.86
Hispanic (209)	497	0.20
Alaska Athabascan (Ala. Nat.) (4)	4	<0.01
Aleut (Alaska Native) (1)	1	<0.01
Apache (15)	43	0.02
Arapaho (2)	3	<0.01
Blackfeet (18)	110	0.04
Canadian/French Am. Ind. (2)	4	<0.01
Central American Ind. (5)	11	<0.01
Cherokee (126)	481	0.19
Cheyenne (2)	6	<0.01
Chickasaw (5)	13	0.01
Chippewa (28)	63	0.02
Choctaw (19)	55	0.02
Colville (0)	0	<0.01
Comanche (3)	4	<0.01
Cree (1)	9	<0.01
Creek (6)	18	0.01
Crow (1)	12	<0.01
Delaware (1)	12	<0.01
Hopi (2)	7	<0.01
Houma (0)	3	<0.01
Inupiat (Alaska Native) (3)	3	<0.01
Iroquois (20)	41	0.02
Kiowa (3)	3	<0.01
Lumbee (1)	2	<0.01
Menominee (0)	1	<0.01
Mexican American Ind. (42)	67	0.03
Navajo (8)	26	0.01
Osage (1)	1	<0.01
Ottawa (9)	15	0.01
Paiute (0)	1	<0.01
Pima (4)	7	<0.01
Potawatomi (7)	26	0.01
Pueblo (2)	7	<0.01
Puget Sound Salish (0)	0	<0.01
Seminole (0)	11	<0.01
Shoshone (0)	0	<0.01
Sioux (21)	68	0.03
South American Ind. (4)	9	<0.01
Spanish American Ind. (2)	3	<0.01
Tlingit-Haida (Alaska Native) (2)	4	<0.01
Tohono O'Odham (0)	0	<0.01
Tsimshian (Alaska Native) (0)	0	<0.01
Ute (1)	2	<0.01
Yakama (0)	0	<0.01
Yaqui (3)	5	<0.01
Yuman (0)	0	<0.01
Yup'ik (Alaska Native) (1)	2	<0.01
Asian (8,379)	9,768	3.85
Not Hispanic (8,279)	9,548	3.76
Hispanic (100)	220	0.09
Bangladeshi (37)	40	0.02
Bhutanese (0)	0	<0.01
Burmese (3,653)	3,819	1.51
Cambodian (38)	46	0.02
Chinese, ex. Taiwanese (493)	643	0.25
Filipino (520)	823	0.32
Hmong (0)	0	<0.01
Indian (1,183)	1,426	0.56
Indonesian (18)	26	0.01
Japanese (128)	252	0.10
Korean (313)	474	0.19
Laotian (290)	369	0.15
Malaysian (19)	41	0.02
Nepalese (10)	11	<0.01
Pakistani (114)	161	0.06
Sri Lankan (17)	19	0.01
Taiwanese (33)	47	0.02
Thai (132)	202	0.08
Vietnamese (818)	939	0.37
Hawaii Native/Pacific Islander (154)	354	0.14
Not Hispanic (91)	249	0.10
Hispanic (63)	105	0.04
Fijian (2)	2	<0.01
Guamanian/Chamorro (67)	102	0.04
Marshallese (1)	1	<0.01
Native Hawaiian (41)	119	0.05
Samoan (13)	38	0.01
Tongan (0)	1	<0.01
White (186,763)	194,759	76.77
Not Hispanic (178,436)	184,757	72.83
Hispanic (8,327)	10,002	3.94

Notes: † The Census 2010 population figure is used to calculate the percentages in the Hispanic Origin and Race categories. Ancestry percentages are based on the 2006-2010 American Community Survey population (not shown); ‡ Numbers in parentheses indicate the number of people reporting a single ancestry; * Numbers in parentheses indicate the number of persons reporting this race alone, not in combination with any other race; Please refer to the Explanation of Data for more information.

Gary

Place Type: City
County: Lake
Population: 80,294

Ancestry	Population	%
Afghan (0)	0	<0.01
African, Sub-Saharan (1,504)	1,824	2.16
African (1,278)	1,527	1.81
Cape Verdean (0)	0	<0.01
Ethiopian (121)	121	0.14
Ghanaian (10)	10	0.01
Kenyan (0)	0	<0.01
Liberian (0)	11	0.01
Nigerian (95)	155	0.18
Senegalese (0)	0	<0.01
Sierra Leonean (0)	0	<0.01
Somalian (0)	0	<0.01
South African (0)	0	<0.01
Sudanese (0)	0	<0.01
Ugandan (0)	0	<0.01
Zimbabwean (0)	0	<0.01
Other Sub-Saharan African (0)	0	<0.01
Albanian (0)	0	<0.01
Alsatian (0)	0	<0.01
American (1,013)	1,013	1.20
Arab (18)	18	0.02
Arab (0)	0	<0.01
Egyptian (0)	0	<0.01
Iraqi (0)	0	<0.01
Jordanian (0)	0	<0.01
Lebanese (0)	0	<0.01
Moroccan (18)	18	0.02
Palestinian (0)	0	<0.01
Syrian (0)	0	<0.01
Other Arab (0)	0	<0.01
Armenian (0)	0	<0.01
Assyrian/Chaldean/Syriac (0)	0	<0.01
Australian (0)	0	<0.01
Austrian (0)	30	0.04
Basque (0)	0	<0.01
Belgian (12)	43	0.05
Brazilian (21)	30	0.04
British (26)	68	0.08
Bulgarian (0)	0	<0.01
Cajun (0)	0	<0.01
Canadian (0)	19	0.02
Carpatho Rusyn (0)	0	<0.01
Celtic (0)	0	<0.01
Croatian (100)	187	0.22
Cypriot (0)	0	<0.01
Czech (24)	24	0.03
Czechoslovakian (0)	0	<0.01
Danish (0)	29	0.03
Dutch (71)	315	0.37
Eastern European (37)	37	0.04
English (724)	1,454	1.72
Estonian (0)	0	<0.01
European (42)	42	0.05
Finnish (7)	7	0.01
French, ex. Basque (15)	207	0.25
French Canadian (10)	19	0.02
German (600)	2,519	2.98
German Russian (0)	0	<0.01
Greek (89)	164	0.19
Guyanese (0)	0	<0.01
Hungarian (65)	167	0.20
Icelander (0)	0	<0.01
Iranian (0)	0	<0.01
Irish (730)	2,537	3.01
Israeli (0)	0	<0.01
Italian (152)	530	0.63
Latvian (0)	0	<0.01
Lithuanian (46)	162	0.19
Luxemburger (0)	0	<0.01
Macedonian (0)	0	<0.01
Maltese (10)	10	0.01
New Zealander (0)	0	<0.01
Northern European (0)	0	<0.01
Norwegian (16)	194	0.23
Pennsylvania German (0)	0	<0.01
Polish (375)	1,164	1.38
Portuguese (0)	0	<0.01
Romanian (0)	9	0.01
Russian (0)	46	0.05
Scandinavian (0)	0	<0.01
Scotch-Irish (34)	169	0.20
Scottish (67)	204	0.24
Serbian (9)	9	0.01
Slavic (0)	12	0.01
Slovak (43)	209	0.25
Slovene (0)	0	<0.01
Soviet Union (0)	0	<0.01
Swedish (27)	98	0.12
Swiss (0)	24	0.03
Turkish (12)	12	0.01
Ukrainian (20)	31	0.04
Welsh (0)	90	0.11
West Indian, ex. Hispanic (198)	265	0.31
Bahamian (0)	0	<0.01
Barbadian (0)	0	<0.01
Belizean (0)	0	<0.01
Bermudan (0)	0	<0.01
British West Indian (0)	0	<0.01
Dutch West Indian (0)	0	<0.01
Haitian (0)	14	0.02
Jamaican (173)	192	0.23
Trinidadian/Tobagonian (0)	0	<0.01
U.S. Virgin Islander (0)	0	<0.01
West Indian (0)	34	0.04
Other West Indian (25)	25	0.03
Yugoslavian (17)	24	0.03

Hispanic Origin	Population	%
Hispanic or Latino (of any race)	4,128	5.14
Central American, ex. Mexican	47	0.06
Costa Rican	0	<0.01
Guatemalan	19	0.02
Honduran	12	0.01
Nicaraguan	2	<0.01
Panamanian	9	0.01
Salvadoran	5	0.01
Other Central American	0	<0.01
Cuban	61	0.08
Dominican Republic	24	0.03
Mexican	2,553	3.18
Puerto Rican	1,223	1.52
South American	14	0.02
Argentinean	1	<0.01
Bolivian	1	<0.01
Chilean	1	<0.01
Colombian	8	0.01
Ecuadorian	0	<0.01
Paraguayan	0	<0.01
Peruvian	2	<0.01
Uruguayan	0	<0.01
Venezuelan	1	<0.01
Other South American	0	<0.01
Other Hispanic or Latino	206	0.26

Race*	Population	%
African-American/Black (68,107)	69,508	86.57
Not Hispanic (67,363)	68,449	85.25
Hispanic (744)	1,059	1.32
American Indian/Alaska Native (241)	760	0.95
Not Hispanic (197)	659	0.82
Hispanic (44)	101	0.13
Alaska Athabascan (Ala. Nat.) (0)	0	<0.01
Aleut (Alaska Native) (0)	0	<0.01
Apache (9)	16	0.02
Arapaho (0)	0	<0.01
Blackfeet (5)	43	0.05
Canadian/French Am. Ind. (0)	1	<0.01
Central American Ind. (2)	3	<0.01
Cherokee (12)	153	0.19
Cheyenne (0)	0	<0.01
Chickasaw (0)	4	<0.01
Chippewa (5)	11	0.01
Choctaw (3)	27	0.03
Colville (0)	0	<0.01
Comanche (1)	2	<0.01
Cree (4)	7	0.01
Creek (2)	20	0.02
Crow (0)	0	<0.01
Delaware (0)	2	<0.01
Hopi (0)	0	<0.01
Houma (4)	4	<0.01
Inupiat (Alaska Native) (0)	0	<0.01
Iroquois (2)	5	0.01
Kiowa (0)	0	<0.01
Lumbee (3)	3	<0.01
Menominee (1)	6	0.01
Mexican American Ind. (6)	15	0.02
Navajo (1)	6	0.01
Osage (0)	0	<0.01
Ottawa (0)	0	<0.01
Paiute (0)	1	<0.01
Pima (0)	0	<0.01
Potawatomi (1)	1	<0.01
Pueblo (0)	0	<0.01
Puget Sound Salish (0)	0	<0.01
Seminole (0)	12	0.01
Shoshone (0)	0	<0.01
Sioux (4)	17	0.02
South American Ind. (1)	3	<0.01
Spanish American Ind. (0)	0	<0.01
Tlingit-Haida (Alaska Native) (0)	0	<0.01
Tohono O'Odham (0)	0	<0.01
Tsimshian (Alaska Native) (0)	0	<0.01
Ute (0)	0	<0.01
Yakama (0)	0	<0.01
Yaqui (0)	0	<0.01
Yuman (0)	0	<0.01
Yup'ik (Alaska Native) (0)	0	<0.01
Asian (164)	345	0.43
Not Hispanic (156)	309	0.38
Hispanic (8)	36	0.04
Bangladeshi (0)	1	<0.01
Bhutanese (0)	0	<0.01
Burmese (0)	0	<0.01
Cambodian (7)	7	0.01
Chinese, ex. Taiwanese (23)	86	0.11
Filipino (42)	75	0.09
Hmong (0)	0	<0.01
Indian (23)	52	0.06
Indonesian (0)	0	<0.01
Japanese (11)	34	0.04
Korean (24)	42	0.05
Laotian (6)	6	0.01
Malaysian (0)	0	<0.01
Nepalese (0)	0	<0.01
Pakistani (6)	9	0.01
Sri Lankan (0)	0	<0.01
Taiwanese (0)	0	<0.01
Thai (2)	4	<0.01
Vietnamese (7)	19	0.02
Hawaii Native/Pacific Islander (8)	46	0.06
Not Hispanic (5)	32	0.04
Hispanic (3)	14	0.02
Fijian (0)	0	<0.01
Guamanian/Chamorro (1)	6	0.01
Marshallese (0)	0	<0.01
Native Hawaiian (1)	4	<0.01
Samoan (3)	15	0.02
Tongan (0)	0	<0.01
White (8,619)	9,685	12.06
Not Hispanic (7,151)	7,969	9.92
Hispanic (1,468)	1,716	2.14

Notes: † The Census 2010 population figure is used to calculate the percentages in the Hispanic Origin and Race categories. Ancestry percentages are based on the 2006-2010 American Community Survey population (not shown); ‡ Numbers in parentheses indicate the number of people reporting a single ancestry; * Numbers in parentheses indicate the number of persons reporting this race alone, not in combination with any other race; Please refer to the Explanation of Data for more information.

Hammond

Place Type: City
County: Lake
Population: 80,830

Ancestry	Population	%
Afghan (0)	0	<0.01
African, Sub-Saharan (354)	421	0.52
African (354)	398	0.49
Cape Verdean (0)	0	<0.01
Ethiopian (0)	0	<0.01
Ghanaian (0)	0	<0.01
Kenyan (0)	0	<0.01
Liberian (0)	0	<0.01
Nigerian (0)	10	0.01
Senegalese (0)	0	<0.01
Sierra Leonean (0)	0	<0.01
Somalian (0)	0	<0.01
South African (0)	0	<0.01
Sudanese (0)	0	<0.01
Ugandan (0)	0	<0.01
Zimbabwean (0)	0	<0.01
Other Sub-Saharan African (0)	13	0.02
Albanian (0)	61	0.08
Alsatian (0)	18	0.02
American (2,149)	2,149	2.64
Arab (180)	272	0.33
Arab (52)	144	0.18
Egyptian (83)	83	0.10
Iraqi (0)	0	<0.01
Jordanian (30)	30	0.04
Lebanese (0)	0	<0.01
Moroccan (0)	0	<0.01
Palestinian (0)	0	<0.01
Syrian (0)	0	<0.01
Other Arab (15)	15	0.02
Armenian (18)	27	0.03
Assyrian/Chaldean/Syriac (7)	7	0.01
Australian (21)	21	0.03
Austrian (8)	59	0.07
Basque (0)	0	<0.01
Belgian (12)	27	0.03
Brazilian (0)	13	0.02
British (30)	79	0.10
Bulgarian (0)	0	<0.01
Cajun (0)	0	<0.01
Canadian (10)	55	0.07
Carpatho Rusyn (0)	0	<0.01
Celtic (0)	7	0.01
Croatian (230)	908	1.12
Cypriot (0)	0	<0.01
Czech (94)	369	0.45
Czechoslovakian (61)	101	0.12
Danish (12)	85	0.10
Dutch (205)	1,088	1.34
Eastern European (180)	180	0.22
English (879)	3,228	3.97
Estonian (0)	18	0.02
European (122)	150	0.18
Finnish (25)	153	0.19
French, ex. Basque (215)	1,407	1.73
French Canadian (103)	345	0.42
German (2,610)	9,601	11.81
German Russian (0)	0	<0.01
Greek (438)	881	1.08
Guyanese (14)	14	0.02
Hungarian (298)	827	1.02
Icelander (0)	0	<0.01
Iranian (0)	0	<0.01
Irish (1,741)	8,337	10.25
Israeli (0)	0	<0.01
Italian (835)	2,841	3.49
Latvian (0)	0	<0.01
Lithuanian (107)	242	0.30
Luxemburger (0)	0	<0.01
Macedonian (0)	9	0.01
Maltese (0)	0	<0.01
New Zealander (0)	0	<0.01
Northern European (49)	49	0.06
Norwegian (77)	322	0.40
Pennsylvania German (18)	76	0.09
Polish (3,706)	7,497	9.22
Portuguese (0)	64	0.08
Romanian (16)	77	0.09
Russian (89)	275	0.34
Scandinavian (17)	65	0.08
Scotch-Irish (223)	574	0.71
Scottish (30)	627	0.77
Serbian (228)	572	0.70
Slavic (0)	22	0.03
Slovak (705)	1,791	2.20
Slovene (0)	0	<0.01
Soviet Union (0)	0	<0.01
Swedish (222)	1,016	1.25
Swiss (12)	81	0.10
Turkish (0)	8	0.01
Ukrainian (129)	244	0.30
Welsh (59)	241	0.30
West Indian, ex. Hispanic (42)	135	0.17
Bahamian (0)	0	<0.01
Barbadian (0)	0	<0.01
Belizean (0)	0	<0.01
Bermudan (0)	0	<0.01
British West Indian (0)	0	<0.01
Dutch West Indian (0)	0	<0.01
Haitian (42)	86	0.11
Jamaican (0)	49	0.06
Trinidadian/Tobagonian (0)	0	<0.01
U.S. Virgin Islander (0)	0	<0.01
West Indian (0)	0	<0.01
Other West Indian (0)	0	<0.01
Yugoslavian (0)	0	<0.01

Hispanic Origin	Population	%
Hispanic or Latino (of any race)	27,563	34.10
Central American, ex. Mexican	526	0.65
Costa Rican	18	0.02
Guatemalan	172	0.21
Honduran	117	0.14
Nicaraguan	19	0.02
Panamanian	21	0.03
Salvadoran	174	0.22
Other Central American	5	0.01
Cuban	140	0.17
Dominican Republic	10	0.01
Mexican	22,684	28.06
Puerto Rican	3,081	3.81
South American	141	0.17
Argentinean	29	0.04
Bolivian	0	<0.01
Chilean	5	0.01
Colombian	36	0.04
Ecuadorian	12	0.01
Paraguayan	1	<0.01
Peruvian	40	0.05
Uruguayan	6	0.01
Venezuelan	12	0.01
Other South American	0	<0.01
Other Hispanic or Latino	981	1.21

Race*	Population	%
African-American/Black (18,224)	19,336	23.92
Not Hispanic (17,568)	18,369	22.73
Hispanic (656)	967	1.20
American Indian/Alaska Native (411)	930	1.15
Not Hispanic (145)	489	0.60
Hispanic (266)	441	0.55
Alaska Athabascan (Ala. Nat.) (0)	0	<0.01
Aleut (Alaska Native) (0)	0	<0.01
Apache (5)	19	0.02
Arapaho (1)	1	<0.01
Blackfeet (7)	24	0.03
Canadian/French Am. Ind. (1)	1	<0.01
Central American Ind. (0)	0	<0.01
Cherokee (40)	182	0.23
Cheyenne (0)	0	<0.01
Chickasaw (0)	2	<0.01
Chippewa (6)	21	0.03
Choctaw (4)	18	0.02
Colville (0)	0	<0.01
Comanche (1)	3	<0.01
Cree (0)	0	<0.01
Creek (8)	10	0.01
Crow (1)	4	<0.01
Delaware (0)	0	<0.01
Hopi (0)	0	<0.01
Houma (0)	0	<0.01
Inupiat (Alaska Native) (0)	0	<0.01
Iroquois (1)	6	0.01
Kiowa (0)	0	<0.01
Lumbee (0)	0	<0.01
Menominee (0)	1	<0.01
Mexican American Ind. (44)	69	0.09
Navajo (1)	4	<0.01
Osage (0)	0	<0.01
Ottawa (2)	3	<0.01
Paiute (0)	0	<0.01
Pima (0)	0	<0.01
Potawatomi (1)	6	0.01
Pueblo (0)	0	<0.01
Puget Sound Salish (0)	2	<0.01
Seminole (0)	3	<0.01
Shoshone (6)	6	0.01
Sioux (7)	12	0.01
South American Ind. (2)	9	0.01
Spanish American Ind. (3)	3	<0.01
Tlingit-Haida (Alaska Native) (0)	0	<0.01
Tohono O'Odham (0)	0	<0.01
Tsimshian (Alaska Native) (0)	0	<0.01
Ute (6)	7	0.01
Yakama (0)	0	<0.01
Yaqui (3)	3	<0.01
Yuman (0)	0	<0.01
Yup'ik (Alaska Native) (0)	0	<0.01
Asian (804)	1,059	1.31
Not Hispanic (753)	931	1.15
Hispanic (51)	128	0.16
Bangladeshi (1)	2	<0.01
Bhutanese (0)	0	<0.01
Burmese (0)	0	<0.01
Cambodian (5)	5	0.01
Chinese, ex. Taiwanese (385)	422	0.52
Filipino (126)	203	0.25
Hmong (0)	0	<0.01
Indian (118)	135	0.17
Indonesian (2)	4	<0.01
Japanese (11)	54	0.07
Korean (34)	55	0.07
Laotian (0)	0	<0.01
Malaysian (0)	0	<0.01
Nepalese (1)	1	<0.01
Pakistani (40)	44	0.05
Sri Lankan (1)	1	<0.01
Taiwanese (3)	3	<0.01
Thai (12)	19	0.02
Vietnamese (35)	48	0.06
Hawaii Native/Pacific Islander (24)	97	0.12
Not Hispanic (9)	47	0.06
Hispanic (15)	50	0.06
Fijian (0)	1	<0.01
Guamanian/Chamorro (4)	9	0.01
Marshallese (0)	0	<0.01
Native Hawaiian (8)	30	0.04
Samoan (8)	21	0.03
Tongan (0)	0	<0.01
White (47,984)	50,206	62.11
Not Hispanic (33,534)	34,532	42.72
Hispanic (14,450)	15,674	19.39

Notes: † The Census 2010 population figure is used to calculate the percentages in the Hispanic Origin and Race categories. Ancestry percentages are based on the 2006-2010 American Community Survey population (not shown); ‡ Numbers in parentheses indicate the number of people reporting a single ancestry; * Numbers in parentheses indicate the number of persons reporting this race alone, not in combination with any other race; Please refer to the Explanation of Data for more information.

Indianapolis

Place Type: City
County: Marion
Population: 820,445

Ancestry	Population	%
Afghan (29)	29	<0.01
African, Sub-Saharan (34,151)	43,672	5.39
African (29,012)	38,288	4.73
Cape Verdean (0)	0	<0.01
Ethiopian (443)	443	0.05
Ghanaian (154)	154	0.02
Kenyan (63)	63	0.01
Liberian (687)	687	0.08
Nigerian (1,907)	2,048	0.25
Senegalese (150)	150	0.02
Sierra Leonean (0)	0	<0.01
Somalian (432)	432	0.05
South African (20)	43	0.01
Sudanese (376)	376	0.05
Ugandan (14)	54	0.01
Zimbabwean (149)	149	0.02
Other Sub-Saharan African (744)	785	0.10
Albanian (51)	105	0.01
Alsatian (0)	12	<0.01
American (52,433)	52,433	6.47
Arab (1,818)	2,776	0.34
Arab (433)	542	0.07
Egyptian (147)	158	0.02
Iraqi (132)	192	0.02
Jordanian (152)	182	0.02
Lebanese (410)	826	0.10
Moroccan (96)	141	0.02
Palestinian (12)	45	0.01
Syrian (77)	239	0.03
Other Arab (359)	451	0.06
Armenian (34)	158	0.02
Assyrian/Chaldean/Syriac (44)	44	0.01
Australian (189)	258	0.03
Austrian (325)	1,084	0.13
Basque (0)	0	<0.01
Belgian (276)	866	0.11
Brazilian (121)	259	0.03
British (1,698)	3,547	0.44
Bulgarian (18)	80	0.01
Cajun (29)	52	0.01
Canadian (702)	1,392	0.17
Carpatho Rusyn (0)	0	<0.01
Celtic (0)	8	<0.01
Croatian (94)	412	0.05
Cypriot (0)	0	<0.01
Czech (366)	1,484	0.18
Czechoslovakian (226)	393	0.05
Danish (513)	1,483	0.18
Dutch (2,739)	11,553	1.43
Eastern European (299)	332	0.04
English (24,751)	67,644	8.35
Estonian (15)	99	0.01
European (7,714)	9,215	1.14
Finnish (177)	436	0.05
French, ex. Basque (3,373)	15,735	1.94
French Canadian (515)	1,565	0.19
German (58,139)	149,656	18.48
German Russian (11)	11	<0.01
Greek (1,089)	2,372	0.29
Guyanese (0)	0	<0.01
Hungarian (951)	2,960	0.37
Icelander (0)	0	<0.01
Iranian (325)	455	0.06
Irish (29,177)	93,959	11.60
Israeli (55)	107	0.01
Italian (7,266)	20,396	2.52
Latvian (142)	275	0.03
Lithuanian (298)	1,175	0.15
Luxemburger (34)	97	0.01
Macedonian (127)	265	0.03
Maltese (22)	56	0.01
New Zealander (35)	35	<0.01
Northern European (560)	584	0.07
Norwegian (967)	3,636	0.45
Pennsylvania German (256)	355	0.04
Polish (3,961)	12,731	1.57
Portuguese (86)	414	0.05
Romanian (629)	1,001	0.12
Russian (1,361)	3,280	0.41
Scandinavian (590)	1,199	0.15
Scotch-Irish (5,103)	10,956	1.35
Scottish (4,801)	14,050	1.73
Serbian (258)	777	0.10
Slavic (134)	455	0.06
Slovak (344)	1,058	0.13
Slovene (203)	497	0.06
Soviet Union (0)	0	<0.01
Swedish (1,395)	5,593	0.69
Swiss (481)	2,276	0.28
Turkish (160)	243	0.03
Ukrainian (395)	792	0.10
Welsh (1,266)	4,603	0.57
West Indian, ex. Hispanic (1,133)	1,846	0.23
Bahamian (8)	8	<0.01
Barbadian (13)	55	0.01
Belizean (28)	51	0.01
Bermudan (0)	0	<0.01
British West Indian (0)	13	<0.01
Dutch West Indian (0)	38	<0.01
Haitian (394)	635	0.08
Jamaican (510)	589	0.07
Trinidadian/Tobagonian (72)	110	0.01
U.S. Virgin Islander (0)	0	<0.01
West Indian (96)	335	0.04
Other West Indian (12)	12	<0.01
Yugoslavian (327)	531	0.07

Hispanic Origin	Population	%
Hispanic or Latino (of any race)	77,352	9.43
Central American, ex. Mexican	7,746	0.94
Costa Rican	125	0.02
Guatemalan	1,616	0.20
Honduran	2,302	0.28
Nicaraguan	668	0.08
Panamanian	274	0.03
Salvadoran	2,695	0.33
Other Central American	66	0.01
Cuban	739	0.09
Dominican Republic	1,124	0.14
Mexican	56,771	6.92
Puerto Rican	3,431	0.42
South American	2,068	0.25
Argentinean	207	0.03
Bolivian	47	0.01
Chilean	83	0.01
Colombian	587	0.07
Ecuadorian	160	0.02
Paraguayan	11	<0.01
Peruvian	611	0.07
Uruguayan	29	<0.01
Venezuelan	314	0.04
Other South American	19	<0.01
Other Hispanic or Latino	5,473	0.67

Race*	Population	%
African-American/Black (225,355)	239,354	29.17
Not Hispanic (223,053)	235,521	28.71
Hispanic (2,302)	3,833	0.47
American Indian/Alaska Native (2,611)	7,323	0.89
Not Hispanic (1,760)	5,844	0.71
Hispanic (851)	1,479	0.18
Alaska Athabascan (Ala. Nat.) (2)	3	<0.01
Aleut (Alaska Native) (12)	14	<0.01
Apache (43)	98	0.01
Arapaho (4)	4	<0.01
Blackfeet (63)	354	0.04
Canadian/French Am. Ind. (10)	22	<0.01
Central American Ind. (6)	11	<0.01
Cherokee (378)	1,682	0.21
Cheyenne (1)	18	<0.01
Chickasaw (6)	12	<0.01
Chippewa (64)	134	0.02
Choctaw (26)	99	0.01
Colville (0)	0	<0.01
Comanche (11)	28	<0.01
Cree (0)	13	<0.01
Creek (14)	31	<0.01
Crow (1)	11	<0.01
Delaware (8)	27	<0.01
Hopi (4)	13	<0.01
Houma (3)	3	<0.01
Inupiat (Alaska Native) (9)	20	<0.01
Iroquois (33)	96	0.01
Kiowa (2)	5	<0.01
Lumbee (8)	17	<0.01
Menominee (4)	5	<0.01
Mexican American Ind. (187)	263	0.03
Navajo (40)	100	0.01
Osage (4)	15	<0.01
Ottawa (3)	15	<0.01
Paiute (0)	5	<0.01
Pima (0)	1	<0.01
Potawatomi (54)	88	0.01
Pueblo (10)	26	<0.01
Puget Sound Salish (0)	0	<0.01
Seminole (2)	17	<0.01
Shoshone (2)	7	<0.01
Sioux (55)	201	0.02
South American Ind. (14)	39	<0.01
Spanish American Ind. (19)	23	<0.01
Tlingit-Haida (Alaska Native) (4)	6	<0.01
Tohono O'Odham (1)	2	<0.01
Tsimshian (Alaska Native) (1)	1	<0.01
Ute (2)	4	<0.01
Yakama (0)	1	<0.01
Yaqui (3)	5	<0.01
Yuman (2)	4	<0.01
Yup'ik (Alaska Native) (0)	2	<0.01
Asian (17,236)	21,294	2.60
Not Hispanic (17,053)	20,777	2.53
Hispanic (183)	517	0.06
Bangladeshi (115)	128	0.02
Bhutanese (0)	0	<0.01
Burmese (3,476)	3,622	0.44
Cambodian (85)	118	0.01
Chinese, ex. Taiwanese (2,666)	3,197	0.39
Filipino (1,628)	2,608	0.32
Hmong (15)	24	<0.01
Indian (4,739)	5,358	0.65
Indonesian (76)	142	0.02
Japanese (517)	1,094	0.13
Korean (1,043)	1,558	0.19
Laotian (115)	142	0.02
Malaysian (29)	44	0.01
Nepalese (45)	46	0.01
Pakistani (544)	625	0.08
Sri Lankan (34)	42	0.01
Taiwanese (144)	160	0.02
Thai (226)	352	0.04
Vietnamese (1,138)	1,347	0.16
Hawaii Native/Pacific Islander (384)	1,129	0.14
Not Hispanic (274)	820	0.10
Hispanic (110)	309	0.04
Fijian (3)	5	<0.01
Guamanian/Chamorro (128)	216	0.03
Marshallese (0)	0	<0.01
Native Hawaiian (114)	361	0.04
Samoan (71)	145	0.02
Tongan (5)	10	<0.01
White (507,005)	526,672	64.19
Not Hispanic (480,960)	496,520	60.52
Hispanic (26,045)	30,152	3.68

Notes: † The Census 2010 population figure is used to calculate the percentages in the Hispanic Origin and Race categories. Ancestry percentages are based on the 2006-2010 American Community Survey population (not shown); ‡ Numbers in parentheses indicate the number of people reporting a single ancestry; * Numbers in parentheses indicate the number of persons reporting this race alone, not in combination with any other race; Please refer to the Explanation of Data for more information.

Lafayette

Place Type: City
County: Tippecanoe
Population: 67,140

Ancestry	Population	%
Afghan (0)	0	<0.01
African, Sub-Saharan (177)	247	0.37
African (66)	105	0.16
Cape Verdean (0)	0	<0.01
Ethiopian (0)	0	<0.01
Ghanaian (0)	0	<0.01
Kenyan (33)	33	0.05
Liberian (32)	32	0.05
Nigerian (23)	23	0.03
Senegalese (0)	0	<0.01
Sierra Leonean (0)	0	<0.01
Somalian (0)	0	<0.01
South African (0)	0	<0.01
Sudanese (0)	0	<0.01
Ugandan (0)	0	<0.01
Zimbabwean (0)	0	<0.01
Other Sub-Saharan African (23)	54	0.08
Albanian (0)	0	<0.01
Alsatian (0)	0	<0.01
American (4,832)	4,832	7.30
Arab (14)	25	0.04
Arab (0)	0	<0.01
Egyptian (0)	0	<0.01
Iraqi (0)	0	<0.01
Jordanian (0)	0	<0.01
Lebanese (14)	14	0.02
Moroccan (0)	0	<0.01
Palestinian (0)	0	<0.01
Syrian (0)	0	<0.01
Other Arab (0)	11	0.02
Armenian (0)	0	<0.01
Assyrian/Chaldean/Syriac (8)	30	0.05
Australian (0)	0	<0.01
Austrian (6)	79	0.12
Basque (0)	0	<0.01
Belgian (20)	100	0.15
Brazilian (8)	31	0.05
British (163)	331	0.50
Bulgarian (0)	0	<0.01
Cajun (11)	22	0.03
Canadian (34)	34	0.05
Carpatho Rusyn (0)	0	<0.01
Celtic (0)	0	<0.01
Croatian (0)	33	0.05
Cypriot (0)	0	<0.01
Czech (40)	84	0.13
Czechoslovakian (0)	36	0.05
Danish (9)	74	0.11
Dutch (663)	2,127	3.22
Eastern European (29)	40	0.06
English (2,659)	6,889	10.41
Estonian (0)	0	<0.01
European (543)	672	1.02
Finnish (40)	63	0.10
French, ex. Basque (322)	1,964	2.97
French Canadian (110)	177	0.27
German (6,095)	16,791	25.38
German Russian (0)	0	<0.01
Greek (94)	147	0.22
Guyanese (0)	0	<0.01
Hungarian (132)	247	0.37
Icelander (0)	0	<0.01
Iranian (0)	0	<0.01
Irish (2,843)	10,032	15.17
Israeli (0)	0	<0.01
Italian (789)	1,624	2.46
Latvian (0)	0	<0.01
Lithuanian (11)	45	0.07
Luxemburger (0)	45	0.07
Macedonian (0)	0	<0.01
Maltese (0)	0	<0.01
New Zealander (68)	68	0.10
Northern European (77)	77	0.12
Norwegian (35)	249	0.38
Pennsylvania German (0)	61	0.09
Polish (693)	1,900	2.87
Portuguese (27)	27	0.04
Romanian (28)	61	0.09
Russian (84)	391	0.59
Scandinavian (26)	36	0.05
Scotch-Irish (519)	1,115	1.69
Scottish (610)	1,572	2.38
Serbian (0)	0	<0.01
Slavic (0)	27	0.04
Slovak (23)	44	0.07
Slovene (0)	0	<0.01
Soviet Union (0)	0	<0.01
Swedish (80)	556	0.84
Swiss (78)	302	0.46
Turkish (49)	49	0.07
Ukrainian (45)	94	0.14
Welsh (88)	360	0.54
West Indian, ex. Hispanic (8)	26	0.04
Bahamian (0)	0	<0.01
Barbadian (0)	0	<0.01
Belizean (0)	0	<0.01
Bermudan (0)	0	<0.01
British West Indian (0)	0	<0.01
Dutch West Indian (0)	8	0.01
Haitian (0)	10	0.02
Jamaican (0)	0	<0.01
Trinidadian/Tobagonian (0)	0	<0.01
U.S. Virgin Islander (8)	8	0.01
West Indian (0)	0	<0.01
Other West Indian (0)	0	<0.01
Yugoslavian (0)	0	<0.01

Hispanic Origin	Population	%
Hispanic or Latino (of any race)	8,107	12.07
Central American, ex. Mexican	283	0.42
Costa Rican	12	0.02
Guatemalan	81	0.12
Honduran	10	0.01
Nicaraguan	16	0.02
Panamanian	26	0.04
Salvadoran	138	0.21
Other Central American	0	<0.01
Cuban	78	0.12
Dominican Republic	33	0.05
Mexican	6,965	10.37
Puerto Rican	253	0.38
South American	130	0.19
Argentinean	16	0.02
Bolivian	12	0.02
Chilean	13	0.02
Colombian	39	0.06
Ecuadorian	23	0.03
Paraguayan	0	<0.01
Peruvian	18	0.03
Uruguayan	0	<0.01
Venezuelan	9	0.01
Other South American	0	<0.01
Other Hispanic or Latino	365	0.54

Race*	Population	%
African-American/Black (4,164)	4,987	7.43
Not Hispanic (4,050)	4,752	7.08
Hispanic (114)	235	0.35
American Indian/Alaska Native (245)	672	1.00
Not Hispanic (171)	544	0.81
Hispanic (74)	128	0.19
Alaska Athabascan (Ala. Nat.) (4)	4	0.01
Aleut (Alaska Native) (1)	2	<0.01
Apache (2)	12	0.02
Arapaho (0)	0	<0.01
Blackfeet (6)	27	0.04
Canadian/French Am. Ind. (2)	3	<0.01
Central American Ind. (0)	0	<0.01
Cherokee (39)	195	0.29
Cheyenne (1)	4	0.01
Chickasaw (0)	3	<0.01
Chippewa (8)	12	0.02
Choctaw (7)	9	0.01
Colville (0)	0	<0.01
Comanche (1)	3	<0.01
Cree (1)	1	<0.01
Creek (0)	4	0.01
Crow (2)	2	<0.01
Delaware (1)	3	<0.01
Hopi (0)	0	<0.01
Houma (6)	6	0.01
Inupiat (Alaska Native) (1)	1	<0.01
Iroquois (8)	14	0.02
Kiowa (0)	0	<0.01
Lumbee (5)	5	0.01
Menominee (0)	0	<0.01
Mexican American Ind. (23)	24	0.04
Navajo (0)	2	<0.01
Osage (0)	0	<0.01
Ottawa (4)	5	0.01
Paiute (0)	0	<0.01
Pima (0)	0	<0.01
Potawatomi (1)	6	0.01
Pueblo (0)	0	<0.01
Puget Sound Salish (0)	0	<0.01
Seminole (0)	5	0.01
Shoshone (0)	0	<0.01
Sioux (12)	23	0.03
South American Ind. (0)	7	0.01
Spanish American Ind. (0)	0	<0.01
Tlingit-Haida (Alaska Native) (0)	5	0.01
Tohono O'Odham (0)	0	<0.01
Tsimshian (Alaska Native) (0)	0	<0.01
Ute (0)	1	<0.01
Yakama (0)	0	<0.01
Yaqui (1)	1	<0.01
Yuman (0)	1	<0.01
Yup'ik (Alaska Native) (0)	0	<0.01
Asian (925)	1,224	1.82
Not Hispanic (908)	1,160	1.73
Hispanic (17)	64	0.10
Bangladeshi (5)	5	0.01
Bhutanese (0)	0	<0.01
Burmese (6)	8	0.01
Cambodian (1)	1	<0.01
Chinese, ex. Taiwanese (188)	226	0.34
Filipino (111)	200	0.30
Hmong (0)	0	<0.01
Indian (196)	225	0.34
Indonesian (9)	9	0.01
Japanese (71)	107	0.16
Korean (190)	239	0.36
Laotian (6)	11	0.02
Malaysian (3)	4	0.01
Nepalese (3)	3	<0.01
Pakistani (10)	13	0.02
Sri Lankan (0)	0	<0.01
Taiwanese (19)	20	0.03
Thai (12)	25	0.04
Vietnamese (63)	79	0.12
Hawaii Native/Pacific Islander (20)	73	0.11
Not Hispanic (14)	55	0.08
Hispanic (6)	18	0.03
Fijian (0)	0	<0.01
Guamanian/Chamorro (17)	20	0.03
Marshallese (0)	0	<0.01
Native Hawaiian (3)	18	0.03
Samoan (0)	13	0.02
Tongan (0)	1	<0.01
White (56,108)	57,759	86.03
Not Hispanic (52,557)	53,754	80.06
Hispanic (3,551)	4,005	5.97

Notes: † The Census 2010 population figure is used to calculate the percentages in the Hispanic Origin and Race categories. Ancestry percentages are based on the 2006-2010 American Community Survey population (not shown); ‡ Numbers in parentheses indicate the number of people reporting a single ancestry; * Numbers in parentheses indicate the number of persons reporting this race alone, not in combination with any other race; Please refer to the Explanation of Data for more information.

Muncie

Place Type: City
County: Delaware
Population: 70,085

Ancestry	Population	%
Afghan (0)	0	<0.01
African, Sub-Saharan (668)	875	1.25
African (546)	737	1.05
Cape Verdean (0)	0	<0.01
Ethiopian (0)	0	<0.01
Ghanaian (0)	0	<0.01
Kenyan (14)	14	0.02
Liberian (0)	0	<0.01
Nigerian (0)	0	<0.01
Senegalese (0)	0	<0.01
Sierra Leonean (0)	0	<0.01
Somalian (0)	0	<0.01
South African (0)	16	0.02
Sudanese (0)	0	<0.01
Ugandan (0)	0	<0.01
Zimbabwean (0)	0	<0.01
Other Sub-Saharan African (108)	108	0.15
Albanian (57)	57	0.08
Alsatian (0)	22	0.03
American (6,079)	6,079	8.68
Arab (7)	204	0.29
Arab (0)	84	0.12
Egyptian (0)	14	0.02
Iraqi (0)	14	0.02
Jordanian (0)	0	<0.01
Lebanese (0)	0	<0.01
Moroccan (0)	13	0.02
Palestinian (7)	7	0.01
Syrian (0)	66	0.09
Other Arab (0)	6	0.01
Armenian (0)	0	<0.01
Assyrian/Chaldean/Syriac (0)	0	<0.01
Australian (14)	27	0.04
Austrian (9)	45	0.06
Basque (0)	0	<0.01
Belgian (0)	110	0.16
Brazilian (0)	0	<0.01
British (225)	372	0.53
Bulgarian (9)	9	0.01
Cajun (0)	0	<0.01
Canadian (125)	194	0.28
Carpatho Rusyn (0)	0	<0.01
Celtic (10)	10	0.01
Croatian (0)	103	0.15
Cypriot (0)	0	<0.01
Czech (63)	87	0.12
Czechoslovakian (0)	0	<0.01
Danish (36)	119	0.17
Dutch (245)	1,417	2.02
Eastern European (0)	0	<0.01
English (2,398)	6,521	9.31
Estonian (0)	0	<0.01
European (449)	525	0.75
Finnish (26)	42	0.06
French, ex. Basque (286)	1,865	2.66
French Canadian (26)	64	0.09
German (5,967)	14,993	21.41
German Russian (0)	0	<0.01
Greek (143)	214	0.31
Guyanese (0)	0	<0.01
Hungarian (78)	175	0.25
Icelander (0)	0	<0.01
Iranian (72)	78	0.11
Irish (2,747)	9,462	13.51
Israeli (13)	24	0.03
Italian (867)	1,965	2.81
Latvian (0)	9	0.01
Lithuanian (64)	77	0.11
Luxemburger (0)	32	0.05
Macedonian (12)	23	0.03
Maltese (0)	0	<0.01
New Zealander (0)	18	0.03
Northern European (17)	17	0.02
Norwegian (47)	422	0.60
Pennsylvania German (0)	14	0.02
Polish (413)	1,148	1.64
Portuguese (0)	12	0.02
Romanian (40)	59	0.08
Russian (59)	162	0.23
Scandinavian (0)	14	0.02
Scotch-Irish (395)	930	1.33
Scottish (318)	1,264	1.81
Serbian (0)	15	0.02
Slavic (22)	22	0.03
Slovak (30)	118	0.17
Slovene (0)	0	<0.01
Soviet Union (0)	0	<0.01
Swedish (144)	494	0.71
Swiss (84)	326	0.47
Turkish (34)	34	0.05
Ukrainian (0)	30	0.04
Welsh (78)	511	0.73
West Indian, ex. Hispanic (41)	41	0.06
Bahamian (0)	0	<0.01
Barbadian (28)	28	0.04
Belizean (0)	0	<0.01
Bermudan (0)	0	<0.01
British West Indian (0)	0	<0.01
Dutch West Indian (0)	0	<0.01
Haitian (0)	0	<0.01
Jamaican (13)	13	0.02
Trinidadian/Tobagonian (0)	0	<0.01
U.S. Virgin Islander (0)	0	<0.01
West Indian (0)	0	<0.01
Other West Indian (0)	0	<0.01
Yugoslavian (12)	27	0.04

Hispanic Origin	Population	%
Hispanic or Latino (of any race)	1,579	2.25
Central American, ex. Mexican	62	0.09
Costa Rican	5	0.01
Guatemalan	9	0.01
Honduran	12	0.02
Nicaraguan	3	<0.01
Panamanian	21	0.03
Salvadoran	11	0.02
Other Central American	1	<0.01
Cuban	38	0.05
Dominican Republic	21	0.03
Mexican	1,061	1.51
Puerto Rican	133	0.19
South American	63	0.09
Argentinean	7	0.01
Bolivian	5	0.01
Chilean	11	0.02
Colombian	6	0.01
Ecuadorian	2	<0.01
Paraguayan	1	<0.01
Peruvian	12	0.02
Uruguayan	2	<0.01
Venezuelan	13	0.02
Other South American	4	0.01
Other Hispanic or Latino	201	0.29

Race*	Population	%
African-American/Black (7,655)	8,829	12.60
Not Hispanic (7,569)	8,664	12.36
Hispanic (86)	165	0.24
American Indian/Alaska Native (203)	650	0.93
Not Hispanic (174)	577	0.82
Hispanic (29)	73	0.10
Alaska Athabascan (Ala. Nat.) (0)	0	<0.01
Aleut (Alaska Native) (0)	0	<0.01
Apache (0)	12	0.02
Arapaho (0)	1	<0.01
Blackfeet (5)	42	0.06
Canadian/French Am. Ind. (0)	0	<0.01
Central American Ind. (0)	0	<0.01
Cherokee (51)	182	0.26
Cheyenne (0)	0	<0.01
Chickasaw (0)	0	<0.01
Chippewa (2)	5	0.01
Choctaw (1)	3	<0.01
Colville (0)	0	<0.01
Comanche (0)	0	<0.01
Cree (1)	5	0.01
Creek (0)	2	<0.01
Crow (2)	2	<0.01
Delaware (0)	2	<0.01
Hopi (0)	0	<0.01
Houma (0)	0	<0.01
Inupiat (Alaska Native) (0)	0	<0.01
Iroquois (5)	7	0.01
Kiowa (0)	0	<0.01
Lumbee (3)	3	<0.01
Menominee (1)	1	<0.01
Mexican American Ind. (9)	11	0.02
Navajo (4)	7	0.01
Osage (0)	1	<0.01
Ottawa (0)	0	<0.01
Paiute (0)	0	<0.01
Pima (0)	0	<0.01
Potawatomi (5)	5	0.01
Pueblo (0)	1	<0.01
Puget Sound Salish (1)	1	<0.01
Seminole (1)	2	<0.01
Shoshone (0)	6	0.01
Sioux (8)	20	0.03
South American Ind. (2)	4	0.01
Spanish American Ind. (2)	2	<0.01
Tlingit-Haida (Alaska Native) (0)	0	<0.01
Tohono O'Odham (0)	0	<0.01
Tsimshian (Alaska Native) (0)	0	<0.01
Ute (0)	0	<0.01
Yakama (0)	0	<0.01
Yaqui (0)	0	<0.01
Yuman (0)	0	<0.01
Yup'ik (Alaska Native) (0)	0	<0.01
Asian (849)	1,173	1.67
Not Hispanic (839)	1,143	1.63
Hispanic (10)	30	0.04
Bangladeshi (21)	23	0.03
Bhutanese (0)	0	<0.01
Burmese (2)	2	<0.01
Cambodian (0)	0	<0.01
Chinese, ex. Taiwanese (250)	282	0.40
Filipino (74)	143	0.20
Hmong (2)	2	<0.01
Indian (196)	248	0.35
Indonesian (2)	2	<0.01
Japanese (48)	86	0.12
Korean (111)	142	0.20
Laotian (2)	3	<0.01
Malaysian (1)	3	<0.01
Nepalese (10)	13	0.02
Pakistani (12)	14	0.02
Sri Lankan (4)	4	0.01
Taiwanese (22)	25	0.04
Thai (9)	16	0.02
Vietnamese (51)	62	0.09
Hawaii Native/Pacific Islander (42)	138	0.20
Not Hispanic (39)	126	0.18
Hispanic (3)	12	0.02
Fijian (0)	1	<0.01
Guamanian/Chamorro (3)	12	0.02
Marshallese (0)	0	<0.01
Native Hawaiian (15)	44	0.06
Samoan (9)	19	0.03
Tongan (1)	3	<0.01
White (58,853)	60,636	86.52
Not Hispanic (58,018)	59,588	85.02
Hispanic (835)	1,048	1.50

Notes: † The Census 2010 population figure is used to calculate the percentages in the Hispanic Origin and Race categories. Ancestry percentages are based on the 2006-2010 American Community Survey population (not shown); ‡ Numbers in parentheses indicate the number of people reporting a single ancestry; * Numbers in parentheses indicate the number of persons reporting this race alone, not in combination with any other race; Please refer to the Explanation of Data for more information.

Noblesville

Place Type: City
County: Hamilton
Population: 51,969

Ancestry	Population	%
Afghan (0)	0	<0.01
African, Sub-Saharan (155)	278	0.57
African (98)	221	0.45
Cape Verdean (0)	0	<0.01
Ethiopian (0)	0	<0.01
Ghanaian (0)	0	<0.01
Kenyan (57)	57	0.12
Liberian (0)	0	<0.01
Nigerian (0)	0	<0.01
Senegalese (0)	0	<0.01
Sierra Leonean (0)	0	<0.01
Somalian (0)	0	<0.01
South African (0)	0	<0.01
Sudanese (0)	0	<0.01
Ugandan (0)	0	<0.01
Zimbabwean (0)	0	<0.01
Other Sub-Saharan African (0)	0	<0.01
Albanian (40)	40	0.08
Alsatian (0)	0	<0.01
American (4,429)	4,429	9.09
Arab (55)	183	0.38
Arab (0)	113	0.23
Egyptian (30)	30	0.06
Iraqi (0)	0	<0.01
Jordanian (0)	0	<0.01
Lebanese (13)	18	0.04
Moroccan (12)	12	0.02
Palestinian (0)	0	<0.01
Syrian (0)	10	0.02
Other Arab (0)	0	<0.01
Armenian (0)	0	<0.01
Assyrian/Chaldean/Syriac (0)	0	<0.01
Australian (14)	14	0.03
Austrian (25)	25	0.05
Basque (0)	0	<0.01
Belgian (32)	247	0.51
Brazilian (28)	28	0.06
British (102)	213	0.44
Bulgarian (29)	41	0.08
Cajun (0)	0	<0.01
Canadian (32)	57	0.12
Carpatho Rusyn (0)	0	<0.01
Celtic (0)	15	0.03
Croatian (17)	56	0.11
Cypriot (0)	0	<0.01
Czech (68)	109	0.22
Czechoslovakian (84)	108	0.22
Danish (24)	71	0.15
Dutch (352)	1,089	2.24
Eastern European (126)	126	0.26
English (1,576)	5,811	11.93
Estonian (0)	0	<0.01
European (875)	1,091	2.24
Finnish (53)	67	0.14
French, ex. Basque (320)	1,734	3.56
French Canadian (90)	186	0.38
German (5,244)	13,766	28.26
German Russian (0)	0	<0.01
Greek (100)	174	0.36
Guyanese (0)	0	<0.01
Hungarian (60)	207	0.42
Icelander (0)	0	<0.01
Iranian (56)	131	0.27
Irish (1,929)	7,262	14.91
Israeli (0)	0	<0.01
Italian (726)	2,728	5.60
Latvian (41)	167	0.34
Lithuanian (9)	46	0.09
Luxemburger (0)	0	<0.01
Macedonian (12)	25	0.05
Maltese (0)	0	<0.01
New Zealander (0)	0	<0.01
Northern European (24)	24	0.05
Norwegian (100)	621	1.27
Pennsylvania German (69)	83	0.17
Polish (653)	1,516	3.11
Portuguese (27)	27	0.06
Romanian (33)	62	0.13
Russian (142)	216	0.44
Scandinavian (14)	83	0.17
Scotch-Irish (220)	817	1.68
Scottish (383)	1,261	2.59
Serbian (24)	70	0.14
Slavic (0)	0	<0.01
Slovak (45)	139	0.29
Slovene (12)	12	0.02
Soviet Union (0)	0	<0.01
Swedish (132)	695	1.43
Swiss (41)	212	0.44
Turkish (26)	52	0.11
Ukrainian (191)	436	0.90
Welsh (132)	497	1.02
West Indian, ex. Hispanic (75)	75	0.15
Bahamian (0)	0	<0.01
Barbadian (0)	0	<0.01
Belizean (0)	0	<0.01
Bermudan (19)	19	0.04
British West Indian (0)	0	<0.01
Dutch West Indian (0)	0	<0.01
Haitian (12)	12	0.02
Jamaican (31)	31	0.06
Trinidadian/Tobagonian (13)	13	0.03
U.S. Virgin Islander (0)	0	<0.01
West Indian (0)	0	<0.01
Other West Indian (0)	0	<0.01
Yugoslavian (121)	121	0.25

Hispanic Origin	Population	%
Hispanic or Latino (of any race)	2,209	4.25
Central American, ex. Mexican	244	0.47
Costa Rican	19	0.04
Guatemalan	59	0.11
Honduran	31	0.06
Nicaraguan	14	0.03
Panamanian	10	0.02
Salvadoran	111	0.21
Other Central American	0	<0.01
Cuban	43	0.08
Dominican Republic	40	0.08
Mexican	1,245	2.40
Puerto Rican	210	0.40
South American	253	0.49
Argentinean	19	0.04
Bolivian	11	0.02
Chilean	11	0.02
Colombian	68	0.13
Ecuadorian	4	0.01
Paraguayan	0	<0.01
Peruvian	41	0.08
Uruguayan	2	<0.01
Venezuelan	97	0.19
Other South American	0	<0.01
Other Hispanic or Latino	174	0.33

Race*	Population	%
African-American/Black (1,896)	2,300	4.43
Not Hispanic (1,840)	2,196	4.23
Hispanic (56)	104	0.20
American Indian/Alaska Native (109)	281	0.54
Not Hispanic (87)	243	0.47
Hispanic (22)	38	0.07
Alaska Athabascan (Ala. Nat.) (0)	0	<0.01
Aleut (Alaska Native) (0)	0	<0.01
Apache (0)	5	0.01
Arapaho (0)	0	<0.01
Blackfeet (6)	16	0.03
Canadian/French Am. Ind. (0)	0	<0.01
Central American Ind. (0)	0	<0.01
Cherokee (13)	58	0.11
Cheyenne (0)	0	<0.01
Chickasaw (0)	0	<0.01
Chippewa (10)	18	0.03
Choctaw (1)	5	0.01
Colville (0)	0	<0.01
Comanche (0)	0	<0.01
Cree (0)	0	<0.01
Creek (4)	8	0.02
Crow (1)	1	<0.01
Delaware (0)	0	<0.01
Hopi (0)	0	<0.01
Houma (0)	0	<0.01
Inupiat (Alaska Native) (0)	1	<0.01
Iroquois (0)	0	<0.01
Kiowa (0)	0	<0.01
Lumbee (0)	0	<0.01
Menominee (0)	0	<0.01
Mexican American Ind. (9)	10	0.02
Navajo (5)	5	0.01
Osage (1)	1	<0.01
Ottawa (0)	0	<0.01
Paiute (0)	0	<0.01
Pima (0)	0	<0.01
Potawatomi (1)	1	<0.01
Pueblo (0)	0	<0.01
Puget Sound Salish (0)	0	<0.01
Seminole (0)	1	<0.01
Shoshone (0)	1	<0.01
Sioux (6)	11	0.02
South American Ind. (1)	2	<0.01
Spanish American Ind. (0)	0	<0.01
Tlingit-Haida (Alaska Native) (0)	0	<0.01
Tohono O'Odham (0)	0	<0.01
Tsimshian (Alaska Native) (0)	0	<0.01
Ute (2)	2	<0.01
Yakama (0)	0	<0.01
Yaqui (0)	1	<0.01
Yuman (0)	0	<0.01
Yup'ik (Alaska Native) (0)	0	<0.01
Asian (874)	1,149	2.21
Not Hispanic (864)	1,128	2.17
Hispanic (10)	21	0.04
Bangladeshi (12)	12	0.02
Bhutanese (0)	0	<0.01
Burmese (0)	0	<0.01
Cambodian (21)	26	0.05
Chinese, ex. Taiwanese (125)	157	0.30
Filipino (114)	198	0.38
Hmong (12)	14	0.03
Indian (241)	262	0.50
Indonesian (12)	15	0.03
Japanese (43)	86	0.17
Korean (94)	143	0.28
Laotian (4)	13	0.03
Malaysian (5)	5	0.01
Nepalese (0)	0	<0.01
Pakistani (11)	12	0.02
Sri Lankan (7)	7	0.01
Taiwanese (2)	2	<0.01
Thai (12)	24	0.05
Vietnamese (123)	139	0.27
Hawaii Native/Pacific Islander (35)	80	0.15
Not Hispanic (24)	61	0.12
Hispanic (11)	19	0.04
Fijian (0)	0	<0.01
Guamanian/Chamorro (2)	7	0.01
Marshallese (1)	1	<0.01
Native Hawaiian (27)	51	0.10
Samoan (3)	11	0.02
Tongan (1)	1	<0.01
White (47,333)	48,170	92.69
Not Hispanic (46,089)	46,797	90.05
Hispanic (1,244)	1,373	2.64

Notes: † The Census 2010 population figure is used to calculate the percentages in the Hispanic Origin and Race categories. Ancestry percentages are based on the 2006-2010 American Community Survey population (not shown); ‡ Numbers in parentheses indicate the number of people reporting a single ancestry; * Numbers in parentheses indicate the number of persons reporting this race alone, not in combination with any other race; Please refer to the Explanation of Data for more information.

South Bend

Place Type: City
County: St. Joseph
Population: 101,168

Ancestry	Population	%
Afghan (0)	0	<0.01
African, Sub-Saharan (979)	1,287	1.26
African (699)	952	0.93
Cape Verdean (0)	0	<0.01
Ethiopian (0)	0	<0.01
Ghanaian (0)	0	<0.01
Kenyan (202)	218	0.21
Liberian (0)	28	0.03
Nigerian (0)	0	<0.01
Senegalese (0)	0	<0.01
Sierra Leonean (0)	11	0.01
Somalian (0)	0	<0.01
South African (0)	0	<0.01
Sudanese (0)	0	<0.01
Ugandan (0)	0	<0.01
Zimbabwean (0)	0	<0.01
Other Sub-Saharan African (78)	78	0.08
Albanian (0)	0	<0.01
Alsatian (0)	0	<0.01
American (3,845)	3,845	3.77
Arab (72)	131	0.13
Arab (27)	27	0.03
Egyptian (0)	0	<0.01
Iraqi (23)	33	0.03
Jordanian (0)	0	<0.01
Lebanese (9)	33	0.03
Moroccan (0)	6	0.01
Palestinian (0)	0	<0.01
Syrian (19)	19	0.02
Other Arab (13)	13	0.01
Armenian (8)	44	0.04
Assyrian/Chaldean/Syriac (0)	0	<0.01
Australian (0)	0	<0.01
Austrian (89)	275	0.27
Basque (0)	0	<0.01
Belgian (397)	871	0.85
Brazilian (10)	50	0.05
British (158)	336	0.33
Bulgarian (22)	47	0.05
Cajun (0)	0	<0.01
Canadian (66)	126	0.12
Carpatho Rusyn (0)	0	<0.01
Celtic (10)	10	0.01
Croatian (23)	295	0.29
Cypriot (0)	0	<0.01
Czech (35)	264	0.26
Czechoslovakian (42)	84	0.08
Danish (20)	88	0.09
Dutch (249)	2,222	2.18
Eastern European (13)	66	0.06
English (1,797)	6,318	6.19
Estonian (0)	8	0.01
European (680)	796	0.78
Finnish (33)	93	0.09
French, ex. Basque (209)	2,323	2.28
French Canadian (84)	422	0.41
German (5,733)	19,199	18.81
German Russian (0)	0	<0.01
Greek (89)	308	0.30
Guyanese (0)	0	<0.01
Hungarian (1,068)	2,904	2.85
Icelander (0)	0	<0.01
Iranian (13)	13	0.01
Irish (2,788)	12,089	11.84
Israeli (0)	0	<0.01
Italian (1,079)	3,341	3.27
Latvian (10)	10	0.01
Lithuanian (55)	176	0.17
Luxemburger (13)	13	0.01
Macedonian (0)	0	<0.01
Maltese (0)	0	<0.01
New Zealander (0)	0	<0.01
Northern European (62)	62	0.06
Norwegian (116)	459	0.45
Pennsylvania German (48)	140	0.14
Polish (4,876)	10,370	10.16
Portuguese (23)	54	0.05
Romanian (68)	88	0.09
Russian (238)	730	0.72
Scandinavian (35)	150	0.15
Scotch-Irish (314)	1,065	1.04
Scottish (213)	1,319	1.29
Serbian (71)	165	0.16
Slavic (10)	10	0.01
Slovak (42)	131	0.13
Slovene (0)	9	0.01
Soviet Union (0)	0	<0.01
Swedish (291)	1,638	1.60
Swiss (141)	343	0.34
Turkish (50)	104	0.10
Ukrainian (58)	214	0.21
Welsh (92)	372	0.36
West Indian, ex. Hispanic (98)	117	0.11
Bahamian (0)	9	0.01
Barbadian (0)	0	<0.01
Belizean (0)	0	<0.01
Bermudan (0)	0	<0.01
British West Indian (15)	15	0.01
Dutch West Indian (11)	11	0.01
Haitian (0)	0	<0.01
Jamaican (12)	12	0.01
Trinidadian/Tobagonian (39)	39	0.04
U.S. Virgin Islander (0)	0	<0.01
West Indian (21)	31	0.03
Other West Indian (0)	0	<0.01
Yugoslavian (364)	514	0.50

Hispanic Origin	Population	%
Hispanic or Latino (of any race)	13,116	12.96
Central American, ex. Mexican	292	0.29
Costa Rican	7	0.01
Guatemalan	66	0.07
Honduran	49	0.05
Nicaraguan	46	0.05
Panamanian	21	0.02
Salvadoran	98	0.10
Other Central American	5	<0.01
Cuban	111	0.11
Dominican Republic	42	0.04
Mexican	11,025	10.90
Puerto Rican	525	0.52
South American	275	0.27
Argentinean	33	0.03
Bolivian	10	0.01
Chilean	27	0.03
Colombian	53	0.05
Ecuadorian	47	0.05
Paraguayan	10	0.01
Peruvian	17	0.02
Uruguayan	5	<0.01
Venezuelan	73	0.07
Other South American	0	<0.01
Other Hispanic or Latino	846	0.84

Race*	Population	%
African-American/Black (26,906)	29,667	29.32
Not Hispanic (26,496)	28,893	28.56
Hispanic (410)	774	0.77
American Indian/Alaska Native (478)	1,334	1.32
Not Hispanic (310)	1,029	1.02
Hispanic (168)	305	0.30
Alaska Athabascan (Ala. Nat.) (0)	0	<0.01
Aleut (Alaska Native) (0)	0	<0.01
Apache (6)	29	0.03
Arapaho (0)	1	<0.01
Blackfeet (14)	74	0.07
Canadian/French Am. Ind. (1)	5	<0.01
Central American Ind. (3)	8	0.01
Cherokee (54)	281	0.28
Cheyenne (0)	1	<0.01
Chickasaw (3)	6	0.01
Chippewa (12)	29	0.03
Choctaw (5)	23	0.02
Colville (1)	1	<0.01
Comanche (0)	1	<0.01
Cree (0)	1	<0.01
Creek (0)	4	<0.01
Crow (0)	0	<0.01
Delaware (1)	1	<0.01
Hopi (0)	0	<0.01
Houma (0)	0	<0.01
Inupiat (Alaska Native) (0)	1	<0.01
Iroquois (0)	4	<0.01
Kiowa (0)	0	<0.01
Lumbee (4)	10	0.01
Menominee (1)	1	<0.01
Mexican American Ind. (31)	54	0.05
Navajo (1)	8	0.01
Osage (0)	0	<0.01
Ottawa (0)	3	<0.01
Paiute (3)	3	<0.01
Pima (0)	0	<0.01
Potawatomi (38)	74	0.07
Pueblo (0)	4	<0.01
Puget Sound Salish (0)	0	<0.01
Seminole (0)	5	<0.01
Shoshone (0)	1	<0.01
Sioux (4)	9	0.01
South American Ind. (2)	3	<0.01
Spanish American Ind. (8)	11	0.01
Tlingit-Haida (Alaska Native) (3)	4	<0.01
Tohono O'Odham (0)	0	<0.01
Tsimshian (Alaska Native) (0)	0	<0.01
Ute (0)	0	<0.01
Yakama (0)	0	<0.01
Yaqui (0)	0	<0.01
Yuman (0)	0	<0.01
Yup'ik (Alaska Native) (0)	0	<0.01
Asian (1,318)	1,824	1.80
Not Hispanic (1,295)	1,742	1.72
Hispanic (23)	82	0.08
Bangladeshi (1)	2	<0.01
Bhutanese (0)	0	<0.01
Burmese (0)	0	<0.01
Cambodian (76)	80	0.08
Chinese, ex. Taiwanese (258)	360	0.36
Filipino (205)	345	0.34
Hmong (2)	2	<0.01
Indian (211)	266	0.26
Indonesian (11)	14	0.01
Japanese (44)	102	0.10
Korean (107)	164	0.16
Laotian (34)	53	0.05
Malaysian (2)	3	<0.01
Nepalese (3)	4	<0.01
Pakistani (12)	16	0.02
Sri Lankan (8)	9	0.01
Taiwanese (17)	19	0.02
Thai (24)	37	0.04
Vietnamese (242)	267	0.26
Hawaii Native/Pacific Islander (64)	185	0.18
Not Hispanic (55)	156	0.15
Hispanic (9)	29	0.03
Fijian (0)	0	<0.01
Guamanian/Chamorro (12)	20	0.02
Marshallese (0)	0	<0.01
Native Hawaiian (17)	55	0.05
Samoan (17)	55	0.05
Tongan (11)	20	0.02
White (61,199)	64,797	64.05
Not Hispanic (56,474)	59,298	58.61
Hispanic (4,725)	5,499	5.44

Notes: † The Census 2010 population figure is used to calculate the percentages in the Hispanic Origin and Race categories. Ancestry percentages are based on the 2006-2010 American Community Survey population (not shown); ‡ Numbers in parentheses indicate the number of people reporting a single ancestry; * Numbers in parentheses indicate the number of persons reporting this race alone, not in combination with any other race; Please refer to the Explanation of Data for more information.

Terre Haute

Place Type: City
County: Vigo
Population: 60,785

Ancestry	Population	%
Afghan (0)	0	<0.01
African, Sub-Saharan (691)	806	1.33
African (685)	800	1.32
Cape Verdean (0)	0	<0.01
Ethiopian (0)	0	<0.01
Ghanaian (0)	0	<0.01
Kenyan (0)	0	<0.01
Liberian (0)	0	<0.01
Nigerian (0)	0	<0.01
Senegalese (0)	0	<0.01
Sierra Leonean (0)	0	<0.01
Somalian (6)	6	0.01
South African (0)	0	<0.01
Sudanese (0)	0	<0.01
Ugandan (0)	0	<0.01
Zimbabwean (0)	0	<0.01
Other Sub-Saharan African (0)	0	<0.01
Albanian (0)	0	<0.01
Alsatian (0)	0	<0.01
American (11,657)	11,657	19.29
Arab (453)	525	0.87
Arab (108)	117	0.19
Egyptian (0)	0	<0.01
Iraqi (0)	0	<0.01
Jordanian (6)	6	0.01
Lebanese (24)	24	0.04
Moroccan (0)	0	<0.01
Palestinian (0)	0	<0.01
Syrian (74)	137	0.23
Other Arab (241)	241	0.40
Armenian (0)	0	<0.01
Assyrian/Chaldean/Syriac (0)	0	<0.01
Australian (0)	0	<0.01
Austrian (25)	85	0.14
Basque (0)	0	<0.01
Belgian (35)	75	0.12
Brazilian (0)	0	<0.01
British (90)	153	0.25
Bulgarian (0)	0	<0.01
Cajun (0)	0	<0.01
Canadian (33)	62	0.10
Carpatho Rusyn (0)	0	<0.01
Celtic (0)	0	<0.01
Croatian (51)	85	0.14
Cypriot (0)	0	<0.01
Czech (69)	232	0.38
Czechoslovakian (43)	53	0.09
Danish (38)	75	0.12
Dutch (335)	1,355	2.24
Eastern European (26)	26	0.04
English (2,093)	5,550	9.18
Estonian (0)	53	0.09
European (396)	484	0.80
Finnish (32)	32	0.05
French, ex. Basque (487)	1,765	2.92
French Canadian (31)	85	0.14
German (5,115)	13,440	22.24
German Russian (0)	0	<0.01
Greek (15)	52	0.09
Guyanese (0)	0	<0.01
Hungarian (135)	438	0.72
Icelander (0)	13	0.02
Iranian (0)	0	<0.01
Irish (2,031)	7,200	11.91
Israeli (13)	13	0.02
Italian (848)	1,814	3.00
Latvian (69)	118	0.20
Lithuanian (33)	110	0.18
Luxemburger (0)	0	<0.01
Macedonian (0)	0	<0.01
Maltese (0)	0	<0.01
New Zealander (0)	0	<0.01
Northern European (0)	3	<0.01
Norwegian (51)	196	0.32
Pennsylvania German (2)	15	0.02
Polish (251)	1,184	1.96
Portuguese (0)	0	<0.01
Romanian (178)	263	0.44
Russian (7)	256	0.42
Scandinavian (41)	50	0.08
Scotch-Irish (308)	884	1.46
Scottish (348)	1,286	2.13
Serbian (24)	66	0.11
Slavic (0)	32	0.05
Slovak (22)	60	0.10
Slovene (16)	16	0.03
Soviet Union (0)	0	<0.01
Swedish (86)	475	0.79
Swiss (42)	165	0.27
Turkish (8)	23	0.04
Ukrainian (20)	20	0.03
Welsh (122)	591	0.98
West Indian, ex. Hispanic (27)	27	0.04
Bahamian (0)	0	<0.01
Barbadian (0)	0	<0.01
Belizean (0)	0	<0.01
Bermudan (0)	0	<0.01
British West Indian (0)	0	<0.01
Dutch West Indian (0)	0	<0.01
Haitian (27)	27	0.04
Jamaican (0)	0	<0.01
Trinidadian/Tobagonian (0)	0	<0.01
U.S. Virgin Islander (0)	0	<0.01
West Indian (0)	0	<0.01
Other West Indian (0)	0	<0.01
Yugoslavian (27)	55	0.09

Hispanic Origin	Population	%
Hispanic or Latino (of any race)	1,893	3.11
Central American, ex. Mexican	63	0.10
Costa Rican	3	<0.01
Guatemalan	16	0.03
Honduran	22	0.04
Nicaraguan	2	<0.01
Panamanian	8	0.01
Salvadoran	12	0.02
Other Central American	0	<0.01
Cuban	46	0.08
Dominican Republic	10	0.02
Mexican	1,469	2.42
Puerto Rican	140	0.23
South American	70	0.12
Argentinean	12	0.02
Bolivian	6	0.01
Chilean	6	0.01
Colombian	28	0.05
Ecuadorian	4	0.01
Paraguayan	0	<0.01
Peruvian	5	0.01
Uruguayan	0	<0.01
Venezuelan	9	0.01
Other South American	0	<0.01
Other Hispanic or Latino	95	0.16

Race*	Population	%
African-American/Black (6,644)	7,819	12.86
Not Hispanic (6,587)	7,705	12.68
Hispanic (57)	114	0.19
American Indian/Alaska Native (259)	685	1.13
Not Hispanic (231)	632	1.04
Hispanic (28)	53	0.09
Alaska Athabascan (Ala. Nat.) (0)	0	<0.01
Aleut (Alaska Native) (0)	0	<0.01
Apache (1)	8	0.01
Arapaho (0)	0	<0.01
Blackfeet (2)	24	0.04
Canadian/French Am. Ind. (1)	1	<0.01
Central American Ind. (0)	0	<0.01
Cherokee (34)	159	0.26
Cheyenne (0)	6	0.01
Chickasaw (0)	4	0.01
Chippewa (2)	3	<0.01
Choctaw (3)	9	0.01
Colville (0)	0	<0.01
Comanche (0)	2	<0.01
Cree (8)	9	0.01
Creek (7)	8	0.01
Crow (0)	0	<0.01
Delaware (0)	1	<0.01
Hopi (0)	0	<0.01
Houma (2)	2	<0.01
Inupiat (Alaska Native) (0)	0	<0.01
Iroquois (0)	4	0.01
Kiowa (2)	2	<0.01
Lumbee (0)	2	<0.01
Menominee (1)	1	<0.01
Mexican American Ind. (13)	20	0.03
Navajo (1)	6	0.01
Osage (1)	1	<0.01
Ottawa (0)	0	<0.01
Paiute (0)	0	<0.01
Pima (0)	0	<0.01
Potawatomi (5)	6	0.01
Pueblo (0)	0	<0.01
Puget Sound Salish (0)	0	<0.01
Seminole (0)	1	<0.01
Shoshone (0)	0	<0.01
Sioux (15)	34	0.06
South American Ind. (0)	0	<0.01
Spanish American Ind. (0)	0	<0.01
Tlingit-Haida (Alaska Native) (0)	1	<0.01
Tohono O'Odham (0)	0	<0.01
Tsimshian (Alaska Native) (0)	0	<0.01
Ute (1)	1	<0.01
Yakama (0)	0	<0.01
Yaqui (0)	3	<0.01
Yuman (0)	0	<0.01
Yup'ik (Alaska Native) (0)	0	<0.01
Asian (879)	1,092	1.80
Not Hispanic (876)	1,081	1.78
Hispanic (3)	11	0.02
Bangladeshi (2)	2	<0.01
Bhutanese (0)	0	<0.01
Burmese (0)	0	<0.01
Cambodian (1)	1	<0.01
Chinese, ex. Taiwanese (222)	254	0.42
Filipino (104)	159	0.26
Hmong (5)	7	0.01
Indian (213)	242	0.40
Indonesian (2)	5	0.01
Japanese (65)	112	0.18
Korean (118)	141	0.23
Laotian (0)	0	<0.01
Malaysian (1)	9	0.01
Nepalese (5)	5	0.01
Pakistani (2)	6	0.01
Sri Lankan (0)	1	<0.01
Taiwanese (52)	55	0.09
Thai (7)	9	0.01
Vietnamese (28)	41	0.07
Hawaii Native/Pacific Islander (26)	79	0.13
Not Hispanic (22)	73	0.12
Hispanic (4)	6	0.01
Fijian (0)	0	<0.01
Guamanian/Chamorro (8)	11	0.02
Marshallese (0)	0	<0.01
Native Hawaiian (10)	44	0.07
Samoan (2)	13	0.02
Tongan (0)	2	<0.01
White (50,750)	52,377	86.17
Not Hispanic (49,456)	50,949	83.82
Hispanic (1,294)	1,428	2.35

Notes: † The Census 2010 population figure is used to calculate the percentages in the Hispanic Origin and Race categories. Ancestry percentages are based on the 2006-2010 American Community Survey population (not shown); ‡ Numbers in parentheses indicate the number of people reporting a single ancestry; * Numbers in parentheses indicate the number of persons reporting this race alone, not in combination with any other race; Please refer to the Explanation of Data for more information.

Ancestry Group Rankings

Afghan

Top 10 Places Sorted by Population
Based on all places, regardless of total population

Place	Population	%
Bloomington (city) Monroe County	59	0.08
York (town) Delaware County	57	0.62
Carmel (city) Hamilton County	37	0.05
Indianapolis (city) Marion County	29	<0.01
Fort Wayne (city) Allen County	20	0.01
Fishers (town) Hamilton County	15	0.02
Portage (city) Porter County	13	0.04
Hanover (town) Jefferson County	12	0.36
Munster (town) Lake County	3	0.01
Aberdeen (cdp) Porter County	0	0.00

Top 10 Places Sorted by Percent of Total Population
Based on all places, regardless of total population

Place	Population	%
York (town) Delaware County	57	0.62
Hanover (town) Jefferson County	12	0.36
Bloomington (city) Monroe County	59	0.08
Carmel (city) Hamilton County	37	0.05
Portage (city) Porter County	13	0.04
Fishers (town) Hamilton County	15	0.02
Fort Wayne (city) Allen County	20	0.01
Munster (town) Lake County	3	0.01
Indianapolis (city) Marion County	29	<0.01
Aberdeen (cdp) Porter County	0	0.00

Top 10 Places Sorted by Percent of Total Population
Based on places with total population of 50,000 or more

Place	Population	%
Bloomington (city) Monroe County	59	0.08
Carmel (city) Hamilton County	37	0.05
Fishers (town) Hamilton County	15	0.02
Fort Wayne (city) Allen County	20	0.01
Indianapolis (city) Marion County	29	<0.01
Anderson (city) Madison County	0	0.00
Elkhart (city) Elkhart County	0	0.00
Evansville (city) Vanderburgh County	0	0.00
Gary (city) Lake County	0	0.00
Hammond (city) Lake County	0	0.00

African, Sub-Saharan

Top 10 Places Sorted by Population
Based on all places, regardless of total population

Place	Population	%
Indianapolis (city) Marion County	43,672	5.39
Fort Wayne (city) Allen County	13,249	5.22
Gary (city) Lake County	1,824	2.16
Lawrence (city) Marion County	1,653	3.72
South Bend (city) St. Joseph County	1,287	1.26
Merrillville (town) Lake County	902	2.62
Muncie (city) Delaware County	875	1.25
Terre Haute (city) Vigo County	806	1.33
Speedway (town) Marion County	709	5.94
Anderson (city) Madison County	648	1.14

Top 10 Places Sorted by Percent of Total Population
Based on all places, regardless of total population

Place	Population	%
Warren Park (town) Marion County	130	9.37
Spring Grove (town) Wayne County	25	7.16
Harmony (town) Clay County	41	6.44
Speedway (town) Marion County	709	5.94
Greenville (town) Floyd County	31	5.48
Indianapolis (city) Marion County	43,672	5.39
Fort Wayne (city) Allen County	13,249	5.22
Stilesville (town) Hendricks County	15	5.21
Hunter (town) Allen County	224	4.76
Lawrence (city) Marion County	1,653	3.72

Top 10 Places Sorted by Percent of Total Population
Based on places with total population of 50,000 or more

Place	Population	%
Indianapolis (city) Marion County	43,672	5.39
Fort Wayne (city) Allen County	13,249	5.22
Gary (city) Lake County	1,824	2.16
Terre Haute (city) Vigo County	806	1.33
South Bend (city) St. Joseph County	1,287	1.26
Muncie (city) Delaware County	875	1.25
Anderson (city) Madison County	648	1.14
Elkhart (city) Elkhart County	409	0.79
Bloomington (city) Monroe County	593	0.76
Hammond (city) Lake County	421	0.52

African, Sub-Saharan: African

Top 10 Places Sorted by Population
Based on all places, regardless of total population

Place	Population	%
Indianapolis (city) Marion County	38,288	4.73
Fort Wayne (city) Allen County	12,753	5.03
Lawrence (city) Marion County	1,595	3.59
Gary (city) Lake County	1,527	1.81
South Bend (city) St. Joseph County	952	0.93
Merrillville (town) Lake County	867	2.52
Terre Haute (city) Vigo County	800	1.32
Muncie (city) Delaware County	737	1.05
Michigan City (city) LaPorte County	629	1.99
East Chicago (city) Lake County	595	1.97

Top 10 Places Sorted by Percent of Total Population
Based on all places, regardless of total population

Place	Population	%
Warren Park (town) Marion County	130	9.37
Spring Grove (town) Wayne County	25	7.16
Harmony (town) Clay County	41	6.44
Greenville (town) Floyd County	31	5.48
Stilesville (town) Hendricks County	15	5.21
Fort Wayne (city) Allen County	12,753	5.03
Speedway (town) Marion County	581	4.87
Hunter (town) Allen County	224	4.76
Indianapolis (city) Marion County	38,288	4.73
Lawrence (city) Marion County	1,595	3.59

Top 10 Places Sorted by Percent of Total Population
Based on places with total population of 50,000 or more

Place	Population	%
Fort Wayne (city) Allen County	12,753	5.03
Indianapolis (city) Marion County	38,288	4.73
Gary (city) Lake County	1,527	1.81
Terre Haute (city) Vigo County	800	1.32
Muncie (city) Delaware County	737	1.05
Anderson (city) Madison County	543	0.96
South Bend (city) St. Joseph County	952	0.93
Bloomington (city) Monroe County	508	0.65
Elkhart (city) Elkhart County	305	0.59
Hammond (city) Lake County	398	0.49

African, Sub-Saharan: Cape Verdean

Top 10 Places Sorted by Population
Based on all places, regardless of total population

Place	Population	%
Dyer (town) Lake County	28	0.18
Aberdeen (cdp) Porter County	0	0.00
Advance (town) Boone County	0	0.00
Akron (town) Fulton County	0	0.00
Alamo (town) Montgomery County	0	0.00
Albany (town) Delaware County	0	0.00
Albion (town) Noble County	0	0.00
Alexandria (city) Madison County	0	0.00
Alfordsville (town) Daviess County	0	0.00
Alton (town) Crawford County	0	0.00

Top 10 Places Sorted by Percent of Total Population
Based on all places, regardless of total population

Place	Population	%
Dyer (town) Lake County	28	0.18
Aberdeen (cdp) Porter County	0	0.00
Advance (town) Boone County	0	0.00
Akron (town) Fulton County	0	0.00
Alamo (town) Montgomery County	0	0.00
Albany (town) Delaware County	0	0.00
Albion (town) Noble County	0	0.00
Alexandria (city) Madison County	0	0.00
Alfordsville (town) Daviess County	0	0.00
Alton (town) Crawford County	0	0.00

Top 10 Places Sorted by Percent of Total Population
Based on places with total population of 50,000 or more

Place	Population	%
Anderson (city) Madison County	0	0.00
Bloomington (city) Monroe County	0	0.00
Carmel (city) Hamilton County	0	0.00
Elkhart (city) Elkhart County	0	0.00
Evansville (city) Vanderburgh County	0	0.00
Fishers (town) Hamilton County	0	0.00
Fort Wayne (city) Allen County	0	0.00
Gary (city) Lake County	0	0.00
Hammond (city) Lake County	0	0.00
Indianapolis (city) Marion County	0	0.00

African, Sub-Saharan: Ethiopian

Top 10 Places Sorted by Population
Based on all places, regardless of total population

Place	Population	%
Indianapolis (city) Marion County	443	0.05
Gary (city) Lake County	121	0.14
Plainfield (town) Hendricks County	82	0.31
Fort Wayne (city) Allen County	47	0.02
Speedway (town) Marion County	46	0.39
Purdue University (cdp) Tippecanoe County	46	0.35
Evansville (city) Vanderburgh County	34	0.03
Hobart (city) Lake County	30	0.11
West Lafayette (city) Tippecanoe County	26	0.09
Anderson (city) Madison County	18	0.03

Top 10 Places Sorted by Percent of Total Population
Based on all places, regardless of total population

Place	Population	%
Speedway (town) Marion County	46	0.39
Purdue University (cdp) Tippecanoe County	46	0.35
Plainfield (town) Hendricks County	82	0.31
Notre Dame (cdp) St. Joseph County	13	0.17
Gary (city) Lake County	121	0.14
Hobart (city) Lake County	30	0.11
West Lafayette (city) Tippecanoe County	26	0.09
Indianapolis (city) Marion County	443	0.05
Crown Point (city) Lake County	13	0.05
Evansville (city) Vanderburgh County	34	0.03

Top 10 Places Sorted by Percent of Total Population
Based on places with total population of 50,000 or more

Place	Population	%
Gary (city) Lake County	121	0.14
Indianapolis (city) Marion County	443	0.05
Evansville (city) Vanderburgh County	34	0.03
Anderson (city) Madison County	18	0.03
Fort Wayne (city) Allen County	47	0.02
Carmel (city) Hamilton County	12	0.02
Bloomington (city) Monroe County	5	0.01
Elkhart (city) Elkhart County	0	0.00
Fishers (town) Hamilton County	0	0.00
Hammond (city) Lake County	0	0.00

African, Sub-Saharan: Ghanaian

Top 10 Places Sorted by Population
Based on all places, regardless of total population

Place	Population	%
Indianapolis (city) Marion County	154	0.02
Mishawaka (city) St. Joseph County	51	0.11
Franklin (city) Johnson County	46	0.20
Merrillville (town) Lake County	18	0.05
Greencastle (city) Putnam County	14	0.14
Schererville (town) Lake County	12	0.04
Columbus (city) Bartholomew County	10	0.02
Gary (city) Lake County	10	0.01
Valparaiso (city) Porter County	7	0.02
Aberdeen (cdp) Porter County	0	0.00

Top 10 Places Sorted by Percent of Total Population
Based on all places, regardless of total population

Place	Population	%
Franklin (city) Johnson County	46	0.20
Greencastle (city) Putnam County	14	0.14
Mishawaka (city) St. Joseph County	51	0.11
Merrillville (town) Lake County	18	0.05
Schererville (town) Lake County	12	0.04
Indianapolis (city) Marion County	154	0.02
Columbus (city) Bartholomew County	10	0.02
Valparaiso (city) Porter County	7	0.02
Gary (city) Lake County	10	0.01
Aberdeen (cdp) Porter County	0	0.00

Top 10 Places Sorted by Percent of Total Population
Based on places with total population of 50,000 or more

Place	Population	%
Indianapolis (city) Marion County	154	0.02
Gary (city) Lake County	10	0.01
Anderson (city) Madison County	0	0.00
Bloomington (city) Monroe County	0	0.00
Carmel (city) Hamilton County	0	0.00
Elkhart (city) Elkhart County	0	0.00
Evansville (city) Vanderburgh County	0	0.00
Fishers (town) Hamilton County	0	0.00
Fort Wayne (city) Allen County	0	0.00
Hammond (city) Lake County	0	0.00

African, Sub-Saharan: Kenyan

Top 10 Places Sorted by Population
Based on all places, regardless of total population

Place	Population	%
South Bend (city) St. Joseph County	218	0.21
Indianapolis (city) Marion County	63	0.01
Elkhart (city) Elkhart County	61	0.12
Noblesville (city) Hamilton County	57	0.12
Anderson (city) Madison County	43	0.08
Goshen (city) Elkhart County	35	0.11
Lafayette (city) Tippecanoe County	33	0.05
West Lafayette (city) Tippecanoe County	29	0.10
Fort Wayne (city) Allen County	27	0.01
Greenwood (city) Johnson County	26	0.05

Top 10 Places Sorted by Percent of Total Population
Based on all places, regardless of total population

Place	Population	%
Bristol (town) Elkhart County	4	0.24
South Bend (city) St. Joseph County	218	0.21
Speedway (town) Marion County	22	0.18
Elkhart (city) Elkhart County	61	0.12
Noblesville (city) Hamilton County	57	0.12
Goshen (city) Elkhart County	35	0.11
West Lafayette (city) Tippecanoe County	29	0.10
Anderson (city) Madison County	43	0.08
Lafayette (city) Tippecanoe County	33	0.05
Greenwood (city) Johnson County	26	0.05

Top 10 Places Sorted by Percent of Total Population
Based on places with total population of 50,000 or more

Place	Population	%
South Bend (city) St. Joseph County	218	0.21
Elkhart (city) Elkhart County	61	0.12
Anderson (city) Madison County	43	0.08
Lafayette (city) Tippecanoe County	33	0.05
Muncie (city) Delaware County	14	0.02
Indianapolis (city) Marion County	63	0.01
Fort Wayne (city) Allen County	27	0.01
Bloomington (city) Monroe County	0	0.00
Carmel (city) Hamilton County	0	0.00
Evansville (city) Vanderburgh County	0	0.00

African, Sub-Saharan: Liberian

Top 10 Places Sorted by Population
Based on all places, regardless of total population

Place	Population	%
Indianapolis (city) Marion County	687	0.08
Lafayette (city) Tippecanoe County	32	0.05
South Bend (city) St. Joseph County	28	0.03
Notre Dame (cdp) St. Joseph County	13	0.17
Gary (city) Lake County	11	0.01
Aberdeen (cdp) Porter County	0	0.00
Advance (town) Boone County	0	0.00
Akron (town) Fulton County	0	0.00
Alamo (town) Montgomery County	0	0.00
Albany (town) Delaware County	0	0.00

Top 10 Places Sorted by Percent of Total Population
Based on all places, regardless of total population

Place	Population	%
Notre Dame (cdp) St. Joseph County	13	0.17
Indianapolis (city) Marion County	687	0.08
Lafayette (city) Tippecanoe County	32	0.05
South Bend (city) St. Joseph County	28	0.03
Gary (city) Lake County	11	0.01
Aberdeen (cdp) Porter County	0	0.00
Advance (town) Boone County	0	0.00
Akron (town) Fulton County	0	0.00
Alamo (town) Montgomery County	0	0.00
Albany (town) Delaware County	0	0.00

Top 10 Places Sorted by Percent of Total Population
Based on places with total population of 50,000 or more

Place	Population	%
Indianapolis (city) Marion County	687	0.08
Lafayette (city) Tippecanoe County	32	0.05
South Bend (city) St. Joseph County	28	0.03
Gary (city) Lake County	11	0.01
Anderson (city) Madison County	0	0.00
Bloomington (city) Monroe County	0	0.00
Carmel (city) Hamilton County	0	0.00
Elkhart (city) Elkhart County	0	0.00
Evansville (city) Vanderburgh County	0	0.00
Fishers (town) Hamilton County	0	0.00

African, Sub-Saharan: Nigerian

Top 10 Places Sorted by Population
Based on all places, regardless of total population

Place	Population	%
Indianapolis (city) Marion County	2,048	0.25
Gary (city) Lake County	155	0.18
Fort Wayne (city) Allen County	138	0.05
Crown Point (city) Lake County	95	0.36
Plainfield (town) Hendricks County	84	0.32
Fishers (town) Hamilton County	79	0.11
West Lafayette (city) Tippecanoe County	49	0.17
Speedway (town) Marion County	40	0.34
Avon (town) Hendricks County	28	0.24
Notre Dame (cdp) St. Joseph County	26	0.35

Top 10 Places Sorted by Percent of Total Population
Based on all places, regardless of total population

Place	Population	%
Rocky Ripple (town) Marion County	3	0.47
Crown Point (city) Lake County	95	0.36
Notre Dame (cdp) St. Joseph County	26	0.35
Speedway (town) Marion County	40	0.34
Plainfield (town) Hendricks County	84	0.32
Indianapolis (city) Marion County	2,048	0.25
Avon (town) Hendricks County	28	0.24
Gary (city) Lake County	155	0.18
Purdue University (cdp) Tippecanoe County	23	0.18
West Lafayette (city) Tippecanoe County	49	0.17

Top 10 Places Sorted by Percent of Total Population
Based on places with total population of 50,000 or more

Place	Population	%
Indianapolis (city) Marion County	2,048	0.25
Gary (city) Lake County	155	0.18
Fishers (town) Hamilton County	79	0.11
Fort Wayne (city) Allen County	138	0.05
Lafayette (city) Tippecanoe County	23	0.03
Bloomington (city) Monroe County	14	0.02
Evansville (city) Vanderburgh County	17	0.01
Hammond (city) Lake County	10	0.01
Anderson (city) Madison County	0	0.00
Carmel (city) Hamilton County	0	0.00

African, Sub-Saharan: Senegalese

Top 10 Places Sorted by Population
Based on all places, regardless of total population

Place	Population	%
Indianapolis (city) Marion County	150	0.02
Greencastle (city) Putnam County	14	0.14
Fishers (town) Hamilton County	13	0.02
Aberdeen (cdp) Porter County	0	0.00
Advance (town) Boone County	0	0.00
Akron (town) Fulton County	0	0.00
Alamo (town) Montgomery County	0	0.00
Albany (town) Delaware County	0	0.00
Albion (town) Noble County	0	0.00
Alexandria (city) Madison County	0	0.00

Top 10 Places Sorted by Percent of Total Population
Based on all places, regardless of total population

Place	Population	%
Greencastle (city) Putnam County	14	0.14
Indianapolis (city) Marion County	150	0.02
Fishers (town) Hamilton County	13	0.02
Aberdeen (cdp) Porter County	0	0.00
Advance (town) Boone County	0	0.00
Akron (town) Fulton County	0	0.00
Alamo (town) Montgomery County	0	0.00
Albany (town) Delaware County	0	0.00
Albion (town) Noble County	0	0.00
Alexandria (city) Madison County	0	0.00

Top 10 Places Sorted by Percent of Total Population
Based on places with total population of 50,000 or more

Place	Population	%
Indianapolis (city) Marion County	150	0.02
Fishers (town) Hamilton County	13	0.02
Anderson (city) Madison County	0	0.00
Bloomington (city) Monroe County	0	0.00
Carmel (city) Hamilton County	0	0.00
Elkhart (city) Elkhart County	0	0.00
Evansville (city) Vanderburgh County	0	0.00
Fort Wayne (city) Allen County	0	0.00
Gary (city) Lake County	0	0.00
Hammond (city) Lake County	0	0.00

African, Sub-Saharan: Sierra Leonean

Top 10 Places Sorted by Population
Based on all places, regardless of total population

Place	Population	%
Mishawaka (city) St. Joseph County	21	0.04
South Bend (city) St. Joseph County	11	0.01
Goshen (city) Elkhart County	9	0.03
Aberdeen (cdp) Porter County	0	0.00
Advance (town) Boone County	0	0.00
Akron (town) Fulton County	0	0.00
Alamo (town) Montgomery County	0	0.00
Albany (town) Delaware County	0	0.00
Albion (town) Noble County	0	0.00
Alexandria (city) Madison County	0	0.00

Top 10 Places Sorted by Percent of Total Population
Based on all places, regardless of total population

Place	Population	%
Mishawaka (city) St. Joseph County	21	0.04
Goshen (city) Elkhart County	9	0.03
South Bend (city) St. Joseph County	11	0.01

Please refer to the Explanation of Data in the front of the book for more detailed information.

Place	Population	%
Aberdeen (cdp) Porter County	0	0.00
Advance (town) Boone County	0	0.00
Akron (town) Fulton County	0	0.00
Alamo (town) Montgomery County	0	0.00
Albany (town) Delaware County	0	0.00
Albion (town) Noble County	0	0.00
Alexandria (city) Madison County	0	0.00

Top 10 Places Sorted by Percent of Total Population
Based on places with total population of 50,000 or more

Place	Population	%
South Bend (city) St. Joseph County	11	0.01
Anderson (city) Madison County	0	0.00
Bloomington (city) Monroe County	0	0.00
Carmel (city) Hamilton County	0	0.00
Elkhart (city) Elkhart County	0	0.00
Evansville (city) Vanderburgh County	0	0.00
Fishers (town) Hamilton County	0	0.00
Fort Wayne (city) Allen County	0	0.00
Gary (city) Lake County	0	0.00
Hammond (city) Lake County	0	0.00

African, Sub-Saharan: Somalian

Top 10 Places Sorted by Population
Based on all places, regardless of total population

Place	Population	%
Indianapolis (city) Marion County	432	0.05
Fort Wayne (city) Allen County	68	0.03
Lawrence (city) Marion County	32	0.07
North Manchester (town) Wabash County	11	0.18
Terre Haute (city) Vigo County	6	0.01
Aberdeen (cdp) Porter County	0	0.00
Advance (town) Boone County	0	0.00
Akron (town) Fulton County	0	0.00
Alamo (town) Montgomery County	0	0.00
Albany (town) Delaware County	0	0.00

Top 10 Places Sorted by Percent of Total Population
Based on all places, regardless of total population

Place	Population	%
North Manchester (town) Wabash County	11	0.18
Lawrence (city) Marion County	32	0.07
Indianapolis (city) Marion County	432	0.05
Fort Wayne (city) Allen County	68	0.03
Terre Haute (city) Vigo County	6	0.01
Aberdeen (cdp) Porter County	0	0.00
Advance (town) Boone County	0	0.00
Akron (town) Fulton County	0	0.00
Alamo (town) Montgomery County	0	0.00
Albany (town) Delaware County	0	0.00

Top 10 Places Sorted by Percent of Total Population
Based on places with total population of 50,000 or more

Place	Population	%
Indianapolis (city) Marion County	432	0.05
Fort Wayne (city) Allen County	68	0.03
Terre Haute (city) Vigo County	6	0.01
Anderson (city) Madison County	0	0.00
Bloomington (city) Monroe County	0	0.00
Carmel (city) Hamilton County	0	0.00
Elkhart (city) Elkhart County	0	0.00
Evansville (city) Vanderburgh County	0	0.00
Fishers (town) Hamilton County	0	0.00
Gary (city) Lake County	0	0.00

African, Sub-Saharan: South African

Top 10 Places Sorted by Population
Based on all places, regardless of total population

Place	Population	%
Carmel (city) Hamilton County	137	0.18
Bloomington (city) Monroe County	63	0.08
Fort Wayne (city) Allen County	52	0.02
Schererville (town) Lake County	43	0.15
Indianapolis (city) Marion County	43	0.01
Ligonier (city) Noble County	40	0.93
Warsaw (city) Kosciusko County	16	0.12
Muncie (city) Delaware County	16	0.02
Greencastle (city) Putnam County	14	0.14
Westfield (town) Hamilton County	10	0.04

Top 10 Places Sorted by Percent of Total Population
Based on all places, regardless of total population

Place	Population	%
Ligonier (city) Noble County	40	0.93
Clear Lake (town) Steuben County	3	0.70
Otterbein (town) Benton County	7	0.62
Fountain City (town) Wayne County	3	0.42
Carmel (city) Hamilton County	137	0.18
Schererville (town) Lake County	43	0.15
Greencastle (city) Putnam County	14	0.14
Warsaw (city) Kosciusko County	16	0.12
Bloomington (city) Monroe County	63	0.08
Peru (city) Miami County	8	0.07

Top 10 Places Sorted by Percent of Total Population
Based on places with total population of 50,000 or more

Place	Population	%
Carmel (city) Hamilton County	137	0.18
Bloomington (city) Monroe County	63	0.08
Fort Wayne (city) Allen County	52	0.02
Muncie (city) Delaware County	16	0.02
Indianapolis (city) Marion County	43	0.01
Anderson (city) Madison County	0	0.00
Elkhart (city) Elkhart County	0	0.00
Evansville (city) Vanderburgh County	0	0.00
Fishers (town) Hamilton County	0	0.00
Gary (city) Lake County	0	0.00

African, Sub-Saharan: Sudanese

Top 10 Places Sorted by Population
Based on all places, regardless of total population

Place	Population	%
Indianapolis (city) Marion County	376	0.05
Chesterton (town) Porter County	19	0.14
Anderson (city) Madison County	18	0.03
Carmel (city) Hamilton County	11	0.01
West Lafayette (city) Tippecanoe County	9	0.03
Aberdeen (cdp) Porter County	0	0.00
Advance (town) Boone County	0	0.00
Akron (town) Fulton County	0	0.00
Alamo (town) Montgomery County	0	0.00
Albany (town) Delaware County	0	0.00

Top 10 Places Sorted by Percent of Total Population
Based on all places, regardless of total population

Place	Population	%
Chesterton (town) Porter County	19	0.14
Indianapolis (city) Marion County	376	0.05
Anderson (city) Madison County	18	0.03
West Lafayette (city) Tippecanoe County	9	0.03
Carmel (city) Hamilton County	11	0.01
Aberdeen (cdp) Porter County	0	0.00
Advance (town) Boone County	0	0.00
Akron (town) Fulton County	0	0.00
Alamo (town) Montgomery County	0	0.00
Albany (town) Delaware County	0	0.00

Top 10 Places Sorted by Percent of Total Population
Based on places with total population of 50,000 or more

Place	Population	%
Indianapolis (city) Marion County	376	0.05
Anderson (city) Madison County	18	0.03
Carmel (city) Hamilton County	11	0.01
Bloomington (city) Monroe County	0	0.00
Elkhart (city) Elkhart County	0	0.00
Evansville (city) Vanderburgh County	0	0.00
Fishers (town) Hamilton County	0	0.00
Fort Wayne (city) Allen County	0	0.00
Gary (city) Lake County	0	0.00
Hammond (city) Lake County	0	0.00

African, Sub-Saharan: Ugandan

Top 10 Places Sorted by Population
Based on all places, regardless of total population

Place	Population	%
Indianapolis (city) Marion County	54	0.01
North Manchester (town) Wabash County	17	0.28
St. Mary of the Woods (cdp) Vigo County	16	1.44
Evansville (city) Vanderburgh County	14	0.01
Mishawaka (city) St. Joseph County	8	0.02
Aberdeen (cdp) Porter County	0	0.00
Advance (town) Boone County	0	0.00
Akron (town) Fulton County	0	0.00
Alamo (town) Montgomery County	0	0.00
Albany (town) Delaware County	0	0.00

Top 10 Places Sorted by Percent of Total Population
Based on all places, regardless of total population

Place	Population	%
St. Mary of the Woods (cdp) Vigo County	16	1.44
North Manchester (town) Wabash County	17	0.28
Mishawaka (city) St. Joseph County	8	0.02
Indianapolis (city) Marion County	54	0.01
Evansville (city) Vanderburgh County	14	0.01
Aberdeen (cdp) Porter County	0	0.00
Advance (town) Boone County	0	0.00
Akron (town) Fulton County	0	0.00
Alamo (town) Montgomery County	0	0.00
Albany (town) Delaware County	0	0.00

Top 10 Places Sorted by Percent of Total Population
Based on places with total population of 50,000 or more

Place	Population	%
Indianapolis (city) Marion County	54	0.01
Evansville (city) Vanderburgh County	14	0.01
Anderson (city) Madison County	0	0.00
Bloomington (city) Monroe County	0	0.00
Carmel (city) Hamilton County	0	0.00
Elkhart (city) Elkhart County	0	0.00
Fishers (town) Hamilton County	0	0.00
Fort Wayne (city) Allen County	0	0.00
Gary (city) Lake County	0	0.00
Hammond (city) Lake County	0	0.00

African, Sub-Saharan: Zimbabwean

Top 10 Places Sorted by Population
Based on all places, regardless of total population

Place	Population	%
Indianapolis (city) Marion County	149	0.02
Elkhart (city) Elkhart County	13	0.03
Aberdeen (cdp) Porter County	0	0.00
Advance (town) Boone County	0	0.00
Akron (town) Fulton County	0	0.00
Alamo (town) Montgomery County	0	0.00
Albany (town) Delaware County	0	0.00
Albion (town) Noble County	0	0.00
Alexandria (city) Madison County	0	0.00
Alfordsville (town) Daviess County	0	0.00

Top 10 Places Sorted by Percent of Total Population
Based on all places, regardless of total population

Place	Population	%
Elkhart (city) Elkhart County	13	0.03
Indianapolis (city) Marion County	149	0.02
Aberdeen (cdp) Porter County	0	0.00
Advance (town) Boone County	0	0.00
Akron (town) Fulton County	0	0.00
Alamo (town) Montgomery County	0	0.00
Albany (town) Delaware County	0	0.00
Albion (town) Noble County	0	0.00
Alexandria (city) Madison County	0	0.00
Alfordsville (town) Daviess County	0	0.00

Top 10 Places Sorted by Percent of Total Population
Based on places with total population of 50,000 or more

Place	Population	%
Elkhart (city) Elkhart County	13	0.03
Indianapolis (city) Marion County	149	0.02
Anderson (city) Madison County	0	0.00
Bloomington (city) Monroe County	0	0.00
Carmel (city) Hamilton County	0	0.00
Evansville (city) Vanderburgh County	0	0.00
Fishers (town) Hamilton County	0	0.00
Fort Wayne (city) Allen County	0	0.00
Gary (city) Lake County	0	0.00
Hammond (city) Lake County	0	0.00

Please refer to the Explanation of Data in the front of the book for more detailed information.

African, Sub-Saharan: Other

Top 10 Places Sorted by Population
Based on all places, regardless of total population

Place	Population	%
Indianapolis (city) Marion County	785	0.10
Fort Wayne (city) Allen County	164	0.06
Muncie (city) Delaware County	108	0.15
South Bend (city) St. Joseph County	78	0.08
West Lafayette (city) Tippecanoe County	65	0.22
Fishers (town) Hamilton County	55	0.08
Lafayette (city) Tippecanoe County	54	0.08
Granger (cdp) St. Joseph County	38	0.13
Elkhart (city) Elkhart County	30	0.06
Anderson (city) Madison County	26	0.05

Top 10 Places Sorted by Percent of Total Population
Based on all places, regardless of total population

Place	Population	%
Austin (city) Scott County	15	0.37
West Lafayette (city) Tippecanoe County	65	0.22
Speedway (town) Marion County	20	0.17
Notre Dame (cdp) St. Joseph County	13	0.17
Muncie (city) Delaware County	108	0.15
Granger (cdp) St. Joseph County	38	0.13
Indianapolis (city) Marion County	785	0.10
South Bend (city) St. Joseph County	78	0.08
Fishers (town) Hamilton County	55	0.08
Lafayette (city) Tippecanoe County	54	0.08

Top 10 Places Sorted by Percent of Total Population
Based on places with total population of 50,000 or more

Place	Population	%
Muncie (city) Delaware County	108	0.15
Indianapolis (city) Marion County	785	0.10
South Bend (city) St. Joseph County	78	0.08
Fishers (town) Hamilton County	55	0.08
Lafayette (city) Tippecanoe County	54	0.08
Fort Wayne (city) Allen County	164	0.06
Elkhart (city) Elkhart County	30	0.06
Anderson (city) Madison County	26	0.05
Hammond (city) Lake County	13	0.02
Evansville (city) Vanderburgh County	8	0.01

Albanian

Top 10 Places Sorted by Population
Based on all places, regardless of total population

Place	Population	%
Indianapolis (city) Marion County	105	0.01
West Lafayette (city) Tippecanoe County	80	0.27
Hammond (city) Lake County	61	0.08
Muncie (city) Delaware County	57	0.08
Noblesville (city) Hamilton County	40	0.08
Greenwood (city) Johnson County	37	0.08
Crawfordsville (city) Montgomery County	34	0.21
Fort Wayne (city) Allen County	33	0.01
Michigan City (city) LaPorte County	26	0.08
Bloomington (city) Monroe County	20	0.03

Top 10 Places Sorted by Percent of Total Population
Based on all places, regardless of total population

Place	Population	%
West Lafayette (city) Tippecanoe County	80	0.27
Ogden Dunes (town) Porter County	3	0.24
Crawfordsville (city) Montgomery County	34	0.21
Rossville (town) Clinton County	3	0.21
Winfield (town) Lake County	7	0.18
Meridian Hills (town) Marion County	3	0.18
Notre Dame (cdp) St. Joseph County	13	0.17
Cedar Lake (town) Lake County	14	0.13
Hammond (city) Lake County	61	0.08
Muncie (city) Delaware County	57	0.08

Top 10 Places Sorted by Percent of Total Population
Based on places with total population of 50,000 or more

Place	Population	%
Hammond (city) Lake County	61	0.08
Muncie (city) Delaware County	57	0.08
Bloomington (city) Monroe County	20	0.03
Indianapolis (city) Marion County	105	0.01

Fort Wayne (city) Allen County	33	0.01
Fishers (town) Hamilton County	10	0.01
Anderson (city) Madison County	0	0.00
Carmel (city) Hamilton County	0	0.00
Elkhart (city) Elkhart County	0	0.00
Evansville (city) Vanderburgh County	0	0.00

Alsatian

Top 10 Places Sorted by Population
Based on all places, regardless of total population

Place	Population	%
Greendale (city) Dearborn County	53	1.16
Aberdeen (cdp) Porter County	48	2.20
Goshen (city) Elkhart County	24	0.08
Muncie (city) Delaware County	22	0.03
Bloomington (city) Monroe County	19	0.02
Hammond (city) Lake County	18	0.02
Auburn (city) DeKalb County	12	0.10
Mishawaka (city) St. Joseph County	12	0.03
Indianapolis (city) Marion County	12	<0.01
Portage (city) Porter County	11	0.03

Top 10 Places Sorted by Percent of Total Population
Based on all places, regardless of total population

Place	Population	%
Aberdeen (cdp) Porter County	48	2.20
Greendale (city) Dearborn County	53	1.16
Shirley (town) Hancock County	3	0.40
Argos (town) Marshall County	4	0.25
George (town) Floyd County	4	0.15
Auburn (city) DeKalb County	12	0.10
Goshen (city) Elkhart County	24	0.08
Muncie (city) Delaware County	22	0.03
Mishawaka (city) St. Joseph County	12	0.03
Portage (city) Porter County	11	0.03

Top 10 Places Sorted by Percent of Total Population
Based on places with total population of 50,000 or more

Place	Population	%
Muncie (city) Delaware County	22	0.03
Bloomington (city) Monroe County	19	0.02
Hammond (city) Lake County	18	0.02
Indianapolis (city) Marion County	12	<0.01
Fort Wayne (city) Allen County	8	<0.01
Anderson (city) Madison County	0	0.00
Carmel (city) Hamilton County	0	0.00
Elkhart (city) Elkhart County	0	0.00
Evansville (city) Vanderburgh County	0	0.00
Fishers (town) Hamilton County	0	0.00

American

Top 10 Places Sorted by Population
Based on all places, regardless of total population

Place	Population	%
Indianapolis (city) Marion County	52,433	6.47
Fort Wayne (city) Allen County	25,688	10.12
Evansville (city) Vanderburgh County	23,162	19.60
Terre Haute (city) Vigo County	11,657	19.29
Kokomo (city) Howard County	6,617	14.42
Muncie (city) Delaware County	6,079	8.68
Anderson (city) Madison County	5,914	10.42
Jeffersonville (city) Clark County	5,374	12.75
Lafayette (city) Tippecanoe County	4,832	7.30
Carmel (city) Hamilton County	4,712	6.14

Top 10 Places Sorted by Percent of Total Population
Based on all places, regardless of total population

Place	Population	%
Williams (cdp) Lawrence County	173	81.60
Marshall (town) Parke County	169	65.25
Jalapa (cdp) Grant County	122	61.62
Mecca (town) Parke County	207	57.66
St. Bernice (cdp) Vermillion County	350	53.52
Montezuma (town) Parke County	392	50.84
Freelandville (cdp) Knox County	195	47.68
Staunton (town) Clay County	308	46.46
Bloomingdale (town) Parke County	153	43.22
Decker (town) Knox County	84	42.86

Top 10 Places Sorted by Percent of Total Population
Based on places with total population of 50,000 or more

Place	Population	%
Evansville (city) Vanderburgh County	23,162	19.60
Terre Haute (city) Vigo County	11,657	19.29
Anderson (city) Madison County	5,914	10.42
Fort Wayne (city) Allen County	25,688	10.12
Muncie (city) Delaware County	6,079	8.68
Lafayette (city) Tippecanoe County	4,832	7.30
Indianapolis (city) Marion County	52,433	6.47
Carmel (city) Hamilton County	4,712	6.14
Fishers (town) Hamilton County	3,929	5.48
Bloomington (city) Monroe County	3,411	4.35

Arab: Total

Top 10 Places Sorted by Population
Based on all places, regardless of total population

Place	Population	%
Indianapolis (city) Marion County	2,776	0.34
Schererville (town) Lake County	668	2.35
Fort Wayne (city) Allen County	664	0.26
Fishers (town) Hamilton County	580	0.81
Carmel (city) Hamilton County	563	0.73
Bloomington (city) Monroe County	548	0.70
Terre Haute (city) Vigo County	525	0.87
Mishawaka (city) St. Joseph County	475	0.99
Highland (town) Lake County	337	1.42
Michigan City (city) LaPorte County	330	1.04

Top 10 Places Sorted by Percent of Total Population
Based on all places, regardless of total population

Place	Population	%
Pottawattamie Park (town) LaPorte County	26	13.13
Versailles (town) Ripley County	97	5.50
Riley (town) Vigo County	11	5.07
Shorewood Forest (cdp) Porter County	127	4.21
Topeka (town) LaGrange County	38	3.02
Campbellsburg (town) Washington County	18	2.86
Dune Acres (town) Porter County	7	2.67
Schererville (town) Lake County	668	2.35
Long Beach (town) LaPorte County	32	2.19
Perrysville (town) Vermillion County	12	2.11

Top 10 Places Sorted by Percent of Total Population
Based on places with total population of 50,000 or more

Place	Population	%
Terre Haute (city) Vigo County	525	0.87
Fishers (town) Hamilton County	580	0.81
Carmel (city) Hamilton County	563	0.73
Bloomington (city) Monroe County	548	0.70
Indianapolis (city) Marion County	2,776	0.34
Hammond (city) Lake County	272	0.33
Muncie (city) Delaware County	204	0.29
Fort Wayne (city) Allen County	664	0.26
Elkhart (city) Elkhart County	109	0.21
South Bend (city) St. Joseph County	131	0.13

Arab: Arab

Top 10 Places Sorted by Population
Based on all places, regardless of total population

Place	Population	%
Indianapolis (city) Marion County	542	0.07
Highland (town) Lake County	326	1.37
Fishers (town) Hamilton County	235	0.33
Fort Wayne (city) Allen County	222	0.09
Schererville (town) Lake County	216	0.76
Bloomington (city) Monroe County	187	0.24
Hammond (city) Lake County	144	0.18
Terre Haute (city) Vigo County	117	0.19
Mishawaka (city) St. Joseph County	116	0.24
Noblesville (city) Hamilton County	113	0.23

Top 10 Places Sorted by Percent of Total Population
Based on all places, regardless of total population

Place	Population	%
Edinburgh (town) Johnson County	65	1.66
Shorewood Forest (cdp) Porter County	50	1.66
Highland (town) Lake County	326	1.37

Please refer to the Explanation of Data in the front of the book for more detailed information.

Place	Population	%
Burns Harbor (town) Porter County	12	0.96
Greencastle (city) Putnam County	91	0.88
Highland (cdp) Vanderburgh County	35	0.83
Oakland City (city) Gibson County	19	0.81
Avon (town) Hendricks County	92	0.79
Schererville (town) Lake County	216	0.76
Koontz Lake (cdp) Starke County	12	0.74

Top 10 Places Sorted by Percent of Total Population
Based on places with total population of 50,000 or more

Place	Population	%
Fishers (town) Hamilton County	235	0.33
Bloomington (city) Monroe County	187	0.24
Terre Haute (city) Vigo County	117	0.19
Hammond (city) Lake County	144	0.18
Carmel (city) Hamilton County	101	0.13
Muncie (city) Delaware County	84	0.12
Fort Wayne (city) Allen County	222	0.09
Indianapolis (city) Marion County	542	0.07
Elkhart (city) Elkhart County	23	0.04
South Bend (city) St. Joseph County	27	0.03

Arab: Egyptian

Top 10 Places Sorted by Population
Based on all places, regardless of total population

Place	Population	%
Carmel (city) Hamilton County	164	0.21
Schererville (town) Lake County	159	0.56
Indianapolis (city) Marion County	158	0.02
Fishers (town) Hamilton County	125	0.17
Hammond (city) Lake County	83	0.10
New Haven (city) Allen County	71	0.51
Versailles (town) Ripley County	62	3.52
Dyer (town) Lake County	52	0.33
Seymour (city) Jackson County	42	0.23
Lebanon (city) Boone County	38	0.24

Top 10 Places Sorted by Percent of Total Population
Based on all places, regardless of total population

Place	Population	%
Versailles (town) Ripley County	62	3.52
Campbellsburg (town) Washington County	18	2.86
Avilla (town) Noble County	19	0.86
Schererville (town) Lake County	159	0.56
New Haven (city) Allen County	71	0.51
Vevay (town) Switzerland County	9	0.45
Dyer (town) Lake County	52	0.33
Lebanon (city) Boone County	38	0.24
Seymour (city) Jackson County	42	0.23
Mitchell (city) Lawrence County	10	0.22

Top 10 Places Sorted by Percent of Total Population
Based on places with total population of 50,000 or more

Place	Population	%
Carmel (city) Hamilton County	164	0.21
Fishers (town) Hamilton County	125	0.17
Hammond (city) Lake County	83	0.10
Bloomington (city) Monroe County	21	0.03
Indianapolis (city) Marion County	158	0.02
Muncie (city) Delaware County	14	0.02
Fort Wayne (city) Allen County	8	<0.01
Anderson (city) Madison County	0	0.00
Elkhart (city) Elkhart County	0	0.00
Evansville (city) Vanderburgh County	0	0.00

Arab: Iraqi

Top 10 Places Sorted by Population
Based on all places, regardless of total population

Place	Population	%
Indianapolis (city) Marion County	192	0.02
Fort Wayne (city) Allen County	54	0.02
Mishawaka (city) St. Joseph County	45	0.09
Versailles (town) Ripley County	35	1.99
South Bend (city) St. Joseph County	33	0.03
Bloomington (city) Monroe County	30	0.04
Evansville (city) Vanderburgh County	16	0.01
Westfield (town) Hamilton County	14	0.05
Muncie (city) Delaware County	14	0.02
Hamilton (town) Steuben County	3	0.19

Top 10 Places Sorted by Percent of Total Population
Based on all places, regardless of total population

Place	Population	%
Versailles (town) Ripley County	35	1.99
Hamilton (town) Steuben County	3	0.19
Churubusco (town) Whitley County	2	0.10
Mishawaka (city) St. Joseph County	45	0.09
Westfield (town) Hamilton County	14	0.05
Bloomington (city) Monroe County	30	0.04
South Bend (city) St. Joseph County	33	0.03
Indianapolis (city) Marion County	192	0.02
Fort Wayne (city) Allen County	54	0.02
Muncie (city) Delaware County	14	0.02

Top 10 Places Sorted by Percent of Total Population
Based on places with total population of 50,000 or more

Place	Population	%
Bloomington (city) Monroe County	30	0.04
South Bend (city) St. Joseph County	33	0.03
Indianapolis (city) Marion County	192	0.02
Fort Wayne (city) Allen County	54	0.02
Muncie (city) Delaware County	14	0.02
Evansville (city) Vanderburgh County	16	0.01
Anderson (city) Madison County	0	0.00
Carmel (city) Hamilton County	0	0.00
Elkhart (city) Elkhart County	0	0.00
Fishers (town) Hamilton County	0	0.00

Arab: Jordanian

Top 10 Places Sorted by Population
Based on all places, regardless of total population

Place	Population	%
Indianapolis (city) Marion County	182	0.02
Greenwood (city) Johnson County	101	0.21
Fishers (town) Hamilton County	37	0.05
Brownsburg (town) Hendricks County	34	0.17
Hammond (city) Lake County	30	0.04
Portage (city) Porter County	28	0.08
Dyer (town) Lake County	25	0.16
Lake Station (city) Lake County	18	0.14
Evansville (city) Vanderburgh County	15	0.01
Purdue University (cdp) Tippecanoe County	13	0.10

Top 10 Places Sorted by Percent of Total Population
Based on all places, regardless of total population

Place	Population	%
Greenwood (city) Johnson County	101	0.21
Brownsburg (town) Hendricks County	34	0.17
Dyer (town) Lake County	25	0.16
Lake Station (city) Lake County	18	0.14
Purdue University (cdp) Tippecanoe County	13	0.10
Portage (city) Porter County	28	0.08
Munster (town) Lake County	13	0.06
Fishers (town) Hamilton County	37	0.05
Hammond (city) Lake County	30	0.04
West Lafayette (city) Tippecanoe County	11	0.04

Top 10 Places Sorted by Percent of Total Population
Based on places with total population of 50,000 or more

Place	Population	%
Fishers (town) Hamilton County	37	0.05
Hammond (city) Lake County	30	0.04
Indianapolis (city) Marion County	182	0.02
Evansville (city) Vanderburgh County	15	0.01
Bloomington (city) Monroe County	10	0.01
Carmel (city) Hamilton County	8	0.01
Terre Haute (city) Vigo County	6	0.01
Fort Wayne (city) Allen County	10	<0.01
Anderson (city) Madison County	0	0.00
Elkhart (city) Elkhart County	0	0.00

Arab: Lebanese

Top 10 Places Sorted by Population
Based on all places, regardless of total population

Place	Population	%
Indianapolis (city) Marion County	826	0.10
Michigan City (city) LaPorte County	288	0.91
Fort Wayne (city) Allen County	235	0.09
Granger (cdp) St. Joseph County	227	0.80
Bloomington (city) Monroe County	167	0.21
Mishawaka (city) St. Joseph County	166	0.35
Carmel (city) Hamilton County	160	0.21
Fishers (town) Hamilton County	135	0.19
Valparaiso (city) Porter County	57	0.18
Notre Dame (cdp) St. Joseph County	52	0.70

Top 10 Places Sorted by Percent of Total Population
Based on all places, regardless of total population

Place	Population	%
Pottawattamie Park (town) LaPorte County	26	13.13
Dune Acres (town) Porter County	7	2.67
Long Beach (town) LaPorte County	32	2.19
Trail Creek (town) LaPorte County	39	1.97
Hebron (town) Porter County	40	1.14
New Ross (town) Montgomery County	3	1.00
Michigan City (city) LaPorte County	288	0.91
Simonton Lake (cdp) Elkhart County	42	0.83
Granger (cdp) St. Joseph County	227	0.80
Meridian Hills (town) Marion County	12	0.74

Top 10 Places Sorted by Percent of Total Population
Based on places with total population of 50,000 or more

Place	Population	%
Bloomington (city) Monroe County	167	0.21
Carmel (city) Hamilton County	160	0.21
Fishers (town) Hamilton County	135	0.19
Indianapolis (city) Marion County	826	0.10
Fort Wayne (city) Allen County	235	0.09
Terre Haute (city) Vigo County	24	0.04
South Bend (city) St. Joseph County	33	0.03
Evansville (city) Vanderburgh County	27	0.02
Lafayette (city) Tippecanoe County	14	0.02
Elkhart (city) Elkhart County	9	0.02

Arab: Moroccan

Top 10 Places Sorted by Population
Based on all places, regardless of total population

Place	Population	%
Indianapolis (city) Marion County	141	0.02
Columbus (city) Bartholomew County	39	0.09
Carmel (city) Hamilton County	36	0.05
Dyer (town) Lake County	30	0.19
Bloomington (city) Monroe County	27	0.03
Franklin (city) Johnson County	24	0.11
Anderson (city) Madison County	24	0.04
Gary (city) Lake County	18	0.02
Elkhart (city) Elkhart County	16	0.03
Bright (cdp) Dearborn County	14	0.27

Top 10 Places Sorted by Percent of Total Population
Based on all places, regardless of total population

Place	Population	%
Gosport (town) Owen County	3	0.31
Bright (cdp) Dearborn County	14	0.27
Gas City (city) Grant County	12	0.20
Dyer (town) Lake County	30	0.19
Franklin (city) Johnson County	24	0.11
Columbus (city) Bartholomew County	39	0.09
Carmel (city) Hamilton County	36	0.05
Anderson (city) Madison County	24	0.04
Bloomington (city) Monroe County	27	0.03
Elkhart (city) Elkhart County	16	0.03

Top 10 Places Sorted by Percent of Total Population
Based on places with total population of 50,000 or more

Place	Population	%
Carmel (city) Hamilton County	36	0.05
Anderson (city) Madison County	24	0.04
Bloomington (city) Monroe County	27	0.03
Elkhart (city) Elkhart County	16	0.03
Indianapolis (city) Marion County	141	0.02
Gary (city) Lake County	18	0.02
Muncie (city) Delaware County	13	0.02
South Bend (city) St. Joseph County	6	0.01
Fort Wayne (city) Allen County	10	<0.01
Evansville (city) Vanderburgh County	0	0.00

Please refer to the Explanation of Data in the front of the book for more detailed information.

Arab: Palestinian

Top 10 Places Sorted by Population
Based on all places, regardless of total population

Place	Population	%
Schererville (town) Lake County	293	1.03
Mishawaka (city) St. Joseph County	119	0.25
Munster (town) Lake County	96	0.41
Crown Point (city) Lake County	71	0.27
Indianapolis (city) Marion County	45	0.01
St. John (town) Lake County	43	0.31
Evansville (city) Vanderburgh County	30	0.03
Columbia City (city) Whitley County	27	0.33
Dyer (town) Lake County	24	0.15
Carmel (city) Hamilton County	24	0.03

Top 10 Places Sorted by Percent of Total Population
Based on all places, regardless of total population

Place	Population	%
Schererville (town) Lake County	293	1.03
Munster (town) Lake County	96	0.41
Columbia City (city) Whitley County	27	0.33
St. John (town) Lake County	43	0.31
Crown Point (city) Lake County	71	0.27
Mishawaka (city) St. Joseph County	119	0.25
Dyer (town) Lake County	24	0.15
New Palestine (town) Hancock County	2	0.09
East Chicago (city) Lake County	18	0.06
New Albany (city) Floyd County	13	0.04

Top 10 Places Sorted by Percent of Total Population
Based on places with total population of 50,000 or more

Place	Population	%
Evansville (city) Vanderburgh County	30	0.03
Carmel (city) Hamilton County	24	0.03
Indianapolis (city) Marion County	45	0.01
Muncie (city) Delaware County	7	0.01
Anderson (city) Madison County	0	0.00
Bloomington (city) Monroe County	0	0.00
Elkhart (city) Elkhart County	0	0.00
Fishers (town) Hamilton County	0	0.00
Fort Wayne (city) Allen County	0	0.00
Gary (city) Lake County	0	0.00

Arab: Syrian

Top 10 Places Sorted by Population
Based on all places, regardless of total population

Place	Population	%
Indianapolis (city) Marion County	239	0.03
Terre Haute (city) Vigo County	137	0.23
Fort Wayne (city) Allen County	104	0.04
Shorewood Forest (cdp) Porter County	77	2.55
Bloomington (city) Monroe County	75	0.10
Merrillville (town) Lake County	66	0.19
Muncie (city) Delaware County	66	0.09
Plainfield (town) Hendricks County	54	0.20
Shelbyville (city) Shelby County	35	0.19
Munster (town) Lake County	35	0.15

Top 10 Places Sorted by Percent of Total Population
Based on all places, regardless of total population

Place	Population	%
Shorewood Forest (cdp) Porter County	77	2.55
Whites (town) Boone County	33	1.72
Knightsville (town) Clay County	13	1.47
Morocco (town) Newton County	10	1.14
Meridian Hills (town) Marion County	17	1.04
Converse (town) Miami County	9	0.69
Rossville (town) Clinton County	9	0.62
Dunlap (cdp) Elkhart County	23	0.40
Fairview Park (town) Vermillion County	5	0.37
Tri-Lakes (cdp) Whitley County	6	0.36

Top 10 Places Sorted by Percent of Total Population
Based on places with total population of 50,000 or more

Place	Population	%
Terre Haute (city) Vigo County	137	0.23
Bloomington (city) Monroe County	75	0.10
Muncie (city) Delaware County	66	0.09
Fort Wayne (city) Allen County	104	0.04
Fishers (town) Hamilton County	32	0.04
Indianapolis (city) Marion County	239	0.03
South Bend (city) St. Joseph County	19	0.02
Evansville (city) Vanderburgh County	11	0.01
Anderson (city) Madison County	0	0.00
Carmel (city) Hamilton County	0	0.00

Arab: Other

Top 10 Places Sorted by Population
Based on all places, regardless of total population

Place	Population	%
Indianapolis (city) Marion County	451	0.06
Terre Haute (city) Vigo County	241	0.40
Granger (cdp) St. Joseph County	73	0.26
Carmel (city) Hamilton County	70	0.09
Elkhart (city) Elkhart County	61	0.12
Greenwood (city) Johnson County	60	0.13
Jasper (city) Dubois County	43	0.30
Topeka (town) LaGrange County	38	3.02
Dyer (town) Lake County	35	0.22
Bloomington (city) Monroe County	31	0.04

Top 10 Places Sorted by Percent of Total Population
Based on all places, regardless of total population

Place	Population	%
Riley (town) Vigo County	11	5.07
Topeka (town) LaGrange County	38	3.02
Perrysville (town) Vermillion County	12	2.11
Berne (town) Adams County	18	0.44
Terre Haute (city) Vigo County	241	0.40
Jasper (city) Dubois County	43	0.30
Granger (cdp) St. Joseph County	73	0.26
Dyer (town) Lake County	35	0.22
Greenwood (city) Johnson County	60	0.13
Griffith (town) Lake County	22	0.13

Top 10 Places Sorted by Percent of Total Population
Based on places with total population of 50,000 or more

Place	Population	%
Terre Haute (city) Vigo County	241	0.40
Elkhart (city) Elkhart County	61	0.12
Carmel (city) Hamilton County	70	0.09
Indianapolis (city) Marion County	451	0.06
Bloomington (city) Monroe County	31	0.04
Fishers (town) Hamilton County	16	0.02
Hammond (city) Lake County	15	0.02
Lafayette (city) Tippecanoe County	11	0.02
Fort Wayne (city) Allen County	21	0.01
South Bend (city) St. Joseph County	13	0.01

Armenian

Top 10 Places Sorted by Population
Based on all places, regardless of total population

Place	Population	%
Chesterton (town) Porter County	207	1.57
Indianapolis (city) Marion County	158	0.02
Fort Wayne (city) Allen County	81	0.03
Evansville (city) Vanderburgh County	78	0.07
South Bend (city) St. Joseph County	44	0.04
Bloomington (city) Monroe County	37	0.05
La Porte (city) LaPorte County	36	0.16
Notre Dame (cdp) St. Joseph County	28	0.38
Columbus (city) Bartholomew County	28	0.06
Hammond (city) Lake County	27	0.03

Top 10 Places Sorted by Percent of Total Population
Based on all places, regardless of total population

Place	Population	%
Chesterton (town) Porter County	207	1.57
Rocky Ripple (town) Marion County	4	0.62
Notre Dame (cdp) St. Joseph County	28	0.38
Porter (town) Porter County	9	0.18
Crothersville (town) Jackson County	3	0.17
La Porte (city) LaPorte County	36	0.16
Madison (city) Jefferson County	15	0.13
Peru (city) Miami County	11	0.10
Schererville (town) Lake County	25	0.09
Crown Point (city) Lake County	24	0.09

Top 10 Places Sorted by Percent of Total Population
Based on places with total population of 50,000 or more

Place	Population	%
Evansville (city) Vanderburgh County	78	0.07
Bloomington (city) Monroe County	37	0.05
South Bend (city) St. Joseph County	44	0.04
Fort Wayne (city) Allen County	81	0.03
Hammond (city) Lake County	27	0.03
Carmel (city) Hamilton County	21	0.03
Indianapolis (city) Marion County	158	0.02
Fishers (town) Hamilton County	10	0.01
Anderson (city) Madison County	0	0.00
Elkhart (city) Elkhart County	0	0.00

Assyrian/Chaldean/Syriac

Top 10 Places Sorted by Population
Based on all places, regardless of total population

Place	Population	%
Aberdeen (cdp) Porter County	61	2.79
Mishawaka (city) St. Joseph County	52	0.11
Indianapolis (city) Marion County	44	0.01
Hobart (city) Lake County	42	0.15
Lafayette (city) Tippecanoe County	30	0.05
Merrillville (town) Lake County	21	0.06
Valparaiso (city) Porter County	20	0.06
Schererville (town) Lake County	19	0.07
Michigan City (city) LaPorte County	18	0.06
West Lafayette (city) Tippecanoe County	15	0.05

Top 10 Places Sorted by Percent of Total Population
Based on all places, regardless of total population

Place	Population	%
Aberdeen (cdp) Porter County	61	2.79
Notre Dame (cdp) St. Joseph County	13	0.17
Hobart (city) Lake County	42	0.15
Jonesboro (city) Grant County	2	0.13
Mishawaka (city) St. Joseph County	52	0.11
Purdue University (cdp) Tippecanoe County	14	0.11
Schererville (town) Lake County	19	0.07
Merrillville (town) Lake County	21	0.06
Valparaiso (city) Porter County	20	0.06
Michigan City (city) LaPorte County	18	0.06

Top 10 Places Sorted by Percent of Total Population
Based on places with total population of 50,000 or more

Place	Population	%
Lafayette (city) Tippecanoe County	30	0.05
Indianapolis (city) Marion County	44	0.01
Hammond (city) Lake County	7	0.01
Fort Wayne (city) Allen County	10	<0.01
Anderson (city) Madison County	0	0.00
Bloomington (city) Monroe County	0	0.00
Carmel (city) Hamilton County	0	0.00
Elkhart (city) Elkhart County	0	0.00
Evansville (city) Vanderburgh County	0	0.00
Fishers (town) Hamilton County	0	0.00

Australian

Top 10 Places Sorted by Population
Based on all places, regardless of total population

Place	Population	%
Indianapolis (city) Marion County	258	0.03
Princeton (city) Gibson County	124	1.44
North Vernon (city) Jennings County	109	1.71
Purdue University (cdp) Tippecanoe County	89	0.69
Fort Wayne (city) Allen County	54	0.02
Bloomington (city) Monroe County	46	0.06
Carmel (city) Hamilton County	42	0.05
Evansville (city) Vanderburgh County	39	0.03
Fishers (town) Hamilton County	36	0.05
Muncie (city) Delaware County	27	0.04

Top 10 Places Sorted by Percent of Total Population
Based on all places, regardless of total population

Place	Population	%
North Vernon (city) Jennings County	109	1.71
Princeton (city) Gibson County	124	1.44
Pine Village (town) Warren County	3	1.35

Please refer to the Explanation of Data in the front of the book for more detailed information.

Ancestry and Ethnicity: Ancestry Group Rankings

Place	Population	%
Spurgeon (town) Pike County	2	1.25
Ashley (town) DeKalb County	10	0.91
Purdue University (cdp) Tippecanoe County	89	0.69
Russellville (town) Putnam County	2	0.68
Spring Lake (town) Hancock County	2	0.68
Southport (city) Marion County	9	0.57
Morocco (town) Newton County	4	0.46

Top 10 Places Sorted by Percent of Total Population
Based on places with total population of 50,000 or more

Place	Population	%
Bloomington (city) Monroe County	46	0.06
Carmel (city) Hamilton County	42	0.05
Fishers (town) Hamilton County	36	0.05
Muncie (city) Delaware County	27	0.04
Indianapolis (city) Marion County	258	0.03
Evansville (city) Vanderburgh County	39	0.03
Hammond (city) Lake County	21	0.03
Fort Wayne (city) Allen County	54	0.02
Anderson (city) Madison County	12	0.02
Elkhart (city) Elkhart County	0	0.00

Austrian

Top 10 Places Sorted by Population
Based on all places, regardless of total population

Place	Population	%
Indianapolis (city) Marion County	1,084	0.13
Bloomington (city) Monroe County	439	0.56
South Bend (city) St. Joseph County	275	0.27
Fort Wayne (city) Allen County	250	0.10
Fishers (town) Hamilton County	233	0.32
Granger (cdp) St. Joseph County	219	0.77
Valparaiso (city) Porter County	192	0.62
Mishawaka (city) St. Joseph County	183	0.38
Carmel (city) Hamilton County	161	0.21
West Lafayette (city) Tippecanoe County	146	0.50

Top 10 Places Sorted by Percent of Total Population
Based on all places, regardless of total population

Place	Population	%
Uniondale (town) Wells County	12	6.78
North Crows Nest (town) Marion County	2	4.76
North Salem (town) Hendricks County	17	4.53
Aberdeen (cdp) Porter County	81	3.71
Dayton (town) Tippecanoe County	24	2.51
Spring Hill (town) Marion County	2	2.38
Dillsboro (town) Dearborn County	29	2.16
Indian Village (town) St. Joseph County	2	2.04
Kennard (town) Henry County	10	2.00
Chalmers (town) White County	9	1.72

Top 10 Places Sorted by Percent of Total Population
Based on places with total population of 50,000 or more

Place	Population	%
Bloomington (city) Monroe County	439	0.56
Fishers (town) Hamilton County	233	0.32
South Bend (city) St. Joseph County	275	0.27
Carmel (city) Hamilton County	161	0.21
Anderson (city) Madison County	103	0.18
Terre Haute (city) Vigo County	85	0.14
Indianapolis (city) Marion County	1,084	0.13
Lafayette (city) Tippecanoe County	79	0.12
Fort Wayne (city) Allen County	250	0.10
Evansville (city) Vanderburgh County	109	0.09

Basque

Top 10 Places Sorted by Population
Based on all places, regardless of total population

Place	Population	%
New Albany (city) Floyd County	17	0.05
Lebanon (city) Boone County	10	0.06
Ogden Dunes (town) Porter County	3	0.24
Gentryville (town) Spencer County	2	0.90
Aberdeen (cdp) Porter County	0	0.00
Advance (town) Boone County	0	0.00
Akron (town) Fulton County	0	0.00
Alamo (town) Montgomery County	0	0.00
Albany (town) Delaware County	0	0.00
Albion (town) Noble County	0	0.00

Top 10 Places Sorted by Percent of Total Population
Based on all places, regardless of total population

Place	Population	%
Gentryville (town) Spencer County	2	0.90
Ogden Dunes (town) Porter County	3	0.24
Lebanon (city) Boone County	10	0.06
New Albany (city) Floyd County	17	0.05
Aberdeen (cdp) Porter County	0	0.00
Advance (town) Boone County	0	0.00
Akron (town) Fulton County	0	0.00
Alamo (town) Montgomery County	0	0.00
Albany (town) Delaware County	0	0.00
Albion (town) Noble County	0	0.00

Top 10 Places Sorted by Percent of Total Population
Based on places with total population of 50,000 or more

Place	Population	%
Anderson (city) Madison County	0	0.00
Bloomington (city) Monroe County	0	0.00
Carmel (city) Hamilton County	0	0.00
Elkhart (city) Elkhart County	0	0.00
Evansville (city) Vanderburgh County	0	0.00
Fishers (town) Hamilton County	0	0.00
Fort Wayne (city) Allen County	0	0.00
Gary (city) Lake County	0	0.00
Hammond (city) Lake County	0	0.00
Indianapolis (city) Marion County	0	0.00

Belgian

Top 10 Places Sorted by Population
Based on all places, regardless of total population

Place	Population	%
Mishawaka (city) St. Joseph County	1,831	3.82
South Bend (city) St. Joseph County	871	0.85
Indianapolis (city) Marion County	866	0.11
Carmel (city) Hamilton County	352	0.46
Granger (cdp) St. Joseph County	347	1.22
Noblesville (city) Hamilton County	247	0.51
Fort Wayne (city) Allen County	220	0.09
Fishers (town) Hamilton County	165	0.23
Bloomington (city) Monroe County	155	0.20
Tell City (city) Perry County	144	1.95

Top 10 Places Sorted by Percent of Total Population
Based on all places, regardless of total population

Place	Population	%
Mishawaka (city) St. Joseph County	1,831	3.82
Albion (town) Noble County	75	2.76
Osceola (town) St. Joseph County	62	2.62
Schneider (town) Lake County	6	2.35
Hudson Lake (cdp) LaPorte County	29	2.16
Indian Village (town) St. Joseph County	2	2.04
Pierceton (town) Kosciusko County	20	1.97
Tell City (city) Perry County	144	1.95
Shelby (cdp) Lake County	7	1.92
Troy (town) Perry County	8	1.82

Top 10 Places Sorted by Percent of Total Population
Based on places with total population of 50,000 or more

Place	Population	%
South Bend (city) St. Joseph County	871	0.85
Carmel (city) Hamilton County	352	0.46
Elkhart (city) Elkhart County	123	0.24
Fishers (town) Hamilton County	165	0.23
Bloomington (city) Monroe County	155	0.20
Muncie (city) Delaware County	110	0.16
Lafayette (city) Tippecanoe County	100	0.15
Terre Haute (city) Vigo County	75	0.12
Indianapolis (city) Marion County	866	0.11
Fort Wayne (city) Allen County	220	0.09

Brazilian

Top 10 Places Sorted by Population
Based on all places, regardless of total population

Place	Population	%
Indianapolis (city) Marion County	259	0.03
Plainfield (town) Hendricks County	149	0.56
West Lafayette (city) Tippecanoe County	104	0.35
Clarksville (town) Clark County	95	0.41
Elkhart (city) Elkhart County	92	0.18
Bloomington (city) Monroe County	69	0.09
Evansville (city) Vanderburgh County	62	0.05
Goshen (city) Elkhart County	59	0.19
Westfield (town) Hamilton County	50	0.18
South Bend (city) St. Joseph County	50	0.05

Top 10 Places Sorted by Percent of Total Population
Based on all places, regardless of total population

Place	Population	%
Plainfield (town) Hendricks County	149	0.56
Meridian Hills (town) Marion County	7	0.43
Clarksville (town) Clark County	95	0.41
West Lafayette (city) Tippecanoe County	104	0.35
Notre Dame (cdp) St. Joseph County	24	0.32
Chesterton (town) Porter County	38	0.29
Kouts (town) Porter County	4	0.22
Goshen (city) Elkhart County	59	0.19
Elkhart (city) Elkhart County	92	0.18
Westfield (town) Hamilton County	50	0.18

Top 10 Places Sorted by Percent of Total Population
Based on places with total population of 50,000 or more

Place	Population	%
Elkhart (city) Elkhart County	92	0.18
Bloomington (city) Monroe County	69	0.09
Evansville (city) Vanderburgh County	62	0.05
South Bend (city) St. Joseph County	50	0.05
Lafayette (city) Tippecanoe County	31	0.05
Gary (city) Lake County	30	0.04
Indianapolis (city) Marion County	259	0.03
Fishers (town) Hamilton County	24	0.03
Hammond (city) Lake County	13	0.02
Fort Wayne (city) Allen County	21	0.01

British

Top 10 Places Sorted by Population
Based on all places, regardless of total population

Place	Population	%
Indianapolis (city) Marion County	3,547	0.44
Fort Wayne (city) Allen County	767	0.30
Bloomington (city) Monroe County	729	0.93
Carmel (city) Hamilton County	626	0.82
Fishers (town) Hamilton County	451	0.63
Evansville (city) Vanderburgh County	446	0.38
Muncie (city) Delaware County	372	0.53
South Bend (city) St. Joseph County	336	0.33
Lafayette (city) Tippecanoe County	331	0.50
Greenwood (city) Johnson County	323	0.68

Top 10 Places Sorted by Percent of Total Population
Based on all places, regardless of total population

Place	Population	%
Clarksburg (cdp) Decatur County	60	49.18
Medaryville (town) Pulaski County	25	5.02
Laconia (town) Harrison County	2	5.00
Carbon (town) Clay County	15	4.66
Mount Auburn (town) Wayne County	7	4.61
Dune Acres (town) Porter County	12	4.58
Chrisney (town) Spencer County	26	4.13
Vallonia (cdp) Jackson County	16	3.40
Woodlawn Heights (town) Madison County	3	3.23
Kimmell (cdp) Noble County	9	2.55

Top 10 Places Sorted by Percent of Total Population
Based on places with total population of 50,000 or more

Place	Population	%
Bloomington (city) Monroe County	729	0.93
Carmel (city) Hamilton County	626	0.82
Fishers (town) Hamilton County	451	0.63
Muncie (city) Delaware County	372	0.53
Lafayette (city) Tippecanoe County	331	0.50
Indianapolis (city) Marion County	3,547	0.44
Evansville (city) Vanderburgh County	446	0.38
South Bend (city) St. Joseph County	336	0.33
Fort Wayne (city) Allen County	767	0.30
Anderson (city) Madison County	153	0.27

Please refer to the Explanation of Data in the front of the book for more detailed information.

Bulgarian

Top 10 Places Sorted by Population
Based on all places, regardless of total population

Place	Population	%
Fort Wayne (city) Allen County	156	0.06
Indianapolis (city) Marion County	80	0.01
Highland (town) Lake County	57	0.24
Munster (town) Lake County	55	0.24
Lebanon (city) Boone County	54	0.34
Merrillville (town) Lake County	50	0.15
South Bend (city) St. Joseph County	47	0.05
Noblesville (city) Hamilton County	41	0.08
West Lafayette (city) Tippecanoe County	38	0.13
Bloomington (city) Monroe County	29	0.04

Top 10 Places Sorted by Percent of Total Population
Based on all places, regardless of total population

Place	Population	%
Arcadia (town) Hamilton County	11	0.74
Melody Hill (cdp) Vanderburgh County	24	0.69
North Terre Haute (cdp) Vigo County	24	0.52
Hope (town) Bartholomew County	8	0.43
Portland (city) Jay County	24	0.37
Lebanon (city) Boone County	54	0.34
North Manchester (town) Wabash County	18	0.30
Bremen (town) Marshall County	14	0.30
Highland (town) Lake County	57	0.24
Munster (town) Lake County	55	0.24

Top 10 Places Sorted by Percent of Total Population
Based on places with total population of 50,000 or more

Place	Population	%
Fort Wayne (city) Allen County	156	0.06
South Bend (city) St. Joseph County	47	0.05
Bloomington (city) Monroe County	29	0.04
Carmel (city) Hamilton County	16	0.02
Indianapolis (city) Marion County	80	0.01
Muncie (city) Delaware County	9	0.01
Anderson (city) Madison County	0	0.00
Elkhart (city) Elkhart County	0	0.00
Evansville (city) Vanderburgh County	0	0.00
Fishers (town) Hamilton County	0	0.00

Cajun

Top 10 Places Sorted by Population
Based on all places, regardless of total population

Place	Population	%
Greenwood (city) Johnson County	72	0.15
Clarksville (town) Clark County	55	0.24
Indianapolis (city) Marion County	52	0.01
Columbus (city) Bartholomew County	36	0.08
Jeffersonville (city) Clark County	29	0.07
Portage (city) Porter County	25	0.07
Plainfield (town) Hendricks County	23	0.09
Lawrenceburg (city) Dearborn County	22	0.44
Fishers (town) Hamilton County	22	0.03
Lafayette (city) Tippecanoe County	22	0.03

Top 10 Places Sorted by Percent of Total Population
Based on all places, regardless of total population

Place	Population	%
Lawrenceburg (city) Dearborn County	22	0.44
Carthage (town) Rush County	3	0.40
Clarksville (town) Clark County	55	0.24
Ingalls (town) Madison County	4	0.21
Huntingburg (city) Dubois County	11	0.19
Salem (city) Washington County	10	0.16
Greenwood (city) Johnson County	72	0.15
Plainfield (town) Hendricks County	23	0.09
Columbus (city) Bartholomew County	36	0.08
Jeffersonville (city) Clark County	29	0.07

Top 10 Places Sorted by Percent of Total Population
Based on places with total population of 50,000 or more

Place	Population	%
Fishers (town) Hamilton County	22	0.03
Lafayette (city) Tippecanoe County	22	0.03
Indianapolis (city) Marion County	52	0.01
Evansville (city) Vanderburgh County	12	0.01
Anderson (city) Madison County	0	0.00
Bloomington (city) Monroe County	0	0.00
Carmel (city) Hamilton County	0	0.00
Elkhart (city) Elkhart County	0	0.00
Fort Wayne (city) Allen County	0	0.00
Gary (city) Lake County	0	0.00

Canadian

Top 10 Places Sorted by Population
Based on all places, regardless of total population

Place	Population	%
Indianapolis (city) Marion County	1,392	0.17
Fort Wayne (city) Allen County	681	0.27
Granger (cdp) St. Joseph County	201	0.71
Fishers (town) Hamilton County	195	0.27
Muncie (city) Delaware County	194	0.28
Greenwood (city) Johnson County	181	0.38
Carmel (city) Hamilton County	166	0.22
Cumberland (town) Marion County	149	2.58
Bloomington (city) Monroe County	138	0.18
South Bend (city) St. Joseph County	126	0.12

Top 10 Places Sorted by Percent of Total Population
Based on all places, regardless of total population

Place	Population	%
Buffalo (cdp) White County	74	10.72
Buck Creek (cdp) Tippecanoe County	30	8.57
Sidney (town) Kosciusko County	4	3.85
Napoleon (town) Ripley County	6	3.16
Cumberland (town) Marion County	149	2.58
State Line City (town) Warren County	3	2.46
La Fontaine (town) Wabash County	17	2.39
Fillmore (town) Putnam County	10	2.23
New Paris (cdp) Elkhart County	28	2.14
Switz City (town) Greene County	8	1.99

Top 10 Places Sorted by Percent of Total Population
Based on places with total population of 50,000 or more

Place	Population	%
Muncie (city) Delaware County	194	0.28
Fort Wayne (city) Allen County	681	0.27
Fishers (town) Hamilton County	195	0.27
Carmel (city) Hamilton County	166	0.22
Bloomington (city) Monroe County	138	0.18
Indianapolis (city) Marion County	1,392	0.17
Elkhart (city) Elkhart County	79	0.15
South Bend (city) St. Joseph County	126	0.12
Terre Haute (city) Vigo County	62	0.10
Anderson (city) Madison County	50	0.09

Carpatho Rusyn

Top 10 Places Sorted by Population
Based on all places, regardless of total population

Place	Population	%
Carmel (city) Hamilton County	16	0.02
Schererville (town) Lake County	13	0.05
Munster (town) Lake County	11	0.05
St. John (town) Lake County	9	0.07
Aberdeen (cdp) Porter County	0	0.00
Advance (town) Boone County	0	0.00
Akron (town) Fulton County	0	0.00
Alamo (town) Montgomery County	0	0.00
Albany (town) Delaware County	0	0.00
Albion (town) Noble County	0	0.00

Top 10 Places Sorted by Percent of Total Population
Based on all places, regardless of total population

Place	Population	%
St. John (town) Lake County	9	0.07
Schererville (town) Lake County	13	0.05
Munster (town) Lake County	11	0.05
Carmel (city) Hamilton County	16	0.02
Aberdeen (cdp) Porter County	0	0.00
Advance (town) Boone County	0	0.00
Akron (town) Fulton County	0	0.00
Alamo (town) Montgomery County	0	0.00
Albany (town) Delaware County	0	0.00
Albion (town) Noble County	0	0.00

Top 10 Places Sorted by Percent of Total Population
Based on places with total population of 50,000 or more

Place	Population	%
Carmel (city) Hamilton County	16	0.02
Anderson (city) Madison County	0	0.00
Bloomington (city) Monroe County	0	0.00
Elkhart (city) Elkhart County	0	0.00
Evansville (city) Vanderburgh County	0	0.00
Fishers (town) Hamilton County	0	0.00
Fort Wayne (city) Allen County	0	0.00
Gary (city) Lake County	0	0.00
Hammond (city) Lake County	0	0.00
Indianapolis (city) Marion County	0	0.00

Celtic

Top 10 Places Sorted by Population
Based on all places, regardless of total population

Place	Population	%
Fort Wayne (city) Allen County	30	0.01
Jeffersonville (city) Clark County	25	0.06
Evansville (city) Vanderburgh County	23	0.02
Plainfield (town) Hendricks County	21	0.08
Franklin (city) Johnson County	17	0.08
Mishawaka (city) St. Joseph County	16	0.03
Highland (cdp) Vanderburgh County	15	0.36
Greencastle (city) Putnam County	15	0.14
Brownsburg (town) Hendricks County	15	0.07
Lawrence (city) Marion County	15	0.03

Top 10 Places Sorted by Percent of Total Population
Based on all places, regardless of total population

Place	Population	%
Worthington (town) Greene County	10	0.51
Rockville (town) Parke County	13	0.49
Shelburn (town) Sullivan County	7	0.47
Highland (cdp) Vanderburgh County	15	0.36
Wanatah (town) LaPorte County	3	0.28
Orleans (town) Orange County	5	0.26
Princes Lakes (town) Johnson County	3	0.26
Burns Harbor (town) Porter County	3	0.24
Oolitic (town) Lawrence County	3	0.22
Cannelton (city) Perry County	2	0.15

Top 10 Places Sorted by Percent of Total Population
Based on places with total population of 50,000 or more

Place	Population	%
Evansville (city) Vanderburgh County	23	0.02
Carmel (city) Hamilton County	14	0.02
Fishers (town) Hamilton County	14	0.02
Anderson (city) Madison County	12	0.02
Fort Wayne (city) Allen County	30	0.01
Muncie (city) Delaware County	10	0.01
South Bend (city) St. Joseph County	10	0.01
Hammond (city) Lake County	7	0.01
Indianapolis (city) Marion County	8	<0.01
Bloomington (city) Monroe County	0	0.00

Croatian

Top 10 Places Sorted by Population
Based on all places, regardless of total population

Place	Population	%
Hammond (city) Lake County	908	1.12
Schererville (town) Lake County	664	2.33
Highland (town) Lake County	663	2.80
Crown Point (city) Lake County	585	2.24
Munster (town) Lake County	516	2.22
Hobart (city) Lake County	483	1.70
Indianapolis (city) Marion County	412	0.05
Merrillville (town) Lake County	359	1.04
St. John (town) Lake County	328	2.39
Portage (city) Porter County	297	0.82

Top 10 Places Sorted by Percent of Total Population
Based on all places, regardless of total population

Place	Population	%
Lake Santee (cdp) Decatur County	61	9.52
Montmorenci (cdp) Tippecanoe County	11	6.51
Aberdeen (cdp) Porter County	118	5.40

516 Ancestry and Ethnicity: Ancestry Group Rankings

Place	Population	%
Ogden Dunes (town) Porter County	51	4.16
Schneider (town) Lake County	10	3.92
La Crosse (town) LaPorte County	22	3.74
Salt Creek Commons (cdp) Porter County	76	3.46
Hebron (town) Porter County	119	3.39
Harmony (town) Clay County	20	3.14
Lakes of the Four Seasons (cdp) Lake County	216	2.86

Top 10 Places Sorted by Percent of Total Population
Based on places with total population of 50,000 or more

Place	Population	%
Hammond (city) Lake County	908	1.12
South Bend (city) St. Joseph County	295	0.29
Carmel (city) Hamilton County	175	0.23
Gary (city) Lake County	187	0.22
Bloomington (city) Monroe County	171	0.22
Muncie (city) Delaware County	103	0.15
Terre Haute (city) Vigo County	85	0.14
Fishers (town) Hamilton County	84	0.12
Fort Wayne (city) Allen County	244	0.10
Anderson (city) Madison County	59	0.10

Cypriot

Top 10 Places Sorted by Population
Based on all places, regardless of total population

Place	Population	%
West Lafayette (city) Tippecanoe County	61	0.21
Aberdeen (cdp) Porter County	0	0.00
Advance (town) Boone County	0	0.00
Akron (town) Fulton County	0	0.00
Alamo (town) Montgomery County	0	0.00
Albany (town) Delaware County	0	0.00
Albion (town) Noble County	0	0.00
Alexandria (city) Madison County	0	0.00
Alfordsville (town) Daviess County	0	0.00
Alton (town) Crawford County	0	0.00

Top 10 Places Sorted by Percent of Total Population
Based on all places, regardless of total population

Place	Population	%
West Lafayette (city) Tippecanoe County	61	0.21
Aberdeen (cdp) Porter County	0	0.00
Advance (town) Boone County	0	0.00
Akron (town) Fulton County	0	0.00
Alamo (town) Montgomery County	0	0.00
Albany (town) Delaware County	0	0.00
Albion (town) Noble County	0	0.00
Alexandria (city) Madison County	0	0.00
Alfordsville (town) Daviess County	0	0.00
Alton (town) Crawford County	0	0.00

Top 10 Places Sorted by Percent of Total Population
Based on places with total population of 50,000 or more

Place	Population	%
Anderson (city) Madison County	0	0.00
Bloomington (city) Monroe County	0	0.00
Carmel (city) Hamilton County	0	0.00
Elkhart (city) Elkhart County	0	0.00
Evansville (city) Vanderburgh County	0	0.00
Fishers (town) Hamilton County	0	0.00
Fort Wayne (city) Allen County	0	0.00
Gary (city) Lake County	0	0.00
Hammond (city) Lake County	0	0.00
Indianapolis (city) Marion County	0	0.00

Czech

Top 10 Places Sorted by Population
Based on all places, regardless of total population

Place	Population	%
Indianapolis (city) Marion County	1,484	0.18
Fort Wayne (city) Allen County	837	0.33
Fishers (town) Hamilton County	513	0.72
Bloomington (city) Monroe County	478	0.61
Hammond (city) Lake County	369	0.45
Crown Point (city) Lake County	361	1.38
West Lafayette (city) Tippecanoe County	342	1.17
Carmel (city) Hamilton County	336	0.44
Valparaiso (city) Porter County	288	0.93
South Bend (city) St. Joseph County	264	0.26

Top 10 Places Sorted by Percent of Total Population
Based on all places, regardless of total population

Place	Population	%
San Pierre (cdp) Starke County	12	13.33
Wolcott (town) White County	40	3.66
Kingsbury (town) LaPorte County	8	3.56
Dune Acres (town) Porter County	9	3.44
Long Beach (town) LaPorte County	50	3.42
North Judson (town) Starke County	54	3.12
Trail Creek (town) LaPorte County	61	3.09
Ogden Dunes (town) Porter County	36	2.94
Roseland (town) St. Joseph County	35	2.93
Culver (town) Marshall County	38	2.63

Top 10 Places Sorted by Percent of Total Population
Based on places with total population of 50,000 or more

Place	Population	%
Fishers (town) Hamilton County	513	0.72
Bloomington (city) Monroe County	478	0.61
Hammond (city) Lake County	369	0.45
Carmel (city) Hamilton County	336	0.44
Terre Haute (city) Vigo County	232	0.38
Elkhart (city) Elkhart County	195	0.38
Fort Wayne (city) Allen County	837	0.33
South Bend (city) St. Joseph County	264	0.26
Indianapolis (city) Marion County	1,484	0.18
Evansville (city) Vanderburgh County	152	0.13

Czechoslovakian

Top 10 Places Sorted by Population
Based on all places, regardless of total population

Place	Population	%
Indianapolis (city) Marion County	393	0.05
Hobart (city) Lake County	178	0.63
Fort Wayne (city) Allen County	130	0.05
Carmel (city) Hamilton County	115	0.15
Noblesville (city) Hamilton County	108	0.22
Portage (city) Porter County	104	0.29
Hammond (city) Lake County	101	0.12
Bloomington (city) Monroe County	85	0.11
South Bend (city) St. Joseph County	84	0.08
Chesterton (town) Porter County	83	0.63

Top 10 Places Sorted by Percent of Total Population
Based on all places, regardless of total population

Place	Population	%
Medaryville (town) Pulaski County	34	6.83
North Salem (town) Hendricks County	7	1.87
Orland (town) Steuben County	11	1.79
Roanoke (town) Huntington County	30	1.66
Cloverdale (town) Putnam County	30	1.28
Hamlet (town) Starke County	10	1.21
Shorewood Forest (cdp) Porter County	30	1.00
Delphi (city) Carroll County	29	0.93
St. Mary of the Woods (cdp) Vigo County	10	0.90
Grabill (town) Allen County	8	0.80

Top 10 Places Sorted by Percent of Total Population
Based on places with total population of 50,000 or more

Place	Population	%
Carmel (city) Hamilton County	115	0.15
Hammond (city) Lake County	101	0.12
Bloomington (city) Monroe County	85	0.11
Terre Haute (city) Vigo County	53	0.09
South Bend (city) St. Joseph County	84	0.08
Evansville (city) Vanderburgh County	73	0.06
Fishers (town) Hamilton County	41	0.06
Indianapolis (city) Marion County	393	0.05
Fort Wayne (city) Allen County	130	0.05
Lafayette (city) Tippecanoe County	36	0.05

Danish

Top 10 Places Sorted by Population
Based on all places, regardless of total population

Place	Population	%
Indianapolis (city) Marion County	1,483	0.18
Fort Wayne (city) Allen County	601	0.24
Carmel (city) Hamilton County	597	0.78
Bloomington (city) Monroe County	353	0.45
Fishers (town) Hamilton County	282	0.39
Valparaiso (city) Porter County	278	0.90
Mishawaka (city) St. Joseph County	245	0.51
Columbus (city) Bartholomew County	222	0.51
Hobart (city) Lake County	169	0.60
Granger (cdp) St. Joseph County	165	0.58

Top 10 Places Sorted by Percent of Total Population
Based on all places, regardless of total population

Place	Population	%
Mexico (cdp) Miami County	36	5.14
Kirklin (town) Clinton County	42	4.60
Spring Hill (town) Marion County	3	3.57
Dayton (town) Tippecanoe County	25	2.61
North Webster (town) Kosciusko County	29	2.50
Kentland (town) Newton County	44	2.20
James (town) Boone County	19	2.13
Hidden Valley (cdp) Dearborn County	107	2.11
Ulen (town) Boone County	3	2.10
Hamlet (town) Starke County	16	1.93

Top 10 Places Sorted by Percent of Total Population
Based on places with total population of 50,000 or more

Place	Population	%
Carmel (city) Hamilton County	597	0.78
Bloomington (city) Monroe County	353	0.45
Fishers (town) Hamilton County	282	0.39
Fort Wayne (city) Allen County	601	0.24
Indianapolis (city) Marion County	1,483	0.18
Muncie (city) Delaware County	119	0.17
Terre Haute (city) Vigo County	75	0.12
Evansville (city) Vanderburgh County	133	0.11
Lafayette (city) Tippecanoe County	74	0.11
Hammond (city) Lake County	85	0.10

Dutch

Top 10 Places Sorted by Population
Based on all places, regardless of total population

Place	Population	%
Indianapolis (city) Marion County	11,553	1.43
Fort Wayne (city) Allen County	3,612	1.42
South Bend (city) St. Joseph County	2,222	2.18
Lafayette (city) Tippecanoe County	2,127	3.22
Evansville (city) Vanderburgh County	1,856	1.57
Carmel (city) Hamilton County	1,777	2.31
Highland (town) Lake County	1,729	7.29
Bloomington (city) Monroe County	1,696	2.16
Anderson (city) Madison County	1,593	2.81
Fishers (town) Hamilton County	1,512	2.11

Top 10 Places Sorted by Percent of Total Population
Based on all places, regardless of total population

Place	Population	%
Monterey (town) Pulaski County	37	19.79
Orland (town) Steuben County	99	16.15
Shepardsville (cdp) Vigo County	10	16.13
New Trenton (cdp) Franklin County	72	16.00
De Motte (town) Jasper County	591	15.82
Bryant (town) Jay County	45	15.00
Lake Village (cdp) Newton County	93	14.05
Merom (town) Sullivan County	24	12.97
San Pierre (cdp) Starke County	11	12.22
Yeoman (town) Carroll County	8	11.94

Top 10 Places Sorted by Percent of Total Population
Based on places with total population of 50,000 or more

Place	Population	%
Lafayette (city) Tippecanoe County	2,127	3.22
Anderson (city) Madison County	1,593	2.81
Elkhart (city) Elkhart County	1,346	2.60
Carmel (city) Hamilton County	1,777	2.31
Terre Haute (city) Vigo County	1,355	2.24
South Bend (city) St. Joseph County	2,222	2.18
Bloomington (city) Monroe County	1,696	2.16
Fishers (town) Hamilton County	1,512	2.11
Muncie (city) Delaware County	1,417	2.02
Evansville (city) Vanderburgh County	1,856	1.57

Please refer to the Explanation of Data in the front of the book for more detailed information.

Profiles of Indiana   Ancestry and Ethnicity: Ancestry Group Rankings   517

Eastern European

Top 10 Places Sorted by Population
Based on all places, regardless of total population

Place	Population	%
Bloomington (city) Monroe County	354	0.45
Indianapolis (city) Marion County	332	0.04
Hammond (city) Lake County	180	0.22
Carmel (city) Hamilton County	164	0.21
Noblesville (city) Hamilton County	126	0.26
Fort Wayne (city) Allen County	110	0.04
Hobart (city) Lake County	78	0.27
Fishers (town) Hamilton County	75	0.10
South Bend (city) St. Joseph County	66	0.06
Zionsville (town) Boone County	63	0.47

Top 10 Places Sorted by Percent of Total Population
Based on all places, regardless of total population

Place	Population	%
River Forest (town) Madison County	7	18.92
Burlington (town) Carroll County	21	2.94
Williams Creek (town) Marion County	4	1.00
Edinburgh (town) Johnson County	37	0.95
Bargersville (town) Johnson County	29	0.75
Meridian Hills (town) Marion County	12	0.74
Zionsville (town) Boone County	63	0.47
Bloomington (city) Monroe County	354	0.45
Whites (town) Boone County	8	0.42
Versailles (town) Ripley County	7	0.40

Top 10 Places Sorted by Percent of Total Population
Based on places with total population of 50,000 or more

Place	Population	%
Bloomington (city) Monroe County	354	0.45
Hammond (city) Lake County	180	0.22
Carmel (city) Hamilton County	164	0.21
Fishers (town) Hamilton County	75	0.10
South Bend (city) St. Joseph County	66	0.06
Lafayette (city) Tippecanoe County	40	0.06
Indianapolis (city) Marion County	332	0.04
Fort Wayne (city) Allen County	110	0.04
Gary (city) Lake County	37	0.04
Terre Haute (city) Vigo County	26	0.04

English

Top 10 Places Sorted by Population
Based on all places, regardless of total population

Place	Population	%
Indianapolis (city) Marion County	67,644	8.35
Fort Wayne (city) Allen County	19,734	7.78
Carmel (city) Hamilton County	11,352	14.79
Evansville (city) Vanderburgh County	9,922	8.40
Fishers (town) Hamilton County	9,173	12.79
Bloomington (city) Monroe County	8,739	11.13
Lafayette (city) Tippecanoe County	6,889	10.41
Muncie (city) Delaware County	6,521	9.31
South Bend (city) St. Joseph County	6,318	6.19
Noblesville (city) Hamilton County	5,811	11.93

Top 10 Places Sorted by Percent of Total Population
Based on all places, regardless of total population

Place	Population	%
Scotland (cdp) Greene County	11	100.00
New Amsterdam (town) Harrison County	6	100.00
Emison (cdp) Knox County	47	60.26
New Goshen (cdp) Vigo County	116	52.02
Toad Hop (cdp) Vigo County	24	47.06
Tennyson (town) Warrick County	127	39.56
Richland (town) Spencer County	154	37.56
Alfordsville (town) Daviess County	49	35.25
Amo (town) Hendricks County	178	34.36
Patriot (town) Switzerland County	93	34.19

Top 10 Places Sorted by Percent of Total Population
Based on places with total population of 50,000 or more

Place	Population	%
Carmel (city) Hamilton County	11,352	14.79
Fishers (town) Hamilton County	9,173	12.79
Bloomington (city) Monroe County	8,739	11.13
Lafayette (city) Tippecanoe County	6,889	10.41
Muncie (city) Delaware County	6,521	9.31
Terre Haute (city) Vigo County	5,550	9.18
Anderson (city) Madison County	4,934	8.69
Evansville (city) Vanderburgh County	9,922	8.40
Indianapolis (city) Marion County	67,644	8.35
Fort Wayne (city) Allen County	19,734	7.78

Estonian

Top 10 Places Sorted by Population
Based on all places, regardless of total population

Place	Population	%
Indianapolis (city) Marion County	99	0.01
Terre Haute (city) Vigo County	53	0.09
Mishawaka (city) St. Joseph County	37	0.08
Munster (town) Lake County	33	0.14
Hammond (city) Lake County	18	0.02
Franklin (city) Johnson County	17	0.08
Bloomington (city) Monroe County	15	0.02
Carmel (city) Hamilton County	13	0.02
Warren Park (town) Marion County	12	0.87
Fort Wayne (city) Allen County	12	<0.01

Top 10 Places Sorted by Percent of Total Population
Based on all places, regardless of total population

Place	Population	%
Crows Nest (town) Marion County	2	2.41
Warren Park (town) Marion County	12	0.87
Darmstadt (town) Vanderburgh County	3	0.23
New Carlisle (town) St. Joseph County	4	0.22
Munster (town) Lake County	33	0.14
Terre Haute (city) Vigo County	53	0.09
Mishawaka (city) St. Joseph County	37	0.08
Franklin (city) Johnson County	17	0.08
West Lafayette (city) Tippecanoe County	8	0.03
Hammond (city) Lake County	18	0.02

Top 10 Places Sorted by Percent of Total Population
Based on places with total population of 50,000 or more

Place	Population	%
Terre Haute (city) Vigo County	53	0.09
Hammond (city) Lake County	18	0.02
Bloomington (city) Monroe County	15	0.02
Carmel (city) Hamilton County	13	0.02
Indianapolis (city) Marion County	99	0.01
South Bend (city) St. Joseph County	8	0.01
Fort Wayne (city) Allen County	12	<0.01
Anderson (city) Madison County	0	0.00
Elkhart (city) Elkhart County	0	0.00
Evansville (city) Vanderburgh County	0	0.00

European

Top 10 Places Sorted by Population
Based on all places, regardless of total population

Place	Population	%
Indianapolis (city) Marion County	9,215	1.14
Fort Wayne (city) Allen County	1,608	0.63
Fishers (town) Hamilton County	1,428	1.99
Bloomington (city) Monroe County	1,404	1.79
Carmel (city) Hamilton County	1,241	1.62
Noblesville (city) Hamilton County	1,091	2.24
South Bend (city) St. Joseph County	796	0.78
Evansville (city) Vanderburgh County	768	0.65
Granger (cdp) St. Joseph County	756	2.67
Lafayette (city) Tippecanoe County	672	1.02

Top 10 Places Sorted by Percent of Total Population
Based on all places, regardless of total population

Place	Population	%
Williams (cdp) Lawrence County	24	11.32
Crandall (town) Harrison County	11	10.19
Ulen (town) Boone County	14	9.79
Metamora (cdp) Franklin County	8	9.52
Homecroft (town) Marion County	41	7.04
Cedar Grove (town) Franklin County	8	7.02
Cadiz (town) Henry County	8	6.78
St. Bernice (cdp) Vermillion County	44	6.73
Galena (cdp) Floyd County	116	6.17
Larwill (town) Whitley County	15	5.54

Top 10 Places Sorted by Percent of Total Population
Based on places with total population of 50,000 or more

Place	Population	%
Fishers (town) Hamilton County	1,428	1.99
Bloomington (city) Monroe County	1,404	1.79
Carmel (city) Hamilton County	1,241	1.62
Indianapolis (city) Marion County	9,215	1.14
Lafayette (city) Tippecanoe County	672	1.02
Terre Haute (city) Vigo County	484	0.80
South Bend (city) St. Joseph County	796	0.78
Muncie (city) Delaware County	525	0.75
Evansville (city) Vanderburgh County	768	0.65
Fort Wayne (city) Allen County	1,608	0.63

Finnish

Top 10 Places Sorted by Population
Based on all places, regardless of total population

Place	Population	%
Indianapolis (city) Marion County	436	0.05
Fort Wayne (city) Allen County	185	0.07
Hammond (city) Lake County	153	0.19
Lawrenceburg (city) Dearborn County	137	2.74
Granger (cdp) St. Joseph County	122	0.43
Portage (city) Porter County	104	0.29
South Bend (city) St. Joseph County	93	0.09
Fishers (town) Hamilton County	83	0.12
Greenwood (city) Johnson County	80	0.17
Evansville (city) Vanderburgh County	80	0.07

Top 10 Places Sorted by Percent of Total Population
Based on all places, regardless of total population

Place	Population	%
Poseyville (town) Posey County	67	6.18
Lawrenceburg (city) Dearborn County	137	2.74
Cedar Grove (town) Franklin County	3	2.63
Michiana Shores (town) LaPorte County	9	2.19
De Motte (town) Jasper County	70	1.87
Galena (cdp) Floyd County	35	1.86
Dana (town) Vermillion County	9	1.77
Fowler (town) Benton County	38	1.65
Sandborn (town) Knox County	6	1.55
Ossian (town) Wells County	47	1.33

Top 10 Places Sorted by Percent of Total Population
Based on places with total population of 50,000 or more

Place	Population	%
Hammond (city) Lake County	153	0.19
Fishers (town) Hamilton County	83	0.12
Lafayette (city) Tippecanoe County	63	0.10
South Bend (city) St. Joseph County	93	0.09
Carmel (city) Hamilton County	70	0.09
Elkhart (city) Elkhart County	48	0.09
Fort Wayne (city) Allen County	185	0.07
Evansville (city) Vanderburgh County	80	0.07
Muncie (city) Delaware County	42	0.06
Anderson (city) Madison County	35	0.06

French, except Basque

Top 10 Places Sorted by Population
Based on all places, regardless of total population

Place	Population	%
Indianapolis (city) Marion County	15,735	1.94
Fort Wayne (city) Allen County	9,917	3.91
Evansville (city) Vanderburgh County	2,952	2.50
Bloomington (city) Monroe County	2,654	3.38
Fishers (town) Hamilton County	2,611	3.64
South Bend (city) St. Joseph County	2,323	2.28
Carmel (city) Hamilton County	2,214	2.88
Lafayette (city) Tippecanoe County	1,964	2.97
Muncie (city) Delaware County	1,865	2.66
Mishawaka (city) St. Joseph County	1,835	3.83

Top 10 Places Sorted by Percent of Total Population
Based on all places, regardless of total population

Place	Population	%
Raglesville (cdp) Daviess County	44	84.62
Griffin (town) Posey County	83	34.30
Stockwell (cdp) Tippecanoe County	152	24.68

Please refer to the Explanation of Data in the front of the book for more detailed information.

Place	Population	%
Collegeville (cdp) Jasper County	10	20.83
West Point (cdp) Tippecanoe County	94	16.46
Alton (town) Crawford County	13	15.29
Colburn (cdp) Tippecanoe County	15	14.02
Zanesville (town) Wells County	105	13.98
New Goshen (cdp) Vigo County	30	13.45
Blountsville (town) Henry County	12	12.12

Top 10 Places Sorted by Percent of Total Population
Based on places with total population of 50,000 or more

Place	Population	%
Fort Wayne (city) Allen County	9,917	3.91
Fishers (town) Hamilton County	2,611	3.64
Bloomington (city) Monroe County	2,654	3.38
Lafayette (city) Tippecanoe County	1,964	2.97
Terre Haute (city) Vigo County	1,765	2.92
Carmel (city) Hamilton County	2,214	2.88
Muncie (city) Delaware County	1,865	2.66
Evansville (city) Vanderburgh County	2,952	2.50
South Bend (city) St. Joseph County	2,323	2.28
Anderson (city) Madison County	1,268	2.23

French Canadian

Top 10 Places Sorted by Population
Based on all places, regardless of total population

Place	Population	%
Indianapolis (city) Marion County	1,565	0.19
Fort Wayne (city) Allen County	813	0.32
South Bend (city) St. Joseph County	422	0.41
Fishers (town) Hamilton County	382	0.53
Hammond (city) Lake County	345	0.42
Kokomo (city) Howard County	324	0.71
Bloomington (city) Monroe County	305	0.39
Greenwood (city) Johnson County	302	0.63
Mishawaka (city) St. Joseph County	278	0.58
Portage (city) Porter County	226	0.62

Top 10 Places Sorted by Percent of Total Population
Based on all places, regardless of total population

Place	Population	%
Howe (cdp) LaGrange County	87	12.79
Country Club Heights (town) Madison County	5	9.80
Pierceton (town) Kosciusko County	40	3.93
Campbellsburg (town) Washington County	23	3.66
Roseland (town) St. Joseph County	39	3.26
Andrews (town) Huntington County	43	3.25
Woodlawn Heights (town) Madison County	3	3.23
Waveland (town) Montgomery County	12	3.10
New (town) Fountain County	4	2.96
Smithville-Sanders (cdp) Monroe County	55	2.20

Top 10 Places Sorted by Percent of Total Population
Based on places with total population of 50,000 or more

Place	Population	%
Fishers (town) Hamilton County	382	0.53
Hammond (city) Lake County	345	0.42
South Bend (city) St. Joseph County	422	0.41
Bloomington (city) Monroe County	305	0.39
Elkhart (city) Elkhart County	203	0.39
Fort Wayne (city) Allen County	813	0.32
Carmel (city) Hamilton County	225	0.29
Lafayette (city) Tippecanoe County	177	0.27
Indianapolis (city) Marion County	1,565	0.19
Terre Haute (city) Vigo County	85	0.14

German

Top 10 Places Sorted by Population
Based on all places, regardless of total population

Place	Population	%
Indianapolis (city) Marion County	149,656	18.48
Fort Wayne (city) Allen County	76,622	30.20
Evansville (city) Vanderburgh County	33,828	28.62
Carmel (city) Hamilton County	21,955	28.60
Fishers (town) Hamilton County	20,883	29.11
Bloomington (city) Monroe County	19,499	24.84
South Bend (city) St. Joseph County	19,199	18.81
Lafayette (city) Tippecanoe County	16,791	25.38
Muncie (city) Delaware County	14,993	21.41
Noblesville (city) Hamilton County	13,766	28.26

Top 10 Places Sorted by Percent of Total Population
Based on all places, regardless of total population

Place	Population	%
Oldenburg (town) Franklin County	485	79.64
St. Meinrad (cdp) Spencer County	266	78.93
Dubois (cdp) Dubois County	204	72.86
Cedar Grove (town) Franklin County	82	71.93
Ferdinand (town) Dubois County	1,534	71.12
Clarksburg (cdp) Decatur County	85	69.67
Shelby (cdp) Lake County	245	67.31
Cannelburg (town) Daviess County	97	66.90
Parkers Settlement (cdp) Posey County	496	65.01
St. Leon (town) Dearborn County	523	63.55

Top 10 Places Sorted by Percent of Total Population
Based on places with total population of 50,000 or more

Place	Population	%
Fort Wayne (city) Allen County	76,622	30.20
Fishers (town) Hamilton County	20,883	29.11
Evansville (city) Vanderburgh County	33,828	28.62
Carmel (city) Hamilton County	21,955	28.60
Lafayette (city) Tippecanoe County	16,791	25.38
Bloomington (city) Monroe County	19,499	24.84
Terre Haute (city) Vigo County	13,440	22.24
Muncie (city) Delaware County	14,993	21.41
Elkhart (city) Elkhart County	9,960	19.21
South Bend (city) St. Joseph County	19,199	18.81

German Russian

Top 10 Places Sorted by Population
Based on all places, regardless of total population

Place	Population	%
Simonton Lake (cdp) Elkhart County	47	0.93
Lawrence (city) Marion County	11	0.02
Indianapolis (city) Marion County	11	<0.01
Mishawaka (city) St. Joseph County	10	0.02
Van Buren (town) Grant County	8	0.91
Hagers (town) Wayne County	6	0.36
Grissom AFB (cdp) Miami County	4	0.22
Aberdeen (cdp) Porter County	0	0.00
Advance (town) Boone County	0	0.00
Akron (town) Fulton County	0	0.00

Top 10 Places Sorted by Percent of Total Population
Based on all places, regardless of total population

Place	Population	%
Simonton Lake (cdp) Elkhart County	47	0.93
Van Buren (town) Grant County	8	0.91
Hagers (town) Wayne County	6	0.36
Grissom AFB (cdp) Miami County	4	0.22
Lawrence (city) Marion County	11	0.02
Mishawaka (city) St. Joseph County	10	0.02
Indianapolis (city) Marion County	11	<0.01
Aberdeen (cdp) Porter County	0	0.00
Advance (town) Boone County	0	0.00
Akron (town) Fulton County	0	0.00

Top 10 Places Sorted by Percent of Total Population
Based on places with total population of 50,000 or more

Place	Population	%
Indianapolis (city) Marion County	11	<0.01
Anderson (city) Madison County	0	0.00
Bloomington (city) Monroe County	0	0.00
Carmel (city) Hamilton County	0	0.00
Elkhart (city) Elkhart County	0	0.00
Evansville (city) Vanderburgh County	0	0.00
Fishers (town) Hamilton County	0	0.00
Fort Wayne (city) Allen County	0	0.00
Gary (city) Lake County	0	0.00
Hammond (city) Lake County	0	0.00

Greek

Top 10 Places Sorted by Population
Based on all places, regardless of total population

Place	Population	%
Indianapolis (city) Marion County	2,372	0.29
Hammond (city) Lake County	881	1.08
Munster (town) Lake County	784	3.37
Fort Wayne (city) Allen County	732	0.29
Crown Point (city) Lake County	661	2.53
Fishers (town) Hamilton County	637	0.89
Schererville (town) Lake County	571	2.01
Bloomington (city) Monroe County	551	0.70
Portage (city) Porter County	528	1.45
Carmel (city) Hamilton County	485	0.63

Top 10 Places Sorted by Percent of Total Population
Based on all places, regardless of total population

Place	Population	%
Shorewood Forest (cdp) Porter County	320	10.61
Manilla (cdp) Rush County	33	10.28
Rocky Ripple (town) Marion County	49	7.61
Bethany (town) Morgan County	9	7.03
River Forest (town) Madison County	2	5.41
Morris (town) Shelby County	40	3.88
Munster (town) Lake County	784	3.37
Ogden Dunes (town) Porter County	37	3.02
Michigan (town) Clinton County	14	2.90
Homecroft (town) Marion County	16	2.75

Top 10 Places Sorted by Percent of Total Population
Based on places with total population of 50,000 or more

Place	Population	%
Hammond (city) Lake County	881	1.08
Fishers (town) Hamilton County	637	0.89
Bloomington (city) Monroe County	551	0.70
Carmel (city) Hamilton County	485	0.63
Muncie (city) Delaware County	214	0.31
South Bend (city) St. Joseph County	308	0.30
Indianapolis (city) Marion County	2,372	0.29
Fort Wayne (city) Allen County	732	0.29
Lafayette (city) Tippecanoe County	147	0.22
Anderson (city) Madison County	126	0.22

Guyanese

Top 10 Places Sorted by Population
Based on all places, regardless of total population

Place	Population	%
Evansville (city) Vanderburgh County	49	0.04
Richmond (city) Wayne County	30	0.08
Hammond (city) Lake County	14	0.02
Goshen (city) Elkhart County	10	0.03
Aberdeen (cdp) Porter County	0	0.00
Advance (town) Boone County	0	0.00
Akron (town) Fulton County	0	0.00
Alamo (town) Montgomery County	0	0.00
Albany (town) Delaware County	0	0.00
Albion (town) Noble County	0	0.00

Top 10 Places Sorted by Percent of Total Population
Based on all places, regardless of total population

Place	Population	%
Richmond (city) Wayne County	30	0.08
Evansville (city) Vanderburgh County	49	0.04
Goshen (city) Elkhart County	10	0.03
Hammond (city) Lake County	14	0.02
Aberdeen (cdp) Porter County	0	0.00
Advance (town) Boone County	0	0.00
Akron (town) Fulton County	0	0.00
Alamo (town) Montgomery County	0	0.00
Albany (town) Delaware County	0	0.00
Albion (town) Noble County	0	0.00

Top 10 Places Sorted by Percent of Total Population
Based on places with total population of 50,000 or more

Place	Population	%
Evansville (city) Vanderburgh County	49	0.04
Hammond (city) Lake County	14	0.02
Anderson (city) Madison County	0	0.00
Bloomington (city) Monroe County	0	0.00
Carmel (city) Hamilton County	0	0.00
Elkhart (city) Elkhart County	0	0.00
Fishers (town) Hamilton County	0	0.00
Fort Wayne (city) Allen County	0	0.00
Gary (city) Lake County	0	0.00
Indianapolis (city) Marion County	0	0.00

Please refer to the Explanation of Data in the front of the book for more detailed information.

Hungarian

Top 10 Places Sorted by Population
Based on all places, regardless of total population

Place	Population	%
Indianapolis (city) Marion County	2,960	0.37
South Bend (city) St. Joseph County	2,904	2.85
Mishawaka (city) St. Joseph County	1,337	2.79
Fort Wayne (city) Allen County	1,122	0.44
Hammond (city) Lake County	827	1.02
Bloomington (city) Monroe County	767	0.98
Valparaiso (city) Porter County	744	2.40
Highland (town) Lake County	707	2.98
Portage (city) Porter County	668	1.84
Granger (cdp) St. Joseph County	655	2.31

Top 10 Places Sorted by Percent of Total Population
Based on all places, regardless of total population

Place	Population	%
Tri-Lakes (cdp) Whitley County	122	7.40
Aberdeen (cdp) Porter County	132	6.04
Roseland (town) St. Joseph County	72	6.03
Lake Village (cdp) Newton County	33	4.98
Trail Creek (town) LaPorte County	94	4.75
Hudson Lake (cdp) LaPorte County	59	4.39
New Carlisle (town) St. Joseph County	76	4.13
Hanna (cdp) LaPorte County	19	4.09
Walkerton (town) St. Joseph County	90	3.92
North Webster (town) Kosciusko County	45	3.88

Top 10 Places Sorted by Percent of Total Population
Based on places with total population of 50,000 or more

Place	Population	%
South Bend (city) St. Joseph County	2,904	2.85
Hammond (city) Lake County	827	1.02
Bloomington (city) Monroe County	767	0.98
Terre Haute (city) Vigo County	438	0.72
Carmel (city) Hamilton County	504	0.66
Fishers (town) Hamilton County	463	0.65
Elkhart (city) Elkhart County	258	0.50
Fort Wayne (city) Allen County	1,122	0.44
Indianapolis (city) Marion County	2,960	0.37
Lafayette (city) Tippecanoe County	247	0.37

Icelander

Top 10 Places Sorted by Population
Based on all places, regardless of total population

Place	Population	%
Bloomington (city) Monroe County	41	0.05
Plainfield (town) Hendricks County	31	0.12
Charlestown (city) Clark County	25	0.33
Purdue University (cdp) Tippecanoe County	18	0.14
Valparaiso (city) Porter County	18	0.06
South Whitley (town) Whitley County	13	0.64
Upland (town) Grant County	13	0.32
Notre Dame (cdp) St. Joseph County	13	0.17
Terre Haute (city) Vigo County	13	0.02
Carmel (city) Hamilton County	12	0.02

Top 10 Places Sorted by Percent of Total Population
Based on all places, regardless of total population

Place	Population	%
South Whitley (town) Whitley County	13	0.64
Charlestown (city) Clark County	25	0.33
Upland (town) Grant County	13	0.32
Notre Dame (cdp) St. Joseph County	13	0.17
Purdue University (cdp) Tippecanoe County	18	0.14
Plainfield (town) Hendricks County	31	0.12
Austin (city) Scott County	5	0.12
Valparaiso (city) Porter County	18	0.06
Bloomington (city) Monroe County	41	0.05
New Haven (city) Allen County	7	0.05

Top 10 Places Sorted by Percent of Total Population
Based on places with total population of 50,000 or more

Place	Population	%
Bloomington (city) Monroe County	41	0.05
Terre Haute (city) Vigo County	13	0.02
Carmel (city) Hamilton County	12	0.02
Fort Wayne (city) Allen County	9	<0.01

Anderson (city) Madison County	0	0.00
Elkhart (city) Elkhart County	0	0.00
Evansville (city) Vanderburgh County	0	0.00
Fishers (town) Hamilton County	0	0.00
Gary (city) Lake County	0	0.00
Hammond (city) Lake County	0	0.00

Iranian

Top 10 Places Sorted by Population
Based on all places, regardless of total population

Place	Population	%
Indianapolis (city) Marion County	455	0.06
Carmel (city) Hamilton County	253	0.33
Bloomington (city) Monroe County	201	0.26
Fishers (town) Hamilton County	181	0.25
Noblesville (city) Hamilton County	131	0.27
Granger (cdp) St. Joseph County	124	0.44
Portage (city) Porter County	99	0.27
Muncie (city) Delaware County	78	0.11
Whiteland (town) Johnson County	68	1.61
Michigan City (city) LaPorte County	44	0.14

Top 10 Places Sorted by Percent of Total Population
Based on all places, regardless of total population

Place	Population	%
Williams Creek (town) Marion County	10	2.50
Burns Harbor (town) Porter County	31	2.48
Spring Hill (town) Marion County	2	2.38
Whiteland (town) Johnson County	68	1.61
Wynnedale (town) Marion County	3	1.28
Riley (town) Vigo County	2	0.92
McCordsville (town) Hancock County	25	0.60
Granger (cdp) St. Joseph County	124	0.44
Bremen (town) Marshall County	19	0.41
Carmel (city) Hamilton County	253	0.33

Top 10 Places Sorted by Percent of Total Population
Based on places with total population of 50,000 or more

Place	Population	%
Carmel (city) Hamilton County	253	0.33
Bloomington (city) Monroe County	201	0.26
Fishers (town) Hamilton County	181	0.25
Muncie (city) Delaware County	78	0.11
Indianapolis (city) Marion County	455	0.06
Evansville (city) Vanderburgh County	20	0.02
South Bend (city) St. Joseph County	13	0.01
Fort Wayne (city) Allen County	8	<0.01
Anderson (city) Madison County	0	0.00
Elkhart (city) Elkhart County	0	0.00

Irish

Top 10 Places Sorted by Population
Based on all places, regardless of total population

Place	Population	%
Indianapolis (city) Marion County	93,959	11.60
Fort Wayne (city) Allen County	28,352	11.17
Evansville (city) Vanderburgh County	14,073	11.91
Carmel (city) Hamilton County	12,211	15.91
South Bend (city) St. Joseph County	12,089	11.84
Bloomington (city) Monroe County	10,941	13.94
Fishers (town) Hamilton County	10,537	14.69
Lafayette (city) Tippecanoe County	10,032	15.17
Muncie (city) Delaware County	9,462	13.51
Hammond (city) Lake County	8,337	10.25

Top 10 Places Sorted by Percent of Total Population
Based on all places, regardless of total population

Place	Population	%
Fish Lake (cdp) LaPorte County	405	45.25
Alton (town) Crawford County	38	44.71
Hayden (cdp) Jennings County	336	44.27
Painted Hills (cdp) Morgan County	187	42.60
Salamonia (town) Jay County	92	42.59
East Enterprise (cdp) Switzerland County	109	39.78
New Goshen (cdp) Vigo County	88	39.46
Notre Dame (cdp) St. Joseph County	2,794	37.61
Buffalo (cdp) White County	243	35.22
Yeoman (town) Carroll County	23	34.33

Top 10 Places Sorted by Percent of Total Population
Based on places with total population of 50,000 or more

Place	Population	%
Carmel (city) Hamilton County	12,211	15.91
Lafayette (city) Tippecanoe County	10,032	15.17
Fishers (town) Hamilton County	10,537	14.69
Bloomington (city) Monroe County	10,941	13.94
Muncie (city) Delaware County	9,462	13.51
Evansville (city) Vanderburgh County	14,073	11.91
Terre Haute (city) Vigo County	7,200	11.91
South Bend (city) St. Joseph County	12,089	11.84
Indianapolis (city) Marion County	93,959	11.60
Anderson (city) Madison County	6,464	11.39

Israeli

Top 10 Places Sorted by Population
Based on all places, regardless of total population

Place	Population	%
Bloomington (city) Monroe County	168	0.21
Indianapolis (city) Marion County	107	0.01
Mount Vernon (city) Posey County	38	0.56
Fort Wayne (city) Allen County	34	0.01
Muncie (city) Delaware County	24	0.03
Fishers (town) Hamilton County	21	0.03
Terre Haute (city) Vigo County	13	0.02
York (town) Delaware County	11	0.12
Portage (city) Porter County	5	0.01
Aberdeen (cdp) Porter County	0	0.00

Top 10 Places Sorted by Percent of Total Population
Based on all places, regardless of total population

Place	Population	%
Mount Vernon (city) Posey County	38	0.56
Bloomington (city) Monroe County	168	0.21
York (town) Delaware County	11	0.12
Muncie (city) Delaware County	24	0.03
Fishers (town) Hamilton County	21	0.03
Terre Haute (city) Vigo County	13	0.02
Indianapolis (city) Marion County	107	0.01
Fort Wayne (city) Allen County	34	0.01
Portage (city) Porter County	5	0.01
Aberdeen (cdp) Porter County	0	0.00

Top 10 Places Sorted by Percent of Total Population
Based on places with total population of 50,000 or more

Place	Population	%
Bloomington (city) Monroe County	168	0.21
Muncie (city) Delaware County	24	0.03
Fishers (town) Hamilton County	21	0.03
Terre Haute (city) Vigo County	13	0.02
Indianapolis (city) Marion County	107	0.01
Fort Wayne (city) Allen County	34	0.01
Anderson (city) Madison County	0	0.00
Carmel (city) Hamilton County	0	0.00
Elkhart (city) Elkhart County	0	0.00
Evansville (city) Vanderburgh County	0	0.00

Italian

Top 10 Places Sorted by Population
Based on all places, regardless of total population

Place	Population	%
Indianapolis (city) Marion County	20,396	2.52
Fort Wayne (city) Allen County	6,703	2.64
Carmel (city) Hamilton County	3,728	4.86
Bloomington (city) Monroe County	3,669	4.67
Fishers (town) Hamilton County	3,343	4.66
South Bend (city) St. Joseph County	3,341	3.27
Hammond (city) Lake County	2,841	3.49
Noblesville (city) Hamilton County	2,728	5.60
Mishawaka (city) St. Joseph County	2,342	4.89
Schererville (town) Lake County	2,160	7.58

Top 10 Places Sorted by Percent of Total Population
Based on all places, regardless of total population

Place	Population	%
Deputy (cdp) Jefferson County	16	59.26
Buck Creek (cdp) Tippecanoe County	119	34.00
Stockwell (cdp) Tippecanoe County	181	29.38

Please refer to the Explanation of Data in the front of the book for more detailed information.

520 Ancestry and Ethnicity: Ancestry Group Rankings — Profiles of Indiana

Place	Population	%
San Pierre (cdp) Starke County	21	23.33
East Enterprise (cdp) Switzerland County	51	18.61
Avoca (cdp) Lawrence County	97	18.44
Blanford (cdp) Vermillion County	63	18.16
Bass Lake (cdp) Starke County	234	16.49
Notre Dame (cdp) St. Joseph County	1,191	16.03
New Goshen (cdp) Vigo County	34	15.25

Top 10 Places Sorted by Percent of Total Population
Based on places with total population of 50,000 or more

Place	Population	%
Carmel (city) Hamilton County	3,728	4.86
Bloomington (city) Monroe County	3,669	4.67
Fishers (town) Hamilton County	3,343	4.66
Hammond (city) Lake County	2,841	3.49
South Bend (city) St. Joseph County	3,341	3.27
Elkhart (city) Elkhart County	1,611	3.11
Terre Haute (city) Vigo County	1,814	3.00
Muncie (city) Delaware County	1,965	2.81
Fort Wayne (city) Allen County	6,703	2.64
Indianapolis (city) Marion County	20,396	2.52

Latvian

Top 10 Places Sorted by Population
Based on all places, regardless of total population

Place	Population	%
Indianapolis (city) Marion County	275	0.03
Noblesville (city) Hamilton County	167	0.34
Carmel (city) Hamilton County	129	0.17
Terre Haute (city) Vigo County	118	0.20
Fort Wayne (city) Allen County	70	0.03
Lake Dalecarlia (cdp) Lake County	47	3.10
Westfield (town) Hamilton County	39	0.14
Griffith (town) Lake County	38	0.22
Munster (town) Lake County	23	0.10
West Lafayette (city) Tippecanoe County	18	0.06

Top 10 Places Sorted by Percent of Total Population
Based on all places, regardless of total population

Place	Population	%
Lake Dalecarlia (cdp) Lake County	47	3.10
Long Beach (town) LaPorte County	11	0.75
Kewanna (town) Fulton County	3	0.53
Frankton (town) Madison County	8	0.41
Attica (city) Fountain County	12	0.37
Bristol (town) Elkhart County	6	0.37
Noblesville (city) Hamilton County	167	0.34
Upland (town) Grant County	13	0.32
Rocky Ripple (town) Marion County	2	0.31
Kentland (town) Newton County	6	0.30

Top 10 Places Sorted by Percent of Total Population
Based on places with total population of 50,000 or more

Place	Population	%
Terre Haute (city) Vigo County	118	0.20
Carmel (city) Hamilton County	129	0.17
Indianapolis (city) Marion County	275	0.03
Fort Wayne (city) Allen County	70	0.03
Fishers (town) Hamilton County	13	0.02
Elkhart (city) Elkhart County	11	0.02
Evansville (city) Vanderburgh County	12	0.01
Bloomington (city) Monroe County	10	0.01
South Bend (city) St. Joseph County	10	0.01
Muncie (city) Delaware County	9	0.01

Lithuanian

Top 10 Places Sorted by Population
Based on all places, regardless of total population

Place	Population	%
Indianapolis (city) Marion County	1,175	0.15
Bloomington (city) Monroe County	362	0.46
Fort Wayne (city) Allen County	278	0.11
Munster (town) Lake County	274	1.18
Valparaiso (city) Porter County	271	0.87
Lakes of the Four Seasons (cdp) Lake County	265	3.51
Schererville (town) Lake County	263	0.92
Highland (town) Lake County	258	1.09
St. John (town) Lake County	242	1.76
Hammond (city) Lake County	242	0.30

Top 10 Places Sorted by Percent of Total Population
Based on all places, regardless of total population

Place	Population	%
Beverly Shores (town) Porter County	144	21.30
Michiana Shores (town) LaPorte County	36	8.76
Dune Acres (town) Porter County	14	5.34
Lakes of the Four Seasons (cdp) Lake County	265	3.51
Star City (cdp) Pulaski County	9	2.94
Monterey (town) Pulaski County	5	2.67
Francesville (town) Pulaski County	20	2.22
Hudson Lake (cdp) LaPorte County	29	2.16
Town of Pines (town) Porter County	15	2.14
Lake Dalecarlia (cdp) Lake County	28	1.85

Top 10 Places Sorted by Percent of Total Population
Based on places with total population of 50,000 or more

Place	Population	%
Bloomington (city) Monroe County	362	0.46
Hammond (city) Lake County	242	0.30
Fishers (town) Hamilton County	166	0.23
Gary (city) Lake County	162	0.19
Terre Haute (city) Vigo County	110	0.18
South Bend (city) St. Joseph County	176	0.17
Carmel (city) Hamilton County	120	0.16
Indianapolis (city) Marion County	1,175	0.15
Fort Wayne (city) Allen County	278	0.11
Muncie (city) Delaware County	77	0.11

Luxemburger

Top 10 Places Sorted by Population
Based on all places, regardless of total population

Place	Population	%
Indianapolis (city) Marion County	97	0.01
Lafayette (city) Tippecanoe County	45	0.07
Fort Wayne (city) Allen County	36	0.01
Muncie (city) Delaware County	32	0.05
Granger (cdp) St. Joseph County	26	0.09
Carmel (city) Hamilton County	22	0.03
Batesville (city) Ripley County	18	0.28
Purdue University (cdp) Tippecanoe County	13	0.10
South Bend (city) St. Joseph County	13	0.01
Lawrence (city) Marion County	12	0.03

Top 10 Places Sorted by Percent of Total Population
Based on all places, regardless of total population

Place	Population	%
Beverly Shores (town) Porter County	5	0.74
St. Mary of the Woods (cdp) Vigo County	8	0.72
Koontz Lake (cdp) Starke County	10	0.62
Morocco (town) Newton County	5	0.57
Wynnedale (town) Marion County	1	0.43
Batesville (city) Ripley County	18	0.28
Roseland (town) St. Joseph County	3	0.25
Ogden Dunes (town) Porter County	3	0.24
Fairview Park (town) Vermillion County	2	0.15
North Judson (town) Starke County	2	0.12

Top 10 Places Sorted by Percent of Total Population
Based on places with total population of 50,000 or more

Place	Population	%
Lafayette (city) Tippecanoe County	45	0.07
Muncie (city) Delaware County	32	0.05
Carmel (city) Hamilton County	22	0.03
Indianapolis (city) Marion County	97	0.01
Fort Wayne (city) Allen County	36	0.01
South Bend (city) St. Joseph County	13	0.01
Anderson (city) Madison County	6	0.01
Bloomington (city) Monroe County	0	0.00
Elkhart (city) Elkhart County	0	0.00
Evansville (city) Vanderburgh County	0	0.00

Macedonian

Top 10 Places Sorted by Population
Based on all places, regardless of total population

Place	Population	%
Crown Point (city) Lake County	901	3.46
Fort Wayne (city) Allen County	580	0.23
Schererville (town) Lake County	401	1.41
Winfield (town) Lake County	385	9.73
Indianapolis (city) Marion County	265	0.03
Hobart (city) Lake County	221	0.78
Portage (city) Porter County	181	0.50
Wheeler (cdp) Porter County	172	38.22
Merrillville (town) Lake County	158	0.46
Munster (town) Lake County	145	0.62

Top 10 Places Sorted by Percent of Total Population
Based on all places, regardless of total population

Place	Population	%
Wheeler (cdp) Porter County	172	38.22
Winfield (town) Lake County	385	9.73
Shorewood Forest (cdp) Porter County	118	3.91
Crown Point (city) Lake County	901	3.46
Schererville (town) Lake County	401	1.41
Lakes of the Four Seasons (cdp) Lake County	79	1.05
St. John (town) Lake County	109	0.79
Hobart (city) Lake County	221	0.78
Dune Acres (town) Porter County	2	0.76
Beverly Shores (town) Porter County	5	0.74

Top 10 Places Sorted by Percent of Total Population
Based on places with total population of 50,000 or more

Place	Population	%
Fort Wayne (city) Allen County	580	0.23
Carmel (city) Hamilton County	104	0.14
Bloomington (city) Monroe County	62	0.08
Indianapolis (city) Marion County	265	0.03
Muncie (city) Delaware County	23	0.03
Fishers (town) Hamilton County	10	0.01
Hammond (city) Lake County	9	0.01
Anderson (city) Madison County	0	0.00
Elkhart (city) Elkhart County	0	0.00
Evansville (city) Vanderburgh County	0	0.00

Maltese

Top 10 Places Sorted by Population
Based on all places, regardless of total population

Place	Population	%
Indianapolis (city) Marion County	56	0.01
Crown Point (city) Lake County	48	0.18
Richmond (city) Wayne County	22	0.06
Leo-Cedarville (town) Allen County	16	0.46
Gary (city) Lake County	10	0.01
Jasper (city) Dubois County	9	0.06
Roanoke (town) Huntington County	8	0.44
Santa Claus (town) Spencer County	5	0.19
Aberdeen (cdp) Porter County	0	0.00
Advance (town) Boone County	0	0.00

Top 10 Places Sorted by Percent of Total Population
Based on all places, regardless of total population

Place	Population	%
Leo-Cedarville (town) Allen County	16	0.46
Roanoke (town) Huntington County	8	0.44
Santa Claus (town) Spencer County	5	0.19
Crown Point (city) Lake County	48	0.18
Richmond (city) Wayne County	22	0.06
Jasper (city) Dubois County	9	0.06
Indianapolis (city) Marion County	56	0.01
Gary (city) Lake County	10	0.01
Aberdeen (cdp) Porter County	0	0.00
Advance (town) Boone County	0	0.00

Top 10 Places Sorted by Percent of Total Population
Based on places with total population of 50,000 or more

Place	Population	%
Indianapolis (city) Marion County	56	0.01
Gary (city) Lake County	10	0.01
Anderson (city) Madison County	0	0.00
Bloomington (city) Monroe County	0	0.00
Carmel (city) Hamilton County	0	0.00
Elkhart (city) Elkhart County	0	0.00
Evansville (city) Vanderburgh County	0	0.00
Fishers (town) Hamilton County	0	0.00
Fort Wayne (city) Allen County	0	0.00
Hammond (city) Lake County	0	0.00

Please refer to the Explanation of Data in the front of the book for more detailed information.

New Zealander

Top 10 Places Sorted by Population
Based on all places, regardless of total population

Place	Population	%
Lafayette (city) Tippecanoe County	68	0.10
Princeton (city) Gibson County	35	0.41
Indianapolis (city) Marion County	35	<0.01
West Lafayette (city) Tippecanoe County	26	0.09
Speedway (town) Marion County	19	0.16
Muncie (city) Delaware County	18	0.03
Fishers (town) Hamilton County	14	0.02
Zionsville (town) Boone County	13	0.10
Fort Wayne (city) Allen County	11	<0.01
Aberdeen (cdp) Porter County	0	0.00

Top 10 Places Sorted by Percent of Total Population
Based on all places, regardless of total population

Place	Population	%
Princeton (city) Gibson County	35	0.41
Speedway (town) Marion County	19	0.16
Lafayette (city) Tippecanoe County	68	0.10
Zionsville (town) Boone County	13	0.10
West Lafayette (city) Tippecanoe County	26	0.09
Muncie (city) Delaware County	18	0.03
Fishers (town) Hamilton County	14	0.02
Indianapolis (city) Marion County	35	<0.01
Fort Wayne (city) Allen County	11	<0.01
Aberdeen (cdp) Porter County	0	0.00

Top 10 Places Sorted by Percent of Total Population
Based on places with total population of 50,000 or more

Place	Population	%
Lafayette (city) Tippecanoe County	68	0.10
Muncie (city) Delaware County	18	0.03
Fishers (town) Hamilton County	14	0.02
Indianapolis (city) Marion County	35	<0.01
Fort Wayne (city) Allen County	11	<0.01
Anderson (city) Madison County	0	0.00
Bloomington (city) Monroe County	0	0.00
Carmel (city) Hamilton County	0	0.00
Elkhart (city) Elkhart County	0	0.00
Evansville (city) Vanderburgh County	0	0.00

Northern European

Top 10 Places Sorted by Population
Based on all places, regardless of total population

Place	Population	%
Indianapolis (city) Marion County	584	0.07
Carmel (city) Hamilton County	105	0.14
Bloomington (city) Monroe County	98	0.12
Fort Wayne (city) Allen County	96	0.04
Granger (cdp) St. Joseph County	85	0.30
Pendleton (town) Madison County	82	1.86
Lawrence (city) Marion County	80	0.18
Lafayette (city) Tippecanoe County	77	0.12
Mishawaka (city) St. Joseph County	73	0.15
South Haven (cdp) Porter County	72	1.35

Top 10 Places Sorted by Percent of Total Population
Based on all places, regardless of total population

Place	Population	%
Indian Village (town) St. Joseph County	4	4.08
Poneto (town) Wells County	5	2.54
Fontanet (cdp) Vigo County	8	2.09
Greens Fork (town) Wayne County	8	1.92
Pendleton (town) Madison County	82	1.86
Ogden Dunes (town) Porter County	20	1.63
Meridian Hills (town) Marion County	24	1.47
Heritage Lake (cdp) Putnam County	38	1.46
South Haven (cdp) Porter County	72	1.35
Millersburg (town) Elkhart County	12	1.32

Top 10 Places Sorted by Percent of Total Population
Based on places with total population of 50,000 or more

Place	Population	%
Carmel (city) Hamilton County	105	0.14
Bloomington (city) Monroe County	98	0.12
Lafayette (city) Tippecanoe County	77	0.12
Indianapolis (city) Marion County	584	0.07

South Bend (city) St. Joseph County	62	0.06
Hammond (city) Lake County	49	0.06
Elkhart (city) Elkhart County	26	0.05
Fort Wayne (city) Allen County	96	0.04
Evansville (city) Vanderburgh County	34	0.03
Fishers (town) Hamilton County	24	0.03

Norwegian

Top 10 Places Sorted by Population
Based on all places, regardless of total population

Place	Population	%
Indianapolis (city) Marion County	3,636	0.45
Fort Wayne (city) Allen County	1,488	0.59
Bloomington (city) Monroe County	1,150	1.47
Carmel (city) Hamilton County	995	1.30
Fishers (town) Hamilton County	843	1.17
Noblesville (city) Hamilton County	621	1.27
Granger (cdp) St. Joseph County	587	2.07
South Bend (city) St. Joseph County	459	0.45
Mishawaka (city) St. Joseph County	428	0.89
Muncie (city) Delaware County	422	0.60

Top 10 Places Sorted by Percent of Total Population
Based on all places, regardless of total population

Place	Population	%
Spring Hill (town) Marion County	5	5.95
Hebron (town) Porter County	162	4.62
Ogden Dunes (town) Porter County	52	4.24
Dune Acres (town) Porter County	10	3.82
Wingate (town) Montgomery County	8	3.64
Springport (town) Henry County	6	3.59
Williams Creek (town) Marion County	14	3.50
Marshall (town) Parke County	9	3.47
Roanoke (town) Huntington County	61	3.38
Winfield (town) Lake County	121	3.06

Top 10 Places Sorted by Percent of Total Population
Based on places with total population of 50,000 or more

Place	Population	%
Bloomington (city) Monroe County	1,150	1.47
Carmel (city) Hamilton County	995	1.30
Fishers (town) Hamilton County	843	1.17
Muncie (city) Delaware County	422	0.60
Fort Wayne (city) Allen County	1,488	0.59
Elkhart (city) Elkhart County	299	0.58
Indianapolis (city) Marion County	3,636	0.45
South Bend (city) St. Joseph County	459	0.45
Hammond (city) Lake County	322	0.40
Lafayette (city) Tippecanoe County	249	0.38

Pennsylvania German

Top 10 Places Sorted by Population
Based on all places, regardless of total population

Place	Population	%
Indianapolis (city) Marion County	355	0.04
Elkhart (city) Elkhart County	347	0.67
Fort Wayne (city) Allen County	255	0.10
Goshen (city) Elkhart County	215	0.69
South Bend (city) St. Joseph County	140	0.14
Mishawaka (city) St. Joseph County	129	0.27
Auburn (city) DeKalb County	85	0.68
Noblesville (city) Hamilton County	83	0.17
Lawrence (city) Marion County	77	0.17
New Paris (cdp) Elkhart County	76	5.80

Top 10 Places Sorted by Percent of Total Population
Based on all places, regardless of total population

Place	Population	%
Burns City (cdp) Martin County	63	43.45
Kingsbury (town) LaPorte County	19	8.44
New Paris (cdp) Elkhart County	76	5.80
Burket (town) Kosciusko County	5	2.69
Lagrange (town) LaGrange County	73	2.66
Hamlet (town) Starke County	21	2.54
Culver (town) Marshall County	31	2.15
Topeka (town) LaGrange County	24	1.91
North Liberty (town) St. Joseph County	26	1.66
Henryville (cdp) Clark County	36	1.64

Top 10 Places Sorted by Percent of Total Population
Based on places with total population of 50,000 or more

Place	Population	%
Elkhart (city) Elkhart County	347	0.67
South Bend (city) St. Joseph County	140	0.14
Fort Wayne (city) Allen County	255	0.10
Hammond (city) Lake County	76	0.09
Lafayette (city) Tippecanoe County	61	0.09
Bloomington (city) Monroe County	58	0.07
Carmel (city) Hamilton County	42	0.05
Indianapolis (city) Marion County	355	0.04
Fishers (town) Hamilton County	27	0.04
Evansville (city) Vanderburgh County	33	0.03

Polish

Top 10 Places Sorted by Population
Based on all places, regardless of total population

Place	Population	%
Indianapolis (city) Marion County	12,731	1.57
South Bend (city) St. Joseph County	10,370	10.16
Hammond (city) Lake County	7,497	9.22
Fort Wayne (city) Allen County	5,438	2.14
Schererville (town) Lake County	4,977	17.48
Mishawaka (city) St. Joseph County	4,612	9.63
Highland (town) Lake County	3,947	16.65
Munster (town) Lake County	3,822	16.44
Bloomington (city) Monroe County	3,792	4.83
Portage (city) Porter County	3,667	10.10

Top 10 Places Sorted by Percent of Total Population
Based on all places, regardless of total population

Place	Population	%
Lake Village (cdp) Newton County	171	25.83
Trail Creek (town) LaPorte County	376	19.02
Shorewood Forest (cdp) Porter County	537	17.81
Schererville (town) Lake County	4,977	17.48
St. John (town) Lake County	2,401	17.48
Lakes of the Four Seasons (cdp) Lake County	1,298	17.20
Highland (town) Lake County	3,947	16.65
Munster (town) Lake County	3,822	16.44
Dyer (town) Lake County	2,496	15.64
Whiting (city) Lake County	781	15.55

Top 10 Places Sorted by Percent of Total Population
Based on places with total population of 50,000 or more

Place	Population	%
South Bend (city) St. Joseph County	10,370	10.16
Hammond (city) Lake County	7,497	9.22
Bloomington (city) Monroe County	3,792	4.83
Carmel (city) Hamilton County	3,117	4.06
Fishers (town) Hamilton County	2,912	4.06
Lafayette (city) Tippecanoe County	1,900	2.87
Elkhart (city) Elkhart County	1,234	2.38
Fort Wayne (city) Allen County	5,438	2.14
Terre Haute (city) Vigo County	1,184	1.96
Muncie (city) Delaware County	1,148	1.64

Portuguese

Top 10 Places Sorted by Population
Based on all places, regardless of total population

Place	Population	%
Indianapolis (city) Marion County	414	0.05
Fort Wayne (city) Allen County	324	0.13
Fishers (town) Hamilton County	185	0.26
Granger (cdp) St. Joseph County	128	0.45
Carmel (city) Hamilton County	112	0.15
Lawrence (city) Marion County	108	0.24
Princeton (city) Gibson County	100	1.16
Evansville (city) Vanderburgh County	95	0.08
Plymouth (city) Marshall County	85	0.85
Greenwood (city) Johnson County	83	0.17

Top 10 Places Sorted by Percent of Total Population
Based on all places, regardless of total population

Place	Population	%
Kingsbury (town) LaPorte County	7	3.11
Rocky Ripple (town) Marion County	14	2.17
Leesburg (town) Kosciusko County	15	2.10

Place	Population	%
Kewanna (town) Fulton County	10	1.76
Orestes (town) Madison County	4	1.40
Princeton (city) Gibson County	100	1.16
Portland (city) Jay County	72	1.11
Plymouth (city) Marshall County	85	0.85
Ingalls (town) Madison County	14	0.74
Flora (town) Carroll County	13	0.61

Top 10 Places Sorted by Percent of Total Population
Based on places with total population of 50,000 or more

Place	Population	%
Fishers (town) Hamilton County	185	0.26
Carmel (city) Hamilton County	112	0.15
Fort Wayne (city) Allen County	324	0.13
Evansville (city) Vanderburgh County	95	0.08
Hammond (city) Lake County	64	0.08
Elkhart (city) Elkhart County	42	0.08
Bloomington (city) Monroe County	52	0.07
Indianapolis (city) Marion County	414	0.05
South Bend (city) St. Joseph County	54	0.05
Anderson (city) Madison County	26	0.05

Romanian

Top 10 Places Sorted by Population
Based on all places, regardless of total population

Place	Population	%
Indianapolis (city) Marion County	1,001	0.12
Fort Wayne (city) Allen County	387	0.15
Schererville (town) Lake County	368	1.29
Bloomington (city) Monroe County	270	0.34
Terre Haute (city) Vigo County	263	0.44
Portage (city) Porter County	233	0.64
Highland (town) Lake County	211	0.89
Carmel (city) Hamilton County	200	0.26
Columbus (city) Bartholomew County	176	0.41
Munster (town) Lake County	153	0.66

Top 10 Places Sorted by Percent of Total Population
Based on all places, regardless of total population

Place	Population	%
Moores Hill (town) Dearborn County	52	6.54
Avoca (cdp) Lawrence County	34	6.46
New Trenton (cdp) Franklin County	19	4.22
Medaryville (town) Pulaski County	19	3.82
Rosedale (town) Parke County	31	3.55
Eaton (town) Delaware County	66	3.50
Rolling Prairie (cdp) LaPorte County	10	2.38
Kouts (town) Porter County	27	1.47
Stilesville (town) Hendricks County	4	1.39
Beverly Shores (town) Porter County	9	1.33

Top 10 Places Sorted by Percent of Total Population
Based on places with total population of 50,000 or more

Place	Population	%
Terre Haute (city) Vigo County	263	0.44
Bloomington (city) Monroe County	270	0.34
Carmel (city) Hamilton County	200	0.26
Fort Wayne (city) Allen County	387	0.15
Fishers (town) Hamilton County	109	0.15
Indianapolis (city) Marion County	1,001	0.12
South Bend (city) St. Joseph County	88	0.09
Hammond (city) Lake County	77	0.09
Lafayette (city) Tippecanoe County	61	0.09
Muncie (city) Delaware County	59	0.08

Russian

Top 10 Places Sorted by Population
Based on all places, regardless of total population

Place	Population	%
Indianapolis (city) Marion County	3,280	0.41
Carmel (city) Hamilton County	1,522	1.98
Bloomington (city) Monroe County	1,268	1.62
Fort Wayne (city) Allen County	913	0.36
South Bend (city) St. Joseph County	730	0.72
West Lafayette (city) Tippecanoe County	545	1.86
Lafayette (city) Tippecanoe County	391	0.59
Evansville (city) Vanderburgh County	381	0.32
Portage (city) Porter County	364	1.00
Fishers (town) Hamilton County	350	0.49

Top 10 Places Sorted by Percent of Total Population
Based on all places, regardless of total population

Place	Population	%
La Paz (town) Marshall County	30	6.05
Orland (town) Steuben County	37	6.04
Brookville (town) Franklin County	155	5.78
Ulen (town) Boone County	7	4.90
Crane (town) Martin County	14	4.76
New Trenton (cdp) Franklin County	19	4.22
Shorewood Forest (cdp) Porter County	114	3.78
Russellville (town) Putnam County	11	3.77
Salt Creek Commons (cdp) Porter County	72	3.28
Beverly Shores (town) Porter County	22	3.25

Top 10 Places Sorted by Percent of Total Population
Based on places with total population of 50,000 or more

Place	Population	%
Carmel (city) Hamilton County	1,522	1.98
Bloomington (city) Monroe County	1,268	1.62
South Bend (city) St. Joseph County	730	0.72
Lafayette (city) Tippecanoe County	391	0.59
Fishers (town) Hamilton County	350	0.49
Terre Haute (city) Vigo County	256	0.42
Indianapolis (city) Marion County	3,280	0.41
Fort Wayne (city) Allen County	913	0.36
Hammond (city) Lake County	275	0.34
Evansville (city) Vanderburgh County	381	0.32

Scandinavian

Top 10 Places Sorted by Population
Based on all places, regardless of total population

Place	Population	%
Indianapolis (city) Marion County	1,199	0.15
Fort Wayne (city) Allen County	269	0.11
Columbus (city) Bartholomew County	229	0.53
Fishers (town) Hamilton County	183	0.26
Bloomington (city) Monroe County	161	0.21
South Bend (city) St. Joseph County	150	0.15
Carmel (city) Hamilton County	90	0.12
Dyer (town) Lake County	85	0.53
Noblesville (city) Hamilton County	83	0.17
Westfield (town) Hamilton County	82	0.30

Top 10 Places Sorted by Percent of Total Population
Based on all places, regardless of total population

Place	Population	%
Fulton (town) Fulton County	18	10.00
Argos (town) Marshall County	47	2.99
Leo-Cedarville (town) Allen County	67	1.93
Dayton (town) Tippecanoe County	18	1.88
Hudson (town) Steuben County	11	1.78
Oakland City (city) Gibson County	36	1.53
Carthage (town) Rush County	11	1.45
Beverly Shores (town) Porter County	8	1.18
Corydon (town) Harrison County	36	1.17
Dune Acres (town) Porter County	3	1.15

Top 10 Places Sorted by Percent of Total Population
Based on places with total population of 50,000 or more

Place	Population	%
Fishers (town) Hamilton County	183	0.26
Bloomington (city) Monroe County	161	0.21
Indianapolis (city) Marion County	1,199	0.15
South Bend (city) St. Joseph County	150	0.15
Anderson (city) Madison County	75	0.13
Carmel (city) Hamilton County	90	0.12
Elkhart (city) Elkhart County	60	0.12
Fort Wayne (city) Allen County	269	0.11
Hammond (city) Lake County	65	0.08
Terre Haute (city) Vigo County	50	0.08

Scotch-Irish

Top 10 Places Sorted by Population
Based on all places, regardless of total population

Place	Population	%
Indianapolis (city) Marion County	10,956	1.35
Fort Wayne (city) Allen County	3,125	1.23
Bloomington (city) Monroe County	2,163	2.76
Evansville (city) Vanderburgh County	1,964	1.66
Carmel (city) Hamilton County	1,430	1.86
Fishers (town) Hamilton County	1,293	1.80
Lafayette (city) Tippecanoe County	1,115	1.69
Columbus (city) Bartholomew County	1,110	2.56
South Bend (city) St. Joseph County	1,065	1.04
Muncie (city) Delaware County	930	1.33

Top 10 Places Sorted by Percent of Total Population
Based on all places, regardless of total population

Place	Population	%
Kent (cdp) Jefferson County	50	26.04
North Crows Nest (town) Marion County	7	16.67
Scipio (cdp) Jennings County	27	13.11
Straughn (town) Henry County	25	12.14
Cannelburg (town) Daviess County	15	10.34
Clarksburg (cdp) Decatur County	12	9.84
Freelandville (cdp) Knox County	40	9.78
Tri-Lakes (cdp) Whitley County	161	9.76
Hamlet (town) Starke County	80	9.66
Brooksburg (town) Jefferson County	7	8.14

Top 10 Places Sorted by Percent of Total Population
Based on places with total population of 50,000 or more

Place	Population	%
Bloomington (city) Monroe County	2,163	2.76
Carmel (city) Hamilton County	1,430	1.86
Fishers (town) Hamilton County	1,293	1.80
Lafayette (city) Tippecanoe County	1,115	1.69
Evansville (city) Vanderburgh County	1,964	1.66
Terre Haute (city) Vigo County	884	1.46
Anderson (city) Madison County	792	1.40
Indianapolis (city) Marion County	10,956	1.35
Muncie (city) Delaware County	930	1.33
Elkhart (city) Elkhart County	647	1.25

Scottish

Top 10 Places Sorted by Population
Based on all places, regardless of total population

Place	Population	%
Indianapolis (city) Marion County	14,050	1.73
Fort Wayne (city) Allen County	4,615	1.82
Carmel (city) Hamilton County	2,632	3.43
Bloomington (city) Monroe County	2,274	2.90
Fishers (town) Hamilton County	2,188	3.05
Evansville (city) Vanderburgh County	2,023	1.71
Lafayette (city) Tippecanoe County	1,572	2.38
Columbus (city) Bartholomew County	1,401	3.23
South Bend (city) St. Joseph County	1,319	1.29
Terre Haute (city) Vigo County	1,286	2.13

Top 10 Places Sorted by Percent of Total Population
Based on all places, regardless of total population

Place	Population	%
Collegeville (cdp) Jasper County	22	45.83
Colburn (cdp) Tippecanoe County	39	36.45
Shepardsville (cdp) Clinton County	11	17.74
Sulphur Springs (town) Henry County	42	14.38
Sims (cdp) Grant County	29	14.08
Kimmell (cdp) Noble County	47	13.31
Orestes (town) Madison County	33	11.54
Arlington (cdp) Rush County	41	10.85
Leesburg (town) Kosciusko County	72	10.07
Gaston (town) Delaware County	82	10.04

Top 10 Places Sorted by Percent of Total Population
Based on places with total population of 50,000 or more

Place	Population	%
Carmel (city) Hamilton County	2,632	3.43
Fishers (town) Hamilton County	2,188	3.05
Bloomington (city) Monroe County	2,274	2.90
Lafayette (city) Tippecanoe County	1,572	2.38
Terre Haute (city) Vigo County	1,286	2.13
Fort Wayne (city) Allen County	4,615	1.82
Muncie (city) Delaware County	1,264	1.81
Indianapolis (city) Marion County	14,050	1.73
Evansville (city) Vanderburgh County	2,023	1.71
Anderson (city) Madison County	861	1.52

Serbian

Top 10 Places Sorted by Population
Based on all places, regardless of total population

Place	Population	%
Munster (town) Lake County	984	4.23
Schererville (town) Lake County	859	3.02
Indianapolis (city) Marion County	777	0.10
Hobart (city) Lake County	614	2.16
Hammond (city) Lake County	572	0.70
St. John (town) Lake County	439	3.20
Valparaiso (city) Porter County	421	1.36
Crown Point (city) Lake County	337	1.29
Portage (city) Porter County	268	0.74
Highland (town) Lake County	259	1.09

Top 10 Places Sorted by Percent of Total Population
Based on all places, regardless of total population

Place	Population	%
Shorewood Forest (cdp) Porter County	139	4.61
Munster (town) Lake County	984	4.23
Reynolds (town) White County	20	3.29
St. John (town) Lake County	439	3.20
Pottawattamie Park (town) LaPorte County	6	3.03
Schererville (town) Lake County	859	3.02
Blanford (cdp) Vermillion County	10	2.88
North Crows Nest (town) Marion County	1	2.38
Hobart (city) Lake County	614	2.16
Whiting (city) Lake County	98	1.95

Top 10 Places Sorted by Percent of Total Population
Based on places with total population of 50,000 or more

Place	Population	%
Hammond (city) Lake County	572	0.70
Bloomington (city) Monroe County	155	0.20
South Bend (city) St. Joseph County	165	0.16
Terre Haute (city) Vigo County	66	0.11
Indianapolis (city) Marion County	777	0.10
Fishers (town) Hamilton County	47	0.07
Carmel (city) Hamilton County	40	0.05
Fort Wayne (city) Allen County	75	0.03
Muncie (city) Delaware County	15	0.02
Anderson (city) Madison County	12	0.02

Slavic

Top 10 Places Sorted by Population
Based on all places, regardless of total population

Place	Population	%
Indianapolis (city) Marion County	455	0.06
Zionsville (town) Boone County	119	0.89
Fort Wayne (city) Allen County	92	0.04
Valparaiso (city) Porter County	82	0.26
Schererville (town) Lake County	67	0.24
Shorewood Forest (cdp) Porter County	62	2.06
Fishers (town) Hamilton County	50	0.07
Chesterton (town) Porter County	42	0.32
Portage (city) Porter County	42	0.12
Highland (town) Lake County	40	0.17

Top 10 Places Sorted by Percent of Total Population
Based on all places, regardless of total population

Place	Population	%
Long Beach (town) LaPorte County	32	2.19
Shorewood Forest (cdp) Porter County	62	2.06
Rocky Ripple (town) Marion County	8	1.24
Dayton (town) Tippecanoe County	11	1.15
Zionsville (town) Boone County	119	0.89
Hebron (town) Porter County	29	0.83
Lagrange (town) LaGrange County	22	0.80
Remington (town) Jasper County	10	0.78
Scottsburg (city) Scott County	38	0.57
Ogden Dunes (town) Porter County	6	0.49

Top 10 Places Sorted by Percent of Total Population
Based on places with total population of 50,000 or more

Place	Population	%
Fishers (town) Hamilton County	50	0.07
Indianapolis (city) Marion County	455	0.06
Terre Haute (city) Vigo County	32	0.05
Fort Wayne (city) Allen County	92	0.04

Place	Population	%
Lafayette (city) Tippecanoe County	27	0.04
Bloomington (city) Monroe County	23	0.03
Hammond (city) Lake County	22	0.03
Muncie (city) Delaware County	22	0.03
Anderson (city) Madison County	13	0.02
Gary (city) Lake County	12	0.01

Slovak

Top 10 Places Sorted by Population
Based on all places, regardless of total population

Place	Population	%
Hammond (city) Lake County	1,791	2.20
Indianapolis (city) Marion County	1,058	0.13
Schererville (town) Lake County	1,051	3.69
Highland (town) Lake County	896	3.78
Munster (town) Lake County	814	3.50
Portage (city) Porter County	766	2.11
Hobart (city) Lake County	689	2.43
Whiting (city) Lake County	584	11.63
Merrillville (town) Lake County	576	1.67
Valparaiso (city) Porter County	530	1.71

Top 10 Places Sorted by Percent of Total Population
Based on all places, regardless of total population

Place	Population	%
Whiting (city) Lake County	584	11.63
Mexico (cdp) Miami County	66	9.43
Alton (town) Crawford County	6	7.06
Hebron (town) Porter County	174	4.96
Highland (town) Lake County	896	3.78
Schererville (town) Lake County	1,051	3.69
Ogden Dunes (town) Porter County	45	3.67
Munster (town) Lake County	814	3.50
St. John (town) Lake County	425	3.09
Pottawattamie Park (town) LaPorte County	6	3.03

Top 10 Places Sorted by Percent of Total Population
Based on places with total population of 50,000 or more

Place	Population	%
Hammond (city) Lake County	1,791	2.20
Carmel (city) Hamilton County	356	0.46
Gary (city) Lake County	209	0.25
Bloomington (city) Monroe County	194	0.25
Fort Wayne (city) Allen County	468	0.18
Muncie (city) Delaware County	118	0.17
Indianapolis (city) Marion County	1,058	0.13
Evansville (city) Vanderburgh County	157	0.13
South Bend (city) St. Joseph County	131	0.13
Terre Haute (city) Vigo County	60	0.10

Slovene

Top 10 Places Sorted by Population
Based on all places, regardless of total population

Place	Population	%
Indianapolis (city) Marion County	497	0.06
Portage (city) Porter County	218	0.60
Carmel (city) Hamilton County	109	0.14
Westfield (town) Hamilton County	84	0.30
Greenwood (city) Johnson County	75	0.16
Bloomington (city) Monroe County	65	0.08
Dyer (town) Lake County	64	0.40
Granger (cdp) St. Joseph County	59	0.21
Fishers (town) Hamilton County	54	0.08
Munster (town) Lake County	51	0.22

Top 10 Places Sorted by Percent of Total Population
Based on all places, regardless of total population

Place	Population	%
Clermont (town) Marion County	34	2.47
Dune Acres (town) Porter County	3	1.15
Indian Village (town) St. Joseph County	1	1.02
Westville (town) LaPorte County	42	0.74
Porter (town) Porter County	36	0.73
Portage (city) Porter County	218	0.60
Columbia City (city) Whitley County	46	0.56
Lakes of the Four Seasons (cdp) Lake County	40	0.53
Dyer (town) Lake County	64	0.40
Ogden Dunes (town) Porter County	4	0.33

Top 10 Places Sorted by Percent of Total Population
Based on places with total population of 50,000 or more

Place	Population	%
Carmel (city) Hamilton County	109	0.14
Bloomington (city) Monroe County	65	0.08
Fishers (town) Hamilton County	54	0.08
Indianapolis (city) Marion County	497	0.06
Elkhart (city) Elkhart County	18	0.03
Terre Haute (city) Vigo County	16	0.03
Anderson (city) Madison County	9	0.02
Fort Wayne (city) Allen County	37	0.01
South Bend (city) St. Joseph County	9	0.01
Evansville (city) Vanderburgh County	0	0.00

Soviet Union

Top 10 Places Sorted by Population
Based on all places, regardless of total population

Place	Population	%
Aberdeen (cdp) Porter County	0	0.00
Advance (town) Boone County	0	0.00
Akron (town) Fulton County	0	0.00
Alamo (town) Montgomery County	0	0.00
Albany (town) Delaware County	0	0.00
Albion (town) Noble County	0	0.00
Alexandria (city) Madison County	0	0.00
Alfordsville (town) Daviess County	0	0.00
Alton (town) Crawford County	0	0.00
Altona (town) DeKalb County	0	0.00

Top 10 Places Sorted by Percent of Total Population
Based on all places, regardless of total population

Place	Population	%
Aberdeen (cdp) Porter County	0	0.00
Advance (town) Boone County	0	0.00
Akron (town) Fulton County	0	0.00
Alamo (town) Montgomery County	0	0.00
Albany (town) Delaware County	0	0.00
Albion (town) Noble County	0	0.00
Alexandria (city) Madison County	0	0.00
Alfordsville (town) Daviess County	0	0.00
Alton (town) Crawford County	0	0.00
Altona (town) DeKalb County	0	0.00

Top 10 Places Sorted by Percent of Total Population
Based on places with total population of 50,000 or more

Place	Population	%
Anderson (city) Madison County	0	0.00
Bloomington (city) Monroe County	0	0.00
Carmel (city) Hamilton County	0	0.00
Elkhart (city) Elkhart County	0	0.00
Evansville (city) Vanderburgh County	0	0.00
Fishers (town) Hamilton County	0	0.00
Fort Wayne (city) Allen County	0	0.00
Gary (city) Lake County	0	0.00
Hammond (city) Lake County	0	0.00
Indianapolis (city) Marion County	0	0.00

Swedish

Top 10 Places Sorted by Population
Based on all places, regardless of total population

Place	Population	%
Indianapolis (city) Marion County	5,593	0.69
Fort Wayne (city) Allen County	1,940	0.76
South Bend (city) St. Joseph County	1,638	1.60
Bloomington (city) Monroe County	1,462	1.86
Carmel (city) Hamilton County	1,414	1.84
Fishers (town) Hamilton County	1,288	1.80
Mishawaka (city) St. Joseph County	1,045	2.18
Hammond (city) Lake County	1,016	1.25
Valparaiso (city) Porter County	906	2.92
Portage (city) Porter County	786	2.17

Top 10 Places Sorted by Percent of Total Population
Based on all places, regardless of total population

Place	Population	%
Point Isabel (cdp) Grant County	9	16.67
State Line City (town) Warren County	17	13.93
Spring Lake (town) Hancock County	35	11.82

Place	Population	%
Shelby (cdp) Lake County	36	9.89
Fish Lake (cdp) LaPorte County	68	7.60
Spring Hill (town) Marion County	6	7.14
Winfield (town) Lake County	258	6.52
Koontz Lake (cdp) Starke County	99	6.10
New Carlisle (town) St. Joseph County	102	5.54
Morocco (town) Newton County	48	5.47

Top 10 Places Sorted by Percent of Total Population
Based on places with total population of 50,000 or more

Place	Population	%
Bloomington (city) Monroe County	1,462	1.86
Carmel (city) Hamilton County	1,414	1.84
Fishers (town) Hamilton County	1,288	1.80
South Bend (city) St. Joseph County	1,638	1.60
Hammond (city) Lake County	1,016	1.25
Lafayette (city) Tippecanoe County	556	0.84
Elkhart (city) Elkhart County	422	0.81
Terre Haute (city) Vigo County	475	0.79
Fort Wayne (city) Allen County	1,940	0.76
Muncie (city) Delaware County	494	0.71

Swiss

Top 10 Places Sorted by Population
Based on all places, regardless of total population

Place	Population	%
Fort Wayne (city) Allen County	2,499	0.98
Indianapolis (city) Marion County	2,276	0.28
Goshen (city) Elkhart County	1,482	4.74
Berne (city) Adams County	1,005	24.67
Fishers (town) Hamilton County	576	0.80
Bluffton (city) Wells County	526	5.52
Elkhart (city) Elkhart County	504	0.97
Bloomington (city) Monroe County	457	0.58
Carmel (city) Hamilton County	431	0.56
South Bend (city) St. Joseph County	343	0.34

Top 10 Places Sorted by Percent of Total Population
Based on all places, regardless of total population

Place	Population	%
Berne (city) Adams County	1,005	24.67
Bryant (town) Jay County	46	15.33
Monroe (town) Adams County	137	15.02
Wakarusa (town) Elkhart County	162	8.86
Vera Cruz (town) Wells County	14	7.73
Geneva (town) Adams County	86	7.00
Waterloo (town) DeKalb County	127	5.82
Bluffton (city) Wells County	526	5.52
Topeka (town) LaGrange County	68	5.41
Shipshewana (town) LaGrange County	32	5.36

Top 10 Places Sorted by Percent of Total Population
Based on places with total population of 50,000 or more

Place	Population	%
Fort Wayne (city) Allen County	2,499	0.98
Elkhart (city) Elkhart County	504	0.97
Fishers (town) Hamilton County	576	0.80
Bloomington (city) Monroe County	457	0.58
Carmel (city) Hamilton County	431	0.56
Muncie (city) Delaware County	326	0.47
Lafayette (city) Tippecanoe County	302	0.46
South Bend (city) St. Joseph County	343	0.34
Indianapolis (city) Marion County	2,276	0.28
Terre Haute (city) Vigo County	165	0.27

Turkish

Top 10 Places Sorted by Population
Based on all places, regardless of total population

Place	Population	%
Indianapolis (city) Marion County	243	0.03
Bloomington (city) Monroe County	111	0.14
South Bend (city) St. Joseph County	104	0.10
West Lafayette (city) Tippecanoe County	99	0.34
Elwood (city) Madison County	73	0.82
Carmel (city) Hamilton County	69	0.09
Noblesville (city) Hamilton County	52	0.11
Lafayette (city) Tippecanoe County	49	0.07
Fort Wayne (city) Allen County	46	0.02
Franklin (city) Johnson County	36	0.16

Top 10 Places Sorted by Percent of Total Population
Based on all places, regardless of total population

Place	Population	%
Universal (town) Vermillion County	13	3.40
Idaville (cdp) White County	9	1.77
Harmony (town) Clay County	11	1.73
Elwood (city) Madison County	73	0.82
Roseland (town) St. Joseph County	8	0.67
Fillmore (town) Putnam County	3	0.67
Dana (town) Vermillion County	3	0.59
West Lafayette (city) Tippecanoe County	99	0.34
Jasonville (city) Greene County	7	0.30
Meridian Hills (town) Marion County	3	0.18

Top 10 Places Sorted by Percent of Total Population
Based on places with total population of 50,000 or more

Place	Population	%
Bloomington (city) Monroe County	111	0.14
South Bend (city) St. Joseph County	104	0.10
Carmel (city) Hamilton County	69	0.09
Lafayette (city) Tippecanoe County	49	0.07
Anderson (city) Madison County	33	0.06
Muncie (city) Delaware County	34	0.05
Terre Haute (city) Vigo County	23	0.04
Indianapolis (city) Marion County	243	0.03
Fort Wayne (city) Allen County	46	0.02
Evansville (city) Vanderburgh County	25	0.02

Ukrainian

Top 10 Places Sorted by Population
Based on all places, regardless of total population

Place	Population	%
Indianapolis (city) Marion County	792	0.10
Noblesville (city) Hamilton County	436	0.90
Fort Wayne (city) Allen County	293	0.12
Carmel (city) Hamilton County	271	0.35
Hammond (city) Lake County	244	0.30
Bloomington (city) Monroe County	232	0.30
South Bend (city) St. Joseph County	214	0.21
Hobart (city) Lake County	157	0.55
Highland (town) Lake County	155	0.65
Portage (city) Porter County	145	0.40

Top 10 Places Sorted by Percent of Total Population
Based on all places, regardless of total population

Place	Population	%
Darlington (town) Montgomery County	29	3.36
Kingman (town) Fountain County	20	3.32
Bourbon (town) Marshall County	41	2.28
New Paris (cdp) Elkhart County	28	2.14
Melody Hill (cdp) Vanderburgh County	73	2.11
Lake Santee (cdp) Decatur County	11	1.72
Shelby (cdp) Lake County	6	1.65
Milford (town) Kosciusko County	25	1.59
Dunlap (cdp) Elkhart County	91	1.57
Otwell (cdp) Pike County	10	1.47

Top 10 Places Sorted by Percent of Total Population
Based on places with total population of 50,000 or more

Place	Population	%
Carmel (city) Hamilton County	271	0.35
Hammond (city) Lake County	244	0.30
Bloomington (city) Monroe County	232	0.30
South Bend (city) St. Joseph County	214	0.21
Fishers (town) Hamilton County	97	0.14
Lafayette (city) Tippecanoe County	94	0.14
Fort Wayne (city) Allen County	293	0.12
Evansville (city) Vanderburgh County	129	0.11
Indianapolis (city) Marion County	792	0.10
Elkhart (city) Elkhart County	39	0.08

Welsh

Top 10 Places Sorted by Population
Based on all places, regardless of total population

Place	Population	%
Indianapolis (city) Marion County	4,603	0.57
Fort Wayne (city) Allen County	1,388	0.55
Fishers (town) Hamilton County	930	1.30
Bloomington (city) Monroe County	840	1.07
Carmel (city) Hamilton County	628	0.82
Terre Haute (city) Vigo County	591	0.98
Muncie (city) Delaware County	511	0.73
Noblesville (city) Hamilton County	497	1.02
Lawrence (city) Marion County	454	1.02
Greenwood (city) Johnson County	412	0.87

Top 10 Places Sorted by Percent of Total Population
Based on all places, regardless of total population

Place	Population	%
Saratoga (town) Randolph County	31	16.49
Ragsdale (cdp) Knox County	16	14.41
Newport (town) Vermillion County	39	10.18
Jalapa (cdp) Grant County	16	8.08
Pennville (town) Jay County	58	7.86
Westphalia (cdp) Knox County	10	6.99
Fowlerton (town) Grant County	18	6.84
Pottawattamie Park (town) LaPorte County	11	5.56
Chrisney (town) Spencer County	32	5.09
Dublin (town) Wayne County	29	5.04

Top 10 Places Sorted by Percent of Total Population
Based on places with total population of 50,000 or more

Place	Population	%
Fishers (town) Hamilton County	930	1.30
Bloomington (city) Monroe County	840	1.07
Terre Haute (city) Vigo County	591	0.98
Carmel (city) Hamilton County	628	0.82
Muncie (city) Delaware County	511	0.73
Anderson (city) Madison County	399	0.70
Indianapolis (city) Marion County	4,603	0.57
Fort Wayne (city) Allen County	1,388	0.55
Lafayette (city) Tippecanoe County	360	0.54
Elkhart (city) Elkhart County	213	0.41

West Indian, excluding Hispanic

Top 10 Places Sorted by Population
Based on all places, regardless of total population

Place	Population	%
Indianapolis (city) Marion County	1,846	0.23
Fort Wayne (city) Allen County	665	0.26
Gary (city) Lake County	265	0.31
Cumberland (town) Marion County	175	3.03
East Chicago (city) Lake County	146	0.48
Hammond (city) Lake County	135	0.17
Elkhart (city) Elkhart County	121	0.23
South Bend (city) St. Joseph County	117	0.11
Bloomington (city) Monroe County	96	0.12
French Lick (town) Orange County	84	4.37

Top 10 Places Sorted by Percent of Total Population
Based on all places, regardless of total population

Place	Population	%
French Lick (town) Orange County	84	4.37
Oolitic (town) Lawrence County	47	3.45
Cumberland (town) Marion County	175	3.03
Ligonier (city) Noble County	75	1.75
Tri-Lakes (cdp) Whitley County	28	1.70
Avon (town) Hendricks County	77	0.66
Utica (town) Clark County	5	0.56
Washington (city) Daviess County	63	0.55
Newburgh (town) Warrick County	18	0.55
Green (town) Howard County	11	0.55

Top 10 Places Sorted by Percent of Total Population
Based on places with total population of 50,000 or more

Place	Population	%
Gary (city) Lake County	265	0.31
Fort Wayne (city) Allen County	665	0.26
Indianapolis (city) Marion County	1,846	0.23
Elkhart (city) Elkhart County	121	0.23
Hammond (city) Lake County	135	0.17
Bloomington (city) Monroe County	96	0.12
South Bend (city) St. Joseph County	117	0.11
Anderson (city) Madison County	56	0.10
Fishers (town) Hamilton County	58	0.08
Carmel (city) Hamilton County	55	0.07

Please refer to the Explanation of Data in the front of the book for more detailed information.

West Indian: Bahamian, excluding Hispanic

Top 10 Places Sorted by Population
Based on all places, regardless of total population

Place	Population	%
Vincennes (city) Knox County	34	0.19
Newburgh (town) Warrick County	18	0.55
Crown Point (city) Lake County	14	0.05
Purdue University (cdp) Tippecanoe County	13	0.10
South Bend (city) St. Joseph County	9	0.01
Indianapolis (city) Marion County	8	<0.01
Aberdeen (cdp) Porter County	0	0.00
Advance (town) Boone County	0	0.00
Akron (town) Fulton County	0	0.00
Alamo (town) Montgomery County	0	0.00

Top 10 Places Sorted by Percent of Total Population
Based on all places, regardless of total population

Place	Population	%
Newburgh (town) Warrick County	18	0.55
Vincennes (city) Knox County	34	0.19
Purdue University (cdp) Tippecanoe County	13	0.10
Crown Point (city) Lake County	14	0.05
South Bend (city) St. Joseph County	9	0.01
Indianapolis (city) Marion County	8	<0.01
Aberdeen (cdp) Porter County	0	0.00
Advance (town) Boone County	0	0.00
Akron (town) Fulton County	0	0.00
Alamo (town) Montgomery County	0	0.00

Top 10 Places Sorted by Percent of Total Population
Based on places with total population of 50,000 or more

Place	Population	%
South Bend (city) St. Joseph County	9	0.01
Indianapolis (city) Marion County	8	<0.01
Anderson (city) Madison County	0	0.00
Bloomington (city) Monroe County	0	0.00
Carmel (city) Hamilton County	0	0.00
Elkhart (city) Elkhart County	0	0.00
Evansville (city) Vanderburgh County	0	0.00
Fishers (town) Hamilton County	0	0.00
Fort Wayne (city) Allen County	0	0.00
Gary (city) Lake County	0	0.00

West Indian: Barbadian, excluding Hispanic

Top 10 Places Sorted by Population
Based on all places, regardless of total population

Place	Population	%
Indianapolis (city) Marion County	55	0.01
Muncie (city) Delaware County	28	0.04
Tri-Lakes (cdp) Whitley County	14	0.85
Aberdeen (cdp) Porter County	0	0.00
Advance (town) Boone County	0	0.00
Akron (town) Fulton County	0	0.00
Alamo (town) Montgomery County	0	0.00
Albany (town) Delaware County	0	0.00
Albion (town) Noble County	0	0.00
Alexandria (city) Madison County	0	0.00

Top 10 Places Sorted by Percent of Total Population
Based on all places, regardless of total population

Place	Population	%
Tri-Lakes (cdp) Whitley County	14	0.85
Muncie (city) Delaware County	28	0.04
Indianapolis (city) Marion County	55	0.01
Aberdeen (cdp) Porter County	0	0.00
Advance (town) Boone County	0	0.00
Akron (town) Fulton County	0	0.00
Alamo (town) Montgomery County	0	0.00
Albany (town) Delaware County	0	0.00
Albion (town) Noble County	0	0.00
Alexandria (city) Madison County	0	0.00

Top 10 Places Sorted by Percent of Total Population
Based on places with total population of 50,000 or more

Place	Population	%
Muncie (city) Delaware County	28	0.04
Indianapolis (city) Marion County	55	0.01
Anderson (city) Madison County	0	0.00
Bloomington (city) Monroe County	0	0.00
Carmel (city) Hamilton County	0	0.00
Elkhart (city) Elkhart County	0	0.00
Evansville (city) Vanderburgh County	0	0.00
Fishers (town) Hamilton County	0	0.00
Fort Wayne (city) Allen County	0	0.00
Gary (city) Lake County	0	0.00

West Indian: Belizean, excluding Hispanic

Top 10 Places Sorted by Population
Based on all places, regardless of total population

Place	Population	%
Indianapolis (city) Marion County	51	0.01
Munster (town) Lake County	31	0.13
Westfield (town) Hamilton County	31	0.11
Lawrence (city) Marion County	25	0.06
Aberdeen (cdp) Porter County	0	0.00
Advance (town) Boone County	0	0.00
Akron (town) Fulton County	0	0.00
Alamo (town) Montgomery County	0	0.00
Albany (town) Delaware County	0	0.00
Albion (town) Noble County	0	0.00

Top 10 Places Sorted by Percent of Total Population
Based on all places, regardless of total population

Place	Population	%
Munster (town) Lake County	31	0.13
Westfield (town) Hamilton County	31	0.11
Lawrence (city) Marion County	25	0.06
Indianapolis (city) Marion County	51	0.01
Aberdeen (cdp) Porter County	0	0.00
Advance (town) Boone County	0	0.00
Akron (town) Fulton County	0	0.00
Alamo (town) Montgomery County	0	0.00
Albany (town) Delaware County	0	0.00
Albion (town) Noble County	0	0.00

Top 10 Places Sorted by Percent of Total Population
Based on places with total population of 50,000 or more

Place	Population	%
Indianapolis (city) Marion County	51	0.01
Anderson (city) Madison County	0	0.00
Bloomington (city) Monroe County	0	0.00
Carmel (city) Hamilton County	0	0.00
Elkhart (city) Elkhart County	0	0.00
Evansville (city) Vanderburgh County	0	0.00
Fishers (town) Hamilton County	0	0.00
Fort Wayne (city) Allen County	0	0.00
Gary (city) Lake County	0	0.00
Hammond (city) Lake County	0	0.00

West Indian: Bermudan, excluding Hispanic

Top 10 Places Sorted by Population
Based on all places, regardless of total population

Place	Population	%
Noblesville (city) Hamilton County	19	0.04
Michigan City (city) LaPorte County	9	0.03
Aberdeen (cdp) Porter County	0	0.00
Advance (town) Boone County	0	0.00
Akron (town) Fulton County	0	0.00
Alamo (town) Montgomery County	0	0.00
Albany (town) Delaware County	0	0.00
Albion (town) Noble County	0	0.00
Alexandria (city) Madison County	0	0.00
Alfordsville (town) Daviess County	0	0.00

Top 10 Places Sorted by Percent of Total Population
Based on all places, regardless of total population

Place	Population	%
Noblesville (city) Hamilton County	19	0.04
Michigan City (city) LaPorte County	9	0.03
Aberdeen (cdp) Porter County	0	0.00
Advance (town) Boone County	0	0.00
Akron (town) Fulton County	0	0.00
Alamo (town) Montgomery County	0	0.00
Albany (town) Delaware County	0	0.00

Top 10 Places Sorted by Percent of Total Population
Based on places with total population of 50,000 or more

Place	Population	%
Albion (town) Noble County	0	0.00
Alexandria (city) Madison County	0	0.00
Alfordsville (town) Daviess County	0	0.00

Top 10 Places Sorted by Percent of Total Population
Based on places with total population of 50,000 or more

Place	Population	%
Anderson (city) Madison County	0	0.00
Bloomington (city) Monroe County	0	0.00
Carmel (city) Hamilton County	0	0.00
Elkhart (city) Elkhart County	0	0.00
Evansville (city) Vanderburgh County	0	0.00
Fishers (town) Hamilton County	0	0.00
Fort Wayne (city) Allen County	0	0.00
Gary (city) Lake County	0	0.00
Hammond (city) Lake County	0	0.00
Indianapolis (city) Marion County	0	0.00

West Indian: British West Indian, excluding Hispanic

Top 10 Places Sorted by Population
Based on all places, regardless of total population

Place	Population	%
Avon (town) Hendricks County	77	0.66
Fort Wayne (city) Allen County	74	0.03
East Chicago (city) Lake County	64	0.21
South Bend (city) St. Joseph County	15	0.01
Fishers (town) Hamilton County	13	0.02
Indianapolis (city) Marion County	13	<0.01
Kokomo (city) Howard County	10	0.02
Purdue University (cdp) Tippecanoe County	8	0.06
Aberdeen (cdp) Porter County	0	0.00
Advance (town) Boone County	0	0.00

Top 10 Places Sorted by Percent of Total Population
Based on all places, regardless of total population

Place	Population	%
Avon (town) Hendricks County	77	0.66
East Chicago (city) Lake County	64	0.21
Purdue University (cdp) Tippecanoe County	8	0.06
Fort Wayne (city) Allen County	74	0.03
Fishers (town) Hamilton County	13	0.02
Kokomo (city) Howard County	10	0.02
South Bend (city) St. Joseph County	15	0.01
Indianapolis (city) Marion County	13	<0.01
Aberdeen (cdp) Porter County	0	0.00
Advance (town) Boone County	0	0.00

Top 10 Places Sorted by Percent of Total Population
Based on places with total population of 50,000 or more

Place	Population	%
Fort Wayne (city) Allen County	74	0.03
Fishers (town) Hamilton County	13	0.02
South Bend (city) St. Joseph County	15	0.01
Indianapolis (city) Marion County	13	<0.01
Anderson (city) Madison County	0	0.00
Bloomington (city) Monroe County	0	0.00
Carmel (city) Hamilton County	0	0.00
Elkhart (city) Elkhart County	0	0.00
Evansville (city) Vanderburgh County	0	0.00
Gary (city) Lake County	0	0.00

West Indian: Dutch West Indian, excluding Hispanic

Top 10 Places Sorted by Population
Based on all places, regardless of total population

Place	Population	%
Oolitic (town) Lawrence County	47	3.45
Indianapolis (city) Marion County	38	<0.01
Bloomington (city) Monroe County	23	0.03
Marion (city) Grant County	19	0.06
Lebanon (city) Boone County	14	0.09
Attica (city) Fountain County	13	0.40
Bedford (city) Lawrence County	11	0.08
Connersville (city) Fayette County	11	0.08
New Castle (city) Henry County	11	0.06
South Bend (city) St. Joseph County	11	0.01

Please refer to the Explanation of Data in the front of the book for more detailed information.

Ancestry and Ethnicity: Ancestry Group Rankings

Top 10 Places Sorted by Percent of Total Population
Based on all places, regardless of total population

Place	Population	%
Oolitic (town) Lawrence County	47	3.45
Burns Harbor (town) Porter County	6	0.48
Attica (city) Fountain County	13	0.40
West Terre Haute (town) Vigo County	5	0.27
Lebanon (city) Boone County	14	0.09
Bedford (city) Lawrence County	11	0.08
Connersville (city) Fayette County	11	0.08
Marion (city) Grant County	19	0.06
New Castle (city) Henry County	11	0.06
Bloomington (city) Monroe County	23	0.03

Top 10 Places Sorted by Percent of Total Population
Based on places with total population of 50,000 or more

Place	Population	%
Bloomington (city) Monroe County	23	0.03
South Bend (city) St. Joseph County	11	0.01
Lafayette (city) Tippecanoe County	8	0.01
Indianapolis (city) Marion County	38	<0.01
Anderson (city) Madison County	0	0.00
Carmel (city) Hamilton County	0	0.00
Elkhart (city) Elkhart County	0	0.00
Evansville (city) Vanderburgh County	0	0.00
Fishers (town) Hamilton County	0	0.00
Fort Wayne (city) Allen County	0	0.00

West Indian: Haitian, excluding Hispanic

Top 10 Places Sorted by Population
Based on all places, regardless of total population

Place	Population	%
Indianapolis (city) Marion County	635	0.08
Fort Wayne (city) Allen County	377	0.15
Cumberland (town) Marion County	175	3.03
Hammond (city) Lake County	86	0.11
Jeffersonville (city) Clark County	32	0.08
Terre Haute (city) Vigo County	27	0.04
Bremen (town) Marshall County	16	0.35
Carmel (city) Hamilton County	16	0.02
La Porte (city) LaPorte County	15	0.07
Goshen (city) Elkhart County	14	0.04

Top 10 Places Sorted by Percent of Total Population
Based on all places, regardless of total population

Place	Population	%
Cumberland (town) Marion County	175	3.03
Bremen (town) Marshall County	16	0.35
North Manchester (town) Wabash County	10	0.17
Fort Wayne (city) Allen County	377	0.15
Hammond (city) Lake County	86	0.11
Indianapolis (city) Marion County	635	0.08
Jeffersonville (city) Clark County	32	0.08
La Porte (city) LaPorte County	15	0.07
Purdue University (cdp) Tippecanoe County	7	0.05
Terre Haute (city) Vigo County	27	0.04

Top 10 Places Sorted by Percent of Total Population
Based on places with total population of 50,000 or more

Place	Population	%
Fort Wayne (city) Allen County	377	0.15
Hammond (city) Lake County	86	0.11
Indianapolis (city) Marion County	635	0.08
Terre Haute (city) Vigo County	27	0.04
Carmel (city) Hamilton County	16	0.02
Gary (city) Lake County	14	0.02
Lafayette (city) Tippecanoe County	10	0.02
Evansville (city) Vanderburgh County	11	0.01
Anderson (city) Madison County	0	0.00
Bloomington (city) Monroe County	0	0.00

West Indian: Jamaican, excluding Hispanic

Top 10 Places Sorted by Population
Based on all places, regardless of total population

Place	Population	%
Indianapolis (city) Marion County	589	0.07
Fort Wayne (city) Allen County	196	0.08
Gary (city) Lake County	192	0.23
Elkhart (city) Elkhart County	121	0.23
French Lick (town) Orange County	84	4.37
Granger (cdp) St. Joseph County	79	0.28
Ligonier (city) Noble County	75	1.75
Washington (city) Daviess County	63	0.55
Bloomington (city) Monroe County	57	0.07
Hammond (city) Lake County	49	0.06

Top 10 Places Sorted by Percent of Total Population
Based on all places, regardless of total population

Place	Population	%
French Lick (town) Orange County	84	4.37
Ligonier (city) Noble County	75	1.75
Utica (town) Clark County	5	0.56
Washington (city) Daviess County	63	0.55
Green (town) Howard County	11	0.55
Jasper (city) Dubois County	47	0.32
Granger (cdp) St. Joseph County	79	0.28
Gary (city) Lake County	192	0.23
Elkhart (city) Elkhart County	121	0.23
Purdue University (cdp) Tippecanoe County	27	0.21

Top 10 Places Sorted by Percent of Total Population
Based on places with total population of 50,000 or more

Place	Population	%
Gary (city) Lake County	192	0.23
Elkhart (city) Elkhart County	121	0.23
Fort Wayne (city) Allen County	196	0.08
Indianapolis (city) Marion County	589	0.07
Bloomington (city) Monroe County	57	0.07
Hammond (city) Lake County	49	0.06
Fishers (town) Hamilton County	45	0.06
Carmel (city) Hamilton County	39	0.05
Anderson (city) Madison County	29	0.05
Evansville (city) Vanderburgh County	44	0.04

West Indian: Trinidadian and Tobagonian, excluding Hispanic

Top 10 Places Sorted by Population
Based on all places, regardless of total population

Place	Population	%
Indianapolis (city) Marion County	110	0.01
South Bend (city) St. Joseph County	39	0.04
East Chicago (city) Lake County	18	0.06
Notre Dame (cdp) St. Joseph County	13	0.17
Portage (city) Porter County	13	0.04
West Lafayette (city) Tippecanoe County	13	0.04
Noblesville (city) Hamilton County	13	0.03
Aberdeen (cdp) Porter County	0	0.00
Advance (town) Boone County	0	0.00
Akron (town) Fulton County	0	0.00

Top 10 Places Sorted by Percent of Total Population
Based on all places, regardless of total population

Place	Population	%
Notre Dame (cdp) St. Joseph County	13	0.17
East Chicago (city) Lake County	18	0.06
South Bend (city) St. Joseph County	39	0.04
Portage (city) Porter County	13	0.04
West Lafayette (city) Tippecanoe County	13	0.04
Noblesville (city) Hamilton County	13	0.03
Indianapolis (city) Marion County	110	0.01
Aberdeen (cdp) Porter County	0	0.00
Advance (town) Boone County	0	0.00
Akron (town) Fulton County	0	0.00

Top 10 Places Sorted by Percent of Total Population
Based on places with total population of 50,000 or more

Place	Population	%
South Bend (city) St. Joseph County	39	0.04
Indianapolis (city) Marion County	110	0.01
Anderson (city) Madison County	0	0.00
Bloomington (city) Monroe County	0	0.00
Carmel (city) Hamilton County	0	0.00
Elkhart (city) Elkhart County	0	0.00
Evansville (city) Vanderburgh County	0	0.00
Fishers (town) Hamilton County	0	0.00
Fort Wayne (city) Allen County	0	0.00
Gary (city) Lake County	0	0.00

West Indian: U.S. Virgin Islander, excluding Hispanic

Top 10 Places Sorted by Population
Based on all places, regardless of total population

Place	Population	%
Lafayette (city) Tippecanoe County	8	0.01
Aberdeen (cdp) Porter County	0	0.00
Advance (town) Boone County	0	0.00
Akron (town) Fulton County	0	0.00
Alamo (town) Montgomery County	0	0.00
Albany (town) Delaware County	0	0.00
Albion (town) Noble County	0	0.00
Alexandria (city) Madison County	0	0.00
Alfordsville (town) Daviess County	0	0.00
Alton (town) Crawford County	0	0.00

Top 10 Places Sorted by Percent of Total Population
Based on all places, regardless of total population

Place	Population	%
Lafayette (city) Tippecanoe County	8	0.01
Aberdeen (cdp) Porter County	0	0.00
Advance (town) Boone County	0	0.00
Akron (town) Fulton County	0	0.00
Alamo (town) Montgomery County	0	0.00
Albany (town) Delaware County	0	0.00
Albion (town) Noble County	0	0.00
Alexandria (city) Madison County	0	0.00
Alfordsville (town) Daviess County	0	0.00
Alton (town) Crawford County	0	0.00

Top 10 Places Sorted by Percent of Total Population
Based on places with total population of 50,000 or more

Place	Population	%
Lafayette (city) Tippecanoe County	8	0.01
Anderson (city) Madison County	0	0.00
Bloomington (city) Monroe County	0	0.00
Carmel (city) Hamilton County	0	0.00
Elkhart (city) Elkhart County	0	0.00
Evansville (city) Vanderburgh County	0	0.00
Fishers (town) Hamilton County	0	0.00
Fort Wayne (city) Allen County	0	0.00
Gary (city) Lake County	0	0.00
Hammond (city) Lake County	0	0.00

West Indian: West Indian, excluding Hispanic

Top 10 Places Sorted by Population
Based on all places, regardless of total population

Place	Population	%
Indianapolis (city) Marion County	335	0.04
East Chicago (city) Lake County	64	0.21
Mishawaka (city) St. Joseph County	35	0.07
Gary (city) Lake County	34	0.04
South Bend (city) St. Joseph County	31	0.03
Valparaiso (city) Porter County	23	0.07
Fort Wayne (city) Allen County	18	0.01
Bloomington (city) Monroe County	16	0.02
Westfield (town) Hamilton County	12	0.04
Columbus (city) Bartholomew County	10	0.02

Top 10 Places Sorted by Percent of Total Population
Based on all places, regardless of total population

Place	Population	%
Jasonville (city) Greene County	5	0.22
East Chicago (city) Lake County	64	0.21
North Manchester (town) Wabash County	7	0.12
Mishawaka (city) St. Joseph County	35	0.07
Valparaiso (city) Porter County	23	0.07
Tell City (city) Perry County	5	0.07
Indianapolis (city) Marion County	335	0.04
Gary (city) Lake County	34	0.04
Westfield (town) Hamilton County	12	0.04
South Bend (city) St. Joseph County	31	0.03

Top 10 Places Sorted by Percent of Total Population
Based on places with total population of 50,000 or more

Place	Population	%
Indianapolis (city) Marion County	335	0.04

Place	Population	%
Gary (city) Lake County	34	0.04
South Bend (city) St. Joseph County	31	0.03
Bloomington (city) Monroe County	16	0.02
Fort Wayne (city) Allen County	18	0.01
Anderson (city) Madison County	0	0.00
Carmel (city) Hamilton County	0	0.00
Elkhart (city) Elkhart County	0	0.00
Evansville (city) Vanderburgh County	0	0.00
Fishers (town) Hamilton County	0	0.00

West Indian: Other, excluding Hispanic

Top 10 Places Sorted by Population
Based on all places, regardless of total population

Place	Population	%
Anderson (city) Madison County	27	0.05
Gary (city) Lake County	25	0.03
Marion (city) Grant County	21	0.07
Tri-Lakes (cdp) Whitley County	14	0.85
Purdue University (cdp) Tippecanoe County	14	0.11
Indianapolis (city) Marion County	12	<0.01
Columbus (city) Bartholomew County	8	0.02
Aberdeen (cdp) Porter County	0	0.00
Advance (town) Boone County	0	0.00
Akron (town) Fulton County	0	0.00

Top 10 Places Sorted by Percent of Total Population
Based on all places, regardless of total population

Place	Population	%
Tri-Lakes (cdp) Whitley County	14	0.85
Purdue University (cdp) Tippecanoe County	14	0.11
Marion (city) Grant County	21	0.07
Anderson (city) Madison County	27	0.05
Gary (city) Lake County	25	0.03
Columbus (city) Bartholomew County	8	0.02
Indianapolis (city) Marion County	12	<0.01
Aberdeen (cdp) Porter County	0	0.00
Advance (town) Boone County	0	0.00
Akron (town) Fulton County	0	0.00

Top 10 Places Sorted by Percent of Total Population
Based on places with total population of 50,000 or more

Place	Population	%
Anderson (city) Madison County	27	0.05
Gary (city) Lake County	25	0.03
Indianapolis (city) Marion County	12	<0.01
Bloomington (city) Monroe County	0	0.00
Carmel (city) Hamilton County	0	0.00
Elkhart (city) Elkhart County	0	0.00
Evansville (city) Vanderburgh County	0	0.00
Fishers (town) Hamilton County	0	0.00
Fort Wayne (city) Allen County	0	0.00
Hammond (city) Lake County	0	0.00

Yugoslavian

Top 10 Places Sorted by Population
Based on all places, regardless of total population

Place	Population	%
Fort Wayne (city) Allen County	1,443	0.57
Indianapolis (city) Marion County	531	0.07
South Bend (city) St. Joseph County	514	0.50
Mishawaka (city) St. Joseph County	446	0.93
Fishers (town) Hamilton County	133	0.19
Dyer (town) Lake County	127	0.80
Noblesville (city) Hamilton County	121	0.25
Brownsburg (town) Hendricks County	119	0.58
Schererville (town) Lake County	110	0.39
Munster (town) Lake County	81	0.35

Top 10 Places Sorted by Percent of Total Population
Based on all places, regardless of total population

Place	Population	%
Gosport (town) Owen County	24	2.48
Springport (town) Henry County	4	2.40
Zanesville (town) Wells County	13	1.73
Town of Pines (town) Porter County	10	1.43
Arcadia (town) Hamilton County	17	1.14
Hanover (town) Jefferson County	34	1.01
Mishawaka (city) St. Joseph County	446	0.93
Winamac (town) Pulaski County	24	0.90
North Webster (town) Kosciusko County	10	0.86
Dyer (town) Lake County	127	0.80

Top 10 Places Sorted by Percent of Total Population
Based on places with total population of 50,000 or more

Place	Population	%
Fort Wayne (city) Allen County	1,443	0.57
South Bend (city) St. Joseph County	514	0.50
Fishers (town) Hamilton County	133	0.19
Carmel (city) Hamilton County	67	0.09
Terre Haute (city) Vigo County	55	0.09
Indianapolis (city) Marion County	531	0.07
Bloomington (city) Monroe County	50	0.06
Muncie (city) Delaware County	27	0.04
Gary (city) Lake County	24	0.03
Anderson (city) Madison County	12	0.02

Hispanic Origin Rankings

Hispanic or Latino (of any race)

Top 10 Places Sorted by Population
Based on all places, regardless of total population

Place	Population	%
Indianapolis (city) Marion County	77,352	9.43
Hammond (city) Lake County	27,563	34.10
Fort Wayne (city) Allen County	20,200	7.96
East Chicago (city) Lake County	15,105	50.86
South Bend (city) St. Joseph County	13,116	12.96
Elkhart (city) Elkhart County	11,451	22.48
Goshen (city) Elkhart County	8,903	28.07
Lafayette (city) Tippecanoe County	8,107	12.07
Portage (city) Porter County	6,044	16.41
Lawrence (city) Marion County	5,155	11.21

Top 10 Places Sorted by Percent of Total Population
Based on all places, regardless of total population

Place	Population	%
Ligonier (city) Noble County	2,270	51.53
East Chicago (city) Lake County	15,105	50.86
Ambia (town) Benton County	104	43.51
Whiting (city) Lake County	2,036	40.74
Hammond (city) Lake County	27,563	34.10
Akron (town) Fulton County	351	30.08
Monon (town) White County	505	28.42
Goshen (city) Elkhart County	8,903	28.07
Lake Station (city) Lake County	3,517	27.97
New Chicago (town) Lake County	558	27.42

Top 10 Places Sorted by Percent of Total Population
Based on places with total population of 50,000 or more

Place	Population	%
Hammond (city) Lake County	27,563	34.10
Elkhart (city) Elkhart County	11,451	22.48
South Bend (city) St. Joseph County	13,116	12.96
Lafayette (city) Tippecanoe County	8,107	12.07
Indianapolis (city) Marion County	77,352	9.43
Fort Wayne (city) Allen County	20,200	7.96
Gary (city) Lake County	4,128	5.14
Anderson (city) Madison County	2,719	4.84
Noblesville (city) Hamilton County	2,209	4.25
Bloomington (city) Monroe County	2,823	3.51

Central American, excluding Mexican

Top 10 Places Sorted by Population
Based on all places, regardless of total population

Place	Population	%
Indianapolis (city) Marion County	7,746	0.94
Fort Wayne (city) Allen County	1,346	0.53
Elkhart (city) Elkhart County	912	1.79
Logansport (city) Cass County	641	3.48
Huntingburg (city) Dubois County	533	8.80
Hammond (city) Lake County	526	0.65
Lawrence (city) Marion County	481	1.05
Jasper (city) Dubois County	342	2.27
Goshen (city) Elkhart County	310	0.98
South Bend (city) St. Joseph County	292	0.29

Top 10 Places Sorted by Percent of Total Population
Based on all places, regardless of total population

Place	Population	%
Monon (town) White County	261	14.69
Huntingburg (city) Dubois County	533	8.80
Alton (town) Crawford County	2	3.64
Logansport (city) Cass County	641	3.48
Jonesville (town) Bartholomew County	6	3.39
Brook (town) Newton County	29	2.91
Sidney (town) Kosciusko County	2	2.41
Jasper (city) Dubois County	342	2.27
Washington (city) Daviess County	237	2.06
Plymouth (city) Marshall County	206	2.05

Top 10 Places Sorted by Percent of Total Population
Based on places with total population of 50,000 or more

Place	Population	%
Elkhart (city) Elkhart County	912	1.79
Indianapolis (city) Marion County	7,746	0.94
Hammond (city) Lake County	526	0.65
Fort Wayne (city) Allen County	1,346	0.53
Noblesville (city) Hamilton County	244	0.47
Lafayette (city) Tippecanoe County	283	0.42
South Bend (city) St. Joseph County	292	0.29
Carmel (city) Hamilton County	181	0.23
Bloomington (city) Monroe County	165	0.21
Fishers (town) Hamilton County	162	0.21

Central American: Costa Rican

Top 10 Places Sorted by Population
Based on all places, regardless of total population

Place	Population	%
Indianapolis (city) Marion County	125	0.02
Fort Wayne (city) Allen County	38	0.01
Bloomington (city) Monroe County	21	0.03
Noblesville (city) Hamilton County	19	0.04
Hammond (city) Lake County	18	0.02
Goshen (city) Elkhart County	14	0.04
Purdue University (cdp) Tippecanoe County	12	0.10
Lafayette (city) Tippecanoe County	12	0.02
Plainfield (town) Hendricks County	11	0.04
West Lafayette (city) Tippecanoe County	10	0.03

Top 10 Places Sorted by Percent of Total Population
Based on all places, regardless of total population

Place	Population	%
Fillmore (town) Putnam County	3	0.56
Tecumseh (cdp) Vigo County	2	0.30
Otwell (cdp) Pike County	1	0.23
Wilkinson (town) Hancock County	1	0.22
Bicknell (city) Knox County	5	0.17
Brooklyn (town) Morgan County	2	0.13
Koontz Lake (cdp) Starke County	2	0.13
Shirley (town) Hancock County	1	0.12
Melody Hill (cdp) Vanderburgh County	4	0.11
Purdue University (cdp) Tippecanoe County	12	0.10

Top 10 Places Sorted by Percent of Total Population
Based on places with total population of 50,000 or more

Place	Population	%
Noblesville (city) Hamilton County	19	0.04
Bloomington (city) Monroe County	21	0.03
Indianapolis (city) Marion County	125	0.02
Hammond (city) Lake County	18	0.02
Lafayette (city) Tippecanoe County	12	0.02
Fort Wayne (city) Allen County	38	0.01
Fishers (town) Hamilton County	9	0.01
Carmel (city) Hamilton County	8	0.01
Evansville (city) Vanderburgh County	7	0.01
South Bend (city) St. Joseph County	7	0.01

Central American: Guatemalan

Top 10 Places Sorted by Population
Based on all places, regardless of total population

Place	Population	%
Indianapolis (city) Marion County	1,616	0.20
Fort Wayne (city) Allen County	729	0.29
Logansport (city) Cass County	412	2.24
Hammond (city) Lake County	172	0.21
Lawrence (city) Marion County	140	0.30
Elkhart (city) Elkhart County	93	0.18
Carmel (city) Hamilton County	87	0.11
Columbus (city) Bartholomew County	82	0.19
Lafayette (city) Tippecanoe County	81	0.12
Goshen (city) Elkhart County	71	0.22

Top 10 Places Sorted by Percent of Total Population
Based on all places, regardless of total population

Place	Population	%
Logansport (city) Cass County	412	2.24
Williams Creek (town) Marion County	3	0.74
Mentone (town) Kosciusko County	7	0.70
Delphi (city) Carroll County	20	0.69
Dale (town) Spencer County	11	0.69
West College Corner (town) Union County	4	0.59
Washington (city) Daviess County	66	0.57
Bourbon (town) Marshall County	8	0.44
Pennville (town) Jay County	3	0.43
Wynnedale (town) Marion County	1	0.43

Top 10 Places Sorted by Percent of Total Population
Based on places with total population of 50,000 or more

Place	Population	%
Fort Wayne (city) Allen County	729	0.29
Hammond (city) Lake County	172	0.21
Indianapolis (city) Marion County	1,616	0.20
Elkhart (city) Elkhart County	93	0.18
Lafayette (city) Tippecanoe County	81	0.12
Carmel (city) Hamilton County	87	0.11
Anderson (city) Madison County	59	0.11
Noblesville (city) Hamilton County	59	0.11
South Bend (city) St. Joseph County	66	0.07
Fishers (town) Hamilton County	54	0.07

Central American: Honduran

Top 10 Places Sorted by Population
Based on all places, regardless of total population

Place	Population	%
Indianapolis (city) Marion County	2,302	0.28
Elkhart (city) Elkhart County	390	0.77
Plymouth (city) Marshall County	199	1.98
Lawrence (city) Marion County	161	0.35
Fort Wayne (city) Allen County	129	0.05
Goshen (city) Elkhart County	124	0.39
Hammond (city) Lake County	117	0.14
Logansport (city) Cass County	54	0.29
Plainfield (town) Hendricks County	52	0.19
South Bend (city) St. Joseph County	49	0.05

Top 10 Places Sorted by Percent of Total Population
Based on all places, regardless of total population

Place	Population	%
Alton (town) Crawford County	2	3.64
Plymouth (city) Marshall County	199	1.98
Dupont (town) Jefferson County	6	1.77
Dubois (cdp) Dubois County	8	1.64
Stilesville (town) Hendricks County	4	1.27
Roseland (town) St. Joseph County	7	1.11
Bourbon (town) Marshall County	15	0.83
Bremen (town) Marshall County	37	0.81
Elkhart (city) Elkhart County	390	0.77
Holland (town) Dubois County	4	0.64

Top 10 Places Sorted by Percent of Total Population
Based on places with total population of 50,000 or more

Place	Population	%
Elkhart (city) Elkhart County	390	0.77
Indianapolis (city) Marion County	2,302	0.28
Hammond (city) Lake County	117	0.14
Noblesville (city) Hamilton County	31	0.06
Fort Wayne (city) Allen County	129	0.05
South Bend (city) St. Joseph County	49	0.05
Terre Haute (city) Vigo County	22	0.04
Evansville (city) Vanderburgh County	31	0.03
Bloomington (city) Monroe County	21	0.03
Anderson (city) Madison County	16	0.03

Central American: Nicaraguan

Top 10 Places Sorted by Population
Based on all places, regardless of total population

Place	Population	%
Indianapolis (city) Marion County	668	0.08
Lawrence (city) Marion County	67	0.15
South Bend (city) St. Joseph County	46	0.05
Fort Wayne (city) Allen County	37	0.01
Evansville (city) Vanderburgh County	35	0.03
Bloomington (city) Monroe County	28	0.03
Carmel (city) Hamilton County	20	0.03
Anderson (city) Madison County	19	0.03
Hammond (city) Lake County	19	0.02
Merrillville (town) Lake County	17	0.05

Top 10 Places Sorted by Percent of Total Population
Based on all places, regardless of total population

Place	Population	%
Royal Center (town) Cass County	3	0.35
Geneva (town) Adams County	3	0.23
Reynolds (town) White County	1	0.19
Lawrence (city) Marion County	67	0.15
Patoka (town) Gibson County	1	0.14
Notre Dame (cdp) St. Joseph County	8	0.13
Milford (town) Kosciusko County	2	0.13
Sheridan (town) Hamilton County	3	0.11
Hagers (town) Wayne County	2	0.11
Indianapolis (city) Marion County	668	0.08

Top 10 Places Sorted by Percent of Total Population
Based on places with total population of 50,000 or more

Place	Population	%
Indianapolis (city) Marion County	668	0.08
South Bend (city) St. Joseph County	46	0.05
Evansville (city) Vanderburgh County	35	0.03
Bloomington (city) Monroe County	28	0.03
Carmel (city) Hamilton County	20	0.03
Anderson (city) Madison County	19	0.03
Elkhart (city) Elkhart County	14	0.03
Noblesville (city) Hamilton County	14	0.03
Hammond (city) Lake County	19	0.02
Lafayette (city) Tippecanoe County	16	0.02

Central American: Panamanian

Top 10 Places Sorted by Population
Based on all places, regardless of total population

Place	Population	%
Indianapolis (city) Marion County	274	0.03
Fishers (town) Hamilton County	39	0.05
Fort Wayne (city) Allen County	38	0.01
West Lafayette (city) Tippecanoe County	28	0.09
Carmel (city) Hamilton County	28	0.04
Lafayette (city) Tippecanoe County	26	0.04
Lawrence (city) Marion County	25	0.05
Evansville (city) Vanderburgh County	24	0.02
Bloomington (city) Monroe County	22	0.03
Hammond (city) Lake County	21	0.03

Top 10 Places Sorted by Percent of Total Population
Based on all places, regardless of total population

Place	Population	%
Sidney (town) Kosciusko County	2	2.41
Lake Santee (cdp) Decatur County	3	0.37
Ogden Dunes (town) Porter County	4	0.36
Bristol (town) Elkhart County	4	0.25
Arcadia (town) Hamilton County	4	0.24
Notre Dame (cdp) St. Joseph County	11	0.18
Akron (town) Fulton County	2	0.17
Speedway (town) Marion County	19	0.16
Dana (town) Vermillion County	1	0.16
Purdue University (cdp) Tippecanoe County	17	0.14

Top 10 Places Sorted by Percent of Total Population
Based on places with total population of 50,000 or more

Place	Population	%
Fishers (town) Hamilton County	39	0.05
Carmel (city) Hamilton County	28	0.04
Lafayette (city) Tippecanoe County	26	0.04
Indianapolis (city) Marion County	274	0.03
Bloomington (city) Monroe County	22	0.03
Hammond (city) Lake County	21	0.03
Muncie (city) Delaware County	21	0.03
Evansville (city) Vanderburgh County	24	0.02
South Bend (city) St. Joseph County	21	0.02
Noblesville (city) Hamilton County	10	0.02

Central American: Salvadoran

Top 10 Places Sorted by Population
Based on all places, regardless of total population

Place	Population	%
Indianapolis (city) Marion County	2,695	0.33
Huntingburg (city) Dubois County	498	8.22
Elkhart (city) Elkhart County	400	0.79
Fort Wayne (city) Allen County	369	0.15
Jasper (city) Dubois County	290	1.93
Monon (town) White County	248	13.96
Hammond (city) Lake County	174	0.22
Logansport (city) Cass County	166	0.90
Washington (city) Daviess County	154	1.34
Lafayette (city) Tippecanoe County	138	0.21

Top 10 Places Sorted by Percent of Total Population
Based on all places, regardless of total population

Place	Population	%
Monon (town) White County	248	13.96
Huntingburg (city) Dubois County	498	8.22
Jonesville (town) Bartholomew County	6	3.39
Brook (town) Newton County	29	2.91
Jasper (city) Dubois County	290	1.93
Chalmers (town) White County	7	1.38
Washington (city) Daviess County	154	1.34
Idaville (cdp) White County	6	1.30
Stinesville (town) Monroe County	2	1.01
Logansport (city) Cass County	166	0.90

Top 10 Places Sorted by Percent of Total Population
Based on places with total population of 50,000 or more

Place	Population	%
Elkhart (city) Elkhart County	400	0.79
Indianapolis (city) Marion County	2,695	0.33
Hammond (city) Lake County	174	0.22
Lafayette (city) Tippecanoe County	138	0.21
Noblesville (city) Hamilton County	111	0.21
Fort Wayne (city) Allen County	369	0.15
South Bend (city) St. Joseph County	98	0.10
Evansville (city) Vanderburgh County	45	0.04
Bloomington (city) Monroe County	31	0.04
Carmel (city) Hamilton County	28	0.04

Central American: Other Central American

Top 10 Places Sorted by Population
Based on all places, regardless of total population

Place	Population	%
Indianapolis (city) Marion County	66	0.01
Elkhart (city) Elkhart County	12	0.02
Westfield (town) Hamilton County	11	0.04
Columbus (city) Bartholomew County	6	0.01
Fort Wayne (city) Allen County	6	<0.01
Hammond (city) Lake County	5	0.01
Evansville (city) Vanderburgh County	5	<0.01
South Bend (city) St. Joseph County	5	<0.01
Fowler (town) Benton County	4	0.17
East Chicago (city) Lake County	4	0.01

Top 10 Places Sorted by Percent of Total Population
Based on all places, regardless of total population

Place	Population	%
Fowler (town) Benton County	4	0.17
Westfield (town) Hamilton County	11	0.04
Osceola (town) St. Joseph County	1	0.04
Elkhart (city) Elkhart County	12	0.02
Avon (town) Hendricks County	3	0.02
Notre Dame (cdp) St. Joseph County	1	0.02
Indianapolis (city) Marion County	66	0.01
Columbus (city) Bartholomew County	6	0.01
Hammond (city) Lake County	5	0.01
East Chicago (city) Lake County	4	0.01

Top 10 Places Sorted by Percent of Total Population
Based on places with total population of 50,000 or more

Place	Population	%
Elkhart (city) Elkhart County	12	0.02
Indianapolis (city) Marion County	66	0.01
Hammond (city) Lake County	5	0.01
Fort Wayne (city) Allen County	6	<0.01
Evansville (city) Vanderburgh County	5	<0.01
South Bend (city) St. Joseph County	5	<0.01
Bloomington (city) Monroe County	4	<0.01
Fishers (town) Hamilton County	3	<0.01
Carmel (city) Hamilton County	1	<0.01
Muncie (city) Delaware County	1	<0.01

Cuban

Top 10 Places Sorted by Population
Based on all places, regardless of total population

Place	Population	%
Indianapolis (city) Marion County	739	0.09
Fort Wayne (city) Allen County	174	0.07
Hammond (city) Lake County	140	0.17
Bloomington (city) Monroe County	126	0.16
South Bend (city) St. Joseph County	111	0.11
Carmel (city) Hamilton County	101	0.13
Fishers (town) Hamilton County	90	0.12
Lafayette (city) Tippecanoe County	78	0.12
Jeffersonville (city) Clark County	72	0.16
Evansville (city) Vanderburgh County	64	0.05

Top 10 Places Sorted by Percent of Total Population
Based on all places, regardless of total population

Place	Population	%
Economy (town) Wayne County	4	2.14
Sidney (town) Kosciusko County	1	1.20
Modoc (town) Randolph County	2	1.02
Notre Dame (cdp) St. Joseph County	55	0.92
Collegeville (cdp) Jasper County	2	0.61
Hayden (cdp) Jennings County	3	0.58
Lewisville (town) Henry County	2	0.55
Hudson Lake (cdp) LaPorte County	7	0.54
New Salisbury (cdp) Harrison County	3	0.49
Shelburn (town) Sullivan County	6	0.48

Top 10 Places Sorted by Percent of Total Population
Based on places with total population of 50,000 or more

Place	Population	%
Hammond (city) Lake County	140	0.17
Bloomington (city) Monroe County	126	0.16
Carmel (city) Hamilton County	101	0.13
Fishers (town) Hamilton County	90	0.12
Lafayette (city) Tippecanoe County	78	0.12
South Bend (city) St. Joseph County	111	0.11
Indianapolis (city) Marion County	739	0.09
Gary (city) Lake County	61	0.08
Terre Haute (city) Vigo County	46	0.08
Noblesville (city) Hamilton County	43	0.08

Dominican Republic

Top 10 Places Sorted by Population
Based on all places, regardless of total population

Place	Population	%
Indianapolis (city) Marion County	1,124	0.14
Fort Wayne (city) Allen County	72	0.03
Fishers (town) Hamilton County	46	0.06
Bloomington (city) Monroe County	43	0.05
Logansport (city) Cass County	42	0.23
South Bend (city) St. Joseph County	42	0.04
Noblesville (city) Hamilton County	40	0.08
Carmel (city) Hamilton County	40	0.05
Lafayette (city) Tippecanoe County	33	0.05
Speedway (town) Marion County	32	0.27

Top 10 Places Sorted by Percent of Total Population
Based on all places, regardless of total population

Place	Population	%
Painted Hills (cdp) Morgan County	2	0.30
Liberty (town) Union County	6	0.28
Speedway (town) Marion County	32	0.27

Ancestry and Ethnicity: Hispanic Origin Rankings

Place	Population	%
Logansport (city) Cass County	42	0.23
Crothersville (town) Jackson County	3	0.19
Avon (town) Hendricks County	23	0.18
Fortville (town) Hancock County	7	0.18
Akron (town) Fulton County	2	0.17
Indianapolis (city) Marion County	1,124	0.14
Brownsburg (town) Hendricks County	23	0.11

Top 10 Places Sorted by Percent of Total Population
Based on places with total population of 50,000 or more

Place	Population	%
Indianapolis (city) Marion County	1,124	0.14
Noblesville (city) Hamilton County	40	0.08
Fishers (town) Hamilton County	46	0.06
Bloomington (city) Monroe County	43	0.05
Carmel (city) Hamilton County	40	0.05
Lafayette (city) Tippecanoe County	33	0.05
South Bend (city) St. Joseph County	42	0.04
Elkhart (city) Elkhart County	19	0.04
Fort Wayne (city) Allen County	72	0.03
Gary (city) Lake County	24	0.03

Mexican

Top 10 Places Sorted by Population
Based on all places, regardless of total population

Place	Population	%
Indianapolis (city) Marion County	56,771	6.92
Hammond (city) Lake County	22,684	28.06
Fort Wayne (city) Allen County	15,545	6.13
East Chicago (city) Lake County	11,819	39.80
South Bend (city) St. Joseph County	11,025	10.90
Elkhart (city) Elkhart County	9,313	18.28
Goshen (city) Elkhart County	7,781	24.53
Lafayette (city) Tippecanoe County	6,965	10.37
Portage (city) Porter County	4,011	10.89
Lawrence (city) Marion County	3,827	8.32

Top 10 Places Sorted by Percent of Total Population
Based on all places, regardless of total population

Place	Population	%
Ligonier (city) Noble County	2,185	49.60
Ambia (town) Benton County	104	43.51
East Chicago (city) Lake County	11,819	39.80
Whiting (city) Lake County	1,765	35.32
Akron (town) Fulton County	342	29.31
Hammond (city) Lake County	22,684	28.06
Goshen (city) Elkhart County	7,781	24.53
Frankfort (city) Clinton County	3,693	22.49
New Chicago (town) Lake County	427	20.98
Lake Station (city) Lake County	2,522	20.06

Top 10 Places Sorted by Percent of Total Population
Based on places with total population of 50,000 or more

Place	Population	%
Hammond (city) Lake County	22,684	28.06
Elkhart (city) Elkhart County	9,313	18.28
South Bend (city) St. Joseph County	11,025	10.90
Lafayette (city) Tippecanoe County	6,965	10.37
Indianapolis (city) Marion County	56,771	6.92
Fort Wayne (city) Allen County	15,545	6.13
Anderson (city) Madison County	2,199	3.92
Gary (city) Lake County	2,553	3.18
Terre Haute (city) Vigo County	1,469	2.42
Noblesville (city) Hamilton County	1,245	2.40

Puerto Rican

Top 10 Places Sorted by Population
Based on all places, regardless of total population

Place	Population	%
Indianapolis (city) Marion County	3,431	0.42
Hammond (city) Lake County	3,081	3.81
East Chicago (city) Lake County	2,528	8.51
Portage (city) Porter County	1,608	4.37
Gary (city) Lake County	1,223	1.52
Fort Wayne (city) Allen County	939	0.37
Hobart (city) Lake County	850	2.93
Lake Station (city) Lake County	843	6.71
Merrillville (town) Lake County	817	2.32
South Bend (city) St. Joseph County	525	0.52

Top 10 Places Sorted by Percent of Total Population
Based on all places, regardless of total population

Place	Population	%
East Chicago (city) Lake County	2,528	8.51
Lake Station (city) Lake County	843	6.71
New Chicago (town) Lake County	98	4.82
Portage (city) Porter County	1,608	4.37
Hammond (city) Lake County	3,081	3.81
Whiting (city) Lake County	163	3.26
Monterey (town) Pulaski County	7	3.21
Hobart (city) Lake County	850	2.93
Cadiz (town) Henry County	4	2.67
Crandall (town) Harrison County	4	2.63

Top 10 Places Sorted by Percent of Total Population
Based on places with total population of 50,000 or more

Place	Population	%
Hammond (city) Lake County	3,081	3.81
Gary (city) Lake County	1,223	1.52
Elkhart (city) Elkhart County	392	0.77
South Bend (city) St. Joseph County	525	0.52
Fishers (town) Hamilton County	349	0.45
Bloomington (city) Monroe County	348	0.43
Indianapolis (city) Marion County	3,431	0.42
Noblesville (city) Hamilton County	210	0.40
Lafayette (city) Tippecanoe County	253	0.38
Fort Wayne (city) Allen County	939	0.37

South American

Top 10 Places Sorted by Population
Based on all places, regardless of total population

Place	Population	%
Indianapolis (city) Marion County	2,068	0.25
Fort Wayne (city) Allen County	651	0.26
Fishers (town) Hamilton County	359	0.47
Bloomington (city) Monroe County	349	0.43
Carmel (city) Hamilton County	310	0.39
South Bend (city) St. Joseph County	275	0.27
Noblesville (city) Hamilton County	253	0.49
West Lafayette (city) Tippecanoe County	241	0.81
Lawrence (city) Marion County	164	0.36
Hammond (city) Lake County	141	0.17

Top 10 Places Sorted by Percent of Total Population
Based on all places, regardless of total population

Place	Population	%
Woodlawn Heights (town) Madison County	1	1.27
Notre Dame (cdp) St. Joseph County	70	1.17
Beverly Shores (town) Porter County	6	0.98
Oakland City (city) Gibson County	21	0.86
Mount Ayr (town) Newton County	1	0.82
West Lafayette (city) Tippecanoe County	241	0.81
Carbon (town) Clay County	3	0.76
Purdue University (cdp) Tippecanoe County	87	0.71
Meridian Hills (town) Marion County	9	0.56
Dune Acres (town) Porter County	1	0.55

Top 10 Places Sorted by Percent of Total Population
Based on places with total population of 50,000 or more

Place	Population	%
Noblesville (city) Hamilton County	253	0.49
Fishers (town) Hamilton County	359	0.47
Bloomington (city) Monroe County	349	0.43
Carmel (city) Hamilton County	310	0.39
South Bend (city) St. Joseph County	275	0.27
Fort Wayne (city) Allen County	651	0.26
Indianapolis (city) Marion County	2,068	0.25
Elkhart (city) Elkhart County	121	0.24
Lafayette (city) Tippecanoe County	130	0.19
Hammond (city) Lake County	141	0.17

South American: Argentinean

Top 10 Places Sorted by Population
Based on all places, regardless of total population

Place	Population	%
Indianapolis (city) Marion County	207	0.03
Bloomington (city) Monroe County	57	0.07
West Lafayette (city) Tippecanoe County	53	0.18
Carmel (city) Hamilton County	38	0.05
Fort Wayne (city) Allen County	36	0.01
South Bend (city) St. Joseph County	33	0.03
Fishers (town) Hamilton County	29	0.04
Hammond (city) Lake County	29	0.04
Noblesville (city) Hamilton County	19	0.04
Columbus (city) Bartholomew County	16	0.04

Top 10 Places Sorted by Percent of Total Population
Based on all places, regardless of total population

Place	Population	%
Dune Acres (town) Porter County	1	0.55
Battle Ground (town) Tippecanoe County	4	0.30
Michigan (town) Clinton County	1	0.21
West Lafayette (city) Tippecanoe County	53	0.18
Winona Lake (town) Kosciusko County	9	0.18
Memphis (cdp) Clark County	1	0.14
Wheatfield (town) Jasper County	1	0.12
Charlestown (city) Clark County	8	0.11
Hebron (town) Porter County	4	0.11
Purdue University (cdp) Tippecanoe County	12	0.10

Top 10 Places Sorted by Percent of Total Population
Based on places with total population of 50,000 or more

Place	Population	%
Bloomington (city) Monroe County	57	0.07
Carmel (city) Hamilton County	38	0.05
Fishers (town) Hamilton County	29	0.04
Hammond (city) Lake County	29	0.04
Noblesville (city) Hamilton County	19	0.04
Indianapolis (city) Marion County	207	0.03
South Bend (city) St. Joseph County	33	0.03
Lafayette (city) Tippecanoe County	16	0.02
Terre Haute (city) Vigo County	12	0.02
Elkhart (city) Elkhart County	10	0.02

South American: Bolivian

Top 10 Places Sorted by Population
Based on all places, regardless of total population

Place	Population	%
Indianapolis (city) Marion County	47	0.01
Goshen (city) Elkhart County	29	0.09
Elkhart (city) Elkhart County	29	0.06
West Lafayette (city) Tippecanoe County	17	0.06
Portage (city) Porter County	17	0.05
Fort Wayne (city) Allen County	15	0.01
Schererville (town) Lake County	13	0.04
Carmel (city) Hamilton County	12	0.02
Lafayette (city) Tippecanoe County	12	0.02
Noblesville (city) Hamilton County	11	0.02

Top 10 Places Sorted by Percent of Total Population
Based on all places, regardless of total population

Place	Population	%
Topeka (town) LaGrange County	5	0.43
Somerset (cdp) Wabash County	1	0.25
Hudson Lake (cdp) LaPorte County	2	0.15
Whites (town) Boone County	3	0.10
Goshen (city) Elkhart County	29	0.09
Highland (cdp) Vanderburgh County	4	0.09
Upland (town) Grant County	3	0.08
Charlestown (city) Clark County	5	0.07
Elkhart (city) Elkhart County	29	0.06
West Lafayette (city) Tippecanoe County	17	0.06

Top 10 Places Sorted by Percent of Total Population
Based on places with total population of 50,000 or more

Place	Population	%
Elkhart (city) Elkhart County	29	0.06
Carmel (city) Hamilton County	12	0.02
Lafayette (city) Tippecanoe County	12	0.02
Noblesville (city) Hamilton County	11	0.02
Indianapolis (city) Marion County	47	0.01
Fort Wayne (city) Allen County	15	0.01
Bloomington (city) Monroe County	11	0.01
South Bend (city) St. Joseph County	10	0.01
Terre Haute (city) Vigo County	6	0.01
Fishers (town) Hamilton County	5	0.01

Please refer to the Explanation of Data in the front of the book for more detailed information.

Ancestry and Ethnicity: Hispanic Origin Rankings

South American: Chilean

Top 10 Places Sorted by Population
Based on all places, regardless of total population

Place	Population	%
Indianapolis (city) Marion County	83	0.01
Bloomington (city) Monroe County	36	0.04
Valparaiso (city) Porter County	30	0.09
South Bend (city) St. Joseph County	27	0.03
Carmel (city) Hamilton County	22	0.03
Fort Wayne (city) Allen County	18	0.01
West Lafayette (city) Tippecanoe County	15	0.05
Fishers (town) Hamilton County	15	0.02
Lafayette (city) Tippecanoe County	13	0.02
Brownsburg (town) Hendricks County	12	0.06

Top 10 Places Sorted by Percent of Total Population
Based on all places, regardless of total population

Place	Population	%
Woodlawn Heights (town) Madison County	1	1.27
Beverly Shores (town) Porter County	6	0.98
Mount Ayr (town) Newton County	1	0.82
Landess (cdp) Grant County	1	0.53
Roseland (town) St. Joseph County	2	0.32
St. Leon (town) Dearborn County	2	0.29
Homecroft (town) Marion County	2	0.28
New Market (town) Montgomery County	1	0.16
St. Mary of the Woods (cdp) Vigo County	1	0.13
Clayton (town) Hendricks County	1	0.10

Top 10 Places Sorted by Percent of Total Population
Based on places with total population of 50,000 or more

Place	Population	%
Bloomington (city) Monroe County	36	0.04
South Bend (city) St. Joseph County	27	0.03
Carmel (city) Hamilton County	22	0.03
Fishers (town) Hamilton County	15	0.02
Lafayette (city) Tippecanoe County	13	0.02
Muncie (city) Delaware County	11	0.02
Noblesville (city) Hamilton County	11	0.02
Indianapolis (city) Marion County	83	0.01
Fort Wayne (city) Allen County	18	0.01
Elkhart (city) Elkhart County	6	0.01

South American: Colombian

Top 10 Places Sorted by Population
Based on all places, regardless of total population

Place	Population	%
Indianapolis (city) Marion County	587	0.07
Fort Wayne (city) Allen County	235	0.09
Fishers (town) Hamilton County	127	0.17
Carmel (city) Hamilton County	125	0.16
West Lafayette (city) Tippecanoe County	94	0.32
Bloomington (city) Monroe County	85	0.11
Noblesville (city) Hamilton County	68	0.13
South Bend (city) St. Joseph County	53	0.05
Lawrence (city) Marion County	41	0.09
Lafayette (city) Tippecanoe County	39	0.06

Top 10 Places Sorted by Percent of Total Population
Based on all places, regardless of total population

Place	Population	%
Carbon (town) Clay County	3	0.76
Notre Dame (cdp) St. Joseph County	27	0.45
Avoca (cdp) Lawrence County	2	0.34
Ingalls (town) Madison County	8	0.33
West Lafayette (city) Tippecanoe County	94	0.32
Uniondale (town) Wells County	1	0.32
Meridian Hills (town) Marion County	5	0.31
Whites (town) Boone County	8	0.28
Bargersville (town) Johnson County	10	0.25
Purdue University (cdp) Tippecanoe County	29	0.24

Top 10 Places Sorted by Percent of Total Population
Based on places with total population of 50,000 or more

Place	Population	%
Fishers (town) Hamilton County	127	0.17
Carmel (city) Hamilton County	125	0.16
Noblesville (city) Hamilton County	68	0.13
Bloomington (city) Monroe County	85	0.11
Fort Wayne (city) Allen County	235	0.09
Indianapolis (city) Marion County	587	0.07
Lafayette (city) Tippecanoe County	39	0.06
South Bend (city) St. Joseph County	53	0.05
Terre Haute (city) Vigo County	28	0.05
Elkhart (city) Elkhart County	24	0.05

South American: Ecuadorian

Top 10 Places Sorted by Population
Based on all places, regardless of total population

Place	Population	%
Indianapolis (city) Marion County	160	0.02
Fort Wayne (city) Allen County	159	0.06
South Bend (city) St. Joseph County	47	0.05
Bloomington (city) Monroe County	30	0.04
Munster (town) Lake County	24	0.10
Lafayette (city) Tippecanoe County	23	0.03
Notre Dame (cdp) St. Joseph County	21	0.35
Dyer (town) Lake County	18	0.11
Merrillville (town) Lake County	18	0.05
Lawrence (city) Marion County	18	0.04

Top 10 Places Sorted by Percent of Total Population
Based on all places, regardless of total population

Place	Population	%
Notre Dame (cdp) St. Joseph County	21	0.35
Whiting (city) Lake County	11	0.22
New Chicago (town) Lake County	3	0.15
Dyer (town) Lake County	18	0.11
Sellersburg (town) Clark County	7	0.11
Munster (town) Lake County	24	0.10
Newburgh (town) Warrick County	3	0.09
Upland (town) Grant County	3	0.08
Purdue University (cdp) Tippecanoe County	9	0.07
Hamilton (town) Steuben County	1	0.07

Top 10 Places Sorted by Percent of Total Population
Based on places with total population of 50,000 or more

Place	Population	%
Fort Wayne (city) Allen County	159	0.06
South Bend (city) St. Joseph County	47	0.05
Bloomington (city) Monroe County	30	0.04
Lafayette (city) Tippecanoe County	23	0.03
Indianapolis (city) Marion County	160	0.02
Carmel (city) Hamilton County	17	0.02
Hammond (city) Lake County	12	0.01
Evansville (city) Vanderburgh County	9	0.01
Fishers (town) Hamilton County	9	0.01
Elkhart (city) Elkhart County	7	0.01

South American: Paraguayan

Top 10 Places Sorted by Population
Based on all places, regardless of total population

Place	Population	%
Indianapolis (city) Marion County	11	<0.01
South Bend (city) St. Joseph County	10	0.01
Bloomington (city) Monroe County	5	0.01
Hidden Valley (cdp) Dearborn County	4	0.07
Granger (cdp) St. Joseph County	4	0.01
Fort Wayne (city) Allen County	4	<0.01
Goshen (city) Elkhart County	3	0.01
Carmel (city) Hamilton County	3	<0.01
Fishers (town) Hamilton County	3	<0.01
Aberdeen (cdp) Porter County	2	0.11

Top 10 Places Sorted by Percent of Total Population
Based on all places, regardless of total population

Place	Population	%
Nashville (town) Brown County	1	0.12
Aberdeen (cdp) Porter County	2	0.11
Hidden Valley (cdp) Dearborn County	4	0.07
Purdue University (cdp) Tippecanoe County	2	0.02
South Bend (city) St. Joseph County	10	0.01
Bloomington (city) Monroe County	5	0.01
Granger (cdp) St. Joseph County	4	0.01
Goshen (city) Elkhart County	3	0.01
St. John (town) Lake County	2	0.01
Greencastle (city) Putnam County	1	0.01

South American: Argentinean

Top 10 Places Sorted by Percent of Total Population
Based on places with total population of 50,000 or more

Place	Population	%
South Bend (city) St. Joseph County	10	0.01
Bloomington (city) Monroe County	5	0.01
Indianapolis (city) Marion County	11	<0.01
Fort Wayne (city) Allen County	4	<0.01
Carmel (city) Hamilton County	3	<0.01
Fishers (town) Hamilton County	3	<0.01
Elkhart (city) Elkhart County	2	<0.01
Evansville (city) Vanderburgh County	2	<0.01
Hammond (city) Lake County	1	<0.01
Muncie (city) Delaware County	1	<0.01

South American: Peruvian

Top 10 Places Sorted by Population
Based on all places, regardless of total population

Place	Population	%
Indianapolis (city) Marion County	611	0.07
Fort Wayne (city) Allen County	128	0.05
Bloomington (city) Monroe County	67	0.08
Plainfield (town) Hendricks County	63	0.23
Fishers (town) Hamilton County	62	0.08
Carmel (city) Hamilton County	49	0.06
Lawrence (city) Marion County	46	0.10
Logansport (city) Cass County	45	0.24
Noblesville (city) Hamilton County	41	0.08
Hammond (city) Lake County	40	0.05

Top 10 Places Sorted by Percent of Total Population
Based on all places, regardless of total population

Place	Population	%
Van Bibber Lake (cdp) Putnam County	2	0.41
Burns Harbor (town) Porter County	4	0.35
Meridian Hills (town) Marion County	4	0.25
Logansport (city) Cass County	45	0.24
Plainfield (town) Hendricks County	63	0.23
Huntingburg (city) Dubois County	12	0.20
Corydon (town) Harrison County	6	0.19
Ferdinand (town) Dubois County	4	0.19
Newburgh (town) Warrick County	6	0.18
Pittsboro (town) Hendricks County	5	0.17

Top 10 Places Sorted by Percent of Total Population
Based on places with total population of 50,000 or more

Place	Population	%
Bloomington (city) Monroe County	67	0.08
Fishers (town) Hamilton County	62	0.08
Noblesville (city) Hamilton County	41	0.08
Indianapolis (city) Marion County	611	0.07
Carmel (city) Hamilton County	49	0.06
Fort Wayne (city) Allen County	128	0.05
Hammond (city) Lake County	40	0.05
Elkhart (city) Elkhart County	20	0.04
Evansville (city) Vanderburgh County	33	0.03
Lafayette (city) Tippecanoe County	18	0.03

South American: Uruguayan

Top 10 Places Sorted by Population
Based on all places, regardless of total population

Place	Population	%
Indianapolis (city) Marion County	29	<0.01
Fort Wayne (city) Allen County	10	<0.01
East Chicago (city) Lake County	7	0.02
Fishers (town) Hamilton County	7	0.01
Hammond (city) Lake County	6	0.01
Mishawaka (city) St. Joseph County	6	0.01
Bloomington (city) Monroe County	5	0.01
South Bend (city) St. Joseph County	5	<0.01
West Lafayette (city) Tippecanoe County	4	0.01
Avon (town) Hendricks County	3	0.02

Top 10 Places Sorted by Percent of Total Population
Based on all places, regardless of total population

Place	Population	%
Napoleon (town) Ripley County	1	0.43
Flora (town) Carroll County	2	0.10
New Paris (cdp) Elkhart County	1	0.07

Please refer to the Explanation of Data in the front of the book for more detailed information.

Place	Population	%
Whiting (city) Lake County	2	0.04
Notre Dame (cdp) St. Joseph County	2	0.03
East Chicago (city) Lake County	7	0.02
Avon (town) Hendricks County	3	0.02
Ellettsville (town) Monroe County	1	0.02
Grissom AFB (cdp) Miami County	1	0.02
Fishers (town) Hamilton County	7	0.01

Top 10 Places Sorted by Percent of Total Population
Based on places with total population of 50,000 or more

Place	Population	%
Fishers (town) Hamilton County	7	0.01
Hammond (city) Lake County	6	0.01
Bloomington (city) Monroe County	5	0.01
Indianapolis (city) Marion County	29	<0.01
Fort Wayne (city) Allen County	10	<0.01
South Bend (city) St. Joseph County	5	<0.01
Carmel (city) Hamilton County	3	<0.01
Muncie (city) Delaware County	2	<0.01
Noblesville (city) Hamilton County	2	<0.01
Elkhart (city) Elkhart County	1	<0.01

South American: Venezuelan

Top 10 Places Sorted by Population
Based on all places, regardless of total population

Place	Population	%
Indianapolis (city) Marion County	314	0.04
Noblesville (city) Hamilton County	97	0.19
Fishers (town) Hamilton County	93	0.12
South Bend (city) St. Joseph County	73	0.07
Bloomington (city) Monroe County	53	0.07
Fort Wayne (city) Allen County	45	0.02
Lawrence (city) Marion County	40	0.09
Carmel (city) Hamilton County	40	0.05
Mishawaka (city) St. Joseph County	36	0.07
Westfield (town) Hamilton County	35	0.12

Top 10 Places Sorted by Percent of Total Population
Based on all places, regardless of total population

Place	Population	%
Oakland City (city) Gibson County	17	0.70
Switz City (town) Greene County	1	0.34
Clear Lake (town) Steuben County	1	0.29
Kentland (town) Newton County	4	0.23
Noblesville (city) Hamilton County	97	0.19
Notre Dame (cdp) St. Joseph County	8	0.13
McCordsville (town) Hancock County	6	0.13
Utica (town) Clark County	1	0.13
Fishers (town) Hamilton County	93	0.12
Westfield (town) Hamilton County	35	0.12

Top 10 Places Sorted by Percent of Total Population
Based on places with total population of 50,000 or more

Place	Population	%
Noblesville (city) Hamilton County	97	0.19
Fishers (town) Hamilton County	93	0.12
South Bend (city) St. Joseph County	73	0.07
Bloomington (city) Monroe County	53	0.07
Carmel (city) Hamilton County	40	0.05
Indianapolis (city) Marion County	314	0.04
Elkhart (city) Elkhart County	22	0.04
Fort Wayne (city) Allen County	45	0.02
Evansville (city) Vanderburgh County	24	0.02
Muncie (city) Delaware County	13	0.02

South American: Other South American

Top 10 Places Sorted by Population
Based on all places, regardless of total population

Place	Population	%
Indianapolis (city) Marion County	19	<0.01
Fishers (town) Hamilton County	9	0.01
Bremen (town) Marshall County	5	0.11
Muncie (city) Delaware County	4	0.01
Hidden Valley (cdp) Dearborn County	3	0.06
La Porte (city) LaPorte County	3	0.01
Mishawaka (city) St. Joseph County	3	0.01
Reynolds (town) White County	2	0.38
Mentone (town) Kosciusko County	2	0.20
Marion (city) Grant County	2	0.01

Top 10 Places Sorted by Percent of Total Population
Based on all places, regardless of total population

Place	Population	%
Reynolds (town) White County	2	0.38
Mentone (town) Kosciusko County	2	0.20
Bremen (town) Marshall County	5	0.11
Hidden Valley (cdp) Dearborn County	3	0.06
Bristol (town) Elkhart County	1	0.06
Edinburgh (town) Johnson County	1	0.02
Porter (town) Porter County	1	0.02
Fishers (town) Hamilton County	9	0.01
Muncie (city) Delaware County	4	0.01
La Porte (city) LaPorte County	3	0.01

Top 10 Places Sorted by Percent of Total Population
Based on places with total population of 50,000 or more

Place	Population	%
Fishers (town) Hamilton County	9	0.01
Muncie (city) Delaware County	4	0.01
Indianapolis (city) Marion County	19	<0.01
Carmel (city) Hamilton County	1	<0.01
Evansville (city) Vanderburgh County	1	<0.01
Fort Wayne (city) Allen County	1	<0.01
Anderson (city) Madison County	0	0.00
Bloomington (city) Monroe County	0	0.00
Elkhart (city) Elkhart County	0	0.00
Gary (city) Lake County	0	0.00

Other Hispanic or Latino

Top 10 Places Sorted by Population
Based on all places, regardless of total population

Place	Population	%
Indianapolis (city) Marion County	5,473	0.67
Fort Wayne (city) Allen County	1,473	0.58
Hammond (city) Lake County	981	1.21
South Bend (city) St. Joseph County	846	0.84
Elkhart (city) Elkhart County	668	1.31
East Chicago (city) Lake County	483	1.63
Lafayette (city) Tippecanoe County	365	0.54
Goshen (city) Elkhart County	340	1.07
Evansville (city) Vanderburgh County	312	0.27
Bloomington (city) Monroe County	286	0.36

Top 10 Places Sorted by Percent of Total Population
Based on all places, regardless of total population

Place	Population	%
Plymouth (city) Marshall County	221	2.20
Monon (town) White County	36	2.03
Windfall City (town) Tipton County	14	1.98
Hamlet (town) Starke County	14	1.75
Bremen (town) Marshall County	78	1.70
East Chicago (city) Lake County	483	1.63
Logansport (city) Cass County	265	1.44
Frankfort (city) Clinton County	235	1.43
Boswell (town) Benton County	11	1.41
Crows Nest (town) Marion County	1	1.37

Top 10 Places Sorted by Percent of Total Population
Based on places with total population of 50,000 or more

Place	Population	%
Elkhart (city) Elkhart County	668	1.31
Hammond (city) Lake County	981	1.21
South Bend (city) St. Joseph County	846	0.84
Indianapolis (city) Marion County	5,473	0.67
Fort Wayne (city) Allen County	1,473	0.58
Lafayette (city) Tippecanoe County	365	0.54
Anderson (city) Madison County	223	0.40
Bloomington (city) Monroe County	286	0.36
Noblesville (city) Hamilton County	174	0.33
Fishers (town) Hamilton County	243	0.32

Racial Group Rankings

African-American/Black

Top 10 Places Sorted by Population
Based on all places, regardless of total population

Place	Population	%
Indianapolis (city) Marion County	239,354	29.17
Gary (city) Lake County	69,508	86.57
Fort Wayne (city) Allen County	44,499	17.54
South Bend (city) St. Joseph County	29,667	29.32
Hammond (city) Lake County	19,336	23.92
Evansville (city) Vanderburgh County	17,089	14.55
Merrillville (town) Lake County	16,337	46.35
East Chicago (city) Lake County	13,135	44.23
Lawrence (city) Marion County	12,900	28.04
Michigan City (city) LaPorte County	9,686	30.77

Top 10 Places Sorted by Percent of Total Population
Based on all places, regardless of total population

Place	Population	%
Gary (city) Lake County	69,508	86.57
Merrillville (town) Lake County	16,337	46.35
East Chicago (city) Lake County	13,135	44.23
Wynnedale (town) Marion County	83	35.93
Michigan City (city) LaPorte County	9,686	30.77
South Bend (city) St. Joseph County	29,667	29.32
Indianapolis (city) Marion County	239,354	29.17
Lawrence (city) Marion County	12,900	28.04
Westville (town) LaPorte County	1,486	25.39
Hammond (city) Lake County	19,336	23.92

Top 10 Places Sorted by Percent of Total Population
Based on places with total population of 50,000 or more

Place	Population	%
Gary (city) Lake County	69,508	86.57
South Bend (city) St. Joseph County	29,667	29.32
Indianapolis (city) Marion County	239,354	29.17
Hammond (city) Lake County	19,336	23.92
Elkhart (city) Elkhart County	9,108	17.88
Fort Wayne (city) Allen County	44,499	17.54
Anderson (city) Madison County	9,500	16.93
Evansville (city) Vanderburgh County	17,089	14.55
Terre Haute (city) Vigo County	7,819	12.86
Muncie (city) Delaware County	8,829	12.60

African-American/Black: Not Hispanic

Top 10 Places Sorted by Population
Based on all places, regardless of total population

Place	Population	%
Indianapolis (city) Marion County	235,521	28.71
Gary (city) Lake County	68,449	85.25
Fort Wayne (city) Allen County	43,301	17.07
South Bend (city) St. Joseph County	28,893	28.56
Hammond (city) Lake County	18,369	22.73
Evansville (city) Vanderburgh County	16,871	14.37
Merrillville (town) Lake County	15,889	45.08
Lawrence (city) Marion County	12,650	27.50
East Chicago (city) Lake County	12,330	41.52
Michigan City (city) LaPorte County	9,477	30.11

Top 10 Places Sorted by Percent of Total Population
Based on all places, regardless of total population

Place	Population	%
Gary (city) Lake County	68,449	85.25
Merrillville (town) Lake County	15,889	45.08
East Chicago (city) Lake County	12,330	41.52
Wynnedale (town) Marion County	83	35.93
Michigan City (city) LaPorte County	9,477	30.11
Indianapolis (city) Marion County	235,521	28.71
South Bend (city) St. Joseph County	28,893	28.56
Lawrence (city) Marion County	12,650	27.50
Westville (town) LaPorte County	1,481	25.30
Grissom AFB (cdp) Miami County	1,286	23.23

African-American/Black: Hispanic

Top 10 Places Sorted by Population
Based on all places, regardless of total population

Place	Population	%
Indianapolis (city) Marion County	3,833	0.47
Fort Wayne (city) Allen County	1,198	0.47
Gary (city) Lake County	1,059	1.32
Hammond (city) Lake County	967	1.20
East Chicago (city) Lake County	805	2.71
South Bend (city) St. Joseph County	774	0.77
Merrillville (town) Lake County	448	1.27
Elkhart (city) Elkhart County	265	0.52
Lawrence (city) Marion County	250	0.54
Lafayette (city) Tippecanoe County	235	0.35

Top 10 Places Sorted by Percent of Total Population
Based on all places, regardless of total population

Place	Population	%
East Chicago (city) Lake County	805	2.71
Gary (city) Lake County	1,059	1.32
Merrillville (town) Lake County	448	1.27
Leavenworth (town) Crawford County	3	1.26
Hammond (city) Lake County	967	1.20
Lake Station (city) Lake County	139	1.11
Whiting (city) Lake County	52	1.04
Elizabeth (town) Bartholomew County	5	0.99
Kewanna (town) Fulton County	6	0.98
Wheeler (cdp) Porter County	4	0.90

Top 10 Places Sorted by Percent of Total Population
Based on places with total population of 50,000 or more

Place	Population	%
Gary (city) Lake County	1,059	1.32
Hammond (city) Lake County	967	1.20
South Bend (city) St. Joseph County	774	0.77
Elkhart (city) Elkhart County	265	0.52
Indianapolis (city) Marion County	3,833	0.47
Fort Wayne (city) Allen County	1,198	0.47
Lafayette (city) Tippecanoe County	235	0.35
Bloomington (city) Monroe County	195	0.24
Muncie (city) Delaware County	165	0.24
Anderson (city) Madison County	124	0.22

American Indian/Alaska Native

Top 10 Places Sorted by Population
Based on all places, regardless of total population

Place	Population	%
Indianapolis (city) Marion County	7,323	0.89
Fort Wayne (city) Allen County	2,669	1.05
South Bend (city) St. Joseph County	1,334	1.32
Hammond (city) Lake County	930	1.15
Evansville (city) Vanderburgh County	916	0.78
Gary (city) Lake County	760	0.95
Elkhart (city) Elkhart County	706	1.39
Bloomington (city) Monroe County	699	0.87
Terre Haute (city) Vigo County	685	1.13
Lafayette (city) Tippecanoe County	672	1.00

Top 10 Places Sorted by Percent of Total Population
Based on all places, regardless of total population

Place	Population	%
Fredericksburg (town) Washington County	6	7.06
Canaan (cdp) Jefferson County	4	4.44
Dunreith (town) Henry County	6	3.39
Jonesville (town) Bartholomew County	6	3.39
Burket (town) Kosciusko County	6	3.08
Alamo (town) Montgomery County	2	3.03
Coalmont (cdp) Clay County	12	2.99
Wheeler (cdp) Porter County	13	2.93
Springport (town) Henry County	4	2.68
Lagro (town) Wabash County	11	2.65

Top 10 Places Sorted by Percent of Total Population
Based on places with total population of 50,000 or more

Place	Population	%
Elkhart (city) Elkhart County	706	1.39
South Bend (city) St. Joseph County	1,334	1.32
Hammond (city) Lake County	930	1.15
Terre Haute (city) Vigo County	685	1.13
Fort Wayne (city) Allen County	2,669	1.05
Lafayette (city) Tippecanoe County	672	1.00
Gary (city) Lake County	760	0.95
Anderson (city) Madison County	528	0.94
Muncie (city) Delaware County	650	0.93
Indianapolis (city) Marion County	7,323	0.89

American Indian/Alaska Native: Not Hispanic

Top 10 Places Sorted by Population
Based on all places, regardless of total population

Place	Population	%
Indianapolis (city) Marion County	5,844	0.71
Fort Wayne (city) Allen County	2,172	0.86
South Bend (city) St. Joseph County	1,029	1.02
Evansville (city) Vanderburgh County	831	0.71
Gary (city) Lake County	659	0.82
Terre Haute (city) Vigo County	632	1.04
Bloomington (city) Monroe County	591	0.74
Muncie (city) Delaware County	577	0.82
Lafayette (city) Tippecanoe County	544	0.81
Mishawaka (city) St. Joseph County	489	1.01

Top 10 Places Sorted by Percent of Total Population
Based on all places, regardless of total population

Place	Population	%
Canaan (cdp) Jefferson County	4	4.44
Dunreith (town) Henry County	6	3.39
Jonesville (town) Bartholomew County	6	3.39
Alamo (town) Montgomery County	2	3.03
Coalmont (cdp) Clay County	12	2.99
Wheeler (cdp) Porter County	13	2.93
Springport (town) Henry County	4	2.68
Lagro (town) Wabash County	11	2.65
Losantville (town) Randolph County	6	2.53
Bethany (town) Morgan County	2	2.47

Top 10 Places Sorted by Percent of Total Population
Based on places with total population of 50,000 or more

Place	Population	%
Terre Haute (city) Vigo County	632	1.04
South Bend (city) St. Joseph County	1,029	1.02
Elkhart (city) Elkhart County	482	0.95
Fort Wayne (city) Allen County	2,172	0.86
Gary (city) Lake County	659	0.82
Muncie (city) Delaware County	577	0.82
Lafayette (city) Tippecanoe County	544	0.81
Anderson (city) Madison County	432	0.77
Bloomington (city) Monroe County	591	0.74
Indianapolis (city) Marion County	5,844	0.71

American Indian/Alaska Native: Hispanic

Top 10 Places Sorted by Population
Based on all places, regardless of total population

Place	Population	%
Indianapolis (city) Marion County	1,479	0.18
Fort Wayne (city) Allen County	497	0.20
Hammond (city) Lake County	441	0.55
South Bend (city) St. Joseph County	305	0.30
Elkhart (city) Elkhart County	224	0.44
East Chicago (city) Lake County	209	0.70
Goshen (city) Elkhart County	137	0.43
Lafayette (city) Tippecanoe County	128	0.19
Lawrence (city) Marion County	118	0.26
Logansport (city) Cass County	111	0.60

Top 10 Places Sorted by Percent of Total Population
Based on all places, regardless of total population

Place	Population	%
Fredericksburg (town) Washington County	4	4.71
Burket (town) Kosciusko County	5	2.56
Akron (town) Fulton County	20	1.71
Mount Ayr (town) Newton County	2	1.64
Reynolds (town) White County	8	1.50
Schneider (town) Lake County	3	1.08
Linden (town) Montgomery County	8	1.05
Whiting (city) Lake County	48	0.96
Francisco (town) Gibson County	4	0.85
New Chicago (town) Lake County	17	0.84

Top 10 Places Sorted by Percent of Total Population
Based on places with total population of 50,000 or more

Place	Population	%
Hammond (city) Lake County	441	0.55
Elkhart (city) Elkhart County	224	0.44
South Bend (city) St. Joseph County	305	0.30
Fort Wayne (city) Allen County	497	0.20
Lafayette (city) Tippecanoe County	128	0.19
Indianapolis (city) Marion County	1,479	0.18
Anderson (city) Madison County	96	0.17
Bloomington (city) Monroe County	108	0.13
Gary (city) Lake County	101	0.13
Muncie (city) Delaware County	73	0.10

Alaska Native: Alaska Athabascan

Top 10 Places Sorted by Population
Based on all places, regardless of total population

Place	Population	%
Cedar Lake (town) Lake County	5	0.04
Lafayette (city) Tippecanoe County	4	0.01
Fort Wayne (city) Allen County	4	<0.01
North Vernon (city) Jennings County	3	0.04
Indianapolis (city) Marion County	3	<0.01
West Terre Haute (town) Vigo County	2	0.09
Brownsburg (town) Hendricks County	2	0.01
Chesterton (town) Porter County	1	0.01
Bloomington (city) Monroe County	1	<0.01
Evansville (city) Vanderburgh County	1	<0.01

Top 10 Places Sorted by Percent of Total Population
Based on all places, regardless of total population

Place	Population	%
West Terre Haute (town) Vigo County	2	0.09
Cedar Lake (town) Lake County	5	0.04
North Vernon (city) Jennings County	3	0.04
Lafayette (city) Tippecanoe County	4	0.01
Brownsburg (town) Hendricks County	2	0.01
Chesterton (town) Porter County	1	0.01
Fort Wayne (city) Allen County	4	<0.01
Indianapolis (city) Marion County	3	<0.01
Bloomington (city) Monroe County	1	<0.01
Evansville (city) Vanderburgh County	1	<0.01

Top 10 Places Sorted by Percent of Total Population
Based on places with total population of 50,000 or more

Place	Population	%
Lafayette (city) Tippecanoe County	4	0.01
Fort Wayne (city) Allen County	4	<0.01
Indianapolis (city) Marion County	3	<0.01
Bloomington (city) Monroe County	1	<0.01
Evansville (city) Vanderburgh County	1	<0.01
Anderson (city) Madison County	0	0.00
Carmel (city) Hamilton County	0	0.00
Elkhart (city) Elkhart County	0	0.00
Fishers (town) Hamilton County	0	0.00
Gary (city) Lake County	0	0.00

Alaska Native: Aleut

Top 10 Places Sorted by Population
Based on all places, regardless of total population

Place	Population	%
Indianapolis (city) Marion County	14	<0.01
Cannelton (city) Perry County	2	0.13
Bloomington (city) Monroe County	2	<0.01
Greenwood (city) Johnson County	2	<0.01
Lafayette (city) Tippecanoe County	2	<0.01
La Paz (town) Marshall County	1	0.18
Rockville (town) Parke County	1	0.04
Auburn (city) DeKalb County	1	0.01
Logansport (city) Cass County	1	0.01
Fort Wayne (city) Allen County	1	<0.01

Top 10 Places Sorted by Percent of Total Population
Based on all places, regardless of total population

Place	Population	%
La Paz (town) Marshall County	1	0.18
Cannelton (city) Perry County	2	0.13
Rockville (town) Parke County	1	0.04
Auburn (city) DeKalb County	1	0.01
Logansport (city) Cass County	1	0.01
Indianapolis (city) Marion County	14	<0.01
Bloomington (city) Monroe County	2	<0.01
Greenwood (city) Johnson County	2	<0.01
Lafayette (city) Tippecanoe County	2	<0.01
Fort Wayne (city) Allen County	1	<0.01

Top 10 Places Sorted by Percent of Total Population
Based on places with total population of 50,000 or more

Place	Population	%
Indianapolis (city) Marion County	14	<0.01
Bloomington (city) Monroe County	2	<0.01
Lafayette (city) Tippecanoe County	2	<0.01
Fort Wayne (city) Allen County	1	<0.01
Anderson (city) Madison County	0	0.00
Carmel (city) Hamilton County	0	0.00
Elkhart (city) Elkhart County	0	0.00
Evansville (city) Vanderburgh County	0	0.00
Fishers (town) Hamilton County	0	0.00
Gary (city) Lake County	0	0.00

American Indian: Apache

Top 10 Places Sorted by Population
Based on all places, regardless of total population

Place	Population	%
Indianapolis (city) Marion County	98	0.01
Fort Wayne (city) Allen County	43	0.02
South Bend (city) St. Joseph County	29	0.03
Evansville (city) Vanderburgh County	23	0.02
Hammond (city) Lake County	19	0.02
Michigan City (city) LaPorte County	17	0.05
Gary (city) Lake County	16	0.02
Lawrence (city) Marion County	12	0.03
Lafayette (city) Tippecanoe County	12	0.02
Muncie (city) Delaware County	12	0.02

Top 10 Places Sorted by Percent of Total Population
Based on all places, regardless of total population

Place	Population	%
Fredericksburg (town) Washington County	6	7.06
Canaan (cdp) Jefferson County	4	4.44
Economy (town) Wayne County	1	0.53
Perrysville (town) Vermillion County	2	0.44
Lyons (town) Greene County	3	0.40
Shirley (town) Hancock County	3	0.36
Swayzee (town) Grant County	3	0.31
Sheridan (town) Hamilton County	8	0.30
St. Leon (town) Dearborn County	2	0.29
Jonesboro (city) Grant County	5	0.28

Top 10 Places Sorted by Percent of Total Population
Based on places with total population of 50,000 or more

Place	Population	%
South Bend (city) St. Joseph County	29	0.03
Fort Wayne (city) Allen County	43	0.02
Evansville (city) Vanderburgh County	23	0.02
Hammond (city) Lake County	19	0.02
Gary (city) Lake County	16	0.02
Lafayette (city) Tippecanoe County	12	0.02
Muncie (city) Delaware County	12	0.02
Anderson (city) Madison County	9	0.02
Indianapolis (city) Marion County	98	0.01
Bloomington (city) Monroe County	11	0.01

American Indian: Arapaho

Top 10 Places Sorted by Population
Based on all places, regardless of total population

Place	Population	%
Indianapolis (city) Marion County	4	<0.01
New Palestine (town) Hancock County	3	0.15
Austin (city) Scott County	3	0.07
Jasper (city) Dubois County	3	0.02
East Chicago (city) Lake County	3	0.01
Fort Wayne (city) Allen County	3	<0.01
Wheatland (town) Knox County	2	0.42
Highland (town) Lake County	2	0.01
Roachdale (town) Putnam County	1	0.11
Shelburn (town) Sullivan County	1	0.08

Top 10 Places Sorted by Percent of Total Population
Based on all places, regardless of total population

Place	Population	%
Wheatland (town) Knox County	2	0.42
New Palestine (town) Hancock County	3	0.15
Roachdale (town) Putnam County	1	0.11
Shelburn (town) Sullivan County	1	0.08
Austin (city) Scott County	3	0.07
Country Squire Lakes (cdp) Jennings County	1	0.03
Smithville-Sanders (cdp) Monroe County	1	0.03
Jasper (city) Dubois County	3	0.02
East Chicago (city) Lake County	3	0.01
Highland (town) Lake County	2	0.01

Top 10 Places Sorted by Percent of Total Population
Based on places with total population of 50,000 or more

Place	Population	%
Indianapolis (city) Marion County	4	<0.01
Fort Wayne (city) Allen County	3	<0.01
Evansville (city) Vanderburgh County	1	<0.01
Hammond (city) Lake County	1	<0.01
Muncie (city) Delaware County	1	<0.01
South Bend (city) St. Joseph County	1	<0.01
Anderson (city) Madison County	0	0.00
Bloomington (city) Monroe County	0	0.00
Carmel (city) Hamilton County	0	0.00
Elkhart (city) Elkhart County	0	0.00

American Indian: Blackfeet

Top 10 Places Sorted by Population
Based on all places, regardless of total population

Place	Population	%
Indianapolis (city) Marion County	354	0.04
Fort Wayne (city) Allen County	110	0.04
South Bend (city) St. Joseph County	74	0.07
Gary (city) Lake County	43	0.05
Muncie (city) Delaware County	42	0.06
Evansville (city) Vanderburgh County	39	0.03
Portage (city) Porter County	35	0.10
Anderson (city) Madison County	32	0.06
Elkhart (city) Elkhart County	31	0.06
Michigan City (city) LaPorte County	28	0.09

Top 10 Places Sorted by Percent of Total Population
Based on all places, regardless of total population

Place	Population	%
Burnettsville (town) White County	2	0.58
Lynnville (town) Warrick County	5	0.56
Laketon (cdp) Wabash County	3	0.48

Please refer to the Explanation of Data in the front of the book for more detailed information.

Place	Population	%
Waveland (town) Montgomery County	2	0.48
Spurgeon (town) Pike County	1	0.48
Carlisle (town) Sullivan County	3	0.43
Decker (town) Knox County	1	0.40
Hayden (cdp) Jennings County	2	0.38
Manilla (cdp) Rush County	1	0.37
Roachdale (town) Putnam County	3	0.32

Top 10 Places Sorted by Percent of Total Population
Based on places with total population of 50,000 or more

Place	Population	%
South Bend (city) St. Joseph County	74	0.07
Muncie (city) Delaware County	42	0.06
Anderson (city) Madison County	32	0.06
Elkhart (city) Elkhart County	31	0.06
Gary (city) Lake County	43	0.05
Indianapolis (city) Marion County	354	0.04
Fort Wayne (city) Allen County	110	0.04
Lafayette (city) Tippecanoe County	27	0.04
Terre Haute (city) Vigo County	24	0.04
Evansville (city) Vanderburgh County	39	0.03

American Indian: Canadian/French American Indian

Top 10 Places Sorted by Population
Based on all places, regardless of total population

Place	Population	%
Indianapolis (city) Marion County	22	<0.01
Granger (cdp) St. Joseph County	12	0.04
Walkerton (town) St. Joseph County	10	0.47
Koontz Lake (cdp) Starke County	7	0.45
East Chicago (city) Lake County	6	0.02
Vincennes (city) Knox County	5	0.03
Schererville (town) Lake County	5	0.02
Elkhart (city) Elkhart County	5	0.01
Jeffersonville (city) Clark County	5	0.01
South Bend (city) St. Joseph County	5	<0.01

Top 10 Places Sorted by Percent of Total Population
Based on all places, regardless of total population

Place	Population	%
Hamlet (town) Starke County	4	0.50
Walkerton (town) St. Joseph County	10	0.47
Koontz Lake (cdp) Starke County	7	0.45
Butlerville (cdp) Jennings County	1	0.35
Camden (town) Carroll County	2	0.33
Markleville (town) Madison County	1	0.19
Chandler (town) Warrick County	4	0.14
Ingalls (town) Madison County	3	0.13
Lakeville (town) St. Joseph County	1	0.13
Shirley (town) Hancock County	1	0.12

Top 10 Places Sorted by Percent of Total Population
Based on places with total population of 50,000 or more

Place	Population	%
Elkhart (city) Elkhart County	5	0.01
Indianapolis (city) Marion County	22	<0.01
South Bend (city) St. Joseph County	5	<0.01
Fort Wayne (city) Allen County	4	<0.01
Lafayette (city) Tippecanoe County	3	<0.01
Evansville (city) Vanderburgh County	2	<0.01
Anderson (city) Madison County	1	<0.01
Bloomington (city) Monroe County	1	<0.01
Gary (city) Lake County	1	<0.01
Hammond (city) Lake County	1	<0.01

American Indian: Central American Indian

Top 10 Places Sorted by Population
Based on all places, regardless of total population

Place	Population	%
Logansport (city) Cass County	27	0.15
Fort Wayne (city) Allen County	11	<0.01
Indianapolis (city) Marion County	11	<0.01
Columbus (city) Bartholomew County	8	0.02
South Bend (city) St. Joseph County	8	0.01
Anderson (city) Madison County	7	0.01
Pittsboro (town) Hendricks County	4	0.14
Seymour (city) Jackson County	4	0.02
Elkhart (city) Elkhart County	4	0.01
Merrillville (town) Lake County	4	0.01

Top 10 Places Sorted by Percent of Total Population
Based on all places, regardless of total population

Place	Population	%
Bourbon (town) Marshall County	3	0.17
Rocky Ripple (town) Marion County	1	0.17
Logansport (city) Cass County	27	0.15
Pittsboro (town) Hendricks County	4	0.14
Newburgh (town) Warrick County	2	0.06
Gas City (city) Grant County	3	0.05
Columbus (city) Bartholomew County	8	0.02
Seymour (city) Jackson County	4	0.02
Avon (town) Hendricks County	2	0.02
Huntingburg (city) Dubois County	1	0.02

Top 10 Places Sorted by Percent of Total Population
Based on places with total population of 50,000 or more

Place	Population	%
South Bend (city) St. Joseph County	8	0.01
Anderson (city) Madison County	7	0.01
Elkhart (city) Elkhart County	4	0.01
Fort Wayne (city) Allen County	11	<0.01
Indianapolis (city) Marion County	11	<0.01
Gary (city) Lake County	3	<0.01
Bloomington (city) Monroe County	2	<0.01
Carmel (city) Hamilton County	2	<0.01
Evansville (city) Vanderburgh County	1	<0.01
Fishers (town) Hamilton County	1	<0.01

American Indian: Cherokee

Top 10 Places Sorted by Population
Based on all places, regardless of total population

Place	Population	%
Indianapolis (city) Marion County	1,682	0.21
Fort Wayne (city) Allen County	481	0.19
Evansville (city) Vanderburgh County	283	0.24
South Bend (city) St. Joseph County	281	0.28
Lafayette (city) Tippecanoe County	195	0.29
Muncie (city) Delaware County	182	0.26
Hammond (city) Lake County	182	0.23
Bloomington (city) Monroe County	161	0.20
Terre Haute (city) Vigo County	159	0.26
Gary (city) Lake County	153	0.19

Top 10 Places Sorted by Percent of Total Population
Based on all places, regardless of total population

Place	Population	%
Fredericksburg (town) Washington County	6	7.06
Deputy (cdp) Jefferson County	2	2.33
Springport (town) Henry County	3	2.01
Medora (town) Jackson County	13	1.88
Wheeler (cdp) Porter County	8	1.81
Losantville (town) Randolph County	4	1.69
Jonesville (town) Bartholomew County	3	1.69
Andrews (town) Huntington County	15	1.31
Vera Cruz (town) Wells County	1	1.25
Bethany (town) Morgan County	1	1.23

Top 10 Places Sorted by Percent of Total Population
Based on places with total population of 50,000 or more

Place	Population	%
Lafayette (city) Tippecanoe County	195	0.29
South Bend (city) St. Joseph County	281	0.28
Muncie (city) Delaware County	182	0.26
Terre Haute (city) Vigo County	159	0.26
Evansville (city) Vanderburgh County	283	0.24
Elkhart (city) Elkhart County	120	0.24
Hammond (city) Lake County	182	0.23
Anderson (city) Madison County	127	0.23
Indianapolis (city) Marion County	1,682	0.21
Bloomington (city) Monroe County	161	0.20

American Indian: Cheyenne

Top 10 Places Sorted by Population
Based on all places, regardless of total population

Place	Population	%
Indianapolis (city) Marion County	18	<0.01
Evansville (city) Vanderburgh County	11	0.01
Terre Haute (city) Vigo County	6	0.01
Fort Wayne (city) Allen County	6	<0.01
Elwood (city) Madison County	5	0.06
Vincennes (city) Knox County	5	0.03
Monticello (city) White County	4	0.07
Logansport (city) Cass County	4	0.02
Anderson (city) Madison County	4	0.01
Lafayette (city) Tippecanoe County	4	0.01

Top 10 Places Sorted by Percent of Total Population
Based on all places, regardless of total population

Place	Population	%
Holton (town) Ripley County	2	0.42
Universal (town) Vermillion County	1	0.28
Geneva (town) Adams County	2	0.15
Monticello (city) White County	4	0.07
Elwood (city) Madison County	5	0.06
Vincennes (city) Knox County	5	0.03
Bicknell (city) Knox County	1	0.03
Country Squire Lakes (cdp) Jennings County	1	0.03
Union City (city) Randolph County	1	0.03
Logansport (city) Cass County	4	0.02

Top 10 Places Sorted by Percent of Total Population
Based on places with total population of 50,000 or more

Place	Population	%
Evansville (city) Vanderburgh County	11	0.01
Terre Haute (city) Vigo County	6	0.01
Anderson (city) Madison County	4	0.01
Lafayette (city) Tippecanoe County	4	0.01
Elkhart (city) Elkhart County	3	0.01
Indianapolis (city) Marion County	18	<0.01
Fort Wayne (city) Allen County	6	<0.01
South Bend (city) St. Joseph County	1	<0.01
Bloomington (city) Monroe County	0	0.00
Carmel (city) Hamilton County	0	0.00

American Indian: Chickasaw

Top 10 Places Sorted by Population
Based on all places, regardless of total population

Place	Population	%
Fort Wayne (city) Allen County	13	0.01
Indianapolis (city) Marion County	12	<0.01
Jeffersonville (city) Clark County	8	0.02
Mishawaka (city) St. Joseph County	7	0.01
South Bend (city) St. Joseph County	6	0.01
Boonville (city) Warrick County	4	0.06
New Albany (city) Floyd County	4	0.01
Terre Haute (city) Vigo County	4	0.01
Gary (city) Lake County	4	<0.01
Bunker Hill (town) Miami County	3	0.34

Top 10 Places Sorted by Percent of Total Population
Based on all places, regardless of total population

Place	Population	%
Bunker Hill (town) Miami County	3	0.34
Richland (town) Spencer County	1	0.24
Cynthiana (town) Posey County	1	0.18
Rolling Prairie (cdp) LaPorte County	1	0.17
Fountain City (town) Wayne County	1	0.13
Centerville (town) Wayne County	3	0.12
Paoli (town) Orange County	3	0.08
Boonville (city) Warrick County	4	0.06
Vevay (town) Switzerland County	1	0.06
Hope (town) Bartholomew County	1	0.05

Top 10 Places Sorted by Percent of Total Population
Based on places with total population of 50,000 or more

Place	Population	%
Fort Wayne (city) Allen County	13	0.01
South Bend (city) St. Joseph County	6	0.01
Terre Haute (city) Vigo County	4	0.01
Indianapolis (city) Marion County	12	<0.01
Gary (city) Lake County	4	<0.01
Evansville (city) Vanderburgh County	3	<0.01
Lafayette (city) Tippecanoe County	3	<0.01
Bloomington (city) Monroe County	2	<0.01
Elkhart (city) Elkhart County	2	<0.01
Hammond (city) Lake County	2	<0.01

American Indian: Chippewa

Top 10 Places Sorted by Population
Based on all places, regardless of total population

Place	Population	%
Indianapolis (city) Marion County	134	0.02
Fort Wayne (city) Allen County	63	0.02
South Bend (city) St. Joseph County	29	0.03
Portage (city) Porter County	26	0.07
Bloomington (city) Monroe County	21	0.03
Hammond (city) Lake County	21	0.03
Kokomo (city) Howard County	19	0.04
Noblesville (city) Hamilton County	18	0.03
Evansville (city) Vanderburgh County	18	0.02
Elkhart (city) Elkhart County	14	0.03

Top 10 Places Sorted by Percent of Total Population
Based on all places, regardless of total population

Place	Population	%
Gentryville (town) Spencer County	4	1.49
Schneider (town) Lake County	3	1.08
San Pierre (cdp) Starke County	1	0.69
Ogden Dunes (town) Porter County	5	0.45
Clifford (town) Bartholomew County	1	0.43
Shelburn (town) Sullivan County	5	0.40
Switz City (town) Greene County	1	0.34
Rocky Ripple (town) Marion County	2	0.33
Collegeville (cdp) Jasper County	1	0.30
Burns Harbor (town) Porter County	3	0.26

Top 10 Places Sorted by Percent of Total Population
Based on places with total population of 50,000 or more

Place	Population	%
South Bend (city) St. Joseph County	29	0.03
Bloomington (city) Monroe County	21	0.03
Hammond (city) Lake County	21	0.03
Noblesville (city) Hamilton County	18	0.03
Elkhart (city) Elkhart County	14	0.03
Indianapolis (city) Marion County	134	0.02
Fort Wayne (city) Allen County	63	0.02
Evansville (city) Vanderburgh County	18	0.02
Lafayette (city) Tippecanoe County	12	0.02
Gary (city) Lake County	11	0.01

American Indian: Choctaw

Top 10 Places Sorted by Population
Based on all places, regardless of total population

Place	Population	%
Indianapolis (city) Marion County	99	0.01
Fort Wayne (city) Allen County	55	0.02
Gary (city) Lake County	27	0.03
South Bend (city) St. Joseph County	23	0.02
Bloomington (city) Monroe County	19	0.02
Hammond (city) Lake County	18	0.02
Jeffersonville (city) Clark County	16	0.04
Evansville (city) Vanderburgh County	16	0.01
Elkhart (city) Elkhart County	12	0.02
New Albany (city) Floyd County	11	0.03

Top 10 Places Sorted by Percent of Total Population
Based on all places, regardless of total population

Place	Population	%
Cedar Grove (town) Franklin County	1	0.64
Memphis (cdp) Clark County	4	0.58
Ashley (town) DeKalb County	3	0.31
Mecca (town) Parke County	1	0.30
Mount Summit (town) Henry County	1	0.28
Waldron (cdp) Shelby County	2	0.25
Lagro (town) Wabash County	1	0.24
Palmyra (town) Harrison County	2	0.22
Hayden (cdp) Jennings County	1	0.19
Bargersville (town) Johnson County	7	0.17

Top 10 Places Sorted by Percent of Total Population
Based on places with total population of 50,000 or more

Place	Population	%
Gary (city) Lake County	27	0.03
Fort Wayne (city) Allen County	55	0.02
South Bend (city) St. Joseph County	23	0.02
Bloomington (city) Monroe County	19	0.02
Hammond (city) Lake County	18	0.02
Elkhart (city) Elkhart County	12	0.02
Anderson (city) Madison County	10	0.02
Indianapolis (city) Marion County	99	0.01
Evansville (city) Vanderburgh County	16	0.01
Carmel (city) Hamilton County	11	0.01

American Indian: Colville

Top 10 Places Sorted by Population
Based on all places, regardless of total population

Place	Population	%
Speedway (town) Marion County	4	0.03
Heritage Lake (cdp) Putnam County	2	0.07
Kokomo (city) Howard County	2	<0.01
Evansville (city) Vanderburgh County	1	<0.01
South Bend (city) St. Joseph County	1	<0.01
Aberdeen (cdp) Porter County	0	0.00
Advance (town) Boone County	0	0.00
Akron (town) Fulton County	0	0.00
Alamo (town) Montgomery County	0	0.00
Albany (town) Delaware County	0	0.00

Top 10 Places Sorted by Percent of Total Population
Based on all places, regardless of total population

Place	Population	%
Heritage Lake (cdp) Putnam County	2	0.07
Speedway (town) Marion County	4	0.03
Kokomo (city) Howard County	2	<0.01
Evansville (city) Vanderburgh County	1	<0.01
South Bend (city) St. Joseph County	1	<0.01
Aberdeen (cdp) Porter County	0	0.00
Advance (town) Boone County	0	0.00
Akron (town) Fulton County	0	0.00
Alamo (town) Montgomery County	0	0.00
Albany (town) Delaware County	0	0.00

Top 10 Places Sorted by Percent of Total Population
Based on places with total population of 50,000 or more

Place	Population	%
Evansville (city) Vanderburgh County	1	<0.01
South Bend (city) St. Joseph County	1	<0.01
Anderson (city) Madison County	0	0.00
Bloomington (city) Monroe County	0	0.00
Carmel (city) Hamilton County	0	0.00
Elkhart (city) Elkhart County	0	0.00
Fishers (town) Hamilton County	0	0.00
Fort Wayne (city) Allen County	0	0.00
Gary (city) Lake County	0	0.00
Hammond (city) Lake County	0	0.00

American Indian: Comanche

Top 10 Places Sorted by Population
Based on all places, regardless of total population

Place	Population	%
Indianapolis (city) Marion County	28	<0.01
Mooresville (town) Morgan County	4	0.04
Fort Wayne (city) Allen County	4	<0.01
Hunter (town) Allen County	3	0.06
Greenwood (city) Johnson County	3	0.01
Lawrence (city) Marion County	3	0.01
Carmel (city) Hamilton County	3	<0.01
Hammond (city) Lake County	3	<0.01
Lafayette (city) Tippecanoe County	3	<0.01
Etna Green (town) Kosciusko County	2	0.34

Top 10 Places Sorted by Percent of Total Population
Based on all places, regardless of total population

Place	Population	%
Etna Green (town) Kosciusko County	2	0.34
Francesville (town) Pulaski County	2	0.23
Medaryville (town) Pulaski County	1	0.16
Roseland (town) St. Joseph County	1	0.16
West College Corner (town) Union County	1	0.15
Bristol (town) Elkhart County	2	0.12
Hunter (town) Allen County	3	0.06
Crothersville (town) Jackson County	1	0.06
Mooresville (town) Morgan County	4	0.04
Fairmount (town) Grant County	1	0.03

Top 10 Places Sorted by Percent of Total Population
Based on places with total population of 50,000 or more

Place	Population	%
Indianapolis (city) Marion County	28	<0.01
Fort Wayne (city) Allen County	4	<0.01
Carmel (city) Hamilton County	3	<0.01
Hammond (city) Lake County	3	<0.01
Lafayette (city) Tippecanoe County	3	<0.01
Elkhart (city) Elkhart County	2	<0.01
Evansville (city) Vanderburgh County	2	<0.01
Gary (city) Lake County	2	<0.01
Terre Haute (city) Vigo County	2	<0.01
South Bend (city) St. Joseph County	1	<0.01

American Indian: Cree

Top 10 Places Sorted by Population
Based on all places, regardless of total population

Place	Population	%
Indianapolis (city) Marion County	13	<0.01
Terre Haute (city) Vigo County	9	0.01
Fort Wayne (city) Allen County	9	<0.01
Gary (city) Lake County	7	0.01
Muncie (city) Delaware County	5	0.01
Elkhart (city) Elkhart County	4	0.01
Plymouth (city) Marshall County	3	0.03
Plainfield (town) Hendricks County	3	0.01
Carmel (city) Hamilton County	3	<0.01
Logansport (city) Cass County	2	0.01

Top 10 Places Sorted by Percent of Total Population
Based on all places, regardless of total population

Place	Population	%
Losantville (town) Randolph County	1	0.42
Boswell (town) Benton County	1	0.13
Mulberry (town) Clinton County	1	0.08
Warren Park (town) Marion County	1	0.07
Plymouth (city) Marshall County	3	0.03
Middlebury (town) Elkhart County	1	0.03
Greendale (city) Dearborn County	1	0.02
Hartford City (city) Blackford County	1	0.02
Terre Haute (city) Vigo County	9	0.01
Gary (city) Lake County	7	0.01

Top 10 Places Sorted by Percent of Total Population
Based on places with total population of 50,000 or more

Place	Population	%
Terre Haute (city) Vigo County	9	0.01
Gary (city) Lake County	7	0.01
Muncie (city) Delaware County	5	0.01
Elkhart (city) Elkhart County	4	0.01
Indianapolis (city) Marion County	13	<0.01
Fort Wayne (city) Allen County	9	<0.01
Carmel (city) Hamilton County	3	<0.01
Evansville (city) Vanderburgh County	2	<0.01
Bloomington (city) Monroe County	1	<0.01
Fishers (town) Hamilton County	1	<0.01

American Indian: Creek

Top 10 Places Sorted by Population
Based on all places, regardless of total population

Place	Population	%
Indianapolis (city) Marion County	31	<0.01
Gary (city) Lake County	20	0.02
Fort Wayne (city) Allen County	18	0.01
Hammond (city) Lake County	10	0.01
Jeffersonville (city) Clark County	9	0.02
Valparaiso (city) Porter County	8	0.03
Noblesville (city) Hamilton County	8	0.02
Portage (city) Porter County	8	0.02
Terre Haute (city) Vigo County	8	0.01
Lake Station (city) Lake County	7	0.06

Top 10 Places Sorted by Percent of Total Population
Based on all places, regardless of total population

Place	Population	%
Laketon (cdp) Wabash County	3	0.48
Grandview (town) Spencer County	3	0.40
Holland (town) Dubois County	2	0.32

Place	Population	%
Roseland (town) St. Joseph County	2	0.32
Michiana Shores (town) LaPorte County	1	0.32
Ferdinand (town) Dubois County	5	0.23
Cannelton (city) Perry County	3	0.19
Monticello (city) White County	6	0.11
Brook (town) Newton County	1	0.10
Green (town) Howard County	2	0.08

Top 10 Places Sorted by Percent of Total Population
Based on places with total population of 50,000 or more

Place	Population	%
Gary (city) Lake County	20	0.02
Noblesville (city) Hamilton County	8	0.02
Fort Wayne (city) Allen County	18	0.01
Hammond (city) Lake County	10	0.01
Terre Haute (city) Vigo County	8	0.01
Bloomington (city) Monroe County	5	0.01
Elkhart (city) Elkhart County	4	0.01
Lafayette (city) Tippecanoe County	4	0.01
Anderson (city) Madison County	3	0.01
Indianapolis (city) Marion County	31	<0.01

American Indian: Crow

Top 10 Places Sorted by Population
Based on all places, regardless of total population

Place	Population	%
Fort Wayne (city) Allen County	12	<0.01
Indianapolis (city) Marion County	11	<0.01
Franklin (city) Johnson County	6	0.03
Ligonier (city) Noble County	5	0.11
Galveston (town) Cass County	4	0.31
Greenfield (city) Hancock County	4	0.02
Elkhart (city) Elkhart County	4	0.01
Hammond (city) Lake County	4	<0.01
Marion (city) Grant County	3	0.01
Bargersville (town) Johnson County	2	0.05

Top 10 Places Sorted by Percent of Total Population
Based on all places, regardless of total population

Place	Population	%
Galveston (town) Cass County	4	0.31
Coalmont (cdp) Clay County	1	0.25
Ligonier (city) Noble County	5	0.11
Bargersville (town) Johnson County	2	0.05
New Palestine (town) Hancock County	1	0.05
Franklin (city) Johnson County	6	0.03
Delphi (city) Carroll County	1	0.03
Greenfield (city) Hancock County	4	0.02
Bremen (town) Marshall County	1	0.02
Gas City (city) Grant County	1	0.02

Top 10 Places Sorted by Percent of Total Population
Based on places with total population of 50,000 or more

Place	Population	%
Elkhart (city) Elkhart County	4	0.01
Fort Wayne (city) Allen County	12	<0.01
Indianapolis (city) Marion County	11	<0.01
Hammond (city) Lake County	4	<0.01
Lafayette (city) Tippecanoe County	2	<0.01
Muncie (city) Delaware County	2	<0.01
Carmel (city) Hamilton County	1	<0.01
Evansville (city) Vanderburgh County	1	<0.01
Noblesville (city) Hamilton County	1	<0.01
Anderson (city) Madison County	0	0.00

American Indian: Delaware

Top 10 Places Sorted by Population
Based on all places, regardless of total population

Place	Population	%
Indianapolis (city) Marion County	27	<0.01
Fort Wayne (city) Allen County	12	<0.01
Bloomington (city) Monroe County	8	0.01
Milroy (cdp) Rush County	6	0.99
Anderson (city) Madison County	6	0.01
Evansville (city) Vanderburgh County	6	0.01
Mishawaka (city) St. Joseph County	6	0.01
Mount Vernon (city) Posey County	4	0.06
Goshen (city) Elkhart County	4	0.01
Clermont (town) Marion County	3	0.22

Top 10 Places Sorted by Percent of Total Population
Based on all places, regardless of total population

Place	Population	%
Milroy (cdp) Rush County	6	0.99
Fontanet (cdp) Vigo County	1	0.24
Richland (town) Spencer County	1	0.24
Clermont (town) Marion County	3	0.22
West Baden Springs (town) Orange County	1	0.17
Patoka (town) Gibson County	1	0.14
Argos (town) Marshall County	2	0.12
Eaton (town) Delaware County	2	0.11
Francesville (town) Pulaski County	1	0.11
Gaston (town) Delaware County	1	0.11

Top 10 Places Sorted by Percent of Total Population
Based on places with total population of 50,000 or more

Place	Population	%
Bloomington (city) Monroe County	8	0.01
Anderson (city) Madison County	6	0.01
Evansville (city) Vanderburgh County	6	0.01
Indianapolis (city) Marion County	27	<0.01
Fort Wayne (city) Allen County	12	<0.01
Lafayette (city) Tippecanoe County	3	<0.01
Fishers (town) Hamilton County	2	<0.01
Gary (city) Lake County	2	<0.01
Muncie (city) Delaware County	2	<0.01
South Bend (city) St. Joseph County	1	<0.01

American Indian: Hopi

Top 10 Places Sorted by Population
Based on all places, regardless of total population

Place	Population	%
Indianapolis (city) Marion County	13	<0.01
Fort Wayne (city) Allen County	7	<0.01
North Salem (town) Hendricks County	4	0.77
Carmel (city) Hamilton County	4	0.01
Richmond (city) Wayne County	3	0.01
Portage (city) Porter County	2	0.01
Bloomington (city) Monroe County	2	<0.01
Kokomo (city) Howard County	2	<0.01
Griffith (town) Lake County	1	0.01
Anderson (city) Madison County	1	<0.01

Top 10 Places Sorted by Percent of Total Population
Based on all places, regardless of total population

Place	Population	%
North Salem (town) Hendricks County	4	0.77
Carmel (city) Hamilton County	4	0.01
Richmond (city) Wayne County	3	0.01
Portage (city) Porter County	2	0.01
Griffith (town) Lake County	1	0.01
Indianapolis (city) Marion County	13	<0.01
Fort Wayne (city) Allen County	7	<0.01
Bloomington (city) Monroe County	2	<0.01
Kokomo (city) Howard County	2	<0.01
Anderson (city) Madison County	1	<0.01

Top 10 Places Sorted by Percent of Total Population
Based on places with total population of 50,000 or more

Place	Population	%
Carmel (city) Hamilton County	4	0.01
Indianapolis (city) Marion County	13	<0.01
Fort Wayne (city) Allen County	7	<0.01
Bloomington (city) Monroe County	2	<0.01
Anderson (city) Madison County	1	<0.01
Evansville (city) Vanderburgh County	1	<0.01
Elkhart (city) Elkhart County	0	0.00
Fishers (town) Hamilton County	0	0.00
Gary (city) Lake County	0	0.00
Hammond (city) Lake County	0	0.00

American Indian: Houma

Top 10 Places Sorted by Population
Based on all places, regardless of total population

Place	Population	%
Lafayette (city) Tippecanoe County	6	0.01
Charlestown (city) Clark County	4	0.05
Evansville (city) Vanderburgh County	4	<0.01
Gary (city) Lake County	4	<0.01
La Fontaine (town) Wabash County	3	0.34
Martinsville (city) Morgan County	3	0.03
Fort Wayne (city) Allen County	3	<0.01
Indianapolis (city) Marion County	3	<0.01
East Chicago (city) Lake County	2	0.01
Portage (city) Porter County	2	0.01

Top 10 Places Sorted by Percent of Total Population
Based on all places, regardless of total population

Place	Population	%
La Fontaine (town) Wabash County	3	0.34
Charlestown (city) Clark County	4	0.05
Martinsville (city) Morgan County	3	0.03
Corydon (town) Harrison County	1	0.03
Lafayette (city) Tippecanoe County	6	0.01
East Chicago (city) Lake County	2	0.01
Portage (city) Porter County	2	0.01
Evansville (city) Vanderburgh County	4	<0.01
Gary (city) Lake County	4	<0.01
Fort Wayne (city) Allen County	3	<0.01

Top 10 Places Sorted by Percent of Total Population
Based on places with total population of 50,000 or more

Place	Population	%
Lafayette (city) Tippecanoe County	6	0.01
Evansville (city) Vanderburgh County	4	<0.01
Gary (city) Lake County	4	<0.01
Fort Wayne (city) Allen County	3	<0.01
Indianapolis (city) Marion County	3	<0.01
Terre Haute (city) Vigo County	2	<0.01
Anderson (city) Madison County	0	0.00
Bloomington (city) Monroe County	0	0.00
Carmel (city) Hamilton County	0	0.00
Elkhart (city) Elkhart County	0	0.00

Alaska Native: Inupiat (Eskimo)

Top 10 Places Sorted by Population
Based on all places, regardless of total population

Place	Population	%
Indianapolis (city) Marion County	20	<0.01
Merrillville (town) Lake County	8	0.02
Frankfort (city) Clinton County	4	0.02
Jeffersonville (city) Clark County	4	0.01
Vallonia (cdp) Jackson County	3	0.89
Hillsboro (town) Fountain County	3	0.56
Pendleton (town) Madison County	3	0.07
Madison (city) Jefferson County	3	0.03
Bloomington (city) Monroe County	3	<0.01
Fort Wayne (city) Allen County	3	<0.01

Top 10 Places Sorted by Percent of Total Population
Based on all places, regardless of total population

Place	Population	%
Vallonia (cdp) Jackson County	3	0.89
Hillsboro (town) Fountain County	3	0.56
Pendleton (town) Madison County	3	0.07
Montpelier (city) Blackford County	1	0.06
Madison (city) Jefferson County	3	0.03
Browns (town) Jackson County	1	0.03
Merrillville (town) Lake County	8	0.02
Frankfort (city) Clinton County	4	0.02
Lowell (town) Lake County	2	0.02
Mooresville (town) Morgan County	2	0.02

Top 10 Places Sorted by Percent of Total Population
Based on places with total population of 50,000 or more

Place	Population	%
Indianapolis (city) Marion County	20	<0.01
Bloomington (city) Monroe County	3	<0.01
Fort Wayne (city) Allen County	3	<0.01
Anderson (city) Madison County	1	<0.01
Carmel (city) Hamilton County	1	<0.01
Evansville (city) Vanderburgh County	1	<0.01
Lafayette (city) Tippecanoe County	1	<0.01
Noblesville (city) Hamilton County	1	<0.01
South Bend (city) St. Joseph County	1	<0.01
Elkhart (city) Elkhart County	0	0.00

Please refer to the Explanation of Data in the front of the book for more detailed information.

American Indian: Iroquois

Top 10 Places Sorted by Population
Based on all places, regardless of total population

Place	Population	%
Indianapolis (city) Marion County	96	0.01
Fort Wayne (city) Allen County	41	0.02
Lafayette (city) Tippecanoe County	14	0.02
Evansville (city) Vanderburgh County	14	0.01
Lawrence (city) Marion County	10	0.02
Bloomington (city) Monroe County	9	0.01
Greenwood (city) Johnson County	8	0.02
Richmond (city) Wayne County	8	0.02
Carmel (city) Hamilton County	8	0.01
Lake Station (city) Lake County	7	0.06

Top 10 Places Sorted by Percent of Total Population
Based on all places, regardless of total population

Place	Population	%
Laurel (town) Franklin County	4	0.78
Grandview (town) Spencer County	4	0.53
Altona (town) DeKalb County	1	0.51
Fish Lake (cdp) LaPorte County	3	0.30
Mulberry (town) Clinton County	3	0.24
Wheeler (cdp) Porter County	1	0.23
Reynolds (town) White County	1	0.19
Medora (town) Jackson County	1	0.14
Town of Pines (town) Porter County	1	0.14
Fountain City (town) Wayne County	1	0.13

Top 10 Places Sorted by Percent of Total Population
Based on places with total population of 50,000 or more

Place	Population	%
Fort Wayne (city) Allen County	41	0.02
Lafayette (city) Tippecanoe County	14	0.02
Indianapolis (city) Marion County	96	0.01
Evansville (city) Vanderburgh County	14	0.01
Bloomington (city) Monroe County	9	0.01
Carmel (city) Hamilton County	8	0.01
Anderson (city) Madison County	7	0.01
Muncie (city) Delaware County	7	0.01
Fishers (town) Hamilton County	6	0.01
Hammond (city) Lake County	6	0.01

American Indian: Kiowa

Top 10 Places Sorted by Population
Based on all places, regardless of total population

Place	Population	%
Indianapolis (city) Marion County	5	<0.01
Fort Wayne (city) Allen County	3	<0.01
Wabash (city) Wabash County	2	0.02
Crawfordsville (city) Montgomery County	2	0.01
Hobart (city) Lake County	2	0.01
Terre Haute (city) Vigo County	2	<0.01
Spring Hill (town) Marion County	1	1.02
Hebron (town) Porter County	1	0.03
Salem (city) Washington County	1	0.02
Greensburg (city) Decatur County	1	0.01

Top 10 Places Sorted by Percent of Total Population
Based on all places, regardless of total population

Place	Population	%
Spring Hill (town) Marion County	1	1.02
Hebron (town) Porter County	1	0.03
Wabash (city) Wabash County	2	0.02
Salem (city) Washington County	1	0.02
Crawfordsville (city) Montgomery County	2	0.01
Hobart (city) Lake County	2	0.01
Greensburg (city) Decatur County	1	0.01
Seymour (city) Jackson County	1	0.01
Indianapolis (city) Marion County	5	<0.01
Fort Wayne (city) Allen County	3	<0.01

Top 10 Places Sorted by Percent of Total Population
Based on places with total population of 50,000 or more

Place	Population	%
Indianapolis (city) Marion County	5	<0.01
Fort Wayne (city) Allen County	3	<0.01
Terre Haute (city) Vigo County	2	<0.01
Anderson (city) Madison County	1	<0.01
Evansville (city) Vanderburgh County	1	<0.01
Fishers (town) Hamilton County	1	<0.01
Bloomington (city) Monroe County	0	0.00
Carmel (city) Hamilton County	0	0.00
Elkhart (city) Elkhart County	0	0.00
Gary (city) Lake County	0	0.00

American Indian: Lumbee

Top 10 Places Sorted by Population
Based on all places, regardless of total population

Place	Population	%
Indianapolis (city) Marion County	17	<0.01
Evansville (city) Vanderburgh County	11	0.01
Bedford (city) Lawrence County	10	0.07
South Bend (city) St. Joseph County	10	0.01
Elkhart (city) Elkhart County	8	0.02
Marion (city) Grant County	6	0.02
Fishers (town) Hamilton County	6	0.01
Lafayette (city) Tippecanoe County	5	0.01
New Whiteland (town) Johnson County	4	0.07
Bloomington (city) Monroe County	4	<0.01

Top 10 Places Sorted by Percent of Total Population
Based on all places, regardless of total population

Place	Population	%
Hatfield (cdp) Spencer County	2	0.25
Clay City (town) Clay County	2	0.23
Poseyville (town) Posey County	2	0.19
Stockwell (cdp) Tippecanoe County	1	0.18
Farmland (town) Randolph County	2	0.15
Parker City (town) Randolph County	2	0.14
Dillsboro (town) Dearborn County	1	0.08
Bedford (city) Lawrence County	10	0.07
New Whiteland (town) Johnson County	4	0.07
Cumberland (town) Marion County	2	0.04

Top 10 Places Sorted by Percent of Total Population
Based on places with total population of 50,000 or more

Place	Population	%
Elkhart (city) Elkhart County	8	0.02
Evansville (city) Vanderburgh County	11	0.01
South Bend (city) St. Joseph County	10	0.01
Fishers (town) Hamilton County	6	0.01
Lafayette (city) Tippecanoe County	5	0.01
Indianapolis (city) Marion County	17	<0.01
Bloomington (city) Monroe County	4	<0.01
Gary (city) Lake County	3	<0.01
Muncie (city) Delaware County	3	<0.01
Carmel (city) Hamilton County	2	<0.01

American Indian: Menominee

Top 10 Places Sorted by Population
Based on all places, regardless of total population

Place	Population	%
Gary (city) Lake County	6	0.01
Indianapolis (city) Marion County	5	<0.01
Whiting (city) Lake County	3	0.06
Elwood (city) Madison County	2	0.02
Hobart (city) Lake County	2	0.01
Munster (town) Lake County	2	0.01
Bloomington (city) Monroe County	2	<0.01
Fishers (town) Hamilton County	2	<0.01
Mishawaka (city) St. Joseph County	2	<0.01
English (town) Crawford County	1	0.16

Top 10 Places Sorted by Percent of Total Population
Based on all places, regardless of total population

Place	Population	%
English (town) Crawford County	1	0.16
Geneva (town) Adams County	1	0.08
Hudson Lake (cdp) LaPorte County	1	0.08
Kingsford Heights (town) LaPorte County	1	0.07
Whiting (city) Lake County	3	0.06
Montpelier (city) Blackford County	1	0.06
Elwood (city) Madison County	2	0.02
Gary (city) Lake County	6	0.01
Hobart (city) Lake County	2	0.01
Munster (town) Lake County	2	0.01

Top 10 Places Sorted by Percent of Total Population
Based on places with total population of 50,000 or more

Place	Population	%
Gary (city) Lake County	6	0.01
Indianapolis (city) Marion County	5	<0.01
Bloomington (city) Monroe County	2	<0.01
Fishers (town) Hamilton County	2	<0.01
Fort Wayne (city) Allen County	1	<0.01
Hammond (city) Lake County	1	<0.01
Muncie (city) Delaware County	1	<0.01
South Bend (city) St. Joseph County	1	<0.01
Terre Haute (city) Vigo County	1	<0.01
Anderson (city) Madison County	0	0.00

American Indian: Mexican American Indian

Top 10 Places Sorted by Population
Based on all places, regardless of total population

Place	Population	%
Indianapolis (city) Marion County	263	0.03
Hammond (city) Lake County	69	0.09
Fort Wayne (city) Allen County	67	0.03
Elkhart (city) Elkhart County	55	0.11
South Bend (city) St. Joseph County	54	0.05
East Chicago (city) Lake County	48	0.16
Goshen (city) Elkhart County	35	0.11
Logansport (city) Cass County	32	0.17
Anderson (city) Madison County	30	0.05
Lafayette (city) Tippecanoe County	24	0.04

Top 10 Places Sorted by Percent of Total Population
Based on all places, regardless of total population

Place	Population	%
Millersburg (town) Elkhart County	5	0.55
Burket (town) Kosciusko County	1	0.51
Delphi (city) Carroll County	11	0.38
Somerset (cdp) Wabash County	1	0.25
New Chicago (town) Lake County	4	0.20
Kingman (town) Fountain County	1	0.20
Dale (town) Spencer County	3	0.19
Logansport (city) Cass County	32	0.17
Bargersville (town) Johnson County	7	0.17
Rocky Ripple (town) Marion County	1	0.17

Top 10 Places Sorted by Percent of Total Population
Based on places with total population of 50,000 or more

Place	Population	%
Elkhart (city) Elkhart County	55	0.11
Hammond (city) Lake County	69	0.09
South Bend (city) St. Joseph County	54	0.05
Anderson (city) Madison County	30	0.05
Lafayette (city) Tippecanoe County	24	0.04
Indianapolis (city) Marion County	263	0.03
Fort Wayne (city) Allen County	67	0.03
Carmel (city) Hamilton County	21	0.03
Terre Haute (city) Vigo County	20	0.03
Gary (city) Lake County	15	0.02

American Indian: Navajo

Top 10 Places Sorted by Population
Based on all places, regardless of total population

Place	Population	%
Indianapolis (city) Marion County	100	0.01
Fort Wayne (city) Allen County	26	0.01
Valparaiso (city) Porter County	12	0.04
Anderson (city) Madison County	11	0.02
Evansville (city) Vanderburgh County	10	0.01
Bloomington (city) Monroe County	9	0.01
South Bend (city) St. Joseph County	8	0.01
Richmond (city) Wayne County	7	0.02
Elkhart (city) Elkhart County	7	0.01
Muncie (city) Delaware County	7	0.01

Top 10 Places Sorted by Percent of Total Population
Based on all places, regardless of total population

Place	Population	%
Patoka (town) Gibson County	6	0.82
Coalmont (cdp) Clay County	3	0.75

Please refer to the Explanation of Data in the front of the book for more detailed information.

Place	Population	%
Elizabeth (town) Harrison County	1	0.62
Odon (town) Daviess County	6	0.44
Kingsbury (town) LaPorte County	1	0.41
Dana (town) Vermillion County	2	0.33
New Salisbury (cdp) Harrison County	2	0.33
Burns Harbor (town) Porter County	3	0.26
Hope (town) Bartholomew County	5	0.24
Clay City (town) Clay County	2	0.23

Top 10 Places Sorted by Percent of Total Population
Based on places with total population of 50,000 or more

Place	Population	%
Anderson (city) Madison County	11	0.02
Indianapolis (city) Marion County	100	0.01
Fort Wayne (city) Allen County	26	0.01
Evansville (city) Vanderburgh County	10	0.01
Bloomington (city) Monroe County	9	0.01
South Bend (city) St. Joseph County	8	0.01
Elkhart (city) Elkhart County	7	0.01
Muncie (city) Delaware County	7	0.01
Gary (city) Lake County	6	0.01
Terre Haute (city) Vigo County	6	0.01

American Indian: Osage

Top 10 Places Sorted by Population
Based on all places, regardless of total population

Place	Population	%
Indianapolis (city) Marion County	15	<0.01
New Haven (city) Allen County	5	0.03
Portage (city) Porter County	5	0.01
Indian Heights (cdp) Howard County	4	0.13
North Terre Haute (cdp) Vigo County	3	0.07
Huntington (city) Huntington County	3	0.02
St. John (town) Lake County	3	0.02
Westfield (town) Hamilton County	3	0.01
Carmel (city) Hamilton County	3	<0.01
Linton (city) Greene County	2	0.04

Top 10 Places Sorted by Percent of Total Population
Based on all places, regardless of total population

Place	Population	%
Medaryville (town) Pulaski County	1	0.16
Indian Heights (cdp) Howard County	4	0.13
Ridgeville (town) Randolph County	1	0.12
Bass Lake (cdp) Starke County	1	0.08
Sweetser (town) Grant County	1	0.08
North Terre Haute (cdp) Vigo County	3	0.07
Fairview Park (town) Vermillion County	1	0.07
Shadeland (town) Tippecanoe County	1	0.06
Cloverdale (town) Putnam County	1	0.05
Linton (city) Greene County	2	0.04

Top 10 Places Sorted by Percent of Total Population
Based on places with total population of 50,000 or more

Place	Population	%
Indianapolis (city) Marion County	15	<0.01
Carmel (city) Hamilton County	3	<0.01
Anderson (city) Madison County	2	<0.01
Bloomington (city) Monroe County	2	<0.01
Evansville (city) Vanderburgh County	2	<0.01
Fort Wayne (city) Allen County	1	<0.01
Muncie (city) Delaware County	1	<0.01
Noblesville (city) Hamilton County	1	<0.01
Terre Haute (city) Vigo County	1	<0.01
Elkhart (city) Elkhart County	0	0.00

American Indian: Ottawa

Top 10 Places Sorted by Population
Based on all places, regardless of total population

Place	Population	%
Fort Wayne (city) Allen County	15	0.01
Indianapolis (city) Marion County	15	<0.01
Elkhart (city) Elkhart County	6	0.01
Mishawaka (city) St. Joseph County	6	0.01
North Judson (town) Starke County	5	0.28
Carmel (city) Hamilton County	5	0.01
Lafayette (city) Tippecanoe County	5	0.01
Edinburgh (town) Johnson County	4	0.09
Jeffersonville (city) Clark County	4	0.01
George (town) Floyd County	3	0.10

Top 10 Places Sorted by Percent of Total Population
Based on all places, regardless of total population

Place	Population	%
Switz City (town) Greene County	1	0.34
North Judson (town) Starke County	5	0.28
Wolcottville (town) Noble County	2	0.20
Warren (town) Huntington County	2	0.16
George (town) Floyd County	3	0.10
Edinburgh (town) Johnson County	4	0.09
Daleville (town) Delaware County	1	0.06
New Carlisle (town) St. Joseph County	1	0.05
Winchester (city) Randolph County	2	0.04
Butler (city) DeKalb County	1	0.04

Top 10 Places Sorted by Percent of Total Population
Based on places with total population of 50,000 or more

Place	Population	%
Fort Wayne (city) Allen County	15	0.01
Elkhart (city) Elkhart County	6	0.01
Carmel (city) Hamilton County	5	0.01
Lafayette (city) Tippecanoe County	5	0.01
Indianapolis (city) Marion County	15	<0.01
Hammond (city) Lake County	3	<0.01
South Bend (city) St. Joseph County	3	<0.01
Bloomington (city) Monroe County	1	<0.01
Fishers (town) Hamilton County	1	<0.01
Anderson (city) Madison County	0	0.00

American Indian: Paiute

Top 10 Places Sorted by Population
Based on all places, regardless of total population

Place	Population	%
Indianapolis (city) Marion County	5	<0.01
Lebanon (city) Boone County	4	0.03
Elkhart (city) Elkhart County	3	0.01
Schererville (town) Lake County	3	0.01
Fishers (town) Hamilton County	3	<0.01
South Bend (city) St. Joseph County	3	<0.01
Dayton (town) Tippecanoe County	1	0.07
Notre Dame (cdp) St. Joseph County	1	0.02
Madison (city) Jefferson County	1	0.01
Fort Wayne (city) Allen County	1	<0.01

Top 10 Places Sorted by Percent of Total Population
Based on all places, regardless of total population

Place	Population	%
Dayton (town) Tippecanoe County	1	0.07
Lebanon (city) Boone County	4	0.03
Notre Dame (cdp) St. Joseph County	1	0.02
Elkhart (city) Elkhart County	3	0.01
Schererville (town) Lake County	3	0.01
Madison (city) Jefferson County	1	0.01
Indianapolis (city) Marion County	5	<0.01
Fishers (town) Hamilton County	3	<0.01
South Bend (city) St. Joseph County	3	<0.01
Fort Wayne (city) Allen County	1	<0.01

Top 10 Places Sorted by Percent of Total Population
Based on places with total population of 50,000 or more

Place	Population	%
Elkhart (city) Elkhart County	3	0.01
Indianapolis (city) Marion County	5	<0.01
Fishers (town) Hamilton County	3	<0.01
South Bend (city) St. Joseph County	3	<0.01
Fort Wayne (city) Allen County	1	<0.01
Gary (city) Lake County	1	<0.01
Anderson (city) Madison County	0	0.00
Bloomington (city) Monroe County	0	0.00
Carmel (city) Hamilton County	0	0.00
Evansville (city) Vanderburgh County	0	0.00

American Indian: Pima

Top 10 Places Sorted by Population
Based on all places, regardless of total population

Place	Population	%
Fort Wayne (city) Allen County	7	<0.01
Cedar Lake (town) Lake County	3	0.03
Clarksville (town) Clark County	3	0.01
Richmond (city) Wayne County	2	0.01
Linton (city) Greene County	1	0.02
Greenfield (city) Hancock County	1	<0.01
Indianapolis (city) Marion County	1	<0.01
Aberdeen (cdp) Porter County	0	0.00
Advance (town) Boone County	0	0.00
Akron (town) Fulton County	0	0.00

Top 10 Places Sorted by Percent of Total Population
Based on all places, regardless of total population

Place	Population	%
Cedar Lake (town) Lake County	3	0.03
Linton (city) Greene County	1	0.02
Clarksville (town) Clark County	3	0.01
Richmond (city) Wayne County	2	0.01
Fort Wayne (city) Allen County	7	<0.01
Greenfield (city) Hancock County	1	<0.01
Indianapolis (city) Marion County	1	<0.01
Aberdeen (cdp) Porter County	0	0.00
Advance (town) Boone County	0	0.00
Akron (town) Fulton County	0	0.00

Top 10 Places Sorted by Percent of Total Population
Based on places with total population of 50,000 or more

Place	Population	%
Fort Wayne (city) Allen County	7	<0.01
Indianapolis (city) Marion County	1	<0.01
Anderson (city) Madison County	0	0.00
Bloomington (city) Monroe County	0	0.00
Carmel (city) Hamilton County	0	0.00
Elkhart (city) Elkhart County	0	0.00
Evansville (city) Vanderburgh County	0	0.00
Fishers (town) Hamilton County	0	0.00
Gary (city) Lake County	0	0.00
Hammond (city) Lake County	0	0.00

American Indian: Potawatomi

Top 10 Places Sorted by Population
Based on all places, regardless of total population

Place	Population	%
Indianapolis (city) Marion County	88	0.01
South Bend (city) St. Joseph County	74	0.07
Mishawaka (city) St. Joseph County	58	0.12
Elkhart (city) Elkhart County	28	0.05
Fort Wayne (city) Allen County	26	0.01
Granger (cdp) St. Joseph County	16	0.05
Carmel (city) Hamilton County	11	0.01
Valparaiso (city) Porter County	10	0.03
Bloomington (city) Monroe County	10	0.01
Anderson (city) Madison County	7	0.01

Top 10 Places Sorted by Percent of Total Population
Based on all places, regardless of total population

Place	Population	%
Bass Lake (cdp) Starke County	4	0.33
Fountain City (town) Wayne County	2	0.25
Hanna (cdp) LaPorte County	1	0.22
New Carlisle (town) St. Joseph County	4	0.21
Wakarusa (town) Elkhart County	3	0.17
Morris (town) Shelby County	2	0.16
Farmland (town) Randolph County	2	0.15
Hudson Lake (cdp) LaPorte County	2	0.15
Darmstadt (town) Vanderburgh County	2	0.14
Kingsford Heights (town) LaPorte County	2	0.14

Top 10 Places Sorted by Percent of Total Population
Based on places with total population of 50,000 or more

Place	Population	%
South Bend (city) St. Joseph County	74	0.07
Elkhart (city) Elkhart County	28	0.05
Indianapolis (city) Marion County	88	0.01
Fort Wayne (city) Allen County	26	0.01
Carmel (city) Hamilton County	11	0.01
Bloomington (city) Monroe County	10	0.01
Anderson (city) Madison County	7	0.01
Fishers (town) Hamilton County	7	0.01
Hammond (city) Lake County	6	0.01
Lafayette (city) Tippecanoe County	6	0.01

American Indian: Pueblo

Top 10 Places Sorted by Population
Based on all places, regardless of total population

Place	Population	%
Indianapolis (city) Marion County	26	<0.01
Fort Wayne (city) Allen County	7	<0.01
Goshen (city) Elkhart County	6	0.02
Lawrence (city) Marion County	5	0.01
South Bend (city) St. Joseph County	4	<0.01
Crawfordsville (city) Montgomery County	3	0.02
Portage (city) Porter County	3	0.01
West Lafayette (city) Tippecanoe County	3	0.01
Bloomington (city) Monroe County	3	<0.01
Evansville (city) Vanderburgh County	3	<0.01

Top 10 Places Sorted by Percent of Total Population
Based on all places, regardless of total population

Place	Population	%
Argos (town) Marshall County	2	0.12
Hartford City (city) Blackford County	2	0.03
Goshen (city) Elkhart County	6	0.02
Crawfordsville (city) Montgomery County	3	0.02
Danville (town) Hendricks County	2	0.02
Lake Station (city) Lake County	2	0.02
Wabash (city) Wabash County	2	0.02
Edinburgh (town) Johnson County	1	0.02
Rensselaer (city) Jasper County	1	0.02
Winona Lake (town) Kosciusko County	1	0.02

Top 10 Places Sorted by Percent of Total Population
Based on places with total population of 50,000 or more

Place	Population	%
Indianapolis (city) Marion County	26	<0.01
Fort Wayne (city) Allen County	7	<0.01
South Bend (city) St. Joseph County	4	<0.01
Bloomington (city) Monroe County	3	<0.01
Evansville (city) Vanderburgh County	3	<0.01
Fishers (town) Hamilton County	1	<0.01
Muncie (city) Delaware County	1	<0.01
Anderson (city) Madison County	0	0.00
Carmel (city) Hamilton County	0	0.00
Elkhart (city) Elkhart County	0	0.00

American Indian: Puget Sound Salish

Top 10 Places Sorted by Population
Based on all places, regardless of total population

Place	Population	%
Bloomington (city) Monroe County	5	0.01
Hammond (city) Lake County	2	<0.01
Mishawaka (city) St. Joseph County	2	<0.01
Muncie (city) Delaware County	1	<0.01
Aberdeen (cdp) Porter County	0	0.00
Advance (town) Boone County	0	0.00
Akron (town) Fulton County	0	0.00
Alamo (town) Montgomery County	0	0.00
Albany (town) Delaware County	0	0.00
Albion (town) Noble County	0	0.00

Top 10 Places Sorted by Percent of Total Population
Based on all places, regardless of total population

Place	Population	%
Bloomington (city) Monroe County	5	0.01
Hammond (city) Lake County	2	<0.01
Mishawaka (city) St. Joseph County	2	<0.01
Muncie (city) Delaware County	1	<0.01
Aberdeen (cdp) Porter County	0	0.00
Advance (town) Boone County	0	0.00
Akron (town) Fulton County	0	0.00
Alamo (town) Montgomery County	0	0.00
Albany (town) Delaware County	0	0.00
Albion (town) Noble County	0	0.00

Top 10 Places Sorted by Percent of Total Population
Based on places with total population of 50,000 or more

Place	Population	%
Bloomington (city) Monroe County	5	0.01
Hammond (city) Lake County	2	<0.01
Muncie (city) Delaware County	1	<0.01
Anderson (city) Madison County	0	0.00

Place	Population	%
Carmel (city) Hamilton County	0	0.00
Elkhart (city) Elkhart County	0	0.00
Evansville (city) Vanderburgh County	0	0.00
Fishers (town) Hamilton County	0	0.00
Fort Wayne (city) Allen County	0	0.00
Gary (city) Lake County	0	0.00

American Indian: Seminole

Top 10 Places Sorted by Population
Based on all places, regardless of total population

Place	Population	%
Indianapolis (city) Marion County	17	<0.01
Gary (city) Lake County	12	0.01
Fort Wayne (city) Allen County	11	<0.01
Lafayette (city) Tippecanoe County	5	0.01
South Bend (city) St. Joseph County	5	<0.01
Linton (city) Greene County	3	0.06
Kokomo (city) Howard County	3	0.01
New Albany (city) Floyd County	3	0.01
Valparaiso (city) Porter County	3	0.01
Bloomington (city) Monroe County	3	<0.01

Top 10 Places Sorted by Percent of Total Population
Based on all places, regardless of total population

Place	Population	%
Boswell (town) Benton County	1	0.13
Orleans (town) Orange County	2	0.09
Topeka (town) LaGrange County	1	0.09
Linton (city) Greene County	3	0.06
Wakarusa (town) Elkhart County	1	0.06
Boonville (city) Warrick County	1	0.02
Grissom AFB (cdp) Miami County	1	0.02
Hunter (town) Allen County	1	0.02
Rensselaer (city) Jasper County	1	0.02
Gary (city) Lake County	12	0.01

Top 10 Places Sorted by Percent of Total Population
Based on places with total population of 50,000 or more

Place	Population	%
Gary (city) Lake County	12	0.01
Lafayette (city) Tippecanoe County	5	0.01
Indianapolis (city) Marion County	17	<0.01
Fort Wayne (city) Allen County	11	<0.01
South Bend (city) St. Joseph County	5	<0.01
Bloomington (city) Monroe County	3	<0.01
Evansville (city) Vanderburgh County	3	<0.01
Hammond (city) Lake County	3	<0.01
Anderson (city) Madison County	2	<0.01
Muncie (city) Delaware County	2	<0.01

American Indian: Shoshone

Top 10 Places Sorted by Population
Based on all places, regardless of total population

Place	Population	%
Indianapolis (city) Marion County	7	<0.01
Hammond (city) Lake County	6	0.01
Muncie (city) Delaware County	6	0.01
Tell City (city) Perry County	4	0.06
Cumberland (town) Marion County	3	0.06
Lanesville (town) Harrison County	2	0.35
St. Mary of the Woods (cdp) Vigo County	2	0.25
Lake Dalecarlia (cdp) Lake County	2	0.15
Michigan City (city) LaPorte County	2	0.01
Greenville (town) Floyd County	1	0.17

Top 10 Places Sorted by Percent of Total Population
Based on all places, regardless of total population

Place	Population	%
Lanesville (town) Harrison County	2	0.35
St. Mary of the Woods (cdp) Vigo County	2	0.25
Greenville (town) Floyd County	1	0.17
Lake Dalecarlia (cdp) Lake County	2	0.15
Tell City (city) Perry County	4	0.06
Cumberland (town) Marion County	3	0.06
Hammond (city) Lake County	6	0.01
Muncie (city) Delaware County	6	0.01
Michigan City (city) LaPorte County	2	0.01
Beech Grove (city) Marion County	1	0.01

American Indian: Sioux

Top 10 Places Sorted by Population
Based on all places, regardless of total population

Place	Population	%
Indianapolis (city) Marion County	201	0.02
Fort Wayne (city) Allen County	68	0.03
Evansville (city) Vanderburgh County	52	0.04
Terre Haute (city) Vigo County	34	0.06
Bloomington (city) Monroe County	24	0.03
Lafayette (city) Tippecanoe County	23	0.03
Elkhart (city) Elkhart County	21	0.04
Muncie (city) Delaware County	20	0.03
Kokomo (city) Howard County	18	0.04
Gary (city) Lake County	17	0.02

Top 10 Places Sorted by Percent of Total Population
Based on all places, regardless of total population

Place	Population	%
San Pierre (cdp) Starke County	1	0.69
Wheeler (cdp) Porter County	3	0.68
Salamonia (town) Jay County	1	0.64
Shelby (cdp) Lake County	3	0.56
Colburn (cdp) Tippecanoe County	1	0.52
Trafalgar (town) Johnson County	5	0.45
Manilla (cdp) Rush County	1	0.37
Royal Center (town) Cass County	3	0.35
Campbellsburg (town) Washington County	2	0.34
Palmyra (town) Harrison County	3	0.32

Top 10 Places Sorted by Percent of Total Population
Based on places with total population of 50,000 or more

Place	Population	%
Terre Haute (city) Vigo County	34	0.06
Evansville (city) Vanderburgh County	52	0.04
Elkhart (city) Elkhart County	21	0.04
Fort Wayne (city) Allen County	68	0.03
Bloomington (city) Monroe County	24	0.03
Lafayette (city) Tippecanoe County	23	0.03
Muncie (city) Delaware County	20	0.03
Indianapolis (city) Marion County	201	0.02
Gary (city) Lake County	17	0.02
Anderson (city) Madison County	11	0.02

American Indian: South American Indian

Top 10 Places Sorted by Population
Based on all places, regardless of total population

Place	Population	%
Indianapolis (city) Marion County	39	<0.01
East Chicago (city) Lake County	18	0.06
Fishers (town) Hamilton County	10	0.01
Hammond (city) Lake County	9	0.01
Fort Wayne (city) Allen County	9	<0.01
Portage (city) Porter County	7	0.02
Lafayette (city) Tippecanoe County	7	0.01
Goshen (city) Elkhart County	6	0.02
Ingalls (town) Madison County	5	0.21
Pittsboro (town) Hendricks County	5	0.17

Top 10 Places Sorted by Percent of Total Population
Based on all places, regardless of total population

Place	Population	%
Ingalls (town) Madison County	5	0.21
Mentone (town) Kosciusko County	2	0.20
Pittsboro (town) Hendricks County	5	0.17

Please refer to the Explanation of Data in the front of the book for more detailed information.

Place	Population	%
Rocky Ripple (town) Marion County	1	0.17
Seelyville (town) Vigo County	1	0.10
Burns Harbor (town) Porter County	1	0.09
Fortville (town) Hancock County	3	0.08
Farmland (town) Randolph County	1	0.08
Hamilton (town) Steuben County	1	0.07
East Chicago (city) Lake County	18	0.06

Top 10 Places Sorted by Percent of Total Population
Based on places with total population of 50,000 or more

Place	Population	%
Fishers (town) Hamilton County	10	0.01
Hammond (city) Lake County	9	0.01
Lafayette (city) Tippecanoe County	7	0.01
Elkhart (city) Elkhart County	4	0.01
Muncie (city) Delaware County	4	0.01
Indianapolis (city) Marion County	39	<0.01
Fort Wayne (city) Allen County	9	<0.01
Bloomington (city) Monroe County	4	<0.01
Evansville (city) Vanderburgh County	4	<0.01
Gary (city) Lake County	3	<0.01

American Indian: Spanish American Indian

Top 10 Places Sorted by Population
Based on all places, regardless of total population

Place	Population	%
Indianapolis (city) Marion County	23	<0.01
Bloomington (city) Monroe County	21	0.03
South Bend (city) St. Joseph County	11	0.01
Lawrence (city) Marion County	9	0.02
Richmond (city) Wayne County	8	0.02
Cumberland (town) Marion County	6	0.12
Goshen (city) Elkhart County	5	0.02
Schererville (town) Lake County	4	0.01
Waveland (town) Montgomery County	3	0.71
Elkhart (city) Elkhart County	3	0.01

Top 10 Places Sorted by Percent of Total Population
Based on all places, regardless of total population

Place	Population	%
Waveland (town) Montgomery County	3	0.71
Cumberland (town) Marion County	6	0.12
Selma (town) Delaware County	1	0.12
Bloomington (city) Monroe County	21	0.03
Lawrence (city) Marion County	9	0.02
Richmond (city) Wayne County	8	0.02
Goshen (city) Elkhart County	5	0.02
Gas City (city) Grant County	1	0.02
Lawrenceburg (city) Dearborn County	1	0.02
Sullivan (city) Sullivan County	1	0.02

Top 10 Places Sorted by Percent of Total Population
Based on places with total population of 50,000 or more

Place	Population	%
Bloomington (city) Monroe County	21	0.03
South Bend (city) St. Joseph County	11	0.01
Elkhart (city) Elkhart County	3	0.01
Indianapolis (city) Marion County	23	<0.01
Fort Wayne (city) Allen County	3	<0.01
Hammond (city) Lake County	3	<0.01
Anderson (city) Madison County	2	<0.01
Carmel (city) Hamilton County	2	<0.01
Muncie (city) Delaware County	2	<0.01
Evansville (city) Vanderburgh County	1	<0.01

Alaska Native: Tlingit-Haida

Top 10 Places Sorted by Population
Based on all places, regardless of total population

Place	Population	%
Indianapolis (city) Marion County	6	<0.01
Highland (town) Lake County	5	0.02
Lafayette (city) Tippecanoe County	5	0.01
Fort Wayne (city) Allen County	4	<0.01
South Bend (city) St. Joseph County	4	<0.01
Winfield (town) Lake County	2	0.05
Greendale (city) Dearborn County	2	0.04
Roseland (town) St. Joseph County	1	0.16
Walton (town) Cass County	1	0.10
French Lick (town) Orange County	1	0.06

Top 10 Places Sorted by Percent of Total Population
Based on all places, regardless of total population

Place	Population	%
Roseland (town) St. Joseph County	1	0.16
Walton (town) Cass County	1	0.10
French Lick (town) Orange County	1	0.06
Winfield (town) Lake County	2	0.05
Greendale (city) Dearborn County	2	0.04
Melody Hill (cdp) Vanderburgh County	1	0.03
Union City (city) Randolph County	1	0.03
Highland (town) Lake County	5	0.02
Hunter (town) Allen County	1	0.02
Lawrenceburg (city) Dearborn County	1	0.02

Top 10 Places Sorted by Percent of Total Population
Based on places with total population of 50,000 or more

Place	Population	%
Lafayette (city) Tippecanoe County	5	0.01
Indianapolis (city) Marion County	6	<0.01
Fort Wayne (city) Allen County	4	<0.01
South Bend (city) St. Joseph County	4	<0.01
Bloomington (city) Monroe County	1	<0.01
Fishers (town) Hamilton County	1	<0.01
Terre Haute (city) Vigo County	1	<0.01
Anderson (city) Madison County	0	0.00
Carmel (city) Hamilton County	0	0.00
Elkhart (city) Elkhart County	0	0.00

American Indian: Tohono O'Odham

Top 10 Places Sorted by Population
Based on all places, regardless of total population

Place	Population	%
Bloomington (city) Monroe County	8	0.01
Whiteland (town) Johnson County	3	0.07
Valparaiso (city) Porter County	3	0.01
Greenwood (city) Johnson County	2	<0.01
Indianapolis (city) Marion County	2	<0.01
Lagrange (town) LaGrange County	1	0.04
Dunlap (cdp) Elkhart County	1	0.02
Vincennes (city) Knox County	1	0.01
Franklin (city) Johnson County	1	<0.01
La Porte (city) LaPorte County	1	<0.01

Top 10 Places Sorted by Percent of Total Population
Based on all places, regardless of total population

Place	Population	%
Whiteland (town) Johnson County	3	0.07
Lagrange (town) LaGrange County	1	0.04
Dunlap (cdp) Elkhart County	1	0.02
Bloomington (city) Monroe County	8	0.01
Valparaiso (city) Porter County	3	0.01
Vincennes (city) Knox County	1	0.01
Greenwood (city) Johnson County	2	<0.01
Indianapolis (city) Marion County	2	<0.01
Franklin (city) Johnson County	1	<0.01
La Porte (city) LaPorte County	1	<0.01

Top 10 Places Sorted by Percent of Total Population
Based on places with total population of 50,000 or more

Place	Population	%
Bloomington (city) Monroe County	8	0.01
Indianapolis (city) Marion County	2	<0.01
Anderson (city) Madison County	0	0.00
Carmel (city) Hamilton County	0	0.00
Elkhart (city) Elkhart County	0	0.00
Evansville (city) Vanderburgh County	0	0.00
Fishers (town) Hamilton County	0	0.00
Fort Wayne (city) Allen County	0	0.00
Gary (city) Lake County	0	0.00
Hammond (city) Lake County	0	0.00

Alaska Native: Tsimshian

Top 10 Places Sorted by Population
Based on all places, regardless of total population

Place	Population	%
Cicero (town) Hamilton County	2	0.04
Indianapolis (city) Marion County	1	<0.01
Schererville (town) Lake County	1	<0.01
Aberdeen (cdp) Porter County	0	0.00
Advance (town) Boone County	0	0.00
Akron (town) Fulton County	0	0.00
Alamo (town) Montgomery County	0	0.00
Albany (town) Delaware County	0	0.00
Albion (town) Noble County	0	0.00
Alexandria (city) Madison County	0	0.00

Top 10 Places Sorted by Percent of Total Population
Based on all places, regardless of total population

Place	Population	%
Cicero (town) Hamilton County	2	0.04
Indianapolis (city) Marion County	1	<0.01
Schererville (town) Lake County	1	<0.01
Aberdeen (cdp) Porter County	0	0.00
Advance (town) Boone County	0	0.00
Akron (town) Fulton County	0	0.00
Alamo (town) Montgomery County	0	0.00
Albany (town) Delaware County	0	0.00
Albion (town) Noble County	0	0.00
Alexandria (city) Madison County	0	0.00

Top 10 Places Sorted by Percent of Total Population
Based on places with total population of 50,000 or more

Place	Population	%
Indianapolis (city) Marion County	1	<0.01
Anderson (city) Madison County	0	0.00
Bloomington (city) Monroe County	0	0.00
Carmel (city) Hamilton County	0	0.00
Elkhart (city) Elkhart County	0	0.00
Evansville (city) Vanderburgh County	0	0.00
Fishers (town) Hamilton County	0	0.00
Fort Wayne (city) Allen County	0	0.00
Gary (city) Lake County	0	0.00
Hammond (city) Lake County	0	0.00

American Indian: Ute

Top 10 Places Sorted by Population
Based on all places, regardless of total population

Place	Population	%
Hammond (city) Lake County	7	0.01
Winamac (town) Pulaski County	4	0.16
Anderson (city) Madison County	4	0.01
Indianapolis (city) Marion County	4	<0.01
Plainfield (town) Hendricks County	3	0.01
Fort Wayne (city) Allen County	2	<0.01
Noblesville (city) Hamilton County	2	<0.01
Fortville (town) Hancock County	1	0.03
Bedford (city) Lawrence County	1	0.01
Chesterton (town) Porter County	1	0.01

Top 10 Places Sorted by Percent of Total Population
Based on all places, regardless of total population

Place	Population	%
Winamac (town) Pulaski County	4	0.16
Fortville (town) Hancock County	1	0.03
Hammond (city) Lake County	7	0.01
Anderson (city) Madison County	4	0.01
Plainfield (town) Hendricks County	3	0.01
Bedford (city) Lawrence County	1	0.01
Chesterton (town) Porter County	1	0.01
New Castle (city) Henry County	1	0.01
Peru (city) Miami County	1	0.01
Speedway (town) Marion County	1	0.01

Top 10 Places Sorted by Percent of Total Population
Based on places with total population of 50,000 or more

Place	Population	%
Hammond (city) Lake County	7	0.01
Anderson (city) Madison County	4	0.01
Indianapolis (city) Marion County	4	<0.01
Fort Wayne (city) Allen County	2	<0.01
Noblesville (city) Hamilton County	2	<0.01
Carmel (city) Hamilton County	1	<0.01
Lafayette (city) Tippecanoe County	1	<0.01
Terre Haute (city) Vigo County	1	<0.01
Bloomington (city) Monroe County	0	0.00
Elkhart (city) Elkhart County	0	0.00

American Indian: Yakama

Top 10 Places Sorted by Population
Based on all places, regardless of total population

Place	Population	%
Bloomington (city) Monroe County	3	<0.01
Mentone (town) Kosciusko County	1	0.10
Avon (town) Hendricks County	1	0.01
Warsaw (city) Kosciusko County	1	0.01
Indianapolis (city) Marion County	1	<0.01
Aberdeen (cdp) Porter County	0	0.00
Advance (town) Boone County	0	0.00
Akron (town) Fulton County	0	0.00
Alamo (town) Montgomery County	0	0.00
Albany (town) Delaware County	0	0.00

Top 10 Places Sorted by Percent of Total Population
Based on all places, regardless of total population

Place	Population	%
Mentone (town) Kosciusko County	1	0.10
Avon (town) Hendricks County	1	0.01
Warsaw (city) Kosciusko County	1	0.01
Bloomington (city) Monroe County	3	<0.01
Indianapolis (city) Marion County	1	<0.01
Aberdeen (cdp) Porter County	0	0.00
Advance (town) Boone County	0	0.00
Akron (town) Fulton County	0	0.00
Alamo (town) Montgomery County	0	0.00
Albany (town) Delaware County	0	0.00

Top 10 Places Sorted by Percent of Total Population
Based on places with total population of 50,000 or more

Place	Population	%
Bloomington (city) Monroe County	3	<0.01
Indianapolis (city) Marion County	1	<0.01
Anderson (city) Madison County	0	0.00
Carmel (city) Hamilton County	0	0.00
Elkhart (city) Elkhart County	0	0.00
Evansville (city) Vanderburgh County	0	0.00
Fishers (town) Hamilton County	0	0.00
Fort Wayne (city) Allen County	0	0.00
Gary (city) Lake County	0	0.00
Hammond (city) Lake County	0	0.00

American Indian: Yaqui

Top 10 Places Sorted by Population
Based on all places, regardless of total population

Place	Population	%
Valparaiso (city) Porter County	5	0.02
Fort Wayne (city) Allen County	5	<0.01
Indianapolis (city) Marion County	5	<0.01
Hammond (city) Lake County	3	<0.01
Terre Haute (city) Vigo County	3	<0.01
Hunter (town) Allen County	2	0.04
Carmel (city) Hamilton County	2	<0.01
Liberty (town) Union County	1	0.05
Greensburg (city) Decatur County	1	0.01
Lake Station (city) Lake County	1	0.01

Top 10 Places Sorted by Percent of Total Population
Based on all places, regardless of total population

Place	Population	%
Liberty (town) Union County	1	0.05
Hunter (town) Allen County	2	0.04
Valparaiso (city) Porter County	5	0.02
Greensburg (city) Decatur County	1	0.01
Lake Station (city) Lake County	1	0.01
Fort Wayne (city) Allen County	5	<0.01
Indianapolis (city) Marion County	5	<0.01
Hammond (city) Lake County	3	<0.01
Terre Haute (city) Vigo County	3	<0.01
Carmel (city) Hamilton County	2	<0.01

Top 10 Places Sorted by Percent of Total Population
Based on places with total population of 50,000 or more

Place	Population	%
Fort Wayne (city) Allen County	5	<0.01
Indianapolis (city) Marion County	5	<0.01
Hammond (city) Lake County	3	<0.01
Terre Haute (city) Vigo County	3	<0.01
Carmel (city) Hamilton County	2	<0.01
Evansville (city) Vanderburgh County	1	<0.01
Lafayette (city) Tippecanoe County	1	<0.01
Noblesville (city) Hamilton County	1	<0.01
Anderson (city) Madison County	0	0.00
Bloomington (city) Monroe County	0	0.00

American Indian: Yuman

Top 10 Places Sorted by Population
Based on all places, regardless of total population

Place	Population	%
Indianapolis (city) Marion County	4	<0.01
Amo (town) Hendricks County	2	0.50
Wabash (city) Wabash County	2	0.02
Lafayette (city) Tippecanoe County	1	<0.01
Aberdeen (cdp) Porter County	0	0.00
Advance (town) Boone County	0	0.00
Akron (town) Fulton County	0	0.00
Alamo (town) Montgomery County	0	0.00
Albany (town) Delaware County	0	0.00
Albion (town) Noble County	0	0.00

Top 10 Places Sorted by Percent of Total Population
Based on all places, regardless of total population

Place	Population	%
Amo (town) Hendricks County	2	0.50
Wabash (city) Wabash County	2	0.02
Indianapolis (city) Marion County	4	<0.01
Lafayette (city) Tippecanoe County	1	<0.01
Aberdeen (cdp) Porter County	0	0.00
Advance (town) Boone County	0	0.00
Akron (town) Fulton County	0	0.00
Alamo (town) Montgomery County	0	0.00
Albany (town) Delaware County	0	0.00
Albion (town) Noble County	0	0.00

Top 10 Places Sorted by Percent of Total Population
Based on places with total population of 50,000 or more

Place	Population	%
Indianapolis (city) Marion County	4	<0.01
Lafayette (city) Tippecanoe County	1	<0.01
Anderson (city) Madison County	0	0.00
Bloomington (city) Monroe County	0	0.00
Carmel (city) Hamilton County	0	0.00
Elkhart (city) Elkhart County	0	0.00
Evansville (city) Vanderburgh County	0	0.00
Fishers (town) Hamilton County	0	0.00
Fort Wayne (city) Allen County	0	0.00
Gary (city) Lake County	0	0.00

Alaska Native: Yup'ik

Top 10 Places Sorted by Population
Based on all places, regardless of total population

Place	Population	%
North Liberty (town) St. Joseph County	3	0.16
Washington (city) Daviess County	3	0.03
Goshen (city) Elkhart County	3	0.01
Fort Wayne (city) Allen County	2	<0.01
Indianapolis (city) Marion County	2	<0.01
Edinburgh (town) Johnson County	1	0.02
Porter (town) Porter County	1	0.02
Rushville (city) Rush County	1	0.02
St. John (town) Lake County	1	0.01
Bloomington (city) Monroe County	1	<0.01

Top 10 Places Sorted by Percent of Total Population
Based on all places, regardless of total population

Place	Population	%
North Liberty (town) St. Joseph County	3	0.16
Washington (city) Daviess County	3	0.03
Edinburgh (town) Johnson County	1	0.02
Porter (town) Porter County	1	0.02
Rushville (city) Rush County	1	0.02
Goshen (city) Elkhart County	3	0.01
St. John (town) Lake County	1	0.01
Fort Wayne (city) Allen County	2	<0.01
Indianapolis (city) Marion County	2	<0.01
Bloomington (city) Monroe County	1	<0.01

Top 10 Places Sorted by Percent of Total Population
Based on places with total population of 50,000 or more

Place	Population	%
Fort Wayne (city) Allen County	2	<0.01
Indianapolis (city) Marion County	2	<0.01
Bloomington (city) Monroe County	1	<0.01
Carmel (city) Hamilton County	1	<0.01
Anderson (city) Madison County	0	0.00
Elkhart (city) Elkhart County	0	0.00
Evansville (city) Vanderburgh County	0	0.00
Fishers (town) Hamilton County	0	0.00
Gary (city) Lake County	0	0.00
Hammond (city) Lake County	0	0.00

Asian

Top 10 Places Sorted by Population
Based on all places, regardless of total population

Place	Population	%
Indianapolis (city) Marion County	21,294	2.60
Fort Wayne (city) Allen County	9,768	3.85
Carmel (city) Hamilton County	7,838	9.90
Bloomington (city) Monroe County	7,368	9.16
West Lafayette (city) Tippecanoe County	5,498	18.58
Fishers (town) Hamilton County	4,930	6.42
Purdue University (cdp) Tippecanoe County	2,973	24.40
Columbus (city) Bartholomew County	2,625	5.96
Greenwood (city) Johnson County	2,170	4.36
South Bend (city) St. Joseph County	1,824	1.80

Top 10 Places Sorted by Percent of Total Population
Based on all places, regardless of total population

Place	Population	%
Purdue University (cdp) Tippecanoe County	2,973	24.40
West Lafayette (city) Tippecanoe County	5,498	18.58
Notre Dame (cdp) St. Joseph County	592	9.91
Carmel (city) Hamilton County	7,838	9.90
Bloomington (city) Monroe County	7,368	9.16
Munster (town) Lake County	1,536	6.51
Fishers (town) Hamilton County	4,930	6.42
Columbus (city) Bartholomew County	2,625	5.96
Roseland (town) St. Joseph County	36	5.71
Granger (cdp) St. Joseph County	1,608	5.28

Top 10 Places Sorted by Percent of Total Population
Based on places with total population of 50,000 or more

Place	Population	%
Carmel (city) Hamilton County	7,838	9.90
Bloomington (city) Monroe County	7,368	9.16
Fishers (town) Hamilton County	4,930	6.42
Fort Wayne (city) Allen County	9,768	3.85
Indianapolis (city) Marion County	21,294	2.60
Noblesville (city) Hamilton County	1,149	2.21
Lafayette (city) Tippecanoe County	1,224	1.82
South Bend (city) St. Joseph County	1,824	1.80
Terre Haute (city) Vigo County	1,092	1.80
Muncie (city) Delaware County	1,173	1.67

Asian: Not Hispanic

Top 10 Places Sorted by Population
Based on all places, regardless of total population

Place	Population	%
Indianapolis (city) Marion County	20,777	2.53
Fort Wayne (city) Allen County	9,548	3.76
Carmel (city) Hamilton County	7,790	9.84
Bloomington (city) Monroe County	7,298	9.08
West Lafayette (city) Tippecanoe County	5,477	18.51
Fishers (town) Hamilton County	4,883	6.36
Purdue University (cdp) Tippecanoe County	2,951	24.22
Columbus (city) Bartholomew County	2,607	5.92
Greenwood (city) Johnson County	2,153	4.32
South Bend (city) St. Joseph County	1,742	1.72

Top 10 Places Sorted by Percent of Total Population
Based on all places, regardless of total population

Place	Population	%
Purdue University (cdp) Tippecanoe County	2,951	24.22
West Lafayette (city) Tippecanoe County	5,477	18.51
Carmel (city) Hamilton County	7,790	9.84

Place	Population	%
Notre Dame (cdp) St. Joseph County	568	9.51
Bloomington (city) Monroe County	7,298	9.08
Munster (town) Lake County	1,514	6.41
Fishers (town) Hamilton County	4,883	6.36
Columbus (city) Bartholomew County	2,607	5.92
Roseland (town) St. Joseph County	36	5.71
Granger (cdp) St. Joseph County	1,594	5.23

Top 10 Places Sorted by Percent of Total Population
Based on places with total population of 50,000 or more

Place	Population	%
Carmel (city) Hamilton County	7,790	9.84
Bloomington (city) Monroe County	7,298	9.08
Fishers (town) Hamilton County	4,883	6.36
Fort Wayne (city) Allen County	9,548	3.76
Indianapolis (city) Marion County	20,777	2.53
Noblesville (city) Hamilton County	1,128	2.17
Terre Haute (city) Vigo County	1,081	1.78
Lafayette (city) Tippecanoe County	1,160	1.73
South Bend (city) St. Joseph County	1,742	1.72
Muncie (city) Delaware County	1,143	1.63

Asian: Hispanic

Top 10 Places Sorted by Population
Based on all places, regardless of total population

Place	Population	%
Indianapolis (city) Marion County	517	0.06
Fort Wayne (city) Allen County	220	0.09
Hammond (city) Lake County	128	0.16
South Bend (city) St. Joseph County	82	0.08
Bloomington (city) Monroe County	70	0.09
Lafayette (city) Tippecanoe County	64	0.10
Carmel (city) Hamilton County	48	0.06
Fishers (town) Hamilton County	47	0.06
Hobart (city) Lake County	41	0.14
Portage (city) Porter County	41	0.11

Top 10 Places Sorted by Percent of Total Population
Based on all places, regardless of total population

Place	Population	%
Kingsford Heights (town) LaPorte County	7	0.49
Dale (town) Spencer County	7	0.44
Montmorenci (cdp) Tippecanoe County	1	0.41
Notre Dame (cdp) St. Joseph County	24	0.40
Corunna (town) DeKalb County	1	0.39
Whiting (city) Lake County	15	0.30
Lynn (town) Randolph County	3	0.27
Utica (town) Clark County	2	0.26
Williams Creek (town) Marion County	1	0.25
Garrett (city) DeKalb County	15	0.24

Top 10 Places Sorted by Percent of Total Population
Based on places with total population of 50,000 or more

Place	Population	%
Hammond (city) Lake County	128	0.16
Lafayette (city) Tippecanoe County	64	0.10
Fort Wayne (city) Allen County	220	0.09
Bloomington (city) Monroe County	70	0.09
South Bend (city) St. Joseph County	82	0.08
Elkhart (city) Elkhart County	35	0.07
Indianapolis (city) Marion County	517	0.06
Carmel (city) Hamilton County	48	0.06
Fishers (town) Hamilton County	47	0.06
Gary (city) Lake County	36	0.04

Asian: Bangladeshi

Top 10 Places Sorted by Population
Based on all places, regardless of total population

Place	Population	%
Indianapolis (city) Marion County	128	0.02
Fort Wayne (city) Allen County	40	0.02
Fishers (town) Hamilton County	35	0.05
Carmel (city) Hamilton County	35	0.04
Purdue University (cdp) Tippecanoe County	31	0.25
Bloomington (city) Monroe County	27	0.03
Muncie (city) Delaware County	23	0.03
West Lafayette (city) Tippecanoe County	21	0.07
Columbus (city) Bartholomew County	17	0.04
Munster (town) Lake County	13	0.06

Top 10 Places Sorted by Percent of Total Population
Based on all places, regardless of total population

Place	Population	%
Purdue University (cdp) Tippecanoe County	31	0.25
West Lafayette (city) Tippecanoe County	21	0.07
Munster (town) Lake County	13	0.06
Fishers (town) Hamilton County	35	0.05
Dyer (town) Lake County	9	0.05
Carmel (city) Hamilton County	35	0.04
Columbus (city) Bartholomew County	17	0.04
Hunter (town) Allen County	2	0.04
McCordsville (town) Hancock County	2	0.04
Bloomington (city) Monroe County	27	0.03

Top 10 Places Sorted by Percent of Total Population
Based on places with total population of 50,000 or more

Place	Population	%
Fishers (town) Hamilton County	35	0.05
Carmel (city) Hamilton County	35	0.04
Bloomington (city) Monroe County	27	0.03
Muncie (city) Delaware County	23	0.03
Indianapolis (city) Marion County	128	0.02
Fort Wayne (city) Allen County	40	0.02
Noblesville (city) Hamilton County	12	0.02
Evansville (city) Vanderburgh County	6	0.01
Lafayette (city) Tippecanoe County	5	0.01
Elkhart (city) Elkhart County	3	0.01

Asian: Bhutanese

Top 10 Places Sorted by Population
Based on all places, regardless of total population

Place	Population	%
Fishers (town) Hamilton County	3	<0.01
Aberdeen (cdp) Porter County	0	0.00
Advance (town) Boone County	0	0.00
Akron (town) Fulton County	0	0.00
Alamo (town) Montgomery County	0	0.00
Albany (town) Delaware County	0	0.00
Albion (town) Noble County	0	0.00
Alexandria (city) Madison County	0	0.00
Alfordsville (town) Daviess County	0	0.00
Alton (town) Crawford County	0	0.00

Top 10 Places Sorted by Percent of Total Population
Based on all places, regardless of total population

Place	Population	%
Fishers (town) Hamilton County	3	<0.01
Aberdeen (cdp) Porter County	0	0.00
Advance (town) Boone County	0	0.00
Akron (town) Fulton County	0	0.00
Alamo (town) Montgomery County	0	0.00
Albany (town) Delaware County	0	0.00
Albion (town) Noble County	0	0.00
Alexandria (city) Madison County	0	0.00
Alfordsville (town) Daviess County	0	0.00
Alton (town) Crawford County	0	0.00

Top 10 Places Sorted by Percent of Total Population
Based on places with total population of 50,000 or more

Place	Population	%
Fishers (town) Hamilton County	3	<0.01
Anderson (city) Madison County	0	0.00
Bloomington (city) Monroe County	0	0.00
Carmel (city) Hamilton County	0	0.00
Elkhart (city) Elkhart County	0	0.00
Evansville (city) Vanderburgh County	0	0.00
Fort Wayne (city) Allen County	0	0.00
Gary (city) Lake County	0	0.00
Hammond (city) Lake County	0	0.00
Indianapolis (city) Marion County	0	0.00

Asian: Burmese

Top 10 Places Sorted by Population
Based on all places, regardless of total population

Place	Population	%
Fort Wayne (city) Allen County	3,819	1.51
Indianapolis (city) Marion County	3,622	0.44
Logansport (city) Cass County	144	0.78

Place	Population	%
Washington (city) Daviess County	80	0.70
Speedway (town) Marion County	42	0.36
Bloomington (city) Monroe County	18	0.02
Carmel (city) Hamilton County	8	0.01
Lafayette (city) Tippecanoe County	8	0.01
Southport (city) Marion County	7	0.41
Topeka (town) LaGrange County	6	0.52

Top 10 Places Sorted by Percent of Total Population
Based on all places, regardless of total population

Place	Population	%
Fort Wayne (city) Allen County	3,819	1.51
Logansport (city) Cass County	144	0.78
Washington (city) Daviess County	80	0.70
Topeka (town) LaGrange County	6	0.52
Indianapolis (city) Marion County	3,622	0.44
Southport (city) Marion County	7	0.41
Speedway (town) Marion County	42	0.36
Melody Hill (cdp) Vanderburgh County	2	0.06
Churubusco (town) Whitley County	1	0.06
Roanoke (town) Huntington County	1	0.06

Top 10 Places Sorted by Percent of Total Population
Based on places with total population of 50,000 or more

Place	Population	%
Fort Wayne (city) Allen County	3,819	1.51
Indianapolis (city) Marion County	3,622	0.44
Bloomington (city) Monroe County	18	0.02
Carmel (city) Hamilton County	8	0.01
Lafayette (city) Tippecanoe County	8	0.01
Fishers (town) Hamilton County	6	0.01
Muncie (city) Delaware County	2	<0.01
Evansville (city) Vanderburgh County	1	<0.01
Anderson (city) Madison County	0	0.00
Elkhart (city) Elkhart County	0	0.00

Asian: Cambodian

Top 10 Places Sorted by Population
Based on all places, regardless of total population

Place	Population	%
Indianapolis (city) Marion County	118	0.01
South Bend (city) St. Joseph County	80	0.08
Goshen (city) Elkhart County	71	0.22
Elkhart (city) Elkhart County	66	0.13
Westfield (town) Hamilton County	58	0.19
Fort Wayne (city) Allen County	46	0.02
Mishawaka (city) St. Joseph County	32	0.07
Noblesville (city) Hamilton County	26	0.05
Carmel (city) Hamilton County	22	0.03
Lawrence (city) Marion County	14	0.03

Top 10 Places Sorted by Percent of Total Population
Based on all places, regardless of total population

Place	Population	%
Corunna (town) DeKalb County	3	1.18
Bristol (town) Elkhart County	9	0.56
Amboy (town) Miami County	1	0.26
Goshen (city) Elkhart County	71	0.22
Westfield (town) Hamilton County	58	0.19
Dunlap (cdp) Elkhart County	9	0.14
Warren Park (town) Marion County	2	0.14
Elkhart (city) Elkhart County	66	0.13
McCordsville (town) Hancock County	6	0.13
Brookville (town) Franklin County	3	0.12

Top 10 Places Sorted by Percent of Total Population
Based on places with total population of 50,000 or more

Place	Population	%
Elkhart (city) Elkhart County	66	0.13
South Bend (city) St. Joseph County	80	0.08
Noblesville (city) Hamilton County	26	0.05
Carmel (city) Hamilton County	22	0.03
Fort Wayne (city) Allen County	46	0.02
Fishers (town) Hamilton County	14	0.02
Indianapolis (city) Marion County	118	0.01
Bloomington (city) Monroe County	9	0.01
Gary (city) Lake County	7	0.01
Hammond (city) Lake County	5	0.01

Please refer to the Explanation of Data in the front of the book for more detailed information.

Asian: Chinese, except Taiwanese

Top 10 Places Sorted by Population
Based on all places, regardless of total population

Place	Population	%
Indianapolis (city) Marion County	3,197	0.39
Carmel (city) Hamilton County	2,754	3.48
Bloomington (city) Monroe County	2,230	2.77
West Lafayette (city) Tippecanoe County	1,852	6.26
Purdue University (cdp) Tippecanoe County	1,285	10.55
Fishers (town) Hamilton County	818	1.07
Fort Wayne (city) Allen County	643	0.25
Columbus (city) Bartholomew County	422	0.96
Hammond (city) Lake County	422	0.52
Granger (cdp) St. Joseph County	420	1.38

Top 10 Places Sorted by Percent of Total Population
Based on all places, regardless of total population

Place	Population	%
Purdue University (cdp) Tippecanoe County	1,285	10.55
West Lafayette (city) Tippecanoe County	1,852	6.26
Carmel (city) Hamilton County	2,754	3.48
Notre Dame (cdp) St. Joseph County	208	3.48
Bloomington (city) Monroe County	2,230	2.77
Howe (cdp) LaGrange County	19	2.35
New Ross (town) Montgomery County	7	2.02
Roseland (town) St. Joseph County	11	1.75
Granger (cdp) St. Joseph County	420	1.38
St. Mary of the Woods (cdp) Vigo County	11	1.38

Top 10 Places Sorted by Percent of Total Population
Based on places with total population of 50,000 or more

Place	Population	%
Carmel (city) Hamilton County	2,754	3.48
Bloomington (city) Monroe County	2,230	2.77
Fishers (town) Hamilton County	818	1.07
Hammond (city) Lake County	422	0.52
Terre Haute (city) Vigo County	254	0.42
Muncie (city) Delaware County	282	0.40
Indianapolis (city) Marion County	3,197	0.39
South Bend (city) St. Joseph County	360	0.36
Lafayette (city) Tippecanoe County	226	0.34
Noblesville (city) Hamilton County	157	0.30

Asian: Filipino

Top 10 Places Sorted by Population
Based on all places, regardless of total population

Place	Population	%
Indianapolis (city) Marion County	2,608	0.32
Fort Wayne (city) Allen County	823	0.32
Carmel (city) Hamilton County	411	0.52
Fishers (town) Hamilton County	391	0.51
South Bend (city) St. Joseph County	345	0.34
Bloomington (city) Monroe County	312	0.39
Munster (town) Lake County	268	1.14
Merrillville (town) Lake County	254	0.72
Evansville (city) Vanderburgh County	248	0.21
Greenwood (city) Johnson County	213	0.43

Top 10 Places Sorted by Percent of Total Population
Based on all places, regardless of total population

Place	Population	%
Blountsville (town) Henry County	3	2.24
Shorewood Forest (cdp) Porter County	45	1.66
Notre Dame (cdp) St. Joseph County	86	1.44
Winfield (town) Lake County	57	1.30
McCordsville (town) Hancock County	62	1.29
Munster (town) Lake County	268	1.14
Salt Creek Commons (cdp) Porter County	24	1.13
Crane (town) Martin County	2	1.09
Dyer (town) Lake County	175	1.07
Bruceville (town) Knox County	5	1.05

Top 10 Places Sorted by Percent of Total Population
Based on places with total population of 50,000 or more

Place	Population	%
Carmel (city) Hamilton County	411	0.52
Fishers (town) Hamilton County	391	0.51
Bloomington (city) Monroe County	312	0.39
Noblesville (city) Hamilton County	198	0.38

South Bend (city) St. Joseph County	345	0.34
Indianapolis (city) Marion County	2,608	0.32
Fort Wayne (city) Allen County	823	0.32
Lafayette (city) Tippecanoe County	200	0.30
Terre Haute (city) Vigo County	159	0.26
Hammond (city) Lake County	203	0.25

Asian: Hmong

Top 10 Places Sorted by Population
Based on all places, regardless of total population

Place	Population	%
Westfield (town) Hamilton County	52	0.17
Carmel (city) Hamilton County	27	0.03
Indianapolis (city) Marion County	24	<0.01
Fort Branch (town) Gibson County	14	0.51
Noblesville (city) Hamilton County	14	0.03
Fishers (town) Hamilton County	11	0.01
Terre Haute (city) Vigo County	7	0.01
Bloomington (city) Monroe County	5	0.01
Lebanon (city) Boone County	4	0.03
Columbus (city) Bartholomew County	4	0.01

Top 10 Places Sorted by Percent of Total Population
Based on all places, regardless of total population

Place	Population	%
Fort Branch (town) Gibson County	14	0.51
Westfield (town) Hamilton County	52	0.17
Hanover (town) Jefferson County	2	0.06
Austin (city) Scott County	2	0.05
Carmel (city) Hamilton County	27	0.03
Noblesville (city) Hamilton County	14	0.03
Lebanon (city) Boone County	4	0.03
Cicero (town) Hamilton County	1	0.02
Fishers (town) Hamilton County	11	0.01
Terre Haute (city) Vigo County	7	0.01

Top 10 Places Sorted by Percent of Total Population
Based on places with total population of 50,000 or more

Place	Population	%
Carmel (city) Hamilton County	27	0.03
Noblesville (city) Hamilton County	14	0.03
Fishers (town) Hamilton County	11	0.01
Terre Haute (city) Vigo County	7	0.01
Bloomington (city) Monroe County	5	0.01
Indianapolis (city) Marion County	24	<0.01
Muncie (city) Delaware County	2	<0.01
South Bend (city) St. Joseph County	2	<0.01
Anderson (city) Madison County	0	0.00
Elkhart (city) Elkhart County	0	0.00

Asian: Indian

Top 10 Places Sorted by Population
Based on all places, regardless of total population

Place	Population	%
Indianapolis (city) Marion County	5,358	0.65
Carmel (city) Hamilton County	2,526	3.19
Fishers (town) Hamilton County	1,785	2.32
West Lafayette (city) Tippecanoe County	1,624	5.49
Fort Wayne (city) Allen County	1,426	0.56
Bloomington (city) Monroe County	1,390	1.73
Columbus (city) Bartholomew County	1,381	3.13
Greenwood (city) Johnson County	1,381	2.77
Munster (town) Lake County	718	3.04
Purdue University (cdp) Tippecanoe County	616	5.06

Top 10 Places Sorted by Percent of Total Population
Based on all places, regardless of total population

Place	Population	%
West Lafayette (city) Tippecanoe County	1,624	5.49
Purdue University (cdp) Tippecanoe County	616	5.06
Carmel (city) Hamilton County	2,526	3.19
Columbus (city) Bartholomew County	1,381	3.13
Munster (town) Lake County	718	3.04
Greenwood (city) Johnson County	1,381	2.77
Fishers (town) Hamilton County	1,785	2.32
Plainfield (town) Hendricks County	595	2.15
Laconia (town) Harrison County	1	2.00
Bloomington (city) Monroe County	1,390	1.73

Top 10 Places Sorted by Percent of Total Population
Based on places with total population of 50,000 or more

Place	Population	%
Carmel (city) Hamilton County	2,526	3.19
Fishers (town) Hamilton County	1,785	2.32
Bloomington (city) Monroe County	1,390	1.73
Indianapolis (city) Marion County	5,358	0.65
Fort Wayne (city) Allen County	1,426	0.56
Noblesville (city) Hamilton County	262	0.50
Terre Haute (city) Vigo County	242	0.40
Muncie (city) Delaware County	248	0.35
Lafayette (city) Tippecanoe County	225	0.34
Evansville (city) Vanderburgh County	369	0.31

Asian: Indonesian

Top 10 Places Sorted by Population
Based on all places, regardless of total population

Place	Population	%
Indianapolis (city) Marion County	142	0.02
Bloomington (city) Monroe County	78	0.10
Fishers (town) Hamilton County	53	0.07
West Lafayette (city) Tippecanoe County	49	0.17
Carmel (city) Hamilton County	41	0.05
Fort Wayne (city) Allen County	26	0.01
Purdue University (cdp) Tippecanoe County	23	0.19
Goshen (city) Elkhart County	17	0.05
Noblesville (city) Hamilton County	15	0.03
Plainfield (town) Hendricks County	14	0.05

Top 10 Places Sorted by Percent of Total Population
Based on all places, regardless of total population

Place	Population	%
Utica (town) Clark County	3	0.39
Pittsboro (town) Hendricks County	8	0.27
Fountain City (town) Wayne County	2	0.25
Purdue University (cdp) Tippecanoe County	23	0.19
West Lafayette (city) Tippecanoe County	49	0.17
Middle (town) Henry County	3	0.13
Bloomington (city) Monroe County	78	0.10
Fishers (town) Hamilton County	53	0.07
Notre Dame (cdp) St. Joseph County	4	0.07
Corydon (town) Harrison County	2	0.06

Top 10 Places Sorted by Percent of Total Population
Based on places with total population of 50,000 or more

Place	Population	%
Bloomington (city) Monroe County	78	0.10
Fishers (town) Hamilton County	53	0.07
Carmel (city) Hamilton County	41	0.05
Noblesville (city) Hamilton County	15	0.03
Indianapolis (city) Marion County	142	0.02
Elkhart (city) Elkhart County	8	0.02
Fort Wayne (city) Allen County	26	0.01
South Bend (city) St. Joseph County	14	0.01
Evansville (city) Vanderburgh County	12	0.01
Lafayette (city) Tippecanoe County	9	0.01

Asian: Japanese

Top 10 Places Sorted by Population
Based on all places, regardless of total population

Place	Population	%
Indianapolis (city) Marion County	1,094	0.13
Carmel (city) Hamilton County	415	0.52
Columbus (city) Bartholomew County	402	0.91
Bloomington (city) Monroe County	395	0.49
Fishers (town) Hamilton County	316	0.41
Fort Wayne (city) Allen County	252	0.10
West Lafayette (city) Tippecanoe County	206	0.70
Evansville (city) Vanderburgh County	135	0.11
Terre Haute (city) Vigo County	112	0.18
Lafayette (city) Tippecanoe County	107	0.16

Top 10 Places Sorted by Percent of Total Population
Based on all places, regardless of total population

Place	Population	%
Dunreith (town) Henry County	5	2.82
Onward (town) Cass County	2	2.00
Roseland (town) St. Joseph County	8	1.27

Place	Population	%
Spring Hill (town) Marion County	1	1.02
Columbus (city) Bartholomew County	402	0.91
St. Joe (town) DeKalb County	4	0.87
Elnora (town) Daviess County	5	0.78
Greencastle (city) Putnam County	77	0.75
Indian Village (town) St. Joseph County	1	0.75
West Lafayette (city) Tippecanoe County	206	0.70

Top 10 Places Sorted by Percent of Total Population
Based on places with total population of 50,000 or more

Place	Population	%
Carmel (city) Hamilton County	415	0.52
Bloomington (city) Monroe County	395	0.49
Fishers (town) Hamilton County	316	0.41
Terre Haute (city) Vigo County	112	0.18
Noblesville (city) Hamilton County	86	0.17
Lafayette (city) Tippecanoe County	107	0.16
Indianapolis (city) Marion County	1,094	0.13
Muncie (city) Delaware County	86	0.12
Evansville (city) Vanderburgh County	135	0.11
Fort Wayne (city) Allen County	252	0.10

Asian: Korean

Top 10 Places Sorted by Population
Based on all places, regardless of total population

Place	Population	%
Bloomington (city) Monroe County	1,807	2.25
Indianapolis (city) Marion County	1,558	0.19
West Lafayette (city) Tippecanoe County	894	3.02
Carmel (city) Hamilton County	684	0.86
Fishers (town) Hamilton County	575	0.75
Purdue University (cdp) Tippecanoe County	542	4.45
Fort Wayne (city) Allen County	474	0.19
Lawrence (city) Marion County	283	0.62
Lafayette (city) Tippecanoe County	239	0.36
Granger (cdp) St. Joseph County	223	0.73

Top 10 Places Sorted by Percent of Total Population
Based on all places, regardless of total population

Place	Population	%
Purdue University (cdp) Tippecanoe County	542	4.45
West Lafayette (city) Tippecanoe County	894	3.02
Bloomington (city) Monroe County	1,807	2.25
Notre Dame (cdp) St. Joseph County	132	2.21
Wynnedale (town) Marion County	4	1.73
Dune Acres (town) Porter County	2	1.10
Schneider (town) Lake County	3	1.08
Freetown (cdp) Jackson County	4	1.04
Utica (town) Clark County	8	1.03
Mackey (town) Gibson County	1	0.94

Top 10 Places Sorted by Percent of Total Population
Based on places with total population of 50,000 or more

Place	Population	%
Bloomington (city) Monroe County	1,807	2.25
Carmel (city) Hamilton County	684	0.86
Fishers (town) Hamilton County	575	0.75
Lafayette (city) Tippecanoe County	239	0.36
Noblesville (city) Hamilton County	143	0.28
Terre Haute (city) Vigo County	141	0.23
Muncie (city) Delaware County	142	0.20
Indianapolis (city) Marion County	1,558	0.19
Fort Wayne (city) Allen County	474	0.19
South Bend (city) St. Joseph County	164	0.16

Asian: Laotian

Top 10 Places Sorted by Population
Based on all places, regardless of total population

Place	Population	%
Fort Wayne (city) Allen County	369	0.15
Indianapolis (city) Marion County	142	0.02
Elkhart (city) Elkhart County	115	0.23
South Bend (city) St. Joseph County	53	0.05
Logansport (city) Cass County	43	0.23
Simonton Lake (cdp) Elkhart County	26	0.56
Fishers (town) Hamilton County	25	0.03
Goshen (city) Elkhart County	23	0.07
Mishawaka (city) St. Joseph County	19	0.04
Granger (cdp) St. Joseph County	18	0.06

Top 10 Places Sorted by Percent of Total Population
Based on all places, regardless of total population

Place	Population	%
Leesburg (town) Kosciusko County	11	1.98
Tecumseh (cdp) Vigo County	5	0.76
Wakarusa (town) Elkhart County	13	0.74
Simonton Lake (cdp) Elkhart County	26	0.56
Bristol (town) Elkhart County	9	0.56
Salt Creek Commons (cdp) Porter County	6	0.28
Dunlap (cdp) Elkhart County	16	0.26
Elkhart (city) Elkhart County	115	0.23
Logansport (city) Cass County	43	0.23
Hunter (town) Allen County	10	0.21

Top 10 Places Sorted by Percent of Total Population
Based on places with total population of 50,000 or more

Place	Population	%
Elkhart (city) Elkhart County	115	0.23
Fort Wayne (city) Allen County	369	0.15
South Bend (city) St. Joseph County	53	0.05
Fishers (town) Hamilton County	25	0.03
Noblesville (city) Hamilton County	13	0.03
Indianapolis (city) Marion County	142	0.02
Lafayette (city) Tippecanoe County	11	0.02
Carmel (city) Hamilton County	9	0.01
Bloomington (city) Monroe County	8	0.01
Gary (city) Lake County	6	0.01

Asian: Malaysian

Top 10 Places Sorted by Population
Based on all places, regardless of total population

Place	Population	%
West Lafayette (city) Tippecanoe County	135	0.46
Bloomington (city) Monroe County	59	0.07
Indianapolis (city) Marion County	44	0.01
Fort Wayne (city) Allen County	41	0.02
Purdue University (cdp) Tippecanoe County	19	0.16
Carmel (city) Hamilton County	17	0.02
Evansville (city) Vanderburgh County	17	0.01
Fishers (town) Hamilton County	10	0.01
Terre Haute (city) Vigo County	9	0.01
Columbus (city) Bartholomew County	6	0.01

Top 10 Places Sorted by Percent of Total Population
Based on all places, regardless of total population

Place	Population	%
West Lafayette (city) Tippecanoe County	135	0.46
Purdue University (cdp) Tippecanoe County	19	0.16
Grabill (town) Allen County	1	0.09
Warren (town) Huntington County	1	0.08
Bloomington (city) Monroe County	59	0.07
North Terre Haute (cdp) Vigo County	3	0.07
Dyer (town) Lake County	5	0.03
Angola (city) Steuben County	3	0.03
Fort Wayne (city) Allen County	41	0.02
Carmel (city) Hamilton County	17	0.02

Top 10 Places Sorted by Percent of Total Population
Based on places with total population of 50,000 or more

Place	Population	%
Bloomington (city) Monroe County	59	0.07
Fort Wayne (city) Allen County	41	0.02
Carmel (city) Hamilton County	17	0.02
Indianapolis (city) Marion County	44	0.01
Evansville (city) Vanderburgh County	17	0.01
Fishers (town) Hamilton County	10	0.01
Terre Haute (city) Vigo County	9	0.01
Noblesville (city) Hamilton County	5	0.01
Lafayette (city) Tippecanoe County	4	0.01
Muncie (city) Delaware County	3	<0.01

Asian: Nepalese

Top 10 Places Sorted by Population
Based on all places, regardless of total population

Place	Population	%
Indianapolis (city) Marion County	46	0.01
Evansville (city) Vanderburgh County	23	0.02
Bloomington (city) Monroe County	19	0.02
Fishers (town) Hamilton County	18	0.02
Munster (town) Lake County	14	0.06
Muncie (city) Delaware County	13	0.02
Carmel (city) Hamilton County	12	0.02
Purdue University (cdp) Tippecanoe County	11	0.09
Fort Wayne (city) Allen County	11	<0.01
Goshen (city) Elkhart County	10	0.03

Top 10 Places Sorted by Percent of Total Population
Based on all places, regardless of total population

Place	Population	%
Mackey (town) Gibson County	1	0.94
North Liberty (town) St. Joseph County	2	0.11
Purdue University (cdp) Tippecanoe County	11	0.09
Oakland City (city) Gibson County	2	0.08
Munster (town) Lake County	14	0.06
Angola (city) Steuben County	4	0.05
Goshen (city) Elkhart County	10	0.03
West Lafayette (city) Tippecanoe County	8	0.03
Warsaw (city) Kosciusko County	4	0.03
Evansville (city) Vanderburgh County	23	0.02

Top 10 Places Sorted by Percent of Total Population
Based on places with total population of 50,000 or more

Place	Population	%
Evansville (city) Vanderburgh County	23	0.02
Bloomington (city) Monroe County	19	0.02
Fishers (town) Hamilton County	18	0.02
Muncie (city) Delaware County	13	0.02
Carmel (city) Hamilton County	12	0.02
Indianapolis (city) Marion County	46	0.01
Terre Haute (city) Vigo County	5	0.01
Fort Wayne (city) Allen County	11	<0.01
South Bend (city) St. Joseph County	4	<0.01
Lafayette (city) Tippecanoe County	3	<0.01

Asian: Pakistani

Top 10 Places Sorted by Population
Based on all places, regardless of total population

Place	Population	%
Indianapolis (city) Marion County	625	0.08
Carmel (city) Hamilton County	211	0.27
Fishers (town) Hamilton County	189	0.25
Fort Wayne (city) Allen County	161	0.06
Plainfield (town) Hendricks County	103	0.37
Purdue University (cdp) Tippecanoe County	93	0.76
Granger (cdp) St. Joseph County	91	0.30
Bloomington (city) Monroe County	87	0.11
West Lafayette (city) Tippecanoe County	74	0.25
Schererville (town) Lake County	64	0.22

Top 10 Places Sorted by Percent of Total Population
Based on all places, regardless of total population

Place	Population	%
Plainville (town) Daviess County	4	0.84
Purdue University (cdp) Tippecanoe County	93	0.76
Dune Acres (town) Porter County	1	0.55
Aberdeen (cdp) Porter County	9	0.48
Avon (town) Hendricks County	53	0.43
Pottawattamie Park (town) LaPorte County	1	0.43
Plainfield (town) Hendricks County	103	0.37
Beverly Shores (town) Porter County	2	0.33
Winfield (town) Lake County	14	0.32
Granger (cdp) St. Joseph County	91	0.30

Top 10 Places Sorted by Percent of Total Population
Based on places with total population of 50,000 or more

Place	Population	%
Carmel (city) Hamilton County	211	0.27
Fishers (town) Hamilton County	189	0.25
Bloomington (city) Monroe County	87	0.11
Indianapolis (city) Marion County	625	0.08
Fort Wayne (city) Allen County	161	0.06
Hammond (city) Lake County	44	0.05
Elkhart (city) Elkhart County	15	0.03
South Bend (city) St. Joseph County	16	0.02
Muncie (city) Delaware County	14	0.02
Lafayette (city) Tippecanoe County	13	0.02

Please refer to the Explanation of Data in the front of the book for more detailed information.

Asian: Sri Lankan

Top 10 Places Sorted by Population
Based on all places, regardless of total population

Place	Population	%
Indianapolis (city) Marion County	42	0.01
West Lafayette (city) Tippecanoe County	40	0.14
Bloomington (city) Monroe County	40	0.05
Carmel (city) Hamilton County	35	0.04
Fort Wayne (city) Allen County	19	0.01
Purdue University (cdp) Tippecanoe County	18	0.15
Fishers (town) Hamilton County	11	0.01
Goshen (city) Elkhart County	10	0.03
Granger (cdp) St. Joseph County	9	0.03
South Bend (city) St. Joseph County	9	0.01

Top 10 Places Sorted by Percent of Total Population
Based on all places, regardless of total population

Place	Population	%
Green (town) Howard County	4	0.17
Purdue University (cdp) Tippecanoe County	18	0.15
West Lafayette (city) Tippecanoe County	40	0.14
Notre Dame (cdp) St. Joseph County	7	0.12
Whites (town) Boone County	2	0.07
Churubusco (town) Whitley County	1	0.06
Bloomington (city) Monroe County	40	0.05
Carmel (city) Hamilton County	35	0.04
Goshen (city) Elkhart County	10	0.03
Granger (cdp) St. Joseph County	9	0.03

Top 10 Places Sorted by Percent of Total Population
Based on places with total population of 50,000 or more

Place	Population	%
Bloomington (city) Monroe County	40	0.05
Carmel (city) Hamilton County	35	0.04
Indianapolis (city) Marion County	42	0.01
Fort Wayne (city) Allen County	19	0.01
Fishers (town) Hamilton County	11	0.01
South Bend (city) St. Joseph County	9	0.01
Noblesville (city) Hamilton County	7	0.01
Elkhart (city) Elkhart County	4	0.01
Muncie (city) Delaware County	4	0.01
Hammond (city) Lake County	1	<0.01

Asian: Taiwanese

Top 10 Places Sorted by Population
Based on all places, regardless of total population

Place	Population	%
Bloomington (city) Monroe County	260	0.32
West Lafayette (city) Tippecanoe County	211	0.71
Carmel (city) Hamilton County	177	0.22
Indianapolis (city) Marion County	160	0.02
Purdue University (cdp) Tippecanoe County	118	0.97
Terre Haute (city) Vigo County	55	0.09
Fort Wayne (city) Allen County	47	0.02
Fishers (town) Hamilton County	45	0.06
Columbus (city) Bartholomew County	30	0.07
Muncie (city) Delaware County	25	0.04

Top 10 Places Sorted by Percent of Total Population
Based on all places, regardless of total population

Place	Population	%
Purdue University (cdp) Tippecanoe County	118	0.97
West Lafayette (city) Tippecanoe County	211	0.71
St. Mary of the Woods (cdp) Vigo County	4	0.50
Williams Creek (town) Marion County	2	0.49
Lagro (town) Wabash County	2	0.48
Bloomington (city) Monroe County	260	0.32
Spring Grove (town) Wayne County	1	0.29
Somerset (cdp) Wabash County	1	0.25
Gosport (town) Owen County	2	0.24
Americus (cdp) Tippecanoe County	1	0.24

Top 10 Places Sorted by Percent of Total Population
Based on places with total population of 50,000 or more

Place	Population	%
Bloomington (city) Monroe County	260	0.32
Carmel (city) Hamilton County	177	0.22
Terre Haute (city) Vigo County	55	0.09
Fishers (town) Hamilton County	45	0.06

Place	Population	%
Muncie (city) Delaware County	25	0.04
Lafayette (city) Tippecanoe County	20	0.03
Indianapolis (city) Marion County	160	0.02
Fort Wayne (city) Allen County	47	0.02
South Bend (city) St. Joseph County	19	0.02
Evansville (city) Vanderburgh County	10	0.01

Asian: Thai

Top 10 Places Sorted by Population
Based on all places, regardless of total population

Place	Population	%
Indianapolis (city) Marion County	352	0.04
Fort Wayne (city) Allen County	202	0.08
Bloomington (city) Monroe County	103	0.13
West Lafayette (city) Tippecanoe County	65	0.22
Fishers (town) Hamilton County	47	0.06
Carmel (city) Hamilton County	42	0.05
Evansville (city) Vanderburgh County	40	0.03
Crown Point (city) Lake County	37	0.14
South Bend (city) St. Joseph County	37	0.04
Purdue University (cdp) Tippecanoe County	32	0.26

Top 10 Places Sorted by Percent of Total Population
Based on all places, regardless of total population

Place	Population	%
Little York (town) Washington County	4	2.08
Cynthiana (town) Posey County	3	0.55
Mill (town) Crawford County	4	0.49
Pine Village (town) Warren County	1	0.46
Ogden Dunes (town) Porter County	5	0.45
Shorewood Forest (cdp) Porter County	11	0.41
Uniondale (town) Wells County	1	0.32
Purdue University (cdp) Tippecanoe County	32	0.26
Henryville (cdp) Clark County	5	0.26
Lake Santee (cdp) Decatur County	2	0.24

Top 10 Places Sorted by Percent of Total Population
Based on places with total population of 50,000 or more

Place	Population	%
Bloomington (city) Monroe County	103	0.13
Fort Wayne (city) Allen County	202	0.08
Fishers (town) Hamilton County	47	0.06
Carmel (city) Hamilton County	42	0.05
Noblesville (city) Hamilton County	24	0.05
Indianapolis (city) Marion County	352	0.04
South Bend (city) St. Joseph County	37	0.04
Lafayette (city) Tippecanoe County	25	0.04
Elkhart (city) Elkhart County	22	0.04
Evansville (city) Vanderburgh County	40	0.03

Asian: Vietnamese

Top 10 Places Sorted by Population
Based on all places, regardless of total population

Place	Population	%
Indianapolis (city) Marion County	1,347	0.16
Fort Wayne (city) Allen County	939	0.37
Fishers (town) Hamilton County	439	0.57
Carmel (city) Hamilton County	279	0.35
South Bend (city) St. Joseph County	267	0.26
Bloomington (city) Monroe County	203	0.25
Evansville (city) Vanderburgh County	194	0.17
Noblesville (city) Hamilton County	139	0.27
Mishawaka (city) St. Joseph County	120	0.25
Columbus (city) Bartholomew County	118	0.27

Top 10 Places Sorted by Percent of Total Population
Based on all places, regardless of total population

Place	Population	%
Hunter (town) Allen County	48	1.00
Roseland (town) St. Joseph County	6	0.95
Shamrock Lakes (town) Blackford County	2	0.87
Notre Dame (cdp) St. Joseph County	48	0.80
Fishers (town) Hamilton County	439	0.57
Middlebury (town) Elkhart County	19	0.56
Garrett (city) DeKalb County	29	0.46
Purdue University (cdp) Tippecanoe County	50	0.41
Wolcottville (town) Noble County	4	0.40
Centerville (town) Wayne County	10	0.39

Top 10 Places Sorted by Percent of Total Population
Based on places with total population of 50,000 or more

Place	Population	%
Fishers (town) Hamilton County	439	0.57
Fort Wayne (city) Allen County	939	0.37
Carmel (city) Hamilton County	279	0.35
Noblesville (city) Hamilton County	139	0.27
South Bend (city) St. Joseph County	267	0.26
Bloomington (city) Monroe County	203	0.25
Evansville (city) Vanderburgh County	194	0.17
Indianapolis (city) Marion County	1,347	0.16
Lafayette (city) Tippecanoe County	79	0.12
Muncie (city) Delaware County	62	0.09

Hawaii Native/Pacific Islander

Top 10 Places Sorted by Population
Based on all places, regardless of total population

Place	Population	%
Indianapolis (city) Marion County	1,129	0.14
Fort Wayne (city) Allen County	354	0.14
South Bend (city) St. Joseph County	185	0.18
Evansville (city) Vanderburgh County	176	0.15
Muncie (city) Delaware County	138	0.20
Bloomington (city) Monroe County	120	0.15
Richmond (city) Wayne County	118	0.32
Hammond (city) Lake County	97	0.12
Lawrence (city) Marion County	94	0.20
Carmel (city) Hamilton County	87	0.11

Top 10 Places Sorted by Percent of Total Population
Based on all places, regardless of total population

Place	Population	%
Bethany (town) Morgan County	2	2.47
Mount Etna (town) Huntington County	2	2.13
Leavenworth (town) Crawford County	5	2.10
Modoc (town) Randolph County	4	2.04
Russellville (town) Putnam County	3	0.84
Medora (town) Jackson County	5	0.72
Beverly Shores (town) Porter County	4	0.65
Collegeville (cdp) Jasper County	2	0.61
Newberry (town) Greene County	1	0.52
New Goshen (cdp) Vigo County	2	0.51

Top 10 Places Sorted by Percent of Total Population
Based on places with total population of 50,000 or more

Place	Population	%
Muncie (city) Delaware County	138	0.20
South Bend (city) St. Joseph County	185	0.18
Evansville (city) Vanderburgh County	176	0.15
Bloomington (city) Monroe County	120	0.15
Noblesville (city) Hamilton County	80	0.15
Indianapolis (city) Marion County	1,129	0.14
Fort Wayne (city) Allen County	354	0.14
Elkhart (city) Elkhart County	71	0.13
Terre Haute (city) Vigo County	79	0.13
Hammond (city) Lake County	97	0.12

Hawaii Native/Pacific Islander: Not Hispanic

Top 10 Places Sorted by Population
Based on all places, regardless of total population

Place	Population	%
Indianapolis (city) Marion County	820	0.10
Fort Wayne (city) Allen County	249	0.10
South Bend (city) St. Joseph County	156	0.15
Evansville (city) Vanderburgh County	150	0.13
Muncie (city) Delaware County	126	0.18
Richmond (city) Wayne County	110	0.30
Bloomington (city) Monroe County	95	0.12
Lawrence (city) Marion County	80	0.20
Mishawaka (city) St. Joseph County	79	0.16
Carmel (city) Hamilton County	77	0.10

Top 10 Places Sorted by Percent of Total Population
Based on all places, regardless of total population

Place	Population	%
Bethany (town) Morgan County	2	2.47
Mount Etna (town) Huntington County	2	2.13

Please refer to the Explanation of Data in the front of the book for more detailed information.

Profiles of Indiana — Ancestry and Ethnicity: Racial Group Rankings

Place	Population	%
Modoc (town) Randolph County	4	2.04
Leavenworth (town) Crawford County	4	1.68
Russellville (town) Putnam County	3	0.84
Medora (town) Jackson County	5	0.72
Beverly Shores (town) Porter County	4	0.65
Collegeville (cdp) Jasper County	2	0.61
Newberry (town) Greene County	1	0.52
New Goshen (cdp) Vigo County	2	0.51

Top 10 Places Sorted by Percent of Total Population
Based on places with total population of 50,000 or more

Place	Population	%
Muncie (city) Delaware County	126	0.18
South Bend (city) St. Joseph County	156	0.15
Evansville (city) Vanderburgh County	150	0.13
Bloomington (city) Monroe County	95	0.12
Terre Haute (city) Vigo County	73	0.12
Noblesville (city) Hamilton County	61	0.12
Indianapolis (city) Marion County	820	0.10
Fort Wayne (city) Allen County	249	0.10
Carmel (city) Hamilton County	77	0.10
Elkhart (city) Elkhart County	44	0.09

Hawaii Native/Pacific Islander: Hispanic

Top 10 Places Sorted by Population
Based on all places, regardless of total population

Place	Population	%
Indianapolis (city) Marion County	309	0.04
Fort Wayne (city) Allen County	105	0.04
Hammond (city) Lake County	50	0.06
South Bend (city) St. Joseph County	29	0.03
Elkhart (city) Elkhart County	27	0.05
Evansville (city) Vanderburgh County	26	0.02
Logansport (city) Cass County	25	0.14
Bloomington (city) Monroe County	25	0.03
Noblesville (city) Hamilton County	19	0.04
Lafayette (city) Tippecanoe County	18	0.03

Top 10 Places Sorted by Percent of Total Population
Based on all places, regardless of total population

Place	Population	%
Leavenworth (town) Crawford County	1	0.42
Corunna (town) DeKalb County	1	0.39
New Chicago (town) Lake County	5	0.25
Wheeler (cdp) Porter County	1	0.23
Huntingburg (city) Dubois County	12	0.20
Whiting (city) Lake County	8	0.16
Logansport (city) Cass County	25	0.14
Pennville (town) Jay County	1	0.14
Bunker Hill (town) Miami County	1	0.11
Burns Harbor (town) Porter County	1	0.09

Top 10 Places Sorted by Percent of Total Population
Based on places with total population of 50,000 or more

Place	Population	%
Hammond (city) Lake County	50	0.06
Elkhart (city) Elkhart County	27	0.05
Indianapolis (city) Marion County	309	0.04
Fort Wayne (city) Allen County	105	0.04
Noblesville (city) Hamilton County	19	0.04
South Bend (city) St. Joseph County	29	0.03
Bloomington (city) Monroe County	25	0.03
Lafayette (city) Tippecanoe County	18	0.03
Evansville (city) Vanderburgh County	26	0.02
Gary (city) Lake County	14	0.02

Hawaii Native/Pacific Islander: Fijian

Top 10 Places Sorted by Population
Based on all places, regardless of total population

Place	Population	%
Marion (city) Grant County	6	0.02
Indianapolis (city) Marion County	5	<0.01
East Chicago (city) Lake County	3	0.01
Princeton (city) Gibson County	2	0.02
Beech Grove (city) Marion County	2	0.01
Fort Wayne (city) Allen County	2	<0.01
Shelbyville (city) Shelby County	1	0.01
Bloomington (city) Monroe County	1	<0.01
Hammond (city) Lake County	1	<0.01
Muncie (city) Delaware County	1	<0.01

Top 10 Places Sorted by Percent of Total Population
Based on all places, regardless of total population

Place	Population	%
Marion (city) Grant County	6	0.02
Princeton (city) Gibson County	2	0.02
East Chicago (city) Lake County	3	0.01
Beech Grove (city) Marion County	2	0.01
Shelbyville (city) Shelby County	1	0.01
Indianapolis (city) Marion County	5	<0.01
Fort Wayne (city) Allen County	2	<0.01
Bloomington (city) Monroe County	1	<0.01
Hammond (city) Lake County	1	<0.01
Muncie (city) Delaware County	1	<0.01

Top 10 Places Sorted by Percent of Total Population
Based on places with total population of 50,000 or more

Place	Population	%
Indianapolis (city) Marion County	5	<0.01
Fort Wayne (city) Allen County	2	<0.01
Bloomington (city) Monroe County	1	<0.01
Hammond (city) Lake County	1	<0.01
Muncie (city) Delaware County	1	<0.01
Anderson (city) Madison County	0	0.00
Carmel (city) Hamilton County	0	0.00
Elkhart (city) Elkhart County	0	0.00
Evansville (city) Vanderburgh County	0	0.00
Fishers (town) Hamilton County	0	0.00

Hawaii Native/Pacific Islander: Guamanian or Chamorro

Top 10 Places Sorted by Population
Based on all places, regardless of total population

Place	Population	%
Indianapolis (city) Marion County	216	0.03
Fort Wayne (city) Allen County	102	0.04
Evansville (city) Vanderburgh County	30	0.03
Lawrence (city) Marion County	28	0.06
Bloomington (city) Monroe County	24	0.03
Lafayette (city) Tippecanoe County	20	0.03
South Bend (city) St. Joseph County	20	0.02
Jeffersonville (city) Clark County	18	0.04
Seymour (city) Jackson County	17	0.10
Elkhart (city) Elkhart County	17	0.03

Top 10 Places Sorted by Percent of Total Population
Based on all places, regardless of total population

Place	Population	%
Corunna (town) DeKalb County	1	0.39
Edwardsport (town) Knox County	1	0.33
Medora (town) Jackson County	2	0.29
Wheeler (cdp) Porter County	1	0.23
Bruceville (town) Knox County	1	0.21
Etna Green (town) Kosciusko County	1	0.17
Roseland (town) St. Joseph County	1	0.16
St. Bernice (cdp) Vermillion County	1	0.15
Fairview Park (town) Vermillion County	2	0.14
Colfax (town) Clinton County	1	0.14

Top 10 Places Sorted by Percent of Total Population
Based on places with total population of 50,000 or more

Place	Population	%
Fort Wayne (city) Allen County	102	0.04
Indianapolis (city) Marion County	216	0.03
Evansville (city) Vanderburgh County	30	0.03
Bloomington (city) Monroe County	24	0.03
Lafayette (city) Tippecanoe County	20	0.03
Elkhart (city) Elkhart County	17	0.03
South Bend (city) St. Joseph County	20	0.02
Muncie (city) Delaware County	12	0.02
Terre Haute (city) Vigo County	11	0.02
Carmel (city) Hamilton County	11	0.01

Hawaii Native/Pacific Islander: Marshallese

Top 10 Places Sorted by Population
Based on all places, regardless of total population

Place	Population	%
Evansville (city) Vanderburgh County	49	0.04
Goshen (city) Elkhart County	4	0.01
Nappanee (city) Elkhart County	3	0.05
Granger (cdp) St. Joseph County	2	0.01
North Manchester (town) Wabash County	1	0.02
Peru (city) Miami County	1	0.01
Elkhart (city) Elkhart County	1	<0.01
Fort Wayne (city) Allen County	1	<0.01
Lawrence (city) Marion County	1	<0.01
Noblesville (city) Hamilton County	1	<0.01

Top 10 Places Sorted by Percent of Total Population
Based on all places, regardless of total population

Place	Population	%
Nappanee (city) Elkhart County	3	0.05
Evansville (city) Vanderburgh County	49	0.04
North Manchester (town) Wabash County	1	0.02
Goshen (city) Elkhart County	4	0.01
Granger (cdp) St. Joseph County	2	0.01
Peru (city) Miami County	1	0.01
Elkhart (city) Elkhart County	1	<0.01
Fort Wayne (city) Allen County	1	<0.01
Lawrence (city) Marion County	1	<0.01
Noblesville (city) Hamilton County	1	<0.01

Top 10 Places Sorted by Percent of Total Population
Based on places with total population of 50,000 or more

Place	Population	%
Evansville (city) Vanderburgh County	49	0.04
Elkhart (city) Elkhart County	1	<0.01
Fort Wayne (city) Allen County	1	<0.01
Noblesville (city) Hamilton County	1	<0.01
Anderson (city) Madison County	0	0.00
Bloomington (city) Monroe County	0	0.00
Carmel (city) Hamilton County	0	0.00
Fishers (town) Hamilton County	0	0.00
Gary (city) Lake County	0	0.00
Hammond (city) Lake County	0	0.00

Hawaii Native/Pacific Islander: Native Hawaiian

Top 10 Places Sorted by Population
Based on all places, regardless of total population

Place	Population	%
Indianapolis (city) Marion County	361	0.04
Fort Wayne (city) Allen County	119	0.05
South Bend (city) St. Joseph County	55	0.05
Noblesville (city) Hamilton County	51	0.10
Columbus (city) Bartholomew County	50	0.11
Evansville (city) Vanderburgh County	49	0.04
Terre Haute (city) Vigo County	44	0.07
Muncie (city) Delaware County	44	0.06
Bloomington (city) Monroe County	37	0.05
Carmel (city) Hamilton County	33	0.04

Top 10 Places Sorted by Percent of Total Population
Based on all places, regardless of total population

Place	Population	%
Leavenworth (town) Crawford County	4	1.68
Beverly Shores (town) Porter County	4	0.65
Medora (town) Jackson County	4	0.58
Stinesville (town) Monroe County	1	0.51
Marengo (town) Crawford County	4	0.48
Bunker Hill (town) Miami County	4	0.45
West College Corner (town) Union County	3	0.44
Elizabeth (town) Bartholomew County	2	0.40
Dublin (town) Wayne County	3	0.38
Edgewood (town) Madison County	7	0.37

Top 10 Places Sorted by Percent of Total Population
Based on places with total population of 50,000 or more

Place	Population	%
Noblesville (city) Hamilton County	51	0.10

Place	Population	%
Terre Haute (city) Vigo County	44	0.07
Muncie (city) Delaware County	44	0.06
Fort Wayne (city) Allen County	119	0.05
South Bend (city) St. Joseph County	55	0.05
Bloomington (city) Monroe County	37	0.05
Indianapolis (city) Marion County	361	0.04
Evansville (city) Vanderburgh County	49	0.04
Carmel (city) Hamilton County	33	0.04
Hammond (city) Lake County	30	0.04

Hawaii Native/Pacific Islander: Samoan

Top 10 Places Sorted by Population
Based on all places, regardless of total population

Place	Population	%
Indianapolis (city) Marion County	145	0.02
South Bend (city) St. Joseph County	55	0.05
Fort Wayne (city) Allen County	38	0.01
Hammond (city) Lake County	21	0.03
Evansville (city) Vanderburgh County	20	0.02
Muncie (city) Delaware County	19	0.03
Lawrence (city) Marion County	18	0.04
Granger (cdp) St. Joseph County	16	0.05
Bloomington (city) Monroe County	16	0.02
Carmel (city) Hamilton County	16	0.02

Top 10 Places Sorted by Percent of Total Population
Based on all places, regardless of total population

Place	Population	%
Bethany (town) Morgan County	2	2.47
Newberry (town) Greene County	1	0.52
New Goshen (cdp) Vigo County	2	0.51
Dillsboro (town) Dearborn County	6	0.45
Arlington (cdp) Rush County	1	0.23
Eaton (town) Delaware County	4	0.22
Idaville (cdp) White County	1	0.22
Williamsport (town) Warren County	4	0.21
Woodburn (city) Allen County	3	0.20
Wanatah (town) LaPorte County	2	0.19

Top 10 Places Sorted by Percent of Total Population
Based on places with total population of 50,000 or more

Place	Population	%
South Bend (city) St. Joseph County	55	0.05
Hammond (city) Lake County	21	0.03
Muncie (city) Delaware County	19	0.03
Indianapolis (city) Marion County	145	0.02
Evansville (city) Vanderburgh County	20	0.02
Bloomington (city) Monroe County	16	0.02
Carmel (city) Hamilton County	16	0.02
Gary (city) Lake County	15	0.02
Lafayette (city) Tippecanoe County	13	0.02
Terre Haute (city) Vigo County	13	0.02

Hawaii Native/Pacific Islander: Tongan

Top 10 Places Sorted by Population
Based on all places, regardless of total population

Place	Population	%
South Bend (city) St. Joseph County	20	0.02
Osceola (town) St. Joseph County	10	0.41
Indianapolis (city) Marion County	10	<0.01
Mishawaka (city) St. Joseph County	8	0.02
Elkhart (city) Elkhart County	6	0.01
Fishers (town) Hamilton County	6	0.01
Elwood (city) Madison County	5	0.06
Logansport (city) Cass County	5	0.03
Kouts (town) Porter County	4	0.21
Muncie (city) Delaware County	3	<0.01

Top 10 Places Sorted by Percent of Total Population
Based on all places, regardless of total population

Place	Population	%
Osceola (town) St. Joseph County	10	0.41
Wheatfield (town) Jasper County	2	0.23
Kouts (town) Porter County	4	0.21
Elwood (city) Madison County	5	0.06
Logansport (city) Cass County	5	0.03
Rensselaer (city) Jasper County	2	0.03
South Bend (city) St. Joseph County	20	0.02
Mishawaka (city) St. Joseph County	8	0.02

Place	Population	%
Batesville (city) Ripley County	1	0.02
Elkhart (city) Elkhart County	6	0.01

Top 10 Places Sorted by Percent of Total Population
Based on places with total population of 50,000 or more

Place	Population	%
South Bend (city) St. Joseph County	20	0.02
Elkhart (city) Elkhart County	6	0.01
Fishers (town) Hamilton County	6	0.01
Indianapolis (city) Marion County	10	<0.01
Muncie (city) Delaware County	3	<0.01
Terre Haute (city) Vigo County	2	<0.01
Fort Wayne (city) Allen County	1	<0.01
Lafayette (city) Tippecanoe County	1	<0.01
Noblesville (city) Hamilton County	1	<0.01
Anderson (city) Madison County	0	0.00

White

Top 10 Places Sorted by Population
Based on all places, regardless of total population

Place	Population	%
Indianapolis (city) Marion County	526,672	64.19
Fort Wayne (city) Allen County	194,759	76.77
Evansville (city) Vanderburgh County	99,372	84.62
Carmel (city) Hamilton County	68,938	87.05
Bloomington (city) Monroe County	68,936	85.74
Fishers (town) Hamilton County	67,165	87.46
South Bend (city) St. Joseph County	64,797	64.05
Muncie (city) Delaware County	60,636	86.52
Lafayette (city) Tippecanoe County	57,759	86.03
Terre Haute (city) Vigo County	52,377	86.17

Top 10 Places Sorted by Percent of Total Population
Based on all places, regardless of total population

Place	Population	%
Dugger (town) Sullivan County	920	100.00
Newport (town) Vermillion County	515	100.00
Wilkinson (town) Hancock County	449	100.00
Troy (town) Perry County	385	100.00
Mooreland (town) Henry County	375	100.00
Lewisville (town) Henry County	366	100.00
Star City (cdp) Pulaski County	344	100.00
Montgomery (town) Daviess County	343	100.00
Blanford (cdp) Vermillion County	342	100.00
Larwill (town) Whitley County	283	100.00

Top 10 Places Sorted by Percent of Total Population
Based on places with total population of 50,000 or more

Place	Population	%
Noblesville (city) Hamilton County	48,170	92.69
Fishers (town) Hamilton County	67,165	87.46
Carmel (city) Hamilton County	68,938	87.05
Muncie (city) Delaware County	60,636	86.52
Terre Haute (city) Vigo County	52,377	86.17
Lafayette (city) Tippecanoe County	57,759	86.03
Bloomington (city) Monroe County	68,936	85.74
Evansville (city) Vanderburgh County	99,372	84.62
Anderson (city) Madison County	45,548	81.15
Fort Wayne (city) Allen County	194,759	76.77

White: Not Hispanic

Top 10 Places Sorted by Population
Based on all places, regardless of total population

Place	Population	%
Indianapolis (city) Marion County	496,520	60.52
Fort Wayne (city) Allen County	184,757	72.83
Evansville (city) Vanderburgh County	97,793	83.28
Carmel (city) Hamilton County	67,446	85.17
Bloomington (city) Monroe County	67,128	83.49
Fishers (town) Hamilton County	65,289	85.02
Muncie (city) Delaware County	59,588	85.02
South Bend (city) St. Joseph County	59,298	58.61
Lafayette (city) Tippecanoe County	53,754	80.06
Terre Haute (city) Vigo County	50,949	83.82

Top 10 Places Sorted by Percent of Total Population
Based on all places, regardless of total population

Place	Population	%
Newport (town) Vermillion County	515	100.00
Blanford (cdp) Vermillion County	342	100.00
Larwill (town) Whitley County	283	100.00
Wingate (town) Montgomery County	263	100.00
Buck Creek (cdp) Tippecanoe County	207	100.00
Westphalia (cdp) Knox County	202	100.00
Cedar Grove (town) Franklin County	156	100.00
Clarksburg (cdp) Decatur County	149	100.00
Springport (town) Henry County	149	100.00
Yeoman (town) Carroll County	139	100.00

Top 10 Places Sorted by Percent of Total Population
Based on places with total population of 50,000 or more

Place	Population	%
Noblesville (city) Hamilton County	46,797	90.05
Carmel (city) Hamilton County	67,446	85.17
Fishers (town) Hamilton County	65,289	85.02
Muncie (city) Delaware County	59,588	85.02
Terre Haute (city) Vigo County	50,949	83.82
Bloomington (city) Monroe County	67,128	83.49
Evansville (city) Vanderburgh County	97,793	83.28
Lafayette (city) Tippecanoe County	53,754	80.06
Anderson (city) Madison County	44,327	78.97
Fort Wayne (city) Allen County	184,757	72.83

White: Hispanic

Top 10 Places Sorted by Population
Based on all places, regardless of total population

Place	Population	%
Indianapolis (city) Marion County	30,152	3.68
Hammond (city) Lake County	15,674	19.39
Fort Wayne (city) Allen County	10,002	3.94
East Chicago (city) Lake County	8,852	29.81
South Bend (city) St. Joseph County	5,499	5.44
Elkhart (city) Elkhart County	4,552	8.93
Goshen (city) Elkhart County	4,029	12.70
Lafayette (city) Tippecanoe County	4,005	5.97
Portage (city) Porter County	3,928	10.67
Hobart (city) Lake County	2,732	9.40

Top 10 Places Sorted by Percent of Total Population
Based on all places, regardless of total population

Place	Population	%
East Chicago (city) Lake County	8,852	29.81
Ligonier (city) Noble County	1,084	24.61
Whiting (city) Lake County	1,166	23.33
Ambia (town) Benton County	55	23.01
Hammond (city) Lake County	15,674	19.39
New Chicago (town) Lake County	327	16.07
Lake Station (city) Lake County	1,914	15.22
Goshen (city) Elkhart County	4,029	12.70
Frankfort (city) Clinton County	1,888	11.50
Plymouth (city) Marshall County	1,104	11.00

Top 10 Places Sorted by Percent of Total Population
Based on places with total population of 50,000 or more

Place	Population	%
Hammond (city) Lake County	15,674	19.39
Elkhart (city) Elkhart County	4,552	8.93
Lafayette (city) Tippecanoe County	4,005	5.97
South Bend (city) St. Joseph County	5,499	5.44
Fort Wayne (city) Allen County	10,002	3.94
Indianapolis (city) Marion County	30,152	3.68
Noblesville (city) Hamilton County	1,373	2.64
Fishers (town) Hamilton County	1,876	2.44
Terre Haute (city) Vigo County	1,428	2.35
Bloomington (city) Monroe County	1,808	2.25

Please refer to the Explanation of Data in the front of the book for more detailed information.

Climate

Indiana Physical Features and Climate Narrative

PHYSICAL FEATURES AND GENERAL CLIMATE. Indiana has an invigorating climate of warm summers and cool winters, because of its location in the middle latitudes in the interior of a large continent. Imposed on the well-known daily and seasonal changes of temperature are changes occurring every few days as surges of polar air move southeastward or air of tropical origin moves northeastward. These outbreaks are more frequent and pronounced in the winter than in the summer. A winter may be unusually cold or a summer cool if the influence of polar air is rather continuous. Likewise, a summer may be unusually warm or a winter mild if air of tropical origin predominates. The action between these two air masses with a contrast in temperature and density fosters the development of low pressure centers which in moving generally eastward frequently pass through or near Indiana, resulting in normally abundant rain. The cyclones are least active and frequently pass north of Indiana in midsummer. Thunderstorms, often local in areal coverage, are important at such times when evaporation and loss of moisture from the soil and vegetation exceeds rainfall. Major climatological variations within the State are caused by differences of latitude, elevation, terrain, soil, and lakes.

The effect of the Great Lakes and more specifically, Lake Michigan, on the climate of northern Indiana is most pronounced just inland from the Lake Michigan shore and diminishes to insignificance in central Indiana. The result of cold air passing over the warmer lake water of Lake Michigan induces precipitation in the lee of Lake Michigan in fall and winter. Average daily minimum temperatures in the fall are higher and daily maximum temperatures in the spring are lower in northwestern Indiana than farther south. Winter precipitation, especially snowfall, is several times greater in the counties of Lake, Porter, and LaPorte as the result of this phenomena. Lake related snowfall and cloudiness often extends to central Indiana in the winter. Very local severe snowstorms have occurred just inland from Lake Michigan.

Another important variable in the composition of Indiana weather is the topography of the State. Elevations range from a little more than 300 feet at the mouth of the Wabash in the southwest corner of the State, to a little over 1,200 feet in the east-central portion (Randolph County) and northeastern section (Steuben County). Differences of terrain affect the climate considerably. South-central Indiana is unglaciated and has the most rugged relief. The Kankakee Valley in the northwest has but little slope to the west and drains what was formerly marshlands. Many small lakes abound in northeastern Indiana among numerous glacial moraines and hills. Most of the north, central, and southwest is rolling country.

TEMPERATURE. Variations of temperature and precipitation occur in short distances where terrain is hilly. On calm, clear nights the valley bottoms have lower temperatures than the slopes and tops of the surrounding hills. Mean maximum as well as mean minimum temperatures decrease from south to north with latitude and decrease from west to east with elevation. Near Lake Michigan temperatures average higher than expected for the latitude in the fall and winter, and lower than expected for the latitude in the spring and summer.

The average date of the last freezing temperature in the spring ranges from the first week of April in the Ohio River Valley of the southwest to the second week of May in the extreme northeast. The usual trend of a later date toward the north is reversed in extreme northwestern Indiana, where the average date is about April 30 near Lake Michigan. In the fall the average date of the first temperature of 32°F. or colder is from October 7 in the extreme northeast to October 26 along the Ohio River in the southwest.

Spring freezes are later in valleys and hollows and fall freezes are earlier. Longer freeze-free periods occur on ridges and hills. Southern Indiana has much of this type of terrain. The gradual slope upward from southwestern Indiana to northeastern Indiana results in lower minimum temperatures and shorter growing seasons in the east compared to the west at the same latitude. In the Kankakee Valley, peat or muck lands experience late spring and early fall frosts because of the radiative characteristic of the soil.

PRECIPITATION. Average annual rainfall ranges from 36 inches in northern Indiana to 43 inches in southern Indiana. July rainfall averages about the same in all areas. The greater precipitation in the south compared with the north comes in the winter months. Southern Indiana has the greatest rainfall in March and the least in October. The wettest month in northern and central Indiana is June and the driest is February. A drought occasionally occurs in the summer when evaporation is highest and dependence on rainfall is greatest.

Most of the state is drained by the Wabash River system. Other river basins are the Maumee in the extreme northeast, the St. Joseph (Lake Michigan) and Kankakee (Illinois River) in the north-central and northwest, and some Ohio River drainage in the extreme south and southeast. Floods occur in some part of the State nearly every year and have occurred in every month of the year. The season of greatest flood frequency is during the winter and spring months. The primary cause of floods is prolonged periods of heavy rains, although occasionally the rains falling on a snow cover and the formation of ice jams are an added factor. The most common type of flood-producing storm in the area is that having a quasi-stationary front oriented from west-southwest to east-northeast with a series of waves or perturbations moving to the east along the front.

Average annual snowfall increases from about 10 inches in southern Indiana to 40 inches in the northern portion of the State and higher in the three county areas along Lake Michigan. From year to year snowfall varies greatly, depending both on temperatures and the frequency of winter storms. At a given latitude in central and southern Indiana snowfall is greatest toward the east because of higher elevation.

OTHER CLIMATIC ELEMENTS. Cloudiness is least in the fall and greatest in the winter. The north is cloudier than the south, particularly in the winter when the Great Lakes have the greatest effect upon the weather.

Average relative humidity differs very little at night over Indiana. During the day relative humidity is usually lower in the south than in the north. This is true for all seasons. However, the simultaneous occurrence of high temperatures and high relative humidity is most frequent in the south.

Prevailing winds are from the southwest quadrant throughout most of the year. Winds from the northern quadrant occur in the winter and persist for a longer time in the north. Along the shore of Lake Michigan the sea-breeze effect is observed in the summer when winds in central United States are light or calm. Vertical currents from the heating of land during the day cause wind near the ground to flow from over water to land reducing the maximum temperature of the day. At night the breezes are in the opposite direction or from the land to water because of land cooling. These breezes are important in limiting extremely high temperatures of a summer day and account for rapid changes in short distances within a mile or so of the lake shore. Winds meet less friction passing over water so off-lake winds have a considerably higher speed than those off or over land.

Severe storms are most frequent in the spring. About one-half of the tornadoes occur between 2 p.m. and 6 p.m. and nearly three-fourths between 10 a.m. and 10 p.m. Hail falls occasionally in very local areas.

Climate: State Reference Map

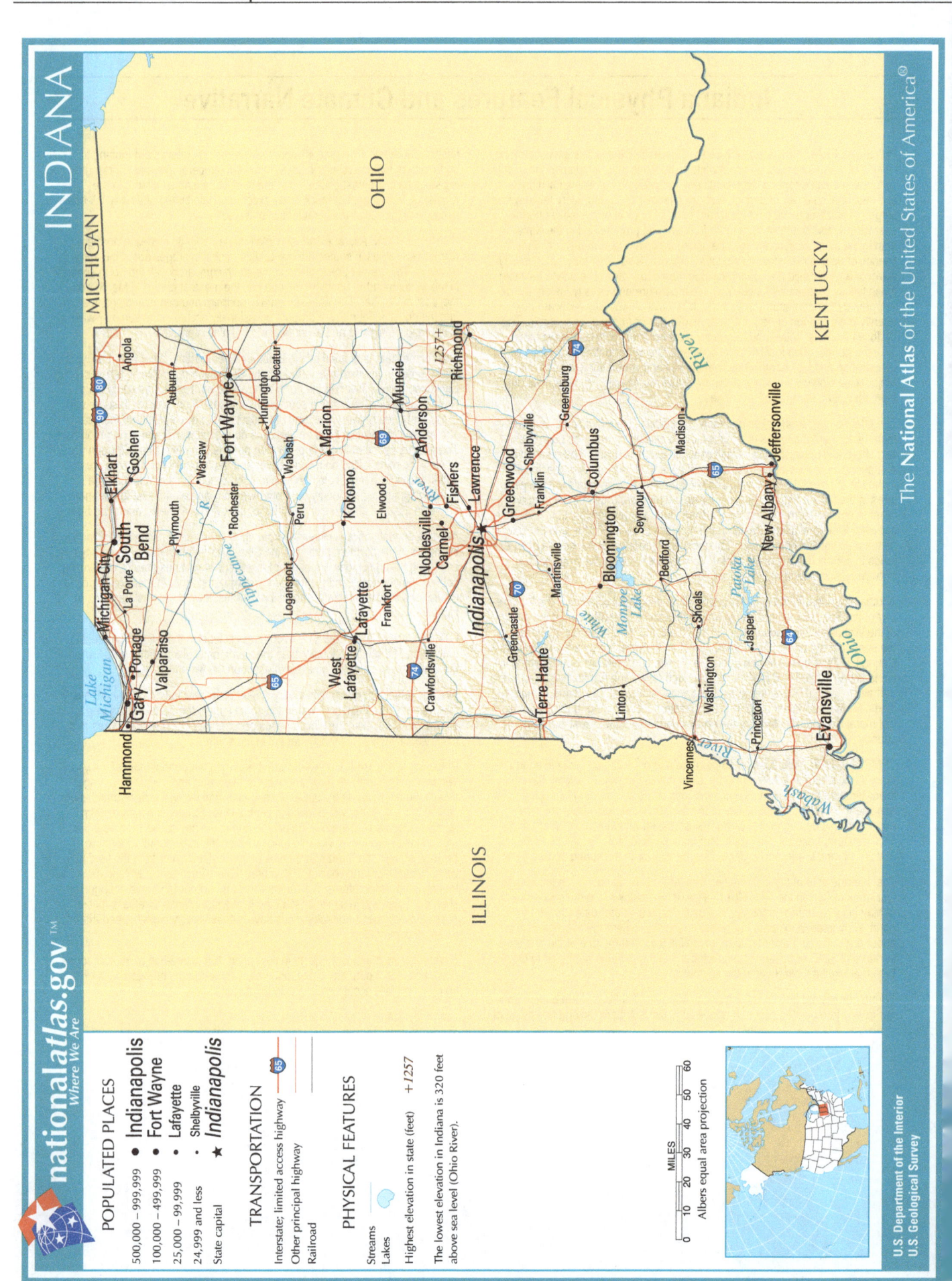

Profiles of Indiana

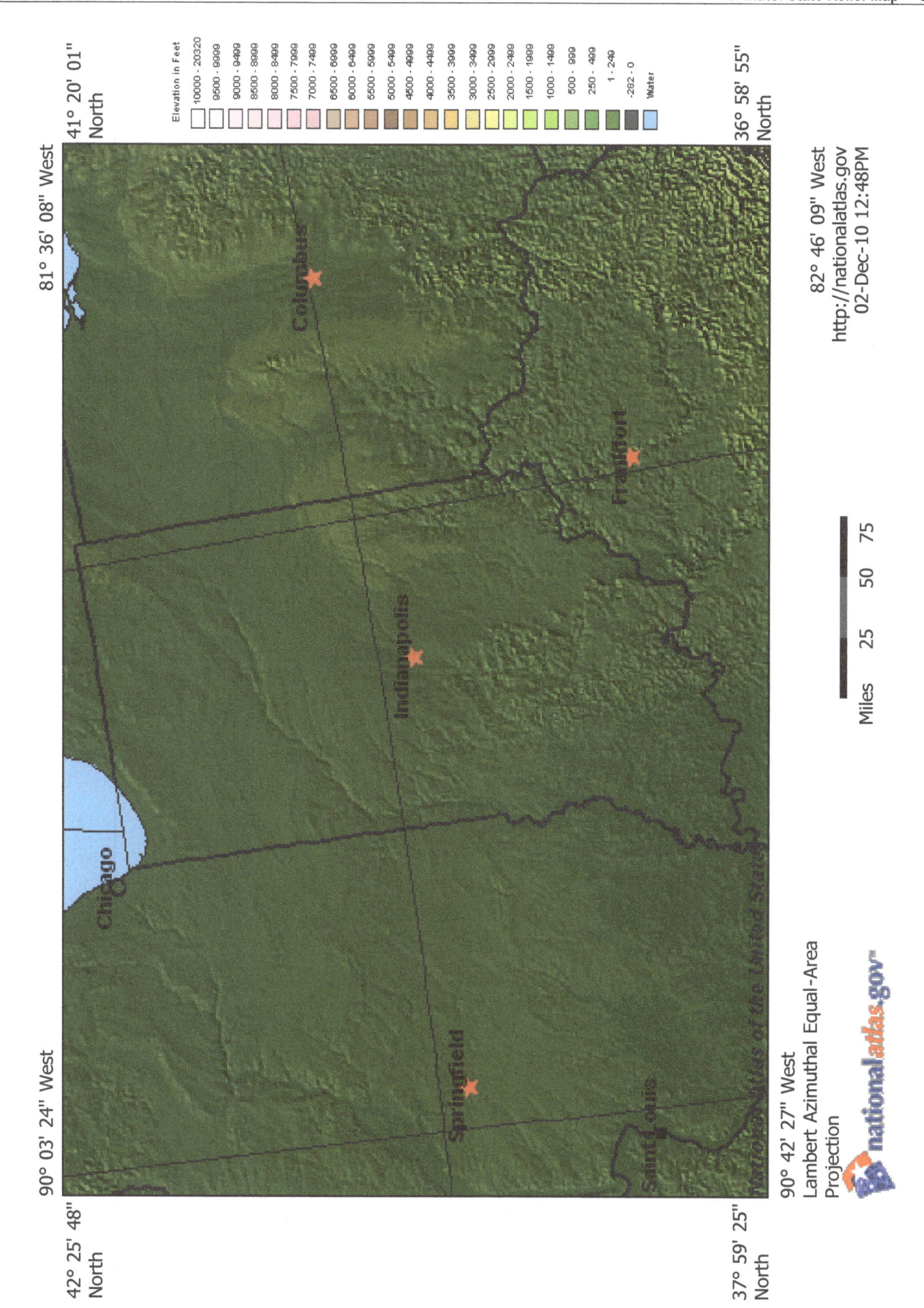

Climate: State Relief Map 553

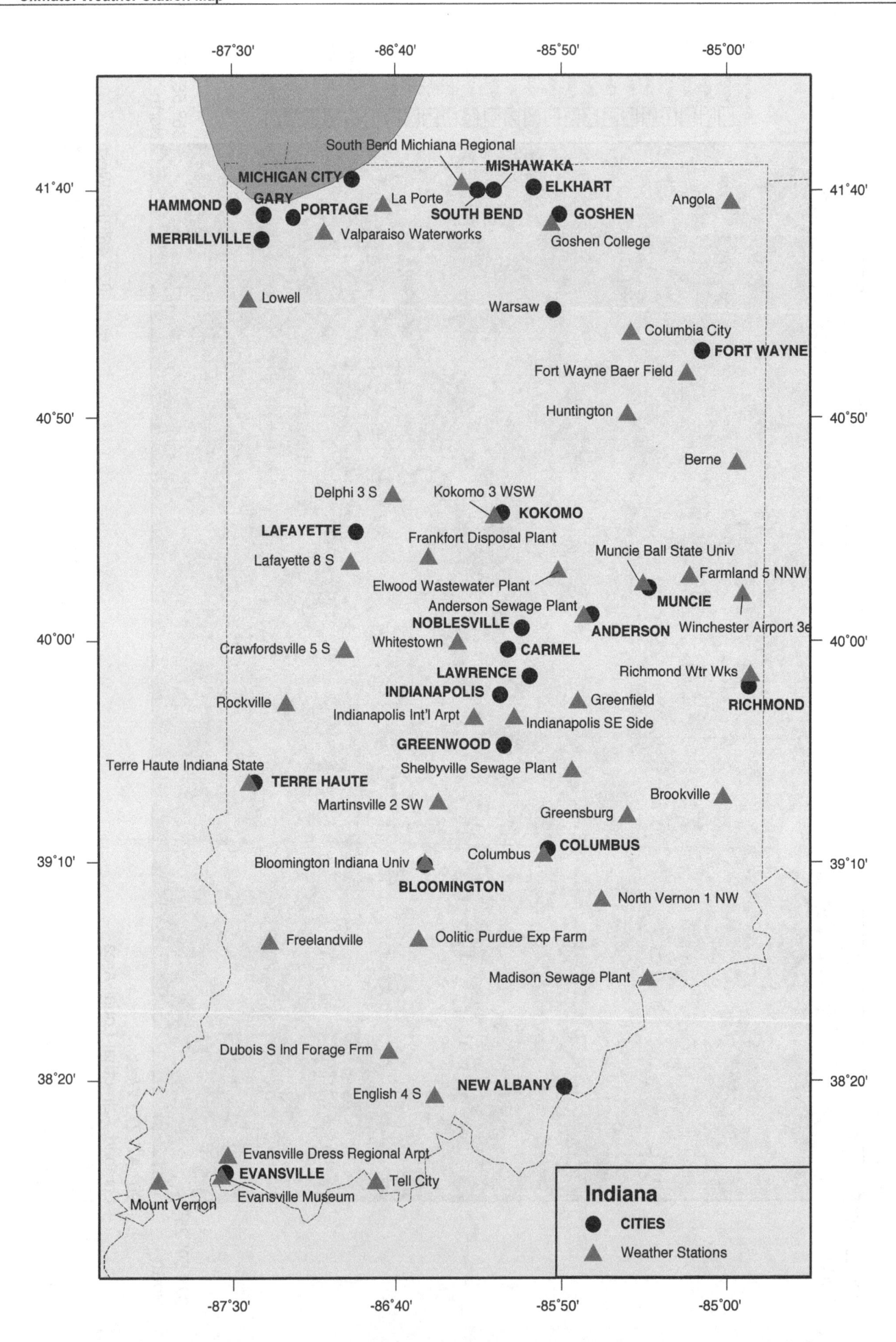

Climate: Weather Station Map

Profiles of Indiana

Indiana Weather Stations by County

County	Station Name
Adams	Berne
Allen	Fort Wayne Baer Field
Bartholomew	Columbus
Boone	Whitestown
Carroll	Delphi 3 S
Clinton	Frankfort Disposal Plant
Crawford	English 4 S
Decatur	Greensburg
Delaware	Muncie Ball State Univ
Dubois	Dubois S Ind Forage Frm
Elkhart	Goshen College
Franklin	Brookville
Hancock	Greenfield
Howard	Kokomo 3 WSW
Huntington	Huntington
Jefferson	Madison Sewage Plant
Jennings	North Vernon 1 NW
Knox	Freelandville
Kosciusko	Warsaw
La Porte	La Porte
Lake	Lowell
Lawrence	Oolitic Purdue Exp Farm
Madison	Anderson Sewage Plant
	Elwood Wastewater Plant
Marion	Indianapolis Int'l Arpt
	Indianapolis SE Side
Monroe	Bloomington Indiana Univ
Montgomery	Crawfordsville 5 S
Morgan	Martinsville 2 SW
Parke	Rockville
Perry	Tell City
Porter	Valparaiso Waterworks
Posey	Mount Vernon

County	Station Name
Randolph	Farmland 5 NNW
	Winchester Airport 3E
Shelby	Shelbyville Sewage Plant
St. Joseph	South Bend Michiana Regional
Steuben	Angola
Tippecanoe	Lafayette 8 S
Vanderburgh	Evansville Dress Regional Arpt
	Evansville Museum
Vigo	Terre Haute Indiana State
Wayne	Richmond Water Works
Whitley	Columbia City

See User Guide for station inclusion criteria.

Indiana Weather Stations by City

City	Station Name	Miles
Anderson	Anderson Sewage Plant	1.9
	Elwood Wastewater Plant	14.6
	Greenfield	22.1
	Muncie Ball State Univ	16.2
Bloomington	Bloomington Indiana Univ	0.5
	Martinsville 2 SW	16.9
	Oolitic Purdue Exp Farm	19.3
Carmel	Anderson Sewage Plant	22.3
	Elwood Wastewater Plant	24.4
	Greenfield	22.9
	Indianapolis Int'l Arpt	19.6
	Indianapolis SE Side	17.8
	Whitestown	13.1
Columbus	Columbus	1.5
	Greensburg	23.4
	North Vernon 1 NW	19.3
	Shelbyville Sewage Plant	21.6
Elkhart	Goshen College	10.2
	South Bend Michiana Regional	18.9
	Three Rivers, MI	24.3
Evansville	Evansville Museum	1.5
	Evansville Dress Regional Arpt	5.1
	Mount Vernon	18.7
	Henderson 7 SSW, KY	16.4
Fishers	Anderson Sewage Plant	18.3
	Elwood Wastewater Plant	22.9
	Greenfield	18.3
	Indianapolis Int'l Arpt	21.5
	Indianapolis SE Side	17.0
	Whitestown	18.2
Fort Wayne	Columbia City	19.5
	Fort Wayne Baer Field	7.1
Gary	Park Forest, IL	18.5
	Lowell	21.9
	Valparaiso Waterworks	16.5
Goshen	Goshen College	3.2
	Warsaw	24.2
Greenwood	Greenfield	22.8
	Indianapolis Int'l Arpt	10.6
	Indianapolis SE Side	7.6
	Martinsville 2 SW	23.1
	Shelbyville Sewage Plant	19.1
Hammond	Chicago Midway Arpt, IL	17.4
	Park Forest, IL	12.3
	Lowell	23.8
	Valparaiso Waterworks	24.5
Indianapolis	Greenfield	20.9
	Indianapolis Int'l Arpt	8.5
	Indianapolis SE Side	6.8
	Whitestown	17.9
Kokomo	Elwood Wastewater Plant	20.9

City	Station Name	Miles
Kokomo (cont.)	Frankfort Disposal Plant	22.2
	Kokomo 3 WSW	1.9
Lafayette	Delphi 3 S	14.0
	Frankfort Disposal Plant	20.6
	Lafayette 8 S	7.6
Lawrence	Anderson Sewage Plant	21.8
	Greenfield	14.1
	Indianapolis Int'l Arpt	17.8
	Indianapolis SE Side	11.0
	Whitestown	21.1
Merrillville	Park Forest, IL	17.2
	Lowell	16.0
	Valparaiso Waterworks	16.5
Michigan City	La Porte	10.0
	Valparaiso Waterworks	15.1
Mishawaka	Goshen College	16.9
	South Bend Michiana Regional	8.7
Muncie	Anderson Sewage Plant	18.3
	Elwood Wastewater Plant	24.6
	Farmland 5 NNW	13.4
	Muncie Ball State Univ	1.9
New Albany	Louisville Standiford Field, KY	9.7
Noblesville	Anderson Sewage Plant	16.7
	Elwood Wastewater Plant	17.6
	Greenfield	23.5
	Indianapolis SE Side	23.1
	Whitestown	17.5
Portage	La Porte	23.6
	Lowell	24.2
	Valparaiso Waterworks	8.8
Richmond	Richmond Water Works	3.8
	Winchester Airport 3E	24.5
South Bend	Goshen College	20.8
	South Bend Michiana Regional	4.6
Terre Haute	Rockville	22.3
	Terre Haute Indiana State	1.4

Note: Miles is the distance between the geographic center of the city and the weather station.

Indiana Weather Stations by Elevation

Feet	Station Name
1,109	Winchester Airport 3E
1,015	Richmond Water Works
1,009	Angola
964	Farmland 5 NNW
939	Muncie Ball State Univ
935	Greensburg
935	Whitestown
875	Goshen College
865	Greenfield
859	Berne
850	Columbia City
845	Anderson Sewage Plant
845	Indianapolis SE Side
839	Elwood Wastewater Plant
834	Frankfort Disposal Plant
830	Bloomington Indiana Univ
819	Kokomo 3 WSW
810	La Porte
810	Warsaw
799	Valparaiso Waterworks
792	Indianapolis Int'l Arpt
791	Fort Wayne Baer Field
772	South Bend Michiana Regional
762	Crawfordsville 5 S
750	Shelbyville Sewage Plant
745	North Vernon 1 NW
732	Lafayette 8 S
725	Huntington
689	Dubois S Ind Forage Frm
689	Rockville
670	Delphi 3 S
665	Lowell
649	Oolitic Purdue Exp Farm
629	Brookville
621	Columbus
609	Martinsville 2 SW
549	Freelandville
509	English 4 S
506	Terre Haute Indiana State
459	Madison Sewage Plant
419	Mount Vernon
399	Tell City
380	Evansville Dress Regional Arpt
379	Evansville Museum

See User Guide for station inclusion criteria.

Evansville Regional Airport

Evansville, Indiana, is located on the Ohio River. The country around Evansville ranges from level to areas of rolling terrain near the river. Dress Regional Airport, where weather observations are taken, is located in a shallow valley with low hills to the east and west which parallel the valley, but slope down to the south. There are hills five miles to the north which are about 100 feet higher than the field. The open end of the valley slopes down and south toward the city of Evansville and the Ohio River.

Prevailing wind direction is from the south-southwest. The strongest winds occur during a deep winter storm passage through the Lower Ohio Valley. Strong and cold north to northwest winds occur from late autumn to early spring, most often, in January and February, as large domes of arctic high pressure moves into the midwest.

Geographically, Evansville lies in the path of moisture-bearing low pressure formations that move from the western Gulf region, northeastward over the Mississippi and Ohio Valleys to the Great Lakes and northern Atlantic Coast. Much of the precipitation results from these storm systems, especially in the cooler part of the year.

Both temperature and precipitation are closely related to the movement of the polar front and the storms which move along the front. This is especially true in the winter and spring months. In summer and early autumn changes are less severe and periods of polar air invasions are less prolonged. There is considerable variation in seasonal and monthly temperature and precipitation from year to year as these factors depend greatly on the frequency of storm and frontal passages.

Convective thunderstorms, developing in the maritime tropical air from the Gulf of Mexico and squall line activity, combine to supply the summer rainfall. The greatest precipitation intensities for short periods of time come in the months of greatest thunderstorm frequency. The greatest intensities for 24 hours or more are confined to the winter months.

Severe storms are rather infrequent but thunderstorms cause some wind damage each year. Hail often occurs with the stronger thunderstorms. Evansville is in tornado alley with the most frequent occurrence in early spring and late fall.

Snowfall varies greatly from season to season, as do rainfall and temperature. Snowfalls of two or more inches are very infrequent, and these amounts are usually melted within a day or two.

The growing season averages 199 days, but has been as long as 250 days and as short as 169 days.

Evansville Regional Airport *Vanderburgh County*   Elevation: 380 ft.   Latitude: 38° 03' N   Longitude: 87° 32' W

	JAN	FEB	MAR	APR	MAY	JUN	JUL	AUG	SEP	OCT	NOV	DEC	YEAR
Mean Maximum Temp. (°F)	41.1	45.8	56.3	67.3	76.7	85.3	88.5	87.8	81.2	69.5	56.3	44.3	66.7
Mean Temp. (°F)	33.0	36.7	46.1	56.1	65.9	74.8	78.3	77.0	69.4	57.8	46.7	36.1	56.5
Mean Minimum Temp. (°F)	24.9	27.7	35.7	44.9	55.0	64.3	68.1	66.0	57.5	46.0	36.9	27.9	46.2
Extreme Maximum Temp. (°F)	71	77	84	91	94	101	102	104	100	93	82	77	104
Extreme Minimum Temp. (°F)	-18	-8	3	23	34	42	51	43	34	23	11	-15	-18
Days Maximum Temp. ≥ 90°F	0	0	0	0	1	9	14	12	5	0	0	0	41
Days Maximum Temp. ≤ 32°F	7	4	1	0	0	0	0	0	0	0	0	5	17
Days Minimum Temp. ≤ 32°F	24	19	13	3	0	0	0	0	0	2	11	21	93
Days Minimum Temp. ≤ 0°F	1	0	0	0	0	0	0	0	0	0	0	1	2
Heating Degree Days (base 65°F)	984	793	585	285	78	5	0	1	41	249	545	889	4,455
Cooling Degree Days (base 65°F)	0	0	0	4	26	113	307	420	378	179	32	1	0	1,460
Mean Precipitation (in.)	3.07	3.16	4.25	4.35	5.39	3.90	3.95	3.02	3.12	3.28	4.12	3.73	45.34
Maximum Precipitation (in.)*	13.5	7.3	12.8	10.3	13.5	6.9	9.7	8.4	7.0	7.9	8.5	8.2	63.1
Minimum Precipitation (in.)*	0.5	0.6	1.3	1.1	0.9	0.6	0.2	0.2	0.5	trace	0.9	0.6	27.9
Extreme Maximum Daily Precip. (in.)	3.72	3.38	6.40	6.04	4.92	3.67	2.95	3.03	2.83	2.45	3.48	2.30	6.40
Days With ≥ 0.1" Precipitation	6	5	7	7	8	6	6	5	5	6	6	7	74
Days With ≥ 0.5" Precipitation	2	2	3	3	4	3	3	2	2	2	3	3	32
Days With ≥ 1.0" Precipitation	1	1	1	1	1	1	1	1	1	1	1	1	12
Mean Snowfall (in.)	3.4	3.8	1.3	0.2	trace	trace	0.0	0.0	trace	0.2	0.1	2.4	11.4
Maximum Snowfall (in.)*	21	18	20	9	0	0	0	0	0	5	7	10	36
Maximum 24-hr. Snowfall (in.)*	8	11	8	9	0	0	0	0	0	4	7	7	11
Maximum Snow Depth (in.)	8	12	10	3	trace	trace	0	0	trace	2	1	7	12
Days With ≥ 1.0" Snow Depth	4	4	1	0	0	0	0	0	0	0	0	3	12
Thunderstorm Days*	1	1	4	5	6	7	7	5	3	2	2	1	44
Foggy Days*	12	12	12	9	11	11	13	16	15	12	11	13	147
Predominant Sky Cover*	OVR	OVR	OVR	OVR	OVR	OVR	SCT	CLR	CLR	CLR	OVR	OVR	OVR
Mean Relative Humidity 7am (%)*	80	80	78	73	75	75	78	82	83	83	80	81	79
Mean Relative Humidity 4pm (%)*	66	61	56	50	52	52	54	54	52	50	59	67	56
Mean Dewpoint (°F)*	24	27	35	44	54	63	67	66	58	46	36	28	46
Prevailing Wind Direction*	NW	NW	NW	SSW	S	SW	SW	SW	S	NW	S	NW	NW
Prevailing Wind Speed (mph)*	12	12	12	13	9	9	8	8	8	7	10	10	10
Maximum Wind Gust (mph)*	55	53	52	63	71	76	56	46	59	52	70	56	76

Note: (*) Period of record is 1948-1995

The period of record for National Weather Service station data is 1980 – 2009 except where noted. See User Guide for detailed explanation of data.

Fort Wayne Baer Field

Fort Wayne is located at the junction of the St. Marys, St. Joseph, and Maumee Rivers in northeastern Indiana. The surrounding area is generally level south and east of the city. Southwest and west, the terrain is somewhat rolling, while to the northwest and a few miles north from the city, it becomes quite hilly. The highest point in the general area is about 40 miles due north of Fort Wayne, near Angola, Indiana. At this point, the elevation rises to 1,060 feet above sea level.

The climate is representative of northeastern Indiana and is influenced to some extent by the Great Lakes. It does not differ greatly from the climates of other midwestern cities of the same general latitude. Temperature differences between daily highs and lows are invigorating and average about 20 degrees. The average occurrence of the last freeze in the spring is late April, and the first freeze in the fall is mid-October, making the average freeze-free period 173 days. The length of the growing season is favorable for the maturing of all crops and vegetables normally grown in the midwest.

Annual precipitation is well distributed, with somewhat larger monthly amounts falling in late spring and early summer. Damaging hailstorms occur at an average of about twice a year. One of the most notable storms caused severe damage to property, many thousands of trees, and power and telephone lines in the area. Severe flooding has also occurred in the area. Snow usually covers the ground for about 30 days during the winter months, but heavy snowstorms are not frequent.

Except for the considerable cloudiness that occurs during the winter months, Fort Wayne enjoys a good midwestern average sunshine. Heavy fog occurrence is infrequent.

Fort Wayne Baer Field *Allen County* Elevation: 791 ft. Latitude: 41° 00' N Longitude: 85° 12' W

	JAN	FEB	MAR	APR	MAY	JUN	JUL	AUG	SEP	OCT	NOV	DEC	YEAR
Mean Maximum Temp. (°F)	32.4	36.1	47.6	60.7	71.6	80.8	84.3	82.1	75.9	63.1	49.6	36.4	60.0
Mean Temp. (°F)	25.2	28.4	38.3	49.9	60.6	70.1	73.7	71.7	64.5	52.7	41.5	29.6	50.5
Mean Minimum Temp. (°F)	17.9	20.6	28.9	39.1	49.5	59.4	63.1	61.2	53.1	42.2	33.4	22.8	40.9
Extreme Maximum Temp. (°F)	66	73	82	88	94	106	102	99	97	89	77	71	106
Extreme Minimum Temp. (°F)	-22	-18	-7	7	27	38	45	40	29	19	10	-18	-22
Days Maximum Temp. ≥ 90°F	0	0	0	0	1	4	6	3	1	0	0	0	15
Days Maximum Temp. ≤ 32°F	15	11	3	0	0	0	0	0	0	0	1	11	41
Days Minimum Temp. ≤ 32°F	28	24	20	7	0	0	0	0	0	4	15	26	124
Days Minimum Temp. ≤ 0°F	4	2	0	0	0	0	0	0	0	0	0	2	8
Heating Degree Days (base 65°F)	1,229	1,029	823	455	183	27	2	9	94	387	697	1,091	6,026
Cooling Degree Days (base 65°F)	0	0	1	9	52	188	279	223	86	10	0	0	848
Mean Precipitation (in.)	2.26	2.08	2.76	3.50	4.13	4.15	4.28	3.68	2.83	2.88	2.98	2.82	38.35
Maximum Precipitation (in.)*	9.7	6.8	5.3	7.1	8.8	8.3	11.0	7.7	6.8	9.3	8.0	7.6	54.6
Minimum Precipitation (in.)*	0.4	0.3	0.7	1.3	1.0	0.8	0.4	0.4	0.3	0.1	0.6	0.4	24.4
Extreme Maximum Daily Precip. (in.)	1.79	3.03	1.96	2.57	4.35	4.40	2.83	3.40	2.13	2.69	2.44	1.79	4.40
Days With ≥ 0.1" Precipitation	5	5	6	8	8	7	7	6	5	6	7	7	77
Days With ≥ 0.5" Precipitation	1	1	2	2	3	3	3	3	2	2	2	2	26
Days With ≥ 1.0" Precipitation	0	0	0	1	1	1	1	1	1	1	1	0	8
Mean Snowfall (in.)	10.2	7.8	4.1	1.1	trace	trace	trace	trace	trace	0.4	2.0	8.2	33.8
Maximum Snowfall (in.)*	30	17	20	12	trace	0	0	0	0	8	14	20	62
Maximum 24-hr. Snowfall (in.)*	11	8	13	6	trace	0	0	0	0	6	6	11	13
Maximum Snow Depth (in.)	12	20	9	6	trace	trace	trace	trace	trace	3	4	9	20
Days With ≥ 1.0" Snow Depth	15	12	4	0	0	0	0	0	0	0	1	9	41
Thunderstorm Days*	< 1	1	2	4	5	7	7	6	4	2	1	< 1	39
Foggy Days*	14	13	13	11	12	10	14	17	14	14	13	15	160
Predominant Sky Cover*	OVR	OVR	OVR	OVR	OVR	OVR	SCT	SCT	OVR	OVR	OVR	OVR	OVR
Mean Relative Humidity 7am (%)*	81	81	80	78	77	78	82	86	87	85	83	83	82
Mean Relative Humidity 4pm (%)*	72	67	62	54	52	52	53	55	53	54	67	74	60
Mean Dewpoint (°F)*	18	20	28	38	48	57	62	61	54	43	33	23	41
Prevailing Wind Direction*	W	W	W	SW	SW	SW	SW	SW	SW	SW	SW	W	SW
Prevailing Wind Speed (mph)*	14	14	14	14	12	12	9	9	10	12	13	13	12
Maximum Wind Gust (mph)*	69	54	59	61	59	64	67	59	53	63	58	58	69

Note: (*) Period of record is 1948-1995

The period of record for National Weather Service station data is 1980 – 2009 except where noted. See User Guide for detailed explanation of data.

Indianapolis Int'l Airport

Indianapolis is located in the central part of the state and is situated on level or slightly rolling terrain. The greater part of the city lies east of the White River which flows in a general north to south direction.

The National Weather Service Forecast Office is located approximately seven miles southwest of the central part of the city at the Indianapolis International Airport. From a field elevation of 797 feet above sea level at the Indianapolis International Airport the terrain slopes gradually downward to a little below 645 feet at the White River, then upward to just over 910 feet in the northwest corner and eastern sections of the county. The street elevation at the former city office located in the Old Federal Building is 718 feet.

Indianapolis has a temperate climate, with very warm summers and without a dry season. Very cold temperatures may be produced by the invasion of continental polar air in the winter from northern latitudes. The polar air can be quite frigid with very low humidity. The arrival of maritime tropical air from the Gulf in the summer brings warm temperatures and moderate humidity. One of the longest and most severe heat waves brought temperatures of 100 degrees or more for nine consecutive days.

Precipitation is distributed fairly evenly throughout the year, and therefore there is no pronounced wet or dry season. Rainfall in the spring and summer is produced mostly by showers and thunderstorms. A rainfall of about two and a half inches in a 24-hour period can be expected about once a year. Snowfalls of three inches or more occur on an average of two or three times in the winter.

Local levees and/or channel improvements now protect some formerly flood-prone areas.

Based on the 1951-1980 period, the average first occurrence of 32 degrees Fahrenheit in the fall is October 20 and the average last occurrence in the spring is April 22.

Indianapolis Int'l Airport *Marion County* Elevation: 792 ft. Latitude: 39° 43' N Longitude: 86° 16' W

	JAN	FEB	MAR	APR	MAY	JUN	JUL	AUG	SEP	OCT	NOV	DEC	YEAR
Mean Maximum Temp. (°F)	36.0	40.5	51.5	63.3	73.1	82.0	85.3	84.1	77.8	65.3	52.3	39.4	62.5
Mean Temp. (°F)	28.3	32.2	42.0	52.9	62.8	72.0	75.5	74.2	67.0	55.0	43.7	32.0	53.1
Mean Minimum Temp. (°F)	20.5	23.8	32.4	42.4	52.5	61.9	65.8	64.3	56.2	44.5	35.0	24.6	43.7
Extreme Maximum Temp. (°F)	68	76	85	86	93	102	103	102	96	91	79	74	103
Extreme Minimum Temp. (°F)	-27	-21	-7	18	29	37	48	42	32	20	10	-23	-27
Days Maximum Temp. ≥ 90°F	0	0	0	0	0	3	7	6	2	0	0	0	18
Days Maximum Temp. ≤ 32°F	12	7	2	0	0	0	0	0	0	0	1	8	30
Days Minimum Temp. ≤ 32°F	26	22	16	4	0	0	0	0	0	3	13	23	107
Days Minimum Temp. ≤ 0°F	2	1	0	0	0	0	0	0	0	0	0	1	4
Heating Degree Days (base 65°F)	1,131	922	709	371	132	15	1	3	66	323	634	1,015	5,322
Cooling Degree Days (base 65°F)	0	0	2	15	72	231	334	296	133	18	0	0	1,101
Mean Precipitation (in.)	2.67	2.35	3.60	3.77	4.98	4.06	4.55	3.39	3.21	3.14	3.60	3.13	42.45
Maximum Precipitation (in.)*	12.7	5.3	10.7	8.1	9.3	7.4	11.8	8.3	8.1	7.8	8.5	7.7	55.8
Minimum Precipitation (in.)*	0.4	0.4	0.9	1.0	1.1	0.4	1.2	0.7	0.2	0.2	0.8	0.4	27.9
Extreme Maximum Daily Precip. (in.)	2.70	2.03	2.54	2.34	3.80	3.09	5.09	3.81	7.20	2.74	4.15	1.74	7.20
Days With ≥ 0.1" Precipitation	6	5	7	8	9	7	7	6	5	5	6	7	78
Days With ≥ 0.5" Precipitation	2	1	2	3	4	3	3	2	2	2	2	2	28
Days With ≥ 1.0" Precipitation	0	0	1	1	1	1	1	1	1	1	1	1	10
Mean Snowfall (in.)	8.5	6.4	2.7	0.3	trace	trace	0.0	trace	trace	0.4	0.8	6.4	25.5
Maximum Snowfall (in.)*	31	18	11	4	trace	0	0	0	0	9	8	28	45
Maximum 24-hr. Snowfall (in.)*	10	8	6	3	trace	0	0	0	0	8	8	10	10
Maximum Snow Depth (in.)	11	13	8	1	trace	trace	0	trace	trace	2	4	9	13
Days With ≥ 1.0" Snow Depth	10	8	2	0	0	0	0	0	0	0	0	6	26
Thunderstorm Days*	1	1	3	5	6	7	8	6	3	2	1	<1	43
Foggy Days*	15	13	13	11	13	12	16	18	15	13	14	15	168
Predominant Sky Cover*	OVR	OVR	OVR	OVR	OVR	OVR	SCT	SCT	CLR	OVR	OVR	OVR	OVR
Mean Relative Humidity 7am (%)*	81	81	79	77	80	80	84	88	87	85	83	83	82
Mean Relative Humidity 4pm (%)*	69	64	59	54	53	53	56	56	53	53	63	70	59
Mean Dewpoint (°F)*	20	23	31	40	51	60	65	64	56	44	34	25	43
Prevailing Wind Direction*	WSW	WNW	WNW	SW	SW	SW	SW	SW	SW	SW	SW	SW	SW
Prevailing Wind Speed (mph)*	12	13	14	13	10	9	8	8	9	10	12	12	10
Maximum Wind Gust (mph)*	60	62	75	75	69	70	81	70	74	64	79	64	81

Note: (*) Period of record is 1948-1995

The period of record for National Weather Service station data is 1980 – 2009 except where noted. See User Guide for detailed explanation of data.

South Bend Michiana Regional

South Bend is located on the Saint Joseph River in the northern portion of Saint Joseph County, situated on mostly level to gently rolling terrain and some former marshland. Drainage for the area is through the Saint Joseph River and Kankakee River.

South Bend is under the climatic influence of Lake Michigan with its nearest shore 20 miles to the northwest. The lake has a moderating effect on the temperature. Temperatures of 100 degrees or higher are rare and cold waves are less severe than at many locations at the same latitude. This results in favorable conditions for orchard and vegetable growth.

Based on the 1951-1980 period, the average first occurrence of 32 degrees Fahrenheit in the fall is October 18 and the average last occurrence in the spring is May 1.

Precipitation is fairly evenly distributed throughout the year with the greatest amounts during the growing season. The predominant snow season is from November through March, although there are also generally lighter amounts in October and April.

Winter is marked by considerable cloudiness and rather high humidity along with frequent periods of snow. Heavy snowfalls, resulting from a cold northwest wind passing over Lake Michigan are not uncommon.

South Bend Michiana Regional *St. Joseph County*   Elevation: 772 ft.   Latitude: 41° 42' N   Longitude: 86° 20' W

	JAN	FEB	MAR	APR	MAY	JUN	JUL	AUG	SEP	OCT	NOV	DEC	YEAR
Mean Maximum Temp. (°F)	31.9	35.6	46.7	59.6	70.5	79.8	83.3	81.2	74.5	61.8	48.5	35.8	59.1
Mean Temp. (°F)	25.0	28.1	37.7	49.2	59.6	69.3	73.3	71.6	64.2	52.3	41.0	29.3	50.1
Mean Minimum Temp. (°F)	18.0	20.6	28.6	38.8	48.7	58.8	63.3	61.9	53.9	42.8	33.5	22.7	41.0
Extreme Maximum Temp. (°F)	65	74	85	89	91	104	102	103	95	88	76	70	104
Extreme Minimum Temp. (°F)	-21	-13	-3	13	26	36	42	42	32	20	7	-15	-21
Days Maximum Temp. ≥ 90°F	0	0	0	0	1	4	6	3	1	0	0	0	15
Days Maximum Temp. ≤ 32°F	16	12	4	0	0	0	0	0	0	0	2	11	45
Days Minimum Temp. ≤ 32°F	28	24	21	8	0	0	0	0	0	3	15	26	125
Days Minimum Temp. ≤ 0°F	3	2	0	0	0	0	0	0	0	0	0	2	7
Heating Degree Days (base 65°F)	1,234	1,035	841	477	211	39	4	11	105	396	712	1,100	6,165
Cooling Degree Days (base 65°F)	0	0	1	10	51	175	270	223	89	10	0	0	829
Mean Precipitation (in.)	2.29	1.95	2.47	3.26	3.68	3.80	3.96	3.99	3.65	3.37	3.23	2.68	38.33
Maximum Precipitation (in.)*	5.3	4.5	8.0	6.0	6.9	10.9	7.5	8.3	9.0	9.8	6.7	5.5	55.6
Minimum Precipitation (in.)*	0.7	0.5	0.5	0.5	0.8	0.5	1.2	0.3	trace	0.4	1.4	0.7	25.1
Extreme Maximum Daily Precip. (in.)	1.80	1.70	1.41	2.48	2.79	3.51	3.64	3.96	6.58	3.47	3.92	2.45	6.58
Days With ≥ 0.1" Precipitation	6	5	6	7	7	7	7	7	6	7	7	7	79
Days With ≥ 0.5" Precipitation	1	1	1	2	3	2	3	3	2	2	2	1	23
Days With ≥ 1.0" Precipitation	0	0	0	1	1	1	1	1	1	1	1	0	8
Mean Snowfall (in.)	20.3	15.1	7.4	1.5	trace	trace	trace	trace	trace	0.5	5.0	17.5	67.3
Maximum Snowfall (in.)*	86	35	34	14	1	0	0	0	0	9	30	42	142
Maximum 24-hr. Snowfall (in.)*	16	12	9	8	1	0	0	0	0	7	15	11	16
Maximum Snow Depth (in.)	18	23	9	6	trace	trace	trace	trace	trace	6	8	14	23
Days With ≥ 1.0" Snow Depth	20	15	5	1	0	0	0	0	0	0	2	12	55
Thunderstorm Days*	<1	<1	2	4	5	8	7	6	4	2	1	<1	39
Foggy Days*	15	14	15	13	13	12	14	18	16	16	15	17	178
Predominant Sky Cover*	OVR	OVR	OVR	OVR	OVR	OVR	OVR	OVR	OVR	OVR	OVR	OVR	OVR
Mean Relative Humidity 7am (%)*	82	82	80	77	76	78	82	86	86	84	83	83	82
Mean Relative Humidity 4pm (%)*	73	69	62	55	53	52	55	57	55	57	68	75	61
Mean Dewpoint (°F)*	18	20	28	37	47	57	62	62	54	43	33	23	41
Prevailing Wind Direction*	SW	SW	SW	NNW	SSW	SSW	SW	SW	SSW	SSW	SW	SW	SW
Prevailing Wind Speed (mph)*	13	13	13	13	12	10	9	9	10	12	12	13	12
Maximum Wind Gust (mph)*	67	58	55	66	86	71	66	59	63	59	74	69	86

Note: (*) Period of record is 1948-1995

Anderson Sewage Plant *Madison County*   Elevation: 845 ft.   Latitude: 40° 06' N   Longitude: 85° 43' W

	JAN	FEB	MAR	APR	MAY	JUN	JUL	AUG	SEP	OCT	NOV	DEC	YEAR
Mean Maximum Temp. (°F)	34.4	39.0	49.2	61.6	71.9	80.7	83.8	82.3	76.2	63.9	50.8	37.9	61.0
Mean Temp. (°F)	27.1	31.2	40.3	51.4	61.7	70.7	74.0	72.5	65.4	53.8	42.8	31.0	51.8
Mean Minimum Temp. (°F)	19.8	23.3	31.4	41.2	51.3	60.6	64.2	62.6	54.7	43.6	34.8	24.0	42.6
Extreme Maximum Temp. (°F)	65	73	81	87	93	101	103	101	95	90	80	75	103
Extreme Minimum Temp. (°F)	-24	-12	-7	17	31	37	45	40	31	20	10	-22	-24
Days Maximum Temp. ≥ 90°F	0	0	0	0	0	4	6	4	1	0	0	0	15
Days Maximum Temp. ≤ 32°F	13	9	3	0	0	0	0	0	0	0	1	10	36
Days Minimum Temp. ≤ 32°F	27	22	18	5	0	0	0	0	0	4	14	24	114
Days Minimum Temp. ≤ 0°F	3	1	0	0	0	0	0	0	0	0	0	1	5
Heating Degree Days (base 65°F)	1,167	952	761	412	164	23	3	7	85	357	659	1,048	5,638
Cooling Degree Days (base 65°F)	0	0	2	12	67	200	289	246	105	17	1	0	939
Mean Precipitation (in.)	2.39	2.28	3.26	3.83	4.39	4.21	4.40	3.49	2.99	3.10	3.66	3.09	41.09
Extreme Maximum Daily Precip. (in.)	3.00	2.37	3.30	2.00	2.69	3.51	3.06	2.70	4.21	1.91	3.42	2.00	4.21
Days With ≥ 0.1" Precipitation	5	5	7	9	8	7	7	6	5	6	6	7	78
Days With ≥ 0.5" Precipitation	2	1	3	3	3	3	4	2	2	2	3	2	30
Days With ≥ 1.0" Precipitation	0	0	1	1	1	1	1	1	1	1	1	1	10
Mean Snowfall (in.)	7.2	4.2	1.6	0.2	0.0	0.0	0.0	0.0	0.0	0.1	0.5	4.1	17.9
Maximum Snow Depth (in.)	*18*	*12*	8	1	0	0	0	0	0	trace	3	*16*	*18*
Days With ≥ 1.0" Snow Depth	*7*	4	2	0	0	0	0	0	0	0	0	4	*17*

Angola *Steuben County*   Elevation: 1,009 ft.   Latitude: 41° 38' N   Longitude: 84° 59' W

	JAN	FEB	MAR	APR	MAY	JUN	JUL	AUG	SEP	OCT	NOV	DEC	YEAR
Mean Maximum Temp. (°F)	30.3	33.9	44.3	57.7	68.8	78.2	81.8	80.1	73.3	60.4	47.4	34.4	57.5
Mean Temp. (°F)	22.5	25.1	34.4	46.7	57.8	67.5	71.3	69.4	61.8	49.6	38.8	27.3	47.7
Mean Minimum Temp. (°F)	14.7	16.3	24.5	35.7	46.7	56.6	60.7	58.6	50.2	38.7	30.1	20.1	37.7
Extreme Maximum Temp. (°F)	63	71	78	85	90	101	98	97	93	86	75	69	101
Extreme Minimum Temp. (°F)	-27	-14	-10	4	22	32	41	37	27	16	9	-19	-27
Days Maximum Temp. ≥ 90°F	0	0	0	0	0	2	3	2	0	0	0	0	7
Days Maximum Temp. ≤ 32°F	18	13	5	0	0	0	0	0	0	0	3	13	52
Days Minimum Temp. ≤ 32°F	29	27	25	12	1	0	0	0	0	9	19	28	150
Days Minimum Temp. ≤ 0°F	5	4	0	0	0	0	0	0	0	0	0	2	11
Heating Degree Days (base 65°F)	1,310	1,122	943	546	250	53	11	23	144	476	781	1,163	6,822
Cooling Degree Days (base 65°F)	0	0	1	6	33	134	212	166	54	4	0	0	610
Mean Precipitation (in.)	2.27	2.10	2.69	3.40	4.25	3.81	4.12	4.18	3.30	3.01	3.07	2.81	39.01
Extreme Maximum Daily Precip. (in.)	1.67	1.75	2.11	2.52	4.10	3.55	3.55	3.78	2.41	3.19	2.35	2.36	4.10
Days With ≥ 0.1" Precipitation	6	5	6	7	8	7	7	7	6	6	7	7	79
Days With ≥ 0.5" Precipitation	1	1	2	2	3	3	3	3	2	2	2	2	26
Days With ≥ 1.0" Precipitation	0	0	0	1	1	1	1	1	1	1	0	0	7
Mean Snowfall (in.)	10.6	8.4	4.8	1.0	trace	0.0	0.0	0.0	0.0	0.3	2.1	9.2	36.4
Maximum Snow Depth (in.)	23	22	13	6	trace	0	0	0	0	0	3	5	20	23
Days With ≥ 1.0" Snow Depth	18	15	6	1	0	0	0	0	0	0	2	11	53

Berne *Adams County*   Elevation: 859 ft.   Latitude: 40° 40' N   Longitude: 84° 57' W

	JAN	FEB	MAR	APR	MAY	JUN	JUL	AUG	SEP	OCT	NOV	DEC	YEAR
Mean Maximum Temp. (°F)	33.7	37.5	48.4	61.1	71.8	81.0	84.6	82.8	76.6	63.7	50.3	37.2	60.7
Mean Temp. (°F)	26.6	29.5	39.0	50.7	61.3	70.9	74.6	72.8	65.7	53.7	42.3	30.4	51.5
Mean Minimum Temp. (°F)	19.4	21.5	29.5	40.2	50.7	60.7	64.6	62.6	54.9	43.7	34.1	23.5	42.1
Extreme Maximum Temp. (°F)	65	74	82	88	94	104	101	99	96	89	77	72	104
Extreme Minimum Temp. (°F)	-24	-13	-4	10	29	39	47	42	31	20	11	-19	-24
Days Maximum Temp. ≥ 90°F	0	0	0	0	0	4	7	4	1	0	0	0	16
Days Maximum Temp. ≤ 32°F	14	10	3	0	0	0	0	0	0	0	1	10	38
Days Minimum Temp. ≤ 32°F	27	23	20	6	0	0	0	0	0	3	14	25	118
Days Minimum Temp. ≤ 0°F	3	2	0	0	0	0	0	0	0	0	0	1	6
Heating Degree Days (base 65°F)	1,185	998	803	435	171	24	2	6	81	361	677	1,067	5,810
Cooling Degree Days (base 65°F)	0	0	2	11	62	207	306	253	109	16	0	0	966
Mean Precipitation (in.)	2.38	2.33	2.75	3.80	3.89	4.31	4.44	3.61	2.78	2.90	3.08	2.79	39.06
Extreme Maximum Daily Precip. (in.)	1.94	1.69	1.95	2.11	2.42	4.20	3.46	3.62	2.45	2.21	2.07	2.02	4.20
Days With ≥ 0.1" Precipitation	6	5	6	8	8	8	7	6	5	6	7	6	78
Days With ≥ 0.5" Precipitation	1	2	2	2	3	3	3	2	2	2	2	2	26
Days With ≥ 1.0" Precipitation	0	0	0	1	1	1	1	1	1	1	1	0	8
Mean Snowfall (in.)	8.2	7.3	4.1	0.8	0.0	0.0	0.0	0.0	0.0	0.3	1.6	5.9	28.2
Maximum Snow Depth (in.)	24	25	11	5	0	0	0	0	0	1	3	9	25
Days With ≥ 1.0" Snow Depth	13	10	4	0	0	0	0	0	0	0	1	8	36

Bloomington Indiana Univ *Monroe County*   Elevation: 830 ft.   Latitude: 39° 10' N   Longitude: 86° 31' W

	JAN	FEB	MAR	APR	MAY	JUN	JUL	AUG	SEP	OCT	NOV	DEC	YEAR
Mean Maximum Temp. (°F)	37.4	42.2	52.2	63.9	73.6	81.8	85.4	84.9	78.2	66.0	53.9	40.8	63.4
Mean Temp. (°F)	29.4	33.0	42.1	53.3	63.2	71.9	75.7	74.6	67.2	55.3	44.9	32.9	53.6
Mean Minimum Temp. (°F)	21.2	23.9	31.9	42.6	52.8	62.0	65.8	64.2	56.1	44.5	35.9	25.0	43.8
Extreme Maximum Temp. (°F)	69	76	83	87	93	101	104	100	98	90	79	74	104
Extreme Minimum Temp. (°F)	-21	-13	-2	18	31	38	48	44	33	23	13	-20	-21
Days Maximum Temp. ≥ 90°F	0	0	0	0	0	3	7	7	2	0	0	0	19
Days Maximum Temp. ≤ 32°F	11	6	2	0	0	0	0	0	0	0	1	8	28
Days Minimum Temp. ≤ 32°F	27	22	17	5	0	0	0	0	0	2	13	23	109
Days Minimum Temp. ≤ 0°F	2	1	0	0	0	0	0	0	0	0	0	1	4
Heating Degree Days (base 65°F)	1,098	896	706	365	126	16	1	3	62	316	596	988	5,173
Cooling Degree Days (base 65°F)	0	0	3	20	78	232	338	307	134	21	1	0	1,134
Mean Precipitation (in.)	3.11	2.72	3.60	4.49	5.80	4.73	4.60	3.62	3.75	3.70	3.81	3.55	47.48
Extreme Maximum Daily Precip. (in.)	2.44	2.14	2.91	3.65	3.50	2.67	3.12	3.75	4.00	4.15	2.98	2.50	4.15
Days With ≥ 0.1" Precipitation	6	6	7	8	9	7	7	5	5	6	6	7	79
Days With ≥ 0.5" Precipitation	2	2	2	3	4	3	3	2	3	3	3	2	32
Days With ≥ 1.0" Precipitation	1	1	1	1	2	1	1	1	1	1	1	1	13
Mean Snowfall (in.)	*5.2*	2.7	0.9	trace	0.0	0.0	0.0	0.0	0.0	0.2	0.0	3.9	*12.9*
Maximum Snow Depth (in.)	*13*	*9*	*14*	1	0	0	0	0	0	2	trace	*15*	*15*
Days With ≥ 1.0" Snow Depth	*6*	4	1	0	0	0	0	0	0	0	0	4	*15*

The period of record for all cooperative weather station data is 1980 – 2009. See User Guide for detailed explanation of data.

Brookville *Franklin County*   Elevation: 629 ft.   Latitude: 39° 25' N   Longitude: 85° 01' W

	JAN	FEB	MAR	APR	MAY	JUN	JUL	AUG	SEP	OCT	NOV	DEC	YEAR
Mean Maximum Temp. (°F)	37.9	42.0	52.6	65.0	74.7	83.3	86.8	86.0	79.6	66.9	54.7	41.3	64.2
Mean Temp. (°F)	28.9	31.8	41.0	52.3	62.1	71.0	74.8	73.8	66.2	53.9	43.8	32.5	52.7
Mean Minimum Temp. (°F)	19.8	21.5	29.3	39.5	49.6	58.6	62.8	61.5	52.8	40.8	32.9	23.7	41.1
Extreme Maximum Temp. (°F)	67	76	84	89	94	102	102	103	99	92	82	76	103
Extreme Minimum Temp. (°F)	-31	-15	-9	16	29	38	45	41	30	17	9	-20	-31
Days Maximum Temp. ≥ 90°F	0	0	0	0	0	6	10	9	3	0	0	0	28
Days Maximum Temp. ≤ 32°F	10	6	1	0	0	0	0	0	0	0	1	7	25
Days Minimum Temp. ≤ 32°F	27	24	20	7	1	0	0	0	0	7	16	24	126
Days Minimum Temp. ≤ 0°F	3	2	0	0	0	0	0	0	0	0	0	1	6
Heating Degree Days (base 65°F)	1,113	931	739	387	146	20	1	5	75	354	629	1,000	5,400
Cooling Degree Days (base 65°F)	0	0	2	12	65	206	312	284	120	18	1	0	1,020
Mean Precipitation (in.)	3.04	2.61	3.64	4.14	5.09	3.72	4.37	3.44	2.62	3.24	3.55	3.40	42.86
Extreme Maximum Daily Precip. (in.)	2.85	2.02	3.18	3.35	4.03	2.35	3.88	3.20	2.94	3.80	2.23	2.57	4.03
Days With ≥ 0.1" Precipitation	6	5	7	9	9	7	7	5	5	6	7	7	80
Days With ≥ 0.5" Precipitation	2	2	2	3	3	3	3	2	2	2	3	2	29
Days With ≥ 1.0" Precipitation	1	0	1	1	1	1	1	1	1	1	1	1	11
Mean Snowfall (in.)	*4.2*	*4.0*	1.5	0.1	trace	0.0	0.0	0.0	0.0	0.1	0.6	*3.7*	*14.2*
Maximum Snow Depth (in.)	*10*	*9*	*7*	*1*	*trace*	*0*	*0*	*0*	*0*	na	*6*	na	na
Days With ≥ 1.0" Snow Depth	*7*	*7*	1	0	0	0	0	0	0	0	0	4	*19*

Columbia City *Whitley County*   Elevation: 850 ft.   Latitude: 41° 09' N   Longitude: 85° 29' W

	JAN	FEB	MAR	APR	MAY	JUN	JUL	AUG	SEP	OCT	NOV	DEC	YEAR
Mean Maximum Temp. (°F)	31.6	35.4	46.4	59.1	70.3	79.5	82.7	81.1	75.0	61.9	49.1	36.2	59.0
Mean Temp. (°F)	24.0	26.8	36.6	48.3	59.2	68.6	72.0	70.3	63.3	50.9	40.3	28.8	49.1
Mean Minimum Temp. (°F)	16.1	18.1	26.9	37.4	48.0	57.7	61.2	59.5	51.6	39.9	31.4	21.3	39.1
Extreme Maximum Temp. (°F)	66	72	80	88	92	103	101	98	95	89	77	70	103
Extreme Minimum Temp. (°F)	-24	-16	-6	7	24	36	44	36	27	17	8	-22	-24
Days Maximum Temp. ≥ 90°F	0	0	0	0	0	3	4	2	1	0	0	0	10
Days Maximum Temp. ≤ 32°F	16	11	4	0	0	0	0	0	0	0	2	11	44
Days Minimum Temp. ≤ 32°F	28	24	23	9	1	0	0	0	0	7	17	26	135
Days Minimum Temp. ≤ 0°F	4	3	0	0	0	0	0	0	0	0	0	2	9
Heating Degree Days (base 65°F)	1,264	1,073	873	503	214	41	7	17	117	437	733	1,117	6,396
Cooling Degree Days (base 65°F)	0	0	1	7	40	157	230	190	74	8	0	0	707
Mean Precipitation (in.)	2.34	1.85	2.79	3.52	4.13	4.41	4.03	3.91	3.33	3.05	3.26	2.85	39.47
Extreme Maximum Daily Precip. (in.)	2.58	1.39	2.14	2.54	2.52	4.48	3.09	4.30	3.20	2.39	3.57	1.70	4.48
Days With ≥ 0.1" Precipitation	6	5	6	7	8	7	7	6	6	6	7	7	78
Days With ≥ 0.5" Precipitation	1	1	2	2	3	3	3	3	2	2	2	2	26
Days With ≥ 1.0" Precipitation	0	0	1	1	1	1	1	1	1	1	1	0	9
Mean Snowfall (in.)	8.8	6.7	3.5	0.7	0.0	0.0	0.0	0.0	0.0	0.2	1.2	6.4	27.5
Maximum Snow Depth (in.)	11	16	7	6	0	0	0	0	0	0	1	4	11	16
Days With ≥ 1.0" Snow Depth	15	10	4	0	0	0	0	0	0	0	1	8	38

Columbus *Bartholomew County*   Elevation: 621 ft.   Latitude: 39° 12' N   Longitude: 85° 55' W

	JAN	FEB	MAR	APR	MAY	JUN	JUL	AUG	SEP	OCT	NOV	DEC	YEAR
Mean Maximum Temp. (°F)	37.6	42.0	52.2	64.1	73.6	82.2	85.4	84.7	78.4	66.5	54.0	41.0	63.5
Mean Temp. (°F)	29.3	32.8	41.8	53.0	63.1	72.0	75.5	74.1	66.8	54.7	44.2	33.0	53.4
Mean Minimum Temp. (°F)	21.0	23.4	31.3	41.9	52.5	61.8	65.5	63.5	55.0	42.9	34.4	24.8	43.2
Extreme Maximum Temp. (°F)	68	76	83	86	91	100	103	103	97	91	80	73	103
Extreme Minimum Temp. (°F)	-26	-14	-6	18	31	41	51	43	34	21	11	-20	-26
Days Maximum Temp. ≥ 90°F	0	0	0	0	0	4	7	7	2	0	0	0	20
Days Maximum Temp. ≤ 32°F	10	6	1	0	0	0	0	0	0	0	1	7	25
Days Minimum Temp. ≤ 32°F	26	23	18	4	0	0	0	0	0	4	14	23	112
Days Minimum Temp. ≤ 0°F	2	1	0	0	0	0	0	0	0	0	0	1	4
Heating Degree Days (base 65°F)	1,099	905	715	367	125	15	1	3	64	329	616	987	5,226
Cooling Degree Days (base 65°F)	0	0	2	15	72	232	332	292	124	18	0	0	1,087
Mean Precipitation (in.)	2.85	2.63	3.71	4.54	5.25	3.87	4.10	3.67	3.05	3.24	3.66	3.45	44.02
Extreme Maximum Daily Precip. (in.)	2.76	2.17	2.67	3.99	3.01	2.72	6.37	4.11	2.72	3.20	2.30	2.25	6.37
Days With ≥ 0.1" Precipitation	5	5	7	8	9	7	6	6	5	5	6	7	76
Days With ≥ 0.5" Precipitation	2	2	3	3	4	3	3	3	2	2	3	3	33
Days With ≥ 1.0" Precipitation	1	0	1	1	1	1	1	1	1	1	1	1	11
Mean Snowfall (in.)	5.1	3.5	2.1	0.1	trace	0.0	0.0	0.0	0.0	0.1	0.1	3.4	14.4
Maximum Snow Depth (in.)	*16*	*9*	*10*	*1*	*trace*	*0*	*0*	*0*	*0*	*0*	*1*	*1*	*19*	*19*
Days With ≥ 1.0" Snow Depth	*6*	*4*	*1*	0	0	0	0	0	0	0	0	4	*15*

Crawfordsville 5 S *Montgomery County*   Elevation: 762 ft.   Latitude: 39° 58' N   Longitude: 86° 56' W

	JAN	FEB	MAR	APR	MAY	JUN	JUL	AUG	SEP	OCT	NOV	DEC	YEAR
Mean Maximum Temp. (°F)	*34.7*	39.0	49.9	62.0	72.0	81.6	84.4	83.2	77.7	65.4	51.2	37.9	*61.6*
Mean Temp. (°F)	25.8	29.3	38.8	50.1	60.1	70.0	72.8	70.9	64.0	52.6	41.3	29.0	*50.4*
Mean Minimum Temp. (°F)	*16.9*	19.5	27.7	38.2	48.1	58.3	61.2	58.7	50.3	39.7	31.4	20.1	*39.2*
Extreme Maximum Temp. (°F)	65	74	83	87	93	102	99	101	96	89	80	74	102
Extreme Minimum Temp. (°F)	-31	-24	-12	3	28	32	41	36	23	18	3	-24	-31
Days Maximum Temp. ≥ 90°F	0	0	0	0	0	4	6	4	2	0	0	0	16
Days Maximum Temp. ≤ 32°F	13	9	3	0	0	0	0	0	0	0	1	10	36
Days Minimum Temp. ≤ 32°F	27	25	22	9	1	0	0	0	1	8	17	26	136
Days Minimum Temp. ≤ 0°F	4	3	0	0	0	0	0	0	0	0	0	3	10
Heating Degree Days (base 65°F)	*1,207*	1,002	806	449	193	31	7	15	109	390	702	1,110	*6,021*
Cooling Degree Days (base 65°F)	*0*	0	1	11	46	187	255	207	85	13	0	0	*805*
Mean Precipitation (in.)	*2.48*	2.46	2.94	4.01	4.66	4.53	4.44	3.70	3.20	3.33	4.16	3.10	*43.01*
Extreme Maximum Daily Precip. (in.)	2.70	2.98	2.10	2.75	3.50	*3.28*	2.71	4.35	2.25	3.76	2.65	3.20	*4.35*
Days With ≥ 0.1" Precipitation	5	5	6	8	9	8	7	5	5	6	7	*7*	*78*
Days With ≥ 0.5" Precipitation	2	2	2	3	3	3	3	3	2	2	2	*2*	*30*
Days With ≥ 1.0" Precipitation	0	1	1	1	1	1	1	1	1	1	1	*0*	*9*
Mean Snowfall (in.)	na	5.4	2.7	0.2	trace	0.0	0.0	0.0	0.0	trace	0.6	*4.7*	na
Maximum Snow Depth (in.)	na	na	na	*3*	*trace*	*0*	*0*	*0*	*0*	*0*	*1*	*5*	na
Days With ≥ 1.0" Snow Depth	na	na	*1*	0	0	0	0	0	0	0	0	4	na

The period of record for all cooperative weather station data is 1980 – 2009. See User Guide for detailed explanation of data.

Delphi 3 S *Carroll County* Elevation: 670 ft. Latitude: 40° 33' N Longitude: 86° 41' W

	JAN	FEB	MAR	APR	MAY	JUN	JUL	AUG	SEP	OCT	NOV	DEC	YEAR
Mean Maximum Temp. (°F)	34.6	39.0	50.7	64.0	74.2	82.8	85.4	83.8	78.3	65.5	52.1	38.3	62.4
Mean Temp. (°F)	26.9	30.5	40.9	52.3	62.5	71.4	74.3	72.6	65.9	54.1	43.4	31.0	52.1
Mean Minimum Temp. (°F)	19.3	22.1	30.9	40.5	50.7	59.9	63.2	61.5	53.5	42.7	34.6	23.6	41.9
Extreme Maximum Temp. (°F)	67	73	84	89	96	105	103	100	96	89	78	71	105
Extreme Minimum Temp. (°F)	-24	-16	0	10	30	36	44	38	27	18	9	-21	-24
Days Maximum Temp. ≥ 90°F	0	0	0	0	1	5	7	5	2	0	0	0	20
Days Maximum Temp. ≤ 32°F	13	8	2	0	0	0	0	0	0	0	1	8	32
Days Minimum Temp. ≤ 32°F	27	23	18	7	0	0	0	0	0	5	13	24	117
Days Minimum Temp. ≤ 0°F	3	2	0	0	0	0	0	0	0	0	0	2	7
Heating Degree Days (base 65°F)	1,174	968	744	389	142	19	2	7	75	347	643	1,048	5,558
Cooling Degree Days (base 65°F)	0	0	2	15	71	216	298	250	109	17	1	0	979
Mean Precipitation (in.)	2.15	2.05	2.76	3.49	4.37	4.00	4.57	3.68	2.74	2.98	3.12	2.61	38.52
Extreme Maximum Daily Precip. (in.)	2.07	2.42	2.03	2.59	3.00	3.00	3.55	2.64	4.78	2.78	2.50	2.44	4.78
Days With ≥ 0.1" Precipitation	5	4	6	7	8	6	7	6	5	6	6	6	72
Days With ≥ 0.5" Precipitation	1	1	2	3	3	3	3	3	2	2	2	2	27
Days With ≥ 1.0" Precipitation	1	0	1	1	1	1	1	1	1	1	1	1	10
Mean Snowfall (in.)	5.6	4.8	2.4	0.5	trace	0.0	0.0	0.0	0.0	0.2	0.5	4.6	18.6
Maximum Snow Depth (in.)	18	17	10	4	trace	0	0	0	0	4	2	9	18
Days With ≥ 1.0" Snow Depth	10	8	2	0	0	0	0	0	0	0	0	6	26

Dubois S Ind Forage Frm *Dubois County* Elevation: 689 ft. Latitude: 38° 27' N Longitude: 86° 42' W

	JAN	FEB	MAR	APR	MAY	JUN	JUL	AUG	SEP	OCT	NOV	DEC	YEAR
Mean Maximum Temp. (°F)	39.6	44.4	54.4	65.4	74.6	82.8	86.4	86.3	79.4	67.8	55.8	43.4	65.0
Mean Temp. (°F)	30.7	34.4	43.6	54.5	63.7	72.2	76.0	75.1	67.7	56.1	45.7	34.3	54.5
Mean Minimum Temp. (°F)	21.7	24.3	32.8	43.5	52.8	61.6	65.5	63.8	55.9	44.4	35.6	25.3	43.9
Extreme Maximum Temp. (°F)	70	76	83	88	92	101	102	102	99	92	81	75	102
Extreme Minimum Temp. (°F)	-25	-12	0	17	29	40	46	42	33	18	10	-20	-25
Days Maximum Temp. ≥ 90°F	0	0	0	0	0	5	9	10	3	0	0	0	27
Days Maximum Temp. ≤ 32°F	8	5	1	0	0	0	0	0	0	0	0	6	20
Days Minimum Temp. ≤ 32°F	26	22	16	4	0	0	0	0	0	4	13	23	108
Days Minimum Temp. ≤ 0°F	2	1	0	0	0	0	0	0	0	0	0	1	4
Heating Degree Days (base 65°F)	1,058	859	659	334	120	15	1	2	60	296	574	944	4,922
Cooling Degree Days (base 65°F)	0	0	4	24	87	238	348	322	147	28	2	0	1,200
Mean Precipitation (in.)	3.27	2.97	4.20	4.63	5.80	4.32	4.31	3.21	3.91	3.73	4.03	3.68	48.06
Extreme Maximum Daily Precip. (in.)	4.20	2.39	4.82	5.66	3.90	5.38	3.45	2.76	3.00	4.12	4.25	3.18	5.66
Days With ≥ 0.1" Precipitation	5	5	7	8	9	7	7	6	5	6	7	6	78
Days With ≥ 0.5" Precipitation	2	2	3	3	4	3	3	2	3	3	3	3	34
Days With ≥ 1.0" Precipitation	1	1	1	1	2	1	1	1	1	1	1	1	13
Mean Snowfall (in.)	2.4	2.7	*1.5*	trace	0.0	0.0	0.0	0.0	0.0	0.2	trace	*2.3*	*9.1*
Maximum Snow Depth (in.)	*8*	10	*14*	trace	0	0	0	*0*	0	0	1	*18*	*18*
Days With ≥ 1.0" Snow Depth	*4*	3	*1*	0	0	0	0	0	0	0	0	*3*	*11*

Elwood Wastewater Plant *Madison County* Elevation: 839 ft. Latitude: 40° 16' N Longitude: 85° 51' W

	JAN	FEB	MAR	APR	MAY	JUN	JUL	AUG	SEP	OCT	NOV	DEC	YEAR
Mean Maximum Temp. (°F)	33.5	38.1	48.8	61.6	72.3	81.3	84.7	83.3	77.5	64.5	51.2	37.6	61.2
Mean Temp. (°F)	25.2	29.1	38.5	50.0	60.9	70.1	73.5	71.7	64.9	52.4	41.7	29.4	50.6
Mean Minimum Temp. (°F)	16.8	20.0	28.2	38.2	49.4	58.8	62.4	60.1	52.2	40.3	32.2	21.3	40.0
Extreme Maximum Temp. (°F)	65	74	81	87	93	102	101	99	96	92	79	72	102
Extreme Minimum Temp. (°F)	-24	-23	-8	12	28	38	44	38	29	18	5	-20	-24
Days Maximum Temp. ≥ 90°F	0	0	0	0	0	4	6	5	2	0	0	0	17
Days Maximum Temp. ≤ 32°F	14	9	3	0	0	0	0	0	0	0	1	9	36
Days Minimum Temp. ≤ 32°F	28	24	21	8	0	0	0	0	0	7	17	26	131
Days Minimum Temp. ≤ 0°F	4	2	0	0	0	0	0	0	0	0	0	2	8
Heating Degree Days (base 65°F)	1,229	1,010	816	454	177	30	3	12	94	394	692	1,095	6,006
Cooling Degree Days (base 65°F)	0	0	1	9	57	189	275	227	96	11	0	0	865
Mean Precipitation (in.)	2.55	2.04	2.87	3.69	4.28	4.36	4.34	3.77	3.35	2.79	3.56	3.02	40.62
Extreme Maximum Daily Precip. (in.)	2.90	1.30	1.95	2.60	2.80	4.65	4.25	3.97	5.01	2.15	3.50	2.50	5.01
Days With ≥ 0.1" Precipitation	5	4	7	8	8	7	7	6	5	5	7	7	76
Days With ≥ 0.5" Precipitation	1	2	2	3	3	3	3	2	2	2	2	2	27
Days With ≥ 1.0" Precipitation	0	0	1	1	1	1	1	1	1	0	1	1	9
Mean Snowfall (in.)	na	na	0.8	trace	0.0	0.0	0.0	0.0	0.0	trace	0.1	2.8	na
Maximum Snow Depth (in.)	na	na	*10*	*4*	*0*	0	0	*0*	0	trace	trace	na	na
Days With ≥ 1.0" Snow Depth	na	na	1	0	0	0	0	0	0	0	0	*2*	na

English 4 S *Crawford County* Elevation: 509 ft. Latitude: 38° 17' N Longitude: 86° 28' W

	JAN	FEB	MAR	APR	MAY	JUN	JUL	AUG	SEP	OCT	NOV	DEC	YEAR
Mean Maximum Temp. (°F)	41.9	48.2	57.6	*68.3*	76.9	84.4	88.0	*87.1*	*80.8*	*69.8*	*57.5*	45.1	*67.1*
Mean Temp. (°F)	32.1	36.9	44.9	*54.7*	63.5	71.6	75.8	*74.2*	*66.8*	*55.5*	*45.9*	35.2	*54.7*
Mean Minimum Temp. (°F)	22.3	25.5	32.1	*40.9*	50.1	58.8	63.5	*61.3*	*52.7*	*41.1*	*34.3*	25.2	*42.3*
Extreme Maximum Temp. (°F)	72	76	85	91	93	102	104	*102*	*98*	*88*	*84*	76	*104*
Extreme Minimum Temp. (°F)	-30	-15	-2	15	26	36	41	*35*	*28*	*14*	*4*	-21	*-30*
Days Maximum Temp. ≥ 90°F	0	0	0	0	0	6	13	*11*	*3*	*0*	*0*	0	*33*
Days Maximum Temp. ≤ 32°F	6	3	0	0	0	0	0	*0*	*0*	*0*	*0*	5	*14*
Days Minimum Temp. ≤ 32°F	25	21	17	7	1	0	0	*0*	*0*	*7*	*14*	22	*114*
Days Minimum Temp. ≤ 0°F	2	1	0	0	0	0	0	*0*	*0*	*0*	*0*	1	*4*
Heating Degree Days (base 65°F)	1,012	789	620	*322*	113	14	1	*3*	*68*	*306*	*566*	919	*4,733*
Cooling Degree Days (base 65°F)	0	0	3	*18*	73	219	341	*295*	*127*	*17*	*1*	1	*1,095*
Mean Precipitation (in.)	3.53	3.54	4.45	4.45	5.66	4.45	4.00	*3.31*	*3.64*	*3.47*	*4.24*	3.91	*48.65*
Extreme Maximum Daily Precip. (in.)	5.50	4.30	3.01	3.82	4.06	3.29	*3.65*	*2.95*	*3.55*	*2.50*	*2.93*	2.65	*5.50*
Days With ≥ 0.1" Precipitation	6	7	8	8	9	7	6	*5*	*5*	*6*	*7*	7	*81*
Days With ≥ 0.5" Precipitation	2	2	3	3	4	3	3	*2*	*2*	*2*	*3*	3	*32*
Days With ≥ 1.0" Precipitation	1	1	1	1	2	1	1	*1*	*1*	*1*	*1*	1	*13*
Mean Snowfall (in.)	*1.0*	na	0.1	trace	0.0	0.0	0.0	*0.0*	*0.0*	trace	trace	2.0	na
Maximum Snow Depth (in.)	*10*	15	*14*	trace	*0*	*0*	*0*	*0*	*0*	*0*	*1*	22	*22*
Days With ≥ 1.0" Snow Depth	*5*	3	*1*	0	0	0	0	*0*	*0*	*0*	*0*	3	*12*

The period of record for all cooperative weather station data is 1980 – 2009. See User Guide for detailed explanation of data.

Evansville Museum *Vanderburgh County* Elevation: 379 ft. Latitude: 37° 58' N Longitude: 87° 34' W

	JAN	FEB	MAR	APR	MAY	JUN	JUL	AUG	SEP	OCT	NOV	DEC	YEAR
Mean Maximum Temp. (°F)	42.9	47.8	59.1	70.2	78.7	87.4	90.0	90.0	83.3	71.6	58.9	46.1	68.8
Mean Temp. (°F)	35.2	38.7	48.5	59.1	68.0	76.7	80.0	79.6	72.2	60.6	49.7	38.2	58.9
Mean Minimum Temp. (°F)	27.2	29.5	38.2	47.9	57.2	66.1	70.0	69.1	61.1	49.4	40.6	30.2	48.9
Extreme Maximum Temp. (°F)	71	78	86	91	95	101	102	102	100	95	85	78	102
Extreme Minimum Temp. (°F)	-17	-8	5	24	36	45	47	46	37	22	13	-15	-17
Days Maximum Temp. ≥ 90°F	0	0	0	0	2	12	17	17	7	1	0	0	56
Days Maximum Temp. ≤ 32°F	5	3	0	0	0	0	0	0	0	0	0	3	11
Days Minimum Temp. ≤ 32°F	21	16	10	1	0	0	0	0	0	1	7	16	72
Days Minimum Temp. ≤ 0°F	1	0	0	0	0	0	0	0	0	0	0	0	1
Heating Degree Days (base 65°F)	917	738	509	216	52	2	0	0	26	186	455	824	3,925
Cooling Degree Days (base 65°F)	0	0	6	44	152	361	473	459	245	56	4	0	1,800
Mean Precipitation (in.)	2.97	3.35	4.48	4.34	4.96	3.55	4.25	3.31	3.57	3.55	4.17	3.79	46.29
Extreme Maximum Daily Precip. (in.)	2.81	2.83	3.84	5.47	2.97	3.77	5.74	4.00	5.34	2.57	4.10	3.15	5.74
Days With ≥ 0.1" Precipitation	5	6	7	7	8	6	6	5	5	6	6	6	73
Days With ≥ 0.5" Precipitation	2	2	3	3	3	2	3	2	2	2	3	2	29
Days With ≥ 1.0" Precipitation	0	1	1	1	1	1	1	1	1	1	1	1	11
Mean Snowfall (in.)	3.1	2.9	1.5	0.1	trace	0.0	0.0	0.0	0.0	trace	0.1	3.3	11.0
Maximum Snow Depth (in.)	6	9	6	trace	trace	0	0	0	0	0	trace	22	22
Days With ≥ 1.0" Snow Depth	3	4	1	0	0	0	0	0	0	0	0	3	11

Farmland 5 NNW *Randolph County* Elevation: 964 ft. Latitude: 40° 15' N Longitude: 85° 09' W

	JAN	FEB	MAR	APR	MAY	JUN	JUL	AUG	SEP	OCT	NOV	DEC	YEAR
Mean Maximum Temp. (°F)	33.9	37.6	48.1	61.0	71.6	80.7	84.0	82.6	76.9	64.4	51.1	37.9	60.8
Mean Temp. (°F)	25.6	28.5	37.9	49.7	60.5	69.9	73.1	71.2	64.2	52.4	41.6	29.8	50.4
Mean Minimum Temp. (°F)	17.3	19.3	27.5	38.5	49.4	58.9	62.1	59.7	51.5	40.4	32.1	21.7	39.9
Extreme Maximum Temp. (°F)	66	74	81	85	94	102	100	98	95	90	79	72	102
Extreme Minimum Temp. (°F)	-25	-21	-16	10	28	37	40	38	27	17	5	-21	-25
Days Maximum Temp. ≥ 90°F	0	0	0	0	0	4	6	5	2	0	0	0	17
Days Maximum Temp. ≤ 32°F	14	10	4	0	0	0	0	0	0	0	1	10	39
Days Minimum Temp. ≤ 32°F	28	25	22	8	1	0	0	0	0	7	17	26	134
Days Minimum Temp. ≤ 0°F	4	2	0	0	0	0	0	0	0	0	0	2	8
Heating Degree Days (base 65°F)	1,214	1,026	836	460	187	33	5	15	106	397	695	1,084	6,058
Cooling Degree Days (base 65°F)	0	0	1	9	54	185	263	214	90	13	0	0	829
Mean Precipitation (in.)	2.11	1.94	2.83	3.65	4.28	4.23	4.77	3.60	2.98	2.95	3.26	2.61	39.21
Extreme Maximum Daily Precip. (in.)	3.31	2.09	2.24	2.36	2.51	3.73	4.40	3.02	3.18	2.73	3.01	2.40	4.40
Days With ≥ 0.1" Precipitation	5	5	7	8	8	7	7	5	5	6	6	6	75
Days With ≥ 0.5" Precipitation	1	1	2	2	3	3	3	3	2	2	2	2	26
Days With ≥ 1.0" Precipitation	0	0	0	1	1	1	1	1	1	1	1	0	8
Mean Snowfall (in.)	7.0	5.9	3.0	0.4	trace	0.0	0.0	0.0	0.0	0.3	1.0	4.8	22.4
Maximum Snow Depth (in.)	16	16	11	5	trace	0	0	0	0	3	4	7	16
Days With ≥ 1.0" Snow Depth	12	10	4	0	0	0	0	0	0	0	1	7	34

Frankfort Disposal Plant *Clinton County* Elevation: 834 ft. Latitude: 40° 19' N Longitude: 86° 30' W

	JAN	FEB	MAR	APR	MAY	JUN	JUL	AUG	SEP	OCT	NOV	DEC	YEAR
Mean Maximum Temp. (°F)	33.9	37.9	49.0	61.8	72.1	81.0	83.9	82.3	76.7	64.0	50.5	37.3	60.9
Mean Temp. (°F)	26.5	29.8	39.6	51.0	61.3	70.5	73.6	72.0	65.2	53.5	42.2	30.1	51.3
Mean Minimum Temp. (°F)	19.0	21.6	30.2	40.2	50.5	59.8	63.4	61.5	53.6	42.9	33.8	22.8	41.6
Extreme Maximum Temp. (°F)	66	73	83	87	92	101	105	98	95	90	77	72	105
Extreme Minimum Temp. (°F)	-25	-14	-13	16	30	36	44	38	28	20	9	-26	-26
Days Maximum Temp. ≥ 90°F	0	0	0	0	0	4	6	4	1	0	0	0	15
Days Maximum Temp. ≤ 32°F	14	9	3	0	0	0	0	0	0	0	1	10	37
Days Minimum Temp. ≤ 32°F	27	24	19	6	0	0	0	0	0	4	14	25	119
Days Minimum Temp. ≤ 0°F	3	2	0	0	0	0	0	0	0	0	0	2	7
Heating Degree Days (base 65°F)	1,188	989	782	422	167	24	3	9	87	364	678	1,076	5,789
Cooling Degree Days (base 65°F)	0	0	1	11	59	195	277	232	99	14	0	0	888
Mean Precipitation (in.)	2.29	2.21	3.01	3.66	4.25	4.42	4.34	3.91	2.96	3.08	3.53	2.94	40.60
Extreme Maximum Daily Precip. (in.)	1.90	3.12	2.80	2.74	3.47	4.30	3.38	4.25	3.50	3.30	3.15	2.27	4.30
Days With ≥ 0.1" Precipitation	5	5	7	8	9	7	7	6	5	6	7	7	79
Days With ≥ 0.5" Precipitation	1	1	2	2	3	3	3	3	2	2	2	2	26
Days With ≥ 1.0" Precipitation	0	0	1	1	1	1	1	1	1	1	1	0	9
Mean Snowfall (in.)	7.5	6.1	2.7	0.4	trace	0.0	0.0	0.0	0.0	0.4	0.5	5.0	22.6
Maximum Snow Depth (in.)	13	18	14	7	trace	0	0	0	0	0	7	3	7	18
Days With ≥ 1.0" Snow Depth	10	8	3	0	0	0	0	0	0	0	0	7	28

Freelandville *Knox County* Elevation: 549 ft. Latitude: 38° 52' N Longitude: 87° 19' W

	JAN	FEB	MAR	APR	MAY	JUN	JUL	AUG	SEP	OCT	NOV	DEC	YEAR
Mean Maximum Temp. (°F)	37.1	41.8	52.5	64.3	73.8	82.7	85.7	84.9	78.5	66.4	53.5	40.1	63.5
Mean Temp. (°F)	29.7	33.4	42.7	53.8	63.7	72.9	76.0	74.6	67.4	55.7	44.6	32.5	53.9
Mean Minimum Temp. (°F)	22.2	24.9	32.9	43.3	53.6	63.1	66.3	64.3	56.2	45.0	35.6	24.9	44.3
Extreme Maximum Temp. (°F)	69	75	82	86	92	101	101	99	97	90	80	72	101
Extreme Minimum Temp. (°F)	-21	-11	7	21	33	41	50	45	35	25	10	-23	-23
Days Maximum Temp. ≥ 90°F	0	0	0	0	0	4	7	6	2	0	0	0	19
Days Maximum Temp. ≤ 32°F	11	6	2	0	0	0	0	0	0	0	1	8	28
Days Minimum Temp. ≤ 32°F	25	22	16	4	0	0	0	0	0	2	12	23	104
Days Minimum Temp. ≤ 0°F	2	1	0	0	0	0	0	0	0	0	0	1	4
Heating Degree Days (base 65°F)	1,089	887	686	347	113	12	1	3	61	305	607	1,000	5,111
Cooling Degree Days (base 65°F)	0	0	3	19	81	257	349	309	139	24	1	0	1,182
Mean Precipitation (in.)	2.77	2.73	3.73	4.16	5.66	3.80	4.77	3.22	3.49	3.93	4.14	3.32	45.72
Extreme Maximum Daily Precip. (in.)	2.57	2.04	2.69	3.14	3.30	3.36	3.37	3.01	3.81	3.52	2.80	2.19	3.81
Days With ≥ 0.1" Precipitation	6	5	7	8	8	7	7	5	5	6	7	7	78
Days With ≥ 0.5" Precipitation	2	2	2	3	4	3	3	2	2	3	3	3	32
Days With ≥ 1.0" Precipitation	1	1	1	1	2	1	1	1	1	1	1	1	13
Mean Snowfall (in.)	4.5	3.5	1.5	trace	0.0	0.0	0.0	0.0	0.0	0.1	0.2	4.1	13.9
Maximum Snow Depth (in.)	11	7	8	trace	0	0	0	0	0	0	2	1	12	12
Days With ≥ 1.0" Snow Depth	5	3	1	0	0	0	0	0	0	0	0	4	13

The period of record for all cooperative weather station data is 1980 – 2009. See User Guide for detailed explanation of data.

Goshen College *Elkhart County* Elevation: 875 ft. Latitude: 41° 33' N Longitude: 85° 53' W

	JAN	FEB	MAR	APR	MAY	JUN	JUL	AUG	SEP	OCT	NOV	DEC	YEAR
Mean Maximum Temp. (°F)	32.2	36.0	47.5	60.6	71.6	80.5	83.6	81.6	75.2	62.5	49.2	35.9	59.7
Mean Temp. (°F)	25.2	28.3	38.2	49.9	60.4	69.8	73.3	71.4	64.4	52.6	41.5	29.5	50.4
Mean Minimum Temp. (°F)	18.2	20.5	28.9	39.1	49.2	58.9	62.8	61.3	53.6	42.7	33.7	23.0	41.0
Extreme Maximum Temp. (°F)	63	73	81	93	92	102	100	99	95	88	76	69	102
Extreme Minimum Temp. (°F)	-24	-14	-3	1	28	37	41	37	29	18	11	-18	-24
Days Maximum Temp. ≥ 90°F	0	0	0	0	0	4	5	3	1	0	0	0	13
Days Maximum Temp. ≤ 32°F	16	11	3	0	0	0	0	0	0	0	1	11	42
Days Minimum Temp. ≤ 32°F	28	24	20	7	0	0	0	0	0	4	14	26	123
Days Minimum Temp. ≤ 0°F	3	2	0	0	0	0	0	0	0	0	0	2	7
Heating Degree Days (base 65°F)	1,228	1,031	825	455	187	30	4	11	98	386	700	1,094	6,049
Cooling Degree Days (base 65°F)	0	0	1	8	52	179	266	217	86	9	0	0	818
Mean Precipitation (in.)	2.17	2.08	2.54	3.47	3.85	3.96	4.28	4.24	3.52	3.23	3.02	2.67	39.03
Extreme Maximum Daily Precip. (in.)	3.02	2.19	2.31	3.18	2.93	3.36	6.65	3.79	3.31	3.05	2.18	2.58	6.65
Days With ≥ 0.1" Precipitation	5	6	7	7	7	7	6	6	6	6	7	7	77
Days With ≥ 0.5" Precipitation	1	1	1	2	3	3	3	3	2	2	2	1	24
Days With ≥ 1.0" Precipitation	0	0	0	1	1	1	1	1	1	1	1	0	8
Mean Snowfall (in.)	10.9	9.0	5.0	1.3	trace	0.0	0.0	0.0	0.0	0.4	3.1	10.6	40.3
Maximum Snow Depth (in.)	17	14	8	4	trace	0	0	0	0	5	4	17	17
Days With ≥ 1.0" Snow Depth	16	12	4	0	0	0	0	0	0	0	1	10	43

Greenfield *Hancock County* Elevation: 865 ft. Latitude: 39° 47' N Longitude: 85° 45' W

	JAN	FEB	MAR	APR	MAY	JUN	JUL	AUG	SEP	OCT	NOV	DEC	YEAR
Mean Maximum Temp. (°F)	34.8	38.9	49.6	62.1	72.2	81.5	84.7	83.6	77.6	65.0	51.5	38.4	61.6
Mean Temp. (°F)	26.8	30.1	39.8	51.6	62.0	71.2	74.6	73.3	66.3	54.0	42.6	30.6	51.9
Mean Minimum Temp. (°F)	18.8	21.3	30.1	41.1	51.7	60.9	64.5	62.9	54.9	42.9	33.6	22.8	42.1
Extreme Maximum Temp. (°F)	65	73	84	87	93	103	102	101	95	90	79	72	103
Extreme Minimum Temp. (°F)	-29	-19	-6	16	30	39	48	41	31	20	10	-19	-29
Days Maximum Temp. ≥ 90°F	0	0	0	0	0	4	6	5	2	0	0	0	17
Days Maximum Temp. ≤ 32°F	13	8	3	0	0	0	0	0	0	0	1	9	34
Days Minimum Temp. ≤ 32°F	27	24	19	6	0	0	0	0	0	4	15	24	119
Days Minimum Temp. ≤ 0°F	3	2	0	0	0	0	0	0	0	0	0	2	7
Heating Degree Days (base 65°F)	1,178	979	774	408	156	23	2	6	74	352	666	1,060	5,678
Cooling Degree Days (base 65°F)	0	0	0	13	69	216	307	270	118	17	0	0	1,011
Mean Precipitation (in.)	2.69	2.36	3.56	4.32	5.48	4.59	5.11	3.86	3.47	3.42	3.82	3.22	45.90
Extreme Maximum Daily Precip. (in.)	2.43	1.67	2.41	3.80	3.41	3.85	4.37	4.71	3.13	4.10	3.00	3.41	4.71
Days With ≥ 0.1" Precipitation	6	5	7	8	9	8	7	6	6	6	7	7	82
Days With ≥ 0.5" Precipitation	2	2	2	3	4	3	4	3	2	2	3	2	32
Days With ≥ 1.0" Precipitation	1	0	1	1	2	1	2	1	1	1	1	0	12
Mean Snowfall (in.)	5.8	3.5	1.7	0.1	0.0	0.0	0.0	0.0	0.0	0.1	0.6	3.9	15.7
Maximum Snow Depth (in.)	15	12	8	3	0	0	0	0	0	3	5	10	15
Days With ≥ 1.0" Snow Depth	10	7	2	0	0	0	0	0	0	0	1	6	26

Greensburg *Decatur County* Elevation: 935 ft. Latitude: 39° 21' N Longitude: 85° 30' W

	JAN	FEB	MAR	APR	MAY	JUN	JUL	AUG	SEP	OCT	NOV	DEC	YEAR
Mean Maximum Temp. (°F)	35.8	40.5	50.6	62.8	72.8	81.6	84.8	83.8	77.4	65.2	52.4	39.7	62.3
Mean Temp. (°F)	28.4	32.0	41.3	52.8	63.0	71.8	75.2	73.9	66.9	54.8	43.8	32.3	53.0
Mean Minimum Temp. (°F)	20.9	23.5	32.0	42.9	53.2	62.0	65.6	63.8	56.2	44.4	35.1	24.8	43.7
Extreme Maximum Temp. (°F)	66	74	82	88	93	101	101	101	96	91	79	73	101
Extreme Minimum Temp. (°F)	-24	-14	-12	19	30	39	46	42	32	17	12	-21	-24
Days Maximum Temp. ≥ 90°F	0	0	0	0	0	4	6	6	1	0	0	0	17
Days Maximum Temp. ≤ 32°F	12	8	2	0	0	0	0	0	0	0	1	8	31
Days Minimum Temp. ≤ 32°F	26	22	17	4	0	0	0	0	0	4	13	24	110
Days Minimum Temp. ≤ 0°F	2	1	0	0	0	0	0	0	0	0	0	1	4
Heating Degree Days (base 65°F)	1,127	925	728	376	133	18	1	5	70	329	631	1,009	5,352
Cooling Degree Days (base 65°F)	0	0	3	18	79	230	324	285	132	21	1	0	1,093
Mean Precipitation (in.)	2.92	2.45	3.69	4.42	5.52	4.45	4.01	3.93	3.08	3.24	3.65	3.38	44.74
Extreme Maximum Daily Precip. (in.)	3.09	2.02	2.48	4.00	2.78	5.00	2.76	4.21	3.54	3.60	2.15	2.25	5.00
Days With ≥ 0.1" Precipitation	6	6	7	9	9	7	7	6	5	6	7	7	82
Days With ≥ 0.5" Precipitation	2	2	3	3	4	3	3	2	2	2	3	2	31
Days With ≥ 1.0" Precipitation	1	0	1	1	1	1	1	1	1	1	1	1	11
Mean Snowfall (in.)	5.5	3.8	2.2	0.3	trace	0.0	0.0	0.0	0.0	0.2	0.2	4.2	16.4
Maximum Snow Depth (in.)	16	8	10	3	0	0	0	0	0	1	1	21	21
Days With ≥ 1.0" Snow Depth	7	5	1	0	0	0	0	0	0	0	0	4	17

Huntington *Huntington County* Elevation: 725 ft. Latitude: 40° 51' N Longitude: 85° 30' W

	JAN	FEB	MAR	APR	MAY	JUN	JUL	AUG	SEP	OCT	NOV	DEC	YEAR
Mean Maximum Temp. (°F)	33.1	37.0	47.6	61.2	72.4	81.7	85.3	83.7	76.9	63.7	50.5	37.1	60.9
Mean Temp. (°F)	25.3	28.0	37.5	49.7	60.4	70.0	73.8	72.2	64.4	52.1	41.4	29.5	50.4
Mean Minimum Temp. (°F)	17.3	18.8	27.5	38.2	48.5	58.3	62.3	60.6	51.8	40.4	32.2	21.8	39.8
Extreme Maximum Temp. (°F)	66	75	82	89	94	105	105	103	96	92	79	71	105
Extreme Minimum Temp. (°F)	-28	-16	-11	6	26	37	43	38	28	16	9	-24	-28
Days Maximum Temp. ≥ 90°F	0	0	0	0	1	5	8	5	2	0	0	0	21
Days Maximum Temp. ≤ 32°F	15	9	3	0	0	0	0	0	0	0	1	10	38
Days Minimum Temp. ≤ 32°F	28	25	22	9	1	0	0	0	0	7	16	26	134
Days Minimum Temp. ≤ 0°F	4	2	0	0	0	0	0	0	0	0	0	2	8
Heating Degree Days (base 65°F)	1,226	1,040	846	462	188	32	3	10	101	404	703	1,094	6,109
Cooling Degree Days (base 65°F)	0	0	1	10	54	191	284	239	90	11	0	0	880
Mean Precipitation (in.)	2.25	2.00	2.62	3.50	4.33	4.17	4.05	3.74	2.99	3.07	3.02	2.69	38.43
Extreme Maximum Daily Precip. (in.)	1.65	2.41	1.94	2.33	2.80	3.08	5.53	4.15	2.80	3.36	3.07	2.21	5.53
Days With ≥ 0.1" Precipitation	6	5	6	8	8	7	6	6	6	6	6	7	77
Days With ≥ 0.5" Precipitation	1	1	2	2	3	3	3	2	2	2	2	2	25
Days With ≥ 1.0" Precipitation	0	0	0	1	1	1	1	1	1	1	1	0	8
Mean Snowfall (in.)	9.7	7.1	3.2	0.8	0.0	0.0	0.0	0.0	0.0	0.2	1.0	7.3	29.3
Maximum Snow Depth (in.)	10	15	10	9	0	0	0	0	0	3	4	8	15
Days With ≥ 1.0" Snow Depth	7	6	2	0	0	0	0	0	0	0	0	6	21

The period of record for all cooperative weather station data is 1980 – 2009. See User Guide for detailed explanation of data.

Climate: Cooperative Weather Stations

Indianapolis SE Side *Marion County*   Elevation: 845 ft.   Latitude: 39° 43' N   Longitude: 86° 04' W

	JAN	FEB	MAR	APR	MAY	JUN	JUL	AUG	SEP	OCT	NOV	DEC	YEAR
Mean Maximum Temp. (°F)	35.0	39.2	49.6	61.9	72.5	81.2	84.3	83.3	77.1	64.7	51.6	38.6	61.6
Mean Temp. (°F)	27.2	30.6	40.0	51.6	61.9	71.2	74.5	73.1	66.0	54.1	42.8	30.9	52.0
Mean Minimum Temp. (°F)	19.4	21.9	30.3	41.4	51.6	61.2	64.7	63.0	54.9	43.4	33.8	23.1	42.4
Extreme Maximum Temp. (°F)	65	74	83	87	92	104	103	100	94	89	82	73	104
Extreme Minimum Temp. (°F)	-22	-12	2	18	29	35	44	45	30	20	8	-20	-22
Days Maximum Temp. ≥ 90°F	0	0	0	0	0	3	6	5	1	0	0	0	15
Days Maximum Temp. ≤ 32°F	13	8	3	0	0	0	0	0	0	0	1	9	34
Days Minimum Temp. ≤ 32°F	27	24	19	5	0	0	0	0	0	4	15	25	119
Days Minimum Temp. ≤ 0°F	3	1	0	0	0	0	0	0	0	0	0	2	6
Heating Degree Days (base 65°F)	1,166	966	772	407	154	22	3	6	78	347	661	1,050	5,632
Cooling Degree Days (base 65°F)	0	0	2	13	66	216	304	265	115	17	0	0	998
Mean Precipitation (in.)	2.33	2.09	3.25	4.10	4.99	4.33	4.71	3.38	2.95	3.24	3.63	3.11	42.11
Extreme Maximum Daily Precip. (in.)	1.94	1.96	2.25	2.80	2.55	3.57	4.16	3.90	4.03	3.04	3.11	2.73	4.16
Days With ≥ 0.1" Precipitation	5	5	7	8	8	7	7	5	5	5	6	7	75
Days With ≥ 0.5" Precipitation	2	1	2	3	4	3	3	2	2	2	3	2	29
Days With ≥ 1.0" Precipitation	1	0	1	1	1	1	1	1	1	1	1	1	11
Mean Snowfall (in.)	*5.0*	3.6	1.0	0.1	trace	0.0	0.0	0.0	0.0	0.2	0.2	3.3	*13.4*
Maximum Snow Depth (in.)	13	12	9	1	0	0	0	0	0	trace	3	15	15
Days With ≥ 1.0" Snow Depth	8	6	2	0	0	0	0	0	0	0	0	5	21

Kokomo 3 WSW *Howard County*   Elevation: 819 ft.   Latitude: 40° 28' N   Longitude: 86° 10' W

	JAN	FEB	MAR	APR	MAY	JUN	JUL	AUG	SEP	OCT	NOV	DEC	YEAR
Mean Maximum Temp. (°F)	32.2	36.3	47.6	61.0	71.4	80.6	83.8	82.3	76.5	63.8	50.2	36.1	60.2
Mean Temp. (°F)	24.3	27.6	37.6	49.6	60.1	69.7	73.0	71.3	64.2	52.2	41.1	28.6	49.9
Mean Minimum Temp. (°F)	16.4	18.8	27.5	38.2	48.8	58.7	62.1	60.2	51.9	40.6	31.8	21.0	39.7
Extreme Maximum Temp. (°F)	65	74	82	88	92	104	102	100	95	91	81	71	104
Extreme Minimum Temp. (°F)	-26	-20	-10	8	28	34	43	37	27	17	3	-24	-26
Days Maximum Temp. ≥ 90°F	0	0	0	0	0	4	6	4	2	0	0	0	16
Days Maximum Temp. ≤ 32°F	16	11	4	0	0	0	0	0	0	0	2	11	44
Days Minimum Temp. ≤ 32°F	28	25	22	9	0	0	0	0	0	7	17	27	135
Days Minimum Temp. ≤ 0°F	5	3	0	0	0	0	0	0	0	0	0	2	10
Heating Degree Days (base 65°F)	1,256	1,051	845	466	194	35	6	14	106	402	712	1,123	6,210
Cooling Degree Days (base 65°F)	0	0	1	11	50	182	260	215	90	13	0	0	822
Mean Precipitation (in.)	2.61	2.48	2.99	3.87	4.47	4.41	4.78	3.98	3.51	3.27	3.56	3.19	43.12
Extreme Maximum Daily Precip. (in.)	1.94	2.66	2.40	2.40	3.54	4.90	8.82	3.56	6.37	3.54	2.83	3.00	8.82
Days With ≥ 0.1" Precipitation	6	6	7	8	9	8	7	6	6	6	7	8	84
Days With ≥ 0.5" Precipitation	1	1	2	3	3	3	3	3	2	2	3	2	28
Days With ≥ 1.0" Precipitation	1	0	0	1	1	1	1	1	1	1	1	1	10
Mean Snowfall (in.)	11.1	10.4	5.2	1.1	trace	0.0	0.0	0.0	0.0	0.4	1.3	8.8	38.3
Maximum Snow Depth (in.)	17	24	14	8	trace	0	0	0	0	7	3	9	24
Days With ≥ 1.0" Snow Depth	14	11	4	0	0	0	0	0	0	0	1	9	39

La Porte *La Porte County*   Elevation: 810 ft.   Latitude: 41° 37' N   Longitude: 86° 44' W

	JAN	FEB	MAR	APR	MAY	JUN	JUL	AUG	SEP	OCT	NOV	DEC	YEAR
Mean Maximum Temp. (°F)	31.3	35.0	45.6	58.4	69.8	78.9	82.3	80.4	74.1	61.7	48.1	35.4	58.4
Mean Temp. (°F)	24.6	28.0	37.3	49.1	59.9	69.5	73.4	71.8	64.7	52.8	41.0	29.1	50.1
Mean Minimum Temp. (°F)	17.8	20.9	29.0	39.8	50.0	60.0	64.4	63.2	55.3	43.8	33.9	22.7	41.7
Extreme Maximum Temp. (°F)	64	71	82	90	91	101	101	100	95	89	75	72	101
Extreme Minimum Temp. (°F)	-23	-16	-6	16	30	38	47	44	35	24	10	-18	-23
Days Maximum Temp. ≥ 90°F	0	0	0	0	0	3	4	3	1	0	0	0	11
Days Maximum Temp. ≤ 32°F	17	12	4	0	0	0	0	0	0	0	2	11	46
Days Minimum Temp. ≤ 32°F	28	24	21	6	0	0	0	0	0	2	14	25	120
Days Minimum Temp. ≤ 0°F	3	2	0	0	0	0	0	0	0	0	0	2	7
Heating Degree Days (base 65°F)	1,247	1,040	852	480	204	37	3	9	94	383	713	1,106	6,168
Cooling Degree Days (base 65°F)	0	0	1	9	52	178	269	228	92	10	0	0	839
Mean Precipitation (in.)	2.63	2.28	2.94	3.55	3.82	4.21	4.26	4.40	3.68	3.75	3.86	3.18	42.56
Extreme Maximum Daily Precip. (in.)	2.34	1.70	1.77	2.56	3.23	3.62	4.59	3.49	6.73	2.81	5.00	2.13	6.73
Days With ≥ 0.1" Precipitation	8	6	7	8	8	7	7	7	6	7	8	8	87
Days With ≥ 0.5" Precipitation	1	1	2	3	3	3	3	3	2	2	2	2	27
Days With ≥ 1.0" Precipitation	0	0	1	1	1	1	1	1	1	1	1	1	10
Mean Snowfall (in.)	20.6	13.9	7.2	1.4	trace	0.0	0.0	0.0	0.0	0.4	3.8	14.9	62.2
Maximum Snow Depth (in.)	18	24	11	6	trace	0	0	0	0	1	10	14	24
Days With ≥ 1.0" Snow Depth	20	14	5	1	0	0	0	0	0	0	2	11	53

Lafayette 8 S *Tippecanoe County*   Elevation: 732 ft.   Latitude: 40° 18' N   Longitude: 86° 54' W

	JAN	FEB	MAR	APR	MAY	JUN	JUL	AUG	SEP	OCT	NOV	DEC	YEAR
Mean Maximum Temp. (°F)	33.4	37.7	48.9	61.5	72.5	81.6	84.3	82.9	77.6	64.8	51.2	37.2	61.1
Mean Temp. (°F)	25.4	28.8	39.2	50.9	61.7	70.9	73.9	72.2	65.6	53.6	42.2	29.4	51.1
Mean Minimum Temp. (°F)	17.3	19.9	29.4	40.1	50.9	60.2	63.5	61.6	53.6	42.4	33.2	21.5	41.1
Extreme Maximum Temp. (°F)	65	74	82	89	93	104	102	98	96	91	80	71	104
Extreme Minimum Temp. (°F)	-25	-19	-8	4	29	36	44	37	26	19	7	-25	-25
Days Maximum Temp. ≥ 90°F	0	0	0	0	1	5	6	4	2	0	0	0	18
Days Maximum Temp. ≤ 32°F	14	10	3	0	0	0	0	0	0	0	1	10	38
Days Minimum Temp. ≤ 32°F	27	25	20	7	0	0	0	0	0	5	15	26	125
Days Minimum Temp. ≤ 0°F	4	3	0	0	0	0	0	0	0	0	0	2	9
Heating Degree Days (base 65°F)	1,221	1,017	796	431	165	27	3	10	87	363	676	1,098	5,894
Cooling Degree Days (base 65°F)	0	0	2	14	70	210	287	241	111	17	0	0	952
Mean Precipitation (in.)	2.07	1.96	2.73	3.37	4.60	4.44	4.08	3.76	2.79	2.81	3.24	2.59	38.44
Extreme Maximum Daily Precip. (in.)	2.30	2.26	3.30	3.44	4.14	4.51	2.50	3.66	3.72	2.19	2.35	2.02	4.51
Days With ≥ 0.1" Precipitation	5	4	6	7	8	7	7	6	5	5	6	6	72
Days With ≥ 0.5" Precipitation	1	1	2	2	3	3	3	2	2	2	2	2	25
Days With ≥ 1.0" Precipitation	0	0	1	1	1	1	1	1	1	1	1	0	7
Mean Snowfall (in.)	6.9	5.3	2.4	0.6	trace	0.0	0.0	0.0	0.0	0.5	0.5	5.1	21.3
Maximum Snow Depth (in.)	18	19	10	5	trace	0	0	0	0	0	5	4	19
Days With ≥ 1.0" Snow Depth	11	9	3	0	0	0	0	0	0	0	0	8	31

The period of record for all cooperative weather station data is 1980 – 2009. See User Guide for detailed explanation of data.

Lowell *Lake County* Elevation: 665 ft. Latitude: 41° 16' N Longitude: 87° 25' W

	JAN	FEB	MAR	APR	MAY	JUN	JUL	AUG	SEP	OCT	NOV	DEC	YEAR
Mean Maximum Temp. (°F)	31.5	35.9	47.5	60.6	71.8	81.0	84.0	82.1	76.5	63.6	49.4	35.4	59.9
Mean Temp. (°F)	23.3	27.0	37.5	49.3	60.0	69.6	73.1	71.2	64.2	52.0	40.4	27.2	49.6
Mean Minimum Temp. (°F)	15.0	18.1	27.6	37.9	48.2	58.2	62.1	60.2	51.9	40.3	31.3	19.3	39.2
Extreme Maximum Temp. (°F)	66	73	84	91	93	104	101	104	98	91	76	69	104
Extreme Minimum Temp. (°F)	-25	-21	-9	7	27	36	42	38	28	18	6	-20	-25
Days Maximum Temp. ≥ 90°F	0	0	0	0	1	5	7	3	2	0	0	0	18
Days Maximum Temp. ≤ 32°F	16	11	3	0	0	0	0	0	0	0	1	11	42
Days Minimum Temp. ≤ 32°F	29	25	23	9	1	0	0	0	0	6	17	27	137
Days Minimum Temp. ≤ 0°F	5	3	0	0	0	0	0	0	0	0	0	3	11
Heating Degree Days (base 65°F)	1,286	1,068	845	474	200	37	5	13	105	408	733	1,165	6,339
Cooling Degree Days (base 65°F)	0	0	1	9	52	182	261	211	88	11	0	0	815
Mean Precipitation (in.)	1.91	1.68	2.65	3.73	4.33	4.53	3.85	4.15	3.23	3.45	3.42	2.52	39.45
Extreme Maximum Daily Precip. (in.)	2.81	1.89	2.19	3.88	2.91	3.85	3.64	3.53	3.20	2.92	5.14	2.96	5.14
Days With ≥ 0.1" Precipitation	5	4	6	7	8	7	7	6	5	6	7	6	74
Days With ≥ 0.5" Precipitation	1	1	2	2	3	2	3	3	2	2	2	1	24
Days With ≥ 1.0" Precipitation	0	0	0	1	1	1	1	1	1	1	1	1	9
Mean Snowfall (in.)	9.4	9.1	3.6	0.3	trace	0.0	0.0	0.0	0.0	0.2	0.8	7.4	30.8
Maximum Snow Depth (in.)	na	na	9	1	trace	0	0	0	0	0	1	4	na
Days With ≥ 1.0" Snow Depth	na	7	2	0	0	0	0	0	0	0	0	8	na

Madison Sewage Plant *Jefferson County* Elevation: 459 ft. Latitude: 38° 44' N Longitude: 85° 24' W

	JAN	FEB	MAR	APR	MAY	JUN	JUL	AUG	SEP	OCT	NOV	DEC	YEAR
Mean Maximum Temp. (°F)	41.0	45.3	55.3	66.5	75.0	83.1	86.7	86.0	79.5	68.2	56.1	44.1	65.6
Mean Temp. (°F)	32.8	35.8	44.8	55.0	64.1	72.5	76.6	75.6	68.6	57.2	46.4	35.9	55.4
Mean Minimum Temp. (°F)	24.5	26.3	34.0	43.5	53.1	61.8	66.4	65.2	57.7	46.0	36.6	27.5	45.2
Extreme Maximum Temp. (°F)	68	76	84	91	93	103	103	104	99	93	84	77	104
Extreme Minimum Temp. (°F)	-17	-8	-2	19	31	40	51	43	33	23	11	-18	-18
Days Maximum Temp. ≥ 90°F	0	0	0	0	0	4	10	9	3	0	0	0	26
Days Maximum Temp. ≤ 32°F	6	4	0	0	0	0	0	0	0	0	0	5	15
Days Minimum Temp. ≤ 32°F	24	20	14	3	0	0	0	0	0	1	11	21	94
Days Minimum Temp. ≤ 0°F	1	0	0	0	0	0	0	0	0	0	0	1	2
Heating Degree Days (base 65°F)	991	820	623	305	105	11	0	1	44	260	553	897	4,610
Cooling Degree Days (base 65°F)	0	0	2	15	82	242	365	338	160	25	1	0	1,230
Mean Precipitation (in.)	3.40	2.96	4.19	4.33	5.32	4.21	4.55	4.11	3.23	3.79	3.69	3.76	47.54
Extreme Maximum Daily Precip. (in.)	4.00	2.60	3.10	2.20	2.80	2.90	3.65	4.97	5.16	5.00	2.80	2.60	5.16
Days With ≥ 0.1" Precipitation	6	6	8	9	9	8	7	6	5	6	7	7	84
Days With ≥ 0.5" Precipitation	2	2	3	3	4	3	3	3	2	3	3	2	33
Days With ≥ 1.0" Precipitation	1	1	1	1	2	1	2	1	1	1	1	1	14
Mean Snowfall (in.)	4.3	3.9	1.3	0.1	trace	0.0	0.0	0.0	0.0	0.1	trace	3.4	13.1
Maximum Snow Depth (in.)	10	16	8	1	trace	0	0	0	0	4	trace	15	16
Days With ≥ 1.0" Snow Depth	4	4	1	0	0	0	0	0	0	0	0	2	11

Martinsville 2 SW *Morgan County* Elevation: 609 ft. Latitude: 39° 24' N Longitude: 86° 27' W

	JAN	FEB	MAR	APR	MAY	JUN	JUL	AUG	SEP	OCT	NOV	DEC	YEAR
Mean Maximum Temp. (°F)	36.6	41.1	51.5	63.2	72.7	81.1	84.7	84.1	78.0	65.5	53.1	40.3	62.7
Mean Temp. (°F)	27.9	31.4	40.6	51.5	61.3	70.2	73.9	72.5	65.1	52.9	42.8	31.7	51.8
Mean Minimum Temp. (°F)	19.1	21.5	29.6	39.7	49.7	59.2	63.0	60.9	52.2	40.3	32.5	23.0	40.9
Extreme Maximum Temp. (°F)	67	75	83	88	92	101	101	100	95	89	81	75	101
Extreme Minimum Temp. (°F)	-35	-20	-15	12	29	35	45	38	28	19	9	-22	-35
Days Maximum Temp. ≥ 90°F	0	0	0	0	0	2	6	6	2	0	0	0	16
Days Maximum Temp. ≤ 32°F	11	7	2	0	0	0	0	0	0	0	1	8	29
Days Minimum Temp. ≤ 32°F	27	24	20	7	1	0	0	0	0	7	16	25	127
Days Minimum Temp. ≤ 0°F	3	2	0	0	0	0	0	0	0	0	0	2	7
Heating Degree Days (base 65°F)	1,145	945	753	411	162	25	3	8	90	380	659	1,027	5,608
Cooling Degree Days (base 65°F)	0	0	1	12	53	187	285	248	101	12	0	0	899
Mean Precipitation (in.)	2.65	2.42	3.42	4.41	5.29	4.57	4.31	3.83	3.50	3.42	3.64	3.23	44.69
Extreme Maximum Daily Precip. (in.)	2.16	2.34	2.20	3.50	2.83	8.02	3.85	5.82	4.12	4.76	3.40	2.92	8.02
Days With ≥ 0.1" Precipitation	5	5	7	8	9	7	7	5	5	5	6	7	76
Days With ≥ 0.5" Precipitation	2	2	2	3	4	3	3	3	2	2	3	2	31
Days With ≥ 1.0" Precipitation	1	0	1	1	1	1	1	1	1	1	1	1	11
Mean Snowfall (in.)	5.6	4.2	2.0	0.1	0.0	0.0	0.0	0.0	0.0	0.2	0.3	3.6	16.0
Maximum Snow Depth (in.)	16	9	10	1	0	0	0	0	0	0	4	13	16
Days With ≥ 1.0" Snow Depth	5	3	1	0	0	0	0	0	0	0	0	3	12

Mount Vernon *Posey County* Elevation: 419 ft. Latitude: 37° 57' N Longitude: 87° 53' W

	JAN	FEB	MAR	APR	MAY	JUN	JUL	AUG	SEP	OCT	NOV	DEC	YEAR
Mean Maximum Temp. (°F)	40.7	45.2	55.1	66.2	76.0	84.7	88.0	87.4	81.2	69.5	56.7	44.3	66.2
Mean Temp. (°F)	32.5	36.2	45.3	55.8	65.9	74.8	78.2	77.0	69.8	58.0	47.3	36.3	56.4
Mean Minimum Temp. (°F)	24.3	27.2	35.3	45.3	55.7	64.9	68.3	66.4	58.4	46.7	37.9	28.2	46.6
Extreme Maximum Temp. (°F)	71	76	83	90	93	101	102	104	99	90	82	77	104
Extreme Minimum Temp. (°F)	-16	-7	7	25	36	44	51	45	32	22	12	-16	-16
Days Maximum Temp. ≥ 90°F	0	0	0	0	1	8	13	12	4	0	0	0	38
Days Maximum Temp. ≤ 32°F	7	5	1	0	0	0	0	0	0	0	0	5	18
Days Minimum Temp. ≤ 32°F	24	19	12	2	0	0	0	0	0	1	10	20	88
Days Minimum Temp. ≤ 0°F	1	1	0	0	0	0	0	0	0	0	0	1	3
Heating Degree Days (base 65°F)	1,000	807	608	295	79	6	0	1	39	246	525	884	4,490
Cooling Degree Days (base 65°F)	0	0	3	26	113	307	416	379	191	34	2	0	1,471
Mean Precipitation (in.)	3.48	3.07	4.26	4.39	5.66	3.94	3.83	2.92	3.02	3.42	4.01	3.92	45.92
Extreme Maximum Daily Precip. (in.)	4.69	2.52	6.29	7.40	3.42	3.73	3.40	3.28	3.57	4.06	3.20	3.70	7.40
Days With ≥ 0.1" Precipitation	5	5	7	7	8	7	6	5	5	5	6	7	73
Days With ≥ 0.5" Precipitation	2	2	3	3	4	3	3	2	2	2	3	3	32
Days With ≥ 1.0" Precipitation	1	1	1	1	2	1	1	1	1	1	1	1	13
Mean Snowfall (in.)	2.3	3.2	1.3	0.1	0.0	0.0	0.0	0.0	0.0	0.1	0.0	1.8	8.8
Maximum Snow Depth (in.)	6	9	8	3	0	0	0	0	0	3	1	6	9
Days With ≥ 1.0" Snow Depth	4	3	1	0	0	0	0	0	0	0	0	2	10

The period of record for all cooperative weather station data is 1980 – 2009. See User Guide for detailed explanation of data.

Muncie Ball State Univ *Delaware County*   Elevation: 939 ft.   Latitude: 40° 13' N   Longitude: 85° 25' W

	JAN	FEB	MAR	APR	MAY	JUN	JUL	AUG	SEP	OCT	NOV	DEC	YEAR
Mean Maximum Temp. (°F)	33.4	38.2	47.9	60.7	71.8	81.0	84.8	82.8	76.5	64.2	50.6	37.9	60.8
Mean Temp. (°F)	25.4	29.5	38.2	50.0	61.4	70.5	74.2	72.1	64.6	52.9	41.6	30.1	50.9
Mean Minimum Temp. (°F)	17.3	20.8	28.6	39.2	51.0	60.1	63.5	61.3	52.7	41.5	32.5	22.1	40.9
Extreme Maximum Temp. (°F)	64	74	80	86	90	102	100	99	96	88	79	71	102
Extreme Minimum Temp. (°F)	-29	-13	-8	10	25	36	40	39	27	18	9	-21	-29
Days Maximum Temp. ≥ 90°F	0	0	0	0	0	4	7	4	2	0	0	0	17
Days Maximum Temp. ≤ 32°F	14	9	4	0	0	0	0	0	0	0	2	9	38
Days Minimum Temp. ≤ 32°F	28	24	21	8	0	0	0	0	0	5	17	26	129
Days Minimum Temp. ≤ 0°F	4	2	0	0	0	0	0	0	0	0	0	2	8
Heating Degree Days (base 65°F)	1,222	997	824	454	170	29	3	9	103	382	696	1,076	5,965
Cooling Degree Days (base 65°F)	0	0	1	10	65	202	294	236	99	14	0	0	921
Mean Precipitation (in.)	1.88	2.12	2.91	3.45	4.56	4.51	4.59	3.14	3.25	2.70	3.52	2.86	39.49
Extreme Maximum Daily Precip. (in.)	1.38	2.05	1.83	na	2.52	4.74	3.10	2.92	4.14	2.13	2.69	3.09	na
Days With ≥ 0.1" Precipitation	5	5	7	7	8	7	7	5	5	5	7	7	75
Days With ≥ 0.5" Precipitation	1	1	2	2	3	3	3	2	2	2	3	2	26
Days With ≥ 1.0" Precipitation	0	0	0	1	1	1	1	1	1	1	1	0	8
Mean Snowfall (in.)	7.4	6.0	2.7	0.5	trace	0.0	0.0	0.0	0.0	0.3	1.0	6.1	24.0
Maximum Snow Depth (in.)	10	16	9	6	trace	0	0	0	0	3	4	10	16
Days With ≥ 1.0" Snow Depth	10	8	3	0	0	0	0	0	0	0	1	7	29

North Vernon 1 NW *Jennings County*   Elevation: 745 ft.   Latitude: 39° 02' N   Longitude: 85° 38' W

	JAN	FEB	MAR	APR	MAY	JUN	JUL	AUG	SEP	OCT	NOV	DEC	YEAR
Mean Maximum Temp. (°F)	40.3	45.2	55.2	67.1	75.0	83.4	86.3	85.2	79.2	67.8	55.4	43.2	65.3
Mean Temp. (°F)	32.0	35.5	44.6	55.2	63.7	72.2	75.6	74.3	67.7	56.3	45.9	34.7	54.8
Mean Minimum Temp. (°F)	23.6	26.0	33.9	43.3	52.2	61.0	64.8	63.3	56.0	44.7	36.3	26.4	44.3
Extreme Maximum Temp. (°F)	67	75	85	87	90	101	102	103	96	91	80	74	103
Extreme Minimum Temp. (°F)	-22	-12	-6	19	30	39	47	40	33	23	8	-22	-22
Days Maximum Temp. ≥ 90°F	0	0	0	0	0	4	8	6	2	0	0	0	20
Days Maximum Temp. ≤ 32°F	7	5	1	0	0	0	0	0	0	0	0	5	18
Days Minimum Temp. ≤ 32°F	23	19	15	4	0	0	0	0	0	4	12	21	98
Days Minimum Temp. ≤ 0°F	1	1	0	0	0	0	0	0	0	0	0	1	3
Heating Degree Days (base 65°F)	1,015	826	630	311	113	11	0	3	55	288	569	932	4,753
Cooling Degree Days (base 65°F)	0	0	5	24	79	235	335	299	139	25	1	0	1,142
Mean Precipitation (in.)	2.40	2.63	3.70	4.49	5.03	3.96	4.44	4.60	3.20	3.69	3.88	3.59	45.61
Extreme Maximum Daily Precip. (in.)	2.09	2.10	3.92	4.00	2.90	3.63	3.47	4.55	3.51	4.02	2.27	2.14	4.55
Days With ≥ 0.1" Precipitation	5	5	6	8	8	6	6	5	4	5	6	7	71
Days With ≥ 0.5" Precipitation	2	2	3	3	3	2	3	3	2	2	3	2	30
Days With ≥ 1.0" Precipitation	1	0	1	1	1	1	1	1	1	1	1	1	11
Mean Snowfall (in.)	2.7	3.1	1.5	trace	trace	0.0	0.0	0.0	0.0	0.0	0.0	3.5	10.8
Maximum Snow Depth (in.)	11	7	12	trace	trace	0	0	0	0	0	1	na	na
Days With ≥ 1.0" Snow Depth	4	4	1	0	0	0	0	0	0	0	0	2	11

Oolitic Purdue Exp Farm *Lawrence County*   Elevation: 649 ft.   Latitude: 38° 53' N   Longitude: 86° 33' W

	JAN	FEB	MAR	APR	MAY	JUN	JUL	AUG	SEP	OCT	NOV	DEC	YEAR
Mean Maximum Temp. (°F)	38.2	43.3	53.0	64.3	73.6	82.0	85.5	84.9	78.8	66.6	54.5	41.7	63.9
Mean Temp. (°F)	29.2	33.0	41.7	52.5	62.1	71.0	74.7	73.5	66.2	54.0	43.9	32.6	52.9
Mean Minimum Temp. (°F)	20.0	22.7	30.3	40.6	50.6	59.9	63.9	62.1	53.6	41.5	33.2	23.5	41.8
Extreme Maximum Temp. (°F)	68	75	82	88	91	102	102	102	99	91	81	75	102
Extreme Minimum Temp. (°F)	-29	-16	-4	15	29	38	47	41	31	16	8	-23	-29
Days Maximum Temp. ≥ 90°F	0	0	0	0	0	3	7	7	2	0	0	0	19
Days Maximum Temp. ≤ 32°F	10	6	1	0	0	0	0	0	0	0	1	7	25
Days Minimum Temp. ≤ 32°F	27	23	19	6	0	0	0	0	0	6	16	24	121
Days Minimum Temp. ≤ 0°F	3	1	0	0	0	0	0	0	0	0	0	2	6
Heating Degree Days (base 65°F)	1,103	898	718	383	144	18	1	4	75	347	628	996	5,315
Cooling Degree Days (base 65°F)	0	0	2	14	62	205	309	275	118	15	0	0	1,000
Mean Precipitation (in.)	2.92	2.74	3.83	4.43	5.76	4.07	4.53	3.65	3.17	3.70	3.70	3.51	46.01
Extreme Maximum Daily Precip. (in.)	3.06	2.67	2.90	4.80	3.18	4.05	3.78	4.61	2.57	3.80	2.83	2.48	4.80
Days With ≥ 0.1" Precipitation	6	5	7	9	8	7	7	6	5	6	7	6	79
Days With ≥ 0.5" Precipitation	2	2	3	3	4	3	3	2	2	3	2	3	32
Days With ≥ 1.0" Precipitation	1	0	1	1	2	1	1	1	1	1	1	1	12
Mean Snowfall (in.)	4.6	4.1	2.0	0.1	trace	0.0	0.0	0.0	0.0	0.1	0.1	3.9	14.9
Maximum Snow Depth (in.)	12	8	10	1	trace	0	0	0	0	1	1	16	16
Days With ≥ 1.0" Snow Depth	7	6	2	0	0	0	0	0	0	0	0	4	19

Richmond Water Works *Wayne County*   Elevation: 1,015 ft.   Latitude: 39° 53' N   Longitude: 84° 53' W

	JAN	FEB	MAR	APR	MAY	JUN	JUL	AUG	SEP	OCT	NOV	DEC	YEAR
Mean Maximum Temp. (°F)	35.6	39.8	50.4	62.7	72.6	81.3	84.5	83.2	76.9	64.5	51.7	39.0	61.8
Mean Temp. (°F)	27.4	30.9	40.2	51.3	61.4	70.1	73.6	72.2	65.0	53.2	42.5	31.2	51.6
Mean Minimum Temp. (°F)	19.2	22.0	30.0	39.9	50.0	58.9	62.6	61.2	53.2	41.9	33.3	23.3	41.3
Extreme Maximum Temp. (°F)	66	74	82	94	92	99	100	100	96	90	78	72	100
Extreme Minimum Temp. (°F)	-27	-20	-9	14	29	37	43	41	32	18	10	-22	-27
Days Maximum Temp. ≥ 90°F	0	0	0	0	0	4	6	5	1	0	0	0	16
Days Maximum Temp. ≤ 32°F	12	8	2	0	0	0	0	0	0	0	1	9	32
Days Minimum Temp. ≤ 32°F	27	23	19	6	0	0	0	0	0	5	15	25	120
Days Minimum Temp. ≤ 0°F	3	2	0	0	0	0	0	0	0	0	0	1	6
Heating Degree Days (base 65°F)	1,159	958	763	412	163	25	2	7	88	372	667	1,041	5,657
Cooling Degree Days (base 65°F)	0	0	1	9	57	185	276	238	96	14	0	0	876
Mean Precipitation (in.)	2.73	2.25	3.19	3.84	4.72	4.30	4.02	3.49	2.75	3.15	3.36	2.90	40.70
Extreme Maximum Daily Precip. (in.)	3.19	1.80	2.12	2.79	2.41	3.12	3.38	2.86	2.41	4.53	2.41	2.27	4.53
Days With ≥ 0.1" Precipitation	6	5	7	8	9	8	6	5	5	6	6	6	77
Days With ≥ 0.5" Precipitation	2	1	2	2	3	3	3	2	2	2	2	2	26
Days With ≥ 1.0" Precipitation	1	0	1	1	1	1	1	1	1	1	1	1	11
Mean Snowfall (in.)	5.9	3.6	1.6	0.2	trace	0.0	0.0	0.0	0.0	0.2	0.4	3.8	15.7
Maximum Snow Depth (in.)	21	13	5	2	trace	0	0	0	0	2	5	20	21
Days With ≥ 1.0" Snow Depth	8	6	1	0	0	0	0	0	0	0	0	5	20

The period of record for all cooperative weather station data is 1980 – 2009. See User Guide for detailed explanation of data.

570 Climate: Cooperative Weather Stations

Rockville *Parke County* Elevation: 689 ft. Latitude: 39° 46' N Longitude: 87° 14' W

	JAN	FEB	MAR	APR	MAY	JUN	JUL	AUG	SEP	OCT	NOV	DEC	YEAR
Mean Maximum Temp. (°F)	36.9	42.0	53.5	66.0	75.7	84.1	86.9	85.5	79.2	67.2	53.6	40.1	64.2
Mean Temp. (°F)	28.8	32.9	43.2	54.4	63.9	72.7	76.0	74.5	67.3	55.8	44.6	32.4	53.9
Mean Minimum Temp. (°F)	20.5	23.8	32.8	42.7	52.1	61.2	64.9	63.5	55.4	44.4	35.5	24.6	43.5
Extreme Maximum Temp. (°F)	66	74	84	89	93	103	104	102	96	90	79	74	104
Extreme Minimum Temp. (°F)	-25	-18	-4	17	27	37	43	41	31	19	8	-21	-25
Days Maximum Temp. ≥ 90°F	0	0	0	0	1	7	10	7	2	0	0	0	27
Days Maximum Temp. ≤ 32°F	11	6	1	0	0	0	0	0	0	0	1	7	26
Days Minimum Temp. ≤ 32°F	26	22	16	5	0	0	0	0	0	4	13	23	109
Days Minimum Temp. ≤ 0°F	3	2	0	0	0	0	0	0	0	0	0	1	6
Heating Degree Days (base 65°F)	1,117	900	673	334	112	12	1	2	59	300	607	1,005	5,122
Cooling Degree Days (base 65°F)	0	0	3	22	86	250	347	304	135	23	1	0	1,171
Mean Precipitation (in.)	2.83	2.51	3.44	4.14	5.39	4.55	5.13	4.01	3.31	3.80	4.21	3.56	46.88
Extreme Maximum Daily Precip. (in.)	2.60	3.18	3.10	2.20	8.05	5.00	3.45	4.73	5.46	3.00	4.15	3.03	8.05
Days With ≥ 0.1" Precipitation	6	5	7	9	9	8	7	6	5	6	7	7	82
Days With ≥ 0.5" Precipitation	2	2	3	3	4	3	3	3	3	3	3	3	35
Days With ≥ 1.0" Precipitation	1	1	1	1	2	1	2	1	1	1	1	1	14
Mean Snowfall (in.)	5.1	2.9	1.6	0.0	trace	0.0	0.0	0.0	0.0	trace	0.1	3.9	13.6
Maximum Snow Depth (in.)	15	18	12	1	trace	0	0	0	0	1	4	12	18
Days With ≥ 1.0" Snow Depth	9	6	1	0	0	0	0	0	0	0	0	6	22

Shelbyville Sewage Plant *Shelby County* Elevation: 750 ft. Latitude: 39° 31' N Longitude: 85° 47' W

	JAN	FEB	MAR	APR	MAY	JUN	JUL	AUG	SEP	OCT	NOV	DEC	YEAR
Mean Maximum Temp. (°F)	36.2	40.4	51.3	63.2	73.1	82.3	85.3	83.7	78.3	66.0	52.8	39.4	62.7
Mean Temp. (°F)	28.0	31.2	41.0	52.4	62.6	71.9	74.9	72.9	66.4	54.3	43.5	31.4	52.5
Mean Minimum Temp. (°F)	19.7	22.0	30.7	41.6	52.1	61.4	64.4	62.0	54.4	42.6	34.2	23.5	42.4
Extreme Maximum Temp. (°F)	66	74	81	85	91	102	102	100	98	90	80	75	102
Extreme Minimum Temp. (°F)	-25	-16	0	17	31	41	48	46	32	20	12	-22	-25
Days Maximum Temp. ≥ 90°F	0	0	0	0	0	4	7	4	2	0	0	0	17
Days Maximum Temp. ≤ 32°F	11	7	2	0	0	0	0	0	0	0	1	8	29
Days Minimum Temp. ≤ 32°F	27	24	19	5	0	0	0	0	0	5	14	25	119
Days Minimum Temp. ≤ 0°F	3	2	0	0	0	0	0	0	0	0	0	1	6
Heating Degree Days (base 65°F)	1,141	950	737	386	137	16	1	6	71	343	638	1,036	5,462
Cooling Degree Days (base 65°F)	0	0	2	14	70	229	314	258	119	17	0	0	1,023
Mean Precipitation (in.)	2.80	2.35	3.28	4.20	4.99	4.11	4.00	3.27	2.99	2.93	3.23	3.00	41.15
Extreme Maximum Daily Precip. (in.)	2.58	2.03	1.84	3.62	3.49	3.54	3.35	3.96	3.15	4.43	2.70	2.50	4.43
Days With ≥ 0.1" Precipitation	6	5	7	8	8	7	7	6	5	5	6	6	76
Days With ≥ 0.5" Precipitation	2	2	3	3	4	3	3	2	2	2	2	2	30
Days With ≥ 1.0" Precipitation	1	0	1	1	1	1	1	1	1	1	1	1	11
Mean Snowfall (in.)	2.4	1.7	0.8	trace	0.0	0.0	0.0	0.0	0.0	trace	trace	0.8	5.7
Maximum Snow Depth (in.)	8	11	7	trace	0	0	0	0	0	0	1	trace	na
Days With ≥ 1.0" Snow Depth	2	2	1	0	0	0	0	0	0	0	0	1	6

Tell City *Perry County* Elevation: 399 ft. Latitude: 37° 57' N Longitude: 86° 46' W

	JAN	FEB	MAR	APR	MAY	JUN	JUL	AUG	SEP	OCT	NOV	DEC	YEAR
Mean Maximum Temp. (°F)	41.9	46.0	56.0	67.1	76.1	84.1	87.5	87.2	80.8	69.5	57.3	45.1	66.5
Mean Temp. (°F)	34.1	37.2	45.9	56.2	65.5	74.1	77.9	76.9	69.8	58.4	48.0	37.3	56.8
Mean Minimum Temp. (°F)	26.3	28.4	35.7	45.2	54.8	64.0	68.3	66.7	58.6	47.2	38.7	29.3	46.9
Extreme Maximum Temp. (°F)	71	74	84	89	91	99	103	100	100	92	83	77	103
Extreme Minimum Temp. (°F)	-17	-5	-1	22	34	43	52	46	36	22	14	-14	-17
Days Maximum Temp. ≥ 90°F	0	0	0	0	0	6	12	11	4	0	0	0	33
Days Maximum Temp. ≤ 32°F	6	4	1	0	0	0	0	0	0	0	0	4	15
Days Minimum Temp. ≤ 32°F	22	19	12	3	0	0	0	0	0	1	8	18	83
Days Minimum Temp. ≤ 0°F	1	0	0	0	0	0	0	0	0	0	0	0	1
Heating Degree Days (base 65°F)	950	779	591	286	85	7	0	1	39	235	505	854	4,332
Cooling Degree Days (base 65°F)	0	0	4	27	107	286	407	378	188	37	3	0	1,437
Mean Precipitation (in.)	3.31	3.18	4.25	4.25	5.78	4.38	4.47	3.35	3.59	3.40	3.78	4.10	47.84
Extreme Maximum Daily Precip. (in.)	3.51	3.09	4.75	3.34	3.93	4.37	3.20	3.27	4.43	2.72	3.10	2.25	4.75
Days With ≥ 0.1" Precipitation	6	6	7	7	9	7	7	5	5	5	6	7	77
Days With ≥ 0.5" Precipitation	2	2	3	3	4	3	3	2	2	2	3	3	32
Days With ≥ 1.0" Precipitation	1	1	1	1	2	1	1	1	1	1	1	1	13
Mean Snowfall (in.)	1.8	2.2	0.4	trace	0.0	0.0	0.0	0.0	0.0	0.0	0.1	0.8	5.3
Maximum Snow Depth (in.)	7	10	5	1	0	0	0	0	0	0	0	trace	21
Days With ≥ 1.0" Snow Depth	2	2	0	0	0	0	0	0	0	0	0	0	4

Terre Haute Indiana State *Vigo County* Elevation: 506 ft. Latitude: 39° 28' N Longitude: 87° 25' W

	JAN	FEB	MAR	APR	MAY	JUN	JUL	AUG	SEP	OCT	NOV	DEC	YEAR
Mean Maximum Temp. (°F)	37.7	42.1	53.3	65.3	75.8	84.4	88.0	86.5	80.7	68.3	54.4	41.1	64.8
Mean Temp. (°F)	28.4	32.2	42.6	54.0	64.0	73.0	76.8	74.8	67.8	55.4	43.9	31.9	53.7
Mean Minimum Temp. (°F)	19.2	22.2	32.3	42.6	52.2	61.4	65.5	63.0	54.9	42.6	33.3	22.6	42.6
Extreme Maximum Temp. (°F)	69	76	84	89	99	102	102	102	100	91	82	74	102
Extreme Minimum Temp. (°F)	-18	-20	1	17	29	36	41	42	27	19	5	-22	-22
Days Maximum Temp. ≥ 90°F	0	0	0	0	1	8	12	10	4	0	0	0	35
Days Maximum Temp. ≤ 32°F	10	6	1	0	0	0	0	0	0	0	1	6	24
Days Minimum Temp. ≤ 32°F	26	23	17	5	0	0	0	0	0	5	15	24	115
Days Minimum Temp. ≤ 0°F	2	2	0	0	0	0	0	0	0	0	0	1	5
Heating Degree Days (base 65°F)	1,125	922	688	346	113	13	1	3	60	312	626	1,017	5,226
Cooling Degree Days (base 65°F)	0	0	2	23	90	259	372	314	149	23	0	0	1,232
Mean Precipitation (in.)	2.56	2.53	3.49	4.49	5.04	4.50	4.42	3.36	3.51	3.65	3.57	3.12	44.24
Extreme Maximum Daily Precip. (in.)	2.50	2.81	2.72	2.87	3.00	4.59	na	2.70	5.30	na	2.00	2.31	na
Days With ≥ 0.1" Precipitation	5	5	6	8	8	6	7	5	5	5	6	5	71
Days With ≥ 0.5" Precipitation	2	2	2	3	3	3	3	2	2	2	2	2	28
Days With ≥ 1.0" Precipitation	1	1	1	1	1	1	1	1	1	1	1	1	12
Mean Snowfall (in.)	3.9	3.3	1.0	0.0	0.0	0.0	0.0	0.0	0.0	0.0	0.3	2.9	11.4
Maximum Snow Depth (in.)	12	na	6	1	0	0	0	0	0	0	2	na	na
Days With ≥ 1.0" Snow Depth	6	na	1	0	0	0	0	0	0	0	0	4	na

The period of record for all cooperative weather station data is 1980 – 2009. See User Guide for detailed explanation of data.

Valparaiso Waterworks *Porter County* Elevation: 799 ft. Latitude: 41° 31' N Longitude: 87° 02' W

	JAN	FEB	MAR	APR	MAY	JUN	JUL	AUG	SEP	OCT	NOV	DEC	YEAR
Mean Maximum Temp. (°F)	31.6	36.9	47.3	60.2	71.2	79.6	83.1	81.0	74.6	63.1	48.9	35.9	59.5
Mean Temp. (°F)	24.4	29.0	38.1	49.6	60.1	68.9	73.2	71.2	64.3	53.0	41.3	29.3	50.2
Mean Minimum Temp. (°F)	17.1	21.1	28.9	39.0	48.9	58.1	63.2	61.5	53.9	42.9	33.5	22.6	40.9
Extreme Maximum Temp. (°F)	63	71	83	88	90	100	99	99	93	85	74	68	100
Extreme Minimum Temp. (°F)	-25	-18	-5	14	30	35	44	39	32	20	8	-20	-25
Days Maximum Temp. ≥ 90°F	0	0	0	0	0	3	4	3	1	0	0	0	11
Days Maximum Temp. ≤ 32°F	17	10	3	0	0	0	0	0	0	0	1	11	42
Days Minimum Temp. ≤ 32°F	28	23	21	7	0	0	0	0	0	4	15	26	124
Days Minimum Temp. ≤ 0°F	4	2	0	0	0	0	0	0	0	0	0	2	8
Heating Degree Days (base 65°F)	1,253	1,011	828	465	197	40	4	12	104	374	706	1,100	6,094
Cooling Degree Days (base 65°F)	0	0	1	10	52	164	264	210	90	10	0	0	801
Mean Precipitation (in.)	2.16	1.91	2.56	3.54	4.13	4.51	4.24	3.91	3.29	3.22	3.81	2.64	39.92
Extreme Maximum Daily Precip. (in.)	1.76	1.59	1.99	2.07	2.20	5.28	7.34	4.42	2.52	2.64	4.05	2.33	7.34
Days With ≥ 0.1" Precipitation	5	5	6	7	8	7	7	6	7	6	7	6	77
Days With ≥ 0.5" Precipitation	1	1	2	2	3	3	3	2	2	2	2	2	25
Days With ≥ 1.0" Precipitation	0	0	0	1	1	1	1	1	1	1	1	1	9
Mean Snowfall (in.)	12.6	8.1	6.0	1.1	trace	0.0	0.0	0.0	0.0	0.2	2.2	9.5	39.7
Maximum Snow Depth (in.)	20	24	16	6	trace	0	0	0	0	3	6	22	24
Days With ≥ 1.0" Snow Depth	20	12	5	0	0	0	0	0	0	0	2	10	49

Warsaw *Kosciusko County* Elevation: 810 ft. Latitude: 41° 14' N Longitude: 85° 52' W

	JAN	FEB	MAR	APR	MAY	JUN	JUL	AUG	SEP	OCT	NOV	DEC	YEAR
Mean Maximum Temp. (°F)	32.3	36.1	47.1	59.7	70.8	79.9	82.9	81.2	74.7	62.3	49.3	36.1	59.4
Mean Temp. (°F)	24.9	28.1	37.9	49.5	59.9	69.3	72.8	71.3	64.0	52.2	41.1	29.3	50.0
Mean Minimum Temp. (°F)	17.5	20.1	28.7	39.2	49.0	58.8	62.7	61.3	53.3	42.1	32.7	22.0	40.6
Extreme Maximum Temp. (°F)	63	73	82	87	91	102	102	98	95	90	76	69	102
Extreme Minimum Temp. (°F)	-25	-13	-9	8	28	37	43	37	29	20	9	-20	-25
Days Maximum Temp. ≥ 90°F	0	0	0	0	0	3	4	2	1	0	0	0	10
Days Maximum Temp. ≤ 32°F	16	11	3	0	0	0	0	0	0	0	1	11	42
Days Minimum Temp. ≤ 32°F	28	24	21	7	0	0	0	0	0	5	16	26	127
Days Minimum Temp. ≤ 0°F	3	2	0	0	0	0	0	0	0	0	0	2	7
Heating Degree Days (base 65°F)	1,236	1,036	834	469	200	32	5	10	107	399	712	1,102	6,142
Cooling Degree Days (base 65°F)	0	0	1	9	49	168	252	213	83	9	0	0	784
Mean Precipitation (in.)	2.10	1.69	2.17	3.58	4.23	4.31	4.05	4.38	3.11	3.29	2.88	2.59	38.38
Extreme Maximum Daily Precip. (in.)	2.20	1.53	1.87	3.42	2.93	4.87	4.32	4.33	2.43	3.69	2.50	3.90	4.87
Days With ≥ 0.1" Precipitation	5	5	5	8	8	7	7	7	6	6	6	6	76
Days With ≥ 0.5" Precipitation	1	1	1	2	3	3	3	3	2	2	2	2	25
Days With ≥ 1.0" Precipitation	0	0	0	1	1	1	1	1	1	1	1	0	8
Mean Snowfall (in.)	na	na	1.7	0.3	0.0	0.0	0.0	0.0	0.0	trace	0.3	4.3	na
Maximum Snow Depth (in.)	na	na	6	4	0	0	0	0	0	0	trace	2	na
Days With ≥ 1.0" Snow Depth	na	na	1	0	0	0	0	0	0	0	0	6	na

Whitestown *Boone County* Elevation: 935 ft. Latitude: 40° 00' N Longitude: 86° 21' W

	JAN	FEB	MAR	APR	MAY	JUN	JUL	AUG	SEP	OCT	NOV	DEC	YEAR
Mean Maximum Temp. (°F)	35.1	40.2	51.4	64.4	74.3	83.0	85.7	84.3	78.5	66.0	52.1	38.6	62.8
Mean Temp. (°F)	27.1	31.2	41.1	52.8	62.8	71.6	74.6	73.0	66.2	54.7	43.2	31.1	52.4
Mean Minimum Temp. (°F)	19.0	22.2	30.8	41.2	51.2	60.2	63.5	61.6	53.9	43.3	34.3	23.5	42.0
Extreme Maximum Temp. (°F)	65	74	82	88	94	104	103	100	96	88	78	73	104
Extreme Minimum Temp. (°F)	-27	-20	-10	15	30	35	43	37	28	20	6	-22	-27
Days Maximum Temp. ≥ 90°F	0	0	0	0	1	5	8	6	2	0	0	0	22
Days Maximum Temp. ≤ 32°F	13	8	2	0	0	0	0	0	0	0	1	9	33
Days Minimum Temp. ≤ 32°F	27	23	18	6	0	0	0	0	0	5	14	24	117
Days Minimum Temp. ≤ 0°F	3	2	0	0	0	0	0	0	0	0	0	2	7
Heating Degree Days (base 65°F)	1,169	949	736	376	138	18	2	7	75	331	648	1,045	5,494
Cooling Degree Days (base 65°F)	0	0	2	17	75	223	307	261	118	19	0	0	1,022
Mean Precipitation (in.)	2.69	2.55	3.40	3.91	4.84	4.06	4.31	3.33	3.39	3.06	3.68	3.29	42.51
Extreme Maximum Daily Precip. (in.)	2.22	3.12	2.66	1.80	2.65	2.95	3.43	3.89	5.46	2.36	3.73	2.45	5.46
Days With ≥ 0.1" Precipitation	6	5	7	9	9	7	7	5	5	6	7	7	80
Days With ≥ 0.5" Precipitation	2	2	2	3	3	3	3	2	3	2	2	2	29
Days With ≥ 1.0" Precipitation	0	0	1	1	1	1	1	1	1	1	1	1	10
Mean Snowfall (in.)	8.0	6.4	2.4	0.3	0.0	0.0	0.0	0.0	0.0	0.3	0.7	5.8	23.9
Maximum Snow Depth (in.)	14	22	11	2	0	0	0	0	0	0	5	2	9	22
Days With ≥ 1.0" Snow Depth	11	8	2	0	0	0	0	0	0	0	0	7	28

Winchester Airport 3E *Randolph County* Elevation: 1,109 ft. Latitude: 40° 11' N Longitude: 84° 55' W

	JAN	FEB	MAR	APR	MAY	JUN	JUL	AUG	SEP	OCT	NOV	DEC	YEAR
Mean Maximum Temp. (°F)	33.0	36.9	47.4	60.4	70.8	79.7	82.9	81.5	75.7	63.1	49.9	37.0	59.9
Mean Temp. (°F)	25.4	28.5	38.2	50.3	60.9	69.9	73.0	71.3	64.8	53.0	41.5	29.7	50.5
Mean Minimum Temp. (°F)	17.8	20.1	28.9	40.1	50.9	60.1	63.1	61.1	53.9	42.7	33.0	22.3	41.2
Extreme Maximum Temp. (°F)	64	73	80	85	89	101	100	97	93	89	77	71	101
Extreme Minimum Temp. (°F)	-26	-15	-11	12	29	40	46	39	29	19	9	-22	-26
Days Maximum Temp. ≥ 90°F	0	0	0	0	0	2	4	2	1	0	0	0	9
Days Maximum Temp. ≤ 32°F	15	10	4	0	0	0	0	0	0	0	2	11	42
Days Minimum Temp. ≤ 32°F	28	25	21	6	0	0	0	0	0	4	16	26	126
Days Minimum Temp. ≤ 0°F	4	2	0	0	0	0	0	0	0	0	0	2	8
Heating Degree Days (base 65°F)	1,220	1,025	826	445	179	31	4	12	95	381	698	1,087	6,003
Cooling Degree Days (base 65°F)	0	0	1	11	58	185	260	216	96	15	0	0	842
Mean Precipitation (in.)	2.07	1.73	2.74	3.71	4.36	4.45	4.36	3.47	2.92	3.04	3.27	2.78	38.90
Extreme Maximum Daily Precip. (in.)	2.64	1.80	2.46	2.58	2.47	6.45	2.90	3.53	3.00	2.68	3.52	2.52	6.45
Days With ≥ 0.1" Precipitation	5	4	6	8	8	7	7	6	5	5	7	6	74
Days With ≥ 0.5" Precipitation	1	1	2	2	3	3	3	2	2	2	2	2	25
Days With ≥ 1.0" Precipitation	1	0	0	1	1	1	1	1	1	1	1	0	9
Mean Snowfall (in.)	5.9	5.4	2.5	0.3	0.0	0.0	0.0	0.0	0.0	0.1	0.5	3.8	18.5
Maximum Snow Depth (in.)	21	19	11	5	0	0	0	0	0	2	2	14	21
Days With ≥ 1.0" Snow Depth	11	10	3	0	0	0	0	0	0	0	1	6	31

The period of record for all cooperative weather station data is 1980 – 2009. See User Guide for detailed explanation of data.

Indiana Weather Station Rankings

Annual Extreme Maximum Temperature

Highest			Lowest		
Rank	Station Name	°F	Rank	Station Name	°F
1	Fort Wayne Baer Field	106	1	Richmond Water Works	100
2	Delphi 3 S	105	1	Valparaiso Waterworks	**100**
2	Frankfort Disposal Plant	105	3	Angola	101
2	Huntington	105	3	Freelandville	101
5	Berne	104	3	Greensburg	101
5	Bloomington Indiana Univ	104	3	La Porte	101
5	English 4 S	**104**	3	Martinsville 2 SW	101
5	Evansville Dress Regional Arpt	104	3	Winchester Airport 3E	101
5	Indianapolis SE Side	104	9	Crawfordsville 5 S	102
5	Kokomo 3 WSW	104	9	Dubois S Ind Forage Frm	102
5	Lafayette 8 S	104	9	Elwood Wastewater Plant	102
5	Lowell	104	9	Evansville Museum	**102**
5	Madison Sewage Plant	104	9	Farmland 5 NNW	102
5	Mount Vernon	104	9	Goshen College	102
5	Rockville	104	9	Muncie Ball State Univ	**102**
5	South Bend Michiana Regional	104	9	Oolitic Purdue Exp Farm	102
5	Whitestown	104	9	Shelbyville Sewage Plant	**102**
18	Anderson Sewage Plant	103	9	Terre Haute Indiana State	**102**
18	Brookville	103	9	Warsaw	102
18	Columbia City	103	20	Anderson Sewage Plant	103
18	Columbus	103	20	Brookville	103
18	Greenfield	103	20	Columbia City	103
18	Indianapolis Int'l Arpt	103	20	Columbus	103
18	North Vernon 1 NW	103	20	Greenfield	103
18	Tell City	103	20	Indianapolis Int'l Arpt	103

Annual Mean Maximum Temperature

Highest			Lowest		
Rank	Station Name	°F	Rank	Station Name	°F
1	Evansville Museum	**68.8**	1	Angola	57.5
2	English 4 S	**67.1**	2	La Porte	58.4
3	Evansville Dress Regional Arpt	66.7	3	Columbia City	59.0
4	Tell City	66.5	4	South Bend Michiana Regional	59.1
5	Mount Vernon	66.2	5	Warsaw	**59.4**
6	Madison Sewage Plant	65.6	6	Valparaiso Waterworks	**59.5**
7	North Vernon 1 NW	**65.3**	7	Goshen College	59.7
8	Dubois S Ind Forage Frm	65.0	8	Lowell	59.9
9	Terre Haute Indiana State	**64.8**	8	Winchester Airport 3E	59.9
10	Brookville	64.2	10	Fort Wayne Baer Field	60.0
10	Rockville	64.2	11	Kokomo 3 WSW	60.2
12	Oolitic Purdue Exp Farm	63.9	12	Berne	60.7
13	Columbus	63.5	13	Farmland 5 NNW	60.8
13	Freelandville	63.5	13	Muncie Ball State Univ	**60.8**
15	Bloomington Indiana Univ	63.4	15	Frankfort Disposal Plant	60.9
16	Whitestown	62.8	15	Huntington	60.9
17	Martinsville 2 SW	62.7	17	Anderson Sewage Plant	61.0
17	Shelbyville Sewage Plant	**62.7**	18	Lafayette 8 S	61.1
19	Indianapolis Int'l Arpt	62.6	19	Elwood Wastewater Plant	61.2
20	Delphi 3 S	62.4	20	Crawfordsville 5 S	**61.6**
21	Greensburg	62.3	20	Indianapolis SE Side	61.6
22	Richmond Water Works	61.8	22	Greenfield	61.7
23	Greenfield	61.7	23	Richmond Water Works	61.8
24	Crawfordsville 5 S	**61.6**	24	Greensburg	62.3
24	Indianapolis SE Side	61.6	25	Delphi 3 S	62.4

Rankings include 25 highest/lowest stations. If state has less than 25 stations, all stations are included. The period of record is 1980–2009. See User Guide for detailed explanation of data.

Annual Mean Temperature

Highest

Rank	Station Name	°F
1	Evansville Museum	**58.9**
2	Tell City	56.8
3	Evansville Dress Regional Arpt	56.5
4	Mount Vernon	56.4
5	Madison Sewage Plant	55.4
6	English 4 S	**54.8**
6	North Vernon 1 NW	**54.8**
8	Dubois S Ind Forage Frm	54.5
9	Freelandville	53.9
9	Rockville	53.9
11	Terre Haute Indiana State	**53.7**
12	Bloomington Indiana Univ	53.6
13	Columbus	53.4
14	Indianapolis Int'l Arpt	53.1
15	Greensburg	53.0
16	Oolitic Purdue Exp Farm	52.9
17	Brookville	52.7
18	Shelbyville Sewage Plant	**52.5**
18	Whitestown	52.5
20	Delphi 3 S	52.2
21	Indianapolis SE Side	52.0
22	Greenfield	51.9
23	Anderson Sewage Plant	51.8
23	Martinsville 2 SW	51.8
25	Richmond Water Works	51.6

Lowest

Rank	Station Name	°F
1	Angola	47.7
2	Columbia City	49.1
3	Lowell	49.6
4	Kokomo 3 WSW	49.9
5	Warsaw	**50.0**
6	La Porte	50.1
6	South Bend Michiana Regional	50.1
8	Valparaiso Waterworks	**50.2**
9	Crawfordsville 5 S	**50.4**
9	Farmland 5 NNW	50.4
9	Goshen College	50.4
9	Huntington	50.4
13	Fort Wayne Baer Field	50.5
13	Winchester Airport 3E	50.5
15	Elwood Wastewater Plant	50.6
16	Muncie Ball State Univ	**50.9**
17	Lafayette 8 S	51.2
18	Frankfort Disposal Plant	51.3
19	Berne	51.5
20	Richmond Water Works	51.6
21	Anderson Sewage Plant	51.8
21	Martinsville 2 SW	51.8
23	Greenfield	51.9
24	Indianapolis SE Side	52.0
25	Delphi 3 S	52.2

Annual Mean Minimum Temperature

Highest

Rank	Station Name	°F
1	Evansville Museum	**48.9**
2	Tell City	46.9
3	Mount Vernon	46.6
4	Evansville Dress Regional Arpt	46.2
5	Madison Sewage Plant	45.2
6	Freelandville	44.4
7	North Vernon 1 NW	**44.3**
8	Dubois S Ind Forage Frm	43.9
9	Bloomington Indiana Univ	43.8
10	Greensburg	43.7
10	Indianapolis Int'l Arpt	43.7
12	Rockville	43.5
13	Columbus	43.2
14	Anderson Sewage Plant	42.6
14	Terre Haute Indiana State	**42.6**
16	Indianapolis SE Side	42.4
16	Shelbyville Sewage Plant	**42.4**
18	English 4 S	**42.3**
19	Berne	42.1
19	Greenfield	42.1
19	Whitestown	42.1
22	Delphi 3 S	41.9
23	Oolitic Purdue Exp Farm	41.8
24	La Porte	41.7
25	Frankfort Disposal Plant	41.6

Lowest

Rank	Station Name	°F
1	Angola	37.8
2	Columbia City	39.1
3	Crawfordsville 5 S	**39.2**
3	Lowell	39.2
5	Kokomo 3 WSW	39.7
6	Huntington	39.8
7	Farmland 5 NNW	39.9
8	Elwood Wastewater Plant	40.0
9	Warsaw	40.6
10	Fort Wayne Baer Field	40.9
10	Martinsville 2 SW	40.9
10	Muncie Ball State Univ	**40.9**
10	Valparaiso Waterworks	**40.9**
14	Goshen College	41.0
14	South Bend Michiana Regional	41.0
16	Brookville	41.1
16	Lafayette 8 S	41.1
18	Winchester Airport 3E	41.2
19	Richmond Water Works	41.3
20	Frankfort Disposal Plant	41.6
21	La Porte	41.7
22	Oolitic Purdue Exp Farm	41.8
23	Delphi 3 S	41.9
24	Berne	42.1
24	Greenfield	42.1

Rankings include 25 highest/lowest stations. If state has less than 25 stations, all stations are included. The period of record is 1980–2009. See User Guide for detailed explanation of data.

Annual Extreme Minimum Temperature

Highest

Rank	Station Name	°F
1	Mount Vernon	-16
2	Evansville Museum	**-17**
2	Tell City	-17
4	Evansville Dress Regional Arpt	-18
4	Madison Sewage Plant	-18
6	Bloomington Indiana Univ	-21
6	South Bend Michiana Regional	-21
8	Fort Wayne Baer Field	-22
8	Indianapolis SE Side	-22
8	North Vernon 1 NW	-22
8	Terre Haute Indiana State	**-22**
12	Freelandville	-23
12	La Porte	-23
14	Anderson Sewage Plant	-24
14	Berne	-24
14	Columbia City	-24
14	Delphi 3 S	-24
14	Elwood Wastewater Plant	-24
14	Goshen College	-24
14	Greensburg	-24
21	Dubois S Ind Forage Frm	-25
21	Farmland 5 NNW	-25
21	Lafayette 8 S	-25
21	Lowell	-25
21	Rockville	-25

Lowest

Rank	Station Name	°F
1	Martinsville 2 SW	-35
2	Brookville	-31
2	Crawfordsville 5 S	-31
4	English 4 S	**-30**
5	Greenfield	-29
5	Muncie Ball State Univ	**-29**
5	Oolitic Purdue Exp Farm	-29
8	Huntington	-28
9	Angola	-27
9	Indianapolis Int'l Arpt	-27
9	Richmond Water Works	-27
9	Whitestown	-27
13	Columbus	-26
13	Frankfort Disposal Plant	-26
13	Kokomo 3 WSW	-26
13	Winchester Airport 3E	-26
17	Dubois S Ind Forage Frm	-25
17	Farmland 5 NNW	-25
17	Lafayette 8 S	-25
17	Lowell	-25
17	Rockville	-25
17	Shelbyville Sewage Plant	**-25**
17	Valparaiso Waterworks	**-25**
17	Warsaw	-25
25	Anderson Sewage Plant	-24

July Mean Maximum Temperature

Highest

Rank	Station Name	°F
1	Evansville Museum	**90.0**
2	Evansville Dress Regional Arpt	88.5
3	English 4 S	88.0
3	Mount Vernon	88.0
3	Terre Haute Indiana State	**88.0**
6	Tell City	87.5
7	Rockville	86.9
8	Brookville	86.8
9	Madison Sewage Plant	86.7
10	Dubois S Ind Forage Frm	86.4
11	North Vernon 1 NW	**86.3**
12	Freelandville	85.7
12	Whitestown	85.7
14	Oolitic Purdue Exp Farm	85.5
15	Bloomington Indiana Univ	85.4
15	Columbus	85.4
15	Delphi 3 S	85.4
18	Huntington	85.3
18	Indianapolis Int'l Arpt	85.3
18	Shelbyville Sewage Plant	85.3
21	Greensburg	84.8
21	Muncie Ball State Univ	**84.8**
23	Elwood Wastewater Plant	84.7
23	Greenfield	84.7
23	Martinsville 2 SW	84.7

Lowest

Rank	Station Name	°F
1	Angola	81.8
2	La Porte	82.3
3	Columbia City	82.7
4	Warsaw	82.9
4	Winchester Airport 3E	82.9
6	Valparaiso Waterworks	**83.1**
7	South Bend Michiana Regional	83.3
8	Goshen College	83.6
9	Anderson Sewage Plant	83.8
9	Kokomo 3 WSW	83.8
11	Frankfort Disposal Plant	83.9
12	Farmland 5 NNW	84.0
12	Lowell	84.0
14	Fort Wayne Baer Field	84.3
14	Indianapolis SE Side	84.3
14	Lafayette 8 S	84.3
17	Crawfordsville 5 S	84.4
18	Richmond Water Works	84.5
19	Berne	84.6
20	Elwood Wastewater Plant	84.7
20	Greenfield	84.7
20	Martinsville 2 SW	84.7
23	Greensburg	84.8
23	Muncie Ball State Univ	**84.8**
25	Huntington	85.3

Rankings include 25 highest/lowest stations. If state has less than 25 stations, all stations are included. The period of record is 1980–2009. See User Guide for detailed explanation of data.

January Mean Minimum Temperature

Highest

Rank	Station Name	°F
1	Evansville Museum	**27.2**
2	Tell City	26.3
3	Evansville Dress Regional Arpt	24.9
4	Madison Sewage Plant	24.5
5	Mount Vernon	24.4
6	North Vernon 1 NW	**23.6**
7	English 4 S	22.3
8	Freelandville	22.2
9	Dubois S Ind Forage Frm	21.7
10	Bloomington Indiana Univ	21.2
11	Columbus	21.0
12	Greensburg	20.9
13	Indianapolis Int'l Arpt	20.5
13	Rockville	20.5
15	Oolitic Purdue Exp Farm	20.1
16	Anderson Sewage Plant	19.8
16	Brookville	19.8
18	Shelbyville Sewage Plant	19.7
19	Berne	19.4
19	Indianapolis SE Side	19.4
21	Delphi 3 S	19.3
22	Richmond Water Works	19.2
22	Terre Haute Indiana State	**19.2**
24	Martinsville 2 SW	19.1
25	Frankfort Disposal Plant	19.0

Lowest

Rank	Station Name	°F
1	Angola	14.7
2	Lowell	15.0
3	Columbia City	16.1
4	Kokomo 3 WSW	16.4
5	Elwood Wastewater Plant	16.8
6	Crawfordsville 5 S	**16.9**
7	Valparaiso Waterworks	17.1
8	Farmland 5 NNW	17.3
8	Huntington	17.3
8	Lafayette 8 S	17.3
8	Muncie Ball State Univ	**17.3**
12	Warsaw	17.5
13	La Porte	17.8
13	Winchester Airport 3E	17.8
15	Fort Wayne Baer Field	17.9
16	South Bend Michiana Regional	18.0
17	Goshen College	18.2
18	Greenfield	18.8
19	Frankfort Disposal Plant	19.0
19	Whitestown	19.0
21	Martinsville 2 SW	19.1
22	Richmond Water Works	19.2
22	Terre Haute Indiana State	**19.2**
24	Delphi 3 S	19.3
25	Berne	19.4

Number of Days Annually Maximum Temperature ≥ 90°F

Highest

Rank	Station Name	Days
1	Evansville Museum	**56**
2	Evansville Dress Regional Arpt	41
3	Mount Vernon	38
4	Terre Haute Indiana State	**35**
5	English 4 S	**33**
5	Tell City	33
7	Brookville	28
8	Dubois S Ind Forage Frm	27
8	Rockville	27
10	Madison Sewage Plant	26
11	Whitestown	22
12	Huntington	21
13	Columbus	20
13	Delphi 3 S	20
13	North Vernon 1 NW	20
16	Bloomington Indiana Univ	19
16	Freelandville	19
16	Oolitic Purdue Exp Farm	19
19	Indianapolis Int'l Arpt	18
19	Lafayette 8 S	18
19	Lowell	18
22	Elwood Wastewater Plant	17
22	Farmland 5 NNW	17
22	Greenfield	17
22	Greensburg	17

Lowest

Rank	Station Name	Days
1	Angola	7
2	Winchester Airport 3E	9
3	Columbia City	10
3	Warsaw	10
5	La Porte	11
5	Valparaiso Waterworks	**11**
7	Goshen College	13
8	Anderson Sewage Plant	15
8	Frankfort Disposal Plant	15
8	Fort Wayne Baer Field	15
8	Indianapolis SE Side	15
8	South Bend Michiana Regional	15
13	Berne	16
13	Crawfordsville 5 S	16
13	Kokomo 3 WSW	16
13	Martinsville 2 SW	16
13	Richmond Water Works	16
18	Elwood Wastewater Plant	17
18	Farmland 5 NNW	17
18	Greenfield	17
18	Greensburg	17
18	Muncie Ball State Univ	**17**
18	Shelbyville Sewage Plant	**17**
24	Indianapolis Int'l Arpt	18
24	Lafayette 8 S	18

Rankings include 25 highest/lowest stations. If state has less than 25 stations, all stations are included. The period of record is 1980–2009. See User Guide for detailed explanation of data.

Number of Days Annually Maximum Temperature ≤ 32°F

Highest

Rank	Station Name	Days
1	Angola	52
2	La Porte	46
3	South Bend Michiana Regional	45
4	Columbia City	44
4	Kokomo 3 WSW	44
6	Goshen College	42
6	Lowell	42
6	Valparaiso Waterworks	42
6	Warsaw	42
6	Winchester Airport 3E	42
11	Fort Wayne Baer Field	41
12	Farmland 5 NNW	39
13	Berne	38
13	Huntington	38
13	Lafayette 8 S	38
13	Muncie Ball State Univ	38
17	Frankfort Disposal Plant	37
18	Anderson Sewage Plant	36
18	Crawfordsville 5 S	36
18	Elwood Wastewater Plant	36
21	Greenfield	34
21	Indianapolis SE Side	34
23	Whitestown	33
24	Delphi 3 S	32
24	Richmond Water Works	32

Lowest

Rank	Station Name	Days
1	Evansville Museum	11
2	English 4 S	14
3	Madison Sewage Plant	15
3	Tell City	15
5	Evansville Dress Regional Arpt	17
6	Mount Vernon	18
6	North Vernon 1 NW	18
8	Dubois S Ind Forage Frm	20
9	Terre Haute Indiana State	24
10	Brookville	25
10	Columbus	25
10	Oolitic Purdue Exp Farm	25
13	Rockville	26
14	Bloomington Indiana Univ	28
14	Freelandville	28
16	Martinsville 2 SW	29
16	Shelbyville Sewage Plant	29
18	Indianapolis Int'l Arpt	30
19	Greensburg	31
20	Delphi 3 S	32
20	Richmond Water Works	32
22	Whitestown	33
23	Greenfield	34
23	Indianapolis SE Side	34
25	Anderson Sewage Plant	36

Number of Days Annually Minimum Temperature ≤ 32°F

Highest

Rank	Station Name	Days
1	Angola	150
2	Lowell	137
3	Crawfordsville 5 S	136
4	Columbia City	135
4	Kokomo 3 WSW	135
6	Farmland 5 NNW	134
6	Huntington	134
8	Elwood Wastewater Plant	131
9	Muncie Ball State Univ	129
10	Martinsville 2 SW	127
10	Warsaw	127
12	Brookville	126
12	Winchester Airport 3E	126
14	Lafayette 8 S	125
14	South Bend Michiana Regional	125
16	Fort Wayne Baer Field	124
16	Valparaiso Waterworks	124
18	Goshen College	123
19	Oolitic Purdue Exp Farm	121
20	La Porte	120
20	Richmond Water Works	120
22	Frankfort Disposal Plant	119
22	Greenfield	119
22	Indianapolis SE Side	119
22	Shelbyville Sewage Plant	119

Lowest

Rank	Station Name	Days
1	Evansville Museum	72
2	Tell City	83
3	Mount Vernon	88
4	Evansville Dress Regional Arpt	93
5	Madison Sewage Plant	94
6	North Vernon 1 NW	98
7	Freelandville	104
8	Indianapolis Int'l Arpt	107
9	Dubois S Ind Forage Frm	108
10	Bloomington Indiana Univ	109
10	Rockville	109
12	Greensburg	110
13	Columbus	112
14	Anderson Sewage Plant	114
14	English 4 S	114
16	Terre Haute Indiana State	115
17	Delphi 3 S	117
17	Whitestown	117
19	Berne	118
20	Frankfort Disposal Plant	119
20	Greenfield	119
20	Indianapolis SE Side	119
20	Shelbyville Sewage Plant	119
24	La Porte	120
24	Richmond Water Works	120

Rankings include 25 highest/lowest stations. If state has less than 25 stations, all stations are included. The period of record is 1980–2009. See User Guide for detailed explanation of data.

Number of Days Annually Minimum Temperature ≤ 0°F

Highest

Rank	Station Name	Days
1	Angola	11
1	Lowell	11
3	Crawfordsville 5 S	10
3	Kokomo 3 WSW	10
5	Columbia City	9
5	Lafayette 8 S	9
7	Elwood Wastewater Plant	8
7	Farmland 5 NNW	8
7	Fort Wayne Baer Field	8
7	Huntington	8
7	Muncie Ball State Univ	8
7	Valparaiso Waterworks	8
7	Winchester Airport 3E	8
14	Delphi 3 S	7
14	Frankfort Disposal Plant	7
14	Goshen College	7
14	Greenfield	7
14	La Porte	7
14	Martinsville 2 SW	7
14	South Bend Michiana Regional	7
14	Warsaw	7
14	Whitestown	7
23	Berne	6
23	Brookville	6
23	Indianapolis SE Side	6

Lowest

Rank	Station Name	Days
1	Evansville Museum	1
1	Tell City	1
3	Evansville Dress Regional Arpt	2
3	Madison Sewage Plant	2
5	Mount Vernon	3
5	North Vernon 1 NW	3
7	Bloomington Indiana Univ	4
7	Columbus	4
7	Dubois S Ind Forage Frm	4
7	English 4 S	4
7	Freelandville	4
7	Greensburg	4
7	Indianapolis Int'l Arpt	4
14	Anderson Sewage Plant	5
14	Terre Haute Indiana State	5
16	Berne	6
16	Brookville	6
16	Indianapolis SE Side	6
16	Oolitic Purdue Exp Farm	6
16	Richmond Water Works	6
16	Rockville	6
16	Shelbyville Sewage Plant	6
23	Delphi 3 S	7
23	Frankfort Disposal Plant	7
23	Goshen College	7

Number of Annual Heating Degree Days

Highest

Rank	Station Name	Num.
1	Angola	6,822
2	Columbia City	6,396
3	Lowell	6,339
4	Kokomo 3 WSW	6,210
5	La Porte	6,168
6	South Bend Michiana Regional	6,165
7	Warsaw	6,142
8	Huntington	6,109
9	Valparaiso Waterworks	6,094
10	Farmland 5 NNW	6,058
11	Goshen College	6,049
12	Fort Wayne Baer Field	6,026
13	Crawfordsville 5 S	6,021
14	Elwood Wastewater Plant	6,006
15	Winchester Airport 3E	6,003
16	Muncie Ball State Univ	5,965
17	Lafayette 8 S	5,894
18	Berne	5,810
19	Frankfort Disposal Plant	5,789
20	Greenfield	5,678
21	Richmond Water Works	5,657
22	Anderson Sewage Plant	5,638
23	Indianapolis SE Side	5,632
24	Martinsville 2 SW	5,608
25	Delphi 3 S	5,558

Lowest

Rank	Station Name	Num.
1	Evansville Museum	3,925
2	Tell City	4,332
3	Evansville Dress Regional Arpt	4,455
4	Mount Vernon	4,490
5	Madison Sewage Plant	4,610
6	English 4 S	4,733
7	North Vernon 1 NW	4,753
8	Dubois S Ind Forage Frm	4,922
9	Freelandville	5,111
10	Rockville	5,122
11	Bloomington Indiana Univ	5,173
12	Columbus	5,226
12	Terre Haute Indiana State	5,226
14	Oolitic Purdue Exp Farm	5,315
15	Indianapolis Int'l Arpt	5,322
16	Greensburg	5,352
17	Brookville	5,400
18	Shelbyville Sewage Plant	5,462
19	Whitestown	5,494
20	Delphi 3 S	5,558
21	Martinsville 2 SW	5,608
22	Indianapolis SE Side	5,632
23	Anderson Sewage Plant	5,638
24	Richmond Water Works	5,657
25	Greenfield	5,678

Rankings include 25 highest/lowest stations. If state has less than 25 stations, all stations are included. The period of record is 1980–2009. See User Guide for detailed explanation of data.

Number of Annual Cooling Degree Days

Highest

Rank	Station Name	Num.
1	Evansville Museum	1,800
2	Mount Vernon	1,471
3	Evansville Dress Regional Arpt	1,460
4	Tell City	1,437
5	Terre Haute Indiana State	1,232
6	Madison Sewage Plant	1,230
7	Dubois S Ind Forage Frm	1,200
8	Freelandville	1,182
9	Rockville	1,171
10	North Vernon 1 NW	1,142
11	Bloomington Indiana Univ	1,134
12	Indianapolis Int'l Arpt	1,101
13	English 4 S	1,095
14	Greensburg	1,093
15	Columbus	1,087
16	Shelbyville Sewage Plant	1,023
17	Whitestown	1,022
18	Brookville	1,020
19	Greenfield	1,011
20	Oolitic Purdue Exp Farm	1,000
21	Indianapolis SE Side	998
22	Delphi 3 S	979
23	Berne	966
24	Lafayette 8 S	952
25	Anderson Sewage Plant	939

Lowest

Rank	Station Name	Num.
1	Angola	610
2	Columbia City	707
3	Warsaw	784
4	Valparaiso Waterworks	801
5	Crawfordsville 5 S	805
6	Lowell	815
7	Goshen College	818
8	Kokomo 3 WSW	822
9	Farmland 5 NNW	829
9	South Bend Michiana Regional	829
11	La Porte	839
12	Winchester Airport 3E	842
13	Fort Wayne Baer Field	848
14	Elwood Wastewater Plant	865
15	Richmond Water Works	876
16	Huntington	880
17	Frankfort Disposal Plant	888
18	Martinsville 2 SW	899
19	Muncie Ball State Univ	921
20	Anderson Sewage Plant	939
21	Lafayette 8 S	952
22	Berne	966
23	Delphi 3 S	979
24	Indianapolis SE Side	998
25	Oolitic Purdue Exp Farm	1,000

Annual Precipitation

Highest

Rank	Station Name	Inches
1	English 4 S	48.65
2	Dubois S Ind Forage Frm	48.06
3	Tell City	47.84
4	Madison Sewage Plant	47.54
5	Bloomington Indiana Univ	47.48
6	Rockville	46.88
7	Evansville Museum	46.29
8	Oolitic Purdue Exp Farm	46.01
9	Mount Vernon	45.92
10	Greenfield	45.90
11	Freelandville	45.72
12	North Vernon 1 NW	45.61
13	Evansville Dress Regional Arpt	45.34
14	Greensburg	44.74
15	Martinsville 2 SW	44.69
16	Terre Haute Indiana State	44.24
17	Columbus	44.02
18	Kokomo 3 WSW	43.12
19	Crawfordsville 5 S	43.01
20	Brookville	42.86
21	La Porte	42.56
22	Whitestown	42.51
23	Indianapolis Int'l Arpt	42.45
24	Indianapolis SE Side	42.11
25	Shelbyville Sewage Plant	41.15

Lowest

Rank	Station Name	Inches
1	South Bend Michiana Regional	38.33
2	Fort Wayne Baer Field	38.35
3	Warsaw	38.38
4	Huntington	38.43
5	Lafayette 8 S	38.44
6	Delphi 3 S	38.52
7	Winchester Airport 3E	38.90
8	Angola	39.01
9	Goshen College	39.03
10	Berne	39.06
11	Farmland 5 NNW	39.21
12	Lowell	39.45
13	Columbia City	39.47
14	Muncie Ball State Univ	39.49
15	Valparaiso Waterworks	39.92
16	Frankfort Disposal Plant	40.60
17	Elwood Wastewater Plant	40.62
18	Richmond Water Works	40.70
19	Anderson Sewage Plant	41.09
20	Shelbyville Sewage Plant	41.15
21	Indianapolis SE Side	42.11
22	Indianapolis Int'l Arpt	42.45
23	Whitestown	42.51
24	La Porte	42.56
25	Brookville	42.86

Rankings include 25 highest/lowest stations. If state has less than 25 stations, all stations are included. The period of record is 1980–2009. See User Guide for detailed explanation of data.

Annual Extreme Maximum Daily Precipitation

Highest

Rank	Station Name	Inches
1	Kokomo 3 WSW	8.82
2	Rockville	8.05
3	Martinsville 2 SW	8.02
4	Mount Vernon	7.40
5	Valparaiso Waterworks	7.34
6	Indianapolis Int'l Arpt	7.20
7	La Porte	6.73
8	Goshen College	6.65
9	South Bend Michiana Regional	6.58
10	Winchester Airport 3E	6.45
11	Evansville Dress Regional Arpt	6.40
12	Columbus	6.37
13	Evansville Museum	5.74
14	Dubois S Ind Forage Frm	5.66
15	Huntington	5.53
16	English 4 S	5.50
17	Whitestown	5.46
18	Madison Sewage Plant	5.16
19	Lowell	5.14
20	Elwood Wastewater Plant	5.01
21	Greensburg	5.00
22	Warsaw	4.87
23	Oolitic Purdue Exp Farm	4.80
24	Delphi 3 S	4.78
25	Tell City	4.75

Lowest

Rank	Station Name	Inches
1	Freelandville	3.81
2	Brookville	4.03
3	Angola	4.10
4	Bloomington Indiana Univ	4.15
5	Indianapolis SE Side	4.16
6	Berne	4.20
7	Anderson Sewage Plant	4.21
8	Frankfort Disposal Plant	4.30
9	Crawfordsville 5 S	4.35
10	Farmland 5 NNW	4.40
10	Fort Wayne Baer Field	4.40
12	Shelbyville Sewage Plant	4.43
13	Columbia City	4.48
14	Lafayette 8 S	4.51
15	Richmond Water Works	4.53
16	North Vernon 1 NW	4.55
17	Greenfield	4.71
18	Tell City	4.75
19	Delphi 3 S	4.78
20	Oolitic Purdue Exp Farm	4.80
21	Warsaw	4.87
22	Greensburg	5.00
23	Elwood Wastewater Plant	5.01
24	Lowell	5.14
25	Madison Sewage Plant	5.16

Number of Days Annually With ≥ 0.1 Inches of Precipitation

Highest

Rank	Station Name	Days
1	La Porte	87
2	Kokomo 3 WSW	84
2	Madison Sewage Plant	84
4	Greenfield	82
4	Greensburg	82
4	Rockville	82
7	English 4 S	81
8	Brookville	80
8	Whitestown	80
10	Angola	79
10	Bloomington Indiana Univ	79
10	Frankfort Disposal Plant	79
10	Oolitic Purdue Exp Farm	79
10	South Bend Michiana Regional	79
15	Anderson Sewage Plant	78
15	Berne	78
15	Columbia City	78
15	Crawfordsville 5 S	78
15	Dubois S Ind Forage Frm	78
15	Freelandville	78
15	Indianapolis Int'l Arpt	78
22	Fort Wayne Baer Field	77
22	Goshen College	77
22	Huntington	77
22	Richmond Water Works	77

Lowest

Rank	Station Name	Days
1	North Vernon 1 NW	71
1	Terre Haute Indiana State	71
3	Delphi 3 S	72
3	Lafayette 8 S	72
5	Evansville Museum	73
5	Mount Vernon	73
7	Evansville Dress Regional Arpt	74
7	Lowell	74
7	Winchester Airport 3E	74
10	Farmland 5 NNW	75
10	Indianapolis SE Side	75
10	Muncie Ball State Univ	75
13	Columbus	76
13	Elwood Wastewater Plant	76
13	Martinsville 2 SW	76
13	Shelbyville Sewage Plant	76
13	Warsaw	76
18	Fort Wayne Baer Field	77
18	Goshen College	77
18	Huntington	77
18	Richmond Water Works	77
18	Tell City	77
18	Valparaiso Waterworks	77
24	Anderson Sewage Plant	78
24	Berne	78

Rankings include 25 highest/lowest stations. If state has less than 25 stations, all stations are included. The period of record is 1980–2009. See User Guide for detailed explanation of data.

Number of Days Annually With ≥ 0.5 Inches of Precipitation

Highest

Rank	Station Name	Days
1	Rockville	35
2	Dubois S Ind Forage Frm	34
3	Columbus	33
3	Madison Sewage Plant	33
5	Bloomington Indiana Univ	32
5	English 4 S	32
5	Evansville Dress Regional Arpt	32
5	Freelandville	32
5	Greenfield	32
5	Mount Vernon	32
5	Oolitic Purdue Exp Farm	32
5	Tell City	32
13	Greensburg	31
13	Martinsville 2 SW	31
15	Anderson Sewage Plant	30
15	Crawfordsville 5 S	30
15	North Vernon 1 NW	30
15	Shelbyville Sewage Plant	30
19	Brookville	29
19	Evansville Museum	29
19	Indianapolis SE Side	29
19	Whitestown	29
23	Indianapolis Int'l Arpt	28
23	Kokomo 3 WSW	28
23	Terre Haute Indiana State	28

Lowest

Rank	Station Name	Days
1	South Bend Michiana Regional	23
2	Goshen College	24
2	Lowell	24
4	Huntington	25
4	Lafayette 8 S	25
4	Valparaiso Waterworks	25
4	Warsaw	25
4	Winchester Airport 3E	25
9	Angola	26
9	Berne	26
9	Columbia City	26
9	Farmland 5 NNW	26
9	Frankfort Disposal Plant	26
9	Fort Wayne Baer Field	26
9	Muncie Ball State Univ	26
9	Richmond Water Works	26
17	Delphi 3 S	27
17	Elwood Wastewater Plant	27
17	La Porte	27
20	Indianapolis Int'l Arpt	28
20	Kokomo 3 WSW	28
20	Terre Haute Indiana State	28
23	Brookville	29
23	Evansville Museum	29
23	Indianapolis SE Side	29

Number of Days Annually With ≥ 1.0 Inches of Precipitation

Highest

Rank	Station Name	Days
1	Madison Sewage Plant	14
1	Rockville	14
3	Bloomington Indiana Univ	13
3	Dubois S Ind Forage Frm	13
3	English 4 S	13
3	Freelandville	13
3	Mount Vernon	13
3	Tell City	13
9	Evansville Dress Regional Arpt	12
9	Greenfield	12
9	Oolitic Purdue Exp Farm	12
9	Terre Haute Indiana State	12
13	Brookville	11
13	Columbus	11
13	Evansville Museum	11
13	Greensburg	11
13	Indianapolis SE Side	11
13	Martinsville 2 SW	11
13	North Vernon 1 NW	11
13	Richmond Water Works	11
13	Shelbyville Sewage Plant	11
22	Anderson Sewage Plant	10
22	Delphi 3 S	10
22	Indianapolis Int'l Arpt	10
22	Kokomo 3 WSW	10

Lowest

Rank	Station Name	Days
1	Angola	7
1	Lafayette 8 S	7
3	Berne	8
3	Farmland 5 NNW	8
3	Fort Wayne Baer Field	8
3	Goshen College	8
3	Huntington	8
3	Muncie Ball State Univ	8
3	South Bend Michiana Regional	8
3	Warsaw	8
11	Columbia City	9
11	Crawfordsville 5 S	9
11	Elwood Wastewater Plant	9
11	Frankfort Disposal Plant	9
11	Lowell	9
11	Valparaiso Waterworks	9
11	Winchester Airport 3E	9
18	Anderson Sewage Plant	10
18	Delphi 3 S	10
18	Indianapolis Int'l Arpt	10
18	Kokomo 3 WSW	10
18	La Porte	10
18	Whitestown	10
24	Brookville	11
24	Columbus	11

Rankings include 25 highest/lowest stations. If state has less than 25 stations, all stations are included. The period of record is 1980–2009. See User Guide for detailed explanation of data.

Annual Snowfall

Highest

Rank	Station Name	Inches
1	South Bend Michiana Regional	67.3
2	La Porte	62.2
3	Goshen College	40.3
4	Valparaiso Waterworks	39.7
5	Kokomo 3 WSW	38.3
6	Angola	36.4
7	Fort Wayne Baer Field	33.8
8	Lowell	30.8
9	Huntington	29.3
10	Berne	28.2
11	Columbia City	27.5
12	Indianapolis Int'l Arpt	25.5
13	Muncie Ball State Univ	24.0
14	Whitestown	23.9
15	Frankfort Disposal Plant	22.6
16	Farmland 5 NNW	22.4
17	Lafayette 8 S	21.3
18	Delphi 3 S	18.6
19	Winchester Airport 3E	18.5
20	Anderson Sewage Plant	17.9
21	Greensburg	16.4
22	Martinsville 2 SW	16.0
23	Greenfield	15.7
23	Richmond Water Works	15.7
25	Oolitic Purdue Exp Farm	14.9

Lowest

Rank	Station Name	Inches
1	Tell City	5.3
2	Shelbyville Sewage Plant	5.7
3	Mount Vernon	8.8
4	Dubois S Ind Forage Frm	9.1
5	North Vernon 1 NW	10.8
6	Evansville Museum	11.0
7	Evansville Dress Regional Arpt	11.4
7	Terre Haute Indiana State	11.4
9	Bloomington Indiana Univ	12.9
10	Madison Sewage Plant	13.1
11	Indianapolis SE Side	13.4
12	Rockville	13.6
13	Freelandville	13.9
14	Brookville	14.2
15	Columbus	14.4
16	Oolitic Purdue Exp Farm	14.9
17	Greenfield	15.7
17	Richmond Water Works	15.7
19	Martinsville 2 SW	16.0
20	Greensburg	16.4
21	Anderson Sewage Plant	17.9
22	Winchester Airport 3E	18.5
23	Delphi 3 S	18.6
24	Lafayette 8 S	21.3
25	Farmland 5 NNW	22.4

Annual Maximum Snow Depth

Highest

Rank	Station Name	Inches
1	Berne	25
2	Kokomo 3 WSW	24
2	La Porte	24
2	Valparaiso Waterworks	24
5	Angola	23
5	South Bend Michiana Regional	23
7	English 4 S	22
7	Evansville Museum	22
7	Whitestown	22
10	Greensburg	21
10	Richmond Water Works	21
10	Tell City	21
10	Winchester Airport 3E	21
14	Fort Wayne Baer Field	20
15	Columbus	19
15	Lafayette 8 S	19
17	Anderson Sewage Plant	18
17	Delphi 3 S	18
17	Dubois S Ind Forage Frm	18
17	Frankfort Disposal Plant	18
17	Rockville	18
22	Goshen College	17
23	Columbia City	16
23	Farmland 5 NNW	16
23	Madison Sewage Plant	16

Lowest

Rank	Station Name	Inches
1	Mount Vernon	9
2	Evansville Dress Regional Arpt	12
2	Freelandville	12
4	Indianapolis Int'l Arpt	13
5	Bloomington Indiana Univ	15
5	Greenfield	15
5	Huntington	15
5	Indianapolis SE Side	15
9	Columbia City	16
9	Farmland 5 NNW	16
9	Madison Sewage Plant	16
9	Martinsville 2 SW	16
9	Muncie Ball State Univ	16
9	Oolitic Purdue Exp Farm	16
15	Goshen College	17
16	Anderson Sewage Plant	18
16	Delphi 3 S	18
16	Dubois S Ind Forage Frm	18
16	Frankfort Disposal Plant	18
16	Rockville	18
21	Columbus	19
21	Lafayette 8 S	19
23	Fort Wayne Baer Field	20
24	Greensburg	21
24	Richmond Water Works	21

Rankings include 25 highest/lowest stations. If state has less than 25 stations, all stations are included. The period of record is 1980–2009. See User Guide for detailed explanation of data.

Number of Days Annually With ≥ 1.0 Inch Snow Depth

Highest

Rank	Station Name	Days
1	South Bend Michiana Regional	55
2	Angola	53
2	La Porte	53
4	Valparaiso Waterworks	49
5	Goshen College	43
6	Fort Wayne Baer Field	41
7	Kokomo 3 WSW	39
8	Columbia City	38
9	Berne	36
10	Farmland 5 NNW	34
11	Lafayette 8 S	31
11	Winchester Airport 3E	31
13	Muncie Ball State Univ	29
14	Frankfort Disposal Plant	28
14	Whitestown	28
16	Delphi 3 S	26
16	Greenfield	26
16	Indianapolis Int'l Arpt	26
19	Rockville	22
20	Huntington	21
20	Indianapolis SE Side	21
22	Richmond Water Works	20
23	Brookville	19
23	Oolitic Purdue Exp Farm	19
25	Anderson Sewage Plant	17

Lowest

Rank	Station Name	Days
1	Tell City	4
2	Shelbyville Sewage Plant	6
3	Mount Vernon	10
4	Dubois S Ind Forage Frm	11
4	Evansville Museum	11
4	Madison Sewage Plant	11
4	North Vernon 1 NW	11
8	English 4 S	12
8	Evansville Dress Regional Arpt	12
8	Martinsville 2 SW	12
11	Freelandville	13
12	Bloomington Indiana Univ	15
12	Columbus	15
14	Anderson Sewage Plant	17
14	Greensburg	17
16	Brookville	19
16	Oolitic Purdue Exp Farm	19
18	Richmond Water Works	20
19	Huntington	21
19	Indianapolis SE Side	21
21	Rockville	22
22	Delphi 3 S	26
22	Greenfield	26
22	Indianapolis Int'l Arpt	26
25	Frankfort Disposal Plant	28

Rankings include 25 highest/lowest stations. If state has less than 25 stations, all stations are included. The period of record is 1980–2009. See User Guide for detailed explanation of data.

Significant Storm Events in Indiana: 2000 – 2009

Location or County	Date	Type	Mag.	Deaths	Injuries	Property Damage ($mil.)	Crop Damage ($mil.)
Kosciusko	10/24/01	Tornado	F1	0	14	2.5	0.0
Marion	09/20/02	Tornado	F2	0	97	40.0	0.0
Johnson	09/20/02	Tornado	F3	0	0	25.0	0.0
Morgan	09/20/02	Tornado	F3	0	28	15.0	0.0
Central Indiana	07/05/03	Flood	na	0	0	41.6	12.0
Carroll, Harold, and Tippecanoe Counties	07/05/03	Flood	na	0	0	24.0	9.0
Howard	07/05/03	Flash Flood	na	0	0	18.0	0.0
Central Indiana	09/01/03	Flood	na	0	0	22.0	0.0
Marion	05/30/04	Tornado	F2	0	26	19.0	0.0
Crawford	05/30/04	Tornado	F3	1	11	5.0	0.0
Warrick	11/06/05	Tornado	F3	4	30	65.0	0.0
Vanderburgh	11/06/05	Tornado	F3	20	200	15.0	0.0
Daviess	11/15/05	Tornado	F3	0	31	11.6	0.0
Marion	05/30/08	Tornado	F2	0	18	29.0	0.0
Vigo	06/01/08	Flood	na	0	0	50.0	50.0
Johnson	06/03/08	Tornado	F2	0	3	23.0	0.0
Morgan	06/04/08	Flood	na	0	0	80.0	100.0
Owen	06/04/08	Flood	na	0	0	50.0	60.0
Clay	06/04/08	Flood	na	0	0	45.0	45.0
Greene	06/04/08	Flood	na	0	0	20.0	60.0
Bartholomew	06/05/08	Flood	na	0	0	150.0	150.0
Jackson	06/05/08	Flood	na	0	0	30.0	30.0
Daviess	06/05/08	Flood	na	0	0	20.0	30.0
Bartholomew	06/07/08	Flash Flood	na	0	0	100.0	0.0
Johnson	06/07/08	Flash Flood	na	0	0	90.0	90.0

Note: Deaths, injuries, and damages are date and location specific.

2016 Title List

Grey House Publishing

Visit www.GreyHouse.com for Product Information, Table of Contents, and Sample Pages.

General Reference
An African Biographical Dictionary
America's College Museums
American Environmental Leaders: From Colonial Times to the Present
Encyclopedia of African-American Writing
Encyclopedia of Constitutional Amendments
Encyclopedia of Gun Control & Gun Rights
An Encyclopedia of Human Rights in the United States
Encyclopedia of Invasions & Conquests
Encyclopedia of Prisoners of War & Internment
Encyclopedia of Religion & Law in America
Encyclopedia of Rural America
Encyclopedia of the Continental Congress
Encyclopedia of the United States Cabinet, 1789-2010
Encyclopedia of War Journalism
Encyclopedia of Warrior Peoples & Fighting Groups
The Environmental Debate: A Documentary History
The Evolution Wars: A Guide to the Debates
From Suffrage to the Senate: America's Political Women
Global Terror & Political Risk Assessment
Nations of the World
Political Corruption in America
Privacy Rights in the Digital Era
The Religious Right: A Reference Handbook
Speakers of the House of Representatives, 1789-2009
This is Who We Were: 1880-1900
This is Who We Were: A Companion to the 1940 Census
This is Who We Were: In the 1910s
This is Who We Were: In the 1920s
This is Who We Were: In the 1940s
This is Who We Were: In the 1950s
This is Who We Were: In the 1960s
This is Who We Were: In the 1970s
U.S. Land & Natural Resource Policy
The Value of a Dollar 1600-1865: Colonial Era to the Civil War
The Value of a Dollar: 1860-2014
Working Americans 1770-1869 Vol. IX: Revolutionary War to the Civil War
Working Americans 1880-1999 Vol. I: The Working Class
Working Americans 1880-1999 Vol. II: The Middle Class
Working Americans 1880-1999 Vol. III: The Upper Class
Working Americans 1880-1999 Vol. IV: Their Children
Working Americans 1880-2015 Vol. V: Americans At War
Working Americans 1880-2005 Vol. VI: Women at Work
Working Americans 1880-2006 Vol. VII: Social Movements
Working Americans 1880-2007 Vol. VIII: Immigrants
Working Americans 1880-2009 Vol. X: Sports & Recreation
Working Americans 1880-2010 Vol. XI: Inventors & Entrepreneurs
Working Americans 1880-2011 Vol. XII: Our History through Music
Working Americans 1880-2012 Vol. XIII: Education & Educators
World Cultural Leaders of the 20th & 21st Centuries

Education Information
Charter School Movement
Comparative Guide to American Elementary & Secondary Schools
Complete Learning Disabilities Directory
Educators Resource Directory
Special Education: A Reference Book for Policy and Curriculum Development

Health Information
Comparative Guide to American Hospitals
Complete Directory for Pediatric Disorders
Complete Directory for People with Chronic Illness
Complete Directory for People with Disabilities
Complete Mental Health Directory
Diabetes in America: Analysis of an Epidemic
Directory of Drug & Alcohol Residential Rehab Facilities
Directory of Health Care Group Purchasing Organizations
Directory of Hospital Personnel
HMO/PPO Directory
Medical Device Register
Older Americans Information Directory

Business Information
Complete Television, Radio & Cable Industry Directory
Directory of Business Information Resources
Directory of Mail Order Catalogs
Directory of Venture Capital & Private Equity Firms
Environmental Resource Handbook
Food & Beverage Market Place
Grey House Homeland Security Directory
Grey House Performing Arts Directory
Grey House Safety & Security Directory
Grey House Transportation Security Directory
Hudson's Washington News Media Contacts Directory
New York State Directory
Rauch Market Research Guides
Sports Market Place Directory

Statistics & Demographics
American Tally
America's Top-Rated Cities
America's Top-Rated Smaller Cities
America's Top-Rated Small Towns & Cities
Ancestry & Ethnicity in America
The Asian Databook
Comparative Guide to American Suburbs
The Hispanic Databook
Profiles of America
"Profiles of" Series – State Handbooks
Weather America

Financial Ratings Series
TheStreet Ratings' Guide to Bond & Money Market Mutual Funds
TheStreet Ratings' Guide to Common Stocks
TheStreet Ratings' Guide to Exchange-Traded Funds
TheStreet Ratings' Guide to Stock Mutual Funds
TheStreet Ratings' Ultimate Guided Tour of Stock Investing
Weiss Ratings' Consumer Guides
Weiss Ratings' Guide to Banks
Weiss Ratings' Guide to Credit Unions
Weiss Ratings' Guide to Health Insurers
Weiss Ratings' Guide to Life & Annuity Insurers
Weiss Ratings' Guide to Property & Casualty Insurers

Bowker's Books In Print® Titles
American Book Publishing Record® Annual
American Book Publishing Record® Monthly
Books In Print®
Books In Print® Supplement
Books Out Loud™
Bowker's Complete Video Directory™
Children's Books In Print®
El-Hi Textbooks & Serials In Print®
Forthcoming Books®
Large Print Books & Serials™
Law Books & Serials In Print™
Medical & Health Care Books In Print™
Publishers, Distributors & Wholesalers of the US™
Subject Guide to Books In Print®
Subject Guide to Children's Books In Print®

Canadian General Reference
Associations Canada
Canadian Almanac & Directory
Canadian Environmental Resource Guide
Canadian Parliamentary Guide
Canadian Venture Capital & Private Equity Firms
Financial Post Directory of Directors
Financial Services Canada
Governments Canada
Health Guide Canada
The History of Canada
Libraries Canada
Major Canadian Cities

Grey House Publishing | Salem Press | H.W. Wilson | 4919 Route, 22 PO Box 56, Amenia NY 12501-0056

SALEM PRESS

SALEM PRESS

2016 Title List

Visit www.SalemPress.com for Product Information, Table of Contents, and Sample Pages.

Science, Careers & Mathematics

- Ancient Creatures
- Applied Science
- Applied Science: Engineering & Mathematics
- Applied Science: Science & Medicine
- Applied Science: Technology
- Biomes and Ecosystems
- Careers in Building Construction
- Careers in Business
- Careers in Chemistry
- Careers in Communications & Media
- Careers in Environment & Conservation
- Careers in Healthcare
- Careers in Hospitality & Tourism
- Careers in Human Services
- Careers in Law, Criminal Justice & Emergency Services
- Careers in Manufacturing
- Careers in Physics
- Careers in Sales, Insurance & Real Estate
- Careers in Science & Engineering
- Careers in Technology Services & Repair
- Computer Technology Innovators
- Contemporary Biographies in Business
- Contemporary Biographies in Chemistry
- Contemporary Biographies in Communications & Media
- Contemporary Biographies in Environment & Conservation
- Contemporary Biographies in Healthcare
- Contemporary Biographies in Hospitality & Tourism
- Contemporary Biographies in Law & Criminal Justice
- Contemporary Biographies in Physics
- Earth Science
- Earth Science: Earth Materials & Resources
- Earth Science: Earth's Surface and History
- Earth Science: Physics & Chemistry of the Earth
- Earth Science: Weather, Water & Atmosphere
- Encyclopedia of Energy
- Encyclopedia of Environmental Issues
- Encyclopedia of Environmental Issues: Atmosphere and Air Pollution
- Encyclopedia of Environmental Issues: Ecology and Ecosystems
- Encyclopedia of Environmental Issues: Energy and Energy Use
- Encyclopedia of Environmental Issues: Policy and Activism
- Encyclopedia of Environmental Issues: Preservation/Wilderness Issues
- Encyclopedia of Environmental Issues: Water and Water Pollution
- Encyclopedia of Global Resources
- Encyclopedia of Global Warming
- Encyclopedia of Mathematics & Society
- Encyclopedia of Mathematics & Society: Engineering, Tech, Medicine
- Encyclopedia of Mathematics & Society: Great Mathematicians
- Encyclopedia of Mathematics & Society: Math & Social Sciences
- Encyclopedia of Mathematics & Society: Math Development/Concepts
- Encyclopedia of Mathematics & Society: Math in Culture & Society
- Encyclopedia of Mathematics & Society: Space, Science, Environment
- Encyclopedia of the Ancient World
- Forensic Science
- Geography Basics
- Internet Innovators
- Inventions and Inventors
- Magill's Encyclopedia of Science: Animal Life
- Magill's Encyclopedia of Science: Plant life
- Notable Natural Disasters
- Principles of Astronomy
- Principles of Chemistry
- Principles of Physics
- Science and Scientists
- Solar System
- Solar System: Great Astronomers
- Solar System: Study of the Universe
- Solar System: The Inner Planets
- Solar System: The Moon and Other Small Bodies
- Solar System: The Outer Planets
- Solar System: The Sun and Other Stars
- World Geography

Literature

- American Ethnic Writers
- Classics of Science Fiction & Fantasy Literature
- Critical Insights: Authors
- Critical Insights: Film
- Critical Insights: Literary Collection Bundles
- Critical Insights: Themes
- Critical Insights: Works
- Critical Survey of Drama
- Critical Survey of Graphic Novels: Heroes & Super Heroes
- Critical Survey of Graphic Novels: History, Theme & Technique
- Critical Survey of Graphic Novels: Independents/Underground Classics
- Critical Survey of Graphic Novels: Manga
- Critical Survey of Long Fiction
- Critical Survey of Mystery & Detective Fiction
- Critical Survey of Mythology and Folklore: Heroes and Heroines
- Critical Survey of Mythology and Folklore: Love, Sexuality & Desire
- Critical Survey of Mythology and Folklore: World Mythology
- Critical Survey of Poetry
- Critical Survey of Poetry: American Poets
- Critical Survey of Poetry: British, Irish & Commonwealth Poets
- Critical Survey of Poetry: Cumulative Index
- Critical Survey of Poetry: European Poets
- Critical Survey of Poetry: Topical Essays
- Critical Survey of Poetry: World Poets
- Critical Survey of Shakespeare's Plays
- Critical Survey of Shakespeare's Sonnets
- Critical Survey of Short Fiction
- Critical Survey of Short Fiction: American Writers
- Critical Survey of Short Fiction: British, Irish, Commonwealth Writers
- Critical Survey of Short Fiction: Cumulative Index
- Critical Survey of Short Fiction: European Writers
- Critical Survey of Short Fiction: Topical Essays
- Critical Survey of Short Fiction: World Writers
- Critical Survey of Young Adult Literature
- Cyclopedia of Literary Characters
- Cyclopedia of Literary Places
- Holocaust Literature
- Introduction to Literary Context: American Poetry of the 20th Century
- Introduction to Literary Context: American Post-Modernist Novels
- Introduction to Literary Context: American Short Fiction
- Introduction to Literary Context: English Literature
- Introduction to Literary Context: Plays
- Introduction to Literary Context: World Literature
- Magill's Literary Annual 2015
- Magill's Survey of American Literature
- Magill's Survey of World Literature
- Masterplots
- Masterplots II: African American Literature
- Masterplots II: American Fiction Series
- Masterplots II: British & Commonwealth Fiction Series
- Masterplots II: Christian Literature
- Masterplots II: Drama Series
- Masterplots II: Juvenile & Young Adult Literature, Supplement
- Masterplots II: Nonfiction Series
- Masterplots II: Poetry Series
- Masterplots II: Short Story Series
- Masterplots II: Women's Literature Series
- Notable African American Writers
- Notable American Novelists
- Notable Playwrights
- Notable Poets
- Recommended Reading: 600 Classics Reviewed
- Short Story Writers

Grey House Publishing | Salem Press | H.W. Wilson | 4919 Route, 22 PO Box 56, Amenia NY 12501-0056

SALEM PRESS

SALEM PRESS

2016 Title List

Visit www.SalemPress.com for Product Information, Table of Contents, and Sample Pages.

History and Social Science
The 2000s in America
50 States
African American History
Agriculture in History
American First Ladies
American Heroes
American Indian Culture
American Indian History
American Indian Tribes
American Presidents
American Villains
America's Historic Sites
Ancient Greece
The Bill of Rights
The Civil Rights Movement
The Cold War
Countries, Peoples & Cultures
Countries, Peoples & Cultures: Central & South America
Countries, Peoples & Cultures: Central, South & Southeast Asia
Countries, Peoples & Cultures: East & South Africa
Countries, Peoples & Cultures: East Asia & the Pacific
Countries, Peoples & Cultures: Eastern Europe
Countries, Peoples & Cultures: Middle East & North Africa
Countries, Peoples & Cultures: North America & the Caribbean
Countries, Peoples & Cultures: West & Central Africa
Countries, Peoples & Cultures: Western Europe
Defining Documents: American Revolution
Defining Documents: Civil Rights
Defining Documents: Civil War
Defining Documents: Emergence of Modern America
Defining Documents: Exploration & Colonial America
Defining Documents: Manifest Destiny
Defining Documents: Postwar 1940s
Defining Documents: Reconstruction
Defining Documents: 1920s
Defining Documents: 1930s
Defining Documents: 1950s
Defining Documents: 1960s
Defining Documents: 1970s
Defining Documents: American West
Defining Documents: Ancient World
Defining Documents: Middle Ages
Defining Documents: Vietnam War
Defining Documents: World War I
Defining Documents: World War II
The Eighties in America
Encyclopedia of American Immigration
Encyclopedia of Flight
Encyclopedia of the Ancient World
Fashion Innovators
The Fifties in America
The Forties in America
Great Athletes
Great Athletes: Baseball
Great Athletes: Basketball
Great Athletes: Boxing & Soccer
Great Athletes: Cumulative Index
Great Athletes: Football
Great Athletes: Golf & Tennis
Great Athletes: Olympics
Great Athletes: Racing & Individual Sports
Great Events from History: 17th Century
Great Events from History: 18th Century
Great Events from History: 19th Century
Great Events from History: 20th Century (1901-1940)
Great Events from History: 20th Century (1941-1970)
Great Events from History: 20th Century (1971-2000)
Great Events from History: Ancient World
Great Events from History: Cumulative Indexes
Great Events from History: Gay, Lesbian, Bisexual, Transgender Events

Great Events from History: Middle Ages
Great Events from History: Modern Scandals
Great Events from History: Renaissance & Early Modern Era
Great Lives from History: 17th Century
Great Lives from History: 18th Century
Great Lives from History: 19th Century
Great Lives from History: 20th Century
Great Lives from History: African Americans
Great Lives from History: American Women
Great Lives from History: Ancient World
Great Lives from History: Asian & Pacific Islander Americans
Great Lives from History: Cumulative Indexes
Great Lives from History: Incredibly Wealthy
Great Lives from History: Inventors & Inventions
Great Lives from History: Jewish Americans
Great Lives from History: Latinos
Great Lives from History: Middle Ages
Great Lives from History: Notorious Lives
Great Lives from History: Renaissance & Early Modern Era
Great Lives from History: Scientists & Science
Historical Encyclopedia of American Business
Issues in U.S. Immigration
Magill's Guide to Military History
Milestone Documents in African American History
Milestone Documents in American History
Milestone Documents in World History
Milestone Documents of American Leaders
Milestone Documents of World Religions
Music Innovators
Musicians & Composers 20th Century
The Nineties in America
The Seventies in America
The Sixties in America
Survey of American Industry and Careers
The Thirties in America
The Twenties in America
United States at War
U.S.A. in Space
U.S. Court Cases
U.S. Government Leaders
U.S. Laws, Acts, and Treaties
U.S. Legal System
U.S. Supreme Court
Weapons and Warfare
World Conflicts: Asia and the Middle East
World Political Yearbook

Health
Addictions & Substance Abuse
Adolescent Health & Wellness
Cancer
Complementary & Alternative Medicine
Genetics & Inherited Conditions
Health Issues
Infectious Diseases & Conditions
Magill's Medical Guide
Psychology & Behavioral Health
Psychology Basics

Grey House Publishing | Salem Press | H.W. Wilson | 4919 Route, 22 PO Box 56, Amenia NY 12501-0056

2016 Title List
Visit www.HWWilsonInPrint.com for Product Information, Table of Contents and Sample Pages

Current Biography
Current Biography Cumulative Index 1946-2013
Current Biography Monthly Magazine
Current Biography Yearbook: 2003
Current Biography Yearbook: 2004
Current Biography Yearbook: 2005
Current Biography Yearbook: 2006
Current Biography Yearbook: 2007
Current Biography Yearbook: 2008
Current Biography Yearbook: 2009
Current Biography Yearbook: 2010
Current Biography Yearbook: 2011
Current Biography Yearbook: 2012
Current Biography Yearbook: 2013
Current Biography Yearbook: 2014
Current Biography Yearbook: 2015

Core Collections
Children's Core Collection
Fiction Core Collection
Graphic Novels Core Collection
Middle & Junior High School Core
Public Library Core Collection: Nonfiction
Senior High Core Collection
Young Adult Fiction Core Collection

The Reference Shelf
Aging in America
American Military Presence Overseas
The Arab Spring
The Brain
The Business of Food
Campaign Trends & Election Law
Conspiracy Theories
The Digital Age
Dinosaurs
Embracing New Paradigms in Education
Faith & Science
Families: Traditional and New Structures
The Future of U.S. Economic Relations: Mexico, Cuba, and Venezuela
Global Climate Change
Graphic Novels and Comic Books
Immigration
Immigration in the U.S.
Internet Safety
Marijuana Reform
The News and its Future
The Paranormal
Politics of the Ocean
Racial Tension in a "Postracial" Age
Reality Television
Representative American Speeches: 2008-2009
Representative American Speeches: 2009-2010
Representative American Speeches: 2010-2011
Representative American Speeches: 2011-2012
Representative American Speeches: 2012-2013
Representative American Speeches: 2013-2014
Representative American Speeches: 2014-2015
Representative American Speeches: 2015-2016
Rethinking Work
Revisiting Gender
Robotics
Russia
Social Networking
Social Services for the Poor
Space Exploration & Development
Sports in America
The Supreme Court
The Transformation of American Cities

U.S. Infrastructure
U.S. National Debate Topic: Surveillance
U.S. National Debate Topic: The Ocean
U.S. National Debate Topic: Transportation Infrastructure
Whistleblowers

Readers' Guide
Abridged Readers' Guide to Periodical Literature
Readers' Guide to Periodical Literature

Indexes
Index to Legal Periodicals & Books
Short Story Index
Book Review Digest

Sears List
Sears List of Subject Headings
Sears: Lista de Encabezamientos de Materia

Facts About Series
Facts About American Immigration
Facts About China
Facts About the 20th Century
Facts About the Presidents
Facts About the World's Languages

Nobel Prize Winners
Nobel Prize Winners: 1901-1986
Nobel Prize Winners: 1987-1991
Nobel Prize Winners: 1992-1996
Nobel Prize Winners: 1997-2001

World Authors
World Authors: 1995-2000
World Authors: 2000-2005

Famous First Facts
Famous First Facts
Famous First Facts About American Politics
Famous First Facts About Sports
Famous First Facts About the Environment
Famous First Facts: International Edition

American Book of Days
The American Book of Days
The International Book of Days

Junior Authors & Illustrators
Eleventh Book of Junior Authors & Illustrations

Monographs
The Barnhart Dictionary of Etymology
Celebrate the World
Guide to the Ancient World
Indexing from A to Z
The Poetry Break
Radical Change: Books for Youth in a Digital Age

Wilson Chronology
Wilson Chronology of Asia and the Pacific
Wilson Chronology of Human Rights
Wilson Chronology of Ideas
Wilson Chronology of the Arts
Wilson Chronology of the World's Religions
Wilson Chronology of Women's Achievements

Grey House Publishing | Salem Press | H.W. Wilson | 4919 Route, 22 PO Box 56, Amenia NY 12501-0056